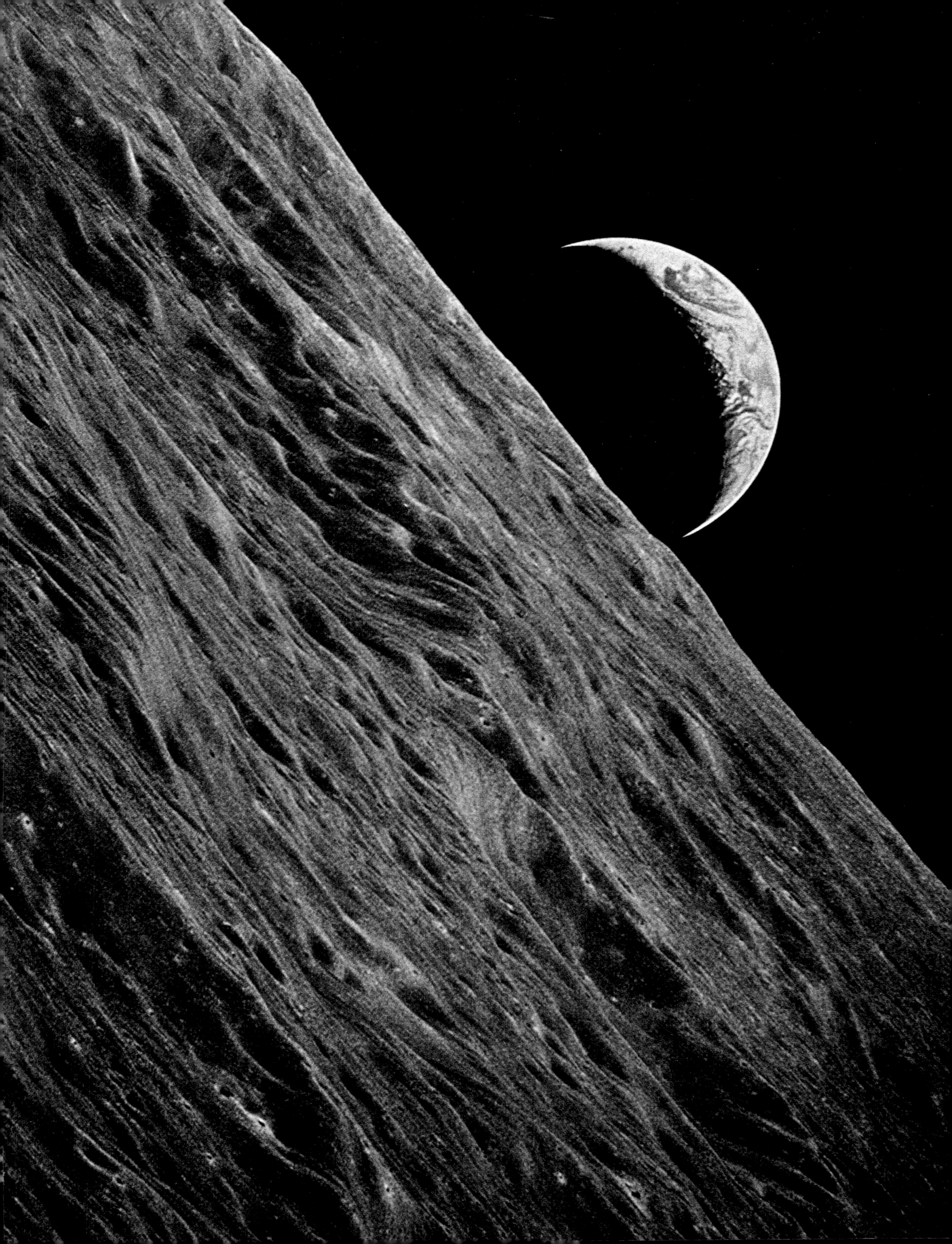

Iceland: Vatnajökull Glacier

The huge ice tongue of the Vatnajökull Glacier extends into the coastal region of southern Iceland. The bluish-black areas are crevasses, glacial debris and ash from previous volcanic eruptions. Filigreed areas at the bottom of the photograph were created by water melting from glaciers.

THE MACMILLAN WORLD ATLAS

MACMILLAN • USA

U.S.A.: New York City

The Greater New York area is one of the world's largest metropolitan areas. Between the Hudson River and the East River lies the borough of Manhattan with the green rectangle of famous Central Park. Brooklyn, the most populous borough, lies on the western tip of Long Island. Sandbars line the southern coast of Long Island.

"The world is a wonderful book, but it is only marginally useful to those who cannot read it."

- Carlo Goldoni

"We live in this world only as long as we love it."

- Rabindranath Tagore

The Earth is our home, both in the region where we happen to live and on the entire planet. We travel to Antarctica or Bali, have friends in Brisbane and Yokohama, place telephone calls to Johannesburg or perhaps even to Tierra del Fuego. Our stereo system was manufactured in Korea, our whiskies were distilled in Scotland or Kentucky. The planet is fast becoming a global village.

For millions of years humankind has been wandering across the face of the Earth, and today global travel has become a familiar feature of life. An increasingly large number of people are spending ever more time and money visiting foreign places. Three decades ago, only seventy million people were counted at international frontier crossings; that number has since increased sevenfold: the world has become mobile.

Modern communications technologies add another dimension to this mobility. An event happening right now in Beijing appears without delay on video screens around the world. No spectacular event can occur without immediately attracting the attention of the world community. Distances have become irrelevant as the continents seem to move closer together. And yet, far too much of the world still remains unknown and foreign to us. The vast expanses of Siberia and Australia, the island world of Oceania, the landscapes of central Africa, the far north and the extreme south of the two American continents: who can claim to have a clear, detailed mental image of these fascinating regions of our planet?

The *Macmillan World Atlas* is designed to meet the changing needs of a changing world. Although it follows in the tradition of Mercator and other cartographers, this new volume is a revolutionary innovation, a trailblazing geographic and cartographic databank. Its fundamental concept reflects two essential goals. First, it is a precise and detailed reference designed to meet the information needs of a contemporary people. It has been created with travelers, both business and leisure, in mind, and it also serves as an invaluable resource for families and students, politicians, scientists, and businesspeople. The maps in this volume have been drawn to depict the actual state of today's world with unprecedented fidelity.

But beyond all that, The *Macmillan World Atlas* hopes to communicate a dream and a fascination: the fascination of our wonderful blue spaceship, a place where life is precious and worthwhile, a threatened oasis whose continued survival depends upon the cooperation and commitment of people around the world.

This book is the creation of the distinguished Bertelsmann Cartographic Institute, which has invested many years and many millions of dollars to create a revolutionary digital cartographic database for a major new atlas series. The 80 to 100 staff members and their expert advisers who have spent years designing (and who continually update) the cartographic database are passionately committed to the goals that define this atlas program. Worldwide cooperation is the guiding principle in all their work. To give just two examples: Chinese geographers and cartographers at the University of Nanking designed the cartography of China: and former employees of Sojus Karta in Moscow helped create the maps of the Commonwealth of Independent States that were born after the collapse of the Soviet Union. These collaborations are all the more remarkable in view of the fact that mapmakers have always been strongly influenced by the complex interplays of military and political forces.

The worldview embodied by *The Macmillan World Atlas* provides other examples of cartographic collaboration as well. New techniques and innovations in cartography have been harnessed in a variety of ways. The revolutionary technique of computer cartography – all map designs were digitally scanned, and all individual map elements are stored in a central databank – permits rapid reaction to changes of every sort. This is a milestone on the path to creating a truly up-to-date cartography commensurate with the actual state of the world.

In creating *The Macmillan World Atlas,* some antiquated cartographic conventions have been abandoned, new methods of representation have been developed, and different informational features have been emphasized. The most obvious example of these improvements lies in the new, more realistic use of color. Subtle gradations of color represent fine distinctions in the world's ecological zones, which are depicted according to their particular climates and characteristic vegetation. Unlike the deserts and mountains in traditional atlases, where color is almost exclusively a function of elevation, the deserts in *The Macmillan World Atlas* are not green and mountains are not brown. Rather, coloration reflects more closely what you would see if you looked down at the Earth from an orbiting spaceship.

The inclusion of a detailed network of transportation arteries is another important feature, and one that will no doubt prove useful to leisure travelers and businesspeople alike. For the first time ever, *The Macmillan World Atlas* presents the world's entire continental network of roads and railways, complete with their exact routes, classifications and numbers. Emphasis has also been given to major cultural or natural sites that are likely to be of interest to tourists.

But perhaps the most important innovation of all has to do with the way we perceive the countries of the world in relation to one another. Previous atlases compel their readers to cope with maps whose scales vary from one page to the next. *The Macmillan World Atlas* puts an end to that by depicting our planet's land surfaces in a single, unified and detailed scale of 1:4.5 million. The scale is the same everywhere, from Nordkapp to Capetown, from Siberia to Australia and Oceania. In order to satisfy the desire for precise and detailed information, *The Macmillan World Atlas* also provides additional larger-scale maps depicting regions of particular interest to its primary audience: a detailed series of maps showing the United States and southern Canada in a scale of 1:2.25 million. As its users will quickly recognize, the policy of treating the continents and their countries with cartographic equality offers obvious practical advantages. Most of us grew up with atlases in which the map of England was nearly as big as the map of China and in which Europe was emphasized at the expense of marginally treated non-European continents. Cartographic misinformation has misled generations of atlas users into forming mistaken notions about the relative sizes of the world's nations and cultural regions.

To deepen our understanding of our home planet and its topographic structures, *The Macmillan World Atlas* offers much more than mere cartography. Selected satellite photographs at the beginning of the volume provide fascinating insights into the world's characteristic natural and cultural landscapes. These images also show the actual models which the map colorations endeavor to represent faithfully.

The Macmillan World Atlas is conceived to serve as the ideal tool for discriminating people with global perspectives in their professional work and personal lifestyles. The atlas sets new standards in graphic design, information density and practical usability. The foundation for this new worldview is an enlightened perspective on humankind's responsibility to the universe. This responsibility involves both an ecologically sensitive attitude and a respect for the fundamental equality of human rights throughout the world. What may seem like a utopia today can and must become a reality – step by step. We hope that the *The Macmillan World Atlas* will help to carry this message.

Table of Contents

Prologue

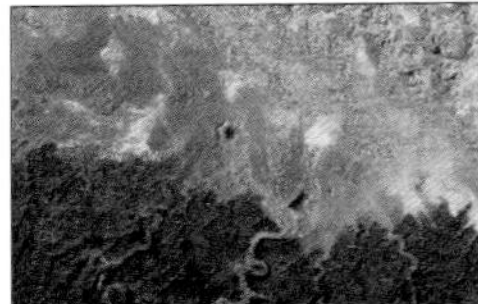

The Earth Seen from the Moon	I
Iceland: Vatnajökull Glacier	II
Title	III
U.S.A.: New York City	IV
Preface	V
Contents	VI – VII
Key to Maps: Continents	VIII – IX
Key to Maps: United States of America and Southern Canada	X
Map Samples	XI
Explanation of Map Symbols	XII – XV
U.S.A.: Mississippi Delta	XVI – XVII
Brazil: Amazon River	XVIII – XIX
Switzerland: Upper Rhône Valley	XX – XXI
Siberia / Russia: Taiga at the Ob River	XXII – XXIII
Sahara Desert / Algeria: Star Dunes	XXIV

The World

1 : 40,000,000

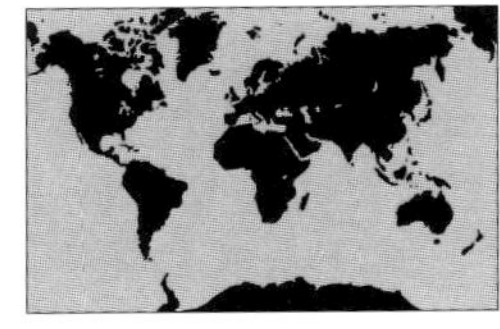

Introduction	1
Satellite Photograph, Key to Maps	2 – 3
North and Middle America	4
South America	5
Atlantic Ocean	6 – 7
Europe	8
Africa	9
Asia	10 – 11
Indian Ocean	12
Australia and Oceania	13
Pacific Ocean (1 : 50,000,000)	14 – 15
The Arctic • Antarctica (1 : 27,000,000)	16

North and Middle America

1 : 4,500,000

Introduction	17
Satellite Photograph, Key to Maps	18 – 19
Alaska	20 – 21
Aleutians	22 – 23
Canada: Arctic Islands	24 – 25
Greenland: Northern Region	26 – 27
Greenland: Southern Region	28 – 29
Canada: Barren Grounds	30 – 31
Canada: British Columbia, Alberta, Saskatchewan	32 – 33
Canada: Manitoba, Ontario	34 – 35
Canada: Labrador	36 – 37
Canada: Atlantic Provinces	38 – 39
U.S.A.: Pacific States	40 – 41
U.S.A.: Central States, North	42 – 43
U.S.A.: Central States, South	44 – 45
U.S.A.: Great Lakes, Northeastern States	46 – 47
U.S.A.: Southeastern States (Inset: Hawaii)	48 – 49
Mexico: Northern Region	50 – 51
Mexico: Southern Region • Central America	52 – 53
Greater Antilles	54 – 55
Lesser Antilles	56

South America

1 : 4,500,000

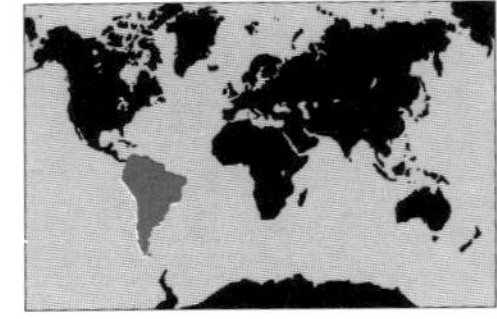

Introduction	57
Satellite Photograph, Key to Maps	58 – 59
Colombia • Venezuela	60 – 61
Guyana • Suriname • Brazil: Northern Region	62 – 63
Ecuador • Peru (Inset: Galápagos Islands)	64 – 65
Brazil: Amazonian Lowlands	66 – 67
Brazil: Northeastern Region	68 – 69
Bolivia • Pantanal	70 – 71
Brazil: Southeastern Region	72 – 73
Brazil: Southern Region • Uruguay	74 – 75
Argentina and Chile: Northern Regions	76 – 77
Argentina and Chile: Central Regions (Inset: Falkland Islands • South Georgia)	78 – 79
Argentina and Chile: Southern Regions	80

Europe

1 : 4,500,000

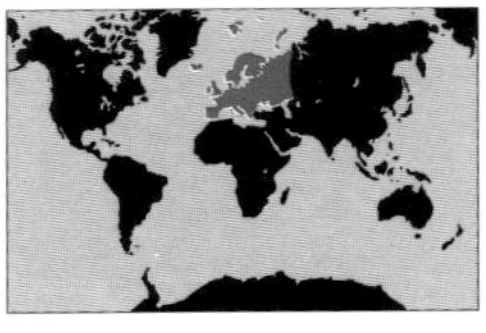

Introduction	81
Satellite Photograph, Key to Maps	82 – 83
Svalbard • Novaya Zemlya	84 – 85
Scandinavia (Inset: Iceland)	86 – 87
Finland • Northern Ural Mountains	88 – 89
Western Europe	90 – 91
Central Europe	92 – 93
Eastern Europe	94 – 95
Ural Mountains	96 – 97
Southwestern Europe	98 – 99
Southern Europe	100 – 101
Southeastern Europe	102 – 103
Caucasus	104

Asia

1 : 4,500,000

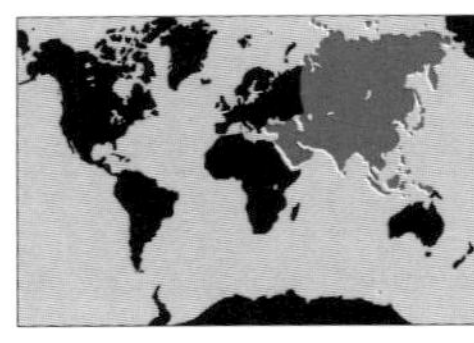

Introduction	105
Satellite Photograph, Key to Maps	106 – 107
Russia: West Siberian Plain, Northern Region	108 – 109
Russia: Central Siberian Plateau, Northern Region	110 – 111
Russia: Siberia, Northeastern Region	112 – 113
Russia: West Siberian Plain, Southern Region	114 – 115
Sayan Mountains • Lake Baikal	116 – 117
Transbaikal Region	118 – 119
Far East: Northern Region • Kamchatka	120 – 121
Far East: Southern Region • Sakhalin	122 – 123
Kazakhstan: The Steppe	124 – 125
Caspian Depression • Aral Sea	126 – 127
Near East	128 – 129

Arabian Peninsula: Northern Region	130 – 131
Arabian Peninsula: Southern Region	132 – 133
Persian Gulf • Plateau of Iran	134 – 135
Central Asia	136 – 137
India: Northwestern Region • Indus Valley	138 – 139
India: Southern Region • Maldives • Sri Lanka	140 – 141
India: Northeastern Region • Bangladesh	142 – 143
Tibet	144 – 145
Sinkiang	146 – 147
Mongolia	148 – 149
Manchuria • Korea	150 – 151
Japan	152 – 153
China: Northern Region	154 – 155
China: Southern Region	156 – 157
Thailand • Cambodia	158 – 159
Philippines	160 – 161
Malaysia • Sumatra	162 – 163
Borneo • Sulawesi	164 – 165
Moluccas • West Irian	166 – 167
Java • Lesser Sunda Islands	168

Australia and Oceania

1 : 4,500,000

Introduction	169
Satellite Photograph, Key to Maps	170 – 171
Australia: Northwestern Region	172 – 173
Australia: Northeastern Region	174 – 175
Australia: Southwestern Region	176 – 177
Australia: Eastern Region	178 – 179
Australia: Southeastern Region,Tasmania	180 – 181
New Zealand	182
Papua New Guinea	183
Solomon Islands • Vanuatu • Fiji • Samoa • Tonga	184

Africa

1 : 4,500,000

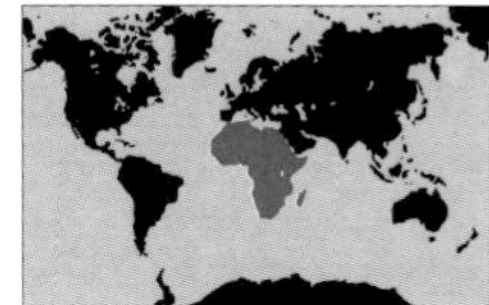

Introduction	185
Satellite Photograph, Key to Maps	186 – 187
Morocco • Canary Islands	188 – 189
Algeria • Tunisia	190 – 191
Libya	192 – 193
Egypt	194 – 195
Mauritania • Mali: Northern Region	196 – 197
Niger • Chad	198 – 199
Sudan: Northern Region • Eritrea	200 – 201
Upper Guinea	202 – 203
Ghana • Togo • Benin • Nigeria • Cameroon	204 – 205
Central African Republic • Sudan: Southern Region	206 – 207
Ethiopia • Somali Peninsula	208 – 209
Lower Guinea	210 – 211
East Africa: Northern Region	212 – 213
East Africa: Southern Region	214 – 215
Angola • Namibia: Northern Region	216 – 217
Zambia • Zimbabwe • Mozambique	218 – 219
South Africa	220 – 221
Madagascar • Comoros	222 – 223
Seychelles • Réunion • Mauritius	224

United States and Southern Canada

1 : 2,250,000

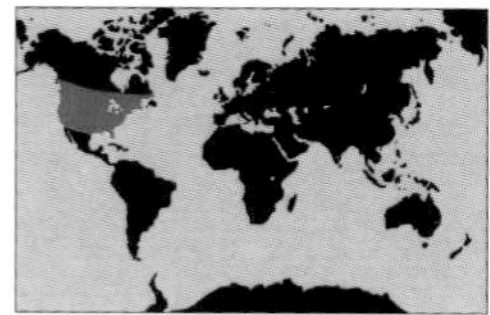

Introduction	225
Satellite Photograph, Key to Maps	226 – 227
British Columbia, Central	228 – 229
British Columbia, South	230 – 231
Alberta and Saskatchewan, South	232 – 233
Manitoba, South • Ontario, West .	234 – 235
Ontario, Central • Québec, Southwest	236 – 237
Ontario and Québec, South	238 – 239
Québec, Southeast • Atlantic Provinces, West	240 – 241
Atlantic Provinces, East	242 – 243
Washington • Oregon	244 – 245
California, North • Nevada	246 – 247
California, South	248 – 249
Idaho, North • Montana	250 – 251
Idaho, South • Wyoming	252 – 253
Utah • Colorado	254 – 255
Arizona • New Mexico	256 – 257
North Dakota	258 – 259
South Dakota	260 – 261
Nebraska • Kansas	262 – 263
Oklahoma • Texas, North	264 – 265
Texas, South	266 – 267
Texas, East • Louisiana • Mississippi	268 – 269
Minnesota • Wisconsin and Michigan, North	270 – 271
Michigan, South • Southern Great Lakes Region	272 – 273
Iowa • Missouri and Illinois, North • Indiana	274 – 275
Missouri, South • Arkansas • Kentucky • Tennessee	276 – 277
New York • Northeastern States	278 – 279
Ohio • Pennsylvania • West Virginia • Maryland • Delaware	280 – 281
West Virginia • Virginia • North Carolina	282 – 283
Alabama • Georgia • South Carolina	284 – 285
Florida (Inset: Puerto Rico, Virgin Islands)	286 – 287
Hawaii	288

Index

Abbreviations	289
Selected References	290 – 291
Index of Map Names	292 – 415
Contributors / Credits	416

Key to Maps: Continents

North and Middle America · 1: 4,500,000

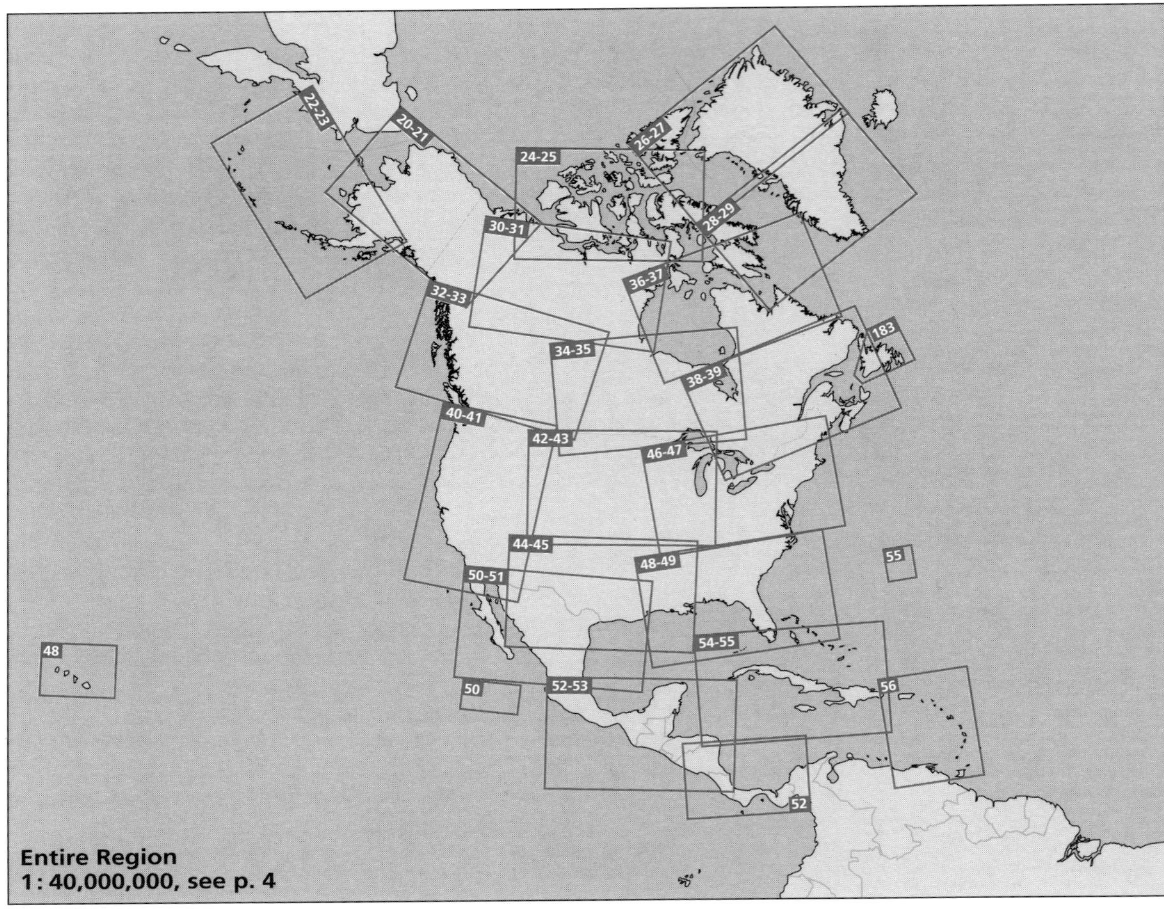

Europe · 1: 4,500,000

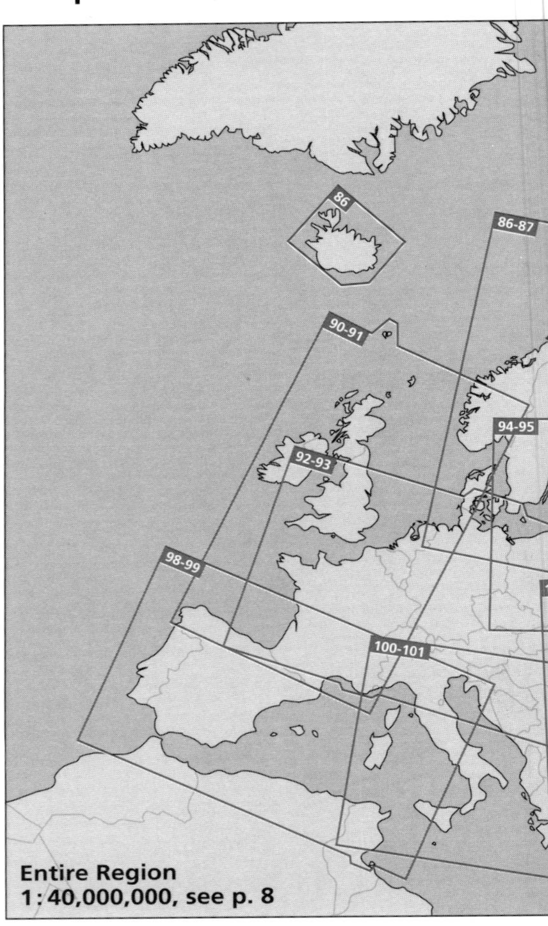

South America · 1: 4,500,000

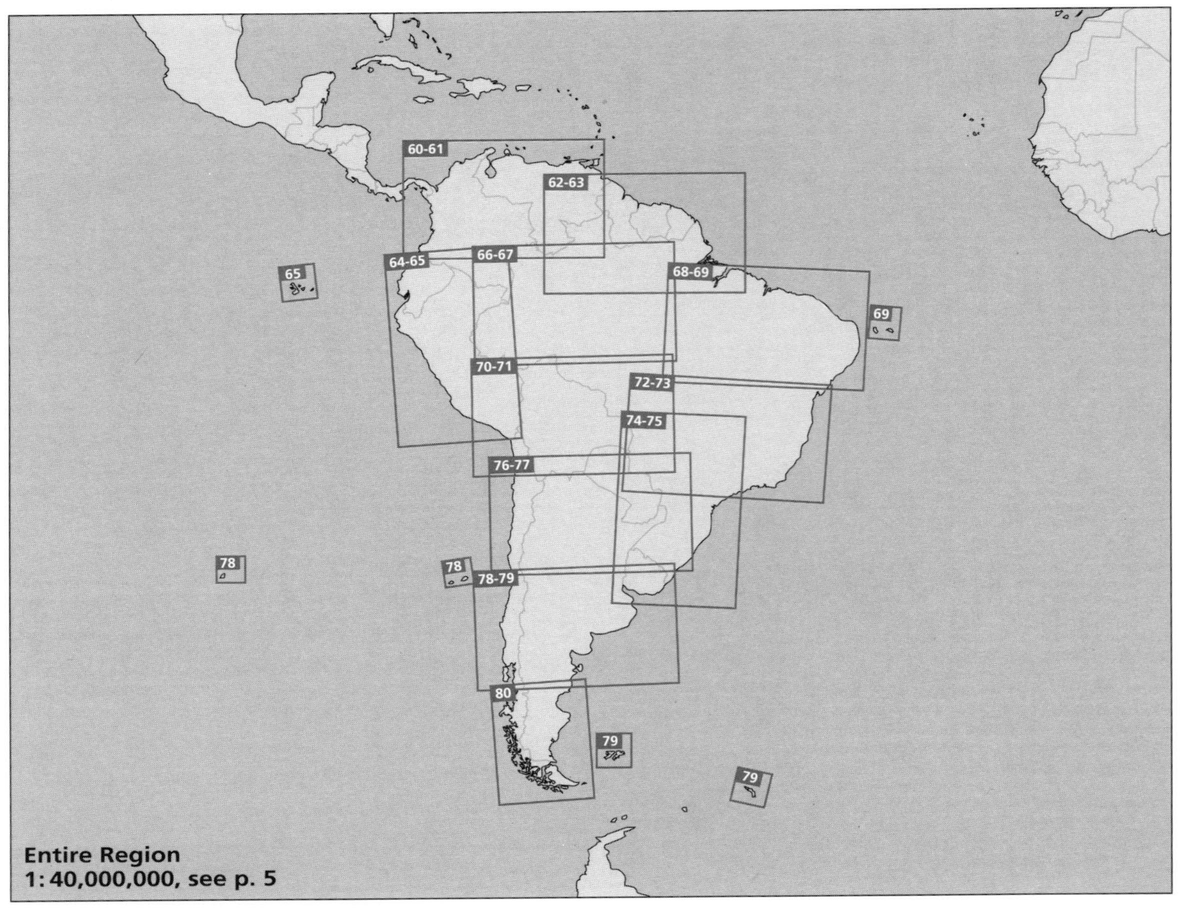

Asia · 1: 4,500,000

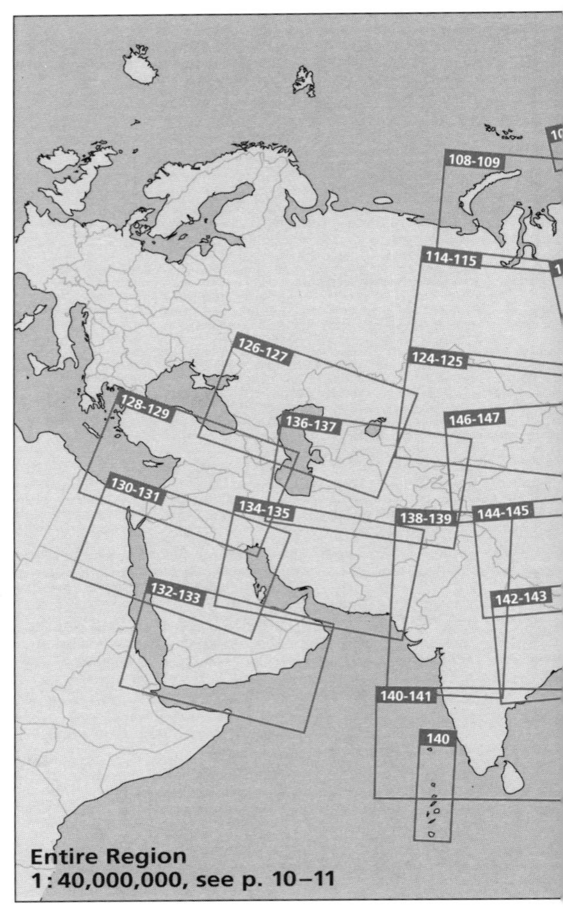

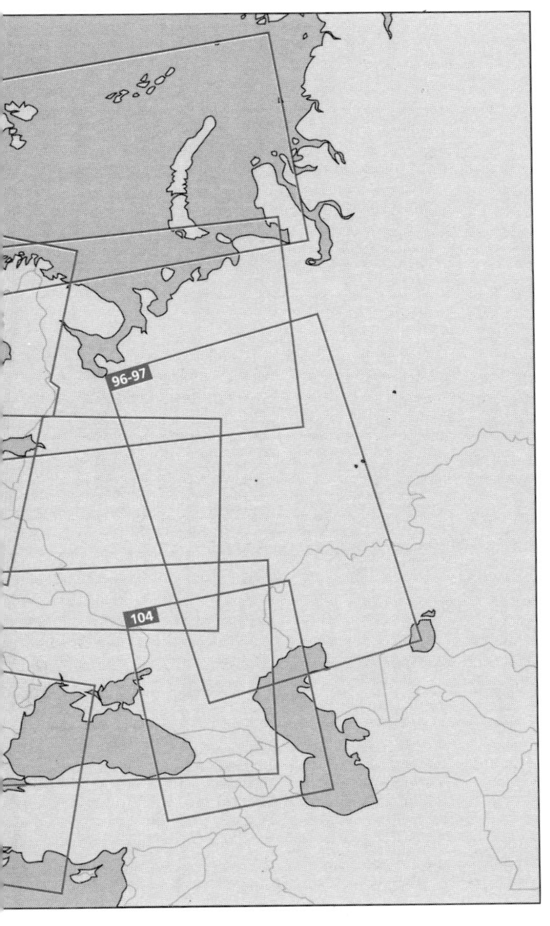

Australia and Oceania · 1:4,500,000

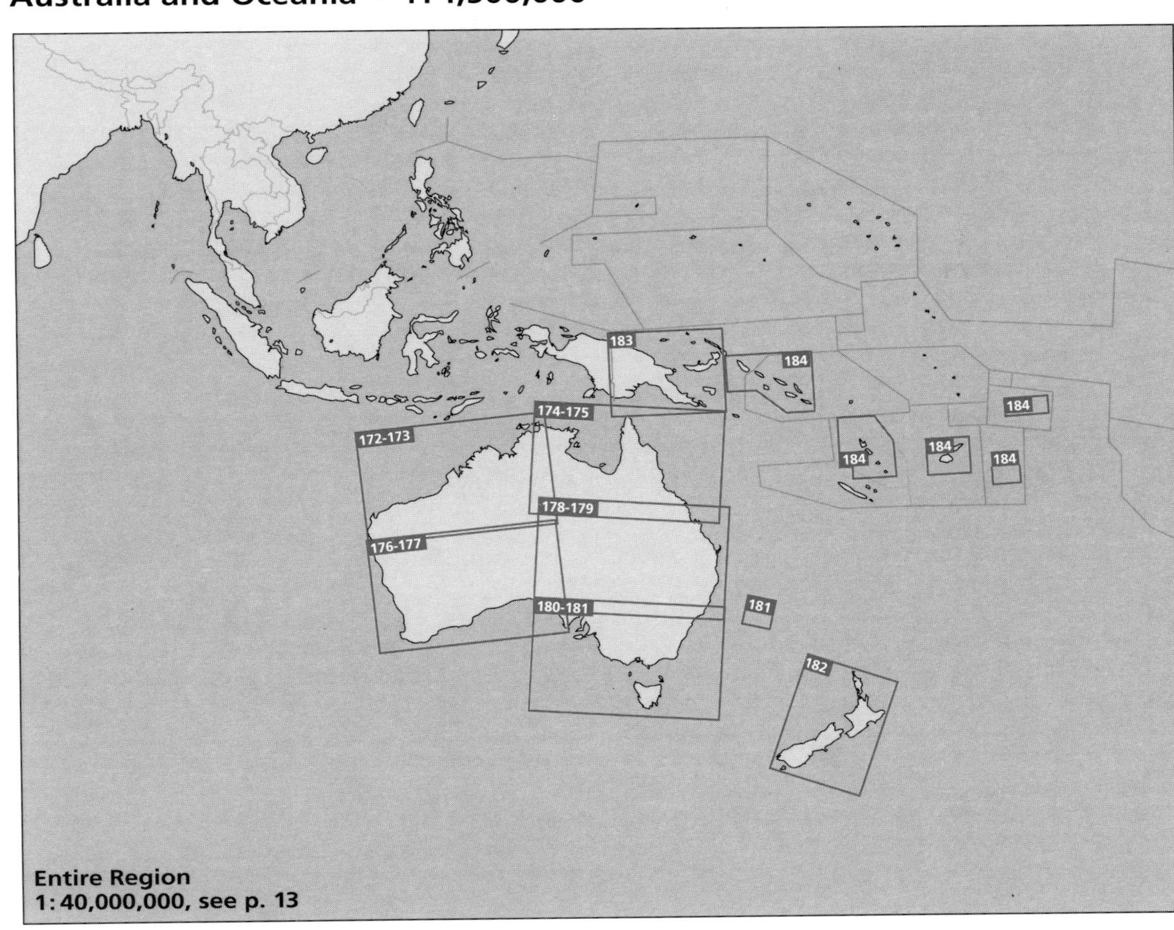

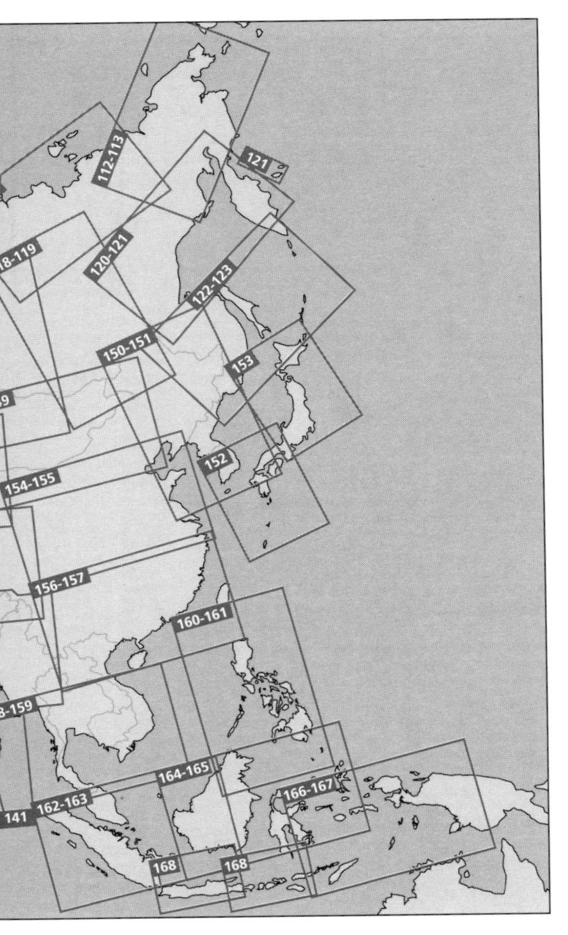

Africa · 1:4,500,000

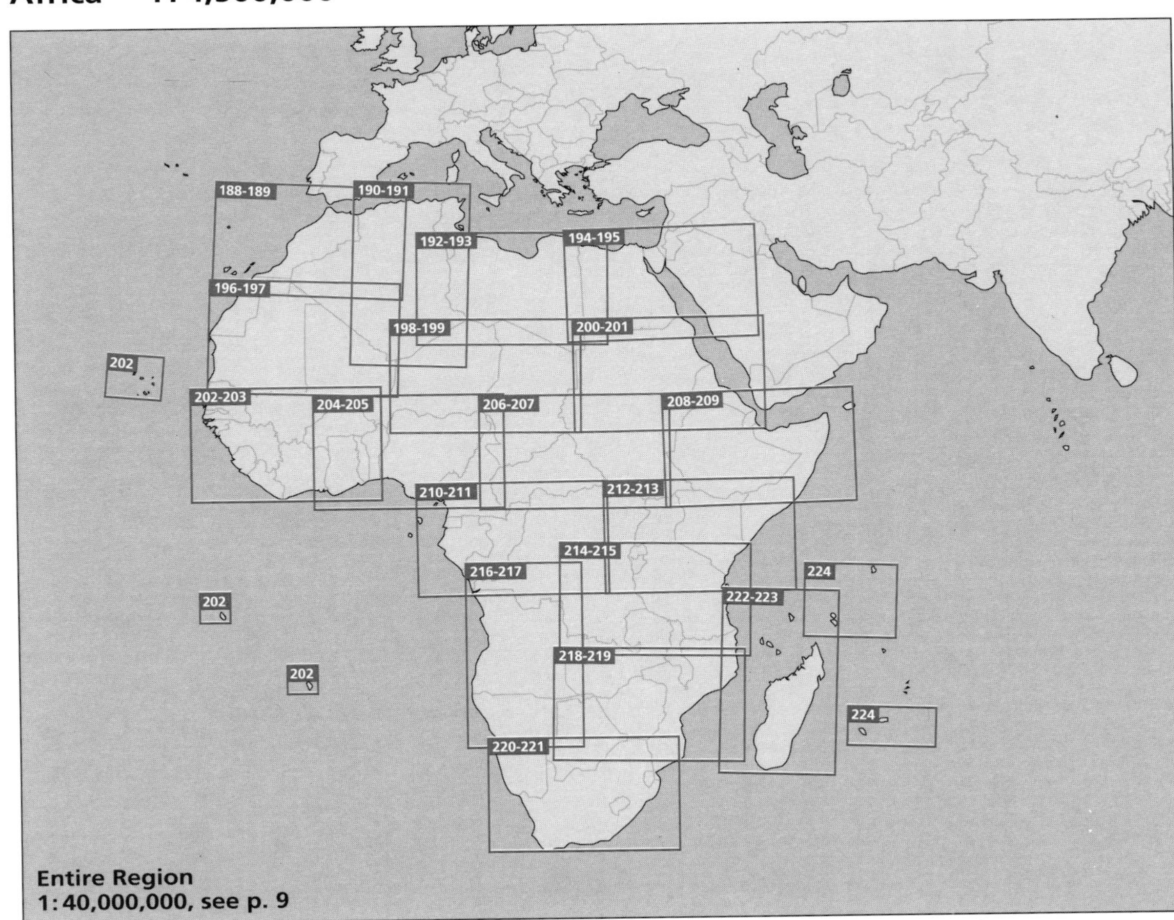

Key to Maps: United States of America and Southern Canada

United States of America and Southern Canada · 1:2,250,000

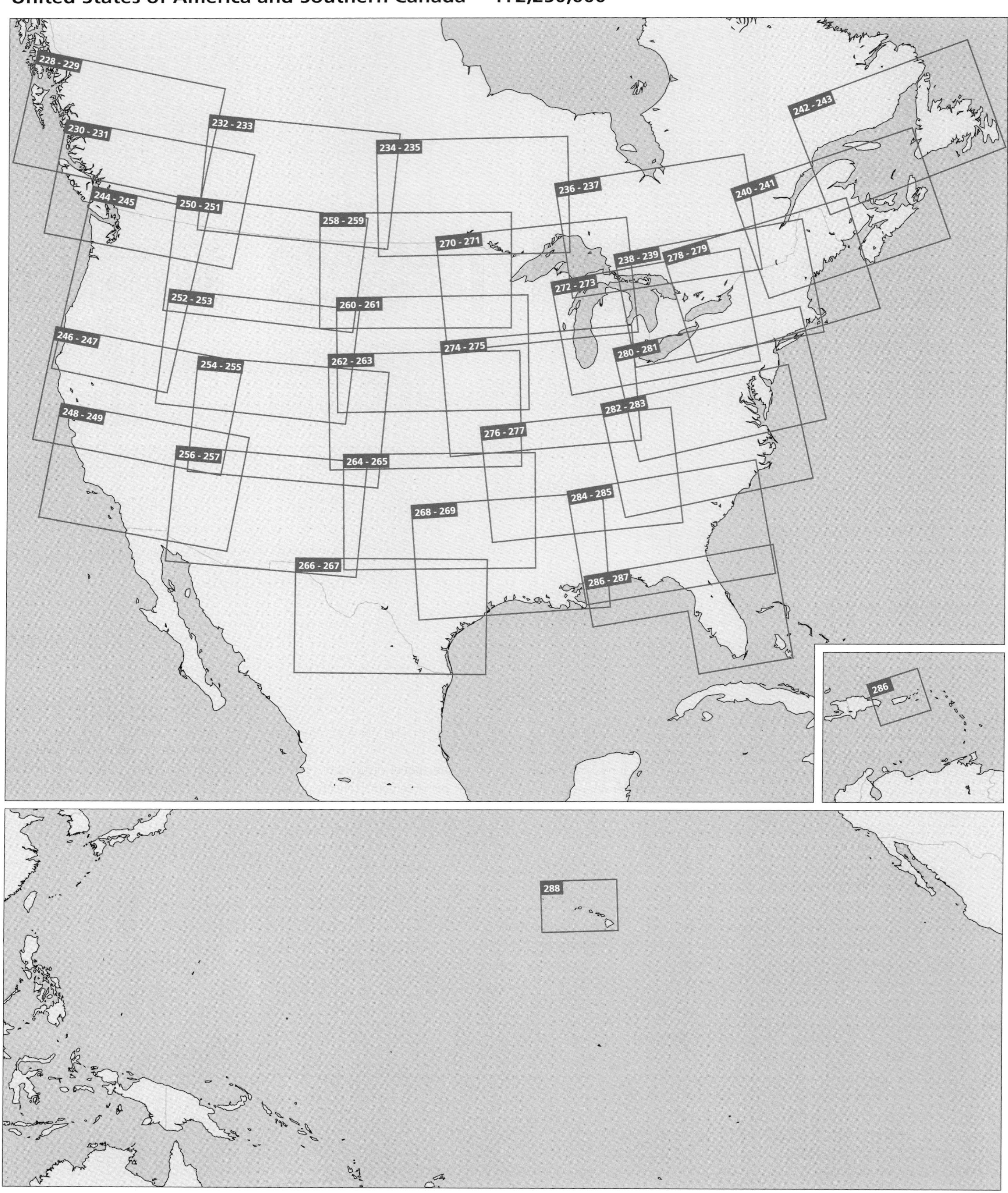

Map Samples

Satellite Imagery

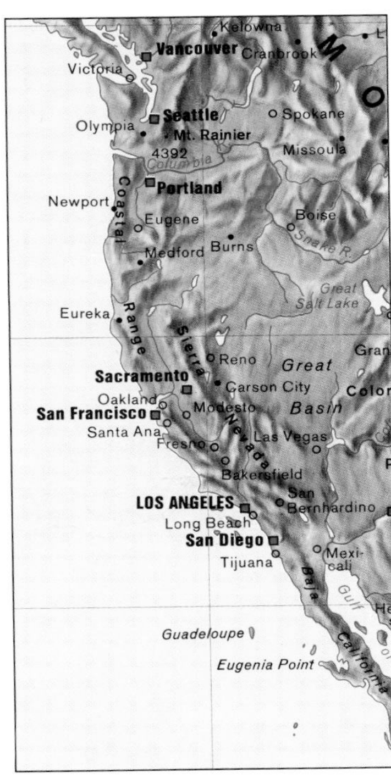

Scale 1 : 40,000,000

Scale 1 : 4,500,000

Scale 1 : 2,250,000

Space travel has provided us with a new image of the Earth. Earth-observation satellites like those in the LANDSAT series orbit the Earth at an altitude of approximately 400 miles (700 kilometers). Sensors on board these satellites detect electromagnetic radiation reflected by the Earth, then transmit this information as photographic data to a global network of ground stations. But to arrive at brilliant satellite images like those selected for inclusion in this book, photographic data received from satellites must first be enhanced in a variety of ways.

Computers help make the gradations of color in the satellite images faithful renditions of their counterparts in nature. Various computer-assisted combinations of individually received spectral bands are used to achieve this accuracy. Filtering and contrast manipulation further enhance the images. Favorable photographic conditions are essential: optimum sunlight, ideal climatic conditions, and a minimum of cloud cover.

Of course, satellite photographs are no substitute for maps, but their multifaceted images do serve as a valuable complement to the cartographic information expressed in maps. Their brilliance is fascinating, and they provide views of the Earth from new and fantastic perspectives.

Space probes can photograph the whole Earth in its entirety as a heavenly body. Satellites in orbit closer to the Earth can photograph areas the size of continents or subcontinents. The view from an airplane reveals individual landscapes. A map's scale expresses the distance between the Earth and an imaginary observer. It determines the extent and contents of the map.

The scale of 1:40,000,000 is suitable for representing the Earth as a whole. The world map shows the Earth's major structures, its division into oceans and landmasses, the continents and their relative positions.

The various colors on the continents indicate major zones of vegetation. Bluish violet and yellowish red represent cold and dry deserts, green tones stand for various kinds of plant life. Since vegetation is largely a function of climate, a bluish green color indicates both coniferous forests and the colder climate of higher latitudes. Deep green, on the other hand, represents tropical rain forests in the hot, humid climate near the equator.

Shadings depict major topographic features of the Earth's crust: chains of folded mountains, highlands and basins, lowlands and low-mountain regions.

The majority of maps in this book are drawn in the scale of 1:4,500,000. All continents are thoroughly depicted in this scale, with the exception of Antarctica and some of the world's smaller islands. Maps on individual pages show parts of the continents. Settlements, transportation routes and political boundaries of various kinds are clearly visible against a color-coded background denoting the various topographies, climates and vegetation zones.

The spatial distribution and extent of settlements reflects population density. The few, widely spaced urban settlements in sparsely settled regions contrast with the urban sprawl of more densely populated regions. Maps also show the density of transportation networks, the presence or absence of roads and the accessibility of various places, as well as the distances between major intersections and the locations of railroads and airports. Political boundaries indicate international frontiers and national administrative subdivisions.

The representation of cultural sights is more than just an aid to tourists and leisure travelers. These sites are often focal points of ethnocultural traditions, important places of religious worship or national identity.

As a complement to the maps of the world and its continents, a special appendix provides maps depicting the United States and southern Canada in detailed scale of 1:2,250,000.

At this scale, maps show a particular wealth of detail. It is possible to distinguish individual forms within the network of rivers and lakes, as well as within the represented relief. These forms range from gently undulating moraine landscapes and lakelands to resurgence valleys in low mountain ranges or individual mountain ranges among high mountains, including their degree of glaciation. The representation of traffic networks shows similar detail. These maps clearly portray the adaptation of towns to the relief or the relationship between their location and other topographic features such as rivers emerging from mountains or mouths of rivers or ocean bays. They also indicate how far cities extend their developed land into the surrounding region. The larger scale permits a greater degree of precision, for example, in the positioning of the numerous topographic map symbols. Other advantages of this scale are the improved definition of locations and greater precision for measuring distances. Large-scale maps are useful for the planning of itineraries.

Explanation of Map Symbols Physical Aspects of the Earth

The Ocean

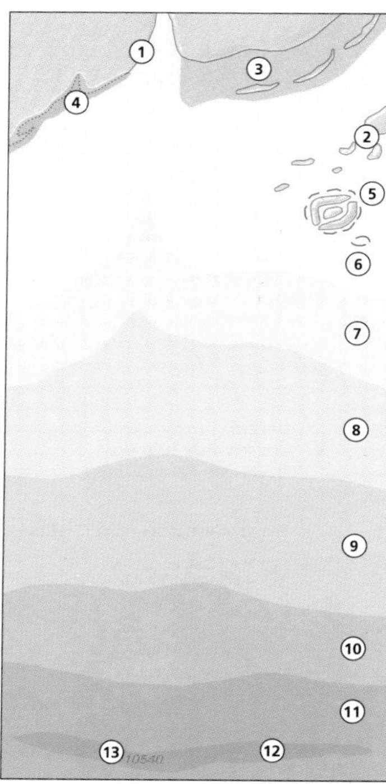

① Coastline, shoreline
② Island(s), archipelago
③ Tidal flat
④ Mangrove coast
⑤ Coral reef

Bathymetric Tints

⑥ 0 – 200 meters
⑦ 200 – 2,000 meters
⑧ 2000 – 4,000 meters
⑨ 4000 – 6,000 meters
⑩ 6000 – 8,000 meters
⑪ 8000 – 10,000 meters
⑫ Deeper than 10,000 meters
⑬ Water depth in meters

Coastlines are drawn with detail and precision in this atlas. As tides ebb and flow, certain sections of coast alternately belong to the mainland and the ocean. This is especially true of tidal flats and mangrove coasts, both of which are specially labeled on the maps.

Coral reefs in tropical oceans are remarkable features. Because of their low tolerance for changes in water temperature, salinity and deterioration in water quality, coral reefs are sensitive indicators of the quality of marine ecosystems.

Ocean depths are represented by bathymetric tints. The epicontinental shelf seas, which attain depths of 656 feet (200 m), are particularly important both politically and economically. During earlier geologic eras, some parts of these zones were dry land. Also known as continental shelves, these regions are rich in economically important resources. The ocean's deepest points are found near the edges of the continents. These deep sea trenches are depicted on individual map pages. Trenches are critical interfaces in the ongoing process of continental genesis and disappearance.

Hydrographic Features

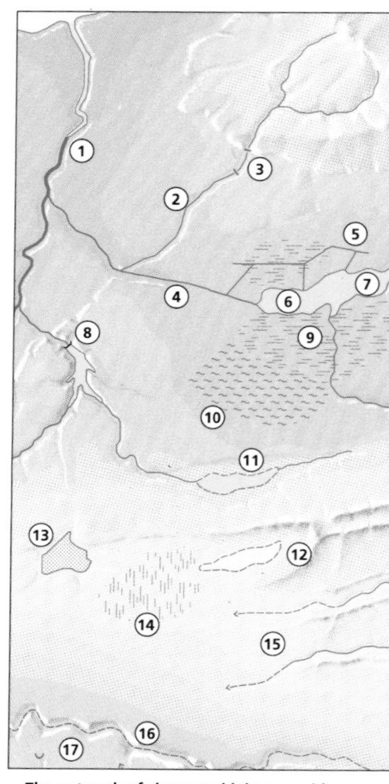

① Perennial stream or river
② Tributary river with headwaters
③ Waterfall, rapids
④ Navigable canal
⑤ Non-navigable canal
⑥ Freshwater lake
⑦ Elevation of lake above sea level and depth of Lake
⑧ Reservoir with dam
⑨ Marsh, moor
⑩ Flood plain
⑪ Lake with variable shoreline

Mostly in Arid Regions

⑫ Seasonal lake
⑬ Salt lake
⑭ Salt swamp
⑮ River, drying up
⑯ Intermittent stream (wadi, arroyo)
⑰ Spring, well

The network of rivers and lakes provides a natural framework for the structures created by human beings in the process of developing and cultivating the land. Rivers and their mouths, bays and lake shores are preferred sites for human settlements. Rivers provide transportation routes, a source of hydroelectric power and water for irrigation. Above all, they supply us with our most basic need - potable water.

The maps depict the catchment areas of larger rivers with the treelike branching of their tributaries. Line thicknesses used in drawing the rivers correspond to their various sizes and to the hierarchy of main artery, major tributaries and headwaters. The paths of the blue lines represent the predominant characteristics of each natural watercourse with its meanders, branches, lakelike widenings and oxbows, as well as the comparatively rigid course of artificial waterways (canals). Agricultural and recreational uses are indicated by reservoirs and dams. The network of rivers and lakes reflects the world's gradient of water resources from abundance to aridity.

Glaciation

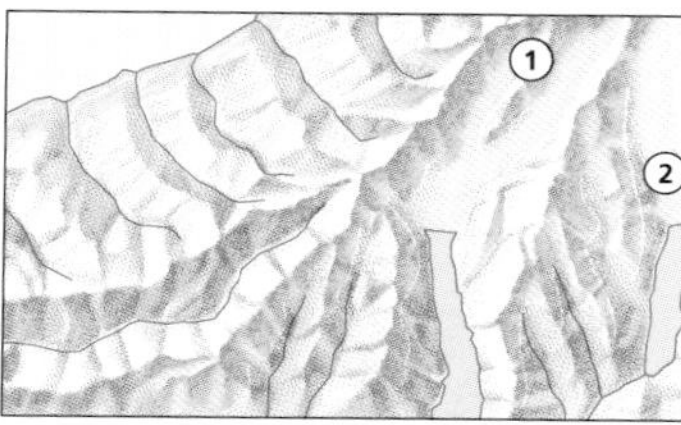

① Glacier in high-mountain range
② Glacial tongue

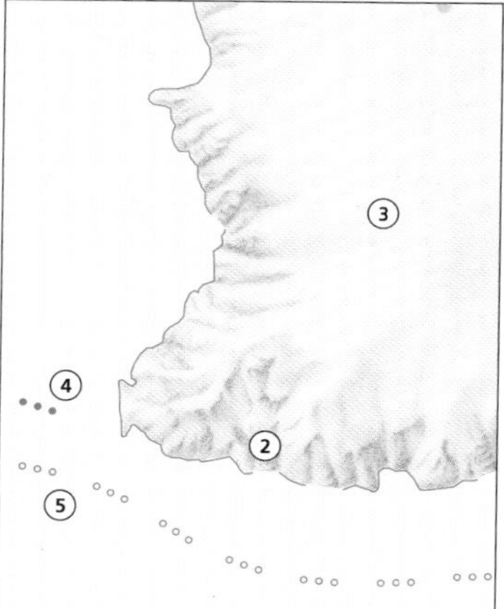

③ Continental ice sheet, icecap
④ Mean pack ice limit in summer
⑤ Mean pack ice limit in winter

The most recent ice age came to an end about 10,000 years ago. Its traces are still visible on roughly one-third of the Earth's landmasses, 11 percent of which are still covered by ice. The depiction of glaciers in the maps shows the worldwide distribution of these icy deserts. Continental ice sheets occupy by far the largest area, covering all of Antarctica and Greenland with sheets of ice as much as 10,000 feet (3,000 m) thick. Extensive surfaces of ocean, especially around the North Pole, are covered by sea or pack ice, and shelf ice is distributed along the edge of the Antarctic ice sheet. Alpine glaciers cover only a relatively insignificant 1 percent of the landmasses.

Glaciers are almost always in motion, usually at a very slow pace. Glacial tongues tend to move more rapidly. Sometimes reaching lengths of more than 125 miles (200 km), these tongues of ice stretch from continental glaciers to the ocean, where they calve icebergs. Glacial tongues are often the most impressive features of alpine glaciers; larger examples of these ice tongues are shown on the maps.

The Topography of the Earth's Surface

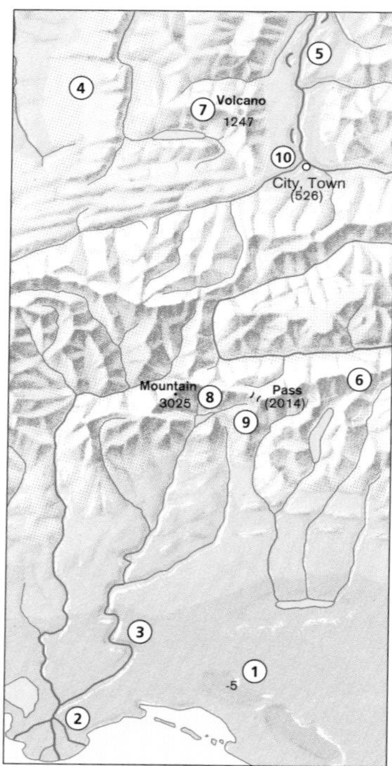

① Depressed region (land below sea level with depth in meters below sea level)
② River delta
③ Plain with depressed river valley
④ Hill country and highlands
⑤ Rift valley
⑥ Mountain range
⑦ Active volcano
⑧ Mountain (with elevation)
⑨ Pass (with elevation)
⑩ Approximate elevation of a city above sea level

Representing the third dimension – the topographic relief of the Earth's surface – is a special challenge for cartographers. The maps in this atlas derive their extraordinary plasticity from "relief shading." Gradations from pale to dark on the two-dimensional surface of the page help users visualize the Earth's actual three-dimensional topography. This impression is quantified with precise information about the elevations above sea level of mountains, passes and major cities.

The network of lakes and rivers is the counterpart to the relief depicted on the map. Waterways mark the locations of valleys that divide the topography. These two phenomena combine to provide an expressive picture of the major geographic regions and their underlying tectonic structures.

Particularly clear examples include the Great Rift Valley (which runs from the Near East to southern East Africa), the gigantic basins and high plateaus of central Asia (surrounded by the world's highest mountains), the generously watered lowlands of North and South America, and the mighty ranges of corrugated mountains that form the Andes.

The Biosphere: Continental Ecological Zones

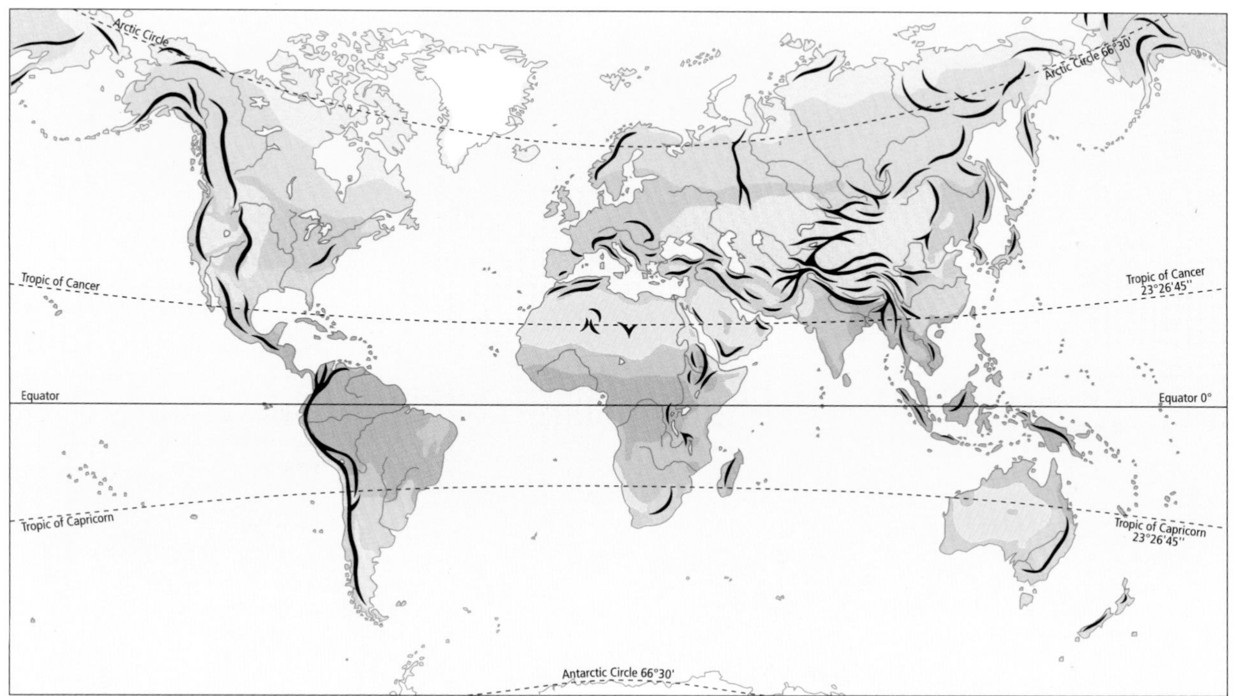

Tropics

I — Perennially humid climates
Tropical rain forest, moist savanna

II — Moist summer climates
Moist and dry savannas, deciduous forests

Subtropics

III — Subtropical-tropical semidesert and desert climates
Thorny scrub, desert

IV — Summer-humid to perennially moist climates
Monsoon forest, shrubs

V — Mediterranean climates with dry summers and moist winters
Shrubs, broadleaved evergreen forests

Temperature zones (middle latitudes)

VI — Winter-cold steppes, semidesert and desert climates
Grasslands (steppe, prairie), desert

VII — Maritime to continental moist climates
Broadleaved deciduous forests, mixed forests

Boreal zone

VIII — Taiga (needleleaved evergreen forests)

Polar and subpolar zone

IX — a: continental ice, ice cap
b: tundra (lichens, mosses, dwarf shrubs)

High Mountains

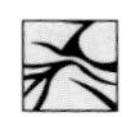
Vertical arrangement of plant communities by altitude

Macroclimates are among the most significant of the many factors affecting the distribution of life on earth. Macroclimates influence soil formation and help shape surface topography, as well as affecting plant growth and animal communities, which in turn determine the suitability of a given geographic region for human habitation. All of these biotic and abiotic factors combine to create a complex web in which each factor influences the others in a variety of ways.

Based on climatic conditions and on the prevailling plant communities determined by those conditions, the earth's landmasses can be subdivided into various habitats and ecozones. The boundaries between these zones, however, are not sharply defined. Instead, each zone emanates from a central region with characteristics typical of that zone, makes a transition across a boundary belt, and then more or less gradually changes into the adjacent landscape zone.

Although the limits of continental ecozones generally correspond to latitude, these zones exhibit two important asymmetries: regions of winter rainfall (Mediterranean climate) occur only along the western edges of the continents; regions with moist summers (or perennially moist tropics) are located exclusively on the eastern edges (so-called "Shanghai climates").

Trees in Eurasia and America cannot grow beyond about 70 degrees of latitude; in South America tree-line occurs at 57 degrees, in New Zealand and Oceania at 48 degrees. The boreal or "northern" band of coniferous forests is entirely absent in the Southern Hemisphere because of the relatively limited extent of land area and the associated dominance of the ocean.

Arrangement of Ecological Zones by Altitude

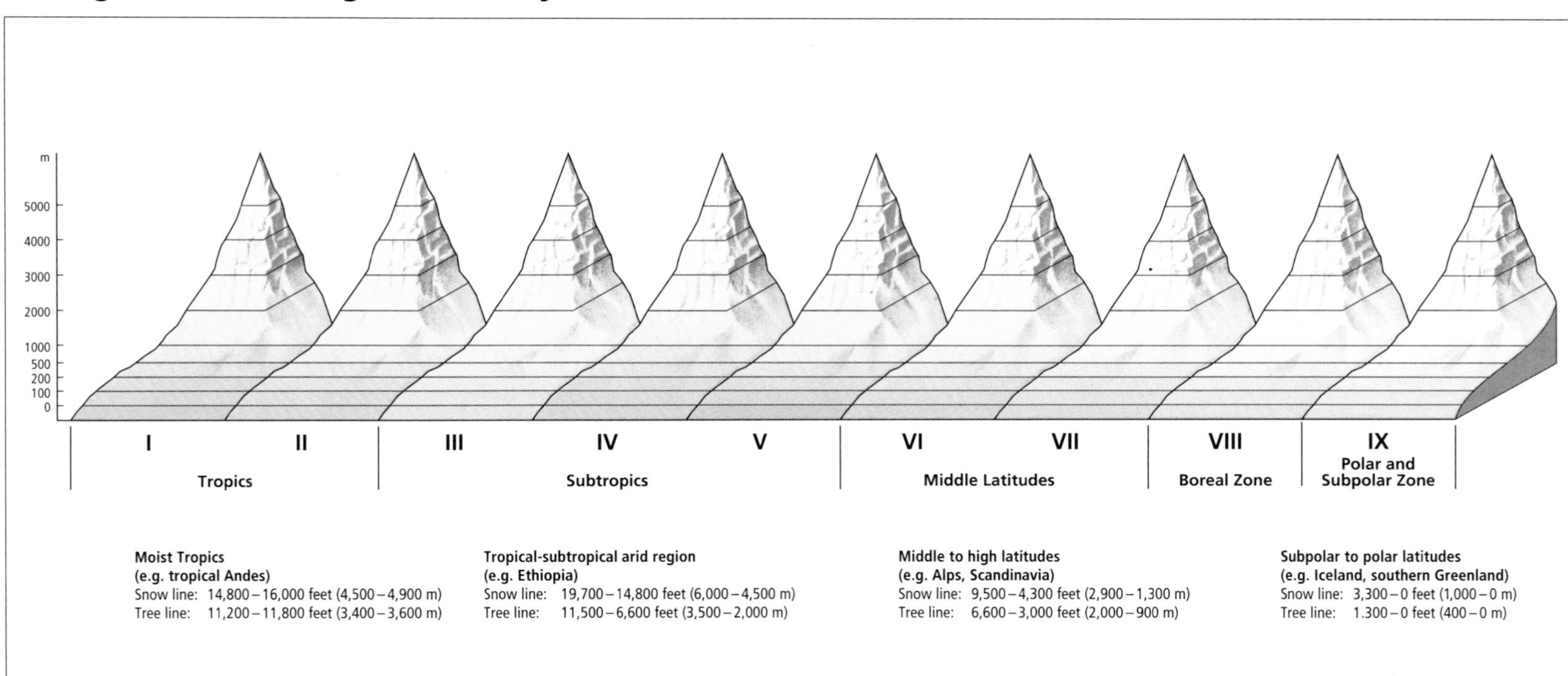

An essential feature of geographic landscapes is their three-dimensional structure. The maps in this atlas provide clearly legible depictions of heights and depths on the face of the Earth. The arrangement of ecological zones is largely dependent upon latitude. This pattern, however, is overlaid by mountain ranges, which cut across latitudinally oriented climatic zones to create their own ecosystems where altitude creates characteristic ecological arrangements. A visible expression of the fact that biological conditions vary with altitude is the vertical arrangement of typical plant communities: generally forest (grassland) – meadows – cliffs (or talus) – ice (or glacier). This arrangement also creates characteristic ecological boundary lines: above, the tree line and the (climatic) snow line; and in arid regions, the lower tree line as well.

Elevations show typical climatic characteristics depending on a mountain range's location in the overall pattern of global climatic zones. Tropical mountains, for example, experience the same diurnal climatic variations typical of their neighboring lowlands.

The upper tree line in mountainous regions is caused by the lack of adequate warmth. The lower tree line found in arid regions is related to the lack of adequate moisture. This combination restricts the growth of forests in arid regions to more or less wide bands along the slopes of mountains.

Where a lower tree line is now found in humid high mountain regions, or where the band of forest is entirely absent in certain places, the causes of this deforestation are likely to be manmade.

Forests in mountainous regions provide absolutely essential protection against avalanches and slope erosion.

The cultivation of crops in mountainous regions is likewise limited by prevailing climatic factors which, in turn, are primarily a function of elevation. In the Andes, for example, grains cannot be cultivated above 5,000 feet (1,500 m), although in the tropical Andes millet can be grown at elevations as high as 14,400 feet (4,400 m). With the exception of mining camps and settlements of shepherds at still higher elevations, these heights mark the upper limits of permanent human settlement.

Explanation of Map Symbols Manmade Features on Earth

The Map Margins

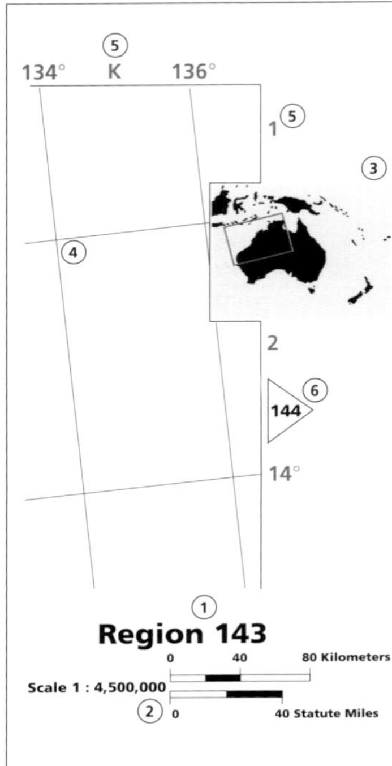

① Page number and short title

② Numeric and graphic map scales (scales in kilometers and miles)

③ Locator map showing the position and extent of continental area covered by that particular map page

④ Map grid (graticule) and its designation

.0 degrees longitude (Meridian of Greenwich) = Gr.

Longitude 180 degrees to 1 degree west of Gr. | Longitude 1 degree to 180 degrees east of Gr.

Latitude 1 degree to 90 degrees north of the equator | Latitude 1 degree to 90 degrees north of the equator

Equator 0 degrees — **Equator 0 degrees**

Latitude 1 degree to 90 degrees south of the Equator | Latitude 1 degree to 90 degrees south of the Equator

Longitude 180 degrees to 1 degree west of Gr. | Longitude 1 degree to 180 degrees east of Gr.

0 degrees longitude of Greenwich = Gr.

⑤ Grid search key as specified for each index entry: Letters at top/bottom
Numbers at left/right with graticule as searching grid

⑥ Page number of adjacent map page

Along with the short title and the page number, further aid in using the atlas is provided by the map overviews in the preface and by the locator maps at the beginning of each series of maps of individual continents. The number inside a small triangle on each map indicates the page where a map of the adjacent region can be found.

A locator map at the top right-hand corner of each double-page spread shows the area within the particular continent depicted by that particular map page. The scale notations in the lower margin are essential for determining geographic distances. They express the relationship between a given distance on the map and a corresponding distance in the real world.

For centuries, the degree-calibrated latitude and longitude grid system has been used to define locations and plot courses on the face of the globe. The red letters along the top and bottom, together with the red numbers along the left and right margins, identify individual fields within the blue search grid.

Settlements and Transportation Routes

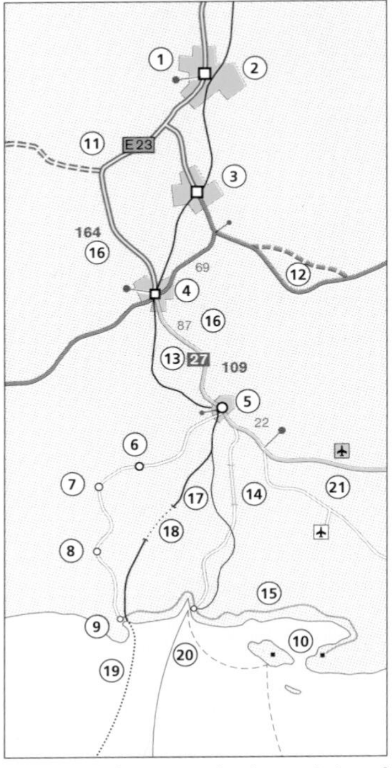

Town Symbols

① Urban area (normally surrounding cities with populations over 100,000)

② Population over 5 million

③ 1,000,000 – 5,000,000

④ 500,000 – 1,000,000

⑤ 100,000 – 500,000

⑥ 50,000 – 100,000

⑦ 10,000 – 50,000

⑧ 5,000 – 10,000

⑨ Population less than 5,000

⑩ Settlement, hamlet, research station (in remote areas often seasonally inhabited only)

Transportation Routes

⑪ Superhighway, four or more lanes, with number in blue

⑫ Highway under construction

⑬ Main road with number

⑭ Other road – road tunnel

⑮ Unpaved road, track

⑯ Distance in kilometers

⑰ Railway: main track – other track

⑱ Railway tunnel

⑲ Railway ferry

⑳ Car ferry – shipping line

㉑ International airport
Domestic airport

Town symbols correspond to the populations of their respective places. The density of these symbols on the map combines with their relative values to indicate a region's population density and settlement structure (urban area or smaller, equally distributed towns).

The representation of urban areas sheds light on the increasing concentration of humanity in major metropolitan areas. According to UNESCO, by the year 2000 approximately half of the world's population will live in cities occupying only about four percent of the Earth's total land area.

In the depiction of transportation routes, special emphasis has been given to the representation of continental road networks. This corresponds to the importance of such networks on the threshold of the 21st century. Transportation of economically important goods, tourism, and the migrations of people searching for work or fleeing disasters all take place primarily over roads. These routes have been classified and numbered according to their relative importance. Distance specifications help map users make accurate calculations of distances.

Political and Other Boundaries

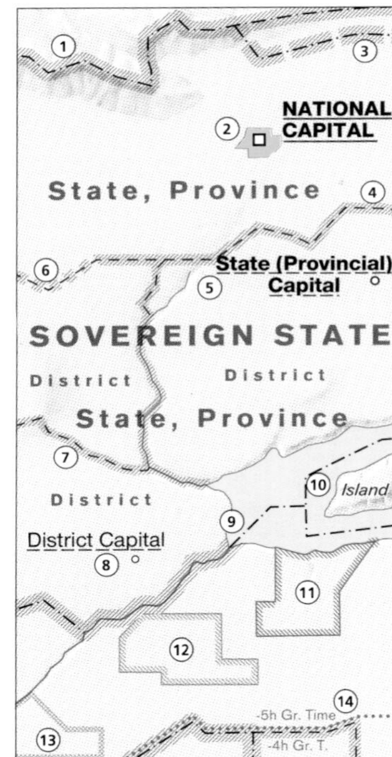

① International boundary

② Capital of a sovereign state

③ Disputed international boundary

④ 1st-order administrative boundary (e.g. region, state, autonomous region, province)

⑤ Capital city (1st-order administrative seat)

⑥ Disputed 1st-order administrative boundary

⑦ 2nd-order administrative boundary (e.g. region, area, province, country)

⑧ 2nd-order administrative seat

⑨ Boundary along watercourses or across bodies of water

⑩ Dependent region and specification of nation with jurisdiction

⑪ National park, national monument

⑫ Reservation

⑬ Restricted area

⑭ Boundary of a time zone with difference between local time and Greenwich Mean Time (GMT)

The documentation of territorial possessions was one of the reasons maps were invented. Maps play a central political role in border disputes and are an indispensable aid in interpreting or representing spatially related statistical data. The vast majority of statistical studies are based on national units or on regions within nations. Regardless of whether population distribution, buying power or cancer-incidence rates are measured, maps are the most convincing method of visually presenting and interpreting data.

International boundaries occupy first place in the hierarchy of political boundaries. They are therefore clearly marked in this atlas. First-order administrative boundaries, which define the limits of the major administrative units within a nation, come next in rank. Secondary boundaries are drawn when their political status merits it, providing their average surface area permits graphic representation on the scale involved. The maps also show capital cities or administrative seats of the depicted administrative entities.

Places and Points of Interest

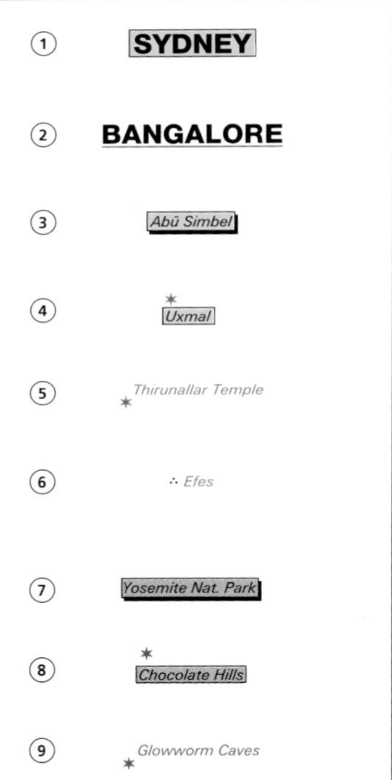

① Place of special interest

② Place of interest

③ UNESCO World Cultural Heritage Site

④ Cultural monument of special interest

⑤ Interesting cultural monument

⑥ Ancient monument or excavation

⑦ UNESCO World Natural Heritage Site

⑧ Natural monument of special interest

⑨ Interesting natural monument

The maps in this atlas provide the reader with a global view of the Blue Planet's most remarkable places and points of interest. These include exceptional monuments of natural or historico-cultural developments. Many of these places are important to national, ethnic or religious identity. This atlas places such sites in their geographical contexts. Graphic distinctions are made between natural and cultural monuments and according to their significance as magnets for tourism. UNESCO, a suborganization of the United Nations, has designated selected cultural sites and natural monuments worldwide as part of the "heritage of mankind" and urged their special preservation. These sites are specially marked in the atlas. The volume thus provides not only an informative manual for globetrotters with widely ranging interests, but also serves as a helpful supplement for students of travel and nature guides or of relevant artistic and historico-cultural literature.

Lettering of Cities and Towns

1	**TEHRĀN** **MONTEVIDEO**
2	**MIAMI** **LE HAVRE**
3	MANHATTAN VAIHINGEN
4	**Darwin** Thimphu
5	Gallipolis Grindelwald Laugarvatn
6	**BOLZANO BOZEN**
7	**HALAP (ALEPPO)**
8	**FRANKFURT am Main**

Type size indicates the relative importance and population of the town

1. City with a population over one million
2. Large city
3. Boroughs of large cities or of cities with populations over one million
4. Medium-sized city
5. Small town, rural community
6. Place names in region with two official languages
7. Place name, alternate or earlier form
8. Official supplement to a place name

This atlas includes carefully selected place names. Type size corresponds to the number of inhabitants; type face indicates the particular significance or function of the place. Place names in capital letters indicate large cities with more than 100,000 inhabitants.

Some names of important places, landscape features and bodies of water are written in the accepted American form, but as a general rule, place names are written in the official national spelling. In the case of countries having two official languages, both versions are given. This rule also applies to all other geographic names.

Letter-oriented transliteration or phonetic transcription is used to spell names from languages with non-Roman alphabets. Wherever possible, the atlas has followed accepted standards for such procedures.

Geographic names can offer valuable insights into historical developments and relationships.

Topographic Typography

1	**CHILE** **Réunion** **(France)**
2	*GOBI* *Cappadocia* *Kimberley*
3	**ANDES** Nan Ling Tibesti
4	Mt. McKinley 6194 Simplonpass (2005) Cabo de Hornos
5	*JAVA* *Galápagos Islands* *York Peninsula*
6	*PACIFIC OCEAN* *Finskij zaliv* *The Channel*
7	*Niger* *Panama Canal* *Taj Hu* *Niagara Falls*
8	*Yucatán Basin* *Cayman Trench*
9	Nazca Ridge Aves Ridge
10	*Aboriginal Land* *Military Training Area*
11	8848 *10540* 398

1. Nation, administrative unit, designation of sovereignty
2. Landscape, historical landscape
3. Mountains, mountain range, highland
4. Mountain with elevation above sea level, pass with elevation above sea level, cape
5. Island, archipelago, peninsula
6. Ocean, sea, gulf, bay, strait
7. River, canal, lake, waterfall
8. Undersea landscapes, trenches
9. Undersea mountains
10. Reservation, restricted areas
11. Elevation in meters above sea level
    Depth in oceans and lakes, elevation of lake surface

Lettering and typeface help explain the various features on a map. They also serve to structure geographic data according to significance and rank. These distinctions are reflected by the use of either all capital letters or mixtures of capital and lower-case letters, and by various type faces and sizes. Color also supports these distinctions: for example, rivers are labeled in blue, political units in gray, and sites of natural interest in green. Colored backgrounds or colored underlining indicates sites of interest to tourists.

Geographic names are one of the ways human beings express their possession of the land. People have given names to the remotest islands, to minor coves in the inhospitable Antarctic and to barely defined coastal promontories. The maps in this atlas, as in any other atlas, can include only the most important of these geographic names. All of them are listed in alphabetical order in the index of geographic names, together with search-grid designations that make it easy to pinpoint them on individual maps.

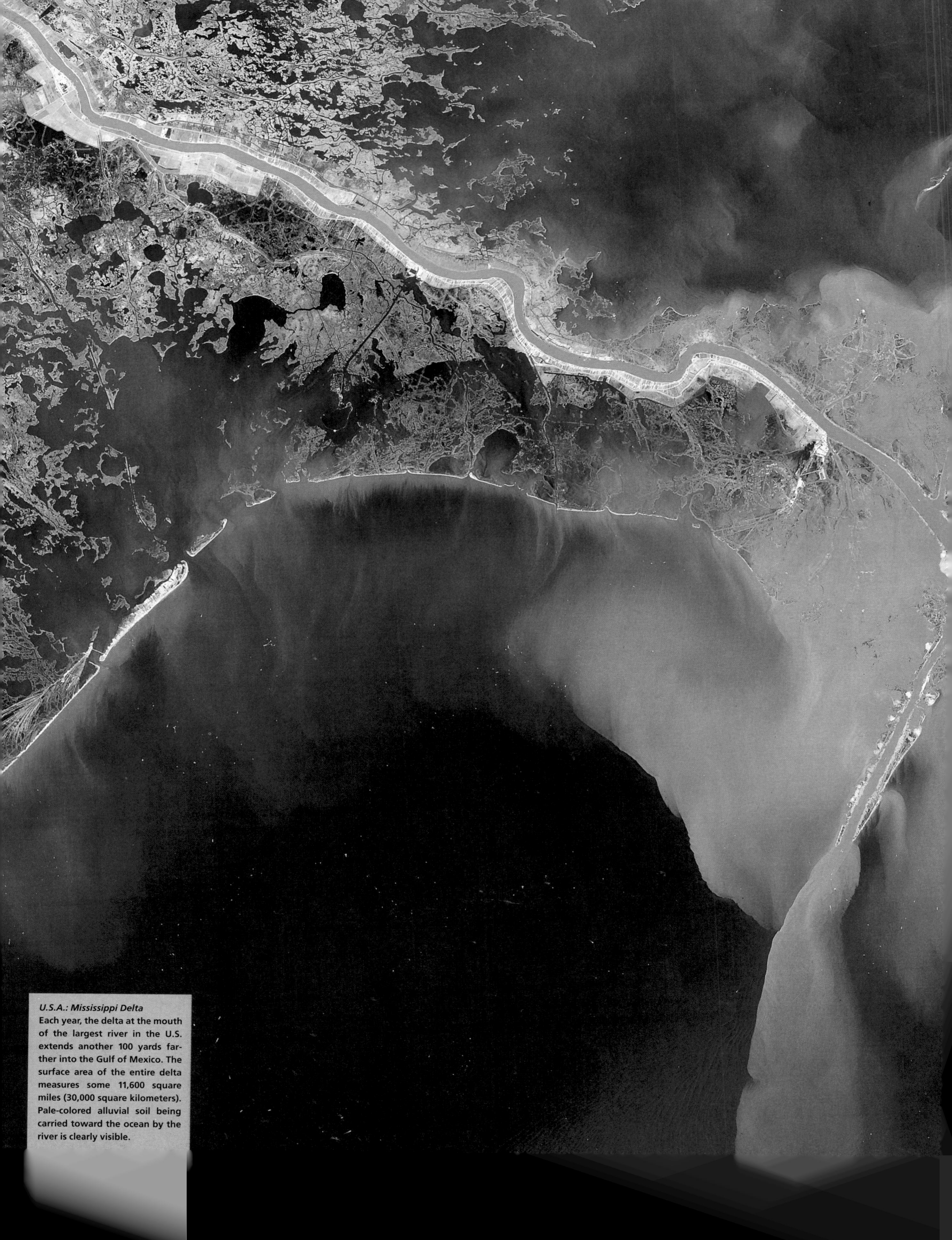

U.S.A.: Mississippi Delta
Each year, the delta at the mouth of the largest river in the U.S. extends another 100 yards farther into the Gulf of Mexico. The surface area of the entire delta measures some 11,600 square miles (30,000 square kilometers). Pale-colored alluvial soil being carried toward the ocean by the river is clearly visible.

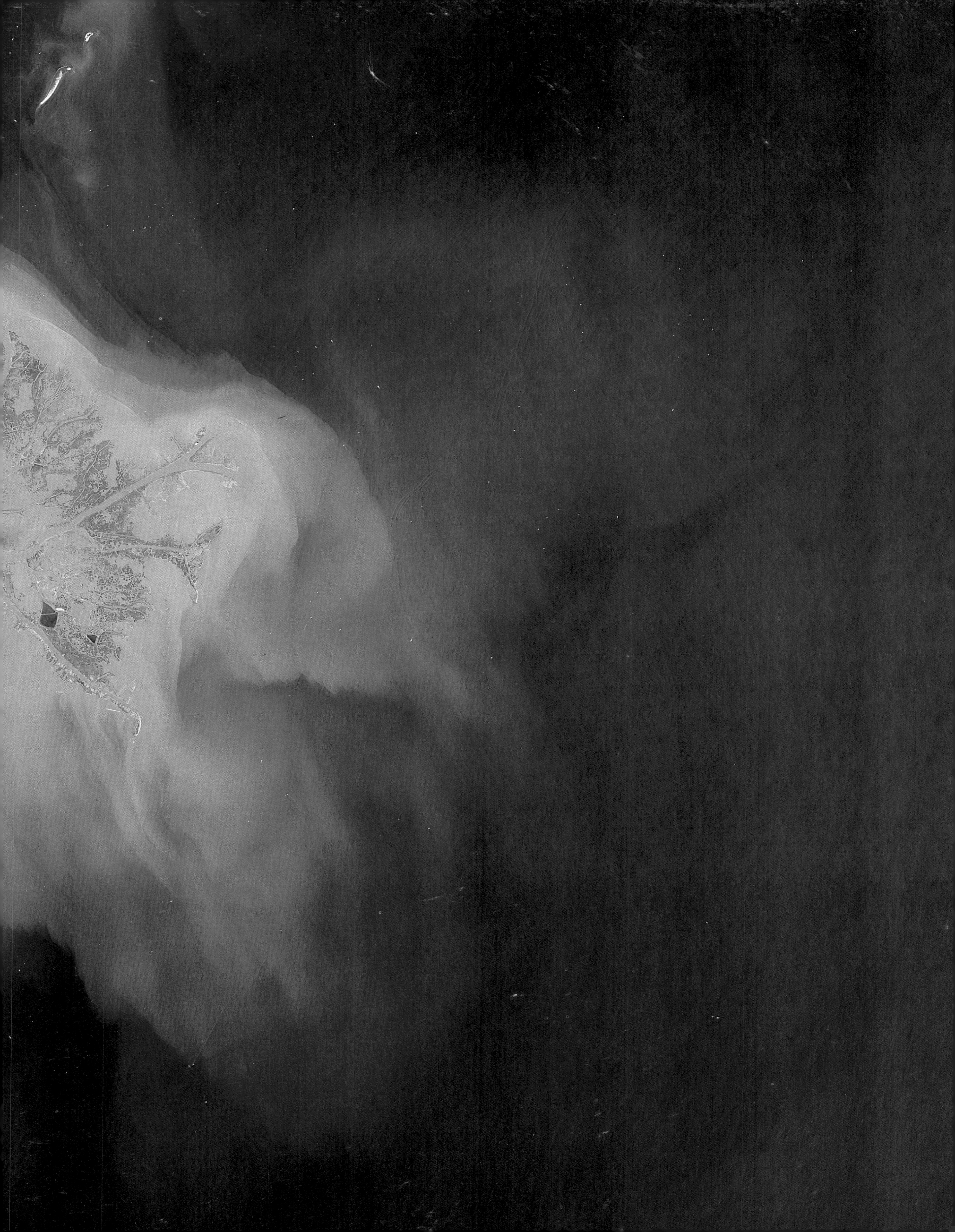

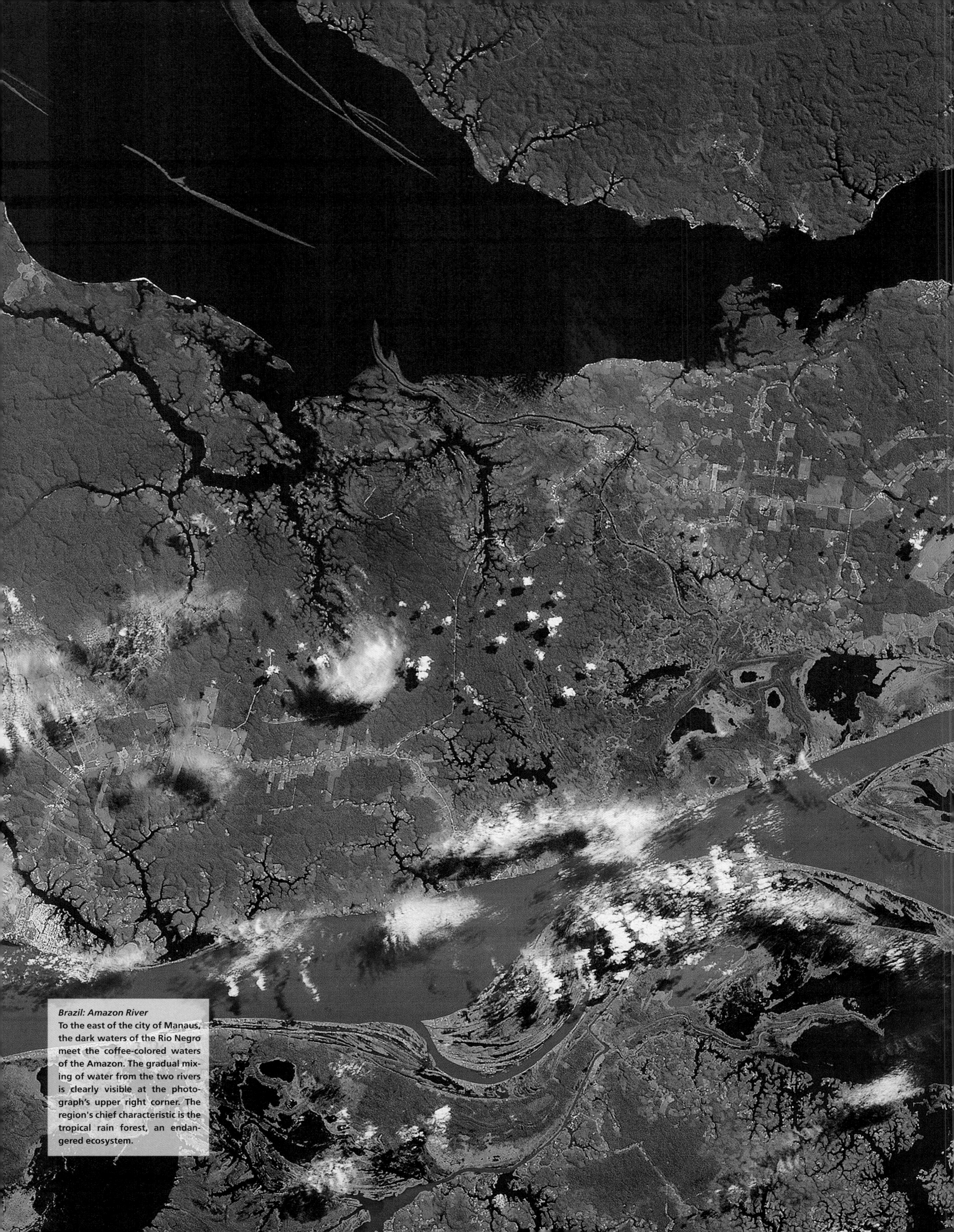

Brazil: Amazon River

To the east of the city of Manaus, the dark waters of the Rio Negro meet the coffee-colored waters of the Amazon. The gradual mixing of water from the two rivers is clearly visible at the photograph's upper right corner. The region's chief characteristic is the tropical rain forest, an endangered ecosystem.

Switzerland: Upper Rhône Valley
The valley of the Upper Rhône crosses the depicted region from the northeast to the southwest. Sickle-shaped Aletsch Glacier, the Alps' largest river of ice, can be seen at the center. Together with its branches, the glacier measures 15 miles (24 km) long with an area of 46 square miles (120 sq. km). Lake Brienz and Lake Thun at the upper left occupy valleys that have been deepened by glacial erosion.

Siberia: Taiga at the Ob River
The pale green region in the left-hand portion of the photograph shows the broad riparian meadows, traversed by the Ob River. The shallow gradient of the land in the west Siberian lowlands allows the river to form many side channels and twisting bends with oxbow lakes and ponds.

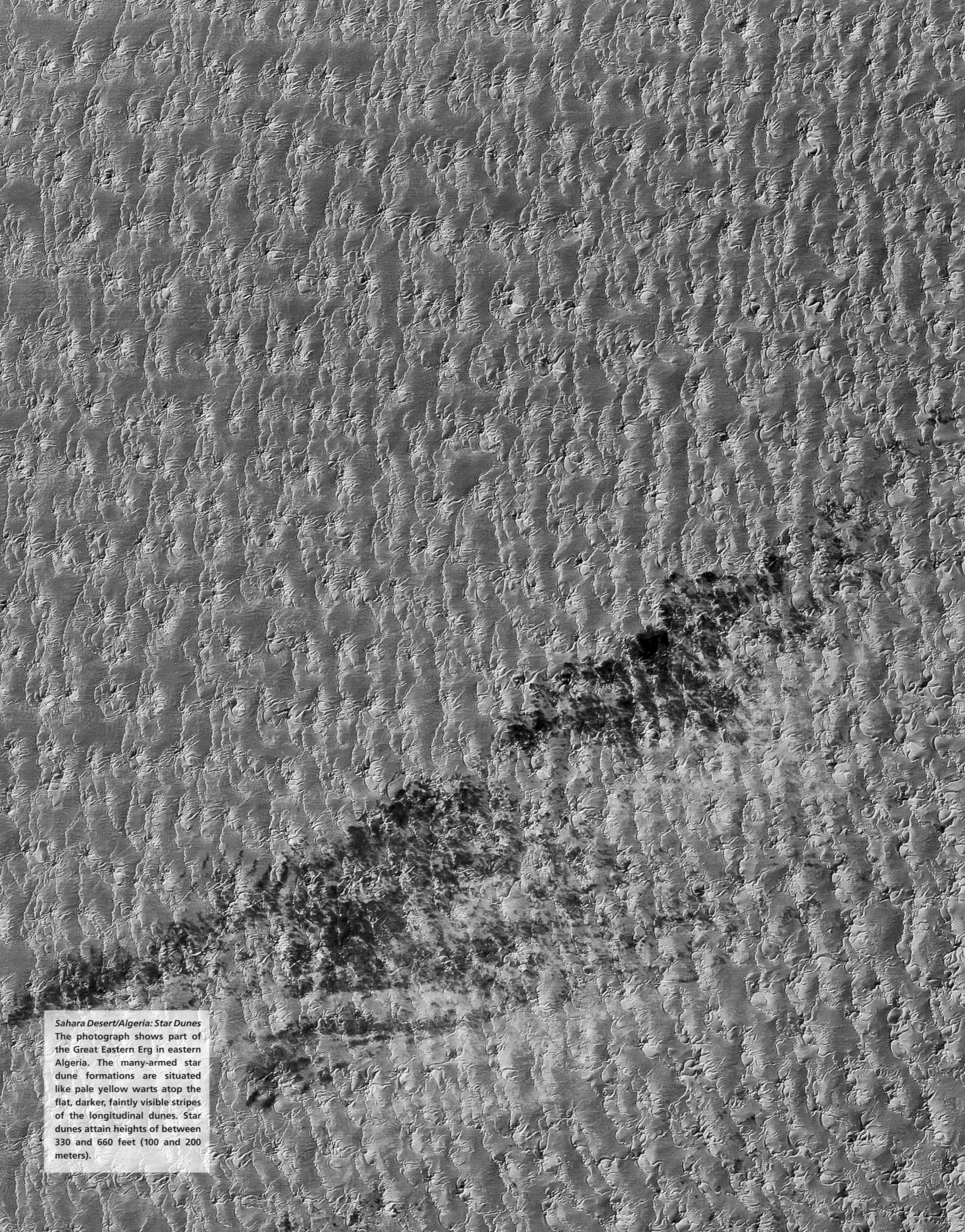

Sahara Desert/Algeria: Star Dunes
The photograph shows part of the Great Eastern Erg in eastern Algeria. The many-armed star dune formations are situated like pale yellow warts atop the flat, darker, faintly visible stripes of the longitudinal dunes. Star dunes attain heights of between 330 and 660 feet (100 and 200 meters).

The World

Among the planets of the solar system, the Earth is unique – not just because of its atmosphere, but above all because of its "face," whose features are the three oceans, occupying over two-thirds of the 196,911,000 square miles (510 million sq. km) of the surface of the Earth, and the seven continents. The Pacific Ocean alone is larger than all land areas together; the largest of these, in turn, is Eurasia, occupying a good third of the total. The highest elevations are reached in the Himalayas, where Mount Everest rises to 29,022 feet (8,846 m). Ten mountains over 26,000 feet can be found in this massive mountain range separating the Indian subcontinent from the rest of Asia. The longest mountain range is the Cordilleras, stretching the entire length of North and South America.

Not entirely up to date: This anonymous woodcut (1530) represents only the continents of the Old World and populates them with fantastic beasts taken from the prophesies of Daniel.

The deepest place on Earth is the Vitiaz Deep (–36,161 feet/ –11,022 m) in the Marianas Trench near the southeast Asian archipelagos. The deepest depression on Earth lies 1,312 feet (400 m) below sea level and is part of a rift valley system that includes the East African faults and the Red Sea. A trench is also the home of the deepest lake with the greatest water volume, Lake Baikal, with a depth of 5,315 feet (1,620 m). The face of the Earth is given further character by volcano chains, such as the Hawaiian Islands, as well as by the icy masses of Antarctica, Greenland and high mountain glaciers.

North and Middle America
p. 4

South America
p. 5

Atlantic Ocean
p. 6–7

Europe
p. 8

Africa
p. 9

Asia
p. 10–11

Indian Ocean
p. 12

Australia and Oceania
p. 13

Pacific Ocean (1 : 50,000,000)
p. 14–15

The Arctic · Antarctica (1 : 27,000,000)
p. 16

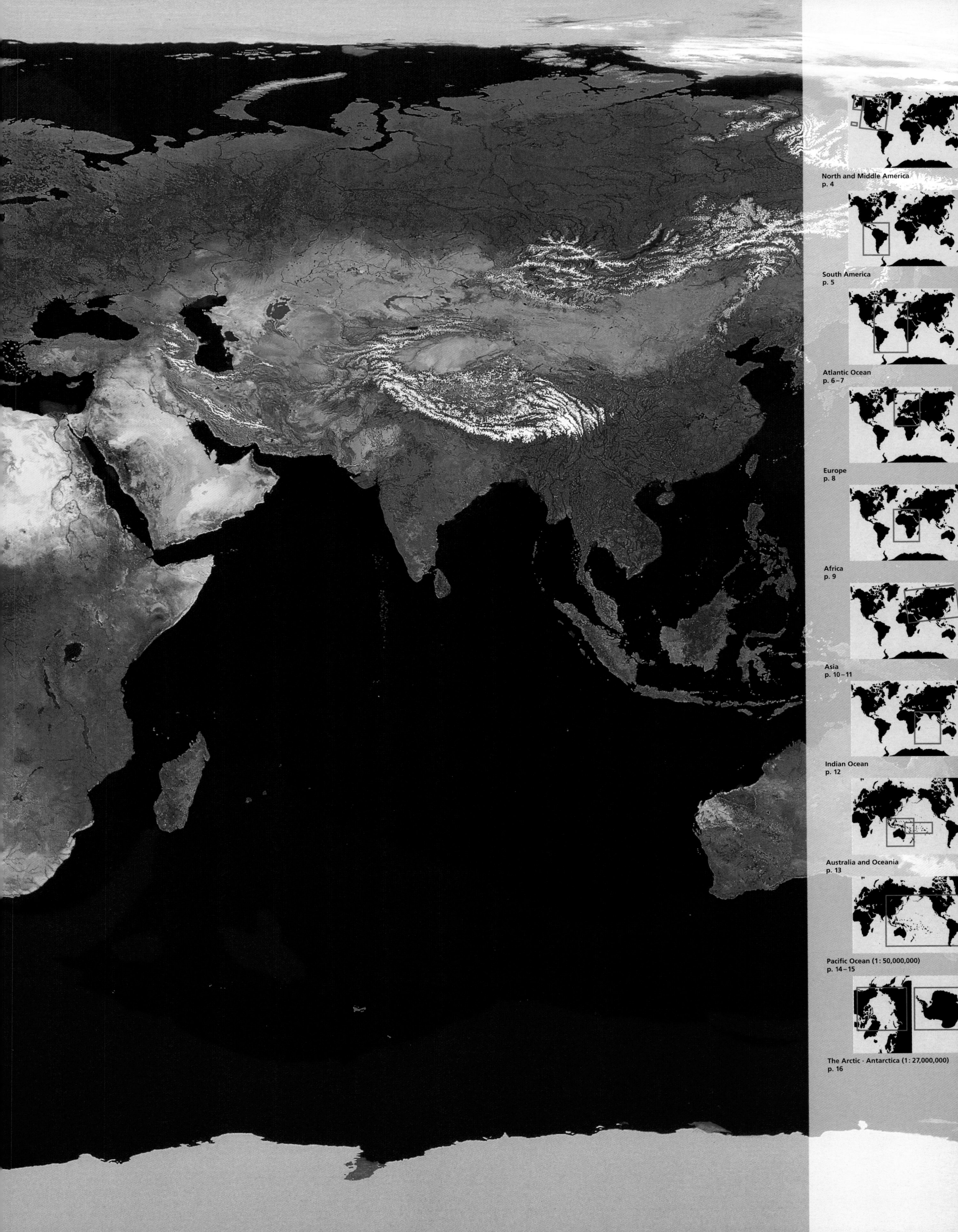

North and Middle America
p. 4
South America
p. 5
Atlantic Ocean
p. 6–7
Europe
p. 8
Africa
p. 9
Asia
p. 10–11
Indian Ocean
p. 12
Australia and Oceania
p. 13
Pacific Ocean (1: 50,000,000)
p. 14–15
The Arctic · Antarctica (1: 27,000,000)
p. 16

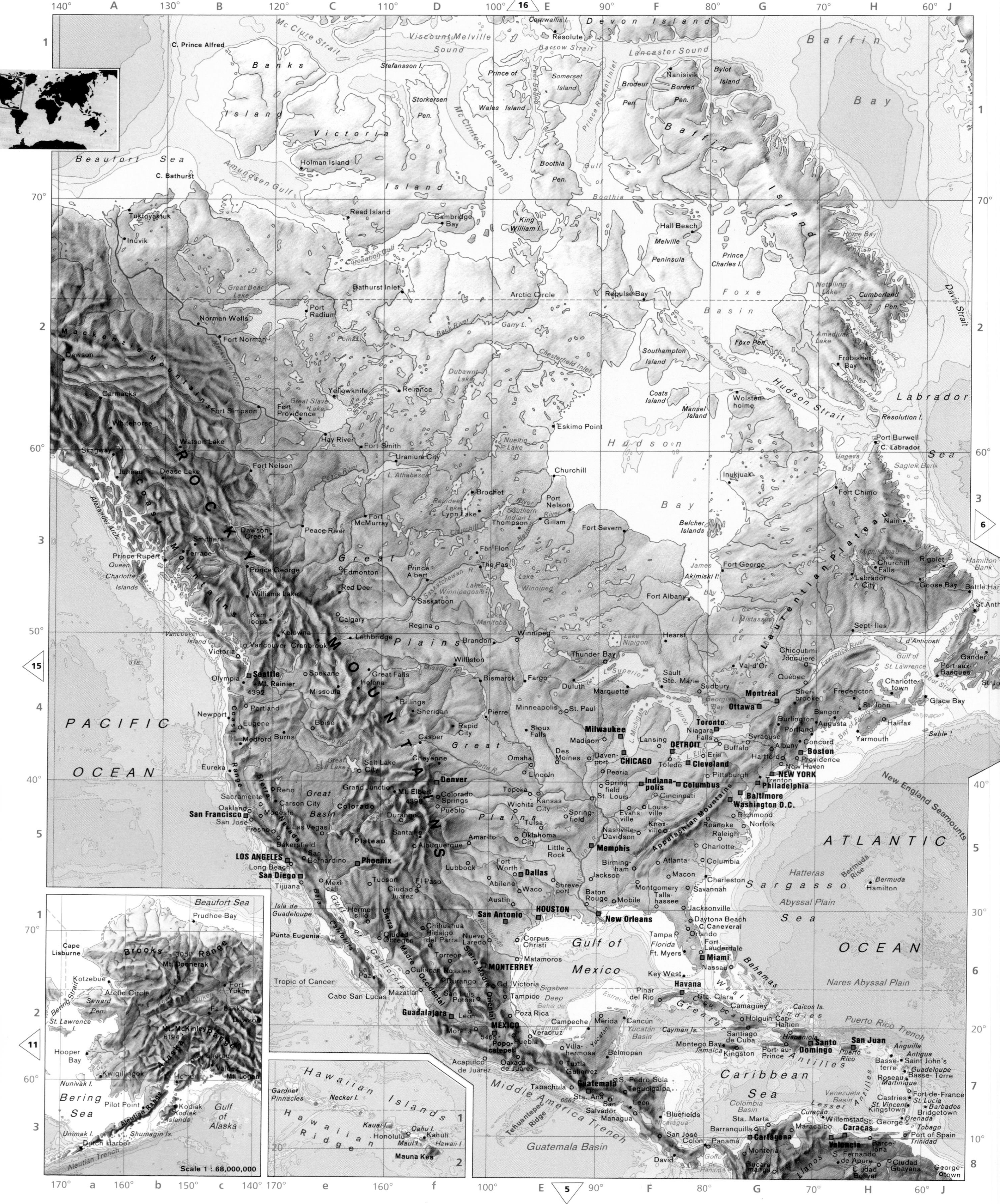

North and Middle America

Scale at the equator 1:40,000,000

ATLANTIC
OCEAN
PACIFIC
OCEAN
Sargasso Sea
Gulf of Mexico
Caribbean Sea
Kane Fracture Zone
Nares Abyssal Plain
Tropic of Cancer
Puerto Rico Trench
Vema Fracture Zone
Demerara Abyssal Plain
Amazon Fan
Four North Fracture Zone
Ceara Abyssal Plain
Equator
Tropic of Capricorn
Middle America Trench
Tehuantepec Ridge
Guatemala Basin
Cocos Ridge
Galápagos Islands
Gofar Fracture Zone
Galapagos Rise
Mendaña Fracture Zone
Peru Basin
Peru-Chile Trench
Nazca Ridge
Chile Basin
Sala y Gomez Ridge
Easter Island
Roggeveen Basin
Is. Juan Fernández
Chile Rise
Valdivia Fracture Zone
Mornington Abyssal Plain
Santos Plateau
Rio Grande Plateau
Argentine Basin
Argentine Abyssal Plain
Argentine Rise
Mar Argentino
Falkland Escarpment
Falkland Plateau
Maurice Ewing Bank
Georgia Basin
Falkland Islands
West Falkland
East Falkland
Stanley
North Scotia Ridge
West Scotia Ridge
South Georgia
Scotia Sea
Yaghan Basin
Drake Passage
Ona Basin
South Orkneys
South Sandwich Islands
Elephant I.
Tierra del Fuego
Cape Horn
Ushuaia
Patagonia
Pampas
Gran Chaco
Pantanal
Brazilian Highlands
Selvas
Llanos
Guiana Highlands
ANDES
Chapada dos Parecis
Trindade
Fernando de Noronha
São Vicente
Caracas
Bogotá
Quito
Lima
La Paz
Santiago
Buenos Aires
Montevideo
Asunción
Brasília
São Paulo
Rio de Janeiro
Belo Horizonte
Salvador
Recife
Fortaleza
Belém
Manaus
Georgetown
Paramaribo
Cayenne
Guayaquil
Medellín
Cali
Cartagena
Barranquilla
Maracaibo
Valencia
Panamá
San José
Managua
Tegucigalpa
San Salvador
Guatemala
Havana
Miami
New Orleans
Houston
San Antonio
Monterrey
México
Guadalajara
Santo Domingo
San Juan
Kingston
Port-au-Prince
Port of Spain
Córdoba
Rosario
Curitiba
Porto Alegre
Mendoza
Aconcagua
Valparaíso
Concepción
Bahía Blanca
Mar del Plata
Comodoro Rivadavia
Río Gallegos
Punta Arenas
Scale at the equator 1:40,000,000

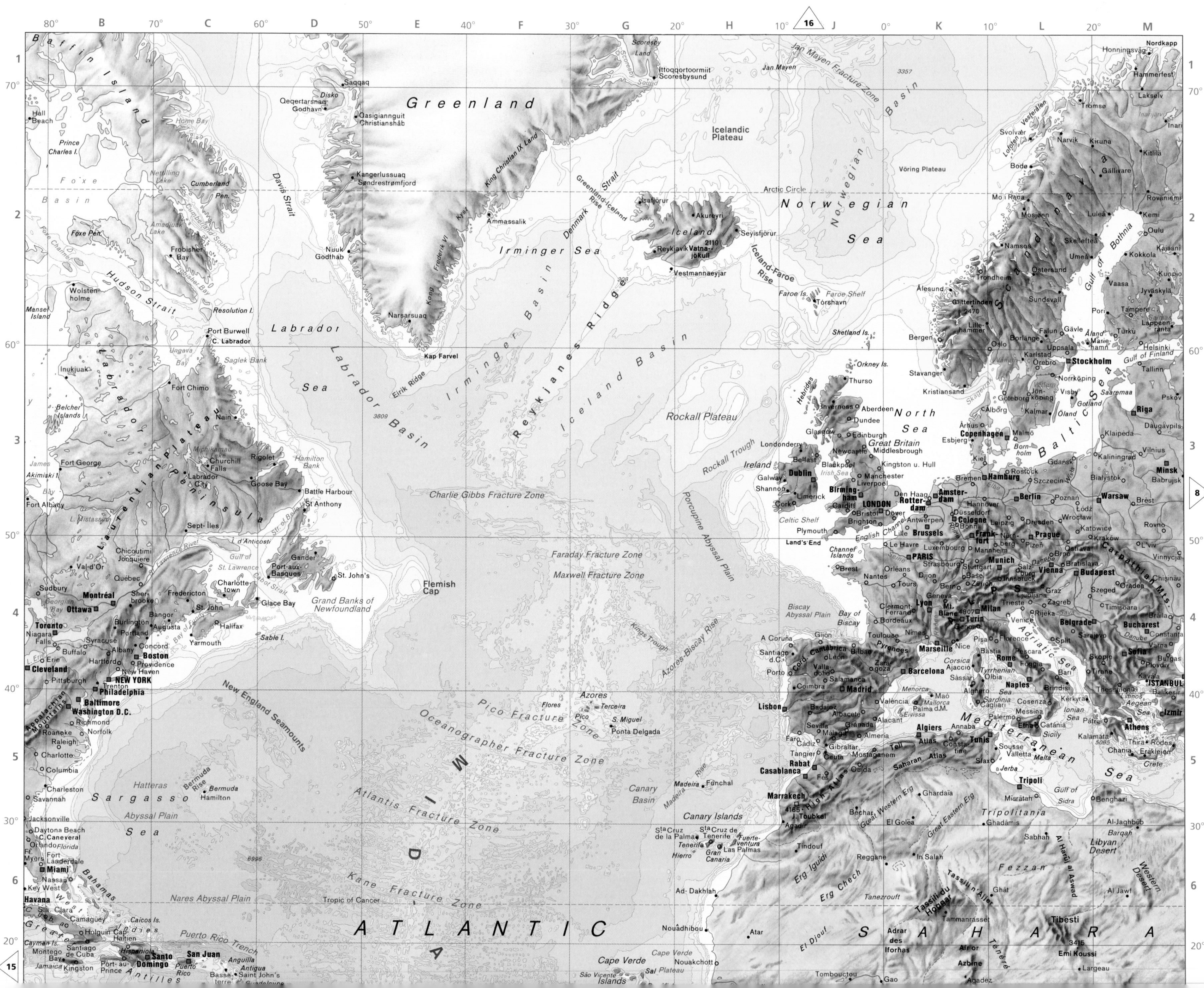

Scale at the equator 1:40,000,000

ATLANTIC OCEAN
MID-ATLANTIC RIDGE
Brazil Basin
Angola Basin
Argentine Basin
Cape Basin
Guinea Basin
Walvis Ridge
Rio Grande Plateau
Santos Plateau
Falkland Escarpment
Georgia Basin
Scotia Sea
South Sandwich Trench
America-Antarctic Ridge
Agulhas Basin
Agulhas Ridge
Discovery Seamounts
Drake Passage
Chile Basin
Peru-Chile Trench
Gulf of Guinea
Tropic of Capricorn
Equator
Mar Argentino
Tierra del Fuego
Cape Town
Luanda
Kinshasa
LAGOS
Accra
Abidjan
RIO DE JANEIRO
SÃO PAULO
Brasília
Salvador
Recife
Fortaleza
Belém
Montevideo
Buenos Aires
Santiago
LIMA
BOGOTÁ
Caracas
Quito
La Paz

Scale at the equator 1:40,000,000

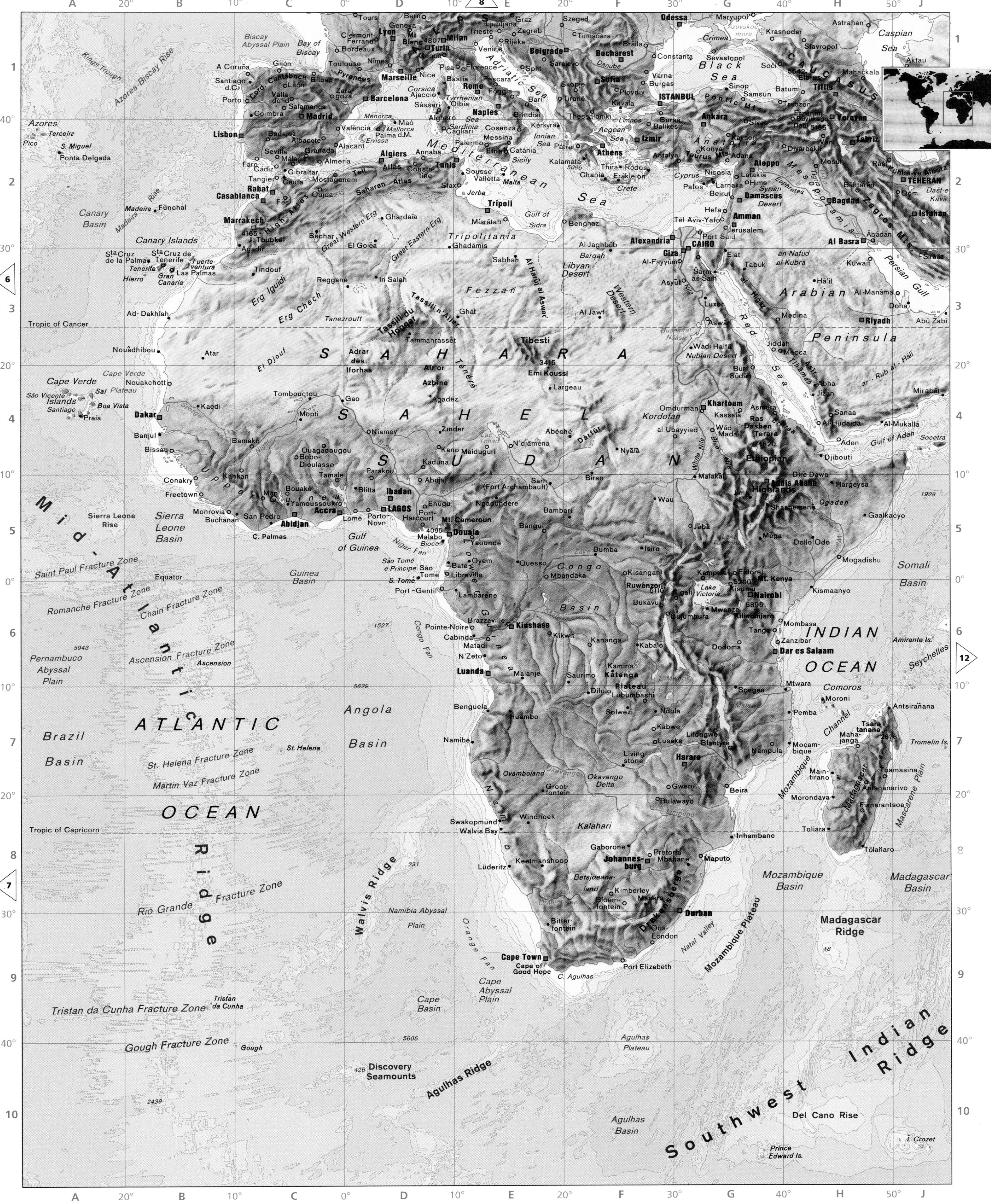

Biscay Abyssal Plain
Bay of Biscay
Kings Trough
Azores-Biscay Rise
Azores
Terceira
Pico
S. Miguel
Ponta Delgada
Madeira
Funchal
Madeira Rise
Canary Basin
Canary Islands
Sta Cruz de la Palma
Sta Cruz de Tenerife
Tenerife
Hierro
Gran Canaria
Las Palmas
Fuerteventura
Tropic of Cancer
Cape Verde
Cape Verde Plateau
São Vicente
Sal
Boa Vista
Santiago
Praia
Sierra Leone Rise
Sierra Leone Basin
Mid-Atlantic Ridge
Saint Paul Fracture Zone
Romanche Fracture Zone
Chain Fracture Zone
Equator
Guinea Basin
Ascension Fracture Zone
Ascension
Pernambuco Abyssal Plain
5943
Brazil Basin
ATLANTIC
OCEAN
St. Helena
St. Helena Fracture Zone
Martin Vaz Fracture Zone
Tropic of Capricorn
Rio Grande Fracture Zone
Ridge
Walvis Ridge
231
Tristan da Cunha Fracture Zone
Tristan da Cunha
Gough Fracture Zone
Gough
5605
Discovery Seamounts
426
2439
Agulhas Ridge
Angola Basin
5629
1527
Congo Fan
Niger Fan
Gulf of Guinea
Namibia Abyssal Plain
Orange Fan
Cape Abyssal Plain
Cape Basin
Agulhas Plateau
Agulhas Basin
Southwest Indian Ridge
Del Cano Rise
Prince Edward Is.
I. Crozet
Madagascar Ridge
Madagascar Basin
Mozambique Basin
Mozambique Plateau
Natal Valley
Mozambique Channel
Mascarene Plain
Tromelin Is.
Comoros
Moroni
Seychelles
Amirante Is.
INDIAN OCEAN
Somali Basin
1928
Gulf of Aden
Socotra
Lisbon
Porto
Coimbra
A Coruña
Santiago d.C.
Gijón
Cord. Cantábrica
León
Bilbao
Valladolid
Salamanca
Madrid
Badajoz
Sevilla
Faro
Cádiz
Málaga
Granada
Gibraltar
Albacete
Alacant
Almería
València
Zaragoza
Barcelona
Pyrenees
Toulouse
Bordeaux
Clermont-Ferrand
Lyon
Nîmes
Marseille
Nice
Tours
Geneva
Bern
Mt Blanc
4807
Turin
Genoa
Milan
Corsica
Ajaccio
Bastia
Sardinia
Sàssari
Olbia
Alghero
Cagliari
Tyrrhenian Sea
Menorca
Mallorca
Palma d.M.
Eivissa
Rome
Florence
Pisa
Pescara
Foggia
Naples
Bari
Brindisi
Cosenza
Messina
Palermo
Catania
Sicily
Malta
Valletta
Ionian Sea
Venice
Trieste
Ljubljana
Graz
Zagreb
Rijeka
Adriatic Sea
Split
Sarajevo
Belgrade
Szeged
Timişoara
Bucharest
Brăila
Constanţa
Danube
Sofia
Skopje
Tirane
Plovdiv
Varna
Burgas
Thessaloníki
Kavála
Kérkyra
Pátrai
Athens
Kalamáta
5095
Aegean Sea
Limnos
Thíra
Ródos
Crete
Chania
Eraklejon
Odessa
Crimea
Sevastopol
Maryupol
Azovskoe more
Krasnodar
Astrakhan'
Stavropol
Soči
Black Sea
CAUCASUS
5642
Elbrus
Mahačkala
Caspian Sea
Aktau
Tiflis
Batumi
Trabzon
Erzurum
Büyükagri Dagi
5165
Yerevan
Tabrīz
ISTANBUL
Bursa
Balıkesir
İzmir
Sinop
Samsun
Pontic Mts.
Ankara
Sivas
Kayseri
Konya
Anatolia
Taurus Mts.
Antalya
Adana
Van
Diyarbakır
Mosul
Rast
Kūhhā-ye Alborz
TEHERAN
Qom
Dasht-e Kavir
Eşfahān
Zagros Mts.
Mesopotamia
Tigris
Euphrates
Syrian Desert
Aleppo
Latakia
Hims
Nicosia
Cyprus
Larnaka
Pafos
Beirut
Damascus
Bagdad
Bahtaran
Hefa
Tel Aviv-Yafo
Amman
Jerusalem
Ābādān
Al Basra
Kuwait
Persian Gulf
Sīraaz
Port Said
Alexandria
CAIRO
Giza
Al-Fayyum
Asyūt
Nile
Sarm as-Saih
Elat
Tabūk
an-Nafūd al-Kubrā
Hā'il
Arabian Peninsula
Al-Manāma
Doha
Riyadh
Abu Zabi
Medina
Red Sea
Hijaz
Jiddah
Mecca
Asir
ar-Rub al-Hali
Abhā
Jīzān
Sanaa
Al-Hudaida
Al-Mukallā
Mirabāt
Aden
Djibouti
Luxor
Aswān
Buhairat Nasir
Wādī Halfā
Nubian Desert
Būr Sūdān
Khartoum
Omdurman
Kassala
Asmera
Eritrea
Ras Dashen Terara
4620
Wad Madani
Blue Nile
White Nile
Ethiopian Highlands
Addis Ababa
Dirē Dawa
Hargeysa
Jima
Ogaden
Shabeelle
Galkacyo
Mogadishu
Dollo Odo
Mega
Juba
Kismaanyo
Tangier
Ceuta
Tell Atlas
Rabat
Casablanca
Fès
Oujda
Mostaganem
Algiers
Annaba
Constantine
Tunis
Sousse
Sfax
Jerba
Saharan Atlas
Atlas
High Atlas
Marrakech
4165
J. Toubkal
Agadir
Béchar
Ghardaïa
Great Western Erg
Great Eastern Erg
El Goléa
Ghadāmis
Tripolitania
Tripoli
Misrātah
Gulf of Sidra
Benghazi
Mediterranean Sea
Al-Jaghbūb
Barqah
Libyan Desert
Western Desert
Tindouf
Erg Iguidi
Erg Chech
Reggane
In Salah
Tanezrouft
Tassili du Hoggar
Tassili n'Ajjer
Ghāt
Tammanrasset
Fezzan
Sabhah
Al Harūj al Aswad
Al Jawf
Tibesti
3415
Emi Koussi
Largeau
Ad- Dakhlah
Nouâdhibou
Atar
El Djouf
Nouakchott
SAHARA
Adrar des Iforhas
Aïr or Azbine
Ténéré
Agadez
Kaedi
Dakar
Senegal
Banjul
Bissau
Tombouctou
Gao
Mopti
SAHEL
Niamey
Zinder
Lac Tchad
N'djamena
Abéché
Darfur
Kordofan
al Ubayyiad
Nyālā
SUDAN
Bamako
Niger
Ouagadougou
Bobo-Dioulasso
Kano
Maiduguri
Kaduna
Conakry
Kankan
Freetown
Monrovia
Buchanan
San Pedro
Upper Guinea
Man
Bouaké
Yamoussoukro
Tamale
Parakou
Blitta
Ibadan
LAGOS
Abuja
Enugu
Accra
Lomé
Porto-Novo
Port-Harcourt
Abidjan
C. Palmas
Mt. Cameroun
4095
Douala
Malabo
Bioco
Yaoundé
Ngaoundéré
Sarh
(Fort Archambault)
Birao
Malakal
Wau
Bambari
Bangui
Bumba
Isiro
São Tomé e Príncipe
São Tomé
S. Tomé
Bata
Oyem
Libreville
Port-Gentil
Lambaréné
Ouesso
Congo Basin
Mbandaka
Kisangani
Ruwenzori
5110
Kampala
Elgon
Mt. Kenya
5200
Lake Victoria
Kisumu
Nairobi
Kigali
Bukavu
Bujumbura
Mwanza
Kilimanjaro
5895
Mombasa
Tanga
Zanzibar
Dar es Salaam
Dodoma
Pointe-Noire
Brazzaville
Kinshasa
Cabinda
Matadi
N'Zeto
Kikwit
Kananga
Kabalo
Luanda
Malanje
Saurimo
Kamina
Katanga Plateau
Dilolo
Lubumbashi
Mtwara
Songea
Solwezi
Ndola
Benguela
Huambo
Kabwe
Lusaka
Lilongwe
Blantyre
Nampula
Pemba
Moçambique
Namibe
Livingstone
Harare
Ovamboland
Okavango
Okavango Delta
Grootfontein
Gweru
Bulawayo
Beira
Limpopo
Swakopmund
Walvis Bay
Windhoek
Namib
Kalahari
Gaborone
Pretoria
Johannesburg
Mbabane
Maputo
Inhambane
Lüderitz
Keetmanshoop
Betsjoeanaland
Kimberley
Bloemfontein
Maseru
Orange River
Drakensberge
Durban
Bitterfontein
East London
Port Elizabeth
Cape Town
Cape of Good Hope
C. Agulhas
Antsirañana
Tsaratanana
2876
Mahajanga
Maintirano
Toamasina
Antananarivo
Madagascar
Morondava
Fianarantsoa
Toliara
Tôlañaro

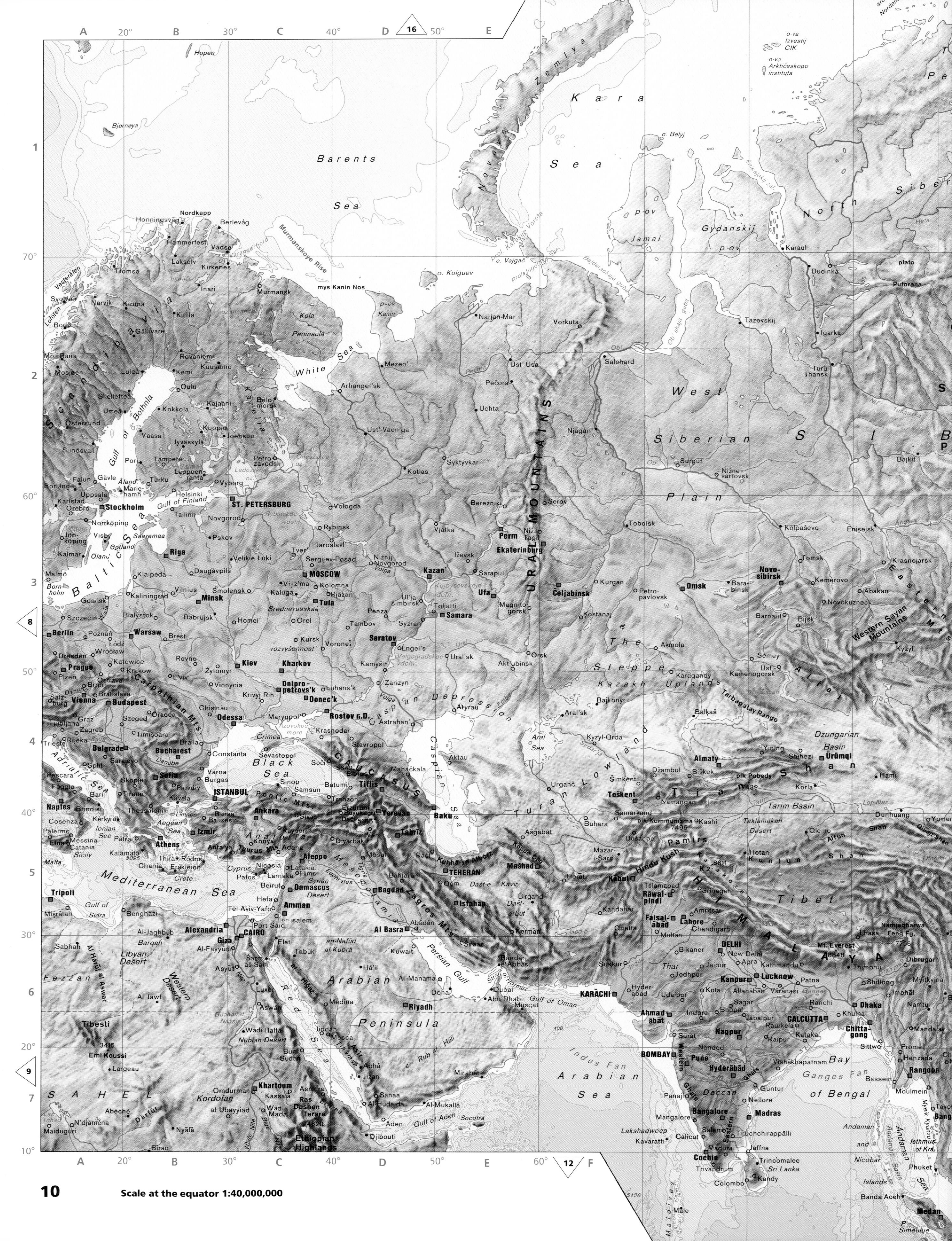

Scale at the equator 1:40,000,000

Laptev
Sea
East Siberian
Sea
Chukchi
Sea
New Siberian Islands
o. Bel'kovskij
o. Kotel'nyj
o. Novaja Sibir'
o. Stolbovoj
Ljahovskie o-va
prol. Dmitrija Lapteva
prol. Sannikova
Lena River Delta
Olenëkskij zaliv
Nordvik
Tit-Ary
Janskij zaliv
Nižnejansk
Čekurovka
Ust'-Kujga
Medvež'i o-va
o. Ajon
o. Vrangelja
proliv Longa
Kolymskaja nizmennost
Čerskij
Cukotskoje nagore
Lowland
Olenëk
Džardžan
Verhojanskij
2389
Žigansk
Družina
Srednekolymsk
Arctic Circle
Cukotskij p-ov
Enmelen
Bering Strait
Anadyrskiy zaliv
Anadyr
hrebet Čerskogo
Pobeda 3147
Ust'-Nera
Ojmjakon
2295
Kolymskoe nagor'e
Susuman
Kamenskoe
Nagornyi
St. Lawrence Island
Korjakskoe nagor'e
Gižiga
Pahači
Viljujsk
Mirnyj
Jakutsk
Lensk
Olëkminsk
Ust'-Maja
Magadan
Gižiginskaja guba
Penžinskaja guba
Korf
m. Oljutorskij
Ohotsk
Sredinnyj hrebet
m. Tolstyj
Tigil'
o. Karaginskij
Bering Sea
Komandorskaya Basin
Aleutian Basin
Pribilof I.
Aldan
Aldanskoe nagor'e
Kirensk
Ust'-Kut
Stanovoe nagor'e
Stanovoj hr.
hr. Džugdžur
Ajan
Kamchatka Peninsula
Ust'-Kamčatsk
o. Bering
Mednyj o.
Komandorskie o-va
Bowers Ridge
o. Bol. Šantar
Sea of Okhotsk
Čumikan
vlk. Korjakskaja Sopka 3456
Ust'-Bol'šereck
Petropavlovsk-Kamčatskij
Aleutian Islands
Attu I.
Agattu I.
Rat Islands
Kiska I.
Andreanof Islands
Atka I.
Umnak I.
7443
7135
3078
Lake Baikal
Angarsk
Ulan-Ude
Čita
Nerčinsk
Jablonovyj hr.
Zeja
Amur
Nikolaevsk-na-Amure
Oha
Svobodnyj
Komsomol'sk-na-Amure
Blagoveščensk
Sakhalin
m. Lopatka
o. Paramušir
o. Onekotan
Obruchev Rise
Emperor Seamount Chain
Ulaanbaatar
Čojbalsan
Habarovsk
Poronajsk
Sihote Alin'
Greater Hinggan Ra.
Qiqihar
Manchuria
Jiamusi
Južno-Sahalinsk
Kuril Basin
Kuril Islands
o. Simušir
Kuril Trench
Harbin
Changchun
Jilin
Wakkanai
o. Kunašir
o. Iturup
o. Urup
9783
Asahikawa
Sapporo
Japan Basin
Kushiro
Hokkaidō
Vladivostok
Chongjin
Hakodate
Chinook Trough
7407
Emperor Trough
Northwest Pacific Basin
Shenyang
Fushun
Anshan
Benxi
Zhangjiakou
Baotou
Hohhot
Datong
Tangshan
Dandong
Hamhung
Aomori
Sea of Japan
PEKING
TIANJIN
Pyongyang
Akita
Morioka
Taiyuan
Dairen
Yellow
SŎUL
Inch'ŏn
Shijiazhuang
Jinan
Handan
Anyang
TSINGTAO
Taejon
Taegu
Niigata
Sendai
Japan Trench
Honshū
3776
TŌKYŌ
8130
Komatsu
Kyōto
Nagoya
Kawasaki
Yokohama
Kobe
Ōsaka
Fuji-san
Lanzhou
Xi'an
Luoyang
Zaozhuang
Kwangyu
Pusan
Hiroshima
Kitakyūshū
Fukuoka
Matsuyama
Shikoku
Xinghua
Cheju Do
Zhengzhou
Huainan
Nanking
Changzhou
Hefei
Wuhu
Wuxi
SHANGHAI
HANGZHOU
Shaoxing
Ningbo
Nagasaki
Kagoshima
Kyūshū
East China Sea
Izu Shoto
Bonin Trench
Yichang
Wuhan
Wan Xian
Chongqing
Luzhou
Huangshi
Nanchang
Changsha
Guiyang
Hengyang
Wuyi Shan
Wenzhou
Amami Shoto
Nansei Shoto
Okinawa I.
Naha
Miyako Jima
9810
Bonin
PACIFIC
OCEAN
Midway I.
Lisianski I.
Guilin
Ganzhou
Fuzhou
Xiamen
Taipei
Taichung
Taiwan
Changhua
Kaohsiung
Volcano Islands
Mapmakers Seamount
Tropic of Cancer
Nanning
Canton
Kowloon
Hong Kong
Victoria
Macao
Beihai
Hà Nôi
Hai Phong
Gulf of Tonkin
Haikou
Hainan Dao
Sanya
Philippine Sea
Luzon Strait
Mid-Pacific Seamounts
Magellan Seamounts
Maug I.
Agrihan
Alamagan
Northern Mariana Islands
Wake I.
Laoag
Tuguegarao
Luzon
Baguio
Quezon City
Manila
Mindoro
Naga
Samar
Philippines
Philippine Trench
Philippine Basin
Hue
Dà Nang
Quy Nho'n
South China Sea
Parece Vela Basin
Saipan
Susupe
Rota
Guam
Agana
Mariana Trench
East Mariana Basin
Marshall Seamounts
Phnum Penh
T. P. Hô Chi Minh
Palawan
Panay
Iloilo
Cebu
10497
Puerto Princesa
11034
Challenger Deep
Yap Is.
Eniwetok
Bikini
Marshall Islands
Ailuk
Sulu Sea
Zamboanga City
Butuan
Davao City
Mindanao
Cotabato City
Talaud I.
Kota Kinabalu
Sandakan
Archipelago
Celebes Sea
Bandar Seri Begawan
Natuna Is.
Tarakan
Anambas Is.
Kuala Lumpur
Singapore
Borneo
Manado
Molucca Sea
Halmahera
130°
140°
150°
160°
170°
180°
N
O
P
Q
R
S
16
13
4
14
1
2
3
5
6
7
70°
60°
50°
40°
30°
20°
10°

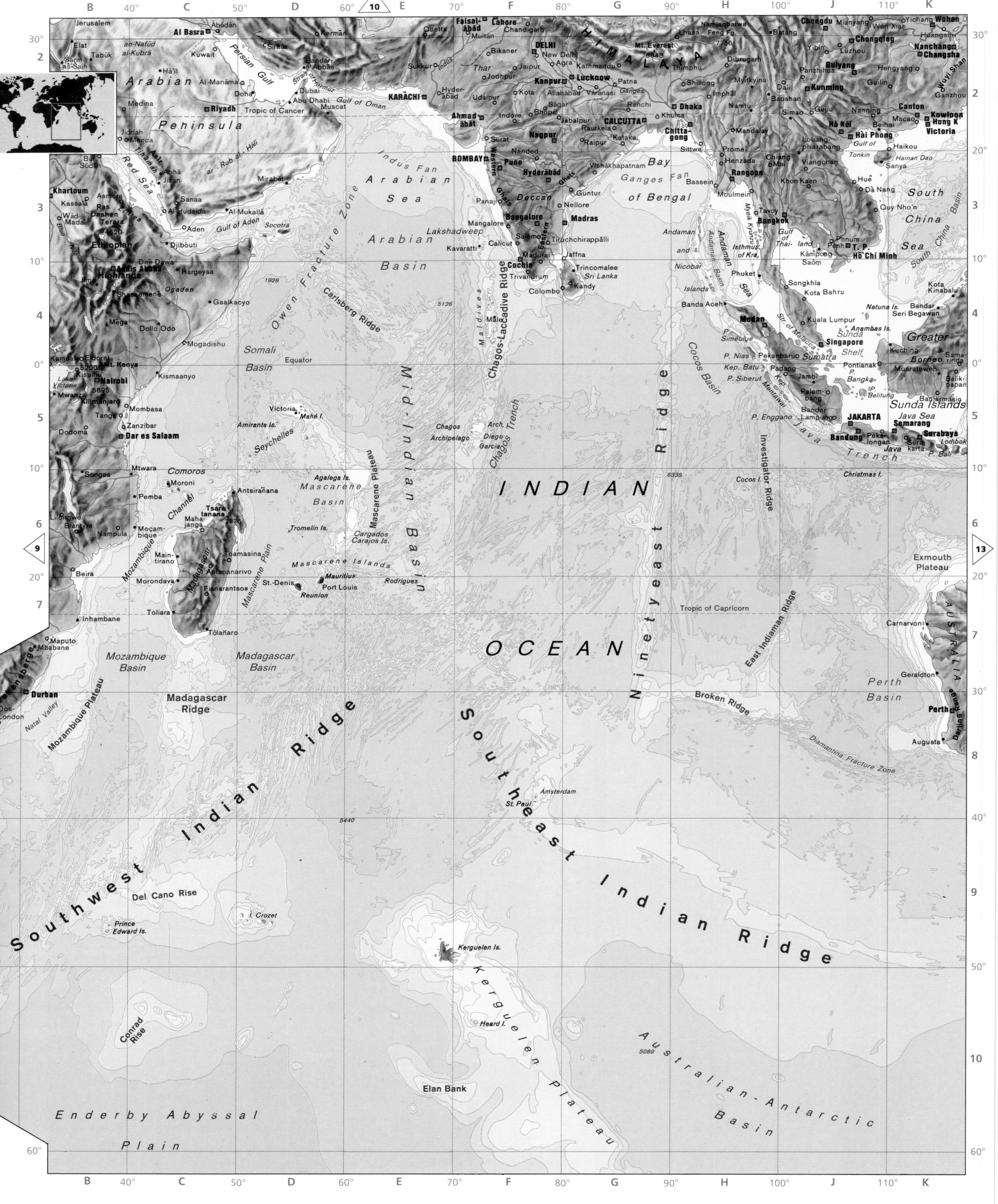

Scale at the equator 1:40,000,000

MICRONESIA
MELANESIA
POLYNESIA
INDIAN OCEAN
PACIFIC OCEAN
AUSTRALIA
South China Sea
Philippines
Celebes Sea
Java Sea
Banda Sea
Arafura Sea
Timor Sea
Coral Sea
Solomon Sea
Tasman Sea
Great Australian Bight
Gulf of Carpentaria
Greater Sunda Islands
Borneo
Sumatra
Java
Sulawesi
Mindanao
Halmahera
New Guinea
Tasmania
New Zealand
North Island
South Island
Fiji
Vanua Levu
Viti Levu
New Caledonia
Gilbert Islands
Marshall Islands
Caroline Islands
Samoa Is.
Tonga Islands
Cook Islands
Society Islands
Tuamotu Archipelago
Marquesas Islands
Line Islands
Tubuai Islands
Phoenix Islands
Hô Chi Minh
Singapore
Kuala Lumpur
JAKARTA
Bandung
Semarang
Surabaya
Davao City
Darwin
Perth
Adelaide
Melbourne
Sydney
Canberra
Brisbane
Newcastle
Hobart
Alice Springs
Ayers Rock
Mount Isa
Cairns
Townsville
Rockhampton
Auckland
Wellington
Christchurch
Dunedin
Great Sandy Desert
Gibson Desert
Great Victoria Desert
Tanami Desert
Barkly Tableland
Great Artesian Basin
Great Dividing Range
Great Barrier Reef
Hamersley Range
Darling Range
Nullarbor Plain
Kosciusko
Mt. Cook
Southern Alps
Tropic of Capricorn
Equator
Java Trench
Tonga Trench
Investigator Ridge
South Australia Basin
Tasman Basin
Lord Howe Rise
Campbell Plateau
South Tasman Rise
Australian-Antarctic Discordance
Diamantina Fracture Zone
Clipperton Fracture Zone
Marquesas Fracture Zone
Austral Fracture Zone

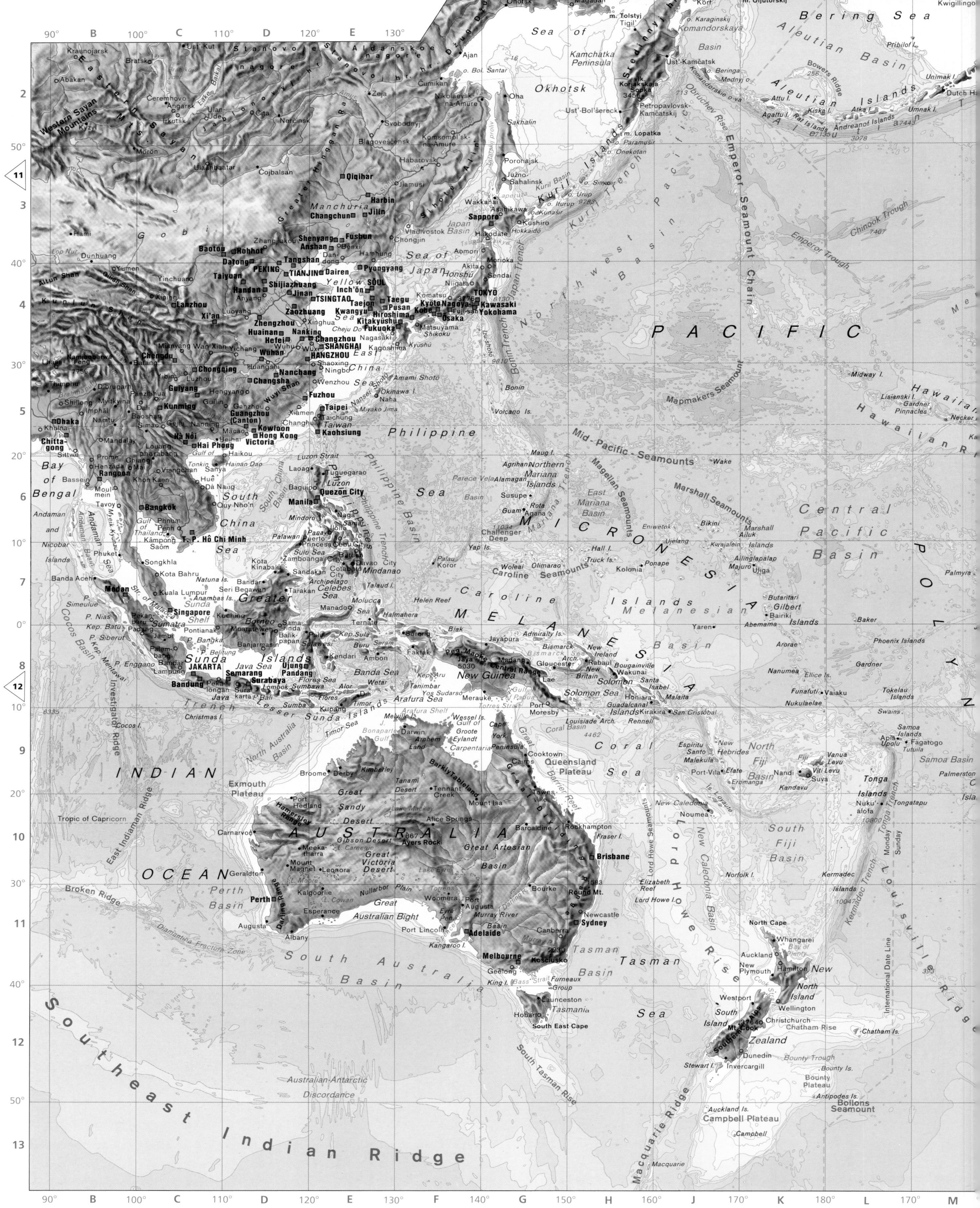

Scale at the equator 1:50,000,000

Gulf of Alaska
Kodiak Island
ROCKY MOUNTAINS
Great Plains
Labrador
Labrador Peninsula
Laurentian Plateau
Gulf of Mexico
Sargasso Sea
Caribbean Sea
Nares Abyssal Plain
Tropic of Cancer
Hatteras Abyssal Plain
New England Seamounts
Bahamas
Greater Antilles
Lesser Antilles
Puerto Rico Trench
Middle America Trench
Guatemala Basin
Cocos Ridge
Galápagos Islands
Galápagos Fracture Zone
Clarion Fracture Zone
Clipperton Fracture Zone
Murray Fracture Zone
Molokai Fracture Zone
Pioneer Fracture Zone
Marquesas Fracture Zone
Marquesas Islands
Tuamotu Archipelago
Society Islands
Tubuai Islands
Austral Fracture Zone
Tiki Basin
Gallego Rise
Wilkes Fracture Zone
Garrett Fracture Zone
Bauer Basin
Galapagos Rise
Mendaña Fracture Zone
Peru Basin
Nazca Ridge
Sala y Gomez Ridge
East Pacific Rise
Roggeveen Basin
Chile Basin
Peru-Chile Trench
Chile Rise
Valdivia Fracture Zone
Agassiz Fracture Zone
Menard Fracture Zone
Eltanin Fracture Zone System
Udintsev Fracture Zone
Heezen Fracture Zone
Tharp Fracture Zone
Mornington Abyssal Plain
Argentine Basin
Argentine Abyssal Plain
Argentine Rise
Falkland Islands
Falkland Plateau
Demerara Abyssal Plain
Selva
Gran Chaco
Pampas
Patagonia
ANDES
Tierra del Fuego
Cape Horn
SOUTH PACIFIC OCEAN
Southwest Pacific Basin
Equator
Seattle
San Francisco
LOS ANGELES
San Diego
Phoenix
Denver
Dallas
HOUSTON
San Antonio
New Orleans
Miami
CHICAGO
DETROIT
Cleveland
Toronto
Montréal
Ottawa
Boston
NEW YORK
Philadelphia
Washington D.C.
Baltimore
Milwaukee
Memphis
MONTERREY
Guadalajara
MÉXICO
Havana
Guatemala
Caracas
Cartagena
Medellín
BOGOTÁ
Quito
Guayaquil
Trujillo
LIMA
La Paz
Santiago
Buenos Aires
Montevideo
Porto Alegre
Curitiba
Córdoba
120° R 110° S 100° T 90° U 80° V 70° W 60° X 50°
N 150° O 140° P 130° Q 120° R 110° S 100° T 90° U 80° V 70° W 60° X 50°

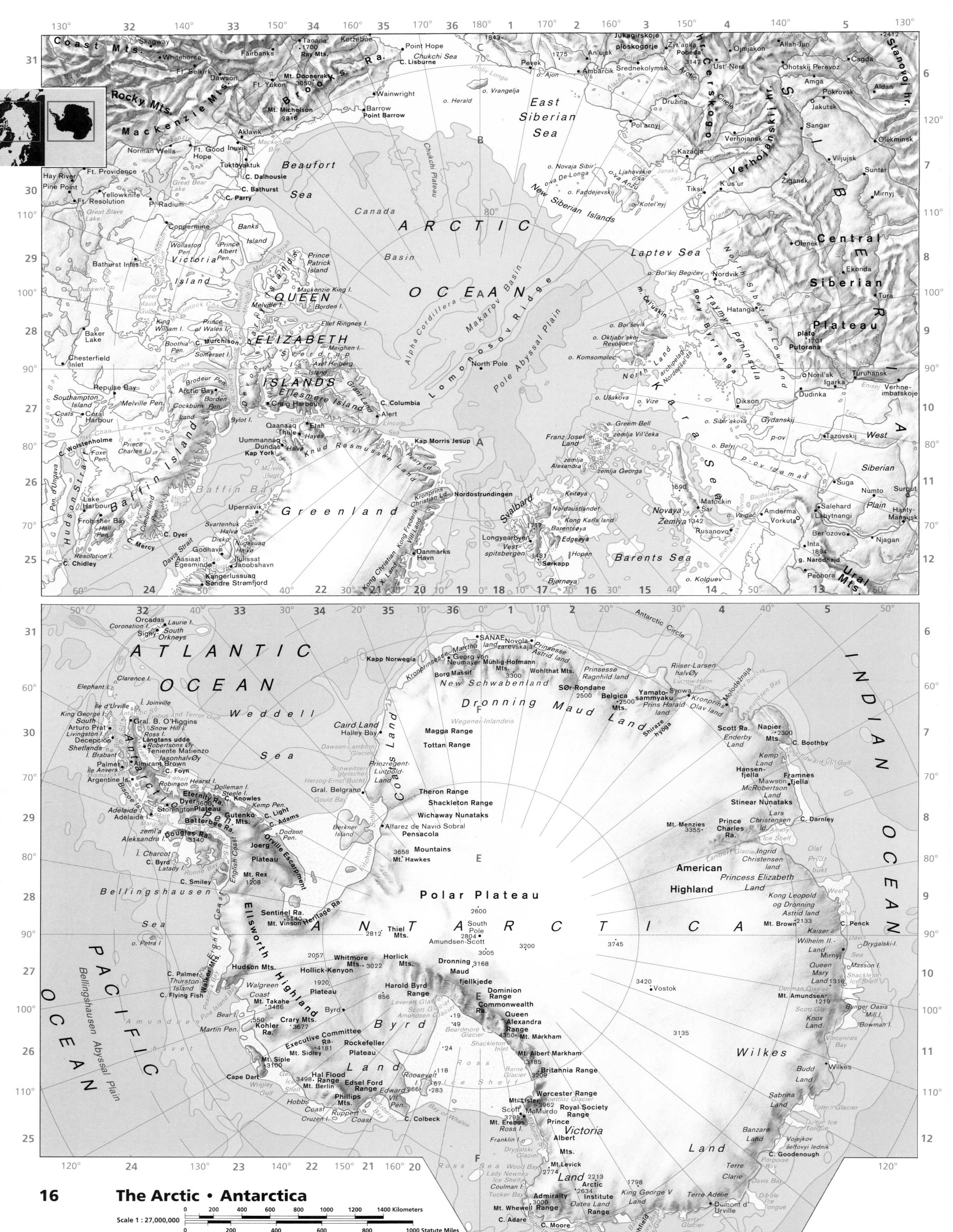

Coast Mts.
Skagway
Whitehorse
Tanana
1700
Ray Mts.
Kotzebue
Point Hope
Chukchi Sea
C. Lisburne
Fairbanks
Dawson
Ft. Selkirk
Ft. Yukon
Brooks Ra.
Mt. Doonerak
3050
Rocky Mts.
Mackenzie Mts.
Mt. Michelson
2816
Wainwright
Barrow
Point Barrow
Aklavik
Inuvik
Norman Wells
Ft. Good Hope
Tuktoyaktuk
C. Dalhousie
C. Bathurst
C. Parry
Beaufort
Sea
Hay River
Pine Point
Ft. Providence
Yellowknife
Ft. Resolution
P. Radium
Great Slave Lake
Great Bear Lake
Coppermine
Banks Island
Wollaston Pen.
Prince Albert Pen.
Victoria Island
Prince Patrick Island
Bathurst Inlet
Canada
Basin
ARCTIC
OCEAN
QUEEN
ELIZABETH
ISLANDS
Mackenzie King I.
Borden I.
Melville I.
Ellef Ringnes I.
King William I.
Prince of Wales I.
C. Murchison
Somerset I.
Boothia Pen.
Baker Lake
Chesterfield Inlet
Meighen I.
Axel Heiberg Island
Ellesmere Island
Grant Land
Craig Harbour
C. Columbia
Alert
Arctic Bay
Borden Pen.
Repulse Bay
Melville Pen.
Southampton Island
Coats
Coral Harbour
Bylot I.
Qaanaaq
Thule
Etah
Hayes
Uummannaq
Dundas
Kap York
Kap Morris Jesup
Knud Rasmussen Land
Peary Ld.
C. Wolstenholme
Prince Charles I.
Foxe Pen.
Baffin Island
Baffin Bay
Melville Bugt
Greenland
Kronprins Christian Ld.
Nordostrundingen
Lake Harbour
Frobisher Bay
Hall Pen.
Cumberland Pen.
C. Mercy
C. Dyer
Upernavik
Svartenhuk Halvø
Disko
Nugssuaq Halvø
Godhavn
Aasiaat
Egesminde
Ilulissat
Jacobshavn
Kangerlussuaq
Søndre Strømfjord
Davis Strait
Hudson Strait
Pen. d'Ungava
Resolution I.
C. Chidley
Kong Christian X. Land
Kong Frederik VIII Land
Danmarks Havn
Chukchi Plateau
Alpha Cordillera
Makarov Basin
Lomonosov Ridge
Pole Abyssal Plain
North Pole
o. Herald
o. Vrangelja
East Siberian Sea
Pevek
o. Ajon
1843
1775
Jukagirskoje ploskogorje
An'ujsk
Ambarčik
Srednekolymsk
Zyr'anka
Pobeda
3147
Ust'-Nera
Ojmjakon
Allah-Jun'
Stanovoj hr.
Čerskogo
Arctic Circle
Družina
Ohotskij Perevoz
Amga
Cagda
Aldan
Pokrovsk
Jakutsk
Sangar
Olekminsk
Verhojansk
Verhojanskij hr.
Pol'arnyj
Kazačje
o. Novaja Sibir'
o-va De-Longa
o-va Anžu
Ljahovskie o-va
o. Faddejevskij
o. Kotel'nyj
New Siberian Islands
Tiksi
K'us'ur
Žigansk
Viljujsk
Suntar
Mirnyj
Olenëk
Central Siberian Plateau
Laptev Sea
o. Bol'šoj Begičev
Nordvik
Ekonda
Tura
Hatanga
m. Čeljuskin
o. Bol'ševik
o. Oktjabr'skoj Revoljucii
o. Komsomolec
North Land
Taymyr Peninsula
gory Byrranga
plato Putorana
1701
North Siberian Lowland
Noril'sk
Igarka
Turuhansk
Verhne-imbatskoje
Dudinka
Dikson
o. Ušakova
o. Vize
o. Greem Bell
zemlja Vil'čeka
Franz Josef Land
zemlja Alexandra
zemlja Georga
o. Sibir'akova
Gydanskij p-ov
Tazovskij
West Siberian Plain
o. Belyj
p-ov Jamal
Kara Sea
Svalbard
Kvitøya
Nordaustlandet
Kong Karls land
Barentsøya
Edgeøya
Longyearbyen
Vestspitsbergen
1717
Hopen
Sørkapp
Bjørnøya
Novaya Zemlya
1590
1342
Matočkin Šar
Rusanovo
Vaigač
Amderma
Vorkuta
Salehard
Labytnangi
Numto
Suga
Surgut
Hanty-Mansijsk
Ber'ozovo
Njagan
Inta
1894
g. Narodnaja
Ural Mts.
Pečora
Barents Sea
o. Kolguev
Orcadas
Laurie I.
Coronation I.
Signy
South Orkneys
ATLANTIC
OCEAN
Clarence I.
Elephant I.
Weddell
Sea
Î. Joinville
Île d'Urville
King George I.
South Shetlands
Arturo Prat
Livingston I.
Decepcion
Gral. B. O'Higgins
Snow Hill I.
Ross I.
Langtans udde
Robertsons Øy
Teniente Matienzo
JasonhalvØy
I. Brabant
Palmer
Île Anvers
Almirante Brown
C. Foyn
Argentine Is.
Antarctic Pen.
Hearst I.
Dolleman I.
Steele I.
Robinson
Eternity Ra.
Dyer Plateau
3600
Stonington
C. Knowles
Kemp Pen.
C. Light
C. Adams
Gutenko Mts.
Adelaide I.
Adelaide
Batterbee Ra.
Marguerite Bay
zemlia
Aleksandra I.
Douglas Ra.
3140
Dodson Pen.
Joerg Plateau
Orville Escarpment
Î. Charcot
C. Byrd
Latady I.
English Coast
Mt. Rex
1208
C. Smiley
Bellingshausen Sea
Ellsworth Highland
Sentinel Ra.
Mt. Vinson
5140
Heritage Ra.
o. Petra I
PACIFIC
OCEAN
Bellingshausen Abyssal Plain
Hudson Mts.
Walker Mts.
Eights Coast
C. Palmer
Thurston Island
C. Flying Fish
Walgreen Coast
Mt. Takahe
3486
Bear I.
Martin Pen.
550
Kohler Ra.
Crary Mts.
3677
Amundsen Sea
Mt. Siple
3100
Cape Dart
Wrigley Gulf
Hobbs Coast
Cruzen I.
Ruppert Coast
Executive Committee Ra.
4181
Mt. Sidley
Hal Flood Range
3498
Mt. Berlin
Edsel Ford Range
Phillips Mts.
Rockefeller Plateau
Byrd Land
Roosevelt I.
Edward VII Pen.
Sulzberger Bay
C. Colbeck
Bay of Whales
Kapp Norwegia
SANAE
Novolazarevskaja
Kronprinsesse Martha land
Georg von Neumayer
Mühlig-Hofmann Mts.
3300
Prinsesse Astrid land
Borg Massif
Wohlthat Mts.
New Schwabenland
Prinsesse Ragnhild land
Sør-Rondane
2500
Belgica Mts.
2500
Dronning Maud Land
Wegener-Inlandeis
Yamato sammyaku
Syowa
Prins Harald land
Riiser-Larsen halvØy
Lutzow-Holm Bukt
Kronprins Olav land
Molodežnaja
Shirase hyoga
Amundsen Bay
Caird Land
Halley Bay
Coats Land
Magga Range
Tottan Range
Dawson-Lambton Glacier
Prinzregent-Luitpold-Land
Schweitzer-gletscher
Herzog-Ernst-Bucht
Gral. Belgrano
Gould Bay
Theron Range
Shackleton Range
Wichaway Nunataks
Berkner Island
Filchner Schelfeis
Alfarez de Navio Sobral
Pensacola
Mountains
3658
Mt. Hawkes
Polar Plateau
2600
ANTARCTICA
South Pole
2804
Amundsen-Scott
2812
Thiel Mts.
3005
3200
3745
2057
Whitmore Mts.
3022
Hollick-Kenyon
Horlick Mts.
Dronning Maud fjellkjede
3168
1920
Plateau
Harold Byrd Range
856
Leverett Glacier
Scott Glacier
Amundsen Glacier
Byrd
19
49
Beardmore Glacier
Dominion Range
Commonwealth Ra.
Queen Alexandra Range
4350
Mt. Markham
24
Shackleton Inlet
Ross Ice Shelf
Mt. Albert Markham
3185
Barne Glacier
Britannia Range
3209
118
67
283
366
Worcester Range
Koettlitz Glacier
Mt. Lister
3962
Scott
McMurdo
3795
Mt. Erebus
Ross I.
Royal Society Range
Prince Albert Mts.
Victoria Land
Franklin I.
Drygalski Glacier
Ross Sea
Wood Bay
Lady Newnes Ice Shelf
Coulman I.
Tucker Bay
Mt. Levick
2774
2213
Arctic Institute Range
2634
1798
King George V Land
Oates Land
Admiralty Range
3000
Mt. Whewell
C. Adare
C. Moore
Terre Adélie
Dumont d'Urville
Mertz Glacier
Dibble Ice Tongue
Mer d'Urville
Freshfield
Scott Ra.
Enderby Land
Napier Mts.
2300
C. Boothby
Kemp Land
King Edward VIII Gulf
Hansen-fjella
Framnes fjella
Mawson
McRobertson Land
Stinear Nunataks
Lars Christensen Id.
C. Darnley
Mt. Menzies
3355
Prince Charles Ra.
Amery Ice Shelf
Lambert Glacier
Ingrid Christensen land
Olaf Prydz bukt
American Highland
Princess Elizabeth Land
Kong Leopold og Dronning Astrid land
West Ice Shelf
Mt. Brown
2133
C. Penck
Kaiser
Wilhelm II.-Land
Davis Sea
Drygalski-I.
Mirnyj
Masson I.
Queen Mary Land
1316
Shackleton Ice Shelf
Denman Glacier
Mt. Amundsen
1219
3420
Vostok
Bunger Oasis
Mill I.
Scott Glacier
Knox Land
Bowman I.
3135
Vincennes Bay
Wilkes
Wilkes
Budd Land
Sabrina Land
Totten Glacier
Dalton Ice Tongue
Banzare Land
Vojejkov šelfovyj lednik
C. Goodenough
Porpoise Bay
Terre Clarie
Davis Bay
INDIAN
OCEAN
Antarctic Circle
Scale 1 : 27,000,000
0 200 400 600 800 1000 1200 1400 Kilometers
0 200 400 600 800 1000 Statute Miles

North and Middle America – one continent, two worlds

The North American continent, including Middle America and the West Indian archipelago, covers an area of 9,266,400 square miles (24 million sq. km). Thus the continent extends from the icy climate of the North Pole to the hot and humid tropics. One-quarter of the area consists of islands and peninsulas: in the north of the Canadian islands and Greenland, the largest island in the world; south of the Tropic of Cancer lie the Greater and Lesser Antilles. The entire area is made up of five elements: the Canadian Shield, the low range of the Appalachian Mountains, the central plains, the high ranges of the Rocky Mountains, and the West Indian islands. Due to the North-South orientation of the mountain ranges, the continent has no mountain barriers to prevent the exchange of polar and tropical air masses. The original population of North, Central and South America originates from Asia and has been displaced, with the exception of a few remaining enclaves, by European immigrants and their descendants. The resulting cultural areas come together at the southern border of the U.S.

"The Newe Islands That Lie Beyond Spain to the East By the Land of India." This depiction of America appeared in Sebastian Münster's "Cosmographia Universalis" (1550).

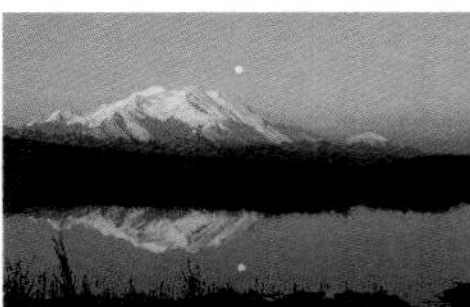
Alaska
p. 20–21

Aleutians
p. 22–23

Canada: Arctic Islands
p. 24–25

Greenland: Northern Region
p. 26–27

Greenland: Southern Region
p. 28–29

Canada: Barren Grounds
p. 30–31

Canada: British Columbia, Alberta, Saskatchewan p. 32–33

Canada: Manitoba, Ontario
p. 34–35

Canada: Labrador
p. 36–37

Canada: Atlantic Provinces
p. 38–39

U.S.A.: Pacific States
p. 40–41

U.S.A.: Central States, North
p. 42–43

U.S.A.: Central States, South
p. 44–45

U.S.A.: Great Lakes, Northeastern States p. 46–47

U.S.A.: Southeastern States (Inset: Hawaii) p. 48–49

Mexico: Northern Region
p. 50–51

Mexico: Southern Region
Central America p. 52–53

Greater Antilles
p. 54–55

Lesser Antilles
p. 56

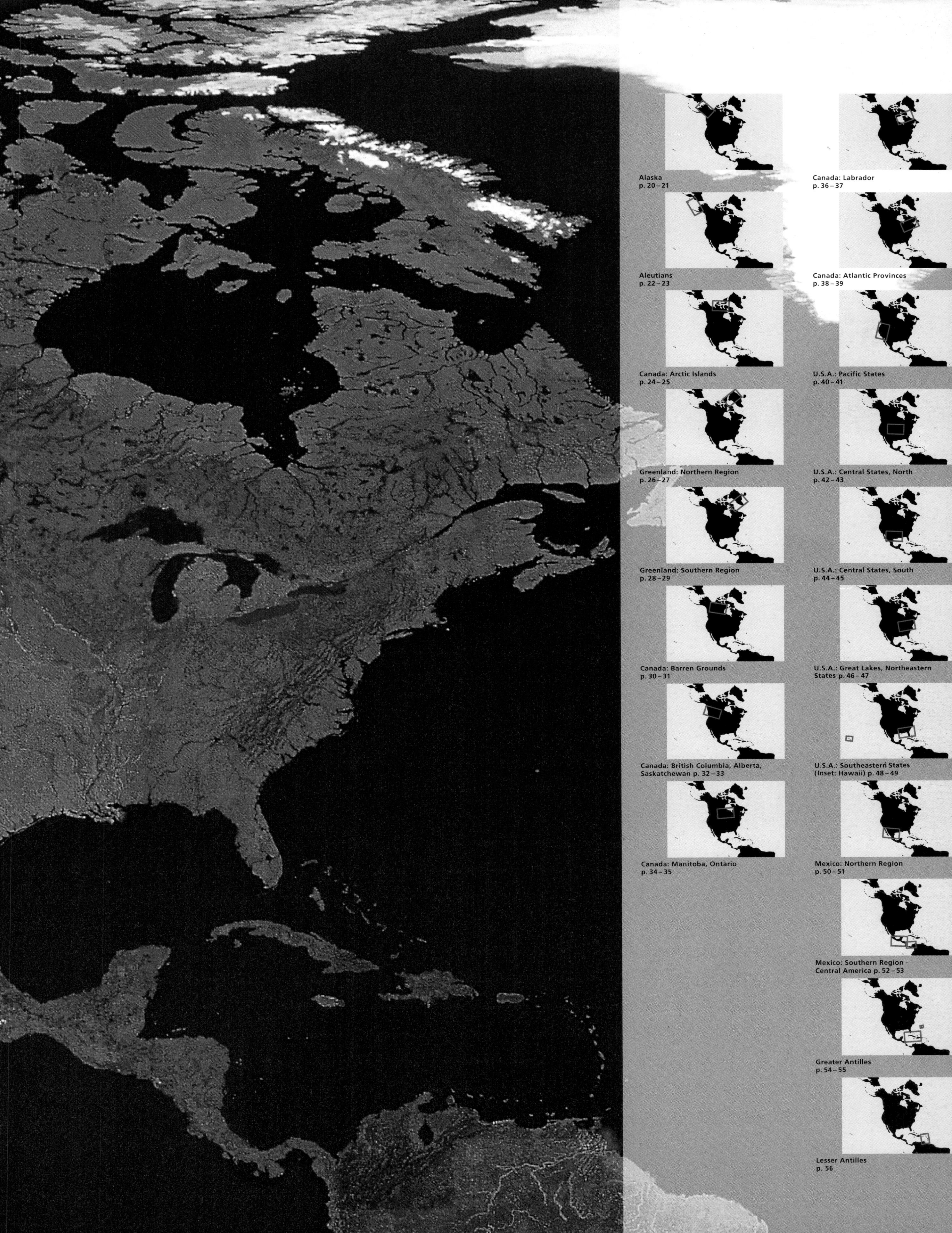
Alaska
p. 20–21
Aleutians
p. 22–23
Canada: Arctic Islands
p. 24–25
Greenland: Northern Region
p. 26–27
Greenland: Southern Region
p. 28–29
Canada: Barren Grounds
p. 30–31
Canada: British Columbia, Alberta,
Saskatchewan p. 32–33
Canada: Manitoba, Ontario
p. 34–35
Canada: Labrador
p. 36–37
Canada: Atlantic Provinces
p. 38–39
U.S.A.: Pacific States
p. 40–41
U.S.A.: Central States, North
p. 42–43
U.S.A.: Central States, South
p. 44–45
U.S.A.: Great Lakes, Northeastern
States p. 46–47
U.S.A.: Southeastern States
(Inset: Hawaii) p. 48–49
Mexico: Northern Region
p. 50–51
Mexico: Southern Region ·
Central America p. 52–53
Greater Antilles
p. 54–55
Lesser Antilles
p. 56

Chukchi Sea
Bering Strait
Bering Sea
Norton Sound
Kotzebue Sound
Kuskokwim Bay
Etolin Strait
RUSSIA
A l a s k a (U. S.)
Brooks Range
North Slope
Seward Peninsula
Baldwin Peninsula
Kenai Peninsula
Saint Lawrence I.
Nunivak I.
Nelson I.
Little Diomede I.
Arctic Circle
International Date Line
+12h Gr.Time
-9h Gr.Time
Knifeblade Ridge
Lookout Ridge
De Long Mts.
Baird Mountains
Igichuk Hills
Mulgrave Hills
Schwatka Mts.
Endicott Mts.
Waring Mountains
Lockwood Hills
Zane Hills
Shekluksuk Range
Ray Mountains
Kokrines Hills
Kaiyuh Mountains
Kuskokwim Mountains
Kilbuck Mountains
Ahklun Mountains
Chigmit Mountains
Kiokluk Mts.
Taylor Mts.
Bendeleben Mts.
Kigluaik Mts.
Darby Mts.
Kookooligit Mts.
Kinipaghulghat Mts.
Askinuk Mts.
Noatak National Preserve
Gates of the Arctic National Park and Preserve
Kobuk Valley Nat. Park
Bering Land Bridge Nat. Reserve
Cape Krusenstern Nat. Mon.
Koyukuk Nat. Wildlife Refuge
Yukon Delta National Wildlife Refuge
Lake Clark Nat. Park and Preserve
Denali National Park and Preserve
Yukon Delta
Yukon R.
Kuskokwim R.
Pt. Barrow
Barrow
Wainwright
Icy Cape
Pt. Lay
C. Lisburne
Pt. Hope
Kivalina
Kotzebue
Noatak
Noorvik
Kiana
Selawik
Ambler
Shungnak
Kobuk
Shishmaref
Wales
Teller
Nome
C. Nome
Solomon
White Mountain
Golovin
Elim
Koyuk
Unalakleet
St. Michael
Stebbins
Gambell
Savoonga
Nulato
Galena
Ruby
Koyukuk
Tanana
Bettles
Allakaket
Hughes
Huslia
McGrath
Aniak
Bethel
Kalskag
Crooked Creek
Stony River
Dillingham
Iliamna Lake
Kenai
Homer
Mt. McKinley 6194
Uelen
Lorino
Lavrentija
Providenija
Enurmino
Neškan
Vankarem
Scale 1 : 4,500,000
0 40 80 120 160 200 Kilometers
0 40 80 120 160 Statute Miles

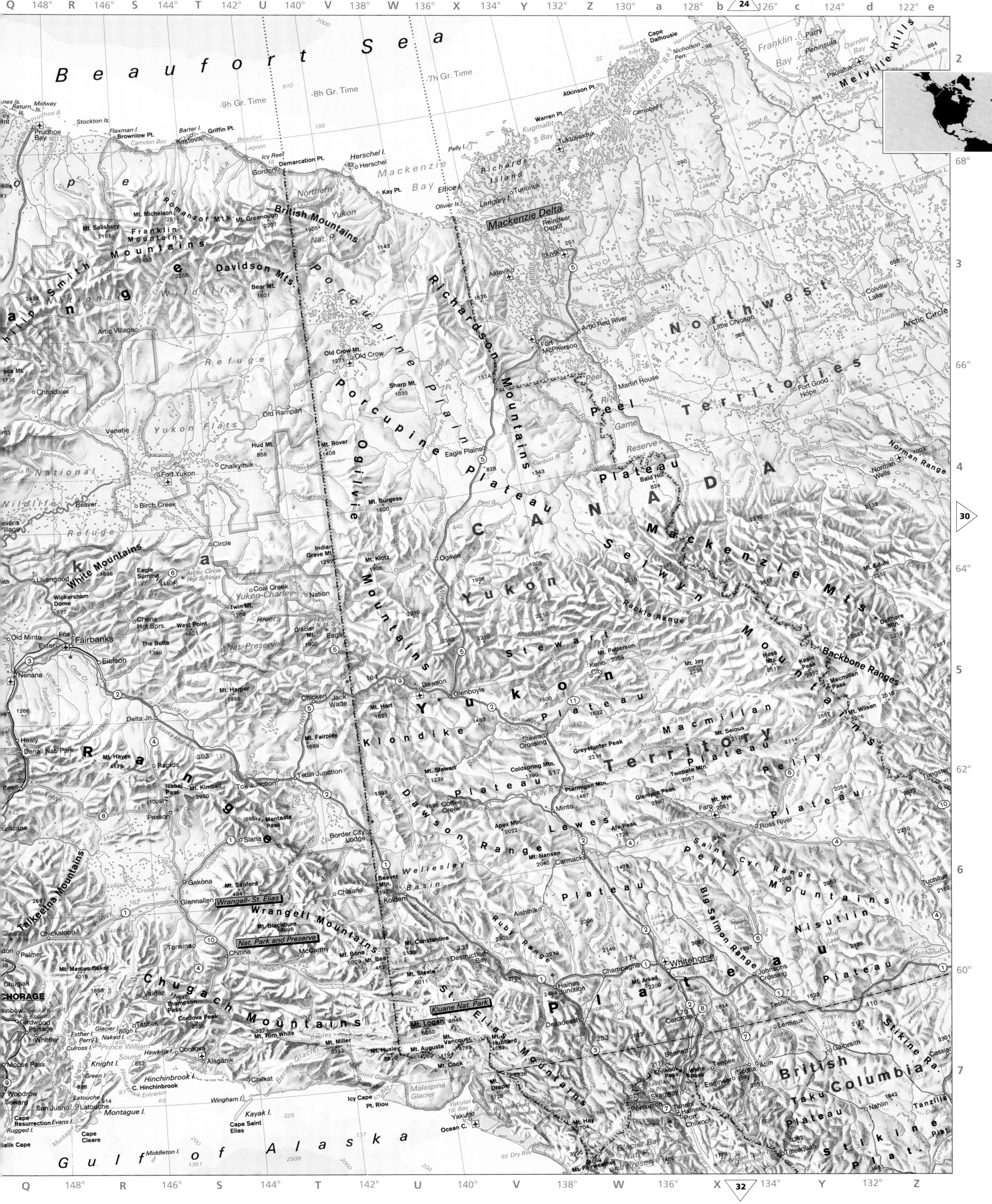

Beaufort Sea
Gulf of Alaska
-9h Gr. Time
-8h Gr. Time
-7h Gr. Time
Prudhoe Bay
Stockton Is.
Flaxman I.
Brownlow Pt.
Barter I.
Kaktovik
Griffin Pt.
Icy Reef
Demarcation Pt.
Herschel I.
Herschel
Mackenzie Bay
Kay Pt.
Eltice I.
Langley I.
Richards Island
Tununuk
Mackenzie Delta
Reindeer Depot
Cape Dalhousie
Nicholson Pen.
Franklin Bay
Parry Peninsula
Darnley Bay
Paulatuk
Melville Hills
Atkinson Pt.
Warren Pt.
Campbell L.
Kugmallit Bay
Tuktoyaktuk
Pelly I.
Olivier Is.
Inuvik
Aklavik
Fort McPherson
Arctic Red River
Martin House
Fort Good Hope
Norman Wells
Norman Range
Colville Lake
Arctic Circle
Northwest Territories
Peel River Game Reserve
Bald Hill
British Mountains
Northern Yukon Nat. P.
Mt. Michelson
Romanzof Mts.
Mt. Greenough
Mt. Salisbury
Franklin Mountains
Davidson Mts.
Bear Mt.
Artic Village
Arctic National Wildlife Refuge
Porcupine Plain
Porcupine Plateau
Richardson Mountains
Old Crow Mt.
Old Crow
Sharp Mt.
Eagle Plains
Ogilvie Mountains
Mt. Rover
Mt. Burgess
Indian Grave Mt.
Mt. Klotz
Ogilvie
Chandalar
Venetie
Old Rampart
Yukon Flats National Wildlife Refuge
Hud Mt.
Chalkyitsik
Fort Yukon
Beaver
Birch Creek
Circle
White Mountains
Eagle Summit
Livengood
Wickersham Dome
Coal Creek
Nation
Yukon-Charley Rivers Nat. Preserve
Twin Mt.
Chena Hot Sprs.
West Point
Old Minto
Fox
Fairbanks
Ester
Eielson
The Butte
Glacier Mt.
Eagle
Nenana
Mt. Harper
Chicken
Jack Wade
Dawson
Glenboyle
Mt. Hart
Klondike
Yukon Plateau
Stewart Plateau
Mt. Patterson
Keno City
Mt. Joy
Hess Mts.
Keele Peak
Backbone Ranges
Macmillan Pass
Mt. Wilson
Mackenzie Mts.
Selwyn Mountains
Rackla Range
Mt. Eduni
Dusthore Mtn.
CANADA
Yukon Territory
Macmillan Plateau
Mt. Selous
Pelly Plateau
Stewart Crossing
Grey Hunter Peak
Coldspring Mtn.
Twopete Mtn.
Ptarmigan Mtn.
Glenlyon Peak
Faro
Mt. Mye
Ross River
Tungsten
Delta Jn.
Healy
Denali Nat. Park
Mt. Hayes
Alaska Range
Rapids
Isabel Pass
Mt. Kimball
Tok Junction
Tetlin Junction
Mt. Fairplay
Mt. Stewart
Dawson Range
Coffee Creek
Apex Mtn.
Mt. Nansen
Carmacks
Minto
Afe Peak
Lewes Plateau
Paxson
Mentasta Pass
Slana
Border City Lodge
Beaver Mtn.
Koidern
Wellesley Basin
Saint Cyr Range
Pelly Mountains
Big Salmon Range
Nisutlin Plateau
Tuchitua
Gakona
Mt. Sanford
Glennallen
Wrangell-St. Elias Nat. Park and Preserve
Wrangell Mountains
Mt. Blackburn
Chisana
Aishihik
Ruby Range
Talkeetna Mountains
Chickaloon
Palmer
Tonsina
Chitina
McCarthy
Mt. Bona
Mt. Bear
Mt. Constantine
Destruction Bay
Mt. Steele
Mt. Marcus Baker
Chugach Mountains
Valdez
Thompson Pass
Cordova Peak
ANCHORAGE
Chugiak
Girdwood
Portage
Whittier
Tatitlek
Glacier I.
Bligh I.
Esther I.
Perry I.
Naked I.
Culross I.
Prince William Sound
Hawkins I.
Cordova
Alaganik
Knight I.
Mt. Tom White
Mt. Miller
Bering Glacier
Mt. Huxley
Mt. Augusta
Mt. Logan
Kluane Nat. Park
Mt. Vancouver
Mt. Hubbard
St. Elias Mountains
Mt. Cook
Haines Junction
Champagne
Mt. Arkell
Whitehorse
Johnsons Crossing
Teslin
Carcross
Dezadeash
Haines
Bennett
Chilkoot Pass
White Pass
Skagway
Port Chilkoot
Atlin
Tagish
Lemieux
Galbraith
Teepee
Engineers
Scotia Bay
British Columbia
Stikine Ra.
Cassiar
Taku Plateau
Nahlin
Tanzilla
Stikine Plat.
Moose Pass
Woodrow
Seward
San Juan
Latouche
Cape Resurrection
Evans I.
Rugged I.
Montague I.
Hinchinbrook I.
C. Hinchinbrook
Chilkat
Malaspina Glacier
Icy Cape
Pt. Riou
Wingham I.
Kayak I.
Cape Saint Elias
Middleton I.
Yakutat
Ocean C.
Yakutat Bay
Mt. Draper
Mt. Hay
Mt. Fairweather
Glacier Bay
Dry Bay
Cape Cleare

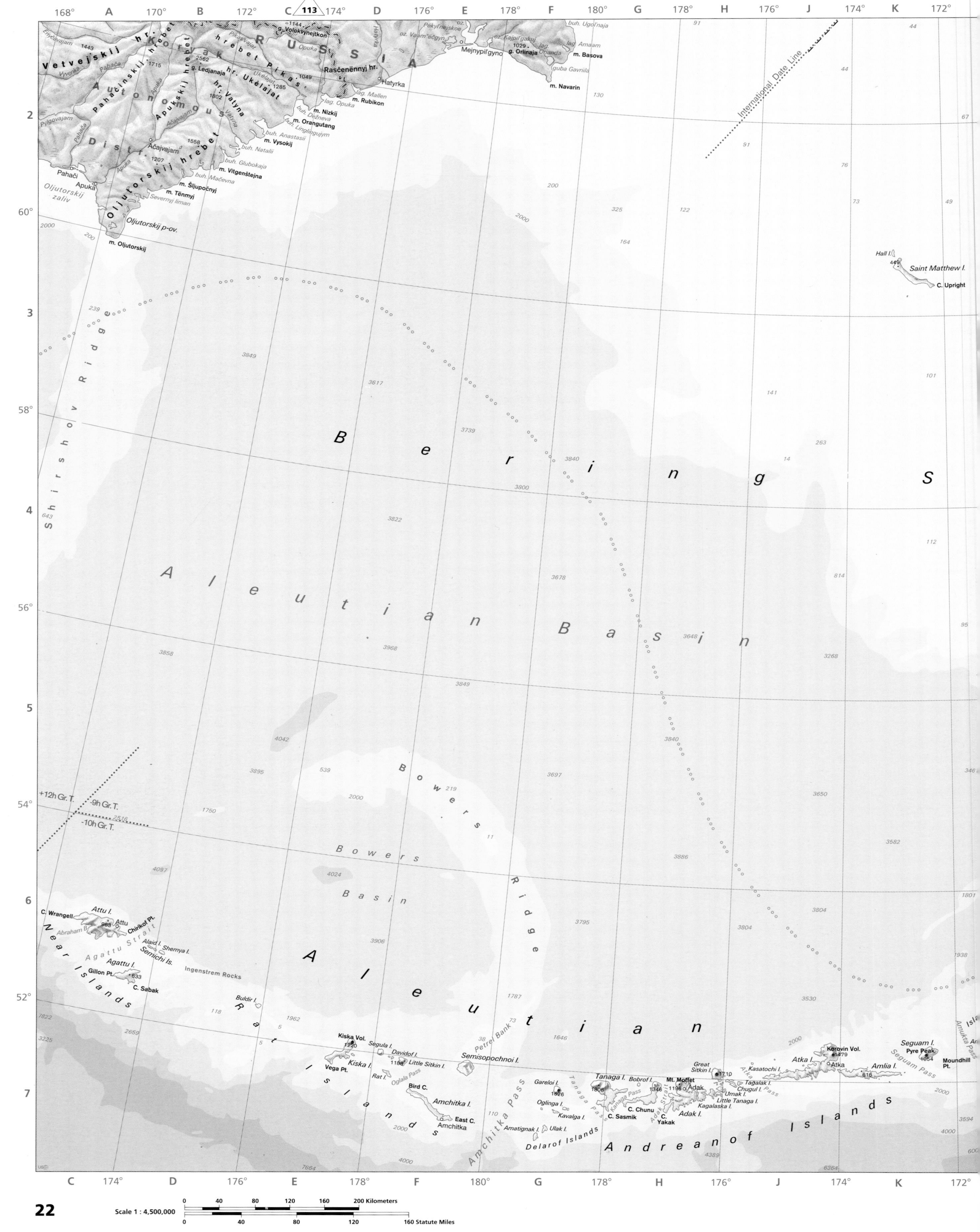

113
R U S S I A
Koryak Autonomous District
Vetvejskij hr.
Korjakskij hrebet
hrebet Pikas
Pahačinskij hr.
hr. Ukèlajat
Apukskij hrebet
hr. Vatyna
Oljutorskij hrebet
g. Ledjanaja
g. Volokvynejtkon
Rasčenënnyj hr.
Hatyrka
lag. Mallen
m. Rubikon
lag. Opuka
m. Nizkij
buh. Dežneva
m. Orangutang
buh. Anastasii
m. Vysokij
buh. Natalii
buh. Glubokaja
m. Vitgenštejna
buh. Mačevna
m. Šljupočnyj
m. Tënmyj
Severnyj liman
Ačajvajam
Pahači
Apuka
Oljutorskij zaliv
Oljutorskij p-ov.
m. Oljutorskij
Mejnypil'gyno
g. Orlinaja
lag. Amaam
m. Basova
guba Gavriila
m. Navarin
buh. Ugol'naja
International Date Line
Hall I.
Saint Matthew I.
C. Upright
Bering Sea
Shirshov Ridge
Aleutian Basin
Bowers Ridge
Bowers Basin
Aleutian Islands
+12h Gr. T.
-9h Gr. T.
-10h Gr. T.
C. Wrangell
Attu I.
Attu
Chirikof Pt.
Abraham B.
Agattu Strait
Alaid I.
Shemya I.
Semichi Is.
Agattu I.
Gillon Pt.
C. Sabak
Near Islands
Ingenstrem Rocks
Buldir I.
Rat Islands
Kiska Vol.
Kiska I.
Vega Pt.
Segula I.
Davidof I.
Little Sitkin I.
Rat I.
Oglala Pass
Bird C.
Amchitka I.
East C.
Amchitka
Petrel Bank
Semisopochnoi I.
Amchitka Pass
Gareloi I.
Ogliuga I.
Kavalga I.
Ulak I.
Amatignak I.
Delarof Islands
Tanaga Pass
Tanaga I.
Kanaga Pass
C. Sasmik
Bobrof I.
C. Chunu
Mt. Moffet
Adak
Adak Strait
Adak I.
C. Yakak
Great Sitkin I.
Andreanof Islands
Kasatochi I.
Tagalak I.
Chugul I.
Umak I.
Little Tanaga I.
Kagalaska I.
Atka Pass
Atka I.
Korovin Vol.
Atka
Amlia I.
Seguam I.
Pyre Peak
Seguam Pass
Moundhill Pt.
Amukta Pass
168° 170° 172° 174° 176° 178° 180° 178° 176° 174° 172°
60° 58° 56° 54° 52°
Scale 1 : 4,500,000
0 40 80 120 160 200 Kilometers
0 40 80 120 160 Statute Miles

Bristol Bay
PACIFIC OCEAN
Aleutian Trench
Fox Islands
Alaska Peninsula
Aleutian Range
Kuskokwim Bay
Etolin Strait
Shelikof Strait
Shumagin Islands
Krenitzin Is.
Sanak Islands
Nunivak I.
Unimak I.
Unalaska I.
Umnak I.
Kodiak Island
Afognak Island
Semidi Is.
Chirikof I.
Trinity Is.
Kenai Peninsula
ANCHORAGE
Yukon Delta
Yukon Delta National Wildlife Refuge
Kilbuck Mountains
Kuskokwim Mts.
Ahklun Mountains
Chigmit Mountains
Lake Clark Nat. Park and Preserve
Katmai Nat. Park and Preserve
Iliamna Lake
Cook Inlet
St. George I.
Pribilof Islands
-10h Gr. T.
-9h Gr. T.

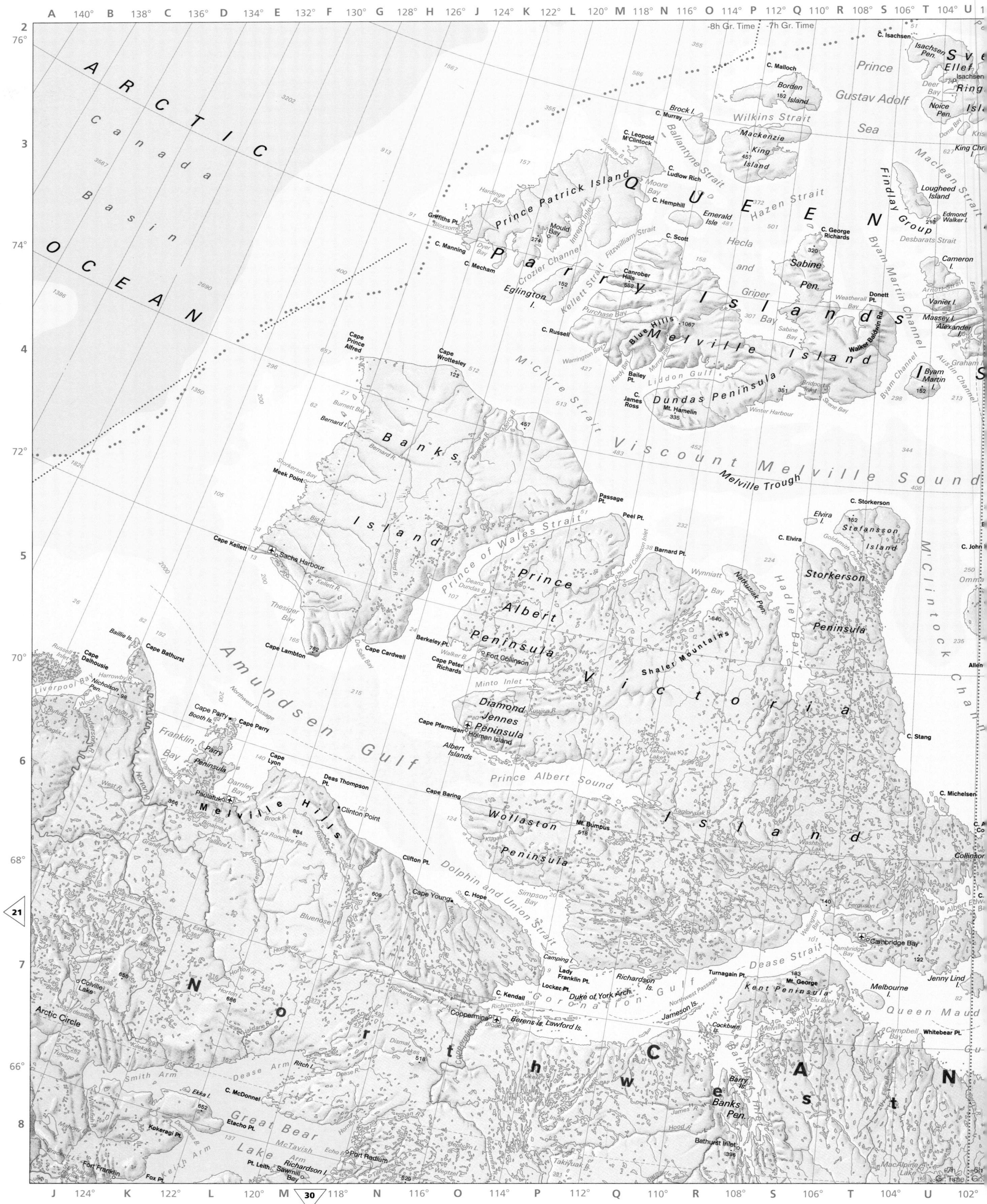

A 140° B 138° C 136° D 134° E 132° F 130° G 128° H 126° J 124° K 122° L 120° M 118° N 116° O 114° P 112° Q 110° R 108° S 106° T 104° U

-8h Gr. Time -7h Gr. Time

ARCTIC OCEAN

Canada Basin

QUEEN ELIZABETH ISLANDS

Parry Islands

Prince Patrick Island

Melville Island

Banks Island

Prince Albert Peninsula

Victoria Island

Amundsen Gulf

Viscount Melville Sound

M'Clure Strait

Melville Trough

Prince of Wales Strait

Prince Gustav Adolf Sea

Wilkins Strait

Ballantyne Strait

Hazen Strait

Byam Martin Channel

Hecla and Griper Bay

Sabine Pen.

Dundas Peninsula

Liddon Gulf

Kellett Strait

Crozier Channel

Fitzwilliam Strait

Intrepid Inlet

Findlay Group

Maclean Strait

Desbarats Strait

Borden Island

Brock I.

Mackenzie King Island

Emerald Isle

Eglinton I.

Lougheed Island

Edmond Walker I.

Cameron I.

Vanier I.

Massey I.

Alexander I.

Byam Martin I.

Ellef Ringnes Island

Isachsen Pen.

C. Isachsen

C. Malloch

C. Murray

C. Leopold M'Clintock

C. Ludlow Rich

C. Hemphill

C. Scott

C. George Richards

Canrober Hills

Blue Hills

C. Russell

C. Manning

C. Mecham

Griffiths Pt.

Mould Bay

Moore Bay

Dyer Bay

Purchase Bay

Warrington Bay

Hardy Bay

Bailey Pt.

C. James Ross

Mt. Hamelin

Winter Harbour

Skene Bay

Bridport Inlet

Weatherall Bay

Donett Pt.

Walker Baldwin Ra.

Arnott Strait

Austin Channel

Cape Prince Alfred

Cape Wrottesley

Burnett Bay

Bernard I.

Bernard R.

Storkerson Bay

Meek Point

Big R.

Cape Kellett

Sachs Harbour

Kellett R.

Thesiger Bay

Cape Lambton

Cape Cardwell

De Salis Bay

Passage Pt.

Peel Pt.

Barnard Pt.

Richard Collinson Inlet

Deans Dundas B.

Wynniatt Bay

Natkusiak Pen.

Hadley Bay

Shaler Mountains

C. Storkerson

Elvira I.

C. Elvira

Stefansson Island

Goldsmith Channel

Storkerson Peninsula

M'Clintock Channel

C. John

Omma...

Allen

C. Stang

C. Michelsen

Collinson

Berkeley Pt.

Walker B.

Fort Collinson

Cape Peter Richards

Minto Inlet

Diamond Jenness Peninsula

Cape Pfarmigan

Holman Island

Albert Islands

Prince Albert Sound

Wollaston Peninsula

Mt. Bumpus

Kagloryuak R.

Washburn L.

Simpson Bay

Dolphin and Union Strait

Ferguson L.

Wellington Bay

Cambridge Bay

Albert Edward Bay

Dease Strait

Turnagain Pt.

Mt. George

Kent Peninsula

Melbourne I.

Jenny Lind I.

Queen Maud Gulf

Campbell Bay

Whitebear Pt.

Coronation Gulf

Northwest Passage

Richardson Is.

Duke of York Arch.

Jameson Is.

Cockburn Is.

Melville Sound

Lady Franklin Pt.

Locker Pt.

Camping I.

C. Kendall

Richardson Bay

Coppermine

Berens Is.

Lawford Is.

Bloody Fall

Baillie Is.

Cape Bathurst

Russell Inlet

Cape Dalhousie

Liverpool Bay

Harrowby B.

Nicholson Pen.

Wood B.

Anderson R.

Mason R.

Cape Parry

Booth Is.

Northwest Passage

Franklin Bay

Parry Peninsula

Langton B.

Darnley Bay

Cape Lyon

Deas Thompson Pt.

Paulatuk

Melville Hills

Clinton Point

Cape Baring

Brock R.

La Roncière Falls

Hornaday R.

Horton R.

Clifton Pt.

Cape Young

C. Hope

Bluenose L.

Croker R.

Kugaluk R.

Rae R.

Richardson R.

Horton L.

Colville Lake

Arctic Circle

Smith Arm

Dease Arm

Ritch I.

Dease R.

Dismal Lakes

Ekka I.

C. McDonnell

Etacho Pt.

Kokeragi Pt.

Great Bear Lake

McTavish Arm

Echo B.

Port Radium

Keith Arm

Fort Franklin

Fox Pt.

Pt. Leith

Richardson I.

Sawmill Bay

Hornby B.

Takiyuak L.

Bathurst Inlet

Barry Is.

Banks Pen.

James R.

Hood R.

MacAlpine Lake

-6h Gr. Time

N o r t h w e s t T e r r i t o r i e s

C A N

2 3 4 5 6 7 8

76° 74° 72° 70° 68° 66°

21

30

J 124° K 122° L 120° M 118° N 116° O 114° P 112° Q 110° R 108° S 106° T 104° U 102°

Scale 1 : 4,500,000

0 40 80 120 160 200 Kilometers

0 40 80 120 160 Statute Miles

Axel Heiberg Island
Ellesmere Island
Raanes Peninsula
Svendsen Peninsula
Amund Ringnes Island
Massey Sound
Hassel Sound
Eureka Sound
Norwegian Bay
Bjorne Peninsula
Cornwall Island
Graham I.
Belcher Channel
Buckingham I.
C. Torrens
Bay
North Lincoln Land
Inglefield Mts.
Grise Fiord
Smith Bay
C. Mouat
C. Combermere
C. Norton Shaw
Phillips Pt.
Coburg Island
Cambridge Pt.
Glacier Strait
Lady Ann Strait
Smith I.
South C.
Mt. Britannia
Grinnel Peninsula
Penny Strait
Colin Archer Pen.
Cape Vera
Jones Sound
C. Sparbo
Belcher Pt.
C. Fitz Roy
C. Becher
Baillie Hamilton I.
Queens Channel
Wellington Channel
Skruis Pt.
Bear Bay
Sverdrup Inlet
Devon Island
Philpots I.
Little Cornwallis I.
Cornwallis Island
McDougall Sound
Dundas Harbour
C. Sherard
C. Capel
Resolute
C. Hotham
C. Ricketts
Fellfoot Pt.
C. Bullen
Lancaster Sound
Baffin Bay
Griffith I.
Lowther I.
Barrow Strait
Northwest Passage
Prince Leopold I.
C. Clarence
C. Crauford
C. Charles Yorke
C. Hay
C. Liverpool
Bylot Island
C. Graham Moore
C. Macculloch
Pond Inlet
Eclipse Sound
Palmerston Pt.
Russell I.
Somerset Island
C. Briggs
Prince of Wales Island
Peel Sound
Prescott I.
Prince Regent Inlet
St. Joseph Plateau
Mt. Sherer
Brodeur Peninsula
Admiralty Inlet
Uluksan Pen.
Arctic Bay
Hartz Mts.
Borden Peninsula
Mt. Emma
Nova Zembla I.
C. Jameson
Dexterity I.
Fury Pt.
Creswell Bay
C. Garry
Magda Plateau
Steensby Peninsula
Mt. Walker
Brentford Bay
C. Farrand
Baffin Island
Barnes Ice Cap
Van Koenig Pt.
Easter C.
Charles Dickens Pt.
C. Hobson
C. Swinburne
Franklin Strait
Boothia Peninsula
C. Allington
Gulf of Boothia
C. St. Catherine
Thom Bay
C. Margaret
C. North Hendon
Astronomical Society Islands
Crown Prince Frederik I.
Pt. Kendall
C. Hallowell
C. Englefield
Fury and Hecla Strait
Ormonde I.
Amherst I.
Sevigny Pt.
Jens Munk I.
C. Konig
Koch I.
Bray I.
Ikpik Bay
C. Thalbitzer
C. Jensen
Igloolik
Rowley I.
Baird Pen.
C. Burpee
Foley I.
North Tweedsmuir I.
South Tweedsmuir I.
Pinger Pt.
Hall Beach
North Spicer I.
South Spicer I.
Prince Charles Island
Air Force I.
Gateshead Island
C. Felix
Franklin Pt.
James Ross Strait
Tennent Is.
Spence Bay
Boothia Isthmus
Matty I.
Harrison Is.
C. Chapman
C. Miles
C. Richardson
Committee Bay
Melville Peninsula
Parry Bay
Amitikoe Pen.
Foxe Basin
King William Island
M'Clintock Pt.
C. Norton
St. Roch Basin
Matheson Pt.
Simpson Peninsula
Pelly Bay
Royal Geographical Society Is.
Gjoa Haven
Rasmussen Basin
Storis Passage
Grant Pt.
Ogle Pt.
Wales I.
C. Penrhyn
Gravell Pt.
Arctic Circle
Adelaide Peninsula
Cowie Pt.
Rae Isthmus
Pt. Elizabeth
Repulse Bay
Beach Pt.
C. Clarke
White I.
C. Martineau
Sturges Is.
Winter I.
Vansittart I.
C. Dorchester
Greenland (Kalaallit Nunaat) (Denmark)
Hayes Halvø
Nordgrønland
Thule
Qaanaaq
Steensby Land
K. Parry
K. Atholt
Dundas
Crimson Cliffs
Carey Øer
Saunders Ø
Wolstenholme Ø
Kap York
Kap Melville
K. Robertson
Herbert Ø
Northumberland Ø
Mt. Leeds
QUEEN ELIZABETH ISLANDS
ARCTIC ARCHIPELAGO
DISTRICT OF FRANKLIN
-4h Gr. Time
-5h Gr. Time
-6h Gr. Time

100° A 98° B 96° C 94° D 92° E 90° F 88° G 86° H 84° J 82° K 80° L 78° M 76° N 74° O 72° P 70° Q 68° R 66° S 64° T 62° U 60° V 58° W 56° X 54° Y 52°

80°
4
78°
5
76°
6
74°
7
72°
8
70°
9

-6h Gr. T.
-5h Gr. T.

A R C T I C
Lincoln Sea
QUEEN ELIZABETH ISLANDS
Ellesmere Island
Axel Heiberg Island
Sverdrup Islands
Princess Margaret Range
Northwest Territories
Grant Land
United States Range
British Empire Range
Conger Range
Krieger Mountains
Victoria and Albert Mts.
Grinnell Land
Fosheim Peninsula
Raanes Peninsula
Svendsen Peninsula
Bjorne Peninsula
Simmon's Peninsula
Johan Peninsula
Judge Daly Promontory
Meighen Island
C. Northwest
C. Thomas Hubbard
Bukken Fiord
Rens Fiord
Nansen Sound
Sverdrup Channel
Li Fiord
Middle Fiord
Audhild Bay
Emma Fiord
Otto Fiord
Phillips Inlet
Yelverton Bay
C. Woods
Alert Pt.
C. Egerton
C. Discovery
Ward Hunt I.
C. Aldrich
C. Colan
Clements Markham Inlet
C. Joseph Henry
Alert
Black Mtn.
Hare Fiord
Schei Pen.
Iceberg Pt.
Trees Pt.
Eureka
Greely Fiord
Elmerson Pen.
Kipley Pt.
Lake Hazen
Tanquary Fiord
Antoinette Bay
Mt. Oxford
Dodge R.
Archer Fiord
C. Baird
Hall Basin
Robeson Channel
Kennedy Channel
Canon Fiord
Massey Sound
Eureka Sound
Bay Fiord
Norwegian Bay
Northeast Pt.
Graham I.
Buckingham I.
C. Torrens
Cardigan Strait
Ammonite Mtn.
Baumann Fiord
Vendom Fiord
Sverdrup Pass
Stygge Glacier
Hayes Fiord
Alexandra Fiord (abandoned)
Mt. Leeds
Cadogan Gl.
Talbot Inlet
Talbot Glacier
Buchanan B.
Parrish Glacier
Cook Pen.
Princess Marie Bay
Bache Pen.
Victoria Head
C. Albert
Pim I.
Dobbin B.
Darling Pen.
C. Hawk's
C. Knorr
C. Collinson
C. Jackson
Franklin I.
Washington L.
Cape Vera
Eidsbotn
West Fiord
Jones Sound
Skruis Pt.
Bear Bay
Sverdrup Inlet
South C.
Lindstrom Pen.
Grise Fiord
North Lincoln Land
Inglefield Mts.
C. Mouat
Smith Bay
C. Combermere
C. Isabella
Smith Sound
Makinson Inlet
Smith I.
C. Sparbo
Glacier Strait
C. Norton Shaw
Devon Island
Lady Ann Strait
Phillips Pt.
Coburg Island
Cambridge Pt.
Belcher Pt.
C. Fitz Roy
C. Bullen
Croker Bay
Hyde Inlet
Dundas Harbour
Philpots I.
C. Sherard
Lancaster Sound
Northwest Passage
C. Crauford
C. Charles Yorke
Hartz Mts.
Borden Peninsula
Navy Board Inlet
C. Hay
Bylot Island
C. Liverpool
Eclipse Sound
Milne Inlet
Mt. Emma
Pond Inlet
C. Graham Moore
Oliver Sound
C. Macculloch
Nova Zembla
C. Jameson
North Arm
Buchan Gulf
Isbjorn Strait
Dexterity I.
Steensby Inlet
Robertson R.
Rowley R.
Scott Inlet
C. Thalbitzer
C. Jensen
Koch I.
Bray I.
Rowley I.
Ikpik Bay
Barnes Ice Cap
Sam Ford Fd.
Erik Pt.
Eglinton Fd.
Clyde
Clyde Inlet
Inugsuin Fd.
CANADA
Baffin Island
Baffin Bay
Baffin Basin
Kane Basin
Kane Bassin
Nares Strait
Nares Stræde
K. Jackson
K. Forbes
Peabody Bugt
Humboldt Gletscher
K. Russell
K. Leiper
K. Inglefield
Inuartigssuaq
Etah
Inglefield Land
Brother John Gl.
K. Alexander
K. Robertson
Marie Jesup Gl.
Siorapaluk
Robertson Fd.
Murchison Sund
Herbert Ø
Qaanaaq
Thule
Northumberland Ø
Hakluyt Ø
K. Powlett
Inglefield Bredning
Harward Øer
Heilprin Gl.
Qeqertat
K. Parry
Steensby Land
Carey Øer
Saunders Ø
Wolstenholme Ø
Wolstenholme Fd.
Uummannaq / Dundas
K. Atholl
Pituffik Gl.
Prudhoe Land
Hayes Halvø
Arktik Hoyland
Crimson Cliffs
Ivnanganek
Kap York
Salve Ø
Meteorit
Kap Melville
Haffner Bjerg
Fisher Øer
Naturreservat Lauge Koch Kyst
Melville Bugt
Nansen Gl.
Kap Seddon
Steenstrup Gl.
Camp Century
Knud Rasmussen Land
K. Brevoort
K. May
K. Dragon
St. George Fd.
Hendrik Ø
Nyeboe Land
Polaris Forland
Newman Bugt
Hall Land
Hall Basin
Petermann Fd.
Petermann Gletscher
Warming Land
Steensby Gl.
John Brown Kyst
Daugaard Jensen Land
Cass Fd.
Ryder Øer
Kullorsuaq
Holms Ø
Igdlulik
Vinter Øer
Cornell Gl.
Vestgrønland
Qutdlikorssuit
Tugtorqortaq
Ikerasârssuk
Tasiussaq
Ivnarssuit
Mamorssoq
Aappilattoq
Upernavik
Nutaarmiut
Kangersuatsiaq
Qeqertarssuaq
Upernavik Kujalleq
Søndre Upernavik
Kigataq
Qeqertaq
Ingnerit
Nunavik
Akuliarusinguaq
Qeqertarsuaq
Nuugaatsiaq
Kanderdlugssuaq
Kap Cranstown
Karrats Fjord
Illorsuit
Ubekendt Ejland
Igdlorssuit Sund
Upernavik
Alfred Wegener Halvø
Ukkusissat
Appat
Niaqornat
Umanak Fd.
Saattut
Maarmorilik

2469 2743 1280 2140 2012 2210 1067 1961 1234 1128 1342 1920 1981 2073 1341 1832 1676 1500 1326 880 1391 999 1887 1097 1036 1250 1067 945 487 1249 1036 1859 1890 2103 1615 1060 975 1159 1804 1214 1150 2210 1189 822 1615 2134 1585 1062 1128 1250 1158 1036 1453 1215 1617 1250 1097 1036 1189 1158 619 1131 1097 1158
87 71 201 298 157 135 338 632 798 334 146 439 187 296 212 329 385 543 535 40 762 639 864 532 196 542 182 108 1062 1550 1054 2473 2000 200 344 2287 1044 138

-5h Gr. Time -4h Gr. Time -4h Gr. Time -3h Gr. Time

25
28

78° M 76° N 74° O 72° P 70° 66° S 64° T 62° U W 56° X 54° Y 52° Z

Scale 1 : 4,500,000
0 40 80 120 160 200 Kilometers
0 40 80 120 160 Statute Miles

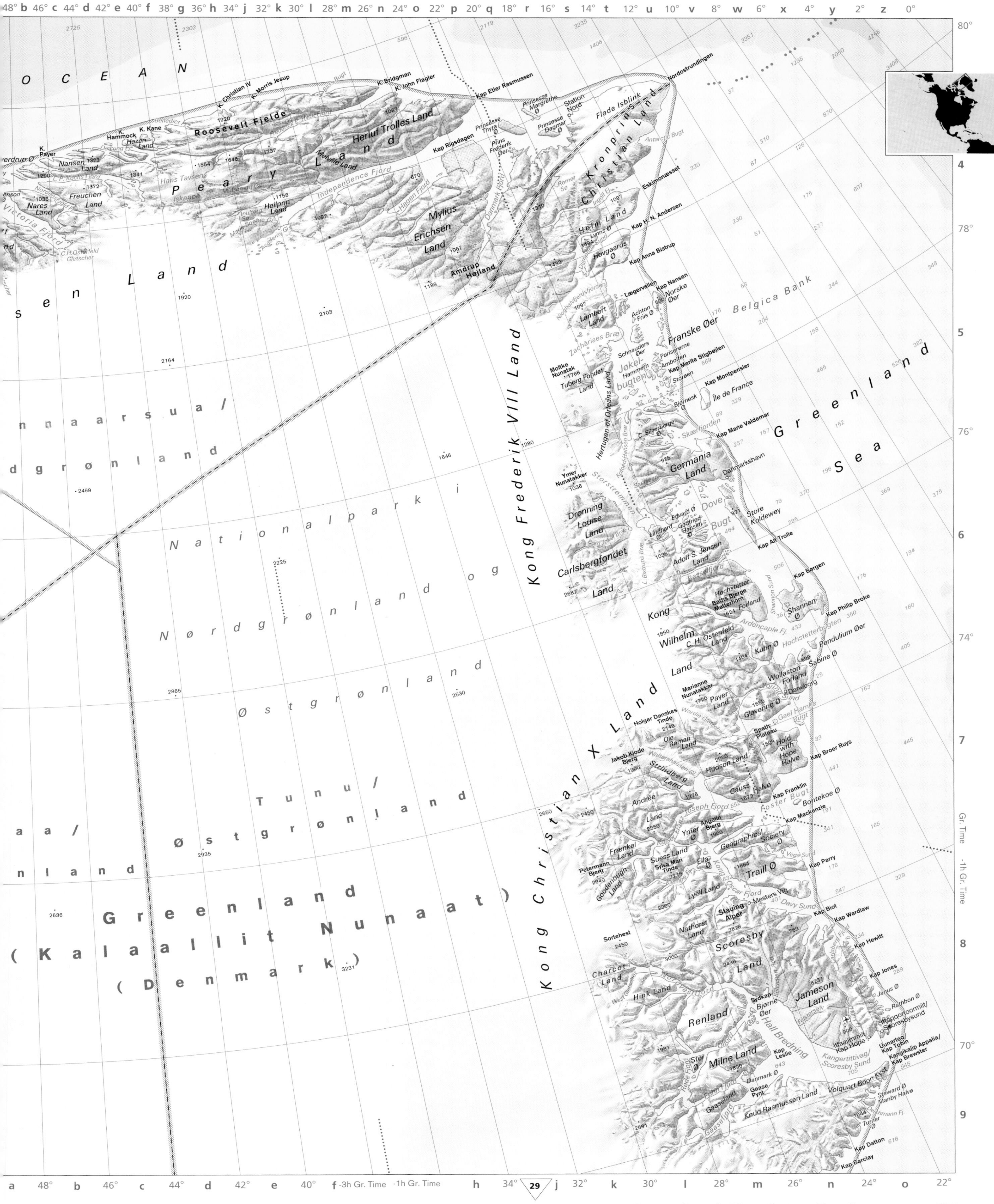

Greenland
(Kalaallit Nunaat)
(Denmark)
Greenland Sea
Peary Land
Kong Frederik VIII Land
Kong Christian X Land
Kronprins Christian Land
Nationalpark i Nordgrønland og Østgrønland
Scoresby Land
Jameson Land
Germania Land
Roosevelt Fjelde
Herluf Trolles Land
Mylius Erichsen Land
Belgica Bank
Franske Øer
Traill Ø
Renland
Milne Land
Ittoqqortoormiit/ Scoresbysund
Kangertittivag/ Scoresby Sund
Danmarkshavn
Station Nord
Nordostrundingen

A 78° B 76° C 25 74° D 72° E 70° F 68° G 66° H 64° 26 J 62° K 60° L 58° M 56° N 54° O 52° P

Baffin Island

CANADA

Northwest Territories

Davis Strait

Labrador Sea

Hudson Strait

Ungava Bay

Frobisher Bay

Cumberland Sound

Cumberland Peninsula

Hall Peninsula

Meta Incognita Peninsula

Great Plain of the Koukdjuak

Prince Charles Island

Air Force I.

Rowley I.

Bray I.

Baird Pen.

C. Burpee

Foley I.

North Tweedsmuir I.

South Tweedsmuir I.

Mid Baffin

Barnes Ice Cap

Clyde

Clyde Inlet

C. Raper

Aulitivik I.

Henry Kater Pen.

C. Henry Kater

Arguyartu Pt.

Home Bay

C. Hooper

Kerkertaluk I.

Kangeeak Pt.

Auyuittuq Nat. Park

Penny Highlands

Penny Ice Cap

Broughton I.

Kekertuk I.

Merchants Bay

Padloping I.

Durban I.

Duck Is.

C. Dyer

Exeter B.

Exeter Sound

C. Walsingham

Angijak I.

Pangnirtung

Usualuk

Tesseralik

Kipisa

Queen C.

Nuvuk Pt.

Hoare Bay

Ilikok I.

Leopold I.

C. Mercy

Lemieux Islands

Leybourne Is.

Hozier Is.

Brevoort I.

C. Murchison

Beekman Pen.

Williams Pen.

C. Haven

C. True

Loks Land

Frobisher Bay

Auyuittuq

Hill I.

Pike-Fletcher

Everett Mts.

Terra Nivea

Potter

East Bluff

Lower Savage Is.

Gabriel Strait

Edgell I.

Resolution Island

Resolution Island

Cockburn I.

Arctic Circle

C. Dominion

Nettilling Lake

Magnetic Pt.

Pingua Hills

Bluegoose Prairie

Amadjuak Lake

Mingo L.

Jubilee L.

Hobart L.

Mac Donald I.

Fair Ness

Crooks Inlet

Big I.

North Bluff

Lake Harbour

Joy Bay

Burgoyne Bay

Québec

Quaqtaq

Diana B.

Eider Is.

Akpatok I.

Button Is.

Gray Strait

Knight Is.

Cape Chidley Is.

C. Labrador

Black Rock Pt.

North Aulatsivik I.

Eclipse Channel

Torngat Mts.

Murphy Head

Seven Islands B.

C. White Handkerchief

Newfoundland

Retchel Hd.

Hopes Advance B.

Pte. Takiyok

Gyrfalcon Is.

Leaf B.

Pte. Stony

Pte. Hubbard

Pte. Congnarauya

C. Kernertut

Kuujjuaq (Fort-Chimo)

Port-Nouveau-Québec

Kelgo B.

Baffin-Greenland Rise

Disko Banke

Store Hellefiske-banke

Lille Hellefiske-banke

Fyllas Banke

Fiskenæs Banke

Danas Banke

Frederikshåbs Banke

Karrats Fjord

Upernavik

Illorsuit

Ubekendt Ejland

Ukkusissat

Niaqornat

Qaarsut

Uummannaq/Umanak

Umanak Fjord

Nuussuaq Halvø

Hare Ø

Sullorsuaq

Vaigat

Qutdligssat

Saqqaq

Disko Ø

Kangerluk/Diskofjord

Disko Fjord

Qeqertarsuaq/Godhavn

Ilulissat/Jakobshavn

Disko Bugt

Ilimanaq/Claushavn

Qasigiannguit/Christianshåb

Egedesminde

Aasiaat/Egedesminde

Ikamiut

Qeersortik

Innalik

Kangaatsiaq

Niaqornaarsuk

Attu

Aqisserniaq

Isortoq

Sisimiut/Holsteinsborg

Kangerlussuaq/Søndre Strømfjord

Camp Lloyd

Sarfannguaq

Itilleq

Sukkertoppen

Simiutaq

Kangaamiut/Gammel Sukkertoppen

Hamborgerland

Maniitsoq

Maniitsoq/Sukkertoppen

Kangerluarsuk

Dronning Ingrid Land

Atammik

Saarloq

Nuuk/Godthåb

Narssaq

Kangerluarsoruseq/Færingehavn

Qeqertarsuatsiaat/Fiskenæsset

F 68° G 66° H -5h Gr. Time -4h Gr. Time J 62° K 37 60° L 58° M 56° N 54° O -4h Gr. Time -3h Gr. Time

Scale 1 : 4,500,000

0 40 80 120 160 200 Kilometers

0 40 80 120 160 Statute Miles

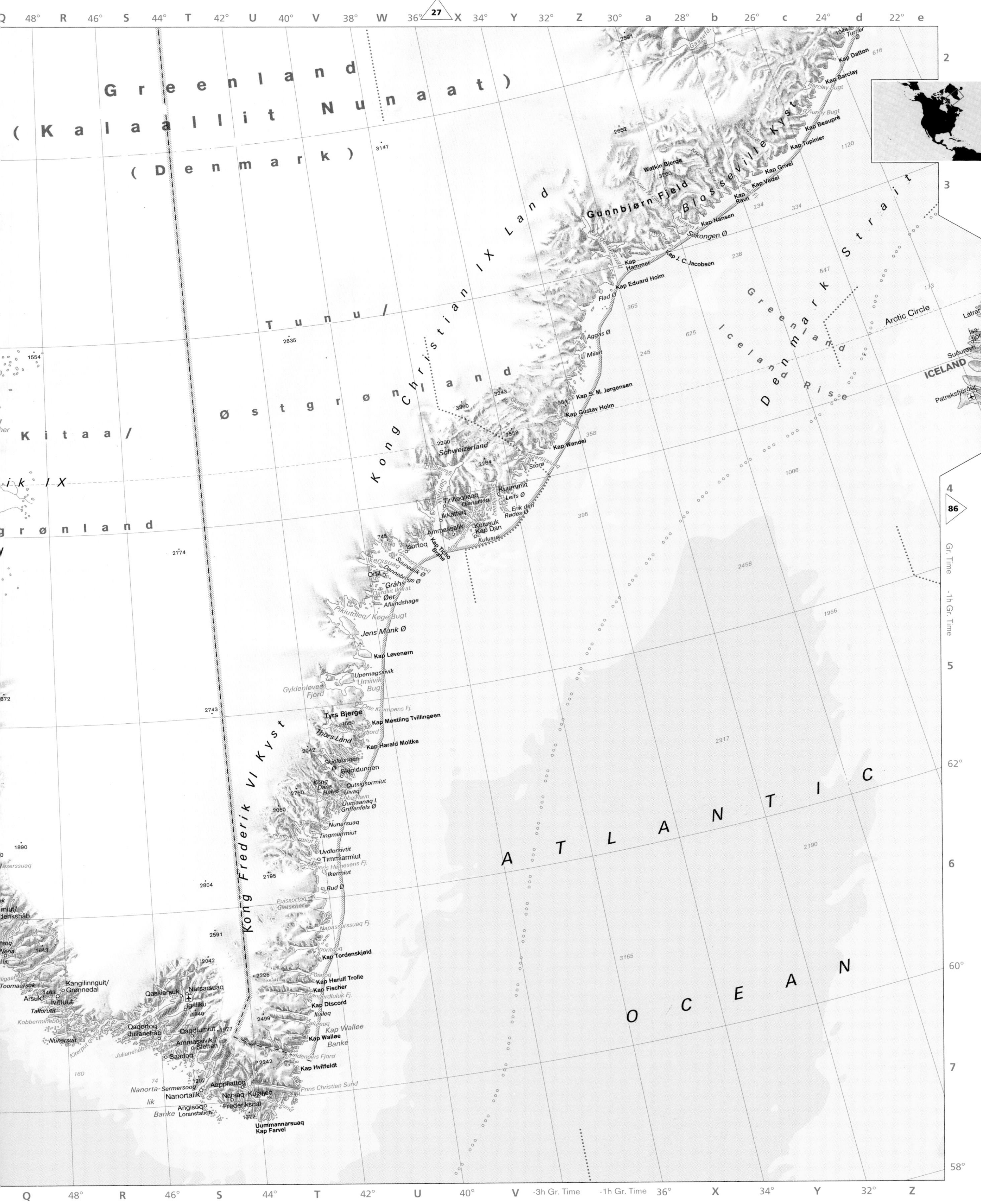

Greenland
(Kalaallit Nunaat)
(Denmark)
Tunu/
Østgrønland
Kitaa/
Kong Christian IX Land
Kong Frederik VI Kyst
Blosseville Kyst
Gunnbjørn Fjeld
Denmark Strait
Greenland-Iceland Rise
Arctic Circle
ICELAND
ATLANTIC
OCEAN
Schweizerland
Ammassalik
Kulusuk
Kap Dan
Tasiilaq
Kap Farvel
Uummannarsuaq
Nanortalik
Qaqortoq
Julianehåb
Narsaq
Narsarsuaq
Ivittuut
Kangilinnguit/Grønnedal
Arsuk
Kap Barclay
Kap Dalton
Kap Beaupré
Kap Tupinier
Kap Grivel
Kap Vedel
Kap Ravn
Kap Nansen
Søkongen Ø
Kap Hammer
Kap J. C. Jacobsen
Kap Eduard Holm
Aggas Ø
Milait
Kap S. M. Jørgensen
Kap Gustav Holm
Kap Wandel
Kap Løvenørn
Jens Munk Ø
Tyrs Bjerge
Kap Møstling Tvillingøen
Thors Land
Kap Harald Moltke
Skjoldungen
Timmiarmiut
Kap Tordenskjøld
Kap Herluf Trolle
Kap Fischer
Kap Walløe
Kap Hvitfeldt
Prins Christian Sund
Watkin Bjerge
-3h Gr. Time
-1h Gr. Time

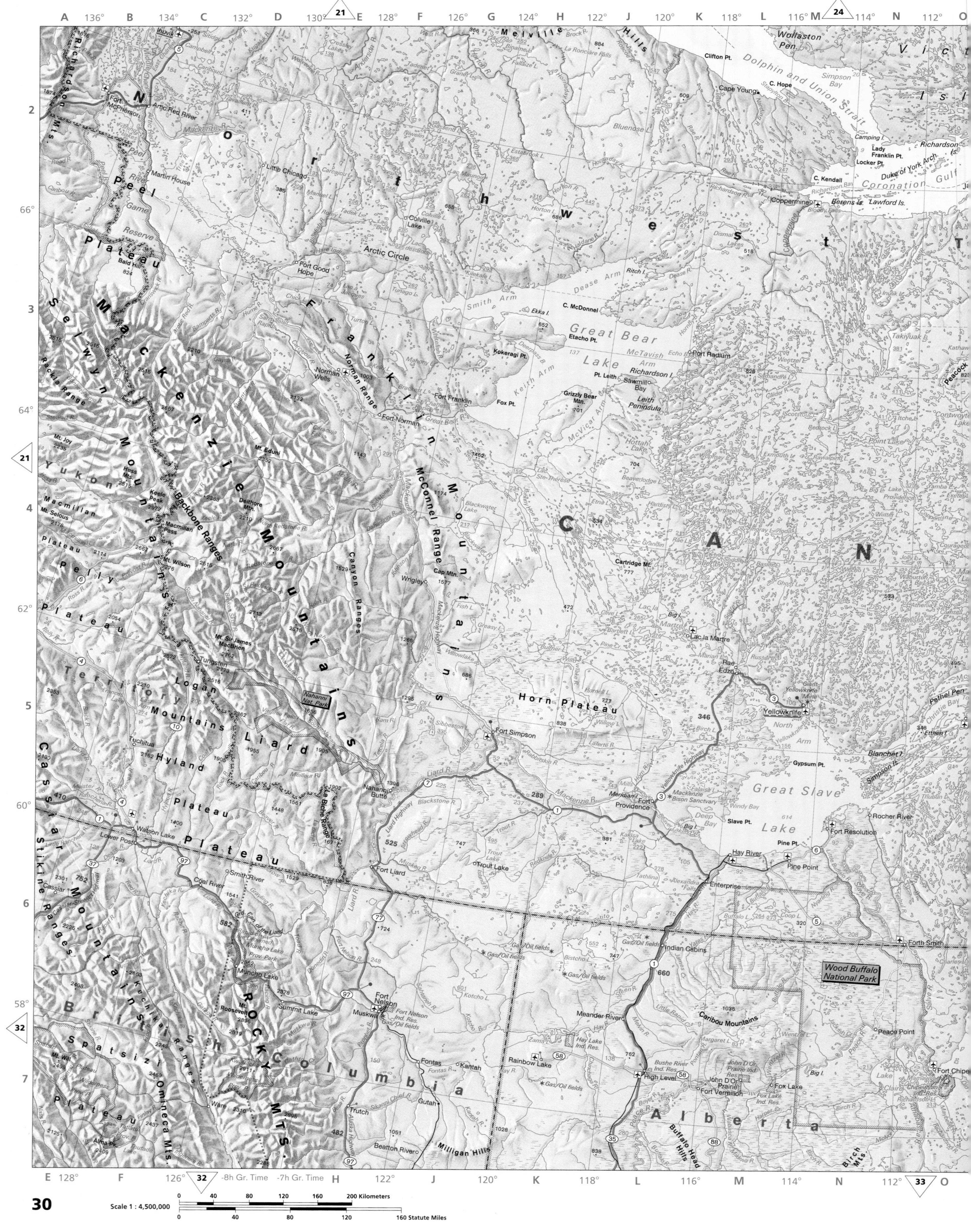

A 136° B 134° C 132° D 130° 21 E 128° F 126° G 124° H 122° J 120° K 118° L 116° M 24 114° N 112° O
E 128° F 126° 32 -8h Gr. Time -7h Gr. Time H 122° J 120° K 118° L 116° M 114° N 112° 33 O
66°
64°
62°
60°
58°
21
32
Inuvik
Fort McPherson
Arctic Red River
Richardson Mts.
Melville Hills
Wollaston Pen.
Clifton Pt.
Dolphin and Union Strait
Cape Young
C. Hope
Simpson Bay
Bluenose L.
Camping I.
Lady Franklin Pt.
Locker Pt.
Richardson Is.
Duke of York Arch.
C. Kendall
Coronation Gulf
Coppermine
Berens Is.
Lawford Is.
Little Chicago
Martin House
Peel Plateau
Peel River Game Reserve
Bald Hill
Colville Lake
Arctic Circle
Fort Good Hope
Dismal Lakes
Smith Arm
Dease Arm
C. McDonnel
Ekka I.
Great Bear Lake
Etacho Pt.
McTavish Arm
Port Radium
Kokeragi Pt.
Richardson I.
Keith Arm
Pt. Leith
Sawmill Bay
Leith Peninsula
Grizzly Bear Mtn.
Fox Pt.
Fort Franklin
McVicar Arm
Norman Wells
Norman Range
Fort Norman
Franklin Mountains
Selwyn Mountains
Mackenzie Mountains
Backbone Ranges
Mt. Joy
Mt. Eduni
Hess Mts.
Keele Peak
Macmillan Pass
Delthore Mtn.
Mt. Selous
Macmillan Plateau
Pelly Plateau
Mt. Wilson
Yukon Plateau
McConnel Range
Canyon Ranges
Blackwater Lake
Cap Mtn.
Wrigley
Cartridge Mt.
Hottah Lake
Lac Ste-Thérèse
Lac la Martre
Rae
Edzo
Yellowknife
Giant Yellowknife Mine
North Arm
Gypsum Pt.
Mt. Sir James MacBrien
Tungsten
Nahanni Nat. Park
Logan Mountains
Liard Range
Horn Plateau
Fort Simpson
Territory
Tuchitua
Hyland Plateau
Nahanni Butte
Liard Highway
Yellowknife Highway
Mackenzie Bison Sanctuary
Fort Providence
Great Slave Lake
Deep Bay
Slave Pt.
Big I.
Rocher River
Fort Resolution
Pine Pt.
Pine Point
Hay River
Enterprise
Cassiar Mountains
Watson Lake
Lower Post
Liard Plateau
La Biche Range
Fort Liard
Trout Lake
Kakisa Lake
Tathlina L.
Smith River
Coal River
Gr. Can. of the Liard
Muncho Lake Prov. Park
Muncho Lake
Stikine Ranges
Gas/Oil fields
Indian Cabins
Buffalo L.
Forth Smith
Wood Buffalo National Park
Caribou Mountains
Peace Point
Meander River
Hay Lake Ind. Res.
Fort Nelson
Muskwa
Fort Nelson Ind. Res.
Summit Lake
Mt. Roosevelt
Kechika Ranges
British Columbia
ROCKY MTS.
Spatsizi Plateau
Omineca Mts.
Mt. Will
Ware
Fontas
Kantah
Rainbow Lake
High Level
Bushe River Ind. Res.
John D'Or Prairie Ind. Res.
John D'Or Prairie
Fort Vermilion
Fox Lake
Fox Lake Ind. Res.
Fort Chipewyan
Gutah
Trutch
Beatton River
Milligan Hills
Buffalo Head Hills
Alberta
Birch Mts.
Alma Pk.
CANADA
Northwest Territories
Scale 1 : 4,500,000
0 40 80 120 160 200 Kilometers
0 40 80 120 160 Statute Miles

King William Island
Queen Maud Gulf
Adelaide Peninsula
Rasmussen Basin
Kent Peninsula
Dease Strait
Cambridge Bay
Gjoa Haven
Melville Pen.
Wager Bay
Roes Welcome Sound
Arctic Circle
B A R R E N   G R O U N D S
Baker Lake
Chesterfield Inlet
Rankin Inlet
Whale Cove
Eskimo Point
Hudson Bay
Dubawnt Lake
Wholdaia Lake
Ennadai
Marjorie Hills
Churchill
Fort Churchill
Manitoba
Saskatchewan
Lake Athabasca
Uranium City
Stony Rapids
Wollaston Lake
Southern Indian Lake
Port Nelson (abandoned)
York Factory (abandoned)
C. Tatnam

Scale 1 : 4,500,000

0 40 80 120 160 200 Kilometers

0 40 80 120 160 Statute Miles

L
118°
M
116°
N
114°
O
112°
P
110°
Q
108°
-7h Gr. Time
-6h Gr. Time
31
104°
T
102°
U
Wood Buffalo National Park
Caribou Mountains
Athabasca
Lake Athabasca
Uranium City
Fort Chipewyan
High Level
Fort Vermilion
Buffalo Head Hills
Birch Mountains
Fort McKay
Fort McMurray
Peace River
Grande Prairie
Swan Hills
Slave Lake
Lesser Slave Lake
Athabasca
La Loche
Buffalo Narrows
La Ronge
Primrose Lake Air Weapons Range
Meadow Lake
Prince Albert
North Battleford
Lloydminster
EDMONTON
Sherwood Park
Spruce Grove
St. Albert
Camrose
Wetaskiwin
Red Deer
Jasper
Hinton
Edson
SASKATOON
REGINA
Moose Jaw
Swift Current
CALGARY
Banff
Lake Louise
Dinosaur Prov. Park
Medicine Hat
Lethbridge
Head-Smashed-in Bison Jump
Cypress Hills
Great Sand Hills
Kelowna
Vernon
Revelstoke
Nelson
Cranbrook
Monashee Mountains
Purcell Mountains
Selkirk Mountains
Yoho Nat. Park
Kootenay Nat. Park
Glacier Nat. Park
Kalispell
Havre
Shelby
Malta
Glasgow
Fort Benton
Piney Buttes
A L B E R T A
S a s k a t c h e w a n
G R E A T   P L A I N S
R O C K Y   M O U N T A I N S
U N I T E D   S T A T E S
M o n t a n a
34
40
42
L
118°
M -8h Gr. Time
-7h Gr. Time
N
114°
O
112°
P
110°
Q
108°
R
106°
S
2
3
4
5
6
7
8
56°
54°
52°
50°
48°
-6h Gr. Time
-7h Gr. Time

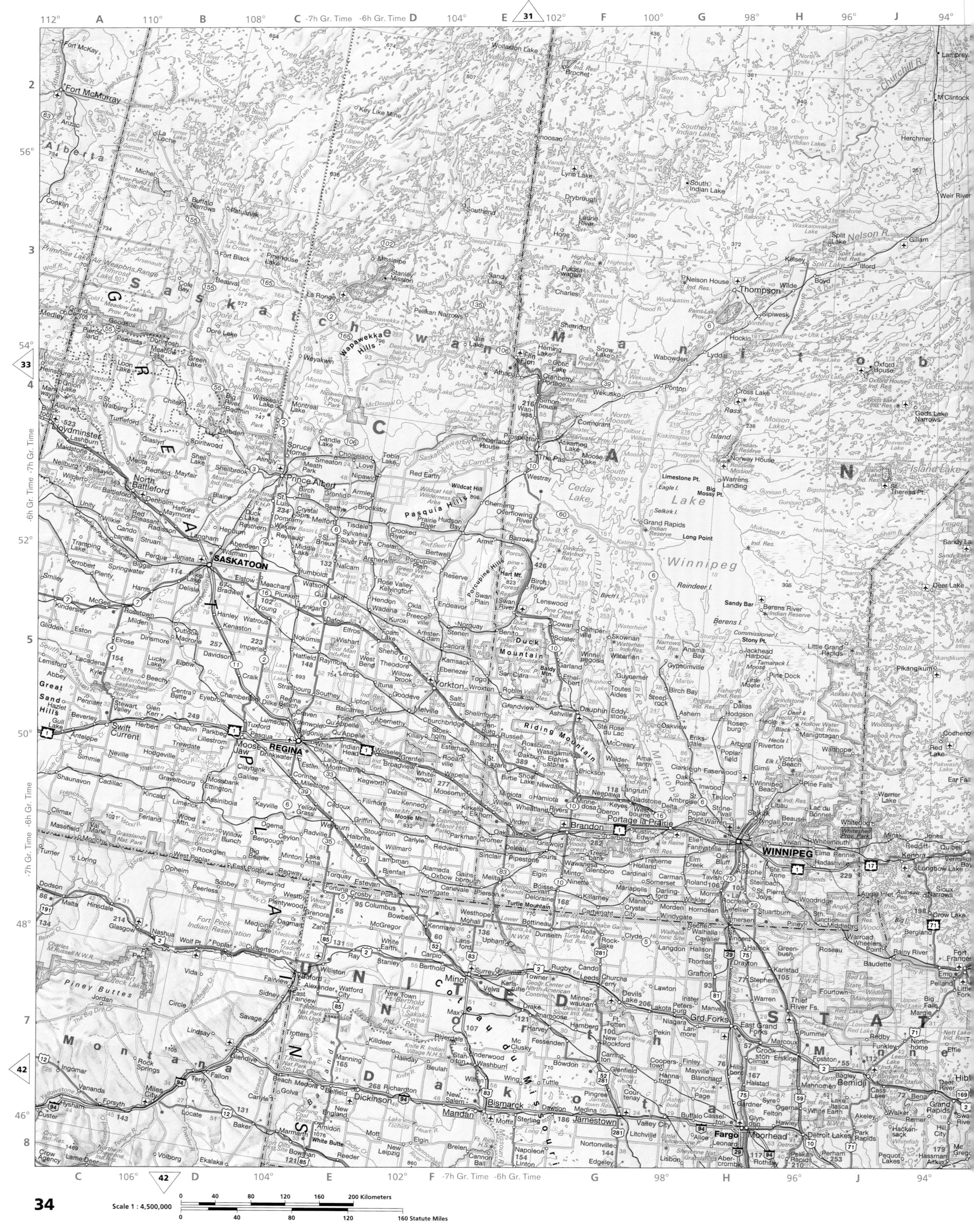
112°
A
110°
B
108°
C -7h Gr. Time
-6h Gr. Time D
104°
E
31
102°
F
100°
G
98°
H
96°
J
94°
2
56°
3
54°
33
4
52°
5
50°
48°
7
42
46°
8
C
106°
42
D
104°
E
102°
F -7h Gr. Time -6h Gr. Time
G
98°
H
96°
J
94°
-6h Gr. Time -7h Gr. Time
-7h Gr. Time -6h Gr. Time
Alberta
Saskatchewan
Manitoba
CANADA
UNITED STATES
Montana
North Dakota
Minnesota
Lake Winnipeg
Lake Winnipegosis
Lake Manitoba
Cedar Lake
SASKATOON
REGINA
WINNIPEG
Scale 1 : 4,500,000
0
40
80
120
160
200 Kilometers
0
40
80
120
160 Statute Miles

Hudson Bay
James Bay
Northwest Territories
Belcher Islands
King George Islands
Sleeper Is.
Akimiski Island
Charlton Island
Polar Bear Provincial Park
Québec
Ontario
CANADA
Clay Belt
Lake Nipigon
Lake Superior
Isle Royale
Keweenaw Pen.
Michigan
Wisconsin
Algoma Upland
THUNDER BAY
Sudbury
North Bay
Timmins
Sault Ste. Marie
Duluth
Superior
Marquette
Moosonee
Fort Severn
Attawapiskat
Kirkland Lake
Kapuskasing
Hearst
Cochrane
Chapleau
Elliot Lake
Nipigon
Marathon
Wawa
Geraldton
Longlac
Red Lake
Sioux Lookout
Big Trout Lake
Sachigo
Kasabonika
Peawanuck
Winisk
C. Henrietta Maria
Poste-de-la-Baleine
Eastmain
Wemindji
Fort Rupert (Waskaganish)
Rouyn-Noranda
Val-d'Or
Amos
Matagami
Val-Paradis
Joutel
Témiscaming
New Liskeard
Mattawa
-6h Gr. Time
-5h Gr. T.

Scale 1 : 4,500,000

0 40 80 120 160 200 Kilometers

0 40 80 120 160 Statute Miles

Labrador Sea
Ungava Bay
Hudson Strait
Cumberland Sound
Frobisher Bay
Cumberland Peninsula
Hall Peninsula
Meta Incognita Peninsula
Torngat Mts.
Greenland (Kalaallit Nunaat) (Denmark)
Vestgronland
Lille Hellefiske-banke
Fyllas Banke
Fiskenæs Banke
Danas Banke
Frederikshåbs Banke
Nuuk/Godthåb
Frobisher Bay
Kuujjuaq (Fort-Chimo)
Port-Nouveau-Quebec
Schefferville
Resolution Island
Akpatok I.
Cape Chidley Is.
C. Labrador
Hebron
Nain
Makkovik
Rigolet
Newfoundland
Labrador
Québec

Scale 1 : 4,500,000
0 40 80 120 160 200 Kilometers
0 40 80 120 160 Statute Miles

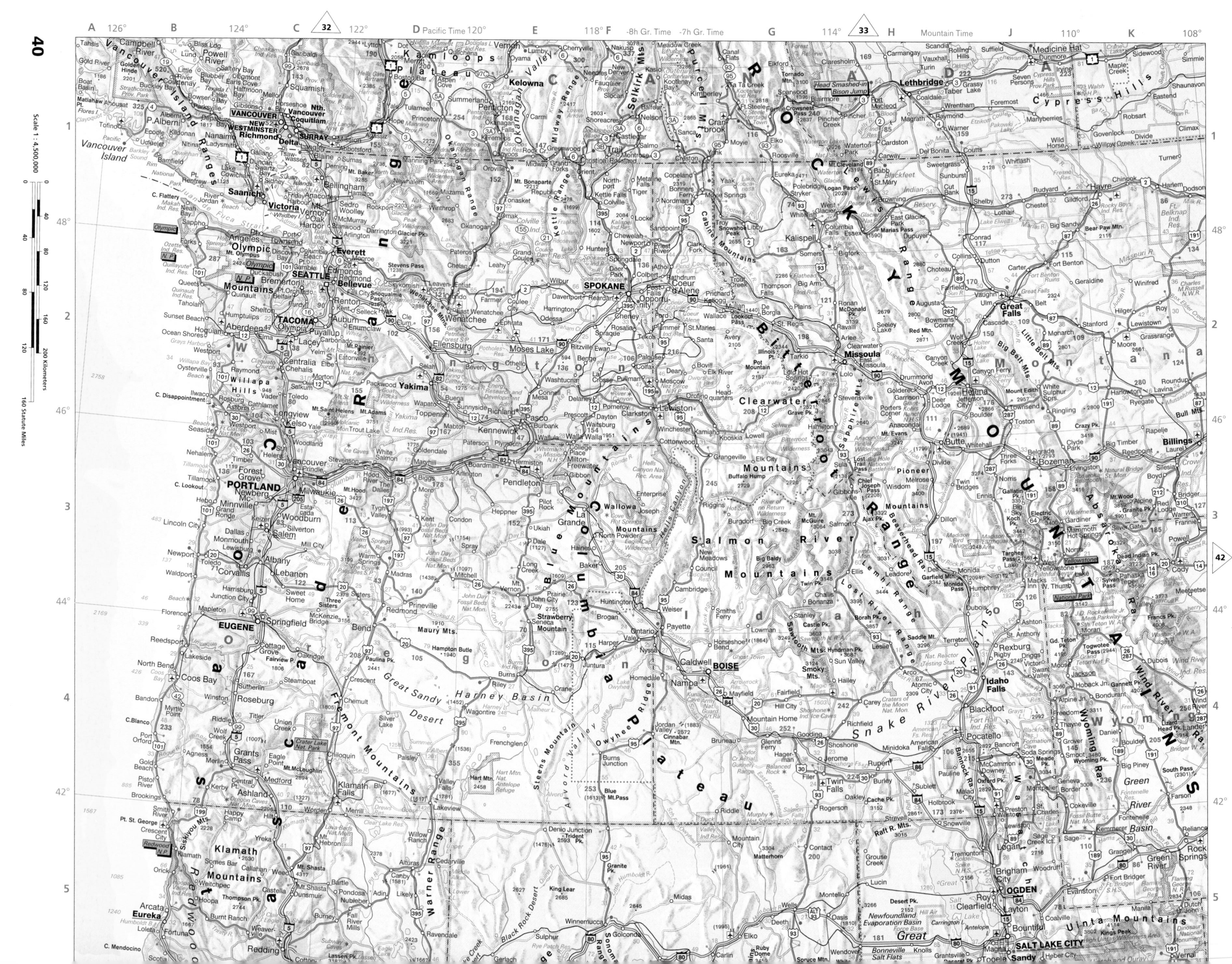

Scale 1 : 4,500,000

0 40 80 120 160 200 Kilometers

0 40 80 120 160 Statute Miles

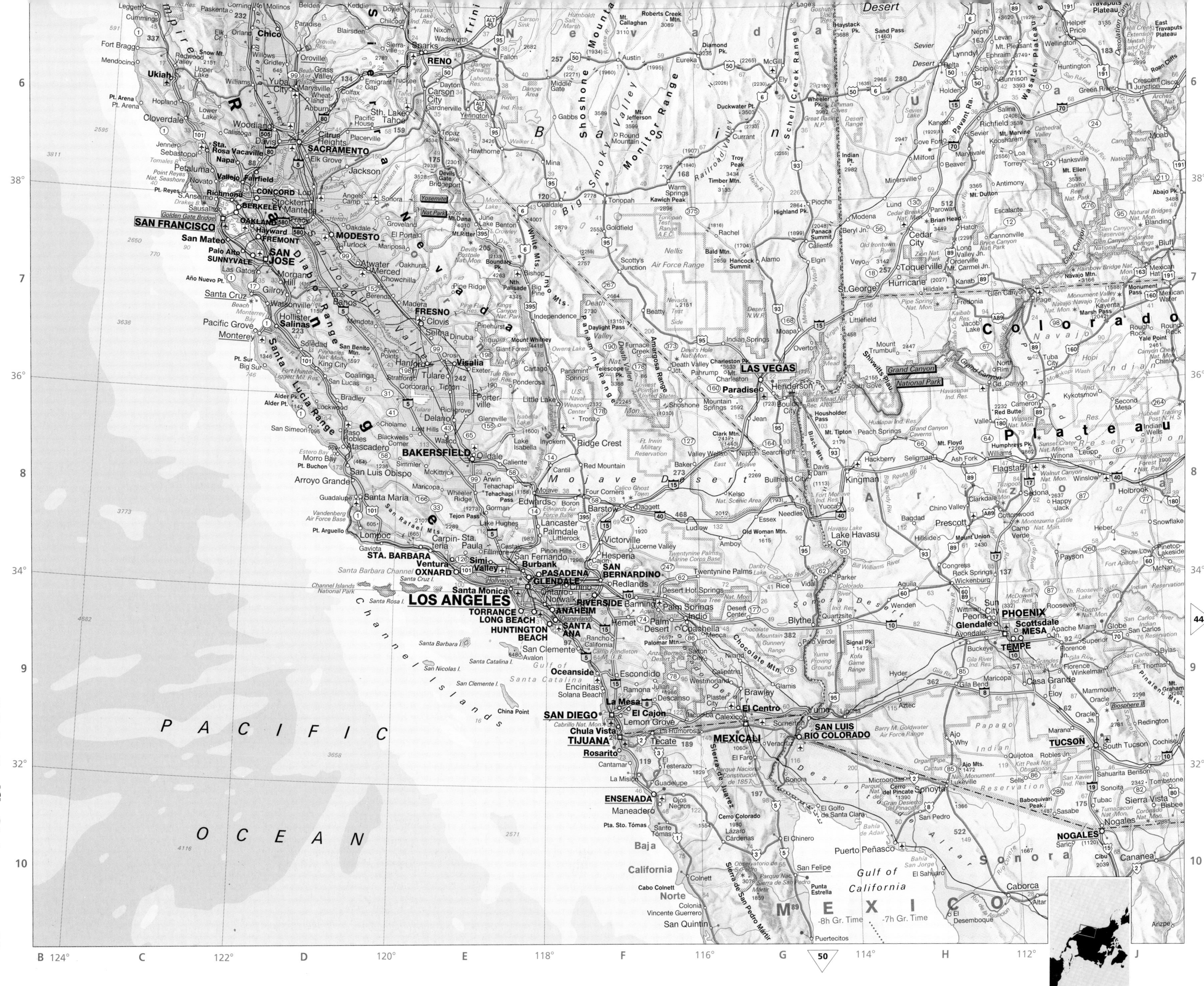
PACIFIC OCEAN
Channel Islands
Gulf of California
MEXICO
LOS ANGELES
SAN FRANCISCO
SAN DIEGO
LAS VEGAS
PHOENIX
TUCSON
SACRAMENTO
FRESNO
BAKERSFIELD
RENO
Mojave Desert
Colorado Plateau
Great Basin
Sierra Nevada
Grand Canyon National Park
Death Valley

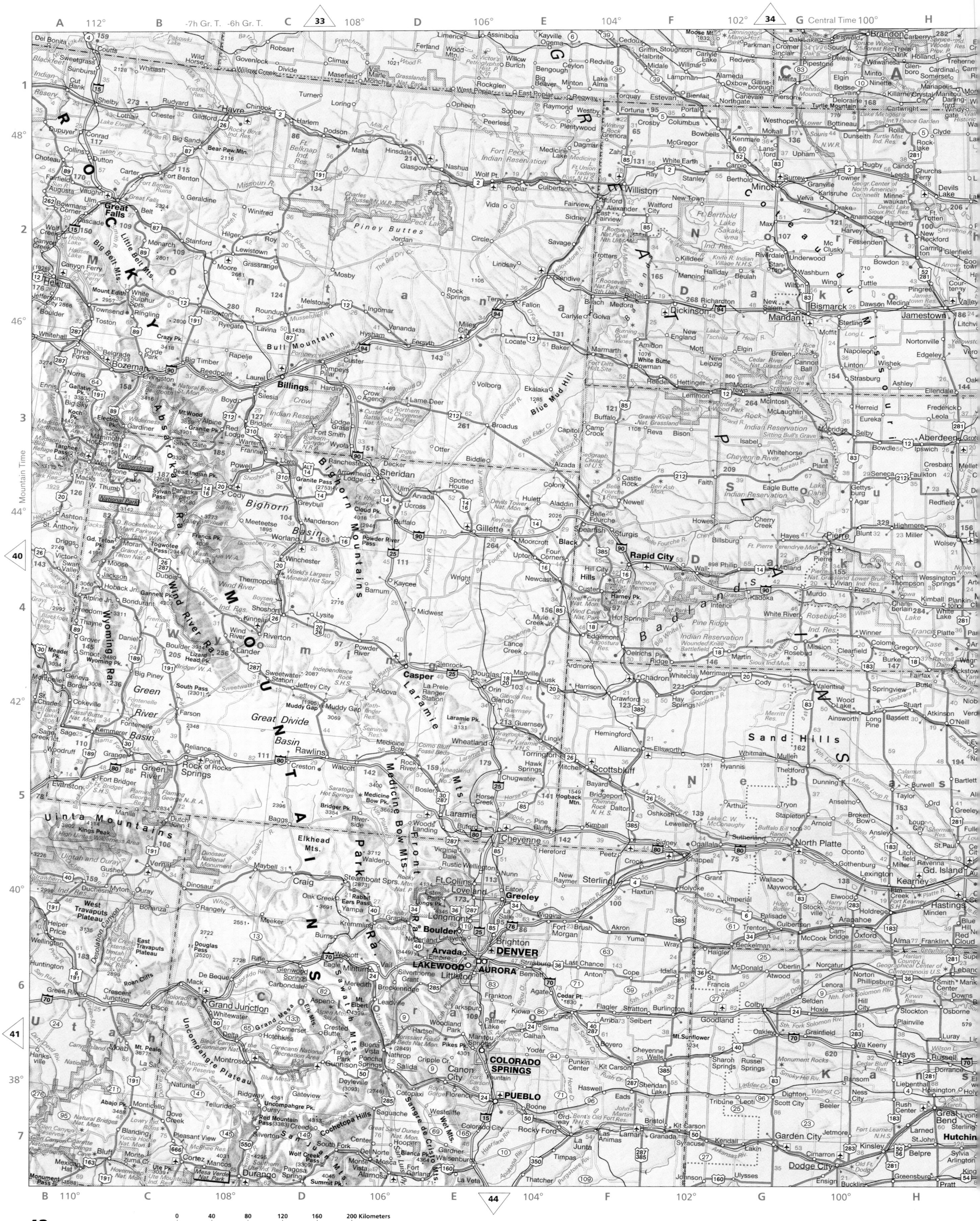

A 112° B -7h Gr. T. -6h Gr. T. C 33 108° D 106° E 104° F 102° 34 G Central Time 100° H

1 48° 2 3 46° 44° 4 42° 5 40° 6 38° 7

Mountain Time

40 41

B 110° C 108° D 106° E 44 104° F 102° G 100° H

Scale 1 : 4,500,000

0 40 80 120 160 200 Kilometers

0 40 80 120 160 Statute Miles

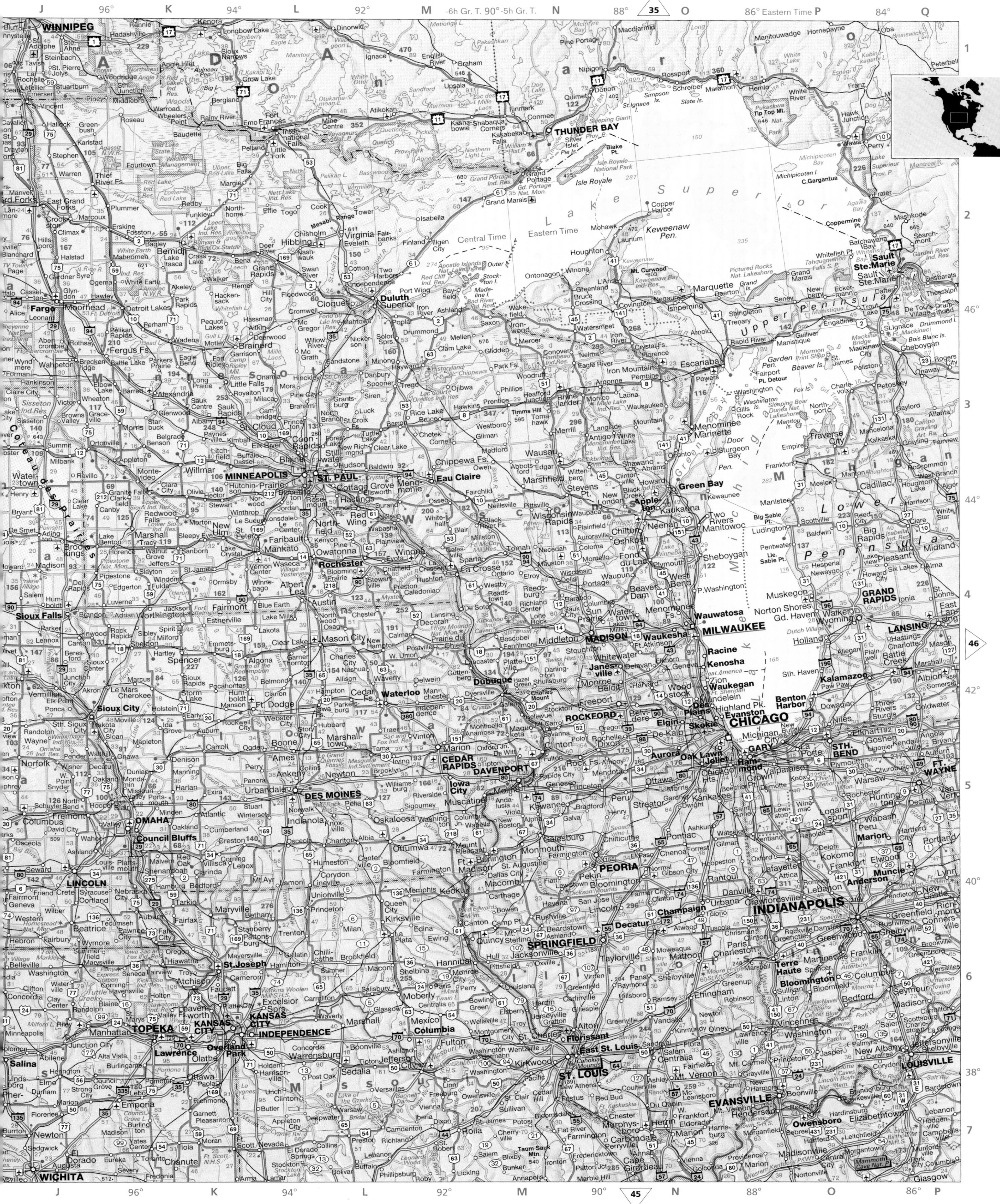

J 96° K 94° L 92° M -6h Gr. T. 90° -5h Gr. T. N 88° 35 O 86° Eastern Time P 84° Q
WINNIPEG
THUNDER BAY
Lake Superior
Isle Royale
Keweenaw Pen.
Central Time
Eastern Time
Duluth
Superior
Sault Ste.Marie
Upper Peninsula
MINNEAPOLIS
ST. PAUL
Green Bay
Lake Michigan
Lower Peninsula
Eau Claire
Rochester
La Crosse
MADISON
MILWAUKEE
Wauwatosa
Waukesha
Racine
Kenosha
ROCKFORD
CHICAGO
GARY
STH. BEND
FT. WAYNE
GRAND RAPIDS
LANSING
Sioux Falls
Sioux City
CEDAR RAPIDS
DAVENPORT
Waterloo
Dubuque
DES MOINES
OMAHA
Council Bluffs
LINCOLN
PEORIA
SPRINGFIELD
Champaign
Decatur
INDIANAPOLIS
St. Joseph
TOPEKA
KANSAS CITY
INDEPENDENCE
Overland Park
Lawrence
Columbia
Jefferson City
ST. LOUIS
East St. Louis
Florissant
EVANSVILLE
Owensboro
LOUISVILLE
Salina
WICHITA
Fargo
Moorhead
Iowa
Illinois
Missouri
Wisconsin
Minnesota
Michigan
Indiana
J 96° K 94° L 92° M 90° 45 N 88° O 86° P
1 2 3 4 5 6 7
46° 44° 42° 40° 38°
46

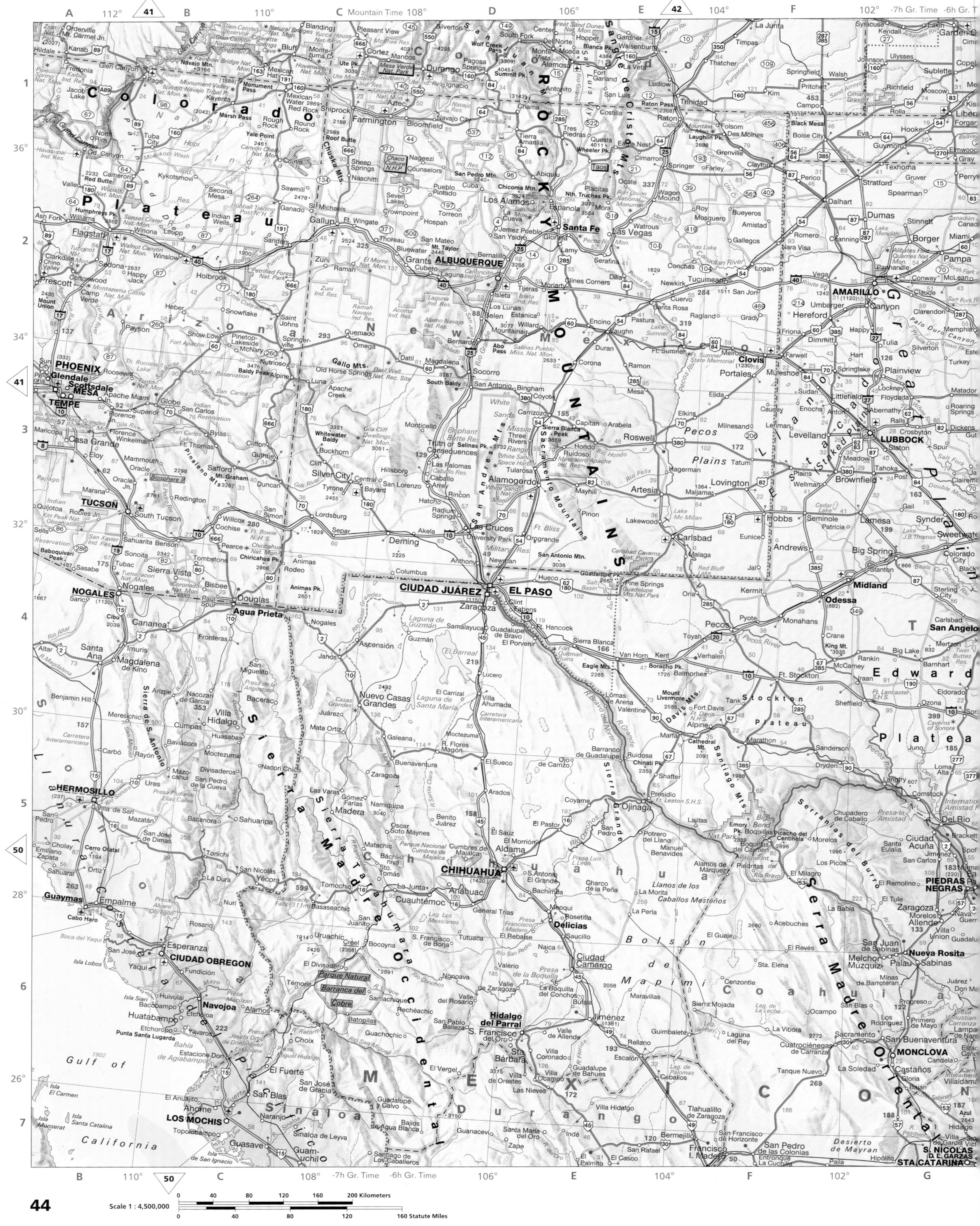

A
112°
41
B
110°
C Mountain Time 108°
D
106°
E
42
104°
F
102° -7h Gr. Time -6h Gr. T
Colorado Plateau
Arizona
New Mexico
ROCKY MOUNTAINS
Sangre de Cristo Mts.
San Juan Mts.
Great Plains
Llano Estacado (Staked Plain)
Pecos Plains
Edwards Plateau
Stockton Plateau
Sierra Madre Occidental
Sierra Tarahumara
Sierra Madre Oriental
Bolsón de Mapimí
Serranías del Burro
Llanura Sonorense
Chihuahua
Coahuila
Durango
Sinaloa
Sonora
MEXICO
Gulf of California
PHOENIX
Glendale
Scottsdale
MESA
TEMPE
Flagstaff
Prescott
TUCSON
NOGALES
Nogales
Douglas
Agua Prieta
ALBUQUERQUE
Santa Fe
Los Alamos
Farmington
Gallup
Durango
Trinidad
Raton
Las Vegas
Tucumcari
Clovis
Portales
Roswell
Carlsbad
Hobbs
Artesia
Alamogordo
Las Cruces
Deming
Lordsburg
Silver City
Socorro
AMARILLO
LUBBOCK
Midland
Odessa
San Angelo
Big Spring
Pecos
Fort Stockton
Alpine
Del Rio
CIUDAD JUÁREZ
EL PASO
CHIHUAHUA
Delicias
Ciudad Camargo
Hidalgo del Parral
Nuevo Casas Grandes
Ojinaga
Cuauhtémoc
HERMOSILLO
Guaymas
Empalme
CIUDAD OBREGON
Navojoa
LOS MOCHIS
Ciudad Acuña
PIEDRAS NEGRAS
MONCLOVA
Nueva Rosita
Sabinas
S. NICOLÁS
D. L. GARZAS
STA. CATARINA
Chaco Culture N.H.P.
Mesa Verde Nat. Park
Taos
Biosphere II
Parque Natural Barranca del Cobre
Carlsbad Caverns Nat. Park
Guadalupe Mts. Nat. Park
White Sands Nat. Mon.
Big Bend Nat. Park
B
110°
50
C
108° -7h Gr. Time -6h Gr. Time
106°
E
104°
F
102°
G
Scale 1 : 4,500,000
0 40 80 120 160 200 Kilometers
0 40 80 120 160 Statute Miles

Central Time
WICHITA
SPRINGFIELD
TULSA
OKLAHOMA CITY
Ozark Plateau
Boston Mts.
Fort Smith
Ouachita Mts.
LITTLE ROCK
MEMPHIS
DALLAS
FT. WORTH
ARLINGTON
GARLAND
Mesquite
SHREVEPORT
JACKSON
ABILENE
Wichita Falls
WACO
AUSTIN
SAN ANTONIO
HOUSTON
BEAUMONT
PASADENA
Galveston
BATON ROUGE
NEW ORLEANS
METAIRIE
Lafayette
Lake Charles
CORPUS CHRISTI
Laredo
Harlingen
BROWNSVILLE
MATAMOROS
REYNOSA
MONTERREY
Padre Island National Seashore
Gulf of Mexico
Mississippi River Delta

A
94° Central Time
B
35
92°
C
-6h Gr. T.
-5h Gr. T.
D
88°
E
86°
F
84°
G
82° Eastern Time
H
THUNDER BAY
Isle Royale
Lake Superior
Central Time
Eastern Time
Keweenaw Pen.
Duluth
Superior
Minnesota
Wisconsin
Michigan
Lake Michigan
Lake Huron
Lake Erie
Ontario
Upper Peninsula
Lower Peninsula
Iowa
Illinois
Indiana
Ohio
Missouri
Kentucky
MINNEAPOLIS
ST. PAUL
Eau Claire
Rochester
Green Bay
MADISON
MILWAUKEE
CHICAGO
ROCKFORD
PEORIA
SPRINGFIELD
DES MOINES
CEDAR RAPIDS
DAVENPORT
GRAND RAPIDS
LANSING
FLINT
DETROIT
WINDSOR
TOLEDO
CLEVELAND
AKRON
YOUNGSTOWN
COLUMBUS
DAYTON
CINCINNATI
INDIANAPOLIS
FT. WAYNE
STH. BEND
GARY
ST. LOUIS
EVANSVILLE
LOUISVILLE
LEXINGTON
LONDON
KITCHENER
Sault Ste. Marie
Manitoulin Is.
Bruce Pen.
Charleston
Huntington
Bristol
43
45
48
46°
44°
40°
38°
36°
2
3
4
5
6
7
8
46
Scale 1 : 4,500,000
0 40 80 120 160 200 Kilometers
0 40 80 120 160 Statute Miles

Québec
Canada
Montréal
Ottawa
Québec
Toronto
Lake Ontario
Adirondack Mountains
New York
Pennsylvania
Massachusetts
Boston
Providence
Hartford
New York
Philadelphia
Baltimore
Washington
Richmond
Gulf of Maine
Atlantic Ocean
Georges Bank
Hudson Canyon
Long Island
Cape Cod
CT = Connecticut
RI = Rhode Island
-5h Gr. Time Eastern Time
-4h Gr. Time Atlantic Time

46
45
54
Boston Mts.
Ouachita Mts.
Muskogee
Fort Smith
Nth. Little Rock
LITTLE ROCK
Hot Springs
Pine Bluff
Texarkana
El Dorado
SHREVEPORT
Monroe
JACKSON
Vicksburg
Natchez
Alexandria
Lafayette
BATON ROUGE
NEW ORLEANS
METAIRIE
Kenner
Lake Charles
BEAUMONT
P. Arthur
Galveston
MEMPHIS
Jonesboro
Tupelo
Columbus
Meridian
Hattiesburg
Gulfport
Biloxi
Pascagoula
MOBILE
Pensacola
Panama City
Tallahassee
Dothan
MONTGOMERY
Tuscaloosa
BIRMINGHAM
HUNTSVILLE
CHATTANOOGA
KNOXVILLE
NASHVILLE
Clarksville
Jackson
Gadsden
Anniston
COLUMBUS
ATLANTA
MACON
Albany
Mississippi River Delta
Chandeleur Islands
Isles Dernieres
Central Time -6h Gr. T.
Eastern Time -5h Gr. T.
Gulf of Mexico
Hawaiian Islands
Hawaiian Ridge
PACIFIC OCEAN
Kauai
Lihue
Niihau
Kauai Channel
Oahu
HONOLULU
Kaneohe
Kailua
Molokai
Kaunakakai
Lanai
Lanai City
Maui
Wailuku
Kahului
Lahaina
Haleakala Crater
Kahoolawe
Alenuihaha Channel
Hawaii
Hilo
Kailua (Kona)
Mauna Kea 4205
Mauna Loa 4170
Hawaii Volcanoes Nat. P.
Ka Lae
Hawaii (U.S.)
Hawaii -10h Gr. Time Hawaiian Time
Scale 1 : 4,500,000
0 40 80 120 160 200 Kilometers
0 40 80 120 160 Statute Miles

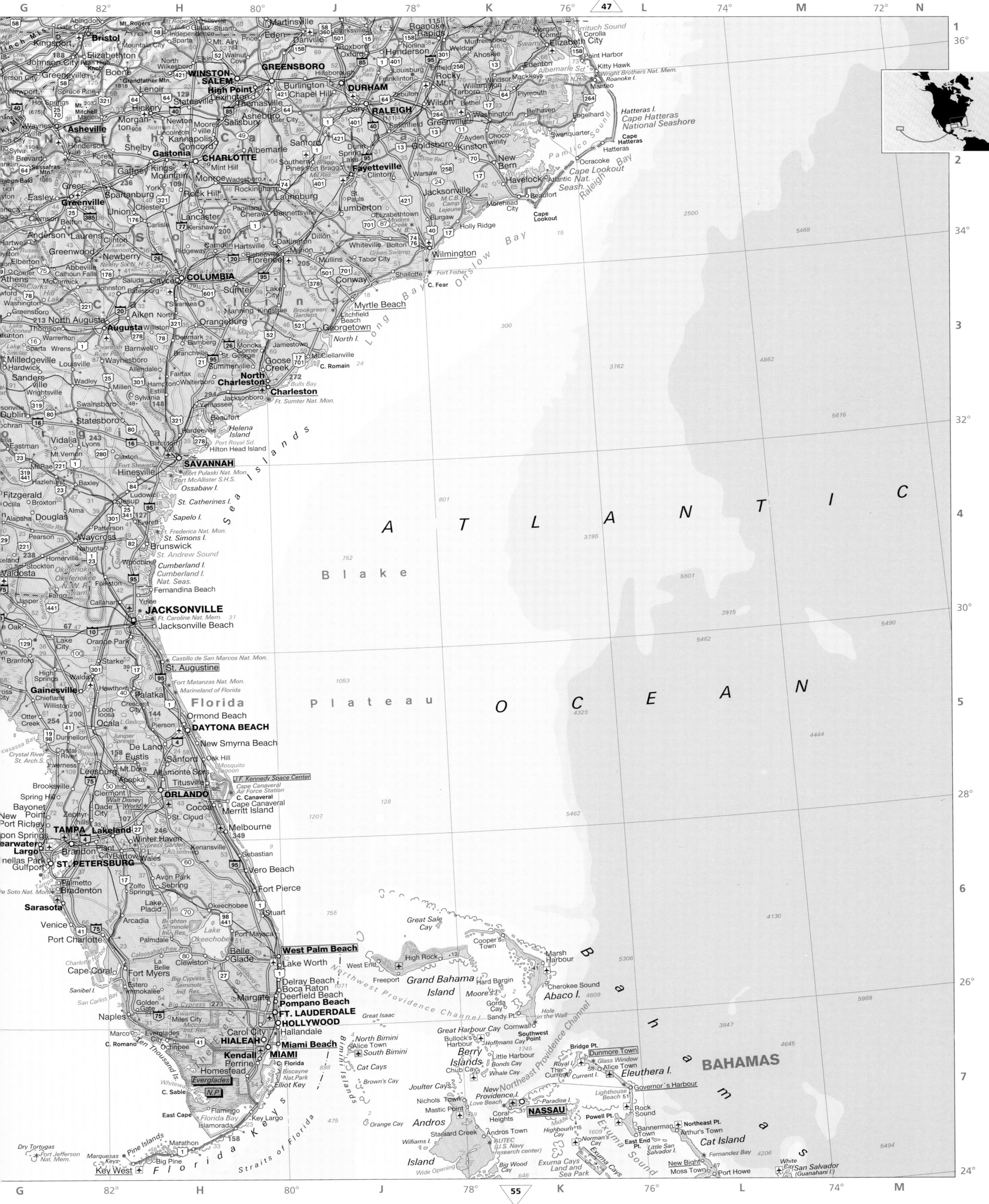

G
82°
H
80°
J
78°
K
76°
47
L
74°
M
72°
N
1
36°
2
34°
3
32°
4
30°
5
28°
6
26°
7
24°
55
A T L A N T I C
O C E A N
Blake
Plateau
Florida
BAHAMAS
Bahamas
Sea Islands
Florida Keys
Straits of Florida
Long Bay
Onslow Bay
Raleigh Bay
Pamlico Sound
Albemarle Sd.
Northwest Providence Channel
Northeast Providence Channel
Exuma Sound
Bristol
Kingsport
Johnson City
Elizabethton
Asheville
Greenville
Spartanburg
Gastonia
CHARLOTTE
WINSTON-SALEM
High Point
GREENSBORO
Burlington
Chapel Hill
DURHAM
RALEIGH
Fayetteville
Danville
Roanoke Rapids
Rocky Mt.
Wilson
Greenville
Goldsboro
Kinston
New Bern
Jacksonville
Elizabeth City
Kitty Hawk
Hatteras I.
Cape Hatteras National Seashore
Ocracoke
Cape Lookout Nat. Seash.
Morehead City
Beaufort
Wilmington
C. Fear
Myrtle Beach
Georgetown
Florence
Sumter
COLUMBIA
Augusta
Aiken
Orangeburg
North Charleston
Charleston
Beaufort
Hilton Head Island
SAVANNAH
Brunswick
Waycross
Valdosta
JACKSONVILLE
Jacksonville Beach
Fernandina Beach
St. Augustine
Gainesville
Ocala
Palatka
DAYTONA BEACH
Ormond Beach
New Smyrna Beach
Sanford
ORLANDO
Titusville
Cape Canaveral
Merritt Island
Melbourne
Vero Beach
Fort Pierce
Stuart
TAMPA
Lakeland
ST. PETERSBURG
Clearwater
Largo
Bradenton
Sarasota
Venice
Port Charlotte
Cape Coral
Fort Myers
Naples
West Palm Beach
Lake Worth
Delray Beach
Boca Raton
Deerfield Beach
Pompano Beach
FT. LAUDERDALE
HOLLYWOOD
Hallandale
HIALEAH
Miami Beach
MIAMI
Kendall
Homestead
Everglades N.P.
Key Largo
Islamorada
Marathon
Key West
Dry Tortugas
Grand Bahama Island
Freeport
Abaco I.
Marsh Harbour
Bimini Islands
Berry Islands
Andros Island
NASSAU
New Providence I.
Eleuthera I.
Governor's Harbour
Cat Island
Exuma Cays
San Salvador

Pacific Time

41

44

PACIFIC OCEAN

Baja California Norte

Baja California Sur

Gulf of California

-8h Greenwich Time
-7h Greenwich Time

Tropic of Cancer

PACIFIC OCEAN

Islas Revilla Gigedo (Mexico)

Isla San Benedicto

Isla Roca Partida

Monte Grijalva

Isla Socorro

Isla Clarión

Revilla Gigedo Islands

-7h Gr. Time
-6h Gr. Time

Scale 1 : 4,500,000

0 40 80 120 160 200 Kilometers

0 40 80 120 160 Statute Miles

Mountain Time
-7h Gr. Time
-6h Gr. Time
Central Time
106°
104°
102°
100°
98°
96°
G
J
K
L
M
H
45
52
1
2
3
4
5
6
7
30°
28°
26°
24°
22°
DALLAS
Richardson
Plano
IRVING
GARLAND
Mesquite
FT. WORTH
ARLINGTON
Waxahachie
Corsicana
WACO
Killeen
Temple
Bryan
College Station
Huntsville
ABILENE
Sweetwater
Big Spring
Midland
Odessa
San Angelo
Lubbock
Pecos
Carlsbad
Hobbs
Artesia
Alamogordo
EL PASO
AUSTIN
SAN ANTONIO
New Braunfels
HOUSTON
PASADENA
Victoria
CORPUS CHRISTI
Laredo
NUEVO LAREDO
Del Rio
Ciudad Acuña
Eagle Pass
PIEDRAS NEGRAS
Nueva Rosita
MONCLOVA
Castaños
MONTERREY
S. NICOLAS D. L. GARZAS
STA. CATARINA
GUADALUPE
SALTILLO
LINARES
REYNOSA
McAllen
Harlingen
BROWNSVILLE
MATAMOROS
CD. VICTORIA
Cd. Mante
CD. MADERO
TAMPICO
CIUDAD VALLES
TAMAZUNCHALE
Tuxpan de R. C.
SAN LUIS POTOSÍ
ZACATECAS
Fresnillo de González Echeverría
AGUASCALIENTES
LEÓN
GUANAJUATO
DOLORES HIDALGO
S. MIGUEL de Allende
DURANGO
GÓMEZ PALACIO
Ciudad Lerdo
TORREÓN
CHIHUAHUA
Delicias
Ciudad Camargo
Hidalgo del Parral
Ojinaga
TEPIC
Edwards Plateau
Stockton Plateau
Balcones Escarpment
Great Plains
Pecos Plains
Llanos de los Caballos Mesteños
Bolsón de Mapimí
Sierra Madre Oriental
Sierra Madre Occidental
Sierra del Burro
Desierto de Mayran
Gulf of Mexico
Padre Island National Seashore
Padre Island
Tropic of Cancer
Río Bravo del Norte
Rio Grande
M E X I C O
T E X A S

A 106° -6h Gr. Time B 104° C 102° D 51 100° E 98° F
Sierra Madre del Sur
MÉXICO
TOLUCA
CUERNAVACA
PUEBLA
GUADALAJARA
AGUASCALIENTES
LEÓN
GUANAJUATO
QUERÉTARO
MORELIA
PUERTO VALLARTA
TEPIC
COLIMA
Manzanillo
ACAPULCO DE JUÁREZ
Chilpancingo de los Bravos
OAXACA DE J.
Tehuacán
PACHUCA DE SOTO
JALAPA
ORIZABA
POZA RICA
Tuxpan de R. C.
Lázaro Cárdenas
Zihuatanejo
Puerto Angel
Pinotepa Nacional
HONDURAS
NICARAGUA
MANAGUA
Granada
Masaya
Matagalpa
Jinotega
Estelí
Bluefields
Puerto Cabezas
Cordillera Isabella
Costa de Miskitos
Lago de Nicaragua
COSTA RICA
SAN JOSÉ
PUERTO LIMÓN
Puntarenas
Cord. de Talamanca
PANAMA
PANAMÁ
Colón
David
Golfo de Panamá
Caribbean Sea
PACIFIC OCEAN
Isla de San Andrés (Col.)
Isla de Providencia (Col.)
Golfo de Papagayo
Golfo de los Mosquitos
-6h Gr. Time -5h Gr. Time
A 86° B 84° C 82° D 80° E 78° F
53
Scale 1 : 4,500,000
0 40 80 120 160 200 Kilometers
0 40 80 120 160 Statute Miles

Gulf of Mexico
Bahía de Campeche
Yucatán Peninsula
Yucatán Channel
Yucatán Basin
Caribbean Sea
Golfo de Tehuantepec
Golfo de Honduras
PACIFIC OCEAN
America Trench
GUATEMALA
BELIZE
HONDURAS
EL SALVADOR
NICARAGUA
COSTA RICA
MERIDA
CAMPECHE
CIUDAD DEL CARMEN
CHETUMAL
Cancún
Cozumel
VILLAHERMOSA
COATZACOALCOS
MINATITLÁN
TUXTLA GUTIÉRREZ
Tapachula
QUEZALTENANGO
GUATEMALA
Cobán
SAN PEDRO SULA
EL PROGRESO
Puerto Cortés
La Ceiba
TEGUCIGALPA
Comayagüela
SAN SALVADOR
SANTA ANA
SAN MIGUEL
LEÓN
Chinandega
MANAGUA
Granada
Masaya
Belize City
Belmopan
Istmo de Tehuantepec
Sierra Madre de Chiapas
Sierra de los Cuchumatanes
Maya Mountains
Meseta de Zohlaguna
SINCELEJO
MONTERIA
CARTAGENA
54
52
60

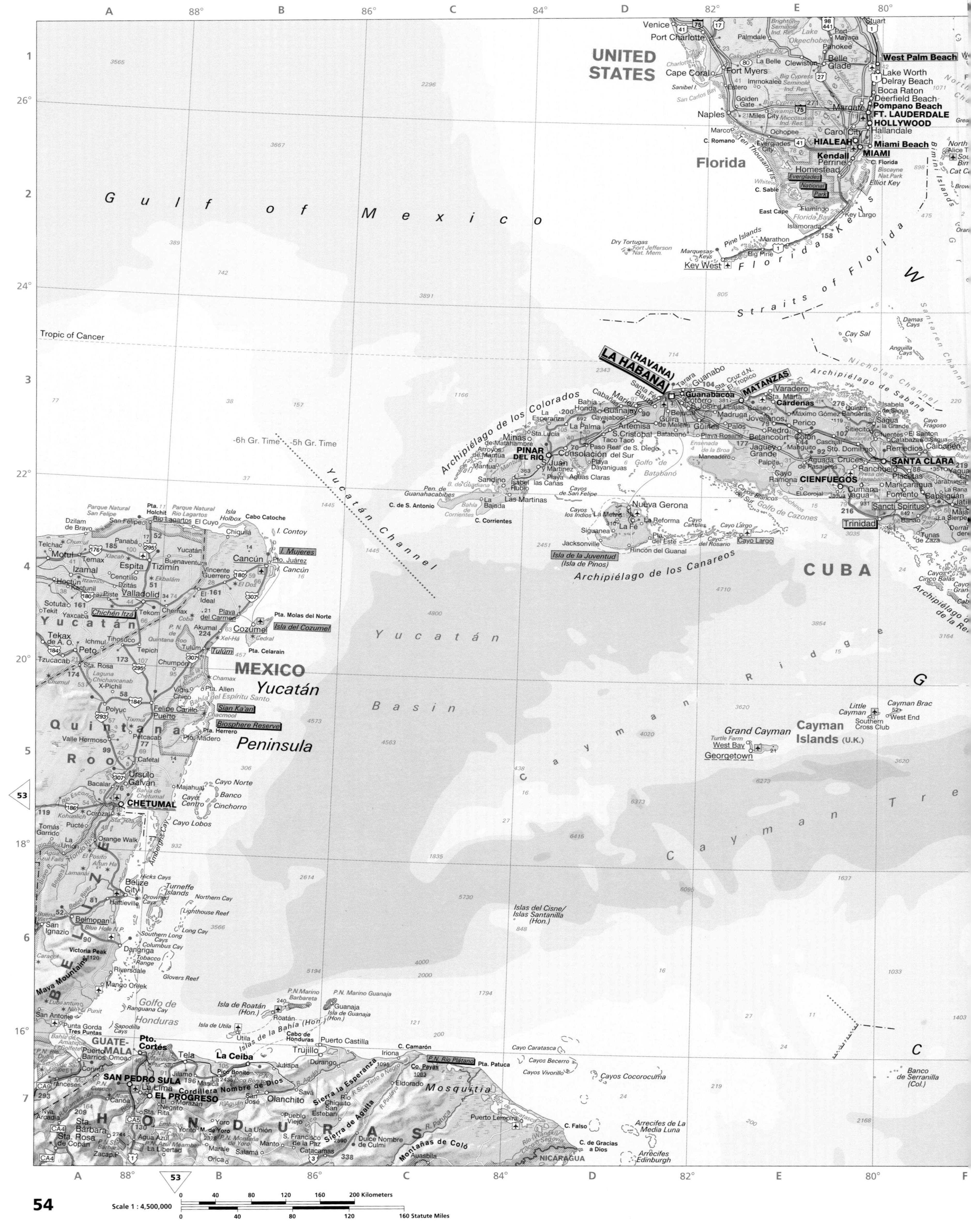

Gulf of Mexico
UNITED STATES
Florida
Venice
Port Charlotte
Palmdale
Lake Okeechobee
Port Mayaca
Pahokee
Stuart
West Palm Beach
Belle Glade
Clewiston
La Belle
Cape Coral
Fort Myers
Immokalee
Sanibel I.
Estero
Lake Worth
Delray Beach
Boca Raton
Deerfield Beach
Pompano Beach
FT. LAUDERDALE
HOLLYWOOD
Hallandale
Naples
Golden Gate
Miles City
Margate
Marco
Ochopee
Carol City
C. Romano
Everglades City
HIALEAH
Miami Beach
Kendall
MIAMI
Perrine
C. Florida
Homestead
Biscayne Nat. Park
Elliot Key
Everglades National Park
C. Sable
East Cape
Flamingo
Florida Bay
Key Largo
Islamorada
Marathon
Big Pine
Pine Islands
Dry Tortugas
Fort Jefferson Nat. Mem.
Marquesas Keys
Key West
Florida Keys
Straits of Florida
Bimini Islands
Damas Cays
Cay Sal
Anguilla Cays
Nicholas Channel
Santaren Channel
Tropic of Cancer
-6h Gr. Time
-5h Gr. Time
Yucatán Channel
(HAVANA)
LA HABANA
MATANZAS
Guanabo
Tarara
Santa Fe
Guanabacoa
Cotorro
Varadero
Cárdenas
Archipiélago de Sabana
Archipiélago de los Colorados
Bahía Honda
Cabañas
Mariel
Guanajay
Artemisa
Bejucal
Güira de Melena
Güines
Madruga
Jovellanos
Colón
Perico
Pedro Betancourt
Batabanó
Playa Rosario
Ensenada de la Broa
Golfo de Batabanó
Jagüey Grande
Palpite
Aguada de Pasajeros
Cruces
Ranchuelo
SANTA CLARA
Remedios
Caibarién
Sagua la Grande
Isabela de Sagua
Cayo Fragoso
Placetas
CIENFUEGOS
Manicaragua
Fomento
Cumanayagua
Sancti Spiritus
Trinidad
Cabaiguán
Jatibonico
Tunas de Zaza
Golfo de Cazones
Cayo Largo
Cayos del Rosario
Cayos Cantiles
Nueva Gerona
La Fe
La Reforma
Siguanea
Jacksonville
Rincón del Guanal
Isla de la Juventud
(Isla de Pinos)
Archipiélago de los Canareos
Cayos de San Felipe
Cayos los Indios
PINAR DEL RIO
Consolación del Sur
San Juan y Martínez
Minas de Matahambre
Mantua
Arroyos de Mantua
Sandino
Isabel Rubio
Las Martinas
La Bajada
Bahía de Corrientes
C. Corrientes
C. de S. Antonio
Pen. de Guanahacabibes
CUBA
Archipiélago de la Reina
Cayos Cinco Balas
Cayman Brac
Little Cayman
West End
Southern Cross Club
Grand Cayman
Turtle Farm
West Bay
Georgetown
Cayman Islands (U.K.)
Cayman Ridge
Cayman Trench
Yucatán Basin
Islas del Cisne/
Islas Santanilla
(Hon.)
MEXICO
Yucatán Peninsula
Yucatán
Quintana Roo
Parque Natural San Felipe
Pta. Holchit
Parque Natural Rio Lagartos
Rio Lagartos
San Felipe
El Cuyo
Isla Holbox
Cabo Catoche
Chiquilá
I. Contoy
I. Mujeres
Pto. Juárez
Cancún
I. Cancún
Dzilam de Bravo
Telchac
Motul
Temax
Panabá
Tizimin
Buenaventura
Espita
Izamal
Cenotillo
Dzitás
Valladolid
Vicente Guerrero
Ekbalám
El Ideal
Hoctún
Kantunil
Piste
Chichén Itzá
Sotuta
Tekit
Yaxcaba
Tekom
Chemax
Playa del Carmen
Pta. Molas del Norte
Isla del Cozumel
Cozumel
Cobá
Akumal
Xel-Há
Pta. Celarain
Tulum
Tekax
Peto
Ichmul
Tihosuco
Tepich
Tzucacab
Sta. Rosa
Chumpón
Laguna Chichancanab
X-Pichil
Chunhuhub
Chamax
Vigia Chico
Pta. Allen
Bahía del Espíritu Santo
Sian Ka'an Biosphere Reserve
Felipe Carillo Puerto
Polyuc
Chacmool
Pta. Herrero
Pto. Madero
Valle Hermoso
Petcacab
Cafetal
Bacalar
Ursulo Galván
Majahual
Cayo Norte
Banco Cinchorro
Cayo Centro
Cayo Lobos
CHETUMAL
Bahía de Chetumal
Corozal
Orange Walk
Tomás Garrido
Pucté
La Unión
Ambergris Cay
Hicks Cays
Turneffe Islands
Northern Cay
Lighthouse Reef
Long Cay
Belize City
Hattieville
Belmopan
San Ignacio
Blue Hole N.P.
Southern Long Cays
Columbus Cay
Dangriga
Tobacco Range
Victoria Peak
Maya Mountains
Riversdale
Glovers Reef
Mango Creek
Golfo de Honduras
Ranguana Cay
Punta Gorda
Sapodilla Cays
San Antonio
GUATEMALA
Puerto Barrios
Omoa
Pto. Cortés
Tela
La Ceiba
Isla de Utila
Utila
Isla de Roatán (Hon.)
Roatán
P.N. Marino Barbareta
P.N. Marino Guanaja
Guanaja
Isla de Guanaja (Hon.)
Islas de la Bahía (Hon.)
Cabo de Honduras
Puerto Castilla
Trujillo
Iriona
C. Camarón
P.N. Río Plátano
Pta. Patuca
Cayo Caratasca
Cayos Becerro
Cayos Vivorillo
Cayos Cocorocuma
SAN PEDRO SULA
EL PROGRESO
La Lima
Jilamo
Pico Bonito
Cordillera Nombre de Dios
Jutiapa
Durango
Savá
Olanchito
Sierra la Esperanza
Eldorado
Mosquitia
Sierra de Agalta
Puerto Lempira
C. Falso
Arrecifes de la Media Luna
C. de Gracias a Dios
Arrecifes Edinburgh
Banco de Serranilla (Col.)
HONDURAS
Santa Bárbara
Sta. Rosa de Copán
Yoro
La Unión
Dulce Nombre de Culmi
Montañas de Coló
Auasbila
NICARAGUA
Manto
Catacamas
Salamá
Marale
Orica
La Libertad
Zacapa
Scale 1 : 4,500,000
0 40 80 120 160 200 Kilometers
0 40 80 120 160 Statute Miles

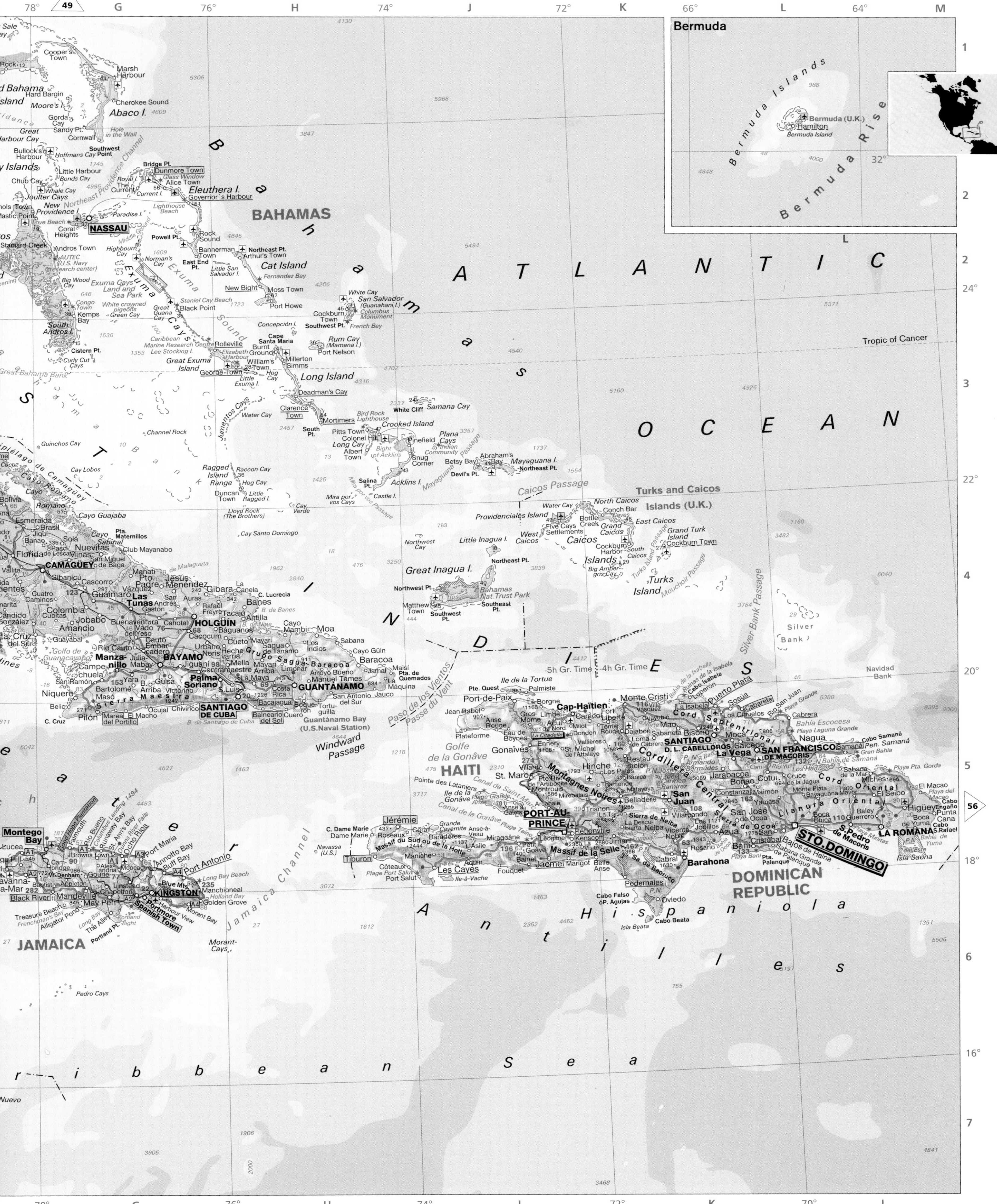

49
56
Bermuda
Bermuda Islands
Bermuda Rise
Bermuda (U.K.)
Hamilton
Bermuda Island
BAHAMAS
Bahamas
ATLANTIC
OCEAN
Tropic of Cancer
Abaco I.
Marsh Harbour
Cherokee Sound
Cooper's Town
Eleuthera I.
Governor's Harbour
Dunmore Town
NASSAU
New Providence I.
Andros Town
Cat Island
Arthur's Town
Exuma Cays
Great Exuma Island
George Town
Long Island
San Salvador (Guanahani I.)
Rum Cay
Crooked Island
Acklins I.
Mayaguana I.
Great Inagua I.
Matthew Town
Little Inagua I.
Samana Cay
Turks and Caicos Islands (U.K.)
North Caicos
Providenciales Island
Caicos Islands
Grand Turk Island
Cockburn Town
Turks Island
Caicos Passage
Silver Bank
Silver Bank Passage
Navidad Bank
Mouchoir Passage
Turks Island Passage
Mayaguana Passage
Crooked Island Passage
Old Bahama Channel
Great Bahama Bank
Jumentos Cays
Ragged Island Range
Cay Santo Domingo
CAMAGÜEY
Nuevitas
Las Tunas
HOLGUÍN
Gibara
BAYAMO
Manzanillo
Palma Soriano
SANTIAGO DE CUBA
GUANTÁNAMO
Baracoa
Sierra Maestra
Guantánamo Bay (U.S.Naval Station)
Windward Passage
Paso de los Vientos
Passe du Vent
-5h Gr. Time
-4h Gr. Time
HAITI
Cap-Haïtien
Port-de-Paix
Île de la Tortue
Gonaïves
Golfe de la Gonâve
Île de la Gonâve
St. Marc
Hinche
PORT-AU-PRINCE
Jérémie
Les Cayes
Jacmel
Massif de la Selle
Massif du Sud
Montagnes Noires
Canal de Saint Marc
Navassa (U.S.)
DOMINICAN REPUBLIC
SANTIAGO
La Vega
SAN FRANCISCO DE MACORIS
Puerto Plata
Monte Cristi
Cordillera Central
Cordillera Septentrional
San Juan
Barahona
Azua
STO. DOMINGO
San Pedro de Macoris
LA ROMANA
Higüey
Samaná
Isla Saona
Cabo Beata
Isla Beata
Hispaniola
Jamaica Channel
JAMAICA
Montego Bay
KINGSTON
Spanish Town
Mandeville
Port Antonio
Morant Cays
Pedro Cays
Greater Antilles
Caribbean Sea

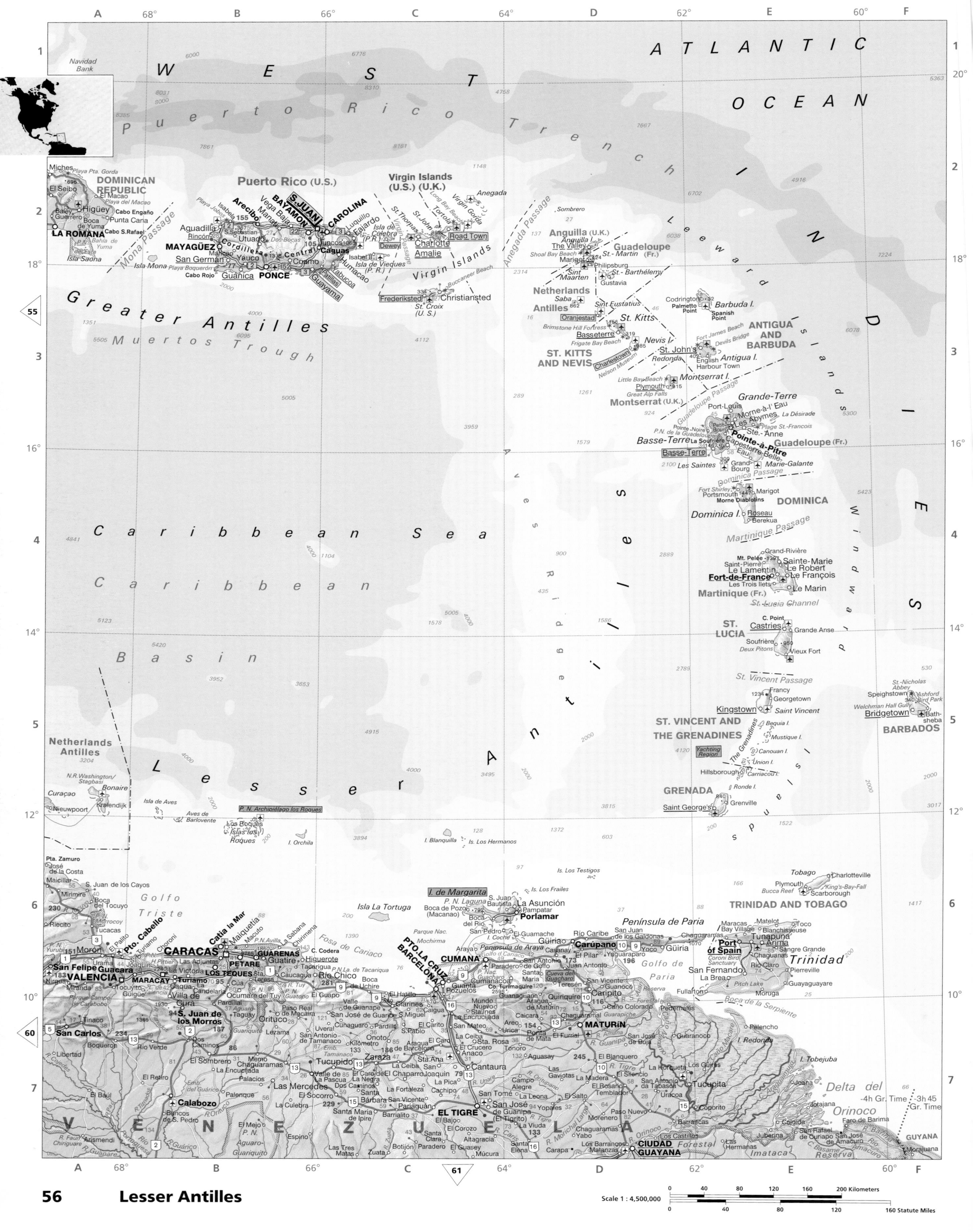
ATLANTIC OCEAN
WEST INDIES
Puerto Rico Trench
Greater Antilles
Muertos Trough
Caribbean Sea
Caribbean Basin
Lesser Antilles
Aves Ridge
Leeward Islands
Windward Islands
Navidad Bank
DOMINICAN REPUBLIC
Puerto Rico (U.S.)
Virgin Islands (U.S.) (U.K.)
Anegada
Anegada Passage
Sombrero
Anguilla (U.K.)
The Valley
Guadeloupe (Fr.)
St.-Martin (Fr.)
Sint Maarten
Philipsburg
St.-Barthélemy
Gustavia
Netherlands Antilles
Saba
Sint Eustatius
Oranjestad
St. Kitts
Basseterre
Nevis
Charlestown
ST. KITTS AND NEVIS
Redonda
Barbuda I.
Codrington
ANTIGUA AND BARBUDA
St. John's
Antigua I.
English Harbour Town
Montserrat I.
Plymouth
Montserrat (U.K.)
Guadeloupe Passage
Grande-Terre
Port-Louis
Les Abymes
Pointe-à-Pitre
Basse-Terre
Les Saintes
Marie-Galante
Grand Bourg
Dominica Passage
Marigot
Portsmouth
Morne Diablotins
DOMINICA
Dominica I.
Roseau
Berekua
Martinique Passage
Grand-Rivière
Mt. Pelée
Saint-Pierre
Sainte-Marie
Le Robert
Le Lamentin
Fort-de-France
Le François
Les Trois Ilets
Le Marin
Martinique (Fr.)
St. Lucia Channel
C. Point
Castries
ST. LUCIA
Grande Anse
Soufrière
Deux Pitons
Vieux Fort
St. Vincent Passage
Francy
Georgetown
Kingstown
Saint Vincent
ST. VINCENT AND THE GRENADINES
Bequia I.
Mustique I.
Canouan I.
Union I.
The Grenadines
Yachting Region
Hillsborough
Carriacou I.
Ronde I.
GRENADA
Saint George's
Grenville
St.-Nicholas Abbey
Speightstown
Bridgetown
Bathsheba
BARBADOS
Netherlands Antilles
Curaçao
Bonaire
Kralendijk
Isla de Aves
Aves de Barlovente
P. N. Archipiélago los Roques
Los Roques
I. Orchila
I. Blanquilla
Is. Los Hermanos
Is. Los Testigos
Is. Los Frailes
Tobago
Charlotteville
Scarborough
TRINIDAD AND TOBAGO
Port of Spain
Trinidad
San Fernando
Golfo de Paria
Península de Paria
I. de Margarita
La Asunción
Porlamar
Isla La Tortuga
CARACAS
VALENCIA
MARACAY
CUMANA
PTO. LA CRUZ
BARCELONA
Carúpano
MATURIN
Tucupita
EL TIGRE
CIUDAD GUAYANA
Delta del Orinoco
Golfo Triste
Pto. Cabello
San Carlos
Calabozo
Barinitas
VENEZUELA
GUYANA
-4h Gr. Time
-3h 45 Gr. Time
Scale 1 : 4,500,000
0 40 80 120 160 200 Kilometers
0 40 80 120 160 Statute Miles

South America – continent of natural highlights

Since most of South America's 6,872,580 square miles (17.8 million sq. km) are located in the Southern Hemisphere, it is considered a southern continent, like Africa. The continent is even connected with the Antarctic via the Southern Antilles and submarine rises. With the exception of the polar ice region, all climatic and vegetation zones are represented on the continent; the tropical climate is predominant, however. The western part of the continent is characterized by the volcano-studded mountain range of the Cordilleras de Los Andes, which is close to 4,660 miles (7,500 km) long and reaches a height of almost 23,000 feet (7,000 m). Parallel to them runs a continuous deep-sea trench in the Pacific Ocean. Over half of the continent's land mass is taken up by the giant lowlands of the Orinoco, the Amazon and the Paraná. Adjacent to the southeastern coast is a broad continental shelf cresting in the Falkland Islands (called Islas Malvinas by Argentina). More animal and plant species are found in South America than anywhere else in the world: More than 250 of the 350 known flowering plant families originate there; it is home to one-third of all bird species, and the number of insect species is beyond estimation. The Amazon Basin not only is the largest river region on Earth but also contains the greatest area of tropical forest.

An early documentation of intercultural encounter: Zacharias Wagner created this depiction of an Indian dance during his sojourn in Brazil (1634–37) and subsequently published it in his "Bestiary."

Colombia · Venezuela
p. 60–61

Guyana · Suriname · Brazil: Northern Region p. 62–63

Ecuador · Peru (Inset: Galápagos Islands)
p. 64–65

Brazil: Amazonian Lowlands
p. 66–67

Brazil: Northeastern Region
p. 68–69

Bolivia · Pantanal
p. 70–71

Brazil: Southeastern Region
p. 72–73

Brazil: Southern Region · Uruguay
p. 74–75

Argentina and Chile: Northern Regions
p. 76–77

Argentina and Chile: Central Regions
p. 78–79

Argentina and Chile: Southern Regions
p. 80

Inset: Falkland Islands · South Georgia
p. 78–79

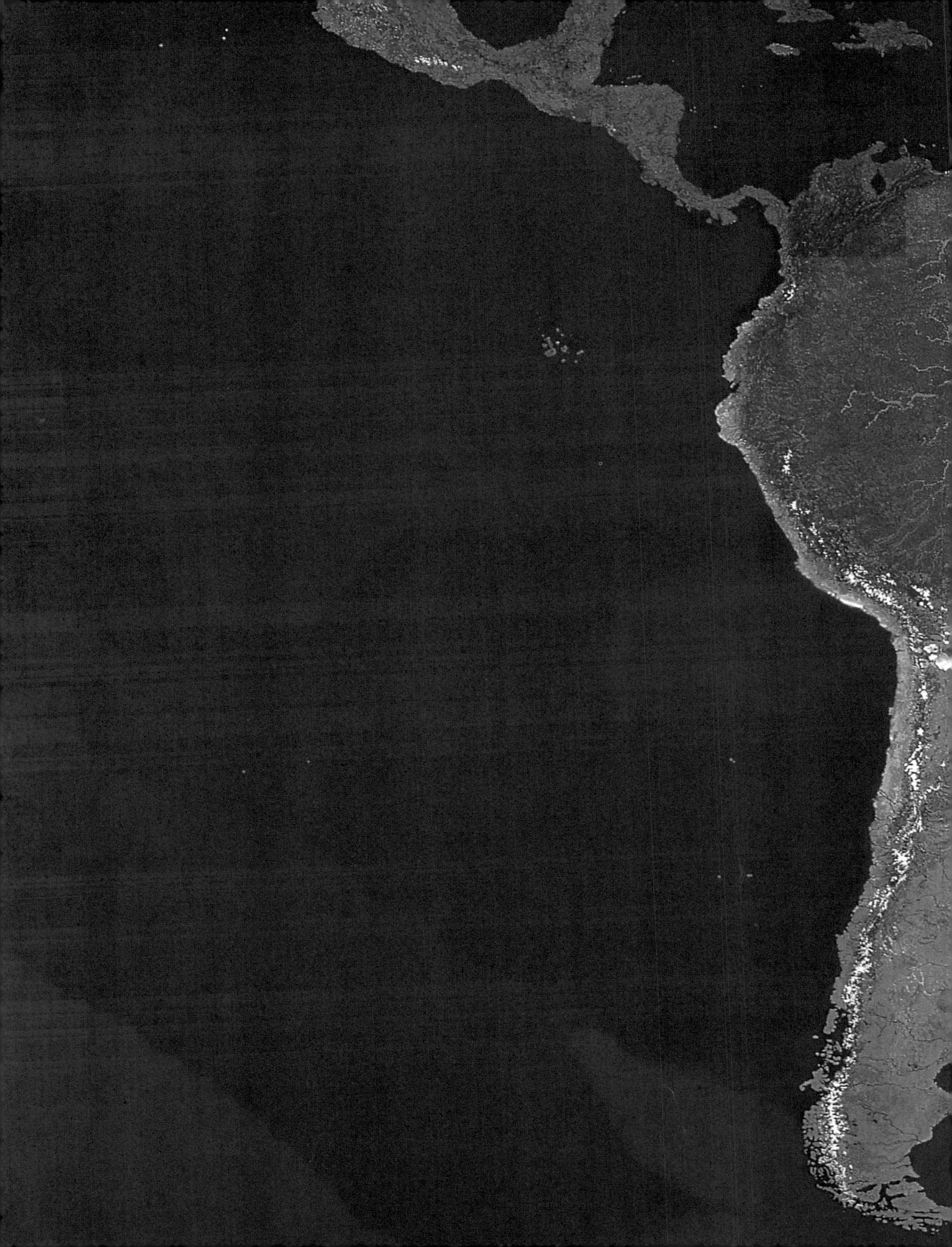

Colombia · Venezuela
p. 60 – 61
Guyana · Suriname · Brazil: Northern Region p. 62 – 63
Ecuador · Peru (Inset: Galápagos Islands)
p. 64 – 65
Brazil: Amazonian Lowlands
p. 66 – 67
Brazil: Northeastern Region
p. 68 – 69
Bolivia · Pantanal
p. 70 – 71
Brazil: Southeastern Region
p. 72 – 73
Brazil: Southern Region · Uruguay
p. 74 – 75
Argentina and Chile: Northern Regions
p. 76 – 77
Argentina and Chile: Central Regions
p. 78 – 79
Argentina and Chile: Southern Regions
p. 80
Inset: Falkland Islands · South Georgia
p. 78 – 79

Scale 1 : 4,500,000

0 40 80 120 160 200 Kilometers

0 40 80 120 160 Statute Miles

70°-4h Gr. Time
G
68°
H
66°
J
64°
56
K
62°
L
Caribbean Sea
Lesser Antilles
Aruba (Neth.)
Oranjestad
Sint Nicolaas
Netherlands Antilles
Curaçao
Willemstad
Bonaire
Kralendijk
Isla de Aves
Aves de Barlovento
Los Roques
Islas los Roques
I. Orchila
P. N. Archipiélago los Roques
I. Blanquilla
Is. Los Hermanos
Is. Los Testigos
SAINT VINCENT AND THE GRENADINES
The Grenadines
Mustique I.
Canouan I.
Union I.
Carriacou I.
Hillsborough
Ronde I.
GRENADA
Saint George's
Grenville
Yachting Region
Tobago
Charlotteville
Plymouth
Scarborough
TRINIDAD AND TOBAGO
Port of Spain
Arima
Trinidad
San Fernando
Península de Paria
Golfo de Paria
Boca de la Serpiente
I. de Margarita
La Asunción
Porlamar
Isla La Tortuga
Golfo Triste
CORO
Pto. Cabello
CARACAS
PETARE
LOS TEQUES
MARACAY
VALENCIA
San Felipe
BARQUISIMETO
PTO.LA CRUZ
BARCELONA
CUMANA
Carúpano
Güiria
MATURIN
Tucupita
CIUDAD GUAYANA
CIUDAD BOLIVAR
Upata
EL TIGRE
Calabozo
S. Fernando de Apure
S. Juan de los Morros
San Carlos
Acarigua
Guanare
Mérida
VENEZUELA
ORINOCO
COLOMBIA
Delta del Orinoco
I. Tobejuba
Pto. Ayacucho
Sierra de Guampí
Sierra de Maigualida
Meseta de Jaua
GUIANA HIGHLANDS
Salto Angel
Canaima
Sierra del Zamuro
Sierra Pacaraima
Serra Parima
Serrania de Imataca
Serrania Turagua
GUYANA
Mt. Roraima
Reserva Florestal Parima
Serra Mucajaí
Sierra de Unturán
Sierra Tapirapeco
Co. de la Neblina
Parque Nacional do Pico da Neblina
Boa Vista
BRAZIL
Amazonas
Roraima
Yanomami
Pico Rondon
S. Carlos de Rio Negro
Pto. Inírida
Serranía de la Cerbatana
Co. Duida
La Esmeralda
Co. Guachamacari
El Callao
Tumeremo
El Dorado
Santa Elena de Uairén
Caracaraí
Mucajaí
62
66
67
1
2
3
4
5
6
7
10°
8°
6°
4°
2°

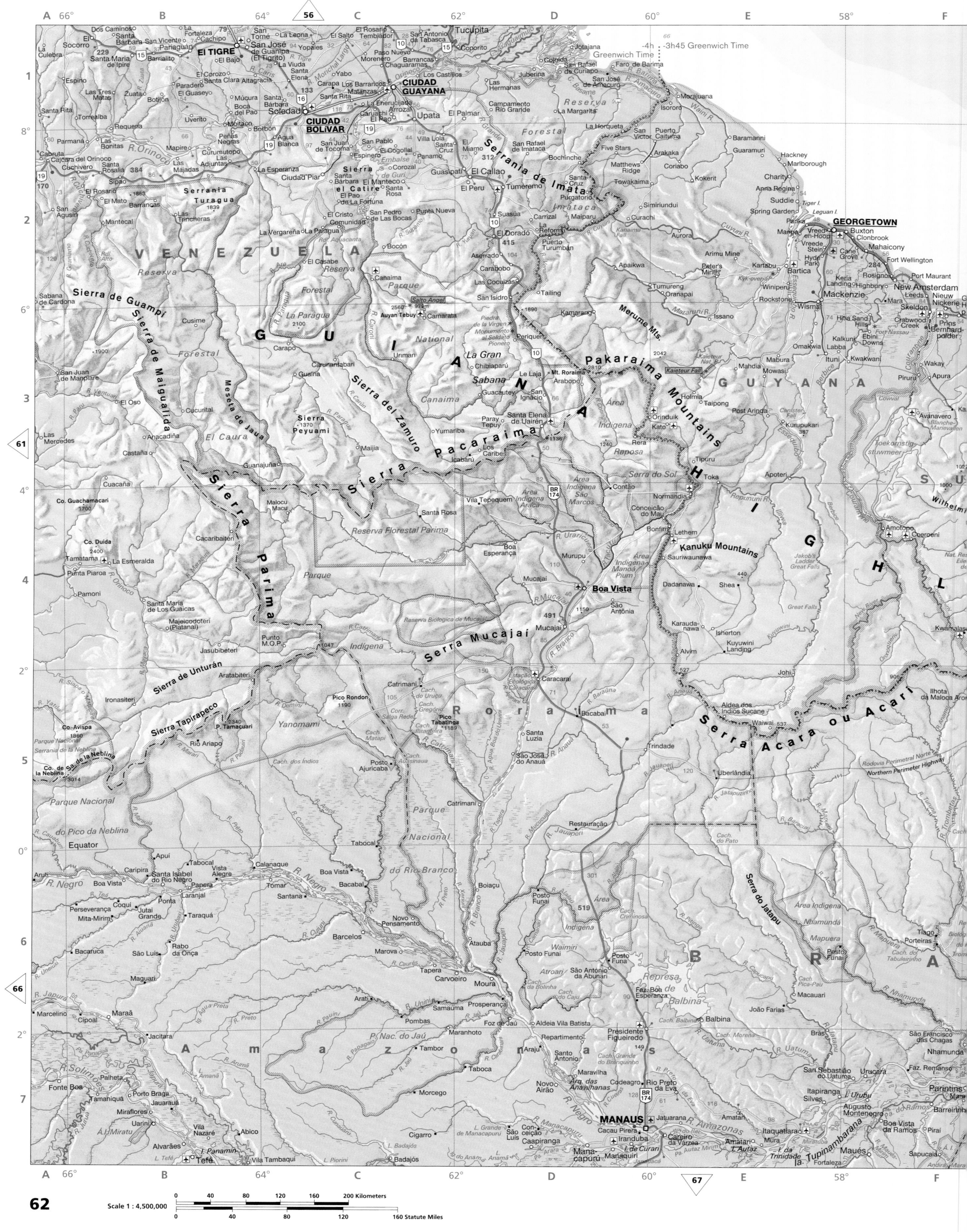

56
61
66
67
-4h -3h45 Greenwich Time
Greenwich Time
Tucupita
EL TIGRE
CIUDAD GUAYANA
CIUDAD BOLÍVAR
Soledad
Upata
El Callao
Tumeremo
El Dorado
Serranía de Imataca
Serranía Turagua
V E N E Z U E L A
Sierra de Guampí
Sierra de Maigualida
Meseta de Jaua
G U I A N A
Sierra del Zamuro
Sierra Pacaraima
Sierra Parima
Salto Angel
Auyan Tebuy
La Gran Sabana
Canaima
Parque Nacional
Santa Elena de Uairén
Mt. Roraima
Pakaraima Mountains
Merume Mts.
Kaieteur Fall
G U Y A N A
GEORGETOWN
New Amsterdam
Linden
Mackenzie
Bartica
Kanuku Mountains
Lethem
Boa Vista
BR 174
Serra Mucajaí
Reserva Florestal Parima
Reserva Biologica de Mucajaí
R o r a i m a
Caracaraí
Sierra de Unturán
Sierra Tapirapecó
Co. de la Neblina
Parque Nacional do Pico da Neblina
Equator
Santa Isabel do Rio Negro
R. Negro
Barcelos
Parque Nacional do Jaú
Serra Acara ou Acari
Serra do Jatapu
Northern Perimeter Highway
Rodovia Perimetral Norte
Represa de Balbina
Presidente Figueiredo
MANAUS
R. Amazonas
Parintins
Itacoatiara
A m a z o n a s
B R A
R. Solimões
Tefé
Coari
Scale 1 : 4,500,000
0 40 80 120 160 200 Kilometers
0 40 80 120 160 Statute Miles

56°
G
54°
H
52°
J
50°
K
48°
L
1
2
3
4
5
6
7
6°
4°
2°
0°
Guiana Plateau
ATLANTIC
OCEAN
4643
1161
3347
4224
62
3691
3264
1622
-3h45 Greenwich Time
-4h Greenwich Time
-3h Greenwich Time
PARA-
MARIBO
Nieuw
Amsterdam
Johan en Margeretha
Tamanredjo
Totness
Bookamp
Bethlehem
Hamburg
Meerzorg
Wriedijk
Lelydorp
Onverwacht
Paranam
Zanderij
Jenny
Mungo
Galibi
Awara
Mana
Albina
St.Laurent-du Maroni
Organabo
Iracoubo
Sinnamary
Îles du Salut
Îles du Diable
Centre Spatial Guyanais
Kourou
Tonate (Macouria)
Cayenne
Remire
Matoury
Roura
Pte. Béhague
Moengo
Sabana
Witagron
Berg en Dal
Victoria
Brokopondo
Afobaka
Langatabiki
Apatou
Dépôt
Lézard Rnes
Santonia
Brownsweg
Pakapaka
Voltzberg
Pokigron
Boslanti
Botopasi
Mgnes. Françaises
Grand-Santi
French
Guiana
Roche Cabrit
Bélizon
Cacao
Regina
Bauge
Ouanary
C. Orange
Saint-Georges
Oiapoque
Ponta dos Índios
Pta. do Costa
C.Caciporé
Irène
Pierrette
Dégrad Saint-Léon
Asindonhopo
Tafelberg
Mt. Cottica
Maripasoula
Dorlin
Mt. Bellevue de l'Inini
Saül
Paleowine (Apetina)
Roseveltpiek
Palumeu
De Goejegeb.
Antecume Pata
Blicade
Dégrad Vitalo
Emerillon
Pierre Hoho
Pelelutepu
Oranje Geb.
Eilerts de Haan Gebergte
Massif Tabulaire
Siminiout
Camopi
Dégrad Claude (Dégrad des Emerillon)
Oscar
Posto Funai
São José do Caciporé
Pta. Cambu
Amazon Canyon
Amazon Shelf
Serra Lombarda
Cunani
Calçoene
Nazaré
Ilakana
Patatpe
Enéné
Patatpe
Maloca Velha
Trios
Sipaliwini
Serra do Tumucumaque
Dégrad Haut Camopi
Trois Sauts
Lourenço
Bela Vista
Pta. da Pescada
Amapá
Maracá
I. de Maracá
Estação Ecológica Maracá-Jipioca
Talimã
Canea
Caneapo
Molocopote
Cabo do Norte
Sucuriju
Amapá
Tartarugalzinho
do Tumucumaque
Aldeia Bona
Iaripo
Aldeia das Canoas
Área Indígena
Waiãpi
São Felício
Aporema
São Miguel
Farol Guará
I. Bailique
Bailique
Uruguinha
Serra do Navio
Ferreira Gomes
Capoeira do Rei
Porto Grande
S. Luzia do Pacuí
I. do Curuá
Limão do Curuá
Estuário do
Pta. de Santarém
I. Janauçu
Rio Amazonas
Maloca
Nauari
Azauri
Paru de Leste
Terceiro Acampamento
Cupixi
Gaivota
S. Antônio
I. Caviana de Dentro
Acampamento Grande
Planalto
Pto. Arari
Macapá
Pta. Rebordelo
I. Caviana de Fora
Tapereba
Camaipi
Maruanum
Santana
Erialé
Rufino
Pancudo
Mazagão
Mazagão Velho
S. Julião do Jurupari
I. da Serraria
Piri Grande
Chaves
I. Mexiana
Nazaré
Equator
Afua
Maracanaquara
Barraca da Boca
Santa Clara
São Tomé
Bom Jardim
Maria
S. Cosme
Ilha de Marajó
Santa Cruz do Arari
Cabo Maguari
Cajuuna
San Marcos
Jenipapo
Salvaterra
Soure
São Caetano de Odivelas
Pta. Curuçá
Cajutuba
Marudá
Pta. de Atalaia
Salinópolis
Marapinim
Curuçá
Magalhães Barata
Maracanã
Vigia
Itatupã
Cach. de S. Antônio Beiradão
Santana
Ipixuna
Punta Alegre
Punto da Barca
Joaquim
Condeixas
Sa. do Almeirim
Monte Dourado
Pagas Divisas
Boca do Jari
I. Grande
São Vicente
Anajás
Boa Vista
Cachoeira do Arari
Colares
Mosqueiro
Santo André
Santarém Novo
Primavera
Japerica
Bragança
Ramos
Coruma
I. Urutai
de Gurupá
I. dos Macacos
São Miguel dos Macacos
Ponta de Pedras
Baía de Marajó
Terra Alta
Igarapé Açu
Peixeboi
Tauari
Nova Macajuba
Cuminá
Serra Paranaquara
Almeirim
Gurupa
Viana
Santa Maria
Muaná
Sta. Isabel do Pará
Castanhal
Nova Timboteua
Capanema
Cumburão
I. Urucuri
Vilarinho do Monte
I. da Laguna
São Sebastião da Boa Vista
BELÉM
Benevides
Inhangapi
Bujaru
Sta. Maria do Pará
Bonito
Ourém
Tentugal
Oriximiná
Curuá
Flexal
Prainha
Is. do Aquiqui
Esperança
Porto de Moz
Melgaço
Breves
Curralinho
Abaetetuba
Barcarena
S. Domingos do Capim
S. Miguel do Guamá
Capitão Poço
Óbidos
Alenquer
Monte Alegre
R. Amazonas
São João da Pracajuba
Portel
Bagre
Limoeiro do Ajuru
Maiauatá
Seguro
Irituia
Juruti
Arapixuna
I. de Santa Rita
Boa Vista
Oeiras do Para
Igarapé Mirim
Acará
Concordia do Pará
Santana
Boa Nova
Curuai
SANTARÉM
Pacoval
I. do Huqui
Marcelo
Acangatá
Aru
Cametá
Trinidade
Curupaiti
Vila Aurora
Alter do Chão
Belterra
Mojui dos Campos
Lago das Pedras
Hidrelétrica Curua-Una
Santa Cruz
Aricari
Senador José Porfírio
Parada
São Pedro
Prainha
Bertinho
Carapajó
Cairari
Mocajuba
Baião
I. do Bacuri
Tomé-Açu
Vicente Franco
S. Francisco
Vila Ipixuna
Nova Olinda
Camarã
Pinhélo
Vitoria
Belo Monte do Pontal
Altamira
Paquiçama
Bailique
São José
Paragominas
S. Bento
Serraria
338
nta Cruz
BR 163
BR 230
BR 156
BR 210
BR 316
BR 010
PA 150
68
Pará
Amapá
SURINAME

68

Scale 1 : 4,500,000

0 40 80 120 160 200 Kilometers

0 40 80 120 160 Statute Miles

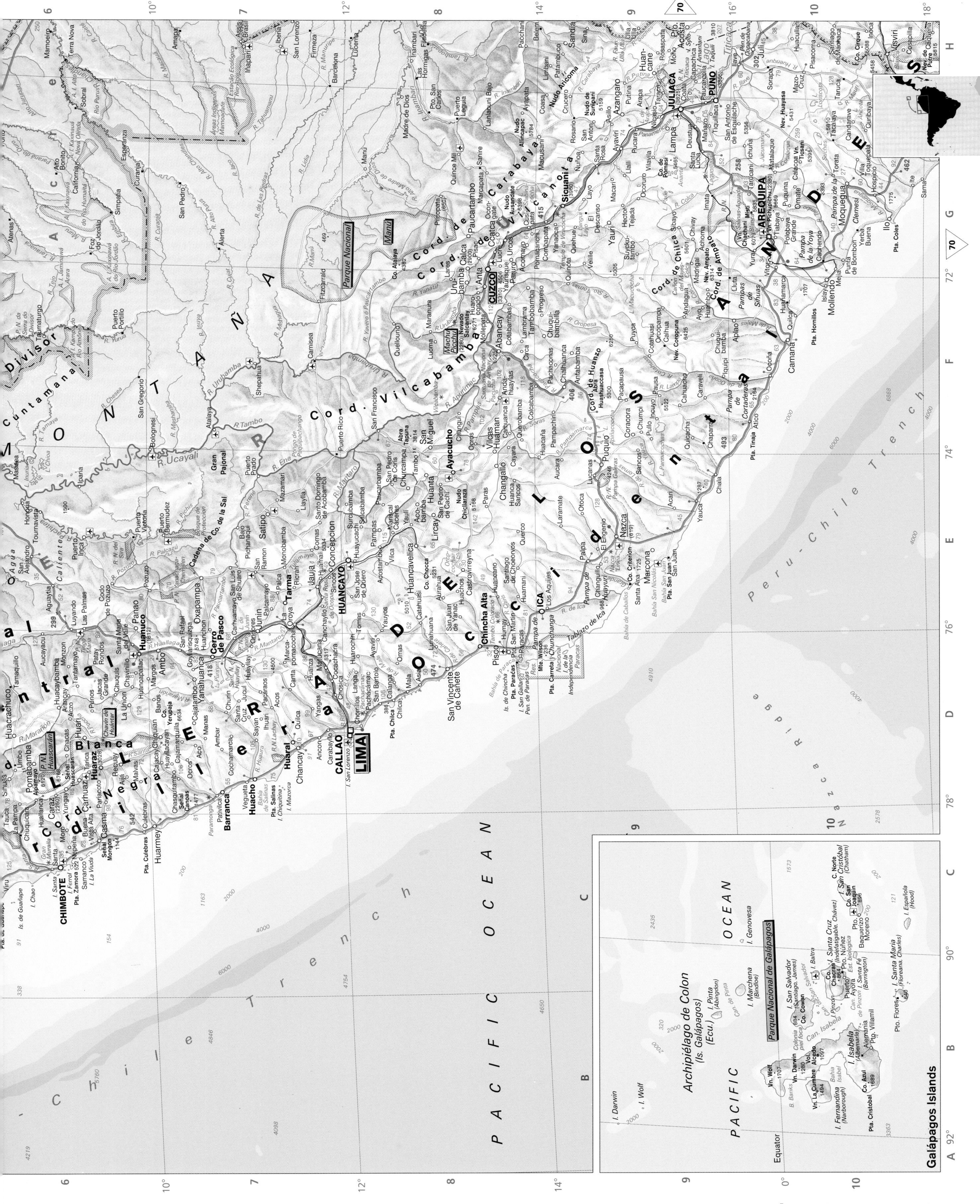

PACIFIC OCEAN
Peru-Chile Trench
Chile Trench
Nazca Ridge
Galápagos Islands
Archipiélago de Colon (Is. Galápagos) (Ecu.)
Parque Nacional de Galápagos
Equator
LIMA
CALLAO
CUZCO
AREQUIPA
JULIACA
PUNO
HUANCAYO
Ayacucho
ICA
Nazca
Huacho
Huaraz
CHIMBOTE
Cerro de Pasco
Huanuco
Chincha Alta
Pisco
Mollendo
Moquegua
Ilo
Cord. Vilcabamba
Cord. de Carabaya
Cord. de Huanzo
Cord. de Chila
Cord. de Ampato
Parque Nacional Manú
Machu Picchu
Lago Titicaca

Scale 1 : 4,500,000

0 40 80 120 160 200 Kilometers

0 40 80 120 160 Statute Miles

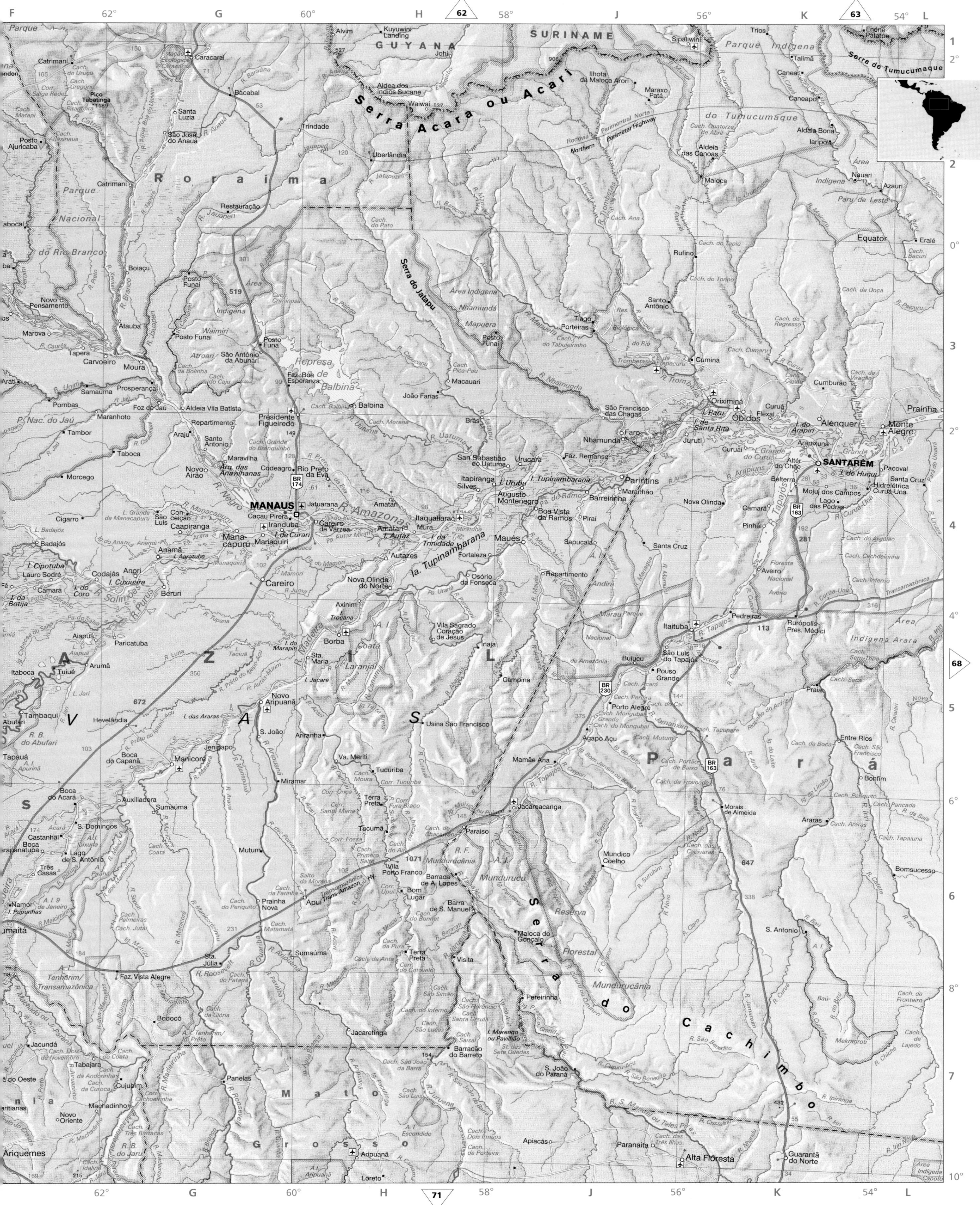

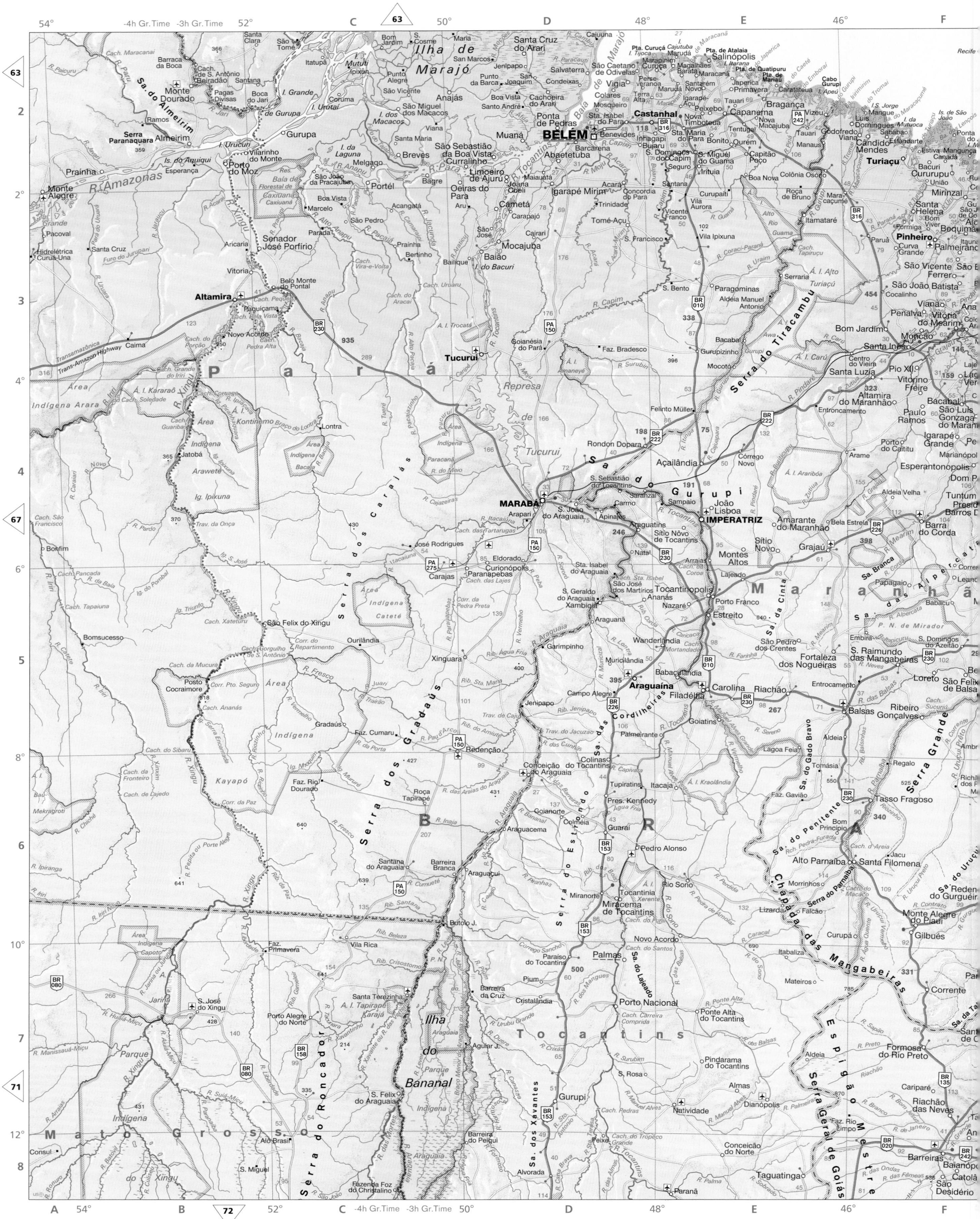

54° -4h Gr.Time -3h Gr.Time 52° C 50° D 48° E 46° F

63

63

67

71

72

Ilha de Marajó

BELÉM

Pará

Maranhão

Tocantins

Mato Grosso

Ilha do Bananal

Serra dos Carajás

Serra dos Gradaús

Serra do Roncador

Serra do Estrondo

Serra do Tiracambu

Serra do Gurupi

Serra Geral de Goiás

Espigão Mestre

Chapada das Mangabeiras

Represa de Tucuruí

Trans-Amazon Highway

A 54° B 52° C -4h Gr.Time -3h Gr.Time 50° D 48° E 46° F

Scale 1 : 4,500,000

0 40 80 120 160 200 Kilometers

0 40 80 120 160 Statute Miles

Fernando de Noronha
Atol das Rocas
I. do Farol (Braz.)
Vila dos Remidos
Ilha Fernando de Noronha (Braz.)
ATLANTIC OCEAN
ATLANTIC OCEAN
FORTALEZA
TERESINA
NATAL
JOÃO PESSOA
OLINDA
RECIFE
MACEIÓ
ARACAJU
MOSSORÓ
CAMPINA GRANDE
CARUARU
ARAPIRACA
JUAZEIRO DO NORTE
FEIRA DE SANTANA
ALAGOINHAS
Sobral
Parnaíba
Caxias
Petrolina
Juazeiro
Paulo Afonso
Garanhuns
Patos
Crato
Iguatu
Picos
Floriano
Camaragibe
Vitória
Chapada Araripe
Raso da Caterina
P. N. da Serra da Capivara
Ceará
Rio Grande do Norte
Paraíba
Pernambuco
Alagoas
Sergipe
Bahia
Piauí
Serra do Boqueirão

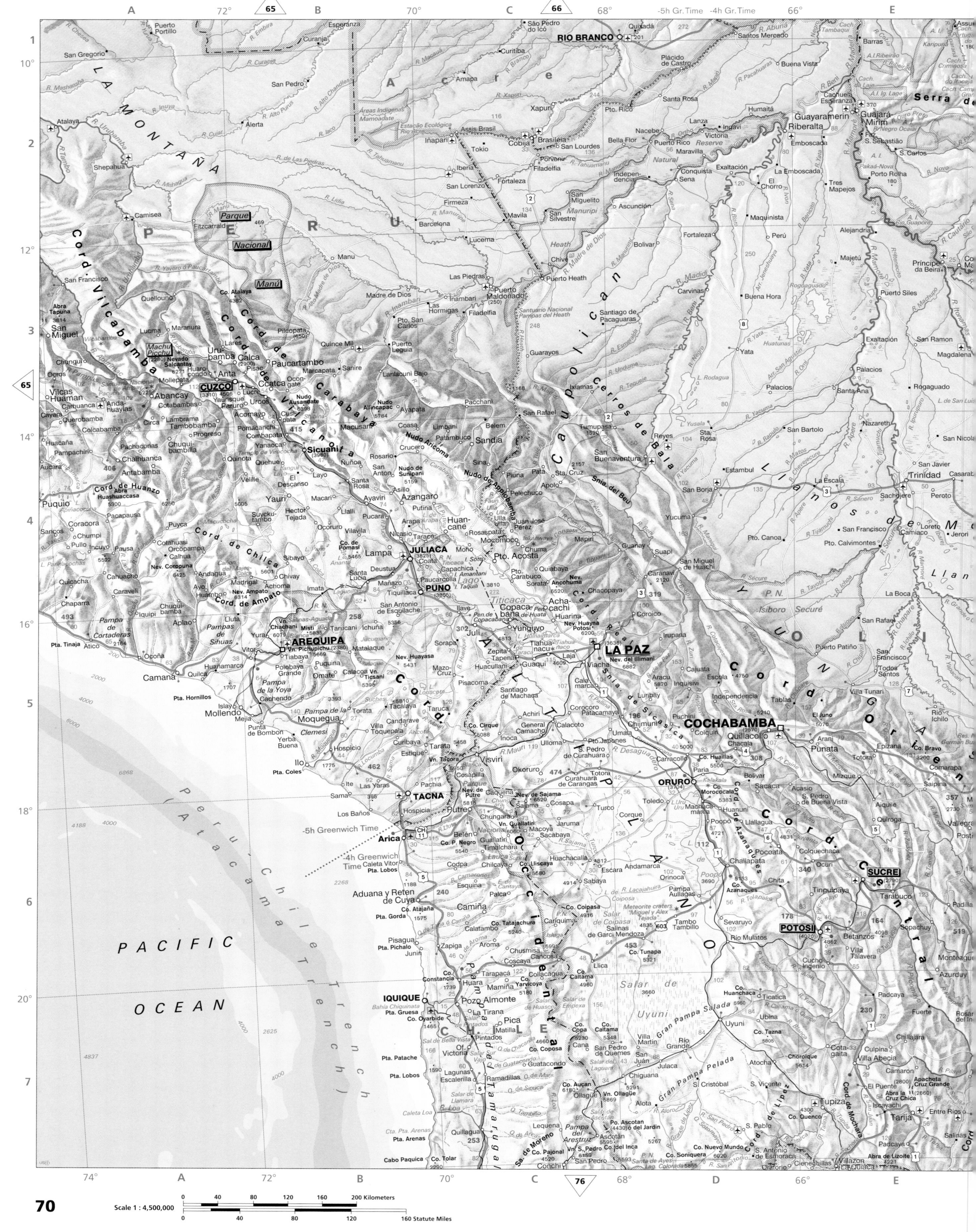

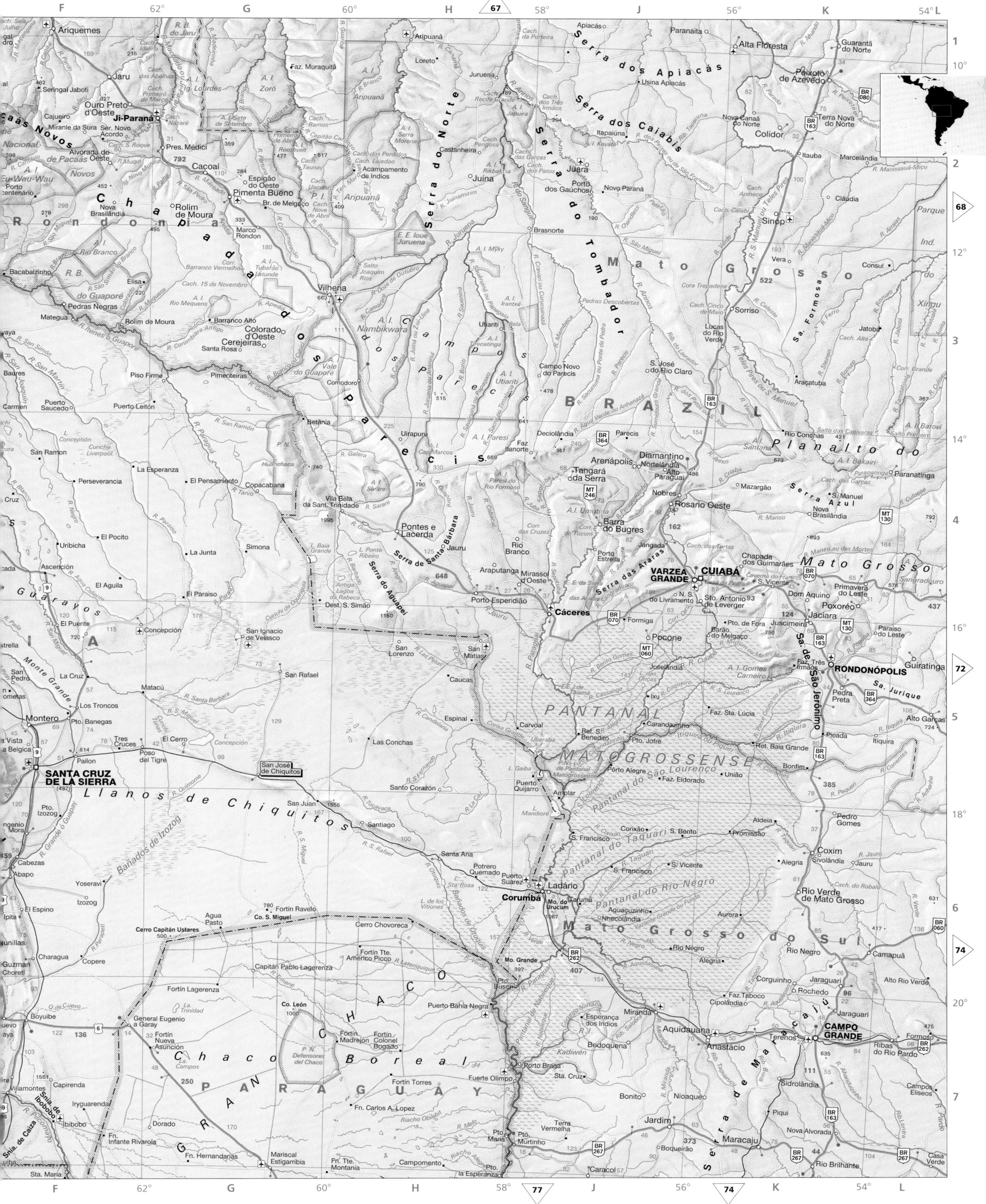

Ariquemes
Jaru
Ji-Paraná
Ouro Preto d'Oeste
Pres. Médici
Cacoal
Pimenta Bueno
Rolim de Moura
Vilhena
Aripuanã
Juína
Juara
Alta Floresta
Peixoto de Azevedo
Sinop
Serra dos Apiacás
Serra dos Caiabis
Serra do Norte
Serra do Tombador
Chapada dos Parecis
Campos Parecis
Mato Grosso
BRAZIL
Planalto do Mato Grosso
Serra Azul
Diamantino
Arenápolis
Tangará da Serra
Rosário Oeste
Barra do Bugres
Pontes e Lacerda
Serra de Santa Bárbara
Serra do Aguapeí
Vila Bela da Sant. Trindade
Cáceres
VARZEA GRANDE
CUIABÁ
Poconé
RONDONÓPOLIS
Jaciara
Pedra Preta
Alto Garças
PANTANAL MATOGROSSENSE
Pantanal do São Lourenço
Pantanal do Taquari
Pantanal do Rio Negro
Coxim
Rio Verde de Mato Grosso
Ladário
Corumbá
Puerto Suárez
Puerto Quijarro
Mato Grosso do Sul
Miranda
Aquidauana
Anastácio
CAMPO GRANDE
Serra de Maracaju
Sidrolândia
Bonito
Jardim
Maracaju
Rio Brilhante
Pto. Murtinho
Porto Esperidião
San Matías
Concepción
San Ignacio de Velasco
San Rafael
Guarayos
SANTA CRUZ DE LA SIERRA
Montero
Cotoca
Pailón
Pto. Banegas
Los Troncos
San José de Chiquitos
Llanos de Chiquitos
Bañados de Izozog
Roboré
Santiago
Santo Corazón
Fortín Ravelo
Cerro Chovoreca
CHACO
Chaco Boreal
GRAN PARAGUAY
Fuerte Olimpo
Puerto Bahía Negra
Boyuibe
Villamontes
Rondônia
Pacaás Novos

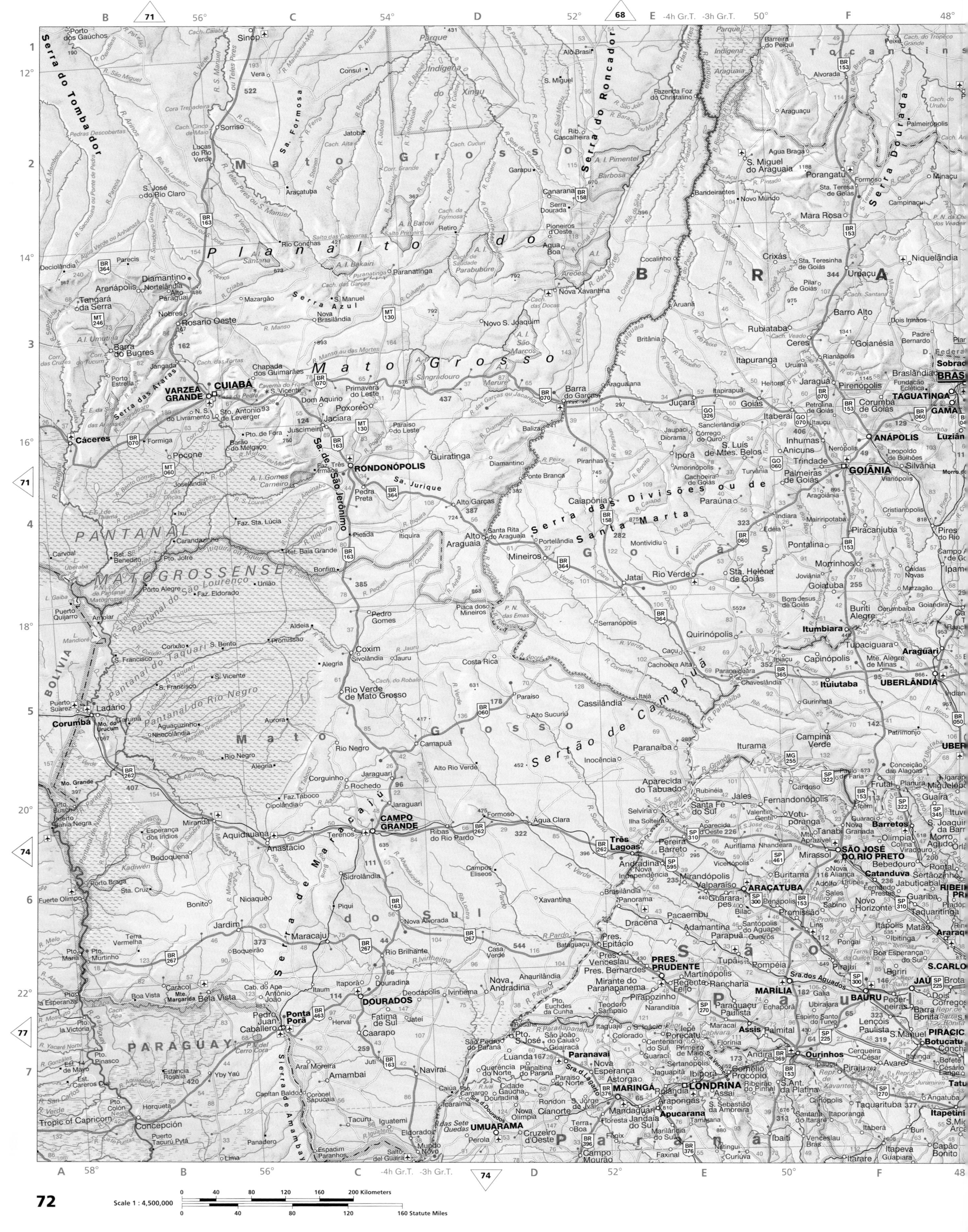

Scale 1 : 4,500,000

0 40 80 120 160 200 Kilometers

0 40 80 120 160 Statute Miles

G
46°
H
44°
J
42°
K
69
40°
L
38°
M
12°
14°
16°
18°
20°
22°
Tropic of Capricorn
B a h i a
BRAZILIAN
HIGHLANDS
Minas
Gerais
Espírito Santo
Serra Geral de Goiás
Espigão Mestre
Chapada Diamantina
Serra da Mantiqueira
Serra do Mar
Serra dos Aimorés
Serra do Chifre
ATLANTIC
OCEAN
Abrolhos
Bank
Arquipélago dos Abrolhos
SALVADOR
FEIRA DE SANTANA
ALAGOINHAS
VITÓRIA DA CONQUISTA
ITABUNA
Ilhéus
Jequié
Porto Seguro
Caravelas
MONTES CLAROS
Diamantina
Teófilo Otoni
GOV. VALADARES
IPATINGA
Itabira
BELO HORIZONTE
CONTAGEM
Ouro Prêto
Congonhas
BARBACENA
JUIZ DE FORA
Linhares
Colatina
VITÓRIA
VILHA VELHA
CACHOEIRO DE ITAPEMIRIM
CAMPOS
Cabo de São Tomé
Macaé
C. Frio
RIO DE JANEIRO
NITERÓI
SÃO GONÇALO
PETRÓPOLIS
VOLTA REDONDA
TAUBATÉ
CAMPINAS
SÃO PAULO
SANTOS
Guarujá
Ubatuba
I. de São Sebastião

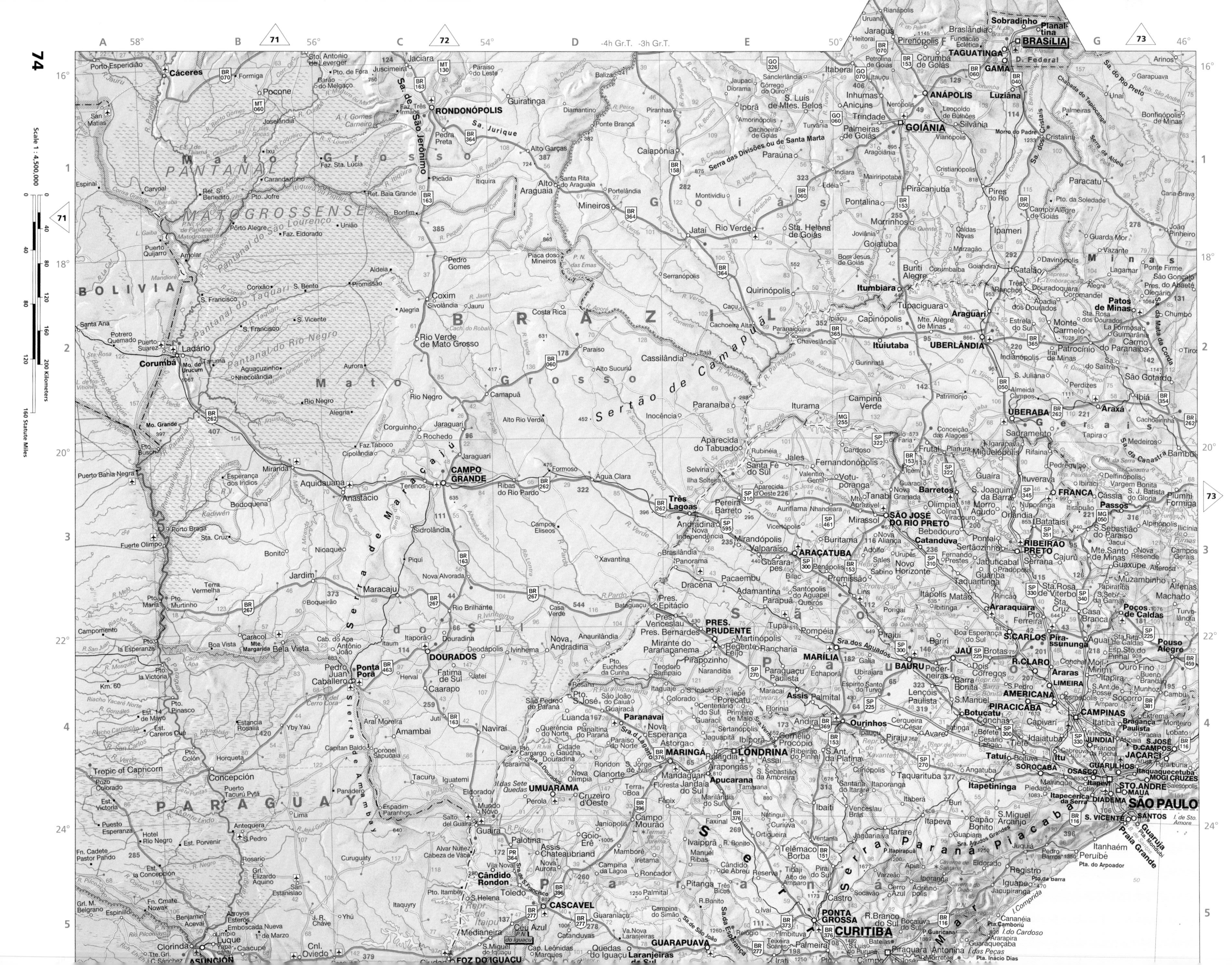

Scale 1 : 4,500,000

0 40 80 120 160 200 Kilometers

0 40 80 120 160 Statute Miles

ATLANTIC
OCEAN
ARGENTINA
URUGUAY
BUENOS AIRES
MONTEVIDEO
PORTO ALEGRE
FLORIANÓPOLIS
PELOTAS
RIO GRANDE
PASSO FUNDO
SANTA MARIA
CAXIAS DO SUL
BLUMENAU
JOINVILLE
CORRIENTES
RESISTENCIA
POSADAS
ENCARNACIÓN
LA PLATA
URUGUAIANA
Garnet Bank

70
78
72°
70°
68°
66°
64°
20°
22°
24°
26°
28°
30°
32°
PACIFIC
OCEAN
Tropic of Capricorn
Peru - Chile Trench
Richards Trench
B O L I V I A
J u j u y
S a l t a
T u c u m á n
C a t a m a r c a
L a R i o j a
S a n J u a n
S a n L u i s
C ó r d o b a
S a n t i a g o d e l E s t e r o
A R G E N T I N A
CORDILLERA DE LOS ANDES
Cordillera Domeyko
Puna de Atacama
Puna de Argentina
Sierra de Calalaste
Sierra de Famatina
Sierra de Velasco
Sierra de la Punilla
Precordillera
Llanos de la Rioja
Salinas Grandes
Salar de Uyuni
Salar de Atacama
Gran Pampa Salada
Gran Pampa Pelada
Pampa del Tamarugal
IQUIQUE
Pozo Almonte
Pica
Tocopilla
María Elena
Chuquicamata
CALAMA
San Pedro de Atacama
ANTOFAGASTA
Mejillones
Taltal
Chañaral
Diego de Almagro
Caldera
Copiapó
Vallenar
Huasco
La Serena
Coquimbo
Vicuña
Ovalle
Monte Patria
Combarbalá
Illapel
Salamanca
Los Vilos
Uyuni
Tupiza
Tarija
Villazón
La Quiaca
Humahuaca
SAN SALVADOR DE JUJUY
Libertador Grl. S. Martín
San Ramón de la Nueva Orán
Tartagal
SALTA
Cafayate
Rosario de la Frontera
Metán
SAN MIGUEL DE TUCUMÁN
Concepción
Monteros
Termas de Río Hondo
SANTIAGO DEL ESTERO
Frías
S. FERN. DEL VALLE DE CATAMARCA
Belén
Tinogasta
Andalgalá
Chilecito
LA RIOJA
Chamical
SAN JUAN
Caucete
Jáchal
Villa Dolores
Deán Funes
Cruz del Eje
Jesús María
CÓRDOBA
Río Segundo
Alta Gracia
Villa María
P. Nat. Prov. Ischigualasto y R. Nac. (Valle de la Luna)
-4h Gr.Time -3h Gr.Time
Scale 1 : 4,500,000
0 40 80 120 160 200 Kilometers
0 40 80 120 160 Statute Miles

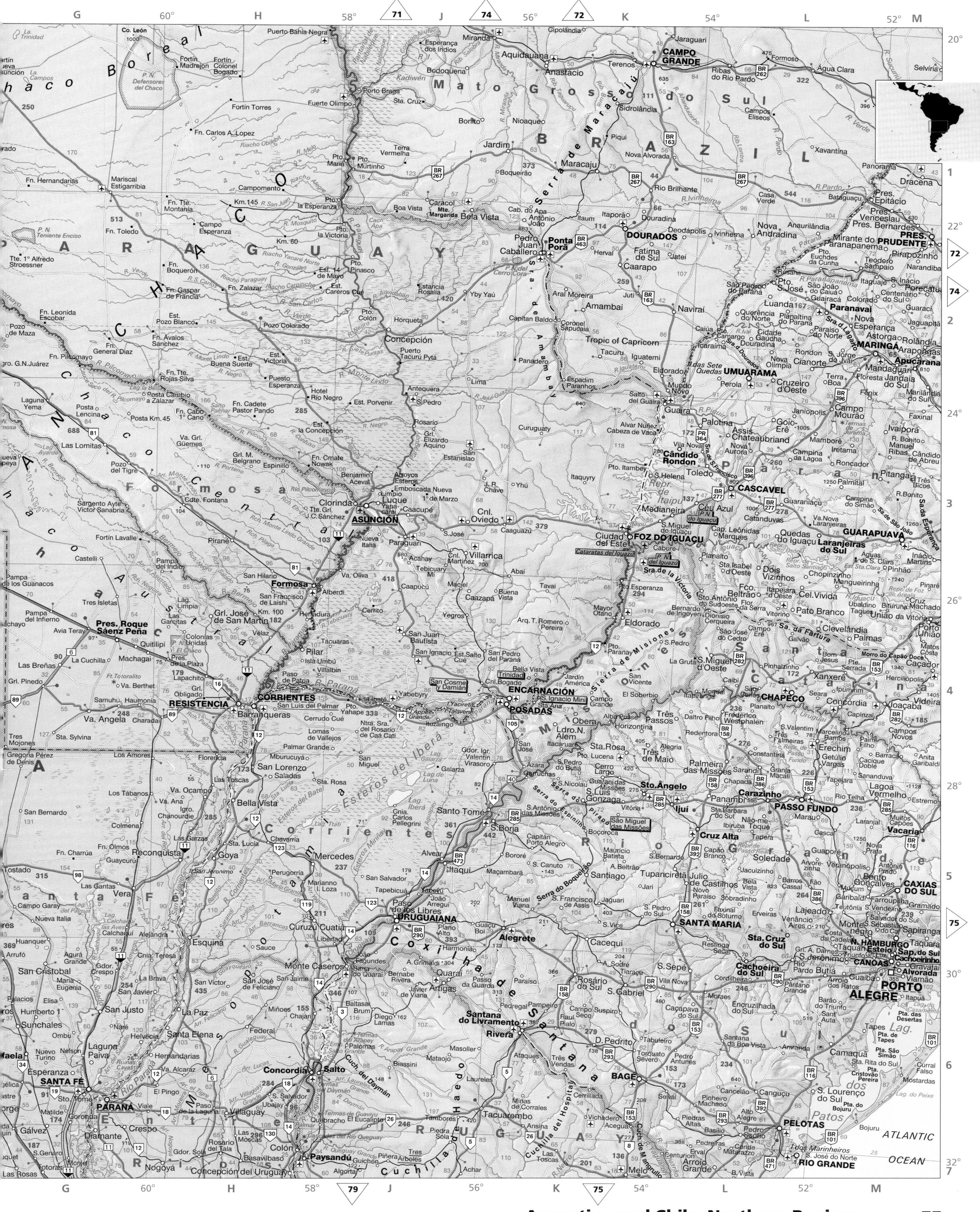

G
H
J
K
L
M
60°
58°
56°
54°
52°
71
74
72
75
79
20°
22°
24°
26°
28°
30°
32°
1
2
3
4
5
6
7
Chaco Boreal
Mato Grosso do Sul
BRAZIL
PARAGUAY
Chaco Central
Chaco Austral
Formosa
Misiones
Santa Catarina
Rio Grande do Sul
Corrientes
Esteros del Iberá
Entre Ríos
Santa Fe
Coxilha de Santana
Cuchilla de Haedo
URUGUAY
Serra de Maracaju
Tropic of Capricorn
ATLANTIC OCEAN
Lag. dos Patos
CAMPO GRANDE
DOURADOS
Ponta Porã
Pedro Juan Caballero
Concepción
ASUNCIÓN
Clorinda
Encarnación
POSADAS
Ciudad del Este
FOZ DO IGUAÇU
CASCAVEL
MARINGÁ
GUARAPUAVA
Formosa
RESISTENCIA
CORRIENTES
Pres. Roque Sáenz Peña
Reconquista
Goya
URUGUAIANA
SANTA MARIA
PASSO FUNDO
CAXIAS DO SUL
PORTO ALEGRE
PELOTAS
RIO GRANDE
BAGÉ
Santana do Livramento
Rivera
Salto
Concordia
Paysandú
PARANÁ
SANTA FE
Tacuarembó
Alegrete
Sto. Ângelo
Cruz Alta
Ijuí
CHAPECÓ
Cataratas del Iguazú
P.N. do Iguaçu
PRES. PRUDENTE
UMUARAMA

Scale 1 : 4,500,000
0 40 80 120 160 200 Kilometers
0 40 80 120 160 Statute Miles

ATLANTIC OCEAN
Falkland Islands
(Islas Malvinas)
(U.K.)
South Georgia
(U.K.)
BUENOS AIRES
MONTEVIDEO
ROSARIO
LA PLATA
MAR DEL PLATA
BAHÍA BLANCA
Falkland Islands
South Georgia

PACIFIC OCEAN
ATLANTIC OCEAN
Mar Argentino
CHILE
ARGENTINA
Patagonia
Chubut
Santa Cruz
Golfo San Jorge
Golfo Corcovado
Golfo de Peñas
Bahía Grande
Archipiélago de los Chonos
Península de Taitao
Isla Wellington
Isla Grande de Tierra del Fuego
Tierra del Fuego
Estrecho de Magallanes
Meseta de Montemayor
Gran Altiplanicie Central
Meseta de la Muerte
Cordillera Darwin
Comodoro Rivadavia
Caleta Olivia
Pto. Deseado
Pto. San Julián
Pto. Santa Cruz
Río Gallegos
Punta Arenas
Pto. Natales
Porvenir
Río Grande
Ushuaia
Pto. Williams
Coihaique
Aisén
Cochrane
Chile Chico
Perito Moreno
El Calafate
Río Turbio
Parque Nacional Los Glaciares
P. N. Torres del Paine
Cabo de Hornos
I. de los Estados
Scale 1 : 4,500,000
200 Kilometers
160 Statute Miles

Europe – a continent with border troubles

With an area of 4,054,050 sq. miles (10.5 million sq. km), Europe is the fourth largest continent. From the point of view of physical geography it merely represents a peninsula of Eurasia, jutting out to the west. Europe and Asia have the least well defined delimitation among all continents. The traditional borderline runs along the Ural Mountains the Ural River, the Caspian Sea, the northern edge of the Caucasus, the Black Sea, the Bosporus and the Aegean Sea. In Russia, which is part European and part Asian, this demarcation line is meaningless. A belt of high mountains in which the Alps are the highest range separates the South from the remainder of the continent. Adjacent to the North is the European medium-height mountainscape followed by a strip of lowlands that widens to the East. The British Isles are, geologically speaking, also part of the northern mountain areas. Its many islands and peninsulas interlace the continent with the Atlantic Ocean and the European Mediterranean Sea. Europe determined the destiny of the world some years into the twentieth century: The scientific research of the planet, the industrial revolution, great inventions and discoveries, but also colonization and thus the transmission of European influences to other parts of the world had their origins here.

An aid to international trade: "New Map of Europe" including "the most noteworthy products and the foremost trading sites." J. Adams made this copperplate engraving in 1787.

Svalbard · Novaya Zemlya
p. 84 – 85

Scandinavia (Inset: Iceland)
p. 86 – 87

Finland · Northern Ural Mountains
p. 88 – 89

Western Europe
p. 90 – 91

Central Europe
p. 92 – 93

Eastern Europe
p. 94 – 95

Ural Mountains
p. 96 – 97

Southwestern Europe
p. 98 – 99

Southern Europe
p. 100 – 101

Southeastern Europe
p. 102 – 103

Caucasus
p. 104

Svalbard · Novaya Zemlya
p. 84–85
Scandinavia (Inset: Iceland)
p. 86–87
Finland · Northern Ural Mountains
p. 88–89
Western Europe
p. 90–91
Central Europe
p. 92–93
Eastern Europe
p. 94–95
Ural Mountains
p. 96–97
Southwestern Europe
p. 98–99
Southern Europe
p. 100–101
Southeastern Europe
p. 102–103
Caucasus
p. 104

2° A 0° B 2° C 4° D 6° E 8° F 10° G 12° H 14° J 16° K 18° L 20° M 22° N 24° O 26° P 28° Q 30° R 32° S 34° T 36° U 38° V 40° W

Greenland Sea

ARCTIC

Greenwich Time

+1h Greenwich Time

+3h Gr. Time

+4h Greenwich Time

Svalbard (Norway)

Spitsbergen

Nordaustlandet

Nordaust-Svalbard nat-res

Kong Karls land

Kvitøya (Nor.)

Edgeøya

Barentsøya

Storfjorden

Olgastretet

Erik Eriksenstretet

Hinlopenstretet

Prins Karls Forland

Storfjordrenna

Storfjordbanken

Hopen

Hopen Radio

Hopenbanken

Bjørnøya Bank

Bjørnøya (Nor.)

Bjørnøy Radio

Tunheim

Perleporten

Norwegian Sea

Barents Sea

Fugløy Bank

London

Murmanskoye Rise

North Kanin Bank

NORWAY

FINLAND

SWEDEN

RUSSIA

Tromsø

Alta

Hammerfest

Nordkapp

Knivskjelodden

Magerøya

Vardø

Vadsø

Kirkenes

Narvik

Harstad

Finnmarksvidda

Varangerhalvøya

Nikel

Zapoljarnyj

Poljarnyj

Murmansk

Kebnekaise

Nordkinnhalvøya

3 4 5 6 7 8 9

78° 76° 74° 72° 70° 68°

K 18° L 20° M +1h Gr. Time N 24° O +2h Gr. Time P 28° Q +3h Gr. Time R 32° S 34° T 36° U 38° V 40° +3h Gr. Time +5h Gr.

86

86

Scale 1 : 4,500,000

0 40 80 120 160 200 Kilometers

0 40 80 120 160 Statute Miles

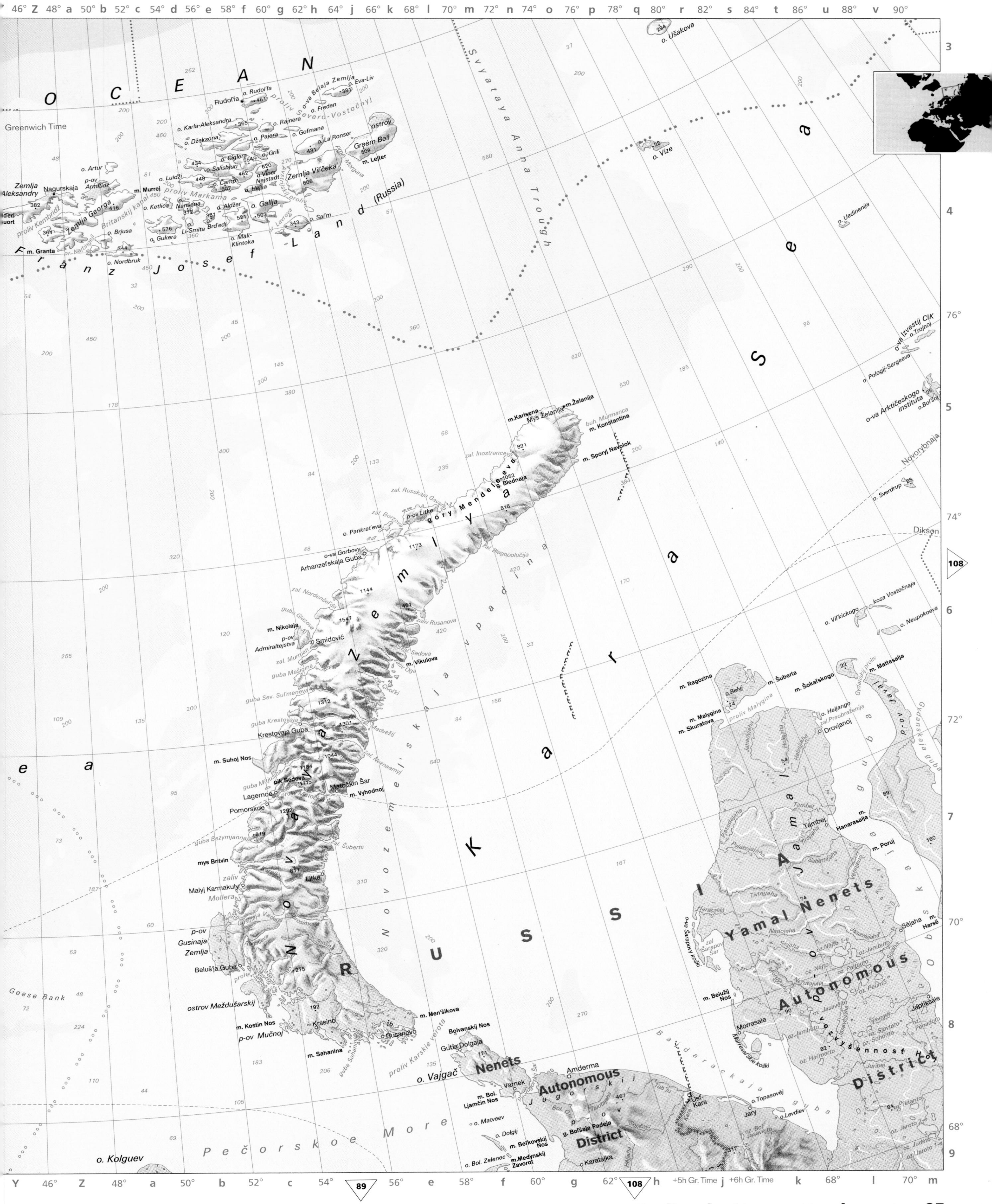

OCEAN
Greenwich Time
Franz Josef Land (Russia)
o. Rudol'fa
o. Eva-Liv
o-va Belaja Zemlja
proliv Severo-Vostočnyj
o. Freden
o. Karla-Aleksandra
o. Rajnera
o. Gofmana
o. Džeksona
o. Pajera
o. La Ronser
ostrov Greem Bell
m. Lejter
o. Artur
Zemlja Aleksandry
Nagurskaja
p-ov Armitidž
o. Ciglera
o. Salisburi
o. Grili
Zemlja Vil'čeka
o. Luidži
proliv Markama
m. Murrej
o. Camp
o. Viner Nejstadt
o. Hejsa
proliv Kembridž
Zemlja Georga
Britanskij kanal
o. Ketlica
Nansena
o. Aldžer
o. Gallja
o. Sal'm
o. Brjusa
Li-Smita
Brd'edi
o. Gukera
o. Mak-Klintoka
m. Granta
o. Nordbruk
o. Ušakova
Svyataya Anna Trough
o. Vize
o. Uedinenija
Kara Sea
o-va Izvestij CIK
o. Trojnoj
o. Pologij-Sergeeva
o-va Arktičeskogo instituta
o. Boršoj
Novorybnaja
o. Sverdrup
Dikson
108
m. Karlsena
Mys Želanija
m. Želanija
buh. Murmanca
m. Konstantina
m. Sporyj Navolok
zal. Inostranceva
gory Mendeleeva
g. Blednaja
zal. Russkaja Gavan'
p-ov Litke
zal. Borzova
o. Pankrat'eva
o-va Gorbovy
Arhanzel'skaja Guba
zal. Blagopolučija
Novaya Zemlya
Vpadina
zal. Nordenšel'da
guba Glazova
zaliv Rusanova
m. Nikolaja
p-ov Admiraltejstva
Smidovič
zal. Murman
zal. Sedova
m. Vikulova
guba Mašigina
guba Sev. Sul'meneva
guba Krestovaja
Krestovaja Guba
zal. Medvežij
m. Suhoj Nos
zal. Neznaemyj
pik Sedova
Matočkin Šar
m. Vyhodnoj
Lagernoe
Pomorskoe
guba Bezymjannaja
zal. Šuberta
mys Britvin
zaliv Mollera
Malyj Karmakuly
Litke
p-ov Gusinaja Zemlja
Beluš'ja Guba
ostrov Meždušarskij
m. Kostin Nos
p-ov Mučnoj
Krasino
m. Men'šikova
Rusanovo
m. Sahanina
guba Savina
Novozemel'skaja Vpadina
proliv Karskie vorota
Bolvanskij Nos
Guba Dolgaja
o. Vajgač
Nenets Autonomous District
Amderma
Jugorskij poluostrov
Varnek
m. Bol. Ljamčin Nos
o. Matveev
o. Dolgij
m. Bel'kovskij Nos
g. Bol'šaja Padeja
o. Bol. Zelenec
m.Medynskij Zavorot
Karatajka
RUSSIA
Pečorskoe More
o. Kolguev
Geese Bank
Bajdarackaja guba
Ust'-Kara
Jary
o. Topasovej
o. Levdiev
m. Ragozina
o. Belyj
m. Šuberta
m. Šokal'skogo
m. Malygina
m. Skuratova
proliv Malygina
o. Haljango
zal. Preobraženija
Drovjanoj
p-ov Javaj
Gydanskij proliv
m. Mattesalja
Gydanskaja guba
Obskaja guba
p-ov Jamal
Tambej
m. Hanarasalja
m. Poruj
Yamal Nenets Autonomous District
Sejaha
m. Harsě
o-va Šarapovy koški
m. Beluži Nos
Morrasale
Marresal'skie koški
ozero Nejto
oz. Jambuto
oz. Jasavejto
Japtiksale
+5h Gr. Time
+6h Gr. Time
89
108

Iceland
Greenland Sea
Arctic Circle
ICELAND
REYKJAVÍK
Akureyri
Vatnajökull
Greenwich Time
Barents Sea
Norwegian Sea
Bottenviken
Gulf of Bothnia
LAPLAND
Finnmarksvidda
Tromsø
Narvik
Bodø
Luleå
Oulu (Uleåborg)
Umeå
TRONDHEIM
MURMANSK
KUOPIO
Scale 1 : 4,500,000
0 40 80 120 160 200 Kilometers
0 40 80 120 160 Statute Miles

A 12° B 14° C 16° D 18° E 20° F 22° G 84 H 26° J 28° K 30° L 32° M 34° N 36° O 38°

+1h Gr. Time +3h Gr. Time

2

68°

3

66°

4

86

64°

5

62°

6

60°

87

7

+1h Gr. Time

20° +3h Gr. Time 22° 94 G 24° H 26° J 28° K 30° L 32° M 34° +3h Gr. Time +4h Gr. Time O 38°

Scale 1 : 4,500,000

0 40 80 120 160 200 Kilometers

0 40 80 120 160 Statute Miles

Novaya Zemlya
Kara Sea
Pečorskoe more
Geese Bank
North Kanin Bank
ostrov Meždušarskij
m. Kostin Nos
p-ov Mučnoj
Krasino
m. Sahanina
Rusanovo
m. Men'šikova
Bolvanskij Nos
Guba Dolgaja
proliv Karskie vorota
o. Vajgač
Amderma
Varnek
m. Bol. Ljamčin Nos
o. Matveev
o. Dolgij
m. Bel'kovskij Nos
m. Medynskij Zavorot
o. Bol. Zelenec
Karatajka
g. Bol'šaja Padeja
Ust'-Kara
Morrasale
+5h Gr. Time
+6h Gr. Time
o. Kolguev
Bugrino
Pesjakov
Varandej
p-ov Russkij Zavorot
o-va Guljaevskie Koški
o. Dolgij
Pečorskaja guba
Pomorskij proliv
Tobseda
o. Sengejskij
mys Kanin Nos
Kanin Nos
o-va Kambal'nickie Koški
g. Mohovaja
Kanin Kamen'
g. Tenja Seda
Jušino
Nar'jan-Mar
Oksino
Indiga
m. Sv. Nos
m. Mikulkin
Šojna
Čëšskaja guba
Velikaja
Timanskij bereg
Malozemel'skaja tundra
Bol'šezemel'skaja tundra
Nenets Autonomous District
Čajcynskij Kamen'
Timanskij krjaž
g. Kovriga
Tošviska
Novyj Bor
Krestovka
Jakšino
Arctic Circle
Horej-Ver
Vorgašor
Severnyj
VORKUTA
Komsomol'skij
Sivomaskinskij
Abez'
Inta
Usinsk
Novikbož
Ust'-Lyža
Pečorskaja grjada
Černyševa grjada
Mutnyj Materik
Kipievo
Synja
Pečora
Kožva
Konecbor
Ust'-Cil'ma
Ščeljajur
Dijur
Ižma
Kadžerom
Ust'-Voja
Iraël'
Kartaël'
Lem''junskaja vozv.
Lemtybož
Podčer'e
Vuktyl
Nenets
Yamal Nenets Autonomous District
Khanty-Mansi Autonomous District
Poljarnyj Ural
Severnyj Ural
g. Narodnaja
g. Neroika
g. Telpoziz
Saranpaul'
Nerohi
Nižnjaja Peša
Oma
Volokovaja
Kaninskaja tundra
m. Konušin
Čiža
m. Orlovskij
m. Voronov
m. Moržovec
Mezenskaja guba
Nes
Tarasovo
Semža
Majda
Kojda
Ručio
Kamenka
Mezen'
Jazevec
Safonovo
Loban
Sojana
Verh. Zolotica
Belomorsko-Kulojskoje-plato
Kepino
Pogorelec
Paluga
Sovpol'e
Bol'šaja Nisogora
Pyl'ema
Palaščel'e
Čubla
Čulasa
Patrakeevka
Pinega
Trufanova
Vožgora
Zasul'e
Segmas
Čëtlasskij Kamen'
Levkinskaja
Verhnevym'skaja grjada
Timanskij kamen'
Myla
Tobysskaja vozvyšennost'
ARHANGEL'SK
SEVERODVINSK
Emeljanovskaja
Holmogory
Kuzomen
Ust'-Pinega
Pirinem
Karpogory
Šardonem'
Čuprovo
Latjuga
Politovo
Važgort
Bol. Čurki
Černutevo
Selib
Koslan
Borovo
Pegyš
UHTA
Sosnogorsk
Vodnyj
Jarega
Niž. Odes
boloto Dž'ërnjur
Savinobor
Vojvož
Troicko-Pečorsk
Pečoro-Ilyčskij zapovednik
Komsomol'sk-na-Pečore
Vojvoždina
Podora
Vol'dino
Požeg
Kur'ja
Vysokaja parma
Holmogorskaja
Brin-Navolok
Sylogа
Verkola
Gorodeck
Njuhča
Ertoma
Razgort
Blagoevo
Samoded
Emeck
Pogost
Kaři
Hetovo
Ust'-Vaen'ga
Osinovo
Bereznik
Ust'-Vaga
Pošegda
Savinskij
Pleseck
Ust'-Vyjskaja
Jarenga
Mikun'
Vesljana
Sindor
Popča
Turja
Trakt
Emva
Sogra
Kondratovskaja
Rakovskaja
Šenkursk
Jarensk
Žešart
Ajkino
Vogvazdino
Časovo
Kortkeros
SYKTYVKAR
Storoževsk
Ust'-Nem
Ust'-Kulom
Koreпino
Nyrob
Krasnovišersk
Čerdyn'
Ivdel'
Severoural'sk
Volčansk
Karpinsk
Šelaša
Makarov Dvor
Rovdino
Njandoma
Berežnaja
Šičuga
Litvinovo
Krasnoborsk
Korjažma
Šipicyno
Kotlas
Vizinga
Černorečenskij
Komi-Permyak Autonomous District
Severnye Uvaly
Vel'sk
Oktjabr'skij
Kizema
Velikij Ustjug
Zanul'e
Kojgorodok
Gajny
Verhnekamskaja vozv.
Kosa
Jukseevo
Kočevo
Jurla
Kudymkar
Jus'va
Lojno
Kirs
Nagorsk
SOLIKAMSK
BEREZNIKI
Usol'e
Jajva
Aleksandrovsk
Kizel
Gubaha
Ugleural'skij
Gremjačinsk
Us'va
Luza
Tarnogskij Gorodok
Moiseevskaja
Igumnovskaja
Dem'janovo
Egošinskaja
Pinjug
Verhnevažskaja vozv.
Esinskaja
Sjamža
Harovskaja grjada
Tot'ma
Kičmengskij Gorodok
Oparino
Murаši
Letka
Knjaževo
Komi
Arkhangel'sk
URAL MOUNTAINS
+4h Gr. Time
+5h Gr. Time
+6h Gr. Time
Q R S T U V W X Y Z a b c d e
42° 44° 46° 48° 50° 52° 54° 56° 58° 60° 62° 64° 66° 68°
60° 64° 66° 68°
85
108
114
95
96
2 3 4 5 6 7

Scale 1 : 4,500,000

0 40 80 120 160 200 Kilometers

0 40 80 120 160 Statute Miles

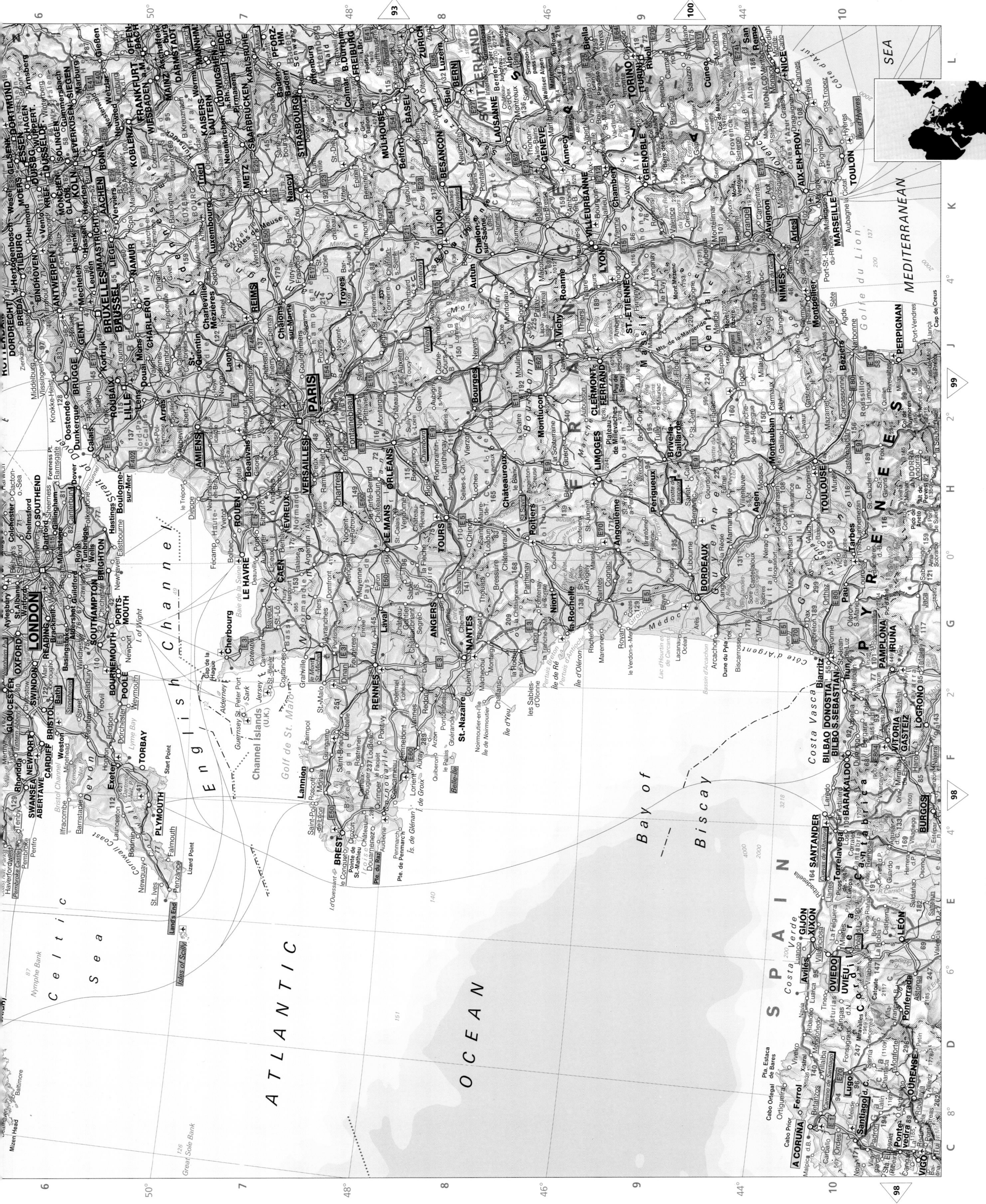
ATLANTIC
OCEAN
Bay of
Biscay
Celtic
Sea
English
Channel
MEDITERRANEAN
SEA
FRANCE
SPAIN
PYRENEES
SWITZERLAND
LONDON
PARIS
BORDEAUX
TOULOUSE
LYON
MARSEILLE
NANTES
RENNES
BREST
BRUXELLES
BRUSSEL
LILLE
STRASBOURG
GENÈVE
TORINO
BILBAO
SANTANDER
OVIEDO
A CORUÑA
PLYMOUTH
SOUTHAMPTON
BRIGHTON
CHERBOURG
LE HAVRE
ROUEN
AMIENS
REIMS
ORLÉANS
TOURS
LIMOGES
CLERMONT-FERRAND
ST.-ÉTIENNE
GRENOBLE
NICE
MONTPELLIER
NÎMES
PERPIGNAN
PAMPLONA
Channel Islands
Bay of
Biscay

North Sea
UNITED KINGDOM
GREAT BRITAIN
IRELAND
Irish Sea
DENMARK
NETHERLANDS
BELGIUM
FRANCE
SPAIN
Celtic Sea
English Channel
ATLANTIC OCEAN
Bay of Biscay
Channel Islands (U.K.)
Golfe de St. Malo
Strait of Dover
Dogger Bank
West Frisian Islands
East Frisian Islands
Deutsche Bucht
Massif Central
Pyrenees
Costa Vasca
DUBLIN
BAILE ATHA CLIATH
LONDON
LIVERPOOL
MANCHESTER
BIRMINGHAM
LEEDS
BRISTOL
CARDIFF
SOUTHAMPTON
PLYMOUTH
SUNDERLAND
MIDDLESBROUGH
KINGSTON UPON HULL
NORWICH
AMSTERDAM
ROTTERDAM
'S-GRAVENHAGE
DEN HAAG
ANTWERPEN
BRUXELLES
BRUSSEL
LILLE
PARIS
VERSAILLES
REIMS
AMIENS
ROUEN
LE HAVRE
CAEN
BREST
RENNES
NANTES
LE MANS
TOURS
ORLÉANS
ANGERS
DIJON
BESANÇON
STRASBOURG
METZ
Nancy
Luxembourg
LYON
VILLEURBANNE
ST.-ETIENNE
GRENOBLE
GENEVE
LAUSANNE
BERN
BASEL
ZÜRICH
TORINO
BORDEAUX
TOULOUSE
LIMOGES
CLERMONT-FERRAND
MONTPELLIER
NÎMES
MARSEILLE
TOULON
NICE
AIX-EN-PROV
BILBAO
BILBO
SANTANDER
DONOSTIA
S.SEBASTIÁN
PAMPLONA
IRUÑA
VITORIA
GASTEIZ
KÖLN
ESSEN
DORTMUND
DÜSSELDORF
FRANKFURT
MAINZ
SAARBRÜCKEN
Gr. Time
+1h Gr. Time (MEZ)
+1h Gr. Time (MEZ) Greenwich Time
Scale 1 : 4,500,000
0 40 80 120 160 200 Kilometers
0 40 80 120 160 Statute Miles

SWEDEN
RUSSIA
LITHUANIA
BELARUS
POLAND
CZECH REPUBLIC
SLOVAKIA
AUSTRIA
HUNGARY
SLOVENIA
CROATIA
BOSNIA AND HERZEGOVINA
YUGOSLAVIA
ROMANIA
UKRAINE
Baltic Sea
Adriatic Sea
COPENHAGEN
MALMÖ
KALININGRAD
KAUNAS
HAMBURG
BERLIN
WARSZAWA (WARSAW)
PRAHA (PRAGUE)
WIEN (VIENNA)
BRATISLAVA
BUDAPEST
BEOGRAD (BELGRADE)
MÜNCHEN
MILANO (MILAN)
VENEZIA (VENICE)
ZAGREB
LJUBLJANA
SARAJEVO
KRAKÓW
WROCŁAW
POZNAŃ
GDAŃSK
ŁÓDŹ
DRESDEN
LEIPZIG
NÜRNBERG
SALZBURG
INNSBRUCK
GRAZ
LVIV
BIAŁYSTOK
LUBLIN
KOŠICE
DEBRECEN
SZEGED
HRODNA
BREST
16°
18°
20°
22°
24°
26°
10°
12°
14°
54°
52°
50°
48°
46°
44°
87
94
100
101
102
+3h Gr. Time
+2h Gr. Time
+2h Gr. Time +1h Gr. Time (MEZ)

+1h Gr.Time (MEZ) +2h Gr.Time
+1h Gr.Time (MEZ) +3h Gr.Time
87
93
102
Gulf of Bothnia
Gulf of Finland
Baltic Sea
Skagerrak
Kattegat
Åland (Ahvenanmaa)
Gotland
Öland
Bornholm (Denmark)
Rügen
Gotska Sandön Nationalpark
Hiiumaa s.
Saaremaa s.
Rigas Jūras Licis
OSLO
STOCKHOLM
GÖTEBORG
HELSINKI HELSINGFORS
S.-PETERBURG (ST.PETERSBURG)
TALLINN
RIGA
KLAIPĖDA
KALININGRAD
VILNIUS
MINSK
KAUNAS
ŠIAULIAI
DAUGAVPILS
TARTU
PSKOV
GDAŃSK
GDYNIA
SZCZECIN
BERLIN
POZNAŃ
WARSZAWA (WARSAW)
ŁÓDŹ
WROCŁAW
KRAKÓW
PRAHA (PRAGUE)
DRESDEN
COPENHAGEN
MALMÖ
HELSINGBORG
L'VIV
BREST
HRODNA
BIAŁYSTOK
LUBLIN
TURKU ÅBO
SWEDEN
FINLAND
ESTONIA
LATVIA
LITHUANIA
RUSSIA
BELARUS
POLAND
DENMARK
GERMANY
CZECH REPUBLIC
SLOVAKIA
UKRAINE
Scale 1 : 4,500,000
0 40 80 120 160 200 Kilometers
0 40 80 120 160 Statute Miles

MOSKVA
(MOSCOW)
NIŽNIJ NOVGOROD
JAROSLAVL'
KOSTROMA
VLADIMIR
IVANOVO
TVER'
RJAZAN'
TULA
KALUGA
SMOLENSK
BRJANSK
OREL
KURSK
BELGOROD
CHARKIV
VORONEŽ
LIPECK
TAMBOV
PENZA
SARATOV
ENGEL'S
ČEBOKSARY
JOŠKAR-OLA
KIROV
VOLOGDA
ČEREPOVEC
RYBINSK
ARZAMAS
SARANSK
KOLOMNA
PODOLSK
SERPUHOV
OBNINSK
SERGIEV-POSAD
DZERŽINSK
MUROM
KOVROV
KINEŠMA
HOMEL'
ČERNIHIV
SUMY
POLTAVA
KAMYŠIN
VOLŽSKIJ
ZARIZYN
MAHILËV
VELIKIE LUKI
KOLPINO
Ladožskoe ozero
Onežskoe ozero
Rybinskoe vodohranilišče
Gor'kovskoe vdhr.
Severnye uvaly
Valdajskaja vozvyšennost'
Smolensko-Moskovskaja vozvyšennost'
Srednerusskaja vozvyšennost'
Donskaja ravnina
Privolžskaja vozv.
Meščerskaja nizmennost'
Mordvinia
Mari-El
Chuvashia
Komi
RUSSIA
UKRAINE
Eastern Europe

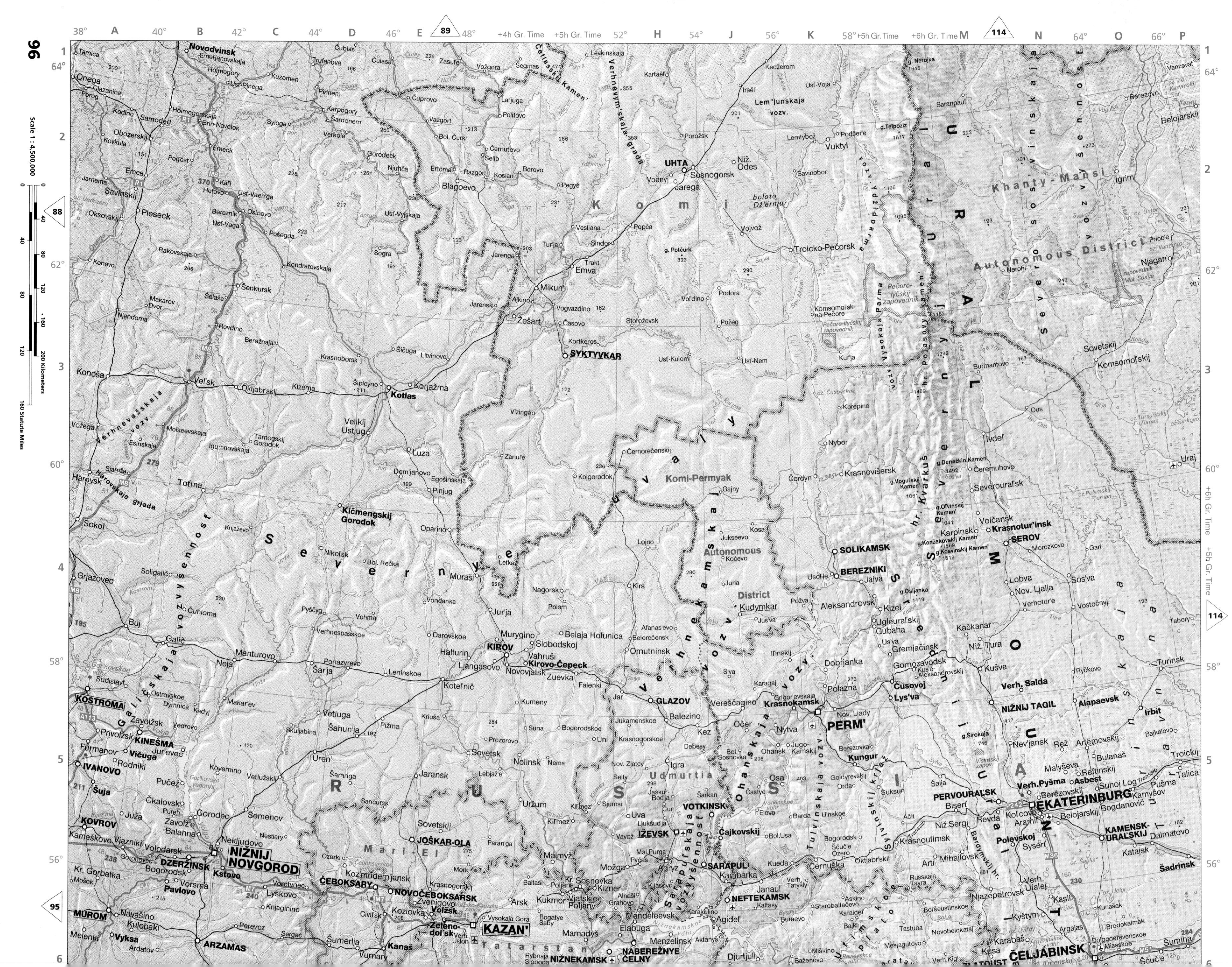

Scale 1 : 4,500,000

0 40 80 120 160 200 Kilometers

0 40 80 120 160 Statute Miles

UFA
SAMARA
ORENBURG
SARATOV
ORAL
AKTÖBE
ATYRAU
ASTRAHAN'
VOLŽSKIJ
ZARIZYN
PENZA
SIMBIRSK
TOLJATTI
SYZRAN'
ENGELS
KAMYŠIN
BALAKOVO
NOVOTROICK
ORSK
MAGNITOGORSK
STERLITAMAK
SALAVAT
OKTJABR'SKIJ
DIMITROVGRAD
NOVOKUJBYŠEVSK
Troick
Buzuluk
Buguruslan
Bugul'ma
Belebej
Kumertau
Beloreck
Sol'-Ileck
Kartaly
Elista
Saransk
Ahtubinsk
K A Z A K H S T A N
Caspian Sea
Aral Sea
UZBEKISTAN
+4h Gr. Time
+5h Gr. Time

Scale 1 : 4,500,000

0 40 80 120 160 200 Kilometers

0 40 80 120 160 Statute Miles

LIPECK
ELEC
VORONEŽ
KURSK
BELGOROD
CHARKIV
SARATOV
ENGEL'S
BALAKOVO
KAMYŠIN
Borisoglebsk
Balašov
Mihajlovka
ZARIZYN
VOLŽSKIJ
Ahtubinsk
KAZAKHSTAN
LUHANS'K
DONEC'K
DNIPROPETROVS'K
ZAPORIŽŽ'A
MARYUPOL'
BERDJANS'K
TAGANROG
ROSTOV-
na-DONU
NOVOČERKASSK
ŠAHTY
VOLGODONSK
Elista
ASTRAHAN'
Kalmykia
Caspian
Sea
Azovskoe
More
KERČ
Feodosija
KRASNODAR
NOVOROSSIJSK
Anapa
Gelendžik
Tuapse
STAVROPOL
ARMAVIR
NEVINNOMYSSK
ČERKESSK
PJATIGORSK
KISLOVODSK
NAL'ČIK
VLADIKAVKAZ
GROZNYJ
Chechenia
MAHAČKALA
Kaspijsk
Dagestan
SOČI
SUCHUMI
Gudauta
Abkhazia
KUTAISI
TBILISI
(TIFLIS)
RUSTAVI
GEORGIA
BATUMI
Poti
AZERBAIJAN
GANŽA
Mingečevir
KIROVAKAN
EREVAN
(YEREVAN)
ARMENIA
Kars
Artvin
TRABZON
Rize
Giresun
ORDU
SAMSUN
Sinop
Bafra
Amasya
Sea
RUSSIA
CAUCASUS

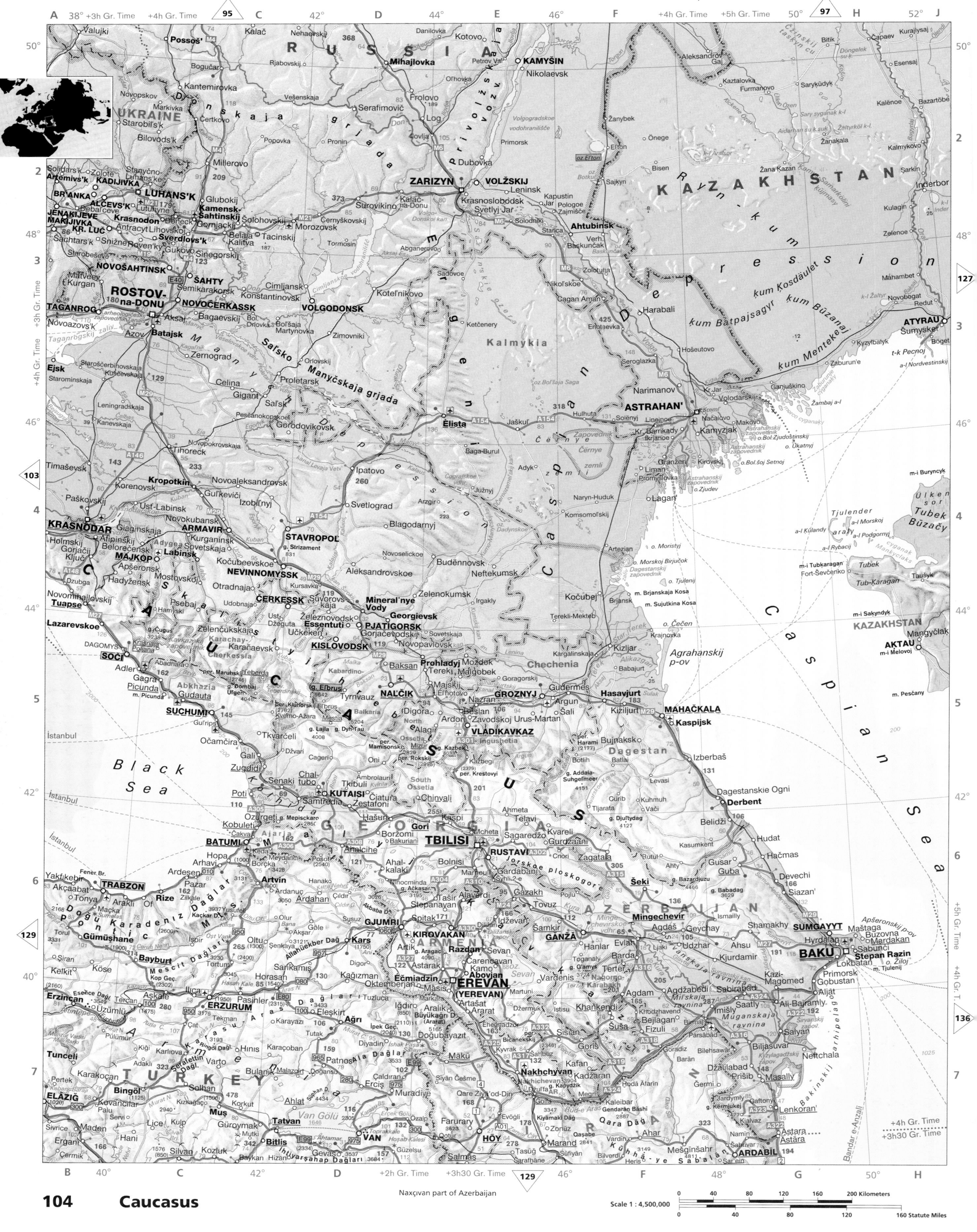

Naxçıvan part of Azerbaijan

Scale 1 : 4,500,000

0 40 80 120 160 200 Kilometers

0 40 80 120 160 Statute Miles

Asia – continent of contrasts

This 17,142,840 square mile (4.4 million sq. km) continent, the largest in the world, incorporates all climatic and vegetation zones from the polar to the tropical region. The major landscapes of Europe continue in Asia to the East: in the North, the western Siberian lowlands, joined by the central Siberian ranges and the eastern Siberian mountains; farther South, the mountain chains converging on the node of Ararat, at the Hindu Kush and in Indochina, encircling several plateaus, including the Tibetan highlands, the highest such feature on Earth at 14,764 feet (4,500 m). South of the mountain chains lie the plateaus of Arabia and the Indian subcontinent. Toward the Pacific the continent is delimited by garlands of islands and by sea trenches.

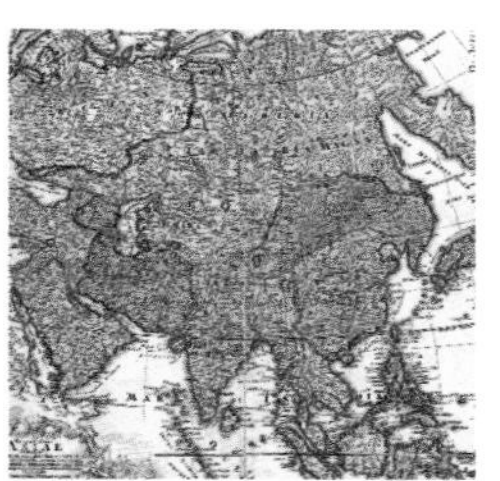
Asia in a copperplate engraving: This detailed map with boundaries and relief features in color was drawn by imperial cartographer Johann Baptist Homann in Nuremberg (circa 1700).

Russia: West Siberian Plain, Northern Region p. 108–109

Russia: Central Siberian Plateau, Northern Region p. 110–111

Russia: Siberia, Northeastern Region p. 112–113

Russia: West Siberian Plain, Southern Region p. 114–115

Sayan Mountains · Lake Baikal p. 116–117

Transbaikal Region p. 118–119

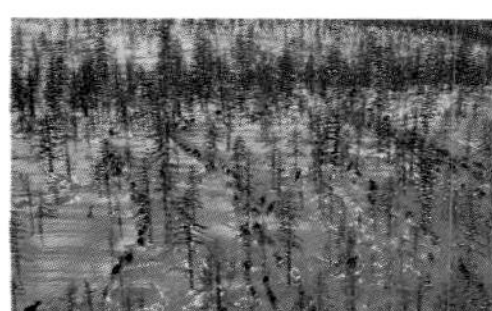
Far East: Northern Region · Kamchatka p. 120–121

Far East: Southern Region · Sakhalin p. 122–123

Kazakhstan: The Steppe p. 124–125

Caspian Depression · Aral Sea p. 126–127

Near East p. 128–129

Arabian Peninsula: Northern Region p. 130–131

Arabian Peninsula: Southern Region p. 132–133

Persian Gulf · Plateau of Iran p. 134–135

Central Asia p. 136–137

India: Northwestern Region · Indus Valley p. 138–139

India: Southern Region · Maldives · Sri Lanka p. 140–141

India: Northeastern Region · Bangladesh p. 142–143

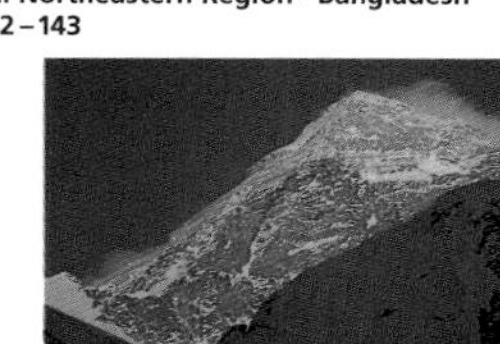
Tibet p. 144–145

Sinkiang p. 146–147

Mongolia p. 148–149

Manchuria · Korea p. 150–151

Japan p. 152–153

China: Northern Region p. 154–155

China: Southern Region p. 156–157

Thailand · Cambodia p. 158–159

Philippines p. 160–161

Malaysia · Sumatra p. 162–163

Borneo · Sulawesi p. 164–165

Moluccas · West Irian p. 166–167

Java · Lesser Sunda Islands p. 168

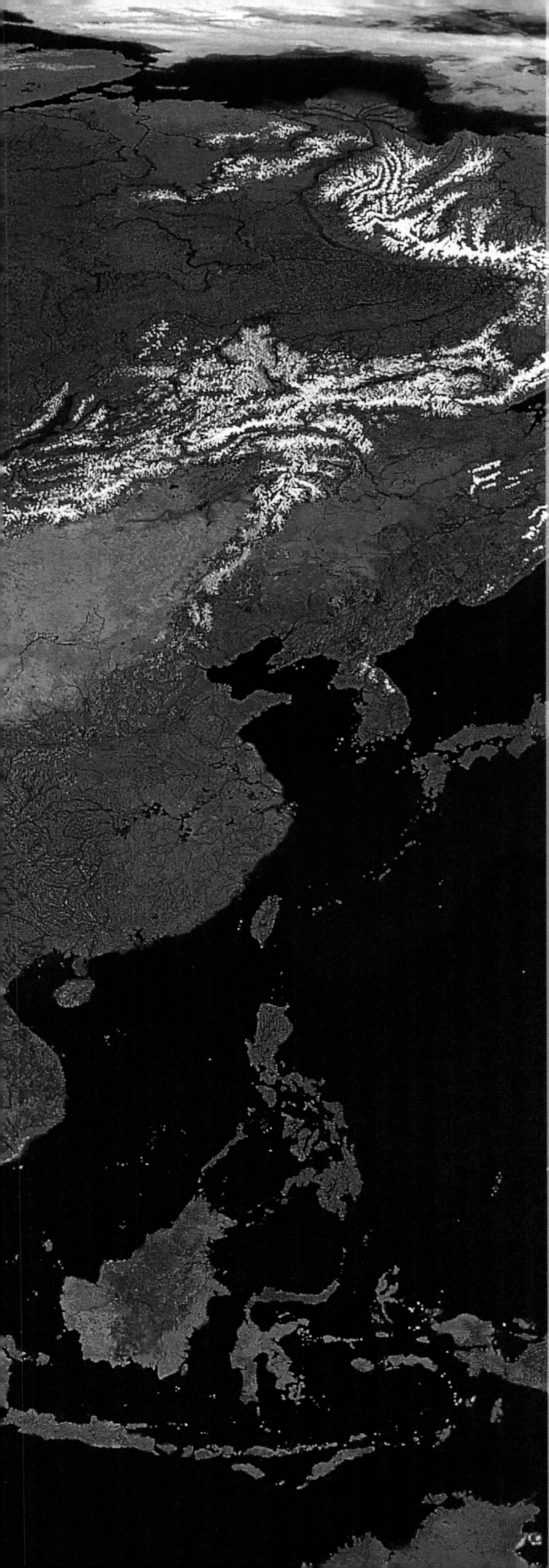

Russia: West Siberian Plain, Northern Region p. 108–109

Russia: Central Siberian Plateau, Northern Region p. 110–111

Russia: Siberia, Northeastern Region p. 112–113

Russia: West Siberian Plain, Southern Region p. 114–115

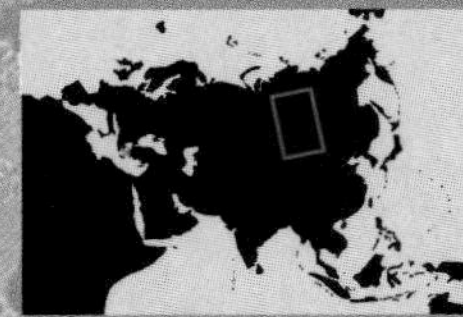

Sayan Mountains · Lake Baikal p. 116–117

Transbaikal Region p. 118–119

Far East: Northern Region · Kamchatka p. 120–121

Far East: Southern Region · Sakhalin p. 122–123

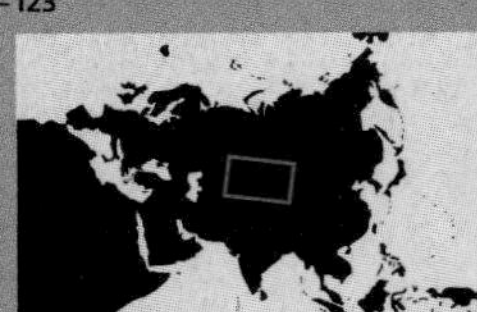

Kazakhstan: The Steppe p. 124–125

Caspian Depression · Aral Sea p. 126–127

Near East p. 128–129

Arabian Peninsula: Northern Region p. 130–131

Arabian Peninsula: Southern Region p. 132–133

Persian Gulf · Plateau of Iran p. 134–135

Central Asia p. 136–137

India: Northwestern Region · Indus Valley p. 138–139

India: Southern Region · Maldives · Sri Lanka p. 140–141

India: Northeastern Region · Bangladesh p. 142–143

Tibet p. 144–145

Sinkiang p. 146–147

Mongolia p. 148–149

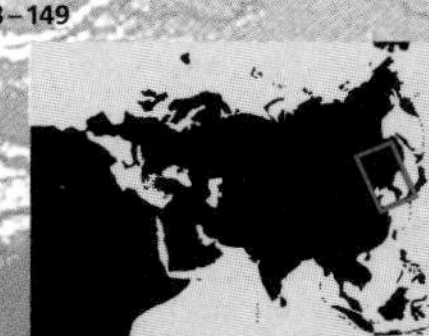

Manchuria · Korea p. 150–151

Japan p. 152–153

China: Northern Region p. 154–155

China: Southern Region p. 156–157

Thailand · Cambodia p. 158–159

Philippines p. 160–161

Malaysia · Sumatra p. 162–163

Borneo · Sulawesi p. 164–165

Moluccas · West Irian p. 166–167

Java · Lesser Sunda Islands p. 168

Severnaya Zemlya
Laptev Sea
Kara Sea
o. Komsomolec
lednik Akademii Nauk
o. Pioner
o. Oktjabr'skoj Revoljucii
o. Bol'ševik
Arhipelag Sedov
m. Arktičeskij
m. Kujbyševa
m. Litvinova
m. Frunze
m. Rozy Ljuksemburg
m. Berga
m. Pesčanyj
m. Cingera
mys Morozova
m. Mednyj
m. Sverdlova
o-va Krasnoflotskie
m. Obryvistyj
o. Voronina
m. Vajgač
m. Tajmyra
Universitetskij
lednik Leningradskij
+8h Gr. Time
Barents Sea
Kara Sea
Novaya Zemlya
Novozemel'skaja vpadina
gory Mendeleeva
Mys Želanija
m. Želanija
m. Karlsena
m. Konstantina
m. Sporyj Navolok
o-va Gorbovy
Arhanzel'skaja Guba
m. Nikolaja
Admiraltejstva
Smidovič
m. Suhoj Nos
Krestovaja Guba
m. Vikulova
Lagernoe
Pomorskoe
Matočkin Šar
m. Vyhodnoj
mys Britvin
Malyj Karmakuly
p-ov Gusinaja Zemlja
Belušja Guba
ostrov Meždušarskij
m. Kostin Nos
p-ov Mučnoj
Krasino
m. Sahanina
Rusanovo
m. Men'šikova
Bolvanskij Nos
Guba Dolgaja
o. Vajgač
proliv Karskie vorota
+5h Gr. Time
+3h Gr. Time
Murmansk
Arhangel'sk
Pečorskoe More
Varnek
Amderma
m. Bol. Ljamčin Nos
o. Matveev
o. Dolgij
m. Bel'kovskij Nos
m. Medynskij Zavorot
Jugorskij p-ov
Varandej
Karatajka
p-ov Russkij Zavorot
o-va Guljaevskie Koški
Pesjakov
Čornaja
Tobseda
Malozemel'skaja tundra
Pečorskaja guba
Narjan-Mar
Nenets Autonomous District
Bol'šezemel'skaja tundra
Arctic Circle
Horej-Ver
Vorgašor
Komsomol'skij
Severnyj
VORKUTA
Černyševa
Usinsk
Inta
Abez'
Sivomaskinskij
Pečorskaja grjada
Pečora
Kožva
Synja
Kožym
Kadžerom
Konecbor
Novikbož
Ust'-Kara
Jary
o. Topasovėj
o. Levdiev
Bajdarackaja guba
g. Očenyrd
Polar Ural
Labytnangi
Salehard
Aksarka
Salemal
Jar-Sale
Nareči
Kutopjugan
Nyda
Novyj Port
Ščuč'e
m. Ostrovnoj
Yamal Nenets Autonomous District
West Siberia
Russia
p-ov Jamal
o. Belyj
m. Ragozina
m. Malygina
m. Skuratova
proliv Malygina
m. Šuberta
m. Šokal'skogo
m. Mattesalja
o. Haljango
Drovjanoj
Tambej
Hanarasalja
m. Poruj
m. Beluži Nos
Morrasale
Mys-Kamennyj
kosa Kamennaja
Japtiksale
Sėjaha
Tadebjajaha
m. Harsė
m. Trehbugornyj
m. Čugor'
Antipajuta
Gydanskij p-ov
Tazovskij
Nahodka
Kara Sea
o. Vil'kickogo
kosa Vostočnaja
o. Neupokoeva
m. Olenij
p-ov Javaj
p-ov Mamonta
Juribejskaja grjada
Scale 1 : 4,500,000
200 Kilometers
160 Statute Miles

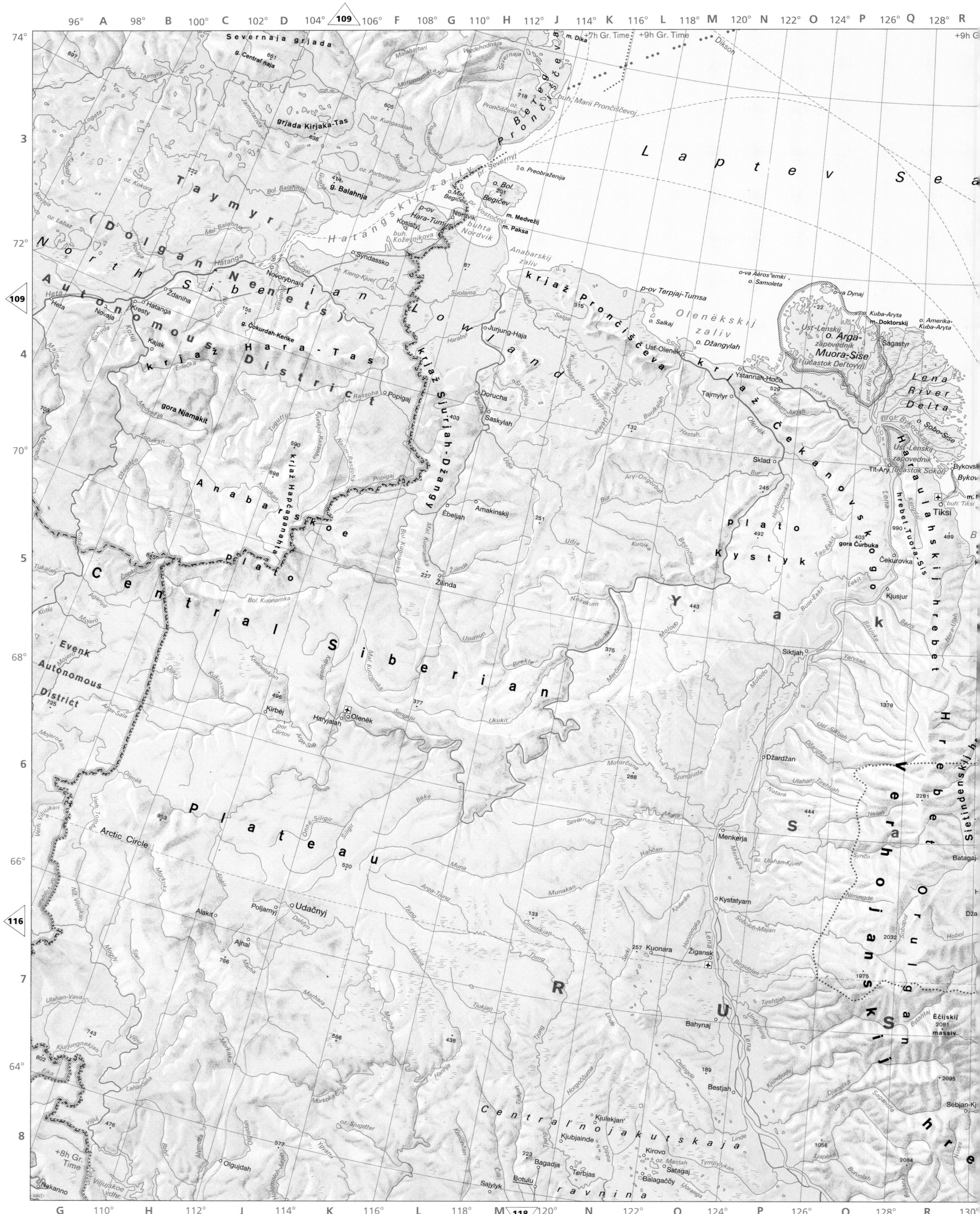

96° A 98° B 100° C 102° D 104° 109 106° F 108° G 110° H 112° J 114° K 116° L 118° M 120° N 122° O 124° P 126° Q 128° R

74° 3 72° 4 70° 5 68° 6 66° 7 64° 8

+7h Gr. Time +9h Gr. Time +9h

Severnaja grjada
g. Central'naja
grjada Kirjaka-Tas
Taymyr (Dolgan-Nenets) Autonomous District
North Siberian Lowland
Hara-Tas krjaž
gora Njamakit
g. Čokurdah-Kerike
Anabarskoe plato
krjaž Hapčaganahja
krjaž Sjurjah-Džangy
Central Siberian Plateau
Evenk Autonomous District
Arctic Circle
Hatangskij zaliv
Anabarskij zaliv
Olenëkskij zaliv
krjaž Prončiščeva
Bereg Prončiščevoj
buh. Marii Prončiščevoj
Laptev Sea
Lena River Delta
Ust'-Lenskij zapovednik (učastok Del'tovyj)
o. Arga-Muora-Sise
Ust'-Lenskij zapovednik (učastok Sokol)
Čekanovskogo krjaž
plato Kystyk
Haraulahskij hrebet
hrebet Tuora-Sis
gora Čurbuka
Hrebet Verhojanskij
Orulgan
Sietindenskij hrebet
Ečijskij massiv
Central'nojakutskaja ravnina
RUSSIA
Yakutsk

Dikson
m. Dika
p-ov Hara-Tumus
o. Bol. Begičev
o. Mal. Begičev
pr. Severnyj
pr. Vostočnyj
buhta Nordvik
Nordvik
m. Medvežij
m. Paksa
Kosistyj
buh. Koževnikova
o. Preobraženija
Syndassko
Novorybnaja
Hatanga
Ždaniha
Kresty
Novaja
Heta
Kajak
Popigaj
Jurjung-Haja
Dorucha
Saskylah
Ebeljah
Amakinskij
Žilinda
Olenëk
Haryjalah
Kirbëj
Udačnyj
Poljarnyj
Alakit
Ajhal
Olgujdah
Nakanno
Ust'-Olenëk
o. Salkaj
o. Džangylah
p-ov Terpjaj-Tumsa
o-va Aèros'emki
o. Samoleta
o. Amerika-Kuba-Aryta
Kuba-Aryta
m. Doktorskij
o. Dynaj
Sagastyr
Sobo-Sise
Tit-Ary
Bykovskij
Tiksi
buh. Tiksi
Čekurovka
Kjusjur
Ystannah-Hočo
Tajmylyr
Sklad
Siktjah
Džardžan
Menkerja
Kystatyam
Kuonara
Žigansk
Bahynaj
Bestjah
Batagaj
Sebjan-Kjuël'
Kjulekjan
Kjubjainde
Kirovo
Sataga
Balagaččy
Terbjas
Bagadja
Botulu
Sajylyk

Lena Olenëk Anabar Popigaj Kotuj Hatanga Heta Viljuj Muna Tjung Linde Molodo Bol. Kuonamka Mal. Kuonamka Markha Ukukit Bur Udja Kuojka Ulahan-Jurjah Omnja Siligir Arga-Sala Mojero

+8h Gr. Time

Scale 1 : 4,500,000

0 40 80 120 160 200 Kilometers

0 40 80 120 160 Statute Miles

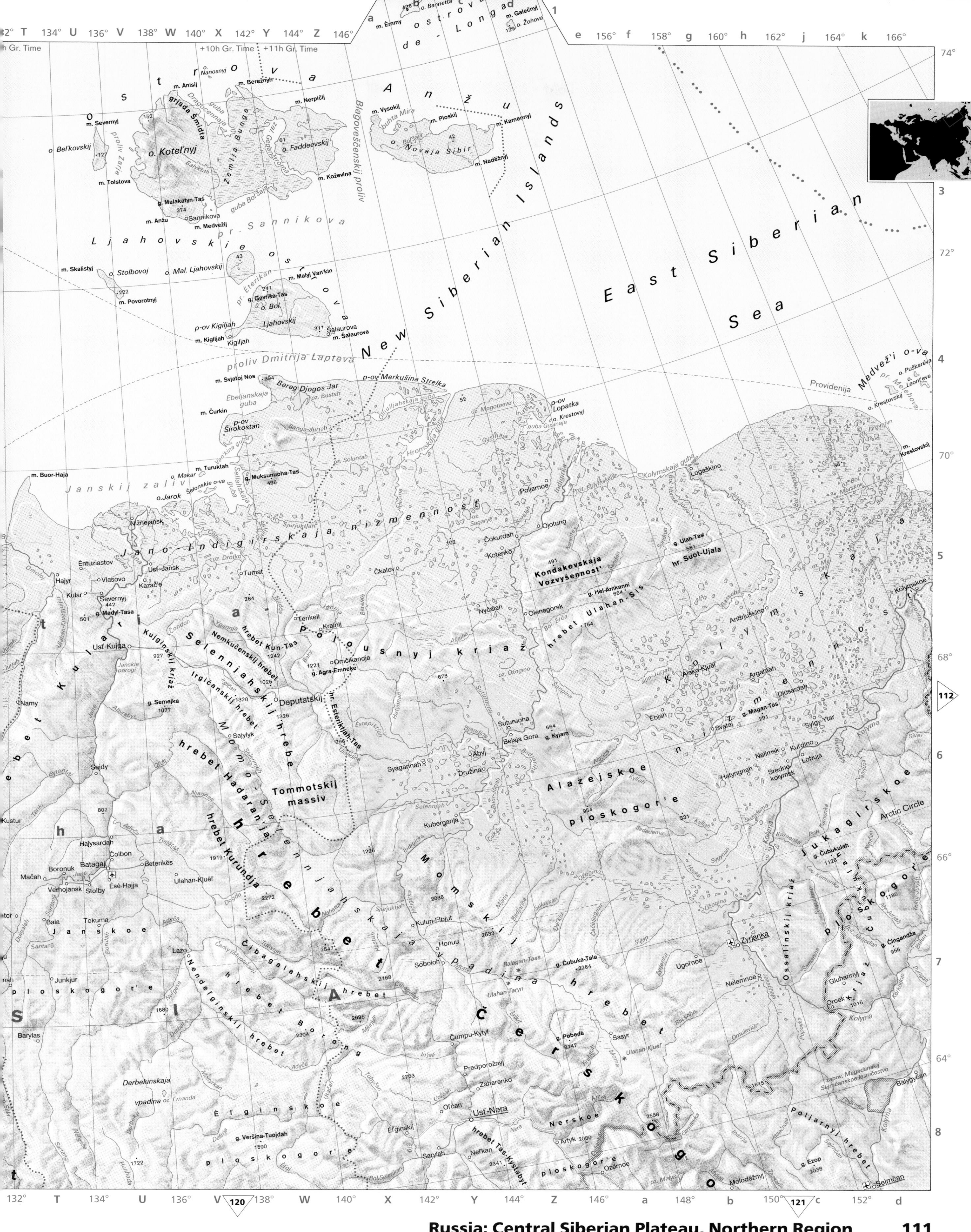

+10h Gr. Time
+11h Gr. Time
New Siberian Islands
East Siberian Sea
o. Kotel'nyj
Zemlja Bunge
o. Faddeevskij
o. Novaja Sibir
Blagoveščenskij proliv
Ljahovskie ostrova
pr. Sannikova
o. Bol. Ljahovskij
o. Mal. Ljahovskij
o. Stolbovoj
o. Bel'kovskij
proliv Dmitrija Lapteva
Medvež'i o-va
Providenija
Janskij zaliv
Jano-Indigirskaja nizmennost'
Kolymskaja nizmennost'
Kondakovskaja Vozvyšennost'
hr. Suot-Ujala
hrebet Ulahan-Sis
Polousnyj krjaž
Selennjahskij hrebet
hrebet Kulartah
Tommotskij massiv
hrebet Hadaranja
hrebet Kurundja
Momo-Selennjahskaja vpadina
Momskij hrebet
Alazejskoe ploskogor'e
Jukagirskoe ploskogor'e
Arctic Circle
Ossalinskij krjaž
Janskoe ploskogor'e
Čibagalahskij hrebet
Nendeginskij hrebet
hrebet Boronog
hrebet Čerskogo
Nerskoe ploskogor'e
Ėl'ginskoe ploskogor'e
Poljarnyj hrebet
hrebet Tas-Kystabyt
g. Pobeda 3147
Verhojansk
Batagaj
Deputatskij
Ust'-Nera
Zyrjanka
Srednekolymsk
Čokurdah
Belaja Gora
Ust'-Kujga
Nižnejansk
Kazač'e
Sejmčan
Balygyčan
Russia

A 142° B 144° C 146° D 148° E 150° 111 152° G 154° H 156° J 158° K 160° L 162° M 164° N 166° O 168° P

East Siberian Sea

Medvežʼi o-va

Yakutia (Sakha)

Polousnyj krjaž

Kondakovskaja Vozvyšennostʼ

hrebet Ulahan-Sis

hr. Suot-Ujala

Kolymskaja nizmennostʼ

Alazejskoe ploskogorʼe

Momskij hrebet

Jukagirskoe ploskogorʼe

Kurʼinskij krjaž

Anjujskij hrebet

Olojskij hrebet

hrebet Uš-Urėkčėn

Kedonskij hrebet

Molongdinskij hr.

Korkodonskij hrebet

Omsukčanskij hrebet

Kolymskoe nagorʼe

Koryak Autonomous District

Korjakskij hrebet

Gižiginskaja guba

Penžinskaja guba

Zaliv Šelihova

Tauiskaja guba

MAGADAN

Arctic Circle

+11h Gr. Time +12h Gr. Time

F 152° G 154° H 156° J 158° K 121 160° L 162° M 164° N 166° O 168° P

Scale 1 : 4,500,000

0 40 80 120 160 200 Kilometers

0 40 80 120 160 Statute Miles

Chukchi Sea
Bering Sea
o. Vrangelja
Anadyrskij zaliv
Bering Strait
Saint Lawrence I.
Saint Matthew I.
Seward Peninsula
Alaska (U.S.)
De Long Mts.
International Date Line
Arctic Circle
+12h Gr. Time
-9h Gr. Time
Anadyr
Providenija
Ugol'nye Kopi
Mys Šmidta
Anadyrskaja nizmennost'
Čukotskij p-ov
Petropavlovsk-Kamčatskij

Scale 1 : 4,500,000

0 40 80 120 160 200 Kilometers

0 40 80 120 160 Statute Miles

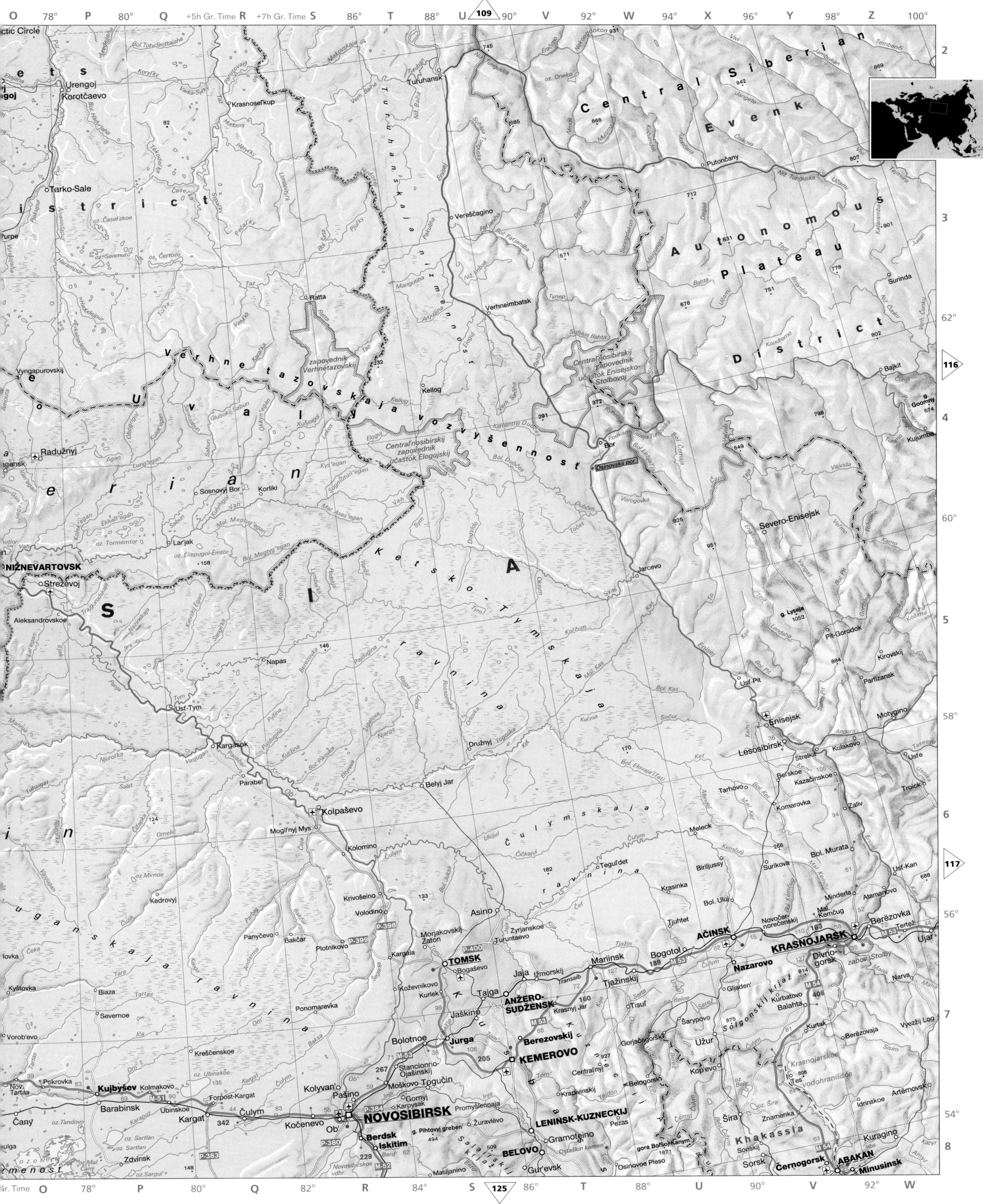

Arctic Circle
Central Siberian Plateau
Evenk Autonomous District
Verhne tazovskaja vozvyšennost
Sibirskie Uvaly
Ketsko-Tymskaja ravnina
Čulymskaja ravnina
Vasjuganskaja ravnina
Kuzneckij Alatau
Salairskij krjaž
Solgonskij krjaž
Khakassia
zapovednik Verhnetazovskij
Central'nosibirskij zapovednik učastok Eloguijskij
Central'nosibirskij zapovednik učastok Enisejsko-Stolbovoj
Krasnojarskoe vodohranilišče
Urengoj
Korotčaevo
Krasnosel'kup
Turuhansk
Tarko-Sale
Vereščagino
Putončany
Surinda
Ratta
Verhneimbatsk
Vyngapurovskij
Kellog
Bajkit
Bor
Osinovskij por.
Radužnyj
Sosnovyj Bor
Korliki
Severo-Enisejsk
Lar'jak
NIŽNEVARTOVSK
Streževoj
Jarcevo
Aleksandrovskoe
g. Lysaja 1052
Pit-Gorodok
Kirovskij
Napas
Ust'-Pit
Partizansk
Ust'-Tym
Enisejsk
Motygino
Kargasok
Družnyj
Lesosibirsk
Kulakovo
Strelka
Bel'skoe
Kazačinskoe
Parabel
Belyj Jar
Tarhovo
Komarovka
Troick
Kolpaševo
Zaliv
Mogil'nyj Mys
Meleck
Kolomino
Bol. Murata
Teguľdet
Biriljussy
Surikova
Ust'-Kan
Krivošeino
Kedrovyj
Volodino
Krasinka
Bol. Uluj
Asino
Minderla
Atamanovo
Tjuhtet
Berëzovka
Zyrjanskoe
Novočerkasskij
Mal. Kemčug
Tertež
Panyčevo
Bakčar
Morjakovskij Zaton
Turuntaevo
AČINSK
Bogotol
KRASNOJARSK
Ujar
Plotnikovo
Kargala
TOMSK
Bogaševo
Mariinsk
Nazarovo
Divnogorsk
Stolby
Jaja
Ižmorskij
Tjažinskij
Narva
Kyštovka
Biaza
Koževnikovo
Kurlek
Tajga
ANŽERO-SUDŽENSK
Krasnyj Jar
Tisul'
Gljaden'
Balahta
Severnoe
Ponomarevka
Jaškino
Šarypovo
Kurtak
Vyezžij Log
Vorob'evo
Bolotnoe
Jurga
Berezovskij
Užur
Berëzovaja
Kreščenskoe
KEMEROVO
Stancionno-Ojašinskij
Gorjačegorsk
Centraľnyj
Kop'evo
Pokrovka
Kujbyšev
Kolmakovo
Forpost-Kargat
Kolyvan'
Pašino
Moškovo
Togučin
Belogorsk
Artëmovsk
Nov. Tartas
Barabinsk
Ubinskoe
Čulym
Gornyj
Karpysak
Krapivinskij
Idrinskoe
Čany
Kargat
Kočenevo
Ob'
NOVOSIBIRSK
Promyšlennaja
Žuravlëvo
LENINSK-KUZNECKIJ
Pezas
Šira
Znamenka
Berdsk
Iskitim
g. Pihtovyj greben
Gramoteino
Kuragino
Zdvinsk
BELOVO
Ostaškin kamen'
gora Bolšoi Kanym 1871
Sonskij
Sorsk
Černogorsk
ABAKAN
Minusinsk
Masljanino
Gur'evsk
Osinovoe Pleso
Obi
Enisej
Angara
Niž. Tunguska
Podkamennaja Tunguska
Čulym
Ket'
Tym
Vah
Vasjugan
Parabel'
Taz
M-51
M-52
M-53
M-54
P-380
P-383
P-384
P-398
P-399
P-400
+5h Gr. Time
+7h Gr. Time
Gr. Time
O 78° P 80° Q R S 86° T 88° U 109 90° V 92° W 94° X 96° Y 98° Z 100°
O 78° P 80° Q 82° R 84° S 125 86° T 88° U 90° V 92° W
2
3
62°
116
4
60°
5
58°
6
117
56°
7
54°
8

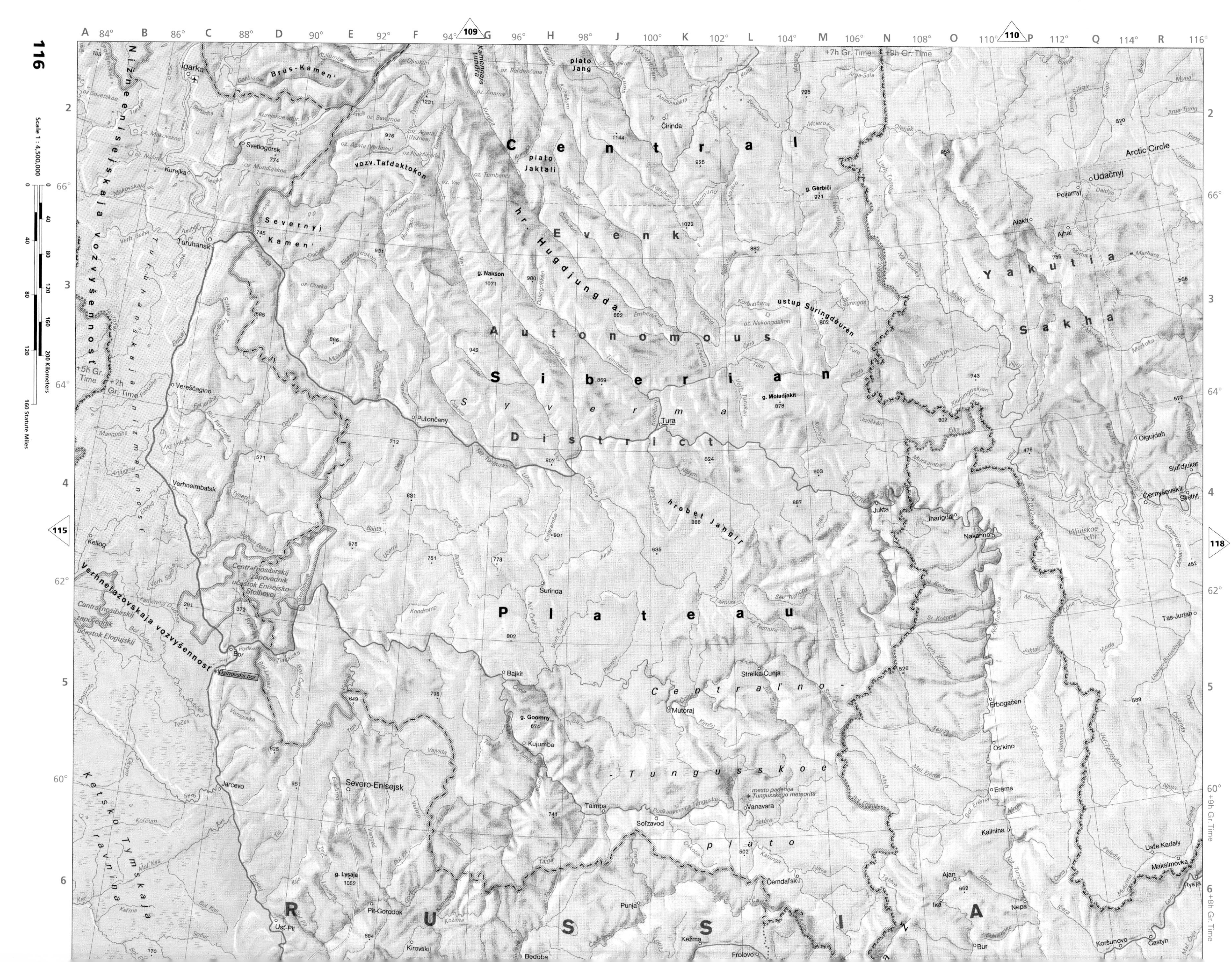

Scale 1 : 4,500,000

0 40 80 120 160 200 Kilometers

0 40 80 120 160 Statute Miles

UST'-ILIMSK
BRATSK
KRASNOJARSK
AČINSK
KANSK
ABAKAN
Minusinsk
Černogorsk
Tulun
Ust'-Ordynsk
Buryat Aut. Dist.
Čeremhovo
USOL'E-SIBIRSKOE
ANGARSK
IRKUTSK
ULAN-UDE
Severobajkal'sk
Ust'-Kut
Kyzyl
Khakassia
East Sayan Mts.
Western Sayan
Tuva
Buryatia
Lake Baikal
MONGOLIA
Hövsgöl
Bulgan
Selenge
Zavhan
Arhangaj
Uvs
Bajan-Ölgij
Hovd
Mörön
Ulaangom
Darhan
Sühbaatar
Erdenet
Kjahta
Gusinoozërsk
Bajkal'skij hrebet
hrebet Ulan-Burgasy
hrebet Akademika Obručeva
hrebet Zapadnyj Tannu-Ola
hrebet Vostočnyj Tannu-Ola
Han Höhijn Nuruu
Bulnajn nuruu
hr. Malyj Hamar-Daban
Todžinskaja kotlovina
Leno-Angarskoe plato
Birjusinskoe plato
Irkutsko-Čeremhovskaja ravnina
Transsib
BAM

Central Siberian Plateau
Central'nojakutskaja ravnina
Verhojanskij hrebet
hrebet Orulgan
Janskoe ploskogorie
Yakutia-Sakha
Prilenskoe plato
Patomskoe
Evenk Autonomous District
JAKUTSK
Lena
Viljuj
Aldan
Mirnyj
Njurba
Viljujsk
Olëkminsk
Lensk
Sangar
Žigansk
Udačnyj
Olenëk
Verhojansk
Arctic Circle
+9h Gr. Time
+10h Gr. Time
+7h Gr. Time
+8h Gr. Time
109
110
111
116
120
Scale 1 : 4,500,000
0 40 80 120 160 200 Kilometers
0 40 80 120 160 Statute Miles

RUSSIA
CHINA
MONGOLIA
+9h Gr. Time
+8h Gr. Time
ČITA
BLAGOVEŠČENSK
Heihe
Tynda
Skovorodino
Nerjungri
Magdagači
Zeja
Svobodnyj
Belogorsk
Lesser Hinggan Ra.
Greater Hinggan Ra.
Amursko-Zejskaja ravnina
Stanovoj hrebet
Stanovoe nagor'e
Jablonovyj hrebet
Borščevočnyj hrebet
Vitimskoe ploskogor'e
Heilongjiang
Inner Mongolia
Nenjiang
JAGDAQI
Oroqen Zizhiqi
Mohe
Ergun Zuoqi
Ergun Youqi
YAKESHI
HAILAR
Chen Barag Qi
MANZHOULI
Krasnokamensk
Zabajkal'sk
Borzja
Sretensk
Nerčinsk
Šilka
Černyševsk
Mogoča
Karymskoe
Aginskoe
Aga Buryat Autonomous Dist.
Dornod
Hilok
Petrovsk-Zabajkal'skij
Severobajkal'sk
Kirensk
Bodajbo
Mama
Taksimo
Novyj Uojan
Barguzin
Lake Baikal

Scale 1 : 4,500,000
0 40 80 120 160 200 Kilometers
0 40 80 120 160 Statute Miles

Commander Islands
Bering Sea
Komandorskie o-va
Kamchatka
Peninsula
Koryak
Autonomous
District
MAGADAN
PETROPAVLOVSK-KAMČATSKIJ
Šelihova zaliv
Gižiginskaja guba
Penžinskaja guba
Karaginskij zaliv
Kamčatskij zaliv
Kronockij zaliv
Komandorskaja Kotlovina
Korjakskoe nagor'e
Kolymskoe nagor'e
Sredinnyj hrebet
Vostočnyj hrebet
Ičigemskij hrebet
Omsukčanskij hrebet
Korkodonskij hrebet
Penžinskij hrebet
Vetvejskij hrebet
Pylginskij hrebet
Parapol'skij dol
Tajgonos p-ov
p-ov Koni
Tauijskaja guba
Jamskaja nizm.
Kilganskij massiv
Susuman
Jagodnoe
Sejmčan
Omsukčan
Evensk
Gižiga
Palana
Ossora
Ust'-Kamčatsk
Ključi
Kozyrevsk
Esso
Mil'kovo
Elizovo
Ust'-Bol'šereck
Nikol'skoe
o. Beringa
o. Mednyj
Ust'-Omčug
Orotukan
Palatka
Sokol
Ola
Arman'
Talon
Jamsk
Manily
Kamenskoe
Tilički
vlk. Ključevskaja Sopka 4750
vlk. Ičinskaja Sopka 3621
vlk. Koriakskaja Sopka 3456
vlk. Ševeluč 3283
+11h Gr. Time
+12h Gr. Time

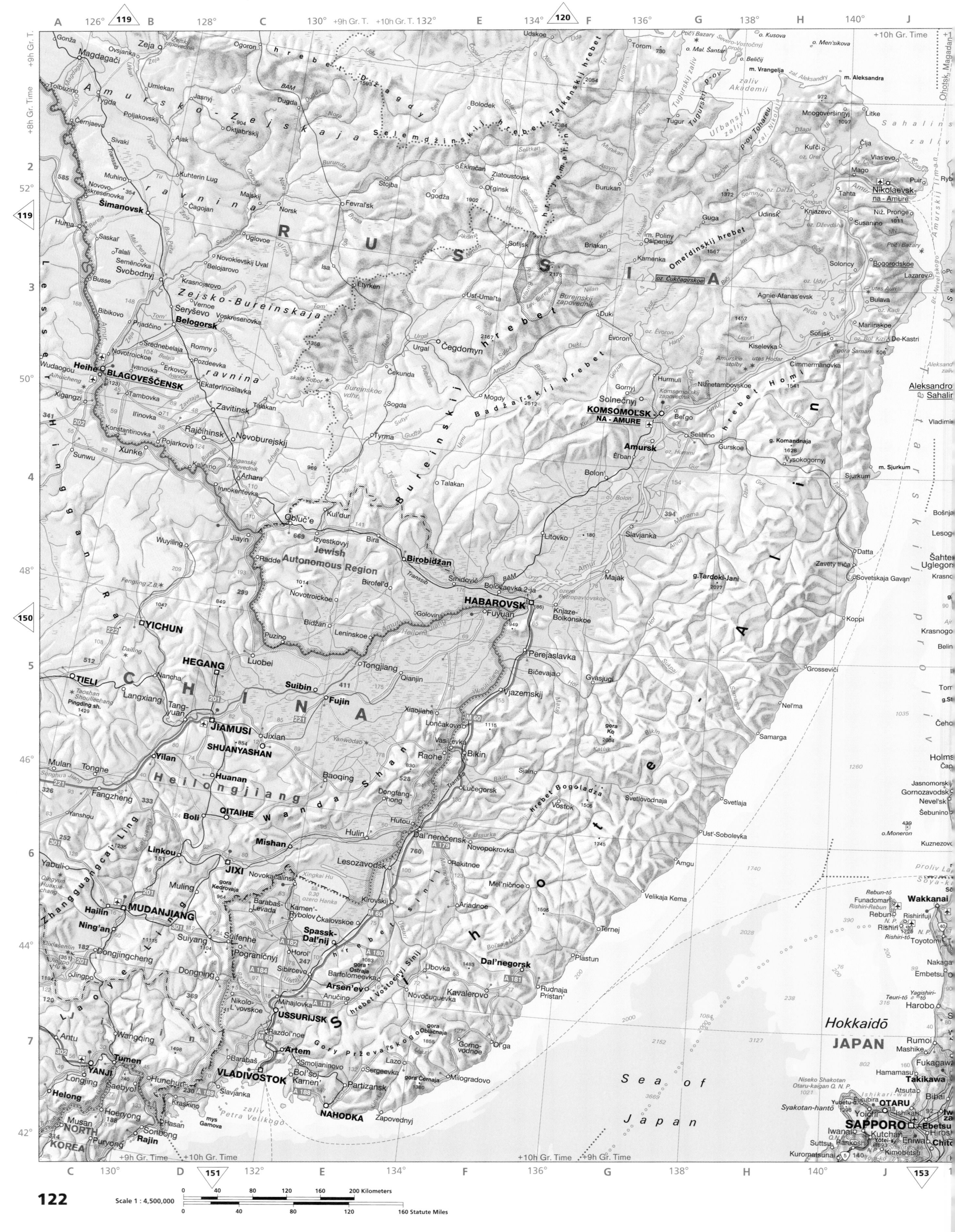

A
126°
119
B
128°
C
130°
+9h Gr. T.
+10h Gr. T.
132°
E
134°
120
F
136°
G
138°
H
140°
J
+10h Gr. Time
+9h Gr. T.
+8h Gr. Time
2
52°
119
3
50°
4
48°
150
5
46°
6
44°
7
42°
RUSSIA
CHINA
Jewish Autonomous Region
Heilongjiang
JAPAN
Hokkaidō
NORTH KOREA
Sea of Japan
Magdagači
Zeja
Tolbuzino
Tygda
Umlekan
Jasnyj
Černjaev
Poljakovskij
Oktjabrskij
Ajak
Sivaki
Kuhterin Lug
Muhino
Novovoskresenovka
Šimanovsk
Čagojan
Majskij
Norsk
Fevral'sk
Stojba
Ogodža
Ekimčan
Zlatoustovsk
Orgïnsk
Uglovoe
Novokievskij Uval
Belojarovo
Svobodnyj
Busse
Krasnojarovo
Vernoe
Seryševo
Voskresenovka
Belogorsk
Bibikovo
Prjadčino
Srednebelaja
Romny
Novotroickoe
Ivanovka
Pozdeevka
Erkovcy
Heihe
BLAGOVEŠČENSK
Wudaogou
Xigangzi
Tambovka
Ekaterinoslavka
Zavitinsk
Il'inovka
Konstantinovka
Rajčihinsk
Novoburejskij
Pojarkovo
Xunke
Sunwu
Kalinino
Arhara
Innokent'evka
Obluč'e
Kul'dur
Izvestkovyj
Bira
Birobidžan
Smidovič
Birofel'd
Novotroickoe
Bidžan
Leninskoe
Jiayin
Radde
Wuyiling
Puzino
Luobei
HABAROVSK
Fuyuan
Knjaze-Bolkonskoe
Perejaslavka
Bičevaja
Gvasjugi
Vjazemskij
YICHUN
HEGANG
TIELI
Nancha
Langxiang
Tang-yuan
JIAMUSI
Suibin
Fujin
Tongjiang
Qianjin
Jixian
SHUANYASHAN
Yilan
Mulan
Tonghe
Huanan
Fangzheng
Baoqing
Dongfanghong
Raohe
Bikin
Vasil'evka
Lončakovo
Xiaojiahe
Lučegorsk
Boli
QITAIHE
Mishan
Hulin
Hutou
Dal'nerečensk
Novopokrovka
Linkou
JIXI
Yabuli
Muling
Hailin
MUDANJIANG
Ning'an
Lesozavodsk
Rakitnoe
Mel'ničnoe
Kirovskij
Ariadnoe
Spassk-Dal'nij
Čkalovskoe
Suifenhe
Suiyang
Pograničnyj
Dongjingcheng
Dongning
Horol'
Sibircevo
Arsen'ev
Anučino
Novočuguevka
Ubovka
Kavalerovo
Dal'negorsk
Rudnaja Pristan'
Plastun
Ternej
Mihajlovka
USSURIJSK
Razdol'noe
Artem
VLADIVOSTOK
Smoljaninovo
Bol'šoj Kamen'
Partizansk
Sergeevka
Lazo
Ol'ga
Milogradovo
NAHODKA
Zapovednyj
Slavjanka
Kraskino
Hasan
Hunchun
Antu
Wangqing
Tumen
YANJI
Longjing
Helong
Hoeryong
Musan
Sonbong
Rajin
Puryong
Ogoron
Udskoe
Torom
Tugur
Čumikan
Burukan
Guga
Udinsk
Briakan
Kamenka
Im. Poliny Osipenko
Sofijsk
Bolodek
Dugda
Ust'-Umal'ta
Čegdomyn
Urgal
Čekunda
Sogda
Mogdy
Tyrma
Talakan
Duki
Evoron
Gornyj
Solnečnyj
Hurmuli
Nižnetambovskoe
KOMSOMOL'SK-NA-AMURE
Bel'go
Selihino
Amursk
Gurskoe
Ėl'ban
Bolon'
Litovko
Slavjanka
Majak
Bolokaevka 2-ja
Mnogoveršinnyj
Litke
Čija
Vlas'evo
Mago
Nikolaevsk-na-Amure
Tahta
Niž. Pronge
Knjazevo
Susanino
Solonci
Bogorodskoe
Lazarev
Bulava
Mariinskoe
Sofijsk
De-Kastri
Kiselevka
Cimmermanovka
Aleksandrovsk-Sahalinskij
Vladimirovo
m. Sjurkum
Sjurkum
Datta
Zavety Il'iča
Sovetskaja Gavan'
Koppi
Grossevići
Nel'ma
Samarga
Svetlaja
Svetlovodnaja
Ust'-Sobolevka
Amgu
Velikaja Kema
Wakkanai
Rishiri
Rebun
Toyotomi
Teshio
Haboro
Rumoi
Mashike
Takikawa
OTARU
SAPPORO
Ebetsu
Iwanai
Kutchan
Eniwa
Chitose
Kiyosato
Suttsu
Kuromatsunai
+9h Gr. Time
+10h Gr. Time
C
130°
D
151
132°
E
134°
F
136°
G
138°
H
140°
J
153
Scale 1 : 4,500,000
0 40 80 120 160 200 Kilometers
0 40 80 120 160 Statute Miles

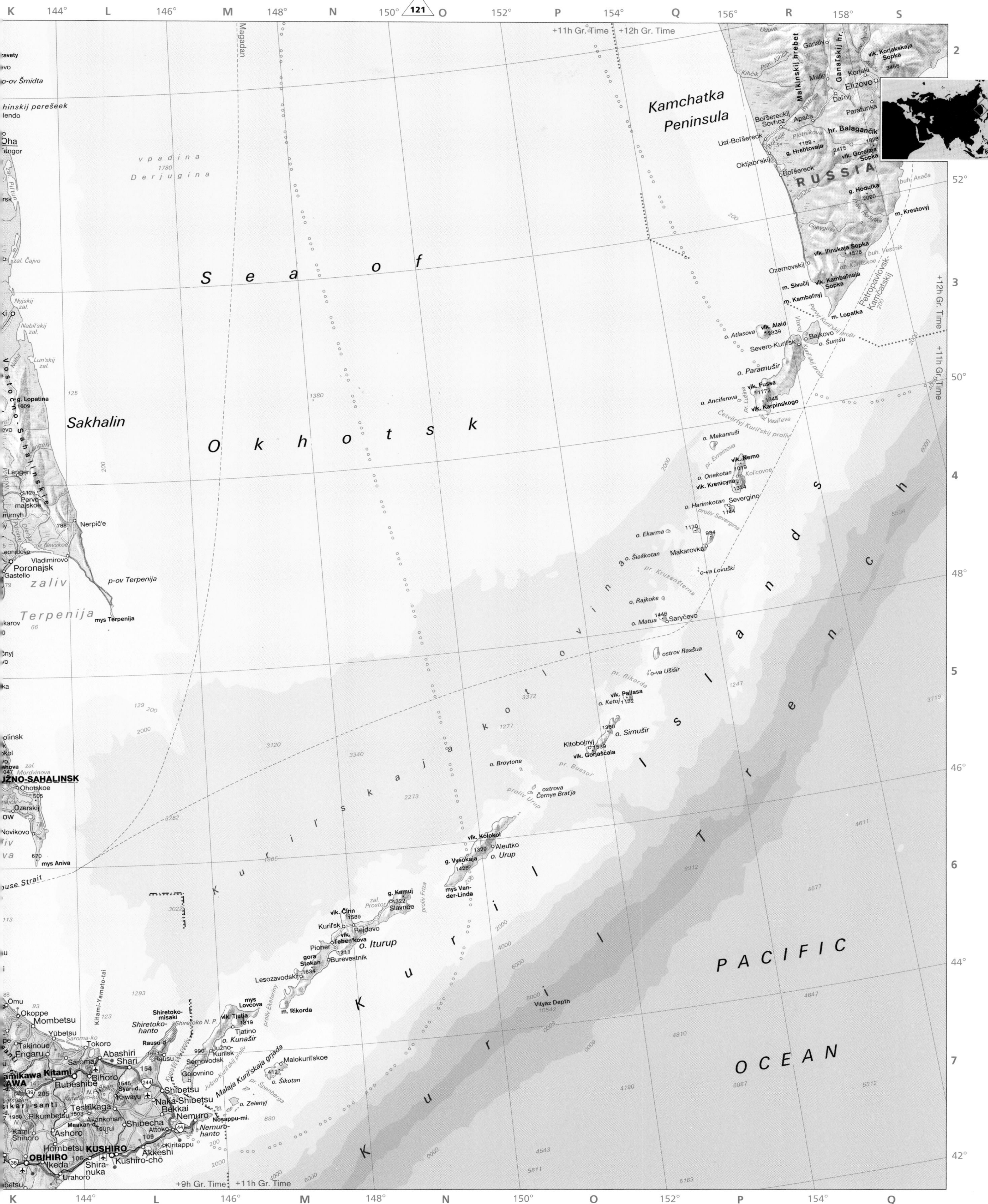
Sea of Okhotsk
Kamchatka Peninsula
RUSSIA
Sakhalin
Kuril'skaja kotlovina
Kuril Islands
Kuril Trench
PACIFIC OCEAN
Vityaz Depth
o. Iturup
o. Urup
o. Kunašir
o. Paramušir
o. Simušir
Južno-Sahalinsk
Petropavlovsk-Kamčatskij
Severo-Kuril'sk
Kuril'sk
Kitami
Kushiro
Obihiro
Nemuro
Abashiri
Poronajsk
zaliv Terpenija
La Perouse Strait
+11h Gr. Time
+12h Gr. Time
+9h Gr. Time

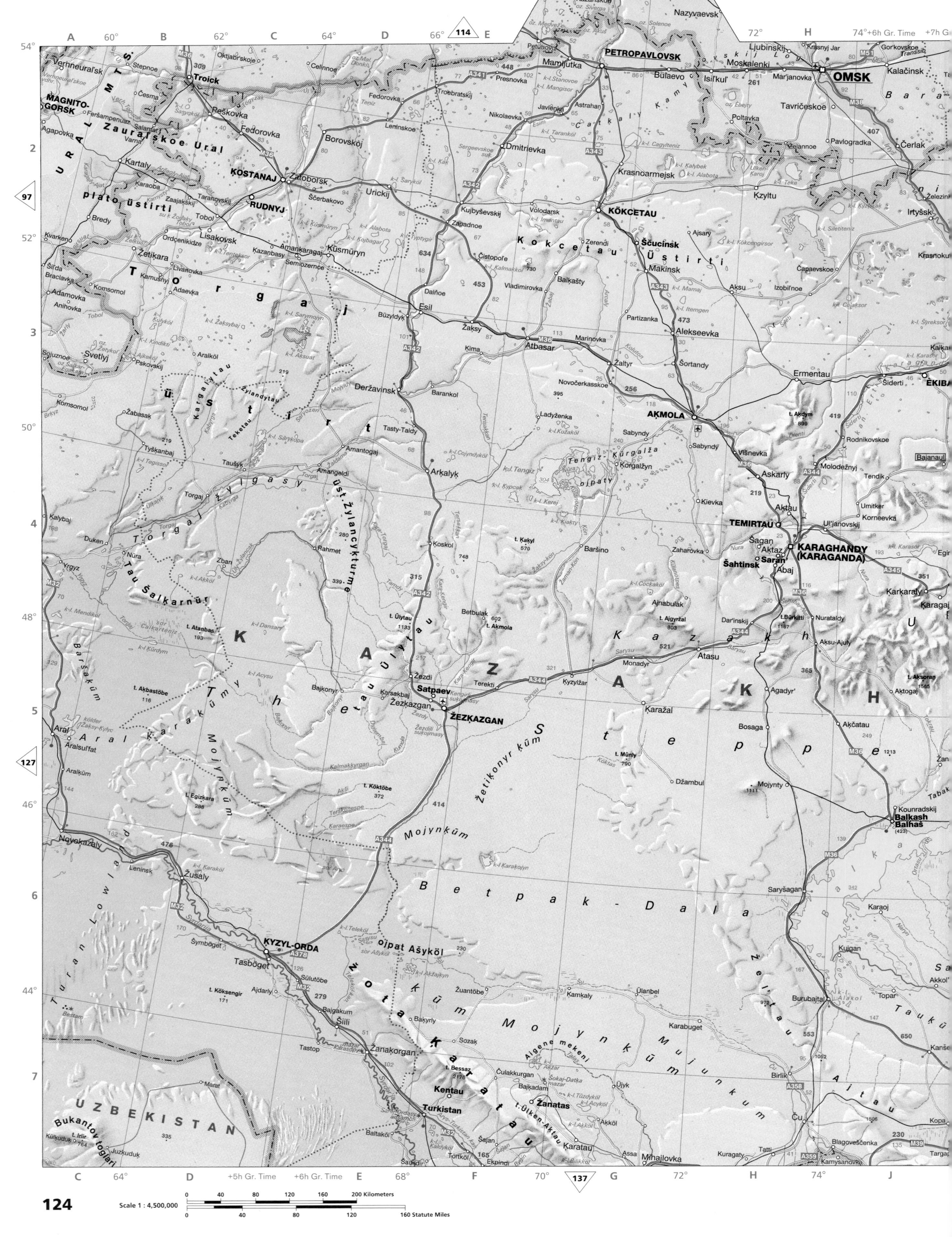

Kazanskoe
Nazyvaevsk
Petuhovo
PETROPAVLOVSK
Mamljutka
Presnovka
Bulaevo
Isil'kul'
Moskalenki
Ljubinskij
Krasnyj Jar
OMSK
Kalačinsk
Gor'kovskoe
Marjanovka
Tavričeskoe
Poltavka
Čerlak
Pavlogradka
Želannoe
Verhneural'sk
Stepnoe
Oktjabr'skoe
Celinnoe
Troick
MAGNITOGORSK
Čes̆ma
Reškovka
Fedorovka
Troebratskij
Nikolaevka
Javlenka
Astrahan
Leninskoe
Borovskoj
Dmitrievka
Krasnoarmejsk
Zauralskoe Ural
Kartaly
KOSTANAJ
Zatobolsk
Urickij
RUDNYJ
Taranovskij
Tobol
Kujbyševskij
Volodarsk
KÖKCETAU
Zapadnoe
Kzyltu
Irtyšsk
Bredy
Lisakovsk
Ordcenikidze
Amankaragaj
Kušmuryn
Semiozernoe
Kazanbasy
Žetikara
Livanovka
Kamyšnyj
Adaevka
Komsomol
Adamovka
Anihovka
Zerendi
Ščucinsk
Makinsk
Čistopoľe
Vladimirovka
Balkašty
Ajsary
Aksu
Izobil'noe
Čapaevskoe
Krasnokut
Kokcetau
Üstirti
Torgaj
Esil
Büzyldyk
Žaksy
Atbasar
Marinovka
Alekseevka
Partizanka
Kima
Žaltyr
Šortandy
Ermentau
Šiderti
EKIBA
Svetlyj
Sojuznoe
Aralköl
Pskovskij
Derzavinsk
Barankol
Novočerkasskoe
AKMOLA
Komsomol
Žabasak
Ladyzenka
Sabyndy
t. Akdym 899
Rodnikovskoe
Tasty-Taldy
Amantogaj
Amangeldi
Tyškanbaj
Taušyk
Arkalyk
Korgalžyn
Tengiz-Kurgalža ojpaty
Višnevka
Askarly
Molodežnyj
Tendik
Bajanaul
Kievka
Torgaj
Žylgasy
Torgaj
üst. Žylancykturme
Aktau
TEMIRTAU
Umitker
Korneevka
Ul'janovskij
Kalybaj
Duken
Rahmet
Koskol
t. Kakyl 570
Baršino
Zaharovka
Sagan
Aktaz
KARAGHANDY (KARAGANDA)
Šahtinsk
Saran
Abaj
Yrgyz
Nüra
Zban
Tau Šalkarnür
t. Atanbas 193
Betbulak
t. Akmola
t. Ülytau 1133
Ajnabulak
t. Ajgyrzal 803
Dar'inskij
t. Burkitti 1187
Nurataldy
Karkaraly
Karagaj
Aksu-Ajuly
Barsakum
K
A
Z
A
K
H
Kazakh Steppe
Atasu
Monadyr
Kyzylžar
Terekti
Žezdi
Bajkonyr
Karsakbaj
Satpaev
Žezkazgan
ŽEZKAZGAN
Agadyr'
t. Aksoran 1565
Aktogaj
t. Akbastöbe 116
Karažal
Bosaga
Akčatau
Aral
Aral karakümy
Aralsul'fat
Aralkum
Mojynkum
t. Egizkara 288
t. Köktöbe 372
Žetikonyr kum
t. Münly 790
Džambul
Mojynty
Kounradskij
Balkash
Balhaš
Novokazaly
Leninsk
Žusaly
Mojynkum
Betpak-Dala
Saryšagan
Karaoj
Kujgan
Akkol'
KYZYL-ORDA
Šymböget
Tasböget
ojpat Ašyköl
Sulutöbe
Ajdarly
t. Köksengir 171
Žuantöbe
Kamkaly
Ulanbel
Bajgakum
Šilli
Bakyrly
Zotakkum
Mojynkum
Mujunkum
Karabuget
Burubajtal
Topar
Tauku
Žel'tau
Ajtau
Tastop
Žanakorgan
Sozak
Algene mekeni
t. Bessaz 2176
Čulakkurgan
Bajkadam
Žanatas
Ujyk
Birlik
Kentau
Turkistan
Karatau
Akköl
Ču
Baltaköl
Šajan
Tortköl
Ekpindi
Assa
Mihajlovka
Kuragaty
Tatti
Blagoveščenka
Kamysanovka
Kopa
UZBEKISTAN
Bukantov toglari
t. Irlir 764
Kulkuduk
Juzkuduk
Marat
Turan Lowland
URAL MTS.
plato Üstirti
Torgaj Üstirti
Torgaj
+5h Gr. Time
+6h Gr. Time
74°+6h Gr. Time
+7h Gr.
97
114
127
137
Scale 1 : 4,500,000
0 40 80 120 160 200 Kilometers
0 40 80 120 160 Statute Miles

Scale 1 : 4,500,000

0 40 80 120 160 200 Kilometers

0 40 80 120 160 Statute Miles

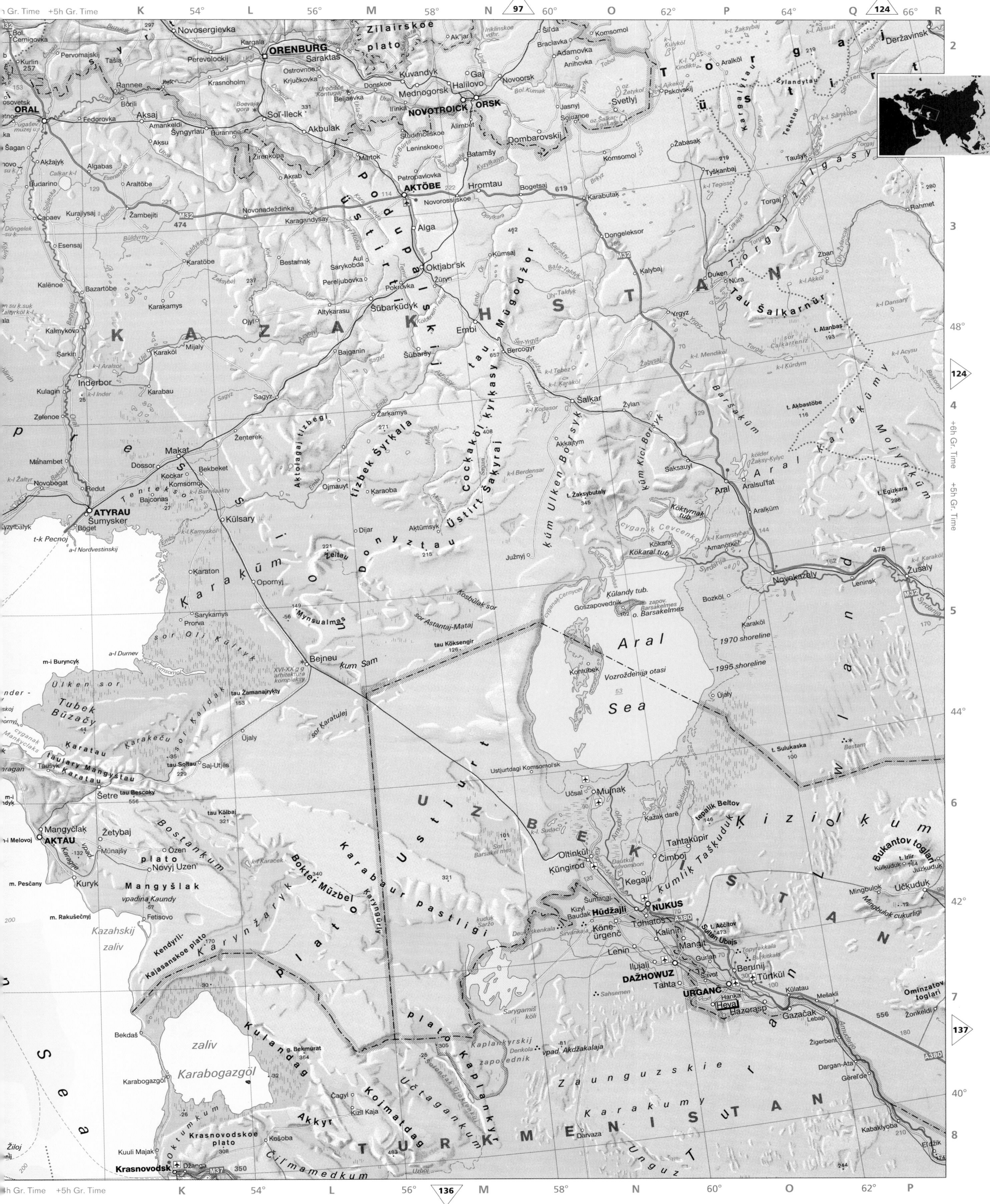

Scale 1 : 4,500,000 — 0 40 80 120 160 200 Kilometers — 0 40 80 120 160 Statute Miles

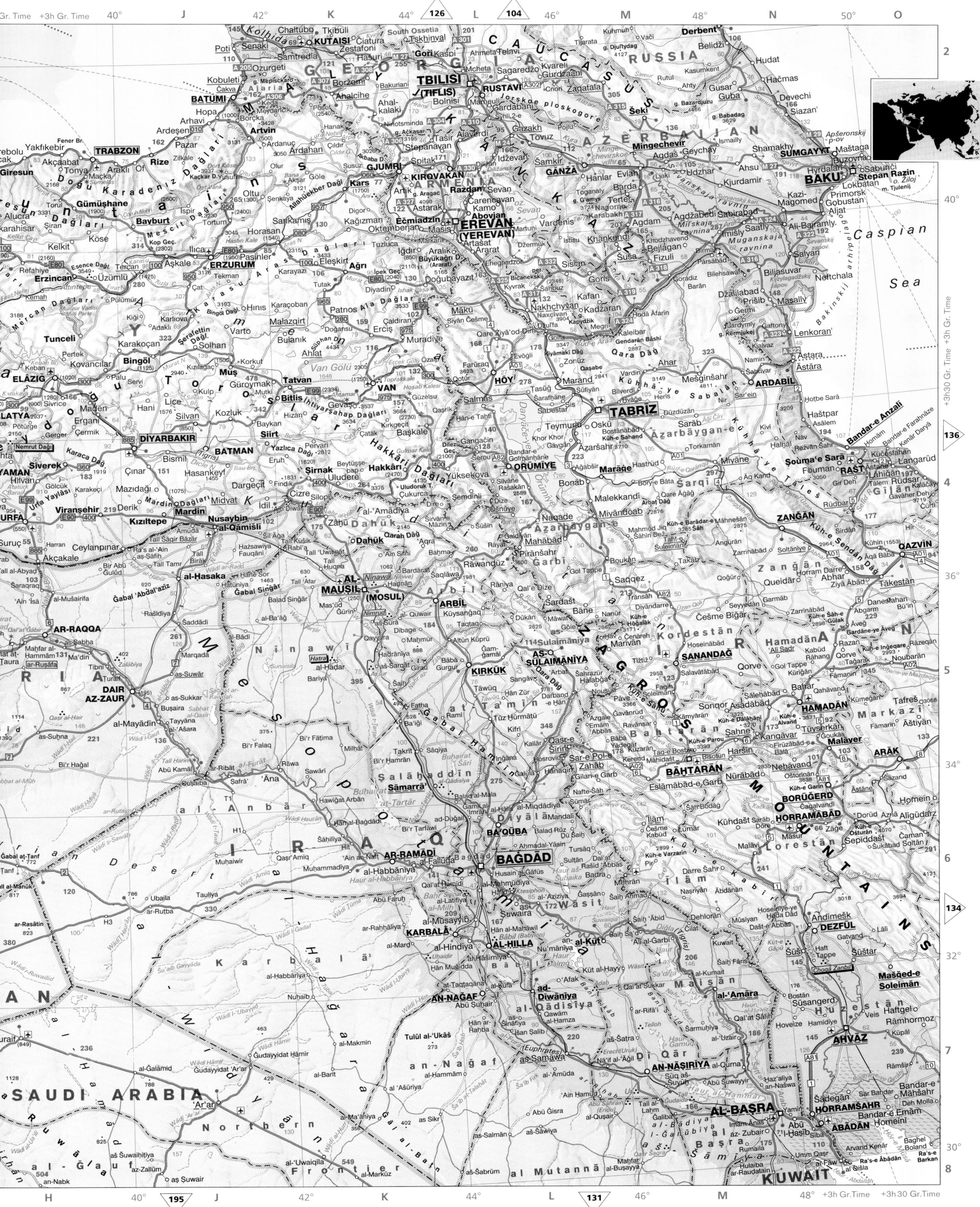

RUSSIA
GEORGIA
ARMENIA
AZERBAIJAN
CAUCASUS
Caspian Sea
TBILISI (TIFLIS)
KUTAISI
BATUMI
RUSTAVI
GJUMRI
KIROVAKAN
EREVAN (YEREVAN)
GĂNZĂ
BAKU
SUMGAYYT
Mingechevir
Derbent
TRABZON
ERZURUM
DIYARBAKIR
BATMAN
Van Gölü
VAN
TABRIZ
ARDABIL
ORŪMIYE
Bandar-e Anzali
RAŠT
ZANĞĀN
QAZVĪN
HAMADĀN
SANANDAĞ
BĀḪTARĀN
ARĀK
BORŪĞERD
ḪORRAMĀBĀD
DEZFŪL
AḪVĀZ
ḪORRAMŠAHR
ĀBĀDĀN
ZAGROS
MOUNTAINS
Kordestān
Lorestān
IRAQ
Mesopotamia
AL-MAUṢIL (MOSUL)
ARBĪL
AS-SULAIMĀNĪYA
KIRKŪK
BA'QŪBA
BAĠDĀD
AR-RAMĀDĪ
KARBALĀ'
AL-ḤILLA
AN-NAĞAF
AD-DĪWĀNĪYA
AL-KŪT
AL-'AMĀRA
AN-NĀṢIRĪYA
AL-BAṢRA
KUWAIT
SAUDI ARABIA
Northern Frontier
AR-RAQQA
DAIR AZ-ZAUR
Syrian Desert
al-Qāmišlī
Nusaybin
Mardin
URFA
Tigris
Euphrates

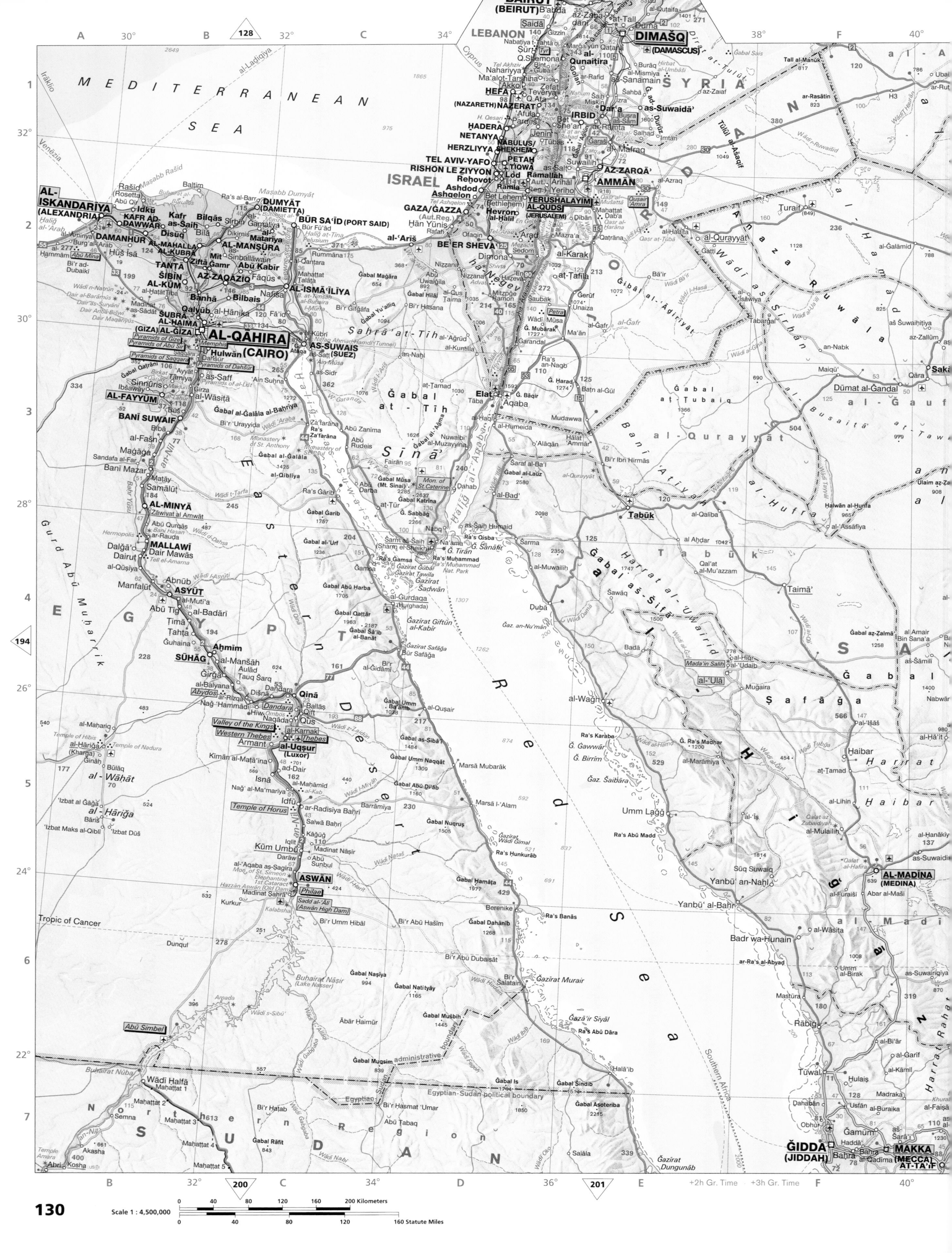

MEDITERRANEAN
SEA
LEBANON
BAIRUT
(BEIRUT)
DIMAŠQ
(DAMASCUS)
SYRIA
ISRAEL
HEFA
TEL AVIV-YAFO
YERUSHALAYIM
AL-QUDS
(JERUSALEM)
'AMMĀN
AZ-ZARQĀ'
IRBID
GAZA/ĠAZZA
BE'ER SHEVA'
AL-ISKANDARĪYA
(ALEXANDRIA)
DUMYĀT
(DAMIETTA)
BŪR SA'ĪD (PORT SAID)
AL-MANṢŪRA
ṬANṬĀ
AZ-ZAQĀZĪQ
AL-ISMĀ'ĪLĪYA
AL-QĀHIRA
(CAIRO)
AL-ĠĪZA
(GIZA)
AS-SUWAIS
(SUEZ)
Ḥulwān
AL-FAYYŪM
BANĪ SUWAIF
AL-MINYĀ
MALLAWĪ
ASYŪṬ
SŪHĀĠ
Qinā
al-Uqṣur
(Luxor)
ASWĀN
Sadd al-'Ālī
(Aswān High Dam)
Abū Simbel
Wādī Ḥalfā
Buḥairat Nāṣir
(Lake Nasser)
Tropic of Cancer
EGYPT
Eastern Desert
SUDAN
Northern Region
Sīnā'
Ǧabal at-Tīh
Elat
'Aqaba
Šarm aš-Šaiḫ
al-Ġurdaqa
(Hurghada)
Red Sea
Tabūk
Taimā'
al-Madīna
(MEDINA)
Yanbū' al-Baḥr
ĞIDDA
(JIDDAH)
MAKKA
(MECCA)
Ḥiǧāz
Ḥalā'ib
Egyptian-Sudan political boundary
Sudan administrative boundary
Scale 1 : 4,500,000
200 Kilometers
160 Statute Miles
+2h Gr. Time
+3h Gr. Time

BAĠDĀD
AR-RAMĀDĪ
al-Falluǧa
KARBALĀ'
AL-HILLA
al-Kūt
AN-NAĞAF
ad-Dīwānīya
al-'Amāra
AN-NĀṢIRĪYA
AL-BAṢRA
DEZFŪL
AHVĀZ
HORRAMŠAHR
ĀBĀDĀN
Behbahān
EṢFAHĀN
NAĞAFĀBĀD
Šahr-e Kord
Kāzerūn
BANDAR-E BŪŠEHR
Z A G R O S   M T S
KUWAIT
AL-KUWAIT
AL-ĠAHRA
Ḥafar al-Bāṭin
Rafḥā
Ḥā'il
BURAIDA
'Unaiza
AR-RIYĀḌ (RIYADH)
ad-Dawādimī
al-Ḫarǧ
AL-HUFŪF
Mubarraz
AD-DAMMĀM
AL-ḪUBAR
AZ-ZAHRĀN (DHAHRAN)
Ra's Tannūra
al-Ǧubail
AL-MANĀMA
BAHRAIN
AD-DAUḤA (DOHA)
QATAR
Persian Gulf
Eastern Province
Tropic of Cancer
Northern Frontier
a d - D i b d i b a
a ṣ - Ṣ u m m ā n
al - Ḥ a s ā '
N a f ū d   a d - D a ḥ ī
G a b a l   T u w a i q
al - Q a s s ī m
ar - R i y ā ḍ
M a k k a
+3h Gr. Time
+3h30 Gr. Time

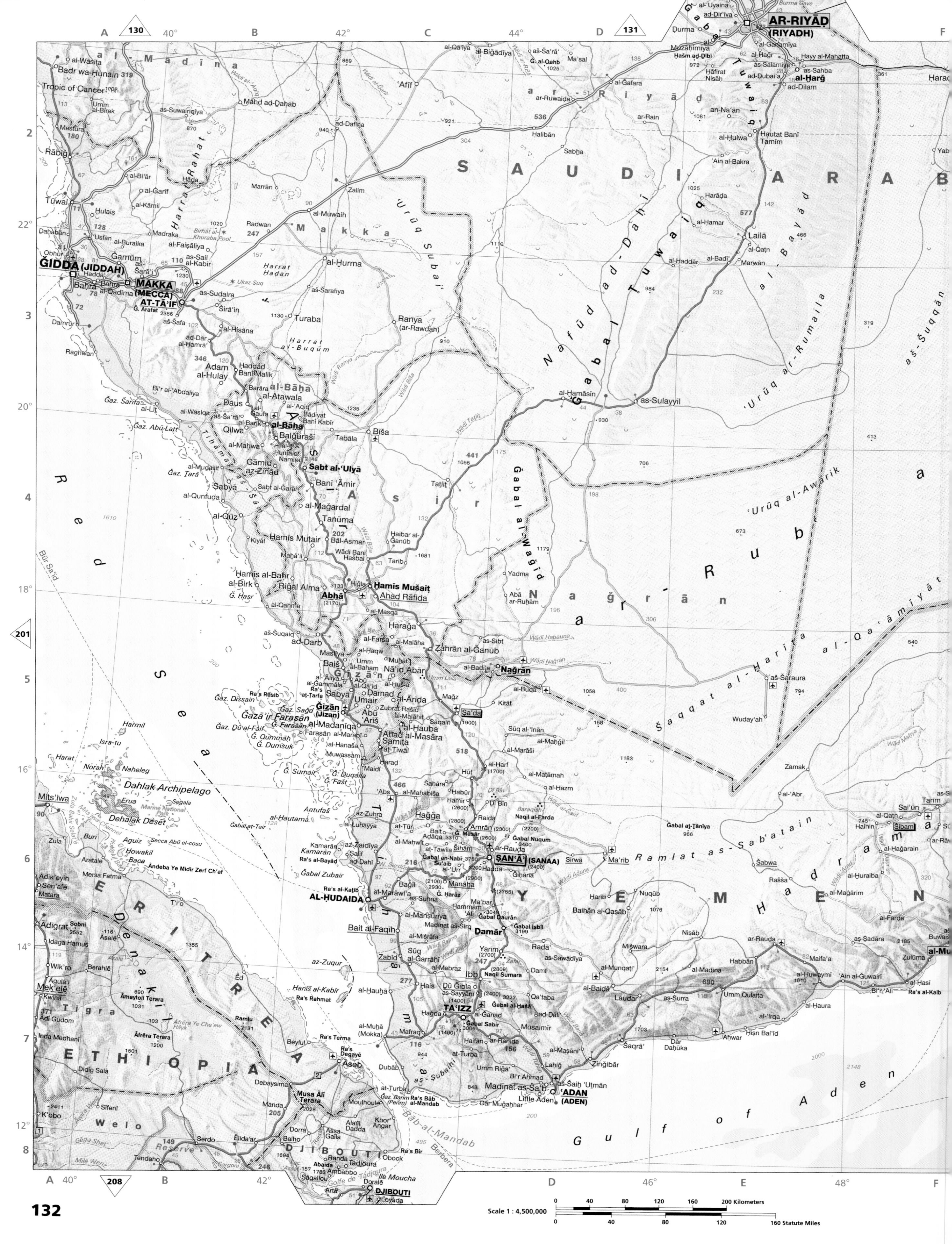

A
130
40°
B
42°
C
44°
D
131
F
AR-RIYĀD
(RIYADH)
al-ʿUyaina
ad-Dirʿiya
Burma Cave
Durma
Muzāhimiya
Ḥašm ad-Ḏibi
al-Ġanamiya
al-Ḥaǧr
Ḥayy al-Mahatta
as-Salamiya
as-Sahba
al-Ḫarǧ
ad-Dilam
Ḥāfirat Nisāḥ
ad-Dubaiʿa
Ġabal Ṭuwaiq
al-Wāsiṭa
Badr wa-Ḥunain
Tropic of Cancer
Umm al-Birak
al-Madina
Mahd ad-Dahab
ʿAfif
al-Qaʿiya
al-Biǧādiya
aš-Šaʿrāʾ
Ġ. al-Qahb
Maʿsal
al-Ġafara
ar-Ruwaida
ar-Riyāḍ
ar-Rain
an-Naʿān
Hautat Bani Tamim
al-Ḥulwa
as-Suwairqiya
Mastūra
Rābiġ
ad-Dafina
Halibān
Šabḥa
ʿAin al-Bakra
S A U D I   A R A B
Harrat Rahat
al-Biʾār
Hāda
al-Ġarif
al-Kāmil
Marrān
Zalim
al-Muwaih
Ṭūwal
Ḫulaiṣ
Dahabān
Radwan
Makka
Birhat al-Ḫurāba Pool
Madraka
ʿUsfān
al-Buraika
al-Faiṣāliya
ʿUrūq Subaiʿ
Harāḍa
al-Hamar
Lailā
al-Qaṭn
al-Badiʿ
Marwān
al-Haddār
Nafūd ad-Daḥi
Ġabal Ṭuwaiq
al-Bayāḍ
Obhur
Ġamūm
as-Sail al-Kabir
Harrat Haḍan
al-Ḥurma
ĠIDDA (JIDDAH)
MAKKA (MECCA)
AṬ-ṬĀʾIF
Ġ. Arafat
Haddā
Bahra
al-Qadima
ʿUkaz Suq
as-Sudaira
Sirā'in
aš-Šarafiya
Turaba
Ranya (ar-Rawdah)
aš-Šafa
Damrūr
al-Hisāna
ad-Dār al-Ḥamrāʾ
Harrat al-Buqūm
Raghwan
Adam al-Hulay
Haddād Bani Malik
Bi'r al-ʿAbdaliya
al-Bāha
Barāra
al-Aṭawala
Ġaz. Šarifa
al-Liṭ
al-Wāsiqa
Daus
al-ʿAqiq
Bādiyat Bani Kabir
Ġaz. Abū Laṭṭ
Qilwa
Balġurasi
Tabāla
Bīša
al-Mahwa
Ġāmid az-Zināḍ
Sabt al-ʿUlyā
Ġaz. Ṭarā
al-Muḏailif
Šabyā
Bani ʿĀmir
al-Qunfuḏa
al-Maġardal
al-Qūz
Tanūma
Bal-Asmar
Ḫamis Muṭair
Kiyāt
Maḥāʾil
Wādi Bani Hašbal
Haibar al-Ġanūb
Tariṯ
Ḫamis al-Baḥr
al-Birk
Riǧāl Alma
Ġ. Ḥasr
Abhā
Ḫamis Mušaiṭ
Ahad Rāfida
al-Qahma
al-Masqa
Harāǧa
aš-Šuqaiq
ad-Darb
Maslya
al-Farša
al-Mālaha
Zahrān al-Ġanūb
Umm
al-Haqw
Baiš
al-Baham
Muhāṭ
Nāʾid ʿAbār
Ǧizān
Sabyā
Umair
Ġaz. Dissain
Ra's Rāsib
Ġaz. Sagid
ĠIZĀN (Jizan)
Abū ʿAriš
Ġazāʾir Farasān
Farasān
Ġ. Qummah
Ġ. Dumsuk
Ḥarmil
Isra-tu
Harat
Norah
Naheleg
Dahlak Archipelago
Mits'iwa
Erua
Segala
Dehalak Desēt
Marine National Park
Zula
Buri
Aguiz
Howakil
Baca
Secca Abū el-cosu
Ândeba Ye Midir Zerf Ch'af
Aratale
Mersa Fatma
Ādik'eyih
Sen'afe
Matara
E R I T R E A
Denakil
Tropic of Cancer
Ādigrat
Sobni
Āsalē
Idaga Hamus
Wik'ro
Berahlē
Mek'elē
Kwiha
Ādi Gudom
Tigra
Inda Medhani
Āmaytoli Terara
Āfrēra Terara
Ramlu
Āfrēra Ye Che'ew Hāyk'
E T H I O P I A
Didig Sala
Sifenī
K'obo
Welo
Serdo
Tendaho
Ēlida'ar
Debaysima
Manda
Musa Ālī Terara
Balho
Dorra
Assa Gaila
Alaili Dadda
Khor Angar
Obock
Ra's Bir
DJIBOUTI
Randa
Tadjoura
Golfe de Tadjoura
Ille Moucha
Dorale
Abaida
Sāgallou
Arta
Loyada
Bāb-al-Mandab
Berbera
Red Sea
Būr Safīd
Ġabal aṭ-Ṭair
az-Zuqur
Ḥaniš al-Kabir
Ra's Rahmat
Antufaš
Kamarān
Ra's al-Bayāḍ
Ġabal Zubair
Ra's al-Kaṯib
AL-ḤUDAIDA
Bait al-Faqih
Zabīd
al-Hauḫa
al-Mūḫa (Mokka)
Ra's Terma
Ra's Degayē
Āseb
Ḏubāb
Mafraq
Ḥais
Ġaz. Barim (Perim)
Ra's Bāb al-Mandab
Tihāma
Nuǧrān
Naǧrān
Yadma
Abā ar-Ruhām
Wādi Habauna
Wādi Naǧrān
al-Badiʿa
aš-Šaraura
al-Buqaʿ
Kitāf
Ṣaʿda
Sāqain
Sūq al-Inān
al-Mahǧil
al-Marāši
al-Harf
al-Maṭamah
Ḥūṯ
al-Ḥazm
Dī Bīn
Baraqiš
Ḥabūr
Hamir
Raida
Amrān
Naqil al-Farda
Ḥaǧǧa
Ġabal Nuqum
Ṣiḥām
ar-Rauḍa
ṢANʿĀʾ (SANAA)
Sirwāḥ
Maʾrib
Ramlat as-Sabʿatain
Ġabal an-Nabi Šuʿaib
Ḥadda
Ḡihāna
Manāḫa
Y E M E N
Ḥadramaut
Ḥarib
Nuqūb
Baiḥān al-Qaṣab
Maʿbar
Ḏamār
Ġabal Isbil
Yarim
Radāʿ
as-Sawādiya
Ibb
Naqil Sumara
Damt
al-Munqaṭiʿ
al-Baiḍā
Ḏū Ǧibla
Qaʿṭaba
TAʿIZZ
Ġabal al-Ḥašāʾ
Ġabal Ṣabir
al-Ġanad
ad-Dāliʿ
Musaimir
Laḥiǧ
al-Masāni
Zinǧibār
Šuqrāʾ
Dār Daḥūka
Madinat aš-Šaʿb
Bir Aḥmad
aš-Šaiḫ ʿUṯmān
ʿADAN (ADEN)
Little Aden
Dār Muġaḫhar
Gulf of Aden
Laudar
aš-Šurra
Umm Qulaita
al-Haura
al-ʿIrqa
Aḥwar
Ḥiṣn Balʿid
Ḥabbān
al-Madina
Miṣwara
Nisāb
ar-Rauḍa
aš-Šadāra
Maifaʿa
al-Ḥuwaymi
ʿAin al-Ġuwairi
Bir ʿAli
Ra's al-Kalb
Zulūma
al-Mukalla
al-Ḥasi
al-Farda
al-Maġārim
al-Ḥuraiba
Raššā
Šabwa
al-Haǧarain
Sayʿūn
Tarim
Šibām
Ḥainin
al-Qaṭn
Zamak
al-ʿAbr
Wādi Maḥyā
Wuday'ah
Šaqqat al-Ḫarīṭa
al-Qaʿāmiyāt
Rubʿ al-Ḫāli
Nafūd
ʿUrūq al-Awārik
ʿUrūq ar-Rumaila
aš-Šuqqān
as-Sulayyil
al-Ḥamāsin
Wādi Taṯliṯ
Taṯliṯ
Ġabal al-Wāǧid
Wādi Bīša
Wādi Ranya
Wādi Tabāla
201
208
45°
46°
48°
E
Scale 1 : 4,500,000
0 40 80 120 160 200 Kilometers
0 40 80 120 160 Statute Miles

ABŪ ZABĪ
(ABU DHABI)
AL-'AIN
Ṣuḥār
Matrah
Masqaṭ (Muscat)
Ruwi
Tropic of Cancer
UNITED ARAB EMIRATES
Baynūna
az-Ẓafra
al-Ǧabal al-Aḫḍar
Nazwā
Bahla
Ḥaǧar aš-Šarqī
Ṣūr
Ramlat al-Wahība
ar-Rabbāḍ
al-Kidan
Umm as-Samīm
Ramlat al-Ǧāfa
Eastern Province
as-Sanām
al-Maḥākik
al-Miḥrāḍ
'Urūq Hibāka
Ḫālī
al-Hibāk
Sabḫat al-'Urūq al-Mu'tariḍa
al-Ḥuqf
Ǧiddat al-Ḥarāsīs
ad-Dikāka
OMAN
Ǧazīrat Maṣīra
Gulf of Maṣīra
Duqm
Ra's Madraka
Sauqira Bay
Arabian Sea
Ẓufār
Ǧabal al-Qarā
Ṣalāla
Mirbāṭ
Ǧazā'ir Ḥuriyā Muriyā
(al-Ḥallānīyāt)
Ǧabal Marat
al-Mahra
Ra's Fartak
INDIAN OCEAN
Ṣuquṭrā (Yemen)
(Socotra)
'Abd al-Kūrī
The Brothers
Samḥa
Darza
+3h Gr. Time
+4h Gr. Time
Karachi
Bombay
Goa
Masqaṭ
Mugdisho
50°
52°
54°
56°
58°
60°
12°
14°
16°
18°
20°
22°
G
H
J
K
L
134
135
209

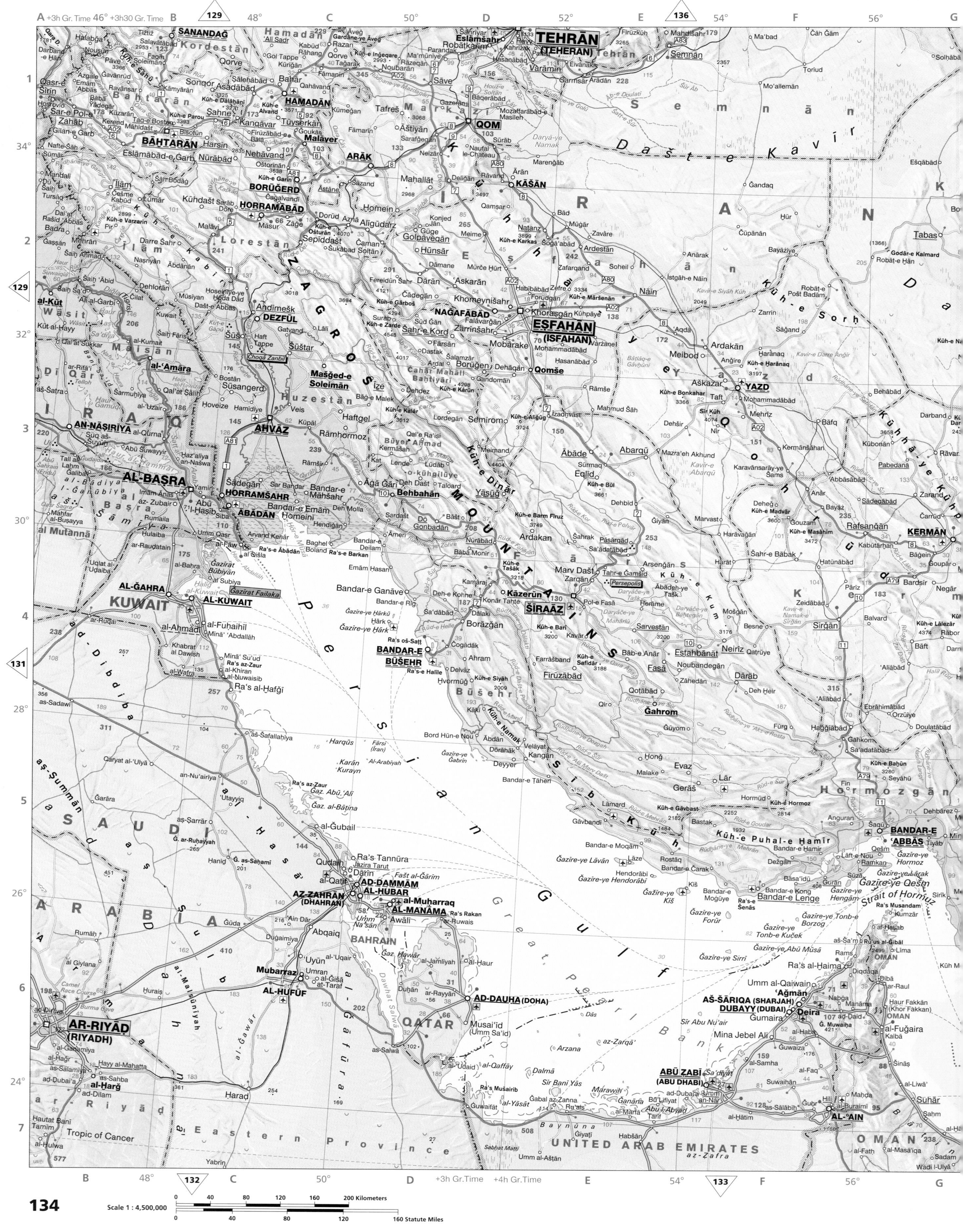

A +3h Gr. Time 46° +3h30 Gr. Time B
129
48°
C
50°
D
52°
E
136
54°
F
56°
G
TEHRĀN
(TEHERAN)
SANANDAĞ
Kordestān
Hamadān
HAMADĀN
BĀHTARĀN
Bāhtarān
QOM
Markazi
ARĀK
KĀŠĀN
Semnān
Dašt-e Kavīr
BORŪĞERD
HORRAMĀBĀD
Lorestān
Īlām
IRAN
DEZFŪL
Šūštar
AHVĀZ
Huzestān
ZAGROS MOUNTAINS
EṢFAHĀN
(ISFAHAN)
NAĞAFĀBĀD
YAZD
Nā'īn
KERMĀN
Kūh-e Sorḫ
Kūhhā-ye Qohrūd
al-Kūt
Wāsit
al-'Amāra
Maisān
AN-NĀṢIRIYA
IRAQ
AL-BAṢRA
HORRAMŠAHR
ĀBĀDĀN
Abū l-Ḫaṣīb
Bandar-e Emām Homeinī
Behbahān
al-Fāw
AL-ĠAHRA
AL-KUWAIT
KUWAIT
al-Aḥmadī
Ġazīrat Failaka
Ġazīrat Būbiyān
Persepolis
ŠĪRĀZ
Kāzerūn
BANDAR-E BŪŠEHR
Būšehr
Fārs
Persian Gulf
Ra's al-Ḫafǧī
ad-Dibdiba
aṣ-Ṣummān
SAUDI ARABIA
al-Ḥasā
Ra's Tannūra
AD-DAMMĀM
AZ-ZAHRĀN
(DHAHRAN)
AL-HUBAR
al-Muḥarraq
AL-MANĀMA
BAHRAIN
Abqaiq
Mubarraz
AL-HUFŪF
AR-RIYĀḌ
(RIYADH)
al-Ḫarǧ
QATAR
AD-DAUHA (DOHA)
Dawḥat Salwā
al-Ǧāfūra
Great Pearl Bank
Kūh-e Puhal-e Hamīr
Hormozgān
BANDAR-E 'ABBĀS
Ġazīre-ye Qešm
Strait of Hormuz
Ra's Musandam
OMAN
Ra's al-Ḫaima
Umm al-Qaiwain
AŠ-ŠĀRIQA (SHARJAH)
DUBAYY (DUBAI)
Deira
al-Fuǧaira
ABŪ ẒABĪ
(ABU DHABI)
AL-'AIN
Ṣuḥār
UNITED ARAB EMIRATES
Eastern Province
Tropic of Cancer
Sirǧān
Lār
Darāb
Fasā
Neiriz
Ardakān
Kāšān
34°
32°
30°
28°
26°
24°
1
2
3
4
5
6
7
129
131
B
48°
132
C
50°
D +3h Gr.Time +4h Gr.Time
E
54°
133
F
56°
G
Scale 1 : 4,500,000
0 40 80 120 160 200 Kilometers
0 40 80 120 160 Statute Miles

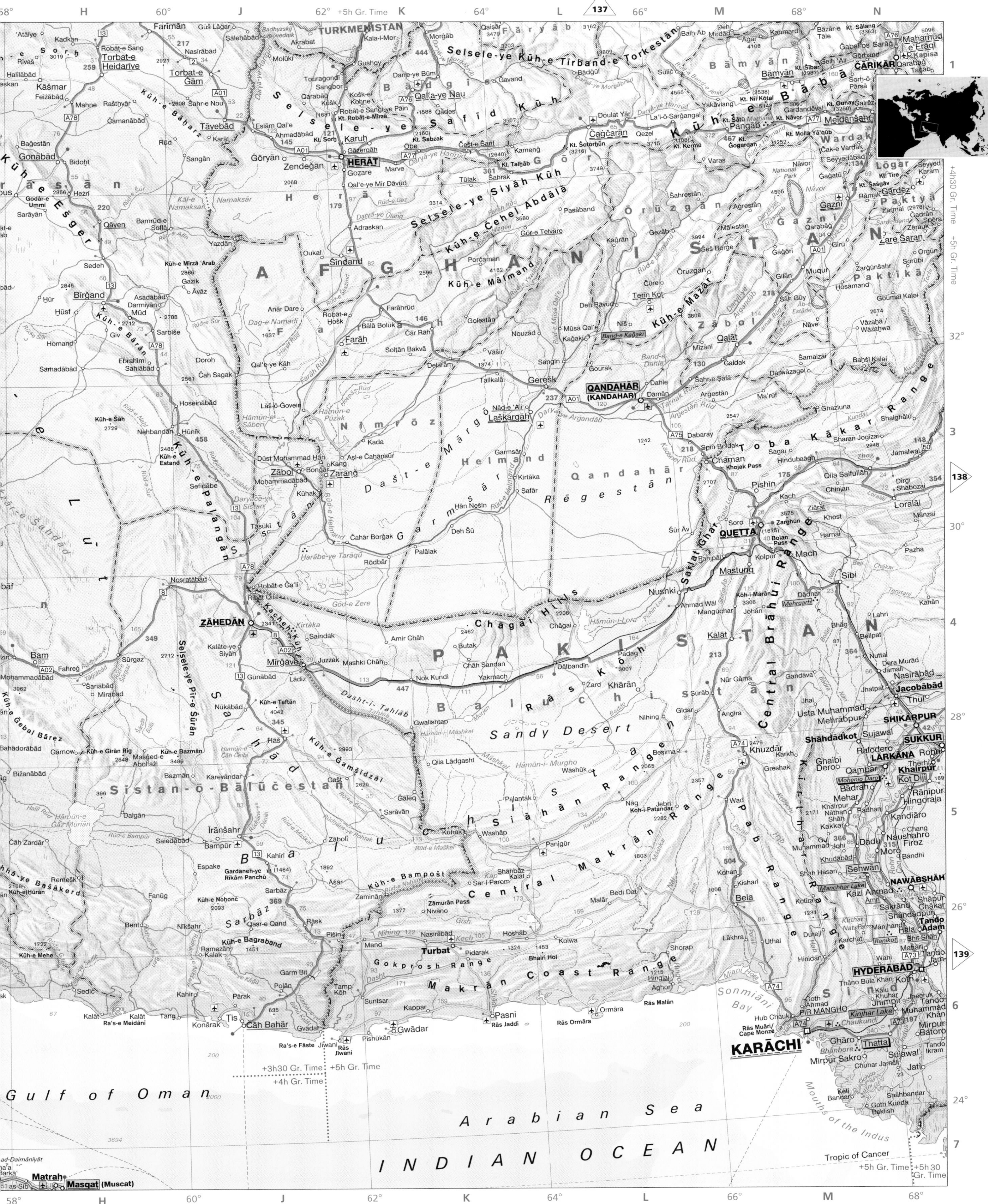

TURKMENISTAN
AFGHANISTAN
PAKISTAN
Sīstan-ō-Bālūčestan
Selsele-ye Kūh-e Tīrband-e Torkestān
Selsele-ye Safīd Kūh
Kūh-e Bābā
Selsele-ye Siyāh Kūh
Kūh-e Čehel Abdālā
Kūh-e Mālmand
Kūh-e Mazār
Kūh-e Bāharz
Kūh-e Bārān
Kūh-e Palangān
Kacheh Kūh
Selsele-ye Pīr-e Šūrān
Kūh-e Gamšīdzāī
Kūh-e Bampošt
Kūh-e Taftān
Herāt
Nīmrōz
Helmand
Qandahār
Rēgestān
Dašt-e Mārgō
Garmsār
Zābol
Oruzgān
Ğaznī
Paktīā
Paktīkā
Wardak
Bāmyān
Bādgīs
Fārāb
Ğōr
Farāh
Sīstān
Dašt-e Lūt
Sarhadd
Baluchistan
Chāgai Hills
Rās Kōh
Sandy Desert
Siāhān Range
Central Makrān Range
Makrān Coast Range
Gokprosh Range
Toba Kākar Range
Central Brāhui Range
Kīrthar Range
Pab Range
Sind
HERĀT
QANDAHĀR (KANDAHAR)
QUETTA
ZĀHEDĀN
KARĀCHI
HYDERĀBĀD
SUKKUR
LĀRKĀNA
SHIKĀRPUR
NAWĀBSHĀH
ČĀRĪKĀR
Masqat (Muscat)
Matrah
Gulf of Oman
Arabian Sea
INDIAN OCEAN
Sonmiāni Bay
Mouths of the Indus
Tropic of Cancer
+5h Gr. Time
+4h30 Gr. Time
+3h30 Gr. Time
+4h Gr. Time
+5h30 Gr. Time
58° H 60° J 62° K 64° L 66° M 68° N
137
138
139

Scale 1 : 4,500,000

0 40 80 120 160 200 Kilometers

0 40 80 120 160 Statute Miles

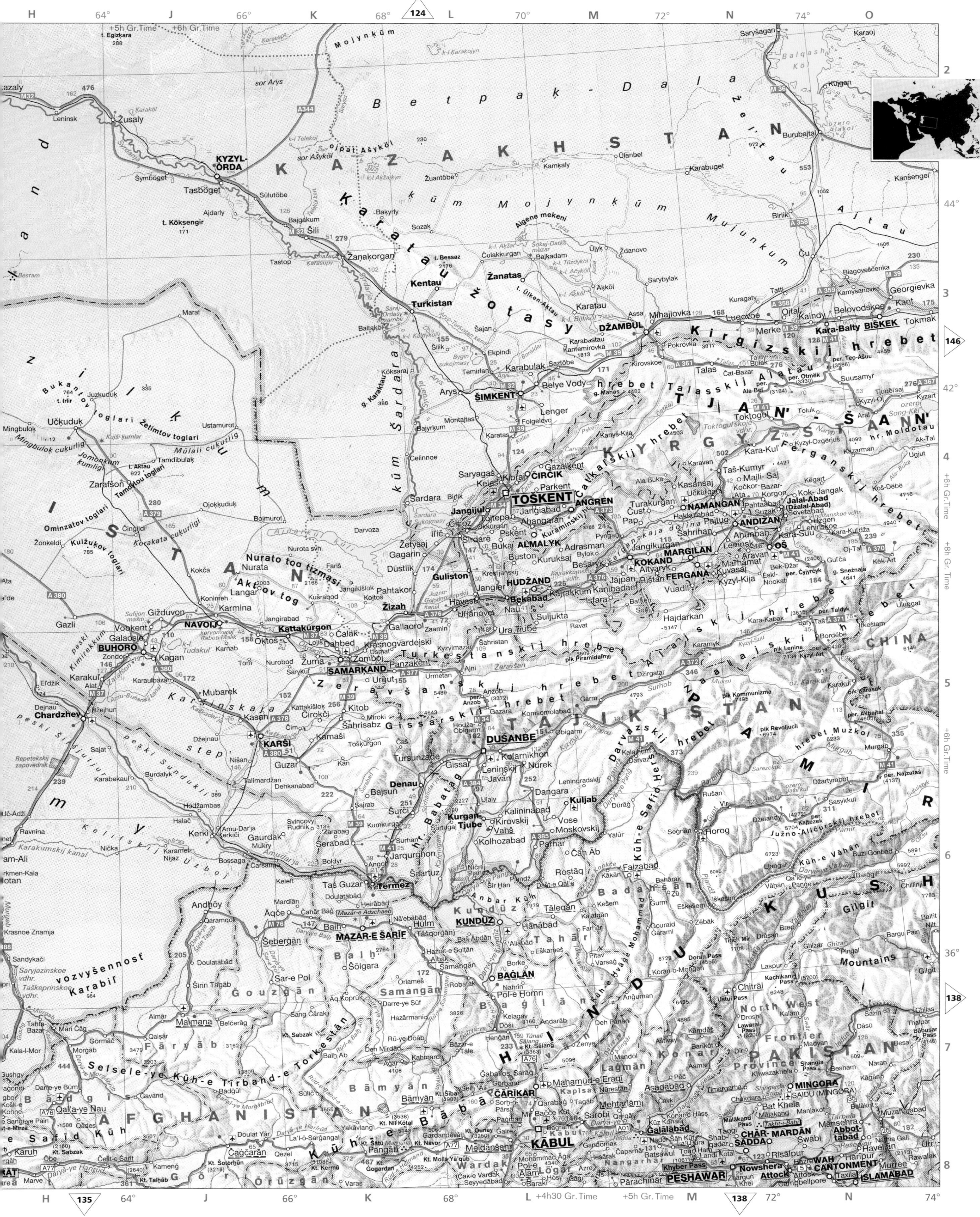
KAZAKHSTAN
Betpak-Dala
Mojynkum
Karatau
Kyzylkum
UZBEKISTAN
KIRGIZSTAN
TJAN'-ŠAN'
TAJIKISTAN
PAMIR
AFGHANISTAN
PAKISTAN
CHINA
HINDU KUSH
Kirgizskij hrebet
Fergans kij hrebet
Alajskij hrebet
Turkestanskij hrebet
Zeravšanskij hrebet
Gissarskij hrebet
Talasskij Alatau
Kūh-e Bābā
Selsele-ye Kūh-e Tirband-e Torkestān
KYZYL-ORDA
DŽAMBUL
BIŠKEK
ŠIMKENT
TOŠKENT
NAMANGAN
ANDIŽAN
FERGANA
KOKAND
MARGILAN
OŠ
HUDŽAND
SAMARKAND
BUHORO
NAVOIJ
KARŠI
DUŠANBE
Turkistan
Termez
MAZĀR-E ŠARĪF
KUNDŪZ
BAGLĀN
KĀBUL
ČĀRĪKĀR
PESHAWAR
ISLAMABAD
MINGORA
Chardzhev
Kurgan-Tjube
Kuljab
Horog
Jalal-Abad
Kara-Balty
Tokmak
+5h Gr.Time
+6h Gr.Time
+8h Gr. Time
+4h30 Gr. Time
H
J
K
L
M
N
O
64°
66°
68°
70°
72°
74°
42°
44°
36°
124
135
138
146

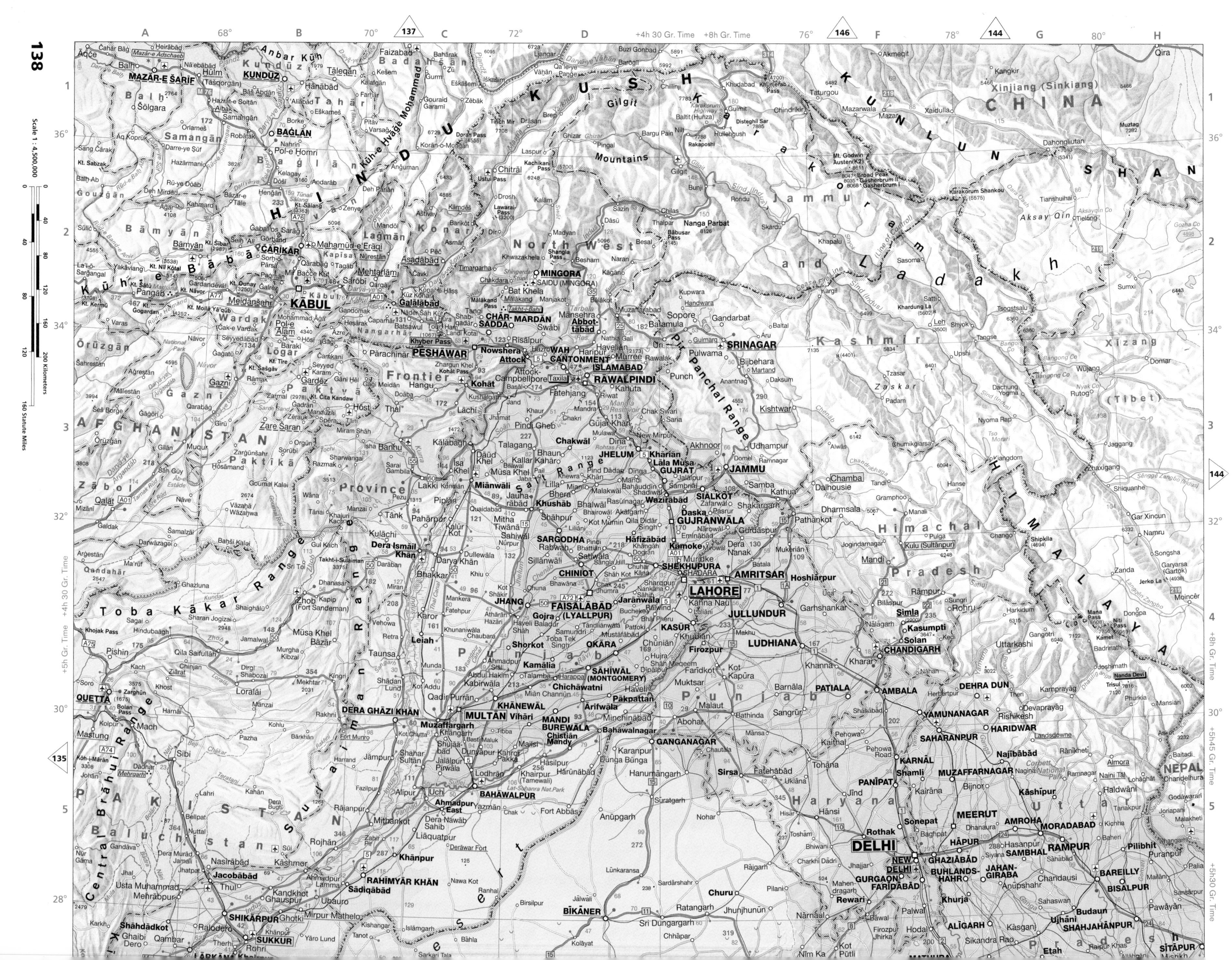

Scale 1 : 4,500,000
0 40 80 120 160 200 Kilometers
0 40 80 120 160 Statute Miles
+4h 30 Gr. Time
+8h Gr. Time
+5h Gr. Time
+5h45 Gr. Time
+5h30 Gr. Time
137
146
144
135
CHINA
Xinjiang (Sinkiang)
Xizang
(Tibet)
NEPAL
AFGHANISTAN
PAKISTAN
Kashmir
Jammu and Ladakh
Himachal Pradesh
Punjab
Haryana
Uttar Pradesh
North West Frontier Province
Baluchistan
HIMALAYA
KUNLUN SHAN
HINDU KUSH
Karakoram
Gilgit
Mountains
Pir Panjal Range
Salt Range
Sulaiman Range
Toba Kakar Range
Central Brahui Range
Nanga Parbat
SRINAGAR
JAMMU
ISLAMABAD
RAWALPINDI
PESHAWAR
KĀBUL
LAHORE
AMRITSAR
JULLUNDUR
LUDHIANA
CHANDIGARH
AMBALA
PATIALA
DELHI
NEW DELHI
MEERUT
MORADABAD
BAREILLY
SHAHJAHANPUR
ALIGARH
DEHRA DUN
HARIDWAR
SAHARANPUR
MUZAFFARNAGAR
FAISALABAD (LYALLPUR)
GUJRANWALA
SIALKOT
SARGODHA
JHANG
MULTAN
BAHAWALPUR
DERA GHAZI KHAN
Dera Ismail Khan
QUETTA
SUKKUR
SHIKARPUR
Jacobabad
BIKANER
Sirsa
GANGANAGAR
KUNDUZ
MAZAR-E SARIF
BAGLAN
CARIKAR
Bamyan
Gazni
Kohat
Bannu
MINGORA
Chitral
Simla

Arabian Sea
Gulf of Kachchh
Gulf of Khambhat
Rann of Kachchh
Tropic of Cancer
Kāthiāwār Peninsula
KARĀCHI
HYDERĀBĀD
BOMBAY
AHMADĀBĀD
VADODARA
SURAT
RĀJKOT
JĀMNAGAR
PORBANDAR
BHAVNAGAR
JODHPUR
AJMER
UDAIPUR
KOTA
GWALIOR
JHĀNSI
KANPUR
SĀGAR
JABALPUR
BHOPĀL
INDORE
UJJAIN
NĀGPUR
NĀSHIK
PUNE
AURANGĀBĀD

For continuation see main map
Arabian Sea
INDIA
Mūlki
Suratkal
MANGALORE
Ullāl
Puttur
Kumbla
Kāsaragod
Hosdrug
Payyānnur
Chetlat I.
Amīndīvi Is.
Cardamum I.
Androth I.
Agatti I.
Kavaratti
Lakshadweep
Cannanore Is.
Kalpeni I.
Nine Degree Channel
Minicoy I.
Eight Degree Channel
+5h30 Gr. Time
+5h Gr. Time
Ihavandiffulu Atoll
Makunudu Atoll
Tiladummati Atoll
Miladummadulu Atoll
North Malosmadulu Atoll
Fadiffolu Atoll
South Malosmadulu Atoll
Horsburgh Atoll
Kardiva Channel
North Male Atoll
Male
Ari Atoll
South Male Atoll
Felidu Atoll
North Nilandu Atoll
South Nilandu Atoll
Mulaku Atoll
Kolumadulu Atoll
Veimandu Channel
Haddumati Atoll
Suvadiva Atoll
MALDIVES
Sea
Maldives
Srīvardhan
Mahād
Wai
Mahābaleshwar
Sātāra
Dāpoli
Khed
Dābhol
Guhāgar
Chiplūn
Karād
Sangameshwar
Ratnāgiri
Sangli
Miraj
Ichalkaranji
Kolhāpur
Bārāmati
Phaltan
Pandharpur
Solāpur
Akalkot
Bijāpur
Nate
Vijayadurg
Mālvan
Vengurla
Belgaum
Māpuca
Panaji
Marmagao
Madgaon
Goa
Cape Rama
Kārwār
Ankola
Kumta
Honāvar
Bhatkal
Coondapoor
Udupi
Dharwad
Hubli
Gadag
Hospet
Haliyāl
Dandeli
Sirsi
Hāvēri
Rānībennur
Harihar
Dāvangere
Shikārpur
Sāgar
Shimoga
Bhadrāvati
Tarikere
Chikmagalūr
Narasimharajapura
Kārkal
Hassan
Sakleshpur
Madikeri
Kalpetta
Cannanore
Mahe
Badagara
Calicut (Kozhikode)
Quilandi
Tirūrangani
Ponnāni
Chavakkad
Kerala
Ernakulam
Cochin
Alleppey
Quilon
Trivandrum
Arabian Sea
Malabar Coast
Western Ghats
Laccadive Sea
Lakshadweep Sea
INDIAN OCEAN
For continuation see inset at left
Scale 1 : 4,500,000
0 40 80 120 160 200 Kilometers
0 40 80 120 160 Statute Miles

HYDERĀBĀD
Secunderābād
WARANGAL
RĀJAHMUNDRY
KĀKINĀDA
VIJAYAWĀDA
ELŪRU
BHĪMAVARAM
GUNTUR
TENĀLI
MACHILĪPATNAM
Ongole
KURNOOL
ĀDONI
PRODDATŪR
CUDDAPAH
NELLORE
TIRUPATI
CHITTOOR
MADRAS
Tāmbaram
KĀNCHIPURAM
VELLORE
PONDICHERRY
CUDDALORE
SALEM
ERODE
TIRUPPUR
KUMBAKONAM
THANJAVUR
TIRUCHIRAPPALLI
DINDIGUL
MADURAI
TUTICORIN
TIRUNELVELI
PALAYANKOTTAI
NĀGERCOIL
Cape Comorin
Gulf of Mannar
Palk Strait
Coromandel Coast
Eastern Ghats
Bay of Bengal
Andaman and Nicobar Islands
SRI LANKA
JAFFNA
Point Pedro
Trincomalee
Anuradhapura
Polonnaruwa
Batticaloa
KANDY
COLOMBO
MORATUWA
Negombo
Galle
Matara
Hambantota
Adam's Peak
MYANMAR (BURMA)
Bogale
Labutta
Erāwadī Myitwanā
Great Coco Island
Coco Channel
+5h30 Gr. Time
+6h30 Gr. Time
North Andaman
Middle Andaman
South Andaman
Andaman Is.
Port Blair
Little Andaman
Duncan Passage
Ten Degree Channel
Andaman Sea
Andaman Basin
Nicobar Islands (India)
Car Nicobar I.
Great Nicobar Island
Indira Point
+5h30 Gr. Time
+7h Gr. Time
Banda Aceh (Baiturahman)
INDONESIA
SUMATRA
INDIAN OCEAN

A
+5h30 Gr.T.
80°
+5h45 Gr.Time
B
82°
144
C
+5h45 Gr.Time
84°
+8h Gr.Time
D
86°
E
88°
F
1
2
3
4
5
6
7
28°
26°
24°
22°
20°
18°
138
139
Xizang (Tibet)
CHINA
HIMALAYA
NEPAL
Churia Range
Uttar Pradesh
Awadh
Bihar
Baghelkhand Plateau
Madhya Pradesh
Chhattisgarh
Orissa
INDIA
Andhra Pradesh
West Bengal
BANGLADESH
Rajmahal Hills
Ranchi Plateau
Khondmal Hills
Bay of Bengal
Mouths of the Ganges
Sundarbans National Park
Royal Chitawan Nat. P.
Sagarmatha National Park
Dhaulagiri Himal
Annapurna Himal
Qomolangma F. Sagarmatha (Mt. Everest)
Kanchenjunga
KATHMANDU
Bhaktapur
Lalitpur
Pokhara
Biratnagar
Thimphu
Gangtok
Darjiling
SHILIBURI
Jalpaiguri
RAMPUR
Pilibhit
BAREILLY
BISALPUR
Budaun
SHAHJAHANPUR
Lakhimpur
SĪTĀPUR
Bahraich
FARRUKHĀBĀD
Gonda
ETAWAH
LUCKNOW
FAIZĀBĀD
Basti
GORAKHPUR
Padrauna
Bettiah
Motihari
KANPUR
Orai
Hamirpur
Fatehpur
Sultanpur
Azamgarh
Mau
MUZAFFARPUR
DARBHANGA
Saharsa
Kishanganj
Rāth
Bānda
ALLAHĀBĀD
VĀRĀNASI
JAUNPUR
Ghāzīpur
Ballia
CHAPRA
ARA
PATNA
Hazipur
Chhatarpur
Khajurāho
Panna
MIRZAPUR
Sasarām
Dehri
GAYA
Mokāma
BHĀGALPUR
KATIHAR
Satna
REWA
Aurangābād
Nawāda
Deoghar
Dumka
Damoh
MURWĀRA
Dāltenganj
Hazāribāg
DHANBĀD
Asansol
DURGAPUR
JABALPUR
Mandla
Shahdol
Ambikāpur
RANCHI
BARDDHAMĀN
Bānkura
JAMSHEDPUR
CHUNCHURA
HAORA
CALCUTTA
Seoni
BILĀSPUR
Raigarh
RAURKELA
Medinipur
KHARAGPUR
Haldia
Diamond Harbour
GONDIA
Bhandāra
BHILAIN-AGAR
RAIPUR
DURG
Rāj-Nāndgaon
SAMBALPUR
Jhārsuguda
Deogarh
Baleshwar
Bhadrak
Dhamtari
Balangīr
Anugul
Dhenkānāl
KATAKA
BHUBANESHWAR
PURI
Konārak
Ashika
BRAHMAPUR
Jagdalpur
JEYPORE
Rāyagada
VIZIANAGARAM
Srikakulam
VISHĀKHAPATNAM
Anakāpalle
Kottagūdem
RAJAHMUNDRY
KAKINĀDA
ELURU
VIJAYAWADA
BHIMAVARAM
KHULNA
JESSORE
PABNA
RAJSHAHI
RANGPUR
SAIDPUR
DHUBURI
+5h30 Gr. Time
+6h Gr. Time
B
141
82°
C
84°
D
86°
E
88°
F
Scale 1 : 4,500,000
0 40 80 120 160 200 Kilometers
0 40 80 120 160 Statute Miles

LHASA
Nyingchi
Medog
Rawu
98°
145
L
100°
M
Zhowagoin
Dêqên
Meili Xue Shan
Pangzulа
Zhongdian
Sichuan
Hengduan Shan
Gaoligong Shan
Nu Shan
Yun Ling
Mianmian Shan
Jinsha Jiang
Yulong Xue Shan
Lijiang
Yongsheng
Huaping
Jianchuan
Heqing
Yunnan
Dayao
Yunlong
Caojian
DALI
Midu
Nanhua
Baoshan
Tengchong
Lianghe
Longling
Changning
Luxi
CHINA
Yunxian
Jingdong
Lincang
Zhenyuan
Zhenkang
Gengma
Tropic of Cancer
Shuangjiang
Jinggu
Cangyuan
Pu'er
Simao
Lancang
Xishuangbanna
Menglian
Jinghong
Menghai
Menglong
156
1
2
3
4
5
26°
24°
22°
Arunachal Pradesh
Rawu
Bruinio
Mainling
Nang Xian
Gyaca
Qusum
Zhanang
Zetang
Gonggar
Qonggyai
Hkakabo Razi
Walung
Dong
Tazungdan
Putao
Langtao
Kumon Taungdan
Shanngaw Taungdan
Myitkyina
Mogaung
Bhamo
Ruili
Namtu
Lashio
Hsipaw
Kyaukme
Mogok
Möng Mit
MANDALAY
Maymyo
AMARAPURA
SUGAING
Ava
Kyaukse
Myittha
Meiktila
Taunggyi
Inle L.
Heho
Kalaw
Yamethin
Pyinmana
Toungoo
Pyu
Kyaikto
Pegu
YANGON (RANGOON)
Syriam
Thaton
MYANMAR (BURMA)
Monywa
Shwebo
Katha
Mawlaik
Kalewa
Kalemyo
Tiddim
Falam
Haka
Gangaw
MYINGYAN
PAKOKKU
Pagan
Chauk
Yenangyaung
MINBU
Magwe
Thayetmyo
PROME
Henzada
PUTHEIN (BASSEIN)
SANDOWAY
Taungup
Ramree
SITTWE (AKYAB)
Paletwa
Kyauktaw
Arakan Yoma
DIBRUGARH
Digboi
North Lakhimpur
Itanagar
Sibsagar
Jorhat
Golaghat
Tezpur
GUWAHATI
Dispur
Nagaon
BARPETA
GOALPARA
SHILLONG
Khasi-Jaintia Hills
Kohima
Dimapur
Nagaland
Manipur
IMPHAL
Silchar
Karimganj
SYLHET
Tripura
AGARTALA
DHAKA
COMILLA
Mizoram
Aizawl
Lunglei
Feni
CHITTAGONG
Cox's Bazar
Kaptai
Rangamati
Bandarban
Bhairab Bazar
MYMENSINGH
Brahmaputra
Manas Wildl. Sanc.
Kaziranga Nat. Park
LAOS
Chiang Rai
Chiang Mai
Lampang
Mae Hong Son
Mae Sai
Phayao
Nan
Phrae
Uttaradit
Sukhothai
Tak
PHITSANULOK
Phichit
Kamphaeng Phet
THAILAND
Salween
Mekong
Irrawaddy
G
92°
H
94°
J
96°
K
98°
158
L
100°

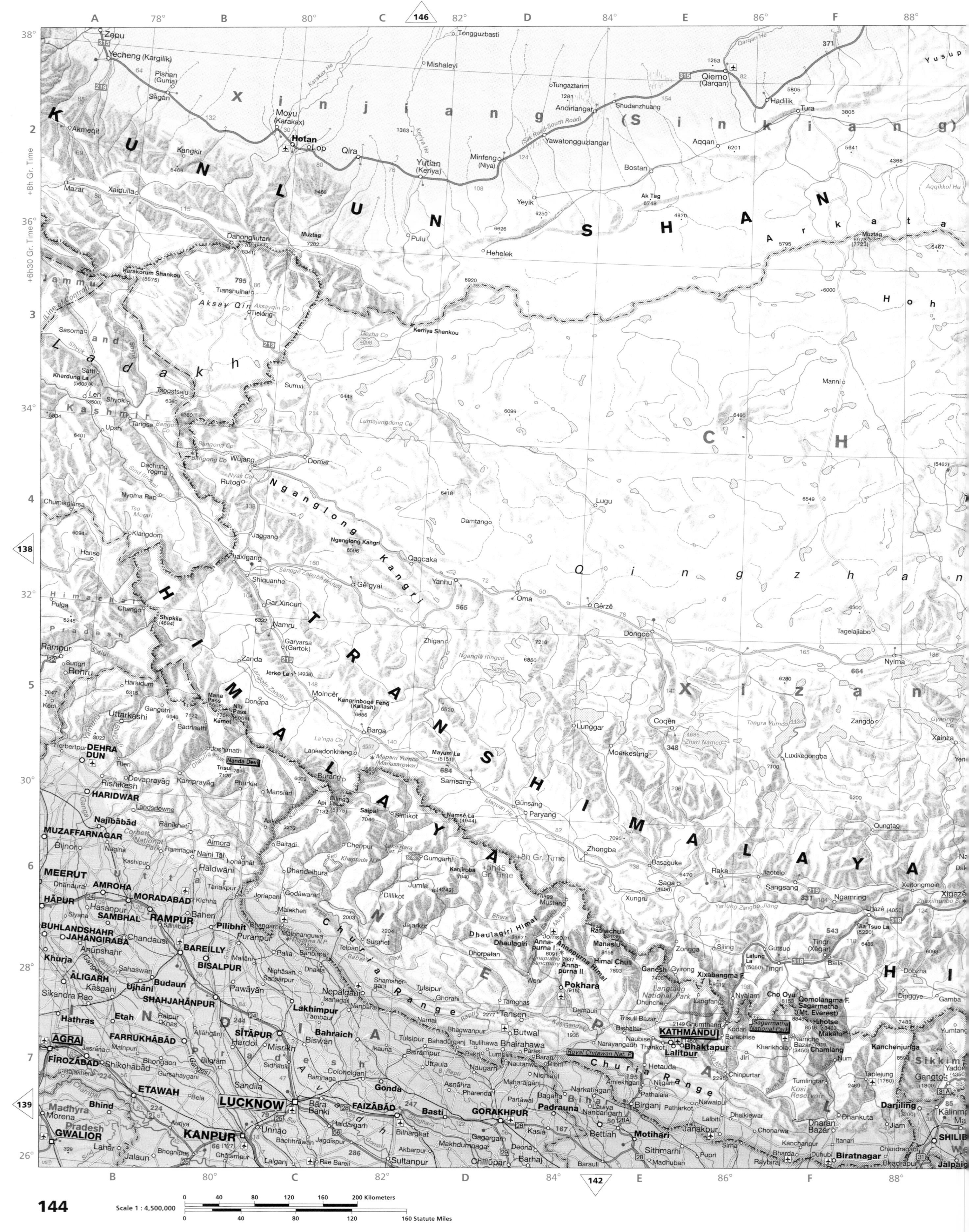

146
138
139
142
Zepu
Yecheng (Kargilik)
Pishan (Guma)
Sagan
Akmeqit
Moyu (Karakax)
Hotan
Lop
Qira
Yutian (Keriya)
Minfeng (Niya)
Yawatongguzlangar
Andirlangar
Shudanzhuang
Tungaztarim
Mishaleyi
Tongguzbasti
Qiemo (Qarqan)
Hadilik
Tura
Aqqan
Bostan
Yeyik
Ak Tag 6748
Muztag (7723)
Kangkir
Mazar
Xaidulla
Dahongliutan
Muztag 7282
Pulu
Hehelek
Karakorum Shankou (5575)
Tianshuihai
Aksay Qin
Tielong
Kerriya Shankou
Sasoma
Satti
Khardung La (5602)
Leh (3500)
Shyok
Tsogstsalu
Tangse
Upshi
Sumxi
Domar
Wujang
Rutog
Dachung Yogma
Nyoma Rap
Chumikglarsa
Kiangdom
Hanse
Jaggang
Zhaxigang
Shiquanhe
Gar Xincun
Namru
Garyarsa (Gartok)
Zanda
Jerko La (4936)
Moincêr
Kangrinboqê Feng (Kailash) 6656
Barga
Lankadonkhang
Mapam Yumco (Mariasarowar)
Mayum La (5151)
Samsang
Gê'gyai
Nganglong Kangri 6596
Qagcaka
Yanhu
Oma
Gêrzê
Dongco
Zhigan
Nganglha Ringco
Lugu
Damtang
Manni
Tagelajiabo
Nyima
Lunggar
Coqên
Zhari Namco
Tangra Yumco
Zangdo
Xainza
Moerkesung
Luxikegongba
Gunsang
Paryang
Zhongba
Basaguke
Raka
Jiaotelo
Saga (4600)
Sangsang
Ngamring
Xungru
Lhazê (4050)
Jia Tsuo La (5220)
Tingri (Xegar)
Xigazê
Qungtag
Xeitongmoin
Shipkila (4694)
Chango
Pulga
Rāmpur
Sungri
Rohru
Harkidum
Kedi
Uttarkashi
Gangotri
Badrinath
Mana Pass (5608)
Niti Pass (5069)
Kamet
Dongpa
Joshimath
Nanda Devi
Trisul 7120
Dehra Dun
Herbertpur
Theri
Devaprayāg
Karnprayāg
Rishikesh
Haridwar
Landsdowne
Rānīkheti
Najībābād
Muzaffarnagar
Corbett National Park
Almora
Naini Tāl
Haldwāni
Bijnor
Meerut
Amroha
Moradabad
Hāpur
Hasanpur
Sambhal
Rampur
Bulandshahr
Jahāngirābād
Chandausi
Bareilly
Bisalpur
Pilibhit
Purānpur
Khurja
Aligarh
Kāsganj
Budaun
Ujhāni
Shahjahānpur
Sikandra Rao
Hathras
Etah
Agra
Firozābād
Farrukhābād
Sītāpur
Hardoi
Misrikh
Bahraich
Lakhimpur
Nepalganj
Etawah
Lucknow
Kanpur
Unnāo
Bhind
Morena
Gwalior
Madhya Pradesh
Faizābād
Basti
Gonda
Gorakhpur
Padrauna
Sultānpur
Rae Bareli
Bettiah
Motihari
Sithmarhi
Janakpur
Birganj
Biratnagar
Darjiling
Kathmandu
Bhaktapur
Lalitpur
Hetauda
Pokhara
Royal Chitawan Nat. P.
Butwal
Bhairahawa
Tansen
Tulsipur
Dhaulagiri Himal
Dhaulagiri 8167
Annapurna I 8091
Annapurna II 7937
Manaslu 8156
Himal Chuli 7893
Ganesh
Xixabangma F.
Langtang National Park
Cho Oyu
Qomolangma F. Sagarmatha (Mt. Everest) 8848
Lhotse
Makalu
Chamlang
Kanchenjunga
Sagarmatha National Park
Sikkim
Gangtok
Dharan Bazar
Dhankuta
Api
Saipal 7040
Simikot
Namsê La (4944)
Jumla
Kanjiroba 7040
Gumgarhi
Mustang
Jomsom
Chenpur
Baitadi
Dhandelhura
Dipayal
Kunlun Shan
Xinjiang (Sinkiang)
Qingzhan
Xizang
Arkatag
Hoh
Kashmir
Ladakh
Jammu
Himachal Pradesh
Trans Himalaya
Nganglong Kangri
Himalaya
Churia Range
Nepal
Bihar
India
Uttar Pradesh
C H
+8h Gr. Time
+5h45 Gr. Time
+6h30 Gr. Time
Line of Control
Scale 1 : 4,500,000
0 40 80 120 160 200 Kilometers
0 40 80 120 160 Statute Miles

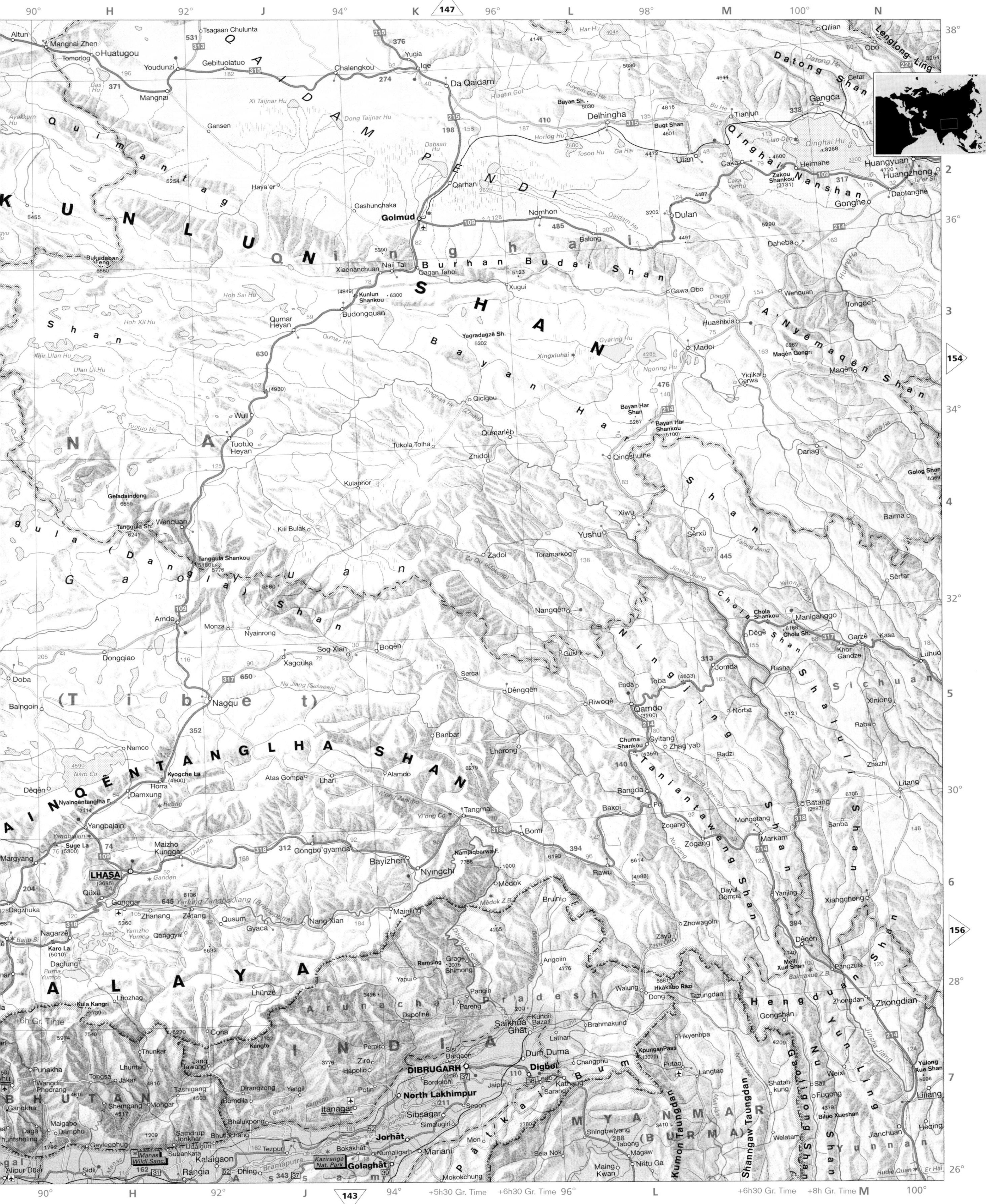

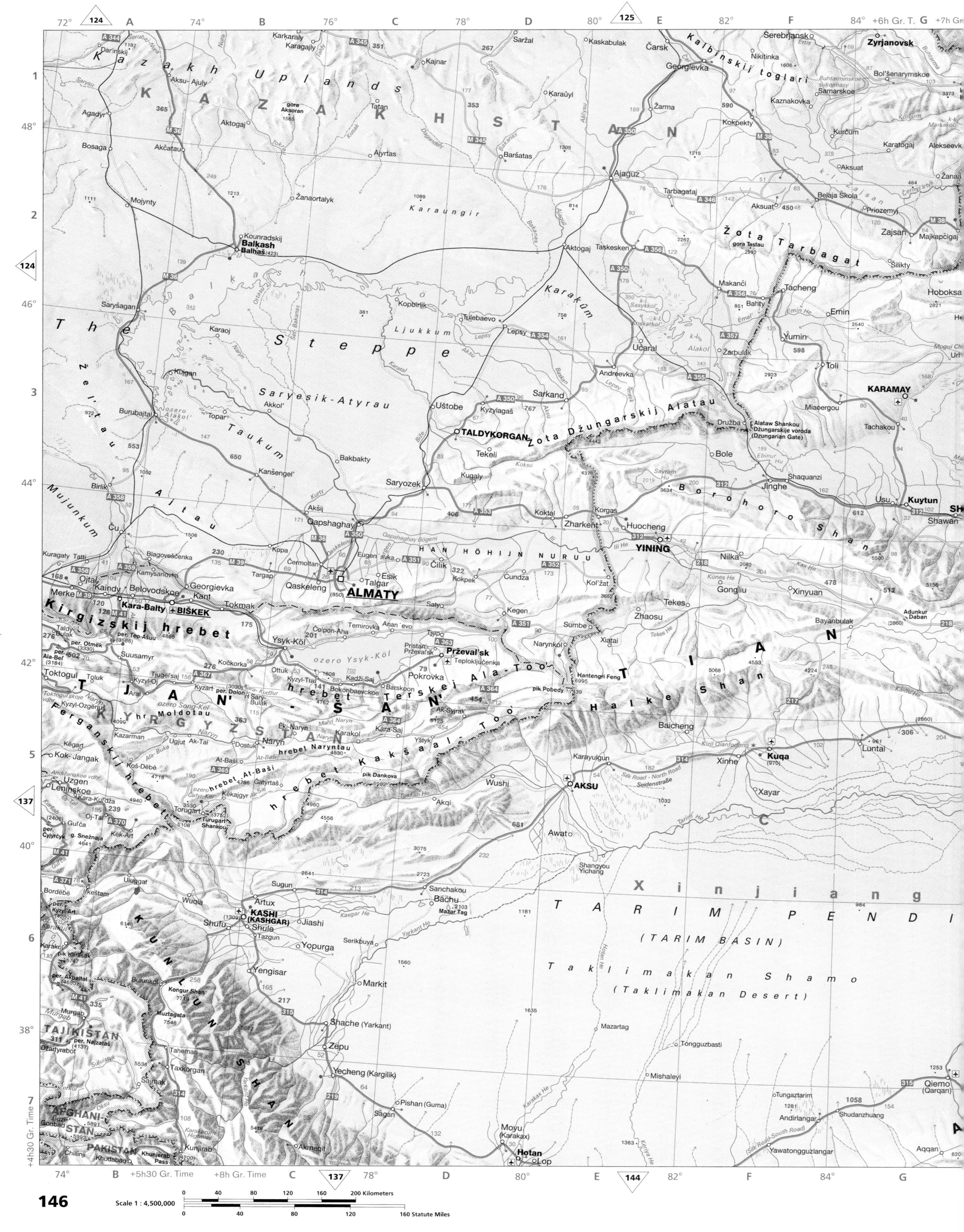
72°
124
A
74°
B
76°
C
78°
D
80°
125
E
82°
F
84°
+6h Gr. T.
G
1
48°
124
46°
2
3
44°
42°
5
137
40°
6
38°
7
+4h30 Gr. Time
K a z a k h U p l a n d s
K A Z A K H S T A N
Karkaraly
Karagajly
Sarzal
Kaskabulak
Čarsk
Serebrjansk
Zyrjanovsk
Darinskij
Kajnar
Georgievka
Kalbinskij toglari
Nikitinka
Bol'šenarymskoe
Samarskoe
Akšu-Ajuly
Karaûyl
Žarma
Kaznakovka
Agadyr'
Tatan
gora Aksoran
Aktogaj
Kokpekty
Kurčum
Karatogaj
Alekseevk
Bosaga
Akčatau
Ajyrtas
Baršatas
Aksuat
Žanaa
Mojynty
Žanaortalyk
Karaungir
Ajaguz
Tarbagataj
Aksuat
Belaja Skola
Priozernyj
Zajsan
Majkapčigaj
Kounradskij
Balkash
Balhaš
Aktogaj
Taskesken
Žota Tarbagat
gora Tastau
Šilikty
Makanči
Tacheng
Bahty
Hoboksa
Saryšagan
Kopbirlik
Tulebaevo
Emin
The
Balkash
Ljukkum
Lepsy
Karakum
Karaoj
Steppe
Učaral
Žarbulak
Yumin
Toli
Andreevka
Kujgan
Saryesik-Atyrau
Sarkand
KARAMAY
Žel'tau
Akkol'
Uštobe
Kyzylagaš
Burubajtal
Topar
Žota Džungarskij Alatau
Družba
Alataw Shankou
Džungarskije vorota
(Dzungarian Gate)
Miaoergou
Tachakou
Taukum
TALDYKORGAN
Tekeli
Bole
Bakbakty
Kanšengel'
Kugaly
Saryozek
Shaquanzi
Jinghe
Boro horo Shan
Birlik
Mujunkum
Ajtau
Akšij
Koktal
Korgas
Zharkent
Huocheng
Usu
Kuytun
Shawan
Ču
Qapshaghay
YINING
Kuragaty
Tatti
Blagoveščenka
Kopa
HAN HÖHIJN NURUU
Čermoltan
Eugen
Čilik
Nilka
Ojtal
Kamysanovka
Targap
Esik
Kokpek
Cundža
Kol'žat
Merke
Kaindy
Belovodskoe
Georgievka
Kant
Qaskeleng
Talgar
ALMATY
Gongliu
Xinyuan
Kara-Balty
BIŠKEK
Tokmak
Saty
Kegen
Tekes
Kirgizskij hrebet
Temirovka
Ananʹevo
Sumbe
Zhaosu
Adunkur Daban
Bayanbulak
Ysyk-Köl
Čolpon-Ata
Pristan'-Prževal'sk
Tjup
Narynkol
Xiatai
Suusamyr
ozero Ysyk-Köl
Prževal'sk
Teploključenka
Kočkorka
Toktogul
Toluk
Kyzyl-Oj
Ottuk
Kadži-Saj
Pokrovka
Hantengri Feng
Kyzyl-Tuu
Bokonbaevskoe
Barskoon
hrebet Terskej Ala-Too
pik Pobedy
Halke Shan
T'JAN'-ŠAN'
Aral
Kyzart
per. Dolon
Sary-Bulak
ozero Song-Köl
Moldotau
Ak-Syirak
KYRGYZSTAN
Baicheng
Kazarman
Eki-Naryn
Karakol
Kara-Saj
Ferganskij hrebet
Kegart
Ak-Tal
Ujgut
Naryn
Dostuk
Ystyk
Kizil Qianfodong
Kok-Jangak
At-Baši
hrebet Naryntau
Karayulgun
Xinhe
Kuqa
Luntai
Koš-Döbö
hrebet At-Baši
pik Dankova
Wushi
Uzgen
Leninskoe
Čatyrtaš
hrebet Kakšaal-Too
Silk Road - North Road
Seidenstraße
AKSU
Xayar
Kara-Kulʹdža
Kekajgyr
Akqi
Oj-Tal
Torugart
Turugart
Shankou
Gulča
Awat
Tarim He
per. Čyjyrčyk
g. Snežnaja
Kek-Art
Shangyou
Yichang
Xinjiang
Bordöbö
Ulugqat
Sugun
Sanchakou
Bachu
Irkeštam
Wuqia
Artux
Mazar Tag
TARIM PENDI
KASHI (KASHGAR)
Shufu
Shule
Jiashi
Kaxgar He
Tazgun
Yopurga
Serikbuya
(TARIM BASIN)
Karakul
pik Karakak
Taklimakan Shamo
per. Akbajtal
Yengisar
Bulunkol
Kongur Shan
Markit
(Taklimakan Desert)
KUNLUN SHAN
Murgab
Muztagata
Mazartag
Shache (Yarkant)
TAJIKISTAN
per. Najzataš
Džartyrabot
Taheman
Zepu
Tongguzbasti
Taxkorgan
Yecheng (Kargilik)
Mishaleyi
Sajmak
Qiemo (Qarqan)
Tungaztarim
AFGHANISTAN
Pishan (Guma)
Andirlangar
Shudanzhuang
Karakax He
Moyu (Karakax)
Sagan
Silk Road - South Road
Yawatongguzlangar
PAKISTAN
Chilinji
Khudabad
Khunjerab Pass
Kunjirab
Akmeqit
Hotan
Lop
Aqqan
74°
B
+5h30 Gr. Time
+8h Gr. Time
C
137
78°
D
80°
E
144
82°
F
84°
G
Scale 1 : 4,500,000
0
40
80
120
160
200 Kilometers
0
40
80
120
160 Statute Miles

RUSSIA
Tasanta
Cagaannuur
Ölgij
Altay
Burqin
Koktokay
Fuyun
Fuhai
Beitun
Qinghe
Hovd
Bajan-hošuu
Har-Us
Hungij
Uliastaj
Buga
Bulgan
Altaj
Tajgan
Zadgaj
Bajanbulag
Tosoncengel
Cavdan
Sogoot
Zagastajn davaa
Otgon Tenger
Bajan
Èèvijn buudal
Sarga
Zujl
Burenhajrhan
Bor-Uzuur
Ertai
Tahilt
Talšand
Zalaa
Bajan-Ovoo
Altan ovoo
Jiangjunmiao
Hutubi
CHANGJI
ÜRÜMQI
Fukang
Jimsar
Qitai
Mori
Bogda Feng
Chaiwopu
Dabancheng
Houxia
Turpan
Toksum
Shanshan
Qijiaojing
Liaodun
Barkol
Yiwu
HAMI
Nom
Atas Bogd
Cagaan Bogd
Hongshishan
Luotuoquanzi
Yandun
Xingxingxia
Weiya
Gongpoquan
Mazong Sh.
Hongliuyuan
Bai Shan
Qiaowan
Anxi
Yumen Zhen
Jinta
Yumenguan
Minghoshan (Dunhuang)
Mogao Ku
YUMEN
Jiayuguan
Jiuquan
Hoxud
Ulanlinggi
Argaybulak Daban
Aqitag
Qongkol
Tikanlik
Argan
Ikanbujimal
Luobuzhuang
Miran
Yandaxkak
Ruoqiang (Qarkilik)
Baxkorgan
Aktaz
Waxxari
Altun
Mangnai Zhen
Huatugou
Mangnai
Youdunzi
Gebituolatuo
Tsagaan Chulunta
Lenghu
Dingzikou
Aksay
Dangjin Shankou
Subei
Huahaizi
Chalengkou
Yugia
Da Qaidam
Delhingha
Ulan
Bugt Shan
Bayan Sh.
Gansen
Tura
Tomorlog
Mongol Altaj Nuruu
Hangajn Nuruu
Bulnajn nuruu
Han Höhijn nuruu
Tarvagatajn Nuruu
Bajan Hongor
Gov'-Altay Nuruu
Az Bogd
Altajn Caadah Gov'
Karlik
Bogda Shan
Baytik Shan
Junggar Pendi
Dzungarian Basin
Gurbantünggüt Shamo
Turpan Pendi
Qoltag
Hami Pendi
Kuruktag
Bei Shan
Inner Mongolia
Qilian Shan
Yema Manshan
Lop Nur
Sinkiang
Altun Shan
Yusupalik Tag
Qaidam Pendi
Qinghai
Qimantag
MONGOLIA

A
94°
B
96°
117
C
106°
H
IRKUTSK
(468)
Šelehov
Tal'jany
Listvjanka
Lake Bajkal
Tanhoj
Babuškin
Ivolginsk
Sljudjanka
Bajkal'sk
Vydrino
g. Sohon
Tarbagataj
Gusinoozersk
Tibel'ti
Kyren
Mondy
gora Munku-Sardyk
3491
Turt
+7h Gr. Time
+8h Gr. Time
gora Munku-Sasan
Boj-šoj Sajan
Hovu-Aksy
Balgazyn
hr. Vostočnyj Tannu-Ola
Toorml
Samagaltaj
Erzin
Naryn
Kungurtug
hrebet Horumnug-Tajga
hrebet Sengilen
gora Taskyl-Sajlyg
2590
Žöölön
Hövsgöl nuur
Hor dil Sar dag
Ulan Tajga
R U S S I A
T u v a
Dalahaj
Hamar Daban
hr. Malyj Hamar Daban
Džida
Povorot
Petropavlovka
Mihajlovka
Zakamensk
Kjahta
Zèltèr
Sühbaatar
Muroči
Džidinskij hrebet
Hatgal
Tsagaan
2524
2
50°
Böörög Dèlijn Èls
Baruunturuun
Han Höhijn Nuruu
U v s
Zur
H ö v s g ö l
Mörön
Šarga
Sèlèngè
Hutag
Darhan
Sèlèngè
3
Cavdan
Sogoot
Halzan Sogootyn davaa
Bulnajn nuruu
Hungij
Tosoncengel
Övögdij
Z a v h a n
B u l g a n
Èrdènèt
Orhon
Baruunharaa
Zuunharaa
Bulgan
Tunhel
Asralt Hairhan
2751
48°
Zagastajn davaa
Tarvagatajn nuruu
Solongotyn davaa
Horgo
Ölzijm
Maan't
Žargalant
Bat-Ölzijt
Ih suuž
Mongol Èls
Buga
Uliastaj
Otgon Tènger
4031
Hangajn Nuruu
A r h a n g a j
Lun
Argalant
ULAANBAATAR
Nalajh
Zuunmod
Suuž
Cècèrlèg
Zögstèj
Altan Ovoo
4
Bajan
Ulaanšiveèt
Ulaanhudag
Bajanbulag
Èèvijn buudal
Šarga
Altaj
Tajgan
Hužirt
Mönhbulag
T ö v
Ihhairhan
46°
Bajan
Zadgaj
Buucagaan
Bajanhongor
Èrdènècogt
Bumbat
Arvajhèèr
G o v ' - A l t a y
Burhan buudaj
3765
M O N G O L
Cagaan-Ovoo
Övör-Hangaj
Sangijn Dalaj
Amardalaj
Tahilt
Talšand
Bajantèèg
Mandalgov'
5
Hongor
Arguut
Ongi
Dundgov'
Suugaant
Äz Bogd
3802
Bajan-Ovoo
Gov'-Altajn nuruu
Orog nuur
Hašaat
147
Zalaa
Hatansuudal
Hovd
Šarhulsan
44°
Nom
Altajn Caadah gov'
Doloon
Bulgan
Uizèn
Yiwu
Atas Bogd
2402
Gurvan Sajchan nuruu
Sajnšand
Dalanzadgad
6
Xinjiang (Sinkiang)
Cagaan Bogd
2480
Urt
Ömnögov'
Ihbulag
Hongshishan
Borzongijn Gov'
42°
Xingxingxia
Gaxun Nur
G O B I
Galbyn Gov'
Gongpoquan
Bei Shan
Mazong Sh.
2583
Saihan Toroi
Ejin Qi
7
Hongliuyuan
NEI MONGOL
Urad Houqi
Lang Shan
Anxi
Qiaowan
Huxi Xincun
ALXA GAOYUAN
Ulan Hu
Hanggin Houqi
Yumen Zhen
Bayan
Gansu
40°
Mogao Ku
Yulin Ku
Badain Jaran Shamo
(Alashan Shamo)
Jinta
Dengkou
YUMEN
Jiayuguan
Jiuquan
(1006)
Bayan Olji
CHINA
QILIAN SHAN
Daler Shan
5483
Jingtie Shan
5205
8
Yema Manshan
Jingtieshan
Qilian Sh.
5547
Hongliuyuan
Qingshui
Gaotai
Linze
Suhait
Jartai
Jartai Yanchi
WUHAI
Zhuozi Shan
Wuda
Yaibrai
Alxa Youqi
Quanzijing
Sanbei Yangchang
Zhangye
Shizuishan
B
96°
C
98°
D
100°
154
E
102°
F
104°
G
106°
H
Scale 1 : 4,500,000
0 40 80 120 160 200 Kilometers
0 40 80 120 160 Statute Miles

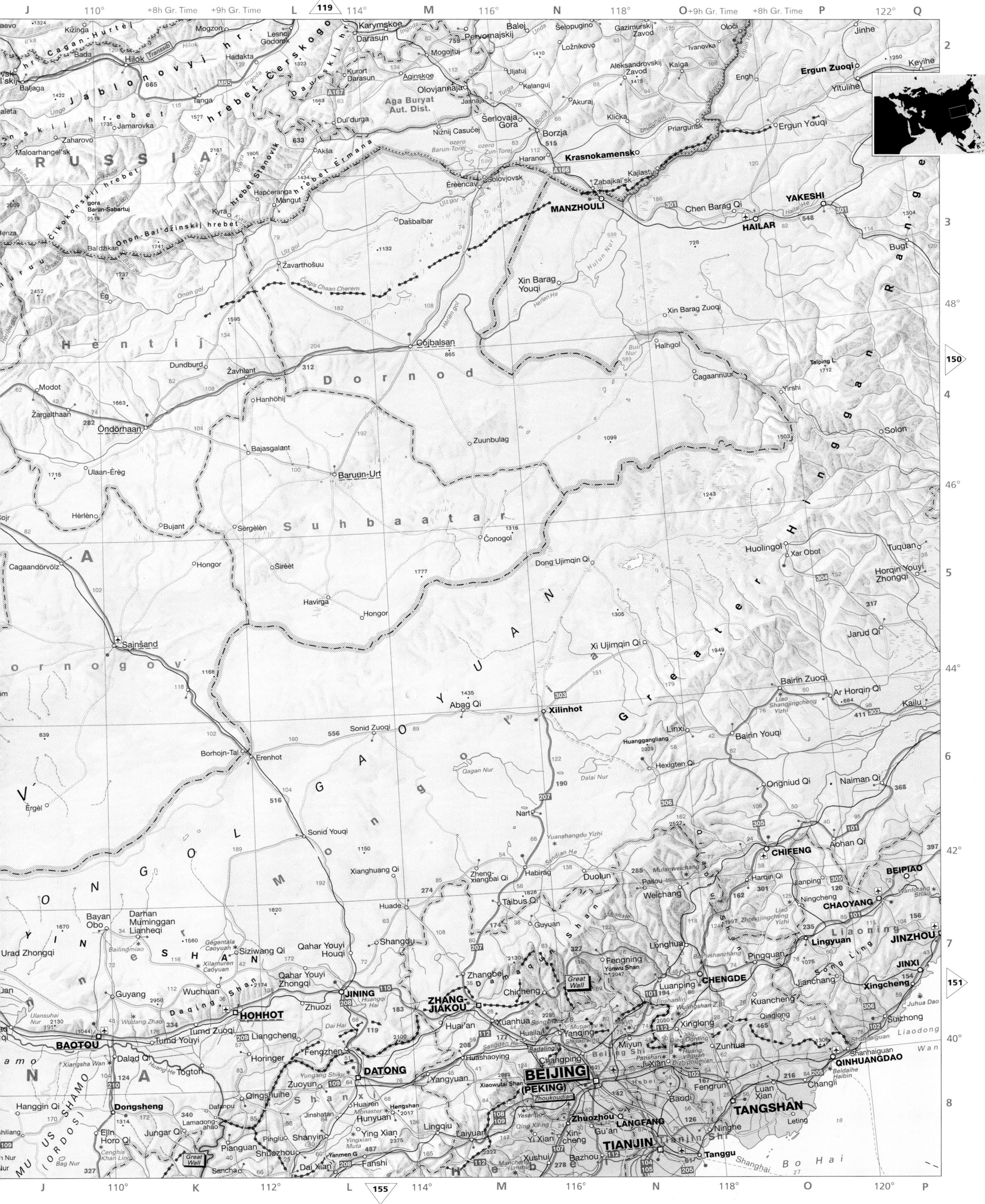

J
110°
+8h Gr. Time
+9h Gr. Time
L
119
114°
M
116°
N
118°
O +9h Gr. Time
+8h Gr. Time
P
122°
Q
Kizinga
Mogzon
Lesnoj Godorok
Karymskoe
Darasun
Pervomajskij
Balej
Selopugino
Gazimurskij Zavod
Oloči
Jinhe
Bada
Hilok
Hadakta
Mogojtuj
Ložnikovo
Ivanovka
Keyihe
Baljaga
Jablonovyj hrebet
Kurort Darasun
Aginskoe
Uljatuj
Aleksandrovskij Zavod
Kalga
Engh
Ergun Zuoqi
Yituliha
Tanga
Olovjannaja
Kalanguj
Aga Buryat Aut. Dist.
Akuraj
Jamarovka
Dul'durga
Jasnaja
Serlovaja Gora
Klička
Priargunsk
Ergun Youqi
Zaharovo
Nižnij Casučej
Borzja
Maloarhangel'sk
RUSSIA
Akša
Haranor
Krasnokamensk
Solovjovsk
Ėrėencav
Zabajkal'sk
Kajlastuj
Hapčeranga
Mangut
MANZHOULI
Chen Barag Qi
YAKESHI
HAILAR
Kyra
Dašbalbar
Bal'džikan
Onon-Bal'džinskij hrebet
Bugt
Žavarthošuu
Xin Barag Youqi
Ėg
Onon gol
Čingis Chaan Cherem
Xin Barag Zuoqi
48°
Hėntij
Čojbalsan
Halhgol
Dundburd
Žavhlant
Dornod
Cagaannuur
Teiping L.
150
Modot
Hanhöhij
Yirshi
4
Žargalthaan
Öndörhaan
Solon
Bajasgalant
Zuunbulag
Ulaan-Ėrėg
Baruun-Urt
46°
Hėrlėn
Bujant
Sergėlėn
Suhbaatar
Čonogol
Huolingol
Xar Obot
Tuquan
Cagaandörvölz
Hongor
Sirėėt
Dong Ujimqin Qi
Horqin Youyi Zhongqi
5
Havirga
Hongor
Jarud Qi
Sajnšand
Xi Ujimqin Qi
44°
Bairin Zuoqi
Ar Horqin Qi
Abag Qi
Xilinhot
Kailu
Sonid Zuoqi
Linxi
Bairin Youqi
Borhojn-Tal
Erenhot
Huanggangliang
Hexigten Qi
6
Qagan Nur
Dalai Nur
Ongniud Qi
Naiman Qi
Ėrgėl
GAOYUAN
Great Hinggan Range
Nart
Sonid Youqi
Aohan Qi
CHIFENG
42°
Xianghuang Qi
Zhengxiangbai Qi
Habirag
Duolun
BEIPIAO
Weichang
Harqin Qi
Jianping
Ningcheng
CHAOYANG
Bayan Obo
Darhan Muminggan Lianheqi
Taibus Qi
Huade
Guyuan
Liaoning
Urad Zhongqi
Siziwang Qi
Qahar Youyi Houqi
Shangdu
Longhua
Lingyuan
JINZHOU
7
Fengning
Pingquan
JINXI
Qahar Youyi Zhongqi
Zhangbei
Great Wall
CHENGDE
Jianchang
Xingcheng
151
Guyang
Wuchuan
JINING
Chicheng
Luanping
Kuancheng
HOHHOT
Zhuozi
ZHANGJIAKOU
Qinglong
Huai'an
Xuanhua
Xinglong
Suizhong
Liaodong Wan
40°
BAOTOU
Tumd Zuoqi
Tumd Youqi
Liangcheng
Yanqing
Miyun
Zunhua
Dalad Qi
Horinger
Fengzhen
Huashaoying
Changping
Shanhaiguan
QINHUANGDAO
Togtoh
DATONG
BEIJING (PEKING)
Ji Xian
Yangyuan
Fengrun
Luan Xian
Changli
Zuoyun
Qingshuihe
Huairen
Hunyuan
Baodi
TANGSHAN
8
Hanggin Qi
Dongsheng
Lamadong
Jinshatan
Zhuozhou
LANGFANG
Leting
Ejin Horo Qi
Jungar Qi
Pinglu
Shanyin
Ying Xian
Lingqiu
Laiyuan
Yi Xian
Xincheng
Ninghe
TIANJIN
Tanggu
Pianguan
Shuozhou
Xushui
Bazhou
Bo Hai
Great Wall
Sancha
Dai Xian
Fanshi
MU US SHAMO (ORDOS)
J
110°
K
112°
L
155
114°
M
116°
N
118°
O
120°
P

Scale 1 : 4,500,000
0 40 80 120 160 200 Kilometers
0 40 80 120 160 Statute Miles

NORTH KOREA
SOUTH KOREA
JAPAN
CHINA
Sea of Japan
Yellow Sea
Korea Bay
Korea Strait
Liaodong Bandao
Shandong Bandao
Bo Hai
Yamato Rise
HONSHŪ
Kyūshū
Shikoku
PYONGYANG
SŎUL
INCH'ŎN
PUSAN
TAEGU
KWANGYU
TAEJŎN
ULSAN
CHONGJIN
HAMHUNG
WONSAN
KAESŎNG
SINUIJU
SHENYANG
FUSHUN
ANSHAN
BENXI
DANDONG
DALIAN (DAIREN)
YANTAI
QINGDAO (TSINGTAO)
JINZHOU
YINGKOU
WEIFANG
HIROSHIMA
FUKUOKA
KITAKYUSHU
NAGASAKI
KUMAMOTO
MATSUE
TOTTORI
OKAYAMA

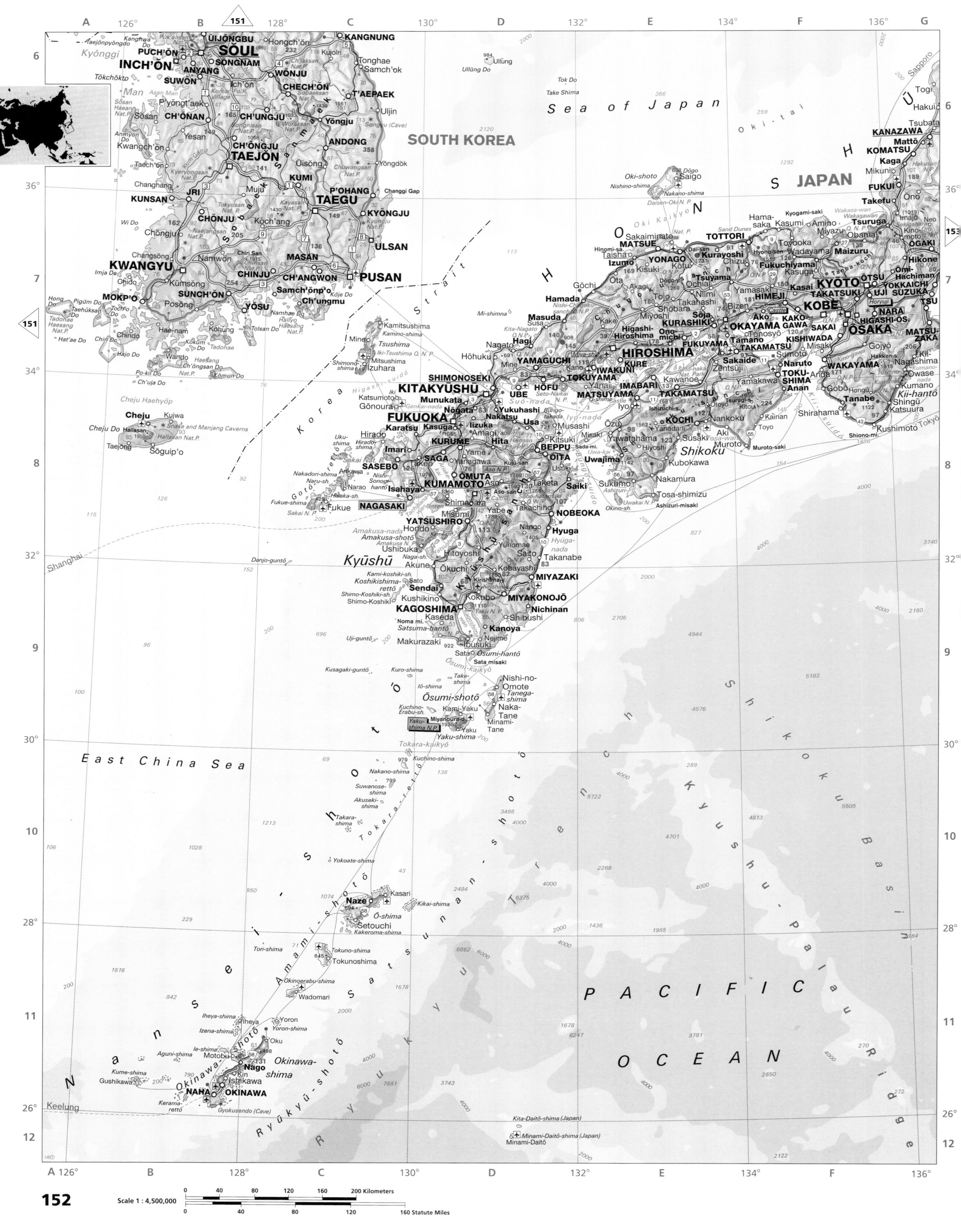

SOUTH KOREA
JAPAN
Sea of Japan
East China Sea
PACIFIC OCEAN
Korea Strait
Kyūshū
Shikoku
Honshū
Nansei-shotō
Ryukyu Trench
Kyushu-Palau Ridge
Shikoku Basin
Satsunan-shotō
Ryūkyū-shotō
Amami-shotō
Okinawa-shotō
Tokara-rettō
Ōsumi-shotō
SŎUL
INCH'ŎN
SUWŎN
ŬIJŎNGBU
SONGNAM
ANYANG
PUCH'ŎN
KANGNUNG
WŎNJU
CHECH'ŎN
CH'ŎNAN
CH'UNGJU
T'AEPAEK
CH'ŎNGJU
TAEJŎN
ANDONG
KUMI
P'OHANG
TAEGU
KYŎNGJU
ULSAN
KUNSAN
IRI
CHŎNJU
KWANGYU
MOKP'O
SUNCH'ŎN
YŎSU
CHINJU
MASAN
CH'ANGWON
PUSAN
Cheju
Cheju Do
Ullŭng Do
Oki-shoto
MATSUE
TOTTORI
YONAGO
KANAZAWA
KOMATSU
FUKUI
KYOTO
KOBE
OSAKA
NARA
HIMEJI
OKAYAMA
KURASHIKI
FUKUYAMA
HIROSHIMA
KURE
IWAKUNI
TOKUYAMA
YAMAGUCHI
SHIMONOSEKI
KITAKYŪSHŪ
UBE
HŌFU
MATSUYAMA
IMABARI
TAKAMATSU
TOKUSHIMA
KŌCHI
WAKAYAMA
FUKUOKA
KURUME
SAGA
SASEBO
NAGASAKI
KUMAMOTO
ŌMUTA
ŌITA
BEPPU
NOBEOKA
MIYAZAKI
MIYAKONOJŌ
YATSUSHIRO
KAGOSHIMA
Sendai
Kanoya
Tsushima
Yaku-shima
Tanega-shima
Naze
Ō-shima
Tokunoshima
Okinawa-shima
Nago
NAHA
OKINAWA
Kita-Daitō-shima (Japan)
Minami-Daitō-shima (Japan)
Shanghai
Keelung
Scale 1 : 4,500,000
0 40 80 120 160 200 Kilometers
0 40 80 120 160 Statute Miles

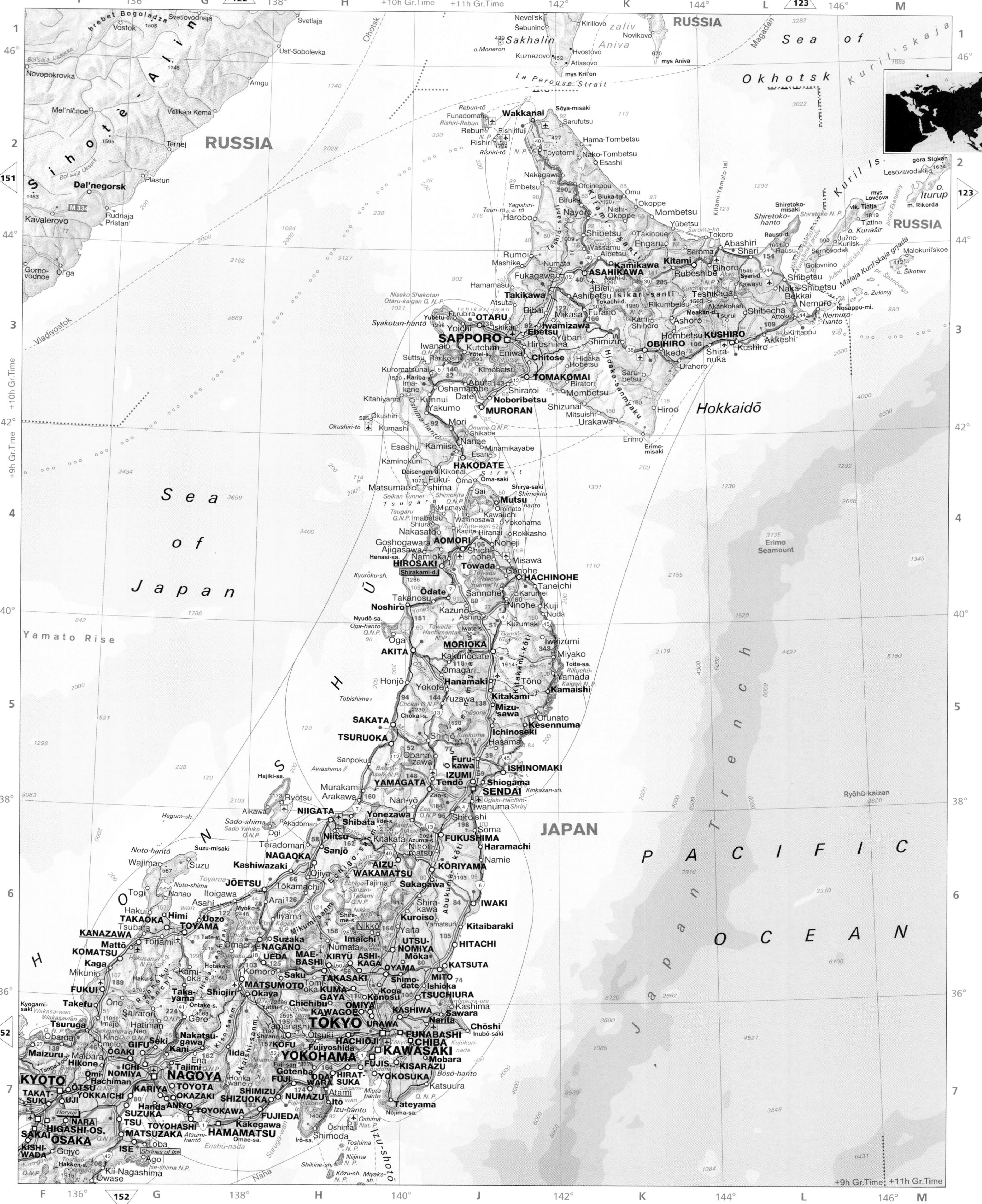

RUSSIA
Sea of Okhotsk
Sakhalin
zaliv Aniva
La Perouse Strait
Sihote-Alin'
Vladivostok
Dal'negorsk
Kuril Is.
Sea of Japan
Yamato Rise
Hokkaidō
Wakkanai
Asahikawa
Sapporo
Otaru
Kushiro
Obihiro
Tomakomai
Muroran
Hakodate
Tsugaru Strait
Honshū
Aomori
Hirosaki
Hachinohe
Morioka
Akita
Sakata
Yamagata
Sendai
Niigata
Fukushima
Kōriyama
Iwaki
Sado-shima
Kanazawa
Toyama
Nagano
Utsunomiya
Mito
Maebashi
Tokyo
Kawasaki
Yokohama
Chiba
Shizuoka
Hamamatsu
Nagoya
Gifu
Kyoto
Osaka
Nara
JAPAN
PACIFIC OCEAN
Japan Trench
Erimo Seamount
Ryōhū-kaizan
Izu-shotō
+9h Gr.Time
+10h Gr.Time
+11h Gr.Time

Scale 1 : 4,500,000
0 40 80 120 160 200 Kilometers
0 40 80 120 160 Statute Miles

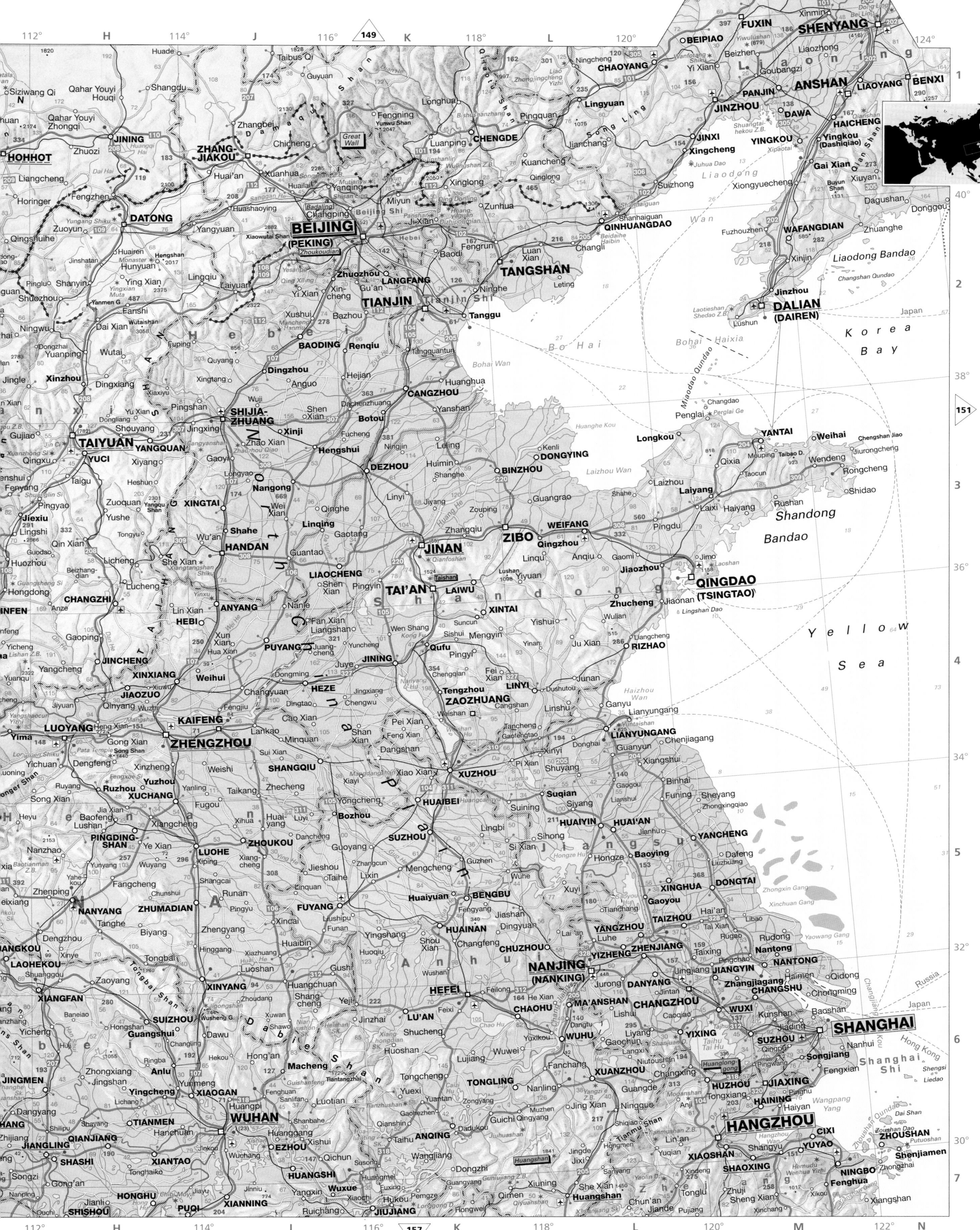

BEIJING
(PEKING)
TIANJIN
Tianjin Shi
Beijing Shi
SHENYANG
FUXIN
BEIPIAO
CHAOYANG
ANSHAN
LIAOYANG
BENXI
PANJIN
JINZHOU
HAICHENG
YINGKOU
Liaodong Bandao
Liaodong Wan
DALIAN
(DAIREN)
Korea Bay
Bohai Haixia
Bo Hai
Bohai Wan
Laizhou Wan
Miaodao Qundao
YANTAI
Weihai
Shandong Bandao
QINGDAO
(TSINGTAO)
Yellow Sea
HOHHOT
JINING
ZHANGJIAKOU
CHENGDE
Great Wall
QINHUANGDAO
TANGSHAN
Tanggu
DATONG
BAODING
CANGZHOU
SHIJIAZHUANG
TAIYUAN
YANGQUAN
YUCI
DEZHOU
BINZHOU
DONGYING
XINGTAI
HANDAN
JINAN
ZIBO
WEIFANG
TAI'AN
LAIWU
LIAOCHENG
CHANGZHI
ANYANG
HEBI
XINXIANG
JIAOZUO
PUYANG
JINING
HEZE
ZAOZHUANG
LINYI
RIZHAO
LIANYUNGANG
XUZHOU
KAIFENG
ZHENGZHOU
LUOYANG
XUCHANG
PINGDINGSHAN
LUOHE
ZHOUKOU
SHANGQIU
HUAIBEI
SUZHOU
BENGBU
HUAINAN
FUYANG
HUAIYIN
YANCHENG
YANGZHOU
ZHENJIANG
NANJING
(NANKING)
HEFEI
CHUZHOU
MA'ANSHAN
CHANGZHOU
WUXI
SUZHOU
SHANGHAI
Shanghai Shi
NANTONG
TAIZHOU
DONGTAI
WUHU
TONGLING
ANQING
XUANZHOU
HUZHOU
JIAXING
HANGZHOU
Hangzhou Wan
SHAOXING
NINGBO
ZHOUSHAN
HUANGSHI
WUHAN
XIAOGAN
XIANTAO
JINGMEN
JIANGLING
SHASHI
XIANGFAN
NANYANG
ZHUMADIAN
XINYANG
LAOHEKOU
JIUJIANG
Huangshan
Taishan
Shandong
Hebei
Henan
Anhui
Jiangsu
Liaoning
Hubei
Taihu
Japan
Russia
Hong Kong
Changjiang Kou
Dabie Shan

CHENGDU
SUINING
CHONGQING
JIULONGPO
FULING
LESHAN
NEIJIANG
ZIGONG
YIBIN
LUZHOU
ZUNYI
GUIYANG
KAILI
DUYUN
ANSHUN
LIUPANSHUI
QUJING
KUNMING
XICHANG
PANZHIHUA
DALI
GEJIU
HUAIHUA
GUILIN
LIUZHOU
NANNING
YULIN
QINZHOU
BEIHAI
ZHANJIANG
HAIKOU
Sanya
Wuzhi Shan
HÀ NỘI
HAI PHONG
HONG GAI
CAMPHA
THÁI NGUYÊN
NAM ĐỊNH
THANH HÓA
VINH
VIETNAM
LAOS
THAILAND
MYANMAR
CAMBODIA
Louangphrabang
VIANGCHAN (VIENTIANE)
Gulf of Tonkin
HAINAN DAO
Hainan SEZ
Leizhou Bandao
Qiongzhou Haixia
Red Basin
Sichuan Basin
Guizhou
Yunnan
Guangxi Zhuangzu Zizhiqu
Yungui Gaoyuan
Miao Ling
Wuling Shan
Daxue Shan
Dalou Shan
Wumeng Shan
Wulian Feng
Shiwan Dashan
Yunkai Dashan
Liuzhao Shan
Luhan Shan
Mianmian Shan
Tropic of Cancer
Xishuangbanna
Stone Forest
Leshan
Emeishan
Ya'an
Mile
Yuxi
Kaiyuan
Mengzi
Wenshan
Bose
Hechi
Heshan
Tongren
Jishou
Enshi
Lichuan
Xiangcheng
Lijiang
Jinghong
Simao
Pu'er
Yuanjiang
Chuxiong
Xingyi
Bijie
Zhaotong
+8h Gr. Time
+7h Gr. Time
Scale 1 : 4,500,000
200 Kilometers
160 Statute Miles

112°
H
114°
155
J
116°
K
118°
L
N
120°
M
160
HANGZHOU
HUZHOU
JIAXING
HAINING
Haiyan
ZHOUSHAN
Shenjiamen
NINGBO
CIXI
YUYAO
SHAOXING
XIAOSHAN
Fenghua
Xiangshan
Sanmen
Linhai
Jiaojiang
Huangyan
Lishui
Wenzhou
WENZHOU
Rui'an
Pingyang
Yueqing
JINHUA
Yiwu
Dongyang
Lanxi
QUZHOU
Jiangshan
Changshan
Yongkang
Z h e j i a n g
WUHAN
EZHOU
HUANGSHI
XIANTAO
XIANNING
HONGHU
SHISHOU
SHASHI
JIANGLING
QIANJIANG
Jinshi
CHANGDE
YUEYANG
Miluo
Yuanjiang
YIYANG
CHANGSHA
XIANGTAN
ZHUZHOU
LIUYANG
LOUDI
Xiangxiang
HENGYANG
Hengshan
Shaodong
Leiyang
CHENZHOU
Yongzhou
JIUJIANG
JINGDEZHEN
Huangshan
Boyang
NANCHANG
FENGCHENG
Zhangshu
YICHUN
XINYU
PINGXIANG
LINCHUAN
SHANGRAO
Yingtan
JI'AN
Jinggangshan
GANZHOU
Ruijin
Jiangxi
Anhui
Yangtze
Poyang Hu
Dongting Hu
NANPING
FUZHOU
Matsu Liehtao (Taiwan)
SANMING
YONG'AN
Fuqing
Putian
Xianyou
QUANZHOU
Shishi
Jinjiang
LONGYAN
ZHANGZHOU
XIAMEN
Chinmen
Chinmen Tao (Taiwan)
Shaowu
Jian'ou
Ningde
Fuding
Fujian
SHAOGUAN
Guangdong
MEIZHOU
CHAOZHOU
SHANTOU
Chaoyang
Jieyang
Chenghai
Raoping
Nan'ao Dao
Shanwei
Lufeng
Huizhou
HUIZHOU
Huiyang
GUANGZHOU (CANTON)
FOSHAN
DONGGUAN
SHUNDE
JIANGMEN
ZHONGSHAN
SHENZHEN
ZHUHAI
KOWLOON (JIULONG)
VICTORIA
MACAO (MACAU)
Macau (Port.)
Hong Kong (U.K.)
ZHAOQING
Qingyuan
Yangjiang
YANGJIANG
Kaiping
Enping
Taishan
Shangchuan Dao
Xiachuan Dao
East China Sea
Taiwan Strait
Penghu Islands (Pescadores)
Makung
Tropic of Cancer
Taiwan Banks
KEELUNG
TAIPEI
TAOYUAN
HSINCHU
Ilan
Suao
Miao Li
FENGYUAN
TAICHUNG
CHANGHUA
HUALIEN
YUANLIN
CHIAYI
TAINAN
KAOHSIUNG
PINGTUNG
FENGSHAN
Taitung
TAIWAN
Lanyu
Hengchun
Oluanpi
Yu Shan
Luzon Strait
Batan Islands
Itbayat I.
Sabtang I.
Balintang Channel
Babuyan Islands
Babuyan Channel
Calayan I.
Dalupiri I.
Fuga I.
Dongsha Qundao
Dongsha Dao
South China Sea
PHILIPPINES
LUZON
LAOAG
Claveria
Pamplona
Abulug
Singapore
Manila
22°
24°
26°
28°
30°
20°
18°

Scale 1 : 4,500,000
0 40 80 120 160 200 Kilometers
0 40 80 120 160 Statute Miles

G
104°
156
H
106°
J
+7h Gr. T.
+8h Gr. T.
108°
K
110°
L
112°
VIENTIANE
VIANGCHAN
Nong Khai
Hà Tĩnh
Yacheng
Sanya
Hainan Dao
(China)
18°
VIET-
NAM
Đồng Hới
Đông Hà
Huế
Khe Sanh
Savannakhet
Mukdahan
Sakhonnakhon
Nakhonphanom
Thakhek
Khon Kaen
Kalasin
Maha Sarakham
Roi Et
Yasothon
Ubon Ratchathani
Pakxé
Champasak
Saravan
Attapu
Đà Nẵng
Hội An
Tam Kỳ
Quảng Ngãi
Kon Tum
Plây Ku
Qui Nhơn
Tuy Hòa
Buôn Ma Thuột
Nha Trang
Đà Lạt
Phan Rang-Tháp Chàm
Phan Thiết
Vũng Tàu
Biên Hòa
Thủ Dầu Một
T. P. HỒ CHÍ MINH
(SAIGON)
Mỹ Tho
Bến Tre
Vĩnh Long
Cần Thơ
Long Xuyên
Châu Đốc
Rạch Giá
Sóc Trăng
Cà Mau
Minh Hải
Côn Đảo
Phnum Pénh
Kâmpóng Cham
Kâmpóng Chhnang
Pouthisăt
Bătdâmbâng
Siĕmréap
Angkor Wat
Sisŏphŏn
Aranyaprathet
Kâmpôt
Krâchéh
Stœng Trêng
Surin
Buri Ram
Si Sa Ket
Tônlé Sab
Chuŏr Phnum Dângrêk
Chuŏr Phnum Krâvanh
Phanom Dong Rak
Plateau des Bolovens
Crescent Group
Xishaqundao
(Paracel Is.)
Cửa Sông Cửu Long
(Mouths of the Mekong)
SOUTH CHINA SEA
Rifleman Bank
Alexander Bank
Vanguard Bank
Scawfell Bank
Charlotte Bank
Roualist Bank
Kota Bharu
+7h Gr. Time
+8h Gr. Time
Singapore
163

Scale 1 : 4,500,000
0 40 80 120 160 200 Kilometers
0 40 80 120 160 Statute Miles

Philippine Trench
MINDANAO
Samar
Leyte
Bohol
Cebu
Negros
Panay
Palawan
Masbate
Visayan Sea
Bohol Sea
Mindanao Sea
Sulu Sea
Celebes Sea
Moro Gulf
Davao Gulf
Leyte Gulf
Palawan Passage
Balabac Strait
Sulu Archipelago
Cuyo East Pass
Cuyo West Pass
Calamian Group
Cuyo Islands
Tubbataha Reefs
Zamboanga Peninsula
Sabah
MALAYSIA
INDONESIA
KALIMANTAN (BORNEO)
Kalimantan Timur
Sulawesi Utara
Kep. Sangir
Kep. Talaud
CEBU CITY
DAVAO CITY
ZAMBOANGA CITY
CAGAYAN DE ORO
ILIGAN
BUTUAN
GENERAL SANTOS
COTABATO CITY
TACLOBAN
ILOILO CITY
BACOLOD
Puerto Princesa
KOTA KINABALU
SANDAKAN
Tawau
Tarakan
Jolo
Dipolog
Dumaguete
Surigao
Tagbilaran

A 96° B 98° 158 C E 104°

141

Ko Tarutao
Ko Rawi
Satun
Na Thawi
Khok Pho
THAILAND
Yala
Pulau Langkawi
Kangar
K.Perlis
Perlis
Jitra
Kuah
Chanlang
Yaha
Ton Sai
Narathiwat
Kg. Pengkalan Kubor
KOTA BHARU
Alor Setar
P. Dayang Bunting
Pokok Sena
Kedah
Nami
Bt. Lata Papalang
Ban Nang Sata
Sungai Ko-lok
Peringat
Kg. Nibong
Pasir Puteh
P. Perhentian Besar
Jertih
P. Redang
Yan
Gurun
Sik
Baling
Betong
Mechang
Jeli
Kuala Krai
Kg. Penarik
Kg. Merang
Batu Rakit
Kuala Terengganu
Sungai Petani
Muka Head
Pulau Penang
GEORGE TOWN
Butterworth
Kulim
Gerik
G. Noring
Kg. Bulon
Kg. S. Ayer Deras
Marang
Wakaf Tapai
Teluk Kumbar
Penang
Nibong Tebal
Tanjung Piandang
Selama
Kemubu
G. Chamah
Kelantan
K.Berang
Terengganu
Kg.Jambu Bongkok
Kota Lenggong
Sungai Siput
Gua Musang
Kg. Jerangau
P. Tenggol
Changkat Jering
Taiping
K.Kangsar
Kg. Kemara
G. Gagau
Kuala Dungan
Ayer Terjun
IPOH
Tanah Rata
Kg. Chenereh
Pantai Remis
Parit
Batu Gajah
Kampar
Merapoh
Taman Negara
Kemasik
Malay
Damar Laut
P. Pangkor
Kampung Koh
Gopeng
K. Tahan
Relok
Kg. Mening
Kg. Ayer Puteh
Chukai
Tapah
Bidor
Kuala Lipis
Kg. Cherating
P.Sembilan
Bagan Datuk
Teluk Intan
Hutan Melintang
Slim River
Benta
Seretang
Jerantut
Tembeling
G. Tapis
Kg. Balok
Raub
G. Benum
S. Lembing
Kuantan
Tanjung Malim
K.Kubu Baharu
Tranum
K. Kerau
Gambang
Kg. Sepat
Kg. Lamir
Pekan
Kg. Sekinchan
Selangor
Bentong
Maran
Tanjung Karang
K. Selangor
Karak
Tasik Chini
Sungai Buloh
Rawang
Temerloh
Peninsu
KUALA LUMPUR
PETALING JAYA
Triang
Nenasi
KLANG
Shah Alam
Kajang
Tasik Bera
Pahang
Banting
SEREMBAN
K.Pilah
Bahau
Kg. Leban Condong
Petoh
Negeri Sembilan
Tanjung Sepat
Port Dickson
Pasir Panjang
Segamat
Pandang Endau
Mersing
P. Tioman
Kg. Tek
Tampin
Gemas
G.Ledang
G.Besar
P. Besar
Jemaluang
Melaka
Tangkak
Labis
Chaah
Paloh
P. Tinggi
P. Sibu
Melaka
Muar
Pagoh
Yong Peng
Johor
Keluang
Ayer Hitam
Batu Pahat
Mawai
Kampur
Kulai
Kota Tinggi
Ulu Tiram
Benut
Pontian Kecil
Kukup
JOHOR BAHRU
SINGAPORE
Nongsa
Pulau
Tanjungpinang

Strait of Malacca

Tanjung Ba'u
P. Weh
P. Breueh
Lambaro Angan
Tg. Bateeputih
Banda Aceh (Baiturahman)
Lampanaih
U. Pidie
Seulimeum
Sigli
Jantho
Meureudu
Lamno
Lammeulo
Keudemane
Tg. Jambuair
Lhokseumawe
Bireuen
Glumpangdua
Bayu
Lhoksukon
Kutabagok
Idi
Tangse
Daerah
Langkahan
Tg. Peureulak
Peureulak
Pameue
Lageuen
Calang
Rumahbaru
Takengon
Oreng
Keudeuteunom
Kualalangsa
Langsa
U. Tamiang
Istimewa
Peg. Pusat Gajo
Terujak
Pantekra
G. Lembu
Kualasimpang
Tanjungmarcang
Meulaboh
Pendeng
Pangkalansusu
Langka
Pangkalanbrandan
Blangkejeren
Kutanibong
Lamainong
Tanjungpura
Blangpidie
G. Leuser
Taring
Hampenanperak
Belawan
Tanjung Raya
Aceh
Genting
Peg. Sergeilsingil
Binjai
Maimoon Palace
Labuhanhaji
Kutacane
MEDAN
Baungan
Lubukpakan
Sungaibamban
Delitua
Bangunpurba
TEBINGTINGGI
Kualatanjung
Indrapura
Tapaktuan
Brastagi
Labuhanruku
Dolok Merawan
Kandang
Perbulan
Kabanjahe
Karo Batak House
Kisaran
Teluknibung
Tg. Dewa
Geloketapang
Barusiahe
Sibolga
Tanjungbalai
Sibolga
Seribudolok
Pematang Purba
PEMATANG SIANTAR
Simpangkawat
Bakungan
Trumon
Danau Toba
Sidikalang
Simanindo
Bandarpasir mandogai
Tanjung Bangsi
P. Simeulue
Ivabah
Kutainang
Rundeng
Pangururan
Ambarita
Prapat
Berembang
Sinabang
Ballasetas
Pulaksama
Tomok
Pulau Samosir
Aekanopan
Labuhanbilik
U. Kakat
P.Bago
Dolok Pinapan
Porsea
Silaen
Alaban
Singkilbaru
Balige
Parsoburan
Negiralama
P. Babi
Bangkaru
P. Tuangku
Onanganjang
Siborongborong
G. Sihabuhabu
Rantauprapat
Bagansiapiapi
Tg. Senebui
Tg. Medang
Kep. Banyak
Barus
Tarutung
Sibalanga
Perbaungan
P. Rupat
Sorkam
Onanhasang
Sipiongot
Kotapinang
Sibolga
Bagansinembah
Batupanjang
P. Musala
Tel. Tapanuli
Sipirok
Langgapayung
Dumai
Sifahandra
Sumatera
Gunungtua
Utara
Sintong
P. Bengkalis
Bengkalis
Huraba
Padang Sidimpuan
Pintupadang
Binanga
Lahewa
Gunungsitoli
Sungaipakning
Duri
P. Padang
Pasarsibuhuan
Daludalu
Titigading
Balaipungut
Selatpanjang
Lemang
P. Karimun
P. Nias
Sirombu
Siabu
G. Malea
P. Rantau (Tebingtinggi)
P. Rangsang
Panyabungan
Pasirpengarayan
Minas
Timun
P. Combol
Muarasoma
Kotanopan
Ujungbatu
Buatan
P. Kundur
Hilismaetano
Nias Settlements
Lagudri
Telukdalam
Natal
Hutanopan
Rao
Rokan
Aliantan
PEKANBARU
P. Sugi
P. Mendol
Batu
Kep.
Panti
Bangkinang
Parit
Airbangis
Talu
Candi Muara Takus
Lancang Kuning
Rantauparangin
Pulau Kateman
Sungaigaiguntung
P. Temiang
P. Buaya
Equator
Pulau Pini
G. Ophir
Lubuksikaping
Bonjol
Reninjauan
Pangkalanpanduk
Ularbemban
Tg. Datuk
P. Bakung
P. Lingga
P.Simuk
Baw
Ofuloa
Pulau Tanahmasa
Mandiangin
Suliki
Harau Canyon
Fort de Kock
Kotabaru
Riau
Tembilahan
Parittanjungmelayu
Kelumpang
Pulau Tanahbala
Bukittinggi
Payakumbuh
Maninjau
G. Merapi
Airmolek
Rengat
P. Basu
Tg. Basu
P. Posik
P. Selayar
P. Cukas
P. Singkep
Mentawai
Tiku
Padangpanjang
Batusangkar
Selat Siberut
Pariaman
Lubukalung
Talawi
Muara
Taluk
Selat Berhala
Indragiri
Singkarak
Solok
Sawahlunto
Banjarkasang
Seberida
PADANG
Lubukbargalung
Tanjungbalai
Sungaidareh
Peg.
Batuampar
Tunkal
Kualatungkal
Telukbayur
Tel. Bayur
Alahanpanjang
Dusunpasirmajang
Tigapulan
Dusunmudo
Simpang
Kagologolo
Pulau Siberut
Tg. Batumandi
U. Teluklembu
D. Dibaru
D. Diatas
Kotabaru
Jambi
Pangkalandurian
Tarusan
Painan
Tel. Painan
Muarasimatalu
Saudaina
Sumatera
Muarasiberut
Barat
Batukangkung
Muarabungo
Muaratebo
Sungaibengkal
Sabulubek
Taibelee
Kambang
Balaisalasa
Tumbijun
G. Kerinci
Sijunjang
JAMBI (TELANAIPURA)
Muaratembesi
Muarabulian
Selat Bungalaut
Sigoisooinan
Sungai Penuh
Siulakderas
Hot Springs
Rantauapanjang
Bangko
Bayunglincir
Siberimanua
Pulau Sipura
Tanjung Batu
Tapan
Pondung
Lamanggang
Jujun
Pauh
Sumate
Kaliet
Dusuntuo
Sarolangun
Tampang
Dabuk
Pasapuat
Mukomuko
G. Masurai
Surulangun
Binginteloh
Babat
Sabeugukgung
Selat Sikakap
Simakalo
Pasarbantal
G. Sebiat
Sukamenang
Muararupit
Sekayu
Talang
P. Pagai Selatan
Tiop
P. Taitaitanopo
Pulau
Lebongtanda
Trawas
Semeteh
Tabingbulang
PALEMBANG
Gelumbang
Muaraaman
Tabahanyer
Angading
Lubuklinggau
Muarabeliti
Pendopo
Belimbing
Selat Sanding
P. Sanding
Ketahun
Tanjung Gold Mines
Lais
Curup
Kepahiang
Tebingtinggi
Bungamas
Muaraenim
Pasarbembah
Tanjung Pagerdunu
Bengkulu
Tanjung Kerbau
Lahat
G. Dempo
Sugihwaras
Pagerdewa
Tais
Pagaralam
Baturaja
Pasartalo
Martapura
Bengkulu
Manna
Padangguci
Pulauberingin
Muaradua
Padanganget
Bintuan
Simpangsender
Liwa
Bambang
Pulau Enggano
Kayaapu
Krui
Ngaras
Tel. Bengkunat
Banding
Kota
Tel. Belimbing
Belimb

Kep. Mentawai
Mentawai Strait
Bukit Barisan
Banjaran Timur
Banjaran Titiwangsa
Java Trench
INDIAN
OCEAN

5077
2693
1759
5304
6048
2000

6° 2 4° 3 2° 4 0° 5 2° 6 4° 7 6°

A 96° B 98° C 100° D 102° E 104°

Scale 1 : 4,500,000
0 40 80 120 160 200 Kilometers
0 40 80 120 160 Statute Miles

SOUTH CHINA SEA
MALAYSIA
Kepulauan Natuna
P. Natuna Besar
Kep. Anambas
Laut Natuna
Karimata Strait
INDONESIA
Kalimantan Barat (BORNEO)
KALIMANTAN
Kalimantan Tengah
Sarawak
BRUNEI
PONTIANAK
Kuching
SIBU
SINGKAWANG
BANJARMASIN
MARTAPURA
JAKARTA
BANDAR LAMPUNG
Pulau Belitung
P. Bangka
PANGKALPINANG
GREATER SUNDA ISLANDS
Java Sea
JAVA
Equator

SOUTH CHINA SEA
MALAYSIA
Sarawak
Sabah
BRUNEI
KALIMANTAN
BORNEO
INDONESIA
Kalimantan Barat
Kalimantan Tengah
Kalimantan Timur
Kalimantan Selatan
Java Sea
Makassar Strait
+8h Gr. Time
+7h Gr. Time
KOTA KINABALU
Bandar Seri Begawan
Kuala Belait
Miri
Bintulu
SIBU
Kuching
SINGKAWANG
PONTIANAK
Equator
Ketapang
Pangkalanbuun
Sampit
Palangkaraya
BANJARMASIN
MARTAPURA
BALIKPAPAN
SAMARINDA
Tarakan
Tanjungredeb
Tawau
SANDAKAN
Labuan
G. Kinabalu
Ban. Crocker
Ban. Kapuas Hulu
Peg. Müller
Peg. Schwaner
Peg. Meratus
Kep. Natuna
Kep. Karimata
Kep. Karimunjawa
P. Laut
Friendship Shoal
North Luconia Shoals
Seahorse Shoal
South Luconia Shoals
Djems Bank
Sel. Karimata
Scale 1 : 4,500,000
0 40 80 120 160 200 Kilometers
0 40 80 120 160 Statute Miles

120°
G
122°
H
161
124°
J
126°
K
128°
L
P H I L I P P I N E S
Jolo
Mindanao Sea
MINDANAO
GENERAL SANTOS
Polomolok
Malapatan
Jose Abad Santos
Glan
Maasim
Kiamba
Maitum
Palimbang
Sarangani Island
Balut I.
Sulu Archipelago
Tapul Group
Tawitawi I.
Bato Bato
Sibutu I.
Philippine Trench
Kep. Nanusa
Kep. Karkaralong
Kep. Talaud
Kep. Karakelong
Melanguane
P. Salibabu
P. Kaburuang
Kep. Sangir
Tahuna
P. Sangir
P. Siau
P. Tahulandang
P. Biaro
+ 8h Gr.Time
+ 9h30h Gr.Time
Celebes Sea
E R S U N D A
P. Morotai
Kep. Loloda Utara
Daruba
Tobelo
P. Halmahera
Ternate
P. Tidore
Soa-Siu (Tidore)
Sulawesi Utara
MANADO
Bitung
Tondano
Airmadidi
P. Lembeh
Tomohon
Amurang
Kotamobagu
Minahasa Semenanjung
GORONTALO
Limboto
Tolitoli
P. Mayu
P. Tifore
Equator
Kep. Togian
Tel. Tomini
Molucca Sea
M O L U C C A S
P. Bacan
Labuha
Tel. Weda
Kep. Widi
Donggala
PALU
Poso
Sulawesi Tengah
Luwuk
Pagimana
P. Peleng
Kep. Banggai
Kep. Sula
P. Taliabu
P. Mangole
Sanana
P. Sanana
P. Obi
Kep. Obi
Ceram Sea
Tel. Tolo
Kolonedale
Kep. Bowokan
Sulawesi Selatan
Palopo
Makale
Rantepao
Sulawesi
M a l u k u
P. Buru
Namlea
North Banda Basin
P. Seram (Ceram)
AMBON
Teluk Bone
Sulawesi Tenggara
Kendari
P. Wowoni
P. Buton
Baubau
P. Muna
Raha
P. Kabaena
Kep. Tukangbesi
Watampone (Bone)
Sinjai
Bulukumba
Jeneponto
P. Selayar
B a n d a   S e a
Kep. Lucipara
Kep. Penyu
166
168

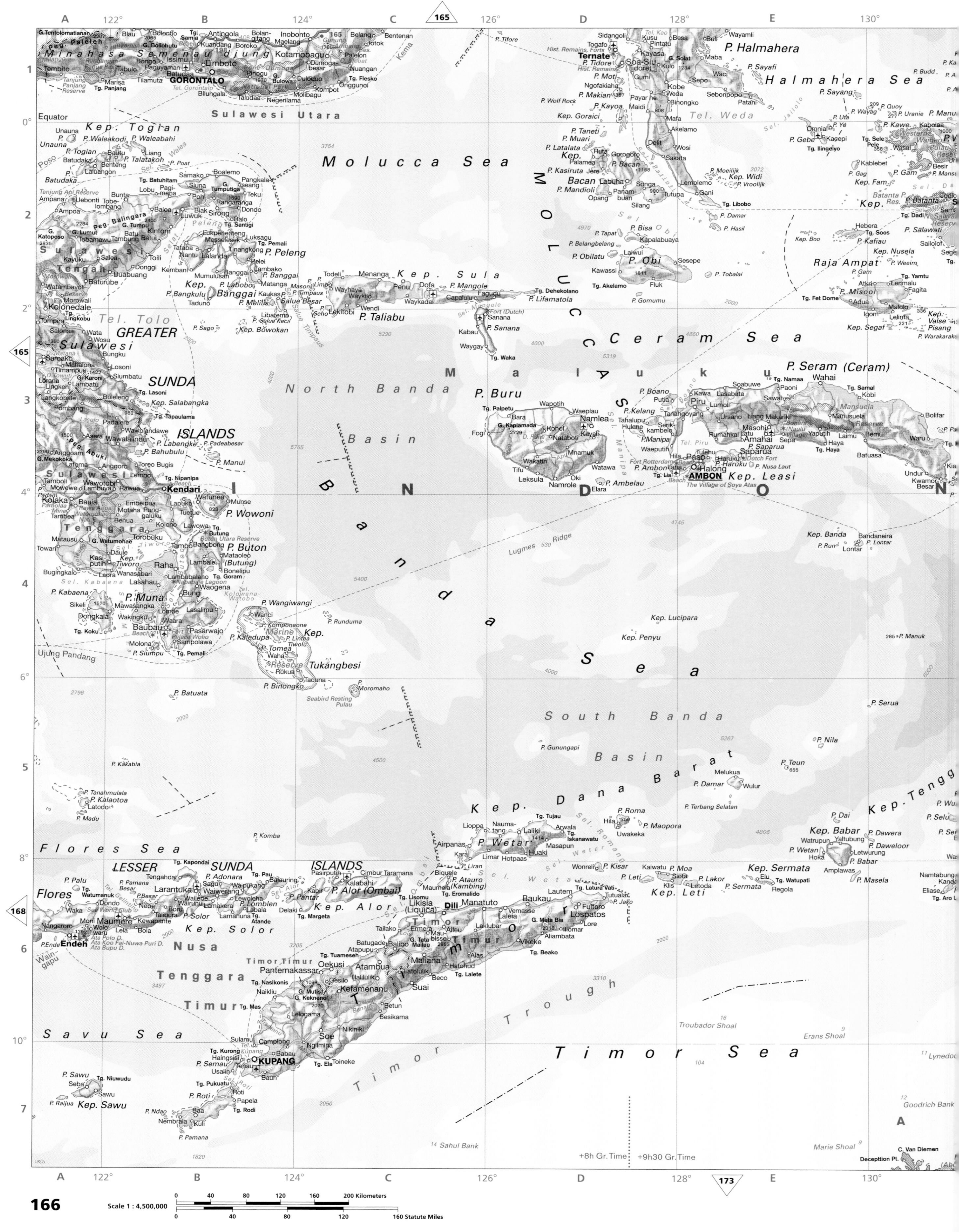

165
Molucca Sea
Sulawesi Utara
Kep. Togian
GORONTALO
Limboto
Kotamobagu
Ternate
P. Tidore
P. Halmahera
Halmahera Sea
Tel. Weda
P. Makian
P. Kayoa
Bacan
P. Obi
Kep. Sula
P. Taliabu
P. Mangole
P. Peleng
Kep. Banggai
Tel. Tolo
GREATER SUNDA ISLANDS
Sulawesi Tengah
Sulawesi Tenggara
Kendari
P. Wowoni
P. Buton
P. Muna
Baubau
Raha
Kep. Tukangbesi
Ujung Pandang
MOLUCCAS
Maluku
Ceram Sea
P. Seram (Ceram)
P. Buru
Namlea
AMBON
Kep. Leasi
Kep. Banda
Raja Ampat
P. Misool
North Banda Basin
BANDA
Banda Sea
South Banda Basin
Kep. Dana Barat
Lugmes Ridge
Kep. Lucipara
P. Wetar
Kep. Babar
Kep. Sermata
Kep. Leti
Flores Sea
Flores
LESSER SUNDA ISLANDS
Larantuka
Maumere
Endeh
Kep. Solor
Kep. Alor
P. Alor (Ombai)
Nusa Tenggara Timur
Timor Timur
Timor
Dili
Baukau
Lospalos
Manatuto
Atambua
Suai
Kefamenanu
Soe
KUPANG
Savu Sea
Kep. Sawu
P. Roti
Timor Trough
Timor Sea
Sahul Bank
+8h Gr. Time
+9h30 Gr. Time
Equator
122°
124°
126°
128°
130°
168
173
Scale 1 : 4,500,000
0 40 80 120 160 200 Kilometers
0 40 80 120 160 Statute Miles

132°
G
134°
H
136°
J
138°
K
140°
L
Kep. Mapia (Indonesia)
+10h Gr. Time
+9h30 Gr. Time
P A C I F I C O C E A N
Equator
New Guinea Trench
Doberai Peninsula (Vogelkop)
Manokwari
Sorong
Warmandi
Koor
Saukorem
Mubrani
Kaironi
Amberbaken
Teminabuan
Inanwatan
Ransiki
Rasiei
P. Numfor
Biak
Kep. Padaido
P. Yapen
Serui
Sarmi
Kep. Podena
JAYAPURA
Vanimo
Tel. Berau
Tel. Bintuni
Bintuni
Babo
Kep. Sariga
Fakfak
Onin (Fakfak) Peninsula
Bomberai Pen.
Kaimana
Kep. Mamboor
Nabire
Enarotali
Tembagapura
Wamena
Puncak Jaya (Pk. Carstensz)
Puncak Trikora
Puncak Mandala
NEW GUINEA
Peg. Van Rees
Foja Mts.
Rouffaer Reserves
Lorentz Reserve
Peg. Jayawijaya
Peg. Sudirman
Peg. Maoke
Timika
Amamapare
Agats
Casuarina Coast
Mapi
Bade
Merauke
P. Dolak
Dolak Pulau Reserve
Kep. Kai
Tual
Kep. Aru
Dobo
South East Aru Marine Reserve
P. Yamdena
Tanimbar
Arafura Sea
PAPUA NEW GUINEA
183
174
A U S T R A L I A
Cobourg Pen.
Wessel Is.
C. Wessel
C. Croker
Smith Pt.
1
2
3
4
5
6
7
2°
4°
6°
8°
10°

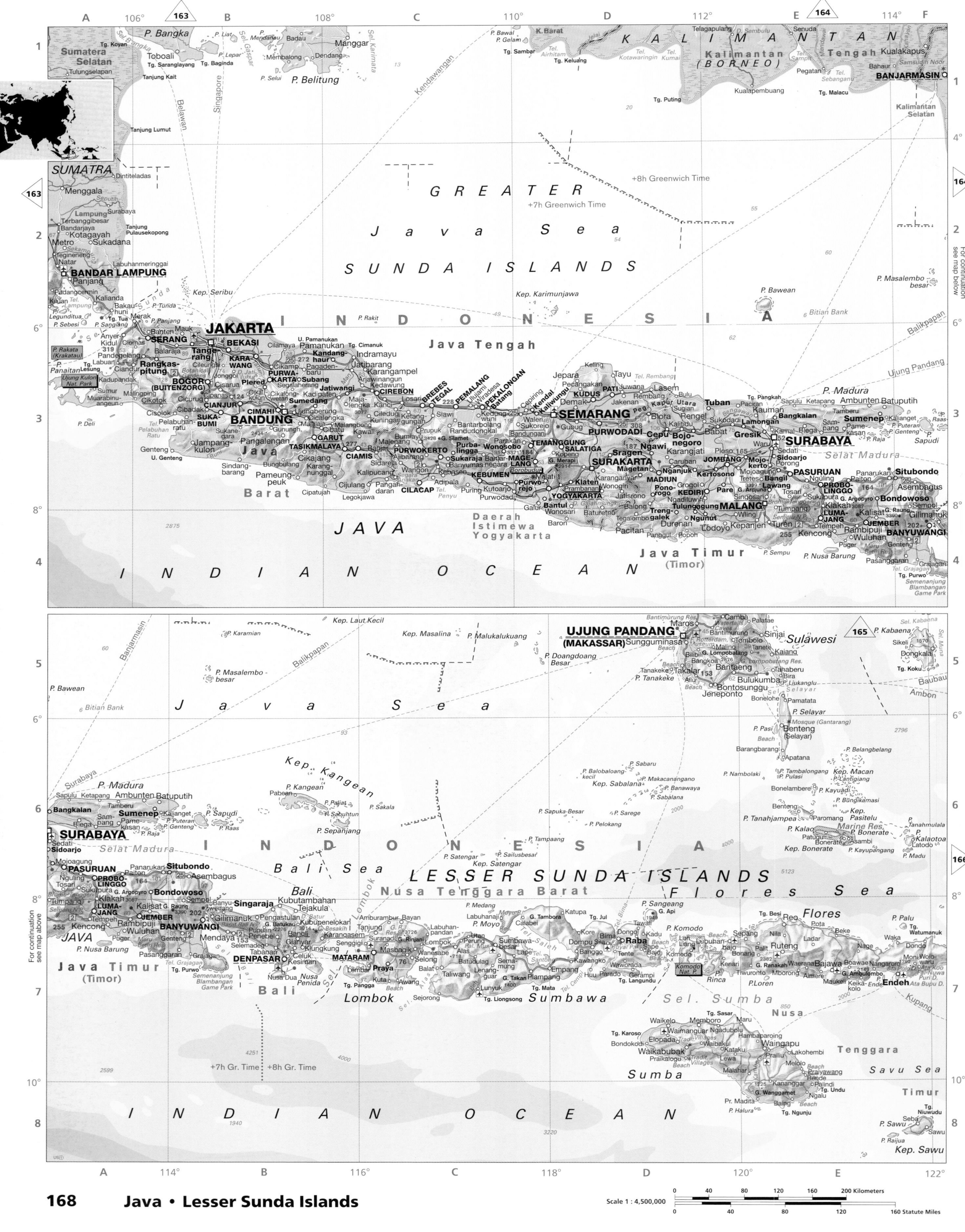

K A L I M A N T A N
Kalimantan (BORNEO)
Kalimantan Tengah
Kalimantan Selatan
BANJARMASIN
Sumatera Selatan
SUMATRA
P. Bangka
P. Belitung
Lampung
BANDAR LAMPUNG
G R E A T E R
S U N D A I S L A N D S
Java Sea
+7h Greenwich Time
+8h Greenwich Time
I N D O N E S I A
JAKARTA
BEKASI
SERANG
BOGOR (BUITENZORG)
BANDUNG
CIREBON
Java Tengah
SEMARANG
SURAKARTA
YOGYAKARTA
Daerah Istimewa Yogyakarta
SURABAYA
MALANG
JEMBER
BANYUWANGI
Java Barat
J A V A
Java Timur (Timor)
P. Madura
Selat Madura
P. Bawean
I N D I A N O C E A N
UJUNG PANDANG (MAKASSAR)
Sulawesi
Bali Sea
Bali
DENPASAR
MATARAM
Lombok
L E S S E R S U N D A I S L A N D S
Nusa Tenggara Barat
Sumbawa
Flores Sea
Flores
Sumba
Nusa Tenggara Timur
Savu Sea
Kep. Sawu
+7h Gr. Time +8h Gr. Time
For continuation see map below
For continuation see map above
Scale 1 : 4,500,000
0 40 80 120 160 200 Kilometers
0 40 80 120 160 Statute Miles

Australia and Oceania – a new world in the Pacific

The smallest continent (2,972,970 square miles/7.7 million sq. km) is also the one farthest from all the others. Australia's distance from Europe and the inaccessibility of its shores, due among other things to the coral reefs that extend north and east, were among the causes for its late exploration. Distinctive features are the western plateau with average heights of between 656 and 1,640 feet (200 – 500 m), the central lowlands with the internal drainage basin of Lake Eyre and the mountain areas in the East including the island of Tasmania. The archipelagos north and east of Australia, including the world's second largest island, New Guinea, and the two-island nation of New Zealand, are sometimes called Oceania, and comprise some 7,500 islands with an area of 501,930 square miles (1.3 million sq. km) dispersed over a sea area of 27,027,000 square miles (70 million sq. km). Melanesia and New Zealand constitute the outer arc of islands, Micronesia and Polynesia the inner. The islands sit partially on old mountains of volcanic origin beneath the sea and partially on elevated coral reefs. The 180th meridian, the dateline, runs through the middle of the region.

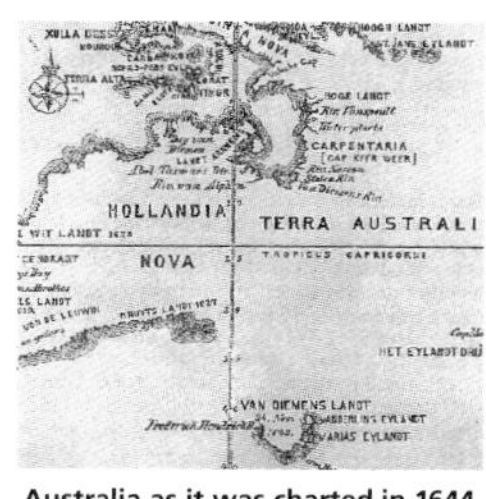

Australia as it was charted in 1644 by the Dutch Abel Tasman. It was not until 1770 that the eastern coast was explored by James Cook.

Australia: Northwestern Region
p. 172 – 173

Australia: Northeastern Region
p. 174 – 175

Australia: Southwestern Region
p. 176 – 177

Australia: Eastern Region
p. 178 – 179

Australia: Southeastern Region, Tasman
p. 180 – 181

New Zealand
p. 182

Papua New Guinea
p. 183

Solomon Islands · Vanuatu · Fiji · Samoa
Tonga p. 184

Australia: Northwestern Region
p. 172–173

Australia: Northeastern Region
p. 174–175

Australia: Southwestern Region
p. 176–177

Australia: Eastern Region
p. 178–179

Australia: Southeastern Region, Tasmania
p. 180–181

New Zealand
p. 182

Papua New Guinea
p. 183

Solomon Islands · Vanuatu · Fiji · Samoa · Tonga p. 184

INDIAN OCEAN
Java Trench
North Australian Basin
Rowley Shoals
Mermaid Reef
Clerke Reef
Imperieuse Reef
Rowley Shelf
Exmouth Plateau
Seringapatam Reef
Scott Reef
Ashmore Reef
Hibernia
Lynher Reef
Beagle R
Churchill Reef
Adele I.
Buccaneer Arch
C. Leveque
Lombadina
Pender Bay
Sunday Strait
Emeriau Pt.
Lacepede Is.
Beagle Bay
King Sound
C. Baskerville
Carnot Bay
Abor. Land
Derby
Coulomb Pt.
C. Bertholet Wildlife Sanct.
Dampier Land
Mowanjum
Kilto
Willare Bridge Roadhouse
Broome
Gantheaume Pt.
Roebuck Roadhouse
Roebuck Bay
Thangoo
Manguel Creek
Cable Beach
C. Latouche Treville
La Grange Bay
La Grange
C. Bossut
Dampier Downs
Nita Downs
Anna Plains
Eighty Mile Beach
Mandora
Wallal Downs
Sandfire Flat Roadhouse
West
Great San
Aust
Poissonnier Point
C. Keraudren
Larrey Pt.
Pardoo Roadhouse
Spit Pt.
Great Northern Hwy.
Port Hedland
C. Thouin
Goldsworthy
Mount Goldsworthy
Shay Gap
Strelley
De Grey Riv.
Callawa
Carlindi
Muccan
Yarrie
Warrawagine
Mundabullangana
Wallareenya
Lalla Rookh
Eginbah
Bamboo Creek
Five Mile Hill
Mt. Edgar
Mount Edgar
Marble Bar
Gillam
Abydos
Yandeearra
Mt. Gratwick
Hillside
Nullagine
Mt. Cooke
Bonney Downs
Mt. McKay
Roy Hill
Mount Divide
Balfour Downs
Ethel Creek
Talawana
Walgun
Jiggalong
Newman
Ophthalmia Ra.
Mt. Whaleback Mining Area
Prairie Downs
Isabelle
Woodi Woodi Mining Centre
Gregory Ra.
Throssell Ra.
Paterson Ra.
Telfer
L. Waukarlycarly
Rudall River National Park
Mt. Connaughton
Hanging Rock
L. Dora
Eva Broadhurst L.
L. Blanche
L. Winifred
McKay Ra.
No. 24 Well
Robertson Ra.
Harbutt Ra.
L. Disappointment
Runton Ra.
Savory Riv.
Legendre I.
Dampier Archipelago
Sloping Pt.
C. Lambert
Pt. Samson
Wickham
Roebourne
Karratha
Dampier
Nickol Bay
Whim Creek
Mallina
Karratha Roadhouse
C. Preston
Montebello Is.
C. Dupuy
Barrow I.
Wapet Camp
Barrow I. Oil Field
South End
Pasco Island
Mardie I.
Barrow I. Shoals
Mardie
Mary Anne Passage
Mary Anne Group
Thevenard I.
Fortescue Riv. Roadhouse
Millstream Chichester Nat. P.
Sherlock Riv.
Yule Riv.
Turner Riv.
Mt. Richthofen
Mount Florance
Pannawonica
Mt. Elvire
Millstream
Tambrey
Yarraloola
Onslow
Beadon Pt.
Muiron Is.
North West C.
U.S. Navy's SRC Base
Exmouth
Exmouth Gulf
Mt. Hollister
C. Range Nat. P.
Learmonth
Peedamulla
Red Hill
Cane River
Hamersley Range
Pilbara
Chichester Ra.
Wittenoom
Wittenoom Gorge
Pk. Hester
Mt. Margaret
Mount Brockman
Hamersley
Mt. Brockman
Mt. Frederick
Mt. Bruce
Mt. George
Mt. Marsh
Tom Price
Mt. Tom Price
Hamersley Range Nat. P.
Juna Downs
Mt. Meharry
Mt. Bennett
Mt. Robinson
Koordarrie
Mt. Stuart
Nanutarra Roadhouse
Ashburton Riv.
Wyloo
Mt. Wall
Rocklea
Kooline
Hardey Riv.
Paraburdoo
Paraburdoo Mining Area
Mt. Palgrave
Ashburton Downs
Turee Cr.
Yanrey
Giralia
Ningaloo
Bullara
Barradale Roadhouse
Uaroo
Coral Bay
Cape Ra.
Giralia Ra.
Towera
Winning
N.W. Coastal Hwy.
Jiggalong Abor. Land
Flora & Fauna Reserve
Scale 1 : 4,500,000
0 40 80 120 160 200 Kilometers
0 40 80 120 160 Statute Miles

Timor Sea
Joseph Bonaparte Gulf
Beagle Gulf
Van Diemen Gulf
Darwin
Katherine
Wyndham
Kununurra
Halls Creek
Fitzroy Crossing
Tennant Creek
Kimberley Plateau
Tanami Desert
Northern Territory
Melville Island
Cobourg Pen.
Kakadu National Park
Arnhem Aboriginal Land
Tropic of Capricorn
+8h Gr. Time
+9h 30 Gr. Time

Scale 1 : 4,500,000
0 40 80 120 160 200 Kilometers
0 40 80 120 160 Statute Miles

183
144°
H
L
PORT MORESBY
NEW GUINEA
PAPUA NEW GUINEA
Owen Stanley Range
Mt. Victory 1891
Mt. Suckling 3676
Cape Nelson
Collingwood Bay
Goodenough Bay
Ward Hunt Strait
Goodenough I.
Fergusson Island
Normanby Island
d'Entrecasteaux Islands
Egum Atoll
Goschen Strait
Milne Bay
Alotau
Sideia I.
Basilaki I.
Kupiano
Magaubo
Suau
Torres Strait
Great Barrier Reef
Section
Marine Park
Far Northern
C. York
C. Grenville
Coral Basin
Osprey Reef
Coral Sea
Coral Sea Island Territory
Bougainville Reef
PACIFIC
Queensland Plateau
Willis Group
Holmes Reef
South West I.
Chilcott I.
Lihou Reefs and Cays
Flinders Reef
OCEAN
Great Barrier Reef
Central Section
Marion Reef
Marine Park
Swain Reefs
Long Reefs
Great Dividing Range
Cape York Peninsula
Cooktown
Wet Tropics
Cairns
of Queensland
Atherton Tableland
Innisfail
Magnetic Island
TOWNSVILLE
Charters Towers
Hughenden
Bowen
Whitsunday I.
Mackay
Clarke Range
Connors Ra.
Denham Range
Percy Isles
Northumberland Isles
Cumberland Is.
1
2
3
4
5
6
7
12°
14°
16°
18°
20°
G
144°
H
146°
179
J
148°
K
150°
L
152°
M

Scale 1 : 4,500,000

0 40 80 120 160 200 Kilometers

0 40 80 120 160 Statute Miles

Tropic of Capricorn
Great Victoria Desert
Nullarbor Plain
Great Australian Bight
INDIAN OCEAN
Northern Territory
South Australia
Alice Springs
Uluru Nat. P.
Ayers Rock
Great Victoria Desert Flora & Fauna Reserve
Tallaringa Conservation Park
Maralinga - Tjarutja Aboriginal Lands
Woomera Prohibited Area
Nullarbor Regional Reserve
Yellabinna Regional Reserve
Eyre Pen.
Ceduna
Port Lincoln
Trans-Australian Railway
+8h Greenwich Time
+9h 30 Greenwich Time

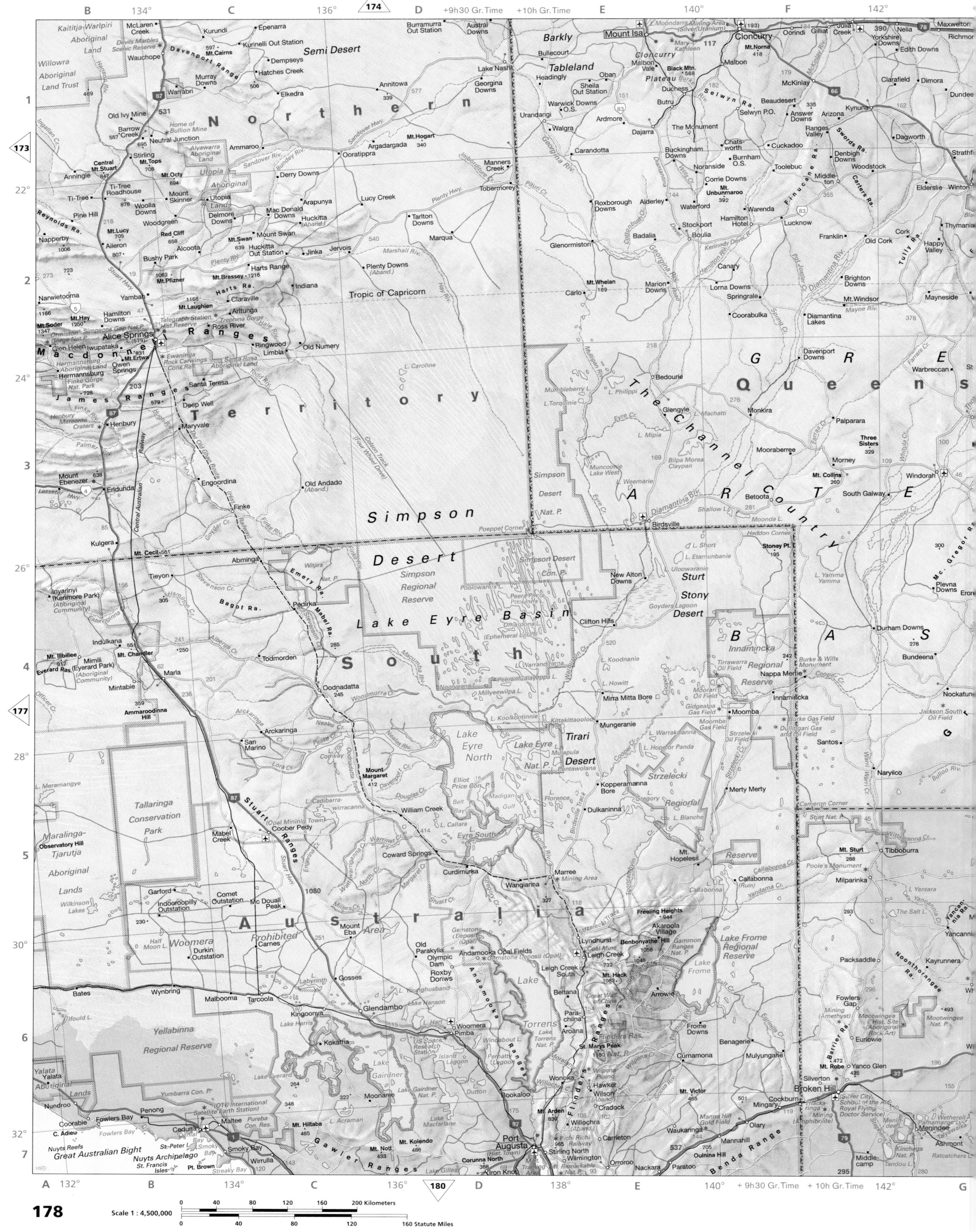

134°
136°
174
+9h30 Gr. Time
+10h Gr. Time
140°
142°
Kaititja-Warlpiri Aboriginal Land
Willowra Aboriginal Land Trust
McLaren Creek
Kurundi
Epenarra
Kurinelli Out Station
Semi Desert
Wauchope
Davenport Range
Dempseys
Hatches Creek
Murray Downs
Warrabri
Elkedra
Annitowa
Burramurra Out Station
Austral Downs
Lake Nash
Georgina Downs
Barkly
Tableland
Bullecourt
Headingly
Mount Isa
Cloncurry
Malbon
Black Mtn.
Duchess
Selwyn Ra.
Selwyn P.O.
Julia Creek
Gilliat
Oorindi
Nelia
Maxwelton
Richmond
Yorkshire Downs
Edith Downs
McKinlay
Clarafield
Dimora
Dundee
Beaudesert
Answer Downs
Arizona
Kynuna
Urandangi
Walgra
Ardmore
Dajarra
Butru
The Monument
Sheila Out Station
Warwick Downs O.S.
Oban
Northern
Territory
Old Ivy Mine
Barrow Creek
Neutral Junction
Home of Bullion Mine
Alyawarra Aboriginal Land
Ammaroo
Argadargada
Mt.Hogart
Sandover Hwy.
Ooratippra
Central Mt.Stuart
Anningie
Stirling
Mt.Tops
Utopia Aboriginal Land
Mt.Octy
Derry Downs
Manners Creek
Tobermorey
Carandotta
Buckingham Downs
Chatsworth
Noranside
Burnham O.S.
Cuckadoo
Toolebuc
Ranges Valley
Denbigh Downs
Woodstock
Dagworth
Swords Ra.
Stratford
Ti-Tree
Ti-Tree Roadhouse
Woolla Downs
Mount Skinner
Arapunya
Lucy Creek
Plenty Hwy.
Corrie Downs
Mt. Unbunmaroo
Middleton
Elderslie
Winton
Pine Hill
Reynolds Ra.
Woodgreen
Delmore Downs
Mac Donald Downs
Huckitta
Tarlton Downs
Roxborough Downs
Alderley
Waterford
Hamilton Hotel
Warenda
Lucknow
Carters Ra.
Napperby
Mt.Lucy
Red Cliff
Mount Swan
Mt.Swan
Marqua
Stockport
Boulia
Badalia
Franklin
Old Cork
Cork
Thymania
Happy Valley
Tully Ra.
Aileron
Alcoota
Huckitta Out Station
Jinka
Jervois
Glenormiston
Bushy Park
Harts Range
Plenty Downs (Aband.)
Canary
Mt.Brassey
Mt.Pfizner
Indiana
Mt.Whelan
Marion Downs
Lorna Downs
Brighton Downs
Narwietooma
Yambah
Claraville
Tropic of Capricorn
Carlo
Springrale
Mt.Windsor
Mayneside
Mt.Laughlen
Arltunga
Hamilton Downs
Mt.Hay
Mt.Soder
Telegraph Station Hist. Reserve
Ross River
Alice Springs
Ringwood
Limbla
Old Numery
Coorabulka
Diamantina Lakes
Macdonnell Ranges
Glen Helen
Iwupataka
Hermannsburg
Owen Springs
Ewaninga Rock Carvings Cons. Res.
Santa Rosa Aboriginal Land
Santa Teresa
L. Caroline
Davenport Downs
Warbreccan
Bedourie
Mumbleberry L.
L. Philippi
L. Torquinie
Glengyle
Monkira
Palparara
Queensland
James Ranges
Deep Well
Henbury
Henbury Meteorite Craters
Maryvale
The Channel Country
Three Sisters
Mooraberree
Morney
Mount Ebenezer
Erldunda
Lasseter Hwy.
Engoordina
Old Andado (Aband.)
Simpson Desert Nat. P.
Muncoonie Lake West
Bilpa Morea Claypan
Mt. Collins
Windorah
Betoota
South Galway
Diamantina Riv.
Finke
Simpson
Desert
Poeppel Corner
Birdsville
Haddon Corner
Stoney Pt.
Kulgera
Mt. Cecil
Abminga
Witjira Nat. P.
Simpson Desert Con. P.
Simpson Regional Reserve
New Alton Downs
L. Short
L. Etamunbanie
Sturt Stony Desert
Tieyon
Emery Ra.
Mc. Gregor Ra.
Plevna Downs
Eromanga
Inyarinyi (Kenmore Park) (Aboriginal Community)
Bagot Ra.
Pedirka
Lake Eyre Basin
Clifton Hills
Goyders Lagoon
Durham Downs
Indulkana
Mt. Illbillee
Mimili
Everard Ras. (Everard Park) (Aboriginal Community)
Mt. Chandler
Todmorden
South
Australia
Innamincka Regional Reserve
Burke & Wills Monument
Nappa Merrie
Bundeena
Marla
Mintabie
Oodnadatta
Mirra Mitta Bore
Innamincka
Nockatunga
Ammaroodinna Hill
L. Koolkootinnie
Kittakittaooloo
Mungeranie
Moomba
Santos
Jackson South Oil Field
Arckaringa
San Marino
Lake Eyre North
Lake Eyre Nat. P.
Tirari Desert
Strzelecki Regional Reserve
Naryilco
Mount Margaret
Elliot Price Con. P.
Kopperamanna Bore
Merty Merty
L. Meramangye
Tallaringa Conservation Park
William Creek
Dulkaninna
Cameron Corner
Maralinga-Tjarutja Aboriginal Lands
Observatory Hill
Mabel Creek
Stuart Ranges
Coober Pedy
Coward Springs
Lake Eyre South
Mt. Hopeless
Mt. Sturt
Tibooburra
Poole's Monument
Milparinka
Curdimurka
Marree
Wangianna
Callabonna
Garford
Comet Outstation
Indooroopilly Outstation
Mc Douall Peak
Freeling Heights
Akaroola Village
Mount Eba
Prohibited Area
Woomera
Carnes
Durkin Outstation
Old Parakylia
Olympic Dam
Roxby Downs
Andamooka Opal Fields
Lyndhurst
Leigh Creek
Leigh Creek South
Gammon Ranges Nat. P.
Lake Frome Regional Reserve
Lake Frome
Packsaddle
Yancannia
Kayrunnera
Noonthorangee Ra.
Bates
Wynbring
Malbooma
Tarcoola
Gosses
Beltana
Arrowie
Mt. Hack
Glendambo
Kingoonya
Lake Torrens
Para-chilna
Aroana
Fowlers Gap
Mootwingee Nat. P.
Mootwingee Hist. Site
Yellabinna Regional Reserve
Kokatha
Pimba
Woomera
Lake Gairdner
Flinders Ranges
St.Marys Peak
Frome Downs
Benagerie
Mulyungarie
Curnamona
Euriowie
Yanco Glen
Mt. Robe
Yalata
Lake Everard
Moonaree
Bookaloo
Wonoka
Hawker
Wilson
Cradock
Mt. Victor
Silverton
Broken Hill
Nundroo
Coorabie
Penong
Fowlers Bay
C. Adieu
Ceduna
Maltee
Smoky Bay
Wirrulla
Mt. Hiltaba
Gawler Ranges
Mt. Nott
Mt. Kolendo
Corunna North
Iron Knob
Port Augusta
Stirling North
Wilmington
Orroroo
Carrieton
Willochra
Mt. Arden
Waukaringa
Mannahill
Olary
Cockburn
Mingary
Menindee
Ashmont
Middle-camp
Paratoo
Nackara
Oulnina Hill
Benda Range
Nuyts Reefs
Great Australian Bight
Nuyts Archipelago
St. Francis Isles
St. Peter I.
Pt. Brown
Streaky Bay
Scale 1 : 4,500,000
0 40 80 120 160 200 Kilometers
0 40 80 120 160 Statute Miles
173
177
180

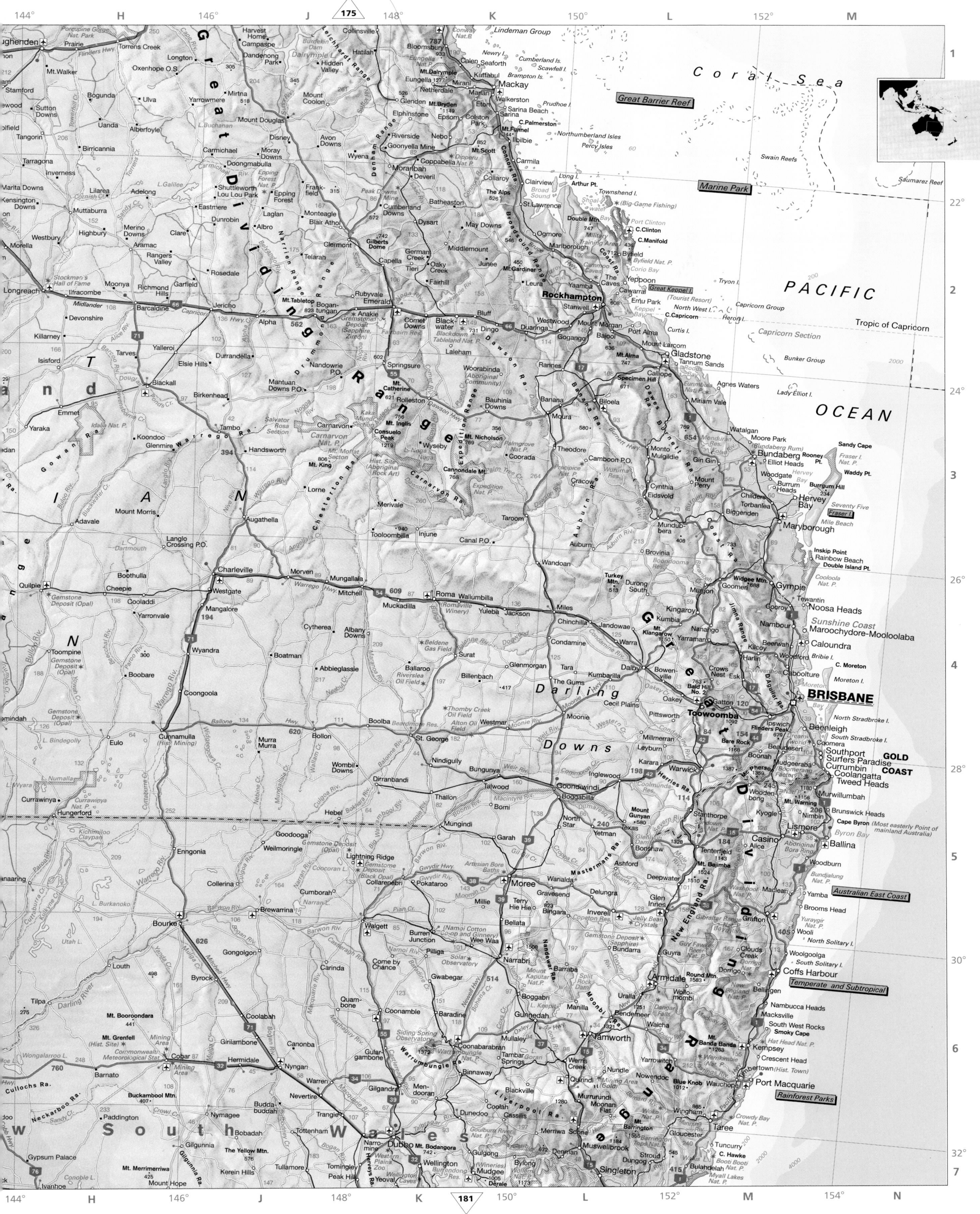
Coral Sea
PACIFIC
OCEAN
Great Barrier Reef
Marine Park
Australian East Coast
Temperate and Subtropical
Rainforest Parks
Tropic of Capricorn
Great Dividing Range
Darling Downs
Drummond Range
Carnarvon Ra.
Expedition Range
Dawson Ra.
Great Dividing Range
South Wales
Lindeman Group
Cumberland Is.
Northumberland Isles
Percy Isles
Swain Reefs
Capricorn Group
Capricorn Section
Bunker Group
Mackay
Rockhampton
Gladstone
Bundaberg
Hervey Bay
Maryborough
Gympie
Noosa Heads
Sunshine Coast
Maroochydore-Mooloolaba
Caloundra
BRISBANE
Toowoomba
Southport
Surfers Paradise
GOLD COAST
Coolangatta
Tweed Heads
Byron Bay
Ballina
Lismore
Grafton
Coffs Harbour
Port Macquarie
Taree
Tamworth
Armidale
Moree
Goondiwindi
Roma
Charleville
St. George
Bourke
Cobar
Dubbo
Longreach
Emerald
Blackall
Cunnamulla
Wallumbilla
Miles
Dalby
Warwick
Fraser I.
Sandy Cape
Double Island Pt.
Cape Byron
North Stradbroke I.
South Stradbroke I.
Moreton I.
Tryon I.
Heron I.
Lady Elliot I.
Saumarez Reef
144°
146°
148°
150°
152°
154°
22°
24°
26°
28°
30°
32°
H
J
K
L
M
N
1
2
3
4
5
6
7
175
181

178
177
A 132°
B
134°
C
136°
D
138°
E
140°
F
142°
G
32°
34°
36°
38°
40°
42°
Yellabinna Regional Reserve
Yalata
Yalata Aboriginal Lands
Yumbarra Con. P.
Lake Everard
Lake Gairdner
Lake Gairdner Nat. P.
Island Lagoon
Lake Torrens
Nundroo
Coorabie
C. Adieu
Fowlers Bay
Penong
Nuyts Reefs
OTC International Satellite Earth Station
Ceduna
Maltee
Pureba Con. Res.
Mt. Hiltaba
L. Acraman
Moonaree
Lake Macfarlane
Dutton
Bookaloo
St. Peter I.
Smoky Bay
Nuyts Archipelago
Pt. Brown
St. Francis Isles
Wirrulla
Streaky Bay
Gawler Ranges
Mt. Nott
Mt. Kolendo
Pinkawillinie Con. P.
Lake Gilles
Corunna North
Iron Knob
Port Augusta
Whyalla
Great Australian Bight
Poochera
Minnipa
Kyancutta
Kimba
Pt. Weyland
Port Kenny
Anxious Bay
Eyre Peninsula
Waddikee
Mt. Wedge
Lock
Darke Peak
Cleve
Cowell
Lucky Bay
Franklin Harbour
Flinders I.
C. Finnis
Elliston
Investigator Group
Sheringa
Rudall
Arno Bay
Mount Hope
Yeelanna
Port Neill
Spencer Gulf
Cummins
Tumby Bay
Coulta
Sir Joseph Banks Group
Greenly I.
Coffin Bay Nat. P.
Whidbey Isles
Port Lincoln
Lincoln Nat. P.
Thistle I.
C. Carnot
West Point
C. Catastrophe
Neptune I.
Wardang Island
Port Victoria
Hardwicke Bay
Minlaton
Warooka
Yorke Peninsula
Yorketown
Formby Bay
Inneston
C. Spencer
Sturt Bay
Investigator Strait
Kangaroo I.
Cape Borda
Flinders Chase Nat. P.
Parndana
Kingscote
Penneshaw
Backstairs Passage
D'Estrees Bay
C. Hart
C. Gantheaume Con. P.
C. Du Couedic
Cape Bouguer
Vivonne Bay
Cape Gantheaume
St. Marys Peak
Flinders Ranges Nat. P.
Wonoka
Hawker
Wilson
Cradock
Mt. Arden
Willochra
Pichi Richi Railway
Stirling North
Wilmington
Carrieton
Orroroo
Mt. Remarkable
Melrose
Murray Town
Wirrabara
Port Germein
Port Pirie
Laura
Jamestown
Gladstone
Crystal Brook
Mt. Bryan
Hallett
Spalding
Peterborough
Terowie
Port Broughton
Tickera
Snowtown
Clare
Burra
Bute
Kadina
Wallaroo
Moonta Bay
Kulpara
Auburn
Port Wakefield
Balaklava
Maitland
Ardrossan
Gulf St. Vincent
Gawler
Virginia
Port Vincent
Port Adelaide
ADELAIDE
Barossa Valley
Hahndorf
Mount Lofty Ranges
Mount Barker
Mc Laren Vale
Murray Bridge
Normanville
Cape Jervis
Victor Harbor
Fleurieu Pen.
Encounter Bay
Goolwa
Milang
Macdonnell Pen.
Coorong Nat. P.
Younghusband Peninsula
Curnamona
Mulyungarie
Mt. Victor
Mingary
Cockburn
Olary
Waukaringa
Manna Hill Gold Field
Mannahill
Oulnina Hill
Nackara
Paratoo
Boiekevie Hill
Benda Range
South Australia
Oakbank
Morgan Vale
Kia Ora
Braemar
Canegrass
Mt. Mary
Eudunda
Morgan
Waikerie
Kingston-on-Murray
Renmark
Barmera
Berri
Loxton
Nuriootpa
Angaston
Sedan
Blanchetown
Swan Reach
Alawoona
Paruna
Purnong
Karoonda
Pinnaroo
Tailem Bend
Sherlock
Geranium
Lameroo
Peake
Meningie
Coonalpyn
Tintinara
Mt. Boothby
Policemans Point
Keith
Ngarkat Con. P.
Bordertown
Lacepede Bay
Kingston S.E.
C. Jaffa
Lucindale
Naracoorte
Naracoorte Caves Con. P.
Robe
C. Dombey
Beachport
Coonawarra
Penola
Millicent
Canunda Nat. P.
C. Banks
Cape Banks
Mount Gambier
Port Mac Donnell
Dingley Dell Cons. P.
Mt. Robe
Yanco Glen
Silverton
Broken Hill
Menindee
Ashmont
Kinchega Nat. P.
Middle-camp
Popilta
Mindona
Travellers L.
Milkengay L.
Pooncarie
Bunnerlingee
Murray River Basin
Darling Riv.
Wentworth
Dareton
Mildura
Red Cliffs
Merbein
Colignan
Robinvale
Hattah
Hattah-Kulkyne Nat. P.
Sunset Country
Murray-Sunset Nat. P.
Meringur
Cullulleraine
Ouyen
Walpeup
Underbool
Murrayville
Big Desert Wilderness
Wyperfeld Nat. P.
Hopetoun
Lascelles
Sea Lake
Big Desert
Yanac
Jeparit
Warracknabeal
Nhill
Dimboola
Little Desert
Kaniva
Wimmera
Murtoa
Horsham
Nautimuk
Goroke
Carpolac
Edenhope
Harrow
Balmoral
Grampians
Stawell
Ararat
Casterton
Coleraine
Dunkeld
Hamilton
Dartmoor
Heywood
Penshurst
Macarthur
Mortlake
Terang
Lower Glenelg Nat. P.
Portland
Portland Bay
Cape Bridgewater
C. Nelson
Port Fairy
Koroit
Warrnambool
Peterborough
Port Campbell Nat. P.
The Twelve Apostles
Timboon
Moonlight Head
Mt. Richmond Nat. P.
Discovery Bay
+9h 30 Greenwich Time
+10h Greenwich Time
South Australia Basin
INDIAN OCEAN
5604
5496
200
2000
4000
Scale 1 : 4,500,000
0 40 80 120 160 200 Kilometers
0 40 80 120 160 Statute Miles

179
South Wales
Great Dividing Range
Victoria
Tasmania
Riverina
SYDNEY
NEWCASTLE
WOLLONGONG
CANBERRA
MELBOURNE
GEELONG
HOBART
Launceston
Ballarat
Bendigo
Wagga Wagga
Albury
Wodonga
Queanbeyan
Goulburn
Bathurst
Orange
Dubbo
Tamworth
Port Macquarie
Taree
Maitland
Cessnock
Gosford
Katoomba
Lithgow
Nowra-Bomaderry
Ulladulla
Batemans Bay
Moruya
Narooma
Bega
Eden
Cooma
Jindabyne
Shepparton-Mooroopna
Wangaratta
Benalla
Seymour
Sale
Traralgon
Morwell
Moe-Yallourn
Bairnsdale
Lakes Entrance
Devonport
Burnie-Somerset
Ulverstone
Kingston
A.C.T.= Australian Capital Territory
Tasman Basin
PACIFIC OCEAN
Tasman Sea
Bass Strait
Banks Strait
Furneaux Group
Flinders I.
King I.
Wilsons Promontory Nat. P.
Blue Mountains Nat. P.
Kosciusko Nat. P.
Mt. Kosciusko 2228
South West Nat. P.
Tasman Pen.
Port Arthur
C. Howe
Lord Howe Island
Lord Howe I.
Ball's Pyramid
144° 146° 148° 150° 152° 154° 156° 158° 160°
34° 36° 38° 40° 32°
H J K L M N
1 2 3 4 5 6 7

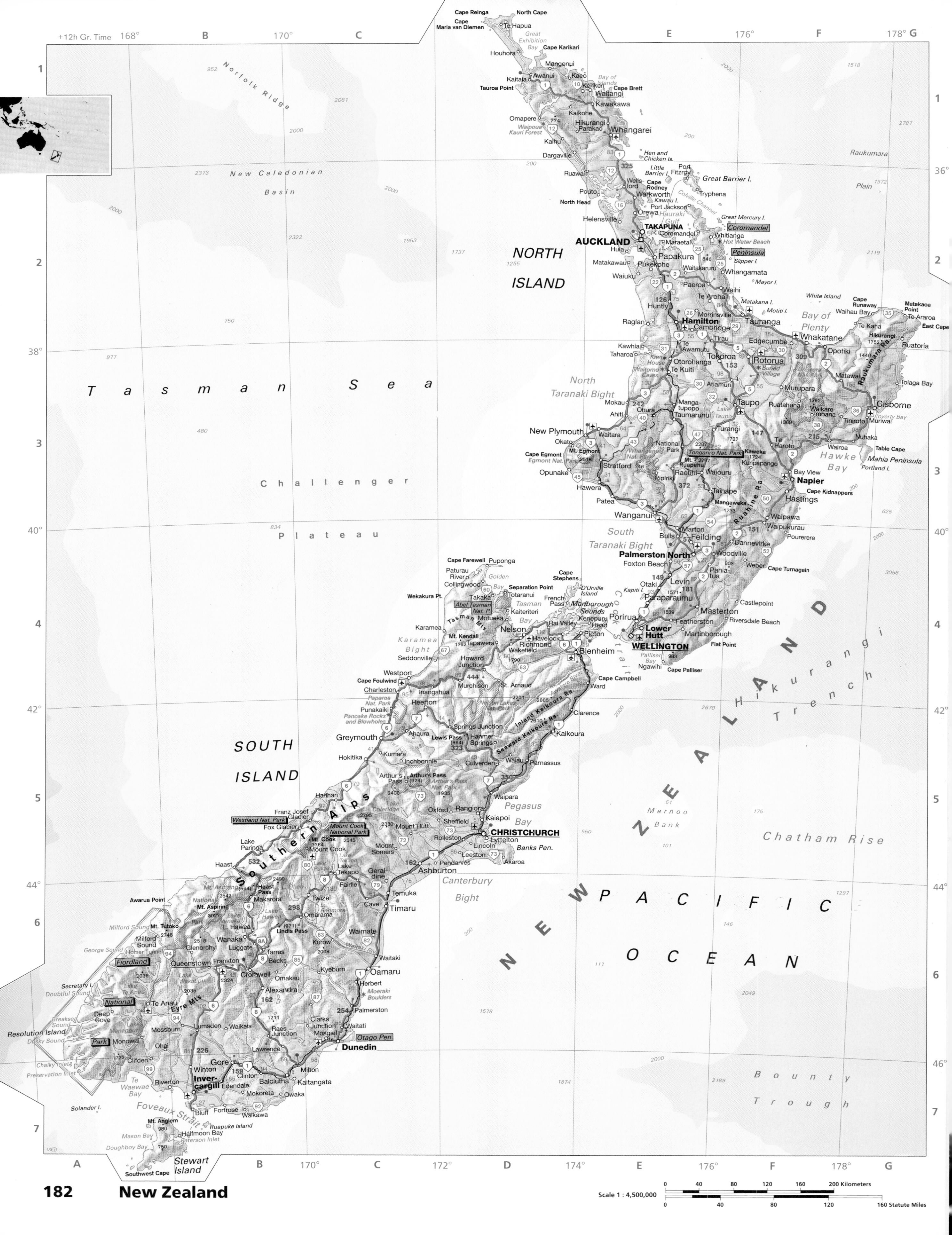
+12h Gr. Time
168°
170°
172°
174°
176°
178°
36°
38°
40°
42°
44°
46°
Cape Reinga
North Cape
Cape Maria van Diemen
Te Hapua
Great Exhibition Bay
Cape Karikari
Houhora
Mangonui
Kaitaia
Awanui
Tauroa Point
Kaeo
Kerikeri
Bay of Islands
Cape Brett
Waitangi
Kawakawa
Kaikohe
Omapere
Waipoua Kauri Forest
Hikurangi
Parakao
Whangarei
Kaihu
Dargaville
Hen and Chicken Is.
Little Barrier I.
Port Fitzroy
Great Barrier I.
Ruawai
Wellsford
Cape Rodney
Warkworth
Kawau I.
Colville Channel
Tryphena
Pouto
North Head
Port Jackson
Orewa
Hauraki Gulf
Helensville
Great Mercury I.
TAKAPUNA
Coromandel
Whitianga
Hot Water Beach
AUCKLAND
Huia
Maraetai
Peninsula
Slipper I.
Matakawau
Pukekohe
Papakura
Waitakaruru
Whangamata
Waiuku
Mayor I.
Paeroa
Waihi
Te Aroha
Matakana I.
Motiti I.
Huntly
Morrinsville
Hamilton
Cambridge
Tauranga
Raglan
Bay of Plenty
White Island
Cape Runaway
Waihau Bay
Matakaoa Point
Te Araroa
East Cape
Te Kaha
Hikurangi
Ruatoria
Whakatane
Edgecumbe
Opotiki
Raukumara Ra.
Kawhia
Taharoa
Te Awamutu
Otorohanga
Kiwi House
Waitomo Caves
Te Kuiti
Tokoroa
Rotorua
Buried Village
Atiamuri
Matawai
Tolaga Bay
Murupara
North Taranaki Bight
Mokau
Manga-tupopo
Taumarunui
Taupo
Ruatahuna
Waikare-moana
Gisborne
Ohura
Ahiti
Lake Taupo
Poverty Bay
Tiniroto
Muriwai
New Plymouth
Waitara
Turangi
Okato
Mt. Egmont
National Park
Tongariro Nat. Park
Kaweka
Nuhaka
Cape Egmont
Egmont Nat. Park
Mt. Ruapehu
Te Haroto
Wairoa
Table Cape
Hawke Bay
Mahia Peninsula
Portland I.
Stratford
Raetihi
Waiouru
Kuripapango
Opunake
Bay View
Napier
Hawera
Taihape
Cape Kidnappers
Hastings
Patea
Mangaweka
Wanganui
Ruahine Ra.
Waipawa
Waipukurau
Pourerere
South Taranaki Bight
Marton
Bulls
Feilding
Dannevirke
Palmerston North
Woodville
Foxton Beach
Pahiatua
Weber
Cape Turnagain
Levin
Otaki
Kapiti I.
Paraparaumu
Castlepoint
Masterton
Porirua
Featherston
Riversdale Beach
Lower Hutt
Martinborough
WELLINGTON
Flat Point
Palliser Bay
Ngawihi
Cape Palliser
Cook Strait
Cape Farewell
Puponga
Paturau River
Golden Bay
Collingwood
Cape Stephens
D'Urville Island
Separation Point
Takaka
Totaranui
French Pass
Marlborough Sounds
Abel Tasman Nat. Park
Kaiteriteri
Tasman Bay
Wekakura Pt.
Tasman Mts.
Motueka
Kenepuru Head
Rai Valley
Karamea
Nelson
Picton
Havelock
Richmond
Wakefield
Mt. Kendall
Tapawera
Karamea Bight
Blenheim
Seddonville
Howard Junction
Cape Campbell
Ward
Westport
Cape Foulwind
Charleston
Murchison
St. Arnaud
Inangahua
Reefton
Paparoa Nat. Park
Punakaiki
Pancake Rocks and Blowholes
Nelson Lakes Nat. Park
Inland Kaikoura Ra.
Clarence
Springs Junction
Greymouth
Ahaura
Lewis Pass
Hanmer Springs
Kaikoura
Seaward Kaikoura Ra.
Hokitika
Kumara
Inchbonnie
Culverden
Waiau
Parnassus
Arthur's Pass
Arthur's Pass Nat. Park
Harihari
Waipara
Pegasus Bay
Franz Josef Glacier
Westland Nat. Park
Fox Glacier
Mount Cook National Park
Oxford
Rangiora
Kaiapoi
Sheffield
Mount Hutt
CHRISTCHURCH
Lyttelton
Rolleston
Lincoln
Banks Pen.
Leeston
Akaroa
Lake Paringa
Mt. Cook
Mount Cook
Mount Somers
Haast
Southern Alps
Lake Pukaki
Lake Tekapo
Geraldine
Ashburton
Pendarves
Canterbury Bight
Fairlie
Temuka
Timaru
Awarua Point
Mt. Aspiring
Haast Pass
Makarora
Twizel
Omarama
Cave
Lake Wanaka
Lake Hawea
L. Hawea
Wanaka
Lindis Pass
Milford Sound
Mt. Tutoko
Glenorchy
Luggate
Tarras
Kurow
Waimate
George Sound
Homer Tunnel
Fiordland
Queenstown
Frankton
Becks
Waitaki
Lake Wakatipu
Cromwell
Omakau
Kyeburn
Oamaru
Secretary I.
Doubtful Sound
Lake Te Anau
National
Te Anau
Eyre Mts.
Alexandra
Herbert
Moeraki Boulders
Deep Cove
Breaksea Sound
Lake Manapouri
Palmerston
Resolution Island
Dusky Sound
Mossburn
Lumsden
Waikaia
Raes Junction
Clarks Junction
Waitati
Park
Monowai
Mosgiel
Otago Pen.
Ohai
Dunedin
Lawrence
Chalky Inlet
Clifden
Preservation Inlet
Gore
Milton
Winton
Clinton
Invercargill
Te Waewae Bay
Riverton
Edendale
Balclutha
Kaitangata
Mokoreta
Owaka
Solander I.
Foveaux Strait
Fortrose
Bluff
Waikawa
Ruapuke Island
Mt. Anglem
Halfmoon Bay
Mason Bay
Paterson Inlet
Doughboy Bay
Stewart Island
Southwest Cape
NORTH ISLAND
SOUTH ISLAND
NEW ZEALAND
Tasman Sea
Norfolk Ridge
New Caledonian Basin
Challenger Plateau
Raukumara Plain
Hikurangi Trench
Mernoo Bank
Chatham Rise
PACIFIC OCEAN
Bounty Trough
Scale 1 : 4,500,000
0 40 80 120 160 200 Kilometers
0 40 80 120 160 Statute Miles

PACIFIC OCEAN
Bismarck Sea
Bismarck Archipelago
Solomon Sea
Coral Sea
Gulf of Papua
Huon Gulf
NEW GUINEA
PAPUA
New Britain
New Ireland
Admiralty Islands
Manus Island
New Hanover
Trobriand Islands
d'Entrecasteaux Islands
Louisiade Archipelago
Torres Strait
Great Barrier Reef
AUSTRALIA
Queensland
PORT MORESBY
Lae
Madang
Wewak
Mount Hagen
Goroka
Rabaul
Kavieng
Vanimo
Daru
Alotau
Central Range
Bismarck Range
Owen Stanley Range
Great Papuan Plateau
Huon Peninsula
Gazelle Pen.
Schouten Is.
Vitiaz Strait
Ysabel Channel
+10h Gr. Time
Scale 1 : 4,500,000
0 40 80 120 160 200 Kilometers
0 40 80 120 160 Statute Miles

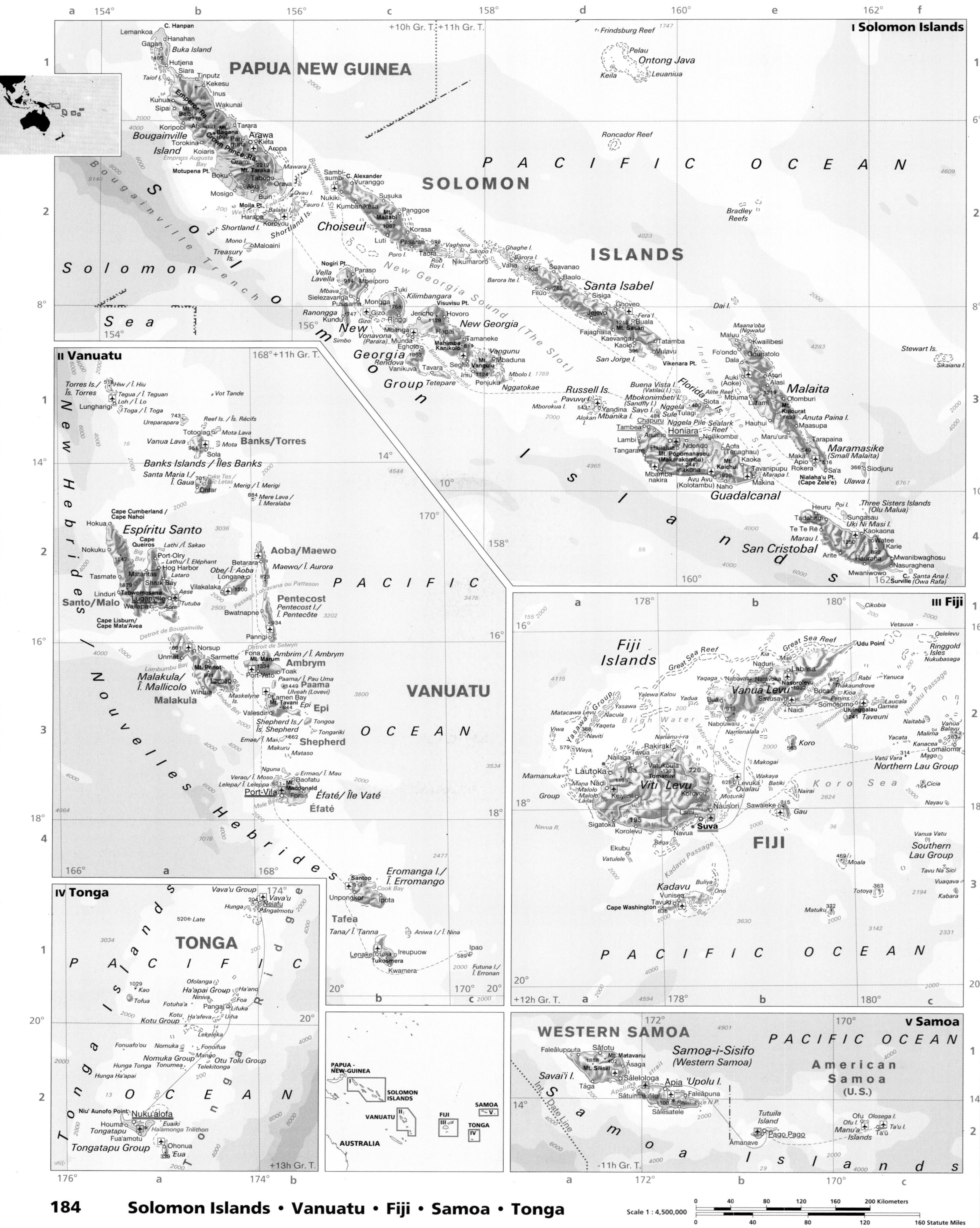
I Solomon Islands
PAPUA NEW GUINEA
SOLOMON ISLANDS
PACIFIC OCEAN
Solomon Sea
II Vanuatu
VANUATU
III Fiji
FIJI
IV Tonga
TONGA
V Samoa
WESTERN SAMOA
American Samoa (U.S.)
Scale 1 : 4,500,000

Africa – a continent of many faces

Africa, the second largest continent on Earth, takes up one-fifth of the total land mass on the planet. It is characterized by a coastline that contains few gulfs and peninsulas, the triangular southern cone with the northern trapeze on top and the division into Upper Africa in the southeast and Lower Africa in the northwest. The highlands with basins and rises as well as an extended rift valley system shape its surface. Africa contains all tropical landscape and climatic areas of the world, distributed primarily along the latitude lines on both sides of the Equator. One-third of Africa is occupied by the largest desert on Earth, the Sahara. This environment, hostile to life, separates white Africa, mostly settled by Islamic Arab peoples, from black Africa, characterized by the Sudanese and Bantu peoples. Ethiopia has unique population and culture. Contrary to the imaginary picture of the "dark continent," Africa has a vibrant culture and history. This is where, over three million years ago, our early ancestors learned to walk upright, and nowadays its melange of peoples, races, languages and traditions is only beginning to be appreciated.

Johann Baptist Homann made this copperplate engraving of Africa around the year 1690, approximately 150 before Europeans first began to explore the continent's interior.

Morocco · Canary Islands
p. 188 – 189

Algeria · Tunisia
p. 190 – 191

Libya
p. 192 – 193

Egypt
p. 194 – 195

Mauritania · Mali: Northern Region
p. 196 – 197

Niger · Chad
p. 198 – 199

Sudan: Northern Region · Eritrea
p. 200 – 201

Upper Guinea
p. 202 – 203

Ghana · Togo · Benin · Nigeria · Cameroon
p. 204 – 205

Central African Republic · Sudan: Southern Region p. 206 – 207

Ethiopia · Somali Peninsula
p. 208 – 209

Lower Guinea
p. 210 – 211

East Africa: Northern Region
p. 212 – 213

East Africa: Southern Region
p. 214 – 215

Angola · Namibia: Northern Region
p. 216 – 217

Zambia · Zimbabwe · Mozambique
p. 218 – 219

South Africa
220 – 221

Madagascar · Comoros
p. 222 – 223

Seychelles · Réunion · Mauritius
p. 224

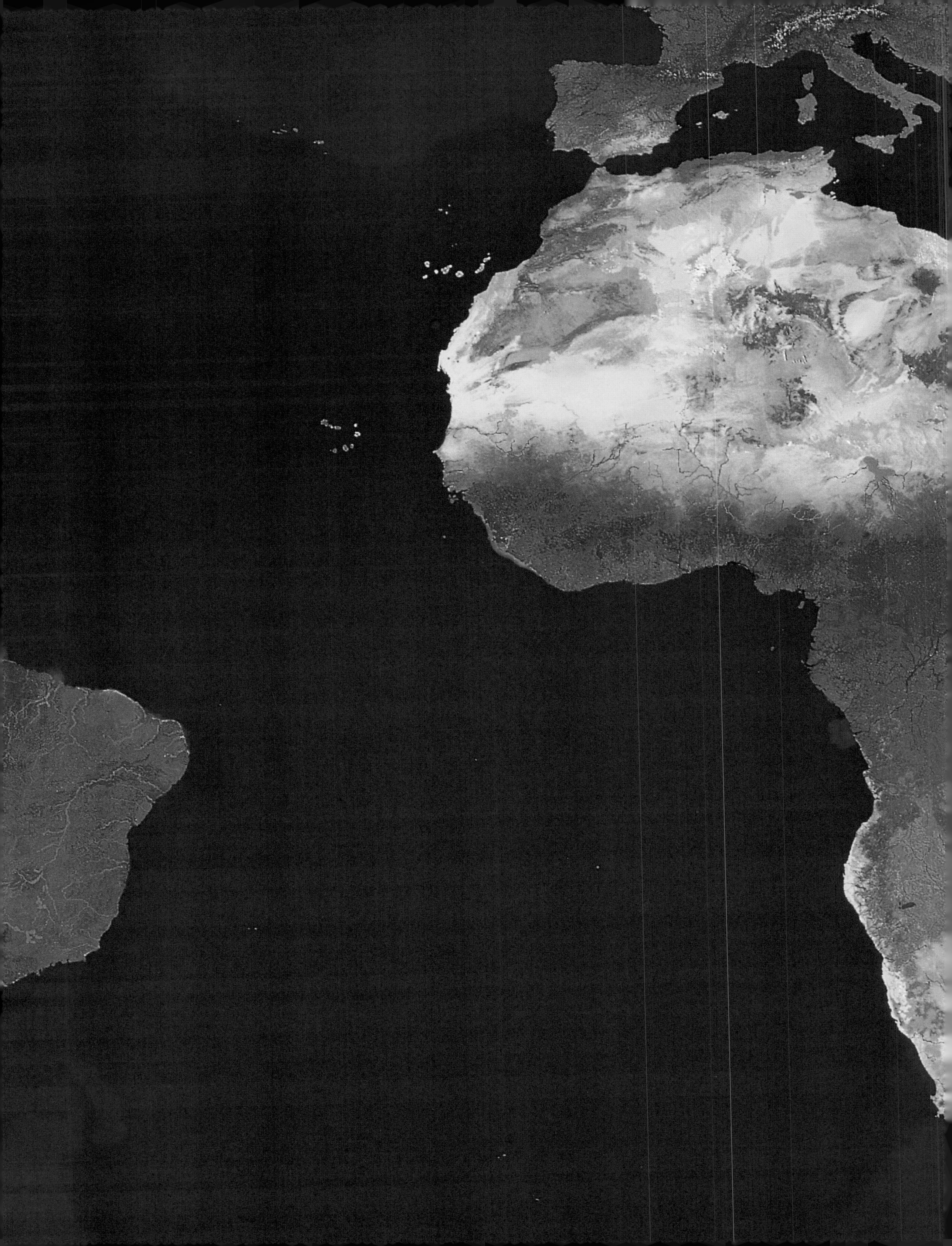

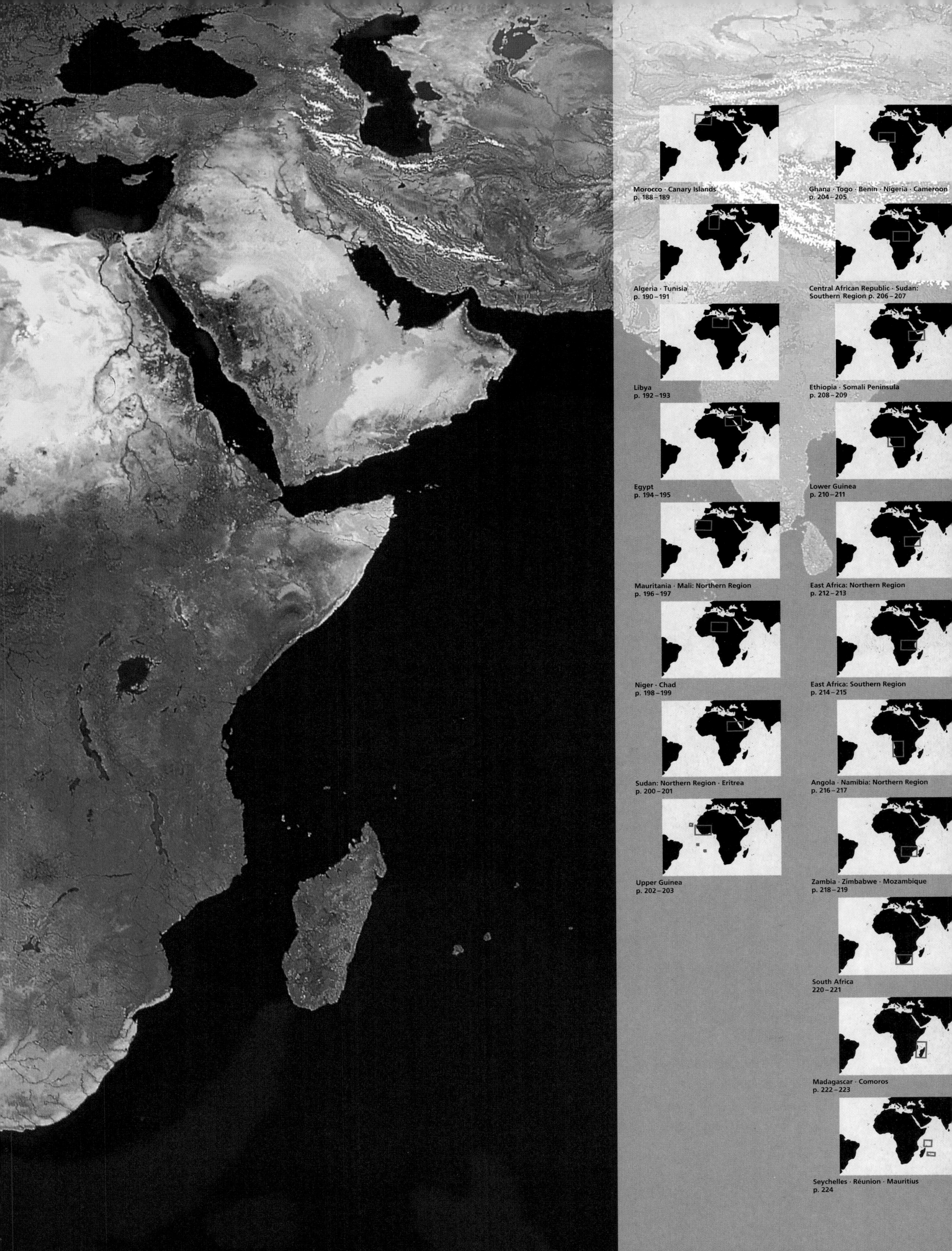

Morocco · Canary Islands
p. 188 – 189

Algeria · Tunisia
p. 190 – 191

Libya
p. 192 – 193

Egypt
p. 194 – 195

Mauritania · Mali: Northern Region
p. 196 – 197

Niger · Chad
p. 198 – 199

Sudan: Northern Region · Eritrea
p. 200 – 201

Upper Guinea
p. 202 – 203

Ghana · Togo · Benin · Nigeria · Cameroon
p. 204 – 205

Central African Republic · Sudan:
Southern Region p. 206 – 207

Ethiopia · Somali Peninsula
p. 208 – 209

Lower Guinea
p. 210 – 211

East Africa: Northern Region
p. 212 – 213

East Africa: Southern Region
p. 214 – 215

Angola · Namibia: Northern Region
p. 216 – 217

Zambia · Zimbabwe · Mozambique
p. 218 – 219

South Africa
220 – 221

Madagascar · Comoros
p. 222 – 223

Seychelles · Réunion · Mauritius
p. 224

Scale 1 : 4,500,000
0 40 80 120 160 200 Kilometers
0 40 80 120 160 Statute Miles

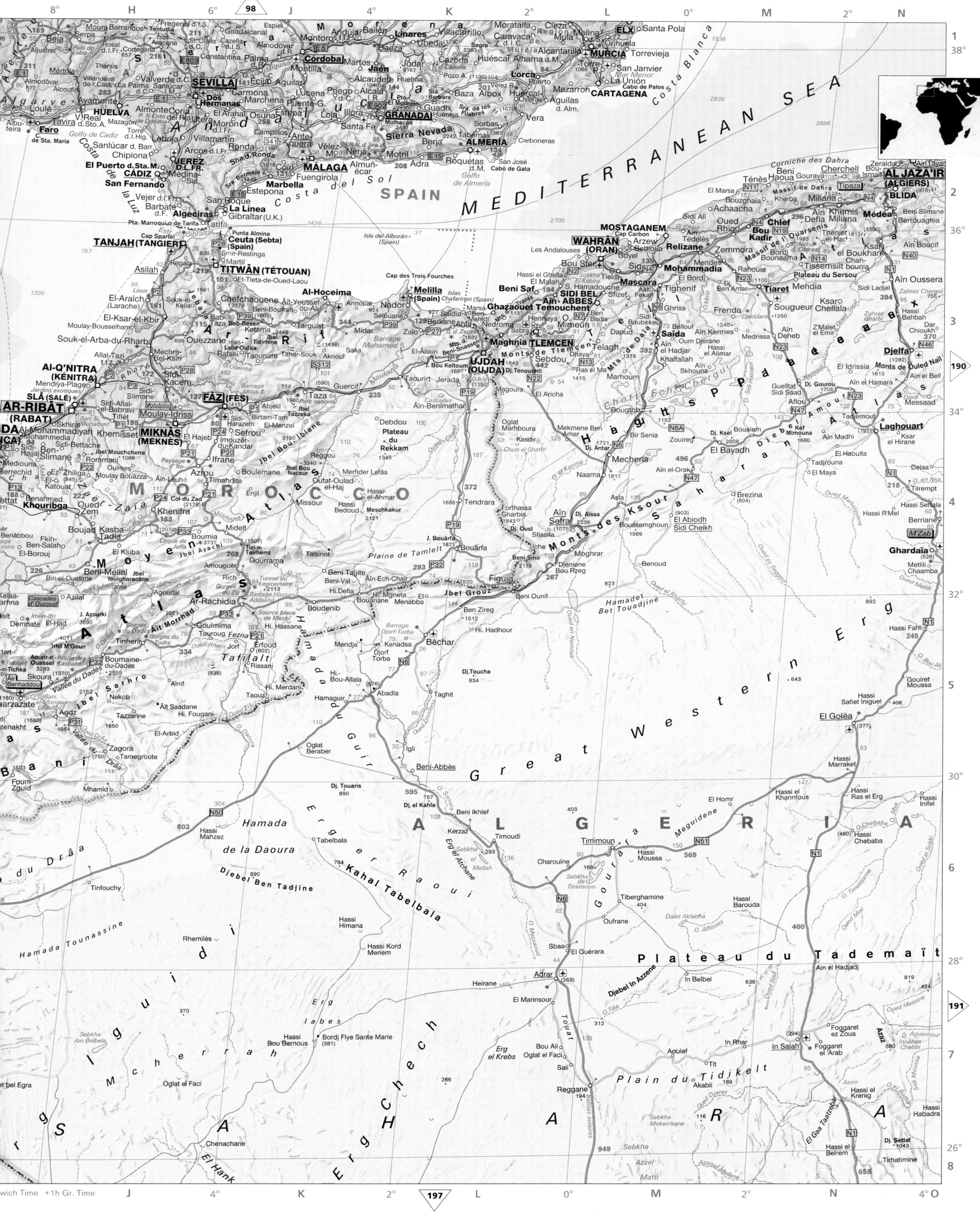

MEDITERRANEAN SEA
SPAIN
MOROCCO
ALGERIA
Great Western Erg
Costa del Sol
Costa Blanca
Andalucía
Sierra Nevada
Rif
Moyen Atlas
Haut Atlas
Hauts Plateaux
Saharan Atlas
Plateau du Tademaït
Plain du Tidikelt
Erg Chech
Hamada de la Daoura
Erg er Raoui
Monts des Ksour
Sevilla
Córdoba
Granada
Málaga
Almería
Cádiz
Murcia
Cartagena
Gibraltar (U.K.)
Tanjah (Tangier)
Ceuta (Sebta) (Spain)
Titwân (Tétouan)
Melilla (Spain)
Al-Hoceima
Faz (Fès)
Miknâs (Meknès)
Ar-Ribât (Rabat)
Al-Q'nitra (Kénitra)
Khouribga
Ujdah (Oujda)
Tlemcen
Wahrân (Oran)
Mostaganem
Sidi Bel Abbès
Mascara
Saïda
Tiaret
Chlef
Médéa
Blida
Al Jaza'ir (Algiers)
Djelfa
Laghouat
Ghardaïa
El Bayadh
Aïn Sefra
Figuig
Bèchar
Beni-Abbès
Timimoun
Adrar
Reggane
In Salah
El Goléa
Ar-Rachidia
Tafilalt
Erfoud
Zagora
97
98
190
191
197

Scale 1 : 4,500,000

0 40 80 120 160 200 Kilometers

0 40 80 120 160 Statute Miles

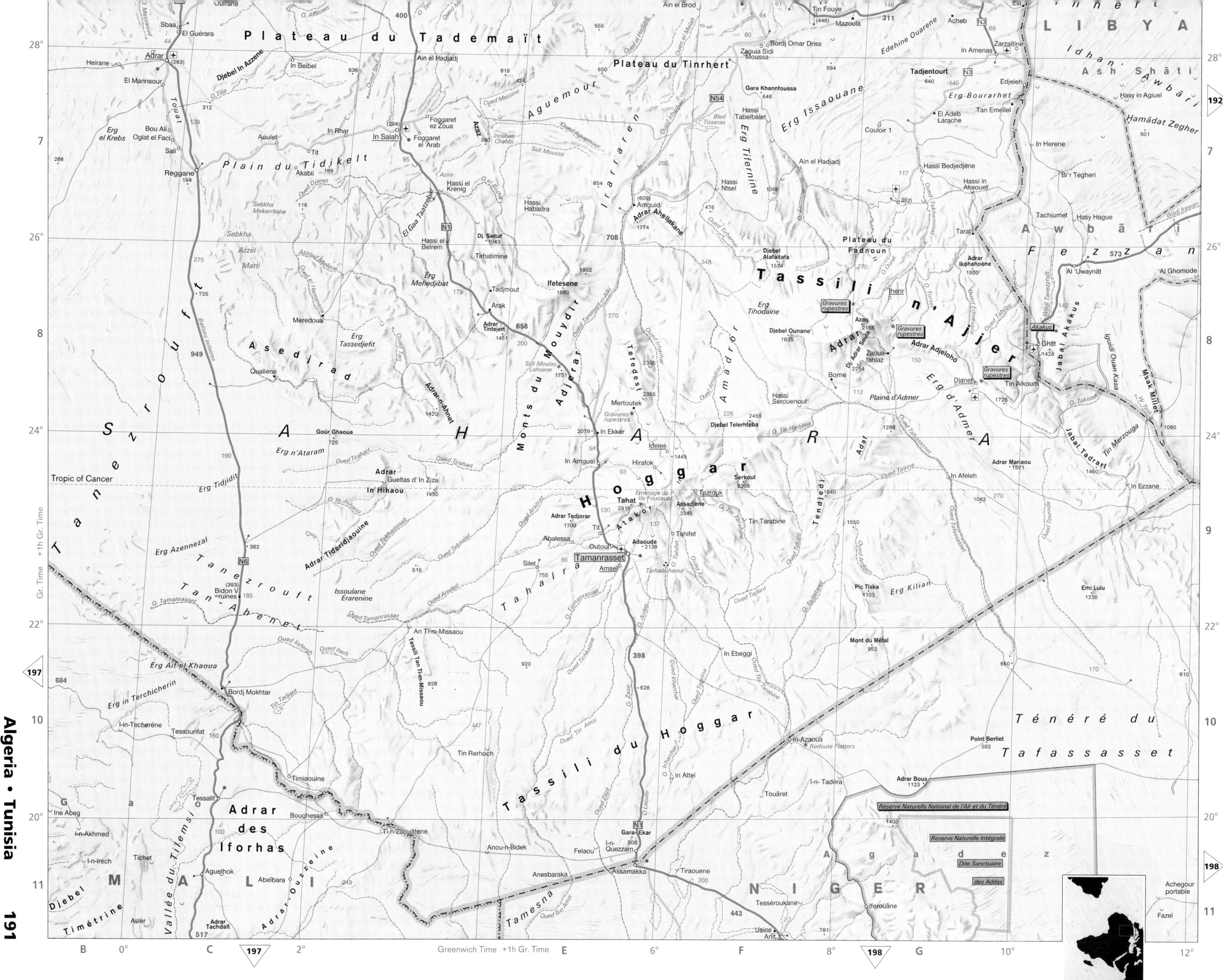
LIBYA
NIGER
MALI
Idhan Awbāri
Ash Shāti
Ḥamādat Zegher
Awbāri
Fezzan
Msak Mallet
Jabal Akakus
Jabal Tadrart
Tassili n'Ajjer
Erg d'Admer
Plaine d'Admer
Adrar Adjeloho
Erg Issaouane
Erg Tifernine
Erg Bourarhet
Plateau du Fadnoun
Plateau du Tinrhert
Plateau du Tademaït
Plain du Tidikelt
Ahaggar
Hoggar
Atakor
Tassili du Hoggar
Tefedest
Amadror
Monts du Mouydir
Adjerar
Asedjrad
Tanezrouft
Tanezrouft-n-Ahenet
Adrar des Iforhas
Vallée du Tilemsi
Ténéré du Tafassasset
Agadez
Adrar Bous
Erg Kilian
Tamanrasset
In Salah
Djanet
Illizi
In Amenas
Ghāt
Adrar
Reggane
Bordj Mokhtar
In Guezzam
Tropic of Cancer
Greenwich Time +1h Gr. Time
Réserve Naturelle National de l'Aïr et du Ténéré
Réserve Naturelle Intégrale
Dite Sanctuaire
des Addax
Gravures rupestres

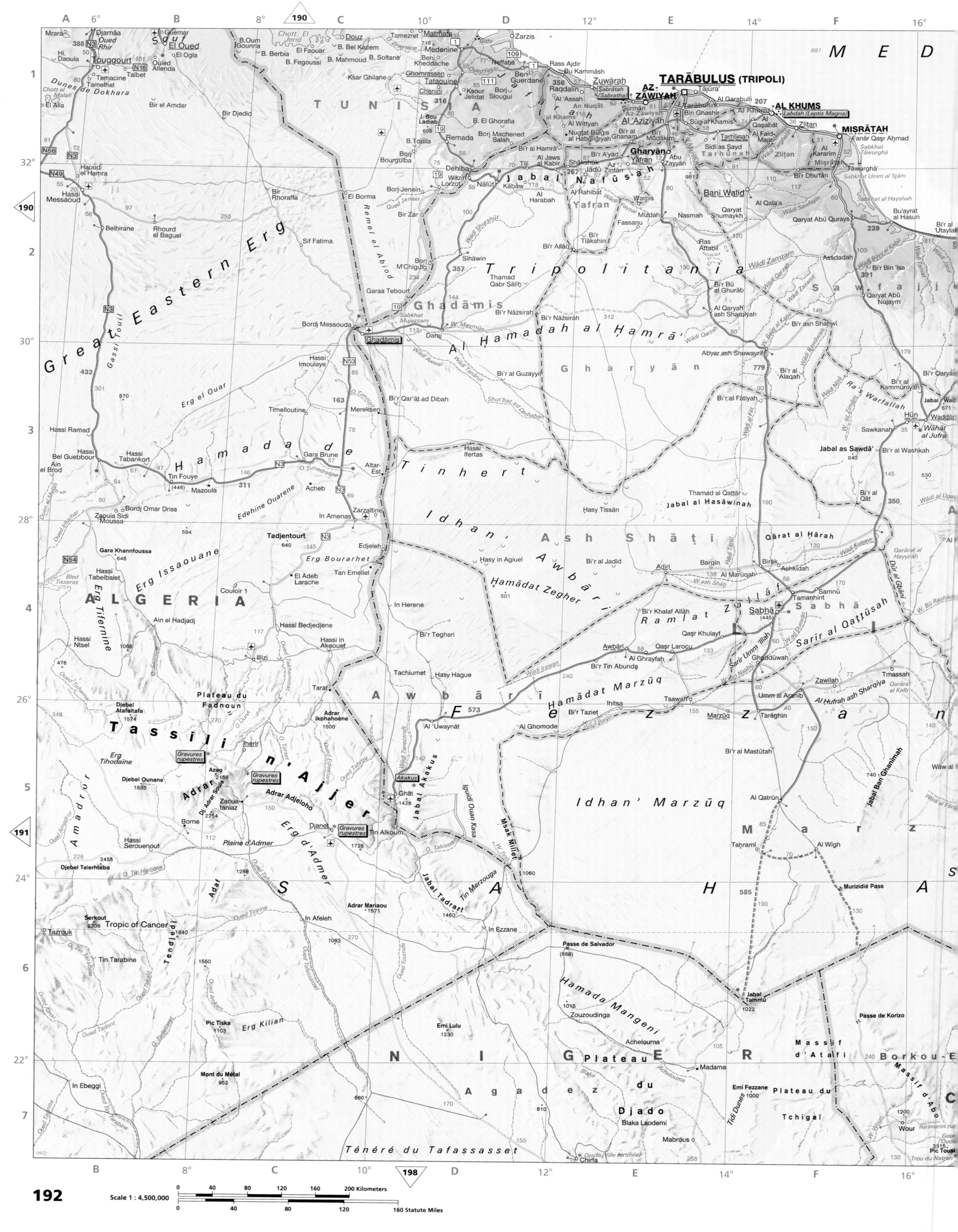

190
191
198
TARĀBULUS (TRIPOLI)
AZ-ZAWIYAH
AL KHUMS
Labdah (Leptis Magna)
MIŞRĀTAH
M E D
T U N I S I A
A L G E R I A
N I G E R
Tripolitania
Great Eastern Erg
Hamada de Tinhert
Al Ḩamādah al Ḩamrā'
Gharyān
Ghadāmis
Jabal Nafūsah
Idhan, Awbārī
Ash Shāṭi
Ramlat Zallāf
Sabhā
Sarīr al Qaṭṭūsah
Idhan' Marzūq
Hamādat Marzūq
Awbārī
Fezzan
Marzūq
Tassili n'Ajjer
Plateau du Fadnoun
Erg d'Admer
Adrar Adjeloho
Jabal Akakus
Ghāt
Djanet
Illizi
In Amenas
Touggourt
El Oued
Zarzis
Medenine
Tataouine
Ben Guerdane
Douz
Gharyān
Yafran
Bani Walid
Zlītan
Nālūt
Ghadāmis
Sabhā
Tropic of Cancer
Massif d'Atafi
Plateau du Djado
Plateau du Tchigaï
Hamada Mangeni
Ténéré du Tafassasset
Agadez
Erg Kilian
Passe de Salvador
Muriziḍié Pass
Passe de Korizo
Madama
Chirfa
Djado
Gravures rupestres
Hassi Messaoud
Erg Issaouane
Erg Tifernine
Amadror
Tahrami
Al Wigh
Al Qaṭrūn
Umm al Aranib
Zawilah
Tmassah
Hūn
Waddān
Jabal as Sawdā'
Scale 1 : 4,500,000
0 40 80 120 160 200 Kilometers
0 40 80 120 160 Statute Miles

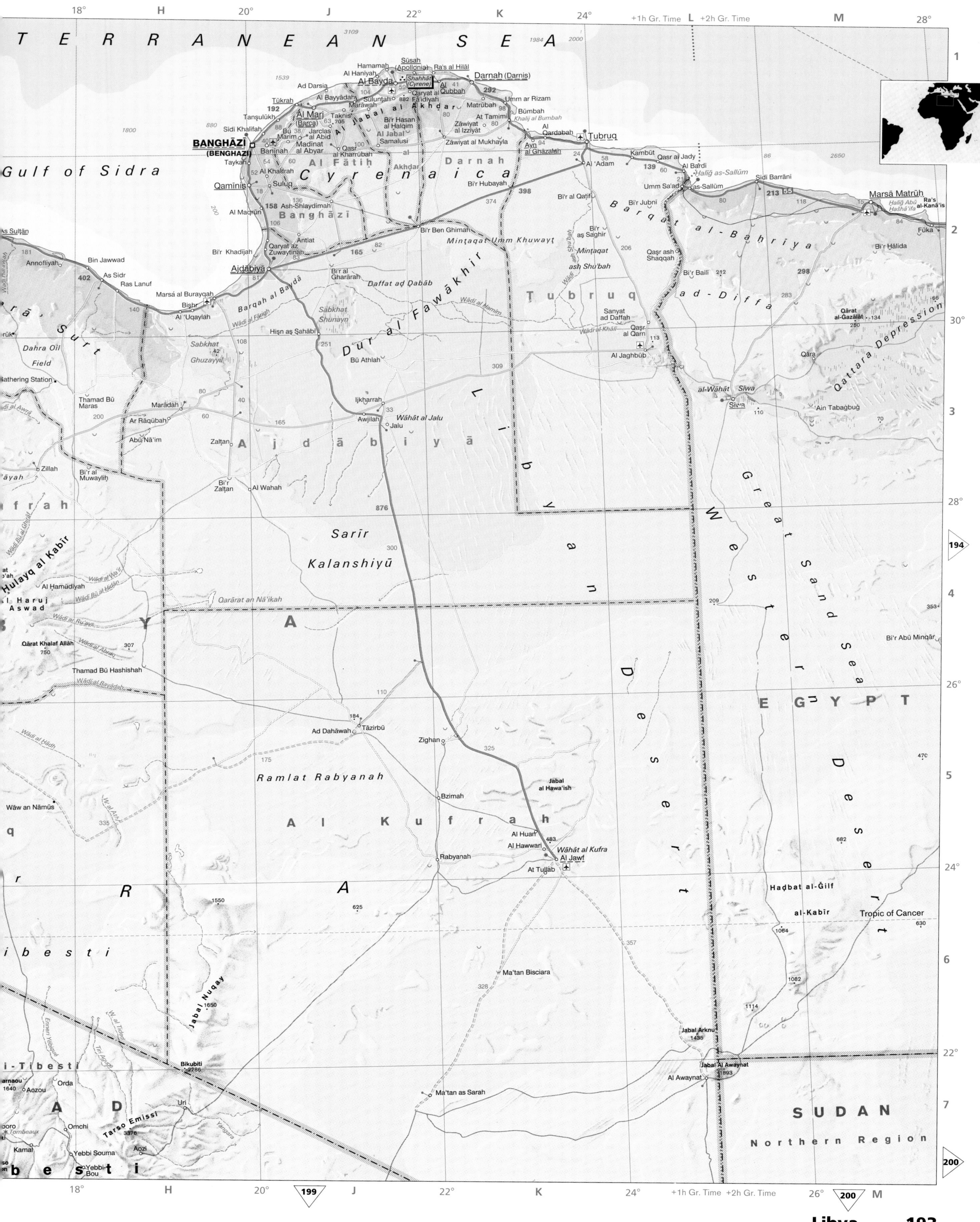

194
199
200
200

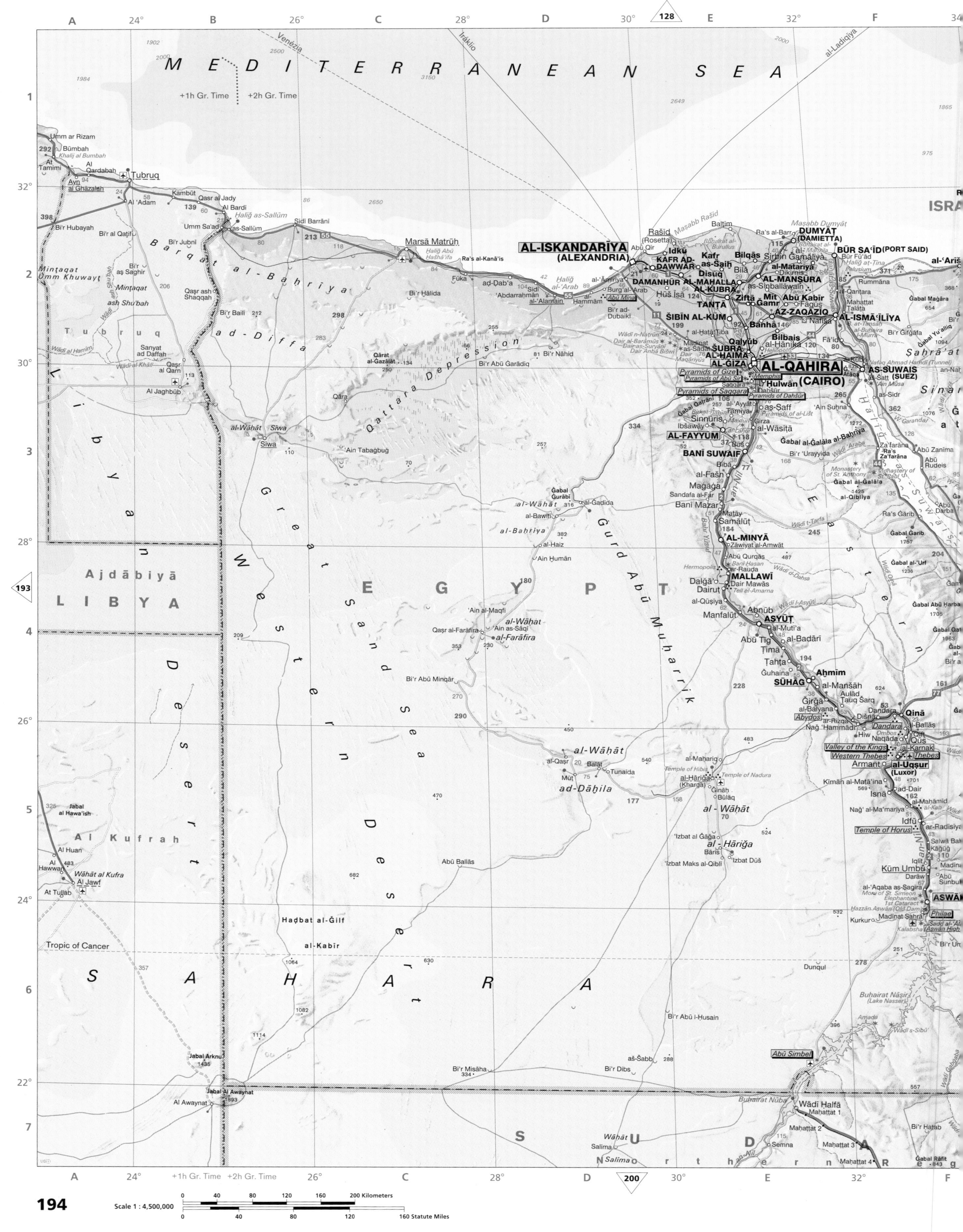

MEDITERRANEAN SEA
+1h Gr. Time
+2h Gr. Time
Venezia
Iraklio
al-Ladiqiya
EGYPT
LIBYA
Ajdābiyā
Great Western Sand Sea
Libyan Desert
Western Desert
SAHARA
Al Kufrah
Tubruq
Tubruq
Barqat al-Bahriya
ad-Diffa
Qattara Depression
Ġurd Abū Muharrik
Eastern Desert
Tropic of Cancer
AL-ISKANDARIYA
(ALEXANDRIA)
AL-QAHIRA
(CAIRO)
AL-GIZA
Pyramids of Gize
Pyramids of Saqqara
Pyramids of Dahšūr
Memphis
Hulwān
AS-SUWAIS
(SUEZ)
BŪR SAʿĪD (PORT SAID)
DUMYĀT
(DAMIETTA)
AL-ISMĀʿĪLIYA
AZ-ZAQĀZIQ
AL-MANSŪRA
AL-MAHALLA AL-KUBRA
TANTA
DAMANHŪR
KAFR AD-DAWWAR
KAFR AŠ-ŠAIḪ
ŠIBĪN AL-KŪM
Banha
Qalyūb
ŠUBRA AL-HAIMA
Bilbais
Rašīd
(Rosetta)
Abū Qīr
Marsā Matrūḥ
Sīdī Barrānī
as-Sallūm
Tubruq
Al Jaghbūb
Siwa
al-Wāhāt Siwa
AL-FAYYŪM
BANĪ SUWAIF
AL-MINYĀ
MALLAWĪ
ASYŪT
SŪHĀG
Aḫmīm
Qinā
Naǧʿ Hammādī
Valley of the Kings
Western Thebes
Thebes
al-Uqsur
(Luxor)
Isnā
Idfū
Temple of Horus
Kūm Umbū
ASWAN
Philae
Abydos
Dandara
al-Wāhāt al-Bahriya
al-Wāhāt al-Farāfira
al-Wāhāt ad-Dāḫila
al-Wāhāt al-Hāriğa
al-Hāriğa
(Kharga)
Hadbat al-Ġilf al-Kabīr
Jabal Al Awaynat
Jabal Arknu
Al Awaynat
Wāḥāt al Kufra
Al Jawf
At Tullab
Abū Simbel
Buhairat Nāṣir
(Lake Nasser)
Buhairat Nūba
Wādī Halfā
SUDAN
Northern
Sinai
ISRAEL
al-ʿAriš
A
B
C
D
E
F
24°
26°
28°
30°
32°
34°
32°
30°
28°
26°
24°
22°
1
2
3
4
5
6
7
128
193
200
+1h Gr. Time +2h Gr. Time
Scale 1 : 4,500,000
0 40 80 120 160 200 Kilometers
0 40 80 120 160 Statute Miles

+2h Gr. Time +3h Gr. Time
129
DIMAŠQ
(DAMASCUS)
S Y R I A
AR-RAMĀDĪ
BAĠDĀD
KARBALĀ'
AL-HILLA
AN-NAĞAF
ad-Dīwānīya
IRBID
AZ-ZARQĀ'
'AMMĀN
YERUSHALAYIM
AL-QUDS
(JERUSALEM)
Syrian Desert
Wādī as-Sirḥān
Turaif
al-Qurayyāt
'Ar'ar
Sakāka
Dūmat al-Ğandal
al-Ğauf
Aqaba
Elat
Tabūk
an-Nafūd al-Kubrā
Northern Frontier
Rafḥā'
Ḥā'il
Ğabal Ağā'
Ğabal Šammar
Taimā'
S A U D I A R A B I A
BURAIDA
'Unaiza
al-Qaṣīm
al-Wağh
Ḥaibar
Ḥarrat Ḫaibar
AL-MADĪNA
(MEDINA)
al-Madīna
Yanbu' al-Baḥr
Yanbu' an-Naḫl
Umm Lağğ
Red Sea
Badr wa-Ḥunain
Rābiġ
Ḥarrat Rahaṭ
Tūwal
ĞIDDA
(JIDDAH)
MAKKA
(MECCA)
AT-TĀ'IF
Turaba
Tropic of Cancer
ar-Riyāḍ
Makka
131
201
132

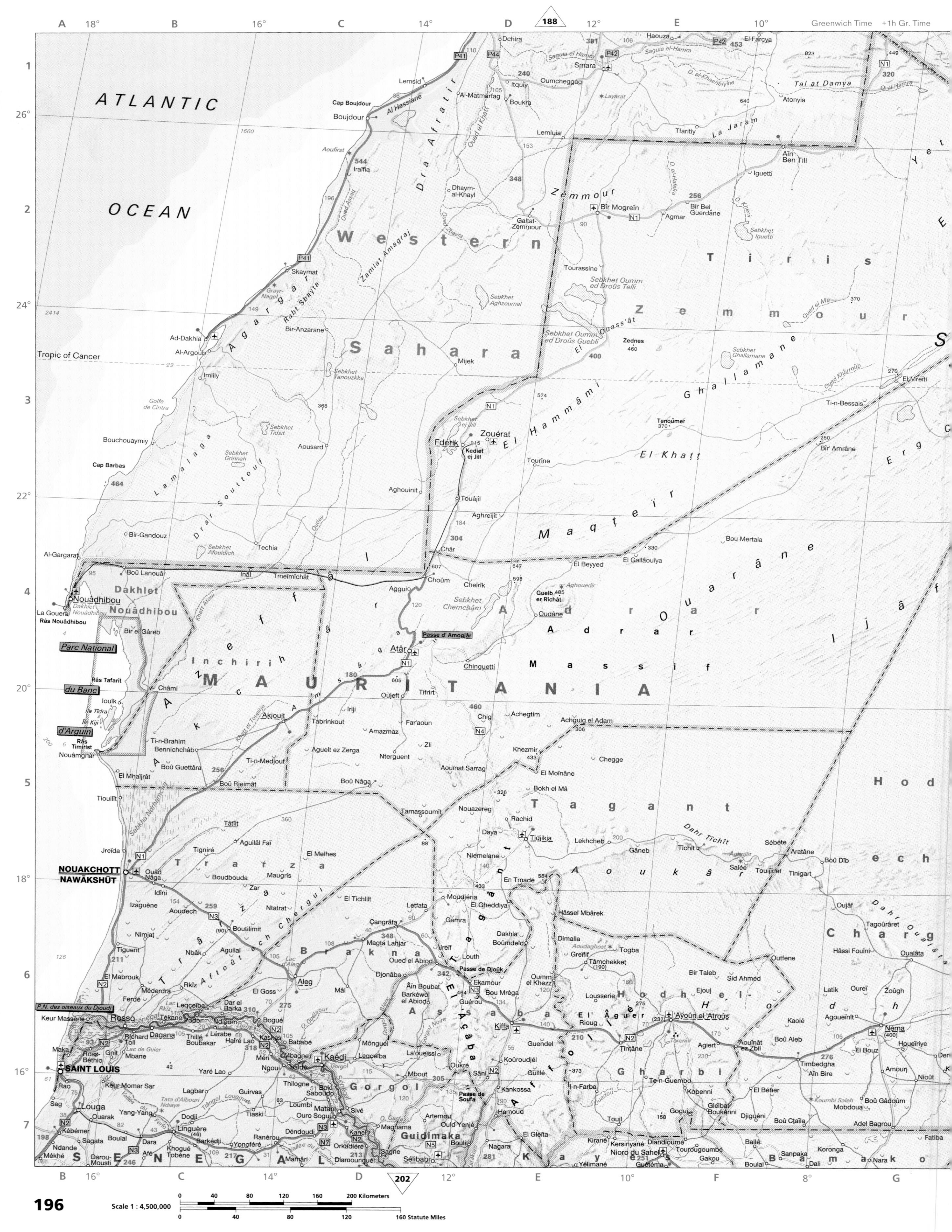

A
18°
B
16°
C
14°
D
188
12°
E
10°
Greenwich Time
+1h Gr. Time
ATLANTIC
OCEAN
Tropic of Cancer
Western
Sahara
MAURITANIA
Tiris
Zemmour
El Hammâmi
El Khaṭṭ
Maqṭeïr
Ouarâne
Adrar
Inchiri
Akjoujt
Tagant
Trarza
Brakna
Aoukâr
Hodh el Gharbi
Assaba
Gorgol
Guidimaka
Tal at Damya
Smara
Boujdour
Cap Boujdour
Lemsid
Al-Matmarfag
Itquiy
Oumcheggag
Boukra
Lemluia
Tfaritiy
Aïn Ben Tili
Iguetti
Bir Mogreïn
Galtat-Zemmour
Agmar
Bir Bel Guerdâne
Tourassine
Skaymat
Ad-Dakhla
Al-Argoub
Bir-Anzarane
Mijek
Imlily
Aousard
Bouchouaymiy
Cap Barbas
Aghouinit
Bir-Gandouz
Techia
Al-Gargarat
Nouâdhibou
La Gouera
Râs Nouâdhibou
Dakhlet Nouâdhibou
Bir el Gâreb
Parc National du Banc d'Arguin
Râs Tafarît
Iouîk
Île Tidra
Râs Timirist
Nouâmghâr
Châmi
Zouérat
Fdérik
Kediet ej Jill
Touâjîl
Aghreijît
Châr
Choûm
Inâl
Tmeimîchât
Boû Lanouâr
Agguio
Atâr
Passe d'Amogjâr
Chinguetti
Oudâne
Guelb er Richât
El Beyyed
El Gallâouîya
Bou Mertala
Tenoumer
Tourîne
Zednes
Bîr Amrâne
Ti-n-Bessais
El Mreïti
Tifrit
Oujeft
Tabrinkout
Achegtim
Achguig el Adam
Chig
Far'aoun
Amazmaz
Zli
Nterguent
Aguelt ez Zerga
Ti-n-Medjouf
Ti-n-Brahim
Bennichchâb
Boû Guettâra
El Mhaijrât
Boû Rjeimât
Boû Nâga
Aouînat Sarrag
Khezmir
El Moïnâne
Chegge
Bokh el Mâ
Tiouilît
Tâtilt
Tamassoumît
Nouazereg
Rachid
Daya
Tidjikja
Lekhcheb
Gâneb
Tichit
Dahr Tichît
Sébéte
Aratâne
Salée
Touijinet
Tinigart
Boû Dîb
Jreïda
NOUAKCHOTT
NAWÂKSHÛT
Tigniré
Aguilâl Faï
El Melhes
Boudbouda
Maugris
Zar
Idîni
Izaguène
Aoudech
Ntatrat
El Tichlilt
Letfata
Moudjéria
El Gheddiya
Niemelane
En Tmadé
Hâssei Mbârek
Boutilimit
Çangrâfa
Gamra
Nimjat
Tiguent
Nbâk
Aguilal
Magtâ Lahjar
Oued el Abiod
Louth
Dakhla
Boûmdeïd
Dimalla
Greïfîf
Tâmchekket
Togba
El Mabrouk
Mederdra
Rkîz
Aleg
Djonâba
Passe de Djoûk
Ekâmour
Oumm el Khezz
Bir Taleb
Sîd Ahmed
Outfene
Oualâta
Hâssi Fouînî
Tagoûrâret
Oujâf
Ferdé
El Goss
Mâl
Âïn Boubat
Barkéwol el Abiod
Bou Mréga
Guérou
Lousserie
Ejouj
Latik
Oureï
Zoûgh
Agoueïnît
Kaolé
Kiffa
El Âguer
Rioug
'Ayoûn el 'Atroûs
Tintâne
Agiert
Aouînât ez Zbil
Boû Aleb
Néma
Houeïriye
El Bouz
Rosso
Keur Massène
Tékane
Dagana
Podor
Ndioum
Lérabe
Haïré Lao
Kaskas
Bogué
Bababé
Mônguel
Maka
Ross-Béthio
Gnit
Mbane
Thillé Boubakar
Mbagne
Kaédi
Leqceiba
La'oueissi
Guendel
Koûroudjél
Sâni
Guillé
Timbedgha
Aïn Bire
Amourj
Nioût
SAINT LOUIS
Rao
Yaré Lao
Ngoui
Mbout
Oukré
Kankossa
Te-n-Guembo
Kobenni
El Béher
Keur Momar Sar
Lagbar
Guirvas
Thilogne
Boki Saboudo
Passe de Soufa
Hamoud
Gogui
Gleïbat Boukenni
Djiguéni
Koumbi Saleh
Boû Gâdoûm
Mobdoua
Sag
Louga
Ouarak
Yang-Yang
Dodji
Tiaski
Loumbi
Matam
Ouro Sogui
Sivé
Artemou
Ould Yenjé
Touil
Boû Çtaïla
Adel Bagrou
Kébémer
Sagata
Boulal
Linguère
Dendoudi
Kanel
Maghama
El Gleïta
Kiranè
Kersinyané
Diandioumé
Ballé
Fatiba
Ndande
Mékhé
Darou-Mousti
Dara
Barkédji
Afé
Khogué
Tobène
Yonoféré
Ranérou
Orkadiéré
Sagne
Sélibabi
Bouli
Nagara
Nioro du Sahel
Touroubgoumbé
Gakou
Sanpaka
Koronga
Dali
Nara
Yélimané
Guetéma
Diamounguel
Mamâri
SENEGAL
Kayes
Bamako
Hodh ech Chargui
B
16°
C
14°
D
202
12°
E
10°
F
8°
G
Scale 1 : 4,500,000
0
40
80
120
160
200 Kilometers
0
40
80
120
160 Statute Miles

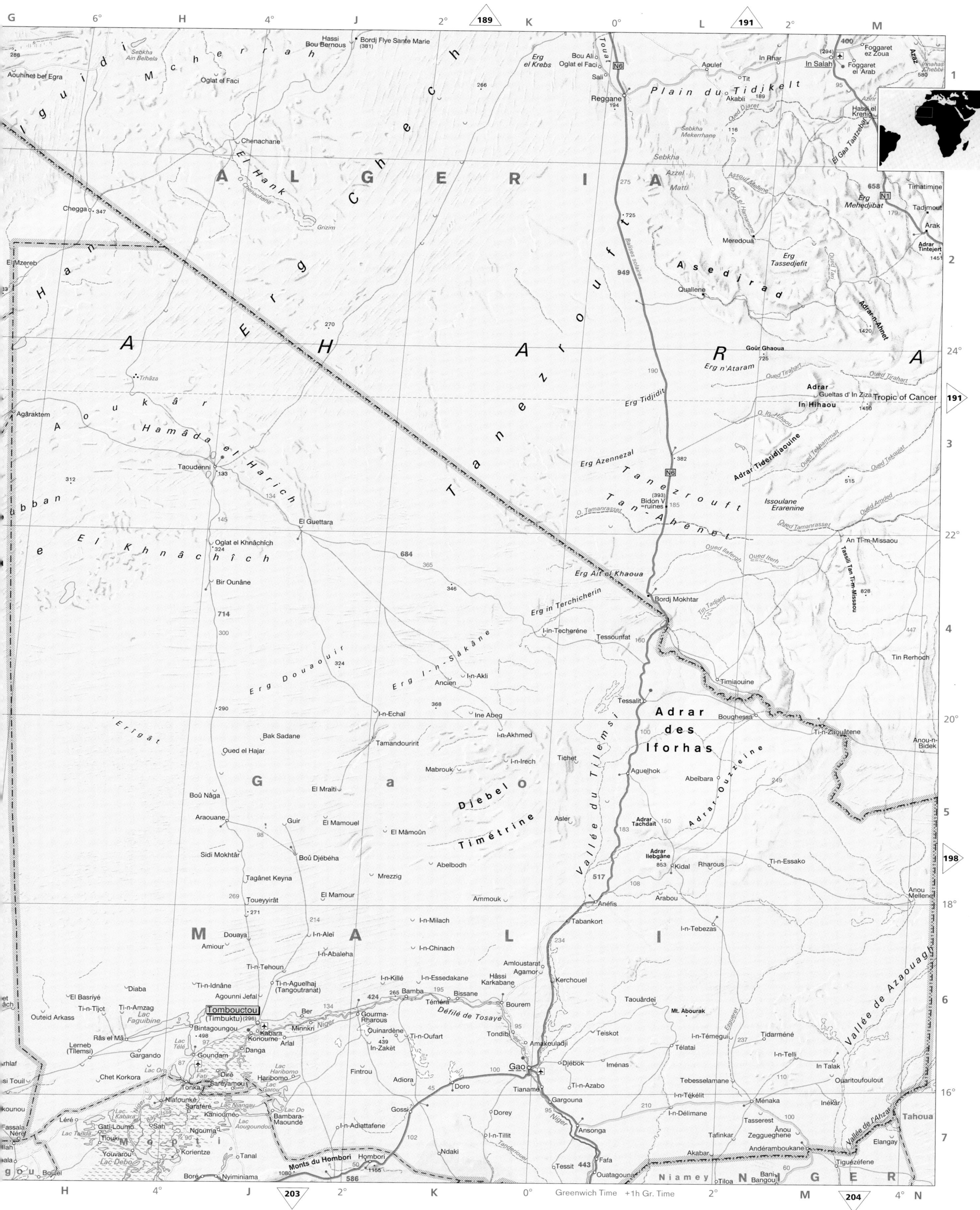
ALGERIA
MALI
Tanezrouft
Erg Chech
Taoudenni
Tombouctou
(Timbuktu)
Gao
Kidal
Adrar des Iforhas
Reggane
Bordj Mokhtar
Tessalit
Aguelhok
Araouane
Ménaka
Niger
Tropic of Cancer
Greenwich Time
+1h Gr. Time

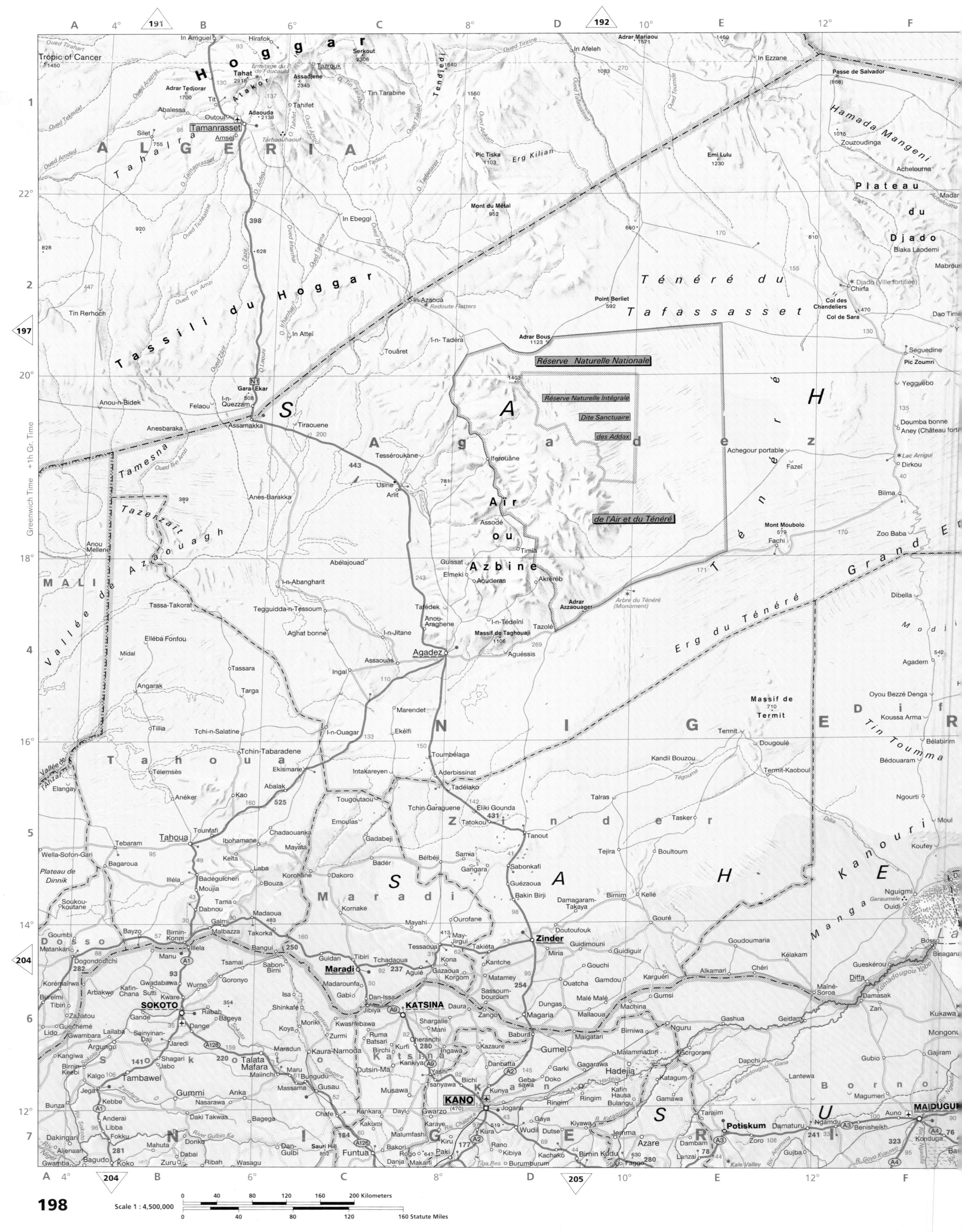

Scale 1 : 4,500,000

0 40 80 120 160 200 Kilometers

0 40 80 120 160 Statute Miles

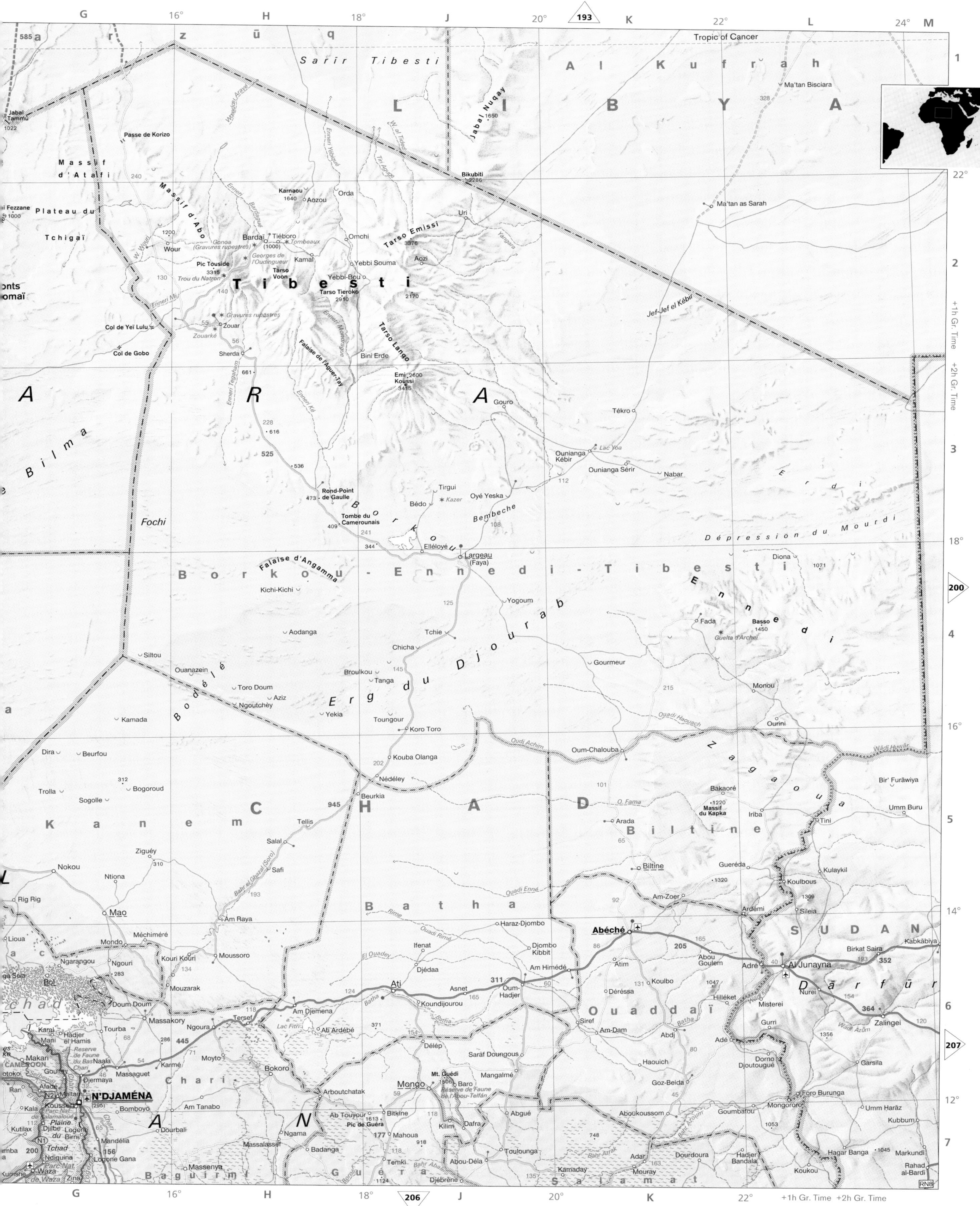

Tropic of Cancer
Sarir Tibesti
Al Kufrah
LIBYA
Jabal Nuqay
Ma'tan Bisciara
Passe de Korizo
Massif d'Atafi
Massif d'Abo
Plateau du Tchigaï
Bikubiti 2286
Karnaou 1640
Aozou
Orda
Ma'tan as Sarah
Uri
Tarso Emissi 3376
Bardaï
Tiéboro
Omchi
Wour
Pic Tousside 3315
Trou du Natron
Tarso Voon
Yebbi Souma
Aozi
Yebbi-Bou
Tibesti
Tarso Tieroko 2910
Jef-Jef el Kébir
Col de Yei Lulu
Zouar
Zouarké
Col de Gobo
Sherda
Tarso Lango
Bini Erde
Falaise de l'Aguer-Tay
Emi Koussi 3415
Gouro
Tékro
Ounianga Kébir
Lac Yoa
Ounianga Sérir
Nabar
Bilma
Fochi
Rond-Point de Gaulle
Tombe du Camerounais
Borkou
Tigui
Bédo
Kazer
Oyé Yeska
Bembeche
Dépression du Mourdi
Erdi
Ellèloyé
Largeau (Faya)
Diona
Falaise d'Angamma
Borkou-Ennedi-Tibesti
Kichi-Kichi
Ennedi
Yogoum
Fada
Basso 1450
Guelta d'Archei
Tchie
Aodanga
Chicha
Siltou
Erg du Djourab
Gourmeur
Ouanazein
Bodélé
Broulkou
Tanga
Toro Doum
Aziz
Ngoutchey
Yekia
Toungour
Monou
Kamada
Koro Toro
Ourini
Ouadi Achim
Oum-Chalouba
Ouadi Hawach
Wādī Huwār
Zagaoua
Dira
Beurfou
Kouba Olanga
Nédéley
Bogoroud
Trolla
Sogolle
Beurkia
Bakaoré
Massif du Kapka
Bir' Furāwiya
Umm Buru
Kanem
CHAD
Tellis
Arada
Iriba
Tini
Biltine
Salal
Ziguéy
Safi
Nokou
Ntiona
Guéréda
Kulaykil
Koulbous
Rig Rig
Am-Zoer
Ardémi
Sileia
Mao
Am Raya
Batha
Ouadi Enné
SUDAN
Haraz-Djombo
Méchiméré
Abéché
Mondo
Ifenat
Djombo Kibbit
Birkat Saira
Kabkābiya
Ngarangou
Ngouri
Kouri Kouri
Moussoro
Djédaa
Am Hirnédé
Abou Goulem
Adré
Al Junayna
Atim
Bol
Mouzarak
Ati
Asnet
Oum-Hadjer
Koulbo
Déressa
Dārfūr
Hillèket
Nurei
Doum Doum
Am Djemena
Koundjourou
Ouaddaï
Misterei
Massakory
Tersef
Karal
Tourba
Ngoura
Ati Ardébé
Siref
Am-Dam
Abdi
Zalingei
Gurri
Adé
Makari
Naala
Karmé
Moyto
Délép
Saraf Doungous
Haouich
Dorno Djoutougué
Garsila
Massaguet
Chari
Bokoro
Mangalmé
Mt. Guédi 1600
Baro
Goz-Beïda
Djermaya
N'DJAMÉNA
Kousseri
Arbouchatak
Mongo
Réserve de Faune de l'Abou-Telfân
Foro Burunga
Bomboyo
Am Tanabo
Ab Touyour
Pic de Guéra
Bitkine
Abguéé
Aboukoussom
Goumbatou
Mongororo
Umm Harāz
Dourbali
Ngama
Mahoua
Kilim
Dafra
Kubbum
Mandélia
Massalassef
Badanga
Toulounga
Logone Gana
Temki
Abou-Déla
Adar
Mouray
Dourdoura
Hadjer Bandala
Hagar Banga
Markundi
Massenya
Kamaday
Koukou
Rahad al-Bardi
Baguirmi
Guéra
Salamat
Djébrène
CAMEROON
+1h Gr. Time +2h Gr. Time

A
24°
+1h Gr. Time
+2h Gr. Time
26°
C
28°
194
D
30°
E
32°
F
Tropic of Cancer
Hadbat al-Ğilf al-Kabīr
E G Y P T
Buhairat Nāṣir (Lake Nasser)
Dunqul
Bi'r Abū l-Husain
Abū Simbel
aš-Šabb
Bi'r Dibs
Bi'r Misāha
Jabal Arknu
Jabal Al Awaynat
Al Awaynat
L I B Y A
Wādī Ḥalfā
Buhairat Nūba
Mahattat 1
Mahattat 2
Mahattat 3
Mahattat 4
Mahattat 5
Mahattat 6
Mahattat 7
Mahattat 8
Mahattat 9
Mahattat 10
Semna
Wāḥāt Salīma
Salīma
Akasha
Temple Amara
Abri
Kosha
Hamid
Temple of Seddenga
Temple of Sulb
Wawa
Ğabal Kuror
Ğabal Rāfit
Bi'r Hatab
Abū Şāri
Temple of Sesibi
Delgo
Laqiyat Arba'īn
Laqiyat 'Umran
Tagab
Kudayn
ash-Shallāl ath-Thālith (3rd Cataract)
Karma
Argū
Gharb Binna
al-Koin
Garada
Temple of Kawa
Donqula (Dongola)
Sahaba
Teiti
Urbi
al-Khandaq
al-Qulayd Bahrī
Amentego
Megauda
Old Dongola
al-Ghāba
ad-Dabba
Abū Dom
Kurī
Kurti
Fagrinkotti
Nukhayla (Merga)
N u b i a n
N u b
Kuhaylī
Shemkhiya
al-Kāb
al-Gamāmīya
Abū Ghirban
Kabna
Umm Rahaw
Umm Mirdi
Birti
ash-Shallāl ar-Rābi' (4th Cataract)
al-Begeir
Karima
Nuri
Marawi (Merowe)
Ğabal Barkal
al-Kurru
az-Zūma
Ghazali
Kanisa
al-Arāk
Hannik
Wādī Abū Dawn
Bi'r al 'Atrun
Rahib
Jabarona
199
193
C H A D
Barriyat al-Bayyūda
Burayqa
Umm Rumetla
Wādī al-Milk
Wādī Muqaddam
Wādī Huwār
S U D A
al-'Ain
Eilai
Qalti al Khudairā
Qalti al Adusa
Umm Qurein
Abū 'Urūq
Rugheiwa
al-Matamma
al-Basabir
Wad Hāmid
al-Huqna
Abū Dawn
Shallāl as-Sablūka (6th Cataract)
al-Gayli
Wādī Seidna
Halfāyat al-Mulūk
UMM DURMĀN (OMDURMAN)
AL-HARṬŪM (KHARTOUM)
Fattasha
Tayyibah
Qalti Immaseri
Ein Mansūr
Megeitia
Bi'r Furāwiya
Musbat
Umm Buru
Miski
N o r t h e r n
R e g
Malha
Ğabal Teljo
Madu
Hamrat al-Wuzz
Faiyiba
Umm Inderaba
Shayhk Sadin
al-Qutayna
Hamrat as Shaykh
Bi'r Abū Zaïma
'Amar Jadīd
Umm Qozein
Sōdiri
Kagmar
Abū Tunaytin
Umm Sayyāla
Ghomera
Ruqayba
Shabasha
Kutum
Mellit
Umm Badr
Umm Dubban
Magrur
Nabalāt
ad-Duwaym
Umm Marahik
Ğabal Gurgei
Khurayt
Abyad
Mazrūb
al-Gabir
Umm Dam
Hashāba
Kabkābiya
Al Fāshir
Hashab
Tawilah
Dirrah
Umm Kaddāda
Ermil Post
Umm Bel
'Iyāl Bakhit
Abdin
Bāra
Umm Būsha
D ā r f ū r
K o r d o f a n
'Ubaid
al Hilla
Balgak
Mahbūb
AL-UBAYYID (EL OBEID)
Kabur
Ğazirat Aba
Darāfisa
Kūsti
Rabak
Ğabal Marra
Suni
Abū Kabisa
Wad Banda
Nebelat el Hagana
'Ati
at-Tayyāra
Umm Segelti
Geifil
Tandalti
Tamaso
Kalokitting
Mellam
Wada'ah
Umm Hawsh
Khasm Elmi
En Nahūd
Umm Ruwāba
al-Ghabsha
Abū Rukba
Fāriq at-Fil
Dibs
Menawashei
Kas
Zarqā
Umm Defeis
ar-Rahad
Ğabal ad-Dair
Semei
Hami Rotoki
at Tuwaysha
Abū Zabad
Sungikai
T i l ā l a n - N ū b a
Keri Kera
ar-Ru'at
NYALA
Ghubaysh
Ogr
al-Udayya
Qadam
Dilling
Kortala
al-'Abbāsiya
Tingal
Mushayfat
Kubbum
Saheib
Muhāgiria
Haskanit
Zarqā' Hadīda
Wad Hassib
al-'Umda
Katla
Dalāmi
Rashād
ar-Rank
Markundi
'Idd al-Ghanam
Bukhit
'Abd ad-Dā'im
Ğaghamni
Kuwāra
Rahad al-Bardi
ad-Du'ayn
Tomat
Kulaykili
Qureida
Kubbi
Babanūsa
Umm Gamāla
al-Lagowa
Umm Hitan
Ğabal al-Liri
Abū Gubayba
Abū Hashim
Haybān
Bagaala
Southern Region
A
24°
B
26°
C
28°
207
D
30°
E
32°
F
Scale 1 : 4,500,000
0 40 80 120 160 200 Kilometers
0 40 80 120 160 Statute Miles

195
130
131
132
208
209
+2h Gr. Time
+3h Gr. Time
36°
38°
40°
42°
44°
20°
18°
16°
14°
12°
SAUDI ARABIA
ERITREA
ETHIOPIA
YEMEN
DJIBOUTI
SOMALIA
Red Sea
Desert
al-Madina
ar-Riyāḍ
Makka
Asir
Tihāmat as-Šām
Ǧabal al-Waǧid
Nağrān
Ǧizān
Dahlak Archipelago
Suakin Archipelago
Danakil
Tigrai
Gonder
Gojam
Wello
Uaza
Bora
Simēn
Dangur
Dindar National Park
T'ana Hayk
Bab al-Mandab
Harrat Rahat
Harrat Hadan
Harrat al-Buqūm
'Urūq Subai'
ĞIDDA (JIDDAH)
MAKKA (MECCA)
AT-TĀ'IF
Rābiġ
Tuwal
Bahra
al-Qunfuda
al-Bāha
Abhā
Hamīs Mušait
Ahad Rafīda
Sabt al-'Ulyā
Ǧizān (Jizan)
Nağrān
Ṣa'da
ṢAN'Ā' (SANAA)
AL-ḤUDAIDA
TA'IZZ
al-Muḫā (Mokka)
Bait al-Faqīh
BŪR SŪDĀN (PORT SUDAN)
Suakin
Tōkar
Haya
KASSALA
al-Qadārif
ar-Ruṣayriṣ
Metema
ASMERA
Keren
Āk'ordat
Mits'iwa
Dek'emhare
Ādī Ugrī
Ādīkwala
Tesenēy
Barentu
Asab
Aksum
Adwa
Ādigrat
Mek'elē
Gonder
Bahir Dar
Debre Tabor
Lalībela
Weldiya
Desē
Kembolcha
Ras Dashen Terara
Simēn Nat Park
Fasil Ghebbi
DJIBOUTI
Tadjoura
Obock
Ali Sabieh
Dikhil
Golfe de Tadjoura
Ra's Dashen Terara 4620

196
MAURITANIA
SENEGAL
DAKAR
THIÈS
Rufisque
Diourbel
KAOLACK
Tambacounda
Kayes
Louga
Banjul
Serekunda
Brikama
GAMBIA
ZIGUINCHOR
GUINEA-BISSAU
BISSAU
Bolama
Bafatá
Gabu
Arquipélago dos Bijagós
GUINEA
CONAKRY
Kindia
LABÉ
Fouta Djallon
Faranah
KANKAN
Kissidougou
Nzérékoré
BAMAKO
SIERRA LEONE
FREETOWN
Makeni
Magburaka
Koidu
Kenema
Bo
LIBERIA
MONROVIA
Buchanan
Harper
Grain Coast
Monts Nimba
ATLANTIC
OCEAN
ATLANTIC OCEAN
-1h Gr. Time
Mindelo
Ilha de Santo Antão
Ilha de São Vicente
Ilha de São Nicolau
Ilha do Sal
Ilha da Boa Vista
Ilhas de Barlavento
Cape Verde Islands
CAPE VERDE
Praia
Ilha de São Tiago
Ilha de Maio
Ilha do Fogo
Ilha Brava
Ilhas de Sotavento
Cape Verde
Greenwich Time
ATLANTIC OCEAN
Georgetown
Ascension
St. Helena (U.K.)
Ascension
Greenwich Time
ATLANTIC OCEAN
Jamestown
Saint Helena
St. Helena (U.K.)
St. Helena
Scale 1 : 4,500,000
0 40 80 120 160 200 Kilometers
0 40 80 120 160 Statute Miles

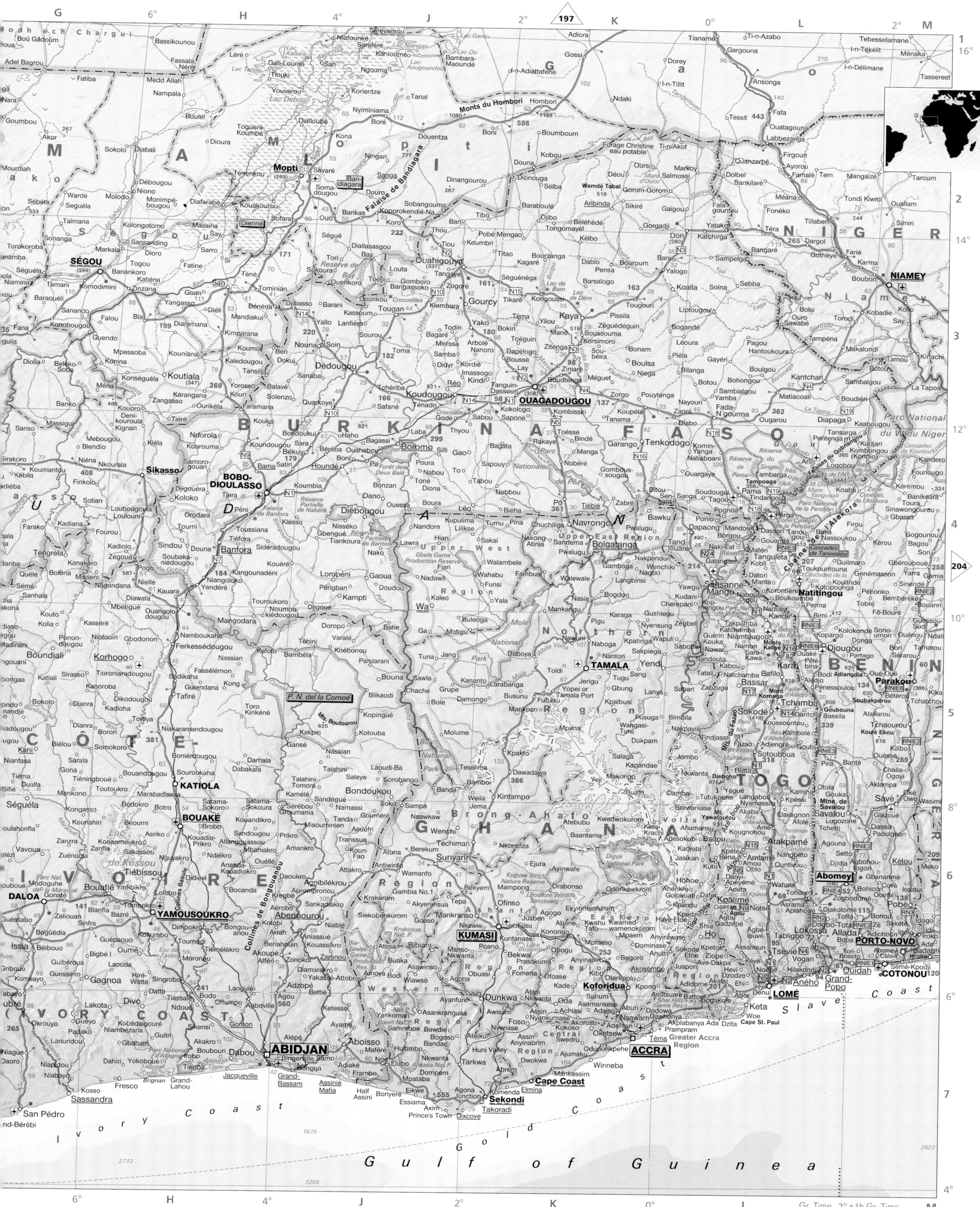

197
204
M A L I
B U R K I N A F A S O
N I G E R
G H A N A
T O G O
B E N I N
N I G E R I A
C Ô T E D'I V O I R E
(I V O R Y C O A S T)
Gulf of Guinea
Gold Coast
Ivory Coast
Slave Coast
SÉGOU
Mopti
Djenné
Bandiagara
Falaise de Bandiagara
Monts du Hombori
NIAMEY
OUAGADOUGOU
Ouahigouya
Koudougou
Kaya
Tenkodogo
Dédougou
BOBO-DIOULASSO
Banfora
Sikasso
Koutiala
Bolgatanga
Navrongo
TAMALA
Wa
Yendi
Sunyani
KUMASI
Koforidua
ACCRA
Téma
Cape Coast
Sekondi
Takoradi
LOMÉ
Aného
Grand-Popo
COTONOU
PORTO-NOVO
Abomey
Parakou
Natitingou
Djougou
Sokodé
Kara
Atakpamé
Kpalimé
Korhogo
KATIOLA
BOUAKÉ
YAMOUSSOUKRO
DALOA
ABIDJAN
Grand-Bassam
Sassandra
San Pédro
P. N. de la Comoé
Greater Accra Region
Gr. Time
2° +1h Gr. Time

197
203
Scale 1 : 4,500,000
0 40 80 120 160 200 Kilometers
0 40 80 120 160 Statute Miles

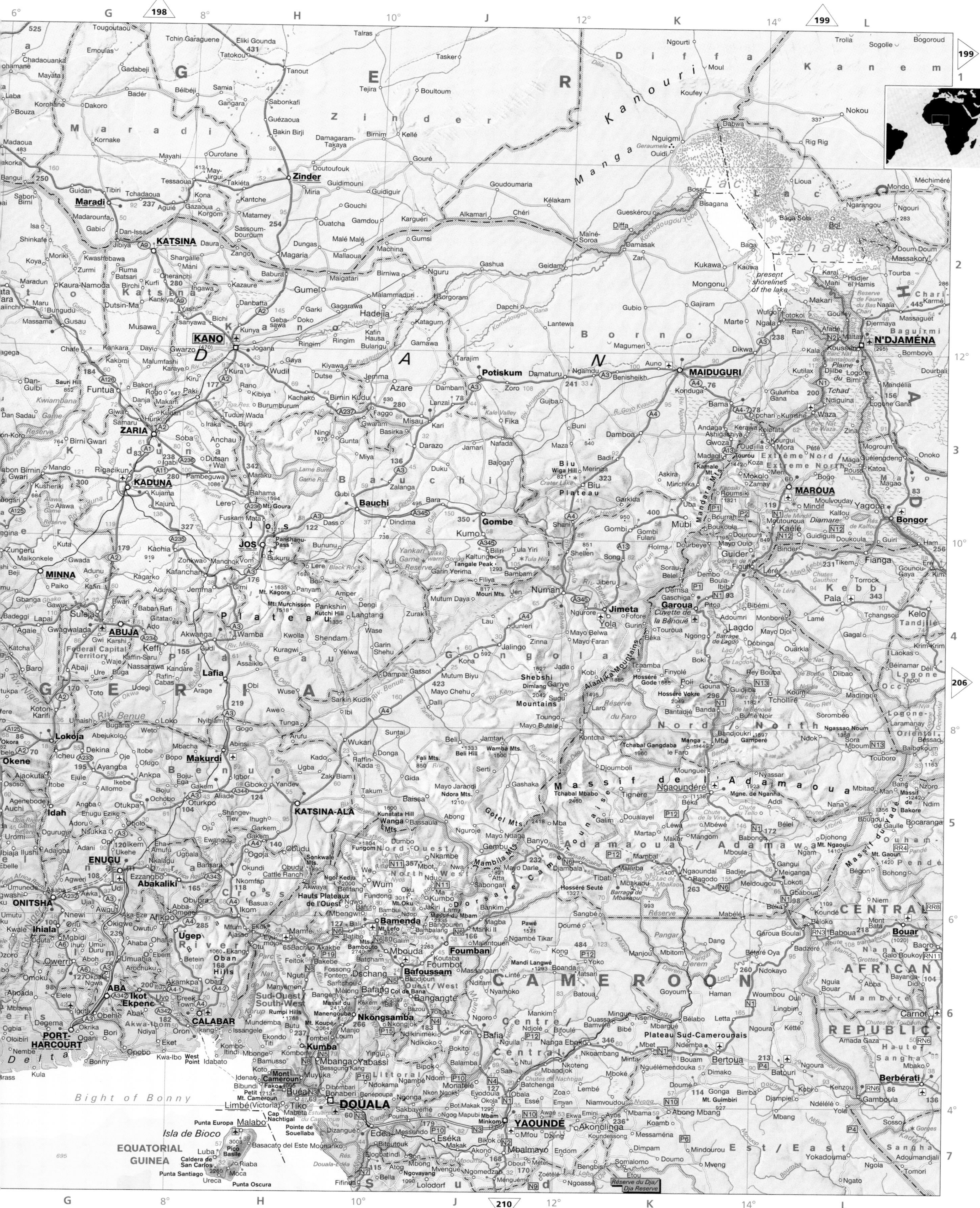

198
199
206
210
G
H
J
K
L
6°
8°
10°
12°
14°
1
2
3
4
5
6
7
Zinder
Maradi
KATSINA
KANO
ZARIA
KADUNA
JOS
Bauchi
Gombe
Potiskum
MAIDUGURI
N'DJAMÉNA
MAROUA
Garoua
Jimeta
Yola
MINNA
ABUJA
Lafia
Makurdi
Lokoja
Okene
KATSINA-ALA
ENUGU
Abakaliki
ONITSHA
Ugep
Ikot Ekpene
ABA
PORT-HARCOURT
CALABAR
Kumba
Bamenda
Foumban
Bafoussam
Nkongsamba
DOUALA
YAOUNDÉ
Bertoua
Berbérati
Bouar
Ngaoundéré
Bongor
Malabo
Buea
Limbé (Victoria)
Mont Cameroun
Isla de Bioco
EQUATORIAL GUINEA
Bight of Bonny
Lac Tchad
present shorelines of the lake
Manga
Kanouri
Diffa
Kanem
Maradi
Zinder
Katsina
Kano
Borno
Bauchi
Plateau
Kaduna
Benue
Gongola
Jos Plateau
Mandara Mts.
Alantika Mountains
Shebshi Mountains
Gotel Mts.
Massif de l'Adamaoua
Adamaoua / Adamawa
Nord / North
Extrême Nord / Extreme North
Nord-Ouest / North West
Ouest / West
Sud-Ouest / South-West
Littoral
Centre / Central
Est / East
Plateau Sud-Camerounais
CAMEROON
CENTRAL AFRICAN REPUBLIC
NIGERIA
NIGER
CHAD
Delta
Riv. Niger
Riv. Benue
Cross River
Oban Hills
Federal Capital Territory
Yankari Game Reserve
Réserve du Faro
Parc Nat. de Waza
Réserve du Dja / Dja Reserve

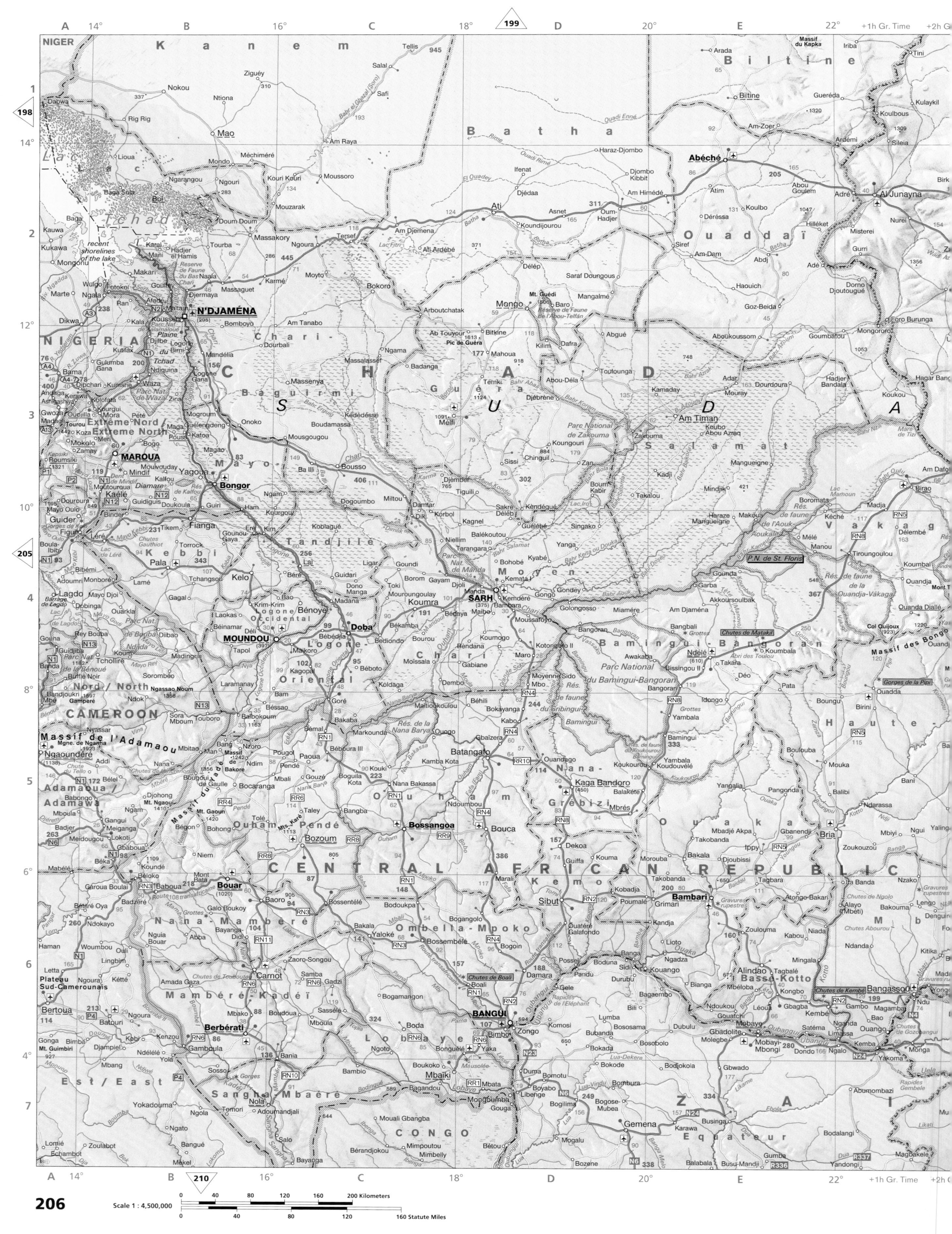

Scale 1 : 4,500,000

0 40 80 120 160 200 Kilometers

0 40 80 120 160 Statute Miles

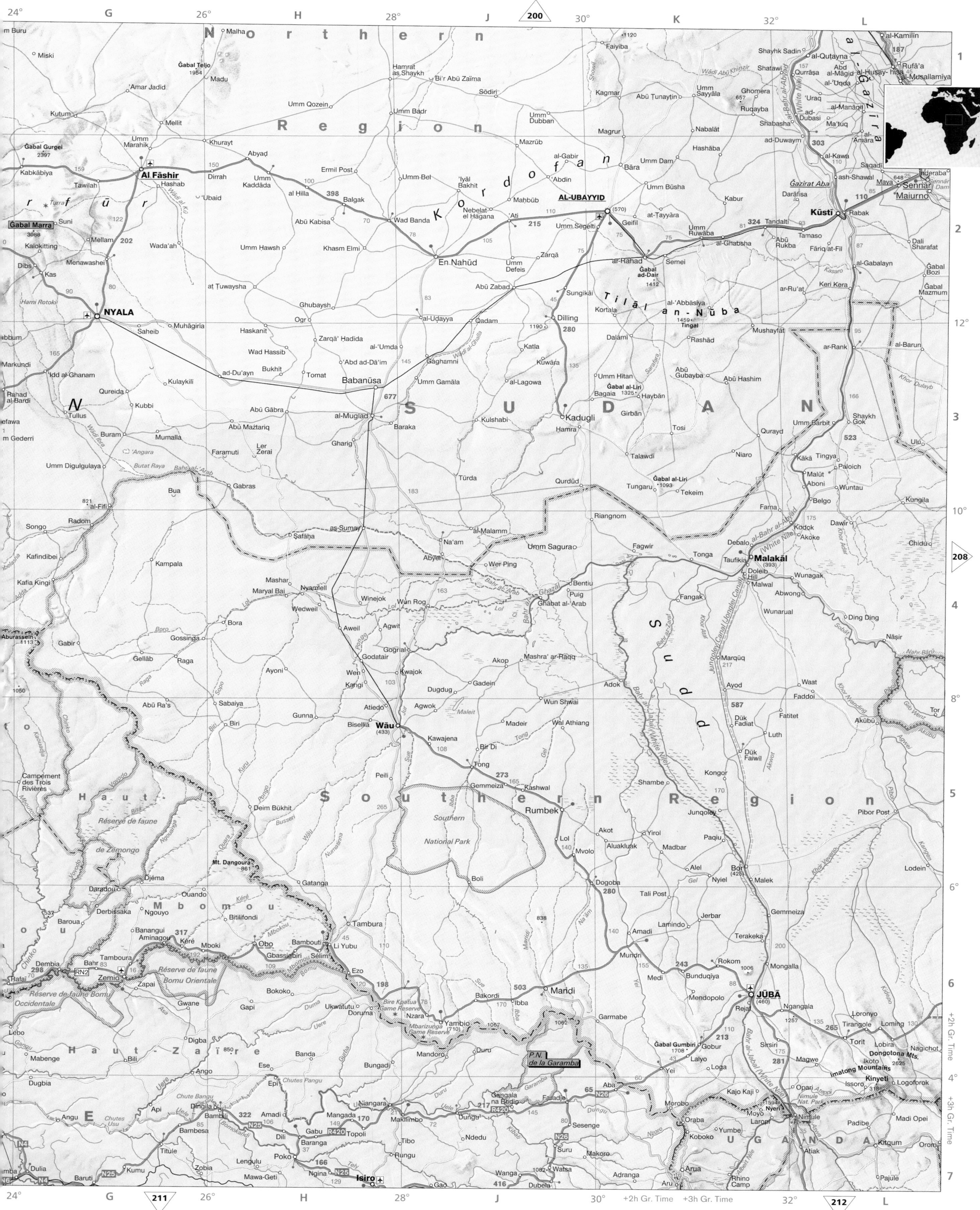

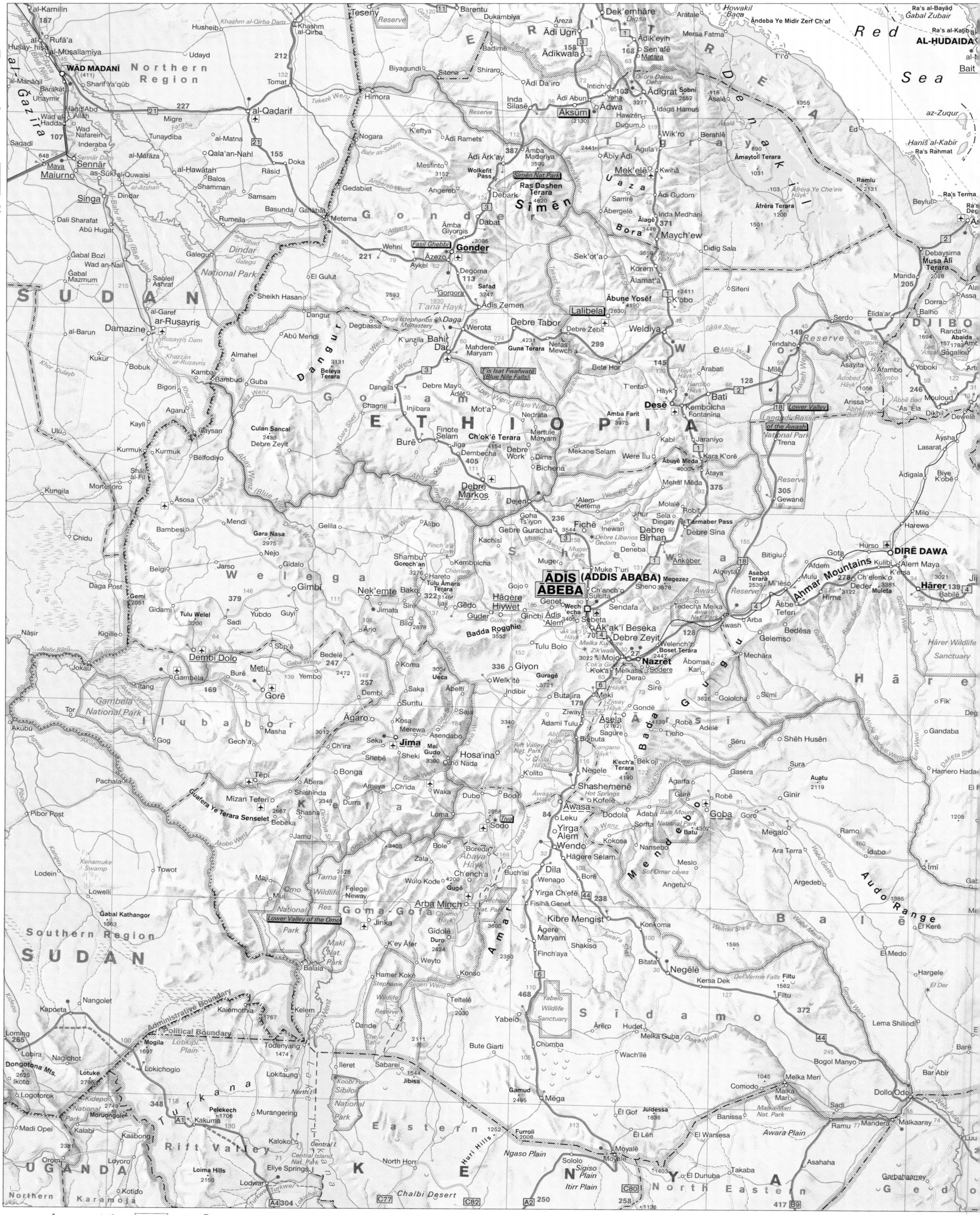

A 34° B +2h Gr. Time +3h Gr. Time C 38° D 40° E 42°

201

200

207

Red Sea

AL-ḪUDAIDA

SUDAN

Northern Region

al-Ǧazira

WĀD MADANĪ

Sennār

Singa

al-Qadarif

Damazine

ar-Ruṣayriṣ

Dindar National Park

ERITREA

Tigray

Dek'emhāre

Ādīgrat

Aksum

Adwa

Mek'elē

Denakil

Gonder

Simēn

Ras Dashen Terara 4620

Simēn Nat. Park

Fasil Ghebbi

T'ana Hayk'

Bahir Dar

Lalibela

Debre Tabor

Weldiya

Desē

Kembolcha

Gojam

ETHIOPIA

Dangur

T'is Isat Fwafwatē (Blue Nile Falls)

Abay Wenz (Blue Nile)

Debre Markos

Welega

Nek'emte

Gimbi

Shewa

ĀDĪS ĀBEBA (ADDIS ABABA)

Debre Zeyit

Nazrēt

Awash

Awash Nat. Park

Lower Valley of the Awash

Ahmar Mountains

DIRĒ DAWA

Hārer

Hārerge

DJIBOUTI

Ilubabor

Gambela National Park

Gambēla

Gorē

Jima

Kefa

Hosa'ina

Arsi

Bale

Goba

Bale Mount. National Park

Shashemenē

Awasa

Dila

Sidamo

Negēlē

Mendebo

Audo Range

Gamo Gofa

Arba Minch

Nech Sar Nat. Park

Omo National Park

Lower Valley of the Omo

Mago Nat. Park

Yabelo Wildlife Sanctuary

Southern Region

SUDAN

Administrative Boundary

Political Boundary

Lotikipi Plain

Turkana

Rift Valley

KENYA

Eastern

North Eastern

Chalbi Desert

Sibiloi National Park

Central Island Nat. Park

Huri Hills

Moyalē

Mandera

Dollo Odo

UGANDA

Northern

Karamoja

Kidepo National Park

A 34° B 36° C 38° D 40° E 42°

212

Scale 1 : 4,500,000

0 40 80 120 160 200 Kilometers

0 40 80 120 160 Statute Miles

YEMEN
Gulf of Aden
INDIAN OCEAN
Socotra
(Yemen)
Qalansiya
Ra's Šu'b
'Abd al-Kūrī
The Brothers
Samḥa
Darza
Ra's Haiṣat an-Naum
al-Mukallā
'ADAN
(ADEN)
TA'IZZ
Ibb
Damār
Yarim
Laḥij
Little Aden
Madinat as-Sa'b
Bāb al-Mandab
Raas Caluula
(Ilaawe)
Caluula
Bereeda
Raas Caseyr
(C. Gwardafuy)
Tooxin
Bargaal
Raas Binna
Qandala
Boosaaso
(Bender Cassim)
Ceelayo
Laasqoray
Maydh
Xiis
Raas Khansiir
Karin
Berbera
Bullaxaar
Lughaye
Saylac
Hargeysa
Galbeed
Burco
Sheekh
Ceerigaabo
Sanaag
Bari
Buuraha Cal Madow
Buuraha Cal Miskaat
Bannaanka Saraar
Bannaanka Dhoodi
Togdheer
Nugaal
Haud
Ogaden
Laascaanood
Garoowe
Qardho
Iskushuban
Handa
Hurdiyo
Raas Xaafuun
Xaafuun
(Dante)
Bandarbeyla
Raas Macbar
Dhuudo
Eyl
Raas Gabbac
Raas Illig
Laas Aano
Jirriiban
Garacad
Gaalkacyo
Mudug
Hobyo
Ceel Huur
Xarardheere
Galguduud
Dhuusa Mareeb
Beledweyne
(Belet Weyne)
Hiiraan
Buulobarde
Bulo Burti
Shabeellaha Dhexe
Bakool
Bay
Godē
K'elafo
Werdēr
Degeh Bur
Shilabo
Mustahil
El Dere
Mareeq
Masagaweyn
Raas Cabaad
Iidaan
SOMALIA

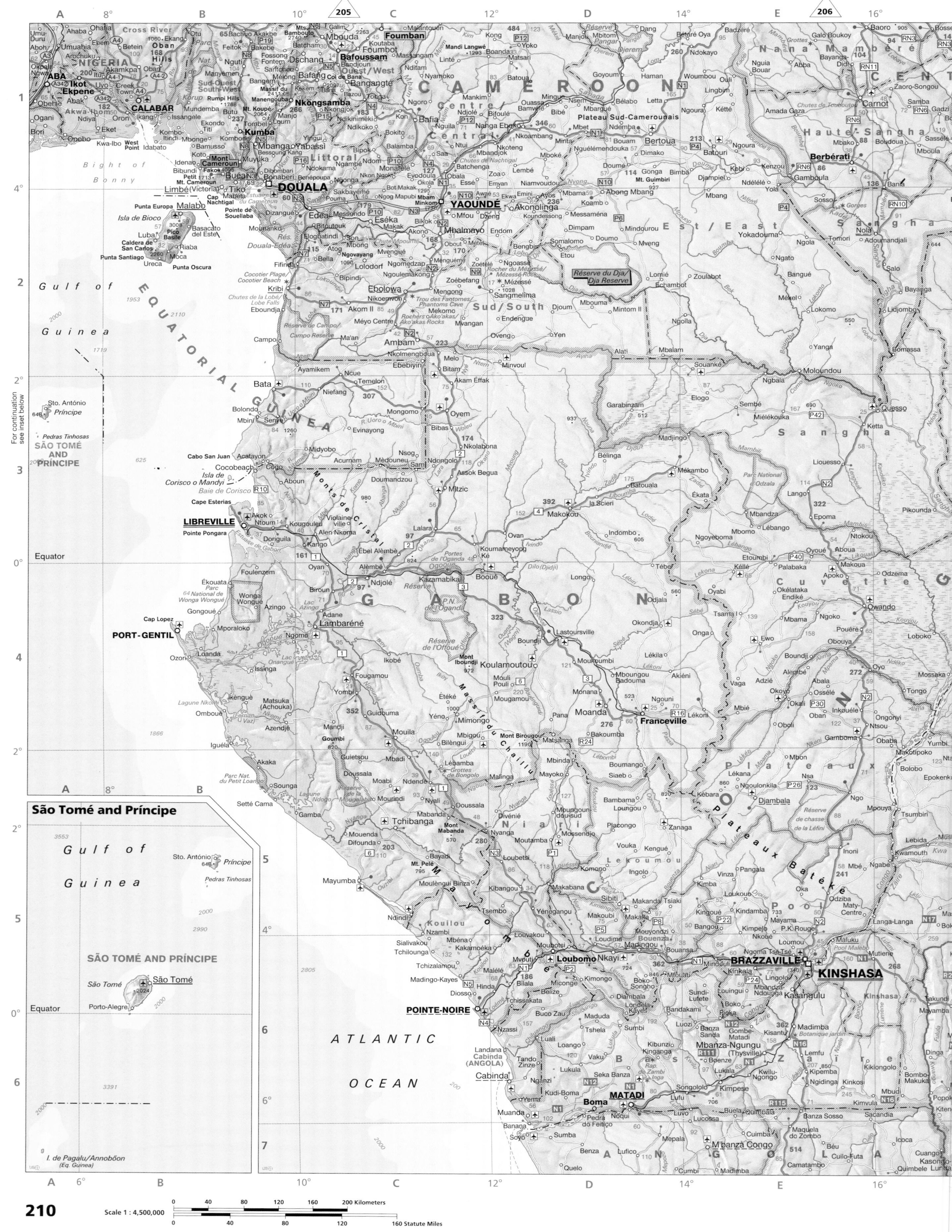

205
206
CAMEROON
NIGERIA
EQUATORIAL GUINEA
GABON
SÃO TOMÉ AND PRÍNCIPE
Gulf of Guinea
Bight of Bonny
ATLANTIC OCEAN
Equator
DOUALA
YAOUNDÉ
LIBREVILLE
PORT-GENTIL
POINTE-NOIRE
BRAZZAVILLE
KINSHASA
MATADI
CALABAR
ABA
Malabo
Bata
Kribi
Ebolowa
Bafoussam
Foumban
Nkongsamba
Kumba
Buea
Limbe (Victoria)
Edéa
Bertoua
Berbérati
Yokadouma
Ouesso
Oyem
Makokou
Lambaréné
Franceville
Koulamoutou
Mouila
Tchibanga
Loubomo
Nkayi
Cabinda
Boma
Owando
Djambala
Mbanza-Ngungu (Thysville)
Est / East
Sud / South
Littoral
Centre / Central
Ouest / West
Sud-Ouest / South-West
Haute-Sangha
Sangha
Cuvette
Plateaux
Plateaux Batéké
Pool
Niari
Lékoumou
Kouilou
Bas-Zaïre
Monts de Cristal
Massif du Chaillu
Mayombe
Réserve du Dja / Dja Reserve
Mont Cameroun
Plateau Sud-Camerounais
For continuation see inset below
São Tomé and Príncipe
São Tomé
Príncipe
Sto. António
Porto-Alegre
Pedras Tinhosas
I. de Pagalu/Annobóon (Eq. Guinea)
Scale 1 : 4,500,000
0 40 80 120 160 200 Kilometers
0 40 80 120 160 Statute Miles

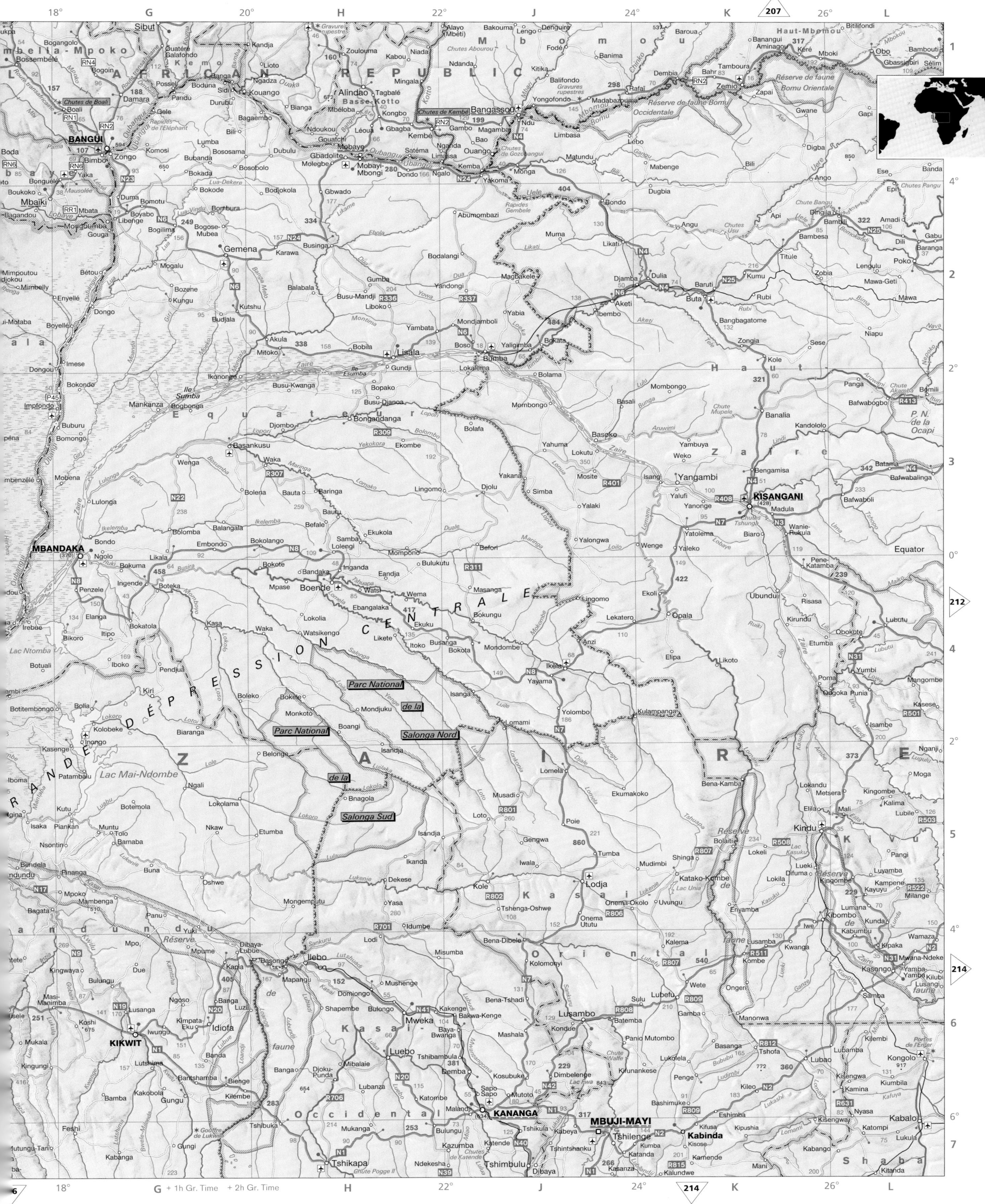

18° G 20° H 22° J 24° K 26° L
207
212
214
Bangui
Bimbo
Zongo
Mbaïki
Sibut
Kandja
Alindao
Basse-Kotto
Mobaye
Gbadolite
Bangassou
Ouango
Kemba
Yakoma
Bondo
Zemio
Obo
Bambouti
Rafaï
Haut-Mbomou
Réserve de faune Bomu Orientale
Réserve de faune Bomu Occidentale
Gemena
Libenge
Gbado-Lite
Businga
Lisala
Bumba
Aketi
Buta
Banalia
Basoko
Yangambi
KISANGANI
Ubundu
Opala
Bongandanga
Basankusu
Ikela
Boende
MBANDAKA
Bikoro
Lac Ntomba
Lac Mai-Ndombe
Inongo
Kiri
Lodja
Lomela
Lusambo
Ilebo
Mweka
Luebo
KANANGA
MBUJI-MAYI
Tshilenge
Kabinda
Tshikapa
Kikwit
Idiofa
Kindu
Kasongo
Kibombo
Kongolo
Kabalo
Lubao
Manono
Parc National de la Salonga Nord
Parc National de la Salonga Sud
DÉPRESSION CENTRALE
Equateur
Haut-Zaïre
Kasai Oriental
Kasai Occidental
Bandundu
Kivu
Shaba
ZAÏRE
CENTRAL AFRICAN REPUBLIC
Zaïre
Ubangi
P. N. de la Ocapi

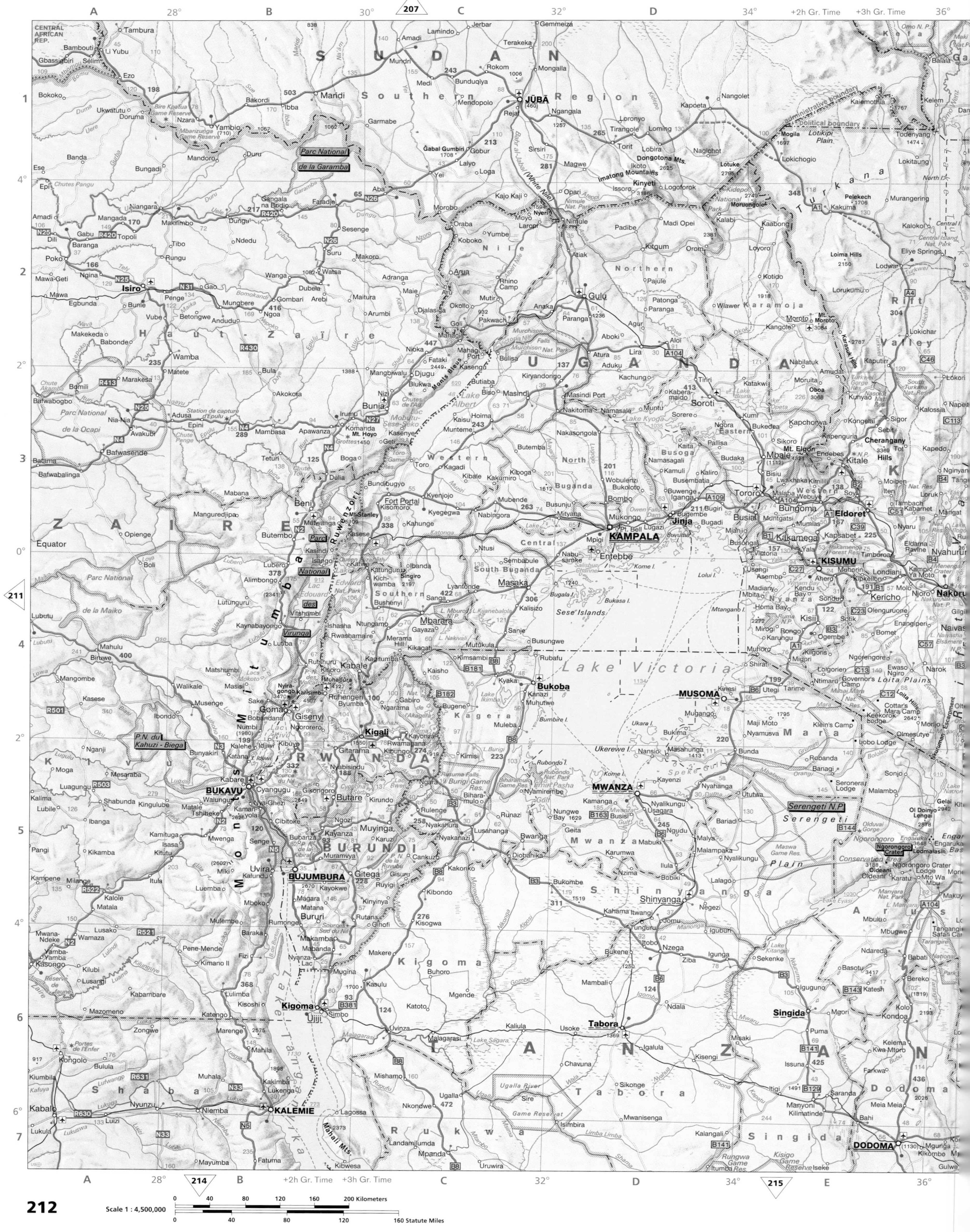

Scale 1 : 4,500,000

0 40 80 120 160 200 Kilometers

0 40 80 120 160 Statute Miles

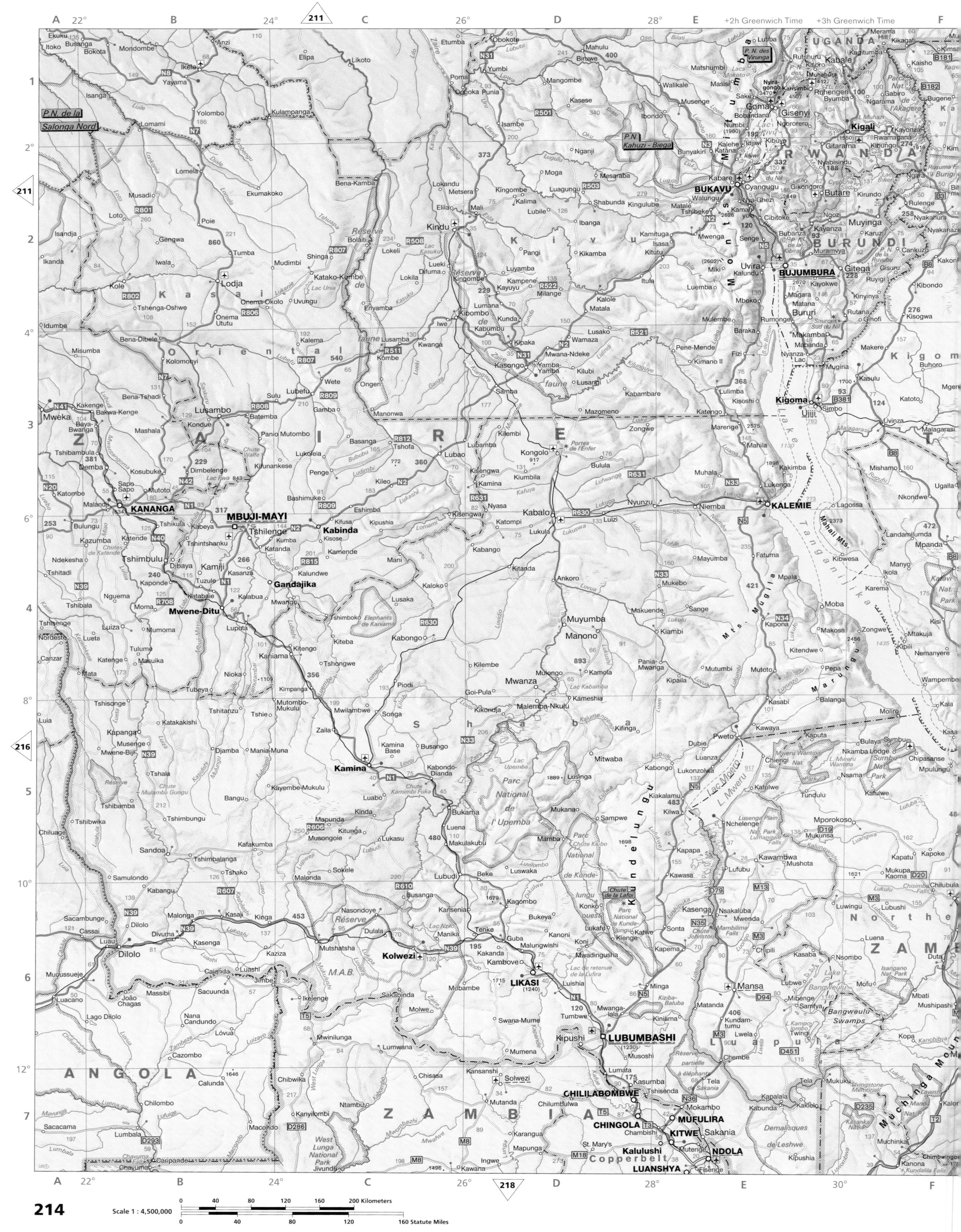

211
+2h Greenwich Time
+3h Greenwich Time
P.N. de la Salonga Nord
P.N. Kahuzi - Biega
P.N. des Virunga
UGANDA
RWANDA
BURUNDI
Z A I R E
K a s a i   O r i e n t a l
K i v u
S h a b a
ANGOLA
ZAMBIA
Kigali
Kabale
Gisenyi
Goma
BUKAVU
Cyangugu
Butare
Gitarama
Muhabura
Kisoro
BUJUMBURA
Gitega
Uvira
Kigoma
Ujiji
Kasulu
KALEMIE
Lake Tanganyika
Mahali Mts
Mts. Mugila
Kindu
Kasongo
Kibombo
Kongolo
Portes de l'Enfer
Kabalo
Nyunzu
Lodja
Lusambo
Mweka
KANANGA
MBUJI-MAYI
Tshilenge
Kabinda
Gandajika
Mwene-Ditu
Tshimbulu
Luiza
Kaniama
Kamina
Kamina Base
Bukama
Manono
Mwanza
Malemba-Nkulu
Mitwaba
Pweto
Moliro
Parc National de l'Upemba
Parc National de Kundelungu
Kundelungu
Lac Moero
L. Mweru
Kilwa
Kasenga
Kolwezi
LIKASI
LUBUMBASHI
Kipushi
Dilolo
Kasaji
Sandoa
Kapanga
CHILILABOMBWE
CHINGOLA
MUFULIRA
KITWE
NDOLA
LUANSHYA
Copperbelt
Solwezi
Mansa
Kawambwa
Bangweulu Swamps
Lake Bangweulu
L u a p u l a
West Lunga National Park
Muchinga Mountains
Northern
218
216
A 22° B 24° C 26° D 28° E 30° F
2° 4° 6° 8° 10° 12°
214
Scale 1 : 4,500,000
0 40 80 120 160 200 Kilometers
0 40 80 120 160 Statute Miles

212
213
219
222
G
H
J
K
L
32°
34°
36°
38°
40°
1
2
3
4
5
6
7
4°
6°
8°
10°
Lake Victoria
MUSOMA
MWANZA
Ukerewe I.
Serengeti N.P.
Serengeti Plain
Ngorongoro Crater
NAIROBI
Thika
Machakos
Kitui
Rift Valley
KENYA
Eastern
Coast
Kilimanjaro
Kilimanjaro N.P.
Kibo
Arusha
Moshi
Tsavo East
Tsavo West
Voi
Malindi
Mombasa Marine National Reserve
MOMBASA
Malindi Marine Nat. Park
Marine Nat. Res.
Watamu Marine National Park
Ras Ngomeni
Lamu
Usambara Mts.
TANGA
Pemba Island
Pemba Channel
Zanzibar and Pemba
ZANZIBAR
Zanzibar
Chwaka Island
Makunduchi
Bagamoyo
DAR ES SALAAM
Mafia Island
Mafia Chan.
Juani Island
Kilwa Kivinje
Kilwa Masoko
Kilwa Kisiwani
Songo Mnara
Masai-Steppe
Arusha
Shinyanga
Tabora
Singida
Dodoma
DODOMA
Morogoro
Uluguru Mts.
Mikumi Nat. Park
Iringa
Ruaha National Park
Rungwa Game Reserve
Kisigo Game Reserve
Selous Game Reserve
Pwani
Lindi
Mtwara
Makonde Plateau
Mbeya
Kipengere Range
Njombe
Songea
Ruvuma
Tunduru
Masasi
Newala
Cabo Delgado
Mocímboa da Praia
Pemba
Mueda
MOZAMBIQUE
Niassa
Lichinga
Lago Niassa
Nkhotakota
Mzuzu
Nkhata Bay
Livingstonia
Nyika Plateau Nat. Park
Viphya Mountains
MALAWI
Northern
Central
Karonga
Chitipa
Lindi Bay
Ungwana Bay
INDIAN OCEAN
+3h Greenwich Time
+2h Greenwich Time

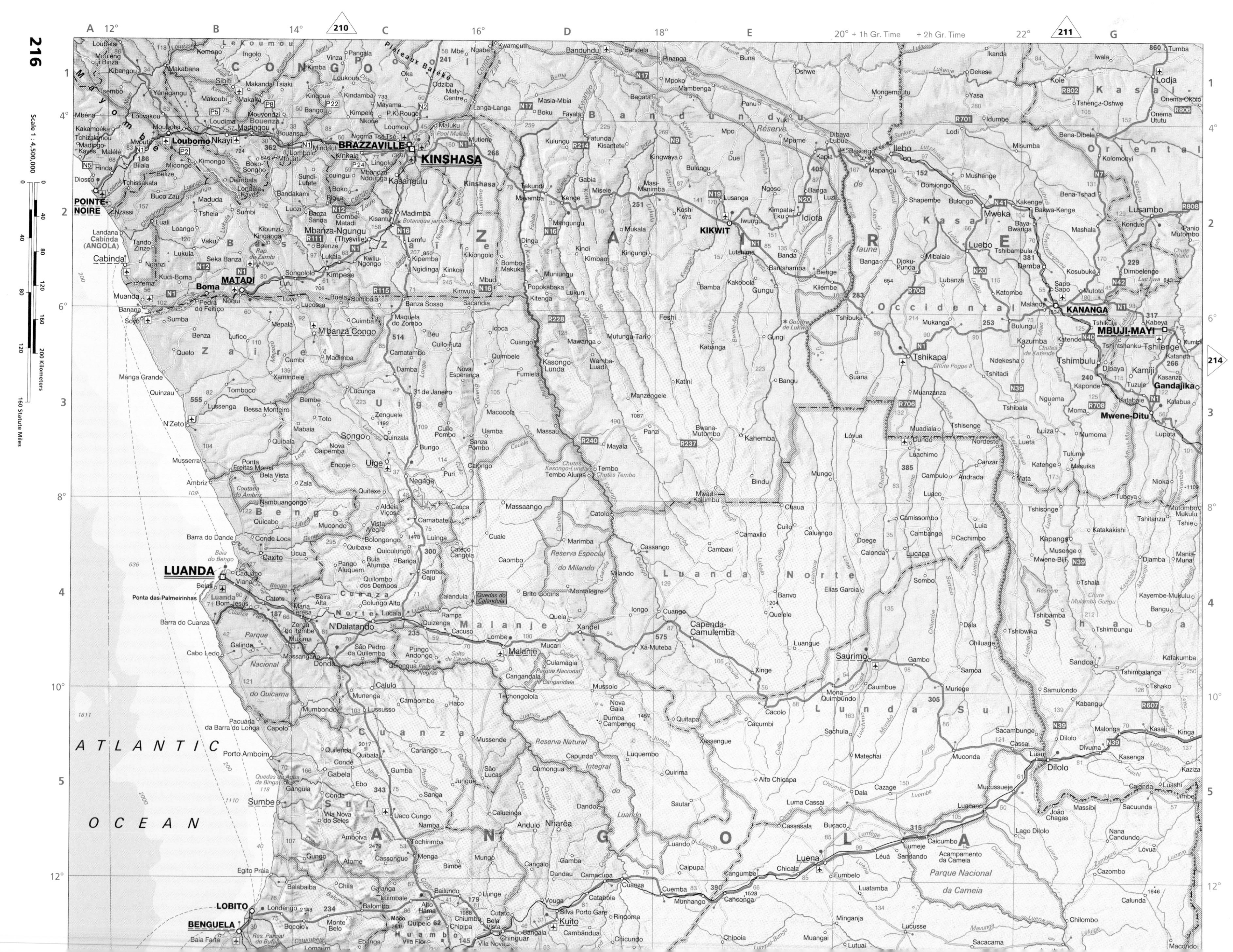

Scale 1 : 4,500,000
0 40 80 120 160 200 Kilometers
0 40 80 120 160 Statute Miles

Z A M B I A
B O T S W A N A
N A M I B I A
Caprivi Strip
O v a m b o l a n d
Etosha National Park
Etosha Pan
Okavango Delta
Moremi Wildlife Reserve
H e r e r o l a n d
K a u k a u v e l d
Ghanzi
Kalahari Desert
Central Kalahari Game Reserve
Skeleton Coast Park
Deserto de Namibe
Plateau
Huíla
WINDHOEK
Khomas Hochland
Grootfontein
Tsumeb
Otjiwarongo
Okahandja
Swakopmund
Walvis Bay
Gobabis
Maun
Rundu
Menongue
Namibe
Lubango
Mongu
Barotske Flood Plain
Coutada Pública do Mucusso
Parque Nacional do Bicuari
Parque Nacional da Mupa

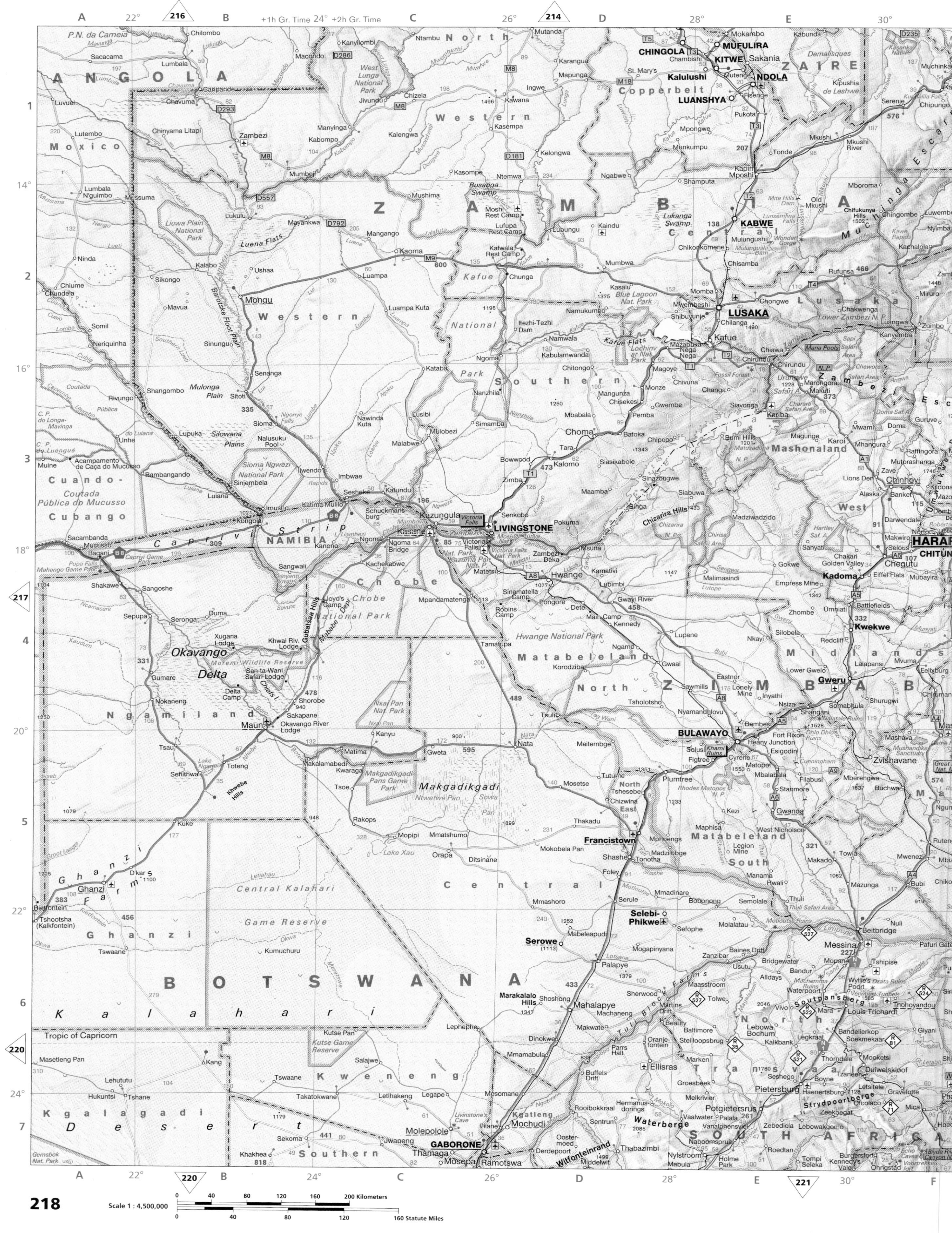

Scale 1 : 4,500,000
0 40 80 120 160 200 Kilometers
0 40 80 120 160 Statute Miles

32°
34°
36°
38°
40°
42°
G
H
J
K
L
M
215
222
223
1
2
3
4
5
6
7
14°
16°
18°
20°
22°
24°
MALAWI
LILONGWE
BLANTYRE
Nkhotakota
Lichinga
Zomba
Tete
Pemba
NAMPULA
Moçambique
Ilha de Moçambique
QUELIMANE
Angoche
BEIRA
Mutare
Inhambane
Maxixe
Quissico
Niassa
Cabo Delgado
Nampula
Zambézia
Tete
Manica
Sofala
Inhambane
Gaza
Mashonaland
Manicaland
Mozambique Channel
Bassas da India
(Fr.) (Réunion)
Île Europa (Fr.)
(Réunion)
Tropic of Capricorn
Parque Nacional de Gorongosa
Parque Nacional de Zinave
Parque Nacional de Banhine
Ilhas do Bazaruto
Parque Nacional de Bazaruto
Reserva do Niassa
Reserva do Gilé
Reserva de Marromeu
Lake Malawi
Cahora Bassa
Mulanje Mts.
Monte Namuli
Mte. Binga
Ponta São Sebastião
Vilanculos
Chimoio
Inhassoro
Xai-Xai
Chinde
Mocuba
Gurué
Cuamba
Montepuez
Mocímboa
Lúrio
Nacala
Ilha de Moma

217

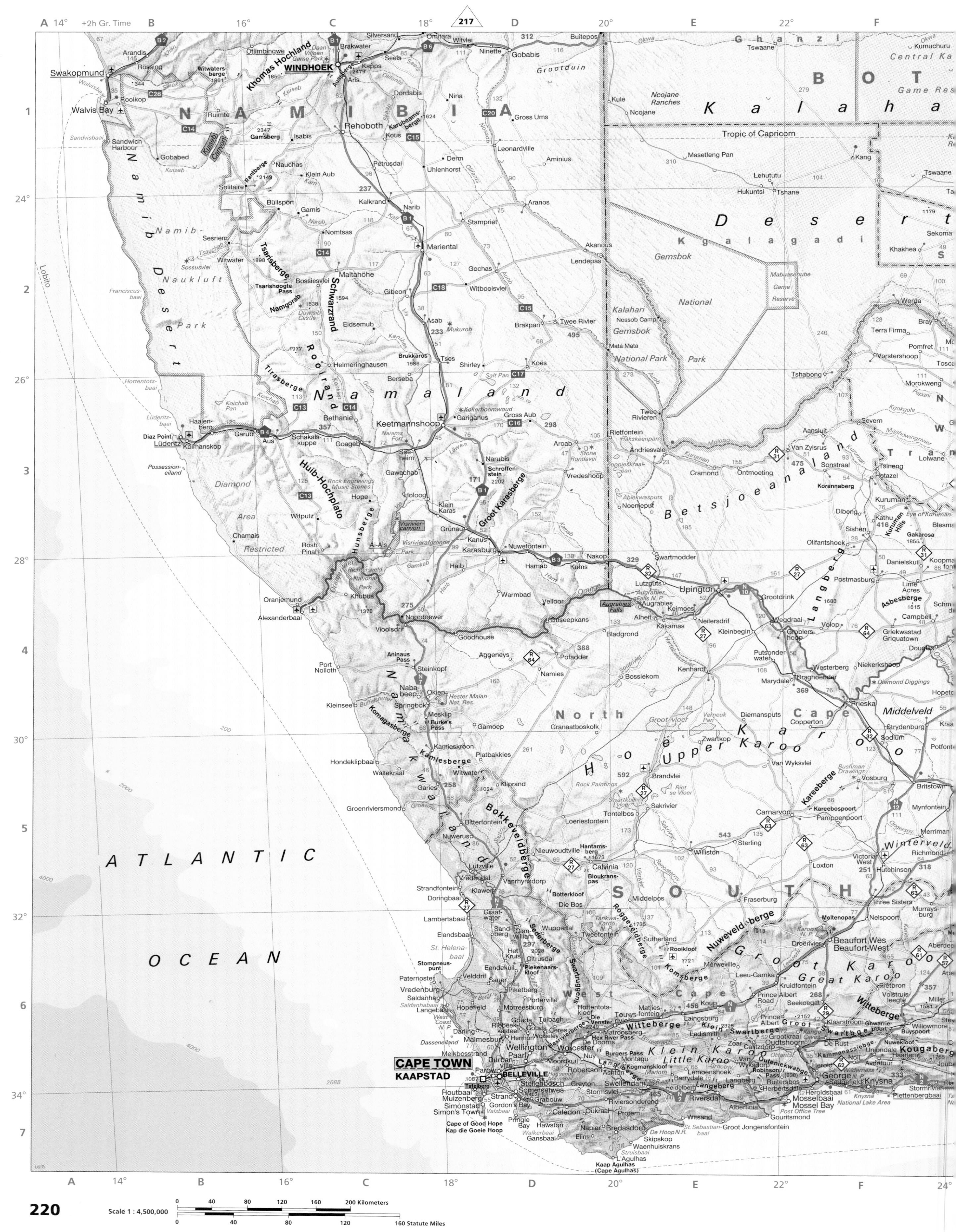

Scale 1 : 4,500,000

0 40 80 120 160 200 Kilometers

0 40 80 120 160 Statute Miles

ZIMBABWE
MOZAMBIQUE
SWAZILAND
LESOTHO
INDIAN
OCEAN
Mozambique Plateau
PWV = Pretoria Witwatersrand Vereeniging
PRETORIA
JOHANNES-BURG
SOWETO
MAPUTO
Mbabane
MASERU
DURBAN
PIETERMARITZ-BURG
KIMBERLEY
BLOEMFONTEIN
WELKOM
GABORONE
PORT ELIZABETH
EAST LONDON
OOS-LONDEN
BISHO
Umtata
Pietersburg
Nelspruit
Xai-Xai
Inhambane
Witwatersrand
Drakensberg
Waterberge
Lebombo
Kruger
National
Park
Giants Castle
Aden, Bur Sa'id

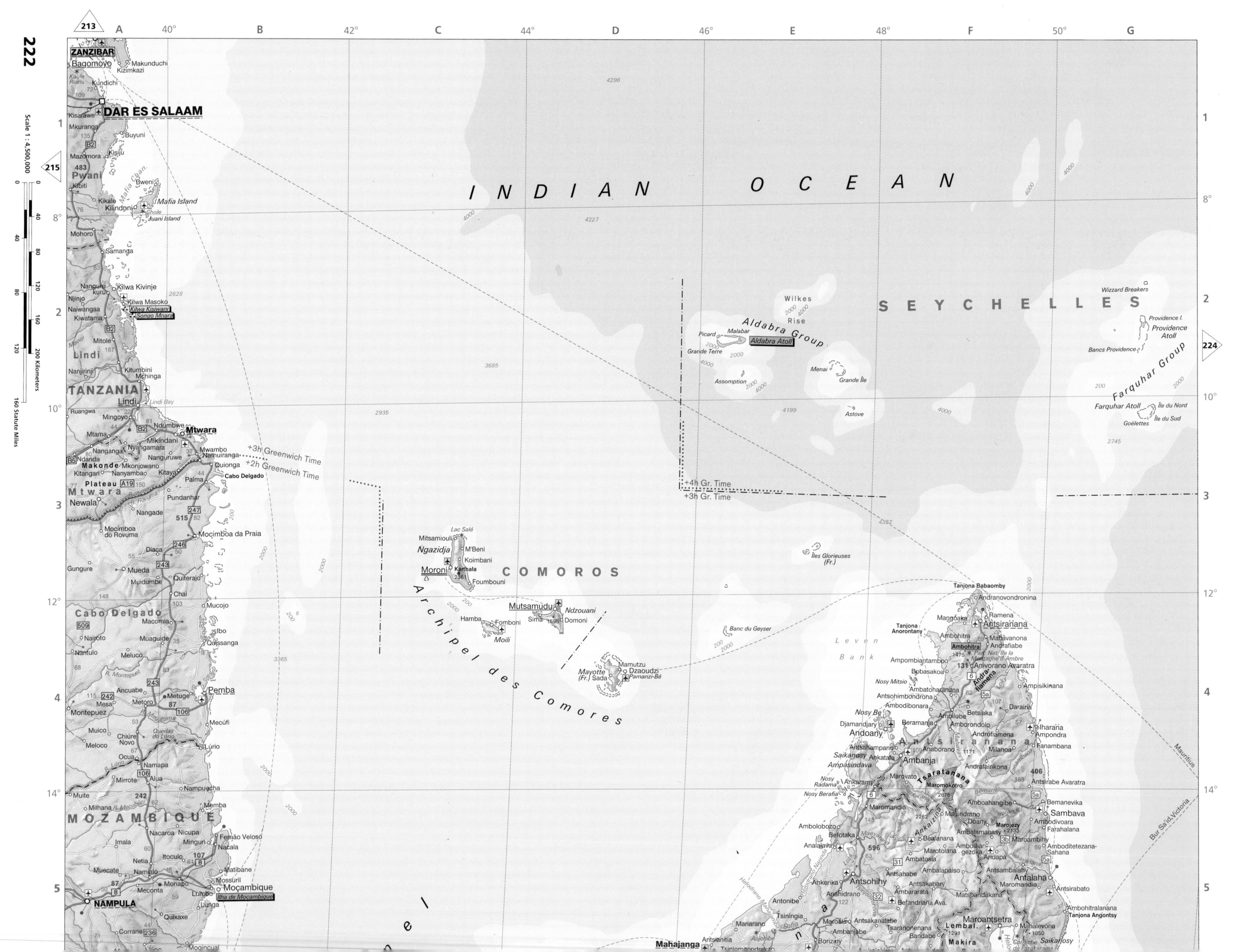
INDIAN OCEAN
SEYCHELLES
COMOROS
Archipel des Comores
Farquhar Group
Aldabra Group
Aldabra Atoll
Wilkes Rise
Providence Atoll
Farquhar Atoll
Îles Glorieuses (Fr.)
Banc du Geyser
Mayotte (Fr.)
Dzaoudzi
Moroni
Ngazidja
Mutsamudu
Ndzouani
Moili
Fomboni
TANZANIA
DAR ES SALAAM
ZANZIBAR
Mafia Island
Mtwara
Lindi
Kilwa Masoko
Cabo Delgado
Pemba
MOZAMBIQUE
NAMPULA
Moçambique
Nacala
Antsiranana
Sambava
Antalaha
Mahajanga
Maroantsetra
Leven Bank
+3h Greenwich Time
+2h Greenwich Time
+4h Gr. Time
+3h Gr. Time
Scale 1 : 4,500,000
200 Kilometers
160 Statute Miles

INDIAN OCEAN
Mozambique Ch
MADAGASCAR
Madagascar Basin
ANTANANARIVO
Toamasina (Tamatave)
Fianarantsoa
Toliara (Tuléar)
Antsirabe
Morondava
Mananjary
Manakara
Farafangana
Tôlañaro
Moramanga
Andringitra
Mahajanga
Toamasina
Antananarivo
Fianarantsoa
Toliara
Tropic of Capricorn
Île Europa (Réunion) (Fr.)
Bassas da India (Réunion) (Fr.)
Île Juan de Nova (Réunion) (Fr.)
Nosy Sainte-Marie
Tsingy de Bemaraha Strict Nature Reserve
Mauritius
Durban
Beira

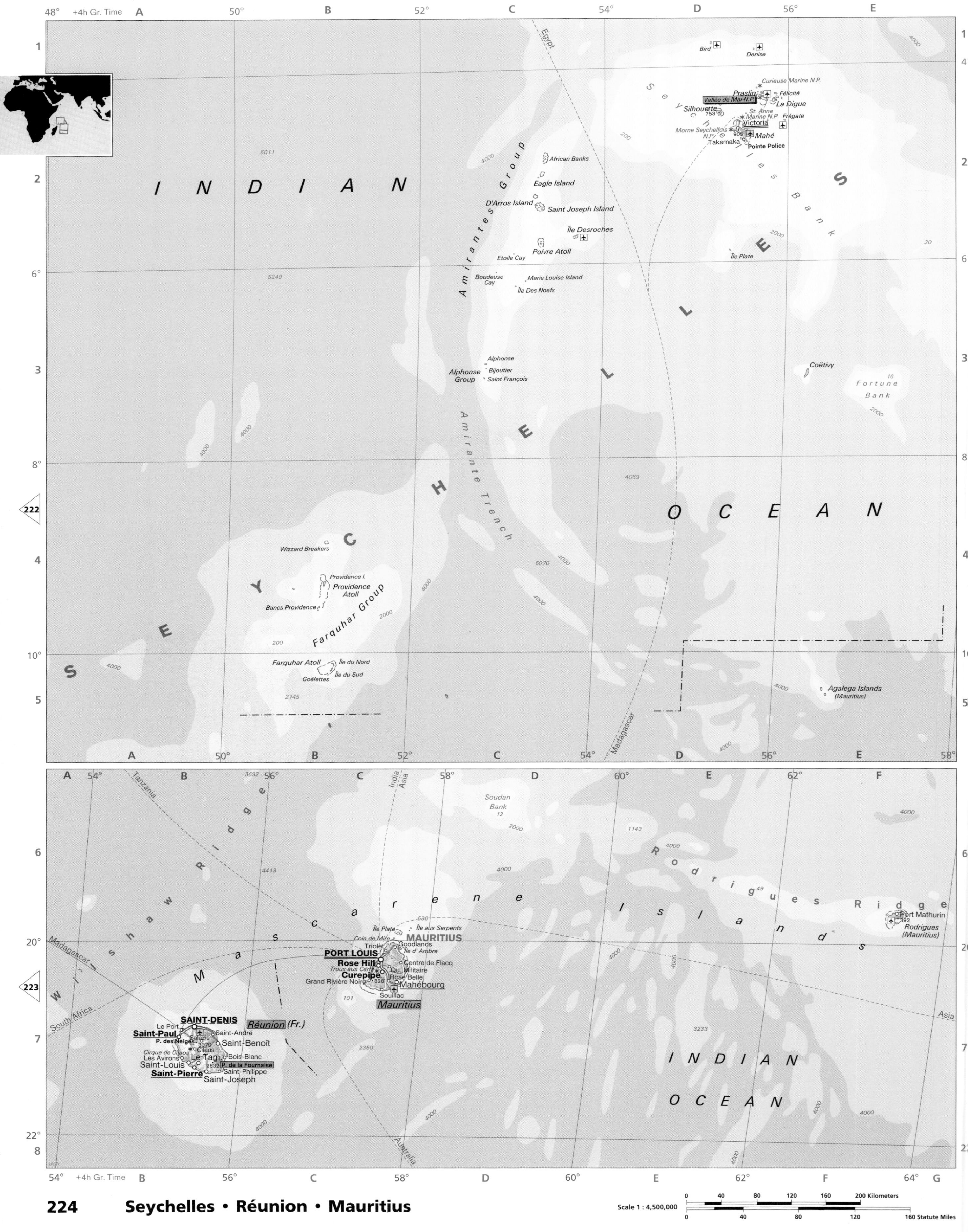

+4h Gr. Time
INDIAN OCEAN
SEYCHELLES
Bird
Denise
Curieuse Marine N.P.
Praslin
Félicité
Vallée de Mai N.P.
La Digue
Silhouette
St. Anne Marine N.P.
Frégate
Morne Seychellois N.P.
Victoria
Mahé
Takamaka
Pointe Police
Seychelles Bank
African Banks
Eagle Island
D'Arros Island
Saint Joseph Island
Île Desroches
Poivre Atoll
Etoile Cay
Boudeuse Cay
Marie Louise Island
Île Des Noefs
Île Plate
Amirantes Group
Alphonse
Bijoutier
Saint François
Alphonse Group
Coëtivy
Fortune Bank
Amirante Trench
Egypt
Madagascar
Wizzard Breakers
Providence I.
Providence Atoll
Bancs Providence
Farquhar Group
Farquhar Atoll
Île du Nord
Île du Sud
Goëlettes
Agalega Islands (Mauritius)
Tanzania
Wishaw Ridge
Mascarene Islands
Rodrigues Ridge
Soudan Bank
India
Asia
Île Plate
Île aux Serpents
Coin de Mire
MAURITIUS
Triolet
Goodlands
Île d'Ambre
PORT LOUIS
Rose Hill
Centre de Flacq
Trous aux Cerfs
Qu. Militaire
Curepipe
Rose Belle
Grand Rivière Noire
Mahébourg
Souillac
Mauritius
Port Mathurin
Rodrigues (Mauritius)
South Africa
Australia
SAINT-DENIS
Réunion (Fr.)
Le Port
Saint-Paul
Saint-André
Salazie
P. des Neiges
Saint-Benoît
Cirque de Cilaos
Cilaos
Les Avirons
Le Tam.
Bois-Blanc
Saint-Louis
P. de la Fournaise
Saint-Philippe
Saint-Pierre
Saint-Joseph
Scale 1 : 4,500,000
200 Kilometers
160 Statute Miles

The U.S.A. and Southern Canada

The United States and the southern provinces of Canada occupy the entire center of North America. A clearly arranged topography characterizes this region between the Atlantic and Pacific Oceans. The mighty Rockies in the west and the narrow chain of the Appalachian Mountains in the east run more or less parallel to one another along their respective meridians of longitude. They enclose a huge plain whose expanse of arable land not only nourishes the native population, but also feeds millions of people in countries with less developed agriculture. Enormous coniferous and mixed forests and more than a million lakes are found in the north. The five Great Lakes lie between the two countries at their most productive point.

The Statue of Liberty, built "to glorify the Republic and Liberty," has become a symbol of freedom throughout the world. This lithography was published in New York one year before "Lady Liberty" was unveiled on 28 October 1886.

British Columbia, Central
p. 228–229

British Columbia, South
p. 230–231

Alberta and Saskatchewan, South
p. 232–233

Manitoba, South · Ontario, West
p. 234–235

Ontario, Central · Québec, Southwest
p. 236–237

Ontario and Québec, South
p. 238–239

Québec, Southeast · Atlantic Provinces, West
p. 240–241

Atlantic Provinces, East
p. 242–243

Washington · Oregon
p. 244–245

California, North · Nevada
p. 246–247

California, South
p. 248–249

Idaho, North · Montana
p. 250–251

Idaho, South · Wyoming
p. 252–253

Utah · Colorado
p. 254–255

Arizona · New Mexico
p. 256–257

North Dakota
p. 258–259

South Dakota
p. 260–261

Nebraska · Kansas
p. 262–263

Oklahoma · Texas, North
p. 264–265

Texas, South
p. 266–267

Texas, East · Louisiana · Mississippi
p. 268–269

Minnesota · Wisconsin and Michigan,
North p. 270–271

Michigan, South · Southern Great Lake
Region p. 272–273

Iowa · Missouri and Illinois, North ·
Indiana p. 274–275

Missouri, South · Arkansas · Kentucky ·
Tennessee p. 276–277

New York · Northeastern States
p. 278–279

Ohio · Pennsylvania · West Virginia ·
Maryland · Delaware p. 280–281

West Virginia · Virginia · North Carolin
p. 282–283

Alabama · Georgia · South Carolina
p. 284–285

Florida (Inset: Puerto Rico, Virgin Islan
p. 286–287

Hawaii
p. 288

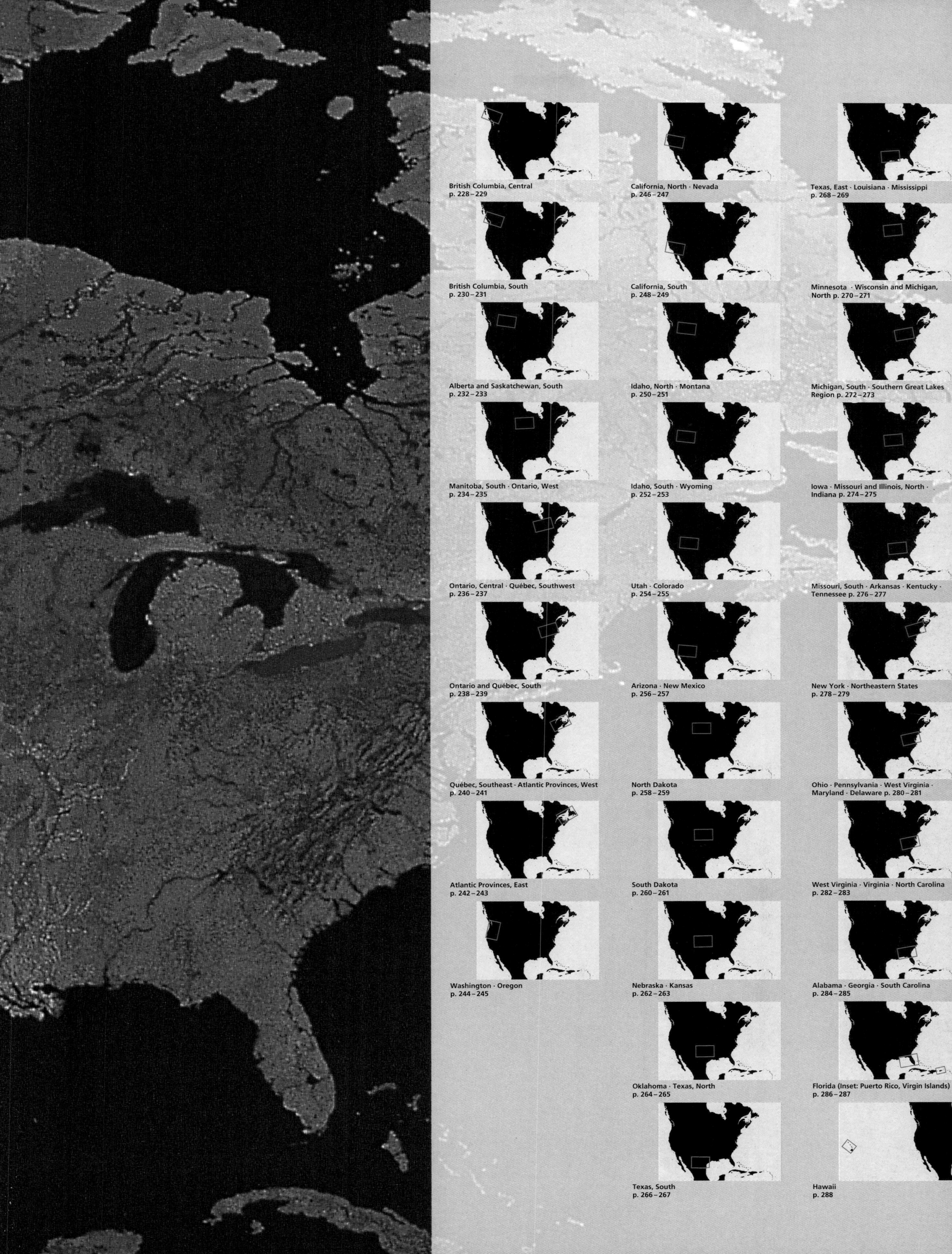
British Columbia, Central
p. 228 – 229

British Columbia, South
p. 230 – 231

Alberta and Saskatchewan, South
p. 232 – 233

Manitoba, South · Ontario, West
p. 234 – 235

Ontario, Central · Québec, Southwest
p. 236 – 237

Ontario and Québec, South
p. 238 – 239

Québec, Southeast · Atlantic Provinces, West
p. 240 – 241

Atlantic Provinces, East
p. 242 – 243

Washington · Oregon
p. 244 – 245

California, North · Nevada
p. 246 – 247

California, South
p. 248 – 249

Idaho, North · Montana
p. 250 – 251

Idaho, South · Wyoming
p. 252 – 253

Utah · Colorado
p. 254 – 255

Arizona · New Mexico
p. 256 – 257

North Dakota
p. 258 – 259

South Dakota
p. 260 – 261

Nebraska · Kansas
p. 262 – 263

Oklahoma · Texas, North
p. 264 – 265

Texas, South
p. 266 – 267

Texas, East · Louisiana · Mississippi
p. 268 – 269

Minnesota · Wisconsin and Michigan, North p. 270 – 271

Michigan, South · Southern Great Lakes Region p. 272 – 273

Iowa · Missouri and Illinois, North · Indiana p. 274 – 275

Missouri, South · Arkansas · Kentucky · Tennessee p. 276 – 277

New York · Northeastern States
p. 278 – 279

Ohio · Pennsylvania · West Virginia · Maryland · Delaware p. 280 – 281

West Virginia · Virginia · North Carolina
p. 282 – 283

Alabama · Georgia · South Carolina
p. 284 – 285

Florida (Inset: Puerto Rico, Virgin Islands)
p. 286 – 287

Hawaii
p. 288

Scale 1 : 2,250,000
0 20 40 60 80 100 Kilometers
0 20 40 60 80 Statute Miles

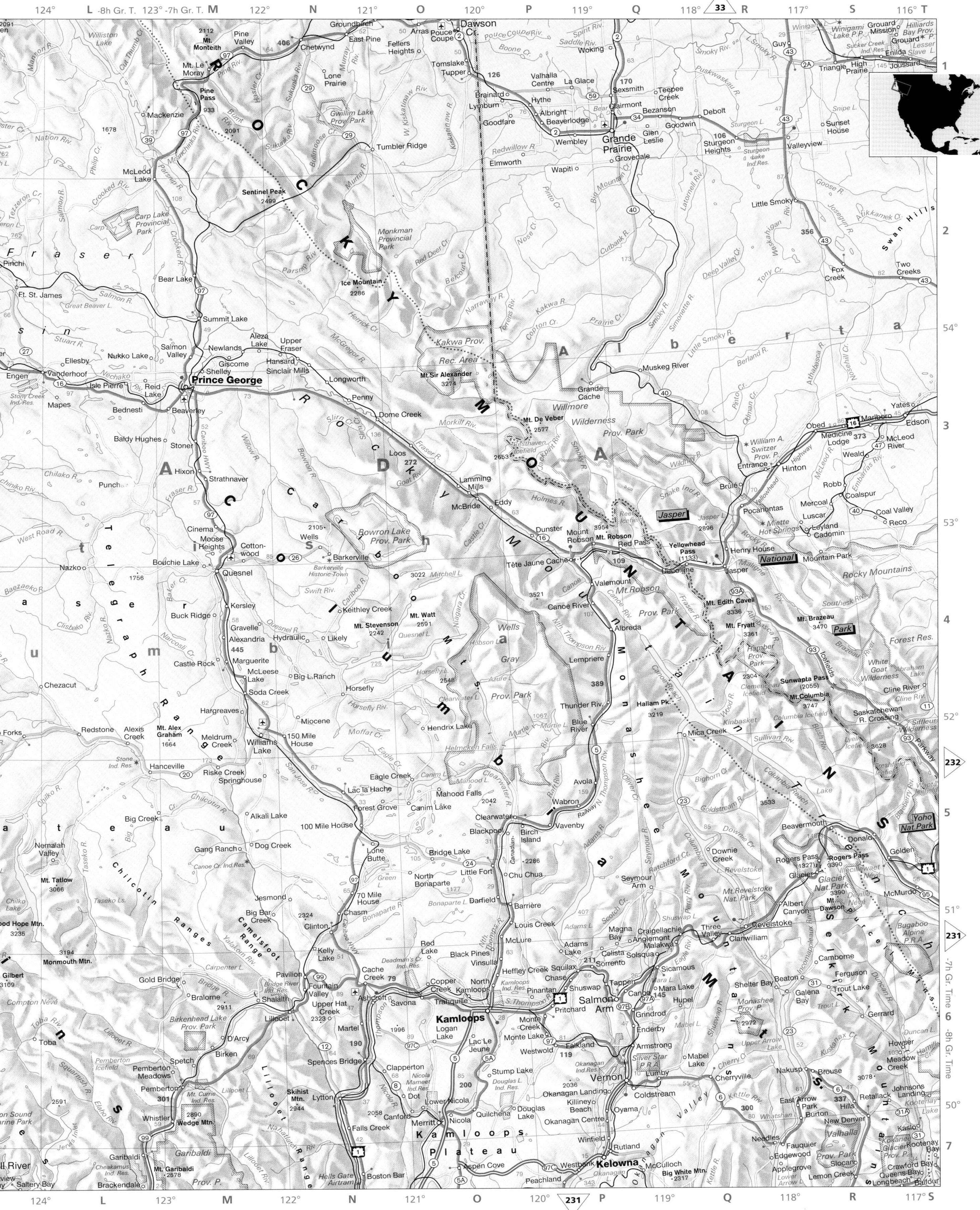

124° L -8h Gr. T. 123° -7h Gr. T. M 122° N 121° O 120° P 119° Q 118° 33 R 117° S 116° T
Rocky Mountains
Alberta
Fraser Basin
Cariboo Mts.
Telegraph Range
Chilcotin Ranges
Camelsfoot Range
Lillooet Range
Monashee Mountains
Selkirk Mountains
Purcell Mts.
Kamloops Plateau
Swan Hills
Okanagan Valley
Dawson Cr.
Pouce Coupe
Arras
Groundbirch
East Pine
Chetwynd
Fellers Heights
Tomslake
Tupper
Pine Valley
Mt. Monteith
Mt. Le Moray
Pine Pass
Mackenzie
Tumbler Ridge
Gwillim Lake Prov. Park
Lone Prairie
Valhalla Centre
La Glace
Sexsmith
Teepee Creek
Brainard
Lymburn
Hythe
Albright
Beaverlodge
Clairmont
Bezanson
Debolt
Goodfare
Wembley
Grande Prairie
Glen Leslie
Goodwin
Sturgeon Heights
Valleyview
Grovedale
Elmworth
Wapiti
Woking
Guy
Winagami Lake P.P.
Grouard Mission
Hilliards Bay Prov. P.
Enilda
Joussard
Triangle
High Prairie
Sunset House
Little Smoky
Fox Creek
Two Creeks
McLeod Lake
Sentinel Peak 2499
Carp Lake Provincial Park
Monkman Provincial Park
Ice Mountain 2286
Pinchi
Bear Lake
Ft. St. James
Summit Lake
Kakwa Prov. Rec. Area
Mt.Sir Alexander 3274
Muskeg River
Grande Cache
Willmore Wilderness Prov. Park
Salmon Valley
Aleza Lake
Upper Fraser
Newlands
Giscome
Shelley
Hansard
Sinclair Mills
Longworth
Nukko Lake
Ellesby
Vanderhoof
Engen
Isle Pierre
Reid Lake
Prince George
Mapes
Bednesti
Beaverley
Penny
Dome Creek
Baldy Hughes
Stoner
Hixon
Strathnaver
Puncha
Loos
Mt. De Veber 2577
Lamming Mills
McBride
Eddy
Dunster
Mount Robson
Mt. Robson 3954
Red Pass
Yellowhead Pass (1133)
Jasper
Tête Jaune Cache
Valemount
Henry House
Mountain Park
Cinema
Moose Heights
Cottonwood
Wells
Barkerville
Bowron Lake Prov. Park
Quesnel
Bouchie Lake
Nazko
Kersley
Buck Ridge
Gravelle
Alexandria
Keithley Creek
Mt. Watt 2591
Mt. Stevenson 2242
Likely
Hydraulic
Castle Rock
Marguerite
McLeese Lake
Big L. Ranch
Soda Creek
Horsefly
Wells Gray Prov. Park
Canoe River
Albreda
Lempriere
Thunder Riv.
Hallam Pk. 3219
Blue River
Mica Creek
Hargreaves
Miocene
Hendrix Lake
Chezacut
Redstone
Alexis Creek
Mt. Alex Graham 1664
Meldrum Creek
Williams Lake
150 Mile House
Hanceville
Riske Creek
Springhouse
Eagle Creek
Lac la Hache
Mahood Falls
Forest Grove
Canim Lake
Avola
Wabron
Vavenby
Clearwater
Birch Island
Blackpool
Big Creek
Alkali Lake
100 Mile House
Gang Ranch
Dog Creek
Lone Butte
Bridge Lake
Little Fort
Chu Chua
North Bonaparte
Nemaiah Valley
Mt. Tatlow 3066
Jesmond
70 Mile House
Darfield
Barrière
Big Bar Creek
Chasm
Clinton
Louis Creek
McLure
Kelly Lake
Red Lake
Black Pines
Vinsulla
Heffley Creek
Squilax
Chase
Adams Lake
Celista
Sorrento
Magna Bay
Anglemont
Craigellachie
Malakwa
Solsqua
Sicamous
Three Valley
Revelstoke
Clanwilliam
Mt. Edith Cavell 3336
Mt. Fryatt 3361
Hamber Prov. Park
Mt. Brazeau 3470
Sunwapta Pass (2055)
Mt. Columbia 3747
Saskatchewan R. Crossing
Cline River
Forest Res.
Beavermouth
Donald
Golden
Rogers Pass (1327)
Glacier
Glacier Nat. Park
Mt. Revelstoke Nat. Park
Albert Canyon
Mt. Dawson
McMurdo
Downie Creek
Seymour Arm
Camborne
Ferguson
Trout Lake
Gerrard
Galena Bay
Beaton
Shelter Bay
Monmouth Mtn. 3194
Pavilion
Gold Bridge
Bralorne
Shalalth
Fountain Valley
Upper Hat Creek
Cache Creek
Ashcroft
Savona
Copper Creek
Tranquille
Kamloops
North Kamloops
Pinantan
Pritchard
Shuswap
Tappen
Salmon Arm
Canoe
Mara Lake
Hupel
Grindrod
Enderby
Lillooet
Birkenhead Lake Prov. Park
D'Arcy
Birken
Toba
Martel
Logan Lake
Lac Le Jeune
Monte Creek
Monte Lake
Westwold
Falkland
Armstrong
Spences Bridge
Pemberton Meadows
Pemberton
Spetch
Clapperton
Stump Lake
Vernon
Lumby
Mabel Lake
Cherryville
Nakusp
Brouse
Howser
Meadow Creek
Whistler
Wedge Mtn. 2890
Skihist Mtn. 2944
Lytton
Lower Nicola
Okanagan Landing
Coldstream
Oyama
Killiney Beach
East Arrow Park
Burton
New Denver
Retallack
Johnsons Landing
Canford
Merritt
Nicola
Quilchena
Douglas Lake
Okanagan Centre
Winfield
Falls Creek
Needles
Fauquier
Edgewood
Applegrove
Lemon Creek
Slocan
Kaslo
Kokanee Glacier Prov. Park
Crawford Bay
Queens Bay
Longbeach
Balfour
Garibaldi
Mt. Garibaldi 2678
Garibaldi Prov. P.
Brackendale
Saltery Bay
Boston Bar
Hells Gate Airtram
Aspen Cove
Peachland
Westbank
Kelowna
McCulloch
Rutland
Big White Mtn. 2317
Obed
Marlboro
Edson
Medicine Lodge
McLeod River
Weald
William A. Switzer Prov. P.
Entrance
Hinton
Brulé
Robb
Coalspur
Mercoal
Luscar
Coal Valley
Pocahontas
Miette Hot Springs
Leyland
Cadomin
Reco
Yates
Jasper National Park
Yoho Nat. Park
Bugaboo Alpine P.R.A.
232
231
-7h Gr. Time -8h Gr. Time
124° L 123° M 122° N 121° O 120° 231 P 119° Q 118° R 117° S

A
128°
B
127°
C
126°
228
D
125°
E
124°
F
123°
G
122°
H
121°
1
2
3
4
5
6
7
52°
51°
50°
49°
48°
47°
Fiordland Provincial Recreation Area
Kimsquit
Tweedsmuir
Prov.
Park
Kalone Pk.
2557
Tsitsuti Pk.
2478
Far Mtn.
2393
Mt. Downton
2365
Nazko
Bouchie Lake
Cottonwood
Quesnel
Barkerville
Barkerville Historic Town
Klemtu
Roderick I.
Swindle I.
Ocean Falls
Price I.
Milbanke Sound
Bella Coola
Hagensborg
Stuie
Firvale
Atnarko
Anahim Lake
Nimpo Lake
Chezacut
Mt. Saugstad
2929
King Island
Waglisla
Bella Bella
Hunter Island
Namu
Hakai Recreation Area
Calvert Island
Cape Calvert
Monarch Mtn.
3533
Chilanko Forks
Redstone
Alexis Creek
Mt. Alex Graham
1664
Tatla Lake
Kleena Kleene
Hanceville
Riske Creek
Springhouse
Williams Lake
150 Mile House
Meldrum Creek
Hargreaves
Miocene
Horsefly
Soda Creek
McLeese Lake
Big L. Ranch
Castle Rock
Marguerite
Alexandria
Hydraulic
Likely
Gravelle
Kersley
Buck Ridge
Keithley Creek
Mt. Stevenson
2242
Dawsons Landing
Duncanby Landing
Goose Bay
Cape Caution
Allison Harbour
Bull Harbour
Scott Is.
C. Scott
Nahwitti
Holberg
Port Hardy
Bear Cove
Fort Rupert
Winter Harbour
Coal Harbour
Rumble Beach
Pt. Alice
Sointula
Alert Bay
Pt.Mc Neill
Beaver Cove
Kokish
Simoon Harbour
Kingcome Inlet
Thompson Sound
Simoon Sound
Minstrel Island
Glendale Cove
Pt. Neville
Jackson Bay
Phillips Arm
Kelsey Bay
Sayward
Blind Channel
Thurlow
Stuart Island
Silverthrone Mtn.
2957
Mt. Waddington
4042
Mt. Queen Bess
3289
Good Hope Mtn.
3235
Mt. Tatlow
3066
Nemaiah Valley
Big Creek
Dog Creek
Gang Ranch
Alkali Lake
100 Mile House
Lac la Hache
Forest Grove
Lone Butte
70 Mile House
Jesmond
Big Bar Creek
Clinton
Chasm
Kelly Lake
Monmouth Mtn.
3194
Mt. Gilbert
3109
Gold Bridge
Bralorne
Pavilion
Cache Creek
Ashcroft
Shalalth
Fountain Valley
Upper Hat Creek
Lillooet
Savona
Martel
D'Arcy
Birken
Spences Bridge
Pemberton Meadows
Pemberton
Whistler
Wedge Mtn.
2890
Skihist Mtn.
2944
Lytton
Canford
Clapperton
Falls Creek
Toba
C. Cook
Kynquot
Chamiss Bay
Fair Harbour
Zeballos
Ceepeecee
Tahsis
Hecate
Gold River
Nootka I.
Nootka
Boat Basin
Estevan Point
Matlahaw Pt.
Stewardson Inlet
Hot Springs Cove
Flores I.
Ahousat
Tofino
Opitsat
Ucluelet
Vancouver
Island
Victoria Pk.
2163
Campbell River
Quathiaski Cove
Black Creek
Merville
Courtenay
Comox
Cumberland
Union Bay
Denman Island
Buckley B.
Fanny Bay
Bowser
Hornby I.
Golden Hinde
2201
Mt. Albert Edward
2094
Strathcoma Prov. Park
Powell River
Westview
Lang Bay
Saltery Bay
Egmont
Earls Cove
Blubber Bay
Texada I.
Gillies Bay
Irvines Landing
Madeira Park
Halfmoon Bay
Sechelt
Port Mellon
Roberts Creek
Langdale
Gibsons
Bowen Island
Squamish
Britannia Beach
Garibaldi
Mt. Garibaldi
2678
Brackendale
Horseshoe Bay
West Vancouver
Nth. Vancouver
Port Moody
Port Coquitlam
VANCOUVER
NEW WESTMINSTER
Richmond
Burnaby
Pitt Meadows
Whonnock
Mission
Delta
SURREY
Langley
Abbotsford
White Rock
Tsawwassen
Blaine
Sumas
Harrison Hot Springs
Harrison Mills
Agassiz
Chilliwack
Sardis
Hope
Laidlaw
Yale
Boston Bar
Great Central
Sproat Lake
P. Alberni
Errington
Parksville
Qualicum Beach
Nanoose Bay
Lantzville
Mt. Arrowsmith
1817
Nanaimo
Departure Bay
Gabriola
Cedar
Cassidy
Nahmint
Kildonan
Port Albion
Ecoole
Bamfield
Sarita
Nitinat
Mt. Whymper
1542
Ladysmith
Chemainus
Youbou
Honeymoon Bay
Lake Cowichan
North Cowichan
Duncan
Thetis Island
Kuper Is.
Ganges
Galiano
Salt Spring
Fulford Harbour
Saturna
South Pender
Pender Is.
Musgrave
Swartz Bay
Sidney
North Saanich
Central Saanich
Malahat
Saanich
Oak Bay
Victoria
Esquimalt
Langford
Metchosin
Sooke
River Jordan
Pt. Renfrew
Clo-oose
Pacific Rim National Park
Barkley Sound
Friday Harbour
Lynden
Kendall
Glacier
Nugents Corner
Ferndale
Deming
Mt. Baker
3285
Bellingham
Acme
Newhalem
Anacortes
Sedro Woolley
Hamilton
Burlington
Mt. Vernon
Oak Harbor
McMurray
Oso
Rockport
Darrington
Arlington
Stanwood
Coupeville
Whidbey I.
Keystone
Port Townsend
Dungeness Spit
Sequim
Pt. Angeles
Joyce
Clallam Bay
Sappho
Forks
La Push
C. Flattery
Neah Bay
Makah Ind. Res.
Olympic National Park
Olympic
Mountains
Mt. Olympus
2424
Hot Springs
Discovery Bay
Quilcene
Brinnon
Duckabush
Lilliwaup
Hoodsport
Kalaloch
Queets
Amanda Park
Neilton
Quinault
Taholah
Humptulips
Pacific Beach
Ocean City
Ocean Shores
Aberdeen
Hoquiam
New London
Montesano
Elma
McCleary
Matlock
Shelton
Olympia
Tumwater
Lacey
Freeland
Columbia Beach
Port Gamble
Silverdale
Poulsbo
Bremerton
Port Orchard
Southworth
Belfair
Dewatto
Allyn
Vaughn
Gig Harbor
Purdy
Bambridge Island
Kingston
Edmonds
Lynnwood
Mukilteo
Everett
Marysville
Lake Stevens
Snohomish
Monroe
Startup
Index
Bothell
Kirkland
SEATTLE
Redmond
Bellevue
Duvall
Fall City
Snoqualmie
North Bend
Issaquah
Renton
Burien
Des Moines
Kent
Maple Valley
Auburn
Fife
TACOMA
Puyallup
Sumner
Enumclaw
Buckley
Carbonado
Orting
Greenwater
Cle Elum
Skykomish
Stevens Pass
Snoqualmie Pass
Monte Cristo
Glacier Pk.
3221
Vancouver
PACIFIC
OCEAN
B
127°
C
126°
D
125°
E
124°
F
123°
244
G
122°
H
121°
Scale 1 : 2,250,000
0
20
40
60
80
100 Kilometers
0
20
40
60
80 Statute Miles

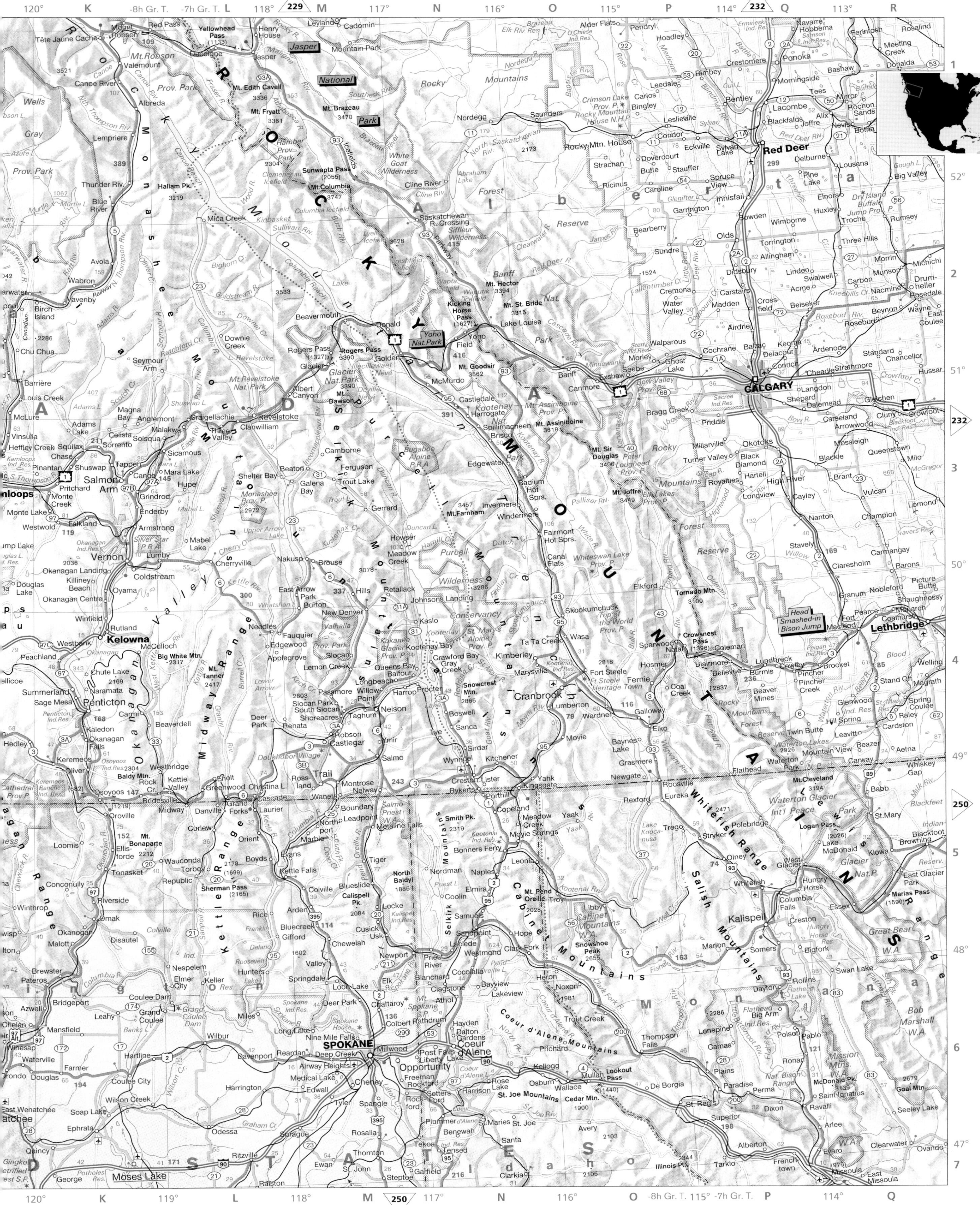

Jasper
National
Park
Rocky
Mountains
ROCKY
MOUNTAINS
Monashee Mountains
Selkirk Mountains
Purcell Mountains
Alberta
Red Deer
CALGARY
Lethbridge
Banff
Lake Louise
Golden
Revelstoke
Kelowna
Vernon
Penticton
Salmon Arm
Nelson
Trail
Cranbrook
Kimberley
Fernie
Kalispell
Whitefish Range
Salish Mountains
Cabinet Mountains
Coeur d'Alene Mountains
St. Joe Mountains
SPOKANE
Coeur d'Alene
Moses Lake
Wenatchee
Okanagan Valley
Kettle Range
Midway Range
Okanogan
Colville
Sandpoint
Yoho Nat.Park
Glacier Nat. Park
Kootenay Nat. Park
Waterton Lakes
Glacier Nat.P.
Mt.Robson
Mt.Columbia
Mt. Assiniboine
Mt.Revelstoke Nat.Park
Head Smashed-in Bison Jump
Idaho
Missoula
120°
119°
118°
117°
116°
115°
114°
113°
52°
51°
50°
49°
48°
47°
229
232
250

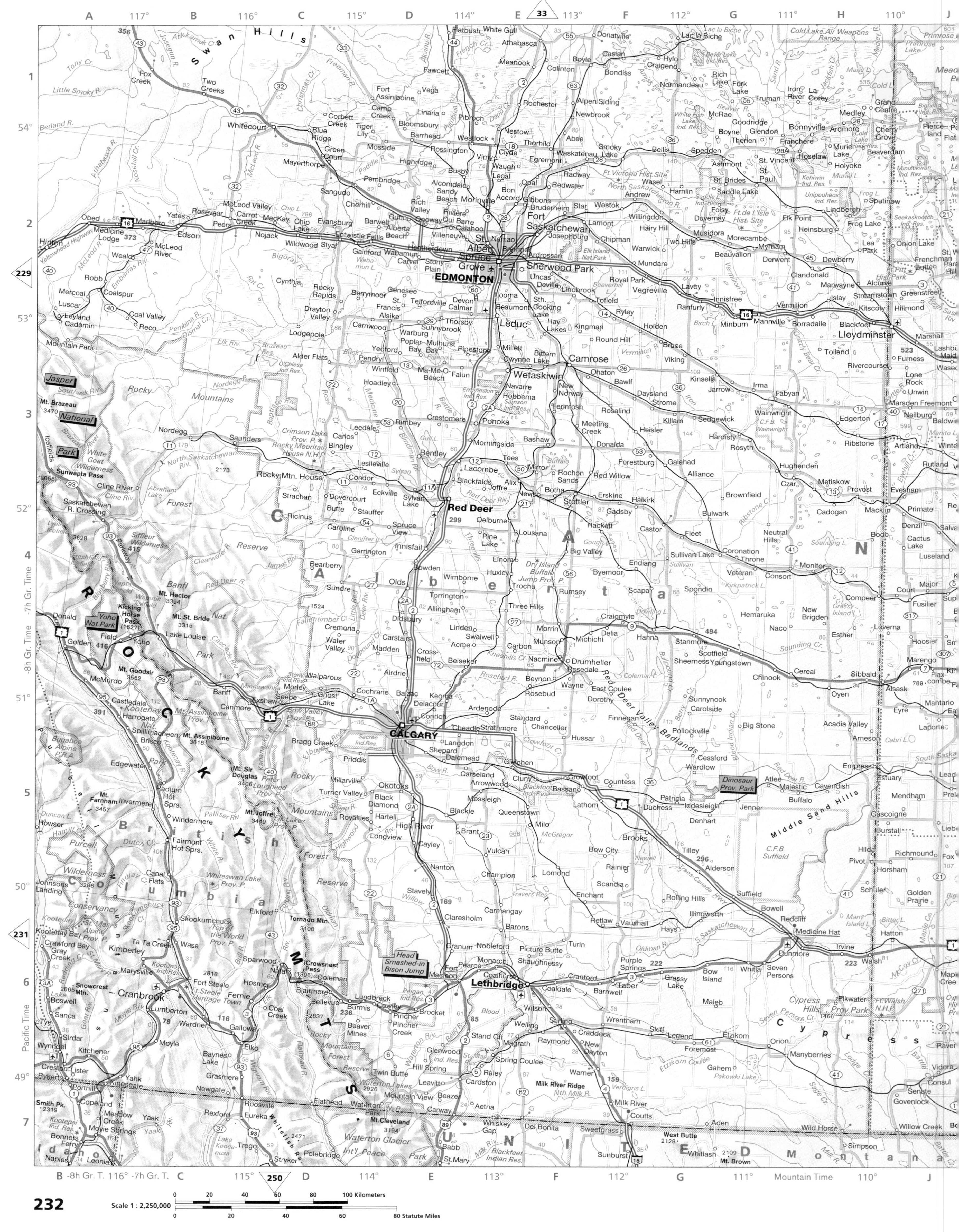

A
117°
B
116°
C
115°
D
114°
E
33
113°
F
112°
G
111°
H
110°
J
1
2
3
4
5
6
7
54°
53°
52°
51°
50°
49°
229
231
Swan Hills
Fox Creek
Two Creeks
Whitecourt
Athabasca
Flatbush
White Gull
Lac la Biche
Donatville
Boyle
Caslan
Colinton
Meanook
Fawcett
Fort Assiniboine
Vega
Rochester
Westlock
Barrhead
Mayerthorpe
Hinton
Obed
Edson
Marlboro
Medicine Lodge
McLeod River
Robb
Coalspur
Cadomin
Luscar
Mercoal
Leyland
Coal Valley
Mountain Park
Evansburg
Entwistle
Wildwood
Stony Plain
St. Albert
Spruce Grove
EDMONTON
Fort Saskatchewan
Sherwood Park
Bon Accord
Gibbons
Redwater
Smoky Lake
Waskatenau
Vegreville
Mundare
Lamont
Chipman
Two Hills
Vermilion
Mannville
Minburn
Lloydminster
Kitscoty
Marwayne
Elk Point
St. Paul
Bonnyville
Ardmore
Cold Lake
Cold Lake Air Weapons Range
Primrose Lake
Leduc
Devon
Calmar
Beaumont
Camrose
Wetaskiwin
Millet
Ponoka
Lacombe
Red Deer
Sylvan Lake
Innisfail
Olds
Didsbury
Carstairs
Airdrie
Cochrane
CALGARY
Okotoks
High River
Nanton
Claresholm
Fort Macleod
Lethbridge
Taber
Medicine Hat
Redcliff
Brooks
Bassano
Strathmore
Drumheller
Hanna
Stettler
Coronation
Consort
Castor
Wainwright
Irma
Provost
Killam
Sedgewick
Rocky Mtn. House
Nordegg
Banff
Canmore
Lake Louise
Jasper National Park
Banff National Park
Yoho Nat. Park
Kootenay Nat. Park
Mt. Brazeau 3470
Mt. Hector 3394
Mt. St. Bride 3315
Mt. Goodsir 3562
Mt. Assiniboine 3618
Mt. Sir Douglas 3406
Mt. Joffre 3449
Mt. Farnham 3457
Kicking Horse Pass (1627)
Golden
Field
Radium Hot Sprs.
Invermere
Windermere
Fairmont Hot Sprs.
Canal Flats
Skookumchuck
Kimberley
Cranbrook
Fort Steele
Fernie
Sparwood
Elkford
Crowsnest Pass
Coleman
Blairmore
Pincher Creek
Cardston
Magrath
Raymond
Milk River
Coutts
Waterton Park
Mt. Cleveland 3194
Head Smashed-in Bison Jump
Dinosaur Prov. Park
Cypress Hills Prov. Park
Ft. Walsh N.H.P.
Middle Sand Hills
C.F.B. Suffield
Red Deer Valley Badlands
Dry Island Buffalo Jump Prov. P.
ROCKY MOUNTAINS
Alberta
British Columbia
Saskatchewan
Cypress Hills
Montana
Idaho
UNITED STATES
Pacific Time
-8h Gr. Time
-7h Gr. Time
Mountain Time
B -8h Gr. T. 116° -7h Gr. T. C
250
Scale 1 : 2,250,000
0 20 40 60 80 100 Kilometers
0 20 40 60 80 Statute Miles

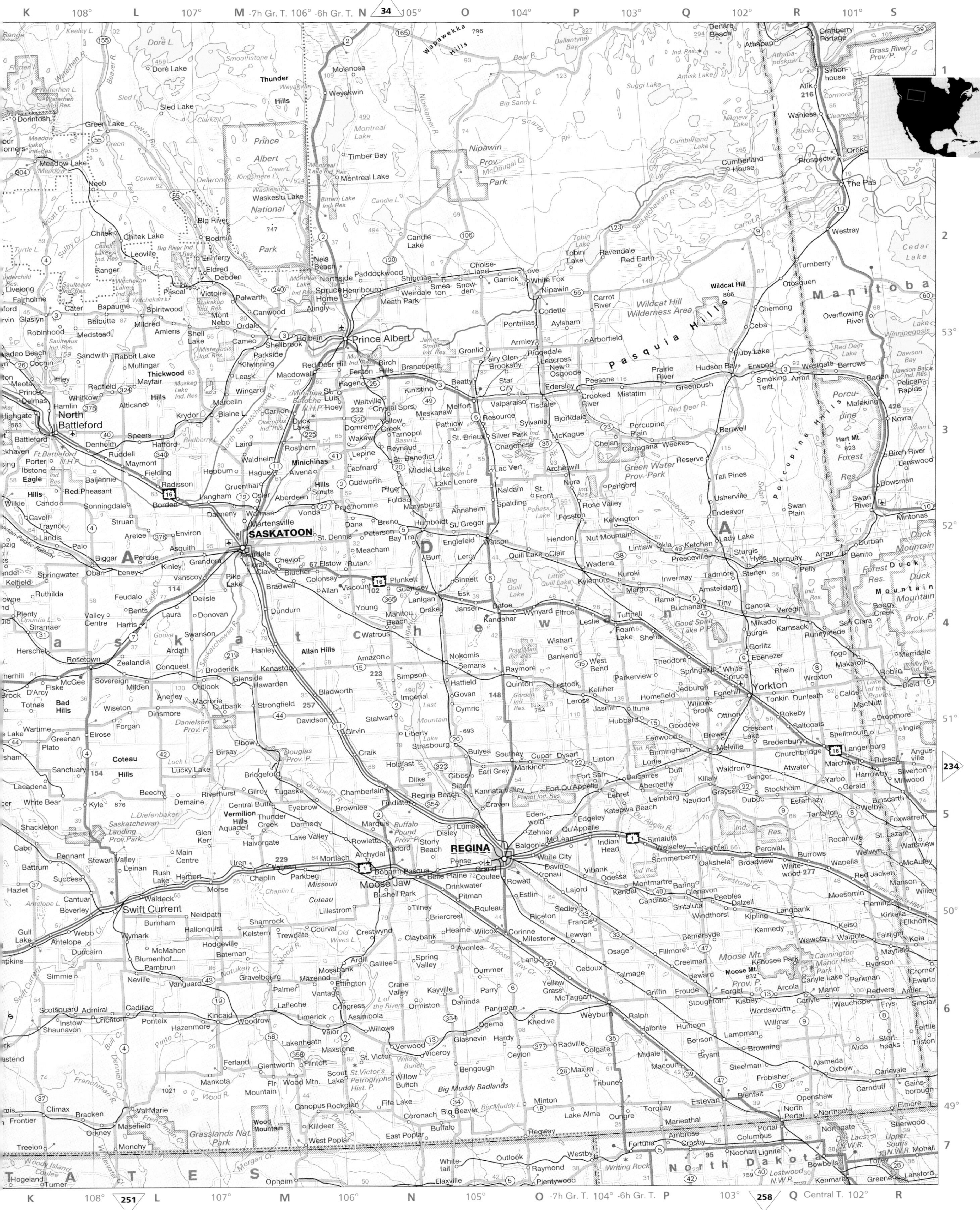

K 108° L 107° M -7h Gr. T. 106° -6h Gr. T. N 34 105° O 104° P 103° Q 102° R 101° S
K 108° 251 L 107° M 106° N 105° O -7h Gr. T. 104° -6h Gr. T. P 103° 258 Q Central T. 102° R
234
53°
52°
51°
50°
49°
1
2
3
4
5
6
7
SASKATOON
REGINA
Prince Albert
North Battleford
Moose Jaw
Swift Current
Yorkton
Melville
Weyburn
Estevan
The Pas
Manitoba
North Dakota
Prince Albert National Park
Thunder Hills
Wapawekka Hills
Pasquia Hills
Porcupine Hills
Nipawin Prov. Park
Wildcat Hill Wilderness Area
Duck Mountain Prov. P.
Moose Mt. Prov. P.
Grasslands Nat. Park
Big Muddy Badlands
Allan Hills
Coteau Hills
Vermilion Hills
Wood Mountain
Cedar Lake
Lake Winnipegosis

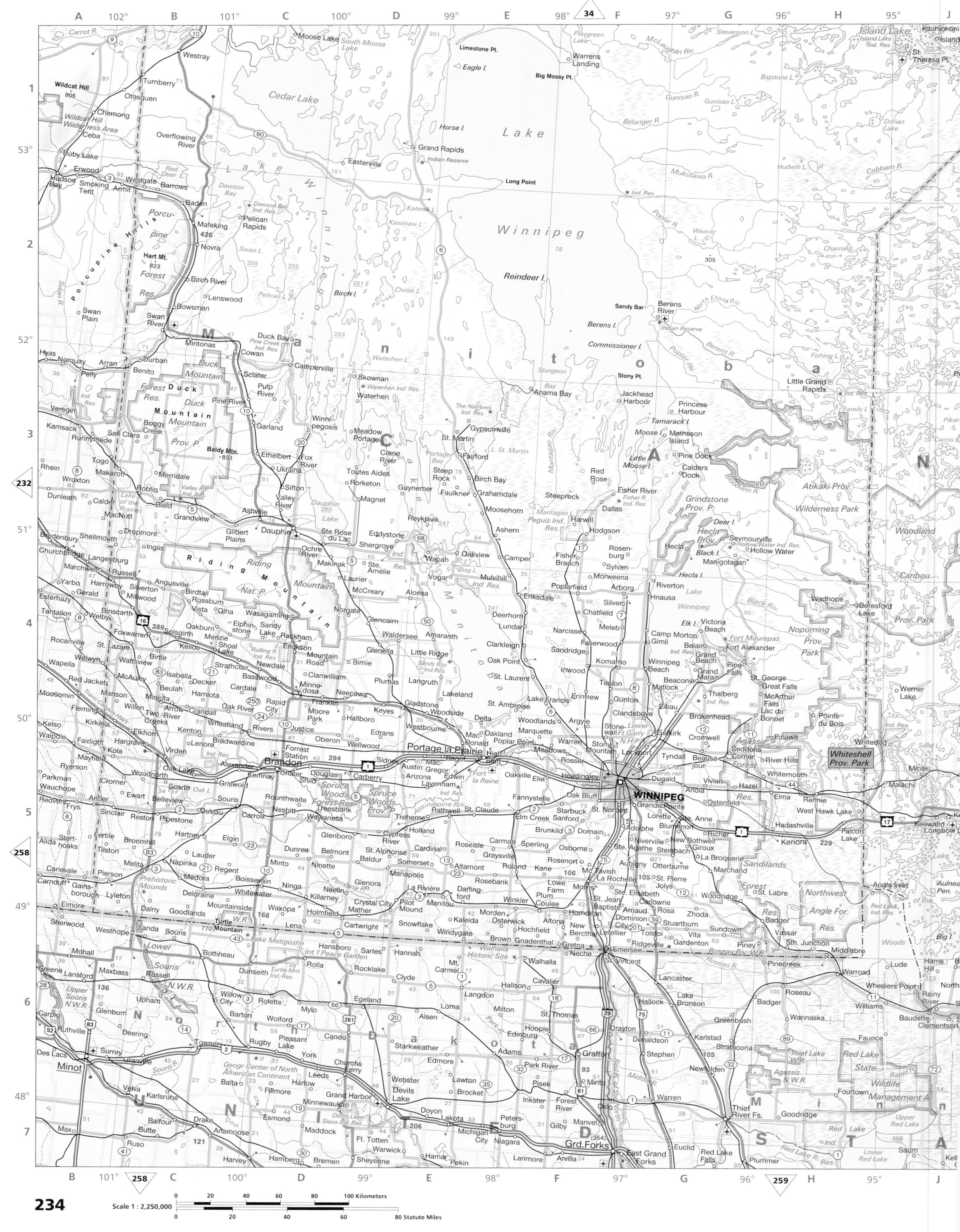

A
102°
B
101°
C
100°
D
99°
E
98°
34
F
97°
G
96°
H
95°
J
1
2
3
4
5
6
7
53°
52°
51°
50°
49°
48°
232
258
Manitoba
North Dakota
United States
Minnesota
Lake Winnipeg
Lake Winnipegosis
Lake Manitoba
Cedar Lake
Porcupine Hills
Porcupine Forest Res.
Duck Mountain Forest Res.
Duck Mountain Prov. P.
Riding Mountain Nat. P.
Spruce Woods Prov. P.
Whiteshell Prov. Park
Atikaki Prov. Wilderness Park
Nopoming Prov. Park
Hecla Prov. P.
Grindstone Prov. P.
Sandilands Forest Res.
Northwest Angle For. Res.
Turtle Mountain
Red Lake
Upper Red Lake
Lower Red Lake
Devils Lake
WINNIPEG
Brandon
Portage la Prairie
Selkirk
Steinbach
Dauphin
Swan River
The Pas
Grand Rapids
Berens River
Gimli
Morden
Winkler
Minot
Grand Forks
Grafton
Thief River Fs.
Kenora
Grd. Forks
Walhalla Historic Site
Int.'l Peace Garden
B
101°
258
C
100°
D
99°
E
98°
F
97°
G
96°
259
H
95°
J
Scale 1 : 2,250,000
0
20
40
60
80
100 Kilometers
0
20
40
60
80 Statute Miles

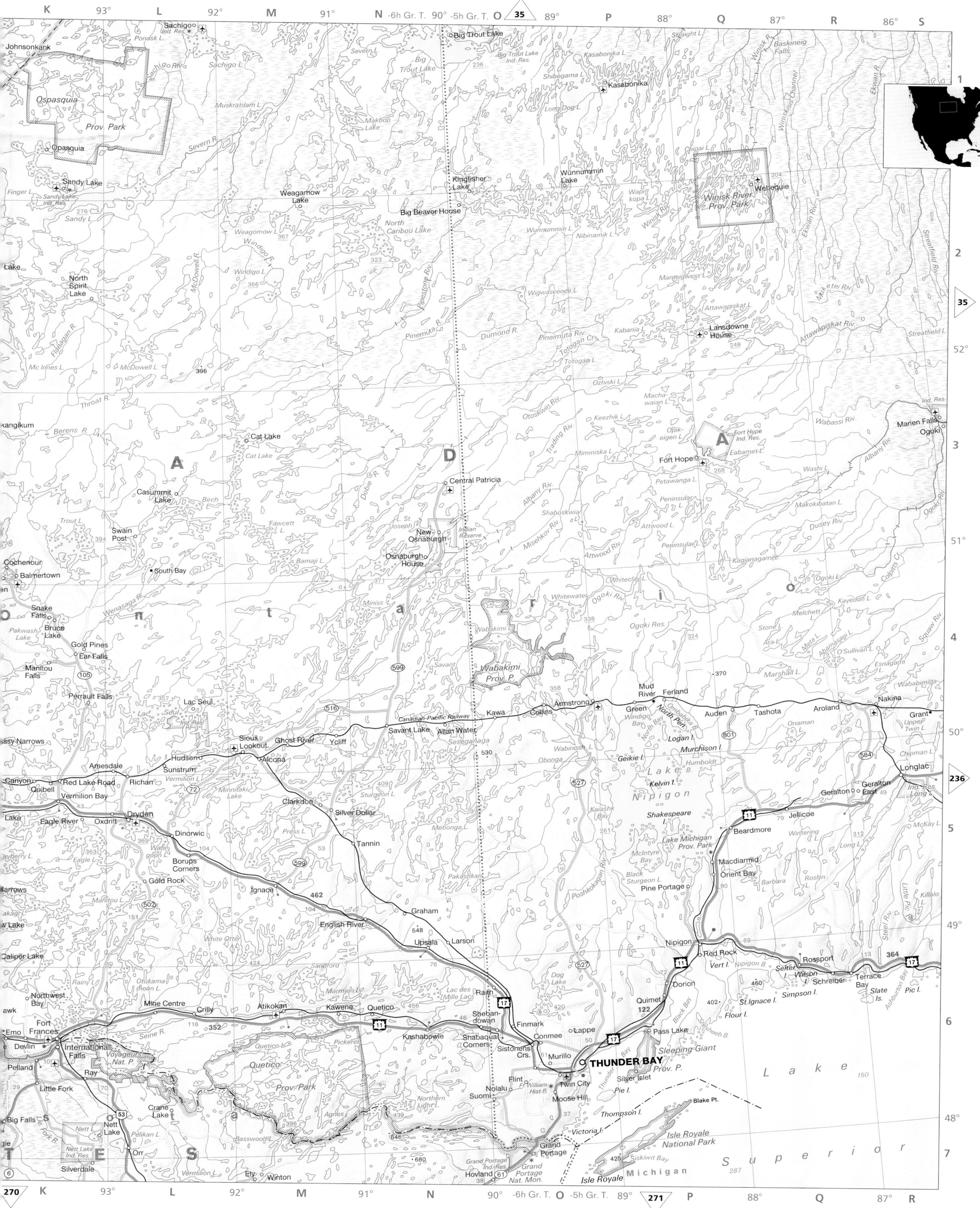

K
93°
L
92°
M
91°
N -6h Gr. T. 90° -5h Gr. T. O
35
89°
P
88°
Q
87°
R
86°
S
Sachigo
Johnsonkank
Ospasquia
Prov. Park
Opasquia
Sandy Lake
Sachigo L.
Muskratdam L.
Severn R.
Severn L.
Big Trout Lake
Big Trout Lake Ind. Res.
Kasabonika L.
Kasabonika
Shibogama L.
Long Dog L.
Baskineig Falls
Winisk R.
Winiskisis Channel
Ekwan R.
Makoop Lake
Kingfisher Lake
Wunnummin Lake
Winisk River Prov. Park
Webequie
Weagamow Lake
Big Beaver House
North Caribou Lake
Weagamow L.
Windigo R.
Windigo L.
McDowell R.
North Spirit Lake
Wunnummin L.
Nibinamik L.
Pipestone Riv.
Pinemuta R.
Wigwascence L.
Attawapiskat L.
Attawapiskat Riv.
Lansdowne House
Dumond R.
Pineimuta Riv.
Totogan Cr.
Totogan L.
Kabania L.
Streatfield Riv.
Streatfield L.
Mc Innes L.
McDowell L.
Throat R.
Berens R.
Cat Lake
Ozhiski L.
Otoskwin Riv.
Keezhik L.
Trading Riv.
Miminiska L.
Fort Hope
Fort Hope Ind. Res.
Eabamet L.
Opikeigen L.
Marien Falls
Ogoki
Wabassi Riv.
Albany Riv.
A
D
A
Casummit Lake
Central Patricia
Petawanga L.
Peninsular L.
Washi L.
Makokibatan L.
Ogoki Riv.
Swain Post
Trout L.
Birch
Fawcett L.
L. St. Joseph
New Osnaburgh
Osnaburgh House
Indian Reserve
Albany Riv.
Shabuskwia L.
Misehkow Riv.
Attwood L.
Attwood Riv.
Dusey Riv.
Cochenour
Balmertown
South Bay
Bamaji L.
Kagianagami L.
Whiteclay L.
Whitewater L.
Ogoki Riv.
Ogoki L.
Snake Falls
Bruce Lake
Pakwash Lake
Wenasaga R.
Miniss L.
Wabakimi L.
Ogoki Res.
Kayedon L.
Melchett L.
O
n
t
a
r
i
o
Gold Pines
Ear Falls
Manitou Falls
Perrault Falls
Lac Seul
Savant L.
Wabakimi Prov. P.
Stone L.
Ara L.
Meta L.
Abamasagi L.
O'Sullivan L.
Esnagami L.
Marshall L.
Wababimiga L.
Mud River
Ferland
Armstrong
Collins
Kawa
Canadian Pacific Railway
Green Windigo Bay
North Bay
Auden
Tashota
Aroland
Nakina
Grant
Upper Twin L.
Savant Lake
Allan Water
Sesaganaga L.
Sioux Lookout
Ghost River
Ycliff
Wabinosh L.
Obonga L.
Logan L.
Murchison L.
Humboldt B.
Chipman L.
Longlac
Hudson
Sunstrum
Alcona
Amesdale
Canyon
Quibell
Red Lake Road
Richan
Vermilion L.
Vermilion Bay
Minnitaki Lake
Clarkdon
Sturgeon L.
Geikie I.
Kelvin I.
Lake Nipigon
Geraldton
Geraldton East
Silver Dollar
Eagle River
Oxdrift
Dryden
Dinorwic
Wabigoon L.
Eagle L.
Press L.
Metionga L.
Shakespeare I.
Beardmore
Jellicoe
Wintering L.
McKay L.
Kaiashk Bay
Lake Michigan Prov. Park
McIntyre Bay
Long L.
Borups Corners
Gold Rock
Tannin
Macdiarmid
Orient Bay
Barbara L.
Roslyn L.
Little Pic Riv.
Killala L.
Manitou L.
Ignace
Pakashkan L.
Black Sturgeon L.
Pine Portage
Poshkokagan Riv.
English River
Graham
Steel Riv.
Upsala
Larson
Nipigon
Red Rock
Caliper Lake
White Otter L.
Sandford L.
Nipigon B.
Vert I.
Rossport
Schreiber
Terrace Bay
Selter I.
Wilson I.
Simpson I.
Slate Is.
Pic I.
Ashburton Bay
Rainy L.
Otukamamoan L.
Marmion L.
Lac des Mille Lacs
Raith
Dog Lake
Dorion
Quimet
Black Bay
St. Ignace I.
Flour I.
Northwest Bay
Mine Centre
Crilly
Atikokan
Kawene
Quetico
Sheban-dowan
Finmark
Lappe
Pass Lake
Fort Frances
Emo
Devlin
International Falls
Seine R.
Kashabowie
Shabaqua Corners
Conmee
Sistonens Crs.
Murillo
Sleeping Giant Prov. P.
Thunder Bay
THUNDER BAY
Voyageurs Nat. P.
Quetico L.
Pickerel L.
Pelland
Ray
Quetico Prov. Park
Flint
Ft. William Hist. B.
Twin City
Silver Islet
Pie I.
Lake Superior
Little Fork
Nolalu
Suomi
Moose Hill
Northern Light L.
Thompson I.
Blake Pt.
Crane Lake
Nett Lake
Nett Lake Ind. Res.
Big Falls
Pelikan L.
Agnes L.
Basswood L.
Victoria I.
Grand Portage
Isle Royale National Park
Siskiwit Bay
Grand Portage Ind. Res.
Grand Portage Nat. Mon.
Hovland
Ely
Winton
Vermilion L.
Orr
Silverdale
Isle Royale
Michigan
S
a
S
E
T
270
K
93°
L
92°
M
91°
N
90° -6h Gr. T. O -5h Gr. T. 89°
271
P
88°
Q
87°
R
1
2
3
4
5
6
7
52°
51°
50°
49°
48°
35
236

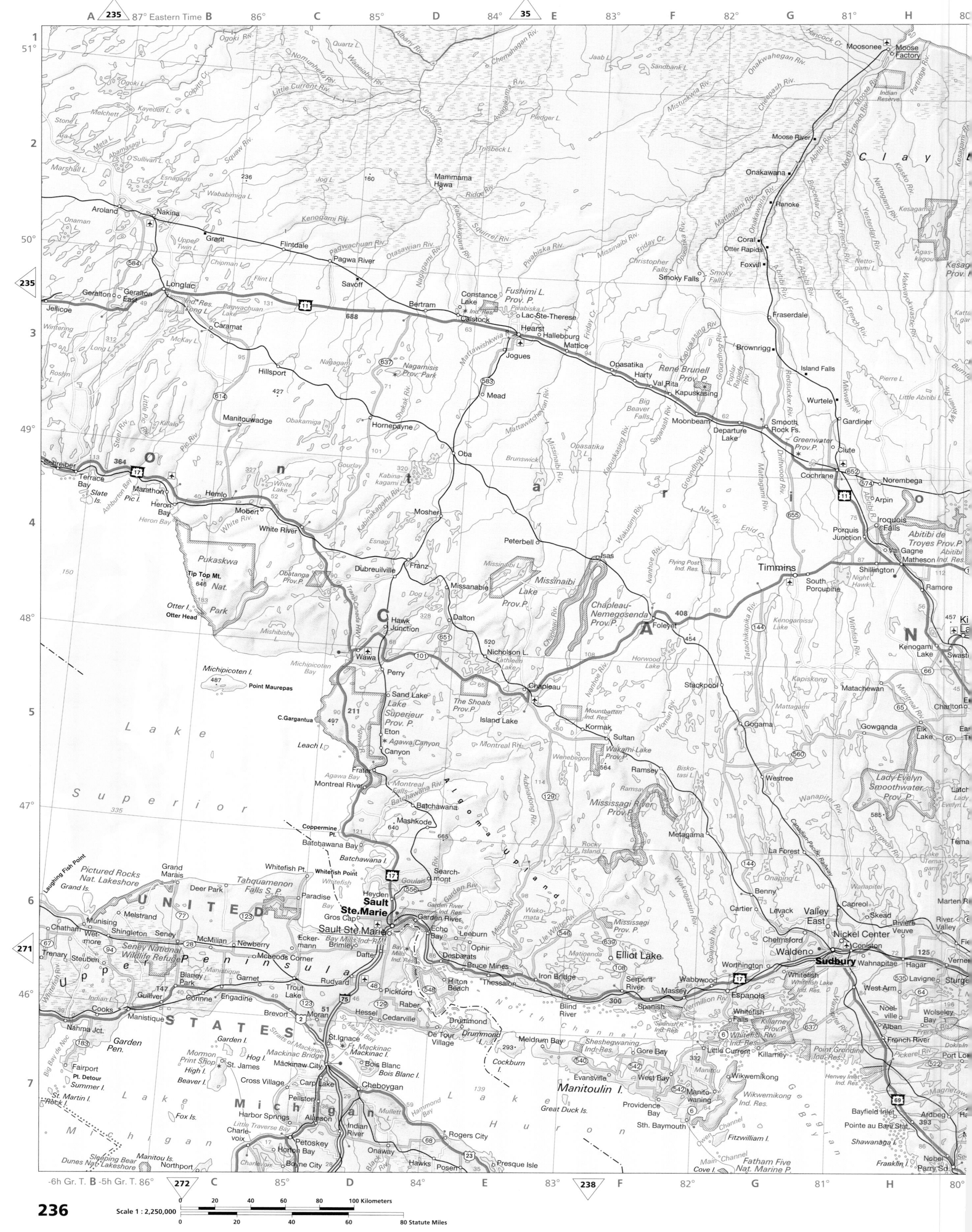

A 235 87° Eastern Time B 86° C 85° D 84° 35 E 83° F 82° G 81° H 80°
51° 50° 49° 48° 47° 46°
235
271
Moosonee
Moose Factory
Moose River
Onakawana
Ranoke
Coral
Otter Rapids
Foxvill
Fraserdale
Brownrigg
Island Falls
Wurtele
Gardiner
Clute
Cochrane
Norembega
Arpin
Iroquois Falls
Porquis Junction
Val Gagne
Matheson
Shillington
Ramore
Timmins
South Porcupine
Kenogami Lake
Matachewan
Charlton
Gowganda
Elk Lake
Gogama
Westree
Lady Evelyn Smoothwater Prov. P.
Metagama
La Forest
Benny
Capreol
Cartier
Levack
Valley East
Chelmsford
Walden
Nickel Center
Coniston
Sudbury
Wahnapitae
Hagar
Worthington
Whitefish
Espanola
Massey
Wabbwood
Spanish
Lavigne
Sturgeon Falls
West Arm
Noelville
Alban
Wolseley Bay
French River
Killarney
Port Loring
Bayfield Inlet
Pointe au Baril Sta.
Ardbeg
Nobel
Parry Sd.
Franklin I.
Shawanaga I.
Manitoulin I.
Little Current
Wikwemikong
Manitowaning
West Bay
Gore Bay
Evansville
Providence Bay
Sth. Baymouth
Great Duck Is.
Fitzwilliam I.
Fatham Five Nat. Marine P.
Cove I.
Georgian Bay
Lake Huron
Meldrum Bay
Cockburn I.
Drummond I.
Blind River
Iron Bridge
Thessalon
Serpent River
Elliot Lake
Mississagi Prov. P.
Bruce Mines
Hilton Beach
Desbarats
Echo Bay
Garden River
Leeburn
Ophir
Sault Ste. Marie
Gros Cap
Heyden
Searchmont
Goulais
Batchawana Bay
Batchawana
Mashkode
Coppermine Pt.
Montreal River
Frater
Canyon
Agawa Canyon
Eton
Lake Superior Prov. P.
Sand Lake
Perry
Wawa
Hawk Junction
Dalton
Nicholson L.
Chapleau
Island Lake
The Shoals Prov. P.
Kormak
Sultan
Wakami Lake Prov. P.
Ramsey
Mississagi River Prov. P.
Algoma Upland
Chapleau-Nemegosenda Prov. P.
Foleyet
Isas
Missinaibi Lake Prov. P.
Missanabie
Franz
Dubreuilville
Peterbell
Mosher
Oba
Hornepayne
Mead
Jogues
Hearst
Hallebourg
Mattice
Opasatika
Harty
Val Rita
Kapuskasing
Rene Brunell Prov. P.
Moonbeam
Departure Lake
Smooth Rock Fs.
Greenwater Prov. P.
Lac-Ste-Therese
Calstock
Constance Lake
Fushimi L. Prov. P.
Bertram
Savoff
Pagwa River
Flintdale
Grant
Nakina
Aroland
Mammama Hawa
Jellicoe
Geralton
Geraldton East
Longlac
Caramat
Hillsport
Nagamisis Prov. Park
Manitouwadge
Schreiber
Terrace Bay
Marathon
Heron Bay
Hemlo
Mobert
White River
Pukaskwa Nat. Park
Otter Head
Michipicoten I.
Point Maurepas
C.Gargantua
Leach I.
Lake Superior
Whitefish Pt.
Whitefish Point
Paradise
Grand Marais
Pictured Rocks Nat. Lakeshore
Grand Is.
Munising
Melstrand
Deer Park
Tahquamenon Falls S.P.
Shingleton
Seney
Seney National Wildlife Refuge
McMillan
Newberry
Mcleods Corner
Ecker-mann
Brimley
Dafter
Rudyard
Pickford
Raber
Cedarville
Hessel
Trout Lake
Garnet
Blaney Park
Gulliver
Corinne
Engadine
Manistique
Cooks
Nahma Jct.
Garden Pen.
Moran
Brevort
St. Ignace
Mackinac Bridge
Mackinaw City
Cheboygan
Bois Blanc I.
De Tour Village
Drummond
St. James
Beaver I.
Fairport
Pt. Detour
Summer I.
St. Martin I.
Rock I.
Cross Village
Pellston
Alanson
Harbor Springs
Petoskey
Charlevoix
Boyne City
Northport
Manitou Is.
Sleeping Bear Dunes Nat. Lakeshore
Indian River
Onaway
Rogers City
Hawks
Posen
Presque Isle
Upper Peninsula
UNITED STATES
Lake Michigan
Ontario
Clay
-6h Gr. T. B -5h Gr. T. 86° 272 C 85° D 84° E 83° 238 F 82° G 81° H 80°
Scale 1 : 2,250,000
0 20 40 60 80 100 Kilometers
0 20 40 60 80 Statute Miles

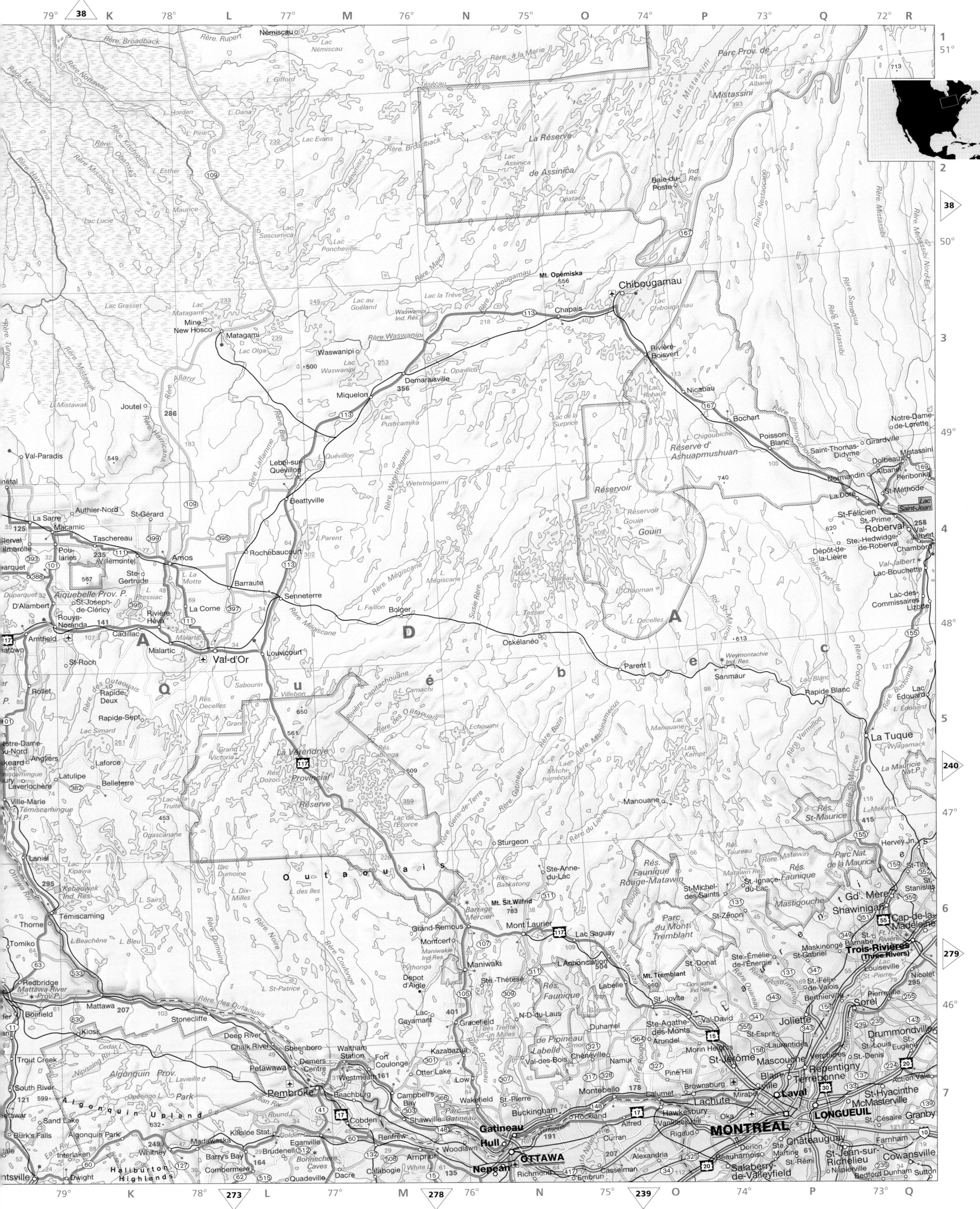

Nemiscau
Lac Némiscau
La Réserve de Assinica
Parc Prov. de Mistassini
Mistassini
Baie-du-Poste
Chibougamau
Mt. Opémiska
Chapais
Rivière-Boisvert
Nicabau
Bochart
Poisson-Blanc
Réserve d' Ashuapmushuan
Matagami
Mine New Hosco
Waswanipi
Demaraisville
Miquelon
Joutel
Val-Paradis
Lebel-sur-Quévillon
Beattyville
La Sarre
Macamic
Authier-Nord
St-Gérard
Taschereau
Amos
Rochebaucourt
Barraute
Senneterre
La Corne
Bolger
Rivière-Héva
Rouyn-Noranda
Aiguebelle Prov. P.
Cadillac
Malartic
Val-d'Or
Louvicourt
Oskélanéo
Parent
Sanmaur
Rapide Blanc
Réservoir Gouin
La Tuque
Roberval
St-Félicien
Normandin
Dolbeau
Mistassini
Rapide-Deux
Rapide-Sept
La Vérendrye Provincial Réserve
Laforce
Belleterre
Latulipe
Angliers
Ville-Marie
Laniel
Témiscaming
Thorne
Manouane
Sturgeon
Ste-Anne-du-Lac
Mt. Sit.Wilfrid
Grand-Remous
Mont Laurier
Lac Saguay
Montcerf
Maniwaki
Mt. Tremblant
Labelle
St. Jovite
Ste-Agathe-des-Monts
St-Jérôme
Mattawa
Stonecliffe
Deep River
Chalk River
Petawawa
Pembroke
Algonquin Prov. Park
Algonquin Upland
Haliburton Highlands
Renfrew
Arnprior
Gatineau
Hull
OTTAWA
Nepean
Buckingham
Rockland
Lachute
Laval
MONTREAL
LONGUEUIL
Châteauguay
Salaberry-de-Valleyfield
Joliette
Sorel
Trois-Rivières (Three Rivers)
Shawinigan
Cap-de-la-Madeleine
Drummondville
St-Hyacinthe
Granby
St-Jean-sur-Richelieu
Québec
Outaouais

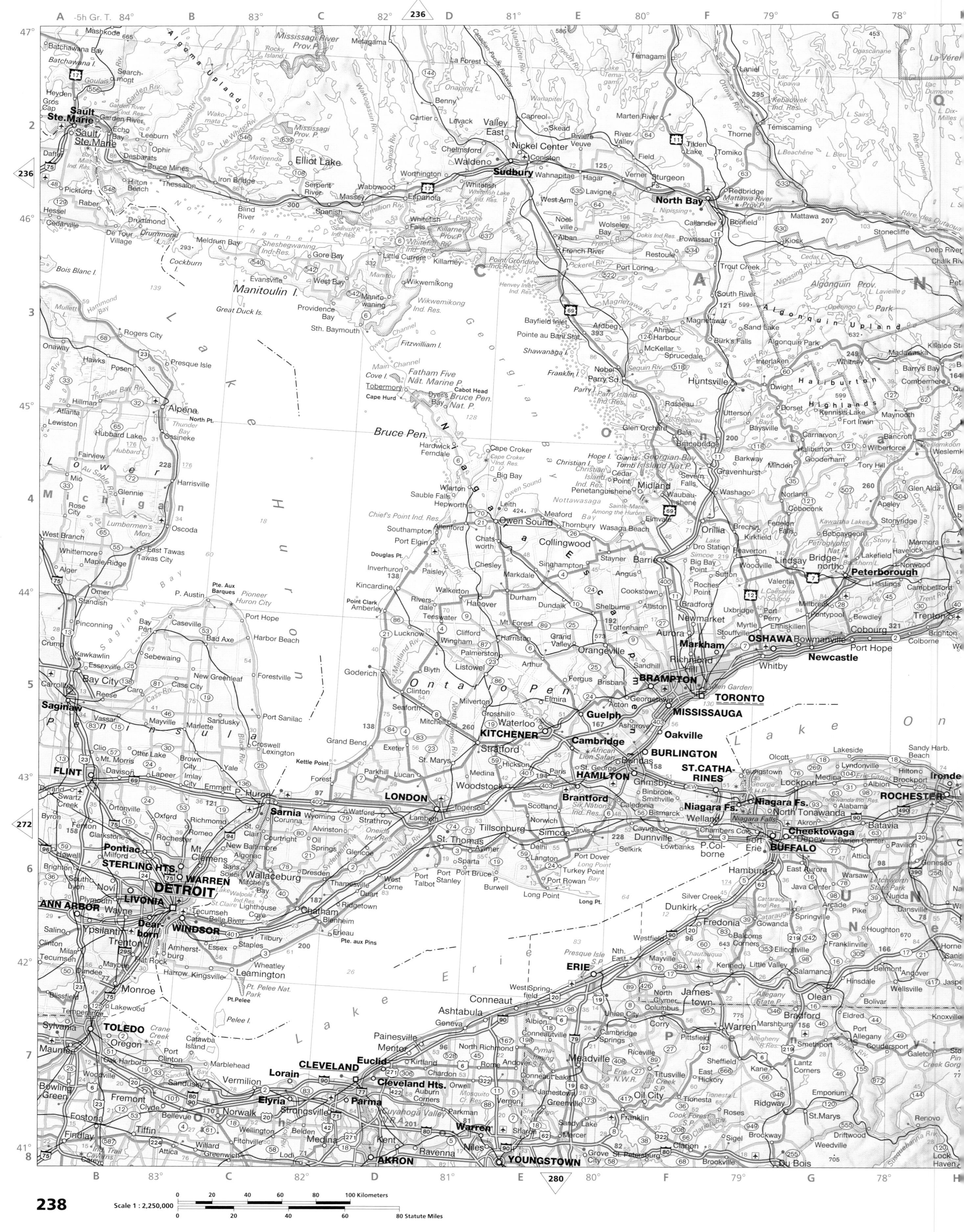

236
272
280
Lake Huron
Georgian Bay
Lake Ontario
Lake Erie
North Channel
Manitoulin I.
Bruce Pen.
Ontario Pen.
Niagara Escarpment
Algonquin Upland
Haliburton Highlands
Algoma Upland
Lower Michigan
Saginaw Bay
Thumb
Sault Ste.Marie
Sudbury
North Bay
Elliot Lake
Espanola
Huntsville
Parry Sd.
Owen Sound
Collingwood
Barrie
Orillia
Peterborough
Oshawa
Markham
Brampton
Toronto
Mississauga
Oakville
Burlington
Hamilton
St.Catharines
Niagara Fs.
Kitchener
Waterloo
Guelph
Cambridge
Brantford
London
Sarnia
Windsor
Detroit
Warren
Sterling Hts.
Pontiac
Livonia
Ann Arbor
Flint
Saginaw
Bay City
Alpena
Toledo
Cleveland
Cleveland Hts.
Euclid
Lorain
Elyria
Parma
Akron
Youngstown
Warren
Erie
Buffalo
Cheektowaga
Rochester
Scale 1 : 2,250,000
100 Kilometers
80 Statute Miles

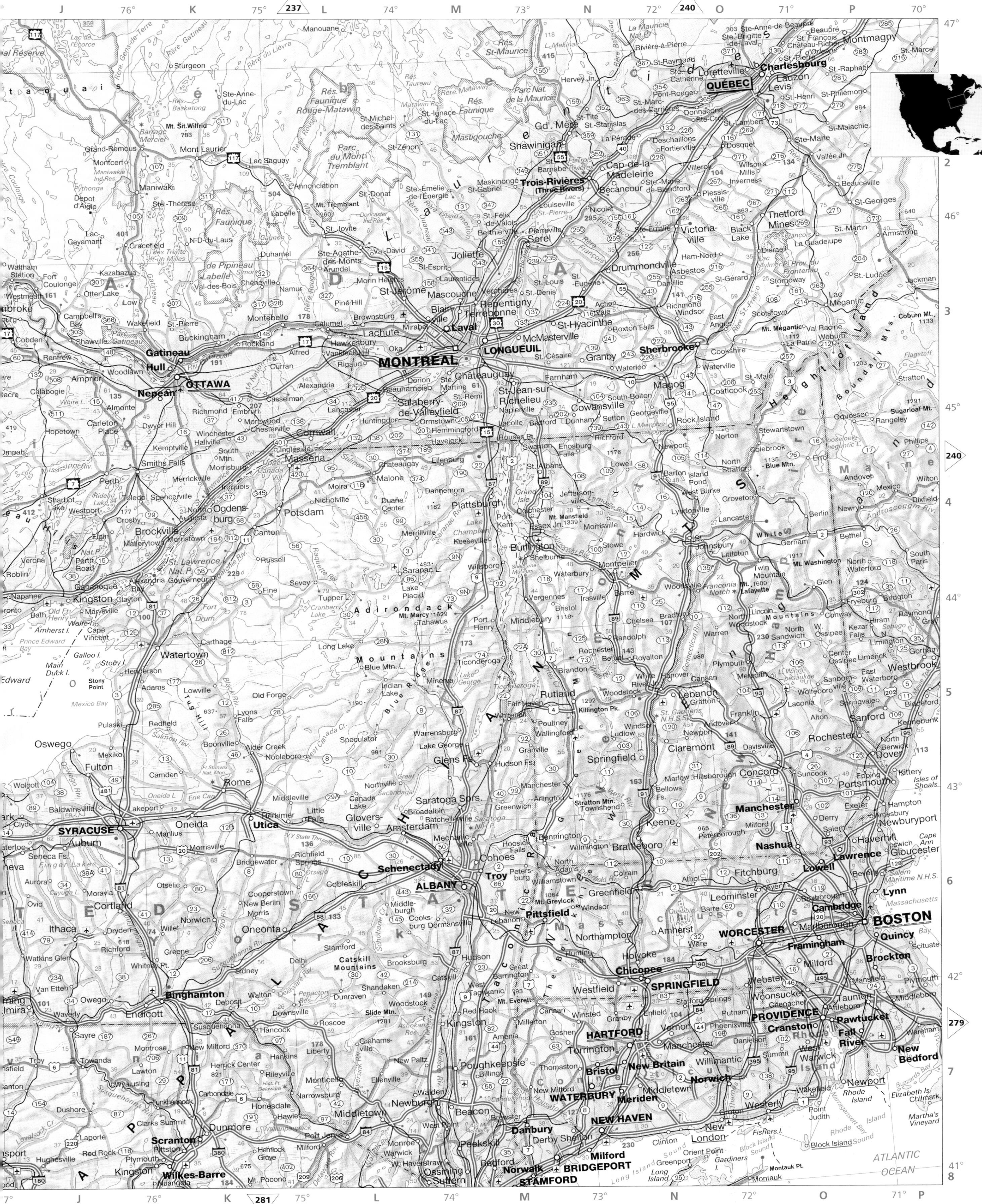
MONTREAL
LONGUEUIL
Laval
QUÉBEC
Charlesbourg
OTTAWA
Gatineau
Hull
Nepean
Trois-Rivières
(Three Rivers)
Sherbrooke
Kingston
SYRACUSE
Utica
ALBANY
Schenectady
Troy
Binghamton
Scranton
Wilkes-Barre
SPRINGFIELD
HARTFORD
New Britain
WATERBURY
NEW HAVEN
BRIDGEPORT
STAMFORD
WORCESTER
PROVIDENCE
Cranston
Pawtucket
BOSTON
Cambridge
Lowell
Lawrence
Manchester
Nashua
Concord
Burlington
Plattsburgh
Adirondack Mountains
ATLANTIC OCEAN

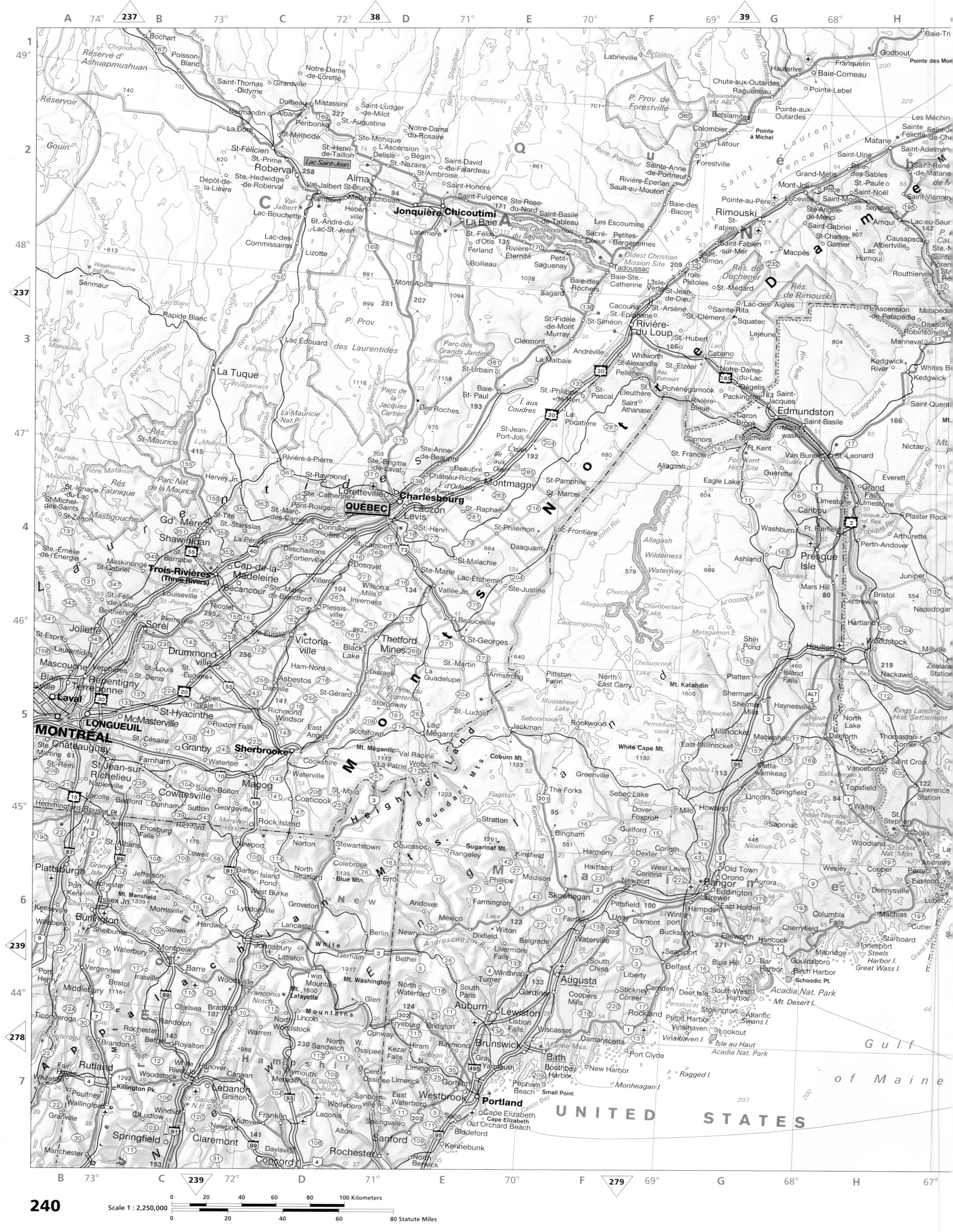

Scale 1 : 2,250,000
0 20 40 60 80 100 Kilometers
0 20 40 60 80 Statute Miles

242
243
Détroit d'Honguedo
Île d'Anticosti
Chicotte
Rivière-aux-Saumons
Baie-du-Renard
Rivière-de-la-Chaloupe
Pointe de l'Est
-5h Gr. Time
-3h30 Gr. T.
-4h Gr. Time
Ruisseau-à-Rebours
Anse-Pleureuse
Madeleine-Centre
Grande-Vallée
Petite-Vallée
La Martre
Marsoui
Cloridorme
Chic Chocs
L'Anse-à-Valleau
Petit-Cap
Rivière-au-Renard
Cap Seize
Mt. Jacques Cartier 1268
Murdochville
P. Nat. de Forillon
L'Anse-au-Griffon
Fontenelle
Jersey Cove
Cap-des-Rosiers
Cap Gaspé
Gaspé
P. Prov. Chic-Choc
Douglastown
Baie de Gaspé
Saint-Georges-de-Malbaie
Péninsule de Gaspé
P. Prov. Baldwin
Bridgeville
Barachois
Rameau
Percé
Cap-d'Espoir
Ste.-Thérèse-de-Gaspé
Réserve faunique de Port-Daniel
Chandler
Saint-Edgar
Port-Daniel
Newport
New Richmond
Saint-Elzéar
L'Anse-aux-Gascons
Maria
Nouvelle
P. Prov. de Miguasha
Dalhousie
Bonaventure
Paspébiac
New Carlisle
Charlo
Benjamin River
Baie des Chaleurs
Chaleur Bay
Jaquet River
Belledune
Petit-Rocher
Miscou Point
Miscou I.
Miscou Centre
Pigeon Hill
Petite-Rivière-de-l'Île
Shippegan I. (Île Lameque)
Ville de Lameque
Grande-Anse
Maisonnette
Caraquet
Bertrand
Beresford
Nepisiguit Bay
Janeville
Shippegan
Acadian Hist. Vill.
Robertville
Caribou Depot
Bathurst
Paquetville
Pokemouche
Losier Settlement
Tracadie
South Tetagouche
Saint-Isidore
Allardville
Tabusintac Ind. Res.
Brantville
Tabusintac
Bathurst Mines
Heath Steele
Lavillette
Neguac
Miramichi Bay
Beaver Brook Station
Wayerton
Barryville
Eel River Bridge
Pt. Escuminac
Escuminac
Big Hole Tract Ind. Res.
Loggieville
Red Bank
Newcastle
Chatham
Bay du Vin
Nelson-Miramichi
Kouchibouguac
Red Bank Ind. Res.
Millerton
Barnaby River
St. Margarets
Kouchibouguac Nat. Park
Renous
Blackville
Rogersville
St.-Louis-de-Kent
Richibucto
Acadie Siding
St.-Ignace
Richibucto-Village
Rexton
Kent Jn.
Molus River
Richibucto 15 Ind. Res.
Doaktown
Buctouche
Smiths Corner
Ste.-Marie-de-Kent
Harcourt
Cocagne
Maximeville
Canaan Station
Gaspereau Forks
Chipman
Moncton
Salisbury
Riverview
Shediac
Cape-Pele
New Canaan
Minto
Youngs Cove
Memramcook
Petitcodiac
St. Joseph
Dorchester
Sackville
Sheffield
Coles I.
Jemseg
Gagetown
Norton
Elgin
Hopewell Cape
Springfield
Sussex
Evandale
Berwick
Caledonia Hills
Riv. Hebert
Hammondvale
Fundy Nat. P.
Alma
Chignecto Game Sanctuary
Hampton
Kingston
Hanford
Apple Riv.
St. Martins
C. Chignecto
Cape Split
Cape d'Or
Scotts Bay
Saint John
Cape Spencer
Musquash
Minas Channel
Minas Basin
Harbourville
Bay of Fundy
North Point
North Cape
Tignish
Alberton
Cascumpeque Bay
Campbellton
O'Leary
Prince Edward Island
Prince Edward I.
Portage
Beach
Derby
Tyne Valley
Malpeque Bay
West Point
Egmont Bay
Malpeque
Prince Edward Island Nat. Park
St. Eleanors
Kensington
Cavendish
Stanhope
New London
Summerside
Central Bedeque
Hunter River
Tracadie
Charlottetown
Borden
Crapaud
Bonshaw
Rocky Point
Ft. Amherst N.H.P.
Hillsborough Bay
Vernon Bridge
Cardigan
Georgetown
Montague
Cambridge
Murray Harbour
High Bank
Belle River
Wood Islands
Northumberland Strait
Port Elgin
Cape Tormentine
Tidnish
Amherst
Oxford
Pugwash
Wallace
Port Philip
Tatamagouche
River John
Seafoam
Scotsburn
Pictou
Pictou I.
Naufrage
St. Peters
Elmira
East Point
Dingwells Mills
Morell
Souris
Wentworth Cen.
Springhill
Southampton
Jackson
Earltown
Central West River
New Glasgow
Thorburn
Stellarton
Cobequid Mts.
Bass River
Parrsboro
Glenholme
Maitland
Truro
Kemptown
Sunnybrae
Lorne
Caledonia
Noel
Walton
Stewiacke
Kennetcook
Shubenacadie Ind. Res.
Upper Rawdon
Gays River
Wolfville
Grand Pré N.H.P.
Kentville
Windsor
Margaretsville
Berwick
Ft. Edwards N.H.S.
Brooklyn
Newport
Wellington
Enfield
Waverley Game Sanctuary
Middleton
Hampton
Bridgetown
Ft. Anne N.H.P.
Annapolis Royal
Victoria Beach
Digby
Albany Cross
Dalhousie Road
Dalhousie West
New Ross
Middle Sackville
Waverley
Musquodoboit Harbour
Gibraltar
Dartmouth
HALIFAX
Cow Bay
Graham Head
Hubbards
Chester
Indian Harb.
Blandford
Peggys Cove
Herring Cove
Portuguese Cove
Sambro
Pennant Point
Terence Bay
Mahone Bay
Lunenburg
Ovens Nat. P.
Kingsburg
La Have
La Have I.
Bridgewater
New Germany
South Brookfield
Baker Settlement
Kejimkujik Nat. P.
Port Royal N.H.P.
Sth. Milford
Weymouth
Corberrie
Tobeatic Game Sanctuary
Indian Gardens
Mill Village
Middlewood
Hectanooga
Kemptville
Milton
West Berlin
Liverpool
Carleton
Middle Ohio
Belleville
Sable River
Houton I.
Shelburne
East Port Hébert
Lockeport
Western Head
Pubnico
Wedge Pt.
Clyde River
Saxon
Barrington
Shag Harbour
Mud I.
Seal I.
Clark's Harbour
Baccaro
Cape Sable
Cape Sable I.
Gulf of Saint Lawrence
Î. Brion
Grosse Île
Grande-Entrée
Îles de la Madelaine
Cap-aux-Meules
Havre-aux-Maisons
Île-d'Entrée
Havre-Aubert
St. Paul I.
Cabot Strait
Newfoundland
Island of Newfoundland
Mainland
Petit Jardin
C. St. George
Cape Anguille
Upper Ferry
St. Andrew's
Cape Ray
C. St. Lawrence
Cape North
St. Margaret Village
Aspy Bay
Dingwall
South Harbour
Neils Harbour
Pleasant Bay
C. Breton Highlands Nat. P.
Ingonish
Ingonish Beach
Petit Étang
Chéticamp
Grand Étang
Wreck Cove
Cape Breton Island
Breton Cove
St. Ann's Bay
Margaree Harbour
Belle Côte
Margaree Forks
Tarbotvale
Dunvegan
Margaree Valley
Sydney Mines
New Waterford
Inverness
Sth. Gut St. Ann's
North Sydney
Reserve Mines
Glace Bay
Strathlorne
Scotsville
Baddeck
Sydney
Port Morien
Black River
Mabou
Ainslie
Wagwalcook
A. G. Bell N.H.P.
Main à Dieu
Westmount
Cape Breton
Port Hood
Whycocomagh
Louisbourg
Christmas Island
Fortress of Louisbourg N.H.P.
Melford
Orangedale
Big Pond
Gabarouse
Bras d'Or L.
Victoria Bridge
Johnstown
McNab Cove
Chapel Island Ind. Res.
Fourchu
C. George
Cape George
St. Craigmore
George's Bay
Malignant Cove
Lismore
Antigonish
Port Hastings
West Bay
Port Hawkesbury
St. Peters
Grant River
Point Michaud
Monastery
Mulgrave
Louisdale
Arichat
North Lochaber
Bolyston
Sand Point
Strait of Canso
Chedabucto Bay
Queensport
Canso
Ogden
Aspen
Whitehead
Seal Harbour
Melrose
Larry's River
Port Hilford
Goose I.
Pt. Bickerton
St. Mary's R.
Liscomb Game Sanct.
Newton Mills
Upper Musquodoboit
Moser River
Liscomb
Liscomb Mills
Liscomb I.
C. St. Mary
Middle Musquodoboit
Sheet Harbour
Port Dufferin
Ship Harbour
Tangier
Sober I.
Taylor Head
Lower Ship Harbour
East Jeddore
Grand Desert
Jeddore C.
Nichol I.
ATLANTIC OCEAN
Sable Island Bank
Sable I.

Scale 1 : 2,250,000

0 20 40 60 80 100 Kilometers

0 20 40 60 80 Statute Miles

Scale 1 : 2,250,000

0 20 40 60 80 100 Kilometers

0 20 40 60 80 Statute Miles

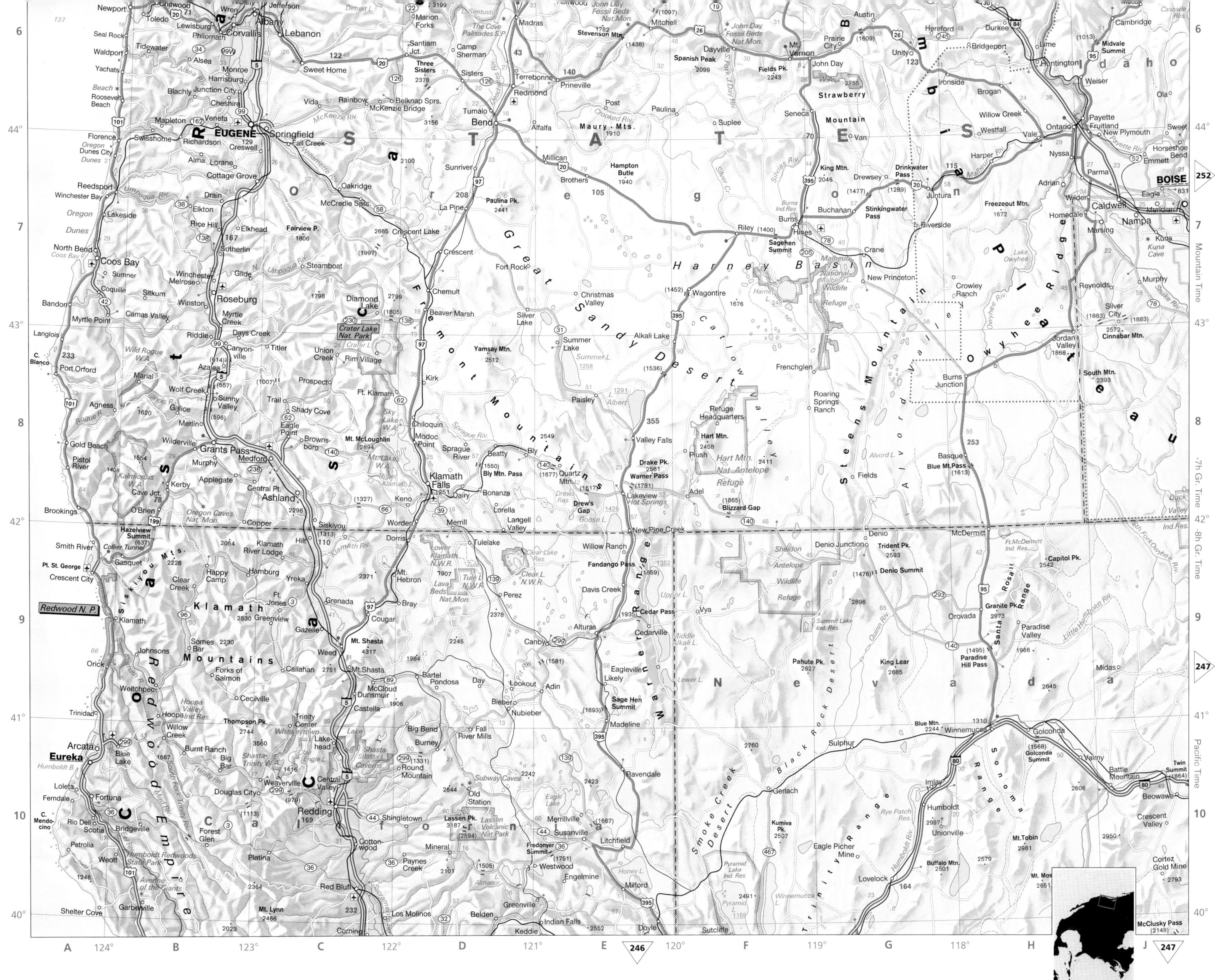

Mountain Time
-7h Gr. Time
-8h Gr. Time
Pacific Time
252
247
246
BOISE
Nampa
Caldwell
Meridian
Kuna
Eagle
Emmett
Payette
Fruitland
New Plymouth
Weiser
Cambridge
Ontario
Nyssa
Vale
Huntington
Burns
Hines
John Day
Prairie City
Mt. Vernon
Dayville
Mitchell
Prineville
Madras
Redmond
Bend
Sisters
La Pine
Crescent
Chemult
Christmas Valley
Summer Lake
Paisley
Lakeview
Valley Falls
Adel
Plush
Frenchglen
Fields
Denio
Burns Junction
Jordan Valley
McDermitt
Orovada
Paradise Valley
Winnemucca
Golconda
Battle Mountain
Lovelock
Gerlach
Cedarville
Alturas
Likely
Madeline
Ravendale
Susanville
Westwood
Burney
Fall River Mills
Bieber
Adin
Canby
Tulelake
Merrill
Bonanza
Bly
Klamath Falls
Chiloquin
Keno
Dorris
Weed
Mt. Shasta
Dunsmuir
McCloud
Yreka
Redding
Cottonwood
Red Bluff
Corning
Weaverville
Happy Camp
Ashland
Medford
Central Pt.
Grants Pass
Cave Jct.
Roseburg
Sutherlin
Myrtle Creek
Canyonville
Cottage Grove
EUGENE
Springfield
Corvallis
Albany
Lebanon
Sweet Home
Florence
Reedsport
Coos Bay
North Bend
Coquille
Bandon
Port Orford
Gold Beach
Brookings
Crescent City
Smith River
Klamath
Orick
Trinidad
Arcata
Eureka
Fortuna
Ferndale
Garberville
Newport
Toledo
Waldport
Yachats
Crater Lake Nat. Park
Redwood N. P.
Lassen Volcanic Nat Park
Mt. Shasta 4317
Harney Basin
Great Sandy Desert
Fremont Mountains
Steens Mountain
Owyhee Ridge
Klamath Mountains
Siskiyou Mts.
Redwood Empire
Black Rock Desert
Smoke Creek Desert
Sonoma Range
Trinity Range
Santa Rosa Range
Warner Range
Catlow Valley
Alvord Valley
Strawberry Mountain
Maury Mts.

Pacific Time
Klamath Mountains
Redwood N. P.
Cascade Range
Redwood Empire
Sacramento Valley
Sierra Nevada
San Joaquin Valley
Diablo Range
Santa Lucia Range
PACIFIC OCEAN
Warner Mountains
Smoke Creek Desert
Black Rock Desert
Brookings
Crescent City
Ashland
Yreka
Mt. Shasta
Weed
Redding
Red Bluff
Chico
Eureka
Arcata
Fortuna
Ukiah
Alturas
Susanville
Lassen Pk.
Lassen Volcanic Nat. Park
Oroville
Yuba City
Marysville
Sparks
RENO
Carson City
Truckee
Sth. Lake Tahoe
Sta. Rosa
Napa
Vacaville
Fairfield
Vallejo
SACRAMENTO
Stockton
Lodi
Richmond
BERKELEY
OAKLAND
SAN FRANCISCO
Golden Gate Bridge
Daly City
Hayward
CONCORD
Walnut
FREMONT
Redwood City
Palo Alto
SUNNYVALE
Milpitas
SAN JOSE
Santa Cruz
Watsonville
Salinas
Monterey
Pacific Grove
Hollister
Gilroy
Morgan Hill
Tracy
MODESTO
Merced
Los Banos
FRESNO
Clovis
Madera
Visalia
Tulare
Hanford
Coalinga
Yosemite Nat. Park
Mono L.
Lee Vining
Bridgeport
Kings Canyon Nat. Park
Sequoia Nat. Park
Scale 1 : 2,250,000
0 20 40 60 100 Kilometers
0 20 40 60 80 Statute Miles

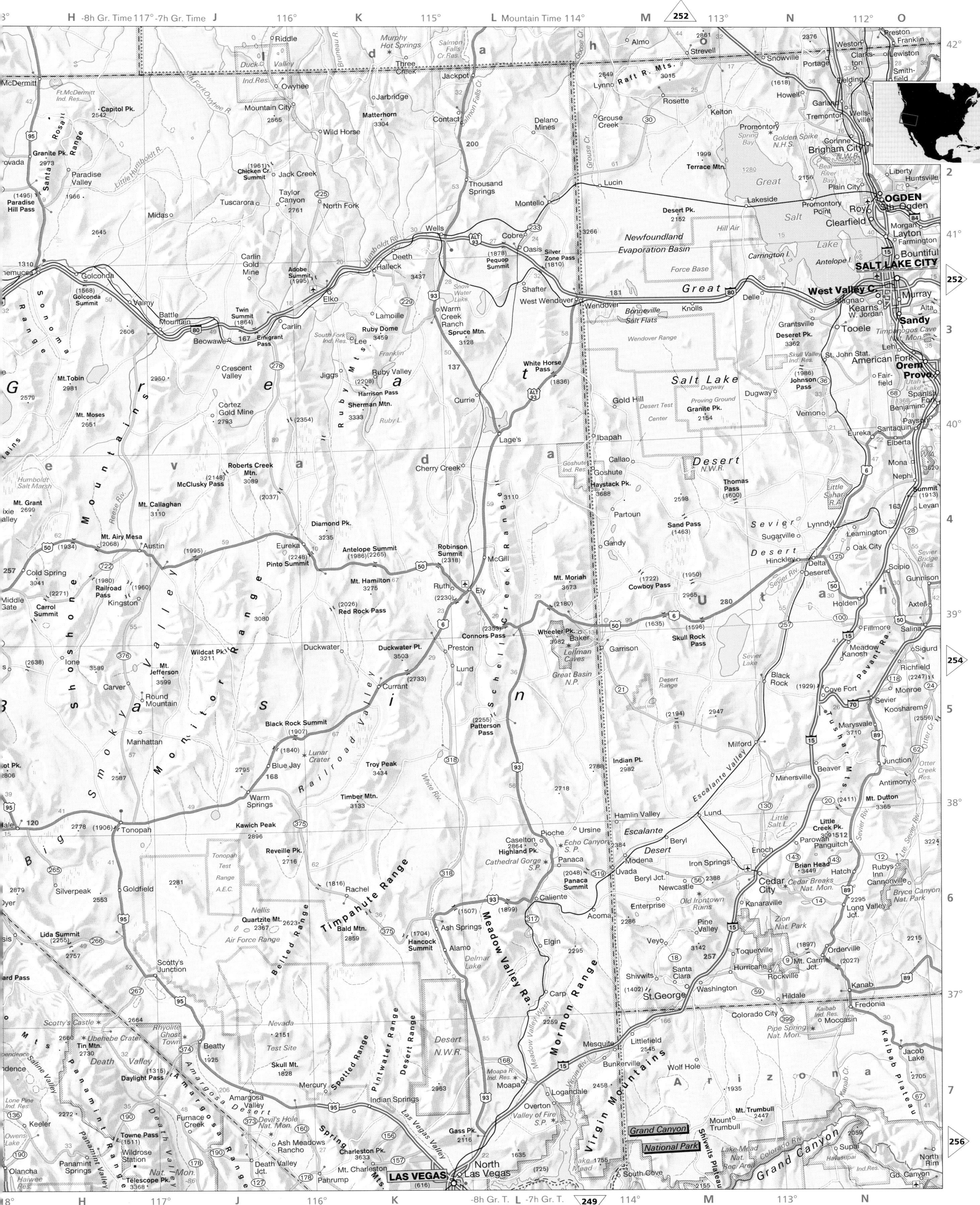

H -8h Gr. Time 117° -7h Gr. Time J
116°
K
115°
L Mountain Time 114°
M
252
113°
N
112°
O
42°
41°
40°
39°
38°
37°
Riddle
Murphy Hot Springs
Salmon Falls Cr. Res.
Almo
Strevell
Snowville
Weston
Preston
Franklin
Lewiston
Clarkston
Portage
Smithfield
McDermitt
Ft. McDermitt Ind. Res.
Duck Valley Ind. Res.
Owyhee
Three Creek
Jackpot
Raft R. Mts.
3015
Lynn
Rosette
Kelton
Howell
Garland
Tremonton
Wellsville
Capitol Pk. 2542
Mountain City
Jarbridge
Matterhorn 3304
Contact
Delano Mines
Grouse Creek
Promontory
Spring Bay
Golden Spike N.H.S.
Corinne
Brigham City
Santa Rosa Range
Granite Pk. 2973
Paradise Valley
Wild Horse
Little Humboldt R.
Chicken Cr. Summit
Jack Creek
Terrace Mtn.
Great
Plain City
Liberty
Huntsville
Paradise Hill Pass
Tuscarora
Taylor Canyon 2761
North Fork
Thousand Springs
Montello
Lucin
Lakeside
Promontory Point
Roy
OGDEN
Sth. Ogden
Midas
Desert Pk. 2152
Salt
Clearfield
Layton
Morgan
Farmington
Bountiful
Wells
Cobre
Oasis
Silver Zone Pass
Newfoundland Evaporation Basin
Hill Air
Force Base
Carrington I.
Lake
Antelope I.
SALT LAKE CITY
Winnemucca
Golconda
Golconda Summit
Carlin Gold Mine
Adobe Summit
Deeth
Halleck
Pequop Summit
Elko
Shafter
West Wendover
Wendover
Great
Delle
West Valley C.
Magna
Kearns
W. Jordan
Murray
Sandy
Valmy
Battle Mountain
Twin Summit
Carlin
Warm Creek Ranch
Lamoille
Bonneville Salt Flats
Knolls
Grantsville
Tooele
Timpanogos Cave Nat. Mon.
Sonoma Range
Beowawe
Emigrant Pass
South Fork Ind. Res.
Ruby Dome 3459
Lee
Spruce Mtn. 3128
Wendover Range
Deseret Pk. 3362
Skull Valley Ind. Res.
St. John Stat.
Lehi
American Fork
Orem
Provo
Crescent Valley
Jiggs
Ruby Valley
White Horse Pass
Salt Lake
Dugway
Johnson Pass
Fairfield
Mt. Tobin 2981
Harrison Pass
Sherman Mtn. 3333
Ruby Mts.
Ruby L.
Currie
Gold Hill
Desert Test Center
Proving Ground
Granite Pk. 2154
Vernon
Spanish Fork
Benjamin
Payson
Cortez Gold Mine
Mt. Moses 2651
Lage's
Ibapah
Santaquin
Elberta
Eureka
Humboldt Salt Marsh
Roberts Creek Mtn. 3089
McClusky Pass
Cherry Creek
Callao
Goshute
Goshute Ind. Res.
Haystack Pk. 3688
Desert N.W.R.
Thomas Pass
Mona
Nephi
Little Sahara R.A.
Mt. Grant 2699
Mt. Callaghan 3110
Partoun
Sand Pass
Levan
Diamond Pk. 3235
Sevier
Sugarville
Lynndyl
Leamington
Oak City
Mt. Airy Mesa
Austin
Eureka
Antelope Summit
Robinson Summit
McGill
Gandy
Desert
Hinckley
Delta
Deseret
Scipio
Sevier Bridge Res.
Gunnison
Cold Spring
Pinto Summit
Railroad Pass
Kingston
Mt. Hamilton 3275
Ruth
Ely
Mt. Moriah 3673
Cowboy Pass
Utah
Holden
Axtell
Carroll Summit
Red Rock Pass
Connors Pass
Wheeler Pk. 3982
Baker
Lehman Caves
Garrison
Skull Rock Pass
Fillmore
Salina
Toiyabe Range
Shoshone Mountains
Wildcat Pk. 3211
Duckwater
Duckwater Pt. 3503
Preston
Lund
Great Basin N.P.
Sevier Lake
Meadow
Kanosh
Sigurd
Richfield
Ione
Mt. Jefferson 3599
Carver
Round Mountain
Currant
Schell Creek Range
Black Rock
Cove Fort
Monroe
Sevier
Koosharem
Desert Range
Pavant Ra.
Black Rock Summit
Patterson Pass
Marysvale
Tushar Mts.
Manhattan
Lunar Crater
Railroad Valley
Milford
Escalante Valley
Junction
Otter Creek Res.
Big Smoky Valley
Monitor Range
Blue Jay
Troy Peak 3434
White Riv.
Indian Pt. 2982
Minersville
Beaver
Antimony
Warm Springs
Timber Mtn. 3133
Mt. Dutton 3365
Tonopah
Kawich Peak 2896
Hamlin Valley
Pioche
Ursine
Escalante Desert
Lund
Little Salt L.
Little Creek Pk.
Parowan
Panguitch
Goldfield
Reveille Pk. 2716
Caselton
Highland Pk.
Echo Canyon S.P.
Cathedral Gorge S.P.
Panaca
Modena
Beryl
Iron Springs
Enoch
Brian Head 3449
Hatch
Rubys Inn
Cannonville
Tonopah Test Range A.E.C.
Timpahute Range
Rachel
Panaca Summit
Uvada
Beryl Jct.
Newcastle
Cedar City
Cedar Breaks Nat. Mon.
Bryce Canyon Nat. Park
Silverpeak
Caliente
Old Irontown Ruins
Kanaraville
Long Valley Jct.
Lida Summit
Quartzite Mt.
Nellis Air Force Range
Bald Mtn. 2859
Hancock Summit
Ash Springs
Alamo
Meadow Valley Ra.
Elgin
Acoma
Enterprise
Pine Valley
Zion Nat. Park
Orderville
Scotty's Junction
Belted Range
Delmar Lake
Mormon Range
Veyo
Toquerville
Hurricane
Mt. Carmel Jct.
Rockville
Shivwits
Santa Clara
St. George
Washington
Hildale
Kanab
Fredonia
Carp
Colorado City
Kaibab Ind. Res.
Moccasin
Pipe Spring Nat. Mon.
Scotty's Castle
Ubehebe Crater
Rhyolite Ghost Town
Tin Mtn.
Death Valley
Beatty
Nevada Test Site
Skull Mt.
Spotted Range
Pintwater Range
Desert Range
Desert N.W.R.
Mesquite
Littlefield
Bunkerville
Wolf Hole
Arizona
Jacob Lake
Kaibab Plateau
Panamint Mts.
Saline Valley
Daylight Pass
Amargosa Range
Amargosa Valley
Amargosa Desert
Mercury
Indian Springs
Moapa
Moapa R. Ind. Res.
Logandale
Virgin Mountains
Mt. Trumbull
Mount Trumbull
Lone Pine Ind. Res.
Keeler
Towne Pass
Wildrose Station
Furnace Creek
Devil's Hole Nat. Mon.
Ash Meadows Rancho
Spring Mts.
Las Vegas Valley
Gass Pk.
Overton
Valley of Fire S.P.
Grand Canyon
National Park
Shivwits Plateau
Supai
Havasupai Ind. Res.
Owens Lake
Panamint Springs
Panamint Range
Telescope Pk. 3368
Death Valley Jct.
Pahrump
Charleston Pk. 3633
Mt. Charleston
LAS VEGAS
North Las Vegas
Lake Mead
South Cove
Lake Mead Nat. Rec. Area
Grand Canyon
North Rim
Gd. Canyon
Olancha
Haiwee Res.
117°
116°
-8h Gr. T. L -7h Gr. T.
249
114°
113°
254
256

Scale 1 : 2,250,000
0 20 40 60 80 100 Kilometers
0 20 40 60 80 Statute Miles

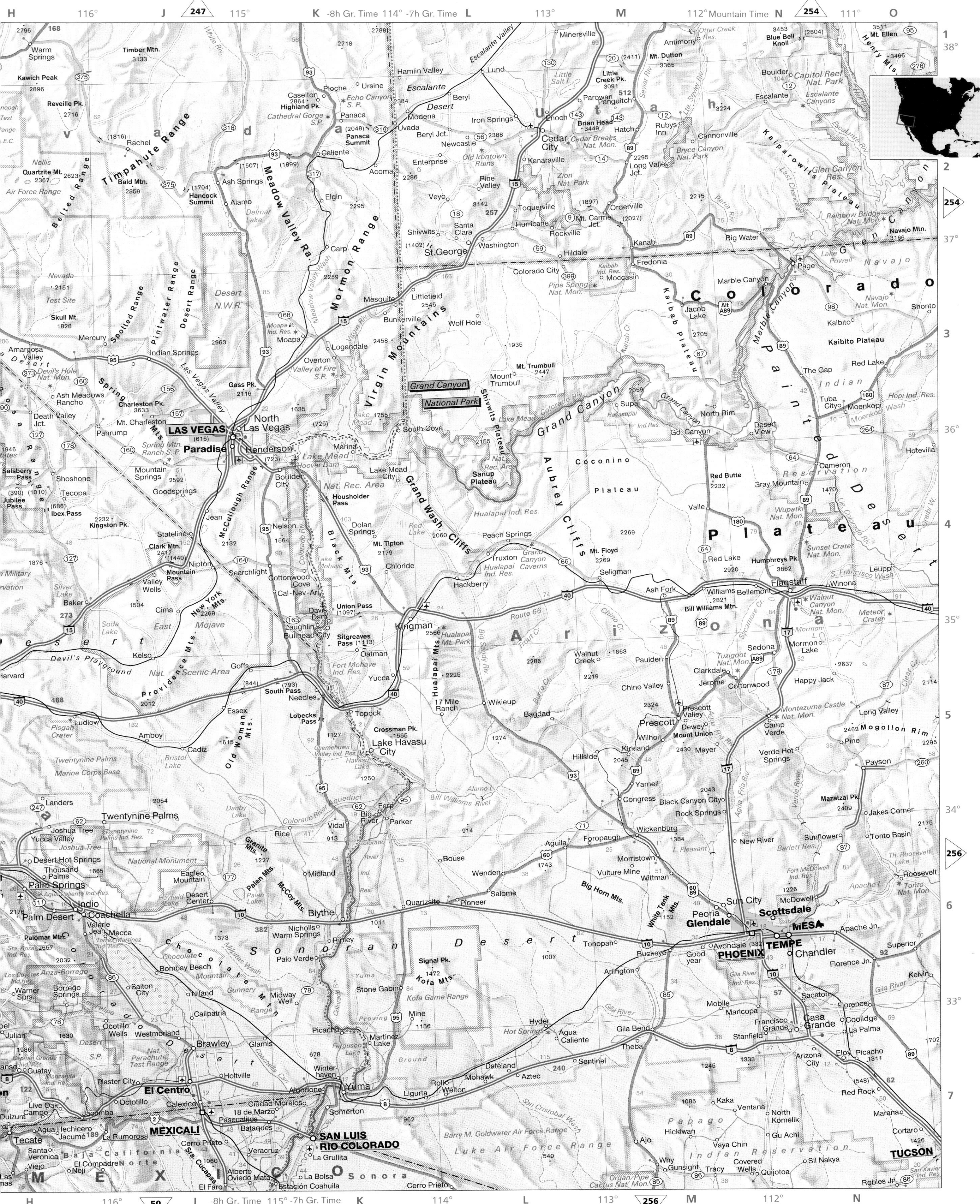

H 116° J 247 115° K -8h Gr. Time 114° -7h Gr. Time L 113° M 112° Mountain Time N 254 111° O
LAS VEGAS
North Las Vegas
Paradise
Henderson
Boulder City
Lake Mead
Hoover Dam
Grand Canyon National Park
Grand Canyon
Coconino Plateau
Colorado Plateau
Painted Desert
Kaibab Plateau
Kaiparowits Plateau
Glen Canyon
Marble Canyon
Page
Kanab
Fredonia
St.George
Cedar City
Mesquite
Virgin Mountains
Mormon Range
Meadow Valley Ra.
Timpahute Range
Grand Wash Cliffs
Aubrey Cliffs
Hualapai Ind. Res.
Kingman
Bullhead City
Laughlin
Needles
Lake Havasu City
Parker
Blythe
Quartzsite
Flagstaff
Williams
Seligman
Sedona
Prescott
Wickenburg
Sun City
Peoria
Glendale
Scottsdale
MESA
TEMPE
PHOENIX
Chandler
Casa Grande
Gila Bend
Yuma
El Centro
Calexico
MEXICALI
SAN LUIS RIO COLORADO
Tecate
Brawley
Indio
Coachella
Palm Springs
Palm Desert
Twentynine Palms
Mojave
East Mojave Nat. Scenic Area
Sonoran Desert
Chocolate Mts.
Kofa Game Range
Luke Air Force Range
Papago Indian Reservation
Sonora
Baja California Norte
MEXICO
Arizona
Utah
Nevada
Colorado
TUCSON
1 38° 2 37° 3 36° 4 35° 5 34° 6 33° 7
H 116° 50 J -8h Gr. Time 115° -7h Gr. Time K 114° L 113° 256 M 112° N

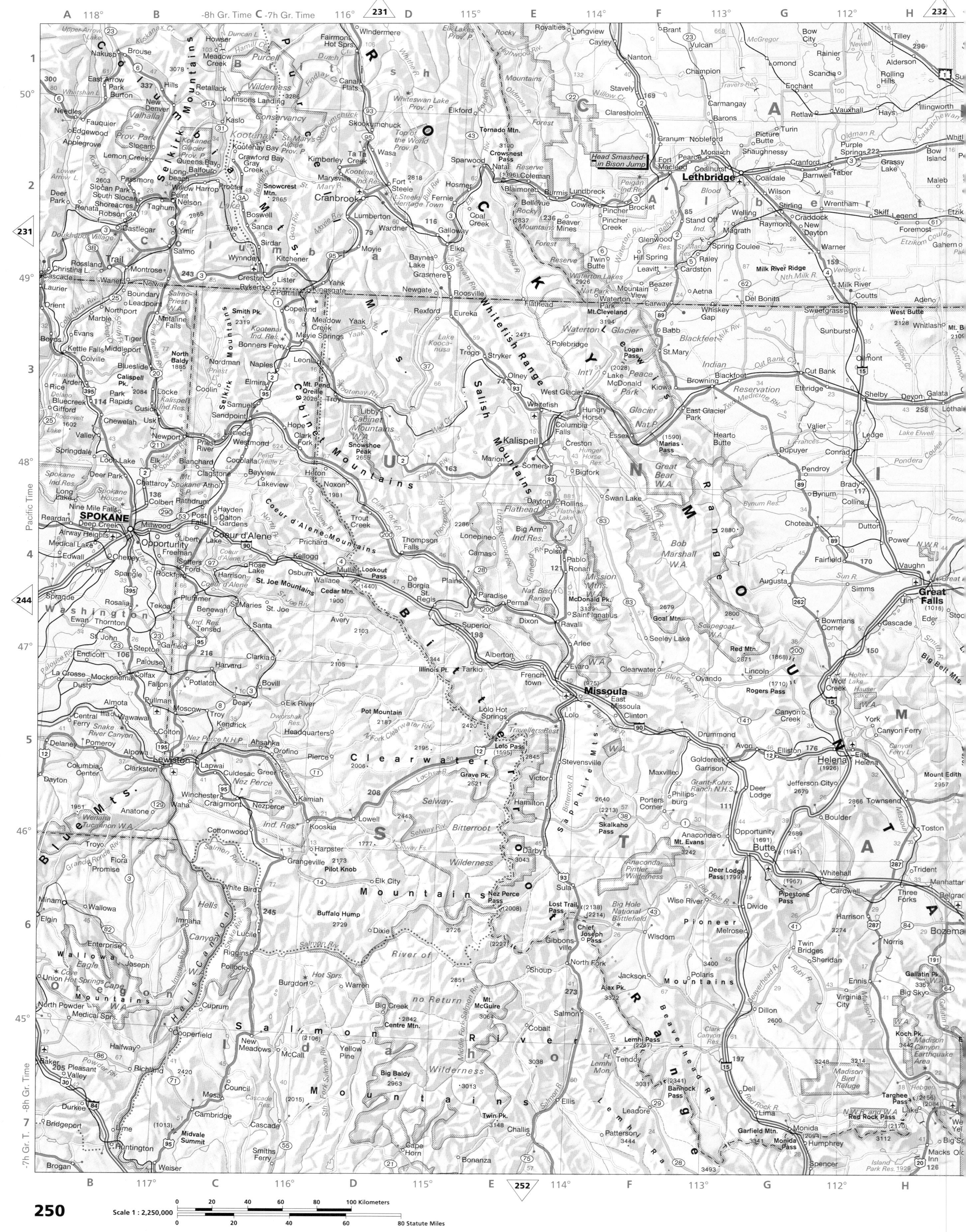

A
118°
B
-8h Gr. Time
C
-7h Gr. Time
116°
231
D
115°
E
114°
F
113°
G
112°
H
232
1
2
3
4
5
6
7
50°
49°
48°
47°
46°
45°
Pacific Time
-7h Gr. T. -8h Gr. Time
231
244
Upper Arrow L.
Nakusp
Brouse
Howser
Duncan L.
Fairmont Hot Sprs.
Windermere
Elk Lakes Prov. P.
Royalties
Longview
Cayley
Brant
Vulcan
Bow City
Tilley
Rainier
Alderson
Meadow Creek
Purcell
Nanton
Champion
Lomond
Scandia
Rolling Hills
East Arrow Park
Burton
Hills
Retallack
Wilderness
Canal Flats
Mountains
Stavely
Enchant
Needles
New Denver
Johnsons Landing
Whiteswan Lake Prov. P.
Claresholm
Carmangay
Barons
Retlaw
Vauxhall
Hays
Illingworth
Fauquier
Edgewood
Applegrove
Valhalla Prov. Park
Kaslo
Conservancy
Skookumchuck
Elkford
Tornado Mtn.
Forest
Granum
Nobleford
Turin
Picture Butte
Purple Springs
Bow Island
Lemon Creek
Slocan
Kokanee Glacier Prov. P.
Kootenay Bay
Crawford Bay
Gray Creek
Queens Bay
Balfour
Longbeach
Top of the World Prov. P.
Wasa
Ta Ta Creek
Kimberley
Sparwood
Crowsnest Pass
Natal
Coleman
Head Smashed-in Bison Jump
Fort Macleod
Pearce
Monarch
Coalhurst
Lethbridge
Shaughnessy
Cranford
Barnwell
Taber
Grassy Lake
Coaldale
Maleb
Deer Park
Slocan Park
South Slocan
Passmore
Willow
Harrop
Procter
Nelson
Shoreacres
Robson
Renata
Taghum
Snowcrest Mtn.
Marysville
Fort Steele
Cranbrook
Fernie
Hosmer
Blairmore
Bellevue
Burmis
Lundbreck
Cowley
Pincher
Pincher Creek
Brocket
Wilson
Stirling
Wrentham
Welling
Skiff
Legend
Etzikom
Castlegar
Ymir
Tye
Boswell
Sanca
Lumberton
Wardner
Coal Creek
Galloway
Beaver Mines
Stand Off
Magrath
Raymond
Craddock
New Dayton
Foremost
Doukhobor Village
Salmo
Sirdar
Kitchener
Moyie
Baynes Lake
Grasmere
Elko
Glenwood
Hill Spring
Spring Coulee
Warner
Gahern
Rossland
Trail
Christina L.
Cascade
Waneta
Montrose
Wynndel
Creston
Rykerts
Lister
Yahk
Kingsgate
Newgate
Roosville
Twin Butte
Waterton Lakes
Leavitt
Raley
Cardston
Milk River Ridge
Milk River
Coutts
Laurier
Orient
Boundary
Leadpoint
Northport
Marble
Evans
Salmo-Priest W.A.
Metaline Falls
Smith Pk.
Porthill
Copeland
Meadow Creek
Moyie Springs
Yaak
Rexford
Eureka
Flathead
Waterton Park
Mountain View
Beazer
Carway
Aetna
Whiskey Gap
Del Bonita
Sweetgrass
West Butte
Aden
Whitlash
Boyds
Kettle Falls
Middleport
Colville
Tiger
Bonners Ferry
Kootenai Ind. Res.
Leonia
Lake Koocanusa
Trego
Stryker
Whitefish Range
Polebridge
Mt.Cleveland
Waterton Glacier
Logan Pass
Babb
St.Mary
Blackfeet
Sunburst
Oilmont
North Baldy
Nordman
Naples
Olney
Indian
Cut Bank
Rice
Arden
Blueslide
Calispell Pk.
Park Rapids
Priest
Elmira
Mt. Pend Oreille
Lake McDonald
Peace
Kiowa
Browning
Blackfoot
Reservation
Ethridge
Shelby
Devon
Galata
Lothair
Bluecreek
Gifford
Cusick
Locke
Kalispell Ind.Res.
Coolin
Samuels
Sandpoint
Troy
Libby
Cabinet Mountains W.A.
Salish
West Glacier
Whitefish
Hungry Horse
Glacier
Nat.P.
East Glacier Park
Two Medicine
Chewelah
Usk
Selkirk Mountains
Hope
Clark Fork
Kalispell
Columbia Falls
Creston
Essex
Marias Pass
Heart Butte
Valier
Ledge
Valley
Newport
Priest River
Laclede
Westmond
Snowshoe Peak
Marion
Somers
Bigfork
Dupuyer
Conrad
Springdale
Loon Lake
Elk
Blanchard
Cocolalla
Pend Oreille
Heron
Bayview
Great Bear W.A.
Pendroy
Brady
Spokane Ind. Res.
Deer Park
Chattaroy
Clagstone
Athol
Lakeview
Noxon
Cabinet Mountains
Bynum
Long Lake
Spokane House
Colbert
Rathdrum
Nine Mile Falls
Coeur d'Alene
Dayton
Rollins
Flathead Lake
Swan Lake
Collins
Reardan
SPOKANE
Deep Creek
Millwood
Post Falls
Hayden
Dalton Gardens
Trout Creek
Thompson Falls
Lonepine
Big Arm
Ind.Res.
Bob Marshall W.A.
Choteau
Dutton
Airway Heights
Medical Lake
Opportunity
Liberty Lake
Freeman
Prichard
Coeur d'Alene Mountains
Camas
Polson
Fairfield
Power
Edwall
Cheney
Tyler
Spangle
Rockford
Harrison
Rose Lake
Kellogg
Osburn
Wallace
Mullan
Lookout Pass
De Borgia
St. Regis
Plains
Pablo
Ronan
Mission Mts.
Augusta
Vaughn
Great Falls
Sprague
Rosalia
Tekoa
Plummer
Benewah
St. Maries
St. Joe
St. Joe Mountains
Cedar Mtn.
Paradise
Perma
Nat. Bison Range
McDonald Pk.
Saint Ignatius
Simms
Ulm
Washington
Ewan
Thornton
Ind. Res.
Tensed
Santa
Avery
Superior
Dixon
Ravalli
Goal Mtn.
Scapegoat W.A.
Bowmans Corner
Cascade
Eder
St. John
Steptoe
Garfield
Clarkia
Alberton
Seeley Lake
Red Mtn.
Endicott
Palouse
Harvard
Illinois Pt.
Tarkio
Frenchtown
Arlee
Evaro
Clearwater
Ovando
Lincoln
Big Belt Mts.
La Crosse
Mockonema
Colfax
Fallon
Potlatch
Bovill
Missoula
East Missoula
Rogers Pass
Wolf Creek
Holter Lake
Hauser Lake
Dusty
Almota
Pullman
Moscow
Deary
Elk River
Pot Mountain
Lolo Hot Springs
Lolo
Clinton
Canyon Creek
York
Central Ferry
Wawawai
Troy
Kendrick
Dworshak Res.
Snake River Canyon
Colton
Headquarters
Travellers Rest
Drummond
Canyon Ferry
Delaney
Pomeroy
Nez Perce N.H.P.
Ahsahka
Orofino
Pierce
Lolo Pass
Stevensville
Goldcreek
Garrison
Avon
Elliston
Helena
East Helena
Alpowa
Lewiston
Clarkston
Lapwai
Culdesac
Greer
Clearwater
Columbia Center
Dayton
Winchester
Craigmont
Nez Perce
Grave Pk.
Maxville
Grant-Kohrs Ranch N.H.S.
Philipsburg
Deer Lodge
Jefferson City
Mount Edith
Townsend
Blue Mts.
Anatone
Waha
Nezperce
Kamiah
Selway-Bitterroot
Victor
Hamilton
Sapphire Mts.
Bitterroot Range
Porters Corner
Skalkaho Pass
Boulder
Wenaha Tucannon W.A.
Cottonwood
Ind. Res.
Kooskia
Lowell
Selway Fs.
Anaconda
Mt. Evans
Opportunity
Butte
Toston
Troy
Flora
Promise
Harpster
Grangeville
Pilot Knob
Wilderness
Darby
Anaconda-Pintler Wilderness
Deer Lodge Pass
Whitehall
Trident
Manhattan
Elk City
Mountains
Nez Perce Pass
Sula
Lost Trail Pass
Big Hole National Battlefield
Wise River
Pipestone Pass
Cardwell
Three Forks
Belgrade
Minam
Wallowa
Elgin
White Bird
Hells Canyon
Buffalo Hump
Dixie
Chief Joseph Pass
Wisdom
Pioneer
Divide
Melrose
Harrison
Bozeman
Enterprise
Joseph
Wallowa
Eagle Cap
Cove
Union
Hot Springs
Lucile
Riggins
Pollock
River of No Return
Gibbonsville
North Fork
Shoup
Jackson
Polaris
Twin Bridges
Sheridan
Norris
Gallatin Pk.
Oregon
Mountains
Cuprum
Burgdorf
Hot Sprs.
Warren
Mt. McGuire
Ajax Pk.
Mountains
Ennis
Big Sky
North Powder
Medical Sprs.
Big Creek
Centre Mtn.
Salmon
Beaverhead
Dillon
Virginia City
Koch Pk.
Madison Canyon Earthquake Area
Cuprum
Cooperfield
Salmon
New Meadows
McCall
Yellow Pine
Middle Fork Salmon Riv.
Cobalt
River
Lemhi Pass
Tendoy
Lemhi Mon.
Clark Canyon Res.
Halfway
Baker
Pleasant Valley
Richland
Big Baldy
Wilderness
Madison Bird Refuge
Council
Mesa
Cascade Res.
Bannock Pass
Dell
Targhee Pass
Durkee
Cambridge
Cascade
Twin Pk.
Challis
Leadore
Lima
Red Rock Pass
Bridgeport
Lime
Huntington
Midvale Summit
Smiths Ferry
Cape Horn
Bonanza
Patterson
Garfield Mtn.
Monida
Monida Pass
Humphrey
Spencer
Island Park Res.
Brogan
Weiser
B
117°
C
116°
D
115°
E
252
114°
F
113°
G
112°
H
Scale 1 : 2,250,000
0
20
40
60
80
100 Kilometers
0
20
40
60
80 Statute Miles

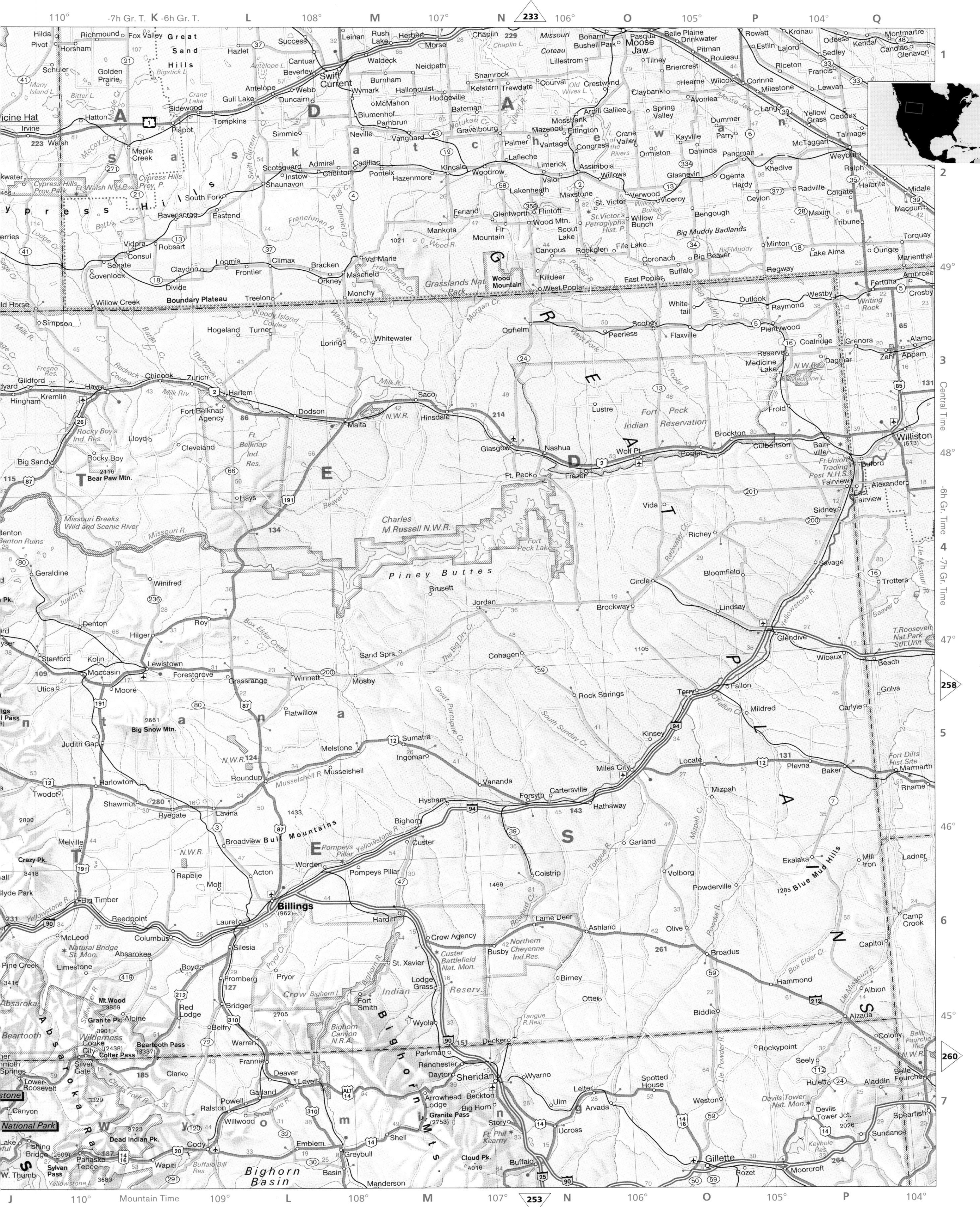

110°
-7h Gr. T. K -6h Gr. T.
L
108°
M
107°
N
233
106°
O
105°
P
104°
Q
Hilda
Pivot
Richmound
Horsham
Fox Valley
Great Sand Hills
Schuler
Golden Prairie
Hazlet
Success
Cantuar
Beverley
Swift Current
Webb
Antelope
Gull Lake
Duncairn
Sidewood
Tompkins
Hatton
Irvine
Walsh
Maple Creek
Piapot
Leinan
Rush Lake
Herbert
Morse
Waldeck
Neidpath
Burnham
Wymark
Hallonquist
McMahon
Hodgeville
Blumenhof
Pambrun
Neville
Simmie
Vanguard
Chaplin
Missouri Coteau
Shamrock
Kelstern
Trewdate
Courval
Bateman
Gravelbourg
Mossbank
Ettington
Mazenod
Vantage
Palmer
Boharm
Bushell Park
Moose Jaw
Lillestrom
Pasqua
Belle Plaine
Drinkwater
Pitman
Rouleau
Tilney
Briercrest
Crestwynd
Claybank
Hearne
Wilcox
Avonlea
Corinne
Milestone
Ardill
Galilee
Spring Valley
Crane Valley
Kayville
Dummer
Parry
Congress
Ormiston
Dahinda
Pangman
Rowatt
Estlin
Lajord
Kronau
Odessa
Sedley
Francis
Riceton
Lewvan
Lang
Yellow Grass
Cedoux
McTaggart
Talmage
Weyburn
Kendal
Montmartre
Candiac
Glenavon
Scotsguard
Admiral
Instow
Shaunavon
Crichton
Cadillac
Ponteix
Hazenmore
Kincaid
Woodrow
Lafleche
Limerick
Assiniboia
Willows
Valor
Glasnevin
Ogema
Khedive
Ralph
Halbrite
Midale
Cypress Hills Prov. Park
Ft. Walsh N.H.S.
Cypress Hills Prov. P.
South Fork
Ravenscrag
Eastend
Lakenheath
Maxstone
St. Victor
Verwood
Viceroy
Hardy
Ceylon
Radville
Colgate
Macoun
Ferland
Glentworth
Flintoft
Wood Mtn.
St. Victor's Petroglyphs Hist. P.
Willow Bunch
Bengough
Maxim
Tribune
Mankota
Fir Mountain
Scout Lake
Big Muddy Badlands
Torquay
Vidora
Consul
Robsart
Canopus
Rockglen
Fife Lake
Minton
Lake Alma
Oungre
Marienthal
Senate
Govenlock
Claydon
Loomis
Frontier
Climax
Bracken
Val Marie
Orkney
Masefield
Monchy
Coronach
Big Beaver
Buffalo
Regway
Ambrose
Divide
Willow Creek
Boundary Plateau
Treelon
Grasslands Nat. Park
Wood Mountain
Killdeer
West Poplar
East Poplar
Fortuna
Crosby
49°
Simpson
Hogeland
Turner
Loring
Whitewater
Opheim
Scobey
Peerless
Flaxville
White-tail
Outlook
Raymond
Westby
Writing Rock
Plentywood
Coalridge
Grenora
Alamo
Appam
Zahl
Reserve
Medicine Lake
Dagmar
Gildford
Havre
Chinook
Zurich
Harlem
Hingham
Kremlin
Fort Belknap Agency
Dodson
Malta
Saco
Hinsdale
Lustre
Fort Peck Indian Reservation
Froid
Rocky Boy's Ind. Res.
Lloyd
Cleveland
Ft. Belknap Ind. Res.
Glasgow
Nashua
Wolf Pt.
Poplar
Brockton
Culbertson
Bainville
Williston
Central Time
48°
Big Sandy
Rocky Boy
Bear Paw Mtn.
Ft. Peck
Frazer
Ft. Union Trading Post N.H.S.
Buford
Fairview
Alexander
East Fairview
-6h Gr. Time
Hays
Missouri Breaks Wild and Scenic River
Charles M. Russell N.W.R.
Fort Peck Lake
Vida
Sidney
Richey
Benton
Geraldine
Winifred
Piney Buttes
Brusett
Circle
Bloomfield
Savage
Trotters
-7h Gr. Time
Denton
Roy
Hilger
Jordan
Brockway
Lindsay
Stanford
Kolin
Lewistown
Moccasin
Forestgrove
Grassrange
Winnett
Sand Sprs.
Mosby
Cohagen
Glendive
T. Roosevelt Nat. Park Sth. Unit
47°
Wibaux
Beach
Utica
Moore
Flatwillow
Rock Springs
Fallon
Terry
Golva
Carlyle
Mildred
258
Big Snow Mtn.
Judith Gap
Melstone
Sumatra
Ingomar
Kinsey
Harlowton
Twodot
Roundup
Musselshell
Vananda
Miles City
Locate
Plevna
Baker
Fort Dilts Hist. Site
Marmarth
Rhame
Shawmut
Ryegate
Lavina
Hysham
Forsyth
Cartersville
Hathaway
Mizpah
Bighorn
Custer
Bull Mountains
Broadview
Pompeys Pillar
Worden
Garland
Ekalaka
Mill Iron
Ladner
46°
Melville
Crazy Pk.
Rapelje
Acton
Molt
Colstrip
Volborg
Powderville
Blue Mud Hills
Big Timber
Billings
Reedpoint
Columbus
Laurel
Hardin
Lame Deer
Ashland
Olive
Camp Crook
McLeod
Natural Bridge St. Mon.
Absarokee
Silesia
Crow Agency
Custer Battlefield Nat. Mon.
Busby
Northern Cheyenne Ind. Res.
Broadus
Capitol
Pine Creek
Limestone
Boyd
Fromberg
Pryor
St. Xavier
Lodge Grass
Birney
Hammond
Albion
Mt. Wood
Red Lodge
Bridger
Fort Smith
Otter
Biddle
Alzada
45°
Alpine
Granite Pk.
Beartooth Pass
Belfry
Warren
Wyola
Bighorn Canyon N.R.A.
Tangue R. Res.
Decker
Rockypoint
Colony
Colter Pass
Cooke City
Silver Gate
Frannie
Parkman
Ranchester
Dayton
Sheridan
Seely
Belle Fourche
260
Deaver
Lovell
Wyarno
Spotted Horse
Hulett
Aladdin
Cowley
Garland
Powell
Arrowhead Lodge
Beckton
Leiter
Weston
Devils Tower Nat. Mon.
Ralston
Big Horn
Granite Pass
Ulm
Arvada
Devils Tower Jct.
Spearfish
Willwood
Story
Ucross
Sundance
Ft. Phil Kearny
Dead Indian Pk.
Cody
Emblem
Shell
Greybull
Wapiti
Pahaska Tepee
Sylvan Pass
Cloud Pk.
Buffalo
Gillette
Moorcroft
Bighorn Basin
Manderson
Basin
Rozet
Bighorn Mts.
Absaroka Range
J
110°
Mountain Time
109°
L
108°
M
107°
253
N
106°
O
105°
P
104°

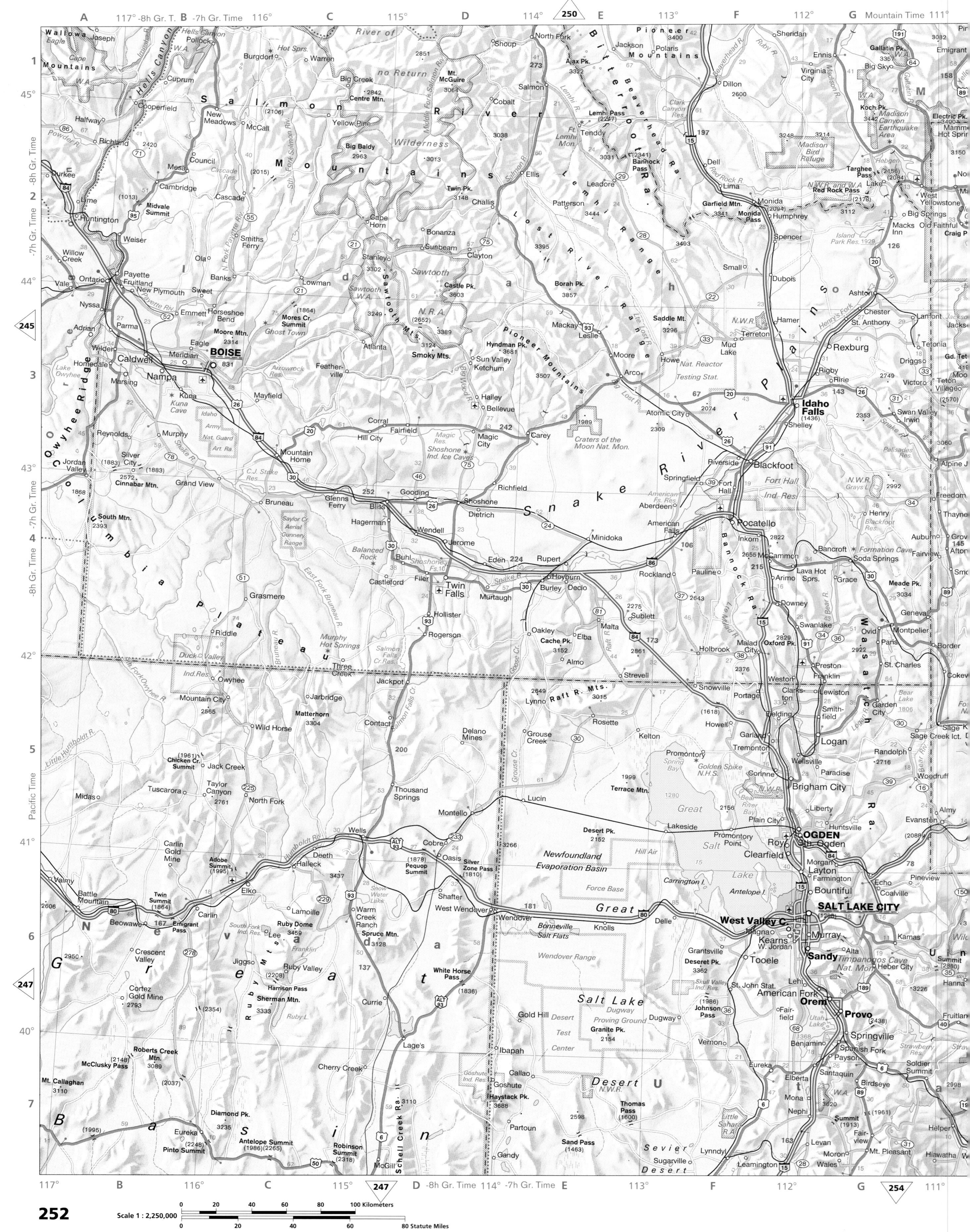

Scale 1 : 2,250,000

0 20 40 60 80 100 Kilometers

0 20 40 60 80 Statute Miles

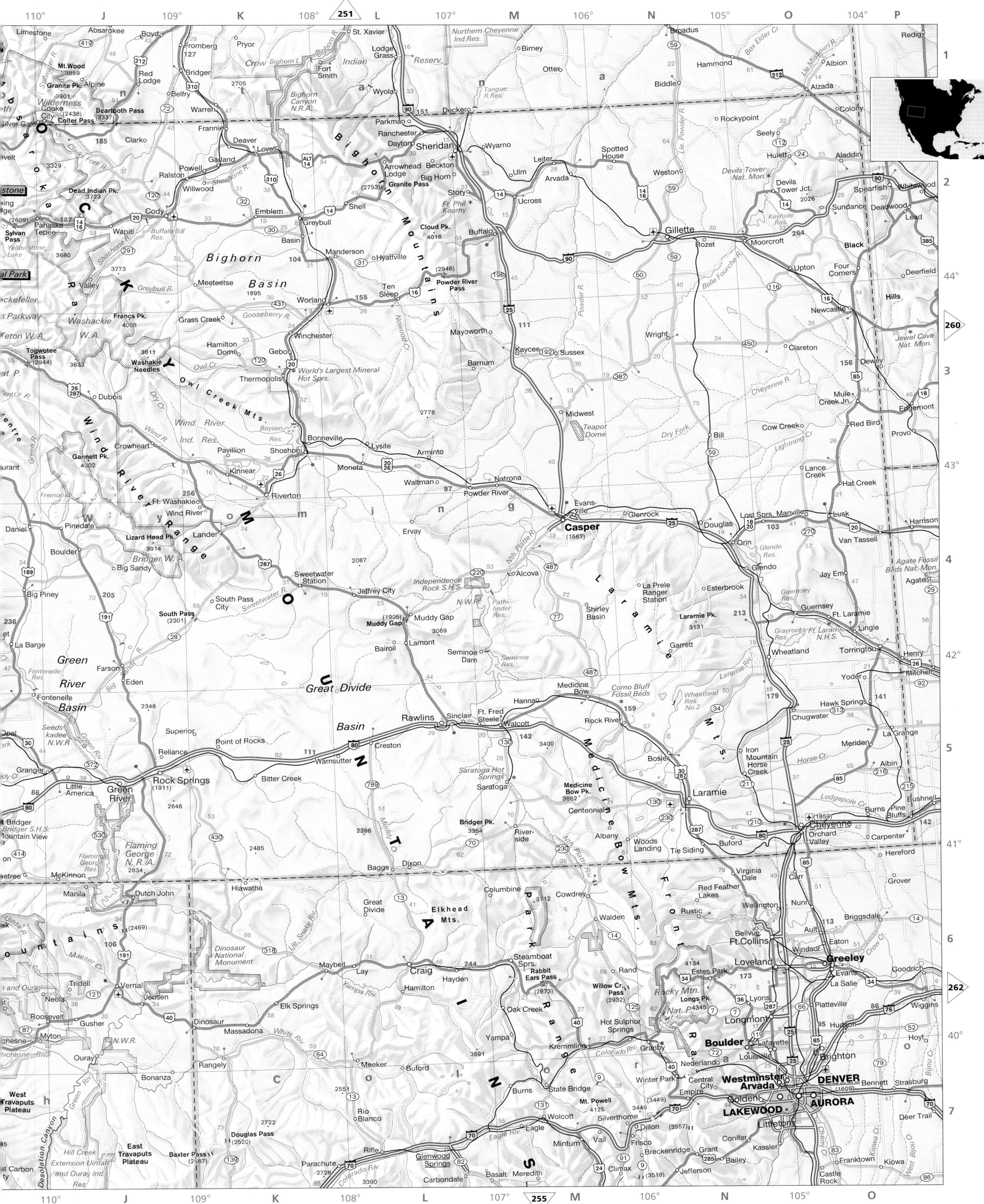

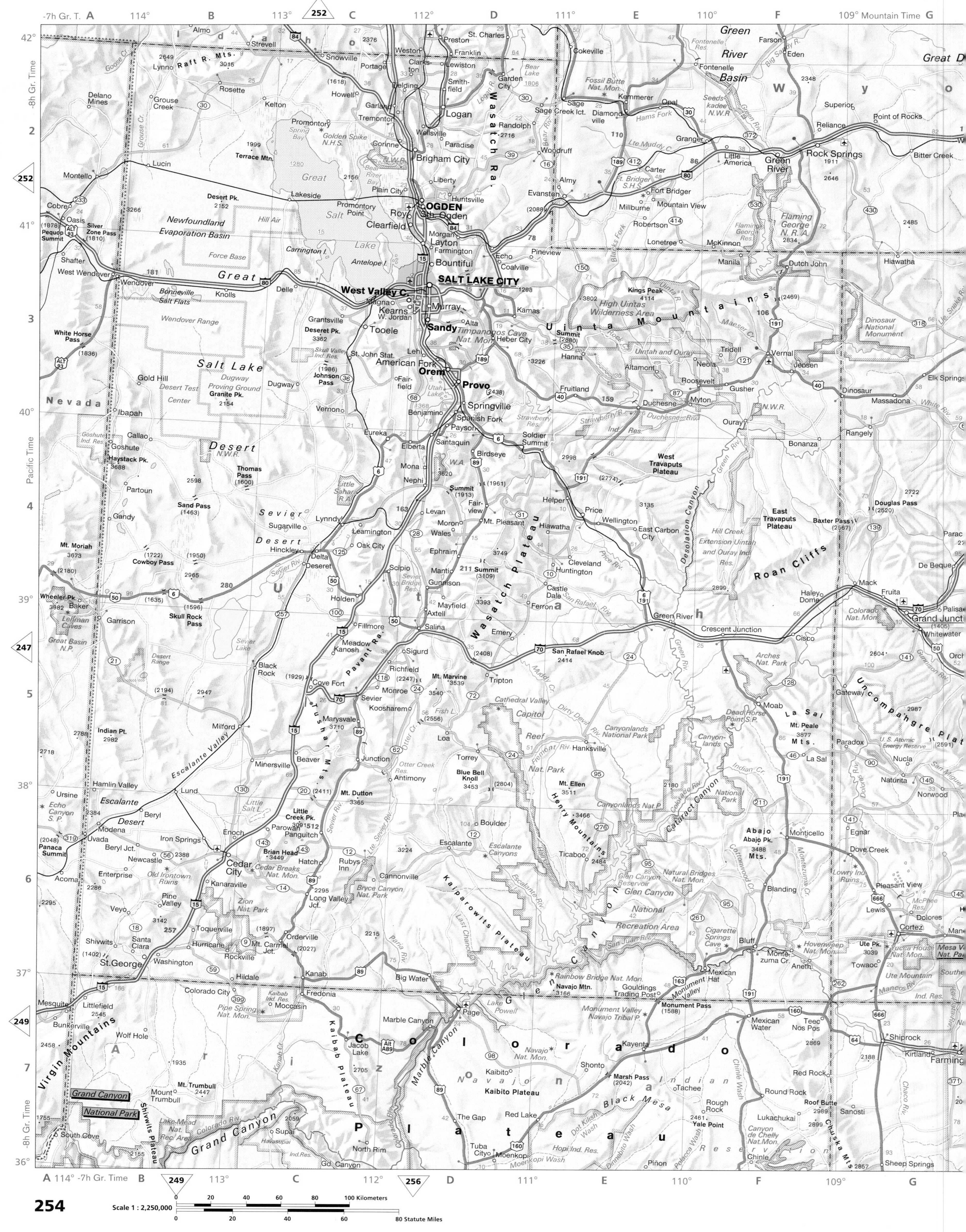

-7h Gr. T. A 114° B 113° 252 C 112° D 111° E 110° F 109° Mountain Time G
-8h Gr. Time
Pacific Time
Idaho
Wyoming
Nevada
Utah
Arizona
Colorado Plateau
Great Salt Lake
Great Salt Lake Desert
Sevier Desert
Escalante Desert
Wasatch Ra.
Wasatch Plateau
Uinta Mountains
High Uintas Wilderness Area
Green River Basin
Great Divide
Raft R. Mts.
Almo
Strevell
Preston
St. Charles
Cokeville
Fontenelle
Farson
Eden
Lynndyl
Snowville
Weston
Franklin
Lewiston
Clarkston
Portage
Fielding
Smithfield
Logan
Garden City
Bear Lake
Kemmerer
Opal
Sage
Sage Creek Jct.
Diamondville
Fossil Butte Nat. Mon.
Seedskadee N.W.R.
Superior
Point of Rocks
Reliance
Rock Springs
Bitter Creek
Green River
Little America
Granger
Lynn
Rosette
Grouse Creek
Delano Mines
Kelton
Howell
Garland
Tremonton
Promontory
Golden Spike N.H.S.
Wellsville
Corinne
Randolph
Woodruff
Paradise
Brigham City
Terrace Mtn.
Lucin
Montello
Liberty
Huntsville
Almy
Evanston
Ft. Bridger S.H.S.
Fort Bridger
Carter
Mountain View
Millburne
Robertson
Lonetree
McKinnon
Manila
Flaming Gorge N.R.A.
Dutch John
Hiawatha
Desert Pk.
Lakeside
Plain City
Promontory Point
OGDEN
Roy
Sth. Ogden
Clearfield
Morgan
Layton
Farmington
Bountiful
Newfoundland Evaporation Basin
Hill Air Force Base
Carrington I.
Antelope I.
Cobre
Oasis
Pequop Summit
Silver Zone Pass
Shafter
West Wendover
Wendover
Bonneville Salt Flats
Knolls
Delle
SALT LAKE CITY
West Valley C.
Magna
Kearns
W. Jordan
Murray
Sandy
Echo
Coalville
Pineview
Kamas
Kings Peak
Wendover Range
White Horse Pass
Grantsville
Deseret Pk.
Tooele
Alta
Timpanogos Cave Nat. Mon.
Heber City
Summit
Hanna
Tridell
Vernal
Dinosaur National Monument
Skull Valley Ind. Res.
St. John Stat.
Lehi
American Fork
Orem
Provo
Johnson Pass
Uintah and Ouray
Altamont
Neola
Roosevelt
Jensen
Elk Springs
Gold Hill
Dugway
Dugway Proving Ground
Desert Test Center
Granite Pk.
Fairfield
Utah Lake
Fruitland
Duchesne
Myton
Gusher
Dinosaur
Massadona
Ibapah
Vernon
Benjamino
Springville
Spanish Fork
Strawberry Res.
Ouray
Rangely
Callao
Goshute
Goshute Ind. Res.
Haystack Pk.
Eureka
Payson
Elberta
Santaquin
Soldier Summit
Bonanza
Desert N.W.R.
Thomas Pass
Birdseye
West Tavaputs Plateau
Mona
Nephi
Partoun
Little Sahara R.A.
Summit
Helper
Price
Wellington
Douglas Pass
Gandy
Sand Pass
Levan
Fairview
Mt. Pleasant
Moroni
Wales
Hiawatha
East Carbon City
East Tavaputs Plateau
Baxter Pass
Sugarville
Leamington
Oak City
Hinckley
Delta
Deseret
Ephraim
Desolation Canyon
Hill Creek Extension Uintah and Ouray Ind. Res.
Roan Cliffs
Mt. Moriah
Cowboy Pass
Scipio
Sevier Bridge Res.
Manti
Cleveland
Huntington
Castle Dale
De Beque
Wheeler Pk.
Baker
Lehman Caves
Great Basin N.P.
Garrison
Skull Rock Pass
Holden
Gunnison
Mayfield
Axtell
Ferron
Green River
Mack
Fruita
Haley Dome
Colorado Nat. Mon.
Grand Junction
Whitewater
Fillmore
Meadow
Kanosh
Pavant Ra.
Salina
Emery
Crescent Junction
Cisco
Sevier Lake
Desert Range
Black Rock
Sigurd
Richfield
San Rafael Knob
Arches Nat. Park
Cove Fort
Mt. Marvine
Monroe
Sevier
Koosharem
Tripton
Cathedral Valley
Capitol Reef Nat. Park
Moab
Gateway
Uncompahgre Plateau
Milford
Indian Pt.
Marysvale
Tushar Mts.
Loa
Dead Horse Point S.P.
Canyonlands National Park
La Sal Mts.
Mt. Peale
La Sal
Paradox
Escalante Valley
Beaver
Junction
Torrey
Hanksville
Minersville
Otter Creek Res.
Antimony
Blue Bell Knoll
Nucla
Naturita
Hamlin Valley
Lund
Little Salt L.
Mt. Dutton
Mt. Ellen
Henry Mountains
Norwood
Ursine
Echo Canyon S.P.
Beryl
Modena
Little Creek Pk.
Panguitch
Boulder
Cataract Canyon
Abajo Mts.
Abajo Pk.
Monticello
Egnar
Uvada
Panaca Summit
Iron Springs
Enoch
Parowan
Escalante
Escalante Canyons
Ticaboo
Beryl Jct.
Newcastle
Cedar City
Brian Head
Hatch
Ruby's Inn
Cannonville
Dove Creek
Enterprise
Old Irontown Ruins
Cedar Breaks Nat. Mon.
Natural Bridges Nat. Mon.
Lowry Ind. Ruins
Acoma
Kanaraville
Bryce Canyon Nat. Park
Glen Canyon Reservoir
Glen Canyon National Recreation Area
Blanding
Pleasant View
Pine Valley
Long Valley Jct.
Kaiparowits Plateau
Veyo
Zion Nat. Park
McPhee Res.
Lewis
Dolores
Toquerville
Orderville
Cortez
Shivwits
Santa Clara
Hurricane
Mt. Carmel Jct.
Cigarette Springs Cave
Bluff
Hovenweep Nat. Mon.
Montezuma Cr.
Aneth
Ute Pk.
Yucca House Nat. Mon.
Towaoc
Mesa Verde Nat. Park
St. George
Washington
Rockville
Ute Mountain Ind. Res.
Hildale
Kanab
Big Water
Rainbow Bridge Nat. Mon.
Navajo Mtn.
Gouldings Trading Post
Mexican Hat
Monument Valley
Mesquite
Littlefield
Colorado City
Kaibab Ind. Res.
Fredonia
Moccasin
Pipe Spring Nat. Mon.
Page
Lake Powell
Monument Pass
Monument Valley Navajo Tribal P.
Mexican Water
Teec Nos Pos
Shiprock
Bunkerville
Wolf Hole
Marble Canyon
Virgin Mountains
Kalbab Plateau
Jacob Lake
Navajo Nat. Mon.
Kayenta
Kirtland
Farmington
Mt. Trumbull
Mount Trumbull
Kaibito
Kaibito Plateau
Shonto
Marsh Pass
Tachee
Red Rock
Round Rock
Roof Butte
Grand Canyon National Park
Shivwits Plateau
Lake Mead Nat. Rec. Area
Grand Canyon
Supai
Havasupai Ind. Res.
The Gap
Red Lake
Black Mesa
Rough Rock
Yale Point
Lukachukai
Sanosti
Canyon de Chelly Nat. Mon.
Chuska Mts.
South Cove
North Rim
Tuba City
Moenkopi
Hopi Ind. Res.
Navajo Indian Reservation
Chinle
Piñon
Gd. Canyon
Sheep Springs
A 114° -7h Gr. Time B 249 113° C 112° 256 D 111° E 110° F 109° G
Scale 1 : 2,250,000
0 20 40 60 80 100 Kilometers
0 20 40 60 80 Statute Miles

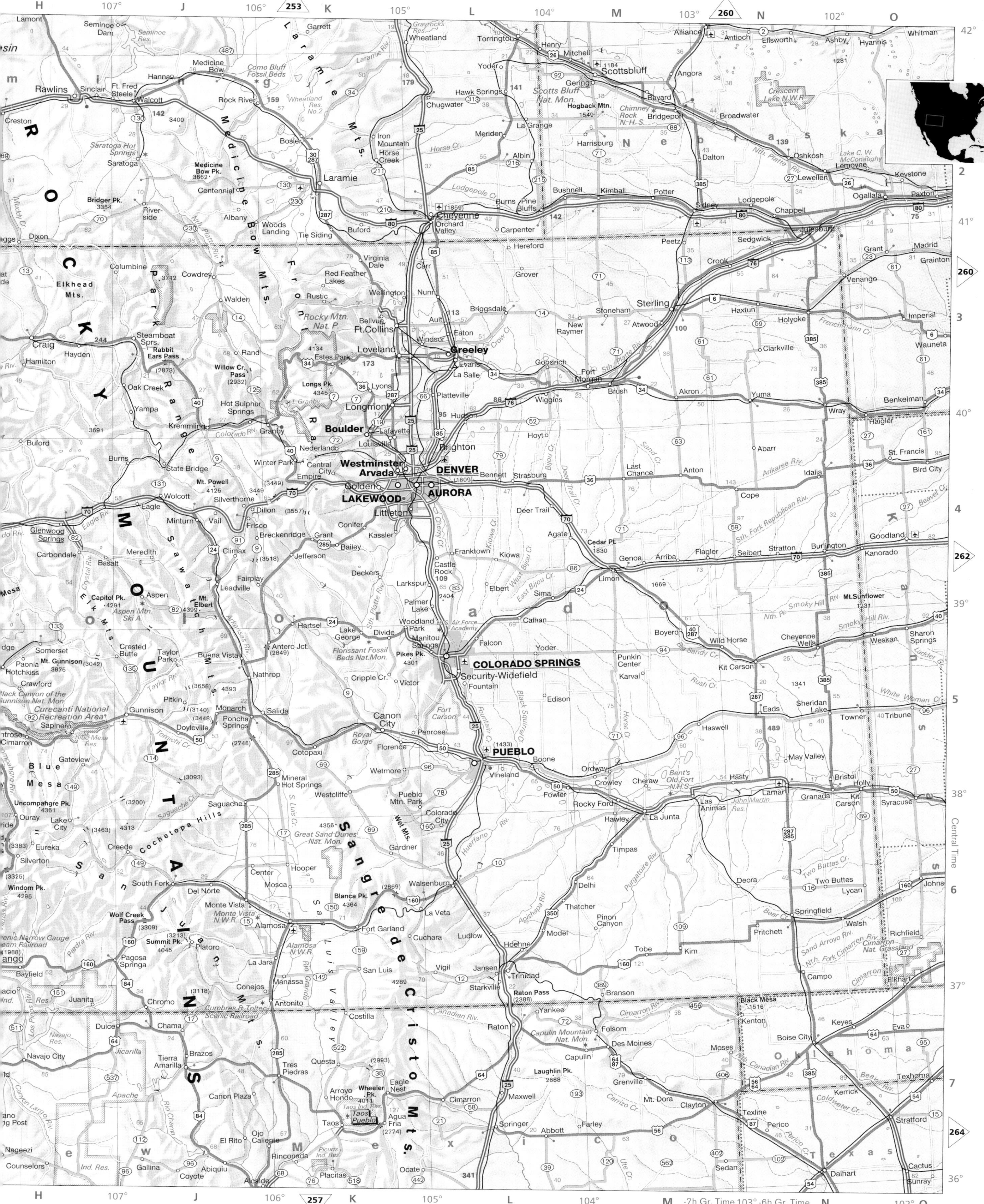

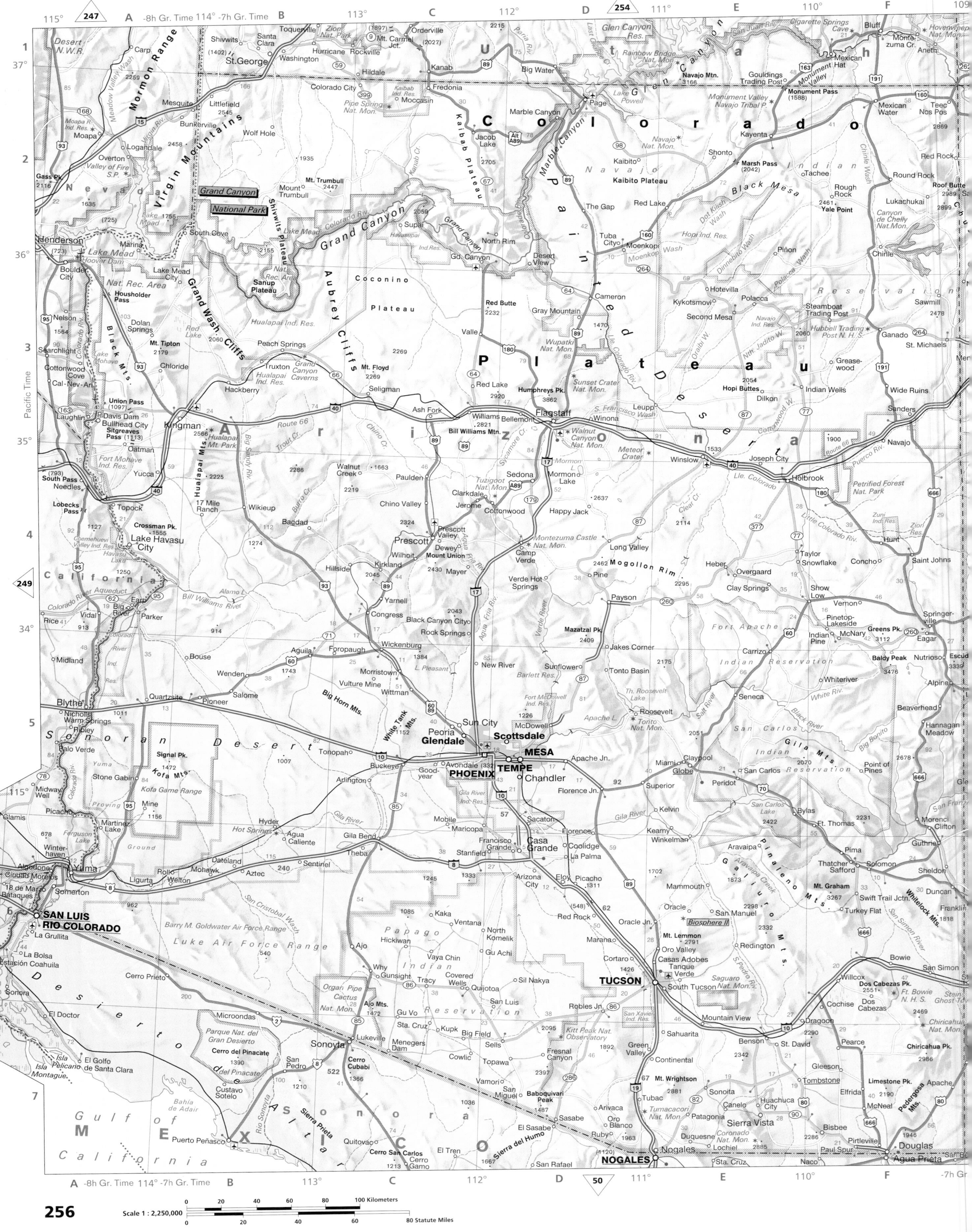

-8h Gr. Time 114° -7h Gr. Time
Utah
Colorado
Plateau
Nevada
Arizona
California
Painted Desert
Sonoran Desert
Desierto de Altar
Sonora
MEXICO
Gulf of California
Grand Canyon National Park
Grand Canyon
Glen Canyon
Glen Canyon Res.
Lake Powell
Lake Mead
Lake Mead Nat. Rec. Area
Virgin Mountains
Mormon Range
Shivwits Plateau
Kaibab Plateau
Coconino Plateau
Aubrey Cliffs
Grand Wash Cliffs
Black Mts.
Hualapai Mts.
Kaibito Plateau
Black Mesa
Navajo Indian Reservation
Hopi Ind. Res.
Hualapai Ind. Res.
Mogollon Rim
Fort Apache Indian Reservation
San Carlos Indian Reservation
Papago Indian Reservation
Luke Air Force Range
Barry M. Goldwater Air Force Range
Kofa Game Range
Big Horn Mts.
White Tank Mts.
Gila Mts.
Pinaleno Mts.
Galiuro Mts.
Whitlock Mts.
Pedregosa Mts.
Colorado Riv.
Gila River
Salt River
Verde River
Little Colorado Riv.
Bill Williams River
Pacific Time
St. George
Kanab
Fredonia
Page
Marble Canyon
Jacob Lake
North Rim
Gd. Canyon
Tuba City
Cameron
Kayenta
Mexican Hat
Bluff
Chinle
Ganado
Window Rock
Henderson
Boulder City
Kingman
Lake Havasu City
Needles
Laughlin
Bullhead City
Seligman
Williams
Flagstaff
Winslow
Holbrook
Sedona
Prescott
Cottonwood
Payson
Show Low
Springerville
Wickenburg
Parker
Quartzsite
Blythe
Yuma
Phoenix
Glendale
Peoria
Sun City
Scottsdale
MESA
TEMPE
Chandler
Gila Bend
Casa Grande
Florence
Globe
Miami
Safford
TUCSON
Nogales
NOGALES
Sierra Vista
Tombstone
Bisbee
Douglas
Agua Prieta
Benson
Willcox
Ajo
Sonoyta
Puerto Peñasco
SAN LUIS RIO COLORADO
Humphreys Pk. 3862
Mt. Trumbull 2447
Mt. Graham 3267
Mt. Lemmon 2791
Baldy Peak 3476
Mt. Wrightson 2881
Scale 1 : 2,250,000
0 20 40 60 80 100 Kilometers
0 20 40 60 80 Statute Miles

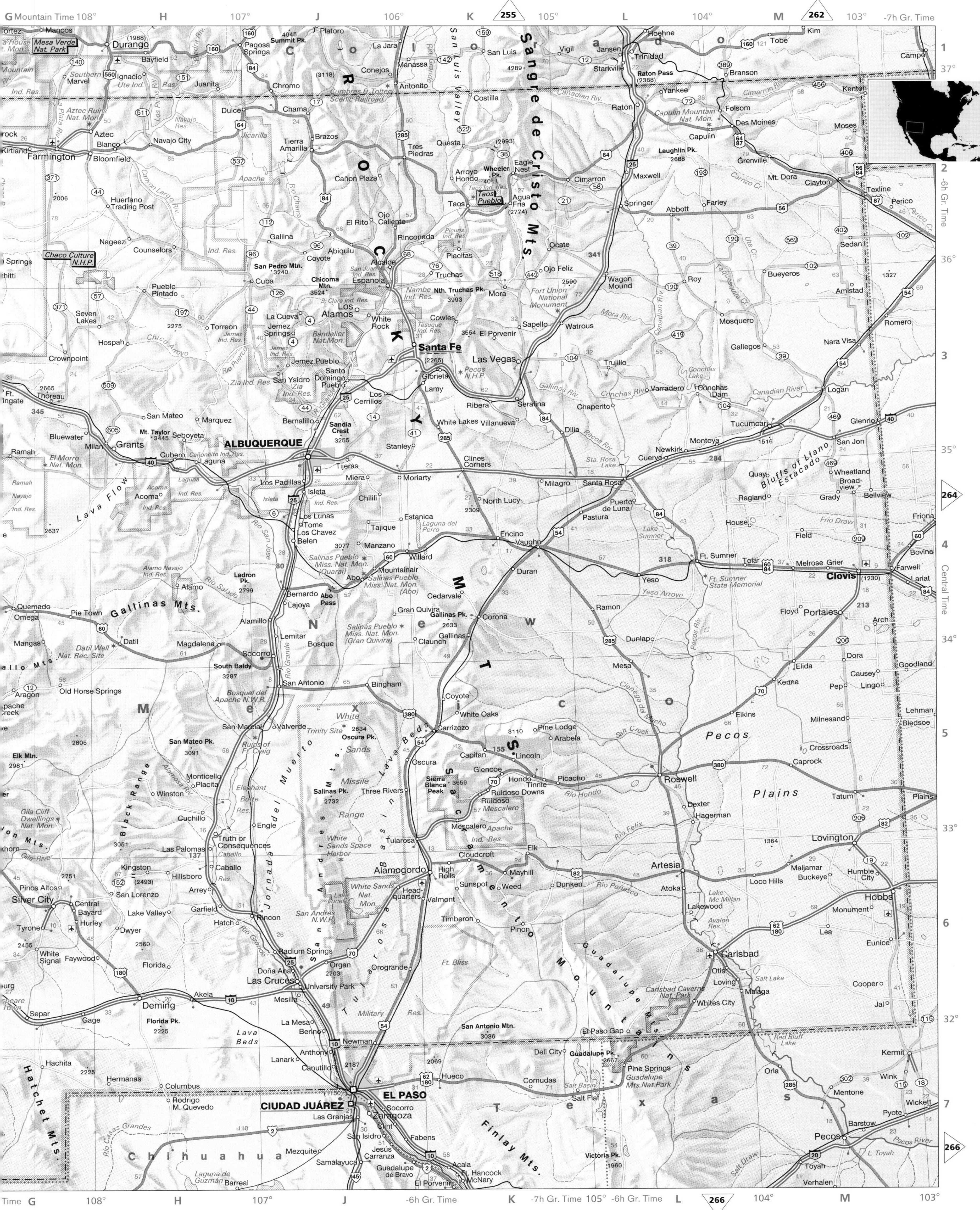

Mountain Time
108°
107°
106°
105°
104°
103°
-7h Gr. Time
-6h Gr. Time
Central Time
255
262
264
266
Durango
Mesa Verde Nat. Park
Pagosa Springs
Summit Pk.
Platoro
La Jara
San Luis
Trinidad
Hoehne
Kim
Tobe
Campo
Manassa
Conejos
Antonito
Chromo
Ignacio
Marvel
Bayfield
Juanita
Raton Pass
Branson
Starkville
Jansen
Vigil
Costilla
Cumbres & Toltec Scenic Railroad
San Luis Valley
Sangre de Cristo Mts.
Aztec Ruins Nat. Mon.
Aztec
Farmington
Kirtland
Bloomfield
Blanco
Navajo City
Dulce
Chama
Tierra Amarilla
Brazos
Tres Piedras
Questa
Raton
Yankee
Folsom
Capulin Mountain Nat. Mon.
Capulin
Des Moines
Moses
Grenville
Laughlin Pk.
Kenton
Maxwell
Mt. Dora
Clayton
Texline
Perico
Arroyo Hondo
Wheeler Pk.
Eagle Nest
Taos
Taos Pueblo
Agua Fria
Cimarron
Springer
Abbott
Farley
Cañon Plaza
Huerfano Trading Post
El Rito
Ojo Caliente
Rinconada
Placitas
Gallina
Nageezi
Counselors
Chaco Culture N.H.P.
Abiquiu
Coyote
Alcalde
Española
Truchas
Ocate
Ojo Feliz
Wagon Mound
Roy
Bueyeros
Amistad
Sedan
San Pedro Mtn.
Cuba
Chicoma Mtn.
Nth. Truchas Pk.
Mora
Fort Union National Monument
Pueblo Pintado
Seven Lakes
Torreon
La Cueva
Jemez Springs
Los Alamos
White Rock
Cowles
Sapello
Watrous
Mosquero
Romero
Hospah
Crownpoint
Bandelier Nat. Mon.
El Porvenir
Santa Fe
Las Vegas
Trujillo
Gallegos
Nara Visa
Jemez Pueblo
Santo Domingo Pueblo
San Ysidro
Zia Ind. Res.
Glorieta
Lamy
Pecos N.H.P.
Logan
Thoreau
Los Cerrillos
Ribera
Serafina
Chaperito
Varradero
Conchas Dam
Canadian River
San Mateo
Marquez
Bernalillo
Sandia Crest
White Lakes
Villanueva
Dilia
Tucumcari
Glenrio
Bluewater
Mt. Taylor
Seboyeta
Milan
Grants
ALBUQUERQUE
Stanley
Montoya
Newkirk
Cuervo
San Jon
Ramah
El Morro Nat. Mon.
Cubero
Laguna
Tijeras
Clines Corners
Sta. Rosa Lake
Bluffs of Llano Estacado
Quay
Wheatland
Broadview
Los Padillas
Miera
Moriarty
Milagro
Santa Rosa
Acoma
Isleta
Chilili
North Lucy
Puerto de Luna
Pastura
Ragland
Grady
Bellview
Lava Flow
Los Lunas
Tome
Los Chavez
Belen
Estancia
Tajique
Encino
Vaughn
Lake Sumner
House
Field
Friona
Bovina
Manzano
Willard
Ft. Sumner
Taiban
Melrose
Grier
Farwell
Clovis
Lariat
Salinas Pueblo Miss. Nat. Mon.
Mountainair
Abo
Duran
Yeso
Ft. Sumner State Memorial
Ladron Pk.
Alamo
Bernardo
Lajoya
Abo Pass
Cedarvale
Ramon
Quemado
Omega
Pie Town
Gallinas Mts.
Gran Quivira
Gallinas Pk.
Corona
Floyd
Portales
Arch
Alamillo
Lemitar
Bosque
Claunch
Dunlap
Mangas
Datil
Datil Well Nat. Rec. Site
Magdalena
Socorro
South Baldy
Mesa
Elida
Dora
Goodland
Causey
Pep
Lingo
Kenna
Aragon
Old Horse Springs
San Antonio
Bingham
Bosque del Apache N.W.R.
Coyote
White Oaks
Elkins
Lehman
Bledsoe
Milnesand
San Marcial
Valverde
Trinity Site
White Sands
Oscura Pk.
Carrizozo
Pine Lodge
Arabela
Pecos
Crossroads
Elk Mtn.
San Mateo Pk.
Capitan
Lincoln
Caprock
Oscura
Monticello
Placita
Winston
Black Range
Sierra Blanca Peak
Glencoe
Hondo
Tinnie
Picacho
Roswell
Plains
Salinas Pk.
Three Rivers
Ruidoso
Ruidoso Downs
Mescalero
Tatum
Dexter
Hagerman
Gila Cliff Dwellings Nat. Mon.
Cuchillo
Engle
Jornada del Muerto
San Andres Mts.
Missile Range
Lovington
Truth or Consequences
Las Palomas
Tularosa
Elk
Cloudcroft
Artesia
Kingston
Hillsboro
Caballo
Alamogordo
High Rolls
Mayhill
Dunken
Maljamar
Buckeye
Humble City
Pinos Altos
Silver City
San Lorenzo
Arrey
White Sands Nat. Mon.
Valmont
Sunspot
Weed
Atoka
Loco Hills
Hobbs
Central
Bayard
Hurley
Lake Valley
Garfield
Rincon
Hatch
Timberon
Pinon
Lakewood
Monument
Tyrone
Dwyer
San Andres N.W.R.
Lea
Eunice
White Signal
Faywood
Radium Springs
Florida
Doña Ana
Organ
Orogrande
Ft. Bliss
Guadalupe Mountains
Carlsbad
Otis
Loving
Malaga
Cooper
Las Cruces
University Park
Tularosa Basin
Akela
Deming
Mesilla
Carlsbad Caverns Nat. Park
Whites City
Jal
Separ
Gage
Florida Pk.
La Mesa
Berino
Military Res.
San Antonio Mtn.
El Paso Gap
Lava Beds
Newman
Red Bluff Lake
Hachita
Anthony
Lanark
Canutillo
Dell City
Guadalupe Pk.
Kermit
Hermanas
Hueco
Cornudas
Pine Springs
Guadalupe Mts. Nat. Park
Orla
Wink
Columbus
Rodrigo M. Quevedo
EL PASO
CIUDAD JUÁREZ
Socorro
Zaragoza
Salt Basin
Salt Flat
Mentone
Wickett
Pyote
Hatchet Mts.
Las Granjas
Clint
Fabens
Finlay Mts.
Barstow
Pecos
Pecos River
L. Toyah
Rio Casas Grandes
Chihuahua
Mezquite
San Isidro
Carranza
Samalayuca
Guadalupe de Bravo
Acala
Ft. Hancock
McNary
Victoria Pk.
Salt Draw
Toyah
Verhalen
Laguna de Guzmán
Barreal
El Porvenir
Texas
Colorado
Rocky Mts.
New Mexico
Oklahoma

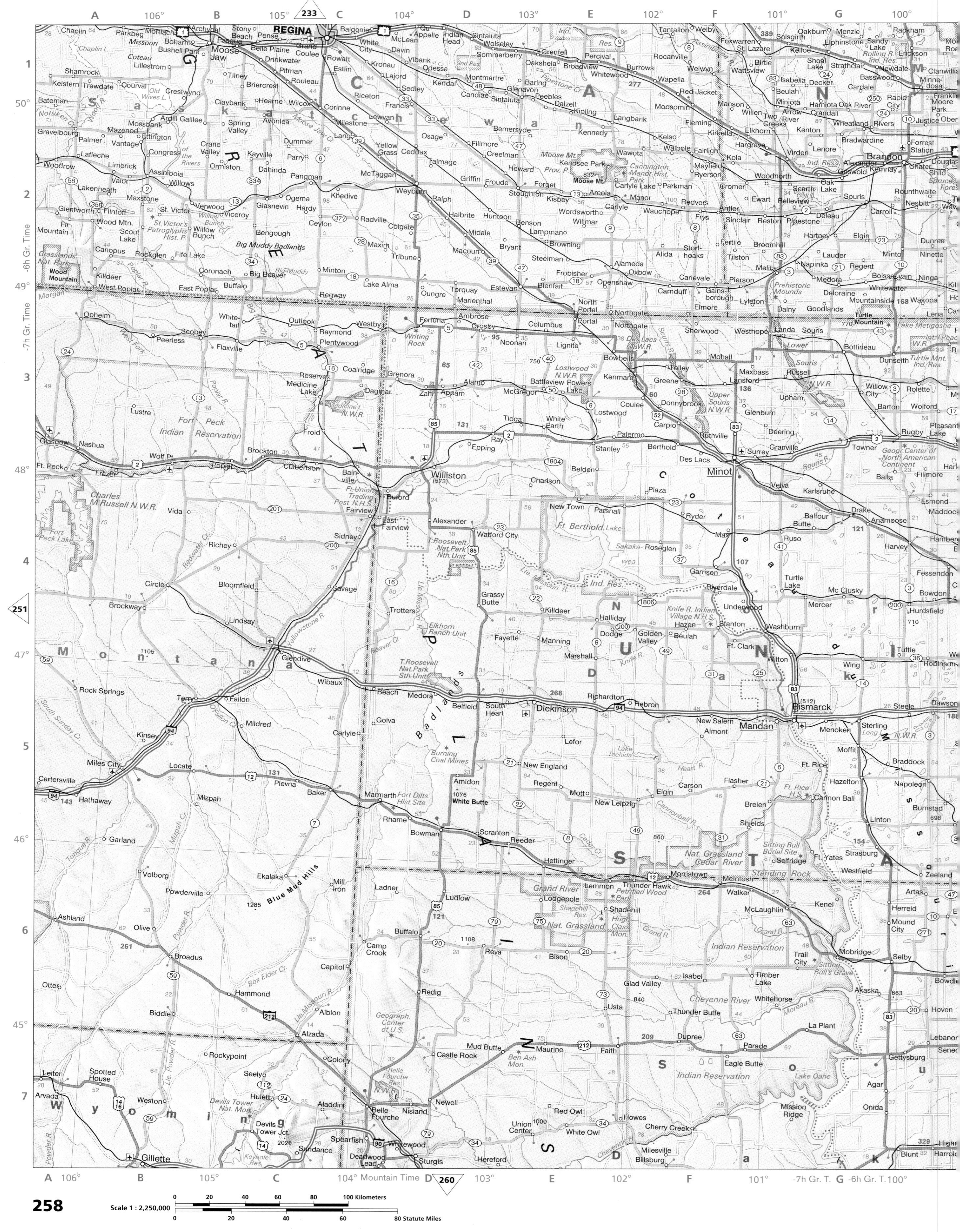

A
106°
B
105°
233
C
104°
D
103°
E
102°
F
101°
G
100°
1
2
3
4
5
6
7
50°
49°
48°
47°
46°
45°
-6h Gr. Time
-7h Gr. Time
251
REGINA
Moose Jaw
Weyburn
Estevan
Brandon
Saskatchewan
Manitoba
Minot
Williston
Bismarck
Mandan
Dickinson
Glendive
Miles City
Gillette
Belle Fourche
Spearfish
Deadwood
Lead
Sturgis
Mobridge
Glasgow
Sidney
Watford City
Big Muddy Badlands
Fort Peck Indian Reservation
Charles M.Russell N.W.R.
T.Roosevelt Nat.Park Nth.Unit
T.Roosevelt Nat.Park Sth.Unit
Badlands
Ft. Berthold Ind. Res.
Lake Sakakawea
Blue Mud Hills
Geograph. Center of U.S.
Standing Rock Indian Reservation
Cheyenne River Indian Reservation
Lake Oahe
Devils Tower Nat. Mon.
Montana
North Dakota
South Dakota
Wyoming
A
106°
B
105°
C
104° Mountain Time
D
260
103°
E
102°
F
101°
-7h Gr. T.
G
-6h Gr. T.
100°
Scale 1 : 2,250,000
0 20 40 60 80 100 Kilometers
0 20 40 60 80 Statute Miles

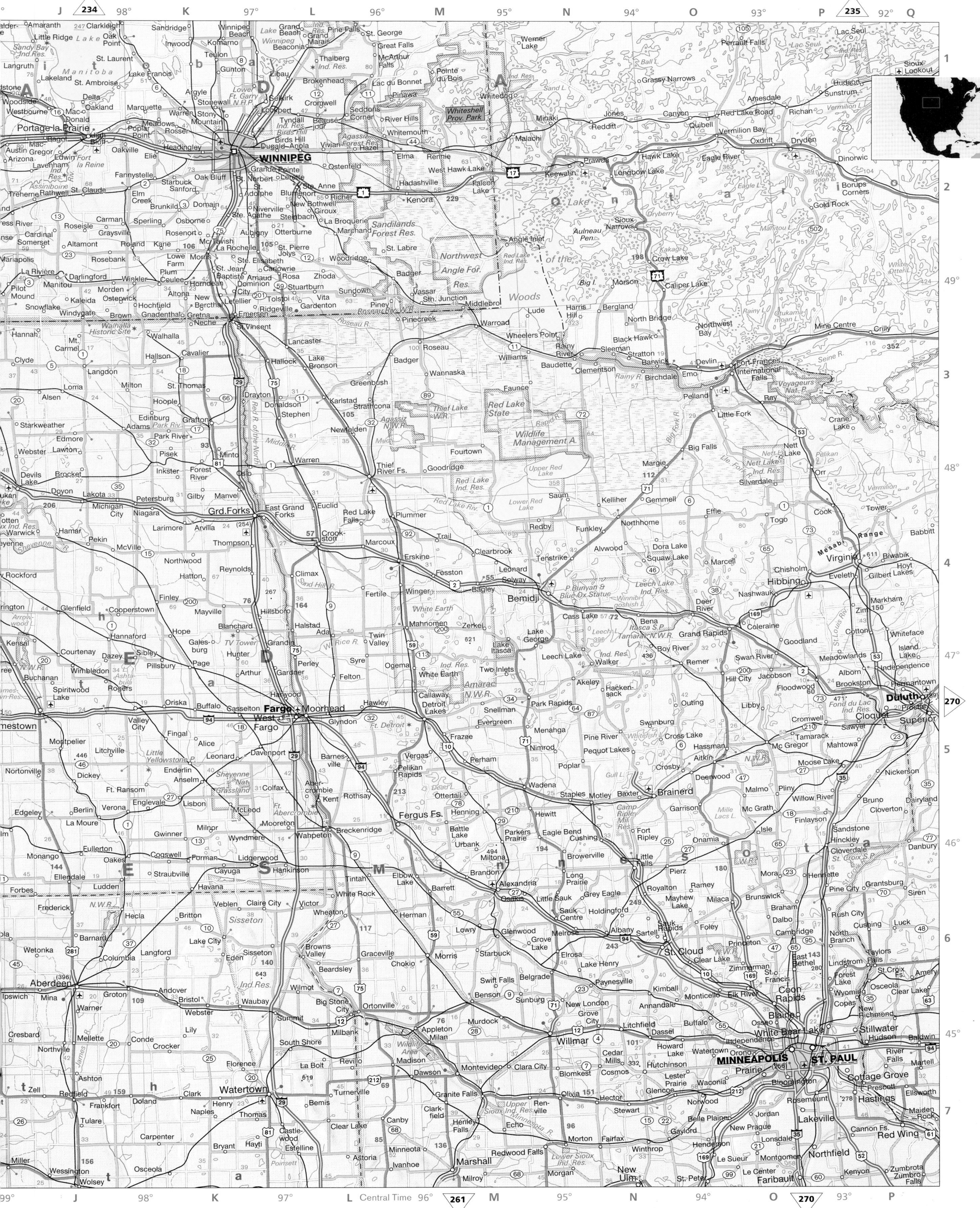
WINNIPEG
Grd.Forks
Fargo
Moorhead
Bemidji
Duluth
Superior
Brainerd
St. Cloud
MINNEAPOLIS
ST. PAUL
Aberdeen
Watertown
Willmar
Marshall
Alexandria
Fergus Fs.
Wahpeton
Thief River Fs.
International Falls
Kenora
Hibbing
Virginia
Grand Rapids
Central Time

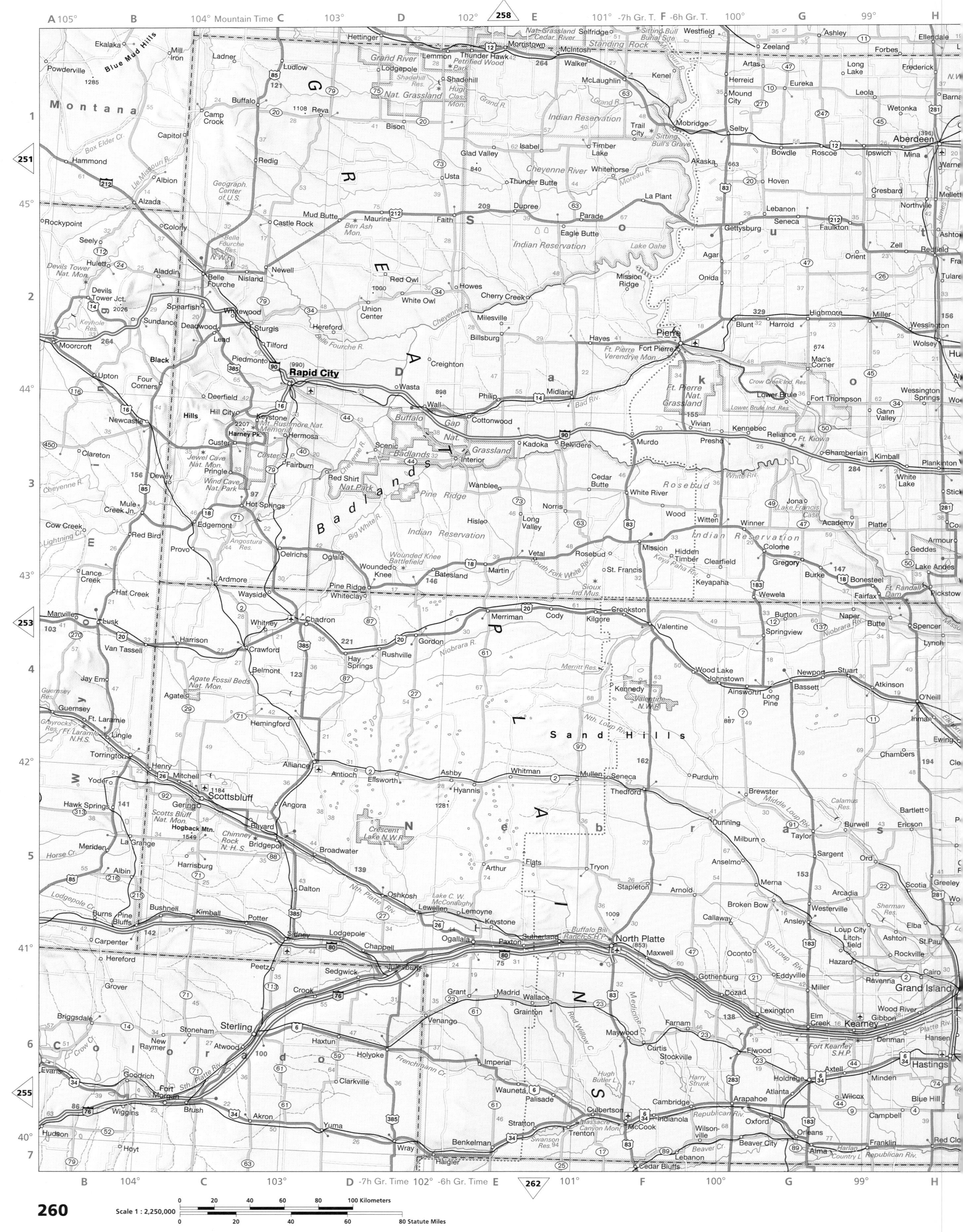

A 105° B 104° Mountain Time C 103° D 102° 258 E 101° -7h Gr. T. F -6h Gr. T. 100° G 99° H
Montana
Ekalaka
Blue Mud Hills
Mill Iron
Powderville
Ladner
Ludlow
Hettinger
Lemmon
Thunder Hawk
Morristown
McIntosh
Nat. Grassland Cedar River
Selfridge
Sitting Bull Burial Site
Westfield
Zeeland
Ashley
Ellendale
Grand River
Lodgepole
Petrified Wood Park
Shadehill Res.
Shadehill
Hugh Glass Mon.
Nat. Grassland
Standing Rock
Walker
McLaughlin
Kenel
Herreid
Artas
Eureka
Long Lake
Forbes
Frederick
Leola
Mound City
Wetonka
Barnard
Buffalo
Camp Crook
Reva
Bison
Indian Reservation
Trail City
Sitting Bull's Grave
Mobridge
Selby
Aberdeen
Capitol
Box Elder Cr.
Hammond
Redig
Isabel
Timber Lake
Glad Valley
Akaska
Bowdle
Roscoe
Ipswich
Mina
Warner
Albion
Alzada
Geograph. Center of U.S.
Usta
Cheyenne River
Whitehorse
Thunder Butte
Moreau R.
Hoven
Cresbard
Mellette
Rockypoint
Colony
Castle Rock
Mud Butte
Maurine
Ben Ash Mon.
Faith
Dupree
La Plant
Parade
Eagle Butte
Lebanon
Gettysburg
Seneca
Faulkton
Northville
Ashton
Seely
Hulett
Devils Tower Nat. Mon.
Belle Fourche Res.
Indian Reservation
Lake Oahe
Agar
Orient
Zell
Redfield
Aladdin
Belle Fourche
Nisland
Newell
Red Owl
Mission Ridge
Onida
Tulare
Devils Tower Jct.
White Owl
Howes
Cherry Creek
Spearfish
Whitewood
Sundance
Deadwood
Sturgis
Keyhole Res.
Union Center
Hereford
Milesville
Cheyenne R.
Belle Fourche R.
Highmore
Miller
Blunt
Harrold
Wessington
Moorcroft
Lead
Tilford
Billsburg
Hayes
Pierre
Fort Pierre
Ft. Pierre Verendrye Mon.
Wolsey
Black
Piedmont
Rapid City
Creighton
Mac's Corner
Upton
Four Corners
Wasta
Ft. Pierre Nat. Grassland
Crow Creek Ind. Res.
Lower Brule
Fort Thompson
Wessington Springs
Deerfield
Philip
Midland
Bad Riv.
Lower Brule Ind. Res.
Gann Valley
Newcastle
Hill City
Keystone
Mt. Rushmore Nat. Memorial
Wall
Cottonwood
Buffalo Gap Nat. Grassland
Vivian
Kennebec
Reliance
Ft. Kiowa
Hills
Harney Pk.
Custer
Hermosa
Kadoka
Belvidere
Murdo
Presho
Chamberlain
Kimball
Plankinton
Clareton
Jewel Cave Nat. Mon.
Custer S.P.
Scenic
Badlands
Interior
Grassland
Pringle
Fairburn
Red Shirt
Nat. Park
White Riv.
Rosebud
White Lake
Cheyenne R.
Dewey
Wind Cave Nat. Park
Cedar Butte
White River
Mule Creek Jn.
Hot Springs
Wanblee
Pine Ridge
Norris
Jona
Lake Francis Case
Stickney
Cow Creek
Edgemont
Badlands
Long Valley
Wood
Witten
Winner
Academy
Platte
Lightning Cr.
Red Bird
Angostura Res.
Big White R.
Hisle
Indian Reservation
Indian Reservation
Armour
Provo
Oelrichs
Oglala
Wounded Knee Battlefield
Vetal
Rosebud
Mission
Hidden Timber
Colome
Geddes
Lance Creek
Ardmore
Wounded Knee
Batesland
Martin
South Fork White Riv.
St. Francis
Keya Paha Riv.
Clearfield
Gregory
Burke
Bonesteel
Lake Andes
Hat Creek
Wayside
Pine Ridge
Whiteclay
Sioux Ind. Mus.
Keyapaha
Wewela
Ft. Randall Dam
Fairfax
Pickstown
Manville
Lusk
Whitney
Chadron
Merriman
Cody
Crookston
Kilgore
Valentine
Burton
Naper
Niobrara Riv.
Butte
Spencer
Harrison
Van Tassell
Crawford
Hay Springs
Rushville
Gordon
Niobrara R.
Springview
Lynch
Belmont
Merritt Res.
Wood Lake
Johnstown
Newport
Stuart
Atkinson
Jay Em
Agate Fossil Beds Nat. Mon.
Agate
Kennedy
Valentine N.W.R.
Ainsworth
Long Pine
Bassett
O'Neill
Guernsey Res.
Guernsey
Ft. Laramie
Grayrocks Res.
Ft. Laramie N.H.S.
Lingle
Hemingford
Nth. Loup Riv.
Sand Hills
Inman
Ewing
Torrington
Henry
Mitchell
Alliance
Antioch
Ellsworth
Ashby
Whitman
Mullen
Seneca
Purdum
Chambers
Yoder
Scottsbluff
Gering
Hyannis
Thedford
Brewster
Calamus Res.
Bartlett
Hawk Springs
Scotts Bluff Nat. Mon.
Angora
Hogback Mtn.
Bayard
Chimney Rock N.H.S.
Bridgeport
Crescent Lake N.W.R.
Dunning
Middle Loup Riv.
Burwell
Ericson
Horse Cr.
Meriden
La Grange
Broadwater
Milburn
Taylor
Harrisburg
Albin
Arthur
Flats
Tryon
Anselmo
Sargent
Ord
Lodgepole Cr.
Dalton
Stapleton
Arnold
Merna
Arcadia
Scotia
Greeley
Burns
Pine Bluffs
Bushnell
Kimball
Potter
Oshkosh
Nth. Platte Riv.
Lake C. W. McConaughy
Lewellen
Lemoyne
Keystone
Broken Bow
Callaway
Westerville
Sherman Res.
Ansley
Loup City
Litchfield
Elba
Ashton
St. Paul
Carpenter
Sidney
Lodgepole
Chappell
Ogallala
Paxton
Sutherland
Buffalo Bill Ranch S.H.P.
North Platte
Maxwell
Oconto
Sth. Loup Riv.
Hazard
Rockville
Hereford
Peetz
Julesburg
Sedgwick
Gothenburg
Eddyville
Ravenna
Cairo
Grand Island
Grover
Crook
Grant
Madrid
Wallace
Grainton
Medicine C.
Cozad
Miller
Lexington
Elm Creek
Kearney
Wood River
Gibbon
Briggsdale
Stoneham
Sterling
Venango
Red Willow C.
Farnam
Maywood
Platte Riv.
Denman
Hansen
New Raymer
Atwood
Haxtun
Holyoke
Frenchman Cr.
Imperial
Curtis
Stockville
Elwood
Fort Kearney S.H.P.
Hastings
Crow Cr.
Colorado
Evans
Goodrich
Sth. Platte Riv.
Fort Morgan
Clarkville
Wauneta
Palisade
Hugh Butler L.
Harry Strunk L.
Holdrege
Axtell
Minden
Atlanta
Wilcox
Blue Hill
Wiggins
Brush
Akron
Yuma
Culbertson
Massacre Canyon Mon.
McCook
Indianola
Cambridge
Arapahoe
Republican Riv.
Campbell
Hudson
Stratton
Trenton
Swanson Res.
Wilsonville
Oxford
Orleans
Beaver Cr.
Beaver City
Benkelman
Wray
Haigler
Lebanon
Alma
Harlan Country L.
Republican Riv.
Franklin
Red Cloud
Hoyt
Cedar Bluffs
B 104° C 103° D -7h Gr. Time 102° -6h Gr. Time E 262 101° F 100° G 99° H
Scale 1 : 2,250,000
0 20 40 60 80 100 Kilometers
0 20 40 60 80 Statute Miles

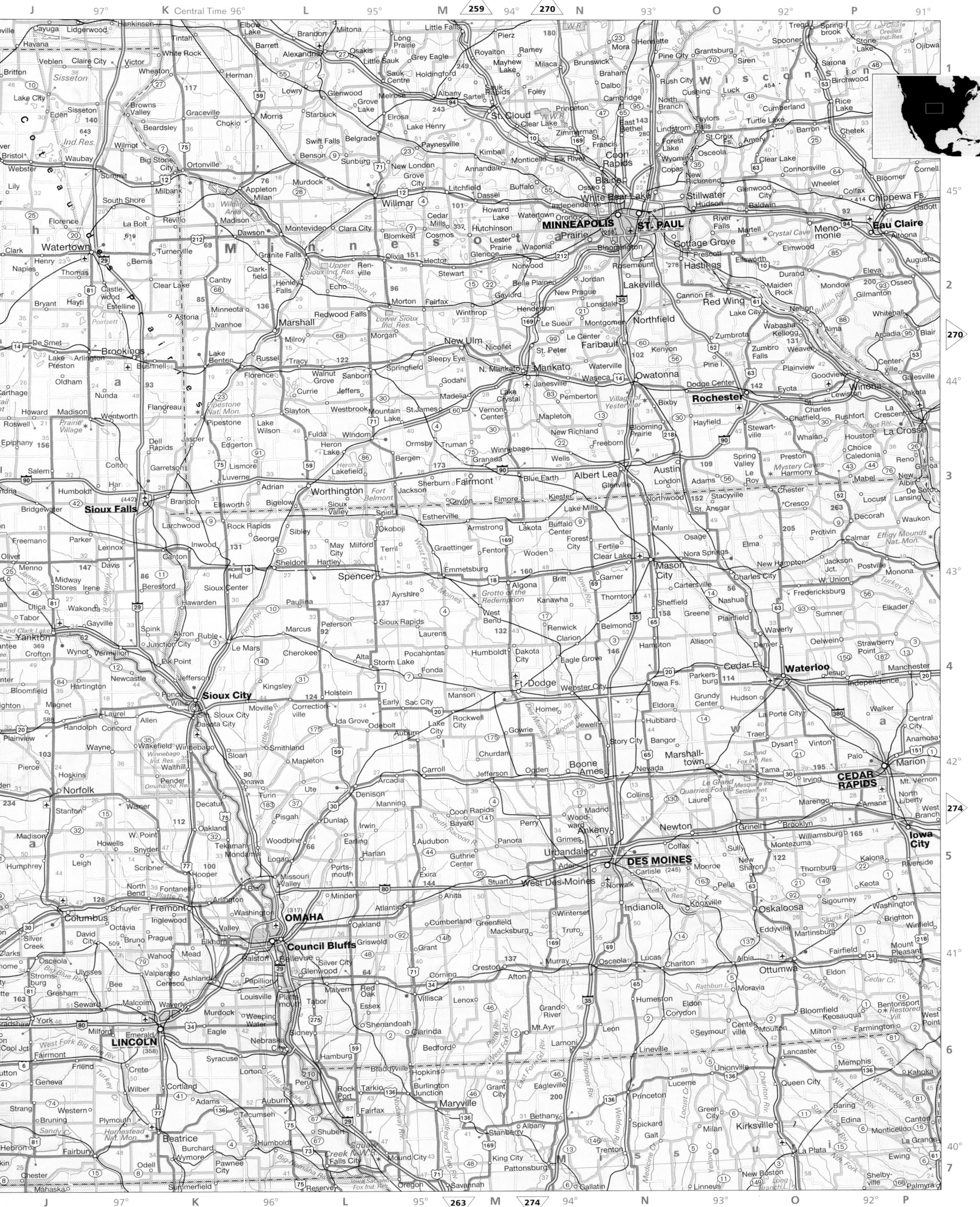
J
97°
K Central Time 96°
L
95°
M
259
94°
270
N
93°
O
92°
P
91°
MINNEAPOLIS
ST. PAUL
Rochester
Eau Claire
Sioux Falls
Sioux City
Waterloo
CEDAR RAPIDS
DES MOINES
OMAHA
Council Bluffs
LINCOLN
Iowa City
263
274
270
274
40°
41°
42°
43°
44°
45°

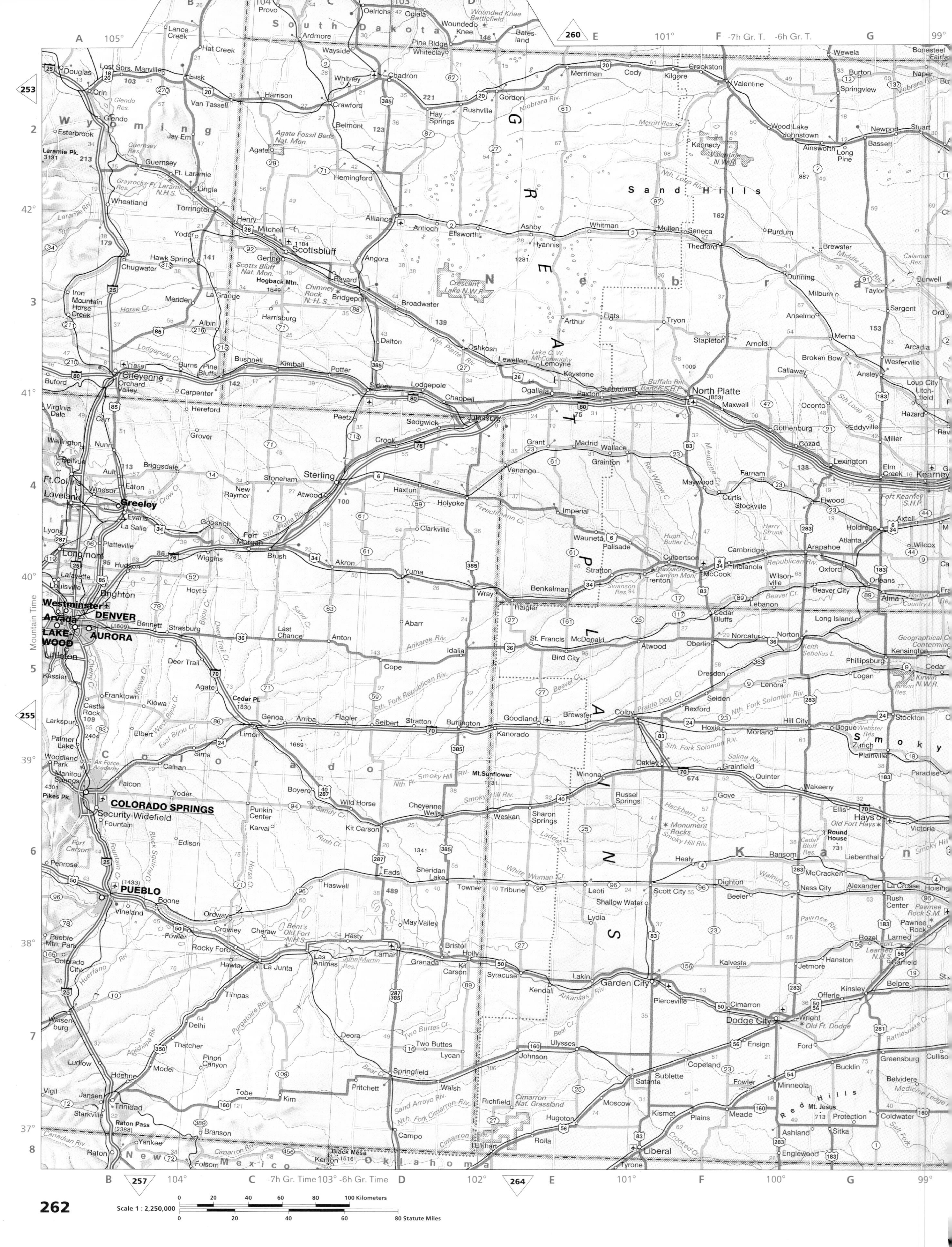

Scale 1 : 2,250,000

0 20 40 60 80 100 Kilometers

0 20 40 60 80 Statute Miles

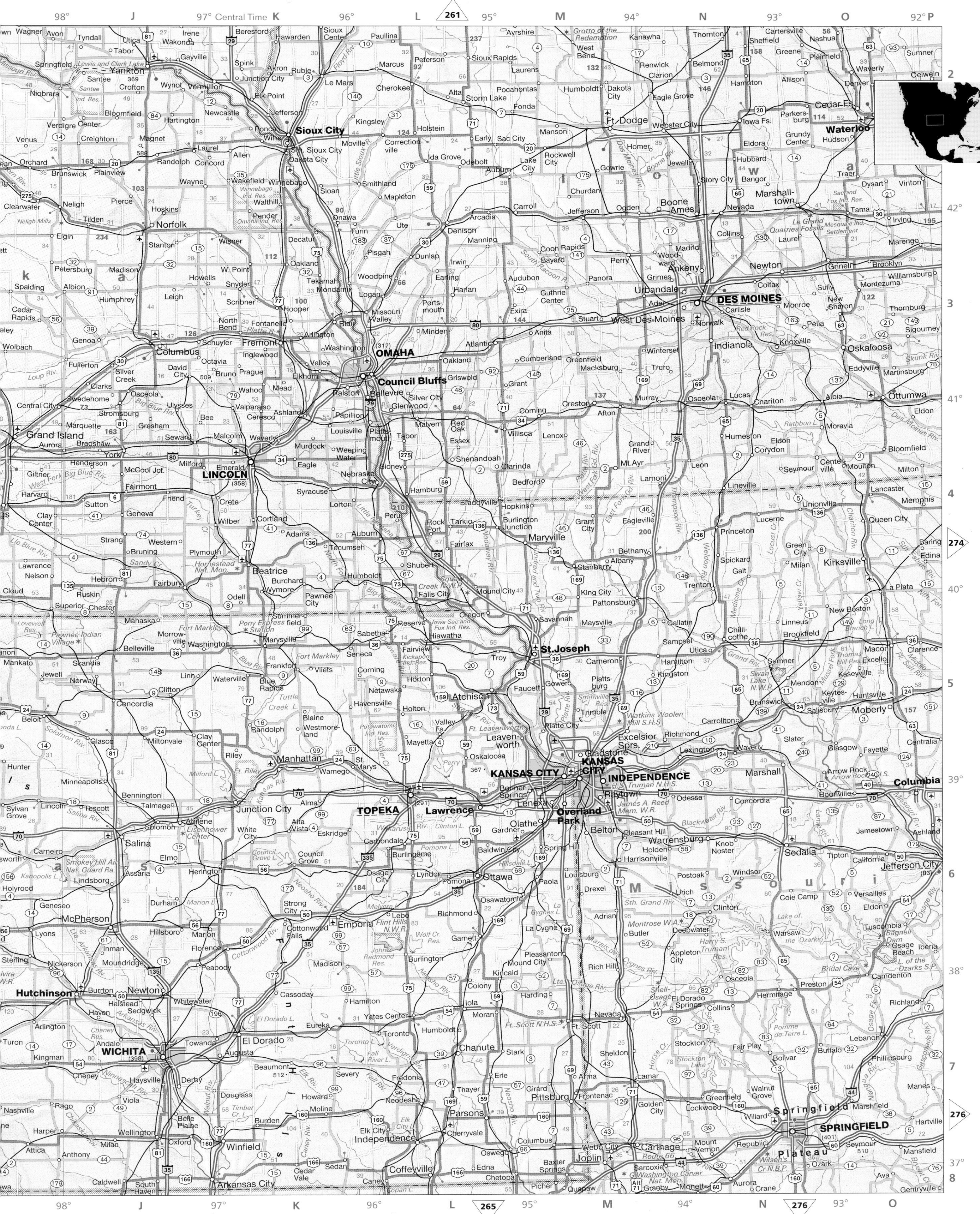
97° Central Time
261
274
276
265
Sioux City
OMAHA
Council Bluffs
LINCOLN
DES MOINES
West Des Moines
Waterloo
Grand Island
Columbus
Fremont
Norfolk
St.Joseph
KANSAS CITY
KANSAS CITY
INDEPENDENCE
Overland Park
TOPEKA
Lawrence
WICHITA
Hutchinson
Salina
Manhattan
Emporia
SPRINGFIELD
Springfield
Columbia
Jefferson City
Joplin
Ottumwa
Ames
Ft. Dodge

255

257

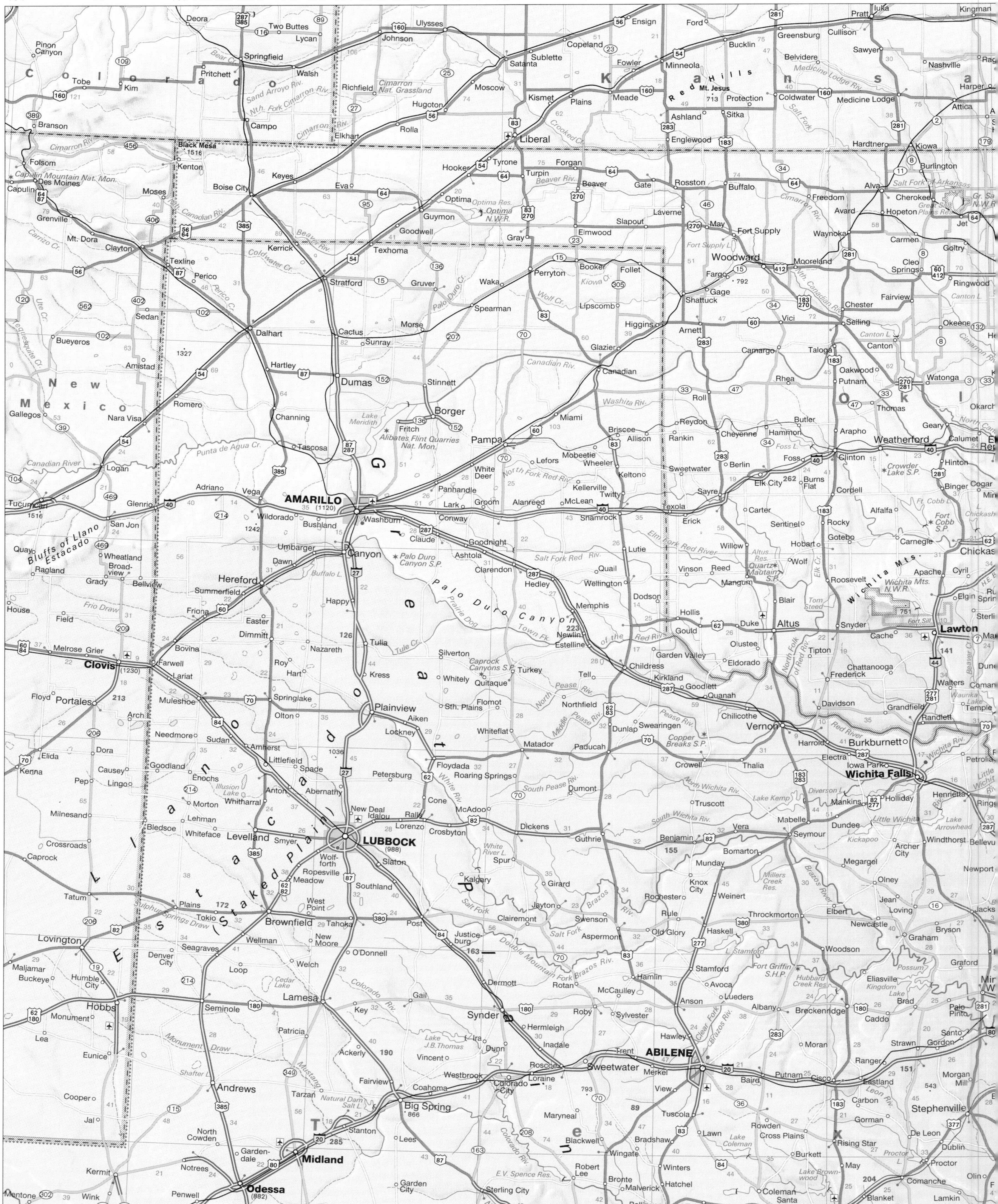

Colorado

Kansas

New Mexico

Oklahoma

Texas

Llano Estacado (Staked Plain)

Great Plains

Bluffs of Llano Estacado

Red Hills

Wichita Mts.

Deora, Two Buttes, Lycan, Ulysses, Johnson, Ensign, Ford, Pratt, Iuka, Kingman, Greensburg, Cullison, Pinon Canyon, Springfield, Copeland, Sublette, Satanta, Fowler, Minneola, Bucklin, Sawyer, Nashville, Pritchett, Walsh, Belvidere, Medicine Lodge Riv., Tobe, Kim, Richfield, Cimarron Nat. Grassland, Moscow, Kismet, Plains, Meade, Mt. Jesus 713, Protection, Coldwater, Medicine Lodge, Harper, Bear Cr., Sand Arroyo Riv., Nth. Fork Cimarron Riv., Hugoton, Ashland, Sitka, Attica

Branson, Campo, Elkhart, Rolla, Liberal, Englewood, Crooked Cr., Salt Fork, Kiowa, Hardtner, Cimarron Riv., Black Mesa 1516, Folsom, Kenton, Hooker, Tyrone, Forgan, Capulin Mountain Nat. Mon., Capulin, Des Moines, Moses, Boise City, Keyes, Eva, Turpin, Beaver, Gate, Rosston, Buffalo, Freedom, Alva, Burlington, Cherokee, Salt Fork of Arkansas, Great Salt Plains N.W.R., Optima, Optima Res., Optima N.W.R., Guymon, Laverne, Avard, Hopeton, Grenville, Nth. Canadian Riv., Slapout, May, Fort Supply, Waynoka, Jet, Mt. Dora, Clayton, Kerrick, Goodwell, Gray, Elmwood, Fort Supply L., Carmen, Goltry, Carrizo Cr., Beaver Riv., Texhoma, Coldwater Cr., Woodward, Mooreland, Cleo Springs, Ringwood

Texline, Perico, Stratford, Gruver, Waka, Perryton, Booker, Follet, Fargo 792, Gage, Shattuck, Fairview, Canton L., Chester, Seiling, Ute Cr., Sedan, Palo Duro Cr., Spearman, Wolf Cr., Lipscomb, Vici, Okeene, Bueyeros, Dalhart, Cactus, Sunray, Morse, Higgins, Arnett, Canton, Amistad, 1327, Glazier, Camargo, Taloga, Hartley, Dumas, Stinnett, Canadian, Canadian Riv., Rhea, Oakwood, Putnam, Watonga, Romero, Gallegos, Nara Visa, Channing, Lake Meridith, Borger, Fritch, Alibates Flint Quarries Nat. Mon., Miami, Roll, Washita Riv., Thomas, Okarche, Geary, Reydon, Cheyenne, Hammon, Butler, Arapho, Weatherford, Calumet, Tascosa, Pampa, Briscoe, Allison, Rankin, Foss L., Foss, Clinton, Hinton, Punta de Agua Cr., Canadian River, Logan, White Deer, Lefors, Mobeetie, Wheeler, Sweetwater, Berlin, Crowder Lake S.P., Tucumcari 1516, Adrian, Vega, Amarillo (1120), Panhandle, Kelton, Elk City, Burns Flat, Binger, Glenrio, Wildorado, Washburn, Lark, Groom, Alanreed, McLean, Kellerville, Twitty, Sayre, Cordell, Alfalfa, Ft. Cobb L., San Jon, Bushland, Conway, Shamrock, Texola, Erick, Carter, Sentinel, Rocky, Ft. Cobb S.P., Quay, Wheatland, Broadview, 1242, Claude, Goodnight, Gotebo, Carnegie, Chickasha, Ragland, Umbarger, Canyon, Palo Duro Canyon S.P., Ashtola, Lutie, Willow, Hobart, Grady, Bellview, Dawn, Clarendon, Salt Fork Red Riv., Elm Fork Red River, Altus Res., Quartz Mountain S.P., Wolf, Hereford, Buffalo L., Hedley, Quail, Vinson, Reed, Mangum, Roosevelt, Apache, Cyril, Summerfield, Wellington, Dodson, Wichita Mts. N.W.R., Elgin, House, Field, Frio Draw, Friona, Happy, Palo Duro Canyon, Prairie Dog Town Fk., Memphis, Hollis, Blair, Tom Steed, Easter, Dimmitt, Newlin, Estelline, Gould, Duke, Altus, Snyder, Lawton, Fort Sill, Melrose, Grier, Clovis (1230), Bovina, Nazareth, Tulia, Tule Cr., Silverton, Garden Valley, Olustee, Eldorado, Tipton, Cache, Farwell, Lariat, Roy, Hart, Kress, Caprock Canyons S.P., Turkey, Childress, Kirkland, Goodlett, Chattanooga, Frederick, Walters, Quitaque, Tell, Quanah, Portales, Floyd, Muleshoe, Springlake, Whitely, Flomot, Pease Riv., Northfield, Chilicothe, Davidson, Grandfield, Temple, Randlett

Arch, Olton, Plainview, Aiken, Sth. Plains, Whiteflat, Dunlap, Swearingen, Vernon, Burkburnett, Needmore, Sudan, Amherst, Lockney, Matador, Paducah, Copper Breaks S.P., Harrold, Elida, Dora, Littlefield, Spade, 1036, Floydada, Roaring Springs, Crowell, Thalia, Electra, Iowa Park, Wichita Falls, Petrolia, Kenna, Causey, Goodland, Enochs, Lingo, Pep, Illusion Lake, Anton, Abernathy, Petersburg, White Riv., South Pease Riv., Dumont, North Wichita Riv., Henrietta, Morton, Whitharral, Cone, Truscott, Lake Kemp, Diversion L., Mankins, Holliday, Milnesand, Lehman, New Deal, Idalou, Ralls, McAdoo, Mabelle, Dundee, Little Wichita, Lake Arrowhead, Bledsoe, Whiteface, Levelland, Smyer, Lubbock (988), Lorenzo, Crosbyton, Dickens, Guthrie, Benjamin, Vera, Seymour, Kickapoo, Windthorst, Bellevue, Crossroads, Caprock, Wolfforth, Slaton, White River L., Spur, Bomarton, Munday, Archer City, Megargel, Newport, Ropesville, Meadow, Kalgary, Girard, Millers Creek Res., Knox City, Weinert, Olney, Tatum, Plains, Southland, West Point, Jayton, Swenson, Rochester, Jean, Loving, Jacksboro, Tokio, Sulphur Springs Draw, Brownfield, Tahoka, Post, Clairemont, Aspermont, Rule, Throckmorton, Elbert, Newcastle, Bryson, Lovington, Wellman, New Moore, Justiceburg, Salt Fork, Old Glory, Haskell, Graham, Seagraves, Denver City, O'Donnell, Double Mountain Fork Brazos Riv., Stamford, Woodson, Maljamar, Buckeye, Humble City, Welch, Loop, Dermott, Rotan, Hamlin, Fort Griffin S.H.P., Hubbard Creek Res., Possum Kingdom Lake, Graford, Eliasville, Cedar Lake, Lamesa, Gail, McCaulley, Avoca, Lueders, Hobbs, Monument, Seminole, Key, Colorado Riv., Snyder, Roby, Sylvester, Anson, Albany, Breckenridge, Brad, Palo Pinto, Caddo, Lea, Patricia, Monument Draw, Hermleigh, Hawley, Clear Fork Brazos Riv., Mineral Wells, Eunice, Ackerly, Lake J.B. Thomas, Ira, Dunn, Inadale, Moran, Strawn, Santo, Gordon, Vincent, Roscoe, Trent, Abilene, Ranger, Shafter L., Andrews, Mustang Draw, Fairview, Westbrook, Colorado City, Loraine, Sweetwater, Merkel, Baird, Putnam, Cisco, Eastland, Morgan Mill, Tarzan, Natural Dam Salt L., Coahoma, Big Spring 866, 793, View, Carbon, Leon Riv., Cooper, Maryneal, Tuscola, Gorman, Stephenville, Jal, Stanton, Blackwell, Bradshaw, Rowden, Cross Plains, De Leon, North Cowden, Lees, Lawn, Lake Coleman, Rising Star, Dublin, Gardendale, Midland, Wingate, Winters, Burkett, Proctor L., Proctor, Kermit, Notrees, E.V. Spence Res., Robert Lee, Lake Brownwood, May, Olin, Odessa (882), Garden City, Bronte, Malverick, Hatchel, Coleman, Santa Anna, Comanche, Mentone, Wink, Penwell, Sterling City, North Concho Riv., Water Valley, Ballinger, Tennyson, Talpa, Valera, Early, Blanket, Lamkin, Pecos Riv., Wickett, Monahans, Midkiff, Rowena, Voss, Bangs, Brownwood, Zephyr, Priddy

Scale 1 : 2,250,000

0 20 40 60 80 100 Kilometers

0 20 40 60 80 Statute Miles

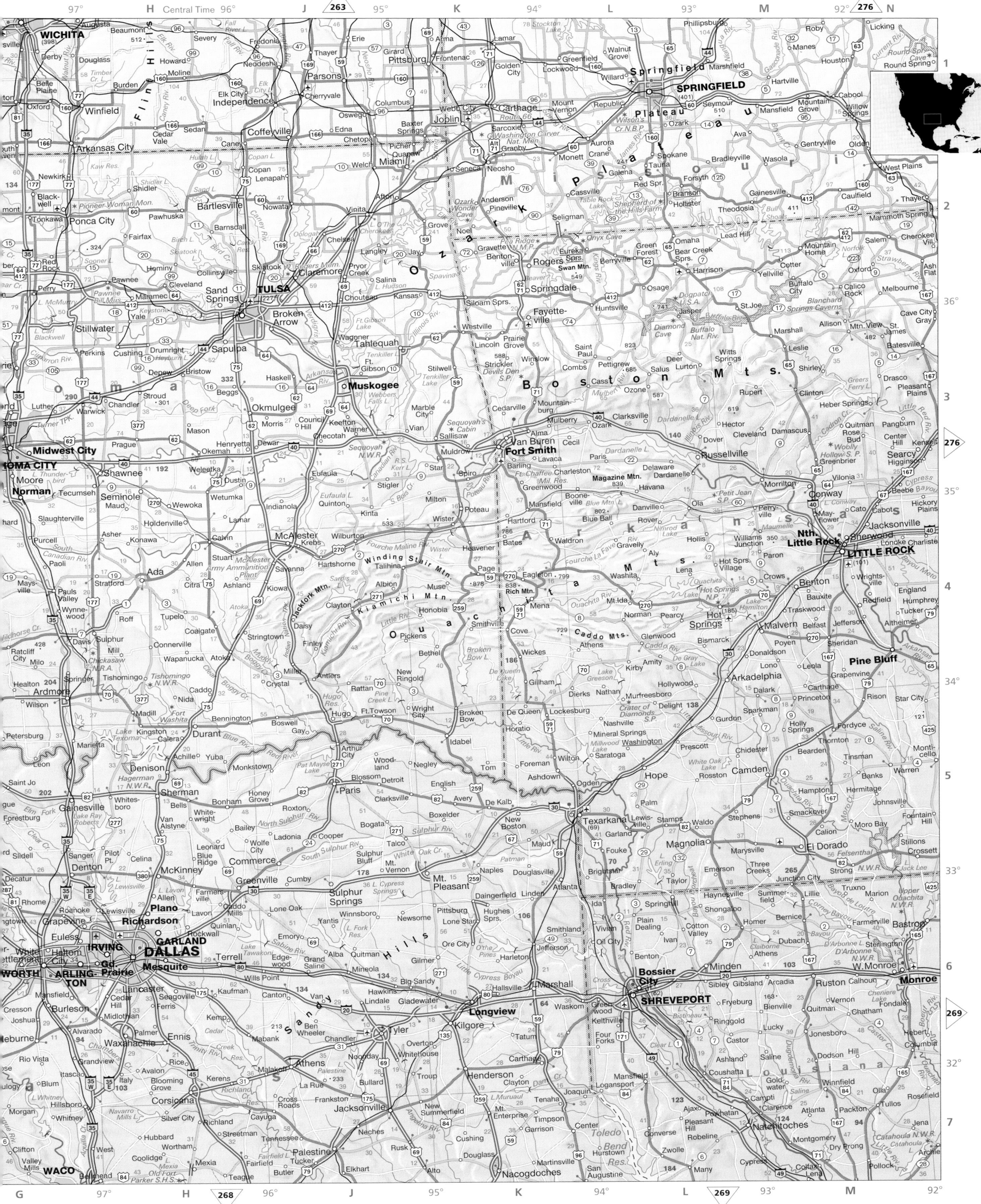
Central Time
WICHITA
Springfield
SPRINGFIELD
Joplin
Independence
Coffeyville
Arkansas City
Bartlesville
Ponca City
TULSA
Broken Arrow
Stillwater
Sapulpa
Muskogee
Okmulgee
Tahlequah
Fayetteville
Springdale
Rogers
Fort Smith
Van Buren
Midwest City
OKLAHOMA CITY
Norman
Shawnee
Seminole
McAlester
Ada
Ardmore
Durant
Denison
Sherman
Paris
Texarkana
Hope
Hot Springs
Nth. Little Rock
LITTLE ROCK
Pine Bluff
El Dorado
Magnolia
Camden
Arkadelphia
Russellville
Conway
Jacksonville
Ozark Plateau
Boston Mts.
Ouachita Mts.
Winding Stair Mtn.
Kiamichi Mtn.
Arkansas
Missouri
Oklahoma
Gainesville
Denton
McKinney
Plano
Richardson
Garland
IRVING
DALLAS
Mesquite
Gd. Prairie
ARLINGTON
FORT WORTH
Waxahachie
Corsicana
WACO
Greenville
Sulphur Springs
Mt. Pleasant
Tyler
Longview
Kilgore
Marshall
Bossier City
SHREVEPORT
Minden
Ruston
Monroe
W. Monroe
Natchitoches
Nacogdoches
Palestine
Jacksonville
Athens
Henderson
Louisiana
Texas
Sandy Hills
263
276
268
269
97°
96°
95°
94°
93°
92°
36°
35°
34°
33°
32°
G
H
J
K
L
M
N
1
2
3
4
5
6
7

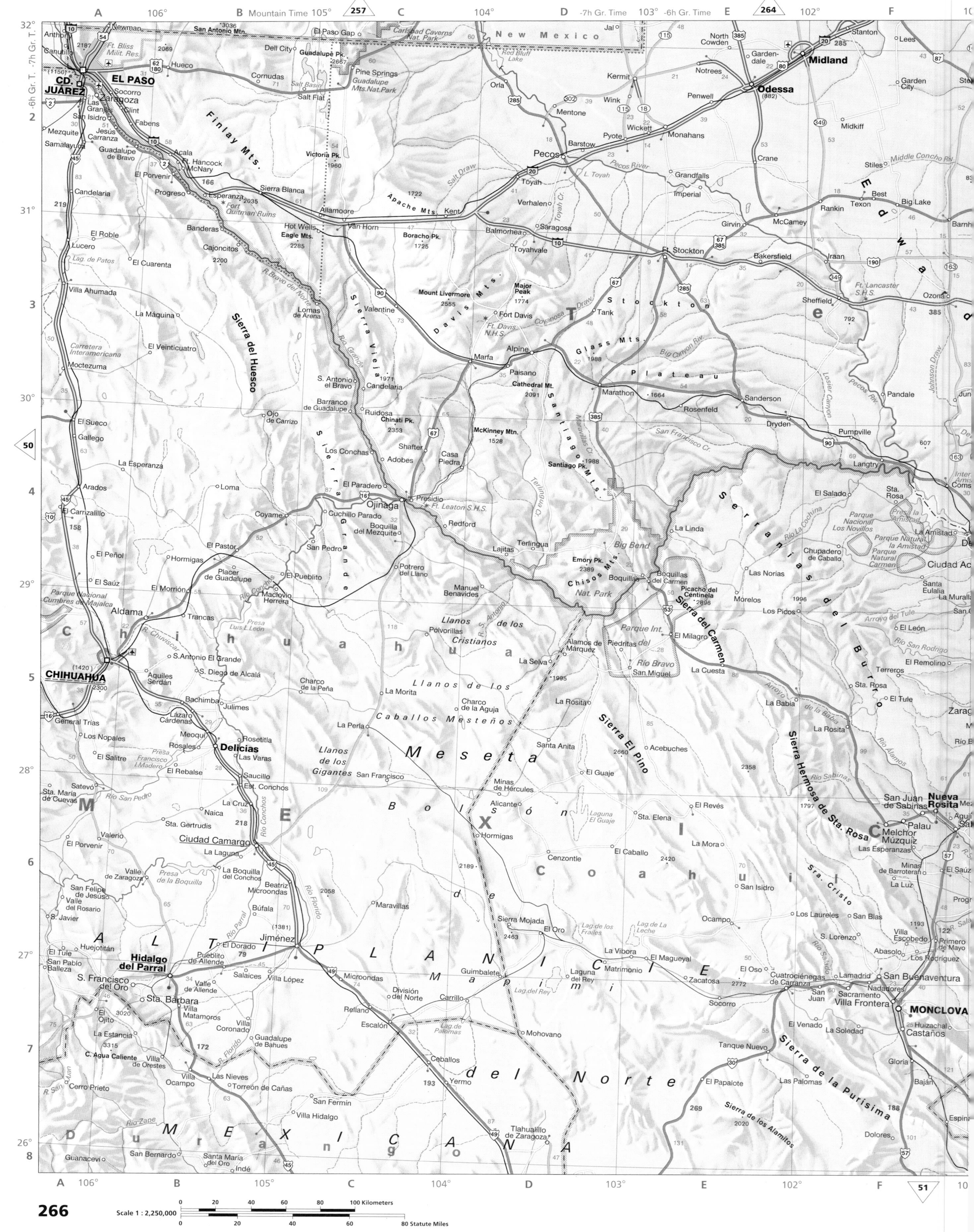

Mountain Time
-7h Gr. Time
-6h Gr. Time
257
264
50
51
New Mexico
El Paso Gap
Carlsbad Caverns Nat. Park
Jal
North Cowden
Stanton
Lees
Newman
Anthony
Canutillo
San Antonio Mtn.
Ft. Bliss Milit. Res.
Dell City
Guadalupe Pk.
Red Bluff Lake
Garden-dale
Midland
Hueco
Pine Springs
Guadalupe Mts. Nat. Park
Kermit
Notrees
Odessa
Garden City
CD. JUÁREZ
EL PASO
Cornudas
Salt Basin
Salt Flat
Orla
Wink
Penwell
Socorro
Zaragoza
Las Granjas
Clint
San Isidro
Fabens
Mentone
Wickett
Monahans
Midkiff
Mezquite
Jesús Carranza
Samalayuca
Finlay Mts.
Pyote
Barstow
Pecos
Crane
Guadalupe de Bravo
Acala
Ft. Hancock
McNary
Victoria Pk.
Pecos River
Stiles
Middle Concho Riv.
El Porvenir
Sierra Blanca
Toyah
L. Toyah
Grandfalls
Imperial
Candelaria
Progreso
Esperanza
Fort Quitman Ruins
Apache Mts.
Kent
Verhalen
Rankin
Best
Big Lake
Texon
Allamoore
Van Horn
Hot Wells
Eagle Mts.
Boracho Pk.
Balmorhea
Saragosa
Girvin
McCamey
Banderas
El Roble
Lucero
Toyahvale
Ft. Stockton
Bakersfield
Iraan
Lag. de Patos
El Cuarenta
Cajoncitos
R. Bravo del Norte
Ft. Lancaster S.H.S.
Villa Ahumada
Mount Livermore
Major Peak
Davis Mts.
Sierra Vieja
Stockton
Sheffield
Ozona
La Máquina
Sierra del Huesco
Lomas de Arena
Valentine
Fort Davis
Ft. Davis N.H.S.
Coyanosa Draw
Tank
Carretera Interamericana
El Veinticuatro
Glass Mts.
Big Canyon Riv.
Moctezuma
Río Grande
Marfa
Alpine
Paisano
Plateau
S. Antonio el Bravo
Candelaria
Cathedral Mt.
Marathon
Santiago Mts.
Sanderson
Pandale
Johnson Draw
Pecos Riv.
Barranco de Guadalupe
Ruidosa
Chinati Pk.
Rosenfeld
Ojo de Carrizo
Dryden
El Sueco
Gallego
McKinney Mtn.
Maravillas Cr.
Pumpville
Shafter
San Francisco Cr.
Los Conchas
Adobes
Casa Piedra
Santiago Pk.
Langtry
La Esperanza
Sierra Grande
El Paradero
Loma
Arados
Ojinaga
Presidio
Ft. Leaton S.H.S.
El Salado
Sta. Rosa
Presa la Amistad
Coyame
Cuchillo Parado
Boquilla del Mezquite
Redford
Serranías del Burro
El Carrizalillo
Terlingua Cr.
Big Bend
La Linda
Parque Nacional Los Novillos
La Amistad
El Pastor
San Pedro
Terlingua
Lajitas
Parque Natural la Amistad
Chupadero de Caballo
Ciudad Acuña
El Peñol
Hormigas
Potrero del Llano
Emory Pk.
Chisos Mts.
Boquillas
Boquillas del Carmen
Las Norias
Placer de Guadalupe
El Pueblito
Nat. Park
Picacho del Centinela
Santa Eulalia
El Saúz
Parque Nacional Cumbres de Majalca
El Morrión
Maclovio Herrera
Río Conchos
Manuel Benavides
Morelos
Los Picos
Aldama
Trancas
Presa Luis L. León
Llanos de los Cristianos
Polvorillas
R. S. Antonio
Parque Int. del Río Bravo
Sierra del Carmen
Arroyo del Tule
El León
Chihuahua
R. Chuviscar
Alamos de Márquez
Piedritas
El Milagro
Río San Rodrigo
S. Antonio El Grande
S. Diego de Alcalá
La Selva
San Miguel
La Cuesta
El Remolino
Terreros
CHIHUAHUA
Aquiles Serdán
Charco de la Peña
La Morita
Llanos de los
Sta. Rosa
Bachimba
Julimes
Charco de la Aguja
La Rosita
Arroyo de la Babia
La Babia
El Tule
General Trias
Lázaro Cárdenas
Caballos Mesteños
La Perla
Sierra El Pino
Acebuches
La Rosita
Meoqui
Rosetitla
Los Nopales
Rosales
Delicias
Las Varas
Santa Anita
El Salitre
Presa Francisco I. Madero
Llanos de los Gigantes
Meseta
El Rebalse
Saucillo
San Francisco
El Guaje
Sierra Hermosa de Sta. Rosa
Río Sabinas
Río Álamos
Est. Conchos
Minas de Hércules
Satevó
Sta. María de Cuevas
Río San Pedro
Bolsón
La Cruz
Naica
Alicante
Laguna El Guaje
Sta. Elena
El Revés
San Juan de Sabinas
Nueva Rosita
Sta. Gertrudis
Valerio
Ciudad Camargo
Hormigas
Palau
Melchor Múzquiz
El Porvenir
La Mora
La Laguna
Cenzontle
El Caballo
Las Esperanzas
Minas de Barroterán
Valle de Zaragoza
La Boquilla del Conchos
Presa de la Boquilla
Coahuila
Sra. Cristo
Río Florido
Beatriz Microondas
San Felipe de Jesús
Valle del Rosario
San Isidro
La Luz
S. Javier
Búfala
Maravillas
Ocampo
Los Laureles
San Blas
Sierra Mojada
Río Parral
Jiménez
El Oro
Lag. de los Frailes
Lag. de La Leche
S. Lorenzo
Villa Escobedo
El Tule
Huejotitán
El Dorado
Altiplanicie
Primero de Mayo
San Pablo Balleza
Hidalgo del Parral
Pueblito de Allende
La Víbora
El Magueyal
Abasolo
Los Rodríguez
Río Salado
Matrimonio
El Oso
S. Francisco del Oro
Valle de Allende
Salaices
Villa López
Guimbalete
Mapimí
Laguna del Rey
Zacatosa
Cuatrociénegas de Carranza
Lamadrid
San Buenaventura
Microondas
Lag. del Rey
Sacramento
Nadadores
Sta. Bárbara
El Ojito
División del Norte
Carrillo
San Juan
Villa Frontera
Villa Matamoros
Rellano
Socorro
MONCLOVA
La Estancia
Villa Coronado
Escalón
Lag. de Palomas
El Venado
La Soledad
Huizachal
Castaños
C. Agua Caliente
Guadalupe de Bahues
Mohovano
Sierra de la Purísima
Villa de Orestes
R. Florido
Tanque Nuevo
Ceballos
Gloria
Villa Ocampo
Las Nieves
Torreón de Cañas
Yermo
del Norte
El Papalote
Las Palomas
Bajan
Cerro Prieto
R. San Juan
San Fermín
Villa Hidalgo
Río Zape
Sierra de los Alamitos
Espinazo
Durango
Mexicana
Tlahualilo de Zaragoza
Dolores
Guanaceví
San Bernardo
Santa María del Oro
Indé
Edwards
Texas
Mexico
Scale 1 : 2,250,000
0 20 40 60 80 100 Kilometers
0 20 40 60 80 Statute Miles

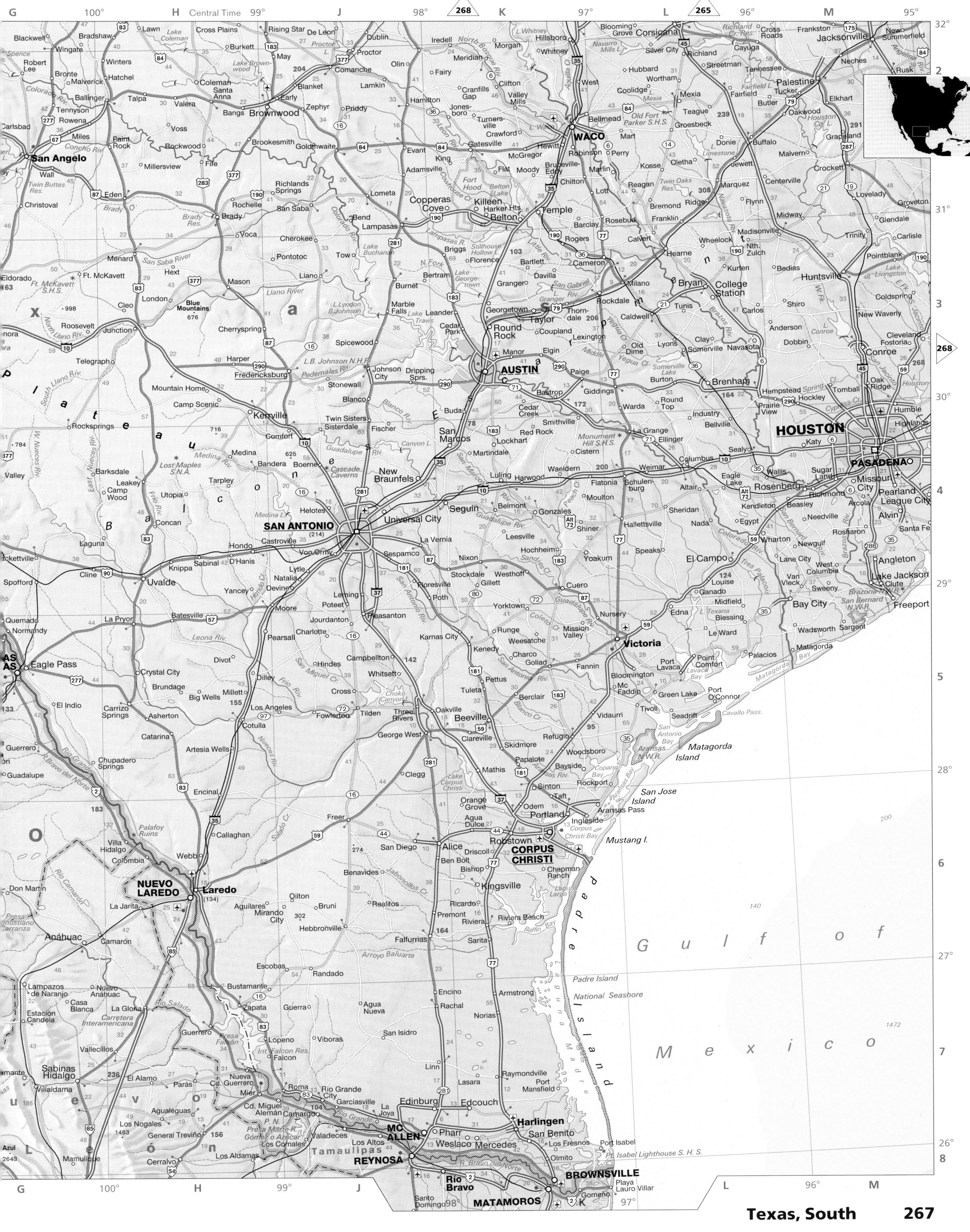

G
100°
H
Central Time
99°
J
98°
268
K
97°
L
265
96°
M
95°
32°
31°
30°
29°
28°
27°
26°
2
3
4
5
6
7
8
San Angelo
Ballinger
Coleman
Brownwood
Brady
Lampasas
Copperas Cove
Killeen
Belton
Temple
WACO
Corsicana
Palestine
Jacksonville
Hillsboro
Fort Hood
Georgetown
Round Rock
Taylor
AUSTIN
Bryan
College Station
Huntsville
Conroe
Navasota
Brenham
Giddings
Bastrop
Fredericksburg
Kerrville
Junction
San Marcos
New Braunfels
Seguin
Luling
Lockhart
SAN ANTONIO
Universal City
Uvalde
Hondo
Castroville
Eagle Pass
Crystal City
Carrizo Springs
Pleasanton
Karnes City
Cuero
Victoria
Yoakum
Hallettsville
Columbus
La Grange
Sealy
Katy
HOUSTON
PASADENA
Missouri City
Rosenberg
Richmond
Pearland
League City
Alvin
Angleton
Lake Jackson
Freeport
Bay City
El Campo
Wharton
Edna
Port Lavaca
Port O'Connor
Matagorda Island
San Jose Island
Aransas Pass
Rockport
Refugio
Beeville
George West
Three Rivers
Cotulla
Alice
Robstown
CORPUS CHRISTI
Portland
Ingleside
Mustang I.
Kingsville
Falfurrias
Hebbronville
Laredo
NUEVO LAREDO
Zapata
Rio Grande City
Edinburg
MC ALLEN
Pharr
Weslaco
Mercedes
Harlingen
San Benito
Port Isabel
BROWNSVILLE
REYNOSA
MATAMOROS
Rio Bravo
Padre Island
Padre Island National Seashore
Laguna Madre
Gulf of Mexico
Edwards Plateau
Balcones Escarpment
Nuevo León
Tamaulipas
Sabinas Hidalgo
Anáhuac
Camargo
Miguel Alemán
Cd. Guerrero
Mier

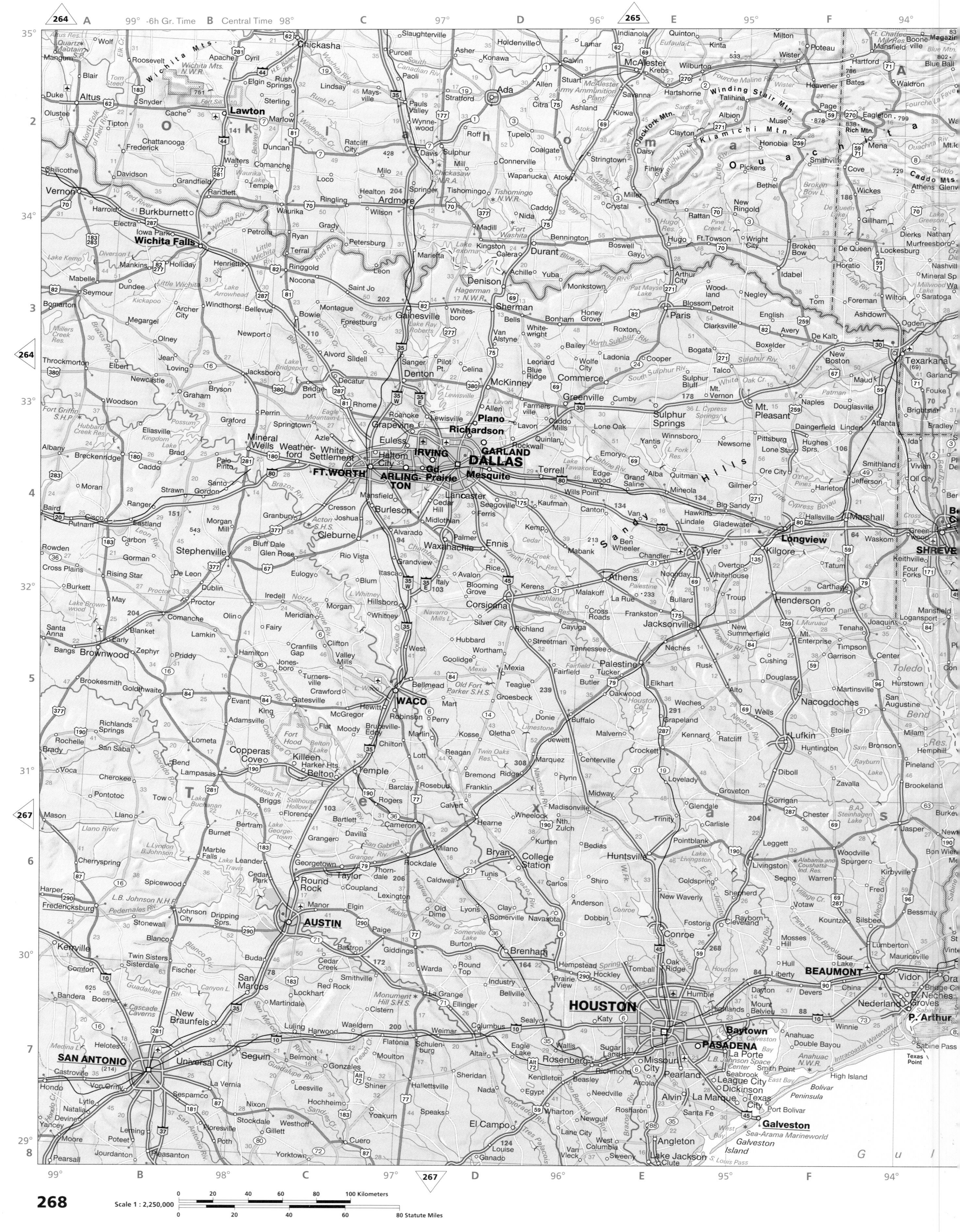

Scale 1 : 2,250,000

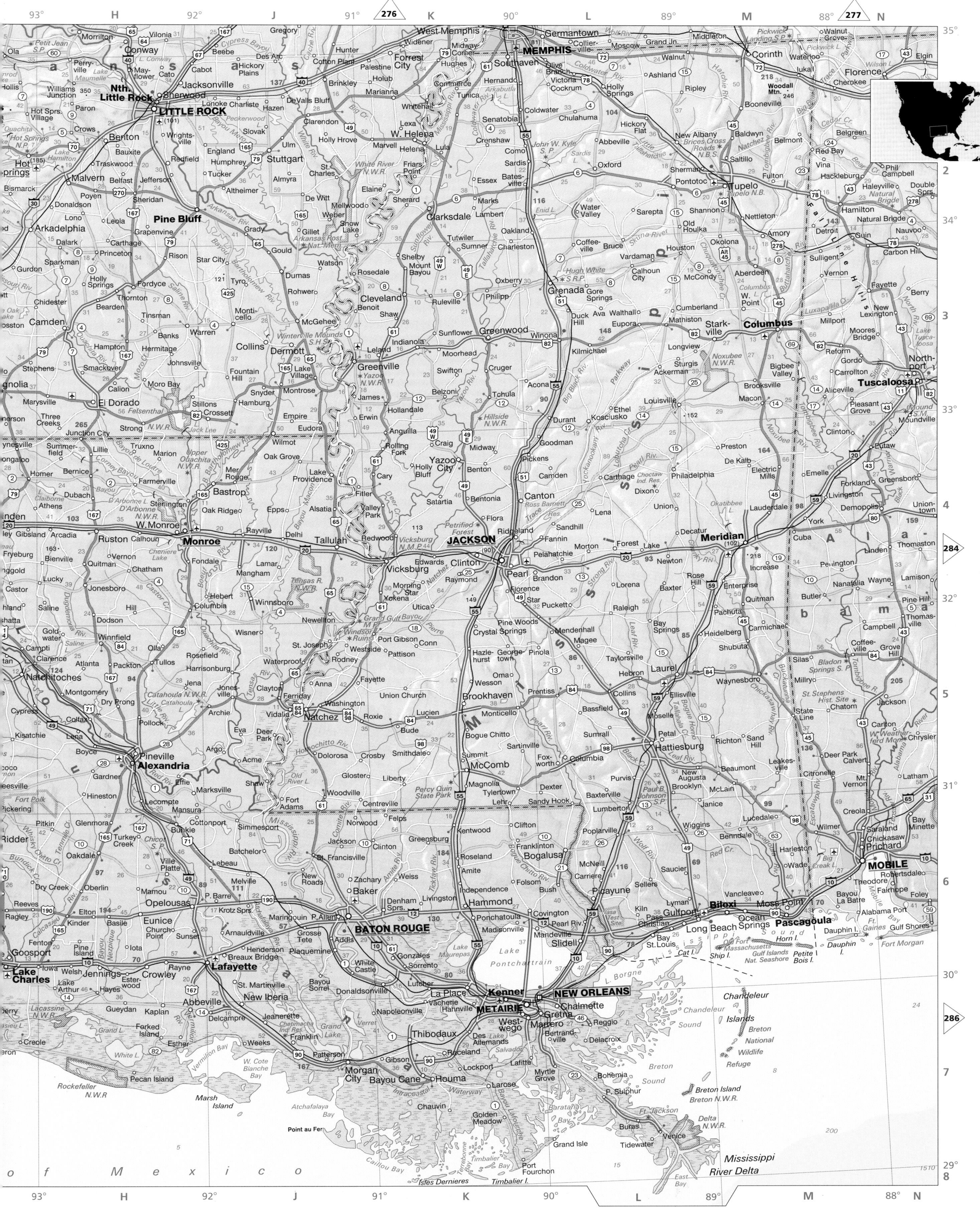
93°
H
92°
J
91°
276
K
90°
L
89°
M
88°
277
N
35°
34°
33°
32°
31°
30°
29°
284
286
LITTLE ROCK
Nth. Little Rock
Conway
Jacksonville
Pine Bluff
Arkadelphia
Camden
El Dorado
Monroe
West Monroe
Ruston
Natchitoches
Alexandria
Pineville
Lafayette
Lake Charles
Opelousas
Crowley
Abbeville
New Iberia
BATON ROUGE
NEW ORLEANS
METAIRIE
Kenner
Chalmette
Houma
Thibodaux
Morgan City
Hammond
Slidell
MEMPHIS
West Memphis
Germantown
Southaven
Tunica
Clarksdale
Greenville
Greenwood
Grenada
Oxford
Tupelo
Corinth
Starkville
Columbus
Tuscaloosa
Northport
Yazoo City
Vicksburg
JACKSON
Clinton
Pearl
Canton
Natchez
Brookhaven
McComb
Meridian
Laurel
Hattiesburg
Gulfport
Biloxi
Pascagoula
MOBILE
Prichard
Lake Pontchartrain
Chandeleur Sound
Chandeleur Islands
Breton National Wildlife Refuge
Breton Sound
Mississippi River Delta
Mississippi Sound
Gulf Islands National Seashore
Atchafalaya Bay
Marsh Island
Rockefeller N.W.R.
Isles Dernieres
Timbalier I.
Grand Isle
o f M e x i c o

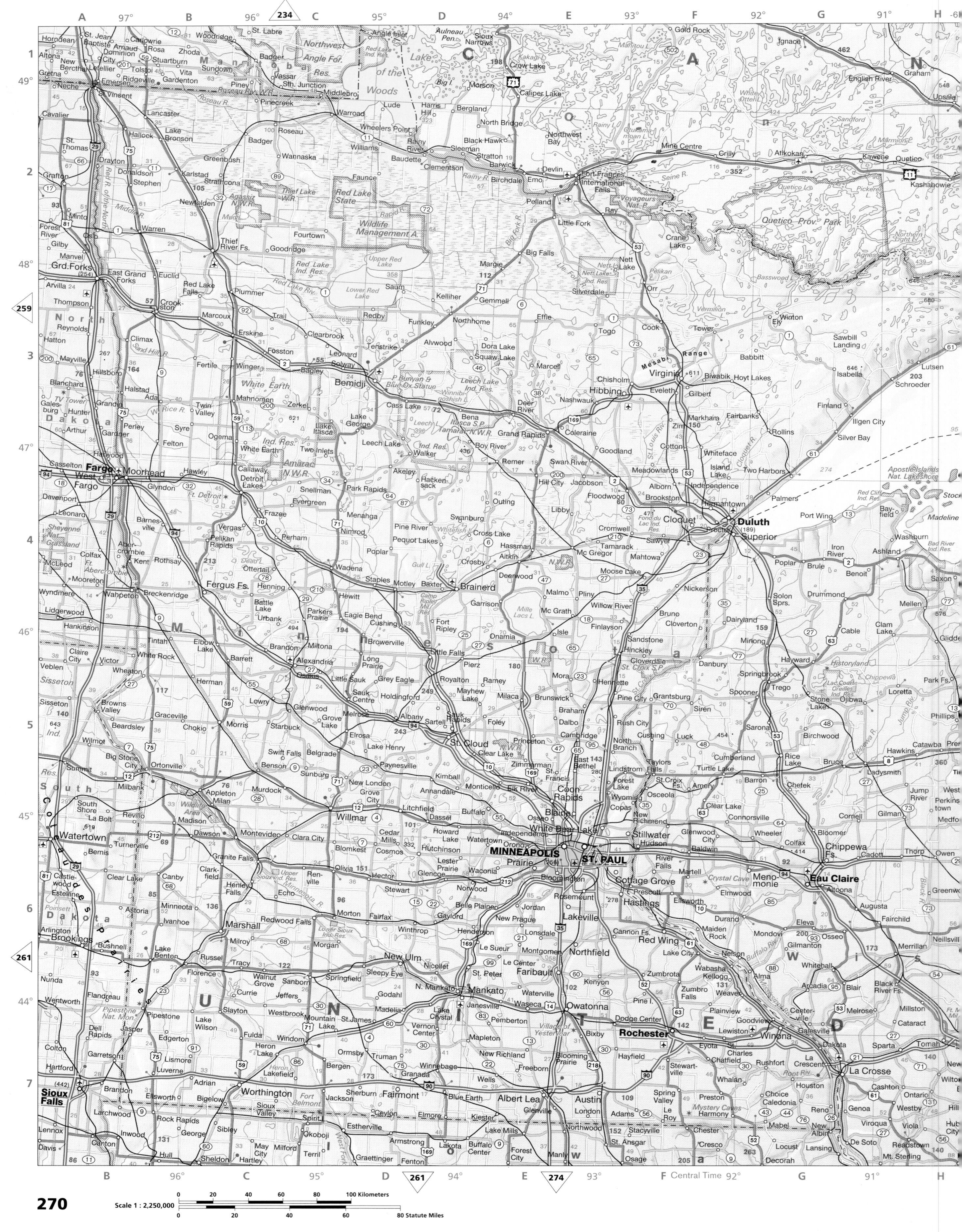

MINNEAPOLIS
ST. PAUL
Duluth
Superior
Fargo
Moorhead
West Fargo
Grd.Forks
East Grand Forks
Rochester
Eau Claire
La Crosse
Sioux Falls
St. Cloud
Mankato
Brainerd
Bemidji
Virginia
Hibbing
Grand Rapids
International Falls
Fort Frances
Thief River Fs.
Fergus Fs.
Alexandria
Willmar
Marshall
New Ulm
Owatonna
Faribault
Northfield
Red Wing
Winona
Austin
Albert Lea
Worthington
Fairmont
Brookings
Watertown
Wahpeton
Breckenridge
Stillwater
Hastings
Lakeville
Chippewa Fs.
Menomonie
Ashland
Lake of the Woods
Red Lake Ind. Res.
Upper Red Lake
Lower Red Lake
Leech Lake Ind. Res.
Mille Lacs L.
Quetico Prov. Park
Voyageurs Nat. P.
Apostle Islands Nat. Lakeshore
Red Lake State Wildlife Management A.
Coteau des Prairies
North Dakota
South Dakota
Minnesota
Central Time
Scale 1 : 2,250,000
0 20 40 60 80 100 Kilometers
0 20 40 60 80 Statute Miles

Lake Superior
Lake Michigan
Lake Huron
Upper Peninsula
Lower Michigan
Algoma Upland
Green Bay
Keweenaw Pen.
Door Pen.
Garden Pen.
Isle Royale National Park
Isle Royale
Sleeping Giant Prov. P.
Pukaskwa Nat. Park
Lake Superieur Prov. P.
Chapleau-Nemegosenda Prov. P.
Missinaibi Lake Prov. P.
Pictured Rocks Nat. Lakeshore
Seney National Wildlife Refuge
Sleeping Bear Dunes Nat. Lakeshore
Michipicoten I.
Mackinac I.
Mackinac Bridge
Drummond I.
THUNDER BAY
Nipigon
Red Rock
Schreiber
Terrace Bay
Marathon
Manitouwadge
Hornepayne
White River
Wawa
Dubreuilville
Chapleau
Sault Ste. Marie
Marquette
Houghton
Hancock
Ontonagon
Ishpeming
Negaunee
Munising
Escanaba
Gladstone
Manistique
Iron Mountain
Menominee
Marinette
Green Bay
Appleton
Oshkosh
Neenah
Manitowoc
Two Rivers
Sheboygan
Fond du Lac
West Bend
Wausau
Stevens Pt.
St. Ignace
Mackinaw City
Cheboygan
Petoskey
Charlevoix
Alpena
Gaylord
Grayling
Traverse City
Cadillac
Manistee
Ludington
Big Rapids
Mt. Pleasant
Midland
Bay City
Saginaw
Oscoda
Tawas City
-6h Gr. Time
-5h Gr. Time
Eastern Time

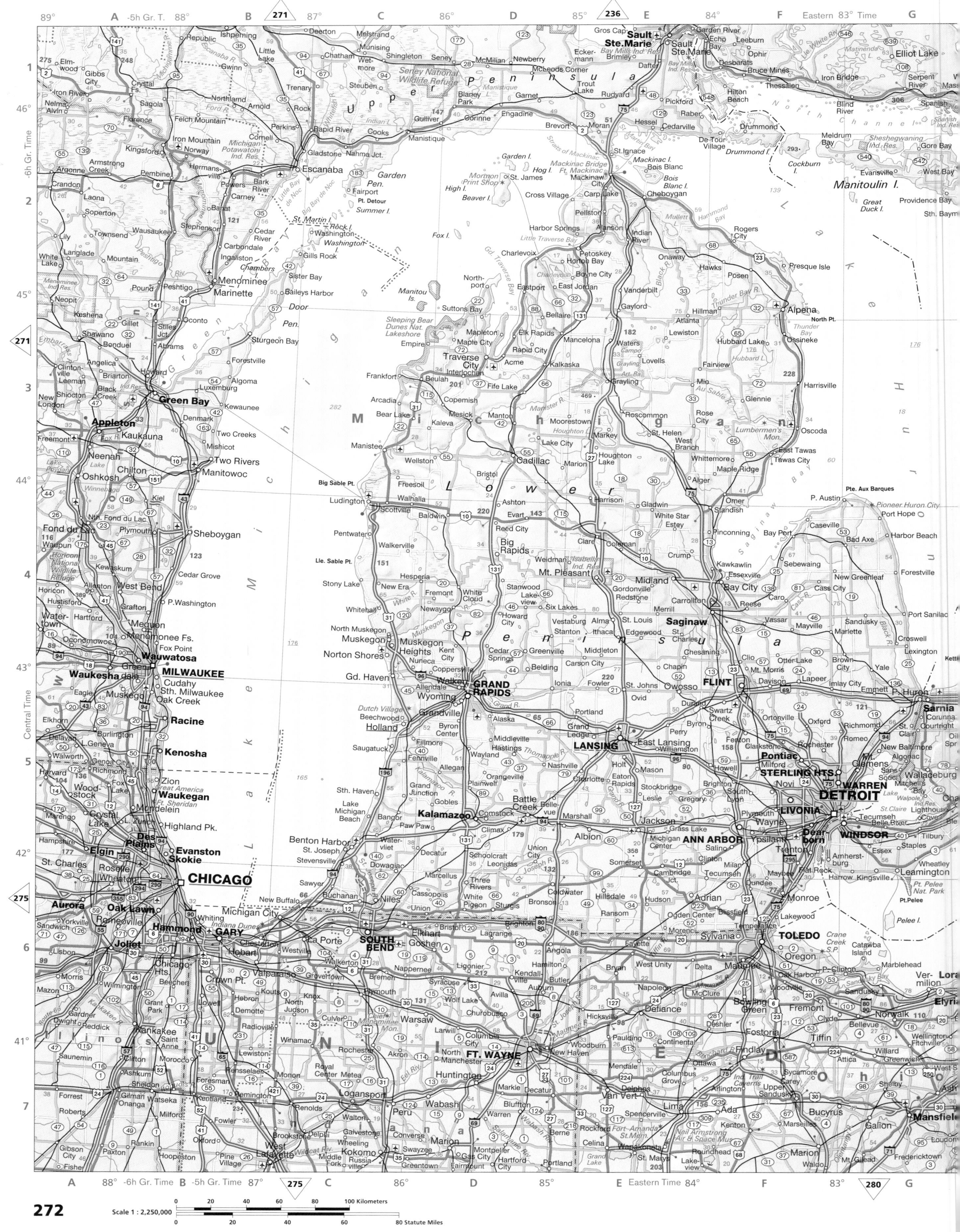

89°
A
-6h Gr. T.
88°
B
271
87°
C
86°
D
85°
236
E
84°
F
Eastern 83° Time
G
46°
45°
44°
43°
42°
41°
-6h Gr. Time
Central Time
Upper Peninsula
Lower Peninsula
Lake Michigan
Green Bay
Lake Huron
Saginaw Bay
North Channel
Manitoulin I.
Seney National Wildlife Refuge
Sleeping Bear Dunes Nat. Lakeshore
Michigan Potawatomi Ind. Res.
Bay Mills Ind. Res.
Straits of Mackinac
Mackinac Bridge
Sault Ste. Marie
Ishpeming
Republic
Munising
Newberry
Escanaba
Manistique
Iron Mountain
Kingsford
Norway
Menominee
Marinette
Green Bay
Appleton
Oshkosh
Fond du Lac
Sheboygan
Manitowoc
Two Rivers
Wauwatosa
MILWAUKEE
Waukesha
Racine
Kenosha
Waukegan
Evanston
Skokie
Des Plaines
Elgin
Aurora
CHICAGO
Joliet
Hammond
GARY
Michigan City
SOUTH BEND
Elkhart
Kankakee
Valparaiso
Mackinaw City
St. Ignace
Cheboygan
Petoskey
Charlevoix
Harbor Springs
Gaylord
Alpena
Traverse City
Cadillac
Ludington
Manistee
Muskegon
Grand Haven
Holland
GRAND RAPIDS
Kalamazoo
Battle Creek
Benton Harbor
St. Joseph
Niles
LANSING
East Lansing
Jackson
ANN ARBOR
Ypsilanti
Livonia
DETROIT
WINDSOR
Dearborn
Warren
Sterling Hts.
Pontiac
Flint
Saginaw
Bay City
Midland
Mt. Pleasant
Port Huron
Sarnia
Monroe
TOLEDO
Sandusky
Findlay
Lima
FT. WAYNE
Huntington
Logansport
Kokomo
West Lafayette
Marion
Mansfield
Bucyrus
Tiffin
Fremont
Norwalk
Defiance
Bowling Green
Adrian
Pelee I.
Leamington
Illinois
Indiana
Ohio
A
88°
-6h Gr. Time
B
-5h Gr. Time
87°
275
C
86°
D
85°
E
Eastern Time 84°
F
83°
280
G
Scale 1 : 2,250,000
0 20 40 60 80 100 Kilometers
0 20 40 60 80 Statute Miles

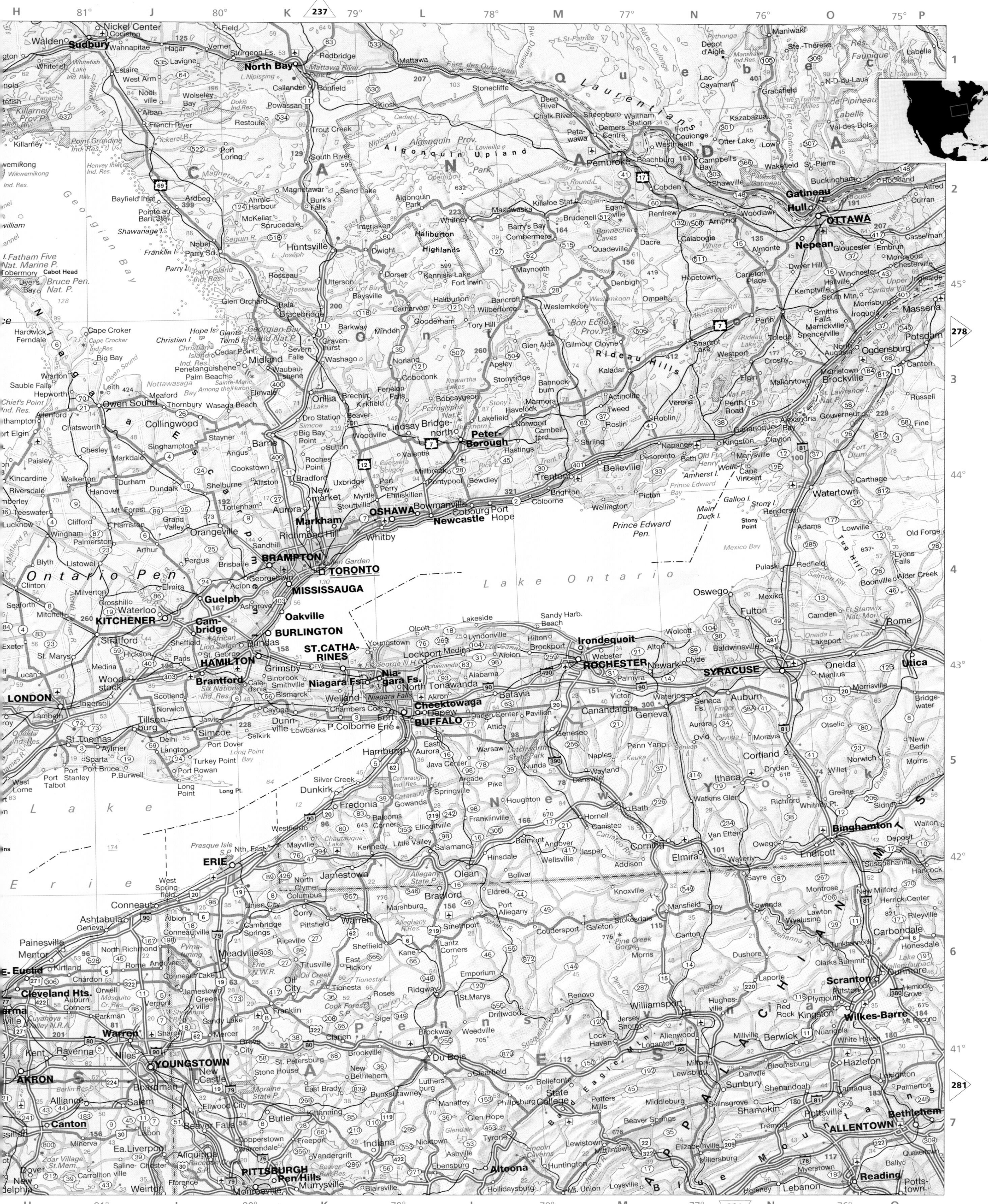

H 81° J 80° K 237 79° L 78° M 77° N 76° O 75° P
Lake Ontario
Lake Erie
Georgian Bay
Ontario Pen
Algonquin Upland
Laurentians
Rideau Hills
Prince Edward Pen.
Algonquin Prov. Park
Haliburton Highlands
Quebec
Canada
New York
Pennsylvania
Appalachian Mts.
Blue Mountains
OTTAWA
TORONTO
MISSISSAUGA
BRAMPTON
HAMILTON
KITCHENER
LONDON
BUFFALO
ROCHESTER
SYRACUSE
ERIE
YOUNGSTOWN
AKRON
PITTSBURGH
ALLENTOWN
OSHAWA
BURLINGTON
ST.CATHARINES
Cheektowaga
Irondequoit
Gatineau
Hull
Nepean
Sudbury
North Bay
Pembroke
Kingston
Belleville
Peterborough
Barrie
Guelph
Cambridge
Brantford
Niagara Falls
Oswego
Utica
Binghamton
Elmira
Williamsport
Scranton
Wilkes-Barre
Bethlehem
Reading
Altoona
State College
Jamestown
Watertown
Brockville
Cornwall
278
281

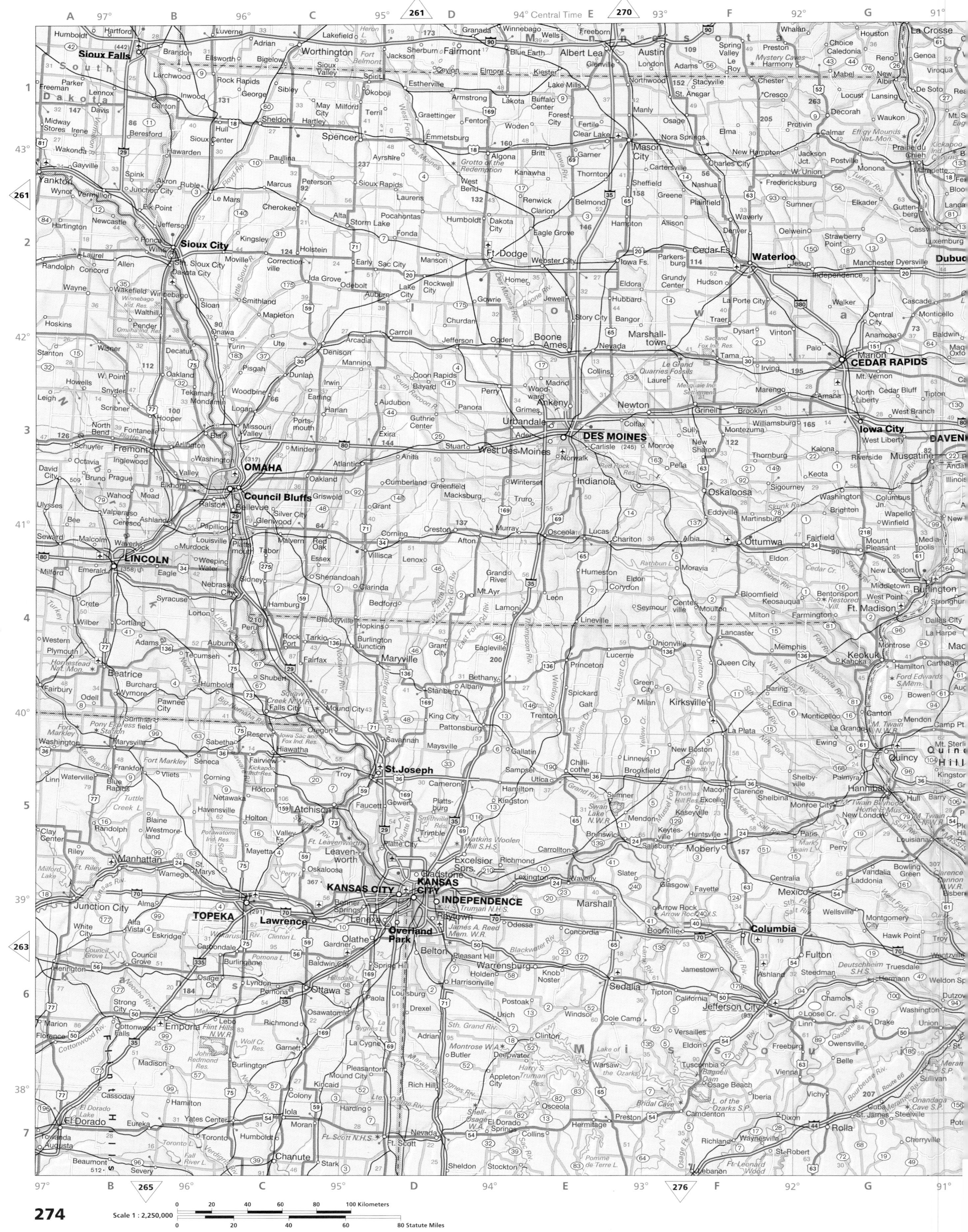
97° 96° 95° 94° Central Time 93° 92° 91°
Minnesota
South Dakota
Iowa
Nebraska
Kansas
Missouri
Sioux Falls
Worthington
Fairmont
Albert Lea
Austin
Yankton
Spencer
Mason City
Sioux City
Ft. Dodge
Waterloo
Cedar Falls
Dubuque
Carroll
Boone
Ames
Marshalltown
CEDAR RAPIDS
Fremont
Ankeny
Urbandale
DES MOINES
West Des Moines
Newton
Iowa City
OMAHA
Council Bluffs
Muscatine
Oskaloosa
Ottumwa
LINCOLN
Burlington
Ft. Madison
Keokuk
Beatrice
Maryville
Kirksville
Quincy
St. Joseph
Hannibal
Atchison
Manhattan
KANSAS CITY
INDEPENDENCE
TOPEKA
Lawrence
Overland Park
Olathe
Columbia
Junction City
Sedalia
Jefferson City
Emporia
Ottawa
Rolla
El Dorado
Chanute
Scale 1 : 2,250,000
0 20 40 60 80 100 Kilometers
0 20 40 60 80 Statute Miles

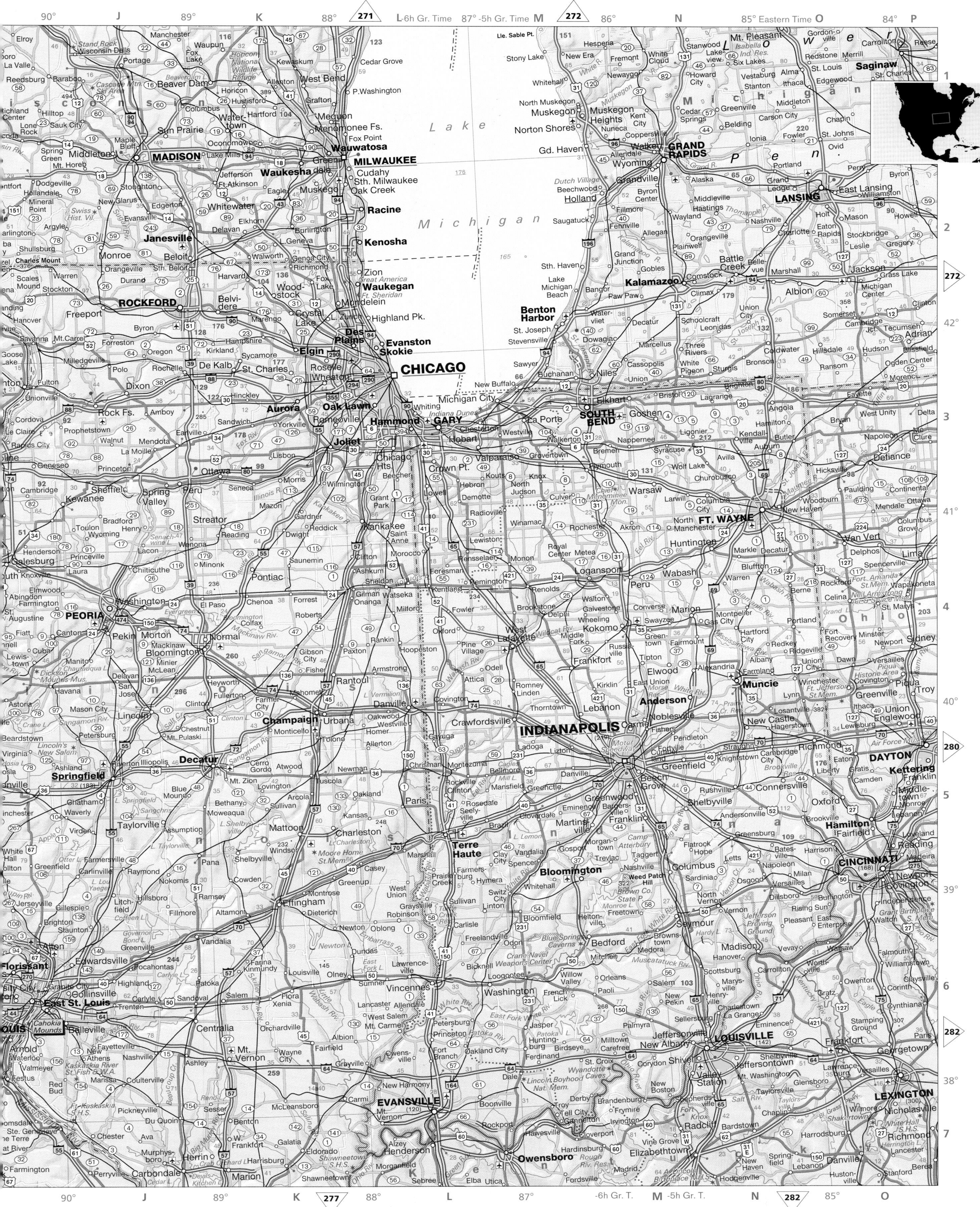

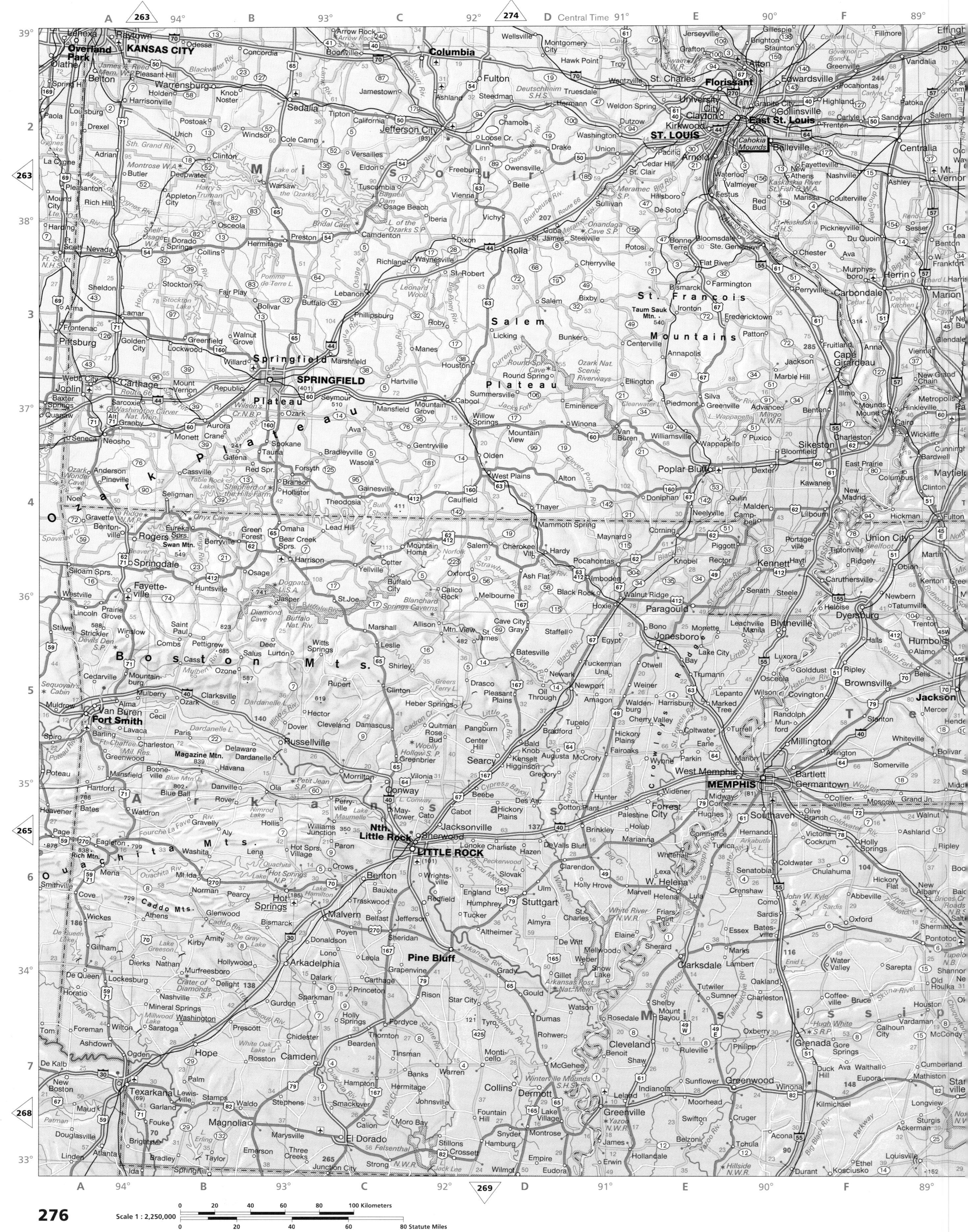
A
263
94°
B
93°
C
92°
274
D Central Time 91°
E
90°
F
89°
39°
38°
37°
36°
35°
34°
33°
KANSAS CITY
Overland Park
Columbia
Jefferson City
ST. LOUIS
East St. Louis
Florissant
Springfield
SPRINGFIELD
Missouri
Ozark Plateau
Salem Plateau
St. Francois Mountains
Boston Mts.
Ouachita Mts.
Arkansas
Fort Smith
LITTLE ROCK
Nth. Little Rock
Pine Bluff
MEMPHIS
Jonesboro
Texarkana
El Dorado
Hot Springs
Jackson
Mississippi
263
265
268
269
Scale 1 : 2,250,000
0 20 40 60 80 100 Kilometers
0 20 40 60 80 Statute Miles

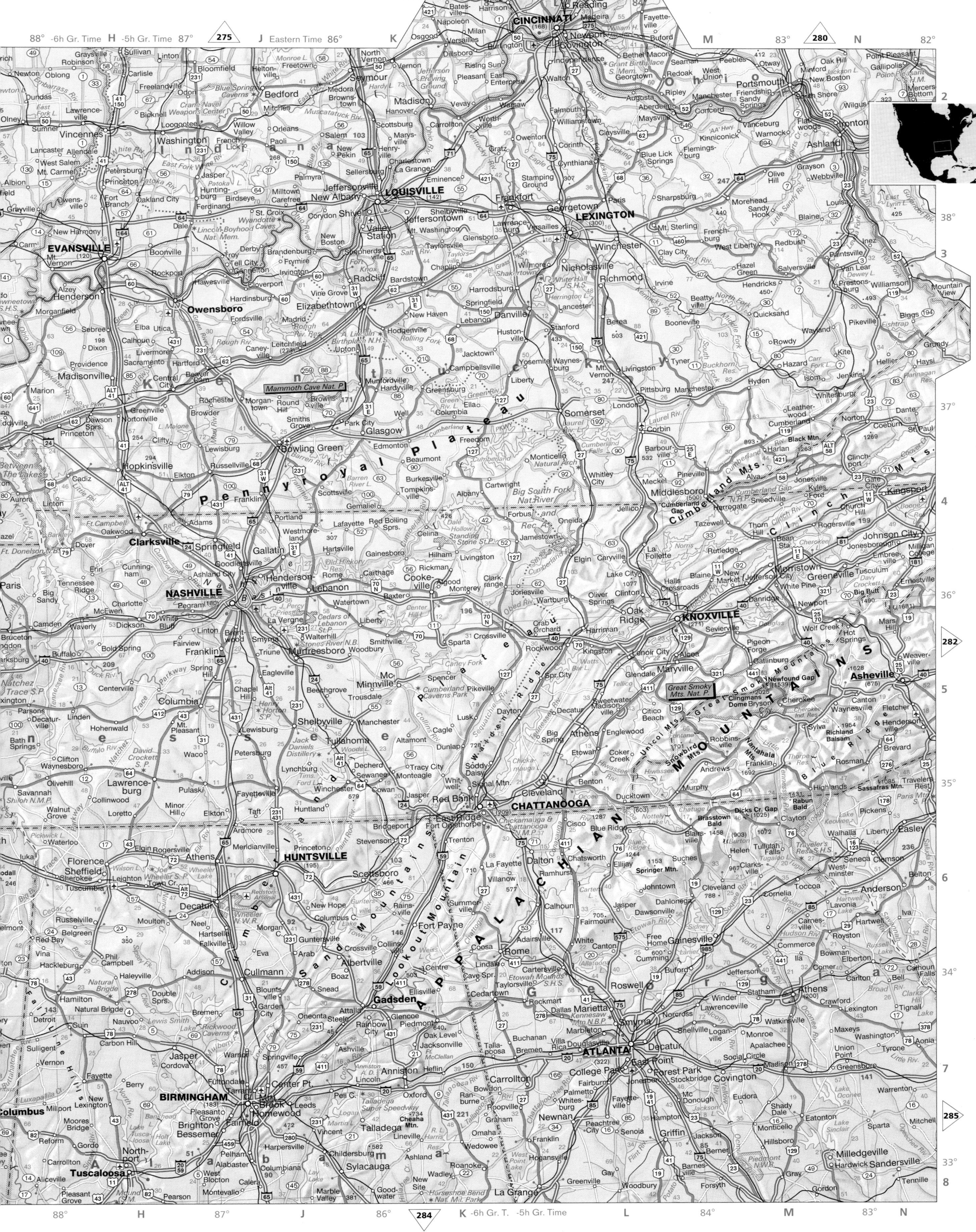

88° -6h Gr. Time H -5h Gr. Time 87°
275
J Eastern Time 86°
K
M 83°
280
N 82°
CINCINNATI
LOUISVILLE
LEXINGTON
EVANSVILLE
Owensboro
Frankfort
Bowling Green
Clarksville
NASHVILLE
KNOXVILLE
CHATTANOOGA
Asheville
HUNTSVILLE
BIRMINGHAM
Tuscaloosa
Gadsden
ATLANTA
Athens
Columbus
Mammoth Cave Nat. P.
Great Smoky Mts. Nat. P.
Pennyroyal Plateau
Cumberland Plateau
APPALACHIAN MOUNTAINS
Cumberland Mts.
Clinch Mts.
Blue Ridge
Sand Mountain
Lookout Mountain
Walden Ridge
38°
37°
36°
35°
34°
33°
282
285
88° H 87° J 86°
284
K -6h Gr. T. -5h Gr. Time
L 84° M 83° N

A
80°
B
79°
C
78°
D
77°
237
E
76°
F
75°
G
74°
H
47°
2
46°
3
238
45°
4
44°
5
273
43°
6
42°
7
280
41°
281
C o u t a o u a i s
N
Q u é b e c
O n t a r i o
La Vérendrye Provincial Réserve
Laurentians
Algonquin Upland
Algonquin Prov. Park
Haliburton Highlands
Rideau Hills
Lake Ontario
Lake Erie
Prince Edward Pen.
Adirondack Mountains
Tug Hill
N e w Y o r k
P e n n s y l v a n i a
U N I T E D S T A T E S
A P P A L A C H I A N M O U N T A I N S
Temagami
Laniel
Témiscaming
Marten River
River Valley
Field
Tilden Lake
Thorne
Tomiko
Verner
Sturgeon Fs.
Lavigne
North Bay
L. Nipissing
Redbridge
Mattawa
Callander
Bonfield
Powassan
Restoule
Trout Creek
Port Loring
South River
Magnetawan
Ahmic Harbour
Burk's Falls
Sand Lake
Ardbeg
McKellar
Sprucedale
Nobel
Parry Sd.
Huntsville
Dwight
Rosseau
Utterson
Glen Orchard
Bala
Bracebridge
Gravenhurst
Midland
Penetanguishene
Orillia
Wasaga Beach
Barrie
Angus
Cookstown
Alliston
Bradford
Tottenham
Newmarket
Aurora
Markham
Richmond Hill
BRAMPTON
Georgetown
TORONTO
MISSISSAUGA
Oakville
BURLINGTON
HAMILTON
ST.CATHARINES
Grimsby
Niagara Fs.
Welland
Dunnville
P.Colborne
Fort Erie
OSHAWA
Whitby
Bowmanville
Newcastle
Cobourg
Port Hope
Colborne
Brighton
Trenton
Belleville
Picton
Wellington
Napanee
Kingston
Gananoque
Brockville
Prescott
Lindsay
Bridgenorth
Peterborough
Hastings
Campbellford
Norwood
Havelock
Marmora
Madoc
Tweed
Bancroft
Haliburton
Minden
Dorset
Whitney
Barry's Bay
Madawaska
Killaloe Stat.
Renfrew
Arnprior
Pembroke
Petawawa
Deep River
Chalk River
Mattawa
Cobden
Shawville
Maniwaki
Mont Laurier
Grand-Remous
Gracefield
Wakefield
Gatineau
Hull
OTTAWA
Nepean
Carleton Place
Almonte
Smiths Falls
Perth
Kemptville
Casselman
Hawkesbury
Lachute
Laval
LONGUEUIL
MONTRÉAL
Salaberry-de-Valleyfield
Cornwall
Massena
Ogdensburg
Potsdam
Canton
Malone
Plattsburgh
Saranac L.
Lake Placid
Tupper L.
Mt. Marcy
Watertown
Carthage
Lowville
Old Forge
Oswego
Fulton
Pulaski
Rome
Utica
Oneida
SYRACUSE
Auburn
Geneva
Canandaigua
ROCHESTER
Irondequoit
Brockport
Batavia
Lockport
Niagara Fs.
North Tonawanda
Cheektowaga
BUFFALO
Depew
Hamburg
Dunkirk
Fredonia
Jamestown
Olean
Salamanca
Bradford
Warren
Hornell
Corning
Elmira
Ithaca
Cortland
Binghamton
Endicott
Owego
Oneonta
Norwich
Cobleskill
Schenectady
ALBANY
Troy
Saratoga Sprs.
Glens Fs.
Amsterdam
Gloversville
Kingston
Poughkeepsie
Newburgh
Beacon
Middletown
Peekskill
Scranton
Wilkes-Barre
Carbondale
Williamsport
Lock Haven
Clearfield
Du Bois
St.Marys
Ridgway
Oil City
Titusville
Bedford
Danbury
BRIDGEPORT
WATERBURY
Sturgeon
Ste-Anne-du-Lac
Mt. Sit.Wilfrid
Lac Saguay
Mt. Tremblant
St.-Jovite
Ste-Agathe-des-Monts
St-Jérôme
Mascouche
Joliette
Manouane
Abitibi
Scale 1 : 2,250,000
0 20 40 60 80 100 Kilometers
0 20 40 60 80 Statute Miles

QUÉBEC
Charlesbourg
Levis
Trois-Rivières
Shawinigan
Cap-de-la-Madeleine
Drummondville
Victoriaville
Thetford Mines
Sherbrooke
Magog
Granby
Edmundston
Saint-Basile
St. Leonard
Presque Isle
Caribou
Houlton
Mt. Katahdin
1605
Millinocket
Bangor
Augusta
Waterville
Lewiston
Auburn
Brunswick
Bath
Portland
Cape Elizabeth
Old Orchard Beach
Saco
Biddeford
Kennebunk
Sanford
Rochester
Dover
Portsmouth
Kittery
Concord
Manchester
Nashua
Lowell
Lawrence
Haverhill
Newburyport
Gloucester
Lynn
BOSTON
Cambridge
Quincy
Brockton
Framingham
Worcester
SPRINGFIELD
PROVIDENCE
Pawtucket
Cranston
Fall River
New Bedford
Newport
Rhode Island
Norwich
New London
New Britain
Hartford
Keene
Brattleboro
Montpelier
Barre
Mt. Washington
1917
White Mountains
Provincetown
Cape Cod
Cape Cod Peninsula
Nat. Seashore
Cape Cod Bay
Hyannis
Falmouth
Martha's Vineyard
Nantucket
Nantucket I.
Monomoy Pt.
Fredericton
Saint John
Oromocto
Woodstock
New Brunswick
Nova Scotia
Yarmouth
Bay of Fundy
Gulf of Maine
ATLANTIC OCEAN
Georges Bank
Platt Bank
Isles of Shoals
Mt. Desert I.
Acadia Nat. Park
Eastern Time -5h Gr. Time
Atlantic Time -4h Gr. Time
Maine
New Hampshire
Massachusetts
Notre Dame Mts.
Height of Land
Boundary Mts.
72°
71°
70°
69°
68°
67°
66°
47°
46°
45°
44°
43°
42°
240
241

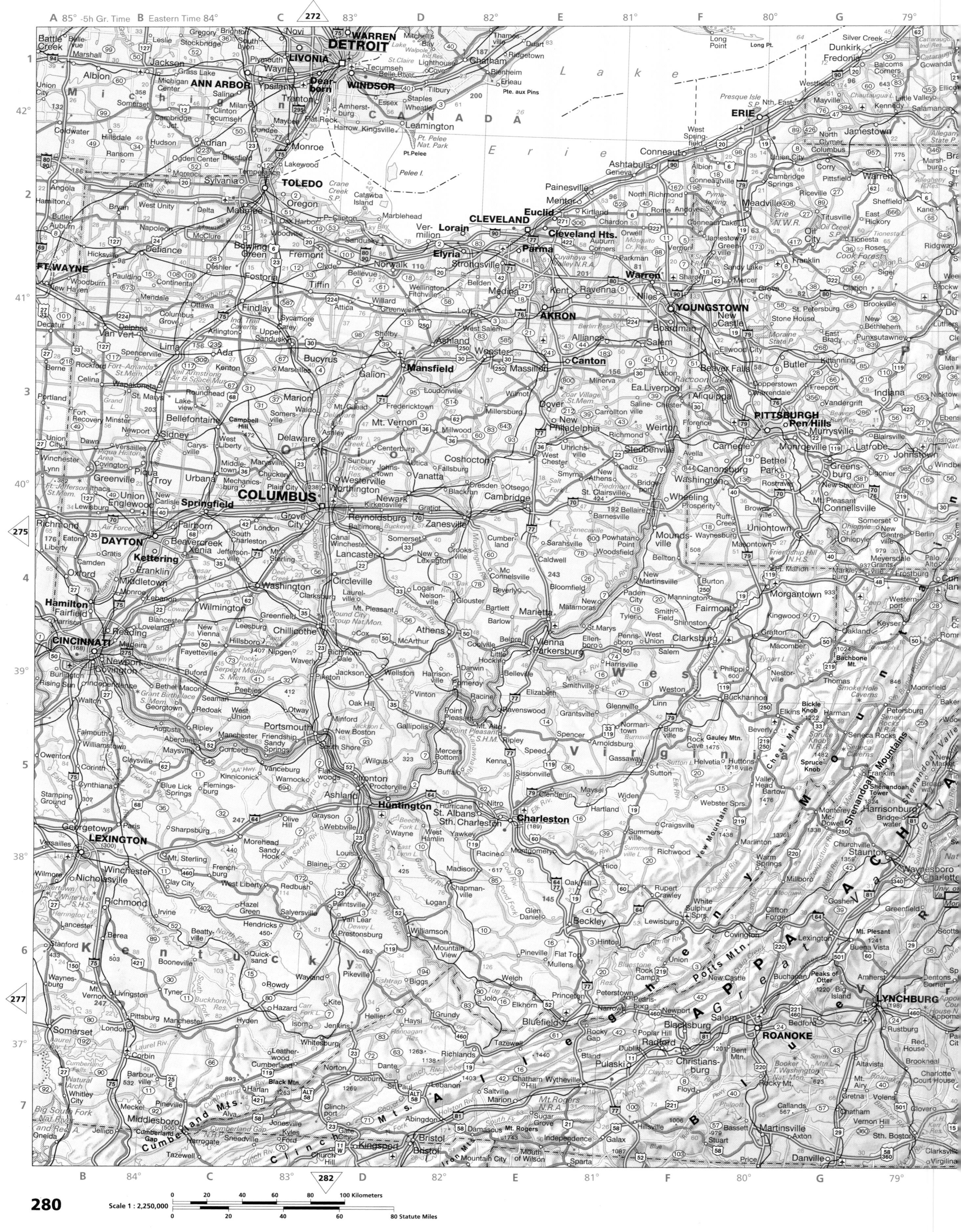

A 85° -5h Gr. Time B Eastern Time 84° C 83° D 82° E 81° F 80° G 79°
272
275
277
282
DETROIT
WARREN
LIVONIA
WINDSOR
ANN ARBOR
TOLEDO
CLEVELAND
Cleveland Hts.
Euclid
Lorain
Elyria
Parma
AKRON
Canton
YOUNGSTOWN
Warren
ERIE
PITTSBURGH
Penn Hills
Mansfield
COLUMBUS
Springfield
DAYTON
Kettering
CINCINNATI
Hamilton
LEXINGTON
Huntington
Charleston
ROANOKE
LYNCHBURG
Ft. WAYNE
Lake Erie
CANADA
Michigan
Ohio
Kentucky
West Virginia
Virginia
Allegheny Mountains
Blue Ridge
Great Appalachian Valley
Shenandoah Mountains
Cumberland Mts.
Clinch Mts.
B 84° C 83° D 82° E 81° F 80° G 79°
Scale 1 : 2,250,000
0 20 40 60 80 100 Kilometers
0 20 40 60 80 Statute Miles

78°
J
77°
273
K
76°
L
75°
278
M
74°
N
73°
O
72°
P
279
1
2
3
4
5
6
7
41°
40°
39°
38°
37°
NEW YORK
PHILADELPHIA
BALTIMORE
WASHINGTON
ARLINGTON
ALEXANDRIA
RICHMOND
HAMPTON
NORFOLK
NEWPORT NEWS
PORTSMOUTH
VIRGINIA BEACH
CHESAPEAKE
HARTFORD
WORCESTER
SPRING-FIELD
Chicopee
WATERBURY
NEW HAVEN
BRIDGEPORT
STAMFORD
YONKERS
New Rochelle
PATERSON
NEWARK
JERSEY CITY
ELIZABETH
ALLENTOWN
Bethlehem
Reading
Harrisburg
Lancaster
Wilmington
Camden
Trenton
Scranton
Wilkes-Barre
Binghamton
Atlantic City
Statue of Liberty
Independence Hall
Long Island
Long Island Sound
Hudson Canyon
Wilmington Canyon
Baltimore Canyon
Washington Canyon
Norfolk Canyon
ATLANTIC
OCEAN
Blue Mountains
78°
283
J
77°
K
76°
L
75°
M
74°
N
73°
O

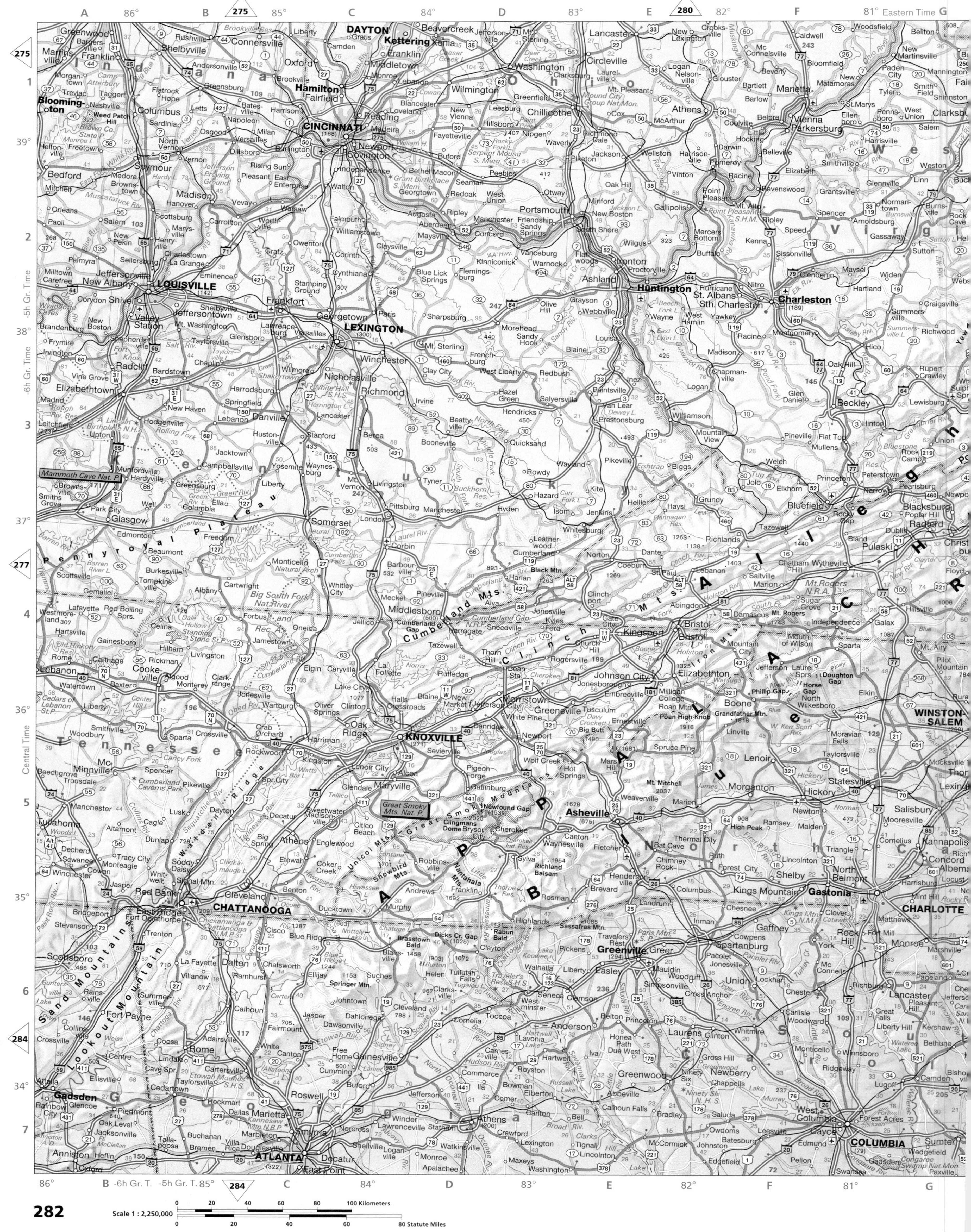

Scale 1 : 2,250,000

0 20 40 60 80 100 Kilometers

0 20 40 60 80 Statute Miles

281
285
BALTIMORE
WASHINGTON
ARLINGTON
ALEXANDRIA
RICHMOND
LYNCHBURG
HAMPTON
NEWPORT NEWS
NORFOLK
PORTSMOUTH
CHESAPEAKE
VIRGINIA BEACH
DURHAM
RALEIGH
GREENSBORO
Fayetteville
Wilmington
ATLANTIC
OCEAN
Atlantic City
Charlottesville
Fredericksburg
Petersburg
Danville
Greenville
New Bern
Jacksonville
Albemarle Sound
Pamlico Sound
Raleigh Bay
Onslow Bay
Hatteras I.
Cape Hatteras National Seashore
Washington Canyon
Norfolk Canyon
Baltimore Canyon

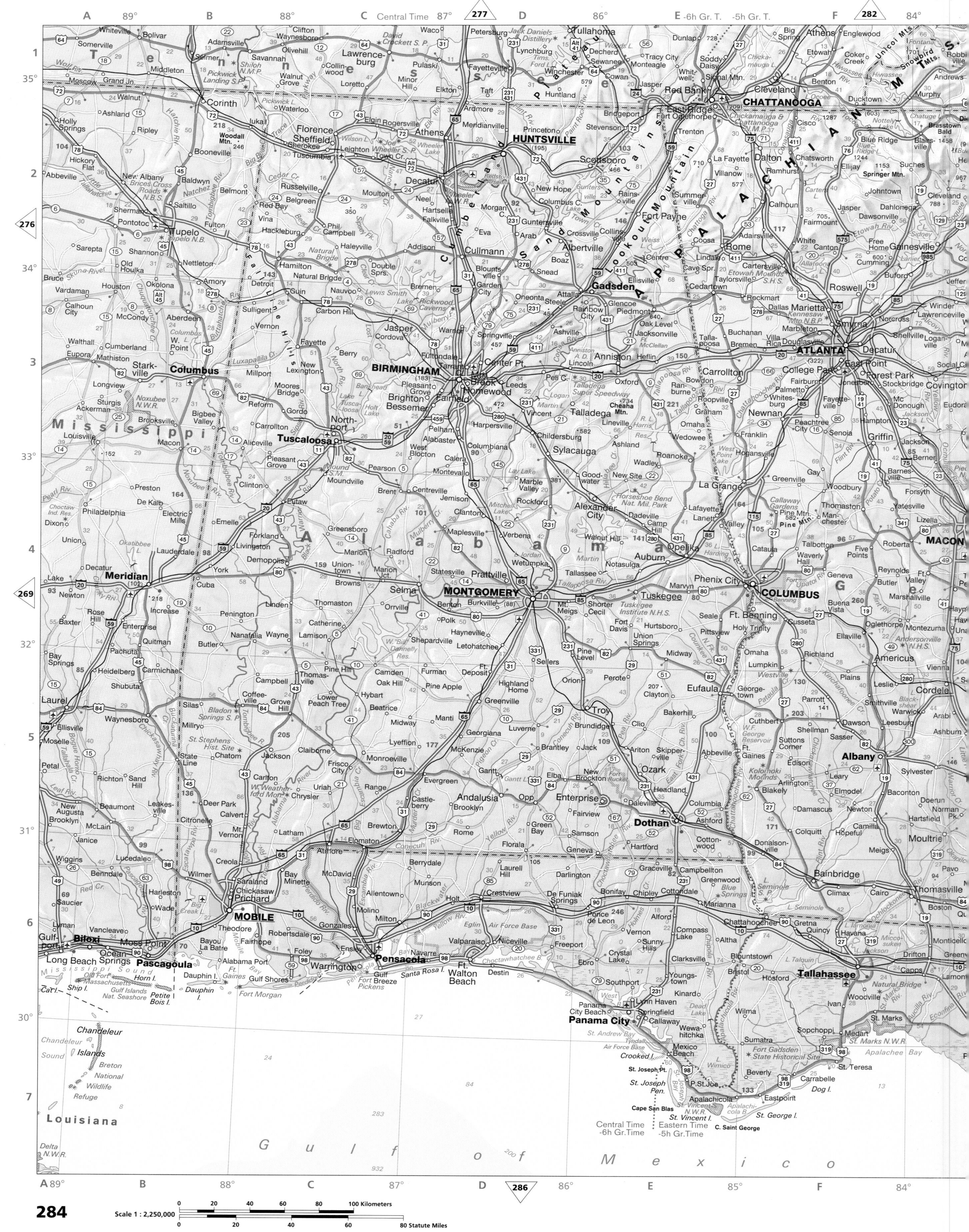
A 89° B 88° C Central Time 87° 277 D 86° E -6h Gr. T. -5h Gr. T. F 282 84°
Tennessee
Alabama
Mississippi
Louisiana
Gulf of Mexico
Cumberland Plateau
Sand Mountains
Lookout Mountain
Appalachian Mts.
Fall Line Hills
Unicoi Mts.
Snowbird Mts.
HUNTSVILLE
CHATTANOOGA
ATLANTA
BIRMINGHAM
MONTGOMERY
COLUMBUS
MOBILE
MACON
Tuscaloosa
Meridian
Columbus
Tupelo
Corinth
Florence
Sheffield
Decatur
Gadsden
Anniston
Rome
Marietta
Dalton
Athens
Cullmann
Jasper
Selma
Auburn
Opelika
Tuskegee
Phenix City
La Grange
Newnan
Dothan
Enterprise
Troy
Eufaula
Albany
Americus
Tallahassee
Pensacola
Panama City
Biloxi
Pascagoula
Gulfport
Laurel
Hattiesburg
Thomasville
Bainbridge
Apalachicola
Chandeleur Islands
Breton National Wildlife Refuge
Gulf Islands Nat. Seashore
Central Time -6h Gr.Time
Eastern Time -5h Gr.Time
C. Saint George
35° 34° 33° 32° 31° 30°
1 2 3 4 5 6 7
276 269 286
Scale 1 : 2,250,000
0 20 40 60 80 100 Kilometers
0 20 40 60 80 Statute Miles

83°
H
82°
J
Eastern Time
81°
K
80°
L
79°
283
M
78°
N
35°
34°
33°
32°
31°
30°
1
2
3
4
5
6
7
283
287
North Carolina
South Carolina
Georgia
Florida
CHARLOTTE
Gastonia
Fayetteville
Greenville
Spartanburg
Anderson
Greenwood
COLUMBIA
Sumter
Florence
Lumberton
Wilmington
Myrtle Beach
Conway
Georgetown
Orangeburg
Aiken
Augusta
North Charleston
Charleston
Mt. Pleasant
James Island
Folly Beach
Beaufort
Hilton Head Island
SAVANNAH
Tybee Island
Statesboro
Vidalia
Hinesville
Waycross
Brunswick
St. Simons Island
Fernandina Beach
JACKSONVILLE
Atlantic Beach
Neptune Beach
Jacksonville Beach
St. Augustine
Gainesville
Palatka
Flagler Beach
Sea Islands
Long Bay
Onslow Bay
ATLANTIC
OCEAN
Blake
Plateau

Puerto Rico • Virgin Islands

Scale 1 : 2,250,000 — 0 20 40 60 80 100 Kilometers; 0 20 40 60 80 Statute Miles

285
Florida
JACKSONVILLE
Fernandina Beach
Atlantic Beach
Neptune Beach
Jacksonville Beach
St. Augustine
Gainesville
Palatka
Flagler Beach
Ormond Beach
DAYTONA BEACH
Port Orange
New Smyrna Beach
Ocala
De Land
Deltona
Sanford
Winter Park
ORLANDO
Walt Disney World
Kissimmee
Titusville
J.F. Kennedy Space Center
Cape Canaveral
Merritt Island
Cocoa Beach
Melbourne
Palm Bay
Lakeland
TAMPA
Clearwater
Largo
ST. PETERSBURG
Bradenton
Sarasota
Venice
Port Charlotte
Fort Myers
Cape Coral
Naples
Vero Beach
Fort Pierce
Port St. Lucie
Lake Okeechobee
West Palm Beach
Boca Raton
Pompano Beach
FT. LAUDERDALE
HOLLYWOOD
HIALEAH
Miami Beach
MIAMI
Kendall
Homestead
Everglades National Park
Key Largo
Key West
Florida Keys
Blake Plateau
ATLANTIC OCEAN
Straits of Florida
Little Bahama Bank
Grand Bahama Island
Northwest Providence Channel
BAHAMAS
Bimini Islands
Berry Islands
Andros Island
54
55

Alaska is presented in the scale 1 : 4,500,000

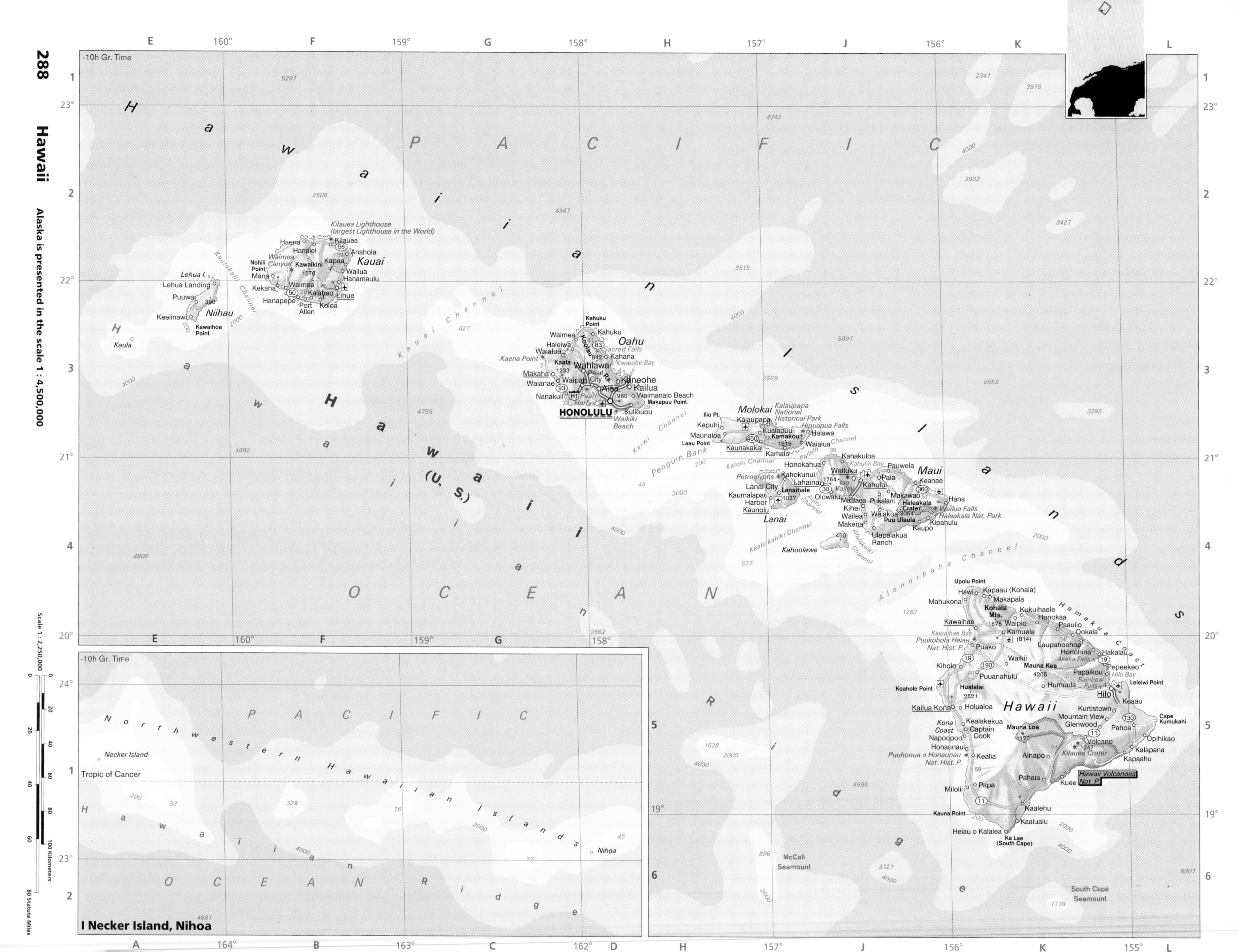

Scale 1 : 2,250,000
0 20 40 60 80 100 Kilometers
0 20 40 60 80 Statute Miles

Abbreviations

A

A. Alm (Ger.) mountain meadow
Abb. Abbaye (Fr.) abbey
Abor. (Engl.) aboriginal
Aç. Açude (Port.) small reservoir
Ad. Adası (Turk.) island
A.F.B. (Engl.) Air Force Base
Ag. Agios (Gr.) saint
Á.I. Área Indígena (Port.) Indian reservation
Ald. Aldeia (Port.) village, hamlet
Arch. (Engl.) archipelago
Arch. Archipiélago (Span.) archipelago
Arh. Arhipelag (Rus.) archipelago
Arq. Arquipélago (Port.) archipelago
Arr. Arroyo (Span.) brook
Art.Ra. (Engl.) artillery range
Aut. (Engl.) autonomous
Aut.Dist. (Engl.) autonomous district
Aut.Reg. (Engl.) autonomous region

B

B. Baie (Fr.) bay
B. Biológica, -o (Span.) biological
Ba. Bahía (Span.) bay
Bal. Balka (Rus.) gorge
Ban. Banjaran (Mal.) mountains
Bel. Belo, -yj, -aja, -oe (Rus.) white
Bk. Bukit (Mal.) mountain, hill
Bol. Boloto (Rus.) swamp
Bol. Bolšoj, -aja, -oe (Rus.) big
Bot. (Engl.) botanical
B.P. (Engl.) battlefield park
Brj. Baraj (Turk.) dam
Buch. Buchta (Ukr.) bay
Buh. Buhta (Rus.) bay

C

C. Cap (Fr.) cape, point
C. Cabo (Port., Span.) cape, point
Cab. Cabeça (Port.) heights, summit
Cach. Cachoeira (Port.) rapids
Cal. Caleta (Span.) bay
Can. Canalul (Rom.) canal
Can. Canal (Span.) canal
Cast. Castello (Ital.) castle, palace
Cd. Ciudad (Span.) city
Cga. Ciénaga (Span.) swamp, moor
Ch. Chenal (Fr.) canal
Chr. Chrebet (Ukr.) mountains
Co. Cerro (Span.) mountain, hill
Col. Colonia (Span.) colony
Conv. Convento (Span.) monastery
Cord. Cordillera (Span.) mountain chain
Corr. Corredeira (Port.) rapids
Cpo. Campo (Port.) field
Cr. (Engl.) creek
Cs. Cerros (Span.) mountain, hill

D

D. Dake (Jap.) mountain
Dağl. Dağlar (Turk.) mountains
Dist. (Engl.) district
Df. Dorf (Ger.) village
Dl. Deal (Rom.) heights, hill

E

Ea. Estancia (Span.) ranch
Ej. Ejido (Span.) common
Emb. Embalse (Span.) reservoir
Ens. Enseada (Port.) small bay
Erm. Ermita (Span.) hermitage
Ero. Estero (Span.) estuary
Esp. España (Span.) Spain
Est. Estación (Span.) railroad terminal
Estr. Estrecho (Span.) straight, sound
Ez. Ezero (Bulg.) lake

F

Faz. Fazenda (Port.) ranch
Fk. (Engl.) fork
Fn. Fortín (Span.) fort
Fr. (Engl.) France
Fs. (Engl.) falls, waterfall
Ft. (Engl.) fort

G

Ǧ. Ǧabal (Arab.) mountain
G. Gawa (Jap.) lagoon
G. Gîtul (Rom.) pass
G. Golfo (Span.) bay, gulf
G. Gora (Rus.) mountain
Gde. Grande (Span.) big
Gds. Grandes (Span.) big
Glac. Glacier (Fr.) glacier
Gos. Gosudarstvennyj, -aja (Rus.) national
Gr. (Engl.) Greece
Gr.Br. (Engl.) Great Britain
Grd. Grand (Fr.) big
Grl. General (Span.) general

H

H. Hora (Ukr.) mountain
H. Hütte (Ger.) mountain hut
Harb. (Engl.) harbor
Hist. (Engl.) historic
Hm. Heim (Ger.) home
Hr. Hrebet (Rus.) mountains
Hte. Haute (Fr.) high
Hwy. (Engl.) highway

I

I. (Engl.) island
Î. Île (Fr.) island
I. Ilha (Port.) island
I. Isla (Span.) island
Igl. Iglesia (Span.) church
In. Insulă (Rom.) island
Ind. (Engl.) Indian
Ind.Res. (Engl.) Indian reservation
Int. (Engl.) international
Is. (Engl.) islands
Is. Islas (Span.) islands

J

Jaz. Jazovir (Bulg.) reservoir
Jct. (Engl.) junction
Jez. Jezero (Slovenian) lake
Juž. Južnyj, -aja (Rus.) southern

K

Kan. Kanal (Ger.) canal
Kep. Kepulauan (Indon.) archipelago
Kg. Kampong (Indon.) village
K-l. Köli (Kazakh.) lake
K-l. Küli (Uzbek.) lake
Kör. Körfez (Turk.) gulf, bay
Kp. Kólpos (Gr.) gulf, bay
Kr. Krasno, -yj, -aja, -oe (Rus.) red

L

L. (Engl.) lake
L. Lac (Fr.) lake
L. Lacul (Rom.) lake
L. Lago (Span.) lake
Lag. Laguna (Rus.) lagoon
Lev. Levyj, -aja (Rus.) left
Lim. Liman (Rus.) lagoon
Lim. Limni (Gr.) lake
Lte. (Engl.) little

M

M. Munte (Rom.) mountain
M. Mys (Rus.) cape, point
Mal. (Engl.) Malaysia
Mal. Malo, -yj, -aja, -oe (Rus.) little
Man. Manastir (Bulg.) monastery
Man. Manastır (Turk.) monastery
Măn. Mănăstire (Rom.) monastery
Mem. (Engl.) memorial
Mgne. Montagne (Fr.) mountain, mountains
Mi. Misaki (Jap.) cape, point
Mil.Res. (Engl.) military reservation
Milli P. Milli Park (Turk.) national park
Min. (Engl.) mineral
Mñas. Montañas (Span.) mountains
Moh. Mohyla (Ukr.) tomb
Mon. Monasterio (Span.) monastery
M.P. (Engl.) military park
Mt. (Engl.) mount
Mte. Monte (Span.) mountain
Mti. Monti (Ital.) mountains
Mtn. (Engl.) mountain
Mtns. (Engl.) mountains
Mtn.S.P. (Engl.) mountain state park
Mts. (Engl.) mountains
Mts. Montes (Span.) mountains
Munţ. Munţii (Rom.) mountains
Mus. (Engl.) museum

N

N. Nehir/ Nehri (Turk.) river, stream
N. Nudo (Span.) peak
Nac. Nacional (Span.) national
Nac. Nacional'nyj, -aja, -oe (Rus.) national
Nat. (Engl.) national
Nat.Mon. (Engl.) national monument
Nat.P. (Engl.) national park
Nat.Seas. (Engl.) national seashore
Naz. Nazionale (Ital.) national
N.B.P. (Engl.) national battlefield park
N.B.S. (Engl.) national battlefield site
Ned. Nederland (Neth.) Netherlands
Nev. Nevado (Span.) snow-capped mountain
N.H.P. (Engl.) national historic park
N.H.S. (Engl.) national historic site
Niž. Niže, -nij, -naja, -neje (Rus.) lower
Nizm. Nizmennost' (Rus.) lowlands
N.M.P. (Engl.) national military park
Nördl. Nördlich (Ger.) northern
Nov. Novo, -yj, -aja, -oe (Rus.) new
N.P. (Engl.) national park
N.R.A. (Engl.) national recreation area
Nsa.Sra. Nossa Senhora (Port.) Our Lady
Nth. (Engl.) north
Ntra.Sra. Nuestra Señora (Span.) Our Lady
Nva. Nueva (Span.) new
Nvo. Nuevo (Span.) new
N.W.R. (Engl.) national wildlife refuge

O

O. Ostrov (Rus.) island
Obl. Oblast (Rus.) district
Ö. Östra (Swed.) eastern
Öv. Övre (Swed.) upper
Of. Oficina (Span.) office
Ostr. Ostrov (Rom.) island
O-va. Ostrova (Rus.) islands
Oz. Ozero (Rus.) lake

P

P. (Engl.) port
P. Passe (Fr.) pass
P. Pico (Span.) peak
P. Pulau (Indon.) island
Peg. Pegunungan (Indon.) mountains
Pen. (Engl.) peninsula
Pen. Península (Span.) peninsula
Per. Pereval (Rus.) pass
Picc. Piccolo (Ital.) little
P-iv. Pivostriv (Ukr.) peninsula
Pk. (Engl.) peak
Pkwy. (Engl.) parkway
Pl. Planina (Bulg.) mountain, mountains
P.N. Parque Nacional (Span.) national park
Po. Paso (Span.) pass
Por. Porog (Rus.) rapids
P-ov. Poluostrov (Rus.) peninsula
Pr. Proliv (Rus.) strait, sound
Pr. Prohod (Bulg.) pass
Presq. Presqu'île (Fr.) peninsula
Prov. (Engl.) provincial
Prov.P. (Engl.) provincial park
Pso. Passo (Ital.) pass
Psto. Puesto (Span.) outpost
Pt. (Engl.) point
Pta. Ponta (Port.) point
Pta. Punta (Span.) point
Pte. Pointe (Fr.) point
Pto. Pôrto (Port.) port
Pto. Puerto (Span.) port, pass
Pzo. Pizzo (Ital.) point

Q

Q.N.P. (Jap.) quasi national park

R

R. Reka (Bulg.) river
R. Reserva (Span.) reservation
R. Rio (Port.) river
R. Río (Span.) river
Ra. (Engl.) range
Rch. Riachão (Port.) small river
Rch. Riacho (Span.) small river
Rdl. Raudal (Span.) stream
Rep. (Engl.) republic
Repr. Represa (Port.) dam
Rère. Rivière (Fr.) river
Res. (Engl.) reservoir
Res. Reserva (Port.) reservation
Resp. Respublika (Rus.) republic
Rib. Ribeira (Port.) shore
Rib. Ribeiro (Port.) small river
Rif. Rifugio (Ital.) mountain hut
Riv. (Engl.) river
Rom. (Engl.) Romania
Rom. Romano, -na (Span.) Roman
Rus. (Engl.) Russia

S

S. San (Jap.) mountain, mountains
S. San (Span.) saint
S. São (Port.) saint
Sa. Saki (Jap.) cape
Sa. Serra (Port.) mountains
Sal. Salar (Span.) salt desert, salt lagoon
Sanm. Sanmyaku (Jap.) mountains
Sd. (Engl.) sound
Sel. Selat (Indon.) road
Sev. Sever, -nyj, -naja, -noe (Rus.) north
Sf. Sfîntu (Rom.) holy
Sh. Shima (Jap.) island
S.H.P. (Engl.) state historic park
S.H.S. (Engl.) state historic site
S.M. (Engl.) state monument
Sna. Salina (Span.) salt flat
Snas. Salinas (Span.) salt flats
Snia. Serranía (Span.) ridge
S.P. (Engl.) state park
Sr. Sredne, -ij, -aja, -ee (Rus.) middle, central
Sra. Sierra (Span.) mountains
St. (Engl.) saint
St. Saint (Fr., Span.) saint
Sta. Santa (Span.) saint
Sta. Staro, -ij, -aja, -oe (Rus.) old
Ste. Sainte (Fr.) saint
Sth. (Engl.) south
St.Mem. (Engl.) state memorial
Sto. Santo (Port.) saint
Str. (Engl.) strait
Suh. Suho, -aja (Rus.) dry
Sv. Svet, -a, -o (Bulg.) saint
Sv. Sveti (Croatian) saint

T

T. Take (Jap.) peak, heights
Tel. Teluk (Indon.) bay
Tg. Tanjung (Indon.) cape
Tg. Tōge (Jap.) pass
Tte. Teniente (Span.) lieutenant

U

Ülk. Ülken (Kazakh.) big
U.K. (Engl.) United Kingdom
U.S. (Engl.) United States

V

V. Vallée (Fr.) valley
Va. Villa (Span.) market town
Vda. Vereda (Port.) path
Vdhr. Vodohranilišče (Rus.) reservoir
Vdp. Vodospad (Ukr.) waterfall
Vel. Veliko, -ij, -aja, -oe (Rus.) big
Verh. Verhnie, -yj, aja, -ee (Rus.) upper
Vf. Vîrf (Rom.) peak, heights
Vill. (Engl.) village
Vis. Visočina (Bulg.) heights
Vjal. Vjalikie (Belarus.) big
Vlk. Vulkan (Ger.) volcano
Vn. Volcán (Span.) volcano
Vod. Vodopad (Rus.) waterfall
Vol. Volcán (Span.) volcano
Vul. Vulcano (Philip.) volcano

W

W.A. (Engl.) wilderness area

Y

Y. Yama (Jap.) mountain, mountains

Z

Zal. Zaliv (Rus.) gulf, bay
Zap. Zapadne, -ij, -aja, -noe (Rus.) west
Zapov. Zapovednik (Rus.) protected area

Selected References

A

Abu Dhabi, sheikhdom of the United Arab Emirates 134
Abyssinia = Ethiopia 208-209
ACP Nations = developing nations of Africa, the Caribbean and the Pacific Islands
Afghanistan 135,137
Africa 185-224
Alaska 20-21
Albania 100-101
Aleutians 22-23
Algeria 190-191
Alpine Nations = Switzerland, Austria, Liechtenstein 92-93
Amazonas 66-67
Anatolia 128-129
Andalusia 98-99
Andes 5
Andorra 98-99
Anglo-America = English-speaking North America 20-49
Angola 216-217
Antarctica = South Polar region 16
Antigua and Barbuda 56
Antilles 54-56
Appennine Peninsula 100-101
Arabia = Arabian Peninsula 130-133
Arctic = North Polar region 16
Arctic Ocean 16
Argentina 76-80
Armenia 129
ASEAN Nations = Brunei, Indonesia, Malaysia, Philippines, Singapore and Thailand 158-167
Asia 105-168
Asia Minor = Asian region of Turkey 128-129
Atlantic Ocean 6-7
Atlas Nations = Algeria, Morocco and Tunisia 188-191
Australia 172-181
Austria 92-93
Azerbaijan 129
Azores 6-7

B

Bahamas 54-55
Bahrain 134
Balkan Peninsula 100-101
Baltic Nations = Estonia, Latvia and Lithuania 94-95
Bangladesh 142-143
Barbados 56
Belarus 94-95
Belgium 90-91
Belize 52-53
Benelux = Belgium, Netherlands, Luxembourg 90-91
Benin 204
Bermuda Islands 55
Bhutan 142-143
Bismarck Archipelago 183
Bolivia 70-71
Borneo = Kalimantan 164-165
Bosnia and Herzegovina ... 100-101
Botswana 218-220
Brazil 66-75
British Isles 90-91
Brunei 164-165
Bulgaria 100-101
Burkina Faso 203
Burma = Myanmar 142,158
Burundi 212

C

California 40-41
Cambodia 158-159
Cameroon 205,209
Canada 30-39
Canary Islands 188
Cape Verde 202
Celebes = Sulawesi 164-165
Central Africa 205-211
Central African Republic ... 206-207
Central America 50-53
Central Asia 124,144
Central Europe 92-93
Ceylon = Sri Lanka 140-141
Chad 199,206
Chile 76-80
China 144-157
Colombia 60-61
Commonwealth of Independent States (CIS) - Formed in 1991 from the republics of the former Soviet Union with the exception of the Baltic States
Commonwealth of Nations = Great Britain and Northern Ireland, Antigua and Barbuda, Australia, Bahamas, Bangladesh, Barbados, Belize, Botswana, Brunei, Canada, Cyprus, Dominica, Gambia, Ghana, Grenada, Guyana, India, Jamaica, Kenya, Kiribati, Lesotho, Malawi, Malaysia, Maldives, Malta, Mauritius, Namibia, Nauru, New Zealand, Nigeria, Pakistan, Papua New Guinea, Saint Kitts and Nevis, Saint Lucia, Saint Vincent and the Grenadines, Samoa, Seychelles, Solomon Islands, South Africa, Sri Lanka, Swaziland, Tanzania, Tonga, Trinidad and Tobago, Tuvalu, Uganda, Vanuatu, Zambia (As of 1995)
Comoros 222
Congo 209-210
Costa Rica 52-53
Côte d'Ivoire (Ivory Coast) 202-203
Croatia 100-101
Cuba 54-55
Cyprus 128-129
Czech Republic 92-93

D

Dahomey = Benin 204
Denmark 86-87
Djibouti 208
Dominica 56
Dominican Republic 54-55
Dubayy = sheikhdom of the United Arab Emirates 134

E

East Asia = eastern China, Japan and Korea 150-157
East Pakistan = Bangladesh 142-143
Ecuador 64-65
Egypt 194-195
El Salvador 52-53
England 90-91
Equatorial Guinea 210
Eritrea 201
Estonia 94-95
Ethiopia 208-209
Europe 81-104
European Union = Austria, Belgium, Denmark, Finland, Germany, France, Greece, Great Britain and Northern Ireland, Ireland, Italy, Luxembourg, Netherlands, Portugal, Spain, Sweden (As of 1995)

F

Far East 120-123
Fiji 184
Finland 88-89
Flanders 92-93
Florida 48-49
Formosa = Taiwan 157
France 90-91
French Guiana 62-63

G

Gabon 210
Gambia 202
Gaza 130
Georgia 126
Germany 92-93
Ghana 203
Gibraltar 98
Gobi 148-155
Great Britain 90-91
Greater Antilles = Cuba, Haiti, Jamaica, Puerto Rico 54-55
Greater Sunda Islands = Borneo/Kalimantan, Java, Sulawesi, Sumatra 162-168
Great Lakes = Lake Erie, Lake Huron, Lake Michigan, Lake Ontario, Lake Superior 46-47
Great Plains 42-45
Greece 100-101
Greenland 26-29
Grenada 56
Guatemala 53
Guinea 201
Guinea-Bissau 201
Gulf States = nations along the Persian Gulf 131-134
Guyana 62-63

H

Haiti 54-55
Hawaii 48
Herzegovina, Bosnia- 100-101
Himalaya 144-145
Hokkaidō 153
Holland 92
Hondo 152
Honduras 52-54
Honshū 152-153
Horn of Africa = Somali Peninsula 209
Hungary 92-93

I

Iberian Peninsula 98-99
Ibero-America = Latin America 50-80
Iceland 86
India 138-143
Indian Ocean 12
Indian Subcontinent 138-143
Indochina 158-159
Indonesia 162-168
Inner Mongolia 148-150
Iran 134-136
Iraq 129-131
Ireland 90-91
Israel 130
Italy 100-101
Ivory Coast = Côte d'Ivoire 202-203

J

Jamaica 54-55
Japan 152-153
Java 168
Jericho 130
Jordan 130-131

K

Kalimantan = Borneo........164-165
Kashmir........138
Kazakhstan........124-127
Kenya........212-213
Korea, Democratic Peoples Republic of = North Korea........150-151
Korea, Republic of = South Korea........150-151
Kurdistan........129
Kuwait........131
Kyrgyzstan........137,146

L

Labrador........36-39
Ladakh........138-139
Laos........156,159
La Plata Nations = Argentina, Paraguay and Uruguay........74-80
Latin America = Spanish- and Portuguese-speaking America........50-80
Latvia........94-95
Lebanon........128
Lesotho........221
Lesser Antilles........56
Lesser Sunda Islands........168
Levant = coastal region of the eastern Mediterranean Sea........128
Liberia........202
Libya........192-193
Liechtenstein........92-93
Lithuania........94-95
Lower Guinea........210-211
Luzon........160-161

M

Madagascar........222-223
Maghreb = Atlas Nations = Algeria, Morocco, Tunisia........188-191
Malawi........215-219
Malaysia........162-165
Maldives........140
Mali........197,203
Malta........100
Manchuria........150-151
Marshall Islands........13
Martinique........56
Mauritania........196-197
Mauritius........224
Mediterranean Sea........8
Melanesia........14-15
Mesopotamia........129
Micronesia........14-15
Middle America........50-56
Middle East........135-138
Mindanao........160-161
Moldova........102-103
Monaco........90-91
Mongolia........147-149
Montenegro........100-101
Morocco........188-189
Mozambique........215,219
Myanmar = Burma........142,158

N

NAFTA Nations = Canada, United States, Mexico........20-53
Namibia........217,220
NATO Nations = Belgium, Canada, Denmark, Germany, Greece, Great Britain and Northern Ireland, Iceland, Italy, Luxembourg, Netherlands, Norway, Portugal, Spain, Turkey, United States
Near East........128-131
Nepal........144-145
Netherlands........92-93
Newfoundland........39
New Guinea........167,183
New World = North and South America and the West Indies........17-80
New Zealand........182
Nicaragua........52-53
Niger........198,205
Nigeria........204-205
North Africa........188-200
North Korea........150-151
North Pole........16
Norway........86-87
Novaya Zemlya........84-85

O

Oceania........13,184
Old World = Europe and Asia........81-168
Oman........132-135
Outer Mongolia........148-149

P

Pacific Ocean........14-15
Pakistan........138-139
Palestine = Land between the Mediterranean Sea and the Jordan River........128-129
Panama........52-53
Papua New Guinea........183
Paraguay........71,77
Patagonia........78-80
Peloponnesus........100-101
Persia = Iran........134-136
Peru........64-65
Philippines........160-161
Poland........92-93
Polynesia........14-15
Portugal........98-99

Q

Qatar........134

R

Red China = unofficial name for China........144-157
Rhodesia = Zimbabwe........218-219
Rocky Mountains........32-33
Romania........102-103
Russia........95,121
Rwanda........212

S

SADC Nations = Angola, Botswana, Lesotho, Malawi, Mozambique, Namibia, South Africa, Swaziland, Tanzania, Zambia, Zimbabwe........214-221
Sahara........188-201
Sahel........196-201
Saint Kitts and Nevis........56
Saint Lucia........56
Saint Vincent and the Grenadines........56
Samoa........184
San Marino........100-101
São Tomé and Príncipe........210
Saudi Arabia........130-133
Scandinavia........86-87
Senegal........196,202
Seychelles........224
Siam = Thailand........158-159
Siberia........108-115
Sierra Leone........202
Singapore........162
Sinkiang (Xinjiang)........146-147
Slovakia........92-93
Slovenia........100-101
Solomon Islands........184
Somalia........209,213
South Africa........220-221
South America........57-80
Southeastern Asia = Brunei, Cambodia, Indonesia, Laos, Malaysia, Myanmar, Philippines, Singapore, Thailand, Vietnam........156-167
South Korea........150-151
South Pole........16
South Seas = South Pacific Ocean........14-15
Southwest Africa = Namibia........217-220
Soviet Union, dissolved in 1991, its former republics (without the Baltic States) formed the Commonwealth of Independent States (CIS)
Spain........98-99
Sri Lanka........140-141
Sudan (nation)........200,207
Sudan (region)........196-201
Sulawesi........164-165
Suriname........62-63
Swaziland........221
Sweden........86-87
Switzerland........92-93
Syria........128-129

T

Taiwan........157
Tajikistan........136-137
Tanganyika = Tanzania........214-215
Thailand........158-159
Tibet........144-145
Togo........204
Tonga........184
Trinidad and Tobago........56
Tunisia........190
Turkey........128-129
Turkmenistan........136-137

U

Uganda........212
Ukraine........102-103
United Arab Emirates........132-135
United Kingdom........90-91
Upper Guinea........202-204
Upper Volta = Burkina Faso........203
Uruguay........75
U.S.A. = United States of America........40-49
Uzbekistan........136-137

V

Vanuatu........184
Vatican City........100-101
Venezuela........60-61
Vietnam........156-159

W

West Africa........202,210
Western Sahara........188-189
West Indies........54-56
White Russia (Belarus)........94-95

Y

Yemen........132-133
Yugoslavia........100-101

Z

Zaire........211,216
Zambia........218-219
Zimbabwe........218-219

Index of Map Names

The index contains all names found on the maps in this atlas. The index's alphabetical listing corresponds to the sequence of letters in the Roman alphabet. Diacritical marks and special letters have been ignored in alphebetizing, e.g.:

A ....Á, À, Â, Ă, Å, Ą, Ā, Ã, Ä, Æ

The ligatures æ, œ are treated as ae and oe in the alphabetical listing.

Names that have been abbreviated on the maps are generally written in full in the index.

Generic concepts follow geographic names, e.g. Mexico, Gulf of; Ventoux, Mont. Exception: colors (e.g. Mount Blanc) and adjectives (e.g. Big, Little) come first. Official additions (e.g. Rothenburg ob der Tauber) are included in the alphabetizing.

To a certain degree, the index also includes official alternate forms, linguistic variants, renamings and other secondary denominations. In such cases, the index refers to names as they appear on the maps, e.g. Meran = Merano, Leningrad = Sankt-Peterburg.

Abbreviations in parentheses help distinguish between places bearing the same names. Abbreviations as used on international motor-vehicle license plates have been given priority; where this is insufficient, administrative information like federal lands, provinces, regions, etc. are indicated.

Icons, which immediately follow the names, are used to indicate fundamental geographic concepts.

New York	o ••	**USA**	(NY)	280-281	N 3
① Search concept	② Icon	③ Nation	④ Administrative unit	⑤ Page	⑥ Search grid designation

② **Icons:**

■ ....Sovereign nation
□ ....Administrative unit
★ ....Capital city (national capital)
☆ ....State (provincial) capital
o ....Place
⩡ ....Landscape
ᴖ ....Island

ᴗ ....Depression
▲▲ ....Mountains
▲ ....Mountain
▲̇ ....Active volcano
≈ ....Ocean, part of an ocean
o ....Lake, salt lake
~ ....River, waterfall

⊂ ....glacier
< ....dam
≃ ....Undersea topography
⊥ ....National park
X ....Reservation
xx ....Military installation
II ....Transportation construction

✈ ....Airport
∴ ....Ruins, ruined city

••• ....World cultural or natural heritage site
•• ....Point of major interest
• ....Point of interest

③ **Souvereign States and Territories (Abbrevations in *italics:* Abbrevation not official)**

A ....Austria
AFG ....Afghanistan
AG ....Antigua and Barbuda
AL ....Albania
AND ....Andorra
ANG ....Angola
AR ....Armenia
ARK ....Antarctica
ARU ....Aruba
AUS ....Australia
AUT ....Autonomous region
AZ ....Azerbaijan
B ....Belgium
BD ....Bangladesh
BDS ....Barbados
BF ....Burkina Faso
BG ....Bulgaria
BH ....Belize
BHT ....Bhutan
BIH ....Bosnia and Herzegovina
BOL ....Bolivia
BR ....Brazil
BRN ....Bahrain
BRU ....Brunei
BS ....Bahamas
BU ....Burundi
BY ....Belarus
C ....Cuba
CAM ....Cameroon
CDN ....Canada
CH ....Switzerland
CI ....Côte d'Ivoire (Ivory Coast)
CL ....Sri Lanka
CO ....Colombia
COM ....Comoros
CR ....Costa Rica
CV ....Cape Verde
CY ....Cyprus
CZ ....Czech Republic
D ....Germany
DJI ....Djibouti
DK ....Denmark
DOM ....Dominican Republic
DVR ....North Korea
DY ....Benin
DZ ....Algeria
E ....Spain
EAK ....Kenya
EAT ....Tanzania
EAU ....Uganda
EC ....Ecuador
ER ....Eritrea
ES ....El Salvador
EST ....Estonia
ET ....Egypt
ETH ....Ethiopia
F ....France
FIN ....Finland
FJI ....Fiji
FL ....Liechtenstein
FR ....Faroe Islands
FSM ....Micronesia
G ....Gabon
GB ....United Kingdom
GBA ....Alderney
GBG ....Guernsey
GBJ ....Jersey
GBM ....Isle of Man
GBZ ....Gibraltar
GCA ....Guatemala
GE ....Georgia
GH ....Ghana
GNB ....Guinea-Bissau
GQ ....Equatorial Guinea
GR ....Greece
GRØ ....Greenland
GUY ....Guyana
H ....Hungary
HK ....Hong Kong
HN ....Honduras
HR ....Croatia
I ....Italy
IL ....Israel
IND ....India
IR ....Iran
IRL ....Ireland
IRQ ....Iraq
IS ....Iceland
J ....Japan
JA ....Jamaika
JOR ....Jordan
K ....Cambodia
KA ....Kazakhstan
KAN ....Saint Kitts and Nevis
KIB ....Kiribati
KS ....Kyrgyzstan
KSA ....Saudi Arabia
KWT ....Kuwait
L ....Luxembourg
LAO ....Laos
LAR ....Libya
LB ....Liberia
LS ....Lesotho
LT ....Lithuania
LV ....Latvia
M ....Malta
MA ....Morocco
MAI ....Marshall Islands
MAL ....Malaysia
MAU ....Mongolia
MC ....Monaco
MD ....Moldova
MEX ....Mexico
MK ....Macedonia
MOC ....Mozambique
MS ....Mauritius
MV ....Maldives
MW ....Malawi
MYA ....Myanmar (Burma)
N ....Norway
NA ....Netherlands Antilles
NAM ....Namibia
NAU ....Nauru
NEP ....Nepal
NIC ....Nicaragua
NL ....Netherlands
NZ ....New Zealand
OM ....Oman
P ....Portugal
PA ....Panama
PAL ....Palau
PE ....Peru
PK ....Pakistan
PL ....Poland
PNG ....Papua New Guinea
PY ....Paraguay
Q ....Qatar
RA ....Argentina
RB ....Botswana
RC ....Taiwan
RCA ....Central African Republic
RCB ....Congo
RCH ....Chile
RG ....Guinea
RH ....Haiti
RI ....Indonesia
RIM ....Mauritania
RL ....Lebanon
RM ....Madagaskar
RMM ....Mali
RN ....Niger
RO ....Romania
ROK ....South Korea
ROU ....Uruguay
RP ....Philippines
RSM ....San Marino
RT ....Togo
RUS ....Russia
RWA ....Rwanda
S ....Sweden
SCV ....Vatican City
SD ....Swaziland
SGP ....Singapore
SK ....Slovakia
SLO ....Slovenia
SME ....Suriname
SN ....Senegal
SOL ....Solomon Islands
SP ....Somalia
STP ....São Tomé and Príncipe
SUD ....Sudan
SY ....Seychelles
SYR ....Syria
TCH ....Chad
THA ....Thailand
TJ ....Tajikistan
TM ....Turkmenistan
TN ....Tunisia
TON ....Tonga
TR ....Turkey
TT ....Trinidad and Tobago
TUV ....Tuvalu
UA ....Ukraine
UAE ....United Arab Emirates
US ....Uzbekistan
USA ....United States
VAN ....Vanuatu
VN ....Vietnam
VRC ....China
WAG ....Gambia
WAL ....Sierra Leone
WAN ....Nigeria
WB ....West Bank
WD ....Dominica
WG ....Grenada
WL ....Saint Lucia
WS ....Western Samoa
WSA ....Western Sahara
WV ....Saint Vincent and the Grenadines
Y ....Yemen
YU ....Yugoslavia
YV ....Venezuela
Z ....Zambia
ZA ....South Africa
ZRE ....Zaire
ZW ....Zimbabwe

AK .... Alaska
AL .... Alabama
AR .... Arkansas
AZ .... Arizona
CA .... California
CO .... Colorado
CT .... Connecticut
DE .... Delaware
FL .... Florida
GA .... Georgia
HI .... Hawaii
IA .... Iowa
ID .... Idaho
IL .... Illinois
IN .... Indiana
KS .... Kansas
KY .... Kentucky
LA .... Louisiana
MA .... Massachusetts
MD .... Maryland
ME .... Maine
MI .... Michigan
MN .... Minnesota
MO .... Missouri
MS .... Mississippi
MT .... Montana
NC .... North Carolina
ND .... North Dakota
NE .... Nebraska
NH .... New Hampshire
NJ .... New Jersey
NM .... New Mexico
NV .... Nevada
NY .... New York
OH .... Ohio
OK .... Oklahoma
OR .... Oregon
PA .... Pennsylvania
RI .... Rhode Island
SC .... South Carolina
SD .... South Dakota
TN .... Tennessee
TX .... Texas
UT .... Utah
VA .... Virginia
VT .... Vermont
WA .... Washington
WI .... Wisconsin
WV .... West Virginia
WY .... Wyoming

A

Aachen o••• D 92-93 J 3
Aačim, mys ▲ RUS 112-113 R 2
Aadan Yabaal o SP 212-213 L 2
'AA' Highway II USA (KY) 276-277 M 2
Äänekoski o FIN 88-89 H 5
Aansluit o ZA 220-221 F 3
Aappilattoq o GRØ (VGR) 26-27 X 7
Aappilattoq o GRØ (VGR) 28-29 S 6
Aar, De o ZA 220-221 G 5
Aaratuba, Ilha ⌒ BR 66-67 G 4
Aarau ☆ CH 92-93 K 5
Aare ~ CH 92-93 J 5
Aasiaat = Egedesminde o GRØ 28-29 Q 2
Aba o VRC 154-155 B 5
Aba o WAN 204-205 G 6
Aba o ZRE 212-213 C 2
Aba, Ğazirat ⌒ SUD 200-201 F 6
Abā ad-Dūd o KSA 130-131 J 4
Abā ar-Ruḥām o KSA 132-133 D 4
Abacaxis, Rio ~ BR 66-67 H 5
Abaco Island ⌒ BS 54-55 G 1
Abadab, Ğabal ▲ SUD 200-201 G 3
Ābādān o• IR 134-135 C 3
Ābādān, Ra's-e ▲ IR 134-135 C 4
Ābāde o• IR 134-135 E 3
Ābādeh-ye Ṭašk o IR 134-135 E 4
Abadhara o GE 126-127 D 6
Abadia dos Dourados o BR 72-73 G 5
Abadla o DZ 188-189 K 5
Abaeté o BR 72-73 H 5
Abaeté, Rio ~ BR 72-73 H 5
Abaetetuba o BR 62-63 K 6
Abag Qi o VRC 148-149 M 5
Abaí o PY 76-77 K 4
Abaida ▲ DJI 208-209 F 3
Abaíra o BR 72-73 K 2
Abaj o KA 124-125 H 4
Abaji o WAN 204-205 G 4
Abajo Mountains ▲ USA (UT) 254-255 F 6
Abajo Peak ▲ USA (UT) 254-255 F 6
Abaj Takalik ∴• GCA 52-53 J 4
Abak o WAN 204-205 G 6
Abakaliki o WAN 204-205 H 5
Abakan ☆ RUS 116-117 E 9
Abakan ~ RUS 116-117 E 9
Abakan ~ RUS 124-125 Q 2
Abakanskij hrebet ▲ RUS 124-125 Q 2
Abala o RCB 210-211 E 4
Abala o RN 204-205 E 1
Abalak o RN 198-199 C 5
Abaleha, I-n- < RMM 196-197 L 6
Abalessa o DZ 190-191 E 9
Abali, Bahr ~ TCH 206-207 D 3
Abamasagi Lake o CDN (ONT) 234-235 Q 4
Aban ☆ RUS 116-117 H 7
Aban ~ RUS 116-117 H 7
Abancay ☆ PE 64-65 F 8
Abanga ~ G 210-211 C 4
Abangharit, I-n- < RN 198-199 C 4
Abapo o BOL 70-71 F 6
Abar al-Maši o KSA 130-131 F 5
Abaré o BR 68-69 J 6
Ābār Ḥaimūr < ET 194-195 F 6
Abarqū o IR 134-135 E 3
Abarqū, Kavīr-e o IR 134-135 E 3
Abarr o USA (CO) 254-255 N 4
Abashiri o J 152-153 L 2
Abasolo o MEX (DGO) 50-51 G 5
Abasolo o MEX (TAM) 50-51 K 5
Abasula < EAK 212-213 G 4
Abatskij ☆ RUS 114-115 L 6
Abaucán, Río ~ RA 76-77 D 5
Abaurai Island ⌒ PNG 183 B 5
Ābaya Hāyk' o ETH 208-209 C 5
Abay Wenz = Blue Nile ~ ETH 208-209 C 3
Abaza o RUS 116-117 E 9
Abba o RCA 206-207 B 6
Abba-Omege o WAN 204-205 H 5
'Abbās, Bandar-e ☆• IR 134-135 G 5
'Abbāsābād o IR (KER) 134-135 F 3
'Abbāsābād o IR (MAZ) 136-137 B 6
'Abbāsābād o IR (SEM) 136-137 E 6
Abbaye, Point ▲ USA (MI) 270-271 K 4
Abbazia della Monte Oliveto Maggiore • I 100-101 C 3
Abbazia di Casamari • I 100-101 D 4
Abbazia di Montecassino • I 100-101 D 4
Abbeville o F 90-91 H 6
Abbeville o USA (AL) 284-285 E 5
Abbeville o USA (GA) 284-285 G 5
Abbeville o USA (LA) 268-269 H 7
Abbeville o USA (MS) 268-269 L 2
Abbeville o USA (SC) 284-285 H 2
Abbey o CDN (SAS) 232-233 K 5
Abbeyfeale = Mainistir na Féile o IRL 90-91 C 5
Abbieglassie o AUS 178-179 J 4
Abbot, Mount ▲ AUS 174-175 J 7
Abbotsford o CDN (BC) 230-231 G 4
Abbotsford o USA (WI) 270-271 H 6
Abbott o USA (NM) 256-257 L 2
Abbottābād o PK 138-139 D 2
'Abd ad-Dā'im o SUD 206-207 H 3
'Abdal'aziz, Ğabal ▲ SYR 128-129 J 4
'Abdaliyah, Bi'r al- o KSA 132-133 B 3
'Abd al-Kūri ⌒ Y 132-133 H 7
'Abdallāh, Minā' o KWT 130-131 L 3
Abd al-Māgid o SUD 200-201 F 5
Ābdān o IR 134-135 D 4
Ābdānān o IR 134-135 B 1
'Abdīn o SUD 200-201 D 6
Abdj o TCH 198-199 K 6
Abdon, Pulau ⌒ RI 166-167 F 1
Abdoulaye, Réserve d' ⊥ RT 202-203 L 5
Abdul Hakim o PK 138-139 D 4
Abdulino ☆ RUS 96-97 H 7
Ābdy Werz ~ ETH 208-209 C 3
Āb-e Bāzoft ~ IR 134-135 C 2
Abéché ☆ TCH 198-199 K 6
Āb-e Estāde o AFG 134-135 M 2
Abeïbara o RMM 196-197 L 5
Abejukolo o WAN 204-205 G 5
Āb-e Kūhrang ~ IR 134-135 D 2
Abélajouad < RN 198-199 C 4
Abelbodh < RMM 196-197 K 5
Abelhas, Cachoeira das ~ BR 70-71 G 2
Abeløya ⌒ N 84-85 R 3
Abel Tasman National Park ⊥ NZ 182 D 4
Ābeltī o ETH 208-209 C 4
Abemama Atoll ⌒ KIB 13 J 3
Abemarre o RI 166-167 L 5
Abene o GH 202-203 K 6
Abengourou ☆• CI 202-203 J 6
Abenójar o E 98-99 E 5
Åbenrå o• DK 86-87 D 9
Abeokuta ☆ WAN 204-205 E 5
Abepura o RI 166-167 L 3
Ābera o ETH 208-209 B 5
Aberaeron o GB 90-91 E 5
Abercrombie o USA (ND) 258-259 L 5
Abercrombie, Fort • USA (ND) 258-259 L 5
Abercrombie Caves • AUS 180-181 K 2
Abercrombie River ~ AUS 180-181 K 3
Aberdare National Park ⊥ EAK 212-213 F 4
Aberdeen o CDN (SAS) 232-233 M 3
Aberdeen o• GB 90-91 F 3
Aberdeen o USA (ID) 252-253 F 4
Aberdeen o USA (MD) 280-281 K 4
Aberdeen o USA (MS) 268-269 M 3
Aberdeen o USA (NC) 282-283 H 5
Aberdeen o USA (OH) 280-281 C 5
Aberdeen o USA (SD) 260-261 H 1
Aberdeen o USA (WA) 244-245 B 4
Aberdeen o ZA 220-221 G 6
Aberdeen Lake o CDN 30-31 U 3
Aberdeen Proving Ground xx USA (MD) 280-281 K 4
Aberdeen Road o ZA 220-221 G 6
Abergavenny-y-Fenni o GB 90-91 F 6
Ābergelē o ETH 200-201 J 6
Abergowrie o AUS 174-175 H 6
Abernathy o USA (TX) 264-265 C 5
Abernethy o CDN (SAS) 232-233 P 5
Abertawe = Swansea o GB 90-91 F 6
Aberystwyth o GB 90-91 E 5
Āb-e Seimarre ~ IR 134-135 B 2
Āb-e Šūr ~ IR 134-135 D 3
Āb-e Šūr ~ IR 134-135 F 4
Abez' o RUS 108-109 J 8
Āb-e Zimkān ~ IR 134-135 B 1
Abganerovo o RUS 96-97 D 9
Abgarm o IR 128-129 N 5
Abgué o TCH 206-207 D 3
Abhā ☆ KSA 132-133 C 4
Abhāna o IND 138-139 G 8
Abhar o IR 128-129 N 4
Abhar Rūd ~ IR 128-129 N 4
Ābhē Bad o DJI 208-209 E 3
Ābhē Bid Hāyk' o ETH 208-209 E 3
Abico o BR 66-67 E 4
'Abīdiyah o SUD 200-201 F 3
Abidjan ☆•• CI 202-203 J 7
Abiekwasputs o ZA 220-221 E 3
Abi Hill ▲ WAN 204-205 F 4
Abilene o USA (KS) 262-263 J 6
Abilene o USA (TX) 264-265 E 6
Abingdon o USA (IL) 274-275 H 4
Abingdon o USA (VA) 280-281 E 7
Abingdon Downs o AUS 174-175 G 5
Abington o GB 90-91 F 4
Abinsi o WAN 204-205 H 5
Abiquiu o USA (NM) 256-257 J 2
Abirāmam o IND 140-141 H 6
Abisko o S 86-87 J 2
Abisko nationalpark ⊥•• S 86-87 J 2
Abitangka o VRC 144-145 G 5
Abitau River ~ CDN 30-31 P 5
Abitibi, Lake o CDN (ONT) 236-237 J 4
Abitibi de Troyes Provincial Park ⊥ CDN (ONT) 236-237 H 4
Abitibi Indian Reservation ✗ CDN (ONT) 236-237 H 4
Abitibi River ~ CDN (ONT) 236-237 G 2
Ābiy Ādī o ETH 200-201 J 6
Abiyata Hāyk' o ETH 208-209 D 5
Abjelil o MA 188-189 J 3
Abkhazia = Abchazskaja Avtonomnaja Respublika ◘ GE 126-127 D 6
Abminga o AUS 178-179 C 4
Abnūb o ET 194-195 E 4
Abo o USA (NM) 256-257 J 4
Abo, Massif d' ▲ TCH 198-199 G 2
Åbo = Turku ☆• FIN 88-89 G 6
Aboabo o RP 160-161 C 8
Aboh o WAN 204-205 G 6
Abohar o IND 138-139 E 4
Aboine, River ~ WAN 204-205 G 5
Aboisso ☆ CI 202-203 J 7
Aboki o EAU 212-213 D 2
Abomey ☆••• DY 202-203 L 6
Abomey-Calavi o DY 204-205 E 5
Ābomsa o ETH 208-209 E 4
Abong o WAN 204-205 J 5
Abong Mbang o CAM 210-211 D 2
Aboni o SUD 206-207 L 3
Abo Pass ▲ USA (NM) 256-257 J 4
Abor o GH 202-203 L 6
Aboriginal Bora Ring ✗ AUS 178-179 M 5
Aboriginal Rock Art • AUS (NT) 172-173 L 2
Aboriginal Rock Art • AUS (QLD) 174-175 H 4
Aborlan o RP 160-161 C 8
Aboua o G 210-211 E 3
Abou-Deïa o TCH 206-207 D 3
Abou Goulem o TCH 198-199 K 6
Aboukoussom o TCH 206-207 E 3
Aboun o G 210-211 B 3
Abourak, Mont ▲ RMM 196-197 L 6
Abourou, Chutes ~ RCA 206-207 F 6
Abou-Telfân, Réserve de Faune de l' ⊥ TCH 198-199 J 6
Abovjan o AR 128-129 L 2
Abqaiq o KSA 130-131 L 5
'Abr, al- o Y 132-133 E 5
Abra, Lago del o RA 78-79 H 6
Abra de Ilog o RP 160-161 D 6
Abra de Lizoite ▲ RA 76-77 E 2
Abraham Bay ≈ 22-23 C 6
Abraham Bay ≈ 36-37 R 2
Abraham Lake o CDN (ALB) 232-233 B 3
Abraham's Bay o BS 54-55 J 3
Abra Huashuaccasa ▲ PE 64-65 F 9
Abraka o WAN 204-205 G 6
Abra la Cruz Chica ▲ BOL 76-77 E 1
Abrams o USA (WI) 270-271 K 6
Abrantes o P 98-99 C 5
Abra Pampa o• RA 76-77 E 2
Abraq, Wādī al ~ LAR 192-193 H 4
Abra Tapuna ▲ PE 64-65 F 8
Abrem o GH 202-203 K 7
Abrene = Pytalovo ☆ LV 94-95 K 3
Abreojos, Punta ▲ MEX 50-51 C 4
Abreus o BR 68-69 H 7
Abri o SUD 200-201 E 2
Abril, 7 de o RA 76-77 E 4
Abrolhos, Arquipélago dos ⌒ BR 72-73 L 4
Abrolhos Bank ≃ 5 H 6
Abrosimova ~ RUS 108-109 F 5
Abrud o RO 102-103 C 4
Abruzzo ◘ I 100-101 D 3
Abruzzo, Parco Nazionale d' ⊥ I 100-101 D 4
'Abs o Y 132-133 C 5
Absaroka-Beartooth Wilderness ⊥ USA (MT) 250-251 J 6
Absaroka Range ▲ USA (WY) 252-253 H 1
Absarokee o USA (MT) 250-251 K 6
Absecon o USA (NJ) 280-281 M 4
Ab Touyour o TCH 206-207 D 3
Abu o GNB 202-203 C 4
Abū 'Alī, Ğazīrat ⌒ KSA 130-131 L 4
Abū 'Ammār o SUD 200-201 G 4
Abū 'Arīš o KSA 132-133 C 5
Abū Ballās < ET 194-195 C 5
Abū Dāra, Ra's ▲ ET 194-195 H 6
Abū Darba o ET 194-195 F 3
Abū Darīḥa o SYR 128-129 G 5
Abū Dā'ūd, Ra's ▲ OM 132-133 L 2
Abū Dawn o SUD 200-201 F 4
Abū Dawn, Wādī ~ SUD 200-201 F 3
Abū ḍ-Ḍuhūr o SYR 128-129 G 5
Abu Dhabi = Abū Ẓabi ★• UAE 134-135 F 6
Abū Dī'āb, Ğabal ▲ ET 194-195 G 5
Abū Dis o SUD 200-201 F 3
Abū Dom o SUD 200-201 E 4
Abū Dubaisāt, Bi'r < ET 194-195 G 6
Abū Dulayq o SUD 200-201 F 5
Abufari o BR 66-67 F 5
Abufari, Reserva Biológica do ⊥ BR 66-67 F 5
Abū Faruḫ o IRQ 128-129 K 6
Abū Gābra o SUD 206-207 H 3
Abū Ğaraīdiq, Bi'r < ET 194-195 D 2
Abugi o WAN 204-205 G 4
Abū Ğisra o IRQ 130-131 J 2
Abū Gubaybah o SUD 206-207 K 3
Abū Ğulūd, Bi'r o SYR 128-129 H 4
Abū Hamad o SUD 200-201 F 3
Abū Ḥarāz o SUD 200-201 F 3
Abū Ḥarba, Ğabal ▲ ET 194-195 F 4
Abū Ḥašhā'ifa, Ḫalīğ ≈ 194-195 C 2
Abū Hashim o SUD 206-207 K 3
Abū Hašim, Bi'r < ET 194-195 G 6
Abū Hugar o SUD 200-201 F 6
Abuja ★ WAN 204-205 G 4
Abū Kabir o ET 194-195 E 2
Abū Kabisa o SUD 200-201 C 6
Abū Kamāl ☆ SYR 128-129 J 5
Abū Khinzir, Wādī ~ SUD 200-201 E 5
Abuki, Pegunungan ▲ RI 164-165 G 5
Abū Kulaywat o SUD 200-201 E 4
Abukuma-gawa ~ J 152-153 J 6
Abukuma-kōti ▲ J 152-153 J 6
Abu l-Abyaḍ ⌒ UAE 134-135 E 6
Abū Latt, Ğazīrat ⌒ KSA 132-133 B 4
Abū l-Ḥaṣīb ☆ IRQ 130-131 K 2
Abū l-Husain, Bi'r < ET 194-195 D 6
Abulug o RP 160-161 D 3
Abulung ~ RP 160-161 D 3
Abū Madd, Ra's ▲ KSA 130-131 E 5
Abū Maṭariq o SUD 206-207 H 3
Abū Mendi o ETH 208-209 B 3
Abū Mina ∴••• ET 194-195 D 2
Abū Minqār, Bi'r < ET 194-195 C 4
Abumombazi o ZRE 210-211 J 2
Abū Muḥarrik, Ğurd ∸ ET 194-195 D 3
Abū Mūsā, Ğazīre-ye ⌒ IR 134-135 F 6
Abunā o BR 66-67 E 7
Abuna, Rio ~ BOL 66-67 D 7
Abunã, Rio ~ BR 70-71 D 2
Abū Nā'im < LAR 192-193 H 3
Ābune Yosēf ▲ ETH 200-201 J 6
Abū Qīr o ET 194-195 E 2
Abū Qurqāṣ o ET 194-195 E 4
Abū Qurun o SUD 200-201 F 3
Abū Ra's o SUD 206-207 G 5
Abū Rasāš, Ra's ▲ OM 132-133 L 3
Aburassein, Mont ▲ RCA 206-207 G 4
Abū Road o IND 138-139 D 7
Abū Rudeis o ET 194-195 F 3
Abū Rukbah o SUD 200-201 E 6
Abū Šaffār o SUD 200-201 F 4
Abū Šağara, Ra's ▲ SUD 200-201 H 2
Abū Šahrain ∴• IRQ 130-131 J 2
Abū Šāri o SUD 200-201 E 2
Abū Simbel ∴••• ET 194-195 E 6
Abū Sir, Pyramids of ∴••• ET 194-195 E 3
Abū Šuhair ☆ IRQ 128-129 L 7
Abū Sunbul o ET 194-195 F 5
Abū Sunt, Khor ~ SUD 200-201 E 4
Abuta o J 152-153 J 3
Abū Ṭabaq < SUD 200-201 G 2
Abū Tig o ET 194-195 E 4
Abū Ṭunayṭin o SUD 200-201 E 5
Abū 'Urūq < SUD 200-201 E 5
Abū Uwaiğila o ET 194-195 G 2
Abū 'Uwaiğila o ET 194-195 G 2
Ābuyē Meda ▲ ETH 208-209 D 3
Abuyog o RP 160-161 F 7
Abū Zabad o SUD 200-201 D 6
Abū Ẓabi ★• UAE 134-135 F 6
Abū Zaima, Bi'r < ET 200-201 D 5
Abū Zanīma o ET 194-195 F 3
Abu Zayyān o LAR 192-193 E 1
Abwong o SUD 206-207 L 4
Aby, Lagune ≈ 202-203 J 7
Abyaḍ o SUD 200-201 C 6
Abyaḍ, ar-Ra's al- ▲ KSA 130-131 F 6
Abyaḍ, Ra's al- ▲ SYR 128-129 H 4
Abyar ash Shuwayrif o LAR 192-193 F 3
Abydos o AUS 172-173 D 6
Abydos ∴••• ET 194-195 E 4
Abyei o SUD 206-207 J 4
Ābyek o IR 136-137 B 6
Abyj o RUS 110-111 Z 5
Abymes, Les o F 56 E 3
Abyrabyt ~ RUS 110-111 U 5
Acacias o CO 60-61 E 6
Academy o USA (SD) 260-261 G 3
Academy Gletscher ⊂ GRØ 26-27 h 3
Acadia, Cape ▲ CDN 36-37 K 4
Acadia National Park ⊥ USA (ME) 278-279 N 4
Acadian Historic Village • CDN (NB) 240-241 L 3
Acadia Valley o CDN (ALB) 232-233 H 4
Acadie ∸ CDN (QUE) 240-241 J 2
Acadie Siding o CDN (NB) 240-241 K 4
Acahay o PY 76-77 J 3
Açailândia o BR 68-69 E 4
Açaí Paraná o BR 66-67 C 2
Acajutla o ES 52-53 K 5
Açajvajam o RUS 112-113 Q 6
Açajvajam ~ RUS 112-113 Q 6
Acala o MEX 52-53 H 3
Acala o USA (TX) 266-267 B 2
Acámbaro o MEX 52-53 D 1
Acambuco, Arroyo ~ RA 76-77 E 2
Acampamento da Cameia o ANG 216-217 F 5
Acampamento de Indios o BR 70-71 H 2
Acampamento Grande o BR 62-63 H 5
Acancéh o MEX 52-53 K 1
Acandí o CO 60-61 C 3
Acangatá o BR 68-69 C 3
Acapetagua o MEX 52-53 H 4
Acaponeta o MEX 50-51 G 6
Acaponeta, Río ~ MEX 50-51 G 6
Acapu, Rio ~ BR 62-63 F 6
Acapulco de Juárez o•• MEX 52-53 E 3
Acará o BR 62-63 K 6
Acará, Cachoeira ~ BR 66-67 J 5
Acará, Lago o BR 66-67 F 6
Acará, Rio ~ BR 62-63 K 6
Acará, Rio ~ BR 66-67 F 6
Acarai, Rio ~ BR 68-69 B 3
Acará-Mirim, Rio ~ BR 68-69 D 3
Acara ou Acarí, Serra ▲ BR 62-63 E 5
Acaraú o BR 68-69 H 3
Acaraú, Rio ~ BR 68-69 H 3
Acari o PE 64-65 E 9
Acari, Rio ~ BR 62-63 E 6
Acari, Rio ~ BR 66-67 H 6
Acari, Rio ~ BR 72-73 H 3
Acarigua o YV 60-61 G 3
Acaso o BOL 70-71 D 5
Acasta River ~ CDN 30-31 L 3
Acatayon o GQ 210-211 B 3
Acatic o MEX 52-53 C 1
Acatlán o MEX 52-53 F 2
Acatlán de Osorio o MEX 52-53 E 2
Acayucan o MEX 52-53 G 3
Aččen, ozero o RUS 112-113 X 4
Aččitov, togi ▲ US 136-137 G 3
Accomac o USA (VA) 280-281 L 6
Accra ★••• GH 202-203 K 7
Aččygyj-Taryn-Jurjah ~ RUS 110-111 Y 7
Acebuches o MEX 50-51 H 3
Aceguá o BR 76-77 K 6
Acequias o YV 60-61 F 3
Acequias, Las o RA 78-79 H 2
Achaacha o DZ 190-191 C 2
Achacachi o BOL 70-71 C 5
Achaguas o YV 60-61 G 4
Achalpur o IND 138-139 F 9
Achao o RCH 78-79 C 7
Achar o ROU 78-79 L 2
Acheb o DZ 190-191 G 6
Achegtim < RIM 196-197 E 5
Achelouma ~ RN 198-199 F 2
Achelouma < RN (AGA) 192-193 E 6
Acheng o VRC 150-151 F 5
Acheron River ~ AUS 180-181 H 4
Achguig el Adam < RIM 196-197 E 5
Achiasi o GH 202-203 K 7
Achibueno, Río ~ RCH 78-79 D 4
Achille o USA (OK) 264-265 H 5
Achill Island ⌒ IRL 90-91 B 5
Achim, Oudi ~ TCH 198-199 J 5
Achinsk = Ačinsk ☆ RUS 116-117 E 7
Achiras o RA 78-79 G 2
Achiri o BOL 70-71 C 5
Achnasheen o GB 90-91 E 3
Achoma o PE 70-71 B 4
Achton Friis Ø ⌒ GRØ 26-27 q 4
Acıgöl o TR 128-129 C 4
Acimā, Igarapé ~ BR 66-67 D 6
Āčin o AFG 138-139 C 2
Āčinsk ☆ RUS 116-117 E 7
Acıpayam ☆ TR 128-129 C 4
Acireale o I 100-101 E 6
Ačit ☆ RUS 96-97 K 5
Ačit nuur o MAU 116-117 E 11
Ačkasar, gora ▲ AR 128-129 L 2
Ackerly o USA (TX) 264-265 C 6
Ackerman o USA (MS) 268-269 L 3
Acklins, Bight of ≈ 54-55 H 3
Acklins Island ⌒ BS 54-55 J 3
Acme o CDN (ALB) 232-233 E 4
Acme o USA (LA) 268-269 J 5
Acme o USA (MI) 272-273 D 3
Acme o USA (WA) 244-245 C 2
Aco o PE 64-65 D 7
Acobamba o PE 64-65 E 8
Acoma o USA (NM) 256-257 H 4
Acoma o USA (NV) 248-249 K 2
Acoma Indian Reservation ✗ USA (NM) 256-257 H 4
Acomayo o PE 70-71 B 3
Acona o USA (MS) 268-269 L 3
Aconcagua, Cerro ▲ RA 78-79 D 2
Aconcagua, Parque Nacional ⊥ RA 78-79 D 2
Aconquija, Sierra del ▲ RA 76-77 D 4
Acopiara o BR 68-69 J 5
Acos o PE 64-65 D 7
Acostambo o PE 64-65 E 8
Acraman, Lake o AUS 178-179 C 6
Acre ◘ BR 66-67 B 7
Acre, Rio ~ BR 66-67 D 7
Acre, Rio ~ BR 70-71 B 2
Actinolite o CDN (ONT) 238-239 H 4
Action Vale o CDN (QUE) 238-239 N 3
Acton o CDN (ONT) 238-239 E 5
Acton o USA (MT) 250-251 L 6
Acton State Historic Site ∴ USA (TX) 264-265 G 6
Actopan o MEX 52-53 E 1
Acuã, Rio ~ BR 66-67 F 6
Açu da Torre o BR 72-73 L 2
Acufre, Paso de ▲ RA 76-77 B 6
Acula o MEX 52-53 G 2
Acul du Nord o RH 54-55 J 5
Acultzingo o MEX 52-53 F 2
Acurnam o GQ 210-211 C 3
Acyköl o KA 136-137 M 3
Acyojyl ~ KA 126-127 L 3
Acysu ~ KA 124-125 J 3
Acysu, köl o KA 124-125 D 5
Aczo o PE 64-65 D 6
Ada o GH 202-203 L 7
Ada o USA (MN) 270-271 B 3
Ada o USA (OH) 280-281 C 3
Ada o USA (OK) 264-265 H 4
Adab ∴• IRQ 128-129 L 7
Ādaba o ETH 208-209 D 5
Adad Cus, Uar < SP 212-213 J 2
Adadikam o RI 166-167 H 2
Adaevka o RUS 124-125 C 3
Adaf ▲ DZ 190-191 G 9
Adaigba o WAN 204-205 G 5
Adair, Bahía de ≈ 50-51 C 2
Adairsville o USA (GA) 284-285 F 2
Adaiso o GH 202-203 K 7
Adaja, Río ~ E 98-99 E 4
Adak o USA 22-23 H 7
Adak Island ⌒ USA 22-23 H 7
Adaklı ☆ TR 128-129 J 3
Adak Strait ≈ 22-23 H 7
Adalei o SP 212-213 K 2
Adam o OM 132-133 K 2
Adam, Mount ▲ GB 78-79 L 6
Adam, Point ▲ USA 22-23 U 3
Adam al-Hulay o KSA 132-133 B 3
Adamantina o BR 72-73 E 6
Adamaoua = Adamawa ◘ CAM 204-205 K 5
Adamaoua, Massif de l' ▲ CAM 204-205 K 5
Adamawa = Adamaoua ◘ CAM 204-205 K 5
Adamello ▲ I 100-101 C 1
Adaminaby o AUS 180-181 K 3
Ādami Tulu o ETH 208-209 D 5
Adams o USA (CA) 246-247 C 5
Adams o USA (MN) 270-271 F 7
Adams o USA (ND) 258-259 J 3
Adams o USA (NE) 262-263 K 4
Adams o USA (NY) 278-279 E 5
Adams o USA (OR) 244-245 G 5
Adams o USA (TN) 276-277 H 4
Adams o USA (WI) 270-271 J 7
Adams, Cape ▲ ARK 16 F 30
Adams, Fort o USA (MS) 268-269 J 5
Adams, Mount ▲ USA (WA) 244-245 D 4
Adams Cove o CDN (NFL) 242-243 P 5
Adams Lake o CDN (BC) 230-231 K 3
Adams Lake o CDN (BC) 230-231 K 2
Adam's Peak ▲•• CL 140-141 J 7
Adams River ~ CDN (BC) 230-231 K 2
Adamsville o USA (TN) 276-277 G 5
Adamsville o USA (TX) 266-267 J 2
'Adan o• Y 132-133 D 7
Adana ☆• TR 128-129 F 4
Adana, Wādī ~ Y 132-133 D 6
Adane o G 210-211 C 4
Adang, Teluk ≈ 164-165 E 4
Adani o WAN 204-205 G 5
Adaouda ▲ DZ 190-191 E 9
Adapazarı = Sakarya o TR 128-129 D 2
Adar o TCH 206-207 E 3
Adar, Khor ~ SUD 206-207 L 4
Adarama o SUD 200-201 G 4
Adarot o SUD 200-201 H 4
Adaut o RI 166-167 F 6
Adavale o AUS 178-179 H 3
Adda ~ I 100-101 B 1
Adda ~ SUD 206-207 G 4
ad-Dab'a o ET 194-195 D 2
ad-Dabbah o SUD 200-201 E 3
Ad Dahāwah < LAR 192-193 J 5
ad-Dāhila, al-Wāhāt ∸• ET 194-195 D 5
ad-Dakhla o MA 196-197 C 3
Addala-Šuhgel'meer, gora ▲ RUS 126-127 G 6
ad-Dāmir o SUD 200-201 F 4
ad-Dammām ☆ KSA 134-135 D 5
Addanki o IND 140-141 H 3
ad-Dār al-Bayda ☆ MA 188-189 H 4
Ad Darsia o LAR 192-193 J 1
ad-Dauḥa ★ Q 134-135 D 6
ad-Dawwār, Kafr o ET 194-195 E 2
Addi o CAM 206-207 B 5
ad-Diffa ∸ ET 192-193 L 2
Addis o USA (LA) 268-269 J 6
Addis Ababa = Ādīs Ābeba ★•• ETH 208-209 D 4
Addison o USA (AL) 284-285 C 2
Addison o USA (NY) 278-279 D 6
Addo o ZA 220-221 G 6
Addoi, Uar < SP 212-213 H 2
Addo-Olifant National Park ⊥ ZA 220-221 G 6
ad-Du'ayn o SUD 206-207 H 3
ad-Dubaiki, Bi'r < ET 194-195 D 2
ad-Dubasi o SUD 200-201 F 5
ad-Duwaym o SUD 200-201 F 5
Adé o TCH 198-199 K 6
Adéane o SN 202-203 B 3
Adel o USA (GA) 284-285 G 5
Adel o USA (IA) 274-275 E 3
Adel o USA (OR) 244-245 F 8
Adelaide ☆• AUS 180-181 E 3
Adelaide o ZA 220-221 H 6
Adelaide Island ⌒ ARK 16 G 30
Adelaide Island ⌒ ARK 16 G 30
Adelaide Peninsula ⌒ CDN 24-25 X 6
Adelaide River o• AUS 172-173 K 2
Adelanto o USA (CA) 248-249 G 5
Adel Bagrou o RIM 196-197 G 7
Adelbert Range ▲ PNG 183 C 3
Adélé o ETH 208-209 D 5
Adele Island ⌒ AUS 172-173 F 3
Adelia María o RA 78-79 G 2
Adélie, Terre ∸ ARK 16 G 15
Adelong o AUS 178-179 H 2
Ademuz o E 98-99 G 4
Aden o CDN (ALB) 232-233 G 6
Aden = 'Adan o• Y 132-133 D 7
Aden, Gulf of ≈ 208-209 G 3
Adendorp o ZA 220-221 G 6
Adentan o GH 202-203 K 7
Aderbissinat o RN 198-199 C 5
Aderpaëta ~ RUS 108-109 Q 7
Aderuba, Ğabal ▲ ER 200-201 H 5
Adéta o RT 202-203 L 6
'Adfā' o KSA 130-131 G 3
Adi, Pulau ⌒ RI 166-167 G 4
Ādī Abun o ETH 200-201 J 5
Adiaké o CI 202-203 J 7
Adiangdia ▲ DY 202-203 L 5
Ādī Ārk'ay o ETH 200-201 H 6
Adicora o YV 60-61 G 2
Ādī Da'iro o ETH 200-201 J 5
Adidome o GH 202-203 L 6
Adieu, Cape ▲ AUS 176-177 M 6
Adieu-Vat o F 62-63 H 3
Ādīgala o ETH 208-209 F 3
Adige ~ I 100-101 D 2
Adige = Etsch ~ I 100-101 C 1
Ādīgrat o ETH 200-201 J 5
Ādī Gudom o ETH 200-201 J 6
Ādīk'eyih o ER 200-201 J 5
Ādīkwala o ER 200-201 J 5
Adilābād o IND 138-139 G 10
Adin o USA (CA) 246-247 E 2
Adiora < RMM 196-197 K 6
Adipala o RI 168 C 3
Adir ☆ LAR 192-193 E 4
Ādī Ramets' o ETH 200-201 H 6
'Ādiriyāt, Ğibāl al- ▲ JOR 130-131 E 2

Adirondack Mountains ▲ USA (NY) 278-279 G 4
Ādīs Ābeba ★·· ETH 208-209 D 4
Ādīs 'Alem ○· ETH 208-209 D 4
Ādīs Zemen ○ ETH 200-201 H 6
Ādī Ugrī ○ ER 200-201 J 5
Adıyaman ☆ TR 128-129 H 4
Adjeloho, Adrar ▲ DZ 190-191 G 8
Adjengré ○ RT 202-203 L 5
Adjerar ▲ DZ 190-191 E 8
Adjiro ~ DY 202-203 L 5
Adjohoun ○ DY 204-205 E 5
Adjud ○ RO 102-103 E 4
Adjuntar, Presa de las < MEX 50-51 K 6
Adjuntas, Las ○ YV (BOL) 60-61 J 4
Adjuntas, Las ○ YV (FED) 60-61 H 2
Adlavik Islands ∩ CDN 36-37 U 7
Adler ○ RUS 126-127 C 6
Admer, Erg d' ∸ DZ 190-191 G 8
Admer, Plaine d' ◡ DZ 190-191 G 8
Admiral ○ CDN (SAS) 232-233 L 6
Admiral Collinson, Cape ▲ CDN 24-25 V 5
Admiral's Beach ○ CDN (NFL) 242-243 P 5
Admiraltejstva, poluostrov ◡ RUS 108-109 G 4
Admiralty Gulf ≈ 172-173 G 3
Admiralty Gulf Aboriginal Land ✕ AUS 172-173 G 3
Admiralty Inlet ≈ 24-25 c 4
Admiralty Inlet ≈ USA 244-245 B 2
Admiralty Island ∩ CDN 24-25 V 6
Admiralty Island ∩ USA 32-33 C 3
Admiralty Island National Monument Kootznoowoo Wilderness ⊥· USA 32-33 C 3
Admiralty Islands ∩ PNG 183 D 2
Admiralty Range ▲ ARK 16 F 17
Admont ○·· A 92-93 N 5
Ado ○ WAN (OGU) 204-205 E 5
Ado ○ WAN (PLA) 204-205 G 4
Ado Awaiye ○ WAN 204-205 E 5
Adobes ○ USA (TX) 266-267 C 4
Adobe Summit ▲ USA (NV) 246-247 K 3
Ado-Ekiti ○ WAN 204-205 F 5
Adok ○ SUD 206-207 K 4
Adolfo ○ BR 72-73 F 6
Adolfo Gonzáles Chaves ○ RA 78-79 J 5
Adolfo López Mateos, Presa < MEX 50-51 F 5
Adolf S. Jensen Land ∸ GRØ 26-27 p 5
Adonara, Pulau ∩ RI 166-167 B 6
Ādoni ○ IND 140-141 G 3
Adorf ○ D 92-93 M 3
Adoru ○ WAN 204-205 G 5
Ado-Tymovo ○ RUS 122-123 K 3
Adoumandjali ○ RCA 210-211 E 2
Adoumri ○ CAM 204-205 K 4
Adour ~ F 90-91 G 10
Adra ○ E 98-99 F 6
Adranga ○ ZRE 212-213 C 2
Adrar ☆· DZ (ADR) 188-189 L 7
Adrar ▲ DZ 190-191 F 8
Adrar Massif ▲ RIM 196-197 E 4
Adraskan ○ AFG 134-135 K 2
Adrasman ○ TJ 136-137 M 4
Adré ○ TCH 198-199 L 6
Adrian ○ USA (GA) 284-285 H 4
Adrian ○ USA (MI) 272-273 E 6
Adrian ○ USA (MN) 270-271 C 7
Adrian ○ USA (MO) 274-275 D 6
Adrian ○ USA (OR) 244-245 H 7
Adrian ○ USA (TX) 264-265 B 3
Adrianópolis ○ BR 74-75 F 5
Adriatic Sea ≈ 100-101 D 2
Adua ○ RI 166-167 E 2
Aduana ○ RCH 78-79 D 3
Aduana y Reten de Cuya ○ RCH 70-71 B 6
Aduku ○ EAU 212-213 D 2
Adunkur Daban ▲ VRC 146-147 G 4
Adunu ○ WAN 204-205 G 4
Adūr ○ IND 140-141 G 6
Adura ○ WAN 204-205 G 4
Adusa ○ ZRE 212-213 B 3
Advance ○ USA (MO) 276-277 F 3
Advat ∴· IL 130-131 D 2
Adventure, Bahía ≈ 80 C 2
Adventure Bank ≃ 100-101 C 6
Ādwa ○ ETH 200-201 J 5
Adwana ○ IND 138-139 B 9
Ady ○ USA (TX) 264-265 B 3
Adyča ~ RUS 110-111 V 6
Adygalah ○ RUS 120-121 M 2
Adygea = Adygè Respublikèm □ RUS 126-127 D 5
Adyk ○ RUS 126-127 F 5
Adzié ○ RCB 210-211 E 4
Adzopé ☆ CI 202-203 J 6
Adz'va ~ RUS 108-109 J 8
Aegean Sea = Egéo Pélagos ≈ 8 F 5
Aegviidu ○ EST 94-95 J 2
Aekanopan ○ RI 162-163 C 3
Ærø ∩ DK 86-87 E 9
Aérobo ○ CI 202-203 J 6
Aèros"emki, ostrova ∩ RUS 110-111 N 3
Aesake, Lake ○ PNG 183 A 4
Aese ∩ VAN 184 II a 2
Aetna ○ CDN (ALB) 232-233 E 6
Aetós ○ GR 100-101 H 4
Afadé ○ CAM 198-199 G 6
'Afak ☆ IRQ 128-129 L 6
Āfambo ○ ETH 208-209 E 3
Afanas'evo ☆ RUS 96-97 H 4
Afanas'evsk, Agnie- ○ RUS 122-123 H 3
'Afar, Tall ○ IRQ 128-129 K 4
Af Barwaarqo ○ SP 208-209 J 5
Āfdem ○ ETH 208-209 E 4
Afé ○ SN 202-203 C 2
Afeleh, In < DZ 190-191 G 9
Afe Peak ▲ CDN 20-21 X 5
Afféri ○ CI 202-203 J 6
Afflisses, Oued ~ DZ 190-191 C 6
Affollé ∸ RIM 196-197 E 6
Affon = Ouémé ~ DY 202-203 L 5
Afghanistan = Afghānistān ■ AFG 134-135 J 2
Afgooye ○ SP 212-213 K 2
'Afif ○ KSA 130-131 H 6
Afikpo ○ WAN 204-205 G 6
Afin, Rūd-e ~ IR 134-135 H 2
Afipinskij ○ RUS 126-127 C 5
Åfjord ○ N 86-87 E 5
Aflandshage ∩ GRØ 28-29 V 4
Aflou ○ DZ 190-191 D 3
Afmadow ○ SP 212-213 J 3
Afobaka ○ SME 62-63 G 3
Afogados da Ingazeira ○ BR 68-69 K 5
Afognak Island ∩ USA 22-23 U 3
Afognak Mountain ▲ USA 22-23 U 3
Afolé ○ RT 202-203 L 6
Afonso Cláudio ○ BR 72-73 K 6
Afore ○ PNG 183 E 5
Afouidich, Sebkhet ○ MA 196-197 C 4
Afrânio ○ BR 68-69 H 6
Āfrēra Terara ▲ ETH 200-201 K 6
Āfrēra Ye Che'ew Hāyk' ○ ETH 200-201 K 6
African Banks ∩ SY 224 C 2
African Lion Safari ⊥ CDN (ONT) 238-239 E 5
Afridi Lake ○ CDN 30-31 P 3
Afrika, mys ▲ RUS 120-121 U 5
'Afrīn ☆ SYR 128-129 G 4
Afşin ☆ TR 128-129 G 3
Afton ○ USA (IA) 274-275 D 3
Afton ○ USA (OK) 264-265 K 2
Afton ○ USA (WY) 252-253 H 4
Afua ○ BR 62-63 J 6
Afua, Rio ~ BR 62-63 K 6
Afuein < SP 212-213 K 3
'Afula ☆ IL 130-131 D 1
Afwein ~ EAK 212-213 G 3
Afyon ☆· TR 128-129 D 3
Aga ~ RUS 118-119 G 10
Aǧā', Ǧabal ▲ KSA 130-131 G 4
Agabama ~ C 54-55 F 4
'Aǧabšīr ○ IR 128-129 L 4
Aga Buryat Autonomous District=Agin. Burj. avt. okrug □ RUS 118-119 F 10
Agač, Koš ☆ RUS 124-125 Q 4
Agadem ○ RN 198-199 F 4
Agadez □ RN 198-199 C 3
Agadez ☆· RN (AGA) 198-199 C 4
Agādir ☆· MA 188-189 G 5
Agadyr' ○ KA 124-125 H 4
Āǧā Ǧārī ○ IR 134-135 C 3
Agaho-gawa ~ J 152-153 H 6
Agaie ○ WAN 204-205 G 4
Again River ~ CDN (ONT) 236-237 J 2
'Aǧā'iz, al- ○ OM 132-133 K 4
Agajakan ~ RUS 120-121 J 2
Agalega Islands ∩ MS 224 E 5
Agalega Islands ∸ MS 12 D 6
Agamor < RMM 196-197 L 6
Agan ~ RUS 114-115 P 3
Agan ~ RUS 114-115 N 4
Aganyli ~ RUS 108-109 f 7
Agapa ~ RUS 108-109 W 6
Agapo Açu ○ BR 66-67 J 5
Agapovka ☆ RUS 96-97 L 7
Āǧar ○ AFG 136-137 K 7
Agar ○ USA (SD) 260-261 F 2
Agâraktem < RIM 196-197 G 3
Āgarfa ○ ETH 208-209 D 5
Agargar ∸ MA 196-197 C 3
Āgaro ○ ETH 208-209 C 5
Āgarsararēn < ETH 208-209 G 5
Agartala ☆ IND 142-143 G 4
Agaru ○ SUD 208-209 B 3
Agaskagou Lake ○ CDN (ONT) 236-237 H 2
Agassiz ○ CDN (BC) 230-231 H 4
Agassiz Forest Reserve ⊥ CDN (MAN) 234-235 G 5
Agassiz Fracture Zone ≃ 14-15 P 11
Agassiz National Wildlife Refuge ⊥ USA (MN) 270-271 C 2
Agastya Malai ▲ IND 140-141 G 6
Agata (Nižnee), ozero ○ RUS 116-117 F 2
Agata (Verhnee), ozero ○ RUS 116-117 F 2
Agate ○ USA (CO) 254-255 M 4
Agate ○ USA (NE) 262-263 C 2
Agate Fossil Beds National Monument ∴ USA (NE) 262-263 C 2
Agats ○ RI 166-167 K 4
Agatti Island ∩ IND 140-141 B 3
Agattu Island ∩ USA 22-23 C 6
Agattu Strait ≈ 22-23 C 6
Agawa Bay ○ CDN (ONT) 236-237 D 5
Agawa Canyon · CDN (ONT) 236-237 D 5
Agawa River ~ CDN (ONT) 236-237 D 5
Agbabu ○ WAN 204-205 F 5
Agbado ~ DY 204-205 E 4
Agbara ○ WAN 204-205 E 5
Agbarha-Otor ○ WAN 204-205 F 6
Agbélouvé ○ RT 202-203 L 6
Agbohoutogon ○ DY 204-205 E 5
Agbor-Bojiboji ○ WAN 204-205 G 5
Agboville ☆ CI 202-203 H 7
Agdam ○ AZ 128-129 M 2
Agdaš = Ağdaş ○ AZ 128-129 M 2
Agde ○ F 90-91 J 10
Agdz ○ MA 188-189 H 5
Agdžabedi = Ağcabadi ○ AZ 128-129 M 2
Agege ○ WAN 204-205 E 5
Agen ○ F 90-91 H 9
Agenebode ○ WAN 204-205 G 5
Āgere Maryam ○ ETH 208-209 D 6
Aggas Ø ∩ GRØ 28-29 Y 3
Aggeneys ○ ZA 220-221 D 4
Aggui ○ RIM 196-197 D 4
Aghat bonne < RN 198-199 C 4
Aghir ○ TN 190-191 H 4
Aghiyuk Island ∩ USA 22-23 S 4
Aghor ○ PK 134-135 L 6
Aghouedir · RIM 196-197 E 4
Aghouinit ○ MA 196-197 D 3
Aghreijīt < RIM 196-197 D 4
Aghrijīt ∴· RIM 196-197 F 5
Aghzoumal, Sebkhet ○ MA 196-197 D 2
Agiabampo, Bahia de ≈ 50-51 E 4
Agía Galíni ○ GR 100-101 K 7
Agia Napa ○· CY 128-129 E 5
Agiapuk River ~ USA 20-21 G 4
Agía Triáda ○ GR 100-101 H 6
Āǧī Čāy ~ IR 128-129 M 4
Agiert ○ RIM 196-197 F 6
Aginskoe ☆ RUS (AGN) 118-119 G 10
Aginskoe ☆ RUS (KRN) 116-117 G 8
Ágio Orous □ GR 100-101 K 4
Ágios Efstrátios ∩ GR 100-101 K 5
Ágios Kírikos ○ GR 100-101 L 6
Ágios Konstantinos ○ GR 100-101 J 5
Agios Nikólaos ○· GR 100-101 K 7
Ágiou Orous, Kólpos ≈ 100-101 J 4
Agita ~ RUS 118-119 H 9
Agiuel, Hasy in < LAR 192-193 D 4
Ağlı ☆ TR 128-129 E 2
Aglipay ○ RP 160-161 D 4
'Aǧlūn, Ǧabal ▲ JOR 130-131 D 1
'Aǧmān ○ UAE 134-135 F 6
Agmar < RIM 196-197 E 2
Agnamala, Mount ▲ RP 160-161 D 3
Agnes ○ USA (TX) 264-265 G 6
Agnes Lake ○ USA (MN) 270-271 G 2
Agness ○ USA (OR) 244-245 A 8
Agnes Waters ○ AUS 178-179 L 3
Agnew ○ AUS 176-177 F 4
Agnibilékrou ○ CI 202-203 J 6
Agnie-Afanas'evsk ○ RUS 122-123 H 3
Agnita ○ RO 102-103 D 5
Agno ~ RP 160-161 D 5
Agnone ○ I 100-101 E 4
Ago ○ J 152-153 G 7
Ago-Are ○ WAN 204-205 E 4
Agogo ○ GH 202-203 K 6
Agona ○ GH 202-203 J 6
Agona Junction ○ GH 202-203 K 7
Agotu ○ PNG 183 C 4
Agou ○ CI 202-203 J 7
Agou, Mont ▲ RT 202-203 L 6
Agoudal ○ MA 188-189 J 4
Agoueïnît ○ RIM 196-197 G 6
Agou Gadzépé ○ RT 202-203 L 6
Agouna ○ DY 202-203 L 6
Agounni Jefal < RMM 196-197 J 6
Agpamiut ○ GRØ 28-29 O 4
Agra ○··· IND 138-139 G 6
Agrado, El ○ CO 60-61 F 4
Agra-Emneke, gora ▲ RUS 110-111 X 5
Agrahanskij poluostrov ◡ RUS 126-127 G 6
Ágreda ○ E 98-99 G 4
Ağrestān ○ AFG 134-135 M 2
Ağrı ☆ TR 128-129 K 3
Agrigento ○ I 100-101 D 6
Agrínio ○ GR 100-101 H 5
Agrio, Río ~ RA 78-79 E 5
Agrirama · USA (GA) 284-285 G 5
Agrópoli ○ I 100-101 E 4
Agryz ☆ RUS 96-97 H 5
Agua Amarga, Pampa del ∸ RA 78-79 E 5
Agua Azúl ○ HN 52-53 L 4
Agua Azúl Cascades ~· MEX 52-53 H 3
Agua Azul Falls ~ BH 52-53 K 3
Agua Blanca ○ YV 60-61 K 4
Água Boa ○ BR 72-73 J 4
Agua Boa ○ BR 72-73 D 3
Agua Boa do Univini, Rio ~ BR 62-63 D 5
Agua Braga ○ BR 72-73 F 2
Água Branca ○ BR 68-69 K 5
Agua Branca, Igarapé ~ BR 66-67 H 7
Agua Caliente ∸ PE 64-65 E 6
Agua Caliente ○ RA 64-65 E 6
Agua Caliente ○ USA (AZ) 256-257 B 6
Agua Caliente, Río ~ BOL 70-71 F 4
Agua Caliente Indian Reservation ✕ USA (CA) 248-249 H 6
Aguacatán ○ GCA 52-53 J 4
Aguachica ○ CO 60-61 E 3
Água Clara ○ BR 72-73 D 6
Aguaçuzinho ○ BR 70-71 J 6
Aguada ○ USA (PR) 286-287 O 2
Aguada de Pasajeros ○ C 54-55 E 3
Aguadas ○ CO 60-61 D 5
Aguadilla ○ USA (PR) 286-287 O 2
Aguados, Serra dos ▲ BR 72-73 E 7
Agua Duke, Caleta ≈ 76-77 B 3
Agua Dulce ○ MEX 52-53 G 2
Aguadulce ○ PA 52-53 D 7
Agua Dulce ○ USA (TX) 266-267 K 6
Agua Escondida ○ RA 78-79 E 4
Água Fria ○ BR 68-69 J 7
Agua Fria ○ USA (NM) 256-257 K 2
Água Fria, Ribeiro ~ BR 68-69 D 5
Agua Fria, Rio ~ BR 72-73 E 2
Agua Fria River ~ USA (AZ) 256-257 C 4
Agua Hedionda, Cerro ▲ RA 78-79 F 2
Aguaí ○ BR 72-73 G 7
Agua Linda ○ YV 60-61 G 2
Aguán, Río ~ HN 52-53 L 4
Aguanaval, Río ~ MEX 50-51 H 5
Agua Negra, Paso del ▲ RA 76-77 C 6
Agua Negra, Río ~ RA 76-77 C 6
Aguanish ○ CDN (QUE) 242-243 F 2
Agua Nueva ○ MEX (COA) 50-51 J 5
Agua Nueva ○ MEX (TAM) 50-51 K 6
Agua Nueva ○ USA (TX) 266-267 J 7
Aguanus, Rivière ~ CDN 38-39 N 3
Aguapai, Rio ~ BR 70-71 H 4
Agua Pasto ○ BOL 70-71 G 6
Aguapei, Serra do ▲ BR 70-71 H 4
Aguapey, Río ~ RA 76-77 J 5
Água Preta, Igarapé ~ BR 66-67 E 3
Agua Prieta ○ MEX 50-51 E 2
Aguara, Río ~ PY 76-77 J 3
Aguaray ○ RA 76-77 F 2
Aguarico, Río ~ EC 64-65 D 1
Aguaro-Guariquito, Parque Nacional ⊥ YV 60-61 H 3
Aguasay ○ YV 60-61 K 3
Águas Belas ○ BR 68-69 K 6
Aguas Blancas ○ BOL 76-77 E 2
Aguas Blancas ○ RCH 76-77 C 3
Aguas Blancas, Cerro ▲ RA 76-77 C 3
Aguas Blancas, Quebrada de ~ RCH 76-77 D 2
Aguás Blancas y Aguás Negras, Reserva Faunística ⊥ YV 60-61 F 3
Aguascalientes □ MEX 50-51 H 6
Aguascalientes ☆· MEX (AGS) 50-51 H 7
Aguas Calientes, Paso de ▲ RA 76-77 C 3
Aguas Calientes, Salar ○ RCH 76-77 D 2
Aguas Calientes, Sierra de ▲ RA 76-77 D 3
Aguas Claras ○ C 54-55 D 3
Aguas Claraso ○ C 54-55 G 4
Águas de São Clara ○ BR 74-75 E 5
Águas Formosas ○ BR 72-73 K 4
Aguas Negras ○ PE 64-65 E 2
Aguateca ∴· GCA 52-53 J 3
Agua Verde ou Anhanazá, Rio ~ BR 70-71 J 4
Agua Viva ○ YV 60-61 F 3
Aguaytia ○ PE 64-65 E 6
Aguaytia, Río ~ PE 64-65 E 6
Aguazul ○ CO 60-61 E 5
Agu Bay ≈ 24-25 c 5
Agudda Cecilio ○ RA 78-79 G 6
Agudos do Sul ○ BR 74-75 F 5
Agudos Grandes, Serra ▲ BR 74-75 F 5
Águeda ○ P 98-99 C 4
Aguelhok ○ RMM 196-197 L 5
Aguelt ez Zerga < RIM 196-197 C 5
Aguemour ∸ DZ 190-191 E 7
Aguemour, Oued ~ DZ 190-191 E 7
Aguer-Tay, Falaise de l' ▲ TCH 198-199 H 2
Aguéssis < RN 198-199 D 4
Agues Verdes, Raudal ~ CO 64-65 F 1
Aguga ~ EAU 212-213 D 2
Águia Branca ○ BR 72-73 K 5
Aguiar Javaés ○ BR 68-69 D 7
Aguié ○ RN 198-199 C 6
Aguieira, Barragem da < P 98-99 C 4
Aguila ○ USA (AZ) 256-257 B 5
Aguila, El ○ BOL 70-71 F 4
Aguila, Gruta C. del · ROU 78-79 L 2
Aguilal < RIM 196-197 C 6
Aguilâl Faï ○ RIM 196-197 C 5
Aguilar ○ E 98-99 E 6
Aguilar, Cerro ▲ RA 76-77 E 2
Aguilar, El ○ RA 76-77 E 2
Aguilar, Salar de ○ RCH 76-77 C 3
Aguilar de Campoo ○ E 98-99 E 3
Aguilares ○ ES 52-53 K 5
Aguilares ○ USA (TX) 266-267 H 6
Águilas ○ E 98-99 G 6
Aguililla ○ MEX 52-53 C 2
Aguirre, Bahía ≈ 80 H 7
Aguiz ∩ ER 200-201 K 5
Aguja, Cerro ▲ RA 78-79 D 7
Aguja, Cerro ▲ RCH 80 F 7
Aguja, Punta ▲ PE 64-65 B 4
Agul ~ RUS 116-117 H 8
Āgula'i ○ ETH 200-201 J 6
Agulhas, Cape = Agulhas, Kaap ▲ ZA 220-221 D 7
Agulhas, L' ○ ZA 220-221 D 7
Agulhas Basin ≃ 6-7 M 13
Agulhas Plateau ≃ 6-7 M 12
Agulhas Ridge ≃ 6-7 K 13
Agumbe ○ IND 140-141 F 4
Aguni-shima ∩ J 152-153 B 11
Agur ○ EAU 212-213 D 2
Agurá Grande ○ RA 76-77 G 6
Agusan ~ RP 160-161 F 8
Agutaya Island ∩ RP 160-161 D 7
Agwampt ~ SUD 200-201 G 3
Agwarra ○ WAN 204-205 F 3
Agweri ○ WAN 204-205 G 5
Agwit ○ SUD 206-207 H 4
Agwok ○ SUD 206-207 J 5
Ahaba ○ WAN 204-205 G 6
Ahaberge ▲ NAM 216-217 F 9
Ahad al-Masāra ○ KSA 132-133 C 5
Aḥad Rāfida ○· KSA 132-133 C 4
Ahalcihe ○· GE 126-127 E 7
Ahalkalaki ○ GE 126-127 E 7
Ahamansu ○ GH 202-203 L 6
Ahanduizinho, Rio ~ BR 70-71 K 7
Ahangaran ○ US 136-137 L 4
Ahar ○· IR 128-129 M 3
Ahaura ○ NZ 182 C 5
Ahča-Kujma ○ TM 136-137 D 5
Aḫḍar, al-Ǧabal al- ▲ OM 132-133 K 2
Ahellakane, Adrar ▲ DZ 190-191 E 7
Ahémè, Lac ○ DY 202-203 L 6
Ahenkro ○ GH 202-203 L 6
Ahero ○ EAK 212-213 E 4
Ahfir ○ MA 188-189 K 3
Ahíllio ○ GR 100-101 J 5
Ahioma ○ PNG 183 F 6
Ahiti ○ NZ 182 E 3
Ahklun Mountains ▲ USA 20-21 M 6
Ahlat ☆· TR 128-129 K 3
Aḥmad, Bi'r ○ Y 132-133 D 7
Aḥmadābād ○ AFG 134-135 J 1
Aḥmadābād ○·· IND 138-139 D 8
Aḥmadal-Yāsin ○ IRQ 128-129 L 6
Aḥmadī, al- □ KWT 130-131 K 3
Aḥmadī, al- ☆ KWT 130-131 L 3
Ahmadnagar ○· IND 138-139 E 10
Ahmadpur ○ IND 138-139 F 10
Ahmadpur East ○ PK 138-139 C 5
Ahmadpur Lamma ○ PK 138-139 C 5
Ahmadpur Siāl ○ PK 138-139 C 4
Ahmad Wāl ○ PK 134-135 L 4
Ahmar Mountains ▲ ETH 208-209 E 4
Ahmatova, zaliv ○ RUS 108-109 e 2
Ahmeta ○ GE 126-127 F 7
Ahmic Harbour ○ CDN (ONT) 238-239 F 3
Aḫmīm ○· ET 194-195 E 4
Ahnet, Adrar n' ▲ DZ 190-191 D 8
Ahoada ○ WAN 204-205 G 6
Ahome ○ MEX 50-51 E 5
Ahoskie ○ USA (NC) 282-283 L 4
Ahousat ○ CDN (BC) 230-231 C 4
Ahram ○ IR 134-135 D 4
Ahraura ○ IND 142-143 C 3
Ahrweiler, Bad Neuenahr- ○ D 92-93 J 3
Ahsahka ○ USA (ID) 250-251 C 5
Ahsu = Ağsu ○ AZ 128-129 N 2
Ahtamar · TR 128-129 K 3
Ahtaranda ~ RUS 118-119 F 4
Ähtäri ○ FIN 88-89 H 5
Ahtarsk, Primorsko- ○ RUS 102-103 L 4
Ahtme, Jõhvi- ○ EST 94-95 K 2
Ahtuba ~ RUS 96-97 E 10
Ahtubinsk ☆ RUS 96-97 E 9
Ahty ○ RUS 126-127 G 7
Ahuacatlan ○ MEX 50-51 K 7
Ahuacatlán ○ MEX 52-53 F 1
Ahuachapán ☆ ES 52-53 K 5
Ahualulco ○ MEX 50-51 J 6
Ahualulco de Mercata ○ MEX 52-53 C 1
Ahuano ○ EC 64-65 D 2
Ahunba ○ US 136-137 N 4
Ahurjan ~ AR 128-129 K 2
Ahus, Pulau ∩ RI 164-165 E 2
Ahvāz ☆· IR 134-135 C 3
Ahvenanmaa = Åland ∩ FIN 88-89 F 6
Ahwa ○ IND 138-139 D 9
Ahwahnee ○ USA (CA) 248-249 E 2
Aḥwar ○ Y 132-133 E 7
Aḥwar, Wādī ~ Y 132-133 E 7
Ahzar, Vallée de l' ∸ RMM 196-197 M 7
Ai-Ais ○· NAM 220-221 C 3
Aiak, Cape ▲ USA 22-23 N 6
Aiaktalik Island ∩ USA 22-23 U 4
Aialik Cape ▲ USA 20-21 Q 7
Aianí ○ GR 100-101 H 4
Aiapuá ○ BR 66-67 F 5
Aiapuá, Lago ○ BR 66-67 F 5
Aiari, Rio ~ BR 66-67 C 2
Aibak ☆· AFG 136-137 K 6
Aibetsu ○ J 152-153 K 3
Aibonito ○ USA (PR) 286-287 P 2
Aichilik River ~ USA 20-21 T 2
Aidarhan su koimašy suk < KA 96-97 F 9
Aiddejavrre Fjellstue ○ N 86-87 L 2
Aiduma, Pulau ∩ RI 166-167 H 3
Aiduna ○ RI 166-167 H 4
Aiea ○ USA (HI) 288 H 3
Aiema River ~ PNG 183 B 4
Aiere ○ WAN 204-205 G 5
Aigene mekeni ∸ KA 124-125 F 6
Aigle, l' ○ F 90-91 H 7
Aigles, Lac-des- ○ CDN (QUE) 240-241 G 3
Aigneau, Lac ○ CDN 36-37 O 6
Aiguá ○ ROU 78-79 M 3
Aiguá, Arroyo del ~ ROU 78-79 M 3
Aigues ~ F 90-91 K 9
Aiguilete, Cerro ▲ RCH 80 D 5
Aihuicheng · VRC 150-151 F 3
Aija ○ PE 64-65 D 6
Aikar, Tanjung ▲ RI 166-167 H 2
Aikawa ○ J 152-153 H 5
Aiken ○ USA (SC) 284-285 J 3
Aiken ○ USA (TX) 264-265 C 4
Aikima ○ RI 166-167 K 4
Ailaoshan Z.B. ⊥· VRC 156-157 B 4
Aileron ○ AUS 178-179 B 2
Aileu ○ RI 166-167 C 6
Ailigandí ○ PA 52-53 E 7
Ailinglapalp ∩ MAI 13 J 2
Aillik ○ CDN 36-37 U 7
Aim ○ RUS 120-121 F 4
Aim ~ RUS 120-121 E 4
Aimere ○ RI 168 E 7
Aimogasta ○ RA 76-77 D 5
Aimorés ○ BR 72-73 K 5
Aimorés, Serra dos ▲ BR 72-73 K 4
Aimorés, Serra dos ▲ BR 72-73 K 5
Ain ~ F 90-91 K 8
'Ain, al- ○ UAE 134-135 F 6
'Ain, Ra's al- ☆ SYR 128-129 J 4
'Ain, Wādī l- ~ OM 132-133 J 2
'Ain al-'Arab ○ SYR 128-129 H 4
'Ain al-Bakra ○ KSA 130-131 K 6
'Ain al-Ǧuwairī ○ Y 132-133 F 6
Āin al-Maqfī < ET 194-195 D 4
'Ain al-Maqfī < ET 194-195 D 4
'Ain an-Nafṭ ○ IRQ 128-129 K 6
Āin as-Sāqī < ET 194-195 D 4
'Ain as-Sāqī < ET 194-195 D 4
Ainaži ○ LV 94-95 J 3
Aïn Beida ○ DZ 190-191 F 3
Aïn Benian ○ DZ 190-191 D 2
Âïn-Benimathar ○ MA 188-189 K 3
Aïn Ben Tili ○ RIM 196-197 F 2
Aïn Bessem ○ DZ 190-191 D 2
'Aïn Bire < RIM 196-197 F 6
Âïn Boubat < RIM 196-197 D 6
Aïn Boucif ○ DZ 190-191 D 3
'Ain Dār ○ KSA 130-131 L 5
Aïn Defla ☆ DZ 190-191 C 2
Aïn Deheb ○ DZ 190-191 C 3
'Ain Diwār ○ SYR 128-129 K 4
Aïn Draham ○ TN 190-191 G 2
Âïn-Ech-Chair ○ MA 188-189 K 4
Aïn El Bell ○ DZ 190-191 D 3
Ain el Brod < DZ 190-191 E 6
Ain el Hadjadj < DZ 190-191 D 6
Ain el Hadjadj < DZ 190-191 F 7
Aïn El Hadjar ○ DZ 190-191 C 3
Aïn El Hadjel ○ DZ 190-191 D 3
Aïn El Hamara ○ DZ 190-191 D 3
Aïn El Melh ○ DZ 190-191 E 3
Aïn el-Orak ○ DZ 190-191 C 4
Aïn Fakroun ○ DZ 190-191 F 3
Aïn Fekan ○ DZ 190-191 C 3
Ainggyi ○ MYA 142-143 J 5
'Ain Ḥamūd ○ IRQ 130-131 J 2
'Ain Ḫumān < ET 194-195 D 4
'Ain Ibn Fuhaid ○ KSA 130-131 J 4
'Ain 'Īsā ○ SYR 128-129 H 4
Aïn Kercha ○ DZ 190-191 F 3
Aïn Kermes ○ DZ 190-191 C 3
Aïn Khadra ○ DZ 190-191 E 3
Âïn-Leuh ○ MA 188-189 J 4
Aïn Madhi ○ DZ 190-191 D 4
Aïn Mansūr < SUD 200-201 C 5
Aïn M'Lila ○ DZ 190-191 F 2
Aïn Oulmene ○ DZ 190-191 E 3
Aïn Oussera ○ DZ 190-191 D 3
Āin Qaiqab < ET 192-193 L 3
Ainsa-Sobrarbe ○ E 98-99 H 3
'Ain Sifnī ○ IRQ 128-129 K 4
Aïn Skhouna ○ DZ 190-191 C 3
Ainslie, Lake ○ CDN (NS) 240-241 O 4
'Ain Suḫna ○ ET 194-195 F 3
Ainsworth ○ USA (NE) 262-263 G 2
Aïn Tamr < TN 190-191 G 4
Aïn Taya ○ DZ 190-191 D 2
Aïn Tédelès ○ DZ 190-191 C 3
Aïn Temouchent ☆ DZ 188-189 L 3
Aiome ○ PNG 183 C 3
Aiome, Mount ▲ PNG 183 C 3
Aiquebelle Provincial Park ⊥ CDN (QUE) 236-237 K 4
Aiquile ○ BOL 70-71 E 6
Aiquiri, Rio ~ BR 66-67 D 7
Airabu, Pulau ∩ RI 162-163 G 3
Airbangis ○ RI 162-163 C 4
Airdrie ○ CDN (ALB) 232-233 D 4
Aire ~ F 90-91 K 7
Aire-sur-la-Lys ○ F 90-91 J 6
Aïr et du Ténéré, Réserve Naturelle Nationale de l' ⊥··· RN 198-199 D 3
Air Force Island ∩ CDN 28-29 C 3
Air Force Museum · USA (OH) 280-281 B 4
Airhitam, Teluk ≈ 162-163 J 6
Airi, Cachoeira do ~ BR 66-67 H 6
Airlie Beach ○ AUS 174-175 K 7
Airlie Gardens · USA (NC) 282-283 K 6
Airmadidi ○· RI 164-165 J 3
Airmolek ○ RI 162-163 E 5
Airpanas ○ RI 166-167 C 5
Air Papan ○ MAL 162-163 E 3
Air Terjung Kaves · RI 164-165 F 6
Airway Heights ○ USA (WA) 244-245 H 3
Airways ○ CDN (ALB) 232-233 G 3
Aisén, Seno ≈ 80 D 2
Aishihik ○ CDN 20-21 W 6
Aishihik Lake ○ CDN 20-21 W 6
Aisne, l' ~ F 90-91 K 7
Aïssa, Djebel ▲ DZ 188-189 L 4
Aitana ▲ E 98-99 G 5
Aitape ○ PNG 183 B 2
Âït-Baha ○ MA 188-189 G 5
Aït el Khaoua, Erg ∸ RMM 196-197 L 4
Aitkin ○ USA (MN) 270-271 E 4
Âït-Melloul ○ MA 188-189 G 5
Âït Morrhad ▲ MA 188-189 J 5
Âït Saadane ○ MA 188-189 J 5
Âït-Youssef-ou-Ali ○ MA 188-189 K 3
Aiuanã, Rio ~ BR 66-67 E 3
Aiuiá-Miçu, Rio ~ BR 68-69 B 7
Aiuruoca ○ BR 72-73 H 6
Aiwan Wan ~ VRC 156-157 M 2
Aiwsa, Danau ○ RI 166-167 H 3
Aix-en-Provence ○· F 90-91 K 10
Aixiós ~ GR 100-101 J 4
Aix-les-Bains ○ F 90-91 K 9
Aiyang, Mount ▲ PNG 183 A 3
Aiyetoro ○ WAN (KWA) 204-205 F 5
Aiyetoro ○ WAN (OGU) 204-205 E 5
Aiyura ○ PNG 183 C 4
Aizanoi ∴· TR 128-129 C 3
Aizawl ☆ IND 142-143 H 4
Aizpute ○·· LV 94-95 G 3
Aizuwakamatsu ○· J 152-153 H 6
Aj ~ RUS 96-97 L 6
Ajaccio ☆· F 98-99 M 4
Ajacuba ○ MEX 52-53 E 1
Ajaguz ○ KA 124-125 M 5
Ajaguz ~ KA 124-125 L 5
Ajajú, Río ~ CO 64-65 F 1
Ajak ○ RUS 118-119 N 9
Ajakli ~ RUS 108-109 b 6
Ajaktal, gory ▲ RUS 108-109 Z 7
Ajalpan ○ MEX 52-53 F 2
Ajan ○ RUS (IRK) 116-117 N 6
Ajan ☆ RUS (HBR) 120-121 H 5
Ajan ~ RUS 108-109 Z 7
Ajan, ozero ~ RUS 108-109 a 7
Ajana ○ AUS 176-177 C 3
Ajan-Jurjah ~ RUS 120-121 M 2
Ajanka ○ RUS 112-113 O 5
Ajanka ~ RUS 112-113 N 4
Ajanta ○· IND 138-139 E 9
Ajanta Caves ··· IND 138-139 E 9
Ajaokuta ○ WAN 204-205 G 5
Ajaria = Adžarskaja Avtonomnaja Respublika □ GE 126-127 D 7
Ajasse ○ WAN 204-205 F 4
Ajasso ○ WAN 204-205 H 6
Ajat ~ KA 124-125 C 2
Ajaturku, ozero ○ RUS 108-109 Y 5
Ajava ~ RUS 116-117 L 6
Ajax ○ USA (TX) 268-269 G 5
Ajax Peak ▲ USA (ID) 250-251 F 6
Ajdābiyā □ LAR 192-193 H 3
Ajdābiyā ☆·· LAR 192-193 J 2
Ajdar ~ UA 102-103 L 3
Ajdarkŭl kŭli ○ US 136-137 K 4
Ajdarkuly, kŭli ○ US 136-137 K 4
Ajdarly ○ KA 124-125 D 6
Ajer' Terjun ○ MAL 162-163 D 2
Ajgyržal, tau ▲ KA 124-125 G 4
Ajhal ○ RUS 110-111 H 7
Aji, Isla ∩ CO 60-61 C 6
Ajibarang ○ RI 168 C 3
Ajigasawa ○ J 152-153 J 4
Ajikagungan ○ RI 162-163 F 7
Ajjer, Tassili n' ▲··· DZ 190-191 F 8
Ajjuva ~ RUS 88-89 X 4
Ajkaegan ~ RUS 114-115 N 3
Ajkeköl ○ KA 126-127 O 2
Ajkino ○ RUS 88-89 U 5
Ajmer ○ IND 138-139 E 6
Ajnabulak ○ KA 124-125 G 4
Ajni ○ TJ 136-137 L 5
Ajnianwāla ○ PK 138-139 D 4
Ajnskoe, ozero ○ RUS 122-123 K 4
Ajo ○ USA (AZ) 256-257 C 6
Ajoda ○ WAN 204-205 F 5
Ajo Mountains ▲ USA (AZ) 256-257 C 6
Ajon ○ RUS 112-113 O 2
Ajon, ostrov ∩ RUS 112-113 P 2
Aj-Pim ~ RUS 114-115 L 3
Ajrag = Cagaandörvölž ○ MAU 148-149 J 5
Ajryk ○ KA 124-125 K 3
Ajsary ○ KA 124-125 G 2
Ajtau ▲ KA 124-125 J 6
Ajtor, ozero ○ RUS 114-115 J 4
Ajtos ○ BG 102-103 E 6
Ajuly, Aksu- ○ KA 124-125 H 4
Ajumaku ○ GH 202-203 K 7
Ajumkan ~ RUS 120-121 D 6
Ajuy ○ RP 160-161 E 7
Ajvasedapur ~ RUS 114-115 O 2
Ajyrtas ○ KA 124-125 K 4
Aka ~ GH 202-203 L 6
Akaba ○ RT 202-203 L 6
Akaba, Réservat d' ⊥ RT 202-203 L 6
Akaba Pass ▲ SUD 200-201 H 3
Akabar < RMM 202-203 L 2
Akabli ○ DZ 190-191 C 7
Akačan ~ RUS 120-121 H 3
Akademii, zaliv ≈ 120-121 G 6
Akademii Nauk, lednik ⊂ RUS 108-109 Z 1
Akademika Obručeva, hrebet ▲ RUS 116-117 G 9
Akadomari ○ J 152-153 H 6
Aka-Eze ○ WAN 204-205 G 6
Akagera ~ RWA 212-213 C 5
Akagera, Parc national de l' ⊥ RWA 212-213 C 4
Akagi ○ J 152-153 E 7
Akaishi-sanmyaku ▲ J 152-153 H 7
Akaka ○ G 210-211 B 5
Akaka Falls ~· USA (HI) 288 K 5
Āk'ak'i Beseka ○ ETH 208-209 D 4
Akakro ○ CI 202-203 H 7
Akakus ··· LAR 190-191 H 8
Akakus, Jabal ▲ LAR 190-191 H 8
Akālgarh ○ PK 138-139 D 3
Akalkot ○ IND 140-141 G 2
Akamba, Chute ~ ZRE 210-211 L 3
Akam Éffak ○ G 210-211 C 3
Akamkpa ○ WAN 204-205 H 6
Akankohan ○ J 152-153 L 3
Akan National Park ⊥ J 152-153 L 3
Akanous ○ NAM 220-221 D 2
Akanyaru ~ RWA 212-213 B 5
Akaroa ○ NZ 182 D 5
Akasame ○ PNG 183 B 2
Akasha ○ SUD 200-201 E 2
Akashi ○ J 152-153 F 7
Akaska ○ USA (SD) 260-261 F 1
Äkäslompolo ○ FIN 88-89 H 3
Akassa ○ WAN 204-205 G 6
Akat Amnuai ○ THA 158-159 G 2
Akatsi ○ GH 202-203 L 6
Akbaba Dağı ▲ TR 128-129 K 2
Akbajtal, pereval ▲ TJ 136-137 N 5
Akbarpur ○ IND (BIH) 142-143 C 3
Akbarpur ○ IND (UTP) 142-143 C 2
Akbastöbe, tau ▲ KA 126-127 P 4
Akbou ○ DZ 190-191 E 2
Akbulak ☆ RUS 96-97 J 8
Akçaabat ☆ TR 128-129 H 2
Akçadağ ☆ TR 128-129 G 3
Akçakale ☆ TR 128-129 H 4
Akçakoca ☆· TR 128-129 D 2
Akçakoca Dağları ▲ TR 128-129 D 2
Akçalı Dağları ▲ TR 128-129 E 4
Akčatau ○ KA 124-125 J 5
Akçay ~ TR 128-129 C 4
Akchâr ∸ RIM 196-197 C 5
Ak Dağlar ▲ TR 128-129 C 4
Ak Dağlar ▲ TR 128-129 F 3
Akdağmadeni ☆ TR 128-129 F 3
Ak-Dovurak ○ RUS 116-117 E 10
Akdym, tau ▲ KA 124-125 H 3
Akdžakala, vpadina ◡ TM 136-137 F 4
Akébou ∸ RT 202-203 L 6
Akela ○ USA (NM) 256-257 H 6
Akelama ~ RI 164-165 L 3
Akelamo ○ RI (MAL) 164-165 L 3
Akelamo ○ RI (MAL) 164-165 K 3
Akelamo ○ RI (MAL) 164-165 K 4
Akelamo, Tanjung ▲ RI 164-165 K 4
Akeley ○ USA (MN) 270-271 D 3
Akeonik ○ USA 20-21 K 1
Akeouet, Hassi in < DZ 190-191 G 7
Akera ~ AZ 128-129 M 3
Åkersberga ☆ S 86-87 J 7
Aketi ○ ZRE 210-211 J 2
Aketi ~ ZRE 210-211 K 2
Akhdar, Al Jabal al □ LAR 192-193 J 1
Akhicha, Daïet ○ DZ 190-191 C 6
Akhiok ○ USA 22-23 T 4
Akhisar ☆ TR 128-129 B 3
Akhmed, I-n- < RMM 196-197 K 5
Akhnoor ○ IND 138-139 E 3
Aki ○ J 152-153 E 8
Akiachak ○ USA 20-21 K 6
Akiéni ○ G 210-211 D 4
Akimiski Island ∩ CDN 34-35 Q 4
Akıncı Burnu ▲ TR 128-129 F 4
Akinum ○ PNG 183 E 4
Akišma ~ RUS 122-123 E 2
Akita ☆ J 152-153 J 5
Ak"jar ☆ RUS 96-97 L 8
Akjoujt ☆ RIM 196-197 C 5
Akkajaure ○ S 86-87 H 3
Akkajtym ○ KA 126-127 N 4
Akkeshi ○ J 152-153 L 3
'Akko ☆·· IL 130-131 D 1
Akkol' ○ KA 124-125 J 6
Akkol' ○ KA (DZA) 136-137 M 3
Akköl ☆ KA (DZM) 136-137 M 3
Akköl ○ KA (DZM) 136-137 M 3
Akköl ○ KA (KST) 126-127 P 3
Akkoursoulbak ○ RCA 206-207 E 4
Akkyr ▲ TM 136-137 D 4
Aklampa ○ DY 204-205 E 4
Aklavik ○ CDN 20-21 X 2
Aklera ○ IND 138-139 F 7
Akli, I-n < RMM 196-197 K 4
Aklim, Adrar-n- ▲ MA 188-189 G 5
Akloa, Cascade d' ~ RT 202-203 L 6
Akmeqit ○ VRC 146-147 C 7
Akmola ○ KA 124-125 G 3
Akmola, tau ▲ KA 124-125 F 4
Akniste ○ LV 94-95 J 3
Aknoul ○ MA 188-189 K 3
Akō ○ J 152-153 F 7
Ako'akas, Rochers = Ako'akas Rocks · CAM 210-211 C 2

Ako'akas Rocks = Rochers Ako'akas • **CAM** 210-211 C 2
Akobo Wenz ∼ **ETH** 208-209 B 5
Ākobo Wenz ∼ **ETH** 208-209 B 5
Ak-Ojuk, gora ▲ **RUS** 124-125 Q 3
Akok ○ **G** 210-211 B 3
Akoke ○ **SUD** 206-207 L 4
Akokora ○ **ZRE** 212-213 B 3
Akola ○ **IND** 138-139 F 9
Akoma ○ **PNG** 183 C 4
Akom II ○ **CAM** 210-211 C 2
Akono ○ **CAM** 210-211 C 2
Akonolinga ○ **CAM** 210-211 D 2
Akop ○ **SUD** 206-207 J 4
Akor ○ **RMM** 202-203 G 2
Āk'ordat ○ **ER** 200-201 H 5
Akoroso ○ **GH** 202-203 K 7
Akosombo ○• **GH** 202-203 L 6
Akot ○ **IND** 138-139 F 9
Akot ○ **SUD** 206-207 K 5
Akoupé ○ **CI** 202-203 J 6
Akpatok Island ∩ **CDN** 36-37 P 4
Akpınar ☆ **TR** 128-129 E 3
Akplabanya ○ **GH** 202-203 L 7
Akposso ∸ **RT** 202-203 L 6
Akqi ○ **VRC** 146-147 D 5
Akrab ○ **KA** 126-127 L 2
Akrabat ○ **TM** 136-137 G 7
Akranes ☆ **IS** 86-87 b 2
Akráta ○ **GR** 100-101 J 5
Akra Ténaro ▲ **GR** 100-101 J 6
Akréréb ○ **RN** 198-199 D 4
Åkrestrømmen ○ **N** 86-87 E 6
Akrokorinthos ·· **GR** 100-101 J 6
Akron ○ **USA** (CO) 254-255 M 3
Akron ○ **USA** (IA) 274-275 B 2
Akron ○ **USA** (IN) 274-275 M 3
Akron ○ **USA** (NY) 278-279 C 5
Akron ○ **USA** (OH) 280-281 E 2
Akša ☆ **RUS** 118-119 F 10
Aksaj ☆ **KA** 96-97 H 8
Ak-Saj ∼ **KS** 146-147 C 5
Aksaj ○ **RUS** (ROS) 102-103 L 4
Aksaj ∼ **RUS** 102-103 M 4
Aksaj ∼ **RUS** 126-127 G 6
Aksaj Esaulovskij ∼ **RUS** 102-103 N 4
Akşar ○ **TR** 128-129 K 2
Aksaray ☆ **TR** 128-129 F 3
Aksarka ○ **RUS** 108-109 N 8
Aksay ○ **VRC** 146-147 M 6
Aksay Qin ∩ **IND** 138-139 G 2
Aksayqin Co ⬭ **VRC** 144-145 B 3
Akşehir ☆ **TR** 128-129 D 3
Akşehir Gölü ⬭ **TR** 128-129 D 3
Akseki ☆ **TR** 128-129 D 4
'Aks-e Rostam, Rūdḫāne-ye ∼ **IR** 134-135 F 4
Akši ∼ **KA** 124-125 D 5
Akšij ○ **KA** 146-147 C 4
Aksoran, gora ▲ **KA** 124-125 J 4
Aksoran, tau ▲ **KA** 124-125 J 4
Aksu ○ **KA** 124-125 G 2
Aksu ○ **KA** (ZPK) 96-97 H 8
Aksu ☆ **KA** 124-125 K 2
Aksu ∼ **KA** 124-125 L 6
Aksu ∼ **KA** 124-125 L 5
Aksu ∼ **KS** 146-147 B 4
Aksu ○ **VRC** 146-147 E 5
Aksu-Ajuly ○ **KA** 124-125 H 4
Aksu-Ajuly ○ **KA** 124-125 H 4
Aksuat ○ **KA** 124-125 N 4
Aksuat, köli ⬭ **KA** 124-125 D 3
Aksubaevo ☆ **RUS** 96-97 G 6
Aksu Çayı ∼ **TR** 128-129 D 4
Aksūm ○··· **ETH** 200-201 J 5
Ak-Syjrak ○ **KS** 146-147 D 5
Ak-Tal ○ **KS** 146-147 B 5
Aktanyš ☆ **RUS** 96-97 J 6
Aktarsk ○ **RUS** 96-97 D 8
Aktaš ○ **RUS** 124-125 P 3
Aktau ○ **KA** (KRG) 124-125 H 3
Aktau ☆ **KA** 126-127 J 6
Aktau ☆ **KA** (MNG) 126-127 J 6
Aktaz ○ **KA** 124-125 H 4
Aktaz ○ **VRC** 146-147 H 6
Aktöbe ☆ **KA** 126-127 M 2
Aktogaj ○ **KA** 124-125 J 4
Aktolagaj tizbegi ⛰ **KA** 126-127 L 4
Aktov tog ⛰ **US** 136-137 J 4
Aktūmsyk ○ **KA** 126-127 M 4
Aku ○ **PNG** 184 I b 2
Akūbū ○ **SUD** 206-207 L 5
Akugdleq, Ikertoog ≈ 28-29 O 3
Akula ○ **ZRE** 210-211 H 2
Akuliarusinguaq ∩ **GRØ** 26-27 Y 8
Akulurak ○ **USA** 20-21 H 5
Akumal ○ **MEX** 52-53 L 1
Akune ○ **J** 152-153 D 8
Akun Island ∩ **USA** 22-23 O 5
Akuraj ○ **RUS** 118-119 H 10
Akure ☆ **WAN** 204-205 F 5
Akureyri ☆ **IS** 86-87 d 2
Akuš, ozero ⬭ **RUS** 114-115 K 7
Akuseki-shima ∩ **J** 152-153 C 10
Akutan ○ **USA** 22-23 O 5
Akutan Island ∩ **USA** 22-23 N 5
Akutan Pass ≈ 22-23 N 5
Akutukpa ○ **WAN** 204-205 G 4
Akvinu River ∼ **CDN** 32-33 N 4
Akwa-Ibom □ **WAN** 204-205 G 6
Akwanga ○ **WAN** 204-205 H 4
Akwatuk Bay ≈ 38-39 E 2
Akwaya ○ **CAM** 204-205 H 5
Akwot ∼ **SUD** 206-207 K 5
Akyab = Sittwe ☆ **MYA** 142-143 H 5
Akžajkyn, köl ⬭ **KA** 124-125 E 6
Akžajyk ○ **KA** 96-97 G 8
Akžar, k-l ⬭ **KA** 136-137 L 3
Akžar, ozero ⬭ **KA** 136-137 L 3
Alabama ○ **USA** (NY) 278-279 C 5
Alabama □ **USA** (AL) 284-285 C 4
Alabama Camp ○ **LB** 202-203 F 5
Alabama & Coushatta Indian Reservation ⨯ **USA** (TX) 268-269 F 6
Alabama Port ○ **USA** (AL) 284-285 B 6
Alabama River ∼ **USA** (AL) 284-285 C 5
Alabaster ○ **USA** (AL) 284-285 D 3
Alabat Island ∩ **RP** 160-161 D 5
al-'Abbāsīyah ○ **SUD** 200-201 E 6
Ala-Bel', pereval ▲ **KS** 136-137 N 3
Alabo ∼ **GH** 202-203 L 6
Alabota, köli ⬭ **KA** (KKC) 124-125 G 2
Alabota, köli ⬭ **KA** (KST) 124-125 D 2
Ala Buka ○ **KS** 136-137 M 4
Ala-Buka ∼ **KS** 146-147 B 5
Alaca ☆ **TR** 128-129 F 2
Alacahöyük ·· **TR** 128-129 F 2
Alacalufe, Reserva Florestal ⊥ **RCH** 80 C 6
Alaçam ☆ **TR** 128-129 F 2
Alacant ☆ **E** 98-99 G 5
Alachua ○ **USA** (FL) 286-287 G 2
Alacranes, Presa < **C** 54-55 E 3
Aladağ ▲ **TR** 128-129 E 4
Ālādāg, Kūh-e ⛰ **IR** 136-137 E 6
Ala Dağlar ⛰ **TR** 128-129 F 4
Ala Dağlar ⛰ **TR** 128-129 K 3
al-'Adam ○ **LAR** 192-193 K 2
Aladdin ○ **USA** (WY) 252-253 O 2
Aladja ○ **WAN** 204-205 F 6
Aladža = Alağa ○ **TM** 136-137 C 5
Alaf Badane < **ETH** 208-209 G 6
Alafiarou ○ **DY** 204-205 E 4
Alaganik ○ **USA** 20-21 S 6
Alagapuram ○ **IND** 140-141 H 5
Ālagē ▲ **ETH** 200-201 J 6
Alagir ○ **RUS** 126-127 F 6
al-'Ağma, Ğabal ⛰ **ET** 194-195 G 3
Alag nuur ⬭ **MAU** 146-147 M 3
Alagoa Grande ○ **BR** 68-69 L 5
Alagoas □ **BR** 68-69 K 6
Alagoinha ○ **BR** 68-69 K 6
Alagoinhas ○ **BR** 72-73 L 2
Alagón ○ **E** 98-99 G 4
Alagón, Río ∼ **E** 98-99 D 4
al-'Ağrūd ○ **ET** 194-195 G 2
Alah ∼ **RP** 160-161 F 9
Alahan Monastir ·· **TR** 128-129 E 4
Alahanpanjang ○ **RI** 162-163 D 5
Alaid, vulkan ▲ **RUS** 122-123 Q 3
Alaid Island ∩ **USA** 22-23 C 6
al-Ain ○··· **OM** 132-133 K 2
al-'Ain < **SUD** 200-201 D 4
Alajärvi ○ **FIN** 88-89 G 5
Alajskij hrebet ⛰ **TJ** 136-137 M 5
Alajuela ☆ **CR** 52-53 B 6
Alakamisy Ambohimaha ○ **RM** 222-223 E 8
Alakamisy Itenina ○ **RM** 222-223 E 8
Alakanuk ○ **USA** 20-21 H 5
Alakit ○ **RUS** 110-111 H 6
Alakit ∼ **RUS** 110-111 H 6
Alakol', köli ⬭ **KA** 124-125 M 5
Alakol', ozero ⬭ **KA** 124-125 J 6
Alaktak ○ **USA** 20-21 N 1
Alakuko ○ **WAN** 204-205 F 5
Alakurtti ○ **RUS** 88-89 L 3
Alalakeiki Channel ≈ **USA** 288 J 4
al-'Alamain ○• **ET** 194-195 D 2
Al 'Alaqah, Bi'r < **LAR** 192-193 F 3
Alalaú, Rio ∼ **BR** 62-63 D 6
'Alālī, al- ○ **RL** 128-129 F 6
al-'Ālī Sadd <·· **ET** 194-195 F 6
Alamar ○ **C** 54-55 D 3
al-'Amārah ○ **SUD** 200-201 F 5
'Alā Marv Dašt, Rūd-e ∼ **IR** 134-135 E 5
Ālamat'ā ○ **ETH** 200-201 J 6
Alameda ○ **CDN** (SAS) 232-233 Q 6
Alameda, La ○ **MEX** 50-51 G 5
Alamikamba ○ **NIC** 52-53 B 5
Alamillo ○ **USA** (NM) 256-257 J 4
Alaminos ○ **RP** 160-161 C 4
al-'Āmiriya ○ **ET** 194-195 D 2
Alamito Creek ∼ **USA** (TX) 266-267 C 4
Alamo ○ **MEX** 52-53 F 1
Alamo ○ **SP** 208-209 F 6
Alamo ○ **USA** (ND) 258-259 D 3
Alamo ○ **USA** (NM) 256-257 H 4
Alamo ○ **USA** (NV) 248-249 J 2
Alamo ○ **USA** (TN) 276-277 F 5
Alamogordo ○ **USA** (NM) 256-257 K 6
Alamo Lake < **USA** (AZ) 256-257 B 4
Alamo Navajo Indian Reservation ⨯ **USA** (NM) 256-257 H 4
Alamor ○ **EC** 64-65 B 4
Alamos ○ **MEX** 50-51 E 4
Alamos, Los ○ **USA** (CA) 248-249 D 5
Alamos, Los ○ **USA** (NM) 256-257 J 3
Álamos, Río de los ∼ **MEX** 50-51 J 3
Alamosa ○ **USA** (CO) 254-255 K 6
Alamosa National Wildlife Refuge ⊥ **USA** (CO) 254-255 K 6
Alamosa River ∼ **USA** (NM) 256-257 H 5
Alamos de Márquez ○ **MEX** 50-51 H 3
Alampur ○ **IND** 140-141 H 3
Åland ∩ **FIN** 88-89 F 6
Aland ○ **IND** 140-141 G 2
Ålands Hav ≈ 86-87 J 6
Alang ○ **IND** 138-139 D 9
Alange ○ **E** 98-99 D 5
Alanreed ○ **USA** (TX) 264-265 D 3
Alanson ○ **USA** (MI) 272-273 E 2
Alantika Mountains ⛰ **WAN** 204-205 K 4
Alanya ○ **TR** 128-129 E 4
Alaolo ∼ **SOL** 184 I e 3
Alaotra ∸ **RM** 222-223 F 6
Alaotra, Farihy ⬭ **RM** 222-223 F 6
Alapa ○ **WAN** 204-205 F 4
Alapaevsk ○ **RUS** 96-97 M 5
Alapaha ○ **USA** (GA) 284-285 G 5
Alapaha River ∼ **USA** (FL) 286-287 F 1
Alapaha River ∼ **USA** (GA) 284-285 G 6
al-'Aqaba, Ḫalīğ ≈ 194-195 G 3
al-'Aqaba as-Ṣagira ○ **ET** 194-195 F 5
'Alāqān ○ **KSA** 130-131 D 3
Alaquines ○ **MEX** 50-51 K 6
al-Arab, Baḥr ∼ **SUD** 206-207 G 3
al-'Arab, Baḥr ∼ **SUD** 206-207 J 4
al-'Arab, Ḫalīğ ≈ 194-195 D 2
al-Arāk ○ **SUD** 200-201 E 3
Alarcón, Embalse de < **E** 98-99 F 5
Alareak Island ∩ **CDN** 36-37 M 2
al-Argoub ○ **MA** 196-197 C 3
al-'Ariš ☆ **ET** 194-195 F 2
al-'Ariš, Wādī ∼ **ET** 194-195 F 2
Alas ○ **RI** (NBA) 168 C 7
Alas ○ **RI** (TIT) 166-167 C 6
Alas ∼ **RI** 162-163 B 3
Alaš ∼ **RUS** 124-125 Q 3
Alas, Hos- ○ **RUS** 110-111 S 6
Alas, Selat ≈ 168 C 7
Alaşehir ☆• **TR** 128-129 C 3
Alašejev buchta ≈ 16 G 5
Alashan Shamo ∩ **VRC** 148-149 E 7
Alasi ○ **SOL** 184 I e 3
al-'Āṣī, Nahr ∼ **SYR** 128-129 G 5
Alaska ○ **USA** (MI) 272-273 D 5
Alaska □ **USA** 20-21 K 4
Alaska ○ **ZW** 218-219 F 3
Alaska, Gulf of ≈ 14-15 O 2
Alaska Highway II **CDN** 32-33 K 3
Alaska Range ⛰ **USA** 20-21 O 6
Al 'Assah ○ **LAR** 192-193 D 1
Alássio ○• **I** 100-101 B 2
Alat ○ **US** 136-137 H 5
Alatau hrebet ⛰ **RUS** 96-97 K 7
Alataw Shankou ▲ **VRC** 146-147 F 3
Al Atazar, Embalse de < **E** 98-99 F 4
Alati ○ **CAM** 210-211 D 2
Alatna River ∼ **USA** 20-21 O 3
al-'Atrun, Bi'r < **SUD** 200-201 C 3
al-Atshan ∼ **SUD** 200-201 G 6
Alatsinainy Bakaro ○ **RM** 222-223 E 7
Alatskivi ○·· **EST** 94-95 K 2
Ālattur ○ **IND** 140-141 G 5
Alatyr' ○ **RUS** 96-97 E 6
Alausí ○ **EC** 64-65 C 3
Alava ○ **RP** 160-161 D 4
Alaverdi ○ **AR** 128-129 L 2
Ala-Vuokki ○ **FIN** 88-89 K 4
Alavus ○ **FIN** 88-89 G 5
Alawa ○ **WAN** 204-205 G 3
Alawa Game Reserve ⊥ **WAN** 204-205 G 3
Alawangandji Aboriginal Land ⨯ **AUS** 174-175 C 4
Al Awaynat ○ **LAR** 200-201 B 2
Al Awaynat, Jabal ▲ **SUD** 200-201 B 2
Alawoona ○ **AUS** 180-181 F 3
Alayo ○ **RCA** 206-207 F 6
al-'Ayun ☆ **MA** 188-189 E 7
al-'Ayyāt ○ **ET** 194-195 E 3
Alazani ∼ **AZ** 128-129 M 2
Alazeja ∼ **RUS** 110-111 b 5
Alazeja ∼ **RUS** 112-113 H 1
Alazejskoe ploskogor'e ⛰ **RUS** 110-111 a 6
Al 'Azīzīyah □ **LAR** 192-193 E 1
Al 'Azīzīyah ☆ **LAR** 192-193 E 1
Alba ○• **I** 100-101 B 2
Alba ○ **USA** (TX) 264-265 J 6
Albacete ○ **E** 98-99 G 5
Albacutya, Lake ⬭ **AUS** 180-181 F 3
al-Badārī ○ **ET** 194-195 E 4
Alba de Tormes ○ **E** 98-99 E 4
Ålbæk Bugt ≈ 86-87 E 8
al-Baḥr al-Azraq ∼ **SUD** 200-201 G 6
al-Baḥrīya, Barqat ∸ **ET** 192-193 L 2
Alba Iulia ☆• **RO** 102-103 C 4
Albāka ○ **IND** 142-143 B 6
al-Balīḫ, Nahr ∼ **SYR** 128-129 H 4
al-Ballāṣ ○ **ET** 194-195 F 4
al-Balyana ○ **ET** 194-195 E 4
Alban ○ **CDN** (ONT) 238-239 E 2
Alban ○ **CO** 60-61 D 5
Alban = San José ○ **CO** 64-65 D 1
Albanel ○ **CDN** (QUE) 240-241 C 2
Albanel, Lac ⬭ **CDN** (QUE) 236-237 P 2
Albania = Shqipëri ■ **AL** 100-101 G 4
Albany ○• **AUS** 176-177 D 7
Albany ○ **USA** (GA) 284-285 F 5
Albany ○ **USA** (IN) 274-275 N 4
Albany ○ **USA** (KY) 276-277 K 4
Albany ○ **USA** (MN) 270-271 D 5
Albany ○ **USA** (MO) 274-275 D 4
Albany ○ **USA** (OR) 244-245 B 6
Albany ○ **USA** (TX) 264-265 E 6
Albany ○ **USA** (WY) 252-253 M 5
Albany ☆• **USA** (NY) 278-279 H 6
Albany Downs ○ **AUS** 178-179 K 4
Albany Highway II **AUS** 176-177 D 6
Albany Island ∩ **CDN** 34-35 Q 4
Albany River ∼ **CDN** 34-35 O 5
Albany River ∼ **CDN** (ONT) 234-235 O 3
Alba Posse ○ **RA** 76-77 K 4
al-Barāmūs, Dair ∴• **ET** 194-195 E 2
Al Bardī ○ **LAR** 192-193 L 2
Albarracín ○• **E** 98-99 G 4
al-Barun ○ **SUD** 208-209 A 3
al-Basabir ○ **SUD** 200-201 F 4
al-Bāṭina, Ğazirat ∩ **KSA** 130-131 L 4
Albatros Bank ≃ 22-23 U 4
Albatross Bay ≈ 174-175 F 3
al-Bauga ○ **SUD** 200-201 F 3
al-Bawītī ○ **ET** 194-195 D 3
Al Bayādah, Wādī ∼ **LAR** 192-193 H 4
Al Bayda □ **LAR** 192-193 J 1
Al Bayda ☆ **LAR** 192-193 J 1
Al Baydā, Barqah ∸ **LAR** 192-193 H 2
Albay Gulf ≈ 160-161 E 6
Al Bayyādah ○ **LAR** 192-193 J 1
Albazino ○ **RUS** 118-119 M 9
al-Begeir ○ **SUD** 200-201 F 3
Albemarle ○ **USA** (NC) 282-283 G 5
Albemarle Sound ≈ 48-49 K 1
Albemarle Sound ≈ **USA** 282-283 L 4
Albenga ○• **I** 100-101 B 2
Alberca, La ○• **E** 98-99 D 4
Alberdi ○ **PY** 76-77 H 4
Alberfoyle ○ **AUS** 178-179 H 1
Alberga Creek ∼ **AUS** 178-179 C 4
Albergaria-a-Velha ○ **P** 98-99 C 4
Alberni ○ **CDN** (BC) 230-231 E 4
Alberni Inlet ≈ **CDN** 230-231 E 4
Alberobello ○• **I** 100-101 F 4
Albert ○ **F** 90-91 J 6
Albert, Cape ▲ **CDN** 26-27 N 4
Albert, Lake ⬭ **AUS** 180-181 E 3
Albert, Lake ⬭ **USA** (OR) 244-245 E 8
Albert, Lake = Lac Mobutu-Sese-Seko ⬭ **EAU** 212-213 C 3
Albert, Port ○• **AUS** 180-181 J 5
Alberta □ **CDN** 32-33 L 4
Alberta ○ **USA** (VA) 280-281 J 7
Alberta Beach ○ **CDN** (ALB) 232-233 D 2
Albert Canyon ○ **CDN** (BC) 230-231 M 2
Albert Edward, Mount ▲ **CDN** (BC) 230-231 D 4
Albert Edward, Mount ▲ **PNG** 183 D 5
Albert Edward Bay ≈ 24-25 U 6
Alberti ○ **RA** 78-79 J 3
Albert I Land ∸ **N** 84-85 G 3
Albertinia ○ **ZA** 220-221 E 7
Albert Law, Mont ▲ **CDN** 36-37 N 4
Albert Lea ○ **USA** (MN) 270-271 E 7
Albert Markham, Mount ▲ **ARK** 16 E 0
Albert Nile ∼ **EAU** 212-213 C 2
Alberto de Agostini, Parque Nacional ⊥ **RCH** 80 E 7
Alberton ○ **CDN** (PEI) 240-241 L 4
Alberton ○ **USA** (MT) 250-251 E 4
Albert River ∼ **AUS** 174-175 E 6
Albert Town ○ **BS** 54-55 H 3
Albert Town ○ **JA** 54-55 G 5
Albertville ○ **CDN** (QUE) 240-241 H 2
Albertville ○• **F** 90-91 L 9
Albertville ○ **USA** (AL) 284-285 D 2
Albi ☆• **F** 90-91 J 10
Albia ○ **USA** (IA) 274-275 F 3
Albin ○ **USA** (WY) 252-253 O 5
Albina ☆ **SME** 62-63 G 3
Albina, Ponta ▲ **ANG** 216-217 A 7
Albion ○ **USA** (CA) 246-247 B 4
Albion ○ **USA** (IL) 274-275 K 6
Albion ○ **USA** (MI) 272-273 E 5
Albion ○ **USA** (MT) 250-251 P 6
Albion ○ **USA** (NE) 262-263 J 3
Albion ○ **USA** (NY) 278-279 C 5
Albion ○ **USA** (OK) 264-265 J 4
Albion ○ **USA** (PA) 280-281 F 2
Alborán, Isla del ∩ **E** 98-99 F 7
Ålborg ○·· **DK** 86-87 D 8
Ålborg Bugt ≈ 86-87 E 8
Alborn ○ **USA** (MN) 270-271 F 4
Alborz, Kūhhā-ye ⛰ **IR** 136-137 B 6
Albox ○ **E** 98-99 F 6
Albreda ○ **CDN** (BC) 228-229 P 4
Albreda ○• **WAG** 202-203 B 3
Albro ○ **AUS** 178-179 J 2
Albufeira ○ **P** 98-99 C 6
Albuquerque ○• **E** 98-99 D 5
Albuquerque ○• **USA** (NM) 256-257 J 3
Albuquerque, Cayos de ∩ **CO** 52-53 D 5
al-Burullus, Buḥairat ⬭ **ET** 194-195 E 2
Albury-Wodonga ○ **AUS** 180-181 J 4
Alcácer do Sal ○ **P** 98-99 C 5
Alcáçovas ○ **P** 98-99 C 5
Alcala ○ **AUS** 174-175 F 6
Alcala ○ **RP** 160-161 D 4
Alcalá de Chivert = Alcalà de Xivert ○ **E** 98-99 H 4
Alcalá de Henares ○• **E** 98-99 F 4
Alcalá del Júcar ○ **E** 98-99 G 5
Alcalà de Xivert ○ **E** 98-99 H 4
Alcalá la Real ○ **E** 98-99 F 6
Alcalde ○ **USA** (NM) 256-257 J 2
Alcalde, Punta ▲ **RCH** 76-77 B 5
Álcamo ○ **I** 100-101 D 6
Alcañices ○ **E** 98-99 D 4
Alcañiz ○ **E** 98-99 G 4
Alcântara ○ **BR** 68-69 F 3
Alcántara ○ **E** 98-99 D 5
Alcantara Lake ⬭ **CDN** 30-31 P 5
Alcantarilla ○ **E** 98-99 G 6
Alcaracejos ○ **E** 98-99 E 5
Alcaraz ○ **E** 98-99 F 5
Alcaraz, Sierra de ⛰ **E** 98-99 F 5
Alcatrazes, Ilha do ∩ **BR** 72-73 H 8
Alcaudete ○ **E** 98-99 E 6
Alcázar ·· **E** 98-99 E 6
Alcázar de San Juan ○ **E** 98-99 F 5
Alcedo, Volcán ▲ **EC** 64-65 B 10
Alcester Island ∩ **PNG** 183 G 5
Alčevs'k ○ **UA** 102-103 L 3
Alcira ○ **RA** 78-79 G 2
Alcoa ○ **USA** (TN) 282-283 D 5
Alcobaça ○··· **P** 98-99 C 5
Alcoi ○ **E** 98-99 G 5
Alcolea del Pinar ○ **E** 98-99 F 4
Alcomdale ○ **CDN** (ALB) 232-233 E 2
Alcona ○ **CDN** (ONT) 234-235 M 4
Alcoota ○ **AUS** 178-179 C 2
Alcorcón ○ **E** 98-99 F 4
Alcorta ○ **RA** 78-79 J 2
Alcott Creek ∼ **CDN** (SAS) 232-233 K 2
Alcoutim ○ **P** 98-99 D 6
Alcova ○ **USA** (WY) 252-253 M 4
Alcovy River ∼ **USA** (GA) 284-285 G 3
Alcoy ○ **RP** 160-161 E 8
Alcoy = Alcoi ○ **E** 98-99 G 5
Alcúdia ○ **E** 98-99 J 5
Alcúdia, l' ○ **E** 98-99 G 5
Alcurve ○ **CDN** (ALB) 232-233 H 2
Aldabra Atoll ∸··· **SY** 222-223 E 2
Aldabra Group ∸ **SY** 222-223 E 2
Aldaia Bona ○ **BR** 62-63 G 5
Aldama ○ **MEX** (CHA) 50-51 G 3
Aldama ○ **MEX** (TAM) 50-51 K 6
Aldamas, Los ○ **MEX** 50-51 K 4
Aldan ☆• **RUS** (SAH) 118-119 M 6
Aldan ∼ **RUS** 118-119 P 4
Aldan ∼ **RUS** 118-119 L 7
Aldan ∼ **RUS** 118-119 N 6
Aldan ∼ **RUS** 120-121 F 2
Aldanskoe nagor'e ⛰ **RUS** 118-119 L 6
Aldea, Isla ∩ **RCH** 80 C 4
Aldea dos Indios Sucane ○ **GUY** 62-63 E 5
Aldehuela Gallinal ○ **ROU** 78-79 M 2
Aldeia ○ **BR** (BAH) 68-69 E 7
Aldeia ○ **BR** (GSU) 70-71 K 6
Aldeia ○ **BR** (MAR) 68-69 E 5
Aldeia, Serra da ⛰ **BR** 72-73 G 4
Aldeia Beltrão ○ **BR** 76-77 K 5
Aldeia das Canoas ○ **BR** 62-63 G 5
Aldeia Grimaldi ○ **BR** 76-77 J 6
Aldeia Manuel Antonio ○ **BR** 68-69 E 3
Aldeia Velha ○ **BR** 68-69 F 4
Aldeia Viçosa ○ **ANG** 216-217 C 4
Aldeia Vila Batista ○ **BR** 62-63 D 6
Alder ○ **USA** (MT) 250-251 G 6
Alder Creek ○ **USA** (NY) 278-279 F 5
Alder Flats ○ **CDN** (ALB) 232-233 D 3
Alderley ○ **AUS** 178-179 E 2
Alderley ○ **ZA** 220-221 J 6
Alderney ∩ **GBA** 90-91 F 7
Alder Peak ▲ **USA** (CA) 248-249 C 4
Alder Point ▲ **USA** (CA) 248-249 C 4
Alderson ○ **CDN** (ALB) 232-233 G 5
Aldoma ○ **RUS** 120-121 H 5
Aldoma ∼ **RUS** 120-121 G 5
Aldrich, Cape ▲ **CDN** 26-27 Q 2
Aldžer, ostrov ∩ **RUS** 84-85 e 2
Alédjo ○ **DY** 202-203 L 5
Alédjo, Faille-d' ▲• **RT** 202-203 L 5
Aledo ○ **USA** (IL) 274-275 H 3
Aleg ☆ **RIM** 196-197 D 6
Aleg, Lac d' ⬭ **RIM** 196-197 D 6
Alegre ○ **BR** (ESP) 72-73 K 6
Alegre ○ **BR** (MIN) 72-73 G 5
Alegre, Riacho ∼ **PY** 76-77 H 1
Alegre, Rio ∼ **BR** 70-71 H 4
Alegres Mountain ▲ **USA** (NM) 256-257 J 4
Alegrete ○ **BR** 76-77 K 5
Alegria ○ **BR** (GSU) 70-71 K 6
Alegria ○ **BR** (RSU) 76-77 K 4
Alegria ○ **RP** 160-161 E 8
Alegro, Ponta ▲ **BR** 74-75 D 9
Alëhovščina ○ **RUS** 94-95 N 1
Aleï, I-n- < **RMM** 196-197 J 6
Aleiandia ○ **CO** 60-61 D 3
Alej ∼ **RUS** 124-125 N 2
Alejandra ○ **RA** 76-77 H 5
Alejandria ○ **BOL** 70-71 E 3
Alejandro Selkirk, Isla ∩ **RCH** 78-79 B 1
Alejsk ○ **RUS** 124-125 N 2
Aleknagik ○ **USA** 22-23 R 3
Aleknagik, Lake ⬭ **USA** 22-23 R 3
Aleko-Kjuël' ○ **RUS** 110-111 d 5
Aleksandovskij, zaliv ⬭ **RUS** 122-123 J 3
Aleksandra, mys ▲ **RUS** 120-121 H 6
Aleksandra I, zeml'a ∸ **ARK** 16 G 29
Aleksandrija = Oleksandrivka ○ **UA** 102-103 H 3
Aleksandrov ☆·· **RUS** 94-95 Q 3
Aleksandrov Gaj ☆ **RUS** 96-97 F 8
Aleksandrovka ☆ **RUS** 96-97 J 7
Aleksandrovsk ○ **RUS** 114-115 D 5
Aleksandrovskij, Kus'e- ○ **RUS** 96-97 L 4
Aleksandrovskoe ○ **RUS** (STA) 126-127 E 5
Aleksandrovskoe ○ **RUS** (TOM) 114-115 O 4
Aleksandrovsk-Sahalinsij ☆• **RUS** 122-123 K 3
Aleksandry, zaliv ⬭ **RUS** 120-121 H 6
Aleksandry, Zemlja ∩ **RUS** 84-85 Z 2
Alekseevaka ○ **RUS** 102-103 L 2
Alekseevka ○ **KA** 124-125 O 4
Alekseevka ☆ **KA** 124-125 G 2
Alekseevka ○ **RUS** 118-119 M 5
Alekseevka ☆ **RUS** (SAM) 96-97 G 7
Alekseevskoe ☆ **RUS** 96-97 G 6
Aleksin ☆• **RUS** 94-95 P 4
Aleksinac ○ **YU** 100-101 H 3
Alel ○ **SUD** 206-207 K 5
Ålem ○ **S** 86-87 H 8
Alemania ○ **EC** 64-65 B 10
Alèmbé ○ **G** 210-211 C 4
Alembé ○ **RCB** 210-211 E 4
'Alem Ketema ○ **ETH** 208-209 D 3
'Alem Maya ○ **ETH** 208-209 E 4
Além-Paraíba ○ **BR** 72-73 J 6
Ålen ☆ **N** 86-87 E 5
Alençon ☆ **F** 90-91 H 7
Alen Nkoma ○ **G** 210-211 C 3
Alenquer ○ **BR** 62-63 G 6
Alentejo ∸ **P** 98-99 C 6
Alenuihaha Channel ≈ 48-49 D 7
Alenuihaha Channel ≈ **USA** 288 J 4
Alépé ○ **CI** 202-203 J 7
Aleppo = Halab ☆··· **SYR** 128-129 G 4
Alerces, Parque Nacional los ⊥ **RA** 78-79 D 7
Aleria ○ **F** 98-99 M 3
Alert ○ **CDN** 26-27 T 2
Alerta ○ **PE** 70-71 B 2
Alert Bay ○ **CDN** (BC) 230-231 C 3
Alert Point ▲ **CDN** 26-27 G 2
Alès ○ **F** 90-91 K 9
Alesandrovskij Zavod ☆ **RUS** 118-119 H 10
Alessándria ☆ **I** 100-101 B 2
Ålesund ☆• **N** 86-87 C 5
Aleutian Basin ≃ 22-23 C 4
Aleutian Islands ∩ **USA** 22-23 H 6
Aleutian Range ⛰ **USA** 22-23 R 4
Aleutian Trench ≃ 22-23 K 7
Aleutko ○ **RUS** 122-123 O 6
Alexander ○ **CDN** (MAN) 234-235 C 5
Alexander ○ **USA** (AK) 20-21 P 6
Alexander ○ **USA** (KS) 262-263 G 6
Alexander ○ **USA** (ND) 258-259 D 4
Alexander, Cape ▲ **SOL** 184 I c 2
Alexander, Kap ▲ **GRØ** 26-27 O 4
Alexander, Point ▲ **AUS** 174-175 D 3
Alexander Archipelago ∩ **USA** 32-33 B 3
Alexanderbaai = Alexander Bay ○ **ZA** 220-221 C 4
Alexander Bay = Alexanderbaai ○ **ZA** 220-221 C 4
Alexander City ○ **USA** (AL) 284-285 E 4
Alexander Graham Bell National Historic Park ⊥• **CDN** (NS) 240-241 P 4
Alexander Inlet ≈ 28-29 G 2
Alexander Island ∩ **CDN** 24-25 U 3
Alexandra ○ **AUS** 180-181 H 4
Alexandra ○ **NZ** 182 B 6
Alexandra, Cape ▲ **GB** 78-79 O 7
Alexandra Bay ≈ 174-175 H 5
Alexandra Channel ≈ 140-141 L 2
Alexandra Falls ∼ **CDN** 30-31 L 5
Alexandra Fiord ○ **CDN** 26-27 N 4
Alexandra River ∼ **AUS** 174-175 F 6
Alexandria ○ **AUS** 174-175 D 6
Alexandria ○ **BR** 68-69 J 5
Alexandria ○ **CDN** (BC) 228-229 M 4
Alexandria ○ **CDN** (ONT) 238-239 L 3
Alexándria ○ **GR** 100-101 J 4
Alexandria ○ **JA** 54-55 G 5
Alexandria ☆• **RO** 102-103 D 6
Alexandria ○ **USA** (IN) 274-275 N 4
Alexandria ○ **USA** (LA) 268-269 H 5
Alexandria ○ **USA** (MN) 270-271 C 5
Alexandria ○ **USA** (SD) 260-261 J 3
Alexandria ○ **USA** (VA) 280-281 J 5
Alexandria ○ **ZA** 220-221 H 6
Alexandria = al-Iskandarīya ☆·· **ET** 194-195 D 2
Alexandria = Iskandarīya, al- ☆·· **ET** 194-195 D 2
Alexandria Bay ○ **USA** (NY) 278-279 F 4
Alexandrina, Lake ⬭ **AUS** 180-181 E 3
Alexandroúpoli ☆ **GR** 100-101 K 4
Alexeck ∼ **NAM** 216-217 E 10
Alex Graham, Mount ▲ **CDN** (BC) 228-229 M 4
Alexis ○ **USA** (IL) 274-275 H 3
Alexis Bay ≈ 38-39 Q 2
Alexis Creek ○ **CDN** (BC) 228-229 L 4
Alexishafen ○ **PNG** 183 C 3
Alexis River ∼ **CDN** 38-39 Q 2
Alex Morrison National Park ⊥ **AUS** 176-177 C 4
Aleza Lake ○ **CDN** (BC) 228-229 M 2
Al Faid-Majir ○ **LAR** 192-193 F 1
Alfalfa ○ **USA** (OK) 264-265 F 3
Alfalfa ○ **USA** (OR) 244-245 D 6
Alfarez de Navio Sobral ○ **ARK** 16 E 0
Alfa River ∼ **CDN** 24-25 f 4
Alfarràs ○ **E** 98-99 H 4
Al Fāshir ○• **SUD** 200-201 B 6
al-Fāshir ○• **SUD** 200-201 B 6
al-Fašn ○ **ET** 194-195 E 3
Al Fāt, Wādī ∼ **LAR** 192-193 F 3
Alfatar ○ **BG** 102-103 E 6
Al Fātiḥ □ **LAR** 192-193 J 1
Al Fātiyah, Bi'r < **LAR** 192-193 F 3
al-Fayyūm ☆·· **ET** 194-195 E 3
Alfenas ○ **BR** 72-73 H 6
al-Fifi ○ **SUD** 206-207 G 3
Alford ○ **USA** (FL) 286-287 D 1
Ålfotbreen ⊂ **N** 86-87 B 6
Alfred ○ **CDN** (ONT) 238-239 L 3
Alfred ○ **USA** (TX) 266-267 K 6
Alfred, Cape ▲ **CDN** 24-25 V 6
Alfred and Marie Range ⛰ **AUS** 176-177 H 2
Alfredo Chaves ○ **BR** 72-73 K 6
Alfredo M. Terrazas ○ **MEX** 50-51 K 7
Alfredo Wagner ○ **BR** 74-75 F 6
Alfred Wegeners Halvø ⌣ **GRØ** 26-27 Z 8
Alf Trolle, Kap ▲ **GRØ** 26-27 q 6
Al Fuqāhā' ○ **LAR** 192-193 G 4
Alga ☆ **KA** 126-127 M 3
al-Gabalayn ○ **SUD** 200-201 F 6
Algabas ○ **KA** 96-97 H 8
al-Gabir ○ **SUD** 200-201 D 6
al-Ğadida ○ **ET** 194-195 D 3
al-Ğāhir, Ğabal ▲ **Y** 132-133 J 7
al-Ğalāla al-Baḥrīya, Ğabal ⛰ **ET** 194-195 E 3
al-Ğalāla al-Qiblīya, Ğabal ⛰ **ET** 194-195 F 3
Algama ∼ **RUS** 118-119 O 8
Algama ∼ **RUS** 120-121 D 5
al-Ğamālīya ○ **ET** 194-195 E 2
al-Gamāmīyah ○ **SUD** 200-201 F 3
Algan ∼ **RUS** 112-113 Q 4
Alganskij krjaž ⛰ **RUS** 112-113 Q 4
Al Garabulli ○ **LAR** 192-193 E 1
al-Garef ○ **SUD** 200-201 G 6
al-Gargarat ○ **MA** 196-197 B 4
Algarrobal, Quebrada ∼ **RCH** 76-77 B 5
Algarrobo ○• **RCH** 78-79 D 2
Algarrobo del Aguila ○ **RA** 78-79 F 4
Algarve ⌣ **E** 98-99 C 6
al-Ğauf □ **KSA** 132-133 F 2
al-Gaylī ○ **SUD** 200-201 F 4
al-Ğazālāt, Qārat ▲ **ET** 194-195 C 2
al-Ğazīra ∸ **SUD** 200-201 F 5
Algeciras ○ **E** 98-99 E 6
Algena ○ **ER** 200-201 J 4
Alger ○ **USA** (MI) 272-273 E 3
Algeria = Al Jazā'ir ■ **DZ** 190-191 B 6
Algerian Provenceal Basin ≃ 98-99 K 4
Algeyta ○ **ETH** 208-209 E 4
al-Ghābah ○ **SUD** 200-201 E 3
al-Ghabshah ○ **SUD** 200-201 E 6
al-Ghalla, Wādī ∼ **SUD** 206-207 J 3
Al Gharārah, Bi'r < **LAR** 192-193 J 2
al-Ghazāl, Baḥr ∼ **SUD** 206-207 J 4
Alghero ○• **I** 100-101 B 4
Al Ghirāf, Wādī Bū ∼ **LAR** 192-193 G 4
Al Ghomode < **LAR** 192-193 D 5
Al Ghrayfah ○ **LAR** 192-193 E 4
al-Ğidāmī, Bi'r < **ET** 194-195 F 4
Algiers = Al Jazā'ir ★··· **DZ** 190-191 D 2
al-Ğilf al-Kabīr, Haḍbat ⛰ **ET** 192-193 L 6
al-Ğīza ☆·· **ET** 194-195 E 2
al-Ğizī, Wādī ∼ **OM** 132-133 K 1
Algoa Bay ≈ 220-221 G 6
Algodón, Río ∼ **PE** 64-65 F 3
Algodone ○ **USA** (CA) 248-249 K 7
Algoma ○ **USA** (WI) 270-271 L 6
Algoma Upland ⛰ **CDN** (ONT) 236-237 E 5
Algona ○ **USA** (IA) 274-275 D 1
Algonac ○ **CDN** (ONT) 238-239 C 6
Algonquin Park ○ **CDN** (ONT) 238-239 G 3
Algonquin Provincial Park ⊥ **CDN** (ONT) 238-239 G 3
Algonquin Upland ⛰ **CDN** (ONT) 238-239 G 3
Algood ○ **USA** (TN) 276-277 K 4
Algorta ○ **ROU** 78-79 L 2
al-Ğurdaqa ☆• **ET** 194-195 F 4
Al Guzayyil, Bi'r < **LAR** 192-193 D 3
al-Ḫābūr, Nahr ∼ **IRQ** 128-129 K 4
Al Hādh, Wādī ∼ **LAR** 192-193 G 5
al-Ḥaiz ○ **ET** 194-195 D 3
Alhama de Murcia ○ **E** 98-99 G 6
Alhambra • **E** 98-99 F 6
Alhambra ○ **USA** (CA) 248-249 F 5
Al Hamīm, Wādī ∼ **LAR** 192-193 K 2
al-Ḥammām ○ **ET** 194-195 D 2
Al Hamrā', Al Hamadah ∸ **LAR** 192-193 D 2
Al Hamrā', Bi'r < **LAR** 192-193 D 1
al-Ḫamsa, Bi'r < **ET** 192-193 L 2
Al Hamūdiyah < **LAR** 192-193 G 4
Alhančurtskij kanal < **RUS** 126-127 F 6
Alhandra ○ **BR** 68-69 L 5
al-Ḫānika ○ **ET** 194-195 E 2
Al Haniyah ○ **LAR** 192-193 J 1
Al Harabah ○ **LAR** 192-193 D 2
Al Hārah, Qārat ⛰ **LAR** 192-193 F 4
al-Ḫāriğa ☆• **ET** 194-195 E 5
al-Ḫāriğa, al-Wāḥāt ∸• **ET** 194-195 E 5
al-Hartūm ★·· **SUD** 200-201 F 5
al-Hartūm Baḥrī ○ **SUD** 200-201 F 5
Al Haruj al Aswad ⛰ **LAR** 192-193 G 4
Al Hasāwinah, Jabal ⛰ **LAR** 192-193 E 3
Al Hassiane ∸ **MA** 188-189 D 7
al-Ḥaṭāṭība ○ **ET** 194-195 E 2
al-Hawad, Wādī ∼ **SUD** 200-201 F 4
Al Hawa'ish, Jabal ⛰ **LAR** 192-193 K 5
al-Hawātah ○ **SUD** 200-201 G 6
Al Hawwari ○ **LAR** 192-193 K 5
Al Hayshah, Sabkhat ⬭ **LAR** 192-193 F 2
Al Hayyirah, Qarārat ∼ **LAR** 192-193 F 4
Alheit ○ **ZA** 220-221 E 4
al-Ḥilla ○ **SUD** 200-201 C 6
Al Hoceima ☆ **MA** 188-189 K 3
Al Huan ○ **LAR** 192-193 K 5
Al Hufrah ash Sharqiyah ∸ **LAR** 192-193 F 4
Al Hulayq al Kabir ⛰ **LAR** 192-193 G 4
al-Ḥuqnah ○ **SUD** 200-201 F 4
Ålhus ○ **N** 86-87 C 6
al-Ḥuṣayhiṣah ○ **SUD** 200-201 F 5
al-Ḫuwair Oilfield ○ **OM** 132-133 J 2
Ali ○ **PNG** 183 B 4
'Alī, Bi'r ○ **Y** 132-133 F 6
'Alīābād ○ **AFG** 136-137 L 6
'Alīābād ○ **IR** 134-135 F 4
Alīābād ○ **IR** 136-137 D 6
Aliade ○ **WAN** 204-205 H 5
Aliaga ○ **E** 98-99 G 4
Aliağa ☆ **TR** 128-129 B 3
Aliákomon ∼ **GR** 100-101 J 4
'Alī al-Ğarbī ☆ **IRQ** 128-129 M 6
Aliambata ○ **RI** 166-167 D 6
Aliança ○ **BR** 66-67 F 7
Aliantan ○ **RI** 162-163 D 4
Alianza, La ○ **CO** 60-61 C 6
Alībāg ○ **IND** 138-139 D 10
Ali-Bajramly = Ali Bayramlı ○ **AZ** 128-129 N 3
Alibates Flint Quarries National Monument ∴ **USA** (TX) 264-265 C 3
Ālībo ○ **ETH** 208-209 C 4
Alibori ∼ **DY** 204-205 E 3
Aliboy Knob ▲ **AUS** 172-173 J 4
Alicante = Alacant ○ **E** 98-99 G 5
Alice ○ **AUS** 178-179 M 5
Alice ○ **USA** (ND) 258-259 K 5
Alice ○ **USA** (TX) 266-267 J 6
Alice ○ **ZA** 220-221 H 6
Alice, Punta ▲ **I** 100-101 F 5
Alice Arm ○ **CDN** 32-33 F 4
Alice River ∼ **AUS** 174-175 G 4
Alice River ∼ **AUS** 178-179 H 2
Alice Springs ☆ **AUS** 176-177 B 2
Alice Town ○ **BS** 54-55 G 2
Alice Town ○ **BS** 54-55 F 2
Aliceville ○ **USA** (AL) 284-285 B 3
Alicia ○ **RP** 160-161 D 4
Alicudi, Ísola di ∩ **I** 100-101 E 5
Alida ○ **CDN** (SAS) 232-233 R 6
Aligarh ○ **IND** 138-139 G 6
Alīgūdarz ○ **IR** 134-135 C 2
'Alīğūg, Kūh-e ▲ **IR** 134-135 D 3
Alikali ○ **WAL** 202-203 E 5
Alikazgan ∼ **RUS** 126-127 G 6
Alikkod ○ **IND** 140-141 F 5
Alima ∼ **RCB** 210-211 E 4
Älimbet ○ **KA** 126-127 N 2
Alimbongo ○ **ZRE** 212-213 B 4
Alim Island ∩ **PNG** 183 D 2
Alindao ○ **RCA** 206-207 E 6
Alīngār, Darre-ye ∼ **AFG** 136-137 M 7
Alingly ○ **CDN** (SAS) 232-233 N 2
Alingsås ☆ **S** 86-87 F 8
Alinshan ▲ **VRC** 144-145 C 4
Alipur ○ **PK** 138-139 C 5
Alipur Duār ○ **IND** 142-143 F 2
Aliquippa ○ **USA** (PA) 280-281 F 3
Aliquisanda ○ **MOC** 214-215 H 7
Alirājpur ○ **IND** 142-143 C 4
Alisaang ○ **RI** 164-165 G 3
Ali Sabīh ○ **DJI** 208-209 F 3
'Alī Sadr ○ **IR** 128-129 N 5
Aliseda ○ **E** 98-99 D 5
Alishan • **RC** 156-157 M 5
al-Iskandarīya = Alexandria ☆·· **ET** 194-195 D 2
Aliskerovo ○ **RUS** 112-113 O 3
al-Ismā'īlīya ☆ **ET** 194-195 F 2
Alitak, Cape ▲ **USA** 22-23 T 4
Alitak Bay ≈ 22-23 T 4
Alite Reef ∩ **SOL** 184 I e 3
Aliulik Peninsula ⌣ **USA** 22-23 U 4
Aliwal-Noord = Aliwal North ○ **ZA** 220-221 H 5
Aliwal North = Aliwal-Noord ○ **ZA** 220-221 H 5
Alix ○ **CDN** (ALB) 232-233 E 3
'Ālīya, al- ○ **KSA** 132-133 C 5
Aliyābād ○ **IND** 140-141 H 4
'Alīyāb Gharb ○ **SUD** 200-201 F 4
'Alīyāb Sharq ○ **SUD** 200-201 F 4
Alīyak, Godār-e ▲ **IR** 136-137 E 6
al-Jabal, Baḥr ∼ **SUD** 206-207 K 6
al-Jabal, Baḥr ∼ **SUD** 206-207 K 5
Al Jabal al Akhdar □ **LAR** 192-193 J 1
Al Jabal al Akhdar ⛰ **LAR** 192-193 J 1
Al Jadid, Bi'r < **LAR** 192-193 E 4
Al Jaghbūb ○ **LAR** 192-193 L 3
Al Jalu, Wāhāt ∸ **LAR** 192-193 J 3
Aljat ○ **AZ** 128-129 N 3
Aljaty ○ **RUS** 116-117 L 9
Al Jawf ☆ **LAR** 192-193 K 5
Al Jaws al Kabír ○ **LAR** 192-193 D 2
Al Jazā'ir ★··· **DZ** 190-191 D 2
Aljenaari ○ **WAN** 204-205 E 3
Aljezur ○ **P** 98-99 C 6
Al Jufra, Wāhāt ∸ **LAR** 192-193 G 3

Al Jufrah □ LAR 192-193 G 3
al-Junaynah o SUD 198-199 L 6
Aljustrel o P 98-99 C 6
al-Kab ∴• ET 194-195 F 5
al-Kāb o SUD 200-201 F 3
Al Kalb, Qarārat o LAR 192-193 G 4
Alkali Lake o CDN (BC) 230-231 H 2
Alkali Lake o USA (OR) 244-245 F 8
Alkamari o RN 198-199 E 6
Alkamergen, köli o KA 124-125 K 3
Alkamergen,köli o KA 124-125 K 3
Alkamergen, ozero = köli Alkamergen o KA 124-125 K 3
al-Kamilin o SUD 200-201 F 5
Al Kammūniyah, Bi'r < LAR 192-193 G 3
al-Kanā'is, Ra's ▲ ET 194-195 C 2
Al Kararim o LAR 192-193 F 1
al-Karnak o• ET 194-195 F 5
al-Kawa o SUD 200-201 F 6
al-Khachbiyine, Oued ~ MA 188-189 F 7
Al Khadrah o LAR 192-193 J 2
Al Khālī, Wādī ~ LAR 192-193 K 2
al-Khāmis, ash-Shallāl = 5th Cataract ~ SUD 200-201 F 3
al-Khandaq o SUD 200-201 E 3
Al Khums □ LAR 192-193 E 1
Al Khums ☆ LAR (Akm) 192-193 F 1
Alkmaar o• NL 92-93 H 2
al-Koin o SUD 200-201 E 3
al-Kū, Wādī ~ SUD 200-201 B 6
al-Kūbrī o ET 194-195 F 2
Al Kufayfiyah o KSA 130-131 J 5
Al Kufra, Wāhāt ⊥ LAR 192-193 K 5
Al Kufrah □ LAR 192-193 J 5
al-Kuntilla o ET 194-195 G 3
al-Kurru • SUD 200-201 E 3
Allada o DY 204-205 E 5
Allagash o USA (ME) 278-279 M 1
Allagash Lake o USA (ME) 278-279 M 2
Allagash River ~ USA (ME) 278-279 M 2
Allagash Wilderness Waterway ⊥ USA (ME) 278-279 M 2
al-Lagowa o SUD 206-207 J 3
Allagudda o IND 140-141 H 3
Allahābād o• IND 142-143 B 3
Allāhganj o IND 138-139 G 6
Allah-Jun' o RUS 120-121 H 3
Allah-Jun' ~ RUS 120-121 F 3
Allahüekber Dağları ▲ TR 128-129 K 2
al-Lāhūn ∴• ET 194-195 E 3
Allaiha ~ RUS 110-111 Z 5
Allakaket o USA 20-21 O 3
Allal-bou-Fenzi o MA 188-189 G 5
Allal-Tazi o MA 188-189 H 3
Allamoore o USA (TX) 266-267 C 2
Allan o CDN (SAS) 232-233 M 4
Allangouassou o CI 202-203 H 6
Allan Hills ▲ CDN (SAS) 232-233 M 4
Allanmyo o MYA 142-143 J 6
Allanridge o ZA 220-221 H 3
Allan Water o CDN (ONT) 234-235 N 4
Allapalli o IND 142-143 B 6
Allard, Lac o CDN (QUE) 242-243 E 2
Allard, Rivière ~ CDN (QUE) 236-237 K 3
Allardville o CDN (NB) 240-241 K 3
Allariz o E 98-99 D 3
Allatoona Lake < USA (GA) 284-285 F 2
Alldays o ZA 218-219 E 6
Ålleberg ▲ S 86-87 F 7
Allegan o USA (MI) 272-273 D 5
Allegany State Park ⊥ USA (NY) 278-279 B 6
Allegheny Mountains ▲ USA (TN) 282-283 F 4
Allegheny River Reservoir < USA (PA) 280-281 H 2
Allemand, Lac o CDN 36-37 M 4
Allemands, Des o USA (LA) 268-269 K 7
Allemanskraaldam < ZA 220-221 H 4
Allen o RP 160-161 F 6
Allen o USA (NE) 262-263 K 2
Allen o USA (OK) 264-265 H 4
Allen o USA (TX) 264-265 H 5
Allendale o USA (IL) 274-275 L 6
Allendale o USA (MI) 272-273 D 5
Allendale o USA (SC) 284-285 J 3
Allende o MEX (COA) 50-51 J 3
Allende o MEX (NL) 50-51 J 5
Allenford o CDN (ONT) 238-239 D 4
Allen Island ʌ AUS 174-175 E 5
Allensworth o USA (CA) 248-249 E 4
Allenton o USA (WI) 274-275 K 1
Allentown o USA (FL) 286-287 B 1
Allentown o• USA (PA) 280-281 L 3
Allenwood o USA (PA) 280-281 K 2
Allen Young Point ▲ CDN 24-25 V 4
Alleppey o IND 140-141 G 6
Allerton o USA (IL) 274-275 L 5
Allgäu ⊥ D 92-93 L 5
Alliance o CDN (ALB) 232-233 G 3
Alliance o USA (NE) 262-263 D 2
Alliance o USA (OH) 280-281 E 3
Allier ~ F 90-91 J 8
Alliford Bay o CDN (BC) 228-229 C 3
Alligator Lake o USA (NC) 282-283 L 5
Alligator Pond o JA 54-55 G 6
Alligator River ~ USA (NC) 282-283 L 5
Allinagaram o IND 140-141 G 5
Allingham o CDN (ALB) 232-233 E 4
Allington, Cape ▲ CDN 24-25 a 5
Allipen, Río ~ RCH 78-79 D 5
al-Līrī, Ǧabal ▲ SUD 206-207 K 3
Allison o USA (AR) 276-277 C 5
Allison o USA (IA) 274-275 F 2
Allison o USA (TX) 264-265 D 3
Allison Harbour o CDN (BC) 230-231 B 2
Allison Pass ▲ CDN (BC) 230-231 J 4
al-Lišt, Pyramids of ∴• ET 194-195 E 3
Alliston o CDN (ONT) 238-239 F 4
Allomo o WAN 204-205 G 5
Allu o RI 164-165 F 6
Allumettes, Île des ʌ CDN (QUE) 238-239 H 3
Allūr o IND 140-141 J 3
Alluttoq ʌ GRØ 28-29 P 2
Alluviaq, Fiord ≈ 36-37 R 5
Alluviaq, Rivière ~ CDN 36-37 R 5
Allyn o USA (WA) 244-245 C 3
Alma o CDN (NB) 240-241 L 5
Alma o CDN (QUE) 240-241 D 2
Al'ma ~ UA 102-103 H 5
Alma o USA (AR) 276-277 A 5
Alma o USA (GA) 284-285 H 5
Alma o USA (KS) 262-263 K 5
Alma o USA (MI) 272-273 E 4
Alma o USA (NE) 262-263 G 4
Alma o USA (OR) 244-245 B 7
Alma o USA (WI) 270-271 G 6
Alma, Mount ▲ AUS 178-179 L 2
Alma-Ata = Almaty ★ KA 146-147 C 4
Almaden o AUS 174-175 H 5
Almadén o E 98-99 E 5
al-Mafāza o SUD 200-201 G 6
Almagro o E 98-99 F 5
Almagro Island ʌ RP 160-161 F 7
al-Mahalla al-Kubrā o ET 194-195 E 2
al-Mahāmid o ET 194-195 F 5
al-Maharig o ET 194-195 E 5
Almahel o ETH 208-209 B 3
Al Majnīnin, Wādī ~ LAR 192-193 E 1
al-Malamm o SUD 206-207 J 4
Almalyk o US 136-137 L 4
Almameda o USA (NM) 256-257 J 3
al-Manāqil o SUD 200-201 F 5
Almanor, Lake o USA (CA) 246-247 D 3
Almansa o E 98-99 G 5
Almansa, Puerto de ▲ E 98-99 G 5
al-Manšāh o ET 194-195 E 4
al-Manšūra ☆ ET 194-195 E 2
al-Manzila, Buhairat o ET 194-195 E 2
Almanzor ▲ E 98-99 E 4
Alma Peak ▲ CDN 32-33 G 3
Al Maqrūn o LAR 192-193 J 2
Almar o AFG 136-137 J 7
Almara o AFG 138-139 B 3
Almarcha, La o E 98-99 F 5
Al Marj ☆•• LAR 192-193 J 1
Al Marūqah o LAR 192-193 F 4
Almas o BR 68-69 E 7
Almas, Rio das ~ BR 72-73 F 2
Almas, Rio das ~ BR 72-73 F 3
al-Massira, Barrage < MA 188-189 H 4
Al Mastūtah, Bi'r < LAR 192-193 F 5
al-Matamma o SUD 200-201 F 4
al-Matariya o ET 194-195 F 2
al-Matmarfag o MA 188-189 E 7
al-Matna o SUD 200-201 G 6
Almaty ★ KA 146-147 C 4
al-Mausil ☆ IRQ 128-129 K 4
Almazán o E 98-99 F 4
Almaznyj o RUS 118-119 G 4
Almeida o P 98-99 D 4
Almeida Campos o BR 72-73 G 5
Almeirim o BR 62-63 H 6
Almeirim o P 98-99 C 5
Almeirim, Serra do ▲ BR 62-63 H 6
Almel o IND 140-141 G 2
Almelo o NL 92-93 J 2
Almenara o BR 72-73 K 4
Almenar de Soria o E 98-99 F 4
Almendralejo o• E 98-99 D 5
Almendrillo o RCH 78-79 D 2
Al'menevo ☆ RUS 114-115 G 7
Almere o NL 92-93 H 2
Almería o E 98-99 F 6
Almería, Golfo de ≈ 98-99 F 6
Al'met'evsk ☆ RUS 96-97 H 6
Al'met'evsk = Al'met'evsk ☆ RUS 96-97 H 6
Älmhult o S 86-87 G 8
al-Milk, Wādī ~ SUD 200-201 E 4
Almina, Punta ▲ E 98-99 E 7
al-Minyā ☆ ET 194-195 E 3
Almirantazgo, Seno ≈ 80 F 7
Almirant Brown o ARK 16 G 30
Almirante o PA 52-53 C 7
Almirante Montt, Golfo ≈ 80 D 5
Almirante Saldanha Seamount ≃ 72-73 M 7
Almirós o GR 100-101 J 5
Almo o USA (ID) 252-253 E 4
Almodôvar o P 98-99 C 6
Almodóvar del Río o E 98-99 E 6
Almond o USA (WI) 270-271 J 6
Almont o USA (ND) 258-259 F 5
Almonte o CDN (ONT) 238-239 J 3
Almonte o E 98-99 D 6
Almonte, Río ~ E 98-99 E 5
Almora o• IND 138-139 G 5
Almota o USA (WA) 244-245 H 4
al-Muglad o SUD 206-207 H 3
al-Muh, Sabhat o SYR 128-129 H 5
al-Muhammadiyah = Mohammedia o MA 188-189 H 4
al-Mukallā o•• Y 132-133 F 6
Almuñécar o E 98-99 F 6
Almunia de Doña Godina, La o E 98-99 G 4
Almus o TR 128-129 G 2
Al Muwaylih, Bi'r < LAR 192-193 H 3
Almy o USA (WY) 252-253 H 5
Almyra o USA (AR) 276-277 D 6
Alnaši ☆ RUS 96-97 H 5
Alness o GB 90-91 E 3
Alnif o MA 188-189 J 5
Alnwick o GB 90-91 G 4
Alóag o EC 64-65 C 2
Alō Brasil o BR 72-73 E 2
Aloi o EAU 212-213 D 2
Aloja o LV 94-95 J 3
Aloma, River ~ WAN 204-205 H 5
Along shan o VRC 150-151 D 2
Alónissos ~ GR 100-101 J 5
Alonon Point ▲ RP 160-161 D 6
Alonsa o CDN (MAN) 234-235 E 4
Alor, Kepulauan ʌ RI 166-167 C 6
Alor, Pulau ʌ RI 166-167 C 6
Alor, Selat ≈ 166-167 B 6
Aloro, Río ~ BOL 76-77 D 1
Alor Setar ☆ MAL 162-163 D 2
Alot o IND 138-139 E 8
Alota o BOL 76-77 D 1
Alotau ☆ PNG 183 F 6
Alpachiri o RA 78-79 H 4
Alpamayo ▲ PE 64-65 D 6
Alpasinche o RA 76-77 D 5
Alpena o USA (MI) 272-273 F 2
Alpena o USA (SD) 260-261 H 2
Alpercata, Rio ~ BR 68-69 F 5
Alpercatas, Serra das ▲ BR 68-69 F 5
Alpha o AUS 178-179 J 2
Alpha o USA (IL) 274-275 H 3
Alpha Cordillera ≃ 16 A 30
Alpha Creek ~ AUS 178-179 J 2
Alphonse Group ʌ SY 224 C 3
Alphonse Island ʌ SY 224 C 3
Alpine o USA (AZ) 256-257 F 5
Alpine o USA (TX) 266-267 D 3
Alpine Junction o USA (WY) 252-253 H 3
Alpine Lakes Wilderness ⊥ USA (WA) 244-245 D 3
Alpine National Park ⊥ AUS 180-181 J 4
Alpinópolis o BR 72-73 G 6
Alpouro ~ DY 204-205 E 4
Alpowa o USA (WA) 244-245 H 4
Alps = Alpen ▲ 92-93 J 6
Alps, The ▲ AUS 178-179 K 2
Alpu ☆ TR 128-129 D 3
al-Qāhira ★••• ET 194-195 E 2
Al Qala'a o LAR 192-193 F 2
al-Qantara o ET 194-195 F 2
Al Qardabah o LAR 192-193 K 1
Al Qasabāt o LAR 192-193 F 1
al-Qāsh, Nahr ~ SUD 200-201 H 5
al-Qasr o ET 194-195 D 5
Al Qāt, Bi'r < LAR 192-193 F 3
Al Qatif, Bi'r < LAR 192-193 L 2
Al Qatrūn o LAR 192-193 F 5
Al Qattūsah, Sarir ⊥ LAR 192-193 F 4
al-Qawz o SUD 200-201 F 4
al-Qirbah Dam, Khashm < SUD 200-201 G 5
al-Q'nitra ☆ MA 188-189 H 3
Al Qubbah o• LAR 192-193 K 1
Alqueva, Barragem do < P 98-99 D 5
Alquízar o C 54-55 D 3
al-Qulayd Bahri o SUD 200-201 E 3
al-Qurayyāt □ KSA 130-131 E 3
al-Qusair o ET 194-195 G 4
al-Qūsīya o ET 194-195 E 4
al-Qus Taima o ET 194-195 G 2
al-Qutaynah o SUD 200-201 F 5
al-Quwaisi o SUD 200-201 G 6
Al Rahibat o LAR 192-193 D 2
Alroy Downs o AUS 174-175 D 6
Alsace o AUS 174-175 E 6
Alsace □ F 90-91 L 8
Alsace ⊥ F 90-91 L 8
Alsask o CDN (SAS) 232-233 J 4
Alsasu o E 98-99 F 3
Alsatia o USA (LA) 268-269 J 4
Alsea o USA (OR) 244-245 B 6
Alsea River ~ USA (OR) 244-245 B 6
Alsek River ~ CDN 20-21 W 6
Alsen o USA (ND) 258-259 J 3
Alshi o EC 64-65 C 3
Alsike o CDN (ALB) 232-233 D 2
Alta o• N 86-87 L 2
Alta o USA (IA) 274-275 C 2
Alta o USA (UT) 254-255 D 3
Alta, Cachoeira ~ BR 70-71 K 3
Alta, Pampa ⊥ RA 78-79 G 4
Alta, Punta ▲ EC 64-65 B 2
Altaelva ~ N 86-87 L 2
Alta Floresta o BR 66-67 K 7
Alta Gracia o RA 76-77 E 6
Altagracia o YV (ANZ) 60-61 J 3
Altagracia o YV (ZUL) 60-61 F 2
Altair o USA (TX) 266-267 L 4
Altaj ▲ KA 124-125 N 3
Altaj ☆ MAU 148-149 C 4
Altaj = Bor-Üzüür o MAU 146-147 L 3
Altajn Caadah Gov' ⊥ MAU 146-147 M 4
Altajsk, Gorno ☆ RUS 124-125 O 3
Altajskij zapovednik ⊥ RUS 124-125 Q 3
Altamachi, Río ~ BOL 70-71 D 5
Altamaha River ~ USA (GA) 284-285 H 5
Altamaha Sound ≈ USA 284-285 J 5
Altamira o BR 68-69 B 3
Altamira o CO 60-61 D 6
Altamira o MEX 50-51 L 6
Altamira o RCH 76-77 C 3
Altamira o YV 60-61 F 3
Altamira, Cuevas de ••• E 98-99 E 3
Altamira do Maranhão o BR 68-69 F 4
Altamirano o MEX 52-53 H 3
Altamont o CDN (MAN) 234-235 E 5
Altamont o USA (IL) 274-275 K 5
Altamont o USA (OR) 244-245 D 8
Altamont o USA (TN) 276-277 K 5
Altamont o USA (UT) 254-255 D 3
Altamonte Springs o USA (FL) 286-287 H 3
Altamura o I 100-101 F 4
Altan Ovoo o MAU 148-149 E 4
Altan ovoo ▲ MAU 146-147 K 3
Altar o MEX 50-51 D 2
Altar, Desierto de ⊥ MEX 50-51 B 1
Altar, Río ~ MEX 50-51 D 2
Altar, Volcán ▲ EC 64-65 C 2
Altar de Sacrificios ∴• GCA 52-53 J 3
Altar-Est o DZ 190-191 G 6
Altata o MEX 50-51 F 5
Alta Vista o USA (KS) 262-263 K 6
Altavista o USA (VA) 280-281 G 6
Altay o VRC 146-147 J 2
Altay Mountains = Altaj ▲ KA 124-125 N 3
Altay Shan ▲ VRC 146-147 H 1
Altdorf ☆• CH 92-93 K 5
Altea o E 98-99 G 5
Altenburg o• D 92-93 M 3
Altér do Chão o BR 66-67 K 4
Alter do Chão o P 98-99 D 5
Alterosa o BR 72-73 G 6
Altevatnet o N 86-87 J 2
Altha o USA (FL) 286-287 D 1
Altheimer o USA (AR) 276-277 D 6
Alticane o CDN (SAS) 232-233 L 3
Al Tidedi, Wādi ~ LAR 192-193 H 6
Al Tikuna Evare, Áreas Indígena X BR 66-67 C 4
Altıntepe ∴• TR 128-129 H 3
Altiplanicie del Payún ▲ RA 78-79 E 4
Altmühl ~ D 92-93 L 4
Alto o USA (TX) 268-269 E 5
Alto, Cerro ▲ RA 78-79 D 6
Alto, El o PE 64-65 B 4
Alto, Raudal ~ YV 60-61 J 4
Alto Alegre o BR (PIA) 68-69 H 4
Alto Alegre o BR (RSU) 74-75 D 8
Alto Anapu, Rio ~ BR 68-69 C 3
Alto Araguaia o BR 72-73 D 4
Alto Bonito o BR 66-67 B 7
Alto Chandless, Río ~ PE 70-71 B 2
Alto Chicapa o ANG 216-217 E 5
Alto de Amparo o BR 74-75 E 5
Alto de Carrizal ▲ CO 60-61 C 4
Alto de la Sierra o RA 76-77 F 2
Alto del Carmen o RCH 76-77 B 5
Alto de los Colorados ▲ RA 76-77 C 4
Alto Garças o BR 72-73 D 4
Alto Hama o ANG 216-217 C 6
Alto Jurupari ~ BR 66-67 B 7
Alto Ligonha o MOC 218-219 K 2
Alto Longá o BR 68-69 G 4
Alto Madre de Dios, Río ~ PE 70-71 B 3
Alto Molócuè o MOC 218-219 J 2
Alton o USA (IA) 274-275 B 2
Alton o USA (IL) 274-275 H 6
Alton o USA (MO) 276-277 D 4
Alton o USA (NH) 278-279 K 5
Alton o USA (NY) 278-279 E 5
Altona o CDN (MAN) 234-235 F 5
Alto Nevado, Cerro ▲ RCH 80 D 2
Altoona o USA (PA) 280-281 H 3
Altoona o USA (WA) 244-245 B 4
Altoona o USA (WI) 270-271 G 6
Alto Pacaja, Rio ~ BR 68-69 C 3
Alto Paraguai o BR 70-71 J 4
Alto Paraíso de Goiás o BR 72-73 G 3
Alto Parnaíba o BR 68-69 F 6
Alto Pencoso o RA 78-79 F 2
Alto Purus, Río ~ PE 70-71 B 2
Alto Quiel o PA 52-53 C 7
Alto Quimari ▲ CO 60-61 C 3
Alto Rabagão, Barragem do < P 98-99 D 4
Alto Rio Guama, Área Indígena X BR 68-69 E 3
Alto Río Mayo o RA 80 E 2
Alto Rio Negro, Área Indígena X BR 66-67 C 3
Alto Rio Novo o BR 72-73 K 5
Alto Rio Purus, Área Indígena X BR 66-67 B 7
Alto Río Senguerr o RA 80 E 2
Alto Rio Verde o BR 72-73 D 5
Altos o BR 68-69 G 4
Altos de Talinay ▲ RCH 76-77 B 6
Alto Sucuriú o BR 72-73 D 5
Altotonga o MEX 52-53 F 2
Alto Turiaçu, Área Indígena X BR 68-69 E 3
Altsohl = Zvolen o SK 92-93 P 4
Altstadt = Staré Město o CZ 92-93 O 4
Altun o VRC 146-147 J 6
Altun Ha ∴• BH 52-53 K 3
Altün Küprü o IRQ 128-129 L 5
Altun Shan ▲ VRC 146-147 G 6
Alturas o USA (CA) 246-247 E 2
Altus o USA (OK) 264-265 E 4
Altus Reservoir < USA (OK) 264-265 E 4
Altvater = Praděd ▲ CZ 92-93 O 3
Altyaryk o US 136-137 M 4
Altyb ~ RUS 116-117 M 5
Altykarasu o KA 126-127 L 3
Alua o MOC 218-219 K 1
Aluakluak o SUD 206-207 K 5
al-Ubayyid = El Obeid ☆• SUD 200-201 E 6
Alučin ~ RUS 112-113 N 3
Alucra ☆ TR 128-129 H 2
al-Udayya o SUD 200-201 D 6
Al Ugayb, Wādi < LAR 192-193 G 3
Aluize, Rio ~ MOC 218-219 G 6
Alūksne ☆•• LV 94-95 K 3
Alum Creek Lake o USA (OH) 280-281 D 3
al-'Umda o SUD 206-207 J 3
Aluminé o RA 78-79 D 5
Aluminé, Río ~ RA 78-79 D 5
A Lu'ó'i ☆ VN 158-159 J 2
Al 'Uqaylah o LAR 192-193 H 2
al-'Uqdah o SUD 200-201 F 5
al-Uqsur o•• ET 194-195 F 5
Alūr o IND 140-141 F 4
Ālūr o IND 140-141 G 3
al-Urdunn, Nahr ~ JOR 130-131 D 2
al-'Urf, Ǧabal ▲ ET 194-195 F 4
Al 'Ushara o SUD 200-201 F 5
Alušta o• UA 102-103 J 5
Al 'Utaylah, Bi'r < LAR 192-193 G 2
al-'Utayshān < SUD 200-201 G 4
al-'Uwaynāt o LAR 190-191 H 8
Al 'Uwaynāt o LAR 192-193 D 5
Alva o USA (KY) 276-277 M 4
Alva o USA (OK) 264-265 F 2
Alvand, Kūh-e ▲ IR 134-135 C 1
Alvarado o CO 60-61 D 5
Alvarado o MEX 52-53 G 2
Alvarado o USA (TX) 264-265 G 6
Alvarães o BR 66-67 E 4
Alvarenga o BR 72-73 K 5
Alvar Nuñez Cabeza de Vaca o PY 76-77 K 3
Alvaro Obregón, Presa o MEX 50-51 E 3
Álvaro Obregón, Presa o MEX 50-51 E 4
Alvdal ☆ N 86-87 E 5
Älvdalen o S 86-87 G 6
Alvear o RA 76-77 J 5
Alvena o CDN (SAS) 232-233 M 3
Alves o BR 72-73 L 2
Alvesta ☆ S 86-87 G 8
Alvin o GUY 62-63 E 4
Alvin o USA (TX) 268-269 E 7
Alvin o USA (WI) 270-271 K 4
Alvinston o CDN (ONT) 238-239 D 6
Alvito o P 98-99 D 5
Älvkarleby ☆• S 86-87 H 6
Alvorada o BR (RSU) 74-75 E 8
Alvorada o BR (TOC) 72-73 F 2
Alvorada do Norte o BR 72-73 G 3
Alvord o USA (TX) 264-265 G 5
Alvord Lake o USA (OR) 244-245 G 8
Alvord Valley ~ USA (OR) 244-245 G 8
Älvsbyn o• S 86-87 K 4
Alwood o USA (MN) 270-271 D 3
Al Wahah o LAR 192-193 J 3
al-Wāhāt al-Bahriya ⊥• ET 194-195 D 3
Al Wa'ir, Wādi ~ LAR 192-193 H 4
Alwar o• IND 138-139 F 6
Alwar Hills ▲ IND 138-139 F 6
Alwās o IND 138-139 F 3
Al Washkah, Bi'r < LAR 192-193 F 3
al-Wāsitā o ET 194-195 E 3
Alwero Wenz ~ ETH 208-209 B 4
Al Wigh o LAR 192-193 F 5
Al Wittyah o LAR 192-193 D 1
Alxa Gaoyuan ⊥ VRC 148-149 E 7
Alxa Youqi o VRC 154-155 B 2
Alxa Zuoqi o VRC 154-155 D 2
Aly o USA (AR) 276-277 B 6
Al Yaman ■ Y 132-133 E 6
Alyangula o AUS 174-175 D 3
Alyawarra Aboriginal Land X AUS 178-179 C 1
Alyeska Resort & Ski Area • USA 20-21 Q 6
Aly-Jurjah ~ RUS 112-113 H 4
Alymdža ~ RUS 118-119 E 4
Alyta, Batagaj- o RUS 110-111 S 6
Alytus ☆ LT 94-95 J 4
Alzada o USA (MT) 250-251 P 6
Alzamaj o RUS 116-117 J 8
Alzey o USA (KY) 276-277 H 3
Alzira o E 98-99 G 5
Ama o PNG 183 A 3
Amaam, laguna o RUS 112-113 U 5
Amacayacu, Parque National ⊥ CO 66-67 B 4
Amaciá o BR 66-67 E 5
Amacuzac, Río ~ MEX 52-53 E 2
Amada ∴• ET 194-195 F 6
Amada Gaza o RCA 206-207 B 6
Amadeus, Lake o AUS 176-177 L 2
Amadi o SUD 206-207 K 6
Amadi o ZRE 210-211 L 2
'Amādiya, al- ☆ IRQ 128-129 K 4
Amadjuak Bay ≈ 36-37 N 3
Amadjuak Lake o CDN 36-37 O 2
Amadjuak River ~ CDN 36-37 O 2
Amado o USA (AZ) 256-257 D 7
Amadora o P 98-99 C 5
Amadror ⊥ DZ 190-191 F 8
Amadror, Oued ~ DZ 190-191 F 8
Amaga o CO 60-61 D 4
Amagi o J 152-153 D 8
Amagon o USA (AR) 276-277 D 5
Amahai o RI 166-167 E 3
Amahtonskij, zaliv o RUS 120-121 N 4
Amair Bin Sana'a, al o KSA 130-131 G 4
Amajac, Río ~ MEX 52-53 E 1
Amaki o PNG 183 B 3
Amakinskij o RUS 110-111 K 4
Amakouladji o RMM 196-197 K 6
Amakusa-nada ≈ 152-153 C 8
Amakusa-shotō ʌ J 152-153 D 8
Åmål ☆ S 86-87 F 7
Amala ~ EAK 212-213 E 4
Amalapuram o IND 140-141 K 2
Amalat ~ RUS 118-119 G 8
Amalfi o•• I 100-101 E 4
Amalia o ZA 220-221 G 3
Amaliáda o GR 100-101 H 6
Amalner o IND 138-139 E 9
Amaluza o EC (CAN) 64-65 C 3
Amaluza o EC (LOJ) 64-65 C 4
Amaluza, Embalse < EC 64-65 C 3
Amamá o RA 76-77 F 4
Amamapare o RI 166-167 J 4
Amamba o MOC 218-219 G 5
Amambai o BR 76-77 K 2
Amambai, Rio ~ BR 76-77 K 2
Amambay, Sierra de ▲ PY 76-77 K 2
Amami-shotō ʌ J 152-153 C 11
Amana o USA (IA) 274-275 G 3
Amanã, Lago o BR 66-67 E 4
Amanã, Rio ~ BR 66-67 J 5
Amana, Río ~ YV 60-61 K 3
Amanab o PNG 183 A 2
Amanave o USA 184 V b 2
Amancio o C 54-55 G 4
Amanda Park o USA (WA) 244-245 A 3
Amaneyé, Área Indígena X BR 68-69 D 3
Amangeldi ☆ KA 124-125 D 3
Amaniú o BR 68-69 H 7
Amankaragaj o KA 124-125 D 2
Amankeldi o KA 96-97 H 8
Amankro o CI 202-203 J 6
Amanötkel' o KA 126-127 O 4
Amantani, Isla ʌ PE 70-71 C 4
Amantea o I 100-101 F 5
Amantenango del Valle o MEX 52-53 H 3
Amantogaj ☆ KA 124-125 D 3
Amanzamnyama ~ ZW 218-219 D 4
Amanzimtoti o ZA 220-221 K 5
Amapá o BR 62-63 J 4
Amapá o BR 70-71 C 2
Amapá □ BR 62-63 H 5
Amapa Grande, Rio ~ BR 62-63 J 4
Amapari, Rio ~ BR 62-63 H 5
Amar ▲ ETH 208-209 C 6
Amar o RI 166-167 F 4
'Amāra, al- ☆• IRQ 128-129 M 7
Amara, Temple • SUD 200-201 E 2
Amarac National Wildlife Refuge ⊥ USA (MN) 270-271 C 3
Amaraji o BR 68-69 L 6
Amaramba, Lago o MOC 218-219 H 2
Amarante o BR 68-69 G 5
Amarante do Maranhão o BR 68-69 E 4
Amaranth o CDN (MAN) 234-235 E 4
Amarapura o MYA 142-143 K 5
Amarapuram o IND 140-141 G 3
Amarāvati o IND 140-141 G 3
Amaravati o• IND 140-141 J 2
Amardalaj o MAU 148-149 H 4
Amarga, Bañados de la o RA 78-79 G 3
Amarga, Laguna la o RA 78-79 F 5
Amargosa Desert ⊥ USA (NV) 248-249 H 3
Amargosa Range ▲ USA (CA) 248-249 H 3
Amargosa River ~ USA (CA) 248-249 H 4
Amargosa Valley o USA (NV) 248-249 H 3
Amarillo o USA (TX) 264-265 C 3
Amarinthos o GR 100-101 J 5
'Amar Jadid o SUD 200-201 B 5
Amarkantak o IND 142-143 B 4
Amarortalik ʌ GRØ 26-27 Y 7
Amaru, Danau o RI 166-167 G 2
Amasu ~ KA 124-125 G 5
Amasya ☆•• TR 128-129 F 2
Amata X AUS 176-177 L 3
Amatari o BR 66-67 H 4
Amates, Los o GCA 52-53 K 4
Amatignak Island ʌ USA 22-23 G 7
Amatique, Bahía de ≈ 52-53 K 4
Amatitlán o• GCA 52-53 J 4
Amatlán de Cañas o MEX 52-53 B 1
Amatura o BR 66-67 C 4
Amau o PNG 183 E 6
Āmaytoli Terara ▲ ETH 200-201 K 6
Amazar o RUS 118-119 K 9
Amazar ~ RUS 118-119 K 9
Amazarskij hrebet ▲ RUS 118-119 K 9
Amazmaz < RIM 196-197 D 5
Amazon o CDN (SAS) 232-233 N 4
Amazonas □ BR 66-67 C 6
Amazon Canyon ≃ 62-63 K 5
Amazon Fan ≃ 62-63 K 4
Amazônia, Parque Nacional de ⊥ BR 66-67 J 5
Amazon Shelf ≃ 62-63 K 4
Ambabbo o DJI 208-209 F 3
Ambad o IND 138-139 E 10
Amba Farit ▲ ETH 208-209 D 3
Āmba Giyorgis o ETH 200-201 H 6
Ambahikily o RM 222-223 C 8
Ambahita o RM 222-223 D 10
Ambājogāi o IND 138-139 F 10
Ambakireny o RM 222-223 E 6
Ambala o IND 138-139 F 4
Ambalabe o RM 222-223 F 7
Ambalajanakomby o RM 222-223 E 6
Ambalakirajy o RM 222-223 F 5
Ambalamanakana o RM 222-223 E 8
Ambalamanasy o RM 222-223 F 5
Ambalamarina o RM 222-223 E 8
Ambalapaiso o RM 222-223 F 5
Ambalarondra o RM 222-223 F 7
Ambalavao o RM 222-223 E 8
Ambam o CAM 210-211 C 2
Āmba Maderiya o ETH 200-201 J 6
Ambang Reserve, Gunung ⊥• RI 164-165 J 3
Ambanja o RM 222-223 F 4
Ambanjabe o RM 222-223 E 5
Ambar o PE 64-65 D 7
Ambarata o RM 222-223 F 5
Ambarčik o RUS (KRN) 116-117 G 8
Ambarčik o RUS (SAH) 112-113 M 2
Ambardah ~ RUS 108-109 d 6
Ambargasta o RA 76-77 F 5
Ambargasta, Salinas de o RA 76-77 E 5
Ambargasta, Sierra ▲ RA 76-77 F 5
Ambarimaninga o RM 222-223 E 6
Ambarita • RI 162-163 C 3
Ambarnyj o RUS 88-89 M 4
Ambato ☆ EC 64-65 C 2
Ambato, Sierra de ▲ RA 76-77 D 5
Ambatoboeny o RM 222-223 E 6
Ambato Finandrahana o RM 222-223 E 8
Ambatoharanana o RM 222-223 F 6
Ambatolahy o RM 222-223 D 8
Ambatolampy o RM 222-223 E 7
Ambatomainty o RM 222-223 D 6
Ambatomanoina o RM 222-223 E 7
Ambatondrazaka o RM 222-223 F 6
Ambatosia o RM 222-223 F 5
Ambatosoratra o RM 222-223 F 6
Ambatovory o RM 222-223 E 8
Ambatry o RM 222-223 D 9
Ambaúba o BR 66-67 D 2
Ambazac o F 90-91 H 9
Ambe ~ ZRE 210-211 K 5
Ambelau, Pulau ʌ RI 166-167 D 3
Amberg o D 92-93 L 4
Ambergris Cay ʌ BH 52-53 L 3
Ambérieu-en-Bugey o F 90-91 K 9
Amberley o CDN (ONT) 238-239 D 4
Ambert o F 90-91 J 9
Ambidédi o RMM 202-203 E 2
Ambikāpur o IND 142-143 C 4
Ambila o RM 222-223 E 8
Ambil Island ʌ RP 160-161 D 6
Ambilobe o RM 222-223 F 4
Ambinanindrano o RM 222-223 F 8
Ambinanínony o RM 222-223 F 7
Ambinanymbazaha o RM 222-223 E 8
Ambition Mountain ▲ CDN 32-33 E 3
Ambitle Island ʌ PNG 183 G 3
Amble-by-the-Sea o GB 90-91 G 4
Ambler o USA 20-21 M 3
Ambler River ~ USA 20-21 M 3
Ambleside o• GB 90-91 F 4
Ambo o PE 64-65 D 7
Amboahangibe o RM 222-223 G 5
Amboahangy o RM 222-223 E 10
Amboasary o RM 222-223 E 10
Amboasary Gara o RM 222-223 F 7
Amboavory o RM 222-223 F 6
Ambodiangezoka o RM 222-223 F 5
Ambodibonara o RM 222-223 F 4
Ambodifototra o RM 222-223 F 6
Ambodiriana o RM 222-223 F 6
Ambodisietezana-Sahana o RM 222-223 G 5
Ambodivoara o RM 222-223 G 5
Ambohibada o RM 222-223 F 4
Ambohibary o RM 222-223 E 7
Ambohidratrimo o RM 222-223 E 7
Ambohijanahary o RM 222-223 F 6
Ambohimahasoa o RM 222-223 E 8
Ambohimanga o RM 222-223 E 7
Ambohinihaonana o RM 222-223 E 8
Ambohipaky o RM 222-223 D 6
Ambohitra o RM (ASA) 222-223 F 4
Ambohitra ▲•• RM (ASA) 222-223 F 4
Ambohitralanana o RM 222-223 G 5
Ambohitrolomahitsy o RM 222-223 E 7
Amboi, Kepulauan ʌ RI 166-167 J 2
Amboise o F 90-91 H 8
Amboiva o ANG 216-217 C 5
Amboli o IND 140-141 E 3
Ambolobozo o RM 222-223 E 5
Ambolomoty o RM 222-223 E 6
Ambolten ʌ GRØ 26-27 q 4
Ambon ☆ RI 166-167 E 3
Ambon, Pulau ʌ RI 166-167 D 3
Ambondro o RM 222-223 D 10
Ambondromamy o RM 222-223 E 6
Ambongo ⊥ RM 222-223 D 6
Amboni o EAT 212-213 G 6
Amboriala o RM 222-223 F 4
Amborompotsy o RM 222-223 E 8
Amborondolo o RM 222-223 F 4
Amboseli, Lake o EAK 212-213 F 5
Amboseli National Park ⊥ EAK 212-213 F 5
Ambositra o RM 222-223 E 8
Ambovombe o RM 222-223 E 10
Amboy o USA (CA) 248-249 J 5
Amboy o USA (IL) 274-275 J 3
Amboy o USA (WA) 244-245 C 5
Amboy Crater • USA (CA) 248-249 J 5
Ambre, Cap d' = Tanjona Babaomby ▲ RM 222-223 F 3
Ambre, Île d' ʌ MS 224 C 7
Ambrim = Île Ambrym ʌ VAN 184 II b 3
Ambriz o ANG 216-217 B 3
Ambriz, Coutada do ⊥ ANG 216-217 B 3
Ambrolauri o GE 126-127 E 6
Ambrose o USA (ND) 258-259 D 3
Ambrósio o BR 68-69 F 5
Ambrym ʌ VAN 184 II b 3
Ambrym, Île = Ambrim ʌ VAN 184 II b 3
Ambuaki o RI 166-167 G 2
Ambulombo, Gunung ▲ RI 168 E 7
Ambulong Island ʌ RP 160-161 D 6
Ambunten o RI 168 E 3
Ambunti o PNG 183 B 3
Ambur o IND 140-141 H 4
Amburambur o RI 168 C 7
Ambuve, Lake o PNG 183 A 4
Amchitka o USA 22-23 F 7
Amchitka Island ʌ USA 22-23 F 7
Amchitka Pass ≈ 22-23 G 7
'Amd, Wādi ~ Y 132-133 F 6
Am Dafok o RCA 206-207 F 3
am-Dam o TCH 198-199 K 6
Amdāpur o IND 138-139 F 9
Amdassa o RI 166-167 F 5
Amded, Oued ~ DZ 190-191 D 9
Amderma o RUS 108-109 J 7
Am Djaména o RCA 206-207 E 4
Am Djemena o TCH 198-199 H 6
Amdo o VRC 144-145 H 4
Amdrup Højland ▲ GRØ 26-27 m 3
Amealco o MEX 52-53 D 1
Ameca o MEX 52-53 B 1
Ameca, Río ~ MEX 52-53 B 1
Amedičí ~ RUS 118-119 L 7
Ameib o NAM 216-217 C 10
Ameland ʌ NL 92-93 H 2
Amelia C.H. o USA (VA) 280-281 J 6
Amellougui o MA 188-189 H 5
Amenia o USA (NY) 280-281 N 2
Amentego o SUD 200-201 E 3
Ameralik ≈ 28-29 P 4
'Ameri o IR 134-135 D 3
América o BR 66-67 E 6
America-Antarctic Ridge ≃ 6-7 H 14
América Dourada o BR 68-69 H 7
Americana o BR 72-73 G 7
American Falls o USA (ID) 252-253 F 4
American Falls Reservoir o USA (ID) 252-253 F 4
American Fork o USA (UT) 254-255 D 3
American Highland ▲ ARK 16 F 8
American Samoa □ USA 184 V c 1
Americus o USA (GA) 284-285 F 4
Amerika-Kuba-Aryta, ostrov ʌ RUS 110-111 R 3
Amersfoort o• NL 92-93 H 2
Amersfoort o ZA 220-221 J 3
Amersham o GB 90-91 G 6
Amery o USA (WI) 270-271 F 5
Amery Ice Shelf ⊂ ARK 16 F 8
Ames o USA (IA) 274-275 E 2
Amesbury o USA (MA) 278-279 L 6
Amesdale o CDN (ONT) 234-235 L 4
Amethi o IND 142-143 B 2
Ameya o ETH 208-209 C 5
Amfilohía o GR 100-101 H 5
Amga ☆ RUS 120-121 D 3
Amga ~ RUS 118-119 L 6
Amga ~ RUS 120-121 D 3
Amginskij hrebet ▲ RUS 118-119 L 6
Amgotro o RI 166-167 L 3
Amgu o RUS 122-123 G 6
Amguèma ~ RUS 112-113 V 3
Amguèma, laguna ≈ 112-113 W 2
Amguemskaja vpadina ⊥ RUS 112-113 U 3
Amguid o DZ 190-191 E 7
Amgun' ~ RUS 122-123 F 3
Amgun ~ RUS 122-123 E 3
Amherst o CDN (NS) 240-241 L 5
Amherst o USA (MA) 278-279 J 6
Amherst o USA (TX) 264-265 B 4
Amherst o USA (VA) 280-281 G 6
Amherst = Kyaikkami o MYA 158-159 D 2
Amherstburg o CDN (ONT) 238-239 C 6
Amherst Island ʌ CDN (NWT) 24-25 e 6
Amherst Island ʌ CDN (ONT) 238-239 J 4
Amherst Junction o USA (WI) 270-271 J 6
Am Himédé o TCH 198-199 K 6
Ami ~ IND 142-143 C 2
Amiata, Monte ▲ I 100-101 C 3

Amidon ○ USA (ND) 258-259 D 5
Amiens ○ CDN (SAS) 232-233 L 2
Amiens ✩··· F 90-91 J 7
Aminagou ○ RCA 206-207 G 6
Amindivi Islands ⌒ IND 140-141 E 5
Aminga ○ RA 76-77 D 5
Aminius ✩ NAM 220-221 D 1
Amino ○ J 152-153 F 7
Amiour < RMM 196-197 J 6
'Amiq, Qasr ○ IRQ 128-129 J 6
'Amiq, Wādi ∼ IRQ 128-129 J 6
Amirābād ○ IR 136-137 D 6
Amirantes Group ⌒ SY 224 C 3
Amirante Trench ≃ 224 C 3
Amir Chāh ○ PK 134-135 K 4
Amisk Lake ○ CDN 34-35 E 3
Amistad ○ USA (NM) 256-257 M 3
Amistad, Parque Internacional La ⊥··· CR 52-53 C 7
Amistad, Presa la < MEX 50-51 J 3
Amite ○ USA (LA) 268-269 K 6
Amite River ∼ USA (LA) 268-269 K 6
Amitikoe Peninsula ⌣ CDN 24-25 f 6
Amity ○ USA (AR) 276-277 B 6
Amityville ○ USA (NY) 280-281 N 3
Amiuté, Ribeiro do ∼ BR 68-69 D 5
Amizmiz ○ MA 188-189 G 5
Amka ∼ RUS 120-121 J 4
Amkunj ○ IND 140-141 L 3
Amla ○ IND 138-139 G 9
Amlāgora ○ IND 142-143 E 4
Amlamé ○ RT 202-203 L 6
Amlapura = Karangasem ○· RI 168 B 7
Amlekhganj ○ NEP 144-145 E 7
Amlia Island ⌒ USA 22-23 K 6
Amloustarat ○ RMM 196-197 L 6
'Ammān ★· JOR 130-131 D 2
Ämmänsaari ○ FIN 88-89 K 4
Ammāpettai ○ IND 140-141 H 5
Ammapettai ○ IND 140-141 G 5
Ammarnäs ○ S 86-87 H 4
Ammaroo ○ AUS 178-179 C 1
Ammaroodinna Hill ▲ AUS 176-177 M 3
Ammassalik ✩ GRØ 28-29 W 4
Ammassivik = Sletten ○ GRØ 28-29 S 6
Ammer ∼ D 92-93 L 4
Ammersee ○ D 92-93 L 5
Ammochostos ○· TR 128-129 E 5
Ammon ○ USA (ID) 252-253 G 3
Ammouk < RMM 196-197 K 5
Amnat Charoen ○ THA 158-159 H 3
Amnja ∼ RUS 114-115 J 3
Amnok Gang ∼ DVR 150-151 E 7
Amnundakta ∼ RUS 116-117 K 2
Amnura ○ BD 142-143 F 3
Amodinonoka ○ RM 222-223 E 8
Amogjār, Passe d' ▲ RIM 196-197 D 4
Āmol ○· IR 136-137 C 6
Amolar ○ BR 70-71 J 6
Amoltepec ○ MEX 52-53 F 3
Amon ○ MA 188-189 F 6
Amontada ○ BR 68-69 J 3
Amores, Arroyo ∼ RA 76-77 H 5
Amores, Los ○ RA 76-77 H 5
Amorgós ○ GR 100-101 K 6
Amorgós ⌒ GR 100-101 K 6
Amorinópolis ○ BR 72-73 E 4
Amory ○ USA (MS) 268-269 M 3
Amos ○ CDN (QUE) 236-237 K 4
Amotape, Cerros de ▲ PE 64-65 B 4
Amotopo ○ SME 62-63 F 4
Amou ∼ RT 202-203 L 6
Amouguèr ○ MA 188-189 J 4
Amou Oblo ○ RT 202-203 L 6
Amour, Djebel ▲ DZ 190-191 C 4
Amourj ○ RIM 196-197 G 6
Amoya ○ GH 202-203 J 6
Amozoc ○ MEX 52-53 E 2
Ampah ○ RI 164-165 D 4
Ampana ○ RI 164-165 G 4
Ampang ○ RI 168 C 7
Ampangalana, Lakandrano < RM 222-223 F 8
Ampanihy ○ RM 222-223 D 10
Amparafaravola ○ RM 222-223 F 6
Amparai ○ CL 140-141 J 7
Amparihy Atsinanana ○ RM 222-223 E 9
Amparo ○ BR 72-73 G 7
Amparo, El ○ YV 60-61 F 4
Ampasamadinika ○ RM 222-223 F 7
Ampasimanolotra ○ RM 222-223 F 7
Ampasimbe ○ RM 222-223 F 6
Ampasinambo ○ RM 222-223 E 8
Ampatakamaroreny ○ RM 222-223 F 6
Ampato, Cordillera de ▲ PE 64-65 F 9
Ampefy ○ RM 222-223 E 7
Amper ○ WAN 204-205 H 4
Ampère Seamount ≃ 188-189 E 3
Amphlett Group ⌒ PNG 183 F 5
Ampibako ○ RI 164-165 G 4
Ampisikinana ○ RM 222-223 F 4
Ampiyacu, Río ∼ PE 64-65 F 3
Amplawas ○ RI 166-167 E 6
Ampoa ○ RI 164-165 G 4
Ampombiantambo ○ RM 222-223 F 4
Ampondra ○ RM 222-223 F 4
Amputa ∼ RUS 114-115 O 3
Amqui ○ CDN (QUE) 240-241 H 2
'Amrān ○· Y 132-133 C 6
Amrâne, Bir' < RIM 196-197 F 3
Amrāvati ○ IND 138-139 F 9
Am Raya < TCH 198-199 H 5
Amreli ○ IND 138-139 C 9
Āmri ○· PK 138-139 B 6
'Amrit ○·· SYR 128-129 F 5
Amritsar ○· IND 138-139 E 4
Amroha ○ IND 138-139 G 5
Amsāga ⊥ RIM 196-197 C 4
Amsel ○· DZ 190-191 E 9
Amsterdam ○ CDN (SAS) 232-233 Q 4
Amsterdam ★·· NL 92-93 H 2
Amsterdam ○ USA (NY) 278-279 G 6
Amsterdam ○ ZA 220-221 K 3
Amsterdam, Fort ∴· NA 56 D 2
Amsterdam, Île ⌒ F 12 F 8
Amstetten ○ A 92-93 N 4
Am Tanabo ○ TCH 198-199 H 6
Am Timan ✩ TCH 206-207 E 3
Amu-Buharskij kanal < US 136-137 H 5
'Āmūdā ○ SYR 128-129 J 4
'Amūda, al- ○ IRQ 128-129 L 7
Amu-Dar'ja ○ TM 136-137 J 6
Amudar'ja ∼ US 136-137 H 4
Amudarjo ∼ US 136-137 F 3
Amudat ○ EAU 212-213 E 3
Amukta Island ⌒ USA 22-23 L 6
Amukta Pass ≈ 22-23 L 6
Amund Ringnes Island ⌒ CDN 24-25 X 1
Amundsen, Mount ▲ ARK 16 G 11
Amundsen Bay ≈ 16 G 5
Amundsen Glacier ⊂ ARK 16 E 0
Amundsen Gulf ≈ 24-25 J 5
Amundsen havet ≈ 16 G 26
Amundsen-Scott ○ ARK 16 E 0
Amungwiwa, Mount ▲ PNG 183 D 4
Amuntai ○ RI 164-165 D 5
Amur ∼ RUS 118-119 K 9
Amur ∼ RUS 122-123 E 4
Amur ∼ RUS 122-123 J 2
'Amūr, Wādi ∼ SUD 200-201 G 3
Amurang ○ RI 164-165 J 3
Amursk ○ RUS 122-123 G 3
Amurskie stolby · RUS 122-123 H 3
Amurskij liman ≈ 122-123 J 2
Amursko-Zejskaja ravnina ⌣ RUS 118-119 M 9
Amutu-Besar, Pulau ⌒ RI 166-167 G 3
Amyderya ∼ TM 136-137 H 5
Amyl ∼ RUS 116-117 F 9
Amzi, Oued Tin ∼ DZ 198-199 B 2
Amzi, Oued Ti-n ∼ RN 198-199 B 3
Am-Zoer ○ TCH 198-199 K 5
'Āna ✩ IRQ 128-129 J 5
Ana, Cachoeira ∼ BR 62-63 F 5
Anabanua ○ RI 164-165 G 5
Anabar ∼ RUS 110-111 J 4
Anabarskij zaliv ≈ 110-111 J 3
Anabarskoe plato ▲ RUS 110-111 F 4
Anabat ○ RP 160-161 D 4
Anaborano ○ RM 222-223 F 4
Anacadiña ○ YV 60-61 J 5
Anacapa Islands ⌒ USA (CA) 248-249 E 5
Anaco ○ YV 60-61 J 3
Anacoco ○ USA (LA) 268-269 G 5
Anacoco, Bayou ∼ USA (LA) 268-269 G 6
Anaconda ○ USA (MT) 250-251 G 5
Anaconda-Pintler Wilderness ⊥ USA (MT) 250-251 F 5
Anacortes ○ USA (WA) 244-245 C 2
Anadarko ○ USA (OK) 264-265 F 3
Anadolu = Anatolia ⊥ 128-129 D 3
Anadyr' ✩· RUS 112-113 T 4
Anadyr ∼ RUS 112-113 S 4
Anadyr ∼ RUS 112-113 Q 3
Anadyr' ∼ RUS 112-113 P 4
Anadyrskaja nizmennost' ⌣ RUS 112-113 S 4
Anadyrskij liman ≈ 112-113 T 4
Anadyrskoe ploskogor'e ⊥ RUS 112-113 P 3
Anadyrskoye Ploskogor'ye = Anadyrskoe ploskogor'e ▲ RUS 112-113 P 3
Anáfi ⌒ GR 100-101 K 6
Anaghit ○· ER 200-201 J 4
Anagni ○· I 100-101 D 4
Anagusa Island ⌒ PNG 183 F 6
Anaharávi ○ GR 100-101 G 5
Anaheim ○ USA (CA) 248-249 G 6
Anahidrano ○ RM 222-223 E 5
Anahim Lake ○ CDN (BC) 228-229 J 4
Anahola ○ USA (HI) 288 F 2
Anáhuac ○ MEX (CHA) 50-51 F 3
Anáhuac ○ MEX (NL) 50-51 J 4
Anahuac ○ USA (TX) 268-269 F 7
Anahuac National Wildlife Refuge ⊥ USA (TX) 268-269 F 7
Anaimālai ○ IND 140-141 G 5
Anai Mudi ▲ IND 140-141 G 5
Anaj ∼ RUS 116-117 N 9
Anajás ○ BR 62-63 K 6
Anajatuba ○ BR 68-69 F 3
Anajé ○ BR 72-73 K 3
Anaka ○ EAU 212-213 C 2
Anakalang ○· RI 168 D 7
Anakāpalle ○ IND 142-143 C 7
Anakch ○ MA 188-189 E 7
Anakdara ○ RI 164-165 G 5
Anakie ○ AUS 178-179 J 2
Anaktuk ○ USA 20-21 L 1
Anaktuvuk Pass ○ USA 20-21 P 2
Anaktuvuk River ∼ USA 20-21 P 2
Analalava ○ RM 222-223 E 5
Analamaitso ▲ RM 222-223 F 6
Analamptsy, Farihy ○ RM 222-223 F 8
Analasarotra ○ RM 222-223 E 5
Analavory ○ RM 222-223 E 7
Anamã ○ BR 66-67 G 4
Anamã, Igarapé do ∼ BR 66-67 G 4
Anamã, Lago ○ BR 66-67 G 4
Anama, ozero ○ RUS 116-117 G 2
Anama Bay ○ CDN (MAN) 234-235 E 3
Ana Maria ○ PE 64-65 E 5
Ana María, Golfo de ≈ 54-55 F 4
Anambas, Kepulauan ⌒ RI 162-163 F 3
Anambra □ WAN 204-205 G 5
Anambra, River ∼ WAN 204-205 G 5
Anamoose ○ USA (ND) 258-259 G 4
Anamosa ○ USA (IA) 274-275 G 2
Anamu, Rio ∼ BR 62-63 F 5
Anamur ✩ TR 128-129 E 4
Anamur Burnu ▲ TR 128-129 E 4
Anan ○ J 152-153 F 8
Ananás ○ BR 68-69 D 5
Ananás, Cachoeira ∼ BR 68-69 B 5
Ananda-Kouadiokro ○ CI 202-203 H 6
Anandpur ○ IND 142-143 E 5
Anan'evo ○ KS 146-147 C 4
Añangu ○ EC 64-65 D 2
Ananta, Lago ○ PE 70-71 B 4
Anantapur ○ IND 140-141 G 3
Anantnag ○ IND 138-139 E 3
Anantsono ○ RM 222-223 C 9
Anantsono, Helodrano ≈ 222-223 C 9
Anapka, zaliv ○ RUS 120-121 V 3
Anápolis ○ BR 72-73 F 4
Anapu, Rio ∼ BR 68-69 C 3
Anār ○ IR 134-135 F 3
Anārak ○ IR 134-135 E 2
Anārbār, Rūd-e ∼ IR 134-135 D 2
Anār Dare ○ AFG 134-135 J 2
Anarjávri = Inarijärvi ○·· FIN 88-89 J 2
Anarjohka ∼ FIN 88-89 H 2
Anarnitsoq ∼ GRØ 28-29 Q 6
Anastácio ○ BR 70-71 K 7
Anastácio, Rio ∼ BR 72-73 E 7
Anastasii, buhta ○ RUS 112-113 R 6
Anatolia = Anadolu ⊥ TR 128-129 D 3
Anatolikí Macedonia Kai Thráki □ GR 100-101 K 4
Anatone ○ USA (WA) 244-245 H 4
Añatuya ○ RA 76-77 F 5
Anauá, Rio ∼ BR 62-63 D 5
Anaunethat Lake ○ CDN 30-31 R 5
Anaurilândia ○ BR 72-73 D 7
Anavgaj ○ RUS 120-121 S 5
Anavilhanas, Arquipélago das ⌒ BR 66-67 G 4
'Anaza Ruwāla ▲ KSA 130-131 E 2
Anbā Bišwi, Dair ∴ ET 194-195 E 2
Anbār, al- □ IRQ 128-129 J 6
Anbar Kūh ▲ AFG 136-137 L 6
Anbyon ○ DVR 150-151 F 8
Anča ∼ RUS 120-121 H 3
An Cabhán = Cavan ✩ IRL 90-91 D 5
An Caisleán Nua = Newcastle West ○ IRL 90-91 C 5
An Caol = Keel ○ IRL 90-91 B 5
Ancasti o del Alto, Sierra de ▲ RA 76-77 E 5
Ancenis ○ F 90-91 G 8
An Chathair = Caher ○ IRL 90-91 D 5
Anchau ○ WAN 204-205 H 3
Ancho ○ USA (NM) 256-257 K 5
Ancho, Canal ≈ 80 C 5
Anchorage ○· USA 20-21 Q 6
Anchorena ○ RA 78-79 G 3
Ancien < RMM 196-197 K 4
Anciferova, ostrov ⌒ RUS 122-123 Q 3
Anclitas, Cayos ⌒ C 54-55 F 4
An Clochán = Clifden ○· IRL 90-91 B 5
Anclote Keys ⌒ USA (FL) 286-287 G 3
An Cóbh = Cobh ○ IRL 90-91 C 6
An Coireán = Waterville ○ IRL 90-91 B 6
Ancon ○ PE 64-65 D 7
Ancon, Punta ▲ EC 64-65 B 3
Ancona ✩· I 100-101 D 3
Anconcito ○ EC 64-65 B 3
Ancón de Sardinas, Bahía de ≈ 64-65 C 1
Ancuabe ○ MOC 214-215 K 7
Ancuaze ○ MOC 218-219 H 3
Ancud ○ RCH 78-79 C 6
Ancud, Golfo de ≈ 78-79 C 6
Anda ○ RP 160-161 C 4
Anda ○ VRC 150-151 E 4
Andacollo ○ RCH 76-77 B 6
Andaga ○ WAN 204-205 K 3
Andagua ○ PE 64-65 F 9
Andahuaylas ○ PE 64-65 F 8
Andaiá, Rio ∼ BR 72-73 H 5
An Daingean = Dingle ○ IRL 90-91 B 5
Andaingo Gara ○ RM 222-223 F 7
Andakalaka ○ RM 222-223 E 5
Andale ○ USA (KS) 262-263 J 7
Andalgala ○ RA 76-77 D 4
Åndalsnes ✩ N 86-87 C 5
Andalucía □ E 98-99 D 6
Andalusia ○ USA (AL) 284-285 D 5
Andalusia ○ USA (IL) 274-275 H 3
Andām, Wādi ∼ OM 132-133 L 3
Andaman and Nicobar Islands □ IND 140-141 L 4
Andaman Basin ≃ 158-159 C 5
Andaman Islands ⌒ IND 140-141 L 3
Andaman Sea ≈ 158-159 C 4
Andamarca ○ BOL 70-71 D 6
Andamooka Opal Fields ○ AUS 178-179 D 6
Andamooka Ranges ▲ AUS 178-179 D 6
Andapa ○ RM 222-223 E 7
Andarāb ○ AFG 136-137 L 7
Andaraí ○ BR 72-73 K 2
Andarma ∼ RUS 114-115 Q 6
Andavaka · RM 222-223 D 10
Āndeba Ye Midir Zerf Ch'af ▲ ER 200-201 K 5
Andelys, les ○ F 90-91 H 7
Andenes ○· N 86-87 H 2
Anderai ○ WAN 204-205 F 3
Anderamboukane ○ RMM 196-197 M 7
Ånderdalen nasjonalpark ⊥ N 86-87 H 2
Andermatt ○ CH 92-93 K 5
Andersen, Salto ∼ RA 78-79 G 5
Anderson ○ USA (IN) 274-275 N 4
Anderson ○ USA (MO) 276-277 A 4
Anderson ○ USA (SC) 284-285 H 2
Anderson ○ USA (TX) 268-269 E 6
Anderson Channel ≈ 36-37 R 3
Anderson Creek ∼ USA (TX) 264-265 K 5
Anderson Gate < NAM 216-217 C 9
Anderson Island ⌒ CDN 36-37 L 6
Anderson River ∼ CDN 20-21 a 2
Anderson River ∼ USA (IN) 274-275 M 6
Andersonville ○ USA (IN) 274-275 N 5
Andersonville National Historic Site · USA (GA) 284-285 F 4
Andes ○ CO 60-61 D 5
Andes = Andes, Cordillera de los ▲ 5 D 8
Andes, Los ○ RCH 78-79 D 2
Andes, Los = Sotomayor ○ CO 64-65 D 1
Andfjorden ≈ 86-87 H 2
Andhōy ○ AFG 136-137 J 6
Andhra Pradesh □ IND 140-141 H 2
Andijskoe Kojsu ∼ RUS 126-127 G 6
Andikithira ⌒ GR 100-101 J 7
Andilamena ○ RM 222-223 F 6
Andimeška ○· IR 134-135 C 2
Anding ○ VRC 156-157 J 4
Andino, Parque Nacional ⊥ RCH 78-79 C 6
Andíparos ⌒ GR 100-101 K 6
Andira ○ BR 72-73 E 7
Andirá, Rio ∼ BR 66-67 J 4
Andirá, Rio ∼ BR 66-67 D 5
Andirá-Marau, Área Indígena ⚔ BR 66-67 J 4
Andırın ✩ TR 128-129 G 4
Andirio ○ GR 100-101 H 5
Andirlangar ○ VRC 144-145 D 2
Andižan ✩ US 136-137 N 4
Andižanskaja oblast' □ US 136-137 M 4
Andižanskoe vodohranilišče < KS 136-137 N 4
Andoain ○ E 98-99 F 3
Andoany ○ RM 222-223 F 4
Andoas ○ PE 64-65 D 3
Andohajango ○ RM 222-223 F 5
Andoi ○ RI 166-167 G 2
Andong ○ ROK 150-151 G 9
Andoom ○ AUS 174-175 F 3
Andorinha ○ BR 68-69 J 7
Andorinha, Cachoeira da ∼ BR 66-67 G 7
Andørja ⌒ N 86-87 H 2
Andorra ■ AND 98-99 H 3
Andorra La Vella ★· AND 98-99 H 3
Andorskaja grjada ▲ RUS 94-95 P 2
Andover ○ USA (ME) 278-279 L 4
Andover ○ USA (NH) 278-279 K 5
Andover ○ USA (NY) 278-279 D 6
Andover ○ USA (OH) 280-281 F 2
Andover ○ USA (SD) 260-261 J 1
Andovoranto ○ RM 222-223 F 7
Andøya ⌒ N 86-87 G 2
Andrada ○ ANG 216-217 F 3
Andradina ○ BR 72-73 E 6
Andrafainkona ○ RM 222-223 F 4
Andrafiabe ○ RM 222-223 F 4
Andrafiamena ▲ RM 222-223 F 4
Andramasina ○ RM 222-223 E 7
Andranavory ○ RM 222-223 D 9
Andranomena ○ RM 222-223 F 7
Andranomita · RM 222-223 D 8
Andranopasy ○ RM 222-223 C 8
Andranovondronina ○ RM 222-223 F 4
Andreafsky River ∼ USA 20-21 J 5
Andreanof Islands ⌒ USA 22-23 H 7
Andrecyk Lake ○ CDN 30-31 R 5
André Land ⊥ GRØ 26-27 m 7
Andrée land ⌣ N 84-85 J 3
Andreevka ○ KA 124-125 M 6
Andreevka ○ RUS 96-97 G 7
Andreevskoe, ozero ○ RUS 114-115 J 6
André Felix, Parc National ⊥ RCA 206-207 F 4
Andre Lake ○ CDN 36-37 R 7
Andrelândia ○ BR 72-73 H 6
Andrequicé ○ BR 72-73 H 5
Andréville ○ CDN (QUE) 240-241 F 3
Andrevo ○ RM 222-223 C 9
Andrew ○ CDN (ALB) 232-233 F 2
Andrew Gordon Bay ≈ 36-37 M 2
Andrew Lake ○ CDN 30-31 O 6
Andrew River ∼ CDN 20-21 a 2
Andrews ○ USA (NC) 282-283 D 5
Andrews ○ USA (SC) 284-285 L 3
Andrews ○ USA (TX) 264-265 B 6
Ándria ○ I 100-101 F 4
Andriamena ○ RM 222-223 E 6
Andriamena, Lavarie d' · RM 222-223 E 6
Andriba ○ RM 222-223 E 6
Andrieskraal ○ ZA 220-221 G 6
Andriesvale ○ ZA 220-221 E 3
Andrijevica ○· YU 100-101 G 3
Andringitra ▲ RM 222-223 E 8
Andrjuškino ○ RUS 112-113 H 2
Androfiamena ○ RM 222-223 F 4
Androhibe ○ RM 222-223 E 5
Androka ○ RM 222-223 D 10
Androna ⊥ RM 222-223 E 5
Andronica Island ⌒ USA 22-23 R 5
Andropov = Rybinsk ✩ RUS 94-95 Q 2
Androranga ∼ RM 222-223 F 5
Ándros ⌒ GR 100-101 K 6
Androscoggin River ∼ USA (ME) 278-279 L 4
Andros Island ⌒ BS 54-55 F 2
Andros Town ○· BS 54-55 G 2
Androth Island ⌒ IND 140-141 E 5
Androy ⊥ RM 222-223 D 10
Andru River ∼ PNG 183 E 4
Andselv ○ N 86-87 J 2
Andudu ○ ZRE 212-213 B 2
Andújar ○ E 98-99 E 5
Andulo ○ ANG 216-217 D 5
Andylivan ∼ RUS 112-113 M 4
Anec, Lake ○ AUS 176-177 K 1
Anecón Chico, Cerro ▲ RA 78-79 E 6
Anecón Grande, Cerro ▲ RA 78-79 D 6
Anéfis ○ RMM 196-197 L 5
Anegada ⌒ GB 56 C 2
Anegada ⌒ GB (VI) 286-287 R 2
Anegada, Bahía ≈ 78-79 H 6
Anegada, Punta ▲ PA 52-53 D 8
Anegada Passage ≈ 56 D 2
Aného ○· RT 202-203 L 6
Anekal ○ IND 140-141 G 4
Anéker ○ RN 198-199 B 5
Añelo ○ RA 78-79 E 5
Anemounon ∴· TR 128-129 E 4
Anepahan ○ RP 160-161 C 8
Anepmete ○ PNG 183 E 3
Anerley ○ CDN (SAS) 232-233 L 4
Anesbaraka < DZ 198-199 B 3
Anes-Barakka < RN 198-199 C 3
Aneth ○ USA (UT) 254-255 F 6
Aneto, Pico de ▲ E 98-99 H 3
Anette Island ⌒ USA 32-33 E 4
Anette Island Indian Reservation ⚔ USA 32-33 E 4
Aney ○ RN 198-199 F 3
Anfeg, Oued ∼ DZ 190-191 E 9
Anfu ○ VRC 156-157 J 3
Anga, Bol'šaja ∼ RUS 116-117 N 8
Angading ○ RI 162-163 E 6
Angajurjualuk Lake ○ CDN 24-25 g 5
Angalimp ○ PNG 183 C 3
Angamāli ○ IND 140-141 G 5
Angamarut ○ PNG 183 A 4
Angamma, Falaise d' ▲ TCH 198-199 H 4
Angamos, Isla ⌒ RCH 80 C 4
Angamos, Punta ▲ RCH 76-77 B 2
Angangueo ○ MEX 52-53 D 2
Ang'ang Xi ∴· VRC 150-151 D 4
Angara ∼ RUS 116-117 F 6
Angara ∼ RUS 116-117 K 6
Angara ∼ RUS 116-117 L 9
'Angara ○ SUD 206-207 G 3
Angaradébou ○ DY 204-205 E 3
Angarakan ○ RUS 118-119 E 8
Angarka ○ RUS 112-113 N 3
Angarka ∼ RUS 112-113 N 3
Angarsk ○ RUS 116-117 L 9
Angarskij krjaž ⊥ RUS 116-117 K 8
Angastaco ○ RA 76-77 D 3
Angaston ○ AUS 180-181 E 3
Angatuba ○ BR 72-73 F 7
Angavo ⊥ RM 222-223 E 7
Angba ○ WAN 204-205 G 5
Angel, El ○ EC 64-65 D 1
Angel, Salto ∼· YV 60-61 K 5
Ángel de la Guarda, Isla ⌒ MEX 50-51 C 3
Angeles ○ RP 160-161 D 5
Angeles, Los ○ RCH 78-79 C 4
Angeles, Los ○ USA (TX) 266-267 H 5
Angeles, Port ○ USA (WA) 244-245 B 2
Ängelholm ○ S 86-87 F 8
Angélica ○ RA 76-77 G 6
Angelica ○ USA (WI) 270-271 K 6
Angelim ○ BR 68-69 K 6
Angelina River ∼ USA (TX) 268-269 E 5
Angelin Bjerg ▲ GRØ 26-27 n 7
Angellala Creek ∼ AUS 178-179 J 4
Angelo River ∼ AUS 176-177 D 1
Ängelsberg ○··· S 86-87 H 7
Angels Camp ○ USA (CA) 246-247 E 5
Angel's Cove ○ CDN (NFL) 242-243 O 5
Angelus Oaks ○ USA (CA) 248-249 H 5
Angemuk, Gunung ▲ RI 166-167 K 3
Angerburg = Węgorzewo ○· PL 92-93 Q 1
Angereb ○ ETH 200-201 H 6
Angereb Wenz ∼ ETH 200-201 H 6
Ångermanälven ∼ S 86-87 H 5
Ångermanland ⊥ S 86-87 H 5
Angermünde ○· D 92-93 N 2
Angers ○ F 90-91 G 8
Ängesån ∼ S 86-87 L 3
Angetu ○ ETH 208-209 D 5
Anggoami ○ RI 164-165 G 5
Anggoro ○ RI 164-165 G 5
Angical ○ BR 68-69 F 7
Angicos ○ BR 68-69 K 4
Angier ○ USA (NC) 282-283 J 5
Angijjak Island ⌒ CDN 36-37 T 2
Angikuni Lake ○ CDN 30-31 U 4
Angira ○ PK 134-135 M 4
Angīre ○ IR 134-135 F 2
Angisoq = Loransation ○ GRØ 28-29 S 7
Angkor Wat ··· K 158-159 H 4
Ângk Tasaôm ○ K 158-159 H 5
Angle Inlet ○ USA (MN) 270-271 C 1
Anglem, Mount ▲ NZ 182 A 7
Anglemont ○ CDN (BC) 230-231 K 3
Anglesea ○ AUS 180-181 H 5
Anglesey ⌒ GB 90-91 E 5
Angleton ○ USA (TX) 268-269 E 7
Angliers ○ CDN (QUE) 236-237 J 5
Angmagssalik Fjord ≈ 28-29 W 4
Ango ○ ZRE 206-207 G 6
Angochagua ○ EC 64-65 C 1
Angoche ○ MOC 218-219 K 3
Angohrān ○ IR 134-135 G 5
Angol ○ RCH 78-79 C 4
Angola ■ ANG 216-217 C 5
Angola ○ USA (IN) 274-275 N 3
Angola Abyssal Plain = Namibia Abyssal Plain ≃ 6-7 K 11
Angola Basin ≃ 6-7 K 10
Angola Swamp ○ USA (NC) 282-283 K 6
Angolin ○ IND 142-143 J 1
Angonia, Planalto de ▲ MOC 218-219 G 2
Angontsy, Tanjona ▲ RM 222-223 G 5
Angoon ○ USA 32-33 C 3
Angor ○ US 136-137 K 6
Angora ○ USA (NE) 262-263 C 3
Angoram ○ PNG 183 C 3
An Gort = Gort ○ IRL 90-91 C 5
Angostura, Presa de la < MEX (CHI) 52-53 H 3
Angostura, Presa de la < MEX (SON) 50-51 E 2
Angostura Reservoir < USA (SD) 260-261 C 3
Angoulême ✩· F 90-91 H 9
Angpawing Bum ▲ MYA 142-143 J 3
Angra dos Reis ○· BR 72-73 H 7
Angramios, Pulau ⌒ RI 166-167 H 3
Angren ○ US 136-137 M 4
Ang Thong Marine National Park ⊥ THA 158-159 E 6
Angu ○ ZRE 210-211 K 2
Anguilla □ GB 56 D 2
Anguilla ○ USA (MS) 268-269 K 3
Anguilla Cays ⌒ BS 54-55 F 3
Anguilla Island ⌒ GB 56 D 2
Anguille, Cape ▲ CDN (NFL) 242-243 J 5
Anguille Mountains ▲ CDN (NFL) 242-243 J 5
Angūman ○ AFG 136-137 M 7
Anguo ○ VRC 154-155 J 2
Angūrān ○ IR 128-129 M 4
Anguran ○ IR 134-135 F 5
Angurugu ✩ AUS 174-175 D 3
Angus ○ CDN (ONT) 238-239 F 4
Angusilla ○ PE 64-65 E 2
Angusko Point ▲ CDN 30-31 X 5
Angusville ○ CDN (MAN) 234-235 B 4
Angwa ∼ ZW 218-219 F 3
An Hải ✩ VN 156-157 E 6
Anhanduí-Guaçu, Rio ∼ BR 76-77 K 1
Anholt ⌒ DK 86-87 E 8
Anhua ○ VRC 156-157 G 2
Anhui □ VRC 154-155 K 5
Ani · TR 128-129 K 2
Aniak ○ USA 20-21 L 6
Aniakchak Crater · USA 22-23 R 4
Aniakchak National Monument and Preserve ⊥ USA 22-23 S 4
Aniak River ∼ USA 20-21 L 6
Aniakshak Bay ≈ 22-23 S 4
Aniassue ○ CI 202-203 J 6
Aníbal Pinto, Lago ○ RCH 80 D 5
Anicuns ○ BR 72-73 F 4
Anié ○ RT (DPL) 202-203 L 6
Anié ∼ RT 202-203 L 5
Anie, Pic d' ▲ F 90-91 G 10
Anihovka ✩ RUS 124-125 B 3
Anikino ○ RUS 118-119 K 9
Anil ○ BR 68-69 F 3
Anil, Igarapé do ∼ BR 66-67 J 7
Animas ○ USA (NM) 256-257 G 7
Animas, Las ○ HN 52-53 L 4
Animas, Punta ▲ RCH 76-77 B 4
Animas, Quebrada de las ∼ RCH 76-77 B 4
Animas Peak ▲ USA (NM) 256-257 G 7
Animas River ∼ USA (CO) 254-255 H 6
Anina ○ RO 102-103 B 5
Aninaus Pass ▲ ZA 220-221 C 4
Anisij, mys ▲ RUS 110-111 W 1
Anita ○ USA (IA) 274-275 D 3
Anita Garibaldi ○ BR 74-75 E 6
Aniuk River ∼ USA 20-21 M 2
Aniva ○ RUS 122-123 K 5
Aniva, mys ▲ RUS 122-123 K 5
Aniva, zaliv ≈ 122-123 K 5
Anivorano Avaratra ○ RM 222-223 F 4
Aniwa ○ USA (WI) 270-271 J 6
Aniwa Island = Île Nina ⌒ VAN 184 II b 4
Aniyo ○ J 152-153 G 7
Anjafy, Lembalemba Ambonin ▲ RM 222-223 E 6
Anjār ○ IND 138-139 C 8
Anji ○ VRC 154-155 L 6
Anjiohibe · RM 222-223 E 5
Anjombony ∼ RM 222-223 F 5
Anjou ⊥ F 90-91 G 8
Anjozorobe ○ RM 222-223 E 7
Anju ○ DVR 150-151 E 8
Anjuj ∼ RUS 122-123 G 4
Anjuj, Bol'šoj ∼ RUS 112-113 M 3
Anjuj, Malyj ∼ RUS 112-113 O 3
Anjujsk ○ RUS 112-113 L 2
Anjujskij hrebet ▲ RUS 112-113 M 3
Anka ○ WAN 198-199 B 6
Ankaboa, Tanjona ▲ RM 222-223 C 8
Ankaimoro, Tombeaux · RM 222-223 E 9
Ankaizina ⊥ RM 222-223 F 5
Ankalalobe ○ RM 222-223 D 7
Ankang ○ VRC 154-155 F 5
Ankara ★· TR 128-129 E 3
Ankaramy ○ RM 222-223 F 4
Ankaratra ▲ RM 222-223 E 7
Ankasa National Park ⊥ GH 202-203 J 7
Ankatafa ○ RM 222-223 F 4
Ankavanana ∼ RM 222-223 F 5
Ankavandra ○ RM 222-223 D 7
Ankazoabo ○ RM 222-223 D 9
Ankazobe ○ RM 222-223 E 7
Ankazobe, Tampoketsan' ▲ RM 222-223 E 6
Ankazomboronza ○ RM 222-223 E 6
Ankazomiriotra ○ RM 222-223 E 7
Ankazondandy ○ RM 222-223 E 7
Ankeny ○ USA (IA) 274-275 E 3
Ankerika ○ RM 222-223 E 5
An Khê ○ VN 158-159 K 4
Ankhalli ○ IND 140-141 F 4
Ankilizato ○ RM 222-223 D 8
Ankirihitra ○ RM 222-223 E 6
Anklam ○ D 92-93 M 2
Ankleshwar ○ IND 138-139 D 9
Ankli ○ IND 140-141 F 2
Ankober ○· ETH 208-209 D 4
Ankobra ∼ GH 202-203 J 7
Ankola ○ IND 140-141 F 3
Ankoro ○ ZRE 214-215 D 4
Ankotrofotsy ○ RM 222-223 D 7
Ankpa ○ WAN 204-205 G 5
An Láithreach = Laragh ○· IRL 90-91 D 5
Anliu ○ VRC 156-157 J 5
Anllóns, Río ∼ E 98-99 C 3
Anlong ○ VRC 156-157 D 4
An Longfort = Longford ✩ IRL 90-91 D 5
Ânlông Vêng ○ K 158-159 H 3
Anlu ○ VRC 154-155 H 6
An Muileann-gCearr = Mullingar ○ IRL 90-91 D 5
Anmyŏn Do ⌒ ROK 150-151 F 9
Ann, Cape ▲ USA (MA) 278-279 L 6
Ann, Cape ▲ ARK 16 G 5
Anna ○ RUS 102-103 M 2
Anna ○ USA (IL) 276-277 F 3
Anna ○ USA (MS) 268-269 J 5
Anna, Lake ○ USA (VA) 280-281 J 5
Annaba ✩· DZ 190-191 F 2
Annaberg ○ PNG 183 C 3
Anna Bistrup, Kap ▲ GRØ 26-27 q 4
an-Nabk ✩ SYR 128-129 G 5
Annaheim ○ CDN (SAS) 232-233 O 3
an-Naḥl ○ ET 194-195 F 3
An Nā'ikah, Qārārat ○ LAR 192-193 H 4
Anna Maria Island ⌒ USA (FL) 286-287 G 4
An Nāmūs, Wāw ○ LAR 192-193 G 5
Annandale ○ USA (MN) 270-271 D 5
Anna Plains ○ AUS 172-173 E 5
Annapolis ○ USA (MO) 276-277 E 3
Annapolis ✩· USA (MD) 280-281 K 5
Annapolis Royal ○ CDN (NS) 240-241 K 6
Annapurna Himal ▲ NEP 144-145 D 6
Annapurna I ▲ NEP 144-145 D 6
Annapurna II ▲ NEP 144-145 E 6
Annapurna Sanctuary ⊥· NEP 144-145 D 6
Ann Arbor ○ USA (MI) 272-273 F 5
Anna Regina ○ GUY 62-63 E 2
An Nás = Naas ✩ IRL 90-91 D 5
Annaville ○ CDN (QUE) 238-239 N 2
Anne, Mount ▲ AUS 180-181 J 7
Annean, Lake ○ AUS 176-177 E 3
Annecy ○ F 90-91 L 9
Annenkov Island ⌒ GB 78-79 O 7
Annigeri ○ IND 140-141 F 3
an-Nil ∼ ET 194-195 E 3
Anning ○ VRC 156-157 C 4
Anningie ○ AUS 178-179 B 1
Anniston ○ USA (AL) 284-285 E 3
Anniston Army Depot xx USA (AL) 284-285 E 3
Annitowa ○ AUS 178-179 D 1
Annofliyah ○ LAR 192-193 G 2
Annonay ○ F 90-91 K 9
Annotto Bay ○ JA 54-55 G 5
Annoual ○ MA 188-189 K 3
an-Nugaym, Bi'r < SUD 200-201 G 3
An Nuqāt al Khams □ LAR 192-193 D 1
Anola ○ CDN (MAN) 234-235 G 5
An Ómaigh = Omagh ✩· GB 90-91 D 4
Año Nuevo, Seno ≈ 80 F 7
Año Nuevo Point ▲ USA (CA) 248-249 B 2
Anony, Farihy ○ RM 222-223 E 10
Anori ○ BR 66-67 G 4
Anoritooq ≈ 28-29 T 6
Anorontany, Tanjona ▲ RM 222-223 F 4
Anosibe An'ala ○ RM 222-223 F 7
Anosy ▲ RM 222-223 E 10
Anpo Gang ∼ VRC 156-157 F 6
Anqing ○ VRC 154-155 K 6
Anqiu ○ VRC 154-155 L 3
Anquincila ○ RA 76-77 E 5
Anranofasika ○ RM 222-223 E 6
Anranomavo ○ RM 222-223 D 6
Anriandampy ○ RM 222-223 D 9
Ansai ○ VRC 154-155 F 3
Ansas ○ RI 166-167 H 2
Ansbach ○· D 92-93 L 4
Anse-à-Galets ○ RH 54-55 J 5
Anse-au-Loup Big Pond, L' ○ CDN (NFL) 242-243 M 1
Anse-à-Veau ○ RH 54-55 J 5
Änseba Shet' ∼ ER 200-201 J 4
Anselm ○ USA (ND) 258-259 K 5
Anselmo ○ USA (NE) 262-263 G 3
Anse-Pleureuse ○ CDN (QUE) 242-243 C 3
Anserma ○ CO 60-61 D 5
Anse Rouge ○ RH 54-55 J 5
Anshan ○ VRC 150-151 D 7
Anshi ○ IND 140-141 F 3
Anshun ○ VRC 156-157 D 3
Ansilta, Cerro de ▲ RA 76-77 C 6
Ansilta, Cordillera de ▲ RA 76-77 C 6
Ansina ○ ROU 76-77 K 6
Ansley ○ USA (NE) 262-263 G 3
Anson ○ USA (TX) 264-265 E 6
Anson Bay ≈ 172-173 J 2
Ansonga ○ RMM 202-203 L 2
Answer Downs ○ AUS 178-179 F 4
Anta ○ PE 64-65 F 8
Anta, Cachoeira da ∼ BR 66-67 H 6
Antabamba ○ PE 64-65 F 9
Antakya = Hatay ✩ TR 128-129 G 4
Antalaha ○ RM 222-223 G 5
Antalya ✩ TR 128-129 D 4
Antalya Körfezi ≈ 128-129 D 4
Antanambao Manampotsy ○ RM 222-223 F 7
Antananarivo □ RM 222-223 D 7
Antananarivo ★· RM (ATN) 222-223 E 7
Antandrokomby ○ RM 222-223 F 7
Antanifotsy ○ RM 222-223 E 7
Antanimora Atsimo ○ RM 222-223 D 10
Antanjombolamena ○ RM 222-223 E 7
An tAonach = Nenagh ○ IRL 90-91 C 5
Antar, Djebel ▲ DZ 188-189 L 4
Antarctica ⊥ ARK 16 F 28
Antarctic Bugt ≈ 26-27 s 3
Antarctic Circle ARK 16 G 3
Antarctic Peninsula ⌣ ARK 16 G 30
Antarctic Sound ≈ 16 G 31
Antares, Gunung ▲ RI 166-167 L 4
Antas ○ BR 68-69 J 7
Antécume Pata ○ F 62-63 G 4
Antelope ○ CDN (SAS) 232-233 K 5
Antelope ○ USA (OR) 244-245 E 6
Antelope Island ⌒ USA (UT) 254-255 C 3
Antelope Lake ○ CDN (SAS) 232-233 K 5
Antelope Mine ○ ZW 218-219 E 5
Antelope Summit ▲ USA (NV) 246-247 K 4
Antelope Valley Indian Museum · USA (CA) 248-249 G 5
Antenor Navarro ○ BR 68-69 J 5
Antequera ○ E 98-99 E 6
Antequera ○ PY 76-77 J 3
Antero Junction ○ USA (CO) 254-255 K 5
Antetezampandrana ○ RM 222-223 F 6
An Thới, Quần Đảo ⌒ VN 158-159 H 6
Anthony ○ USA (KS) 262-263 H 7
Anthony ○ USA (TX) 256-257 A 2
Anthony Island ⌒··· CDN (BC) 228-229 C 4
Anthony Lagoon ○ AUS 174-175 C 5
Anthropological Museum ·· RI 166-167 L 3
Anti Atlas ▲ MA 188-189 G 6
Anticosti, Île d' ⌒ CDN (QUE) 242-243 E 3
Antiga Lagoa da Rabeca ○ BR 70-71 H 4
Antigo ○ BR 72-73 J 7
Antigo ○ USA (WI) 270-271 J 5
Antigonish ○ CDN (NS) 240-241 N 5
Antigua ○· MEX 52-53 F 2
Antigua, Salina la ○ RA 76-77 E 5
Antigua and Barbuda ■ AG 56 E 3
Antigua Guatemala ✩··· GCA 52-53 J 4
Antigua Island ⌒ AG 56 E 3
Antiguo Cauce del Río Bermejo ∼ RA 76-77 F 4
Antiguo Morelos ○ MEX 50-51 K 6
Antilla ○ C 54-55 H 4
Antimari, Rio ∼ BR 66-67 C 7
An Ti-m-Missaou < DZ 196-197 M 4
Antimonan ○ RP 160-161 D 6
Antimony ○ USA (UT) 254-255 D 5

Antinaëtajaha ~ RUS 108-109 R 7
An tInbhear Mór = Arklow o IRL 90-91 D 5
Antingola o RI 164-165 H 3
Antioch o USA (NE) 262-263 D 2
Antioquia o CO 60-61 D 4
Antipajuta o RUS 108-109 R 7
Antipodes Islands ⌒ NZ 13 J 7
Antisana, Volcán ▲ EC 64-65 C 2
Antissa o GR 100-101 K 5
An tIúr = Newry o GB 90-91 D 4
Antiwirifo o GH 202-203 J 6
Antlat o LAR 192-193 J 2
Antler o CDN (SAS) 232-233 R 6
Antlers o USA (OK) 264-265 J 4
Antofagasta ☆ RCH 76-77 B 2
Antofagasta de la Sierra o RA 76-77 D 4
Antofalla, Salar de ⊙ RA 76-77 D 4
Antofalla, Volcán ▲ RA 76-77 D 3
Antoinette Bay ≈ 26-27 L 3
Anton o USA (CO) 254-255 M 4
Anton o USA (TX) 264-265 B 5
Antongil, Helodrano ≈ 222-223 F 5
Antongomena-Bevary o RM 222-223 D 5
Antonibe o RM 222-223 E 5
Antonina o BR (CEA) 68-69 J 5
Antonina o BR (PAR) 74-75 F 5
Antonio de Biedma o RA 80 G 3
Antônio Dias o BR 72-73 J 5
Antônio Gonçalves o BR 68-69 H 7
Antônio João o BR 76-77 K 2
Antônio Martins o BR 68-69 K 5
Antônio Prado o BR 74-75 E 7
Antonio Varas, Península ⌒ RCH 80 D 5
Antonito o USA (CO) 254-255 J 6
Antón Lizardo o MEX 52-53 F 2
Antracyt o UA 102-103 L 3
Antrim o • GB 90-91 D 4
Antrim Mountains ▲ GB 90-91 D 4
Antsahabe o RM 222-223 F 5
Antsahampano o RM 222-223 F 4
Antsakabary o RM 222-223 F 5
Antsakanalabe o RM 222-223 F 5
Antsalova o RM 222-223 D 7
Antsambalahy o RM 222-223 F 5
Antsaravibe o RM 222-223 F 4
Antsatramidola o RM 222-223 F 5
Antsiafabositra o RM 222-223 E 6
Antsianitia o RM 222-223 E 5
Antsirabato o RM 222-223 G 5
Antsirabe o RM 222-223 E 7
Antsirabe Afovoany o RM 222-223 F 5
Antsirabe Avaratra o RM 222-223 F 4
Antsiranana ◻ RM 222-223 F 4
Antsiranana ☆ RM 222-223 F 4
Antsla o EST 94-95 K 3
Antsoha o RM 222-223 D 7
Antsohihy o RM 222-223 E 5
Antsohimbondrona o RM 222-223 F 4
Antsondrodava o RM 222-223 D 7
Antu o VRC 150-151 G 6
Antuco o RCH 78-79 D 4
Antuco, Volcán ▲ RCH 78-79 D 4
Antufaš ⌒ Y 132-133 C 6
Antwerpen ☆ •• B 92-93 H 3
Antykan o RUS 120-121 F 6
An Uaimh = Navan o IRL 90-91 D 5
Anuajito, El o MEX 50-51 E 5
Anučino o RUS 122-123 E 7
Añueque, Sierra ▲ RA 78-79 E 6
Anugul o IND 142-143 D 5
Anuj ~ RUS 124-125 O 2
Anum o GH 202-203 L 6
Anumma, River ~ WAN 204-205 J 3
Anūpgarh o IND 138-139 D 5
Anūpshahr o IND 138-139 G 5
Anuradhapura o ••• CL 140-141 J 6
Anvak Island ⌒ USA 22-23 P 5
Anvers = Antwerpen ☆ •• B 92-93 H 3
Anvers, Île ⌒ ARK 16 G 30
Anvik o USA 20-21 K 5
Anvik River ~ USA 20-21 K 5
Anxi o VRC (GAN) 146-147 M 5
Anxi o VRC (JXI) 156-157 J 2
An Xian o VRC 154-155 D 6
Anxious Bay ≈ 180-181 C 2
Anyang o ROK 150-151 F 9
Anyang o VRC 154-155 J 3
A'nyêmaqên Shan ▲ VRC 144-145 M 3
Anyer-Kidul o RI 168 A 3
Anyinam o GH 202-203 K 6
Anyirawase o GH 202-203 L 6
Anykščiai ☆ •• LT 94-95 J 4
Anyuan o VRC 156-157 J 4
Anyue o VRC 154-155 D 6
Anza-Borrego Desert State Park ⊥ USA (CA) 248-249 H 6
Anzac o CDN 32-33 P 3
Anzali, Bandar-e o • IR 128-129 N 4
Anze o VRC 154-155 H 3
Anžero-Sudžensk o RUS 114-115 T 6
Anzerskij, ostrov ⌒ RUS 88-89 O 4
Anzhero Sudzhensk = Anžero-Sudžensk o RUS 114-115 T 6
Anzi o ZRE 210-211 J 4
Ânzio o I 100-101 D 4
Anzoategui o CO 60-61 D 5
Anzob o TJ 136-137 L 5
Anzob, pereval ▲ TJ 136-137 L 5
Anžu, mys ▲ RUS 110-111 V 2
Anžu, ostrova ⌒ RUS 110-111 U 1
Aoba, Île = Obe ⌒ VAN 184 II a 2
Aoba/ Maewo ◻ VAN 184 II b 2
Ao Ban Don ≈ 158-159 E 6
Aodanga < TCH 198-199 H 4
Aohan Qi o VRC 148-149 O 6
'Aoînât ez Zbil o RIM 196-197 F 6
Aoiz o E 98-99 G 3
Aoke = Auki ☆ SOL 184 I e 3
Aola = Tenaghau o SOL 184 I e 3
Aomen = Macao o P 156-157 H 5
Aomori o J 152-153 J 4
Aonia o USA (GA) 284-285 H 3
Ao Phangnga National Park ⊥ THA 158-159 E 6
Aore ⌒ VAN 184 II a 2
Ao Sawi ≈ 158-159 E 5
Aosta o I 100-101 A 2
Aosta, Valle d' = Vallé d'Aoste ◻ I 100-101 A 2
Aoste, Vallée d' = Valle d'Aosta ◻ I 100-101 A 2
Ao Trat ≈ 158-159 G 4
Aouara o F 62-63 H 3
Aoudaghost ∴• RIM 196-197 E 6
Aoudech < RIM 196-197 C 6
Aouderas o RN 198-199 D 4
Aoufirst • MA 196-197 C 2
Aougoundou, Lac ⊙ RMM 202-203 J 2
Aouhinet bel Egra < DZ 188-189 H 7
Aouînat Sarrag < RIM 196-197 D 5
Aouk, Bahr ~ TCH 206-207 D 4
Aoukalé ~ TCH 206-207 E 3
Aouk-Aoukale, Réserve de faune de l' ⊥ RCA 206-207 E 4
Aoukâr ∸ RIM 196-197 E 5
Aoukâr ∸ RMM 196-197 H 3
Aoulef o DZ 190-191 C 7
Aoulime, Ibel ▲ MA 188-189 G 5
Aoulouz o MA 188-189 G 5
Aourir n' Ouassel ▲ MA 188-189 H 5
Aourou o RMM 202-203 E 2
Aousard o MA 196-197 C 3
Aozi o TCH 198-199 J 2
Aozou o • TCH 198-199 H 2
Apača o RUS 122-123 R 2
Apache o USA (AZ) 256-257 F 7
Apache o USA (OK) 264-265 F 4
Apache Creek o USA (NM) 256-257 G 5
Apache Junction o USA (AZ) 256-257 D 5
Apache Lake o USA (AZ) 256-257 D 5
Apache Mountains ▲ USA (TX) 266-267 C 2
Apacheta Cruz Grande ▲ BOL 76-77 E 1
Apaikwa o GUY 62-63 D 2
Apakapur ~ RUS 114-115 O 3
Apalachee o USA (GA) 284-285 G 3
Apalachee Bay ≈ 48-49 F 5
Apalachee Bay ≈ USA 286-287 E 2
Apalachee River ~ USA (GA) 284-285 G 3
Apalachicola o USA (FL) 286-287 E 2
Apalachicola Bay ≈ USA 286-287 D 2
Apalachicola River ~ USA (FL) 286-287 D 1
Apan o MEX 52-53 E 2
Apapel'gino o RUS 112-113 Q 2
Apaporis, Río ~ CO 66-67 B 3
Aparados da Serra ▲ BR 74-75 F 7
Aparados da Serra, Parque Nacional ⊥ •• BR 74-75 E 7
Aparecida d'Oeste o BR 72-73 E 6
Aparecida do Tabuado o BR 72-73 E 6
Aparri o RP 160-161 D 3
Apastovo ☆ RUS 96-97 F 6
Apatana o RI 168 E 6
Apatity o RUS 88-89 M 3
Apatou o F 62-63 G 3
Apatzingán de la Constitución o MEX 52-53 C 2
Apauwar o RI 166-167 K 2
Apauwar ~ RI 166-167 K 3
Apawanza o ZRE 212-213 B 3
Apaxtla de Castrejón o MEX 52-53 E 2
Ape o LV 94-95 K 3
Apediá, Rio ~ BR 70-71 G 3
Apeldoorn o • NL 92-93 H 2
Apeleg, Arroyo ~ RA 80 E 2
Apennines = Appennini ▲ I 100-101 B 2
Apere, Río ~ BOL 70-71 E 4
Apesokubi o GH 202-203 L 6
Apetina = Puleowine o SME 62-63 G 4
Apeú, Ilha ⌒ BR 68-69 E 2
Apex o USA (NC) 282-283 J 5
Apex Mountain ▲ CDN 20-21 V 5
Aphrodisias •• TR 128-129 C 4
Api ▲ NEP 144-145 C 5
Api o ZRE 210-211 K 2
Api, Gunung ▲ RI 168 D 7
Apia o CO 60-61 D 5
Apia ★ WS 184 V b 1
Apiacás o BR 66-67 J 7
Apiaí o BR 74-75 F 5
Apinaco, Cachoeira ~ BR 70-71 K 2
Apiñacoccha, Lago ⊙ PE 64-65 F 9
Apinajes o BR 68-69 D 4
Apio o SOL 184 I e 3
Apishapa River ~ USA (CO) 254-255 L 6
Apitpac o MEX 52-53 H 3
Aplahoué o DY 202-203 L 6
Aplao o PE 70-71 A 5
Apo, Mount ▲ RP 160-161 F 9
Apódaca o MEX 50-51 J 5
Apodi o BR 68-69 K 4
Apodi, Chapada do ▲ BR 68-69 J 4
Apodi, Rio ~ BR 68-69 J 4
Apo East Pass ≈ 160-161 D 6
Apoko o RCB 210-211 E 4
Apolima Strait ≈ 184 V a 1
Apolinario Saravia o RA 76-77 F 3
Apollo Bay o AUS 180-181 G 5
Apollonia = Sūsah o • LAR 192-193 J 1
Apolo o BOL 70-71 C 4
Apolu o WAN 204-205 F 4
Apopa o ES 52-53 K 5
Apopka o USA (FL) 286-287 H 3
Apopka, Lake ⊙ USA (FL) 286-287 H 3
Apoquitaua, Rio ~ BR 66-67 J 5
Aporá o BR 68-69 J 7
Aporé, Rio ~ BR 72-73 E 5
Apo Reef National Park ⊥ RP 160-161 D 6
Aporema o BR 62-63 J 5
Apostle Islands National Lakeshore ⊥ USA (WI) 270-271 H 3
Apostolos Andreas, Cape ▲ TR 128-129 F 5
Apostolove o UA 102-103 H 4
Apoteri o GUY 62-63 E 3
Appalachian Mountains ▲ USA 46-47 J 7
Appam o USA (ND) 258-259 D 3
Appat ⌒ GRØ 26-27 Z 8
Appê Grande, Ilha ⌒ RA 76-77 J 4
Appelton City o USA (MO) 274-275 D 6
Appennino Abruzzese ▲ I 100-101 D 3
Apple Creek ~ USA (IL) 274-275 H 5
Applegate o USA (OR) 244-245 B 8
Applegrove o CDN (BC) 230-231 L 4
Apple River o CDN (NS) 240-241 L 5
Apple Springs o USA (TX) 268-269 F 5
Appleton o • JA 54-55 G 5
Appleton o USA (MN) 270-271 B 5
Appleton o USA (WI) 270-271 K 6
Appleton City o USA (MO) 274-275 E 6
Apple Valley o USA (CA) 248-249 G 5
Appomattox o USA (VA) 280-281 H 6
Appomattox Court House National Historic Park • USA (VA) 280-281 H 6
Appomattox River ~ USA (VA) 280-281 H 6
Approuague ~ F 62-63 H 4
Apraksin Bor o RUS 94-95 M 2
Aprel'sk o RUS 118-119 G 6
Apricena o I 100-101 E 4
Aprilia o I 100-101 D 4
April River ~ PNG 183 B 3
Apromprom o CI 202-203 J 6
Apšeronsk o RUS 126-127 C 5
Apšeronskij poluostrov ⌒ AZ 128-129 N 2
Apsley o CDN (ONT) 238-239 G 4
Apsley River ~ AUS 178-179 L 6
Apt o F 90-91 K 10
Aptos o USA (CA) 248-249 C 3
Apu ~ RI 166-167 D 3
Apucarana o BR 72-73 E 7
Apuí o BR (AMA) 66-67 E 3
Apuí o BR (AMA) 66-67 H 6
Apuka o RUS 112-113 P 6
Apuka ~ RUS 112-113 Q 6
Apukskij hrebet ▲ RUS 112-113 Q 6
Apura o SME 62-63 F 3
Apurahuan o RP 160-161 C 8
Apure o CO 60-61 D 3
Apure, Río ~ YV 60-61 F 4
Apurimac, Río ~ PE 64-65 F 8
Apurinã, Área Indígena ✕ BR 66-67 F 6
Apurinã Peneri, Área Indígena ✕ BR 66-67 D 7
Apurito o YV 60-61 G 4
Apurlec • PE 64-65 C 5
Apuseni, Munţii ▲ RO 102-103 C 4
'Aqaba ☆ JOR 130-131 D 3
Aqaba, Gulf of = 'Aqaba, Ḫalīǧ al- ≈ ET 130-131 D 3
Āqā Bābā o IR 128-129 N 4
Āqče o AFG 136-137 K 6
'Aqdā o IR 134-135 E 2
'Aqiq, al- o KSA 132-133 B 3
'Aqiq, Wādī al- ~ KSA 130-131 G 5
Aqissermiaq o GRØ 28-29 O 3
Aqitag ▲ VRC 146-147 K 5
Āq Kand o IR 128-129 N 4
Āq Koprük o AFG 136-137 K 6
Āq Qal'e o IR 136-137 D 6
Aqqan o VRC 144-145 E 2
Aqqikkol Hu ⊙ VRC 144-145 G 2
'Aqra ☆ IRQ 128-129 K 4
Āq Šū ~ IRQ 128-129 L 5
Aqtaū = Aktau ☆ KA 126-127 J 6
Aqtöbe = Aktöbe ☆ KA 126-127 M 2
Aqua Caliente Indian Reservation ✕ USA (CA) 248-249 H 6
Aquacanta, Raudal ~ YV 60-61 K 4
Aquadell o CDN (SAS) 232-233 M 5
Aquadeo Beach o CDN (SAS) 232-233 K 2
Água Fria, Ribeiro ~ BR 68-69 D 6
Aquanga o USA (CA) 248-249 H 6
Água Quente, Rio ~ BR 68-69 F 6
Aquatuk River ~ CDN 34-35 O 3
Aquidabán, Río ~ PY 76-77 J 2
Aquidauana o BR 70-71 K 7
Aquidauana, Rio ~ BR 70-71 J 6
Aquijes, Los o PE 64-65 E 9
Aquila o MEX 52-53 C 2
Aquilla Creek ~ USA (TX) 266-267 K 2
Aquin o RH 54-55 J 5
Aquiqui, Ilhas do ⌒ BR 62-63 H 6
Aquitaine ◻ F 90-91 G 10
Ara o IND 142-143 D 3
'Arab ~ SUD 200-201 G 4
Arab o USA (AL) 284-285 D 2
'Arab, 'Ain al- o SYR 128-129 H 4
'Araba, Wādī ~ ET 194-195 F 3
'Araba, Wādī l- ~ JOR 130-131 D 2
'Arabābād o IR 134-135 G 2
Araban ☆ TR 128-129 G 4
Arabati o ETH 208-209 D 3
Arabats'ka zatoka ≈ 102-103 J 5
Arabela o USA (NM) 256-257 K 5
Arabi o USA (GA) 284-285 G 5
Arabian Basin ≃ 12 E 3
Arabian Oryx Sanctuary ⊥ ••• OM 132-133 K 4
Arabian Peninsula ⌒ KSA 10-11 C 6
Arabian Sea ≈ 12 E 3
Arabiya, al- ⌒ KSA 134-135 D 5
Arabopó o YV 62-63 D 3
Arabos, Los o C 54-55 E 3
Arabou < RMM 196-197 L 5
Araç ☆ TR 128-129 E 2
Araca o BOL 70-71 D 5
Aracá, Área Indígena ✕ BR 62-63 D 4
Aracá, Rio ~ BR 66-67 F 2
Aracai, Cachoeira do ~ BR 68-69 C 3
Aracaju ☆ • BR 68-69 K 7
Aracati o BR 68-69 K 4
Araci o BR 72-73 K 3
Araçatuba o BR (MAT) 70-71 K 3
Araçatuba o BR (PAU) 72-73 E 6
Araceli o RP 160-161 C 7
Aracena o E 98-99 D 6
Araci o BR 68-69 J 7
Araçu, Rio ~ BR 66-67 H 5
Araçuaí o BR 72-73 J 4
Araçuaí, Rio ~ BR 72-73 J 4
'Arad o IL 130-131 D 2
Arad ☆ • RO 102-103 B 4
Arad, Tel ∴• IL 130-131 D 2
Arada o TCH 198-199 K 5
'Arāda o UAE 132-133 H 2
Ārādān o IR 136-137 C 7
Aradan o RUS 116-117 F 9
Arados o MEX 50-51 F 3
Arafura Sea ≈ 166-167 G 6
Aragac o AR 128-129 K 2
Aragac, gora ▲ AR 128-129 L 2
Arage o WAN 204-205 H 4
Araghene, Anou- o RN 198-199 C 4
Aragoiânia o BR 72-73 F 4
Aragón ◻ E 98-99 G 4
Aragon o USA (NM) 256-257 G 5
Aragón, Río ~ E 98-99 G 3
Araguacema o BR 68-69 D 6
Araguaçu o BR 72-73 F 2
Araguaçui o BR 68-69 D 6
Aragua de Barcelona o YV 60-61 J 3
Aragua de Maturín o YV 60-61 K 3
Araguaia, Parque Indígena ✕ BR 68-69 C 7
Araguaia, Parque Nacional do ⊥ BR 68-69 C 7
Araguaia, Rio ~ BR 68-69 D 5
Araguaiana o BR 72-73 E 3
Araguaimujo, Caño ~ YV 60-61 L 3
Araguaina o BR 68-69 D 5
Araguanã o BR 68-69 D 5
Araguari o BR 72-73 F 5
Araguari, Rio ~ BR 62-63 J 5
Araguari, Rio ~ BR 72-73 F 5
Araguatins o BR 68-69 D 4
Arahal o E 98-99 E 6
Arai o BR 72-73 G 2
Arai o J 152-153 H 6
Araias do Araguaia, Rio das ~ BR 68-69 C 6
Arail Khan ~ BD 142-143 G 4
Araioses o BR 68-69 H 3
Araju o BR 66-67 G 4
Arak o DZ 190-191 D 8
Arāk ☆ • IR 134-135 C 1
Arakaka o GUY 62-63 D 2
Arakamčečen, ostrov ⌒ RUS 112-113 Y 4
Arakan Yoma = Ragaing Yōma ▲ MYA 142-143 J 6
Arakawa o J 152-153 H 5
Arakawa-gawa ~ J 152-153 H 5
Araklı ☆ TR 128-129 J 2
Arak's ~ AR 128-129 L 2
Aral ☆ KA 126-127 O 4
Aral o KS 146-147 B 5
Ara Lake ⊙ CDN (ONT) 234-235 Q 4
Aralık ☆ TR 128-129 L 3
Aral karakůmy ∸ KA 126-127 P 4
Aralköl o KA 124-125 C 3
Aralkům o KA 126-127 P 4
Aral Moreira o BR 76-77 K 2
Aral Sea ⊙ 126-127 N 5
Aral'sk ☆ KA 126-127 O 4
Aralsor, köl ⊙ KA (ZPK) 96-97 H 9
Aralsor, köl ⊙ KA (ZPK) 96-97 F 9
Aralsul'fat o KA 126-127 O 4
Araltöbe o KA 96-97 H 8
Aramac o AUS 178-179 H 2
Aramaca, Ilha ⌒ BR 66-67 C 5
Arame o BR 68-69 E 4
Aramia River ~ PNG 183 B 4
Aramil' o RUS 96-97 M 5
Ārān o IR 134-135 D 1
Arancay o PE 64-65 D 6
Aranda de Duero o E 98-99 F 4
Arandai o RI 166-167 G 3
Arandas o MEX 52-53 C 1
Arandis o NAM 216-217 C 11
Arani o BOL 70-71 E 5
Ārani o IND 140-141 H 4
Aran Islands ⌒ • IRL 90-91 C 5
Aranjuez o E 98-99 F 4
Aranos o NAM 220-221 D 2
Aransas Bay ≈ USA 266-267 K 6
Aransas National Wildlife Refuge ⊥ USA (TX) 266-267 L 5
Aransas Pass o USA (TX) 266-267 K 6
Aransas River ~ USA (TX) 266-267 K 5
Arantangi o IND 140-141 H 5
Arantes, Ribeiro ~ BR 72-73 E 5
Aranyaprathet o THA 158-159 G 4
Araouane o RMM 196-197 J 5
Aráoz o RA 76-77 E 4
Arapa o PE 70-71 B 4
Arapa, Lago de ⊙ PE 70-71 B 4
Arapahoe o USA (NE) 262-263 G 4
Arapari o BR (AMA) 66-67 D 4
Arapari o BR (P) 68-69 D 4
Arapey Grande, Río ~ ROU 76-77 J 6
Arapho o USA (OK) 264-265 F 3
Arapicos o EC 64-65 D 2
Arapiraca o BR 68-69 K 6
Arapiri, Ilha do ⌒ BR 66-67 K 4
Arapiuns, Rio ~ BR 66-67 K 4
Arapixi o BR 66-67 D 7
Arapixuna o BR 66-67 K 4
Arapkir ☆ TR 128-129 H 3
Arapongas o BR 72-73 E 7
Arapunya o AUS 178-179 C 2
Araputanga o BR 70-71 H 4
Araquaia, Rio ~ BR 68-69 D 6
'Ar'ar ☆ KSA 130-131 G 2
'Ar'ar, Wādī ~ KSA 130-131 G 2
Arara, Área Indígena ✕ BR 66-67 K 5
Arara, Paraná ~ BR 66-67 G 4
Araracuara o CO 64-65 F 2
Arara Igarapé Humaitá, Área Indígena ✕ BR 64-65 F 6
Araranguá o BR 74-75 F 7
Ararapira o BR 74-75 F 5
Araraquara o BR 72-73 F 6
Araras o BR (P) 66-67 K 6
Araras o BR (PAU) 72-73 G 7
Araras, Cachoeira ~ BR 66-67 K 6
Araras, Ilha das ⌒ BR 66-67 G 5
Araras, Serra das ▲ BR 70-71 J 4
Ararat o AR 128-129 L 3
Ararat o AUS 180-181 G 4
Araraú o BR 68-69 H 3
Ararenda o BR 68-69 H 4
Arari o BR 68-69 F 3
Araria o IND 142-143 E 2
Araribóia, Área Indígena ✕ BR 68-69 E 4
Araripe o BR 68-69 H 5
Araripina o BR 68-69 H 5
Araruama o BR 72-73 J 7
Araruama, Lagoa ⊙ BR 72-73 J 7
Aras, Rūd-e ~ IR 128-129 M 3
Arasālu o IND 140-141 F 4
Aras Nehri ~ TR 128-129 J 3
Aras Nehri ~ TR 128-129 K 2
Aratabiteri o YV 66-67 E 2
Aratale o ER 200-201 K 5
Araṭāne < RIM 196-197 F 5
Ara Terra o ETH 208-209 E 5
Arati o BR 66-67 F 3
Araticu, Rio ~ BR 68-69 D 3
Araua, Rio ~ BR 66-67 F 7
Arauá, Rio ~ BR 66-67 E 5
Arauá, Rio ~ BR 66-67 G 6
Arauca ☆ CO 60-61 F 4
Arauca, Rio ~ YV 60-61 H 4
Araucária o BR 74-75 F 5
Arauco o RCH 78-79 C 4
Arauco, Golfo de ≈ 78-79 C 4
Araure o YV 60-61 G 3
'Arava, ha ∸ IL 130-131 D 2
Aravaipa o USA (AZ) 256-257 E 6
Aravaipa Creek ~ USA (AZ) 256-257 E 6
Arāvalli Range ▲ IND 138-139 D 7
Aravan o KS 136-137 N 4
Aravete o EST 94-95 J 2
Arawa ☆ PNG 184 I b 2
Arawale National Reserve ⊥ EAK 212-213 H 4
Arawe Islands ⌒ PNG 183 E 4
Araweté Igarapé Ipixuna, Área Indígena ✕ BR 68-69 B 4
Araxá o BR 72-73 G 5
Araya o YV 60-61 J 2
Araya, Península de ⌣ YV 60-61 J 2
Arayé, Wādi ~ TCH 192-193 G 6
Araz ~ AZ 128-129 N 3
Arazraz, Oued ~ DZ 190-191 E 9
Arbadin < SP 212-213 J 3
Arbakwe o WAN 198-199 B 6
Arba Minch ☆ ETH 208-209 C 6
'Arbat o IRQ 128-129 L 5
Arbatax o • I 100-101 B 5
Arbat Dāġ ▲ IR 128-129 M 4
Arbau o RI 166-167 F 4
Arbi ~ RUS 118-119 N 9
Arbil ◻ IRQ 128-129 K 4
Arbil ☆ IRQ (ARB) 128-129 L 4
Arboga ☆ • S 86-87 G 7
Arbolé o BF 202-203 J 3
Arboledas o CO 60-61 E 4
Arboledas o RA 78-79 J 4
Arboletes o CO 60-61 C 3
Arbor o ZA 220-221 J 3
Arborfield o CDN (SAS) 232-233 P 2
Arborg o CDN (MAN) 234-235 F 4
Arboutchatak o TCH 198-199 H 6
Arbre du Ténéré • RN 198-199 D 4
Arbroath o GB 90-91 F 3
Arbuckle o USA (CA) 246-247 C 4
Arbutla ~ RUS 120-121 Q 3
Arc, Des o USA (AR) 276-277 D 6
Arcabuco o CO 60-61 E 5
Arcachon o F 90-91 G 9
Arcade o USA (NY) 278-279 C 6
Arcadia o USA (FL) 286-287 H 4
Arcadia o USA (IA) 274-275 C 2
Arcadia o USA (LA) 268-269 H 4
Arcadia o USA (MI) 272-273 C 3
Arcadia o USA (NE) 262-263 G 3
Arcadia o USA (WI) 270-271 G 6
Arčagly-Ajat ~ RUS 124-125 B 2
Arcahaie o RH 54-55 J 5
Arcaly ~ KA 124-125 F 2
Arcángelo, Monte ▲ I 100-101 E 4
Arcas, Quebradas de ~ RCH 76-77 C 1
Arcata o USA (CA) 246-247 A 3
Arcelia o MEX 52-53 D 2
Arc-et-Senans o ••• F 90-91 K 8
Arch o USA (NM) 256-257 M 4
Arch Cape o USA (OR) 244-245 B 5
Archdale o USA (NC) 282-283 H 5
Archei, Guelta d' • TCH 198-199 K 4
Archer o USA (FL) 286-287 G 2
Archer Bay ≈ 174-175 F 3
Archer Bend National Park ⊥ AUS 174-175 G 3
Archer City o USA (TX) 264-265 F 5
Archer Fiord ≈ 26-27 Q 3
Archer's Post o EAK 212-213 F 3
Archerwill o CDN (SAS) 232-233 P 3
Arches National Park ⊥ USA (UT) 254-255 F 5
Archie o USA (LA) 268-269 J 5
Archipelago of the Recherche ⌒ AUS 176-177 G 7
Archipel-de-Mingan, Réserve de Parc Nacional de L' ⊥ CDN (QUE) 242-243 E 2
Archipiélago de las Guaitecas, Parque Nacional ⊥ RCH 80 C 2
Archipiélago los Roques, Parque Nacional ⊥ •• YV 60-61 H 2
Archydal o CDN (SAS) 232-233 N 5
Arckaringa o AUS 178-179 C 4
Arckaringa Creek ~ AUS 178-179 C 4
Arčman o TM 136-137 E 5
Arco o USA (ID) 252-253 E 3
Arco, El o MEX 50-51 C 3
Arco, Paso del ▲ RA 78-79 D 5
Arcola o CDN (SAS) 232-233 Q 6
Arcola o USA (IL) 274-275 K 5
Arcola o USA (MS) 268-269 K 3
Arcos o BR 72-73 H 6
Arcos de la Frontera o E 98-99 E 6
Arcoverde o BR 68-69 K 6
Arctic Bay o CDN 24-25 d 4
Arctic Circle 16 C 4
Arctic Circle Hot Springs • USA 20-21 S 4
Arctic Harbour ≈ 28-29 G 2
Arctic Institute Range ▲ ARK 16 F 16
Arctic Ocean ≈ 16 B 33
Arctic Red River ~ CDN 20-21 Z 4
Arcturus o ZW 218-219 F 3
Arcyz ☆ UA 102-103 F 5
Ardabil o • IR 128-129 N 3
Ardahan o • TR 128-129 K 2
Ardakān o IR 134-135 E 2
Ardakan o IR 134-135 D 3
Ardal o IR 134-135 D 3
Ardanuç o TR 128-129 K 2
Ardath o CDN (SAS) 232-233 L 4
Ardatov o RUS 94-95 S 4
Ardavidu o IND 140-141 H 3
Ardbeg o CDN (ONT) 238-239 E 3
Ardébé, Ati o TCH 198-199 H 6
Ardee = Baile Átha Fhirdhia o IRL 90-91 D 5
Ardémi o TCH 198-199 L 5
Arden o USA (TX) 266-267 G 2
Arden o USA (WA) 244-245 H 2
Arden, Mount ▲ AUS 180-181 D 2
Ardencaple Fjord ≈ 26-27 p 6
Ardennes ▲ B 92-93 H 4
Ardenode o CDN (ALB) 232-233 E 4
Ardenvoir o USA (WA) 244-245 E 3
Ardeşen ☆ TR 128-129 J 2
Ardestān o • IR 134-135 E 2
Ardila, Ribeira de ~ P 98-99 D 5
Ardila, Río ~ E 98-99 D 5
Ardiles o RA 76-77 E 4
Ardill o CDN (SAS) 232-233 N 6
Ardilla, Cerro La ▲ MEX 50-51 H 6
Ardiṭ o OM 132-133 K 5
Ardlethan o AUS 180-181 J 3
Ard Mhacha = Armagh ☆ • GB 90-91 D 4
Ardmore o AUS 178-179 E 1
Ardmore o USA (AL) 284-285 D 2
Ardmore o USA (OK) 264-265 G 4
Ardmore o USA (SD) 260-261 C 3
Ardon o RUS 126-127 F 6
Ardon ~ RUS 126-127 F 6
Ardrossan o AUS 180-181 D 3
Ardrossan o CDN (ALB) 232-233 E 2
Ardrossan o GB 90-91 E 4
Åre o • S 86-87 F 5
Arebi o ZRE 212-213 B 2
Arecibo o USA (PR) 286-287 P 2
Areco, Río ~ RA 78-79 K 3
Aredo o RI 166-167 G 3
Aregičinskij, mys ▲ RUS 120-121 Q 3
Areia, Cachoeira d' ~ BR 68-69 F 6
Areia, Ribeira da ~ BR 72-73 H 3
Areia Branca o BR 68-69 K 4
Areias, Rio ~ BR 68-69 D 7
Areka o ETH 208-209 C 5
Arelee o CDN (SAS) 232-233 L 3
Arena, Isla ⌒ MEX 50-51 C 4
Arena, La o RCH 78-79 C 6
Arena, Point o USA (CA) 246-247 B 5
Arena, Point ▲ USA (CA) 246-247 B 5
Arenal, Volcán ▲ CR 52-53 B 6
Arenales o RCH 76-77 D 2
Arenales, Cerro ▲ RCH 80 D 3
Arena Point ▲ RP 160-161 E 6
Arenápolis o BR 70-71 J 4
Arenas o PA 52-53 D 8
Arenas, Punta de ▲ RCH 76-77 B 1
Arenas, Punta de ▲ RA 80 F 6
Arendal ☆ N 86-87 D 7
Arenillas o EC 64-65 B 3
Arenosa o PA 52-53 E 7
Areo o YV 60-61 K 3
Areópoli o GR 100-101 J 6
Areôs, Área Indígena ✕ BR 72-73 D 3
Arequipa ☆ • PE 70-71 B 5
Arêro o ETH 208-209 D 6
Arerunguа, Arroyo ~ ROU 76-77 J 6
Arestruz, Pampa del ∸ RCH 76-77 C 1
Arévalo o E 98-99 E 4
Áreza o ER 200-201 J 5
Arezzo o I 100-101 C 3
Arfersiorfik ≈ 28-29 O 2
'Arġa o KSA 130-131 J 5
Argada ~ RUS 118-119 E 8
Argadargada o AUS 178-179 D 1
Argahtah o RUS 110-111 d 5
Argajaš ☆ RUS 96-97 M 6
Arga Jurjah ~ RUS 110-111 c 5
Arga-Jurjah ~ RUS 110-111 S 5
Argalant o MAU 148-149 G 4
Argalasti o GR 100-101 J 5
Arga-Muora-Sise, ostrov ⌒ RUS 110-111 P 3
Argan o VRC 146-147 J 5
Arganda o E 98-99 F 4
Arġandāb, Daryā-ye ~ AFG 134-135 M 2
Argao o RP 160-161 E 8
Argas o RUS 118-119 N 4
Arga Sala ~ RUS 110-111 F 5
Arga-Sala ~ RUS 116-117 M 2
Arga-Tjung ~ RUS 110-111 K 6
Argaybulak Daban ▲ VRC 146-147 J 4
Argazinskoe vodohranilišče < RUS 96-97 M 6
Argedeb o ETH 208-209 E 5
Argelia o CO 60-61 C 6
Argent, Côte d' ⌣ F 90-91 G 10
Argenta o I 100-101 C 2
Argentan o F 90-91 G 7
Argentia o CDN (NFL) 242-243 P 5
Argentina ▪ RA 76-77 F 5
Argentina ■ RA 78-79 K 4
Argentina, La o CO 60-61 C 6
Argentina, Laguna la ⊙ RA 78-79 L 4
Argentina, Puna de ∸ RA 76-77 C 4
Argentine Rise ≃ 6-7 D 13
Argentine Abyssal Plain ≃ 6-7 D 13
Argentine Basin ≃ 6-7 D 13
Argentine Islands o ARK 16 G 30
Argentino, Lago ⊙ RA 80 D 5
Argentino, Mar ≈ 80 H 5
Argentino, Paso ▲ RA 78-79 E 2
Argenton-sur-Creuse o F 90-91 H 8
Argeş ~ RO 102-103 E 5
Argestān o AFG 134-135 M 3
Argestān Rūd ~ AFG 134-135 M 3
Argi ~ RUS 120-121 C 6
Argo o USA (LA) 268-269 J 5
Argoim o BR 72-73 L 2
Argolão, Cachoeira do ~ BR 66-67 K 4
Argolikos Kólpos ≈ 100-101 J 6
Argonne o USA (WI) 270-271 K 5
Argopyro, Gunung ▲ RI 168 E 3
Árgos o • GR 100-101 J 6
Argos o USA (IN) 274-275 M 3
Árgos Orestikó o GR 100-101 H 4
Argostóli o GR 100-101 H 5
Arguello, Point ▲ USA (CA) 248-249 D 5
Arguelo Canyon ≃ 248-249 C 5
Argun o RUS (CEC) 126-127 F 6
Argun' ~ RUS 118-119 J 11
Argun' ~ RUS 118-119 K 10
Argun ~ RUS 126-127 F 6
Argungu o WAN 198-199 B 6
Arguut o MAU 148-149 F 5
Arguvan ☆ TR 128-129 H 3
Arguyartu Point ▲ CDN 28-29 G 2
Argyle o CDN (MAN) 234-235 F 4
Argyle o USA (WI) 274-275 J 2
Argyle, Lake ⊙ AUS 172-173 J 4
Arhangaj ◻ MAU 148-149 D 4
Arhangel'sk ☆ RUS 88-89 Q 4
Arhangel'skoe ☆ RUS 96-97 K 6
Arhanzel'skaja Guba o RUS 108-109 H 4
Arhara o RUS 122-123 D 4
Arhara ~ RUS 122-123 D 4
Arhavi o TR 128-129 J 2
arheologičeskij zapovednik Tanais • RUS 102-103 L 4
Arhipelag Sedova ⌒ RUS 108-109 Y 2
Arhipovka o RUS 94-95 M 4
Ar Horqin Qi o VRC 150-151 C 6
Århus o DK 86-87 E 8
Ariadnoe o RUS 122-123 F 6
Ariake-kai ≈ 152-153 D 8
Ariamsvlei o NAM 220-221 D 4
Ariano Irpino o I 100-101 E 4
Ariari, Río ~ CO 60-61 E 6
Aria River ~ PNG 183 E 3
Arias o RA 78-79 H 2
Ari Atoll ⌒ MV 140-141 B 6
Aribinda o • BF 202-203 K 2
Arica o RCH 70-71 B 6
Aricapampa o PE 64-65 D 5
Aricaria o BR 68-69 B 3
Arichat o CDN (NS) 240-241 O 5
Arichuna o YV 60-61 H 4
Aricota, Lago ⊙ PE 70-71 B 5
Arid, Cape ▲ AUS 176-177 G 7
Arida o J 152-153 F 7
'Arīda o OM 132-133 H 5
'Ariḍa, al- o KSA 132-133 C 5
Aridéa o GR 100-101 J 4
Ariège ~ F 90-91 H 10
Ariel o RA 78-79 K 4
Ārifwāla o PK 138-139 D 4
Arig gol ~ MAU 148-149 E 2
Ariḥā ☆ •• AUT 130-131 D 2
Arinhanha, Rio ~ BR 72-73 D 4
Arikaree River ~ USA (CO) 254-255 N 4
Arikawa o J 152-153 C 8
Arikok, National Reservaat ⊥ ARU 60-61 G 1
Arima o • TT 60-61 L 2
Arimao ~ C 54-55 E 3
Arimo o USA (ID) 252-253 F 4
Arimu Mine o GUY 62-63 E 2
Arinos o BR 72-73 G 3
Arinos, Rio ~ BR 70-71 J 3
Ariogala o LT 94-95 H 4
Aripeka o USA (FL) 286-287 G 3
Ariporo, Río ~ CO 60-61 F 4
Aripuanã o BR 66-67 H 7
Aripuanã, Área Indígena ✕ BR 70-71 H 2
Aripuanã, Parque Indígena ✕ BR 70-71 G 2
Aripuanã, Rio ~ BR 66-67 G 6
Ariquemes o BR 66-67 F 7
Ariranha o BR 68-69 H 5
Aris o NAM 216-217 D 11
Arish, El o AUS 174-175 J 5
Arismendi o YV 60-61 G 3
Arissa o ETH 208-209 E 3
Aristazabal Island ⌒ CDN (BC) 228-229 E 4
Aristizábal, Cabo ▲ RA 80 G 2
Aristoménis o GR 100-101 J 6
Aritao o RP 160-161 D 4
Arite o SOL 184 I e 4
Ariton o USA (AL) 284-285 E 5
Arivaca o USA (AZ) 256-257 D 7
Arivaca Junction o USA (AZ) 256-257 D 7
Arivonimamo o RM 222-223 E 7
Ariyadka o IND 140-141 F 4
Ariyalur o IND 140-141 H 5
Ariza o E 98-99 F 4
Arizaro, Salar de ⊙ RA 76-77 D 3
Arizona o AUS (QLD) 174-175 F 6
Arizona o AUS (QLD) 178-179 F 1
Arizona o CDN (MAN) 234-235 E 5
Arizona o RA 78-79 F 3
Arizona ◻ USA (AZ) 256-257 B 3
Arizona City o USA (AZ) 256-257 D 6
Arizpe o MEX 50-51 D 2
Arjäng ☆ S 86-87 F 7
Arjawinangun o RI 168 C 3
Arjeplog o S 86-87 H 3
Arjo o ETH 208-209 C 4
Arjona o CO 60-61 D 2
Arjuna, Gunung ▲ RI 168 E 3
Arjuni o IND 142-143 B 5
Arka o RUS 120-121 K 3
Arka ~ RUS 120-121 J 3
Arkabutla Lake < USA (MS) 268-269 K 2
Arkadak o RUS 102-103 N 2
Arkadelphia o USA (AR) 276-277 B 6
Arkalgūd o IND 140-141 G 4
Arkalyk ☆ KA 124-125 E 3
Arkansas o USA (AR) 276-277 B 6
Arkansas City o USA (AR) 276-277 D 7
Arkansas City o USA (KS) 262-263 K 7
Arkansas Post National Memorial • USA (AR) 276-277 D 6
Arkansas River ~ USA (AR) 276-277 D 6
Arkansas River ~ USA (CO) 254-255 J 4
Arkansas River ~ USA (KS) 262-263 E 7
Arkansas River ~ USA (OK) 264-265 J 3
Arka-Pojlovajaha ~ RUS 108-109 Q 8
Arkaroola Village o AUS 178-179 E 6
Arka-Tab"jaha ~ RUS 108-109 Q 8
Arkatag ▲ VRC 144-145 F 2
Arkell, Mount ▲ CDN 20-21 X 6

Arkhangel'sk = Arhangel'sk ☆ RUS 88-89 Q 4
Arklow = An tInbhear Mór ○ IRL 90-91 D 5
Arknu, Jabal ▲ LAR 192-193 L 6
Arkona, Kap ▲ • D 92-93 M 1
Arkonam ○ IND 140-141 H 4
Arktičeskij, mys ▲ RUS 108-109 b 1
Arktičeskogo instituta, ostrova ⌒ RUS 108-109 T 4
Arktik Hoyland ⩡ GRØ 26-27 R 5
Arlal ○ RMM 196-197 J 6
Arlan, gora ▲ TM 136-137 D 5
Arlanza, Río ∼ E 98-99 F 3
Arlanzón ○ E 98-99 F 3
Arlanzón, Río ∼ E 98-99 F 3
Arlee ○ USA (MT) 250-251 E 4
Arles ○ ••• F 90-91 K 10
Arli ○ BF 202-203 L 4
Arli, Parc National de l' ⊥ BF 202-203 L 4
Arli, Réserve de l' ⊥ BF 202-203 L 4
Arlington ○ USA (AZ) 256-257 C 5
Arlington ○ USA (GA) 284-285 F 5
Arlington ○ USA (KS) 262-263 H 7
Arlington ○ USA (NE) 262-263 K 3
Arlington ○ USA (OH) 280-281 C 3
Arlington ○ USA (OR) 244-245 E 5
Arlington ○ USA (SD) 260-261 J 2
Arlington ○ USA (TN) 276-277 F 5
Arlington ○ USA (TX) 264-265 G 6
Arlington ○ USA (VA) 280-281 J 5
Arlington ○ USA (VT) 278-279 H 5
Arlington ○ USA (WA) 244-245 C 2
Arlington ○ ZA 220-221 H 4
Arlit ○ RN 198-199 C 3
Arlon ☆ • B 92-93 H 4
Arltunga ○ • AUS 178-179 C 2
'Armā' ⩡ KSA 130-131 K 5
Arma ○ USA (KS) 262-263 M 7
Armacão dos Búzios ○ BR 72-73 K 7
Armagh ☆ • GB 90-91 D 4
Armagnac ⩡ F 90-91 H 10
Arma Konda ▲ IND 142-143 C 6
Arman' ○ RUS 120-121 O 4
Arman' ∼ RUS 120-121 O 3
Armanda ○ BR 74-75 D 8
Armando Bermúdes, Parque Nacional ⊥ DOM 54-55 K 5
Armant ○ • ET 194-195 F 5
Armark Lake ○ CDN 30-31 T 2
Armark River ∼ CDN 30-31 T 2
Armas, Las ○ RA 78-79 L 4
Armavir ○ RUS 126-127 D 5
Armavir ○ RUS (STV) 102-103 M 5
Armenia ☆ CO 60-61 D 5
Armenia = Armenija ⩡ 128-129 J 3
Armenia = Armenija ■ AR 128-129 L 2
Armeria ○ MEX 52-53 C 2
Armero ○ CO 60-61 D 5
Armidale ○ AUS 178-179 L 6
Armil Lake ○ CDN 30-31 Y 3
Arminavallen ∼ SME 62-63 G 3
Arminto ○ USA (WY) 252-253 L 3
Armit ○ CDN (SAS) 232-233 R 3
Armitidž, poluostrov ⌣ RUS 84-85 a 2
Armit Range ⩓ PNG 183 C 4
Armjans'k ○ UA 102-103 H 4
Armley ○ CDN (SAS) 232-233 O 2
Armour ○ USA (SD) 260-261 H 3
Armraynald ○ AUS 174-175 E 5
Arm River ∼ CDN (SAS) 232-233 N 5
Armstrong ○ CDN (BC) 230-231 K 3
Armstrong ○ CDN (ONT) 234-235 O 4
Armstrong ○ CDN (QUE) 240-241 E 5
Armstrong ○ USA (IA) 274-275 D 1
Armstrong ○ USA (IL) 274-275 L 4
Armstrong ○ USA (TX) 266-267 K 7
Armstrong Creek ○ USA (WI) 270-271 K 5
Armstrong River ∼ AUS 172-173 K 4
Ārmūr ○ IND 138-139 G 10
Arnaud ○ CDN (MAN) 234-235 F 5
Arnaud (Payne), Rivière ∼ CDN 36-37 O 4
Arnaudville ○ USA (LA) 268-269 J 6
Arnedo ○ E 98-99 F 3
Arneiroz ○ BR 68-69 H 5
Arneson ○ CDN (ALB) 232-233 H 4
Arnett ○ USA (OK) 264-265 E 2
Arnhem ☆ • NL 92-93 H 2
Arnhem, Cape ▲ AUS 174-175 D 3
Arnhem Aboriginal Land ⩡ AUS 174-175 B 3
Arnhem Bay ≈ 174-175 D 3
Arnhem Highway II AUS 172-173 K 2
Arnhem Land ⩡ AUS 174-175 B 3
Arno ∼ I 100-101 C 3
Arno Bay ○ AUS 180-181 D 2
Arnold ○ USA (CA) 246-247 E 5
Arnold ○ USA (MI) 270-271 L 4
Arnold ○ USA (MO) 274-275 H 6
Arnold ○ USA (NE) 262-263 F 3
Arnold River ∼ AUS 174-175 C 5
Arnoldsburg ○ USA (WV) 280-281 E 5
Arnold's Cove ○ CDN (NFL) 242-243 P 5
Arnott Strait ≈ 24-25 U 2
Arnøy ⌒ N 86-87 K 1
Arnprior ○ CDN (ONT) 238-239 J 3
Arnsberg ○ • D 92-93 K 3
Arnstadt ○ • D 92-93 L 3
Arntfield ○ CDN (QUE) 236-237 J 4
Aro, Río ∼ YV 60-61 J 4
Aroa ○ YV 60-61 G 2
Aroab ○ NAM 220-221 D 3
Arochuku ○ WAN 204-205 G 6
Aroeiras ○ BR 68-69 L 5
Arokam, Oued ∼ DZ 190-191 G 9
Aroland ○ CDN (ONT) 236-237 B 2
Arolik River ∼ USA 22-23 Q 3
Aroma ○ PNG 183 E 6
Aroma ○ RCH 70-71 C 6
Aroma ○ SUD 200-201 H 5
Aroma, Quebrada de ∼ RCH 70-71 C 6
Aroona ○ AUS 178-179 E 6
Aroostock River ∼ USA (ME) 278-279 N 2
Aropa ○ PNG 184 I b 2
Aropuk Lake ○ USA 20-21 H 6
Arorae ⌒ KIB 13 J 3
Aroroy ○ RP 160-161 E 6
Aro Usu, Tanjung ▲ RI 166-167 F 6
Arpa Çayı ∼ TR 128-129 K 2
Arpajon ○ F 90-91 J 7
Arpangasia ∼ BD 142-143 F 4
Arpin ○ CDN (ONT) 236-237 H 4
Arpoador, Ponta do ▲ BR 74-75 G 5
Arq. T. Romero Pereira ○ PY 76-77 K 4
Arqū ○ SUD 200-201 E 3
Arque, Río ∼ BOL 70-71 D 5
Arra ∼ PK 134-135 L 5
ar-Rābi', ash-Shallāl = 4th Cataract ∼ SUD 200-201 F 3
Ar-Rachidia ☆ MA 188-189 J 5
ar-Radd, Wādī ∼ SYR 128-129 J 4
ar-Radisiya Bahrī ○ ET 194-195 F 5
ar-Rafid ○ SYR 128-129 F 6
Arraga ○ RA 76-77 E 5
Arrah ○ CI 202-203 J 6
ar-Rahad ○ SUD 200-201 E 6
ar-Rahad ∼ SUD 200-201 G 6
Arraial do Cabo ○ BR 72-73 J 7
Arraias ○ BR (MAR) 68-69 E 4
Arraias ○ BR (TOC) 72-73 G 2
Arraias, Rio ∼ BR 68-69 A 7
Arraida ○ OM 132-133 J 5
Arran ○ CDN (SAS) 232-233 R 4
Arran ⌒ GB 90-91 E 4
Arrandale ○ CDN (BC) 228-229 E 2
ar-Rank ○ SUD 206-207 L 3
Ar Rāqūbah ○ LAR 192-193 H 3
Arras ○ CDN 32-33 K 4
Arras ☆ • F 90-91 J 6
Ar Rashidiyah = Ar Rachidia ☆ MA 188-189 J 5
ar-Rauda ○ ET 194-195 E 4
ar-Rawdah = Ranya ○ KSA 132-133 C 3
ar-Rawdah, Sabhat ○ SYR 128-129 J 5
ar-Rawgal ○ SUD 200-201 G 3
Arrecife ○ E 188-189 E 6
Arrecifes ○ RA 78-79 J 3
Arrecifes, Río ∼ RA 78-79 K 3
Arrecifes de la Media Luna ⌒ NIC 54-55 D 7
Arreti ○ PA 52-53 F 8
Arrey ○ USA (NM) 256-257 H 6
Arriaga ○ • MEX 52-53 H 3
Arrias, Las ○ RA 76-77 F 6
Arriba ○ USA (CO) 254-255 M 4
ar-Ribāt ☆ •• MA 188-189 H 4
Arrieros, Quebrada de los ∼ RCH 76-77 C 2
ar-Rif ⩓ MA 188-189 J 3
Arrigetch Peaks ▲ USA 20-21 N 3
Arrigui, Lac ○ • RN 198-199 F 3
ar-Rizqa ○ ET 194-195 F 4
Arroio dos Ratos ○ BR 74-75 E 8
Arroio Grande ○ BR 74-75 D 9
Arrojado, Rio ∼ BR 72-73 H 2
Arrojolândia ○ BR 72-73 H 2
Arros Island, D' ⌒ SY 224 C 2
Arrowhead, Lake < USA (TX) 264-265 F 5
Arrowhead Lodge ○ USA (WY) 252-253 L 2
Arrowhead River ∼ CDN 30-31 H 5
Arrowie ○ AUS 178-179 E 6
Arrow River ○ CDN (MAN) 234-235 C 4
Arrow Rock ○ USA (MO) 274-275 F 5
Arrowrock Reservoir ○ USA (ID) 252-253 C 3
Arrow Rock State Historic Site ∴ USA (MO) 274-275 F 5
Arrowsmith, Mount ▲ CDN (BC) 230-231 F 4
Arrowsmith River ∼ CDN 30-31 Y 2
Arrowwood ○ CDN (ALB) 232-233 E 5
Arrowwood Lake ○ USA (ND) 258-259 J 4
Arroyito ○ RA (COD) 76-77 F 6
Arroyito ○ RA (MEN) 78-79 F 2
Arroyo Bueno ○ C 54-55 H 4
Arroyo de la Ventana ○ RA 78-79 F 6
Arroyo de los Huesos ○ RA 78-79 K 4
Arroyo Grande ○ USA (CA) 248-249 D 4
Arroyo Hondo ○ USA (NM) 256-257 K 2
Arroyos de Mantua ○ C 54-55 C 3
Arroyos Esteros ○ PY 76-77 J 3
Arrozal ○ YV 60-61 K 3
ar-Ru'at ○ SUD 200-201 F 6
Ar Ru'ays, Wādī ∼ LAR 192-193 G 4
Arrufó ○ RA 76-77 G 6
ar-Ruṣayriṣ ○ SUD 208-209 B 3
Arsameia • TR 128-129 H 4
Arsan ○ RUS 116-117 J 9
Arsenault Lake ○ CDN 32-33 Q 4
Arsen'ev ○ RUS 122-123 E 6
Arsen'evka ∼ RUS 122-123 E 7
Arsenǧān ○ IR 134-135 E 4
Arsent'evka ○ RUS 122-123 K 5
Ārsī ◘ ETH 208-209 D 5
Arsikeri ○ IND 140-141 G 4
Arsk ☆ RUS 96-97 F 5
Arso ○ RI 166-167 L 3
Arsuk ○ GRØ 28-29 Q 6
Arta ○ DJI 208-209 F 3
Árta ○ GR 100-101 H 5
Artas ○ USA (SD) 260-261 G 1
Artašat ○ AR 128-129 L 3
Artawi, al- ○ KSA 130-131 J 5
Artāwiya, al- ○ KSA 130-131 J 4
Arteaga ○ MEX (COA) 50-51 J 5
Arteaga ○ MEX (MIC) 52-53 C 2
Arteaga ○ RA 78-79 J 2
Artem ○ RUS 122-123 E 7
Artemisa ○ C 54-55 D 3
Artemivs'k ○ UA 102-103 L 3
Artem-Ostrov ○ AZ 128-129 O 2
Artemou ○ RIM 196-197 D 7
Artëmovsk ○ RUS 116-117 F 8
Artemovsk = Artemivs'k ○ UA 102-103 L 3
Artëmovskij ☆ RUS 96-97 M 5
Artesia ○ USA (NM) 256-257 L 6
Artesian ○ USA (SD) 260-261 J 2
Artesian Bore Baths • AUS 178-179 K 5
Artesia Wells ○ USA (TX) 266-267 H 5
Artezian ○ RUS 126-127 G 5
Arthur ○ CDN (ONT) 238-239 E 5
Arthur ○ USA (ND) 258-259 K 4
Arthur ○ USA (NE) 262-263 E 3
Arthur, Port ○ AUS 180-181 J 7
Arthur City ○ USA (TX) 264-265 J 5
Arthurette ○ CDN (NB) 240-241 H 4
Arthur Point ▲ AUS 178-179 L 2
Arthur River ○ AUS 176-177 D 6
Arthur's Pass ○ NZ 182 C 5
Arthur's Pass ▲ NZ 182 C 5
Arthur's Pass National Park ⊥ NZ 182 C 5
Arthur's Town ○ BS 54-55 H 2
Arti ☆ RUS 96-97 L 5
Artic ○ USA (OR) 244-245 B 4
Artic National Wildlife Refuge ⊥ USA 20-21 R 2
Artic Red River ○ CDN (NWT) 20-21 Y 3
Artic Red River ∼ CDN 20-21 Y 3
Artic Village ○ USA 20-21 S 2
Artigas ☆ ROU 76-77 J 6
Artik ○ AR 128-129 K 2
Artillery Lake ○ CDN 30-31 Q 4
Artjugina ∼ RUS 114-115 T 3
Artland ○ CDN (SAS) 232-233 J 3
Artois ⩡ F 90-91 H 6
Artur, ostrov ⌒ RUS 84-85 b 2
Arturo Prat ○ ARK 16 G 30
Artux ○ VRC 146-147 C 6
Artvin ☆ TR 128-129 J 2
Artybaš ○ RUS 124-125 P 3
Artyk ○ RUS 110-111 Z 7
Artyk ∼ RUS 110-111 a 7
Artyk ○ TM 136-137 F 6
Artyšta ○ RUS 124-125 P 1
Aru ○ BR (AMA) 66-67 D 2
Aru ○ BR (P) 68-69 D 3
Aru ○ IND 138-139 E 2
Aru ○ ZRE 212-213 C 2
Aru, Kepulauan ⩡ RI 166-167 H 5
Aru, Tanjung ▲ RI 164-165 E 5
Arua ☆ EAU 212-213 C 2
Aruã, Rio ∼ BR 66-67 J 4
Aruanã ○ BR 72-73 E 3
Aruba ◘ ARU 60-61 G 1
Aruba Lodge ○ EAK 212-213 G 5
Arufi ○ PNG 183 A 5
Arufu ○ WAN 204-205 H 5
Aruja ○ BR 72-73 G 7
Aruliho ○ SOL 184 I d 3
Arumã ○ BR 66-67 F 5
Arumã, Rio ∼ BR 66-67 E 4
Arumbi ○ ZRE 212-213 C 2
Ārumuganeri ○ IND 140-141 H 6
Arun ∼ NEP 144-145 F 7
Arunāchal Pradesh ◘ IND 142-143 H 1
Arundel ○ CDN (QUE) 238-239 L 3
Arundel = Kohinggo ⌒ SOL 184 I c 3
Arun Qi ○ VRC 150-151 D 3
Arupukkottai ○ IND 140-141 H 6
Aruri, Rio ∼ BR 66-67 K 5
Aruri, Selat ≈ 166-167 H 2
Arus, Tanjung ▲ RI 164-165 G 3
Arusha ◘ EAT 212-213 E 5
Arusha ☆ • EAT (ARU) 212-213 F 5
Arusha Chini ○ EAT 212-213 F 5
Arusha National Park ⊥ EAT 212-213 F 5
Aruti ○ BR 66-67 D 3
Aruwimi ∼ ZRE 210-211 L 3
Arvada ○ USA (CO) 254-255 K 4
Arvada ○ USA (WY) 252-253 M 2
Arvajhèèr ☆ MAU 148-149 F 4
Arvand Kenār ○ IR 134-135 C 4
Arvi ○ IND 138-139 G 9
Arvidsjaur ○ S 86-87 J 4
Arvika ☆ • S 86-87 F 7
Årviksand ○ N 86-87 K 1
Arvilla ○ USA (ND) 258-259 K 4
Arvorezinha ○ BR 74-75 D 7
Arwala ○ RI 166-167 D 5
Arwin ○ USA (CA) 248-249 F 4
Ary, Tit- ○ RUS (SAH) 110-111 Q 3
Ary, Tit- ○ RUS (SAH) 118-119 N 5
Arykbalı ○ RUS 118-119 M 4
Ary-Ongorbut ∼ RUS 110-111 M 4
Arys ○ KA 136-137 L 3
Arys' ○ KA 136-137 L 3
Arys ∼ KA 136-137 L 3
Arys, sor ○ KA 124-125 E 6
Arys-Turkistan kanal < KA 136-137 L 3
Arzamas ○ RUS 94-95 S 4
Arzana ⌒ UAE 134-135 E 6
Arzgir ○ RUS 126-127 F 5
Arzon ○ F 90-91 F 8
As ○ B 92-93 H 3
Aša ☆ RUS 96-97 K 6
Asa ∼ ZRE 206-207 G 6
Asab ○ NAM 220-221 D 2
Asaba ○ WAN 204-205 G 5
Asadābād ☆ • AFG 138-139 C 2
Asadābād ○ IR (HAM) 134-135 C 1
Asadābād ○ IR (HOR) 134-135 J 2
Asad Buhairat al- < SYR 128-129 H 4
Āsaga ○ WS 184 V a 1
Aşağı Pınarbaşı ○ TR 128-129 E 3
Asagny, Parc National d' ⊥ CI 202-203 H 7
Asahaha < EAK 212-213 H 2
Asahi ○ J 152-153 G 6
Asahi-dake ▲ J 152-153 K 3
Asahi-gawa ∼ J 152-153 E 7
Asahikawa ○ J 152-153 K 3
Āsalē ○ ETH 200-201 K 5
Asālem ○ IR 128-129 N 4
Asamankese ○ GH 202-203 K 7
Asambi ○ RI 168 E 6
Asankranguaa ○ GH 202-203 J 7
Asan Man ≈ 150-151 F 9
Asansol ○ IND 142-143 E 4
Āsār ○ IR 134-135 J 5
'Asara, al- ○ SYR 128-129 J 5
Asaro ○ PNG 183 C 4
Asaro River ∼ PNG 183 C 4
Asawinso ○ GH 202-203 J 6
Asayita ○ ETH 208-209 E 3
Asbesberge ⩓ ZA 220-221 F 4
Asbest ○ RUS 96-97 M 5
Asbestos ○ CDN (QUE) 238-239 O 3
Asbe Teferi ○ ETH 208-209 E 4
Asbury Park ○ USA (NJ) 280-281 M 3
Ascención ○ BOL 70-71 F 4
Ascención, Bahía de la ≈ MEX 52-53 L 2
Ascension ⌒ GB 202-203 B 7
Ascensión ○ MEX 50-51 F 2
Ascension Fracture Zone ⩳ 6-7 H 9
Aschaffenburg ○ D 92-93 K 4
Aschersleben ○ • D 92-93 L 3
Ascochinga ○ RA 76-77 E 6
Áscoli Piceno ☆ • I 100-101 D 3
Ascope ○ PE 64-65 C 5
Ascotán ○ RCH 76-77 C 1
Ascotán, Salar de ○ RCH 76-77 C 1
Ascunción ○ BOL 70-71 D 2
Aščykoľ, ozero ○ KA 136-137 M 3
Aščysu ∼ KA 124-125 L 4
Aščysu ∼ KA 124-125 J 3
Aščyšu ∼ KA 124-125 J 3
Aše ○ RUS 126-127 C 6
Āseb ○ ER 200-201 L 6
Asebot Terara ▲ ETH 208-209 E 4
Asedjrad ⩓ DZ 190-191 C 8
Asekeevo ☆ RUS 96-97 H 7
Aseki ○ PNG 183 D 4
As Ela ○ DJI 208-209 F 3
Āsela ☆ ETH 208-209 D 5
Åsele ○ • S 86-87 H 4
Asembagus ○ RI 168 B 6
Asembo ○ EAK 212-213 E 4
Asendabo ○ ETH 208-209 C 5
Asenovgrad ○ BG 102-103 D 6
Asera ○ RI 164-165 G 5
Asermanuevo ○ CO 60-61 D 5
Aserrado ○ YV 62-63 D 2
Asfi ☆ MA 188-189 G 4
Ašgabat ★ • TM 136-137 F 6
Åsgårdfonna ⊂ N 84-85 K 3
Ash ○ USA (NC) 282-283 J 6
Asha ○ WAN 204-205 E 5
Ašhabad = Ašgabat ★ TM 136-137 F 6
Āšhāne ○ IR 136-137 E 6
Ashangé Hayk' ○ ETH 200-201 J 6
Ashanti Region ◘ GH 202-203 J 6
Ašhara, al- ○ OM 132-133 L 3
Ashburn ○ USA (GA) 284-285 G 5
Ashburton ○ NZ 182 C 5
Ashburton Bay ≈ CDN 236-237 B 4
Ashburton Downs ○ AUS 176-177 D 1
Ashburton River ∼ AUS 172-173 B 7
Ashby ○ USA (NE) 262-263 E 2
Ashcroft ○ CDN (BC) 230-231 H 3
Ashdod ☆ IL 130-131 D 2
Ashdown ○ USA (AR) 276-277 A 7
Asheboro ○ USA (NC) 282-283 H 5
Asher ○ USA (OK) 264-265 H 4
Ashern ○ CDN (MAN) 234-235 E 3
Asherton ○ USA (TX) 266-267 H 5
Asheville ○ • USA (NC) 282-283 E 5
Asheweig River ∼ CDN 34-35 N 3
Ashewele ○ WAN 204-205 F 5
Ash Flat ○ USA (AR) 276-277 D 4
Ashford ○ AUS 178-179 L 5
Ashford ○ USA (AL) 284-285 E 5
Ashford Bird Park ⊥ • BDS 56 F 5
Ash Fork ○ USA (AZ) 256-257 C 3
Ashgabat = Ašgabat ★ • TM 136-137 F 6
Ashgrove ○ CDN (ONT) 238-239 F 5
Ashibetsu ○ J 152-153 K 3
Ashigashiya ○ WAN 204-205 K 3
Ashika ○ IND 142-143 D 6
Ashikaga ○ J 152-153 H 6
Ashiro ○ J 152-153 J 4
Ashizuri-misaki ▲ J 152-153 E 8
Ashizuri-Uwakai National Park ⊥ J 152-153 E 8
Ashkidah ○ LAR 192-193 F 4
Ashkum ○ USA (IL) 274-275 L 4
Ashland ○ USA (AL) 284-285 E 3
Ashland ○ USA (IL) 274-275 H 5
Ashland ○ USA (KS) 262-263 G 7
Ashland ○ USA (KY) 276-277 N 2
Ashland ○ USA (LA) 268-269 G 4
Ashland ○ USA (ME) 278-279 N 2
Ashland ○ USA (MO) 274-275 F 6
Ashland ○ USA (MS) 268-269 L 2
Ashland ○ USA (MT) 250-251 N 6
Ashland ○ USA (NE) 262-263 K 3
Ashland ○ USA (OH) 280-281 D 3
Ashland ○ USA (OK) 264-265 H 4
Ashland ○ USA (OR) 244-245 C 8
Ashland ○ USA (VA) 280-281 J 6
Ashland ○ USA (WI) 270-271 H 4
Ashland City ○ USA (TN) 276-277 H 4
Ashley ○ USA (IL) 274-275 J 6
Ashley ○ USA (ND) 258-259 H 5
Ashley ○ USA (OH) 280-281 D 3
Ash Meadows Rancho ○ USA (NV) 248-249 H 3
Ashmont ○ AUS 180-181 G 2
Ashmont ○ CDN 32-33 P 4
Ashmore Reef ⌒ AUS 172-173 F 2
Ashmore Reef ⌒ PNG 183 C 6
Ashokan Reservoir ○ USA (NY) 280-281 M 2
Ashoknagar ○ IND 138-139 F 7
Ashoro ○ J 152-153 K 3
Ashqelon ☆ • IL 130-131 D 2
Ashqelon, Tel ∴ • IL 130-131 C 2
Ash Shahwī, Bi'r < LAR 192-193 F 2
ash-Shallāl ath-Thālith = 3rd Cataract ∼ SUD 200-201 E 3
ash-Sharmah ○ SUD 200-201 G 5
Ash Shāṭī ◘ LAR 192-193 D 3
ash-Shawal ○ SUD 200-201 F 6
ash-Shlaydimah ○ LAR 192-193 J 2
Ash Shu'ban, Wādī ∼ LAR 192-193 K 2
Ash Shubayrimah, Wādī ∼ LAR 192-193 G 4
ash-Shuheit ∼ SUD 200-201 G 6
ash-Shurayk ○ SUD 200-201 F 3
Ash Springs ○ USA (NV) 248-249 J 3
Ashta ○ IND 138-139 F 8
Ashtabula ○ USA (OH) 280-281 F 2
Ashtabula, Lake ○ USA (ND) 258-259 J 4
Ashtola ○ USA (TX) 264-265 C 3
Ashton ○ USA (ID) 252-253 G 2
Ashton ○ USA (NE) 262-263 H 3
Ashton ○ USA (SD) 260-261 H 1
Ashton ○ ZA 220-221 E 6
Ashuanipi Lake ○ CDN 38-39 L 2
Ashville ○ CDN (MAN) 234-235 C 3
Ashville ○ USA (AL) 284-285 D 3
Ashville ○ USA (PA) 280-281 H 3
Ashwaraopet ○ IND 142-143 B 7
Ashwood ○ USA (OR) 244-245 E 6
Asia ○ PE 64-65 D 8
Asia, Estrecho ≈ 80 C 5
Asiak River ∼ CDN 30-31 N 2
Asid Gulf ≈ 160-161 E 6
Asientos, Los ○ PA 52-53 D 8
Asif Melloul ∼ MA 188-189 H 4
Asilah ○ • MA 188-189 H 3
Asile, L' ○ RH 54-55 J 5
Asillo ○ PE 70-71 B 4
Asinara, Golfo dell' ≈ 100-101 B 4
Asinara, Ísola ⌒ I 100-101 B 4
Asindonhopo ○ SME 62-63 G 4
Asi Nehri ∼ TR 128-129 G 4
Asino ☆ RUS 114-115 T 6
Asir ◘ KSA 132-133 C 4
'Asis, Ra's ▲ SUD 200-201 J 3
Aşkale ☆ TR 128-129 J 3
'Askarān ○ IR 134-135 D 2
Askarly ☆ KA 124-125 H 3
Askarovo ☆ RUS 96-97 L 7
Aškazar ○ IR 134-135 F 3
Askeaton ○ ZA 220-221 H 5
Asker ☆ N 86-87 E 7
Askersund ☆ • S 86-87 G 7
Askim ☆ N 86-87 E 7
Askino ☆ RUS 96-97 K 5
Askinuk Mountains ⩓ USA 20-21 H 6
Askira ○ WAN 204-205 K 3
Askiz ☆ RUS 116-117 E 9
Åsköping ○ S 86-87 H 7
Askot ○ IND 144-145 C 6
Askøy ○ N 86-87 B 6
Asla ○ DZ 188-189 L 4
Aşl-e Čahānsūr ○ AFG 134-135 K 3
Asler < RMM 196-197 L 5
Asmār ○ AFG 136-137 M 7
Āsmara ★ ER 200-201 J 5
Asmara, Wādī ∼ KSA 130-131 G 4
Asmat Woodcarvings ○ • RI 166-167 K 4
Āsmera = Āsmara ★ ER 200-201 J 5
Ašmjany ☆ BY 94-95 K 4
Asnāhra ○ IND 142-143 C 2
Asnet ○ TCH 198-199 J 6
Ásni ○ MA 188-189 H 5
Aso ○ J 152-153 D 8
Aso National Park ⊥ •• J 152-153 D 8
Asori ○ RI 166-167 J 4
Āsosa ○ ETH 208-209 B 3
Aso-san ⩞ J 152-153 D 8
Asoteriba, Ǧabal ▲ SUD 200-201 H 2
Aspāla ○ IND 142-143 B 7
Aspen ○ CDN (NS) 240-241 N 5
Aspen ○ USA (CO) 254-255 J 4
Aspen Cove ○ CDN (BC) 230-231 J 4
Aspendos •• TR 128-129 D 4
Aspen Mountain Ski Area • USA (CO) 254-255 J 4
Aspermont ○ USA (TX) 264-265 D 5
Aspiring, Mount ▲ NZ 182 B 6
Aspy Bay ≈ 38-39 O 5
Aspy Bay ≈ CDN 240-241 P 4
Asquith ○ CDN (SAS) 232-233 L 3
Asrama ○ RT 202-203 L 6
Asriko ○ CI 202-203 H 6
Assa ○ KA 134-137 M 3
Assa ∼ KA 136-137 M 3
Assa ○ MA 188-189 G 6
Assaba ◘ RIM 196-197 D 6
As Sab'ah, Qārat ▲ LAR 192-193 G 4
aš-Šabb < ET 194-195 D 6
as-Sablūkah, Shallāl = 6th Cataract ∼ SUD 200-201 F 4
Assadjene ▲ DZ 190-191 F 9
aş-Şaff ○ ET 194-195 E 3
'Assāfiya, al- ○ KSA 130-131 F 3
As Saghir, Bi'r < LAR 192-193 L 2
as-Sāhiliya, Ǧabal ⩓ SYR 128-129 G 5
Assahoun ○ RT 202-203 L 6
Assaí ○ BR 72-73 E 7
Assaikio ○ WAN 204-205 H 4
Assaka ○ MA 188-189 G 6
Assal, Lac ○ DJI 208-209 F 3
as-Salam, Bahr ∼ SUD 200-201 D 6
as-Sallūm ○ ET 192-193 L 2
as-Sallūm, Ḫalīǧ ≈ 192-193 L 2
Assam ◘ IND 142-143 H 2
aš-Šām, Ǧabal ▲ OM 132-133 K 2
Assamakka ○ RN 198-199 B 3
Assaouas ○ RN 198-199 C 4
Assaq, Oued ∼ MA 196-197 C 2
Assaré ○ BR 68-69 J 5
Assaria ○ USA (KS) 262-263 J 6
Assateague Islands National Seashore ⊥ USA (VA) 280-281 L 5
aš-Šaṭṭ ○ ET 194-195 F 3
As Sawdā', Jabal ⩓ LAR 192-193 F 3
As Sawdāyah ⩡ LAR 192-193 G 3
as-Sawirah ☆ • MA 188-189 G 5
Assdadah ○ LAR 192-193 F 2
Asse, River ∼ WAN 204-205 G 6
Assegai ∼ SD 220-221 K 3
Assegaon ○ IND 138-139 F 9
Assen ☆ NL 92-93 J 2
Assen ○ ZA 220-221 H 2
as-Sibā'i, Ǧabal ▲ ET 194-195 G 5
As Sibā'n ○ KSA 130-131 G 4
as-Sidr ○ ET 194-195 F 3
As Sidr ○ LAR 192-193 H 3
Assin Anyinabrim ○ GH 202-203 K 7
Assina River ∼ PNG 183 B 2
as-Sinballāwain ○ ET 194-195 E 2
Assiniboia ○ CDN (SAS) 232-233 N 6
Assiniboine, Fort ○ CDN 32-33 N 4
Assiniboine, Mount ▲ CDN (BC) 230-231 O 3
Assiniboine River ∼ CDN (MAN) 234-235 E 5
Assiniboine River ∼ CDN (MAN) 234-235 B 4
Assiniboine River ∼ CDN (SAS) 232-233 Q 3
Assinica, Lac ○ CDN (QUE) 236-237 N 2
Assinica, La Réserve de ⊥ CDN (QUE) 236-237 O 2
Assinié Mafia ○ • CI 202-203 J 7
Assin Nyankumase ○ GH 202-203 K 7
Assis ○ BR 72-73 E 7
Assis Brasil ○ BR 70-71 C 2
Assis Chateaubriand ○ BR 74-75 D 5
Assisi ○ •• I 100-101 D 3
Assodé < RN 198-199 D 3
Assok Begua ○ G 210-211 C 3
Assomption, Rivière l' ∼ CDN (QUE) 238-239 M 2
Assomption Island ⌒ SY 222-223 E 2
Assos •• TR 128-129 B 3
Assu ○ BR 68-69 K 4
Assu, Rio ∼ BR 68-69 K 4
as-Sūki ○ SUD 200-201 F 6
as-Sulayyil ○ KSA 132-133 D 3
As Sulṭān ○ LAR 192-193 G 2
as-Sumay ○ SUD 206-207 H 4
Assumption ○ USA (IL) 274-275 J 5
Assunção ○ BR 66-67 E 7
Assur ∴ •• IRQ 128-129 K 5
as-Suryāni, Dair ∴ ET 194-195 E 2
as-Sūs ⩡ MA 188-189 G 5
as-Suwais ☆ ET 194-195 F 3
as-Suwais, Ḫalīǧ ≈ 194-195 F 3
as-Suwais, Qanāt < ET 194-195 F 2
Assyni ∼ RUS 122-123 F 2
Astakós ○ GR 100-101 H 5
Aštān, Umm al- ○ UAE 132-133 H 2
Āstane ○ IR 128-129 N 4
Āstāne ○ IR 134-135 C 2
Astantaj-Mataj, sor ⩡ KA 126-127 M 5
Astara ○ AZ 128-129 N 3
Āstārā ○ • IR 128-129 N 3
Astarak ○ AR 128-129 L 2
Asti ☆ • I 100-101 B 2
Astillero,El ○ E 98-99 F 3
Astipálea ○ GR 100-101 L 6
Astipálea ⌒ GR 100-101 L 6
Aštivay ○ AFG 136-137 M 7
Āštiyān ○ IR 134-135 C 1
Astorga ○ BR 72-73 E 7
Astorga ○ • E 98-99 D 3
Astoria ○ USA (IL) 274-275 H 4
Astoria ○ USA (SD) 260-261 K 2
Astoria ○ • USA (OR) 244-245 B 4
Astor Park ○ USA (FL) 286-287 H 2
Astove Island ⌒ SY 222-223 E 3
Astrahan ○ KA 124-125 F 1
Astrahan' ☆ RUS 96-97 E 10
Astrahanskij zapovednik ⊥ RUS 126-127 G 5
Astrahanskij zapovednik ⊥ RUS (AST) 96-97 F 10
Astrakhan' = Astrahan' ☆ RUS 126-127 H 4
Astray ○ CDN 36-37 Q 7
Astrolabe Bay ≈ 183 C 3
Astronomical Society Islands ⌒ CDN 24-25 a 6
Ástros ○ GR 100-101 J 6
Astrovna ○ BY 94-95 L 4
Astura, gora ▲ RUS 108-109 e 3
Asturias ◘ E 98-99 D 3
Asuéfri ○ CI 202-203 J 6
Asunción ○ CR 52-53 C 7
Asunción ★ • PY 76-77 J 3
Asunción, La ☆ YV 60-61 K 2
Asuncion, Rio de la ∼ MEX 50-51 C 2
Asunción Nochixtlán ○ MEX 52-53 F 3
Asundi ○ IND 140-141 F 3
'Asūriya, al- ○ IRQ 128-129 K 7
Asustado, Arroyo el ∼ RA 76-77 G 4
Asutsuare ○ GH 202-203 L 6
Aswa ∼ EAU 212-213 D 2
Aswān ☆ •• ET 194-195 F 5
Aswān High Dam = Sadd al-Ālī < •• ET 194-195 F 6
Asÿköl, sor ○ KA 124-125 E 6
Asÿköl ojpat ⩡ KA 124-125 E 6
Asyma ○ RUS 118-119 N 4
Asyūt ☆ • ET 194-195 E 4
Asyūṭī, Wādī ∼ ET 194-195 E 4
Ata, Qiryat ○ IL 130-131 D 1
Ataa ○ GRØ 28-29 P 2
Ata Bupu Danau • RI 168 E 7
Atacama, Desierto de ⩡ RCH 76-77 B 4
Atacama, Puna de ⩡ RA 76-77 C 4
Atacama, Salar de ○ RCH 76-77 C 2
Atacama Trench ⩳ 70-71 A 5
Atacames ○ EC 64-65 C 1
Atafaitafa, Djebel ▲ DZ 190-191 F 8
Atafi, Massif d' ⩓ RN 192-193 F 6
'Aṭāiye ○ IR 136-137 F 7
Atajaña, Cerro ▲ RCH 70-71 B 6
Atakakup Indian Reservation ⵋ CDN (SAS) 232-233 M 2
Ata Koo Fai-Nuwa Puri Danau • RI 168 E 7
Atakor ⩓ DZ 190-191 E 9
Atakora, Chaîne de l' ⩓ DY 202-203 L 4
Atakora, Zone Cynégétique de l' ⊥ DY 202-203 L 4
Atakpamé ☆ RT 202-203 L 6
Atalaia ○ BR 68-69 K 6
Atalaia, Ponta de ▲ BR 68-69 E 2
Atalaia do Norte ○ BR 66-67 B 5
Atalaya ○ PE 64-65 F 7
Atalaya, Cerro ▲ PE 70-71 B 3
Ataléia ○ BR 72-73 K 5
Atamanovo ○ RUS 116-117 F 7
Atambua ○ RI 166-167 C 6
Atami ○ • J 152-153 H 7
Atammik ○ GRØ 28-29 O 4
Atanbas, tau ▲ KA 126-127 P 3
Atande, Tanjung ▲ RI 166-167 B 6
Atanik ○ USA 20-21 L 1
Atapange ○ RI 164-165 G 6
Ata Polo Danau • RI 168 E 7
Atapupu ○ RI 166-167 C 6
'Ataqa, Ǧabal ▲ ET 194-195 F 3
Ataques ○ ROU 76-77 K 6
Atār ☆ RIM 196-197 D 4
Atar, Khor ∼ SUD 206-207 K 4
Ataram, Erg n' ⩡ DZ 190-191 C 9
Atas Bogd ▲ MAU 148-149 C 6
Atascadero ○ PE 64-65 B 4
Atascadero ○ USA (CA) 248-249 D 4
Atascosa River ∼ USA (TX) 266-267 J 4
Atasi Nkwanta ○ GH 202-203 K 7
Atasta ○ MEX 52-53 H 2
Atasu ○ KA 124-125 G 4
Atatürk Barajı < TR 128-129 H 4
Atauba ○ BR 62-63 D 6
Atauro, Pulau (Kambing) ⌒ RI 166-167 C 6
Atawala, al- ○ KSA 132-133 B 3
Ātaya ○ ETH 208-209 D 3
'Atbara ∼ ETH 200-201 H 6
'Atbara ☆ SUD 200-201 G 4
'Atbara ∼ SUD 200-201 G 5
Atbasar ☆ KA 124-125 F 3
At-Baši ○ KS 146-147 B 5
At-Baši, hrebet ⩓ KS 146-147 B 5
Atchafalaya Bay ≈ 44-45 M 5
Atchafalaya Bay ≈ USA 268-269 J 7
Atchafalaya River ∼ USA (LA) 268-269 J 6
Atchane, Erg el ⩡ DZ 188-189 L 6
Atchane, Hamadet el ⩡ DZ 190-191 E 6
Atchison ○ USA (KS) 262-263 L 5
Atchuelinguk River ∼ USA 20-21 K 5
Atebubu ○ GH 202-203 K 6
Ateiku ○ GH 202-203 K 7
Aten, Río ∼ BOL 70-71 C 4
Atenango del Río ○ MEX 52-53 E 2
Atenas ○ BR 66-67 B 7
Atencingo ○ MEX 52-53 E 2
Atequiza ○ MEX 52-53 C 1
Aterau ☆ KA 96-97 H 10
Aterau = Aterau ☆ KA 126-127 H 4
Atesa ○ GH 202-203 J 6
Athabasca ○ CDN 32-33 O 4
Athabasca, Lake ○ CDN 30-31 P 6
Athabasca River ∼ CDN 32-33 O 4
Athabasca River ∼ CDN (ALB) 228-229 R 3
Athamánon ▲ GR 100-101 H 5
Athamar • TR 128-129 K 3
Athapap ○ CDN 34-35 F 3
Athapapuskow Lake ○ CDN 34-35 F 3
Athārān Hazārī ○ PK 138-139 D 4
Athenia Lake ○ CDN 30-31 O 4
Athens ○ USA (AL) 284-285 D 2
Athens ○ USA (AR) 276-277 B 6
Athens ○ USA (GA) 284-285 G 3
Athens ○ USA (LA) 268-269 G 4
Athens ○ USA (OH) 280-281 D 4
Athens ○ USA (TN) 282-283 C 5
Athens ○ USA (TX) 264-265 J 6
Athens = Athína ★ ••• GR 100-101 J 6
Atherton ○ AUS 174-175 H 5
Atherton Tableland ⩡ AUS 174-175 H 5
Athgarh ○ IND 142-143 D 5
Athi ∼ EAK 212-213 F 4
Athiémè ○ DY 202-203 L 6
Athienou ○ CY 128-129 E 5
Athi River ○ EAK 212-213 F 4
Athl, Wādī al ∼ LAR 192-193 H 5
Athlone = Baile Átha Luain ○ IRL 90-91 D 5
Athni ○ IND 140-141 F 2
Athol ○ USA (ID) 250-251 C 4
Athol ○ USA (MA) 278-279 J 6
Atholl, Kap ▲ GRØ 26-27 P 5
Áthos ▲ ••• GR 100-101 K 4
'Ati ○ SUD 200-201 D 6
Ati ☆ TCH 198-199 J 6
Atiak ○ EAU 212-213 D 2
Atiamuri ○ NZ 182 F 3
Atibaia ○ BR 72-73 G 7
Atico ○ PE 70-71 A 5
Atienza ○ E 98-99 F 4
Atijere ○ WAN 204-205 F 5
Atik ○ CDN (MAN) 234-235 B 2
Atikaki Provincial Wilderness Park ⊥ CDN (MAN) 234-235 H 3
Atikameg Lake ○ CDN 34-35 F 3
Atikameg River ∼ CDN 34-35 P 4
Atikī ◘ GR 100-101 J 5
Atikokan ○ CDN (ONT) 234-235 M 6
Atikonak Lake ○ CDN 38-39 M 2
Atim ○ TCH 198-199 K 6
Atinia, Nakong- ○ GH 202-203 K 4
Atitlán, Lago de ○ • GCA 52-53 J 4
Atitlán, Volcán ▲ GCA 52-53 J 4
Atka ○ RUS 120-121 O 3
Atka ○ USA 22-23 J 6
Atka Island ⌒ USA 22-23 J 6
Atkamba Mission ○ PNG 183 A 3
Atka Pass ≈ 22-23 J 6
Atkins ○ USA (AR) 276-277 C 5
Atkinson ○ USA (NC) 282-283 J 6
Atkinson ○ USA (NE) 262-263 H 2
Atkinson Lake ○ CDN 30-31 R 5
Atkinson Point ▲ CDN 20-21 Z 2
Atkot ○ IND 138-139 C 8
Atkri ○ RI 166-167 F 2
Atlacomulco ○ MEX 52-53 E 2
Atlanta ○ USA (ID) 252-253 C 3
Atlanta ○ USA (LA) 268-269 H 5
Atlanta ○ USA (MI) 272-273 E 2
Atlanta ○ USA (NE) 262-263 G 4
Atlanta ○ USA (TX) 264-265 K 5
Atlanta ☆ • USA (GA) 284-285 F 3
Atlantic ○ USA (IA) 274-275 C 3
Atlantic ○ USA (ME) 278-279 N 4
Atlantic ○ USA (NC) 282-283 L 6
Atlantic Beach ○ USA (FL) 286-287 H 1
Atlantic City ○ • USA (NJ) 280-281 M 4
Atlantic Ocean ≈ 6-7 D 6
Atlantida ○ ROU 78-79 M 3
Atlantis Fracture Zone ⩳ 6-7 D 5
Atlasova, ostrov ⌒ RUS 122-123 Q 3
Atlasovo ○ RUS (KMC) 120-121 S 6
Atlasovo ○ RUS (SHL) 122-123 K 5
Atlee ○ CDN (ALB) 232-233 H 5
Atlee Creek ∼ AUS 172-173 K 6
Atlin ○ CDN 20-21 Y 7
Atlin Lake ○ CDN 20-21 Y 7
Atlin Provincial Park ⊥ CDN 32-33 D 2
Atlixco ○ MEX 52-53 E 2
Ātmakūr ○ IND 140-141 H 3
Atmakur ○ IND (ANP) 140-141 G 2

Atmakur o IND (ANP) 140-141 H 3
Atmis ~ RUS 94-95 S 5
Atmore o CDN 32-33 O 4
Atmore o USA (AL) 284-285 C 5
Atna Peak ▲ CDN (BC) 228-229 F 3
Atna Range ▲ CDN 32-33 G 4
Atnarko o CDN (BC) 228-229 J 4
Atnbrua o N 86-87 E 6
Atocha o BOL 70-71 D 7
Atog o CAM 210-211 C 2
Atoka o USA (NM) 256-257 L 6
Atoka o USA (OK) 264-265 H 4
Atoka Lake < USA (OK) 264-265 H 4
Atome o ANG 216-217 C 5
Atomic City o USA (ID) 252-253 F 3
Atongo-Bakari o RCA 206-207 E 6
Atonyia < MA 188-189 G 7
Atori o SOL 184 I e 3
Atotonilco o MEX 52-53 E 2
Atotonilco el Alto o MEX 52-53 C 1
Atotonilco El Grande o MEX 52-53 E 1
Atouat, Mount ▲ LAO 158-159 J 3
Atoyac, Río ~ MEX 52-53 E 2
Atoyac, Río ~ MEX 52-53 F 3
Atoyac de Alvarez o MEX 52-53 D 3
Atoyatempan o MEX 52-53 F 2
Atpadi o IND 140-141 F 2
Atqasuk o USA 20-21 M 1
Atrai ~ BD 142-143 F 3
Atrak, Rūd-e ~ IR 136-137 E 6
Ätran ~ S 86-87 F 8
Atrato, Río ~ CO 60-61 C 4
Atrek ~ TM 136-137 D 6
Atsion o USA (NJ) 280-281 M 4
Atsumi-hantō ⌒ J 152-153 G 7
Atsuta o J 152-153 J 3
Atsy o RI 166-167 K 4
Atta o CAM 204-205 J 5
Attakro o CI 202-203 J 6
Attalla o USA (AL) 284-285 D 2
at-Tamad o ET 194-195 G 3
At Tamimi o LAR 192-193 K 1
at-Tanf, Ǧabal ▲ SYR 128-129 H 6
Attāni o IND 140-141 G 5
Attapu o LAO 158-159 J 3
Attar, Oued el ~ DZ 190-191 E 4
Attawapiskat o CDN 34-35 P 4
Attawapiskat Lake o CDN (ONT) 234-235 Q 2
Attawapiskat River ~ CDN 34-35 O 4
Attawapiskat River ~ CDN (ONT) 234-235 R 2
Attayampatti o IND 140-141 H 5
at-Taiyārah o SUD 200-201 E 6
Attéï, In < DZ 198-199 C 2
Atterbury Reserve Training Center xx USA (IN) 274-275 M 5
Attica o USA (IN) 274-275 L 4
Attica o USA (KS) 262-263 H 7
Attica o USA (NY) 278-279 C 6
Attica o USA (OH) 280-281 D 2
at-Tih, Ǧabal ▲ ET 194-195 F 3
at-Tih, Ṣaḥrā' ⊥ ET 194-195 F 2
Attikamagen Lake o CDN 36-37 Q 7
at-Tina, Ḫaliǧ ≈ 194-195 F 2
Attingal o IND 140-141 G 6
Attipāra o IND 140-141 G 6
Attleboro o USA (RI) 278-279 K 7
Attobrou, Yakass- o CI 202-203 J 6
Attock o• PK 138-139 D 3
Attock-Campbellpore o PK 138-139 D 3
Attoko o J 152-153 L 3
Attoyac River ~ USA (TX) 268-269 F 5
Attu o GRØ 28-29 O 3
Attu o USA 22-23 C 6
Attu Island ⌒ USA 22-23 C 6
At Tullab o LAR 192-193 K 5
at-Tūr ☆ ET 194-195 F 3
Attur o IND 140-141 H 5
at-Tuwayshah o SUD 200-201 C 6
Attwood Lake o CDN (ONT) 234-235 P 3
Attwood River ~ CDN (ONT) 234-235 P 3
Attykeveem ~ RUS 112-113 N 2
Atucatiquini, Rio ~ BR 66-67 C 6
Atuel, Río ~ RA 78-79 E 3
Atuka o RI 166-167 J 4
Atuna o GH 202-203 J 6
Atuntaqui o EC 64-65 C 1
Atura o EAU 212-213 D 2
Atures o YV 60-61 H 5
Atutia, Rio ~ RA 76-77 B 6
Åtvidaberg ☆ S 86-87 H 7
Atwa, al- o KSA 130-131 H 3
Atwater o CDN (SAS) 232-233 Q 5
Atwater o USA (CA) 248-249 D 2
Atwood o USA (CO) 254-255 M 3
Atwood o USA (IL) 274-275 K 5
Atwood o USA (KS) 262-263 E 5
Atwood Cay = Samana Cays ⌒ BS 54-55 J 3
Atykan, ostrov ⌒ RUS 120-121 Q 4
Atžaksy ~ KA 126-127 M 3
Atzinging Lake o CDN 30-31 S 5
Aû, Chutes de l' ~• ZRE 212-213 C 3
Aua River ~ CDN 24-25 e 7
Auasberge ▲ NAM 216-217 D 11
Auasbila o HN 52-53 B 4
Auasinaua, Cachoeira ~ BR 66-67 F 2
Auatu ▲ ETH 208-209 E 5
Auau Channel ≈ USA 288 J 4
Aubagne o F 90-91 K 10
Aube ~ F 90-91 K 8
Aúbe o MOC 218-219 K 3
Aubenas o F 90-91 K 9
Aubigny o CDN (MAN) 234-235 F 5
Aubigny-sur-Nère o F 90-91 J 8
Aubinadong River ~ CDN (ONT) 236-237 E 5
Aubrey Cliffs ▲ USA (AZ) 256-257 B 3
Aubry Lake o CDN 30-31 G 2
Auburn o AUS (QLD) 178-179 L 3
Auburn o AUS (SA) 180-181 E 3
Auburn o USA (AL) 284-285 E 4
Auburn o USA (CA) 246-247 D 5
Auburn o USA (IA) 274-275 D 2
Auburn o USA (IN) 274-275 N 3
Auburn o USA (ME) 278-279 L 4
Auburn o USA (NE) 262-263 L 4
Auburn o USA (NY) 278-279 E 6
Auburn o USA (WA) 244-245 C 3
Auburn o USA (WY) 252-253 H 4
Auburn Corners o USA (OH) 280-281 E 2
Auburndale o USA (FL) 286-287 H 3
Auburn Range ▲ AUS 178-179 L 3
Auburn River ~ AUS 178-179 L 3
Aubusson o F 90-91 J 9
Auca Mahuida, Sierra de ▲ RA 78-79 E 4
Auçan, Cerro ▲ RCH 76-77 C 1
Aucara o PE 64-65 E 9
Aucayacu o PE 64-65 D 6
Auch ☆• F 90-91 H 10
Auchi o WAN 204-205 G 5
Aucilla River ~ USA (FL) 286-287 F 1
Auckland o NZ 182 E 2
Auckland Bay ≈ 158-159 E 4
Auckland Island ⌒ NZ 13 H 8
Aude ~ F 90-91 J 10
Auden o CDN (ONT) 234-235 Q 4
Audhild Bay ≈ 26-27 E 3
Audierne o F 90-91 E 7
Audo Range ▲ ETH 208-209 E 5
Audru o• EST 94-95 J 2
Audubon o USA (IA) 274-275 D 3
Aue o D 92-93 M 3
Augathella o AUS 178-179 J 3
Augrabies o ZA 220-221 E 4
Augrabies Falls ~•• ZA 220-221 E 4
Augrabies Falls National Park ⊥ ZA 220-221 E 4
Augsburg o•• D 92-93 L 4
Aug Thong o THA 158-159 F 3
Augusta o• AUS 176-177 C 7
Augusta o I 100-101 E 6
Augusta o USA (AR) 276-277 D 5
Augusta o USA (GA) 284-285 J 3
Augusta o USA (IL) 274-275 H 4
Augusta o USA (KS) 262-263 K 7
Augusta o USA (MT) 250-251 G 4
Augusta o USA (OH) 280-281 B 5
Augusta o USA (WI) 270-271 G 6
Augusta ☆ USA (ME) 278-279 M 4
Augusta, Cabo ▲ CO 60-61 D 2
Augusta, Mount ▲ CDN 20-21 U 6
Augustín Libarona o RA 76-77 F 4
Augustín Codazzi o CO 60-61 E 2
Augustine Island ⌒ USA 22-23 U 3
Augusto Montenegro o BR 66-67 J 4
Augusto Severo o BR 68-69 K 4
Augustów o PL 92-93 R 2
Augustus, Mount ▲ AUS 176-177 D 2
Augustus Downs o AUS 174-175 E 6
Augustus Island ⌒ AUS 172-173 G 3
Augustus Island ⌒ CDN 36-37 Q 3
Auiita, Rio ~ BR 72-73 D 2
Auke Bay o USA 32-33 C 2
Auki = Aoke ☆ SOL 184 I e 3
Aukpar River ~ CDN 36-37 N 2
Aulād Tauq Šarq o ET 194-195 F 4
Aulander o USA (NC) 282-283 K 4
Auld, Lake o AUS 172-173 F 7
Auliräipāra o IND 142-143 G 4
Aulitivik Island ⌒ CDN 28-29 G 2
Auliyā Dam < SUD 200-201 F 5
Aulneau Peninsula ⌒ CDN (ONT) 234-235 J 5
Aul Sarykobda o KA 126-127 M 3
Ault o USA (CO) 254-255 L 3
Aumo o PNG 183 E 3
Auna o WAN 204-205 F 3
Aundah o IND 138-139 F 10
Auno o WAN 204-205 K 3
Auob ~ NAM 220-221 D 2
Aupwel o PNG 183 B 3
Aur, Pulau ⌒ MAL (KED) 162-163 F 3
Aura o USA (MI) 270-271 K 4
Aurahua o PE 64-65 E 8
Auram ~ NAM 220-221 C 3
Aurangābād o IND 142-143 D 3
Aurangābād o• IND 138-139 E 10
Auras o C 54-55 G 4
Auray o F 90-91 F 8
Aurbunak, Gunung ▲ RI 164-165 D 5
Aure ☆ N 86-87 D 5
Aure River ~ PNG 183 C 4
Aures, Massif de l' ▲ DZ 190-191 F 3
Aure Scarp ▲ PNG 183 C 4
Auri, utes • RUS 122-123 J 2
Aurich (Ostfriesland) o D 92-93 J 2
Auriflama o BR 72-73 E 6
Aurillac ☆ F 90-91 J 9
Auriya o IND 138-139 G 6
Aurlandsvangen o N 86-87 C 6
Auro o PNG 183 E 5
Aurora o BR (CEA) 68-69 J 5
Aurora o BR (GSU) 70-71 K 6
Aurora o CDN (ONT) 238-239 F 5
Aurora o CDN (ONT) 238-239 F 4
Aurora o GUY 62-63 E 2
Aurora o RP (ISA) 160-161 D 4
Aurora o RP (ZAS) 160-161 E 9
Aurora o USA (AK) 20-21 H 4
Aurora o USA (CO) 254-255 L 4
Aurora o USA (IL) 274-275 K 3
Aurora o USA (KY) 276-277 G 4
Aurora o USA (ME) 278-279 N 4
Aurora o USA (MO) 276-277 B 4
Aurora o USA (NE) 262-263 H 4
Aurora o USA (NY) 278-279 E 6
Aurora, Île = Maewo ⌒ VAN 184 II b 2
Aurora, La o RA 76-77 E 4
Aurora do Tocantins o BR 72-73 G 2
Auroraville o USA (WI) 270-271 K 6
Aurukun Ⅹ AUS 174-175 F 3
Aurukun Aboriginal Land Ⅹ AUS 174-175 F 3
Aus o NAM 220-221 C 3
Ausa o IND 138-139 F 10
Au Sable River ~ USA (MI) 272-273 F 3
Auschwitz = Oświęcim o••• PL 92-93 P 3
Ausentes o BR 74-75 E 7
Ausis < NAM 216-217 B 9
Aussig = Ústí nad Labem o CZ 92-93 N 3
Austerlitz = Slavkov u Brna o CZ 92-93 O 4
Austfonna ⊂ N 84-85 N 3
Austin o CDN (MAN) 234-235 E 5
Austin o USA (MN) 270-271 F 7
Austin o USA (NV) 246-247 H 4
Austin o USA (OR) 244-245 G 6
Austin ☆ USA (TX) 266-267 K 3
Austin, Lake o AUS 176-177 E 3
Austin, Point ▲ AUS 174-175 F 5
Austin Channel ≈ 24-25 U 3
Austin Island ⌒ CDN 30-31 X 5
Austral Downs o AUS 174-175 D 7
Austral Fracture Zone ≃ 14-15 Q 9
Australia ◼ AUS 180-181 K 3
Australia ⊥ AUS 13 D 5
Australian-Antarctic Basin ≃ 12 G 10
Australian-Antarctic Discordance ≃ 13 C 7
Australian Capital Territory ◻ AUS 180-181 K 3
Australind o AUS 176-177 C 6
Austria = Österreich ◼ A 92-93 M 5
Austvågøy ⌒ N 86-87 G 2
Austwell o USA (TX) 266-267 L 5
Autás-Mirim, Rio ~ BR 66-67 G 5
Autaz, Ilha ⌒ BR 66-67 H 4
Autazes o BR 66-67 H 4
Autaz Mirim, Paraná ~ BR 66-67 H 4
Autec ∴• BS 54-55 G 2
Authier-Nord o CDN (QUE) 236-237 K 4
Autlán de Navarro o MEX 52-53 B 2
Autridge Bay ≈ 24-25 d 5
Autun o• F 90-91 K 8
Auvergne o AUS 172-173 J 3
Auvergne ◻ F 90-91 J 9
Aux Barques, Pointe ▲ USA (MI) 272-273 G 3
Auxerre ☆• F 90-91 J 8
Auxiliadora o BR 66-67 G 6
Auyan Tebuy ▲ YV 60-61 K 5
Auyuittug National Park ⊥ CDN 28-29 G 3
Ava o MYA 142-143 J 5
Ava o USA (IL) 276-277 F 3
Ava o USA (MO) 276-277 C 4
Ava o USA (MS) 268-269 L 3
Avača ~ RUS 120-121 S 7
Avá-Canoeiro, Área Indígena Ⅹ BR 72-73 F 2
Avačinskaja, guba o RUS 120-121 S 7
Avačinskij zaliv ≈ 120-121 S 7
Avadh ⊥ IND 142-143 B 2
Avadi o IND 140-141 J 4
Avakubi o ZRE 210-211 L 3
Avalik River ~ USA 20-21 L 1
Avaljak hrebet ▲ RUS 96-97 L 6
Avallon o F 90-91 J 8
Avalon o USA (CA) 248-249 F 6
Avalon o USA (TX) 264-265 H 6
Avalon Peninsula ⌒ CDN (NFL) 242-243 P 5
Avalon Reservoir ~ USA (NM) 256-257 L 6
Avalos, Arroyo ~ RA 76-77 H 5
Avanavero o SME 62-63 F 3
Avannaarsua = Nordgrønland ◻ GRØ 26-27 V 4
Avard o USA (OK) 264-265 F 2
Avare o BR 72-73 F 7
Avarskoe Kojsu ~ RUS 126-127 G 6
Avatanak Island ⌒ USA 22-23 O 5
Avatanak Strait ≈ 22-23 O 5
Āvāz o IR 134-135 J 2
Ave, Rio ~ P 98-99 C 4
Ave-Dakpa o GH 202-203 L 6
Āveǧ o IR 128-129 N 5
Āveǧ, Gardāne-ye ▲ IR 128-129 N 5
Aveiro o BR 66-67 K 4
Aveiro ☆• P 98-99 C 4
Avekova ~ RUS 112-113 L 5
Avelino Lopes o BR 68-69 G 7
Avella o USA (PA) 280-281 F 3
Avellaneda o RA 78-79 K 3
Avellino ☆ I 100-101 E 4
Avenal o USA (CA) 248-249 D 3
Avenne of the Giants • USA (CA) 246-247 B 3
Avery o USA (ID) 250-251 D 4
Avery o USA (TX) 264-265 K 5
Aves, Isla de ⌒ YV 56 D 4
Aves, Islas de ⌒ YV 60-61 H 1
Aves de Barlovente ⌒ YV 60-61 H 2
Aves Ridge ≃ 56 D 5
Aveyron ~ F 90-91 J 9
Avezzano o I 100-101 D 3
Avia Teray o RA 76-77 G 4
Avignon o•• F 90-91 K 10
Ávila de los Caballeros o••• E 98-99 E 4
Avilés o•• E 98-99 E 3
Avilla o USA (IN) 274-275 N 3
Avilla, Parque Nacional ⊥ YV 60-61 H 2
Avinurme o EST 94-95 K 2
Avirons, Les o F 224 B 7
Avis o P 98-99 D 5
Avispa, Cerro ▲ YV 66-67 E 2
Avissawella o CL 140-141 J 7
Avlandja, Bofšaja ~ RUS 112-113 L 5
Avoca o AUS (TAS) 180-181 J 6
Avoca o AUS (VIC) 180-181 G 4
Avoca o USA (TX) 264-265 E 6
Avoca River ~ AUS 180-181 G 4
Avola o CDN (BC) 230-231 K 2
Avon o USA (MT) 250-251 G 5
Avon o USA (NC) 282-283 M 5
Avon o USA (SD) 260-261 H 3
Avon, Lake < AUS 180-181 L 3
Avondale o USA (AZ) 256-257 C 5
Avon Downs o AUS (NT) 174-175 D 7
Avon Downs o AUS (QLD) 178-179 J 1
Avonia o USA (PA) 280-281 F 1
Avon Park o USA (FL) 286-287 H 4
Avon Park Air Force Range xx USA (FL) 286-287 H 4
Avon River ~ AUS 176-177 D 6
Avontuur o ZA 220-221 F 6
Avranches o F 90-91 G 7
Avstrijskij proliv ≈ 84-85 f 2
Avu Avu = Kolotambu o SOL 184 I e 3
'Awābi o OM 132-133 K 2
Awaé o CAM 210-211 C 2
Awagakama River ~ CDN (ONT) 236-237 E 2
Awa Gurupi, Área Indígena Ⅹ BR 68-69 E 3
Awai, Pulau ⌒ RI 166-167 J 2
Awaji-shima ⌒ J 152-153 F 7
Awakaba o RCA 206-207 E 4
'Awālī o BRN 134-135 D 5
Awang o RI 168 C 7
Awanui o NZ 182 D 1
Awar o PNG 183 C 3
Awara Plain ⊥ EAK 212-213 H 2
Awara soela ~ SME 62-63 G 4
Āwarē o ETH 208-209 G 4
Awarua Point ▲ NZ 182 B 6
Āwasa ☆ ETH 208-209 D 5
Āwasa Häyk' o ETH 208-209 D 5
Awashima ⌒ J 152-153 H 5
Āwash National Park ⊥ ETH 208-209 D 4
Āwash Reserve ⊥ ETH 208-209 D 4
Āwash Wenz ~ ETH 208-209 E 3
Awat o VRC 146-147 E 5
Āwat'a Shet' ~ ETH 208-209 D 6
Awatere River ~ NZ 182 D 4
Awbāri o LAR 190-191 H 7
Awbāri ☆ LAR 192-193 E 4
Awdheegle o SP 212-213 K 3
Awdiinle o SP 212-213 J 2
Awe o WAN 204-205 H 4
Aweil o SUD 206-207 H 4
Awendaw o USA (SC) 284-285 L 3
Awgu o WAN 204-205 G 5
Awio o PNG 183 F 4
Awio River ~ PNG 183 F 4
Āwira Wenz ~ ETH 200-201 K 6
Awisam o GH 202-203 K 7
Awisang o RI 164-165 F 4
Awjilah o LAR 192-193 J 3
Awka o WAN 204-205 G 5
Awrā, Wādī al ~ LAR 192-193 G 3
Awu, Gunung ▲ RI 164-165 J 2
Awun, River ~ WAN 204-205 F 4
Awuna River ~ USA 20-21 M 2
Awungi o PNG 183 F 3
Awura, Tanjung ▲ RI 166-167 H 4
Awwal, Wādī al ~ LAR 190-191 H 6
Axe Hill ▲ AUS 176-177 J 3
Axel Heiberg Island ⌒ CDN 26-27 C 3
Axim o GH 202-203 J 7
Axinim o BR 66-67 H 5
Axtell o USA (NE) 262-263 G 4
Axtell o USA (UT) 254-255 D 4
Axton o USA (VA) 280-281 G 7
Axui o BR 68-69 G 3
Ayabaca o PE 64-65 C 4
Ayachi, Ibel ▲ MA 188-189 J 4
Ayacucho ☆ PE 64-65 E 8
Ayacucho o RA 78-79 K 4
Ayakkum Hu o VRC 144-145 G 2
Ayamé o CI 202-203 J 7
Ayami, Tanjung ▲ RI 166-167 H 3
Ayamikem o GQ 210-211 C 2
Ayamonte o• E 98-99 D 6
Ayancık ☆ TR 128-129 F 2
Ayanfure o GH 202-203 K 7
Ayangba o WAN 204-205 G 5
Ayapata o PE 70-71 B 3
Ayapel o CO 60-61 D 3
Ayapel, Serranía de ▲ CO 60-61 D 4
Ayapunga, Cerro ▲ EC 64-65 C 3
Ayarde, Laguna o RA 76-77 G 3
Ayas o TR 128-129 E 2
Ayaviri o PE (LIM) 64-65 D 8
Ayaviri o PE (PUN) 70-71 B 4
Ayden o USA (NC) 282-283 K 5
Aydın ☆ TR 128-129 B 4
Aydın Dağları ▲ TR 128-129 B 4
Aydingkol Hu o VRC 146-147 J 4
Ayer o USA (MA) 278-279 K 6
Ayerbe o E 98-99 G 3
Ayer Deras, Kampung Sungai o MAL 162-163 E 2
Ayer Hitam o• MAL 162-163 E 4
Ayer Puteh, Kampung o MAL 162-163 E 2
Ayers Rock ▲•• AUS 176-177 L 2
Ayilūr o IND 140-141 H 5
Ayina ~ G 210-211 D 2
Ayinwafe o GH 202-203 K 6
Ayiyak River ~ USA 20-21 O 2
Aykel o ETH 200-201 H 6
Aylesbury o GB 90-91 G 6
Āylet o ER 200-201 J 5
Ayllón o E 98-99 F 4
Aylmer o CDN (ONT) 238-239 E 6
Aylmer, Lac o CDN (QUE) 238-239 O 3
Aylmer Lake o CDN 30-31 P 3
Aylsham o CDN (SAS) 232-233 P 2
Aymat o• ER 200-201 J 4
Ayn al Ghazalah o LAR 192-193 K 1
Aynor o USA (SC) 284-285 L 3
Ayo o PE 64-65 F 9
Ayod o SUD 206-207 K 4
Ayoni o SUD 206-207 H 4
Ayopaya, Río ~ BOL 70-71 D 5
Ayorou o RN 202-203 L 2
Ayos o CAM 210-211 D 2
'Ayoûn el 'Atroûs ☆ RIM 196-197 F 6
Ayr o AUS 174-175 J 6
Ayr o• GB 90-91 E 4
Ayr Lake o CDN 26-27 Q 8
Ayrshire o USA (IA) 274-275 D 1
Āysha o ETH 208-209 F 3
Ayu, Kepulanan ⌒ RI 166-167 F 1
Ayu, Pulau ⌒ RI 166-167 F 1
Ayu, Tanjung ▲ RI 164-165 E 4
Ayungon o RP 160-161 E 8
Ayutla o MEX 52-53 B 1
Ayutla de los Libres o MEX 52-53 E 3
Ayvacık o EC 64-65 D 3
Ayvacık ☆ TR 128-129 G 2
Ayvacık ☆ TR 128-129 B 3
Ayvalık ☆ TR 128-129 B 3
Ayyampettai o IND 140-141 H 5
Ažabač'e, ozero o RUS 120-121 T 5
Azad Kashmir ⊥ IND 138-139 D 3
Āzād Šar o IR 136-137 D 6
Azahar, Costa del ▲ E 98-99 H 5
Azaila o E 98-99 G 4
Azalea o USA (OR) 244-245 B 8
Āzamgarh o IND 142-143 C 2
Azanaques, Cerro ▲ BOL 70-71 D 6
Azanaques, Cordillera de ▲ BOL 70-71 D 6
Azangaro o PE 70-71 B 4
Azao ▲ DZ 190-191 G 8
Azaouak, Vallée de l' ⊥ RMM 196-197 M 6
Azara o RA 76-77 K 5
Āzarbāyǧān-e Ġarbī ◻ IR 128-129 L 3
Āzarbāyǧān-e Šarqī ◻ IR 128-129 M 4
Azare o WAN 204-205 J 3
Āzaršahr o IR 128-129 L 4
Azas ~ RUS 116-117 H 9
Azas, ozero = Todža, ozero o RUS 116-117 H 9
Azauri o BR 62-63 G 5
Azaz ▲ DZ 190-191 D 7
A'zāz ☆ SYR 128-129 G 4
Azazga o DZ 190-191 E 2
Azbine, Aïr ou ⊥• RN 198-199 D 3
Až Bogd ▲ MAU 146-147 M 3
Azeffāl ⊥ RIM 196-197 C 5
Azemmour o MA 188-189 G 4
Azendjé o G 210-211 B 4
Azennezal, Erg ⊥ DZ 190-191 C 9
Azerbaijan = Azerbajdžan ◼ AZ 128-129 M 2
Azero, Río ~ BOL 70-71 F 6
Azevedo Sodré o BR 76-77 K 6
Āzezo o ETH 200-201 H 6
Azgale o IR 134-135 A 1
Azilal ☆ MA 188-189 H 5
Azingo o G 210-211 B 4
Azingo, Lac o G 210-211 B 4
Azirir o DZ 190-191 D 7
Aziz < TCH 198-199 H 4
'Azīzīya, al- o IRQ 128-129 L 6
'Azīzīyah, Al ◻ LAR 192-193 E 1
'Azīzīyah, Al ☆ LAR 192-193 E 1
Azlam, Wādī ~ KSA 130-131 E 4
Azle o USA (TX) 264-265 G 6
Azná o IR 134-135 C 2
Aznakaevo ☆ RUS 96-97 H 6
Azogues ☆ EC 64-65 C 3
Azoren ⊥ P 6-7 E 6
Azores = Açores, Archipélago dos ⌒ P 188-189 C 4
Azores-Biscaya Rise ≃ 6-7 G 4
Azores-Cape Saint Vincent Ridge ≃ 188-189 D 2
Azoum, Bahr ~ TCH 206-207 E 3
Azourki, Ibel ▲ MA 188-189 H 5
Azov o• RUS 102-103 L 4
Azov, Sea of = Azovskoe more ≈ RUS 102-103 J 4
Azovskoe More ≈ 102-103 J 4
Azovy o RUS 114-115 H 2
Azpeitia o E 98-99 F 3
Azrak, Bahr ~ TCH 206-207 E 3
Azraq, al- o JOR 130-131 E 2
Āzre o AFG 138-139 B 2
Azrou o MA 188-189 J 4
Azrou, Oued ~ DZ 190-191 F 9
Aztec o USA (AZ) 256-257 B 6
Aztec o USA (NM) 256-257 H 2
Aztecas, Los o MEX 50-51 K 6
Aztec Ruins National Monument ∴ USA (NM) 256-257 H 2
Azua ☆ DOM 54-55 K 5
Azuaga o• E 98-99 E 5
Azúcar o EC 64-65 B 3
Azuer, Río ~ E 98-99 F 5
Azuero, Península de ⌒ PA 52-53 D 8
Azufral, Volcán ▲ CO 64-65 D 1
Azufre, Paso del ▲ RA 76-77 C 3
Azufre ó Copiapo, Cerro ▲ RCH 76-77 C 4
Azul ▲ MEX 50-51 J 4
Azul o RA 78-79 K 4
Azul, Arroyo del ~ RA 78-79 K 4
Azul, Cerro ▲ CR 52-53 B 7
Azul, Cerro ▲ EC 64-65 B 10
Azul, Cerro ▲ RA 78-79 D 6
Azul, Rio ~ BR 64-65 F 5
Azul, Río ~ MEX 52-53 E 3
Azul, Río ~ MEX 52-53 K 3
Azul, Serra ▲ BR 70-71 K 4
Azúl Meambar, Parque Nacional ⊥ HN 52-53 L 4
Azūm, Wādī ~ SUD 198-199 L 6
Azuma-san ▲ J 152-153 J 6
Azurduy o BOL 70-71 E 6
Azure Lake o CDN (BC) 228-229 O 4
Azwell o USA (WA) 244-245 F 3
Azzaba o DZ 190-191 F 2
az-Zāb al-Kabīr, Nahr ~ IRQ 128-129 K 5
az-Zāb aṣ-Ṣaǧīr, Nahr ~ IRQ 128-129 L 5
az-Zahrān o KSA 134-135 D 5
Azzaouager, Adrar ▲ RN 198-199 D 4
az-Zaqāzīq ☆ ET 194-195 E 2
az-Zaraf, Bahr ~ SUD 206-207 K 4
az-Zarqā' ⌒ UAE 134-135 E 6
az-Zāwiyah ◻ LAR 192-193 E 1
az-Zāwiyah ☆ LAR 192-193 E 1
Azzel Matti, Sebkha o DZ 190-191 C 7
Az Zimām, Wādī ~ LAR 192-193 F 3
Az Zintān o LAR 192-193 E 2
az-Zūmah o SUD 200-201 E 3

B

Ba o FJI 184 III a 2
Baa o• RI 166-167 B 7
Ba'āǧ, al- o IRQ 128-129 J 4
Ba'ā'iṭ, al- o KSA 130-131 G 4
Baantama o GH 202-203 K 6
Baardheere o SP 212-213 J 2
Bāb, al- ☆ SYR 128-129 G 4
Baba o EC 64-65 C 2
Baba ~ RCA 206-207 C 6
Bābā, Kūh-e ▲ AFG 134-135 M 1
Bababé o RIM 196-197 D 6
Baba Burnu ▲ TR 128-129 B 3
Babacu o BR 68-69 F 5
Babaçulândia o BR 68-69 E 5
Babadag o• RO 102-103 F 5
Babadag, gora ▲ AZ 128-129 N 2
Babadayhan o TM 136-137 G 6
Babaera o ANG 216-217 C 6
Babaeski ☆ TR 128-129 B 2
Babaevo o RUS 94-95 O 2
Bābā Gurgur o IRQ 128-129 L 5
Babahoyo ☆ EC 64-65 C 2
Babai ~ NEP 144-145 C 6
Babajurt o RUS 126-127 G 6
Babalegi o ZA 220-221 J 2
Bāb al-Mandab ≈ 132-133 C 7
Bāb al-Mandab, Ra's ▲ Y 132-133 C 7
Bābā Monir o IR 134-135 D 3
Babana o RI 164-165 F 5
Babana o WAN 204-205 E 3
Baban Rafi o WAN 204-205 G 4
Babanty, gory ▲ RUS 118-119 F 8
Babanūsa o SUD 206-207 H 3
Babao o VRC 156-157 D 5
Babaomby, Tanjona ▲ RM 222-223 F 3
Babar, Kepulauan ⌒ RI 166-167 E 5
Babar, Pulau ⌒ RI 166-167 E 5
Babasa Island ⌒ PNG 183 G 3
Babat o RI (JTI) 168 E 3
Babat o RI (SUS) 162-163 F 6
Babat o RI (SUS) 162-163 E 6
Babatag, hrebet ▲ US 136-137 K 6
Babati o EAT 212-213 E 6
Babau o RI 166-167 B 7
Bābā Yādegār o IR 128-129 L 4
Babb o USA (MT) 250-251 E 3
Babbage River ~ CDN 20-21 V 2
Bab-Besen ▲ MA 188-189 J 3
Babbitt o USA (MN) 270-271 G 3
Babbitt o USA (NV) 246-247 G 5
Babcock o USA (FL) 286-287 H 5
B'abdā ☆ RL 128-129 F 6
Bab'e, ozero o RUS 88-89 P 3
Bāb-e Anār o IR 134-135 E 4
Babel, Mont de ▲ CDN 38-39 K 3
Băbeni o RO 102-103 D 5
Baberu o IND 142-143 B 3
Babetville o RM 222-223 E 7
Babi, Pulau ⌒ RI 162-163 B 3
Babia, La o MEX 50-51 H 3
Bābil o IRQ 128-129 L 6
Bābil (Babylon) ∴• IRQ 128-129 L 6
Babilē o ETH 208-209 F 4
Babina o IND 138-139 G 7
Babinda o AUS 174-175 H 5
Babine Lake o CDN (BC) 228-229 J 2
Babine Mountains Provincial Recreation Area ⊥ CDN (BC) 228-229 G 2
Babine Range ▲ CDN 32-33 G 4
Babine River ~ CDN 32-33 G 4
Babo o RI 166-167 G 3
Bābol o• IR 136-137 C 6
Bābolsar o• IR 136-137 C 6
Babonde o ZRE 212-213 A 2
Babongo o CAM 206-207 B 5
Baboquivari Peak ▲ USA (AZ) 256-257 D 7
Babor, Djebel ▲ DZ 190-191 E 2
Baboua o RCA 206-207 B 6
Băbra o IND 138-139 C 9
Babrongan Tower ▲ AUS 172-173 F 5
Babrujsk ☆ BY 94-95 L 5
Babruysk = Babrujsk ☆ BY 94-95 L 5
Babtai o LT 94-95 H 4
Bab-Taza o MA 188-189 J 3
Babura o WAN 198-199 D 6
Băbusar Pass ▲ PK 138-139 E 2
Babuškin o RUS 116-117 N 10
Babuškina, mys ▲ RUS 120-121 Q 4
Babuškina, zaliv o RUS 120-121 P 4
Babuyan Channel ≈ 160-161 D 3
Babuyan Island ⌒ RP 160-161 D 3
Babuyan Islands ⌒ RP 160-161 D 3
Baca ⌒ ER 200-201 K 5
Bacaadweyn o SP 208-209 H 5
Bacabal o BR (AMA) 66-67 F 3
Bacabal o BR (MAR) 68-69 F 4
Bacabal o BR (MAR) 68-69 F 3
Bacabal o BR (ROR) 62-63 D 5
Bacabalzinho o BR 70-71 F 3
Bacada o BR 66-67 E 6
Bacaja, Área Indígena Ⅹ BR 68-69 C 4
Bacaja, Rio ~ BR 68-69 C 3
Bacajagua o C 54-55 H 5
Bacalar o MEX 52-53 K 2
Bacan, Kepulauan ⌒ RI 164-165 K 4
Bacan, Pulau ⌒ RI 164-165 K 4
Bacanora o MEX 50-51 E 3
Bacaruca o BR 66-67 E 3
Bacateiro o BR 68-69 F 3
Bacău ☆• RO 102-103 E 4
Bắc Binh o VN 158-159 K 5
Baccaro o CDN (NS) 240-241 K 7
Bacchus Marsh o AUS 180-181 H 4
Bacerac o MEX 50-51 E 2
Bắc Giang ☆ VN 156-157 E 6
Bắc Hà ☆ VN 156-157 D 5
Bachalo o WAL 202-203 D 6
Bachaquero o YV 60-61 F 3
Bachčysaraj ☆•• UA 102-103 H 5
Bache Peninsula ⌒ CDN 26-27 M 4
Bachhrāwān o IND 142-143 B 2
Bachimba o MEX 50-51 G 3
Bachiniva o MEX 50-51 F 3
Bachmač o UA 102-103 H 2
Bach Thông o VN 156-157 D 5
Bachu o VRC 146-147 D 6
Bachuo Akakbe o CAM 204-205 H 6
Bačka Palanka o YU 100-101 G 2
Bačka Topola o YU 100-101 G 2
Back Bay ≈ USA 280-281 L 7
Back Bay National Wildlife Refuge ⊥ USA (VA) 280-281 L 7
Backbone Mountain ▲ USA (MD) 280-281 G 4
Backbone Ranges ▲ CDN 30-31 E 4
Bäckefors o S 86-87 F 7
Bäckhammar o S 86-87 G 7
Back River ~ CDN 30-31 S 3
Backstairs Passage ≈ 180-181 D 3
Bắc Lạc o VN 156-157 D 5
Bắc Mê ☆ VN 156-157 D 5
Bắc Ngư'ờ'n o VN 156-157 D 5
Bắc Ninh ☆ VN 156-157 E 6
Baco, Mount ▲ RP 160-161 D 6
Bacobampo o MEX 50-51 E 4
Bacolod ☆ RP 160-161 E 7
Baconton o USA (GA) 284-285 F 5
Bắc Quang o VN 156-157 D 5
Bacqueville, Lac o CDN 36-37 M 5
Bactili o SP 212-213 H 3
Bacuag o RP 160-161 F 8
Bacungan o RP 160-161 C 8
Bacuri o BR 68-69 F 2
Bacuri, Cachoeira ~ BR 62-63 H 6
Bacuri, Ilha do ⌒ BR 68-69 D 3
Bacuri, Lago de o BR 68-69 G 3
Bād o IR 134-135 D 2
Bad', al- o KSA 130-131 D 3
Bada ▲ ETH 208-209 D 5
Badā o KSA 130-131 E 4
Bada o RUS 118-119 D 10
Bada Barabil o IND 142-143 D 4
Badagangshan Z.B. ⊥• VRC 156-157 F 2
Badagara o IND 140-141 F 5
Badago o RMM 202-203 F 4
Badagri o WAN 204-205 E 5
Badahšān ◻ AFG 136-137 M 6
Badā'i', al- o KSA 130-131 H 4
Badain Jaran Shamo ⊥ VRC 148-149 E 7
Badajós o BR 66-67 F 4
Badajós, Lago o BR 66-67 F 4
Badajoz o•• E 98-99 D 5
Badalia o AUS 178-179 E 2
Badaling • VRC 154-155 J 1
Badam ~ KA 136-137 L 3
Badanga o TCH 206-207 C 3
Badas, Kepulauan ⌒ RI 162-163 G 4
Badau o RI 162-163 J 6
Bada Valley ∴• RI 164-165 G 4
Bad Axe o USA (MI) 272-273 G 4
Badda Rogghie ▲ ETH 208-209 C 4
Baddeck o CDN (NS) 240-241 P 4
Baddo ~ PK 134-135 L 4
Bad Dürrheim o D 92-93 K 4
Badeggi o WAN 204-205 G 4
Badéguicheri o RN 198-199 B 5
Baden o A 92-93 O 5
Baden o CDN (MAN) 234-235 B 2
Baden o CH 92-93 K 5
Badena ~ SP 212-213 H 4
Baden-Baden o• D 92-93 K 4
Baden-Württemberg ◻ D 92-93 K 4
Bādepalli o IND 140-141 H 2
Badér o RN 198-199 C 3
Badgastein o• A 92-93 M 5
Badger o CDN (MAN) 234-235 H 5
Badger o CDN (NFL) 242-243 M 4
Badger o USA (MN) 270-271 B 2
Badgingarra o AUS 176-177 C 5
Badgingarra National Park ⊥ AUS 176-177 C 5
Bādgīs ◻ AFG 136-137 H 7
Bādgūl ⌒ AFG 136-137 J 7
Bad Hersfeld o D 92-93 K 3
Bad Hills ▲ CDN (SAS) 232-233 K 4
Badhyzskij zapovednik ⊥ TM 136-137 G 7
Badi, al- o IRQ 128-129 J 5
Badī', al- o KSA 130-131 K 6
Badī'a, al- o KSA 132-133 D 5
Badiara ~ SN 202-203 D 2
Badikaha o CI 202-203 H 5
Badime o ETH 200-201 H 5
Badin o PK 138-139 B 7
Badinko o RMM 202-203 F 3
Badinko, Reserve du ⊥ RMM 202-203 F 3
Badin Lake < USA (NC) 282-283 G 5
Badinn-Ko ~ RMM 202-203 F 3
Badir o WAN 204-205 K 3
Bad Ischl o•• A 92-93 M 5
Bādiyat Bani Kabir o KSA 132-133 B 3
Badjariha ~ RUS 110-111 Z 6
Badjer o CAM 204-205 K 5
Bad Kissingen o D 92-93 L 3
Bad Kreuznach o D 92-93 J 4
Badlands ⊥ USA (ND) 258-259 D 5
Badlands ⊥ USA (SD) 260-261 D 3
Badlands National Park ⊥ USA (SD) 260-261 D 3
Badnāwar o IND 138-139 E 8
Badnera o IND 138-139 F 9
Bad Neuenahr-Ahrweiler o• D 92-93 J 3
Bado o RI 166-167 K 5
Badoc o RP 160-161 D 4
Ba Đông o VN 158-159 J 6
Badong o VRC 154-155 G 6
Badou o RT 202-203 L 6
Badoumbé o RMM 202-203 E 3
Badplaas o ZA 220-221 K 2
Badra ☆ IRQ 128-129 L 6
Bādra ~ PK 134-135 M 4
Bad Radkersburg o A 92-93 N 5
Bādrah o PK 138-139 B 6
Badrānlū o IR 136-137 E 6
Bad Rapids ~ CDN 32-33 N 3
Bad Reichenhall o D 92-93 M 5
Badrinath o IND 138-139 G 4
Bad River ~ USA (SD) 260-261 E 2
Bad River Indian Reservation Ⅹ USA (WI) 270-271 H 4
Badr wa-Hunain o KSA 130-131 F 6
Bad Segeberg o• D 92-93 L 2
Bad Tölz o D 92-93 L 5
Badu o VRC 156-157 J 3
Badu Island ⌒ AUS 174-175 G 2
Badulla o CL 140-141 J 7
Badvel o IND 140-141 H 3
Badwater River ~ CDN 30-31 R 6
Badžal ~ RUS 122-123 F 3
Badžal'skij hrebet ▲ RUS 122-123 E 3
Badzéré o CAM 206-207 B 6
Baediam o RIM 202-203 E 2
Baer o VRC 144-145 B 4
Baerskin Lake o CDN 34-35 L 4
Baeza o E 98-99 F 6
Baeza o EC 64-65 D 2

Baezaeko River ~ CDN (BC) 228-229 K 4
Bafang o CAM 204-205 J 6
Bafata ☆ GNB 202-203 C 3
Baffin Basin ≃ 26-27 R 7
Baffin Bay ≈ 26-27 P 7
Baffin Bay ≈ 44-45 J 6
Baffin Bay ≈ USA 266-267 K 6
Baffin-Greenland Rise ≃ 28-29 L 3
Baffin Island ⌒ CDN 24-25 e 5
Bafia o CAM 204-205 J 6
Bafilo o RT 202-203 L 5
Bafing ~ RMM 202-203 E 3
Bafing-Makana o RMM 202-203 E 3
Bafodia o WAL 202-203 E 5
Bafoulabé o RMM 202-203 E 3
Bafoussam ☆ CAM 204-205 J 6
Bāfq o IR 134-135 F 3
Bafra ☆ TR 128-129 F 2
Bafra Burnu ▲ TR 128-129 F 2
Bāft o IR 134-135 G 4
Bafu Bay ≈ 202-203 F 7
Bafut o• CAM 204-205 J 5
Bafwabalinga o ZRE 212-213 A 3
Bafwabogbo o ZRE 210-211 L 3
Bafwaboli o ZRE 210-211 L 3
Bafwasende o ZRE 212-213 A 3
Baga o WAN 198-199 F 6
Bagabag o RP 160-161 D 4
Bagabag Island ⌒ PNG 183 D 3
Baga-Burul o RUS 126-127 F 5
Bagaces o CR 52-53 B 6
Bagadja o RUS 118-119 J 3
Bagaembo o ZRE 206-207 E 6
Bagaevskij = stanica Bagaevskaja o RUS 102-103 M 4
Bagagem, Rio ~ BR 68-69 D 7
Bagai o PNG 183 E 3
Bagalkot o IND 140-141 F 2
Bāgalūr o IND 140-141 G 4
Bagamanoc o RP 160-161 F 6
Bagan Datuk o MAL 162-163 D 2
Bagandou o RCA 210-211 F 2
Bagani o NAM 216-217 F 9
Bagansiapiapi o RI 162-163 D 3
Bagansinembah o RI 162-163 D 4
Baganuur = Nuurst o MAU 148-149 J 4
Bagaré o BF 202-203 J 3
Bagaroua o RN 198-199 B 5
Bagasin o PNG 183 C 3
Baga Sola o TCH 198-199 G 6
Bagassi o BF 202-203 J 4
Bagata o BF 202-203 K 4
Bagata o ZRE 210-211 F 5
Bagazan o PE 64-65 F 4
Bagbe ~ WAL 202-203 E 5
Bagdād ▫ IRQ 128-129 L 6
Bagdād ★•• IRQ 128-129 L 6
Bagdad o USA (AZ) 256-257 B 4
Bagdarin ☆ RUS 118-119 F 8
Bagé o BR 76-77 K 6
Bagega o WAN 204-205 F 3
Bāqein o IR 134-135 G 3
Bāq-e Malek o IR 134-135 C 3
Bāgepalli o IND 140-141 G 4
Baqestān o IR 134-135 H 1
Bageya o WAN 198-199 B 6
Bāggirān o IR 136-137 F 6
Baggs o USA (WY) 252-253 L 5
Baghdad = Bagdād ★•• IRQ 128-129 L 6
Baghel Boland o IR 134-135 C 3
Baghelkhand Plateau ▲ IND 142-143 B 4
Bagherhat o•• BD 142-143 F 4
Baghmara o IND 142-143 G 3
Baghpat o IND 138-139 F 5
Bağil o Y 132-133 C 6
Baginda, Tanjung ▲ RI 162-163 G 6
Baglān ▫ AFG 136-137 L 7
Baglān ☆ AFG 136-137 L 6
Bagley o USA (MN) 270-271 C 3
Bagley Icefield ⊂ USA 20-21 T 6
Bagnell Dam • USA (MO) 274-275 F 6
Bagnères-de-Bigorre o F 90-91 H 10
Bago o RP 160-161 E 7
Bago, Pulau ⌒ RI 162-163 B 3
Bagodar o IND 142-143 D 3
Bagodo o CAM 204-205 K 5
Bagodra o IND 138-139 D 8
Bagoé ~ RMM 202-203 G 3
Bagomoyo o• EAT 214-215 K 4
Bagoosaar o SP 208-209 G 6
Bagot o CDN (MAN) 234-235 E 5
Bagot Range ▲ AUS 178-179 C 4
Bagou o DY 204-205 E 3
Bagraband, Kūh-e ▲ IR 134-135 J 5
Bagrāmi o AFG 138-139 B 2
Bagrationovsk ☆•• RUS 94-95 G 4
Bagre o BR 62-63 J 6
Bag Tug ~ VRC 154-155 F 2
Bagua o PE 64-65 C 4
Bagua Grande o PE 64-65 C 4
Baguales, Cerro ▲ RA 80 F 4
Báguanos o C 54-55 G 4
Bagudo o WAN 204-205 F 3
Baguinéda o RMM 202-203 G 3
Baguio o RP (DAO) 160-161 F 9
Baguio o•• RP (BEN) 160-161 D 4
Bagyrlaj ~ KA 96-97 G 9
Bāha, al- ▫ KSA 132-133 B 3
Bāha, al- ☆ KSA 132-133 B 3
Bahādorābād o IR 134-135 G 4
Bahadurabad Ghat o BD 142-143 F 3
Bahādurganj o IND 142-143 E 2
Baham, Umm al- o KSA 132-133 C 5
Bahamas = Bahamas, The ■ BS 54-55 J 4
Bahamas National Trust Park ⊥ BS 54-55 J 4
Bahapča ~ RUS 120-121 O 3
Bahār o IR 134-135 C 1
Bahārāgora o IND 142-143 E 4
Baharak o AFG 136-137 M 6
Baharampur o IND 142-143 F 3
Baharden o TM 136-137 E 5
Bahardok o TM 136-137 F 5
Bahariya Oasis = Bahriya, al-Wāhāt al- ⚍• ET 194-195 D 3
Bāharz, Kūh-e ▲ IR 136-137 F 7
Bahau o MAL 162-163 E 3
Bahaur o RI 164-165 D 5
Bahāwalnagar o PK 138-139 D 5
Bahāwalpur o• PK 138-139 C 5
Bahay o RP 160-161 E 6
Bahçe ☆ TR 128-129 G 4
Baheri o IND 138-139 G 5
Bahi o EAT 212-213 E 6
Bahia ▫ BR 68-69 H 7
Bahia ▫ BR 72-73 H 2
Bahía, Islas de la ⌒ HN 52-53 L 3
Bahia, Tanjung ▲ RI 166-167 H 4
Bahía Asunción o MEX 50-51 B 4
Bahía Blanca o RA 78-79 H 5
Bahía Bustamante o RA 80 G 2
Bahía Creek o RA 78-79 H 6
Bahía de Caráquez o EC 64-65 B 2
Bahía de Los Angeles o MEX 50-51 C 3
Bahía Honda o C 54-55 D 3
Bahía Kino o MEX 50-51 D 3
Bahía Laura o RA 80 G 4
Bahía Mansa o RCH 78-79 C 6
Bahías, Cabo dos ▲ RA 80 H 2
Bahía Solano o CO 60-61 C 4
Bahía Tortugas o MEX 50-51 B 4
Bahir, Che'w o ETH 208-209 C 6
Bahir Dar o ETH 208-209 C 3
Bāhla o IND 138-139 C 6
Bahla o••• OM 132-133 K 2
Bahma o IRQ 128-129 L 4
Bahn o LB 202-203 F 6
Bahr o RCA 206-207 G 6
Bahra o KSA 132-133 A 3
Bahra, al- o KWT 130-131 K 3
Bahra al-Qadima o KSA 132-133 A 3
Bahraich o IND 142-143 B 2
Bahrain = Bahrain, al- ■ BRN 134-135 D 6
Bahr al-Milh ‹ IRQ 128-129 K 6
Bahret Lut = Yam Hamelah ⊖ JOR 130-131 D 2
Bahši Kalai o AFG 138-139 B 4
Bahta ~ RUS 114-115 U 3
Bahta ~ RUS 116-117 F 4
Bāhtarān ▫ IR 134-135 B 1
Bāhtarān ☆• IR (BAH) 134-135 B 1
Bahtegān, Daryāče-ye ⊖ IR 134-135 E 4
Bahtemir ~ RUS 126-127 G 5
Bahty o KA 124-125 N 5
Bahubulu, Pulau ⌒ RI 164-165 H 5
Bāhū Kalāt, Rūdhāne-ye ~ IR 134-135 J 6
Bahusuai o RI 164-165 G 5
Bahynaj o RUS 110-111 O 6
Baia o PNG 183 F 3
Baía, Rio da ~ BR 68-69 B 5
Baía dos Tigres o ANG 216-217 A 8
Baia Farta o ANG 216-217 B 6
Baia Formosa o BR 68-69 L 5
Baia Grande, Lago ⊖ BR 70-71 G 4
Baia Mare ☆• RO 102-103 C 4
Baianópolis o BR 72-73 H 2
Baião o BR 68-69 D 3
Baia River ~ PNG 183 B 4
Baibokoum o TCH 206-207 B 5
Baicheng o VRC (JIL) 150-151 D 5
Baicheng o VRC (XUZ) 146-147 E 5
Băicoi o RO 102-103 D 5
Baidā', al- o Y 132-133 D 7
Baidā' Natil o KSA 130-131 G 4
Baidi Cheng • VRC 154-155 F 6
Baïdou ~ RCA 206-207 E 6
Baie, La o CDN (QUE) 240-241 E 2
Baie-Comeau o CDN 38-39 K 4
Baie-des-Bacon o CDN (QUE) 240-241 F 2
Baie-des-Rochers o CDN (QUE) 240-241 F 3
Baie-des-Sables o CDN (QUE) 240-241 H 2
Baie-du-Poste o CDN (QUE) 236-237 P 2
Baie-du-Renard o CDN (QUE) 242-243 G 3
Baie Johan Beetz o CDN (QUE) 242-243 F 2
Baie-Sainte-Catherine o CDN (QUE) 240-241 F 2
Baie-Sainte-Claire o CDN (QUE) 242-243 D 3
Baie-Trinité o CDN (QUE) 242-243 A 3
Ba'iği o IRQ 128-129 K 5
Baihān al-Qasāb o Y 132-133 D 6
Baihe o VRC (JIL) 150-151 G 6
Baihe o VRC (SXI) 154-155 G 5
Baikal, Lake = Bajkal, ozero ⊖ RUS 116-117 N 9
Baikal-Amur-Magistrale = BAM II RUS 118-119 E 7
Baikoré, Bahr ~ TCH 206-207 E 3
Baikunthpur o IND 142-143 C 4
Baila o SN 202-203 B 3
Baila o VRC 144-145 F 6
Bailang o VRC 156-157 E 4
Baile Átha Cliath = Dublin ★•• IRL 90-91 D 5
Baile Átha Fhirdhia = Ardee o IRL 90-91 D 5
Baile Átha Luain = Athlone o IRL 90-91 D 5
Baile Átha Troim = Trim ☆• IRL 90-91 D 5
Baile Brigin = Balbriggan o IRL 90-91 D 5
Baile Chaisleáin Bhéarra = Castletown Bearhaven o IRL 90-91 C 6
Baile Chathail = Charlestown o IRL 90-91 C 5
Băile Herculane o RO 102-103 C 5
Baile Locha Riach = Loughrea o IRL 90-91 C 5
Baile Mhistéala = Mitchelstown o IRL 90-91 C 5
Bailén o E 98-99 F 5
Băilești o RO 102-103 C 5
Bailey o USA (CO) 254-255 K 4
Bailey o USA (TX) 264-265 H 5
Bailey Point ▲ CDN 24-25 O 3
Bailey Range ▲ AUS 176-177 G 4
Baileys Harbor o USA (WI) 270-271 L 5
Bail Hongal o IND 140-141 F 3
Baili, Bi'r ‹ ET 192-193 L 2
Bailidujuan • VRC 156-157 E 3
Bailin o VRC 156-157 H 3
Bailingmiao • VRC 148-149 K 7
Bailique o BR (APA) 62-63 J 5
Bailique o BR (P) 68-69 D 3
Bailique, Ilha ⌒ BR 62-63 K 5
Baillargeon, Réserve ⊥ CDN (QUE) 240-241 L 2
Bailleul o F 90-91 J 6
Ba Illi o TCH 206-207 C 3
Ba Illi ~ TCH 206-207 C 3
Baillie Hamilton Island ⌒ CDN 24-25 Z 3
Baillie Islands ⌒ CDN 24-25 G 5
Baillie River ~ CDN 30-31 R 3
Bailong Jiang ~ VRC 154-155 D 5
Bailundo o ANG 216-217 C 6
Baima o VRC 154-155 B 5
Baimaxue Shan Z.B. ⊥• VRC 144-145 M 6
Baimka o RUS 112-113 N 3
Baimun o RI 166-167 H 5
Baimuru o PNG 183 C 4
Baina o PNG 183 B 4
Bainbridge o USA (GA) 284-285 F 6
Bainbridge Island o USA (WA) 244-245 C 3
Baines Drift o RB 218-219 E 6
Bainet o RH 54-55 J 5
Baing o RI 168 E 8
Baingoin o VRC 144-145 H 5
Baining Mountains ▲ PNG 183 G 3
Bainville o USA (MT) 250-251 P 3
Baiona o E 98-99 C 3
Baiquan o VRC 150-151 F 4
Bā'ir o JOR 130-131 E 2
Bā'ir, Wādi ~ JOR 130-131 E 2
Baird o USA (TX) 264-265 E 6
Baird, Cape ▲ CDN 26-27 S 3
Baird Inlet ≈ 20-21 H 6
Baird Mountains ▲ USA 20-21 K 3
Baird Peninsula ⌣ CDN 24-25 h 6
Bairds Table Mountain ▲ AUS 174-175 G 6
Baire o C 54-55 G 4
Bairiki ★ KIB 13 J 2
Bairin Youqi o VRC 148-149 O 6
Bairin Zuoqi o VRC 148-149 O 5
Bairnsdale o• AUS 180-181 J 4
Bairoil o USA (WY) 252-253 L 4
Bairūt ★ RL 128-129 F 6
Baiš o KSA 132-133 C 5
Bais o RP 160-161 E 8
Baiš, Wādi ~ KSA 132-133 C 5
Baïse ~ F 90-91 H 10
Baisha o VRC (HAI) 156-157 F 7
Baisha o VRC (SIC) 156-157 E 2
Baishan o VRC 150-151 F 6
Bai Shan ▲ VRC 146-147 L 4
Baishanzu ▲ VRC 156-157 L 3
Baishilazi Z.B. ⊥• VRC 150-151 E 7
Baishiling • VRC 156-157 G 4
Baishui o VRC 154-155 F 4
Baishuijiang Z.B. ⊥• VRC 154-155 D 5
Baisogala o•• LT 94-95 H 4
Baissa o WAN 204-205 J 5
Bait Adāqa o Y 132-133 C 6
Baitadi o NEP 144-145 C 6
Bait al-Faqih o• Y 132-133 C 6
Bait Lahm = Bet Lehem ☆•• WB 130-131 D 2
Bait Range ▲ CDN 32-33 G 4
Baixa do Tubarã, Rio ~ BR 68-69 J 7
Baixa Grande o BR 68-69 H 7
Baixão o BR 72-73 K 2
Baixo Guandu o BR 72-73 K 5
Baixo Longa o ANG 216-217 E 7
Baiyang Gou • VRC 146-147 H 4
Baiyan Temple o VRC 154-155 G 3
Baiyer River o PNG 183 C 3
Baiyer River National Park ⊥ PNG 183 C 3
Baiyi o VRC 154-155 E 6
Baiyin o VRC 154-155 D 3
Baizeklik Qianfodong • VRC 146-147 J 4
Baja o H 92-93 P 5
Baja, Punta ▲ MEX (BCN) 50-51 B 3
Baja, Punta ▲ MEX (SON) 50-51 D 3
Baja California ⌣ MEX 50-51 B 2
Baja California Norte ▫ MEX 50-51 B 2
Baja California Sur ▫ MEX 50-51 C 4
Bajada, La o C 54-55 C 4
Bajada del Agrio o RA 78-79 D 5
Bajaga ~ RUS 120-121 E 2
Bajan o MAU 146-147 M 2
Baján o MEX 50-51 J 4
Bajanaul ☆•• KA 124-125 J 3
Bajanbulag o MAU 148-149 D 4
Bajančandman = Ih suuž o MAU 148-149 H 4
Bajandaj ☆ RUS 116-117 M 9
Bajandèlgèr =Širèèt o MAU 148-149 L 5
Bajangol=Baruunharaa o MAU 148-149 H 3
Bajan-Hongor ▫ MAU 148-149 D 4
Bajanhongor ☆ MAU 148-149 E 4
Bajanhošuu o MAU 146-147 K 1
Bajanlig = Hatansuudal o MAU 148-149 E 5
Bajanmönh = Ulaan-Èrèg o MAU 148-149 J 4
Bajan-Ölgijo ▫ MAU 146-147 J 1
Bajan-Öndör = Bumbat o MAU 148-149 G 4
Bajan-Önzuul = Ihhairhan o MAU 148-149 H 4
Bajan-Ovoo o MAU 146-147 M 3
Bajan-Ovoo = Žavhlant o MAU 148-149 L 4
Bajantèèg o MAU 148-149 E 5
Bajan Uul = Bajan o MAU 146-147 M 2
Bajan-Uul = Žavarthošuu o MAU 148-149 L 3
Bajasgalant o MAU 148-149 L 4
Bajawa o RI 168 E 7
Bajdarackaja guba ≈ 108-109 L 7
Bajdarata ~ RUS 108-109 M 8
Bajdrag gol ~ MAU 148-149 D 4
Bajganin ☆ KA 126-127 M 3
Bajie o VRC 156-157 D 4
Bajimba, Mount ▲ AUS 178-179 M 5
Bajina Bašta o• YU 100-101 G 3
Bajio de Ahuichila o MEX 50-51 H 5
Bajios de Agua Blanca o MEX 50-51 F 5
Bajkadam o KA 136-137 L 3
Bajkadam ☆ KA 136-137 L 3
Bajkal o RUS 116-117 M 10
Bajkal, zaliv ⊖ RUS 122-123 K 2
Bajkalovo o RUS 114-115 J 6
Bajkalovsk o RUS 108-109 U 6
Bajkal'sk o RUS 116-117 L 10
Bajkal'skij hrebet ▲ RUS 116-117 O 8
Bajkal'skij zapovednij ⊥ RUS 116-117 M 10
Bajkal'skoe o RUS 118-119 D 8
Bajki o RUS 96-97 K 6
Bajkit o RUS 116-117 H 5
Bajkonyr o KA 124-125 E 5
Bajkonyr ~ KA 124-125 D 5
Bajkovo o RUS 122-123 R 3
Bajmak ☆ RUS 96-97 L 7
Bajo o RI 168 D 7
Bajo, El o YV 60-61 J 3
Bajo Caracoles o RA 80 E 3
Bajoga o WAN 204-205 J 3
Bajo Hondo o RA 76-77 D 6
Bajo Nuevo ⌒ CO 54-55 F 7
Bajool o AUS 178-179 L 2
Bajo Pichanaqui o PE 64-65 E 7
Bajos de Haina o DOM 54-55 K 5
Bajram-Ali o TM 136-137 H 6
Bajsa o RUS 118-119 F 8
Bajsun o US 136-137 K 5
Bajugan o RI 164-165 G 3
Bajyrkům o KA 136-137 L 3
Baká o NIC 52-53 B 5
Bakaba o TCH 206-207 C 5
Bakairi, Área Indígena ⚔ BR 70-71 K 4
Bakal o RUS 96-97 L 6
Bakala o RCA (OMB) 206-207 C 6
Bakala o RCA (Oua) 206-207 E 5
Bakali ~ ZRE 210-211 F 6
Bakaly ☆ RUS 96-97 H 6
Bakanas ~ KA 124-125 L 5
Bakaoré o TCH 198-199 K 5
Bakau o• WAG 202-203 B 3
Bakaucengal o RI 164-165 E 5
Bakauhuni o RI 162-163 F 7
Bakayan, Gunung ▲ RI 164-165 E 2
Bakbakty o KA 124-125 K 6
Bakčar o RUS 114-115 R 6
Bakčar ~ RUS 114-115 R 6
Bakebe o CAM 204-205 H 6
Bakel o• SN 202-203 D 2
Bakelalan o MAL 164-165 D 2
Baker o USA (CA) 248-249 H 4
Baker o USA (LA) 268-269 J 6
Baker o USA (MT) 250-251 P 5
Baker o USA (NV) 246-247 L 4
Baker o USA (OR) 244-245 H 6
Baker o USA (WV) 280-281 H 4
Baker, Canal ≈ 80 C 3
Baker, Mount ▲ USA (WA) 244-245 D 2
Baker Creek ~ CDN (BC) 228-229 M 4
Bakerhill o USA (AL) 284-285 E 5
Baker Island ⌒ USA 13 K 2
Baker Island ⌒ USA 32-33 D 4
Baker Lake o AUS 176-177 J 3
Baker Lake o CDN (NWT) 30-31 V 3
Baker Lake ⊖ CDN (NWT) 30-31 W 3
Baker Lake ⊖ USA (WA) 244-245 D 2
Baker Range ▲ AUS 176-177 H 2
Bakers Dozen Islands ⌒ CDN 36-37 K 6
Baker Settlement o CDN (NS) 240-241 L 6
Bakersfield o USA (CA) 248-249 F 4
Bakersfield o USA (TX) 266-267 E 3
Bakerville o ZA 220-221 H 2
Ba Khe o VN 156-157 D 6
Bakhtiyārpur o IND 142-143 D 3
Baki ★• AZ 128-129 N 2
Bakin Birji o RN 198-199 D 5
Bakinskij arhipelago ⌒ AZ 128-129 N 3
Bakırçay ~ TR 128-129 B 3
Bakkafjörður o IS 86-87 f 1
Bakkejord o N 86-87 J 2
Baknars Tāl o IND 142-143 C 2
Bako o CI 202-203 G 5
Bako o ETH 208-209 C 4
Bako National Park ⊥ MAL 162-163 J 4
Bakong, Pulau ⌒ RI 162-163 F 4
Bakongan o RI 162-163 B 3
Bakool ▫ SP 208-209 F 6
Bakop o PNG 183 G 3
Bakordi o SUD 206-207 J 6
Bakore, Massif de ▲ RCA 206-207 B 5
Bakori o WAN 204-205 G 3
Bakouma o RCA 206-207 F 6
Bakoumba o G 210-211 D 4
Bakoye ~ RMM 202-203 F 3
Baksa ~ RUS 114-115 R 7
Bak Sadane ‹ RMM 196-197 J 5
Baksaj ~ KA 96-97 G 10
Baksan o RUS 126-127 E 6
Baksan ~ RUS 126-127 E 6
Baktalórántháza o H 92-93 R 5
Baku = Bakı ★• AZ 128-129 N 2
Bakulu o RI 164-165 K 3
Bakung, Pulau ⌒ RI 162-163 F 4
Bakuriani o GE 126-127 E 7
Bakwa-Kenge o ZRE 210-211 J 6
Baky ~ RUS 110-111 X 5
Bakyrly o KA 124-125 E 6
Bakyrly o KA 124-125 E 6
Bala o CDN (ONT) 238-239 F 3
Bala o RUS 110-111 T 6
Bala o SN 202-203 D 2
Balâ ☆ TR 128-129 E 3
Bala o WAN 204-205 F 4
Bala, Cerros de ▲ BOL 70-71 C 3
Balabac o RP 160-161 B 9
Balabac Island ⌒ RP 160-161 B 9
Balabac Strait ≈ 160-161 B 9
Balabagan o RP 160-161 F 9
Balabaiba o ANG 216-217 B 6
Ba'labakk ☆••• RL 128-129 G 5
Balabala o ZRE 210-211 H 2
Balabalangan, Kepulauan ⌒ RI 164-165 E 5
Bālā Bolūk o AFG 134-135 K 2
Balad al-Mala o IRQ 128-129 L 5
Balade o IR 136-137 B 6
Baladjie Lake ⊖ AUS 176-177 E 5
Balad Rūz o IRQ 128-129 L 6
Balad Sinğār o IRQ 128-129 J 4
Balagaččy o RUS 118-119 L 3
Balaganah o RUS 118-119 H 6
Balagančik, hrebet ▲ RUS 122-123 R 2
Balagannoe o RUS 120-121 N 4
Balagansk o RUS 116-117 L 9
Balagan-Taas • RUS 110-111 Z 6
Balaguer o E 98-99 H 4
Balahna o RUS 94-95 S 3
Balahnja, Bol'šaja ~ RUS 108-109 f 5
Balahnja, gora ▲ RUS 110-111 F 3
Balahta ☆ RUS 116-117 E 8
Ba Lai, Sông ~ VN 158-159 J 5
Balai Berkuak o RI 162-163 J 5
Balaikarangan o RI 162-163 J 4
Balaipunguț o RI 162-163 D 4
Balaiselasa o RI 162-163 D 5
Balaka o MW 218-219 H 2
Balakbal ∴• MEX 52-53 K 3
Balakété o RCA 206-207 D 5
Balaki o RG 202-203 E 3
Balaklava o AUS 180-181 E 3
Balaklija o UA 102-103 K 3
Balākot o PK 138-139 D 2
Balakovo ☆ RUS 96-97 E 7
Balala o ETH 208-209 B 6
Balalai Island ⌒ SOL 184 I b 2
Balama o MOC 218-219 K 1
Balamba o CAM 204-205 J 6
Balambangan, Pulau ⌒ MAL 160-161 B 9
Balam Tākli o IND 138-139 E 10
Balancán de Domínguez o MEX 52-53 J 3
Balanced Rock ∴• USA (ID) 252-253 D 4
Balandou o RG 202-203 F 4
Balanga ☆ RP 160-161 D 5
Balanga o ZRE 214-215 E 5
Balangala o ZRE 210-211 G 3
Ba Làng An, Mūi ▲ VN 158-159 K 3
Balāngir o IND 142-143 C 5
Balangkayan o RP 160-161 F 7
Balangoda o CL 140-141 J 7
Balao o EC 64-65 C 3
Balaoan o RP 160-161 D 4
Balapitiya o CL 140-141 J 7
Balaraja o RI 168 B 3
Balarāmpur o IND 142-143 E 4
Balasan o RP 160-161 E 7
Balašiha ☆ RUS 94-95 P 4
Bal-Asmar o KSA 132-133 C 4
Balašov o RUS 102-103 N 2
Balassagyarmat o H 92-93 P 4
Balāt o ET 194-195 D 5
Balat (Labuhanbalat) o RI 168 C 7
Bala-Tal'dyk ~ KA 126-127 N 3
Balatan o RP 160-161 E 6
Balaton ⊖ H 92-93 O 5
Balatonfüred o H 92-93 O 5
Balauring o RI 166-167 B 6
Balavé o BF 202-203 H 3
Balaya o RG 202-203 D 4
Balazote o E 98-99 F 5
Balbalan o RP 160-161 D 4
Balbalasang o RP 160-161 D 4
Balbao o• PA 52-53 E 7
Balbi, Mount ▲ PNG 184 I b 1
Balbina o BR 62-63 E 6
Balbina, Cachoeira ~ BR 62-63 E 6
Balbina, Represa de ‹ BR 62-63 E 6
Balboa o CO 60-61 D 5
Balbriggan = Baile Brigin o IRL 90-91 D 5
Balcad o SP 212-213 K 2
Balcarce o RA 78-79 K 4
Balcarres o CDN (SAS) 232-233 P 5
Bălcești o RO 102-103 C 5
Balchaš, ozero = Balqash Köl ⊖ KA 124-125 H 6
Balčik o BG 102-103 F 6
Balclutha o NZ 182 B 7
Balcoms Corners o USA (NY) 278-279 B 6
Balcones Escarpment ▲ USA (TX) 266-267 H 4
Bald Eagle Mountain ▲ USA (PA) 280-281 J 3
Balde de la Mora o RA 76-77 E 6
Baldenburg = Biały Bór o• PL 92-93 O 2
Bald Head ▲ AUS 176-177 E 7
Bald Hill ▲ CDN 20-21 Z 4
Bald Hill No. 2 ▲ AUS 178-179 L 4
Bald Knob o USA (AR) 276-277 D 5
Bald Mountain ▲ USA (NV) 248-249 J 2
Baldock Lake ⊖ CDN 34-35 H 2
Baldur o CDN (MAN) 234-235 D 5
Baldwin o USA (FL) 286-287 H 1
Baldwin o USA (IA) 274-275 H 2
Baldwin o USA (MI) 272-273 D 4
Baldwin o USA (WI) 270-271 F 6
Baldwin, Parc Provincial ⊥ CDN (QUE) 240-241 K 2
Baldwin Bank ~ AUS 172-173 H 2
Baldwin City o USA (KS) 262-263 L 6
Baldwin Peninsula ⌣ USA 20-21 J 3
Baldwinsville o USA (NY) 278-279 E 5
Baldwinton o CDN (SAS) 232-233 J 3
Baldwyn o USA (MS) 268-269 M 2
Baldy Hughes o CDN (BC) 228-229 M 3
Baldy Mountain ▲ CDN (BC) 230-231 K 4
Baldy Mountain ▲ CDN (MAN) 234-235 C 3
Baldy Peak ▲ USA (AZ) 256-257 F 5
Bal'dźikan o RUS 118-119 E 11
Bale o ANG 216-217 D 7
Bale ▫ ETH 208-209 E 6
Balé ~ RG 202-203 E 4
Bale ~ RMM 202-203 F 4
Bâle = Basel ☆• CH 92-93 J 5
Baleares, Islas ▫ E 98-99 H 5
Balearic Islands = Balears, Illes ⌒ E 98-99 J 5
Balease ~ RI 164-165 G 5
Balease, Gunung ▲ RI 164-165 G 5
Baleh ~ MAL 162-163 K 4
Baleia, Ponta da ▲ BR 72-73 L 4
Baleine, Rivière à la ~ CDN 36-37 Q 5
Balej ☆ RUS 118-119 H 10
Balékoutou o TCH 206-207 D 4
Balelesberge ▲ ZA 220-221 K 3
Bale Mount National Park ⊥ ETH 208-209 D 5
Baleno o RP 160-161 E 6
Baler o RP 160-161 D 5
Baler Bay ≈ 160-161 D 5
Baleshwar o IND 142-143 E 5
Balestrand ☆• N 86-87 C 6
Baléya o RMM 202-203 F 3
Baleyara o RN 204-205 E 2
Baley Guerrero o DOM 54-55 L 5
Balezino ☆ RUS 96-97 H 5
Balfour o AUS 180-181 H 6
Balfour o CDN (BC) 230-231 N 4
Balfour o USA (ND) 258-259 G 4
Balfour o ZA (CAP) 220-221 H 6
Balfour o ZA (TRA) 220-221 J 3
Balfour Downs o AUS 172-173 E 7
Balgak o SUD 200-201 C 6
Balgazyn o RUS 116-117 G 10
Balgo ⚔ AUS 172-173 J 6
Balgonie o CDN (SAS) 232-233 O 5
Balguntay o VRC 146-147 H 4
Balğurasi o KSA 132-133 B 4
Balh o AFG 136-137 K 6
Balh ▫ AFG 136-137 K 6
Balh, Daryā-ye ~ AFG 136-137 K 6
Balh Ab o AFG 136-137 K 7
Balh Ab, Rūd-e ~ AFG 136-137 K 7
Balhaš = Balkash o KA 124-125 J 5
Balhaš, ozero = Balkash köl ⊖ KA 124-125 J 5
Balho o DJI 200-201 L 6
Bali o CAM 204-205 J 6
Bali o IND 142-143 F 4
Bali ▫ RI 168 B 6
Bali, Laut ≈ 168 B 6
Bali, Pulau ⌒ RI 168 B 7
Bali, Selat ≈ 168 B 7
Balibi o RCA 206-207 E 5
Balibo o RI 166-167 C 6
Baliem ~ RI 166-167 K 4
Baliem Valley ⌣ RI 166-167 K 3
Balifondo o RCA 206-207 F 6
Balige o RI 162-163 C 3
Balıkesir ☆ TR 128-129 B 3
Balikpapan o RI 164-165 E 4
Balikpapary, Teluk ≈ 164-165 E 4
Balimela Reservoir ‹ IND 142-143 C 6
Balimo o PNG 183 B 5
Baling o MAL 162-163 D 2
Balingara, Pegunungan ▲ RI 164-165 G 4
Balingian o MAL 162-163 K 3
Balinn ~ RMM 202-203 E 3
Balintang Channel ≈ 160-161 D 3
Baliza o BR 72-73 D 4
Baljaga o RUS 116-117 O 10
Baljennie o CDN (SAS) 232-233 L 3
Balkan Mountains = Stara Planina ▲ BG 102-103 C 6
Balkaš o KA 124-125 J 5
Balkash köl ⊖ KA 124-125 H 6
Balkašty ☆ KA 124-125 F 2
Balkon-Myl'k, gora ▲ RUS 88-89 O 2
Ball, Mount ▲ AUS 172-173 H 5
Balladonia Motel o AUS 176-177 G 6
Ballangen o N 86-87 H 2
Ballantyne, Lac o CDN 36-37 P 5
Ballantyne Strait ≈ 24-25 O 2
Ballarat o AUS 180-181 G 4
Ballard, Lake o AUS 176-177 F 4
Ballaroo o AUS 178-179 K 4
Ballasetas o RI 162-163 B 3
Ballater o GB 90-91 F 3
Ballé o RMM 202-203 F 2
Ballena, Punta ▲ EC 64-65 B 2
Ballenas, Canal de ≈ 50-51 C 3
Ballenero, Canal ≈ 80 E 7
Ballia o IND 142-143 D 3
Ballidu o AUS 176-177 D 5
Ballina o AUS 178-179 M 5
Ballina = Béal an Átha o IRL 90-91 C 4
Ballinasloe = Béal Átha na Sluaighe o IRL 90-91 C 5
Ballinger o USA (TX) 266-267 H 2
Ball Lake o CDN (ONT) 234-235 K 4
Ballone Highway II AUS 178-179 J 4
Balloul o DZ 190-191 C 3
Ball's Pyramid ⌒ AUS 180-181 N 7
Bally o USA (PA) 280-281 L 3
Ballycastle o GB 90-91 D 4
Ballyshannon o IRL 90-91 C 4
Balmacara o GB 90-91 E 3
Balmaceda o RCH 80 E 2
Balmaceda, Cerro ▲ RCH 80 D 5
Balmaceda, Parque Nacional ⊥ RCH 80 D 5
Balmaceda, Sierra ▲ RCH 80 F 6
Balmertown o CDN (ONT) 234-235 K 3
Balmoral o AUS 180-181 F 4
Balmoral o ZA 220-221 J 2
Balmorhea o USA (TX) 266-267 D 2
Balnearia o RA 76-77 F 6
Balneário Camboriú o BR 74-75 F 6
Balneario del Sol o•• C 54-55 H 5
Balneario las Grutas o RA 78-79 G 6
Balneario Massini o RA 78-79 H 6
Balo o RI 164-165 H 4
Baloa o RI 164-165 H 4
Balobaloang-Kecil, Pulau ⌒ RI 168 D 6
Balod o IND 142-143 B 5
Balohan, Teluk ≈ 162-163 A 2
Balok, Kampung o MAL 162-163 E 3
Balombo o ANG 216-217 C 6
Balombo ~ ANG 216-217 C 6
Balong o RI 168 D 3
Balong o VRC 144-145 L 2
Balonne River ~ AUS 178-179 K 5
Balotra o IND 138-139 D 7
Balqash Köl = Balkaš köl ⊖ KA 124-125 H 6
Balrāmpur o IND 142-143 C 2
Balranald o AUS 180-181 G 3
Balș o RO 102-103 D 5
Balsa Nova o BR 74-75 F 5
Balsapuerto o PE 64-65 D 4
Balsas o BR 68-69 E 5
Balsas o MEX 52-53 E 2
Balsas o PE 64-65 D 5
Balsas, Río ~ MEX 52-53 E 3
Balsas, Rio das ~ BR 68-69 F 5
Balsas, Rio das ~ BR 68-69 E 7
Balsinhas, Ribeiro ~ BR 68-69 F 5
Balta ☆ UA 102-103 F 4
Balta o USA (ND) 258-259 G 3
Balta Brăilei ⚍ RO 102-103 E 5
Baltakōl o KA 136-137 K 3
Baltakol' o KA 136-137 K 3
Baltal o IND 138-139 E 2
Baltasar Brum o ROU 76-77 J 6
Baltasi ☆ RUS 96-97 G 5
Baltazar o YV 60-61 H 6
Bălți ☆ MD 102-103 E 4
Baltic Sea ≈ 86-87 H 9
Baltijsk ☆ RUS 94-95 F 4
Baltīm o ET 194-195 E 2
Baltimore o USA (OH) 280-281 D 4
Baltimore o• USA (MD) 280-281 K 4
Baltimore o ZA 218-219 E 6
Baltimore = Dún na Séad o IRL 90-91 C 6
Baltit o PK 138-139 E 1
Baltiysk = Baltijsk o RUS 94-95 F 4
Baltra, Isla ⌒ EC 64-65 B 10
Baltrum ⌒ D 92-93 J 2
Ba Lụa, Quần Đảo ⌒ VN 158-159 H 5
Baluan Island ⌒ PNG 183 D 2
Baluarte, Arroyo ~ USA (TX) 266-267 J 6
Bālūčestān, Sīstān -ō- ▫ IR 134-135 H 5
Baluchistan ▫ PK 134-135 K 4
Baluchistan = Bālūčestan ⚍ IR 134-135 K 4
Balud o RP 160-161 E 6
Balui ~ MAL 164-165 D 2
Balūr o IND 140-141 F 4
Baluran Game Park ⊥ RI 168 B 6
Balut Island ⌒ RP 160-161 F 10
Balvard o IR 134-135 G 4
Balvi ☆•• LV 94-95 K 3
Balwāda o IND 138-139 E 8
Balwina Aboriginal Land ⚔ AUS 172-173 J 6
Balygyčan o RUS 112-113 H 5
Balygyčan ~ RUS 112-113 H 5
Balygyčan, Verhnij o RUS 112-113 H 5
Balyhta o RUS 116-117 M 8
Balykča o RUS 124-125 P 3
Balyktah ~ RUS 110-111 W 2
Balyktyg-Hem ~ RUS 116-117 H 10
Balzac o CDN (ALB) 232-233 D 4
Balzar o EC 64-65 C 2
Balzas o EC 64-65 C 3
Balž gol ~ MAU 148-149 K 3
Bam o IR 134-135 H 4
Bam o TCH 206-207 C 4
BAM = Baikal-Amur-Magistrale II RUS 118-119 E 7
Bam, Lac de o BF 202-203 K 3
Bama o• BF 202-203 H 4
Bama o VRC 156-157 E 4
Bama o WAN 204-205 K 3
Bamaba o ZRE 210-211 G 5
Bamaga ⚔ AUS 174-175 G 2
Bamaji Lake ⊖ CDN (ONT) 234-235 M 3
Bamake o LB 202-203 G 7
Bamako ▫ RMM 202-203 F 2
Bamako ★ RMM (BAM) 202-203 F 3
Bamba o EAK 212-213 G 5
Bamba ~ RCA 206-207 D 6
Bamba o RMM 196-197 K 6
Bamba o ZRE 210-211 G 6
Bambadinca o GNB 202-203 C 3
Bambak o PNG 183 E 3
Bambalang o CAM 204-205 J 6
Bambam o WAN 204-205 J 4
Bambama o RCB 210-211 D 5
Bambamarca o PE 64-65 C 5
Bambana, Río ~ NIC 52-53 B 5
Bambang o RI 162-163 E 7
Bambang o RP 160-161 D 4
Bambangan o MAL 160-161 B 10
Bambangando o ANG 218-219 B 3
Bambara o TCH 206-207 D 4
Bambara-Maoundé o RMM 202-203 J 2
Bambari ☆ RCA 206-207 E 6
Bambaroo o AUS 174-175 J 6
Bambéla o CI 202-203 J 5
Bamberg o•• D 92-93 L 4
Bamberg o USA (SC) 284-285 J 3
Bambesa o ZRE 210-211 K 2
Bambesi o ETH 208-209 B 4
Bambey o• SN 202-203 B 2
Bambila o RMM 202-203 E 2
Bambili o ZRE 210-211 L 2
Bambio o RCA 210-211 F 2
Bamboesberg ▲ ZA 220-221 G 5
Bamboi o GH 202-203 J 5
Bamboo Creek o AUS 172-173 E 6
Bambouk ⚍ RMM 202-203 E 2
Bambouti o RCA 206-207 H 6
Bamboutos, Monts ▲ CAM 204-205 J 6
Bambudi o ETH 208-209 B 3
Bambui o BR 72-73 H 6
Bambui o CAM 204-205 J 5
Bambujka ~ RUS 118-119 G 8
Bamenda ☆ CAM 204-205 J 6
Bamendjing, Lac de ‹ CAM 204-205 J 6
Bame Town o LB 202-203 F 7
Bamfield o CDN (BC) 230-231 D 5
Bami o TM 136-137 E 5
Bamingui o RCA 206-207 E 5
Bamingui ~ RCA 206-207 E 5
Bamingui-Bangoran ▫ RCA 206-207 D 4
Bamingui-Bangoran, Parc National du ⊥ RCA 206-207 D 4
Bamio o PNG 183 B 4

Bam Island ⌒ PNG 183 C 2
Bamkeri o RI 166-167 F 2
Bampošt, Kūh-e ▲ IR 134-135 K 5
Bampūr o IR 134-135 J 5
Bampūr, Rūd-e ~ IR 134-135 H 5
Bamra Hills ▲ IND 142-143 D 5
Bamrūd-e Softā o IR 134-135 J 2
Bamu River ~ PNG 183 B 4
Bamusso o CAM 204-205 H 6
Bāmyān ◘ AFG 134-135 M 1
Bāmyān ☆ • AFG (BM) 134-135 M 1
Bāmyān ~ AFG 136-137 K 7
Bamyili ✕ AUS 172-173 L 3
Ban o BF 202-203 J 2
Bana o CAM 204-205 J 6
Bana ∴ • TR 128-129 K 2
Bana, Col de ▲ CAM 204-205 J 6
Banā, Wādi ~ Y 132-133 D 7
Banaadir ◘ SP 212-213 K 2
Banabuiú, Açude < BR 68-69 J 4
Banabuiú, Rio ~ BR 68-69 J 4
Bana Daniéd o SN 202-203 D 2
Banagi o EAT 212-213 E 5
Banaigarh o IND 142-143 D 5
Banalia o ZRE 210-211 K 3
Banama o RG 202-203 F 5
Banamba o RMM 202-203 G 3
Banana o AUS 178-179 L 3
Banana o ZRE 216-217 B 3
Bananal, Ilha do ⌒ BR 68-69 C 7
Bananal, Rio ~ BR 68-69 D 6
Banana Range ▲ AUS 178-179 L 3
Banana River ≈ USA 286-287 J 3
Banandjé o CI 202-203 G 5
Bananeiras o BR 68-69 L 5
Banantara o RG 202-203 F 4
Banangui o RCA 206-207 G 6
Banankoro o RG 202-203 F 5
Banankoro o RMM (SÉ) 202-203 G 3
Banankoro o RMM (SIK) 202-203 F 4
Banao o C (CG) 54-55 G 4
Banao o C (SS) 54-55 F 4
Banapur o IND 142-143 D 6
Banās ~ IND 138-139 E 7
Banas ~ IND 138-139 D 7
Banas ~ IND 142-143 B 3
Banās, Ra's ▲ ET 194-195 G 6
Banat o USA (MI) 270-271 L 5
Banaue ☆ RP 160-161 D 4
Banaz ☆ TR 128-129 C 3
Banaz Çayı ~ TR 128-129 C 3
Banba o RMM 202-203 G 4
Ban Bakha o LAO 156-157 D 7
Ban Ban o AUS 178-179 G 3
Ban Ban o LAO 156-157 C 7
Ban Ban o VN 156-157 D 7
Banbar o VRC 144-145 K 5
Banbaran o RMM 202-203 F 3
Banbirpur o IND 144-145 C 6
Ban Boun Tai o LAO 156-157 B 6
Banbridge o GB 90-91 D 4
Banbury o GB 90-91 G 5
Bancauan Island ⌒ RP 160-161 C 9
Banc d'Arguin, Parc National du ⊥ ••• RIM 196-197 B 4
Ban Chamrung o THA 158-159 G 4
Ban Chiang o••• THA 158-159 G 2
Banco, El o CO 60-61 E 3
Bancoran Island ⌒ RP 160-161 C 9
Bancos de San Pedro o YV 60-61 H 3
Bancroft o CDN (ONT) 238-239 H 3
Bancroft o USA (ID) 252-253 G 4
Bancs Providence ⌒ SY 224 B 4
Banda o CAM 204-205 K 4
Banda o GH 202-203 J 5
Banda o IND 138-139 G 7
Bānda o IND 142-143 B 3
Banda o ZRE (BAN) 210-211 G 6
Banda o ZRE (Hau) 206-207 H 6
Banda, Kepulauan (Nutmeg Kepulauan) ⌒ •• RI 166-167 E 4
Banda, La o RA 76-77 E 4
Banda Aceh = Baiturahman ☆ RI 162-163 A 2
Banda Banda, Mount ▲ AUS 178-179 M 6
Bandabe o RM 222-223 F 5
Banda del Río Salí o RA 76-77 E 4
Bandae o GH 202-203 J 7
Banda Elat o RI 166-167 G 4
Bandafassi o SN 202-203 D 3
Bandai-Asahi National Park ⊥ J (NII) 152-153 H 6
Bandai-Asahi National Park ⊥ J (YAM) 152-153 H 5
Bandak ⊂ N 86-87 D 7
Bandaka o ZRE 210-211 H 4
Bandakani o ZRE 210-211 D 6
Ban Dakchoun o LAO 158-159 J 3
Bandama ~ CI 202-203 H 6
Bandama Blanc ~ CI 202-203 H 5
Bandama Rouge ~ CI 202-203 G 5
Bandaneira o• RI 166-167 E 4
Bāndanwāra o IND 138-139 E 6
Bandar o MOC 218-219 H 3
Bandar o RI 168 C 3
Bandaragama o CL 140-141 H 7
Bandarban o BD 142-143 H 4
Bandarbeyla o SP 208-209 K 4
Bandar-e 'Abbās ☆ • IR 134-135 G 5
Bandar-e Anzalī o • IR 128-129 N 4
Bandar-e Būšehr ☆ • IR 134-135 D 4
Bandar-e Čarak o IR 134-135 F 5
Bandar-e Deilam o IR 134-135 D 3
Bandar-e Emām Ḫomeinī o IR 134-135 C 3
Bandar-e Ganāve o IR 134-135 D 4
Bandar-e Gaz o IR 136-137 C 6
Bandar-e Golmānḫāne o IR 128-129 L 4
Bandar-e Ḫamīr o IR 134-135 F 5
Bandar-e Kong o IR 134-135 F 5
Bandar-e Lenge o • IR 134-135 F 5
Bandar-e Māhšahr o IR 134-135 C 3
Bandar-e Moġūye o IR 134-135 F 5
Bandar-e Moqām o IR 134-135 E 5
Bandar-e Rig o IR 134-135 D 4
Bandarian Balagra o IND 138-139 D 3
Bandarjaya o RI 162-163 F 7
Bandar Lampung ☆ RI 162-163 F 7
Bandar Murcaayo o SP 208-209 K 3
Bandarpasirmandogai o RI 162-163 C 3
Bandar Seri Begawan ☆ •• BRU 164-165 D 1
Bandar Sri Aman (Simanggang) o MAL 162-163 J 4
Bandar Wanaag o SP 208-209 G 4
Banda Sea = Banda, Laut ≈ 166-167 C 3
Band-e Amir, Rūd-e ~ AFG 136-137 K 7
Bandeira o BR 72-73 K 3
Bandeira, Pico da ▲ BR 72-73 K 6
Bandeirante, Rio ~ BR 72-73 E 7
Bandeirantes o BR (GOI) 72-73 E 2
Bandeirantes o BR (MAT) 70-71 J 2
Bandelierkop o ZA 218-219 E 6
Bandelier National Monument ∴ USA (NM) 256-257 J 3
Bandera o RA 76-77 F 5
Bandera o USA (TX) 266-267 H 4
Bandera Bajada o RA 76-77 F 4
Banderantes, Ilha dos ⌒ BR 72-73 D 7
Banderas, Bahía de ≈ 52-53 B 1
Banderilla o MEX 52-53 F 2
Bandhavagarh National Park ⊥ IND 142-143 B 4
Bāndhi o PK 138-139 B 6
Bandia ~ IND 142-143 B 6
Bandiagara o••• RMM 202-203 J 2
Bandiagara, Falaise de ▲ RMM 202-203 J 2
Banding o RI 162-163 F 7
Bandipur National Park ⊥ • IND 140-141 G 5
Bandırma ☆ TR 128-129 B 2
Bandjoukri o CAM 204-205 K 4
Bandjoun o CAM 204-205 J 6
Bandon o USA (OR) 244-245 A 7
Ba'n Đôn o VN 158-159 J 4
Bandon = Droichead na Bandan o IRL 90-91 C 6
Bandua o MOC 218-219 H 4
Bandula o MOC 218-219 G 4
Bandundu ◘ ZRE 210-211 F 5
Bandundu ☆ ZRE (Ban) 210-211 F 5
Bandung ☆ RI 168 B 3
Ban Dung o THA 158-159 G 2
Bandungan o• RI 168 D 3
Bandur o ZA 218-219 E 6
Bandurrias, Caleta ≈ 76-77 B 3
Bandya o AUS 176-177 G 3
Bāne o IR 128-129 L 4
Bāneasa o RO 102-103 E 5
Ba'n E. Klōp o VN 158-159 K 4
Banes o C 54-55 H 4
Banes, Bahía de ≈ 54-55 H 4
Banfèlè o RG 202-203 E 4
Banff o CDN (ALB) 232-233 C 4
Banff o• GB 90-91 F 3
Banff National Park ⊥ CDN (ALB) 232-233 B 4
Banfora o• BF 202-203 H 4
Banfora, Falaise de ▲ BF 202-203 H 4
Bang o RCA 206-207 B 5
Banga o ANG 216-217 C 4
Banga o BD 142-143 G 4
Banga o RCA (Kem) 206-207 D 6
Banga ~ RCA 206-207 F 5
Banga o RP 160-161 F 9
Banga o ZRE (BAN) 210-211 G 6
Banga o ZRE (KOC) 210-211 H 6
Bangabong o RP 160-161 D 6
Bangala, Lake ⊂ ZW 218-219 F 5
Bangalore ☆ • IND 140-141 G 4
Banga Melo ~ ZRE 210-211 H 2
Bangana o RCA 206-207 F 5
Banganapalle o IND 140-141 H 3
Bangangté o CAM 204-205 J 6
Bangaon o IND 142-143 G 4
Bangar o RP 160-161 D 4
Bangaré o RN 202-203 L 3
Bangarpet o IND 140-141 H 4
Bangassoko o BF 202-203 J 3
Bangassou ☆ RCA 206-207 F 6
Bangba o RCA 206-207 C 5
Bangbagatome o ZRE 210-211 K 2
Bangbali o RCA 206-207 E 4
Bangbong o RI 164-165 H 6
Bangda o VRC 144-145 L 5
Bangem o CAM 204-205 H 6
Banggai o RI 164-165 H 4
Banggai, Kepulauan ⌒ RI 164-165 H 4
Banggai, Pulau ⌒ RI 164-165 H 4
Banggi, Pulau ⌒ MAL 160-161 B 9
Banggo o RI 168 D 7
Ban Ghanimah, Jabal ▲ LAR 192-193 F 5
Banghāzī ◘ LAR 192-193 J 2
Banghāzī ☆ LAR 192-193 J 1
Banghiang ~ LAO 158-159 J 2
Bangil o RI 168 E 3
Bangka, Pulau ⌒ RI (SLU) 164-165 J 3
Bangka, Pulau ⌒ RI (SUS) 162-163 G 6
Bangka, Selat ≈ 162-163 F 6
Bangkai, Tanjung ▲ RI 162-163 H 4
Bangkalan o RI 168 E 3
Bangkaru, Pulau ⌒ RI 162-163 B 3
Bangkudulis, Pulau ⌒ RI 164-165 E 2
Bangkinang o RI 162-163 D 4
Bangkir o RI 164-165 G 3
Bangko o RI 162-163 E 6
Bangkoa o RI 164-165 F 6
Bangkok ☆ THA 158-159 F 4
Bangkok, Bight of ≈ 158-159 F 4
Bangkulu, Pulau ⌒ RI 164-165 H 4
Bangladesh ■ BD 142-143 F 3
Bang Lamung o THA 158-159 F 4
Bang Len o THA 158-159 F 3
Bangli o• RI 168 B 7
Bang O o THA 158-159 E 6
Bangolo o CI 202-203 G 6
Bangong Co o IND 138-139 G 3
Bangong Co o VRC (XIZ) 144-145 B 4
Bangong Co • VRC (XIZ) 144-145 B 4
Bangor o CDN (SAS) 232-233 Q 5
Bangor o• GB (NIR) 90-91 E 4
Bangor o• GB (WAL) 90-91 E 5
Bangor o USA (IA) 274-275 E 2
Bangor o USA (ME) 278-279 N 4
Bangor o USA (MI) 272-273 C 5
Bangor o USA (PA) 280-281 L 3
Bangoran o RCA 206-207 D 4
Bangoran o RCA (Bam) 206-207 E 4
Bangoran ~ RCA 206-207 D 4
Bangou o RCB 210-211 E 5
Bangourèn o CAM 204-205 J 6
Bang Pakong o THA 158-159 F 4
Bangs o USA (TX) 266-267 H 2
Bangsalsembera o RI 164-165 E 4
Bang Saphan o THA 158-159 E 5
Bangsi, Tanjung ▲ RI 162-163 D 3
Bangsund o N 86-87 E 4
Bangu o ZRE (BAN) 216-217 E 3
Bangu o ZRE (SHA) 214-215 B 5
Bangu, Chute ~ ZRE 210-211 L 2
Bangué o CAM 210-211 E 2
Bangued ☆ RP 160-161 D 4
Banguey Barat Parit ≈ 160-161 B 9
Bangui ☆ • RCA 206-207 D 6
Bangui o RN 198-199 C 6
Bangui Bay ≈ 160-161 D 3
Bangui Kété ~ RCA 206-207 E 6
Bangui-Motaba o RCB 210-211 F 2
Bangula o MW 218-219 H 3
Bangun o VRC 156-157 E 5
Bangunpurba o RI 162-163 C 3
Bangweulu, Lake ⊂ Z 214-215 E 6
Bangweulu Swamps ⁓ Z 214-215 E 6
Banhā ☆ ET 194-195 E 2
Ban Haew Ta Bua o THA 158-159 F 3
Ban Hat Lek o THA 158-159 G 5
Banhine, Parque Nacional de ⊥ MOC 218-219 G 6
Ban Hinkhan o LAO 158-159 H 2
Ban Houayxay ☆ LAO 142-143 M 5
Bani o BF 202-203 K 3
Bani o CI 202-203 G 5
Baní ☆ DOM 54-55 K 5
Bani o RCA 206-207 F 5
Bani ~ RMM 202-203 H 3
Bani, Ibel ▲ MA 188-189 G 6
Bani, Playa ⁓ • DOM 54-55 K 5
Bania o RCA 206-207 C 6
Bani 'Āmir o KSA 132-133 C 4
Bani 'Atiya ⁓ KSA 130-131 E 3
Bani-Bangou o RN 204-205 E 1
Bánica o DOM 54-55 K 5
Banifing ~ RMM 202-203 G 4
Banifing ~ RMM 202-203 H 3
Bani Hasan ∴ • ET 194-195 E 4
Bani Hašbal, Wādi o KSA 132-133 C 4
Bani Island ⌒ RP 160-161 F 6
Banija ▲ BIH 100-101 E 2
Banikoara o DY 204-205 E 3
Banima o RCA 206-207 F 6
Bani-Mallāl = Beni-Mellal ☆ MA 188-189 H 4
Bani Mazar o ET 194-195 E 3
Baninah o LAR 192-193 J 1
Bani Rikāb ⁓ IRQ 128-129 L 7
Banir River ~ PNG 183 B 4
Bani Sa'īd ⁓ IRQ 128-129 M 7
Banissa o EAK 212-213 H 2
Banister River ~ USA (VA) 280-281 G 7
Bani Suwaif ☆ ET 194-195 E 3
Bani Walīd ☆ LAR 192-193 E 2
Bāniyās o• IRQ 128-129 F 5
Banja Luka o• BIH 100-101 F 2
Banjar o RI 168 C 3
Banjaran Bintang ▲ MAL 162-163 D 2
Banjaran Brassey ▲ MAL 160-161 B 10
Banjaran Timur ▲ MAL 162-163 E 2
Banjaran Titiwangsa ▲ MAL 162-163 D 3
Banjarbaru o RI 164-165 D 5
Banjarkasang o RI 162-163 D 5
Banjarmasin ☆ RI 164-165 D 5
Banjarnegara o RI 168 C 3
Banjia o VRC 142-143 L 4
Banjul ☆ • WAG 202-203 B 3
Bank o AZ 128-129 N 3
Bānka o IND 142-143 E 3
Banka Banka o AUS 174-175 C 6
Bankapur o IND 140-141 F 3
Bankas o RMM 202-203 J 2
Bankberg ▲ ZA 220-221 G 6
Bankend o CDN (SAS) 232-233 P 4
Banket o ZW 218-219 F 3
Ban Khamphô o LAO 158-159 J 3
Bankilaré o RN 202-203 L 2
Bankim o CAM 204-205 J 5
Banko o RG 202-203 E 4
Banko o RMM 202-203 G 3
Bankon o RG 202-203 F 4
Bankoumana o RMM 202-203 F 3
Banks o USA (AR) 276-277 C 7
Banks o USA (ID) 252-253 B 2
Banks, Cape ▲ AUS 180-181 F 4
Banks, Îles = Banks Island ⌒ VAN 184 II a 2
Banks, Point ▲ USA 22-23 U 3
Banks/ Torres ◘ VAN 184 II b 1
Banks Island ⌒ CDN (BC) 228-229 D 3
Banks Island ⌒ CDN (NWT) 24-25 L 4
Banks Islands = Îles Banks ⌒ VAN 184 II a 2
Banks Lake ⊂ CDN 30-31 W 4
Banks Lake ⊂ USA (GA) 284-285 G 6
Banks Lake ⊂ USA (WA) 244-245 F 3
Banks Peninsula ⁀ CDN 30-31 P 2
Banks Peninsula ⁀ NZ 182 D 5
Banks Strait ≈ 180-181 J 6
Bānkura o IND 142-143 E 4
Ban Lam Narai o THA 158-159 F 3
Ban La Pha o LAO 158-159 H 2
Banli o VRC 156-157 E 5
Banmankhi o IND 142-143 E 3
Banmauk o MYA 142-143 J 3
Ban Mouang o LAO 156-157 B 7
Ban Na Inh Noi o LAO 156-157 D 7
Bannaja ~ RUS 112-113 L 3
Ban Nakala o LAO 158-159 H 2
Ban Na Mang o LAO 156-157 D 6
Ban Nambak o LAO 156-157 C 6
Ban Nang Sata o THA 158-159 F 7
Ban Napè o LAO 156-157 D 7
Ban Na Phao o LAO 158-159 H 2
Ban Na Sam o THA 158-159 E 6
Bannerman Town o BS 54-55 G 2
Banner Reef ⌒ JA 54-55 F 6
Bannikoppa o IND 140-141 F 3
Banning o USA (CA) 248-249 H 6
Bannockburn o CDN (ONT) 238-239 H 4
Bannock Pass ▲ USA (MT) 250-251 F 7
Bannock Range ▲ USA (ID) 252-253 F 4
Ban Nong Chaeng o THA 158-159 F 3
Ban Nong Phu o THA 158-159 H 3
Ban Nongsim o LAO 158-159 H 3
Bannu o• PK 138-139 C 3
Bannur o IND 140-141 G 4
Baños o EC 64-65 C 2
Banos o PE 64-65 D 7
Baños, Los o PE 70-71 B 6
Banos, Los o USA (CA) 248-249 D 2
Ban Pa Daeng o THA 142-143 M 6
Ban Pak Bat o THA 158-159 F 2
Ban Pakbông o LAO 158-159 J 3
Ban Phai o THA 158-159 G 2
Ban Phon o LAO 158-159 J 3
Ban Phu o THA 158-159 G 2
Ban Pong o THA 158-159 E 4
Banqiao o VRC 154-155 H 6
Ban Rai o THA 158-159 E 3
Ban San Chao Po o THA 158-159 F 3
Bansara o WAN 204-205 H 5
Ban Sènkhan o LAO 156-157 C 6
Banská Bystrica o SK 92-93 P 4
Banská Štiavnica o••• SK 92-93 P 4
Bānswāra o IND 138-139 E 8
Banta o SP 212-213 J 3
Banta, Pulau ⌒ RI 168 D 7
Ban Tabôk o LAO 156-157 C 7
Bantadjé o CAM 204-205 K 4
Bantaeng o RI 164-165 F 6
Bantakoto o RMM 202-203 E 3
Bantala ~ RG 202-203 D 4
Bantarbolang o RI 168 C 3
Bantarkawung o RI 168 C 3
Bantaya Island ⌒ RP 160-161 E 7
Bantayan o RP 160-161 E 7
Banté o DY 202-203 L 5
Banten o• RI 168 B 3
Ban Tha Rae o THA 158-159 H 2
Ban Tha Song Yang o THA 158-159 D 2
Ban Thieng o LAO 156-157 C 7
Bantimurung o RI 164-165 F 6
Bantimurung Reserve ⊥ • RI 164-165 F 6
Banting o MAL 162-163 D 3
Bantioli, Réserve Partielle de ⊥ BF 202-203 J 4
Bantola o RI 164-165 F 3
Banton Island ⌒ RP 160-161 E 6
Bantry = Beanntraí o IRL 90-91 C 6
Bantshamba o ZRE 210-211 G 6
Bantul o RI 168 D 3
Ban Tung o LAO 158-159 H 2
Banua o RP 160-161 B 8
Banvo o ANG 216-217 E 4
Ban Xang o VN 156-157 D 7
Ban Xésavang o LAO 158-159 H 2
Banyak, Kepulauan ⌒ RI 162-163 B 4
Banynasin ~ RI 162-163 F 6
Banyo o CAM 204-205 J 5
Banyoles o• E 98-99 J 3
Banyumas o RI 168 C 3
Banyuwangi o RI 168 B 7
Banyuwedang o RI 168 B 7
Banz o PNG 183 C 3
Banzana o RMM 202-203 G 4
Banzare Land ⁓ ARK 16 G 13
Banza Sanda o ZRE 210-211 E 6
Banza Sosso o ANG 216-217 C 2
Banzi o CI 202-203 G 5
Bao o RCA 206-207 F 6
Bao o TCH 206-207 C 4
Bao, Río ~ DOM 54-55 K 5
Baode o VRC 154-155 G 2
Baodi o VRC 154-155 K 2
Baoding o VRC 154-155 J 2
Baodingchan Temple o VRC 156-157 D 2
Baofatu o VAN 184 II b 3
Baofeng o VRC 154-155 H 5
Baoji o VRC 154-155 E 4
Baojing o VRC 156-157 F 2
Baojiqu o VRC 154-155 D 3
Baokang o VRC 154-155 G 6
Bao Khao Sai o THA 158-159 F 2
Baolo o SOL 184 I d 2
Bảo Lộc o VN 158-159 J 5
Baoqing o VRC 150-151 J 4
Baoro o RCA 206-207 B 6
Baoruco, Parque Nacional Sierra de ⊥ DOM 54-55 K 5
Baoruco, Sierra de ▲ DOM 54-55 K 5
Baoshan o VRC (SGH) 154-155 M 6
Baoshan o VRC (YUN) 142-143 L 3
Baota Shan o VRC 154-155 F 3
Baotianman Z.B. ⊥ • VRC 154-155 G 5
Baoting o VRC 156-157 F 7
Baotou o VRC 154-155 F 1
Baoulé ~ RMM 202-203 F 3
Baoulé ~ RMM 202-203 G 4
Baoule, Collines ▲ CI 202-203 H 6
Baoxu o VRC 156-157 G 5
Bảo Yên o VN 156-157 D 5
Bảo Yên o VN 156-157 D 5
Baoying o VRC 154-155 L 5
Bāp o IND 138-139 D 6
Bāpatla o IND 140-141 J 3
Bapaume o CDN (SAS) 232-233 L 2
Bappagaj ~ RUS 118-119 M 4
Bapsfontein o ZA 220-221 J 2
Baptist o JA 54-55 G 5
Baptiste River ~ CDN (ALB) 232-233 C 3
Baq'ā' o KSA 130-131 H 4
Baqên o VRC 144-145 K 5
Bāqerābād o IR 134-135 D 1
Bāqir, Ġabal ▲ JOR 130-131 D 3
Ba'qūba ☆ IRQ 128-129 L 6
Baquedano o RCH 76-77 C 2
Baquerizo o EC 64-65 C 2
Bar o YU 100-101 G 3
Bara o RG 202-203 D 3
Bara o RI 166-167 D 3
Bara o WAN 204-205 J 3
Baraawe o SP 212-213 K 3
Baraba, gora ▲ RUS 120-121 R 6
Barabai o RI 164-165 D 5
Barabaš o RUS 122-123 D 7
Barabaš-Levada o RUS 122-123 D 6
Barabinsk o RUS 114-115 P 7
Barabinskaja nizmenost' ⁀ RUS 124-125 J 1
Barabinskaya Step' = Barabinskaja nizmenost' ⁀ RUS 124-125 J 1
Bar Abir < ETH 208-209 F 6
Baraboo o USA (WI) 274-275 J 1
Baraboulé o BF 202-203 K 2
Baracaju ou Maracaja, Rio ~ BR 72-73 E 2
Barachois o CDN (QUE) 240-241 L 2
Barachois Pond Provincial Park ⊥ CDN (NFL) 242-243 K 4
Baracoa o C 54-55 H 4
Barādar-e Šāh, Kūh-e ▲ IR 128-129 M 4
Baradères o RH 54-55 J 5
Baradero o RA 78-79 K 2
Baradine o AUS 178-179 K 6
Baradine Creek ~ AUS 178-179 K 6
Baraga o USA (MI) 270-271 K 4
Baragoi o EAK 212-213 F 3
Bārah o SUD 200-201 E 6
Barahan o RP 160-161 D 6
Barāhanagar o IND 142-143 F 4
Barahona ☆ DOM 54-55 K 5
Barahona, Paso de ▲ RA 76-77 B 6
Barail Range ▲ IND 142-143 H 3
Bara-Issa ~ RMM 202-203 H 2
Barajy ~ RUS 120-121 E 2
Baraka ~ ER 200-201 H 5
Baraka o ZRE 212-213 B 6
Baraka, Khor ~ SUD 200-201 H 4
Barakaldo o E 98-99 F 3
Barakan o RI 166-167 H 5
Barakāt Sharif Ya'qūb o SUD 200-201 F 5
Baraki o AFG 138-139 B 3
Baral ~ BD 142-143 F 3
Baralzon Lake ⊂ CDN 30-31 V 5
Baram ~ MAL 164-165 D 1
Baram, Tanjung ▲ MAL 162-163 K 2
Baramani o GUY 62-63 E 2
Baramata o PNG 183 E 6
Bārāmati o IND 138-139 E 10
Barambah Creek ~ AUS 178-179 L 4
Baramula o IND 138-139 E 2
Bārān o IND 138-139 F 7
Barān o IR 128-129 M 3
Bārān, Kūh-e ▲ IR 134-135 H 2
Baranavichy = Baranavičy ☆ BY 94-95 K 5
Baranavičy ☆ BY 94-95 K 5
Baranga o ZRE 210-211 L 2
Barangbarang o RI 168 E 6
Barani o BF 202-203 J 3
Baraniha o RUS 112-113 P 2
Barankol o KA 124-125 E 3
Baranoa o CO 60-61 D 2
Baranof o USA 32-33 C 3
Baranof Island ⌒ USA 32-33 C 3
Baranoviči = Baranavičy ☆ BY 94-95 K 5
Barão de Grajaú o BR 68-69 G 5
Barão de Melgaço o BR 70-71 G 2
Barão do Melgaço o BR 70-71 K 5
Barão do Triunfo o BR 74-75 E 8
Baraouéli o RMM 202-203 G 3
Baraqish ∴ • Y 132-133 D 6
Barāra o KSA 132-133 B 3
Bararati, Rio ~ BR 66-67 H 6
Bararis, togga ~ SP 208-209 G 3
Barataria Bay ≈ 48-49 D 5
Barataria Bay ≈ USA 268-269 L 7
Barat Bali National Park ⊥ RI 168 B 7
Barauli o IND 142-143 D 2
Barauna, Rio ~ BR 62-63 D 5
Baraya o CO 60-61 D 6
Barbacena o BR 72-73 J 6
Barbacoas o CO 64-65 C 1
Barbadan o SP 212-213 J 2
Barbado o BR 66-67 D 7
Barbado, Rio ~ BR 70-71 H 4
Barbados ■ BDS 56 F 5
Barbágia Belvì ⁓ I 100-101 B 5
Barbalha o BR 68-69 J 5
Barbar o SUD 200-201 G 3
Barbara Lake ⊂ CDN (ONT) 234-235 Q 5
Barbastro o E 98-99 H 3
Barbate de Franco o E 98-99 E 6
Barbaza o RP 160-161 E 7
Bārbele o LV 94-95 J 3
Barberton o ZA 220-221 K 2
Barberville o USA (FL) 286-287 H 2
Barbes, Cap ▲ MA 196-197 B 3
Barbitaj ~ RUS 116-117 J 9
Barbosa o CO 60-61 E 5
Barbour Bay ≈ 30-31 X 4
Barbourville o USA (KY) 276-277 M 4
Barbuda Island ⌒ AG 56 E 3
Barbwire Range ▲ AUS 172-173 G 5
Barca = Al Marj ☆ •• LAR 192-193 J 1
Barca, La o MEX 52-53 C 1
Barcaldine o AUS 178-179 H 2
Barcarena o BR 62-63 K 6
Barcarrota o E 98-99 D 5
Barcelona o BR 68-69 L 4
Barcelona ☆••• E 98-99 J 4
Barcelona o PE 70-71 C 2
Barcelona ☆ YV 60-61 J 2
Barcelonnette o• F 90-91 L 9
Barcelos o BR 66-67 F 3
Barciany o PL 92-93 Q 1
Barclay o USA (TX) 266-267 K 2
Barclay, Kap ▲ GRØ 28-29 c 2
Barclay Bugt ≈ 28-29 c 2
Barco o USA (NC) 282-283 M 4
Barcoo River ~ AUS 178-179 G 3
Barcs o H 92-93 O 6
Barcyŋ ☆ KA 124-125 F 4
Barda ☆ RUS 96-97 J 5
Barda, Arroyo de la ~ RA 78-79 F 4
Barda = Barda o AZ 128-129 M 2
Bardaale o SP 208-209 H 5
Barda del Medio o RA 78-79 E 5
Bardagué ~ TCH 198-199 H 2
Bardaï o TCH 198-199 H 2
Bardārāš o IRQ 128-129 K 4
Bårdarbunga ▲ IS 86-87 e 2
Bardas Blancas o RA 78-79 E 3
Barddhamān o IND 142-143 E 4
Bardejov o SK 92-93 Q 4
Bardeskan o IR 136-137 E 7
Bardoli o IND 138-139 D 9
Bardsir o IR 134-135 G 4
Bardstown o USA (KY) 276-277 K 3
Barduelva ~ N 86-87 J 2
Bardula o IND 142-143 C 5
Bardwell o USA (KY) 276-277 F 4
Bardymskij hrebet ▲ RUS 96-97 L 5
Barē o ETH 208-209 F 6
Bāre o IND 140-141 F 3
Bareilly o IND 138-139 G 5
Bareli o IND 138-139 G 8
Barentsburg o N 84-85 J 3
Barentsøya ⌒ N 84-85 N 3
Barents Sea ≈ 84-85 O 6
Barentu o ER 200-201 H 5
Bareo o MAL 164-165 D 2
Bare Rock ▲ AUS 178-179 M 4
Barfolomeevsk o RUS 122-123 E 6
Bārgā o IR 134-135 G 5
Barga o• VRC 144-145 C 5
Bargaal o SP 208-209 K 3
Bargarh o IND 142-143 C 5
Barge Bay o CDN (NFL) 242-243 M 1
Bargersville o USA (IN) 274-275 M 5
Barğovein, Kūh-e ▲ IR 136-137 E 6
Barguzin ☆ RUS 118-119 D 9
Barguzin ~ RUS 118-119 E 8
Barguzin, Ust'- o RUS 116-117 O 9
Barguzinskij, zapovednik ⊥ RUS 118-119 D 8
Barguzinskij hrebet ▲ RUS 118-119 D 9
Bārh o IND 142-143 D 3
Bar Harbor o USA (ME) 278-279 N 4
Barhi o IND 142-143 D 3
Bari ☆ • I 100-101 F 4
Bāri o IND 138-139 F 6
Bari ◘ SP 208-209 K 3
Bari o WAN 204-205 F 3
Bari, Kūh-e ▲ IR 134-135 E 4
Bariadi o EAT 212-213 D 5
Baricho o EAK 212-213 G 5
Barik, al- o KSA 132-133 B 3
Barika o DZ 190-191 E 3
Barika ~ DZ 190-191 E 3
Barikōt o AFG 136-137 M 7
Barillas o GCA 52-53 J 4
Baril Station, Pointe au o CDN (ONT) 238-239 E 3
Barim, Ğazirat ⌒ Y 132-133 C 7
Barinas ☆ YV 60-61 F 3
Baring o CDN (SAS) 232-233 P 5
Baring o USA (MO) 274-275 F 4
Baring, Cape ▲ CDN 24-25 N 5
Baringa o ZRE 210-211 H 3
Baring Channel ≈ 24-25 W 4
Baringo, Lake ⊂ EAK 212-213 F 3
Baripāda o IND 142-143 E 5
Bariri o BR 72-73 F 7
Bariri, Represa < BR 72-73 F 7
Bāris o ET 194-195 E 5
Bari Sādri o IND 138-139 E 7
Barisal o BD 142-143 G 4
Barisan, Pegunungan ▲ RI 162-163 D 5
Barit, al- o IRQ 128-129 K 7
Barito ~ RI 164-165 D 4
Baritu, Parque Nacional ⊥ RA 76-77 E 2
Bariya < IRQ 128-129 K 5
Barjūj, Wādi ~ LAR 192-193 E 5
Barkā' o OM 132-133 K 2
Barkal, Ġabal • SUD 200-201 E 3
Barkam o VRC 154-155 C 6
Barkan, Ra's-e ▲ IR 134-135 C 4
Barkava o LV 94-95 K 3
Barkédji o SN 202-203 C 2
Barkerville o• CDN (BC) 228-229 N 3
Barkerville Historic Town • CDN (BC) 228-229 N 3
Barkéwol Abiod o RIM 196-197 D 6
Bārkhān o PK 138-139 B 5
Barkley, Lake ⊂ USA (KY) 276-277 H 4
Barkley Sound ≈ 32-33 H 7
Barkley Sound ≈ CDN 230-231 D 5
Barkly Downs o AUS 174-175 E 7
Barkly East o ZA 220-221 H 5
Barkly Highway II AUS 174-175 D 6
Barkly Homestead Roadhouse o AUS 174-175 C 6
Barkly Pass o ZA 220-221 H 5
Barkly Tableland ▲ AUS 174-175 C 5
Barkly West o ZA 220-221 G 4
Barkol o VRC 146-147 L 4
Barkol, Wādi ~ SUD 200-201 E 4
Barkol Hu ⊂ VRC 146-147 L 4
Bark River o USA (MI) 270-271 L 5
Barksdale o USA (TX) 266-267 G 4
Barkway o CDN (ONT) 238-239 F 4
Barlavento, Ilhas de ⌒ CV 202-203 B 5
Bar-le-Duc ☆ • F 90-91 K 7
Barlee, Lake ⊂ AUS 176-177 E 4
Barlee Range ▲ AUS 176-177 D 1
Barletta o• I 100-101 F 4
Barlett Reservoir ⊂ USA (AZ) 256-257 D 5
Barling o USA (AR) 276-277 A 5
Barlow o USA (OH) 280-281 E 4
Barlo Warf o WAL 202-203 D 5
Barlowerie, Mount ▲ AUS 176-177 D 3
Barlyk ~ RUS 116-117 E 10
Barma o RI 166-167 G 2
Barmedman o AUS 180-181 J 3
Barmer o IND 138-139 C 7
Barmera o AUS 180-181 F 3
Barm Firuz, Kūh-e ▲ IR 134-135 D 3
Barnaby River o CDN (NB) 240-241 K 4
Barnāla o IND 138-139 E 4
Barnard o USA (SD) 260-261 H 1
Barnard Castle o• GB 90-91 G 4
Barnard Point ▲ CDN 24-25 P 4
Barnard River ~ AUS 178-179 L 6
Barnato o AUS 178-179 H 6
Barnaul ☆ RUS 124-125 N 2
Barnaulka ~ RUS 124-125 N 2
Barnegat Light o USA (NJ) 280-281 M 4
Barne Glacier ⊂ ARK 16 E 0
Barnes Ice Cap ⊂ CDN 26-27 O 8
Barnes Sound ≈ USA 286-287 J 6
Barnesville o USA (GA) 284-285 F 3
Barnesville o USA (MN) 270-271 B 4
Barnesville o USA (OH) 280-281 E 4
Barneys Brook ~ CDN (NFL) 242-243 M 3
Barneys Lake ⊂ AUS 180-181 H 2
Barnhart o USA (TX) 266-267 F 2
Barnsdall o USA (OK) 264-265 H 2
Barnstable o USA (MA) 278-279 L 7
Barnstaple o• GB 90-91 E 6
Barnum o USA (WY) 252-253 M 3
Barnwell o CDN (ALB) 232-233 F 6
Barnwell o USA (SC) 284-285 J 3
Baro o TCH 198-199 J 6
Baro o WAN 204-205 G 4
Baroe o ZA 220-221 G 6
Barōgil o AFG 136-137 N 6
Baron o RI (JTI) 168 E 3
Baron o RI (YOG) 168 D 4
Barons o CDN (ALB) 232-233 E 5
Barora Island ⌒ SOL 184 I d 2
Barora Ite Island ⌒ SOL 184 I d 2
Barossa Valley ⁀ AUS 180-181 E 3
Barotac Nuevo o RP 160-161 E 7
Barotske Floot Plain ⁓ Z 218-219 B 2
Baroua o RCA 206-207 G 6
Barouda, Hassi < DZ 190-191 C 6
Baro Wenz ~ ETH 208-209 B 4
Barpeta o IND 142-143 G 2
Barqah ⁓ LAR 192-193 J 2
Barquisimeto ☆ YV 60-61 G 2
Barra o BR (BAH) 68-69 G 7
Barra o BR (CAT) 74-75 F 7
Barra ⌒ GB 90-91 D 3
Barra o WAG 202-203 B 3
Barra, Ponta da ▲ BR 74-75 G 5
Barraba o AUS 178-179 L 6
Barra Bonita o BR 72-73 F 7
Barra Bonita, Represa de < BR 72-73 F 7
Barraca da Boca o BR 62-63 H 6
Barraca de A. Lopes o BR 66-67 H 6
Barracão o BR 74-75 E 6
Barracão do Barreto o BR 66-67 H 7
Barracas o E 98-99 G 4
Barracouta Shoal ~ AUS 172-173 G 2
Barra da Estiva o BR 72-73 K 2
Barradale Roadhouse o AUS 172-173 B 7
Barra del Chuy o ROU 74-75 D 9
Barra de Mamanguape o BR 68-69 L 5
Barra de Santa Rosa o BR 68-69 K 5
Barra de São Francisco o BR 72-73 K 5
Barra de São Manuel o BR 66-67 H 6
Barra de São Miguel o BR (ALA) 68-69 L 6
Barra de São Miguel o BR (PA) 68-69 K 5
Barra de Tuxpan o MEX 52-53 F 1
Barra do Bugres o BR 70-71 J 4
Barra do Corda o BR 68-69 F 4
Barra do Cuanza o ANG 216-217 B 4
Barra do Dande o ANG 216-217 B 4
Barra do Garças o BR 72-73 D 3
Barra do Mendes o BR 68-69 G 7
Barra do Ouro o BR 74-75 E 7
Barra do Piraí o BR 72-73 J 7
Barra do Quaraí o BR 76-77 J 6
Barrage Mercier • CDN (QUE) 238-239 K 2
Barra Longa o BR 72-73 J 6
Barra Mansa o BR 72-73 H 7
Barrāmiya o ET 194-195 F 5
Barranca o PE (LIM) 64-65 D 7
Barranca o PE (LOR) 64-65 D 4
Barrancabermeja o CO 60-61 E 4
Barranca del Cobre, Parque Natural ⊥ MEX 50-51 F 4
Barranca de Upía = Cumaral o CO 60-61 E 5
Barrancas o YV (BOL) 60-61 J 4
Barrancas o YV (MON) 60-61 K 3
Barrancas, Arroyo ~ RA 76-77 H 5
Barrancas, Río ~ RA 78-79 D 4
Barranco Alto o BR 70-71 G 3
Barranco de Guadalupe o MEX 50-51 G 2
Barranco de Loba o CO 60-61 D 3
Barranco Picure o CO 60-61 G 6
Barrancos o P 98-99 D 5
Barrancos, Los o YV 60-61 K 3
Barrancoso, Arroyo ~ RA 78-79 J 2
Barranco Vermelho, Corredeira ~ BR 70-71 G 3
Barranqueras o RA 76-77 H 4
Barranquilla ☆ CO 60-61 D 2
Barranquilla o RCH 76-77 B 4
Barranquitas o USA (PR) 286-287 P 2
Barranquitas o YV 60-61 E 2
Barras o BR 66-67 E 7
Barra Seca o BR 72-73 K 6
Barraute o CDN (QUE) 236-237 L 4
Barr'd Harbour o CDN (NFL) 242-243 L 2
Barre o USA (MA) 278-279 J 6
Barre o USA (VT) 278-279 J 4
Barre, Port o USA (LA) 268-269 J 6
Barreal o RA 76-77 C 6
Barreal, El o MEX 50-51 F 2
Barreal, El o RA 76-77 D 5
Barreira Branca o BR 68-69 C 6
Barreira da Cruz o BR 68-69 D 7
Barreira do Peiqui o BR 72-73 F 2
Barreiras o BR 72-73 H 2
Barreiras, Rio das ~ BR 68-69 D 6
Barreirinha o BR 66-67 J 4
Barreirinhas o BR 68-69 G 3
Barreiro o P 98-99 C 5
Barreiros o BR 68-69 L 6
Barrelville o USA (SC) 284-285 K 4
Barrême o F 90-91 L 10
Barren, Nosy ⌒ RM 222-223 C 7
Barren Grounds ⁓ CDN 30-31 O 2
Barren Island ⌒ IND 140-141 L 3
Barren Island, Cape ▲ AUS 180-181 K 6
Barren Islands ⌒ USA 22-23 U 3

Barren River ~ **USA** (KY) 276-277 J 4
Barren River Lake ⬭ **USA** (KY) 276-277 J 4
Barreras Blancas, Antiplano ∸ **RA** 80 F 5
Barretal, El o **MEX** 50-51 K 5
Barretos o **BR** 72-73 F 6
Barrett o **USA** (MN) 270-271 C 5
Barrett Lake o **CDN** (BC) 228-229 H 2
Barrhead o **CDN** 32-33 N 4
Barrialito o **YV** 60-61 J 3
Barrie o **CDN** (ONT) 238-239 F 4
Barrie Island ⌒ **CDN** (ONT) 238-239 C 3
Barrière o **CDN** (BC) 230-231 J 2
Barrier Highway II **AUS** 178-179 G 6
Barrier Inlet ≈ 36-37 P 3
Barrier Range ⛰ **AUS** 178-179 F 6
Barrier River ~ **CDN** (SAS) 232-233 O 3
Barril, El o **MEX** 50-51 H 6
Barriles, Los o **MEX** 50-51 E 6
Barrington o **CDN** (NS) 240-241 K 7
Barrington, Mount ▲ **AUS** 180-181 L 2
Barrington Lake ⬭ **CDN** 34-35 F 2
Barrington Tops National Park ⊥ **AUS** 178-179 L 6
Barriyat al-Bayyūda ∸ **SUD** 200-201 F 4
Barro Alto o **BR** 72-73 F 3
Barro Duro o **BR** 68-69 G 4
Barron o **USA** (WI) 270-271 G 5
Barros o **BR** 68-69 G 4
Barros, Lagoa dos ⬭ **BR** 74-75 E 7
Barros, Los o **RCH** 78-79 D 4
Barros Arana, Cerro ▲ **RCH** 78-79 C 7
Barros Cassal o **BR** 74-75 D 7
Barrow ~ **IRL** 90-91 D 5
Barrow o **USA** 20-21 M 1
Barrow, Point ▲ **USA** 20-21 M 1
Barrow Creek o **AUS** 178-179 B 1
Barrow-in-Furness o **GB** 90-91 F 4
Barrow Island ⌒ **AUS** 172-173 B 6
Barrow Island Oil Field • **AUS** 172-173 B 6
Barrow Island Shoals ⌒ **AUS** 172-173 B 6
Barrow Peninsula ⌣ **CDN** 36-37 Q 3
Barrow River ~ **CDN** 24-25 e 7
Barrows o **CDN** (MAN) 234-235 B 2
Barrow Strait ≈ 24-25 Y 3
Barru o **RI** 164-165 F 6
Barry o **USA** (IL) 274-275 G 5
Barry Caves • **AUS** 174-175 D 7
Barrydale o **ZA** 220-221 E 6
Barry Islands ⌒ **CDN** 30-31 P 2
Barry's Bay o **CDN** (ONT) 238-239 H 3
Barryville o **CDN** (NB) 240-241 K 3
Barsa ∸ **SYR** 128-129 H 4
Barsakelmes, ostrov ⌒ **KA** 126-127 O 5
Barsakel mes, Sor ⬭ **US** 136-137 E 3
Barsakelmes, sor ⬭ **US** 136-137 E 3
Barsakelmes zapovednik ⊥ **KA** 126-127 N 5
Baršaķūm ∸ **KA** 126-127 O 4
Barsalogo o **BF** 202-203 K 3
Barsaloi o **EAK** 212-213 F 3
Baršatas o **KA** 124-125 L 4
Bārsi o **IND** 138-139 E 10
Baršino o **KA** 124-125 F 4
Barskoon o **KS** 146-147 C 4
Barsovo o **RUS** 114-115 M 4
Barstow o **USA** (CA) 248-249 G 5
Barstow o **USA** (TX) 266-267 D 2
Bar-sur-Aube o **F** 90-91 K 7
Bartang ~ **TJ** 136-137 M 5
Bartel o **USA** (CA) 246-247 D 2
Barten = Barciany o **PL** 92-93 Q 1
Barter Island ⌒ **USA** 20-21 T 1
Barthel o **CDN** (SAS) 232-233 K 2
Bartica ☆ **GUY** 62-63 E 2
Bartın ☆ **TR** 128-129 E 2
Bartle o **USA** (CA) 246-247 D 2
Bartle Frere ▲ **AUS** 174-175 H 5
Bartlesville o **USA** (OK) 264-265 J 2
Bartlett o **USA** (NE) 262-263 H 3
Bartlett o **USA** (OH) 280-281 E 4
Bartlett o **USA** (TN) 276-277 F 5
Bartlett o **USA** (TX) 266-267 K 3
Bartlett, Cape ▲ **CDN** 36-37 K 6
Bartlett Lake ⬭ **CDN** 30-31 K 4
Bartletts Harbour o **CDN** (NFL) 242-243 L 2
Bartok Lake, De ⬭ **CDN** 30-31 U 5
Bartolomé Masó o **C** 54-55 G 4
Barton o **RP** 160-161 C 7
Barton o **USA** (ND) 258-259 G 3
Barton o **USA** (VT) 278-279 J 4
Bartoszyce o **PL** 92-93 Q 1
Bartow o **USA** (FL) 286-287 H 4
Bartow o **USA** (WV) 280-281 G 5
Bartyłaakty, köl ⬭ **KA** 96-97 H 10
Baru o **CO** 60-61 D 2
Baru o **RI** (IRJ) 166-167 G 2
Baru o **RI** (MAL) 164-165 K 3
Bārū, Nahr ~ **SUD** 208-209 A 4
Baru, Punta ▲ **CO** 60-61 D 2
Barukova, mys ▲ **RUS** 112-113 U 5
Barumun ~ **RI** 162-163 D 3
Barun-Torej, ozero ⬭ **RUS** 118-119 G 10
Barus o **RI** 162-163 C 3
Barusiahe o **RI** 162-163 C 3
Baruti o **ZRE** 210-211 K 2
Baruunharaa o **MAU** 148-149 H 3
Baruunturuun o **MAU** 116-117 G 11
Baruun-Urt ☆ **MAU** 148-149 L 4
Barva, Volcán ▲ **CR** 52-53 B 6
Barvinkove o **UA** 102-103 K 3
Barwāni o **IND** 138-139 E 8
Barwick o **CDN** (ONT) 234-235 K 6
Barwidgi o **AUS** 174-175 H 5
Barwon River ~ **AUS** 178-179 J 5
Barycz ~ **PL** 92-93 O 3
Barylas o **RUS** 110-111 T 7
Baryš o **RUS** 96-97 E 7
Barysav ☆ **BY** 94-95 L 4
Barysaw = Barysav ☆ **BY** 94-95 L 4
Bāš Ābdān o **AFG** 136-137 L 6
Basacato del Este o **GQ** 210-211 B 2
Basaguke o **VRC** 144-145 E 6
Bāsa'idū o **IR** 134-135 F 5
Basāk ~ **K** 158-159 H 5
Basakan, Gunung ▲ **RI** 164-165 E 2
Bašākerd, Kūhhā-ye ⛰ **IR** 134-135 G 5
Basāl o **PK** 138-139 D 3
Baš-Alatau hrebet ⛰ **RUS** 96-97 K 7
Basali o **ZRE** 210-211 J 3
Basalt o **USA** (CO) 254-255 H 4
Basame, Caño ~ **YV** 60-61 L 3
Basanga o **ZRE** 210-211 K 6
Basankusu o **ZRE** 210-211 G 3
Basarabi o **RO** 102-103 F 5
Basaseachic o **MEX** 50-51 E 3
Basaseachi Falls ~ **MEX** 50-51 E 3
Basavana Bāgevādi o **IND** 140-141 F 2
Basavilbaso o **RA** 78-79 K 2
Basay o **RP** 160-161 E 8
Bascán, Río ~ **MEX** 52-53 H 3
Bašcelakskij hrebet ⛰ **RUS** 124-125 N 3
Bas Chari, Reserve de faune du ⊥ **TCH** 198-199 G 6
Bascombe Well Conservation Park ⊥ **AUS** 180-181 C 2
Base Casamance, Parc National du ⊥ **SN** 202-203 B 3
Basel ☆ • **CH** 92-93 J 5
Basettihalli o **IND** 140-141 G 4
Bashaw o **CDN** (ALB) 232-233 F 3
Bashee Bridge o **ZA** 220-221 J 5
Basheerivier ~ **ZA** 220-221 H 5
Bashi Haixia ≈ 156-157 M 6
Bashimuke o **ZRE** 210-211 K 6
Bashkortostan = Respublika Baškortostan □ **RUS** 96-97 J 6
Basi o **IND** 138-139 F 4
Basiano o **RI** 164-165 H 4
Basilaki Island ⌒ **PNG** 183 F 6
Basilan Island ⌒ **RP** 160-161 D 9
Basilan Strait ≈ 160-161 D 9
Basile o **USA** (LA) 268-269 H 6
Basile, Pico ▲ **GQ** 210-211 B 2
Basilicata □ **I** 100-101 E 4
Basílio o **BR** 74-75 D 8
Basin o **USA** (WY) 252-253 K 2
Basingstoke o **GB** 90-91 G 6
Basin Lake ⬭ **CDN** (SAS) 232-233 N 3
Başīrī, al- o **SYR** 128-129 G 5
Basirka o **WAN** 204-205 J 3
Baška o **HR** 100-101 E 2
Baskahegan Lake ⬭ **USA** (ME) 278-279 O 3
Başkale ☆ **TR** 128-129 L 3
Baskan ~ **KA** 124-125 L 6
Baskatong, Réservoir ⬭ **CDN** (QUE) 238-239 K 2
Baškaus ~ **RUS** 124-125 Q 3
Baškaus ~ **RUS** 124-125 Q 3
Baskerville, Cape ▲ **AUS** 172-173 F 4
Baskineig Falls ~ **CDN** 34-35 N 4
Baškirskij zapovednik ⊥ **RUS** 96-97 K 7
Baskunčak, ozero ⬭ **RUS** 96-97 E 9
Basler Lake ⬭ **CDN** 30-31 M 4
Basmat o **IND** 138-139 F 10
Bašnja Šamilja • **RUS** 102-103 J 2
Bāsoda o **IND** 138-139 F 8
Basoko o **ZRE** 210-211 J 3
Basongo o **ZRE** 210-211 H 6
Basotu o **EAT** 212-213 E 6
Basova, mys ▲ **RUS** 112-113 U 5
Basque o **USA** (OR) 244-245 H 8
Başra, al- □ **IRQ** 130-131 K 2
Başra, al- ☆ **IRQ** 130-131 K 2
Bassano o **CDN** (ALB) 232-233 F 5
Bassano del Grappa o **I** 100-101 C 2
Bassar o **RT** 202-203 L 5
Bassas da India ⌒ **F** 218-219 K 5
Bassaula o **WAN** 204-205 J 5
Bassein ~ **MYA** 158-159 C 2
Bassein = Puthein o **MYA** 158-159 C 2
Basse-Kotto □ **RCA** 206-207 E 6
Basse-Normandie □ **F** 90-91 G 7
Basse Santa Su ☆ • **WAG** 202-203 C 3
Basse-Terre ☆ •• **F** 56 E 3
Basse-Terre ⌒ **F** 56 E 3
Basseterre ★ **KAN** 56 D 3
Bassett o **USA** (NE) 262-263 G 2
Bassett o **USA** (VA) 280-281 G 7
Bassfield o **USA** (MS) 268-269 L 5
Bass Highway II **AUS** 180-181 H 6
Bassikounou o **RIM** 196-197 H 7
Bassila o **DY** 202-203 L 5
Basso o **DY** 204-205 E 3
Basso ▲ **TCH** 198-199 L 4
Bassoues o **F** 98-99 H 3
Bass River o **CDN** (NS) 240-241 M 5
Bass Strait ≈ 180-181 H 5
Basswood o **CDN** (MAN) 234-235 C 4
Basswood Lake ⬭ **USA** (MN) 270-271 G 2
Bāšt o **IR** 134-135 D 3
Bastak o **IR** 134-135 F 5
Baštanka o **UA** 102-103 H 4
Bastar ∸ **IND** 142-143 B 6
Baštau hrebet ⛰ **RUS** 96-97 K 7
Bastenaken = Bastogne o **B** 92-93 H 3
Bastia ☆ • **F** 98-99 M 3
Basti Maluk o **PK** 138-139 C 5
Bastogne o **B** 92-93 H 3
Bastrop o **USA** (LA) 268-269 J 4
Bastrop o **USA** (TX) 266-267 K 3
Basu, Pulau ⌒ **RI** 162-163 E 5
Basu, Tanjung ▲ **RI** 162-163 E 5
Basua o **WAN** 204-205 H 5
Basunda o **SUD** 200-201 G 6
Başyurt Tepe ▲ **TR** 128-129 D 3
Bas-Zaïre □ **ZRE** 210-211 D 6
Bat ••• **OM** 132-133 K 2
Bata ☆ **GQ** 210-211 B 3
Batabanó o **C** 54-55 D 3
Batabanó, Golfo de ≈ 54-55 D 3
Batabi o **WAN** 204-205 F 4
Bataf o **RI** 166-167 K 3
Batagaj o **RUS** 110-111 U 6
Batagaj-Alyta o **RUS** 110-111 S 6
Batag Island ⌒ **RP** 160-161 F 6
Bataguaçu o **BR** 72-73 D 6
Batajka ~ **RUS** 108-109 Z 6
Batajsk o **RUS** 102-103 L 4
Batakan o **RI** 164-165 D 5
Bataker Palace • **RI** 162-163 C 3
Batak Houses • **RI** 162-163 C 3
Batala o **IND** 138-139 E 4
Batalha o **BR** (ALA) 68-69 K 6
Batalha o **BR** (PIA) 68-69 G 4
Batalha, Mosteiro de ••• **P** 98-99 C 5
Batam, Pulau ⌒ **RI** 162-163 E 4
Batama o **ZRE** 210-211 L 3
Batamaj o **RUS** 118-119 O 4
Batâmbali Beafada o **GNB** 202-203 C 4
Batamšy ☆ **KA** 126-127 N 2
Batan o **VRC** 154-155 B 4
Batang o **RI** 168 C 3
Batang o **VRC** 144-145 M 6
Batangafo o **RCA** 206-207 D 5
Batangas ☆ **RP** 160-161 D 6
Batan Island ⌒ **RP** (ALB) 160-161 F 6
Batan Island ⌒ **RP** (BTN) 160-161 E 2
Batan Islands ⌒ **RP** 160-161 D 2
Batanta, Pulau ⌒ **RI** 166-167 F 2
Batanta Pulau Reserve ⊥ • **RI** 166-167 F 2
Batas Island ⌒ **RP** 160-161 C 7
Batatais o **BR** 72-73 G 6
Batavia o **USA** (NY) 278-279 C 5
Batavia = Jakarta ★ **RI** 168 B 3
Batavia Downs o **AUS** 174-175 G 3
Bat Cave o **USA** (NC) 282-283 E 5
Batcham o **CAM** 204-205 J 6
Batchawana o **CDN** (ONT) 236-237 D 5
Batchawana Bay o **CDN** (ONT) 236-237 D 6
Batchawana Island ⌒ **CDN** (ONT) 236-237 D 6
Batchawana River ~ **CDN** (ONT) 236-237 D 5
Batchellerville o **USA** (NY) 278-279 H 5
Batchelor o **AUS** 172-173 K 2
Batchelor o **USA** (LA) 268-269 J 6
Batchenga o **CAM** 204-205 J 6
Bătdâmbâng o **K** 158-159 G 4
Bateckij o **RUS** 94-95 M 2
Bateeputih, Tanjung ▲ **RI** 162-163 A 2
Bateias o **BR** 74-75 F 5
Batéké, Plateaux ⛰ **RCB** 210-211 E 5
Batel, Esteros del ⬭ **RA** 76-77 H 5
Batelito, Arroyo ~ **RA** 76-77 H 5
Bateman o **CDN** (SAS) 232-233 M 6
Batemans Bay o **AUS** 180-181 L 3
Batemba o **ZRE** 210-211 J 6
Baté-Nafadj o **RG** 202-203 F 4
Batería, Cerro de la • **RA** 78-79 D 4
Bates o **AUS** 176-177 M 5
Bates o **USA** (AR) 276-277 A 6
Batesburg o **USA** (SC) 284-285 J 3
Batesland o **USA** (SD) 260-261 D 3
Batesville o **USA** (AR) 276-277 D 5
Batesville o **USA** (IN) 274-275 N 5
Batesville o **USA** (MS) 268-269 L 2
Batesville o **USA** (TX) 266-267 H 5
Bath o **CDN** (ONT) 238-239 J 4
Bath o ••• **GB** 90-91 F 6
Bath o **JA** 54-55 G 6
Bath o **USA** (NC) 282-283 L 5
Bath o **USA** (NY) 278-279 D 6
Bath o • **USA** (ME) 278-279 M 5
Batha □ **TCH** 198-199 J 5
Batha ~ **TCH** 198-199 J 6
Bathā, Wādī- ~ **OM** 132-133 L 2
Batha de Laïri ~ **TCH** 206-207 C 3
Batheaston o **AUS** 178-179 K 2
Bathinda o **IND** 138-139 E 4
Baths, The ∸ **GB** 56 C 2
Baths Bjerge Matterhorn ▲ **GRØ** 26-27 p 6
Bathsheba o **BDS** 56 F 5
Bath Springs o **USA** (TN) 276-277 G 5
Bá Thu'ó'c ☆ **VN** 156-157 D 6
Bathurst o **AUS** 180-181 K 2
Bathurst o **CDN** (NB) 240-241 K 3
Bathurst o **ZA** 220-221 H 6
Bathurst = Banjul ★ • **WAG** 202-203 B 3
Bathurst, Cape ▲ **CDN** 24-25 H 5
Bathurst Inlet ≈ 30-31 P 2
Bathurst Inlet o **CDN** 30-31 P 2
Bathurst Island ⌒ **AUS** 172-173 K 1
Bathurst Island ⌒ **CDN** 24-25 V 3
Bathurst Mines o **CDN** (NB) 240-241 K 3
Bati o **ETH** 208-209 E 3
Batia o **DY** 202-203 L 4
Batibati o **RI** 164-165 D 5
Batibo o **CAM** 204-205 H 6
Batié o **BF** 202-203 J 5
Batiki ⌒ **FJI** 184 III b 2
Bāṭin, Wādī al- ~ **KSA** 130-131 J 3
Bāṭina ∸ **OM** 132-133 K 1
Batinga o **BR** 72-73 K 4
Batiscan, Rivière ~ **CDN** (QUE) 240-241 C 3
Bat Island ⌒ **PNG** 183 D 2
Batkanu o **WAL** 202-203 D 5
Batken o **KS** 136-137 M 4
Batkes o **RI** 166-167 F 5
Bat Khela o **PK** 138-139 C 2
Batlai o **RUS** 126-127 G 6
Bāṭlāq-e Gāvḫūni ⬭ **IR** 134-135 E 2
Batlow o **AUS** 180-181 K 3
Batman ☆ **TR** 128-129 J 4
Baṭn, Ğāl al- ⛰ **IRQ** 130-131 H 2
Batna ☆ **DZ** 190-191 F 3
Baṭn al-Ġūl o **JOR** 130-131 D 3
Batnorov = Dundburd o **MAU** 148-149 K 4
Bato o **RP** 160-161 E 6
Ba To' o **VN** 158-159 K 3
Bato Bato ☆ **RP** 160-161 C 10
Batoka o **Z** 218-219 D 3
Bat-Ölzijt o **MAU** 148-149 G 3
Batomga o **RUS** 120-121 G 5
Batomga ~ **RUS** 120-121 F 5
Baton Rouge ☆ • **USA** (LA) 268-269 J 6
Batopilas o • **MEX** 50-51 F 4
Batoua o **CAM** 204-205 K 6
Batouala o **G** 210-211 D 3
Batouri o **CAM** 206-207 B 6
Batovi, Área Indígena X **BR** 72-73 D 2
Batovil, Rio ~ **BR** 72-73 D 2
Ba Town o **LB** 202-203 F 6
Batpajsagyr, kum ∸ **KA** 96-97 F 10
Ba Tri o **VN** 158-159 J 5
Batsari o **WAN** 198-199 C 6
Batsawul o **AFG** 138-139 C 2
Båtsfjord o **N** 86-87 O 1
Batteau o **CDN** 38-39 R 2
Batterbee Range ⛰ **ARK** 16 F 30
Batticaloa o • **CL** 140-141 J 7
Batti Malv Island ⌒ **IND** 140-141 L 5
Battleboro o **USA** (NC) 282-283 K 4
Battle Camp o **AUS** 174-175 H 4
Battle Creek ~ **CDN** (SAS) 232-233 J 6
Battle Creek o **USA** (MI) 272-273 E 5
Battle Creek ~ **USA** (MT) 250-251 K 3
Battlefields o **ZW** 218-219 E 4
Battleford o **CDN** (SAS) 232-233 K 3
Battle Ground o **USA** (WA) 244 245 C 5
Battle Harbour o **CDN** 38-39 R 2
Battle Lake o **USA** (MN) 270-271 C 4
Battle Mountain o **USA** (NV) 246-247 J 3
Battle River ~ **CDN** (ALB) 232-233 H 3
Battleview o **USA** (ND) 258-259 E 3
Battor o **GH** 202-203 L 6
Battrum o **CDN** (SAS) 232-233 K 5
Batu ▲ **ETH** 208-209 D 5
Batu, Bukit ▲ **MAL** 162-163 K 3
Batu, Kepulauau ⌒ **RI** 162-163 C 4
Batu, Tanjung ▲ **RI** (KTI) 164-165 F 2
Batu, Tanjung ▲ **RI** (SUB) 162-163 D 6
Batuaga o **RI** 164-165 H 6
Batuampar o **RI** 162-163 E 5
Batuamparan o **RI** 164-165 D 5
Batuasa o **RI** 166-167 F 3
Batuata, Pulau ⌒ **RI** 166-167 B 5
Batubatu o **RI** 164-165 F 6
Batuberagam, Tanjung ▲ **RI** 162-163 F 7
Batu Buteh, Gunung ▲ **MAL** 162-163 D 2
Batudaa o **RI** 164-165 H 3
Batudaka o **RI** 164-165 G 4
Batudaka, Pulau ⌒ **RI** 164-165 G 4
Batu Danau o **MAL** 164-165 D 1
Batudulag o **RI** 168 C 7
Batugade o **RI** 166-167 C 6
Batu Gajah o **MAL** 162-163 D 2
Batuhitam, Tanjung ▲ **RI** 164-165 H 4
Batui o **RI** 164-165 H 4
Batukangkung o **RI** 162-163 D 5
Batukau, Gunung ▲ **RI** 168 B 7
Batulicin o **RI** 164-165 D 5
Batumandi, Tanjung ▲ **RI** 162-163 D 5
Batumi ☆ • **GE** 126-127 D 7
Batu Pahat o • **MAL** 162-163 E 4
Batupanjang o **RI** 162-163 D 4
Batu Puteh, Gunung ▲ **MAL** 162-163 D 2
Batuputih o **RI** (JTI) 168 E 3
Batuputih o **RI** (KTI) 164-165 F 3
Batur, Danau ⬭ **RI** 168 B 7
Baturaja o **RI** 162-163 F 7
Batu Rakit o **MAL** 162-163 E 2
Baturetno o **RI** 168 D 3
Baturi o **MEX** 50-51 E 5
Baturube o **RI** 164-165 G 4
Batusangkar o • **RI** 162-163 D 5
Batu Satu o **MAL** 162-163 K 2
Batusitanduk o **RI** 164-165 G 5
Batu Tambung o **RI** 164-165 H 4
Batutua o **RI** 166-167 B 7
Baty-Jurjah ~ **RUS** 108-109 c 6
Batyr ~ **RUS** 118-119 E 4
Batyrevo o **RUS** 96-97 E 6
Bau o **MAL** 162-163 J 4
Bau o **RI** 164-165 F 5
Baú, Rio ~ **BR** 66-67 K 6
Baú, Rio do ~ **BR** 66-67 K 7
Ba'u, Tanjung ▲ **RI** 162-163 A 2
Bauana, Rio ~ **BR** 66-67 E 4
Baubau o **RI** 164-165 H 6
Bauchi □ **WAN** 204-205 H 3
Bauchi ☆ **WAN** (BAU) 204-205 H 3
Baudette o **USA** (MN) 270-271 D 2
Baudisson Island ⌒ **PNG** 183 F 2
Baudó, Serranía de ⛰ **CO** 60-61 C 4
Bauer Basin ≃ 14-15 S 9
Baugé o **F** 62-63 H 3
Bauhinia Downs o **AUS** (NT) 174-175 C 5
Bauhinia Downs o **AUS** (QLD) 178-179 K 3
Bauia o **RI** 164-165 G 6
Baukau o **RI** 166-167 D 6
Baúl, El ∴ • **GCA** 52-53 J 4
Baúl, El o **YV** 60-61 G 3
Bauld, Cape ▲ **CDN** (NFL) 242-243 N 1
Baule-Escoublac, la o • **F** 90-91 F 8
Baumann Fiord ≈ 24-25 d 2
Baú-Mekragroti, Área Indígena X **BR** 66-67 K 6
Baun o **RI** 166-167 B 7
Baungan o **RI** 162-163 C 3
Baun Pulau Reserve ⊥ • **RI** 166-167 H 5
Baunra o **IND** 142-143 E 4
Baunt o **RUS** 118-119 F 8
Baunt, ozero ⬭ **RUS** 118-119 F 8
Baures o **BOL** 70-71 F 3
Bauru o **BR** 72-73 F 7
Bauru o **ZRE** 210-211 H 3
Bauska ☆ •• **LV** 94-95 J 3
Bauta o **C** 54-55 D 3
Bauta o **ZRE** 210-211 H 3
Bautu o **RI** 164-165 H 4
Bautzen o •• **D** 92-93 N 3
Bauxite o **USA** (AR) 276-277 C 6
Baviácora o **MEX** 50-51 D 3
Bavispe, Rio ~ **MEX** 50-51 E 2
Bavly ☆ **RUS** 96-97 H 6
Bavon o **USA** (VA) 280-281 K 6
Bawa o **RP** 160-161 E 3
Bāwal o **IND** 138-139 F 5
Bawal, Pulau ⌒ **RI** 162-163 J 6
Bawanbir o **IND** 138-139 F 9
Bawang, Tanjung ▲ **RI** 162-163 H 5
Bawangling Z.B. ⊥ • **VRC** 156-157 F 7
Bawāti, Ğabal ▲ **SUD** 200-201 H 3
Baw Baw National Park ⊥ **AUS** 180-181 J 4
Bawdie o **GH** 202-203 J 7
Bawe o **RI** (IRJ) 166-167 F 2
Bawe o **RI** (IRJ) 166-167 H 3
Bawean, Pulau ⌒ **RI** 168 E 2
Bawen o **RI** 168 D 3
Bawku o **GH** 202-203 K 4
Bawlake o **MYA** 142-143 K 6
Bawlf o **CDN** (ALB) 232-233 F 3
Bawo o **LB** 202-203 F 7
Bawo Ofuloa o **RI** 162-163 C 5
Ba Xay o **LAO** 156-157 C 6
Baxkorgan o **VRC** 146-147 K 6
Baxley o **USA** (GA) 284-285 H 5
Baxoi o **VRC** 144-145 L 5
Baxter o **USA** (FL) 286-287 G 1
Baxter o **USA** (MN) 270-271 D 4
Baxter o **USA** (MS) 268-269 L 4
Baxter o **USA** (TN) 276-277 K 4
Baxter Cliffs ∸ **AUS** 176-177 H 6
Baxter Pass ▲ **USA** (CO) 254-255 G 4
Baxter Springs o **USA** (KS) 262-263 M 7
Baxterville o **USA** (MS) 268-269 L 5
Bay o **RMM** 202-203 J 3
Bay □ **SP** 212-213 J 2
Bay o **USA** (AR) 276-277 E 5
Bay, Reserve de ⊥ **RMM** 202-203 J 3
Baya-Bwanga o **ZRE** 210-211 J 6
Bayāḍ, al- ∸ **KSA** 132-133 E 3
Bayāḍ, Ra's al- ▲ **Y** 132-133 C 6
Bayadi o **G** 210-211 C 5
Bayaguana o **DOM** 54-55 L 5
Bayamo ☆ **C** 54-55 G 4
Bayamon o **USA** (PR) 286-287 P 2
Bayan o **VRC** 150-151 F 4
Bayanbulak o **VRC** 146-147 G 4
Bayanbulak Z.B. II **VRC** 146-147 G 4
Bayanga o **RCA** 210-211 F 2
Bayanga-Didi o **RCA** 206-207 B 6
Bayan Har Shan ⛰ **VRC** 144-145 K 3
Bayan Har Shankou ▲ **VRC** 144-145 L 3
Bayan Obo o **VRC** 148-149 J 7
Bayan Olji o **VRC** 154-155 D 1
Bayan Shan ▲ **VRC** 144-145 L 2
Bayard o **USA** (IA) 274-275 D 3
Bayard o **USA** (NE) 262-263 C 3
Bayard o **USA** (NM) 256-257 G 6
Bayat ☆ **TR** 128-129 F 2
Bayawan o **RP** 160-161 E 8
Bayāż o **IR** 134-135 F 3
Bayāżīye o **IR** 134-135 F 2
Baybay o **RP** 160-161 F 7
Bayboro o **USA** (NC) 282-283 L 5
Bay Bulls o **CDN** (NFL) 242-243 Q 5
Bayburt ☆ • **TR** 128-129 J 2
Bay City o **USA** (MI) 272-273 F 4
Bay City o **USA** (OR) 244-245 B 5
Bay de Verde o **CDN** (NFL) 242-243 Q 4
Baydhabo ☆ **SP** 212-213 J 2
Bay du Vin o **CDN** (NB) 240-241 K 3
Bayerischer Wald ∸ **D** 92-93 M 4
Bayern □ **D** 92-93 L 4
Bayeux o **BR** 68-69 L 5
Bayeux o • **F** 90-91 G 7
Bayfield o **USA** (CO) 254-255 H 6
Bayfield o **USA** (WI) 270-271 H 4
Bayfield Inlet o **CDN** (ONT) 238-239 E 3
Bay Fiord ≈ 26-27 J 4
Bãy Háp, Cử'a Sông ≈ 158-159 H 6
Bayındır ☆ **TR** 128-129 B 3
Bāyir Ğovein, Kūh-e ⛰ **IR** 136-137 E 6
Bayizhen o **VRC** 144-145 K 6
Baykan ☆ **TR** 128-129 J 3
Baykonyr = Bajķoņyr o **KA** 124-125 E 5
Bay Mills Indian Reservation X **USA** (MI) 270-271 O 4
Baynes Lake o **CDN** (BC) 230-231 O 4
Baynes Mountains ⛰ **NAM** 216-217 B 8
Baynūna ∸ **UAE** 132-133 H 2
Bayo, Cerro ▲ **RCH** 80 D 2
Bayobar o **PE** 64-65 B 4
Bay of Whales ≈ 16 F 20
Bayog o **RP** 160-161 E 9
Bayombong ☆ **RP** 160-161 D 4
Bayo Mesa, Cerro ▲ **RA** 78-79 E 5
Bayonet Point o **USA** (FL) 286-287 G 3
Bayon Macon ~ **USA** (LA) 268-269 J 4
Bayonne o • **F** 90-91 G 10
Bayou Bartholomew River ~ **USA** (AR) 276-277 D 7
Bayou Cane o **USA** (LA) 268-269 K 7
Bayou D'Arbonne Lake < **USA** (LA) 268-269 H 4
Bayou de Loutre ~ **USA** (LA) 268-269 H 4
Bayou de View ~ **USA** (AR) 276-277 D 5
Bayou Dorcheat ~ **USA** (LA) 268-269 G 4
Bayou La Batre o **USA** (AL) 284-285 B 6
Bayou La Grune ~ **USA** (AR) 276-277 D 6
Bayou Meto o **USA** (AR) 276-277 D 6
Bayou Pierre ~ **USA** (MS) 268-269 K 4
Bayou Sorrel o **USA** (LA) 268-269 J 6
Bay Port o **USA** (MI) 272-273 F 4
Bayramiç ☆ **TR** 128-129 B 3
Bayreuth o **D** 92-93 L 4
Bays, Lake of ⬭ **CDN** (ONT) 238-239 F 3
Bay Shore o **USA** (NY) 280-281 N 3
Bayside o **USA** (TX) 266-267 K 5
Bay Springs o **USA** (MS) 268-269 L 5
Baysville o **CDN** (ONT) 238-239 F 3
Baytik Shan ⛰ **VRC** 146-147 K 3
Baytown o **USA** (TX) 268-269 E 7
Bay Trail o **CDN** (SAS) 232-233 N 3
Bay Tree o **CDN** 32-33 L 4
Bayu o **RI** (ACE) 162-163 B 2
Bayu o **RI** (STG) 164-165 H 5
Bayugan o **RP** 160-161 F 8
Bayunglincir o **RI** 162-163 E 6
Bayun Gol He ~ **VRC** 144-145 L 2
Bayur, Tanjung ▲ **RI** 164-165 E 4
Bayur, Teluk ≈ 162-163 D 5
Bay View o **NZ** 182 F 3
Bayview o **USA** (ID) 250-251 C 4
Bay View o **USA** (MI) 272-273 E 2
Bayy al Kabīr, Wādī ~ **LAR** 192-193 F 2
Bayy al Kabír, Wādí ~ **LAR** 192-193 F 2
Bayzo o **RN** 198-199 B 6
Baza o **E** 98-99 F 6
Bazardjuzu, gora ▲ **RUS** 126-127 G 7
Bāzār-e Tāle o **AFG** 136-137 L 7
Bāzārgān o **IR** 128-129 L 3
Bazar-Korgon o **KS** 136-137 N 4
Bazarnye Mataki ☆ **RUS** 96-97 F 6
Bazartöbe o **KA** 96-97 H 9
Bazaruto, Ilhas do ⌒ **MOC** 218-219 H 5
Bazaruto, Parque Nacional de ⊥ **MOC** 218-219 H 5
Bazavluk ~ **UA** 102-103 J 4
Baženovo o **RUS** 96-97 J 6
Bazhong o **VRC** 154-155 E 6
Bazhou o **VRC** 154-155 K 2
Bazin, Rivière ~ **CDN** (QUE) 236-237 N 5
Bazmān o **IR** 134-135 J 5
Bazmān, Kūh-e ▲ **IR** 134-135 H 4
Bazou o **CAM** 204-205 J 6
Bazré o **CI** 202-203 H 6
Be, Nosy ⌒ **RM** 222-223 F 4
Beach ∸ **CDN** (PEI) 240-241 L 4
Beach o **USA** (ND) 258-259 D 5
Beach • **USA** (DE) 280-281 L 5
Beachburg o **CDN** (ONT) 238-239 J 3
Beachêne, Lac ⬭ **CDN** (QUE) 238-239 G 2
Beach Point ▲ **CDN** 24-25 d 7
Beachport o • **AUS** 180-181 E 4
Beach River ~ **USA** (TN) 276-277 G 5
Beacon o **AUS** 176-177 D 5
Beacon o **USA** (NY) 280-281 N 2
Beacon Bay o **ZA** 220-221 H 6
Beaconia o **CDN** (MAN) 234-235 G 4
Beadell, Mount ▲ **AUS** 176-177 H 2
Beadle o **CDN** (SAS) 232-233 K 4
Beadon Point ▲ **AUS** 172-173 B 6
Beafada, Batâmbali o **GNB** 202-203 C 4
Beagle, Canal ≈ 80 F 7
Beagle Bay ≈ 172-173 F 4
Beagle Bay X **AUS** 172-173 F 4
Beagle Bay Aboriginal Land X **AUS** 172-173 F 4
Beagle Gulf ≈ 172-173 J 2
Beagle Island ⌒ **AUS** 176-177 C 4
Beagle Reef ⌒ **AUS** 172-173 F 3
Beako, Tanjung ▲ **RI** 166-167 D 6
Bealanana o **RM** 222-223 F 5
Béal an Atha = Ballina o **IRL** 90-91 C 4
Béal an Mhuirthead = Belmullet o **IRL** 90-91 C 4
Béal Átha na Sluaighe = Ballinasloe o **IRL** 90-91 C 5
Beale Air Force Base • **USA** (CA) 246-247 D 4
Bealeton o **USA** (VA) 280-281 J 5
Beals Creek ~ **USA** (TX) 264-265 C 6
Beampingaratra ⛰ **RM** 222-223 E 10
Beanntraí = Bantry o **IRL** 90-91 C 6
Bean Station o **USA** (TN) 282-283 D 4
Bear, Mount ▲ **USA** 20-21 U 6
Bear Bay ≈ 24-25 c 3
Bearberry o **CDN** (ALB) 232-233 D 4
Bear Cove o **CDN** (BC) 230-231 B 3
Bear Cove o **CDN** (NFL) 242-243 M 3
Bear Cove ⬭ **CDN** (NWT) 36-37 G 3
Bear Cove Point ▲ **CDN** 36-37 H 3
Bear Creek ~ **USA** (AL) 284-285 C 2
Bear Creek ~ **USA** (CO) 254-255 N 6
Bear Creek ~ **USA** (KS) 262-263 E 7
Bear Creek Springs o **USA** (AR) 276-277 B 4
Bearden o **USA** (AR) 276-277 C 7
Beardmore o **CDN** (ONT) 234-235 Q 5
Beardmore Glacier ⊂ **ARK** 16 E 0
Beardmore Reservoir < **AUS** 178-179 K 4
Beardsley o **USA** (MN) 270-271 B 5
Beardstown o **USA** (IL) 274-275 H 4
Beardy River ~ **AUS** 178-179 L 5
Bearhead Creek ~ **CDN** 32-33 M 4
Bear Island ⌒ **ARK** 16 F 26
Bear Island ⌒ **CDN** 34-35 Q 3
Bear Islands = Medvež'i ostrova ⌒ **RUS** 112-113 L 1
Bear Lake o **CDN** (BC) 228-229 M 2
Bear Lake ⬭ **CDN** 34-35 H 3
Bear Lake o **USA** (MI) 272-273 C 3
Bear Lake ⬭ **USA** (ID) 252-253 G 5
Bear Lake ⬭ **USA** (UT) 254-255 D 2
Bear Mount ▲ **USA** 20-21 T 2
Bearpaw Mount ▲ **USA** 20-21 P 4
Bear Paw Mountain ▲ **USA** (MT) 250-251 K 3
Bear River ~ **CDN** 34-35 D 3
Bear River ~ **USA** (ID) 252-253 G 4
Bear River ~ **USA** (UT) 254-255 D 2
Bear River Bay ≈ **USA** 254-255 C 2
Bearskin Lake o **CDN** 34-35 L 4
Beartooth Pass ▲ **USA** (MT) 250-251 K 6
Bear Valley o **USA** (CA) 246-247 E 5
Beas ~ **IND** 138-139 E 4
Beas de Segura o **E** 98-99 F 5
Beasley o **USA** (TX) 268-269 E 7
Beata, Cabo ▲ **DOM** 54-55 K 6
Beata, Isla ⌒ **DOM** 54-55 K 6
Beaton o **CDN** (BC) 230-231 M 3
Beatrice o **USA** (AL) 284-285 C 5
Beatrice o **USA** (NE) 262-263 K 4
Beatrice o **ZW** 218-219 F 4
Beatrice, Cape ▲ **AUS** 174-175 D 4
Beatton River o **CDN** 32-33 K 3
Beatton River ~ **CDN** 32-33 K 3
Beatty o **CDN** (SAS) 232-233 O 3
Beatty o **USA** (NV) 248-249 H 3
Beatty o **USA** (OR) 244-245 D 8
Beattyville o **CDN** (QUE) 236-237 L 4
Beattyville o **USA** (KY) 276-277 M 3
Beauceville o **CDN** (QUE) 240-241 E 4
Beauchêne Island ⌒ **GB** 78-79 L 7
Beaucoup Creek ~ **USA** (IL) 276-277 F 3
Beaudesert o **AUS** (QLD) 178-179 M 5
Beaudesert o **AUS** (QLD) 178-179 F 1
Beaufield o **CDN** (SAS) 232-233 J 4
Beaufort o **AUS** 180-181 G 4
Beaufort o **MAL** 160-161 A 10
Beaufort o **USA** (NC) 282-283 L 6
Beaufort o **USA** (SC) 284-285 K 4
Beaufort Lagoon ⬭ **USA** 20-21 U 2
Beaufort Sea ≈ 20-21 Q 1
Beaufort-Wes = Beaufort West o **ZA** 220-221 F 6
Beaufort West = Beaufort-Wes o **ZA** 220-221 F 6
Beaugency o **F** 90-91 H 8
Beauharnois o **CDN** (QUE) 238-239 M 3
Beaulieu River ~ **CDN** 30-31 N 4
Beauly o • **GB** 90-91 E 3
Beaumont o **CDN** (ALB) 232-233 E 2
Beaumont o **USA** (CA) 248-249 H 6
Beaumont o **USA** (KS) 262-263 K 7
Beaumont o **USA** (KY) 276-277 K 4
Beaumont o **USA** (MS) 268-269 M 5
Beaumont o **USA** (TX) 268-269 F 6
Beaumont-de-Lomagne o **F** 90-91 H 10
Beaumont-sur-Oise o **F** 90-91 J 7
Beaune o **F** 90-91 K 8
Beaupré o **CDN** (QUE) 240-241 E 3
Beaupré, Kap ▲ **GRØ** 28-29 c 2
Beauséjour o **CDN** (MAN) 234-235 G 4
Beauséjour National Historical Park, Fort • **CDN** (NB) 240-241 L 5
Beauty o **ZA** 218-219 D 6
Beauvais ☆ • **F** 90-91 J 7
Beauvais Lake ⬭ **CDN** 30-31 R 5
Beauval o **CDN** 34-35 C 3
Beauvallon o **CDN** (ALB) 232-233 G 2
Beauveau, Lac ⬭ **CDN** 38-39 G 2
Beaver o **USA** (AK) 20-21 R 3
Beaver o **USA** (OK) 264-265 D 2
Beaver o **USA** (OR) 244-245 B 5
Beaver o **USA** (UT) 254-255 C 5
Beaver Brook Station o **CDN** (NB) 240-241 K 3
Beaver City o **USA** (NE) 262-263 G 4
Beaver Cove o **CDN** (BC) 230-231 C 3
Beavercreek o **USA** (OH) 280-281 B 4
Beaver Creek ~ **USA** 20-21 R 4
Beaver Creek ~ **USA** (KS) 262-263 E 5
Beaver Creek ~ **USA** (MT) 250-251 L 4
Beaver Creek ~ **USA** (ND) 258-259 D 4
Beaver Creek ~ **USA** (NE) 262-263 F 4
Beaver Creek ~ **USA** (OK) 264-265 F 4
Beaver Creek Mountain ⛰ **USA** (AL) 284-285 D 3
Beaver Dam o **USA** (KY) 276-277 J 3
Beaver Dam o **USA** (WI) 274-275 K 1
Beaverdam Lake ⬭ **USA** (WI) 274-275 K 1
Beaverdell o **CDN** (BC) 230-231 K 4
Beaver Falls o **USA** (PA) 280-281 F 3
Beaverhead o **USA** (AZ) 256-257 F 5
Beaverhead Range ⛰ **USA** (MT) 250-251 F 6
Beaverhead River ~ **USA** (MT) 250-251 G 6
Beaverhill Lake ⬭ **CDN** (ALB) 232-233 F 2
Beaverhill Lake ⬭ **CDN** (MAN) 34-35 J 3
Beaverhill Lake ⬭ **CDN** (NWT) 30-31 R 4
Beaver Island ⌒ **USA** (MI) 272-273 D 2
Beaver Lake ⬭ **CDN** 30-31 L 5
Beaver Lake ⬭ **USA** (AR) 276-277 A 4
Beaverley o **CDN** (BC) 228-229 M 3
Beaverlodge Lake ⬭ **CDN** (NWT) 30-31 K 3
Beaverlodge Lake ⬭ **CDN** (SAS) 30-31 P 6
Beaver Marsh o **USA** (OR) 244-245 D 7
Beaver Mines o **CDN** (ALB) 232-233 D 6
Beaver Mountain ▲ **CDN** 20-21 U 5
Beavermouth o **CDN** (BC) 230-231 M 2
Beaver River ~ **CDN** 30-31 G 5
Beaver River ~ **CDN** 32-33 P 4
Beaver River ~ **CDN** 34-35 C 3
Beaver River ~ **CDN** 34-35 M 3
Beaver River ~ **CDN** 38-39 E 2
Beaver River ~ **USA** (OK) 264-265 D 2
Beaver Run Reservoir ⬭ **USA** (PA) 280-281 G 3
Beaver Springs o **USA** (PA) 280-281 J 3
Beaverstone River ~ **CDN** 34-35 L 3
Beaverton o **CDN** (ONT) 238-239 F 4
Beaverton o **USA** (OR) 244-245 C 5
Beāwar o **IND** 138-139 E 6
Beazer o **CDN** (ALB) 232-233 E 6
Beazley o **RA** 78-79 F 2
Bebarama o **CO** 60-61 C 4
Bébédjia o **TCH** 206-207 C 4
Bebedouro o **BR** 72-73 F 6
Bebeka o **ETH** 208-209 B 5
Bebenaro o **RI** 166-167 C 6
Bebisa o **PNG** 183 B 4
Béboto o **TCH** 206-207 C 4
Béboura III o **RCA** 206-207 C 5
Bebra o **D** 92-93 K 3
Becal o • **MEX** 52-53 J 1
Becan ∴ • **MEX** 52-53 K 2
Becanchén o **MEX** 52-53 K 2
Bécancour o **CDN** (QUE) 238-239 N 2
Bécard, Lac ⬭ **CDN** 36-37 N 4
Bečenča o **RUS** 118-119 G 5
Becerreá o **E** 98-99 D 3
Becerro, Cayos ⌒ **HN** 54-55 D 7
Béchar ☆ **DZ** 188-189 K 5
Becharof Lake ⬭ **USA** 22-23 S 4
Becher, Cape ▲ **CDN** 24-25 Y 2
Becher Peninsula ⌣ **CDN** 36-37 P 3
Bechevin Bay ≈ 22-23 P 5
Becilla de Valderaduey o **E** 98-99 E 3
Beckley o **USA** (WV) 280-281 E 6
Becks o **NZ** 182 B 6
Beckton o **USA** (WY) 252-253 L 2
Beckwourth Pass ▲ **USA** (CA) 246-247 E 4
Beco o **RI** 166-167 C 6
Bedarra Island ⌒ **AUS** 174-175 J 6
Bédaya o **TCH** 206-207 C 4
Beddovza, Cap ▲ **MA** 188-189 G 4
Bedelē o **ETH** 208-209 C 4
Bedēsa o **ETH** 208-209 E 4
Bedford o **CDN** (QUE) 238-239 N 3
Bedford o **GB** 90-91 G 5
Bedford o **USA** (IA) 274-275 D 4
Bedford o **USA** (IN) 274-275 M 6
Bedford o **USA** (NY) 280-281 N 2
Bedford o **USA** (PA) 280-281 H 4
Bedford o **USA** (VA) 280-281 G 6
Bedford o **ZA** 220-221 H 6
Bedford, Cape ▲ **AUS** 174-175 H 4
Bedford, Lake ⬭ **AUS** 176-177 G 3
Bedford, Mount ▲ **AUS** 172-173 H 4
Bedford Downs o **AUS** 172-173 H 4
Bediako o **GH** 202-203 J 6

Bediani ○ GE 126-127 F 7
Bedias ○ USA (TX) 268-269 E 6
Bedi Dat ○ PK 134-135 L 5
Bediondo ○ TCH 206-207 C 4
Bedjedjene, Hassi < DZ 190-191 G 7
Bednesti ○ CDN (BC) 228-229 L 3
Bednodem'janovsk ○ RUS 94-95 S 5
Bédo < TCH 198-199 J 3
Bedoba ○ RUS 116-117 H 6
Bédouaram < RN 198-199 F 5
Bedoud, Hassi < MA 188-189 K 4
Bee ○ USA (NE) 262-263 J 4
Beebe ○ USA (AR) 276-277 D 5
Beechal River ∼ AUS 178-179 H 4
Beecher ○ USA (IL) 274-275 L 3
Beechey Lake ○ CDN 30-31 Q 3
Beechey Point ○ USA 20-21 Q 1
Beech Fork Lake ○ USA (WV) 280-281 D 5
Beech Grove ○ USA (IN) 274-275 M 5
Beechgrove ○ USA (TN) 276-277 J 5
Beech Island ○ USA (SC) 284-285 J 3
Beechwood ○ USA (MI) 272-273 C 5
Beechworth ○ • AUS 180-181 J 4
Beechy ○ CDN (SAS) 232-233 L 5
Beekman Peninsula ⌣ CDN 36-37 R 3
Beeler ○ USA (KS) 262-263 F 6
Beenčime ∼ RUS 110-111 N 4
Beenleigh ○ AUS 178-179 M 4
Be'ér Sheva' ☆ IL 130-131 D 2
Beerwah ○ AUS 178-179 M 4
Beeskow ○ • D 92-93 N 2
Beestekraal ○ ZA 220-221 H 2
Beetaloo ○ AUS 174-175 B 5
Beeville ○ USA (TX) 266-267 K 5
Befale ○ ZRE 210-211 H 3
Befandefa ○ RM 222-223 C 9
Befandriana Atsimo ○ RM 222-223 C 9
Befandriana Avaratra ○ RM 222-223 F 5
Befasy ○ RM 222-223 D 8
Beffa ∼ DY 204-205 E 4
Befori ○ ZRE 210-211 J 3
Beforona ○ RM 222-223 F 7
Befotaka ○ RM 222-223 E 9
Bega ○ AUS 180-181 K 4
Beggs ○ USA (OK) 264-265 H 3
Begičeva, grjada ▲ RUS 108-109 X 5
Begidzjan ∼ RUS 110-111 P 6
Bégin ○ CDN (QUE) 240-241 D 2
Begna ∼ N 86-87 D 6
Begogo ○ RM 222-223 E 9
Bégon ○ RCA 206-207 B 5
Begoro ○ GH 202-203 K 6
Begunicy ○ RUS 94-95 L 2
Begusarai ○ IND 142-143 E 3
Beh ∼ RI 168 C 7
Behābād ○ IR 134-135 G 3
Béhague, Pointe ▲ F 62-63 J 3
Behara ○ RM 222-223 E 10
Behbahān ○ • IR 134-135 D 3
Beheloka ○ RM 222-223 C 9
Behenjy ○ RM 222-223 E 7
Béhili ○ RCA 206-207 D 5
Behm Canal ≈ 32-33 E 4
Behring Point ○ BS 54-55 G 2
Behšahr ○ • IR 136-137 C 6
Bei'an ○ VRC 150-151 F 3
Béibouo ○ CI 202-203 G 6
Beibu Wan ≈ 156-157 E 6
Beichuan ○ VRC 154-155 D 6
Beida = Goz ○ TCH 198-199 K 6
Beidaihe Haibin • VRC 154-155 L 2
Beidaneikechuke ○ VRC 144-145 F 5
Beidou ○ VRC 156-157 H 6
Beigi ○ ETH 208-209 B 4
Beihai ○ VRC 156-157 F 6
Bei Jiang ∼ VRC 156-157 H 4
Bei Jiao ⌒ VRC 158-159 L 2
Beijing ★ ··· VRC 154-155 K 2
Beijin Gang ∼ VRC 156-157 H 6
Beijing Shi ▫ VRC 154-155 K 2
Bei Ling • VRC 150-151 D 7
Beiliu ○ VRC 156-157 G 5
Béinamar ○ TCH 206-207 B 4
Beipan Jiang ∼ VRC 156-157 D 4
Beipiao ○ VRC 150-151 C 7
Beira ☆ MOC 218-219 H 4
Beira Alta ○ ANG 216-217 C 4
Beiradão ○ BR 62-63 H 6
Beirut = Bairūt ★ RL 128-129 F 6
Beiseker ○ CDN (ALB) 232-233 E 4
Bei Shan ▲ VRC 146-147 M 5
Beishan • VRC (JIL) 150-151 E 6
Beishan • VRC (ZHE) 156-157 L 2
Beitan ○ VRC 156-157 F 6
Beitau ○ VRC 156-157 F 6
Beitbridge ○ ZW 218-219 F 6
Beitstadfjorden ≈ 86-87 E 5
Beitun ○ VRC 146-147 H 2
Beizhangdian ○ VRC 154-155 H 3
Beizhen ○ VRC 150-151 C 7
Beja ○ ·· P 98-99 D 5
Beja ☆ TN 190-191 G 2
Bejaia ☆ · DZ 190-191 E 2
Béjar ○ • E 98-99 E 4
Bejarn ○ N 86-87 G 3
Beji ∼ PK 138-139 B 5
Beji ○ WAN 204-205 G 4
Bejlagan = Beylagan ○ AZ 128-129 M 3
Bejneu ☆ KA 126-127 L 5
B.E. Jordan Lake ○ USA (NC) 282-283 H 5
Bejsug ∼ RUS 102-103 L 5
Bejsugskij liman ≈ 102-103 L 4
Bejucal ○ C 54-55 D 3
Bek ∼ CAM 210-211 E 2
Béka ○ CAM (ADA) 204-205 K 5
Béka ○ CAM (ADA) 206-207 B 5
Béka ○ CAM (NOR) 204-205 K 4
Bekabad ○ US 136-137 L 4
Békamba ○ TCH 206-207 C 4
Bekasi ○ RI 168 B 3
Bekati ○ US 136-137 K 4
Bekbeket ○ KA 96-97 H 10
Bekdaš ○ TM 136-137 C 4
Bek-Džar ○ KS 136-137 N 4
Beke ○ RI 168 E 7
Bèkè ∼ RUS 110-111 K 6
Beke ○ ZRE 214-215 D 5
Bekenu ○ MAL 162-163 K 2
Békés ○ H 92-93 Q 5
Békéscsaba ○ H 92-93 Q 5
Bekily ○ RM (TLA) 222-223 D 10
Bekipay ○ RM 222-223 E 6
Bekitro ○ RM 222-223 D 10
Bekkai ○ J 152-153 L 3
Bekmurat, gora ▲ TM 136-137 D 4
Bekodoka ○ RM 222-223 D 6
Bek'oji ○ ETH 208-209 D 5
Bekopaka ○ RM 222-223 D 7
Békuy ○ BF 202-203 J 4
Bekwai ○ GH 202-203 K 6
Bekyem ○ GH 202-203 J 6
Bela ∼ BR 70-71 H 3
Bela ○ IND 142-143 C 3
Bela ○ PK 134-135 M 5
Bélabirim < RN 198-199 F 5
Bélabo ○ CAM 204-205 K 6
Bela Estrela ○ BR 68-69 E 4
Belaga ○ MAL 162-163 K 3
Belair ○ CDN (MAN) 234-235 G 4
Bel Air ○ USA (MD) 280-281 K 4
Belaja ∼ RUS 96-97 J 6
Belaja ∼ RUS 112-113 O 5
Belaja ∼ RUS 112-113 R 4
Belaja ∼ RUS 116-117 L 9
Belaja ∼ RUS 122-123 C 3
Belaja ∼ RUS 126-127 D 5
Belaja, gora ▲ RUS 112-113 S 4
Belaja, Ust'- ○ RUS 112-113 R 4
Belaja Berëzka ○ RUS 94-95 N 5
Belaja Cerkov' = Bila Cerkva ☆ UA 102-103 G 3
Belaja Gora ○ RUS 110-111 a 5
Belaja Holunica ☆ RUS 96-97 G 4
Belaja Kalitva ○ RUS 102-103 M 3
Belaja Škola ○ KA 124-125 N 5
Belajau, Danau ○ RI 162-163 K 6
Belaja Zemlja, ostrova ⌒ RUS 84-85 g 2
Belalcázar ○ E 98-99 E 5
Bela Lorena ○ BR 72-73 G 3
Belamoty ○ RM 222-223 D 9
Belang ○ RI 164-165 J 3
Belangan ○ RI 162-163 K 6
Belangbelang, Pulau ⌒ RI (MAL) 164-165 K 4
Belangbelang, Pulau ⌒ RI (SSE) 168 E 6
Belanger Island ⌒ CDN 36-37 L 6
Belanger River ∼ CDN 34-35 H 4
Bela Palanka ○ • YU 100-101 J 3
Belarus = Belarus' ■ BY 94-95 K 5
Belas ○ ANG 216-217 B 4
Beláti ○ IND 140-141 F 2
Bela Vista ○ ANG (BGO) 216-217 B 3
Bela Vista ○ ANG (HBO) 216-217 D 6
Bela Vista ○ BR (APA) 62-63 J 4
Bela Vista ○ BR (GSU) 76-77 J 2
Bela Vista ○ BR (RSU) 74-75 D 7
Bela Vista ○ MOC 220-221 L 3
Bela Vista, Cachoeira ∼ BR 68-69 C 5
Belawan ○ RI 162-163 C 3
Belayan ∼ RI 164-165 E 3
Bélbéji ○ RN 198-199 C 5
Belbela, Sebkha Aïn ○ DZ 188-189 J 7
Belbutte ○ CDN (SAS) 232-233 L 2
Bèl'c' = Bălţi ☆ MD 102-103 E 4
Belčerāg ○ AFG 136-137 J 7
Bełchatów ○ PL 92-93 P 3
Belcher Channel ≈ 24-25 X 2
Belcher Islands ○ CDN (NWT) 36-37 K 6
Belcher Islands ⌒ CDN (NWT) 36-37 J 6
Belcher Point ▲ CDN 24-25 g 3
Belchite ○ E 98-99 G 4
Belcourt Creek ∼ CDN (BC) 228-229 O 2
Bel'cy = Bălţi ☆ MD 102-103 E 4
Belda ○ IND 142-143 E 4
Belden ○ USA (CA) 246-247 D 3
Belden ○ USA (ND) 258-259 E 3
Belden ○ USA (OH) 280-281 D 2
Belding ○ USA (MI) 272-273 D 4
Bel'dir, Uš ○ RUS 116-117 J 10
Bel'dunčana, ozero ○ RUS 116-117 G 2
Bele, ozero ○ RUS 116-117 E 8
Belebej ☆ RUS 96-97 J 6
Belebelka ○ RUS 94-95 M 3
Beledweyne ☆ SP 208-209 G 6
Bélèhédé ○ BF 202-203 K 2
Beléko-Soba ○ RMM 202-203 G 3
Bélel ○ CAM 206-207 B 5
Belel ○ WAN 204-205 K 4
Belele ○ AUS 176-177 D 3
Belém ○ BR (AMA) 66-67 C 5
Belém ○ BR (PA) 68-69 L 5
Belém ☆ • BR (P) 62-63 K 6
Belem ○ PE 70-71 C 4
Belem de São Francisco ○ BR 68-69 J 6
Belen ○ CO 60-61 E 4
Belen ∼ PA 52-53 D 7
Belén ○ RA 76-77 D 4
Belén ○ RCH 70-71 C 6
Belen ○ USA (NM) 256-257 J 4
Belén, Río ∼ RA 76-77 D 4
Belen'kij ○ RUS 118-119 M 8
Belesc Cogani ○ SP 212-213 H 3
Beles Wenz ∼ ETH 208-209 C 3
Belet Weyne = Beledweyne ☆ SP 208-209 G 6
Beleuli ∴ • US 136-137 E 2
Belev ☆ RUS 94-95 P 5
Bélèya ○ RG 202-203 E 4
Beleya Terara ▲ ETH 208-209 C 3
Beleza, Ribeiro ∼ BR 68-69 C 6
Belezma, Monts de ▲ DZ 190-191 E 3
Belfast ☆ • GB 90-91 E 4
Belfast ○ USA (AR) 276-277 C 6
Belfast ○ USA (ME) 278-279 M 4
Belfast ○ USA (OH) 280-281 C 4
Belfast ○ ZA 220-221 K 2
Belfield ○ USA (ND) 258-259 E 5
Bēlfodiyo ○ ETH 208-209 B 3
Belfort ☆ • F 90-91 L 8
Belfry ○ USA (MT) 250-251 K 6
Belgaum ○ • IND 140-141 F 3
Belgica, La ○ BOL 70-71 F 5
Belgica Bank ≈ 26-27 s 4
Belgica Mountains ▲ ARK 16 F 3
Belgium = België = Belgique ■ B 92-93 G 3
Bel'go ○ RUS 122-123 G 3
Belgo ○ SUD 206-207 L 3
Belgorod ○ RUS 102-103 K 2
Belgorod-Dnestrovskij ☆ UA 102-103 G 4
Belgrade ○ USA (ME) 278-279 M 4
Belgrade ○ USA (MN) 270-271 C 5
Belgrade ○ USA (MT) 250-251 H 6
Belgrade = Beograd ★ ·· YU 100-101 H 2
Belgrano ○ RA 76-77 F 3
Belgrano, Cerro ▲ RA 80 E 3
Belgreen ○ USA (AL) 284-285 B 2
Bel Guerdāne, Bir < RIM 196-197 E 2
Belhatti ○ IND 140-141 F 3
Belhaven ○ USA (NC) 282-283 L 5
Belhe ○ IND 138-139 E 10
Belhirane ○ DZ 190-191 F 5
Béli ∼ BF 202-203 K 2
Béli ○ GNB 202-203 D 4
Beli ○ WAN 204-205 J 5
Belic ○ C 54-55 G 5
Bélice ∼ I 100-101 D 6
Beličij, ostrov ⌒ RUS 120-121 G 6
Belidži ○ RUS 126-127 H 7
Belifang ○ CAM 204-205 J 5
Beli Hill ▲ WAN 204-205 J 5
Belimbing ○ RI (LAM) 162-163 F 7
Belimbing ○ RI (SUS) 162-163 F 6
Belimbing, Tanjung ▲ RI 162-163 F 7
Belimbing, Teluk ≈ 162-163 F 7
Bélinga ○ G 210-211 D 3
Belinskij ○ RUS 94-95 R 5
Belinskoe ○ RUS 122-123 K 4
Belinyu ○ RI 162-163 F 5
Belitung, Pulau ⌒ RI 162-163 H 6
Belize ○ ANG 210-211 D 6
Belize ■ BH 52-53 K 3
Belize City ○ BH 52-53 K 3
Belize River ∼ BH 52-53 K 3
Bélizon ○ F 62-63 H 3
Beljaevka ☆ RUS 96-97 K 8
Beljaka, kosa ⌣ RUS 112-113 X 3
Beljanica ▲ YU 100-101 H 2
Beljanka ∼ RUS 118-119 O 4
Bel Kacem, Bir < TN 190-191 G 4
Bel'kači ∼ RUS 120-121 D 4
Bel'kači ∼ RUS 120-121 D 4
Belkar ○ IND 140-141 E 2
Belknap Springs ○ USA (OR) 244-245 C 6
Bel'kovskij, ostrov ⌒ RUS 110-111 U 2
Bel'kovskij Nos, mys ▲ RUS 108-109 J 7
Bell ○ USA (FL) 286-287 G 2
Bell ○ USA (GA) 284-285 H 3
Bell ○ ZA 220-221 H 6
Bell, Rivière ∼ CDN (QUE) 236-237 L 3
Bella ○ CAM 210-211 C 2
Bella, Laguna la ○ RA 76-77 G 3
Bella Bella ○ CDN (BC) 228-229 F 4
Bellac ○ F 90-91 H 8
Bella Coola ○ CDN (BC) 228-229 H 4
Bella Coola River ∼ CDN (BC) 228-229 H 4
Belladère ○ RH 54-55 J 5
Bella Flor ○ BOL 70-71 D 2
Bellaire ○ USA (MI) 272-273 D 3
Bellaire ○ USA (OH) 280-281 F 3
Bellary ○ IND 140-141 G 3
Bellata ○ AUS 178-179 K 5
Bellavista ○ EC 64-65 B 10
Bellavista ○ PE (CAJ) 64-65 C 4
Bellavista ○ PE (MAR) 64-65 D 5
Bella Vista ○ PY 76-77 K 4
Bella Vista ○ RA 76-77 H 5
Bella Vista, Salar de ○ RCH 70-71 C 7
Bell Bay ≈ 24-25 e 5
Bellburns ○ CDN (NFL) 242-243 L 2
Belle ○ USA (MO) 274-275 G 6
Belle, La ○ USA (FL) 286-287 H 5
Belle Anse ○ RH 54-55 J 5
Belle Bay ≈ 38-39 R 5
Belle Côte ○ CDN (NS) 240-241 O 4
Belledune ○ CDN (NB) 240-241 K 3
Bellefontaine ○ USA (OH) 280-281 C 3
Bellefonte ○ USA (PA) 280-281 J 3
Belle Fourche ○ USA (SD) 260-261 C 2
Belle Fourche Reservoir ○ USA (SD) 260-261 C 2
Belle Fourche River ∼ USA (WY) 252-253 N 3
Belle Glade ○ USA (FL) 286-287 J 5
Belle-Île ⌒ F 90-91 F 8
Belle Isle ○ CDN (NFL) 242-243 N 1
Belle Isle ⌒ CDN 38-39 R 3
Belle Isle, Strait of ≈ 38-39 Q 3
Belle Isle, Strait of ≈ CDN 242-243 M 1
Bellemont ○ USA (AZ) 256-257 D 3
Bellenden Ker ○ AUS 174-175 H 5
Bellenden Ker National Park ⊥ AUS 174-175 H 5
Belleoram ○ CDN (NFL) 242-243 N 5
Belle Plaine ○ CDN (SAS) 232-233 N 5
Belle Plaine ○ USA (KS) 262-263 J 7
Belle Plaine ○ USA (MN) 270-271 E 6
Belle River ○ CDN (ONT) 238-239 C 6
Belle River ○ CDN (PEI) 240-241 N 4
Belleterre ○ CDN (QUE) 236-237 K 5
Belleview ○ CDN (MAN) 234-235 C 5
Belleville ○ CDN (NS) 240-241 K 7
Belleville ○ CDN (ONT) 238-239 H 4
Belleville ○ USA (IL) 274-275 J 6
Belleville ○ USA (KS) 262-263 J 5
Belleville ○ USA (TX) 266-267 L 4
Belleville ○ USA (WV) 280-281 E 4
Bellevue ○ AUS 174-175 H 5
Bellevue ○ CDN (ALB) 232-233 D 6
Bellevue ○ USA (IA) 274-275 H 2
Bellevue ○ USA (ID) 252-253 D 3
Bellevue ○ USA (MI) 272-273 D 5
Bellevue ○ USA (NE) 262-263 L 3
Bellevue ○ USA (OH) 280-281 D 2
Bellevue ○ USA (TX) 264-265 F 5
Bellevue ○ USA (WA) 244-245 C 3
Bellevue de-Inini, Mont ▲ F 62-63 H 4
Bellingen ○ AUS 178-179 M 6
Bellinger, Lac ○ CDN 38-39 G 3
Bellingham ○ USA (WA) 244-245 C 2
Bellingshausen Abyssal Plain ≈ ARK 16 G 27
Bellingshausen Sea ≈ ARK 16 G 28
Bellinzona ☆ • CH 92-93 K 5
Bell-Irving River ∼ CDN 32-33 F 3
Bell Irving River ∼ CDN 32-33 F 3
Bell Island ⌒ CDN (NFL) 242-243 P 5
Bell Island ⌒ CDN (NFL) 242-243 N 2
Bell Island Hot Springs ○ USA 32-33 E 4
Bellmead ○ USA (TX) 266-267 K 2
Bellmore ○ USA (IN) 274-275 L 5
Bell National Historic Park, Alexander Graham • CDN (NS) 240-241 P 4
Bello ○ CO 60-61 D 4
Bellocq ○ RA 78-79 J 3
Bellona Island ⌒ SOL 184 I d 4
Bellota ○ USA (CA) 246-247 D 5
Bellows Falls ○ USA (NH) 278-279 J 5
Bellpat ○ PK 138-139 B 5
Bell Peninsula ⌣ CDN 36-37 H 3
Bell River ∼ AUS 180-181 K 2
Bell River ∼ CDN 20-21 W 3
Bells ○ USA (TN) 276-277 F 5
Bells ○ USA (TX) 264-265 H 5
Bellsund ≈ N (SVA) 84-85 H 4
Bellton ○ USA (WV) 280-281 F 4
Belluno ☆ I 100-101 D 1
Bellview ○ USA (NM) 256-257 M 4
Bell Ville ○ RA 78-79 H 2
Bellville ○ ZA 220-221 D 6
Bellvue ○ USA (CO) 254-255 K 3
Belly River ∼ CDN (ALB) 232-233 E 6
Belmond ○ USA (IA) 274-275 E 2
Belmont ○ AUS 180-181 L 2
Belmont ○ CDN (MAN) 234-235 D 5
Belmont ○ USA (MS) 268-269 M 2
Belmont ○ USA (NE) 262-263 C 2
Belmont ○ USA (NY) 278-279 C 6
Belmont ○ USA (TX) 266-267 K 4
Belmont ○ ZA 220-221 G 4
Belmont, Fort • USA (MN) 270-271 G 7
Belmonte ○ BR 72-73 L 3
Belmopan ★ BH 52-53 K 3
Belmore Creek ∼ AUS 174-175 F 6
Belmullet = Béal an Mhuirthead ○ IRL 90-91 C 4
Belo ○ RM 222-223 D 8
Belobaka ○ RM 222-223 D 7
Belobrova, proliv ≈ 108-109 Z 1
Belo Campo ○ BR 72-73 K 3
Beloe, ozero ○ RUS 94-95 P 1
Beloe, ozero ○ RUS 114-115 U 7
Belogolovaja ∼ RUS 120-121 R 5
Belogorsk ○ RUS (AMR) 122-123 C 3
Belogorsk ○ RUS (KMR) 114-115 U 7
Belogorskij materik ⊥ RUS 114-115 J 3
Belogorskij materik, vozvšennost' ▲ RUS 114-115 J 3
Beloha ○ RM 222-223 D 10
Belo Horizonte ☆ BR 72-73 J 5
Beloit ○ USA (KS) 262-263 H 5
Beloit ○ USA (WI) 274-275 J 2
Belo Jardim ○ BR 68-69 K 6
Belojarovo ○ RUS 122-123 C 3
Belojarskij ○ RUS 114-115 J 3
Belojarskij ☆ RUS (SVR) 96-97 M 5
Béloko ○ RCA 206-207 B 6
Belokuriha ○ RUS 124-125 O 3
Belo Monte ○ BR (ALA) 68-69 K 6
Belo Monte ○ BR (AMA) 66-67 E 6
Belo Monte do Pontal ○ BR 68-69 C 3
Belomorsk ○ RUS 88-89 N 4
Belomorsko-Baltijskij kanal < RUS 88-89 N 4
Belomorsko-Kulojskoje-plato ▲ RUS 88-89 Q 4
Belonge ○ ZRE 210-211 H 5
Belopa ○ RI 164-165 G 5
Belorečensk ○ RUS 126-127 C 5
Beloreck ☆ RUS 96-97 L 7
Belot, Lac ○ CDN 30-31 G 2
Belo Tsiribihina ○ RM 222-223 D 7
Belousovka ○ KA 124-125 N 3
Belovo ☆ RUS 114-115 T 7
Belovodskoe ○ KS 146-147 B 4
Beloye Ozero = Beloe, ozero ○ RUS 94-95 P 1
Belozerskoe ○ RUS 94-95 P 1
Belozerskoe ☆ RUS 114-115 H 7
Belozersko-Kirillovskie grjady ▲ RUS 94-95 P 1
Belpre ○ USA (KS) 262-263 G 7
Belpre ○ USA (OH) 280-281 E 4
Belrem, Hassi el < DZ 190-191 D 7
Bel'skaja vozvyšennost' ▲ RUS 94-95 N 4
Bel'skie, Ust'-gory ▲ RUS 112-113 R 4
Bel'skoe ○ RUS 116-117 F 7
Belt ○ USA (MT) 250-251 J 4
Belt Bay ○ AUS 178-179 D 5
Belted Range ▲ USA (NV) 248-249 H 2
Belterra ○ BR 66-67 K 4
Belton ○ USA (MO) 274-275 D 6
Belton ○ USA (SC) 284-285 H 2
Belton ○ USA (TX) 266-267 K 2
Belton Lake < USA (TX) 266-267 K 2
Beltov tepalik ∴ US 136-137 G 3
Belubula River ∼ AUS 180-181 K 2
Beluga Lake ○ USA 20-21 P 6
Beluha, gora ▲ KA 124-125 P 4
Beluran ○ MAL 160-161 B 10
Beluru ○ MAL 164-165 D 2
Belus'e ○ RUS 88-89 T 3
Belus Guba ○ RUS 108-109 E 6
Belužij Nos, mys ▲ RUS 108-109 M 6
Belvedere Marittimo ○ I 100-101 E 5
Belvidere ○ USA (IL) 274-275 K 2
Belvidere ○ USA (KS) 262-263 G 7
Belvidere ○ USA (SD) 260-261 E 3
Belwa, River ∼ WAN 204-205 J 4
Belwali ○ LB 202-203 F 6
Belyando River ∼ AUS 178-179 J 2
Belye Vody ☆ KA 136-137 L 3
Belyj ☆ RUS 94-95 N 4
Belyj, ostrov ⌒ RUS 108-109 O 5
Belyj Čulym ∼ RUS 114-115 U 7
Belyj Jar ☆ RUS 114-115 S 5
Belyj Urjum ∼ RUS 118-119 H 9
Belyj, Ostrov = Belyj, ostrov ⌒ RUS 108-109 O 5
Bełżec ○ PL 92-93 R 3
Belzoni ○ USA (MS) 268-269 K 3
Béma ○ RMM 202-203 F 2
Bémal ○ RCA 206-207 C 5
Bemanevika ○ RM 222-223 G 5
Bemaraha ⊥ RM 222-223 D 7
Bemarivo ∼ RM 222-223 E 6
Bembe ○ ANG 216-217 C 3
Bembeche ⊥ TCH 198-199 J 3
Bembèrèkè ○ DY 204-205 E 3
Bembesi ○ ZW 218-219 E 4
Bemersyde ○ CDN (SAS) 232-233 Q 6
Bemetára ○ IND 142-143 B 5
Bemidji ○ USA (MN) 270-271 D 3
Bemis ○ USA (SD) 260-261 K 2
Bemonto ○ RM 222-223 D 7
Bemu ○ RI 166-167 E 3
Ben ○ BF 202-203 H 3
Bena ○ USA (MN) 270-271 D 3
Bena ○ WAN 204-205 F 3
Benabarre ○ • E 98-99 H 3
Benada ○ IND 138-139 G 9
Bena-Dibele ○ ZRE 210-211 J 6
Benagerie ○ AUS 178-179 F 6
Benahmed ○ MA 188-189 H 4
Benahouin ○ CI 202-203 J 6
Benain ∼ RI 166-167 C 6
Bena-Kamba ○ ZRE 210-211 K 5
Benalla ○ AUS 180-181 H 4
Ben Ash Monument • USA (SD) 260-261 D 1
Benato-Toby ○ RM 222-223 D 9
Bena-Tshadi ○ ZRE 210-211 J 6
Benaule ○ PNG 183 F 3
Benavente ○ • E 98-99 E 3
Benavides ○ USA (TX) 266-267 J 6
Ben Bolt ○ USA (TX) 266-267 J 6
Benbonyathe Hill ▲ AUS 178-179 E 6
Ben Boyd National Park ⊥ AUS 180-181 K 4
Benbrook Lake < USA (TX) 264-265 G 6
Bencubbin ○ AUS 176-177 D 5
Bend ○ USA (OR) 244-245 D 6
Bend ○ USA (TX) 266-267 J 2
Bèndana ○ TCH 206-207 D 4
Benda Range ▲ AUS 180-181 E 2
Bendel ▫ WAN 204-205 F 5
Bendela ○ ZRE 210-211 F 5
Bendeleben Mountains ▲ USA 20-21 H 4
Bendemeer ○ AUS 178-179 L 6
Bender = Tighina ○ MD 102-103 F 4
Bender Cassim = Boosaaso = Bender Qaasim ☆ SP 208-209 J 3
Bender Qaasim = Boosaaso ☆ SP 208-209 J 3
Bendery = Tighina ○ MD 102-103 F 4
Bendieuta Creek ∼ AUS 178-179 E 6
Bendigo ○ • AUS 180-181 H 4
Bend of the Boyne ··· IRL 90-91 D 5
Bendugu ○ WAL 202-203 E 5
Bene ○ MOC 218-219 G 2
Benedict, Mount ▲ CDN 36-37 U 7
Benedict Fjord ≈ 26-27 f 2
Benedictine Monastery • AUS 176-177 D 5
Benedito Leite ○ BR 68-69 F 5
Bénéna ○ RMM 202-203 H 3
Benenitra ○ RM 222-223 D 9
Benešov ○ CZ 92-93 N 4
Benevento ☆ • I 100-101 E 4
Benevides ○ BR 62-63 K 6
Benewah ○ USA (ID) 250-251 C 4
Benfica ○ BR 72-73 J 6
Benga ○ MOC 218-219 G 3
Benga ○ MW 218-219 H 1
Bengābād ○ IND 142-143 E 3
Bengal, Bay of ≈ 12 G 3
Bengala ○ CO 60-61 E 5
Bengāla ○ IND 140-141 J 5
Bengalun, Tanjung ▲ RI 164-165 E 3
Bengamisa ○ ZRE 210-211 K 3
Bengawan ∼ RI 168 E 3
Bengbis ○ CAM 210-211 D 2
Bengbu ○ VRC 154-155 K 5
Benge ○ USA (WA) 244-245 G 4
Benghazi = Banghāzi ☆ LAR 192-193 J 1
Bengkalis ○ RI 162-163 E 4
Bengkalis, Pulau ⌒ RI 162-163 E 4
Bengkayang ○ RI 162-163 H 4
Bengkulu ▫ RI 162-163 E 6
Bengkulu ☆ RI 162-163 E 6
Bengkunat, Teluk ≈ 162-163 F 7
Bengo ▫ ANG 216-217 B 4
Bengo ∼ ANG 216-217 B 4
Bengo, Baia do ≈ 216-217 B 4
Bengough ○ CDN (SAS) 232-233 N 6
Benguela ○ ANG 216-217 B 6
Benguela ☆ ANG (BGU) 216-217 B 6
Ben Guerdane ○ TN 190-191 H 4
Benguerir ○ MA 188-189 H 4
Benguérua, Ilha ⌒ MOC 218-219 H 5
Beni ○ ZRE 212-213 B 3
Beni, Río ∼ BOL 70-71 D 3
Beni-Abbès ○ • DZ 188-189 K 5
Beniah Lake ○ CDN 30-31 N 4
Beni-Boufrah ○ MA 188-189 J 3
Benicarló ○ E 98-99 H 4
Benicasim = Benicàssim ○ E 98-99 H 4
Benicia ○ USA (CA) 246-247 C 5
Benicito, Río ∼ BOL 70-71 E 2
Benidorm ○ E 98-99 G 5
Beni Hammad ··· DZ 190-191 E 3
Beni Haoua ○ DZ 190-191 C 2
Beni Ikhlef ○ DZ 188-189 L 6
Beni Kheddache ○ TN 190-191 H 4
Beni-Mellal ☆ MA 188-189 H 4
Benin ■ DY 204-205 D 4
Benin, Bight of ≈ 204-205 E 6
Benin, River ∼ WAN 204-205 F 6
Benin City ☆ • WAN 204-205 F 5
Beni Ounif ○ DZ 188-189 L 4
Beni Saf ○ DZ 188-189 L 3
Benisheikh ○ WAN 204-205 K 3
Beni Slimane ○ DZ 190-191 D 2
Beni-Smir ▲ DZ 188-189 L 4
Beni-Snassen, Monts des ▲ MA 188-189 K 3
Beni Tajjite ○ MA 188-189 K 4
Benito ○ CDN (MAN) 234-235 B 3
Benito Juárez ○ MEX 50-51 F 3
Benito Juárez ○ RA 78-79 K 4
Benito Juárez, Parque Nacional ⊥ MEX 52-53 F 3
Benito Juárez, Presa < MEX 52-53 G 3
Beni-Val < MA 188-189 K 4
Benjamin ○ USA (TX) 264-265 E 5
Benjamin ○ USA (UT) 254-255 D 3
Benjamin, Isla ⌒ RCH 80 C 2
Benjamin Aceval ○ PY 76-77 J 3
Benjamin Constant ○ BR 66-67 B 5
Benjamin Hill ○ MEX 50-51 D 2
Benjamin River ○ CDN (NB) 240-241 J 3
Benjina ○ RI 166-167 H 5
Benkelman ○ USA (NE) 262-263 E 4
Ben Lawers ▲ GB 90-91 E 3
Ben Loganbil ○ LB 202-203 E 6
Ben Lomond ▲ AUS 180-181 J 6
Ben Macdui ▲ GB 90-91 F 3
Ben Mehidi ○ DZ 190-191 F 2
Ben More ▲ GB 90-91 E 3
Benmore, Lake ○ NZ 182 C 6
Benndale ○ USA (MS) 268-269 M 6
Bennett ○ USA (CO) 254-255 L 4
Bennett ○ USA (NC) 282-283 H 5
Bennett ○ USA (NM) 256-257 M 6
Bennett, Lake ○ AUS 172-173 K 7
Bennett, Mount ▲ AUS 172-173 C 7
Bennetta, ostrov ⌒ RUS 110-111 b 1
Bennett Lake ○ CDN 20-21 X 6
Bennettsville ○ USA (SC) 284-285 L 2
Ben Nevis ▲ ·· GB 90-91 E 3
Bennichāb ○ RIM 196-197 C 5
Bennington ○ USA (KS) 262-263 J 6
Bennington ○ USA (OK) 264-265 H 4
Bennington ○ USA (VT) 278-279 H 6
Benny ○ CDN (ONT) 238-239 D 2
Benoit ○ USA (MS) 268-269 J 3
Benoit ○ USA (WI) 270-271 G 4
Benoit's Cove ○ CDN (NFL) 242-243 K 3
Benoni ○ ZA 220-221 J 3
Benoud < DZ 190-191 C 4
Bénoué ∼ CAM 204-205 K 5
Bénoué, Cuvette de la ⊥ CAM 204-205 K 4
Bénoué, Parc National de la ⊥ CAM 204-205 K 4
Bénoye ○ TCH 206-207 C 4
Ben Quang ○ VN 158-159 J 2
Bến Quang ○ VN 158-159 J 2
Ben Rinnes ▲ GB 90-91 F 3
Bensbach River ∼ PNG 183 A 5
Bensékou ○ DY 204-205 E 3
Ben-Slimane ☆ MA 188-189 H 4
Benson ○ CDN (SAS) 232-233 P 6
Benson ○ USA (AZ) 256-257 E 7
Benson ○ USA (MN) 270-271 C 5
Ben S'Rour ○ DZ 190-191 E 3
Bent ○ IR 134-135 H 5
Bent, Rūdḫāne-ye ∼ IR 134-135 H 5
Ben Tadjine, Djebel ▲ DZ 188-189 K 6
Benta Seberang ○ MAL 162-163 D 2
Bentenan ○ RI 164-165 J 3
Benteng ○ RI (SLT) 164-165 G 4
Benteng ○ RI (SSE) 168 E 6
Benteng Tanahjampea ○ RI 168 E 6
Bentiaba ∼ ANG 216-217 B 7
Bentick Island ⌒ MYA 158-159 E 5
Bentinck Island ⌒ AUS 174-175 E 5
Bentinck Sound ≈ 158-159 D 3
Bentiu ○ SUD 206-207 J 4
Bentley ○ CDN (ALB) 232-233 D 3
Bent Mountain ○ USA (VA) 280-281 F 6
Bento Gomes, Rio ∼ BR 70-71 J 5
Bento Gonçalves ○ BR 74-75 E 7
Benton ○ USA (AL) 284-285 D 4
Benton ○ USA (AR) 276-277 C 6
Benton ○ USA (CA) 248-249 F 2
Benton ○ USA (IL) 276-277 G 3
Benton ○ USA (KY) 276-277 G 4
Benton ○ USA (LA) 268-269 G 4
Benton ○ USA (MO) 276-277 F 3
Benton ○ USA (MS) 268-269 K 4
Benton ○ USA (TN) 282-283 C 5
Benton City ○ USA (WA) 244-245 F 4
Bentong ○ MAL 162-163 D 3
Benton Harbor ○ USA (MI) 272-273 C 5
Bentonia ○ USA (MS) 268-269 K 4
Bentonsport ○ USA (IA) 274-275 G 4
Bentonville ○ USA (AR) 276-277 A 4
Bentonville ○ • USA (NC) 282-283 J 5
Bentota ○ CL 140-141 H 7
Bến Tre ☆ VN 158-159 J 5
Bents ○ CDN (SAS) 232-233 L 4
Bent's Old Fort National Historic Site • USA (CO) 254-255 M 5
Bentuka ○ MAL 160-161 A 10
Benty ○ RG 202-203 D 5
Benua ○ RI 164-165 H 6
Benua, Pulau ⌒ RI 162-163 G 4
Benualawas ○ RI 164-165 D 5
Benue ▫ WAN 204-205 G 5
Benue, River ∼ WAN 204-205 G 4
Benum, Gunung ▲ MAL 162-163 E 3
Benum,Gunung ▲ MAL 162-163 E 3
Benut ○ MAL 162-163 E 4
Ben Wheeler ○ USA (TX) 264-265 J 6
Benxi ○ VRC 150-151 D 7
Benxi Shuidong • VRC 150-151 E 7
Benye ○ ZRE 210-211 F 4
Ben Zireg ○ DZ 188-189 L 5
Beo ○ RI 164-165 K 1
Beoga ○ RI 166-167 J 3
Beograd ★ ·· YU 100-101 H 2
Beoumi ○ CI 202-203 H 6
Beowawe ○ USA (NV) 246-247 J 3
Bepondi, Pulau ⌒ RI 166-167 H 2
Beppu ○ • J 152-153 D 8
Beqa ⌒ FJI 184 III b 3
Beque, De ○ USA (CO) 254-255 G 4
Bequia Island ⌒ WV 56 E 5
Bequimão ○ BR 68-69 F 3
Ber ○ RMM 196-197 J 6
Berabevú ○ RA 78-79 J 2
Berafia, Nosy ⌒ RM 222-223 E 4
Berahle ○ ETH 200-201 K 6
Beraketa ○ RM 222-223 D 10
Beramanja ○ RM 222-223 F 4
Bérandjokou ○ RCB 210-211 F 2
Berangas ○ RI 164-165 E 5
Beráni ○ PK 138-139 B 7
Berat ☆ ·· AL 100-101 G 4
Berau ∼ RI 164-165 E 2
Berau, Teluk ≈ 166-167 G 3
Beraun = Beroun ○ CZ 92-93 N 4
Beravina ○ RM 222-223 D 7
Beravy ○ RM 222-223 D 8
Berazino ☆ BY 94-95 L 5
Berbera ○ SP 208-209 G 3
Berbérati ☆ RCA 206-207 B 6
Berbia, Bir < TN 190-191 G 4
Berbice ∼ GUY 62-63 E 4
Berchtesgaden ○ D 92-93 M 5
Berclair ○ USA (TX) 266-267 K 5
Bercogyi ○ KA 126-127 N 3
Berd' ∼ RUS 114-115 S 7
Berd' ∼ RUS 124-125 N 1
Berdaale ○ SP 212-213 J 2
Berd'ans'ka kosa ⌣ UA 102-103 K 4
Berdensar, kōl ○ KA 126-127 N 4
Berdičev = Berdyčiv ☆ UA 102-103 F 3
Berdigestjah ☆ RUS 118-119 N 4
Berdjans'k ○ UA 102-103 K 4
Berdsk ○ RUS 124-125 N 1
Berdyans'k = Berdjans'k ○ UA 102-103 K 4
Berdyčiv ☆ UA 102-103 F 3
Béré ○ TCH 206-207 C 4
Berea ○ USA (KY) 276-277 L 3
Berea ○ USA (NC) 282-283 J 4
Béréba ○ BF 202-203 J 4
Berebere ○ RI 164-165 L 2
Bereeda ○ SP 208-209 K 3
Bereg Djogos Jar ⌣ RUS 110-111 X 3
Bereg Haritona Lapteva ⌣ RUS 108-109 W 4
Beregovoe ○ RUS 124-125 M 2
Beregovoj ○ RUS 118-119 N 8
Bereg Prončiščeva ⌣ RUS 108-109 h 3
Berehove ☆ UA 102-103 C 3
Bereina ○ PNG 183 D 5
Bereja ∼ RUS 122-123 B 3
Bereku ○ EAT (DOD) 212-213 E 6
Berekua ○ WD 56 E 4
Berekum ○ GH 202-203 J 6
Bërëlëh ∼ RUS 110-111 b 4
Bërëlëh ∼ RUS 120-121 M 2
Berembang ○ RI 162-163 D 3
Berenda ○ USA (CA) 248-249 D 2
Berendi ○ TR 128-129 F 4
Berenike ○ ET 194-195 G 6
Berens Island ⌒ CDN (MAN) 234-235 F 2
Berens Islands ⌒ CDN 30-31 N 2
Berens River ○ CDN (MAN) 234-235 F 2
Berens River ∼ CDN (MAN) 234-235 F 2
Berens River ∼ CDN (ONT) 234-235 K 3
Bereš ∼ RUS 114-115 U 7
Beresford ○ CDN (NB) 240-241 K 3
Beresford ○ USA (SD) 260-261 K 3
Beresford Lake ○ CDN (MAN) 234-235 H 4
Berettyóújfalu ○ H 92-93 Q 5
Berezivka ○ UA 102-103 G 4
Berežnaja ○ RUS 88-89 R 6
Bereznehuvate ○ UA 102-103 H 4
Bereznik ○ RUS 88-89 R 5
Berezniki ○ RUS 114-115 D 5
Berežnyh, mys ▲ RUS 110-111 X 1
Berezova ○ RUS 88-89 M 4
Berëzovaja ○ RUS 116-117 F 8
Berëzovaja ∼ RUS 112-113 R 5
Berëzovka ☆ RUS (KRN) 116-117 F 7
Berezovka ☆ RUS (PRM) 96-97 K 5
Berëzovka ∼ RUS 112-113 K 3
Berëzovka ∼ RUS 112-113 J 3
Berezovka ∼ RUS 114-115 R 5
Berezovka ∼ RUS 114-115 D 4
Berezovo ☆ RUS 114-115 H 3
Berëzovskij ○ RUS 114-115 T 7
Berëzovskij ☆ RUS 96-97 M 5
Berg ○ N 86-87 H 2
Berga ○ E 98-99 H 3
Berga, mys ▲ RUS 108-109 c 1
Bergama ☆ • TR 128-129 B 3
Bèrgamo ☆ • I 100-101 B 2
Bergara ○ E 98-99 F 3
Bergen ☆ ··· N 86-87 B 6
Bergen ○ • NL 92-93 H 2
Bergen ○ USA (MN) 270-271 D 7
Bergen (Rügen) ○ D 92-93 M 1
Berg en Dal ○ SME 62-63 G 3
Bergerac ○ F 90-91 H 9
Bergland ○ CDN (ONT) 234-235 J 6
Bergland ○ USA (MI) 270-271 J 4
Bergsig ○ NAM 216-217 C 10
Bergville ○ ZA 220-221 J 4
Berhait ○ IND 142-143 E 3
Berhala, Selat ≈ 162-163 F 5
Berhampur = Brahmapur ○ IND 142-143 D 6
Berikat, Tanjung ▲ RI 162-163 G 6
Berilo ○ BR 72-73 J 4
Beringa, mogila • RUS 120-121 V 6
Beringa, mys ▲ RUS 112-113 X 4
Beringa, ostrov ⌒ RUS 120-121 W 6
Beringarra ○ AUS 176-177 D 3
Bering Glacier ⊂ USA 20-21 T 6
Bering Land Bridge Nature Reserve ⊥ USA 20-21 G 4
Bering Sea = Beringovo more ≈ 22-23 D 3
Bering Strait = Beringov proliv ≈ 112-113 a 4
Berino ○ USA (NM) 256-257 J 6
Beripeta ○ IND 140-141 J 4
Beris ∼ RUS 110-111 Q 4
Berisso ○ RA 78-79 L 3
Beriza ○ BR 72-73 K 3
Berja ○ E 98-99 F 6
Berkåk ☆ N 86-87 E 5
Berkane ○ MA 188-189 K 3
Berkeley ○ USA (CA) 248-249 B 2
Berkeley, Cape ▲ CDN 24-25 V 4
Berkeley Point ▲ CDN 24-25 M 5
Berkeley River ∼ AUS 172-173 H 3
Berkeley Sound ≈ 78-79 M 6
Berkley Group ⌒ CDN 24-25 V 2

Berkner Island ⌒ ARK 16 F 30
Berkovica o BG 102-103 C 6
Berland River ~ CDN (ALB) 228-229 R 3
Berlengas, Rio ~ BR 68-69 G 5
Berlevåg o N 86-87 O 1
Berliet, Point ▲ RN 198-199 D 2
Berlin ★ ··· D 92-93 M 2
Berlin o USA (MD) 280-281 L 5
Berlin o USA (ND) 258-259 J 5
Berlin o USA (NH) 278-279 K 4
Berlin o USA (NJ) 280-281 M 4
Berlin o USA (OK) 264-265 E 3
Berlin o USA (PA) 280-281 H 4
Berlin o USA (WI) 270-271 K 7
Berlin, Mount ▲ ARK 16 F 23
Berlinguet Inlet ≈ 24-25 d 5
Berlin Reservoir < USA (OH) 280-281 E 3
Bermagui o AUS 180-181 L 4
Bermego, Río ~ RA 76-77 C 5
Bermeja, Sierra ▲ E 98-99 E 6
Bermejillo o MEX 50-51 H 5
Bermejo, Isla ⌒ RA 78-79 J 5
Bermejo, Río ~ RA 76-77 D 6
Bermejo, Río ~ RA 76-77 F 2
Bermuda Island ⌒ GB 54-55 L 1
Bermuda Islands ⌒ GB 54-55 L 2
Bermuda Rise ≃ 6-7 C 5
Bern ★ ··· CH 90-91 J 5
Bernabe Rivera o ROU 76-77 J 6
Bernalillo o USA (NM) 256-257 J 3
Bernam ~ MAL 162-163 D 3
Bernard Island ⌒ CDN 24-25 J 4
Bernardo o USA (NM) 256-257 J 4
Bernardo de Irigoyen o RA 74-75 D 6
Bernardo O'Higgins, Parque Nacional ⊥ RCH 80 C 5
Bernardo Sacuita, Ponta do ▲ BR 68-69 F 2
Bernard River ~ CDN 24-25 K 4
Bernay o F 90-91 H 7
Bernburg (Saale) o · D 92-93 L 3
Berne o USA (IN) 274-275 O 4
Berne o USA (WA) 244-245 D 3
Berner o USA (GA) 284-285 G 3
Berner Alpen ▲ CH 92-93 J 5
Bernice o USA (LA) 268-269 H 4
Bernier, Cape ▲ AUS 172-173 H 3
Bernier Bay ≈ 24-25 b 5
Bernier Island ⌒ AUS 176-177 B 2
Bernina, Piz ▲ CH 92-93 K 5
Berninapass ▲ CH 92-93 L 5
Bernstorffs Isfjord ≈ 28-29 U 5
Bero ~ ANG 216-217 B 7
Beroroha o RM 222-223 D 8
Beroun o CZ 92-93 N 4
Berounka ~ CZ 92-93 M 4
Berrahal o DZ 190-191 F 2
Berrechid o MA 188-189 H 4
Berrekhem, Hassi < DZ 190-191 E 4
Berri o AUS 180-181 F 3
Berriane o DZ 190-191 D 3
Berridale o AUS 180-181 K 4
Berrigan o AUS 180-181 H 3
Berriwillock o AUS 180-181 G 3
Berrouaghia o DZ 190-191 D 2
Berrugas o CO 60-61 D 3
Berry ▲ F 90-91 H 8
Berry o USA (AL) 284-285 C 3
Berry, De o USA (TX) 264-265 K 6
Berry Creek ~ CDN (ALB) 232-233 G 4
Berrydale o USA (FL) 286-287 B 1
Berryessa, Lake o USA (CA) 246-247 C 5
Berry Head o CDN (NFL) 242-243 K 4
Berry Islands ⌒ BS 54-55 F 2
Berrymoor o CDN (ALB) 232-233 D 2
Berryville o USA (AR) 276-277 B 4
Berryville o USA (VA) 280-281 J 4
Berseba o NAM 220-221 C 3
Berté, Lac o CDN 38-39 K 3
Berthierville o CDN (QUE) 238-239 M 2
Berthold o USA (ND) 258-259 F 3
Bertiehaugh o AUS 174-175 G 3
Bertinho o BR 68-69 C 3
Bertolínia o BR 68-69 G 5
Bertoua ☆ CAM 204-205 K 6
Bertram o CDN (ONT) 236-237 D 3
Bertram o USA (TX) 266-267 J 3
Bertrand o CDN (NB) 240-241 K 3
Bertrandville o USA (LA) 268-269 L 7
Bertwell o CDN (SAS) 232-233 Q 3
Beruniy ☆ US 136-137 G 4
Beruri o BR 66-67 G 4
Beruwala o CL 140-141 H 7
Berwick o CDN (NB) 240-241 K 5
Berwick o CDN (NS) 240-241 L 5
Berwick o USA (PA) 280-281 K 2
Berwick-upon-Tweed o · GB 90-91 F 4
Beryl o USA (UT) 254-255 B 6
Beryl Junction o USA (UT) 254-255 B 6
Beryslav o UA 102-103 H 4
Besa o RI 164-165 K 3
Besal o PK 138-139 D 2
Besalampy o RM 222-223 D 6
Besançon ☆ ·· F 90-91 L 8
Bešankovičy ☆ BY 94-95 L 4
Besar, Gunung ▲ MAL 162-163 E 3
Besar, Gunung ▲ RI 164-165 D 5
Besar, Pulau ⌒ RI 166-167 B 6
Besarabca o MD 102-103 F 4
Besarabjaska = Besarabca o MD 102-103 F 4
Besar Hantu, Gunung ▲ MAL (SEL) 162-163 D 3
Besa River ~ CDN 32-33 J 3
Bešaryk o US 136-137 M 4
Besbes, Oued ~ DZ 190-191 E 3
Besboro Island ⌒ USA 20-21 K 4
Bescoky, tau ▲ KA 126-127 K 5
Besedz' ~ BY 94-95 M 5
Besham o PK 138-139 D 2
Beshlo ~ ETH 208-209 D 3
Besi, Tanjung ▲ RI 168 E 7
Besikama o RI 166-167 C 6
Besima o PK 134-135 L 5
Besir o RI 166-167 F 2
Bėsjuke ~ RUS 110-111 Q 4
Beskid Mountains = Beskidy ▲ PL 92-93 P 4
Beskidy Zachodnie ▲ PL 92-93 P 4
Beslan o RUS 126-127 F 6
Besnard Lake o CDN 34-35 D 3
Besne o IR 134-135 F 4
Besni ☆ TR 128-129 G 4
Bessa Monteiro o ANG 216-217 B 3
Béssao o TCH 206-207 B 5
Bessarabia = Bessarabija ⊥ MD 102-103 E 3
Bessarabka = Aul Sarykobda o KA 126-127 M 3
Bessarabka = Besarabca o MD 102-103 F 4
Bessaz, gora ▲ KA 136-137 L 3
Bessaz, togi ▲ KA 136-137 L 3
Besselfjord ≈ 26-27 p 6
Bessemer o USA (AL) 284-285 D 3
Bessemer o USA (MI) 270-271 H 4
Bessmay o USA (TX) 268-269 G 6
Bessoung Kang o CAM 204-205 H 6
Best o USA (TX) 266-267 F 2
Bestām o · IR 136-137 D 6
Bestam ∴ · KA 136-137 H 3
Bestamak o KA 126-127 L 3
Bestjah o RUS (SAH) 110-111 P 7
Bestjah o RUS (SAH) 118-119 O 5
Beswick o AUS 174-175 B 4
Beswick Aboriginal Land ✗ AUS 172-173 L 3
Betafo o RM 222-223 E 7
Betalevana o RM 222-223 F 6
Betanantanana o RM 222-223 D 7
Betânia o BR (MAT) 70-71 G 4
Betânia o BR (PER) 68-69 J 6
Betânia, Área Indígena ✗ BR 66-67 C 4
Betanty o RM 222-223 D 10
Betanzos o BOL 70-71 E 6
Betanzos o E 98-99 C 3
Betarara o VAN 184 II b 2
Bétaré Oya o CAM 206-207 B 6
Betbakdala ⊥ KA 124-125 E 6
Betbulak o KA 124-125 F 4
Bete Grise Bay ≈ USA 270-271 L 3
Bete Hor o ETH 208-209 D 3
Betein o WAN 204-205 H 6
Betenkës o RUS 110-111 U 6
Bétérou o DY 204-205 E 4
Bethal o ZA 220-221 J 3
Bethanie ☆ NAM 220-221 C 3
Bethany o USA (IL) 274-275 K 5
Bethany o USA (MO) 274-275 D 4
Bethany o USA (OK) 264-265 G 3
Bethany Beach o USA (DE) 280-281 L 5
Bethel o USA (AK) 20-21 K 6
Bethel o USA (ME) 278-279 L 4
Bethel o USA (NC) 282-283 K 5
Bethel o USA (OH) 280-281 B 5
Bethel o USA (OK) 264-265 K 4
Bethel o USA (VT) 278-279 J 5
Bethel Park o USA (PA) 280-281 F 3
Bethesdaweg o ZA 220-221 G 5
Bethlehem o SME 62-63 G 3
Bethlehem o USA (PA) 280-281 L 3
Bethlehem o ZA 220-221 J 4
Bethlehem = Bet Leḥem ☆ ·· IL 130-131 D 2
Bethulie o ZA 220-221 G 5
Bethune o USA (SC) 284-285 K 2
Betinče ~ RUS 118-119 G 5
Betioky o RM 222-223 D 9
Bet Leḥem ☆ ·· WB 130-131 D 2
Beton o MAL 162-163 J 4
Betong o THA 158-159 F 8
Betongwe o ZRE 212-213 B 2
Betoota o AUS 178-179 F 3
Bétou o RCB 210-211 G 2
Be Town o LB 202-203 F 6
Betpak Dala = Betbakdala ⊥ KA 124-125 E 6
Betrandraka o RM 222-223 E 6
Betroka o RM 222-223 E 9
Bet She'an o IL 130-131 D 1
Betsiaka o RM 222-223 F 4
Betsiamites o CDN (QUE) 240-241 G 2
Betsiamites, Rivière ~ CDN 38-39 J 3
Betsiamites Indian Réserve ✗ CDN 38-39 K 4
Betsiboka ~ RM 222-223 E 6
Betsjoeanaland ⊥ ZA 220-221 E 3
Betsy Bay o BS 54-55 J 3
Bettiah o IND 142-143 D 2
Bettié o CI 202-203 J 6
Bettiesdam o ZA 220-221 J 3
Bettioua o DZ 188-189 L 3
Bettles o USA 20-21 P 3
Bet Touadjine, Hamadet ⊥ DZ 190-191 C 5
Betty, Lake o AUS 172-173 H 5
Betül o IND 138-139 F 9
Betulia o CO (ANT) 60-61 D 4
Betulia o CO (SAN) 60-61 E 4
Betun o RI 166-167 C 6
Betuwe ~ RI 164-165 F 5
Betwa ~ IND 138-139 G 7
Betwa ~ IND 142-143 B 3
Béu o ANG 216-217 C 3
Beu, Serranía del ▲ BOL 70-71 C 4
Beulah o AUS 180-181 G 3
Beulah o CDN (MAN) 234-235 B 4
Beulah o USA (MI) 272-273 C 3
Beulah o USA (ND) 258-259 F 4
Beulaville o USA (NC) 282-283 K 6
Beurfou < TCH 198-199 G 5
Beurkia o TCH 198-199 H 5
B. Everette Jordan Lake o USA (NC) 282-283 J 5
Bever Lake Indian Reserve ✗ CDN 32-33 P 4
Beverley o AUS 176-177 D 6
Beverley o CDN (SAS) 232-233 L 5
Beverley o · GB 90-91 G 5
Beverley, Lake o USA 22-23 R 3
Beverley Springs o AUS 172-173 G 4
Beverly o USA (FL) 286-287 E 2
Beverly o USA (MA) 278-279 L 6
Beverly o USA (OH) 280-281 E 4
Beverly o USA (WA) 244-245 F 4
Beverly o USA (WV) 280-281 G 5
Beverly Beach o USA (MD) 280-281 K 5
Beverly Lake o CDN 30-31 T 3
Beveromay ▲ RM 222-223 E 6
Beveromay, Tampoketsan'i ▲ RM 222-223 E 6
Bevoalava Andrefana o RM 222-223 D 10
Bevoay o RM 222-223 C 8
Bewani o PNG 183 A 2
Bewani Mountains ▲ PNG 183 A 2
Bewar o IND 138-139 G 6
Bewdley o CDN (ONT) 238-239 G 4
Bewick Lake o CDN 30-31 R 4
Bexley o USA (OH) 280-281 D 3
Bey Dağ ▲ TR 128-129 G 3
Bey Dağları ▲ TR 128-129 D 4
Beyla o RG 202-203 F 5
Beylul o ER 200-201 L 6
Beylul Bahire Sekat'e ≈ 200-201 L 6
Beynon o CDN (ALB) 232-233 F 4
Beypazarı o · TR 128-129 D 2
Beyra o SP 208-209 H 5
Beyşehir ☆ TR 128-129 D 4
Beyşehir Gölü o TR 128-129 D 4
Beytüşşebap ☆ TR 128-129 K 4
Bezaha o RM 222-223 D 9
Bežanicy ☆ RUS 94-95 L 3
Bežeck ☆ RUS 94-95 P 3
Bežeckij verh ▲ RUS 94-95 P 3
Bezenčuk ☆ RUS 96-97 F 7
Bezergen o US 136-137 G 4
Bezerra ou Montes Claros, Rio ~ BR 72-73 G 2
Béziers o · F 90-91 J 10
Bezmein o TM 136-137 F 5
Bezymjannaja, guba o RUS 108-109 E 5
Bhābhar o IND 138-139 C 7
Bhadgaon o IND 138-139 E 9
Bhador ~ IND 138-139 C 9
Bhadrāchalam o IND 142-143 B 7
Bhadrak o IND 142-143 E 5
Bhadra Reservoir o IND 140-141 F 4
Bhadrāvati o IND 140-141 F 4
Bhadwan o IND 140-141 F 2
Bhāg o PK 134-135 M 4
Bhāgalpur o IND 142-143 E 3
Bhāgirathi ~ IND 138-139 G 4
Bhagirathi ~ IND 142-143 F 3
Bhagirathi ~ VRC 144-145 B 5
Bhāgvati o IND 140-141 F 3
Bhagwanpur o NEP 144-145 D 7
Bhagyakul o BD 142-143 G 4
Bhainsrorgarh o IND 138-139 E 7
Bhāi Pheru o PK 138-139 D 4
Bhairab Bazar o BD 142-143 G 3
Bhairahawa o NEP 144-145 D 7
Bhairi Hol ▲ PK 134-135 L 6
Bhairowāl o PK 138-139 D 3
Bhaisa o IND 138-139 F 10
Bhakkar o PK 138-139 C 4
Bhaktapur o · NEP 144-145 E 7
Bhālki o IND 138-139 F 10
Bhaluka o BD 142-143 G 3
Bhalukpong o IND 142-143 H 2
Bhalwāl o PK 138-139 D 3
Bhamo o MYA 142-143 K 3
Bhanas o IND 138-139 E 10
Bhanbore ∴ · PK 134-135 M 6
Bhandāra o IND 138-139 G 9
Bhanjanagar o IND 142-143 D 6
Bhānpura o IND 138-139 E 7
Bharatpur o IND 140-141 L 3
Bharatpur o · IND 138-139 F 6
Bhareli ~ IND 142-143 H 2
Bharūch o IND 138-139 D 9
Bhata o NEP 144-145 E 7
Bhatiapara o BD 142-143 F 4
Bhatkal o IND 140-141 F 3
Bhātpāra o IND 142-143 F 4
Bhaun o PK 138-139 D 3
Bhavāni o IND 140-141 G 5
Bhavnagar o · IND 138-139 D 9
Bhawāna o PK 138-139 D 4
Bhawānipatna o IND 142-143 C 6
Bhera o PK 138-139 D 3
Bheri ~ NEP 144-145 C 6
Bhiavan o IND 138-139 E 10
Bhilainagar o · IND 142-143 B 5
Bhilwāra o IND 138-139 E 7
Bhima ~ IND 138-139 D 10
Bhima ~ IND 140-141 F 2
Bhimāshankar o IND 138-139 D 10
Bhimavaram o IND 140-141 J 2
Bhimunipatnam o IND 142-143 C 7
Bhind o IND 138-139 G 6
Bhinmāl o IND 138-139 D 7
Bhit Shāh o PK 138-139 B 7
Bhiwandi o IND 138-139 D 10
Bhognipur o IND 138-139 G 6
Bhokar o IND 138-139 F 10
Bhol Aha o BD 142-143 F 3
Bhongaon o IND 138-139 G 6
Bhongir o IND 140-141 H 2
Bhopāl ☆ ·· IND 138-139 F 8
Bhopālpatnam o IND 142-143 B 6
Bhowali o IND 138-139 G 5
Bhuban o IND 142-143 D 5
Bhubaneshwar o ·· IND 142-143 D 5
Bhuj o IND 138-139 B 8
Bhusāwal o IND 138-139 E 9
Bhutan ■ BHT 142-143 F 2
Biá, Rio ~ BR 66-67 D 5
Biafra ⊥ WAN 204-205 H 6
Biak o RI (IRJ) 166-167 J 2
Biak o RI (SLT) 164-165 H 4
Biak, Pulau ⌒ RI 166-167 J 2
Biała, Bielsko- ☆ PL 92-93 P 4
Biała Podlaska ☆ PL 92-93 R 2
Białogard o PL 92-93 N 1
Białowieski Park Narodowy ⊥ ··· PL 92-93 R 2
Biały Bór o · PL 92-93 O 2
Białystok ☆ · PL 92-93 R 2
Bian ~ RI 166-167 L 5
Biang o RI 164-165 K 3
Bianga o RCA 206-207 E 6
Biankouma ☆ CI 202-203 G 6
Biaora o IND 138-139 F 8
Biar o PK 138-139 C 2
Bi'ār, al- o KSA 130-131 F 6
Biaranga o ZRE 210-211 G 4
Biārğmand o IR 136-137 D 6
Biaro o ZRE 210-211 K 3
Biaro, Pulau ⌒ RI 164-165 J 2
Biarritz o · F 90-91 G 10
Bias Fortes o BR 72-73 J 6
Biasi ~ ZRE 212-213 A 4
Biassini o ROU 76-77 J 6
Biata, Rio ~ BOL 70-71 D 2
Bia-Tawya Game Production Reserve ⊥ GH 202-203 J 6
Biau ~ RI 166-167 K 6
Biaza o RUS 114-115 P 6
Bibā o ET 194-195 E 3
Bibai o J 152-153 J 3
Bibala o ANG 216-217 B 7
Biban, Chaîne de ▲ DZ 190-191 E 2
Bibas o G 210-211 C 3
Bibbiena o I 100-101 C 3
Bibby Island ⌒ CDN 30-31 X 5
Bibé o CAM 204-205 K 6
Bibémi o CAM 204-205 K 4
Biberach an der Riß o D 92-93 K 4
Bibiani o GH 202-203 J 6
Bibikovo o RUS 122-123 B 3
Bibirevo o RUS 94-95 N 3
Biblian o EC 64-65 C 3
Biboohra o AUS 174-175 H 5
Bibundi o CAM 204-205 H 6
Bičanekskij, pereval ▲ AZ 128-129 L 3
Bicas o BR 72-73 J 6
Bičevaja o RUS 122-123 F 5
Biche, Lac la o CDN 32-33 O 4
Bichena o ETH 208-209 D 3
Biche Range, La ▲ CDN 30-31 G 5
Biche River, La ~ CDN 30-31 G 5
Bichhua o IND 138-139 G 9
Bichi o WAN 198-199 D 6
Bići ~ RUS 122-123 G 3
Bickerton Island ⌒ AUS 174-175 D 3
Bickle Knob ▲ USA (WV) 280-281 G 5
Bickleton o USA (WA) 244-245 E 4
Bicknell o USA (IN) 274-275 L 6
Bicuari, Parque Nacional do ⊥ ANG 216-217 C 7
Bičura ☆ RUS 116-117 N 10
Bida o WAN 204-205 G 4
Bidadari, Tanjung ▲ MAL 160-161 C 10
Bidal o · IND 140-141 G 2
Bidbid o OM 132-133 L 2
Bidde o SP 212-213 J 3
Biddeford o USA (ME) 278-279 L 5
Biddle o USA (MT) 250-251 O 6
Bide Arm o CDN (NFL) 242-243 M 2
Bideford o · GB 90-91 E 6
Bidek, Anou-n- < DZ 198-199 B 3
Bidjovagge o N 86-87 L 2
Bidoḫt o IR 134-135 H 1
Bidon V o DZ 190-191 C 9
Bidor o MAL 162-163 D 2
Bidukbiduk o RI 164-165 F 3
Bidžan o RUS 122-123 D 5
Bié ⊓ ANG 216-217 D 6
Bieber o USA (CA) 246-247 D 2
Biéha o BF 202-203 K 4
Biei o J 152-153 K 3
Biel o · CH 92-93 J 5
Bield o CDN (MAN) 234-235 B 3
Bielefeld o D 92-93 K 2
Bieler Lake o CDN 26-27 O 8
Biella ☆ · I 100-101 B 2
Biélou o CI 202-203 G 5
Bielsa o E 98-99 H 3
Bielsko-Biała ☆ PL 92-93 P 4
Bielsk Podlaski o PL 92-93 R 2
Biên Đông ≈ 158-159 J 7
Bienfait o CDN (SAS) 232-233 Q 6
Bienge o ZRE 210-211 G 6
Biên Hòa ☆ · VN 158-159 J 5
Bienne = Biel o · CH 92-93 J 5
Bienville o USA (LA) 268-269 H 4
Bienville, Lac o CDN 36-37 N 7
Bierdnačokka ▲ N 86-87 G 3
Biertan o ··· RO 102-103 D 4
Biesiesvlei o ZA 220-221 G 3
Bieszczadzki Park Narodowy ⊥ PL 92-93 R 4
Bifoulé o CAM 204-205 K 6
Bifuka o J 152-153 K 2
Biga ☆ TR 128-129 B 2
Bigadiç ☆ TR 128-129 C 3
Biğâdiya, al- o KSA 130-131 H 5
Big Ambergris Cay ⌒ GB 54-55 K 4
Bigand o RA 78-79 J 2
Big Arm o USA (MT) 250-251 E 4
Biga Yarımadası ⌣ TR 128-129 B 3
Big Bald Mountain ▲ CDN (NB) 240-241 J 3
Big Baldy ▲ USA (ID) 252-253 C 2
Big Bar o USA (CA) 246-247 B 3
Big Bar Creek o CDN (BC) 230-231 G 2
Big Bay ☆ 36-37 T 7
Big Bay ≈ 184 II a 2
Big Bay o CDN (ONT) 238-239 E 4
Big Bay o USA (MI) 270-271 L 4
Big Bay de Noc ≈ USA 270-271 M 5
Big Bay Point o CDN (ONT) 238-239 F 4
Big Bear City o USA (CA) 248-249 H 5
Big Bear Creek ~ USA (MS) 268-269 M 2
Big Bear Lake o USA (CA) 248-249 H 5
Big Beaver o CDN (SAS) 232-233 N 6
Big Beaver Falls ~ CDN (ONT) 236-237 F 3
Big Beaver House o CDN (ONT) 234-235 O 2
Bigbee Valley o USA (MS) 268-269 M 3
Bigbé I o CI 202-203 H 6
Big Bell o AUS 176-177 D 3
Big Belt Mountains ▲ USA (MT) 250-251 H 4
Big Bend o SD 220-221 K 3
Big Bend o USA (CA) 246-247 D 2
Big Bend o USA (LA) 268-269 J 5
Big Bend National Park ⊥ USA (TX) 266-267 D 4
Big Black River ~ USA (MS) 268-269 L 3
Big Blue River ~ USA (IN) 274-275 N 5
Big Blue River ~ USA (KS) 262-263 J 3
Big Brook o CDN (NFL) 242-243 M 1
Big Brush Creek ~ USA (AL) 284-285 C 4
Big Butt ▲ USA (TN) 282-283 E 4
Big Canyon River ~ USA (TX) 266-267 E 3
Bigcedar Creek ~ CDN (ONT) 236-237 G 2
Big Creak Lake < USA (AL) 284-285 B 6
Big Creek o CDN (BC) 230-231 H 2
Big Creek ~ CDN (BC) 230-231 F 2
Big Creek o USA (ID) 250-251 D 6
Big Creek ~ USA (AL) 284-285 D 5
Big Creek ~ USA (AR) 276-277 D 6
Big Creek ~ USA (LA) 268-269 J 4
Big Cypress Seminole Indian Reservation ✗ USA (FL) 286-287 H 5
Big Cypress Swamp o USA (FL) 286-287 H 5
Big Desert ⊥ AUS 180-181 F 3
Big Desert Wilderness ⊥ AUS 180-181 F 3
Big Dry Creek, The ~ USA (MT) 250-251 M 4
Big Eau Plaine Reservoir < USA (WI) 270-271 J 6
Bigelow o USA (MN) 270-271 C 7
Bigene o GNB 202-203 C 3
Big Escambia Creek ~ USA (AL) 284-285 C 5
Big Falls o USA (MN) 270-271 E 2
Big Falls o USA (WI) 270-271 J 6
Big Field o USA (AZ) 256-257 C 7
Bigfork o USA (MT) 250-251 E 3
Big Fork River ~ USA (MN) 270-271 E 2
Big Frog Mountain ▲ USA (TN) 282-283 C 6
Biggar o CDN (SAS) 232-233 L 3
Bigge Island ⌒ AUS 172-173 G 3
Biggenden o AUS 178-179 M 3
Biggs o USA (KY) 276-277 N 3
Biggs o USA (OR) 244-245 E 5
Big Hips Island ⌒ CDN 30-31 W 3
Big Hole · ZA 220-221 G 4
Big Hole National Battlefield · USA (MT) 250-251 F 6
Big Hole River ~ USA (MT) 250-251 F 6
Big Hole Tract Indian Reserve ✗ · CDN (NB) 240-241 K 3
Bighorn o USA (MT) 250-251 M 5
Big Horn o USA (WY) 252-253 M 2
Bighorn Basin ⊥ USA (WY) 252-253 K 2
Bighorn Canyon National Recreation Area ⊥ USA (MT) 250-251 L 6
Bighorn Creek ~ CDN (BC) 230-231 L 2
Bighorn Lake o USA (MT) 250-251 L 6
Big Horn Mountains ▲ USA (AZ) 256-257 B 5
Bighorn Mountains ▲ USA (WY) 252-253 L 2
Bighorn River ~ USA (MT) 250-251 M 6
Bighorn Wildland Recreation Area ⊥ CDN (ALB) 232-233 B 3
Bight, The o BS 54-55 H 2
Big Island ⌒ CDN (ALB) 30-31 N 6
Big Island ⌒ CDN (NFL) 36-37 S 5
Big Island ⌒ CDN (NWT) 30-31 L 4
Big Island ⌒ CDN (NWT) 30-31 L 5
Big Island ⌒ CDN (NWT) 36-37 O 3
Big Island ⌒ CDN (ONT) 234-235 J 5
Big Island ⌒ CDN (QUE) 36-37 Q 5
Big Island o USA (VA) 280-281 G 6
Big John Creek ~ AUS 178-179 E 6
Big Kalzas Lake o CDN 20-21 X 5
Big Koniuji Island ⌒ USA 22-23 R 5
Big Lake o CDN 30-31 N 3
Big Lake o USA (TX) 266-267 F 2
Big Lake o USA (ME) 278-279 O 3
Big Lake Ranch o CDN (BC) 228-229 N 4
Big Lost River ~ USA (ID) 252-253 E 3
Big Mossy Point ▲ CDN 34-35 G 4
Big Mountain Creek ~ CDN (ALB) 228-229 Q 2
Big Muddy Badlands ⊥ CDN (SAS) 232-233 N 6
Big Muddy Creek ~ USA (MT) 250-251 O 3
Big Muddy Lake o CDN (SAS) 232-233 O 6
Big Muddy River ~ USA (IL) 276-277 F 3
Big Nemaha River ~ USA (NE) 262-263 L 4
Bignona o SN 202-203 B 3
Bigoray River ~ CDN (ALB) 232-233 C 2
Bigori o SUD 208-209 B 3
Big Pine o USA (CA) 248-249 F 2
Big Pine o USA (FL) 286-287 H 7
Big Pine Mountain ▲ USA (CA) 248-249 E 5
Big Piney o USA (WY) 252-253 H 4
Big Piney River ~ USA (MO) 276-277 C 3
Big Piskwanish Point ▲ CDN 34-35 Q 5
Big Pond o CDN (NS) 240-241 P 5
Big Quill Lake o CDN (SAS) 232-233 O 4
Big Rapids o USA (MI) 272-273 D 4
Big River o CDN (SAS) 232-233 L 2
Big River ~ CDN 24-25 K 4
Big River ~ CDN 36-37 U 7
Big River ~ CDN (SAS) 232-233 L 2
Big River o USA (CA) 248-249 K 5
Big River ~ USA (MO) 274-275 H 6
Big River Indian Reserve ✗ CDN (SAS) 232-233 L 2
Big Sable Point ▲ USA (MI) 272-273 C 3
Big Salmon Range ▲ CDN 20-21 Y 6
Big Salmon River ~ CDN 20-21 X 6
Big Sand Lake o CDN 34-35 G 2
Big Sandy o USA (MT) 250-251 J 3
Big Sandy o USA (TN) 276-277 G 4
Big Sandy o USA (TX) 264-265 J 6
Big Sandy o USA (WY) 252-253 J 4
Big Sandy Creek ~ USA (CO) 254-255 M 5
Big Sandy Creek ~ USA (TX) 264-265 G 5
Big Sandy Lake o CDN 34-35 D 3
Big Sandy River ~ USA (AZ) 256-257 B 4
Big Sandy River ~ USA (KY) 276-277 N 2
Big Sandy River ~ USA (WY) 252-253 J 5
Big Satilla Creek ~ USA (GA) 284-285 H 5
Big Sky o USA (MT) 250-251 H 6
Big Slough Creek ~ USA (GA) 284-285 F 5
Big Smoky Valley ⌣ USA (NV) 246-247 H 6
Big Snow Mountain ▲ USA (MT) 250-251 K 5
Big South Fork National River and Recreation Area ⊥ USA (TN) 276-277 K 4
Big South Fork National River and Recreation Area ⊥ USA (TN) 282-283 C 4
Big Spring o USA (TN) 282-283 C 5
Big Spring o USA (TX) 264-265 C 6
Big Springs o USA (ID) 252-253 G 2
Bigstick Lake o CDN (SAS) 232-233 J 5
Big Stone o CDN (ALB) 232-233 G 4
Big Stone City o USA (SD) 260-261 K 1
Bigstone Lake o CDN 34-35 H 4
Big Stone Lake o USA (MN) 270-271 B 5
Bigstone River ~ CDN 34-35 J 3
Big Suehn o LB 202-203 F 7
Big Sur o USA (CA) 248-249 C 3
Big Timber o USA (MT) 250-251 K 6
Big Trout Lake o CDN (ONT) 34-35 M 4
Big Trout Lake o CDN (ONT) 34-35 L 4
Big Trout Lake Indian Reservation ✗ CDN 34-35 M 4
Big Valley o CDN (ALB) 232-233 F 3
Big Warrambool River ~ AUS 178-179 K 5
Big Water o USA (UT) 254-255 D 6
Big White Mountain ▲ CDN (BC) 230-231 L 4
Big White River ~ USA (SD) 260-261 D 3
Big Willow River ~ CDN 34-35 P 4
Big Wood Cay ⌒ BS 54-55 G 2
Big Wood River ~ USA (ID) 252-253 D 3
Bihać o · BIH 100-101 E 2
Bihar ⊓ IND 142-143 C 3
Biharamulo o EAT 212-213 C 5
Biharamulo Game Reservat ⊥ EAT 212-213 C 5
Bihār Sharīf o · IND 142-143 D 3
Bihoro o J 152-153 L 3
Bihorului, Muntii ▲ RO 102-103 C 4
Bihta o IND 142-143 D 3
Bija ~ RUS 124-125 O 2
Bija ~ RUS 124-125 P 3
Bijagos, Arquipélago dos ⌒ GNB 202-203 B 4
Bijāpur o ·· IND 140-141 F 2
Bijbehara o IND 138-139 E 3
Bijelo Polje o YU 100-101 G 3
Bijie o VRC 156-157 D 3
Bijlikol', ozero o KA 136-137 M 3
Bijnor o IND 138-139 G 5
Bijou Creek ~ USA (CO) 254-255 L 4
Bijoutier Island ⌒ SY 224 C 3
Bijsk ☆ RUS 124-125 O 2
Bijskaja Griva, hrebet ▲ RUS 124-125 P 2
Bikāner o · IND 138-139 D 5
Bikin o RUS 122-123 F 5
Bikin ~ RUS 122-123 G 5
Bikita o ZW 218-219 F 5
Bikok o CAM 210-211 C 2
Bikoro o ZRE 210-211 G 4
Bikou o VRC 154-155 D 5
Bikramganj o IND 142-143 D 3
Bikubiti ▲ LAR 198-199 J 2
Bilā o ET 194-195 E 2
Bila ~ RI 162-163 C 3
Bilaat Point ▲ RP 160-161 F 8
Bilac o BR 72-73 E 6
Bila Cerkva ☆ UA 102-103 G 3
Bilād Bani Bū Ḥasan o OM 132-133 L 2
Bilala o RCB 210-211 D 6
Bilang, Teluk ≈ 164-165 G 3
Bilanga o BF 202-203 K 3
Bilap Bay ≈ 140-141 L 4
Bilāsipāra o IND 142-143 G 2
Bilāspur o IND (MAP) 142-143 C 4
Bilāspur o IND (UTP) 138-139 G 5
Bilassana o RG 202-203 F 5
Bilatē Shet' ~ ETH 208-209 D 5
Bilati ~ ZRE 212-213 B 4
Bila Tserkva = Bila Cerkva ☆ UA 102-103 G 3
Bilauri o NEP 144-145 C 6
Bilāwal o PK 138-139 C 3
Bilbais o ET 194-195 E 2
Bilbao = Bilbo o E 98-99 F 3
Bilberatha Hill ▲ AUS 176-177 D 4
Bilbo = Bilbao o · E 98-99 F 3
Bilecik ☆ TR 128-129 C 2
Bilehsawār o IR 128-129 N 3
Bilėngui o G 210-211 C 4
Bilesha Plain ⊥ EAK 212-213 H 3
Biłgoraj o · PL 92-93 R 3
Bilgrām o IND 142-143 B 2
Bilhorod-Dnistrovs'kyj ☆ UA 102-103 G 4
Bili o ZRE 206-207 D 6
Bili o ZRE (Hau) 206-207 G 6
Bili ~ ZRE 206-207 F 6
Bilibili o RI 164-165 F 6
Bilibino o · RUS 112-113 O 2
Bilikkol' o KA 136-137 M 3
Bilimora o IND 138-139 D 9
Bilin o MYA 158-159 D 2
Biling La ▲ NEP 144-145 C 5
Biliran Island ⌒ RP 160-161 F 7
Biliri o WAN 204-205 J 4
Biljasuvar = Bilasuvar o AZ 128-129 N 3
Bill o USA (WY) 252-253 N 3
Billabong Creek ~ AUS 180-181 H 3
Billefjorden ≈ 84-85 K 3
Billenbach o AUS 178-179 K 4
Billete, Cerro El ▲ MEX 52-53 D 2
Billiat Conservation Park ⊥ AUS 180-181 F 3
Billiluna o AUS 172-173 H 5
Billings o RUS 112-113 S 2
Billings o USA (MT) 250-251 L 6
Billings o USA (NY) 280-281 N 2
Billingsa, mys ▲ RUS 112-113 T 2
Billjah ~ RUS 110-111 S 6
Billsburg o USA (SD) 260-261 E 2
Billund o DK 86-87 D 9
Bill Williams Mountain ▲ USA (AZ) 256-257 C 3
Bill Williams River ~ USA (AZ) 256-257 B 4
Billy, Chutes de ~ · RMM 202-203 F 3
Bilma o RN 198-199 F 3
Bilma, Grand Erg de ⊥ RN 198-199 F 4
Bilo o ETH 208-209 C 4
Biloela o AUS 178-179 L 3
Bilohors'k ☆ · UA 102-103 J 5
Biloo o SP 212-213 J 3
Bilopil'a o UA 102-103 J 2
Bilou o CI 202-203 G 5
Bilovods'k o UA 102-103 L 3
Biloxi o USA (MS) 268-269 M 6
Bilpa Morea Claypan o AUS 178-179 E 3
Bilqās o ET 194-195 E 2
Bilthara o IND 142-143 C 2
Biltine ⊓ TCH 198-199 K 5
Biltine ☆ TCH 198-199 K 5
Bilugyun ⌒ MYA 158-159 D 2
Bilungala o RI 164-165 H 3
Biluo Xueshan ▲ VRC 142-143 L 2
Bilverdi o IR 128-129 M 3
Bilyj Čeremoš ~ UA 102-103 D 4
Bima o RI 168 D 7
Bima ~ ZRE 210-211 L 2
Bimba o CAM 206-207 B 6
Bimbe o ANG 216-217 C 5
Bimberi Peak ▲ AUS 180-181 K 3
Bimbijy o AUS 176-177 E 4
Bimbila o GH 202-203 L 5
Bimbo ☆ RCA 206-207 D 6
Bimi, Sabon- o WAN 198-199 C 6
Bimini Islands ⌒ BS 54-55 F 2
Bina o IND 138-139 G 7
Binaluan o RP 160-161 C 7
Biname Lake o CDN 24-25 K 6
Binanga o RI 162-163 C 4
Binbee o AUS 174-175 J 7
Binbrook o CDN (ONT) 238-239 F 5
Bindé o BF 202-203 K 4
Bindegolly, Lake o AUS 178-179 H 5
Binder o TCH 206-207 B 4
Bindi Bindi o AUS 176-177 D 5
Bindu o ZRE 216-217 E 3
Bindura ☆ ZW 218-219 F 3
Bin-el-Ouidane o MA 188-189 H 4
Binga o ZW 218-219 D 3
Binga, Monte ▲ MOC 218-219 G 4
Binga, Quedas de Agua ~ ANG 216-217 C 5
Bingara o AUS 178-179 L 5
Bingassi o RMM 202-203 E 3
Bing Bong o AUS 174-175 D 4
Binger o USA (OK) 264-265 F 3
Bingerville o CI 202-203 J 7
Bingham o USA (ME) 278-279 M 3
Bingham o USA (NM) 256-257 J 5
Binghamton o USA (NY) 278-279 F 6
Bin Ghashīr o LAR 192-193 E 1
Bingintelok o RI 162-163 E 6
Bingley o CDN (ALB) 232-233 D 3
Binglingsi Shankou · VRC 154-155 C 4
Bingöl ☆ TR 128-129 J 3
Bingöl Dağları ▲ TR 128-129 J 3
Binhai o VRC 154-155 L 4
Binh Chánh o VN 158-159 J 5
Binh Châu o VN 158-159 J 5
Binh Định o VN 158-159 K 4
Binh Giá o VN 158-159 J 5
Binh Gia ☆ VN 156-157 E 6
Binh Lâm o VN 158-159 K 3
Binh Long o VN 158-159 J 5
Bin-Hoyé o CI 202-203 F 6
Binibihali o PNG 183 F 6
Bini Drosso < TCH 198-199 J 3
Bini Erde < TCH 198-199 J 2
Bin 'Isa, Bi'r < LAR 192-193 F 2
Binjai o RI 162-163 C 3
Bin Jawwad o LAR 192-193 H 2
Binjuda ~ RUS 108-109 X 5
Binkolo o WAL 202-203 E 5
Binnaway o AUS 178-179 K 6
Binongko o RI 164-165 K 3
Binongko, Pulau ⌒ RI 164-165 H 6
Binscarth o CDN (MAN) 234-235 B 4
Bintagoungou o RMM 196-197 J 6
Bintan, Pulau ⌒ RI 162-163 F 4
Bintang, Banjaran ▲ MAL 162-163 D 2
Bint Ğubail ☆ RL 128-129 F 6
Binthalya o AUS 176-177 C 2
Bintuan o RI 162-163 E 7
Bintulu o MAL 162-163 K 3
Bintuni o RI 166-167 G 3
Bintuni, Teluk ≈ 166-167 G 3
Binuang o RI 164-165 D 5
Bin Xian o VRC 150-151 F 5
Binyang o VRC 156-157 F 5
Binz, Ostseebad o D 92-93 M 1
Binzhou o VRC 154-155 K 3
Biobío, Río ~ RCH 78-79 C 4
Bio Caddo o SP 212-213 K 2
Bioco, Isla de ⌒ GQ 210-211 B 2
Biograd na Moru o HR 100-101 E 3
Biokovo ▲ HR 100-101 F 3
Biorra = Birr o IRL 90-91 D 5
Biosphere II ·· USA (AZ) 256-257 E 6
Biot, Kap ▲ GRØ 26-27 o 8
Biougra o MA 188-189 G 5
Bipi Island ⌒ PNG 183 D 2
Bipindi o CAM 210-211 C 2
Bipok o CAM 204-205 J 6
Biquele o RI 166-167 C 6

Bir ○ IND 138-139 E 10
Bir, Ras ▲ DJI 200-201 L 6
Bira ○ RI 164-165 G 6
Bira ○ RUS 122-123 E 4
Bi'r Abū Ğulūd ○ SYR 128-129 H 4
Birāk ○ LAR 192-193 F 4
Birāk, Tall ○ SYR 128-129 J 4
Birak, Umm al- ○ KSA 130-131 F 6
Bir al Ghanam ○ LAR 192-193 E 1
Bir Ali Ben Khelifa ○ TN 190-191 H 3
Bi'r Allāq ○ LAR 192-193 D 2
Bir-Anzarane ○ MA 196-197 C 3
Birao ☆ • RCA 206-207 F 3
Biratnagar ○ NEP 144-145 F 7
Biratori ○ J 152-153 K 3
Bi'r A'yād ○ LAR 192-193 E 1
Bi'r Ben Ghimah ○ LAR 192-193 J 2
Birca ○ RO 102-103 C 6
Birch Bay ○ CDN (MAN) 234-235 E 3
Birch Creek ○ USA 20-21 S 3
Birch Creek ~ USA 20-21 S 3
Birch Creek ~ USA 20-21 P 5
Birch Creek ~ USA (OR) 244-245 F 5
Birchdale ○ USA (MN) 270-271 D 2
Birchenough Bridge ○ ZW 218-219 G 4
Birches ○ USA 20-21 O 4
Birch Harbor ○ USA (ME) 278-279 N 4
Birch Hills ○ CDN (SAS) 232-233 N 3
Birchi ○ WAN 198-199 C 6
Birchip ○ AUS 180-181 G 3
Birch Island ○ CDN (BC) 230-231 K 2
Birch Island ⌒ CDN (MAN) 234-235 D 2
Birch Lake ⊖ CDN (ALB) 232-233 G 2
Birch Lake ⊖ CDN (NWT) 30-31 L 4
Birch Lake ⊖ CDN (ONT) 234-235 L 3
Birch Lake ⊖ USA (OK) 264-265 H 2
Birch Mountains ▲ CDN 32-33 N 3
Birch River ○ CDN (MAN) 234-235 B 2
Birch River ~ CDN 32-33 O 3
Birchwood ○ USA (WI) 270-271 G 5
Bircot ○ ETH 208-209 F 5
Bird Cape ▲ USA 22-23 F 7
Bird City ○ USA (KS) 262-263 E 5
Bird Creek ~ USA (OK) 264-265 H 2
Bi'r Dhu'fān ○ LAR 192-193 F 2
Bi'r Di ○ SUD 206-207 J 5
Bird Island ⌒ GB 78-79 N 7
Bird Island ⌒ SY 224 D 1
Bird Island ⌒ USA 22-23 R 5
Bird Rock Lighthouse • BS 54-55 H 3
Birdseye ○ USA (IN) 274-275 M 6
Birdseye ○ USA (UT) 254-255 D 4
Birds Hill ○ CDN (MAN) 234-235 F 5
Birdsville ○ AUS 178-179 E 3
Birdsville Track • AUS 178-179 E 5
Birdtail ○ CDN (MAN) 234-235 C 4
Birdum ○ AUS 174-175 B 4
Birdum Creek ~ AUS 172-173 L 3
Bi'r Durb ○ KSA 130-131 G 4
Birecik ☆ • TR 128-129 G 4
Bire Kpatua Game Reserve ⊥ SUD 206-207 J 6
Birekte ~ RUS 110-111 L 5
Bir El Ater ○ DZ 190-191 G 3
Bireuen ○ RI 162-163 B 2
Bi'r Falaq < IRQ 128-129 J 5
Bi'r Fāṭima < IRQ 128-129 K 5
Birğand ○ • IR 134-135 H 2
Bir-Gandouz ○ MA 196-197 B 4
Birganj ○ NEP 144-145 E 7
Bi'r Ğuraibī'āt ○ IRQ 130-131 J 3
Bi'r Haġal < SYR 128-129 H 5
Bi'r Ḥamrān < IRQ 128-129 K 5
Bi'r Hasana ○ ET 194-195 F 2
Birhat al-Khuraba Pool • KSA 130-131 G 6
Biri ○ SUD (SR) 206-207 H 5
Biri ~ SUD 206-207 H 5
Biri Island ⌒ RP 160-161 F 6
Biriljussy ○ RUS 116-117 E 7
Birini ○ RCA 206-207 F 5
Biritinga ○ BR 68-69 J 7
Birjuk ~ RUS 118-119 J 5
Birjusa ~ RUS 116-117 H 7
Birjusa = Ona ~ RUS 116-117 G 7
Birjusinsk ○ RUS 116-117 H 8
Birjusinskoe plato ⊥ RUS 116-117 J 7
Birk, al- ○ KSA 132-133 B 4
Birka ••• S 86-87 H 7
Birkat al-'Amyā' ○ IRQ 130-131 H 3
Birkat Saira ○ SUD 198-199 L 6
Birkelane ○ SN 202-203 C 2
Birken ○ CDN (BC) 230-231 G 3
Birkenhead ○ AUS 178-179 J 3
Birkenhead ○ GB 90-91 F 5
Birkenhead Lake Provincial Park ⊥ CDN (BC) 230-231 G 3
Bi'r Khadījah ○ LAR 192-193 J 2
Birlad ○ RO 102-103 E 4
Birlad ~ RO 102-103 E 4
Birlik ○ KA 124-125 H 6
Birlik ○ KA (JUK) 136-137 L 4
Birma ~ RUS 122-123 C 3
Birma = Myanmar ■ MYA 142-143 J 4
Birmaqi ○ AZ 128-129 M 3
Birmingham ○ CDN (SAS) 232-233 P 5
Birmingham ○ GB 90-91 G 5
Birmingham ○ USA (AL) 284-285 D 3
Bir Mogreïn ○ RIM 196-197 E 2
Birnagar ○ IND 142-143 F 4
Birney ○ USA (MT) 250-251 N 6
Birni ○ DY 202-203 L 5
Birnie ○ CDN (MAN) 234-235 D 4
Birni Gwari ○ WAN 204-205 G 3
Birnim ○ RN 198-199 D 5
Birnin-Gaoure ○ RN 204-205 E 2
Birnin-Kebbi ○ WAN 198-199 B 6
Birnin Konni ○ RN 198-199 B 6
Birnin Kudu ○ WAN 204-205 H 3
Birnin-Yauri ○ WAN 204-205 F 3
Birniwa ○ WAN 198-199 E 6
Biro ○ DY 204-205 E 4
Birobidžan ○ RUS 122-123 E 4
Birofeľd ○ RUS 122-123 E 4
Biromba ~ RUS 116-117 G 4
Biron ○ CDN (QUE) 240-241 J 2
Birougou, Mont ▲ G 210-211 D 4
Biroun ○ G 210-211 C 4
Birqin ○ LAR 192-193 E 4
Birr = Biorra ○ IRL 90-91 D 5
Birricannia ○ AUS 178-179 H 1
Birrim, Ğazirat ⌒ KSA 130-131 E 5
Birrimba Out Station ○ AUS 172-173 L 3
Birrindudu ○ AUS 172-173 J 5
Birsay ○ CDN (SAS) 232-233 M 4
Birsilpur ○ IND 138-139 D 5
Birsk ☆ RUS 96-97 J 6
Birsuat ~ RUS 124-125 B 2
Birtam-Tam ○ MA 188-189 J 4
Bi'r Ṭarfāwi < IRQ 128-129 K 6
Birti ○ SUD 200-201 F 3
Birtle ○ CDN (SAS) 232-233 R 5
Biruaca ○ YV 60-61 H 4
Birufu ○ RI 166-167 K 4
Birūr ○ IND 140-141 F 4
Biržai ☆ •• LT 94-95 J 3
Bir Zar ○ TN 190-191 H 5
Biša ○ KSA 132-133 C 3
Bisa, Pulau ⌒ RI 164-165 K 4
Bīša, Wādī ~ KSA 132-133 C 3
Bisagana ○ WAN 198-199 F 6
Bisalpur ○ IND 138-139 G 5
Bisanadi National Reserve ⊥ EAK 212-213 G 3
Bisbee ○ USA (AZ) 256-257 F 7
Biscarrosse ○ F 90-91 G 9
Biscay, Bay of ≈ 90-91 E 9
Biscay Abyssal Plain ≃ 6-7 J 4
Biscayne Bay ≈ 48-49 H 7
Biscayne Bay ≈ USA 286-287 J 6
Biscayne National Park ⊥ USA (FL) 286-287 J 6
Bischofshofen ○ A 92-93 M 5
Biscoe ○ USA (NC) 282-283 H 5
Biscoe Islands ⌒ ARK 16 G 30
Biscucuy ○ YV 60-61 G 3
Bisellia ○ SUD 206-207 H 5
Bisen ○ KA 96-97 E 9
Bisert' ○ RUS 96-97 L 5
Bisha ○ ER 200-201 H 5
Bishaltar ○ NEP 144-145 E 7
Bishan ○ VRC 156-157 E 2
Bishkek = Biškek ★ KS 146-147 B 4
Bishkhali ~ BD 142-143 G 4
Bishnupur ○ IND 142-143 E 4
Bisho ○ ZA 220-221 H 6
Bishop ○ USA (CA) 248-249 F 2
Bishop ○ USA (TX) 266-267 K 6
Bishop Hill State Historic Park • USA (IL) 274-275 H 3
Bishop Range ▲ AUS 172-173 H 6
Bishop's Falls ○ CDN (NFL) 242-243 N 3
Bishopville ○ USA (SC) 284-285 K 2
Bişhr ○ LAR 192-193 H 2
Bishushanzhang • VRC 148-149 N 7
Bisina, Lake ⊖ EAU 212-213 E 3
Bisiu ○ EAU 212-213 E 3
Biškek ★ KS 146-147 B 4
Biskotasi Lake ⊖ CDN (ONT) 236-237 G 5
Biskra ☆ • DZ 190-191 E 3
Biskupiec ○ PL 92-93 Q 2
Bismarck ○ CDN (ONT) 238-239 F 5
Bismarck ○ USA (AR) 276-277 B 6
Bismarck ○ USA (MO) 276-277 E 3
Bismarck ☆ USA (ND) 258-259 G 5
Bismarck Archipelago ⌒ PNG 183 E 2
Bismarck Range ▲ PNG 183 C 3
Bismarck Sea ≈ 183 D 2
Bismarckstraße ≈ 16 G 30
Bismil ☆ TR 128-129 J 4
Biso ○ EAU 212-213 C 3
Bison ○ USA (SD) 260-261 D 1
Bisonó ○ DOM 54-55 K 5
Bisotūn ○ IR 134-135 B 1
Bispgården ○ S 86-87 H 5
Bissane ○ RMM 196-197 K 6
Bissau ★ • GNB 202-203 C 4
Bisset Lake ⊖ CDN 30-31 W 4
Bissikrima ○ RG 202-203 E 4
Bissingou II ○ RCA 206-207 E 4
Bissora ☆ GNB 202-203 C 3
Bistcho Lake ⊖ CDN 30-31 K 6
Bistineau, Lake ⊖ USA (LA) 268-269 G 4
Bistriţa ☆ • RO 102-103 D 4
Biswān ○ IND 142-143 B 2
Bita ~ RCA 206-207 G 5
Bita, Rio ~ CO 60-61 G 4
Bitam ○ G 210-211 C 2
Bitangor ○ MAL 162-163 J 3
Bitata ○ ETH 208-209 D 6
Bitencourt ○ BR 66-67 C 3
Bitian Bank ≃ 168 E 2
Bitigiu ○ ETH 208-209 E 4
Bitik ○ KA 96-97 G 8
Bitilifondi ○ RCA 206-207 H 6
Bitjug ~ RUS 94-95 R 5
Bitjug ~ RUS 102-103 M 2
Bitkine ○ TCH 206-207 D 3
Bitlis ☆ • TR 128-129 K 3
Bitola ○ •• MK 100-101 H 4
Bitou ○ BF 202-203 K 4
Bitoutouk ○ CAM 210-211 C 2
Bitter Creek ○ USA (WY) 252-253 K 5
Bitter Creek ~ USA (WY) 252-253 J 5
Bitterfeld ○ D 92-93 M 3
Bitterfontein ○ ZA 220-221 D 5
Bitter Lake ⊖ CDN (SAS) 232-233 J 5
Bittern Lake ○ CDN (ALB) 232-233 E 3
Bittern Lake Indian Reservation ⅩCDN (SAS) 232-233 N 2
Bitterroot Range ▲ USA (ID) 250-251 D 4
Bitterroot River ~ USA (MT) 250-251 E 5
Bitui River ~ PNG 183 B 5
Bitumount ○ CDN 32-33 P 3
Bitung ○ RI 164-165 J 3
Bituruna ○ BR 74-75 E 6
Bitzshtini Mount ▲ USA 20-21 P 4
Biu ○ WAN 204-205 K 3
Biuka-tōge ▲ J 152-153 K 2
Biu Plateau ▲ WAN 204-205 K 3
Biwabik ○ USA (MN) 270-271 F 3
Biwa-ko ⊖ J 152-153 G 7
Biwako Quasi National Park ⊥ J 152-153 F 7
Biwat ○ PNG 183 B 3
Bixby ○ USA (MN) 270-271 E 7
Bixby ○ USA (MO) 276-277 D 3
Biyagundi ○ ER 200-201 H 5
Biyang ○ VRC 154-155 H 5
Biye K'obē ○ ETH 208-209 F 3
Bijsk = Bijsk ☆ RUS 124-125 O 2
Bizana ○ ZA 220-221 J 5
Bižanābād ○ IR 134-135 H 5
Bižbuljak ☆ RUS 96-97 J 7
Bize ~ KA 124-125 K 6
Bizen ○ J 152-153 F 7
Bizerte ☆ • TN 190-191 G 2
Bizigui ~ BF 202-203 K 3
Bjahomľ ○ BY 94-95 L 4
Bjala ○ BG 102-103 D 6
Bjala Slatina ○ BG 102-103 C 6
Bjarėzina ~ BY 94-95 L 5
Bjarezinski zapavednik ⊥ BY 94-95 L 4
Bjargtangar ▲ IS 86-87 a 2
Bjaroza ○ BY 94-95 J 5
Bjas'-Kjuël' ○ RUS (SAH) 118-119 J 6
Bjas'-Kjuël' ○ RUS (SAH) 118-119 N 4
Bjästa ○ S 86-87 J 5
Bjelašnica ▲ BIH 100-101 G 3
Bjelovar ○ HR 100-101 F 2
Bjerkvik ○ N 86-87 H 2
Bjorkdale ○ CDN (SAS) 232-233 P 3
Björna ○ S 86-87 J 5
Bjørnafjorden ≈ 86-87 B 6
Bjørne Øer ⌒ GRØ 26-27 n 8
Bjørne Peninsula ⌒ CDN 24-25 c 2
Bjørnesk Ø ⌒ GRØ 26-27 q 5
Bjørnøya ⌒ N 84-85 L 5
Bjørnøya Bank ≃ 84-85 M 5
Bjørnøy Radio ○ N 84-85 L 5
Bjurholm ○ • S 86-87 J 5
Bjutejdjah ○ • RUS 120-121 D 3
Bla ○ RMM 202-203 H 3
Blachly ○ USA (OR) 244-245 B 6
Black ○ USA 20-21 K 5
Blackall ○ AUS 178-179 H 3
Black Bay ⊖ CDN (ONT) 234-235 P 6
Black Bear Creek ~ USA (OK) 264-265 G 2
Black Bear River ~ CDN 34-35 L 3
Blackbear River ~ CDN 34-35 M 3
Black Bear River ~ CDN 38-39 Q 2
Black Birch Lake ⊖ CDN 34-35 C 2
Black Braes ○ AUS 174-175 H 6
Blackbull ○ AUS 174-175 F 5
Blackburn, Mount ▲ USA 20-21 T 6
Black Canyon City ○ USA (AZ) 256-257 C 4
Black Canyon of the Gunnison National Monument ∴ USA (CO) 254-255 H 5
Black Cape ▲ USA 22-23 U 3
Black Creek ○ CDN (BC) 230-231 D 4
Black Creek ○ USA (WI) 270-271 K 6
Black Creek ~ USA (MS) 268-269 L 5
Black Diamond ○ CDN (ALB) 232-233 D 5
Blackdown ○ AUS 174-175 G 5
Blackdown Tableland National Park ⊥ AUS 178-179 K 2
Blackfalds ○ CDN (ALB) 232-233 E 3
Blackfeet Indian Reservation Ⅹ USA (MT) 250-251 F 3
Blackfoot ○ CDN (ALB) 232-233 H 2
Blackfoot ○ USA (ID) 252-253 F 3
Blackfoot ○ USA (MT) 250-251 G 3
Blackfoot Indian Reserve Ⅹ CDN (ALB) 232-233 F 5
Blackfoot Reservoir ⊖ USA (ID) 252-253 G 4
Blackfoot River ~ USA (MT) 250-251 F 5
Black Forest = Schwarzwald ▲ D 92-93 K 4
Black Hawk ○ CDN (ONT) 234-235 K 6
Black Hills ▲ USA (SD) 260-261 B 2
Blackie ○ CDN (ALB) 232-233 E 5
Black Island ⌒ • CDN (MAN) 234-235 G 3
Black Lake ○ CDN (QUE) 238-239 O 2
Black Lake ○ CDN (SAS) 30-31 R 6
Black Lake ⊖ USA 22-23 R 4
Black Mesa ▲ USA (OK) 264-265 B 2
Black Mesa ⊥ USA (AZ) 256-257 E 2
Black Mountain ▲ AUS 178-179 E 1
Black Mountain ▲ CDN 26-27 G 3
Black Mountain ▲ USA (VA) 280-281 D 7
Black Mountains ▲ USA (AZ) 256-257 A 3
Black Nossob ~ NAM 216-217 E 10
Black Pines ○ CDN (BC) 230-231 K 3
Black Point ○ BS 54-55 G 2
Black Point ▲ USA 22-23 U 4
Blackpool ○ CDN (BC) 230-231 J 2
Blackpool ○ • GB 90-91 F 5
Black Range ▲ USA (NM) 256-257 H 5
Black River ○ CDN (NS) 240-241 O 4
Black River ~ CDN 20-21 X 3
Black River ~ CDN (MAN) 234-235 G 4
Black River ~ CDN (ONT) 238-239 F 4
Black River ○ •• JA 54-55 G 6
Black River ~ USA 20-21 T 3
Black River ~ USA (AR) 276-277 D 5
Black River ~ USA (AZ) 256-257 E 5
Black River ~ USA (FL) 286-287 H 1
Black River ~ USA (MI) 272-273 F 2
Black River ~ USA (MI) 272-273 G 4
Black River ~ USA (MO) 276-277 E 4
Black River ~ USA (NC) 282-283 J 6
Black River ~ USA (NM) 256-257 L 6
Black River ~ USA (NY) 278-279 F 5
Black River ~ USA (OH) 280-281 D 2
Black River ~ USA (SC) 284-285 L 3
Black River ~ USA (SC) 284-285 K 2
Black River ~ USA (WI) 270-271 H 6
Black River Falls ○ USA (WI) 270-271 H 6
Black Rock ○ USA (AR) 276-277 D 4
Black Rock ○ USA (UT) 254-255 C 5
Black Rock Desert ⊥ USA (NV) 246-247 F 3
Black Rock Point ▲ CDN 36-37 R 4
Black Rocks ▲ • WAN 204-205 H 4
Black Rocks Landing ○ AUS 174-175 D 4
Black Rock Summit ▲ USA (NV) 246-247 J 5
Blackrun ○ USA (OH) 280-281 D 3
Blacksburg ○ USA (VA) 280-281 F 6
Black Sea ≈ 102-103 G 6
Blacks Fork ~ USA (UT) 254-255 E 3
Blacks Harbour ○ CDN (NB) 240-241 J 5
Blackshear ○ USA (GA) 284-285 H 5
Blackshear, Lake < USA (GA) 284-285 G 5
Black Squirrel Creek ~ USA (CO) 254-255 L 5
Blackstone ○ USA (VA) 280-281 H 6
Blackstone River ~ CDN 20-21 V 4
Blackstone River ~ CDN 30-31 H 5
Blackstone River ~ CDN (ALB) 232-233 B 3
Black Sturgeon Lake ⊖ CDN (ONT) 234-235 P 5
Blackville ○ AUS 178-179 L 6
Blackville ○ CDN (NB) 240-241 K 4
Blackville ○ USA (SC) 284-285 J 3
Black Volta ~ GH 202-203 J 5
Black Warrior River ~ USA (AL) 284-285 C 4
Blackwater ○ AUS 178-179 K 2
Blackwater ~ USA (FL) 286-287 C 1
Blackwater Creek ~ AUS 178-179 H 3
Blackwater Creek ~ AUS 180-181 L 2
Blackwater Lake ⊖ CDN 30-31 H 3
Blackwater National Wildlife Refuge Ⅹ USA (MD) 280-281 K 5
Blackwater River ~ CDN 30-31 H 4
Blackwater River ~ USA (MO) 274-275 E 6
Blackwell ○ USA (OK) 264-265 G 2
Blackwell ○ USA (TX) 264-265 D 6
Blackwells Corner ○ USA (CA) 248-249 E 4
Blackwood River ~ AUS 176-177 D 6
Bladenboro ○ USA (NC) 282-283 J 6
Bladensburg National Park ⊥ AUS 178-179 G 2
Bladgrond ○ ZA 220-221 D 4
Bladon Springs State Park ⊥ • USA (AL) 284-285 B 5
Bladworth ○ CDN (SAS) 232-233 M 4
Blaeberry River ~ CDN (BC) 230-231 N 2
Blåfjellet ▲ N 86-87 F 4
Blagodarnyj ○ RUS 102-103 N 5
Blagoevgrad ○ BG 102-103 C 6
Blagoevo ○ RUS 88-89 T 5
Blagopolučija, zaliv ○ RUS 108-109 K 4
Blagoveščenka ○ KA 146-147 B 4
Blagoveščenka ☆ RUS 124-125 L 2
Blagoveščenka ○ • RUS 122-123 B 3
Blagoveščensk ☆ RUS (BAS) 96-97 J 6
Blagoveščenskij proliv ≈ 110-111 Z 2
Blagoveshchensk = Blagoveščensk ☆ RUS 118-119 N 10
Blaine ○ USA (KS) 262-263 K 5
Blaine ○ USA (KY) 276-277 N 2
Blaine ○ USA (MN) 270-271 E 5
Blaine ○ USA (TN) 282-283 D 4
Blaine ○ USA (WA) 244-245 C 2
Blaine Lake ○ CDN (SAS) 232-233 M 3
Blainville ○ CDN (QUE) 238-239 M 3
Blair ○ USA (NE) 262-263 K 3
Blair ○ USA (OK) 264-265 E 4
Blair ○ USA (WI) 270-271 G 6
Blair Athol ○ AUS 178-179 J 2
Blairbeth ○ ZA 220-221 H 2
Blairgowrie ○ GB 90-91 F 3
Blairmore ○ CDN (ALB) 232-233 D 6
Blairsden ○ USA (CA) 246-247 E 4
Blairsville ○ USA (GA) 284-285 G 2
Blairsville ○ USA (PA) 280-281 G 3
Blaka ~ RN 198-199 F 2
Blaka Laodemi < RN 198-199 F 2
Blake Bay ≈ 24-25 e 7
Blakely ○ USA (GA) 284-285 F 5
Blake Plateau ≃ 48-49 J 4
Blake Plateau ≃ 286-287 K 1
Blake Point ▲ USA (MI) 270-271 K 2
Blamo ○ WAL 202-203 E 6
Blanc, Lac ⊖ CDN (QUE) 236-237 P 5
Blanc, le ○ F 90-91 H 8
Blanca, Bahía ≈ 78-79 H 5
Blanca, Cordillera ▲ PE 64-65 D 6
Blanca, Lago ○ RCH 70-71 C 5
Blanca, Laguna ⊖ RCH 80 E 6
Blanca, Punta ▲ MEX 50-51 B 3
Blanca, Río ~ BOL 70-71 D 7
Blanca, Sierra ▲ USA (NM) 256-257 K 5
Blanca Grande, Laguna la ⊖ RA 78-79 H 5
Blanca Peak ▲ USA (CO) 254-255 K 6
Blancas, Sierras ▲ RA 78-79 F 6
Blancester ○ USA (OH) 280-281 C 4
Blanchard ○ USA (ID) 250-251 C 3
Blanchard ○ USA (ND) 258-259 K 4
Blanchard ○ USA (OK) 264-265 G 3
Blanchard River ~ USA (OH) 280-281 C 2
Blanchard Springs Caverns ∴ USA (AR) 276-277 C 5
Blanche, Lake ⊖ AUS (SA) 178-179 E 5
Blanche, Lake ⊖ AUS (WA) 172-173 F 7
Blanche Channel ≈ 184 I c 3
Blanche-Marievallen ~ SME 62-63 F 3
Blanchet Island ⌒ CDN 30-31 N 4
Blanchetown ○ AUS 180-181 E 3
Blanchisseuse ○ TT 60-61 L 2
Blanco ○ USA (NM) 256-257 H 2
Blanco ○ USA (TX) 266-267 J 3
Blanco, Cabo ▲ CR 52-53 B 7
Blanco, Cape ▲ USA (OR) 244-245 A 8
Blanco, Cerro ▲ RA 78-79 D 6
Blanco, Lago ○ RA 80 E 2
Blanco, Lago ○ RCH 80 F 7
Blanco, Río ~ BOL 70-71 E 3
Blanco, Río ~ PE 64-65 F 4
Blanco, Río ~ RA 76-77 C 5
Blanco, Río ~ RA 76-77 C 6
Blanco, Río ~ RA 76-77 B 6
Blanco, Río ~ RA 78-79 D 2
Blanco, Río ~ RCH 80 D 2
Blanco Creek ~ USA (TX) 266-267 K 5
Blanco River ~ USA (TX) 266-267 J 3
Blancos, Los ○ RA 76-77 F 2
Blancos del Sur, Cayos ⌒ C 54-55 E 3
Blanc Sablon ○ CDN 38-39 Q 3
Bland ○ USA (VA) 280-281 E 6
Blandá ~ IS 86-87 d 2
Bland Creek ~ AUS 180-181 J 2
Blandford ○ CDN (NS) 240-241 L 6
Blanding ○ USA (IL) 274-275 H 2
Blanding ○ USA (UT) 254-255 F 6
Blanes ○ E 98-99 J 4
Blaney Park ○ USA (MI) 270-271 N 4
Blanfla ○ CI 202-203 H 6
Blangkejeren ○ RI 162-163 B 2
Blangpidie ○ RI 162-163 B 3
Blanket ○ USA (TX) 266-267 J 2
Blanquero, El ○ YV 60-61 K 3
Blanquilla, Isla ⌒ YV 60-61 J 2
Blanquillo ○ ROU 78-79 M 2
Blantyre ☆ • MW 218-219 H 2
Blåsjøen ⊖ N 86-87 C 7
Blau ○ RI 164-165 H 3
Blåvands Huk ⌒ DK 86-87 D 9
Blaye ○ F 90-91 G 9
Blayney ○ AUS 180-181 K 2
Bleaker Island ⌒ GB 78-79 L 7
Blebo ○ LB 202-203 G 7
Blednaja, gory ▲ RUS 108-109 L 3
Bledsoe ○ USA (TX) 264-265 A 5
Bled Tisseras ⊖ DZ 190-191 E 7
Blega ○ RI 168 E 3
Bleikvassli ○ N 86-87 F 4
Blendio ○ RMM 202-203 G 4
Blenheim ○ CDN (ONT) 238-239 D 6
Blenheim ○ NZ 182 D 4
Blenheim ○ USA (SC) 284-285 L 2
Blenheim Palace ••• GB 90-91 G 6
Blesmanspos ○ ZA 220-221 G 3
Blessing ○ USA (TX) 266-267 L 5
Bleu, Lac ⊖ CDN (QUE) 238-239 G 2
Bleus, Monts ▲ ZRE 212-213 C 3
Blewett ○ USA (WA) 244-245 E 3
Blicade ○ F 62-63 H 4
Blida ☆ DZ 190-191 D 2
Bligh Island ⌒ USA 20-21 R 6
Bligh Water ≈ 184 III a 2
Blikadi ○ CI 202-203 J 5
Blina ○ AUS 172-173 G 4
Blina Oil Field • AUS 172-173 G 4
Blind Channel ○ CDN (BC) 230-231 D 3
Blindman River ~ CDN (ALB) 232-233 D 3
Blind River ○ CDN (ONT) 238-239 C 2
Blinisht ○ AL 100-101 G 4
Blipi ○ LB 202-203 F 6
Bliss ○ USA (ID) 252-253 D 4
Bliss Bugt ≈ 26-27 I 2
Blissfield ○ USA (MI) 272-273 F 6
Bliss Landing ○ CDN (BC) 230-231 E 3
Blissville ○ CDN (NB) 240-241 J 5
Blitchton ○ USA (GA) 284-285 J 4
Blitta ○ RT 202-203 L 5
Blizzard Gap ▲ USA (OR) 244-245 F 8
Bloedel ○ CDN (BC) 230-231 D 3
Bloemfontein ☆ ZA 220-221 H 4
Bloemhof ○ ZA 220-221 G 3
Bloemhof Dam < ZA 220-221 G 3
Blois ☆ • F 90-91 H 8
Bloléquin ○ CI 202-203 G 6
Blomkest ○ USA (MN) 270-271 C 6
Blommesteinmeer, W.J. van ⊖ SME 62-63 G 3
Blönduós ☆ IS 86-87 c 2
Blood Indian Creek ~ CDN (ALB) 232-233 G 4
Blood Indian Reserve Ⅹ CDN (ALB) 232-233 E 6
Blood River Monument • ZA 220-221 K 4
Bloodvein River ~ CDN (MAN) 234-235 G 3
Bloody Falls ~ CDN 30-31 M 2
Bloomer ○ USA (WI) 270-271 G 5
Bloomfield ○ USA (IA) 274-275 F 4
Bloomfield ○ USA (IN) 274-275 M 5
Bloomfield ○ USA (MO) 276-277 F 4
Bloomfield ○ USA (MT) 250-251 P 4
Bloomfield ○ USA (NE) 262-263 J 2
Bloomfield ○ USA (NM) 256-257 H 2
Bloomfield ○ USA (OH) 280-281 E 4
Bloomfield River Ⅹ AUS 174-175 H 4
Blooming Grove ○ USA (TX) 264-265 H 6
Blooming Prairie ○ USA (MN) 270-271 E 7
Bloomington ○ USA (IL) 274-275 J 4
Bloomington ○ USA (IN) 274-275 M 5
Bloomington ○ USA (MN) 270-271 E 6
Bloomington ○ USA (TX) 266-267 L 5
Bloomington ○ USA (WI) 274-275 H 2
Bloomington, Lake ⊖ USA (IL) 274-275 K 4
Bloomsburg ○ USA (PA) 280-281 K 2
Bloomsbury ○ AUS 174-175 K 7
Bloomsdale ○ USA (MO) 274-275 H 6
Blora ○ RI 168 D 3
Blosseville Kyst ⊥ GRØ 28-29 a 2
Blossom ○ USA (TX) 264-265 J 5
Blossom, mys ▲ RUS 112-113 U 1
Bloukranspas ▲ ZA 220-221 D 5
Blount Mountains ▲ USA (AL) 284-285 D 3
Blountstown ○ USA (FL) 286-287 D 1
Blountsville ○ USA (AL) 284-285 D 2
Blowering Reservoir < AUS 180-181 K 3
Blower Rock ⌒ JA 54-55 G 6
Blow River ~ CDN 20-21 W 2
Bloxsome Bay ≈ 24-25 K 2
Blubber Bay ○ CDN (BC) 230-231 E 4
Blucher ○ CDN (SAS) 232-233 M 3
Blucher Range ▲ PNG 183 A 3
Bludnaja ~ RUS 110-111 G 3
Bludnaja ~ RUS 118-119 E 10
Blue Ball ○ USA (AR) 276-277 B 6
Blue Bell Knoll ▲ USA (UT) 254-255 D 5
Blueberry River ~ CDN 32-33 K 3
Bluecreek ○ USA (WA) 244-245 H 2
Blue Cypress Lake ⊖ USA (FL) 286-287 J 4
Blue Earth ○ USA (MN) 270-271 D 7
Bluefield ○ USA (WV) 280-281 E 6
Bluefields ☆ NIC 52-53 C 5
Bluefields, Bahía de ≈ 52-53 C 6
Bluefish River ~ CDN 30-31 F 2
Bluegoose Prairie ⊥ CDN 36-37 N 2
Bluegoose River ~ CDN 36-37 N 2
Blue Grass Parkway II USA (KY) 276-277 L 3
Blue Hill ○ USA (ME) 278-279 N 4
Blue Hill ○ USA (NE) 262-263 H 4
Blue Hills ▲ CDN 24-25 O 3
Blue Hills of Couteau ▲ CDN (NFL) 242-243 L 5
Blue Hole National Park ⊥ BH 52-53 K 3
Blue Jay ○ USA (NV) 246-247 J 5
Blue Knob ▲ AUS 178-179 M 6
Blue Lagoon National Park ⊥ Z 218-219 D 2
Blue Lake ○ USA (CA) 246-247 B 3
Blue Licks Spring ○ USA (KY) 276-277 L 2
Blue Mesa ▲ USA (CO) 254-255 H 5
Blue Mesa Reservoir ⊖ USA (CO) 254-255 H 5
Blue Mound ○ USA (IL) 274-275 J 5
Blue Mountain ▲ IND 142-143 H 4
Blue Mountain ▲ USA (AR) 276-277 A 6
Blue Mountain ▲ USA (NH) 278-279 K 4
Blue Mountain ▲ USA (NV) 246-247 G 3
Blue Mountain Lake ○ USA (NY) 278-279 G 5
Blue Mountain Lake < USA (AR) 276-277 B 5
Blue Mountains ▲ JA 54-55 G 5
Blue Mountains ▲ USA (OR) 244-245 G 6
Blue Mountains ▲ USA (PA) 280-281 J 3
Blue Mountains ▲ USA (TX) 266-267 H 3
Blue Mountains National Park ⊥ •• AUS 180-181 L 2
Blue Mount Pass ▲ USA (OR) 244-245 H 8
Blue Mud Bay ≈ 174-175 C 3
Blue Mud Hills ▲ USA (MT) 250-251 P 6
Blue Nile = Abay Wenz ~ ETH 208-209 C 3
Blue Nile Falls = T'is Isat Fwafwatē ~ •• ETH 208-209 C 3
Bluenose Lake ⊖ CDN 24-25 M 6
Blue Rapids ○ USA (KS) 262-263 K 5
Blue Ridge ○ USA (GA) 284-285 F 2
Blue Ridge ○ USA (TX) 264-265 H 5
Blue Ridge ▲ USA (NY) 278-279 G 5
Blue Ridge Lake < USA (GA) 284-285 F 2
Blue Ridge Parkway II USA (NC) 282-283 F 4
Blue Ridge Parkway II USA (VA) 280-281 F 7
Blue River ○ CDN (BC) 228-229 P 4
Blue River ~ USA (AZ) 256-257 F 5
Blue River ~ USA (IN) 274-275 M 6
Blue River ~ USA (TX) 264-265 H 5
Blue Robin Hill ▲ AUS 176-177 H 4
Blueslide ○ USA (WA) 244-245 H 2
Blue Springs ∴ USA (FL) 286-287 D 1
Blue Springs Caverns • USA (IN) 274-275 M 6
Bluestone Reservoir ⊖ USA (WV) 280-281 F 6
Bluewater ○ AUS 174-175 J 6
Bluewater ○ USA (NM) 256-257 H 3
Bluff ○ AUS 178-179 K 2
Bluff ○ NZ 182 B 7
Bluff ○ USA (AK) 20-21 J 4
Bluff ○ USA (UT) 254-255 F 6
Bluff, Cape ▲ CDN 38-39 R 2
Bluff, The ○ BS 54-55 G 2
Bluff Dale ○ USA (TX) 264-265 F 6
Bluff Face Range ▲ AUS 172-173 H 4
Bluff Point ▲ AUS 176-177 C 3
Bluff Point ▲ USA (NC) 282-283 L 5
Bluffs of Llano Estacado ⊥ USA (NM) 256-257 M 4
Bluffton ○ USA (IN) 274-275 N 4
Blukwa ○ ZRE 212-213 C 3
Blum ○ USA (TX) 264-265 G 6
Blumenau ○ • BR 74-75 F 6
Blumenhof ○ CDN (SAS) 232-233 L 5
Blumenort ○ CDN (MAN) 234-235 G 5
Blunt ○ USA (SD) 260-261 G 2
Blunt Peninsula ~ CDN 36-37 R 3
Blup Blup Island ⌒ PNG 183 C 2
Bly ○ USA (OR) 244-245 D 8
Blyde River Canyon Nature Reserve ⊥ ZA 220-221 K 2
Bly Mountain Pass ▲ USA (OR) 244-245 D 8
Blyth ○ CDN (ONT) 238-239 D 5
Blythe ○ USA (CA) 248-249 K 6
Blytheville ○ USA (AR) 276-277 F 5
Blyth Lagoon ⊖ AUS 176-177 H 2
Blyth River ~ AUS 174-175 C 3
Bnagola ○ ZRE 210-211 H 3
B'Nom So'Ro'Long ▲ VN 158-159 J 5
Bo ☆ N 86-87 D 7
Bo ☆ WAL 202-203 E 6
Boa ~ CI 202-203 G 5
Boac ☆ RP 160-161 D 6
Boaco ☆ NIC 52-53 B 5
Boa Esperança ○ BR (AMA) 66-67 E 6
Boa Esperança ○ BR (MIN) 72-73 H 6
Boa Esperança ○ BR (ROR) 62-63 D 4
Boa Esperança do Sul ○ BR 72-73 F 6
Boa Fé ○ BR 66-67 F 4
Boagis ○ PNG 183 G 5
Boalemo ○ RI 164-165 H 4
Boali ○ RCA 206-207 D 6
Boali, Chutes de ~ RCA 206-207 D 6
Boanamary ○ RM 222-223 E 5
Boanda ○ CAM 204-205 K 6
Boane ○ MOC 220-221 L 3
Boangi ○ ZRE 210-211 F 4
Boang Island ⌒ PNG 183 G 2
Boano, Pulau ⌒ RI 166-167 D 3
Boano, Selat ≈ 166-167 D 3
Boa Nova ○ BR (P) 68-69 E 2
Boa Nova ○ BR (RON) 66-67 F 7
Boardman ○ USA (OH) 280-281 F 2
Boardman ○ USA (OR) 244-245 F 5
Boas River ~ CDN 36-37 G 3
Boat Basin ○ CDN (BC) 230-231 C 4
Boatman ○ AUS 178-179 J 4
Boat of Garten ○ • GB 90-91 F 3
Boatswain, Baie ≈ 38-39 E 3
Boa Viagem ○ BR 68-69 J 4
Boa Vista ○ BR (AMA) 66-67 E 5
Boa Vista ○ BR (AMA) 66-67 C 6
Boa Vista ○ BR (AMA) 66-67 F 3
Boa Vista ○ BR (AMA) 66-67 E 4
Boa Vista ○ BR (GSU) 76-77 J 2
Boa Vista ○ BR (P) 62-63 K 6
Boa Vista ○ BR (P) 68-69 C 3
Boa Vista ○ BR (RSU) 74-75 D 9
Boa Vista ☆ BR (ROR) 62-63 D 4
Boa Vista, Ilha de ⌒ CV 202-203 C 5
Boa Vista das Palmas ○ BR 72-73 H 4
Boa Vista da Ramos ○ BR 66-67 J 4
Boa Vista do Tupim ○ BR 72-73 K 2
Boawae ○ RI 168 E 7
Boaz ○ USA (AL) 284-285 D 2
Bobadah ○ AUS 180-181 J 2
Bobai ○ VRC 156-157 F 5
Bobandana ○ ZRE 212-213 B 4
Bobasakoa ○ RM 222-223 F 4
Bobbie Burns Creek ~ CDN (BC) 230-231 N 3
Bobbili ○ IND 142-143 C 6
Bobcaygeon ○ CDN (ONT) 238-239 G 4
Bobila ○ ZRE 210-211 H 2
Bob Marshall Wilderness Area ⊥ USA (MT) 250-251 F 4
Bob Marshall Wilderness Area ⊥ USA (MT) 250-251 F 3
Bobo ~ RCA 206-207 C 5
Bobo-Dioulasso ☆ BF 202-203 H 4
Bobolice ○ PL 92-93 O 2
Bobonaza, Río ~ EC 64-65 D 2
Bobonong ○ RB 218-219 E 5
Bobopayo ○ RI 164-165 K 3
Bobr ○ BY 94-95 L 4
Bóbr ~ PL 92-93 N 3
Bobrof Island ⌒ USA 22-23 H 7
Bobrov ○ RUS 102-103 L 2
Bobrujsk = Babrujsk ☆ BY 94-95 L 5
Bobrynec' ○ UA 102-103 H 3
Bobuk ○ SUD 208-209 B 3
Bobures ○ YV 60-61 F 3
Boby ▲ RM 222-223 E 9
Boca, Cachoeira da ~ BR 66-67 K 5
Boca, La ○ BOL 70-71 E 4
Boca Arenal ○ CR 52-53 B 6
Boca Candelaria ⌒ CO 60-61 C 6
Boca Caragual ⌒ CO 60-61 C 5
Boca Chica ○ • DOM 54-55 L 6
Boca de Anaro ○ YV 60-61 F 4
Boca de Arguaca ○ YV 60-61 H 4
Boca de la Serpiente ≈ 60-61 L 3
Boca del Pao ○ YV 60-61 J 3
Boca del Río ○ MEX 52-53 F 2
Boca del Río ○ YV 60-61 J 2
Boca del Río Indio ○ PA 52-53 D 7
Boca del Tocuyo ○ YV 60-61 G 2
Boca de Pozo ○ YV 60-61 J 2
Boca de Sábelo ○ PA 52-53 E 7
Boca de Uchire ○ YV 60-61 J 2
Boca de Yuma ○ DOM 54-55 L 5
Boca do Acará ○ BR 66-67 F 6
Boca do Acre ○ BR 66-67 D 7
Boca do Capanã ○ BR 66-67 G 6
Boca do Carapanatuba ○ BR 66-67 F 6
Boca do Iaco ○ BR 66-67 C 7
Boca do Jari ○ BR 62-63 J 6
Bocaina de Minas ○ BR 72-73 H 7
Bocaino do Sul ○ BR 74-75 F 6
Bocaiúva ○ BR 72-73 J 4
Bocaiúva do Sul ○ BR 74-75 F 5
Bocana, La ○ MEX 50-51 B 3
Bocanda ○ CI 202-203 H 6
Bocaranga ○ RCA 206-207 B 5
Boca Raton ○ USA (FL) 286-287 J 5
Bocas del Toro ☆ PA 52-53 C 7
Bocas del Toro, Archipiélago de ⌒ PA 52-53 C 7
Bocay, Río ~ NIC 52-53 B 5
Bochart ○ CDN (QUE) 236-237 P 3
Bochinche ○ YV 62-63 D 2
Bocholt ○ D 92-93 J 3
Bocoio ○ ANG 216-217 C 6
Bocón ○ YV 60-61 K 4
Bocon, Caño ~ CO 60-61 G 6
Bocono ○ YV 60-61 F 3
Boçoroca ○ BR 76-77 K 5
Bocoyna ○ MEX 50-51 F 4
Boda ○ RCA 206-207 C 6
Böda ○ S 86-87 H 8
Bodajbo ☆ RUS 118-119 G 7
Bodalangi ○ ZRE 210-211 J 2
Bodalla ○ AUS 180-181 L 4
Bodallin ○ AUS 176-177 E 5
Bodangora, Mount ▲ AUS 180-181 K 2
Boddington ○ AUS 176-177 D 6
Bodega Bay ○ USA (CA) 246-247 B 5
Bodélé ⊥ TCH 198-199 H 4
Boden ○ • S 86-87 K 4
Bodensee ⊖ CH 92-93 K 5
Bode-Shadu ○ WAN 204-205 F 4
Bodfish ○ USA (CA) 248-249 F 4
Bodhan ○ IND (ANP) 138-139 F 10
Bodhan ○ IND (KAR) 140-141 G 2
Bodhei ○ EAK 212-213 H 4
Bodh Gayav ○ IND 142-143 D 3
Bodi ○ DY 202-203 L 5
Bodi ○ DY 202-203 J 6
Bodie ○ USA (CA) 246-247 F 5
Bodinguė ~ RCA 210-211 F 2
Boditi ○ ETH 208-209 C 5
Bod'ja, Jaškur- ☆ RUS 96-97 H 5
Bodjokola ○ ZRE 210-211 H 2
Bodmin ○ CDN (SAS) 232-233 M 2
Bodmin ○ GB 90-91 E 6
Bodo ○ CDN (ALB) 232-233 H 3
Bodo ○ CI 202-203 H 7

Bodø ☆ N 86-87 G 3
Bodoco o BR 66-67 G 7
Bodocó o BR 68-69 J 5
Bodokro o CI 202-203 H 6
Bodoquena o BR 70-71 J 7
Bodoukpa o RCA 206-207 C 6
Bodrum ☆· TR 128-129 B 4
Bodum o S 86-87 H 5
Boduna o RCA 206-207 D 6
Boé o· GNB 202-203 C 4
Boëkovo ~ RUS 112-113 L 2
Boende o ZRE 210-211 H 4
Boenze o ZRE 210-211 E 6
Boerne o USA (TX) 266-267 J 4
Boesmansrivier ~ ZA 220-221 H 6
Boesmansriviermond o ZA 220-221 H 6
Boeuf River ~ USA (LA) 268-269 J 4
Boevaja gora · RUS 96-97 J 8
Bofete o BR 72-73 F 7
Boffa o RG 202-203 C 4
Bofossou o RG 202-203 F 5
Boga o ZRE 212-213 B 3
Bogal, Lagh ~ EAK 212-213 H 3
Bogale o MYA 158-159 C 2
Bogalusa o USA (LA) 268-269 L 6
Bogamangon o RCA 206-207 C 6
Bogandé o BF 202-203 K 3
Bogan Gate o AUS 180-181 J 2
Bogangolo o RCA 206-207 D 6
Boganida ~ RUS 108-109 c 5
Bogan River ~ AUS 178-179 J 6
Bogantungan o AUS 178-179 J 2
Bogaševo o RUS 114-115 S 6
Bogata o USA (TX) 264-265 J 5
Bogatoe ☆ RUS 96-97 G 7
Bogatye Saby ☆ RUS 96-97 G 6
Boğazkale ☆· TR 128-129 F 2
Boğazlıyan ☆ TR 128-129 F 3
Bogbonga o ZRE 210-211 G 3
Bogcang Zangpo ~ VRC 144-145 F 5
Bogd = Hovd o MAU 148-149 F 5
Bogda Feng ▲ VRC 146-147 J 4
Bogdanovič ☆ RUS 114-115 G 6
Bogdanovka o RUS 96-97 G 7
Bogda Shan ▲ VRC 146-147 J 4
Bogdoo o GH 202-203 K 4
Böget o KA 96-97 G 10
Bogetsaj o KA 126-127 N 2
Boggabilla o AUS 178-179 L 5
Boggabri o AUS 178-179 L 6
Boggola, Mount ▲ AUS 176-177 D 1
Boggy Creek o CDN (MAN) 234-235 B 3
Bogia o PNG 183 C 3
Bogilima o ZRE 210-211 G 2
Bogīnūrd o· IR 136-137 E 6
Bogo o CAM 206-207 B 3
Bogo o RP 160-161 F 7
Bogoin o RCA 206-207 D 6
Bogoladza, hrebet ▲ RUS 122-123 F 5
Bogol Manyo o ETH 208-209 E 6
Bogong, Mount ▲ AUS 180-181 J 4
Bogong National Park ⊥ AUS 180-181 J 4
Bogor (Buitenzorg) o RI 168 B 3
Bogoria, Lake ⊖· EAK 212-213 F 3
Bogorodick ☆·· RUS 94-95 Q 5
Bogorodsk o RUS 94-95 S 3
Bogorodsk o RUS (PRM) 96-97 K 5
Bogorodskoe ☆ RUS (KIR) 96-97 G 5
Bogorodskoe ☆ RUS 122-123 J 2
Bogoroud < TCH 198-199 G 5
Bogose-Mubea o ZRE 210-211 G 2
Bogoslof Island ⌒ USA 22-23 N 6
Bogoso o GH 202-203 J 7
Bogotá ☆· CO 60-61 D 5
Bogotol ☆ RUS 114-115 U 6
Bogra o BD 142-143 F 3
Bogučany ☆ RUS 116-117 H 6
Bogučar o RUS 102-103 M 3
Bogué o RIM 196-197 C 6
Bogue o USA (KS) 262-263 G 5
Bogue Banks ≃ 282-283 L 6
Bogue Chitto o USA (MS) 268-269 K 5
Bogue Chitto River ~ USA (LA) 268-269 K 6
Bogüédia o CI 202-203 G 6
Bogue Homo ~ USA (MS) 268-269 L 5
Bogueloosa Creek ~ USA (AL) 284-285 B 5
Boguila Kota o RCA 206-207 C 5
Bogunda o AUS 178-179 H 1
Bo Hai ≈ 154-155 L 2
Bohai Haixia ≈ 150-151 C 8
Bohai Wan ≈ 154-155 K 2
Boharm o CDN (SAS) 232-233 N 5
Bohemia o USA (LA) 268-269 L 7
Bohemia Downs o AUS 172-173 H 5
Bohena Creek ~ AUS 178-179 K 6
Bohicon o DY 204-205 E 5
Böhmisch-Trübau = Česká Třebová o· CZ 92-93 O 4
Bohobé o TCH 206-207 D 4
Bohodou o RG 202-203 F 5
Bohoduchiv o UA 102-103 J 2
Bohol ⌒ RP 160-161 F 8
Bohol Sea ≈ 160-161 F 8
Bohol Strait ≈ 160-161 E 8
Bohong o RCA 206-207 B 5
Bohongou o BF 202-203 L 3
Böhönye o H 92-93 O 5
Bohorods'kyj Kostel · UA 102-103 D 2
Böhöt o MAU 148-149 J 5
Boi o WAN 204-205 H 4
Boi, Ponta do ▲ BR 72-73 H 7
Bóia, Rio ~ BR 66-67 C 5
Boiaçu o BR 62-63 D 6
Boiekevie Hill ▲ AUS 180-181 E 2
Boiestown o CDN (NB) 240-241 J 4
Boigu Island ⌒ AUS 183 B 5
Boiken o PNG 183 B 2
Boila o MOC 218-219 K 3
Boileau o CDN (QUE) 240-241 E 2
Boina ≐ RM 222-223 E 6
Boipárigüda o IND 142-143 C 6
Boipeba, Ilha de ⌒ BR 72-73 L 2
Bois, Lac des ⊖ CDN 30-31 G 2
Bois, Ribeiro dos ~ BR 68-69 D 6
Bois, Rio dos ~ BR 72-73 F 2
Bois, Rio dos ~ BR 72-73 F 4
Bois-Blanc o F 224 B 7
Bois Blanc o USA (MI) 272-273 E 2
Bois Blanc Island ⌒ USA (MI) 272-273 E 2
Bois d'Arc Creek ~ USA (TX) 264-265 H 5
Boise ☆· USA (ID) 252-253 B 3
Boise City o USA (OK) 264-265 B 2
Boissevain o CDN (MAN) 234-235 C 5
Boituva o BR 72-73 G 7
Boja o RI 168 D 3
Bojano o I 100-101 E 4
Bojarka ~ RUS 108-109 b 6
Bojarsk o RUS 116-117 N 7
Bojčinovci o BG 102-103 C 6
Bojkov, liman ≈ 102-103 K 5
Bojmurot o US 136-137 K 4
Bojonegoro o RI 168 D 3
Boju o WAN 204-205 G 5
Boju-Ega o WAN 204-205 H 5
Bojuru o BR 74-75 E 8
Bojuru, Ponta do ▲ BR 74-75 E 8
Bokada o ZRE 206-207 D 6
Bokākhāt o IND 142-143 H 2
Boka Kotorska ≈·· 100-101 G 3
Bokala o ZRE 210-211 F 5
Bokata o ZRE 210-211 J 2
Bokatola o ZRE 210-211 G 4
Bokayanga o RCA 206-207 D 5
Boké ◻ RG 202-203 C 4
Boké ☆ RG 202-203 C 4
Bokele o ZRE 210-211 H 4
Bokhara River ~ AUS 178-179 J 5
Bokh el Mâ < RIM 196-197 E 5
Bokhol Plain ≐ EAK 212-213 G 2
Boki o CAM 204-205 K 4
Bokin o BF 202-203 K 3
Boki Saboudo o RIM 196-197 D 7
Bokito o CAM 204-205 J 6
Bokkeveldberge ▲ ZA 220-221 D 5
Boknafjorden ≈ 86-87 B 7
Boko o RCB 210-211 E 6
Bokode o ZRE 210-211 G 2
Bokoko o ZRE 206-207 H 6
Bokolako o SN 202-203 D 3
Bokolango o ZRE 210-211 H 3
Bokolo o CI 202-203 G 5
Bokonbaevckoe o KS 146-147 C 4
Bokondo o ZRE 210-211 G 3
Bokoro o TCH 198-199 H 6
Boko-Songho o RCB 210-211 D 6
Bokota o ZRE 210-211 J 4
Bokote o ZRE 210-211 H 4
Boksburg o ZA 220-221 J 3
Boksitogorsk ☆ RUS 94-95 N 2
Bokter Müzbel ▲ KA 126-127 L 6
Boktor ~ RUS 122-123 G 3
Boku o PNG 184 I b 2
Bokungu o ZRE 210-211 F 5
Bokuma o ZRE 210-211 G 4
Bokungu o ZRE 210-211 J 4
Bol ☆ TCH 198-199 G 6
Bola o RI 166-167 B 6
Bola, Bahr ~ TCH 206-207 D 3
Bolafa o ZRE 210-211 J 3
Bolaiti o ZRE 210-211 K 5
Bolama ☆· GNB 202-203 C 4
Bolama o ZRE 210-211 J 3
Bolān ~ PK 134-135 M 4
Boland Lake ⊖ CDN 30-31 U 5
Bolangitang o RI 164-165 H 3
Bolaños, Río ~ MEX 50-51 H 7
Bolan Pass ▲ PK 134-135 M 4
Bolbec o F 90-91 H 7
Bolbolo o RP 160-161 D 4
Bolčiha o RUS 124-125 M 2
Bold Point ▲ RP 160-161 C 7
Bold Spring o USA (TN) 276-277 H 5
Boldyr o US 136-137 K 6
Bole o ETH 208-209 C 5
Bole o GH 202-203 J 5
Bole o VRC 146-147 F 3
Boleko o ZRE 210-211 G 4
Boleko o ZRE 210-211 G 3
Bolesławiec o· PL 92-93 N 3
Bolgart o AUS 176-177 D 5
Bolgatanga ☆· GH 202-203 K 4
Bolger o CDN (QUE) 236-237 M 4
Bolhov ☆· RUS 94-95 O 5
Bolhrad ☆ UA 102-103 F 5
Boli o SUD 206-207 J 5
Boli o VRC 150-151 H 5
Boli o ZRE 210-211 L 4
Bolia o IND 138-139 E 7
Bolia o ZRE 210-211 G 4
Boliche = Pedro J. Montero o EC 64-65 C 3
Boliden o S 86-87 K 4
Bolifar o RI 166-167 F 3
Bolinha, Cachoeira da ~ BR 62-63 D 6
Bolintin-Vale o RO 102-103 D 5
Boliohutu, Gunung ▲ RI 164-165 H 3
Bolivar o BOL (COC) 70-71 D 5
Bolivar o BOL (PAN) 70-71 D 3
Bolívar o CO 60-61 C 7
Bolívar o PE 64-65 D 5
Bolivar o USA (MO) 276-277 B 3
Bolivar o USA (NY) 278-279 C 6
Bolivar o USA (TN) 276-277 G 5
Bolívar, Pico ▲·· YV 60-61 F 3
Bolivar Peninsula ⌣ USA (TX) 268-269 F 7
Bolivia ■ BOL 70-71 D 5
Bolivia o C 54-55 F 3
Boljevac o YU 100-101 H 3
Boljoon o RP 160-161 E 8
Bolkar Dağları ▲ TR 128-129 F 4
Bollène o F 90-91 K 9
Bollnäs o S 86-87 H 6
Bollock, Mount ▲ CDN 24-25 W 3
Bollon o AUS 178-179 J 5
Bollons Seamount ≃ 14-15 L 13
Bolmen ⊖ S 86-87 F 8
Bolnisi o GE 126-127 F 7
Bolobo o ZRE 210-211 F 5
Boločaevka 2-ja o RUS 122-123 F 4
Bolodek o RUS 122-123 E 2
Bologna ☆·· I 100-101 C 2
Bolognesi o PE 64-65 E 7
Bologoe ☆ RUS 94-95 O 3
Bololedi ~ EAT 212-213 E 5
Bolomba o ZRE 210-211 G 3
Bolombo ~ ZRE 210-211 H 3
Bolon' o RUS 122-123 G 4
Bolon', ozero ⊖ RUS 122-123 G 4
Bolona o BF 202-203 G 4
Bolonchén ∴· MEX 52-53 K 2
Bolonchén de Rejón o· MEX 52-53 K 1
Bolondo o GQ 210-211 B 3
Bolongongo o ANG 216-217 C 4
Bolonguera o ANG 216-217 B 6
Bolontio o RI 164-165 H 3
Bolotnoe ☆ RUS 114-115 S 7
Bolovens, Plateau des ▲ LAO 158-159 J 3
Bol'šaja ~ RUS 110-111 a 2
Bol'šaja ~ RUS 122-123 K 2
Bol'šaja ~ RUS 122-123 R 2
Bol'šaja, guba ≈ 110-111 X 2
Bol'šaja Belaja ~ RUS 116-117 K 9
Bol'šaja Bi'ca ~ RUS 114-115 L 6
Bol'šaja Birjusa ~ RUS 116-117 H 8
Bol'šaja Bootankaga ~ RUS 108-109 b 4
Bol'šaja Černaja ~ RUS 116-117 E 5
Bol'šaja Černigovka ☆ RUS 96-97 G 7
Bol'šaja Erëma ~ RUS 116-117 N 5
Bol'šaja Glušica ☆ RUS 96-97 G 7
Bol'šaja Horga, ozero ⊖ RUS 118-119 E 9
Bol'šaja Ket' ~ RUS 116-117 E 7
Bol'šaja Kof-Tajga, gora ▲ RUS 124-125 Q 2
Bol'šaja Kuropatoč'ja ~ RUS 112-113 J 1
Bol'šaja Lebjaž'ja ~ RUS 116-117 E 5
Bol'šaja Martynovka = S'loboda Bol'šaja Martynovka o RUS 102-103 M 4
Bol'šaja Murata ☆ RUS 116-117 F 7
Bol'šaja Mutnaja ~ RUS 88-89 X 3
Bol'šaja Nisogora o RUS 88-89 S 4
Bol'šaja Orlovka o RUS 102-103 M 4
Bol'šaja Padeja, gora ▲ RUS 108-109 J 7
Bol'šaja Pera ~ RUS 122-123 C 3
Bol'šaja Pula ~ RUS 88-89 V 3
Bol'šaja Rečka o RUS 96-97 E 4
Bol'šaja Saga, ozero ⊖ RUS 96-97 D 10
Bol'šaja Sosnovka ☆ RUS 96-97 J 5
Bol'šaja Tira ~ RUS 116-117 M 7
Bol'šaja Usa o RUS 96-97 J 5
Bol'šaja Ussurka ~ RUS 122-123 F 6
Bol'šaja Uzen' ~ RUS 96-97 F 8
Bol'šaja Vladimirovka o KA 124-125 L 3
Bol'šakovo o RUS 94-95 G 4
Bolsena, Lago di ⊖ I 100-101 C 3
Bol'šenarymskoe o KA 124-125 O 4
Bol'šereč'e ☆ RUS 114-115 N 6
Bol'šereck o RUS 122-123 R 2
Bol'šereck, Ust'- ☆ RUS 122-123 R 2
Bol'šereckij Sovhoz o RUS 122-123 R 2
Bol'šeustinskoe ☆ RUS 96-97 L 6
Bol'ševik o RUS 120-121 M 2
Bol'ševik, ostrov ⌒ RUS 108-109 d 2
Bol'šezemel'skaja tundra ≐ RUS 88-89 W 3
Bolsi o RN 202-203 L 3
Bolsico o RCH 76-77 B 2
Bol'šie Čukkuri, gora ▲ RUS 88-89 M 4
Bol'šie Hatymi o RUS 118-119 M 7
Bol'šoe Eravnoe, ozero ⊖ RUS 118-119 E 9
Bol'šoe Jarovoe ozero ⊖ RUS 124-125 K 2
Bol'šoe Jasavèjto, ozero ⊖ RUS 108-109 M 7
Bol'šoe Kizi, ozero ⊖ RUS 122-123 J 3
Bol'šoe Morskoe, ozero ⊖ RUS 112-113 K 1
Bol'šoe Nagatkino ☆ RUS 96-97 F 6
Bol'šoe Sorokino ☆ RUS 114-115 K 6
Bol'šoe Toko, ozero ⊖ RUS 120-121 D 6
Bol'šoe Topol'noe ozero ⊖ RUS 124-125 K 2
Bol'šoe Zaborov'e o RUS 94-95 N 2
Bol'šoj, ostrov ⌒ RUS 108-109 U 4
Bol'šoj Abakan ~ RUS 124-125 Q 2
Bol'šoj Abakan ~ RUS 124-125 Q 3
Bol'šoj Aim ~ RUS 120-121 E 5
Bol'šoj Akzar o KA 124-125 L 3
Bol'šoj Amalat ~ RUS 118-119 F 9
Bol'šoj Anjuj ~ RUS 112-113 L 2
Bol'šoj Atlym ~ RUS 114-115 J 3
Bol'šoj Avam ~ RUS 108-109 Z 6
Bol'šoj Balhan, hrebet ▲ TM 136-137 D 5
Bol'šoj Baranov, mys ▲ RUS 112-113 M 2
Bol'šoj Begičev, ostrov ⌒ RUS 110-111 J 2
Bol'šoj Čeremšan ~ RUS 96-97 G 6
Bol'šoj Čurki o RUS 88-89 T 5
Bol'šoj Dubčes ~ RUS 114-115 T 4
Bol'šoj Enisej ~ RUS 116-117 G 10
Bol'šoj Homus Jurjah ~ RUS 110-111 d 4
Bol'šoj Ik ~ RUS 96-97 K 7
Bol'šoj Ik ~ RUS 96-97 L 6
Bol'šoj Irakan ~ RUS 120-121 C 6
Bol'šoj Iremel', gora ▲ RUS 96-97 L 6
Bol'šoj Irgiz ~ RUS 96-97 F 8
Bol'šoj Jarhodon ~ RUS 112-113 H 4
Bol'šoj Jarudej ~ RUS 108-109 P 8
Bol'šoj Jugan ~ RUS 114-115 M 4
Bol'šoj Kamen' o RUS 122-123 E 7
Bol'šoj Karaman ~ RUS 96-97 E 8
Bol'šoj Kas ~ RUS 116-117 E 6
Bol'šoj Kazymskij Sor, ozero ⊖ RUS 114-115 J 3
Bol'šoj Kemčug ~ RUS 116-117 F 7
Bol'šoj Kèpèrveem ~ RUS 112-113 O 2
Bol'šoj Kinel' ~ RUS 96-97 H 7
Bol'šoj Kujbiveem ~ RUS 112-113 P 5
Bol'šoj Kumak ~ RUS 96-97 L 8
Bol'šoj Kun"jak ~ RUS 114-115 L 5
Bol'šoj Ljahovskij, ostrov ⌒ RUS 110-111 X 3
Bol'šoj Ljamčin Nos, mys ▲ RUS 108-109 H 7
Bol'šoj Loptjuga ~ RUS 88-89 U 5
Bol'šoj Megtyg"egan ~ RUS 114-115 R 4
Bol'šoj Nimnyr o RUS 118-119 M 6
Bol'šoj Nimnyr ~ RUS 118-119 M 6
Bol'šoj Oju ~ RUS 108-109 J 7
Bol'šoj Ol'doj ~ RUS 118-119 L 8
Bol'šoj On o RUS 124-125 Q 2
Bol'šoj On o RUS 124-125 Q 2
Bol'šoj Ous ~ RUS 114-115 F 4
Bol'šoj Patom ~ RUS 118-119 G 5
Bol'šoj Peledon ~ RUS 112-113 O 3
Bol'šoj Pit ~ RUS 116-117 F 6
Bol'šoj Pykarvaam ~ RUS 112-113 S 3
Bol'šoj Rautan, ostrov ⌒ RUS 112-113 Q 2
Bol'šoj Sajan ▲ RUS 116-117 J 9
Bol'šoj Salym ~ RUS 114-115 L 4
Bol'šoj Šantar o RUS 120-121 G 6
Bol'šoj Šantar, ostrov ⌒ RUS 120-121 G 6
Bol'šoj Selerikan ~ RUS 110-111 X 7
Bol'šoj Setnoj, ostrov ⌒ RUS 126-127 H 5
Bol'šoj Šiskaryn ozero ⊖ RUS 114-115 K 6
Bol'šoj Šor o KA 126-127 J 5
Bol'šoj Tap ~ RUS 114-115 H 4
Bol'šoj Turtas ~ RUS 114-115 L 5
Bol'šoj Tyrkan ~ RUS 120-121 E 5
Bol'šoj Uluj ☆ RUS 116-117 E 7
Bol'šoj Urkan ~ RUS 118-119 M 8
Bol'šoj Uvat ozero ⊖ RUS 114-115 L 6
Bol'šoj Uzen' ~ RUS 96-97 F 8
Bol'šoj Yllymah ~ RUS 118-119 N 6
Bol'šoj Zelenoc, ostrov ⌒ RUS 108-109 H 7
Bol'šoj Zelenzuk ~ RUS 126-127 D 5
Bol'šoj Zjudostinskij, ostrov ⌒ RUS 126-127 H 5
Bol'šoj Žužmuj, ostrov ⌒ RUS 88-89 N 4
Bolsón de Mapimí ≐ MEX 50-51 G 3
Boltodden ▲ N 84-85 L 4
Bolton o GB 90-91 F 5
Bolton o USA (NC) 282-283 J 6
Bolu ☆ TR 128-129 D 2
Bolubolu o PNG 183 F 5
Bolvaninka ~ RUS 116-117 N 6
Bolvanskij Nos ▲ RUS 108-109 H 6
Bolyston o CDN (NS) 240-241 O 5
Bolzano = Bozen ☆ I 100-101 C 1
Boma o ZRE 210-211 D 6
Bomaderry, Nowra- o AUS 180-181 L 3
Bomadi o WAN 204-205 F 6
Bomarton o USA (TX) 264-265 E 5
Bomassa o RCB 210-211 F 2
Bombabasua o RI 164-165 F 4
Bombala o AUS 180-181 K 4
Bombay ☆·· IND 138-139 D 10
Bombay Beach o USA (CA) 248-249 J 6
Bomberai ~ RI 166-167 G 3
Bomberai Peninsula ⌣ RI 166-167 G 3
Bombo ☆ EAU 212-213 D 3
Bombo ~ ZRE 210-211 E 6
Bömbögör = Zadgaj o MAU 148-149 D 4
Bombo-Makuka o ZRE 210-211 F 6
Bombonal o CO 64-65 F 1
Bomboyo o TCH 198-199 G 6
Bombura o ZRE 210-211 G 2
Bom Comercio o BR 66-67 E 7
Bom Conselho o BR 68-69 K 6
Bom Despacho o BR 72-73 H 5
Bomdila o· IND 142-143 H 2
Bomet o EAK 212-213 E 4
Bomi o AUS 178-179 K 5
Bomi o VRC 144-145 K 6
Bomili o ZRE 212-213 A 3
Bom Intento o BR 66-67 F 5
Bom Jardim o BR (MAR) 68-69 F 3
Bom Jardim o BR (P) 62-63 J 6
Bom Jardim o BR (RIO) 72-73 J 7
Bom Jardim de Minas o BR 72-73 H 6
Bom Jardim ou Bacabal, Igarapé ~ BR 66-67 J 5
Bom Jesus o ANG 216-217 B 4
Bom Jesus o BR (CAT) 74-75 D 6
Bom Jesus o BR (PIA) 68-69 F 6
Bom Jesus o BR (RSU) 74-75 E 7
Bom Jesus, Rio ~ BR 68-69 F 7
Bom Jesus da Gurguéira, Serra ▲ BR 68-69 G 6
Bom Jesus da Lapa o BR 72-73 J 2
Bom Jesus da Penha o BR 72-73 G 6
Bom Jesus de Goiás o BR 72-73 F 5
Bom Jesus do Amparo o BR 72-73 J 5
Bom Jesus do Galho o BR 72-73 J 5
Bom Jesus do Itabapoana o BR 72-73 K 6
Bømlo ⌒ N 86-87 B 7
Bom Lugar o BR 66-67 H 6
Bomnak o RUS 118-119 O 8
Bomokandi ~ ZRE 210-211 L 2
Bomongo o ZRE 210-211 G 2
Bom Princípio o BR 68-69 E 6
Bomsucesso o BR 68-69 B 5
Bom Sucesso o BR (MIN) 72-73 H 6
Bom Sucesso o BR (PA) 68-69 K 5
Bomu ~ ZRE 206-207 F 6
Bomu Occidentale, Réserve de faune ⊥ ZRE 206-207 G 6
Bomu Orientale, Réserve de faune ⊥ ZRE 206-207 G 6
Bom Viver o BR 68-69 F 3
Bon, Cap ▲ TN 190-191 H 2
Bona, Mount ▲ USA 20-21 U 6
Bonāb o IR 128-129 M 4
Bonaberi o CAM 204-205 H 6
Bona Bona Island ⌒ PNG 183 E 6
Bon Accord o CDN (ALB) 232-233 E 2
Bonaire ⌒ NL 60-61 G 1
Bonam o BF 202-203 K 3
Bonampak ∴·· MEX 52-53 J 3
Bonang o AUS 180-181 K 4
Bonang o RI 168 E 7
Bonanza o NIC 52-53 B 4
Bonanza o USA (ID) 252-253 D 2
Bonanza o USA (OR) 244-245 D 8
Bonanza o USA (UT) 254-255 F 3
Bonao ☆ DOM 54-55 K 5
Bonapabli o LB 202-203 F 6
Bonaparte, Mount ▲ USA (WA) 244-245 F 2
Bonaparte Archipelago ⌒ AUS 172-173 G 3
Bonaparte Lake ⊖ CDN (BC) 230-231 J 2
Bonaparte River ~ CDN (BC) 230-231 H 2
Bonar o E 98-99 E 3
Bonara (Naulu Village) ⊥·· RI 166-167 E 3
Bonaventure o CDN (QUE) 240-241 K 2
Bonaventure, Rivière ~ CDN (QUE) 240-241 K 2
Bonavista o CDN (NFL) 242-243 P 4
Bonavista, Cape ▲·· CDN (NFL) 242-243 P 4
Bonavista Bay ≈ 38-39 S 4
Bonavista Bay ≈ CDN 242-243 P 4
Bonavista Peninsula ⌣·· CDN (NFL) 242-243 P 4
Boncuk Dağı ▲ TR 128-129 C 4
Bondari o RUS 94-95 S 5
Bond Lake, Governor ⊖ USA (IL) 274-275 J 6
Bondo o ZRE (EQU) 210-211 G 3
Bondo o ZRE (Hau) 210-211 J 2
Bondoc Peninsula ⌣ RP 160-161 E 6
Bondokodi o RI 168 D 7
Bondoukou ☆· CI 202-203 J 5
Bondoukui o BF 202-203 J 4
Bondowoso o RI 168 E 3
Bonds Cay ⌒ BS 54-55 G 2
Bonduel o USA (WI) 270-271 K 6
Bondurant o USA (WY) 252-253 H 3
Boné o RG 202-203 E 4
Bone ~ RI 164-165 H 3
Bone = Watampone o RI 164-165 G 6
Bonebone o·· RI 164-165 G 5
Bon Echo Provincial Park ⊥ CDN (ONT) 238-239 H 4
Bone Creek ~ CDN (SAS) 232-233 K 6
Bone-Dumoga National Park ⊥·· RI 164-165 H 3
Bonelambere o RI 168 E 6
Bonelipu o RI 164-165 H 6
Bonelohe o RI 164-165 G 6
Bonépoupa o CAM 204-205 J 6
Bonerate o RI 168 E 6
Bonerate, Kepulauan ⌒ RI 168 E 6
Bonerate, Pulau ⌒ RI 168 E 6
Bonesteel o USA (SD) 260-261 H 3
Bonete, Cerro ▲ RA 76-77 C 4
Bonete, Río ~ RA 76-77 C 5
Bone Teluk ≈ 164-165 G 5
Bonfield o CDN (ONT) 238-239 F 2
Bonfim o BR (AMA) 66-67 D 6
Bonfim o BR (MAT) 70-71 K 5
Bonfim o BR (P) 66-67 K 5
Bonfim o BR (ROR) 62-63 E 4
Bonfinópolis de Minas o BR 72-73 H 4
Bonga o ETH 208-209 C 5
Bonga o PNG 183 D 4
Bongabon o RP 160-161 D 5
Bongandanga o ZRE 210-211 H 3
Bongaon o IND 142-143 F 4
Bongār o IR 134-135 J 3
Bông Hu'ng ☆ VN 156-157 E 6
Bongka ~ RI 164-165 G 4
Bongo o RI 164-165 H 3
Bongo, Massif des ▲ RCA 206-207 F 4
Bongolava ≐ RM 222-223 D 7
Bongolo, Grottes de · G 210-211 C 5
Bongor ☆ TCH 206-207 B 3
Bongouanou ☆ CI 202-203 H 6
Bongouanou, Collines de ▲ CI 202-203 H 6
Bonguélé o RCA 206-207 D 6
Bonham o USA (TX) 264-265 H 5
Boni o BF 202-203 J 4
Boni o RMM 202-203 J 2
Boniérdougou o CI 202-203 H 5
Bonifacio o· F 98-99 M 4
Bonifacio o RP 160-161 E 8
Bonifacio, Bocche di ≈ 100-101 B 4
Bonifacio, Bouches de ≈ 98-99 M 4
Bonifay o USA (FL) 286-287 D 1
Boninal o BR 72-73 K 2
Boni National Reserve ⊥ EAK 212-213 H 4
Bonin National Park ⊥ GH 202-203 J 7
Bonin Trench ≃ 14-15 G 4
Bonita o USA (AZ) 256-257 F 6
Bonita, La o EC 64-65 D 1
Bonitas, Las o YV 60-61 J 4
Bonita Springs o USA (FL) 286-287 H 5
Bonito o BR (BAH) 68-69 H 7
Bonito o BR (GSU) 76-77 J 1
Bonito o BR (MIN) 72-73 H 3
Bonito o BR (P) 68-69 E 2
Bonito o BR (PER) 68-69 L 6
Bonito, Big ~ USA (AZ) 256-257 F 5
Bonito, Pico ▲ HN 52-53 L 4
Bonito, Rio ~ BR 72-73 E 4
Bonito Pico, Parque Nacional ⊥ HN 52-53 L 4
Bonjol o RI 162-163 D 4
Bonkahar, Kūh-e ▲ IR 134-135 E 3
Bonkoukou o RN 204-205 E 1
Bonn o· D 92-93 J 3
Bonneau o USA (SC) 284-285 L 3
Bonne Bay ≈ 38-39 P 4
Bonne Bay ≈ CDN 242-243 K 3
Bonnechere Caves ∴· CDN (ONT) 238-239 H 3
Bonners Ferry o USA (ID) 250-251 C 3
Bonner Springs o USA (KS) 262-263 M 5
Bonnet, Cachoeira do ~ BR 66-67 H 6
Bonne Terre o USA (MO) 276-277 E 3
Bonnet Plume River ~ CDN 20-21 Y 4
Bonneville o USA (OR) 244-245 D 5
Bonneville o USA (WY) 252-253 K 3
Bonneville Salt Flats ≐ USA (UT) 254-255 B 3
Bonney, Lake ⊖ AUS 180-181 F 4
Bonney Downs o AUS 172-173 D 7
Bonnie Rock o AUS 176-177 E 5
Bonnissant, Pointe ▲ CDN 36-37 K 5
Bonny o WAN 204-205 G 6
Bonny, Bight of ≈ 204-205 G 6
Bonnyville o CDN 32-33 P 4
Bono o USA (AR) 276-277 E 5
Bonoi o RI 166-167 J 2
Bonou o DY 204-205 E 5
Bonoua o CI 202-203 J 7
Bonsall o USA (CA) 248-249 G 6
Bon Secour Bay ≈ USA 284-285 C 6
Bonshaw o AUS 178-179 L 5
Bonshaw o CDN (PEI) 240-241 M 4
Bonsoaga ~ BF 202-203 L 3
Bontang o RI 164-165 E 3
Bontekoe Ø ⌒ GRØ 26-27 p 7
Bonthe o WAL 202-203 D 6
Bontoc ☆ RP 160-161 D 4
Bontoc Point ▲ RP 160-161 E 6
Bontosunggu o RI 164-165 F 6
Bontosunggu-Jeneponto o RI 164-165 F 6
Bonvouloir Islands ⌒ PNG 183 F 6
Bon Wier o USA (TX) 268-269 G 6
Bonyere o GH 202-203 J 7
Bonyhád o H 92-93 P 5
Bonzan o BF 202-203 J 4
Boo, Kepulauan ⌒ RI 166-167 E 2
Boobare o AUS 178-179 H 4
Boodi Boodi Range ▲ AUS 176-177 G 2
Bookaloo o AUS 178-179 D 6
Booker o USA (TX) 264-265 D 2
Booko o CI 202-203 G 5
Boola o RG 202-203 F 5
Boolardy o AUS 176-177 D 3
Boolba o AUS 178-179 K 4
Booligal o AUS 180-181 H 2
Booltharda Hill ▲ AUS 176-177 D 3
Boomarra o AUS 174-175 F 6
Boomi River ~ AUS 178-179 K 5
Boonah o AUS 178-179 M 4
Bööncagaan nuur ⊖ MAU 148-149 D 5
Boondooma Reservoir ⊖ AUS 178-179 L 4
Boone o USA (CO) 254-255 L 5
Boone o USA (IA) 274-275 E 2
Boone o USA (NC) 282-283 F 4
Boone Reservoir ⊖ USA (TN) 282-283 E 4
Boone River ~ USA (IA) 274-275 E 2
Booneville o USA (AR) 276-277 B 5
Booneville o USA (KY) 276-277 M 3
Booneville o USA (MS) 268-269 M 2
Boongaree Island ⌒ AUS 172-173 G 3
Boonsboro o USA (MD) 280-281 J 4
Boonville o USA (CA) 246-247 B 4
Boonville o USA (IN) 274-275 L 6
Boonville o USA (MO) 274-275 F 6
Boonville o USA (NY) 278-279 F 5
Boopi, Río ~ BOL 70-71 D 4
Boorabbin o AUS 176-177 F 5
Boorabbin National Park ⊥ AUS 176-177 F 5
Boorama o SP 208-209 F 4
Bööròg Dèlijn Èls ≐ MAU 116-117 F 10
Booroondara, Mount ▲ AUS 178-179 H 6
Boorowa o AUS 180-181 K 3
Boort o AUS 180-181 G 4
Boosaaso = Bender Qaasim ☆ SP 208-209 J 3
Boothbay Harbor o USA (ME) 278-279 M 5
Boothby, Cape ▲ ARK 16 G 6
Boothby, Mount ▲ AUS 180-181 E 3
Boothia, Gulf of ≈ 24-25 a 5
Boothia Isthmus ⌣ CDN 24-25 Z 6
Boothia Peninsula ⌣ CDN 24-25 Y 5
Booth Islands ⌒ CDN 24-25 J 5
Booth's River ~ BH 52-53 K 3
Boothulla o AUS 178-179 H 4
Booti Booti National Park ⊥ AUS 180-181 M 2
Boot Key ⌒ USA (FL) 286-287 H 7
Booué o G 210-211 C 4
Booylgoo Spring o AUS 176-177 E 3
Bopa o DY 202-203 L 6
Bopako o ZRE 210-211 H 3
Bophuthatswana (former Homel., now part of North-West) ◻ ZA 220-221 F 3
Bopo o WAN 204-205 G 5
Boqên o VRC 144-145 K 5
Boqueirão o BR (ACR) 64-65 F 5
Boqueirão o BR (BAH) 68-69 G 7
Boqueirão o BR (GSU) 76-77 J 1
Boqueirão o BR (PA) 68-69 K 5
Boqueirão, Serra do ▲ BR 68-69 G 7
Boqueirão, Serra do ▲ BR 72-73 H 2
Boqueirão, Serra do ▲ BR 76-77 K 5
Boqueirão Cesário o BR 68-69 J 4
Boquerón o C 54-55 H 5
Boquerón o USA (PR) 286-287 O 2
Boqueron o YV 60-61 G 3
Boquerón, Playa ≐ USA (PR) 286-287 O 2
Boquete, Cerro ▲ RA 78-79 E 7
Boquilla, Presa de la < MEX 50-51 G 4
Boquilla del Conchos, La o MEX 50-51 G 4
Boquillas o USA (TX) 266-267 E 4
Boquillas del Carmen o MEX 50-51 H 3
Boquira o BR 72-73 J 2
Bor o RUS 116-117 E 5
Bor o RUS (GOR) 96-97 D 5
Bor o SUD 206-207 K 5
Bor ☆· TR 128-129 F 4
Bor, Lagh ~ EAK 212-213 G 2
Bora ▲ ETH 200-201 J 6
Bora o PNG 183 B 4
Bora o SUD 206-207 H 4
Borabu o THA 158-159 G 2
Borabu Park ⊥· THA 158-159 G 2
Boracho Peak ▲ USA (TX) 266-267 C 3
Borah Peak ▲ USA (ID) 252-253 D 2
Boraldaj ~ KA 136-137 L 3
Boraldaj, žota ▲ KA 136-137 L 3
Borang, Tanjung ▲ RI 166-167 G 4
Borås ☆ S 86-87 F 8
Borāzjān o IR 134-135 D 4
Borba o BR 66-67 H 5
Borbon o RP 160-161 F 7
Borbón o YV 60-61 J 4
Borborema, Planalto da ≐ BR 68-69 K 5
Borçka ☆ TR 128-129 J 2
Borde Alto del Payún ▲ RA 78-79 E 4
Bordeaux ☆· F 90-91 G 9
Bordëbë o KS 136-137 N 5
Borden o AUS 176-177 E 7
Borden o CDN (PEI) 240-241 M 4
Borden o CDN (SAS) 232-233 L 3
Borden Island ⌒ CDN 24-25 Q 1
Borden Peninsula ⌣ CDN 24-25 e 4
Borden River ~ CDN 30-31 Z 3
Border o USA (WY) 252-253 H 4
Border, Pegunungan ▲ RI 166-167 L 3
Border City Lodge o USA 20-21 U 5
Bordertown o AUS 180-181 F 4
Borðeyri o IS 86-87 c 2
Bord Hûn-e Nou o IR 134-135 D 4
Bordighera o I 100-101 A 3
Bordj Bou Arreridj ☆ DZ 190-191 E 2
Bordj Bounaama o DZ 190-191 C 3
Bordj Flye Sainte Marie o DZ 188-189 K 7
Bordj Messouda o DZ 190-191 G 5
Bordj Mokhtar o DZ 196-197 L 4
Bordj Omar Driss o DZ 190-191 F 6
Bordo, El = Patía o CO 60-61 C 6
Bordoloni o IND 142-143 J 2
Borë o ETH 208-209 D 5
Boré o RMM 202-203 J 2
Boreda o ETH 208-209 C 5
Borensberg o S 86-87 G 7
Boren Xuanguan ∴· VRC 156-157 D 2
Borgå = Porvoo o FIN 88-89 H 6
Borgampād o IND 142-143 B 7
Borgarfjörður o IS 86-87 g 2
Borgarnes ☆ IS 86-87 c 2
Børgefjellet ▲ N 86-87 F 4
Børgefjell nasjonalpark ⊥ N 86-87 F 4
Børgen, Kap ▲ GRØ 26-27 q 6
Borger o USA (TX) 264-265 C 3
Borgholm ☆· S 86-87 H 8
Borgi o IND 142-143 B 6
Borgia, De o USA (MT) 250-251 D 4
Borg Jøkel Bræ ⊂ GRØ 26-27 n 5
Borg Massif = Borgmassivet ▲ ARK 16 F 36
Borgne, Lake ⊖ USA (MS) 268-269 L 6
Borgne, Le o RH 54-55 J 5
Borgomanero o I 100-101 B 2
Borgo San Lorenzo o I 100-101 C 3
Borgou ◻ RT 202-203 L 4
Borgou ≐ DY 204-205 E 3
Borgu Game Reserve ⊥ WAN 204-205 E 3
Borgund o N 86-87 C 6
Borgund stavkirke ·· N 86-87 C 6
Borhojn-Tal o MAU 148-149 K 6
Bori o DY 204-205 E 4
Bori o IND 138-139 G 9
Bori o WAN 204-205 G 6
Boria Tibhu o IND 142-143 B 5
Borigumma o IND 142-143 C 6
Börili o KA 96-97 H 8
Borisoglebsk o RUS 102-103 N 2
Borisov = Barysav ☆ BY 94-95 L 4
Borisova, mys ▲ RUS 120-121 G 6
Borisovka o RUS 102-103 K 2
Borisovo-Sudskoe o RUS 94-95 P 2
Boriziny o RM 222-223 E 5
Borja o PE 64-65 D 4
Borj Bourguiba o TN 190-191 G 4
Borjhar o IND 138-139 E 8
Borj Jenein o TN 190-191 H 5
Borj Machened Salah o TN 190-191 H 4
Borj M'Chiguig o TN 190-191 H 5
Borj Slougui < TN 190-191 H 4
Borke o AFG 136-137 L 6
Borkou ≐ TCH 198-199 H 3
Borkou-Ennedi-Tibesti ◻ TCH 198-199 H 4
Borkum ⌒ D 92-93 J 2
Borlänge ☆ S 86-87 G 6
Borne o DZ 190-191 F 8
Borneo = Kalimantan ⌒ 164-165 B 4
Bornholm ⌒· DK 86-87 G 9
Bornholmsgattet ≈ 86-87 G 9
Borno ◻ WAN 198-199 E 6
Boro ~ RB 218-219 B 4
Boro ~ SUD 206-207 G 4
Borobudur ··· RI 168 D 3
Borodale Creek ~ AUS 176-177 G 4
Borodino o RUS 116-117 G 8
Borogoncy ☆· RUS 118-119 P 4
Borohoro Shan ▲ VRC 146-147 E 3
Borojó o YV 60-61 F 2
Boroko o RI 164-165 H 3
Borol ~ TCH 206-207 C 3
Borom o TCH 206-207 C 4
Boromata o RCA 206-207 E 3
Boromo o· BF 202-203 J 4
Boron o CI 202-203 H 5
Boron o RMM 202-203 G 2
Boron o USA (CA) 248-249 G 5
Bor-Öndör = Hèrlèn o MAU 148-149 J 4
Borong, hrebet ▲ RUS 110-111 V 6
Borònono o RM 222-223 E 5
Boronuk o RUS 110-111 T 6
Bororé o BR 76-77 K 5
Borovići ☆ RUS (PSK) 94-95 L 3
Boroviči ☆ RUS (NVG) 94-95 N 2
Borovo o RUS 88-89 U 5
Borovoj o RUS 88-89 M 4
Borovsk ☆ RUS 94-95 P 4
Borovskoj ☆ KA 124-125 C 2
Borradaile o CDN (ALB) 232-233 H 2
Borrego Springs o USA (CA) 248-249 H 6
Borrero o EC 64-65 C 3
Borroloola X AUS 174-175 D 5
Borroloola Aboriginal Land X AUS 174-175 C 4
Borşa o RO 102-103 D 4
Borsad o IND 138-139 D 8
Borsa-kelmas Šuri ⊖ US 136-137 E 3
Borščevočnyj, hrebet ▲ RUS 118-119 H 10
Borskoe ☆ RUS 96-97 G 7

Bort-les-Orgues ○ F 90-91 J 9
Börtnan ○ S 86-87 F 5
Boru ○ RI 166-167 B 6
Boruambe ~ ZRE 210-211 F 5
Borūğen ○ • IR 134-135 D 3
Borūğerd ○ • IR 134-135 C 2
Borulah ~ RUS 110-111 U 6
Borulah ~ RUS 118-119 O 5
Borups Corners ○ CDN (ONT) 234-235 L 5
Bor-Üzuur ○ MAU 146-147 L 3
Bory, Tianguel- ○ RG 202-203 D 4
Boryspil' ○ UA 102-103 G 2
Borzja ★ RUS 118-119 H 10
Borzja ~ RUS 118-119 G 10
Borzna ○ UA 102-103 H 2
Boržomi ○ • GE 126-127 E 7
Borzongijn Gov' ⊥ MAU 148-149 G 6
Borzova, zaliv ≈ RUS 108-109 J 3
Bosa ○ • I 100-101 B 4
Bosaga ○ KA 124-125 H 5
Bosanska Brod ○ BIH 100-101 G 2
Bosanska Krupa ○ BIH 100-101 F 2
Bosanski Novi ○ BIH 100-101 F 2
Bosanski Petrovac ○ BIH 100-101 F 2
Bosanski Šamac ○ BIH 100-101 G 2
Bosavi, Mount ▲ PNG 183 B 4
Boscobel ○ USA (WI) 274-275 H 1
Bosconia ○ CO 60-61 E 2
Bose ○ VRC 156-157 E 5
Bosencheve, Parque Nacional ⊥ MEX 52-53 D 2
Boset Terara ▲ ETH 208-209 D 4
Boshoek ○ ZA 220-221 H 2
Boshof ○ ZA 220-221 G 4
Bô Sinh ○ VN 156-157 C 6
Boskamp ○ SME 62-63 G 3
Boslanti ○ SME 62-63 G 3
Bosler ○ USA (WY) 252-253 N 5
Bosmediano ○ PE 64-65 F 4
Bosna ~ BIH 100-101 G 2
Bosnia and Herzegovina = Bosna i Hercegovina ■ BIH 100-101 F 2
Bosnik ○ RI 166-167 J 2
Bošnjakovo ○ RUS 122-123 K 4
Boso ○ ZRE 210-211 J 2
Bosobolo ○ ZRE 206-207 D 6
Bōsō-hanto ∪ J 152-153 H 7
Bososama ○ ZRE 206-207 E 6
Bosporus = İstanbul Boğazi ≈ 128-129 C 2
Bosporus = Karadeniz Boğazi ≈ 128-129 C 2
Bosque ○ USA (NM) 256-257 J 4
Bosque del Apache National Wildlife Refuge ⊥ • USA (NM) 256-257 H 5
Bošrūye ○ IR 134-135 G 2
Bossaga ○ TM 136-137 J 6
Bossangoa ★ RCA 206-207 C 5
Bossembélé ○ RCA 206-207 C 6
Bossentélé ○ RCA 206-207 C 6
Bossiekom ○ ZA 220-221 E 4
Bossier City ○ USA (LA) 268-269 G 4
Bossieslvei ○ NAM 220-221 C 2
Bosso ○ RN 198-199 F 6
Bosso ~ RN 204-205 E 1
Bosso, Dallol ~ BF 204-205 E 2
Bossut, Cape ▲ AUS 172-173 E 5
Bostān ○ IR 134-135 B 3
Bostan ○ VRC 144-145 E 2
Bostānābād ○ IR 128-129 M 4
Bostankum ⊥ KA 126-127 K 6
Bosten Hu • VRC 146-147 H 5
Boston ○ GB 90-91 G 5
Boston ○ USA (GA) 284-285 G 6
Boston ★ • USA (MA) 278-279 K 6
Boston Bar ○ CDN (BC) 230-231 H 4
Boston Mountains ▲ USA (AR) 276-277 A 5
Bostonnais, Rivière ~ CDN (QUE) 240-241 C 3
Bosumba ~ ZRE 210-211 G 3
Bosumtwi, Lake ⊂ GH 202-203 K 6
Boswell ○ CDN (BC) 230-231 N 4
Boswell ○ USA (OK) 264-265 J 4
Botād ○ IND 138-139 C 8
Botafogo ○ BR 66-67 B 5
Botalón, El ○ YV 60-61 F 2
Botan Çayı ~ TR 128-129 K 4
Botany Bay ≈ 180-181 L 2
Botare ○ RI 166-167 G 3
Botata ○ LB 202-203 F 6
Bote ○ IND 138-139 E 10
Boteka ○ ZRE 210-211 G 4
Botemola ○ ZRE 210-211 G 5
Boteti ~ RB 218-219 B 5
Botev ▲ BG 102-103 D 6
Botha ○ CDN (ALB) 232-233 F 3
Bothasberg ▲ ZA 220-221 J 3
Bothaville ○ ZA 220-221 H 3
Bothell ○ USA (WA) 244-245 C 3
Bothwell ○ AUS 180-181 J 7
Botija, Ilha da ⌒ BR 66-67 F 4
Botijón ○ YV 60-61 J 3
Botín, El ○ YV 60-61 F 2
Botitembongo ○ ZRE 210-211 G 4
Botkul', ozero ○ RUS 96-97 E 9
Botlih ○ RUS 126-127 G 6
Bot Makak ○ CAM 210-211 C 2
Botolan ○ RP 160-161 D 5
Botomoju ~ RUS 118-119 J 4
Botopasi ○ SME 62-63 G 3
Botoşani ★ • RO 102-103 E 4
Botou ○ BF (EST) 202-203 L 3
Botou ○ BF (EST) 204-205 E 2
Botou ○ VRC 154-155 K 2
Botro ○ CI 202-203 H 6
Botswana ■ RB 218-219 B 6
Bottenhavet ≈ 86-87 J 6
Bottenviken ≈ 86-87 L 4
Botterkloof ▲ ZA 220-221 D 5
Bottineau ○ USA (ND) 258-259 G 3
Bottle Creek ○ GB 54-55 K 4
Botuali ○ ZRE 210-211 F 4
Botucatu ○ BR 72-73 F 7
Botulu ○ • RUS 118-119 J 3
Botumirim ○ BR 72-73 J 4
Botuobuja, Ulahan ~ RUS 118-119 E 5
Botwood ○ CDN (NFL) 242-243 N 3
Bou ~ CI 202-203 H 5
Bou ○ RI 164-165 G 3
Bouaflé ★ CI 202-203 H 6
Bou Akba < DZ 188-189 H 6
Bouaké ★ • CI 202-203 H 6
Boû Aleb < RIM 196-197 F 6
Boualem ○ DZ 190-191 C 4
Bou Ali ○ DZ 188-189 L 7
Bou Ali, Oued ~ DZ 190-191 D 5
Bou-Allala, Hassi < DZ 188-189 K 5
Bouam ○ CAM 204-205 K 6
Bouânane ○ MA 188-189 K 4
Bouandougou ∪ CI 202-203 H 5
Bouanri ○ DY 204-205 E 3
Bouansa ○ RCB 210-211 D 6
Bouar ★ • RCA 206-207 B 6
Bouârfa ○ MA 188-189 L 4
Bouârfa, Jbel ▲ MA 188-189 L 4
Bouba Ndjida, Parc National de ⊥ CAM 206-207 B 4
Boubela ○ CI 202-203 G 7
Bou Bernous, Hassi < DZ 188-189 K 7
Boubon ○ RN 202-203 L 3
Boubouri ○ CI 202-203 H 7
Bouca ○ RCA 206-207 D 5
Boucaut Bay ≈ 174-175 C 2
Bouchard ○ RA 78-79 H 3
Bouchette, Lac- ○ CDN (QUE) 240-241 C 2
Bouchie Lake ○ CDN (BC) 228-229 M 3
Bouchouaymiy ○ MA 196-197 B 2
Boucle du Baoulé, Parc National de la ⊥ RMM 202-203 F 2
Boû Çtaïla ○ RIM 196-197 F 7
Boudamassa ○ TCH 206-207 C 3
Boudbouda < RIM 196-197 C 5
Boudenib ○ MA 188-189 K 5
Boudeuse Cay ⌒ SY 224 C 3
Boû Dîb ○ RIM 196-197 F 5
Boudiéri ○ BF 202-203 K 3
Boû Djébéha < RMM 196-197 J 5
Boudo ○ ANG 216-217 E 8
Boudoua ○ RCA 206-207 C 6
Boudtenga ○ BF 202-203 K 3
Boudinguidi ~ G 210-211 D 4
Bouenza ■ RCB 210-211 D 6
Bouenza ~ RCB 210-211 D 5
Bougaa ○ DZ 190-191 E 2
Boû Gâdoûm ○ RIM (HCH) 196-197 G 7
Boû Gâdoûm ○ RIM (HCH) 202-203 G 2
Bougainville, Cape ▲ AUS 172-173 H 2
Bougainville, Cape ▲ GB 78-79 L 6
Bougainville Island ⌒ PNG 184 I b 2
Bougainville Reef ⌒ AUS 174-175 J 4
Bougainville Strait ≈ 184 I c 2
Bougainville Trench ≃ 183 G 3
Bougaroun, Cap ▲ DZ 190-191 F 2
Boughessa ○ RMM 196-197 M 4
Bougouï ○ RCA 206-207 B 5
Bougouni ○ RMM 202-203 G 4
Bougouriba ~ BF 202-203 J 4
Bougouso ○ CI 202-203 G 5
Bougtob ○ DZ 190-191 C 3
Bouguer, Cape ▲ AUS 180-181 D 4
Boû Guettâra < RIM 196-197 C 5
Bou Hadjar ○ DZ 190-191 G 2
Bou Iblane, Jbel ▲ MA 188-189 J 4
Bou-Izakarn ○ MA 188-189 G 6
Boujad ○ MA 188-189 H 4
Boujdour ○ MA 188-189 D 7
Boujdour, Cap ▲ MA 188-189 D 7
Bou Kadir ○ DZ 190-191 C 2
Bou Kahil, Djebel ▲ DZ 190-191 D 3
Boukān ○ IR 128-129 M 4
Bou Kouture, Jbel ▲ MA 188-189 K 3
Boukoko ○ RCA 210-211 F 2
Boukoula ○ CAM 204-205 K 3
Boukoumbé ○ DY 202-203 L 4
Boukra ○ MA 188-189 E 7
Bou Ladiab, Jebel ▲ TN 190-191 H 4
Boulai-Ibib ○ CAM 204-205 K 5
Boulal ○ RMM 202-203 F 2
Boulal ○ SN 202-203 C 2
Boû Lanouâr ○ RIM 196-197 B 4
Boulâouane • MA 188-189 G 4
Boulder ○ USA (CO) 254-255 K 3
Boulder ○ USA (MT) 250-251 G 5
Boulder ○ USA (UT) 254-255 D 6
Boulder ○ USA (WY) 252-253 J 4
Boulder, Kalgoorli- ○ AUS 176-177 F 5
Boulder City ○ USA (NV) 248-249 K 4
Boulder Creek ○ USA (CA) 248-249 B 2
Boulel ○ RMM 202-203 H 2
Boulel ○ SN 202-203 C 2
Boulemane ★ MA 188-189 J 4
Boulgou ○ BF 202-203 L 3
Bouli ~ DY 204-205 E 3
Bouli ○ RIM 196-197 E 7
Boulia ○ AUS 178-179 E 2
Boulogne-sur-Mer ○ • F 90-91 H 6
Bouloüba ○ RCA 206-207 E 5
Boulouli ○ RMM 202-203 F 3
Boulsa ○ BF 202-203 K 3
Boulsmail ○ DZ 190-191 D 2
Boultoum ○ RN 198-199 E 5
Boumaine-du-Dades ○ MA 188-189 J 5
Boumango ○ G 210-211 D 5
Boumba ~ CAM 210-211 E 2
Boumbé I ~ RCA 206-207 B 6
Boumbé II ~ CAM 206-207 B 6
Boumbia ○ CI 202-203 G 7
Boumboum ○ RMM 202-203 K 2
Boumba National Park ⊥ AUS 180-181 K 4
Boûmdeïd ○ RIM 196-197 E 6
Boumerdes ★ DZ 190-191 D 2
Bou Mertala < RIM 196-197 F 6
Boumia ○ MA 188-189 J 4
Boum Kabir ○ TCH 206-207 D 3
Bou Mréga < RIM 196-197 E 6
Bouna ★ CI 202-203 J 5
Bou Naceur, Jbel ▲ MA 188-189 K 4
Boû Nâga ○ RIM 196-197 D 5
Boû Nâga < RMM 196-197 J 6
Boundary ○ CDN 32-33 E 3
Boundary ○ USA (WA) 244-245 H 2
Boundary Mountains ▲ USA (ME) 278-279 L 3
Boundary Peak ▲ USA (CA) 248-249 F 2
Boundary Plateau ▲ CDN (SAS) 232-233 J 6
Boundary Ranges ▲ CDN 32-33 E 3
Boundiali ★ CI 202-203 G 5
Boundji ○ G 210-211 D 4
Boundji ○ RCB 210-211 E 4
Boungo ~ RCA 206-207 F 4
Boungou ~ RCA 206-207 E 5
Boungu ○ RCA 206-207 F 5
Bouniandjé ~ G 210-211 D 3
Bounkiling ○ SN 202-203 C 3
Bounoum ~ SN 202-203 C 2
Bountiful ○ USA (UT) 254-255 D 3
Bountiful Islands ⌒ AUS 174-175 E 5
Bounty Islands ⌒ NZ 13 J 7
Bounty Plateau ≃ 13 J 7
Bounty Trough ≃ 13 J 7
Bouquet ○ RA 78-79 J 2
Boura ○ BF 202-203 J 4
Bourarhet, Erg ⊥ DZ 190-191 G 7
Bourbeuse River ~ USA (MO) 274-275 G 6
Bourbonnais ⊥ F 90-91 J 8
Bourdel, Lac ⊂ CDN 36-37 M 6
Bourem ○ RMM 196-197 K 6
Bourg, Lac ⊂ CDN 36-37 N 6
Bourg-en-Bresse ★ • F 90-91 K 8
Bourges ★ ••• F 90-91 J 8
Bourgogne ■ F 90-91 J 8
Bourgogne ⊥ F 90-91 K 8
Bourgoin-Jallieu ○ F 90-91 K 9
Bourg-Saint-Maurice ○ F 90-91 L 9
Bouria ★ DZ 190-191 D 2
Boû Rjeïmât < RIM 196-197 C 5
Bourke ○ AUS 178-179 H 6
Bournemouth ○ GB 90-91 G 6
Bourou ○ TCH 206-207 C 4
Bouroum ○ BF 202-203 K 3
Bourrah ○ CAM 204-205 K 3
Bourzanga ○ BF 202-203 K 3
Bous, Adrar ▲ RN 198-199 D 2
Bou Saada ○ • DZ 190-191 E 3
Bouse ○ USA (AZ) 256-257 B 5
Bou Sellam ~ DZ 190-191 E 2
Bou Sfer ○ DZ 188-189 L 3
Boussé ○ BF 202-203 K 3
Boussemghoun ○ DZ 190-191 C 4
Bousso ○ TCH 206-207 C 3
Bousso River ~ CDN 30-31 M 4
Boussouma ○ BF 202-203 K 3
Boutilimit ○ RIM 196-197 C 6
Boutougou Fara ○ SN 202-203 D 3
Boutourou, Monts ▲ CI 202-203 J 5
Bouza ○ RN 198-199 C 5
Bouzghaïa ★ DZ 190-191 C 2
Bovill ○ USA (ID) 250-251 C 5
Bovina ○ USA (TX) 264-265 B 4
Bowbells ○ USA (ND) 258-259 E 3
Bow City ○ CDN (ALB) 232-233 F 5
Bowden ○ CDN (ALB) 232-233 D 4
Bowdle ○ USA (SD) 260-261 G 1
Bowdon ○ USA (GA) 284-285 E 3
Bowdon ○ USA (ND) 258-259 H 4
Bowell ○ CDN (ALB) 232-233 H 5
Bowell Islands ⌒ CDN 30-31 W 3
Bowen ○ AUS 174-175 K 7
Bowen ○ RA 78-79 E 3
Bowen ○ USA (IL) 274-275 G 4
Bowen, Cape ▲ AUS 174-175 H 4
Bowens Island ○ CDN (BC) 230-231 F 4
Bowens Hill ○ USA (GA) 284-285 F 5
Bowenville ○ AUS 178-179 L 4
Bowers Basin ≃ 22-23 E 5
Bowers Ridge ≃ 22-23 E 5
Bowie ○ USA (AZ) 256-257 F 6
Bowie ○ USA (MD) 280-281 K 5
Bowie ○ USA (TX) 264-265 G 5
Bowie National Historic Site, Fort • USA (AZ) 256-257 F 6
Bow Island ○ CDN (ALB) 232-233 G 6
Bowler ○ USA (WI) 270-271 K 6
Bowling Green ○ USA (FL) 286-287 H 4
Bowling Green ○ USA (KY) 276-277 J 4
Bowling Green ○ USA (MO) 274-275 G 5
Bowling Green ○ USA (OH) 280-281 C 2
Bowling Green ○ USA (VA) 280-281 J 5
Bowling Green Bay ≈ 174-175 J 6
Bowling Green Bay National Park ⊥ AUS 174-175 J 6
Bowman ○ USA (GA) 284-285 G 2
Bowman ○ USA (ND) 258-259 D 5
Bowman Bay ≈ 36-37 N 2
Bowman Island ⌒ ARK 16 G 11
Bowmans Corner ○ USA (MT) 250-251 G 4
Bowmanville ○ CDN (ONT) 238-239 G 5
Bowokan, Kepulauan ⌒ RI 164-165 H 5
Bowral ○ AUS 180-181 L 3
Bow River ~ AUS 172-173 J 4
Bow River ~ CDN (ALB) 232-233 E 5
Bowron Lake Provincial Park ⊥ CDN (BC) 228-229 N 3
Bowron Lake Provincial Park ⊥ CDN (BC) 228-229 O 3
Bowron River ~ CDN (BC) 228-229 N 3
Bowser ○ CDN (BC) 230-231 E 4
Bowsman ○ CDN (MAN) 234-235 B 2
Bowutu Mountains ▲ PNG 183 D 4
Bow Valley Provincial Park ⊥ CDN (ALB) 232-233 C 4
Boxwood ○ Z 218-219 D 3
Boxborough ○ USA (MA) 278-279 K 6
Boxelder ○ USA (TX) 264-265 K 5
Box Elder Creek ~ USA (MT) 250-251 L 4
Box Elder Creek ~ USA (MT) 250-251 P 6
Box Lake ⊂ CDN 30-31 Q 6
Boxwood Hill ○ AUS 176-177 E 7
Boyabat ○ TR 128-129 F 2
Boyabo ○ ZRE 210-211 G 2
Boyacá ○ CO (BOL) 60-61 D 3
Boyacá ○ CO (BOY) 60-61 E 5
Boyang ○ VRC 156-157 K 2
Boyce ○ USA (LA) 268-269 H 5
Boyce Thompson Arboretum • USA (AZ) 256-257 D 5
Boyd ○ CDN 34-35 H 3
Boyd ○ USA (MT) 250-251 K 6
Boyd, Lac ⊂ CDN 38-39 F 2
Boyd Lake ⊂ CDN 30-31 S 5
Boyd River ~ AUS 178-179 M 5
Boyds ○ USA (WA) 244-245 G 2
Boyellé ○ RCB 210-211 G 2
Boyero ○ USA (CO) 254-255 M 5
Boyer River ~ CDN 30-31 L 6
Boyer River ~ USA (IA) 274-275 C 3
Boykin ○ USA (AL) 284-285 C 4
Boykins ○ USA (VA) 280-281 J 7
Boyle ○ CDN 32-33 O 4
Boyle = Mainistir na Búille ○ IRL 90-91 C 5
Boylston ○ CDN (NS) 240-241 O 5
Boyne ○ ZA 218-219 E 6
Boyne City ○ USA (MI) 272-273 E 2
Boyne Valley ••• IRL 90-91 D 5
Boynton Beach ○ USA (FL) 286-287 J 5
Boyolali ○ RI 168 D 3
Boy River ○ USA (MN) 270-271 D 3
Boysen Reservoir ⊂ USA (WY) 252-253 K 3
Boys Ranch ○ USA (TX) 264-265 B 3
Boyte ○ CDN 32-33 O 4
Boyuibe ○ BOL 70-71 F 7
Boyup Brook ○ AUS 176-177 D 6
Bozburun ○ TR 128-129 C 4
Bozcaada ⌒ TR 128-129 B 3
Bozdağlar ▲ TR 128-129 B 3
Božedomova, mys ▲ RUS 120-121 T 3
Bozeman ○ USA (MT) 250-251 H 6
Bozeman Pass ▲ USA (MT) 250-251 J 6
Bozen = Bolzano ★ I 100-101 C 1
Bozene ○ ZRE 210-211 G 2
Bozġān ○ IR 136-137 F 6
Bozhou ○ VRC 154-155 J 5
Bozkır ★ TR 128-129 E 4
Bozkól ○ KA 126-127 O 5
Bozok Yaylâsı ▲ TR 128-129 F 3
Bozoum ★ • RCA 206-207 C 5
Bozova ★ TR 128-129 H 4
Bozüyük ★ TR 128-129 D 3
Bozyazı ★ TR 128-129 E 4
Brabant, Île ⌒ ARK 16 G 30
Brač ⌒ HR 100-101 F 3
Bracciano, Lago di ⊂ I 100-101 D 3
Bracebridge ○ CDN (ONT) 238-239 F 3
Bräcke ○ S 86-87 G 5
Bracken ○ CDN (SAS) 232-233 K 6
Brackendale ○ CDN (BC) 230-231 F 4
Brackett Lake ⊂ CDN 30-31 G 3
Brackettville ○ USA (TX) 266-267 G 4
Bracknell ○ GB 90-91 G 6
Braćavka ○ RUS 124-125 B 3
Braço do Lontra ~ BR 68-69 C 4
Braço do Norte ○ BR 74-75 F 7
Braço Menor do Araguaia ou Jauaés ~ BR 68-69 D 7
Brad ○ RO 102-103 C 4
Brad ○ USA (TX) 264-265 F 6
Brádano ~ I 100-101 E 4
Braddock ○ USA (ND) 258-259 G 5
Braddyville ○ USA (IA) 274-275 C 4
Bradenton ○ USA (FL) 286-287 G 4
Bradford ○ CDN (ONT) 238-239 F 4
Bradford ○ GB 90-91 G 5
Bradford ○ USA (AR) 276-277 D 5
Bradford ○ USA (IL) 274-275 J 3
Bradford ○ USA (PA) 280-281 H 2
Bradford ○ USA (VT) 278-279 J 4
Bradley ○ USA (AR) 276-277 B 7
Bradley ○ USA (CA) 248-249 D 4
Bradley ○ USA (SC) 284-285 H 2
Bradleyville ○ USA (MO) 276-277 C 4
Bradore, Baie ≈ 38-39 Q 3
Bradshaw ○ USA (NE) 262-263 J 4
Bradshaw ○ USA (TX) 264-265 E 6
Bradwardine ○ CDN (MAN) 234-235 C 5
Bradwell ○ CDN (SAS) 232-233 M 4
Brady ○ USA (MT) 250-251 H 3
Brady ○ USA (TX) 266-267 H 2
Brady Creek ~ USA (TX) 266-267 H 2
Brady Glacier ⊂ USA 32-33 B 2
Brady Reservoir < USA (TX) 266-267 H 2
Braemar ○ AUS 180-181 E 2
Braemar ○ GB 90-91 F 3
Braga ○ •• P 98-99 C 4
Bragado ○ RA 78-79 J 3
Bragança ○ BR 68-69 E 2
Bragança ○ P 98-99 D 4
Bragança Paulista ○ BR 72-73 G 7
Bragg, Fort ○ USA (CA) 246-247 B 4
Bragg Creek ○ CDN (ALB) 232-233 D 5
Braham ○ USA (MN) 270-271 E 5
Brahestad ○ FIN 88-89 H 4
Brahim, Hassi < MA 188-189 G 6
Brahmani ~ IND 142-143 D 5
Brahmapur ○ IND 142-143 D 6
Brahmaputra ~ 142-143 H 2
Braidwood ○ AUS 180-181 K 3
Brăila ★ • RO 102-103 E 5
Brainard ○ CDN 32-33 L 4
Brainerd ○ USA (MN) 270-271 D 4
Braintree ○ GB 90-91 H 6
Brajarājnagar ○ IND 142-143 C 5
Braka ⊂ RIM 196-197 D 6
Brakpan ○ NAM 220-221 D 2
Brakpan ○ ZA 220-221 J 3
Brakspruit ○ ZA 220-221 H 3
Brakwater ○ NAM 216-217 D 11
Bralorne ○ CDN (BC) 230-231 G 3
Brālos ○ GR 100-101 J 5
Bramhapuri ○ IND 138-139 G 9
Brampton ○ CDN (ONT) 238-239 F 5
Brampton Islands ⌒ AUS 174-175 K 7
Bramwell ○ AUS 174-175 G 3
Branca, Serra ▲ BR 68-69 F 5
Brancepeth ○ CDN (SAS) 232-233 N 2
Branch ○ CDN (NFL) 242-243 P 6
Branch Creek ~ AUS 174-175 E 6
Branchville ○ USA (SC) 284-285 K 3
Branco, Ilhéu ⌒ CV 202-203 B 5
Branco, Rio ~ BR 62-63 D 4
Branco, Rio ~ BR 66-67 B 5
Branco, Rio ~ BR 66-67 B 5
Branco, Rio ~ BR 66-67 F 4
Branco, Rio ~ BR 66-67 E 7
Branco, Rio ~ BR 68-69 F 7
Branco, Rio ~ BR 70-71 F 3
Branco, Rio ~ BR 70-71 G 2
Branco, Rio ~ BR 70-71 H 2
Branco ou Cabixi, Rio ~ BR 70-71 G 3
Brandberg •• NAM 216-217 C 10
Brandberg Wes ○ NAM 216-217 C 10
Brandbu ★ N 86-87 E 6
Brande ○ DK 86-87 D 9
Brandenburg ■ D 92-93 M 3
Brandenburg ○ USA (KY) 276-277 J 3
Brandenburg an der Havel ○ • D 92-93 M 2
Brandenton Beach ○ USA (FL) 286-287 G 4
Brandfort ○ ZA 220-221 H 4
Brandon ○ CDN (MAN) 234-235 D 5
Brandon ○ USA (FL) 286-287 G 4
Brandon ○ USA (MN) 270-271 C 5
Brandon ○ USA (MS) 268-269 L 4
Brandon ○ USA (SD) 260-261 K 3
Brandon ○ USA (VT) 278-279 H 5
Brandsen ○ RA 78-79 K 3
Brandvlei ○ ZA 220-221 E 5
Brandýs nad Labem-Stará Boleslav ○ CZ 92-93 N 3
Brandywine ○ USA (MD) 280-281 K 5
Branford ○ USA (FL) 286-287 G 2
Brang, Kuala ○ MAL 162-163 E 2
Braniewo ○ • PL 92-93 P 1
Br'anka ○ UA 102-103 L 3
Branqueada do Salto ○ BR 74-75 D 9
Bransan ○ SN 202-203 D 3
Bransfield Strait ≈ 16 G 30
Branson ○ USA (CO) 254-255 M 6
Branson ○ USA (MO) 276-277 B 4
Brant ○ CDN (ALB) 232-233 E 5
Brantford ○ CDN (ONT) 238-239 E 5
Brantley ○ USA (AL) 284-285 D 5
Brantôme ○ F 90-91 H 9
Brantville ○ CDN (NB) 240-241 L 3
Brás ○ BR 66-67 H 4
Bras d'Or Lake ⊂ CDN (NS) 240-241 P 5
Brasil ○ C 54-55 G 4
Brasilândia ○ BR 72-73 D 6
Brasiléia ○ BR 70-71 C 2
Brasília ★ ••• BR 72-73 G 3
Brasília, Lago de ⊂ BR 72-73 G 3
Brasília de Minas ○ BR 72-73 H 4
Braslândia ○ BR 72-73 F 3
Braslav ○ BY 94-95 K 4
Brasnorte ○ BR 70-71 H 2
Braşov ★ •• RO 102-103 D 5
Brass ○ WAN 204-205 G 6
Brasschaat ○ B 92-93 H 3
Brassey, Banjaran ▲ MAL 160-161 B 10
Brassey, Mount ▲ AUS 178-179 C 2
Brassey Range ▲ AUS 176-177 G 2
Brasstown Bald ▲ USA (GA) 284-285 G 2
Brastagi ○ • RI 162-163 C 3
Bratislava ★ •• SK 92-93 O 4
Bratovoești ○ RO 102-103 C 5
Bratsk ★ RUS 116-117 K 7
Bratskoe vodohranilišče < RUS 116-117 K 8
Bratskoye Vodokhranilishche = Bratskoe vodohranilišče < RUS 116-117 K 8
Brattleboro ○ USA (VT) 278-279 J 6
Braulio Carrillo, Parque Nacional ⊥ CR 52-53 C 6
Braúnas ○ BR 72-73 J 5
Braunau am Inn ○ A 92-93 M 4
Braunlage ○ D 92-93 L 3
Braunschweig ○ •• D 92-93 L 2
Brava, Ilha ⌒ CV 202-203 B 6
Brava, La ○ RA 76-77 G 6
Brava, Laguna la ⊂ RA 78-79 H 2
Bravo, Cerro ▲ BOL (COC) 70-71 E 5
Bravo, Cerro ▲ BOL (POT) 76-77 D 2
Bravo, Cerro ▲ RCH 76-77 C 4
Bravo, El ○ RA 76-77 F 4
Bravo del Norte, Río ~ MEX 50-51 J 3
Bravo River ~ BH 52-53 K 3
Brawley ○ USA (CA) 248-249 J 7
Bray ○ USA (CA) 246-247 D 2
Bray ○ ZA 220-221 F 2
Bray = Bré ○ IRL 90-91 D 5
Bray Island ⌒ CDN 24-25 h 6
Bray-sur-Seine ○ F 90-91 J 7
Brazeau, Mount ▲ CDN (ALB) 228-229 R 4
Brazeau Reservoir < CDN (ALB) 232-233 C 3
Brazeau River ~ CDN (ALB) 228-229 R 4
Brazeau River ~ CDN (ALB) 232-233 C 3
Brazil ○ USA (IN) 274-275 L 5
Brazil = Brasil ■ BR 74-75 C 2
Brazil Basin = Brasil Basin ≃ 6-7 G 10
Brazilian Highlands = Brasileiro, Planalto ⊥ BR 72-73 G 3
Brazo Aná Cuá ~ PY 76-77 J 4
Brazo de Loba ~ CO 60-61 D 3
Brazos ○ USA (NM) 256-257 J 2
Brazos River ~ USA (TX) 264-265 E 5
Brazos River ~ USA (TX) 266-267 L 3
Brazo Sur del Río Coig ~ RA 80 E 5
Brazzaville ★ • RCB 210-211 E 6
Brčko ○ BIH 100-101 G 2
Brdy ▲ CZ 92-93 M 4
Bré = Bray ○ IRL 90-91 D 5
Brea, Cordillera de la ▲ RA 76-77 C 5
Brea, La ○ TT 60-61 L 2
Breaden, Lake ⊂ AUS 176-177 H 2
Breaksea Sound ≈ 182 A 6
Brea Pozo ○ RA 76-77 F 5
Breas, Las ○ RCH 76-77 B 5
Breaux Bridge ○ USA (LA) 268-269 J 6
Brebes ○ RI 168 C 3
Brechin ○ CDN (ONT) 238-239 F 4
Breckenridge ○ USA (CO) 254-255 J 4
Breckenridge ○ USA (MN) 270-271 B 4
Breckenridge ○ USA (TX) 264-265 F 6
Breckinridge Mountain ▲ USA (CA) 248-249 F 4
Brecknock, Península ∪ RCH 80 E 7
Brecon ○ • GB 90-91 F 6
Brecon Beacons National Park ⊥ GB 90-91 F 6
Breda ○ • NL 92-93 H 3
Bredasdorp ○ ZA 220-221 E 7
Bredbo ○ AUS 180-181 K 3
Bredbyn ○ S 86-87 J 5
Bredenbury ○ CDN (SAS) 232-233 Q 5
Brēdi, ostrov ⌒ RUS 84-85 d 2
Bredsel ○ S 86-87 K 4
Bredy ★ RUS 124-125 B 2
Breede ~ ZA 220-221 E 7
Breeza Plains Out Station ○ AUS 174-175 H 4
Bregalnica ~ MK 100-101 J 4
Bregenz ★ A 92-93 K 5
Bregovo ○ BG 102-103 C 5
Bréhal ○ F 90-91 G 7
Brehat ○ CDN (NFL) 242-243 N 1
Brehovskie ostrova ⌒ RUS 108-109 U 6
Breiðafjörður ≈ 86-87 b 2
Breien ○ USA (ND) 258-259 G 5
Breivikbotn ○ N 86-87 L 1
Brejão da Caatinga ○ BR 68-69 H 7
Brejo ○ BR 68-69 G 3
Brejo, Riachão do ~ BR 68-69 G 6
Brejo da Madre de Deus ○ BR 68-69 K 6
Brejo de São Félix ○ BR 68-69 G 4
Brejo do Cruz ○ BR 68-69 K 5
Brejo do Serra ○ BR 68-69 G 7
Brejo Grande ○ BR (CEA) 68-69 J 5
Brejo Grande ○ BR (SER) 68-69 K 7
Brejolândia ○ BR 72-73 J 2
Brejo Velho, Riachão ~ BR 72-73 J 2
Brekken ○ N 86-87 E 5
Brekstad ○ N 86-87 D 5
Brelen ○ USA (ND) 258-259 G 5
Bremangerlandet ⌒ N 86-87 B 6
Bremen ★ •• D 92-93 K 2
Bremen ○ USA (AL) 284-285 D 3
Bremen ○ USA (GA) 284-285 E 3
Bremen ○ USA (IN) 274-275 M 3
Bremen ○ USA (ND) 258-259 H 4
Bremer Bay ≈ 176-177 E 7
Bremer Bay ○ AUS 176-177 E 7
Bremerhaven ○ D 92-93 K 2
Bremer Island ⌒ AUS 174-175 D 3
Bremer Range ▲ AUS 176-177 F 6
Bremerton ○ USA (WA) 244-245 C 3
Bremervörde ○ D 92-93 K 2
Bremner ○ CDN (ALB) 232-233 E 2
Bremond ○ USA (TX) 266-267 L 2
Brenãs, Las ○ RA 76-77 G 4
Brenham ○ USA (TX) 266-267 L 3
Brennerpaß = Passo del Brennero ▲ A 92-93 L 5
Brennevinsfjorden ≈ 84-85 L 2
Brent ○ USA (AL) 284-285 C 4
Brenta ~ I 100-101 C 2
Brentford Bay ≈ 24-25 Z 5
Brentwood ○ USA (TN) 276-277 J 4
Brenzia ○ DZ 190-191 C 4
Brep ○ PK 138-139 D 1
Bresaylor ○ CDN (SAS) 232-233 K 3
Bréscia ○ • I 100-101 C 2
Bresnahan, Mount ▲ AUS 176-177 D 1
Bressanone = Brixen ○ I 100-101 C 1
Bressuire ○ F 90-91 G 8
Brèst ○ BY 94-95 H 5
Brest ○ F 90-91 E 7
Brest = Brèst ○ BY 94-95 H 5
Bretagne ■ F 90-91 E 7
Bretaña ○ PE 64-65 E 4
Breteuil ○ F 90-91 J 7
Breton, Cape ▲ CDN (NS) 240-241 Q 5
Breton, Playa El ⊥ • DOM 54-55 L 5
Breton Cove ○ CDN (NS) 240-241 P 4
Breton Island ⌒ USA (LA) 268-269 L 7
Breton National Wildlife Refuge ⊥ USA (LA) 268-269 M 7
Breton N. W. R. ⊥ USA (LA) 268-269 L 7
Breton Sound ≈ 48-49 D 5
Breton Sound ≈ USA 268-269 L 7
Brett, Cape ▲ NZ 182 E 1
Breueh, Pulau ⌒ RI 162-163 A 2
Brevard ○ USA (NC) 282-283 E 5
Breverville ○ LB 202-203 E 6
Breves ○ BR 62-63 J 6
Brevoort, Kap ▲ GRØ 26-27 U 3
Brevoort Island ⌒ CDN 36-37 R 3
Brevort ○ USA (MI) 270-271 N 4
Brewaniase ○ GH 202-203 L 5
Brewarrina ○ AUS 178-179 J 5
Brewer ○ CDN (SAS) 232-233 Q 4
Brewer ○ USA (ME) 278-279 N 4
Brewster ○ USA (KS) 262-263 E 5
Brewster ○ USA (NE) 262-263 G 3
Brewster ○ USA (NY) 280-281 N 2
Brewster ○ USA (WA) 244-245 F 2
Brewster, Lake ⊂ AUS 180-181 H 2
Brewton ○ USA (AL) 284-285 C 5
Breynat ○ CDN 32-33 O 4
Breyten ○ ZA 220-221 J 3
Brezina ○ DZ 190-191 C 4
Brežnev = Naberežnye Čelny ★ RUS 96-97 H 6
Brezovo Polje ▲ HR 100-101 F 2
Bria ★ RCA 206-207 E 5
Briakan ○ RUS 122-123 F 2
Briançon ○ • F 90-91 L 9
Brian Head ▲ USA (UT) 254-255 C 6
Briarton ○ USA (WI) 270-271 K 6
Bribie Island ⌒ AUS 178-179 M 4
Bribri ○ CR 52-53 C 7
Bričany = Briceni ★ MD 102-103 E 3
Bričen' = Briceni ★ MD 102-103 E 3
Briceni ★ MD 102-103 E 3
Brices Cross Roads National Battlefield Site ∴ USA (MS) 268-269 M 2
Briconnet, Lac ⊂ CDN 38-39 O 3
Bridal Cave ∴ USA (MO) 274-275 F 6
Bridesville ○ CDN (BC) 230-231 K 4
Bridge City ○ USA (TX) 268-269 G 6
Bridgeford ○ CDN (SAS) 232-233 M 5
Bridge Lake ○ CDN (BC) 230-231 J 2
Bridgenorth ○ CDN (ONT) 238-239 G 4
Bridge over the River Kwai • THA 158-159 E 3
Bridge Point ▲ BS 54-55 G 2
Bridgeport ○ USA (AL) 284-285 E 2
Bridgeport ○ USA (CA) 246-247 F 5
Bridgeport ○ USA (CT) 280-281 N 2
Bridgeport ○ USA (NE) 262-263 C 3
Bridgeport ○ USA (OH) 280-281 F 3
Bridgeport ○ USA (OR) 244-245 H 6
Bridgeport ○ USA (TX) 264-265 G 5
Bridgeport ○ USA (WA) 244-245 F 2
Bridgeport, Lake ⊂ USA (TX) 264-265 G 5
Bridger ○ USA (MT) 250-251 L 6
Bridge River ~ CDN (BC) 230-231 G 3
Bridge River Indian Reservation ✗ CDN (BC) 230-231 G 3
Bridger Peak ▲ USA (WY) 252-253 L 5
Bridger State Historic Site, Fort • USA (WY) 252-253 H 5
Bridger Wilderness Area ⊥ USA (WY) 252-253 J 4
Bridgeton ○ USA (NJ) 280-281 L 4
Bridgetown ○ AUS 176-177 D 6
Bridgetown ★ BDS 56 F 5
Bridgetown ○ CDN (NS) 240-241 K 6
Bridgeville ○ CDN (QUE) 240-241 L 2
Bridgeville ○ USA (CA) 246-247 B 3
Bridgewater ○ AUS (TAS) 180-181 J 7
Bridgewater ○ AUS (VIC) 180-181 G 4
Bridgewater ○ CDN (NS) 240-241 L 6
Bridgewater ○ USA (NY) 278-279 F 6
Bridgewater ○ USA (SD) 260-261 J 3
Bridgewater ○ USA (VA) 280-281 H 5
Bridgewater ○ ZA 218-219 E 6
Bridgewater, Cape ▲ AUS 180-181 F 5
Bridgman, Kap ▲ GRØ 26-27 m 2
Bridgton ○ USA (ME) 278-279 L 4
Bridlington ○ GB 90-91 G 4
Bridport ○ AUS 180-181 J 6
Bridport ○ GB 90-91 F 6
Bridport Inlet ≈ 24-25 R 3
Brie ⊥ • F 90-91 J 7
Brieg = Brzeg ○ • PL 92-93 O 3
Brier Creek ~ USA (GA) 284-285 H 3
Briercrest ○ CDN (SAS) 232-233 N 5
Brier Island ⌒ CDN (NS) 240-241 J 6
Brig ○ • CH 92-93 J 5
Brig Bay ○ CDN (NFL) 242-243 M 1
Briggs ○ USA (TX) 266-267 K 3
Briggs, Cape ▲ CDN 24-25 Y 4
Briggsdale ○ USA (CO) 254-255 L 3
Brigham City ○ USA (UT) 254-255 C 2
Bright ○ • AUS 180-181 J 4
Brighton ○ CDN (ONT) 238-239 H 4
Brighton ○ GB 90-91 G 6
Brighton ○ USA (AL) 284-285 C 3
Brighton ○ USA (CO) 254-255 L 4
Brighton ○ USA (FL) 286-287 H 4
Brighton ○ USA (IA) 274-275 G 3
Brighton ○ USA (IL) 274-275 H 5
Brighton ○ USA (IN) 274-275 N 3
Brighton ○ USA (MI) 272-273 F 5
Brighton Downs ○ AUS 178-179 F 2
Brighton Seminole Indian Reservation ✗ USA (FL) 286-287 H 4
Brightsand Lake ⊂ CDN (SAS) 232-233 K 2
Brightstar ○ USA (AR) 276-277 B 7
Brigida, Riachão ou ~ BR 68-69 J 6
Brignan ∪ CI 202-203 H 7
Brignoles ○ F 90-91 L 10
Brikama ○ WAG 202-203 B 3
Brilhante, Rio ~ BR 76-77 K 1
Brilon ○ D 92-93 K 3
Brimley ○ USA (MI) 270-271 O 4
Brimstone Hill Fortress ∴ KAN 56 D 3
Brinawa ○ AUS 174-175 E 6
Brinckheuvel, National Reservaat ⊥ SME 62-63 G 3
Brindakit ○ RUS 120-121 G 3
Bríndisi ★ • I 100-101 F 4
Brinkley ○ USA (AR) 276-277 D 6
Brinkleyville ○ USA (NC) 282-283 K 4
Brin-Navolok ○ RUS 88-89 Q 5
Brinnon ○ USA (WA) 244-245 C 3
Brion, Île ⌒ CDN (QUE) 242-243 G 5
Brisbane ★ • AUS 178-179 M 4
Brisbane ○ CDN (ONT) 238-239 E 5
Brisbane River ~ AUS 178-179 M 4
Brisco ○ CDN (BC) 230-231 N 3
Briscoe ○ USA (TX) 264-265 D 3
Brisson, Lac ⊂ CDN 36-37 R 6
Bristol ○ CDN (NB) 240-241 H 4
Bristol ○ • GB 90-91 F 6
Bristol ○ USA (CO) 254-255 N 5
Bristol ○ USA (CT) 280-281 O 2
Bristol ○ USA (FL) 286-287 E 1
Bristol ○ USA (GA) 284-285 H 5
Bristol ○ USA (IN) 274-275 N 3
Bristol ○ USA (MI) 272-273 D 3
Bristol ○ USA (SD) 260-261 J 1
Bristol ○ USA (TN) 282-283 E 4
Bristol ○ USA (VA) 280-281 D 7
Bristol ○ USA (VT) 278-279 H 4
Bristol Bay ≈ 22-23 Q 4
Bristol Channel ≈ 90-91 E 6
Bristol Lake ⊂ USA (CA) 248-249 J 5
Bristow ○ USA (OK) 264-265 H 3
Britânia ○ BR 72-73 E 3
Britannia ○ CDN (NFL) 242-243 P 4
Britannia, Mount ▲ CDN 24-25 Y 2
Britannia Beach ○ CDN (BC) 230-231 F 4
Britannia Range ▲ ARK 16 E 0
Britanskij kanal ≈ 84-85 b 2
British Columbia ■ CDN 32-33 F 3
British Empire Range ▲ CDN 26-27 K 2
British Mountains ▲ USA 20-21 U 2
British Virgin Islands ■ GB 56 C 2
Brito Godins ○ ANG 216-217 D 4
Brits ○ ZA 220-221 H 2
Britstown ○ ZA 220-221 F 5
Britt ○ USA (IA) 274-275 E 1
Britton ○ USA (SD) 260-261 J 1
Britvin, mys ▲ RUS 108-109 F 5
Brive-la-Gaillarde ○ F 90-91 H 9
Brixen = Bressanone ○ I 100-101 C 1
Brjanka = Br'anka ○ UA 102-103 L 3
Brjansk ○ RUS 94-95 O 5
Brjansk ○ RUS 126-127 G 5
Brjanskaja Kosa, mys ▲ RUS 126-127 G 5
Brjanskoe ○ RUS 122-123 K 5
Brjanta ~ RUS 118-119 N 8

Brjungjade ~ RUS 120-121 J 2
Brjusa, ostrov ⌒ RUS 84-85 b 2
Brno o CZ 92-93 O 4
Broa, Ensenada de la ≈ 54-55 D 3
Broadacres o CDN (SAS) 232-233 K 3
Broadalbin o USA (NY) 278-279 G 5
Broad Arrow ∴ AUS 176-177 F 5
Broadback Rivière ~ CDN (QUE) 236-237 M 2
Broadford o AUS 180-181 H 4
Broad Peak ▲ IND 138-139 F 2
Broad River ~ USA (GA) 284-285 H 3
Broad River ~ USA (GA) 284-285 G 2
Broad River ~ USA (SC) 284-285 J 2
Broad Sound ≈ 178-179 K 2
Broadsound Range ▲ AUS 178-179 K 2
Broadus o USA (MT) 250-251 O 6
Broadview o CDN (SAS) 232-233 Q 5
Broadview o USA (MT) 250-251 L 5
Broadview o USA (NM) 256-257 M 4
Broadview Acton o USA (MT) 250-251 L 5
Broadwater o USA (NE) 262-263 D 3
Broadway o USA (VA) 280-281 H 5
Brobo o CI 202-203 H 6
Brochant, Rivière ~ CDN 36-37 O 5
Brochet o CDN 34-35 F 2
Brochet, Lac o CDN 30-31 T 6
Brochet, Lac du o CDN 38-39 K 4
Brock o CDN (SAS) 232-233 K 4
Brocken ▲ D 92-93 L 3
Brocket o CDN (ALB) 232-233 E 6
Brocket o USA (ND) 258-259 J 3
Brock Island ⌒ CDN 24-25 O 2
Brockman, Mount ▲ AUS 172-173 C 7
Brockport o USA (NY) 278-279 D 5
Brock River ~ CDN 24-25 L 6
Brockton o USA (MA) 278-279 K 6
Brockton o USA (MT) 250-251 P 3
Brockville o CDN (ONT) 238-239 K 4
Brockway o USA (MT) 250-251 O 4
Brockway o USA (PA) 280-281 H 2
Broco o USA (FL) 286-287 G 3
Brodec'ke o UA 102-103 F 3
Broderick o CDN (SAS) 232-233 M 4
Brodeur Peninsula ⌣ CDN 24-25 b 4
Brodeur River ~ CDN 24-25 b 4
Brodick o GB 90-91 E 4
Brodie Bay ≈ 28-29 G 2
Brodnica o • PL 92-93 P 2
Brodokalmak o RUS 114-115 G 7
Brody o UA 102-103 D 2
Broer Ruys, Kap ▲ GRØ 26-27 p 7
Brogan o USA (OR) 244-245 H 6
Broke Inlet ≈ 176-177 D 7
Broken Arrow o USA (OK) 264-265 J 2
Broken Bay ≈ 180-181 L 2
Broken Bow o USA (NE) 262-263 G 3
Broken Bow o USA (OK) 264-265 K 4
Broken Bow Lake o USA (OK) 264-265 K 4
Brokenburg o USA (VA) 280-281 J 5
Brokenhead o CDN (MAN) 234-235 G 4
Broken Hill o • AUS 178-179 F 6
Broken Ridge ≃ 12 H 7
Broken River ~ AUS 180-181 H 4
Broken Skull River ~ CDN 30-31 E 4
Broken Water Bay ≈ 183 C 2
Brokopondo ☆ SME 62-63 G 3
Bromby Islands ⌒ AUS 174-175 D 2
Bromley o ZW 218-219 F 3
Bromo, Gunung ▲ RI 168 E 3
Bromo-Tengger-Semeru National Park ⊥ RI 168 E 3
Bromsi, Pulau ⌒ RI 166-167 J 2
Brønderslev o DK 86-87 D 8
Brong-Ahafo Region ◻ GH 202-203 J 6
Bronkhorstspruit o ZA 220-221 J 2
Bronnicy o • RUS 94-95 Q 4
Brønnøysund o N 86-87 F 4
Bronson o USA (FL) 286-287 G 2
Bronson o USA (MI) 272-273 D 6
Bronson o USA (TX) 268-269 F 5
Bronte o USA (TX) 266-267 G 2
Brook, Lake ~ CDN 36-37 J 3
Brookeland o USA (TX) 268-269 G 5
Brookesmith o USA (TX) 266-267 H 2
Brooke's Point o RP 160-161 B 8
Brookfield o USA (MO) 274-275 E 5
Brookgreen Gardens • USA (SC) 284-285 L 3
Brookhaven o USA (MS) 268-269 K 5
Brookings o USA (OR) 244-245 A 8
Brookings o USA (SD) 260-261 K 2
Brooklet o USA (GA) 284-285 J 4
Brooklyn o CDN (NS) 240-241 L 5
Brooklyn o USA (AL) 284-285 D 5
Brooklyn o USA (IA) 274-275 F 3
Brooklyn o USA (MS) 268-269 L 5
Brooklyn (River cruises) • AUS 180-181 L 2
Brookneal o USA (VA) 280-281 H 6
Brooks o CDN (ALB) 232-233 G 5
Brooksburg o USA (NY) 278-279 G 6
Brooksby o CDN (SAS) 232-233 O 3
Brooks Mount ▲ USA 20-21 G 4
Brooks Nek o ZA 220-221 J 5
Brooks Peninsula Provincial Recreation Area ⊥ CDN (BC) 230-231 B 3
Brooks Range ▲ USA 20-21 K 2
Brookston o USA (MN) 270-271 F 4
Brookstone o USA (IN) 274-275 M 4
Brooksville o USA (FL) 286-287 G 3
Brooksville o USA (MS) 268-269 M 3
Brookton o AUS 176-177 D 6
Brookville o AUS 174-175 J 7
Brookville o USA (IN) 274-275 N 5
Brookville o USA (PA) 280-281 G 2
Brookville Reservoir < USA (IN) 274-275 O 5
Broome o • AUS 172-173 F 4
Broomhill o CDN (MAN) 234-235 B 5
Brooms Head o AUS 178-179 M 5
Brotas o BR 72-73 F 7
Brotas de Macaúbas o BR 68-69 G 7
Brother John Gletscher ⊂ GRØ 26-27 O 4
Brothers o USA (OR) 244-245 E 7
Brothers, The ⌒ Y 132-133 H 7
Broughton Island ⌒ CDN (NWT) 28-29 J 3
Broughton Island ⌒ CDN (NWT) 36-37 L 6
Broulkou < TCH 198-199 J 4
Brouse o CDN (BC) 230-231 M 3
Brovary o UA 102-103 G 2
Brovinia o AUS 178-179 L 3
Browder o USA (KY) 276-277 H 3
Browerville o USA (MN) 270-271 D 4
Brown o CDN (MAN) 234-235 E 5
Brown, Mount ▲ ARK 16 F 9
Brown, Mount ▲ USA (MT) 250-251 H 3
Brown, Point ▲ AUS 176-177 M 6
Brown Bank ≃ 160-161 B 7
Brown City o USA (MI) 272-273 G 4
Brown Co. State Park ⊥ USA (IN) 274-275 M 5
Browne o USA 20-21 Q 4
Browne Bay ≈ 24-25 X 4
Browne Range ▲ AUS 176-177 H 2
Brownfield o CDN (ALB) 232-233 G 3
Brownfield o USA (TX) 264-265 B 5
Browning o CDN (SAS) 232-233 Q 6
Browning o USA (MT) 250-251 G 3
Brown Lake o CDN 30-31 Y 3
Brownlee o CDN (SAS) 232-233 N 5
Brownlow Point ▲ USA 20-21 S 1
Brownrigg o CDN (ONT) 236-237 G 3
Brown River ~ AUS 178-179 K 3
Brown River ~ PNG 183 D 5
Browns o USA (AL) 284-285 C 4
Brownsberg, National Reservaat ⊥ SME 62-63 G 3
Brownsboro o USA (OR) 244-245 C 8
Brownsburg o CDN (QUE) 238-239 L 3
Brownsburg o USA (IN) 274-275 M 5
Brown's Cay ⌒ BS 54-55 F 2
Brown's Cove o CDN (NFL) 242-243 M 3
Browns Town o JA 54-55 G 5
Brownstown o USA (IN) 274-275 M 6
Browns Valley o USA (MN) 270-271 B 5
Brownsville o USA (KY) 276-277 J 3
Brownsville o USA (TN) 276-277 F 5
Brownsville o USA (TX) 266-267 K 8
Brownsweg o SME 62-63 G 3
Brownton o USA (GA) 284-285 J 5
Brownwood o USA (TX) 266-267 J 2
Brownwood, Lake < USA (TX) 266-267 H 2
Browse Island ⌒ AUS 172-173 F 3
Broxton o USA (GA) 284-285 H 5
Broytona, ostrov ⌒ RUS 122-123 O 5
Bruce o CDN (ALB) 232-233 F 2
Bruce o USA (MS) 268-269 L 3
Bruce o USA (WI) 270-271 G 5
Bruce, Mount ▲ AUS 172-173 D 7
Bruce Crossing o USA (MI) 270-271 J 4
Bruce Highway II AUS 178-179 K 2
Bruce Lake o CDN (ONT) 234-235 K 4
Bruce Mines o CDN (ONT) 238-239 B 2
Bruce Peninsula ⌣ CDN (ONT) 238-239 D 3
Bruce Peninsula National Park ⊥ CDN (ONT) 238-239 D 3
Bruce Rock o AUS 176-177 E 5
Bruceton o USA (TN) 276-277 G 4
Bruceville-Eddy o USA (TX) 266-267 K 2
Bruck an der Leitha o A 92-93 O 5
Bruck an der Mur o A 92-93 N 5
Brudenell o CDN (ONT) 238-239 H 3
Bruderheim o CDN (ALB) 232-233 F 2
Brug, De o ZA 220-221 G 4
Bruges = Brugge ☆ • B 92-93 G 3
Brugge ☆ • B 92-93 G 3
Brühl o • D 92-93 J 3
Bruini o IND 144-145 L 6
Bruit, Pulau ⌒ MAL 162-163 J 3
Brujas o CO 60-61 G 6
Brujas, Cueva de las • RA 78-79 E 3
Brujas, Las o MEX 50-51 K 6
Brukkaros ▲ NAM 220-221 C 2
Brûlé o CDN (ALB) 228-229 R 3
Brule o USA (WI) 270-271 G 4
Brûle, Lac = Burnt Lake o CDN 38-39 N 2
Brumadinho o BR 72-73 H 6
Brumado o BR 72-73 K 3
Brumunddal ☆ N 86-87 E 6
Brunchilly o AUS 174-175 C 6
Brundage o USA (TX) 266-267 H 5
Brundidge o USA (AL) 284-285 E 5
Bruneau o USA (ID) 252-253 C 4
Bruneau River ~ USA (ID) 252-253 C 4
Brunei ■ BRU 164-165 D 1
Brunei = Bandar Seri Begawan ★ • BRU 164-165 D 1
Brunei, Teluk ≈ 160-161 A 10
Brunette Downs o AUS 174-175 C 6
Brunette Island ⌒ CDN (NFL) 242-243 M 5
Brunflo o S 86-87 G 5
Bruni o USA (TX) 266-267 J 6
Bruning o USA (NE) 262-263 J 4
Brunkild o CDN (MAN) 234-235 F 5
Brünn = Brno o CZ 92-93 O 4
Bruno o CDN (SAS) 232-233 N 3
Bruno o USA (MN) 270-271 F 4
Bruno o USA (NE) 262-263 K 3
Brunswick o USA (GA) 284-285 J 5
Brunswick o USA (MD) 280-281 J 4
Brunswick o USA (ME) 278-279 M 5
Brunswick o USA (MN) 270-271 E 5
Brunswick o USA (MO) 274-275 E 5
Brunswick o USA (OH) 280-281 E 2
Brunswick = Braunschweig o • D 92-93 L 2
Brunswick, Península ⌣ RCH 80 E 6
Brunswick Bay ≈ 172-173 G 3
Brunswick Heads o AUS 178-179 M 5
Brunswick Lake o CDN (ONT) 236-237 E 4
Bruntál o CZ 92-93 O 4
Bruny Island ⌒ AUS 180-181 J 7
Brus o YU 100-101 H 3
Brusett o USA (MT) 250-251 M 4
Brush o USA (CO) 254-255 M 3
Brus-Kamen' ▲ RUS 108-109 X 8
Brusque o BR 74-75 F 6
Brussel = Bruxelles ★ • B 92-93 H 3
Brussels = Bruxelles = Brussel ★ • B 92-93 H 3
Brüx = Most o CZ 92-93 M 3
Bruzual o YV 60-61 G 3
Bryan o USA (OH) 280-281 B 2
Bryan o USA (TX) 266-267 L 3
Bryan, Mount ▲ AUS 180-181 E 2
Bryansk = Brjansk o RUS 94-95 O 5
Bryant o CDN (SAS) 232-233 P 6
Bryant o USA (AR) 276-277 C 6
Bryant o USA (SD) 260-261 J 2
Bryant Creek ~ USA (MO) 276-277 C 4
Bryce Canyon National Park ∴ USA (UT) 254-255 C 6
Bryden, Mount ▲ AUS 178-179 K 1
Brylivka o UA 102-103 H 4
Bryne ☆ N 86-87 B 7
Bryson o USA (TX) 264-265 F 5
Bryson City o USA (NC) 282-283 D 5
Brzeg o • PL 92-93 O 3
Brześć Kujawski o PL 92-93 P 2
Brzesko o PL 92-93 Q 4
Bširri ☆ RL 128-129 G 5
Bua o FJI 184 III b 2
Bua ~ MW 218-219 G 1
Bua < SUD 206-207 G 3
Bua Bay ≈ 184 III b 2
Buabuang o RI 164-165 H 4
Buafri o GH 202-203 K 5
Buaka o GH 202-203 J 6
Buala o SOL 184 I d 3
Bū al Ghurāb, Bi'r < LAR 192-193 E 2
Bū al Hidān, Wādī ~ LAR 192-193 H 4
Buan, Pulau ⌒ RI 162-163 H 5
Buatan o RI 162-163 D 4
Bū Athlah < LAR 192-193 J 3
Buaya, Pulau ⌒ RI 162-163 F 4
Buaya Channel ≈ 166-167 K 6
Bu'ayrat al Hasun o LAR 192-193 F 2
Buba o GNB 202-203 C 4
Buba, Rio Grande de ~ GNB 202-203 C 4
Bubanda o ZRE 206-207 D 6
Bubanza o BU 212-213 B 5
Bubaque o • GNB 202-203 C 4
Bubi o ZW (Mvi) 218-219 F 5
Bubi ~ ZW 218-219 E 4
Bubi ~ ZW 218-219 F 5
Bubiai o • LT 94-95 H 4
Bubiki o EAT 212-213 D 5
Būbiyān, Ğazirat ⌒ KWT 130-131 L 3
Bublitz = Bobolice o PL 92-93 O 2
Bublos ∴ • RL 128-129 F 5
Bubu ~ EAT 214-215 H 4
Bubu o PNG 183 F 3
Bubudu ~ ZRE 210-211 K 6
Buburu o ZRE 210-211 G 3
Buca o FJI 184 III b 2
Buçaco o ANG 216-217 F 5
Bucak ☆ TR 128-129 D 4
Bucalemu o RCH 78-79 C 3
Bucaramanga ☆ CO 60-61 E 4
Bucareli Bay ≈ 32-33 D 4
Bucas Grande Island ⌒ RP 160-161 F 8
Buccaneer Archipelago ⌒ AUS 172-173 F 3
Buccaneer Beach ⊥ USA (VI) 286-287 R 3
Buchan o AUS 180-181 K 4
Buchanan o CDN (SAS) 232-233 Q 4
Buchanan ☆ LB 202-203 E 7
Buchanan o USA (GA) 284-285 E 3
Buchanan o USA (MI) 272-273 C 6
Buchanan o USA (ND) 258-259 J 4
Buchanan o USA (OR) 244-245 G 7
Buchanan o USA (VA) 280-281 G 6
Buchanan, Lake o AUS 178-179 H 1
Buchanan, Lake < USA (TX) 266-267 J 3
Buchanan Bay ≈ 26-27 N 4
Buchanan Highway II AUS 172-173 J 4
Buchan Caves • AUS 180-181 K 4
Buchan Gulf ≈ 26-27 O 8
Buchans o CDN (NFL) 242-243 M 4
Buchans Junction o CDN (NFL) 242-243 M 4
Bucharest = Bucureşti ★ • RO 102-103 D 5
Bucheke o PK 138-139 D 4
Buchenwald o • D 92-93 L 3
Buch'isi o ETH 208-209 C 5
Buchon, Point ▲ USA (CA) 248-249 D 4
Buchwa o ZW 218-219 F 5
Buck, Lake o AUS 172-173 K 5
Buckambool Mountain ▲ AUS 178-179 H 6
Buckatunna Creek ~ USA (MS) 268-269 M 5
Buck Creek ~ CDN (BC) 228-229 H 2
Buck Creek ~ USA (KY) 276-277 L 3
Buck Creek ~ USA (TX) 264-265 D 4
Buckeye o USA (AZ) 256-257 C 5
Buckeye o USA (NM) 256-257 M 6
Buckeye Lake o USA (OH) 280-281 D 4
Buckhannon o USA (WV) 280-281 F 4
Buckhorn o USA (NM) 256-257 G 5
Buckhorn Draw ~ USA (TX) 266-267 G 3
Buckhorn Lake o CDN (ONT) 238-239 G 4
Buckhorn Reservoir < USA (KY) 276-277 M 3
Buckingham o CDN (QUE) 238-239 K 3
Buckingham Bay ≈ 174-175 C 3
Buckingham Downs o AUS 178-179 E 2
Buckingham Island ⌒ CDN 24-25 a 2
Buck Lake o CDN (ALB) 232-233 D 2
Buckland o USA 20-21 K 4
Buckland, Monte ▲ RA 80 H 7
Buckland River ~ USA 20-21 K 4
Buckley o USA (WA) 244-245 C 3
Buckley Bay ≈ 16 G 15
Buckley Bay o CDN (BC) 230-231 E 4
Buckley River ~ AUS 174-175 E 7
Bucklin o USA (KS) 262-263 G 7
Buckmuische = Ezernieki o LV 94-95 K 3
Buckner Creek ~ USA (KS) 262-263 F 7
Buck Ridge o CDN (BC) 228-229 M 4
Bucksport o USA (ME) 278-279 N 4
Buck Valley o USA (PA) 280-281 H 4
Buco Zau o ANG 210-211 D 6
Buctouche o CDN (NB) 240-241 L 4
Bucureşti ★ • RO 102-103 E 5
Bucyrus o USA (OH) 280-281 D 3
Buda o USA (TX) 266-267 K 3
Budaka o EAU 212-213 D 3
Budalin o MYA 142-143 J 4
Bù Dăngo o VN 158-159 J 5
Budapest ★ • H 92-93 P 5
Búðardalur ☆ IS 86-87 c 2
Budarino o KA 96-97 G 8
Budaun o IND 138-139 G 5
Budawang Range ▲ AUS 180-181 L 3
Bud Bud o SP 208-209 H 6
Budd, Pulau ⌒ RI 166-167 F 1
Buddabadah o AUS 178-179 J 6
Buddha Park • THA 158-159 H 3
Budd Land ⊥ ARK 16 G 12
Bude o USA (MS) 268-269 K 5
Budënnovsk o RUS 126-127 F 5
Budennovsk o RUS 126-127 F 5
Budhi Gandaki ~ NEP 144-145 E 6
Budi, Lago o RCH 78-79 C 5
Budibudi Islands ⌒ PNG 183 G 5
Buding o RI 162-163 G 6
Buðir o IS 86-87 b 2
Budjala o ZRE 210-211 G 2
Budogošč' o RUS 94-95 N 2
Budongquan o VRC 144-145 J 3
Budu o MAL 162-163 J 4
Budu, Tanjung ▲ MAL 162-163 J 3
Budungbudung ~ RI 164-165 F 5
Budva o • YU 100-101 G 3
Budweis = České Budějovice o CZ 92-93 N 4
Buéa ☆ • CAM 204-205 H 6
Buedu o WAL 202-203 E 5
Buefjorden ≈ 86-87 B 6
Buela o ANG 216-217 C 2
Buena o USA (WA) 244-245 E 4
Buena Esperanza o RA 78-79 G 3
Buena Hora o BOL 70-71 D 3
Buenaventura o C 54-55 G 4
Buenaventura o CO 60-61 C 6
Buenaventura o MEX (CHA) 50-51 F 3
Buenaventura o MEX (YUC) 52-53 L 1
Buenaventura, Bahía de ≈ 60-61 C 6
Buena Vista ∴ • BH 52-53 K 3
Buena Vista o BOL (PAN) 70-71 D 2
Buena Vista o BOL (SAC) 70-71 F 5
Buenavista o CO 60-61 E 5
Buena-vista o CO 60-61 D 3
Buenavista o MEX (CHI) 52-53 H 3
Buenavista o MEX (SIN) 50-51 E 5
Buena Vista o PY 76-77 J 4
Buena Vista o RA 76-77 D 4
Buenavista o RP (MAR) 160-161 D 6
Buenavista o RP (ZAS) 160-161 E 9
Buena Vista o USA (CO) 254-255 J 5
Buena Vista o USA (GA) 284-285 F 4
Buena Vista o USA (VA) 280-281 G 6
Buena Vista o YV 60-61 G 4
Buena Vista, Bahía ≈ 54-55 F 3
Buena Vista Alta o PE 64-65 C 6
Buena Vista Island = Vatilau Island ⌒ SOL 184 I d 3
Buena Vista Lake o USA (CA) 248-249 E 4
Buenavista Tomatlán o MEX 52-53 C 2
Buendía, Embalse de < E 98-99 F 4
Buenga ~ ANG 216-217 C 3
Bueno, Río ~ RCH 78-79 C 6
Bueno Brandão o BR 72-73 G 7
Buenópolis o BR 72-73 H 4
Buenos Aires o CO (AMA) 66-67 B 4
Buenos Aires o CO (MET) 60-61 E 6
Buenos Aires o CO (TOL) 60-61 D 5
Buenos Aires o CO (VAU) 64-65 F 1
Buenos Aires o CR 52-53 C 7
Buenos Aires o MEX 50-51 K 6
Buenos Aires ◻ RA 78-79 H 3
Buenos Aires ★ • RA 78-79 K 3
Buenos Aires, Lago o RA 80 E 3
Buenos Aires Lérida o CO 66-67 B 2
Buen Pasto o RA 80 F 2
Buesaco o CO 64-65 D 1
Buet, Rivière ~ CDN 36-37 O 4
Buey o CO 60-61 C 4
Buey Arriba o C 54-55 G 4
Bueyeros o USA (NM) 256-257 M 3
Bueyes, Cerro de los ▲ RA 78-79 D 4
Búfala o MEX 50-51 G 4
Bufalo, Reserva Parcial do ⊥ ANG 216-217 B 6
Bufareh o RI 166-167 K 3
Buffalo o CDN (ALB) 232-233 H 5
Buffalo o CDN (SAS) 232-233 N 6
Buffalo o USA (IA) 274-275 H 3
Buffalo o USA (MN) 270-271 E 5
Buffalo o USA (MO) 276-277 B 3
Buffalo o USA (ND) 258-259 K 4
Buffalo o USA (OK) 264-265 E 2
Buffalo o USA (SD) 260-261 C 1
Buffalo o USA (TN) 276-277 G 5
Buffalo o USA (TX) 266-267 L 2
Buffalo o USA (WV) 280-281 E 5
Buffalo o USA (WY) 252-253 M 2
Buffalo o • USA (NY) 278-279 C 6
Buffalo Bill Ranch State Historic Park ∴ USA (NE) 262-263 F 3
Buffalo Bill Reservoir o USA (WY) 252-253 J 2
Buffalo Center o USA (IA) 274-275 E 1
Buffalo City o USA (AR) 276-277 C 4
Buffalo Creek ~ CDN 32-33 O 3
Buffalo Gap National Grassland ⊥ USA (SD) 260-261 D 3
Buffalo Head Hills ▲ CDN 32-33 M 3
Buffalo Hump ▲ USA (ID) 250-251 D 6
Buffalo Lake o CDN (ALB) 232-233 F 3
Buffalo Lake o CDN (NWT) 30-31 M 5
Buffalo Lake o USA (TX) 264-265 B 4
Buffalo Mountain ▲ USA (NV) 246-247 G 3
Buffalo Narrows o CDN 32-33 Q 4
Buffalo National River ⊥ USA (AR) 276-277 C 5
Buffalo Pound Provincial Park ⊥ CDN (SAS) 232-233 N 5
Buffalo River ~ CDN 30-31 M 6
Buffalo River ~ CDN 32-33 M 3
Buffalo River ~ USA (AR) 276-277 C 4
Buffalo River ~ USA (MS) 268-269 J 5
Buffalo River ~ USA (TN) 276-277 G 5
Buffalo River ~ USA (WI) 270-271 G 6
Buffalo Springs National Reserve ⊥ EAK 212-213 F 3
Buff Bay o JA 54-55 G 5
Buffels Drift o ZA 218-219 D 6
Buffelsrivier ~ ZA 220-221 K 4
Buffelsrivier ~ ZA 220-221 C 4
Bufflé Noir o CAM 204-205 K 4
Buford o USA (CO) 254-255 H 4
Buford o USA (GA) 284-285 F 2
Buford o USA (ND) 258-259 D 3
Buford o USA (OH) 280-281 C 4
Buford o USA (WY) 252-253 N 5
Buftea o RO 102-103 D 5
Bug ~ PL 92-93 R 2
Buga o CO 60-61 C 6
Buga o MAU 146-147 M 2
Buga o WAN 204-205 G 4
Bugaboo Alpine Provincial Recreation Area ⊥ CDN (BC) 230-231 N 3
Bugadi o EAU 212-213 D 3
Bugala Island ⌒ EAU 212-213 D 4
Bugana o WAN 204-205 G 5
Bugant o MAU 148-149 H 3
Bugdajly o TM 136-137 D 5
Buge o VRC 144-145 M 5
Bugembe o EAU 212-213 D 3
Bugene o EAT 212-213 C 4
Buggs Island Lake o USA (VA) 280-281 H 7
Bugi o • RI 166-167 K 3
Bugingkalo o RI 164-165 G 6
Bugiri o EAU 212-213 D 3
Bugojno o BIH 100-101 F 2
Bugrino o RUS 88-89 U 2
Bugsuk Island ⌒ RP 160-161 B 8
Bugt o VRC 150-151 C 3
Buguey o RP 160-161 D 3
Bugui Point ▲ RP 160-161 E 6
Bugul'ma ☆ RUS 96-97 H 6
Bugul'minsko-Belebeevskaja vozvyšennost' ▲ RUS 96-97 H 6
Bugunda o RUS 118-119 G 9
Buguruslan ☆ RUS 96-97 H 7
Buhara = Buhoro ☆ • US 136-137 J 5
Buharskaja oblast' ◻ US 136-137 H 4
Bu He ~ VRC 144-145 M 2
Buhera o ZW 218-219 F 4
Buhl o USA (ID) 252-253 D 4
Buhlandshahr o IND 138-139 F 5
Buhoro ☆ • US 136-137 J 5
Buhtarma ~ KA 124-125 O 4
Buhtarminskoe sukojmasy < KA 124-125 N 4
Buhta Sytygan-Tala ≈ 110-111 S 4
Buhu ~ EAT 212-213 E 6
Buick o CDN 32-33 K 3
Buiko o EAT 212-213 G 6
Builth Wells o GB 90-91 F 5
Bū'in o IR 136-137 B 7
Buin o PNG 184 I b 2
Bui National Park ⊥ GH 202-203 J 5
Buinsk ☆ RUS 96-97 F 6
Buir Nur o VRC 148-149 N 4
Buitenzorg = Bogor o RI 168 B 3
Buitepos o NAM 216-217 E 11
Buiucu o BR 66-67 J 5
Buj o RUS 94-95 R 2
Buj ~ RUS 96-97 J 5
Bujanovac o YU 100-101 H 3
Bujant o MAU 148-149 C 4
Bujant gol ~ MAU 148-149 C 4
Bujaraloz o E 98-99 G 4
Bujaru o BR 62-63 K 6
Bujaru, Rio ~ BR 68-69 E 2
Bujnaksk o RUS 126-127 G 6
Bujukly o RUS 122-123 K 4
Bujumbura ★ BU 212-213 B 5
Bujunda ~ RUS 120-121 P 3
Buk o PNG 183 B 5
Buka o US 136-137 L 4
Bukaan o RI 164-165 G 3
Bukačača o RUS 118-119 H 9
Bukadaban Feng ▲ VRC 144-145 H 2
Bukairiya, al- o KSA 130-131 H 4
Buka Island ⌒ PNG 184 I b 1
Bukama o ZRE 214-215 C 5
Bu Kammāsh o LAR 192-193 D 1
Bukantov toglari ▲ US 136-137 H 3
Bukasa Island ⌒ EAU 212-213 D 4
Bukat, Pulau ⌒ RI 164-165 E 2
Bukaua o PNG 183 D 4
Bukavu ☆ ZRE 212-213 B 5
Bukedea o EAU 212-213 E 3
Bukene o EAT 212-213 D 6
Bukeya o ZRE 214-215 D 6
Bukhit o SUD 206-207 H 3
Bukhoro = Buhoro ☆ • US 136-137 J 5
Bukima o EAT 212-213 D 4
Bukitkemuning o RI 162-163 F 7
Bukit Lata Papalang ▲ MAL 162-163 D 2
Bukittinggi ☆ • RI 162-163 D 5
Bükk ▲ H 92-93 Q 4
Bukkapatna o IND 140-141 G 4
Bukken Fiord ≈ 26-27 C 3
Bükki Nemzeti Park ⊥ H 92-93 Q 4
Bukoba ☆ EAT 212-213 C 4
Bukoloto o EAU 212-213 D 3
Bukombe o EAT 212-213 D 5
Bukrane o RI 166-167 F 5
Bukuru o WAN 204-205 H 4
Būl, Kūh-e ▲ IR 134-135 E 3
Bula o GNB 202-203 C 3
Bula o PNG 183 A 5
Bula o ZRE 212-213 B 3
Bula, Cachoeira ~ BR 66-67 C 2
Bula Atumba o ANG 216-217 C 4
Bulacaue Point ▲ RP 160-161 E 7
Bulacle o SP 208-209 H 6
Bulaevo ☆ KA 124-125 G 1
Bulag o MAU 148-149 J 3
Bulagansk o RUS 118-119 E 9
Bulagi o RI 164-165 H 4
Bulahdelah o AUS 180-181 M 2
Bulaka ~ RI 166-167 K 5
Bulalacao Island ⌒ RP 160-161 D 7
Bulalakao o RP 160-161 D 6
Bulan o RP 160-161 E 6
Bulanaš o RUS 96-97 M 5
Bulancak ☆ TR 128-129 H 2
Bulanghe o VRC 154-155 F 2
Bulangu o WAN 198-199 E 6
Bulanik ☆ TR 128-129 K 3
Būlāq o ET 194-195 E 5
Bulava o RUS 122-123 J 3
Bulawa, Gunung ▲ RI 164-165 H 3
Bulawayo ☆ ZW 218-219 E 5
Bulaya o Z 214-215 F 5
Bulbodney Creek ~ AUS 180-181 J 2
Bul'buhta o RUS 118-119 H 6
Bulbuta o ETH 208-209 D 5
Buldan ☆ TR 128-129 C 3
Buldāna o IND 138-139 F 9
Buldibuyo o PE 64-65 D 6
Buldir Island ⌒ USA 22-23 D 6
Buldyrtty ~ KA 96-97 H 9
Buleleng o RI 164-165 H 5
Bulenga o GH 202-203 J 5
Bulga Downs o AUS 176-177 E 4
Bulgan o MAU 146-147 L 2
Bulgan o MAU (ÖMN) 148-149 F 5
Bulgan ◻ MAU 148-149 F 3
Bulgan ☆ MAU (BUL) 148-149 F 3
Bulgan = Burènhajrhan o MAU 146-147 K 2
Bulgan = Šargalant o MAU 146-147 K 2
Bulgan gol ~ MAU 146-147 K 2
Bulgar ☆ RUS 96-97 F 6
Bulgaria = Bălgarija ■ BG 102-103 C 6
Bulgnéville o F 90-91 K 7
Buli o RI 164-165 L 3
Bū Lifiyat o UAE 134-135 E 6
Buliluyan, Cape ▲ RP 160-161 B 8
Bulimba o AUS 174-175 G 5
Bulisa o EAU 212-213 C 2
Buliya ⌒ FJI 184 III b 3
Bulkley Ranges ▲ CDN (BC) 228-229 G 2
Bulkley River ~ CDN 32-33 G 4
Bullabulling o AUS 176-177 F 5
Bullara o AUS 172-173 B 7
Bullard o USA (TX) 264-265 J 6
Bulla Regia ∴ • TN 190-191 G 2
Bullaxaar o SP 208-209 G 3
Bull Bay o JA 54-55 G 6
Bull Creek ~ CDN (SAS) 232-233 L 6
Bullecourt o AUS 174-175 E 7
Bullen, Cape ▲ CDN 24-25 d 3
Bullen River ~ CDN 30-31 S 3
Buller, Mount ▲ AUS 180-181 J 4
Bullfinch o AUS 176-177 E 5
Bull Harbour o CDN (BC) 230-231 B 3
Bullhead City o USA (AZ) 256-257 A 3
Bulli o AUS 180-181 L 3
Bull Island ⌒ USA (SC) 284-285 L 4
Bullita Out Station o AUS 172-173 K 4
Bull Lake o CDN 30-31 R 5
Bullmoose Creek ~ CDN 32-33 K 4
Bull Mountains ▲ USA (MT) 250-251 L 5
Bullock o USA (NC) 282-283 J 4
Bullock's Harbour o BS 54-55 G 2
Bulloo Downs o AUS 176-177 E 2
Bulloo River ~ AUS 178-179 H 4
Bullo River o AUS 172-173 J 3
Bullpound Creek ~ CDN (ALB) 232-233 G 4
Bull River o CDN (BC) 230-231 O 4
Bulls o NZ 182 E 4
Bulls Bay ≈ 48-49 J 3
Bulls Bay ≈ USA 284-285 L 4
Bull Shoals Lake o USA (AR) 276-277 C 4
Büllsport o NAM 220-221 C 2
Bulmer Lake o CDN 30-31 J 4
Bulnajn Nuruu ▲ MAU 148-149 C 3
Bulnes o RCH 78-79 C 4
Bulo Balamal o SP 212-213 J 2
Buloke, Lake o AUS 180-181 G 4
Bulolo o PNG 183 D 4
Bulolo River ~ PNG 183 D 4
Bulongo o ZRE 210-211 H 6
Buloo River ~ AUS 178-179 H 3
Bulqizë o • AL 100-101 H 4
Bultfontein o ZA 220-221 H 4
Bulu o RI 168 D 3
Buluan o RP 160-161 F 9
Buluan ~ RP 160-161 F 9
Buluan Lake o RP 160-161 F 9
Bulukumba o RI 164-165 G 6
Bulukutu o ZRE 210-211 H 4
Bulula o ZRE 212-213 A 6
Bulumuri o PNG 183 F 3
Bulun o RUS (SAH) 120-121 E 2
Bulun ~ RUS 112-113 H 4
Bulungu o ZRE (Ban) 210-211 G 6
Bulungu o ZRE (KOC) 216-217 F 3
Bulupulu, Tanjung ▲ RI 164-165 G 5
Bulus o RUS 118-119 O 4
Bulusan o RP 160-161 F 6
Bulusan Vulcano ▲ RP 160-161 F 6
Bulwark o CDN (ALB) 232-233 G 3
Bulwer o ZA 220-221 J 4
Bulyea o CDN (SAS) 232-233 O 4
Buma ~ ZRE 210-211 F 6
Bū Maras, Thamad < LAR 192-193 H 3
Bū Marim o LAR 192-193 J 1
Bumba o ZRE 210-211 J 2
Bumbah o LAR 192-193 K 1
Bumbat o MAU 148-149 G 4
Bumbire Island ⌒ EAT 212-213 C 4
Bumble Bee o USA (AZ) 256-257 C 4
Bum Bum, Pulau ⌒ MAL 160-161 C 10
Bumbuna o WAL 202-203 E 5
Bumi Hills o ZW 218-219 E 3
Bumijawa o RI 168 C 3
Bumpus, Mount ▲ CDN 24-25 P 6
Buna o EAK 212-213 G 2
Buna o ZRE 210-211 G 5
Bunabun o PNG 183 C 3
Bunam o PNG 183 C 3
Bunapas o PNG 183 C 3
Bunbury o AUS 176-177 C 6
Bunda o EAT 212-213 D 5
Bundaberg o AUS 178-179 M 3
Bunda Bunda o AUS 174-175 G 7
Bundarra o AUS 178-179 L 6
Bundeena o AUS 178-179 G 4
Bundey, Mount ▲ AUS 172-173 K 2
Bundey River ~ AUS 178-179 C 1
Bündi o IND 138-139 E 7
Bundi o PNG 183 C 3
Bundibugyo o EAU 212-213 C 3
Bundick Creek ~ USA (LA) 268-269 G 6
Bundjalung National Park ⊥ AUS 178-179 M 5
Bunduqiya o SUD 206-207 K 6
Bunga ~ ZRE 210-211 K 3
Bunga, River ~ WAN 204-205 H 3
Bungadi o ZRE 206-207 H 6
Bungalaut, Selat ≈ 162-163 C 6
Bungamas o RI 162-163 E 6
Bungbulang o RI 168 B 3
Bunger Oasis ⌒ ARK 16 G 11
Bungi o RI 164-165 H 6
Bungikamasi, Pulau ⌒ RI 168 E 6
Bungil Creek ~ AUS 178-179 K 4
Bungku o RI 164-165 G 5
Bungle Bungle National Park ⊥ AUS 172-173 J 4
Bungle Bungle Range ▲ AUS 172-173 J 4
Bungo o ANG 216-217 C 3
Bungoma o EAK 212-213 E 3
Bungo-suido ≈ 152-153 E 8
Bungo-takada ⌣ J 152-153 D 8
Bung Sam Phan o THA 158-159 F 3
Bungtlang o IND 142-143 H 4
Bungudu o WAN 198-199 C 6
Bunguruya o AUS 178-179 K 5
Bunguran, Pulau ⌒ RI 162-163 G 2
Buni o WAN 204-205 K 3
Bunia o ZRE 212-213 C 3
Bunie o ZRE 212-213 A 2
Buninyong o AUS 180-181 G 4
Bunji o IND 138-139 E 2
Bunker o USA (MO) 276-277 D 3
Bunker Group ⌒ AUS 178-179 M 2
Bunker Hill o USA 20-21 H 4
Bunkerville o USA (NV) 248-249 K 3
Bunkie o USA (LA) 268-269 H 6
Bunnell o USA (FL) 286-287 H 2
Bunneringee o AUS 180-181 F 2
Bunsuru ~ WAN 198-199 C 6
Bunta o RI 164-165 H 4
Buntharig o THA 158-159 H 3
Buntu o RI 168 C 3
Bununu o WAN 204-205 H 4
Bunut o BRU 164-165 D 1
Bunyakiri o ZRE 212-213 B 5
Bünyan ☆ TR 128-129 F 3
Bunyan, Paul & Blue Ox Statue • USA (MN) 270-271 D 3
Bunyanyi, Lake o EAU 212-213 B 4
Bunyu, Pulau ⌒ RI 164-165 E 2
Bunza o WAN 204-205 E 2
Buolkalah ~ RUS 110-111 M 3
Buôn Ma Thuôt ☆ • VN 158-159 K 4
Buor-Èekit ~ RUS 110-111 P 4
Buor-Haja, guba ≈ 110-111 R 4
Buor-Haja, mys ▲ RUS 110-111 T 4
Buor-Jurjah ~ RUS 110-111 Z 6
Buotama ~ RUS 118-119 N 5
Buptgang Zangpo ~ VRC 144-145 E 5
Bupul o RI 166-167 L 5
Buqa', al- o KSA 132-133 D 5
Buqda Caqable o SP 208-209 G 6
Bur o RUS (IRK) 116-117 N 6
Bur ~ RUS 110-111 O 4
Bura o EAK 212-213 G 4
Buraan o SP 208-209 J 3
Buraatyn davaa ▲ MAU 146-147 K 1
Buraevo ☆ RUS 96-97 J 6
Buraida ☆ KSA 130-131 J 4
Buraika, al- o KSA 132-133 A 3
Buraimi, al- o OM 134-135 F 6
Burakin o AUS 176-177 D 5
Būrālān o IR 128-129 L 3
Buram o SUD 206-207 G 3
Burang o VRC 144-145 C 5
Buranhem, Rio ~ BR 72-73 L 4
Burannoe o RUS 96-97 J 8
Buras o USA (LA) 268-269 L 7
Bū Rashādah, Wādī < LAR 192-193 G 4
Burauen o RP 160-161 F 7
Burayqah < SUD 200-201 E 4
Burbank o USA (CA) 248-249 F 5
Burbank o USA (WA) 244-245 G 4
Burchard o USA (NE) 262-263 K 4
Burcher o AUS 180-181 J 2
Burco ☆ SP 208-209 G 4
Burdalyk o TM 136-137 J 5
Burdekin Dam < AUS 174-175 J 7
Burden o USA (KS) 262-263 K 7
Burdulba o AUS 172-173 L 2
Burdur ☆ • TR 128-129 D 4
Burdur Gölü o TR 128-129 D 4
Burdwood Bank ≃ 5 E 10
Burē o ETH (Ilu) 208-209 B 4
Burē o ETH (Wel) 208-209 C 3
Bureau, Lac o CDN (QUE) 236-237 N 4
Bureimi o RN 204-205 E 2
Bureinskij hrebet ▲ RUS 122-123 E 4
Bureinskij Khrebet = Bureinskij hrebet ▲ RUS 122-123 E 4
Bureija < SUD 200-201 E 4
Bureja ~ RUS 122-123 C 4
Burejnskij zapovednik ⊥ RUS 122-123 F 3
Burejnskoe vodohranilišče < RUS 122-123 D 3
Burengapara o IND 142-143 G 3
Burènhajrhan o MAU 146-147 K 2
Bureo, Río ~ RCH 78-79 C 4
Burera, Lac o RWA 212-213 B 4
Burevestnik o RUS 122-123 M 6
Bürfell o IS 86-87 d 2
Būr Fu'ād o ET 194-195 F 2
Burğ o OM 132-133 H 5
Burgagylkan ~ RUS 120-121 M 3
Burgal-'Arab o ET 194-195 D 2
Burgas o BG 102-103 E 6

Bur Gavo o SP 212-213 H 4
Burgaw o USA (NC) 282-283 K 6
Burgdorf o USA (ID) 250-251 D 6
Burgdorf Hot Springs • USA (ID) 250-251 D 6
Burgenland ◻ A 92-93 O 5
Burgeo o CDN (NFL) 242-243 L 5
Burgeo Bank ≃ 38-39 P 5
Burgeo Bank ≃ 242-243 K 5
Burgersdorp o ZA 220-221 H 5
Burgersfort o ZA 220-221 K 2
Burgers Pass ▲ ZA 220-221 D 6
Burges, Mount ▲ AUS 176-177 F 5
Burgess o USA (VA) 280-281 J 6
Burgess, Mount ▲ CDN 20-21 V 3
Burgis o CDN (SAS) 232-233 Q 4
Burgo de Osma, El o E 98-99 F 4
Burgos o••• E 98-99 F 3
Burgos o RP 160-161 C 4
Burgoyne Bay ≈ 36-37 O 4
Burgsvik o S 86-87 J 8
Burhala o RUS 120-121 N 2
Burhan Budai Shan ▲ VRC 144-145 K 3
Burhan buudaj ▲ MAU 148-149 C 5
Burhaniye o TR 128-129 B 3
Burhānpur o IND 138-139 F 9
Burhi Rapti ~ IND 142-143 C 2
Buri o BR 72-73 F 7
Buri ∩ ER 200-201 J 5
Burias Island ∩ RP 160-161 E 6
Burias Pass ≈ 160-161 E 6
Burica, Punta ▲ PA 52-53 C 7
Buried Village • NZ 182 F 3
Burien o USA (WA) 244-245 C 3
Burigi, Lake ⊖ EAT 212-213 C 5
Burigi Game Reservat ⊥ EAT 212-213 C 5
Burin o CDN (NFL) 242-243 N 5
Burin Peninsula ⌣ CDN (NFL) 242-243 N 5
Buri Ram o THA 158-159 G 3
Buritaca • CO 60-61 E 2
Buritama o BR 72-73 E 6
Buriti, Ribeiro ~ BR 70-71 K 7
Buriti, Rio ~ BR 68-69 G 3
Buriti, Rio ~ BR 70-71 H 3
Buriti Alegre o BR 72-73 F 5
Buriti Bravo o BR 68-69 G 4
Buriticupu, Rio ~ BR 68-69 E 4
Buriti dos Lopes o BR 68-69 H 3
Buritirama o BR 68-69 G 7
Buritis o BR 72-73 G 3
Burjassot o E 98-99 G 5
Burji o WAN 204-205 H 3
Burkand'ja o RUS 120-121 M 2
Burkanoko, Lake ⊖ AUS 178-179 H 5
Burkburnett o USA (TX) 264-265 F 4
Burke o USA (SD) 260-261 G 3
Burke and Wills Roadhouse o AUS 174-175 F 6
Burke Channel ≈ 32-33 G 6
Burke Channel ≈ CDN 230-231 B 2
Burke Development Road II AUS 174-175 F 6
Burke River ~ AUS 178-179 E 1
Burke's Pass ▲ ZA 220-221 C 4
Burkesville o USA (KY) 276-277 K 4
Burketown o AUS 174-175 E 5
Burkett o USA (TX) 264-265 E 6
Burkeville o USA (TX) 268-269 G 6
Burkeville o USA (VA) 280-281 H 6
Burke & Wills Monument • AUS 178-179 F 4
Burkina Faso ■ BF 202-203 H 4
Burkitkala ∴• US 136-137 G 4
Bürkitti, tau ▲ KA 124-125 H 4
Burkot o RUS 120-121 P 3
Burk's Falls o CDN (ONT) 238-239 F 3
Burkville o USA (AL) 284-285 D 4
Burla ~ RUS 124-125 M 2
Burleigh o AUS 174-175 G 7
Burleson o USA (TX) 264-265 G 6
Burley o USA (ID) 252-253 E 4
Burlingame o USA (KS) 262-263 L 6
Burlington o CDN (NFL) 242-243 M 3
Burlington o CDN (ONT) 238-239 F 5
Burlington o USA (CO) 254-255 N 4
Burlington o USA (IA) 274-275 G 4
Burlington o USA (KS) 262-263 L 6
Burlington o USA (KY) 276-277 L 1
Burlington o USA (NC) 282-283 H 4
Burlington o USA (OK) 264-265 F 2
Burlington o USA (VT) 278-279 H 4
Burlington o USA (WA) 244-245 C 2
Burlington o USA (WI) 274-275 K 2
Burlington Junction o USA (MO) 274-275 C 4
Burma = Myanmar ■ MYA 142-143 J 4
Burma Cave • KSA 130-131 K 5
Burmantovo o RUS 114-115 F 4
Burmis o CDN (ALB) 232-233 D 6
Burnaby o CDN (BC) 230-231 G 4
Burndoo o AUS 180-181 G 2
Burnet o USA (TX) 266-267 J 3
Burnett Bay ≈ 24-25 J 4
Burnett Highway II AUS 178-179 L 3
Burnett Lake ⊖ CDN 30-31 S 6
Burnett Range ▲ AUS 178-179 L 3
Burnett River ~ AUS 178-179 L 3
Burney o USA (CA) 246-247 D 3
Burney, Monte ▲ RCH 80 D 6
Burnham o CDN (SAS) 232-233 L 5
Burnham Out Station o AUS 178-179 F 2
Burnie-Somerset o AUS 180-181 H 6
Burni Gandak ~ IND 142-143 D 2
Burning Coal Mines ∴ USA (ND) 258-259 D 5
Burnley o GB 90-91 F 5
Burnpur o IND 142-143 E 4
Burns o USA (CO) 254-255 J 4
Burns o USA (OR) 244-245 F 7
Burns o USA (WY) 252-253 O 5
Burns Flat o USA (OK) 264-265 E 3
Burnside o CDN (NFL) 242-243 P 4
Burnside, Lake ⊖ AUS 176-177 G 2
Burnside River ~ CDN 30-31 P 2
Burns Indian Reservation ✗ USA (OR) 244-245 F 7
Burns Junction o USA (OR) 244-245 H 8
Burns Lake o CDN (BC) 228-229 J 2
Burnsville o USA (WV) 280-281 F 5
Burnsville Lake ⊖ USA (WV) 280-281 F 5
Burntbush River ~ CDN (ONT) 236-237 J 3
Burnt Creek o CDN 36-37 Q 7
Burnt Ground o BS 54-55 H 3
Burnt Islands o CDN (NFL) 242-243 K 5
Burnt Lake ⊖ CDN 38-39 N 2
Burnt Lake = Lac Brulé ⊖ CDN 38-39 N 2
Burnt Ranch o USA (CA) 246-247 B 3
Burntwood Lake ⊖ CDN 34-35 F 3
Burntwood River ~ CDN 34-35 G 3
Buro ~ RUS 108-109 W 6
Burpee, Cape ▲ CDN 24-25 j 6
Burqin o VRC 146-147 H 2
Burr o CDN (SAS) 232-233 N 3
Burra o AUS 180-181 E 2
Burracoppin o AUS 176-177 E 5
Burramurra Out Station o AUS 174-175 D 7
Burras, Rio de las ~ RA 76-77 D 2
Burrel ☆•• AL 100-101 H 4
Burrell Creek ~ CDN (BC) 230-231 L 4
Burrendong Reservoir < AUS 180-181 K 2
Burren Junction o AUS 178-179 K 6
Burr Ferry o USA (LA) 268-269 G 5
Burrgum Hill ▲ AUS 178-179 M 3
Burrinjuck Reservoir < AUS 180-181 K 3
Burro, El o YV 60-61 H 4
Burro, Serranías del ▲ MEX 50-51 H 3
Burr Oak Reservoir ⊖ USA (OH) 280-281 D 4
Burro Creek ~ USA (AZ) 256-257 B 4
Burro Peak ▲ USA (NM) 256-257 G 6
Burrows o CDN (SAS) 232-233 Q 5
Burr Point ▲ USA 22-23 U 3
Burrton o USA (KS) 262-263 J 6
Burrumbeet, Lake ⊖ AUS 180-181 G 4
Burrum Heads o AUS 178-179 M 3
Burrwood o USA (LA) 268-269 L 8
Bursa ☆•• TR 128-129 C 2
Būr Safāğa o ET 194-195 F 4
Būr Sa'īd ☆ ET 194-195 F 2
Burstall o CDN (SAS) 232-233 J 5
Bursting Brook ~ CDN 36-37 G 3
Būr Sūdān ☆• SUD 200-201 H 3
Būr Taufiq o ET 194-195 F 3
Bur Tinle o SP 208-209 H 5
Burton o CDN (BC) 230-231 M 3
Burton o USA (NE) 262-263 G 2
Burton o USA (TX) 266-267 L 3
Burton o USA (WV) 280-281 F 4
Burton, Baie de ⊖ ZRE 212-213 B 6
Burton, Lac ⊖ CDN 36-37 K 7
Burton, Lake < USA (GA) 284-285 G 2
Burton upon Trent o GB 90-91 G 5
Burträsk o S 86-87 K 4
Buru, Pulau ∩ RI 166-167 D 3
Burubajtal o KA 124-125 J 6
Buru Island ∩ AUS 183 B 5
Burukan o RUS 122-123 F 2
Burumburum o WAN 204-205 H 3
Burunda ~ RUS 122-123 D 2
Burundi ■ BU 212-213 B 5
Buruntuma o GNB 202-203 D 3
Buruolah ~ RUS 118-119 N 3
Bururi o BU 212-213 B 5
Bururi o PNG 183 B 2
Burutu o WAN 204-205 F 6
Burwash Bay ≈ 36-37 O 2
Burwell o USA (NE) 262-263 G 3
Burwick o GB 90-91 F 2
Buryatia = Respublika Burjatija ◻ RUS 116-117 K 9
Buryn' o UA 102-103 H 2
Burynсyk mujisi ▲ KA 126-127 J 5
Burynšik, mys ▲ KA 126-127 J 5
Bury Saint Edmunds o• GB 90-91 H 5
Būš o ET 194-195 E 3
Buşaira o SYR 128-129 J 5
Busaitā', al- ∸ KSA 130-131 F 3
Busang ~ RI 162-163 K 4
Busanga o ZRE (EQU) 210-211 J 4
Busanga o ZRE (SHA) 214-215 C 6
Busanga Swamp ⌣ Z 218-219 C 2
Busango o ZRE 214-215 C 5
Buşayya, Maḥfar al- o IRQ 130-131 K 2
Busby o CDN (ALB) 232-233 E 2
Busby o USA (MT) 250-251 N 6
Būšehr ◻ IR 134-135 D 4
Būšehr, Bandar-e ☆• IR 134-135 D 4
Busembatia o EAU 212-213 D 3
Bush o USA (LA) 268-269 L 6
Bushat o AL 100-101 G 4
Bushell o CDN 30-31 P 6
Bushell Park o CDN (SAS) 232-233 N 5
Bushenyi o EAU 212-213 C 4
Bushe River Indian Reserve ✗ CDN 30-31 L 6
Bushland o USA (TX) 264-265 B 3
Bushman Drawings • ZA 220-221 F 5
Bushman Paintings • SD 220-221 K 3
Bushman Paintings • ZA 220-221 J 4
Bushnell o USA (FL) 286-287 G 3
Bushnell o USA (IL) 274-275 H 4
Bushnell o USA (NE) 262-263 C 3
Bushnell o USA (SD) 260-261 K 2
Bush River ~ CDN (BC) 228-229 R 4
Bushy Park o AUS 178-179 B 2
Busia o EAU 212-213 E 3
Businga o ZRE 210-211 H 2
Busira ~ ZRE 210-211 G 4
Busisi o EAT 212-213 D 5
Bus'k ☆ UA 102-103 D 3
Busoga ◻ EAU 212-213 D 3
Busonga o EAK 212-213 E 3
Buṣra aš-šām o••• SYR 128-129 G 6
Busse o RUS 122-123 B 3
Busselton o AUS 176-177 C 6
Busseri ~ SUD 206-207 H 5
Bussol', proliv ≈ RUS 122-123 O 5
Bustah, ozero o RUS 110-111 Y 3
Bustamante o MEX 50-51 K 6
Bustamante o USA (TX) 266-267 H 7
Bustamante, Punta ▲ RA 80 F 5
Busto Arsizio o I 100-101 B 2
Buston o TJ 136-137 L 4
Busu o RI 164-165 L 4
Busuanga o RP 160-161 C 6
Busuanga Island ∩ RP 160-161 D 6
Busu-Djanoa o ZRE 210-211 H 3
Busu-Kwanga o ZRE 210-211 H 3
Busu-Mandji o ZRE 210-211 H 2
Busungwe o EAU 212-213 C 4
Busunju o EAU 212-213 D 3
Busunu o GH 202-203 K 5
But o PNG 183 B 2
Buta o ZRE 210-211 K 2
Butahuao, Cerro ▲ RA 78-79 D 5
Butain, al o KSA 130-131 H 4
Butajira o ETH 208-209 D 4
Butak o PK 134-135 K 4
Buta Mallin, Paso de ▲ RA 78-79 D 4
Buta Ranquil o RA 78-79 E 4
Butare o• RWA 212-213 B 5
Butaritari Island ∩ KIB 13 J 2
Butaš, ozero o RUS 114-115 G 7
Butat Raya o SUD 206-207 G 3
Bute o AUS 180-181 D 2
Butedale o CDN (BC) 228-229 F 3
Bute Giarti o ETH 208-209 C 6
Bute Inlet ≈ 32-33 H 6
Bute Inlet ≈ CDN 230-231 D 3
Butemba o EAU 212-213 C 3
Butembo o ZRE 212-213 B 3
Butha-Buthe o LS 220-221 J 4
Buthidaung o MYA 142-143 H 5
Buthurst Inlet ≈ 30-31 Q 2
Butiá o BR 74-75 E 8
Butiaba o EAU 212-213 C 3
Butler o USA (AL) 284-285 B 4
Butler o USA (GA) 284-285 F 4
Butler o USA (IN) 274-275 O 3
Butler o USA (MO) 274-275 D 6
Butler o USA (OK) 264-265 E 3
Butler o USA (PA) 280-281 G 3
Butler o USA (TX) 268-269 E 5
Butler Creek ~ CDN 34-35 Q 5
Butolo ⊥ o BR 68-69 C 6
Buton, Pulau ∩ RI 164-165 H 6
Buton, Selat ≈ 164-165 H 6
Buton Utara Reserve ⊥ RI 164-165 H 6
Butro River ~ LB 202-203 F 7
Butrint ∴•• AL 100-101 H 5
Butru o AUS 178-179 E 1
Buttahatchee River ~ USA (MS) 268-269 M 3
Butte o CDN (ALB) 232-233 D 3
Butte o USA (MT) 250-251 G 5
Butte o USA (ND) 258-259 G 4
Butte o USA (NE) 262-263 H 2
Butte, The ▲ USA 20-21 S 4
Butte Creek ~ USA (CA) 246-247 D 4
Butter Creek Pass ▲ USA (OR) 244-245 E 6
Butterpot Provincial Park ⊥ CDN (NFL) 242-243 P 5
Butterworth o MAL 162-163 D 2
Butterworth o ZA 220-221 J 6
Buttle Lake ⊖ CDN (BC) 230-231 D 4
Butt of Lewis ▲ GB 90-91 D 2
Button Islands ∩ CDN 36-37 R 4
Buttonwillow o USA (CA) 248-249 E 4
Butu o CAM 204-205 H 6
Butu o RI 164-165 F 5
Butuan ☆ RP 160-161 F 8
Butuan Bay ≈ 160-161 F 8
Butuí, Rio ~ BR 76-77 J 5
Butung = Pulau Buton ∩ RI 164-165 H 6
Butung, Tanjung ▲ RI 164-165 H 6
Butuo o VRC 156-157 C 3
Buturlinovka o RUS 102-103 M 2
Butwal o NEP 144-145 D 7
Buucagaan o MAU 148-149 D 4
Buulobarde o SP 212-213 K 2
Buur Hakkaba o SP 212-213 K 2
Buvuma Island ∩ EAU 212-213 D 3
Buwaiš o Y 132-133 F 6
Buwenge o EAU 212-213 D 3
Buxar o IND 142-143 D 3
Buxton o GUY 62-63 E 2
Buxton o USA (OR) 244-245 B 5
Büyer Ahmad-o-Kūhgīlūye ◻ IR 134-135 D 3
Buyo o CI 202-203 G 6
Buyo, Lac du < CI 202-203 G 6
Buyspoort ▲ ZA 220-221 F 6
Büyük Ada o TR 128-129 C 2
Büyükağrı Dağı (Ararat) ▲•• TR 128-129 L 3
Büyük-menderes N. ~ TR 128-129 B 4
Büyük Menderes Nehri ~ TR 128-129 C 3
Buyuni o EAT 214-215 K 4
Buyun Shan ▲ VRC 150-151 D 7
Buzači, poluostrov ⌣ KA 126-127 J 5
Buzan ~ RUS 96-97 F 10
Büzanaj, kum ∸ KA 96-97 F 10
Buzău ☆• RO 102-103 E 5
Buzdjak ☆ RUS 96-97 J 6
Buzi o MOC 218-219 H 4
Buzi, Rio ~ MOC 218-219 H 4
Buzi Gonbad o AFG 146-147 B 7
Búzios, Cabo dos ▲ BR 72-73 K 7
Buzluk Mağarası • TR 128-129 H 3
Buzovna o AZ 128-129 O 2
Buzuluk ☆ RUS 96-97 H 7
Buzuluk ~ RUS 102-103 N 2
Buzūn, al- o Y 132-133 G 6
Büzyldyk o KA 124-125 E 3
Bwadela o PNG 183 F 5
Bwana-Mutombo o ZRE 216-217 E 3
Bwanga o EAT 212-213 C 5
Bwari o WAN 204-205 G 4
Bwatnapne o VAN 184 II b 2
Bwea Town o LB 202-203 F 7
Bwele-Milonda ~ ZRE 216-217 E 3
Bweni o EAT 214-215 K 4
Bwiam o WAG 202-203 B 3
Byadgi o IND 140-141 F 3
Byam Channel ≈ 24-25 T 3
Byam Martin Channel ≈ 24-25 S 2
Byam Martin Island ∩ CDN 24-25 T 3
Bydgoszcz ☆• PL 92-93 P 2
Byemoor o CDN (ALB) 232-233 F 4
Byers o USA (TX) 264-265 F 4
Byfield o AUS 178-179 L 2
Byfield National Park ⊥ AUS 178-179 L 2
Byford o AUS 176-177 D 6
Bygdeå o• S 86-87 K 4
Bygin ~ KA 136-137 L 3
Bygin sukojmasy < KA 136-137 L 3
Bygland ☆ N 86-87 C 7
Bykle o N 86-87 C 7
Bykovskaja, protoka ~ RUS 110-111 Q 3
Bykovskij o RUS 110-111 R 3
Bykovskij poluostrov ⌣ RUS 110-111 R 4
Bylas o USA (AZ) 256-257 E 5
Bylok o TJ 136-137 M 4
Bylong o AUS 180-181 L 2
Bylot Island ∩ CDN 24-25 g 4
Bylyra ~ RUS 118-119 E 11
Bynoe River ~ AUS 174-175 F 5
Bynum o USA (MT) 250-251 G 4
Bynum Reservoir ⊖ USA (MT) 250-251 G 4
Byohori o IND 142-143 B 3
Byrakan ~ RUS 118-119 K 4
Byrd o ARK 16 F 25
Byrd Land ∸ ARK 16 E 0
Byro o AUS 176-177 D 3
Byrock o AUS 178-179 J 6
Byron o USA (IL) 274-275 J 2
Byron o USA (MI) 272-273 F 5
Byron, Cape ▲ AUS 178-179 M 5
Byron, Isla ∩ RCH 80 C 3
Byron Bay ≈ 36-37 V 7
Byron Bay ≈ 178-179 M 5
Byron Center o USA (MI) 272-273 D 5
Byron Sound ≈ 78-79 K 6
Byrranga, Gory ▲ RUS 108-109 U 5
Byske o S 86-87 K 4
Byskeälven ~ S 86-87 K 4
Byssa ~ RUS 122-123 D 2
Bystraja ~ RUS 108-109 V 5
Bystraja ~ RUS 120-121 S 6
Bystrinskij hrebet ▲ RUS 120-121 S 5
Bystrjanka o RUS 124-125 O 2
Bystryj Istok ☆ RUS 124-125 O 2
Bystryj Tanyp ~ RUS 96-97 J 6
Bystrzyca ~ PL 92-93 O 3
Bysyttah o RUS 118-119 H 4
Bytantaj ~ RUS 110-111 T 5
Bytom o PL 92-93 P 3
Bytów o• PL 92-93 O 1
Byumba o RWA 212-213 C 4
Byxelkrok o S 86-87 H 8
Byzanz = İstanbul ☆••• TR 128-129 C 2
Bzimah o LAR 192-193 K 5
Bzyb' ~ GE 126-127 D 6

C

Caača o TM 136-137 G 6
Caacupé ☆ PY 76-77 J 3
Caaguazú o PY 76-77 J 3
Caala o ANG 216-217 C 6
Caamaño Sound ≈ 32-33 F 5
Caamaño Sound ≈ CDN 228-229 E 4
Caapiranga o BR 66-67 G 4
Caapucu o PY 76-77 J 4
Caarapo o BR 76-77 K 2
Caatiba o BR 72-73 K 3
Caatingas ∸ BR 68-69 G 7
Caazapá ☆ PY 76-77 J 4
Cab o RP 160-161 D 4
Cabaad, Raas ▲ SP 208-209 J 5
Cabacal, Rio ~ BR 70-71 H 4
Cabaceiras o BR 68-69 K 5
Cabadbaran o RP 160-161 F 8
Cabaiguán o C 54-55 F 3
Caballo o USA (NM) 256-257 H 6
Caballococha o PE 66-67 B 4
Caballones, Cayo ∩ C 54-55 F 4
Caballo Reservoir < USA (NM) 256-257 H 6
Caballos, Bahía de ≈ 64-65 E 9
Caballos Mesteños, Llanos de los ∸ MEX 50-51 G 3
Cabañas o C 54-55 D 3
Cabanatuan o RP 160-161 D 5
Cabangtohan o RP 160-161 D 7
Cabano o• CDN (QUE) 240-241 G 3
Cabarete o DOM 54-55 K 5
Cabarete, Punta ▲• DOM 54-55 K 5
Cabatuan o RP 160-161 D 4
Čabda ~ RUS 120-121 F 4
Cabecea do Salsa, Igarapé ~ BR 66-67 F 5
Cabeceiras o BR (GOI) 72-73 G 3
Cabeceiras o BR (PIA) 68-69 G 4
Cabeceiras de Basto o P 98-99 D 4
Cabeço do Apa o BR 76-77 K 2
Cabedelo o BR 68-69 L 5
Cabeza da Velha, Baía ≈ 68-69 F 2
Cabeza del Este, Cayo ∩ C 54-55 F 4
Cabeza del Mar o RCH 80 E 6
Cabeza Mechuda, Punta ▲ MEX 50-51 D 5
Cabezas o BOL 70-71 F 6
Cabezas de San Juan ▲ USA (PR) 286-287 Q 2
Cabildo o RCH 78-79 D 2
Cabimas o YV 60-61 F 2
Cabinda ◻ ANG 210-211 C 6
Cabinda ☆ ANG (Cab) 210-211 D 6
Cabinet Mountains ▲ USA (MT) 250-251 C 3
Cabinet Mountains Wilderness Area ⊥ USA (MT) 250-251 D 3
Cabingaan Island ∩ RP 160-161 D 10
Cabitutu, Rio ~ BR 66-67 J 6
Cable o USA (WI) 270-271 G 4
Cable Beach ⊥ AUS 172-173 F 5
Cabo o BR 68-69 L 6
Cabo Blanco o RA 80 H 3
Cabo de Hornos, Parque Nacional ⊥ RCH 80 G 7
Cabo Delgado ◻ MOC 214-215 K 7
Cabo Frio, Ilha do ∩ BR 72-73 K 7
Čáboksar o IR 136-137 B 6
Cabo Ledo o ANG 216-217 B 4
Cabonga, Réservoir ⊖ CDN (QUE) 236-237 M 5
Cabool o USA (MO) 276-277 C 3
Caboolture o AUS 178-179 M 4
Cabo Orange, Parque Nacional do ∴ BR 62-63 J 3
Cabo Polonio, Parque Forestal de ⊥ ROU 74-75 D 10
Cabora Bassa, Lago de < MOC 218-219 F 2
Caborca o• MEX 50-51 C 2
Cabo San Lucas o MEX 50-51 E 6
Cabot o USA (AR) 276-277 C 6
Cabot Head ▲ CDN (ONT) 238-239 D 3
Cabot Strait ≈ 38-39 O 5
Cabra Corral, Embalse < RA 76-77 E 3
Cabra Island ∩ RP 160-161 D 6
Cabral o DOM 54-55 K 5
Cabral, Serra do ▲ BR 72-73 H 4
Cabramurra o AUS 180-181 K 3
Cabrera o CO 60-61 D 6
Cabrera o• DOM 54-55 L 5
Cabreras, Las ~ C 54-55 G 4
Cabrero o RCH 78-79 C 4
Cabreúva o BR 72-73 G 7
Cabri o CDN (SAS) 232-233 K 5
Cabri Lake ⊖ CDN (SAS) 232-233 J 4
Cabrillo National Monument • USA (CA) 248-249 G 7
Cabrobó o BR 68-69 J 6
Cabruta o YV 60-61 H 4
Cabuca o GNB 202-203 C 3
Cabudare o YV 60-61 G 2
Cabugao o RP 160-161 D 4
Cabure o YV 60-61 G 2
Cabure, El o RA 76-77 F 4
Cabure-i o RA 76-77 K 3
Caburgua, Lago ⊖ RCH 78-79 D 5
Cabuyaro o CO 60-61 E 5
Čača ~ RUS 118-119 J 9
Caça do Mucusso, Acampamento de o ANG 216-217 F 8
Caçador o BR 74-75 E 6
Čačak o• YU 100-101 H 3
Cacao o F 62-63 H 3
Caçapava do Sul o BR 74-75 D 8
Cacaribaiteri o YV 60-61 J 6
Cacau Pirera o BR 66-67 G 4
Cáccia, Capo ▲ I 100-101 B 4
Cacequi o BR 76-77 K 5
Cáceres o BR 70-71 J 5
Cáceres o••• E 98-99 D 5
Čačevičy o BY 94-95 L 5
Cachachi o PE 64-65 C 5
Cachapoal, Rio ~ RCH 78-79 D 3
Cachari o RA 78-79 K 4
Cache o USA (OK) 264-265 F 4
Cache Creek o CDN (BC) 230-231 H 3
Cache Creek ~ USA (OK) 264-265 F 4
Cache Creek, West ~ USA (OK) 264-265 F 4
Cachendo o PE 70-71 B 5
Cache Peak ▲ USA (ID) 252-253 E 4
Cache River ~ USA (AR) 276-277 D 5
Cacheu ☆ GNB 202-203 B 3
Cacheu, Rio ~ GNB 202-203 C 3
Cachi o• RA 76-77 D 3
Cá Chiên, Sông ~ VN 158-159 J 6
Cachimbo o ANG 216-217 F 4
Cachimbo, Serra do ▲ BR 66-67 J 6
Cachina, Quebrada ~ RCH 76-77 B 3
Cachingues o ANG 216-217 D 6
Cachipo o YV 60-61 J 3
Cachira o CO 60-61 E 4
Cachoeira o BR (AMA) 66-67 C 2
Cachoeira o• BR (BAH) 72-73 L 2
Cachoeira Alta o BR 72-73 E 5
Cachoeira de Goiás o BR 72-73 E 4
Cachoeira do Arari o BR 62-63 K 6
Cachoeira do Sul o BR 74-75 D 8
Cachoeira de Macacu o BR 72-73 J 7
Cachoeirinha o BR 72-73 G 5
Cachoeirinha, Cachoeira ~ BR 66-67 K 4
Cachoeirinha, Corredeira ~ BR 66-67 G 7
Cachoeirinho o BR 74-75 E 7
Cachoeiro de Itapemirim o BR 72-73 K 6
Cachos, Punta ▲ RCH 76-77 B 4
Cachueca o ANG 216-217 D 7
Cachuela Esperanza o BOL 70-71 E 2
Cachuma, Lake ⊖ USA (CA) 248-249 E 5
Cacimba de Dentro o BR 68-69 L 5
Cacina o GNB 202-203 C 4
Caciporé, Cabo ▲ BR 62-63 J 4
Caciporé, Rio ~ BR 62-63 J 4
Cacique Doble o BR 74-75 E 6
Cacoal o BR 70-71 G 2
Cacocum o C 54-55 G 4
Cacolo o ANG 216-217 E 5
Caconda o ANG 216-217 C 6
Cacouna o CDN (QUE) 240-241 F 3
Cactus o USA (TX) 264-265 C 2
Cactus Lake ⊖ CDN (SAS) 232-233 J 3
Caçu o BR 72-73 E 5
Cacuaco o ANG 216-217 B 4
Cacuchi ~ ANG 216-217 D 6
Caculo ~ ANG 216-217 E 4
Cacula o ANG 216-217 C 7
Caculé o BR 72-73 J 3
Cacumba, Ilha ∩ BR 72-73 L 4
Cacumbi o ANG 216-217 E 5
Cacuria o BR 66-67 E 6
Cacuso o ANG 216-217 C 4
Cada, Rio ~ CO 60-61 F 6
Cadaadley o SP 208-209 G 4
Cadaado o SP 208-209 H 5
Cadale o SP 212-213 L 2
Čadan ☆ RUS 116-117 E 10
Cadariri, Rio ~ BR 66-67 J 6
Caddo o USA (OK) 264-265 H 4
Caddo o USA (TX) 264-265 F 6
Caddo Mills o USA (TX) 264-265 H 5
Caddo Mountains ▲ USA (AR) 276-277 B 6
Caddo River ~ USA (AR) 276-277 B 6
Čādegān o IR 134-135 D 2
Cadena, Arroyo de la ~ MEX 50-51 G 5
Cadereyta o MEX 50-51 J 5
Cadibarrawirracanna, Lake ⊖ AUS 178-179 C 5
Cadillac o CDN (QUE) 236-237 K 4
Cadillac o CDN (SAS) 232-233 L 6
Cadillac o USA (MI) 272-273 D 3
Cadillal, Embalse el < RA 76-77 E 4
Cádiz o E 98-99 D 6
Cadiz o RP 160-161 E 7
Cadiz o USA (CA) 248-249 J 5
Cadiz o USA (KY) 276-277 H 4
Cadiz o USA (OH) 280-281 E 3
Cádiz, Golfo de ≈ 98-99 D 6
Cadlao Island ∩ RP 160-161 C 7
Čadman = Urd gol o MAU 146-147 L 2
Čadobec ~ RUS 116-117 J 6
Cadogan o CDN (ALB) 232-233 H 3
Cadogan Glacier ⊂ CDN 26-27 L 4
Cadogan Inlet ≈ 26-27 M 4
Cadomin o CDN (ALB) 228-229 R 3
Cadott o USA (WI) 270-271 G 6
Cadotte Lake o CDN 32-33 M 3
Cadotte River ~ CDN 32-33 M 3
Cadoux o AUS 176-177 D 5
Cadron Creek ~ USA (AR) 276-277 C 5
Caduman Point ▲ RP 160-161 F 7
Cadwell o USA (GA) 284-285 G 4
Caek o KS 146-147 B 5
Caen ☆• F 90-91 G 7
Caerdydd = Cardiff o GB 90-91 F 6
Caerfyrddin = Carmarthen o GB 90-91 E 6
Caernarfon o••• GB 90-91 E 5
Caerphilly Castle •• GB 90-91 F 6
Caesarea Scugog, Lake ⊖ CDN (ONT) 238-239 G 4
Caesar Creek Lake < USA (OH) 280-281 C 4
Caetas o BR 68-69 K 6
Caeté o BR 72-73 J 5
Caeté, Baía do ≈ 68-69 E 2
Caeté, Rio ~ BR 66-67 C 7
Caetité o BR 72-73 J 3
Čaevo o RUS 94-95 P 2
Cafamaum o BR 68-69 H 7
Cafayate o• RA 76-77 E 4
Cafema, Serra ▲ ANG 216-217 B 8
Cafetal o MEX 52-53 K 2
Cafuma ~ ANG 216-217 E 8
Cagaan Bogd ▲ MAU 148-149 D 6
Cagaandörvölž o MAU 148-149 J 5
Cagaannuur o MAU 146-147 J 1
Cagaan-Ovoo o MAU 148-149 E 5
Cagaan-Uul = Šarga o MAU 148-149 D 3
Čagalvandi o IR 134-135 C 2
Cagan o KA 124-125 L 3
Čagan ~ RUS 96-97 G 8
Cagan Aman ☆ RUS 96-97 E 10
Cagayan ~ RP 160-161 D 3
Cagayan de Oro ☆ RP 160-161 F 8
Cagayan de Tawi Tawi Island ∩ RP 160-161 C 9
Cagayan Islands ∩ RP 160-161 D 8
Čağčarān o• AFG 134-135 L 1
Čagda o RUS (SAH) 118-119 M 4
Čagda o RUS (SAH) 120-121 D 4
Cageri o GE 126-127 E 6
Cagle o USA (TN) 276-277 K 5
Cagles Mill Lake ⊖ USA (IN) 274-275 M 5
Cágliari o I 100-101 B 5
Cágliari, Golfo di ≈ 100-101 B 5
Čaglinka ~ KA 124-125 F 2
Cagnano Varano o I 100-101 E 4
Čagojan o RUS 122-123 C 2
Čagra ~ RUS 96-97 F 7
Cagraray Island ∩ RP 160-161 E 6
Caguán, Rio ~ CO 64-65 E 1
Caguana, La o USA (PR) 286-287 P 2
Caguas o USA (PR) 286-287 P 2
Čagyl o TM 136-137 D 4
Čagyltenįz, köli o KA 124-125 F 1
Čah Āb o AFG 136-137 L 6
Cahaba River ~ USA (AL) 284-285 C 4
Cahabón, Rio ~ GCA 52-53 K 4
Cahama o ANG 216-217 C 8
Čahār Bāğ o AFG 136-137 K 6
Čahār Borğak o AFG 134-135 K 3
Čahār Maḥāll-o-Baḫtiyāri ◻ IR 134-135 D 3
Čāh Bahār o IR 134-135 J 6
Čāh Bahār, Bandar-e ≈ 134-135 J 6
Čāh Bahār, Ra's-e ▲ IR 134-135 J 6
Čāh Čeibi, Hāmūn-e ⊖ IR 134-135 J 4
Caher = An Chathair o IRL 90-91 D 5
Čāh Ğam o IR 136-137 D 7
Cahkwaktolik o USA 20-21 J 6
Cahobas, Las o RH 54-55 K 5
Cahokia Mounds •• USA (IL) 274-275 H 6
Cahors ☆• F 90-91 H 9
Cahotal o C 54-55 G 4
Čāh Sagak o IR 134-135 J 2
Cahuacho o PE 64-65 F 9
Cahuapanas o PE 64-65 D 4
Cahuilla Indian Reservation ✗ USA (CA) 248-249 H 6
Cahuinari, Rio ~ CO 66-67 B 3
Cahul ☆ MD 102-103 F 5
Čāh Zardār o IR 134-135 H 5
Caí, Cachoeira do ~ BR 66-67 J 5
Caia o MOC 218-219 H 3
Caiabi, Cachoeira ~ BR 70-71 K 2
Caiabis, Serra dos ▲ BR 70-71 J 2
Caiambé o BR 66-67 E 4
Caianda o ANG 214-215 B 6
Caiapó, Rio ~ BR 68-69 D 6
Caiapó, Rio ~ BR 72-73 E 4
Caiapônia o BR 72-73 E 4
Caibarién o C 54-55 F 3
Caibi o BR 74-75 D 6
Caibiran o RP 160-161 F 7
Caicara o YV 60-61 H 4
Caiçara do Rio do Vento o BR 68-69 K 4
Caicedo o CO 60-61 D 4
Caicedonia o CO 60-61 D 5
Caico o BR 68-69 K 5
Caicos Islands ∩ GB 54-55 J 4
Caicos Passage ≈ 54-55 J 3
Caicumbo o ANG 216-217 F 5
Cái Đầu o VN 158-159 H 5
Caigua o YV 60-61 J 3
Cai Hu ~ VRC 154-155 K 6
Cái Lậy o VN 158-159 J 5
Caillou Bay ≈ 44-45 M 5
Caillou Bay ≈ USA 268-269 K 7
Caima o BR 68-69 B 3
Caimanero o MEX 50-51 F 6
Caimanero, Laguna del ⊖ MEX 50-51 F 6
Caimbambo o ANG (BGU) 216-217 C 6
Caimbambo ~ ANG 216-217 B 6
Caimito o CO 60-61 D 3
Caín, El o RA 78-79 E 6
Caine, Rio ~ BOL 70-71 E 6
Cainta o RP 160-161 D 5
Caiongo o ANG 216-217 C 3
Caipe o RA 76-77 C 3
Caipupa o ANG 216-217 E 5
Cairari o BR 68-69 D 3
Cairn, Île ∩ CDN 36-37 L 6
Cairn Mountain ▲ USA 20-21 N 6
Cairns o•• AUS 174-175 H 5
Cairns, Mount ▲ AUS 174-175 C 7
Cairns Lake ⊖ CDN (ONT) 234-235 J 3
Cairns Section ⊥ AUS 174-175 J 4
Cairo o USA (GA) 284-285 F 6
Cairo o USA (KY) 276-277 F 4
Cairo o USA (NE) 262-263 H 3
Cairo = al-Qāhira ☆••• ET 194-195 E 2
Cairo, Cape ▲ CDN 24-25 V 1
Cairu o BR 72-73 L 2
Caiseal = Cashel o• IRL 90-91 D 5
Caisleán an Bharraigh = Castlebar ☆ IRL 90-91 C 5
Caititu, Área Indígena ✗ BR 66-67 E 6
Caitou o ANG 216-217 B 7
Caiúa o BR 72-73 D 7
Caiundo o ANG 216-217 D 7
Caixa, Rio de ~ BR 72-73 J 2
Caiyuan o VRC 156-157 C 3
Caiza, Serranía de ▲ BOL 76-77 F 1
Čaja ~ RUS 114-115 R 5
Čaja ~ RUS 118-119 D 6
Čaja-Ajan, gory ▲ RUS 108-109 Z 7
Cajabamba o EC 64-65 C 2
Cajabamba o PE 64-65 C 5
Cajacay o PE 64-65 D 7
Cajamarca ☆• PE 64-65 C 5
Cajamarquilla o PE 64-65 D 7
Čajan o KA 136-137 L 3
Čajanda ~ RUS 118-119 F 5
Cajatambo o PE 64-65 D 7
Cajazeiras o BR 68-69 J 5
Cajazeiras, Rio ~ BR 68-69 C 4
Čajbuha o RUS 120-121 T 3
Cajcara del Orinoco o YV 60-61 H 4
Čajcyns'kij Kamen' ▲ RUS 88-89 U 3
Čajetina o YU 100-101 G 3
Cajidiocan o RP 160-161 E 6
Čajkovskij ☆ RUS 96-97 J 5
Cajobabo o C 54-55 H 4
Cajon o USA (CA) 248-249 G 5
Cajon, El o USA (CA) 248-249 H 7
Cajón, Embalse el < HN 52-53 L 4
Cajón del Maipo • RCH 78-79 D 2
Cajones, Rio ~ MEX 52-53 F 3
Cajon Pass ▲ USA (CA) 248-249 G 5
Cajon Troncoso ~ RCH 78-79 D 4
Caju, Cachoeira do ~ BR 62-63 D 6
Cajuapara, Rio ~ BR 68-69 E 4
Cajuata o BOL 70-71 D 5
Cajueiro o BR (MIN) 72-73 H 3
Cajueiro o BR (RON) 70-71 F 2
Cajuru o BR 72-73 G 6
Cajuti, Cachoeira ~ BR 62-63 G 6
Cajutuba, Ilha ∩ BR 68-69 E 2
Cajuuna o BR 62-63 K 6
Čajvo, zaliv ≈ RUS 122-123 K 2
Caka o VRC 144-145 M 2
Caka Yanhu ⊖ VRC 144-145 M 2
Čak-e Vardak o AFG 138-139 B 2
Čakne-ye Pāin o IR 136-137 F 6
Čakranegara o• RI 168 C 7
Čakva o• GE 126-127 D 7
Čakyja ~ RUS 118-119 O 4
Čāl o AFG 136-137 L 6
Çal ☆ TR 128-129 C 3
Cal, Rio La ~ BOL 70-71 H 6
Cala o ZA 220-221 H 5
Calabar ☆ WAN 204-205 H 6
Calabazar de Sagua o C 54-55 F 3
Calabei o RI 168 C 7
Calabogie o CDN (ONT) 238-239 J 3
Calabozo o YV 60-61 H 3
Calabria ◻ I 100-101 E 5
Calabria, Parco Nazionale della ⊥ I 100-101 F 5
Calacoa o PE 70-71 B 5
Calacoto o BOL 70-71 C 5
Calafat o RO 102-103 C 6
Calafate, El o RA 80 D 5
Calafquen, Lago ⊖ RCH 78-79 C 5
Calagua Islands ∩ RP 160-161 E 5
Calahoo o CDN (ALB) 232-233 E 2
Calahorra o• E 98-99 G 3
Calai o ANG 216-217 E 8
Calais o• F 90-91 H 6
Calais o USA (ME) 278-279 O 3
Čalak o US 136-137 K 5
Calalaste, Sierra de ▲ RA 76-77 D 4
Calalzo di Cadore o I 100-101 D 1
Calama o BR 66-67 F 7
Calama o RCH 76-77 C 2
Calamar o CO (ATL) 60-61 D 2
Calamar o CO (VAU) 60-61 E 7
Calamarca o BOL 70-71 D 5
Calamba o• RP 160-161 D 5
Calamian Group ∩ RP 160-161 C 6
Calamocha o E 98-99 G 4
Calamus o USA (IA) 274-275 H 3
Calamus Reservoir ⊖ USA (NE) 262-263 G 3
Calamuya ∴• HN 52-53 L 4
Calanaque o BR 66-67 E 3

Calandula ○ ANG 216-217 C 4
Calandula, Quedas do ∼ ·· ANG 216-217 D 4
Calang ○ RI 162-163 A 2
Calanga ○ PE 64-65 D 8
Calanus Bay ≈ 36-37 H 3
Calapan ☆ RP 160-161 D 6
Cala Rajada ○ E 98-99 J 5
Călăraşi ☆ MD 102-103 F 4
Călăraşi ☆ RO 102-103 E 5
Calarca ○ CO 60-61 D 5
Calatambo ○ RCH 70-71 C 6
Calatayud ○ E 98-99 G 4
Calatrava ○ RP 160-161 E 7
Calavite Passage ≈ 160-161 D 6
Calayan Island ⌒ RP 160-161 D 3
Calbayog ○ RP 160-161 F 6
Calbore ○ PA 52-53 D 7
Calbuco ○ RCH 78-79 C 6
Calbuco, Volcán ▲ RCH 78-79 C 6
Calca ○ PE 70-71 B 3
Calcasieu Lake ⬭ USA (LA) 268-269 G 7
Calcasieu River ∼ USA (LA) 268-269 H 6
Calceta ○ EC 64-65 B 2
Calchaquí ○ RA 76-77 G 5
Calchaquí, Río ∼ RA 76-77 G 6
Calchaquí, Río ∼ RA 76-77 D 3
Calchaquí las Aves, Laguna ⬭ RA 76-77 G 5
Calçoene ○ BR 62-63 J 4
Calçoene, Rio ∼ BR 62-63 J 4
Calcutta ☆ ·· IND 142-143 F 4
Caldas ○ CO 60-61 D 4
Caldas Novas ○ BR 72-73 F 4
Caldeiras ○ BR 72-73 J 2
Calder ○ CDN (SAS) 232-233 R 4
Caldera ○ CR 52-53 B 7
Caldera ○ RCH 76-77 B 4
Caldera de Taburiente, Parque Nacional de la ⊥ E 188-189 C 6
Calderon, Cerro ▲ RA 78-79 E 6
Calder River ∼ CDN 30-31 M 3
Calders Dock ○ CDN (MAN) 234-235 G 3
Çaldıran ☆ TR 128-129 K 3
Caldonia ○ USA (MN) 270-271 G 7
Caldwell ○ USA (ID) 252-253 B 3
Caldwell ○ USA (KS) 262-263 J 7
Caldwell ○ USA (NC) 282-283 H 4
Caldwell ○ USA (OH) 280-281 E 4
Caldwell ○ USA (TX) 266-267 L 3
Calebee Creek ∼ USA (AL) 284-285 E 4
Caledon ○ ZA 220-221 D 7
Caledon Bay ≈ 174-175 D 3
Caledonia ○ CDN (NS) 240-241 N 5
Caledonia ○ CDN (ONT) 238-239 F 5
Caledonia ○ USA (MN) 270-271 G 7
Caledonia Hills ▲ CDN (NB) 240-241 K 5
Caledonrivier ∼ ZA 220-221 H 4
Calen ○ AUS 174-175 K 7
Calequisse ○ GNB 202-203 B 3
Calera ○ USA (AL) 284-285 D 3
Calera ○ USA (OK) 264-265 H 5
Calera, La ○ RCH 78-79 D 2
Caleta Josefina ○ RCH 80 F 6
Caleta Olivia ○ RA 80 G 3
Caleta Vitor ○ RCH 70-71 B 6
Caleufú ○ RA 78-79 G 3
Caleufú, Río ∼ RA 78-79 D 6
Calexico ○ USA (CA) 248-249 J 7
Calfpen Swamp ⬭ USA (SC) 284-285 K 4
Calgary ○· CDN (ALB) 232-233 D 4
Calhan ○ USA (CO) 254-255 L 4
Calhoun ○ USA (GA) 284-285 F 2
Calhoun ○ USA (KY) 276-277 H 3
Calhoun ○ USA (LA) 268-269 H 4
Calhoun City ○ USA (MS) 268-269 L 3
Calhoun Falls ○ USA (SC) 284-285 H 2
Calhua ○ PE 64-65 F 9
Cali ☆ CO 60-61 C 6
Calicoan Island ⌒ RP 160-161 F 7
Calico Ghost Town · USA (CA) 248-249 H 5
Calico Rock ○ USA (AR) 276-277 C 4
Calicut ○· IND 140-141 F 5
Caliente ○ USA (CA) 248-249 F 4
Caliente ○ USA (NV) 248-249 K 2
California ○ BR 66-67 B 7
California ○ CO 60-61 E 4
California ○ USA (MO) 274-275 F 6
California ◘ USA (CA) 246-247 D 3
California, Gulf of = California, Golfo de ≈ MEX 50-51 B 2
California Aqueduct < USA (CA) 248-249 C 2
California City ○ USA (CA) 248-249 G 4
Calik ∼ RI 162-163 F 6
Calilegua, Parque Nacional ⊥ RA 76-77 E 2
Calima = Darien ○ CO 60-61 C 6
Călimani, Munţii ▲ RO 102-103 D 4
Calingasta ○ RA 76-77 C 6
Calingasta, Valle de ⌣ RA 76-77 C 6
Calingiri ○ AUS 176-177 D 5
Calintaan ○ RP 160-161 D 6
Calion ○ USA (AR) 276-277 C 7
Calipatria ○ USA (CA) 248-249 J 6
Caliper Lake ○ CDN (ONT) 234-235 K 5
Calipuy, Reserva Nacional ⊥ PE 64-65 C 6
Calispell Peak ▲ USA (WA) 244-245 H 2
Calistoga ○ USA (CA) 246-247 C 5
Calitzdorp ○ ZA 220-221 E 6
Calķar köl ⬭ KA 96-97 G 8
Calķarteniz, sor ⬭ KA 126-127 P 3
Calkiní ○ MEX 52-53 J 1
Callabonna ○ AUS 178-179 F 5
Callabonna, Lake ⬭ AUS 178-179 F 5
Callabonna Creek ∼ AUS 178-179 F 5
Callaghan ○ USA (TX) 266-267 H 6
Callagiddy ○ AUS 176-177 C 2
Callahan ○ USA (CA) 246-247 C 2
Callahan ○ USA (FL) 286-287 H 1
Callahan, Mount ▲ USA (NV) 246-247 J 4
Callama ó Quirce, Río ∼ BOL 70-71 D 7
Callana, Río ∼ PE 64-65 E 5
Callander ○ CDN (ONT) 238-239 F 2
Callands ○ USA (VA) 280-281 G 7
Callanish ○ GB 90-91 D 2
Callao ○ PE 64-65 D 8
Callao ○ USA (UT) 254-255 B 4
Callao ○ USA (VA) 280-281 K 6
Callao, El ○ YV 62-63 D 2
Callaqui, Volcán ▲ RCH 78-79 D 4
Callara, Lake ⬭ AUS 178-179 D 5
Callatharra Springs ○ AUS 176-177 C 2
Callawa ○ AUS 172-173 E 6
Callaway ○ USA (FL) 286-287 D 1
Callaway ○ USA (MN) 270-271 C 4
Callaway ○ USA (NE) 262-263 G 3
Callaway Gardens · USA (GA) 284-285 F 4
Calle Calle, Río ∼ RCH 78-79 C 5
Calles ○ MEX 50-51 K 6
Calling Lake ⬭ CDN 32-33 O 4
Calling River ∼ CDN 32-33 O 4
Calliope ○ AUS 178-179 L 3
Callon ○ USA (WI) 270-271 J 6
Cal Madow, Buuraha ▲ SP 208-209 J 3
Calmar ○ CDN (ALB) 232-233 E 2
Calmar ○ USA (IA) 274-275 G 1
Cal Miskaat, Buuraha ▲ SP 208-209 J 3
Calm Point ▲ USA 22-23 Q 3
Čalna ○ RUS 88-89 N 6
Cal-Nev-Ari ○ USA (NV) 248-249 K 4
Calombo ○ ANG 216-217 C 6
Calonda ○ ANG 216-217 F 4
Calonga ∼ ANG 216-217 C 7
Caloosahatchee River ∼ USA (FL) 286-287 H 5
Caloto ○ CO 60-61 C 6
Caloundra ○ AUS 178-179 M 4
Calpet ○ USA (WY) 252-253 H 4
Calpon, Cerro ▲ PE 64-65 C 5
Calpulalpan ○ MEX 52-53 E 1
Calstock ○ CDN (ONT) 236-237 D 3
Caltagirone ○ I 100-101 E 6
Caltama, Cerro ▲ BOL 70-71 C 7
Caltanissetta ○ I 100-101 E 6
Calton Hills ○ AUS 174-175 E 7
Ca Lu ○ VN 158-159 J 2
Caluango ○ ANG 216-217 E 4
Calucinga ○ ANG 216-217 D 5
Calulo ○ ANG 216-217 C 4
Calumet ○ USA (OK) 264-265 F 3
Calunda ○ ANG 214-215 B 7
Caluquembe ○ ANG 216-217 C 6
Čalūs ○· IR 136-137 B 6
Caluula ○ SP 208-209 K 3
Calvert ○ USA (AL) 284-285 B 5
Calvert ○ USA (TX) 266-267 L 2
Calvert, Cape ▲ CDN (BC) 230-231 B 2
Calvert Hills ○ AUS 174-175 D 5
Calvert Island ⌒ CDN (BC) 230-231 A 2
Calvi ○·· F 98-99 M 3
Calvillo ○ MEX 50-51 H 7
Calvin ○ USA (OK) 264-265 H 4
Calvinia ○ ZA 220-221 D 5
Calwa ○ USA (CA) 248-249 E 3
Calzada de Calatrava ○ E 98-99 F 5
Camabatela ○ ANG 216-217 C 4
Camacã ○ BR 72-73 L 3
Camaça, Rio ∼ BR 66-67 D 6
Camaçari ○ BR 68-69 K 7
Camachi, Lac ⬭ CDN (QUE) 236-237 M 5
Camacupa ○ ANG 216-217 D 6
Camaguan ○ YV 60-61 H 3
Camagüey ☆· C 54-55 G 4
Camagüey, Archipiélago de ⌒ C 54-55 F 3
Camaipi ○ BR 62-63 J 5
Camaiú, Rio ∼ BR 66-67 H 5
Camalote ○ C 54-55 G 4
Camamu ○ BR 72-73 L 2
Camana ○ PE 70-71 A 5
Čamanābād ○ IR 134-135 H 1
Camanaú, Rio ∼ BR 62-63 D 6
Čaman Bīd ○ IR 136-137 E 6
Camandog Island ⌒ RP 160-161 F 7
Čaman Soltān ○ IR 134-135 C 2
Camapuã ○ BR 70-71 K 6
Camaquã ○ BR 74-75 E 8
Camará ○ BR (AMA) 66-67 F 4
Camará ○ BR (P) 66-67 K 4
Camaragibe ○ BR 68-69 L 6
Camaraipi, Rio ∼ BR 68-69 C 3
Camararé, Rio ∼ BR 70-71 H 3
Camarata ○ YV 60-61 K 5
Camargo ○ MEX 50-51 K 4
Camargo ○ USA (OK) 264-265 E 2
Camaron ○ BOL 76-77 E 1
Camarón, Cabo ▲ HN 54-55 C 7
Camarones ○ RA 80 H 2
Camarones, Bahía ≈ 80 H 2
Camarones, Río ∼ RCH 70-71 C 6
Camaruã ○ BR 66-67 E 5
Camarvik Creek ∼ CDN 30-31 Z 3
Camas ○ USA (MT) 250-251 E 4
Camas ○ USA (WA) 244-245 C 5
Camas Valley ○ USA (OR) 244-245 B 7
Camata, Río ∼ BOL 70-71 C 4
Camatambo ○ ANG 216-217 C 3
Cà Mau ○ VN 158-159 H 6
Camaxilo ○ ANG 216-217 E 4
Camba ○ RI 164-165 F 6
Čamba ∼ RUS 116-117 L 5
Cambahee River ∼ USA (SC) 284-285 K 4
Cambaju ○ GNB 202-203 C 3
Camballin ○ AUS 172-173 G 4
Cambândua ○ ANG 216-217 D 6
Cambange ○ ANG 216-217 F 4
Cambao ○ CO 60-61 D 5
Cambará do Sul ○ BR 74-75 E 7
Cambaxi ○ ANG 216-217 E 4
Cambellford ○ CDN (ONT) 238-239 H 4
Cambo ∼ ANG 216-217 D 4
Cambodia = Kâmpŭchéa ■ K 158-159 G 4
Camboeiro, Riachão do ∼ BR 68-69 F 7
Cambombo ○ ANG 216-217 C 5
Camboon P.O. ○ AUS 178-179 L 3
Camboriú, Ponta ▲ BR 74-75 G 5
Camborne ○ CDN (BC) 230-231 M 3
Cambrai ○· F 90-91 J 6
Cambria ○ USA (CA) 248-249 C 4
Cambrian Mountains ▲ GB 90-91 F 5
Cambridge ○ CDN (NS) 240-241 N 4
Cambridge ○ CDN (ONT) 238-239 E 5
Cambridge ○·· GB 90-91 H 5
Cambridge ○ JA 54-55 G 5
Cambridge ○ NZ 182 E 2
Cambridge ○ USA (ID) 252-253 B 2
Cambridge ○ USA (IL) 274-275 H 3
Cambridge ○ USA (MA) 278-279 K 6
Cambridge ○ USA (MD) 280-281 K 5
Cambridge ○ USA (MN) 270-271 E 5
Cambridge ○ USA (NE) 262-263 F 4
Cambridge ○ USA (OH) 280-281 E 3
Cambridge Bay ≈ 24-25 T 6
Cambridge Bay ○ CDN 24-25 U 6
Cambridge City ○ USA (IN) 274-275 N 5
Cambridge Gulf ≈ 172-173 J 3
Cambridge Junction ○ USA (MI) 272-273 E 5
Cambridge Point ▲ CDN 24-25 g 3
Cambridge Springs ○ USA (PA) 280-281 F 2
Cambrils ○ E 98-99 H 4
Cambu, Rio ∼ BR 62-63 K 6
Cambuí ○ BR 72-73 G 7
Cambulo ○ ANG 216-217 F 3
Camburinga X AUS 174-175 D 3
Cambutal ○ PA 52-53 D 8
Camden ○ USA (AL) 284-285 C 5
Camden ○ USA (AR) 276-277 C 7
Camden ○ USA (ME) 278-279 M 4
Camden ○ USA (MS) 268-269 L 4
Camden ○ USA (NC) 282-283 L 4
Camden ○ USA (NJ) 280-281 L 4
Camden ○ USA (NY) 278-279 F 5
Camden ○ USA (OH) 280-281 B 4
Camden ○ USA (TN) 276-277 G 4
Camden ○· USA (SC) 284-285 K 2
Camden Bay ≈ 20-21 S 1
Camdenton ○ USA (MO) 274-275 F 6
Cameia, Parque Nacional da ⊥ ANG 216-217 F 5
Camel Back Mountain ▲ CDN (NB) 240-241 J 3
Camel Creek ○ AUS 174-175 H 6
Çameli ○ TR 128-129 C 4
Camel Race Course · KSA 130-131 K 5
Camelsfoot Range ▲ CDN (BC) 230-231 G 2
Cameo ○ CDN (SAS) 232-233 M 2
Cameron ○ USA (AZ) 256-257 D 3
Cameron ○ USA (LA) 268-269 G 7
Cameron ○ USA (MO) 274-275 D 5
Cameron ○ USA (SC) 284-285 K 3
Cameron ○ USA (TX) 266-267 L 3
Cameron Corner · AUS 178-179 F 5
Cameron Island ⌒ CDN 24-25 U 2
Cameron River ∼ CDN 30-31 N 4
Cameroon = Cameroun ■ CAM 204-205 J 6
Cameroon, Mount = Mont Cameroun ▲·· CAM 204-205 H 6
Cameroun, Estuaire du ≈ 210-211 B 2
Cameroun, Mont = Mount Cameroon ▲·· CAM 204-205 H 6
Cametá ○ BR 68-69 D 3
Camfield ○ AUS 172-173 K 4
Camiaco ○ BOL 70-71 E 4
Camiguin Island ⌒ RP (CAG) 160-161 D 3
Camiguin Island ⌒ RP (MSO) 160-161 F 8
Camiling ○ RP 160-161 D 5
Camilla ○ USA (GA) 284-285 F 5
Camiña ○ RCH 70-71 C 6
Caming ○ RI 164-165 G 6
Caminha ○ P 98-99 C 4
Camino de Santiago ··· E 98-99 D 3
Caminos, Dos ○ YV 60-61 J 3
Camisea ○ PE 64-65 F 7
Camissombo ○ ANG 216-217 F 4
Čamkanī ○ AFG 138-139 B 3
Çamlıdere ☆ TR 128-129 E 2
Cammarata, Monte ▲ I 100-101 D 6
Cammoo Caves · AUS 178-179 L 2
Camocim ○ BR 68-69 H 3
Camocim de São Felix ○ BR 68-69 L 6
Camogton ○ RP 160-161 E 6
Camongua ○ ANG 216-217 D 5
Camooweal ○ AUS 174-175 E 6
Camooweal Caves National Park ⊥ AUS 174-175 E 6
Camopi ○ F 62-63 H 4
Camopi ∼ F 62-63 H 4
Camorta Island ⌒ IND 140-141 L 5
Camotes Islands ⌒ RP 160-161 F 7
Camotes Sea ≈ 160-161 F 7
Čamp, ostrov ⌒ RUS 84-85 e 2
Campamento ○ HN 52-53 L 4
Campamento Río Grande ○ YV 60-61 L 3
Campana, Cerro la ▲ RCH 80 D 5
Campana, Isla ⌒ RCH 80 C 4
Campana, Monte ▲ RA 80 H 7
Campana, Parque Nacional la ⊥ RCH 78-79 D 2
Campanario ○ BR 72-73 K 5
Campanarío, Cerro ▲ RA 78-79 D 3
Campanas ○ RA 76-77 D 5
Campania ◘ I 100-101 E 4
Campania Island ⌒ CDN (BC) 228-229 E 3
Campanilla ○ PE 64-65 D 5
Campanquiz, Cerros ▲ PE 64-65 D 4
Campaspe ○ AUS 174-175 J 7
Campbell ○ USA (AL) 284-285 C 5
Campbell ○ USA (MO) 276-277 E 4
Campbell ○ USA (NE) 262-263 H 4
Campbell ○ ZA 220-221 F 4
Campbell, Cape ▲ NZ 182 E 4
Campbell Bay ≈ 24-25 U 6
Campbell Hill ▲ USA (OH) 280-281 C 3
Campbell Island ⌒ CDN 24-25 G 6
Campbell Lake ⬭ CDN (NWT) 20-21 Y 2
Campbell Lake ⬭ CDN (NWT) 30-31 Q 4
Campbell Plateau ≃ 13 H 7
Campbell River ○ CDN (BC) 230-231 D 3
Campbell's Bay ○ CDN (QUE) 238-239 J 3
Campbellsville ○ USA (KY) 276-277 K 3
Campbellton ○ CDN (NB) 240-241 J 3
Campbellton ○ CDN (PEI) 240-241 L 4
Campbellton ○ USA (FL) 286-287 D 1
Campbellton ○ USA (TX) 266-267 J 5
Campbell Town ○ AUS 180-181 J 6
Campbeltown ○ GB 90-91 E 4
Camp Century ○ GRØ 26-27 U 5
Camp Crook ○ USA (SD) 260-261 C 1
Campeana ○ GNB 202-203 C 4
Campeche ◘ MEX 52-53 J 2
Campeche ☆· MEX 52-53 J 2
Campeche, Bahía de ≈ 52-53 G 2
Campechuela ○ C 54-55 G 4
Camper ○ CDN (MAN) 234-235 E 3
Camperdown ○ AUS 180-181 G 5
Camperdown ○ ZA 220-221 K 4
Camperville ○ CDN (MAN) 234-235 C 3
Camp Gagetown xx CDN (NB) 240-241 J 5
Cẩm Phả ☆ VN 156-157 E 6
Camp Hill ○ USA (AL) 284-285 E 4
Campidano ⌣ I 100-101 B 5
Campillos ○ E 98-99 E 6
Campín, El ○ CO 60-61 F 5
Campina ○ BR 66-67 J 5
Campina da Lagoa ○ BR 74-75 D 5
Campina do Simão ○ BR 74-75 E 5
Campina Grande ○ BR 68-69 L 5
Campinas ○ BR (BAH) 72-73 J 2
Campinas ○ BR (PAU) 72-73 G 7
Campinas, Área Indígena X BR 64-65 F 5
Campina Verde ○ BR 72-73 F 5
Camping Island ⌒ CDN 24-25 P 6
Campinho ○ BR (BAH) 72-73 J 2
Campinho ○ BR (BAH) 72-73 L 2
Camp Lloyd ○ GRØ 28-29 P 3
Camplong ○ RI 166-167 B 7
Campo ○· CAM 210-211 B 2
Campo ○ MOC 218-219 J 3
Campo ○ USA (CA) 248-249 H 7
Campo ○ USA (CO) 254-255 N 6
Campo, El ○ USA (TX) 266-267 L 4
Campo, Réserve de = Campo Reserve ⊥ CAM 210-211 B 2
Campo Alegre ○ BR (ALA) 68-69 K 6
Campo Alegre ○ BR (PIA) 68-69 H 6
Campo Alegre ○ BR (TOC) 68-69 D 5
Campoalegre ○ CO 60-61 D 6
Campo Alegre ○ YV 60-61 K 3
Campo Alegre de Goiás ○ BR 72-73 G 4
Campo Alegre de Lourdes ○ BR 68-69 G 6
Campobasso ☆ I 100-101 E 4
Campo Belo ○ BR 72-73 H 6
Campo Bernal ○ YV 60-61 E 3
Campo Camalajue ○ MEX 50-51 B 3
Campo de Carabobo, Parque · YV 60-61 G 2
Campo de Talampaya · RA 76-77 D 5
Campo do Padre, Morro ▲ BR 74-75 F 6
Campo Erê ○ BR 74-75 D 6
Campo Esperanza ○ PY 76-77 H 2
Campo Gallo ○ RA 76-77 F 4
Campo Garay ○ RA 76-77 G 5
Campo Grande ☆ BR 70-71 K 7
Campo Grande ○ RA 76-77 K 4
Campo Grande, Cachoeira ∼ BR 70-71 F 2
Campo Grayling Artillery Range xx USA (MI) 272-273 E 3
Campo Largo ○ BR 74-75 F 5
Campo Maior ○ BR 68-69 G 4
Campo Maior ○ P 98-99 D 5
Campomento ○ PY 76-77 H 1
Campo Mourão ○ BR 74-75 D 5
Campo Novo do Parecis ○ BR 70-71 J 3
Campo Nuevo ○ MEX 50-51 B 3
Campo Reserve = Réserve de Campo ⊥ CAM 210-211 B 2
Campos ○ BR 72-73 K 6
Campos ⁐ BR 68-69 G 7
Campos, Laguna ⬭ PY 70-71 G 7
Campos, Tierra de ▲ E 98-99 E 4
Campos Belos ○ BR 72-73 G 2
Campos do Jordão ○ BR 72-73 H 7
Campos dos Parecis ⁐ BR 70-71 H 3
Campo Seco ○ BR 76-77 K 6
Campos Eliseos ○ BR 72-73 D 6
Campo Serio ○ PE 64-65 E 2
Campos Gerais ○ BR 72-73 H 6
Campos Novos ○ BR 74-75 E 6
Campos Sales ○ BR 68-69 H 5
Camp Peary xx USA (VA) 280-281 K 6
Camp Pendleton Marine Corps Base · USA (CA) 248-249 G 6
Camp Point ○ USA (IL) 274-275 G 4
Camp Ripley Military Reservation xx USA (MN) 270-271 D 4
Camp Roberts Military Reservation xx USA (CA) 248-249 D 4
Camp Scenic ○ USA (TX) 266-267 H 3
Camp Sherman ○ USA (OR) 244-245 D 6
Campti ○ USA (LA) 268-269 G 5
Camp Verde ○ USA (AZ) 256-257 D 4
Camp Wood ○ USA (TX) 266-267 H 4
Cam Ranh ○ VN 158-159 K 5
Camrose ○ CDN (ALB) 232-233 F 2
Camsell Bay ⬭ CDN 28-29 F 3
Camsell Lake ⬭ CDN 30-31 O 4
Camú, Río ∼ DOM 54-55 K 5
Camucio ○ ANG 216-217 B 7
Camulemba, Capenda- ○ ANG 216-217 E 4
Camuy ○ USA (PR) 286-287 P 2
Camuya, Río ∼ CO 64-65 F 1
Čamzihka ○ RUS 96-97 D 6
Čamzinka ○ RUS 96-97 D 6
Çan ☆ TR 128-129 B 2
Cana ○ BOL 70-71 C 7
Caña, La ○ CO 60-61 C 3
Canaã ○ BR 68-69 F 5
Canaã, Rio ∼ BR 70-71 F 2
Canaan ○ USA (NH) 278-279 J 5
Canaan River ∼ CDN (NB) 240-241 K 4
Canaan Station ○ CDN (NB) 240-241 K 4
Canabal ○ E 98-99 D 3
Cana-Brava ○ BR 72-73 H 4
Cana Brava, Rio ∼ BR 72-73 F 2
Cana-Brava, Serra da ▲ BR 72-73 K 4
Canadá ○ BR 68-69 F 2
Canada ■ CDN 38-39 D 3
Cañada, La ○ RA (COD) 76-77 F 6
Cañada, La ○ RA (SAE) 76-77 F 4
Canada Basin ≃ 16 B 33
Canada Bay ≈ 38-39 Q 3
Canada Bay ≈ CDN 242-243 M 2
Cañada de Gómez ○ RA 78-79 J 2
Cañada de Luque ○ RA 76-77 F 6
Canada Harbour ○ CDN (NFL) 242-243 M 2
Canada Lake ○ USA (NY) 278-279 G 5
Cañada Rosquín ○ RA 78-79 J 2
Cañada Seca ○ RA 78-79 H 3
Canadian ○ USA (TX) 264-265 D 3
Canadian-Pacific-Railway II CDN 232-233 K 3
Canadian River ∼ USA (NM) 256-257 M 3
Canadian River ∼ USA (OK) 264-265 J 3
Canadian River ∼ USA (TX) 264-265 D 3
Cañadon El Pluma ∼ RA 80 E 3
Cañadón Lagarto ○ RA 80 F 2
Cañadón Sacho ∼ RA 80 E 2
Cañadón Seco ∼ RA 80 E 2
Canadys ○ USA (SC) 284-285 K 3
Canagu, Río ∼ YV 60-61 F 3
Canaima ○ YV 60-61 K 4
Canaima, Parque National ⊥ YV 60-61 K 5
Çanakkale ☆· TR 128-129 B 2
Çanakkale Boğazı ≈ 128-129 B 2
Canal de Tūnis ≃ 100-101 C 6
Canale di Sicilia ≃ 100-101 C 6
Canal Flats ○ CDN (BC) 230-231 O 3
Canalí ○ MEX 52-53 E 1
Canal P.O. ○ AUS 178-179 K 3
Canals ○ RA 78-79 H 2
Canal Winchester ○ USA (OH) 280-281 D 4
Canamã, Rio ∼ BR 70-71 H 2
Cananari, Río ∼ CO 66-67 B 2
Canandaigua ○ USA (NY) 278-279 D 6
Cananea ○ MEX 50-51 D 2
Cananéia ○ BR 74-75 G 5
Canar ○ EC 64-65 C 3
Canarana ○ BR (BAH) 68-69 H 7
Canarana ○ BR (MAT) 72-73 D 2
Canárias, Ilha das ⌒ BR 68-69 H 3
Canarreos, Archipiélago de los ⌒ C 54-55 D 4
Canary ○ AUS 178-179 F 2
Canary Islands = Canarias, Islas ⌒ E 188-189 C 6
Cañas ○ MEX 52-53 D 2
Cañas, Bahía las ≈ 78-79 C 3
Cañas, Las ○ CR 52-53 B 6
Cañas, Playa las ○ C 54-55 D 3
Cañas, Río ∼ RA 76-77 E 2
Cañasgordas ○ CO 60-61 C 4
Canastra, Rio ∼ BR 68-69 D 7
Canastra, Serra da ▲ BR 68-69 J 7
Canastra, Serra da ▲ BR 72-73 G 6
Canatián ○ MEX 50-51 G 5
Canatiba ○ BR 72-73 J 2
Canaveral ○ EC 64-65 B 3
Canaveral, Cape ▲ USA (FL) 286-287 J 3
Canaveral National Seashore ⊥ USA (FL) 286-287 J 3
Cañaveras ○ E 98-99 F 4
Canavieiras ○ BR 72-73 L 3
Canayan ○ RP 160-161 E 8
Cañazas ○ PA (Pan) 52-53 E 7
Cañazas ○ PA (Ver) 52-53 D 7
Canberra ★· AUS 180-181 K 3
Canberra Space Centre · AUS 180-181 K 3
Canby ○ USA (CA) 246-247 E 2
Canby ○ USA (MN) 270-271 B 6
Canby ○ USA (OR) 244-245 C 5
Cancela ○ BR 68-69 G 3
Cancelão ○ BR 74-75 D 8
Canchayllo ○ PE 64-65 E 7
Canchungo ○ GNB 202-203 B 3
Canconga ○ ANG 216-217 E 6
Cancosa ○ RCH 70-71 C 6
Cancuc ○ MEX 52-53 H 3
Cancuén ∴· GCA 52-53 J 3
Cancún ○· MEX 52-53 L 1
Cancún, Isla ⌒ MEX 52-53 L 1
Candarave ○ PE 70-71 B 5
Çandarlı Körfezi ≈ 128-129 B 3
Candeado ○ MOC 218-219 G 4
Candeias ○ BR 72-73 L 2
Candeias, Rio ∼ BR 66-67 F 7
Candela ○ MEX 50-51 J 4
Candelaria ○· MEX 52-53 J 2
Candelaria ○ USA (TX) 266-267 C 3
Candelaria, La ○ CO 60-61 F 5
Candelaria, La ○ YV 60-61 H 2
Candelaria, Río ∼ BOL 70-71 H 5
Candelaria, Río ∼ MEX 52-53 J 2
Candeleda ○ E 98-99 E 4
Candelwood, Lake ⬭ USA (CT) 280-281 N 2
Candi · RI (LAM) 162-163 E 7
Candi · RI (RIA) 162-163 D 4
Candiac ○ CDN (SAS) 232-233 P 5
Candi Besakih · RI 168 B 7
Cândido de Abreu ○ BR 74-75 E 5
Cándido González ○ C 54-55 F 4
Cândido Mendes ○ BR 68-69 F 2
Cândido Rondon ○ BR 76-77 K 3
Cândido Sales ○ BR 72-73 K 3
Candi Mendut · RI 168 D 3
Candi Pura · RI 168 B 7
Candi Sukuh · RI 168 D 3
Candle ○ USA 20-21 K 4
Candle Lake ○ CDN (SAS) 232-233 N 2
Candle Lake ⬭ CDN (SAS) 232-233 N 2
Čandman' = Talšand ○ MAU 148-149 C 5
Cando ○ CDN (SAS) 232-233 K 3
Cando ○ USA (ND) 258-259 H 3
Candon ○ RP 160-161 D 4
Candover ○ ZA 220-221 K 3
Candulo ○ MOC 214-215 J 6
Cẩn Đước ○ VN 158-159 J 5
Cẩn Du'ó'c ○ VN 158-159 J 5
Candy Reservoir ⬭ USA (OK) 264-265 H 2
Canea ○ BR 62-63 G 5
Caneapo ○ BR 62-63 G 5
Canegrass ○ AUS 180-181 F 2
Cane Grove ○ GUY 62-63 F 2
Canela, La ○ C 54-55 H 4
Canela Baja ○ RCH 76-77 B 6
Canelo ○ USA (AZ) 256-257 E 7
Canelones ☆ ROU 78-79 L 3
Canelos ○ EC 64-65 D 2
Canelos, Los ○ RCH 80 E 6
Cane River ○ AUS 172-173 B 7
Cane River ∼ AUS 172-173 B 7
Cañete ○ E 98-99 G 4
Cañete ○· RCH 78-79 C 4
Cañete, Río de ∼ PE 64-65 D 8
Caney ○ USA (KS) 262-263 L 7
Caney Fork ∼ USA (TN) 276-277 K 5
Caney River ∼ USA (KS) 262-263 K 7
Caney River ∼ USA (OK) 264-265 J 2
Caneyville ○ USA (KY) 276-277 J 3
Canford ○ CDN (BC) 230-231 J 3
Čangada ∼ RUS 108-109 c 7
Cangaime, Río ∼ EC 64-65 D 3
Cangala ○ ANG 216-217 D 6
Cangallo ○ PE 64-65 E 8
Cangalo ○ ANG 216-217 D 5
Cangandala ○ ANG 216-217 D 4
Cangandala, Parque Nacional de ⊥ ANG 216-217 D 4
Cangas ○ E 98-99 C 3
Cangas del Narcea ○ E 98-99 D 3
Cangjie Temple · VRC 154-155 F 4
Cangoa ○ ANG 216-217 E 6
Cango Caves · ZA 220-221 F 6
Cangombe ○ ANG 216-217 F 7
Cangrejo, Cerro ▲ RA 80 D 4
Cangshan ○ VRC 154-155 L 4
Canguaretama ○ BR 68-69 L 5
Canguçu ○ BR 74-75 D 8
Čangūle, Rūdhāne-ye ∼ IRQ 128-129 M 6
Cangumbe ○ ANG 216-217 E 5
Cangxi ○ VRC 154-155 D 6
Cangyanshan · VRC 154-155 J 3
Cangyuan ○ VRC 142-143 L 4
Cangzhou ○ VRC 154-155 K 2
Can Hasan Höyügü ∴· TR 128-129 E 4
Canhotinho ○ BR 68-69 K 6
Caniapiscau, Lac ⬭ CDN 36-37 P 7
Caniapiscau, Réservoir de < CDN 36-37 P 7
Caniapiscau, Rivière ∼ CDN 36-37 P 7
Canicattì ○ I 100-101 D 6
Canigao Channel ≈ 160-161 F 7
Canik Dağları ▲ TR 128-129 G 2
Canim Lake ○ CDN (BC) 230-231 J 2
Canim Lake ⬭ CDN (BC) 230-231 J 2
Canindé ○ BR 68-69 J 4
Canindé, Rio ∼ BR 68-69 G 5
Caninde de São Francisco ○ BR 68-69 K 6
Canipo Island ⌒ RP 160-161 D 7
Canisteo ○ USA (NY) 278-279 D 6
Canisteo River ∼ USA (NY) 278-279 D 6
Canister Fall ∼ GUY 62-63 E 3
Canit Point ▲ RP 160-161 E 6
Canjime ○ ANG 216-217 E 8
Çankırı ☆· TR 128-129 E 2
Cankuzo ○ BU 212-213 C 5
Canlaon, Mount ▲ RP 160-161 E 7
Canmang ○ VRC 156-157 G 2
Canmore ○ CDN (ALB) 232-233 C 4
Cann, Mount ▲ AUS 180-181 K 4
Cannac Island ⌒ PNG 183 G 5
Cannanore ○· IND 140-141 F 5
Cannanore Islands ⌒ IND 140-141 E 5
Cannelton ○ USA (IN) 274-275 M 7
Cannes ○· F 90-91 L 10
Canning Hill ▲ AUS 176-177 D 4
Canning River ∼ USA 20-21 R 2
Canning Stock Route II AUS 172-173 G 7
Cannon Ball ○ USA (ND) 258-259 G 5
Cannonball River ∼ USA (ND) 258-259 F 5
Cannon Beach ○ USA (OR) 244-245 B 5
Cannondale Mount ▲ AUS 178-179 K 3
Cannon Falls ○ USA (MN) 270-271 F 6
Cannonville ○ USA (UT) 254-255 C 6
Cann River ○ AUS (VIC) 180-181 K 4
Cann River ∼ AUS 180-181 K 4
Caño, El ○ PA 52-53 D 7
Caño, Isla de ⌒ CR 52-53 C 7
Cano, Pico do ▲ CV 202-203 B 6
Canoa ○ HN 52-53 K 4
Canoas ○ BR 74-75 E 7
Canoas ○ MEX 50-51 K 6
Canoas, Punta ▲ MEX 50-51 B 3
Canobie ○ AUS 174-175 F 6
Canobolas, Mount ▲ AUS 180-181 K 2
Canochee River ∼ USA (GA) 284-285 J 4
Canoe ○ CDN (BC) 230-231 K 3
Canoe Creek Indian Reserve X CDN (BC) 230-231 G 2
Canoe Lake ⬭ CDN 32-33 Q 4
Canoe Reach ∼ CDN (BC) 228-229 Q 4
Canoe River ○ CDN (BC) 228-229 P 4
Canoe River ∼ CDN (BC) 228-229 P 4
Caño Hondo, Cuevas de ∴· DOM 54-55 L 5
Canoinhas ○ BR 74-75 E 6
Cañon · DZ 190-191 F 3
Canonaco, Río ∼ EC 64-65 D 2
Canonba ○ AUS 178-179 J 6
Cañoncito Indian Reservation X USA (NM) 256-257 H 3
Canon City ○ USA (CO) 254-255 K 5
Cañon del Sumidero, Parque Nacional ⊥ MEX 52-53 H 3
Cañon de Río Blanco, Parque Nacional ⊥ MEX 52-53 F 2
Cañon Fiord ≈ 26-27 J 3
Cañon Plaza ○ USA (NM) 256-257 J 2
Canonsburg ○ USA (PA) 280-281 F 3
Canoochee ○ USA (GA) 284-285 H 4
Canopus ○ CDN (SAS) 232-233 M 6
Canora ○ CDN (SAS) 232-233 Q 4
Canosa di Púglia ○· I 100-101 F 4
Canouan Island ⌒ WV 56 E 5
Canowindra ○ AUS 180-181 K 2
Canquel, Meseta del ⁐ RA 80 F 2
Canrober Hills ▲ CDN 24-25 N 2
Canso ○ CDN (NS) 240-241 O 5
Canso, Strait of ≈ 38-39 O 6
Canso, Strait of ≈ CDN 240-241 O 5
Canso Channel ≈ 28-29 J 3
Canta ○ PE 64-65 D 7
Cantabria ◘ E 98-99 E 3
Cantábrica, Cordillera ▲ E 98-99 D 3
Cantador, Cerro el ▲ MEX 52-53 C 2
Cantagalo, Ponta ▲ BR 74-75 F 6
Cantalejo ○ E 98-99 F 4
Cantalpino ○ E 98-99 E 4
Čantal'skij hrebet ▲ RUS 112-113 T 3
Čantal'vèrgyrgyn ∼ RUS 112-113 U 3
Cantamar ○ MEX 50-51 A 1
Cantanal, Sierra de ▲ RA 76-77 D 6
Cantário, Rio ∼ BR 70-71 F 2
Cantaura ○ YV 60-61 J 3
Canterbury ○··· GB 90-91 H 6
Canterbury Bight ≈ 182 D 5
Cần Thơ' ○· VN 158-159 H 5
Canthyuaya, Cerros de ▲ PE 64-65 E 5
Cantil ○ USA (CA) 248-249 G 4
Cantilan ○ RP 160-161 F 8
Cantiles, Cayo ⌒ C 54-55 D 4
Canto del Agua ○ RCH 76-77 B 5
Canto do Buriti ○ BR 68-69 G 6
Canton ○ USA (GA) 284-285 F 2
Canton ○ USA (IL) 274-275 J 4
Canton ○ USA (MO) 274-275 G 4
Canton ○ USA (MS) 268-269 K 4
Canton ○ USA (NC) 282-283 E 5
Canton ○ USA (NY) 278-279 F 4
Canton ○ USA (OK) 264-265 F 2
Canton ○ USA (PA) 280-281 K 2
Canton ○ USA (SD) 260-261 K 3
Canton ○ USA (TX) 264-265 J 6
Canton ○· USA (OH) 280-281 E 3
Canton, El ○ YV 60-61 F 4
Canton = Guangzhou ☆·· VRC 156-157 H 5
Canton Lake ⬭ USA (OK) 264-265 F 2
Cantuar ○ CDN (SAS) 232-233 K 5
Cantwell ○ USA 20-21 Q 5
Canudos ○ BR 68-69 J 6
Cañuelas ○ RA 78-79 K 3
Canumã, Rio ∼ BR 66-67 H 5
Canunda National Park ⊥ AUS 180-181 F 4
Canutama ○ BR 66-67 E 6
Canutillo ○ USA (TX) 266-267 A 2
Canwood ○ CDN (SAS) 232-233 M 2
Canxixe ○ MOC 218-219 H 3
Čany ☆ RUS 114-115 O 7
Čany, ozero ⬭ RUS 124-125 K 1
Canyon ○ CDN (ONT) 234-235 K 5
Canyon ○ CDN (ONT) 236-237 D 5
Canyon ⁐·· RI 166-167 K 4
Canyon ○ USA (TX) 264-265 C 4
Canyon ○ USA (WY) 252-253 H 2
Canyon Creek ○ USA (MT) 250-251 G 5
Canyon de Chelly National Monument ∴ USA (AZ) 256-257 F 2
Canyon Ferry ○ USA (MT) 250-251 H 5
Canyon Ferry Lake ⬭ USA (MT) 250-251 H 5
Canyon Lake ⬭ USA (TX) 266-267 J 4
Canyonlands National Park ⊥ USA (UT) 254-255 F 5
Canyon Largo River ∼ USA (NM) 256-257 H 2
Canyon Ranges ▲ CDN 30-31 G 4
Canyon River ∼ CDN 36-37 G 2
Canyonville ○ USA (OR) 244-245 B 8
Canzar ○ ANG 216-217 F 3
Cao Bằng ☆· VN 156-157 E 5
Caohekou ○ VRC 150-151 D 7
Caojian ○ VRC 142-143 L 3
Cao Lãnh ○ VN 158-159 H 5
Caombo ○ ANG 216-217 D 4
Caonao ∼ C 54-55 F 4
Caoqiao ○ VRC 154-155 L 6
Cáorle ○ I 100-101 D 2
Cao Xian ○ VRC 154-155 J 4
Čapa ∼ RUS 116-117 F 5
Capachica ○ PE 70-71 C 4
Čapaev = Čapaevo ☆ KA 96-97 G 8
Čapaevka ∼ RUS 96-97 G 7
Čapaevo ☆ KA 96-97 G 8
Čapaevo ○ RUS 118-119 H 5
Čapaevskoe ○ KA 124-125 H 2
Capahuari, Río ∼ EC 64-65 D 3
Capaias ○ RP 160-161 C 7
Capalonga ○ RP 160-161 E 5
Capalulu ○ RI 164-165 J 4
Capana ○ BR 66-67 C 3
Capana, Punta ▲ YV 60-61 F 2
Capanema ○ BR 68-69 E 2
Capão Alto ○ BR 74-75 E 6
Capão Bonito ○ BR 72-73 F 7
Capão Branco ○ BR 74-75 D 7
Capão da Canoa ○ BR 74-75 E 7
Capão Doce, Morro do ▲ BR 74-75 E 6
Caparaó, Parque Nacional do ⊥ BR 72-73 K 6
Čaparhār ○ AFG 138-139 C 2
Capas ○ RP 160-161 D 5
Capauari, Rio ∼ BR 66-67 C 3
Capauari, Serra do ▲ BR 66-67 C 3
Cap-aux-Meules ○ CDN (QUE) 242-243 G 5
Capay ○ RP 160-161 E 6
Capbreton ○ F 90-91 G 10
Cap-Chat ○ CDN (QUE) 242-243 B 3
Cap-de-la-Madeleine ○ CDN (QUE) 238-239 N 2

Cap-de-Rabast ○ CDN (QUE) 242-243 D 3
Cap-d'Espoir ○ CDN (QUE) 240-241 L 2
Cape Abyssal Plain ≃ 6-7 L 12
Cape Adare ▲ ARK 16 F 18
Cape Alexander ▲ SOL 184 I c 2
Cape Anguille ○ CDN (NFL) 242-243 J 5
Cape Arid National Park ⊥ AUS 176-177 G 6
Cape Basin ≃ ZA 6-7 K 12
Cape Bertholet Wildlife Sanctuary ⊥ AUS 172-173 F 4
Cape Borda ○ AUS 180-181 D 3
Cape Breton Highlands National Park ⊥ CDN (NS) 240-241 O 4
Cape Breton Island ⌒ CDN (NS) 240-241 P 4
Cape Byrd ▲ ARK 16 G 8
Cape Canaveral ○ USA (FL) 286-287 J 3
Cape Canaveral Air Force Station xx USA (FL) 286-287 J 3
Cape Charles ○ USA (VA) 280-281 K 6
Cape Chidley Islands ⌒ CDN 36-37 R 4
Cape Coast ☆ • GH 202-203 K 7
Cape Cod Bay ≈ 46-47 N 5
Cape Cod Bay ≈ USA 278-279 L 7
Cape Cod Peninsula ⊥ USA (MA) 278-279 M 7
Cape Colbeck ▲ ARK 16 F 21
Cape Coral ○ USA (FL) 286-287 H 5
Cape Crawford ○ AUS 174-175 C 5
Cape Croker ○ CDN (ONT) 238-239 D 4
Cape Croker Indian Reserve ⊼ CDN (ONT) 238-239 E 4
Cape Dart ▲ ARK 16 F 24
Cape Dorset ○ CDN 36-37 L 2
Cape Elizabeth ○ USA (ME) 278-279 L 5
Cape Fear River ~ USA (NC) 282-283 J 6
Cape Fear River ~ USA (NC) 282-283 J 5
Cape Flying Fish ▲ ARK 16 F 26
Cape Freshfield ▲ ARK 16 G 16
Cape Gantheaume Conservation Park ⊥ AUS 180-181 D 4
Cape George ○ CDN (NS) 240-241 O 5
Cape Girardeau ○ USA (MO) 276-277 F 3
Cape Girgir ▲ PNG 183 C 2
Cape Hope Islands ⌒ CDN 38-39 E 2
Cape Horn ○ USA (ID) 252-253 C 2
Cape Horn = Hornos, Cabo de ▲ RCH 80 G 8
Cape Island ⌒ USA (SC) 284-285 L 3
Cape Jervis ○ AUS 180-181 E 3
Cape Krusenstern National Monument ⊥ USA 20-21 H 3
Capel ○ AUS 176-177 C 6
Capel, Cape ▲ CDN 24-25 X 3
Capela do Mato Verde ○ BR 72-73 H 4
Cape Le Grand National Park ⊥ AUS 176-177 G 6
Capelinha ○ BR 72-73 J 4
Capel'ka ○ RUS 94-95 L 2
Capella ○ AUS 178-179 K 2
Capelle, la ○ F 90-91 J 7
Cape Lookout National Seashore ⊥ USA (NC) 282-283 L 6
Cape May ○ USA (NJ) 280-281 M 5
Capembe ~ ANG 216-217 F 8
Cape Melville National Park ⊥ AUS 174-175 H 4
Cape Monze = Rās Muari ▲ PK 134-135 M 6
Cape Moore ▲ ARK 16 F 17
Capenda-Camulemba ○ ANG 216-217 E 4
Cape of Good Hope ▲ • ZA 220-221 D 7
Cape of Good Hope = Kaap die Goeie Hoop ▲ • ZA 220-221 D 7
Cape Palmer ▲ ARK 16 F 27
Cape Parry ○ CDN 24-25 K 5
Cape-Pele ○ CDN (NB) 240-241 L 4
Cape Peninsula ⌣ ZA 220-221 D 7
Cape Pole ○ USA 32-33 D 3
Cape Race ○ CDN (NFL) 242-243 P 6
Cape Rama ○ IND 140-141 E 3
Cape Range ▲ AUS 172-173 A 7
Cape Range National Park ⊥ AUS 172-173 A 7
Cape Ray ○ CDN (NFL) 242-243 J 5
Cape River ~ AUS 174-175 H 7
Cape Romain National Wildlife Refuge ⊥ USA (SC) 284-285 L 4
Cape Sable Island ⌒ CDN (NS) 240-241 K 7
Cape Saint Francis ▲ CDN (NFL) 242-243 Q 5
Cape Saint Francis ○ ZA 220-221 G 7
Cape Saint John ▲ CDN (NFL) 242-243 N 2
Cape Scott Provincial Park ⊥ CDN (BC) 230-231 A 3
Čāpešlū ○ IR 136-137 F 6
Cape Smiley ▲ ARK 16 F 29
Capesterre-Belle-Eau ○ F 56 E 3
Cape Surville ▲ SOL 184 I f 4
Cape Tormentine ○ CDN (NB) 240-241 M 4
Cape Town ☆ •• ZA 220-221 D 6
Cape Town = Cape Town = Kaapstad ☆ •• ZA 220-221 D 7
Cape Tribulation National Park ⊥ AUS 174-175 H 5
Cape Upstart National Park ⊥ AUS 174-175 J 6
Cape Verde = Cabo Verde ■ CV 202-203 B 6
Cape Verde Islands = Cabo Verde, Arquipélago de ⌒ CV 202-203 B 6
Cape Verde Plateau ≃ 6-7 G 7
Cape Vincent ○ USA (NY) 278-279 E 4
Cape Washington ▲ FJI 184 III a 3
Cape York Peninsula ⌣ AUS 174-175 G 3
Cape Young ○ CDN 24-25 O 6
Cape Zele'e = Nialaha'u Point ▲ SOL 184 I e 3
Cap-Haïtien ☆ RH 54-55 J 5
Capiá, Rio ~ BR 68-69 K 6
Capibaribe, Rio ~ BR 68-69 L 5
Capilla del Monte ○ RA 76-77 E 6
Capim, Rio ~ BR 62-63 K 6
Capim Grosso ○ BR 68-69 H 7
Capinópolis ○ BR 72-73 F 5
Capinzal ○ BR 74-75 E 6
Capirenda ○ BOL 76-77 F 1
Cap Island ⌒ RP 160-161 D 10
Capissayan ○ RP 160-161 D 3
Capistrano ○ BR 68-69 J 4
Capitachouane, Rivière ~ CDN (QUE) 236-237 M 5
Capitan ○ USA (NM) 256-257 K 5
Capitán Aracena, Isla ⌒ RCH 80 E 7
Capitan Baldo ○ PY 76-77 K 2
Capitan Grande Indian Reservation ⊼ USA (CA) 248-249 H 7
Capitán Pablo Lagerenza ☆ PY 70-71 G 6
Capitão Porto Alegre ○ BR 76-77 K 5
Capitán Sarmiente ○ RA 78-79 K 3
Capitán Ustares, Cerro ▲ BOL 70-71 G 6
Capitão, Igarapé ~ BR 66-67 E 6
Capitão Cardoso, Rio ~ BR 70-71 G 2
Capitão de Campos ○ BR 68-69 H 4
Capitão Enéas ○ BR 72-73 J 4
Capitão Leônidas Marques ○ BR 74-75 D 5
Capitão Poço ○ BR 68-69 E 2
Capitán Rivadenaira ○ EC 64-65 E 2
Capitol ○ USA (MT) 250-251 P 6
Capitol Peak ▲ USA (CO) 254-255 H 4
Capitol Peak ▲ USA (NV) 246-247 H 2
Capitol Reef National Park ⊥ USA (UT) 254-255 D 5
Capivara, Represa < BR 72-73 E 7
Capivara, Rio ~ BR 68-69 D 6
Capivaras, Cachoeira das ~ BR 66-67 K 6
Capivaras, Salto das ~ BR 70-71 K 3
Capivari ○ BR 72-73 G 7
Capivari, Rio ~ BR 70-71 J 6
Capixaba ○ BR 68-69 G 7
Čaplanovo ○ RUS 122-123 K 5
Čaplino ○ RUS 112-113 Y 4
Čaplino, Novoe ○ RUS 112-113 Y 4
Čapljina ○ BIH 100-101 F 3
Čaplygin ○ RUS 94-95 Q 5
Čaplynka ○ UA 102-103 H 4
Cap Marcos, Área Indígena ⊼ BR 70-71 H 4
Cap Mountain ▲ CDN 30-31 H 4
Capoche ~ MOC 218-219 G 2
Capoeira do Rei ○ BR 62-63 J 5
Capolo ○ ANG 216-217 B 5
Čapoma ~ RUS 88-89 P 3
Caponda ○ MOC 218-219 F 2
Čapo-Ologo ○ RUS 118-119 J 7
Capo Rizzuto ○ I 100-101 F 5
Capot Blanc, Lac ○ CDN 30-31 O 4
Capoto, Área Indígena ⊼ BR 68-69 B 6
Capotoan, Mount ▲ RP 160-161 F 6
Cappadocia = Capadocia ⊥ TR 128-129 F 3
Cappahayden ○ CDN (NFL) 242-243 Q 6
Capps ○ USA (FL) 286-287 F 1
Capráia, Ísola di ⌒ I 100-101 B 3
Capreol ○ CDN (ONT) 238-239 E 2
Capri, Ísola di ⌒ •• I 100-101 E 4
Capricorn, Cape ▲ AUS 178-179 L 2
Capricorn Group ⌒ AUS 178-179 L 2
Capricorn Highway II AUS 178-179 H 2
Capricorn Section ⊥ AUS 178-179 M 2
Caprivi Game Park ⊥ NAM 218-219 B 4
Caprivi Strip = Caprivistrook ⊥ NAM 218-219 B 3
Caprock ○ USA (NM) 256-257 M 5
Caprock Canyons State Park ⊥ • USA (TX) 264-265 C 4
Capron ○ USA (VA) 280-281 J 7
Cap Seize ○ CDN (QUE) 242-243 B 3
Captain Cook ○ USA (HI) 288 K 5
Captains Flat ○ AUS 180-181 K 3
Captiva ○ USA (FL) 286-287 G 5
Captiva Island ⌒ USA (FL) 286-287 G 5
Capua ○ ANG 216-217 E 7
Capucapu, Rio ~ BR 62-63 E 6
Capulin ○ USA (NM) 256-257 M 2
Capulin Mountain National Monument • USA (NM) 256-257 M 2
Capul Island ⌒ RP 160-161 F 6
Capunda ○ ANG 216-217 D 5
Cap Wom National Park ⊥ PNG 183 B 2
Čaqlāve, Čam-e ~ IRQ 128-129 L 5
Caqua ○ YV 60-61 H 2
Caquena ○ RCH 70-71 C 6
Caquetá, Río ~ CO 66-67 B 3
Caqueza ○ CO 60-61 E 5
Car ~ KA 124-125 M 4
Čara ☆ RUS (CTN) 118-119 J 7
Čara ~ RUS 118-119 H 7
Čara ~ RUS 118-119 K 5
Čara ~ RUS 118-119 J 6
Carabao Island ⌒ RP 160-161 D 6
Carabaya, Cordillera de ▲ PE 70-71 B 3
Carabaya, Río ~ PE 70-71 C 4
Carabayllo ○ PE 64-65 D 7
Carabinani, Rio ~ BR 66-67 G 4
Carabobo ○ YV 62-63 D 2
Caracal ○ RO 102-103 D 5
Caracal, Rio ~ BR 68-69 E 6
Caracara, Estação Ecológica ⊥ BR 62-63 D 5
Caracaraí ○ BR 62-63 D 5
Caracas ★ • YV 60-61 H 2
Caracol ∴ • BH 52-53 K 3
Caracól ○ BR 68-69 G 6
Caracol ○ BR 76-77 J 2
Caracol ~ MEX 50-51 D 5
Caracoli ○ CO 60-61 E 2
Caracuja Falls ~ CDN 30-31 F 3
Caraculo ○ ANG 216-217 B 7
Carad ○ RH 54-55 J 5
Caraguatá, Arroyo ~ ROU 78-79 M 2
Caraí ○ BR 72-73 K 4
Caraiari, Rio ~ BR 68-69 B 4
Caraíva ○ BR 72-73 L 4
Carajas ○ BR 68-69 C 5
Carajás, Serra dos ▲ BR 68-69 C 5
Čarak, Bandar-e ○ IR 134-135 F 5
Caramat ○ CDN (ONT) 236-237 B 3
Caramelo ○ CO 60-61 D 3
Caramoan ○ RP 160-161 E 6
Caramoan Peninsula ⌣ RP 160-161 E 6
Caraná, Rio ~ BR 70-71 H 3
Caranavi ○ BOL 70-71 D 4
Carandaí ○ BR 72-73 J 6
Carandazinho ○ BR 70-71 J 5
Carandotta ○ AUS 178-179 E 1
Carangola ○ BR 72-73 J 6
Caransebeș ○ RO 102-103 C 5
Carapa ○ YV 60-61 K 3
Carapajó ○ BR 68-69 D 3
Carapán ○ MEX 52-53 C 2
Cara-Paraná, Río ~ CO 64-65 F 2
Carapé, Sierra de ▲ ROU 78-79 M 3
Carapebus ○ BR 72-73 K 7
Carapo ○ YV 60-61 K 5
Caraquet ○ • CDN (NB) 240-241 L 3
Carara Puca ○ BR 66-67 D 2
Carat, Tanjung ▲ RI 162-163 F 6
Caratasca, Cayo ⌒ HN 54-55 D 6
Caratasca, Laguna de ≈ 54-55 C 7
Carateteua ○ BR 68-69 E 2
Caratinga ○ BR 72-73 J 5
Carauari ○ BR 66-67 D 5
Caraúbas ○ BR 68-69 K 4
Caravaca de la Cruz ○ E 98-99 G 5
Caravela ○ GNB 202-203 B 4
Caravelas ○ BR 72-73 L 4
Caraveli ○ PE 64-65 F 9
Caravelle ⊥ F 56 E 3
Caraz ○ PE 64-65 D 6
Carazinho ○ BR (CAT) 74-75 E 7
Carazinho ○ BR (RSU) 74-75 D 7
Carballino, O ○ E 98-99 C 3
Carballo ○ E 98-99 C 3
Carberry ○ CDN (MAN) 234-235 D 5
Carbet, Chutes du ~ • F 56 E 3
Carbine ○ AUS 176-177 F 5
Carbó ○ MEX 50-51 D 3
Carbon ○ CDN (ALB) 232-233 E 4
Carbon ○ USA (TX) 264-265 F 6
Carbonado ○ USA (WA) 244-245 C 3
Carbonara, Capo ▲ I 100-101 B 5
Carbondale ○ USA (CO) 254-255 H 4
Carbondale ○ USA (IL) 276-277 F 3
Carbondale ○ USA (KS) 262-263 L 6
Carbondale ○ USA (MI) 270-271 L 5
Carbondale ○ USA (PA) 280-281 L 2
Carbonear ○ CDN (NFL) 242-243 P 5
Carbonera, La ○ MEX 50-51 L 5
Carboneras ○ E 98-99 G 6
Carbon Hill ○ USA (AL) 284-285 C 3
Carbónia ○ I 100-101 B 5
Carbonita ○ BR 72-73 J 4
Carcajou Lake ○ CDN 30-31 F 2
Carcajou River ~ CDN 30-31 F 3
Carcar ○ RP 160-161 E 7
Carcaraña, Río ~ RA 78-79 J 2
Carcassonne ☆ •• F 90-91 J 10
Carcross ○ CDN 20-21 X 6
Çardak ☆ TR 128-129 C 4
Cardale ○ CDN (MAN) 234-235 C 4
Cardamon Hills ▲ IND 140-141 G 5
Cardamum Island ⌒ IND 140-141 E 5
Cardeña ○ E 98-99 E 5
Cárdenas ○ C 54-55 E 3
Cárdenas ○ MEX (SLP) 50-51 K 6
Cárdenas ○ • MEX (TAB) 52-53 H 2
Cardenyabba Creek ~ AUS 178-179 G 5
Cardiel, Lago ○ RA 80 E 4
Cardiff ○ GB 90-91 F 6
Cardiff Hall ⊥ • JA 54-55 G 5
Cardigan ○ CDN (NS) 240-241 N 4
Cardigan ○ GB 90-91 E 5
Cardigan Bay ≈ 90-91 E 5
Cardigan Strait ≈ 24-25 a 2
Cardinal ○ CDN (MAN) 234-235 E 5
Cardona ○ E 98-99 H 4
Cardona ○ ROU 78-79 L 2
Cardón del Plata ▲ RA 78-79 E 2
Cardoso ○ BR 72-73 F 6
Cardoso, Ilha do ⌒ BR 74-75 G 5
Cardston ○ CDN (ALB) 232-233 E 6
Cardwell ○ AUS 174-175 J 6
Cardwell ○ USA (MT) 250-251 H 6
Cardwell, Cape ▲ CDN 24-25 L 5
Cardwell Range ▲ AUS 174-175 H 6
Čardzouskaja oblast' ■ TM 136-137 G 4
Careen Lake ○ CDN 32-33 Q 3
Carefree ○ USA (IN) 274-275 M 6
Carei ○ RO 102-103 C 4
Careiro ○ BR 66-67 G 4
Careiro da Várzea ○ BR 66-67 H 4
Carén ○ RCH 76-77 B 6
Čarencavan ○ AR 128-129 L 2
Carentan ○ F 90-91 G 7
Carevo ○ BG 102-103 E 6
Carey ○ USA (ID) 252-253 E 3
Carey ○ USA (OH) 280-281 C 3
Carey, Lake ○ AUS 176-177 G 4
Carey Downs ○ AUS 176-177 C 2
Carey Lake ○ CDN 30-31 S 4
Carey Øer ⌒ GRØ 26-27 O 5
Careysburg ○ LB 202-203 E 6
Careys Cave • AUS 180-181 K 3
Cargados Carajos Islands ⊥ MS 12 D 6
Čarh ○ AFG 138-139 B 3
Carhaix-Plouguer ○ F 90-91 F 7
Carhuamayo ○ PE 64-65 D 7
Carhuanca ○ PE 64-65 F 8
Carhuaz ○ PE 64-65 D 6
Carhué ○ RA 78-79 H 4
Cariaco, Golfo de ≈ 60-61 J 2
Cariamanga ○ EC 64-65 C 4
Cariango ○ ANG 216-217 C 5
Cariati ○ I 100-101 F 5
Caribaná, Punta ▲ CO 60-61 C 3
Caribbean Basin ≃ 56 A 4
Caribbean Marine Research Centre Lee Stocking Island ⊥ • BS 54-55 G 3
Caribbean Sea ≈ 56 A 4
Caribe, Río ~ MEX 52-53 J 2
Caribes, Los ○ YV 62-63 D 3
Caribia ○ CO 60-61 C 3
Cariboo Highway • CDN (BC) 230-231 H 2
Cariboo Mountains ▲ CDN (BC) 228-229 N 3
Caribou ○ CDN 30-31 V 6
Caribou ○ USA (ME) 278-279 O 2
Caribou Depot ○ CDN (NB) 240-241 J 3
Caribou Island ⌒ CDN 36-37 J 2
Caribou Lake ○ CDN (MAN) 30-31 W 6
Caribou Lake ○ CDN (NWT) 20-21 Y 2
Caribou Lake ○ CDN (ONT) 234-235 O 4
Caribou Mount ▲ USA 20-21 P 3
Caribou Mountains ▲ CDN 30-31 M 6
Caribou River ~ CDN 20-21 X 3
Caribou River ~ CDN 30-31 W 6
Caribou River ~ CDN 30-31 F 5
Caribou River ~ CDN (BC) 228-229 N 4
Caribou River ~ USA 22-23 Q 5
Caricaca, Rio ~ BR 68-69 E 5
Carié ○ BR 68-69 K 6
Carievale ○ CDN (SAS) 232-233 R 6
Carigara ○ RP 160-161 F 7
Čārīkār ☆ AFG 138-139 B 2
Cari Laufquen, Bajo de ⊥ RA 78-79 E 6
Cari Laufquen Grande, Laguna ○ RA 78-79 E 6
Carinda ○ AUS 178-179 J 6
Cariñena ○ E 98-99 G 4
Carinhanha ○ BR 72-73 J 3
Carinhanha, Rio ~ BR 72-73 H 3
Caripande ○ ANG 214-215 B 7
Caripare ○ BR 68-69 F 7
Caripé, Rio ~ BR 68-69 D 3
Caripira ○ BR 66-67 E 3
Caripito ○ YV 60-61 K 2
Cariquima ○ RCH 70-71 C 6
Carira ○ BR 68-69 K 7
Cariré ○ BR 68-69 H 3
Cariris Novos, Serra dos ▲ BR 68-69 H 5
Caritaya, Embalse de < RCH 70-71 C 6
Caritianas ○ BR 66-67 F 7
Carito, El ○ YV 60-61 J 3
Carius ○ BR 68-69 J 5
Čarky (Muolakan) ~ RUS 110-111 V 6
Carl Blackwell, Lake ○ USA (OK) 264-265 G 2
Carleton ○ CDN (NS) 240-241 K 6
Carleton, Mount ▲ CDN (NB) 240-241 J 3
Carleton Place ○ CDN (ONT) 238-239 J 3
Carletonville ○ ZA 220-221 H 3
Carlin ○ USA (NV) 246-247 J 3
Carlindi ○ AUS 172-173 D 6
Carlin Gold Mine ○ USA (NV) 246-247 J 3
Carlinville ○ USA (IL) 274-275 J 5
Carlisle ○ GB 90-91 F 4
Carlisle ○ USA (IA) 274-275 E 3
Carlisle ○ USA (IN) 274-275 L 6
Carlisle ○ USA (PA) 280-281 J 3
Carlisle ○ USA (SC) 284-285 J 2
Carlisle ○ USA (TX) 268-269 E 6
Carlisle Island ⌒ USA 22-23 L 6
Carlisle Lakes ○ AUS 176-177 J 4
Carlo ○ AUS 178-179 E 2
Carloforte ○ I 100-101 B 5
Carlópolis ○ BR 72-73 F 7
Carlos ○ CDN (ALB) 232-233 D 3
Carlos ○ USA (TX) 266-267 L 3
Carlos Casares ○ RA 78-79 J 3
Carlos Chagas ○ BR 72-73 K 4
Carlos Tejedor ○ RA 78-79 H 3
Carlota, La ○ RA 78-79 H 2
Carlow = Ceatharlach ○ IRL 90-91 D 5
Carlowrie ○ CDN (MAN) 234-235 G 5
Carlsbad ○ USA (CA) 248-249 G 6
Carlsbad ○ USA (NM) 256-257 L 6
Carlsbad ○ USA (TX) 266-267 G 2
Carlsbad Caverns National Park ⊥ USA (NM) 256-257 L 6
Carlsberg Fjord ≈ 26-27 o 8
Carlsbergfondet Land ⊥ GRØ 26-27 n 5
Carlsberg Ridge ≃ 12 D 4
Carlton ○ CDN (SAS) 232-233 M 3
Carlton ○ USA (AL) 284-285 C 5
Carlton ○ USA (GA) 284-285 G 2
Carlton ○ USA (OR) 244-245 B 5
Carlton ○ USA (WA) 244-245 E 2
Carlyle ○ CDN (SAS) 232-233 Q 6
Carlyle ○ USA (IL) 274-275 J 6
Carlyle ○ USA (MT) 250-251 P 5
Carlyle Lake ○ CDN (SAS) 232-233 Q 6
Carlyle Lake ○ USA (IL) 274-275 J 6
Carmacks ○ CDN 20-21 W 5
Carmagnola ○ I 100-101 A 2
Carman ○ CDN (MAN) 234-235 E 5
Carmangay ○ CDN (ALB) 232-233 E 5
Carmanville ○ CDN (NFL) 242-243 O 3
Carmarthen ○ GB 90-91 E 6
Carmaux ○ F 90-91 J 9
Carmel ○ USA (IN) 274-275 M 5
Carmelita ○ GCA 52-53 J 3
Carmelo ○ ROU 78-79 K 3
Carmen ○ RP 160-161 F 8
Carmen ○ USA (OK) 264-265 F 2
Carmen, El ○ BOL 70-71 F 3
Carmen, El ○ CO 60-61 B 6
Carmen, El ○ EC 64-65 C 2
Carmen, El ○ GCA 52-53 H 4
Carmen, El ○ RA 76-77 E 3
Carmen, Isla del ⌒ MEX 52-53 J 2
Carmen, Isla El ⌒ MEX 50-51 D 5
Carmen, Laguna del ≈ 52-53 H 2
Carmen, Río del ~ RCH 76-77 B 5
Carmen de Areco ○ RA 78-79 K 3
Carmen de Bolívar, El ○ CO 60-61 D 3
Carmen de Patagones ○ RA 78-79 H 6
Carmen Silva, Sierra de ▲ RCH 80 F 6
Carmi ○ CDN (BC) 230-231 K 4
Carmi ○ USA (IL) 274-275 K 6
Carmichael ○ AUS 178-179 J 1
Carmichael ○ USA (CA) 246-247 D 5
Carmichael ○ USA (MS) 268-269 M 5
Carmichael Craq ▲ AUS 176-177 L 2
Carmichael River ~ AUS 178-179 J 2
Carmila ○ AUS 178-179 K 1
Carmo ○ BR 68-69 D 4
Carmo de Mata ○ BR 72-73 H 6
Carmo de Minas ○ BR 72-73 H 7
Carmo do Paranaíba ○ BR 72-73 G 5
Carmody, Lake ○ AUS 176-177 E 6
Carmona ○ CR 52-53 B 7
Carmona ○ •• E 98-99 E 6
Carnage, Mount ▲ AUS 176-177 F 5
Carnaíba ○ BR 68-69 K 5
Carnamah ○ AUS 176-177 C 4
Carnarvon ○ AUS (QLD) 178-179 J 3
Carnarvon ○ AUS (WA) 176-177 B 2
Carnarvon ○ CDN (ONT) 238-239 G 3
Carnarvon ○ ZA 220-221 F 5
Carnarvon National Park ⊥ AUS 178-179 J 3
Carnarvon Range ▲ AUS 176-177 F 2
Carnarvon Range ▲ AUS 178-179 K 3
Carnatic Shoal ≃ 160-161 B 7
Carndonagh ○ IRL 90-91 D 4
Carnduff ○ CDN (SAS) 232-233 R 6
Carnegie ○ AUS 176-177 G 2
Carnegie ○ USA (OK) 264-265 F 3
Carnegie ○ USA (PA) 280-281 G 3
Carnegie ○ USA (PA) 280-281 F 3
Carnegie, Lake ○ AUS 176-177 G 3
Carn Eige ▲ GB 90-91 E 3
Carneiro ○ USA (KS) 262-263 H 6
Carnera, Punta ▲ EC 64-65 B 3
Carnes ○ AUS 178-179 C 6
Carnesville ○ USA (GA) 284-285 G 2
Carney ○ USA (MI) 270-271 L 5
Car Nicobar Island ⌒ IND 140-141 L 5
Carnikava ○ LV 94-95 J 3
Carnot ○ • RCA 206-207 B 6
Carnot, Cape ▲ AUS 180-181 C 3
Carnot Bay ≈ 172-173 F 4
Carnsore Point ▲ IRL 90-91 D 5
Carnwath River ~ CDN 30-31 F 2
Carnwood ○ CDN (ALB) 232-233 D 2
Caro ○ USA (MI) 272-273 F 4
Caro, El ○ YV 60-61 J 3
Caro de La Negra, El ○ YV 60-61 J 3
Carol City ○ USA (FL) 286-287 J 6
Carolina ○ BR 68-69 E 5
Carolina ○ CO 60-61 D 4
Carolina ○ E 98-99 F 5
Carolina ○ RCH 76-77 B 2
Carolina ○ USA (PR) 286-287 Q 2
Carolina ○ ZA 220-221 K 3
Carolina Sandhills National Wildlife Refuge ⊥ USA (SC) 284-285 K 2
Caroline ○ CDN (ALB) 232-233 D 3
Caroline, Lake ○ AUS 178-179 D 3
Caroline Beach ○ USA (NC) 282-283 K 6
Caroline Island ⌒ KIB 13 M 3
Caroline Islands ⌒ FSM 13 M 3
Caroline National Memorial, Fort • USA (FL) 286-287 H 1
Caroline Seamounts ≃ 13 F 2
Carolside ○ CDN (ALB) 232-233 G 4
Caron ○ AUS 176-177 D 4
Caron Brook ○ CDN (NB) 240-241 G 3
Caroni, Río ~ YV 60-61 K 5
Carora ○ YV 60-61 F 2
Carp ○ USA (NV) 248-249 K 2
Carpathian Mountains = Karpaty ▲ 102-103 B 3
Carpații Orientali ▲ RO 102-103 D 4
Carpentaria, Gulf of ≈ AUS 174-175 D 3
Carpentaria Highway II AUS 174-175 B 5
Carpenter ○ USA (SD) 260-261 J 2
Carpenter ○ USA (WY) 252-253 O 5
Carpenter Lake ○ CDN (BC) 230-231 G 3
Carpentras ○ F 90-91 K 9
Carpi ○ I 100-101 C 2
Carpina ○ BR 68-69 L 5
Carpincho, Riacho ~ PY 76-77 H 2
Carpinteria ○ USA (CA) 248-249 E 5
Carpio ○ USA (ND) 258-259 F 3
Carp Lake ○ CDN (BC) 228-229 L 2
Carp Lake ○ USA (MI) 272-273 E 2
Carp Lake Provincial Park ⊥ CDN (BC) 228-229 L 2
Carpolac ○ AUS 180-181 F 4
Carr ○ USA (CO) 254-255 L 3
Carrabelle ○ USA (FL) 286-287 E 2
Carracollo ○ BOL 70-71 D 5
Carragana ○ CDN (SAS) 232-233 P 3
Čār Rāh ○ AFG 134-135 K 2
Carraipia ○ CO 60-61 E 2
Carranya ○ AUS 172-173 H 5
Carrapatal ○ BR 68-69 G 3
Carrapatal, Ilha ⌒ BR 68-69 G 3
Carrara ○ I 100-101 C 2
Carrasquero ○ YV 60-61 E 2
Carr Boyd Ranges ▲ AUS 172-173 J 4
Carreira Comprida, Cachoeira ~ BR 68-69 D 7
Carrere, Cerro ▲ RA 78-79 E 4
Carreta, Punta ▲ PE 64-65 D 9
Carretera Interamericana II MEX 50-51 F 2
Carretero, Puerto de ▲ E 98-99 F 6
Carr Fork Lake ○ USA (KY) 276-277 M 3
Carriacou Island ⌒ WG 56 E 5
Carrical ○ CV 202-203 B 5
Carrick ○ IRL 90-91 C 4
Carriere ○ USA (MS) 268-269 L 6
Carrieton ○ AUS 180-181 E 2
Carril, El ○ RA 76-77 E 3
Carrington ○ USA (ND) 258-259 H 4
Carrington Island ⌒ USA (UT) 254-255 C 3
Carrión, Río ~ E 98-99 E 3
Carriringue ○ RCH 78-79 D 5
Carrizal ○ CO 60-61 E 1
Carrizal ○ RA 76-77 D 5
Carrizal ○ YV 62-63 D 2
Carrizal, El ○ MEX 50-51 F 2
Carrizal, Punta ▲ RCH 76-77 B 5
Carrizal, Quebrada ~ RCH 76-77 B 5
Carrizal Bajo ○ RCH 76-77 B 5
Carrizo ○ USA (AZ) 256-257 E 5
Carrizo, Quebrada del ~ RCH 76-77 C 3
Carrizo Creek ~ USA (NM) 256-257 M 2
Carrizo Springs ○ USA (TX) 266-267 H 5
Carrizozo ○ USA (NM) 256-257 K 5
Carroll ○ CDN (MAN) 234-235 C 5
Carroll ○ USA (IA) 274-275 D 2
Carrollton ○ USA (AL) 284-285 B 3
Carrollton ○ USA (GA) 284-285 E 3
Carrollton ○ USA (IL) 274-275 H 5
Carrollton ○ USA (KY) 276-277 K 2
Carrollton ○ USA (MI) 272-273 F 4
Carrollton ○ USA (MO) 274-275 E 5
Carrollton ○ USA (MS) 268-269 L 3
Carrollton ○ USA (OH) 280-281 E 3
Carrol Summit ▲ USA (NV) 246-247 H 4
Carrot Creek ○ CDN (ALB) 232-233 C 2
Carrot River ○ CDN (SAS) 232-233 P 2
Carrot River ~ CDN (SAS) 232-233 Q 2
Carrozas ○ CO 60-61 E 6
Čarrūd ○ IR 134-135 G 3
Carruthers ○ CDN (SAS) 232-233 J 3
Çarşamba ☆ TR 128-129 G 2
Čaršanga ○ TM 136-137 K 6
Carseland ○ CDN (ALB) 232-233 E 5
Carsk ○ KA 124-125 M 4
Carson ○ USA (ND) 258-259 F 5
Carson, Fort • USA (CO) 254-255 L 5
Carson City ○ USA (MI) 272-273 E 4
Carson City ☆ USA (NV) 246-247 F 4
Carson River ~ AUS 172-173 H 3
Carson Sink ○ USA (NV) 246-247 G 4
Carstairs ○ CDN (ALB) 232-233 D 4
Cartagena ☆ ••• CO 60-61 D 2
Cartagena ○ E 98-99 G 6
Cartagena del Chaira ○ CO 64-65 E 1
Cartago ○ CO 60-61 D 5
Cartago ☆ CR 52-53 C 7
Cartago ○ USA (CA) 248-249 F 3
Carta Valley ○ USA (TX) 266-267 G 4
Carter ○ USA (MT) 250-251 J 4
Carter ○ USA (OK) 264-265 E 3
Carter ○ USA (WY) 252-253 H 5
Carter, Mount ▲ AUS 174-175 G 3
Carters Lake ○ USA (GA) 284-285 F 2
Carter Spit ▲ USA 22-23 P 3
Carters Range ▲ AUS 178-179 F 2
Cartersville ○ USA (GA) 284-285 F 2
Cartersville ○ USA (IA) 274-275 E 2
Cartersville ○ USA (MT) 250-251 N 5
Carthage ∴ ••• TN 190-191 H 2
Carthage ○ USA (AR) 276-277 C 6
Carthage ○ USA (IL) 274-275 G 4
Carthage ○ USA (MO) 276-277 A 3
Carthage ○ USA (MS) 268-269 L 4
Carthage ○ USA (NC) 282-283 H 5
Carthage ○ USA (NY) 278-279 F 5
Carthage ○ USA (SD) 260-261 J 2
Carthage ○ USA (TN) 276-277 K 4
Carthage ○ USA (TX) 264-265 K 6
Cartier ○ CDN (ONT) 238-239 D 2
Cartier, Port- ○ CDN (QUE) 242-243 B 2
Cartier Islet ⌒ AUS 172-173 F 2
Carti Suitupo ○ PA 52-53 E 7
Cartridge Mount ▲ CDN 30-31 K 4
Cartwright ○ CDN (MAN) 234-235 D 5
Cartwright ○ USA (KY) 276-277 K 4
Carú, Área Indígena ⊼ BR 68-69 F 3
Caru, Rio ~ BR 68-69 E 3
Caruachi ○ YV 60-61 K 3
Caruaru ○ BR 68-69 L 6
Caruban ○ RI 168 D 3
Carún, Río ~ YV 60-61 K 5
Carunantabari ○ YV 60-61 K 5
Carúpano ○ YV 60-61 K 2
Carurai ○ RP 160-161 C 7
Caruthersville ○ USA (MO) 276-277 F 4
Čarvakskoe vodohranilišče < US 136-137 M 4
Carvel ○ CDN (ALB) 232-233 D 2
Carver ○ USA (NV) 246-247 H 5
Carvinas ○ BOL 70-71 D 3
Carvoal ○ BR 70-71 J 5
Carvoeiro ○ BR 62-63 D 6
Carway ○ CDN (ALB) 232-233 E 6
Cary ○ USA (MS) 268-269 K 4
Cary ○ USA (NC) 282-283 J 5
Caryčanka ○ UA 102-103 J 3
Caryš ~ RUS 124-125 O 3
Caryš ~ RUS 124-125 N 2
Carysfort, Cape ▲ GB 78-79 M 6
Caryškoe ○ RUS 124-125 N 3
Carysville ○ USA (OH) 280-281 C 3
Caryville ○ USA (TN) 282-283 C 4
Čaš ○ US 136-137 K 5
Casabe, El ○ YV 60-61 K 4
Casabindo ○ RA 76-77 E 2
Casablanca ○ RCH 78-79 D 2
Casablanca = Ad-Dār-al-Bayda ☆ • MA 188-189 H 4
Casa Branca ○ BR 72-73 G 6
Casa da Pedra • BR 70-71 K 4
Casadepaga ○ USA 20-21 H 4
Casa de Piedra ○ RA 78-79 F 5
Casa Grande ○ USA (AZ) 256-257 D 6
Casa Grandes Ruins National Monument • USA (AZ) 256-257 D 5
Casale Monferrato ○ I 100-101 B 2
Casalins ○ RA 78-79 K 4
Casamance ⊥ SN 202-203 B 3
Casamance ~ SN 202-203 B 3
Casamento, Lagoa do ○ BR 74-75 E 8
Casamozza ○ F 98-99 M 3
Casanare ○ CO 60-61 G 5
Casanare, Río ~ CO 60-61 F 4
Casanay ○ YV 60-61 K 2
Casa Nova ○ BR 68-69 H 6
Casa Piedra ○ USA (TX) 266-267 C 4
Casarabi ○ BOL 70-71 E 4
Casares ○ NIC 52-53 L 6
Casas ○ MEX 50-51 K 6
Casas Adobes ○ USA (AZ) 256-257 E 6
Casas Grandes ∴ MEX 50-51 F 2
Casas Grandes, Río ~ MEX 50-51 F 2
Casa Verde ○ BR 72-73 D 6
Casavieja ○ • E 98-99 E 4
Casazinc ○ CO 60-61 E 6
Casca ○ BR (RSU) 74-75 E 8
Casca ○ BR (RSU) 74-75 E 7
Cascade ○ CDN (BC) 230-231 L 4
Cascade ○ USA (IA) 274-275 G 2
Cascade ○ USA (ID) 252-253 B 2
Cascade ○ USA (MT) 250-251 H 4
Cascade Caverns ∴ USA (TX) 266-267 J 4
Cascade Mountain Ski Area • USA (WI) 274-275 J 1
Cascade Range ▲ USA (CA) 246-247 C 2
Cascade Reservoir ○ USA (ID) 252-253 B 2
Cascade River ~ CDN (ALB) 232-233 C 4
Cascades ○ AUS 176-177 F 6
Cascais ○ P 98-99 C 5
Cascajal ○ C 54-55 E 3
Cascajal, Río ~ PE 64-65 B 4
Cascapédia, Rivière ~ CDN (QUE) 240-241 J 2
Cascas ○ PE 64-65 C 5
Cascavel ○ BR (CEA) 68-69 J 4
Cascavel ○ BR (PAR) 74-75 D 5
Casco, El ○ MEX 50-51 G 5
Casco Bay ≈ USA 278-279 L 5
Cascorro ○ C 54-55 G 4
Cascumpeque Bay ≈ 38-39 N 5
Cascumpeque Bay ≈ CDN 240-241 M 4
Časeľka ~ RUS 114-115 Q 2
Časeľskoe, ozero ○ RUS 114-115 P 2
Caselton ○ USA (NV) 248-249 K 2
Caserta ☆ I 100-101 E 4
Caseville ○ USA (MI) 272-273 F 4
Casey ○ USA (IL) 274-275 L 5
Caseyr, Raas = Gwardafuy ▲ SP 208-209 K 3
Cashel ○ ZW 218-219 G 4
Cashel = Caiseal ○ • IRL 90-91 D 5
Cashmere Downs ○ AUS 176-177 E 4
Cashton ○ USA (WI) 270-271 H 7
Casian Island ⌒ RP 160-161 C 7
Casigua ○ YV 60-61 F 2
Casiguran ○ RP 160-161 E 4
Casilda ○ RA 78-79 J 2
Casimiro de Abreu ○ BR 72-73 J 7
Casino ○ AUS 178-179 M 5
Casinos ○ E 98-99 G 5
Casiquiare, Río ~ YV 60-61 H 6
Casma ○ PE 64-65 C 6
Časniki ☆ BY 94-95 L 4
Časovaja ○ RUS 118-119 J 9
Časovo ○ RUS 88-89 V 5
Caspana ○ RCH 76-77 C 2
Caspe ○ E 98-99 G 4
Casper ○ USA (WY) 252-253 M 4
Caspian ○ USA (MI) 270-271 K 4
Caspian Depression = Prikaspijskaja nizmennost' ⌣ 126-127 F 5
Caspian Sea ≈ 10-11 D 4
Cass ○ RCH 76-77 D 2
Cass ○ USA (AR) 276-277 B 5
Cassacatiza ○ MOC 218-219 G 2
Cassai ○ ANG 216-217 F 5
Cassai ~ ANG 216-217 F 5
Cassamba ○ ANG 216-217 F 6
Cassange, Rio ~ BR 70-71 J 5
Cassango ○ ANG 216-217 D 4
Cassasala ○ ANG 216-217 E 5
Cass City ○ USA (MI) 272-273 F 4
Casselman ○ CDN (ONT) 238-239 K 3
Casselton ○ USA (ND) 258-259 K 5
Cass Fjord ≈ 26-27 S 3
Cássia ○ BR 72-73 G 6
Cassiar ○ CDN 30-31 E
Cassiar Mountains ▲ CDN 30-31 D 5
Cassiar-Stewart Highway II CDN 32-33 E 3
Cassidy ○ CDN (BC) 230-231 F 4
Cassilândia ○ BR 72-73 E 5
Cassilis ○ AUS 180-181 K 2
Cassinga ○ ANG 216-217 D 7
Cassino ○ I 100-101 D 4
Cass Lake ○ USA (MN) 270-271 D 3
Cassoday ○ USA (KS) 262-263 K 6
Cassongue ○ ANG 216-217 C 5
Cassopolis ○ USA (MI) 272-273 C 6
Cass River ~ USA (MI) 272-273 F 4
Cassville ○ USA (MO) 276-277 B 4
Cassville ○ USA (WI) 274-275 H 2
Cast ▲ MAU 146-147 K 1
Castaic ○ USA (CA) 248-249 F 5
Castaña ○ YV 60-61 J 5
Castanhal ○ BR (AMA) 66-67 F 6
Castanhal ○ BR (P) 68-69 E 2
Castanheira ○ BR 70-71 H 2
Castaños ○ MEX 50-51 J 4
Castaño Viejo ○ RA 76-77 C 6
Castèl del Monte •• I 100-101 F 4
Castelhanos, Ponta dos ▲ BR (ESP) 72-73 K 6
Castelhanos, Ponta dos ▲ BR (RIO) 72-73 H 7
Casteljaloux ○ F 90-91 H 9
Castella ○ USA (CA) 246-247 C 2
Castellana, Grotte di •• I 100-101 F 4
Castellana, La ○ RP 160-161 E 7
Castellar de Santisteban ○ E 98-99 F 5
Castelldefels ○ E 98-99 H 4
Castelli ○ RA (BUA) 78-79 L 4
Castelli ○ RA (CHA) 76-77 G 3
Castelló de la Plana ○ E 98-99 G 5
Castellón de la Plana = Castelló de la Plana ○ E 98-99 G 5
Castelnaudary ○ • F 90-91 H 10
Castelnau-Magnoac ○ F 90-91 H 10
Castelo ○ BR 72-73 K 6
Castelo Branco ☆ • P 98-99 D 5
Castelo do Piauí ○ BR 68-69 H 4
Castelsardo ○ • I 100-101 B 4
Castelsarrasin ○ F 90-91 H 9
Castelvetrano ○ I 100-101 D 6
Casterton ○ AUS 180-181 F 4
Castilla ○ PE 64-65 B 4
Castilla ○ RA 78-79 K 3
Castilla la Mancha ■ E 98-99 F 5
Castilla y León ■ E 98-99 D 3
Castilletes ○ CO 60-61 F 2
Castillo, El ○ • NIC 52-53 B 6
Castillo, Pampa del ⊥ RA 80 F 2
Castillo de Bayuela ○ E 98-99 E 4
Castillo de San Marcos National Monument • USA (FL) 286-287 H 2
Castillos ○ ROU 74-75 D 10

Castillos, Laguna de ○ ROU 74-75 D 10
Castle ○ USA (MT) 250-251 J 5
Castlebar = Caisleán an Bharraigh ○ IRL 90-91 C 5
Castleberry ○ USA (AL) 284-285 C 5
Castle Cape ▲ USA 22-23 R 4
Castle Creek ~ CDN (BC) 228-229 O 3
Castledale ○ CDN (BC) 230-231 N 2
Castle Dale ○ USA (UT) 254-255 E 4
Castleford ○ USA (ID) 252-253 D 4
Castlegar ○ CDN (BC) 230-231 M 4
Castle Island ⌒ BS 54-55 H 3
Castle Island ○ CDN (NFL) 38-39 R 3
Castle Island ○ CDN (NFL) 242-243 N 1
Castle Island ⌒ CDN (NWT) 36-37 L 7
Castlemaine ○ • AUS 180-181 H 4
Castle Mountain ▲ USA (CA) 248-249 D 4
Castle Peak ▲ USA (ID) 252-253 D 2
Castlepoint ○ NZ 182 F 4
Castlereagh Bay ≈ 174-175 C 3
Castlereagh River ~ AUS 178-179 K 6
Castle Rock ○ CDN (BC) 228-229 M 4
Castle Rock ○ USA (CO) 254-255 L 4
Castle Rock ○ USA (SD) 260-261 C 2
Castle Rock ○ USA (WA) 244-245 C 4
Castleton ○ • JA 54-55 G 5
Castletown ○ GBM 90-91 E 4
Castletown Bearhaven = Baile Chaisleáin Bhéarra ○ IRL 90-91 C 6
Castle Windsor •• GB 90-91 G 6
Castlewood ○ USA (SD) 260-261 J 2
Castolon ○ USA (TX) 266-267 D 4
Castor ○ CDN (ALB) 232-233 G 3
Castor ○ USA (LA) 268-269 G 4
Castor Creek ~ USA (LA) 268-269 H 4
Castor River ~ USA (MO) 276-277 E 3
Castres ○ F 90-91 J 10
Castries ★ WL 56 E 4
Castro ○ BR (BAH) 72-73 L 2
Castro ○ BR (PAR) 74-75 E 5
Castro ○ RCH 78-79 C 7
Castro, Canal ≈ 80 C 5
Castro, Punta ▲ RA 78-79 G 7
Castro Barras ○ RA 76-77 E 6
Castro Daire ○ P 98-99 D 4
Castrovillari ○ I 100-101 F 5
Castroville ○ USA (TX) 266-267 J 4
Castrovirreyna ○ PE 64-65 E 8
Castuera ○ E 98-99 E 5
Čaštye ☆ RUS 96-97 J 5
Častyh ○ RUS 118-119 E 6
Casuarina Coast ∪ RI 166-167 J 4
Casummit Lake ○ CDN (ONT) 234-235 L 3
Caswell ○ USA 20-21 Q 6
Čat ☆ TR 128-129 J 3
Catabola ○ ANG (BIE) 216-217 D 6
Catabola ○ ANG (HBO) 216-217 C 6
Cataby Roadhouse ○ AUS 176-177 C 5
Catacamas ○ HN 52-53 B 4
Catacaos ○ PE 64-65 B 4
Catache ○ PE 64-65 C 5
Catacocha ○ EC 64-65 C 4
Cataguases ○ BR 72-73 J 6
Catahoula Lake ○ USA (LA) 268-269 H 5
Catahoula National Wildlife Refuge ⊥ USA (LA) 268-269 H 5
Catahuasi ○ PE 64-65 E 8
Cataingan ○ RP 160-161 E 6
Çatak ☆ TR 128-129 K 3
Çatak Çayı ~ TR 128-129 K 3
Catalão ○ BR 72-73 G 5
Çatalhöyük ∴ • TR 128-129 E 4
Catalina ○ CDN (NFL) 242-243 P 4
Catalina ○ RCH 76-77 C 3
Catalina, Punta ▲ RCH 80 F 6
Catalunya ◘ E 98-99 J 4
Catama ○ SP 212-213 H 2
Catamarca ◘ RA 76-77 D 4
Catamarca = San Fernando del Valle de Catamarca ☆ • RA 76-77 E 5
Catamayo ○ EC 64-65 C 3
Catambué ○ ANG 216-217 E 8
Catanacuname ○ CO 60-61 H 6
Catandica ○ MOC 218-219 G 4
Catanduanes ⌒ RP 160-161 F 6
Catanduva ○ BR 72-73 F 6
Catanduvas ○ BR 74-75 D 5
Catánia ○ I 100-101 E 6
Catán Lil ○ RA 78-79 D 5
Cataño ○ USA (PR) 286-287 P 2
Catanzaro ○ I 100-101 F 5
Cataract ○ USA (WI) 270-271 H 6
Cataract, 1st ~ ET 194-195 F 5
Cataract, 3rd = ash-Shallāl ath-Thālith ~ SUD 200-201 E 3
Cataract, 4th = ash Shallāl ar-Rābi' ~ SUD 200-201 F 3
Cataract, 5th = ash-Shallāl al-Khāmis ~ SUD 200-201 F 3
Cataract, 6th = Shallal as-Sablūkah ~ SUD 200-201 F 4
Cataract Canyon ∪ USA (UT) 254-255 E 6
Cataractes • RM 222-223 F 7
Cataraugus Creek ~ USA (NY) 278-279 C 6
Catarina ○ USA (TX) 266-267 H 5
Catarman ☆ RP 160-161 F 6
Catastrophe, Cape ▲ AUS 180-181 D 3
Catata-a-Nova ○ ANG 216-217 C 6
Catatumbo, Río ~ YV 60-61 E 3
Cataula ○ USA (GA) 284-285 F 4
Cataviña ○ MEX 50-51 B 3
Catawba ○ USA (WI) 270-271 H 5
Catawba Island ○ USA (OH) 280-281 D 2
Catawba Lake < USA (NC) 282-283 F 5
Catawba River ~ USA (SC) 284-285 K 2
Cataxa ○ MOC 218-219 G 2
Catazaja ○ MEX 52-53 H 3
Catbalogan ☆ RP 160-161 F 7
Čat-Bazar ○ KS 136-137 N 3
Cat Cays ⌒ BS 54-55 F 2
Cateau-Cambrésis, le ○ F 92-93 G 3
Cateco Cangola ○ ANG 216-217 C 4
Catemaco ○ MEX 52-53 G 2
Catemaco, Laguna de ○ • MEX 52-53 G 2
Catembe ○ MOC 220-221 L 3
Catende ○ BR 68-69 L 6
Catengue ○ ANG 216-217 B 6
Cater ○ CDN (SAS) 232-233 K 2
Catete ○ ANG 216-217 B 4
Catetê, Área Indígena ⅄ BR 68-69 C 5
Catete, Rio ~ BR 66-67 K 6
Cathair na Mart = Westport ○ • IRL 90-91 C 5
Cathay ○ USA (ND) 258-259 H 4
Cathcart ○ ZA 220-221 H 6
Cathedral Gorge State Park • USA (NV) 248-249 K 2
Cathedral Mountain ▲ USA (TX) 266-267 D 3
Cathedral Peak ○ ZA 220-221 J 4
Cathedral Provincial Park ⊥ CDN (BC) 230-231 J 4
Cathedral Valley ∴ USA (UT) 254-255 D 5
Catherine ○ USA (AL) 284-285 C 4
Catherine, Mount ▲ AUS 178-179 K 3
Cathlamet ○ USA (WA) 244-245 B 4
Catia la Mar ○ YV 60-61 H 2
Catió ☆ GNB 202-203 C 4
Catire, Sierra el ▲ YV 60-61 K 4
Cat Island ⌒ BS 54-55 H 2
Cat Island ⌒ USA (MS) 268-269 L 6
Catitas, Las ○ RA 78-79 E 2
Čatkal'skij hrebet ▲ US 136-137 M 4
Čatkaly Kamyčlovskij Log ≟ KA 124-125 F 1
Cat Lake ○ CDN (ONT) 234-235 M 3
Cat Lake ○ CDN (ONT) 234-235 M 3
Catlettsburg ○ USA (KY) 276-277 N 2
Catlow Valley ∪ USA (OR) 244-245 F 7
Cato ○ USA (AR) 276-277 C 6
Catoche, Cabo ▲ MEX 52-53 L 1
Catolândia ○ BR 72-73 H 2
Catolé do Rocha ○ BR 68-69 K 5
Catolo ○ ANG 216-217 D 4
Caton Island ⌒ USA 22-23 P 5
Catoute ▲ E 98-99 D 3
Cátria, Monte ▲ I 100-101 D 3
Catriel ○ RA 78-79 F 4
Catrilo ○ RA 78-79 H 4
Catrimani ○ BR (ROR) 62-63 D 5
Catrimani ○ BR (ROR) 66-67 F 2
Catrimani, Rio ~ BR 60-61 K 6
Catskill ○ USA (NY) 278-279 H 6
Catskill Mountains ▲ USA (NY) 278-279 G 6
Cattaraugus Indian Reservation ⅄ USA (NY) 278-279 C 6
Cattle Creek ~ AUS 172-173 K 4
Cattle Creek Out Station ○ AUS 172-173 K 4
Catuane ○ MOC 220-221 L 3
Catumbela ~ ANG 216-217 C 6
Caturiá, Ilha ⌒ BR 66-67 C 4
Catyr-Kël, ozero ○ KS 146-147 B 5
Čatyrtaš ○ KS 146-147 C 5
Cauaburi, Rio ~ BR 66-67 D 2
Cauale ~ ANG 216-217 D 3
Cauayan ○ RP 160-161 E 7
Cauca ○ ANG 216-217 C 4
Cauca, Río ~ CO 60-61 D 3
Caucagua ○ YV 60-61 H 2
Caucaia ○ BR 68-69 J 3
Caucas ○ BOL 70-71 H 5
Caucasia ○ CO 60-61 D 3
Caucasus = Boľšoj Kavkaz ▲ RUS 126-127 C 5
Cauce Seco del Rio Pilcomayo ~ RA 76-77 G 2
Caucete ○ RA 76-77 C 6
Cauchari ○ RA 76-77 D 3
Cauchari, Salar de ○ RA 76-77 D 2
Caucomgiomoc Lake ○ USA (ME) 278-279 M 2
Caulfield ○ USA (MO) 276-277 C 4
Caumbue ○ ANG 216-217 F 4
Čaun ~ RUS 112-113 Q 2
Čauns kaja guba ≈ 112-113 P 2
Caupolican ≟ BOL 70-71 C 4
Cauquenes ○ RCH 78-79 C 3
Caurés, Rio ~ BR 66-67 F 3
Causabiscau, Lac ○ CDN 38-39 F 2
Causapscal ○ CDN (QUE) 240-241 H 2
Causapscal, Parc Provincial ⊥ CDN (QUE) 240-241 H 2
Căușeni ☆ MD 102-103 F 4
Causey ○ USA (NM) 256-257 M 5
Cautário, Rio ~ BR 70-71 E 3
Cautín, Río ~ RCH 78-79 C 5
Caution, Cape ▲ CDN (BC) 230-231 B 2
Caution Point ▲ AUS 172-173 K 1
Cauto ~ C 54-55 G 4
Cauto Cristo ○ C 54-55 G 4
Cauto Embarcadero ○ C 54-55 G 4
Cauvery ~ IND 140-141 F 4
Cauvery ~ IND 140-141 G 5
Cavalier ○ USA (ND) 258-259 K 3
Cavalla River ~ LB 202-203 G 7
Cavallo Passage ≈ USA 266-267 L 5
Cavalonga, Sierra ▲ RA 76-77 D 2
Cavan = An Cabhán ☆ IRL 90-91 D 5
Cavdan ○ MAU 148-149 C 3
Çavdarhisar ☆ TR 128-129 C 3
Cave ○ NZ 182 C 6
Cave City ○ USA (AR) 276-277 D 5
Cave Junction ○ USA (OR) 244-245 B 8
Cavendish ○ AUS 180-181 G 4
Cavendish ○ CDN (ALB) 232-233 H 5
Cavendish ○ CDN (PEI) 240-241 M 4
Caverns of Sonora ∴ • USA (TX) 266-267 G 3
Caves, The ○ AUS 178-179 L 2
Cave Spring ○ USA (GA) 284-285 E 2
Caviana de Dentro, Ilha ⌒ BR 62-63 J 5
Caviana de Fora, Ilha ⌒ BR 62-63 J 5
Cavite ○ RP 160-161 D 5
Čavki ○ AFG 138-139 C 2
Cawayan ○ RP 160-161 E 7
Caxambu ○ BR 72-73 H 6
Caxias ○ BR 68-69 G 4
Caxias do Sul ○ BR 74-75 E 7
Caxito ☆ ANG 216-217 B 4
Caxiuanã, Baía de ○ BR 62-63 J 6
Caxiuanã, Reserva Florestal de ⊥ BR 62-63 J 6
Caxuxa ○ BR 68-69 F 4
Çay ☆ • TR 128-129 D 3
Cayajabos ○ C 54-55 D 3
Cayambe ○ EC 64-65 C 1
Cayambe, Volcán ▲ EC 64-65 D 1
Cayambre, Isla ⌒ CO 60-61 C 6
Cayara ○ PE 64-65 F 8
Cayastá, Ruinas • RA 76-77 G 6
Cayce ○ USA (SC) 284-285 J 3
Cây Du'o'ng, Vũng ≈ 158-159 H 5
Cayenne ☆ F 62-63 H 3
Cayes, Les ☆ • RH 54-55 J 5
Cayley ○ CDN (ALB) 232-233 E 5
Cayman Brac ⌒ GB 54-55 F 5
Cayman Ridge ≃ 54-55 D 5
Cayman Trench ≃ 54-55 D 5
Caynabo ○ SP 208-209 H 4
Cayo, El ∴ • MEX 52-53 J 3
Cayo Guillermo ○ •• C 54-55 F 3
Cayo Güin ○ C 54-55 H 4
Cayo Largo ○ •• C 54-55 E 4
Cayo Mambi ○ C 54-55 H 4
Cayo Ramona ○ C 54-55 E 3
Cayos Arcas, Isla ⌒ MEX 52-53 J 1
Cay Sal Bank ⌒ BS 54-55 E 3
Cayucos ○ USA (CA) 248-249 D 4
Cayuga ○ CDN (ONT) 238-239 F 6
Cayuga ○ USA (IN) 274-275 L 5
Cayuga ○ USA (ND) 258-259 K 5
Cayuga ○ USA (TX) 268-269 E 5
Cayuga Lake ○ USA (NY) 278-279 E 6
Cayuse Pass ▲ USA (WA) 244-245 D 4
Cazage ○ ANG 216-217 F 5
Cazalla de la Sierra ○ E 98-99 E 6
Čažma, mys ▲ RUS 120-121 T 6
Cazombo ○ ANG 214-215 B 6
Cazones, Golfo de ≈ 54-55 E 4
Cazorla ○ E 98-99 F 6
Cazorla ○ YV 60-61 H 3
Cazorla, Segura y Las Villas Parque Nacional de ⊥ E 98-99 F 5
Cazula ○ MOC 218-219 G 2
Ccatca ○ PE 70-71 B 3
Cea, Río ~ E 98-99 E 3
Ceará ◘ BR 68-69 H 4
Ceara Abyssal Plain = Ceará Abyssal Plain ≃ 6-7 H 8
Ceará-Mirim ○ BR 68-69 L 4
Ceatharlach = Carlow ○ IRL 90-91 D 5
Ceba ○ CDN (SAS) 232-233 Q 2
Ceballos ○ MEX 50-51 G 4
Čebarkuľ ☆ RUS 96-97 M 6
Čeboksarskoe vodohranilišče < RUS 96-97 E 5
Čeboksary ☆ RUS 96-97 E 5
Cebollati ○ ROU 74-75 D 9
Ceboruco, Cerro ▲ MEX 52-53 B 2
Cebu ⌒ RP 160-161 E 8
Cebu City ☆ •• RP 160-161 E 7
Čečeljugjun ~ RUS 110-111 a 6
Čečen, ostrov ⌒ RUS 126-127 G 5
Cècèrlèg ☆ MAU 148-149 E 4
Čechy ≟ CZ 92-93 N 4
Cecil ○ USA (AL) 284-285 E 4
Cecil ○ USA (AR) 276-277 B 5
Cecil ○ USA (OR) 244-245 E 5
Cecil, Mount ▲ AUS 176-177 M 2
Cecil Goodman ○ AUS 172-173 K 2
Cecil Plains ○ AUS 178-179 L 4
Cecil Rhodes, Mount ▲ AUS 176-177 F 2
Cecilville ○ USA (CA) 246-247 B 2
Cecina ○ I 100-101 C 3
Čečuj ~ RUS 118-119 D 7
Čečujsk ○ RUS 116-117 O 6
Cedar ○ CDN (BC) 230-231 F 4
Cedar ○ USA (KS) 262-263 H 5
Cedar Bluff ○ USA (IA) 274-275 G 3
Cedar Bluff Reservoir ○ USA (KS) 262-263 G 6
Cedar Bluffs ○ USA (KS) 262-263 F 5
Cedar Breaks National Monument ∴ USA (UT) 254-255 C 6
Cedar Butte ○ USA (SD) 260-261 E 3
Cedar City ○ USA (UT) 254-255 B 6
Cedar Creek ○ USA (TX) 266-267 K 3
Cedar Creek ~ USA (AL) 284-285 B 2
Cedar Creek ~ USA (AL) 284-285 D 4
Cedar Creek ~ USA (IA) 274-275 G 4
Cedar Creek ~ USA (ND) 258-259 F 5
Cedar Creek Reservoir ○ USA (TX) 264-265 H 6
Cedaredge ○ USA (CO) 254-255 H 5
Cedar Falls ○ USA (IA) 274-275 F 2
Cedar Grove ○ USA (TN) 276-277 G 5
Cedar Grove ○ USA (WI) 274-275 L 1
Cedar Hill ○ USA (MO) 274-275 H 6
Cedar Hill ○ USA (TX) 264-265 H 6
Cedar Island ⌒ USA (NC) 282-283 L 6
Cedar Island National Wildlife Refuge ⊥ USA (NC) 282-283 L 6
Cedar Key ○ USA (FL) 286-287 F 2
Cedar Lake ○ CDN 34-35 F 4
Cedar Lake ○ CDN (QUE) 238-239 G 2
Cedar Lake ○ USA (IL) 276-277 F 3
Cedar Lake ○ USA (TX) 264-265 B 6
Cedar Mills ○ USA (MN) 270-271 D 6
Cedar Mountain ▲ USA (MT) 250-251 D 4
Cedar Park ○ USA (TX) 266-267 K 3
Cedar Pass ▲ USA (CA) 246-247 E 2
Cedar Point ○ CDN (ONT) 238-239 E 4
Cedar Point ▲ USA (CO) 254-255 M 4
Cedar Rapids ○ USA (IA) 274-275 G 3
Cedar Rapids ○ USA (NE) 262-263 H 3
Cedar River ~ CDN (BC) 228-229 F 2
Cedar River ~ USA (MI) 270-271 L 5
Cedar River ~ USA (IA) 274-275 G 3
Cedar River National Grassland ⊥ USA (ND) 258-259 F 5
Cedars of Lebanon State Park ⊥ USA (TN) 276-277 J 4
Cedar Springs ○ USA (MI) 272-273 D 4
Cedartown ○ USA (GA) 284-285 E 2
Cedar Vale ○ USA (KS) 262-263 K 7
Cedarvale ○ USA (NM) 256-257 K 4
Cedarville ○ USA (AR) 276-277 A 5
Cedarville ○ USA (CA) 246-247 E 2
Cedarville ○ USA (MI) 270-271 O 4
Cedarville ○ ZA 220-221 J 5
Cedeño ○ HN 52-53 L 5
Cedoux ○ CDN (SAS) 232-233 P 6
Cedral ○ BR 68-69 F 3
Cedral ○ MEX (SLP) 50-51 J 6
Cedral ∴ • MEX (QR) 52-53 L 1
Cèdres, Parque National des ⊥ DZ 190-191 C 3
Cedro ○ BR 68-69 J 5
Cedros ○ MEX (DGO) 50-51 J 5
Cedros ○ MEX (SON) 50-51 E 4
Cedros, Isla ⌒ MEX 50-51 B 3
Ceduna ○ AUS 176-177 M 6
Ceek ○ SP 208-209 G 4
Ceel Afweyn ○ SP 208-209 H 4
Ceelayo ○ SP 208-209 J 3
Ceelbuur ○ SP 208-209 H 6
Ceel Dheere ○ SP 208-209 H 6
Ceel Duubo ○ SP 212-213 K 2
Ceel Gaal ○ SP 208-209 K 3
Ceel Garas ○ SP 208-209 G 6
Ceel Huur ○ SP 208-209 J 6
Ceel Madoobe, togga ~ SP 208-209 J 4
Ceepeecee ○ CDN (BC) 230-231 C 4
Ceerigaabo ☆ SP 208-209 H 3
Cefalù ○ I 100-101 E 5
Cega, Río ~ E 98-99 E 4
Čegdomyn ○ RUS 122-123 E 3
Čegitun ~ RUS 112-113 Z 3
Cegléd ○ H 92-93 P 5
Cegonha, Corredeira da ~ BR 72-73 E 7
Čehel Abdālān, Kūh-e ▲ AFG 134-135 K 2
Ceheng ○ VRC 156-157 D 4
Čehov ○ RUS 122-123 K 5
Čehov ☆ • RUS (Mos) 94-95 P 4
Čehova, gora ▲ RUS 122-123 K 5
Ceiba, La ☆ HN 52-53 L 4
Ceiba, La ○ YV (ANZ) 60-61 J 3
Ceiba, La ○ YV (TRU) 60-61 F 3
Ceibal, El ∴ • GCA 52-53 J 3
Ceibalito ○ RA 76-77 E 3
Ceibas ○ RA 78-79 K 2
Ceja, La ○ CO 60-61 D 4
Cejas, Las ○ RA 76-77 E 4
Čeka ~ RUS 114-115 O 6
Čekanovskij ○ RUS 116-117 K 7
Čekanovskogo, krjaž ▲ RUS 110-111 N 3
Çekerek ☆ TR 128-129 F 2
Çekerek Irmağı ~ TR 128-129 G 2
Çekerek Irmağı ~ TR 128-129 F 2
Čekmaguš ☆ RUS 96-97 J 6
Čekunda ○ RUS 122-123 E 3
Čekurdah ○ RUS 110-111 a 4
Čekurovka ○ RUS 110-111 Q 4
Celaque, Parque Nacional ⊥ HN 52-53 K 4
Celarain, Punta ▲ MEX 52-53 L 1
Čelasin ~ RUS 120-121 G 5
Celaya ○ MEX 52-53 D 1
Čelbas ~ RUS 102-103 M 5
Čeldonka ○ RUS 118-119 J 9
Celebes Basin ≃ 14-15 E 7
Celebes Sea ≈ 164-165 G 2
Celeiro Murta ○ BR 72-73 J 4
Čeleken ○ TM 136-137 C 5
Celendín ○ PE 64-65 C 5
Celeste, Rio ~ BR 70-71 K 3
Celestún ○ • MEX 52-53 J 1
Celica ○ EC 64-65 C 4
Celina ○ RUS 102-103 M 4
Celina ○ USA (OH) 280-281 B 3
Celina ○ USA (TN) 276-277 K 4
Celina ○ USA (TX) 264-265 H 5
Celinnoe ○ KA 136-137 L 4
Celinnoe ☆ RUS (ALT) 124-125 O 2
Celinnoe ☆ RUS (KRG) 114-115 G 7
Celinograd = Akmola ○ KA 124-125 G 3
Celista ○ CDN (BC) 230-231 K 3
Čeljabinsk ☆ RUS 96-97 M 6
Celje ○ SLO 100-101 E 1
Čeljuskin, mys ▲ RUS 108-109 f 3
Čeljuskin, poluostrov ⌒ RUS 108-109 e 3
Celle ○ • D 92-93 L 2
Čeľmana, ostrova ⌒ RUS 108-109 V 4
Čelno-Veršiny ☆ RUS 96-97 G 6
Čelomdža ~ RUS 120-121 M 3
Čelončèn ~ RUS 118-119 G 6
Celorico da Beira ○ P 98-99 D 4
Celtic Shelf ≃ 8 B 3
Çeltik ☆ TR 128-129 D 3
Celuk ○ RI 168 B 7
Čema ~ RUS 88-89 T 4
Čemal ○ RUS 124-125 P 3
Cemara ~ RI 166-167 J 4
Čemdaľsk ○ RUS 116-117 L 6
Čemoltan ○ KA 146-147 C 4
Cempi, Teluk ≈ 168 D 7
Cenajo, Embalse del < E 98-99 G 5
Čenárán ○ IR 136-137 F 6
Čenáreh ○ IR 128-129 M 5
Cenderawasih, Teluk ≈ 166-167 H 3
Cenderawasih Marine Reserve ⊥ • RI 166-167 H 3
Cenepa, Río ~ PE 64-65 C 4
Cengel = Hösööt ○ MAU 146-147 J 1
Cenghis Khan Ling • VRC 154-155 F 2
Cènhèr = Altan Ovoo ○ MAU 148-149 E 4
Cènhèrmandal = Modot ○ MAU 148-149 J 4
Cennet ve Cehennem • TR 128-129 F 4
Cenotillo ○ MEX 52-53 K 1
Centani ○ ZA 220-221 J 6
Centenario, El ○ MEX 50-51 D 5
Centenário do Sul ○ BR 72-73 E 7
Centenary ○ USA (SC) 284-285 L 2
Centenary ○ ZW 218-219 F 3
Centennial ○ USA (WY) 252-253 M 5
Center ○ USA (CO) 254-255 J 6
Center ○ USA (NE) 262-263 J 2
Center ○ USA (TX) 268-269 F 5
Center, Le ○ USA (MN) 270-271 E 6
Centerburg ○ USA (OH) 280-281 D 3
Center Hill ○ USA (AR) 276-277 D 5
Center Hill Lake ○ USA (TN) 276-277 K 4
Center Ossipee ○ USA (NH) 278-279 K 5
Center Point ○ USA (AL) 284-285 D 3
Centerville ○ USA (IA) 274-275 F 4
Centerville ○ USA (MO) 276-277 E 3
Centerville ○ USA (NC) 282-283 J 4
Centerville ○ USA (TN) 276-277 H 5
Centerville ○ USA (TX) 268-269 E 5
Centerville ○ USA (WI) 270-271 G 6
Centinela, Cerro ▲ RA 78-79 D 4
Centinela, Picacho del ▲ MEX 50-51 H 3
Centinela, Sierra del ▲ RA 76-77 E 3
Central ○ BR 68-69 G 7
Central ◘ EAK 212-213 F 4
Central ◘ MW 218-219 G 1
Central ◘ RB 218-219 C 5
Central ○ USA (AL) 284-285 E 2
Central ○ USA (NM) 256-257 G 6
Central ◘ Z 218-219 D 2
Central = Centre ◘ CAM 204-205 J 6
Central, Cordillera ▲ BOL 70-71 D 6
Central, Cordillera ▲ CO 60-61 C 6
Central, Cordillera ▲ CR 52-53 B 6
Central, Cordillera ▲ DOM 54-55 K 5
Central, Cordillera ▲ PE 64-65 C 5
Central, Cordillera ▲ USA (PR) 286-287 P 2
Central African Republic = Centrafricaine, République ■ RCA 206-207 C 5
Central Australia Aboriginal Land ⅄ AUS 172-173 J 6
Central Bedeque ○ CDN (PEI) 240-241 M 4
Central Brāhui Range ▲ PK 134-135 M 4
Central Butte ○ CDN (SAS) 232-233 M 5
Central City ○ USA (CO) 254-255 K 4
Central City ○ USA (IA) 274-275 G 2
Central City ○ USA (KY) 276-277 H 3
Central City ○ USA (NE) 262-263 J 3
Central de Minas ○ BR 72-73 K 5
Central Desert Aboriginal Land ⅄ AUS 172-173 K 5
Central Eastern Australian Rainforest ⊥ ••• AUS 178-179 M 5
Central Ferry ○ USA (WA) 244-245 H 4
Centralia ○ USA (IL) 274-275 J 6
Centralia ○ USA (MO) 274-275 F 6
Centralia ○ USA (WA) 244-245 C 4
Central Island ⌒ EAK 212-213 F 2
Central Island National Park ⊥ EAK 212-213 F 2
Central Kalahari Game Reserve ⊥ RB 218-219 B 5
Central los Molles ○ RCH 76-77 B 6
Central Makrān Range ▲ PK 134-135 J 5
Central Mount Stuart ▲ AUS 178-179 B 1
Central Mount Wedge ▲ AUS 172-173 K 7
Centraľnaja, gora ▲ RUS 108-109 e 4
Centraľnojakutskaja ravnina ∪ RUS 118-119 J 3
Centraľnolesnoj zapovednik ▲ RUS 94-95 N 3
Centraľnosibirskij zapovednik ⊥ RUS (KRN) 114-115 U 3
Centraľnosibirskij zapovednik ⊥ RUS (KRN) 114-115 S 4
Centraľno-Tungusskoe, plato ≟ RUS 116-117 K 5
Centraľnye Karakumy ≟ TM 136-137 E 5
Centraľnyj ○ RUS 114-115 T 7
Central Pacific Basin ≃ 14-15 K 6
Central Patricia ○ CDN (ONT) 234-235 N 3
Central Point ○ USA (OR) 244-245 C 8
Central Range ▲ LS 220-221 J 4
Central Range ▲ PNG 183 B 3
Central Region ◘ GH 202-203 K 7
Central Saanich ○ CDN (BC) 230-231 F 5
Central Siberian Plateau = Srednesibirskoe ploskogor'e ≟ RUS 10-11 J 2
Central Valley ○ USA (CA) 246-247 C 3
Central West Goldfields • AUS 180-181 K 2
Central West River ○ CDN (NS) 240-241 N 5
Centre ◘ F 90-91 H 8
Centre ○ USA (AL) 284-285 E 2
Centre = Central ◘ CAM 204-205 J 6
Centre de Flacq ○ MS 224 C 7
Centre Island ⌒ AUS 174-175 D 4
Centre Mountain ▲ USA (ID) 250-251 D 6
Centre Spatial Guyanais • F 62-63 H 3
Centreville ○ CDN (NB) 240-241 H 4
Centreville ○ CDN (NFL) 242-243 P 4
Centreville ○ USA (AL) 284-285 C 4
Centreville ○ USA (MD) 280-281 K 4
Centreville ○ USA (MS) 268-269 J 5
Centro, Cayo ⌒ MEX 52-53 L 2
Centro, El ○ USA (CA) 248-249 J 7
Centro do Vieira ○ BR 68-69 F 3
Centurion ○ ROU 74-75 D 9
Century ○ USA (FL) 286-287 B 1
Cenxi ○ VRC 156-157 G 5
Cenzontle ○ MEX 50-51 H 4
Čepca ~ RUS 96-97 J 5
Čepeck, Kirovo- ☆ RUS 96-97 G 4
Cepiring ○ RI 168 D 3
Cepu ○ RI 168 D 3
Ceram = Pulau Seram ⌒ RI 166-167 E 3
Ceram Sea = Seram, Laut ≈ RI 166-167 D 3
Cerbatana, Serrania de la ▲ YV 60-61 H 4
Cercado, El ○ DOM 54-55 K 5
Čerdakly ☆ RUS 96-97 F 6
Čerdyn' ☆ RUS 114-115 D 4
Cereal ○ CDN (ALB) 232-233 H 4
Cerejeiras ○ BR 70-71 G 3
Čeremhovo ☆ RUS 116-117 L 9
Čeremhovskaja, Irkutsko, ravnina ∪ RUS 116-117 K 8
Čeremšan ☆ RUS 96-97 G 6
Čeremuhovo ○ RUS 114-115 F 4
Čeremuški ○ RUS 116-117 E 9
Čerendej ~ RUS 118-119 J 5
Čerepanovo ☆ RUS 124-125 N 1
Čerepovec ☆ RUS 94-95 P 2
Ceres ○ BR 72-73 F 3
Ceres ○ RA 76-77 G 5
Ceres ○ ZA 220-221 D 6
Ceresco ○ USA (NE) 262-263 K 3
Cerete ○ CO 60-61 D 3
Cerezo de Abajo ○ E 98-99 F 4
Čerga ○ RUS 124-125 O 3
Cerignola ○ I 100-101 E 4
Čeriktej ○ RUS 118-119 P 4
Čerkasskoe ○ RUS 96-97 E 7
Čerkassy = Čerkasy ☆ UA 102-103 H 3
Čerkasy ☆ UA 102-103 H 3
Çerkeş ☆ TR 128-129 E 2
Čerkessk ☆ RUS 126-127 E 5
cerkva Česnoho chresta • UA 102-103 G 3
Čerlak ☆ RUS 124-125 J 1
Çermik ☆ TR 128-129 H 3
Cerna ○ RO 102-103 F 5
Černaja ~ RUS 112-113 L 5
Černaja ~ RUS 112-113 P 5
Černaja ~ RUS 118-119 J 9
Černaja, gora ▲ RUS 122-123 F 7
Cernavodă ○ RO 102-103 F 5
Černenko = Šarypovo ○ RUS 114-115 U 7
Černigov = Černihiv ○ • UA 102-103 G 2
Černihiv ○ • UA 102-103 G 2
Černihivs'ke polissja ≟ UA 102-103 G 2
Černivci ☆ UA 102-103 D 3
Černjachiv ○ UA 102-103 F 2
Černjaevo ○ RUS 118-119 N 9
Černjahovsk ☆ •• RUS 94-95 G 4
Černjanka ○ RUS 102-103 K 2
Černogorsk ○ RUS 116-117 E 9
Černorečenskij ○ RUS 96-97 H 3
Černovcy = Černivci ☆ UA 102-103 D 3
Černovka ○ RUS 124-125 M 1
Černozemeľskij kanal ○ RUS 126-127 F 5
Černuška ☆ RUS 96-97 K 5
Černuťevo ○ RUS 88-89 U 5
Černycev cyganak ≈ 126-127 N 5
Černye Braťja, ostrova ⌒ RUS 122-123 O 5
Čërnye zemli ≟ RUS 96-97 D 10
Čërnyj Čulym ~ RUS 114-115 U 7
Černyj Irtyš = Qara Ertis ~ KA 124-125 O 5
Čërnyj Urjum ~ RUS 118-119 J 9
Černyševa, grjada ▲ RUS 108-109 H 9
Černyševskij ○ RUS 118-119 F 4
Černyškovskij ○ RUS 102-103 N 3
Černyšova, hrebet ▲ RUS 118-119 L 8
Cero, Corredeira ~ BR 70-71 J 5
Cerqueira César ○ BR 72-73 F 7
Cerralvo ○ MEX 50-51 K 4
Cerralvo, Isla ⌒ MEX 50-51 E 5
Cërrik ○ • AL 100-101 G 4
Cerrillada ○ ROU 76-77 K 6
Cerrillos ○ RCH 76-77 C 2
Cerrito ○ PY 76-77 J 4
Cerrito, El ○ CO 60-61 C 6
Cerritos ○ MEX 50-51 J 6
Cerro, El ○ BOL 70-71 G 5
Cerro Azul ○ BR 74-75 F 5
Cerro Blanco ○ RA 80 G 3
Cerro Blanco ○ RCH 76-77 B 5
Cerro Chato ○ ROU 78-79 M 2
Cerro Chovoreca ○ PY 70-71 H 6
Cerro Colorado ○ ROU 78-79 M 2
Cerro-Cora ○ BR 68-69 K 5
Cerro Cora, Parque Nacional del ⊥ PY 76-77 J 2
Cerro de Pasco ☆ PE 64-65 D 7
Cerro Gordo ○ USA (IL) 274-275 K 5
Cerro Largo ○ BR 76-77 K 5
Cerro Mangote ∴ PA 52-53 D 7
Cerrón, Cerro ▲ YV 60-61 F 2
Cerro Pintado • YV 60-61 H 5
Cerro Policia ○ RA 78-79 E 5
Cerro Punta ○ PA 52-53 C 7
Cerro Rico ○ RA 76-77 E 5
Cerros Colorados, Embalse < RA 78-79 E 5
Cerros de Amotape, Parque Nacional ⊥ PE 64-65 B 3
Cerro Vera ○ ROU 78-79 L 2
Cerrudo Cué ○ RA 76-77 J 4
Čerskij ○ RUS 112-113 L 2
Čerskogo, hrebet ▲ RUS 110-111 W 5
Čerskogo, hrebet ▲ RUS 118-119 E 10
Čertala ~ RUS 114-115 O 6
Certaldo ○ I 100-101 C 3
Cértegui ○ CO 60-61 C 5
Čertkovo ○ RUS 102-103 M 3
Čertov, porog ~ RUS 110-111 H 5
Čertovo, ozero ○ RUS 114-115 Q 2
Cervantes ○ AUS 176-177 C 5
Cervati, Monte ▲ I 100-101 E 4
Červen' ☆ BY 94-95 L 5
Cervera ○ E 98-99 H 4
Cervera de Pisuerga ○ E 98-99 E 3
Cerveteri ○ • I 100-101 D 4
Cérvia ○ I 100-101 D 2
Cervino, Monte = Matterhorn ▲ •• I 100-101 A 1
Červjanka ○ RUS 116-117 J 7
Červonograd = Červonohrad ○ UA 102-103 D 2
Červonohrad ○ UA 102-103 D 2
Červonoznam'janka ○ UA 102-103 G 4
Cerwa ○ VRC 144-145 M 3
Čeryševsk ○ RUS 118-119 H 9
César, Río ~ CO 60-61 E 3
Césares, Isla de los ⌒ RA 78-79 H 6
Cesário Lange ○ BR 72-73 G 7
Cesena ○ I 100-101 D 2
Cesira, La ○ RA 78-79 H 2
Cēsis ☆ •• LV 94-95 J 3
Česká Třebová ○ CZ 92-93 O 4
České Budějovice ○ CZ 92-93 N 4
Českomoravská vrchovina ▲ CZ 92-93 N 4
Český Krumlov ○ ••• CZ 92-93 N 4
Český Šternberk •• CZ 92-93 N 4
Český Těšín ○ CZ 92-93 P 4
Česma ☆ RUS 124-125 B 2
Çeşme ☆ TR 128-129 B 3
Česme Bīğār ○ IR 128-129 M 5
Česme Kabūd ○ IR 134-135 B 2
Cess, River ○ LB 202-203 F 7
Cessford ○ CDN (ALB) 232-233 G 5
Čëšskaja guba ≈ 88-89 S 3
Cessnock ○ AUS 180-181 L 2
Češt-e Šarif ○ • AFG 134-135 K 1
Cestos Bay ≈ 202-203 F 7
Cestos River ~ LB 202-203 F 7
Cesvaine ☆ •• LV 94-95 K 3
Čet' ~ RUS 114-115 T 6
Cetaceo, Mount ▲ RP 160-161 E 4
Cētar ○ VRC 154-155 B 3
Četlasskij Kamen' ▲ RUS 88-89 U 4
Cetraro ○ I 100-101 E 5
Četvërtyj Kuriľskij proliv ○ RUS 122-123 Q 3
Četyrëhstolbovoj, ostrov ⌒ RUS 112-113 M 1
Céu Azul ○ BR 74-75 D 5
Čeugda ○ RUS 122-123 D 3
Ceuta ○ E 98-99 E 7
Ceuta ○ YV 60-61 F 3
Cevcenko, cyganak ≈ 126-127 O 4
Cévennes ≟ F 90-91 J 9
Cévennes, Parc National des ⊥ • F 90-91 J 9
Ceyhan ☆ TR 128-129 F 4
Ceyhan Nehri ~ TR 128-129 F 4
Ceylanpınar ☆ TR 128-129 J 4
Ceylon ○ CDN (SAS) 232-233 O 6
Ceylon ○ USA (MN) 270-271 D 7
Chaah ○ MAL 162-163 E 3
Cha-am ○ THA 158-159 E 4
Cha'anpu ○ VRC 156-157 G 2
Chabbie Lake ○ CDN (ONT) 236-237 J 3
Chabet El Akra • DZ 190-191 E 2
Chablé ○ MEX 52-53 J 3
Chabyêr Caka ○ VRC 144-145 E 5
Chacabuco ○ RA 78-79 J 3
Chacahua, Laguna de ≈ • 52-53 F 4
Chacala ○ BOL 70-71 D 5
Chacane ○ MOC 218-219 H 7
Chacao ○ RCH 78-79 C 6
Chacao, Canal de ≈ 78-79 C 6
Chacarilla, Quebrada de ~ RCH 70-71 C 7
Chacarrão, Cachoeira do ~ BR 66-67 H 6
Chacas ○ PE 64-65 D 6
Chacay, Arroyo el ~ RA 78-79 E 3
Chacay Alto ○ RCH 76-77 B 5
Chacayan ○ PE 64-65 D 7
Chachani, Volcán ▲ PE 70-71 B 5
Chachapoyas ☆ PE 64-65 D 5
Cháchar ~ PK 138-139 C 5
Chacharramendi ○ RA 78-79 G 4
Chache ○ GH 202-203 J 5
Chacho, El ○ RA 76-77 E 6
Chachoengsao ○ THA 158-159 F 4
Chāchro ○ • PK 138-139 C 7
Chacmool ∴ • MEX 52-53 L 2
Chaco ◘ RA 76-77 G 3
Chaco, Quebrada de ~ RCH 76-77 C 3
Chaco Austral ≟ RA 76-77 G 3
Chaco Boreal ≟ PY 70-71 G 7
Chaco Central ≟ PY 76-77 G 3
Chaco Culture National Historic Park ⊥ ••• USA (NM) 256-257 H 2
Chacon, Cape ▲ USA 32-33 E 4
Chacopaya ○ BOL 70-71 C 4
Chaco River ~ USA (NM) 256-257 G 2
Chacras, Cerro ▲ EC 64-65 B 10
Chad, Lake = Tchad, Lac ○ 198-199 F 6
Chad = Tchad ■ TCH 198-199 G 5
Chadaouanka ○ RN 198-199 C 5
Chadayang ○ VRC 156-157 K 5
Chadbourn ○ USA (NC) 282-283 J 6
Chadin ○ PE 64-65 C 5
Chadiza ○ Z 218-219 G 2
Chadron ○ USA (NE) 262-263 D 2
Chafarinas, Islas ⌒ E 98-99 F 7
Chafe ○ WAN 204-205 G 3
Chaffee Military Reservation, Fort xx • USA (AR) 276-277 A 5
Chaffers, Isla ⌒ RCH 80 C 2
Chafo ○ WAN 204-205 F 3
Chafurray ○ CO 60-61 E 6
Chāgai ○ PK 134-135 L 4
Chāgai Hills ▲ PK 134-135 K 4
Chāgalamarri ○ IND 140-141 H 3
Chaghat ~ BD 142-143 F 3
Chagne ○ ETH 208-209 C 3
Chagoness ○ CDN (SAS) 232-233 O 3
Chagos Archipel ~ GB 12 F 5
Chagos Archipelago ~ GB 12 F 5
Chagos-Laccadive Ridge ≃ 12 F 5
Chagos Trench ≃ 12 F 5
Chaguanas ○ TT 60-61 L 2
Chaguaramal ○ YV 60-61 K 3
Chaguaramas ○ YV 60-61 L 2
Chaguaramas ○ YV (GUA) 60-61 H 3
Chaguaramas ○ YV (MON) 60-61 K 3
Chaguarpambo ○ EC 64-65 C 3
Chagulak Island ⌒ USA 22-23 L 6
Chagyúmgoinba ○ VRC 144-145 H 5
Chahbounia ○ DZ 190-191 D 3
Chāh Sandan ○ PK 134-135 K 4
Chai ○ MOC 214-215 L 6
Chaiba, Col de ▲ DZ 190-191 E 3
Chāibāsa ○ IND 142-143 D 4
Chaigneau, Islas ⌒ RCH 80 C 6
Chaillu, Massif du ▲ G 210-211 C 4
Chai Nat ○ THA 158-159 F 3
Chain Fracture Zone ≃ 6-7 H 9
Chaira, La ○ CO 64-65 E 1
Chaitén ○ RCH 78-79 C 7
Chaitén, Ensenada ≈ 78-79 C 7
Chaiwopu ○ VRC 146-147 H 4
Chaiya ○ THA 158-159 E 6
Chaiyaphum ○ THA 158-159 G 3
Chajarí ○ RA 76-77 H 6

Chak o PK 138-139 D 5
Chakachamna Lake ⊂ USA 20-21 O 6
Chakachatna River ~ USA 20-21 O 6
Chākāi o IND 142-143 E 3
Chakaktolik o USA 20-21 J 6
Chākar ~ PK 138-139 B 5
Chakari o ZW 218-219 E 4
Chakdara o • PK 138-139 D 2
Chake Chake o EAT 212-213 G 6
Chakia o IND 142-143 C 3
Chak Jhumra o PK 138-139 D 4
Chakkrarat o THA 158-159 G 3
Chakonipau, Lac ⊂ CDN 36-37 P 6
Chakri o PK 138-139 D 3
Chak Swari o IND 138-139 D 3
Chakwāl o PK 138-139 D 3
Chakwenga o Z 218-219 E 2
Chala o EAT 214-215 F 4
Chala o PE 64-65 E 9
Chalaco o PE 64-65 C 4
Chalais o F 90-91 H 9
Chalalou o PNG 183 D 2
Chalanta o RA 78-79 G 2
Chalatenango ☆ ES 52-53 K 4
Chalaua o MOC 218-219 K 3
Chalawa, River ~ WAN 204-205 H 3
Chalbi Desert ⊥ EAK 212-213 F 2
Chalchuapa o ES 52-53 K 5
Chalengkou o VRC 146-147 L 6
Chaleur Bay ≈ 38-39 M 4
Chaleur Bay ≈ CDN 240-241 K 3
Chaleurs, Baie des ≈ 38-39 M 4
Chaleurs, Baie des ≈ CDN 240-241 K 3
Chalhuanca o PE 64-65 F 9
Chalía o Shehuen, Río ~ RA 80 E 4
Chaling o VRC 156-157 H 3
Chalinze o EAT 214-215 K 4
Chālisgaon o IND 138-139 E 9
Chalk River o CDN (ONT) 238-239 H 2
Chalky Inlet ≈ 182 A 7
Chalkyitsik o USA 20-21 T 3
Challakere o IND 140-141 G 3
Challans o F 90-91 G 8
Challa-Ogoyi o DY 204-205 E 4
Challapata o BOL 70-71 D 6
Challenger Deep ≃ 14-15 G 6
Challenger Plateau ≃ 182 B 3
Challis o USA (ID) 252-253 D 2
Chalmette o USA (LA) 268-269 L 7
Châlons-sur-Marne ☆ • F 90-91 K 7
Chalon-sur-Saône o F 90-91 K 8
Chalouba = Oum o TCH 198-199 K 5
Chaltel o Fitz Roy, Cerro ▲ RA 80 D 4
Chaltubo o • GE 126-127 E 6
Chá Lugela o MOC 218-219 J 3
Cham o D 92-93 M 4
Chàm ⌒ VN 158-159 K 3
Chama o USA (NM) 256-257 J 2
Chama o Z 214-215 G 6
Chama, Rio ~ USA (NM) 256-257 J 2
Chamah, Gunung ▲ MAL (PEK) 162-163 D 2
Chamais < NAM 220-221 B 3
Chaman o PK 134-135 M 3
Chamax ∴ • MEX 52-53 L 2
Chamaya, Río ~ PE 64-65 C 5
Chamba o EAT 214-215 J 6
Chamba o •• IND 138-139 F 3
Chambal ~ IND 138-139 G 6
Chambas o C 54-55 F 3
Chamberlain o CDN (SAS) 232-233 N 5
Chamberlain o USA (SD) 260-261 G 3
Chamberlain Island ⌒ CDN 36-37 M 2
Chamberlain Lake ⊂ USA (ME) 278-279 M 2
Chamberlain River ~ AUS 172-173 H 4
Chambers o USA (NE) 262-263 H 2
Chambers Bay ≈ 172-173 K 2
Chambersburg o USA (PA) 280-281 J 4
Chambers Cois o CDN (ONT) 238-239 F 6
Chambers Creek ~ USA (TX) 264-265 H 6
Chambers Island ⌒ USA (WI) 270-271 L 5
Chambéry ☆ • F 90-91 K 9
Chambeshi ~ Z 214-215 F 6
Chambi, Jebel ▲ TN 190-191 G 3
Chambira, Río ~ PE 64-65 E 4
Chambishi o Z 214-215 E 7
Chambo o EC 64-65 C 2
Chambord o CDN (QUE) 240-241 C 2
Chambord, Château ••• F 90-91 H 8
Chambrey o RP 160-161 E 7
Chambri Lakes ⊂ PNG 183 B 3
Chame o PA 52-53 E 7
Chamelecón, Río ~ HN 52-53 K 4
Chametengo o MOC 218-219 H 3
Chameza o CO 60-61 E 5
Chāmi < RIM 196-197 C 4
Chamical o RA 76-77 D 6
Chamiss Bay o CDN (BC) 230-231 B 3
Cham Kha o THA 142-143 L 6
Chamlang ▲ NEP 144-145 F 7
Ch'amo Hāyk' ⊂ ETH 208-209 C 6
Chamois o USA (MO) 274-275 G 6
Chamouchouane, Rivière ~ CDN (QUE) 236-237 P 3
Champ, Lac ⊂ CDN 36-37 R 7
Champagne o CDN 20-21 W 6
Champagne ⊥ • F 90-91 K 7
Champagne-Ardenne ◘ F 90-91 K 8
Champaign o USA (IL) 274-275 K 4
Champaqui, Cerro ▲ RA 76-77 E 6
Champasak o LAO 158-159 H 3
Champerico o GCA 52-53 J 4
Champhai o IND 142-143 H 4
Champion o CDN (ALB) 232-233 E 5
Champion o USA (MI) 270-271 L 4
Champlain o USA (NY) 278-279 H 4
Champlain, Lake ⊂ USA (NY) 278-279 H 4
Champotón o • MEX 52-53 J 2
Chāmrājnagar o IND 140-141 G 5
Chana, Kafin- o WAN 198-199 B 6
Chanachane, Oued ~ DZ 196-197 H 2
Chañaral o RCH 76-77 B 4
Chañaral, Isla ⌒ RCH 76-77 B 5
Chança, Rio ~ P 98-99 D 6
Chancani o RA 76-77 E 6
Chancay o PE 64-65 D 7
Chancay, Río ~ PE 64-65 C 5
Chancaybaños o PE 64-65 C 5
Chancellor o CDN (ALB) 232-233 F 4
Chan-Chan ••• PE 64-65 C 6
Ch'anch'o o ETH 208-209 D 4
Chanco o RCH 78-79 C 3
Chanco, Bahía ≈ 78-79 C 3
Chanda o IND 142-143 C 2
Chandalar River ~ USA 20-21 Q 3
Chandaler o USA 20-21 Q 3
Chandannagar o IND 142-143 F 4
Chandarpur o IND 142-143 C 5
Chandausi o IND 138-139 G 5
Chāndbāli o IND 142-143 E 5
Chandeleur Islands ⌒ USA (LA) 268-269 M 7
Chandeleur Sound ≈ 48-49 D 5
Chandeleur Sound ≈ USA 268-269 L 7
Chandeliers, Col des ▲ RN 198-199 F 2
Chanderi o IND 138-139 G 7
Chandgad o IND 140-141 F 3
Chandigarh ☆ •• IND 138-139 F 4
Chandipur o IND 142-143 E 5
Chandla o IND 142-143 B 3
Chandler o CDN (QUE) 240-241 L 2
Chandler o USA (AZ) 256-257 D 5
Chandler o USA (OK) 264-265 H 3
Chandler o USA (TX) 264-265 J 6
Chandler, Mount ▲ AUS 176-177 M 3
Chandler Lake ⊂ USA 20-21 O 2
Chandler River ~ USA 20-21 P 2
Chandless, Rio ~ BR 66-67 C 7
Chandless, Rio ~ BR 70-71 J 2
Chandpur o BD 142-143 G 4
Chandrabhāga ~ IND 138-139 F 3
Chandragadi o NEP 144-145 G 7
Chandrapur o IND 138-139 G 10
Chandrasekharapuram o IND 140-141 H 3
Chanduy o EC 64-65 B 3
Chandvad o IND 138-139 E 9
Chandwa o IND 142-143 D 4
Chang o PK 138-139 B 6
Changa o Z 218-219 E 3
Changadae Dan ▲ DVR 150-151 G 8
Changamba o ANG 216-217 E 6
Changamwe o EAK 212-213 G 6
Changanācheri o IND 140-141 G 6
Changane, Rio ~ MOC 218-219 G 6
Changara o MOC 218-219 G 3
Changar Char o BD 142-143 G 4
Changbai o VRC 150-151 G 7
Changbai Shan ▲ VRC 150-151 F 7
Changbaishan • VRC 150-151 G 6
Changbaishan Z.B. ⊥ • VRC 150-151 F 6
Changcheng o VRC 156-157 F 7
Chang Chenmo ~ IND 138-139 G 2
Changchun ☆ VRC 150-151 E 6
Changdao o VRC 154-155 M 3
Changde o VRC 156-157 G 2
Changdianhekou o VRC 150-151 E 7
Changfeng o VRC 154-155 K 5
Changgi Gap ▲ ROK 150-151 G 9
Changhang o ROK 150-151 F 9
Changhua o RC 156-157 M 4
Changji o VRC 146-147 H 3
Changjiang o VRC 156-157 F 7
Chang Jiang ~ VRC 154-155 L 6
Changjiang Kou ≈ 154-155 N 6
Changjiang Sanxia ⌣ •• VRC 154-155 F 6
Changjin o DVR 150-151 F 7
Changjin Gang ~ DVR 150-151 F 7
Changjin Ho ⊂ DVR 150-151 F 7
Changkat Jering o MAL 162-163 D 2
Changle o VRC (FUJ) 156-157 L 4
Changle o VRC (SIC) 154-155 E 6
Changli o VRC 154-155 L 2
Changling o VRC (HUB) 154-155 H 6
Changling o VRC (JIL) 150-151 E 5
Changlun o MAL 162-163 D 2
Changma He ~ VRC 146-147 N 6
Changmar o VRC 144-145 C 3
Changning o VRC (HUN) 156-157 H 3
Changning o VRC (SIC) 156-157 D 2
Changning o VRC (YUN) 142-143 L 3
Chango o IND 138-139 G 4
Changoti o IND 138-139 E 5
Changpin o RC 156-157 M 5
Changping o VRC 154-155 K 1
Changsan Got ▲ DVR 150-151 E 8
Changsha ☆ • VRC 156-157 H 2
Changshan o VRC 156-157 L 2
Changshan Qundao ⌒ VRC 150-151 D 8
Changshou o VRC 156-157 E 2
Changshu o VRC 154-155 M 6
Changshun o VRC 156-157 E 3
Changsong o DVR 150-151 E 7
Changsŏng o ROK 150-151 F 10
Changtai o VRC 156-157 K 4
Changting o VRC 156-157 K 4
Changtu o VRC 150-151 E 6
Changuillo o PE 64-65 E 9
Ch'angwon o ROK 150-151 G 10
Changwu o VRC 156-157 G 5
Changxing o VRC 154-155 L 6
Changyang o VRC 156-157 D 3
Changyon o DVR 150-151 E 8
Changyuan o VRC 154-155 J 4
Changzhi o VRC 154-155 H 3
Changzhou o VRC 154-155 L 6
Chankanai o CL 140-141 H 6
Chanler's Falls ~ EAK 212-213 G 3
Channapatna o IND 140-141 G 4
Channarāyapatna o IND 140-141 G 4
Channel Country, The ⌣ AUS 178-179 E 3
Channel Islands ◘ GB 90-91 F 7
Channel Islands ⌒ USA (CA) 248-249 D 6
Channel Islands National Park ⊥ USA (CA) 248-249 D 6
Channel-Port-aux-Basques o CDN (NFL) 242-243 J 5
Channel Rock ⌒ BS 54-55 G 3
Channing o USA (TX) 264-265 B 3
Chantada o E 98-99 D 3
Chanthaburi o THA 158-159 G 4
Chantrey Inlet ≈ 30-31 W 2
Chanu Daro ∴ • PK 138-139 B 6
Chanute o USA (KS) 262-263 L 7
Chany, Ozero = Čany, ozero ⊂ RUS 124-125 K 1
Chao, Isla ⌒ PE 64-65 C 6
Chaohu o VRC 154-155 K 6
Chao Hu • VRC 154-155 K 6
Chaouia ⊥ MA 188-189 H 4
Chaoyang o VRC 150-151 C 7
Chaozhou o VRC 156-157 K 5
Chapacura, Cachoeira ~ BOL 70-71 F 4
Chapada o BR 74-75 D 7
Chapada Diamantina ▲ BR 72-73 J 2
Chapada Diamantina, Parque Nacional ⊥ BR 72-73 K 2
Chapada do Araripe ▲ BR 68-69 H 5
Chapada dos Guimarães o BR 70-71 K 4
Chapada dos Veadeiros, Parque Nacional da ⊥ BR 72-73 G 3
Chapada Grande ▲ BR 68-69 G 5
Chapadinha o BR 68-69 G 3
Chapais o CDN (QUE) 236-237 O 3
Chapala o MEX 52-53 C 1
Chapala, Lago de ⊂ MEX 52-53 C 1
Chapalcó, Valle de ⌣ RA 78-79 G 4
Chaparaó, Serra do ▲ BR 72-73 J 6
Chapare, Río ~ BOL 70-71 E 5
Chaparra o PE 64-65 F 9
Chaparral o CO 60-61 D 6
Chaparrito o CO 60-61 F 5
Chaparro, El o YV 60-61 J 3
Chapas, Las o RA 78-79 F 7
Chapeco o BR 74-75 D 6
Chapel Hill o USA (NC) 282-283 H 5
Chapel Hill o USA (TN) 276-277 J 5
Chapel Island Indian Reserve ⚔ • CDN (NS) 240-241 P 5
Chapelle, La o RH 54-55 J 5
Chapelton o JA 54-55 G 5
Chaperito o USA (NM) 256-257 L 3
Chapin o USA (MI) 272-273 E 4
Chapleau o CDN (ONT) 236-237 E 5
Chapleau-Nemegosenda Provincial Park ⊥ CDN (ONT) 236-237 F 4
Chapleau River ~ CDN (ONT) 236-237 E 4
Chaplin o CDN (SAS) 232-233 M 5
Chaplin o USA (KY) 276-277 K 3
Chaplin Lake ⊂ CDN (SAS) 232-233 M 5
Chapman, Cape ▲ CDN 24-25 b 5
Chapman, Lac ⊂ CDN (QUE) 236-237 O 4
Chapman Ranch o USA (TX) 266-267 K 6
Chapmanville o USA (WV) 280-281 D 6
Chapo, Lago ⊂ RCH 78-79 C 6
Chappell o USA (NE) 262-263 D 3
Chappells o USA (SC) 284-285 J 2
Chapra o IND (BIH) 142-143 D 3
Chapra o IND (MAP) 138-139 F 8
Chã Preta o BR 68-69 K 6
Chaptico o USA (MD) 280-281 K 5
Chapuru o • SOL 184 I d 3
Chapuy o RA 78-79 J 2
Châr < RIM 196-197 D 4
Charache o YV 60-61 F 3
Charadai o RA 76-77 H 4
Charagua o BOL 70-71 F 6
Charala o CO 60-61 E 4
Charancho, El o RA 78-79 G 4
Charara Safari Area ⊥ ZW 218-219 E 3
Charcas o MEX 50-51 J 6
Charco o USA (TX) 266-267 K 5
Charco, El o RA 76-77 E 4
Charco de la Peña o MEX 50-51 G 3
Charcot, Île ⌒ ARK 16 G 23
Charcot Land ⊥ GRØ 26-27 I 7
Chardon o USA (OH) 280-281 E 2
Chardzhev ☆ TM 136-137 H 5
Charef, Oued ~ MA 188-189 K 4
Charente ~ F 90-91 H 8
Charentes ~ F 90-91 G 9
Chari ~ TCH 206-207 C 3
Chari-Baguirmi ◘ TCH 206-207 C 3
Charité-sur-Loire, la o F 90-91 J 8
Chariton o USA (IA) 274-275 E 3
Chariton River ~ USA (MO) 274-275 F 4
Charity o GUY 62-63 E 2
Charkhi Dādri o IND 138-139 F 5
Charkiv o UA 102-103 K 3
Charleroi o B 92-93 H 3
Charles o CDN 34-35 F 3
Charles, Cape ▲ USA (VA) 280-281 L 6
Charles, Mount ▲ AUS (WA) 176-177 J 2
Charles, Mount ▲ AUS (WA) 176-177 D 3
Charles, Peak ▲ AUS 176-177 F 6
Charles Bay ≈ 36-37 M 3
Charlesbourg o CDN (QUE) 238-239 O 2
Charles City o USA (IA) 274-275 F 1
Charles City o USA (VA) 280-281 J 6
Charles Dickens Point ▲ CDN 24-25 X 5
Charles Fuhr o RA 80 E 5
Charles Island ⌒ CDN 36-37 M 3
Charles Knob ▲ AUS 176-177 H 2
Charles Lake ⊂ CDN 30-31 O 6
Charles Lighthouse, Cape • USA (VA) 280-281 L 6
Charles Mound ▲ USA (IL) 274-275 H 2
Charles M. Russell National Wildlife Refuge ⊥ USA (MT) 250-251 M 4
Charleston o NZ 182 C 4
Charleston o USA (AR) 276-277 A 5
Charleston o USA (IL) 274-275 K 5
Charleston o USA (MO) 276-277 F 4
Charleston o USA (MS) 268-269 K 2
Charleston o • USA (SC) 284-285 L 4
Charleston ☆ USA (WV) 280-281 E 5
Charleston, Lake ⊂ USA (IL) 274-275 L 5
Charleston Peak ▲ USA (NV) 248-249 J 3
Charlestown o •• KAN 56 D 3
Charlestown o USA (IN) 274-275 N 6
Charles Town o USA (WV) 280-281 J 4
Charlestown = Baile Chathail o IRL 90-91 C 5
Charles Yorke, Cape ▲ CDN 24-25 f 4
Charleville o AUS 178-179 J 4
Charleville-Mézières ☆ F 90-91 K 7
Charlevoix o USA (MI) 272-273 D 2
Charlevoix, Lake ⊂ USA (MI) 272-273 D 2
Charlie Gibbs Fracture Zone ≃ 6-7 E 3
Charliste o USA (AR) 276-277 D 6
Charlo o CDN (NB) 240-241 J 3
Charloit, Lac de ⊂ CDN 30-31 Q 4
Charlotte o USA (MI) 272-273 E 5
Charlotte o USA (NC) 282-283 G 5
Charlotte o USA (TN) 276-277 H 4
Charlotte o USA (TX) 266-267 J 5
Charlotte, Lake ⊂ CDN (NS) 240-241 M 6
Charlotte Amalie ☆ • USA (VI) 286-287 R 2
Charlotte Bank ≈ 158-159 J 7
Charlotte Court House o USA (VA) 280-281 H 6
Charlotte Harbor ≈ 48-49 G 6
Charlotte Harbor ≈ USA 286-287 G 5
Charlotte Lake ⊂ CDN (BC) 228-229 J 4
Charlottesville o ••• USA (VA) 280-281 H 5
Charlottetown ☆ • CDN (PEI) 240-241 M 4
Charlotteville o TT 60-61 L 2
Charlson o USA (ND) 258-259 E 3
Charlton o AUS 180-181 G 4
Charlton o CDN (ONT) 236-237 J 5
Charlton Island ⌒ CDN 38-39 E 2
Charnley River ~ AUS 172-173 G 4
Charouine o DZ 188-189 L 6
Charron Lake ⊂ CDN (MAN) 234-235 H 2
Chārsadda o • PK 138-139 C 2
Charters Towers o • AUS 174-175 J 7
Chartres ☆ ••• F 90-91 H 7
Chás o IND 142-143 E 4
Chaschuil o RA 76-77 C 4
Chaschuil, Valle de ⌣ RA 76-77 C 4
Chaschuil o Guanchin, Rio ~ RA 76-77 C 4
Chascomús o RA 78-79 K 3
Chase o CDN (BC) 230-231 K 3
Chase City o USA (VA) 280-281 H 7
Chasicó o RA (BUA) 78-79 H 5
Chasicó o RA (RIN) 78-79 E 6
Chasicó, Arroyo ~ RA 78-79 H 5
Chasicó, Laguna ⊂ RA 78-79 H 5
Chasm o CDN (BC) 230-231 H 2
Chasong o DVR 150-151 F 7
Chasquitambo o PE 64-65 D 7
Chassahowitzka o USA (FL) 286-287 G 3
Chassahowitzka Bay ≈ USA 286-287 G 3
Chassahowitzka National Wildlife Refuge ⊥ USA (FL) 286-287 G 3
Chasse, Réserve de ⊥ MA 188-189 J 3
Châtaigneraie, la o F 90-91 G 8
Chatanika River ~ USA 20-21 R 4
Chateau o CDN (NFL) 242-243 N 1
Châteaubriant o F 90-91 G 8
Château Chambord ••• F 90-91 H 8
Château-d'Oex o CH 92-93 J 5
Châteaudun o F 90-91 H 7
Chateaugay o USA (NY) 278-279 G 4
Château-Gontier o F 90-91 G 8
Châteauguay o CDN (QUE) 238-239 M 3
Chateauguay, Lac ⊂ CDN 36-37 P 6
Châteaulin o F 90-91 E 7
Châteauneuf-sur-Charente o F 90-91 G 9
Châteauneuf-sur-Loire o F 90-91 J 8
Château-Renault o F 90-91 H 8
Château-Richer o CDN (QUE) 238-239 O 2
Châteauroux ☆ F 90-91 H 8
Château-Thierry o F 90-91 J 7
Châtellerault o F 90-91 H 8
Chater o CDN (MAN) 234-235 D 5
Chatfield o CDN (MAN) 234-235 F 4
Chatfield o USA (MN) 270-271 F 7
Chatham o CDN (NB) 240-241 K 3
Chatham o CDN (ONT) 238-239 C 6
Chatham o USA (AK) 32-33 C 3
Chatham o USA (IL) 274-275 J 5
Chatham o USA (LA) 268-269 H 4
Chatham o USA (MI) 270-271 M 4
Chatham o USA (VA) 280-281 G 7
Chatham, Isla ⌒ RCH 80 C 5
Chatham Hill o USA (VA) 280-281 E 7
Chatham Island ⌒ AUS 176-177 D 7
Chatham Islands ⌒ NZ 13 K 7
Chatham Rise ≃ 182 F 5
Chatham Sound ≈ 32-33 E 4
Chatham Sound ≈ CDN 228-229 D 2
Chatham Strait ≈ 32-33 C 3
Châtillon o I 100-101 A 2
Châtillon-sur-Seine o • F 90-91 K 8
Chato, Cerro ▲ RA 78-79 C 7
Chatom o USA (AL) 284-285 B 5
Chatra o IND 142-143 D 3
Chatrapur o IND 142-143 D 6
Chatsworth o AUS 178-179 F 1
Chatsworth o CDN (ONT) 238-239 E 4
Chatsworth o USA (GA) 284-285 F 2
Chattahoochee o USA (FL) 286-287 E 1
Chattahoochee River ~ USA (AL) 284-285 E 5
Chattahoochee River ~ USA (GA) 284-285 E 3
Chattanooga o USA (OK) 264-265 F 4
Chattanooga o • USA (TN) 276-277 K 5
Chattaroy o USA (WA) 244-245 H 3
Chattoga River ~ USA (GA) 284-285 E 2
Chattooga River ~ USA (GA) 284-285 G 2
Chatuge Lake < USA (GA) 284-285 G 2
Chaua o ANG 216-217 E 4
Chaubara o PK 138-139 C 4
Chaudepalle o IND 140-141 H 4
Chaudière, Rivière ~ CDN (QUE) 238-239 O 2
Châu Đốc o • VN 158-159 H 5
Chauk o MYA 142-143 J 5
Chaukundi ∴ • PK 134-135 M 6
Chaumont o F 90-91 K 7
Chaumont o F 90-91 H 8
Chauncey o USA (GA) 284-285 G 4
Chauques, Islas ⌒ RCH 78-79 C 7
Chaura Island ⌒ IND 140-141 L 5
Chauri o • IND 140-141 F 3
Chautara o NEP 144-145 E 7
Chautauqua Lake ⊂ USA (IL) 274-275 J 4
Chautauqua Lake ⊂ USA (NY) 278-279 B 6
Chauvin o USA (LA) 268-269 K 7
Chavakachcheri o CL 140-141 J 6
Chāvakkād o IND 140-141 G 5
Chaval o BR 68-69 H 3
Chavarria o RA 76-77 H 5
Cha-Vat o THA 158-159 F 7
Chaves o BR 62-63 K 6
Chaves o • P 98-99 D 4
Chaveslândia o BR 72-73 E 5
Chavez, Los o USA (NM) 256-257 J 4
Chavigny, Lac ⊂ CDN 36-37 M 5
Chavín de Huántar ••• PE 64-65 D 6
Chavinillo o PE 64-65 D 6
Chavón, Río ~ DOM 54-55 L 5
Chavuma o Z 218-219 B 1
Chavuma Falls ~ Z 218-219 B 1
Chavuna o EAT 212-213 D 6
Chayanta, Río ~ BOL 70-71 D 6
Chazón o RA 78-79 H 2
Chazón, Arroyo ~ RA 78-79 H 2
Cheadle o CDN (ALB) 232-233 E 4
Cheaha Mountain ▲ USA (AL) 284-285 E 3
Cheakamus Indian Reserve ⚔ CDN (BC) 230-231 F 4
Cheat Lake ⊂ USA (WV) 280-281 G 4
Cheat Mountain ▲ USA (WV) 280-281 G 5
Cheat River ~ USA (WV) 280-281 G 4
Cheb o CZ 92-93 M 3
Chebaba, Hassi < DZ 190-191 D 6
Chebba o TN 190-191 H 3
Chebbi, Erg ⊥ MA 188-189 K 5
Chebogue Point o CDN (NS) 240-241 J 7
Cheboksary = Čeboksary ☆ RUS 96-97 E 5
Cheboygan o USA (MI) 272-273 E 2
Checa o E 98-99 G 4
Chech, Erg ⊥ DZ 196-197 J 2
Chech, Erg ⊥ RIM 196-197 G 3
Ché Ché o GNB 202-203 C 4
Checheng o RC 156-157 M 5
Chechenia = Nohčijčo' Respublika ◘ RUS 126-127 F 6
Cheche Pass ▲ LS 220-221 J 4
Chech'ŏn o ROK 150-151 G 9
Checotah o USA (OK) 264-265 J 3
Chedabucto Bay ≈ 38-39 O 6
Chedabucto Bay ≈ CDN 240-241 O 5
Chéddra o TCH 198-199 H 6
Cheding o VRC 144-145 G 6
Cheduba = Man'aung o MYA 142-143 H 6
Cheduba Island = Man'aung Kyun ⌒ MYA 142-143 H 6
Cheduba Strait ≈ 142-143 H 6
Cheecham o CDN 32-33 P 3
Cheektowaga o USA (NY) 278-279 C 6
Cheepash River ~ CDN (ONT) 236-237 G 2
Cheepie o AUS 178-179 H 4
Cheesman Peak ▲ AUS 176-177 L 3
Chefchaouene ☆ MA 188-189 J 3
Chefornak o USA 20-21 H 6
Chéfu, Rio ~ MOC 194-195 F 6
Chegga o DZ 190-191 E 3
Chegga o RIM 196-197 H 2
Chegge < RIM 196-197 E 5
Chegutu o ZW 218-219 F 4
Chehalis o USA (WA) 244-245 C 4
Chehalis River ~ USA (WA) 244-245 B 4
Chehaw Indian Monument • USA (GA) 284-285 F 5
Chehong Jiang ~ VRC 156-157 C 3
Chejchila, La o RA 76-77 E 4
Cheju o ROK 150-151 F 11
Cheju Do ⌒ ROK 150-151 F 11
Cheju Haehyŏp ≈ 150-151 F 11
Chela, Serra da ▲ ANG 216-217 B 8
Chelan o CDN (SAS) 232-233 P 3
Chelan o USA (WA) 244-245 E 3
Chelan, Lake ⊂ USA (WA) 244-245 E 2
Chelaslie River ~ CDN (BC) 228-229 H 3
Chelatna Lake ⊂ USA 20-21 P 5
Ch'elenk'o o ETH 208-209 E 4
Chelforó o RA 78-79 F 5
Chelforo, Arroyo ~ RA 78-79 K 4
Chelghoum El Aïd o DZ 190-191 F 2
Chelia, Djebel ▲ DZ 190-191 F 3
Chelif, Oued ~ DZ 190-191 C 3
Chelinda o MW 214-215 G 6
Cheline o MOC 218-219 H 6
Chellal o DZ 190-191 E 3
Chelm ☆ PL 92-93 R 3
Chelmno o • PL 92-93 P 2
Chelmsford o CDN (ONT) 238-239 D 2
Chelmsford Dam < ZA 220-221 J 4
Chelmża o • PL 92-93 P 2
Chelsea o USA (OK) 264-265 J 2
Chelsea o USA (VT) 278-279 J 5
Cheltenham o • GB 90-91 F 6
Chelvai o IND 142-143 B 6
Chelyabinsk = Čeljabinsk ☆ RUS 96-97 M 6
Chemaïa o MA 188-189 G 4
Chemainus o CDN (BC) 230-231 F 5
Chemax o MEX 52-53 L 1
Chemba o MOC 218-219 H 3
Chembe o Z 214-215 E 6
Chemchâm, Sebkhet ⊂ RIM 196-197 D 4
Chemehuevi Valley Indian Reservation ⚔ USA (CA) 248-249 K 5
Chemillé o F 90-91 G 8
Chemnitz o D 92-93 M 3
Chemong o CDN (SAS) 232-233 Q 2
Chemult o USA (OR) 244-245 D 7
Chemung River ~ USA (NY) 278-279 E 6
Chenab ~ IND 138-139 E 3
Chenāb ~ PK 138-139 D 3
Chenachen < DZ 188-189 J 7
Chena Hot Springs o USA 20-21 R 4
Chenango River ~ USA (NY) 278-279 F 6
Chena River ~ USA 20-21 R 4
Chen Barag Qi o VRC 150-151 B 3
Ch'ench'a o ETH 208-209 C 5
Chencoyi o MEX 52-53 J 2
Chenereh, Kampung o MAL 162-163 E 2
Chénéville o CDN (QUE) 238-239 K 3
Cheney o USA (KS) 262-263 J 7
Cheney o USA (WA) 244-245 H 3
Cheney Reservoir ⊂ USA (KS) 262-263 J 7
Chengalpattu o IND 140-141 H 4
Chengam o IND 140-141 H 4
Chengannūr o IND 140-141 G 6
Chengbu o VRC 156-157 F 3
Chengcheng o VRC 154-155 F 4
Chengde o VRC 154-155 K 1
Chengdu ☆ VRC 154-155 D 6
Chenggu o VRC 154-155 E 5
Chenghai o VRC 156-157 K 5
Cheng Hai ⊂ VRC 142-143 M 2
Chengkung o RC 156-157 M 5
Chengmai o VRC 156-157 G 7
Chengqian o VRC 154-155 K 4
Chengshan Jiao ▲ VRC 154-155 N 3
Chengwu o VRC 154-155 J 4
Cheng Xian o VRC 154-155 D 5
Cheniere Lake < USA (LA) 268-269 H 4
Chenik o USA 22-23 T 3
Chenini o • TN 190-191 H 4
Chenjiagang o VRC 154-155 L 4
Chenoa o USA (IL) 274-275 K 4
Chenpur o NEP 144-145 C 6
Chenque, Cerro ▲ RA 80 G 2
Chenxi o VRC (HUN) 156-157 G 2
Chenxi o VRC (SIC) 154-155 E 6
Chenzhou o VRC 156-157 H 4
Cheo Reo o VN 158-159 K 4
Chepachet o USA (RI) 278-279 K 7
Chepen o PE 64-65 C 5
Chepes o RA 76-77 D 6
Chepes, Sierra de ▲ RA 76-77 D 6
Chepo o • PA 52-53 E 7
Chepstow o GB 90-91 F 6
Chequamegon Bay ⊂ USA (WI) 270-271 H 4
Cheran o MEX 52-53 D 2
Cheranchi o WAN 198-199 C 6
Cherangany Hills ▲ EAK 212-213 E 3
Cheraw o USA (CO) 254-255 M 5
Cheraw o USA (SC) 284-285 L 2
Cherbourg o F 90-91 G 7
Cherchell o • DZ 190-191 D 2
Cherepani o GH 202-203 L 4
Cherepovets = Čerepovec ☆ RUS 94-95 P 2
Cherful, Cape ▲ USA 22-23 N 5
Chergui, Aftoût ech ⊥ RIM 196-197 C 6
Chergui, Zahrez ⊂ DZ 190-191 D 3
Cherhill o CDN (ALB) 232-233 D 2
Chéri o RN 198-199 E 6
Cheria o DZ 190-191 F 3
Cheriāl o IND 140-141 H 2
Cherkasy = Čerkasy ☆ UA 102-103 H 3
Chernabura Island ⌒ USA 22-23 R 5
Chernihiv = Černihiv o • UA 102-103 G 2
Cherni Island ⌒ USA 22-23 P 5
Chernivtsi = Černivci ☆ UA 102-103 D 3
Chernobyl = Čornobyl' o UA 102-103 G 2
Chernyakhovsk = Černjahovsk ☆ •• RUS 94-95 G 4
Cherokee o BS 54-55 G 1
Cherokee o USA (AL) 284-285 B 2
Cherokee o USA (IA) 274-275 C 2
Cherokee o USA (NC) 282-283 D 5
Cherokee o USA (OK) 264-265 F 2
Cherokee o USA (TX) 266-267 J 2
Cherokee Indian Reservation ⚔ USA (NC) 282-283 D 5
Cherokee Lake ⊂ USA (TN) 282-283 D 4
Cherokee Sound o BS 54-55 G 1
Cherokee Village o USA (AR) 276-277 D 4
Cherrabun o AUS 172-173 G 5
Chérrepe, Punta de ▲ PE 64-65 C 5
Cherry Creek ~ CDN (BC) 230-231 L 3
Cherry Creek o USA (NV) 246-247 L 4
Cherry Creek ~ USA (SD) 260-261 E 2
Cherry Creek ~ USA (CO) 254-255 L 4
Cherryfield o USA (ME) 278-279 O 4
Cherry Hill o USA (VA) 280-281 J 7
Cherryspring o USA (TX) 266-267 J 3
Cherryvale o USA (KS) 262-263 L 7
Cherry Valley o USA (AR) 276-277 E 5
Cherryville o CDN (BC) 230-231 L 3
Cherryville o USA (MO) 276-277 D 3
Cherskogo, Khrebet = Čerskogo, hrebet ▲ RUS 110-111 W 5
Cherson ☆ • UA 102-103 H 4
Chesaning o USA (MI) 272-273 E 4
Chesapeake Bay Bridge Tunnel II USA (VA) 280-281 L 6
Chesapeake o USA (VA) 280-281 K 7
Chesapeake Bay ≈ 46-47 K 6
Chesapeake Bay ≈ USA 280-281 K 5
Chesapeake Beach o USA (MD) 280-281 K 5
Chesea, Rio ~ PE 64-65 F 6
Cheshire o USA (OR) 244-245 B 6
Chëshskaya Guba = Češskaja guba ≈ RUS 88-89 S 3
Cheslatta Lake ⊂ CDN (BC) 228-229 J 3
Chesley o CDN (ONT) 238-239 D 4
Chesnee o USA (SC) 284-285 J 1
Chester o CDN (NS) 240-241 L 6
Chester o •• GB 90-91 F 5
Chester o USA (IA) 274-275 F 1
Chester o USA (ID) 252-253 G 3
Chester o USA (IL) 276-277 F 3
Chester o USA (MT) 250-251 J 3
Chester o USA (NE) 262-263 J 4
Chester o USA (OH) 280-281 F 3
Chester o USA (OK) 264-265 F 2
Chester o USA (PA) 280-281 L 4
Chester o USA (SC) 284-285 J 2
Chester o USA (TX) 268-269 F 6
Chester o USA (VA) 280-281 J 6
Chesterfield o GB 90-91 G 5
Chesterfield o USA (SC) 284-285 K 2
Chesterfield Inlet ≈ 30-31 X 4
Chesterfield Inlet o CDN 30-31 Y 4
Chesterton o USA (IN) 274-275 L 3
Chesterton Range ▲ AUS 178-179 J 3
Chestertown o USA (MD) 280-281 K 4
Chesterville o CDN (ONT) 238-239 K 3
Chestnut o USA (IL) 274-275 J 4
Chesuncook Lake ⊂ USA (ME) 278-279 M 3
Chetaibi o • DZ 190-191 F 2
Chetek o USA (WI) 270-271 G 5
Chéticamp o CDN (NS) 240-241 P 4
Cheticamp River ~ CDN (NS) 240-241 P 4
Chetimacha Indian Reservation ⚔ USA 268-269 J 7
Chet Korkora < RMM 196-197 H 6
Chetlat Island ⌒ IND 140-141 E 5
Chetopa o USA (KS) 262-263 L 7
Chetumal ☆ • MEX 52-53 K 2
Chetumal, Bahía de ≈ 52-53 K 2
Chetwynd o CDN 32-33 K 4
Chevak o USA 20-21 H 6
Chevejecure, Río ~ BOL 70-71 D 4
Cheviot o CDN (SAS) 232-233 M 3
Cheviot Hills, The ▲ GB 90-91 F 4
Cheviot Range ▲ AUS 178-179 G 3
Chewack River ~ USA (WA) 244-245 E 2
Chewelah o USA (WA) 244-245 H 2
Chewore Safari Area ⊥ ZW 218-219 E 3
Cheyenne o USA (OK) 264-265 E 3
Cheyenne ☆ USA (WY) 252-253 O 5
Cheyenne Bottoms ⊂ USA (KS) 262-263 H 6
Cheyenne River ~ USA (SD) 260-261 D 2
Cheyenne River ~ USA (WY) 252-253 O 3
Cheyenne River Indian Reservation ⚔ USA (SD) 260-261 E 1
Cheyenne Wells o USA (CO) 254-255 N 5
Cheyūr o IND 140-141 J 4
Chezacut o CDN (BC) 228-229 L 4
Chhāpar o IND 138-139 E 6
Chhatak o BD 142-143 G 3
Chhatarpur o IND 138-139 G 7
Chhattisgarh ⊥ IND 142-143 B 5
Chhaygaon o IND 142-143 G 2
Chheharta o IND 138-139 E 4
Chhindwāra o IND 138-139 G 8
Chhota Udepur o IND 138-139 E 8
Chhukha o BHT 142-143 F 2
Chhura o IND 142-143 C 5
Chiachi Island ⌒ USA 22-23 R 5
Ch'iaksan National Park ⊥ ROK 150-151 G 9
Chiamboni o SP 212-213 H 4
Chiangchün o RC 156-157 M 5
Chiang Dao o THA 142-143 L 6
Chiang Kan o THA 158-159 F 2
Chiang Kham o THA 142-143 M 6
Chiang Khong o THA 142-143 M 5
Chiang Mai ☆ THA 142-143 L 6
Chiang Rai o THA 142-143 L 6
Chian Muan o THA 142-143 M 6
Chiapa, Río ~ MEX 52-53 H 3
Chiapa de Corzo o • MEX 52-53 H 3
Chiapas ◘ MEX 52-53 H 3
Chiari o I 100-101 B 2
Chiasien o RC 156-157 M 5
Chiautla o MEX 52-53 E 2
Chiávari o • I 100-101 B 2
Chiavenna o I 100-101 B 1
Chiawa o Z 218-219 E 2
Chiayi o RC 156-157 M 5
Chiba ☆ J 152-153 J 7
Chibabava o MOC 218-219 G 5
Chibembe o Z 218-219 G 1
Chibia o ANG 216-217 B 7
Chibiapari o YV 62-63 D 3
Chibi Moya • VRC 156-157 H 2
Chibougamau o CDN (QUE) 236-237 O 3
Chibougamau, Lac ⊂ CDN (QUE) 236-237 O 3
Chibougamau, Rivière ~ CDN (QUE) 236-237 N 3
Chibuto o MOC 220-221 L 2
Chibuzhanghu ⊂ VRC 144-145 H 4
Chibwika o Z 214-215 C 7
Chica, Sierra ▲ RA 76-77 E 6
Chicago o • USA (IL) 274-275 L 3
Chicago Heights o USA (IL) 274-275 L 3
Chicala o ANG (BIE) 216-217 D 6
Chicala o ANG (MOX) 216-217 E 5
Chicamba o MOC 218-219 G 4
Chicamba Real, Barragem de < MOC 218-219 G 4
Chicambi o ANG 216-217 B 6
Chicaná ∴ • MEX 52-53 K 2
Chicapa ~ ANG 216-217 F 3
Chicas, Salinas ⊂ RA 78-79 H 5
Chicbul o MEX 52-53 J 2
Chic-Choc, Parc Provincial ⊥ CDN (QUE) 240-241 K 2
Chic-Chocs, Monts ▲ CDN (QUE) 240-241 H 2
Chicha < TCH 198-199 J 4
Chichagof o USA 32-33 B 3
Chichagof Island ⌒ USA 32-33 B 3
Chichancanab, Laguna ⊂ • MEX 52-53 K 2
Chichaoua o MA 188-189 G 5
Chicharrona, La o MEX 50-51 H 6
Chichāwatni o PK 138-139 D 4
Chiché, Rio ~ BR 68-69 B 6
Chicheng o VRC 154-155 J 1
Chichén Itzá ∴ ••• MEX 52-53 K 1
Chichester Range ▲ AUS 172-173 D 7

Chichibu ○ J 152-153 H 6
Chichibu-Tama National Park ⊥ J 152-153 H 7
Chichigalpa ○ NIC 52-53 L 5
Chichirate ○ EC 64-65 D 3
Chichón, Volcán ▲ MEX 52-53 H 3
Chickaloon ○ USA 20-21 Q 6
Chickamauga & Chattanooga National Military Park • USA (GA) 284-285 E 2
Chickamauga Lake < USA (TN) 282-283 C 5
Chickasaw ○ USA (AL) 284-285 B 6
Chickasaw Bogue ∼ USA (AL) 284-285 C 4
Chickasawhatchee Creek ∼ USA (GA) 284-285 F 5
Chickasawhay River ∼ USA (MS) 268-269 M 5
Chickasaw National Recreation Area ⊥• USA (OK) 264-265 H 6
Chickasha ○ USA (OK) 264-265 G 3
Chickasha, Lake < USA (OK) 264-265 F 3
Chic Kata ○ RH 54-55 J 5
Chicken ○ USA 20-21 U 4
Chicken Creek Summit ▲ USA (NV) 246-247 J 2
Chick Lake ⊂ CDN 30-31 F 3
Chiclayo ☆ PE 64-65 C 5
Chico ○ MOC 218-219 G 5
Chico ○ USA (CA) 246-247 D 4
Chico, Arroyo ∼ RA 78-79 L 4
Chico, Río ∼ RA 76-77 E 4
Chico, Río ∼ RA 78-79 D 7
Chico, Río ∼ RA 80 F 5
Chico, Río ∼ RA 80 F 4
Chico, Río ∼ RA 80 G 2
Chicoa ○ MOC 218-219 G 2
Chico Arroyo ∼ USA (NM) 256-257 H 3
Chicoasén ○ MEX 52-53 H 3
Chicoasén, Presa <• MEX 52-53 H 3
Chicoca ○ ANG 216-217 F 7
Chicomba ○ ANG 216-217 C 7
Chicomo ○ MOC 220-221 M 2
Chicomoztoc ∴• MEX 50-51 H 6
Chicomuselo ○ MEX 52-53 H 4
Chiconduа ∼ ANG 216-217 B 7
Chicontepec de Tejeda ○ MEX 52-53 E 1
Chicopee ○ USA (MA) 278-279 J 6
Chicoral ○ CO 60-61 D 5
Chicot State Park ⊥ USA (LA) 268-269 H 6
Chicotte ○ CDN (QUE) 242-243 E 3
Chicoutimi ○ CDN (QUE) 240-241 D 2
Chicualacuala ○ MOC 218-219 F 6
Chicuma ○ ANG 216-217 C 6
Chicundo ○ ANG 216-217 D 6
Chicupa ○ ANG 216-217 E 7
Ch'ida ○ ETH 208-209 C 5
Chidambaram ○•• IND 140-141 H 5
Chidenguele ○ MOC 220-221 M 2
Chidester ○ USA (AR) 276-277 B 7
Chido ○ ROK 150-151 F 10
Chiede ○ ANG 216-217 C 8
Chief Joseph Pass ▲ USA (MT) 250-251 F 6
Chiefland ○ USA (FL) 286-287 G 2
Chief Menominee Monument • USA (IN) 274-275 M 3
Chiefs Island ⌒ RB 218-219 B 4
Chief's Point Indian Reservation ⚔ CDN (ONT) 238-239 D 4
Chiemsee ⊂ D 92-93 M 5
Chiengi ○ Z 214-215 E 5
Chiêng Khu'o'ng ○ VN 156-157 C 6
Chiengo ○ ANG 216-217 D 7
Chieo Lan Reservoir < THA 158-159 E 6
Chiese ∼ I 100-101 C 2
Chieti ☆ I 100-101 E 3
Chifango ○ ANG 216-217 D 7
Chifeng ○ VRC 148-149 O 6
Chifre, Serra do ▲ BR 72-73 K 4
Chifu ○ WAN 204-205 F 3
Chifukunya Hills ▲ Z 218-219 E 2
Chifumage ∼ ANG 216-217 F 5
Chifunda ○ Z 214-215 G 6
Chifunde ○ MOC 218-219 G 2
Chig < RIM 196-197 D 5
Chigamane ○ MOC 218-219 G 5
Chiginagak, Mount ▲ USA 22-23 S 4
Chiginagak Bay ≈ 22-23 S 4
Chigmit Mountains ▲ USA 22-23 U 3
Chignecto, Cape ▲ CDN (NB) 240-241 K 5
Chignecto Bay ≈ 38-39 M 6
Chignecto Bay ≈ CDN 240-241 L 5
Chignecto Game Sanctuary ⊥ CDN (NS) 240-241 L 5
Chignik ○ USA 22-23 R 4
Chignik Bay ≈ 22-23 R 4
Chigombe, Rio ∼ MOC 218-219 G 6
Chigorodó ○ CO 60-61 C 4
Chigoubiche, Lac ⊂ CDN (QUE) 236-237 P 3
Chiguana ○ BOL 70-71 D 7
Chigubo ○ MOC 218-219 G 6
Chihli, Gulf of = Bo Hai ≈ VRC 154-155 L 2
Chihsing Yen ⌒ RC 156-157 M 6
Chihuahua ◘ MEX 50-51 F 3
Chihuahua ☆ MEX (CHA) 50-51 F 3
Chihuido de Medio, Cerro ▲ RA 78-79 E 5
Chijmuni ○ BOL 70-71 D 5
Chikanda ○ WAN 204-205 E 4
Chikaskia River ∼ USA (KS) 262-263 J 7
Chik Ballāpur ○ IND 140-141 G 4
Chikhli ○ IND (GUJ) 138-139 D 9
Chikhli ○ IND (MAH) 138-139 F 9
Chikhli ○ IND (MAP) 138-139 G 8
Chikjajur ○ IND 140-141 G 3
Chikmagalūr ○ IND 140-141 F 4
Chiknāyakanhalli ○ IND 140-141 G 4
Chikodi ○ IND 140-141 F 2
Chikombedzi ○ ZW 218-219 F 5
Chikonkomene ○ Z 218-219 E 2
Chikuma-gawa ∼ J 152-153 H 6
Chikuminuk Lake ⊂ USA 20-21 L 6
Chikwa ○ Z 214-215 G 6
Chikwawa ○ MW 218-219 H 3
Chikwina ○ MW 214-215 H 6
Chikyu-misaki ▲ J 152-153 J 3
Chila ○ ANG 216-217 C 6
Chila ○ MEX 52-53 F 3
Chila, Laguna ⊂ MEX 50-51 K 6
Chilakalūrupet ○ IND 140-141 J 2
Chilako River ∼ CDN (BC) 228-229 L 3
Chilan ○ RC 156-157 M 4
Chi Lăng ○ VN 156-157 E 6
Chilanga ○ Z 218-219 E 2
Chilanko Forks ○ CDN (BC) 228-229 K 4
Chilanko River ∼ CDN (BC) 228-229 K 4
Chilapa ○ MEX 52-53 E 3
Chilapa de Díaz ○ MEX 52-53 F 3
Chilas ○• IND 138-139 E 2
Chilaw ○ CL 140-141 H 7
Chilca ○ PE 64-65 D 8
Chilca, Punta ▲ PE 64-65 D 8
Chilcas ○ RA 76-77 E 4
Chilcaya ○ RCH 70-71 C 6
Chilcoot ○ USA (CA) 246-247 E 4
Chilcotin Ranges ▲ CDN (BC) 230-231 F 2
Chilcotin River ∼ CDN (BC) 230-231 G 2
Chilcott Island ⌒ AUS 174-175 L 5
Childers ○ AUS 178-179 M 3
Childersburg ○ USA (AL) 284-285 D 3
Childress ○ USA (TX) 264-265 D 4
Chile ■ RCH 78-79 C 5
Chile Basin ≃ 5 D 7
Chile Chico ○ RCH 80 E 3
Chilecito ○• RA 76-77 D 5
Chileka ○ MW 218-219 H 2
Chilembwe ○ Z 218-219 F 1
Chilena, Cordillera ▲ RCH 80 D 6
Chilengue, Serra do ▲ ANG 216-217 C 6
Chile Rise ≃ 5 B 8
Chiles, Los ○ CR 52-53 B 6
Chilesburg ○ USA (VA) 280-281 J 5
Chilete ○ PE 64-65 C 5
Chili, Gulf of = Bo Hai ≈ 154-155 L 2
Chilikadrotna River ∼ USA 20-21 N 6
Chililabombwe ○ Z 214-215 D 7
Chilili ○ USA (NM) 256-257 J 4
Chilkat ○ USA 20-21 S 6
Chilkat Bald Eagle Preserve ⊥ USA 20-21 W 7
Chilkat Inlet ≈ 20-21 X 7
Chilko Lake ⊂ CDN (BC) 230-231 E 2
Chilkoot Pass ▲ USA 20-21 X 7
Chilko River ∼ CDN (BC) 230-231 E 2
Chilla ○ EC 64-65 C 3
Chillagoe ○ AUS 174-175 H 5
Chillajara ○ BOL 70-71 E 7
Chillán ○ RCH 78-79 C 4
Chillán, Río ∼ RCH 78-79 D 4
Chillán, Volcán ▲ RCH 78-79 D 4
Chillar ○ RA 78-79 J 4
Chilla Well ○ AUS 172-173 K 6
Chillicothe ○ USA (IL) 274-275 J 4
Chillicothe ○ USA (MO) 274-275 E 5
Chillicothe ○ USA (OH) 280-281 D 4
Chillicothe ○ USA (TX) 264-265 E 4
Chillinji ○ IND 138-139 E 1
Chilliwack ○ CDN (BC) 230-231 H 4
Chillūa Tāl ○ IND 142-143 C 2
Chillūpar ○ IND 142-143 C 2
Chilmari ○ BD 142-143 F 3
Chilmark ○ USA (MA) 278-279 L 7
Chiloango ∼ ANG 210-211 D 6
Chilobwe ○ MW 218-219 G 1
Chiloé, Isla de ⌒ RCH 78-79 C 7
Chiloé, Parque Nacional ⊥ RCH 78-79 B 7
Chilombo ○ ANG 214-215 B 6
Chilongozi ○ Z 218-219 F 1
Chiloquin ○ USA (OR) 244-245 D 8
Chilpancingo de los Bravos ☆ MEX 52-53 E 3
Chilpi ○ IND 142-143 B 4
Chiltepec ○ MEX 52-53 H 2
Chillicothe ○ USA (IL) 274-275 J 4
Chilton ○ USA (TX) 266-267 K 2
Chilton ○ USA (WI) 270-271 K 6
Chiluage ○ ANG 216-217 F 4
Chilubula ○ Z 214-215 F 6
Chilumba ○ MW 214-215 H 6
Chilumbulwa ○ Z 214-215 D 7
Chilwa, Lake ⊂ MW 218-219 H 2
Chimala ○ EAT 214-215 H 5
Chimaliro ▲ MW 214-215 H 6
Chimaltenango ☆ GCA 52-53 J 4
Chimán ○ PA 52-53 E 7
Chimanimani ○• ZW 218-219 G 4
Chimanimani National Park ⊥ ZW 218-219 G 4
Chimasula ○ Z 218-219 F 2
Chimban ○ PE 64-65 C 5
Chimbangombe ○ ANG 216-217 D 6
Chimbarongo ○ RCH 78-79 D 3
Chimbinde ○ ANG 216-217 E 6
Chimbo, Río ∼ EC 64-65 C 3
Chimborazo, Volcán ▲ EC 64-65 C 2
Chimbote ○ PE 64-65 C 6
Chimbwingombi ▲ Z 218-219 F 1
Chiméal ○ K 158-159 G 5
Chimney Rock • USA (NC) 282-283 E 5
Chimney Rock National Historic Site ∴ USA (NE) 262-263 C 3
Chimoio ☆ MOC 218-219 G 4
Chimumo ∼ ANG 216-217 D 8
Chin ○ MEX 50-51 K 5
China ○ USA (TX) 268-269 F 6
China = Zhongguo ■ VRC 144-145 E 6
Chinach, I-n- < RMM 196-197 K 6
Chinacota ○ CO 60-61 E 4
Chinake ○ IND 140-141 F 2
China Lake ⊂ USA (CA) 248-249 G 4
China Lake Naval Weapons Center ✕✕ USA (CA) 248-249 G 4
Chinampas ○ MEX 50-51 J 7
China Muerte, Arroyo ∼ RA 78-79 E 5
Chinandega ☆ NIC 52-53 L 5
China Point ≃ 248-249 F 7
Chinati Peak ▲ USA (TX) 266-267 C 4
Chincha, Islas de ⌒ PE 64-65 D 8
Chincha Alta ○ PE 64-65 D 8
Chinchaga River ∼ CDN 30-31 K 6
Chinchilla ○ AUS 178-179 L 4
Chinchilla de Monte Aragón ○ E 98-99 G 5
Chinchina ○ CO 60-61 D 5
Chinchin Straits ≈ 162-163 C 2
Chinchorro, Banco ⌒ MEX 52-53 L 2
Chincolco ○ RCH 78-79 D 2
Chincoteague ○ USA (VA) 280-281 L 6
Chincoteague Bay ≈ 46-47 L 6
Chincoteague Bay ≈ USA 280-281 L 5
Chincultic ∴• MEX 52-53 J 3
Chinde ○ MOC 218-219 J 4
Chindo ○ ROK 150-151 F 10
Chin Do ⌒ ROK 150-151 F 10
Chindwin Myit ∼ MYA 142-143 J 3
Chinengue ○ MOC 218-219 H 1
Chinero, El ○ MEX 50-51 B 2
Chingaza, Parque Nacional ⊥ CO 60-61 E 5
Chingo ○ ANG 216-217 B 7
Chingola ○ Z 214-215 D 7
Chingombe ○ Z 218-219 F 2
Chinguar ○ ANG 216-217 D 6
Chingueia ○ ANG 216-217 D 6
Chinguetti ○• RIM 196-197 D 4
Chinguil ○ TCH 206-207 D 3
Chingwin Bum ▲ MYA 142-143 L 3
Chinhama ○ ANG 216-217 D 6
Chinhanda ○ MOC 218-219 G 2
Chinhanguanine ○ MOC 220-221 L 2
Chin Hills ▲ MYA 142-143 H 4
Chinhoyi ☆• ZW 218-219 F 3
Chiniak, Cape ▲ USA 22-23 U 4
Chiniak Bay ≈ 22-23 U 4
Chiniot ○• PK 138-139 D 4
Chinitna Point ▲ USA 22-23 U 3
Chinjan ○ PK 134-135 M 3
Chinkapook ○ AUS 180-181 G 3
Chinko ∼ RCA 206-207 G 6
Chinle ○ USA (AZ) 256-257 F 2
Chinle Wash ∼ USA (AZ) 256-257 F 2
Chinmen ○ RC 156-157 L 4
Chinmen Tao ⌒ RC 156-157 L 4
Chinnūr ○ IND 138-139 G 10
Chino ○ USA (CA) 248-249 G 5
Chino Creek ∼ USA (AZ) 256-257 C 3
Chinon ○ F 90-91 H 8
Chinook ○ CDN (ALB) 232-233 H 4
Chinook ○ USA (MT) 250-251 K 3
Chinook ○ USA (WA) 244-245 B 4
Chinook Trough ≃ 14-15 L 3
Chinook Valley ○ CDN 32-33 M 3
Chino Valley ○ USA (AZ) 256-257 C 4
Chinpurtar ○ NEP 144-145 E 7
Chinquite ○ ANG 216-217 B 6
Chinsali ○ Z 214-215 G 6
Chintāmani ○ IND 140-141 H 4
Chinteche ○ MW 214-215 H 6
Chinturu ○ IND 142-143 B 7
Chinvali ○ GE 126-127 F 6
Chinyama Litapi ○ Z 218-219 B 1
Chioa, Lago ⊂ PE 64-65 E 8
Chioco ○ MOC 218-219 G 3
Chióggia ○• I 100-101 D 2
Chipai Lake ⊂ CDN 34-35 N 4
Chipanga ○ MOC 218-219 H 3
Chipasanse ○ Z 214-215 F 5
Chipata ☆ Z 218-219 G 1
Chipepo ○ Z 218-219 D 3
Chiperone, Monte ▲ MOC 218-219 H 3
Chipewyan Indian Reserve ⚔ CDN 30-31 O 6
Chipewyan River ∼ CDN 32-33 O 3
Chipili ○ Z 214-215 E 6
Chipinda Pools ○ ZW 218-219 F 5
Chipindo ○ ANG 216-217 C 6
Chipinga Safari Area ⊥ ZW 218-219 G 5
Chipinge ○ ZW 218-219 G 5
Chipiona ○ E 98-99 D 6
Chipipa ○ ANG 216-217 C 6
Chipiriri, Río ∼ BOL 70-71 E 5
Chip Lake ⊂ CDN (ALB) 232-233 C 2
Chip Lake ⊂ CDN (ALB) 232-233 C 2
Chipley ○ USA (FL) 286-287 D 1
Chiplūn ○ IND 140-141 E 2
Chipman ○ CDN (ALB) 232-233 F 2
Chipman ○ CDN (NB) 240-241 K 4
Chipman Lake ⊂ CDN (ONT) 236-237 B 3
Chipman River ∼ CDN 30-31 R 6
Chipogolo ○ EAT 214-215 J 4
Chipoia ○ ANG 216-217 E 6
Chipoka ○ MW 218-219 H 1
Chipola River ∼ USA (FL) 286-287 D 1
Chippenham ○ GB 90-91 F 6
Chippewa, Lake ⊂ USA (WI) 270-271 G 5
Chippewa Falls ○ USA (WI) 270-271 G 6
Chippewa River ∼ USA (WI) 270-271 G 5
Chipungo ○ Z 218-219 F 1
Chiputneticook Lakes ∼ USA (ME) 278-279 O 3
Chiputo ○ MOC 218-219 G 2
Chiquian ○ PE 64-65 D 7
Chiquilá ○ MEX 52-53 L 1
Chiquimula ☆ GCA 52-53 K 4
Chiquimulilla ○ GCA 52-53 J 4
Chiquinata, Bahía ≈ 70-71 B 7
Chiquinquirá ○ CO 60-61 E 5
Chiquitina, Isla ⌒ PE 64-65 D 7
Chiquitos, Llanos de ⊥ BOL 70-71 F 6
Ch'ira ○ ETH 208-209 C 5
Chira, Río ∼ PE 64-65 B 4
Chirāla ○ IND 140-141 J 3
Chiramba ○ MOC 218-219 H 3
Chiredzi ○ ZW 218-219 F 5
Chireno ○ USA (TX) 268-269 F 5
Chirfa ○ RN 198-199 F 2
Chiriacu ○ PE 64-65 C 4
Chiribiquete, Raudal ∼ CO 64-65 F 1
Chiricahua Peak ▲ USA (AZ) 256-257 F 7
Chiriguare, Reserva Faunística ⊥ YV 60-61 G 3
Chirikof Island ⌒ USA 22-23 T 5
Chirikof Point ▲ USA 22-23 C 6
Chirimena ○ YV 60-61 H 2
Chiriquí, Golfo de ≈ 52-53 C 7
Chiriquí, Laguna de ≈ 52-53 C 7
Chiriquí Grande ○ PA 52-53 C 7
Chiris, Río ∼ PE 64-65 E 8
Chiri San ▲ ROK 150-151 F 10
Chirisan National Park ⊥• ROK 150-151 F 10
Chirisa Safari Area ⊥ ZW 218-219 E 3
Chirima River ∼ PNG 183 D 5
Chiromo ○ MW 218-219 H 3
Chirripó, Río ∼ CR 52-53 C 6
Chirripó del Atlántico, Río ∼ CR 52-53 C 7
Chirripó Grande, Cerro ▲ CR 52-53 C 7
Chirumanzu ○ ZW 218-219 F 4
Chirundu ○ Z 218-219 E 3
Chirundu ○ ZW 218-219 E 3
Chisamba ○ Z 218-219 E 2
Chisana ○ USA 20-21 U 5
Chisana River ∼ USA 20-21 U 5
Chisasa ○ Z 214-215 C 7
Chisasibi ○ CDN 38-39 E 2
Chisec ○ GCA 52-53 J 4
Chisekesi ○ Z 218-219 D 3
Chisenga ○ MW 214-215 G 5
Chishan ○ RC 156-157 M 5
Chishang ○ RC 156-157 M 5
Chisholm ○ USA (MN) 270-271 F 3
Chishui ○ VRC 156-157 D 2
Chishuihe ○ VRC 156-157 D 3
Chishui He ∼ VRC 156-157 D 2
Chisik Island ⌒ USA 20-21 O 6
Chisimba Falls ∼ Z 214-215 F 6
Chişinău ★ MD 102-103 F 4
Chişineu-Criş ○ RO 102-103 B 4
Chisos Mountains ▲ USA (TX) 266-267 D 4
Chissano ○ MOC 220-221 L 2
Chissibuca ○ MOC 220-221 M 2
Chissinguane ○ MOC 218-219 H 5
Chistiān Mandy ○ PK 138-139 D 5
Chisumbanje ○ ZW 218-219 G 5
Chita ○ BOL 70-71 D 6
Chita ○ EAT 214-215 H 5
Chita = Čita ☆• RUS 118-119 F 9
Chitado ○ ANG 216-217 B 8
Chitaga ○ CO 60-61 E 4
Chitāpur ○ IND 140-141 G 2
Chitek ○ CDN (SAS) 232-233 L 2
Chitek Lake ○ CDN (SAS) 232-233 L 2
Chitek Lake ⊂ CDN (MAN) 234-235 D 2
Chitek Lake Indian Reservation ⚔ CDN (SAS) 232-233 L 2
Chitembo ○ ANG 216-217 D 6
Chí Thanh ○ VN 158-159 K 4
Chitina ○ USA 20-21 S 6
Chitina River ∼ USA 20-21 T 6
Chitipa ○ MW 214-215 G 5
Chito ○ EC 64-65 C 4
Chitobe ○ MOC 218-219 G 5
Chitongo ○ Z 218-219 D 3
Chitose ○ J 152-153 J 3
Chitowe ○ EAT 214-215 K 6
Chitradurga ○• IND 140-141 G 3
Chitrakūt ○ IND 142-143 B 3
Chitré ☆ PA 52-53 D 8
Chittagong ○• BD 142-143 G 4
Chittaurgarh ○• IND 138-139 E 7
Chittivalasa ○ IND 142-143 C 7
Chittoor ○ IND 140-141 H 4
Chitungwiza ○ ZW 218-219 F 3
Chitwood ○ USA (OR) 244-245 B 6
Chityal ○ IND 140-141 H 2
Chiu Chiu ○ RCH 76-77 C 2
Chiulezi, Rio ∼ MOC 214-215 J 6
Chiumbe ∼ ANG 216-217 F 4
Chiumbo ○ ANG 216-217 D 6
Chiume ○ ANG 216-217 F 7
Chiúre Novo ○ MOC 218-219 K 1
Chivacoa ○ YV 60-61 G 2
Chivasing ○ PNG 183 D 4
Chivasso ○ I 100-101 A 2
Chivato ○ RCH 76-77 B 4
Chivay ○ PE 70-71 B 4
Chivé ○ BOL 70-71 C 3
Chivhu ○ ZW 218-219 F 4
Chivicahua National Monument ∴ USA (AZ) 256-257 F 6
Chivilcoy ○ RA 78-79 K 3
Chivirico ○ C 54-55 G 5
Chiviriga Falls ∼ ZW 218-219 F 5
Chivuna ○ Z 218-219 D 3
Chiweta ○ MW 214-215 H 6
Chixoy o Negro, Río ∼ GCA 52-53 J 4
Chizarira Hills ▲ ZW 218-219 D 3
Chizarira National Park ⊥ ZW 218-219 D 3
Chizela ○ Z 218-219 C 1
Chizu ○ J 152-153 F 7
Chizwina ○ RB 218-219 D 5
Chlef ☆ DZ 190-191 C 2
Chloride ○ USA (AZ) 256-257 A 3
Chmel'nyc'kyj ☆ UA 102-103 E 3
Chmel'nyc'kyj, Perejaslav- ○ UA 102-103 G 2
Chnattisgarh ∴ IND 142-143 B 5
Chŏâm Khsant ○ K 158-159 H 3
Choapa, Río ∼ RCH 76-77 B 6
Choapan ○ MEX 52-53 G 3
Choapas, Las ○ MEX 52-53 G 3
Choate ○ CDN (BC) 230-231 H 4
Chobe ∼ NAM 218-219 C 3
Chobe ◘ RB 218-219 C 4
Chobe National Park ⊥ RB 218-219 C 4
Chocca, Cerro ▲ PE 64-65 E 8
Chocolate Hills ⊥•• RP 160-161 F 8
Chocolate Mountain Gunnery Range • USA (CA) 248-249 J 6
Chocolate Mountains ▲ USA (CA) 248-249 J 6
Choconta ○ CO 60-61 E 5
Chocope ○ PE 64-65 C 5
Chocowinity ○ USA (NC) 282-283 K 5
Choctawhatchee Bay ≈ 48-49 E 4
Choctawhatchee Bay ≈ USA 286-287 C 1
Choctawhatchee River ∼ USA (FL) 286-287 C 1
Choctawhatchee River, East Fork ∼ USA (AL) 284-285 E 5
Choctawhatchee River, West Fork ∼ USA (AL) 284-285 E 5
Choctaw Indian Reservation ⚔ USA (MS) 268-269 L 4
Chodavaram ○ IND 142-143 C 7
Cho Do ⌒ DVR 150-151 E 8
Chodzież ○• PL 92-93 O 2
Choele Choel ○ RA 78-79 G 5
Chofombo ○ MOC 218-219 F 2
Choice ○ USA (MN) 270-271 G 7
Choichuff, Lagh ∼ EAK 212-213 F 2
Choiseland ○ CDN (SAS) 232-233 O 2
Choiseul ⌒ SOL 184 I c 2
Choiseul Sound ≈ 78-79 L 6
Choix ○ MEX 50-51 E 4
Choix, Port aux ○ CDN (NFL) 242-243 L 2
Chojnice ○ PL 92-93 O 2
Chojniki ○ BY 94-95 M 6
Chōkai Quasi National Park ⊥ J 152-153 J 5
Chōkai-san ▲ J 152-153 J 5
Chok Chai ○ THA 158-159 G 3
Choke Canyon Lake < USA (TX) 266-267 J 5
Ch'ok'ē Terara ▲ ETH 208-209 C 3
Chokio ○ USA (MN) 270-271 B 5
Chókué ○ MOC 220-221 L 2
Cholame ○ USA (CA) 248-249 D 4
Chola Shan ▲ VRC 144-145 M 4
Chola Shankou ▲ VRC 144-145 M 5
Cholay ○ MEX 50-51 D 3
Cholchol, Río ∼ RCH 78-79 C 5
Chole • EAT 214-215 K 4
Cholet ○ F 90-91 G 8
Choluteca ☆ HN 52-53 L 5
Choluteca, Río ∼ HN 52-53 L 5
Ch'ŏlwŏn ○ ROK 150-151 F 8
Choma ○ Z 218-219 D 3
Chom Bung ○ THA 158-159 E 4
Chom Phra ○ THA 158-159 G 3
Chom Tong ○ THA 142-143 L 6
Chomūn ○ IND 138-139 E 6
Chona ∼ EAT 212-213 D 6
Ch'ŏnan ○ ROK 150-151 F 9
Chonarwa ○ NEP 144-145 F 7
Chon Buri ○ THA 158-159 F 4
Chonchi ○ RCH 78-79 C 7
Chonchon ○ DVR 150-151 F 7
Chone ○ EC 64-65 B 2
Chongchon Gang ∼ DVR 150-151 E 8
Chongjin ☆ DVR 150-151 G 7
Chŏngju ○ ROK 150-151 F 10
Chongming ○ VRC 154-155 M 6
Chongoene ○ MOC 220-221 L 2
Chongoróì ○ ANG 216-217 B 6
Chongoyape ○ PE 64-65 C 5
Chong Phan ≈ 158-159 E 6
Chongpyong ○ DVR 150-151 F 8
Chongqing ○ VRC (SIC) 154-155 C 6
Chongqing ○• VRC (SIC) 156-157 E 2
Chongren ○ VRC 156-157 K 3
Chong Samui ≈ 158-159 E 6
Ch'ŏngsan Do ⌒ ROK 150-151 F 10
Chong Tao ≈ 158-159 E 6
Chongwe ○ Z 218-219 E 2
Chongwe ∼ Z 218-219 E 2
Chongyang ○ VRC 156-157 J 2
Chongyi ○ VRC 156-157 J 4
Chŏnju ○ ROK 150-151 F 9
Chonos, Archipiélago de los ⌒ RCH 80 C 2
Chontaleña, Cordillera ▲ NIC 52-53 B 6
Chontali ○ PE 64-65 C 4
Chontalpa ○ MEX 52-53 H 3
Cho'n Thành ○ VN 158-159 J 5
Cho Oyu ▲ NEP 144-145 F 6
Chopda ○ IND 138-139 E 9
Chopinzinho ○ BR 74-75 D 5
Choptank River ∼ USA (MD) 280-281 L 5
Choqā Zanbil ∴••• IR 134-135 C 2
Choras, Isla ⌒ RCH 76-77 B 5
Choreti ○ BOL 70-71 F 7
Chorkbak Inlet ≈ 36-37 M 2
Choró ○ BR 68-69 J 4
Choro, Río ∼ BOL 70-71 E 5
Choro, Rio ∼ BR 68-69 J 4
Chorol ○ UA 102-103 H 3
Chorolque ▲ BOL 70-71 E 7
Choromoro ○ RA 76-77 E 4
Choroní ○ YV 60-61 H 2
Chorregon ○ AUS 178-179 G 2
Chorrera, La ○ CO 64-65 F 2
Chorrera, La ○ PA 52-53 E 7
Chorrillos ○ PE 64-65 D 8
Chorro, El ○ RA 76-77 E 5
Chorro la Libertad ∼ CO 66-67 C 3
Chorzung ○ VRC 144-145 L 5
Chosan ○ DVR 150-151 E 7
Chōshi ○ J 152-153 J 7
Chosica ○ PE 64-65 D 7
Chos Malal ○ RA 78-79 D 4
C. H. Ostenfeld Gletscher ⊂ GRØ 26-27 c 3
C. H. Ostenfeld Land ⊥ GRØ 26-27 o 3
Chota ○ PE 64-65 C 5
Choteau ○ USA (MT) 250-251 G 4
Choûm ○ RIM 196-197 D 4
Chouteau ○ USA (OK) 264-265 J 2
Chowan River ∼ USA (NC) 282-283 L 4
Chowchilla ○ USA (CA) 248-249 D 2
Chowduar ○ IND 142-143 D 5
Chowiet Island ⌒ USA 22-23 S 4
Chozi ∼ Z 214-215 G 5
Chreirîk < RIM 196-197 D 4
Chrisman ○ USA (IL) 274-275 L 5
Chrissiesmeer ○ ZA 220-221 K 3
Christchurch ○•• NZ 182 D 5
Christiana ○ ZA 220-221 G 3
Christian Island ⌒ CDN (ONT) 238-239 E 4
Christian Island Indian Reservation ⚔ CDN (ONT) 238-239 E 4
Christian IV, Kap ▲ GRØ 26-27 h 2
Christian IV Gletscher ⊂ GRØ 28-29 Z 2
Christian River ∼ USA 20-21 S 3
Christiansburg ○ USA (VA) 280-281 F 6
Christianshåb = Qasigiannguit ○ GRØ 28-29 P 2
Christian Sound ≈ 32-33 C 3
Christiansted ○ USA (VI) 286-287 R 3
Christie Bay ⊂ CDN 30-31 O 4
Christie Lake ⊂ CDN 24-25 c 7
Christina Lake ○ CDN (BC) 230-231 L 4
Christina River ∼ CDN 32-33 P 3
Christino Castro ○ BR 68-69 F 6
Christmas, Islas ⌒ RCH 80 E 7
Christmas Creek ○ AUS 172-173 G 5
Christmas Creek ∼ AUS 172-173 H 5
Christmas Island ⌒ AUS 13 B 4
Christmas Island ○ CDN (NS) 240-241 P 5
Christmas Valley ○ USA (OR) 244-245 E 7
Christopher Falls ∼ CDN (ONT) 236-237 F 2
Christopher Lake ⊂ AUS 176-177 J 2
Christoval ○ USA (TX) 266-267 G 2
Chrome ○ USA (CA) 246-247 C 4
Chromer ○• GB 90-91 H 5
Chromo ○ USA (CO) 254-255 J 6
Chrysler ○ USA (AL) 284-285 C 5
Chuali, Lagoa ⊂ MOC 220-221 L 2
Chuave ○ PNG 183 C 4
Chub Cay ○ BS 54-55 G 2
Chubu-Sangaku National Park ⊥ J 152-153 G 6
Chubut ◘ RA 78-79 D 7
Chubut, Río ∼ RA 78-79 E 7
Chuchi Lake ⊂ CDN 32-33 H 4
Chuchiliga ○ GH 202-203 K 4
Chu Chua ○ CDN (BC) 230-231 J 2
Chuckery ○ USA (OH) 280-281 C 3
Chucuma ○ RA 76-77 D 6
Chucunaque ∼ PA 52-53 E 7
Chu Dang Sin ▲ VN 158-159 K 4
Chudleigh ○ CDN (ONT) 238-239 E 2
Chudskoye Ozero = Čudskoe ozero ⊂ RUS 94-95 K 2
Chugach Islands ⌒ USA 22-23 V 3
Chugach Mountains ▲ USA 20-21 R 6
Chugchug, Cerros de ▲ RCH 76-77 C 2
Chugchug, Quebrada ∼ RCH 76-77 C 2
Chugiak ○ USA 20-21 Q 6
Chuginadak Island ⌒ USA 22-23 L 6
Chugoku-sanchi ▲ J 152-153 E 7
Chugul Island ⌒ USA 22-23 J 7
Chugwater ○ USA (WY) 252-253 O 5
Chuhar Jamāli ○ PK 134-135 M 6
Chuhar Kāna ○ PK 138-139 D 4
Ch'uja Do ⌒ ROK 150-151 F 11
Chuka ○ EAK 212-213 F 4
Chukai ○ MAL 162-163 E 2
Chukchi Autonomous District = Čukotskij avtonomnyj okrug ◘ RUS 112-113 N 3
Chukchi Plateau ≃ 16 B 35
Chukchi Sea ≈ 112-113 X 1
Chukotat, Rivière ∼ CDN 36-37 L 4
Chukotskiy Poluostrov = Čukotskij poluostrov ⌒ RUS 112-113 W 3
Chula ○ USA (GA) 284-285 G 5
Chulahuma ○ USA (MS) 268-269 L 2
Chulas, Raudal las ∼ CO 60-61 F 6
Chula Vista ○ USA (CA) 248-249 G 7
Chulitna River ∼ USA 20-21 Q 5
Chulucanas ○ PE 64-65 B 4
Chuma ○ BOL 70-71 C 4
Chuma Shankou ▲ VRC 144-145 L 5
Chumba ○ ETH 208-209 D 6
Chumbicha ○ RA 76-77 D 5
Chumbo ○ BR 72-73 G 5
Chumikgarsa ○ IND 138-139 F 3
Chumphae ○ THA 158-159 G 2
Chumphon ○ THA 158-159 E 5
Chumpi ○ PE 64-65 F 9
Chumpón ○ MEX 52-53 L 2
Chumsaeng ○ THA 158-159 F 3
Chumul ∴• MEX (YUC) 52-53 K 2
Chumul ∴• MEX (YUC) 52-53 K 1
Chun ○ THA 142-143 M 6
Chuna ○ PK 138-139 D 4
Chunăn ○ VRC 156-157 L 2
Chuncar ○ PE 64-65 B 4
Chunchanga, Pampa de ⊥ PE 64-65 E 9
Chunchi ○ EC 64-65 C 3
Ch'unch'ŏn ○ ROK 150-151 F 9
Chunchura ○ IND 142-143 F 4
Chundela ○ ANG 216-217 F 7
Chunga ○ Z 218-219 D 2
Chungara ○ RCH 70-71 C 6
Chungara, Lago ⊂ RCH 70-71 C 6
Chunggang ○ DVR 150-151 F 7
Ch'ungju ○ ROK 150-151 F 9
Ch'ungmu ○ ROK 150-151 G 10
Chungu ○ Z 214-215 G 6
Chungui ○ PE 64-65 F 8
Chungyang Shanmo ▲ RC 156-157 M 5
Chuniān ○ PK 138-139 D 4
Chuniespoort ○ ZA 220-221 J 2
Chunky River ∼ USA (MS) 268-269 M 4
Chunshui ○ VRC 154-155 H 5
Chunu, Cape ▲ USA 22-23 H 7
Chunwan ○ VRC 156-157 G 5
Chunya ○ EAT 214-215 G 5
Chuŏr Phnum Dângrek ▲ K 158-159 G 3
Chuŏr Phnum Krvanh ▲ K 158-159 G 4
Chupabe, Caño ∼ CO 60-61 G 6
Chupadero de Caballo ○ MEX 50-51 J 3
Chupadero Springs ○ USA (TX) 266-267 G 5
Chu' Pha ○ VN 158-159 J 4
Chu' Prŏng ○ VN 158-159 J 4
Chuquatonchee Creek ∼ USA (MS) 268-269 M 3
Chuquibamba ○ PE 64-65 F 9
Chuquibambilla ○ PE 64-65 F 9
Chuquicamata ○ RCH 76-77 C 2
Chuquicara ○ PE 64-65 C 6
Chuquisaca ◘ BOL 70-71 E 7
Chuquis ○ PE 64-65 D 6
Chur ☆• CH 92-93 K 5
Churachāndpur ○ IND 142-143 H 3
Churcampa ○ PE 64-65 E 8
Church ○ USA (VA) 280-281 J 6
Churchbridge ○ CDN (SAS) 232-233 R 5
Church Hill ○ USA (TN) 282-283 E 4
Churchill ○• CDN 30-31 W 6
Churchill, Cap ▲ CDN 30-31 X 6
Churchill Falls ○ CDN 38-39 M 2
Churchill Lake ⊂ CDN 32-33 Q 3
Churchill Lake ⊂ USA (ME) 278-279 M 2
Churchill Reef ⌒ AUS 172-173 F 3
Churchill River ∼ CDN 32-33 Q 4
Churchill River ∼ CDN 34-35 E 3
Churchill River ∼ CDN 34-35 J 2
Churchill River ∼ CDN 38-39 N 2
Churchill Sound ≈ 36-37 J 7
Church Point ○ USA (LA) 268-269 H 6
Churchs Ferry ○ USA (ND) 258-259 H 3
Churchville ○ USA (VA) 280-281 G 5
Churdan ○ USA (IA) 274-275 D 2
Chureo o Deshecho, Paso ▲ RA 78-79 D 4
Churia Range ▲ NEP 144-145 E 7
Churin ○ PE 64-65 D 7
Churubusco ○ USA (IN) 274-275 N 3
Churu ○ IND 138-139 E 5
Churuguara ○ YV 60-61 G 2
Chu' Sê ○ VN 158-159 K 4
Chuska Mountains ▲ USA (AZ) 256-257 F 2
Chusmisa ○ RCH 70-71 C 6
Chūsonji • J 152-153 J 5
Chust ☆ UA 102-103 C 3
Chute-des-Passes ○ CDN 38-39 J 4
Chute Lake ○ CDN (BC) 230-231 K 4
Chutine Landing ○ CDN 32-33 E 3
Chuvashia = Čavaš respubliki ◘ RUS 96-97 E 6
Chuwangsan National Park ⊥• ROK 150-151 G 9
Chuxiong ○ VRC 156-157 B 4
Chuy ○ ROU 74-75 D 9
Chuzhou ○ VRC 154-155 L 5
Chwaka ○ EAT 214-215 K 4
Chyulu Hills ▲ EAK 212-213 F 5
Ciágola, Monte ▲ I 100-101 E 5
Ciamis ○ RI 168 C 3
Ciandur ○ RI 168 A 3
Cianjur ○ RI 168 B 3
Ciano ○ EC 64-65 C 3
Cianorte ○ BR 72-73 D 7
Čiatura ○ GE 126-127 E 6
Cibadak ○ RI 168 B 3
Čibagalah ∼ RUS 110-111 Y 6
Čibagalahskij hrebet ▲ RUS 110-111 W 6
Cibatu ○ RI 168 B 3
Cibit ○ RUS 124-125 P 3
Čibit ○ RUS 124-125 P 3
Cibitoke ○ BU 212-213 B 5
Cibu ▲ MEX 50-51 D 2
Cicalengka ○ RI 168 B 3
Čičatka, Bol'šaja ∼ RUS 118-119 K 8
Cícero Dantas ○ BR 68-69 J 7
Cicia ⌒ FJI 184 III c 2
Čičkajul ∼ RUS 114-115 T 6
Cicurug ○ RI 168 B 3
Cidade Gaúcha ○ BR 72-73 D 7
Cide ☆ TR 128-129 E 2
Ciechanów ☆• PL 92-93 Q 2
Ciego, El ○ C 54-55 G 4
Ciego de Ávila ☆ C 54-55 F 4
Ciempozuelos ○ E 98-99 F 4
Ciénaga ○ CO 60-61 D 2
Cienaga, La ○ RA 76-77 C 5
Ciénaga Grande de Santa Marta ≈ 60-61 D 2
Cieneguillas ○ RA 76-77 E 2
Cienfuegos ☆ C 54-55 E 3
Cieszanów ○ PL 92-93 R 3
Cieza ○ E 98-99 G 5
Çifteler ☆ TR 128-129 D 3
Cifuentes ○ C 54-55 E 3
Cifuentes ○ E 98-99 F 4
Cifuncho ○ RCH 76-77 B 3
Cigarette Spring Cave ∴ USA (UT) 254-255 F 6
Cigarro ○ BR 66-67 F 4
Ciglera, ostrov ⌒ RUS 84-85 e 2
Cihanbeyli ☆ TR 128-129 E 3
Cihanbeyli Yaylâsı ▲ TR 128-129 E 3
Cihuatlán ○ MEX 52-53 B 2
Čili ○ KA 124-125 E 6
Cíjara, Reserva Nacional de ⊥ E 98-99 E 5
Cijulang ○ RI 168 C 3
Cikajang ○ RI 168 B 3
Cikalongkulon ○ RI 168 B 3
Cikalongwetan ○ RI 168 B 3
Cikampek ○ RI 168 B 3
Čikoj ○ RUS 116-117 N 10
Čikoj ∼ RUS 116-117 O 10
Čikoj ∼ RUS 116-117 N 10
Čikoj ∼ RUS 118-119 E 11
Čikoj ∼ RUS 118-119 E 10
Čikokon ∼ RUS 118-119 E 10
Čikokonskij, hrebet ▲ RUS 118-119 D 11
Cikotok ○• RI 168 B 3
Čikšina ∼ RUS 88-89 Y 4
Čikšina ∼ RUS 114-115 D 2
Cilacap ○ RI 168 C 3
Cilamaya ○ RI 168 B 3
Cilaos ○ F 224 B 7
Cilaos, Cirque de • F 224 B 7
Cilat ○ IRQ 128-129 M 6
Čilči ○ RUS 118-119 L 7
Çıldır ○ TR 128-129 K 2
Çıldır Gölü ⊂ TR 128-129 K 2
Ciledug ○ RI 168 C 3
Cileungsi ○ RI 168 B 3
Cili ○ VRC 156-157 G 2
Cilibia ○ RO 102-103 E 5
Čilik ○ KA 146-147 D 4
Čilik ∼ KA 146-147 C 4
Cilipi ○ HR 100-101 G 3
Cill Airne = Killarney ○• IRL 90-91 C 5
Cill Bheagáin = Kilbeggan ○ IRL 90-91 D 5
Cill Chainnigh = Kilkenny ☆• IRL 90-91 D 5
Cill Chaoi = Kilkee ○ IRL 90-91 C 5
Cill Dara = Kildare ○ IRL 90-91 D 5

Čilli ∼ RUS 118-119 J 3
Cill Mhantáin = Wicklow ☆ IRL 90-91 D 5
Cill Orglan = Killorglin o IRL 90-91 C 5
Cill Rois = Kilrush o IRL 90-91 C 5
Čil'ma ∼ RUS 88-89 U 4
Čil'ma ∼ RUS 88-89 V 4
Čil'mamedkum ∸ TM 136-137 D 4
Cima o USA (CA) 248-249 J 4
Cimahi o RI 168 B 3
Cimanggu o RI 168 A 3
Cimanuk, Tanjung ▲ RI 168 C 3
Cimarron o USA (CO) 254-255 H 5
Cimarron o USA (KS) 262-263 F 7
Cimarron o USA (NM) 256-257 L 2
Cimarron National Grassland ⊥ USA (KS) 262-263 E 7
Cimarron River ∼ USA (CO) 254-255 N 6
Cimarron River ∼ USA (NM) 256-257 M 2
Cimarron River ∼ USA (OK) 264-265 G 3
Čimbaj o US 136-137 F 3
Čimboj ☆ US 136-137 F 3
Cimbur o RI 166-167 C 6
Čimčememel' ∼ RUS 112-113 O 3
Čimidikjan ∼ RUS 110-111 M 6
Cimişlia ☆ MD 102-103 F 4
Cimitarra o CO 60-61 E 4
Čimljansk o RUS 102-103 N 4
Cimljanskoe vodohranilišče < RUS 102-103 N 4
Cimmermanovka o RUS 122-123 H 3
Cîmpeni o RO 102-103 C 4
Cîmpina o· RO 102-103 D 5
Cimpu o RI 164-165 G 5
Cîmpulung o· RO 102-103 D 5
Cîmpulung Moldovenesc o· RO 102-103 D 4
Čina ∼ RUS 116-117 L 3
Čina ∼ RUS 118-119 F 8
Cina, Tanjung ▲ RI 162-163 F 7
Çınar ☆ TR 128-129 J 4
Cinaruco, Río ∼ YV 60-61 H 4
Cincel, Río ∼ RA 76-77 D 2
Cincinnati o USA (OH) 280-281 B 4
Cinco Balas, Cayos ⌒ C 54-55 F 4
Cinco de Maio, Cachoeira ∼ BR 70-71 K 3
Çine ☆· TR 128-129 C 4
Činejveem ∼ RUS 112-113 Q 3
Cinema o CDN (BC) 228-229 M 3
Cingaly o RUS 114-115 K 4
Čingandža, gora ▲ RUS 112-113 H 4
Čingera, mys ▲ RUS 108-109 f 2
Čingildi o US 136-137 J 4
Cingirlau o KA 96-97 H 8
Čingis Chaan Cherem ∴· MAU 148-149 L 3
Cinnabar Mountain ▲ USA (ID) 252-253 B 4
Činoz ☆ US 136-137 L 4
Činozero, ozero ⊖ RUS 88-89 M 5
Cinque Island ⌒ IND 140-141 L 4
Cinta, Serra da ▲ BR 68-69 E 5
Cintalapa de Figueroa o MEX 52-53 H 3
Cinto, Monte ▲ F 98-99 M 3
Cintra o RA 78-79 H 2
Cintra, Golfe de ≈ 196-197 B 3
Cinuelos, Los o DOM 54-55 K 5
Cinzas, Rio das ∼ BR 72-73 E 7
Ciotat, la o F 90-91 K 10
Cipa ∼ RUS 118-119 G 8
Cipanda o RUS 120-121 F 4
Cipatujah o RI 168 C 3
Cipikan o RUS 118-119 F 8
Cipikan ∼ RUS 118-119 E 8
Cipó, Rio ∼ BR 72-73 J 5
Cipoal o BR 66-67 E 3
Cipolândia o BR 70-71 K 7
Cipolletti o RA 78-79 F 5
Cipotuba, Ilha ⌒ BR 66-67 F 4
Čir ∼ RUS 102-103 N 3
Circa o PE 64-65 F 8
Čirčik o US 136-137 L 4
Čirčik ∼ US 136-137 L 4
Circle o USA (AK) 20-21 S 4
Circle o USA (MT) 250-251 O 4
Circleville o USA (OH) 280-281 D 4
Circular Head ▲ AUS 180-181 H 6
Circular Reef ⌒ PNG 183 D 2
Cirebon o· RI 168 C 3
Čirikovo o RUS 94-95 P 4
Čirin, vulkan ▲ RUS 122-123 M 6
Čirinda o RUS 116-117 K 2
Ciriquiri, Rio ∼ BR 66-67 E 7
Čirka Kem' ∼ RUS 88-89 M 5
Cir Kud o SP 212-213 J 2
Čirkuo ∼ RUS 118-119 D 4
Cirò o I 100-101 F 5
Čirokči o US 136-137 K 5
Čirpan o BG 102-103 D 6
Cirque, Cerro ▲ BOL 70-71 C 5
Cirque Mountain ▲ CDN 36-37 S 5
Ciruelo, El o MEX 50-51 D 5
Cisarua o RI 168 B 3
Cisco o USA (GA) 284-285 F 2
Cisco o USA (TX) 264-265 F 6
Cisco o USA (UT) 254-255 F 5
Ciskei (former Homeland, now part of East-Cape) ◘ ZA 220-221 H 5
Čiskova ∼ RUS 116-117 G 3
Čišmy ☆ RUS 96-97 J 6
Cisne, Islas del = Islas Santanilla ⌒ HN 54-55 D 6
Cisne, Laguna del o RA 76-77 F 5
Cisne, Santuario del · EC 64-65 C 3
Cisnes, Río ∼ RCH 80 E 2
Cisnes Medio o RCH 80 D 2
Cisolok o RI 168 B 3
Cisséla o RG 202-203 E 4
Cistern o USA (TX) 266-267 K 4
Cistern Point ▲ BS 54-55 G 3
Cistierna o E 98-99 E 3
Čistoe, ozero ⊖ RUS 120-121 O 4
Čistopol' ☆ RUS 96-97 G 6
Čistopol'e ☆ KA 124-125 E 2
Čita ☆· RUS 118-119 F 9
Čita ∼ RUS 118-119 F 9
Citadelle, La ∴··· RH 54-55 J 5
Čita Kandaw, Kōtal-e ▲ AFG 138-139 B 3
Citaré, Rio ∼ BR 62-63 G 5
Citiari, Igarapé ∼ BR 66-67 E 6
Citico Beach o USA (TN) 282-283 C 5
Citra o USA (FL) 286-287 G 2
Citra o USA (OK) 264-265 H 4
Citronelle o USA (AL) 284-285 B 5
Citrusdal o ZA 220-221 D 6
Citrus Heights o USA (CA) 246-247 D 5
Città del Vaticano ★··· SCV 100-101 D 4
Cittanova o I 100-101 F 5
Ciu o RI 164-165 L 2
Ciudad o MEX 50-51 G 6
Ciudad Acuña o MEX 50-51 J 3
Ciudad Altamirano o MEX 52-53 D 2
Ciudad Bolívar ☆· YV 60-61 K 3
Ciudad Camargo o· MEX 50-51 G 4
Ciudad Colón o CR 52-53 B 7
Ciudad Constitución o· MEX 50-51 D 5
Ciudad Cortés o CR 52-53 C 7
Ciudad Cuauhtémoc o MEX 52-53 J 4
Ciudad Darío o· NIC 52-53 L 5
Ciudad de Guatemala = Guatemala ★·· GCA 52-53 J 4
Ciudad del Carmen o· MEX 52-53 J 2
Ciudad del Este ☆ PY 76-77 K 3
Ciudad del Maíz o MEX 50-51 K 6
Ciudad de México = México ★··· MEX 52-53 E 2
Ciudad de Nutria o YV 60-61 G 3
Ciudad Guayana o· YV 60-61 K 3
Ciudad Guzmán o· MEX 52-53 C 2
Ciudad Hidalgo o MEX 52-53 D 2
Ciudad Ixtepec o MEX 52-53 G 3
Ciudad Juárez o· MEX 50-51 F 2
Ciudad Lerdo o MEX 50-51 H 5
Ciudad López Mateos o MEX 52-53 E 2
Ciudad Madero o MEX 50-51 L 6
Ciudad Mante o MEX 50-51 K 6
Ciudad Melchor de Mencos o GCA 52-53 K 3
Ciudad Mutis = Bahía Solano o CO 60-61 C 4
Ciudad Neily o CR 52-53 C 7
Ciudad Nezahualcóyotl o MEX 52-53 E 2
Ciudad Obregón o MEX 50-51 E 4
Ciudad Ojeda o YV 60-61 F 2
Ciudad Pemex o MEX 52-53 H 3
Ciudad Piar o YV 60-61 K 4
Ciudad Quesada o CR 52-53 B 6
Ciudad Real o· E 98-99 F 5
Ciudad-Rodrigo o·· E 98-99 D 4
Ciudad Sahagún o MEX 52-53 E 2
Ciudad Serdán o MEX 52-53 F 2
Ciudad Valles o MEX 50-51 K 7
Ciudad Victoria ☆· MEX 50-51 K 6
Ciutadella o E 98-99 J 5
Civil'sk o RUS 96-97 E 6
Civita Castellana o· I 100-101 D 3
Civitanova Marche o I 100-101 D 3
Civitavecchia o I 100-101 C 3
Civol'ki, zaliv ⊖ RUS 108-109 H 4
Çivril ☆ TR 128-129 C 3
Ciwidey o RI 168 B 3
Cixi o VRC 154-155 M 6
Čiža o RUS 88-89 S 3
Čižapka ∼ RUS 114-115 P 5
Čižinskij taskyn cu ⊖ KA 96-97 F 8
Cizre ☆ TR 128-129 K 4
C.J. Strike Reservoir ⊖ USA (ID) 252-253 C 4
Čjurupyns'k o UA 102-103 H 4
Čkalov o RUS 110-111 Z 4
Čkalovsk o RUS 94-95 S 3
Clacton-on-Sea o GB 90-91 H 6
Clagstone o USA (ID) 250-251 C 3
Claiborne o USA (AL) 284-285 C 5
Claiborne, Lake < USA (LA) 268-269 H 4
Clain ∼ F 90-91 H 8
Clair o CDN (SAS) 232-233 O 3
Claire, Lake ⊖ CDN 30-31 N 6
Claire City o USA (SD) 260-261 J 1
Clairemont o USA (TX) 264-265 D 5
Clair Engle Lake ⊖ USA (CA) 246-247 C 3
Clair Falls ∼ CDN 30-31 K 3
Clairview o AUS 178-179 K 2
Clallam Bay o USA (WA) 244-245 A 2
Clamecy o F 90-91 J 8
Clam Lake o USA (WI) 270-271 H 4
Clandonald o CDN (ALB) 232-233 H 2
Clanton o USA (AL) 284-285 D 4
Clanville o ZA 220-221 H 5
Clanwilliam o CDN (BC) 230-231 L 3
Clanwilliam o CDN (MAN) 234-235 D 4
Clanwilliam o ZA 220-221 D 6
Clapperton o CDN (BC) 230-231 H 3
Claquato Church · USA (WA) 244-245 B 4
Clara o USA (MS) 268-269 M 5
Clara, Punta ▲ RA 78-79 G 7
Clara City o USA (MN) 270-271 C 6
Clarafield o AUS 178-179 G 4
Clara Island ⌒ MYA 158-159 D 5
Claravale o AUS 172-173 K 3
Claraville o AUS (NT) 178-179 C 2
Claraville o AUS (QLD) 174-175 F 6
Clare o AUS (QLD) 174-175 J 6
Clare o AUS (QLD) 178-179 H 2
Clare o AUS (SA) 180-181 E 2
Clare o USA (MI) 272-273 E 4
Claremont o USA (NH) 278-279 J 5
Claremore o USA (OK) 264-265 J 2
Clarence o NZ 182 D 5
Clarence o USA (LA) 268-269 G 5
Clarence o USA (MO) 274-275 F 5
Clarence, Cape ▲ CDN 24-25 b 4
Clarence, Isla ⌒ RCH 80 E 6
Clarence, Port ≈ 20-21 G 4
Clarence Cannon National Wildlife Refuge ⊥ USA (IL) 274-275 H 5
Clarence Island ⌒ ARK 16 G 31
Clarence River ∼ AUS 178-179 M 5
Clarence Strait ≈ 32-33 D 3
Clarence Strait ≈ 172-173 K 2
Clarence Town o· BS 54-55 H 3
Clarendon o USA (AR) 276-277 D 6
Clarendon o USA (TX) 264-265 D 4
Clarens o ZA 220-221 J 4
Clarenville o CDN (NFL) 242-243 O 4
Claresholm o CDN (ALB) 232-233 E 5
Clareton o USA (WY) 252-253 O 3
Clareville o USA (TX) 266-267 K 5
Clarie, Terre ∸ ARK 16 G 14
Clarinda o USA (IA) 274-275 C 4
Clarines o· YV 60-61 J 3
Clarion o USA (IA) 274-275 E 2
Clarion o USA (PA) 280-281 G 2
Clarión, Isla ⌒ MEX 50-51 A 7
Clarion Fracture Zone ≃ 14-15 O 6
Clarion River ∼ USA (PA) 280-281 G 2
Clark o USA (SD) 260-261 J 2
Clark o USA (WY) 252-253 J 2
Clark, Lake ⊖ USA 20-21 N 6
Clark, Point ▲ CDN (ONT) 238-239 D 4
Clark Canyon Reservoir < USA (MT) 250-251 G 7
Clarkdale o USA (AZ) 256-257 C 4
Clarkdon o CDN (ONT) 234-235 M 5
Clarke, Cape ▲ CDN 24-25 d 7
Clarke City o CDN (QUE) 242-243 B 2
Clarke Island ⌒ AUS 180-181 K 6
Clarke Lake ⊖ CDN 34-35 C 3
Clarke Range ▲ AUS 174-175 J 7
Clarke River ∼ AUS 174-175 H 6
Clarke River ∼ CDN 30-31 S 4
Clarke River P.O. o AUS 174-175 H 6
Clarkfield o USA (MN) 270-271 C 6
Clark Fork o USA (ID) 250-251 C 3
Clark Fork River ∼ USA (MT) 250-251 D 4
Clark Fork River ∼ USA (MT) 250-251 F 5
Clarkia o USA (ID) 250-251 C 4
Clarkleigh o CDN (MAN) 234-235 E 4
Clark Mountain ▲ USA (CA) 248-249 J 4
Clarkrange o USA (TN) 276-277 K 4
Clarks o USA (NE) 262-263 J 3
Clarksburg o USA (OH) 280-281 C 4
Clarksburg o USA (TN) 276-277 G 5
Clarksburg o USA (WV) 280-281 F 4
Clarksdale o USA (MS) 268-269 K 2
Clarks Fork River ∼ USA (WY) 252-253 J 2
Clark's Harbour o CDN (NS) 240-241 K 7
Clarks Hill o USA (SC) 284-285 H 3
Clarks Hill Lake < USA (GA) 284-285 H 3
Clarks Junction o NZ 182 C 6
Clarkson o ZA 220-221 G 6
Clarks Point o USA 22-23 R 3
Clarks Summit o USA (PA) 280-281 L 2
Clarkston o USA (UT) 254-255 C 2
Clarkston o USA (WA) 244-245 H 4
Clarkstone o USA (MI) 272-273 F 5
Clarksville o USA (AR) 276-277 B 5
Clarksville o USA (FL) 286-287 D 1
Clarksville o USA (GA) 284-285 G 2
Clarksville o USA (TN) 276-277 H 4
Clarksville o USA (TX) 264-265 J 5
Clarksville o USA (VA) 280-281 H 7
Clarkton o USA (NC) 282-283 J 6
Clarkville o USA (CO) 254-255 N 3
Clarno o USA (OR) 244-245 E 6
Claro, Rio ∼ BR 66-67 K 6
Claro, Rio ∼ BR 72-73 D 4
Claro, Rio ∼ BR 72-73 E 4
Claromecó o RA 78-79 J 5
Claros, Los o YV 60-61 F 2
Clatskanie o USA (OR) 244-245 B 4
Clatsop National Memorial, Fort · USA (OR) 244-245 B 4
Claude o USA (TX) 264-265 C 3
Cláudia o BR 70-71 K 2
Claudio Gay, Cordillera ▲ RCH 76-77 C 4
Claunch o USA (NM) 256-257 K 4
Claushavn = Ilimanaq o GRØ 28-29 P 2
Claveria o RP (CAG) 160-161 D 3
Claveria o RP (MAS) 160-161 E 6
Clavet o CDN (SAS) 232-233 M 3
Claxton o USA (GA) 284-285 J 4
Clay o USA (CA) 246-247 D 5
Clay o USA (TX) 266-267 L 3
Claybank o CDN (SAS) 232-233 N 5
Clay Belt ∸ CDN (ONT) 236-237 H 2
Clay Center o USA (KS) 262-263 J 5
Clay Center o USA (NE) 262-263 H 4
Clay City o USA (IN) 274-275 L 5
Clay City o USA (KY) 276-277 M 3
Claydon o CDN (SAS) 232-233 J 6
Clayoquot Sound ≈ 32-33 G 7
Clayoquot Sound ≈ CDN 230-231 C 4
Claypool o USA (AZ) 256-257 E 5
Clay River ∼ PNG 183 C 3
Clay Springs o USA (AZ) 256-257 E 4
Claysville o USA (KY) 276-277 L 2
Clayton o USA (AL) 284-285 E 5
Clayton o USA (GA) 284-285 G 2
Clayton o USA (ID) 252-253 D 2
Clayton o USA (LA) 268-269 J 5
Clayton o USA (MO) 274-275 H 6
Clayton o USA (NM) 256-257 M 2
Clayton o USA (NY) 278-279 E 4
Clayton o USA (OK) 264-265 J 4
Clayton o USA (TX) 264-265 K 6
Claytor Lake ⊖ USA (VA) 280-281 F 6
Clear Boggy Creek ∼ USA (OK) 264-265 H 4
Clearbrook o USA (MN) 270-271 C 3
Clear Creek o USA (CA) 246-247 B 2
Clear Creek ∼ USA 20-21 R 4
Clear Creek ∼ USA (AL) 284-285 C 2
Clear Creek ∼ USA (AZ) 256-257 E 4
Clear Creek ∼ USA (TX) 264-265 G 5
Cleardale o CDN 32-33 L 3
Cleare, Cape ▲ USA 20-21 R 7
Clearfield o USA (PA) 280-281 H 2
Clearfield o USA (SD) 260-261 F 3
Clearfield o USA (UT) 254-255 C 2
Clear Fork ∼ USA (TX) 264-265 G 6
Clear Fork Brazos ∼ USA (TX) 264-265 E 6
Clear Hills ▲ CDN 32-33 L 3
Clearlake o USA (CA) 246-247 C 5
Clear Lake o USA (IA) 274-275 E 1
Clear Lake o USA (MN) 270-271 D 5
Clear Lake o USA (SD) 260-261 K 2
Clear Lake o USA (WI) 270-271 F 5
Clear Lake ⊖ USA (CA) 246-247 C 4
Clear Lake ⊖ USA (LA) 268-269 G 4
Clear Lake National Wildlife Refuge ⊥ USA (CA) 246-247 D 2
Clear Lake Reservoir ⊖ USA (CA) 246-247 D 2
Clear Prairie o CDN 32-33 L 3
Clearwater o CDN (BC) 230-231 J 2
Clearwater o USA (FL) 286-287 G 4
Clearwater o USA (MT) 250-251 F 4
Clearwater o USA (NE) 262-263 H 2
Clearwater Creek ∼ CDN 30-31 F 4
Clearwater Lake ⊖ CDN 34-35 F 3
Clearwater Lake ⊖ CDN (BC) 228-229 O 4
Clearwater Lake ⊖ USA (MO) 276-277 E 3
Clearwater Mountains ▲ USA (ID) 250-251 D 5
Clearwater Provincial Park ⊥ CDN 34-35 F 3
Clearwater River ∼ CDN 32-33 P 3
Clearwater River ∼ CDN (ALB) 232-233 C 4
Clearwater River ∼ CDN (BC) 230-231 J 2
Clearwater River ∼ USA (ID) 250-251 C 5
Cleburne o USA (TX) 264-265 G 6
Cle Elum o USA (WA) 244-245 E 3
Clegg o USA (TX) 266-267 J 5
Clematis Creek ∼ AUS 178-179 K 3
Clemenceau Icefield ⊂ CDN (BC) 228-229 R 4
Clements, Port o CDN (BC) 228-229 B 3
Clements Markham Inlet ≈ 26-27 R 2
Clementson o USA (MN) 270-271 D 2
Clemesi, Pampa de la ∸ PE 70-71 B 5
Clemson o USA (SC) 284-285 H 2
Clendenin o USA (WV) 280-281 E 5
Cleo o USA (TX) 266-267 H 3
Cleopatra Needle ▲ RP 160-161 C 7
Cleo Springs o USA (OK) 264-265 F 2
Clephane Bay ≈ 28-29 J 3
Clerke Reef ⌒ AUS 172-173 D 4
Clerke Rocks ⌒ GB 78-79 P 7
Clermont o AUS 178-179 J 2
Clermont o CDN (QUE) 240-241 E 3
Clermont o F 90-91 J 7
Clermont o USA (FL) 286-287 H 3
Clermont-Ferrand ☆· F 90-91 J 9
Clermont-l'Hérault o F 90-91 J 10
Clerval o CDN (QUE) 236-237 J 4
Cleugh Passage ≈ 140-141 L 3
Cleve o AUS 180-181 D 2
Cleveland o USA (AR) 276-277 C 5
Cleveland o USA (GA) 284-285 G 2
Cleveland o USA (MS) 268-269 K 3
Cleveland o USA (MT) 250-251 K 3
Cleveland o USA (ND) 258-259 H 5
Cleveland o USA (OK) 264-265 H 2
Cleveland o USA (TN) 282-283 C 5
Cleveland o USA (TX) 268-269 E 6
Cleveland o USA (UT) 254-255 E 4
Cleveland o· USA (OH) 280-281 E 2
Cleveland, Kap ▲ GRØ 26-27 P 5
Cleveland, Mount ▲ USA (AK) 22-23 M 6
Cleveland, Mount ▲ USA (MT) 250-251 F 3
Cleveland Heights o USA (OH) 280-281 E 2
Clevelândia o BR 74-75 D 6
Cleveland Peninsula ⌣ USA 32-33 D 4
Cleveland River ∼ CDN 36-37 G 2
Clewiston o USA (FL) 286-287 J 5
Clifden o NZ 182 A 7
Clifden = An Clochán o· IRL 90-91 B 5
Cliff o USA (NM) 256-257 G 6
Cliff o USA (NM) 256-257 G 5
Cliffdell o USA (WA) 244-245 D 4
Clifford o CDN (ONT) 238-239 E 5
Cliffs of Moher ·· IRL 90-91 C 5
Clifton o USA (AZ) 256-257 F 5
Clifton o USA (IL) 274-275 L 4
Clifton o USA (KS) 262-263 J 5
Clifton o USA (LA) 268-269 K 6
Clifton o USA (TN) 276-277 G 5
Clifton o USA (TX) 266-267 K 2
Clifton Forge o USA (VA) 280-281 G 6
Clifton Hills o AUS 178-179 E 4
Clifton Point ▲ CDN 24-25 N 6
Clifty o USA (KY) 276-277 H 3
Cli Lake ⊖ CDN 30-31 H 4
Climax o CDN (SAS) 232-233 K 6
Climax o USA (CO) 254-255 J 4
Climax o USA (GA) 284-285 F 6
Climax o USA (MI) 272-273 D 5
Climax o USA (MN) 270-271 B 3
Clinch Mountains ▲ USA (TN) 282-283 D 4
Clinchport o USA (VA) 280-281 D 7
Clinch River ∼ USA (TN) 282-283 D 4
Clinch River ∼ USA (TN) 282-283 C 5
Clinch River ∼ USA (VA) 280-281 D 7
Cline o USA (TX) 266-267 G 4
Cline River o CDN (ALB) 232-233 B 3
Cline River ∼ CDN (ALB) 232-233 B 3
Clines Corners o USA (NM) 256-257 K 3
Clingmans Dome ▲ USA (NC) 282-283 D 5
Clint o USA (TX) 266-267 A 2
Clinton o CDN (BC) 230-231 H 2
Clinton o CDN (ONT) 238-239 D 5
Clinton o NZ 182 B 7
Clinton o USA (AL) 284-285 C 4
Clinton o USA (AR) 276-277 C 5
Clinton o USA (CT) 280-281 O 2
Clinton o USA (IA) 274-275 H 3
Clinton o USA (IL) 274-275 K 4
Clinton o USA (IN) 274-275 L 5
Clinton o USA (KY) 276-277 G 4
Clinton o USA (LA) 268-269 J 6
Clinton o USA (MI) 272-273 F 5
Clinton o USA (MO) 274-275 E 6
Clinton o USA (MS) 268-269 K 4
Clinton o USA (MT) 250-251 F 5
Clinton o USA (NC) 282-283 J 6
Clinton o USA (OK) 264-265 F 3
Clinton o USA (SC) 284-285 J 2
Clinton o USA (TN) 282-283 C 4
Clinton, Cape ▲ AUS 178-179 L 2
Clinton, Port ≈ 178-179 L 2
Clinton-Colden Lake ⊖ CDN 30-31 Q 3
Clinton Lake ⊖ USA (IL) 274-275 K 4
Clinton Lake ⊖ USA (KS) 262-263 L 6
Clinton Point o CDN 24-25 M 6
Clintonville o USA (WI) 270-271 K 6
Clio o USA (AL) 284-285 E 5
Clio o USA (MI) 272-273 F 4
Clio o USA (SC) 284-285 L 2
Cliong Karik Tagh ▲ VRC 144-145 H 2
Clipperton Fracture Zone ≃ 14-15 O 7
Clisbako River ∼ CDN (BC) 228-229 L 4
Clive Lake ⊖ CDN 30-31 K 4
Čija o RUS 122-123 J 2
Čija, ozero ⊖ RUS 122-123 J 2
Cloan o CDN (SAS) 232-233 K 3
Clocolan o ZA 220-221 H 4
Clodomira o RA 76-77 E 4
Clonagh o AUS 174-175 F 7
Clonbrook o GUY 62-63 F 2
Cloncurry o AUS 174-175 F 7
Cloncurry Plateau ∸ AUS 178-179 E 1
Cloncurry River ∼ AUS 174-175 F 6
Clonmacnoise o·· IRL 90-91 D 5
Clonmel = Cluain Meala o IRL 90-91 D 5
Clo-oose o CDN (BC) 230-231 E 5
Cloppenburg o D 92-93 K 2
Cloquet o USA (MN) 270-271 F 4
Cloquet River ∼ USA (MN) 270-271 F 3
Clore River ∼ CDN (BC) 228-229 G 2
Cloridorme o CDN (QUE) 242-243 D 3
Clorinda o RA 76-77 J 3
Cloudcroft o USA (NM) 256-257 K 6
Cloud Peak ▲ USA (WY) 252-253 L 2
Clouds Creek o AUS 178-179 M 6
Cloudy Mountain ▲ USA 20-21 M 5
Clover o USA (SC) 284-285 J 1
Clover o USA (VA) 280-281 H 7
Cloverdale o USA (CA) 246-247 B 5
Cloverdale o USA (IN) 274-275 M 5
Cloverdale o USA (MN) 270-271 F 4
Cloverport o USA (KY) 276-277 J 3
Cloverton o USA (MN) 270-271 F 4
Clovis o USA (CA) 248-249 E 3
Clovis o USA (NM) 256-257 M 4
Cloyne o CDN (ONT) 238-239 H 4
Cluain Meala = Clonmel o IRL 90-91 D 5
Club Mayanabo o C 54-55 G 4
Cluj-Napoca ☆· RO 102-103 C 4
Cluny o CDN (ALB) 232-233 F 5
Clute o CDN (ONT) 236-237 G 3
Clute o USA (TX) 268-269 E 7
Clyde o CDN (ALB) 32-33 O 4
Clyde o CDN (NWT) 26-27 Q 8
Clyde ∼ GB 90-91 F 4
Clyde o USA (ND) 258-259 J 3
Clyde o USA (NY) 278-279 E 5
Clyde o USA (OH) 280-281 D 2
Clyde o USA (TX) 264-265 E 6
Clyde Inlet ≈ 26-27 Q 8
Clyde Park o USA (MT) 250-251 J 6
Clyde River o CDN (NS) 240-241 K 7
Clyde River ∼ CDN (NS) 240-241 K 7
Clyo o USA (GA) 284-285 J 4
Cna ∼ RUS 94-95 R 5
Cnori o GE 126-127 F 7
Coachella o USA (CA) 248-249 H 6
Coachella Canal < USA (CA) 248-249 J 7
Coachman's Cove o CDN (NFL) 242-243 M 2
Coahoma o USA (TX) 264-265 C 6
Coahuayana o MEX 52-53 C 2
Coahuayutla o MEX 52-53 D 2
Coahuila ◘ MEX 50-51 H 4
Coalcomán, Río ∼ MEX 52-53 C 2
Coalcomán de Matamoros o MEX 52-53 C 2
Coal Creek o CDN (BC) 230-231 P 4
Coal Creek o USA 20-21 T 4
Coaldale o CDN (ALB) 232-233 F 6
Coaldale o USA (NV) 246-247 H 5
Coalgate o USA (OK) 264-265 H 4
Coal Harbour o CDN (BC) 230-231 B 3
Coal Hill o USA (AR) 276-277 B 5
Coalhurst o CDN (ALB) 232-233 E 6
Coalinga o USA (CA) 248-249 D 3
Coal Mine · AUS 178-179 E 6
Coalmont o CDN (BC) 230-231 J 4
Coalridge o USA (MT) 250-251 P 3
Coal River o CDN (BC) 30-31 F 6
Coal River ∼ CDN 30-31 F 5
Coal River ∼ USA (WV) 280-281 E 5
Coalspur o CDN (ALB) 228-229 R 3
Coal Valley o CDN (ALB) 232-233 B 2
Coalville o USA (UT) 254-255 D 3
Coamo o USA (PR) 286-287 P 2
Coaraci o BR 72-73 L 3
Coari o BR 66-67 F 5
Coari, Lago de ⊖ BR 66-67 F 5
Coari, Rio ∼ BR 66-67 F 5
Coasa o PE 70-71 B 4
Coast ◘ EAK 212-213 G 5
Coastal Plains Research Station o AUS 172-173 K 2
Coast Mountains ▲ CDN 32-33 D 2
Coast of Labrador ∸ CDN 36-37 R 5
Coast Range ▲ AUS 178-179 L 2
Coast Range ▲ AUS 178-179 L 3
Coast Range ▲ USA 40-41 C 3
Coata o PE 70-71 C 4
Coatá, Cachoeira ∼ BR 66-67 G 6
Coatá, Cachoeira do ∼ BR 66-67 F 7
Coatá Laranjal, Área Indígena X BR 66-67 H 5
Coatbridge o GB 90-91 E 4
Coatepec o MEX 52-53 F 2
Coatepeque o GCA 52-53 J 4
Coatesville o USA (PA) 280-281 L 4
Coaticook o CDN (QUE) 238-239 O 3
Coats Bay ≈ 36-37 K 6
Coats Island ⌒ CDN 36-37 H 3
Coats Land ∸ ARK 16 F 34
Coatzacoalcos o· MEX 52-53 G 2
Coatzacoalcos, Río ∼ MEX 52-53 G 3
Coba ∴· MEX 52-53 L 1
Cobadin o RO 102-103 F 5
Cobalt o CDN (ONT) 236-237 J 5
Cobalt o USA (ID) 250-251 E 6
Cobán ☆ GCA 52-53 J 4
Cobar o AUS 178-179 H 6
Cobargo o AUS 180-181 K 4
Cobb, Lake ⊖ AUS 176-177 J 2
Cobberas, Mount ▲ AUS 180-181 K 4
Cobb Highway II AUS 180-181 G 2
Cobb Island ⌒ USA (VA) 280-281 L 6
Cobbs Arm o CDN (NFL) 242-243 O 3
Cobden o AUS 180-181 G 5
Cobden o CDN (ONT) 238-239 J 3
Cobequid Mountains ▲ CDN (NS) 240-241 L 5
Cobh = An Cóbh o IRL 90-91 C 6
Cobham River ∼ CDN 34-35 J 4
Cobija ☆ BOL 70-71 C 2
Cobija, Punta ▲ RCH 76-77 B 2
Cobleskill o USA (NY) 278-279 G 6
Coboconk o CDN (ONT) 238-239 G 4
Cobourg o CDN (ONT) 238-239 G 5
Cobourg Peninsula ⌣ AUS 172-173 K 1
Cobquecura o RCH 78-79 C 4
Cobra o AUS 176-177 D 2
Cobre o USA (NV) 246-247 L 2
Cobre, El o RCH 76-77 B 3
Cobre, Sierra del ▲ RA 76-77 D 2
Cobuè o MOC 214-215 H 7
Coburg o· D 92-93 L 3
Coburg Island ⌒ CDN 24-25 h 2
Coburg Marine Park ⊥ AUS 172-173 K 1
Coburn o AUS 176-177 C 3
Coburn Mount ▲ USA (ME) 278-279 L 3
Coca = Puerto Francisco de Orellana o EC 64-65 D 2
Coca, Río ∼ EC 64-65 D 2
Cocachacra o PE 64-65 D 7
Cocagne o CDN (NB) 240-241 L 4
Cocal o BR 68-69 H 3
Cocalinho o BR (MAR) 68-69 F 3
Cocalinho o BR (MAT) 72-73 E 3
Cocha, La o RA 76-77 E 4
Cochabamba ☆ BOL 70-71 D 5
Cochabamba o PE 64-65 C 5
Cochagne o CDN (NB) 240-241 L 4
Cochagón, Cerro ▲ NIC 52-53 B 5
Cochamarca o PE 64-65 D 7
Cochamó o RCH 78-79 C 6
Cochaquingu o EC 64-65 D 2
Coche, Isla ⌒ YV 60-61 K 2
Cochem o· D 92-93 J 3
Cochenour o CDN (ONT) 234-235 K 3
Cochetopa Hills ▲ USA (CO) 254-255 J 6
Cochico, Sierra de ▲ RA 78-79 D 4
Cochiguas, Río ∼ RCH 76-77 B 6
Cochin o CDN (SAS) 232-233 K 2
Cochin o·· IND 140-141 G 6
Cochinos, Bahía de ≈ 54-55 E 3
Cochise o USA (AZ) 256-257 F 6
Cochran o USA (GA) 284-285 G 4
Cochrane o CDN (ALB) 232-233 D 4
Cochrane o CDN (ONT) 236-237 H 3
Cochrane o RCH 80 D 3
Cochrane, Cerro ▲ RCH 80 D 3
Cochrane, Lago ≈ 80 D 3
Cockaköl ⊖ KA 124-125 G 4
Cockaköl kyrkasy ▲ KA 126-127 N 4
Cockburn o AUS 180-181 F 2
Cockburn, Canal ≈ 80 E 7
Cockburn, Cape ▲ CDN 24-25 V 3
Cockburn, Mount ▲ AUS (NT) 172-173 K 7
Cockburn, Mount ▲ AUS (NT) 176-177 K 2
Cockburn Harbor o GB 54-55 K 4
Cockburn Island ⌒ CDN (ONT) 238-239 B 3
Cockburn Islands ⌒ CDN 24-25 R 6
Cockburn North, Mount ▲ AUS 172-173 J 3
Cockburn Town o BS 54-55 H 2
Cockburn Town ☆ GB 54-55 K 4
Cocklebiddy Cave · AUS 176-177 H 5
Cocklebiddy Motel o AUS 176-177 J 6
Cockram Strait ≈ 28-29 C 3
Cockrum o USA (MS) 268-269 L 2
Coco, Cayo ⌒ C 54-55 F 3
Coco, El o CR 52-53 B 6
Coco, Punta ▲ CO 60-61 C 6
Coco, Río ∼ NIC 52-53 L 5
Côco, Rio do ∼ BR 68-69 D 6
Cocoa o USA (FL) 286-287 J 3
Cocoa Beach o USA (FL) 286-287 J 3
Cocobeach o G 210-211 B 3
Coco Channel ≈ 140-141 L 3
Cococi o BR 68-69 H 5
Cocodrie o USA (LA) 268-269 K 7
Cocolalla o USA (ID) 250-251 C 3
Coconho, Ponta ▲ BR 68-69 L 4
Coconino Plateau ▲ USA (AZ) 256-257 C 3
Coco o Segovia = Río Wangkí ∼ HN 52-53 B 4
Cocoparra National Park ⊥ AUS 180-181 J 3
Cocorna o CO 60-61 D 4
Cocorocuma, Cayos ⌒ NIC 54-55 D 7
Côcos o BR 72-73 H 2
Cocos o BR (BAH) 72-73 H 3
Cocos o BR (MAR) 68-69 G 4
Cocos Basin ≃ 12 H 4
Cocos Island ⌒ AUS 12 H 6
Cocos Ridge ≃ 5 C 4
Cocotier Beach = Cocotier Plage ∸· CAM 210-211 B 2
Cocotier Plage = Cocotier Beach ∸· CAM 210-211 B 2
Cocuí, Parque Nacional el ⊥ CO 60-61 E 4
Cocuizas, Las o YV 62-63 D 2
Cocula o MEX 52-53 C 1
Cod, Cape ▲ USA (MA) 278-279 L 6
Codajás o BR 66-67 D 4
Codeagro o BR 66-67 G 4
Codera, Cabo ▲ YV 60-61 H 2
Codette o CDN (SAS) 232-233 O 2
Cod Island ⌒ CDN 36-37 T 6
Cod National Seashore, Cape ⊥ USA (MA) 278-279 M 6
Codó o BR 68-69 G 4
Codo de Pozuzo o PE 64-65 E 6
Codora o USA (CA) 246-247 C 4
Codorniz, Paso ▲ RCH 80 D 3
Codozinho o BR 68-69 F 4
Codpa o RCH 70-71 C 6
Codrii ▲ MD 102-103 E 3
Codrington o AG 56 E 3
Codru-Moma, Munţii ▲ RO 102-103 C 4
Cody o USA (NE) 262-263 E 2
Cody o USA (WY) 252-253 J 2
Coeburn o USA (VA) 280-281 D 7
Coelemu o RCH 78-79 C 4
Coelho Neto o BR 68-69 G 4
Coen o AUS 174-175 G 3
Coerney o ZA 220-221 G 6
Coeroeni o SME 62-63 F 4
Coesfeld o· D 92-93 J 3
Coëtivy Island ⌒ SY 224 E 3
Coeur d'Alene o USA (ID) 250-251 C 4
Coeur d'Alene Indian Reservation X USA (ID) 250-251 C 4
Coeur d'Alene Lake ⊖ USA (ID) 250-251 C 4
Coeur d'Alene Mountains ▲ USA (ID) 250-251 C 4
Coeur d'Alene River ∼ USA (ID) 250-251 C 4
Coevorden o NL 92-93 J 2
Coffee Bay o ZA 220-221 J 5
Coffee Creek o CDN 20-21 V 5
Coffeen Lake ⊖ USA (IL) 274-275 J 5
Coffeeville o USA (AL) 284-285 B 5
Coffeeville o USA (MS) 268-269 L 3
Coffeyville o USA (KS) 262-263 L 7
Coffin Bay ≈ 180-181 C 3
Coffin Bay National Park ⊥ AUS 180-181 C 3
Coffs Harbour o AUS 178-179 M 6
Cofimvaba o ZA 220-221 H 6
Čogādāk o IR 134-135 D 4
Čogar ∼ RUS 120-121 E 6
Cogar o USA (OK) 264-265 F 3
Cogotí, Embalse < RCH 76-77 B 6
Coghlan o ZA 220-221 J 5
Cognac o· F 90-91 G 9
Cogo o GQ 210-211 B 3
Cogollal, El o YV 60-61 K 4
Cogotí, Río ∼ RCH 76-77 B 6
Čograjskoe vodohranilišče ⊖ RUS 126-127 F 5
Cogswell o USA (ND) 258-259 K 5
Cogt = Tahilt o MAU 148-149 C 5
Cogt-Ovoo = Doloon o MAU 148-149 G 5
Coguno o MOC 220-221 M 2
Cohade, Rivière ∼ CDN 36-37 N 5
Cohagen o USA (MT) 250-251 N 4
Cohocton River ∼ USA (NY) 278-279 D 6
Cohoes o USA (NY) 278-279 H 6
Cohutta Mountain ▲ USA (GA) 284-285 F 2
Coiba, Isla de ⌒ PA 52-53 D 8
Coig, Río ∼ RA 80 E 5
Coihaique ☆ RCH 80 D 2
Coihaique Alto o RCH 80 E 2
Coihué o RCH 78-79 C 4
Coihueco o RCH 78-79 D 4
Coimbatore o IND 140-141 G 5
Coimbra o BR 72-73 J 6
Coimbra ☆·· P 98-99 C 4
Coín o E 98-99 E 6
Coin de Mire ⌒ MS 224 C 6
Coipasa, Cerro ▲ BOL 70-71 C 6
Coipasa, Salar de ⊖ BOL 70-71 C 6
Coiposa, Lago de ⊖ BOL 70-71 C 6
Čojbalsan ☆ MAU 148-149 M 3
Cojedes, Río ∼ YV 60-61 G 3
Cojimíes o EC 64-65 B 1
Cojoida o YV 60-61 L 3
Čojr o MAU 148-149 J 4
Cojúa o YV 60-61 F 2
Cojudo Blanco, Cerro ▲ RA 80 F 3
Cojutepeque ☆ ES 52-53 K 5
Cojyndykol ⊖ KA 124-125 E 3
Coker Creek o USA (TN) 282-283 C 5
Cokeville o USA (WY) 252-253 H 4
Čokrakbejik, Gora ▲ TM 136-137 F 5
Čokurdah-Kerike, gora ▲ RUS 110-111 F 3
Colac o AUS 180-181 G 5
Colakšor, köli ⊖ KA 124-125 J 2
Colan, Cape ▲ CDN 26-27 R 2
Colán Conhué o RA 78-79 E 7
Colangüil, Cordillera de la ▲ RA 76-77 C 5
Colares o BR 62-63 K 6
Colasi Point ▲ RP 160-161 F 7
Colatina o BR 72-73 K 5
Colazo o RA 76-77 F 6
Colbert o USA (WA) 244-245 H 3
Colbon o RUS 110-111 U 6
Colborne o CDN (ONT) 238-239 H 4
Colborne, Port o CDN (ONT) 238-239 F 6
Colby o USA (KS) 262-263 E 5
Colca, Río ∼ PE 64-65 F 9
Colcabamba o PE 64-65 F 9
Colchester o· GB 90-91 H 6
Colchester o USA (VT) 278-279 H 4
Colchester o ZA 220-221 G 6
Cold Bay o USA 22-23 P 5
Cold Lake o CDN 32-33 Q 4
Cold Spring o USA (NV) 246-247 H 4
Coldspring o USA (TX) 268-269 E 6
Coldspring Mountain ▲ CDN 20-21 W 5
Coldstream o CDN (BC) 230-231 K 3
Coldstream o GB 90-91 F 4
Coldwater o USA (KS) 262-263 G 7
Coldwater o USA (MI) 272-273 D 6
Coldwater o USA (MS) 268-269 L 2
Coldwater Creek ∼ USA (TX) 264-265 B 2
Coldwater River ∼ USA (MS) 268-269 K 2
Coleambally o AUS 180-181 H 3
Coleambally Creek ∼ AUS 180-181 H 3
Cole Bay o CDN 32-33 Q 4
Colebrook o USA (NH) 278-279 K 4
Cole Camp o USA (MO) 274-275 E 6

Coleen River ~ USA 20-21 T 3
Colekeplaas o ZA 220-221 G 6
Coleman o CDN (ALB) 232-233 D 6
Coleman o USA (MI) 272-273 E 4
Coleman o USA (TX) 266-267 H 2
Coleman, Lake < USA (TX) 264-265 E 6
Coleman Lake ⊂ CDN (ALB) 232-233 G 4
Coleman River ~ AUS 174-175 F 4
Colenso o ZA 220-221 J 4
Colerain o USA (NC) 282-283 L 4
Coleraine o AUS 180-181 F 4
Coleraine o GB 90-91 D 4
Coleraine o USA (MN) 270-271 E 3
Coleridge, Lake ⊂ NZ 182 C 5
Coleroon ~ IND 140-141 H 5
Coles, Punta ▲ PE 70-71 B 5
Colesberg o ZA 220-221 G 5
Coles Island o CDN (NB) 240-241 K 5
Coleto Creek ~ USA (TX) 266-267 K 5
Coleville o CDN (SAS) 232-233 J 4
Colfax o USA (CA) 246-247 E 4
Colfax o USA (IA) 274-275 E 3
Colfax o USA (IL) 274-275 K 4
Colfax o USA (LA) 268-269 H 5
Colfax o USA (ND) 258-259 L 5
Colfax o USA (WA) 244-245 H 4
Colfax o USA (WI) 270-271 G 6
Colga Downs o AUS 176-177 E 3
Colgate o CDN (SAS) 232-233 P 6
Colguula o SP 208-209 H 5
Colhué Huapi, Lago ⊂ RA 80 F 2
Colidor o BR 70-71 K 2
Colignan o AUS 180-181 G 3
Coligny o ZA 220-221 H 3
Colima ▫ MEX 52-53 B 2
Colima ☆ • MEX (COL) 52-53 C 2
Colina o BR 72-73 F 6
Colin Archer Peninsula ⌣ CDN 24-25 a 2
Colinas o BR 68-69 F 5
Colinas do Tocantins o BR 68-69 D 6
Colindina, Mount ▲ AUS 176-177 G 4
Colinet o CDN (NFL) 242-243 P 5
Coliseo o C 54-55 E 3
Coll ⌒ GB 90-91 D 3
Collacagua o RCH 70-71 C 7
Colladere o RH 54-55 J 5
Collado-Villalba o E 98-99 F 4
Collarenebri o AUS 178-179 K 5
Collaroy o AUS 178-179 K 2
Collbran o USA (CO) 254-255 H 4
Collector o AUS 180-181 K 3
College Park o USA (GA) 284-285 F 3
College Place o USA (WA) 244-245 G 4
College Station o USA (TX) 266-267 L 3
Collerina o AUS 178-179 J 5
Colleymount o CDN (BC) 228-229 H 2
Collie o AUS 176-177 D 6
Collier Bay ≈ 172-173 G 4
Collier Bay Aboriginal Land ⅹ AUS 172-173 F 4
Collier Range ▲ AUS 176-177 E 2
Collier Range National Park ⊥ AUS 176-177 E 2
Collier Tunnel II USA (CA) 246-247 B 2
Collierville o USA (TN) 276-277 F 5
Collingwood o CDN (ONT) 238-239 E 4
Collingwood o NZ 182 D 4
Collingwood Bay ≈ 183 E 5
Collins o CDN (ONT) 234-235 O 4
Collins o USA (AR) 276-277 D 7
Collins o USA (IA) 274-275 E 3
Collins o USA (MO) 276-277 B 3
Collins o USA (MS) 268-269 L 5
Collins o USA (MT) 250-251 H 4
Collins, Mount ▲ AUS 178-179 F 3
Collinson, Cape ▲ CDN 26-27 P 3
Collinson Peninsula ⌣ CDN 24-25 V 5
Collins River ~ USA (TN) 276-277 K 5
Collinsville o AUS 174-175 J 7
Collinsville o USA (AL) 284-285 E 2
Collinsville o USA (CA) 246-247 D 5
Collinsville o USA (IL) 274-275 J 6
Collinsville o USA (OK) 264-265 J 2
Collinwood o USA (TN) 276-277 G 5
Collipulli o RCH 78-79 C 4
Collo o DZ 190-191 F 2
Collón Curá, Río ~ RA 78-79 D 6
Colly Creek ~ USA (NC) 282-283 J 6
Colmar ☆ • F 90-91 L 7
Colméia o BR 68-69 D 6
Colmena o RA 76-77 G 5
Colmenar Viejo o E 98-99 F 4
Colnett o MEX 50-51 A 2
Colnett, Cabo ▲ MEX 50-51 A 2
Cologne = Köln o•• D 92-93 J 3
Cololo, Arroyo ~ ROU 78-79 L 2
Coloma o USA (WI) 270-271 J 6
Colombia o C 54-55 G 4
Colombia o CO 60-61 D 6
Colombia ■ CO 60-61 D 6
Colombia o MEX 50-51 K 4
Colombia Basin ≃ 5 D 3
Colombier o CDN (QUE) 240-241 G 2
Colombo o BR 68-69 F 3
Colombo ★ CL 140-141 H 7
Colome o USA (SD) 260-261 G 3
Colomiers o F 90-91 H 10
Colón o C 54-55 E 3
Colón ☆ PA 52-53 E 7
Colón o RA (BUA) 78-79 J 2
Colón o RA (ERI) 78-79 K 2
Colón, Archipiélago de = Islas Galápagos ⌒ EC 64-65 B 9
Colonelganj o IND 142-143 B 2
Colonel Hill o BS 54-55 H 3
Colonia 10 de Julio o RA 76-77 F 6
Colonia Angamos o PE 64-65 F 4
Colonia Carlos Pellegrini o RA 76-77 J 5
Colonia del Sacramento ☆ • ROU 78-79 L 3
Colonia Dora o RA 76-77 F 5
Colonial Beach o USA (MD) 280-281 K 5
Colônia Leopoldina o BR 68-69 L 6
Colonial Heights o USA (VA) 280-281 J 6
Colonial National Historic Park • USA (VA) 280-281 K 6
Colônia Osório o BR 68-69 E 2
Colonia piel foca • EC 64-65 B 10
Colonia Prosperidad o RA 76-77 F 6
Colonias o USA (NM) 256-257 L 3
Colonias Unidas o RA 76-77 H 4
Colonia Teresa o RA 76-77 H 6
Colonia Vicente Guerrero o MEX 50-51 B 2
Colon Ridge ≃ 5 B 4
Colonsay o CDN (SAS) 232-233 N 4
Colony o USA (KS) 262-263 L 6
Colony o USA (WY) 252-253 O 2
Colorada, Laguna ⊂ BOL 76-77 D 2
Colorada, Sierra ▲ RA 76-77 E 3
Colorado o BR 72-73 E 7
Colorado o C 54-55 F 4
Colorado o CR 52-53 B 6
Colorado ▫ USA (CO) 254-255 H 4
Colorado, Caño o YV 60-61 K 3
Colorado, Cerro ▲ MEX 50-51 B 2
Colorado, Cerro ▲ RA (CHU) 80 F 2
Colorado, Cerro ▲ RA (LAR) 76-77 D 5
Colorado, Cerro ▲ RCH 80 E 2
Colorado, El o RA 76-77 F 4
Colorado, Punta ▲ MEX 50-51 C 3
Colorado, Rio ~ BR 70-71 F 3
Colorado, Río ~ RA 76-77 D 4
Colorado, Río ~ RA 76-77 D 6
Colorado, Río ~ RA 76-77 E 2
Colorado, Río ~ RA 78-79 F 5
Colorado, Río ~ RCH 78-79 D 2
Colorado City o USA (AZ) 256-257 C 2
Colorado City o USA (CO) 254-255 L 6
Colorado City o USA (TX) 264-265 D 6
Colorado Desert ⊥ USA (CA) 248-249 H 6
Colorado d'Oeste o BR 70-71 G 3
Colorado National Monument • USA (CO) 254-255 G 4
Colorado Plateau ▲ USA (AZ) 256-257 D 2
Colorado River ~ USA (AZ) 256-257 B 2
Colorado River ~ USA (CA) 248-249 K 6
Colorado River ~ USA (CO) 254-255 G 4
Colorado River ~ USA (TX) 264-265 D 6
Colorado River ~ USA (TX) 266-267 J 2
Colorado River ~ USA (UT) 254-255 E 5
Colorado River Aqueduct < USA (CA) 248-249 K 5
Colorado River Indian Reservation ⅹ USA (AZ) 256-257 A 5
Colorados, Archipiélago de los ⌒ C 54-55 C 3
Colorados, Cerros ▲ RA 78-79 E 6
Colorado Springs o• USA (CO) 254-255 L 5
Colotlan o MEX 50-51 H 6
Coloitlipa o MEX 52-53 E 3
Colpitts Creek ~ CDN (ONT) 236-237 B 2
Colpon-Ata o KS 146-147 C 4
Colquechaca o BOL 70-71 D 6
Colquen, Cerro ▲ RCH 78-79 C 4
Colquiri o BOL 70-71 D 5
Colquitt o USA (GA) 284-285 F 5
Colrain o USA (MA) 278-279 J 6
Colson Track II AUS 178-179 D 3
Colston Park o AUS 178-179 K 1
Colstrip o USA (MT) 250-251 N 6
Colter Pass ▲ USA (MT) 250-251 K 6
Colton o USA (SD) 260-261 K 3
Colton o USA (UT) 254-255 E 4
Colton o USA (WA) 244-245 H 4
Coltons Point o USA (MD) 280-281 K 5
Coltwater o USA (AR) 276-277 E 5
Columbia o USA (AL) 284-285 E 5
Columbia o USA (KY) 276-277 K 3
Columbia o USA (LA) 268-269 H 4
Columbia o USA (MD) 280-281 K 4
Columbia o USA (MO) 274-275 F 6
Columbia o USA (MS) 268-269 L 5
Columbia o USA (NC) 282-283 L 5
Columbia o USA (PA) 280-281 K 3
Columbia o USA (SD) 260-261 H 1
Columbia o USA (TN) 276-277 H 5
Columbia ☆ USA (SC) 284-285 J 3
Columbia, Mount ▲ CDN (BC) 228-229 R 4
Columbia Beach o USA (WA) 244-245 C 3
Columbia Center o USA (WA) 244-245 H 4
Columbia City o USA (FL) 286-287 G 1
Columbia City o USA (IN) 274-275 N 3
Columbia Falls o USA (ME) 278-279 O 4
Columbia Falls o USA (MT) 250-251 E 3
Columbia Glacier ⊂ USA 20-21 R 6
Columbia Icefield ⊂ CDN (ALB) 228-229 R 4
Columbia Mountains ▲ CDN (BC) 228-229 M 3
Columbiana o USA (AL) 284-285 D 3
Columbia National Wildlife Refuge ⊥ USA (WA) 244-245 F 4
Columbia Plateau ▲ USA (OR) 40-41 E 3
Columbia Reach ~ CDN (BC) 230-231 M 2
Columbia River ~ CDN (BC) 230-231 L 2
Columbia River ~ USA (WA) 244-245 D 5
Columbine o USA (CO) 254-255 J 3
Columbus o USA (GA) 284-285 F 4
Columbus o USA (IN) 274-275 N 5
Columbus o USA (KS) 262-263 M 7
Columbus o USA (KY) 276-277 F 4
Columbus o USA (MS) 268-269 M 3
Columbus o USA (MT) 250-251 K 6
Columbus o USA (NC) 282-283 E 5
Columbus o USA (ND) 258-259 E 3
Columbus o USA (NE) 262-263 J 3
Columbus o USA (NM) 256-257 H 7
Columbus o USA (PA) 280-281 G 2
Columbus o USA (TX) 266-267 L 4
Columbus o USA (WI) 274-275 J 1
Columbus ☆ USA (OH) 280-281 D 4
Columbus Cay ⌒ BH 52-53 L 3
Columbus City o USA (AL) 284-285 D 2
Columbus Grove o USA (OH) 280-281 B 3
Columbus Junction o USA (IA) 274-275 G 3
Columbus Lake < USA (MS) 268-269 M 3
Columbus Landing 5/ 4th./ 1494 • JA 54-55 G 5
Columbus Monument • BS 54-55 H 2
Columbus Point ▲ BS 54-55 H 2
Columna, Pico ▲ PA 52-53 E 7
Coluna o BR 72-73 J 5
Colup, Cerro ▲ RCH 76-77 C 2
Colusa o USA (CA) 246-247 C 4
Colville o USA (WA) 244-245 H 2
Colville Channel ≈ 182 E 2
Colville Indian Reservation ⅹ USA (WA) 244-245 F 2
Colville Lake o CDN (NWT) 30-31 F 2
Colville Lake ⊂ CDN (NWT) 30-31 G 2
Colville River ~ USA 20-21 L 2
Coma, La o MEX 50-51 K 5
Comácchio o I 100-101 D 2
Comácha o MOC 218-219 G 3
Comalcalco o MEX (TAB) 52-53 H 2
Comalcalco ∴ • MEX (TAB) 52-53 H 2
Comallo o RA 78-79 D 6
Comallo, Arroyo ~ RA 78-79 D 6
Comanche o USA (OK) 264-265 G 4
Comanche o USA (TX) 266-267 J 2
Comandante Fontana o RA 76-77 H 3
Comandante Giribone o RA 78-79 L 3
Comandante Luis Piedra Buena o RA 80 F 4
Comănești o RO 102-103 E 4
Comarapa o BOL 70-71 E 5
Comas o PE 64-65 E 7
Comau, Fiordo ≈ 78-79 C 7
Comayagua ☆ • HN 52-53 L 4
Comayagua, Montañas de ▲ HN 52-53 L 4
Comayagüela o HN 52-53 L 4
Combapata o PE 70-71 B 4
Combarbala o RCH 76-77 B 6
Combermere o CDN (ONT) 238-239 H 3
Combermere, Cape ▲ CDN 24-25 g 2
Combermere Bay ≈ 142-143 H 6
Combo, Selat ≈ 162-163 F 4
Combol, Pulau ⌒ RI 162-163 E 4
Combomune o MOC 218-219 G 6
Combs o USA (AR) 276-277 B 5
Comè o DY 202-203 L 6
Come by Chance o AUS 178-179 K 6
Comechingones, Sierra de ▲ RA 78-79 G 2
Comedero o MEX 50-51 F 5
Comemoração, Rio ~ BR 70-71 G 2
Comer o USA (GA) 284-285 G 2
Comerio o USA (PR) 286-287 P 2
Comer Strait ≈ 36-37 G 2
Comerzinho o BR 72-73 K 4
Comet Downs o AUS 178-179 K 2
Cometela o MOC 218-219 H 5
Comet Outstation o AUS 178-179 C 5
Comet River ~ AUS 178-179 K 3
Comfort o USA (TX) 266-267 J 4
Comfort, Cape ▲ CDN 36-37 H 2
Comfort, Point o USA (TX) 266-267 L 5
Comfort Bight o CDN 38-39 R 2
Comicó, Arroyo ~ RA 78-79 F 6
Comilla o BD 142-143 G 4
Comino, Capo ▲ I 100-101 B 4
Comitán de Domínguez o MEX 52-53 H 3
Comite River ~ USA (LA) 268-269 J 6
Commander Islands = Komandorskie ostrova ⌒ RUS 120-121 W 6
Commee o CDN (ONT) 234-235 O 6
Commerce o USA (GA) 284-285 G 2
Commerce o USA (MS) 268-269 K 2
Commerce o USA (TX) 264-265 J 5
Commissioner Island ⌒ CDN (MAN) 234-235 F 2
Committee Bay ≈ 24-25 c 6
Commodore Reef ⌒ 160-161 A 8
Commonwealth Meteorological Station • AUS 178-179 H 6
Commonwealth Range ▲ ARK 16 E 0
Commoron Creek ~ AUS 178-179 L 5
Como ☆ • I 100-101 B 2
Como ~ RCB 210-211 E 3
Como o USA (MS) 268-269 L 2
Como o USA (TX) 264-265 J 5
Como, Lago di ⊂ I 100-101 B 2
Comoapa o NIC 52-53 B 5
Como Bluff Fossil Beds ∴ USA (WY) 252-253 N 5
Comodo o ETH 208-209 E 6
Comodoro o BR 70-71 H 3
Comodoro Rivadavia o RA 80 G 2
Comoé ~ CI 202-203 J 6
Comoé, Parc National de la ⊥ ••• CI 202-203 H 5
Comonfort o MEX 52-53 D 1
Comorin, Cape ▲ IND 140-141 G 6
Comoros = Comores ■ COM 222-223 C 3
Comoros = Comores, Archipel des ⌒ COM 222-223 C 3
Comox o CDN (BC) 230-231 E 4
Compass Lake o USA (FL) 286-287 D 1
Compeer o CDN (ALB) 232-233 H 4
Compiègne o• F 90-91 J 7
Complejo Ferrovial Zárate-Brazo Largo • RA 78-79 K 2
Čompolo ~ RUS 118-119 L 6
Compostela o MEX 50-51 G 7
Comprida, Ilha ⌒ BR 74-75 G 5
Compton o USA (CA) 248-249 F 6
Compton Névé ~ CDN (BC) 230-231 E 3
Comrat o MD 102-103 F 4
Comstock o USA (MI) 272-273 D 5
Comstock o USA (TX) 266-267 F 4
Côm Thiêu, Mũi ▲ VN 158-159 J 5
Comunidad o CR 52-53 B 6
Comunidad o YV (AMA) 60-61 H 6
Comunidad o YV (BOL) 60-61 K 4
Comunidad de Madrid ▫ E 98-99 F 4
Čona ~ RUS 118-119 D 5
Cona o VRC 144-145 H 7
Conakry ▫ RG 202-203 D 5
Conakry ★ • RG 202-203 D 5
Conambo, Río ~ EC 64-65 D 3
Conasauga River ~ USA (GA) 284-285 F 2
Conay o RCH 76-77 B 5
Conay, Río ~ RCH 76-77 B 5
Concan o USA (TX) 266-267 H 4
Concarán o RA 78-79 G 2
Concarneau o• F 90-91 F 8
Conceição o BR (AMA) 66-67 G 4
Conceição o BR (PA) 68-69 J 5
Conceiçao, Riachão ~ BR 68-69 H 5
Conceição da Barra o BR 72-73 L 5
Conceiçao das Alagoas o BR 72-73 F 5
Conceicão de Macabu o BR 72-73 K 7
Conceição do Araguaia o BR 68-69 D 6
Conceição do Canindé o BR 68-69 H 5
Conceição do Coité o BR 68-69 J 7
Conceição do Mato Dentro o BR 72-73 J 5
Conceição do Mau o BR 62-63 E 4
Conceicão do Norte o BR 72-73 G 2
Concepción o BOL 70-71 F 5
Concepcion o CO 64-65 F 2
Concepcion o PE 64-65 E 7
Concepción ☆ PY 76-77 J 2
Concepción o RA 76-77 E 4
Concepción ☆ RCH 78-79 C 4
Concepción, Canal ≈ 80 C 5
Concepción, La o EC 64-65 C 1
Concepcion, La o PA 52-53 C 7
Concepcion, La o YV 60-61 F 2
Concepción, Lago ⊂ BOL 70-71 G 5
Concepción, Punta ▲ MEX 50-51 D 4
Concepción, Volcán ▲ NIC 52-53 B 6
Concepcion de Buenos Aires o MEX 52-53 C 2
Concepción del Oro o MEX 50-51 J 5
Concepción del Uruguay o RA 78-79 K 2
Concepción Island ⌒ BS 54-55 H 3
Conception o RP 160-161 D 5
Conceptión, Lago ⊂ BOL 70-71 F 4
Conception, Point ▲ USA (CA) 248-249 D 5
Conception Bay ≈ 38-39 S 5
Conception Bay ≈ CDN 242-243 P 5
Conch o IND 138-139 G 7
Conchal o BR 72-73 G 7
Conchali, Bahía ≈ 76-77 B 6
Conchas o BR 72-73 G 7
Conchas o USA (NM) 256-257 L 3
Conchas, Las o BOL 70-71 H 5
Conchas Lake ⊂ USA (NM) 256-257 L 3
Conchas River ~ USA (NM) 256-257 L 3
Conch Bar o GB 54-55 K 4
Conche o CDN (NFL) 242-243 N 2
Conchi o RCH 76-77 C 2
Concho o USA (AZ) 256-257 F 4
Concho River ~ USA (TX) 266-267 G 2
Concho River, Middle ~ USA (TX) 266-267 F 2
Concho River, North ~ USA (TX) 266-267 G 2
Conchos, Río ~ MEX 50-51 K 5
Conchos, Río ~ MEX 50-51 F 4
Concón o RCH 78-79 D 2
Concón, Punta de ▲ RCH 78-79 D 2
Conconully o USA (WA) 244-245 F 2
Concord o USA (CA) 248-249 C 2
Concord o USA (KY) 276-277 M 2
Concord o USA (NC) 282-283 G 5
Concord o USA (NE) 262-263 K 2
Concord ☆ USA (NH) 278-279 K 5
Concórdia o BR 74-75 D 6
Concordia o MEX 50-51 F 6
Concordia o PE 64-65 E 4
Concordia o RA 76-77 H 6
Concordia o USA (KS) 262-263 J 5
Concordia o USA (MO) 274-275 E 6
Concordia o ZA 220-221 C 4
Concordia, La o MEX 52-53 H 3
Concordia do Pará o BR 68-69 E 2
Concord Point ▲ USA 22-23 M 6
Con Cuông ☆ VN 156-157 D 7
Conda o ANG 216-217 C 5
Conda o USA (ID) 252-253 G 4
Condal, Cañada ~ RA 76-77 F 2
Condamine o AUS 178-179 L 4
Condamine River ~ AUS 178-179 L 4
Côn Đảo ~ VN (Con) 158-159 J 6
Côn Đảo ⌒ VN (Con) 158-159 J 6
Condé o ANG 216-217 C 5
Conde o BR 68-69 K 7
Conde o USA (SD) 260-261 H 1
Condédezi, Rio ~ MOC 218-219 G 2
Condega o NIC 52-53 L 5
Condeixas o BR 62-63 K 6
Conde Loca o ANG 216-217 B 4
Conde Matarazzo o BR 74-75 D 9
Condeúba o BR 72-73 K 3
Condingup o AUS 176-177 G 6
Condobolin o AUS 180-181 J 2
Condom o F 90-91 H 10
Čondon ~ RUS 110-111 V 4
Condon o USA (OR) 244-245 E 5
Condor o CDN (ALB) 232-233 D 3
Cóndor, Cerro el ▲ RA 76-77 C 4
Condor, Cordillera del ▲ PE 64-65 C 4
Cone o USA (TX) 264-265 C 5
Conecuh River ~ USA (AL) 284-285 E 5
Conecuh River ~ USA (AL) 284-285 C 5
Conejo, El o MEX 50-51 D 5
Conejos o USA (CO) 254-255 J 6
Cone Peak ▲ AUS 174-175 G 3
Conesa o RA 78-79 J 2
Conestogo River ~ CDN (ONT) 238-239 E 5
Confluencia o RA 78-79 D 6
Confolens o F 90-91 H 8
Confusion Bay ≈ 38-39 R 3
Confusion Bay ≈ CDN 242-243 N 2
Confuso, Río ~ PY 76-77 H 3
Congaree River ~ USA (SC) 284-285 K 3
Congaree Swamp National Monument ⊥ USA (SC) 284-285 K 3
Congaz o MD 102-103 F 4
Congerenge o MOC 218-219 H 2
Conger Range ▲ CDN 26-27 J 3
Conghua o VRC 156-157 H 5
Congjiang o VRC 156-157 F 4
Congnarauya, Pointe ▲ CDN 36-37 Q 5
Congo o BR 68-69 K 5
Congo ■ RCB 210-211 D 5
Congo ~ RCB 210-211 F 5
Congo Basin = Grande Dépression Centrale ⊥ ZRE 210-211 F 5
Congo Fan ≃ 6-7 K 9
Congonhas o••• BR 72-73 H 6
Congonhas do Norte o BR 72-73 J 5
Congo Town o• BS 54-55 G 2
Congress o CDN (SAS) 232-233 N 6
Congress o USA (AZ) 256-257 C 4
Conguillo los Paraguas, Parque Nacional ⊥ RCH 78-79 D 5
Conhello o RA 78-79 G 4
Conifer o USA (CO) 254-255 K 4
Coniston o AUS 172-173 L 7
Coniston o CDN (ONT) 238-239 E 2
Conitaca o MEX 50-51 F 5
Conjo ~ ANG 216-217 D 5
Conjuboy o AUS 174-175 H 6
Conjuror Bay ⊂ CDN 30-31 K 3
Conkal o MEX 52-53 K 1
Conklin o CDN 32-33 P 4
Conlara, Río ~ RA 78-79 G 2
Conmee o CDN (ONT) 234-235 O 6
Conn o USA (MS) 268-269 K 5
Connaughton, Mount ▲ AUS 172-173 F 7
Conneaut o USA (OH) 280-281 F 2
Conneaut Lake o USA (PA) 280-281 F 2
Conneautville o USA (PA) 280-281 F 2
Connecticut ▫ USA (CT) 280-281 N 2
Connecticut River ~ USA 278-279 J 5
Connecticut River ~ USA (CT) 280-281 O 2
Connell o USA (WA) 244-245 G 4
Connellsville o USA (PA) 280-281 G 3
Connelly, Mount ▲ AUS 172-173 H 3
Connels Lagoon Conservation Reserve ⊥ AUS 174-175 D 6
Conner o RP 160-161 D 4
Conner, Mount ▲ AUS 176-177 L 2
Conne River o CDN (NFL) 242-243 N 5
Conner Prairie • USA (IN) 274-275 N 4
Connersville o USA (IN) 274-275 N 5
Connerville o USA (OK) 264-265 H 4
Conn Lake ⊂ CDN 26-27 O 8
Connor, Mount ▲ AUS 172-173 H 3
Connors o CDN (NB) 240-241 G 3
Connors Pass ▲ USA (NV) 246-247 L 4
Connors Range ▲ AUS 178-179 K 1
Connors River ~ AUS 178-179 K 2
Connorsville o USA (WI) 270-271 F 5
Conoble Lake ⊂ AUS 180-181 H 2
Conodoguinet Creek ~ USA (PA) 280-281 J 3
Čonogol o MAU 148-149 M 5
Cononaco o EC 64-65 E 2
Conover o USA (MI) 270-271 J 4
Conquest o CDN (SAS) 232-233 L 4
Conquet o F 90-91 E 7
Conquista o BOL 70-71 D 2
Conrad o USA (MT) 250-251 H 3
Conrad Rise ≃ 12 B 10
Conran, Cape ▲ AUS 180-181 K 4
Conrana ~ RI 164-165 G 6
Conrich o CDN (ALB) 232-233 E 4
Conroe o USA (TX) 268-269 E 6
Conroe, Lake < USA (TX) 268-269 E 6
Consata, Río ~ BOL 70-71 C 4
Conselheiro Lafaiete o BR 72-73 J 6
Conselho, Ponta do ▲ BR 72-73 L 2
Consett o GB 90-91 G 4
Consolación del Sur o C 54-55 D 3
Consort o CDN (ALB) 232-233 H 4
Constance, Lac de = Bodensee ⊂ CH 92-93 K 5
Constance Bay ≈ 140-141 L 4
Constance Headland ▲ AUS 176-177 G 2
Constance Lake o CDN (ONT) 236-237 D 3
Constancia, Cerro ▲ RCH 70-71 C 7
Constanța ☆ • RO 102-103 F 5
Constantina o BR 74-75 D 6
Constantina o E 98-99 E 6
Constantine ☆ •• DZ 190-191 F 2
Constantine, Cape ▲ USA 22-23 R 3
Constantine, Mount ▲ CDN 20-21 U 6
Constanza o•• DOM 54-55 K 5
Constitución o RCH 78-79 C 3
Constitución de 1857, Parque Nacional ⊥ MEX 50-51 B 1
Consuelo Peak ▲ AUS 178-179 K 3
Consul o BR 70-71 K 3
Consul o CDN (SAS) 232-233 J 6
Consul River ~ CDN 30-31 T 3
Contact o USA (NV) 246-247 L 2
Contagem o BR 72-73 H 5
Contamana o PE 64-65 E 5
Contamana, Sierra ▲ PE 64-65 F 6
Contão o BR 62-63 D 4
Contas, Rio de ~ BR 72-73 L 3
Contendas do Sincorá o BR 72-73 K 2
Continental o USA (AZ) 256-257 E 7
Continental o USA (OH) 280-281 B 2
Contoy, Isla ⌒ MEX 52-53 L 1
Contramaestre o C 54-55 G 4
Contrato, Rio ~ BR 68-69 F 6
Con Trau, Hòn ⌒ VN 158-159 K 4
Contreras, Isla ⌒ RCH 80 C 6
Contuboel o GNB 202-203 C 3
Contumaza o PE 64-65 C 5
Contwoyto Lake ⊂ CDN 30-31 O 3
Conucos, Los o YV 60-61 E 3
Convencion o CO 60-61 E 3
Convento, Cerro ▲ RA 80 F 5
Convento, Montañas de ▲ EC 64-65 C 2
Converse o USA (IN) 274-275 N 4
Converse o USA (LA) 268-269 G 5
Conway o USA (AR) 276-277 C 5
Conway o USA (NH) 278-279 K 5
Conway o USA (SC) 284-285 L 3
Conway o USA (TX) 264-265 C 3
Conway o ZA 220-221 G 5
Conway, Lake ⊂ AUS 178-179 C 5
Conway, Lake < USA (AR) 276-277 C 5
Conway National Park ⊥ AUS 174-175 K 7
Coober Pedy o• AUS 178-179 C 5
Coocoran Lake ⊂ AUS 178-179 J 5
Cooinda Motel o AUS 172-173 L 2
Cook o AUS 176-177 L 5
Cook o USA (MN) 270-271 F 3
Cook, Cape ▲ CDN (BC) 230-231 A 3
Cook, Mount ▲ NZ 182 C 5
Cook, Mount ▲ USA 20-21 U 6
Cook Bay ≈ 16 G 16
Cook Bay ≈ 184 II b 4
Cooke, Mount ▲ AUS (WA) 172-173 E 7
Cooke, Mount ▲ AUS (WA) 176-177 D 6
Cooke City o USA (MT) 250-251 K 6
Cookeville o USA (TN) 276-277 K 4
Cook Forest State Park ⊥ USA (PA) 280-281 G 2
Cookhouse o ZA 220-221 G 6
Cooking Lake o CDN (ALB) 232-233 E 2
Cook Inlet ≈ 22-23 U 3
Cook Islands ⌒ NZ 13 L 4
Cook Lake ⊂ CDN 30-31 P 4
Cook Peninsula ⌣ CDN 26-27 M 4
Cooks o USA (MI) 270-271 M 5
Cooksburg o USA (NY) 278-279 G 6
Cooks Harbour o CDN (NFL) 242-243 N 1
Cookshire o CDN (QUE) 238-239 O 3
Cookstown o CDN (ONT) 238-239 F 4
Cookstown o GB 90-91 D 4
Cook Strait ≈ 182 E 4
Cooktown o•• AUS 174-175 H 4
Cool, Tanjung ▲ RI 166-167 K 6
Coolabah o AUS 178-179 J 6
Cooladdi o AUS 178-179 H 4
Coolah o AUS 178-179 K 6
Coolamon o AUS 180-181 J 3
Coolangatta o AUS 178-179 M 5
Coolgardie o AUS 176-177 F 5
Coolidge o USA (AZ) 256-257 D 6
Coolidge o USA (TX) 266-267 L 2
Coolin o USA (ID) 250-251 C 3
Coolmunda Reservoir < AUS 178-179 L 5
Cooloola National Park ⊥ AUS 178-179 M 4
Coolville o USA (OH) 280-281 E 4
Cooma o AUS 180-181 K 4
Coombes Cove o CDN (NFL) 242-243 N 5
Coomera o AUS 178-179 M 4
Coonabarabran o AUS 178-179 K 6
Coonalpyn o AUS 180-181 E 3
Coonamble o AUS 178-179 K 6
Coonawarra o• AUS 180-181 F 4
Coondapoor o IND 140-141 F 4
Coongan River ~ AUS 172-173 D 6
Coongoola o AUS 178-179 H 4
Coon Rapids o USA (IA) 274-275 D 3
Coon Rapids o USA (MN) 270-271 E 5
Cooper o USA (ME) 278-279 O 4
Cooper o USA (NM) 256-257 M 6
Cooper o USA (TX) 264-265 J 5
Cooper Creek ~ AUS 178-179 F 4
Cooper Creek ~ AUS 178-179 E 5
Cooperfield o USA (OR) 244-245 J 6
Cooper River ~ USA (SC) 284-285 L 3
Coopers Island ⌒ CDN 36-37 T 6
Coopers Mills o USA (ME) 278-279 M 4
Cooper's Town o BS 54-55 G 1
Cooperstown o USA (ND) 258-259 J 4
Cooperstown o USA (NY) 278-279 G 6
Coop Lake ⊂ CDN 30-31 M 5
Coorabie o AUS 176-177 M 5
Coorabulka o AUS 178-179 F 2
Coorada o AUS 178-179 K 3
Coordewandy ▲ AUS 176-177 D 2
Coorong National Park ⊥ AUS 180-181 E 4
Coorow o AUS 176-177 D 4
Cooroy o AUS 178-179 M 4
Coosa o USA (GA) 284-285 E 2
Coosa River ~ USA (AL) 284-285 D 3
Coosawattee River ~ USA (GA) 284-285 F 2
Coosawhatchie River ~ USA (SC) 284-285 J 4
Coos Bay ≈ 40-41 B 4
Coos Bay o USA (OR) 244-245 A 7
Coos Bay ≈ USA 244-245 A 7
Cootamundra o AUS 180-181 K 3
Coover Creek ~ USA (VA) 280-281 D 7
Čop o UA 102-103 C 3
Copa, Cerro ▲ BOL 70-71 C 7
Copacabana o BOL (PAZ) 70-71 C 5
Copacabana o BOL (SAC) 70-71 G 4
Copacabana o CO 60-61 D 4
Copacabana, Península de ⌣ BOL 70-71 C 5
Copahué o RA 78-79 D 4
Copahué, Paso ▲ RCH 78-79 D 4
Copahué, Volcán ▲ RCH 78-79 D 4
Copal Urco o PE 64-65 F 3
Copán ∴ ••• HN 52-53 K 4
Copan o USA (OK) 264-265 J 2
Copan Lake ⊂ USA (OK) 264-265 J 2
Copano Bay ≈ 44-45 J 5
Copano Bay ≈ USA 266-267 K 5
Copán Ruinas o HN 52-53 K 4
Copas o USA (MN) 270-271 F 5
Cope o USA (CO) 254-255 N 4
Copé, El o PA 52-53 D 7
Copeland o USA (ID) 250-251 C 3
Copeland o USA (KS) 262-263 F 7
Copemish o USA (MI) 272-273 D 3
Copenhagen = København ★ •• DK 86-87 F 9
Copere o BOL 70-71 F 6
Copeton Reservoir < AUS 178-179 L 5
Copeyal o YV 60-61 G 2
Copiapó ☆ RCH 76-77 B 4
Copiapó, Río ~ RCH 76-77 B 4
Čopko ~ RUS 108-109 f 7
Čopko ~ RUS 108-109 Z 6
Coporito o YV 60-61 L 3
Coporolo ~ ANG 216-217 B 6
Coposa, Cerro ▲ RCH 70-71 C 7
Coppabella o AUS 178-179 K 1
Coppename Monding, National Reservaat ⊥ SME 62-63 G 2
Coppenamerivier ~ SME 62-63 F 3
Copper o USA (OR) 244-245 B 8
Copperas Cove o USA (TX) 266-267 K 2
Copperbelt ▫ Z 218-219 D 1
Copper Breaks State Park ⊥ • USA (TX) 264-265 E 4
Copper Creek o CDN (BC) 230-231 J 3
Copper Harbor o USA (WI) 270-271 L 3
Coppermine o CDN 30-31 M 2
Coppermine Point ▲ CDN (ONT) 236-237 D 5
Coppermine River ~ CDN 30-31 M 2
Copper Mines • AUS 180-181 H 7
Copperneedle River ~ CDN 30-31 W 4
Copper River ~ USA 20-21 S 5
Copperstown o USA (PA) 280-281 G 3
Coppersville o USA (MI) 272-273 D 4
Copperton o ZA 220-221 F 4
Copton Creek ~ CDN (ALB) 228-229 P 2
Coqên o VRC 144-145 E 5
Coqueiro, Ribeiro ~ BR 70-71 J 5
Coqueiros, Ponta dos ▲ BR 68-69 L 5
Coqui o BR 66-67 E 3
Coqui o CO 60-61 C 5
Coquilhatville = Mbandaka ☆ ZRE 210-211 G 3
Coquille o USA (OR) 244-245 A 7
Coquimatlán o MEX 52-53 C 2
Coquimbo o RCH 76-77 B 5
Coquimbo, Bahía ≈ 76-77 B 5
Corabia o RO 102-103 D 6
Coração de Jesus o BR 72-73 H 4
Coraci-Paraná, Rio ~ BR 68-69 E 3
Coracora o PE 64-65 F 9
Corail o RH 54-55 J 5
Corais, Ilha dos ⌒ BR 74-75 F 5
Coral o CDN (ONT) 236-237 G 2
Coralaque, Río ~ PE 70-71 B 5
Coral Basin ≃ 13 F 4
Coral Bay ≈ 160-161 B 8
Coral Gables o USA (FL) 286-287 J 6
Coral Harbour o CDN 36-37 H 2
Coral Heights o BS 54-55 G 2
Coral Sea ≈ 13 G 4
Coral Springs o USA (FL) 286-287 J 5
Corangamite, Lake ⊂ AUS 180-181 G 5
Coranzuli o RA 76-77 D 2
Corapeake o USA (NC) 282-283 L 4
Cora Trepadeira ~ BR 70-71 K 3
Corazón, El o EC 64-65 C 2
Corberrie o CDN (NS) 240-241 K 6
Corbett Inlet ≈ 30-31 X 4
Corbett National Park ⊥ • IND 138-139 G 5
Corbin o USA (KY) 276-277 L 4
Corby o GB 90-91 G 5
Corcaigh = Cork ☆ IRL 90-91 C 6
Corcoran o USA (CA) 248-249 E 3
Corcovada, Park Nacional ⊥ CR 52-53 C 7
Corcovado o RA 78-79 D 7
Corcovado, Golfo ≈ 78-79 C 7
Corcovado, Volcán ▲ RCH 78-79 C 7
Corcubión o E 98-99 C 3
Corda, Ribeiro ~ BR 68-69 D 5
Corda, Rio ~ BR 68-69 F 5
Cordeiro o BR 72-73 J 7
Cordeiro, Rio ~ BR 68-69 K 5
Cordele o USA (GA) 284-285 G 5
Cordell o USA (OK) 264-265 F 3
Cordilheira o BR 74-75 D 8
Cordilheiras, Serra das ▲ BR 68-69 D 5
Cordillera Cantábrica ▲ E 98-99 D 3
Cordillera Central ▲ E 98-99 E 4
Cordillera Central ▲ RP 160-161 D 4
Cordillera de la Costa ▲ YV 60-61 H 2
Cordillera de los Picachos, Parque Nacional ⊥ CO 60-61 D 6
Cordilleras Range ▲ RP 160-161 E 7
Cordisburgo o BR 72-73 H 5
Córdoba o••• E 98-99 E 6
Córdoba o MEX 52-53 F 2
Córdoba ▫ RA 78-79 G 2
Córdoba ☆ • RA 76-77 E 6
Córdoba, Sierra de ▲ RA 78-79 G 2
Cordobés, Arroyo del ~ ROU 78-79 M 2
Cordobés, Cerro ▲ RA 76-77 C 5
Cordón Alto ⊥ RA 80 F 4
Cordón de las Llarretas ▲ RA 78-79 E 3
Cordon de Puntas Negras ▲ RCH 76-77 D 2
Cordón Seler ▲ RCH 80 D 3
Cordova o USA 20-21 S 6
Cordova o USA (AL) 284-285 C 3
Cordova o USA (IA) 274-275 H 3
Córdova, Península ⌣ RCH 80 D 6
Cordova Bay ≈ 32-33 D 4
Cordova Peak ▲ USA 20-21 S 6
Coreaú, Rio ~ BR 68-69 H 3
Coremas o BR 68-69 K 5
Corey, La o CDN 32-33 P 4
Corfield o AUS 178-179 G 1
Corfu = Kérkira ⌒ GR 100-101 G 5
Corguinho o BR 70-71 K 6
Coria o•• E 98-99 D 5
Coriabo o GUY 62-63 E 2
Coria del Río o E 98-99 D 6
Coribe o BR 72-73 H 2
Corico, Lago ⊂ RCH 78-79 C 5
Coricó, Laguna ⊂ RA 78-79 F 6
Coricudgy, Mount ▲ AUS 180-181 L 2
Co' Rinh, Ngoc ▲ VN 158-159 K 3
Corinna o AUS 180-181 H 6
Corinna o USA (ME) 278-279 M 4
Corinne o CDN (SAS) 232-233 O 5
Corinne o USA (MI) 270-271 N 4
Corinne o USA (UT) 254-255 C 2
Corinth o USA (KY) 276-277 L 2
Corinth o USA (ME) 278-279 N 3
Corinth o USA (MS) 268-269 M 2
Corinto o BR 72-73 H 5
Corinto o CO 60-61 C 6
Corinto o HN 52-53 K 4
Corinto o NIC 52-53 L 5
Corio Bay ≈ 178-179 L 2
Corisco, Baie de ≈ 210-211 B 3

Corisco o Mandyi, Isla de ⌒ GQ 210-211 B 3
Corixa Grande ~ BR 70-71 J 5
Corixão o BR 70-71 J 6
Corixão, Rio ~ BR 70-71 J 6
Cork o AUS 178-179 G 2
Cork ☆ IRL 90-91 C 6
Corleone o I 100-101 D 6
Çorlu ☆ TR 128-129 B 2
Corme e Laxe, Ría de ≈ 98-99 C 3
Cormorant o CDN 34-35 F 3
Cormorant Forest Reserve ⊥ CDN 34-35 F 3
Cormorant Lake ⊖ CDN 34-35 F 3
Čornae, vozero ⊖ BY 94-95 J 5
Čornaja o RUS 88-89 Y 2
Čornaja ~ RUS 88-89 Y 2
Cornate, le ▲ I 100-101 C 3
Corn Creek ~ USA (AZ) 256-257 E 3
Cornelia o USA (GA) 284-285 G 2
Cornelia o ZA 220-221 J 3
Cornelio o MEX 50-51 D 3
Cornélio Procópio o BR 72-73 E 7
Cornelius o USA (NC) 282-283 G 5
Cornelius Grinnell Bay ≈ 36-37 R 3
Cornell o USA (MI) 270-271 L 5
Cornell o USA (WI) 270-271 G 5
Cornell Gletscher ⊂ GRØ 26-27 W 6
Čorne more ≈ 102-103 G 5
Corner Brook o CDN (NFL) 242-243 L 4
Corner Inlet ≈ 180-181 J 5
Corner River ~ CDN (ONT) 236-237 J 2
Corney Bayou ~ USA (LA) 268-269 H 4
Corning o USA (AR) 276-277 E 4
Corning o USA (CA) 246-247 C 4
Corning o USA (IA) 274-275 D 4
Corning o USA (KS) 262-263 K 5
Corning o USA (NY) 278-279 D 6
Cornish, Mount ▲ AUS 172-173 H 6
Cornish Creek ~ AUS 178-179 H 2
Corn Islands = Islas del Maíz ⌒ NIC 52-53 C 5
Čornobyl' o UA 102-103 G 2
Čornomors'ke ☆ UA 102-103 H 5
Cornouaille ∸ F 90-91 E 7
Cornudas o USA (TX) 266-267 B 2
Cornwall o BS 54-55 G 2
Cornwall o CDN (ONT) 238-239 L 3
Cornwall ∸ GB 90-91 E 6
Cornwall Coast ⌣·· GB 90-91 E 6
Cornwallis Island ⌒ CDN 24-25 Y 3
Cornwall Island ⌒ CDN 24-25 Y 2
Čornyj Čeremoš ~ UA 102-103 D 3
Coro ☆··· YV 60-61 G 2
Coro, Golfete de ≈ 60-61 F 2
Coro, Ilha do ⌒ BR 66-67 F 4
Coro, Raudal ~ CO 66-67 B 3
Coroa, Cachoeira de ~ BR 68-69 E 5
Coroatá o BR 68-69 F 4
Corocoro o BOL 70-71 C 5
Coroico o BOL 70-71 D 5
Coroico, Río ~ BOL 70-71 D 4
Corojal, El o C 54-55 E 3
Corolla o USA (NC) 282-283 M 4
Coromandel o BR 72-73 G 5
Coromandel o NZ 182 E 2
Coromandel Coast ⌣ IND 140-141 J 6
Coromandel Peninsula ⌣·· NZ 182 E 2
Coron o RP 160-161 D 7
Corona o USA (CA) 248-249 G 6
Corona o USA (NM) 256-257 K 4
Corona, Cerro ▲ RA 78-79 D 6
Corona, Río ~ MEX 50-51 K 6
Coronach o CDN (SAS) 232-233 N 6
Coronado, Bahía de ≈ 52-53 C 7
Coronado National Monument · USA (AZ) 256-257 E 7
Coronation o CDN (ALB) 232-233 G 3
Coronation Gulf ≈ 24-25 P 6
Coronation Gulf ≈ CDN 24-25 O 6
Coronation Island ⌒ ARK 16 G 32
Coronation Islands ⌒ AUS 172-173 G 3
Coronation Island Wilderness ⊥ USA 32-33 C 4
Coron Bay ≈ 160-161 D 7
Coronda o RA 76-77 G 6
Coronel o RCH 78-79 C 4
Coronel Bogado o PY 76-77 J 4
Coronel Dorrego o RA 78-79 J 5
Coronel Martínez o PY 76-77 J 3
Coronel Moldes o RA 78-79 G 2
Coronel Oviedo ☆ PY 76-77 J 3
Coronel Pringles o RA 78-79 J 4
Coronel Rodolfo Bunge o RA 78-79 J 4
Coronel Sapucaia o BR 76-77 K 2
Coronel Suárez o RA 78-79 J 4
Coronel Vidal o RA 78-79 L 4
Coronel Vivida o BR 74-75 D 5
Coroni Bird Sanctuary ⊥ TT 60-61 L 2
Coron Island ⌒ RP 160-161 D 7
Corowa-Wahgunyah o AUS 180-181 J 4
Corozal o BH 52-53 K 2
Corozal o YV 60-61 K 4
Corozo, El o YV 60-61 J 3
Corpus Christi o USA (TX) 266-267 K 6
Corpus Christi, Lake ⊖ USA (TX) 266-267 K 5
Corpus Christi Bay ≈ 44-45 J 6
Corpus Christi Bay ≈ USA 266-267 K 6
Corque o BOL 70-71 D 6
Corral o RCH 78-79 C 5
Corral o USA (ID) 252-253 D 3
Corral de Bustos o RA 78-79 H 2
Corralejo o E 188-189 E 6
Corrales o CO 60-61 E 5
Corrales, Los (Los Corralles de Buelna) o E 98-99 E 3
Corralillo o C 54-55 E 3
Corrane o MOC 218-219 K 2
Correctionville o USA (IA) 274-275 C 2
Corregidor Island ⌒ RP 160-161 D 5
Córrego do Ouro o BR 72-73 E 4
Córrego Novo o BR 68-69 E 4
Correia Pinto o BR 74-75 E 6
Corrente o BR 68-69 F 7
Corrente, Rio ~ BR 68-69 F 5
Corrente, Rio ~ BR 68-69 G 4
Corrente, Rio ~ BR 72-73 E 5
Corrente, Rio ~ BR 72-73 J 2
Correntes o BR 68-69 K 6
Correntes, Riachão ~ BR 68-69 H 4
Correntina o BR 72-73 H 2
Correntinho o BR 68-69 F 4
Correntoso o RA 78-79 D 6
Corrib, Lough ⊖ IRL 90-91 C 5
Corrida de Cori ▲ RA 76-77 C 3
Corrie Downs o AUS 178-179 F 2
Corrientes ◘ RA 76-77 H 5
Corrientes ☆ RA 76-77 H 4
Corrientes, Bahía de ≈ 54-55 C 4
Corrientes, Cabo ▲ C 54-55 C 4
Corrientes, Cabo ▲ CO 60-61 C 5
Corrientes, Cabo ▲ MEX 52-53 B 1
Corrientes, Río ~ PE 64-65 E 3
Corrientes, Río ~ RA 76-77 H 5
Corrigan o USA (TX) 268-269 F 5
Corrigin o AUS 176-177 D 6
Corry o USA (PA) 280-281 G 2
Corryong o AUS 180-181 J 4
Corse ◘ F 98-99 M 3
Corse, Cap ▲ F 98-99 M 3
Corsica o USA (SD) 260-261 H 3
Corsica = Corse ⌒ F 98-99 M 4
Corsicana o USA (TX) 264-265 H 6
Cortadera, La o RA 78-79 E 4
Cortaderal, Cerro ▲ RCH 76-77 C 3
Cortaderas, Pampa de ∸ PE 70-71 A 5
Cortaro o USA (AZ) 256-257 D 6
Corte o· F 98-99 M 3
Cortegana o E 98-99 D 6
Cortez o USA (CO) 254-255 G 6
Cortez Gold Mine o USA (NV) 246-247 J 3
Cortina d'Ampezzo o I 100-101 D 1
Čortkiv ☆ UA 102-103 D 3
Cortland o USA (NE) 262-263 K 4
Cortland o USA (NY) 278-279 E 6
Cortona o· I 100-101 C 3
Coruage, Cachoeira ~ BR 68-69 B 4
Corubal, Rio ~ GNB 202-203 C 4
Coruche o P 98-99 C 5
Çoruh Nehri ~ TR 128-129 J 2
Çoruh Neri ~ TR 128-129 J 2
Çorum ☆· TR 128-129 F 2
Coruma o BR 62-63 J 6
Corumbá o BR 70-71 J 6
Corumba, Rio ~ BR 72-73 G 4
Corumbá de Goiás o BR 72-73 F 3
Corumbaíba o BR 72-73 F 5
Corumbaú, Ponta de ▲ BR 72-73 L 4
Corumbiara Antigo, Rio ~ BR 70-71 G 3
Coruña, A ☆·· E 98-99 C 3
Corunna o CDN (ONT) 238-239 C 6
Corunna North ▲ AUS 180-181 D 2
Čoruoda ~ RUS 118-119 K 7
Corupá o BR 74-75 F 6
Coruto, Laguna ⊖ BOL 76-77 D 2
Corutuba, Rio ~ BR 72-73 J 3
Corvallis o USA (OR) 244-245 B 6
Corvette, Rivière ~ CDN 38-39 G 2
Corwen o GB 90-91 F 5
Corwin o USA 20-21 H 2
Corwin, Cape ▲ USA 22-23 O 3
Cory Bay ≈ 36-37 M 2
Corydon o USA (IA) 274-275 E 4
Corydon o USA (IN) 274-275 M 6
Cosa · I 100-101 C 3
Cosamaloapan o MEX 52-53 G 2
Cosapa o BOL 70-71 C 6
Cosapilla o RCH 70-71 C 5
Coscaya o RCH 70-71 C 6
Cosenza o I 100-101 F 5
Coșești o RO 102-103 D 5
Coshocton o USA (OH) 280-281 E 3
Cosigüina, Punta ▲ NIC 52-53 L 5
Cosigüina, Volcán ▲ NIC 52-53 L 5
Cosmoledo Atoll ∸ SY 222-223 E 2
Cosmo Newbery Aboriginal Land X AUS 176-177 G 4
Cosmo Newbery Mission X AUS 176-177 G 4
Cosmópolis o BR 72-73 G 7
Cosmos o USA (MN) 270-271 D 6
Cosne-Cours-sur-Loire o F 90-91 J 8
Cosoleacaque o MEX 52-53 G 2
Cosos, Cordillera de la ▲ RCH 78-79 C 4
Costa, La o MEX 52-53 J 1
Costa, Ponta do ▲ BR 62-63 J 3
Costa Blanca ⌣ E 98-99 G 6
Costa Brava ⌣ E 98-99 J 4
Costa da Cadeia o BR 74-75 E 7
Costa Daurada ⌣ E 98-99 H 4
Costa de Araujo o RA 78-79 E 2
Costa de la Luz ⌣ E 98-99 D 6
Costa del Sol ⌣ E 98-99 E 6
Costa de Prata ⌣ P 98-99 C 5
Costa Island, La ⌒ USA (FL) 286-287 G 5
Costa Marques o BR 70-71 E 3
Costa Rica o BR 72-73 D 5
Costa Rica o C 54-55 H 4
Costa Rica ■ CR 52-53 B 7
Costa Vasca ⌣ E 98-99 F 3
Costa Verde ⌣ E 98-99 D 3
Costera del Golfo, Llanura ⌣ MEX 50-51 K 5
Costera del Pacífico, Llanura ⌣ MEX 50-51 D 3
Costești o MD 102-103 E 4
Costești o RO 102-103 D 5
Costilla o USA (NM) 256-257 K 2
Cota o CO 60-61 D 5
Cotabambas o PE 64-65 F 8
Cotabato City ☆ RP 160-161 F 9
Cotacachi, Cerro ▲ EC 64-65 C 1
Cotacachi-Cayapas, Reserva Ecológica ⊥ EC 64-65 C 1
Cotacajes, Río ~ BOL 70-71 D 5
Cotagaita o BOL 70-71 E 7
Cotahuasi o PE 64-65 F 9
Cotahuasi, Río ~ PE 64-65 F 9
Cotaxe, Rio ~ BR 72-73 K 5
Cotazar o MEX 52-53 D 1
Coteau des Prairies ▲ USA (SD) 260-261 J 1
Coteau du Missouri ▲ USA (ND) 258-259 F 3
Coteau Hills ▲ CDN (SAS) 232-233 L 4
Côteaux o RH 54-55 H 5
Côte d'Azur ⌣· F 90-91 L 10
Côte d'Ivoire = Côte-d'Ivoire ■ CI 202-203 G 5
Cotejipe o BR 72-73 H 2
Cote Nord ∸ CDN 38-39 L 3
Cotentin ∸ F 90-91 G 7
Côtes de Fer o RH 54-55 J 5
Coti, Rio ~ BR 66-67 E 7
Cotia o BR 72-73 G 7
Cotia, Rio ~ BR 66-67 E 7
Cotija de la Paz o MEX 52-53 C 2
Cotingo, Rio ~ BR 62-63 D 3
Coto de Doñana, Parque Nacional ⊥ E 98-99 D 6
Cotonou ☆ DY 204-205 E 5
Cotopaxi o USA (CO) 254-255 K 5
Cotopaxi, Volcán ▲ EC 64-65 C 2
Cotorro o C 54-55 D 3
Cotovelo, Corredeira do ~ BR 66-67 H 6
Cotronei o I 100-101 F 5
Cottage Grove o USA (MN) 270-271 F 6
Cottage Grove o USA (OR) 244-245 B 7
Cottageville o USA (SC) 284-285 K 4
Cottar's Mara Camp o EAK 212-213 E 4
Cottbus o D 92-93 N 3
Cotter o USA (AR) 276-277 C 4
Cottica, Mont ▲ F 62-63 G 4
Cotton o USA (MN) 270-271 F 3
Cottonbush Creek ~ AUS 178-179 E 2
Cottondale o USA (FL) 286-287 D 1
Cotton Draw ~ USA (TX) 266-267 C 2
Cotton Plant o USA (AR) 276-277 D 5
Cottonport o USA (LA) 268-269 H 6
Cotton Valley o USA (LA) 268-269 G 4
Cottonwood o CDN (BC) 228-229 M 3
Cottonwood o USA (AL) 284-285 E 5
Cottonwood o USA (AZ) 256-257 C 4
Cottonwood o USA (CA) 246-247 C 3
Cottonwood o USA (ID) 250-251 C 5
Cottonwood o USA (SD) 260-261 E 3
Cottonwood Cove o USA (NV) 248-249 K 4
Cottonwood Creek ~ USA (MT) 250-251 H 3
Cottonwood Creek ~ USA (UT) 254-255 F 6
Cottonwood Falls o USA (KS) 262-263 K 6
Cottonwood River ~ USA (KS) 262-263 K 6
Cottonwood River ~ USA (MN) 270-271 C 6
Cottonwood Wash ~ USA (AZ) 256-257 E 3
Cotuhe, Río ~ PE 66-67 B 4
Cotui ☆ DOM 54-55 K 5
Cotulla o USA (TX) 266-267 H 5
Couchman Range ▲ AUS 172-173 H 3
Coudersport o USA (PA) 280-281 H 2
Coudres, Île aux ⌒ CDN (QUE) 240-241 E 3
Couëron o F 90-91 G 8
Cougar o USA (CA) 246-247 C 2
Couhé o F 90-91 H 8
Coulee o USA (ND) 258-259 F 3
Coulee City o USA (WA) 244-245 F 3
Coulee Dam o USA (WA) 244-245 G 3
Coulman Island ⌒ ARK 16 F 18
Couloir 1 < DZ 190-191 G 7
Coulomb Point ▲ AUS 172-173 F 4
Coulommiers o F 90-91 J 7
Coulonge, Rivière ~ CDN (QUE) 238-239 J 2
Coulta o AUS 180-181 C 3
Coulterville o USA (CA) 248-249 D 2
Coulterville o USA (IL) 274-275 J 6
Council o USA (AK) 20-21 J 4
Council o USA (ID) 252-253 B 2
Council Bluffs o USA (IA) 274-275 C 3
Council Grove o USA (KS) 262-263 K 6
Council Grove Lake ⊖ USA (KS) 262-263 K 6
Council Hill o USA (OK) 264-265 J 3
Counselors o USA (NM) 256-257 H 2
Countess o CDN (ALB) 232-233 F 5
Country Force Base Suffield xx CDN (ALB) 232-233 H 5
Country Harbour ≈ CDN 240-241 O 5
Coupeville o USA (WA) 244-245 C 2
Coupland o USA (TX) 266-267 K 3
Courageous Lake ⊖ CDN 30-31 O 4
Courantyne ~ GUY 62-63 F 4
Courmayeur o I 100-101 A 2
Cours, Cours-sur-Loire- o F 90-91 J 8
Court o CDN (SAS) 232-233 J 4
Courtenay o CDN (BC) 230-231 E 4
Courtenay o USA (ND) 258-259 J 4
Courtis River ~ CDN 24-25 c 7
Courtright o CDN (ONT) 238-239 C 6
Courval o CDN (SAS) 232-233 M 5
Coushatta o USA (LA) 268-269 G 4
Coushatta Indian Reservation, & Alabama X USA (TX) 268-269 F 6
Coutances o F 90-91 G 7
Couto de Magalhães, Rio ~ BR 72-73 D 2
Couto de Magelhães de Minas o BR 72-73 J 5
Coutras o F 90-91 G 9
Coutts o CDN (ALB) 232-233 G 6
Couture, Lac ⊖ CDN 36-37 M 4
Cova Figueira o CV 202-203 B 6
Covè o DY 204-205 E 5
Cove o USA (AR) 276-277 A 6
Cove Fort o USA (UT) 254-255 C 5
Cove Island ⌒ CDN (ONT) 238-239 D 3
Covelo o USA (CA) 246-247 B 4
Coventry o GB 90-91 G 5
Coventry Lake ⊖ CDN 30-31 R 5
Cove Palisades State Park, The ⊥· USA (OR) 244-245 D 6
Covered Wells o USA (AZ) 256-257 C 6
Covilhã o P 98-99 D 4
Covington o USA (GA) 284-285 G 3
Covington o USA (IN) 274-275 L 4
Covington o USA (KY) 276-277 L 1
Covington o USA (LA) 268-269 K 6
Covington o USA (MI) 270-271 K 4
Covington o USA (OH) 280-281 B 3
Covington o USA (OK) 264-265 G 2
Covington o USA (TN) 276-277 F 5
Covington o USA (VA) 280-281 F 6
Covunco, Arroyo ~ RA 78-79 E 5
Cowal, Lake ⊖ AUS 180-181 J 2
Cowal Creek X AUS 174-175 G 2
Cowan o CDN (MAN) 234-235 C 2
Cowan o USA (TN) 276-277 K 5
Cowan, Cerro ▲ EC 64-65 B 10
Cowan, Lake ⊖ AUS 176-177 G 5
Cowan Downs o AUS 174-175 F 6
Cowan Hill ▲ AUS 176-177 F 5
Cowan Lake ⊖ USA (OH) 280-281 C 4
Cowansville o CDN (QUE) 238-239 N 3
Coward o USA (SC) 284-285 L 3
Coward Springs o AUS 178-179 D 5
Cow Bay o CDN (NS) 240-241 M 6
Cowboy Pass ▲ USA (UT) 254-255 B 4
Cowcowing Lakes ⊖ AUS 176-177 D 5
Cow Creek o USA (WY) 252-253 O 3
Cow Creek ~ USA (WA) 244-245 G 4
Cowden o USA (IL) 274-275 K 5
Cowdrey o USA (CO) 254-255 J 3
Cowell o AUS 180-181 D 2
Cow Head o CDN (NFL) 242-243 L 3
Cowhouse Creek ~ USA (TX) 266-267 K 2
Cowichan Lake ⊖ CDN (BC) 230-231 E 5
Cowie Point ▲ CDN 24-25 c 7
Cowles o USA (NM) 256-257 K 3
Cowley o CDN (ALB) 232-233 D 6
Cowlic o USA (AZ) 256-257 C 7
Cowlitz River ~ USA (WA) 244-245 C 4
Cowpasture River ~ USA (VA) 280-281 G 5
Cowpens o USA (SC) 284-285 J 1
Cowra o AUS 180-181 K 2
Cowval ~ GUY 62-63 F 4
Cox o USA (OH) 280-281 D 4
Coxilha de Santana ▲ BR 76-77 J 5
Coxim o BR 70-71 K 6
Cox Island ⌒ CDN 36-37 K 5
Cox River ~ AUS 174-175 C 4
Cox's Bazar o· BD 142-143 H 5
Cox's Cove o CDN (NFL) 242-243 K 3
Coxs Creek ~ AUS 178-179 K 6
Coyaguaima, Cerro ▲ RA 76-77 D 2
Coyah o RG 202-203 D 5
Coyaima o CO 60-61 D 6
Coyame o MEX 50-51 G 3
Coyanosa Draw ~ USA (TX) 266-267 D 3
Coy City o USA (TX) 266-267 J 5
Coyoacan o MEX 52-53 E 2
Coyolate, Río ~ GCA 52-53 J 4
Coyolito o HN 52-53 L 5
Coyote o USA (NM) 256-257 K 5
Coyote o USA (NM) 256-257 J 2
Coyote, Bahía ≈ 50-51 D 5
Coyote, Río ~ MEX 50-51 C 2
Coyotitán o MEX 50-51 F 6
Coyte, El o RA 80 E 2
Coyuca de Benítez o MEX 52-53 D 3
Cozad o USA (NE) 262-263 G 4
Cozes o F 90-91 G 9
Cozumel o· MEX 52-53 L 1
Cozumel, Isla del ⌒·· MEX 52-53 L 1
Crab Orchard o USA (TN) 282-283 C 5
Crab Orchard Lake ⊖ USA (IL) 276-277 F 3
Crabwood Creek o GUY 62-63 F 3
Cracow o AUS 178-179 L 3
Cracroft Island ⌒ CDN (BC) 230-231 D 3
Craddock o CDN (ALB) 232-233 F 6
Cradle Mountain Lake St. Clair National Park ⊥ AUS 180-181 H 6
Cradle Valley o AUS 180-181 H 6
Cradock o AUS 180-181 E 2
Cradock o ZA 220-221 G 6
Craig o USA (AK) 32-33 D 4
Craig o USA (CO) 254-255 H 3
Craig o USA (FL) 286-287 J 7
Craig o USA (MS) 268-269 K 4
Craig Creek ~ USA (VA) 280-281 F 6
Craigellachie o CDN (BC) 230-231 L 3
Craigend o CDN 32-33 P 4
Craig Harbour o CDN 24-25 f 3
Craigie o AUS 174-175 H 6
Craigieburn o AUS 180-181 H 4
Craigmont o USA (ID) 250-251 C 5
Craigmore o CDN (NS) 240-241 O 5
Craigmyle o CDN (ALB) 232-233 F 4
Craignure o GB 90-91 E 4
Craig Pass ▲ USA (WY) 252-253 H 2
Craigsville o USA (WV) 280-281 F 5
Craik o CDN (SAS) 232-233 N 4
Craiova ☆· RO 102-103 C 5
Cramond o ZA 220-221 E 3
Cranberry Junction o CDN 32-33 F 4
Cranberry Lake o USA (NY) 278-279 G 4
Cranberry Portage o CDN 34-35 F 3
Cranbourne o AUS 180-181 H 5
Cranbrook o AUS 176-177 D 7
Cranbrook o CDN (BC) 230-231 O 4
Crandall o CDN (MAN) 234-235 C 4
Crandon o USA (WI) 270-271 K 5
Crane o USA (MO) 276-277 B 4
Crane o USA (OR) 244-245 G 7
Crane o USA (TX) 266-267 E 2
Crane Creek State Park ⊥ USA (OH) 280-281 C 2
Crane Lake o CDN (SAS) 232-233 J 5
Crane Lake o USA (MN) 270-271 F 2
Crane Lake ⊖ USA (IL) 274-275 H 4
Crane River o CDN (MAN) 234-235 D 3
Crane Valley o CDN (SAS) 232-233 N 6
Cranfills Gap o USA (TX) 266-267 K 2
Cranford o CDN (ALB) 232-233 F 6
Cranston o USA (RI) 278-279 K 7
Cranstown, Kap ▲ GRØ 26-27 X 8
Cranswick River ~ CDN 20-21 Y 4
Crapaud o CDN (PEI) 240-241 M 4
Crary Mountains ▲ ARK 16 F 25
Crasna ~ RO 102-103 C 4
Crater Lake o USA (OR) 244-245 C 8
Crater Lake ·· WAN 204-205 K 3
Crater Lake National Monument ∴ USA (OR) 244-245 C 8
Crater Lake National Park ⊥·· USA (OR) 244-245 C 8
Crater Mountain ▲ USA 20-21 M 5
Crater of Diamonds State Park ∴· USA (AR) 276-277 B 6
Craters of the Moon National Monument ∴ USA (ID) 252-253 E 3
Cratéus o BR 68-69 H 4
Crati ~ I 100-101 F 5
Crato o BR 68-69 J 5
Crauford, Cape ▲ CDN 24-25 e 4
Cravari ou Curucuinazá, Rio ~ BR 70-71 J 3
Craven o CDN (SAS) 232-233 O 5
Cravo Norte o CO 60-61 F 4
Crawford o USA (CO) 254-255 H 5
Crawford o USA (GA) 284-285 G 3
Crawford o USA (NE) 262-263 C 2
Crawford o USA (TX) 266-267 K 2
Crawford Bay o CDN (BC) 230-231 N 4
Crawfordsville o USA (IN) 274-275 M 4
Crawley o USA (WV) 280-281 F 6
Crazy Peak ▲ USA (MT) 250-251 J 5
Creede o USA (CO) 254-255 J 6
Creedmoor o USA (NC) 282-283 J 4
Creek Town o WAN 204-205 H 6
Creel o· MEX 50-51 F 4
Cree Lake ⊖ CDN 34-35 C 2
Creelman o CDN (SAS) 232-233 P 6
Creen Lake ⊖ CDN 34-35 C 3
Creighton o USA (NE) 262-263 J 2
Creighton o USA (SD) 260-261 D 2
Creil o F 90-91 J 7
Cremona o CDN (ALB) 232-233 D 4
Cremona ☆ I 100-101 C 2
Crenshaw o USA (MS) 268-269 K 2
Creola o USA (AL) 284-285 B 6
Creole o USA (LA) 268-269 G 7
Crepori, Rio ~ BR 66-67 J 6
Cres o HR 100-101 E 2
Cres ∸ HR 100-101 E 2
Cresbard o USA (SD) 260-261 H 1
Crescent o USA (OK) 264-265 G 3
Crescent o USA (OR) 244-245 D 7
Crescent, La o USA (MN) 270-271 G 7
Crescent City o USA (CA) 246-247 A 2
Crescent City o USA (FL) 286-287 H 2
Crescent Group = Yongle Qundao ⌒ VRC 158-159 L 2
Crescent Head o AUS 178-179 M 6
Crescent Junction o USA (UT) 254-255 F 5
Crescent Lake o CDN (SAS) 232-233 Q 5
Crescent Lake o USA (OR) 244-245 D 7
Crescent Lake ⊖ USA (FL) 286-287 H 2
Crescent Lake National Wildlife Refuge ⊥ USA (NE) 262-263 D 3
Crescent Valley o USA (NV) 246-247 J 3
Cresco o USA (IA) 274-275 F 1
Crespo o RA 78-79 J 2
Cresson o USA (TX) 264-265 G 6
Crest o F 90-91 K 9
Crested Butte o USA (CO) 254-255 J 5
Crestline o USA (CA) 248-249 G 5
Crestomere o CDN (ALB) 232-233 E 3
Creston o CDN (BC) 230-231 N 4
Creston o USA (CA) 248-249 D 4
Creston o USA (IA) 274-275 D 3
Creston o USA (MT) 250-251 E 3
Creston o USA (WY) 252-253 L 5
Crestón, Cerro ▲ RA 76-77 E 3
Crestview o USA (FL) 286-287 C 1
Crestwynd o CDN (SAS) 232-233 N 5
Creswell o USA (OR) 244-245 B 7
Creswell Bay ≈ 24-25 Z 4
Creswell Downs o AUS 174-175 C 5
Crete o USA (NE) 262-263 K 4
Crete = Kriti ⌒ GR 100-101 K 7
Crete, Sea of = Kritiko Pélagos ≈ GR 100-101 J 6
Creus, Cap de ▲ E 98-99 J 3
Creuse ~ F 90-91 J 8
Crewe o GB 90-91 F 5
Crewe o USA (VA) 280-281 H 6
Criaba, Rio ~ BR 70-71 J 4
Crichton o CDN (SAS) 232-233 L 6
Criciúma o BR 74-75 F 7
Crieff o GB 90-91 F 3
Crikvenica o HR 100-101 E 2
Crilly o CDN (ONT) 234-235 L 6
Crimea = Krym, Respublika ◘ UA 102-103 H 5
Crimea = Kryms'kyj pivostriv ⌣ UA 102-103 H 5
Criminosa, Cachoeira ~ BR 62-63 D 6
Criminosa, Cachoeira ~ BR 70-71 E 2
Crimson Cliffs ▲ GRØ 26-27 R 5
Crimson Lake Provincial Park ⊥ CDN (ALB) 232-233 C 3
Criolla, Cerro la ▲ RA 80 E 5
Cripple o USA 20-21 M 5
Cripple Creek o USA (CO) 254-255 K 5
Criș, Chișineu- o RO 102-103 B 4
Crisfield o USA (MD) 280-281 L 6
Crisóstomo, Ribeiro ~ BR 68-69 C 7
Crispín, El o RA 76-77 F 6
Cristais, Serra dos ▲ BR 72-73 G 4
Cristal, Monts de ▲ G 210-211 C 3
Cristalândia o BR 68-69 D 7
Cristalina o BR 72-73 G 4
Cristalino, Rio ~ BR 66-67 K 7
Cristalino, Rio ~ BR 72-73 E 2
Cristiano Muerto, Arroyo ~ RA 78-79 K 5
Cristianópolis o BR 72-73 F 4
Cristianos, Los o E 188-189 C 6
Cristo, El o YV 60-61 K 4
Cristóbal, Punta ▲ EC 64-65 B 10
Cristóbal Cólon, Pico ▲·· CO 60-61 E 2
Cristoffel, National Reservaat ⊥ NL 60-61 G 1
Cristópolis o BR 72-73 H 2
Cristovão Pereira, Ponta ▲ BR 74-75 E 8
Criterion, Cerro ▲ PE 64-65 E 9
Criterion Pass ▲ USA (OR) 244-245 D 5
Crixás o BR 72-73 F 3
Crixás, Rio ~ BR 68-69 D 7
Crixas Açu, Rio ~ BR 72-73 E 2
Crixas Mirim, Rio ~ BR 72-73 E 2
Crna gora ▲ MK 100-101 H 3
Crni vrh ▲ BIH 100-101 F 2
Croajingolong National Park ⊥ AUS 180-181 K 4
Croatá o BR 68-69 H 4
Croatan Sound ≈ USA 282-283 M 5
Croatia = Hrvatska ■ HR 100-101 E 2
Croche, Rivière ~ CDN (QUE) 240-241 C 3
Crocker o USA (SD) 260-261 J 1
Crocker, Banjaran ▲ MAL 160-161 A 10
Crocker Range National Park ⊥ MAL 160-161 B 10
Crockett o USA (TX) 268-269 E 5
Crocodile Camp o EAK 212-213 G 5
Crocodile Farm · AUS 172-173 K 2
Crocodiles · BF 202-203 J 3
Crofton o USA (NE) 262-263 J 2
Croher River ~ CDN 24-25 M 6
Croix, Lac à la ⊖ CDN 38-39 J 3
Croix des Bouquets o RH 54-55 J 5
Croix-de-Vie, Saint-Gilles- o F 90-91 G 8
Croker, Cape ▲ AUS 172-173 L 1
Croker Bay ≈ 24-25 e 3
Croker Island ⌒ AUS 172-173 L 1
Cromer o CDN (MAN) 234-235 B 5
Cromwell o CDN (MAN) 234-235 G 4
Cromwell o NZ 182 B 6
Cromwell o USA (MN) 270-271 F 4
Crông Kno ~ VN 158-159 K 4
Cronin, Mount ▲ CDN (BC) 228-229 H 2
Crook o USA (CO) 254-255 N 3
Crooked Creek o USA 20-21 L 6
Crooked Creek ~ USA (KS) 262-263 F 7
Crooked Island ⌒ BS 54-55 H 3
Crooked Island ⌒ USA 22-23 Q 3
Crooked Island ⌒ USA (FL) 286-287 D 2
Crooked Island Passage ≈ 54-55 H 3
Crooked Lake ⊖ CDN 24-25 E 6
Crooked River o CDN (SAS) 232-233 P 3
Crooked River ~ CDN (BC) 228-229 M 2
Crooked River ~ USA (OR) 244-245 E 6
Crooks Inlet ≈ 36-37 O 3
Crookston o USA (MN) 270-271 B 3
Crookston o USA (NE) 262-263 F 2
Crooksville o USA (OH) 280-281 D 4
Crookwell o AUS 180-181 K 3
Croppa Creek ~ AUS 178-179 L 5
Croque o CDN (NFL) 242-243 N 1
Crosby o CDN (ONT) 238-239 J 4
Crosby o USA (MN) 270-271 E 4
Crosby o USA (MS) 268-269 J 5
Crosby o USA (ND) 258-259 D 3
Crosbyton o USA (TX) 264-265 C 5
Cross o USA (SC) 284-285 K 3
Cross o USA (TX) 266-267 J 5
Cross, Cape = Kaap Kruis ▲ NAM 216-217 B 10
Cross Anchor o USA (SC) 284-285 J 2
Cross City o USA (FL) 286-287 F 2
Crosse, La o USA (WA) 244-245 H 4
Crossett o USA (AR) 276-277 D 7
Crossfield o CDN (ALB) 232-233 D 4
Crosshill o CDN (ONT) 238-239 E 5
Cross Hill o USA (SC) 284-285 J 2
Cross Lake o CDN (MAN) 34-35 H 3
Cross Lake ⊖ CDN (MAN) 34-35 H 3
Cross Lake o USA (MN) 270-271 D 4
Cross Lake < USA (LA) 268-269 G 4
Crossley Lakes ⊖ CDN 20-21 a 2
Crossman Peak ▲ USA (AZ) 256-257 A 4
Cross Plains o USA (TX) 264-265 E 6
Cross River ◘ WAN 204-205 H 5
Cross River ~ WAN 204-205 H 6
Crossroads o USA (NM) 256-257 M 5
Cross Roads o USA (TX) 264-265 J 6
Cross Sound ≈ USA 32-33 B 2
Cross Village o USA (MI) 272-273 D 2
Crossville o USA (AL) 284-285 E 2
Crossville o USA (TN) 276-277 K 5
Crosswind Lake ⊖ USA 20-21 S 5
Croswell o USA (MI) 272-273 G 4
Croton Creek ~ USA (TX) 264-265 D 5
Crotone o I 100-101 F 5
Crouse o CDN (NFL) 242-243 N 2
Crow Agency o USA (MT) 250-251 M 6
Crow Creek ~ USA (CO) 254-255 L 3
Crow Creek Indian Reservation X USA (SD) 260-261 G 2
Crowder Lake State Park ⊥· USA (OK) 264-265 F 3
Crowdy Bay National Park ⊥ AUS 178-179 M 6
Crowell o USA (TX) 264-265 E 5
Crowe River ~ CDN (ONT) 238-239 H 4
Crowfoot o CDN (ALB) 232-233 F 5
Crowfoot Creek ~ CDN (ALB) 232-233 F 5
Crowheart o USA (WY) 252-253 J 3
Crow Indian Reservation X USA (MT) 250-251 L 6
Crow Lake o CDN (ONT) 234-235 K 5
Crowl Creek ~ AUS 180-181 H 2
Crowley o USA (CO) 254-255 M 5
Crowley o USA (LA) 268-269 H 6
Crowley, Lake ⊖ USA (CA) 248-249 F 2
Crowley Ridge ▲ USA (AR) 276-277 E 5
Crown Island ⌒ PNG 183 D 3
Crown Point o USA (IN) 274-275 L 3
Crownpoint o USA (NM) 256-257 G 3
Crown Prince Christian Land = Kronprins Christian Land ∸ GRØ 26-27 q 3
Crown Prince Frederik Island ⌒ CDN 24-25 c 6
Crown Prince Range ▲ PNG 184 I b 2
Crow River ~ CDN 30-31 G 6
Crows o USA (AR) 276-277 C 6
Crows Nest o AUS 178-179 M 4
Crowsnest Pass ▲ CDN (BC) 230-231 P 4
Croydon o AUS 174-175 G 6
Croydon o SD 220-221 K 3
Crozet, Îles ⌒ F 9 J 10
Crozier Channel ≈ 24-25 M 3
Crozon o F 90-91 E 7
Cruce, El o GCA 52-53 K 3
Cruce de la Jagua o DOM 54-55 L 5
Crucero o PE 70-71 B 4
Crucero, El o MEX 50-51 B 3
Crucero, El o YV 60-61 J 3
Cruces o C 54-55 E 3
Cruces, Las o MEX 52-53 H 3
Cruces, Las o USA (NM) 256-257 J 6
Cruces, Punta ▲ CO 60-61 C 4
Crucetillas, Puerto de las ▲ E 98-99 F 5
Crucita o EC 64-65 B 2
Cruger o USA (MS) 268-269 K 3
Cruillas o MEX 50-51 K 5
Crump o USA (MI) 272-273 E 4
Crump Lake ⊖ USA (OR) 244-245 F 8
Cruz, Bahía ≈ 80 H 2
Cruz, Cabo ▲ C 54-55 G 5
Cruz, Ilha ⌒ BR 72-73 L 3
Cruz, La o BOL (SAC) 70-71 F 5
Cruz, La o BOL (SAC) 70-71 F 4
Cruz, La o CR 52-53 B 6
Cruz, La o MEX (SIN) 50-51 F 6
Cruz, La o MEX (TAM) 50-51 L 6
Cruz, La o RA 78-79 G 2
Cruz Alta o BR 74-75 D 7
Cruz Bay o USA (VI) 286-287 R 2
Cruz de Elorza o MEX 50-51 J 6
Cruz del Eje o RA 76-77 E 6
Cruz de Loreto, La o MEX 52-53 B 2
Cruz de Taratara, La o YV 60-61 G 2
Cruzeiro o BR 72-73 H 7
Cruzeiro o MOC 218-219 H 5
Cruzeiro d'Oeste o BR 72-73 D 7
Cruzeiro do Nordeste o BR 68-69 K 6
Cruzeiro do Sul o BR 64-65 F 5
Cruzen Island ⌒ ARK 16 F 23
Cruzes, Corredeira das ~ BR 70-71 J 4
Cruz Grande o MEX 52-53 E 3
Cruzinha da Garca o CV 202-203 B 5
Cruz Machado o BR 74-75 E 6
Crysdale, Mount ▲ CDN 32-33 J 4
Crystal o USA (OK) 264-265 J 4
Crystal Bay ≈ 48-49 G 5
Crystal Bay ≈ USA 286-287 G 3
Crystal Brook o AUS 180-181 E 2
Crystal Cave ∴ USA (WI) 270-271 F 6
Crystal City o CDN (MAN) 234-235 E 5
Crystal City o USA (TX) 266-267 H 5
Crystal Creek National Park ⊥ AUS 174-175 J 6
Crystal Falls o USA (MI) 270-271 K 4
Crystal Lake o USA (FL) 286-287 D 1
Crystal Lake o USA (IL) 274-275 K 2
Crystal Lake Cave ∴ USA (IA) 274-275 H 2
Crystal River o USA (FL) 286-287 G 3
Crystal River ~ USA (CO) 254-255 H 4
Crystal River State Archaeological Site · USA (FL) 286-287 G 3
Crystal Springs o CDN (SAS) 232-233 N 3
Crystal Springs o USA (MS) 268-269 K 5
Cserhát ∸ H 92-93 P 5
C. Silverberge Ø ⌒ GRØ 26-27 p 5
Csorna o H 92-93 O 5
Cu ~ KA 124-125 H 6
Ču ~ KS 146-147 B 4
Cúa o YV 60-61 H 2
Cù'a Bày Hóp ≈ 158-159 H 6
Cuacaña o YV 60-61 J 5
Cuácua, Rio ~ MOC 218-219 J 3
Cù'a Cung Hầu ≈ 158-159 J 6
Cuaio ~ ANG 216-217 F 7
Cuajinicuilapa o MEX 52-53 E 3
Cuale o ANG 216-217 D 4
Cuamato o ANG 216-217 C 8
Cuamba o MOC 218-219 J 2
Cuanavale ~ ANG 216-217 E 7
Cuando ~ ANG 216-217 F 7
Cuando-Cubango ◘ ANG 216-217 E 7
Cuangar o ANG 216-217 E 8
Cuango o ANG 216-217 D 3
Cuango o ANG (LUN) 216-217 E 4
Cuango ~ ANG 216-217 D 4
Cuanza o ANG (BIE) 216-217 D 5
Cuanza ~ ANG 216-217 D 4
Cuanza Norte ◘ ANG 216-217 C 4
Cuanza Sul ◘ ANG 216-217 C 5
Cuao, Río ~ YV 60-61 H 5
Cuareim, Río ~ ROU 76-77 J 6
Cuarinuma o CO 60-61 G 6
Cuaró Grande, Arroyo ~ ROU 76-77 J 6
Cuarto, Río ~ RA 78-79 G 2
Cù'a Soi Rap ≈ 158-159 J 5
Cuatir ~ ANG 216-217 E 8
Cuatro Bocas, Las o YV 60-61 F 2
Cuatro Caminos o C 54-55 G 4
Cuatrociénegas de Carranza o MEX 50-51 H 4
Cuauhtémoc o MEX (CHA) 50-51 F 3
Cuauhtémoc o MEX (TAM) 50-51 K 6
Cuautitlán o MEX 52-53 E 2
Cuautla o MEX 52-53 B 1
Cuautla de Morelos o MEX 52-53 E 2
Cuba ■ C 54-55 E 4
Cuba ⌒ C 5 C 2
Cuba o USA (AL) 284-285 B 4
Cuba o USA (IL) 274-275 H 4
Cuba o USA (MO) 274-275 G 6
Cuba o USA (NM) 256-257 J 2
Cuba City o USA (WI) 274-275 H 2
Cù Bai o VN 158-159 J 2
Cubal o ANG (BGU) 216-217 C 6
Cubal ~ ANG 216-217 C 5
Cubal ~ ANG 216-217 B 7
Cubango o ANG 216-217 D 7
Cubango ~ ANG 216-217 E 8
Cubaté, Rio ~ BR 66-67 D 2
Cubati ~ ANG 216-217 D 7
Cube o EC 64-65 C 1
Cubero o USA (NM) 256-257 H 3
Cubia ~ ANG 216-217 F 7
Cubitas o C 54-55 G 4
Čublas o RUS 88-89 S 4
Çubuk ☆ TR 128-129 E 2
Čubuka-Tala, gora ▲ RUS 110-111 a 7
Čubukulah, gora ▲ RUS 110-111 d 6
Čubukulah, krjaž ▲ RUS 110-111 d 7

Cubulco ○ GCA 52-53 J 4
Cuchara ○ USA (CO) 254-255 K 6
Cuchi ○ ANG (CUA) 216-217 D 7
Cuchi ~ ANG 216-217 D 6
Cuchilla, La ○ RA 76-77 G 4
Cuchillo ○ USA (NM) 256-257 H 5
Cuchillo-Co ○ RA 78-79 G 5
Cuchivero ○ YV 60-61 J 4
Cuchivero, Río ~ YV 60-61 J 4
Cucho Ingenio ○ BOL 70-71 E 6
Cuchumatanas, Parque Nacional Los ⊥ • GCA 52-53 J 4
Cuchumatanas, Sierra de los ▲ GCA 52-53 J 4
Cuckadoo ○ AUS 178-179 F 1
Cuckoo ○ USA (VA) 280-281 J 6
Cucuí ○ BR 66-67 D 2
Cucumbi ~ ANG 216-217 E 4
Cucuri, Cachoeira ~ BR 72-73 D 2
Cucurital ○ YV 60-61 J 5
Cucuta ★ CO 60-61 E 4
Cudahy ○ USA (WI) 274-275 L 2
Cuddalore ○ IND 140-141 H 5
Cuddapah ○ IND 140-141 H 3
Čudovo ○ RUS 94-95 M 2
Čudskoe ozero ○ RUS 94-95 K 2
Cudworth ○ CDN (SAS) 232-233 N 3
Čudzjavr, ozero ○ RUS 88-89 N 2
Cue ○ AUS 176-177 D 3
Cuebe ~ ANG 216-217 D 7
Cueio ~ ANG 216-217 D 7
Cueiras, Rio ~ BR 66-67 G 4
Cuélab • PE 64-65 D 5
Cuelei ~ ANG 216-217 D 7
Cuéllar ○ E 98-99 E 4
Cuemba ○ ANG 216-217 E 6
Cuenca ○ E 98-99 F 4
Cuenca ★ •• EC 64-65 C 3
Cuenca, Serranía de ▲ E 98-99 F 4
Cuenca del Añelo ⊥ • RA 78-79 E 5
Cuencamé ○ MEX 50-51 H 5
Cuengo ~ ANG 216-217 E 4
Cueramaro ○ MEX 52-53 D 1
Cuernavaca ★ • MEX 52-53 E 2
Cuero ○ C 54-55 H 5
Cuero ○ USA (TX) 266-267 K 4
Cuervo ○ USA (NM) 256-257 L 3
Cueto ○ C 54-55 H 4
Cuetzalń ○ • MEX 52-53 F 1
Cueva de la Quebrada del Toro, Parque Nacional ⊥ YV 60-61 G 2
Cuevas, Las ○ RA 78-79 D 2
Cuevas o de las Cañas, Rio ~ RA 76-77 E 3
Cuevo ○ BOL 70-71 F 7
Cuevo, Quebrada de ~ BOL 70-71 F 7
Čuga ~ RUS 118-119 L 7
Čuginskoe ploskogor'e ▲ RUS 118-119 K 7
Cugo ~ ANG 216-217 D 3
Čugor', mys ▲ RUS 108-109 Q 7
Čugor'jaha ~ RUS 108-109 Q 7
Čuguš, gora ▲ RUS 126-127 D 6
Čuhloma ○ RUS 94-95 S 2
Čuhujiv ○ UA 102-103 K 3
Cuiabá ○ BR (AMA) 66-67 C 4
Cuiabá ★ BR (MAT) 70-71 J 4
Cuiabá, Rio ~ BR 70-71 J 5
Cuije ~ ANG 216-217 D 4
Cuilapa ★ GCA 52-53 J 4
Cuilo ○ ANG 216-217 E 4
Cuilo ~ ANG 216-217 C 3
Cuilo ~ ANG 216-217 E 4
Cuilo ~ ANG 216-217 E 5
Cuilo-Futa ○ ANG 216-217 C 3
Cuilo Pombo ○ ANG 216-217 C 3
Cuima ○ ANG 216-217 C 6
Cuimba ○ ANG 216-217 C 3
Cuio ○ ANG 216-217 B 6
Cuira o Monos ○ CO 64-65 F 2
Cuiriri ~ ANG 216-217 E 7
Cuito ~ ANG 216-217 E 8
Cuito Cuanavale ○ ANG 216-217 E 7
Cuiubi ○ BR 66-67 C 2
Cuiuni, Rio ~ BR 66-67 F 3
Cuivre River ~ USA (IL) 274-275 H 5
Cuiyun Lang • VRC 154-155 D 5
Čuja ~ RUS 118-119 F 6
Čuja ~ RUS 124-125 Q 3
Čuja ~ RUS 124-125 P 3
Čuja, Boľšaja ~ RUS 118-119 E 7
Cujar, Río ~ PE 64-65 F 7
Čujskij, Gorno ○ RUS 118-119 E 7
Cujubim ○ BR 66-67 G 7
Čukar ○ RUS 118-119 H 4
Cukas, Pulau ⌒ RI 162-163 F 5
Čukča ~ RUS 110-111 Z 6
Čukčagirskoe, ozero ○ RUS 122-123 G 3
Čukoč'e, ozero ○ RUS 112-113 L 2
Čukoč'ja, Boľšaja ~ RUS 112-113 K 2
Čukotskij, mys ▲ RUS 112-113 Y 4
Čukotskij polustrov ⌣ RUS 112-113 W 3
Čukotskoe more ≈ 112-113 V 1
Čukša ~ RUS 116-117 J 7
Çukurca ★ TR 128-129 K 4
Cula ~ MD 102-103 F 4
Čulakan ~ RUS 116-117 M 6
Čulakkurgan ○ KA 136-137 L 3
Culamagia ○ ANG 216-217 D 4
Cu Lao Thu ⌒ VN 158-159 K 5
Cù Lao Thu = Phú Qúy ⌒ VN 158-159 K 5
Čulas ~ RUS 88-89 T 4
Čulasa ○ RUS 88-89 T 4
Culasi ○ RP 160-161 E 7
Culbertson ○ USA (MT) 250-251 P 3
Culbertson ○ USA (NE) 262-263 F 4
Culdesac ○ USA (ID) 250-251 C 5
Culebra, Isla de ⌒ USA (PR) 286-287 Q 2
Culebra, La ○ YV 60-61 H 3
Culebras ○ PE 64-65 C 6
Culebras, Punta ▲ PE 64-65 C 6
Culgoa River ~ AUS 178-179 J 5
Culiacán Rosales ★ MEX 50-51 F 5
Culion ○ RP 160-161 D 7
Culion Island ⌒ RP 160-161 C 7
Culiseu, Rio ~ BR 72-73 D 2
Cullen Garden • CDN (ONT) 238-239 F 5
Cullera ○ E 98-99 G 5
Cullinan ○ ZA 220-221 J 2
Cullison ○ USA (KS) 262-263 H 7
Cullmann ○ USA (AL) 284-285 D 2
Culluleraine ○ AUS 180-181 F 3
Čuľman ○ RUS 118-119 M 7
Čuľman ~ RUS 118-119 M 7
Culpeper ○ USA (VA) 280-281 J 5
Culpina ○ BOL 70-71 E 7
Culross Island ⌒ USA 20-21 R 6
Culuene, Rio ~ BR 72-73 D 2
Čuluunhoroom = Érèèncav ○ MAU 148-149 M 3
Čuluut gol ~ MAU 148-149 E 3
Culver ○ USA (IN) 274-275 M 3
Culver, Point ▲ AUS 176-177 H 6
Culverden ○ NZ 182 D 5
Čulym ★ RUS (NVS) 114-115 Q 7
Čulym ~ RUS 114-115 U 6
Čulym ~ RUS 116-117 E 8
Čulym ~ RUS 124-125 L 1
Čulymskaja, ravnina ⌣ RUS 114-115 T 6
Čulyšman ~ RUS 124-125 Q 3
Čulyšman ~ RUS 124-125 P 3
Čulyšmanskoe, nagor'e ⊥ •• RUS 124-125 Q 3
Čulyšmanskoe nagorie ▲ RUS 124-125 P 3
Cuma ○ ANG 216-217 C 6
Cumã, Baía do ≈ 68-69 F 3
Cuma, Cachoeira ~ BR 66-67 C 2
Cumana ★ • YV 60-61 J 2
Cumanacoa ○ YV 60-61 K 2
Cumanayagua ○ C 54-55 E 3
Cumanda ○ EC 64-65 C 3
Cumaral ○ CO 60-61 E 5
Cumaral = Barranca de Upía ○ CO 60-61 E 5
Cumaral, Raudal ~ CO 60-61 F 6
Cumaribo ○ CO 60-61 G 5
Cumaru, Cachoeira ~ BR 62-63 G 6
Cumbe ○ EC 64-65 C 3
Cumberland ○ CDN (BC) 230-231 D 4
Cumberland ○ USA (IA) 274-275 D 3
Cumberland ○ USA (IN) 274-275 N 5
Cumberland ○ USA (KY) 276-277 N 4
Cumberland ○ USA (MD) 280-281 H 4
Cumberland ○ USA (MS) 268-269 L 3
Cumberland ○ USA (OH) 280-281 E 4
Cumberland ○ USA (VA) 280-281 H 6
Cumberland ○ USA (WI) 270-271 F 5
Cumberland, Cape = Cape Nahoi ▲ VAN 184 II a 2
Cumberland, Lake ⊂ USA (KY) 276-277 K 4
Cumberland Bay ≈ 78-79 O 7
Cumberland Caverns Park ⚔ USA (TN) 276-277 K 5
Cumberland City Reservoir ⊂ USA (PA) 280-281 H 4
Cumberland Downs ○ AUS 178-179 J 2
Cumberland Falls ~ USA (KY) 276-277 L 4
Cumberland Gap ▲ USA (TN) 282-283 D 4
Cumberland Gap National Historic Park ∴ USA (KY) 276-277 M 4
Cumberland House ○ CDN (SAS) 232-233 Q 2
Cumberland Island ⌒ USA (GA) 284-285 J 6
Cumberland Island National Seashore ⊥ USA (GA) 284-285 J 6
Cumberland Islands ⌒ AUS 174-175 K 7
Cumberland Lake ○ CDN 34-35 E 3
Cumberland Mountains ▲ USA (TN) 282-283 D 4
Cumberland Parkway II USA (KY) 276-277 K 3
Cumberland Peninsula ⌣ CDN 28-29 G 3
Cumberland River ~ USA (KY) 276-277 M 4
Cumberland River ~ USA (TN) 276-277 K 4
Cumberland Sound ≈ 36-37 R 2
Cumbi ○ ANG 216-217 B 3
Cumborah ○ AUS 178-179 J 5
Cumbre, Paso de la ▲ RA 78-79 E 2
Cumbre, Volcán La ▲ EC 64-65 B 10
Cumbrera, Cerro ▲ RCH 80 D 4
Cumbres and Toltec Scenic Railroad • USA (CO) 254-255 J 6
Cumbres de Majalca ○ MEX 50-51 F 3
Cumbres de Majalca, Parque Nacional ⊥ MEX 50-51 F 3
Cumbrian Mountains ▲ GB 90-91 F 4
Cumbum ○ IND 140-141 H 3
Cumburão ○ BR 62-63 G 6
Cumby ○ USA (TX) 264-265 J 5
Čumikan ★ RUS 120-121 F 6
Čumikan ~ RUS 120-121 F 5
Cuminá ○ BR 62-63 F 6
Cuminá, Rio ~ BR 62-63 F 5
Cuminapanema, Rio ~ BR 62-63 G 6
Cumming ○ USA (GA) 284-285 F 2
Cummings ○ USA (CA) 246-247 B 4
Cummins ○ AUS 180-181 C 3
Cummins Range ▲ AUS 172-173 H 5
Cumnock ○ GB 90-91 E 4
Čumpu-Kytyl ○ RUS 110-111 Y 7
Çumra ★ TR 128-129 E 4
Cumshewa Head ▲ CDN (BC) 228-229 C 3
Cumshewa Inlet ≈ CDN 228-229 C 3
Cumueté, Rio ~ BR 68-69 C 6
Čumyš ~ RUS 124-125 P 2
Čumyš ~ RUS 124-125 N 2
Čuna ~ RUS 116-117 H 7
Cunaguaro ○ YV 60-61 J 3
Cunani ○ BR 62-63 J 4
Cuñare ○ CO 64-65 F 1
Cunarno ○ RCH 78-79 C 6
Cunauaru, Rio ~ BR 66-67 F 4
Cund ~ ANG 216-217 D 6
Cunday ○ CO 60-61 D 5
Cundeelee ⚔ AUS 176-177 G 5
Cundeelee Aboriginal Land ⚔ AUS 176-177 G 5
Cunderdin ○ AUS 176-177 D 5
Cunduacán ○ MEX 52-53 H 2
Cundza ○ KA 146-147 D 4
Cunene ○ ANG 216-217 C 7
Cunene ◘ ANG 216-217 C 8
Cunene ~ ANG 216-217 C 8
Cunene ~ ANG 216-217 D 7
Cúneo ★ I 100-101 A 2
Cung Hầu, Cửa ≈ 158-159 J 6
Cunha ○ BR 72-73 H 7
Cunhãs, Rio das ~ BR 68-69 D 5
Cunhinga ~ ANG 216-217 D 5
Cunia, Estação Ecológica ⊥ BR 66-67 F 7
Cuniuá, Rio ~ BR 66-67 D 6
Čunja ~ RUS 116-117 K 5
Čunja, Strelka ○ RUS 116-117 L 5
Cunjamba ○ ANG 216-217 F 7
Cunnamulla ○ • AUS 178-179 H 5
Cunningham ○ USA (KY) 276-277 G 4
Cunningham ○ USA (TN) 276-277 H 4
Cunningham ○ USA (TX) 264-265 J 5
Cunningham, Lake ○ ZW 218-219 E 5
Cunningham Islands ⌒ AUS 174-175 D 2
Cunningham Lake ○ CDN (BC) 228-229 J 2
Čunskij ○ RUS 116-117 H 7
Čun'skij ★ RUS 116-117 J 7
Cuntima ○ GNB 202-203 C 3
Čuokkarašša ▲ N 86-87 M 2
Čupa ○ RUS 88-89 M 3
Čūpānān ○ IR 134-135 F 2
Cupar ○ CDN (SAS) 232-233 O 5
Cupari, Rio ~ BR 66-67 K 4
Cupertino ○ USA (CA) 248-249 B 2
Cupica ○ CO 60-61 C 4
Cupica, Golfo de ≈ 60-61 C 4
Cupisnique, Cerro ▲ PE 64-65 C 5
Cupixi ○ BR 62-63 J 5
Čuprovo ○ RUS 88-89 T 4
Cuprum ○ USA (ID) 250-251 C 6
Cuptano, Isla ⌒ RCH 80 D 2
Curaça ○ BR 68-69 J 6
Curaça, Rio ~ BR 68-69 J 6
Curaçao ⌒ NL 60-61 G 1
Curacautín ○ RCH 78-79 D 5
Curacaví ○ RCH 78-79 D 2
Curachi ○ GUY 62-63 D 2
Curácuaro de Morelos ○ MEX 52-53 D 2
Curahuara de Carangas ○ BOL 70-71 C 5
Curale ○ ETH 208-209 G 5
Cura Malal, Sierra de ▲ RA 78-79 H 4
Curanilahué ○ RCH 78-79 C 4
Curanja ○ BR 66-67 B 7
Curanja, Río ~ PE 70-71 B 2
Čurapča ★ • RUS 120-121 E 3
Curaray ○ EC 64-65 D 2
Curaray ○ PE 64-65 E 3
Curaray, Río ~ PE 64-65 E 3
Curari, Ilha de ⌒ BR 66-67 G 4
Curaru ○ RA 78-79 H 3
Curauaí, Rio ~ BR 66-67 H 5
Čurbuka, gora ▲ RUS 110-111 Q 4
Čurbukan ~ RUS 116-117 H 2
Curdimurka ○ AUS 178-179 D 5
Čure ○ AFG 134-135 M 2
Curecanti National Recreation Area ⊥ • USA (CO) 254-255 H 5
Curepipe ○ MS 224 C 7
Curepto ○ RCH 78-79 C 3
Curib ○ RUS 126-127 G 6
Curibaya ○ PE 70-71 B 5
Curiche Liverpool ○ BOL 70-71 F 4
Curichi de Oquiriquia ~ BOL 70-71 G 5
Curichi Tunas ~ BOL 70-71 G 5
Curico ○ RCH 78-79 D 3
Curicuriari, Rio ~ BR 66-67 C 3
Curieuse Marine National Park ⊥ SY 224 D 2
Curi Leuvú, Arroyo ~ RA 78-79 D 4
Curimatá ○ BR 68-69 F 7
Curimatá, Rio ~ BR 68-69 F 6
Curimatá de Baixo, Rio ~ BR 66-67 E 5
Curimávida, Cerro de ▲ RCH 76-77 B 6
Curionópolis ○ BR 68-69 D 5
Curitiba ○ BR (ACR) 70-71 C 2
Curitiba ★ • BR (PAR) 74-75 F 5
Curitibanos ○ BR 74-75 E 6
Curiúva ○ BR 74-75 E 5
Čurkin, mys ▲ RUS 110-111 W 3
Curlew ○ USA (WA) 244-245 G 2
Curly Cut Cays ⌒ BS 54-55 G 3
Curnamona ○ AUS 178-179 E 6
Čuro ~ RUS 118-119 F 7
Curoca ~ ANG 216-217 B 8
Curoca, Cachoeira da ~ BR 66-67 G 7
Currais Novos ○ BR 68-69 K 5
Curral Alto ○ BR 74-75 D 9
Currais ○ BR 74-75 E 8
Curralinho ○ BR 62-63 K 6
Curral Novo ○ BR 68-69 H 6
Curral Velho ○ BR 72-73 H 2
Curral Velho ○ CV 202-203 C 5
Curran ○ CDN (ONT) 238-239 L 3
Currant ○ USA (NV) 246-247 K 5
Currarehue ○ RCH 78-79 D 5
Currawinya ○ AUS 178-179 H 5
Currawinya National Park ⊥ AUS 178-179 H 5
Current Island ⌒ BS 54-55 G 2
Current River ~ USA (MO) 276-277 D 3
Currie ○ AUS 180-181 G 5
Currie ○ USA (MN) 270-271 C 6
Currie ○ USA (NV) 246-247 L 3
Currie Indian Reserve, Mount ⚔ CDN (BC) 230-231 G 3
Currituck Sound ≈ 46-47 L 7
Currituck ○ USA (NC) 282-283 L 4
Currituck Sound ★ USA 280-281 L 7
Curtea de Argeș ○ • RO 102-103 D 5
Čürti ○ IR 136-137 B 6
Curtin ○ AUS 176-177 G 5
Curtin Springs ○ AUS 176-177 L 2
Curtis ○ USA (NE) 262-263 F 4
Curtis Island ⌒ AUS 178-179 L 2
Curtis Lake ○ CDN 30-31 Z 2
Curtis River ~ CDN 30-31 Z 2
Curu, Rio ~ BR 68-69 J 3
Curuá ○ BR 62-63 G 6
Curuá, Ilha do ⌒ BR 62-63 J 5
Curuá, Rio ~ BR 62-63 G 6
Curuá, Rio ~ BR 66-67 K 7
Curuaés, Rio ~ BR 66-67 K 7
Curuaí ○ BR 66-67 K 4
Curuá ou Cururu, Rio ~ BR 72-73 D 3
Curuá-Una, Rio ~ BR 66-67 K 4
Curuá-Una, Rio ~ BR 66-67 K 4
Curuçá ○ BR 68-69 E 2
Curuçá, Ponta ▲ BR 68-69 E 2
Curuça, Rio ~ BR 64-65 F 4
Curuduri, Rio ~ BR 66-67 F 2
Curuguaty ○ PY 76-77 K 3
Curuma la Grande, Cerro ▲ RA 78-79 H 4
Curumutopo ○ YV 60-61 J 4
Curup ○ RI 162-163 E 6
Curupá ○ BR 68-69 F 6
Curupaiti ○ BR 68-69 E 3
Curupira ○ BR 68-69 J 4
Curuquetê, Rio ~ BR 66-67 E 7
Cururu, Raudal ~ CO 66-67 B 2
Cururu-Açu, Rio ~ BR 66-67 J 7
Cururu ou Cururuí, Rio ~ BR 66-67 J 7
Cururupu ○ BR 68-69 F 2
Curuzú Cuatiá ○ RA 76-77 H 5
Curva del Turco ○ RA 76-77 F 3
Curva Grande ○ BR 68-69 C 3
Curvelo ○ BR 72-73 H 5
Curwood, Mount ▲ USA (MI) 270-271 K 4
Cushabatay, Río ~ PE 64-65 E 5
Cushamen ○ RA 78-79 D 7
Cushing ○ USA (MN) 270-271 D 4
Cushing ○ USA (OK) 264-265 H 3
Cushing ○ USA (TX) 268-269 F 5
Cushing ○ USA (WI) 270-271 F 5
Cusick ○ USA (WA) 244-245 H 2
Cusime ○ YV 60-61 J 5
Cusipata ○ PE 70-71 B 3
Cusis, Río ~ BOL 70-71 H 5
Čusovaja ~ RUS 96-97 L 5
Čusovoj ★ RUS 96-97 K 4
Čusovskoe, ozero ○ RUS 114-115 D 4
Cusseta ○ USA (GA) 284-285 F 4
Cussivi ~ ANG 216-217 F 7
Cusso ~ ANG 216-217 C 7
Cusson, Pointe ▲ CDN 36-37 K 4
Čust ○ US 136-137 M 4
Custer ○ USA (MT) 250-251 M 5
Custer ○ USA (SD) 260-261 C 3
Custer Battlefield National Monument ∴ USA (MT) 250-251 M 6
Custer State Park ⊥ USA (SD) 260-261 C 3
Custódia ○ BR 68-69 K 6
Cusuco, Parque Nacional ⊥ HN 52-53 K 4
Cutato ○ ANG (BIE) 216-217 D 6
Cutato ○ ANG (CUA) 216-217 D 7
Cutato ~ ANG 216-217 D 5
Cutato ~ ANG 216-217 D 7
Cutbank ○ CDN (SAS) 232-233 M 4
Cut Bank ○ USA (MT) 250-251 G 3
Cut Bank Creek ~ USA (MT) 250-251 G 3
Cutbank River ~ CDN (ALB) 228-229 P 2
Cutenda ○ ANG 216-217 C 7
Cutervo ○ PE 64-65 C 5
Cutervo, Parque Nacional de ⊥ PE 64-65 C 5
Cuthbert ○ USA (GA) 284-285 F 5
Cutknife ○ CDN (SAS) 232-233 K 3
Cutler ○ USA (ME) 278-279 O 4
Čutove ○ UA 102-103 J 3
Cuttaburra Creek ~ AUS 178-179 H 5
Cutta Cutta Caves • AUS 172-173 L 3
Cuttak=Kataka ○ IND 142-143 D 5
Cutzamala de Pinzón ○ MEX 52-53 D 2
Cửu Long, Cửa Sông ≈ VN 158-159 J 6
Čuvanajskie gory ▲ RUS 112-113 O 3
Čuvanskij hrebet ▲ RI 112-113 O 4
Čuvanskoe ○ RUS 112-113 O 4
Cuvelai ○ ANG 216-217 C 7
Cuvelai ~ ANG 216-217 D 7
Cuvette ◘ RCB 210-211 E 4
Cuvo ~ ANG 216-217 C 5
Cuxhaven ○ D 92-93 K 2
Cuxiuara, Ilha ⌒ BR 66-67 G 4
Cuy, El ○ RA 78-79 E 5
Cuyabeno, Reserva Faunística ⊥ EC 64-65 E 2
Cuyahoga Valley National Recreation Area ⊥ USA (OH) 280-281 E 2
Cuyama ○ USA (CA) 248-249 E 5
Cuyo, El ○ MEX 52-53 L 1
Cuyo East Pass ≈ 160-161 D 7
Cuyo 'English Game' Subterranean National Park ⊥ RP 160-161 D 7
Cuyo Island ⌒ RP 160-161 D 7
Cuyo Islands ⌒ RP 160-161 D 7
Cuyo West Pass ≈ 160-161 D 7
Cuyuni, Rio ~ YV 62-63 D 2
Cuzco ★ ••• PE 70-71 B 3
Čuzik ~ RUS 114-115 P 6
Čvrisnica ▲ BIH 100-101 F 3
Cyama River ~ USA (CA) 248-249 E 4
Cyangugu ○ RWA 212-213 B 5
Čyappara ○ RUS 118-119 P 4
Čyb ~ RUS 88-89 V 5
Čybyda ~ RUS 118-119 K 4
Cyclades = Kikládes ⌒ GR 100-101 K 6
Cycloop, Pegunungan ▲ RI 166-167 L 3
Cyclop Mountains Reserve ⊥ • RI 166-167 L 3
Čyhyryn ○ UA 102-103 H 3
Čyjyrčyk, pereval ▲ KS 136-137 N 4
Čym ○ RUS 108-109 K 8
Cymric ○ CDN (SAS) 232-233 O 4
Čyna ~ RUS 118-119 M 5
Cynthia ○ AUS 178-179 L 3
Cynthia ○ CDN (ALB) 232-233 C 2
Cynthiana ○ USA (KY) 276-277 L 2
Cyohoha Sud, Lac ○ BU 212-213 C 5
Cypnavolok, mys ▲ RUS 88-89 M 2
Cypress ○ USA (LA) 268-269 G 5
Cypress Bayou ~ USA (AR) 276-277 D 5
Cypress Creek ~ USA (TX) 268-269 E 7
Cypress Gardens ∴ • USA (FL) 286-287 H 4
Cypress Hills ▲ CDN (SAS) 232-233 J 6
Cypress Hills Provincial Park ⊥ CDN (ALB) 232-233 H 6
Cypress Hills Provincial Park ⊥ CDN (SAS) 232-233 J 6
Cypress Provincial Park ⊥ CDN (BC) 230-231 F 4
Cypress River ○ CDN (MAN) 234-235 D 5
Cypress Springs, Lake ⊂ USA (TX) 264-265 J 5
Cyprus = Kypros ■ CY 128-129 E 5
Čyra ~ RUS 118-119 M 5
Cyrene ○ ZW 218-219 E 5
Cyrene = Shahhât ∴ ••• LAR 192-193 J 1
Cyril ○ USA (OK) 264-265 F 4
Cyrus Field Bay ≈ 36-37 R 3
Čyrvonae, vozero ○ BY 94-95 L 5
Cytherea ○ AUS 178-179 J 4
Czaplinek ○ • PL 92-93 O 2
Czar ○ CDN (ALB) 232-233 H 3
Czarnków ○ PL 92-93 O 2
Czech Republic = Česká Republika ■ CZ 92-93 M 4
Czersk ○ PL 92-93 O 2
Częstochowa ★ •• PL 92-93 P 3
Człuchów ○ • 92-93 O 2

D

Da'an ○ VRC 150-151 E 5
Daanbantayan ○ RP 160-161 F 7
Daan Viljoen Game Park ⊥ NAM 216-217 D 11
Daaquam ○ CDN (QUE) 240-241 E 4
Ḍab'a, Maḥaṭṭat ○ JOR 130-131 E 2
Dabadougou ○ CI 202-203 G 5
Dabaga ○ EAT 214-215 H 5
Dabai ○ WAN 204-205 F 3
Dabajuro ○ YV 60-61 F 2
Dabakala ★ CI 202-203 H 5
Dabancheng ○ VRC 146-147 J 4
Dabaray ○ AFG 134-135 M 3
Dabaro ○ SP 208-209 J 5
Daba Shan ▲ VRC 154-155 F 5
Dabassi ○ RG 202-203 C 4
Dabat ○ ETH 200-201 H 6
Dabatou ○ RG 202-203 E 4
Dabeiba ○ CO 60-61 C 4
Daben ○ VRC 156-157 F 3
Dābhāde ○ IND 138-139 D 10
Dabhoi ○ IND 138-139 D 8
Dābhol ○ IND 140-141 E 2
Dabie Shan ▲ VRC 154-155 J 6
Dablo ○ BF 202-203 K 3
Dabnou ○ RN 198-199 B 5
Dabo ○ SN 202-203 C 3
Dabola ○ RG 202-203 E 4
Dabou ○ CI 202-203 H 7
Daboya ○ GH 202-203 K 5
Dabra ○ IND 138-139 G 7
Dabsan Hu ○ VRC 144-145 K 2
Dabuk ○ RI 162-163 E 6
Dabus Wenz ~ ETH 208-209 B 3
Dabwa ○ TCH 198-199 F 5
Dacca = Dhaka ★ BD 142-143 G 4
Đắc Glei ○ VN 158-159 J 3
Dachau ○ D 92-93 L 4
Dacheng ○ VRC 156-157 J 2
Dachenzhuang ○ VRC 154-155 K 2
Dachigam National Park ⊥ IND 138-139 E 2
Dachsteingruppe ▲ A 92-93 M 5
Dachung Yogma ○ IND 138-139 G 3
Dacia Seamount ≃ 188-189 E 5
Đắc Mil ○ VN 158-159 J 4
Dacre ○ CDN (ONT) 238-239 J 3
Đắc Song ○ VN 158-159 J 4
Đắc Tô ○ VN 158-159 J 3
Dadanawa ○ GUY 62-63 E 4
Dade City ○ USA (FL) 286-287 G 3
Dades, Gorges du •• MA 188-189 J 5
Dades, Oued ~ MA 188-189 J 5
Dadès, Vallée du ⊥ MA 188-189 H 5
Dadeville ○ USA (AL) 284-285 E 4
Dādhar ○ PK 134-135 M 4
Dadi, Tanjung ▲ RI 166-167 F 2
Dadong ○ VRC 156-157 F 5
Dadonghai • VRC 156-157 F 7
Dadra and Nagar Haveli ◘ IND 138-139 D 9
Dādu ○ PK 134-135 M 5
Daduan ○ VRC 156-157 J 2
Dādu Canal ~ PK 134-135 M 5
Dadu He ~ VRC 154-155 C 6
Dadukou ○ VRC 154-155 K 6
Dadynskoe, ozero ○ RUS 126-127 F 5
Daerah Istimewa Aceh ◘ RI 162-163 A 2
Daerah Istimewa Yogyakarta ◘ RI 168 C 4
Daet ★ RP 160-161 E 5
Dafang ○ VRC 156-157 D 3
Dafanpu ○ VRC 154-155 G 2
Dafeng ○ VRC 154-155 M 5
Dafengding Natural Biosystem Reserves ⊥ VRC 156-157 C 2
Daffat ad Dabāb ⊥ LAR 192-193 J 2
Dafina, ad- ○ KSA 130-131 H 6
Dafoe ○ CDN (SAS) 232-233 O 4
Dafoe River ~ CDN 34-35 J 3
Dafor ○ GH 202-203 L 6
Dafra ○ TCH 206-207 D 3
Dafter ○ USA (MI) 270-271 O 4
Daga ○ BHT 142-143 F 2
Daga ⌒ ETH 208-209 C 3
Daga ~ SUD 208-209 A 4
Dagaari ○ SP 208-209 H 5
Dagaldyn ~ RUS 108-109 c 7
Dagami ○ RP 160-161 F 7
Dagana ○ • SN 196-197 C 6
Dagandely ~ KA 124-125 K 4
Dagasuli, Pulau ⌒ RI 164-165 K 2
Dagda ○ LV 94-95 K 3
Dages Range ▲ PNG 183 F 3
Dagestan = Dagestan, Respublika ◘ RUS 126-127 H 6
Dagestan, Respublika ◘ RUS 126-127 G 5
Dagestanskie Ogni ○ RUS 126-127 H 6
Dagestanskij zapovednik ⊥ RUS 126-127 G 5
Daggaboersnek ▲ ZA 220-221 G 6
Daggett ○ USA (CA) 248-249 H 5
Daggyai Co ○ VRC 144-145 E 6
Dagida Game Reserve ⊥ WAN 204-205 F 4
Daginggou ⊥ • VRC 150-151 C 6
Daglung ○ VRC 144-145 H 6
Dagmar ○ OM 132-133 L 2
Dagmar ○ USA (MT) 250-251 P 3
Dagö = Hiiumaa saar ⊥ EST 94-95 H 2
Dagomys ○ RUS 126-127 C 6
Dagoudane-Pickine ○ SN 202-203 B 2
Dagua ○ CO 60-61 C 6
Daguan ○ VRC (SIC) 156-157 C 2
Daguan ○ VRC (YUN) 156-157 C 3
D'Aguilar Range ▲ AUS 178-179 M 4
Dagupan ★ RP 160-161 E 5
Daguragu-Kurintji Aboriginal Land ⚔ AUS 172-173 K 4
Dagushan ○ VRC 150-151 D 8
Dagu Shan ⌒ VRC 154-155 N 6
Dagworth ○ AUS (QLD) 174-175 G 5
Dagworth ○ AUS (QLD) 178-179 G 1
Dagzhuka ○ VRC 144-145 G 6
Dah ○ RI 166-167 K 5
Ḍahab ○ ET 194-195 G 3
Ḍahabān ○ KSA 132-133 A 3
Dahadinni River ~ CDN 30-31 G 4
Dahānib, Ġabal ▲ ET 194-195 G 6
Dahbed ○ US 136-137 K 5
Daheba ○ VRC 144-145 M 3
Dahequ ○ VRC 154-155 C 3
Ḍahi, aḍ- ○ Y 132-133 C 6
Dahinda ○ CDN (SAS) 232-233 N 6
Dahiri ○ CI 202-203 H 7
Dahlak Archipelago ⌒ ER 200-201 K 5
Dahle ○ AFG 134-135 L 3
Dahle, Band-e ⊂ AFG 134-135 M 3
Dahlonega ○ USA (GA) 284-285 G 2
Dahmani ○ TN 190-191 G 3
Dahnā', aḍ- ▲ KSA 130-131 H 3
Dahnā', aḍ- ⊥ KSA 130-131 J 4
Dāhod ○ IND 138-139 E 8
Dahongliutan ○ VRC 144-145 B 3
Dahra, Corniche des ⌣ DZ 190-191 C 2
Dahra, Massif de ▲ DZ 190-191 C 2
Dahra Oil Field ⊥ LAR 192-193 G 3
Dahsa, Wādī d- ~ ET 194-195 E 4
Dahšūr ○ ET 194-195 E 3
Dahšūr, Pyramids of ∴ ••• ET 194-195 E 3
Dahūk ◘ IRQ 128-129 K 4
Dahūk ★ IRQ (DAH) 128-129 K 4
Đại, Cửa ≈ 158-159 J 5
Dai, Pulau ⌒ RI 166-167 E 5
Daïa, Monts de ▲ DZ 188-189 L 3
Ḍaid, aḍ- ○ UAE 134-135 F 6
Dai Hai ○ VRC 154-155 H 1
Dai Island ⌒ SOL 184 I e 2
Dailing • VRC 150-151 G 4
Đại Lộc ○ VN 156-157 D 7
Daimāniyāt, ad- ⌒ OM 132-133 K 2
Daimiel ○ E 98-99 F 5
Daingerfield ○ USA (TX) 264-265 K 5
Daintree ○ AUS 174-175 H 5
Daintree National Park ⊥ AUS 174-175 H 5
Dair, aḍ- ○ ET 194-195 F 5
Dair, Ġabal aḍ- ▲ SUD 200-201 E 6
Dairana ○ RM 222-223 F 4
Dā'irat ar-Riyy ○ IRQ 128-129 L 6
Dair az-Zaur ★ SYR 128-129 J 5
Daireaux ○ RA 78-79 J 4
Dairen = Dalian ○ VRC 150-151 C 8
Dair Ḥāfir ○ SYR 128-129 G 4
Dair Mawās ○ ET 194-195 E 4
Dairūṭ ○ ET 194-195 E 4
Dairy ○ USA (OR) 244-245 D 8
Dairy Creek ○ AUS 176-177 C 2
Dairyland ○ USA (WI) 270-271 F 4
Dai-sen ▲ J 152-153 E 7
Daisengen-dake ▲ J 152-153 J 4
Daisen-Oki National Park ⊥ J 152-153 E 6
Daisetsuzan National Park ⊥ J 152-153 K 3
Dai Shan ⌒ VRC 154-155 M 6
Daisy ○ USA (OK) 264-265 J 4
Đại Từ ★ VN 156-157 D 6
Dai Xian ○ VRC 154-155 H 2
Daiyun Shan ▲ VRC 156-157 K 4
Dajabón ★ DOM 54-55 K 5
Dājal ○ PK 138-139 C 5
Dajan nuur ○ MAU 146-147 J 1
Dajarra ○ AUS 178-179 E 1
Dajiuba ○ VRC 144-145 G 2
Daka ~ GH 202-203 K 5
Dakar ★ • SN 202-203 B 2
Dakataua, Lake ○ PNG 183 F 3
Dakawa ○ EAT 214-215 J 4
Dakelangsi ○ VRC 144-145 G 6
Dakeshi ○ VRC 144-145 G 6
Daketa Shet' ~ ETH 208-209 F 5
Dakhla ⊂ RIM 196-197 E 6
Dakhlet Nouâdhibou ≈ 196-197 B 4
Dakhlet Nouâdhibou ◘ RIM 196-197 B 4
Dakingari ○ WAN 204-205 F 3
Daki Takwas ○ WAN 204-205 F 3
Đắk Nông ○ VN 158-159 J 4
Dako, Gunung ▲ RI 164-165 G 3
Dākoānk ○ IND 140-141 L 6
Dakoro ○ RN 198-199 C 5
Dakota ○ USA (MN) 270-271 G 7
Dakota City ○ USA (IA) 274-275 D 2
Dakota City ○ USA (NE) 262-263 K 2
Dakovica ○ YU 100-101 H 3
Đakovo ○ • HR 100-101 G 2
Daksum ○ IND 138-139 E 3
Dala ○ ANG (LUS) 216-217 F 4
Dala ○ ANG (LUS) 216-217 F 5
Dala ○ SOL 184 I e 3
Dalaba ○ • RG 202-203 D 4
Dalaba ○ SN 202-203 D 3
Dalad Qi ○ VRC 154-155 G 1
Dalahaj ○ RUS 116-117 L 10
Dālāhāni, Kūh-e ▲ IR 134-135 B 1
Dalai Nur ○ VRC 148-149 N 6
Dālaki ○ IR 134-135 D 4
Dālaki, Rūdhāne-ye ~ IR 134-135 D 4
Dalälven ~ S 86-87 H 6
Dalaman Çayı ~ TR 128-129 C 4
D'Alembert ○ CDN (QUE) 236-237 J 4
Dalāmi ○ SUD 206-207 K 3
Dalandolé ⊂ SP 212-213 K 2
Dalangyun ○ MYA 142-143 J 6
Dalanzadgad ★ MAU 148-149 G 6
Dala River ~ CDN (BC) 228-229 F 3
Dalark ○ USA (AR) 276-277 C 6
Dalarna ⊥ S 86-87 F 6
Dalat ○ MAL 162-163 J 3
Đà Lạt ★ •• VN 158-159 K 5
Dal'at Rašid 'Abbās ○ IRQ 128-129 L 6
Dālbandin ○ PK 134-135 L 4
Dalbeg ○ AUS 174-175 J 7
Dalbo ○ USA (MN) 270-271 E 5
Dalby ○ AUS 178-179 L 4
Dalcahue ○ RCH 78-79 C 7
Dale ○ N (HOR) 86-87 B 6
Dale ★ N (FJO) 86-87 B 6
Dale ○ USA (IN) 274-275 M 6
Dale ○ USA (OR) 244-245 G 6
Dale Hollow Lake ○ USA (TN) 276-277 K 4
Dalei Shan ▲ VRC 146-147 N 6
Dalemead ○ CDN (ALB) 232-233 E 5
Daletme ○ MYA 142-143 H 5
Daleville ○ USA (AL) 284-285 E 5
Dalğā' ○ ET 194-195 E 4
Dalgān ○ IR 134-135 H 5
Dalgaranga Hill ▲ AUS 176-177 D 3
Dalgety Brook ~ AUS 176-177 D 2
Dalgonally ○ AUS 174-175 F 7
Dălgopol ○ BG 102-103 E 6
Dalgyn ~ RUS 110-111 J 6
Dalhart ○ USA (TX) 264-265 B 2
Dalhousie ○ CDN (NB) 240-241 J 2
Dalhousie ○ IND 138-139 F 3
Dalhousie, Cape ▲ CDN 24-25 G 5
Dalhousie Road ○ CDN (NS) 240-241 L 6
Dalhousie West ○ CDN (NS) 240-241 K 6
Dali ○ RMM 202-203 G 2
Dali ○ VRC (SXI) 154-155 F 4
Dali ○ • VRC (YUN) 142-143 M 3
Ḍāli', aḍ- ○ • Y 132-133 D 7
Dalian ○ VRC 150-151 C 8
Daliang Shan ▲ VRC 156-157 C 2
Dālimb ○ IND 140-141 G 2
Dali Sharafat ○ SUD 200-201 F 6
Dalkola ○ IND 142-143 E 3
Dall, Mount ▲ USA 20-21 O 5
Dallas ○ CDN (MAN) 234-235 F 3
Dallas ○ USA (GA) 284-285 F 3
Dallas ○ USA (OR) 244-245 B 6
Dallas ○ • USA (TX) 264-265 H 6
Dallas City ○ USA (IL) 274-275 G 4
Dalles, The ○ USA (OR) 244-245 D 5
Dalli ○ WAN 204-205 J 4
Dall Island ⌒ USA 32-33 D 4
Dall Lake ○ USA 20-21 J 6
Dalmā ⌒ UAE 134-135 E 6
Dalmacija ⊥ HR 100-101 E 3
Dalmacio Vélez Sarsfield ○ RA 78-79 H 2
Dalmas, Lac ○ CDN 38-39 J 2
Dalmatia = Dalmacija ⊥ HR 100-101 E 3
Dalmatovo ★ RUS 114-115 G 6
Dalmeny ○ CDN (SAS) 232-233 M 3
Dalmīg, Haur ○ IRQ 128-129 L 6
Dal'nee ○ RUS 122-123 K 5
Dal'negorsk ○ RUS 122-123 F 6
Dal'nerečensk ○ RUS 122-123 E 6
Dal'nij ○ RUS 120-121 R 7
Dal'nije Zelency ○ RUS 88-89 O 2
Dalñoe ○ KA 124-125 E 2
Dalny ○ CDN (MAN) 234-235 C 5
Daloa ★ CI 202-203 G 6
Dalong ○ VRC 156-157 F 3
Dalrymple, Mount ▲ AUS 178-179 K 1
Dalrymple Lake ⊂ AUS 174-175 J 7
Dalsland ⊥ S 86-87 F 7
Dalsmynni ○ IS 86-87 c 2
Dāltenganj ○ IND 142-143 D 3
Dalton ○ CDN (ONT) 236-237 D 4
Dalton ○ USA (GA) 284-285 F 2
Dalton ○ USA (NE) 262-263 D 3
Dalton Gardens ○ USA (ID) 250-251 C 4
Dalton Ice Tongue ⊂ ARK 16 G 13
Daltro Filho ○ BR 74-75 D 6
Dalu ○ VRC 154-155 D 3
Daludalu ○ RI 162-163 D 4
Dalugama ○ CL 140-141 H 7
Dalupiri Island ⌒ RP (CAG) 160-161 D 3
Dalupiri Island ⌒ RP (NSA) 160-161 F 6
Dalu Shan ▲ VRC 156-157 E 2
Dalvík ○ IS 86-87 d 2
Dalwallinu ○ AUS 176-177 D 5
Dalwhinnie ○ GB 90-91 E 3
Daly Bay ≈ 30-31 Z 4
Dalyr ○ RUS 118-119 K 4
Daly River ⚔ AUS (NT) 172-173 K 2
Daly River ~ AUS 172-173 K 2
Daly River Aboriginal Land ⚔ AUS 172-173 J 2
Daly River Wildlife Sanctuary ⊥ AUS 172-173 J 2
Daly Waters ○ AUS 174-175 B 5
Dal'ža, ozero ○ RUS 122-123 H 2
Dalzell ○ CDN (SAS) 232-233 Q 5
Damā, Wādī ~ KSA 130-131 E 4
Damad ○ KSA 132-133 C 5
Damagaram-Takaya ○ RN 198-199 D 5
Damaguete ★ RP 160-161 E 8
Damamgani ○ PK 138-139 B 5
Dāmān ○ AFG 134-135 L 3
Damān ★ IND 138-139 D 9
Damān and Diu ◘ IND 138-139 D 9
Dāmane ○ IR 134-135 D 2
Damanhūr ★ ET 194-195 E 2
Damant Lake ○ CDN 30-31 R 5

Damaqun Shan ▲▲ **VRC** 148-149 M 7
Ḑamār o **Y** 132-133 D 6
Damar, Kepulauan ⌒ **RI** 166-167 E 5
Damar, Pulau ⌒ **RI** (MAL) 164-165 L 4
Damar, Pulau ⌒ **RI** (MAL) 166-167 E 5
Damara o **RCA** 206-207 D 6
Damaraland ∸ **NAM** 216-217 B 9
Damardatar o **RI** 164-165 D 5
Damariscotta o **USA** (ME) 278-279 M 4
Damar Laut o **MAL** 162-163 D 2
Damasak o **WAN** 198-199 F 6
Damas Cays ⌒ **BS** 54-55 F 3
Damascus o **USA** (AR) 276-277 C 5
Damascus o **USA** (GA) 284-285 F 5
Damascus o **USA** (VA) 280-281 E 7
Damascus = Dimašq ★ ··· **SYR** 128-129 G 6
Damaturu o **WAN** 204-205 J 3
Damauli o **NEP** 144-145 E 7
Damāvand o **IR** 136-137 C 7
Damāvand, Kūh-e ▲ ·· **IR** 136-137 C 7
Damazine o **SUD** 208-209 B 3
Damba o **ANG** 216-217 C 3
Dambai o **GH** 202-203 L 5
Dambam o **WAN** 204-205 J 3
Damboa o **WAN** 204-205 K 3
Dambulla o ··· **CL** 140-141 J 7
Dam Creek ~ **USA** (TX) 264-265 K 6
Dãm Do'i o **VN** 158-159 H 6
Dame Marie o **RH** 54-55 H 5
Dame Marie, Cape ▲ **RH** 54-55 H 5
Dāmgān o • **IR** 136-137 D 6
Damietta = Dumyāṭ ☆ **ET** 194-195 E 2
Dāmin, Rūdḫāne-ye ~ **IR** 134-135 J 5
Damji o **BHT** 142-143 F 2
Dammām, ad- ☆ **KSA** 134-135 D 5
Dāmnagar o **IND** 138-139 C 9
Dāmodar ~ **IND** 142-143 E 4
Damo Debir, Debre • **ETH** 200-201 J 5
Damoh o **IND** 138-139 G 8
Damongo o **GH** 202-203 K 5
Damortis o **RP** 160-161 D 4
Dampar o **WAN** 204-205 J 4
Dampelas, Tanjung ▲ **RI** 164-165 F 3
Damphu o **BHT** 142-143 G 2
Dampier o **AUS** 172-173 C 6
Dampier Archipelago ⌒ **AUS** 172-173 C 6
Dampier Downs o **AUS** 172-173 F 5
Dampier Land ∸ **AUS** 172-173 F 4
Dampier Strait ≈ 183 E 3
Dampir, Selat ≈ 166-167 F 2
Damqaut o **Y** 132-133 H 5
Dam Qu ~ **VRC** 144-145 J 4
Damrūr o **KSA** 132-133 A 3
Damt o **Y** 132-133 D 6
Damtang o **VRC** 144-145 D 4
Damtar o **TCH** 206-207 C 3
Damu Yang ~ **VRC** 156-157 N 2
Damwal o **ZA** 220-221 J 2
Damxung o **VRC** 144-145 H 5
Dana o **CDN** (SAS) 232-233 N 3
Dana, Lac ⬭ **CDN** (QUE) 236-237 L 2
Dana, Mount ▲ **USA** (CA) 248-249 E 2
Dana-Barat, Kepulauan ⌒ **RI** 166-167 C 5
Danané ☆ **CI** 202-203 F 6
Đà Nẵng ☆ • **VN** 158-159 K 2
Danao o **RP** 160-161 F 7
Danas Banke ≃ 28-29 P 5
Danau Rombebai ⬭ **RI** 166-167 J 2
Danau Toba • **RI** 162-163 C 3
Danba o **VRC** 154-155 B 6
Danbatta o **WAN** 198-199 D 6
Danbury o **USA** (CT) 280-281 N 2
Danbury o **USA** (WI) 270-271 F 4
Danby Lake ⬭ **USA** (CA) 248-249 J 6
Dan Chang o **THA** 158-159 E 3
Dancheng o **VRC** 154-155 J 5
Dandara o **ET** (QIN) 194-195 F 4
Dandara ∴ ·· **ET** (QIN) 194-195 F 4
Dandaragan o **AUS** 176-177 C 5
Dandau o **ANG** 216-217 D 5
Dande o **ETH** 208-209 C 6
Dandeli o **IND** 140-141 F 3
Dandenong o **AUS** 180-181 H 4
Dandenong Park o **AUS** 174-175 J 7
Dandenong Range National Park ⊥ **AUS** 180-181 H 4
Dando o **ANG** 216-217 D 5
Dandong o **VRC** 150-151 E 7
Daneborg o **GRØ** 26-27 p 6
Danesfahan o **IR** 128-129 N 5
Danfeng o **VRC** 154-155 G 5
Danforth o **USA** (ME) 278-279 O 3
Dang o **CAM** 204-205 K 6
Danga o **RMM** 196-197 J 6
Dangara o **TJ** 136-137 L 5
Dangar Falls ~ • **AUS** 178-179 L 6
Dangchang o **VRC** 154-155 D 4
Dange ~ **ANG** 216-217 C 4
Dange o **WAN** 198-199 B 6
Danger Area xx **USA** (NV) 246-247 G 4
Dangerous Cape ▲ **USA** 22-23 U 4
Danggali Conservation Park ⊥ **AUS** 180-181 F 2
Dangila o **ETH** 208-209 C 3
Dangjin Shankou ▲ **VRC** 146-147 M 6
Dangoura, Mont ▲ **RCA** 206-207 H 5
Dangriga o **BH** 52-53 K 3
Dangshan o **VRC** 154-155 K 4
Dangtu o **VRC** 154-155 L 6
Dan-Gulbi o **WAN** 204-205 G 3
Dangur o **ETH** 200-201 G 6
Dangur ▲▲ **ETH** 208-209 B 3
Dangyang o **VRC** 154-155 G 6
Daniel o **USA** (WY) 252-253 H 4
Daniel's Harbour o **CDN** (NFL) 242-243 L 2
Danielskuil o **ZA** 220-221 F 4
Danielson o **USA** (CT) 278-279 K 7
Danielson Provincial Park ⊥ **CDN** (SAS) 232-233 M 4
Danilov o **RUS** 94-95 R 2
Danilovka o **RUS** 96-97 D 8
Danilovskaja vozvyšennost' ▲▲ **RUS** 94-95 Q 2
Daning o **VRC** 154-155 G 3
Daninghe • **VRC** 154-155 F 6
Dan-Issa o **RN** 198-199 C 6
Danja o **WAN** 204-205 G 3
Danjiangkou o **VRC** 154-155 G 5
Danjiankou Sk. ⬭ **VRC** 154-155 G 5
Danjo-guntō ⌒ **J** 152-153 C 8
Ḑank o **OM** 132-133 K 2
Dankov o **RUS** 94-95 Q 5
Dankova, pik ▲ **KS** 146-147 C 5
Danli o **HN** 52-53 L 4
Danmark Fjord ≈ 26-27 o 3
Danmark Ø ⌒ **GRØ** 26-27 m 8
Danmarkshavn o **GRØ** 26-27 q 5
Dannebrogs Ø ⌒ **GRØ** 28-29 V 4
Dannemora o **USA** (NY) 278-279 H 4
Dannenberg (Elbe) o **D** 92-93 L 2
Dannevirke o **NZ** 182 F 4
Dannhauser o **ZA** 220-221 K 4
Dano o **BF** 202-203 J 4
Danot o **ETH** 208-209 G 5
Danridge o **USA** (TN) 282-283 D 4
Dan River ~ **USA** (NC) 282-283 H 4
Dan Sadau o **WAN** 204-205 G 3
Dansary, köl ⬭ **KA** 124-125 D 4
Danskøya ⌒ **N** 84-85 G 3
Dansville o **USA** (NY) 278-279 D 6
Dānta o **IND** 138-139 D 7
Dantalpalli o **IND** 140-141 H 2
Dantcho o **RT** 202-203 L 5
Dante o **USA** (VA) 280-281 D 7
Dante = Xaafuun o **SP** 208-209 K 3
Danube = Donau ~ **D** 92-93 L 4
Danubyu o **MYA** 158-159 C 2
Danum Valley Conservation Area ⊥ **MAL** 160-161 B 10
Danville o **CDN** (QUE) 238-239 N 3
Danville o **USA** (AR) 276-277 B 5
Danville o **USA** (GA) 284-285 G 4
Danville o **USA** (IL) 274-275 L 4
Danville o **USA** (IN) 274-275 M 5
Danville o **USA** (KY) 276-277 L 3
Danville o **USA** (PA) 280-281 K 3
Danville o **USA** (VA) 280-281 G 7
Danville o **USA** (WA) 244-245 G 2
Dan Xian o **VRC** 156-157 F 7
Danxiashan • **VRC** 156-157 H 4
Danyang o **VRC** 154-155 L 5
Danyi-Apéyémé o **RT** 202-203 L 6
Danzhai o **VRC** 156-157 E 3
Danzhou o **VRC** 156-157 F 4
Đao Lý So'n ⌒ **VN** 158-159 K 3
Daoro o **CI** 202-203 G 7
Daotanghe o **VRC** 154-155 B 3
Dao Thô Chu' ⌒ **VN** 158-159 G 6
Dao Timi o **RN** 198-199 F 2
Daoud o **DZ** 188-189 L 3
Daoukro o **CI** 202-203 J 6
Daoula, Hassi < **DZ** 190-191 E 4
Daoura, Hamada de la ∸ **DZ** 188-189 K 6
Daoura, Oued ~ **DZ** 188-189 K 5
Daowadung Cave • **THA** 158-159 F 3
Dao Xian o **VRC** 156-157 G 4
Daozhen o **VRC** 156-157 E 2
Dapaong ☆ **RT** 202-203 L 4
Dapchi o **WAN** 198-199 E 6
Dapélogo o **BF** 202-203 K 3
Đa Phúc ☆ **VN** 156-157 D 6
Dapitan o **RP** 160-161 E 8
Dāpoli o **IND** 140-141 E 2
Dapsang = K2 ▲ **PK** 138-139 F 2
Dapuchaihe o **VRC** 150-151 G 6
Da Qaidam o **VRC** 144-145 K 2
Daqiao o **VRC** 156-157 C 3
Daqing o **VRC** 150-151 E 4
Daqinggou ⊥ • **VRC** 150-151 C 6
Daqing Shan ▲▲ **VRC** 154-155 G 1
Dara o **SN** 202-203 C 2
Dar'a ☆ **SYR** 128-129 G 6
Dārāb o • **IR** 134-135 F 4
Darab ∸ **SP** 212-213 H 3
Darāban o **PK** 138-139 C 4
Daradou o **RCA** 206-207 G 6
Daraj o **LAR** 190-191 H 5
Dār al-Ḥamrā', ad- o **KSA** 132-133 B 3
Dārān o **IR** 134-135 D 2
Darapap o **PNG** 183 C 2
Darasun o **RUS** 118-119 F 10
Darasun, Kurort o **RUS** 118-119 F 10
Darasunskij, Veršino o **RUS** 118-119 G 9
Darauli o **IND** 142-143 D 2
Darāw o **ET** 194-195 F 5
Darazo o **WAN** 204-205 J 3
Darb, ad- o **KSA** 132-133 C 5
Darband o **IR** 134-135 G 3
Darband, Kūh-e ▲ **IR** 134-135 G 3
Darband-e Ḫān o **IRQ** 128-129 M 5
Darband Sar ▲ **IR** 136-137 B 6
Darbhanga o **IND** 142-143 D 2
D'Arbonne National Wildlife Refuge ⊥ **USA** (LA) 268-269 H 4
Darby o **USA** (MT) 250-251 E 5
Darby, Cape ▲ **USA** 20-21 J 4
Darby Creek ~ **USA** (OH) 280-281 C 4
Darby Mountains ▲▲ **USA** 20-21 J 4
Dar Chioukh o **DZ** 190-191 D 3
D'Arcy o **CDN** (BC) 230-231 G 3
D'Arcy o **CDN** (SAS) 232-233 K 4
Darda o **AUS** 176-177 F 3
Dār Daḥūka o **Y** 132-133 E 7
Dardanelle o **USA** (AR) 276-277 B 5
Dardanelle Lake ⬭ **USA** (AR) 276-277 B 5
Dareda o **EAT** (ARU) 212-213 E 6
Dar el Barka o **RIM** 196-197 C 6
Darende ☆ **TR** 128-129 G 3
Dar es Salaam ☆ • **EAT** 214-215 K 4
Dareton o **AUS** 180-181 G 3
Darfield o **CDN** (BC) 230-231 J 2
Dārfūr ∸ **SUD** 200-201 A 6
Dargan-Ata o **US** 136-137 H 4
Dargaville o **NZ** 182 D 1
Dargeçit ☆ **TR** 128-129 J 4
Dargo o **AUS** 180-181 J 4
Dargol o **RN** 202-203 L 3
Darhala o **CI** 202-203 H 5
Darhan o **MAU** 148-149 G 3
Darhan Muminggan Lianheqi o **VRC** 148-149 K 7
Darién ∸ **PA** 60-61 C 4
Darien o **USA** (GA) 284-285 J 5
Darien = Calima o **CO** 60-61 C 6
Darien, El o **CO** 60-61 E 4
Darién, Golfo del ≈ 60-61 C 3
Darién, Parque Nacional de ⊥ ··· **PA** 52-53 F 8
Darién, Serrania del ▲▲ **PA** 52-53 E 7
Darien Center o **USA** (NY) 278-279 C 6
Darīḫa, Abū o **SYR** 128-129 G 5
Dārin o **KSA** 134-135 D 5
Dar'inskij ☆ **KA** 124-125 H 4
Dario Meira o **BR** 72-73 L 3
Dārjiling o **IND** 142-143 F 2
Dārjing o **IND** 142-143 D 5
Darkan o **AUS** 176-177 D 6
Darke Peak o **AUS** 180-181 D 2
Darkylah o **RUS** 120-121 D 3
Darling o **ZA** 220-221 D 6
Darling, Mount ▲ **AUS** 180-181 K 3
Darling Downs ∸ **AUS** 178-179 L 4
Darlingford o **CDN** (MAN) 234-235 E 5
Darling Peninsula ⌣ **CDN** 26-27 O 4
Darling Range ▲▲ **AUS** 176-177 D 5
Darling River ~ **AUS** 178-179 H 6
Darling River ~ **AUS** 180-181 G 2
Darlington o **GB** 90-91 G 4
Darlington o **USA** (FL) 286-287 C 1
Darlington o **USA** (SC) 284-285 L 2
Darlington o **USA** (WI) 274-275 H 2
Darlington Point o **AUS** 180-181 H 3
Darlot, Lake ⬭ **AUS** 176-177 F 3
Darłowo o • **PL** 92-93 O 1
Darmazār o **IR** 134-135 G 4
Darmiyān o **IR** 134-135 H 2
Darmody o **CDN** (SAS) 232-233 M 5
Darmstadt o • **D** 92-93 K 4
Darnah □ **LAR** 192-193 K 1
Darnah ☆ **LAR** 192-193 K 1
Darnall o **ZA** 220-221 K 4
Darnétal o **F** 90-91 H 7
Darnick o **AUS** 180-181 G 2
Darnis = Darnah ☆ **LAR** 192-193 K 1
Darnley, Cape ▲ **ARK** 16 G 7
Darnley Bay ≈ 24-25 K 6
Darnley Island ⌒ **AUS** 183 B 5
Daro o **MAL** 162-163 J 3
Daroca o **E** 98-99 G 4
Darouma ~ **RMM** 202-203 F 2
Darou-Mousti o **SN** 202-203 B 2
Darovskoe o **RUS** 96-97 E 4
Darre Anğir, Kavīr-e ⬭ **IR** 134-135 F 2
Darregaz o **IR** 136-137 F 6
Darregueira o **RA** 78-79 H 4
Darre Qeyād ~ **IR** 134-135 C 2
Darre Šahr o **IR** 134-135 B 2
Darre-ye Būm o **AFG** 136-137 H 7
Darre-ye Ṣūf o **AFG** 136-137 K 7
Darrington o **USA** (WA) 244-245 D 2
Darr River ~ **AUS** 178-179 G 2
Darrūd o **IR** 136-137 F 6
Darsana o **BD** 142-143 F 4
Dartford o **GB** 90-91 H 6
Dartmoor o **AUS** 180-181 F 4
Dartmoor National Park ⊥ **GB** 90-91 F 6
Dartmouth o **CDN** (NS) 240-241 M 6
Dartmouth, Lake ⬭ **AUS** 178-179 H 4
Dartmouth Reservoir < **AUS** 180-181 J 4
Daru o **PNG** 183 B 5
Daru o **WAL** 202-203 E 6
Daruba o **RI** 164-165 L 2
Darubia o **PNG** 183 F 5
Daru Island ⌒ **PNG** 183 B 5
Daruvar o **HR** 100-101 F 2
Darvaza o **TM** 136-137 F 4
Darvazskij hrebet ▲▲ **TJ** 136-137 M 5
Darvel, Teluk ≈ 160-161 C 10
Darvi = Bulgan o **MAU** 146-147 L 2
Darvills o **USA** (VA) 280-281 J 6
Darvinskij zapovednik ⊥ **RUS** 94-95 P 2
Darvoza o **US** 136-137 K 4
Darwaz o **AFG** 136-137 M 5
Darwāzagai o **AFG** 134-135 M 3
Darwell o **CDN** (ALB) 232-233 D 2
Darwendale o **ZW** 218-219 F 3
Dārwha o **IND** 138-139 F 9
Darwin ☆ **AUS** 172-173 K 2
Darwin o **GB** 78-79 L 6
Darwin o **USA** (OH) 280-281 D 4
Darwin, Bahía ≈ 80 C 2
Darwin, Canal ≈ 80 C 2
Darwin, Cordillera ▲▲ **RCH** 80 E 7
Darwin, Cordillera de ▲▲ **RCH** 76-77 C 4
Darwin, Isla ⌒ **EC** 64-65 B 9
Darwin, Volcán ▲ **EC** 64-65 B 10
Darwin River o **AUS** 172-173 K 2
Daryāče-ye Ṭašk ⬭ **IR** 134-135 E 4
Darya Khān o **PK** 138-139 C 4
Daryaleh o **SP** 208-209 G 4
Daryāpur o **IND** 138-139 F 9
Daryā-ye Hazar ≈ 136-137 B 7
Daryā-ye Vāḫān ~ **AFG** 136-137 N 6
Darza ⌒ **Y** 132-133 H 7
Dārzīn o **IR** 134-135 H 4
Dās ⌒ **UAE** 134-135 E 6
Dasāda o **IND** 138-139 C 8
Dašbalbar o **MAU** 148-149 M 3
Dashan o **VRC** 156-157 D 3
Dashapalla o **IND** 142-143 D 5
Dashennongjia ▲ **VRC** 154-155 G 6
Dashennongjio ▲▲ **VRC** 154-155 G 6
Dashen Terara, Ras ▲ **ETH** 200-201 J 6
Dashhowuz = Dažhovuz ☆ **TM** 136-137 F 4
Dashuikeng o **VRC** 154-155 E 3
Dashwood o **CDN** (BC) 230-231 E 4
Dašinčilèn = Suuž o **MAU** 148-149 G 4
Daska o **PK** 138-139 E 3
Dasol Bay ≈ 160-161 C 5
Dass o **WAN** 204-205 H 3
Dassa o **DY** 204-205 E 5
Dassari o **DY** 202-203 L 4
Dassel o **USA** (MN) 270-271 D 5
Dasseneiland ⌒ **ZA** 220-221 D 6
Dastak o **IR** 134-135 D 2
Dašt-e 'Abbās o **IR** 134-135 B 1
Dašt-e Palang, Rūd-e ~ **IR** 134-135 D 4
Dašt-e Qal'e o • **AFG** 136-137 L 6
Dāsū o **PK** 138-139 D 2
Datang o **VRC** (GXI) 156-157 F 4
Datang o **VRC** (GXI) 156-157 F 5
Data Temple • **VRC** 154-155 H 4
Datça ☆ **TR** 128-129 B 4
Date o **J** 152-153 J 3
Dateland o **USA** (AZ) 256-257 B 6
Datian o **VRC** 156-157 K 4
Datian Ding ▲ **VRC** 156-157 G 5
Datian Z.B. ⊥ • **VRC** 156-157 F 7
Datil o **USA** (NM) 256-257 H 4
Datil Well National Recreation Site • **USA** (NM) 256-257 H 4
Dating o **VRC** 156-157 E 4
Datkan o **MYA** 142-143 J 6
Datong o **VRC** (QIN) 154-155 B 3
Datong o **VRC** (SHA) 154-155 H 1
Datong o **VRC** (XUZ) 146-147 C 7
Datong He ~ **VRC** 154-155 B 3
Datong Shan ▲▲ **VRC** 144-145 M 2
Datori o **DY** 202-203 L 4
Dato Temple o **VRC** (SIC) 156-157 D 2
Dato Temple o **VRC** (SIC) 156-157 C 2
Datta o **CI** 202-203 H 7
Datta o **RUS** 122-123 J 4
Datton, Kap ▲ **GRØ** 28-29 c 2
Datu, Tanjung ▲ **RI** 162-163 H 3
Datu, Teluk ≈ 162-163 J 4
Datuk, Tanjung ▲ **RI** 162-163 E 4
Datu Piang o **RP** 160-161 F 9
Dau o **RP** 160-161 D 5
Daub o **RI** 166-167 L 6
Dāūd Khel o **PK** 138-139 C 3
Daudmannsodden ▲ **N** 84-85 H 3
Daudnagar o **IND** 142-143 D 3
Daugaard Jensen Land ∸ **GRØ** 26-27 T 3
Daugava ~ **LV** 94-95 K 3
Daugavpils ☆ ·· **LV** 94-95 K 4
Dauḥa, ad- ★ **Q** 134-135 D 6
Dauka o **OM** 132-133 J 4
Daule o **EC** 64-65 C 2
Daule o **RI** 164-165 H 6
Daule, Río ~ **EC** 64-65 B 2
D'Aunay Bugt ≈ 28-29 c 2
Daund o **IND** 138-139 E 10
Daung Kyun ⌒ **MYA** 158-159 E 4
Dauphin o **CDN** (MAN) 234-235 C 3
Dauphin o **CDN** (MAN) 234-235 C 2
Dauphiné ∸ **F** 90-91 K 9
Dauphin Island o **USA** (AL) 284-285 B 6
Dauphin Island ⌒ **USA** (AL) 284-285 B 6
Dauphin Lake ⬭ **CDN** (MAN) 234-235 D 3
Dauphin River ~ **CDN** (MAN) 234-235 E 3
Daura o **WAN** 198-199 D 6
Ḍaurān, Ǧabal ▲ **Y** 132-133 D 6
Daur'an, Wādī ~ **Y** 132-133 F 6
Daurkina, poluostrov ⌣ **RUS** 112-113 Y 3
Daus o **KSA** 132-133 B 3
Dausa o **IND** 138-139 F 6
Dâu Tiêng o **VN** 158-159 J 5
Dautkŭl suvombori < **US** 136-137 F 3
Đá Vách, Mũi ▲ **VN** 158-159 K 5
Dāvangere o **IND** 140-141 F 3
Davao City o **RP** 160-161 F 9
Davao Gulf ≈ 160-161 F 9
Dāvari o **IR** 134-135 G 5
Dāvarzan o **IR** 136-137 E 6
Davenda o **RUS** 118-119 J 9
Davenport o **USA** (CA) 248-249 B 2
Davenport o **USA** (IA) 274-275 H 3
Davenport o **USA** (ND) 258-259 K 5
Davenport o **USA** (WA) 244-245 G 3
Davenport Creek ~ **AUS** 178-179 D 5
Davenport Downs o **AUS** 178-179 F 3
Davenport Range ▲▲ **AUS** 174-175 C 7
David ☆ ·· **PA** 52-53 C 7
David City o **USA** (NE) 262-263 J 3
David Crockett State Park ⊥ **USA** (TN) 276-277 H 5
Davidof Island ⌒ **USA** 22-23 F 7
Davidson o **CDN** (SAS) 232-233 N 4
Davidson o **USA** (OK) 264-265 E 4
Davidson, Mount ▲ **AUS** 172-173 K 6
Davidson Bank ≃ 22-23 O 6
Davidson Mountains ▲▲ **USA** 20-21 T 2
Davieau Island ⌒ **CDN** 36-37 L 6
Davilla o **USA** (TX) 266-267 K 3
Davin o **CDN** (SAS) 232-233 O 5
Davinópolis o **BR** 72-73 G 5
Davis o **USA** (CA) 246-247 D 5
Davis o **USA** (OK) 264-265 G 4
Davis o **USA** (SD) 260-261 J 3
Davis, Fort o **USA** (TX) 266-267 D 3
Davis Bay ≈ 16 G 14
Davis Creek o **USA** (CA) 246-247 E 2
Davis Dam o **USA** (AZ) 256-257 A 3
Davis Mountains ▲▲ **USA** (TX) 266-267 C 3
Davis National Historic Site, Fort ∴ **USA** (TX) 266-267 D 3
Davison o **USA** (MI) 272-273 F 4
Davis River ~ **AUS** 172-173 E 7
Davis Sea ≈ 16 G 10
Davis Strait ≈ 28-29 K 2
Davisville o **USA** (NH) 278-279 K 5
Daviumbu, Lake ⬭ **PNG** 183 A 4
Davlekanovo ☆ **RUS** 96-97 J 6
Davo ~ **CI** 202-203 G 7
Davos o • **CH** 92-93 K 5
Davša o **RUS** 118-119 D 8
Davy Crockett Lake ⬭ **USA** (TN) 282-283 E 4
Davy Lake ⬭ **CDN** 30-31 P 6
Davy Sund ≈ 26-27 o 7
Dawa o **VRC** 150-151 D 7
Dawadawa o **GH** 202-203 K 5
Dawa Dawa o **RP** 160-161 E 9
Dawādimī, ad- o • **KSA** 130-131 J 5
Dawangstan ~ **VRC** 156-157 F 5
Dawa Wenz ~ **ETH** 208-209 D 6
Daweloor, Pulau ⌒ **RI** 166-167 F 5
Dawera, Pulau ⌒ **RI** 166-167 E 5
Dawes Range ▲▲ **AUS** 178-179 L 3
Dawhat Salwā ≈ 134-135 D 6
Dawhenya o **GH** 202-203 L 7
Dawn o **USA** (OH) 280-281 B 3
Dawn o **USA** (TX) 264-265 B 4
Dawn o **USA** (VA) 280-281 J 6
Dawson o **CDN** 20-21 V 4
Dawson o **USA** (GA) 284-285 F 5
Dawson o **USA** (MN) 270-271 B 6
Dawson o **USA** (ND) 258-259 H 5
Dawson, Isla ⌒ **RCH** 80 E 6
Dawson, Mount ▲ **CDN** (BC) 230-231 M 2
Dawson Bay ⬭ **CDN** (MAN) 234-235 C 2
Dawson Bay Indian Reserve X **CDN** (MAN) 234-235 C 2
Dawson Creek o **CDN** 32-33 K 4
Dawson Highway II **AUS** 178-179 K 3
Dawson-Lambton Glacier ⊂ **ARK** 16 F 33
Dawson Range ▲▲ **AUS** 178-179 K 2
Dawson Range ▲▲ **CDN** 20-21 V 5
Dawson River ~ **AUS** 178-179 K 3
Dawsons Landing o **CDN** (BC) 230-231 B 2
Dawson Springs o **USA** (KY) 276-277 H 3
Dawsonville o **CDN** (NB) 240-241 J 3
Dawsonville o **USA** (GA) 284-285 F 2
Dawu o **VRC** (HUB) 154-155 J 6
Dawu o **VRC** (SIC) 154-155 B 6
Daww, ad- ∸ **SYR** 128-129 G 5
Dax o **F** 90-91 G 10
Daxi o **VRC** 156-157 M 2
Da Xian o **VRC** 154-155 E 6
Daxin o **VRC** 156-157 E 5
Daxue Shan ▲▲ **VRC** 154-155 B 6
Day o **USA** (CA) 246-247 D 2
Daya < **RIM** 196-197 E 5
Dayang Bunting, Pulau ⌒ **MAL** (KED) 162-163 C 2
Dayangshu o **VRC** 150-151 E 3
Dayao o **VRC** 156-157 B 4
Daya Wan ≈ 156-157 J 5
Daybabān, Shut'bat ad ~ **LAR** 192-193 D 3
Dayi ~ **GH** 202-203 L 6
Dayi o **VRC** 154-155 C 6
Dayi o **WAN** 204-205 G 3
Daylesford o **AUS** 180-181 H 4
Daylight Pass ▲ **USA** (CA) 248-249 H 3
Daymán, Cuchilla del ▲▲ **ROU** 76-77 J 6
Daymán, Río ~ **ROU** 76-77 J 6
Daymán, Termas del • **ROU** 76-77 J 6
Dayong o **VRC** 156-157 G 2
Days Creek o **USA** (OR) 244-245 B 8
Daysland o **CDN** (ALB) 232-233 F 3
Dayton o **USA** (MT) 250-251 E 4
Dayton o **USA** (NV) 246-247 F 4
Dayton o **USA** (OH) 280-281 B 4
Dayton o **USA** (OR) 244-245 B 5
Dayton o **USA** (TN) 276-277 K 5
Dayton o **USA** (TX) 268-269 F 6
Dayton o **USA** (WA) 244-245 H 4
Dayton o **USA** (WY) 252-253 L 2
Daytona Beach o **USA** (FL) 286-287 H 2
Dayu o **RI** 164-165 D 4
Dayu o **VRC** 156-157 J 4
Da Yunhe ~ **VRC** 154-155 J 3
Dayville o **USA** (OR) 244-245 F 6
Dazey o **USA** (ND) 258-259 J 4
Dazhou Dao ⌒ **VRC** 156-157 G 7
Dažhovuz ☆ **TM** 136-137 F 4
Dazhu o **VRC** 154-155 E 6
Dazkırı ☆ **TR** 128-129 C 4
Dazu o **VRC** 156-157 D 2
Dazu Shike • **VRC** 156-157 D 2
Dchira o **MA** 188-189 E 7
Dead Horse Point State Park • **USA** (UT) 254-255 F 5
Dead Indian Peak ▲ **USA** (WY) 252-253 J 2
Dead Lake ⬭ **USA** (MN) 270-271 C 4
Dead Lake < **USA** (FL) 286-287 D 1
Deadman Bay ≈ 48-49 G 5
Deadman Bay ≈ **USA** 286-287 F 2
Deadman's Bay o **CDN** (NFL) 242-243 P 3
Deadman's Cay o • **BS** 54-55 H 3
Deadmans Cove o **CDN** (NFL) 242-243 M 1
Deadman's Creek Indian Reserve X **CDN** (BC) 230-231 J 3
Deadman Summit ▲ **USA** (CA) 248-249 E 2
Dead Sea = Yam Hamelah = Bahret Lut ⬭ **JOR** 130-131 D 2
Deadwood o **USA** (SD) 260-261 C 2
Deakin o **AUS** 176-177 K 5
Dealesville o **ZA** 220-221 G 4
Déali o **SN** 202-203 C 2
De'an o **VRC** 156-157 J 2
Dean, Mount ▲ **AUS** 176-177 G 6
Dean Channel ≈ 32-33 G 5
Dean Channel ≈ **CDN** 228-229 G 4
Deán Funes o **RA** 76-77 E 6
Dean River ~ **CDN** (BC) 228-229 J 4
Deans Dundas Bay ≈ 24-25 N 4
Dearborn o **USA** (MI) 272-273 F 5
Deary o **USA** (ID) 250-251 C 5
Dease Arm ⬭ **CDN** 30-31 J 2
Dease Inlet ≈ 20-21 N 1
Dease Lake o **CDN** (BC) 32-33 E 2
Dease Lake ⬭ **CDN** (BC) 32-33 E 2
Dease River ~ **CDN** 30-31 L 2
Dease River ~ **CDN** 30-31 E 6
Dease Strait ≈ 24-25 S 6
Deas Thompson Point ▲ **CDN** 24-25 L 6
Death Valley ⌣ **USA** (CA) 248-249 G 3
Death Valley Junction o **USA** (CA) 248-249 H 3
Death Valley National Monument ⊥ • **USA** (CA) 248-249 G 3
Deatsville o **USA** (AL) 284-285 D 4
Deauville o ·· **F** 90-91 H 7
Deaver o **USA** (WY) 252-253 K 2
Debak o **MAL** 162-163 J 4
Debal'ceve o **UA** 102-103 L 3
Debalo o **SUD** 206-207 K 4
Debao o **VRC** 156-157 E 5
Debar o • **MK** 100-101 H 4
Debark o **ETH** 200-201 H 6
Debauch Mountain ▲ **USA** 20-21 L 4
Debaysima o **ER** 200-201 L 6
Debden o **CDN** (SAS) 232-233 M 2
Debdirge o **RUS** 120-121 E 2
Debdou o **MA** 188-189 K 4
Debed ~ **AR** 128-129 L 2
Debepare o **PNG** 183 A 4
Débéré ~ **BF** 202-203 J 3
Debesa o **AUS** 172-173 G 4
Debesy ☆ **RUS** 96-97 H 5
Debin o **RUS** 120-121 O 2
Debin ~ **RUS** 120-121 N 2
Debo, Lac ⬭ **RMM** 202-203 H 2
Debolt o **CDN** 32-33 M 4
Deborah East, Lake ⬭ **AUS** 176-177 E 5
Deborah West, Lake ⬭ **AUS** 176-177 E 5
Débougou o **RMM** 202-203 H 2
Debre Birhan o **ETH** 208-209 D 4
Debrecen o **H** 92-93 Q 5
Debre Markos ☆ **ETH** 208-209 C 3
Debre May o **ETH** 208-209 C 3
Debre Sina o **ETH** 208-209 D 4
Debre Tabor o **ETH** 208-209 D 3
Debre Work' o **ETH** 208-209 D 3
Debre Zebit o **ETH** 208-209 D 3
Debre Zeyit o **ETH** (Goj) 208-209 B 3
Debre Zeyit o **ETH** (She) 208-209 D 4
Decatur o **USA** (AL) 284-285 D 2
Decatur o **USA** (GA) 284-285 F 3
Decatur o **USA** (IL) 274-275 K 5
Decatur o **USA** (IN) 274-275 O 4
Decatur o **USA** (MI) 272-273 D 5
Decatur o **USA** (MS) 268-269 L 4
Decatur o **USA** (NE) 262-263 K 3
Decatur o **USA** (TN) 282-283 C 5
Decatur o **USA** (TX) 264-265 G 5
Decaturville o **USA** (TN) 276-277 G 5
Decazeville o **F** 90-91 J 9
Deccan ∸ **IND** 10-11 G 7
Decelles, Lac ⬭ **CDN** (QUE) 236-237 O 4
Decelles, Réservoir ⬭ **CDN** (QUE) 236-237 L 5
Decepcion o **ARK** 16 G 30
Déception o **CDN** 36-37 M 3
Déception, Rivière ~ **CDN** 36-37 M 3
Déception Bay ≈ 36-37 M 3
Deception Bay ≈ 183 C 4
Deception Lake ⬭ **CDN** 34-35 D 2
Deception Point ▲ **AUS** 172-173 K 1
Dechang o **VRC** 156-157 C 3
Decherd o **USA** (TN) 276-277 J 5
Dechu o **IND** 138-139 D 6
Děčín o **CZ** 92-93 N 3
Deciolândia o **BR** 70-71 J 4
Decize o **F** 90-91 J 8
Decker o **CDN** (MAN) 234-235 C 4
Decker o **USA** (MT) 250-251 N 6
Decker Field o **AUS** 176-177 H 2
Decker Lake o **CDN** (BC) 228-229 J 2
Deckers o **USA** (CO) 254-255 K 4
Declo o **USA** (ID) 252-253 E 4
Decoigne o **CDN** (ALB) 228-229 Q 4
Decorah o **USA** (IA) 274-275 G 1
Dedegöl Dağları ▲▲ **TR** 128-129 D 4
Deder o **ETH** 208-209 E 4
Dediāpāda o **IND** 138-139 D 9
Dedo, Cerro ▲ **RA** 80 E 2
Dédougou ☆ **BF** 202-203 J 3
Dedoviči ☆ **RUS** 94-95 L 3
Dedza o **MW** 218-219 H 2
Dee ~ **GB** 90-91 F 5
Dee ~ **GB** 90-91 F 3
Deep Bay ⬭ **CDN** 30-31 L 5
Deep Cove o **NZ** 182 A 6
Deep Creek o **USA** (WA) 244-245 H 3
Deep Creek, South Fork ~ **USA** (WA) 244-245 H 2
Deep Creek Lake < **USA** (MD) 280-281 G 4
Deep Fork ~ **USA** (OK) 264-265 H 3
Deep River o **CDN** (ONT) 238-239 H 2
Deep River ~ **CDN** (NFL) 242-243 M 2
Deep River ~ **USA** (NC) 282-283 H 5
Deep Rose Lake ⬭ **CDN** 30-31 U 3
Deep Valley Creek ~ **CDN** (ALB) 228-229 R 2
Deepwater o **AUS** 178-179 L 5
Deepwater o **USA** (MO) 274-275 E 6
Deep Well o **AUS** 178-179 C 3
Deer o **USA** (AR) 276-277 B 5
Deer Bay ≈ 24-25 T 1
Deer Creek ~ **USA** (MS) 268-269 K 4
Deer Creek Lake ⬭ **USA** (OH) 280-281 C 4
Deerfield o **USA** (SD) 260-261 C 2
Deerfield Beach o **USA** (FL) 286-287 J 5
Deerfield River ~ **USA** (MA) 278-279 J 6
Deer Fork ~ **USA** (TN) 276-277 F 5
Deerhorn o **CDN** (MAN) 234-235 E 4
Deering o **USA** 20-21 J 3
Deering o **USA** (ND) 258-259 F 3
Deering, Mount ▲ **AUS** 176-177 K 2
Deer Island ⌒ **CDN** (MAN) 234-235 G 3
Deer Island ⌒ **USA** 22-23 P 5
Deer Isle o **USA** (ME) 278-279 N 4
Deer Lake o **CDN** (NFL) 242-243 L 3
Deer Lake o **CDN** (ONT) 234-235 J 2
Deer Lake ⬭ **CDN** (NFL) 242-243 L 3
Deer Lodge o **USA** (MT) 250-251 G 5
Deer Lodge Pass ▲ **USA** (MT) 250-251 G 6
Deer Park o **CDN** (BC) 230-231 L 4
Deer Park o **USA** (AL) 284-285 B 5
Deer Park o **USA** (LA) 268-269 J 5
Deer Park o **USA** (MI) 270-271 N 4
Deer Park o **USA** (WA) 244-245 H 3
Deerpass Bay ⬭ **CDN** 30-31 J 3
Deer Pond ⬭ **CDN** (NFL) 242-243 O 4
Deer River ~ **CDN** 34-35 J 2
Deer River o **USA** (MN) 270-271 E 3
Deerton o **USA** (MI) 270-271 L 4
Deer Trail o **USA** (CO) 254-255 L 4
Deer Trail Creek ~ **USA** (CO) 254-255 M 4
Deerwood o **USA** (MN) 270-271 E 4
Deeth o **USA** (NV) 246-247 K 2
Defensores del Chaco, Parque Nacional ⊥ **PY** 70-71 G 7
Defferrari o **RA** 78-79 K 5
Defia, Hassi < **MA** 188-189 K 4
Defiance o **USA** (OH) 280-281 B 2
Défilé de Tosaye ∸ **RMM** 196-197 K 6
Degache o **TN** 190-191 G 4
Degali ~ **RUS** 116-117 F 4
Degayê, Ra's ▲ **ER** 200-201 L 6
Dêgê o **VRC** 144-145 M 5
Degeh Bur o **ETH** 208-209 F 4
Degeh Medo o **ETH** 208-209 F 5
Dégelis o **CDN** (QUE) 240-241 G 3
Degema o **WAN** 204-205 G 6
Deggendorf o **D** 92-93 M 4
Degollado o **MEX** 52-53 C 1
Degoma o **ETH** 200-201 H 6
Dégrad Claude o **F** 62-63 H 4
Dégrad des Emerillon = Dégrad Claude o **F** 62-63 H 4
Dégrad Haut Camopi o **F** 62-63 H 4
Dégrad Saint-Léon o **F** 62-63 H 4
Dégrad Vitalo o **F** 62-63 H 4
De Grau o **CDN** (NFL) 242-243 J 4
De Grey River ~ **AUS** 172-173 D 6
Dehalak Desēt ⌒ **ER** 200-201 K 5
Dehāqān o **IR** 134-135 D 3
Dehbārez o **IR** 134-135 G 5
Dehbid o **IR** 134-135 E 3
Deh Dašt o **IR** 134-135 D 3
Dehdez o **IR** 134-135 D 3
Deheğ o **IR** 134-135 F 3
Dehej o **IND** 138-139 D 9
Deh-e Kohne o **IR** 134-135 D 4
Dehekolano, Tanjung ▲ **RI** 164-165 K 4
Dehepodo o **RI** 164-165 K 3
Deh Ḫeir o **IR** 134-135 F 4
Dehibai o **TN** 190-191 H 4
Dehkanabad o **US** 136-137 K 5
Dehlorān o **IR** 134-135 B 1
Deh Mirdād o **AFG** 136-137 K 7
Deh Molla o **IR** 134-135 C 3
Deh Pariān o **AFG** 136-137 L 7
Dehra Dun o ·· **IND** 138-139 G 4
Deh Rāvūd o **AFG** 134-135 L 2
Dehri o **IND** 142-143 D 3
Dehšir o **IR** 134-135 E 3
Deh Šū o **AFG** 134-135 K 3
Dehua o **VRC** 156-157 L 4
Dehui o **VRC** 150-151 E 5
Deilam, Bandar-e o **IR** 134-135 D 3
Deim Būkhit o **SUD** 206-207 H 5
Deira o **UAE** 134-135 F 6
Dej o **RO** 102-103 C 4
Dejen o **ETH** 208-209 D 3
Dejian o **VRC** 156-157 F 2
Dejnau o **TM** 136-137 H 5
De Jongs, Tanjung ▲ **RI** 166-167 K 5
De-Kastri o **RUS** 122-123 J 3
Dek'emhāre o **ER** 200-201 J 5
Dekese o **ZRE** 210-211 H 5
Dekina o **WAN** 204-205 G 5
Dekoa o **RCA** 206-207 D 5
Delaa o **DZ** 190-191 D 4
Delacour o **CDN** (ALB) 232-233 E 4
Delacroix o **USA** (LA) 268-269 L 7
Delaki o **RI** 166-167 C 6
Delaney o **USA** (WA) 244-245 H 4
Delanggu o **RI** 168 D 3
Delano o **USA** (CA) 248-249 E 4
Delārām o **AFG** 134-135 K 2
Delareyville o **ZA** 220-221 G 3
Delarof Islands ⌒ **USA** 22-23 G 7
Delaronde Lake ⬭ **CDN** 34-35 C 3
Delavan o **USA** (IL) 274-275 J 4
Delavan o **USA** (WI) 274-275 K 2
Delaware o **USA** (AR) 276-277 B 5
Delaware o **USA** (OH) 280-281 C 3
Delaware □ **USA** (DE) 280-281 L 4
Delaware Bay ≈ 46-47 L 6
Delaware Bay ≈ **USA** 280-281 L 4
Delaware Creek ~ **USA** (TX) 266-267 C 2
Delaware Lake ⬭ **USA** (OH) 280-281 C 3
Delaware River ~ **USA** (KS) 262-263 L 5
Delaware River ~ **USA** (NY) 278-279 F 6
Delaware River ~ **USA** (PA) 280-281 M 2
Delbi o **SN** 202-203 C 2
Del Bonita o **CDN** (ALB) 232-233 F 6
Delburne o **CDN** (ALB) 232-233 E 3
Delcampre o **USA** (LA) 268-269 J 7
Del Cano Rise ≃ 9 H 10
Delčevo o • **MK** 100-101 J 4
Delco o **USA** (NC) 282-283 J 6
Deleau o **CDN** (MAN) 234-235 C 5
Deleg o **EC** 64-65 C 3
Delegate River o **AUS** 180-181 K 4
Délembé o **RCA** 206-207 F 4
Délép o **TCH** 198-199 J 6
Delfino o **BR** 68-69 H 7
Delfinópolis o **BR** 72-73 G 6
Delft o • **NL** 92-93 H 2
Delfus o **PE** 64-65 D 4
Delfzijl o **NL** 92-93 J 2
Dèlgèr = Tajgan o **MAU** 148-149 C 4
Dèlgèrèh = Hongor o **MAU** 148-149 K 5
Dèlgèrhangaj = Hašaat o **MAU** 148-149 G 5
Dèlgèr mörön ~ **MAU** 148-149 D 3
Delgo o **SUD** 200-201 E 2
Delhi o **CDN** (ONT) 238-239 E 6
Delhi ☆ ·· **IND** 138-139 F 5
Delhi o **USA** (CO) 254-255 L 6
Delhi o **USA** (LA) 268-269 J 4
Delhi o **USA** (NY) 278-279 G 6
Déli o **TCH** 206-207 B 4
Deli, Pulau ⌒ **RI** 168 A 3
Delia o **CDN** (ALB) 232-233 F 4
Delicias o **CO** 64-65 E 2
Delicias o **MEX** 50-51 G 3
Delicias, Las o **CO** 60-61 F 5
Deliğān o **IR** 134-135 D 1
Delight o **USA** (AR) 276-277 B 6
Délimane, I-n- < **RMM** 202-203 L 2
Delingdè ~ **RUS** 110-111 O 7
Delingdèkèn ~ **RUS** 116-117 H 3
Delingha o **VRC** 144-145 L 2
Delin'ja ~ **RUS** 110-111 V 7
Delisle o **CDN** (QUE) 240-241 D 2
Delisle o **CDN** (SAS) 232-233 L 4
Delissaville X **AUS** 172-173 K 2
Delitua o **RI** 162-163 C 3
Deliverence Island ⌒ **AUS** 183 A 5
Deljankir ~ **RUS** 110-111 a 7

Del'kju-Ohotskaja ∼ RUS 120-121 J 3
Dèl'ku ∼ RUS 110-111 a 6
Dell ○ USA (MT) 250-251 G 7
Dell City ○ USA (TX) 266-267 B 2
Delle ○ USA (UT) 254-255 C 3
Dell Rapids ○ USA (SD) 260-261 K 3
Dellys ○ DZ 190-191 D 2
Delmar Lake ○ USA (NV) 248-249 K 2
Delmarva Peninsula ⌣ USA (MD) 280-281 L 4
Delmas ○ CDN (SAS) 232-233 K 3
Delmas ○ ZA 220-221 J 3
Delmenhorst ○ D 92-93 K 2
Delmont ○ USA (NJ) 280-281 M 4
Delmore Downs ○ AUS 178-179 C 2
Del Norte ○ USA (CO) 254-255 J 6
De-Longa, ostrova ⌒ RUS 110-111 b 1
Deloraine ○ AUS 180-181 J 6
Deloraine ○ CDN (MAN) 234-235 C 5
Delos ∴ GR 100-101 K 6
Delphi ∴ GR 100-101 J 5
Delphi ○ USA (IN) 274-275 M 4
Delphos ○ USA (OH) 280-281 B 3
Delportshoop ○ ZA 220-221 G 4
Delray Beach ○ USA (FL) 286-287 J 5
Del Rio ○ USA (TX) 266-267 G 4
Delsbo ○ S 86-87 H 6
Del Sur ○ USA (CA) 248-249 F 5
Delta ○ CDN (BC) 230-231 G 4
Delta ○ CDN (MAN) 234-235 E 4
Delta ○ USA (CO) 254-255 G 5
Delta ○ USA (OH) 280-281 B 2
Delta ○ USA (UT) 254-255 C 4
Delta Camp < RB 218-219 B 4
Delta del Tigre ○ ROU 78-79 L 3
Delta Downs ○ AUS 174-175 F 5
Delta Dunării ∴ RO 102-103 F 5
Delta Junction ○ USA 20-21 S 4
Delta Mendota Canal < USA (CA) 248-249 D 3
Delta National Wildlife Refuge ⊥ USA (LA) 268-269 L 7
Delthore Mountain ▲ CDN 30-31 F 4
Deltona ○ USA (FL) 286-287 H 3
Del'tula ∼ RUS 116-117 E 3
Delungra ○ AUS 178-179 L 5
Dèluun = Rašaant ○ MAU 146-147 K 2
Del Verme Falls ∼ ETH 208-209 E 6
Dèm, Lac de ○ BF 202-203 K 3
Dema ∼ RUS 96-97 J 6
Demagiri ○ IND 142-143 H 4
Demaine ○ CDN (SAS) 232-233 L 5
Demak ○ RI 168 D 3
Demalisques de Leshwe ⊥ ZRE 214-215 E 7
Demaraisville ○ CDN (ONT) 236-237 M 3
Demarcation Point ▲ USA 20-21 U 2
Demba ○ ZRE 210-211 J 6
Demba Koli ○ SN 202-203 D 3
Dembecha ○ ETH 208-209 C 3
Dembi ○ ETH 208-209 C 4
Dembia ○ RCA 206-207 G 6
Dembi Dolo ○ ETH 208-209 B 4
Dembo ○ CAM 204-205 K 4
Dembo ○ TCH 206-207 C 4
Demensk, Spas- ○ RUS 94-95 O 4
Demerara Abyssal Plain ≃ 6-7 D 7
Demers, Pointe ▲ CDN 36-37 K 4
Demers Centre ○ CDN (QUE) 238-239 H 3
Demidov ☆ RUS 94-95 M 4
Deming ○ USA (NM) 256-257 H 6
Deming ○ USA (WA) 244-245 C 2
Demini, Rio ∼ BR 66-67 F 3
Demirci ○ TR 128-129 C 3
Dem'janka ∼ RUS 114-115 K 5
Dem'janka ∼ RUS 114-115 N 5
Dem'janovo ○ RUS 96-97 E 3
Demjansk ☆ RUS 94-95 N 3
Dem'janskoe ○ RUS 114-115 K 5
Demmin ○ D 92-93 M 2
Demnate ○ MA 188-189 H 5
Demopolis ○ USA (AL) 284-285 C 4
Demotte ○ USA (IN) 274-275 L 3
Dempo, Gunung ▲ RI 162-163 E 6
Dempo, Selat ≈ 162-163 F 4
Dempseys ○ AUS 174-175 C 7
Dempster Highway II CDN 20-21 V 4
Dempta ○ RI 166-167 L 3
Dêmqog ○ IND 138-139 G 3
Demsa ○ CAM 204-205 K 4
Denakil ∴ ETH 200-201 K 5
Denali Highway II USA 20-21 Q 5
Denali National Park ○ USA 20-21 Q 5
Denali National Park and Preserve ⊥ USA 20-21 P 5
Denan ○ ETH 208-209 F 5
Denau ○ US 136-137 K 5
Denbigh ○ CDN (ONT) 238-239 H 3
Denbigh, Cape ▲ USA 20-21 K 4
Denbigh Downs ○ AUS 178-179 F 2
Den Chai ○ THA 158-159 F 2
Dendang ○ RI 162-163 G 6
Dendâra ○ RIM 196-197 G 6
Déndoudi ○ SN 202-203 D 2
Deneba ○ ETH 208-209 D 4
Denežkin Kamen', gora ▲ RUS 114-115 E 4
Dengfeng ○ VRC 154-155 H 4
Dengi ○ WAN 204-205 H 4
Dengkou ○ VRC 154-155 E 1
Dengqên ○ VRC 144-145 K 5
Denguiro ○ RCA 206-207 F 6
Dengyuan ○ VRC 156-157 D 2
Dengzhou ○ VRC 154-155 H 5
Den Haag = 's-Gravenhage ☆ NL 92-93 H 2
Denham ○ AUS 176-177 B 2
Denham, Mount ▲ JA 54-55 G 5
Denham Island ⌒ AUS 174-175 E 5
Denham Range ▲ AUS 178-179 J 2
Denham Sound ≈ 176-177 B 2
Denham Springs ○ USA (LA) 268-269 K 6
Denhart ○ CDN (ALB) 232-233 G 5
Den Helder ○ NL 92-93 H 2
Denholm ○ CDN (SAS) 232-233 L 3
Deni, Área Indígena ☒ BR 66-67 C 6
Denia ○ E 98-99 H 5
Denial Bay ≈ 176-177 M 6
Denikourcula ○ RMM 202-203 H 4
Deniliquin ○ AUS 180-181 H 3
Denio ○ USA (NV) 246-247 G 2
Denio Junction ○ USA (NV) 246-247 G 2
Denio Summit ▲ USA (NV) 246-247 G 2
Denise Island ⌒ SY 224 D 1
Denison ○ USA (IA) 274-275 C 2
Denison ○ USA (TX) 264-265 H 5
Denison Range ▲ AUS 172-173 J 5
Denizli ☆ TR 128-129 C 4
Denkanikota ○ IND 140-141 G 4
Denkola ∴ TM 136-137 E 4
Denman ○ AUS 180-181 L 2
Denman ○ USA (NE) 262-263 H 4
Denman Glacier ⊂ ARK 16 G 10
Denman Island ○ CDN (BC) 230-231 E 4
Denmark ○ AUS 176-177 D 7
Denmark ○ USA (SC) 284-285 J 3
Denmark ○ USA (WI) 270-271 L 6
Denmark = Danmark ■ DK 86-87 C 9
Denmark Strait ≈ 6-7 F 2
Denmark Strait ≈ 6-7 G 2
Denniel Creek ∼ CDN (SAS) 232-233 L 6
Dennis, Lake ○ AUS 172-173 J 6
Dennysville ○ USA (ME) 278-279 O 4
Den Oever ○ NL 92-93 H 2
Denpasar ☆ RI 168 B 7
Dent, La ▲ CI 202-203 G 6
Denton ○ USA (GA) 284-285 H 5
Denton ○ USA (MD) 280-281 L 5
Denton ○ USA (MT) 250-251 K 4
Denton ○ USA (NC) 282-283 G 5
Denton ○ USA (TX) 264-265 G 5
Denton Creek ∼ USA (TX) 264-265 G 5
Dentons Corner ○ USA (VA) 280-281 H 6
D'Entrecasteaux, Point ▲ AUS 176-177 D 7
D'Entrecasteaux Islands ⌒ PNG 183 F 5
D'Entrecasteaux National Park ⊥ AUS 176-177 C 7
Denu ○ GH 202-203 L 6
Denver ○ USA (IA) 274-275 F 2
Denver ☆ USA (CO) 254-255 L 4
Denver City ○ USA (TX) 264-265 B 6
Denzil ○ CDN (SAS) 232-233 J 3
Déo ○ RCA 206-207 E 4
Déo, Mayo ∼ CAM 204-205 K 5
Deoband ○ IND 138-139 F 5
Deodápolis ○ BR 76-77 K 2
Deogarh ○ IND 142-143 D 5
Deogarh Peak ▲ IND 142-143 C 4
Deoghar ○ IND 142-143 E 3
Deolāli ○ IND 138-139 D 10
Deoli ○ IND 138-139 G 9
Deolia ○ IND 138-139 E 7
Deora ○ USA (CO) 254-255 N 6
Deori ○ IND 142-143 B 5
Déou ○ BF 202-203 K 2
Dep ∼ RUS 118-119 N 9
Dep ∼ RUS 122-123 C 2
Dep, River ∼ WAN 204-205 H 4
Depālpur ○ IND 138-139 E 8
De Panne ○ B 92-93 G 3
Depapre ○ RI 166-167 L 3
Departure Bay ○ CDN (BC) 230-231 F 4
Departure Lake ○ CDN (ONT) 236-237 G 3
Depew ○ USA (NY) 278-279 C 6
Depew ○ USA (OK) 264-265 H 3
Deposit ○ USA (NY) 278-279 F 6
Depot d'Aigle ○ CDN (QUE) 238-239 J 2
Dépôt-de-la-Lièvre ○ CDN (QUE) 240-241 C 2
Dépôt Lézard Rnes ○ F 62-63 H 3
Deptumala ∼ RUS 108-109 a 5
Deputatskij ☆ RUS 110-111 W 5
Dêqên ○ VRC (XIZ) 144-145 K 5
Dêqên ○ VRC (YUN) 144-145 M 6
Deqing ○ VRC 156-157 G 5
Dera ○ ETH 208-209 D 4
Dera ∼ SP 212-213 J 3
Dera Bugti ○ PK 138-139 B 5
Dera Ghāzi Khān ○ PK 138-139 C 4
Dera Ismāīl Khān ○ PK 138-139 C 4
Derale ▲ AUS 180-181 K 2
Dera Murād Jamali ○ PK 138-139 B 5
Dera Nānak ○ IND 138-139 E 3
Dera Nawāb Sāhib ○ PK 138-139 C 5
Đeravica ▲ YU 100-101 H 3
Derāwar Fort ○ PK 138-139 C 5
Derbeikan, Wādi ∼ SUD 200-201 G 3
Derbeke ∼ RUS 110-111 U 7
Derbekinskaja vpadina ⌣ RUS 110-111 U 7
Derbent ○ RUS 126-127 H 6
Derbissaka ○ RCA 206-207 G 6
Derby ○ AUS (TAS) 180-181 J 6
Derby ○ AUS (WA) 172-173 F 4
Derby ○ CDN (PEI) 240-241 L 4
Derby ○ GB 90-91 G 5
Derby ○ USA (IN) 274-275 M 6
Derby ○ USA (KS) 262-263 J 7
Derby ○ ZA 220-221 H 2
Derby Lake ○ CDN 30-31 X 2
Derby Shelton ○ USA (CT) 280-281 N 2
Derdepoort ○ ZA 220-221 H 2
Dereli ☆ TR 128-129 H 2
Deren, Adrar-n- ▲ MA 188-189 G 5
Deréssa ○ TCH 198-199 K 6
Derewo ∼ RI 166-167 J 3
Derg, Lough ○ IRL 90-91 C 5
Dergači ☆ RUS 96-97 F 8
Derhačy ○ UA 102-103 K 2
Derickson Seamount ≃ 22-23 Q 6
Derik ☆ TR 128-129 J 4
Derjugina, vpadina ≃ 122-123 L 2
Derkül ∼ KA 96-97 G 8
Derm ○ NAM 220-221 D 1
Dermitt ○ USA (TX) 264-265 C 6
Dermott ○ USA (AR) 276-277 D 7
Dernieres, Isles ⌒ USA (LA) 268-269 K 7
Deroche ○ CDN (BC) 230-231 G 4
Derramadero ○ C 54-55 F 4
Derre ○ MOC 218-219 J 3
Derri ○ SP 208-209 H 6
Derry ○ USA (NH) 278-279 K 6
Derry Doire = Londonderry ☆ GB 90-91 D 4
Derry Downs ○ AUS 178-179 C 2
Derudeb ○ SUD 200-201 H 4
Derval ○ F 90-91 G 8
Derville, Rivière ∼ CDN 36-37 L 3
Derwent ○ AUS 176-177 M 1
Derwent ○ CDN (ALB) 232-233 H 2
Derwent, River ∼ AUS 180-181 J 7
Deržavinsk ☆ KA 124-125 E 3
Deržavnyj zapovednyk Dunajskie plavni ∴ UA 102-103 F 5
Desaguadero, Río ∼ BOL 70-71 D 5
Desaguadero, Río ∼ RA 78-79 F 2
Desagües de los Colorados ○ RA 76-77 D 5
Desaru ○ MAL 162-163 F 4
Desbarats ○ CDN (ONT) 238-239 B 2
Desbarats Strait ≈ 24-25 T 2
Descabezado Grande, Volcán ▲ RCH 78-79 D 3
Descanso ○ USA (CA) 248-249 H 7
Descanso, El ○ PE 70-71 B 4
Deschaillons ○ CDN (QUE) 238-239 N 2
Deschambault Lake ○ CDN 34-35 D 3
Descharme River ∼ CDN 32-33 Q 3
Deschutes River ∼ USA (OR) 244-245 E 5
Deschutes River ∼ USA (OR) 244-245 D 6
Descoberto ○ BR 72-73 H 2
Descubierta, La ○ DOM 54-55 K 5
Desē ☆ ETH 208-209 D 3
Deseado, Cabo ▲ RCH 80 C 6
Deseado, Río ∼ RA 80 G 3
Desecheo, Isla ⌒ USA (PR) 286-287 O 2
Desecho ○ YV 60-61 H 6
Desemboque, El ○ MEX 50-51 C 2
Desengaño, Punta ▲ RA 80 G 4
Desenzano del Garda ○ I 100-101 C 2
Deseret ○ USA (UT) 254-255 C 4
Deseret Peak ▲ USA (UT) 254-255 C 3
Desertas, Ilhas ⌒ P 188-189 C 4
Desertas, Ponta das ▲ BR 74-75 E 8
Desert Center ○ USA (CA) 248-249 J 6
Desert Hot Springs ○ USA (CA) 248-249 H 6
Desert National Park ⊥ IND 138-139 C 6
Desert National Wildlife Refuge ⊥ USA (NV) 248-249 J 3
Desert Peak ▲ USA (UT) 254-255 B 2
Desert Range ▲ USA (NV) 248-249 J 3
Desert Range ✕✕ USA (UT) 254-255 B 5
Desert Test Center ✕✕ USA (UT) 254-255 B 3
Desert View ○ USA (AZ) 256-257 D 2
Deshler ○ USA (OH) 280-281 C 2
Desiderio Tello ○ RA 76-77 D 6
Desierto, Canal al < RA 76-77 F 4
Desierto Central de Baja California, Parque Nacional del ⊥ MEX 50-51 B 3
Desirade, La ⌒ F 56 E 3
Des Lacs ○ USA (ND) 258-259 F 3
Des Lacs National Wildlife Refuge ⊥ USA (ND) 258-259 E 3
Desmarais Lake ○ CDN 30-31 R 5
Des Moines ○ USA (WA) 244-245 C 3
Des Moines ☆ USA (IA) 274-275 E 3
Des Moines River ∼ USA (IA) 274-275 F 4
Desna ∼ RUS 94-95 N 4
Desna ∼ UA 102-103 G 2
Desna ∼ UA 102-103 H 2
Desnățui ∼ RO 102-103 C 5
Desolación, Isla ⌒ RCH 80 C 6
Desolation Canyon ⌣ USA (UT) 254-255 E 4
Desolation Point ▲ RP 160-161 F 7
Desolation Sound Provincial Marine Park ⊥ CDN (BC) 230-231 E 3
Desoronto ○ CDN (ONT) 238-239 H 4
De Soto National Monument ∴ USA (FL) 286-287 G 4
Despatch ○ ZA 220-221 G 6
Despeñaderos ○ RA 76-77 E 6
Despotovac ○ YU 100-101 H 2
Des Roches ○ CDN (QUE) 240-241 D 3
Desroches, Île ⌒ SY 224 C 2
Dessau ○ D 92-93 M 3
Destacado Island ⌒ RP 160-161 F 6
Destacamento São Simão ○ BR 70-71 G 4
Desterro ○ BR 66-67 C 6
Destin ○ USA (FL) 286-287 C 1
D'Estrees Bay ≈ 180-181 D 3
Destruction Bay ○ CDN 20-21 V 6
Desvelos, Bahía ≈ 80 G 4
Dete ○ ZW 218-219 D 4
Detmold ○ D 92-93 K 3
Detour, Point ▲ USA (MI) 270-271 M 5
Detpa ○ AUS 180-181 F 4
Detrin ∼ RUS 120-121 N 3
Detroit ○ USA (AL) 284-285 B 2
Detroit ○ USA (OR) 244-245 C 6
Detroit ○ USA (TX) 264-265 J 5
Detroit ○ USA (MI) 272-273 F 5
Detroit, Fort ∴ USA (MN) 270-271 C 4
Détroit de Bougainville ≈ 184 II a 2
Détroit de Jaques-Cartier ≈ 38-39 N 4
Détroit d'Honguedo ≈ 38-39 M 4
Detroit Lake ○ USA (OR) 244-245 C 6
Detroit Lakes ○ USA (MN) 270-271 C 4
Dettifoss ∼ IS 86-87 e 2
Det Udom ○ THA 158-159 H 3
Detuo ○ VRC 156-157 C 2
Deua National Park ⊥ AUS 180-181 K 3
Deukeskenkala ∴ TM 136-137 F 3
Deustua ○ PE 70-71 B 4
Deutsch Brod = Havlíčkův Brod ○ CZ 92-93 N 4
Deutsche Bucht ≈ D 92-93 J 1
Deutschheim State Historic Site ∴ USA (MO) 274-275 G 6
Deux Balé, Forêt des ⊥ BF 202-203 J 4
Deux Bassins, Col de ⊥ DZ 190-191 D 2
Deux Pietons ∴ WL 56 E 5
Deva ☆ RO 102-103 C 5
Devadurg ○ IND 140-141 G 2
Devakottai ○ IND 140-141 H 6
Devanhalli ○ IND 140-141 G 4
Devar Hipparg ○ IND 140-141 G 2
Devarkonda ○ IND 140-141 H 2
Devarshola ○ IND 140-141 G 5
De Veber, Mount ▲ CDN (ALB) 228-229 P 3
Devechi = Davaçi ○ AZ 128-129 N 2
Deveci Dağı ▲ TR 128-129 F 2
Develi ☆ TR 128-129 F 3
Deveril ○ AUS 178-179 K 2
Devers ○ USA (TX) 268-269 F 6
Devgarh ○ IND 138-139 D 7
Deviation Peak ▲ USA 20-21 K 3
Devica ∼ RUS 102-103 L 2
Deville ○ CDN (ALB) 232-233 F 2
Deville Névé ∼ CDN (BC) 230-231 M 2
Devil Mountain ▲ USA 20-21 H 3
Devil Mountain Lake ○ USA 20-21 H 3
Devils Bridge ∴ AG 56 E 3
Devils Den ○ USA (CA) 248-249 E 4
Devils Den State Parks ⊥ USA (AR) 276-277 A 5
Devils Gate ▲ USA (CA) 246-247 F 5
Devil's Hole ≃ 90-91 H 3
Devil's Hole National Monument ∴ USA (NV) 248-249 H 3
Devil's Island = Diable, Île du ⌒ F 62-63 H 3
Devils Kitchen Lake ○ USA (IL) 276-277 F 3
Devils Lake ○ USA (ND) 258-259 J 3
Devils Lake Sioux Indian Reservation ☒ USA (ND) 258-259 J 4
Devils Marbles Scenic Reserve ∴ AUS 174-175 C 7
Devil's Playground ∴ USA (CA) 248-249 H 4
Devil's Point ▲ BS 54-55 J 3
Devils Postpile National Monument ∴ USA (CA) 248-249 E 2
Devils River ∼ USA (TX) 266-267 F 3
Devils Tower Junction ○ USA (WY) 252-253 O 2
Devils Tower National Monument ∴ USA (WY) 252-253 O 2
Devin ○ BG 102-103 D 7
Devine ○ USA (TX) 266-267 J 4
Devipattinam ○ IND 140-141 H 6
Devli ○ IND 138-139 E 7
Devlin ○ CDN (ONT) 234-235 K 6
Devnja ○ BG 102-103 E 6
Devoll, Lumi ∼ AL 100-101 H 4
Devon ○ CDN (ALB) 232-233 E 2
Devon ∴ GB 90-91 E 6
Devon ○ USA (MT) 250-251 H 3
Devon ○ ZA 220-221 J 3
Devon 30 Indian Reserve ☒ CDN (NB) 240-241 J 4
Devon Island ⌒ CDN 24-25 b 3
Devonport ○ AUS 180-181 H 6
Devonshire ○ AUS 178-179 H 2
Devrek ☆ TR 128-129 D 2
Devure ∼ ZW 218-219 F 4
Dewa, Tanjung ▲ RI (ACE) 162-163 A 3
Dewa, Tanjung ▲ RI (KSE) 164-165 E 5
Dewar ○ USA (OK) 264-265 J 3
Dewās ○ IND 138-139 F 8
Dewatto ○ USA (WA) 244-245 C 3
Dewberry ○ CDN (ALB) 232-233 H 2
Dewdney ○ CDN (BC) 230-231 G 4
Dewelē ○ ETH 208-209 F 3
Dewetsdorp ○ ZA 220-221 H 4
Dewey ○ USA (AZ) 256-257 C 4
Dewey ○ USA (SD) 260-261 B 3
Dewey ○ USA (PR) 286-287 Q 2
Dewey Lake ○ USA (KY) 276-277 N 3
Dexing ○ VRC 156-157 K 2
Dexter ○ USA (ME) 278-279 M 3
Dexter ○ USA (MO) 276-277 F 4
Dexter ○ USA (MS) 268-269 L 5
Dexter ○ USA (NM) 256-257 L 5
Dexterity Island ⌒ CDN 26-27 O 8
Deyang ○ VRC 154-155 D 6
Dey-Dey, Lake ○ AUS 176-177 L 4
Deyhūk ○ IR 134-135 G 2
Deyyer ○ IR 134-135 D 5
Dez, Rūd-e ∼ IR 134-135 C 2
Dezadeash ○ CDN 20-21 W 6
Dezadeash Lake ○ CDN 20-21 W 6
Dezfūl ○ IR 134-135 C 2
Dežgān ○ IR 134-135 F 5
Dezhneva, Mys = Dežneva, mys ▲ RUS 112-113 a 3
Dezhou ○ VRC 154-155 K 3
Dežneva, buhta ≈ RUS 112-113 R 6
Dežneva, mys ▲ RUS 112-113 a 3
Dezong ○ VRC 144-145 H 4
Dhahran = az-Zahrān ○ KSA 134-135 D 5
Dhahran = Zahrān, az- ○ KSA 134-135 D 5
Dhaka ★ BD 142-143 G 4
Dhakia ○ IND 144-145 C 6
Dhaleswari ∼ BD 142-143 F 3
Dhanāna ○ IND 138-139 C 6
Dhanasar ○ PK 138-139 B 4
Dhanaura ○ IND 138-139 G 5
Dhanbād ○ IND 142-143 E 4
Dhandelhura ○ NEP 144-145 C 6
Dhandhuka ○ IND 138-139 C 8
Dhangarhi ○ NEP 144-145 C 6
D'Hanis ○ USA (TX) 266-267 H 4
Dhankuta ○ NEP 144-145 F 7
Dhanpuri ○ IND 142-143 B 4
Dhanushkodi ○ IND 140-141 H 6
Dhār ○ IND 138-139 E 8
Dharampur ○ IND 138-139 D 9
Dharan Bazar ○ NEP 144-145 F 7
Dhārāpuram ○ IND 140-141 G 5
Dhāri ○ IND 138-139 C 9
Dhāriwal ○ IND 138-139 E 4
Dharla ∼ BD 142-143 F 3
Dharmapuri ○ IND 140-141 H 4
Dharmastala ○ IND 140-141 F 4
Dharmavaram ○ IND 140-141 G 3
Dharmsala ○ IND 138-139 F 3
Dhāmi ○ IND 138-139 F 9
Dharwad ○ IND 140-141 F 3
Dhasān ∼ IND 138-139 G 7
Dhaulagiri ▲ NEP 144-145 D 6
Dhaulagiri Himal ▲ NEP 144-145 D 6
Dhauliganga ∼ IND 138-139 G 4
Dhaulpur ○ IND 138-139 F 6
Dhaya ○ DZ 188-189 L 3
Dhaym-al-Khayl ○ MA 196-197 D 2
Dhebar Lake ○ IND 138-139 D 7
Dhekelia Sovereign Base Area (GB) ✕✕ CY 128-129 E 5
Dhenkānāl ○ IND 142-143 D 5
Dhiinsoor ○ SP 212-213 J 2
Dhing ○ IND 142-143 H 2
Dhlo Dhlo Ruins ∴ ZW 218-219 E 4
Dholera ○ IND 138-139 D 8
Dhone ○ IND 140-141 G 3
Dhoodi, Bannaanka ∴ SP 208-209 H 4
Dhorpatan ○ NEP 144-145 D 6
Dhrāngadhra ○ IND 138-139 C 8
Dhubbato ○ SP 208-209 G 4
Dhuburi ○ IND 142-143 F 2
Dhud, togga ∼ SP 208-209 J 3
Dhule ○ IND 138-139 E 9
Dhulian ○ BD 142-143 F 3
Dhull ○ IND 138-139 D 3
Dhunat ○ BD 142-143 F 3
Dhunche ○ NEP 144-145 E 6
Dhūndār ∴ IND 138-139 E 7
Dhurbo ○ SP 208-209 K 3
Dhuudo ○ SP 208-209 K 4
Dhuudo, togga ∼ SP 208-209 K 4
Dhuusa Mareeb ☆ SP 208-209 H 6
Di ○ BF 202-203 J 3
Dia ○ LB 202-203 E 6
Diaba < RMM 196-197 H 6
Diabakania ○ RG 202-203 E 4
Diabali ○ RMM 202-203 G 2
Diable, Île du ⌒ F 62-63 H 3
Diablo, Punta del ▲ ROU 74-75 D 10
Diablo Range ▲ USA (CA) 248-249 C 2
Diablotins, Morne ▲ WD 56 E 4
Diabo ○ BF 202-203 K 3
Diabo, Caverna do ∴ BR 74-75 F 5
Diabugu ○ WAG 202-203 C 3
Diaca ○ MOC 214-215 K 6
Diadema ○ BR 72-73 G 7
Diadi ○ RP 160-161 D 4
Diadioumbéra ○ RMM 202-203 E 2
Diafarabé ○ RMM 202-203 H 2
Diaka ∼ RMM 202-203 H 2
Diakon ○ RMM 202-203 E 2
Dialafara ○ RMM 202-203 E 3
Dialaka ○ RMM 202-203 E 2
Dialakoto ○ SN 202-203 D 3
Diallassagou ○ RMM 202-203 J 3
Dialloubé ○ RMM 202-203 H 2
Diamante ○ RA 78-79 J 2
Diamante, Pampa del ∴ RA 78-79 E 3
Diamante, Río ∼ RA 78-79 F 3
Diamante, Río ∼ RA 78-79 F 3
Diamantina ○ BR 72-73 J 5
Diamantina, Chapada da ▲ BR 68-69 H 7
Diamantina Development Road II AUS 178-179 E 2
Diamantina Fracture Zone ≃ 12 J 8
Diamantina Lakes ○ AUS 178-179 F 2
Diamantina River ∼ AUS 178-179 E 3
Diamantino ○ BR (MAT) 70-71 J 4
Diamantino ○ BR (MAT) 72-73 D 4
Diamantino, Rio ∼ BR 72-73 D 4
Diamarakro ○ CI 202-203 J 6
Diamare ∴ CAM 206-207 B 3
Diambala ○ RCB 210-211 D 6
Diamond Area Restricted ✕✕ NAM 220-221 B 3
Diamond Cave ∴ USA (AR) 276-277 B 5
Diamond Diggings ∴ ZA 220-221 F 4
Diamond Islands ⌒ CDN 36-37 M 2
Diamond Jennes Peninsula ⌣ CDN 24-25 N 5
Diamond Lake ○ USA (OR) 244-245 C 7
Diamond Peak ▲ USA (NV) 246-247 K 4
Diamondville ○ USA (WY) 252-253 H 5
Diamou ○ RMM 202-203 E 2
Diamounguél ○ SN 202-203 D 2
Diana ○ SN 202-203 D 3
Diana Bay ≈ 36-37 P 4
Dianbai ○ VRC 156-157 G 6
Dianbé ○ RMM 202-203 H 2
Diancang Shan ▲ VRC 142-143 M 3
Dian Chi ○ VRC 156-157 C 4
Dianda, Kabondo- ○ ZRE 214-215 C 5
Diandian ○ RG 202-203 D 4
Diandioumé ○ RMM 202-203 F 2
Diangounté Kamara ○ RMM 202-203 F 2
Dianké Makam ○ SN 202-203 D 3
Dianópolis ○ BR 68-69 E 7
Dianra ○ CI 202-203 G 5
Diapaga ○ BF 202-203 L 3
Diaramana ○ RMM 202-203 H 3
Dias ○ MOC 218-219 H 1
Diassa = Madina ○ RMM 202-203 G 4
Diatas, Danau ○ RI 162-163 D 5
Diavlos Zakinthou ≈ 100-101 H 6
Diawala ○ CI 202-203 H 4
Díaz Ordaz ○ MEX 50-51 C 4
Diaz Point ▲ NAM 220-221 B 3
Dibā ○ UAE 134-135 G 6
Dibage ○ IRQ 128-129 K 5
Dībān ○ JOR 130-131 D 2
Dibaru, Danau ○ RI 162-163 D 5
Dibaya ○ ZRE 214-215 B 4
Dibaya-Lubue ○ ZRE 210-211 G 6
Dibble Ice Tongue ⊂ ARK 16 G 14
Dib Dabiib < SP 212-213 J 2
Dibdiba, ad- ▲ KSA 130-131 K 3
Dibella < RN 198-199 F 4
Dibeng ○ ZA 220-221 F 3
Dibia ○ WAL 202-203 E 6
Di Bin ○ Y 132-133 D 6
Di Bin ∴ Y 132-133 D 5
Dibin, ad- ○ Y 132-133 G 5
Dibiri Island ⌒ PNG 183 B 5
Dibni ○ NEP 144-145 D 7
Diboll ○ USA (TX) 268-269 F 5
Dibombari ○ CAM 204-205 H 6
Dibrugarh ○ IND 142-143 J 2
Dibs ○ SUD 200-201 B 6
Dibs, Bi'r < ET 194-195 D 6
Dick, Mount ▲ AUS 174-175 H 7
Dickens ○ USA (TX) 264-265 D 5
Dickey ○ USA (ND) 258-259 J 5
Dickeyville ○ USA (WI) 274-275 H 2
Dickinson ○ USA (ND) 258-259 E 5
Dickinson ○ USA (TX) 268-269 E 7
Dicks Creek Gap ▲ USA (GA) 284-285 G 2
Dickson ○ USA (AK) 20-21 H 4
Dickson ○ USA (TN) 276-277 H 4
Dickson Land ∴ N 84-85 J 3
Dickson Mounds Museum ∴ USA (IL) 274-275 H 4
Dicle Nehri ∼ TR 128-129 J 3
Dicle Nehri ∼ TR 128-129 J 4
Dico Leopoldino ○ BR 68-69 H 4
Dida Galgalu Desert ∴ EAK 212-213 G 2
Didah ○ KSA 130-131 H 4
Didēsa Wenz ∼ ETH 208-209 B 4
Didiéni ○ RMM 202-203 F 3
Didiévi ○ CI 202-203 H 6
Didig Sala ○ ETH 200-201 K 6
Didimótiho ○ GR 100-101 L 4
Didsbury ○ CDN (ALB) 232-233 D 4
Didwāna ○ IND 138-139 E 6
Didy ○ RM 222-223 F 7
Didyma ∴ TR 128-129 B 4
Didyr ○ BF 202-203 J 3
Die Bos ○ ZA 220-221 D 5
Diébougou ○ BF 202-203 J 4
Dieciocho de Marco ○ MEX 50-51 L 5
Dieciocho de Marzo ○ MEX 52-53 J 2
Diécké ○ RG 202-203 F 6
Diefenbaker, Lake ○ CDN (SAS) 232-233 L 5
Diego de Almagro ○ RCH 76-77 B 4
Diego de Almagro, Isla ⌒ RCH 80 C 5
Diego de Alvear ○ RA 78-79 H 3
Diego Garcia, Archipelago ⌒ GB 12 F 5
Diego Lamas ○ ROU 76-77 J 6
Diégo Suarez = Antsiranana ☆ RM 222-223 F 4
Diéli ○ RMM 202-203 H 3
Diéma ○ RMM 202-203 F 2
Diemals ○ AUS 176-177 E 4
Diemansputs ○ ZA 220-221 E 4
Điện Biên ☆ VN 156-157 C 6
Diễn Châu ☆ VN 156-157 D 7
Dieng Plateau ∴ RI 168 C 3
Diên Khánh ○ VN 158-159 K 4
Dienné ○ RMM 202-203 H 3
Diepholz ○ D 92-93 K 2
Dieppe ○ F 90-91 H 7
Dierks ○ USA (AR) 276-277 A 6
Dieterich ○ USA (IL) 274-275 K 5
Dietrich ○ USA (ID) 252-253 D 4
Die Venster ▲ ZA 220-221 D 6
Dif ○ EAK 212-213 H 3
Diffa ■ RN 198-199 F 4
Diffa ☆ RN (DIF) 198-199 F 6
Difounda ○ G 210-211 C 5
Difuma ○ ZRE 210-211 K 5
Dig ○ IND 138-139 F 6
Digba ○ ZRE 206-207 G 6
Digboi ○ IND 142-143 J 2
Digby ○ CDN (NS) 240-241 K 6
Digges ○ CDN 30-31 W 6
Digges Islands ⌒ CDN 36-37 K 3
Digges Sound ⌒ CDN 36-37 K 3
Dighanchi ○ IND 140-141 F 2
Dighton ○ USA (KS) 262-263 F 6
Diğla ∼ IRQ 128-129 M 6
Diglūr ○ IND 138-139 F 10
Digne-les-Bains ○ F 90-91 L 9
Digoin ○ F 90-91 K 8
Digor ☆ TR 128-129 K 2
Digora ○ RUS 126-127 F 6
Digos ☆ RP 160-161 F 9
Digri ○ PK 138-139 B 7
Digsa ∴ ER 200-201 J 5
Digua ○ RCH 78-79 D 4
Digue Island, La ⌒ SY 224 D 2
Diguillín, Río ∼ RCH 78-79 D 4
Digul ∼ RI 166-167 L 5
Digya National Park ⊥ GH 202-203 K 6
Dihang or Siang ∼ IND 142-143 J 1
Diibao ○ CAM 206-207 B 4
Dijar ○ KA 126-127 M 4
Dijmphna Sund ≈ 26-27 p 4
Dijon ☆ F 90-91 K 8
Dijon ∼ RG 202-203 F 5
Dijur ○ RUS 88-89 W 4
Dik ○ TCH 206-207 C 4
Dika, mys ▲ RUS 108-109 k 3
Dikāka, ad- ∴ KSA 132-133 G 4
Dikanäs ○ S 86-87 G 4
Dikhil ○ DJI 208-209 F 3
Dikhu ∼ IND 142-143 J 2
Dikili ☆ TR 128-129 B 3
Dikimdja ○ RUS 118-119 K 6
Dikirnis ○ ET 194-195 E 2
Dikodougou ○ CI 202-203 H 5
Dikson ☆ RUS 108-109 T 5
Dikson, ostrov ⌒ RUS 108-109 T 5
Dikulwe ∼ ZRE 214-215 D 6
Dikwa ○ WAN 198-199 F 6
Đila ○ AFG 138-139 B 3
Dila ○ ETH 208-209 D 5
Dilam, ad- ○ KSA 130-131 K 6
Dilezi Geçidi ▲ TR 128-129 L 4
Dili ☆ RI 166-167 C 6
Dili ○ ZRE 210-211 L 2
Dilia ∼ RN 198-199 F 5
Dilia ○ USA (NM) 256-257 K 3
Di Linh ○ VN 158-159 K 5
Dilīžan ○ AR 128-129 L 2
Diližanskij zapovednik ⊥ AR 128-129 L 2
Dilj ▲ HR 100-101 F 2
Dilke ○ CDN (SAS) 232-233 N 5
Dilkon ○ USA (AZ) 256-257 E 3
Dilley ○ USA (TX) 266-267 H 5
Dilli ○ RMM 202-203 G 2
Dillikot ○ NEP 144-145 C 6
Dilling ○ SUD 200-201 D 6
Dillingham ○ USA 22-23 R 3
Dillon ○ USA (CO) 254-255 J 4
Dillon ○ USA (MT) 250-251 G 6
Dillon ○ USA (SC) 284-285 L 2
Dillon Lake ○ USA (OH) 280-281 E 3
Dillon River ∼ CDN 32-33 P 4
Dillsboro ○ USA (IN) 274-275 N 5
Dillsburg ○ USA (PA) 280-281 J 3
Dilo = Djidji ∼ G 210-211 D 4
Dilolo ○ ZRE 214-215 B 6
Dilts Historic Site, Fort ∴ USA (ND) 258-259 D 5
Dima ○ ETH 208-209 D 3
Dimako ○ CAM 204-205 K 6
Dimalla < RIM 196-197 E 6
Dimāpur ○ IND 142-143 H 3
Dimašq ★ SYR 128-129 G 6
Dimbaza ○ ZA 220-221 H 6
Dimbelenge ○ ZRE 210-211 J 6
Dimbokro ☆ CI 202-203 H 6
Dimboola ○ AUS 180-181 G 4
Dimbulah ○ AUS 174-175 H 5
Dimissi ○ PNG 183 B 5
Dimitrievka ○ RUS 94-95 R 5
Dimitrovgrad ○ BG 102-103 D 6
Dimitrovgrad ☆ RUS 96-97 F 6
Dimitrovgrad ○ YU 100-101 J 3
Dimlang ▲ WAN 204-205 J 4
Dimlao ○ RP 160-161 B 6
Dimlik ∼ TCH 206-207 C 4
Dimma Lake ○ CDN 30-31 T 5
Dimmitt ○ USA (TX) 264-265 B 4
Dimona ☆ IL 130-131 D 2
Dimora ○ AUS 178-179 G 1
Dimovo ○ BG 102-103 C 6
Dimpam ○ CAM 210-211 D 2
Dina ○ PK 138-139 D 3
Dinagat ○ RP 160-161 F 8
Dinagat Island ⌒ RP 160-161 F 7
Dinajpur ○ BD 142-143 F 3
Dinalongan ○ RP 160-161 D 4
Dinan ○ F 90-91 F 7
Dinangourou ○ RMM 202-203 J 2
Dinant ○ B 92-93 H 3
Dinapigui ○ RP 160-161 E 4
Dinar ☆ TR 128-129 D 3
Dinār, Kūh-e ▲ IR 134-135 D 3
Dinara ▲ YU 100-101 F 2
Dinchiya Shet' ∼ ETH 208-209 C 5
Dindar ∼ SUD 200-201 F 6
Dindar National Park ⊥ SUD 200-201 G 6
Dinder Wenz ∼ ETH 208-209 B 3
Dindi ○ ZW 218-219 G 3
Dindigul ○ IND 140-141 G 5
Dindima ○ WAN 204-205 J 3
Dindori ○ IND 142-143 B 4
Dindoudi Séydi ○ SN 202-203 D 2
Dinga ○ PK 138-139 D 3
Dinga ○ ZRE 210-211 F 6
Dingalan Bay ≈ 160-161 D 5
Ding'an ○ VRC 156-157 D 4
Dingbian ○ VRC 154-155 E 3
Ding Ding ○ SUD 206-207 L 4
Dinge ○ ANG 216-217 B 7
Dinggye ○ VRC 144-145 F 6
Dinghushan ∴ VRC 156-157 H 5
Dinghushan Z.B. ⊥ VRC 156-157 H 5
Dingila ○ ZRE 210-211 L 2
Dingjie ○ VRC 144-145 G 6
Dingle = An Daingean ○ IRL 90-91 B 5
Dingle Bay ≈ 90-91 B 5
Dingley Dell Cons. P. ∴ AUS 180-181 F 5
Dingnan ○ VRC 156-157 J 4
Dingo ○ ANG 216-217 F 8
Dingo ○ AUS 178-179 K 2
Dingtao ○ VRC 154-155 J 4
Dinguiraye ○ RG 202-203 E 4
Dingwall ○ CDN (NS) 240-241 P 4
Dingwall ○ GB 90-91 E 3
Dingwells Mills ○ CDN (NS) 240-241 N 4
Dingxi ○ VRC 154-155 D 4
Dingxiang ○ VRC 154-155 H 2
Dingyuan ○ VRC 154-155 K 5
Dingzhou ○ VRC 154-155 J 2
Dingzikou ○ VRC 146-147 L 6
Dinhata ○ IND 142-143 F 2
Đinh Lập ☆ VN 156-157 E 6
Dinnebito Wash ∼ USA (AZ) 256-257 E 2
Dinnik, Plateau de ▲ RN 204-205 E 1
Dinokwe ○ RB 218-219 D 6
Dinorwic ○ CDN (ONT) 234-235 L 5
Dinosaur ○ USA (CO) 254-255 G 3
Dinosaur National Monument ∴ USA (CO) 254-255 G 3
Dinosaur Provincial Park ⊥ CDN (ALB) 232-233 G 5
Dinosaurusspore ∴ NAM 216-217 D 10
Dinsmore ○ CDN (SAS) 232-233 L 4
Dintiteladas ○ RI 162-163 F 7
Dinuba ○ USA (CA) 248-249 E 3
d'In Ziza, Gueltas < DZ 190-191 D 9
Diolla ○ RMM 202-203 G 3
Diokana ○ TCH 198-199 H 6
Diomandou ○ RG 202-203 F 5
Diona ○ BF 202-203 J 4
Diona < TCH 198-199 L 4
Diongoï ○ RMM 202-203 F 2
Dionisio ○ BR 72-73 J 5
Dionísio Cerqueira ○ BR 74-75 D 6
Dionouga ○ BF 202-203 K 2
Diorama ○ BR 72-73 E 4
Dios, Canal de < RA 76-77 F 3
Diosso ○ RCB 210-211 C 6
Diou ○ F 90-91 J 8
Dioulatiédougou ○ CI 202-203 G 5
Dioulouiou ○ SN 202-203 B 3
Dioumara ○ RMM 202-203 F 2
Dioundiou ○ RN 204-205 E 2
Dioura ○ RMM 202-203 H 2
Diourbel ☆ SN 202-203 B 2
Diourou ○ RMM 202-203 H 3
Dipālpur ○ PK 138-139 D 4
Dipchari ○ WAN 204-205 K 3
Diphu ○ IND 142-143 H 3
Dipkun ○ RUS 118-119 N 8
Diplo ○ PK 138-139 B 7
Dipolog ☆ RP 160-161 E 8
Dippa ∼ RUS 118-119 K 3
Dipper Lake ○ CDN 34-35 C 3
Dipperu National Park ⊥ AUS 178-179 K 1
Dī Qār ■ IRQ 128-129 M 7

Diqdāqa o UAE 134-135 F 6
Dira < TCH 198-199 G 5
Dirat at-Tulūl ∴ SYR 128-129 G 6
Dire o IRQ 128-129 L 4
Diré o RMM 196-197 J 6
Direction, Cape ▲ AUS 174-175 G 3
Dirē Dawa o • ETH 208-209 E 4
Dirgi Shabozai o PK 138-139 B 4
Diriamba o NIC 52-53 L 6
Dirico o ANG 216-217 F 8
Dir'iya, ad- o KSA (QAS) 130-131 H 5
Dir'iya, ad- o • KSA (RIY) 130-131 K 5
Dirk Hartog Island ⌒ AUS 176-177 B 2
Dirkou o RN 198-199 F 3
Dirrah o SUD 200-201 C 6
Dirranbandi o AUS 178-179 K 5
Dirty Devil River ~ USA (UT) 254-255 E 5
Disa o IND 138-139 D 7
Disang ~ IND 142-143 J 2
Disappointment, Cape ▲ GB 78-79 O 7
Disappointment, Cape ▲ USA (WA) 244-245 A 4
Disappointment, Lake ⊂ AUS 176-177 G 1
Disautel o USA (WA) 244-245 F 2
Discovery, Cape ▲ CDN 26-27 M 2
Discovery Bay ≈ 180-181 F 5
Discovery Bay o USA (WA) 244-245 C 3
Discovery Reef = Huaguang Jiao ⌒ VRC 158-159 L 2
Discovery Seamounts ≃ 6-7 K 13
Dishkakat o USA 20-21 M 5
Dishna River ~ USA 20-21 M 5
Disko Banke ≃ 28-29 M 2
Disko Bugt ≈ 28-29 O 2
Disko Fjord ≈ 28-29 N 2
Diskofjord = Kangerluk o GRØ 28-29 N 2
Disko Ø ⌒ GRØ 28-29 N 2
Disley o CDN (SAS) 232-233 N 5
Dismal Creek ~ CDN (ALB) 232-233 B 2
Dismal Lakes ⊂ CDN 30-31 L 2
Dīšnā o ET 194-195 F 4
Disney o AUS 178-179 J 1
Disneyland •• USA (CA) 248-249 G 6
Disney World, Walt • USA (FL) 286-287 H 3
Dispur ☆ IND 142-143 G 2
Disputada, La o RCH 78-79 D 2
Disraeli o CDN (QUE) 238-239 O 3
Disraeli Fiord ≈ 26-27 O 2
Diss o GB 90-91 H 5
Dissain, Ğazirat ⌒ KSA 132-133 B 5
Disteghil Sar ▲ IND 138-139 E 1
District of Columbia = D.C., Washington □ USA (DC) 280-281 J 5
Distrito Federal □ BR 72-73 F 3
Distrito Federal □ MEX 52-53 E 2
Disūq o ET 194-195 E 2
Ditang o VRC 156-157 F 2
Ditinn o RG 202-203 D 4
Ditsinane < RB 218-219 C 5
Ditu, Mwene- o ZRE 214-215 B 4
Diu o IND 138-139 C 9
Divāndarre o IR 128-129 M 5
Divénié o RCB 210-211 D 5
Diverson Lake < USA (TX) 264-265 F 5
Divide o CDN (SAS) 232-233 J 6
Divide o USA (CO) 254-255 K 5
Divide o USA (MT) 250-251 G 6
Divilican o RP 160-161 E 4
Divilican Bay ≈ 160-161 E 4
Divinhe o MOC 218-219 H 5
Divinolândia de Minas o BR 72-73 J 5
Divinópolis o BR 72-73 H 6
Divisa o PA 52-53 D 7
Divisadero, El o MEX 50-51 F 4
Divisaderos o MEX 50-51 E 3
Divisões ou de Santa Marta, Serra das ▲ BR 72-73 D 4
Divisópolis o BR 72-73 K 3
Divisor, Serra de ▲ BR 64-65 F 5
Divisoria o RP 160-161 F 7
Divisorio, El o RA 78-79 J 5
Divnogorsk o RUS 116-117 F 8
Divo ☆ CI 202-203 H 7
Divor, Ribeira do ~ P 98-99 C 5
Divot o USA (TX) 266-267 H 5
Divriği ☆ ••• TR 128-129 H 3
Divuma o ZRE 214-215 B 6
Diwāniya, ad- ☆ IRQ 128-129 L 7
Diwopu J. II VRC 146-147 H 4
Diwouni, Mare o DY 202-203 L 4
Dixcove o GH 202-203 K 7
Dixfield o USA (ME) 278-279 L 4
Dixiasenlin • VRC 150-151 G 5
Dixie o USA (ID) 250-251 D 6
Dixie o USA (WA) 244-245 G 4
Dixie Valley o USA (NV) 246-247 G 4
Dix-Milles, Lac ⊂ CDN (QUE) 238-239 H 2
Dixmont o USA (ME) 278-279 M 4
Dixon o USA (CA) 246-247 D 5
Dixon o USA (IL) 274-275 J 3
Dixon o USA (KY) 276-277 H 3
Dixon o USA (MO) 276-277 C 3
Dixon o USA (MS) 268-269 L 4
Dixon o USA (MT) 250-251 E 4
Dixon o USA (WY) 252-253 L 5
Dixon Entrance ≈ 32-33 D 4
Dixon Entrance ≈ CDN 228-229 B 2
Dixonville o CDN 32-33 M 3
Dixonville o RA 78-79 G 3
Diyadin ☆ TR 128-129 K 3
Diyālā □ IRQ 128-129 L 6
Diyarbakır o •• TR 128-129 J 4
Dizangué o CAM 210-211 C 2
Dize o IR 128-129 L 4
Dizhipoumian ⊥ • VRC 154-155 K 1
Dja ~ CAM 210-211 D 2
Dja, Réserve du = Dja Reserve ⊥ ••• CAM 210-211 D 2
Djado ∴• RN 198-199 F 2
Djado, Plateau du ▲ RN 198-199 F 1
Djakarta = Jakarta ★ RI 168 B 3
Djakotomè o DY 202-203 L 6
Djalasiga o ZRE 212-213 C 2
Djale ~ ZRE 210-211 J 5
Djalon, Fouta ∴ RG 202-203 D 4
Djaluwon Creek ~ AUS 172-173 H 6
Djamâa o DZ 190-191 E 4
Djamandjary o RM 222-223 F 4
Djamba o ZRE (HAU) 210-211 K 2
Djamba o ZRE (SHA) 214-215 B 5
Djambala o CAM 204-205 K 5
Djambala ☆ RCB 210-211 E 5
Djampiel o CAM 206-207 B 6
Djanet ☆ • DZ 190-191 G 8
Djangylah, ostrov ⌒ RUS 110-111 N 3
Djanyška ~ RUS 110-111 Q 7
Djara ~ RUS 110-111 F 5
Dja Reserve = Réserve du Dja ⊥ ••• CAM 210-211 D 2
Djaret, Oued ~ DZ 190-191 C 7
Djarua ~ RI 166-167 G 3
Djat'kovo o RUS 94-95 O 5
Djeboho ▲ GH 202-203 L 5
Djebok o RMM 196-197 L 6
Djébrène o TCH 206-207 D 3
Djédaa o TCH 198-199 J 6
Djeddars • DZ 190-191 D 3
Djedi, Oued ~ DZ 190-191 E 3
Djedid, Bir < DZ 190-191 F 4
Djelfa ☆ • DZ 190-191 D 3
Djéma o RCA 206-207 G 5
Djemadja, Pulau ⌒ RI 162-163 F 3
Djèmber o TCH 206-207 C 3
Djemila ∴ ••• DZ 190-191 E 2
Djems Bank ≃ 162-163 K 3
Djerem ~ CAM 204-205 K 6
Djérem ~ CAM 204-205 K 5
Djermaya o TCH 198-199 G 6
Djibasso o BF 202-203 H 3
Djibo o BF 202-203 K 2
Djiborosso o CI 202-203 G 5
Djibouti ■ DJI 208-209 F 3
Djibouti ☆ DJI 208-209 F 3
Djidja o DY 202-203 L 6
Djidji = Dilo ~ G 210-211 D 4
Djigoué o BF 202-203 J 4
Djigouéra o BF 202-203 H 4
Djiguéni o RIM 196-197 F 7
Djilbe o CAM 206-207 B 3
Djillali Ben Amar o DZ 190-191 C 3
Djiroutou o CI 202-203 G 7
Djohong o CAM 206-207 B 5
Djoku-Punda o ZRE 210-211 H 6
Djoli o TCH 206-207 D 4
Djolu o ZRE 210-211 J 3
Djombo o ZRE 210-211 H 3
Djombo = Haraz o TCH 198-199 J 6
Djombo Kibbit o TCH 198-199 J 6
Djona, Zone Cynégétique de ⊥ DY 204-205 E 3
Djonâba o RIM 196-197 D 6
Djorf Torba < DZ 188-189 K 5
Djorf-Torba, Barrage < DZ 188-189 K 5
Djoua ~ G 210-211 D 3
Djoubissi o RCA 206-207 E 5
Djoudj, Parc National des oiseaux du ⊥ ••• SN 196-197 B 6
Djoué ~ RCB 210-211 E 5
Djougou o DY 202-203 L 5
Djoûk, Passe de ▲ RIM 196-197 D 6
Djoum o CAM 210-211 D 2
Djoumboli o CAM 204-205 K 5
Djourab, Erg du ∴ TCH 198-199 H 4
Djoutou-Pétel o RG 202-203 D 4
Djugadjak ~ RUS 112-113 K 4
Djugu o ZRE 212-213 C 3
Djuljukju o RUS 118-119 K 4
Djuľtydag, gora ▲ RUS 126-127 G 7
Djúpivogur o IS 86-87 f 2
Djupkun, ozero ⊂ RUS (EVN) 108-109 c 7
Djupkun, ozero ⊂ RUS (EVN) 116-117 F 2
Djura, Kytyl- o RUS 118-119 M 5
Djurdjura, Djebel ▲ DZ 190-191 E 2
Djurtjuli ☆ RUS 96-97 J 6
D'kar o RB 216-217 F 10
Dla ~ RMM 202-203 F 3
Dlinnyj, ostrov ⌒ RUS 108-109 Y 2
Dłoławana o ZA 220-221 K 4
Dmitrievka o KA 124-125 E 2
Dmitriev-L'govskij o RUS 94-95 O 5
Dmitrija Lapteva, proliv ≈ 110-111 W 3
Dmitrov ☆ • RUS 94-95 P 3
Dmytrivka o UA 102-103 H 2
Dnepr ~ RUS 94-95 M 4
Dneprodzeržinsk = Dniprodzeržyns'k o UA 102-103 J 3
Dnepropetrovsk = Dnipropetrovs'k ☆ UA 102-103 J 3
Dnestr = Dnister ~ UA 102-103 E 3
Dnestr = Nistru ~ MD 102-103 F 4
Dnipro ~ UA 102-103 J 3
Dnipro ~ UA 102-103 G 2
Dniprodzeržyns'k o UA 102-103 J 3
Dniprodzherzhyns'k = Dniprodzeržyns'k o UA 102-103 J 3
Dnipropetrovs'k ☆ UA 102-103 J 3
Dniprorudne o UA 102-103 J 4
Dniprovs'kyj lyman ≈ 102-103 G 4
Dniprovs'kyj lyman ≈ 102-103 H 4
Dnister ~ UA 102-103 E 3
Dnistrovs'kyj lyman ≈ 102-103 G 4
Dnjapro ~ BY 94-95 M 5
Dnjaprovska-Buhski, Kanal < BY 94-95 J 5
Dno ☆ RUS 94-95 L 3
Do, Lac ⊂ RMM 202-203 J 2
Doa o MOC 218-219 H 3
Doāba o PK 138-139 C 3
Doaktown o CDN (NB) 240-241 J 4
Doangdoangan Besar, Pulau ⌒ RI 164-165 E 6
Doany o RM 222-223 F 5
Doba ☆ TCH 206-207 C 4
Doba o VRC 144-145 G 5
Dobbiaco = Toblach o I 100-101 D 1
Dobbin o USA (TX) 268-269 E 6
Dobbin Bay ≈ 26-27 N 4
Dobbs, Cape ▲ CDN 36-37 F 2
Dobbspet o IND 140-141 G 4
Dobbyn o AUS 174-175 F 6
Dobele o •• LV 94-95 H 3
Doberai Peninsula ⌣ RI 166-167 F 2
Dobie River ~ CDN (ONT) 234-235 N 3
Dobinga o CAM 204-205 K 4
Doblas o RA 78-79 G 4
Dobo o •• RI 166-167 H 4
Doboj o • BIH 100-101 G 2
Doboy Sound ≈ USA 284-285 J 5
Dobre Miasto o • PL 92-93 Q 2
Dobrič o BG 102-103 E 6
Dobrich = Dobrič o BG 102-103 E 6
Dobrinka o RUS 94-95 R 5
Dobrjanka ☆ RUS 96-97 K 4
Dobromyľ o UA 102-103 C 3
Dobron' o UA 102-103 C 3
Dobropillja o UA 102-103 K 3
Dobrotești o RO 102-103 D 5
Dobruči o RUS 94-95 K 2
Dobruš o BY 94-95 M 5
Dobržanskogo, ostrov ⌒ RUS 112-113 M 5
Dobzha o VRC 144-145 G 6
Docas, Cachoeira das ~ BR 72-73 D 3
Doc Can Island ⌒ RP 160-161 C 10
Doce, Rio ~ BR 72-73 K 5
Doce, Rio ~ BR 72-73 E 4
Dochigam National Park ⊥ IND 138-139 E 2
Docker River ⊼ AUS (NT) 176-177 K 2
Docker River ~ AUS 176-177 K 2
Docking o GB 90-91 H 5
Dock Junction o USA (GA) 284-285 J 5
Dockrell, Mount ▲ AUS 172-173 H 5
Dockyard, The ∴ AG 56 E 3
Doctor Arroyo o MEX 50-51 J 6
Doctor González o MEX 50-51 K 5
Doctor Mora o MEX 50-51 J 7
Doctor Pedro P. Peña ☆ PY 76-77 F 2
Doda o EAT 212-213 G 6
Doda o RI 164-165 G 4
Dodaga o RI 164-165 L 3
Dod Ballapur o IND 140-141 G 4
Dodecanese = Dodekanissa ⌒ GR 100-101 L 6
Døde Fjord, De ≈ 26-27 R 5
Dodge o USA (ND) 258-259 E 4
Dodge Center o USA (MN) 270-271 F 6
Dodge City o • USA (KS) 262-263 F 7
Dodge Lake ⊂ CDN 30-31 R 6
Dodge River ~ CDN 26-27 P 3
Dodinga o RI 164-165 K 3
Dodji o SN 202-203 C 2
Dodol < SP 212-213 J 2
Dodola o ETH 208-209 D 5
Dodoma □ EAT 212-213 E 6
Dodoma ★ • EAT (DOD) 214-215 H 4
Dodori ~ EAK 212-213 H 4
Dodori National Reserve ⊥ EAK 212-213 H 4
Dodowa o GH 202-203 K 7
Dodsland o CDN (SAS) 232-233 K 4
Dodson o USA (LA) 268-269 H 4
Dodson o USA (MT) 250-251 L 3
Dodson o USA (TX) 264-265 D 4
Dodson Peninsula ⌣ ARK 16 F 30
Doege o ANG 216-217 F 4
Doembang Nangbuat o THA 158-159 F 3
Doerun o USA (GA) 284-285 G 5
Dofa o RI 164-165 J 4
Dōgā'i o IR 136-137 F 6
Dogai Coring ⊂ VRC 144-145 G 3
Dogal'dyn ~ RUS 108-109 a 7
Doğanşehir ☆ TR 128-129 G 3
Doğansu o TR 128-129 K 3
Dogbo-Tota o DY 202-203 L 6
Dog Creek o CDN (BC) 230-231 G 2
Dogdo ~ RUS 110-111 V 6
Dog Island ⌒ CDN 36-37 T 6
Dog Island ⌒ USA (FL) 286-287 E 2
Dog Lake ⊂ CDN (MAN) 234-235 E 4
Dog Lake ⊂ CDN (ONT) 234-235 O 6
Dog Lake ⊂ CDN (ONT) 236-237 D 4
Dōgo ⌒ J 152-153 E 6
Dogo o RMM 202-203 G 4
Dogoba o SUD 206-207 J 5
Do Gonbadān o • IR 134-135 D 3
Dogondoutchi o RN 198-199 B 6
Dogoumbo o TCH 206-207 C 3
Dōgo-yama ▲ J 152-153 E 7
Dogpatch U.S.A. • USA (AR) 276-277 B 4
Dogpound Creek ~ CDN (ALB) 232-233 D 4
Dog Salmon River ~ USA 22-23 S 4
Doğubayazıt ☆ TR 128-129 L 3
Doğu Karadeniz Dağlari ▲ TR (61) 128-129 H 2
Doğu Menteşe Dağları ▲ TR 128-129 C 4
Dogura o PNG 183 F 6
Dogwalo, River ~ WAN 204-205 H 3
Dogwood Creek ~ AUS 178-179 K 4
Dogyaling o VRC 144-145 G 5
Dogyldo ~ RUS 114-115 U 4
Doha = ad-Dauḥa ★ Q 134-135 D 6
Doha = Dauḥa, ad- ★ Q 134-135 D 6
Doi, Pulau ⌒ RI 164-165 K 2
Doigan ▲ EAK 212-213 F 3
Doig River ~ CDN 32-33 K 3
Doi Inthanon ▲ THA 142-143 L 6
Doi Inthanon National Park ⊥ THA 142-143 L 6
Đōi Mōi, Hòn ⌒ VN 158-159 H 6
Dois Córregos o BR 72-73 F 7
Dois de Novembro, Cachoeira ~ BR 66-67 F 7
Dois Irmãos o BR 72-73 F 3
Dois Irmãos, Cachoeira ~ BR 66-67 H 7
Dois Riachos, Rio ~ BR 68-69 K 6
Doi Suthep-Poi National Park ⊥ THA 142-143 L 6
Dois Vizinhos o BR 74-75 D 5
Doi Tachi ▲ THA 158-159 E 2
Doka o RI 166-167 H 5
Doka o SUD 200-201 G 6
Dokhara, Dunes de ∴ DZ 190-191 E 4
Dokis Indian Reserve ⊼ CDN (ONT) 238-239 F 2
Doko o RG 202-203 F 4
Doko o WAN 198-199 D 6
Dokpam o GH 202-203 K 5
Doktorskij, mys ▲ RUS 110-111 Q 3
Dokučaevs'k o UA 102-103 K 4
Dokui o BF 202-203 H 3
Dolak, Pulau ⌒ RI 166-167 K 5
Dolak Pulau Reserve ⊥ • RI 166-167 J 5
Doland o USA (SD) 260-261 H 2
Dolan Springs o USA (AZ) 256-257 A 3
Dolavon o RA 78-79 G 7
Dolbeau o CDN (QUE) 240-241 C 2
Dolbel o RN 202-203 L 2
Dolby Lake ⊂ CDN 30-31 R 5
Dole o F 90-91 K 8
Doleib Hill o SUD 206-207 K 4
Dolenci o MK 100-101 H 4
Dolgellau o GB 90-91 F 5
Dolgij, ostrov ⌒ RUS 108-109 H 7
Dolgij, ostrov ⌒ RUS (NAO) 88-89 X 2
Dolgij Most o RUS 116-117 H 7
Dolgoderevenskoe ☆ RUS 96-97 M 6
Dolgoi Island ⌒ USA 22-23 Q 5
Dolia o IND 138-139 C 8
Dolina gejzerov •• RUS 120-121 S 6
Dolinovka o RUS 120-121 S 6
Dolinsk o RUS 122-123 K 5
Dolit o RI 164-165 K 4
Dolleman Island ⌒ ARK 16 F 30
Dollo Odo o ETH 208-209 F 6
Dolni Lom o BG 102-103 C 6
Dolný Kubín o SK 92-93 P 4
Dolo o RI 164-165 F 4
Dolokmerawan o RI 162-163 C 3
Dolok Pinapan ▲ RI 162-163 C 3
Dolomiti = Dolomiten ▲ I 100-101 C 1
Dolon, pereval ▲ KS 146-147 B 5
Dolong o RI 164-165 H 4
Doloon o MAU 148-149 G 5
Dolores o CO 60-61 D 6
Dolores o GCA 52-53 K 3
Dolores o RA 78-79 L 4
Dolores o ROU 78-79 K 2
Dolores ~ RP 160-161 F 6
Dolores o USA (CO) 254-255 G 6
Dolores o YV 60-61 G 3
Dolores Creek ~ USA (TX) 266-267 H 6
Dolores Hidalgo o • MEX 50-51 J 7
Dolores River ~ USA (CO) 254-255 G 5
Doloroso o USA (MS) 268-269 J 5
Dolphin, Cape ▲ GB 78-79 L 6
Dolphin and Union Strait ≈ 24-25 O 6
Đồ Lu'o'ng ☆ VN 156-157 D 7
Dolyna ☆ UA 102-103 D 3
Dolyns'ka o UA 102-103 H 3
Dom, Gunung ▲ RI 166-167 J 3
Doma o ZW 218-219 F 3
Domain o CDN (MAN) 234-235 F 5
Domaine de chasse d'Iguéla ⊥ G 210-211 B 4
Dom Aquino o BR 70-71 K 4
Domar o VRC 144-145 C 4
Doma Safari Area ⊥ ZW 218-219 F 3
Domažlice o CZ 92-93 M 4
Dombaj Ul'gen, gora ▲ RUS 126-127 D 6
Dombarovskij ☆ RUS 126-127 N 2
Dombås o N 86-87 D 5
Dombe o MOC 218-219 G 4
Dombe Grande o ANG 216-217 B 6
Dombey, Cape ▲ AUS 180-181 E 4
Dombo o RI 166-167 J 2
Domboshawa o • ZW (Mle) 218-219 F 3
Domboshawa ▲ ZW (Mle) 218-219 F 3
Dombóvár o H 92-93 P 5
Dom Cavati o BR 72-73 J 5
Dome Bay ≈ 24-25 U 1
Dome Creek o CDN (BC) 228-229 N 3
Domel o IND 138-139 E 3
Domeyko o RCH 76-77 B 5
Domeyko, Cordillera de ▲ RCH 76-77 C 3
Domfront o F 90-91 G 7
Dominase o GH 202-203 K 6
Domingos Martins o BR 72-73 K 6
Domingos Mourão o BR 68-69 H 4
Dominica ■ WD 56 E 4
Dominica Island ⌒ WD 56 E 4
Dominical o CR 52-53 C 7
Dominican Republic = Republica Dominicana ■ DOM 54-55 K 6
Dominica Passage ≈ 56 E 4
Dominion City o CDN (MAN) 234-235 F 5
Dominion Range ▲ ARK 16 E 0
Domiongo o ZRE 210-211 H 6
Domkonda o IND 138-139 G 10
Domo o ETH 208-209 H 5
Domodedovo ☆ RUS 94-95 P 4
Domodóssola o I 100-101 B 1
Domoni o COM 222-223 D 4
Dom Pedrito o BR 76-77 K 6
Dom Pedro o BR 68-69 F 4
Dompem o GH 202-203 J 7
Dompu o RI 168 D 7
Domremy o CDN (SAS) 232-233 N 3
Dom Silvério o BR 72-73 J 6
Domuyo, Volcán ▲ RA 78-79 D 4
Don ~ GB 90-91 F 3
Don ~ RUS 94-95 Q 5
Don ~ RUS 102-103 L 2
Doña Ana o USA (NM) 256-257 J 6
Doña Ana, Cerro ▲ RCH 76-77 B 5
Doña Inés, Cerro ▲ RCH 76-77 C 4
Doña Juana, Volcán ▲ CO 64-65 D 1
Donald o AUS 180-181 G 4
Donald o CDN (BC) 230-231 M 2
Donalda o CDN (ALB) 232-233 F 3
Donald Landing o CDN (BC) 228-229 J 2
Donaldson o USA (AR) 276-277 C 6
Donaldson o USA (MN) 270-271 B 2
Donaldsonville o USA (LA) 268-269 K 6
Donalsonville o USA (GA) 284-285 F 5
Doña Rosa, Cordillera ▲ RCH 76-77 B 6
Donau ~ 8 E 4
Donau ~ D 92-93 L 4
Donauwörth o • D 92-93 L 4
Don Benito o E 98-99 E 5
Doncaster o AUS 174-175 G 7
Doncaster o GB 90-91 G 5
Doncaster Indian Réserve ⊼ CDN (QUE) 238-239 L 2
Doncello, El o CO 64-65 E 1
Dondaicha o IND 138-139 E 9
Donderkamp o SME 62-63 F 3
Don Diego o CO 60-61 E 2
Dondo o ANG 216-217 C 4
Dondo o MOC 218-219 H 4
Dondo o RI (NTI) 168 E 7
Dondo o RI (SLT) 164-165 H 4
Dondo o ZRE 206-207 E 6
Dondo, Teluk ≈ 164-165 G 3
Don Dol o EAK 212-213 F 3
Dondon o RH 54-55 J 5
Đo'n Du'o'ng o VN 158-159 K 5
Donec ~ RUS 102-103 K 2
Doneck o RUS 102-103 L 3
Donec'k ☆ UA 102-103 K 4
Doneck = Donec'k ☆ UA 102-103 K 4
Donegal o • IRL 90-91 C 4
Donegal Bay ≈ 90-91 C 4
Donelson National Battlefield, Fort • USA (AR) 276-277 H 4
Don Esteban, Arroyo ~ ROU 78-79 L 2
Donets Basin = Donec'kyj krjaž ▲ UA 102-103 K 3
Donets'k = Donec'k ☆ UA 102-103 K 4
Donett Point ▲ CDN 24-25 S 2
Dong o IND 144-145 L 6
Donga o DY 202-203 L 5
Donga o WAN 204-205 J 5
Donga, River ~ WAN 204-205 J 5
Dong'an o VRC 156-157 G 3
Dongane, Lagoa ⊂ MOC 218-219 H 7
Dongara o AUS 176-177 C 4
Dongargarh o IND 142-143 B 5
Dongchuan o VRC 156-157 C 3
Dongco o VRC 144-145 E 4
Dông Đăng ☆ VN 156-157 E 6
Dongeleksor o KA 126-127 O 3
Döngelek su kojmasy < KA 96-97 G 8
Dongfang o VRC (HAI) 156-157 F 7
Dongfang o VRC (HUN) 156-157 F 2
Dongfanghong o VRC 150-151 J 4
Dongfeng o VRC 150-151 E 6
Donggala o •• RI 164-165 F 4
Donggi o RI 164-165 H 4
Donggi Cona ⊂ VRC 144-145 M 3
Donggou o VRC 150-151 E 8
Dongguan o VRC 156-157 B 5
Dongguan o VRC (GDG) 156-157 H 5
Đông Hà ☆ VN 158-159 J 2
Dong Hai ≈ 154-155 N 6
Donghai o VRC 154-155 L 4
Donghai Dao ⌒ VRC 156-157 G 6
Đong Hới ☆ VN 158-159 J 2
Donghuang ~ VRC 156-157 J 5
Dongji Liedao ⌒ VRC 156-157 M 2
Dongjingcheng o VRC 150-151 G 5
Dongkait, Tanjung ▲ RI 164-165 F 5
Dongkala o RI 164-165 H 6
Dongkeng o VRC 156-157 L 3
Dongkou o VRC 156-157 G 3
Donglan o VRC 156-157 E 4
Dongliang o VRC 154-155 H 2
Dong Ling • VRC 150-151 D 7
Dongmen o VRC 156-157 E 5
Dongming o VRC 154-155 J 4
Dongning o VRC 150-151 H 5
Dongo o ANG 216-217 C 7
Dongo o ZRE 210-211 G 2
Dongola = Donqula ☆ SUD 200-201 E 3
Dongou o RCB 210-211 G 2
Dong Phaya Yen ▲ THA 158-159 F 2
Đông Phú o VN 158-159 J 5
Dongpo o VRC 144-145 C 5
Dongqiao o VRC 144-145 H 5
Dongsha Dao ⌒ VRC 156-157 K 6
Dongshanling • VRC 156-157 G 4
Dongshan Wan ~ VRC 156-157 K 5
Dongsha Qundao ⌒ VRC 156-157 K 6
Dongsheng o VRC 154-155 F 2
Dongtai o VRC 154-155 M 5
Dong Taijnar Hu ⊂ VRC 144-145 K 2
Dongting Hu ⊂ VRC 156-157 H 2
Đông Triều ☆ VN 156-157 E 6
Dongue o ANG 216-217 C 7
Donguila o G 210-211 B 3
Dong Ujimqin Qi o VRC 148-149 N 5
Donguz ~ RUS 96-97 J 8
Đông Van o VN 156-157 D 5
Dongwe ~ Z 218-219 C 1
Dongxing o VRC 156-157 F 7
Dongyang o VRC 156-157 M 2
Dongying o VRC 154-155 L 3
Dongzhai o VRC 156-157 G 2
Dongzhaigang Z.B. ⊥ • VRC 156-157 G 7
Dongzhi o VRC 154-155 K 6
Donie o USA (TX) 266-267 L 2
Doniphan o USA (MO) 276-277 E 4
Donjek River ~ CDN 20-21 V 6
Donji Vakuf o BIH 100-101 F 2
Don Juan o DOM 54-55 L 5
Donkar o BHT 142-143 G 2
Donkerpoort o ZA 220-221 G 5
Donko o WAN 204-205 F 3
Don Martín o MEX 50-51 J 4
Donmatia o IND 142-143 G 3
Dønna ⌒ N 86-87 F 3
Donnacona o CDN (QUE) 238-239 O 2
Donnelly o CDN 32-33 M 4
Donner Pass ▲ USA (CA) 246-247 E 4
Donnybrook o AUS 176-177 C 6
Donnybrook o USA (ND) 258-259 F 3
Donnybrook o ZA 220-221 J 4
Dono Manga o TCH 206-207 C 4
Donon ▲ F 90-91 L 7
Donostia-San Sebastián o •• E 98-99 G 3
Donovan o CDN (SAS) 232-233 L 4
Đon Quê o VN 158-159 J 2
Donqula ☆ SUD 200-201 E 3
Don River ~ AUS 174-175 J 7
Donskaja grjada ▲ RUS 102-103 L 3
Donskaja ravnina ▲ RUS 94-95 R 5
Donskoe o RUS 96-97 K 8
Donskoj o RUS 94-95 Q 5
Donyztau ▲ KA 126-127 M 4
Doolgunna o AUS 176-177 E 2
Doomadgee ⊼ AUS 174-175 E 5
Doomadgee Aboriginal Land ⊼ AUS 174-175 E 5
Doonerak, Mount ▲ USA 20-21 P 3
Doongmabulla o AUS 178-179 J 2
Doornik = Tournai o • B 92-93 G 3
Doorns, De o ZA 220-221 D 6
Door Peninsula ⌣ USA (WI) 270-271 L 6
Dora o USA (NM) 256-257 M 5
Dora, Lake ⊂ AUS 172-173 F 7
Dora, Mount ▲ AUS 176-177 G 3
Dorada, La o CO 60-61 D 5
Dorado o PY 76-77 G 1
Dorado, El o MEX 50-51 F 5
Dorado, El o YV 62-63 D 2
Dorado, Río ~ RA 76-77 F 3
Doraga o RP 160-161 E 6
Dōrāhāk o IR 134-135 D 5
Dora Lake o USA (MN) 270-271 D 3
Doralé o DJI 208-209 F 3
Doranāla o IND 140-141 H 3
Doran Lake ⊂ CDN 30-31 Q 5
Dorbod o VRC 150-151 E 4
Dorchester o CDN (NB) 240-241 L 5
Dorchester ☆ • GB 90-91 F 6
Dorchester, Cape ▲ CDN 36-37 L 2
Dordabis o NAM 216-217 D 11
Dordogne ~ F 90-91 H 9
Dordrecht o • NL 92-93 H 3
Dordrecht o ZA 220-221 H 5
Doreen, Mount ▲ AUS 172-173 K 7
Doré Lake o CDN (SAS) 34-35 C 3
Doré Lake ⊂ CDN (SAS) 34-35 C 3
Dores do Indaiá o BR 72-73 H 5
Dores do Rio Preto o BR 72-73 K 6
Dores Turvo o BR 72-73 J 6
Dorey o RMM 202-203 K 2
Dörgön = Seer o MAU 146-147 L 1
Dori ☆ BF 202-203 K 2
Doringbaai o ZA 220-221 D 5
Doringrivier ~ ZA 220-221 D 6
Dorintosh o CDN 32-33 Q 4
Dorion o CDN (ONT) 234-235 P 6
Dorion o CDN (QUE) 238-239 L 3
Dorisvale o AUS 172-173 K 3
Dorlin o F 62-63 H 4
Dormansville o USA (NY) 278-279 H 6
Dormentes o BR 68-69 H 6
Dornakal o IND 142-143 B 7
Dornoch o GB 90-91 E 3
Dornod □ MAU 148-149 L 4
Dorno Djoutougué o TCH 198-199 L 6
Dornogov' □ MAU 148-149 J 5
Doro o RMM 196-197 K 6
Dorogobuž o RUS 94-95 N 4
Doroh o IR 134-135 J 2
Dorohoi o RO 102-103 E 4
Dorohovo o RUS 94-95 P 4
Dorolamo o RI 164-165 L 3
Doroninskoe o RUS 118-119 F 10
Döröö nuur ⊂ MAU 146-147 L 2
Doropo o CI 202-203 J 5
Dorotea o S 86-87 H 4
Dorothy o CDN (ALB) 232-233 F 4
Dorowa o ZW 218-219 F 4
Doroznyj o RUS 118-119 G 5
Dorra o DJI 200-201 L 6
Dorrance o USA (KS) 262-263 H 6
Dorreen o CDN (BC) 228-229 F 2
Dorre Island ⌒ AUS 176-177 B 2
Dorrigo o AUS 178-179 M 6
Dorrigo National Park ⊥ AUS 178-179 M 6
Dorris o USA (CA) 246-247 D 2
Dorsale Camerounaise ▲ CAM 204-205 J 5
Dorset o CDN (ONT) 238-239 G 3
Dorset o CDN (ONT) 238-239 G 3
Dorset Island ⌒ CDN 36-37 L 2
Dört Kilise ∴• TR 128-129 J 2
Dortmund o • D 92-93 J 3
Dörtyol ☆ • TR 128-129 G 4
Dorucha o RUS 110-111 J 3
Dorūd o IR 134-135 C 2
Doruma o ZRE 206-207 H 6
Dörvölžin = Buga o MAU 146-147 M 2
Dos, El ∴• MEX 52-53 L 1
Dos Bocas ∴• USA (PR) 286-287 P 2
Dos Cabezas o USA (AZ) 256-257 F 6
Dos Cabezas Peak ▲ USA (AZ) 256-257 F 6
Dos Caminos o C 54-55 H 4
Dos Caminos o YV 60-61 H 3
Dos de Mayo o PE 64-65 E 5
Doseo, Bahr ~ TCH 206-207 D 4
Dos Hermanas o E 98-99 E 6
Dōšī o AFG 136-137 L 7
Dos Lagunas o GCA 52-53 K 3
Dos Lagunas, Parque Nacional ⊥ RCH 80 E 2
Đô So'n ☆ VN 156-157 E 6
Dospat o BG 102-103 D 7
Dosquet o CDN (QUE) 238-239 O 2
Dos Rios o CO 64-65 F 1
Dos Rios o USA (CA) 246-247 B 4
Dosso □ RN 204-205 E 2
Dosso ☆ RN (DOS) 204-205 E 2
Dossor o KA 96-97 H 10
Dostuk o KS 146-147 B 5
Doswell o USA (VA) 280-281 J 6
Dot o CDN (BC) 230-231 H 3
Dothan o USA (AL) 284-285 E 5
Dot Klish Wash ~ USA (AZ) 256-257 E 2
Dotswood o AUS 174-175 J 6
Douai o F 90-91 J 6
Douala ☆ CAM 204-205 H 6
Douala-Edéa, Réserve ⊥ CAM 210-211 C 2
Doualayel o CAM 204-205 K 5
Douaouir, Erg ∴ RMM 196-197 J 4
Douarnenez o F 90-91 E 7
Douaya < RMM 196-197 J 6
Doubabougou o RMM 202-203 G 2
Double Bayou o USA (TX) 268-269 F 7
Double Island Point ▲ AUS 178-179 M 3
Double Mer ⊂ CDN 36-37 U 7
Double Mountain ▲ AUS 178-179 L 2
Double Mountain Fork Brazos River ~ USA (TX) 264-265 C 5
Double Springs o USA (AL) 284-285 C 2
Doubodo ~ BF 202-203 L 4
Doubs ~ F 90-91 L 8
Doubtful Bay ≈ 172-173 G 4
Doubtful Island Bay ≈ 176-177 E 7
Doubtful Sound ≈ 182 A 6
Douchuishan • VRC 154-155 D 5
Doudou o BF 202-203 J 4
Doué ~ SN 196-197 C 6
Douélé o CI 202-203 G 6
Douentza o RMM 202-203 J 2
Dougga ∴•• TN 190-191 G 2
Doughboy Bay ≈ 182 A 7
Dougherty o USA (TX) 264-265 C 5
Doughton Gap ▲ USA (NC) 282-283 F 4
Douglas o AUS 172-173 K 2
Douglas o CDN (MAN) 234-235 D 5
Douglas o GB 78-79 L 6
Douglas ☆ • GBM 90-91 E 4
Douglas o USA (AK) 32-33 C 2
Douglas o USA (AZ) 256-257 F 7
Douglas o USA (GA) 284-285 H 5
Douglas o USA (WA) 244-245 E 3
Douglas o USA (WY) 252-253 N 4
Douglas o ZA 220-221 F 4
Douglas, Cape ▲ USA 22-23 U 3
Douglas, Mount ▲ USA 22-23 U 3
Douglas Channel ≈ 32-33 F 5
Douglas Channel ≈ CDN 228-229 E 3
Douglas City o USA (CA) 246-247 C 3
Douglas Creek ~ USA 178-179 D 5
Douglas Flat o USA (CA) 246-247 E 5
Douglas Lake o CDN (BC) 230-231 J 3
Douglas Lake ⊂ CDN 30-31 Q 4
Douglas Lake ⊂ USA (TN) 282-283 D 5
Douglas Lake Indian Reserve ⊼ CDN (BC) 230-231 J 3
Douglas Pass ▲ USA (CO) 254-255 G 4
Douglas Peninsula ⌣ CDN 30-31 P 4
Douglas Point ▲ CDN (ONT) 238-239 D 4
Douglas Ponds Creek ~ AUS 178-179 H 3
Douglas Provincial Park ⊥ CDN (SAS) 232-233 M 4
Douglas Range ▲ ARK 16 G 29
Douglass o USA (KS) 262-263 J 7
Douglass o USA (TX) 268-269 F 5
Douglastown o CDN (QUE) 240-241 L 2
Douglasville o USA (GA) 284-285 F 3
Douglasville o USA (TX) 264-265 K 5
Dougmuge o VRC 156-157 C 5
Dougoulé < RN 198-199 E 5
Douhongpo ▲ VRC 156-157 D 4
Douka o RG 202-203 E 4
Douka, Bahr Keita ou ~ TCH 206-207 D 4
Doukhobor Village • CDN (BC) 230-231 M 4
Doukoula o CAM 206-207 B 3
Doulatābād o AFG (BAL) 136-137 K 6
Doulatābād o AFG (FĀ) 136-137 J 6
Doulatābād o IR 134-135 G 4
Doulati, Āb-e ~ IR 136-137 C 7
Doulat Yār o AFG 134-135 L 1
Doullens o F 90-91 J 6
Doumandzou o G 210-211 C 3
Doumba bonne < RN 198-199 F 3
Doum Doum o TCH 198-199 G 6
Doumé o CAM 204-205 K 6
Doumé ~ CAM 206-207 B 6
Doumen o VRC 156-157 H 5
Doumo o CAM 210-211 D 2
Douna o BF 202-203 H 4
Douna o RMM 202-203 K 2
Doundé Bagué o SN 202-203 D 2
Dounet o RG 202-203 E 4
Dounguél-Sigon o RG 202-203 D 4
Dounkassa o DY 204-205 E 3
Dounkou o BF 202-203 J 3
Douqing o VRC 156-157 F 4
Dourada, Serra ▲ BR 72-73 F 2
Douradina o BR (GSU) 76-77 K 2
Douradina o BR (PAR) 72-73 D 7
Douradoquara o BR 72-73 G 5
Dourados o BR 76-77 K 2
Dourados, Rio ~ BR 76-77 K 2
Dourados, Serra dos ▲ BR 72-73 D 7
Dour Bābā o AFG 138-139 C 2
Dourbali o TCH 206-207 B 3
Dourbeye o CAM 204-205 K 4
Dourdoura o TCH 206-207 E 3
Douro o RMM 202-203 J 2
Douro ~ RMM 202-203 J 2
Douro, Rio ~ P 98-99 D 4
Douroum o CAM 204-205 K 3
Doussala o G 210-211 C 5
Doutoufouk o RN 198-199 D 6
Douz o • TN 190-191 G 4
Dove o PNG 183 E 5
Dove Bugt ≈ 26-27 q 5
Dove Creek o USA (CO) 254-255 G 6
Dover o AUS 180-181 J 7
Dover o CDN (NFL) 242-243 P 4
Dover o • GB 90-91 H 6
Dover o USA (AR) 276-277 B 5
Dover o USA (NH) 278-279 L 5
Dover o USA (NJ) 280-281 M 3
Dover o USA (OH) 280-281 E 3
Dover o USA (TN) 276-277 H 4
Dover ☆ USA (DE) 280-281 L 4
Dover, Point ▲ AUS 176-177 H 6
Dover, Strait of ≈ 90-91 H 6
Dovercourt o CDN (ALB) 232-233 D 3
Dover-Foxcroft o USA (ME) 278-279 M 3
Dover River ~ CDN 32-33 O 3
Dovrefjell ▲ N 84-85 H 3
Dovsk o BY 94-95 M 5
Dowa o MW 218-219 G 1
Dowagiac o USA (MI) 272-273 C 6
Dowerin o AUS 176-177 D 5
Dowi, Mount ▲ PNG 183 D 3
Dowling Lake ⊂ CDN (ALB) 232-233 F 4
Downe o CDN (SAS) 232-233 K 4
Downey o USA (ID) 252-253 F 4
Downie Creek o CDN (BC) 230-231 L 2
Downie Creek ~ CDN (BC) 230-231 L 2
Downieville o USA (CA) 246-247 E 4
Downs o USA (KS) 262-263 H 5
Downsville o USA (NY) 278-279 F 6

Downton, Mount ▲ CDN (BC) 228-229 K 4
Doyle o USA (CA) 246-247 E 3
Doylestown o USA (PA) 280-281 L 3
Doyleville o USA (CO) 254-255 J 5
Doyon o USA (ND) 258-259 J 3
Doze de Outubro, Rio ~ BR 70-71 H 3
Dozgah, Rūdḫāne-ye ~ IR 134-135 E 4
Dozois, Réservoir ⊂ CDN (QUE) 236-237 L 5
Drâa, Cap ▲ MA 188-189 F 6
Drâa, Hamada du ⩶ DZ 188-189 G 6
Drâa, Oued ~ MA 188-189 G 6
Drâa, Vallée du ⌣•• MA 188-189 H 5
Dra Afratir ⩶ MA 196-197 D 2
Drabonso o GH 202-203 K 6
Dracena o BR 72-73 E 6
Drachten o NL 92-93 J 2
Drăgănești-Olt o RO 102-103 D 5
Drăgănești-Vlașca o RO 102-103 D 5
Drăgășani o RO 102-103 D 5
Draghoender o ZA 220-221 F 4
Dragocennaja, guba ≈ 110-111 W 1
Dragon, Kap ▲ GRØ 26-27 Y 2
Dragoon o USA (AZ) 256-257 E 6
Draguignan o F 90-91 L 10
Drahičyn o BY 94-95 J 5
Drain o USA (OR) 244-245 B 7
Drake o CDN (SAS) 232-233 N 4
Drake o USA (MO) 274-275 G 6
Drake o USA (ND) 258-259 G 4
Drakensberge ▲ ZA 220-221 J 4
Drake Passage ≈ 9 E 10
Drake Peak ▲ USA (OR) 244-245 E 8
Drakes Bay ≈ 40-41 C 7
Drakes Bay ≈ USA 248-249 B 2
Dráma o GR 100-101 K 4
Drammen ☆ N 86-87 E 7
Drangajökull ⊂ IS 86-87 b 1
Dranoz ▲ TR 128-129 F 2
Draper, Mount ▲ USA 20-21 V 7
Drar Souttouf ⩶ MA 196-197 C 4
Drāsan o PK 138-139 D 1
Drasco o USA (AR) 276-277 C 5
Drava ~ HR 100-101 F 2
Drawa ~ PL 92-93 N 2
Drawsko Pomorskie o PL 92-93 N 2
Drayton o USA (ND) 258-259 K 3
Drayton Valley o CDN (ALB) 232-233 D 2
Dreamworld • AUS 178-179 M 4
Dréan o DZ 190-191 F 2
Dreikikir o PNG 183 B 2
Dremsel, Mount ▲ PNG 183 D 2
Drennan o ZA 220-221 G 6
Dresden o CDN (ONT) 238-239 C 6
Dresden ☆•• D 92-93 M 3
Dresden o USA (KS) 262-263 F 5
Dresden o USA (OH) 280-281 D 3
Dresden o USA (TN) 276-277 G 4
Dreux o F 90-91 H 7
Drevsjø o N 86-87 F 6
Drew o USA (MS) 268-269 K 3
Drewsey o USA (OR) 244-245 G 7
Drew's Gap ▲ USA (OR) 244-245 E 8
Drews Reservoir ⊂ USA (OR) 244-245 E 8
Drexel o USA (MO) 274-275 D 6
Drezdenko o PL 92-93 N 2
Driffield o GB 90-91 G 4
Drifton o USA (FL) 286-287 F 1
Driftpile River ~ CDN 32-33 N 4
Driftpile River Indian Reserve ⊼ CDN 32-33 N 4
Driftwood o CDN 32-33 G 4
Driftwood o USA (PA) 280-281 H 2
Driftwood Creek ~ CDN (BC) 228-229 G 2
Driftwood River ~ CDN 32-33 N 4
Driftwood River ~ CDN (ONT) 236-237 G 3
Driggs o USA (ID) 252-253 G 3
Drimiopsis o NAM 216-217 E 11
Drin, Lumi ~ AL 100-101 G 3
Drina ~ YU 100-101 G 3
Drinkwater o CDN (SAS) 232-233 N 5
Drinkwater Pass ▲ USA (OR) 244-245 G 7
Dripping Springs o USA (TX) 266-267 J 3
Driscoll o USA (TX) 266-267 K 6
Drjanovo o BG 102-103 D 6
Drniš o HR 100-101 F 3
Drobeta-Turnu Severin o• RO 102-103 C 5
Drobin o PL 92-93 P 2
Droërivier o ZA 220-221 F 6
Drogheda = Droichead Átha o IRL 90-91 D 5
Drogobyč = Drohobyč ☆ UA 102-103 C 3
Drohobyč ☆ UA 102-103 C 3
Droichead Átha = Drogheda o IRL 90-91 D 5
Droichead na Bandan = Bandan o IRL 90-91 C 6
Drôme ~ F 90-91 K 9
Drome o PNG 183 B 2
Dromedary, Cape ▲ AUS 180-181 L 4
Dronne ~ F 90-91 H 9
Dronning Ingrid Land ⩶ GRØ 28-29 P 4
Dronning Louise Land ⩶ GRØ 26-27 n 5
Dronning Maud fjellkjede ▲ ARK 16 E 0
Dronning Maud land ⩶ ARK 16 F 36
Dronten o NL 92-93 H 2
Dropmore o CDN (MAN) 234-235 B 3
Drossopigí o GR 100-101 H 5
Dro Station o CDN (ONT) 238-239 F 4
Drottningholm ••• S 86-87 H 7
Drovers Cave National Park ⊥ AUS 176-177 C 5
Drovjanoj o RUS 108-109 P 5
Drowned Cays ⌒ BH 52-53 K 3
Drowning River ~ CDN (ONT) 236-237 C 2
Dr. Petru Groza = Ștei o RO 102-103 C 4
Druid o CDN (SAS) 232-233 K 4
Drumduff o AUS 174-175 G 5
Drume o YU 100-101 G 3
Drumheller o CDN (ALB) 232-233 F 4
Drummond o USA (MI) 270-271 P 4
Drummond o USA (MT) 250-251 F 5
Drummond o USA (WI) 270-271 G 4
Drummond Island ⌒ USA (MI) 272-273 F 2
Drummond Range ▲ AUS 178-179 J 2
Drummondville o CDN (QUE) 238-239 N 3
Drumochter, Pass of ▲ GB 90-91 E 3
Drumright o USA (OK) 264-265 H 3
Druskininkai o•• LT 94-95 H 4
Druza, gora ▲ RUS 120-121 K 3
Druzba o KA 146-147 F 3
Družina o RUS 110-111 Z 5
Družkivka o UA 102-103 K 3
Družkovka = Družkivka o UA 102-103 K 3
Družnyj o RUS 114-115 T 5
Dry Bay ≈ 20-21 V 7
Dryberry Lake ⊂ CDN (ONT) 234-235 K 5
Drybrough o CDN 34-35 F 2
Dry Creek o USA (LA) 268-269 G 6
Dry Creek ~ USA (WY) 252-253 J 3
Dryden o CDN (ONT) 234-235 L 5
Dryden o USA (NY) 278-279 E 6
Dryden o USA (TX) 266-267 E 3
Dry Fork ~ USA (WY) 252-253 N 3
Drygalski Glacier ⊂ ARK 16 F 17
Drygalski-Island ⌒ ARK 16 G 10
Drygalskis Halvø ⌣ GRØ 28-29 P 1
Dry Hartsrivier ~ ZA 220-221 G 3
Dry Island Buffalo Jump Provincial Park ⊥ CDN (ALB) 232-233 F 4
Dry Prong o USA (LA) 268-269 H 5
Dry River ~ AUS 172-173 L 3
Drysdale Island ⌒ AUS 174-175 C 2
Drysdale River o AUS (WA) 172-173 H 3
Drysdale River ~ AUS 172-173 H 3
Drysdale River National Park ⊥ AUS 172-173 H 3
Dry Tortugas ⌒ USA (FL) 286-287 G 7
Drytown o USA (CA) 246-247 E 5
Dschang o CAM 204-205 J 6
Dtscord, Kap ▲ GRØ 28-29 T 6
Dua ~ ZRE 210-211 J 2
Duaca o YV 60-61 G 2
Duale ~ ZRE 210-211 J 3
Ḍū al-Faif, Ğazīrat ⌒ KSA 132-133 B 5
Dualla o CI 202-203 G 5
Du'an o VRC 156-157 F 5
Duane Center o USA (NY) 278-279 G 4
Duangua, Rio ~ MOC 218-219 F 2
Duanshan o VRC 156-157 E 4
Duaringa o AUS 178-179 K 2
Duart o CDN (ONT) 238-239 D 6
Duarte o MEX 50-51 J 7
Duas Barras do Morro o BR 68-69 H 7
Duau, Mount ▲ PNG 183 C 4
Ḍubā o KSA 130-131 D 4
Duba o WAN 204-205 F 4
Ḍubāb o• Y 132-133 C 7
Dubach o USA (LA) 268-269 H 4
Dubai'a, ad- o KSA 130-131 K 5
Dubai'a, ad- o UAE 134-135 F 6
Dubăsari ☆ MD 102-103 F 4
Dubawnt Lake ⊂ CDN 30-31 S 4
Dubawnt River ~ CDN 30-31 T 3
Dubayy = Dubai o• UAE 134-135 F 6
Dubbo o AUS 180-181 K 2
Dubčes ~ RUS 114-115 U 4
Dubec o RUS 94-95 Q 2
Dubela o ZRE 212-213 B 2
Dubėsar' = Dubăsari ☆ MD 102-103 F 4
Dubie o ZRE 214-215 E 5
Dublikan ~ RUS 122-123 E 3
Dublin o GA (GA) 284-285 H 4
Dublin o USA (TX) 264-265 F 6
Dublin o USA (VA) 280-281 F 6
Dublin = Baile Átha Cliath ☆•• IRL 90-91 D 5
Dubli River ~ USA 20-21 N 4
Dubna o RUS 94-95 P 3
Dubno o UA 102-103 D 2
Dubois o USA (ID) 252-253 F 2
Du Bois o USA (PA) 280-281 H 2
Dubois o USA (WY) 252-253 J 3
Du Bose o CDN (BC) 228-229 F 2
Dubossary = Dubăsari ☆ MD 102-103 F 4
Dubovka o RUS 96-97 D 9
Dubréka o RG 202-203 D 5
Dubreuilville o CDN (ONT) 236-237 D 4
Dubrovnik o••• HR 100-101 G 3
Dubrovycja o UA 102-103 E 2
Dubulu o ZRE 206-207 E 6
Dubuque o• USA (IA) 274-275 H 2
Dubwe o LB 202-203 G 7
Đức Hạnh o VN 158-159 J 5
Duchener, Réserve de ⊥ CDN (QUE) 240-241 G 2
Duchesne o USA (UT) 254-255 E 3
Duchesne River ~ USA (UT) 254-255 E 3
Duchess o AUS 178-179 E 1
Duchess o CDN (ALB) 232-233 G 5
Duck Bay o CDN (MAN) 234-235 C 2
Duck Creek ~ AUS 172-173 C 7
Duck Hill o USA (MS) 268-269 L 3
Duck Islands ⌒ CDN (NWT) 28-29 J 3
Duck Islands ⌒ CDN (ONT) 238-239 C 3
Duck Lake o CDN (SAS) 232-233 M 3
Duck Mountain ▲ CDN (MAN) 234-235 B 3
Duck Mountain Forest Reserve ⊥ CDN (MAN) 234-235 B 3
Duck Mountain Provincial Park ⊥ CDN (MAN) 234-235 B 3
Duck River o USA (TN) 276-277 H 5
Duck River ~ USA (TN) 276-277 H 5
Ducktown o USA (TN) 282-283 C 5
Duck Valley Indian Reservation ⊼ USA (NV) 246-247 J 1
Duckwater o USA (NV) 246-247 K 5
Duckwater Point ▲ USA (NV) 246-247 K 5
Duc Lâp ☆ VN 158-159 J 2
Đức Liêu o VN 158-159 J 5
Dục Mỹo o VN 158-159 K 4
Ducor o USA (CA) 248-249 E 4
Du Couedic, Cape ▲ AUS 180-181 D 4
Đức Phổ o VN 158-159 K 3
Đức Phổ o VN 158-159 K 3
Đức Tho ☆ VN 156-157 D 7
Đức Trọng o VN 158-159 K 5
Duda, Río ~ CO 60-61 D 6
Dudduumo o SP 212-213 J 3
Düdensuyu Mağarası •• TR 128-129 D 4
Dudhani o IND 140-141 G 2
Dūdhi o IND 142-143 C 3
Dudh Kosi ~ NEP 144-145 F 7
Dudhwa National Park ⊥ IND 144-145 C 6
Dudignac o RA 78-79 J 3
Dudinka ☆ RUS 108-109 W 7
Dudinka ~ RUS 108-109 W 7
Dudley o GB 90-91 F 5
Dudorovskij o RUS 94-95 O 5
Dūdu o IND 138-139 E 6
Dudub o ETH 208-209 H 5
Dudypta ~ RUS 108-109 b 5
Due o ZRE 210-211 G 6
Duékoué o CI 202-203 G 6
Duere, Rio ~ BR 68-69 D 7
Duero, Río ~ E 98-99 F 4
Duette o USA (FL) 286-287 G 4
Due West o USA (SC) 284-285 H 2
Duff o CDN (SAS) 232-233 P 5
Dufreboy, Lac ⊂ CDN 36-37 O 5
Dufrost, Pointe ▲ CDN 36-37 L 4
Dufur o USA (OR) 244-245 D 5
Dugda ~ RUS 122-123 F 3
Dugi Otok ⌒ HR 100-101 E 2
Dugum o ETH 200-201 J 6
Dugway o USA (UT) 254-255 C 3
Dugwaya o SUD 200-201 G 4
Dugway Proving Ground xx USA (UT) 254-255 B 3
Duhamel o CDN (QUE) 238-239 K 2
Duḫān o Q 134-135 D 6
Duhau o RA 78-79 H 4
Du He ~ VRC 154-155 G 5
Duḫna o KSA 130-131 H 5
Duhovnickoe ☆ RUS 96-97 F 7
Duhovščina ☆ RUS 94-95 N 4
Duhubi o NEP 144-145 F 7
Duḫūr, Abū ḍ- o SYR 128-129 G 5
Duida, Cerro ▲ YV 60-61 J 6
Duifken Point ▲ AUS 174-175 F 3
Duisburg o D 92-93 J 3
Duitama o CO 60-61 E 5
Duiwelskloof o ZA 218-219 F 6
Dujiangyan o VRC 154-155 C 6
Dujiang Yan • VRC 154-155 C 6
Dukambiya o ER 200-201 H 5
Dūkān o IRQ 128-129 L 5
Dūkān Buhairat ⊂ IRQ 128-129 L 4
Duke o USA (OK) 264-265 E 4
Duke Island ⌒ USA 32-33 E 4
Duken o KA 126-127 O 3
Duke of York Archipelago ⌒ CDN 24-25 P 6
Duke of York Bay ≈ 36-37 G 2
Duke of York Island ⌒ PNG 183 G 3
Dūk Fadiat o SUD 206-207 K 5
Dūk Faiwil o SUD 206-207 K 5
Duki o RUS 122-123 F 3
Duki ~ RUS 122-123 F 3
Dukkālah ⩶ MA 188-189 G 4
Dukku o WAN 204-205 F 3
Dukoa, ozero ⊂ RUS 112-113 J 2
Dūkštas o LT 94-95 K 4
Duku o WAN 204-205 J 3
Dulac o USA (LA) 268-269 K 7
Dulaihān o KSA 130-131 G 4
Dulaimiya, ad- o KSA 130-131 H 4
Dulai' Rašid o KSA 130-131 H 5
Dulala o ZRE 214-215 C 6
Dulamaya o RI 164-165 H 3
Dulan o VRC 144-145 M 2
Dulayb, Khor ~ SUD 208-209 A 3
Dulce o USA (NM) 256-257 J 2
Dulce, Arroyo ~ RA 78-79 L 4
Dulce, Golfo ≈ 52-53 C 7
Dulce, Laguna la ⊂ RA 78-79 F 4
Dulce, Río ~ GCA 52-53 K 4
Dulce, Río ~ RA 76-77 F 5
Dulce Nombre de Culmí o HN 54-55 C 7
Dul'durga ☆ RUS 118-119 F 10
Dulgalah ~ RUS 110-111 S 6
Dulgalah ~ RUS 118-119 P 3
Dulhunty River ~ AUS 174-175 G 2
Dulia o ZRE (HAU) 210-211 K 2
Dulia o ZRE (KIV) 212-213 B 3
Dulkaninna o AUS 178-179 E 5
Dullewala o PK 138-139 C 4
Dullingari Gas and Oil Field • AUS 178-179 F 5
Dulovo o BG 102-103 E 6
Duluth o USA (MN) 270-271 F 4
Dulzura o USA (CA) 248-249 H 7
Duma ~ EAT 212-213 D 5
Duma o RB 218-219 B 4
Dūmā ☆ SYR 128-129 G 6
Duma o ZRE (Equ) 210-211 G 2
Duma ~ ZRE 206-207 H 6
Dumai o RI 162-163 D 4
Dumaran Island ⌒ RP 160-161 C 7
Dumaresq River ~ AUS 178-179 L 5
Dumas o USA (AR) 276-277 D 7
Dumas o USA (TX) 264-265 C 3
Dumas, Península ⌣ RCH 80 F 7
Dūmat al-Ğandal o• KSA 130-131 F 3
Dumba Cambango o ANG 216-217 D 5
Dumbleyung o AUS 176-177 D 6
Dumbleyung Lake ⊂ AUS 176-177 D 6
Dumbo o CAM 204-205 J 5
Dum Duma o IND 142-143 J 2
Dume, Point ▲ USA (CA) 248-249 F 5
Dumfries o• GB 90-91 F 4
Dumfries o USA (VA) 280-281 J 5
Dumjala o NEP 144-145 D 6
Dummer o CDN (SAS) 232-233 O 6
Dumogabesar o RI 164-165 J 3
Dumoine, Lac ⊂ CDN (QUE) 238-239 H 2
Dumoine, Rivière ~ CDN (QUE) 238-239 H 2
Dumond River ~ CDN (ONT) 234-235 O 2
Dumont o USA (TX) 264-265 D 5
Dumont d'Urville o ARK 16 G 15
Dumore o USA (PA) 280-281 L 2
Dumpu o PNG 183 C 3
Dumrān, Wādī ad ~ LAR 192-193 F 4
Dumri o IND 142-143 E 4
Dumsuk, Ğazīrat ⌒ KSA 132-133 C 5
Dumyāṭ ☆ ET 194-195 E 2
Dumyāṭ, Maṣabb ~ ET 194-195 E 2
Duna o ANG 216-217 F 6
Dunaföldvár o H 92-93 P 5
Dunai o NEP 144-145 D 6
Dunaj ~ UA 102-103 F 5
Dunajivci ☆ UA 102-103 E 3
Dunajská Streda o SK 92-93 O 5
Dunalley o AUS 180-181 J 7
Dunărea ~ RO 102-103 C 5
Dunaújváros o H 92-93 P 5
Dunav ~ BG 102-103 D 6
Dunav ~ YU 100-101 G 2
Dunbar o AUS 174-175 G 5
Dunbar o GB 90-91 F 4
Dunbrody Abbey •• IRL 90-91 D 5
Duncairn o CDN (SAS) 232-233 K 5
Duncan o CDN (BC) 230-231 F 5
Duncan o USA (AZ) 256-257 F 6
Duncan o USA (OK) 264-265 G 4
Duncan, Cape ▲ CDN 34-35 Q 4
Duncan, Lac ⊂ CDN 38-39 E 2
Duncanby Landing o CDN (BC) 230-231 B 2
Duncan Highway II AUS 172-173 H 5
Duncan Lake ⊂ CDN 30-31 N 4
Duncan Lake ⊂ CDN (BC) 230-231 N 3
Duncan Passage ≈ 140-141 L 4
Duncan River ~ CDN (BC) 230-231 M 3
Duncansby Head ▲ GB 90-91 F 2
Duncan Town o BS 54-55 H 3
Dundaga o• LV 94-95 H 3
Dundalk o CDN (ONT) 238-239 E 4
Dundalk o• IRL 90-91 D 4
Dundalk o USA (MD) 280-281 K 4
Dundangan Island ⌒ RP 160-161 D 10
Dundas o CDN (ONT) 238-239 F 5
Dundas o GRØ 26-27 Q 5
Dundas o USA (IL) 274-275 K 6
Dundas, Lake ⊂ AUS 176-177 F 6
Dundas Harbour o CDN 24-25 f 3
Dundas Island ⌒ CDN (BC) 228-229 D 2
Dundas Peninsula ⌣ CDN 24-25 P 3
Dundas Strait ≈ 172-173 K 1
Dundburd o MAU 148-149 K 4
Dún Dealgan = Dundalk o• IRL 90-91 D 4
Dundee o AUS 178-179 G 1
Dundee o GB 90-91 F 3
Dundee o USA (MI) 272-273 F 6
Dundee o USA (TX) 264-265 F 5
Dundee o ZA 220-221 K 4
Dundgov' ■ MAU 148-149 G 5
Dundo o ANG 216-217 F 3
Dundoboo Range ▲ AUS 180-181 H 2
Dundret ▲•• S 86-87 K 3
Dundurn o CDN (SAS) 232-233 M 4
Dunedin o NZ 182 C 6
Dunedin o USA (FL) 286-287 G 3
Dunedin River ~ CDN 30-31 G 6
Dunedoo o AUS 180-181 K 2
Dunes City o USA (OR) 244-245 A 7
Dunfermline o GB 90-91 F 3
Dünga Büngə o PK 138-139 C 5
Dungan, Kuala o• MAL 162-163 E 2
Dungannon o GB 90-91 D 4
Dún Garbhán = Dungarvan o IRL 90-91 D 5
Düngarpur o IND 138-139 D 8
Dungarvan = Dún Garbhán o IRL 90-91 D 5
Dungas o RN 198-199 D 6
Dungeness, Punta ▲ RA 80 F 6
Dungeness Spit ▲ USA (WA) 244-245 B 2
Dungog o AUS 180-181 L 2
Dungu o ZRE 212-213 B 2
Dungu ~ ZRE 212-213 B 2
Dungunāb o SUD 200-201 H 2
Dungunāb, Ğazīrat ⌣ SUD 200-201 H 2
Dunham o CDN (QUE) 238-239 N 3
Dunham River ~ AUS (WA) 172-173 J 4
Dunham River ~ AUS 172-173 J 4
Dunhua o VRC 150-151 G 6
Dunhuang = Minghoshan o• VRC 146-147 M 5
Dunière, Parc Provincial de ⊥ CDN (QUE) 240-241 J 2
Dunkeld o AUS 180-181 G 4
Dunken o USA (NM) 256-257 K 6
Dunkerque o F 90-91 J 6
Dunkirk o USA (NY) 278-279 B 6
Dunk Island ⌒ AUS 174-175 J 5
Dunkwa o GH 202-203 K 7
Dun Laoghaire o IRL 90-91 D 5
Dunlap o USA (IA) 274-275 C 3
Dunlap o USA (NM) 256-257 L 4
Dunlap o USA (TN) 276-277 K 5
Dunlap o USA (TX) 264-265 D 4
Dunleath o CDN (SAS) 232-233 Q 4
Dunmarra o AUS 174-175 B 5
Dunmore o CDN (ALB) 232-233 H 6
Dunmore o USA (PA) 280-281 L 2
Dunmore Town o•• BS 54-55 G 2
Dunn o USA (NC) 282-283 J 5
Dunn o USA (TX) 264-265 D 6
Dún na Séad = Baltimore o IRL 90-91 C 6
Dunnellon o USA (FL) 286-287 G 2
Dunne River ~ CDN 36-37 L 2
Dunnigan o USA (CA) 246-247 D 5
Dunning o USA (NE) 262-263 F 3
Dunns River Falls ~• JA 54-55 G 5
Dunnville o CDN (ONT) 238-239 F 6
Dunolly o AUS 180-181 G 4
Dunqul < ET 194-195 E 6
Dunraven o USA (NY) 278-279 G 6
Dunrea o CDN (MAN) 234-235 D 5
Dunrobin o AUS 178-179 J 2
Dunsborough o AUS 176-177 C 6
Dunseith o USA (ND) 258-259 G 3
Dunster o CDN (BC) 228-229 P 3
Dunvegan o CDN 32-33 L 4
Dunvegan o CDN (NS) 240-241 O 4
Dunvegan Historic Site ∴ CDN 32-33 L 4
Dunvegan Lake ⊂ CDN 30-31 Q 5
Dunville o CDN (NFL) 242-243 P 5
Dunyāpur o PK 138-139 C 5
Duolun o VRC 148-149 N 6
Du'o'ng Đông o• VN 158-159 G 5
Duparquet o CDN (QUE) 236-237 J 4
Duparquet, Lac ⊂ CDN (QUE) 236-237 J 4
Dupnica o BG 102-103 C 6
Du Pont o USA (GA) 284-285 H 6
Dupree o USA (SD) 260-261 E 1
Dupuy, Cape ▲ AUS 172-173 B 6
Dupuyer o USA (MT) 250-251 G 3
Duqaila, Ğazīrat ⌒ KSA 132-133 C 5
Duqm o OM 132-133 K 4
Duque de York, Isla ⌒ RCH 80 C 5
Duquesne o USA (AZ) 256-257 E 7
Dura, La o MEX 50-51 E 3
Dūr Abū Arhlah o IRQ 128-129 F 2
Durack Range ▲ AUS 172-173 H 4
Durack River ~ AUS 172-173 H 4
Dūrāğ o AFG 136-137 M 6
Durağan ☆ TR 128-129 F 2
Dur al Fawākhir ⩶ LAR 192-193 J 3
Dūr al Ghānī ⩶ LAR 192-193 F 4
Duran o USA (NM) 256-257 K 4
Durán = Eloy Alfaro o EC 64-65 C 3
Durance ~ F 90-91 L 9
Durand o USA (IL) 274-275 J 2
Durand o USA (MI) 272-273 F 5
Durand o USA (WI) 270-271 G 6
Durango o• E 98-99 F 3
Durango o HN 54-55 C 7
Durango ■ MEX 50-51 G 5
Durango ☆•• MEX 50-51 G 5
Durango o USA (CO) 254-255 H 6
Durango, Victoria de = Durango ☆• MEX 50-51 G 5
Durañona o RA 78-79 J 4
Durant o USA (MS) 268-269 L 3
Durant o USA (OK) 264-265 H 5
Durazno ☆ ROU 78-79 L 2
Durban o CDN (MAN) 234-235 B 3
Durban o• ZA 220-221 K 4
Durban Island ⌒ CDN 28-29 J 3
Durbanville o ZA 220-221 D 6
Durbet-Daba, pereval ▲ MAU 146-147 J 1
Durdur ~ SP 208-209 F 3
Dureji o PK 134-135 M 6
Durenan o RI 168 D 4
Durg o IND 142-143 B 5
Durgāpur o• IND 142-143 E 4
Durgarajupatnam o IND 140-141 J 4
Durham o CDN (ONT) 238-239 E 4
Durham ☆••• GB 90-91 G 4
Durham o USA (KS) 262-263 J 6
Durham o USA (NC) 282-283 J 4
Durham Downs o AUS 178-179 F 4
Duri o RI 162-163 D 4
Durian, Selat ≈ 162-163 E 4
Durika, Cerro ▲ CR 52-53 C 7
Durjela o RI 166-167 H 4
Durkee o USA (OR) 244-245 H 6
Durkin Outstation o AUS 176-177 M 5
Durlas = Thurles o IRL 90-91 D 5
Durma o KSA 130-131 K 5
Durmitor ▲ YU 100-101 G 3
Durmitor Nacionalni park ⊥••• YU 100-101 G 3
Durness o GB 90-91 E 2
Durnev, aral ⌒ KA 96-97 H 10
Duro ▲ ETH 208-209 C 6
Duroa o RI 166-167 G 4
Durong South o AUS 178-179 L 4
Duro Tara o ETH 208-209 C 5
Durrandella o AUS 178-179 J 3
Durrës ☆•• AL 100-101 G 4
Duru o ZRE 206-207 J 6
Duru ~ ZRE 212-213 B 2
Durubu o ZRE 206-207 D 6
Durūz, Ğabal ad ▲ SYR 128-129 G 6
D'Urville, Tanjung ▲ RI 166-167 J 2
D'Urville Island ⌒ NZ 182 D 4
Duruy San ▲ DVR 150-151 G 7
Duš, 'Izbat o ET 194-195 E 5
Ḍū Šaiḥ o IRQ 128-129 L 6
Dušak o TM 136-137 G 6
Dušanbe ★• TJ 136-137 L 5
Dusey River ~ CDN (ONT) 234-235 Q 3
Dushan o VRC 156-157 E 4
Dushanbe = Dušanbe ☆• TJ 136-137 L 5
Dushore o USA (PA) 280-281 K 2
Dusin o PNG 183 C 3
Dusky Sound ≈ 182 A 6
Dusseljour, Cape ▲ AUS 172-173 J 3
Düsseldorf ☆• D 92-93 J 3
Dussoumbidiagna o RMM 202-203 E 2
Dustin o USA (OK) 264-265 H 3
Düstlik ☆ US 136-137 L 4
Düst Mohammad Hān o IR 134-135 J 3
Dusty o USA (WA) 244-245 H 4
Dusunmudo o RI 162-163 E 5
Dusunpasirmayang o RI 162-163 E 5
Dusuntuo o RI 162-163 D 6
Duta o Z 214-215 F 6
Dutch Creek ~ CDN (BC) 230-231 N 3
Dutch Fort ∴• RI (MAL) 166-167 E 3
Dutch Fort ∴• RI (SLT) 164-165 G 3
Dutch Harbour o USA 22-23 N 6
Dutch Village • USA (MI) 272-273 C 5
Dutsan Wai o WAN 204-205 H 3
Dutse o WAN 204-205 H 3
Dutsin-Ma o WAN 198-199 C 6
Duttaluru o IND 140-141 H 3
Dutton o USA (MT) 250-251 H 4
Dutton, Lake ⊂ AUS 178-179 D 6
Dutton, Mount ▲ USA (UT) 254-255 C 5
Dutzow o USA (MO) 274-275 H 6
Duvall o USA (WA) 244-245 D 3
Duvefjorden ≈ 84-85 N 2
Duvernay o CDN (ALB) 232-233 G 2
Duvno o BIH 100-101 F 3
Duwisib Castle • NAM 220-221 C 2
Duwwa o OM 132-133 L 3
Duxbury, Lac ⊂ CDN 38-39 F 2
Duye ~ ZRE 212-213 B 3
Duyun o VRC 156-157 E 3
Düzce ☆ TR 128-129 D 2
Düzdüzān o IR 128-129 M 4
Düziçi o TR 128-129 G 4
Duziguo Gang ▲ VRC 156-157 C 2
Dvinskaja guba ≈ 88-89 P 4
Dvinskaya Guba = Dvinskaja guba ≈ RUS 88-89 P 4
Dwarsberg o ZA 220-221 H 2
Dwellingup o AUS 176-177 D 6
Dwesa-natuurreservaat ⊥ ZA 220-221 J 6
Dwight o CDN (ONT) 238-239 G 3
Dwight o USA (IL) 274-275 K 3
Dwokwa o GH 202-203 K 7
Dworshak Reservoir ⊂ USA (ID) 250-251 C 5
Dwyer o USA (NM) 256-257 H 6
Dwyer Hill o CDN (ONT) 238-239 K 3
Dwyka ~ ZA 220-221 E 6
Dyaul Island ⌒ PNG 183 F 2
Dyer o USA (NV) 248-249 F 2
Dyer, Cabo ▲ RCH 80 C 4
Dyer, Cape ▲ CDN 28-29 K 3
Dyer Bay ≈ 24-25 L 3
Dyer Plateau ▲ ARK 16 G 30
Dyer's Bay o CDN (ONT) 238-239 D 3
Dyersburg o USA (TN) 276-277 F 4
Dyersville o USA (IA) 274-275 G 2
Dygdal o RUS 118-119 P 4
Dyh-Tau, gora ▲ RUS 126-127 E 6
Dyje ~ CZ 92-93 N 4
Dyjsembaj ~ KA 124-125 E 5
Dyke Ackland Bay ≈ 183 E 5
Dymond Lake ⊂ CDN 30-31 Q 5
Dynaj, ostrova ⌒ RUS 110-111 P 3
Dyrhólaey ▲ IS 86-87 d 3
Dyryn-Jurjah ~ RUS 118-119 K 7
Dysart o AUS 178-179 K 2
Dysart o CDN (SAS) 232-233 O 5
Dysart o USA (IA) 274-275 F 2
Dytikí o GR 100-101 H 5
Dytikí Makedonía ■ GR 100-101 H 4
Džagdy, hrebet ▲ RUS 122-123 C 2
Džagyn ~ RUS 112-113 H 5
Džalal-Abad = Jalal-Abad o KS 136-137 N 4
Džalilabad = Çalilabad o AZ 128-129 N 3
Džambul o KA 124-125 G 5
Džambul ☆ KA 136-137 M 3
Džana ~ RUS 120-121 F 6
Džanda ~ RUS 120-121 D 4
Džanga o TM 136-137 C 4
Džangylah, ostrov ⌒ RUS 110-111 N 3
Džankoj ☆ UA 102-103 J 5
Dzaoudzi o COM 222-223 D 4
Džapi ~ RUS 122-123 H 2
Džardžan o RUS 110-111 P 5
Džardžan ~ RUS 110-111 P 5
Džargalah o RUS 110-111 S 6
Džarkurgan = Jarqurghon o US 136-137 K 6
Džartyrabot o TJ 136-137 N 6
Dzata Ruins ∴• ZA 218-219 F 6
Džaur ~ RUS 122-123 H 4
Džebariki-Haja o RUS 120-121 F 2
Džebel = Ğebel o TM 136-137 D 5
Džebrail o AZ 128-129 M 3
Džejhun o TM 136-137 H 5
Džejnau o US 136-137 J 5
Džeksona, ostrov ⌒ RUS 84-85 d 2
Dželandy o TJ 136-137 N 6
Dželgala o RUS 120-121 N 2
Dželonda o RUS 118-119 J 9
Dželtulah ~ RUS 118-119 N 6
Dželtulinskij stanovik ▲ RUS 118-119 L 8
Dzeng o CAM 210-211 C 2
Džerba ~ RUS 118-119 H 5
Džermuk o AR 128-129 L 3
Džërnjur, boloto ⩶ RUS 88-89 X 5
Dzerzhinsk = Dzeržinsk o RUS 94-95 S 3
Dzeržinsk o RUS 94-95 S 3
Dzeržyns'k o UA 102-103 K 3
Dževdaha, ozero ⊂ RUS 122-123 H 2
Dzhugdzhur, Khrebet = Džug-Džur, hrebet ▲ RUS 120-121 F 6
Działdowo o• PL 92-93 Q 2
Dzibalchén o MEX 52-53 K 2
Dzibilchaltún ∴• MEX 52-53 K 1
Džida o RUS 116-117 N 10
Džida ~ RUS 116-117 L 10
Džidinskij hrebet ▲ MAU 148-149 F 2
Dzierżoniów o• PL 92-93 O 3
Džigda o RUS 120-121 F 5
Džila ~ RUS 118-119 F 10
Dzilam de Bravo o MEX 52-53 K 1
Džilinda, Ust'- o RUS 118-119 E 9
Dzioua o DZ 190-191 E 4
Džirgatal' o TJ 136-137 M 5
Dzisna ~ BY (VTB) 94-95 L 4
Dzisna ~ BY 94-95 K 4
Dzita o GH 202-203 L 7
Dzitás o MEX 52-53 K 1
Džizakskaja oblast' ■ US 136-137 K 4
Dzjaržynsk ☆ BY 94-95 K 5
Džjunekjan ~ RUS 120-121 F 3
Dzodze o GH 202-203 L 6
Džogdžo ~ RUS 108-109 e 6
Džubga o RUS 126-127 C 5
Džug-Džur, hrebet ▲ RUS 120-121 F 6
Džugdžurskij zapovednik ⊥ RUS 120-121 F 6
Džuk ~ RUS 122-123 H 2
Džul'fa = Culfa o AZ (NAH) 128-129 L 3
Dzungarian Basin = Junggar Pendi ⩶ VRC 146-147 H 3
Džungarskij Alatau, žota ▲ KA 124-125 L 6
Dzungarskije voroda ▲ KA 146-147 F 3
Džurak-Sal ~ RUS 102-103 N 4
Džuryn o UA 102-103 F 3
Dzvari o GE 126-127 E 6
Dźwierzuty o PL 92-93 Q 2

E

Ea A Dun ~ VN 158-159 K 3
Eabamet Lake ⊂ CDN (ONT) 234-235 Q 3
Eades o CDN (ONT) 236-237 J 4
Eads o USA (CO) 254-255 N 5
Eadytown o USA (SC) 284-285 K 3
Eagar o USA (AZ) 256-257 F 4
Eagle o USA (AK) 20-21 U 4
Eagle o USA (CO) 254-255 J 4
Eagle o USA (ID) 252-253 B 3
Eagle o USA (NE) 262-263 K 4
Eagle o USA (WI) 274-275 K 2
Eagle Bend o USA (MN) 270-271 C 4
Eagle Butte o USA (SD) 260-261 E 2
Eagle Cape Wilderness Area ⊥ USA (OR) 244-245 H 5
Eagle Cap Wilderness Area • USA (OR) 244-245 H 5
Eagle Cave ∴ USA (WI) 274-275 H 1
Eagle Creek o CDN (BC) 230-231 J 2
Eagle Creek ~ CDN (BC) 228-229 N 4
Eagle Creek ~ CDN (SAS) 232-233 L 4
Eagle Creek o USA (OR) 244-245 C 5
Eagle Creek ~ USA (KY) 276-277 L 2
Eagle Grove o USA (IA) 274-275 E 2
Eagle Harbor o USA (MI) 270-271 K 3
Eagle Hills ▲ CDN (SAS) 232-233 K 3
Eagle Island ⌒ CDN 34-35 G 4
Eagle Island ⌒ SY 224 C 2
Eagle Lake ⊂ CDN (ONT) 234-235 K 5
Eagle Lake o USA (ME) 278-279 N 1
Eagle Lake o USA (TX) 266-267 L 4
Eagle Lake ⊂ USA (CA) 246-247 E 3
Eagle Mountain o USA (CA) 248-249 J 6
Eagle Mountain Lake < USA (TX) 264-265 G 6
Eagle Mountains ▲ USA (TX) 266-267 B 3
Eagle Nest o USA (NM) 256-257 K 2
Eagle Pass o USA (TX) 266-267 G 5
Eagle Passage ≈ 78-79 L 7
Eagle Picher Mine o USA (NV) 246-247 G 3
Eagle Plains o CDN 20-21 W 3
Eagle Point ▲ PNG 183 E 6
Eagle Point o USA (OR) 244-245 C 8
Eagle River o CDN (ONT) 234-235 K 5
Eagle River ~ CDN 20-21 W 3
Eagle River ~ CDN 38-39 P 2
Eagle River ~ CDN (BC) 230-231 L 3
Eagle River o USA (WI) 270-271 J 5
Eagle River ~ USA (CO) 254-255 H 4
Eagle Summit ▲ USA 20-21 S 4
Eagleton o USA (AR) 276-277 A 6
Eagleville o USA (CA) 246-247 E 2
Eagleville o USA (MO) 274-275 E 4
Eagleville o USA (TN) 276-277 J 5
Ea H'leo o VN 158-159 K 4
Eandja o ZRE 210-211 H 4
Earaheedy o AUS 176-177 F 2
Ear Falls o CDN (ONT) 234-235 K 4
Earle o USA (AR) 276-277 E 5
Earl Grey o CDN (SAS) 232-233 O 5
Earling o USA (IA) 274-275 C 3
Earls Cove o CDN (BC) 230-231 F 4
Earlton o CDN (ONT) 236-237 J 5
Earltown o CDN (NS) 240-241 M 5
Earlville o USA (IL) 274-275 K 3
Early o USA (IA) 274-275 C 2
Early o USA (TX) 266-267 J 2
Earn ~ GB 90-91 F 3
Earn Lake ⊂ CDN 20-21 X 5
Earp o USA (CA) 248-249 K 5
Easley o USA (SC) 284-285 H 2
East = Est ■ CAM 210-211 D 2
East, Mount ▲ AUS 176-177 G 5
East Alligator River ~ AUS 174-175 B 3
East Amatuli Island ⌒ USA 22-23 V 3
East Angus o CDN (QUE) 238-239 O 3
East Arm ⊂ CDN 30-31 E 5
East Arrow Park o CDN (BC) 230-231 M 3
East Aurora o USA (NY) 278-279 C 6
East Bay ≈ 36-37 J 2
East Bay o CDN (ONT) 234-235 P 5
East Bay ≈ USA 268-269 L 7
East Bay ≈ USA 268-269 F 7
East Bethel o USA (MN) 270-271 E 5
East Bijou Creek ~ USA (CO) 254-255 L 4
East Bluff ▲ CDN 36-37 R 4
Eastbourne o GB 90-91 H 6
East Brady o USA (PA) 280-281 G 3
East Broughton o CDN (QUE) 238-239 O 2
East Caicos ⌒ GB 54-55 K 4
East Cape ▲ NZ 182 G 2
East Cape ▲ USA (AK) 22-23 F 7
East Cape ▲ USA (FL) 286-287 H 6
East-Cape Province ■ ZA 220-221 H 5
East Carbon City o USA (UT) 254-255 E 4
East Cay ⌒ AUS 183 C 5
East Channel ~ CDN 20-21 Y 3
East China Sea ≈ 10-11 M 5
East Chugach Island ⌒ USA 22-23 V 3
East Coulee o CDN (ALB) 232-233 F 4
East Dereham o GB 90-91 H 5
Eastend o CDN (SAS) 232-233 K 6
East End Point ▲ BS 54-55 G 2
East Enterprise o USA (IN) 274-275 O 6

Easter o USA (TX) 264-265 B 4
Easter Cape ▲ CDN 24-25 b 5
Easter Group ⌒ AUS 176-177 B 4
Easter Island = Pascua, Isla de ⌒ RCH 78-79 B 2
Eastern □ EAK 212-213 F 4
Eastern □ EAU 212-213 D 3
Eastern □ Z 218-219 F 1
Eastern Bay ≈ USA 280-281 K 5
Eastern Blue Pond ⊂ CDN (NFL) 242-243 L 2
Eastern Desert = Şaḥrā' aš-Šarqīya, as- ∸ ET 194-195 F 3
Eastern Fields ⌒ PNG 183 C 6
Eastern Ghāts ▲ IND 140-141 G 5
Eastern Group ⌒ AUS 176-177 H 6
Eastern Meelpaeg ⊂ CDN (NFL) 242-243 O 4
Eastern Neck Island National Wildlife Refuge ⊥ USA (MD) 280-281 K 5
Eastern Province □ KSA 132-133 F 3
Eastern Region □ GH 202-203 K 6
Eastern Sayan Mountains = Vostočnyj Sajan ▲ RUS 116-117 F 8
East Fairview o USA (ND) 258-259 D 4
East Falkland ⌒ GB 78-79 L 6
East Fork ~ USA (AL) 284-285 C 2
East Fork Andreafsky ~ USA 20-21 J 5
East Fork Bruneau River ~ USA (ID) 252-253 C 4
East Fork Chandalar ~ USA 20-21 S 2
East Fork Grand River ~ USA (MO) 274-275 D 4
East Fork Lake ⊂ USA (IL) 274-275 K 6
East Fork White River ~ USA (IN) 274-275 M 6
East Frisian Islands = Ostfriesische Inseln ∸ D 92-93 J 2
East Glacier Park o USA (MT) 250-251 F 3
East Grand Forks o USA (MN) 270-271 A 3
East Hampton o USA (NY) 280-281 O 3
East Haydon o AUS 174-175 F 5
East Helena o USA (MT) 250-251 H 5
East Hickory o USA (PA) 280-281 G 2
East Holden o USA (ME) 278-279 N 4
East Holothuria Reef ⌒ AUS 172-173 H 2
East Hyden Wheat Bin o AUS 176-177 E 6
East Indiaman Ridge ≃ 12 H 7
East Islands ⌒ PNG 183 F 2
East Jeddore o CDN (NS) 240-241 M 6
East Jordan o USA (MI) 272-273 D 2
East Lake Tohopekaliga ⊂ USA (FL) 286-287 H 3
Eastland o USA (TX) 264-265 F 6
East Lansing o USA (MI) 272-273 E 5
East Liverpool o USA (OH) 280-281 F 3
East London = Oos-Londen o• ZA 220-221 H 6
East Lynn Lake ⊂ USA (WV) 280-281 D 5
Eastmain o CDN 38-39 E 2
Eastmain, Rivière ~ CDN 38-39 F 2
Eastman o USA (GA) 284-285 G 4
East Mariana Basin ≃ 14-15 H 6
Eastmere o AUS 178-179 H 2
East Millinocket o USA (ME) 278-279 N 3
East Missoula o USA (MT) 250-251 F 5
East Mojave National Scenic Area ⊥ • USA (CA) 248-249 J 4
Eastnor o ZW 218-219 E 4
East Novaya Zemlya Trough = Novozemel'skaja vpadina ≃ RUS 108-109 G 6
Easton o USA (MD) 280-281 K 5
Easton o USA (PA) 280-281 L 3
East Pacific Rise ≃ 14-15 Q 12
East Palatka o USA (FL) 286-287 H 2
East Pen Island ⌒ CDN 34-35 M 2
East Point ▲ CDN (ONT) 38-39 E 3
East Point ▲ CDN (PEI) 240-241 O 4
Eastpoint o USA (FL) 286-287 E 2
East Point o USA (GA) 284-285 F 3
Eastpoort o ZA 220-221 G 6
East Poplar o CDN (SAS) 232-233 N 6
East Porcupine River ~ CDN 20-21 V 4
Eastport o CDN (NFL) 242-243 P 4
Eastport o USA (ME) 278-279 O 4
Eastport o USA (MI) 272-273 D 2
East Port Hébert ▲ CDN (NS) 240-241 L 7
East Prairie o USA (MO) 276-277 F 4
East Prairie River ~ CDN 32-33 M 4
East Ridge o USA (TN) 276-277 K 5
East River ~ CDN (ONT) 238-239 F 3
East Saint Louis o USA (IL) 274-275 H 6
East Sepik □ PNG 183 A 3
East Siberian Sea = Vostočno-Sibirskoe more ≈ RUS 10-11 Q 1
East Tawas o USA (MI) 272-273 F 3
East Transvaal Province □ ZA 220-221 J 3
East Travaputs Plateau ▲ USA (UT) 254-255 F 4
East Union o USA (IN) 274-275 M 4
East Waterboro o USA (ME) 278-279 L 5
East Wenatchee o USA (WA) 244-245 E 3
Ea Sup o VN 158-159 J 4
Eateringinna Creek ~ AUS 176-177 M 3
Eaton o USA (CO) 254-255 L 3
Eaton o USA (OH) 280-281 B 4
Eatonia o CDN (SAS) 232-233 J 4
Eaton Rapids o USA (MI) 272-273 E 5
Eatonton o USA (GA) 284-285 G 3
Eatonville o USA (WA) 244-245 C 4
Eau Claire o USA (WI) 270-271 G 6
Eau Claire, Lac à l' ⊂ CDN 36-37 M 6
Eau Claire, Rivière à l' ~ CDN 36-37 M 6
Eau Claire River ~ USA (WI) 270-271 J 5
Eau de Boynes o RH 54-55 J 5
Eauripik Rise ≃ 166-167 K 1
Ebagoola o AUS 174-175 G 4
Ebala o PNG 183 C 4
Eban o WAN 204-205 F 4
Ebanga o ANG 216-217 C 6
Ebangalaka o ZRE 210-211 H 4
Ebano o• MEX 50-51 K 6
Ebba Havn ≈ 28-29 U 5
Ebba Ksour = Dahmani o TN 190-191 G 3
Ebe o RI 166-167 J 3
Ebebiyin o G 210-211 C 2
Ebeggi, In < DZ 198-199 C 2
Ébejty, ozero ⊂ RUS 124-125 G 1
Ébel Alèmbe o G 210-211 C 3
Ébeljah o RUS 110-111 J 4
Ébeljanskaja guba ≈ 110-111 W 3
Ebelle o WAN 204-205 G 5
Ebeltoft o DK 86-87 E 8
Ebem o WAN 204-205 G 6
Ebenezer o CDN (SAS) 232-233 Q 4
Ebensburg o• USA (PA) 280-281 H 3
Ebe River ~ WAN 204-205 H 6
Eberswalde o D 92-93 M 2
Ebetsu o J 152-153 J 3
Ebian o VRC 156-157 C 2
Ebini Downs o GUY 62-63 F 3
Ebinur Hu ⊂ VRC 146-147 F 3
Ebja o RUS 118-119 L 4
Ebjah o RUS 110-111 c 5
Ebo o ANG 216-217 C 5
Ebola ~ ZRE 210-211 H 2
Éboli o I 100-101 E 4
Ebolowa ☆ CAM 210-211 C 2
Ebony o NAM 216-217 C 11
Ebounda o CAM 210-211 B 2
Ebrāhīmābād o IR 134-135 G 4
Ebrahimi o IR 134-135 H 2
Ebre, l' ~ E 98-99 H 4
Ebrié, Lagune ≈ 202-203 H 7
Ebro o USA (FL) 286-287 D 1
Ebro, Río ~ E 98-99 G 4
Ébručorr, gora ▲ RUS 88-89 M 3
Ecatepec de Morelos o MEX 52-53 E 2
Echaï, In- < RMM 196-197 K 4
Echambot o CAM 210-211 D 2
Echaporã o BR 72-73 E 7
Ech Chergui, Chott ⊂ DZ 190-191 C 3
Echeconnee Creek ~ USA (GA) 284-285 G 4
Echigo-sanmyaku ▲ J 152-153 H 6
Echigo-Sanzan-Tadami Quasi National Park ⊥ J 152-153 H 6
Echo o USA (MN) 270-271 C 6
Echo o USA (UT) 254-255 D 2
Echo Bay o CDN (ONT) 236-237 D 6
Echo Bay o CDN 30-31 L 2
Echo Canyon State Park ⊥ • USA (NV) 248-249 K 2
Echoing River ~ CDN 34-35 L 3
Echouani, Lac ⊂ CDN (QUE) 236-237 N 5
Echuca-Moama o• AUS 180-181 H 4
Écija o E 98-99 E 6
Ėcijskij massiv ▲ RUS 110-111 R 6
Ecilda Paullier o ROU 78-79 L 3
Eckengrafen = Viesite o LV 94-95 J 3
Ecker, Río ~ RA 80 E 3
Eckermann o USA (MI) 270-271 N 4
Eckernförde o D 92-93 K 1
Eckerö o FIN 88-89 F 6
Eckville o CDN (ALB) 232-233 D 3
Eclectic o USA (AL) 284-285 D 4
Eclipse Channel ≈ 36-37 R 5
Eclipse Island ⌒ AUS 176-177 D 7
Eclipse River ~ CDN 36-37 R 5
Eclipse Sound ≈ 24-25 g 4
Ėčmiadzin o AR 128-129 L 2
Econfina Creek ~ USA (FL) 286-287 D 1
Econfina River ~ USA (FL) 286-287 F 1
Ecoole o CDN (BC) 230-231 D 5
Ecorce, Lac de l' ⊂ CDN (QUE) 236-237 M 5
Ecrevisses, Cascade aux ~ F 56 E 3
Ecrins, Barre des ▲ F 90-91 L 9
Écrins, Parc National des ⊥ • F 90-91 L 9
Ecstall River ~ CDN (BC) 228-229 E 3
Ecuador ■ EC 64-65 B 2
Écueils, Pointe aux ▲ CDN 36-37 K 5
Ed o ER 200-201 K 6
Edalābād o IND 138-139 F 9
Edam o CDN (SAS) 232-233 K 2
Edam o• NL 92-93 H 2
Edappalli o IND 140-141 G 5
Edarma ~ RUS 116-117 K 6
Edcouch o USA (TX) 266-267 K 7
Eddies Cove o CDN (NFL) 242-243 M 1
Eddies Cove West o CDN (NFL) 242-243 L 2
Eddington o USA (ME) 278-279 N 4
Ed Douakel, Hamada ∸ DZ 188-189 H 7
Eddy o CDN (BC) 228-229 O 3
Eddystone o CDN (MAN) 234-235 D 3
Eddyville o USA (IA) 274-275 F 3
Eddyville o USA (KY) 276-277 G 3
Eddyville o USA (NE) 262-263 G 3
Ede o WAN 204-205 F 5
Edéa o CAM 210-211 C 2
Edefors o S 86-87 K 3
Edehine Ouarene ∸ DZ 190-191 G 6
Edehon Lake ⊂ CDN 30-31 V 5
Edéia o BR 72-73 F 4
Eden o AUS 180-181 K 4
Eden o USA (ID) 252-253 D 4
Eden o USA (NC) 282-283 H 4
Eden o USA (SD) 260-261 J 1
Eden o USA (TX) 266-267 H 2
Eden o USA (WY) 252-253 J 4
Edenburg o ZA 220-221 G 4
Edendale o NZ 182 B 7
Edendale o ZA 220-221 K 4
Edenhope o AUS 180-181 F 4
Edenton o USA (NC) 282-283 L 4
Edenville o ZA 220-221 H 3
Edenwold o CDN (SAS) 232-233 O 5
Ede Point ▲ CDN 24-25 V 4
Eder o USA (MT) 250-251 H 4
Edersley o CDN (SAS) 232-233 P 3
Édessa o• GR 100-101 J 4
Edgar o USA (WI) 270-271 J 6
Edgar, Mount ▲ AUS 172-173 E 6
Edgar Ranges ▲ AUS 172-173 F 5
Edgartown o USA (MA) 278-279 L 7
Edgecumbe o NZ 182 F 2
Edgefield o USA (SC) 284-285 J 3
Edgeley o CDN (SAS) 232-233 O 5
Edgeley o USA (ND) 258-259 J 5
Edgell Island ⌒ CDN 36-37 R 4
Edgemont o USA (SD) 260-261 C 3
Edgeøya ⌒ N 84-85 M 4
Edgeøyjøkulen ⊂ N 84-85 N 4
Edgerton o CDN (ALB) 232-233 H 3
Edgerton o USA (MN) 270-271 B 7
Edgerton o USA (WI) 274-275 J 2
Edgertown o USA (VA) 280-281 J 7
Edgewater o CDN (BC) 230-231 N 3
Edgewater o USA (FL) 286-287 J 3
Edgewood o CDN (BC) 230-231 L 4
Edgewood o USA (MD) 280-281 K 4
Edgewood o USA (MI) 272-273 E 4
Edgewood o USA (TX) 264-265 J 6
Ediessane, Oued ~ DZ 190-191 G 8
Edillilie o AUS 180-181 C 3
Edina o USA (MO) 274-275 F 4
Edinburg o USA (ND) 258-259 K 3
Edinburg o USA (TX) 266-267 J 7
Edinburgh ☆ •• GB 90-91 F 4
Edinburgh o USA (IN) 274-275 N 5
Edincy = Edineț ☆ MD 102-103 E 3
Edinec = Edineț ☆ MD 102-103 E 3
Edineț ☆ MD 102-103 E 3
Edingeni o MW 214-215 G 7
Edirne ☆ •• TR 128-129 B 2
Edison o USA (CO) 254-255 L 5
Edison o USA (GA) 284-285 F 5
Edisto Beach o USA (SC) 284-285 K 4
Edisto Island ⌒ USA (SC) 284-285 K 4
Edisto River ~ USA (SC) 284-285 K 3
Edisto River, North Fork ~ USA (SC) 284-285 J 3
Edisto River, South Fork ~ USA (SC) 284-285 J 3
Edith, Mount ▲ USA (MT) 250-251 H 5
Edith Cavell, Mount ▲ CDN (ALB) 228-229 Q 4
Edith Downs o AUS 174-175 G 7
Edith Falls o AUS 172-173 L 3
Edithvale o AUS 172-173 K 3
Edjeleh o DZ 190-191 G 7
Edkins Range ▲ AUS 172-173 G 4
Edmond o USA (OK) 264-265 G 3
Edmonds o USA (WA) 244-245 C 3
Edmond Walker Island ⌒ CDN 24-25 U 2
Edmonton ☆ • CDN (ALB) 232-233 E 2
Edmonton o USA (KY) 276-277 K 4
Edmore o USA (ND) 258-259 J 3
Edmund o USA (SC) 284-285 J 3
Edmund Lake ⊂ CDN 34-35 K 3
Edmundston o CDN (NB) 240-241 G 3
Edna o USA (KS) 262-263 L 7
Edna o USA (TX) 266-267 L 4
Édolo o I 100-101 C 1
Édouard, Lac ⊂ CDN (QUE) 240-241 C 3
Édouard, Lac ⊂ CDN (QUE) 240-241 C 3
Edouard, Lac = Lake Edward ⊂ ZRE 212-213 B 4
Edough, Djebel ▲ DZ 190-191 F 2
Edrans o CDN (MAN) 234-235 D 4
Edremit o TR 128-129 K 3
Edremit o• TR 128-129 B 3
Edremit Körfezi ≈ 128-129 B 3
Edremo o ETH 208-209 B 5
Edsbyn o S 86-87 G 6
Edsel Ford Range ▲ ARK 16 F 23
Edson o CDN (ALB) 232-233 B 2
Edson River ~ CDN (ALB) 232-233 B 2
Eduard Holm, Kap ▲ GRØ 28-29 Y 3
Eduni, Mount ▲ CDN 30-31 E 3
Edvard Ø ⌒ GRØ 26-27 p 5
Edwall o USA (WA) 244-245 H 3
Edward, Lake = Lac Edouard ⊂ ZRE 212-213 B 4
Edward Island ⌒ AUS 174-175 C 4
Edward River ⊼ AUS 174-175 F 4
Edward River ~ AUS 180-181 G 3
Edward River Kowanyama Aboriginal Land ⊼ AUS 174-175 F 4
Edwards o USA (CA) 248-249 G 5
Edwards o USA (MS) 268-269 K 4
Edwards Air Force Base • USA (CA) 248-249 G 5
Edwards Plateau ▲ USA (TX) 266-267 F 2
Edwards State Memorial, Fort ∴ • USA (IL) 274-275 G 4
Edwardsville o USA (IL) 274-275 J 6
Edward VIIth Peninsula ⌒ ARK 16 F 22
Edwin o CDN (MAN) 234-235 E 5
Edziza Peak ▲ CDN 32-33 E 3
Edzna ∴ •• MEX 52-53 J 2
Edzo o CDN 30-31 M 4
Eek o USA 20-21 J 6
Eek Island ⌒ USA 20-21 J 6
Éekit ~ RUS 110-111 P 4
Eeklo o B 92-93 G 3
Eek River ~ USA 20-21 K 6
Eel River ~ USA (CA) 246-247 B 3
Eel River ~ USA (IN) 274-275 N 4
Eel River ~ USA (IN) 274-275 L 5
Eel River Bridge o CDN (NB) 240-241 K 3
Eendekuil o ZA 220-221 D 6
Èèvijn buudal o MAU 146-147 M 2
Éfaté ⌒ VAN 184 II b 3
Éfaté = Île Vaté ⌒ VAN 184 II b 3
Efes ∴ •• TR 128-129 B 3
Effie o USA (MN) 270-271 E 3
Effigy Mounds National Monument • USA (IA) 274-275 G 1
Effingham o USA (IL) 274-275 K 5
Efimovskij o RUS 94-95 O 2
Efon Alaye o WAN 204-205 F 5
Eforie Nord o• RO 102-103 F 5
Efremov o RUS 94-95 Q 5
Efremova ~ RUS 108-109 T 5
Efremova, buhta ⊂ RUS 108-109 T 5
Ég o MAU 148-149 K 3
Égadi, Ísole ⌒ I 100-101 D 6
Eganville o CDN (ONT) 238-239 H 3
Egari o PNG 183 B 4
Egayit o MYA 142-143 J 6
Egbe o WAN 204-205 F 4
Egbunda o ZRE 210-211 L 2
Ege Denizi ≈ 128-129 A 3
Egedesminde ≈ 28-29 O 2
Egedesminde = Aasiaat o GRØ 28-29 O 2
Egeland o USA (ND) 258-259 H 3
Egenolf Lake ⊂ CDN 30-31 U 6
Egeo Pelagos ≈ 100-101 K 5
Eger o H 92-93 Q 5
Eger = Cheb o CZ 92-93 M 3
Eger = Ohře ~ CZ 92-93 M 3
Egersund ☆ N 86-87 C 7
Egerton, Cape ▲ CDN 26-27 K 2
Egerton, Mount ▲ AUS 176-177 D 2
Eggenfelden o D 92-93 M 4
Egg Lake ⊂ CDN 34-35 D 3
Ėg gol ~ MAU 148-149 F 3
Egholo o SOL 184 I c 3
Egilsstaðir o IS 86-87 f 2
Egina o GR 100-101 J 6
Égina ⌒ GR 100-101 J 6
Eginbah o AUS 172-173 D 6
Egindybulak o KA 124-125 K 4
Égio o GR 100-101 J 5
Eğirdir ☆ • TR 128-129 D 4
Eğirdir Gölü ⊂ TR 128-129 D 3
Egito Praia o ANG 216-217 B 5
Egizkara, tau ▲ KA 124-125 D 5
Eglin Air Force Base xx USA (FL) 286-287 C 1
Eglinton Island ⌒ CDN 24-25 M 3
Eglinton Fiord ≈ 26-27 Q 8
Egmont o CDN (BC) 230-231 F 4
Egmont, Cape ▲ NZ 182 D 3
Egmont, Mount ▲ NZ 182 E 3
Egmont Bay ≈ 38-39 M 5
Egmont Bay ≈ CDN 240-241 L 4
Egmont National Park ⊥ NZ 182 E 3
Egnar o USA (CO) 254-255 G 6
Egolf'jah ~ RUS 114-115 N 5
Egor'evsk ☆ • RUS 94-95 Q 4
Egorlyk ~ RUS 102-103 M 5
Egošinskaja o RUS 96-97 F 3
Egra o IND 142-143 E 5
Eğriğöz Dağı ▲ TR 128-129 C 3
Eguia o RP 160-161 C 5
Égujja, gora ▲ RUS 120-121 P 4
Egum Atoll ⌒ PNG 183 F 5
Ėgvekinot o RUS 112-113 V 3
Egypt o USA (AR) 276-277 E 5
Egypt o USA (TX) 266-267 L 4
Egypt = al-Miṣr ■ ET 194-195 C 4
Egypt, Lake of ⊂ USA (IL) 276-277 G 3
Eha-Amufu o WAN 204-205 G 5
Ehegnadzor o AR 128-129 L 3
Eh-Eh, Riacho ~ RA 76-77 H 3
Ehi o GH 202-203 L 6
Ehodak o N 86-87 L 2
Eholt o CDN (BC) 230-231 L 4
Ehrhardt o USA (SC) 284-285 J 3
Eibi, Bur ▲ SP 212-213 K 2
Eichstätt o D 92-93 L 4
Eide ☆ N 86-87 C 5
Eider Island ⌒ CDN 36-37 P 4
Eidsbotn West Fiord ≈ 24-25 b 2
Eidsemub < NAM 220-221 C 2
Eidsvold o AUS 178-179 L 3
Eielson o USA 20-21 R 4
Eifel ▲ D 92-93 J 3
Eiffel Flats o ZW 218-219 E 4
Eiger ▲ CH 92-93 J 5
Eight Degree Channel ≈ 140-141 E 6
Eights Coast ∸ ARK 16 F 27
Eighty Mile Beach ∸ AUS 172-173 E 5
Eikefjord o N 86-87 B 6
Eikwe o GH 202-203 J 7
Eilai < SUD 200-201 E 4
Eildon o AUS 180-181 H 4
Eildon, Lake ⊂ AUS 180-181 H 4
Eileen Lake ⊂ CDN 30-31 Q 4
Eilerts de Haan, National Reservaat ⊥ SME 62-63 F 4
Eilerts de Haan Gebergte ▲ SME 62-63 F 4
Einasleigh o AUS 174-175 H 6
Einasleigh River ~ AUS 174-175 G 5
Eindayaza o MYA 158-159 E 3
Eindhoven o NL 92-93 H 3
Einme o MYA 158-159 C 2
Eirik Ridge ≃ 6-7 E 3
Eiríksjökull ⊂ IS 86-87 c 2
Eirunepé o BR 66-67 C 6
Eiseb ~ NAM 216-217 F 10
Eisenach o• D 92-93 L 3
Eisenerz o A 92-93 N 5
Eisenhower, Mount ▲ CDN (ALB) 232-233 C 4
Eisenhower Center • USA (KS) 262-263 J 6
Eisenstadt ☆ A 92-93 O 5
Eišiškės o LT 94-95 J 4
Eivānakī o IR 136-137 C 7
Eivissa o• E (BAL) 98-99 H 5
Eivissa ⌒ E (BAL) 98-99 H 5
Eja ~ RUS 102-103 L 4
Ejea de los Caballeros o E 98-99 G 3
Ejeda o RM 222-223 D 10
Ejer Bavnehøj ▲ DK 86-87 D 9
Ejido o YV 60-61 F 3
Ejidogari o WAN 204-205 G 4
Ejido Pancho Villa o MEX 50-51 C 5
Ėjim ~ RUS 118-119 L 4
Ejin Horo Qi o VRC 154-155 F 2
Ejin Qi o VRC 148-149 E 7
Ejirin o WAN 204-205 E 5
Ejisu o GH 202-203 K 6
Ej-Jemâa o MA 188-189 G 5
Ej Jill, Kediet ▲ RIM 196-197 D 3
Ej Jill, Sebkhet ⊂ RIM 196-197 D 3
Ėjka ~ RUS 116-117 M 4
Ėjna o RUS 88-89 M 2
Ejouj < RIM 196-197 F 6
Ėjrinejskaja guba ⊂ RUS 120-121 L 4
Ejsk o RUS 102-103 L 4
Ėjt'ja ~ RUS 114-115 G 4
Ejule o WAN 204-205 G 5
Ejura o GH 202-203 K 6
Ejutla o MEX 52-53 F 3
Ekalaka o USA (MT) 250-251 P 6
Ekalluk River ~ CDN 24-25 T 5
Ekalugad Fiord ≈ 28-29 F 2
Ekamour o RIM 196-197 E 6
Ekang o WAN 204-205 H 6
Ekar, Gara- ▲ DZ 198-199 B 3
Ėkarjaujaha ~ RUS 108-109 T 6
Ėkarma, ostrov ⌒ RUS 122-123 P 4
Ėkata o G 210-211 E 3
Ekaterinburg ☆ RUS 96-97 M 5
Ekaterinoslavka o RUS 122-123 C 3
Ekaterinovka o RUS 96-97 D 7
Ekateriny, proliv ⊂ RUS 122-123 M 6
Ekbalám ∴ • MEX 52-53 K 1
Ekblaw Glacier ⊂ CDN 26-27 M 4
Ekélfi < RN 198-199 C 4
Ekenäs o• FIN 88-89 G 7
Eket o WAN 204-205 G 6
Ėkibastūz ☆ KA 124-125 J 3
Ekibastuz = Ėkibastūz ☆ KA 124-125 J 3
Ėkimčan ☆ RUS 122-123 E 2
Ekismane < RN 198-199 C 5
Ėkityki ~ RUS 112-113 V 3
Ėkityki, ozero ⊂ RUS 112-113 U 3
Ėkitykskij hrebet ▲ RUS 112-113 T 3
Ekjuččju o RUS 110-111 S 6
Ekka Islands ⌒ CDN 30-31 J 2
Ėkkan"egan ~ RUS 114-115 P 4
Ekker, In o DZ 190-191 E 8
Eklingli o IND 138-139 D 7
Ekok o CAM 204-205 H 6
Ekoli o ZRE 210-211 K 4
Ekom, Chutes, d' ~ • CAM 204-205 J 6
Ekombe o ZRE 210-211 H 3
Ekondo Titi o CAM 204-205 H 6
Ekor o RI 164-165 K 3
Ekpe < WAN 204-205 G 6
Ekpindi o KA 136-137 L 3
Ekshärad o S 86-87 F 6
Eksjö ☆ • S 86-87 G 8
Ektrema o BR 72-73 G 7
Eku o WAN 204-205 F 6
Eku, River ~ WAN 204-205 F 4
Ekubu o FJI 184 III a 3
Ėkugvaam ~ RUS 112-113 W 3
Ekukola o ZRE 210-211 H 3
Ekuku o ZRE 210-211 H 4
Ekuma ~ NAM 216-217 C 9
Ekumakoko o ZRE 210-211 J 5
Ėkvyvatapskij hrebet ▲ RUS 112-113 S 2
Ėkvyvatop ~ RUS 112-113 T 2
Ekwa o CAM 210-211 D 2
Ekwan Point ▲ CDN 34-35 P 4
Ekwan River ~ CDN 34-35 O 4
Ekwan River ~ CDN (ONT) 234-235 R 2
Ekyiomenfurom o GH 202-203 K 6
Ela, Tanjung ▲ RI 166-167 C 7
El Abiodh Sidi Cheikh o DZ 190-191 C 4
El Ābrēd o ETH 208-209 G 6
Elabuga ☆ RUS 96-97 H 6
El 'Açâba ▲ RIM 196-197 D 6
Elada o GR 100-101 H 5
Eláda Steireá □ GR 100-101 H 5
El Adeb Larache o DZ 190-191 G 7
Elahera o CL 140-141 J 7
el-Ahmar, Hassi < MA 188-189 K 4
Elaho River ~ CDN (BC) 230-231 F 3
Elaine o USA (AR) 276-277 E 6
el-Aïoun o MA 188-189 K 3
El Alia o DZ 190-191 E 4
El Alimar, Hassi < DZ 190-191 C 3
el-Amarna, Tell ∴ • ET 194-195 E 4
El Amdar, Bir < DZ 190-191 F 4
Elan' o RUS 102-103 N 2
Elan Bank = Élan Bank ≃ 12 F 10
Elandsbaai o ZA 220-221 D 6
Elands Height o ZA 220-221 J 5
Elandslaagte o ZA 220-221 J 4
Elandsrivier ~ ZA 220-221 J 2
Elanga o ZRE 210-211 G 4
Elangay < RN 196-197 M 7
Elanka o RUS 114-115 N 7
Elan'-Kolenovskij o RUS 102-103 M 2
El Aouinet o DZ 190-191 G 3
El Âquer ▲ RIM 196-197 E 6
Elara o RI 166-167 D 3
El Arab, Oued ~ DZ 190-191 F 3
El Araïch o MA 188-189 H 3
el-Arbid < MA 188-189 G 5
El Arhlaf < RIM 196-197 H 6
El Aricha o DZ 188-189 L 3
El Arrouch o DZ 190-191 F 2
El Asli, Bir < TN 190-191 F 4
Elassóna o GR 100-101 J 5
Elat ☆ IL 130-131 D 3
Élavagnon o RT 202-203 L 6
Elâzığ ☆ TR 128-129 H 3
Elba o USA (AL) 284-285 D 5
Elba o USA (ID) 252-253 E 4
Elba o USA (KY) 276-277 H 3
Elba o USA (NE) 262-263 H 3
Elba, Ísola d' ⌒ I 100-101 C 3
Él'ban o RUS 122-123 G 3
Elbasan ☆ •• AL 100-101 H 4
El Basrīyé < RMM 196-197 H 6
El Bayadh ☆ DZ 190-191 C 4
Elbe ~ D 92-93 K 2
Elbe o USA (WA) 244-245 C 4
Elbe = Labe ~ CZ 92-93 N 3
El Béher o RIM 196-197 F 7
El Beid ~ WAN 198-199 G 6
Elbert o USA (CO) 254-255 L 4
Elbert o USA (TX) 264-265 F 5
Elbert, Mount ▲ USA (CO) 254-255 J 4
Elberta o USA (UT) 254-255 D 4
Elberton o USA (GA) 284-285 H 2
El Beru Hagia o SP 212-213 H 2
Elbeuf o F 90-91 H 7
El Beyyed < RIM 196-197 E 4
El Bioba o ETH 208-209 F 6
Elbistan ☆ TR 128-129 G 3
Elbjut, Kulun o RUS 110-111 Y 6
Elbląg ☆ • PL 92-93 P 1
El Bordj o DZ 190-191 D 3
El Borma o TN 190-191 G 5
el-Borouj o MA 188-189 H 4
El Botha, Oued ~ DZ 190-191 D 7
El Bouz < RIM 196-197 G 6
Elbow o CDN (SAS) 232-233 M 4
Elbow Lake o USA (MN) 270-271 C 5
Elbow River ~ CDN (ALB) 232-233 D 5
Él'brus o RUS 126-127 E 6
Él'brus, gora ▲ •• RUS 126-127 E 6
El Capitan Peak ▲ USA (NM) 256-257 K 5
El Capitan Reservoir < USA (CA) 248-249 H 7
El Caura, Reserva Forestal ⊥ YV 60-61 J 4
El Cerrito o USA (CA) 248-249 B 2
El Chaco, Parque Nacional ⊥ RA 76-77 H 4
Elche = Elx o E 98-99 G 5
Elche de la Sierra o E 98-99 F 5
Elcho o USA (WI) 270-271 J 5
Elcho Island ⌒ AUS 174-175 C 2
El Cobias o SP 212-213 K 2
Él'cy o RUS 94-95 N 3
Elda o E 98-99 G 5
Eldama Ravine o EAK 212-213 E 3
El Der • ETH 208-209 F 6
El Dere o SP 208-209 H 7
Élderslie o AUS 178-179 G 2
Él'dikan o RUS 120-121 F 3
Eldjarnsstaðir o IS 86-87 d 2
Eldon o USA (IA) 274-275 F 4
Eldon o USA (MO) 274-275 F 6
Eldora o USA (IA) 274-275 E 2
Eldorado o BR (GSU) 76-77 K 2
Eldorado o BR (P) 68-69 D 4
Eldorado o BR (PAU) 74-75 F 5
Eldorado o HN 54-55 C 7
Eldorado o RA 76-77 K 4
El Dorado o USA (AR) 276-277 C 7
Eldorado o USA (IL) 276-277 G 3
El Dorado o USA (KS) 262-263 K 7
Eldorado o USA (OK) 264-265 E 4
Eldorado o USA (TX) 266-267 G 3
El Dorado Lake ⊂ USA (KS) 262-263 K 7
El Dorado Springs o USA (MO) 276-277 A 3
Eldoret o EAK 212-213 E 3
Eldred o CDN (SAS) 232-233 M 2
Eldred o USA (PA) 280-281 H 2
Eldridge o USA (IA) 274-275 H 3
El Dunuba o EAK 212-213 G 2
El'džik o TM 136-137 H 5
Elec o RUS 94-95 Q 5
Elečej o RUS 120-121 D 3
Eleckij o RUS 108-109 L 8
Electra o USA (TX) 264-265 F 4
Electric Mills o USA (MS) 268-269 M 4
Electric Peak ▲ USA (MT) 250-251 J 6
Elefantes, Fiordo ≈ 80 C 3
Elefantes, Rio dos ~ MOC 218-219 G 6
Eleja o• LV 94-95 J 3
Elektrėnai o LT 94-95 J 4
Elektrostal' o RUS 94-95 Q 4
Elektrostal' = Ėlektrostal' o RUS 94-95 Q 4
Eleku ~ ZRE 210-211 G 3
Elele o WAN 204-205 G 6
Eléphant, Île = Lathu ⌒ VAN 184 II a 2
Elephanta Caves ••• IND 138-139 D 10
Elephant Butte Reservoir < USA (NM) 256-257 H 5
Elephantine ∴ • ET 194-195 F 5
Elephant Island ⌒ ARK 16 G 31
Elephant Point o BD 142-143 H 5
Elephant Point o USA 20-21 K 3
Eléphants de Kaniama, Réserve ⊥ ZRE 214-215 C 4
Elesbão Veloso o BR 68-69 G 5
Eleşkirt ☆ TR 128-129 K 3
Elesvaram o IND 142-143 C 7
El Eulma o DZ 190-191 E 2
Eleuthera Island ⌒ BS 54-55 G 2
Eleva o USA (WI) 270-271 G 6
Eleven Point River ~ USA (MO) 276-277 D 4
El Fahl, Oued ~ DZ 190-191 D 5
El Fahs o TN 190-191 G 2
El Faouar o TN 190-191 G 4
El Farcya o MA 188-189 G 7
El Fedjaj, Chott ⊂ TN 190-191 G 4
Elfin Cove o USA 32-33 B 2
El Fouz < RIM 196-197 E 6
Elfrida o USA (AZ) 256-257 F 7
Elfros o CDN (SAS) 232-233 P 4
El Fud o ETH 208-209 F 5
El Gaa Taatzebar ∸ DZ 190-191 D 7
El Gal < EAK 212-213 G 3
El Gallaoulya < RIM 196-197 E 4
El Gambole < SP 212-213 K 2
El Gareb, Bir < RIM 196-197 B 4
Él'gen o RUS 120-121 O 2
El Gharsa, Chott ⊂ TN 190-191 F 3
El Ghazal, Bahr ~ TCH 198-199 H 5
El Gheddiya o RIM 196-197 E 6
El Ghorafia, Bir < TN 192-193 D 1
Él'gi ~ RUS 110-111 X 7
El Giara o SP 212-213 H 4
Elgin o CDN (MAN) 234-235 C 5
Elgin o CDN (NB) 240-241 K 5
Elgin o CDN (ONT) 238-239 J 4
Elgin o• GB 90-91 F 3
Elgin o USA (AL) 284-285 C 2
Elgin o USA (IL) 274-275 K 2
Elgin o USA (ND) 258-259 F 5
Elgin o USA (NE) 262-263 H 3
Elgin o USA (NV) 248-249 K 2
Elgin o USA (OK) 264-265 F 4
Elgin o USA (OR) 244-245 H 5
Elgin o USA (SC) 284-285 K 2
Elgin o USA (TN) 282-283 C 4
Elgin o USA (TX) 266-267 K 3
Él'ginskij o RUS 110-111 X 7
Él'ginskoe ploskogor'e ▲ RUS 110-111 V 7
Él'gjaj o RUS 118-119 H 4
El Gleïta o RIM 196-197 E 7
Él Gof o ETH 208-209 D 7
El Goléa o DZ 190-191 D 5
Elgon, Mount ▲ EAU 212-213 E 3
Él'goras, gora ▲ RUS 88-89 L 2
El Goss < RIM 196-197 C 6
El Goûfi, Djebel ▲ DZ 190-191 F 2
El Guérara o DZ 188-189 L 6
El Guetar o TN 190-191 G 3
El Guettara < RMM 196-197 J 3
Él'gygytgyn, ozero ⊂ RUS 112-113 R 3
Él'gykakvym ~ RUS 112-113 Q 2
el-Had o MA 188-189 H 5
El Hadjar o DZ 190-191 F 2
el-Hafeïra, Oued ~ RIM 196-197 E 2
El Haggounia o MA 188-189 E 7
El Hajeb o MA 188-189 J 4
El Hallail, Oued ~ DZ 190-191 F 3
El Ham, Oued ~ DZ 190-191 D 3
El Hamanene, Oued ~ DZ 190-191 C 8
El Hamel o DZ 190-191 E 3
El Hamma o TN 190-191 G 4
El Hammâmi ∸ RIM 196-197 D 3
el-Hamra, Oued ~ RIM 188-189 G 7
El Hamurre o SP 208-209 J 5
El Han ∸ DZ 196-197 G 2
El Hank ∸ DZ 196-197 H 2
El Haouaria o TN 190-191 H 2
El Haouita o DZ 190-191 D 4
El Harar < SP 212-213 J 3
El Harich, Hamâda ∸ RIM 196-197 H 3
El Haricha, Hamâda ∸ RMM 196-197 H 3
El Harrach, Oued ~ DZ 190-191 D 2
El Homr o DZ 190-191 E 6
Él'hotovo o RUS 126-127 F 6
Elhovka o RUS 96-97 G 7
Elhovo o BG 102-103 E 6
Elias, Cerro ▲ RA 80 G 2
Eliase o RI 166-167 F 6
Elias Garcia o ANG 216-217 F 4
Eliasville o USA (TX) 264-265 F 6
Elida o USA (NM) 256-257 M 5
Élida'ar o ETH 200-201 K 6
El Idrissia o DZ 190-191 D 3
Elie o CDN (MAN) 234-235 F 5
Elif ∴ • TR 128-129 G 4
Élikčan ~ RUS 112-113 J 5
Eliki Gounda < RN 198-199 D 5
Elila o ZRE 210-211 K 5
Elila ~ ZRE 210-211 L 5
Elim o USA 20-21 J 4
Elim o ZA 220-221 D 7
Eliot, Mount ▲ CDN 36-37 S 5
Elipa o ZRE 210-211 K 4
Elisa o BR 70-71 F 3
Elisa o RA 76-77 G 6
Eliseu Martins o BR 68-69 G 6
Élista ☆ RUS 96-97 D 10
Ėlistratova, poluostrov ⌒ RUS 120-121 U 3
Eliye Springs o EAK 212-213 F 2
Eliza, Lake ⊂ AUS 180-181 E 4
Elizabeth o USA (NJ) 280-281 M 3
Elizabeth o USA (WV) 280-281 E 4
Elizabeth, Cape ▲ USA (ME) 278-279 L 5
Elizabeth, Lac ⊂ CDN 36-37 M 7
Elizabeth Point ▲ CDN 24-25 e 7
Elizabeth City o USA (NC) 282-283 L 4
Elizabeth Downs o AUS 172-173 K 2
Elizabeth Harbour • BS 54-55 H 3
Elizabeth Island ⌒ USA 22-23 U 3
Elizabeth Islands ⌒ USA (MA) 278-279 L 7
Elizabeth Reef ⌒ 13 G 5
Elizabethton o USA (TN) 282-283 E 4
Elizabethtown o USA (KY) 276-277 K 3
Elizabethtown o USA (NC) 282-283 J 6
Elizabethville o USA (PA) 280-281 K 3
Elizavety, mys ▲ RUS 120-121 K 6
Elizovo ☆ RUS 120-121 S 7
el-Jadida ☆ • MA 188-189 G 4
El Jem o•• TN 190-191 H 3
El Jerid, Chott ⊂ TN 190-191 G 4
Elk o PL 92-93 R 2
Elk o USA (NM) 256-257 K 6
Elk o USA (WA) 244-245 H 2
Elkader o USA (IA) 274-275 G 2
El Kahla, Djebel ▲ DZ 188-189 L 6
El Kala ☆ DZ 190-191 G 2
El Kantara o DZ 190-191 E 3
El Kantour, Col d' ▲ DZ 190-191 F 2
El Kataoui o TN 190-191 H 3
el-Katouat o MA 188-189 H 4
Elk City o USA (ID) 250-251 D 6
Elk City o USA (KS) 262-263 L 7
Elk City o USA (OK) 264-265 E 3
Elk City Lake ⊂ USA (KS) 262-263 L 7
Elk Creek o USA (CA) 246-247 C 4
Elk Creek ~ USA (OK) 264-265 E 3
El Kebir, Oued ~ TN 190-191 G 3
Elkedra o AUS 178-179 C 1
El Kef ☆ TN 190-191 G 2
el-Kelaa-des-Srarhna ☆ MA 188-189 H 4
Él Kerē o ETH 208-209 F 6
el-Kerma, Hassi < MA 188-189 G 6
Elkford o CDN (BC) 230-231 P 3
Elk Grove o USA (CA) 246-247 D 5
El Khannfous, Hassi < DZ 190-191 B 6
el-Khaoula o MA 188-189 F 6
Elkhart o USA (IN) 274-275 N 3
Elkhart o USA (KS) 262-263 E 7
Elkhart o USA (TX) 268-269 E 5
El Khatt ∸ RIM 196-197 E 3
El Khatt, Oued ~ MA 196-197 D 2
Elkhead o USA (OR) 244-245 B 7
Elkhead Mounts ▲ USA (CO) 254-255 H 3
El Khnâchich ∸ RMM 196-197 H 4
Elkhorn o CDN (MAN) 234-235 B 5
Elkhorn o USA (NE) 262-263 K 3
Elkhorn o USA (WI) 274-275 K 2
Elkhorn o USA (WV) 280-281 E 6
Elkhorn Ranch Unit ⊥ USA (ND) 258-259 D 4
El Khroub o DZ 190-191 F 2
Elkin o USA (NC) 282-283 G 4
Elkins o USA (NM) 256-257 L 5
Elkins o USA (WV) 280-281 G 5
Elk Island ⌒ CDN (MAN) 234-235 G 4
Elk Island National Park ⊥ CDN (ALB) 232-233 F 2
Elk Lake o CDN (ONT) 236-237 H 5

Elk Lakes Provincial Park ⊥ CDN (BC) 230-231 O 3
Elk Mountain ▲ USA (NM) 256-257 G 5
Elk Mountains ▲ USA (CO) 254-255 H 4
Elko o CDN (BC) 230-231 O 4
Elko o• USA (NV) 246-247 K 3
Ėl'konka ~ RUS 118-119 N 6
Ēl K'oran o ETH 208-209 G 6
Elk Point o CDN (ALB) 232-233 H 2
Elk Point o USA (SD) 260-261 K 4
Elk Rapids o USA (MI) 272-273 D 3
El Krebs, Erg ⩲ DZ 188-189 L 7
El Krenig, Hassi < DZ 190-191 D 7
Elk River ~ CDN (ALB) 232-233 C 3
Elk River ~ CDN (BC) 230-231 O 4
Elk River o USA (ID) 250-251 C 5
Elk River o USA (MN) 270-271 E 5
Elk River ~ USA (AL) 284-285 C 2
Elk River ~ USA (KS) 262-263 K 7
Elk River ~ USA (MO) 276-277 A 4
Elk River ~ USA (TN) 276-277 J 5
Elk River ~ USA (WV) 280-281 F 5
Elk River ~ USA (WV) 280-281 E 5
El Ksar el Kbir o MA 188-189 J 3
EL Kseur o DZ 190-191 E 2
El Ksiba o MA 188-189 J 4
Elk Springs o USA (CO) 254-255 G 3
Elkton o USA (KY) 276-277 H 4
Elkton o USA (MD) 280-281 L 4
Elkton o USA (OR) 244-245 B 7
Elkton o USA (TN) 276-277 J 5
Elkton o USA (VA) 280-281 H 5
Elkwater o CDN (ALB) 232-233 H 6
Ella o USA (KY) 276-277 K 3
Ella Ø ⌒ GRØ 26-27 n 7
Ellaville o USA (FL) 286-287 F 1
Ellaville o USA (GA) 284-285 F 4
Ell Bay ≈ 36-37 F 2
Elléba Fonfou < RN 198-199 B 4
Ellef Ringnes Island ⌒ CDN 24-25 U 1
Ēl Lēh o ETH 208-209 D 7
El Lein < EAK 212-213 H 4
Elléloyé o TCH 198-199 J 4
Ellen, Mount ▲ USA (UT) 254-255 E 5
Ellenboro o USA (WV) 280-281 E 4
Ellenburg o USA (NY) 278-279 H 4
Ellendale o USA (ND) 258-259 J 5
Ellensburg o USA (WA) 244-245 E 3
Ellenville o USA (NY) 280-281 M 2
Ellepugol-Ėmtor, ozero o RUS 114-115 Q 4
Ellerbe o USA (NC) 282-283 H 5
Ellery, Mount ▲ AUS 180-181 K 4
Ellesby o CDN (BC) 228-229 L 2
Ellesmere Island ⌒ CDN 24-25 e 2
Ellice Islands ⌒ TUV 13 J 3
Ellice River ~ CDN 30-31 R 2
Ellicott City o USA (MD) 280-281 K 4
Ellicottville o USA (NY) 278-279 C 6
Ellijay o USA (GA) 284-285 F 2
Ellinger o USA (TX) 266-267 L 4
Ellington o USA (MO) 276-277 E 3
Ellinwood o USA (KS) 262-263 H 6
Elliot o ZA 220-221 H 5
Elliot, Mount ▲ AUS 174-175 J 6
Elliot Lake o CDN (ONT) 238-239 C 2
Elliot Price Conservation Park ⊥ AUS 178-179 D 5
Elliott o AUS 174-175 B 5
Elliott o USA (MD) 280-281 L 5
Elliott, Mount ▲ AUS 172-173 H 6
Elliott Key ⌒ USA (FL) 286-287 J 6
Ellis o USA (ID) 252-253 D 2
Ellis o USA (KS) 262-263 G 6
Ellisforde o USA (WA) 244-245 F 2
Ellisras o ZA 218-219 D 6
Elliston o AUS 180-181 C 2
Elliston o CDN (NFL) 242-243 P 4
Elliston o USA (MT) 250-251 G 5
Ellisville o USA (AL) 284-285 E 2
Ellisville o USA (MS) 268-269 L 5
Ellora o• IND 138-139 E 9
Ellora Caves ··· IND 138-139 E 9
Ellsworth o USA (KS) 262-263 H 6
Ellsworth o USA (ME) 278-279 N 4
Ellsworth o USA (MN) 270-271 B 7
Ellsworth o USA (NE) 262-263 D 2
Ellsworth o USA (WI) 270-271 F 6
Ellsworth Highland ▲ ARK 16 F 28
Ellwood City o USA (PA) 280-281 F 3
Elma o CDN (MAN) 234-235 H 5
Elma o USA (IA) 274-275 F 1
Elma o USA (WA) 244-245 B 3
El Ma, Oued ~ RIM 196-197 F 2
El Maad o DZ 190-191 E 2
El Mabrouk < RIM 196-197 C 6
Elmadağ o TR 128-129 E 3
Elma Dağı ▲ TR 128-129 E 3
El Mahbas o MA 188-189 G 7
Elma Labiod o DZ 190-191 G 3
El Malah o DZ 188-189 L 3
El Malah, Chott ⊖ DZ 190-191 E 4
Elmalı ☆• TR 128-129 C 4
El Mallaile o ETH 208-209 F 6
El Mamouel < RMM 196-197 J 5
El Mâmoûn < RMM 196-197 K 5
El Mamour < RMM 196-197 J 5
El Mannsour o DZ 188-189 L 7
el-Mansour-Eddahbi, Barrage < MA 188-189 H 5
El Marsa o DZ 190-191 C 2
El Maya o DZ 190-191 D 4
Elm Creek o CDN (MAN) 234-235 F 5
Elm Creek o USA (NE) 262-263 G 4
El Medo o ETH 208-209 E 6
El Meghaier o DZ 190-191 E 4
Elmeki o RN 198-199 D 4
El Melah, Ouen < DZ 190-191 E 6
El Melhes < RIM 196-197 D 5
El Mellah, Sebkha ⊖ DZ 188-189 L 6
El Menabba o DZ 188-189 K 5
el-Menzel o MA 188-189 J 4
Elmer o USA (OK) 264-265 E 4
Elmer City o USA (WA) 244-245 G 2
Elmerson Peninsula ⌒ CDN 26-27 J 3
Elm Fork ~ USA (TX) 264-265 G 5
Elm Fork Red River ~ USA (TX) 264-265 D 3
Elm Grove o USA (LA) 268-269 G 4
El Mhaïjrât o RIM 196-197 B 5
El Milia o DZ 190-191 F 2
Elmina o• GH 202-203 K 7
Elmira o CDN (ONT) 238-239 E 5
Elmira o CDN (PEI) 240-241 N 4
Elmira o USA (ID) 250-251 C 3
Elmira o USA (NY) 278-279 E 6
Elmo o USA (KS) 262-263 J 6
Elmodel o USA (GA) 284-285 F 5
El Moïnâne < RIM 196-197 E 5
Elmore o AUS 180-181 H 4
Elmore o CDN (SAS) 232-233 R 6
Elmore o USA (MN) 270-271 D 7
El Morro National Monument ∴ USA (NM) 256-257 G 3
El Mounir, Hassi < DZ 188-189 H 6
El Mraïti < RMM 196-197 J 5
El Mreïti < RIM 196-197 G 3
Elmvale o CDN (ONT) 238-239 F 4
Elmwood o USA (IL) 274-275 J 4
Elmwood o USA (MI) 270-271 K 4
Elmwood o USA (OK) 264-265 D 2
Elmwood o USA (WI) 270-271 F 6
El Nido o•• RP 160-161 C 7
Elnja o RUS 94-95 N 4
Elnora o CDN (ALB) 232-233 E 4
El Obeid = al-Ubayyid ☆• SUD 200-201 E 6
El Obeid = Ubayyid, al- ☆• SUD 200-201 E 6
Elogbatindi o CAM 210-211 C 2
El Ogla o DZ 190-191 F 4
El Ogla Gasses o DZ 190-191 F 3
Elogo o RCB 210-211 E 3
Ėloguj ~ RUS 114-115 S 3
Ėlogujskij, učastok ⊥ RUS 114-115 S 4
Ėlojaha ~ RUS 108-109 R 8
Elopada o RI 168 D 7
Elora o USA (TN) 276-277 J 5
Elorza o YV 60-61 G 4
Elota o MEX 50-51 F 6
El Ouadey ~ TCH 198-199 J 6
el-Oualidia o MA 188-189 G 4
El Ouar, Erg ⩲ DZ 190-191 F 6
El Ouass'ât ⩲ RIM 196-197 E 3
El Oued ☆• DZ 190-191 F 4
Ėlovaja, Bol'šaja (Tet) ~ RUS 114-115 U 5
Ėlovka ~ RUS 120-121 T 5
Ėlovo ☆ RUS 96-97 J 5
Eloy o USA (AZ) 256-257 D 6
Eloy Alfaro o EC (GUA) 64-65 C 3
Eloy Alfaro o EC (MAN) 64-65 B 2
El Paso o• USA (TX) 266-267 A 2
El Paso Gap o USA (NM) 256-257 L 6
El Paso Mountains ▲ USA (CA) 248-249 G 4
Elphant, Rapides de l' ~ ZRE 206-207 D 6
Elphinstone o AUS 178-179 K 1
Elphinstone o CDN (MAN) 234-235 C 4
Elpitiya o CL 140-141 J 7
El Portal o USA (CA) 248-249 E 2
El Porvenir o USA (NM) 256-257 K 3
Elquí, Río ~ RCH 76-77 B 6
El Rharbi, Oued ~ DZ 190-191 C 4
Elrosa o USA (MN) 270-271 D 5
Elrose o CDN (SAS) 232-233 K 4
Elroy o USA (WI) 270-271 H 7
El Salvador ■ ES 52-53 K 5
Elsamere National Park ⊥ EAK 212-213 F 4
Elsberry o USA (MO) 274-275 H 5
Elsey o AUS 174-175 B 4
Elsey Cemetery • AUS 174-175 B 4
Elsey National Park ⊥ AUS 174-175 B 4
El Sharana Mine • AUS 172-173 L 2
Elsie Hills o AUS 178-179 J 3
Elsie Island ⌒ CDN 36-37 K 5
Elsinore, Lake ⊖ USA (CA) 248-249 G 6
Elstad o N 86-87 E 6
Elstow o CDN (SAS) 232-233 M 3
Eltanin Fracture Zone System ≃ 14-15 O 13
El Tarf o TN 190-191 G 2
Eltice Island ⌒ CDN 20-21 X 2
El Tichlitt < RIM 196-197 D 6
Elton o RUS 96-97 E 9
Elton o USA (LA) 268-269 H 6
Elton, ozero ⊖• RUS 96-97 E 9
Eltopia o USA (WA) 244-245 F 4
El Tuparro, Parque Nacional ⊥ CO 60-61 G 5
Eltyreva ~ RUS 114-115 R 5
Elu o RI 166-167 E 6
Elubo o GH 202-203 J 7
Elu Inlet ≈ 24-25 T 6
El Ure < SP 212-213 J 2
Elūru o IND 140-141 J 2
Elva o•• EST 94-95 K 2
Ėlva ~ RUS 88-89 V 5
Elvas o•• P 98-99 D 5
Elverum ☆ N 86-87 E 6
Elvira o RA 78-79 K 3
Elvira, Cape ▲ CDN 24-25 S 4
Elvira Island ⌒ CDN 24-25 S 4
Elvire, Mount ▲ AUS 172-173 C 6
Elvire River ~ AUS 172-173 J 5
Elvita, Río ~ CO 60-61 F 5
El Wak o EAK 212-213 H 2
El Warsesa < EAK 212-213 G 2
Elwell, Lake ⊖ USA (MT) 250-251 H 3
Elwood o USA (IN) 274-275 N 4
Elwood o USA (NE) 262-263 G 4
Elx o E 98-99 G 5
Ely o• GB 90-91 H 5
Ely o USA (MN) 270-271 G 3
Ely o USA (NV) 246-247 L 4
Elyria o USA (OH) 280-281 D 2
Emae = Île Mai ⌒ VAN 184 II b 3
Emali o EAK 212-213 F 5
Emām 'Abbās o IR 134-135 A 1
Emām Ḥasan o IR 134-135 D 4
Emām Ḥomeini, Bandar-e o IR 134-135 C 3
Emām Tāqi o IR 136-137 F 7
Emån ~ S 86-87 G 8
Ėmanda, ozero ⊖ RUS 110-111 U 7
Emanželinsk o RUS 96-97 M 6
Emas, Parque Nacional das ⊥ BR 72-73 D 5
Embarcación o RA 76-77 E 2
Embarras River ~ CDN (ALB) 228-229 R 3
Embarrass River ~ USA (IL) 274-275 K 5
Embarrass River ~ USA (WI) 270-271 K 6
Ėmbenčimė ~ RUS 116-117 J 3
Embetsu o J 152-153 J 2
Embi ☆ KA 126-127 N 3
Embi ~ KA 156-157 L 3
Embi ~ RUS 96-97 H 10
Embi, Mount ▲ PNG 183 B 3
Embilipitiya o CL 140-141 J 7
Embira o BR 68-69 F 5
Embira, Rio ~ BR 66-67 B 6
Emblem o USA (WY) 252-253 K 2
Embocada o BOL 70-71 F 4
Embondo o ZRE 210-211 G 3
Emboracação, Represa < BR 72-73 G 5
Emboraí, Baía do ≈ 68-69 E 2
Emboscada o BOL 70-71 E 2
Emboscada, La o BOL 70-71 D 2
Emboscada Nueva o PY 76-77 J 3
Embreeville o USA (TN) 282-283 E 4
Embrun o CDN (ONT) 238-239 K 3
Embu ☆ EAK 212-213 F 4
Embudo, Raudal del ~ CO 64-65 F 1
Embundo o ANG 216-217 D 8
Emca o RUS 88-89 Q 5
Emca ~ RUS 88-89 Q 5
Emcisweni o MW 214-215 G 6
Emden o• D 92-93 J 2
Emeck o RUS 88-89 Q 5
Emeishan o VRC (SIC) 156-157 C 2
Emeishan •• VRC (SIC) 156-157 C 2
Ėmel' ~ KA 124-125 N 5
Emeljanovskaja o RUS 88-89 Q 4
Emelle o USA (AL) 284-285 B 4
Emerald o AUS 178-179 K 2
Emerald o USA (NE) 262-263 K 4
Emerald Bank ≃ 38-39 N 7
Emerald Isle ⌒ CDN 24-25 P 2
Emeriau Point ▲ AUS 172-173 F 4
Emerillon o F 62-63 H 4
Emersen o CDN (MAN) 234-235 F 5
Emerson o USA (AR) 276-277 B 7
Emery o USA (UT) 254-255 D 5
Emery Range ▲ AUS 178-179 C 4
Emet ☆ TR 128-129 C 3
Emeti o PNG 183 B 4
Emigrant o USA (MT) 250-251 J 6
Emigrant Gap o USA (CA) 246-247 E 4
Emigrant Pass ▲ USA (NV) 246-247 J 3
Emilia, La o YV 60-61 H 4
Emiliano Zapata o MEX (CHI) 52-53 J 3
Emiliano Zapata o MEX (COA) 50-51 H 5
Emiliano Zapata o MEX (SON) 50-51 D 3
Emilia-Romagna □ I 100-101 B 2
Emin o VRC 146-147 F 2
Emīnābād o PK 138-139 E 3
Eminee o RI 166-167 K 5
Eminence o USA (IN) 274-275 M 5
Eminence o USA (KY) 276-277 K 2
Eminence o USA (MO) 276-277 D 3
Emin He ~ VRC 146-147 F 2
Emini o CAM 210-211 D 2
Emin Pasha Gulf ⊖ EAT 212-213 C 5
Emirdağ ☆ TR 128-129 D 3
Emirgazi ☆ TR 128-129 E 4
Emlinskaja, buhta ⊖ RUS 120-121 Q 3
Emma, Mount ▲ CDN 24-25 g 4
Emmaboda ☆ S 86-87 G 8
Emma Fiord ≈ 26-27 E 3
Emmen o NL 92-93 J 2
Emmet o AUS 178-179 H 3
Emmetsburg o USA (IA) 274-275 D 1
Emmett o USA (ID) 252-253 B 3
Emmett o USA (MI) 272-273 G 5
Emmiganuru o IND 140-141 G 3
Emmitsburg o USA (MD) 280-281 J 4
Emmonak o USA 20-21 H 5
Ėmmy, mys ▲ RUS 110-111 a 1
Emo o CDN (ONT) 234-235 K 6
Emory o USA (TX) 264-265 J 6
Emory Pass ▲ USA (NM) 256-257 H 6
Emory Peak ▲ USA (TX) 266-267 D 4
Emoulas < RN 198-199 C 5
Empalme o MEX 50-51 D 4
Empalme, El = Velasco Ibarra o EC 64-65 C 2
Empangeni o ZA 220-221 K 4
Empedrado o RCH 78-79 C 3
Emperado, El o YV 60-61 F 3
Emperor Range ▲ PNG 184 I b 1
Emperor Seamount Chain ≃ 14-15 K 3
Emperor Trough ≃ 14-15 K 3
Empexa, Salar de ⊖ BOL 70-71 C 7
Empire o USA (AR) 276-277 D 7
Empire o USA (CA) 248-249 D 2
Empire o USA (CO) 254-255 K 4
Empire o USA (MI) 272-273 C 3
Emporia o USA (KS) 262-263 K 6
Emporia o USA (VA) 280-281 J 7
Emporium o USA (PA) 280-281 H 2
Empress o CDN (ALB) 232-233 H 5
Empress Augusta Bay ≈ 184 I b 2
Empress Mine o ZW 218-219 E 4
Ems ~ D 92-93 J 2
Emu Park o• AUS 178-179 L 2
Emure o WAN 204-205 F 5
Emva o RUS 88-89 V 5
Emvan o CAM 204-205 K 6
Ena o J 152-153 G 7
Enakievo = Jenakijeve o UA 102-103 L 3
Enangiperi o EAK 212-213 E 4
Enarotali o RI 166-167 J 3
Enašimo ~ RUS 116-117 F 5
Encantado o BR 68-69 J 4
Encantado, Valle ⩲ RA 78-79 D 6
Encanto, Cape ▲ RP 160-161 D 5
Encanto, El o CO 64-65 F 2
Encarnación ☆ PY 76-77 K 4
Encarnacion de Díaz o MEX 50-51 H 7
Enchant o CDN (ALB) 232-233 F 5
Encinal o USA (TX) 266-267 H 5
Encinal, El o MEX 50-51 K 5
Encinitas o USA (CA) 248-249 G 7
Encino o CO 60-61 E 4
Encino o USA (NM) 256-257 K 4
Encino o USA (TX) 266-267 J 7
Encoje o ANG 216-217 C 3
Encon o RA 78-79 F 2
Encontrados o YV 60-61 E 3
Encounter Bay ≈ 180-181 E 3
Encrucijada, La o YV 60-61 J 3
Encruzilhada o BR 72-73 K 3
Encruzilhada do Sul o BR 74-75 D 8
Encucijada, La o YV 60-61 H 3
Enda o VRC 144-145 L 5
Endako o CDN (BC) 228-229 J 2
Endau o EAK (EAS) 212-213 G 4
Endau ▲ EAK (EAS) 212-213 G 4
Ėndė ~ RUS 116-117 E 2
Ende, Pulau ⌒ RI 168 E 7
Endeavor o CDN (SAS) 232-233 Q 3
Endeavour Strait ≈ 174-175 G 2
Endebes o EAK 212-213 E 3
Endeh o RI 168 E 7
Endengue o CAM 210-211 D 2
Enderby o CDN (BC) 230-231 K 3
Enderby Abyssal Plain ≃ 12 B 10
Enderby Land ⩲ ARK 16 G 6
Enderlin o USA (ND) 258-259 K 5
Endiang o CDN (ALB) 232-233 F 4
Endicott o USA (NY) 278-279 E 6
Endicott o USA (WA) 244-245 H 4
Endicott Arm ≈ 32-33 D 3
Endicott Mountains ▲ USA 20-21 N 3
Endicott Mountains Range ▲ USA 20-21 N 3
Endiké o RCB 210-211 E 4
Endimari, Rio ~ BR 66-67 D 7
Endom o CAM 210-211 D 2
Endra, ozero o RUS 114-115 J 4
Endyalgout Island ⌒ AUS 172-173 L 1
Ene, Río ~ PE 64-65 E 7
Eneabba o AUS 176-177 C 4
Enemawira o RI 164-165 J 2
Enemy, Lake of the ⊖ CDN 30-31 O 4
Énéné Patatpe o F 62-63 G 4
Energia o RA 78-79 K 5
Enerucijada, La o YV 60-61 K 3
Enez ☆ TR 128-129 B 2
Enfer, Portes de l' ~• ZRE 212-213 A 6
Enfield o CDN (NS) 240-241 M 6
Enfield o USA (CT) 280-281 O 2
Enfield o USA (NC) 282-283 K 4
Enfok o IND 140-141 E 4
Engadin ⩲ CH 92-93 K 5
Engadine o USA (MI) 270-271 N 4
Engaño, Cabo ▲ DOM 54-55 L 5
Engaru o J 152-153 K 2
Engaruka o EAT (ARV) 212-213 E 5
Engaruka ∴• EAT (MA) 212-213 E 5
Engaruka Basin ⩲ EAT 212-213 F 5
Engcobo o ZA 220-221 H 5
En Gedi • IL 130-131 D 2
Engelhard o USA (NC) 282-283 M 5
Engelmine o USA (CA) 246-247 E 3
Ėngel's o RUS 96-97 E 8
Engels = Ėngel's o RUS 96-97 E 8
Engelsberg bruk ••• S 86-87 H 7
Engen o CDN (BC) 228-229 K 2
Engenheiro Navarro o BR 72-73 J 4
Engenio, El o PE 64-65 E 9
Engerina Creek ~ AUS 178-179 C 5
Enggano, Pulau ⌒ RI 162-163 E 7
Engh o VRC 150-151 B 2
Engida ~ RUS 116-117 G 5
Engineer o CDN 20-21 X 7
Engineer Group ⌒ PNG 183 F 6
Engkilili o MAL 162-163 J 4
England □ GB 90-91 F 5
England o USA (AR) 276-277 D 6
Engle o USA (NM) 256-257 H 5
Englee o CDN (NFL) 242-243 M 2
Englefeld o CDN (SAS) 232-233 O 3
Englefield, Cape ▲ CDN 24-25 d 6
Englefield Bay ≈ CDN 228-229 B 4
Englehart o CDN (ONT) 236-237 J 5
Englevale o USA (ND) 258-259 K 5
Englewood o USA (FL) 286-287 G 5
Englewood o USA (KS) 262-263 G 7
Englewood o USA (OH) 280-281 B 4
Englewood o USA (TN) 282-283 C 5
English o USA (TX) 264-265 K 5
English Channel = English Channel = La Manche ≈ 90-91 G 6
English Coast ⩲ ARK 16 F 29
English Company's Islands, The ⌒ AUS 174-175 D 3
English Harbour East o CDN (NFL) 242-243 O 5
English Harbour Town o AG 56 E 3
English Harbour West o CDN (NFL) 242-243 N 5
English River o CDN (ONT) 234-235 N 5
Engoordina o AUS 178-179 C 3
Engozero o RUS 88-89 M 4
Engure o LV 94-95 H 3
Enid o USA (OK) 264-265 G 2
Enid Creek ~ CDN (ONT) 236-237 G 4
Enid Lake < USA (MS) 268-269 L 2
Enid Mining Area, Mount • AUS 172-173 C 6
Enisej ⌒ 10-11 H 2
Enisej ~ RUS 10-11 H 2
Enisejsk ☆ RUS 116-117 F 6
Enisejskij zaliv ≈ 108-109 S 5
Enisejsko-Stolbovoj, učastok ⊥ RUS 114-115 U 3
Eniwa o J 152-153 J 3
Enjil o MA 188-189 J 4
Enjukovo o RUS 94-95 P 2
Ėnkėn, mys ▲ RUS 120-121 J 5
Enkhuizen o• NL 92-93 H 2
Enköping ☆ S 86-87 H 7
Enmelen o RUS 112-113 T 4
Enmelen ~ RUS 112-113 X 4
Ėnmyvaam ~ RUS 112-113 R 3
Enna o I 100-101 E 6
Ennadai o CDN 30-31 T 5
Ennadai Lake ⊖ CDN 30-31 T 5
En Naga, Oued ~ DZ 188-189 H 6
En Nahūd o SUD 200-201 D 6
Enné, Ouadi ~ TCH 198-199 J 5
Ennedi ▲ TCH 198-199 K 4
Ennery o RH 54-55 J 5
Enngonia o AUS 178-179 H 5
Ennis o USA (MT) 250-251 H 6
Ennis o USA (TX) 264-265 H 6
Ennis = Inis ☆• IRL 90-91 C 5
Enniscorthy = Inis Córthaidh o IRL 90-91 D 5
Enniskillen o CDN (ONT) 238-239 G 4
Enniskillen ☆• GB 90-91 D 4
En Noual, Sebkhet ⊖ TN 190-191 G 3
Enns ~ A 92-93 N 5
En Nsa, Oued ~ DZ 190-191 E 4
Enoch o USA (UT) 254-255 B 6
Enochs o USA (TX) 264-265 B 5
Enontekiö o FIN 88-89 G 2
Enoree River ~ USA (SC) 284-285 J 2
Enosburg Falls o USA (VT) 278-279 J 4
Enotaevka ☆ RUS 96-97 E 10
Enozero ⊖ RUS 88-89 O 2
Enping o VRC 156-157 H 5
Enrekang o RI 164-165 F 5
Enridaville o TN 190-191 H 2
Enrile o RP 160-161 D 4
Enriquillo, Lago ⊖ DOM 54-55 K 5
Enschede o NL 92-93 J 2
Ensenada o• MEX 50-51 A 2
Ensenada o RCH 78-79 C 6
Enshi o VRC 154-155 F 6
Enshū-nada ≈ 152-153 G 7
Ensign o USA (KS) 262-263 F 7
Ensley o USA (FL) 286-287 B 1
Ėnstor, ozero ⊖ RUS 114-115 K 4
Entebang, Rumah o MAL 162-163 K 3
Entebbe o EAU 212-213 D 3
Enterprise o CDN 30-31 L 5
Enterprise o USA (AL) 284-285 E 5
Enterprise o USA (MS) 268-269 M 4
Enterprise o USA (OR) 244-245 H 5
Enterprise o USA (UT) 254-255 B 6
Enterprise Point ▲ RP 160-161 C 7
Entiako River ~ CDN (BC) 228-229 J 3
Entiat o USA (WA) 244-245 E 3
Ėntf-Imijagun ~ RUS 114-115 M 3
En Tmadé < RIM 196-197 E 5
Entrada, Punta ▲ RA 80 F 5
Entrance o CDN (ALB) 228-229 R 3
Entre Lagos o RCH 78-79 C 6
Entre Ríos o BOL 76-77 E 1
Entre Rios o BR 66-67 K 5
Entre-Rios o BR 68-69 J 7
Entre Ríos □ RA 76-77 H 6
Entre Ríos, Cordillera ▲ HN 52-53 B 4
Entriken o USA (PA) 280-281 H 3
Entrocamento o BR 68-69 F 5
Entroncamento o BR 68-69 E 4
Entronque La Cuchilla o MEX 50-51 H 5
Entropo o RI 166-167 L 3
Entumeni o ZA 220-221 K 4
Ėntuziastov o RUS 110-111 U 4
Entwistle o CDN (ALB) 232-233 D 2
Enu, Pulau ⌒ RI 166-167 H 5
Enugu ☆ WAN 204-205 G 5
Enugu Ezike o WAN 204-205 G 5
Enumclaw o USA (WA) 244-245 D 3
Ėnurmino o RUS 112-113 Z 3
Envigado o CO 60-61 D 4
Envira o BR 66-67 B 6
Environ o CDN (SAS) 232-233 L 3
Enxudé o GNB 202-203 C 4
Enyamba o ZRE 210-211 K 5
Enyčavajam ~ RUS 112-113 O 6
Enyellé o RCB 210-211 G 2
Ėnyngvajam ~ RUS 120-121 V 3
Eo, Río ~ E 98-99 D 3
Eochaill = Youghal o IRL 90-91 D 6
Eola o USA (TX) 266-267 G 2
Eólie o Lipari, Ísole ⌒ I 100-101 E 5
Epako o NAM 216-217 D 10
Epanomí o GR 100-101 J 4
Epatlán o MEX 52-53 E 2
Epe o WAN 204-205 E 5
Epecuén, Laguna ⊖ RA 78-79 H 4
Epembe o NAM 216-217 B 8
Epéna o RCB 210-211 F 3
Epenarra o AUS 174-175 C 7
Épernay o• F 90-91 J 7
Ephesus = Efes ∴•• TR 128-129 B 3
Ephraim o USA (UT) 254-255 D 4
Ephrata o USA (WA) 244-245 F 3
Ephrata o USA (PA) 280-281 K 3
Epi □ VAN 184 II b 3
Epi ⌒ VAN (EPI) 184 II b 3
Epi o ZRE 210-211 L 2
Epidauros ••• GR 100-101 J 6
Épinal ☆• F 90-91 L 7
Epini o ZRE 212-213 B 3
Epiphany o USA (SD) 260-261 J 3
Epizana o BOL 70-71 E 5
Epokenkoso o ZRE 210-211 F 5
Epoma o RCB 210-211 E 3
Epping o USA (ND) 258-259 D 3
Epping o USA (NH) 278-279 L 5
Epping Forest o AUS 178-179 J 2
Epping Forest National Park ⊥ AUS 178-179 J 2
Epps o USA (LA) 268-269 J 4
Epsom o AUS 178-179 K 1
Epu, River ~ WAN 204-205 G 4
Epukiro o NAM 216-217 E 10
Epukiro ~ NAM 216-217 F 10
Epulu ~ ZRE 212-213 B 3
Epulu, Station de capture d' • ZRE 212-213 B 3
Epupa Falls ~ NAM 216-217 B 8
Epuyén o RA 78-79 D 7
Eqlid o IR 134-135 E 3
Equateur □ ZRE 210-211 G 3
Equator 14-15 O 7
Equatorial Guinea = Guinea Ecuatorial ■ GQ 210-211 B 2
Eračimo ~ RUS 116-117 E 3
Erahtur o RUS 94-95 R 4
Eralé o BR 62-63 H 6
Eram o PNG 183 B 3
Eran Bay ≈ 160-161 B 8
Era River ~ PNG 183 C 4
Erātini o GR 100-101 J 5
Erave o PNG 183 B 4
Erave River ~ PNG 183 B 4
Eravur o CL 140-141 J 7
Erāwadi Myit ~ MYA 142-143 J 5
Erāwadi Myitwanyā ⌒ MYA 158-159 C 3
Erawan National Park ⊥• THA 158-159 E 3
Erba, Ğabal ▲ SUD (Ahm) 200-201 H 2
Erba, Ğabal ▲ SUD (Ahm) 200-201 G 3
Erbaa ☆ TR 128-129 G 2
Erbogačen ☆ RUS 116-117 N 5
Ėrča, Bol'šaja ~ RUS 110-111 b 5
Erçek Gölü ⊖ TR 128-129 K 3
Erciş ☆ TR 128-129 K 3
Erciyes Dağı ▲ TR 128-129 F 3
Erdaobaihe o VRC 150-151 G 6
Erdek ☆• TR 128-129 B 2
Erdemli ☆ TR 128-129 F 4
Ėrdėnėcagaan = Čonogol o MAU 148-149 M 5
Ėrdėnėcogt o MAU 148-149 E 4
Ėrdėnėdalaj = Sangijn Dalaj o MAU 148-149 G 4
Ėrdėnėmandal = Ölzijt o MAU 148-149 E 3
Ėrdėnėsant = Ulaanhudag o MAU 148-149 G 4
Ėrdėnėt o MAU 148-149 G 3
Ėrdėni Cu • MAU 148-149 F 4
Erdi ⩲ TCH 198-199 L 3
Eré o TCH 206-207 B 4
Erebus, Mount ⩲ ARK 16 F 17
Erebus and Terror Gulf ≈ 16 G 31
Erebus Bay ≈ 24-25 W 6
Erech ∴• IRQ 128-129 L 7
Erechim o BR 74-75 D 6
Ėrėėncav o MAU 148-149 M 3
Ereğli ☆ TR 128-129 D 2
Ereğli ☆ TR 128-129 F 4
Eréké ~ RCA 206-207 C 5
Ėrėma o RUS 116-117 N 5
Ėrėma, Bol'šaja ~ RUS 116-117 M 5
Erenhot o VRC 148-149 K 6
Erepecuru, Lago de ⊖ BR 62-63 F 6
Ereré o BR 68-69 J 3
Ērer Wenz ~ ETH 208-209 F 5
Erevan ☆ AR 128-129 L 2
Erfenisdam < ZA 220-221 H 4
Erfoud o MA 188-189 J 5
Erfurt ☆•• D 92-93 L 3
Erganı ☆ TR 128-129 H 3
Ėrgėl o MAU 148-149 J 6
Ėrgėlėh o RUS 118-119 O 4
Ergene Çayı ~ TR 128-129 B 2
Ergene Nehri ~ TR 128-129 B 2
Ergeni ▲ RUS 96-97 D 9
Ērģli o LV 94-95 J 3
Erguig, Bahr ~ TCH 206-207 C 3
Ergun He ~ VRC 150-151 C 1
Ergun Youqi o VRC 150-151 C 2
Ergun Zuoqi o VRC 150-151 C 2
Ėrguveem ~ RUS 112-113 X 4
Er Hai ⊖ VRC 142-143 M 3
Eri, River ~ WAN 204-205 E 4
Ería, Río ~ E 98-99 D 3
Eriba o SUD 200-201 H 4
Eric o CDN 38-39 M 3
Erica o AUS 180-181 J 5
Erichsen Lake ⊖ CDN 24-25 f 5
Erick o USA (OK) 264-265 E 3
Erickson o CDN (MAN) 234-235 D 4
Ericson o USA (NE) 262-263 H 3
Eridu = Abū Šahrain ∴• IRQ 130-131 J 2
Erie o USA (IA) 274-275 H 3
Erie o USA (KS) 262-263 L 7
Erie o USA (PA) 280-281 F 1
Erie, Lake ⊖ 46-47 G 5
Erie, Lake ⊖ 280-281 D 2
Erieau o CDN (ONT) 238-239 D 6
Erie Canal ~ USA (NY) 278-279 C 5
Erie Canal < USA (NY) 278-279 F 5
Ėriečka ~ RUS 108-109 e 6
Erie National Wildlife Refuge ⊥ USA (PA) 280-281 G 2
'Erîgât ⩲ RMM 196-197 H 5
Erik den Rødes Ø ⌒ GRØ 28-29 W 4
Erik Eriksenstretet ≈ 84-85 O 3
Erikit ~ RUS 110-111 Z 7
Erik Point ▲ CDN 26-27 Q 8
Eriksdale o CDN (MAN) 234-235 E 4
Eriksmåla o S 86-87 G 8
Erimo o J 152-153 K 4
Erimo-misaki ▲ J 152-153 K 4
Erimo Seamount ≃ 152-153 L 4
Erin o USA (TN) 276-277 H 4
Erinferry o CDN (SAS) 232-233 M 2
Erith River ~ CDN (ALB) 232-233 B 2
Eritrea ■ ER 200-201 H 5
Erkalnadejpur ~ RUS 114-115 P 3
Erkovcy o RUS 122-123 C 3
Erkowit o SUD 200-201 H 3
Erlangen o D 92-93 L 4
Erlang Shan ▲ VRC 156-157 C 2
Erldunda o AUS 176-177 M 2
Erling, Lake < USA (AR) 276-277 B 7
Erlistoun Creek ~ AUS 176-177 F 3
Erlongshan • VRC 150-151 F 5
Ermaki o RUS 116-117 N 7
Ermao = Île Mau ⌒ VAN 184 II b 3
Ermelo o ZA 220-221 J 3
Ėrmeneevo ☆ RUS 96-97 H 6
Ermenek ☆ TR 128-129 E 4
Ermentau ☆ KA 124-125 H 3
Ermera o RI 166-167 C 6
Ermil Post o SUD 200-201 C 6
Ermineskin Indian Reservation ⚔ CDN (ALB) 232-233 E 3
Ermoúpoli o• GR 100-101 K 6
Ernakulam o IND 140-141 G 6
Ernée o F 90-91 G 7
Ernest Giles Range ▲ AUS 176-177 G 3
Ernest Sound ≈ 32-33 D 4
Ernestville o USA (TN) 282-283 E 4
Ernul o USA (NC) 282-283 K 5
Erode o IND 140-141 G 5
Erofej Pavlovič o RUS 118-119 L 8
Eromalido, Tanjung ▲ RI 166-167 C 6
Eromanga o AUS 178-179 G 4
Eromanga Island = Île Erromango ⌒ VAN 184 II b 4
Eromohon ~ RUS 116-117 L 2
Erongoberg ▲ NAM 216-217 C 10
Erong Springs o AUS 176-177 D 2
Eröö = Bugant o MAU 148-149 H 3
Eröö gol ~ MAU 148-149 H 3
Eropol ~ RUS 112-113 O 4
Eroro o PNG 183 E 5
Errabiddy o AUS 176-177 D 2
Erragondapālem o IND 140-141 H 2
Er Raoui, Erg ⩲ DZ 188-189 K 6
Errego o MOC 218-219 J 3
er-Remla o TN 190-191 H 3
Er Richât, Guelb ▲ RIM 196-197 E 4
Errigal Mountain ▲ IRL 90-91 C 4
Errington o CDN (BC) 230-231 E 4
Erris Head ▲ IRL 90-91 B 4
Errittau o PNG 183 C 4
Errol o USA (NH) 278-279 K 4
Erromango, Île = Eromanga Island ⌒ VAN 184 II b 4
Erronan, Île = Futuna Island ⌒ VAN 184 II c 4
Ersa ~ RUS 88-89 W 3
Ersekë ☆• AL 100-101 H 4
Erši o RUS 94-95 O 4
Erskine o CDN (ALB) 232-233 F 3
Erskine o USA (MN) 270-271 B 3
Erskine Inlet ≈ 24-25 V 2
Eršov ☆ RUS 96-97 F 8
Eršova o RUS 116-117 L 7
Ert o RUS 118-119 M 4
Ertai o VRC 146-147 K 2
Ertil' o RUS 102-103 M 2
Ertis ~ KA 124-125 L 3
Ertis-Karaganda kanal < KA 124-125 H 3
Ertix He ~ VRC 146-147 G 2
Ėrtom ~ RUS 88-89 T 5
Ėrtoma o RUS 88-89 T 5
Ertwa, Mount ▲ AUS 176-177 M 1
Erua ⌒ ER 200-201 K 5
Erufa o WAN 204-205 F 4
Eruh ☆ TR 128-129 K 4
Eruki, Mount ▲ PNG 183 C 4
Erundu o NAM 216-217 D 10
Eruslan ~ RUS 96-97 E 8
Eruwa o WAN 204-205 E 5
Erval o BR 74-75 D 9
Ervay o USA (WY) 252-253 L 4
Erveiras o BR 74-75 D 7
Ervent o TM 136-137 F 5
Erwin o USA (MS) 268-269 J 3
Erwin o USA (NC) 282-283 J 5
Erwood o CDN (SAS) 232-233 Q 3
Erzgebirge ▲ D 92-93 M 3
Ėrzin ☆ RUS 116-117 G 10
Ėrzin ~ RUS 116-117 G 10
Erzincan ☆ TR 128-129 H 3
Erzurum ☆• TR 128-129 J 3
Eržvilkas o LT 94-95 H 4
Esa, Isanlu- o WAN 204-205 F 4
Esa'ala o PNG 183 F 5
Esan o J 152-153 J 4
Esang o RI 164-165 K 1
Esashi o J (HOK) 152-153 K 2
Esashi o J (HOK) 152-153 J 4
Esayoo Bay ≈ 26-27 J 3
Esbjerg o• DK 86-87 D 9
Esbo = Espoo o FIN 88-89 H 6
Escada o BR 68-69 L 6
Escala, La o BOL 70-71 E 4
Escalante o RP 160-161 E 7
Escalante o USA (UT) 254-255 D 6
Escalante Canyons • USA (UT) 254-255 D 6
Escalante Desert ⩲ USA (UT) 254-255 B 6
Escalante River ~ USA (UT) 254-255 D 6
Escalante Valley ⌣ USA (UT) 254-255 B 5
Escalerilla o RCH 76-77 C 1
Escalón o MEX 50-51 G 4
Escalon o USA (CA) 248-249 D 2
Escambia River ~ USA (FL) 286-287 B 1
Escanaba o USA (MI) 270-271 L 5
Escanaba River ~ USA (MI) 270-271 L 4
Escara o BOL 70-71 C 6
Escárcega o• MEX 52-53 J 2
Escarpada Point ▲ RP 160-161 E 3
Escatawpa River ~ USA (AL) 284-285 B 6
Eschscholtz Bay ≈ 20-21 K 3
Eschwege o• D 92-93 L 3
Escobas o USA (TX) 266-267 J 6
Escocesa, Bahía ≈ 54-55 L 5
Escola o BOL 70-71 D 5
Escondida, La o MEX 50-51 K 5
Escondida, Punta ▲ MEX 52-53 F 4
Escondido o USA (CA) 248-249 G 6
Escondido, Área Indígena ⚔ BR 66-67 H 7
Escondido, Río ~ MEX 52-53 K 2
Escondido, Río ~ NIC 52-53 B 5
Escoporanga o BR 72-73 K 5
Escorial, El o••• E 98-99 E 4
Escott o AUS 174-175 E 5
Escoumins, Les o CDN (QUE) 240-241 F 2
Escravos ~ WAN 204-205 F 6
Escudilla Mountain ▲ USA (AZ) 256-257 F 5
Escuinapa de Hidalgo o MEX 50-51 G 6
Escuintla ☆ GCA 52-53 J 4
Escuminac o• CDN (NB) 240-241 L 3
Escuminac, Point ▲ CDN (NB) 240-241 L 3
Ese o ZRE 206-207 H 6
Ėsė-Hajja o RUS 110-111 U 6
Eséka o CAM 210-211 C 2
Eseli o PNG 183 E 4
Esenanhaty ~ KA 96-97 H 8
Eşen Çayı ~ TR 128-129 C 4
Esence Dağları ▲ TR 128-129 H 3
Esensaj o KA 96-97 G 9
Esenyurt o TR 128-129 G 3
Eşfahān □ IR 134-135 D 2
Eşfahān ☆••• IR (ESF) 134-135 D 2
Esfarāyen o IR 136-137 E 6

Esfolado, Rio ~ BR 68-69 G 5
Ešger, Kūh-e ⛰ IR 134-135 H 1
Eshan o VRC 156-157 C 4
Eshimba o ZRE 210-211 K 6
Eshowe o ZA 220-221 K 4
Esigodini o ZW 218-219 E 5
Esik o KA 146-147 C 4
Esil ☆ KA 124-125 E 3
Esim ~ KA 124-125 F 1
Esinskaja o RUS 94-95 R 1
Esira o RM 222-223 E 10
Esjajaha ~ RUS 108-109 S 6
Esk o AUS 178-179 M 4
Esk o CDN (SAS) 232-233 O 4
Eškameš o AFG 136-137 L 6
Eškāšem o AFG 136-137 M 6
Eskdale o AUS 180-181 J 4
Esker o CDN 38-39 L 2
Eskifjörður ☆ IS 86-87 f 2
Eskil ☆ TR 128-129 E 3
Eskilstuna ☆ S 86-87 H 7
Eskimo Lakes ⊖ CDN 20-21 Y 2
Eskimonæsset ▲ GRØ 26-27 s 3
Eskimo Point o CDN (NWT) 30-31 W 5
Eskimo Point ▲ CDN (MAN) 30-31 W 6
Eski-Nookat o KS 136-137 N 4
Eskişehir ☆ TR 128-129 D 3
Eskridge o USA (KS) 262-263 K 6
Esla, Río ~ E 98-99 E 3
Eslāmābād-e Ğarb o IR 134-135 B 1
Eslām Qal'e o AFG 134-135 J 1
Eslām Qal'e o IR 136-137 F 7
Eslāmšahr o IR 136-137 B 7
Eslöv o S 86-87 F 9
Eşme ☆ TR 128-129 C 3
Esmeralda o AUS 174-175 G 6
Esmeralda o C 54-55 F 4
Esmeralda, Isla ⌒ RCH 80 C 4
Esmeralda, La o YV (AMA) 60-61 J 6
Esmeralda, La o YV (BAR) 60-61 F 3
Esmeralda, Río ~ BOL 70-71 D 3
Esmeraldas o BR 72-73 H 5
Esmeraldas ☆ • EC 64-65 C 1
Esmeraldas, Río ~ EC 64-65 C 1
Esmond o USA (ND) 258-259 H 3
Esnagami Lake ⊖ CDN (ONT) 236-237 B 2
Esnagi Lake ⊖ CDN (ONT) 236-237 D 4
Espadim Paranhos o BR 76-77 K 2
Espake o IR 134-135 J 5
Espalion o F 90-91 J 9
España o RP 160-161 E 6
Espanola o CDN (ONT) 238-239 D 2
Espanola o USA (NM) 256-257 J 3
Española, Isla ⌒ EC 64-65 C 10
Esparto o USA (CA) 246-247 C 5
Espavelta o PA 52-53 D 8
Espenberg o USA 20-21 J 3
Espenberg, Cape ▲ USA 20-21 J 3
Esperança o BR (P) 62-63 H 6
Esperança o BR (PA) 68-69 L 5
Esperança, Serra da ⛰ BR 74-75 E 5
Esperança dos Indios o BR 70-71 J 7
Esperance o AUS 176-177 F 6
Esperance Bay ≈ 176-177 F 6
Esperantina o BR 68-69 G 3
Esperantinopolis o BR 68-69 F 4
Esperanza o BR (AMA) 66-67 C 5
Esperanza o BR (UCA) 66-67 B 7
Esperanza o C 54-55 E 3
Esperanza o MEX 50-51 E 4
Esperanza o RA (SAC) 80 E 5
Esperanza o RA (SAF) 76-77 G 6
Esperanza o USA (TX) 266-267 B 2
Esperanza, La o BOL 70-71 F 4
Esperanza, La o C 54-55 D 3
Esperanza, La ☆ • HN 52-53 K 4
Esperanza, La o RA 78-79 E 6
Esperanza, La o YV 60-61 J 4
Esperanza, Sierra la ⛰ HN 54-55 C 7
Esperanza Inlet ≈ CDN 230-231 B 4
Espichel, Cabo ▲ P 98-99 C 5
Espiel o E 98-99 E 5
Espigão, Serra do ⛰ BR 74-75 E 6
Espigão do Oeste o BR 70-71 G 2
Espigão Mestre ⛰ BR 68-69 E 7
Espinal o BOL 70-71 H 5
Espinal o CO 60-61 D 5
Espinal, El o PA 52-53 D 8
Espinero o YV 60-61 K 4
Espinhaço, Serra do ⛰ BR 72-73 J 6
Espinheira o ANG 216-217 B 8
Espinho o P 98-99 C 4
Espinilho, Serra do ⛰ BR 76-77 K 5
Espinillo o RA 76-77 H 3
Espino o CO 60-61 E 4
Espino o YV 60-61 H 3
Espino, El o BOL 70-71 F 6
Espino, El o PA 52-53 E 7
Espinosa o BR 72-73 J 3
Espírito Santo o BR 66-67 C 4
Espírito Santo ■ BR 72-73 K 5
Espírito Santo do Turvo o BR 72-73 F 7
Espiritu Santo o MEX 50-51 J 6
Espiritu Santo ⌒ VAN 184 II a 2
Espiritu Santo, Bahía del ≈ MEX 52-53 L 2
Espiritu Santo, Isla ⌒ MEX 50-51 D 5
Espírito Santo do Pinhal o BR 72-73 G 7
Espita o MEX 52-53 K 1
Esplanada o BR 68-69 K 7
Espoo o FIN 88-89 H 6
Espungabera o MOC 218-219 G 5
Esqābād o IR 134-135 G 1
Esquel o RA 78-79 D 7
Esquibel, Gulf of ≈ 32-33 D 4
Esquimalt o CDN (BC) 230-231 F 5
Esquina o RA 76-77 H 6
Esquina o RCH 70-71 C 6
Esquiú o RA 76-77 E 5
Ėss ~ RUS 114-115 G 4
Essaouira = As-Sawirah ☆ • MA 188-189 G 5
Essé o CAM 204-205 J 6
Es-Sed, Oued ~ TN 190-191 H 4
Essendakane, In- < RMM 196-197 K 6
Es Seggeur, Oued ~ DZ 190-191 C 4
Essej o RUS 108-109 e 7
Essej, ozero ⊖ RUS 108-109 e 7
Essen o B 92-93 H 3
Essen o • D 92-93 J 3
Essendon, Mount ▲ AUS 176-177 F 2
Essentuki o RUS 126-127 E 5
Essequibo ~ GUY 62-63 E 5
Essequibo River ~ GUY 62-63 E 2
Essex o CDN (ONT) 238-239 C 6
Essex o USA (CA) 248-249 J 5
Essex o USA (IA) 274-275 C 4
Essex o USA (MD) 280-281 K 4
Essex o USA (MS) 268-269 K 2
Essex o USA (MT) 250-251 F 3
Essex Junction o USA (VT) 278-279 H 4
Essexville o USA (MI) 272-273 F 4
Essiama o GH 202-203 J 7
Essington, Port ≈ 172-173 K 1
Esslingen am Neckar o • D 92-93 K 4
Ėsso ☆ RUS 120-121 S 6
Est = East ■ CAM 210-211 E 2
Est, Pointe de l' ▲ CDN (QUE) 242-243 G 3
Estabrook Lake ⊖ CDN 24-25 K 6
Estacada o USA (OR) 244-245 C 5
Estaca de Bares, Punta de ▲ E 98-99 D 3
Estação Catur o MOC 218-219 H 1
Estacia Camacho o MEX 50-51 H 5
Estación 14 de Mayo o PY 76-77 H 2
Estación Atamisqui o RA 76-77 F 5
Estacion biologica • EC 64-65 B 10
Estación Buena Suerte o PY 76-77 H 2
Estación Candela o MEX 50-51 J 4
Estación Careros Cué o PY 76-77 H 2
Estacione Don o MEX 50-51 E 4
Estación Km. 329 o ROU 78-79 M 2
Estación la Concepción o PY 76-77 H 3
Estación Pozo Blanco o PY 76-77 H 2
Estación Salto Cué o PY 76-77 J 4
Estación Santa Clara • BR 74-75 E 5
Estación Simón o MEX 50-51 H 5
Estación Vanegas o MEX 50-51 J 6
Estación Victoria o PY 76-77 H 2
Estado Cañitas de Felipe Pescador o MEX 50-51 H 6
Estado de Guerrero, Parque Natural del ⊥ MEX 52-53 E 3
Estado la Calle o MEX 52-53 D 1
Estado Las Tablas o MEX 50-51 K 6
Estado Pabellones o MEX 50-51 H 6
Estados, Isla de los ⌒ RA 80 H 7
Estados, Parque Nacional de los ⊥ RA 80 H 7
Eṣṭahbānāt o • IR 134-135 F 4
Estambul o BOL 70-71 D 4
Estância o BR 68-69 K 7
Estancia Camerón o RCH 80 F 6
Estancia Carmen o RA 80 F 7
Estancia el Durazno o RA 76-77 C 6
Estancia Invierno o RCH 80 E 6
Estancia la Federica o RA 80 D 4
Estancia Laguna Union o RA 80 D 5
Estancia la Jerónima o RA 80 D 5
Estancia la Julia o RA 80 F 4
Estancia la Oriental o RA 80 D 3
Estancia las Cumbres o RCH 80 D 5
Estancia María Esther o RA 80 F 4
Estancia María Luisa o RA 80 G 7
Estancia Marina o RA 80 F 7
Estancia Moat o RA 80 G 7
Estancia Monte Dinero o RA 80 F 6
Estancia Policarpo o RA 80 H 7
Estancia Rocallosa o RCH 80 E 6
Estancia Rosalía o PY 76-77 J 2
Estancia San Justo o RA 80 F 7
Estand, Kūh-e ▲ IR 134-135 J 3
Estandarte o BR 68-69 F 2
Estanica o USA (NM) 256-257 J 4
Estanques o YV 60-61 F 3
Estarca, Río ~ BOL 76-77 D 1
Estcourt o ZA 220-221 J 4
Estcourt, Réserve ⊥ CDN (QUE) 240-241 F 3
Este, Laguna del ≈ 52-53 J 2
Este, Parque nacional del ⊥ DOM 54-55 L 5
Este, Punta del ▲ ROU 78-79 M 3
Esteban, Canal ≈ 80 C 5
Estehārd o IR 136-137 B 7
Esteio o BR 74-75 E 7
Esteli ☆ NIC 52-53 L 5
Estelline o USA (SD) 260-261 K 2
Estelline o USA (TX) 264-265 D 4
Estépar o E 98-99 F 3
Estepiktjah ~ RUS 110-111 Y 5
Estepona o E 98-99 E 6
Ester o USA 20-21 R 4
Esterbrook o USA (WY) 252-253 N 4
Esterhazy o CDN (SAS) 232-233 Q 5
Esteriktjah-Tas, hrebet ⛰ RUS 110-111 X 5
Estero o USA (FL) 286-287 H 5
Estero Bay ≈ 40-41 D 8
Estero Bay ≈ USA 248-249 D 4
Estero Blanco ~ RCH 76-77 B 5
Estero de Boca o EC 64-65 B 3
Esterwood o USA (LA) 268-269 H 6
Estes Park o USA (CO) 254-255 K 3
Estevan o CDN (SAS) 232-233 Q 6
Estevan Group ⌒ CDN (BC) 228-229 D 3
Estevan Point o CDN (BC) 230-231 C 4
Estey o USA (MI) 272-273 E 4
Esther o CDN (ALB) 232-233 H 4
Esther o USA (LA) 268-269 H 7
Esther Island ⌒ USA 20-21 R 6
Esther Lac ⊖ CDN (ONT) 236-237 K 2
Estherville o USA (IA) 274-275 D 1
Estill o USA (SC) 284-285 J 4
Estima o MOC 218-219 G 2
Estique o PE 70-71 B 5
Estirão do Equador o BR 66-67 B 5
Estiva o BR 68-69 F 2
Estiva, Riachão da ~ BR 68-69 F 5
Estivane o MOC 218-219 H 6
Estlin o CDN (SAS) 232-233 O 5
Esto o USA (LA) 268-269 G 5
Eston o CDN (SAS) 232-233 K 4
Estonia = Eesti ■ EST 94-95 J 2
Estor, El o GCA 52-53 K 4
Estrecho, El o CO 60-61 C 7
Estreito o BR 68-69 E 5
Estrela, Serra da ⛰ P 98-99 C 4
Estrela do Sul o BR 72-73 G 5
Estrella, La o BOL 70-71 F 5
Estrella, La o RA 76-77 E 2
Estrella, Punta ▲ MEX 50-51 B 2
Estrelto, Serra do ⛰ BR 68-69 G 7
Estremadura ⌄ P 98-99 C 5
Estremo o BR 74-75 E 7
Estremoz o • P 98-99 D 5
Estrondo, Serra do ⛰ BR 68-69 D 6
Estuary o CDN (SAS) 232-233 J 5
Esumba, Île ⌒ ZRE 210-211 H 3
Esztergom o H 92-93 P 5
Etacho Point ▲ CDN 30-31 J 2
Etah o GRØ 26-27 O 4
Etah o IND 138-139 G 6
Etaka ~ NAM 216-217 C 9
Étampes o F 90-91 J 7
Etamunbanie, Lake ⊖ AUS 178-179 E 4
Etawah o IND 138-139 G 6
Etchojoa o MEX 50-51 E 4
Etchoropo o MEX 50-51 E 4
Étéké o G 210-211 C 4
Éterikan, proliv ≈ 110-111 X 3
Eternity Range ⛰ ARK 16 G 30
Ethel o USA (MS) 268-269 L 3
Ethelbert o CDN (MAN) 234-235 C 3
Ethel Creek o AUS 172-173 E 7
Etheldale o AUS 174-175 G 6
Ethel Lake ⊖ CDN 20-21 W 5
Ethel River ~ AUS 176-177 E 2
Ethiopia = Ītyopya ■ ETH 208-209 C 3
Ethridge o USA (MT) 250-251 G 3
Etivluk River ~ USA 20-21 M 2
Etler Rasmussen, Kap ▲ GRØ 26-27 p 2
Etna, Monte ⛰ I 100-101 E 6
Etna Lake ⊖ CDN 30-31 K 3
Etoile o USA (TX) 268-269 F 5
Etoile Cay ⌒ SY 224 C 2
Etolin, Cape ▲ USA 20-21 G 6
Etolin Island ⌒ USA 32-33 D 3
Etolin Point ▲ USA 22-23 R 3
Etolin Strait ≈ 20-21 H 6
Eton o AUS 178-179 K 1
Eton o CDN (ONT) 236-237 D 5
Etorohaberge ⛰ NAM 216-217 B 8
Etosha Lookout • NAM 216-217 D 9
Etosha National Park ⊥ NAM 216-217 C 9
Etosha Pan ⊖ NAM 216-217 D 9
Etou o CAM 210-211 D 2
Etoumbi o RCB 210-211 E 3
Etowah o USA (TN) 282-283 C 5
Etowah Mounds State Historic Site ∴ • USA (GA) 284-285 F 2
Etowah River ~ USA (GA) 284-285 F 2
Etropole o BG 102-103 D 6
Ettaiyāpuram o IND 140-141 G 6
Etta Plains o AUS 174-175 F 6
Et Tarf, Garaet ⊖ DZ 190-191 F 3
Etthen Island ⌒ CDN 30-31 O 4
Ettington o CDN (SAS) 232-233 M 6
et-Tleta-de-Oved-Laov o MA 188-189 J 3
et-Tnine o MA 188-189 G 5
Ettumanur o IND 140-141 G 6
Etumba o ZRE (BAN) 210-211 H 5
Etumba o ZRE (HAU) 210-211 K 4
Ėturerveem ~ RUS 112-113 X 3
Eturnagaram o IND 142-143 B 6
Ėtyrkėn o RUS 122-123 D 3
Etzatlan o MEX 52-53 B 1
Etzikom o CDN (ALB) 232-233 G 6
Etzikom Coulee ⊖ CDN (ALB) 232-233 G 6
'Eua ⌒ TON 184 IV a 2
Euabalong o AUS 180-181 J 2
Euaiki ⌒ TON 184 IV a 2
Euca o BR 62-63 J 4
Eucalipto, El o ROU 76-77 J 6
Euchiniko River ~ CDN (BC) 228-229 K 3
Eucla Basin ⊥ AUS 176-177 H 6
Eucla Motels o AUS 176-177 K 5
Euclid o USA (MN) 270-271 B 3
Euclid o USA (OH) 280-281 E 2
Euclides da Cunha o BR 68-69 J 7
Eucumbene, Lake ⊖ AUS 180-181 K 4
Eudistes, Lac des ⊖ CDN (QUE) 242-243 C 2
Eudora o USA (AR) 276-277 D 7
Eudora o USA (GA) 284-285 G 3
Eudunda o AUS 180-181 E 3
Eufaula o USA (AL) 284-285 E 5
Eufaula o USA (OK) 264-265 J 3
Eufaula Lake ⊖ USA (OK) 264-265 J 3
Eufrasio Loza o RA 76-77 F 5
Eugene o USA (OR) 244-245 B 6
Eugene McDermott Shoal ⌒ AUS 172-173 G 2
Eugênia, Rio da ~ BR 70-71 H 2
Eugowra o AUS 180-181 K 2
Euless o USA (TX) 264-265 G 6
Eulo o AUS 178-179 H 5
Eulogy o USA (TX) 264-265 G 6
Eumara Springs o AUS 174-175 H 6
Eunápolis o BR 72-73 L 4
Eungella o AUS 178-179 K 1
Eungella National Park ⊥ AUS 174-175 K 7
Eunice o USA (LA) 268-269 H 6
Eunice o USA (NM) 256-257 M 6
Eupen o B 92-93 J 3
Euphrat ~ 128-129 L 7
Euphrates = Furāt, al- ~ SYR 128-129 L 7
Eupora o USA (MS) 268-269 L 3
Eura o FIN 88-89 G 6
Eureka o CDN 26-27 H 4
Eureka o USA (CO) 254-255 H 6
Eureka o USA (KS) 262-263 K 7
Eureka o USA (MT) 250-251 D 3
Eureka o USA (NV) 246-247 K 4
Eureka o USA (SD) 260-261 G 1
Eureka o USA (UT) 254-255 C 4
Eureka o USA (WA) 244-245 G 4
Eureka o • USA (CA) 246-247 A 3
Eureka Sound ≈ 26-27 G 3
Eureka Springs o USA (AR) 276-277 B 4
Eurimbula National Park ⊥ AUS 178-179 L 3
Eurinilla Creek ~ AUS 178-179 F 6
Euriowie o AUS 178-179 F 6
Euroa o AUS 180-181 H 4
Euromos • TR 128-129 B 4
Europa, Île ⌒ F 218-219 L 6
Europa, Picos de ⛰ E 98-99 E 3
Europa, Punta ▲ GQ 210-211 B 2
Europoort ⊥ NL 92-93 H 3
Eurotunnel II • 90-91 H 6
Euskadi ■ E 98-99 F 3
Euskadi Pis -Vasco •• E 98-99 F 3
Eustis o USA (FL) 286-287 H 3
Eutaw o USA (AL) 284-285 C 4
Euthini o MW 214-215 G 6
Eutin o • D 92-93 L 1
Eutsuk Lake ⊖ CDN (BC) 228-229 H 3
Eva o USA (AL) 284-285 D 2
Eva o USA (LA) 268-269 J 5
Eva o USA (OK) 264-265 C 2
Eva Broadhurst Lake ⊖ AUS 172-173 F 7
Eva Downs o AUS 174-175 C 6
Evale o ANG 216-217 C 8
Eva-Liv, ostrov ⌒ RUS 84-85 h 2
Evandale o CDN (NB) 240-241 J 5
Evander o ZA 220-221 J 3
Evans o USA (CO) 254-255 L 3
Evans o USA (WA) 244-245 H 2
Evans, Lac ⊖ CDN (QUE) 236-237 L 2
Evans, Mount ▲ USA (MT) 250-251 F 5
Evansburg o CDN (ALB) 232-233 C 2
Evans Island ⌒ USA 20-21 Q 7
Evans Shoal ≃ 166-167 E 6
Evans Strait ≈ 36-37 H 3
Evanston o USA (IL) 274-275 L 2
Evanston o USA (WY) 252-253 H 5
Evansville o CDN (ONT) 238-239 C 3
Evansville o USA (IN) 274-275 L 7
Evansville o USA (WI) 274-275 J 2
Evansville o USA (WY) 252-253 M 4
Evant o USA (TX) 266-267 J 2
Evaro o USA (MT) 250-251 E 4
Evart o USA (MI) 272-273 D 4
Evaton o ZA 220-221 H 3
Eva Valley o AUS 172-173 L 3
Evaz o IR 134-135 E 5
Eveleth o USA (MN) 270-271 F 3
Evelyn o CDN (BC) 228-229 G 2
Evelyn, Mount ▲ AUS 172-173 L 2
Evenk Autonomous District = Ėvenkijskij avtonomnyj okrug ■ RUS 116-117 G 2
Ėvensk ☆ RUS 120-121 S 3
Everard, Lake ⊖ AUS 178-179 C 6
Everard Junction o AUS 176-177 H 2
Everard Ranges ⛰ 176-177 M 3
Everest, Mount ▲ NEP 144-145 F 7
Everett o CDN (NB) 240-241 H 3
Everett o USA (GA) 284-285 J 5
Everett o USA (WA) 244-245 C 3
Everett, Mount ▲ USA (MA) 278-279 H 6
Everett Mountains ⛰ CDN 36-37 Q 3
Everglades, The ⊥ USA (FL) 286-287 J 6
Everglades City o USA (FL) 286-287 H 6
Everglades National Park ⊥ ••• USA (FL) 286-287 J 6
Everglades Reclamation State Historic Site • USA (FL) 286-287 J 5
Evergreen o USA (AL) 284-285 D 5
Evergreen o USA (MN) 270-271 C 4
Evergreen Lake ⊖ USA (IL) 274-275 J 4
Evesham o AUS 178-179 G 2
Evesham o CDN (SAS) 232-233 J 3
Evgen'evka o KA 146-147 C 4
Évia ⌒ GR 100-101 J 5
Evijärvi o FIN 88-89 G 5
Evinayong o GQ 210-211 C 3
Evje ☆ N 86-87 C 7
Evlah = Yevlax o AZ 128-129 M 2
Evodoula o CAM 204-205 J 6
Evōglī o IR 128-129 L 3
Évora o ••• P 98-99 D 5
Évoron o RUS 122-123 G 3
Évoron, ozero ⊖ RUS 122-123 G 3
Évota, gora ▲ RUS 118-119 M 7
Evpatorija = Jevpatorija ☆ • UA 102-103 H 5
Evreinova, mys ▲ RUS 120-121 P 4
Evreinova, proliv ⊖ RUS 122-123 Q 4
Évreux ☆ F 90-91 H 7
Evron o F 90-91 G 7
Évur ~ RUS 122-123 G 3
Évva ~ RUS 88-89 U 5
Ewan o USA (WA) 244-245 H 3
Ewango o WAN 204-205 H 5
Ewarton o JA 54-55 G 5
Ewaso Ngiro ~ EAK (RIF) 212-213 E 4
Ewaso Ngiro ~ EAK 212-213 F 3
Ewasse o PNG 183 F 3
Ewell o USA (MD) 280-281 K 6
Ewing o USA (MO) 274-275 G 4
Ewing o USA (NE) 262-263 H 2
Ewing o USA (NJ) 280-281 M 3
Ewo o RCB 210-211 E 4
Exaltación o BOL (BEN) 70-71 E 3
Exaltación o BOL (PAN) 70-71 D 2
Excell o USA (TX) 264-265 C 3
Excello o USA (MO) 274-275 F 5
Excelsior o ZA 220-221 H 4
Excelsior Springs o USA (MO) 274-275 D 5
Exchamsiks River ~ CDN (BC) 228-229 E 2
Executive Committee Range ⛰ ARK 16 F 24
Exeter o CDN (ONT) 238-239 D 5
Exeter o • GB 90-91 F 6
Exeter o USA (CA) 248-249 E 3
Exeter o USA (NH) 278-279 L 6
Exeter Bay ≈ 28-29 K 3
Exeter Lake ⊖ CDN 30-31 O 3
Exeter Sound ≈ 28-29 K 3
Exira o USA (IA) 274-275 D 3
Exmoor National Park ⊥ GB 90-91 F 6
Exmore o USA (VA) 280-281 L 6
Exmouth o AUS 172-173 B 6
Exmouth Gulf ≈ 172-173 B 7
Exmouth Lake ⊖ CDN 30-31 M 3
Exmouth Plateau ≃ 13 C 4
Expedition National Park ⊥ AUS 178-179 K 3
Expedition Range ⛰ AUS 178-179 K 3
Expedito Lopes Francisco Santos, D. o BR 68-69 H 5
Exploits, Bay of ≈ 38-39 R 4
Exploits, Bay of ≈ CDN 242-243 N 3
Exploits Islands ⌒ CDN (NFL) 242-243 N 3
Exploits River ~ CDN (NFL) 242-243 M 4
Explorer Mountain ▲ USA 22-23 Q 3
Exshaw o CDN (ALB) 232-233 C 4
Exstew o CDN (BC) 228-229 E 2
Extremadura ■ E 98-99 D 5
Extrême Nord = Extreme North ■ CAM 206-207 B 3
Extreme North = Extrême Nord ■ CAM 206-207 B 3
Exu o BR 68-69 J 5
Exuma Cays ⌒ BS 54-55 G 2
Exuma Cays Land and Sea Park • BS 54-55 G 2
Exuma Sound ≈ 54-55 G 2
Eyasi, Lake ⊖ EAT 212-213 E 5
Eyeberry Lake ⊖ CDN 30-31 R 4
Eyebrow o CDN (SAS) 232-233 M 5
Eyehill Creek ~ CDN (SAS) 232-233 J 3
Eye of Kuruman • ZA 220-221 F 3
Eyl o SP 208-209 J 5
Eyota o USA (MN) 270-271 F 7
Eyre o CDN (SAS) 232-233 J 4
Eyre, Seno ≈ 80 C 4
Eyre Creek ~ AUS 178-179 E 3
Eyre Highway II AUS 176-177 H 6
Eyre Mountains ⛰ NZ 182 B 6
Eyre North, Lake ⊖ AUS 178-179 D 5
Eyre Peninsula ⌄ AUS 180-181 C 2
Eyre South, Lake ⊖ AUS 178-179 D 5
Eyumojok o CAM 204-205 H 6
Ezequiel Montes o MEX 52-53 E 1
Ezequiel Ramos Mexia, Embalse < RA 78-79 E 5
Ezere o •• LV 94-95 H 3
Ezernieki o LV 94-95 K 3
Ezgueret ~ RMM 196-197 M 6
Ezhou o VRC 154-155 J 6
Ezibeleni o ZA 220-221 H 5
Ezike, Enugu o WAN 204-205 G 5
Ezine ☆ TR 128-129 B 3
Ezo o SUD 206-207 H 6
Ėzop, gora ▲ RUS 120-121 O 2
Ėžuga ~ RUS 88-89 S 4
Ezzane, In < DZ 192-193 D 6
Ezzangbo o WAN 204-205 G 5
ez-Zhiliga o MA 188-189 H 4

F

Fabens o USA (TX) 266-267 A 2
Faber Lake ⊖ CDN 30-31 L 4
Fåborg o DK 86-87 E 9
Fabriano o I 100-101 D 3
Fabyan o CDN (ALB) 232-233 H 3
Facatativá o CO 60-61 D 5
Fachi o RN 198-199 E 3
Fāchūd o IND 138-139 E 10
Facundo o RA 80 F 2
Fada o TCH 198-199 K 4
Fada-Ngourma o BF 202-203 L 3
Faddeevskij, ostrov ⌒ RUS 110-111 Y 2
Faddeja, ostrova ⌒ RUS 108-109 h 3
Faddeja, zaliv ≈ 108-109 g 3
Faddoi o SUD 206-207 L 4
Faden o CDN 36-37 Q 7
Fadiadougou o CI 202-203 G 5
Fadiffolu Atoll ⌒ MV 140-141 B 5
Fadnoun, Plateau du ⛰ DZ 190-191 G 7
Fadugu o WAL 202-203 E 5
Fa'er o VRC 156-157 D 3
Færingehavn = Kangerluarsoruseq o GRØ 28-29 P 5
Færøerne = Føroyar ⌒ FR 90-91 D 1
Faeroe Shelf ≃ 6-7 J 2
Fafa ~ RCA 206-207 D 5
Fafa o RMM 202-203 L 2
Fafadun o SP 212-213 H 2
Fafakourou o SN 202-203 C 3
Fafen Shet' ~ ETH 208-209 G 5
Făgăraş o • RO 102-103 D 5
Fagatogo ☆ USA 184 V b 2
Fagernes o N 86-87 D 6
Făget o RO 102-103 C 5
Făget, Munţii ⛰ RO 102-103 C 4
Faggo o WAN 204-205 H 3
Fagita o RI 166-167 F 2
Fagnano o Cami, Lago ⊖ RCH 80 F 7
Fago ~ BF 202-203 L 3
Fağr, Wādī ~ KSA 130-131 E 3
Fagrinkotti o SUD 200-201 E 3
Fagudu o RI 164-165 K 4
Faguibine, Lac ⊖ RMM 196-197 H 6
Fagurhólsmýri o IS 86-87 e 3
Fahl, Hassi < DZ 190-191 D 5
Fahliyān, Rūd-e ~ IR 134-135 D 3
Fahreğ o IR 134-135 H 4
Fā'id o ET 194-195 E 2
Faid o TN 190-191 G 3
Faidami, al- o Y 132-133 H 5
Failaka, Ğazirat ⌒ •• KWT 130-131 L 3
Faillon, Lac ⊖ CDN (QUE) 236-237 M 4
Fairān o ET 194-195 F 3
Fairān, Wādī ~ ET 194-195 F 3
Fairbairn Reservoir < AUS 178-179 K 2
Fairbank o USA (MD) 280-281 K 5
Fairbanks o USA (MN) 270-271 G 3
Fairbanks o • USA 20-21 R 4
Fair Bluff o USA (NC) 282-283 H 6
Fairborn o USA (OH) 280-281 B 4
Fairburn o USA (GA) 284-285 F 3
Fairburn o USA (SD) 260-261 C 3
Fairbury o USA (NE) 262-263 J 4
Fair Cape ▲ AUS 174-175 G 3
Fairchild o USA (WI) 270-271 H 6
Fairfax o USA (MN) 270-271 D 6
Fairfax o USA (MO) 274-275 C 4
Fairfax o USA (OK) 264-265 H 2
Fairfax o USA (SC) 284-285 J 4
Fairfax o USA (SD) 260-261 H 3
Fairfax o USA (VA) 280-281 J 5
Fairfield o USA (AL) 284-285 D 3
Fairfield o USA (CA) 246-247 C 5
Fairfield o USA (IA) 274-275 G 4
Fairfield o USA (IA) 274-275 F 4
Fairfield o USA (ID) 252-253 D 3
Fairfield o USA (IL) 274-275 K 6
Fairfield o USA (ME) 278-279 M 4
Fairfield o USA (MT) 250-251 H 4
Fairfield o USA (NC) 282-283 L 5
Fairfield o USA (OH) 280-281 B 4
Fairfield o USA (TX) 266-267 L 2
Fairfield o USA (UT) 254-255 C 3
Fairfield Lake < USA (TX) 266-267 L 2
Fairford o CDN (MAN) 234-235 E 3
Fair Harbour o CDN (BC) 230-231 B 3
Fairhaven o CDN (NFL) 242-243 P 5
Fair Haven o USA (VT) 278-279 H 5
Fairhill o AUS 178-179 K 2
Fairholme o CDN (SAS) 232-233 K 2
Fairhope o USA (AL) 284-285 C 6
Fair Isle ⌒ GB 90-91 G 2
Fairlie o NZ 182 C 6
Fairlight o CDN (SAS) 232-233 R 6
Fairmont o USA (MN) 270-271 D 7
Fairmont o USA (NC) 282-283 H 6
Fairmont o USA (NE) 262-263 J 4
Fairmont o USA (WV) 280-281 F 4
Fairmont Hot Springs o CDN (BC) 230-231 O 3
Fairmount o CDN (SAS) 232-233 J 4
Fairmount o USA (GA) 284-285 F 2
Fairmount o USA (IN) 274-275 N 4
Fair Ness ▲ CDN 36-37 N 3
Fairo o WAL 202-203 E 6
Fair Oaks o USA (AR) 276-277 D 5
Fairoaks o USA (AR) 276-277 E 5
Fairplay o USA (CO) 254-255 J 4
Fair Play o USA (MO) 276-277 B 3
Fairplay, Mount ▲ USA 20-21 T 5
Fairview o AUS 174-175 H 4
Fairview o CDN 32-33 L 3
Fairview o USA (AL) 284-285 D 5
Fairview o USA (CA) 248-249 F 4
Fairview o USA (KS) 262-263 L 5
Fairview o USA (MI) 272-273 E 3
Fairview o USA (MT) 250-251 P 4
Fairview o USA (OK) 264-265 F 2
Fairview o USA (TN) 276-277 H 5
Fairview o USA (TX) 264-265 C 6
Fairview o USA (UT) 254-255 D 4
Fairview o USA (WY) 252-253 H 4
Fairview Peak ▲ USA (OR) 244-245 C 7
Fairweather, Cape ▲ USA 32-33 A 2
Fairweather, Mount ▲ USA 32-33 B 2
Fairy o USA (TX) 266-267 K 2
Fairy, Port o AUS 180-181 G 5
Fairy Glen o CDN (SAS) 232-233 O 2
Faisalābād o PK 138-139 D 4
Faisaliya, al- o KSA 132-133 B 3
Faith o USA (SD) 260-261 D 1
Faiyiba o SUD 200-201 E 5
Faizabad ☆ AFG 136-137 M 6
Faizābād o IND 142-143 C 2
Fajaghalia o SOL 184 I d 3
Fajardo o USA (PR) 286-287 Q 2
Faje o WAN 204-205 F 4
Fakenham o GB 90-91 H 5
Fakfak o RI 166-167 G 3
Fakfak, Pegunungan ⛰ RI 166-167 G 3
Fako ▲ CAM 204-205 H 6
Fakse Bugt ≈ 86-87 F 9
Fak Tha o THA 158-159 F 2
Faku o VRC 150-151 D 6
Fala ~ RMM 202-203 H 2
Falaba o WAL 202-203 E 5
Falagountou o BF 202-203 L 2
Falaise o F 90-91 G 7
Falaise Lake ⊖ CDN 30-31 L 5
Falam ☆ MYA 142-143 H 4
Falaq, Bi'r < IRQ 128-129 J 5
Falāvarğān o IR 134-135 D 2
Falcão o BR 68-69 E 6
Falcon o USA (CO) 254-255 L 5
Falcon o USA (TX) 266-267 H 7
Falcón, Fiordo ≈ 80 C 4
Falcón, Presa < MEX 50-51 K 4
Falcon Lake o CDN (MAN) 234-235 H 5
Falda, La o RA 76-77 E 6
Faléa o RMM 202-203 E 3
Faleālupouta o WS 184 V a 1
Faleāpuna o WS 184 V b 1
Falémé ~ SN 202-203 E 3
Falenki ☆ RUS 96-97 G 4
Falfurrias o USA (TX) 266-267 J 6
Falima ~ WAL 202-203 E 5
Fali Mountains ⛰ WAN 204-205 J 5
Falkat ~ ER 200-201 J 4
Falkenberg ☆ • S 86-87 F 8
Falkenberg (Elster) o D 92-93 M 3
Falkland o CDN (BC) 230-231 K 3
Falkland o USA (NC) 282-283 K 5
Falkland Escarpment ≃ 6-7 E 13
Falkland Islands ⌒ GB 78-79 L 6
Falkland Plateau ≃ 6-7 D 14
Falkland Sound ≈ 78-79 K 7
Falköping ☆ S 86-87 F 7
Falkville o USA (AL) 284-285 D 2
Fallaize Lake ⊖ CDN 24-25 K 6
Fall City o USA (WA) 244-245 D 3
Fall Creek o USA (OR) 244-245 C 7
Fallentimber Creek ~ CDN (ALB) 232-233 C 4
Fallis o CDN (ALB) 232-233 D 2
Fall Line Hills ⛰ USA (AL) 284-285 B 2
Fallon o USA (MT) 250-251 O 5
Fallon o USA (NV) 246-247 G 4
Fallon o USA (WA) 244-245 H 4
Fall River o USA (MA) 278-279 K 7
Fall River ~ USA (KS) 262-263 L 7
Fall River Lake ⊖ USA (KS) 262-263 K 7
Fall River Mills o USA (CA) 246-247 D 2
Fallsburg o USA (OH) 280-281 D 3
Falls City o USA (NE) 262-263 L 5
Falls Creek o • AUS 180-181 J 4
Falls Creek o CDN (BC) 230-231 H 3
Falls Lake Reservoir ⊖ USA (NC) 282-283 J 4
Fallūğa, al- ☆ IRQ 128-129 K 6
Falmey o RN 204-205 E 2
Falmouth o • GB 90-91 E 6
Falmouth o JA 54-55 G 5
Falmouth o USA (KY) 276-277 L 2
Falmouth o USA (MA) 278-279 L 7
Falou o RMM (BAM) 202-203 G 2
Falou o RMM (SIK) 202-203 G 3
Falsa, Bahía ≈ 78-79 H 5
Falsa Calera, Punta ▲ RCH 78-79 C 5
False, Rivière ~ CDN 36-37 P 6
False Bay ≈ 220-221 D 7
False Bay o CDN (BC) 230-231 E 4
False Cape ▲ USA (DE) 280-281 L 5
False Pass o USA 22-23 P 5
False Point ▲ IND 142-143 E 5
Falsino, Rio ~ BR 62-63 J 5
Falso, Cabo ▲ HN 54-55 D 7
Falso Cabo de Hornos ▲ RCH 80 F 7
Falso ÓP. Aguja, Cabo ▲ DOM 54-55 K 6
Falster ⌒ DK 86-87 E 9
Falsterselv ~ GRØ 26-27 n 8
Falterona, Monte ▲ I 100-101 C 3
Falun o CDN (ALB) 232-233 E 3
Falun o S 86-87 G 6
Fam = Fafa ~ RCA 206-207 D 5
Fam, Kepulauan ⌒ RI 166-167 F 2
Fama o SUD 206-207 K 3
Fama, Ouidi ~ TCH 198-199 K 5
Famaillá o RA 76-77 E 4
Famalé o RN 202-203 L 2
Fāmanin o IR 128-129 N 5
Fāmarin o IR 134-135 C 1
Famatina, Sierra de ⛰ RA 76-77 D 5
Fambusi o GH 202-203 K 4
Famen Si • VRC 154-155 E 4
Fame Range ⛰ AUS 176-177 G 2
Family Lake ⊖ CDN (MAN) 234-235 G 3
Fana o RMM 202-203 G 3
Fanado, Rio ~ BR 72-73 J 4
Fanambana o RM (ASA) 222-223 F 4
Fanambana ~ RM 222-223 F 4
Fanār Qaşr Ahmad o LAR 192-193 F 1
Fanchang o VRC 154-155 L 6
Fandango Pass ⛰ USA (CA) 246-247 E 2
Fandriana o RM 222-223 E 8
Fang o THA 142-143 L 6
Fangak o SUD 206-207 K 4
Fangamadou o RG 202-203 E 5
Fangcheng o VRC (GXI) 156-157 F 6
Fangcheng o VRC (HEN) 154-155 H 5
Fangliao o RC 156-157 M 5
Fang Xian o VRC 154-155 G 5
Fangzheng o VRC 150-151 G 5
Fanjingshan • VRC 156-157 F 3
Fanjingshan z.B. ⊥ • VRC 156-157 F 3
Fannin o USA (MS) 268-269 L 4
Fannin ~ USA (TX) 266-267 K 5
Fanning River o AUS 174-175 J 6
Fanny Bay o CDN (BC) 230-231 E 4
Fannystelle o CDN (MAN) 234-235 F 5
Fanø ⌒ DK 86-87 D 9
Fano o I 100-101 D 3
Fanshi o VRC 154-155 H 2
Fanti o LB 202-203 F 6
Fantomes, Trou des = Phantoms Cave • CAM 210-211 C 2
Fanūğ o IR 134-135 H 5
Fan Xian o VRC 154-155 J 4
Fanxue o VRC 154-155 E 3
Fão o BR 74-75 D 7
Fao, Koun- o CI 202-203 J 6
Faouët, le o F 90-91 F 7
Faq', al- o UAE 134-135 F 6
Faqih Soleimān o IR 128-129 M 5
Fāqūs o ET 194-195 E 2
Faraba o RMM 202-203 E 3
Farab-Pristan' = Džejhun o TM 136-137 H 5
Faraday Fracture Zone ≃ 6-7 F 4
Faradje o ZRE 212-213 B 2
Farafangana o RM 222-223 E 9
Farafara Oasis = Farāfira, al-Wāḥāt al- ⊥ ET 194-195 D 4
Farafenni o WAG 202-203 C 3
Farāfira, al-Wāḥāt al- ⊥ ET 194-195 C 4
Faragouaran o RMM 202-203 G 4
Farāh ■ AFG 134-135 J 2
Farāh ☆ AFG (FA) 134-135 K 2
Farahābād o IND 140-141 H 2
Farahalana o RM 222-223 G 5
Farahnāze, Bandar-e o IR 128-129 N 4
Farāhrūd o AFG 134-135 K 2
Farāh Rūd ~ AFG 134-135 K 2
Farakaraina, Corniche de • RM 222-223 F 5
Farako o RMM 202-203 G 4
Farallones de Cali, Parque Nacional ⊥ CO 60-61 C 6
Faramana o BF 202-203 H 3
Faramuti < SUD 206-207 H 3
Faranah ■ RG 202-203 E 4
Faranah ☆ RG 202-203 E 4
Faraony ~ RM 222-223 E 8
Far'aoun < RIM 196-197 D 5
Farasān o KSA 132-133 C 5
Farasān, Ğazā'ir ⌒ KSA 132-133 B 5
Farasān, Ğazirat ⌒ KSA 132-133 B 5
Faratsiho o RM 222-223 E 7
Farda, al- o Y 132-133 F 6
Farda, Naqil al- ▲ Y 132-133 D 6
Farewell o USA 20-21 O 5
Farewell, Cape ▲ NZ 182 D 4
Fargha ~ SUD 200-201 G 6
Fargo o USA (GA) 284-285 H 6
Fargo o USA (ND) 258-259 L 5
Fargo o USA (OK) 264-265 E 2
Farğār o AFG 136-137 L 6
farhar ai o EAU 212-213 D 3
Fari o RMM 202-203 E 3
Farias Brito o BR 68-69 J 5
Faribault o USA (MN) 270-271 E 6
Faribault, Lac ⊖ CDN 36-37 O 5
Farīdābād o IND 138-139 F 5
Faridkot o IND 138-139 E 4
Faridpur o BD 142-143 F 4

Farié ○ RN 202-203 L 3
Fārigh, Wādi al ~ LAR 192-193 G 5
Fārigh, Wādi al ~ LAR 192-193 H 2
Farim ○ GNB 202-203 C 3
Farimān ○ IR 136-137 F 7
Farina ○ USA (IL) 274-275 K 6
Farinha, Cachoeira da ~ BR 66-67 H 6
Farinha, Rio ~ BR 68-69 E 5
Fariš ○ US 136-137 K 4
Färjestaden ○ S 86-87 H 8
Farka ○ RN 204-205 E 1
Fārkawn ○ IND 142-143 H 4
Farley ○ USA (NM) 256-257 L 2
Farmer ○ USA (WA) 244-245 F 3
Farmer City ○ USA (IL) 274-275 K 4
Farmer Island ⌒ CDN 36-37 J 5
Farmersburg ○ USA (IN) 274-275 L 5
Farmersville ○ USA (IL) 274-275 J 5
Farmersville ○ USA (TX) 264-265 H 5
Farmerville ○ USA (LA) 268-269 H 4
Farmington ○ USA (CA) 248-249 D 2
Farmington ○ USA (IA) 274-275 G 4
Farmington ○ USA (IL) 274-275 H 4
Farmington ○ USA (ME) 278-279 L 4
Farmington ○ USA (MO) 276-277 E 3
Farmington ○ USA (NM) 256-257 G 2
Farmington ○ USA (UT) 254-255 D 3
Farmland ○ USA (IN) 274-275 N 4
Farmoreah ○ RG 202-203 D 5
Far Mountain ▲ CDN (BC) 228-229 J 4
Farmville ○ USA (NC) 282-283 K 5
Farmville ○ USA (VA) 280-281 H 6
Farnam ○ USA (NE) 262-263 F 4
Farnham ○ CDN (QUE) 238-239 N 3
Farnham, Lake ○ AUS 176-177 J 2
Farnham, Mount ▲ CDN (BC) 230-231 N 3
Far Northern Section ⊥ AUS 174-175 G 3
Faro ○ BR 66-67 J 4
Faro ~ CAM 204-205 K 4
Faro ○ CDN 20-21 Y 5
Faro ○• P 98-99 D 6
Faro, El ○ MEX 50-51 B 1
Faro, le ○ CAM 204-205 K 5
Faro, Réserve du ⊥ CAM 204-205 K 4
Faroe Bank ≃ 90-91 C 1
Faroe Islands = Føroyar ⌒ FR 90-91 D 1
Faroe Shelf ≃ 6-7 J 2
Farofa, Serra da ▲ BR 74-75 E 7
Farol, Ilha do ⌒ BR 68-69 L 3
Farol das Canárias ○ BR 68-69 H 3
Farol Guará ○ BR 62-63 K 5
Fårösund ○ S 86-87 J 8
Farquhar Atoll ⌒ SY 224 B 5
Farquhar Group ⌒ SY 224 B 4
Farquharson, Mount ▲ AUS 172-173 K 4
Farquharson Tableland ∴ AUS 176-177 G 3
Farrand, Cape ▲ CDN 24-25 Z 5
Farrars Creek ~ AUS 178-179 G 3
Farrāšband ○ IR 134-135 E 4
Farras Creek ~ AUS 178-179 F 3
Farroupilha ○ BR 74-75 E 7
Farrukhābād ○ IND 138-139 G 6
Farrukhnagar ○ IND 140-141 H 2
Fārs ■ IR 134-135 D 4
Fārs, Ḫalīğ-e • IR 134-135 C 4
Farša, al- ○ KSA 132-133 C 5
Fársala ○ GR 100-101 J 5
Fārsān ○ IR 134-135 D 2
Fārsi ⌒ IR 134-135 D 5
Farson ○ USA (WY) 252-253 J 4
Fartak, Ra's ▲ Y 132-133 H 6
Fartura, Serra da ▲ BR 74-75 D 6
Fārūğ ○ IR 136-137 F 6
Faruraq ○ IR 128-129 L 3
Farvel, Kap = Ummannarsuaq ▲ GRØ 28-29 T 7
Farwell ○ USA (TX) 264-265 B 4
Fāryāb ■ AFG 136-137 J 7
Fasā ○ IR 134-135 E 4
Fasad ○ OM 132-133 H 4
Fašam ○ IR 136-137 B 7
Fasama ○ LB 202-203 F 6
Fasano ○ I 100-101 F 4
Fås Boye ○ SN 202-203 B 2
Faserwood ○ CDN (MAN) 234-235 F 4
Fashe ○ WAN 204-205 F 4
Fashola ○ WAN 204-205 E 5
Fasil Ghebbi ••• ETH 200-201 H 6
Fask ○ MA 188-189 G 6
Fassala Néré ○ RIM 196-197 H 7
Fassanu ○ LAR 192-193 E 2
Fassélémon ○ CI 202-203 H 5
Fašt, Ğazirat ⌒ KSA 132-133 C 5
Fašt al-Ğārim ⌒ KSA 134-135 D 5
Fāste, Ra's-e ▲ IR 134-135 J 6
Fastiv ○ UA 102-103 F 2
Fastov = Fastiv ○ UA 102-103 F 2
Fatagar-Tuting, Tanjung ▲ RI 166-167 F 3
Fataki ○ ZRE 212-213 C 2
Fatao ○ RMM 202-203 F 2
Fatehābād ○ IND 138-139 E 5
Fatehjang ○ PK 138-139 D 3
Fatehpur ○ IND 142-143 B 3
Fatehpur ○ PK 138-139 C 4
Fatehpur Sikri ○••• IND 138-139 F 6
Fatepur ○ BD 142-143 G 3
Fatež ○ RUS 94-95 O 5
Fatḥ, al- ○ OM 132-133 K 2
Fatha ○ IRQ 128-129 K 5
Fathom Five National Marine Park ⊥ CDN (ONT) 238-239 D 3
Fati, Lac ○ RMM 196-197 J 6
Fatiba < RMM 202-203 G 2
Fatick ☆ SN 202-203 B 2
Fátima ○• P 98-99 C 5
Fāṭima, Bi'r < IRQ 128-129 K 5
Fatima de Sul ○ BR 76-77 K 2
Fatine ○ RMM 202-203 H 3
Fatitet ○ SUD 206-207 K 5
Fat'janiha ~ RUS 114-115 U 2
Fat'janiha, Bol'šaja ~ RUS 114-115 U 3
Fatki ~ BD 142-143 F 4
Fatolulik ○ RI 166-167 C 6
Fatsa ☆ TR 128-129 G 2
Fatujuring (Village of pearl trade) ○•• RI 166-167 H 5
Faturna ○ ZRE 214-215 E 4
Fatunda ○ ZRE 210-211 F 6
Fatural ○ RI 166-167 H 5
Faucett ○ USA (MO) 274-275 D 5
Faulkner ○ CDN (MAN) 234-235 E 3
Faulkton ○ USA (SD) 260-261 G 1
Faunce ○ USA (MN) 270-271 D 2
Fauquier ○ CDN (BC) 230-231 L 4
Faure Island ⌒ AUS 176-177 B 2
Fauresmith ○ ZA 220-221 G 4
Fauro Island ⌒ SOL 184 I c 2
Fauske ○ N 86-87 G 3
Faux Cap = Betanty ○ RM 222-223 D 10
Favignana ○ I 100-101 D 6
Fāw, al- ☆ IRQ 130-131 L 3
Fawcett ○ CDN 32-33 N 4
Fawcett Lake ○ CDN (ONT) 234-235 M 3
Fawnie Range ▲ CDN (BC) 228-229 J 3
Fawnleas ○ ZA 220-221 K 4
Fawn Point ▲ USA 22-23 P 5
Fawn River ~ CDN 34-35 M 3
Fawwāra, al- ○ KSA 130-131 H 4
Faxaflói ≈ 86-87 b 2
Faxälven ~ S 86-87 H 5
Faxinal ○ BR 74-75 E 5
Faxinal do Soturno ○ BR 74-75 D 7
Faya ~ RMM 202-203 G 3
Faya = Largeau ☆ TCH 198-199 J 4
Fayala ○ ZRE 210-211 F 5
Fayette ○ USA (AL) 284-285 C 3
Fayette ○ USA (MO) 274-275 F 5
Fayette ○ USA (MS) 268-269 J 5
Fayette ○ USA (ND) 258-259 E 4
Fayette ○ USA (OH) 280-281 B 2
Fayette, La ○ USA (GA) 284-285 E 2
Fayetteville ○ USA (AR) 276-277 A 4
Fayetteville ○ USA (GA) 284-285 F 3
Fayetteville ○ USA (IL) 274-275 J 6
Fayetteville ○ USA (NC) 282-283 J 5
Fayetteville ○ USA (OH) 280-281 C 4
Fayetteville ○ USA (TN) 276-277 J 5
Fayhān, Wādi ~ KSA 130-131 H 3
Faysal, Wādi ~ LAR 192-193 E 2
Faywood ○ USA (NM) 256-257 G 6
Fāz ☆••• MA 188-189 J 3
Fazao ○ RT 202-203 L 5
Fazao, Monts du ▲ RT 202-203 L 5
Fazao Malfakassa, Parc National de ⊥ RT 202-203 L 5
Fazei < RN 198-199 E 3
Fazenda Boa Esperanza ○ BR 62-63 D 6
Fazenda Bradesco ○ BR 68-69 D 3
Fazenda Cumaru ○ BR 68-69 C 5
Fazenda Eldorado ○ BR 70-71 J 5
Fazenda Foz do Christalino ○ BR 72-73 E 2
Fazenda Gavião ○ BR 68-69 E 6
Fazenda Itanorte ○ BR 70-71 J 4
Fazenda Muraquitā ○ BR 70-71 G 2
Fazenda Narciso ○ BR 66-67 D 2
Fazenda Primavera ○ BR 68-69 B 7
Fazenda Remanso ○ BR 66-67 J 4
Fazenda Rio Dourado ○ BR 68-69 C 6
Fazenda Rio Limpo ○ BR 68-69 F 7
Fazenda Santa Lúcia ○ BR 70-71 K 5
Fazenda São Sebastião ○ BR 70-71 E 2
Fazenda Taboco ○ BR 70-71 K 7
Fazenda Três Irmãos ○ BR 70-71 K 5
Fazenda Vista Alegre ○ BR 66-67 G 7
Fazilpur ○ PK 138-139 C 5
Fdérik ☆ RIM 196-197 D 3
Fé, La ○ C 54-55 D 4
Fear, Cape ▲ USA (NC) 282-283 K 7
Feather Falls ○ USA (CA) 246-247 D 4
Featherston ○ NZ 182 E 4
Feathertop, Mount ▲ AUS 180-181 J 4
Featherville ○ USA (ID) 252-253 C 3
Fécamp ○ F 90-91 H 7
Federal ○ RA 76-77 H 6
Federal Capital ■ RA 78-79 K 3
Federal Capital Territory ■ WAN 204-205 G 4
Federalsburg ○ USA (MD) 280-281 L 5
Fedjour, Col de ▲ DZ 190-191 F 2
Fedorovka ○ KA (KST) 124-125 D 1
Fedorovka ○ KA (KST) 124-125 C 2
Fedorovka ☆ KA (ZPK) 96-97 H 8
Fedorovka ☆ RUS 96-97 J 7
Fedotova kosa ~ UA 102-103 J 4
Feestone ○ USA (CA) 246-247 B 5
Féfiné, Rio ~ GNB 202-203 D 4
Fegoh, Wādi ~ ET 194-195 G 6
Fegoussi, Bir < TN 190-191 G 4
Fehmarn ⌒ D 92-93 L 1
Feia, Lagoa ○ BR 72-73 K 6
Feidh el Botma ○ DZ 190-191 D 3
Feidong ○ VRC 154-155 K 6
Feijó ○ BR 66-67 B 7
Feilai Xia • VRC 156-157 H 5
Feilding ○ NZ 182 E 4
Feio ou Aguapei, Rio ~ BR 72-73 E 6
Feira de Santana ○ BR 72-73 L 2
Feitok ○ CAM 204-205 H 6
Feixi ○ VRC 154-155 K 6
Fei Xian ○ VRC 154-155 K 4
Feizābād ○ IR 134-135 H 1
Feke ☆ TR 128-129 F 4
Feklistova, ostrov ⌒ RUS 120-121 G 6
Felaou < DZ 198-199 B 3
Felch Mountain ○ USA (MI) 270-271 L 4
Feldberg ▲•• D 92-93 J 5
Feldioara ○• RO 102-103 D 5
Feldkirch ○ A 92-93 K 5
Felege Neway ○ ETH 208-209 C 6
Felguera, La ○ E 98-99 E 3
Feliciano, Arroyo ~ RA 76-77 H 6
Félicité Island ⌒ SY 224 D 2
Felidu Atoll ⌒ MV 140-141 B 6
Felinto Müller ○ BR 68-69 E 4
Felipe, San ~ USA (CA) 248-249 H 6
Felipe Carillo Puerto ○• MEX 52-53 K 2
Felix, Cape ▲ CDN 24-25 X 6
Felix, Rio ~ USA (NM) 256-257 L 5
Felixburg ○ ZW 218-219 F 4
Felixlândia ○ BR 72-73 H 5
Felixstowe ○ GB 90-91 H 6
Felizardo ○ BR 68-69 J 5
Fellfoot Point ▲ CDN 24-25 b 3
Fellsmere ○ USA (FL) 286-287 J 4
Félou, Chutes de ~• RMM 202-203 E 2
Felps ○ USA (LA) 268-269 K 6
Felsenthal, Lake < USA (AR) 276-277 C 7
Felton ○ USA (MN) 270-271 B 3
Feltre ○ I 100-101 C 1
Fêmeas, Rio das ~ BR 72-73 H 2
Femund ○ N 86-87 E 5
Femundsmarka nationalpark ⊥ N 86-87 F 5
Fence Lake ○ USA (NM) 256-257 G 4
Fenelon Falls ○ CDN (ONT) 238-239 G 4
Fener Burnu ▲ TR 128-129 H 2
Feng'an ○ VRC 156-157 J 5
Fengcheng ○ VRC (JXI) 156-157 J 2
Fengcheng ○ VRC (LIA) 150-151 E 7
Fengdu ○ VRC 156-157 E 2
Fenggang ○ VRC 156-157 E 3
Fenghua ○ VRC 156-157 M 2
Fenghuang ○ VRC (GDG) 156-157 K 5
Fenghuang ○ VRC (HUB) 154-155 J 6
Fenghuang ○ VRC (HUN) 156-157 F 3
Fenghuangshan • VRC 150-151 E 7
Fengjie ○ VRC 154-155 F 6
Fengkang ○ RC 156-157 M 5
Fengliang ○ VRC 156-157 K 5
Fengling Guan ▲ VRC 156-157 L 2
Fengling Z.B. ⊥• VRC 150-151 G 3
Fengning ○ VRC 148-149 N 7
Fengpin ○ RC 156-157 M 5
Fengpo ○ VRC 156-157 E 5
Fengqiu ○ VRC 154-155 J 4
Fengrun ○ VRC 154-155 L 2
Fengshan ○ RC 156-157 M 5
Fengshan ○ VRC 156-157 E 4
Fengshui Shan ▲ VRC 150-151 D 1
Fengshun ○ VRC 156-157 K 5
Fengtongzhai Giant panda Reserves ⊥ VRC 154-155 C 6
Fengtou SK ~ VRC 156-157 F 2
Fengxian ○ VRC 154-155 M 6
Feng Xian ○ VRC (JIA) 154-155 K 4
Feng Xian ○ VRC (SXI) 154-155 E 5
Fengxiang ○ VRC 154-155 E 4
Fengxin ○ VRC 156-157 J 2
Fengxue Si • VRC 154-155 H 4
Fengyang ○ VRC 154-155 K 5
Fengyuan ○ RC 156-157 M 4
Fengzhen ○ VRC 154-155 H 1
Feni ○ BD 142-143 G 4
Feniak Lake ○ USA 20-21 L 2
Feni Islands ⌒ PNG 183 G 3
Fênix ○ BR 72-73 E 7
Fennimore ○ USA (WI) 274-275 H 2
Fennville ○ USA (MI) 272-273 C 5
Fenoarivo Atsinanana ○ RM 222-223 F 6
Fenoarivo Be ○ RM 222-223 E 7
Fenshui Guan ▲ VRC 156-157 K 3
Fenton ○ CDN (SAS) 232-233 N 3
Fenton ○ USA (IA) 274-275 D 1
Fenton ○ USA (LA) 268-269 H 6
Fenton ○ USA (MI) 272-273 F 5
Fenwood ○ CDN (SAS) 232-233 P 4
Fenyang ○ VRC 154-155 G 3
Feodosija ☆• UA 102-103 J 5
Feodosijs'ka zatoka ≈ 102-103 J 5
Ferapontovo ○ RUS 94-95 Q 2
Ferdé < RIM 196-197 C 6
Ferdinand ○ USA (IN) 274-275 M 6
Ferdjioua ○ DZ 190-191 E 2
Ferdo, Le ∴ SN 202-203 C 2
Ferdous ○ IR 134-135 H 1
Fereidūnkenār ○ IR 136-137 C 6
Fereidūn Šahr ○ IR 134-135 D 2
Fērfēr ○ ETH 208-209 G 6
Fergana ☆ US 136-137 M 4
Ferganskaja dolina ∴ US 136-137 M 4
Ferganskaja oblast ■ US 136-137 M 4
Ferganskij hrebet ▲ KS 136-137 N 4
Fergus ○ CDN (ONT) 238-239 E 5
Fergus Falls ○ USA (MN) 270-271 B 4
Ferguson ○ CDN (BC) 230-231 M 3
Ferguson Lake ○ CDN (NWT) 24-25 T 6
Ferguson Lake ○ CDN (NWT) 30-31 V 4
Ferguson Lake ○ USA (CA) 248-249 K 7
Ferguson River ~ CDN 30-31 X 4
Fergusson Island ⌒ PNG 183 F 5
Fergusson River ○ AUS 172-173 K 3
Feriana ○ TN 190-191 G 3
Ferintosh ○ CDN (ALB) 232-233 F 3
Ferkessédougou ☆ CI 202-203 H 5
Ferland ○ CDN (ONT) 234-235 P 4
Ferland ○ CDN (QUE) 240-241 E 2
Ferland ○ CDN (SAS) 232-233 M 6
Ferlo, Vallée du ~ SN 202-203 C 2
Ferma ○ LT 94-95 J 4
Fermeuse ○ CDN (NFL) 242-243 Q 6
Fermoselle ○ E 98-99 D 4
Fermoy = Mainistir Fhear Maí ○ IRL 90-91 C 5
Fernandez Bay ∴• BS 54-55 H 2
Fernandina, Isla ⌒ EC 64-65 B 10
Fernandina Beach ○ USA (FL) 286-287 H 1
Fernando de Magallanes, Parque Nacional ⊥ RCH 80 D 6
Fernando de Noronha, Ilha ⌒ BR 68-69 L 1
Fernandópolis ○ BR 72-73 E 6
Fernando Prestes ○ BR 72-73 F 6
Fernane, Djebel ▲ DZ 190-191 E 3
Fernan Vaz = Lagune Nkomi ○ G 210-211 B 4
Fernão Veloso ○ MOC 218-219 L 2
Ferndale ○ USA (CA) 246-247 A 3
Ferndale ○ USA (WA) 244-245 C 2
Fernie ○ CDN (BC) 230-231 O 4
Fernley ○ USA (NV) 246-247 F 4
Ferokh ○ IND 140-141 F 5
Ferrara ☆• I 100-101 C 2
Ferreira ○ ZA 220-221 H 4
Ferreira do Alentejo ○ P 98-99 C 5
Ferreira Gomes ○ BR 62-63 J 5
Ferreñafe ○ PE 64-65 C 5
Ferriday ○ USA (LA) 268-269 J 5
Ferris ○ USA (TX) 264-265 H 6
Ferro, Corredeira do ~• BR 72-73 D 7
Ferro, Rio ~ BR 70-71 K 3
Ferrol ○ E 98-99 C 3
Ferrol, Isla ⌒ PE 64-65 C 6
Ferron ○ USA (UT) 254-255 D 4
Ferryland ○ CDN (NFL) 242-243 Q 5
Feršampenuaz ☆ RUS 96-97 L 7
Ferté-Bernard, la ○ F 90-91 H 7
Fértil, Valle ~ RA 76-77 D 6
Fertile ○ CDN (SAS) 232-233 R 6
Fertile ○ USA (IA) 274-275 E 1
Fertile ○ USA (MN) 270-271 B 3
Fès = Fāz ☆••• MA 188-189 J 3
Fès = Fāz ☆••• MA 188-189 J 3
Feshi ○ ZRE 216-217 E 3
Fessenden ○ USA (ND) 258-259 H 4
Fessi, Oued ~ TN 190-191 H 4
Festus ○ USA (MO) 274-275 H 6
Fet Dome, Tanjung ▲ RI 166-167 E 2
Fété Bowé ○ SN 202-203 D 2
Fetești ○ RO 102-103 F 5
Fethiye ☆• TR 128-129 C 4
Fetisovo ○ KA 126-127 K 6
Fetlar ⌒ GB 90-91 G 1
Feudal ○ CDN (SAS) 232-233 L 4
Feuilles, Lac aux ○ CDN 36-37 P 5
Feuilles, Rivière aux ~ CDN 36-37 O 5
Feurs ○ F 90-91 K 9
Fevral'sk ○ RUS 122-123 D 2
Fezna ⌒ MA 188-189 J 5
Fezzan = Fazzān ∴ LAR 192-193 D 5
Fezzane, Emi ▲ RN 198-199 G 2
F.G. Villarreal ○ MEX 50-51 L 5
Fiadanana ○ RM 222-223 E 7
Fiambalá ○ RA 76-77 D 4
Fiambala, Río ~ RA 76-77 D 4
Fian ○ GH 202-203 J 4
Fianarantsoa ■ RM 222-223 D 8
Fianarantsoa ☆• RM (Fns) 222-223 E 8
Fianga ○ TCH 206-207 B 4
Fiatt ○ USA (IL) 274-275 H 4
Fiché ○ ETH 208-209 D 4
Fichot Islands ○ CDN (NFL) 242-243 N 1
Fichtelgebirge ▲ D 92-93 L 3
Ficksburg ○ ZA 220-221 H 4
Fidenza ○• I 100-101 C 2
Field ○ CDN (BC) 230-231 N 2
Field ○ CDN (ONT) 238-239 E 2
Field ○ USA (NM) 256-257 M 4
Fielding ○ CDN (SAS) 232-233 L 3
Fielding ○ USA (UT) 254-255 C 2
Fields ○ USA (OR) 244-245 G 8
Fields Peak ▲ USA (OR) 244-245 F 6
Fier ☆•• AL 100-101 G 4
Fierenana ○ RM 222-223 D 7
Fiery Creek ~ AUS 174-175 E 6
Fierzë, Liqeni i ~ AL 100-101 H 3
Fifa ○ RG 202-203 F 4
Fife ○ USA (TX) 266-267 H 2
Fife ○ USA (WA) 244-245 C 3
Fife Lake ○ CDN (SAS) 232-233 N 6
Fife Lake ○ USA (MI) 272-273 D 3
Fifinda ○ CAM 210-211 C 2
Figeac ○ F 90-91 J 9
Figtree ○ ZW 218-219 E 5
Figueira da Foz ○ P 98-99 C 4
Figueira de Castelo Rodrigo ○ P 98-99 D 4
Figueira Torta ○ BR 74-75 D 9
Figueres ○ E 98-99 J 3
Figueroa, Bañado de ~ RA 76-77 F 4
Figuig ○ MA 188-189 L 4
Figuil ○ CAM 204-205 K 4
Fiherenana ~ RM 222-223 D 9
Fiji ■ FJI 184 III b 3
Fiji Islands ⌒ FJI 184 III a 2
Fik' ○ ETH 208-209 F 4
Fika ○ WAN 204-205 J 3
Filabres, Sierra de los ▲ E 98-99 F 6
Filabusi ○ ZW 218-219 E 5
Filadelfia ○ BOL 70-71 C 2
Filadélfia ○ BR (BAH) 68-69 H 7
Filadélfia ○ BR (TOC) 68-69 E 5
Filadélfia ○ CR 52-53 B 6
Filadelfia ○ PE 70-71 C 3
Filamane ○ RMM 202-203 G 4
Filchner-Schelfeis ⊂ ARK 16 E 30
Filer ○ USA (ID) 252-253 D 4
Filiaşi ○ RO 102-103 C 5
Filiatrá ○ GR 100-101 H 6
Filicudi, Ísola ⌒ I 100-101 E 5
Filim ○ OM 132-133 L 3
Filingué ○ RN 204-205 E 1
Filippova ~ RUS 112-113 L 2
Filipstad ☆ S 86-87 G 7
Filiya ○ WAN 204-205 J 4
Fillmore ○ CDN (SAS) 232-233 P 6
Fillmore ○ USA (CA) 248-249 F 5
Fillmore ○ USA (IL) 274-275 J 5
Fillmore ○ USA (MI) 272-273 C 5
Fillmore ○ USA (ND) 258-259 H 3
Fillmore ○ USA (UT) 254-255 C 5
Filomena ○ RP 160-161 D 4
Filtu ○ ETH 208-209 E 6
Filuo ○ SOL 184 I d 2
Fimi ~ ZRE 210-211 F 5
Fin ○ IR 134-135 F 5
Fina, Réserve de ⊥ RMM 202-203 F 3
Finca 7 ○ CR 52-53 C 7
Finca de Chañaral ○ RCH 76-77 C 4
Finch'a'ā Dam < ETH 208-209 C 4
Finch'aya ○ ETH 208-209 D 4
Finchburg ○ USA (AL) 284-285 C 5
Findik ○ TR 128-129 J 4
Findlater ○ CDN (SAS) 232-233 N 5
Findlay ○ USA (OH) 280-281 C 2
Findlay Group ⌒ CDN 24-25 S 2
Fine ○ USA (NY) 278-279 F 4
Fingal ○ AUS 180-181 J 6
Fingal ○ USA (ND) 258-259 K 5
Finger Hill Island ⌒ CDN 36-37 S 5
Finger Lake ○ CDN 34-35 K 4
Finger Lakes ○ USA (NY) 278-279 E 6
Fingoe ○ MOC 218-219 F 2
Finike ☆• TR 128-129 D 4
Finisterra, Cabo ▲ E 98-99 C 3
Finisterre Range ▲ PNG 183 D 3
Fink Creek ○ USA 20-21 J 4
Finke ○ AUS 178-179 C 3
Finke Bay ≈ 172-173 K 2
Finke Gorge National Park ⊥ AUS 176-177 M 2
Finke River ~ AUS 176-177 M 2
Finke River ~ AUS 178-179 C 4
Finkolo ○ RMM 202-203 G 4
Finland ○ USA (MN) 270-271 G 3
Finland, Gulf of ≈ 88-89 H 7
Finland = Suomi ■ FIN 88-89 H 5
Finlay Forks ○ CDN 32-33 J 4
Finlay Mountains ▲ USA (TX) 266-267 B 2
Finlay Ranges ▲ CDN 32-33 H 3
Finlay River ~ CDN 32-33 H 3
Finlayson ○ USA (MN) 270-271 F 4
Finlayson Channel < CDN (BC) 228-229 F 4
Finley ○ AUS 180-181 H 3
Finley ○ USA (ND) 258-259 K 4
Finley ○ USA (OK) 264-265 J 4
Finmark ○ CDN (ONT) 234-235 O 6
Finnegan ○ CDN (ALB) 232-233 F 4
Finnie Bay ≈ 36-37 L 2
Finnigan, Mount ▲ AUS 174-175 H 4
Finnis, Cape ▲ AUS 180-181 C 2
Finnmarksvidda ∴ N 86-87 L 2
Finn Mount ▲ USA 20-21 M 6
Finnsnes ○ N 86-87 H 2
Finote Selam ○ ETH 208-209 C 3
Finschhafen ○ PNG 183 D 4
Finspång ☆ S 86-87 G 7
Finsteraarhorn ▲ CH 92-93 K 5
Finsterwalde ○ D 92-93 M 3
Fintrou < RMM 196-197 K 6
Finucane Range ▲ AUS 178-179 F 2
Finyolé ○ CAM 204-205 K 4
Fiordland National Park ••• NZ 182 A 6
Fiordland Provincial Recreation Area ⊥ CDN (BC) 228-229 F 4
Firat Nehri ~ TR 128-129 J 3
Firebag River ~ CDN 32-33 P 3
Firebaugh ○ USA (CA) 248-249 D 3
Firedrake Lake ○ CDN 30-31 R 5
Fire Island ⌒ USA 20-21 P 6
Fire Island National Seashore ⊥ USA (NY) 280-281 O 3
Firenze ○••• I 100-101 C 3
Firestone Plantation • LB 202-203 E 6
Firgoun ○ RN 202-203 L 2
Firjuza ○ TM 136-137 F 6
Firk, Ša'īb ~ IRQ 130-131 J 2
Firmat ○ RA 78-79 J 2
Firmeza ○ PE 70-71 C 2
Firminy ○ F 90-91 K 9
Fir Mountain ○ CDN (SAS) 232-233 M 6
Firou ○ DY 202-203 L 4
Firozābād ○ IND 138-139 G 6
Firozpur ○ IND 138-139 E 4
Firsovo ○ RUS 122-123 K 5
First Broad River ~ USA (NC) 282-283 F 5
Firth of Clyde ≈ 90-91 E 4
Firth of Forth ≈ 90-91 F 3
Firth of Tay ≈ 90-91 F 3
Firth River ~ CDN 20-21 V 2
Firūzābād ○• IR 134-135 E 4
Firūzābād-e Bālā ○ IR 134-135 C 1
Firūzkūh ○ IR 136-137 C 7
Firvale ○ CDN (BC) 228-229 H 4
Fischell ○ CDN (NFL) 242-243 K 4
Fischer ○ USA (TX) 266-267 J 4
Fischer, Kap ▲ GRØ 28-29 T 6
Fisenge ○ Z 218-219 E 1
Fish Camp ○ USA (CA) 248-249 E 2
Fish Cove Point ▲ CDN 36-37 V 7
Fish Creek ~ USA 20-21 P 1
Fisheating Creek ~ USA (FL) 286-287 H 4
Fisher ○ AUS 176-177 L 5
Fisher ○ USA (AR) 276-277 E 5
Fisher ○ USA (IL) 274-275 K 4
Fisher, Lake O.C. < USA (TX) 266-267 G 2
Fisher Branch ○ CDN (MAN) 234-235 F 3
Fisher Øer ⌒ GRØ 26-27 U 5
Fisher River ○ CDN (MAN) 234-235 F 3
Fisher River ~ USA (MT) 250-251 D 3
Fisher River Indian Reserve X CDN (MAN) 234-235 F 3
Fishers ○ USA (IN) 274-275 M 5
Fishers Island ⌒ USA (NY) 280-281 P 2
Fisher Strait ≈ 36-37 G 3
Fishguard ○ GB 90-91 E 6
Fishing Bridge ○ USA (WY) 252-253 H 2
Fishing Creek ○ USA (MD) 280-281 K 5
Fishing Lake ○ CDN (MAN) 234-235 H 2
Fishing Lakes ○ CDN 20-21 Y 3
Fishing River ~ USA (NC) 282-283 K 4
Fish Lake ○ CDN 30-31 H 4
Fish Lake ○ USA (UT) 254-255 D 5
Fish River ~ AUS 174-175 D 5
Fish River ~ USA 20-21 J 4
Fish River ~ USA (AL) 284-285 C 6
Fishtrap Lake ○ USA (KY) 276-277 N 3
Fishā Genet ○ ETH 208-209 D 5
Fiskå ☆ N 86-87 B 5
Fiske ○ CDN (SAS) 232-233 K 4
Fiskenæs Banke ≃ 28-29 O 5
Fiskenæsset = Qeqertarsuatsiaat ○ GRØ 28-29 P 5
Fissoa ○ PNG 183 F 2
Fišt, gora ▲ RUS 126-127 C 6
Fitampito ○ RM 222-223 E 8
Fitchburg ○ USA (MA) 278-279 K 6
Fitchville ○ USA (OH) 280-281 D 2
Fitler ○ USA (MS) 268-269 J 4
Fitri, Lac ○ TCH 198-199 J 6
Fitzcarrald ○ PE 64-65 F 7
Fitzgerald ○ USA (GA) 284-285 G 5
Fitzgerald River National Park ⊥ AUS 176-177 E 6
Fitzmaurice River ~ AUS 172-173 K 3
Fitzroy ○ AUS 172-173 K 3
Fitzroy ○ GB 78-79 L 6
Fitz Roy ○ RA 80 G 3
Fitz Roy, Cape ▲ CDN 24-25 g 3
Fitzroy Crossing ○ AUS 172-173 G 5
Fitzroy Island ⌒ AUS 174-175 J 5
Fitzroy River ~ AUS 172-173 H 4
Fitzroy River ~ AUS 172-173 F 4
Fitzroy River ~ AUS 178-179 K 2
Fitzwilliam Island ⌒ CDN (ONT) 238-239 D 3
Fitzwilliam Strait ≈ 24-25 N 2
Fiume = Rijeka ○ HR 100-101 E 2
Five Cays Settlements ○ GB 54-55 J 4
Five Mile Hill ▲ AUS 172-173 E 6
Five Points ○ USA (CA) 248-249 D 3
Five Points ○ USA (GA) 284-285 F 4
Five Stars ○ GUY 62-63 D 2
Fizi ○ ZRE 212-213 B 6
Fizuli = Füzuli ○ AZ 128-129 M 3
Fjällnes ○ S 86-87 F 5
Fjerritslev ○ DK 86-87 D 8
Fkih-Ben-Salah ○ MA 188-189 H 4
Flade Isblink ∴ GRØ 26-27 r 3
Flad Ø ⌒ GRØ 28-29 Y 3
Flagler ○ USA (CO) 254-255 M 4
Flagler Beach ○ USA (FL) 286-287 H 2
Flagstaff ○• USA (AZ) 256-257 D 3
Flagstaff ○ ZA 220-221 J 5
Flagstaff Lake ○ USA (ME) 278-279 L 3
Flaherty Island ⌒ CDN 36-37 J 7
Flåm ○ N 86-87 C 6
Flamborough Head ▲ GB 90-91 G 4
Flamenco, Isla ⌒ RA 78-79 H 6
Flamencos, Parque Nacional los ⊥•• CO 60-61 E 2
Fläming ∴ D 92-93 M 2
Flaming Gorge National Rercreation Area ⊥ USA (WY) 252-253 J 5
Flaming Gorge Reservoir ~ USA (WY) 252-253 J 5
Flamingo ○ USA (FL) 286-287 J 6
Flampleu ○ CI 202-203 F 6
Flanagan River ~ CDN (ONT) 234-235 K 2
Flandreau ○ USA (SD) 260-261 K 2
Flannagan Reservoir ○ USA (VA) 280-281 D 6
Flasher ○ USA (ND) 258-259 F 5
Flåsjön ○ S 86-87 G 4
Flat ○ USA 20-21 L 5
Flat ○ USA (TX) 266-267 K 2
Flat Bay ○ CDN (NFL) 242-243 K 4
Flatey ⌒ IS 86-87 b 2
Flathead ○ CDN (BC) 230-231 P 4
Flathead Indian Reservation X USA (MT) 250-251 E 4
Flathead Lake ○ USA (MT) 250-251 E 4
Flathead River ~ CDN (BC) 230-231 P 4
Flathead River ~ USA (MT) 250-251 F 4
Flathead River, South Fork ~ USA (MT) 250-251 F 4
Flat Island ⌒ 160-161 A 7
Flatonia ○ USA (TX) 266-267 K 4
Flatow = Złotów ○• PL 92-93 O 2
Flat Point ▲ NZ 182 E 4
Flat River ~ CDN 30-31 F 5
Flat River ○ USA (MO) 276-277 E 3
Flatrock ○ USA (IN) 274-275 N 5
Flat Rock ○ USA (MI) 272-273 F 5
Flats ○ USA (NE) 262-263 E 3
Flattery, Cape ▲ AUS 174-175 H 4
Flattery, Cape ▲ USA (WA) 244-245 A 2
Flat Top ○ USA (WV) 280-281 E 6
Flatwillow ○ USA (MT) 250-251 L 5
Flatwoods ○ USA (KY) 276-277 N 2
Flaxcombe ○ CDN (SAS) 232-233 J 4
Flaxman Island ⌒ USA 20-21 S 1
Flaxville ○ USA (MT) 250-251 O 3
Flé ~ RG 202-203 F 4
Flecha Point ▲ RP 160-161 E 9
Flèche, la ○ F 90-91 G 8
Fleet ○ CDN (ALB) 232-233 G 3
Fleetwood ○ GB 90-91 F 5
Flekkefjord ☆ N 86-87 C 7
Fleming ○ CDN (SAS) 232-233 R 5
Flemingsburg ○ USA (KY) 276-277 M 2
Flemington ○ USA (NJ) 280-281 M 3
Flemish Cap ≃ 6-7 E 4
Flenelon Falls ○ CDN (ONT) 238-239 G 4
Flensburg ○• D 92-93 K 1
Flers ○ F 90-91 G 7
Flesko, Tanjung ▲ RI 164-165 J 3
Fletcher Island ⌒ CDN 36-37 Q 3
Fletcher Lake ○ CDN 30-31 P 4
Fletscher ○ USA (NC) 282-283 E 5
Flett Lake ○ CDN 30-31 R 5
Fleurance ○ F 90-91 H 10
Fleur de Lys ○ CDN (NFL) 242-243 M 2
Fleur de May, Lac ○ CDN 38-39 M 3
Fleurieu Peninsula ~ AUS 180-181 E 3
Flexal ○ BR 62-63 G 6
Flinders Bay ≈ 176-177 C 7
Flinders Chase National Park ⊥ AUS 180-181 D 3
Flinders Group ⌒ AUS 174-175 H 4
Flinders Highway II AUS 174-175 H 7
Flinders Island ⌒ AUS (SA) 180-181 C 2
Flinders Island ⌒ AUS (TAS) 180-181 J 5
Flinders Peak ▲ AUS 178-179 M 4
Flinders Ranges ▲ AUS 180-181 E 2
Flinders Ranges National Park ⊥ AUS 178-179 E 6
Flinders Reef ⌒ AUS 174-175 K 5
Flinders River ~ AUS 174-175 F 7
Flin Flon ○ CDN 34-35 F 3
Flint ○ CDN (ONT) 234-235 O 6
Flint ○ USA (MI) 272-273 F 4
Flintdale ○ CDN (ONT) 236-237 C 2
Flint Hills ▲ USA (KS) 262-263 K 6
Flint Hills National Wildlife Refuge • USA (KS) 262-263 L 6
Flint Lake ○ CDN 28-29 C 3
Flint Lake ○ CDN (ONT) 236-237 C 3
Flintoft ○ CDN (SAS) 232-233 M 6
Flint Rapids ~ CDN 34-35 P 4
Flint River ~ USA (AL) 284-285 D 2
Flint River ~ USA (GA) 284-285 E 5
Flint River ~ USA (GA) 284-285 F 4
Flint River ~ USA (GA) 284-285 F 3
Flisa ☆ N 86-87 F 6
Flix ○ E 98-99 H 4
Flomaton ○ USA (AL) 284-285 C 5
Flomot ○ USA (TX) 264-265 D 4
Floods ○ CDN (BC) 230-231 H 4
Floodwood ○ USA (MN) 270-271 F 4
Flora ○ USA (IL) 274-275 K 6
Flora ○ USA (MS) 268-269 K 4
Flora ○ USA (OR) 244-245 H 5
Flora & Fauna Reserve ⊥ AUS 172-173 D 6
Floral ○ CDN (SAS) 232-233 M 3
Florala ○ USA (AL) 284-285 D 5
Floral City ○ USA (FL) 286-287 G 3
Flora Valley ○ AUS 172-173 J 5
Floraville ○ AUS 174-175 E 6
Flor da Serra ○ BR 74-75 D 6
Flor de Agosto ○ PE 64-65 F 3
Flor del Desierto ○ RCH 76-77 C 2
Flor de Punga ○ PE 64-65 E 4
Florence ○ USA (AL) 284-285 C 2
Florence ○ USA (AZ) 256-257 D 5
Florence ○ USA (CO) 254-255 K 5
Florence ○ USA (KS) 262-263 K 6
Florence ○ USA (MN) 270-271 B 6
Florence ○ USA (MS) 268-269 K 4
Florence ○ USA (OR) 244-245 A 6
Florence ○ USA (PA) 280-281 F 3
Florence ○ USA (SC) 284-285 L 2
Florence ○ USA (SD) 260-261 J 1
Florence ○ USA (TX) 266-267 K 3
Florence ○ USA (WI) 270-271 K 5
Florence = Firenze ☆••• I 100-101 C 3
Florence, Lake ○ AUS 178-179 E 5
Florence Junction ○ USA (AZ) 256-257 D 5
Florencia ☆ CO 64-65 E 1
Florencia ○ RA 76-77 H 5
Florencio Sanches ○ ROU 78-79 L 2
Florens, mys ▲ RUS 112-113 U 1
Florentino Ameghino, Embalse < RA 78-79 F 7
Flores ○ BR 68-69 K 5
Flores ☆• GCA 52-53 K 3
Flores ⌒ P 6-7 E 7
Flores ⌒ RI 168 E 7
Flores, Arroyo de las ~ RA 78-79 J 4
Flôres, Igarapé ~ BR 70-71 F 3
Flores, Las ○ CO 60-61 E 2
Flores, Las ○ RA (BUA) 78-79 K 4
Flores, Las ○ RA (SAJ) 76-77 C 6
Flores de Goiás ○ BR 72-73 G 3
Flores do Piauí ○ BR 68-69 G 5
Flores Gracía ○ MEX 50-51 H 6
Flores Island ⌒ CDN (BC) 230-231 C 4
Flores Sea = Flores, Laut ≈ RI 168 D 6
Florešť = Florești ☆ MD 102-103 F 4
Floresta ○ BR (PAR) 72-73 D 7
Floresta ○ BR (PER) 68-69 J 6
Floresta Nacional Aveiro ⊥ BR 66-67 K 4
Florești ☆ MD 102-103 F 4
Florešty = Florești ☆ MD 102-103 F 4
Floresville ○ USA (TX) 266-267 J 4
Florian ○ CO 60-61 E 5
Floriano ○ BR 68-69 G 5
Floriano Peixoto ○ BR 66-67 D 7
Florianópolis ☆• BR 74-75 F 6
Florida ○ C 54-55 F 4
Florida ○ CO 60-61 C 6
Florida ○ RCH 78-79 C 4
Florida ☆ ROU 78-79 L 3
Florida ○ USA (NM) 256-257 H 6
Florida ■ USA (FL) 286-287 J 2
Florida, Cape ▲ USA (FL) 286-287 J 6
Florida, Estrecho de la = Florida, Straits of ≈ 54-55 E 3
Florida, La ○ CO 64-65 D 1
Florida, La ∴• GCA 52-53 J 3
Florida, La ○ PE 64-65 C 5
Florida, La ○ YV 60-61 G 3
Florida Bay ≈ 48-49 H 7
Florida Bay ≈ USA 286-287 J 6
Floridablanca ○ CO 60-61 E 4
Florida City ○ USA (FL) 286-287 J 6
Florida Islands ⌒ SOL 184 I e 3
Florida Keys ⌒ USA (FL) 286-287 H 7
Florida Peak ▲ USA (NM) 256-257 H 6
Florida's Turnpike II USA (FL) 286-287 H 3
Florido, Río ~ MEX 50-51 G 4
Florien ○ USA (LA) 268-269 G 5
Florin ○ USA (CA) 246-247 D 5
Flórina ○ GR 100-101 H 4
Florínia ○ BR 72-73 E 7
Florissant ○ USA (MO) 274-275 H 6
Florissant Fossil Beds National Monument ∴ USA (CO) 254-255 K 5
Florø ☆ N 86-87 B 6
Flour Island ⌒ CDN (ONT) 234-235 P 6
Floyd ○ USA (NM) 256-257 M 4
Floyd ○ USA (VA) 280-281 F 7
Floyd, Mount ▲ USA (AZ) 256-257 C 3
Floydada ○ USA (TX) 264-265 C 5
Floyd River ~ USA (IA) 274-275 B 2
Flu ○ LB 202-203 G 7
Fluk ○ RI 164-165 K 4
Flumendosa ~ I 100-101 B 5
Fluvanna ○ USA (TX) 264-265 C 6
Flying Fox Creek ~ AUS 174-175 B 4
Flying Post Indian Reserve X CDN (ONT) 236-237 F 4
Flynn ○ USA (TX) 266-267 L 2
Fly River ~ PNG 183 A 4
Fly River ~ PNG 183 B 5
Foa ⌒ TON 184 IV a 1
Foam Lake ○ CDN (SAS) 232-233 P 4
Fô-Bouré ○ DY 204-205 E 3
Foča ○• BIH 100-101 G 3
Foça ☆ TR 128-129 B 3
Foca, Isla ⌒ PE 64-65 B 4
Foca, Punta ▲ RA 80 H 3
Fochi ∴ TCH 198-199 G 3
Focșani ☆ RO 102-103 E 5
Fodé ○ RCA 206-207 F 6
Fodekaria ○ RG 202-203 F 4
Fofore ○ WAN 204-205 K 4
Fogang ○ VRC 156-157 H 5
Fog Bay ≈ 172-173 K 2
Fogelevo ○ KA 136-137 L 3

Foggaret el 'Arab ○ DZ 190-191 D 7
Foggaret ez Zoua ○ DZ 190-191 D 7
Fóggia ☆ I 100-101 E 4
Foggy Cape ▲ USA 22-23 S 4
Fogi ○ RI 166-167 D 3
Fogo ○ CDN (NFL) 242-243 O 3
Fogo, Ilha de ⌒ CV 202-203 B 6
Fogo Island ⌒ CDN (NFL) 242-243 O 3
Føhn Fjord ≈ 26-27 m 8
Föhr ⌒ D 92-93 K 1
Fóia ▲ P 98-99 C 6
Foisy ○ CDN (ALB) 232-233 G 2
Foix ○ F 90-91 H 10
Foja, Pegunungan ▲ RI 166-167 K 3
Fokina ∼ RUS 108-109 W 7
Fokino ○ RUS 94-95 O 5
Fokku ○ WAN 204-205 F 3
Folda ≈ 86-87 G 3
Foldereid ○ N 86-87 F 4
Foley ○ RB 218-219 D 5
Foley ○ USA (AL) 284-285 C 6
Foley ○ USA (MN) 270-271 E 5
Foleyet ○ CDN (ONT) 236-237 F 4
Foley Island ⌒ CDN 24-25 j 6
Folgares ○ ANG 216-217 C 7
Folgefonni ⊂ N 86-87 C 7
Foligno ○ I 100-101 D 3
Folkestone ○ • GB 90-91 H 6
Folkston ○ USA (GA) 284-285 H 6
Folkstone ○ USA (NC) 282-283 K 6
Folldal ☆ N 86-87 D 5
Follett ○ USA (TX) 264-265 D 2
Follette, La ○ USA (TN) 282-283 C 4
Föllinge ○ S 86-87 G 5
Follónica ○ I 100-101 C 3
Folly Beach ○ USA (SC) 284-285 L 4
Folly Island ⌒ USA (SC) 284-285 L 4
Folsom ○ USA (LA) 268-269 K 6
Folsom ○ USA (NM) 256-257 M 2
Fomboni ○ COM 222-223 C 4
Fome, Rio da ∼ BR 68-69 G 3
Fomena ○ GH 202-203 K 6
Fomento ○ C 54-55 F 3
Fomič ∼ RUS 110-111 F 4
Fona ○ VAN 184 II b 3
Fonda ○ USA (IA) 274-275 D 2
Fondale ○ USA (LA) 268-269 H 4
Fond-du-Lac ○ CDN 30-31 Q 6
Fond du Lac ∼ CDN 30-31 Q 6
Fond du Lac ○ USA (WI) 270-271 K 7
Fond du Lac Indian Reservation ⚔ USA (MN) 270-271 F 4
Fond du Lac River ∼ CDN 30-31 R 6
Fonehill ○ CDN (SAS) 232-233 Q 4
Fonéko ○ RN 202-203 L 2
Fongolembi ○ SN 202-203 D 3
Fonni ○ I 100-101 B 4
Fonoifua ⌒ TON 184 IV a 2
Fonsagrada, A ○ E 98-99 D 3
Fonseca ○ CO 60-61 E 2
Fonseca, Golfo de ≈ 52-53 L 5
Fonsecas, Serra dos ▲ BR 72-73 H 4
Fontaine Lake ○ CDN 30-31 Q 6
Fontana, Lago ○ RA 80 E 2
Fontana Lake < USA (NC) 282-283 D 5
Fontanelle ○ USA (NE) 262-263 K 3
Fontanina ○ ETH 208-209 D 3
Fontas ○ CDN 30-31 J 6
Fontas River ∼ CDN 30-31 J 6
Fonte Boa ○ BR 66-67 D 4
Fontenay, Abbaye de ••• F 90-91 K 8
Fontenay-le-Comte ○ F 90-91 G 8
Fonteneau, Lac ○ CDN 38-39 O 3
Fontenelle ○ CDN (QUE) 240-241 L 2
Fontenelle ○ USA (WY) 252-253 H 5
Fontenelle Reservoir ○ USA (WY) 252-253 H 4
Fontibón ○ CO 60-61 D 5
Fontur ▲ IS 86-87 f 1
Fonuafo'ou ⌒ TON 184 IV a 2
Fonualei ⌒ TON 184 IV a 1
Fo'ondo ○ SOL 184 I e 3
Foping ○ VRC 154-155 E 5
Foping Z.B. ⊥ • VRC 154-155 E 5
Forage Christine eau potable < BF 202-203 K 2
Forari ○ VAN 184 II b 3
Forbes ○ AUS 180-181 K 2
Forbes ○ USA (ND) 258-259 J 6
Forbes, Kap ▲ GRØ 26-27 R 4
Forbus ○ USA (TN) 276-277 K 4
Forcados ○ WAN 204-205 F 6
Ford ○ USA (ID) 250-251 B 4
Ford ○ USA (KS) 262-263 G 7
Ford, Cape ▲ AUS 172-173 J 2
Ford, Cerro el ▲ RCH 80 E 6
Fordate, Pulau ⌒ RI 166-167 F 5
Ford Costantine ○ AUS 174-175 F 7
Førde ☆ N 86-87 B 6
Ford Falls ∼ CDN 30-31 R 4
Fording River ∼ CDN (BC) 230-231 P 4
Ford River ∼ CDN 36-37 H 2
Ford River ∼ USA (MI) 270-271 L 5
Fordsville ○ USA (KY) 276-277 J 3
Fordyce ○ USA (AR) 276-277 C 7
Forécariah ○ RG 202-203 D 5
Foreman ○ USA (AR) 276-277 A 7
Foremost ○ CDN (ALB) 232-233 G 6
Foresman ○ USA (IN) 274-275 L 4
Forest ○ CDN (ONT) 238-239 D 5
Forest ○ USA (MS) 268-269 L 4
Forest, Lac la ○ CDN 36-37 O 7
Forest Acres ○ USA (SC) 284-285 K 2
Forestburg ○ CDN (ALB) 232-233 F 3
Forestburg ○ USA (TX) 264-265 G 5
Forest City ○ USA (IA) 274-275 E 1
Forest City ○ USA (NC) 282-283 F 5
Forestdale ○ CDN (BC) 228-229 H 2
Forest Glen ○ USA (CA) 246-247 B 3
Forest Grove ○ CDN (BC) 230-231 H 2
Forestgrove ○ USA (MT) 250-251 K 4
Forest Grove ○ USA (OR) 244-245 B 5
Forest Home ○ AUS 174-175 G 6
Forestier, Cape ▲ AUS 180-181 K 7
Forest Lake ○ USA (MN) 270-271 F 5
Forest Park ○ USA (GA) 284-285 F 3
Forest River ○ USA (ND) 258-259 K 3
Forest Strait ≈ 158-159 E 5
Forestville ○ CDN (QUE) 240-241 F 2
Forestville ○ USA (MI) 272-273 G 4
Forestville ○ USA (WI) 270-271 L 6
Forfar ○ GB 90-91 F 3
Forgan ○ CDN (SAS) 232-233 L 4
Forgan ○ USA (OK) 264-265 D 2
Forges-les-Eaux ○ F 90-91 H 7
Forget ○ CDN (SAS) 232-233 Q 6
Forillon, Parc National de ⊥ CDN (QUE) 240-241 L 2
Fork ○ USA (SC) 284-285 L 2
Forked Island ○ USA (LA) 268-269 H 7
Fork Lake ○ CDN 32-33 P 4
Forkland ○ USA (AL) 284-285 C 4
Fork Reservoir, Lake ○ USA (TX) 264-265 J 6
Forks ○ USA (WA) 244-245 A 3
Forks of Cacapon ○ USA (WV) 280-281 H 4
Forks of Salmon ○ USA (CA) 246-247 B 2
Fork Union ○ USA (VA) 280-281 H 6
Forlandet nasjonalpark ⊥ N 84-85 G 3
Forlandsundet ≈ 84-85 G 3
Forlì ○ I 100-101 D 2
Forman ○ USA (ND) 258-259 K 5
Formation Cave ∴ USA (ID) 252-253 G 4
Formby Bay ≈ 180-181 D 3
Formentera, Illa de ⌒ E 98-99 H 5
Formentor, Cap de ▲ •• E 98-99 J 5
Formia ○ I 100-101 D 4
Formiga ○ BR (MAR) 68-69 F 3
Formiga ○ BR (MIN) 72-73 H 6
Formosa ○ BR 72-73 G 3
Formosa ■ RA 76-77 G 3
Formosa ☆ RA (FOR) 76-77 H 4
Formosa, Cachoeira da ∼ BR 72-73 D 2
Formosa, Ilha ⌒ GNB 202-203 B 4
Formosa, La ○ BR 72-73 G 5
Formosa, Serra ▲ BR 70-71 K 3
Formosa do Rio Preto ○ BR 68-69 F 7
Formoso ○ BR (GOI) 72-73 F 2
Formoso ○ BR (GSU) 72-73 D 6
Formoso ○ BR (MIN) 72-73 G 3
Formoso, Cape ▲ WAN 204-205 G 6
Formoso, Rio ∼ BR 68-69 D 7
Formoso, Rio ∼ BR 72-73 H 2
Formoso, Rio ∼ BR 72-73 H 4
Formoso, Rio ∼ BR 72-73 D 5
Fornæs ▲ DK 86-87 E 8
Fornells ○ E 98-99 K 4
Fornos ○ MOC 218-219 H 6
Foro Burunga ○ SUD 198-199 L 6
Foroko ○ PNG 183 C 3
Forolshogna ▲ N 86-87 E 5
Foropaugh ○ USA (AZ) 256-257 B 5
Foros ○ • UA 102-103 H 5
Forpost-Kargat ○ RUS 114-115 Q 7
Forres ○ RA 76-77 F 4
Forrest ○ AUS (VIC) 180-181 G 5
Forrest ○ AUS (WA) 176-177 K 5
Forrest ○ USA (IL) 274-275 K 4
Forrest, Mount ▲ AUS 176-177 E 4
Forrest City ○ USA (AR) 276-277 E 5
Forrest Lakes ○ AUS 176-177 K 4
Forreston ○ USA (IL) 274-275 J 2
Forrest River Aboriginal Land ⚔ AUS 172-173 H 3
Forrest Station ○ CDN (MAN) 234-235 D 5
Forsayth ○ AUS 174-175 G 6
Forshaga ☆ S 86-87 F 7
Forsnes ○ N 86-87 D 5
Forssa ○ FIN 88-89 G 6
Forsyth ○ USA (GA) 284-285 G 3
Forsyth ○ USA (MO) 276-277 B 4
Forsyth ○ USA (MT) 250-251 N 5
Forsyth Island ⌒ AUS 174-175 E 5
Forsyth Range ▲ AUS 178-179 G 2
Fort (Dutch) •• RI 164-165 J 5
Fort Abbās ○ PK 138-139 D 5
Fort Abercrombie • USA (ND) 258-259 L 5
Fort Albany ○ CDN 34-35 Q 4
Fort Albercrombie State Historical Park • USA 22-23 U 4
Fortale, Caño la ∼ CO 60-61 F 5
Fort Alexander ○ CDN (MAN) 234-235 G 4
Fortaleza ○ BOL 70-71 D 3
Fortaleza ○ BR (ACR) 66-67 B 7
Fortaleza ○ BR (AMA) 66-67 C 6
Fortaleza ○ BR (AMA) 66-67 H 4
Fortaleza ○ BR (RON) 66-67 E 7
Fortaleza ☆ • BR (CEA) 68-69 J 3
Fortaleza, La ○ YV 60-61 J 3
Fortaleza dos Nogueiras ○ BR 68-69 E 5
Fort Amanda State Memorial • USA (OH) 280-281 B 3
Fort Amherst National Historic Park • CDN (PEI) 240-241 M 4
Fort Anne National Historic Park • CDN (NS) 240-241 K 6
Fort Apache Indian Reservation ⚔ USA (AZ) 256-257 E 4
Fort Atkinson ○ USA (WI) 274-275 K 2
Fort Augustus ○ • GB 90-91 E 3
Fort Battleford National Historic Park • CDN (SAS) 232-233 K 3
Fort Beaufort ○ ZA 220-221 H 6
Fort Belknap Agency ○ USA (MT) 250-251 L 3
Fort Belknap Indian Reservation ⚔ USA (MT) 250-251 L 3
Fort Belmont • USA (MN) 270-271 C 7
Fort Belvoir ✕✕ USA (VA) 280-281 J 5
Fort Benning ○ USA (GA) 284-285 F 4
Fort Benning ✕✕ USA (GA) 284-285 F 4
Fort Benton ○ USA (MT) 250-251 J 4
Fort Benton Ruins • USA (MT) 250-251 J 4
Fort Berthold Indian Reservation ⚔ USA (ND) 258-259 E 4
Fort Black ○ CDN 34-35 C 3
Fort Bliss Military Reservation ✕✕ USA (NM) 256-257 J 6
Fort Bragg ○ USA (NC) 282-283 J 5
Fort Bragg Military Reservation ✕✕ USA (NC) 282-283 H 5
Fort Branch ○ USA (IN) 274-275 L 6
Fort Bridger ○ USA (WY) 252-253 H 5
Fort-Chimo = Kuujjuaq ○ CDN 36-37 P 5
Fort Chipewyan ○ CDN 30-31 O 6
Fort Churchill ○ CDN 30-31 X 6
Fort Clark ○ USA (ND) 258-259 F 4
Fort Cobb ○ USA (OK) 264-265 F 3
Fort Cobb Reservoir < USA (OK) 264-265 F 3
Fort Cobb State Park ⊥ • USA (OK) 264-265 F 3
Fort Collins ○ USA (CO) 254-255 K 3
Fort Collinson ○ CDN 24-25 N 5
Fort Coulonge ○ CDN (QUE) 238-239 J 3
Fort Craig, Ruins of • USA (NM) 256-257 H 5
Fort-Dauphin = Tôlanaro ○ • RM 222-223 E 10
Fort Davis ○ USA (AL) 284-285 E 4
Fort de Cock • RI 162-163 D 5
Fort-de-France ☆ F 56 E 4
Fort Deposit ○ USA (AL) 284-285 D 5
Fort Dodge ○ USA (IA) 274-275 D 2
Fort Drum • USA (NY) 278-279 F 4
Forteau ○ CDN (NFL) 242-243 M 1
Fort Edward National Historic Site • CDN (NS) 240-241 L 6
Fort Egbert National Historic Site • USA 20-21 U 4
Fort Erie ○ CDN (ONT) 238-239 G 6
Fortescue River ∼ AUS 172-173 C 6
Fortescue River Roadhouse ○ AUS 172-173 C 6
Fort Eustis ✕✕ USA (VA) 280-281 K 6
Fort Fisher • USA (NC) 282-283 K 7
Fort Frances ○ CDN (ONT) 234-235 K 6
Fort Franklin ○ CDN 30-31 H 3
Fort Fraser ○ CDN (BC) 228-229 K 2
Fort Fred Steele ○ USA (WY) 252-253 M 5
Fort Gadsden State Historical Site • USA (FL) 286-287 E 2
Fort Gaines ○ USA (GA) 284-285 E 5
Fort Garland ○ USA (CO) 254-255 K 6
Fort George ○ CDN 38-39 E 2
Fort George National Historic Park • CDN (ONT) 238-239 F 5
Fort George River = La Grande Rivière ∼ CDN 38-39 G 2
Fort Gibson ○ USA (OK) 264-265 J 3
Fort Gibson Lake ○ USA (OK) 264-265 J 2
Fort Glenn ○ USA 22-23 N 6
Fort Good Hope ○ CDN 30-31 E 2
Fort Gordon ✕✕ USA (GA) 284-285 H 3
Fort Griffin State Historic Park ⊥ USA (TX) 264-265 E 6
Fort Hall ○ CDN 30-31 T 6
Fort Hall ○ USA (ID) 252-253 F 3
Fort Hall Indian Reservation ⚔ USA (ID) 252-253 F 3
Fort Hancock ○ USA (TX) 266-267 B 2
Forthassa Gharbia ○ DZ 188-189 L 4
Fort Hope ○ CDN (ONT) 234-235 P 3
Fort Hope Indian Reserve ⚔ CDN (ONT) 234-235 Q 3
Fort Huachuca • USA (AZ) 256-257 E 7
Fort Hunter Liggett Military Reservation ✕✕ USA (CA) 248-249 C 3
Fortierville ○ CDN (QUE) 238-239 N 2
Fortín 1° de Mayo ○ RA 78-79 D 5
Fortín, El ○ RA 76-77 F 6
Fortín Avalos Sanchez ○ PY 76-77 G 2
Fortín Boquerón ○ PY 76-77 H 2
Fortín Cabo 1° Cano ○ PY 76-77 H 3
Fortín Cadete Pastor Pando ○ PY 76-77 H 3
Fortín Carlos A. Lopez ○ PY 76-77 H 1
Fortín Charrúa ○ RA 76-77 G 5
Fortín Crnate Nowak ○ PY 76-77 H 3
Fortín Colonel Bogado ○ PY 70-71 H 7
Fortín de las Flores ○ MEX 52-53 F 2
Fort Independence Indian Reservation ⚔ USA (CA) 248-249 F 3
Fortín Gaspar de Francia ○ PY 76-77 H 2
Fortín General Díaz ○ PY 76-77 G 2
Fortín Guanacos • RA 78-79 D 4
Fortín Hernandarias ○ PY 76-77 G 1
Fortín Infante Rivarola ○ PY 76-77 F 1
Fortín Lagerenza ○ PY 70-71 G 7
Fortín Lavalle ○ RA 76-77 G 3
Fortín Leonida Escobar ○ PY 76-77 G 2
Fortín Madrejón ○ PY 70-71 H 7
Fortín Malargüe • RA 78-79 E 3
Fortín Nueva Asunción ○ PY 70-71 G 7
Fortín Olmos ○ RA 76-77 G 5
Fortín Pilcomayo ○ RA 76-77 G 2
Fortín Pozo Hondo ○ PY 76-77 F 2
Fortín Ravelo ○ BOL 70-71 G 6
Fortín Teniente Américo Picco ○ PY 70-71 H 6
Fortín Teniente Montania ○ PY 76-77 H 2
Fortín Teniente Rojas Silva ○ PY 76-77 G 2
Fortín Toledo ○ PY 76-77 G 2
Fortín Torres ○ PY 76-77 H 1
Fortín Zalazar ○ PY 76-77 H 2
Fort Irwin ○ CDN (ONT) 238-239 G 3
Fort Jackson ∴ USA (SC) 284-285 K 2
Fort Jones ○ USA (CA) 246-247 C 2
Fort Kearney State Historic Park ∴ • USA (NE) 262-263 G 4
Fort Kent ○ USA (ME) 278-279 N 1
Fort Kent Historic Site • USA (ME) 278-279 N 1
Fort Kissimmee ○ USA (FL) 286-287 H 4
Fort Klamath ○ USA (OR) 244-245 C 8
Fort Knox ✕✕ USA (KY) 276-277 K 3
Fort Langley National Historic Park • CDN (BC) 230-231 G 4
Fort Laramie ○ USA (WY) 252-253 O 4
Fort la Reine • CDN (MAN) 234-235 E 5
Fort Lauderdale ○ USA (FL) 286-287 J 5
Fort Lemhi Monument • USA (ID) 252-253 E 2
Fort Lewis • USA (WA) 244-245 C 4
Fort Liard ○ CDN 30-31 H 5
Fort Liberté ☆ RH 54-55 K 5
Fort MacKavett ○ USA (TX) 266-267 G 3
Fort MacKay ○ CDN 32-33 P 3
Fort Mackinac • USA (MI) 272-273 E 2
Fort Madison ○ USA (IA) 274-275 G 4
Fort Matanzas National Monument • USA (FL) 286-287 H 2
Fort Maurepas • CDN (MAN) 234-235 G 4
Fort McClellan ✕✕ USA (AL) 284-285 E 3
Fort McCoy Military Reservation ✕✕ USA (WI) 270-271 H 6
Fort McHenry • USA (MD) 280-281 K 4
Fort McKavett State Historic Site • USA (TX) 266-267 G 3
Fort McMurray ○ • CDN 32-33 P 3
Fort McPherson ○ CDN 20-21 Y 3
Fort Meade ○ USA (FL) 286-287 H 4
Fort Mill ○ USA (SC) 284-285 K 1
Fort Mohave Indian Reservation ⚔ USA (AZ) 256-257 A 4
Fort Morgan ○ USA (CO) 254-255 M 3
Fort Morgan • USA (AL) 284-285 B 6
Fort Mtobeni ○ ZA 220-221 K 4
Fort Munro ○ • PK 138-139 B 5
Fort Myers ○ USA (FL) 286-287 H 5
Fort Nelson ○ CDN 30-31 H 6
Fort Nelson Indian Reserve ⚔ CDN 30-31 H 6
Fort Nelson River ∼ CDN 30-31 H 6
Fort Norman ○ CDN 30-31 G 3
Fort Oglethorpe ○ USA (GA) 284-285 E 2
Fort Payne ○ USA (AL) 284-285 E 2
Fort Peck ○ USA (MT) 250-251 N 3
Fort Peck Indian Reservation ⚔ USA (MT) 250-251 O 3
Fort Pickett ✕✕ USA (VA) 280-281 J 6
Fort Pierce ○ USA (FL) 286-287 J 4
Fort Pierre ○ USA (SD) 260-261 F 2
Fort Pierre National Grassland ⊥ USA (SD) 260-261 F 2
Fort Pierre Verendrye Monument • USA (SD) 260-261 F 2
Fort Pitt Historic Park • CDN (SAS) 232-233 J 2
Fort Portal ☆ EAU 212-213 C 3
Fort Prince of Wales National Historic Park • CDN 30-31 W 6
Fort Providence ○ CDN 30-31 L 5
Fort Qu'Appelle ○ CDN (SAS) 232-233 P 5
Fort Ransom ○ USA (ND) 258-259 K 5
Fort Recovery ○ USA (OH) 280-281 B 3
Fort Resolution ○ CDN 30-31 N 5
Fortress • RI 162-163 C 3
Fortress of Louisbourg National History Park • CDN (NS) 240-241 P 5
Fort Rice ○ USA (ND) 258-259 G 5
Fort Rice Historic Site • USA (ND) 258-259 G 5
Fort Ripley ○ USA (MN) 270-271 D 4
Fort Rixon ○ ZW 218-219 E 5
Fort Rock ○ USA (OR) 244-245 D 7
Fortrose ○ NZ 182 B 7
Fort Rotterdam ∴ • RI 166-167 D 3
Fort Rotterdam, Museum ∴ • RI 164-165 F 6
Fort Rucker ✕✕ USA (AL) 284-285 E 5
Fort Rupert ○ CDN 38-39 E 3
Fort Rupert ○ CDN (BC) 230-231 B 3
Fort Saint James ○ CDN (BC) 228-229 K 2
Fort Saint James • CDN (BC) 228-229 K 2
Fort Saint James National Historic Park ∴ • CDN (BC) 228-229 K 2
Fort Saint John ○ CDN 32-33 K 3
Fort San ○ CDN (SAS) 232-233 P 5
Fort Sandeman = Zhob ○ PK 138-139 B 4
Fort Saskatchewan ○ CDN (ALB) 232-233 E 2
Fort Scott ○ USA (KS) 262-263 M 7
Fort-Ševčenko ○ KA 126-127 J 5
Fort Severn ○ CDN 34-35 N 3
Fort Sheridan • USA (IL) 274-275 L 2
Fort Simpson ○ CDN 30-31 J 5
Fort Smith ○ CDN 30-31 O 5
Fort Smith ○ USA (AR) 276-277 A 5
Fort Smith ○ USA (MT) 250-251 M 6
Fort Steele Heritage Town • CDN (BC) 230-231 O 4
Fort Stewart ✕✕ USA (GA) 284-285 J 4
Fort Stockton ○ USA (TX) 266-267 E 3
Fort Supply ○ USA (OK) 264-265 E 2
Fort Supply Lake ○ USA (OK) 264-265 E 2
Fort Témiscamingue National Historic Park • CDN (QUE) 236-237 J 5
Fort Thomas ○ USA (AZ) 256-257 F 5
Fort Thompson ○ USA (SD) 260-261 G 2
Fort Totten ○ USA (ND) 258-259 J 4
Fort Towson ○ USA (OK) 264-265 J 4
Fort Trois Rivières • CDN (QUE) 238-239 N 2
Fortuna ○ BR 68-69 F 4
Fortuna ○ USA (CA) 246-247 A 3
Fortuna ○ USA (ND) 258-259 D 3
Fortuna, La ○ MEX 50-51 E 6
Fortuna, Rio ∼ BR 70-71 G 2
Fortuna de Minas ○ BR 72-73 H 5
Fortuna de San Carlos ○ CR 52-53 B 6
Fortuna Ledge ○ USA 20-21 J 6
Fortune ○ CDN (NFL) 242-243 N 5
Fortune Bank ≃ 224 E 3
Fortune Bay ≈ 38-39 R 5
Fortune Bay ≈ CDN 242-243 N 5
Fortune Harbour ○ CDN (NFL) 242-243 N 3
Fort Union Trading Post National Historic Site ∴ USA (MT) 250-251 P 3
Fort Valley ○ USA (GA) 284-285 G 4
Fort Vasquez State Museum • USA (CO) 254-255 L 3
Fort Vermilion ○ CDN 30-31 M 6
Fort Victoria Historic Site ∴ • CDN 32-33 O 4
Fortville ○ USA (IN) 274-275 N 5
Fort Walsh National Historic Park • CDN (SAS) 232-233 J 6
Fort Walton Beach ○ USA (FL) 286-287 C 1
Fort Washakie ○ USA (WY) 252-253 K 4
Fort Wayne ○ USA (IN) 274-275 N 3
Fort Wellington ○ GUY 62-63 F 2
Fort William ○ GB 90-91 E 3
Fort William Historic Park • CDN (ONT) 234-235 O 6
Fort Wingate ○ USA (NM) 256-257 G 3
Fort Worth ○ USA (TX) 264-265 G 6
Fort Yates ○ USA (ND) 258-259 G 5
Fortymile River ∼ USA 20-21 U 4
Fort Yukon ○ USA 20-21 S 3
Fort Yuma Indian Reservation ⚔ USA (CA) 248-249 K 7
Forūdgāh ○ IR 134-135 D 2
Forūmad ○ IR 136-137 E 6
Forūr, Ğazīre-ye ⌒ IR 134-135 F 5
Forvik ○ N 86-87 F 4
Fosa de Cariaco ≈ 60-61 J 2
Fosca ○ CO 60-61 E 5
Foshan ○ • VRC 156-157 H 5
Fosheim Peninsula ⌣ CDN 26-27 H 4
Fosnavåg ☆ N 86-87 B 5
Foso ○ GH 202-203 K 7
Foss ○ USA (OK) 264-265 E 3
Fossa, Corredeira ∼ BR 66-67 H 6
Fossil ○ USA (OR) 244-245 E 5
Fossil Butte National Monument ∴ USA (WY) 252-253 H 5
Fossil Downs ○ • AUS 172-173 G 5
Foss Lake < USA (OK) 264-265 E 3
Fossong Fontem ○ CAM 204-205 H 6
Fosston ○ CDN (SAS) 232-233 P 3
Fosston ○ USA (MN) 270-271 C 3
Foster ○ AUS 180-181 J 5
Foster Bay ≈ 24-25 f 6
Foster Bugt ≈ 26-27 o 7
Fostoria ○ USA (OH) 280-281 C 2
Fostoria ○ USA (TX) 268-269 E 6
Fotadrevo ○ RM 222-223 D 10
Fotiná ○ GR 100-101 J 4
Fotokol ○ CAM 198-199 G 6
Fotuha'a ⌒ TON 184 IV a 1
Foucauld, Ermitage du P. de • DZ 190-191 E 9
Fouénan ○ CI 202-203 G 5
Fougamou ○ G 210-211 C 4
Fougani, Hassi < MA 188-189 J 5
Fougères ○ • F 90-91 G 7
Fouîni, Hâssi < RIM 196-197 G 6
Fouke ○ USA (AR) 276-277 B 7
Foula ⌒ GB 90-91 F 1
Foulabala ○ RMM 202-203 G 4
Foulamory ○ RG 202-203 D 3
Foul Bay ≈ 194-195 G 6
Foulenzem ○ G 210-211 B 4
Foulwind, Cape ▲ NZ 182 C 4
Fouman ○ IR 128-129 N 4
Foumbadou ○ RG 202-203 F 5
Foumban ○ •• CAM 204-205 J 6
Foumbot ○ CAM 204-205 J 6
Foumbouni ○ COM 222-223 C 3
Foum-el-Hassan • MA 188-189 G 6
Foum-Zguid ○ MA 188-189 H 5
Foundiougne ○ SN 202-203 B 2
Founougo ○ DY 204-205 E 3
Fountain ○ USA (CO) 254-255 L 5
Fountain Creek ∼ USA (CO) 254-255 L 5
Fountain Hill ○ USA (AR) 276-277 D 7
Fountain Inn ○ USA (SC) 284-285 H 2
Fountains Abbey ••• GB 90-91 G 4
Fountain Valley ○ CDN (BC) 230-231 H 3
Fouquet ○ RH 54-55 J 5
Four Archers, The • AUS 174-175 C 4
Fourche La Fave River ∼ USA (AR) 276-277 B 6
Fourche Maline River ∼ USA (OK) 264-265 J 4
Fourche Mountain ▲ USA (AR) 276-277 B 6
Fourchu ○ CDN (NS) 240-241 P 5
Four Corners ○ USA (CA) 248-249 G 5
Four Corners ○ USA (WY) 252-253 O 2
Fourcroy, Cape ▲ AUS 172-173 K 1
Four Forks ○ USA (LA) 268-269 G 4
Fouriesburg ○ ZA 220-221 J 4
Four Mountains, Islands of the ⌒ USA 22-23 L 6
Fournaise, Piton de la ▲ F 224 B 7
Four North Fracture Zone ≃ 6-7 F 8
Fourou ○ RMM 202-203 G 4
Fourteen Mile Point ▲ USA (MI) 270-271 J 3
Fourtown ○ USA (MN) 270-271 C 2
Foveaux Strait ≈ 182 A 7
Fowler ○ USA (CO) 254-255 L 5
Fowler ○ USA (IN) 274-275 L 4
Fowler ○ USA (KS) 262-263 F 7
Fowler ○ USA (MI) 272-273 E 4
Fowler ○ USA (SC) 284-285 L 3
Fowlers Bay ≈ 176-177 M 6
Fowlers Bay ○ AUS 176-177 M 5
Fowlers Gap ○ AUS 178-179 F 6
Fowlerton ○ USA (TX) 266-267 J 5
Fox ○ USA 20-21 R 4
Fox Cove ○ CDN (NFL) 242-243 N 5
Fox Creek ○ CDN 32-33 M 4
Foxe Basin ≈ 24-25 g 6
Foxe Channel ≈ 36-37 J 2
Foxe Peninsula ⌣ CDN 36-37 L 2
Fox Glacier ○ NZ 182 C 5
Fox Islands ⌒ USA (AK) 22-23 M 6
Fox Islands ⌒ USA (MI) 272-273 D 2
Fox Lake ○ CDN 30-31 M 6
Fox Lake ○ USA (IL) 274-275 K 2
Fox Lake ○ USA (WI) 274-275 K 1
Fox Lake Indian Reserve ⚔ CDN 30-31 M 6
Fox Point ▲ CDN 30-31 J 3
Fox Point ○ USA (WI) 274-275 L 1
Fox River ○ CDN (MAN) 234-235 C 3
Fox River ∼ CDN 34-35 J 3
Fox River ∼ USA (IL) 274-275 K 3
Fox River ∼ USA (MO) 274-275 G 4
Fox River ∼ USA (WI) 270-271 K 6
Foxton Beach ○ NZ 182 E 4
Fox Valley ○ CDN (SAS) 232-233 J 5
Foxvill ○ CDN (ONT) 236-237 G 2
Foxwarren ○ CDN (MAN) 234-235 B 4
Foxworth ○ USA (MS) 268-269 L 5
Foyle, Lough ≈ 90-91 D 4
Foyn, Cape ▲ ARK 16 G 30
Foynøya ⌒ N 84-85 P 2
Foz de Areala, Represa de < BR 74-75 E 5
Foz de Jaú ○ BR 62-63 D 6
Foz do Cunene ○ ANG 216-217 A 8
Foz do Iguaçu ○ BR 76-77 K 3
Foz do Jordão ○ BR 66-67 B 7
Foz do Mamoriá ○ BR 66-67 D 4
Foz Jurupari ○ BR 66-67 B 6
Frænkel Land ⊥ GRØ 26-27 m 7
Fraga ○ E 98-99 H 4
Fragoso, Cayo ⌒ C 54-55 F 3
Fraile Muerto ○ ROU 78-79 M 2
Frailes, Islas Los ⌒ YV 60-61 K 2
Frambo ○ CI 202-203 J 7
Framingham ○ USA (MA) 278-279 K 6
Framnesfjella ▲ ARK 16 G 7
Franca ○ BR 72-73 G 6
Francavilla Fontana ○ I 100-101 F 4
France ■ F 90-91 H 8
France, Glacier de ⊂ GRØ 28-29 X 3
France, Île de ⌒ 26-27 r 5
Francés, Caverna do • BR 70-71 K 4
Frances, Lake ○ USA (MT) 250-251 G 3
Franceses ○ GCA 52-53 K 4
Frances Lake ○ CDN 30-31 E 5
Frances River ∼ CDN 30-31 E 5
Francés Viejo, Cabo ▲ DOM 54-55 L 5
Franceville ☆ G 210-211 D 4
Franche-Comté ■ F 90-91 K 8
Francia, La ○ RA 76-77 F 6
Francis ○ CDN (SAS) 232-233 P 5
Francis Case, Lake ○ USA (SD) 260-261 G 3
Francisco Aires ○ BR 68-69 G 5
Francisco Beltrão ○ BR 74-75 D 6
Francisco de Vitoria ○ RA 78-79 H 3
Francisco Dumont ○ BR 72-73 H 4
Francisco Grande ○ USA (AZ) 256-257 D 6
Francisco I. Madero ○ MEX (COA) 50-51 H 5
Francisco I. Madero ○ MEX (DGO) 50-51 G 5
Francisco I. Madero, Presa < MEX 50-51 G 3
Francisco Perito Moreno, Parque Nacional ⊥ RA 80 D 3
Francisco Rueda ○ MEX 52-53 H 3
Francisco Sá ○ BR 72-73 J 4
Franciscusbaai ≈ 220-221 B 2
Francistown ☆ RB 218-219 D 5
Franco da Rocha ○ BR 72-73 G 7
Franco de Orellana ○ PE 64-65 F 3
François ○ CDN (NFL) 242-243 M 5
François, Le ○ F 56 E 4
Francois Lake ○ CDN (BC) 228-229 J 2
Francois Lake ○ CDN (BC) 228-229 J 3
Franconia Notch • USA (NH) 278-279 K 4
Franc Peak ▲ USA (WY) 252-253 J 3
Frankel City ○ USA (TX) 264-265 B 6
Frankfield ○ AUS 178-179 J 2
Frankfort ○ USA (IN) 274-275 M 4
Frankfort ○ USA (KS) 262-263 K 5
Frankfort ○ USA (MI) 272-273 C 3
Frankfort ○ USA (SD) 260-261 H 2
Frankfort ☆ USA (KY) 276-277 L 2
Frankfort ○ ZA 220-221 J 3
Frankfurt (Oder) ○ • D 92-93 N 2
Frankfurt am Main ○ D 92-93 K 3
Frank Hann National Park ⊥ AUS 176-177 F 6
Fränkische Alb ▲ D 92-93 L 4
Fränkische Saale ∼ D 92-93 K 3
Franklin ○ AUS 178-179 F 2
Franklin ○ CDN (MAN) 234-235 D 4
Franklin ○ USA (GA) 284-285 E 3
Franklin ○ USA (ID) 252-253 G 4
Franklin ○ USA (IN) 274-275 M 5
Franklin ○ USA (KY) 276-277 J 4
Franklin ○ USA (LA) 268-269 J 7
Franklin ○ USA (NC) 282-283 D 5
Franklin ○ USA (NE) 262-263 H 4
Franklin ○ USA (NH) 278-279 K 5
Franklin ○ USA (NM) 256-257 F 6
Franklin ○ USA (OH) 280-281 B 4
Franklin ○ USA (PA) 280-281 G 2
Franklin ○ USA (TN) 276-277 J 5
Franklin ○ USA (TX) 266-267 L 2
Franklin ○ USA (VA) 280-281 K 7
Franklin ○ USA (WV) 280-281 G 5
Franklin ○ ZA 220-221 J 5
Franklin, Kap ▲ GRØ 26-27 o 7
Franklin, Point ▲ USA 20-21 L 1
Franklin Bay ≈ 24-25 J 6
Franklin D. Roosevelt Lake ○ USA (WA) 244-245 G 2
Franklin Glacier ⊂ CDN (BC) 230-231 D 2
Franklin Harbour ≈ 180-181 D 2
Franklin Island ⌒ ARK 16 F 17
Franklin Island ⌒ CDN (ONT) 238-239 E 3
Franklin Lake ○ CDN (NWT) 30-31 V 2
Franklin Lake ○ CDN (SAS) 30-31 S 6
Franklin Lake ○ USA (NV) 246-247 K 3
Franklin Lower Gordon Wild Rivers Nationalpark ⊥ AUS 180-181 H 7
Franklin Mountains ▲ CDN 30-31 F 3
Franklin Mountains ▲ USA 20-21 S 2
Franklin Ø ⌒ GRØ 26-27 R 3
Franklin Point ▲ CDN 24-25 W 6
Franklin Strait ≈ 24-25 X 5
Franklinton ○ USA (LA) 268-269 K 6
Franklinton ○ USA (NC) 282-283 J 4
Franklinville ○ USA (NY) 278-279 C 6
Frankston ○ USA (TX) 264-265 J 6
Frankton ○ NZ 182 B 6
Franktown ○ USA (CO) 254-255 L 4
Frannie ○ USA (WY) 252-253 K 2
Franquelin ○ CDN (QUE) 242-243 A 3
Fransfontein ○ NAM 216-217 C 10
Fransfonteinberge ▲ NAM 216-217 C 10
Franske Øer ⌒ GRØ 26-27 q 4
Frånsta ○ S 86-87 H 5
Franz ○ CDN (ONT) 236-237 D 4
Franz Josef Glacier ○ NZ 182 C 5
Franz Josef Land = Franca-Iosifa, Zemlja ⌒ RUS 84-85 Y 2
Frascati ○ I 100-101 D 4
Fraser, Mount ▲ AUS 176-177 E 2
Fraser Basin ⌣ CDN (BC) 228-229 K 2
Fraserburg ○ ZA 220-221 E 5
Fraserburgh ○ GB 90-91 F 3
Fraserdale ○ CDN (ONT) 236-237 G 3
Fraser Island ⌒ ••• AUS 178-179 M 3
Fraser Island National Park ⊥ AUS 178-179 M 3
Fraser Lake ○ CDN (BC) 228-229 K 2
Fraser Lake ○ CDN (BC) 228-229 K 2
Fraser Lake ○ CDN (NFL) 36-37 S 7
Fraser National Park ⊥ AUS 180-181 H 4
Fraser Plateau ▲ CDN (BC) 228-229 J 4
Fraser Range ○ AUS 176-177 G 6
Fraser River ∼ CDN 36-37 S 6
Fraser River ∼ CDN (BC) 228-229 Q 4
Fraser River ∼ CDN (BC) 228-229 M 4
Fraser River ∼ CDN (BC) 230-231 H 4
Frater ○ CDN (ONT) 236-237 D 5
Fraustro ○ MEX 50-51 J 5
Fray Bentos ☆ ROU 78-79 K 2
Fray Jorge ○ RCH 76-77 B 6
Fray Jorge, Parque Nacional ⊥ RCH 76-77 B 6
Fray Marcos ○ ROU 78-79 M 3
Frazee ○ USA (MN) 270-271 C 4
Frazer ○ USA (MT) 250-251 N 3
Frazier Park ○ USA (CA) 248-249 F 5
Freakly Point ▲ CDN 36-37 K 7
Frebag River ∼ CDN 32-33 Q 3
Fred ○ USA (TX) 268-269 F 6
Freden, ostrov ⌒ RUS 84-85 g 2
Frederica National Monument, Fort • USA (GA) 284-285 J 5
Fredericia ○ • DK 86-87 D 9
Frederick ○ USA (MD) 280-281 J 4
Frederick ○ USA (OK) 264-265 E 4
Frederick ○ USA (SD) 260-261 H 1
Frederick, Mount ▲ AUS (NT) 172-173 J 5
Frederick, Mount ▲ AUS (WA) 172-173 D 7
Frederick E. Hyde Fjord ≈ 26-27 j 2
Fredericksburg ○ USA (IA) 274-275 F 2
Fredericksburg ○ USA (TX) 266-267 J 3
Fredericksburg ○ USA (VA) 280-281 J 5
Frederick Sound ≈ 32-33 C 3
Fredericton ○ CDN (NFL) 242-243 O 3
Fredericktown ○ USA (MD) 280-281 L 4
Fredericktown ○ USA (MO) 276-277 E 3
Fredericktown ○ USA (OH) 280-281 D 3
Frederico Westphalen ○ BR 74-75 D 6
Fredericton ☆ CDN (NB) 240-241 J 5
Frederik Henrik Island = Pulau Dolak ⌒ RI 166-167 K 5
Frederiksdal = Narsaq Kujalleg ○ GRØ 28-29 S 6
Frederikshåb = Paamiut ○ GRØ 28-29 Q 5
Frederikshåbs Banke ≃ 28-29 P 5
Frederikshavn ○ DK 86-87 E 8
Frederiksted ○ • USA (VI) 286-287 R 3
Fredonia ○ CO 60-61 D 5
Fredonia ○ USA (AZ) 256-257 C 2
Fredonia ○ USA (KS) 262-263 L 7
Fredonia ○ USA (NY) 278-279 B 6
Fredonyer Summit ▲ USA (CA) 246-247 E 3
Fredrika ○ S 86-87 J 4
Fredriksberg ○ S 86-87 G 6
Fredrikstad ☆ N 86-87 E 7
Freeborn ○ USA (MN) 270-271 E 7
Freeburg ○ USA (MO) 274-275 G 6
Freedom ○ USA (CA) 248-249 C 3
Freedom ○ USA (KY) 276-277 K 4
Freedom ○ USA (OK) 264-265 E 2
Freedom ○ USA (WY) 252-253 H 4
Freehold ○ USA (NJ) 280-281 M 3
Free Home ○ USA (GA) 284-285 F 2
Freeland ○ USA (WA) 244-245 C 2
Freelandville ○ USA (IN) 274-275 L 6
Freeling Heights ▲ AUS 178-179 E 6
Freels, Cape ▲ CDN (NFL) 242-243 P 3
Freeman ○ USA (SD) 260-261 J 3
Freeman ○ USA (WA) 244-245 H 3
Freeman River ∼ CDN 32-33 N 4
Freemansundet ≈ 84-85 M 3
Freemont ○ CDN (SAS) 232-233 J 3
Freeport ○ BS 54-55 F 1
Freeport ○ CDN (NS) 240-241 J 6
Freeport ○ USA (FL) 286-287 C 1
Freeport ○ USA (IL) 274-275 J 2
Freeport ○ USA (PA) 280-281 G 3
Freeport ○ USA (TX) 266-267 M 5
Freer ○ USA (TX) 266-267 J 6
Freesoil ○ USA (MI) 272-273 C 3
Freetown ○ USA (IN) 274-275 M 6
Freetown ★ • WAL 202-203 D 5
Freezeout Mountain ▲ USA (OR) 244-245 H 7
Frégate Island ⌒ SY 224 D 2
Fregenal de la Sierra ○ • E 98-99 D 5
Fregon ⚔ AUS 176-177 M 3
Freiberg ○ • D 92-93 M 3
Freiburg im Breisgau ○ • D 92-93 J 5
Frei Inocêncio ○ BR 72-73 K 5
Frei Orlando ○ BR 72-73 H 5
Freire ○ RCH 78-79 C 5
Freirina ○ RCH 76-77 B 5
Freising ○ D 92-93 L 4
Freiwaldau = Jeseník ○ CZ 92-93 O 3
Fréjus ○ F 90-91 L 10
Fremantle ○ AUS 176-177 C 6
Fremont ○ USA (CA) 248-249 C 2
Fremont ○ USA (MI) 272-273 D 4
Fremont ○ USA (NC) 282-283 K 5
Fremont ○ USA (NE) 262-263 K 3
Fremont ○ USA (OH) 280-281 C 2
Fremont ○ USA (WI) 270-271 K 6
Fremont Lake ○ USA (WY) 252-253 J 3
Fremont Mountains ▲ USA (OR) 244-245 D 7

Fremont River ~ USA (UT) 254-255 D 5
French Bay ⊥• BS 54-55 H 3
Frenchburg o USA (KY) 276-277 M 3
French Cove o CDN (NFL) 242-243 N 2
French Creek ~ USA (PA) 280-281 F 2
Frenchglen o USA (OR) 244-245 G 8
French Guiana = Guyane Française ▫ F 62-63 H 3
French Hills ▲ AUS 172-173 H 6
French Lick o USA (IN) 274-275 M 6
Frenchman Butte o CDN (SAS) 232-233 J 2
Frenchman Creek ~ CDN (SAS) 232-233 L 6
Frenchman Creek ~ USA (NE) 262-263 D 4
Frenchman River ~ CDN (SAS) 232-233 K 6
Frenchman's Bay ≈• 54-55 G 6
Frenchman's Cove Provincial Park ⊥ CDN (NFL) 242-243 N 5
French Pass o NZ 182 D 4
French River o CDN (ONT) 238-239 E 2
French River ~ CDN (ONT) 238-239 E 2
Frenchtown o USA (MT) 250-251 E 4
Frenchville o USA (ME) 278-279 N 1
Frenda o DZ 190-191 C 3
Frere o ZA 220-221 J 4
Fresco o CI 202-203 H 7
Fresco, Rio ~ BR 68-69 C 5
Freshfield Icefield ⊂ CDN (ALB) 232-233 B 4
Freshwater o CDN (NFL) 242-243 P 5
Freshwater Point ▲ AUS 176-177 C 4
Fresia o RCH 78-79 C 6
Fresnal Canyon o USA (AZ) 256-257 D 7
Fresnillo de González Echeverría o MEX 50-51 H 6
Fresno o USA (CA) 248-249 E 3
Fresno Reservoir o USA (MT) 250-251 J 3
Freuchen Bay ≈ 24-25 f 7
Freuchen Land ⊥ GRØ 26-27 c 2
Freudenthal = Bruntál o CZ 92-93 O 4
Freundschaftsinseln = Tonga ⌒ TON 184 IV a 2
Frewena o AUS 174-175 C 6
Freycinet Estuary ≈ 176-177 B 3
Freycinet National Park ⊥ AUS 180-181 K 7
Freycinet Peninsula ⌣ AUS 180-181 J 7
Fria o RG 202-203 D 4
Fria, Kaap ▲ NAM 216-217 A 9
Fria, La o YV 60-61 E 3
Friant o USA (CA) 248-249 E 3
Friars Point o USA (MS) 268-269 K 2
Frías o RA 76-77 E 5
Friday Creek ~ CDN (ONT) 236-237 F 2
Friday Harbour o USA (WA) 244-245 B 2
Friedberg (Hessen) o D 92-93 K 3
Friedrichshafen o D 92-93 K 5
Friend o USA (NE) 262-263 J 4
Friendship o USA (AR) 276-277 B 6
Friendship o USA (OH) 280-281 C 5
Friendship Hill National Historic Site • USA (PA) 280-281 G 4
Friendship Shoal ≃ 162-163 K 2
Friesach o A 92-93 N 5
Frigate, Lac o CDN 38-39 G 2
Frigate Bay Beach ⊥ KAN 56 D 3
Friggesund o S 86-87 H 6
Frindsburg Reef ⌒ SOL 184 I d 1
Frio, Cabo ▲ BR 72-73 K 7
Frio Draw ~ USA (NM) 256-257 M 4
Friona o USA (TX) 264-265 B 4
Frio River ~ USA (TX) 266-267 J 5
Frisco o USA (CO) 254-255 J 4
Frisco City o USA (AL) 284-285 C 5
Fritch o USA (TX) 264-265 C 3
Fritz Hugh Sound ≈ 32-33 G 6
Fritz Hugh Sound ≈ CDN 230-231 B 2
Friuli-Venézia Giúlia ▫ I 100-101 D 1
Friza, proliv ≈ RUS 122-123 N 6
Frobisher o CDN (SAS) 232-233 Q 6
Frobisher Bay ≈ 36-37 Q 3
Frobisher Bay o CDN 36-37 P 3
Frobisher Lake o CDN 32-33 Q 3
Frog Lake o CDN (ALB) 232-233 H 2
Frog Lake o CDN (ALB) 232-233 H 2
Frog River ~ CDN 32-33 G 3
Frog River ~ CDN 34-35 M 3
Frohavet ≈ 86-87 D 5
Froid o USA (MT) 250-251 P 3
Frolovo o RUS 116-117 L 6
Frolovo o RUS (VLG) 102-103 N 3
Fromberg o USA (MT) 250-251 L 6
Frome, Lake o AUS 178-179 E 6
Frome Downs o AUS 178-179 E 6
Fronteiro, Cachoeira da ~ BR 68-69 B 6
Frontenac o USA (KS) 262-263 M 7
Frontera o E 188-189 C 7
Frontera o• MEX 52-53 H 2
Frontera, Punta ▲ MEX 52-53 H 2
Frontera Comalapa o MEX 52-53 H 4
Fronteras o MEX 50-51 E 2
Frontier o CDN (SAS) 232-233 K 6
Front Range ▲ USA (CO) 254-255 K 3
Front Royal o USA (VA) 280-281 H 5
Frosinone ☆ I 100-101 D 4
Frostburg o USA (MD) 280-281 H 4
Frostproof o USA (FL) 286-287 H 4
Froude o CDN (SAS) 232-233 P 6
Frøya ⌒ N 86-87 D 5
Frozen Strait ≈ 24-25 d 7
Fruita o USA (CO) 254-255 G 4
Fruitland o USA (ID) 252-253 B 3
Fruitland o USA (MO) 276-277 F 3
Fruitland o USA (UT) 254-255 E 3
Frunze = Biškek ★ KS 146-147 B 4
Frunze, mys ▲ RUS 108-109 Y 1
Fruta de Leite o BR 72-73 J 4
Frutal o BR 72-73 F 6
Frutillar o RCH 78-79 C 6
Fryatt, Mount ▲ CDN (ALB) 228-229 R 4
Fryeburg o USA (LA) 268-269 G 4
Fryeburg o USA (ME) 278-279 L 4
Frymire o USA (KY) 276-277 J 3
Frys o CDN (SAS) 232-233 R 6
Fua'amotu o TON 184 IV a 2
Fucheng o VRC 154-155 K 3
Fuding o VRC 156-157 M 3
Fududa < EAK 212-213 G 5
Fuego, Tierra del ⊥ RCH 80 E 7
Fuencaliente o E 188-189 C 6
Fuencaliente de la Palma o E 188-189 C 6
Fuengirola o E 98-99 E 6
Fuente de Cantos o E 98-99 D 5
Fuente del Fresno o E 98-99 F 5
Fuente de San Esteban, La o E 98-99 D 4
Fuente Obejuna o E 98-99 E 5
Fuentesaúco o E 98-99 E 4
Fuerte o BOL 70-71 E 7
Fuerte, El o MEX 50-51 E 4
Fuerte, Río ~ MEX 50-51 E 4
Fuerte Bulnes o RCH 80 E 6
Fuerte Olimpo ☆ PY 76-77 J 1
Fuerte Quemado o RA 76-77 D 4
Fuerte San Lorenzo ∴•• PA 52-53 E 7
Fuerte San Rafael • RA 78-79 E 3
Fuerteventura ⌒ E 188-189 D 6
Fufeng o VRC 154-155 E 4
Fufulsu o GH 202-203 K 5
Fuğaira, al- o UAE 134-135 G 6
Fuga Island ⌒ RP 160-161 D 3
Fuglasker ⌒ IS 86-87 b 3
Fuglehuken ▲ N 84-85 G 3
Fugløy Bank ≃ 86-87 J 1
Fuğma o Y 132-133 F 5
Fugong o VRC 142-143 L 2
Fugou o VRC 154-155 J 4
Fugu o VRC 154-155 G 2
Fuhai o VRC 146-147 H 2
Fuhaihil, al- o KWT 130-131 L 3
Fuji o J 152-153 H 7
Fujian ▫ VRC 156-157 K 3
Fu Jiang ~ VRC 154-155 D 6
Fujieda o J 152-153 H 7
Fuji-gawa ~ J 152-153 H 7
Fuji-Hakone-Izu National Park ⊥ J 152-153 H 7
Fujin o VRC 150-151 J 4
Fuji-san ▲•• J 152-153 H 7
Fujisawa o J 152-153 H 7
Fujiyoshida o J 152-153 H 7
Fūka o ET 194-195 C 2
Fukagawa o J 152-153 K 3
Fukang o VRC 146-147 H 3
Fukuchiyama o J 152-153 F 7
Fukue o J 152-153 C 8
Fukuei Chiao ▲ RC 156-157 M 4
Fukue-shima ⌒ J 152-153 C 8
Fukui ☆ J 152-153 G 6
Fukuoka ☆• J 152-153 D 8
Fukushima o J (HOK) 152-153 J 4
Fukushima ☆ J (FUK) 152-153 J 6
Fukuyama o J 152-153 E 7
Fulacunda o GNB 202-203 C 4
Fulda o CDN (SAS) 232-233 N 3
Fulda o•• D (HES) 92-93 K 3
Fulda ~ D 92-93 K 3
Fulda o USA (MN) 270-271 C 7
Fulford Harbour o CDN (BC) 230-231 F 5
Fuli o RC 156-157 M 5
Fuling o VRC 156-157 E 2
Fullarton o TT 60-61 L 2
Fullerborn o PNG 183 F 4
Fullerton o USA (IL) 274-275 K 4
Fullerton o USA (ND) 258-259 J 5
Fullerton o USA (NE) 262-263 J 3
Fulton o USA (AR) 276-277 B 7
Fulton o USA (IL) 274-275 H 3
Fulton o USA (KY) 276-277 G 4
Fulton o USA (MO) 274-275 G 6
Fulton o USA (MS) 268-269 M 2
Fulton o USA (NY) 278-279 E 5
Fultondale o USA (AL) 284-285 D 3
Fulton River ~ CDN (BC) 228-229 H 2
Fultoro o RI 166-167 D 6
Fulula ~ ZRE 210-211 F 6
Fulunäs o S 86-87 F 6
Fumbelo o ANG 216-217 E 5
Fumel o F 90-91 H 9
Fumiela o ANG 216-217 D 3
Funabashi o J 152-153 H 7
Funadomari o J 152-153 J 2
Funafuti Atoll ⌒ TUV 13 J 3
Funan o VRC 154-155 J 5
Funäsdalen o S 86-87 F 5
Funchal o P 188-189 C 4
Fundacão Eclética o BR 72-73 F 3
Fundación o CO 60-61 D 2
Fundão o BR 72-73 K 5
Fundão o P 98-99 D 4
Fundición o MEX 50-51 E 4
Fundo, Rio ~ BR 68-69 G 6
Fundo das Figueiras o CV 202-203 C 5
Fundong o CAM 204-205 J 5
Fundy, Bay of ≈ 38-39 L 6
Fundy, Bay of ≈ CDN 240-241 J 6
Fundy National Park ⊥ CDN (NB) 240-241 K 5
Fungom ▲ CAM 204-205 H 5
Funhalouro o MOC 218-219 H 6
Funiak Springs, De o USA (FL) 286-287 C 1
Funing o VRC (JIA) 154-155 L 5
Funing o VRC (YUN) 156-157 D 5
Funkley o USA (MN) 270-271 D 3
Funsi o GH 202-203 K 4
Funtua o WAN 204-205 G 3
Funzi Island ⌒ EAK 212-213 G 6
Fuping o VRC (HEB) 154-155 J 2
Fuping o VRC (SXI) 154-155 F 4
Fuqing o VRC 156-157 L 4
Fuquan o VRC 156-157 E 3
Fuquay Varina o USA (NC) 282-283 H 5
Fura Braço, Correduira ~ BR 66-67 H 6
Furaiši, al- o KSA 130-131 F 5
Furancungo o MOC 218-219 G 2
Furano o J 152-153 K 3
Furano, Kami- o J 152-153 K 3
Furāt, al- ~ IRQ 128-129 L 7
Furāwiya, Bi'r < SUD 198-199 L 5
Furdale o CDN (SAS) 232-233 M 3
Fürg o IR 134-135 F 4
Furkwa o EAT (DOD) 212-213 E 6
Furman o USA (AL) 284-285 D 5
Furmanov ☆ RUS 94-95 R 3
Furmanovo ☆ KA 96-97 F 9
Furnace Creek o USA (CA) 248-249 H 3
Furnas, Represa de < BR 72-73 G 6
Furneaux Group ⌒ AUS 180-181 K 6
Furness o CDN (SAS) 232-233 J 2
Furo Carandazinho ~ BR 70-71 J 5
Furo do Jurupari ~ BR 68-69 B 3
Furo do Tajapuru ~ BR 62-63 J 6
Furqlūs o SYR 128-129 G 5
Furrial, El o YV 60-61 K 3
Furroli ▲ ETH 208-209 D 7
Fürstenfeld o A 92-93 O 5
Fürstenwalde (Spree) o• D 92-93 N 2
Fürth o D 92-93 L 4
Furubira o J 152-153 J 3
Furukawa o J 152-153 J 5
Fury and Hecla Strait ≈ 24-25 e 6
Fury Point ▲ CDN 24-25 a 4
Fusagasuga o CO 60-61 D 5
Fushimi Lake Provincial Park ⊥ CDN (ONT) 236-237 E 3
Fushui o VRC 154-155 F 4
Fushun o VRC 150-151 D 7
Fusilier o CDN (SAS) 232-233 J 4
Fuskam Mata o WAN 204-205 H 3
Fusong o VRC 150-151 F 6
Fussa, vulkan ▲ RUS 122-123 Q 3
Füssen o• D 92-93 L 5
Fusui o VRC 156-157 E 5
Futa, Cuilo- o ANG 216-217 C 3
Futalaufquen, Lago o RA 78-79 D 7
Futaleufú o RCH 78-79 D 7
Futaleufú, Río ~ RA 78-79 D 7
Futrono o RCH 78-79 C 6
Futuna Island = Île Erronan ⌒ VAN 184 II c 4
Fu Xian o VRC 154-155 F 4
Fuxian Hu o VRC 156-157 C 4
Fuxin o VRC 150-151 C 6
Fuxing o VRC 156-157 J 2
Fuyang o VRC 154-155 J 5
Fuyu o VRC (HEI) 150-151 E 4
Fuyu o VRC (JIL) 150-151 E 5
Fuyuan o VRC (HEI) 150-151 K 3
Fuyuan o VRC (YUN) 156-157 D 4
Fuyun o VRC 146-147 J 2
Fuzhou ☆• VRC 156-157 L 3
Fuzhouzhen o VRC 150-151 C 8
Fwa, Lac o• ZRE 210-211 J 6
Fyllas Banke ≃ 28-29 O 5
Fyn ⌒ DK 86-87 E 9
Fyresvatn o N 86-87 D 7

G

Ga o GH 202-203 J 5
Gaalkacyo ☆ SP 208-209 H 5
Gaamodebli o LB 202-203 F 6
Gaasefjord ≈ 26-27 m 8
Gaaseland ⊥ GRØ 26-27 m 8
Gaase Pynt ▲ GRØ 26-27 m 8
Ġāb, al- ⊥ SYR 128-129 G 5
Gaba o ETH 208-209 F 5
Gabagaba o PNG 183 D 5
Ġabal, al-al-Aḫḍar ▲ OM 132-133 K 2
Ġabala o• SYR 128-129 F 5
Ġabal 'Abdal'aziz ▲ SYR 128-129 J 4
Ġabalatuai o LB 202-203 F 6
Ġabal Auliyā o SUD 200-201 F 5
Ġabal Bozi o SUD 200-201 F 6
Gabaldon o RP 160-161 D 5
Ġabal Mazmum o SUD 200-201 F 6
Ġabal os Sarāğ o AFG 136-137 L 7
Gabargaon o BD 142-143 F 3
Gabarouse o CDN (NS) 240-241 P 5
Gabbac, Raas ▲ SP 208-209 K 4
Gabba Island ⌒ AUS 183 B 5
Gabbro Lake o CDN 38-39 M 2
Gabbs o USA (NV) 246-247 H 5
Ġabbūl, Sabḫat al- o SYR 128-129 G 4
Gabela o ANG 216-217 C 5
Gabensis o PNG 183 D 4
Gabes ☆ TN 190-191 H 4
Gabes = Gabès ☆ TN 190-191 H 3
Gabes, Golfe de ≈ 190-191 H 3
Gabes, Gulf of = Gabès, Golfe de ≈ TN 190-191 H 3
Gabèt al-Ma'ādin o SUD 200-201 H 2
Gabgāba, Wādi ~ SUD 200-201 F 2
Gabi o RN 198-199 C 6
Gabia o ZRE 210-211 F 6
Gabiane o TCH 206-207 D 4
Gabir o SUD 206-207 G 4
Ġābir, Qal'at • SYR 128-129 H 5
Gabon, Estuaire de ≈ 210-211 B 3
Gabo Island ⌒ AUS 180-181 K 4
Gabon ■ G 210-211 C 4
Gaborone ★ RB 220-221 G 2
Gabras o SUD 206-207 H 3
Gabreševci o BG 102-103 C 6
Gabriel, Lac o CDN 36-37 P 5
Gabriel Strait ≈ 36-37 R 4
Gabriel Vera o BOL 70-71 E 6
Gabriel Zamora o MEX 52-53 C 2
Ġabrik, Rūd-e ~ IR 134-135 H 5
Ġabrin, Ġazire-ye ⌒ IR 134-135 D 5
Gabriola o CDN (BC) 230-231 F 4
Gabrovo o BG 102-103 D 6
Gabú ☆ GNB 202-203 C 3
Gabu o ZRE 212-213 A 2
Gacheta o CO 60-61 E 5
Gackle o USA (ND) 258-259 H 5
Gacko o BIH 100-101 G 3
Gačsar o IR 136-137 B 6
Gadabeji o RN 198-199 C 5
Gadaf, Wādi l- ~ JOR 130-131 E 2
Gadag o IND 140-141 F 3
Gadaisu o PNG 183 E 6
Gadamai o SUD 200-201 H 4
Gada-Oundou o RG 202-203 E 4
Gäddede o S 86-87 G 4
Gadein o SUD 206-207 J 4
Gado Bravo, Serra do ▲ BR 68-69 E 6
Gādra o PK 138-139 C 7
Ġadrān o AFG 138-139 B 3
Gadsby o CDN (ALB) 232-233 F 3
Gadsden o USA (AL) 284-285 D 3
Gadsden o USA (SC) 284-285 K 3
Ġadūn, Wādi ~ OM 132-133 H 4
Gadwāl o IND 140-141 G 2
Gadzi o RCA 206-207 C 6
Gael Hamke Bugt ≈ 26-27 p 6
Găești o RO 102-103 D 5
Gaeta, Golfo di ≈ 100-101 D 4
Ġafara, al- o KSA 130-131 J 6
Ġa'farābād = Abgarm o IR 128-129 N 5
Ġafāt, al- o OM 132-133 K 2
Gaffney o USA (SC) 284-285 J 1
Ġafr, al- o JOR (MAA) 130-131 E 2
Ġafr, al- o JOR (MAA) 130-131 E 2
Gafsa ☆• TN 190-191 G 3
Gaftony o AZ 128-129 N 3
Ġāfūra, al- ⊥ KSA 134-135 D 6
Gag, Pulau ⌒ RI 166-167 E 2
Gagal o TCH 206-207 B 4
Gagan o PNG 184 I b 1
Gagarawa o WAN 198-199 D 6
Gagargarh o IND 142-143 C 2
Gagarin o• RUS 94-95 O 4
Gagarin ☆ US 136-137 L 4
Ġāğarm o IR 136-137 E 6
Ġağarm, Kāl-e Šūr ~ IR 136-137 E 6
Ġagatū o AFG 138-139 B 3
Gagau, Gunung ▲ MAL (PAH) 162-163 E 2
Gage o USA (NM) 256-257 G 6
Gage o USA (OK) 264-265 E 2
Gagere ~ WAN 198-199 C 6
Gagetown o CDN (NB) 240-241 J 5
Gaggabutan o RP 160-161 D 4
Ġağğağa, Nahr ~ SYR 128-129 J 4
Gaghamni o SUD 206-207 J 3
Ġāği o AFG 138-139 B 3
Ġāği Meidān o AFG 138-139 C 3
Ġagin, Rūd-e ~ IR 134-135 G 6
Gagnoa ☆ CI 202-203 H 6
Gagnon o CDN 38-39 K 3
Gagnon, Lac o CDN (QUE) 238-239 K 2
Ġāğori o AFG 134-135 M 2
Gagra o• GE 126-127 D 6
Ġağrūd, Rūdḫāne-ye ~ IR 136-137 B 7
Ga Hai ~ VRC 144-145 L 2
Gahern o CDN (ALB) 232-233 G 6
Gahkom o IR 134-135 F 4
Ġahnin o OM 132-133 J 5
Ġahra, al- o• KWT 130-131 K 3
Ġahrom o• IR 134-135 E 4
Gaiba, Lago o BOL 70-71 J 5
Gaibanda o BD 142-143 F 3
Gaida, al- o Y 132-133 H 5
Gaida, al- o Y 132-133 G 6
Gaigou o BF 202-203 K 3
Gail ~ A 92-93 M 5
Gail o USA (TX) 264-265 C 6
Gail, al- o Y 132-133 G 6
Gail Bāwazir o• Y 132-133 F 6
Gaillac o F 90-91 H 10
Gaillimh = Galway ☆• IRL 90-91 C 5
Gaiman o RA 78-79 G 7
Gaimonaki o PNG 183 E 5
Gaines, Fort • USA (AL) 284-285 B 6
Gainesboro o USA (TN) 276-277 K 4
Gainesville o USA (FL) 286-287 G 2
Gainesville o USA (GA) 284-285 G 2
Gainesville o USA (MO) 276-277 C 4
Gainesville o USA (TX) 264-265 G 5
Gainford o CDN (ALB) 232-233 D 2
Gainsborough o CDN (SAS) 232-233 R 6
Gairdner, Lake o AUS 178-179 C 6
Gairdner River ~ AUS 176-177 E 6
Gaire o PNG 183 D 5
Gairesi ~ ZW 218-219 G 3
Gairo o EAT (MOR) 214-215 J 4
Gaital, Cerro ▲ PA 52-53 D 7
Gaithersburg o USA (MD) 280-281 J 4
Gaivota o BR 62-63 J 5
Gai Xian o VRC 150-151 D 7
Gaj ☆ RUS 96-97 L 8
Gaja, Pulau ⌒ MAL 160-161 C 10
Gajah, Kampung o MAL 162-163 D 2
Gajahmungkur, Danau o RI 168 D 3
Gajčaveem ~ RUS 112-113 O 5
Gajendragarh o IND 140-141 F 3
Gaji, River ~ WAN 204-205 J 3
Gajiram o WAN 198-199 F 6
Gajny ☆ RUS 96-97 J 3
Gajwel o IND 140-141 H 2
Gakarosa ▲ ZA 220-221 F 3
Gakem o WAN 204-205 H 5
Gakona o USA 20-21 S 5
Gakona River ~ USA 20-21 S 5
Gakou o RMM 202-203 F 2
Gakuch o IND 138-139 D 1
Gala o VRC 144-145 G 6
Galachipa ~ BD 142-143 G 4
Gal Adhale o SP 208-209 H 5
Ġalāģil o KSA 130-131 J 5
Galahad o CDN (ALB) 232-233 G 3
Galal, togga ~ SP 208-209 K 3
Ġalālābād ☆• AFG 138-139 C 2
Galam ~ RUS 122-123 E 2
Galam, Selat ≈ 162-163 E 4
Ġalāmid, al- o KSA 130-131 G 2
Galán o CO 60-61 E 4
Galán, Cerro ▲ RA 76-77 D 3
Galana ~ EAK 212-213 G 5
Galandūk o IR 136-137 B 7
Galanga o ANG 216-217 C 6
Galangachi o RT 202-203 L 4
Galangue o ANG 216-217 D 6
Galaosiē o US 136-137 J 5
Galápagos, Islas = Archipiélago de Colón ⌒ EC 64-65 B 9
Galápagos, Parque Nacional de ⊥••• EC 64-65 B 9
Galápagos Fracture Zone = Galapagos Fracture Zone ≃ 14-15 P 8
Galápagos Islands = Islas Galápagos ⌒ EC 64-65 B 9
Galapagos Rise = Galápagos Rise ≃ 5 B 4
Galarza o RA 76-77 J 5
Galarza, Laguna o RA 76-77 J 5
Galas ~ MAL 162-163 D 2
Galashiels o GB 90-91 F 4
Galata o CY 128-129 E 5
Galata o USA (MT) 250-251 H 3
Galați ☆• RO 102-103 F 5
Galatia o USA (IL) 276-277 G 3
Galax o USA (VA) 280-281 F 7
Galbraith o AUS 174-175 F 5
Galbraith o CDN 20-21 Y 7
Galbyn Gov' ⊥ MAU 148-149 H 6
Ġaldak o AFG 134-135 M 3
Gáldar o E 188-189 D 6
Galdhøpiggen ▲•• N 86-87 D 6
Ġaldiyan o IR 128-129 L 4
Galé o RMM 202-203 E 3
Galeana o MEX (CHA) 50-51 F 2
Galeana o MEX (NL) 50-51 J 5
Galečnyj, mys ▲ RUS 110-111 d 1
Galegu o SUD (Naz) 200-201 G 6
Galegu ~ SUD 200-201 G 6
Galela o RI 164-165 K 3
Galela, Teluk ≈ 164-165 K 3
Galena o USA (AK) 20-21 M 4
Galena o USA (IL) 274-275 H 2
Galena o USA (MO) 276-277 B 4
Galena Bay o CDN (BC) 230-231 M 3
Galenbindunuwewa o CL 140-141 J 6
Galeo o LB 202-203 G 7
Ġāleq o IR 134-135 K 5
Galera o EC 64-65 B 1
Galera, Punta ▲ EC 64-65 B 1
Galera, Rio ~ BR 70-71 H 4
Galesburg o USA (IL) 274-275 H 4
Galesburg o USA (ND) 258-259 K 4
Galesong o RI 164-165 F 6
Galesville o USA (WI) 270-271 G 6
Galēti Shet' ~ ETH 208-209 E 4
Galeton o USA (PA) 280-281 J 2
Galgamuwa o CL 140-141 J 7
Gal'gavaam ~ RUS 112-113 J 1
Galguduud ▫ SP 208-209 H 6
Gal Hareeri o SP 208-209 H 6
Galheirão, Rio ~ BR 72-73 H 2
Galheiros o BR 72-73 G 2
Gali o GE 126-127 D 6
Galia o BR 72-73 F 7
Galiano o CDN (BC) 230-231 F 5
Ġaliba o IRQ 130-131 K 2
Galibi o SME 62-63 G 3
Galibi, National Reservaat ⊥ SME 62-63 G 3
Galič o• RUS 94-95 S 2
Galice o USA (OR) 244-245 B 8
Galicia ▫ E 98-99 C 3
Galičskaja vozvyšennost' ▲ RUS 94-95 R 3
Galilee o CDN (SAS) 232-233 N 6
Galilee, Lake o AUS 178-179 H 2
Galiléia o BR 72-73 K 5
Galilo o PNG 183 F 3
Galim o CAM (ADA) 204-205 K 5
Galim o CAM (OUE) 204-205 J 6
Galimovskij hrebet ▲ RUS 112-113 H 5
Galimyj o RUS 112-113 H 5
Galina • JA 54-55 G 5
Galinda o ANG 216-217 B 4
Galinhas, Ilha das ⌒ GNB 202-203 C 4
Galion o USA (OH) 280-281 D 3
Galite, La ⌒ TN 190-191 G 2
Galiuro Mountains ▲ USA (AZ) 256-257 E 6
Galivedu o IND 140-141 H 4
Galiwinku ✕ AUS 174-175 C 3
Ġallābāt o SUD 200-201 H 6
Gallants o CDN (NFL) 242-243 K 4
Gallaorol ☆ US 136-137 K 5
Gallatin o USA (MO) 274-275 E 5
Gallatin o USA (TN) 276-277 J 4
Gallatin Peak ▲ USA (MT) 250-251 H 6
Gallatin River ~ USA (MT) 250-251 H 6
Galle o•• CL 140-141 J 7
Gállego, Río ~ E 98-99 G 3
Gallego Rise ≃ 14-15 R 8
Gallegos o USA (NM) 256-257 M 3
Gallegos, Río ~ RA 80 F 5
Galleguillos o RCH 76-77 B 4
Gallina o USA (NM) 256-257 J 2
Gallinas o USA (NM) 256-257 K 4
Gallinas, Punta ▲ CO 60-61 F 1
Gallinas Mountains ▲ USA (NM) 256-257 H 4
Gallinas Peak ▲ USA (NM) 256-257 K 4
Gallinas River ~ USA (NM) 256-257 K 3
Gallinero, Cerro ▲ YV 60-61 H 5
Gallipoli o AUS 174-175 D 6
Gallipoli o I 100-101 F 4
Gallipolis o USA (OH) 280-281 D 5
Gällivare o• S 86-87 K 3
Gallix o CDN (QUE) 242-243 B 2
Gallja, ostrov ⌒ RUS 84-85 e 2
Galljaaral o US 136-137 K 4
Gallo Arroyo ~ USA (NM) 256-257 K 4
Gallo Mountains ▲ USA (NM) 256-257 G 4
Galloo Island ⌒ USA (NY) 278-279 E 5
Galloway o CDN (BC) 230-231 O 4
Galloway ⊥ GB 90-91 E 4
Gallup o USA (NM) 256-257 G 3
Galma, River ~ WAN 204-205 H 3
Galma Galla < EAK 212-213 H 4
Galmi o RN 198-199 B 6
Galo Boukoy o RCA 206-207 B 6
Gal Oya National Park ⊥ CL 140-141 J 7
Galpón, El o RA 76-77 E 3
Ġālrēz o AFG 138-139 B 2
Galšar = Bujant o MAU 148-149 K 4
Galt o USA (CA) 246-247 D 5
Galt o USA (MO) 274-275 E 4
Gal Tardo o SP 212-213 K 2
Galtat-Zemmour o MA 196-197 D 2
Ġalūgāh o IR 136-137 C 6
Ġalūlā' o IRQ 128-129 L 5
Galung o RI 164-165 F 5
Galur o RI 168 D 3
Galva o USA (IL) 274-275 H 3
Galvão o BR 74-75 D 6
Gálves o RA 78-79 J 2
Galveston o• USA (TX) 268-269 F 7
Galveston Bay ≈ USA 268-269 F 7
Galvestone o USA (IN) 274-275 M 4
Galveston Island ⌒ USA (TX) 268-269 F 7
Galvez, Río ~ PE 64-65 F 4
Galway = Gaillimh ☆• IRL 90-91 C 5
Galway Bay ≈ 90-91 C 5
Galway's Soufrière ⊥ GB 56 D 3
Gam, Pulau ⌒ RI 166-167 F 2
Gama o BR 72-73 F 3
Gama o RG 202-203 F 6
Gama, Isla ⌒ RA 78-79 H 6
Gamaches o F 90-91 H 7
Ġamāġim, Umm al- o KSA 130-131 J 4
Gamana, River ~ WAN 204-205 H 5
Gama River ~ PNG 183 B 4
Ġamāsāb, Rūd-e ~ IR 134-135 B 1
Gamawa o WAN 198-199 E 6
Gamba o ANG 216-217 D 5
Gamba o G 210-211 C 5
Gamba o VRC 144-145 G 6
Gamba o ZRE 210-211 K 6
Gambaga o GH 202-203 K 4
Gambang o MAL 162-163 E 3
Gambara o MEX 52-53 C 2
Gambēla o ETH 208-209 B 4
Gambela National Park ⊥ ETH 208-209 A 5
Gambell o USA 20-21 E 5
Gambia ■ WAG 202-203 B 3
Gambia, River ~ WAG 202-203 B 3
Gambia No.1 o GH 202-203 J 6
Gambie ~ SN 202-203 D 3
Gambier Islands ⌒ AUS 180-181 D 3
Gambo o ANG 216-217 F 4
Gambo o CDN (NFL) 242-243 O 4
Gambo o RCA 206-207 F 6
Gamboa o PA 52-53 E 7
Gamboma o RCB 210-211 E 4
Gamboula o RCA 206-207 B 6
Gamčen, hrebet ▲ RUS 120-121 T 6
Gamčen, vulkan ▲ RUS 120-121 T 6
Gamdou o RN 198-199 D 6
Gameleir, Ribeiro ~ BR 68-69 C 7
Gameleira, Serra da ▲ BR 68-69 G 5
Gameleira da Lapa o BR 72-73 J 2
Gameleiras o BR 72-73 J 3
Gameteira, Riachão ~ BR 68-69 H 6
Ġamğamāl ☆ IRQ 128-129 L 5
Ġanūbiya, al-Bādiya l- ⊥ IRQ 130-131 K 2
Ganxi o VRC 156-157 F 2
Gānid o DY 204-205 E 3
Ġāmid az-Zinād o KSA 132-133 B 4
Ġamil al-'Imrān o IRQ 128-129 L 6
Gamis o NAM 220-221 C 2
Gamkab ~ NAM 220-221 C 4
Gamkahe o RI 164-165 K 3
Gamkarivier ~ ZA 220-221 E 6
Ġammāla, al- o KSA 132-133 C 5
Gammelstaden o• S 86-87 L 4
Gammel Sukkertoppen = Kangaamiut o GRØ 28-29 O 4
Gammon Ranges National Park ⊥ AUS 178-179 E 6
Gammouda = Sidi Bouzid ☆ TN 190-191 G 3
Gamoep o ZA 220-221 D 4
Gamo-Gofa ▫ ETH 208-209 C 6
Gamova, mys ▲ RUS 122-123 D 7
Gamperé ▲ CAM 206-207 B 5
Gamping o RI 168 D 3
Gamra < RIM 196-197 D 6
Ġamsa o ET 194-195 F 4
Ġamsa, Ra's ▲ ET 194-195 F 4
Gamsberg ▲ NAM 220-221 C 1
Gamsby River ~ CDN (BC) 228-229 G 3
Ġamšīdzāi, Kūh-e ▲ IR 134-135 J 4
Ġamūd ▲ ETH 208-209 D 6
Ġamūm o KSA 132-133 A 3
Gamvik o N 86-87 O 1
G'amys, gora ▲ AZ 128-129 M 2
Gana, Komadougou ~ WAN 198-199 E 6
Ġanad, al- o Y 132-133 D 7
Ganado o USA (AZ) 256-257 F 3
Ganado o USA (TX) 266-267 L 4
Ganai o PNG 183 G 3
Ganal'skij hrebet ▲ RUS 120-121 R 7
Ganaly o RUS 120-121 R 7
Ġanamiya, al- o KSA 130-131 K 5
Ġanāna ⌒ UAE 134-135 E 6
Gananoque o CDN (ONT) 238-239 J 4
Ganāve, Bandar-e o IR 134-135 D 4
Gancheng o VRC 156-157 F 7
Gand = Gent ☆• B 92-93 G 3
Ganda o ANG 216-217 C 6
Gandaba o ETH 208-209 F 5
Gandadiwata, Gunung ▲ RI 164-165 F 5
Gandajika o ZRE 214-215 B 4
Gandak ~ IND 142-143 D 2
Gandaq o IR 134-135 F 1
Gandara o RP 160-161 F 6
Gandarbat o IND 138-139 E 2
Gandāva o PK 134-135 M 4
Gande o WAN 198-199 B 6
Ganden • VRC 144-145 H 6
Gander o CDN (NFL) 242-243 O 4
Gander Bay o CDN (NFL) 242-243 O 3
Gander Lake o CDN (NFL) 242-243 O 4
Gander River ~ CDN (NFL) 242-243 O 3
Gāndhi Dhām o• IND 138-139 C 8
Gāndhinagar ☆ IND 138-139 D 8
Gāndhi Sāgar o IND 138-139 E 7
Gandia o E 98-99 G 5
Gandiaye o SN 202-203 B 2
Gandō-ko < J 152-153 J 5
Gandomak o AFG 138-139 C 2
Gandomān o IR 134-135 D 3
Gandu o BR 72-73 L 2
Gandy o USA (UT) 254-255 B 4
Ganeb < RIM 196-197 E 5
Ganespur o IND 142-143 B 2
Ganga, Mouths of the ≈ 142-143 F 5
Gangaćin o IR 128-129 L 4
Gangākher o IND 138-139 F 10
Gangala na Bodio o ZRE 212-213 B 2
Gan Gan o RA 78-79 E 7
Gangan ▲ RG 202-203 D 4
Ganganagar o IND 138-139 D 5
Gangāpur o IND (RAJ) 138-139 F 6
Gangāpur o IND (RAJ) 138-139 E 7
Gangara o RN 198-199 D 5
Gangaw o MYA 142-143 J 4
Gangca o VRC 154-155 B 3
Gangchang o VRC 154-155 F 6
Ganges o CDN (BC) 230-231 F 5
Ganges o F 90-91 J 10
Ganges ~ IND 10-11 H 6
Ganges = Ganga ~ IND 10-11 H 6
Ganges, Mouths of the ≈ 142-143 F 5
Ganges Fan = Bengal Fan ≃ 12 G 3
Ganges River Delta = Ganga Delta ⊥ IND 142-143 F 4
Gangīr, Rūdḫāne-ye ~ IR 134-135 A 2
Gangkha o BHT 142-143 F 2
Gango ~ ANG 216-217 C 5
Gangoli o IND 140-141 F 4
Gangotri o• IND 138-139 G 4
Gang Ranch o CDN (BC) 230-231 G 2
Gangtok ☆• IND 142-143 F 2
Gangu ~ ZRE 206-207 F 6
Gangui o CAM 206-207 B 5
Gangula o ANG 216-217 B 5
Ganhe o VRC 150-151 D 2
Gani o RI 164-165 L 4
Gāni Ĝēl o AFG 138-139 B 3
Gan Jiang ~ VRC 156-157 J 3
Ganjuškino ☆ KA 96-97 F 10
Ganlanba • VRC 156-157 B 6
Ganluo o VRC 156-157 C 2
Gannan o VRC 150-151 D 4
Gannat o F 90-91 J 8
Gannett Peak ▲ USA (WY) 252-253 J 3
Ganquan o VRC 154-155 F 3
Gansbaai o ZA 220-221 D 7
Gansé o CI 202-203 J 5
Gansen o VRC 144-145 J 2
Gansu ▫ VRC 148-149 D 7
Ganta o LB 202-203 F 6
Gantang o VRC 154-155 D 3
Gantas, Las o RA 76-77 G 5
Gantheaume, Cape ▲ AUS 180-181 D 4
Gantheaume Bay ≈ 176-177 C 3
Gantheaume Point ▲ AUS 172-173 F 4
Ganti o RI 168 C 7
Gantira o RI 164-165 G 5
Gantisan o MAL 160-161 B 9
Gantt o USA (AL) 284-285 D 5
Gantt Lake < USA (AL) 284-285 D 5
Ġanūbiya, al-Bādiya l- ⊥ IRQ 130-131 K 2
Ganxi o VRC 156-157 F 2
Ganye o WAN 204-205 K 4
Ganyesa o ZA 220-221 G 3
Ganyh ~ AZ 128-129 M 2
Ganyu o VRC 154-155 L 4
Ganža o• AZ 128-129 M 2
Ganze ~ ZRE 210-211 K 6
Ganzhou o VRC 156-157 J 4
Gao o BF 202-203 J 4
Gao ▫ RMM 196-197 J 5
Gao ☆• RMM (GAO) 196-197 K 6
Gao o ZRE 212-213 B 2
Gao'an o VRC 156-157 J 2
Gaochang Gucheng ∴• VRC 146-147 J 4
Gaochun o VRC 154-155 L 6
Gaofengtao o VRC 154-155 L 4
Gaogou o VRC 154-155 L 4
Gaohezhen o VRC 154-155 K 6
Gaojiabu o VRC 154-155 G 2
Gaolan o VRC (GAN) 154-155 C 3
Gaolan • VRC (HUB) 154-155 G 6
Gaoligong Shan ▲ VRC 142-143 L 2
Gaomi o VRC 154-155 L 3
Gaoping o VRC 154-155 H 4
Gaotai o VRC 154-155 A 2
Gaotang o VRC 154-155 K 3
Gaotou o VRC 154-155 A 2
Gaoua ☆ BF 202-203 J 4
Gaoual o RG 202-203 D 3
Gaoun, Mont ▲ RCA 206-207 B 5
Gao Xian o VRC 156-157 D 2
Gaoyi o VRC 154-155 J 3
Gaozhou o VRC 156-157 G 6
Gap o F 90-91 L 9
Gap, Pico ▲ RCH 80 F 6
Gapi o ZRE 206-207 H 6
Gapuwiyak ✕ AUS 174-175 C 3
Gar' ~ RUS 122-123 C 2
Garaa Tebourt < TN 190-191 H 5
Garabinzam o RCB 210-211 D 3
Ġarābļus ☆ SYR 128-129 H 4
Garabogazköl o TM (KRS) 136-137 C 4
Gara Brune o DZ 190-191 G 6
Garacad o SP 208-209 J 5
Garachico o E 188-189 C 6
Garada o SUD 200-201 E 3
Garadag o SP 208-209 H 4
Gara Dragoman o BG 102-103 C 6
Ġarāģir, Wādi al- ~ KSA 130-131 H 4
Garagoa o CO 60-61 E 5
Garaguene, Tchin < RN 198-199 D 5
Garagum ⊥ TM 136-137 E 4
Garah o AUS 178-179 K 5
Garaina o PNG 183 D 4
Garajonay, Parque Nacional de ⊥••• E 188-189 C 6
Garalo o RMM 202-203 G 4
Garamba ~ ZRE 212-213 B 2
Garamba, Parc National de la ⊥••• ZRE 206-207 J 6
Garampani o IND 142-143 H 2
Ġarandal o JOR 130-131 D 2
Garandal, Wādi ~ ET 194-195 F 3
Garango o BF 202-203 K 4
Garanhuns o BR 68-69 K 6
Ga-Rankuwa o ZA 220-221 H 2
Garapa, Serra do ▲ BR 72-73 J 2
Garapu o BR 72-73 D 2
Garapuava o BR 72-73 G 4
Ġarārā o KSA 130-131 K 4
Garara o PNG 183 E 5
Ġaraš o•• JOR 130-131 D 1
Garawe o LB 202-203 G 7
Garayalde o RA 80 G 2
Garba o RCA 206-207 E 4
Garbahaarrey ☆ SP 212-213 J 2
Garba Tula o EAK 212-213 G 3
Garber o USA (OK) 264-265 G 2

Garberville o USA (CA) 246-247 B 3
Garbi, 'Alī al- ☆ IRQ 128-129 M 6
Gārboš, Kūh-e ▲ IR 134-135 D 2
Garças, Cachoeira das ~ BR 70-71 K 4
Garças, Cachoeira das ~ BR 70-71 H 2
Garças ou Jacaréqueau, Rio das ~ BR 72-73 D 3
Garchitorena o RP 160-161 E 6
Garciasville o USA (TX) 266-267 J 7
Garcitas, Las o RA 76-77 H 4
Garco o VRC 144-145 G 4
Garda o I 100-101 C 2
Gardabani o GE 126-127 F 7
Gardandēwāl o AFG 138-139 B 2
Garde Lake o CDN 30-31 Q 4
Gardelegen o• D 92-93 L 2
Garden City o USA (AL) 284-285 D 2
Garden City o USA (GA) 284-285 J 4
Garden City o USA (KS) 262-263 F 7
Garden City o USA (TX) 266-267 F 2
Garden City o USA (UT) 254-255 D 2
Garden Cove o CDN (NFL) 242-243 O 5
Gardendale o USA (TX) 264-265 B 6
Gardenia Lake o CDN 30-31 R 4
Garden Island ⌒ USA (MI) 272-273 D 2
Garden Peninsula ⌣ USA (MI) 270-271 M 5
Garden River o CDN (ONT) 236-237 D 6
Garden River ~ CDN (ONT) 238-239 B 2
Garden River Indian Reserve ⅄ CDN (ONT) 236-237 D 6
Gardens Corner o USA (SC) 284-285 K 4
Garden State Parkway II USA (NJ) 280-281 M 4
Gardenton o CDN (MAN) 234-235 G 5
Garden Valley o USA (TX) 264-265 D 4
Gardēz ☆ AFG 138-139 B 3
Gardi o USA (GA) 284-285 J 5
Gardiner o CDN (ONT) 236-237 G 3
Gardiner o USA (ME) 278-279 M 4
Gardiner o USA (MT) 250-251 J 6
Gardiner, Mount ▲ AUS 178-179 K 2
Gardiners Island ⌒ USA (NY) 280-281 O 2
Gardner ⌒ KIB 13 K 3
Gardner o USA (CO) 254-255 K 6
Gardner o USA (FL) 286-287 H 4
Gardner o USA (IL) 274-275 K 3
Gardner o USA (KS) 262-263 M 6
Gardner o USA (LA) 268-269 H 5
Gardner o USA (ND) 258-259 L 4
Gardner Canal < CDN (BC) 228-229 F 3
Gardner Pinnacles ⌒ USA 14-15 M 5
Gardner Plateau ⊥ AUS 172-173 G 3
Gardner Range ▲ AUS 172-173 J 5
Gardnerville o USA (NV) 246-247 F 5
Gardunha, Serra da ▲ P 98-99 D 4
Garei ~ BD 142-143 F 4
Gareloi Island ⌒ USA 22-23 G 7
Gare Tigre o F 62-63 H 3
Garfa, Oued ~ RIM 196-197 D 7
Garfield o AUS 178-179 H 2
Garfield o USA (KS) 262-263 G 6
Garfield o USA (NM) 256-257 H 6
Garfield o USA (WA) 244-245 H 3
Garfield Mountain ▲ USA (MT) 250-251 G 7
Garford o AUS 176-177 M 4
Gargamelle o CDN (NFL) 242-243 L 2
Gargando o RMM 196-197 H 6
Gargano, Promontorio del ▲ I 100-101 E 4
Gargantua, Cape ▲ CDN (ONT) 236-237 C 5
Gargaris o PNG 183 G 2
Gargnäs o S 86-87 H 4
Gargouna o RMM 202-203 L 2
Gargždai ☆• LT 94-95 G 4
Garhjāt Hills ▲ IND 142-143 D 5
Garhshankar o IND 138-139 F 4
Gari ☆ RUS 114-115 G 5
Gariāband o IND 142-143 C 5
Gariau o RI 166-167 H 3
Gārib, Ra's ▲ ET 194-195 F 3
Garibaldi o BR 74-75 E 7
Garibaldi o CDN (BC) 230-231 F 4
Garibaldi o USA (OR) 244-245 B 5
Garibaldi, Mount ▲ CDN (BC) 230-231 F 4
Garibaldi Provincial Park ⊥ CDN (BC) 230-231 G 4
Garies o ZA 220-221 C 5
Garif, al- o KSA 130-131 F 6
Gariganus o NAM 220-221 D 3
Garimpinho o BR 68-69 D 5
Garīn, Kūh-e ▲ IR 134-135 C 2
Garin Shehu o WAN 204-205 J 4
Garin Yerima o WAN 204-205 J 4
Ġarīr, Wādī al- ~ KSA 130-131 H 5
Garissa ☆ EAK 212-213 G 4
Garkem o WAN 204-205 H 5
Garki o WAN 198-199 D 6
Garkida o WAN 204-205 K 3
Garladinne o IND 140-141 G 3
Garland o CDN (MAN) 234-235 C 3
Garland o USA (AR) 276-277 B 7
Garland o USA (MT) 250-251 O 5
Garland o USA (NC) 282-283 J 6
Garland o USA (TX) 264-265 H 6
Garland o USA (UT) 254-255 C 2
Garland o USA (WY) 252-253 K 2
Garm o TJ 136-137 M 5
Garmāb o IR 128-129 N 5
Garmabe o SUD 206-207 K 6
Garmanda o RUS 112-113 K 5
Garmanda, Bol'šaja ~ RUS 112-113 K 5
Garm Bīt o IR 134-135 J 6
Garme o IR 136-137 E 6
Garmisch-Partenkirchen o• D 92-93 L 5
Garmsār o AFG 134-135 L 3
Garmsār ⊥ AFG 134-135 K 3
Garmsār o IR 136-137 C 7
Garner o USA (IA) 274-275 E 1
Garner o USA (NC) 282-283 J 5
Garnet o USA (MI) 270-271 N 4
Garnet Bank ≃ 74-75 F 9
Garnet Bay ≈ 36-37 M 2
Garnett o USA (KS) 262-263 L 6
Garnett o USA (SC) 284-285 J 4
Garnish o CDN (NFL) 242-243 N 5
Garnpung, Lake o AUS 180-181 G 2
Garonne ~ F 90-91 H 9
Garoowe ☆ SP 208-209 J 4
Garou o DY 204-205 E 3
Garou, Lac o RMM 196-197 J 6
Garoua ☆ CAM 204-205 K 4
Garoua Boulai o CAM 206-207 B 6
Garove Island ⌒ PNG 183 E 3
Garré o RA 78-79 H 4
Garretson o USA (SD) 260-261 K 3
Garrett o USA (WY) 252-253 N 4
Garrett Fracture Zone ≃ 14-15 R 9
Garrick o CDN (SAS) 232-233 O 2
Garrido, Isla ⌒ RCH 80 C 2
Garrington o CDN (ALB) 232-233 D 4
Garrison o USA (MN) 270-271 E 4
Garrison o USA (MT) 250-251 G 5
Garrison o USA (ND) 258-259 F 4
Garrison o USA (NV) 246-247 M 5
Garrison o USA (TX) 268-269 F 5
Garro o MEX 52-53 G 2
Garrobo, El o NIC 52-53 B 5
Garruchas o BR 76-77 K 5
Garry, Cape ▲ CDN 24-25 Z 4
Garry Bay ≈ 24-25 d 6
Garry Lake o CDN 30-31 T 3
Garsala o SP 212-213 K 2
Garsen o EAK 212-213 H 5
Garsila o SUD 198-199 L 6
Garson Lake o CDN 32-33 Q 3
Gartempe ~ F 90-91 H 8
Gartok = Garyarsa o VRC 144-145 C 5
Garu o PNG 183 E 3
Garuahi o PNG 183 F 6
Garub o NAM 220-221 C 3
Ġarūb o Y 132-133 H 5
Garuma o RCH 76-77 C 2
Garupá, Rio ~ BR 76-77 J 6
Garut o• RI 168 B 3
Garuva o BR 74-75 F 6
Garwa o IND 142-143 C 3
Garwolin o PL 92-93 Q 3
Gar Xincun o VRC 144-145 C 4
Gary o USA (IN) 274-275 L 3
Garyarsa o VRC 144-145 C 5
Garysburg o USA (NC) 282-283 K 4
Garza o RA 76-77 F 5
Garzas, Las o RA 76-77 H 5
Garzê o VRC 144-145 M 5
Garzón o CO 60-61 D 6
Gasan Kuli o TM 136-137 C 6
Gasan-Kulijskijučastok Krasnovodskogo zapovednik ⊥ TM 136-137 C 6
Gaschiga o CAM 204-205 K 4
Gas City o USA (IN) 274-275 N 4
Gascogne ⊥ F 90-91 G 10
Gascoigne o CDN (SAS) 232-233 J 5
Gasconade River ~ USA (MO) 274-275 G 6
Gasconade River ~ USA (MO) 276-277 C 3
Gascoyne, Mount ▲ AUS 176-177 D 2
Gascoyne Junction o AUS 176-177 C 2
Gascoyne River ~ AUS 176-177 C 2
Gasera o ETH 208-209 E 5
Gash ~ ER 200-201 H 5
Gashaka o WAN 204-205 J 5
Gasherbrum I ▲ PK 138-139 F 2
Gasherbrum II ▲ PK 138-139 F 2
Gas Hu o VRC 146-147 K 6
Gashua o WAN 198-199 E 6
Gashunchaka o VRC 144-145 K 2
Gasim o RI 166-167 F 2
Ġāsk o IR 134-135 G 6
Ġāsk, Ḫalīǧ-e ≈ 134-135 G 6
Gaskačokka ▲ N 86-87 H 3
Gasmata o PNG 183 F 4
Gaspar, Selat ≈ 162-163 G 6
Gaspar Hernández o DOM 54-55 K 5
Gasparilla Island ⌒ USA (FL) 286-287 G 5
Gaspé o CDN (QUE) 240-241 L 2
Gaspé, Baie de ≈ 38-39 M 4
Gaspé, Baie de ≈ CDN 240-241 L 2
Gaspé, Cape ▲ CDN (QUE) 240-241 L 2
Gaspé, Péninsule de ⌣ CDN (QUE) 240-241 J 2
Gaspereau Forks o CDN (NB) 240-241 J 4
Gaspésie, Parc de la ⊥ CDN (QUE) 240-241 J 2
Gasquet o USA (CA) 246-247 B 2
Gassan o BF 202-203 J 3
Ġassān o IRQ 128-129 L 6
Gassan ▲ J 152-153 H 5
Gassane o SN 202-203 C 2
Gassaway o USA (WV) 280-281 F 5
Gassend Lake o CDN 24-25 J 6
Gassi Touil ⊥ DZ 190-191 F 6
Gassol o WAN 204-205 J 4
Gass Peak ▲ USA (NV) 248-249 J 3
Gašt o IR 134-135 J 5
Gastello o RUS 122-123 K 4
Gastón o C 54-55 G 4
Gastona, Río ~ RA 76-77 E 4
Gastonia o USA (NC) 282-283 F 5
Gastre o RA 78-79 E 7
Ġāṭ, al- o KSA 130-131 J 4
Gata o CV 202-203 C 5
Gata, Cabo de ▲ E 98-99 F 6
Gata, Sierra de ▲ E 98-99 D 4
Gataga River ~ CDN 30-31 F 6
Gatanga o SUD 206-207 H 5
Gatčina ☆ RUS 94-95 M 2
Gate o USA (OK) 264-265 D 2
Gate City o USA (VA) 280-281 D 7
Gatehouse of Fleet o GB 90-91 E 4
Gatentiri o RI 166-167 L 5
Gates o USA (NC) 282-283 L 4
Gateshead Island ⌒ CDN 24-25 W 5
Gates of the Artic National Park and Preserve ⊥ USA 20-21 N 2
Gatesville o USA (TX) 266-267 K 2
Gateview o USA (CO) 254-255 H 5
Gateway o USA (CO) 254-255 G 5
Gateway National Recreation Area • USA (NY) 280-281 N 3
Gathto Creek ~ CDN 30-31 G 6
Gati-Loumo o RMM 202-203 H 2
Gatin, Rivière ~ CDN 36-37 M 4
Gatineau o CDN (QUE) 238-239 K 3
Gatineau, Rivière ~ CDN (QUE) 236-237 N 5
Gatineau, Rivière ~ CDN (QUE) 238-239 K 3
Gatlinburg o USA (TN) 282-283 D 5
Gatos, Los o USA (CA) 248-249 C 2
Ġaṭṭi o KSA 130-131 E 2
Gatton o AUS 178-179 M 4
Gatún, Lago o• PA 52-53 E 7
Gatuncito o PA 52-53 D 7
Gatvand o IR 134-135 C 2
Gau ⌒ FJI 184 III b 3
Gaua, Île = Santa Maria Island ⌒ VAN 184 II a 2
Gaudan o TM 136-137 F 6
Gaudan, pereval ▲ TM 136-137 F 6
Gauer Lake o CDN 34-35 H 2
Ġauf, al- o KSA 130-131 F 2
Ġauf, Wādī al- ~ Y 132-133 D 5
Ġaufa, al- o KSA 132-133 B 3
Gaujas nacionālais parks ⊥ LV 94-95 J 3
Gaula ~ N 86-87 E 5
Gaulay River ~ USA (WV) 280-281 E 5
Gauley Mountain ▲ USA (WV) 280-281 F 5
Gaulim o PNG 183 G 3
Gaulle, De o RCA 206-207 B 5
Gaultois o CDN (NFL) 242-243 N 5
Gaurdak o TM 136-137 K 6
Gauribidanur o IND 140-141 G 4
Gauss Halvø ⊥ GRØ 26-27 o 7
Gausta ▲ N 86-87 D 7
Gauthiot, Chutes ~• TCH 206-207 B 4
Gauttier, Pegunungan ▲ RI 166-167 K 3
Ġavāher Deh o IR 136-137 B 6
Ġavand o AFG 136-137 J 7
Ġavānrūd o IR 134-135 B 1
Ġāvbandī o IR 134-135 E 5
Gāvbast, Kūh-e ▲ IR 134-135 E 5
Gávdos ⌒ GR 100-101 K 7
Gave de Pau ~ F 90-91 G 10
Gāve Rūd ~ IR 134-135 B 1
Gāvgān o IR 128-129 L 4
Gavião o BR 68-69 J 7
Gavião o P 98-99 D 5
Gavião, Rio ~ BR 72-73 K 3
Gavien o PNG 183 C 2
Gaviota o USA (CA) 248-249 D 5
Gaviota Beach • USA (CA) 248-249 D 5
Gaviota Pass ▲ USA (CA) 248-249 D 5
Gaviotas, Las o YV 60-61 K 3
Gävle ☆ S 86-87 H 6
Gavrilla, guba o RUS 112-113 U 5
Gavrilov -Jam ☆ RUS 94-95 Q 3
Gávrio o GR 100-101 K 6
Gavriša-Tas, gora ▲ RUS 110-111 X 3
Gavunipalli o IND 140-141 H 4
Gawachab o NAM 220-221 C 3
Gawa Island ⌒ PNG 183 F 5
Gawalisi, Gunung ▲ RI 164-165 F 4
Gawa Obo o VRC 144-145 M 3
Ġawār,al- ⊥ UAE 130-131 L 5
Gāwilgarh Hills ▲ IND 138-139 F 9
Gawler o AUS 180-181 E 3
Gawler Ranges ▲ AUS 180-181 C 2
Gawu o WAN 204-205 G 4
Ġawwār, Ġazirat ⌒ KSA 130-131 E 5
Gaxun Nur o VRC 148-149 E 6
Gay o USA (GA) 284-285 F 3
Gay o USA (OK) 264-265 J 5
Gaya o• IND 142-143 D 3
Gaya o MAL 160-161 B 9
Gaya o RN 204-205 E 3
Gaya o WAN 204-205 H 3
Gaya, Pulau ⌒ MAL 160-161 B 9
Gayam o TCH 206-207 C 4
Gayamcam o RP 160-161 E 9
Gayaza o EAU 212-213 C 4
G'Aydat Al Ihoucha ⊥ MA 188-189 F 7
Gayéri o BF 202-203 L 3
Gay Head ▲ USA (MA) 278-279 L 7
Gaylord o USA (MI) 272-273 E 2
Gaylord o USA (MN) 270-271 D 6
Gaylord o USA (VA) 280-281 J 4
Gayna River ~ CDN 30-31 E 3
Gays River o CDN (NS) 240-241 M 5
Gayville o USA (SD) 260-261 J 4
Ġayyāda, Šu'aib ~ IRQ 128-129 J 6
Gaz, Rūd-e ~ AFG 134-135 K 2
Gaza ▫ MOC 218-219 G 6
Gaza/ Ġazza ☆ AUT 130-131 C 2
Gazačak o TM 136-137 G 4
Gaz-Ačak = Gazačak o TM 136-137 G 4
Gazakh = Qazax o• AZ 128-129 L 2
Ġazala, al- o KSA 130-131 G 4
Gazalkent o US 136-137 L 4
Gazanak o IR 136-137 C 7
Gazankulu (former Homel., now part of North-Transvaal) ▫ ZA 218-219 D 6
Gazaoua o RN 198-199 C 6
Gazara o TJ 136-137 L 5
Gazelle o USA (CA) 246-247 C 2
Gazelle Channel ≈ 183 F 2
Gazelle Peninsula ⌣ PNG 183 F 3
Gazerān o IR 136-137 B 6
Gāzergāh o• AFG 134-135 K 1
Gazi o EAK 212-213 G 6
Gazi Antep ☆ TR 128-129 G 4
Gazik o IR 134-135 J 2
Gazimur ~ RUS 118-119 J 9
Gazimurskij Zavod ☆ RUS 118-119 J 10
Gazipaşa ☆ TR 128-129 E 4
Gazipur o BD 142-143 G 4
Gazli o US 136-137 H 4
Ġaz Mūrān, Hāmūn-e o IR 134-135 H 5
Gazni ▫ AFG 134-135 M 2
Gaznī ☆• AFG 138-139 B 3
Gazni, Daryā-ye ~ AFG 138-139 B 3
Gbabam o CI 202-203 H 7
Gbaboua o CAM 206-207 B 5
Gbadolite o ZRE 206-207 E 6
Gbagba o RCA 206-207 D 6
Gbaizera o RCA 206-207 D 5
Gbako, River ~ WAN 204-205 G 4
Gbananmè o DY 204-205 E 5
Gbanendji o RCA 206-207 E 5
Gbanga ☆ LB 202-203 F 6
Gbanga o WAN 204-205 G 4
Gbangbatok o WAL 202-203 D 6
Gbanhala ~ RG 202-203 F 5
Gbapleu o CI 202-203 F 6
Gbassa o DY 204-205 E 3
Gbassigbiri o RCA 206-207 H 6
Gbatala o LB 202-203 F 6
Gbele Game Production Reserve ⊥ GH 202-203 J 4
Gbengué o BF 202-203 J 4
Gbentu o WAL 202-203 E 5
Gberia Timbako o WAL 202-203 E 5
Gbéroubouè o DY 204-205 E 3
Gbibo o LB 202-203 F 7
Gbodonon o CI 202-203 H 5
Gboko o WAN 204-205 H 5
Gbongaa o CI 202-203 G 5
Gbongan o WAN 204-205 F 5
Gbung o GH 202-203 K 5
Gbwado o ZRE 210-211 H 2
Gdańsk ☆•• PL 92-93 P 1
Gdańsk, Gulf of = Gdańska, Zatoka ≈ PL 92-93 P 1
Gdańska, Zatoka ≈ 92-93 P 1
Gdov ☆ RUS 94-95 K 2
Gdyel o DZ 188-189 L 3
Gdynia o•• PL 92-93 P 1
Geary o CDN (NB) 240-241 J 5
Geary o USA (OK) 264-265 F 3
Gêba, Canal do ≈ 202-203 B 4
Geba, Rio ~ GNB 202-203 C 3
Ġebal Bārez, Kūh-e ▲ IR 134-135 G 4
Gebasawa o WAN 198-199 D 6
Geba Wenz ~ ETH 208-209 B 4
Gebe, Pulau ⌒ RI 166-167 E 2
Gebeit o SUD 200-201 H 3
Gebeledan o CI 202-203 F 5
Gebituolatuo o VRC 146-147 L 6
Gebo o USA (WY) 252-253 K 3
Gebre Guracha o ETH 208-209 D 4
Gebze ☆ TR 128-129 C 2
Gech'a o ETH 208-209 B 5
Gedabiet o ETH 200-201 H 6
Geddes o USA (SD) 260-261 H 3
Gedenštroma, zaliv ≈ 110-111 Y 2
Gedi o EAK 212-213 H 5
Gedi National Monument • EAK 212-213 H 5
Gediz ☆ TR 128-129 C 3
Gediz Nehri ~ TR 128-129 C 3
Gedlegube o ETH 208-209 G 5
Gēdo o ETH 208-209 C 4
Gedo ▫ SP 212-213 H 2
Gedongratu o RI 162-163 F 7
Gedser o DK 86-87 E 9
Geegully Creek ~ AUS 172-173 F 5
Geel o B 92-93 H 3
Geelong o• AUS 180-181 H 5
Geelvink Channel ≈ 176-177 B 4
Geesaley o SP 208-209 K 3
Geese Islands ⌒ USA 22-23 U 4
Geeveston o AUS 180-181 J 7
Gēga Shet' ~ ETH 208-209 E 3
Gegbwema o WAL 202-203 E 6
Gegentala Caoyuan • VRC 148-149 K 7
Gê'gyai o VRC 144-145 C 4
Geidam o WAN 198-199 E 6
Geifil o SUD 200-201 E 6
Geikie Island ⌒ CDN (ONT) 234-235 P 4
Geikie River ~ CDN 34-35 D 2
Geiki Gorge National Park ⊥ AUS 172-173 G 5
Geillini Lake o CDN 30-31 W 5
Geillini River ~ CDN 30-31 W 5
Geilo o N 86-87 D 6
Geirangerfjorden ≈•• 86-87 C 5
Geiser del Tatio o• RCH 76-77 C 2
Geita o EAT 212-213 D 5
Gejberga, ostrova ⌒ RUS 108-109 c 3
Gejiu o VRC 156-157 C 5
Geka, mys ▲ RUS 112-113 U 4
Gel ~ SUD 206-207 J 5
Gela o I 100-101 E 6
Geladangong ▲ VRC 144-145 H 4
Geladī o ETH 208-209 H 5
Gelai ▲ EAT 212-213 F 5
Gelam, Pulau ⌒ RI 162-163 J 6
Gele o ZRE 206-207 D 6
Gelemso o ETH 208-209 E 4
Gelendžik o RUS 126-127 C 5
Gel Gulbis < EAK 212-213 G 2
Gelibolu ☆• TR 128-129 B 2
Gelila o ETH 208-209 C 4
Gelinting, Teluk ≈ 166-167 B 6
Gellāb o SUD 206-207 G 4
Gellinsor o SP 208-209 H 5
Geloketapang o RI 162-163 A 3
Gelot' o RUS 116-117 L 7
Gelsenkirchen o D 92-93 J 3
Gelumbang o RI 162-163 F 6
Gemaliel o USA (KY) 276-277 K 4
Gemas o MAL 162-163 E 3
Gembele, Rapides ~ ZRE 210-211 J 2
Gembogl o PNG 183 C 3
Gembu o WAN 204-205 J 5
Geme o RI 164-165 K 1
Gemena o ZRE 210-211 G 2
Gemerek ☆ TR 128-129 G 3
Gemeri Hāyk' o ETH 208-209 E 3
Gemi ▲ ETH 208-209 B 4
Gemlik ☆ TR 128-129 C 2
Gemlik Körfezi ≈ 128-129 C 2
Gemmeiza o SUD 200-201 G 4
Gemmell o USA (MN) 270-271 D 3
Gemona del Friuli o I 100-101 D 1
Gempol o RI 168 E 3
Gemsbok National Park ⊥ RB 220-221 E 2
Gemsbokvlakte o ZA 220-221 G 2
Genalē Wenz ~ ETH 208-209 E 6
Genali, Danau o RI 162-163 K 4
Gendarān Bāshī ▲ IR 128-129 M 3
Genémasson o DY 204-205 E 3
General Acha o RA 78-79 G 4
General A. Dames o BR 74-75 E 7
General Alvear o RA (BUA) 78-79 J 4
General Alvear o RA (MEN) 78-79 F 3
General Arenales o RA 78-79 J 3
General Arnulfo R. Gómez o MEX 50-51 G 5
General Ballivián o RA 76-77 F 2
General Belgrano o RA 78-79 K 3
General Bravo o MEX 50-51 K 5
General Cabrera o RA 78-79 H 2
General Camacho o BOL 70-71 C 5
General Carrera, Lago o RCH 80 D 3
General Cepeda o MEX 50-51 J 5
General Conesa o RA (BUA) 78-79 L 4
General Conesa o RA (RIN) 78-79 G 6
General Elizardo Aquino o PY 76-77 J 3
General Enrique Martinez o ROU 74-75 D 9
General Enrique Mosconi o RA 76-77 F 2
General Eugenio a Garay ☆ PY 70-71 F 7
General Francisco Murguía o MEX 50-51 H 5
General Güemes o RA 76-77 E 3
General Ignacio Zaragoza o MEX 50-51 K 6
General José de San Martín o RA 76-77 H 4
General Juan Madariaga o RA 78-79 L 4
General la Madrid o RA 78-79 J 4
General Levalle o RA 78-79 H 3
General L. Plaza Gutiérrez o EC 64-65 C 3
General Luz o BR 74-75 E 7
General Mansilla o RA 78-79 L 3
General M. Belgrano o RA 76-77 H 3
General Mosconi o RA 76-77 F 2
General Obligado o RA 76-77 H 4
General Pico o RA 78-79 H 3
General Pinedo o RA 76-77 G 4
General Roca o RA 78-79 F 5
General Sampaio o BR 68-69 J 4
General San Martin o RA 78-79 H 4
General Santos ☆ RP 160-161 F 9
General Simón Bolívar o MEX 50-51 H 5
General Terán o MEX 50-51 K 5
General Tiburcio o BR 68-69 H 3
General Toševo o BG 102-103 F 6
General Treviño o MEX 50-51 K 4
General Trías o MEX 50-51 F 3
General Villegas o RA 78-79 H 3
General Vintter, Lago o RA 78-79 D 7
Genesee o CDN (ALB) 232-233 D 2
Genesee o USA (ID) 250-251 C 5
Geneseo o USA (IL) 274-275 H 3
Geneseo o USA (KS) 262-263 H 6
Geneseo o USA (NY) 278-279 D 6
Genet o ETH 208-209 D 4
Geneva o USA (AL) 284-285 E 5
Geneva o USA (GA) 284-285 F 4
Geneva o USA (ID) 252-253 G 4
Geneva o USA (NE) 262-263 J 4
Geneva o USA (NY) 278-279 E 6
Geneva o USA (OH) 280-281 F 2
Geneva = Genève ☆•• CH 92-93 J 5
Geneva, Lake = Léman, Lac o CH 92-93 J 5
Genève ☆•• CH 92-93 J 5
Genévriers, Île des ⌒ CDN 38-39 P 3
Genf = Genève ☆•• CH 92-93 J 5
Genfer See = Lac Léman o CH 92-93 J 5
Gengma o VRC 142-143 L 4
Gengwa o ZRE 210-211 J 5
Genil, Río ~ E 98-99 E 6
Genk o B 92-93 H 3
Genkai-nada ≈ 152-153 D 8
Genkanyj, hrebet ▲ RUS 112-113 Y 3
Gennargentu, Monti del ▲ I 100-101 B 4
Genoa o AUS 180-181 K 4
Genoa o USA (CO) 254-255 M 4
Genoa o USA (NE) 262-263 J 3
Genoa o USA (NV) 246-247 F 4
Genoa o USA (WI) 270-271 G 7
Genoa = Génova ☆•• I 100-101 B 2
Genoa City o USA (WI) 274-275 K 2
Génova ☆•• I 100-101 B 2
Genova, Golfo di ≈ 100-101 B 2
Genovesa, Isla ⌒ EC 64-65 C 9
Gens-de-Terre, Rivière ~ CDN (QUE) 236-237 M 5
Gent ☆•• B 92-93 G 3
Genteng o RI 168 B 3
Genteng, Pulau ⌒ RI 168 E 3
Genteng, Ujung ▲ RI 168 B 3
Genteng Game Park ⊥ RI 168 B 3
Genting o RI 162-163 C 3
Gentios, Isla dos ⌒ BR 70-71 E 3
Gentryville o USA (MO) 276-277 C 4
Genyem o RI 166-167 L 3
Geographe Bay ≈ 176-177 C 6
Geographe Channel ≈ 176-177 B 2
Geographical Center of Conterminous United States • USA (KS) 262-263 H 5
Geographical Center of North American Continent ∴ USA (ND) 258-259 H 3
Geographical Center of the United States ∴ USA (SD) 260-261 C 1
Geographical Society Ø ⌒ GRØ 26-27 o 7
Geok-Tepe o TM 136-137 E 5
Geologičeskaja, grjada ▲ RUS 108-109 Z 4
Geologičeskij o RUS 112-113 V 3
Georga, Zemlja ⌒ RUS 84-85 a 2
George o USA (IA) 274-275 C 1
George o USA (WA) 244-245 F 3
George o ZA 220-221 F 6
George, Cape ▲ CDN (BC) 228-229 D 3
George, Cape ▲ CDN (NS) 240-241 N 5
George, Lake o AUS (NSW) 180-181 K 3
George, Lake o AUS (SA) 180-181 E 4
George, Lake o AUS (WA) 172-173 F 7
George, Lake o EAU 212-213 C 3
George, Lake o USA (FL) 286-287 H 2
George, Lake o USA (NY) 278-279 H 5
George, Mount ▲ AUS 172-173 D 7
George, Mount ▲ CDN 24-25 S 6
George, Rivière ~ CDN 36-37 R 6
George Gill Range ▲ AUS 176-177 L 2
George Island ⌒ CDN 36-37 V 7
George Island ⌒ GB 78-79 L 7
George National Historic Park, Fort • CDN (ONT) 238-239 F 5
George Reservoir, Walter F. < USA (AL) 284-285 E 5
George Richards, Cape ▲ CDN 24-25 R 2
George River ~ USA 20-21 M 5
George R. Parks Highway II USA 20-21 P 5
Georges Bank ≃ 46-47 P 5
Georges Bank ≃ 278-279 O 7
Georges de l'Oudingueur • TCH 198-199 H 2
George Sound ≈ 182 A 6
Georges Tavern o USA (VA) 280-281 H 6
Georgetown o AUS 174-175 G 6
George Town o AUS 180-181 J 6
George Town o• BS 54-55 H 3
Georgetown o CDN (NS) 240-241 N 4
Georgetown o CDN (ONT) 238-239 F 5
Georgetown o GB (STH) 202-203 B 7
Georgetown ☆ GB 54-55 E 5
Georgetown ★ GUY 62-63 E 2
Georgetown o USA (CA) 246-247 E 5
Georgetown o USA (DE) 280-281 L 5
Georgetown o USA (GA) 284-285 E 5
Georgetown o USA (KY) 276-277 L 2
Georgetown o USA (MS) 268-269 K 5
Georgetown o USA (OH) 280-281 C 5
Georgetown o USA (TX) 266-267 K 3
Georgetown o• USA (SC) 284-285 L 3
Georgetown ☆• WAG 202-203 C 3
Georgetown o WV 56 E 5
Georgetown, Lake < USA (TX) 266-267 K 3
Georgeville o CDN (QUE) 238-239 N 3
George Washington Carver National Monument ∴ USA (MO) 276-277 A 3
George West o USA (TX) 266-267 J 5
Georgia ▫ USA (GA) 284-285 F 4
Georgia = Gruzija ■ GE 126-127 E 7
Georgia, Strait of ≈ CDN 230-231 E 4
Georgia Basin ≃ 6-7 F 14
Georgiana o USA (AL) 284-285 D 5
Georgian Bay o CDN (ONT) 238-239 D 3
Georgian Bay Island National Park ⊥ CDN (ONT) 238-239 F 4
Georgian Bay Islands National Park ⊥ CDN (ONT) 238-239 F 3
Georgievka o KA 124-125 M 4
Georgievka o KA 146-147 B 4
Georgievsk o RUS 126-127 E 5
Georgina Downs o AUS 178-179 D 1
Georgina River ~ AUS 178-179 E 2
Georgiu-Dež = Liski o RUS 102-103 L 2
Georg von Neumayer o ARK 16 F 36
Gera o• D 92-93 M 3
Gerace o I 100-101 F 5
Gerachiné o PA 52-53 E 7
Geráki o GR 100-101 J 6
Geral, Serra ▲ BR 72-73 K 2
Geral, Serra ▲ BR 74-75 E 5
Gerald o CDN (SAS) 232-233 R 5
Gerard, ostrov ⌒ RUS 112-113 X 1
Geral de Goiás, Serra ▲ BR 72-73 G 2
Geraldine o NZ 182 C 6
Geraldine o USA (MT) 250-251 J 4
Geraldo, Furo do ~ BR 66-67 F 5
Geral do Paraná ou do Veadeiros, Serra ▲ BR 72-73 G 3
Geraldton o AUS 176-177 C 4
Geraldton o CDN (ONT) 236-237 B 3
Geralton o CDN (ONT) 236-237 B 3
Geralton East o CDN (ONT) 236-237 B 3
Geralzinho o BR 72-73 K 3
Gerampi o RI 168 D 7
Geranium o AUS 180-181 F 3
Geräš o IR 134-135 F 5
Geraumele ∴ RN 198-199 F 5
Gerbiči, gora ▲ RUS 116-117 M 2
Gerdau o ZA 220-221 H 3
Gerdine, Mount ▲ USA 20-21 O 6
Gerede ☆ TR 128-129 E 2
Gerede Çayı ~ TR 128-129 E 2
Gerel'de o US 136-137 H 4
Gereshk o AFG 134-135 L 3
Gerger ☆ TR 128-129 H 3
Gerihun o WAL 202-203 E 6
Gerik o• MAL 162-163 D 2
Gering o USA (NE) 262-263 C 3
Gerisa o SP 208-209 F 3
Gerlach o USA (NV) 246-247 F 3
Germakolo o RI 166-167 G 2
German Busch, Reserva Busch ⊥ BOL 70-71 F 5
German Creek o AUS 178-179 K 2
Germania o RA 78-79 H 3
Germania Land ⊥ GRØ 26-27 p 5
Germansen Landing o CDN 32-33 H 4
Germantown o USA (TN) 276-277 F 5
Germany = Deutschland ■ D 92-93 J 4
Germencik ☆ TR 128-129 B 4
Ġermi o IR 128-129 N 3
Germiston o ZA 220-221 J 3
Gernika-Lumo o E 98-99 F 3
Gero o J 152-153 G 7
Gerolimenas o GR 100-101 J 6
Gerona o RP 160-161 D 5
Gerona = Girona o E 98-99 J 4
Gerrard o CDN (BC) 230-231 M 3
Gers ~ F 90-91 H 10
Ġerūf o JOR 130-131 D 2
Gerung o RI 168 C 7
Gerze ☆ TR 128-129 F 2
Gêrzê o VRC 144-145 E 4
Gesa ~ RI 166-167 J 3
Gesellschafts-Inseln ⌒ F 13 M 4
Gestro, Wabē ~ ETH 208-209 E 5
Getafe o E 98-99 F 4
Geti o ZRE 212-213 C 3
Getkan ~ RUS 118-119 L 8
Gëtljangën, laguna ≈ 112-113 Y 4
Getta o BHT 142-143 F 2
Gettysburg o USA (PA) 280-281 J 4
Gettysburg o USA (SD) 260-261 G 1
Gettysburg National Military Park • USA (PA) 280-281 J 4
Gettysburg Seamount ≃ 188-189 F 2
Getúlio Vargas o BR 74-75 D 6
Getz Ice Shelf ⊂ ARK 16 F 24
Geva§ ☆ TR 128-129 K 3
Gevgelija o MK 100-101 J 4
Gevrai o IND 138-139 E 10
Gewanē o ETH 208-209 E 3
Geychay = Göyçay o AZ 128-129 M 2
Geyik Dağları ▲ TR 128-129 D 4
Geylegphug o BHT 142-143 G 2
Geyser o USA (MT) 250-251 J 4
Geyser, Banc du ⌒ RM 222-223 E 4
Geyserville o USA (CA) 246-247 C 5
Geyve ☆ TR 128-129 D 2
Gezāb o AFG 134-135 M 2
Gezhou Ba • VRC 154-155 G 6
Ghābat al-'Arab o SUD 206-207 J 4
Ghadāmis ▫ LAR 190-191 H 5
Ghadāmis ☆••• LAR 190-191 G 5
Ghaddūwah o LAR 192-193 F 4
Ghaghara ~ IND 142-143 C 2
Ghaghat ~ BD 142-143 F 3
Ghaghe Island ⌒ SOL 184 I d 2
Ghāghra o IND 142-143 D 4
Ghaibi Dero o PK 134-135 M 5
Ghallamane ⊥ RIM 196-197 E 3
Ghallamane, Sebkhet o RIM 196-197 E 3
Ghana ■ GH 204-205 B 5
Ghangmi o RI 166-167 K 4
Ghansali o IND 138-139 G 4
Ghanzi ▫ RB 216-217 F 11
Ghanzi ☆ RB 216-217 F 10
Ghanzi Farms ⊥ RB 216-217 F 10
Ghaoua, Goûr ▲ DZ 190-191 D 9
Gharb Binna o SUD 200-201 E 3
Gharbi, Chott el o DZ 188-189 L 4
Gharbi, Zahrez o DZ 190-191 D 3
Ghardaïa ☆• DZ 190-191 D 4
Ghardimaou o TN 190-191 G 2
Gharig o SUD 206-207 H 3
Ghāro o PK 134-135 M 6
Gharyān ▫ LAR 192-193 E 3
Gharyān ☆ LAR 192-193 E 1
Ghāt o LAR 190-191 H 8
Ghātāl o IND 142-143 E 4
Ghātampur o IND 142-143 B 2
Ghātsila o IND 142-143 E 4
Ghauspur o PK 138-139 B 5
Ghawdex = Gozo ⌒ M 100-101 E 6
Ghazaouet o DZ 188-189 L 3
Ghāziābād o IND 138-139 F 5
Ghāzipur o IND 142-143 C 3
Ghazluna o PK 134-135 M 3
Gheorghe Gheorghiu-Dej = Onești o RO 102-103 E 4
Gheorgheni o RO 102-103 D 4
Gherdi o IND 140-141 F 2
Gherla o RO 102-103 C 4
Ghilarza o I 100-101 B 4
Ghimpați o RO 102-103 D 5
Ghio, Lago o RA 80 E 3
Ghizar o IND 138-139 D 1
Ghizar ~ IND 138-139 D 1
Gho Dôn o VN 156-157 D 5
Ghogha o IND 138-139 D 9
Ghomrassen o TN 190-191 H 4
Ghorahi o NEP 144-145 D 6
Ghosla o IND 138-139 E 8
Ghost Lake o CDN (ALB) 232-233 D 4
Ghost Lake o CDN 30-31 M 4
Ghost River o CDN (ONT) 234-235 M 4
Ghost River Wilderness ⊥ CDN (ALB) 232-233 C 4
Ghost Town • USA (ID) 252-253 C 3
Ghot o IND 142-143 B 6
Ghotanu o IND 138-139 C 6
Ghotki o• PK 138-139 B 6
Ghoveo o SOL 184 I d 3
Ghriss o DZ 190-191 C 3
Ghuar o IND 138-139 B 8
Ghubaysh o SUD 200-201 C 6
Ghugri ~ IND 142-143 E 3
Ghutkel o IND 142-143 B 5
Ghuzayyil, Sabkhat o LAR 192-193 H 3
Ghwarriepoort ▲ ZA 220-221 F 6
Gialalassi o SP 212-213 K 2
Giàng o VN 158-159 J 3
Giang Trung o VN 158-159 K 4
Giannitsá o GR 100-101 J 4
Giant Forest o USA (CA) 248-249 F 3
Giants Castle ▲• ZA 220-221 J 4
Giants Castle Game Reserve ⊥ ZA 220-221 J 4
Giant's Causeway ••• GB 90-91 D 4
Giants Tomb Island ⌒ CDN (ONT) 238-239 E 4
Giant Yellowknife Mine • CDN 30-31 M 4
Gianyar o RI 168 B 7
Gia Rai o VN 158-159 H 6
Giarre o I 100-101 E 6
Gia Vực o VN 158-159 K 3
Giba o I 100-101 B 5
Gibara o C 54-55 G 4
Gibbon o USA (NE) 262-263 H 4
Gibbon o USA (OR) 244-245 G 5
Gibbons o CDN (ALB) 232-233 E 2
Gibbonsville o USA (ID) 250-251 F 6
Gibb River o AUS (WA) 172-173 H 4
Gibb River ~ AUS 172-173 H 3
Gibbs o CDN (SAS) 232-233 O 5
Gibbs City o USA (MI) 270-271 K 4
Gibeon o NAM 220-221 C 2
Gibeon Station o NAM 220-221 C 2
Gibe Shet' ~ ETH 208-209 C 5
Gibē Wenz ~ ETH 208-209 C 4
Ġibla, Dū o• Y 132-133 D 7
Gibraltar o CDN (NS) 240-241 M 6
Gibraltar o GBZ 98-99 E 6
Gibraltar, Estrecho de ≈ 188-189 J 3
Gibraltar Range National Park ⊥ AUS 178-179 M 5
Gibsland o USA (LA) 268-269 G 4
Gibson o USA (LA) 268-269 K 7
Gibson City o USA (IL) 274-275 K 4
Gibson Desert ⊥ AUS 172-173 G 7
Gibson Desert Nature Reserve ⊥ AUS 176-177 H 2
Gibson Island o USA (MD) 280-281 K 4

Gibson Lake ⊂ CDN 30-31 X 4
Gibsons o CDN (BC) 230-231 F 4
Gibsonville o USA (NC) 282-283 H 4
Gida o WAN 204-205 J 5
Gidalo o ETH 208-209 B 4
Gidami o ETH 208-209 B 4
Gidar o PK 134-135 M 4
Gidar Dhor ~ PK 134-135 M 4
Ġidda o • KSA 132-133 A 3
Giddalur o IND 140-141 H 3
Ġiddat al-Ḥarāsis ∸ OM 132-133 K 4
Giddings o USA (TX) 266-267 L 3
Gideån ~ S 86-87 J 5
Gidgealpa Gas Field • AUS 178-179 F 4
Gidgee o AUS 176-177 E 3
Gidgi, Lake ⊂ AUS 176-177 H 4
Gidolē o ETH 208-209 C 6
Gielnaga del Coro o RA 76-77 E 6
Gien o F 90-91 J 8
Gieseckes Isfjord ≈ 26-27 X 7
Gießen o D 92-93 K 3
Gifford o USA (FL) 286-287 J 4
Gifford o USA (WA) 244-245 G 2
Gifford Creek o AUS 176-177 D 2
Gifford Fiord ≈ 24-25 f 5
Gifford River ~ CDN 24-25 f 5
Ġifġāfa, Bi'r o ET (SIN) 194-195 F 2
Gift Lake o CDN 32-33 N 4
Giftūn al-Kabīr, Ġazīrat ⌒ ET 194-195 F 4
Gifu ☆ J 152-153 G 7
Gigant o RUS 102-103 M 4
Giganta, Cerro ▲ MEX 50-51 D 4
Giganta, Sierra de la ▲ MEX 50-51 D 4
Gigante o CO 60-61 D 6
Gig Harbor o USA (WA) 244-245 C 3
Gigi, Danau o RI 166-167 G 2
Giglio, Isola del ⌒ I 100-101 C 3
Gigüela, Río ~ E 98-99 F 5
Ġihāna o Y 132-133 D 6
Gihofi o BU 212-213 C 5
Giir Forest National Park ⊥ IND 138-139 C 9
Giir Hills ▲ IND 138-139 C 9
Gijón = Xixón o • E 98-99 E 3
Gikongoro o RWA 212-213 B 5
Gila o USA (NM) 256-257 G 6
Gila, Tanjung ▲ RI 164-165 L 3
Gila Bend o USA (AZ) 256-257 C 6
Gila Cliff Dwellings National Monument • USA (NM) 256-257 G 5
Gila Mountains ▲ USA (AZ) 256-257 E 5
Gilān o AFG 134-135 M 2
Ġilān o IR 136-137 D 6
Gilān ▫ IR 128-129 N 3
Gilan-e Garb o IR 134-135 A 1
Gila River ~ USA (AZ) 256-257 D 5
Gila River ~ USA (NM) 256-257 G 6
Gila River Indian Reservation ⵝ USA (AZ) 256-257 C 5
Gilbert o USA (MN) 270-271 F 3
Gilbert, Islas ⌒ RCH 80 E 7
Gilbert, Mount ▲ CDN (BC) 230-231 E 3
Gilbert Islands ⌒ KIB 13 J 2
Gilbert Lake ⊂ CDN 38-39 Q 2
Gilberton o AUS 174-175 G 6
Gilbert Plains o CDN (MAN) 234-235 C 3
Gilbert River o AUS (QLD) 174-175 G 6
Gilbert River ~ AUS 174-175 F 5
Gilberts Dome ▲ AUS 178-179 J 2
Gilbués o BR 68-69 F 6
Gilby o USA (ND) 258-259 K 3
Gildford o USA (MT) 250-251 J 3
Gilé o MOC 218-219 K 3
Giles, Lake ⊂ AUS 176-177 E 4
Giles Meteorological Station o AUS 176-177 K 2
Ġilf al-Kabīr, Haḍbat al- ▲ ET 192-193 L 6
Gilford Island ⌒ CDN (BC) 230-231 C 3
Gilgandra o AUS 178-179 K 6
Gilgil o EAK 212-213 F 4
Gil Gil Creek ~ AUS 178-179 K 5
Gilgit o IND 138-139 E 2
Gilgit ~ IND 138-139 E 2
Gilgit Mountains ▲ IND 138-139 D 1
Gilgunnia o AUS 180-181 J 2
Gilgunnia Range ▲ AUS 180-181 H 2
Gili, Reserva do ⊥ MOC 218-219 K 3
Gilimanuk o RI 168 B 7
Gil Island ⌒ CDN (BC) 228-229 E 3
Giljuj ~ RUS 118-119 M 8
Gillam o AUS 172-173 D 6
Gillam o CDN 34-35 J 2
Gillams o CDN (NFL) 242-243 K 3
Gilleleje o DK 86-87 F 8
Gillen, Lake ⊂ AUS 176-177 H 3
Gilles, Lake ⊂ AUS 180-181 D 2
Gillespie o USA (IL) 274-275 J 5
Gillet o USA (AR) 276-277 D 6
Gillet o USA (WI) 270-271 K 6
Gillett o USA (TX) 266-267 K 4
Gillette o USA (WY) 252-253 N 2
Gillham o USA (AR) 276-277 A 6
Gillian Lake ⊂ CDN 24-25 j 6
Gilliat o AUS 174-175 F 7
Gilliat River ~ AUS 174-175 F 7
Gillies Bay o CDN (BC) 230-231 E 4
Gilliss Island ⌒ CDN 36-37 L 6
Gillingham o GB 90-91 H 6
Gillon Point ▲ USA 22-23 C 6
Gills Rock o USA (MI) 270-271 L 5
Gilman o USA (IL) 274-275 L 4
Gilman o USA (WI) 270-271 H 5
Gilmanton o USA (WI) 270-271 G 6
Gilmer o USA (TX) 264-265 K 6
Gil'mitka ~ RUS 112-113 O 5
Gilmore, Lake ⊂ AUS 176-177 F 6
Gilmour o CDN (ONT) 238-239 H 4
Gilmour Island ⌒ CDN 36-37 J 5
Gilo Wenz ~ ETH 208-209 A 5
Gilpo o LB 202-203 G 6
Gilroy o CDN (SAS) 232-233 M 5
Gilroy o USA (CA) 248-249 C 2
Giluth, Mount ▲ AUS 174-175 B 3
Giltner o USA (NE) 262-263 H 4
Giluwe, Mount ▲ PNG 183 B 4
Gima o EC 64-65 C 3
Ġimāl, Umm al ∴ • JOR 130-131 E 1
Gimbi o ETH 208-209 B 4
Gimi o WAN 204-205 H 4
Gimli o CDN (MAN) 234-235 G 4
Gimo o S 86-87 J 6
Gimpu o RI 164-165 G 4
Gina, Wādī al- ~ KSA 130-131 F 2
Ġināh o ET 194-195 E 5
Ginchi o ETH 208-209 D 4
Ginda o ER 200-201 J 5
Gineta, La o E 98-99 G 5
Ginevrabotnen ≈ 84-85 L 3
Gingin o AUS 176-177 C 5
Gin Gin o AUS 178-179 L 3
Gingindlovu o ZA 220-221 K 4
Gingko Petrified Forest State Park • USA (WA) 244-245 E 4
Gingoog o RP 160-161 F 8
Gingoog Bay ≈ 160-161 F 8
Ginir o ETH 208-209 E 5
Giòia del Colle o I 100-101 F 4
Giòia Tàuro o I 100-101 E 5
Giralia o AUS 172-173 B 7
Giralia Range ▲ AUS 176-177 C 1
Girān Rig, Kūh-e ▲ IR 134-135 H 4
Girard o USA (KS) 262-263 M 7
Girard o USA (TX) 264-265 D 5
Girardot o CO 60-61 D 5
Girardville o CDN (QUE) 240-241 C 2
Gira River ~ PNG 183 D 5
Girau o IRQ 128-129 K 5
Giraul ~ ANG 216-217 B 7
Gir Deh o IR 128-129 N 4
Girdwood o USA 20-21 Q 6
Giresun ☆ TR 128-129 H 2
Giresun Dağları ▲ TR 128-129 H 2
Ġirġā o ET 194-195 E 4
Giri ~ ZRE 210-211 G 2
Giridih o IND 142-143 E 3
Girilambone o AUS 178-179 J 6
Giro o WAN 204-205 F 3
Giron o EC 64-65 C 3
Girona o • E 98-99 J 4
Gironde ~ F 90-91 G 9
Giroux o CDN (MAN) 234-235 G 5
Girū o AFG 138-139 B 3
Giru o AUS 174-175 J 6
Girvan o GB 90-91 E 4
Girvin o CDN (SAS) 232-233 N 4
Girvin o USA (TX) 266-267 E 2
Girza o ET 194-195 E 3
Ġīšā, al- o KSA 130-131 L 5
Gisasa River ~ USA 20-21 L 4
Gisborne o AUS 180-181 H 4
Gisborne o NZ 182 G 3
Gisborne Lake ⊂ CDN (NFL) 242-243 O 5
Giscome o CDN (BC) 228-229 M 2
Gisenyi o • RWA 212-213 B 4
Gisi o RI 164-165 K 2
Gislaved ☆ S 86-87 F 8
Gisors o F 90-91 H 7
Ġisr aš-Šuġūr o SYR 128-129 G 5
Gissar o TJ 136-137 L 5
Gissarskij hrebet ▲ US 136-137 K 5
Gisuru o BU 212-213 C 5
Gita, Danau o RI 166-167 G 2
Gitagum o RP 160-161 F 8
Gitarama o RWA 212-213 B 5
Gitata o WAN 204-205 G 4
Gitega o BU 212-213 B 5
Githi • TN 190-191 H 4
Githio o GR 100-101 J 6
Gitnadoix River Provincial Recreation Area ⊥ CDN (BC) 228-229 E 2
Giulianova o I 100-101 D 3
Giurgiu ☆ • RO 102-103 D 6
Givi o IR 134-135 H 2
Givet o F 90-91 K 6
Giwa o WAN 204-205 G 3
Ġiyān o IR 134-135 E 3
Giyani ☆ ZA 218-219 F 6
Ġiyatj o UAE 132-133 H 2
Giylana, al- o KSA 130-131 K 5
Giyon o ETH 208-209 C 4
Ġiz', Wādī al- ~ Y 132-133 G 5
Ġiza, al- ☆ •• ET 194-195 E 2
Giza = Ġiza, al- ☆ •• ET 194-195 E 2
Giza, Pyramids of ∴ ••• ET 194-195 E 3
Ġizān o KSA 132-133 C 5
Ġizān ☆ KSA 132-133 C 5
Gižduvon ☆ US 136-137 J 4
Gize, Pyramids of ∴ •• ET 194-195 E 3
Gižiga o RUS (MAG) 120-121 T 3
Gižiga ~ RUS 112-113 L 5
Gižiginskaja guba ≈ 120-121 R 3
Gižiginskaja ravina ~ RUS 112-113 L 5
Ġizl, Wādī al- ~ KSA 130-131 E 4
Gizo ☆ SOL (Wes) 184 I c 3
Gizo ⌒ SOL (Wes) 184 I c 3
Giżycko o • PL 92-93 Q 1
Gizzin ☆ RL 128-129 F 6
Gjandža = Ganža o • AZ 128-129 M 2
Gjiri i Drinit ≈ 100-101 G 4
Gjirokastër ☆ • AL 100-101 H 4
Gjoa Haven o CDN 24-25 Y 6
Gjógur ▲ IS 86-87 c 1
Gjoklenkul, Solončak o TM 136-137 E 4
Gjøvik ☆ N 86-87 E 6
Gjuhëzës, Kepi i ▲ AL 100-101 G 4
Gjumri o AR 128-129 K 2
Glace, La o CDN 32-33 L 4
Glace Bay o CDN (NS) 240-241 Q 4
Glaciares, Parque Nacional los ⊥ ••• RA 80 D 4
Glaciar Perito Moreno •• RA 80 D 5
Glaciar Upsala • RCH 80 D 4
Glacier o CDN (BC) 230-231 M 2
Glacier o USA (WA) 244-245 D 2
Glacier Bay ≈ 32-33 B 2
Glacier Bay National Park and Preserve ⊥ USA 32-33 B 2
Glacier Island ⌒ USA 20-21 R 6
Glacier Mount ▲ USA 20-21 U 4
Glacier National Park ⊥ CDN (BC) 230-231 M 2
Glacier National Park ⊥ USA (MT) 250-251 F 3
Glacier Peak ▲ USA (WA) 244-245 D 2
Glacier Peak Wilderness Area ⊥ USA (WA) 244-245 D 2
Glacier Strait ≈ 24-25 g 2
Gladewater o USA (TX) 264-265 K 6
Gladstad o N 86-87 E 4
Gladstone o AUS (QLD) 178-179 L 2
Gladstone o AUS (SA) 180-181 E 2
Gladstone o AUS (TAS) 180-181 J 6
Gladstone o CDN (MAN) 234-235 E 4
Gladstone o USA (MI) 270-271 L 5
Gladstone o USA (MO) 274-275 D 5
Gladstone o USA (OR) 244-245 C 5
Glad Valley o USA (SD) 260-261 E 1
Gladwin o USA (MI) 272-273 E 4
Gladys Lake ⊂ CDN 20-21 Y 7
Glåma ▲ IS 86-87 b 2
Glåma ~ N 86-87 E 6
Glamis o USA (CA) 248-249 J 6
Glamoč o BIH 100-101 F 2
Glan o RP 160-161 F 10
Glarner Alpen ▲ CH 92-93 K 5
Glasco o USA (KS) 262-263 J 5
Glasgow ☆ • GB 90-91 E 4
Glasgow o USA (KY) 276-277 K 3
Glasgow o USA (MO) 274-275 F 5
Glasgow o USA (MT) 250-251 N 3
Glaslyn o CDN (SAS) 232-233 K 2
Glasnevin o CDN (SAS) 232-233 N 6
Glassboro o USA (NJ) 280-281 L 4
Glass Mountains ▲ USA (TX) 266-267 D 3
Glass Window • BS 54-55 G 2
Glavering Ø ⌒ GRØ 26-27 p 6
Glavinica o BG 102-103 E 6
Glavnaja, grjada ▲ RUS 108-109 Z 5
Glavnij Survanskij kanal < AZ 128-129 M 2
Glazaniha o RUS 88-89 P 5
Glazier o USA (TX) 264-265 D 2
Glazoué o DY 204-205 E 5
Glazov ☆ RUS 96-97 H 4
Glazova, guba o RUS 108-109 G 4
Gleeson o USA (AZ) 256-257 F 7
Gleïbat Boukenni o RIM 202-203 F 2
Gleichen o CDN (ALB) 232-233 E 5
Gleisdorf o A 92-93 N 5
Glélé o CI 202-203 G 7
Glen o AUS 176-177 D 3
Glen o USA (NH) 278-279 K 4
Glen o ZA 220-221 H 4
Glen Alda o CDN (ONT) 238-239 H 4
Glénan, Îles de ⌒ F 90-91 F 8
Glenannan o CDN (BC) 228-229 K 2
Glenavon o CDN (SAS) 232-233 P 5
Glenayle o AUS 176-177 G 2
Glenboro o CDN (MAN) 234-235 D 5
Glenboyle o CDN 20-21 V 5
Glenbrook o USA (NV) 246-247 F 4
Glenburgh o AUS 176-177 D 2
Glenburn o USA (ND) 258-259 F 3
Glencairn o CDN (MAN) 234-235 D 4
Glen Canyon ~ USA (UT) 254-255 E 6
Glen Canyon National Recreation Area ∴ USA (UT) 254-255 E 6
Glen Canyon Reservoir < USA (UT) 254-255 E 6
Glencoe o CDN (NB) 240-241 J 3
Glencoe o CDN (ONT) 238-239 D 6
Glencoe o USA (AL) 284-285 E 3
Glencoe o USA (MN) 270-271 D 6
Glencoe o USA (NM) 256-257 K 5
Glencoe o ZA 220-221 K 4
Glen Cove o USA (NY) 280-281 N 3
Glendale o USA (AZ) 256-257 C 5
Glendale o USA (CA) 248-249 F 5
Glendale o USA (IL) 276-277 G 3
Glendale o USA (TN) 282-283 C 5
Glendale o USA (TX) 268-269 E 5
Glendale o ZW 218-219 F 3
Glendale Cove o CDN (BC) 230-231 D 3
Glendale Lake ⊂ USA (PA) 280-281 H 3
Glendambo o AUS 178-179 C 6
Glen Daniel o USA (WV) 280-281 E 6
Glenden o AUS 178-179 K 1
Glendive o USA (MT) 250-251 P 4
Glendo o USA (WY) 252-253 N 4
Glendora o USA (CA) 248-249 G 5
Glendo Reservoir < USA (WY) 252-253 O 4
Glenelg River ~ AUS 180-181 F 4
Glenella o CDN (MAN) 234-235 D 4
Glenfield o USA (ND) 258-259 J 4
Glengyle o AUS 178-179 E 3
Glen Helen o AUS 176-177 M 1
Glenholme o CDN (NS) 240-241 M 5
Glen Hope o USA (PA) 280-281 H 3
Gleniffer Lake ⊂ CDN (ALB) 232-233 D 3
Glen Innes o AUS 178-179 L 5
Glen Kerr o CDN (SAS) 232-233 L 5
Glenlivet < ZW 218-219 F 5
Glenlyon Dam < AUS 178-179 L 5
Glenmire o AUS 178-179 H 3
Glen Mor ∸ GB 90-91 E 3
Glenmora o USA (LA) 268-269 H 6
Glen More ⌵ GB 90-91 E 3
Glenmorgan o AUS 178-179 K 4
Glennallen o USA 20-21 S 5
Glenn Highway II USA 20-21 R 6
Glennie o USA (MI) 272-273 F 3
Glenns o USA (VA) 280-281 K 6
Glenns Ferry o USA (ID) 252-253 C 4
Glennville o USA (CA) 248-249 F 4
Glennville o USA (GA) 284-285 J 5
Glenora o AUS 174-175 G 6
Glenora o CDN (MAN) 234-235 D 5
Glen Orchard o CDN (ONT) 238-239 F 3
Glenorchy o AUS 180-181 J 7
Glenorchy o NZ 182 B 6
Glenore o AUS 174-175 F 5
Glenormiston o AUS 178-179 E 2
Glen Raven o USA (NC) 282-283 H 4
Glenrio o USA (NM) 256-257 M 3
Glenrock o USA (WY) 252-253 N 4
Glen Rose o USA (TX) 264-265 G 6
Glensboro o USA (KY) 276-277 K 2
Glens Falls o USA (NY) 278-279 H 5
Glenside o CDN (SAS) 232-233 M 4
Glenties o IRL 90-91 C 4
Glentworth o CDN (SAS) 232-233 M 6
Glenville o USA (MN) 270-271 E 7
Glenville o USA (WV) 280-281 F 5
Glenwood o CDN (ALB) 232-233 E 6
Glenwood o CDN (NFL) 242-243 O 4
Glenwood o USA (AR) 276-277 B 6
Glenwood o USA (HI) 288 K 5
Glenwood o USA (IA) 274-275 C 3
Glenwood o USA (MN) 270-271 C 5
Glenwood o USA (NM) 256-257 G 5
Glenwood o USA (OR) 244-245 C 5
Glenwood City o USA (WI) 270-271 F 5
Glenwood Springs o • USA (CO) 254-255 H 4
Glidden o CDN (SAS) 232-233 J 4
Glidden o USA (WI) 270-271 H 4
Glide o USA (OR) 244-245 B 7
Glina o HR 100-101 F 2
Glittertinden ▲ N 86-87 D 6
Gliwice o • PL 92-93 P 3
Gljaden' o RUS 116-117 E 8
Gljadjanskoe ☆ RUS 114-115 H 7
Globe o • USA (AZ) 256-257 E 5
Głogów o • PL 92-93 O 3
Gloie o LB 202-203 F 6
Glomfjord o N 86-87 F 3
Glommersträsk o S 86-87 J 4
Gloria o MEX 50-51 J 4
Gloria, Bahia de la ≈ 54-55 G 4
Glória, Cachoeira da ~ BR 66-67 G 7
Gloria, La o CO 60-61 E 3
Gloria, La o MEX 50-51 K 4
Gloria, Sierra de la ▲ RCH 76-77 B 4
Glorias, Las o MEX 50-51 E 5
Glorieta o USA (NM) 256-257 K 3
Glorieuses, Îles ⌒ F 222-223 E 3
Gloster o USA (MS) 268-269 J 5
Gloucester o AUS 180-181 L 2
Gloucester o GB 90-91 F 6
Gloucester o PNG 183 E 3
Gloucester o USA (MA) 278-279 L 6
Gloucester o USA (VA) 280-281 K 6
Gloucester Island ⌒ AUS 174-175 K 7
Gloucester Point o USA (VA) 280-281 K 6
Glouster o USA (OH) 280-281 D 4
Glover Island ⌒ CDN (NFL) 242-243 L 4
Glovers Reef ⌒ BH 52-53 L 3
Gloversville o USA (NY) 278-279 G 5
Glovertown o CDN (NFL) 242-243 O 4
Głubczyce o • PL 92-93 O 3
Glubokaja, buhta o RUS 112-113 R 6
Glubokaja, laguna o RUS 112-113 U 5
Glubokij o RUS 102-103 M 3
Glubokij Poluj ~ RUS 114-115 K 2
Glubokij Sabun ~ RUS 114-115 Q 3
Glubokoe, ozero o RUS 108-109 Y 7
Gluharinyj o RUS 110-111 d 7
Glumpangdua o RI 162-163 B 2
Glymur ~ IS 86-87 c 2
Glyndon o USA (MN) 270-271 B 4
Gmünd o • A 92-93 N 4
Gmunden o A 92-93 M 5
Gnadenthal o CDN (MAN) 234-235 F 5
Gnaraloo o AUS 176-177 B 1
Gnarp o S 86-87 H 5
Gnibi o SN 202-203 C 2
Gniezno o •• PL 92-93 O 2
Gnit o SN 196-197 C 6
Gnjilane o YU 100-101 H 3
Gnowangerup o AUS 176-177 D 6
Gnows Nest Range ▲ AUS 176-177 D 4
Goa ▫ IND 140-141 E 3
Goageb o NAM 220-221 C 3
Goal Mountain ▲ USA (MT) 250-251 F 4
Goālpāra o IND 142-143 G 3
Goaltor o IND 142-143 E 4
Goa Mampu Caves • RI 164-165 G 6
Goan o RMM 202-203 H 3
Goari o PNG 183 C 4
Goaso o GH 202-203 J 6
Goat River ~ CDN (BC) 228-229 O 3
Goat River ~ CDN (BC) 230-231 N 4
Goat Rocks Wilderness ⊥ USA (WA) 244-245 D 4
Goba ☆ ETH 208-209 D 5
Goba o MOC 220-221 L 3
Gobabed o NAM 220-221 B 1
Gobabis ☆ NAM 216-217 E 11
Goba Fronteira o MOC 220-221 L 3
Gobālpur o IND 142-143 E 3
Gobari ~ ZRE 210-211 G 6
Gobe o PNG 183 E 5
Gobēlē Wenz ~ ETH 208-209 E 4
Gobernador Crespo o RA 76-77 G 6
Gobernador Gregores o RA 80 E 4
Gobernador Ingeniero Valentín Virasoro o RA 76-77 J 5
Gobernador Moyano o RA 80 F 3
Gobernador Piedrabuena o RA 76-77 E 4
Gobernador Solá o RA 78-79 K 2
Gobi = Gov' ∸ MAU 148-149 F 6
Gobles o USA (MI) 272-273 D 5
Gobnangou, Falaises du ▲ •• BF 202-203 L 4
Gobō o J 152-153 F 8
Gobo, Col de ▲ RN 198-199 G 2
Gobourno ~ RCA 210-211 F 2
Gobur o SUD 206-207 K 6
Gobustan o AZ 128-129 N 2
Gobustan ∸ AZ 128-129 N 2
Goce Delčev o BG 102-103 C 7
Gochas o NAM 220-221 D 2
Go Công o VN 158-159 J 5
Gò Công Đông o VN 158-159 J 5
Godafoss ∸ 86-87 e 2
Godahl o USA (MN) 270-271 D 6
Godatair o SUD 206-207 H 4
Godāvari ~ IND 138-139 E 10
Godāvari ~ IND 142-143 B 7
Godāwari o NEP 144-145 C 6
Godbout o CDN (QUE) 242-243 A 3
Godbout, Rivière ~ CDN (QUE) 242-243 A 3
Godda o IND 142-143 E 3
Godē o ETH 208-209 F 6
Godé o RMM 202-203 J 3
Gode, Hosséré ▲ CAM 204-205 K 4
Godegode o EAT 214-215 J 4
Goderich o CDN (ONT) 238-239 D 5
Godfreys Tank < AUS 172-173 H 6
Godfried Hansen Ø ⌒ GRØ 26-27 p 5
Godhavn = Qeqertarsuaq o GRØ 28-29 O 2
Godhra o IND 138-139 D 8
Godhyogol o SP 208-209 F 4
Godi, Mayo ~ CAM 206-207 B 4
Göding = Hodonín o CZ 92-93 O 4
Godinlabe o SP 208-209 H 6
Godofredo Viana o BR 68-69 F 2
Godong o RI 168 D 3
Godong Kangri ▲ VRC 144-145 D 5
Godoy Cruz o RA 78-79 E 2
Gods Lake ⊂ CDN 34-35 J 3
Gods Lake Indian Reserve ⵝ CDN 34-35 J 3
Gods Lake Narrows o CDN 34-35 J 3
Gods Mercy, Bay of ≈ 36-37 F 3
Gods River ~ CDN 34-35 K 2
Godthåb = Nuuk ☆ GRØ 28-29 P 4
Godwin Austen, Mount = K2 ▲ PK 138-139 F 2
Goe o PNG 183 A 5
Goeie Hoop, Kaap die = Cape of Good Hope ▲ • ZA 220-221 D 7
Goejegebergte, De ▲ SME 62-63 G 4
Goéland, Lac ⊂ CDN (QUE) 236-237 M 3
Goëlettes ⌒ SY 224 B 5
Goeree ∸ NL 92-93 G 3
Goes o NL 92-93 G 3
Goeygina ~ RUS 122-123 R 3
Gofar Fracture Zone ≃ 14-15 S 8
Goffs o USA (CA) 248-249 J 5
Gofmana, ostrov ⌒ RUS 84-85 g 2
Goft'ima Sebeka o ETH 208-209 C 3
Gog o ETH 208-209 B 5
Gogama o CDN (ONT) 236-237 G 5
Gogango o AUS 178-179 L 2
Gogardan, Kōtal-e ▲ AFG 134-135 M 1
Gō-gawa ~ J 152-153 E 7
Gogebic, Lake ⊂ USA (MI) 270-271 J 4
Gogland, ostrov ⌒ RUS 94-95 K 1
Gogo o AUS 172-173 G 5
Gogo o WAN 204-205 H 4
Gogogogo o RM 222-223 D 10
Gogói o MOC 218-219 G 5
Gogorrón, Parque Natural ⊥ MEX 50-51 J 7
Gogounou o DY 204-205 E 3
Gogrial o SUD 206-207 J 4
Gogui o RMM 196-197 F 7
Goh o IND 142-143 D 3
Goha Ts'iyon o ETH 208-209 D 3
Goiana o BR 68-69 L 5
Goiandira o BR 72-73 F 5
Goianésia o BR 72-73 F 3
Goianésia do Pará o BR 68-69 D 3
Goiânia ☆ BR 72-73 F 4
Goianinha o BR 68-69 L 5
Goianorte o BR 68-69 D 6
Goiás o • BR 72-73 E 3
Goiás ▫ BR 72-73 D 4
Goiatins o BR 68-69 E 5
Goiatuba o BR 72-73 F 5
Goio, Rio ~ BR 72-73 D 7
Goio-Erê o BR 74-75 D 5
Goi-Pula o ZRE 214-215 D 4
Gojeb Wenz ~ ETH 208-209 C 5
Gojo o ETH 208-209 D 4
Gojra o PK 138-139 D 4
Gojyō o J 152-153 F 7
Gökçeada ⌒ TR 128-129 A 2
Gökırmak ~ TR 128-129 F 2
Gökova o TR 128-129 C 4
Gökova Körfezi ≈ 128-129 B 4
Gokprosh Range ▲ PK 134-135 K 5
Göksu Çayı ~ TR 128-129 G 3
Göksun ☆ TR 128-129 G 3
Göksu Nehri ~ TR 128-129 E 4
Gokteik Viadukt • MYA 142-143 K 4
Gokwe o ZW 218-219 E 4
Gol ☆ N 86-87 D 6
Golaghāt o IND 142-143 H 2
Gola Hills ▲ WAL 202-203 E 6
Golaja, gora ▲ RUS 112-113 K 4
Golan ▲ SYR 128-129 F 6
Golana Gof ~ EAK 212-213 G 3
Golbāf o IR 134-135 G 4
Gölbaşı o TR 128-129 E 3
Gölbaşı ☆ TR 128-129 G 4
Golconda o USA (IL) 276-277 G 3
Golconda o USA (NV) 246-247 H 3
Golconda Summit ▲ USA (NV) 246-247 H 3
Gol'covaja ~ RUS 108-109 f 3
Gölcük o TR 128-129 H 4
Gölcük ☆ TR 128-129 C 2
Gołdap o PL 92-93 R 1
Gold Bar o CDN 32-33 J 3
Gold Beach o USA (OR) 244-245 A 8
Gold Bridge o CDN (BC) 230-231 G 3
Gold Coast ⌵ AUS 178-179 N 4
Gold Coast ⌵ GH 202-203 K 7
Golddust o USA (TN) 276-277 F 5
Golden o CDN (BC) 230-231 N 2
Golden o USA (CO) 254-255 K 4
Golden Bay ≈ 182 D 4
Golden City o USA (MO) 276-277 A 3
Goldendale o USA (WA) 244-245 E 5
Golden Ears Provincial Park ⊥ CDN (BC) 230-231 G 4
Golden Gate o USA (FL) 286-287 H 5
Golden Gate Bridge •• USA (CA) 248-249 B 2
Golden Grove o JA 54-55 G 6
Golden Hinde ▲ CDN (BC) 230-231 D 4
Golden Lake o CDN (ONT) 238-239 H 3
Golden Meadow o USA (LA) 268-269 K 7
Golden Prairie o CDN (SAS) 232-233 J 5
Golden Spike National Historic Site ∴ USA (UT) 254-255 C 2
Golden Valley o USA (ND) 258-259 E 4
Golden Valley o ZW 218-219 E 4
Goldereck o USA 250-251 F 5
Goldfield o USA (NV) 248-249 G 2
Gold Hill o USA (UT) 254-255 B 3
Goldokita ~ RUS 116-117 E 4
Gold Pines o CDN (ONT) 234-235 K 4
Gold River o CDN (BC) 230-231 C 4
Gold Rock o CDN (ONT) 234-235 L 5
Goldsand Lake ⊂ CDN 34-35 F 2
Goldsboro o USA (MD) 280-281 L 4
Goldsboro o USA (NC) 282-283 K 5
Goldsmith Channel ≈ 24-25 T 4
Goldstream River ~ CDN (BC) 230-231 L 2
Goldsworthy o AUS 172-173 D 6
Goldsworthy, Mount ▲ AUS 172-173 D 6
Goldthwaite o USA (TX) 266-267 J 2
Goldwater o USA (LA) 268-269 H 5
Goldyrevskij o RUS 96-97 K 5
Göle o IRQ 128-129 L 5
Göle ☆ TR 128-129 K 2
Goleniów o PL 92-93 N 2
Goleniščeva, mys ▲ RUS 120-121 V 4
Golestān o AFG 134-135 K 2
Golfa o • IR 128-129 L 3
Golfete, El o GCA 52-53 K 4
Golfito o • CR 52-53 C 7
Golfo Aranci o I 100-101 B 4
Golfo de Santa Clara, El o MEX 50-51 B 2
Golfo Nuevo ≈ 78-79 G 7
Gölgeli Dağları ▲ TR 128-129 C 4
Gol Gol o AUS 180-181 G 2
Gölhisar ☆ TR 128-129 C 4
Goli o EAU 212-213 C 2
Goliad o USA (TX) 266-267 K 5
Golija ▲ • YU 100-101 H 3
Goliševa o LV 94-95 K 3
Gölköy ☆ TR 128-129 G 2
Golmānḫāne, Bandar-e o IR 128-129 L 4
Gölmarmara ☆ TR 128-129 B 3
Golmud o VRC 144-145 K 2
Golodnaja Guba, ozero o RUS 88-89 W 3
Golog Shan ▲ VRC 154-155 B 5
Golo Island ⌒ RP 160-161 D 6
Golokuati o GH 202-203 L 6
Golol o SP 212-213 J 2
Gololcha o ETH 208-209 E 4
Golomoti o MW 218-219 H 2
Golongosso o RCA 206-207 D 4
Goloustnaja ~ RUS 116-117 M 9
Golovin o USA 20-21 J 4
Golovin Bay ≈ 20-21 J 4
Golovin Mission o USA 20-21 J 4
Golovino o RUS 122-123 E 4
Golovnino o RUS 122-123 L 7
Golpāyegān o • IR 134-135 D 2
Gol Tappe o IR (AZG) 128-129 L 4
Gol Tappe o IR (HAM) 128-129 N 5
Goľtjavino o RUS 116-117 J 6
Goltry o USA (OK) 264-265 F 2
Golū, Rūdḫāne-ye ~ IR 136-137 B 7
Golungo o ANG 216-217 C 4
Golva o USA (ND) 258-259 D 5
Golweyn o SP 212-213 K 3
Golyšmanovo ☆ RUS 114-115 K 6
Goma o ZRE 212-213 B 4
Goma-Gofa ▫ ETH 208-209 C 6
Gomati ~ IND 142-143 C 3
Gomati ~ IND 144-145 C 6
Gombari o ZRE 212-213 B 2
Gombe o WAN 204-205 J 3
Gombe-Matadi o ZRE 210-211 E 6
Gombi o WAN 204-205 K 3
Gombi Fulani o WAN 204-205 K 3
Gombo ~ RG 202-203 E 4
Gomboro o BF 202-203 J 3
Gomboussougou o BF 202-203 K 4
Gomel' = Homel' ☆ BY 94-95 M 5
Gomera, La ⌒ E 188-189 C 6
Gomes Carneiro, Área Indígena ⵝ BR 70-71 K 5
Gómez, Laguna de o RA 78-79 J 3
Gómez Farías o MEX (CHA) 50-51 F 3
Gómez Farías o MEX (TAM) 50-51 K 6
Gómez Palacio o MEX 50-51 H 5
Gómez Rendón o EC 64-65 B 3
Ġomišān o IR 136-137 D 6
Gomon o • CI 202-203 H 7
Gomontang Caves • MAL 160-161 C 10
Gomorovići o RUS 94-95 O 1
Gomumu, Pulau ⌒ RI 164-165 K 4
Gona o CI 202-203 G 5
Gonābād o • IR 134-135 H 1
Gonaïves ☆ RH 54-55 J 5
Gonam ~ RUS 118-119 M 8
Gonam ~ RUS 120-121 D 5
Gonamskij, Sutamo-hrebet ▲ RUS 118-119 N 7
Gonarezhou National Park ⊥ ZW 218-219 F 5
Gonaté o CI 202-203 G 6
Gonâve, Canal de la ≈ 54-55 J 5
Gonâve, Golfe de la ≈ 54-55 J 5
Gonâve, Ile de la ⌒ RH 54-55 J 5
Gonbad-e Kabūd o IR 136-137 F 6
Gonbad-e Qabūs o • IR 136-137 D 6
Gonçalo, Canal de < BR 74-75 D 9
Gonçalves Dias o BR 68-69 F 4
Gonda o IND 142-143 B 2
Gondal o IND 138-139 C 9
Gondē o ETH 208-209 D 4
Gonder ▫ ETH 200-201 H 6
Gonder ☆ • ETH 200-201 H 6
Gondey o TCH 206-207 D 4
Gondia o IND 142-143 B 5
Gondola o MOC 218-219 G 4
Gondolahun o LB 202-203 E 6
Gondomar o • P 98-99 C 4
Gönen ☆ TR 128-129 B 2
Gonga o CAM 204-205 K 6
Gong'an o VRC 154-155 H 6
Gongbo'gyamda o VRC 144-145 J 6
Gongchen o VRC 156-157 G 4
Gongda ~ RUS 108-109 b 7
Gonggar o VRC 144-145 H 6
Gongga Shan ▲ VRC 156-157 B 2
Gongguan o VRC 156-157 F 6
Gonghe o VRC 154-155 B 3
Gongliu o VRC 146-147 F 4
Gongo o TCH 206-207 D 4
Gongola ▫ WAN 204-205 J 4
Gongola, River ~ WAN 204-205 K 4
Gongolgon o AUS 178-179 J 6
Gongoué o G 210-211 B 4
Gongpoquan o VRC 148-149 C 7
Gongshan o VRC 142-143 L 2
Gong Xian o VRC (HEN) 154-155 H 4
Gong Xian o VRC (SIC) 156-157 D 2
Gongzhuling o VRC 150-151 E 6
Gonikoppla o IND 140-141 F 4
Gono, togga ~ SP 208-209 K 4
Gonoa • TCH 198-199 H 2
Gonohe o J 152-153 J 4
Gonoruwa o CL 140-141 J 7
Gōnoura o J 152-153 C 8
Gonža o RUS 118-119 M 9
Gonzales o USA (CA) 248-249 C 3
Gonzales o USA (FL) 286-287 B 1
Gonzales o USA (LA) 268-269 K 6
Gonzales o USA (TX) 266-267 K 4
Gonzáles, Río ~ PY 76-77 H 2
Gonzáles Moreno o RA 78-79 H 3
Gonzales Suares o PE 64-65 E 3
González o MEX 50-51 K 6
Gonzanamá o EC 64-65 C 4
Goobang Creek ~ AUS 180-181 J 2
Goobies o CDN (NFL) 242-243 P 5
Gooch Range ▲ AUS 176-177 C 1
Goode, Mount ▲ AUS 176-177 F 3
Goodenough, Cape ▲ ARK 16 G 13
Goodenough Bay ≈ 183 E 5
Goodenough Island ⌒ PNG 183 F 5
Goodenough Land ⌒ GRØ 26-27 l 7
Gooderham o CDN (ONT) 238-239 G 4
Goodeve o CDN (SAS) 232-233 P 4
Good Hope, Cape of ▲ • ZA 220-221 D 7
Good Hope Mountain ▲ CDN (BC) 230-231 E 2
Good Hope Plantation •• JA 54-55 G 5
Goodhouse o ZA 220-221 D 4
Gooding o USA (ID) 252-253 D 4
Goodland o USA (KS) 262-263 E 5
Goodland o USA (MN) 270-271 E 3
Goodland o USA (TX) 264-265 B 5
Goodlands o CDN (MAN) 234-235 C 5
Goodlands o MS 224 C 7
Goodlett o USA (TX) 264-265 E 4
Goodlettsville o USA (TN) 276-277 J 4
Goodman o USA (MS) 268-269 L 4
Goodnews Mining Camp o USA 22-23 Q 3
Goodnight o USA (TX) 264-265 C 3
Goodnoe Hills o USA (WA) 244-245 E 5
Goodooga o AUS 178-179 J 5
Goodparla o AUS 172-173 L 2
Goodpaster River ~ USA 20-21 S 4
Goodrich o USA (CO) 254-255 L 3
Goodrich Bank ≃ 166-167 F 7
Goodridge o USA (MN) 270-271 C 2
Goodsir, Mount ▲ CDN (BC) 230-231 N 2
Goodsoil o CDN 32-33 Q 4
Good Spirit Lake ⊂ CDN (SAS) 232-233 Q 4
Good Spirit Lake Provincial Park ⊥ CDN (SAS) 232-233 Q 4
Goodsprings o USA (NV) 248-249 J 4
Goodview o USA (MN) 270-271 G 6
Goodwater o USA (AL) 284-285 D 3
Goodwell o USA (OK) 264-265 C 2
Goodwin o CDN 32-33 L 4
Goodyear o USA (AZ) 256-257 C 5
Goold Island ⌒ AUS 174-175 J 6
Goole o GB 90-91 G 5
Goolgowi o AUS 180-181 H 2
Goolwa o AUS 180-181 E 3
Goomader River ~ AUS 174-175 B 3
Goomalling o AUS 176-177 D 5
Goomeri o AUS 178-179 M 4
Goomny, gora ▲ RUS 116-117 H 5
Goondiwindi o AUS 178-179 L 5
Goongarrie, National Park ⊥ AUS 176-177 F 4
Goonyella Mine o AUS 178-179 K 1
Goorly, Lake ⊂ AUS 176-177 D 5
Goornong o AUS 180-181 H 4
Goose Bay o CDN (BC) 230-231 B 2
Goose Bay o CDN (NFL) 38-39 O 2
Goose Bay o CDN (NFL) 38-39 O 2
Gooseberry River ~ USA (WY) 252-253 K 2
Goose Cove o CDN (NFL) 242-243 N 1
Goose Creek ~ CDN 34-35 N 3
Goose Creek o USA (SC) 284-285 K 4
Goose Creek ~ USA (ID) 252-253 E 4
Goose Island ⌒ CDN (NS) 240-241 O 5
Goose Lake ⊂ CDN (SAS) 232-233 L 4
Goose Lake o USA (IA) 274-275 H 3
Goose Lake ⊂ USA (CA) 246-247 E 2
Goose River ~ CDN 32-33 M 4
Goose River ~ CDN 38-39 O 2
Goosport o USA (LA) 268-269 G 6
Gooty o IND 140-141 G 3
Gopalganj o IND 142-143 D 2
Gopichettipalaiyam o IND 140-141 G 5
Goplo, Jezioro o PL 92-93 P 2
Goppe Bazar o MYA 142-143 H 5
Gō Quao o VN 158-159 H 6
Gōr ▫ AFG 134-135 K 1
Goradiz o AZ 128-129 M 3
Goragorskij o RUS 126-127 F 6
Gorahun o WAL 202-203 E 6
Goraici, Kepulauan ⌒ RI 164-165 K 4
Góra Kalwaria o PL 92-93 Q 3
Gorakhpur o IND 142-143 C 2
Goram, Tanjung ▲ RI 164-165 H 6
Goran, Lake ⊂ AUS 178-179 L 6
Goranlega ~ SP 212-213 H 4
Gorantla o IND 140-141 G 4
Goražde o BIH 100-101 G 3
Görband o AFG 138-139 B 2
Gorbea o RCH 78-79 C 5
Gorbi ~ RUS 120-121 G 4
Gorbiačin ~ RUS 108-109 X 8
Gorbica o RUS 118-119 J 9
Gorbilok ~ RUS 116-117 G 6
Gorbita ~ RUS 108-109 a 5
Gorbovy, ostrova ⌒ RUS 108-109 H 4
Gorbyľ ~ RUS 122-123 C 3
Gorda, Punta ▲ NIC 52-53 C 4
Gorda, Punta ▲ RCH 70-71 B 6
Gorda Cay o BS 54-55 G 1
Gördes ☆ TR 128-129 C 3

Gordo o USA (AL) 284-285 C 3
Gordon o USA (AK) 20-21 U 2
Gordon o USA (GA) 284-285 G 4
Gordon o USA (NE) 262-263 D 2
Gordon o USA (TX) 264-265 F 6
Gordon, Isla ⌒ RCH 80 F 7
Gordon, Lake o AUS 180-181 J 7
Gordon, Mount ▲ AUS 176-177 F 6
Gordon Downs o AUS 172-173 J 5
Gordonia Alatamaha State Park ⊥ • USA (GA) 284-285 H 4
Gordon Indian Reservation ✗ CDN (SAS) 232-233 O 4
Gordon Lake o CDN (ALB) 32-33 P 3
Gordon Lake o CDN (NWT) 30-31 N 4
Gordon River ~ CDN 30-31 Z 3
Gordon's Bay o ZA 220-221 D 7
Gordonsville o USA (VA) 280-281 H 5
Gordonvale o AUS 174-175 H 5
Gordonville o USA (MI) 272-273 E 4
Gorë o ETH 208-209 B 4
Gore o NZ 182 B 7
Goré o TCH 206-207 C 5
Gore Bay ≈ 24-25 d 7
Gore Bay o CDN (ONT) 238-239 C 3
Gorée, Île de ⌒ ••• SN 202-203 B 2
Gorelaja Sopka, vulkan ▲ RUS 120-121 S 7
Göreme o••• TR 128-129 F 3
Gore Point ▲ USA 22-23 V 3
Gore Springs o USA (MS) 268-269 L 3
Gōr-e Teivāre o • AFG 134-135 L 2
Gorgadji o BF 202-203 K 2
Gorgān o • IR 136-137 D 6
Gorgān, Rūdḫāne-ye ~ IR 136-137 D 6
Gorgol ◘ RIM 196-197 D 6
Gorgol ~ RIM 196-197 D 7
Gorgol Blanc ~ RIM 196-197 D 6
Gorgol Noire ~ RIM 196-197 D 6
Gorgora o • ETH 200-201 H 6
Gorgoram o WAN 198-199 E 6
Gorgulho de São Antônio, Cachoeira ~ BR 68-69 C 5
Gorham o USA (ME) 278-279 L 5
Gorham o USA (NH) 278-279 K 4
Gorhiar o PK 138-139 C 7
Gori o • GE 126-127 F 7
Goricy o RUS 94-95 P 3
Gori Hills ▲ WAL 202-203 E 5
Gorinchem o NL 92-93 H 3
Goris o AR 128-129 M 3
Gorizia ☆ I 100-101 D 2
Gorjačegorsk o RUS 114-115 U 7
Gorjačevodskij o RUS 126-127 E 5
Gorjačij Ključ o RUS 126-127 C 5
Gorjaščaja, vulkan ▲ RUS 122-123 O 5
Gorjun ~ RUS 122-123 G 3
Gorka, mys ▲ RUS 120-121 R 3
Gor'kaja Balka < RUS 126-127 F 5
Gor'kij = Nižnij Novgorod ☆ •• RUS 94-95 S 3
Gorkij = Nižnij Novgorod ☆ •• RUS 94-95 S 3
Gor'koe, ozero o RUS 124-125 M 2
Gor'koe-Pereščečnoe, ozero o RUS 124-125 M 3
Gor'kovskoe ☆ RUS 114-115 N 7
Gorkovskoye Vodokhranilishche = Gor'kovskoe vodohranilišče < RUS 94-95 S 3
Gorlice o • PL 92-93 Q 4
Gorlitz o CDN (SAS) 232-233 Q 4
Görlitz o •• D 92-93 N 3
Gorlovka = Horlivka o UA 102-103 L 3
Gormač o AFG 136-137 H 7
Gorman o USA (CA) 248-249 F 5
Gorman o USA (TX) 264-265 F 6
Gornaja Ob' ~ RUS 114-115 H 2
Gorna Mitropolia o BG 102-103 D 6
Gornjackij o RUS 102-103 M 3
Gornjak o RUS 124-125 M 3
Gorno-Altajsk ☆ RUS 124-125 O 3
Gorno-Altay = Gornyj Altaj, Respublika ◘ RUS 124-125 P 3
Gorno-Čujskij o RUS 118-119 E 7
Gornoslinkino o RUS 114-115 K 5
Gornovodnoe o RUS 122-123 F 7
Gornozavodsk o RUS 122-123 J 5
Gornozavodsk ☆ RUS (PRM) 96-97 L 4
Gorny Altaj, Respublika ◘ RUS 124-125 P 3
Gornyj o RUS (HBR) 122-123 G 3
Gornyj o RUS (NVS) 114-115 R 7
Gornyj ☆ RUS (SAR) 96-97 F 8
Goro o ETH 208-209 E 5
Goroch'an ▲ ETH 208-209 C 4
Gorodec o RUS 94-95 S 3
Gorodeck o RUS 88-89 S 5
Gorodišče o RUS 96-97 D 7
Gorodok, Lesnoj o RUS 118-119 F 10
Gorodovikovsk o RUS 102-103 M 4
Gorogoro o RI 164-165 K 4
Goroh, Tanjung ▲ RI 162-163 F 5
Gorohovec o RUS 94-95 S 3
Goroka ☆ • PNG 183 C 4
Goroke o AUS 180-181 F 4
Gorom-Gorom o BF 202-203 K 2
Gorona, Isla ⌒ CO 60-61 B 6
Gorong, Kepulauan ⌒ RI 166-167 F 4
Gorong, Pulau ⌒ RI 166-167 F 3
Gorongosa o MOC (Sof) 218-219 H 4
Gorongosa ▲ MOC (Sof) 218-219 H 4
Gorongosa, Parque Nacional de ⊥ MOC 218-219 H 4
Gorongosa, Rio ~ MOC 218-219 H 5
Gorontalo o RI 164-165 H 3
Gorontalo, Teluk ≈ 164-165 H 3
Goronyo o WAN 198-199 B 6
Gororos o BR 72-73 J 5
Goroubi ~ RN 202-203 L 3
Gorouol ~ BF 202-203 K 2
Gorrie o AUS 172-173 L 3
Goršečnoe o RUS 102-103 L 2
Gort = An Gort o IRL 90-91 C 5
Gōryān o AFG 134-135 J 1
Gorzów Wielkopolski ☆ • PL 92-93 N 2
Goschen Strait ≈ 183 F 6
Gosford-Woy Woy o • AUS 180-181 L 2
Goshen o USA (CA) 248-249 E 3
Goshen o USA (CT) 280-281 N 2
Goshen o USA (IN) 274-275 N 3
Goshen o USA (VA) 280-281 G 6
Goshogawara o J 152-153 J 4
Goshute o USA (NV) 246-247 L 4
Goshute Indian Reservation ✗ USA (NV) 246-247 L 4
Goslar o ••• D 92-93 L 3
Gospić o HR 100-101 E 2
Gosport o USA (IN) 274-275 M 5
Gossas o SN 202-203 B 2
Gosses o AUS 178-179 C 6
Gossi o RMM 202-203 K 2
Gossinga o SUD 206-207 G 4
Gostivar o • MK 100-101 H 4
Gostynin o PL 92-93 P 2
Goszapovednik o KA 126-127 N 5
Gota o • ETH 208-209 E 4
Göta älv ~ S 86-87 F 8
Götaland ⊥ S 86-87 F 8
Gotebo o USA (OK) 264-265 F 3
Göteborg ☆ •• S 86-87 E 8
Gotel Mountains ▲ WAN 204-205 J 5
Gotenba o J 152-153 H 7
Gotera = San Francisco ☆ ES 52-53 K 5
Gotha o • D 92-93 L 3
Goth Ahmad o PK 134-135 M 6
Gothenburg o USA (NE) 262-263 F 4
Gothèye o RN 202-203 L 3
Goth Kunda Bakhsh o PK 134-135 M 6
Gotland ⌒ •• S 86-87 J 8
Gotō-rettō ⌒ J 152-153 C 8
Gotska Sandön ⌒ • S 86-87 J 7
Gotska Sandön Nationalpark ⊥ S 86-87 J 7
Göttingen o • D 92-93 K 3
Gottwaldov = Zlín o CZ 92-93 O 4
Gotval'd = Zmijiv o UA 102-103 K 3
Gouandé o DY 202-203 L 4
Gouatchi o RCA 206-207 E 6
Gouaya ~ BF 202-203 K 3
Goubangzi o VRC 150-151 C 7
Goubi o RT 202-203 L 5
Goubouna ▲ DY 202-203 L 5
Gouburn River ~ AUS 180-181 L 2
Gouchi o RN 198-199 D 6
Gouda o • NL 92-93 H 2
Gouda o ZA 220-221 D 6
Goudar, Rūd-e ~ IR 134-135 F 5
Goudiri o SN 202-203 D 2
Goudoumaria o RN 198-199 E 6
Gouera, La o RIM 196-197 B 4
Gouga o RCA 210-211 G 2
Gough Fracture Zone ≃ 6-7 H 13
Gough Lake o CDN (ALB) 232-233 F 3
Gouin, Réservoir ⊥ CDN (QUE) 236-237 O 4
Gouin, Réservoir o CDN (QUE) 236-237 O 4
Gouina, Chutes de ~ • RMM 202-203 E 2
Gouiret Moussa < DZ 190-191 D 5
Gouka o DY 202-203 L 5
Goukār o IR 134-135 C 1
Goulahonfla o CI 202-203 G 6
Goulais River ~ CDN (ONT) 236-237 D 6
Goulburn o AUS 180-181 K 3
Goulburn Island, North ⌒ AUS 174-175 B 2
Goulburn Island, South ⌒ AUS 174-175 B 2
Goulburn River ~ AUS 180-181 H 4
Goulburn River National Park ⊥ AUS 180-181 K 2
Gould o USA (AR) 276-277 D 7
Gould o USA (OK) 264-265 E 4
Gould, Mount ▲ AUS 176-177 D 2
Gould Bay ≈ 16 F 32
Gouldings Trading Post o USA (UT) 254-255 E 6
Gouldsboro o USA (ME) 278-279 N 4
Goulfey o CAM 198-199 G 6
Goulia o CI 202-203 G 4
Goulimine ☆ MA 188-189 F 6
Goulmima o MA 188-189 J 5
Goulou D. • VRC 156-157 G 5
Goumal Kalai o AFG 138-139 B 3
Goumal Rūd ~ AFG 138-139 B 3
Goumbatou o TCH 206-207 F 3
Goumbi ▲ G 210-211 C 4
Goumbi o RN 198-199 B 6
Goumbou o RMM 202-203 G 2
Gouméré o CI 202-203 J 6
Gouna o CAM 204-205 K 4
Gounatolo o SOL 184 I e 3
Gounda o RCA 206-207 E 4
Gounda ~ RCA 206-207 E 4
Goundam o RMM 196-197 J 6
Goundi o TCH 206-207 C 4
Gounou-Gaya o TCH 206-207 B 4
Goupār o IR 134-135 G 3
Goúra o GR 100-101 J 6
Goura, Mount ▲ WAN 204-205 H 3
Gouraid Garami o AFG 136-137 M 6
Gourak o AFG 134-135 L 2
Gourara ⊥ DZ 190-191 C 6
Gouraya o DZ 190-191 C 2
Gourcy o BF 202-203 J 3
Gourdon o F 90-91 H 9
Gourdon, Cape ▲ PNG 183 C 3
Gouré o RN 198-199 E 6
Gourey o RIM 202-203 D 2
Gourie o • JA 54-55 G 5
Gourits ~ ZA 220-221 E 6
Gouritsmond o ZA 220-221 E 7
Gourjhamar o IND 138-139 G 8
Gourlay Lake o CDN (ONT) 236-237 D 4
Gourma ⊥ BF 202-203 L 4
Gourma-Rharous o RMM 196-197 K 6
Gourmeur < TCH 198-199 K 4
Gouro o TCH 198-199 J 3
Gourou, Djebel ▲ DZ 190-191 D 3
Gourrama o MA 188-189 J 4
Gouvêa o BR 72-73 J 5
Gouverneur o USA (NY) 278-279 F 4
Gouzam o IR 134-135 F 3
Gouzé o RCA 206-207 C 5
Gouzgān ◘ AFG 136-137 J 6
Gouzon o F 90-91 J 8
Gov' ⊥ MAU 148-149 F 6
Gov'-Altaj ◘ MAU 146-147 M 3
Gov' Altajn nuruu ▲ MAU 148-149 D 5
Govan o CDN (SAS) 232-233 O 4
Gove o USA (KS) 262-263 F 6
Govena, mys ▲ RUS 112-113 O 7
Govena, poluostrov ⌒ RUS 112-113 O 7
Govenlock o CDN (SAS) 232-233 J 6
Gove Peninsula ⌒ AUS 174-175 D 3
Governador Eugênio o BR 68-69 F 4
Governador Valadares o BR 72-73 K 5
Governor's Camp o EAK 212-213 E 4
Governor's Harbour o • BS 54-55 G 2
Govind Ballabh Pant Sāgar < IND 142-143 C 3
Govind Sagar o IND 138-139 F 4
Gowanda o USA (NY) 278-279 C 6
Gowan Range ▲ AUS 178-179 H 3
Gowan River ~ CDN 34-35 J 4
Gower o USA (MO) 274-275 D 5
Gowers Corners o USA (FL) 286-287 G 3
Gowganda o CDN (ONT) 236-237 H 5
Gowrie o USA (IA) 274-275 D 2
Goya o RA 76-77 H 5
Goyder Creek ~ AUS 178-179 C 3
Goyder River ~ AUS 174-175 C 3
Goyders Lagoon o AUS 178-179 E 4
Goyelle, Lac o CDN (QUE) 242-243 H 2
Goyllarisquizga o PE 64-65 D 7
Goyo Kyauwo, River ~ WAN 204-205 K 3
Goyoum o CAM 204-205 K 6
Gozare o AFG 134-135 K 1
Goz-Beïda o TCH 198-199 K 6
Gozha Co o VRC 144-145 C 3
Gozo ⌒ M 100-101 E 6
Gozobangui, Chutes de ~ ZRE 206-207 F 6
Graaff-Reinet o • ZA 220-221 G 6
Graafwater o ZA 220-221 D 6
Grabo o CI 202-203 G 7
Grabo, Collines de ▲ CI 202-203 G 7
Grabouw o ZA 220-221 D 7
Grace o USA (ID) 252-253 G 4
Grace (South), Lake o AUS 176-177 E 6
Gracefield o CDN (QUE) 238-239 J 2
Graceville o USA (FL) 286-287 D 1
Graceville o USA (MN) 270-271 B 5
Gračevka ☆ RUS 96-97 H 7
Gracho Cardoso o BR 68-69 K 7
Gracias ☆ HN 52-53 K 4
Gracias a Dios, Cabo de ▲ HN 54-55 D 7
Gradaús o BR 68-69 C 5
Gradaus, Serra dos ▲ BR 68-69 C 6
Grado, Embalse de El < E 98-99 H 3
Gradsko o MK 100-101 H 4
Grady o USA (AR) 276-277 D 6
Grady o USA (NM) 256-257 M 4
Grady o USA (OK) 264-265 G 4
Grady Harbour o CDN 38-39 Q 2
Grady Island ⌒ CDN 38-39 Q 2
Grædefjorden ≈ GRØ 28-29 P 5
Graettinger o USA (IA) 274-275 D 1
Graford o USA (TX) 264-265 F 6
Grafton o AUS 178-179 M 5
Grafton o USA (IL) 274-275 H 6
Grafton o USA (ND) 258-259 K 3
Grafton o USA (NH) 278-279 K 5
Grafton o USA (WI) 274-275 L 1
Grafton o USA (WV) 280-281 F 4
Gragnon Lake o CDN 30-31 O 5
Graham o CDN (ONT) 234-235 N 5
Graham o USA (AL) 284-285 E 3
Graham o USA (TX) 264-265 F 5
Graham, Mount ▲ USA (AZ) 256-257 F 6
Graham Creek ~ USA (WA) 244-245 G 3
Grahamdale o CDN (MAN) 234-235 E 3
Graham Head ▲ CDN (NS) 240-241 M 6
Graham Island ⌒ CDN (BC) 228-229 B 3
Graham Island ⌒ CDN (NWT) 24-25 a 2
Graham Lake o CDN 32-33 N 3
Graham Lake o USA (ME) 278-279 N 4
Graham Moore, Cape ▲ CDN 24-25 j 4
Graham Moore Bay ≈ 24-25 j 4
Graham River ~ CDN 32-33 J 3
Grahamstad = Grahamstown o ZA 220-221 H 6
Grahamstown = Grahamstad o ZA 220-221 H 6
Grahamsville o USA (NY) 280-281 M 2
Grahovo ☆ RUS 96-97 H 5
Grǻhs Øer ⌒ GRØ 28-29 V 4
Grain Coast ⌒ LB 202-203 E 7
Graines, Rivière-aux- o CDN (QUE) 242-243 C 2
Grainfield o USA (KS) 262-263 F 5
Grainton o USA (NE) 262-263 E 4
Grajagan o RI 168 B 7
Grajagan, Teluk ≈ 168 B 7
Grajaú o BR 68-69 E 4
Grajaú, Rio ~ BR 68-69 F 3
Grajewo o PL 92-93 R 2
Grajvoron o RUS 102-103 J 2
Gramado o • BR 74-75 E 7
Gramilla o RA 76-77 E 4
Grammos ▲ GR 100-101 H 4
Gramoteino o RUS 114-115 T 7
Gramphoo o IND 138-139 F 3
Grampianfjella ▲ N 84-85 G 3
Grampian Mountains ▲ GB 90-91 E 3
Grampians National Park ⊥ AUS 180-181 G 4
Gramsh ☆ • AL 100-101 H 4
Granaatboskolk o ZA 220-221 D 5
Granada o CO (ANT) 60-61 D 4
Granada o CO (MET) 60-61 E 6
Granada o ••• E 98-99 F 6
Granada ☆ •• NIC 52-53 B 6
Granada o USA (CO) 254-255 N 5
Granada o USA (MN) 270-271 D 7
Granada II, Cerro ▲ RA 76-77 D 2
Gran Altiplanicie Central ⊥ RA 80 E 4
Gran Bahia ⊥ • DOM 54-55 L 5
Gran Bajo del Gualicho ⊥ RA 78-79 G 6
Gran Bajo de San Julián ⊥ RA 80 F 4
Granbury o USA (TX) 264-265 G 6
Granby o CDN (QUE) 238-239 N 3
Granby o USA (CO) 254-255 K 3
Granby o USA (CT) 280-281 O 2
Granby o USA (MO) 276-277 A 4
Granby River ~ CDN (BC) 230-231 L 4
Gran Canaria ⌒ E 188-189 D 7
Gran Chaco ⊥ RA 76-77 F 3
Grand Bahama Island ⌒ BS 54-55 F 1
Grand Ballon, le ▲ F 90-91 L 8
Grand Bank o CDN (NFL) 242-243 N 5
Grand Banks of Newfoundland ≃ 6-7 D 4
Grand-Bassam o • CI 202-203 J 7
Grand Bay o CDN (NB) 240-241 J 5
Grand Beach o CDN (MAN) 234-235 G 4
Grand Bend o CDN (ONT) 238-239 D 5
Grand-Bérébi o CI 202-203 G 7
Grand Bérébi o CI 202-203 G 7
Grand-Bourg o F 56 E 4
Grand Bruit o CDN (NFL) 242-243 K 5
Grandby, Lake o USA (CO) 254-255 K 3
Grand Caicos ⌒ GB 54-55 K 4
Grand Canal < IRL 90-91 D 5
Grand Canyon o USA (AZ) 256-257 C 2
Grand Canyon ⌒ USA (AZ) 256-257 B 2
Grand Canyon Caverns ∴ USA (AZ) 256-257 B 3
Grand Canyon National Park ⊥ ••• USA (AZ) 256-257 B 2
Grand Canyon of the Liard ⌒ CDN 30-31 G 6
Grand Cayman ⌒ GB 54-55 E 5
Grand Centre o CDN 32-33 P 4
Grand Cess o LB 202-203 F 7
Grand-Combe, la o F 90-91 K 9
Grand Coulee o CDN (SAS) 232-233 O 5
Grand Coulee o USA (WA) 244-245 G 3
Grand Coulee Dam < • USA (WA) 244-245 G 3
Grand Desert o CDN (NS) 240-241 M 6
Grande, Arroyo ~ RA 78-79 K 4
Grande, Arroyo ~ ROU 78-79 L 2
Grande, Bahía ≈ 80 F 5
Grande, Cañada ~ RA 76-77 F 2
Grande, Cayo ⌒ C 54-55 F 4
Grande, Ciénaga o CO 60-61 D 3
Grande, Corredeira ~ BR 70-71 K 3
Grande, Cuchilla ▲ ROU 78-79 M 2
Grande, Ilha ⌒ BR 72-73 H 7
Grande, La o USA (OR) 244-245 G 5
Grande, Lago o BR 66-67 K 4
Grande, Lago o RA 80 G 3
Grande, Monte ▲ BR 70-71 J 6
Grande, Playa ⊥ • DOM 54-55 L 5
Grande, Ponta ▲ CV 202-203 B 5
Grande, Punta ▲ PE 64-65 D 9
Grande, Punta ▲ RCH 76-77 B 3
Grande, Rio ~ BOL 70-71 E 6
Grande, Rio ~ BR 68-69 G 7
Grande, Rio ~ BR 72-73 H 2
Grande, Rio ~ BR 72-73 F 6
Grande, Rio ~ GCA 52-53 J 4
Grande, Rio ~ PE 64-65 E 9
Grande, Rio ~ RA 76-77 E 2
Grande, Rio ~ RA 76-77 D 4
Grande, Rio ~ RA 78-79 E 4
Grande, Rio ~ RA 80 F 6
Grande, Rio ~ RCH 76-77 B 6
Grande, Rio ~ USA (TX) 266-267 G 5
Grande, Rio ~ YV 60-61 L 3
Grande, Rivière la ~ CDN 38-39 E 2
Grande, Salar o RCH 76-77 C 4
Grande, Serra ▲ BR 68-69 H 4
Grande, Serra ▲ BR 68-69 F 6
Grande, Sierra ▲ MEX 50-51 G 3
Grande, Sierra ▲ RA 76-77 E 6
Grande-Anse o CDN (NB) 240-241 K 3
Grande Anse o WL 56 E 4
Grande Anse, Plage ⊥ • RH 54-55 J 5
Grande Cache o CDN (ALB) 228-229 P 3
Grande Casse, Pointe de la ▲ F 90-91 L 9
Grande Cayemite ⌒ RH 54-55 J 5
Grande de Gurupa, Ilha ⌒ BR 62-63 J 6
Grande del Durazno, Cuchilla ▲ ROU 78-79 L 2
Grande de Lipez, Rio ~ BOL 76-77 D 1
Grande de Manacapuru, Lago o BR 66-67 G 4
Grande de Manati, Rio ~ USA (PR) 286-287 P 2
Grande de Matagalpa, Rio ~ NIC 52-53 C 5
Grande de Santiago, Rio ~ MEX 50-51 G 7
Grande de São Isabel, Ilha ⌒ BR 68-69 H 3
Grande de Tarija, Rio ~ RA 76-77 E 2
Grande deValle Hermoso, Rio ~ RA 76-77 C 5
Grande do Branquinho, Cachoeira ~ BR 66-67 G 4
Grande do Curuai, Lago o BR 66-67 K 4
Grande do Iriri, Cachoeira ~ BR 68-69 B 3
Grande-Entrée o CDN (QUE) 242-243 G 5
Grande Île ⌒ SY 222-223 E 2
Grande Inferior, Cuchilla ▲ ROU 78-79 L 2
Grande Kabylie ⊥ DZ 190-191 D 2
Grande Miquelon ⌒ F 38-39 Q 5
Grande Miquelon ⌒ F (975) 242-243 M 6
Grande o Guapay, Rio ~ BOL 70-71 F 6
Grande o Guapay, Rio ~ BOL 70-71 E 5
Grande o Guasamayo, Rio ~ RA 76-77 D 4
Grande Pointe o CDN (MAN) 234-235 G 5
Grande Prairie o CDN 32-33 L 4
Grande Quatre, Réservoir de la < CDN 36-37 N 7
Grand Erg de Bilma ⊥ RN 198-199 F 4
Grande Rivière, La = Fort George River ~ CDN 38-39 G 2
Grande Rivière de la Baleine ~ CDN 36-37 L 7
Grande Ronde River ~ USA (OR) 244-245 H 5
Grandes, Salinas o RA (CAT) 76-77 E 5
Grandes, Salinas o RA (LAP) 78-79 H 5
Grandes, Salinas o RA (LAP) 78-79 H 4
Grandes, Salinas o RA (SAL) 76-77 D 2
Grandes Cascades ~ MA 188-189 K 3
Grande Sido ~ TCH 206-207 D 4
Gran Desierto Del Pinacate, Parque Natural del ⊥ MEX 50-51 C 2
Grand Étang o CDN (NS) 240-241 O 4
Grande-Terre ⌒ F 56 E 3
Grande Terre ⌒ SY 222-223 E 2
Grande-Vallée o CDN (QUE) 242-243 C 3
Grand Falls o CDN (NFL) 242-243 N 4
Grand Falls o • CDN (NB) 240-241 H 3
Grand Falls ~ EAK 212-213 F 4
Grandfalls o USA (TX) 266-267 E 2
Grandfather Mountain ▲ USA (NC) 282-283 F 4
Grandfield o USA (OK) 264-265 F 4
Grand Forks o CDN (BC) 230-231 L 4
Grand Forks o USA (ND) 258-259 K 4
Grand Gulf Military Park • USA (MS) 268-269 J 4
Grand Harbor o USA (ND) 258-259 J 3
Grand Haven o USA (MI) 272-273 C 4
Grandin o USA (ND) 258-259 L 4
Grandin, Lac o CDN 30-31 K 3
Grand Island o USA (NE) 262-263 H 4
Grand Island ⌒ USA (MI) 270-271 M 4
Grand Isle o USA (LA) 268-269 L 7
Grand Isle ⊥ USA (VT) 278-279 H 4
Grand Junction o USA (MI) 272-273 C 5
Grand Junction o USA (TN) 276-277 F 5
Grand Junction o • USA (CO) 254-255 G 4
Grand Lac Victoria o CDN (QUE) 236-237 L 5
Grand-Lahou o CI 202-203 H 7
Grand Lake o CDN (NB) 240-241 J 5
Grand Lake o CDN (NFL) 38-39 O 2
Grand Lake o CDN (NFL) 242-243 L 4
Grand Lake o USA (LA) 268-269 H 7
Grand Lake o USA (ME) 278-279 O 3
Grand Lake o USA (OH) 280-281 B 3
Grand Ledge o USA (MI) 272-273 E 5
Grand le Pierre o CDN (NFL) 242-243 O 5
Grand Manan Channel ≈ CDN 240-241 H 6
Grand Manan Island ⌒ CDN (NB) 240-241 J 6
Grand Marais o CDN (MAN) 234-235 G 4
Grand Marais o USA (MI) 270-271 N 4
Grand Marais o USA (MN) 270-271 H 3
Grand Mécatina, Ile du ⌒ CDN (QUE) 242-243 K 2
Grand-Mère o CDN (QUE) 238-239 N 2
Grand Mesa ▲ USA (CO) 254-255 H 4
Grand-Métis o CDN (QUE) 240-241 G 2
Grandois o CDN (NFL) 242-243 N 1
Grândola o P 98-99 C 5
Grandora o CDN (SAS) 232-233 M 3
Grand Pacific Glacier ⊂ CDN 20-21 W 7
Grand-Popo o • DY 202-203 L 6
Grand Portage o USA (MN) 270-271 J 3
Grand Portage Indian Reservation ✗ USA (MN) 270-271 J 3
Grand Portage National Monument ∴ USA (MN) 270-271 J 3
Grand Prairie o USA (TX) 264-265 G 6
Grand Pré National Historical Park • CDN (NS) 240-241 L 5
Grand Quarries Fossils, Le • USA (IA) 274-275 F 2
Grand Rapids o CDN (MAN) 34-35 G 4
Grand Rapids ~ CDN 32-33 O 3
Grand Rapids o USA (MI) 272-273 D 5
Grand Rapids o USA (MN) 270-271 E 3
Grand-Remous o CDN (QUE) 238-239 K 2
Grand River o USA (IA) 274-275 E 4
Grand River ~ USA (MI) 272-273 E 5
Grand River ~ USA (MI) 272-273 D 5
Grand River ~ USA (MI) 272-273 D 4
Grand River ~ USA (MO) 274-275 E 5
Grand River ~ USA (SD) 260-261 E 1
Grand River National Grassland ⊥ USA (SD) 260-261 D 1
Grand-Rivière o F 56 E 4
Grand Rivière Noire o MS 224 C 7
Grand Ronde o USA (OR) 244-245 B 5
Grand Saline o USA (TX) 264-265 J 6
Grand-Santi o F 62-63 G 3
Grands Jardins, Parc des ⊥ CDN (QUE) 240-241 E 3
Grand Teton National Park ⊥ USA (WY) 252-253 H 3
Grand Teton Peak ▲ USA (WY) 252-253 H 3
Grand Traverse Bay o USA (MI) 272-273 D 2
Grand Turk Island ⌒ GB 54-55 K 4
Grand Valley o CDN (ONT) 238-239 E 5
Grandview o CDN (MAN) 234-235 C 3
Grand View o USA (ID) 252-253 B 4
Grandview o USA (TX) 264-265 G 6
Grandview o USA (WA) 244-245 F 4
Grandville o USA (MI) 272-273 D 5
Grand Wash Cliffs ▲ USA (AZ) 256-257 B 3
Granet, Lac o CDN (QUE) 236-237 L 5
Granet Lake o CDN 24-25 J 6
Grange o USA (GA) 284-285 H 3
Grange, La o USA (GA) 284-285 E 3
Grange, La o USA (KY) 276-277 K 2
Grange, La o USA (MO) 274-275 G 4
Grange, La o USA (NC) 282-283 K 5
Grange, La o USA (TX) 266-267 L 4
Grange Hill o JA 54-55 F 5
Granger o USA (TX) 266-267 K 3
Granger o USA (WA) 244-245 E 4
Granger o USA (WY) 252-253 J 5
Granger, Lake < USA (TX) 266-267 K 3
Grangeville o USA (ID) 250-251 C 6
Granisle o CDN (BC) 228-229 H 2
Granite o USA (OR) 244-245 G 6
Granite Bay o CDN (BC) 230-231 D 3
Granite City o USA (IL) 274-275 H 6
Granite Falls o USA (MN) 270-271 C 6
Granite Island ⌒ USA (MI) 270-271 L 4
Granite Lake o CDN (NFL) 242-243 L 4
Granite Mountains ▲ USA (CA) 248-249 J 5
Granite Pass ▲ USA (WY) 252-253 L 2
Granite Peak ▲ AUS 176-177 D 7
Granite Peak ▲ USA (MT) 250-251 K 6
Granite Peak ▲ USA (NV) 246-247 H 2
Granite Peak ▲ USA (UT) 254-255 B 3
Granites Mine, The ∴ AUS 172-173 K 6
Granito o BR 68-69 J 5
Granja o BR 68-69 H 3
Granja Macali o BR 74-75 D 6
Gran Laguna Salada o RA 80 G 2
Gran Muralla • PE 64-65 C 6
Gränna o • S 86-87 G 7
Granollers o E 98-99 J 4
Gran Pajatén ••• PE 64-65 D 5
Gran Pajonal ▲ PE 64-65 E 7
Gran Pampa Pelada ⊥ BOL 76-77 D 1
Gran Pampa Salada ⊥ BOL 70-71 D 7
Gran Paradiso ▲ I 100-101 A 2
Gran Quivira o USA (NM) 256-257 J 4
Gran Rio ~ SME 62-63 F 4
Gran Sabana, La ⊥ YV 62-63 D 3
Gran Sasso d'Italia ▲ I 100-101 D 3
Grant o CDN (ONT) 236-237 B 2
Grant o USA (CO) 254-255 K 4
Grant o USA (IA) 274-275 D 3
Grant o USA (NE) 262-263 E 4
Grant, Lake o USA (OH) 280-281 C 5
Grant, Mount ▲ USA (NV) 246-247 H 4
Grant, Mount ▲ USA (NV) 246-247 G 5
Granta, mys ▲ RUS 84-85 Z 2
Gran Tarajal o E 188-189 D 6
Grant City o USA (MO) 274-275 D 4
Grantham o GB 90-91 G 5
Grant-Kohrs Ranch National Historic Site • USA (MT) 250-251 G 5
Grant Lake o CDN 30-31 L 3
Grant Park o USA (IL) 274-275 L 3
Grant Point ▲ CDN 24-25 X 6
Grant River o CDN (NS) 240-241 P 5
Grants o USA (NM) 256-257 H 3
Grant's Birthplace, U.S. • USA (OH) 280-281 B 5
Grantsburg o USA (WI) 270-271 F 5
Grants Pass o USA (OR) 244-245 B 8
Grant Suttie Bay ≈ 24-25 h 6
Grantsville o USA (MD) 280-281 G 4
Grantsville o USA (UT) 254-255 C 3
Grantsville o USA (WV) 280-281 E 5
Granum o CDN (ALB) 232-233 E 6
Granville o F 90-91 G 7
Granville o USA (ND) 258-259 G 3
Granville o USA (NY) 278-279 H 5
Granville Lake o CDN 34-35 F 2
Grão-Mogol o BR 72-73 J 4
Grapeland o USA (TX) 268-269 E 5
Grapevine o USA (AR) 276-277 C 6
Grapevine o USA (CA) 248-249 F 5
Grapevine o USA (TX) 264-265 G 6
Gras, Lac de o CDN 30-31 O 3
Grasa, Cerro la ▲ RA 78-79 D 5
Graskop o ZA 220-221 K 2
Grasmere o CDN (BC) 230-231 O 4
Grasmere o USA (ID) 252-253 C 4
Grass Creek o USA (WY) 252-253 K 3
Grasse o F 90-91 L 10
Grasset, Lac o CDN (QUE) 236-237 K 3
Grass Lake o USA (MI) 272-273 E 5
Grassland o CDN 32-33 O 4
Grassland o USA (TX) 264-265 C 5
Grasslands National Park ⊥ CDN (SAS) 232-233 L 6
Grassrange o USA (MT) 250-251 L 4
Grassridgedam < ZA 220-221 G 5
Grass River ~ CDN 34-35 G 3
Grass River Provincial Park ⊥ CDN 34-35 F 3
Grass Valley o USA (CA) 246-247 D 4
Grass Valley o USA (OR) 244-245 E 5
Grassy o AUS 180-181 H 6
Grassy Butte o USA (ND) 258-259 D 4
Grassy Island Lake o CDN (ALB) 232-233 H 4
Grassy Lake o CDN (ALB) 232-233 G 6
Grassy Narrows o CDN (ONT) 234-235 K 4
Grassy Plains o CDN (BC) 228-229 J 3
Grates Cove o CDN (NFL) 242-243 Q 4
Grates Point ▲ CDN (NFL) 242-243 Q 4
Gratiot o USA (OH) 280-281 D 4
Gratis o USA (OH) 280-281 B 4
Gratwick, Mount ▲ AUS 172-173 D 6
Gratz o USA (KY) 276-277 L 2
Gravata o BR 68-69 L 6
Gravataí o BR 74-75 E 7
Gravataí, Termas do • BR 74-75 F 7
Gravelbourg o CDN (SAS) 232-233 M 6
Gravel Hill Lake o CDN 30-31 S 4
Gravelle o CDN (BC) 228-229 M 4
Gravelly o USA (AR) 276-277 B 6
Gravelotte o ZA 218-219 F 6
Gravenhage, 's- = Den Haag ☆ •• NL 92-93 H 2
Gravenhurst o CDN (ONT) 238-239 F 4
Grave Peak ▲ USA (ID) 250-251 E 5
Gravesend o AUS 178-179 L 5
Graves Strait ≈ 36-37 R 4
Gravette o USA (AR) 276-277 A 4
Gray o F 90-91 K 8
Gray o USA (AR) 276-277 D 5
Gray o USA (GA) 284-285 G 3
Gray o USA (ME) 278-279 L 5
Gray o USA (OK) 264-265 D 2
Gray o USA (TX) 264-265 D 3
Gray Creek o CDN (BC) 230-231 N 4
Gray Lake, De < USA (AR) 276-277 B 6
Grayland o USA (WA) 244-245 A 4
Grayling o USA (MI) 272-273 E 3
Grayling Fork ~ USA 20-21 U 3
Grayling River ~ CDN 30-31 G 6
Gray Mountain o USA (AZ) 256-257 D 3
Grayr-Nagel • MA 196-197 C 2
Grayrocks Reservoir < USA (WY) 252-253 O 4
Grays o USA (SC) 284-285 J 4
Grays Harbor ≈ 40-41 B 2
Grays Harbor ≈ USA 244-245 A 4
Grays Lake o USA (ID) 252-253 G 3
Grayson o CDN (SAS) 232-233 Q 5
Grayson o USA (KY) 276-277 N 2
Grays River o USA (WA) 244-245 B 4
Gray Strait ≈ 36-37 R 4
Graysville o CDN (MAN) 234-235 E 5
Graysville o USA (IN) 274-275 L 5
Grayville o USA (IL) 274-275 K 6
Graz ☆ •• A 92-93 N 5
Grease River ~ CDN 30-31 Q 6
Greasewood o USA (AZ) 256-257 F 3
Greasy Lake o CDN 30-31 H 4
Great Abaco Island ⌒ BS 54-55 G 1
Great Alp Falls ⊥ GB 56 D 3
Great America ∴ • USA (IL) 274-275 L 2
Great Artesian Basin ⌒ AUS 178-179 F 3
Great Australian Bight ≈ AUS 176-177 K 6
Great Bahama Bank ≃ BS 54-55 F 2
Great Barasway o CDN (NFL) 242-243 O 5
Great Barrier Island ⌒ NZ 182 E 2
Great Barrier Reef ⊥ ••• AUS 174-175 K 6
Great Barrier Reef Marine Park ⊥ ••• AUS 174-175 L 6
Great Barrington o USA (MA) 278-279 H 6
Great Basalt Wall National Park ⊥ AUS 174-175 H 6
Great Basin ⌒ USA (NV) 246-247 H 3
Great Basin National Park ⊥ USA (NV) 246-247 L 5
Great Bear Lake o CDN 30-31 J 2
Great Bear River ~ CDN 30-31 H 3
Great Bear Wilderness Area ⊥ USA (MT) 250-251 F 3
Great Beaver Lake o CDN (BC) 228-229 L 2
Great Bend o USA (KS) 262-263 H 6
Great Bend o USA (ND) 258-259 L 5
Great Bitter Lake = Murra, al-Buhaira l- < ET 130-131 C 2
Great Britain ⊥ GB 90-91 G 3
Great Central o CDN (BC) 230-231 E 4
Great Coco Island ⌒ MYA 140-141 L 2
Great Dismal Swamp National Wildlife Refuge ⊥ USA (VA) 280-281 K 7
Great Divide o USA (CO) 254-255 H 3
Great Divide Basin ⌒ USA (WY) 252-253 K 4
Great Dividing Range ▲ AUS 178-179 K 4
Great Duck Islands ⌒ CDN (ONT) 238-239 B 3
Great Eastern Erg = Grand Erg Oriental ⊥ DZ 190-191 E 6
Great Eastern Highway II AUS 176-177 E 5
Greater Accra Region ◘ GH 202-203 K 7
Greater Antilles ⌒ 4 F 6
Greater Hinggan Range = Da Hinggan Ling ▲ VRC 148-149 N 5
Greater Sunda Islands = Sunda Besar, Kepulauan ⌒ RI 14-15 D 8
Great Exhibition Bay ≈ 182 D 1
Great Exuma Island ⌒ BS 54-55 G 3
Great Falls o CDN (MAN) 234-235 G 4
Great Falls ~ GUY 62-63 E 4
Great Falls o USA (MT) 250-251 H 4
Great Falls o USA (SC) 284-285 K 2
Great Falls ~ USA (MD) 280-281 J 4
Great Falls ~ USA (MT) 250-251 H 4
Great Guana Cay ⌒ BS 54-55 G 2
Great Harbour Cay ⌒ BS 54-55 F 2
Great Inagua Island ⌒ BS 54-55 J 4
Great Isaac ⌒ BS 54-55 F 1
Great Kambung Swamp o AUS 180-181 G 3
Great Karoo = Groot Karoo ⊥ ZA 220-221 E 6
Great Keppel Island ⌒ AUS 178-179 L 2
Great Lake o AUS 180-181 J 6
Great Lake o USA (NC) 282-283 K 6
Great Mercury Island ⌒ NZ 182 E 2
Great Nicobar Island ⌒ IND 140-141 L 6
Great North East Channel ≈ 183 B 5
Great Northern Highway II AUS 176-177 E 2
Great Ocean Road • AUS 180-181 G 5
Great Ouse ~ GB 90-91 G 5
Great Palm Island ⌒ AUS 174-175 J 6
Great Papuan Plateau ▲ PNG 183 B 4
Great Pearl Bank ⌒ UAE 134-135 D 5
Great Plains ⊥ CDN 32-33 O 3
Great Point ▲ USA (MA) 278-279 L 7
Great Porcupine Creek ~ USA (MT) 250-251 M 5
Great Rattling Brook ~ CDN (NFL) 242-243 N 4
Great Ruaha ~ EAT 214-215 J 4
Great Ruaha ~ EAT 214-215 H 4
Great Sacandaga Lake o USA (NY) 278-279 G 5
Great Salt Lake o USA (UT) 254-255 C 2
Great Salt Lake Desert ⊥ USA (UT) 254-255 B 3
Great Salt Plains National Wildlife Refuge ⊥ USA (OK) 264-265 F 2
Great Salt Plains Reservoir o USA (OK) 264-265 F 2
Great Sand Dunes National Monument ∴ USA (CO) 254-255 K 6
Great Sand Hills ▲ CDN (SAS) 232-233 J 5
Great Sand Sea = Bahr ar Ramla al Kabir ⊥ ET 194-195 B 3
Great Sandy Desert ⊥ AUS 172-173 F 6
Great Sandy Desert ⊥ USA (OR) 244-245 D 7
Great Sea Reef ⌒ FJI 184 III b 2
Great Sitkin Island ⌒ USA 22-23 H 6
Great Slave Lake o CDN 30-31 M 5
Great Smoky Mountains ▲ USA (NC) 282-283 D 5

Great Smoky Mountains National Park ⊥ ••• USA (TN) 282-283 D 5
Great Sole Bank ≃ 90-91 B 7
Great Swamp ⊖ USA (NC) 282-283 L 5
Great Valley ∪ USA (VA) 280-281 F 6
Great Victoria Desert ∸ AUS 176-177 J 3
Great Victoria Desert Flora & Fauna Reserve ⊥ AUS 176-177 K 4
Great Wall = Great Wall, The ••• VRC 154-155 K 1
Great Wass Island ⌒ USA (ME) 278-279 O 4
Great Western Erg = Grand Erg Occidental ∸ DZ 188-189 L 5
Great Western Torres Island ⌒ MYA 158-159 D 5
Great Yarmouth o GB 90-91 H 5
Great Zimbabwe National Monument ∴ ••• ZW 218-219 F 5
Gredos, Coto Nacional de ⊥ E 98-99 E 4
Greece = Elláς ■ GR 100-101 H 5
Greeley o USA (CO) 254-255 L 3
Greeley o USA (NE) 262-263 H 3
Greeleyville o USA (SC) 284-285 L 3
Greely Fiord ≈ 26-27 H 3
Greém Bell, ostrov ⌒ RUS 84-85 h 2
Green o CDN (ONT) 234-235 P 4
Green o PNG 183 A 2
Greenan o CDN (SAS) 232-233 K 4
Green Bank ≃ 38-39 R 6
Green Bay ≈ 38-39 R 4
Green Bay ≈ CDN 242-243 N 3
Green Bay o USA (AL) 284-285 D 5
Green Bay o USA (WI) 270-271 K 6
Green Bay ≈ USA (WI) 270-271 L 6
Greenbrier o USA (AR) 276-277 C 5
Greenbrier River ~ USA (WV) 280-281 F 6
Greenbrier River ~ USA (WV) 280-281 F 5
Greenbush o CDN (SAS) 232-233 Q 3
Greenbush o USA (MN) 270-271 B 2
Green Cape ▲ AUS 180-181 K 4
Greencastle o USA (IN) 274-275 M 5
Greencastle o USA (PA) 280-281 J 4
Green Cay ⌒ BS 54-55 G 2
Green City o USA (MO) 274-275 F 4
Green Cove Springs o USA (FL) 286-287 H 2
Greendale o USA (OH) 280-281 B 4
Greendale o USA (WI) 274-275 K 2
Greene o USA (IA) 274-275 F 2
Greene o USA (ND) 258-259 F 3
Greene o USA (NY) 278-279 F 6
Greeneville o USA (TN) 282-283 E 4
Greenfield o USA (CA) 248-249 C 3
Greenfield o USA (IA) 274-275 D 3
Greenfield o USA (IL) 274-275 H 5
Greenfield o USA (IN) 274-275 N 5
Greenfield o USA (MA) 278-279 J 6
Greenfield o USA (MO) 276-277 B 3
Greenfield o USA (OH) 280-281 C 4
Greenfield o USA (TN) 276-277 G 4
Greenfield o USA (VA) 280-281 H 6
Green Forest o USA (AR) 276-277 B 4
Green Head o AUS 176-177 C 5
Greenhill River ~ CDN (ONT) 236-237 E 4
Greenhorn Mountains ⛰ USA (CA) 248-249 F 4
Green Island ⌒ AUS 174-175 J 5
Green Island ⌒ USA 20-21 R 6
Green Island Bay ≈ 160-161 C 7
Green Lake o CDN 34-35 C 3
Green Lake ⊖ CDN (BC) 230-231 H 2
Green Lake o USA (TX) 266-267 L 5
Greenland o USA (MI) 270-271 J 4
Greenland = Grønland ◻ GRØ 26-27 C 7
Greenland = Grønland ∸ GRØ 6-7 E 2
Greenland-Iceland Rise ≃ 6-7 G 2
Greenland Sea ≈ 26-27 s 5
Greenly Island ⌒ AUS 180-181 C 3
Green Mountain ⛰ USA (VT) 278-279 J 5
Greenock o GB 90-91 E 4
Greenough o AUS 176-177 C 4
Greenough, Mount ▲ USA 20-21 U 2
Greenough River ~ AUS 176-177 C 4
Greenport o USA (NY) 280-281 O 2
Green River o USA (UT) 254-255 E 4
Green River o USA (WY) 252-253 J 5
Green River ~ USA (IL) 274-275 J 3
Green River ~ USA (KY) 276-277 K 3
Green River ~ USA (UT) 254-255 E 4
Green River ~ USA (WY) 252-253 J 5
Green River Basin ∪ USA (WY) 252-253 J 4
Green River Lake ⊖ USA (KY) 276-277 K 3
Green River Parkway II USA (KY) 276-277 J 3
Greensboro o USA (AL) 284-285 C 4
Greensboro o USA (FL) 286-287 E 1
Greensboro o USA (GA) 284-285 G 3
Greensboro o USA (NC) 282-283 H 4
Greensburg o USA (IN) 274-275 N 5
Greensburg o USA (KS) 262-263 G 7
Greensburg o USA (KY) 276-277 K 3
Greensburg o USA (LA) 268-269 K 6
Greensburg o USA (PA) 280-281 G 3
Greens Peak ▲ USA (AZ) 256-257 F 4
Greenstreet o CDN (SAS) 232-233 J 2
Green Swamp ⊖ USA (NC) 282-283 J 6
Greentown o USA (IN) 274-275 N 4
Greenup o USA (IL) 274-275 K 5
Greenvale o AUS 174-175 H 6
Green Valley o USA (AZ) 256-257 E 7
Greenview o USA (CA) 246-247 C 2
Greenville ☆ LB 202-203 F 7
Greenville o USA (AL) 284-285 D 5
Greenville o USA (CA) 246-247 E 3
Greenville o USA (FL) 286-287 F 1
Greenville o USA (GA) 284-285 F 3
Greenville o USA (IL) 274-275 J 6
Greenville o USA (KY) 276-277 H 3
Greenville o USA (ME) 278-279 M 3
Greenville o USA (MI) 272-273 D 4
Greenville o USA (MO) 276-277 E 3
Greenville o USA (MS) 268-269 J 3
Greenville o USA (NC) 282-283 K 5
Greenville o USA (OH) 280-281 B 3
Greenville o USA (PA) 280-281 F 2
Greenville o USA (SC) 284-285 H 2
Greenville o USA (TN) 282-283 K 5
Greenville o USA (TX) 264-265 H 5
Greenwater o USA (WA) 244-245 D 3
Green Water Provincial Park ⊥ CDN (SAS) 232-233 P 3
Greenwater Provincial Park ⊥ • CDN (ONT) 236-237 G 3
Greenwich o GB 90-91 H 6
Greenwich o USA (CT) 280-281 N 2
Greenwich o USA (NJ) 280-281 L 4
Greenwich o USA (NY) 278-279 H 5
Greenwich o USA (OH) 280-281 D 2
Greenwood o CDN (BC) 230-231 L 4
Greenwood o USA (AR) 276-277 A 5
Greenwood o USA (FL) 286-287 D 1
Greenwood o USA (IN) 274-275 M 5
Greenwood o USA (LA) 268-269 G 4
Greenwood o USA (MS) 268-269 K 3
Greenwood o USA (SC) 284-285 H 2
Greenwood o USA (WI) 270-271 H 6
Greenwood, Lake < USA (SC) 284-285 H 2
Greer o USA (ID) 250-251 C 5
Greer o USA (SC) 284-285 H 2
Greers Ferry Lake ⊖ USA (AR) 276-277 C 5
Greeshield Lake ⊖ CDN 28-29 G 3
Greeson, Lake ⊖ USA (AR) 276-277 B 6
Gregoria Pérez de Denis o RA 76-77 G 5
Gregório, Cachoeira ~ BR 66-67 F 2
Gregório, Rio ~ BR 66-67 B 6
Gregório, Rio ~ BR 66-67 B 7
Gregorio Aznarez o ROU 78-79 M 3
Gregorio Méndez o MEX 52-53 J 3
Gregory o USA (AR) 276-277 D 5
Gregory o USA (MI) 272-273 E 5
Gregory o USA (SD) 260-261 G 3
Gregory, Lake ⊖ AUS (SA) 178-179 E 5
Gregory, Lake ⊖ AUS (WA) 176-177 E 2
Gregory Creek ~ AUS 178-179 D 5
Gregory Development Road II AUS 174-175 J 7
Gregory Downs o AUS 174-175 E 6
Gregory Lake ⊖ AUS 172-173 H 6
Gregory National Park ⊥ AUS 172-173 K 4
Gregory Range ⛰ AUS 172-173 E 6
Gregory Range ⛰ AUS 174-175 G 6
Gregory River ~ AUS 174-175 E 6
Gregory Springs o AUS 174-175 H 6
Greifit < RIM 196-197 E 6
Greifswald o • D 92-93 M 1
Greig Bank ≃ 162-163 H 5
Greiz o • D 92-93 M 3
Gremiha o RUS 88-89 P 2
Gremjač'e o RUS 102-103 L 2
Gremjačinsk ☆ RUS 96-97 K 4
Grenå o DK 86-87 E 8
Grenada o USA (CA) 246-247 C 2
Grenada o USA (MS) 268-269 L 3
Grenada ■ WG 56 D 5
Grenada ⌒ WG 56 E 5
Grenadines, The ⌒ WV 56 E 5
Grenen ∸ •• DK 86-87 E 8
Grenfell o AUS 180-181 K 2
Grenfell o CDN (SAS) 232-233 Q 5
Grenfell, Mount ▲ AUS 178-179 H 6
Grenivík o IS 86-87 d 2
Grenoble ☆ F 90-91 K 9
Grenora o USA (ND) 258-259 D 3
Grense Jakobselv o N 86-87 P 2
Grenville o USA (NM) 256-257 M 2
Grenville o WG 56 E 5
Grenville, Cape ▲ AUS 174-175 G 2
Grenville Channel ≈ CDN 228-229 D 3
Greshak o PK 134-135 M 5
Gresham o USA (NE) 262-263 J 3
Gresham o USA (OR) 244-245 C 5
Gresik o RI 168 E 3
Gressåmoen nasjonalpark ⊥ N 86-87 F 4
Gretna o CDN (MAN) 234-235 F 5
Gretna o USA (FL) 286-287 E 1
Gretna o USA (LA) 268-269 K 7
Gretna o USA (VA) 280-281 G 7
Grevená o GR 100-101 H 4
Grevy, Isla ⌒ RCH 80 G 7
Grey, Cape ▲ AUS 174-175 D 3
Greybull o USA (WY) 252-253 K 2
Greybull River ~ USA (WY) 252-253 J 2
Grey Eagle o USA (MN) 270-271 D 5
Grey Hunter Peak ▲ CDN 20-21 X 5
Greylingstad o ZA 220-221 J 3
Greylock, Mount ▲ USA (MA) 278-279 H 6
Greymouth o NZ 182 C 5
Grey Range ⛰ AUS 178-179 G 4
Grey River o CDN (NFL) 242-243 L 5
Grey River ~ CDN (NFL) 242-243 L 5
Greys Point o USA (VA) 280-281 K 6
Greyton o ZA 220-221 D 7
Greytown o ZA 220-221 K 4
Griba, La • TN 190-191 H 4
Gribanovskij o RUS 102-103 M 2
Gribbell Island ⌒ CDN (BC) 228-229 E 3
Gribingui ~ RCA 206-207 D 5
Gribingui-Bamingui, Réserve de faune du ⊥ RCA 206-207 D 5
Griboue o CI 202-203 G 6
Gridino o RUS 88-89 N 4
Gridley o USA (CA) 246-247 D 4
Griekwastad = Griquatown o ZA 220-221 F 4
Grier o USA (NM) 256-257 M 4
Griffenfelds Ø = Uumaanaq ⌒ GRØ 28-29 U 5
Griffin o CDN (SAS) 232-233 P 6
Griffin o USA (GA) 284-285 F 3
Griffin, Lake ⊖ USA (FL) 286-287 H 3
Griffin Lake ⊖ CDN 30-31 U 5
Griffin Point ▲ USA 20-21 T 1
Griffith o AUS 180-181 J 3
Griffith Island ⌒ CDN 24-25 Y 3
Griffiths Point ▲ CDN 24-25 K 2
Grifton o USA (NC) 282-283 K 5
Griggsville o USA (IL) 274-275 H 5
Grigor'evka o RUS 116-117 F 9
Grigor'evskaja o RUS 96-97 J 4
Grijalva, Monte ▲ MEX 50-51 C 7
Grijalva, Río ~ MEX 52-53 H 2
Grili, ostrov ⌒ RUS 84-85 f 2
Grillon, Mount ▲ USA 32-33 B 2
Grimes o USA (IA) 274-275 E 3
Grimiari o RCA 206-207 E 6
Grimma o D 92-93 M 3
Grimmington Bay ≈ 38-39 E 2
Grimmington Island ⌒ CDN 36-37 T 6
Grimsby o CDN (ONT) 238-239 F 5
Grimsby o • GB 90-91 G 5
Grimselpass ▲ •• CH 92-93 K 5
Grimsey ⌒ IS 86-87 e 1
Grimshaw o CDN 32-33 M 3
Grímsstaðir o IS 86-87 e 2
Grímsvötn ▲ IS 86-87 e 2
Grindavík o IS 86-87 b 3
Grindrod o CDN (BC) 230-231 K 3
Grindsted o DK 86-87 D 9
Grindstone Provincial Park ⊥ CDN (MAN) 234-235 G 3
Grinell o USA (IA) 274-275 F 3
Grinnah, Sebkhet ⊖ MA 196-197 C 3
Grinnel Land ∸ CDN 26-27 L 3
Grinnell Glacier ⊂ CDN 36-37 Q 3
Grinnel Peninsula ∪ CDN 24-25 Y 2
Griquatown = Griekwastad o ZA 220-221 F 4
Griquet o CDN (NFL) 242-243 N 1
Grise Fiord o CDN 24-25 f 2
Grisslehamn o S 86-87 J 6
Griswold o CDN (MAN) 234-235 C 5
Griswold o USA (IA) 274-275 C 3
Grita, La o YV 60-61 E 3
Grivel, Kap ▲ GRØ 28-29 b 2
Grivița o RO 102-103 E 5
Grizim o DZ 196-197 J 2
Grizzly Bear Creek ~ CDN (ALB) 232-233 H 2
Grizzly Bear Mountain ▲ CDN 30-31 K 3
Grjazi o RUS 94-95 Q 5
Grjazovec o RUS 94-95 R 2
Groais Island ⌒ CDN (NFL) 242-243 N 2
Groaras, Rio ~ BR 68-69 H 4
Grobin = Grobiņa ☆ •• LV 94-95 G 3
Grobiņa ☆ •• LV 94-95 G 3
Groblersdal o ZA 220-221 J 2
Groblershoop o ZA 220-221 E 4
Grodno = Hrodna ☆ BY 94-95 H 5
Groenlo o NL 92-93 J 2
Groenrivier ~ ZA 220-221 C 5
Groenriviersmond o ZA 220-221 C 5
Groesbeck o USA (TX) 266-267 L 2
Groesbeek o ZA 218-219 E 6
Grogol o RI 168 D 3
Groix, Île de ⌒ F 90-91 F 8
Grójec o PL 92-93 Q 3
Grombalia o TN 190-191 H 2
Grong o N 86-87 F 4
Groningen ☆ • NL 92-93 J 2
Gronlid o CDN (SAS) 232-233 O 2
Grønlingrotten • N 86-87 G 3
Grønnedal = Kangilinnguit o GRØ 28-29 Q 6
Groom o USA (TX) 264-265 C 3
Grootberg ⛰ NAM 216-217 C 9
Groot Bergrivier ~ ZA 220-221 D 6
Grootdraaidam < ZA 220-221 J 3
Grootdrink o ZA 220-221 E 4
Grootduin ∸ NAM 216-217 E 11
Groote Eylandt ⌒ AUS 174-175 D 3
Grootfontein ☆ NAM 216-217 E 9
Groot Henarpolder o SME 62-63 F 3
Groot Jongensfontein o ZA 220-221 E 7
Groot Karasberge ⛰ NAM 220-221 D 3
Groot Karoo = Great Karoo ∸ ZA 220-221 E 6
Groot Kei ~ ZA 220-221 H 6
Grootkraal o ZA 220-221 F 6
Groot Laagte ~ RB 216-217 F 10
Groot Letaba ~ ZA 218-219 F 6
Groot Marico o ZA 220-221 H 2
Grootmis o ZA 220-221 C 4
Groot Rietrivier ~ ZA 220-221 E 5
Grootrivier ~ ZA 220-221 F 6
Groot Swartberge ⛰ ZA 220-221 F 6
Groot Visrivier ~ ZA 220-221 H 6
Grootvloer ⊖ ZA 220-221 E 4
Groot Waterberg ⛰ NAM 216-217 D 10
Groot Winterhoekberge ⛰ ZA 220-221 G 6
Gropakehn o LB 202-203 G 7
Gros Cap o CDN (ONT) 236-237 D 6
Gros Morne ▲ CDN (NFL) 242-243 L 3
Gros-Morne o RH 54-55 J 5
Gros Morne National Park ⊥ ••• CDN (NFL) 242-243 L 3
Gros Pate ▲ CDN (NFL) 242-243 L 2
Grossa da Marambaia, Ponta ▲ BR 72-73 J 7
Gross Aub o NAM 220-221 D 3
Gross Barmen, Warmbron • NAM 216-217 D 11
Großer Arber ▲ D 92-93 M 4
Großer Ötscher ▲ A 92-93 N 5
Großer Schwielowsee ⊖ D 92-93 N 2
Grosse Sundainseln ⌒ RI 164-165 E 2
Grosse Tete o USA (LA) 268-269 J 6
Grosseto ☆ I 100-101 C 3
Grossevičí o RUS 122-123 H 5
Großglockner ▲ A 92-93 M 5
Gross Ums o NAM 220-221 D 1
Gros Ventre Range ⛰ USA (WY) 252-253 H 3
Gros Ventre River ~ USA (WY) 252-253 H 3
Groswater Bay ≈ 36-37 V 7
Groton o USA (CT) 280-281 O 2
Groton o USA (SD) 260-261 H 1
Grotto o USA (WA) 244-245 D 3
Grotto of the Redemption • USA (ID) 274-275 D 2
Groué, Oued ~ MA 188-189 H 4
Grouard o CDN 32-33 M 4
Groumania o CI 202-203 J 6
Groundbirch o CDN 32-33 K 4
Groundhog River ~ CDN (ONT) 236-237 F 4
Grouse Creek o USA (UT) 254-255 B 2
Grouse Creek ~ USA (UT) 254-255 B 2
Groust, Rivière ~ CDN 36-37 N 4
Grouz, Ibel ⛰ DZ 188-189 L 4
Grove o USA (OK) 264-265 K 2
Grove City o USA (MN) 270-271 D 5
Grove City o USA (OH) 280-281 C 4
Grove City o USA (PA) 280-281 F 2
Grove Hill o USA (AL) 284-285 C 5
Grove Lake o USA (MN) 270-271 C 5
Groveland o USA (CA) 248-249 D 2
Grover o USA (CO) 254-255 L 3
Grover o USA (WY) 252-253 H 4
Grovertown o USA (IN) 274-275 M 3
Groves o USA (TX) 268-269 G 7
Groveton o USA (NH) 278-279 K 4
Groveton o USA (TX) 268-269 E 5
Groznyj ☆ RUS 126-127 F 6
Grudovo = Sredec o BG 102-103 E 6
Grudziądz o • PL 92-93 P 2
Gruenthal o CDN (SAS) 232-233 M 3
Gruesa, Cerro Punta ▲ RA 80 D 5
Gruesa, Punta ▲ RCH 70-71 B 7
Grulla o USA (TX) 266-267 J 7
Grullo, El o MEX 52-53 B 2
Grumantbyen o N 84-85 J 3
Grumo Áppula o I 100-101 F 4
Grums ☆ S 86-87 F 7
Grünau o NAM 220-221 D 3
Grundarfjörður o IS 86-87 b 2
Grundy o USA (VA) 280-281 D 6
Grundy Center o USA (IA) 274-275 F 2
Grupe o GH 202-203 J 5
Gruszka, Lake ⊖ AUS 176-177 H 2
Gruta, La o RA 74-75 D 6
Grutas de Juxtlahuaca, Parque Natural ⊥ MEX 52-53 E 3
Gruver o USA (TX) 264-265 C 2
Gruzdžiai o LT 94-95 H 3
Gryfice o PL 92-93 N 2
Gryllefjord o N 86-87 H 2
Gryt o S 86-87 H 7
Grytøya ⌒ N 86-87 H 2
Grytviken o GB 78-79 O 7
Guabito o PA 52-53 C 7
Guabo, El o PA 52-53 D 7
Guabún o RCH 78-79 C 6
Guacamaya, Raudal ~ CO 60-61 G 6
Guacamayas o CO (CA) 60-61 D 6
Guacamayas o CO (VIC) 60-61 F 5
Guacara o YV 60-61 H 2
Guacautey o YV 62-63 D 3
Guachamacari, Cerro ▲ YV 60-61 J 6
Guachara o YV 60-61 G 4
Guacharo, Cueva del • YV 60-61 K 2
Guacharo, Parque Nacional ⊥ YV 60-61 K 2
Gu Achi o USA (AZ) 256-257 C 6
Guachochic o MEX 50-51 F 4
Guachucal o CO 64-65 D 1
Guaco o CO 60-61 F 6
Guaçu Boi o BR 76-77 J 5
Guadajoz, Río ~ E 98-99 E 6
Guadalajara o E 98-99 F 4
Guadalajara ☆ •• MEX 52-53 C 1
Guadalcanal o E 98-99 E 5
Guadalcanal ⌒ SOL 184 I d 3
Guadalcázar o MEX 50-51 J 6
Guadalimar, Río ~ E 98-99 F 5
Guadalmez, Río ~ E 98-99 E 5
Guadalope, Río ~ E 98-99 G 4
Guadalupe o BR 68-69 G 5
Guadalupe o ••• E 98-99 E 5
Guadalupe o MEX (COA) 50-51 J 3
Guadalupe o MEX (NL) 50-51 J 5
Guadalupe o MEX (ZAC) 50-51 H 6
Guadalupe ~ MEX 50-51 D 5
Guadalupe o PE 64-65 C 5
Guadalupe o USA (CA) 248-249 D 5
Guadalupe de Bahues o MEX 50-51 G 4
Guadalupe de Bravo o MEX 50-51 F 2
Guadalupe Mountains ⛰ USA (NM) 256-257 L 6
Guadalupe Mountains National Park ⊥ USA (TX) 266-267 C 2
Guadalupe Peak ▲ USA (TX) 266-267 C 2
Guadalupe River ~ USA (TX) 266-267 K 4
Guadalupe Victoria o MEX (DGO) 50-51 G 5
Guadalupe Victoria o MEX (TAM) 50-51 L 5
Guadalupe y Calvo o MEX 50-51 F 4
Guadarrama, Sierra de ⛰ E 98-99 E 4
Guadeloupe ◻ F 56 E 3
Guadeloupe ⌒ F 56 D 2
Guadeloupe, Parc National de la ⊥ F 56 E 3
Guadeloupe Passage ≈ 56 E 3
Guadelupe o MEX 50-51 A 1
Guadelupe, La o CDN (QUE) 240-241 E 5
Guadiana, Bahía de ≈ 54-55 C 3
Guadiana, Río ~ E 98-99 E 5
Guadiana Menor, Río ~ E 98-99 F 6
Guadix o E 98-99 F 6
Guaduas o CO 60-61 D 5
Guafera Ye Terara Senselet ⛰ ETH 208-209 B 5
Guafo, Isla ⌒ RCH 78-79 B 7
Guaíba o BR 74-75 E 8
Guaicuí o BR 72-73 H 4
Guáimaro o C 54-55 G 4
Guaina o YV 60-61 K 5
Guainía, Río ~ CO 60-61 G 6
Guaíra o BR (PAR) 76-77 K 3
Guaíra o BR (PAU) 72-73 F 6
Guaira, La o YV 60-61 H 2
Guairacá o BR 72-73 D 7
Guaitecas, Islas ⌒ RCH 78-79 C 7
Guajaba, Cayo ⌒ C 54-55 G 4
Guajará o BR 64-65 F 5
Guajará-Mirim o BR 70-71 E 2
Guaje, El o MEX 50-51 H 3
Guajeru o BR 72-73 K 3
Guajira, Península de la ∪ CO 60-61 F 1
Gualacéo o EC 64-65 C 3
Gualala o USA (CA) 246-247 B 5
Gualán o GCA 52-53 K 4
Gualaquiza o EC 64-65 C 3
Gualcuna o RCH 76-77 B 5
Gualeguay o RA 78-79 K 2
Gualeguay, Río ~ RA 78-79 K 2
Gualeguaychu o RA 78-79 K 2
Gualeguaychu, Río ~ RA 78-79 K 2
Gualicho, Bajo del ∸ RA 78-79 G 7
Gualicho, Salina del ⊖ RA 78-79 G 6
Gualjaina o RA 78-79 D 7
Guallatiri o RCH 70-71 C 6
Guallatiri, Volcán ▲ RCH 70-71 C 6
Gualmatan o CO 64-65 D 1
Guamache, El o YV 60-61 K 2
Guamal o CO (MAG) 60-61 D 3
Guamal o CO (MET) 60-61 E 6
Guamani, Cordillera de ⛰ PE 64-65 C 4
Guamblin, Isla ⌒ RCH 80 C 2
Guaminí o RA 78-79 H 4
Guamo o CO 60-61 D 5
Guamo, El o CO 60-61 E 3
Guamote o EC 64-65 C 2
Guamúchil o MEX 50-51 E 5
Guamués, Río ~ CO 64-65 D 1
Gua Musang o MAL 162-163 E 2
Gu'an o VRC 154-155 K 2
Guanabacoa o C 54-55 D 3
Guanabo o C 54-55 D 3
Guanacaste, Cordillera de ⛰ CR 52-53 B 6
Guanacayabo, Golfo de ≈ 54-55 G 4
Guanaceví o MEX 50-51 G 5
Guanaco Muerto o RA 76-77 E 6
Guanaco Sombriana o RA 76-77 E 5
Guanaguana o YV 60-61 K 2
Guanahacabibes, Península de ∪ C 54-55 C 4
Guanahani Island = San Salvador ⌒ BS 54-55 H 3
Guanaja o HN 54-55 C 6
Guanaja, Isla de ⌒ HN 54-55 C 6
Guanajay o C 54-55 D 3
Guanajuato ◻ MEX 52-53 D 1
Guanajuato ☆ ••• MEX (GTO) 50-51 J 7
Guanajuña o YV 60-61 K 5
Guanambi o BR 72-73 J 3
Guañape, Islas de ⌒ PE 64-65 C 6
Guañape, Punta ▲ 64-65 C 6
Guanaquero, Bahía ≈ 76-77 B 6
Guanare ☆ YV 60-61 G 3
Guanare, Río ~ YV 60-61 G 3
Guanarito o YV 60-61 G 3
Guanay o BOL 70-71 D 4
Guanay, Cerro ▲ YV 60-61 H 5
Guandacol o RA 76-77 C 5
Guandi, Rio ~ BR 72-73 K 5
Guandiping o VRC 156-157 G 2
Guang'an o VRC 154-155 E 6
Guangchang o VRC 156-157 K 3
Guangde o VRC 154-155 L 6
Guangdong ◻ VRC 156-157 H 4
Guanghai o VRC 156-157 H 6
Guanghan o VRC 154-155 D 6
Guangji o VRC 154-155 D 6
Guangmao Shan ▲ VRC 142-143 M 2
Guangning o VRC 156-157 H 5
Guangrao o VRC 154-155 L 3
Guangsheng Si • VRC 154-155 G 3
Guangshui o VRC 154-155 H 6
Guangshun o VRC 156-157 E 3
Guangxi Zhuangzu Zizhiqu ◻ VRC 156-157 E 4
Guangyang o VRC 156-157 K 2
Guangyuan o VRC 154-155 D 5
Guangze o VRC 156-157 K 3
Guangzhou ☆ •• VRC 156-157 H 5
Guanhães o BR 72-73 J 5
Guaniamo, Río ~ YV 60-61 J 4
Guánica o • USA (PR) 286-287 P 3
Guanipa, Río ~ YV 60-61 K 3
Guanling o VRC 156-157 D 4
Guanocó o YV 60-61 K 2
Guanqiao o VRC 154-155 D 3
Guanta o RCH 76-77 B 5
Guanta o YV 60-61 J 2
Guantánamo ☆ C 54-55 H 4
Guantánamo Bay xx USA 54-55 H 5
Guantao o VRC 154-155 J 3
Guanumbi o BR 68-69 K 6
Guanyun o VRC 154-155 L 4
Guapa o CO 60-61 C 4
Guapi o CO 60-61 C 6
Guapiara o BR 74-75 F 5
Guápiles o CR 52-53 C 6
Guapo, El o YV 60-61 J 2
Guaporé o BR 74-75 E 7
Guaporé, Reserva Biológica do ⊥ BR 70-71 F 3
Guaporé, Río ~ BOL 70-71 G 3
Guaqui o BOL 70-71 C 5
Guará, Rio ~ BR 72-73 H 2
Guarabira o BR 68-69 L 5
Guaraci o BR (PAR) 72-73 E 7
Guaraci o BR (PAU) 72-73 F 6
Guaraí o BR 68-69 D 6
Guarajambala, Río ~ HN 52-53 K 4
Guaramuri o GUY 62-63 E 2
Guaranda ☆ EC 64-65 C 2
Guaraniaçu o BR 74-75 D 5
Guarani das Missões o BR 76-77 K 5
Guaranoco o YV 60-61 K 3
Guarantã do Norte o BR 66-67 K 7
Guarapari o BR 72-73 K 6
Guarapiche, Reserva Forestal ⊥ YV 60-61 K 2
Guarapuava o BR 74-75 E 5
Guaraqueçaba o BR 74-75 F 5
Guarará o BR 72-73 J 6
Guararapes o BR 72-73 E 6
Guaratinga o BR 72-73 L 4
Guaratinguetá o BR 72-73 H 7
Guaratuba o BR 74-75 F 5
Guarayos o BOL 70-71 C 3
Guarayos, Llanos de ∸ BOL 70-71 E 4
Guarda ☆ • P 98-99 D 4
Guarda, A o E 98-99 C 4
Guarda Mor o BR 72-73 G 4
Guardia, La o RA 76-77 E 5
Guardia, La o RCH 76-77 C 4
Guardia, Paso de la ▲ RA 76-77 B 6
Guardia Mitre o RA 78-79 H 6
Guardián, Cabo ▲ RA 80 G 4
Guardian Brito, Isla ⌒ RCH 80 D 7
Guardo o E 98-99 E 3
Guarei, Rio ~ BR 72-73 D 7
Guarenas o YV 60-61 H 2
Guari o PNG 183 D 5
Guaria o CR 52-53 C 7
Guariba o BR 72-73 F 6
Guariba, Rio ~ BR 66-67 G 6
Guaribas, Cachoeira ~ BR 68-69 B 4
Guaricana, Pico ▲ BR 74-75 F 5
Guárico, Embalse del < YV 60-61 H 3
Guárico, Río ~ YV 60-61 H 3
Guarittico, Caño ~ YV 60-61 G 4
Guarujá o BR 74-75 G 5
Guarulhos o BR 72-73 G 7
Guasave o MEX 50-51 E 5
Guasca o CO 60-61 E 5
Guascama, Punta ▲ CO 60-61 B 6
Guasey, El o YV 60-61 J 3
Guasipati o YV 62-63 D 2
Guasopa o PNG 183 G 5
Guatacondo o RCH 70-71 C 7
Guatacondo, Quebrada de ~ RCH 70-71 C 7
Guataquí o CO 60-61 D 5
Guatay o USA (CA) 248-249 H 7
Guatemala ■ GCA 52-53 J 4
Guatemala, Ciudad de = Guatemala ★ •• GCA 52-53 J 4
Guatemala = Guatemala, Ciudad de ★ •• GCA 52-53 J 4
Guatemala Basin ≃ 5 B 4
Guatimape, Laguna ⊖ MEX 50-51 G 5
Guatín o RCH 76-77 C 2
Guatire o YV 60-61 H 2
Guatopo, Parque Nacionale ⊥ YV 60-61 H 2
Guaviare, Río ~ CO 60-61 G 6
Guaviyu, Termas de • ROU 76-77 J 6
Guaxupe o BR 72-73 G 6
Guayabal o C 54-55 G 4
Guayabal o YV 60-61 H 3
Guayabero, Río ~ CO 60-61 E 6
Guayabo, El o YV 60-61 E 3
Guayaguas o RA 76-77 D 6
Guayaguayare o TT 60-61 L 2
Guayalejo, Río ~ MEX 50-51 K 6
Guayama o •• USA (PR) 286-287 P 3
Guayaneco, Archipiélago ⌒ RCH 80 C 3
Guayapán, Quebrada de ~ MEX 50-51 F 5
Guayape, Río ~ HN 52-53 L 4
Guayapo, Río ~ YV 60-61 H 5
Guayaquil ☆ • EC 64-65 C 3
Guayaquil, Golfo de ≈ 64-65 B 3
Guayaramerín o BOL 70-71 E 2
Guayas, Río ~ CO 64-65 E 1
Guayatayoc, Salinas de ⊖ RA 76-77 E 2
Guaycurú o RA 76-77 G 5
Guayllabamba, Río ~ EC 64-65 C 1
Guayllabamba o EC 64-65 C 2
Guaymallén o RA 78-79 E 2
Guaymas o • MEX 50-51 D 4
Guaynabo o USA (PR) 286-287 P 2
Guayquiraró, Río ~ RA 76-77 H 6
Guayubín o DOM 54-55 K 5
Guayzimi o EC 64-65 C 4
Guba o ETH 208-209 B 3
Guba o ZRE 214-215 D 6
Guba = Quba o • AZ 128-129 N 2
Guba Dolgaja o RUS 108-109 H 6
Gubaha ☆ RUS 96-97 K 4
Gubail ☆ • RL 128-129 F 5
Gubail, al- o KSA 130-131 L 4
Gübäl, Ğazirat ⌒ ET 194-195 F 4
Guban ∸ ETH 208-209 F 3
Gubat o RP 160-161 F 6
Gubato, Bannaanka ∸ SP 208-209 H 4
Gubatsaa Hills ⛰ RB 218-219 B 4
Ğubba o KSA 130-131 G 3
Gubbi o IND 140-141 G 4
Gúbbio o I 100-101 D 3
Guben o D 92-93 N 3
Gubi o WAN 204-205 H 3
Gubio o WAN 198-199 F 6
Gubkin o RUS 102-103 K 2
Gubug o RI 168 D 3
Gucha ~ EAK 212-213 E 4
Gucheng o VRC (HUB) 154-155 G 5
Gucheng o VRC (SHA) 154-155 G 4
Gučin-Us = Argut o MAU 148-149 F 5
Ğuda o KSA 130-131 L 5
Gudalur o IND 140-141 G 5
Gudalur o IND 140-141 G 6
Gudauta o • GE 126-127 D 6
Ğudayyidat 'Ar'ar o KSA 130-131 G 2
Ğudayyidat Ḥamir o IRQ 128-129 J 7
Gudbrandsdalen ∸ N 86-87 D 6
Guddekoppa o IND 140-141 F 4
Gudekota o IND 140-141 G 3
Gudenå ~ DK 86-87 D 8
Guder o ETH 208-209 C 4
Guder Falls ~ ETH 208-209 C 4
Gudermes o RUS 126-127 G 6
Gudgaon o IND 138-139 F 9
Gudi o WAN 204-205 H 4
Gudibanda o IND 140-141 G 4
Gudiña, A o E 98-99 D 3
Gudivāda o IND 140-141 J 2
Gudiyattam o IND 140-141 H 4
Gudong o VRC 142-143 L 3
Gudryolum o TM 136-137 D 6
Güdür o IND 140-141 H 3
Gudvangen o N 86-87 C 6
Gudžal ~ RUS 122-123 E 3
Gue, Rivière du ~ CDN 36-37 N 6
Guechémé o RN 204-205 E 2
Guéckedou o WAL 202-203 E 5
Guédi, Mont ▲ TCH 198-199 J 6
Güéjar, Río ~ CO 60-61 E 6
Guéké o RG 202-203 F 5
Guélaour, Oued ~ RIM 196-197 D 6
Guéléhé o TCH 206-207 D 4
Guélengdeng o TCH 206-207 B 3
Guéléninkoro o RMM 202-203 F 4
Guelma ☆ DZ 190-191 F 2
Guelph o CDN (ONT) 238-239 E 5
Gueltat Sidi Saad o DZ 190-191 C 3
Guémar o DZ 190-191 F 4
Guembou, Te-n- o RIM 196-197 F 6
Guendel < RIM 196-197 E 6
Guendo o RMM 202-203 G 3
Guéné o DY 204-205 E 3
Guénéto o SN 202-203 D 3
Guenguel, Río ~ RA 80 E 3
Guenguel, Meseta del ∸ RA 80 E 3
Guenté Paté o SN 202-203 C 2
Guépaouo o CI 202-203 H 6
Güeppi o PE 64-65 E 2
Guéra ◻ TCH 206-207 C 3
Guéra, Pic de ▲ TCH 206-207 D 3
Güer Aike o RA 80 F 5
Guérande o F 90-91 F 8
Guerara o DZ 190-191 E 4
Guercif o MA 188-189 K 3
Guéréda o TCH 198-199 L 5
Guéret ☆ F 90-91 H 8
Guerette o USA (ME) 278-279 N 1
Guérin Kouka o RT 202-203 L 5
Guerneville o USA (CA) 246-247 B 5
Guernsey o CDN (SAS) 232-233 N 4
Guernsey ⌒ GBG 90-91 F 7
Guernsey o USA (WY) 252-253 O 4
Guernsey Reservoir < USA (WY) 252-253 O 4
Guérou o RIM 196-197 E 6
Guerra o USA (TX) 266-267 J 7
Guerrero o MEX (COA) 50-51 J 3
Guerrero o MEX (TAM) 50-51 K 4
Guerrero ◻ MEX 52-53 D 3
Guerrero, Cayos ⌒ NIC 52-53 C 5
Guerrero Negro o • MEX 50-51 B 4
Gueskérou o RN 198-199 F 6
Guéssabo o CI 202-203 G 6
Guéssésso o CI 202-203 G 6
Guessihio o CI 202-203 H 6
Guessou-Sud o DY 204-205 E 3
Guestecitas o CO 60-61 E 2
Guétéma o RMM 202-203 F 2
Gueydan o USA (LA) 268-269 H 6
Guéyo o CI 202-203 G 7
Guézaoua o RN 198-199 D 5
Guga o RUS 122-123 G 2
Gugě ▲ ETH 208-209 C 5
Güge o IR 134-135 D 2
Gugu ⛰ ETH 208-209 D 4
Guguang, Gunung ▲ RI 164-165 E 2
Guhāgar o IND 140-141 E 2
Ğuhaina o ET 194-195 E 4
Ğuhr o UAE 134-135 F 6
Guiana Highlands = Guayana, Macizo de ⛰ 5 E 4
Guiana Plateau ≃ 62-63 G 1
Guiba, Jasiira ⌒ SP 212-213 J 4
Guibéroua o CI 202-203 G 6
Guibu, Plage ∸ • RH 54-55 J 5
Guichaud, Rivière ~ CDN 36-37 L 3
Guichi o VRC 154-155 K 6
Guichón o ROU 78-79 L 2
Guidan o RN 198-199 C 6
Guidari o TCH 206-207 C 4
Guider o CAM 204-205 K 4
Guidiguir o RN 198-199 D 6
Guidiguis o CAM 206-207 B 3
Guidimaka ◻ RIM 196-197 D 7
Guidimouni o RN 198-199 D 6
Guiding o VRC 156-157 E 3
Guidjiba o CAM 204-205 K 4
Guidong o VRC 156-157 H 3
Guidouma o G 210-211 C 4
Guiendana o CI 202-203 H 5
Guier, Lac de ⊖ SN 196-197 C 6
Guietsou o G 210-211 C 5
Guifeng • VRC 156-157 K 2
Guiffa o RCA 206-207 E 5
Guigang o VRC 156-157 F 5
Guiglo o CI 202-203 G 6
Güigüe o YV 60-61 H 2
Guihua o VRC 154-155 D 6
Guihulngan o RP 160-161 E 7
Guijá o MOC 220-221 L 2
Guijuelo o E 98-99 E 4
Guilderton o AUS 176-177 C 5
Guildford o • GB 90-91 G 6
Guilford o USA (ME) 278-279 M 3
Guilford Courthouse National Military Park • USA (NC) 282-283 H 4
Guilin o • VRC 156-157 G 4
Guillaume-Delisle, Lac ⊖ CDN 36-37 L 6
Guillé < RIM 196-197 E 6
Guillemard Bay ≈ 24-25 X 5
Guillestre o F 90-91 L 9
Guilmaro o DY 202-203 L 4
Guimarães o BR 68-69 F 3
Guimarães o P 98-99 C 4
Guimarânia o BR 72-73 G 5
Guimaras Island ⌒ RP 160-161 E 7
Guimaras Strait ≈ 160-161 E 7
Guimba o RP 160-161 D 5
Guimbaleta o MEX 50-51 H 4
Guimbiri, Mont ▲ CAM 204-205 K 6
Guin o USA (AL) 284-285 C 3
Guinagourou o DY 204-205 E 4
Guinchos Cay ⌒ BS 54-55 G 3
Guinda o USA (CA) 246-247 C 5
Guindelman o RP 160-161 F 8
Guiné o BR 72-73 K 2
Guinea = Guinée ■ RG 202-203 D 4
Guinea, Gulf of ≈ 9 D 5
Guinea Basin ≃ 9 C 5
Guinea-Bissau ■ GNB 202-203 B 3
Güines o C 54-55 D 3
Guingamp o F 90-91 F 7
Guinguinéo o SN 202-203 C 2
Guintinua Island ⌒ RP 160-161 E 5
Guiones, Punta ▲ CR 52-53 B 7
Guiping o VRC 156-157 G 5
Guir < RMM 196-197 J 5
Guir, Hamada du ∸ DZ 188-189 K 5
Guir, Oued ~ MA 188-189 K 5
Güira de Melena o C 54-55 D 3
Guiratinga o BR 72-73 D 4
Güires, Los o YV 60-61 L 3

Guiri ○ CAM 206-207 B 3
Güiria ○ YV 60-61 K 2
Guirripa, Caño ∼ CO 60-61 F 5
Guirvas ○ SN 196-197 C 7
Guisa ○ C 54-55 G 4
Guishanfeng • VRC 154-155 J 6
Guishi SK ∼ VRC 156-157 G 4
Guissat < RN 198-199 D 4
Guissèr ○ MA 188-189 H 4
Guissoumalé ○ RMM 202-203 F 3
Guitri ○ CI 202-203 H 7
Guiuan ○ RP 160-161 F 7
Guixi ○ VRC 156-157 K 2
Guiyang ○ VRC (HUN) 156-157 H 4
Guiyang ☆ VRC (GZH) 156-157 E 3
Guizhou ▫ VRC 156-157 D 3
Gujarat ▫ IND 138-139 C 8
Gūjar Khān ○ PK 138-139 D 3
Gujba ○ WAN 204-205 J 3
Gujiao ○ VRC 154-155 H 3
Gujrānwāla ○ PK 138-139 E 3
Gujrāt ○ PK 138-139 E 3
Gujri ○ IND 138-139 E 8
Gukera, ostrov ⌒ RUS 84-85 c 2
Gulang ○ VRC 154-155 C 3
Gulargambone ○ AUS 178-179 K 6
Gulbarga ○• IND 140-141 G 2
Gulbene ☆ LV 94-95 K 3
Gulbin Ka, River ∼ WAN 204-205 F 3
Gul'ča ○ KS 136-137 N 4
Gul'ča ∼ KS 136-137 N 5
Guledagudda ○ IND 140-141 F 2
Gulf Breeze ○ USA (FL) 286-287 B 1
Gulf Development Road II AUS 174-175 G 6
Gulf Islands National Seashore ⊥ USA (MS) 268-269 M 6
Gulflander (Historical Railway) • AUS 174-175 F 5
Gulf of Bothnia = Bothnia, Gulf of ≈ 86-87 J 6
Gulf of Finland ≈ FIN 86-87 M 7
Gulfport ○ USA (FL) 286-287 G 4
Gulfport ○ USA (MS) 268-269 L 6
Gulf Shores ○ USA (AL) 284-285 C 6
Gulgong ○ AUS 180-181 K 2
Gulir ○ RI 166-167 F 4
Gulistan = Guliston ☆ US 136-137 L 4
Guliston ☆ US 136-137 L 4
Guliya Shan ▲ VRC 150-151 D 3
Gulja ○ RUS 118-119 K 8
Guljaevskie Koški, ostrova ⌒ RUS 88-89 X 2
Guljanci ○ BG 102-103 D 6
Gul Kach ○ PK 138-139 B 4
Gulkana River ∼ USA 20-21 S 5
Gul'keviči ○ RUS 102-103 M 5
Güllab Dere ∼ TR 128-129 H 4
Gull Bay ○ CDN (ONT) 234-235 O 5
Gullfoss •• IS 86-87 c 2
Gull Lake ○ CDN (SAS) 232-233 K 5
Gull Lake ○ CDN (ALB) 232-233 E 3
Gull Lake ○ USA (MN) 270-271 D 4
Gull Pond ○ CDN (NFL) 242-243 M 3
Gullrock Lake ○ CDN (ONT) 234-235 K 4
Güllük Körfezi ≈ 128-129 B 4
Gully, The ≈ 38-39 P 6
Gulmarg ○• IND 138-139 E 2
Gulmar Kale ∴• TR 128-129 K 4
Gulmit ○ PK 138-139 E 1
Gul Muhammad ○ PK 134-135 M 5
Gülnar ☆ TR 128-129 E 4
Gülpınar ☆ TR 128-129 B 3
Gul'rips ○ GE 126-127 D 6
Gülşehir ☆ TR 128-129 F 3
Gulu ☆ EAU 212-213 D 2
Gulumba Gana ○ WAN 206-207 B 3
Gulūr ○ IND 140-141 G 4
Guluwuru Island ⌒ AUS 174-175 D 2
Gulwe ○ EAT 214-215 J 4
Ğumaira ○ UAE 134-135 F 6
Gumal ∼ PK 138-139 B 3
Gumal ∼ PK 138-139 C 4
Gumani Hurasagar ∼ BD 142-143 F 3
Gumare ○ RB 218-219 B 4
Gumawana Island ⌒ PNG 183 F 5
Gumba ○ ANG 216-217 C 5
Gumba ○ ZRE 210-211 H 2
Gumbiri, Ğabal ▲ SUD 206-207 K 6
Gumbiro ○ EAT 214-215 H 6
Gumbo Gumbo Creek ∼ AUS 178-179 G 4
Gumel ○ WAN 198-199 D 6
Gumgarhi ○ NEP 144-145 D 6
Gumi ○ RI 164-165 K 3
Gumine ○ PNG 183 C 4
Gumla ○ IND 142-143 D 4
Gumlu ○ AUS 174-175 J 6
Gummersbach ○ D 92-93 J 3
Gummi ○ WAN 198-199 B 6
Gumpolds = Humpolec ○ CZ 92-93 N 4
Gums, The ○ AUS 178-179 L 4
Gumsi ○ WAN 198-199 E 6
Gum Swamp Creek ∼ USA (GA) 284-285 G 4
Gümüşhane ☆ TR 128-129 H 2
Gumu Uen, Uar < SP 212-213 J 3
Gumzai ○ RI 166-167 H 4
Günäbäd ○ IR 134-135 J 4
Guna Terara ▲ ETH 208-209 D 3
Gunbar ○ AUS 180-181 H 3
Gundagai ○• AUS 180-181 K 3
Gundāla ○ IND 142-143 B 7
Gundji ○ ZRE 210-211 H 2
Gundlupet ○ IND 140-141 G 5
Gündoğmuş ☆ TR 128-129 E 4
Güneydoğu Toroslar ▲ TR 128-129 G 4
Gunga ○ ANG 216-217 E 7
Gungi ○ ZRE 216-217 E 3
Gungo ○ ANG 216-217 C 5
Gungu ○ ZRE 210-211 G 6
Gungure ○ MOC 214-215 K 6
Gunisao Lake ○ CDN 34-35 H 4
Gunisao River ∼ CDN 34-35 H 4
Guniujiang Z.B. ⊥• VRC 156-157 K 2
Gūniya ☆ RL 128-129 F 6
Gunn ○ CDN (ALB) 232-233 D 2
Gunna ○ SUD 206-207 H 5
Gunnaramby Swamp ○ AUS 180-181 G 2
Gunnarn ○ S 86-87 H 4
Gunnawarra ○ AUS 174-175 H 5
Gunnbjørn Fjeld ▲ GRØ 28-29 Y 2
Gunnedah ○ AUS 178-179 L 6
Gunning ○ AUS 180-181 K 3
Gunningbar Creek ∼ AUS 178-179 J 6
Gunnison ○ USA (CO) 254-255 J 5
Gunnison ○ USA (UT) 254-255 D 4
Gunnison, Mount ▲ USA (CO) 254-255 H 5
Gunnison River ∼ USA (CO) 254-255 G 5
Gunpowder ○ AUS 174-175 E 6
Günsang ○ VRC 144-145 D 5
Gunsight ○ USA (AZ) 256-257 C 6
Gunt ∼ TJ 136-137 N 6
Gunta ○ WAN 204-205 H 3
Guntakal ○ IND 140-141 G 3
Guntersville ○ USA (AL) 284-285 D 2
Guntersville Lake < USA (AL) 284-285 D 2
Gunton ○ CDN (MAN) 234-235 F 4
Guntur ○ IND 140-141 J 2
Gununa ○ AUS 174-175 E 5
Gunung, Tanjung ▲ RI 162-163 H 4
Gunungapi, Pulau ⌒ RI 166-167 D 5
Gunung Gading National Park ⊥ MAL 162-163 H 4
Gununghalum ○ RI 168 B 3
Gunung-Leuser, National-Reservation- ⊥ RI 162-163 C 3
Gunung Leuser Nature Reserve ⊥ RI 162-163 B 3
Gunung Lompobatang Reserve ⊥• RI 164-165 G 6
Gunung Meja Reserve ⊥• RI 166-167 G 2
Gunung Mulu National Park ⊥• MAL 164-165 D 1
Gunung Rinjani Reserve ⊥• RI 168 C 7
Gunungsitoli ○ RI 162-163 B 4
Gunungtua ○ RI 162-163 C 4
Gunupur ○ IND 142-143 C 6
Gunyan, Mount ▲ AUS 178-179 L 5
Gunzenhausen ○ D 92-93 L 4
Guocheng ○ VRC 154-155 D 3
Guocun ○ VRC 154-155 B 5
Guodao ○ VRC 154-155 H 3
Guoguo Wenwu • VRC 154-155 G 4
Guo He ∼ VRC 154-155 K 5
Guoju ○ VRC 156-157 N 2
Guoquanyan ▲ VRC 154-155 C 6
Guoyang ○ VRC 154-155 K 5
Gur ∼ RUS 122-123 H 4
Gurābi, Ğabal ▲ ET 194-195 D 3
Gurabo ○ USA (PR) 286-287 Q 2
Guragē ▲ ETH 208-209 D 4
Gurān ○• IR 134-135 F 5
Gurara, River ∼ WAN 204-205 G 4
Gurba ∼ ZRE 206-207 H 6
Gurbantünggut Shamo ∴ VRC 146-147 H 3
Gurdāspur ○ IND 138-139 E 3
Gurdon ○ USA (AR) 276-277 B 7
Gurdzaani ○• GE 126-127 F 7
Gurē ○ ETH 208-209 D 5
Gur'ev = Atyrau ☆ KA 96-97 H 10
Gur'evsk ☆ RUS 114-115 S 7
Gurgaon ○ IND 138-139 F 5
Gurgei, Ğabal ▲ SUD 200-201 B 6
Gurguéia, Rio ∼ BR 68-69 G 5
Gurguéira, Rio ∼ BR 68-69 F 5
Guri, Embalse de < YV 60-61 K 4
Gurib ∼ NAM 220-221 C 3
Gurig National Park ⊥ AUS 172-173 K 1
Gurijuba, Canal do ∼ BR 62-63 J 5
Gūrīn ○ IRQ 128-129 K 4
Gurin ○ WAN 204-205 K 4
Gurinhatã ○ BR 72-73 F 5
Gurlan ○ US 136-137 G 4
Ğurm ○ AFG 136-137 M 6
Gurner ○ AUS 172-173 K 7
Guro ○ MOC 218-219 G 3
Güroymak ☆ TR 128-129 K 3
Gurri ○ SUD 198-199 L 6
Gurskoe ○ RUS 122-123 G 3
Guru ○ VRC 144-145 G 6
Guruè ○ MOC 218-219 J 2
Gurumeti ∼ EAT (MA) 212-213 E 5
Gurun ○ MAL 162-163 D 2
Gürün ☆ TR 128-129 G 3
Gurupa ○ BR 62-63 J 6
Gurupi ○ BR 68-69 D 7
Gurupi, Baía do ≈ 68-69 E 2
Gurupi, Cabo ▲ BR 68-69 E 2
Gurupi, Rio ∼ BR 68-69 E 3
Gurupi, Serra do ▲ BR 68-69 D 4
Gurupizinho ○ BR 68-69 E 3
Guru Sikhar ▲ IND 138-139 D 7
Guruve ○ ZW 218-219 F 3
Guruzāla ○ IND 140-141 H 2
Gurvan Sajchan ▲ MAU 148-149 F 6
Gurvansajhan = Suugaant ○ MAU 148-149 H 5
Gurvantès = Urt ○ MAU 148-149 E 6
Gurydangdan, peski ∴ TM 136-137 F 6
Gusar = Qusar ○ AZ 128-129 N 2
Gusau ○ WAN 198-199 C 6
Gusev ○ RUS 94-95 H 4
Gushan • VRC 156-157 L 3
Gusher ○ USA (UT) 254-255 F 3
Gushgy ○ TM 136-137 H 7
Gushgy ∼ TM 136-137 H 7
Gushi ○ VRC (HEN) 154-155 J 5
Gushi ○ VRC (QIN) 144-145 L 5
Gushiegu ○ GH 202-203 K 5
Gushie Point ▲ CDN 36-37 K 6
Gushikawa ○ J 152-153 B 11
Gus'-Hrustal'nyj ☆• RUS 94-95 R 4
Gusi ○ RI 166-167 G 3
Gusika ∼ RUS 110-111 F 3
Gusinaja ∼ RUS 110-111 a 4
Gusinaja, guba ≈ 110-111 b 4
Gusinaja Vadega ∼ RUS 108-109 E 5
Gusinaja Zemlja, poluostrov ⌒ RUS 108-109 D 6
Gusinoe, ozero ○•• RUS 116-117 M 10
Gusinoozërsk ☆ RUS 116-117 N 10
Gūš Lāgar ○ IR 136-137 G 7
Gusmp, ostrov ⌒ RUS 112-113 L 2
Gūspini ○ I 100-101 B 5
Gustav Adolf Land ⌒ N 84-85 M 3
Gustavfjellet ▲ N 84-85 K 4
Gustav Holm, Kap ▲ GRØ 28-29 X 3
Gustavia ☆ F 56 D 3
Gustavo A. Madero ○ MEX 52-53 E 2
Gustavsberg ☆ S 86-87 J 7
Gustavus ○ USA 32-33 C 2
Gustav V land ≈ 84-85 L 2
Gustine ○ USA (CA) 248-249 D 2
Güstrow ○• D 92-93 M 2
Gutah ○ CDN 32-33 K 3
Gutara ∼ RUS 116-117 H 8
Gutarskij hrebet ▲ RUS 116-117 H 8
Gutenko Mountains ▲ ARK 16 F 30
Gütersloh ○ D 92-93 K 3
Guthalungra ○ AUS 174-175 J 6
Guthrie ○ USA (AZ) 256-257 F 6
Guthrie ○ USA (OK) 264-265 G 3
Guthrie ○ USA (TX) 264-265 D 5
Guthrie Center ○ USA (IA) 274-275 D 3
Gutian ○ VRC 156-157 L 3
Gutiérrez Zamora ○ MEX 52-53 F 1
Gut River ○ JA 54-55 G 6
Gutsuo ○ VRC 144-145 F 6
Guttaiyūr ○ IND 140-141 G 5
Guttenberg ○ USA (IA) 274-275 G 2
Guttstadt = Dobre Miasto ○• PL 92-93 Q 2
Gutu ○ ZW 218-219 F 4
Gu Vo ○ USA (AZ) 256-257 C 6
Guwahati ☆ IND 142-143 G 2
Ğuwaifāt ○ UAE 134-135 D 6
Ğuwaiza ○ UAE 134-135 F 6
Guwayr ○ SUD 200-201 F 4
Guy ○ CDN 32-33 M 4
Guyana ■ GUY 62-63 E 3
Guyandot River ∼ USA (WV) 280-281 D 5
Guyang ○ VRC 148-149 J 7
Guyenne ∴ F 90-91 G 9
Guy Fawkes River National Park ⊥ AUS 178-179 M 6
Guyi ○ ETH 208-209 B 4
Guymon ○ USA (OK) 264-265 C 2
Gūyom ○ IR 134-135 E 4
Guyot Glacier ⊂ USA 20-21 U 6
Guyra ○ AUS 178-179 L 6
Guyton ○ USA (GA) 284-285 J 4
Guyuan ○ VRC (HEB) 148-149 M 7
Guyuan ○ VRC (NIN) 154-155 E 4
Guzar ○ US 136-137 K 5
Güzeloluk ○ TR 128-129 F 4
Güzelsu ○ TR 128-129 K 3
Guzhen ○ VRC (ANH) 154-155 K 5
Guzhen ○ VRC (FUJ) 156-157 M 3
Guzmán ○ MEX 50-51 F 2
Guzmán, Laguna de ○ MEX 50-51 F 2
Gvādar ○ IR 134-135 J 6
Gvardejsk ☆ RUS 94-95 G 4
Gvardeysk = Gvardejsk ☆ RUS 94-95 G 4
Gvasjugi ○ RUS 122-123 G 5
Gwa ○ MYA 158-159 C 2
Gwaai ○ ZW 218-219 D 4
Gwabegar ○ AUS 178-179 K 6
Gwada ○ WAN 204-205 G 4
Gwadabawa ○ WAN 198-199 B 6
Gwādar ○ PK 134-135 K 6
Gwagwalada ○ WAN 204-205 G 4
Gwalia ∴ AUS 176-177 F 4
Gwalior ○• IND 138-139 G 6
Gwalishtap ○ PK 134-135 K 4
Gwamba ○ WAN 204-205 F 3
Gwambara ○ WAN 198-199 B 6
Gwanda ☆ ZW 218-219 E 5
Gwane ○ ZRE 206-207 G 6
Gwaram ○ WAN 204-205 H 3
Gwardafuy = Raas Caseyr ▲ SP 208-209 K 3
Gwarif ○ RI 166-167 K 3
Gwarzo ○ WAN 204-205 G 3
Gwasero ○ WAN 204-205 E 4
Gwayi ∼ ZW 218-219 D 4
Gwayi River ○ ZW 218-219 D 4
Gweedore ○ IRL 90-91 C 4
Gwembe ○ Z 218-219 D 3
Gweru ☆ ZW (Mid) 218-219 E 4
Gweru ∼ ZW 218-219 E 4
Gweta ○ RB 218-219 C 5
Gwi ○ WAN 204-205 G 4
Gwillim River ∼ CDN 34-35 C 2
Gwinn ○ USA (MI) 270-271 L 4
Gwinner ○ USA (ND) 258-259 K 5
Gwoza ○ WAN 204-205 K 3
Gwydir Highway II AUS 178-179 K 5
Gwydir River ∼ AUS 178-179 L 6
Gwynne ○ CDN (ALB) 232-233 E 2
Gwynn Island ⌒ USA (VA) 280-281 K 6
Gyaca ○ VRC 144-145 J 6
Gya'gya = Saga ○ VRC 144-145 E 6
Gyalshing ○ IND 142-143 F 2
Gyandzha = Ganca ○• AZ 128-129 M 2
Gyangzê ○• VRC 144-145 G 6
Gyaring Co ○ VRC 144-145 G 5
Gyaring Hu ○ VRC 144-145 L 3
Gyda ○ RUS 108-109 S 6
Gydanskaja grjada ▲ RUS 108-109 Q 7
Gydanskaja guba ≈ 108-109 R 5
Gydanskij poluostrov ⌒ RUS 108-109 Q 6
Gydanskij proliv ○ RUS 108-109 Q 5
Gydanskiy Poluostrov = Gydanskij poluostrov ⌒ RUS 108-109 Q 6
Gyêsar Co ○ VRC 144-145 E 5
Gyirong ○ VRC 144-145 E 6
Gyitang ○ VRC 144-145 L 5
Gyldenløves Fjord ≈ 28-29 U 4
Gympie ○• AUS 178-179 M 4
Gynym ∼ RUS 118-119 O 7
Gynym ∼ RUS 120-121 E 5
Gyobinchan ○ MYA 142-143 J 6
Gyokusendo • J 152-153 B 11
Gyöngyös ○ H 92-93 P 5
Győr ○ H 92-93 O 5
Gypsum Palace ○ AUS 180-181 H 2
Gypsum Point ▲ CDN 30-31 M 5
Gypsumville ○ CDN (MAN) 234-235 E 3
Gyrfalcon Islands ⌒ CDN 36-37 P 5
Gyrgyčan ○ RUS 112-113 Q 2

H

H1 ○ IRQ 128-129 J 6
H3 ○ IRQ 128-129 H 6
Häädemeeste ○ EST 94-95 J 2
Ha'afeva ⌒ TON 184 IV a 1
Haag, Den = 's-Gravenhage ☆•• NL 92-93 H 2
Haakon VII Land ∴ N 84-85 H 3
Haalenberg ○ NAM 220-221 B 3
Ha'amonga Trilithon • TON 184 IV a 2
Ha'ano ⌒ TON 184 IV a 1
Ha'apai Group ⌒ TON 184 IV a 1
Haapajärvi ○ FIN 88-89 H 5
Haapsalu ☆ EST 94-95 H 2
Haarlem ☆•• NL 92-93 H 2
Haarlem ○ ZA 220-221 F 6
Haast ○ NZ 182 B 5
Haastberget ▲ N 84-85 M 3
Haast Bluff ⊼ AUS 176-177 L 1
Haast Pass ▲ NZ 182 B 6
Haasts Bluff Aboriginal Land ⊼ AUS 176-177 K 1
Hab ∼ PK 134-135 M 6
Haba, al- ○ UAE 134-135 F 6
Habadra, Hassi < DZ 190-191 E 7
Habahe ○ VRC 146-147 H 1
Habana, La ☆••• C 54-55 D 3
Habarane ○ CL 140-141 J 6
Habar Cirir ○ SP 208-209 H 6
Habarovsk ○ RUS 122-123 F 4
Ḥabarūt ○ OM 132-133 H 5
Habaswein ○ EAK 212-213 G 3
Ḥabauna, Wādī ∼ KSA 132-133 D 5
Habay ○ SP 212-213 J 3
Ḫabbā, al- ○ KSA 130-131 G 4
Ḥabbān ○ Y 132-133 E 6
Ḥabbānīya, al- ○ IRQ 128-129 K 6
Ḥabbārīya, al- ○ IRQ 128-129 K 6
Habejjaha ∼ RUS 108-109 O 5
Ḥabībābād ○ IR 134-135 D 2
Habirag ○ VRC 148-149 M 6
Ḥable Rūd, Rūdḫāne-ye ∼ IR 136-137 C 7
Habob ∼ SUD 200-201 G 3
Habraykhoun ○ LAO 158-159 H 3
Habšān ○ UAE 132-133 H 2
Habūr ○ Y 132-133 C 5
Ḫābūr, al- ∼ SYR 128-129 J 5
Ḫābūr, Nahr al- ∼ SYR 128-129 J 4
Ḫabūra, al- ○ OM 132-133 K 2
Hacari ○ CO 60-61 E 3
Hacha, Raudal ∼ CO 64-65 F 1
Hachinohe ○ J 152-153 J 4
Hachiōji ○ J 152-153 H 7
Hachirōgata-ko ○ J 152-153 J 5
Hachita ○ USA (NM) 256-257 G 7
Hack, Mount ▲ AUS 178-179 E 6
Hackberry ○ USA (AZ) 256-257 B 3
Hackberry ○ USA (LA) 268-269 G 7
Hackberry Creek ∼ USA (KS) 262-263 F 6
Hackensack ○ USA (MN) 270-271 D 4
Hackett ○ CDN (ALB) 232-233 F 3
Hackettstown ○ USA (NJ) 280-281 M 3
Hackleburg ○ USA (AL) 284-285 B 2
Hackney ○ GUY 62-63 E 2
Hačmas = Xaçmaz ○ AZ 128-129 N 2
Haco ○ ANG 216-217 C 5
Hacufera ○ MOC 218-219 G 5
Hadaaftimo ○ SP 208-209 J 3
Hadagalli ○ IND 140-141 F 3
Hadakta ○ RUS 118-119 F 10
Hadaliya ○ SUD 200-201 H 4
Hadama ○ RUS 116-117 J 9
Ḥadar, al- ☆ IRQ 128-129 K 5
Hadaran'ja, hrebet ▲ RUS 110-111 V 5
Hadashville ○ CDN (MAN) 234-235 H 5
Ḥadbaram ○ OM 132-133 J 5
Ḥadd, al- ○ OM 132-133 L 2
Ḥadd, Ra's al- ▲ OM 132-133 L 2
Hadda ∴• AFG 138-139 C 2
Ḥaddā' ○ KSA 132-133 A 3
Ḥaddād Banī Malik ○ KSA 132-133 B 3
Ḥaddār, al- ○ KSA 132-133 D 3
Haddington • GB 90-91 F 4
Haddon Corner • AUS 178-179 F 4
Haddummati Atoll ⌒ MV 140-141 B 7
Hadejia ○ WAN (KAN) 198-199 E 6
Hadejia ∼ WAN 198-199 D 6
Hadera ☆ IL 130-131 D 1
Haderslev ○• DK 86-87 D 9
Hadhf ○ NZ 134-135 F 6
Hadhour, Hassi < DZ 188-189 L 5
Hadibū ○ Y 132-133 H 7
Hadīga ○ SUD 200-201 G 4
Hadilik ○ VRC 144-145 F 2
Hadim ☆ TR 128-129 E 4
Ḥadīṯa, al- ○ KSA 130-131 E 2
Hadjač ○ UA 102-103 H 2
Hadjadj, Oued el ∼ DZ 190-191 E 6
Hadjer = Oum ○ TCH 198-199 J 6
Hadjer Bandala ○ TCH 206-207 E 3
Hadjer el Hamis ○ TCH 198-199 G 6
Hadley ○ USA (WA) 244-245 G 4
Hadley Bay ≈ 24-25 R 4
Ḥadnān ○ IRQ 128-129 K 4
Hà Đông ☆ VN 156-157 D 6
Ḥadrā', al- ○ KSA 130-131 H 3
Ḥaḍramaut ∴ Y 132-133 E 6
Ḥaḍramaut, Wādī ∼ Y 132-133 F 5
Hadrametum = Sousse ☆• TN 190-191 H 3
Ḥadrāniya ○ IRQ 128-129 K 5
Hadrian's Wall ••• GB 90-91 F 4
Hadseløya ⌒ N 86-87 G 2
Hadsund ○ DK 86-87 E 8
Hadudejpur ∼ RUS 114-115 P 3
Hadutte ∼ RUS 108-109 R 8
Hadweenzie River ∼ USA 20-21 Q 3
Hadyjah ∼ RUS 114-115 K 2
Hadyr'jaha, Bol'šaja ∼ RUS 114-115 P 2
Hadytajha ∼ RUS 108-109 N 8
Hadyžensk ○ RUS 126-127 C 5
Hae ○ THA 142-143 M 6
Haedo, Cuchilla de ▲ ROU 78-79 L 2
Haeju ○ DVR 150-151 E 8
Haena ○ USA (HI) 288 F 2
Haenam ○ ROK 150-151 F 10
Haenertsburg ○ ZA 218-219 E 6
Ḥafar al-Bāṭin ○ KSA 130-131 J 3
Haffa, al- ○ SYR 128-129 G 5
Haffner Bjerg ▲ GRØ 26-27 T 5
Hafford ○ CDN (SAS) 232-233 L 3
Haffouz ○ TN 190-191 G 3
Ḫafǧī, Ra's al- ○ KSA 130-131 L 3
Hafik ☆ TR 128-129 G 3
Ḥāfirat Nisāh ○ KSA 130-131 K 5
Ḥāfizābād ○ PK 138-139 D 3
Hafnarfjörður ☆ IS 86-87 c 2
Haftgel ○ IR 134-135 C 3
Haft Tappe ○ IR 134-135 C 2
Hagadera ○ EAK 212-213 H 3
Ḥağal Bi'r < SYR 128-129 H 5
Hagar ○ CDN (ONT) 238-239 E 2
Ḥağar, al- ▲ OM 132-133 K 2
Ḥağara, al ∴ IRQ 128-129 K 6
Ḥağara, al- ▲ KSA 130-131 H 2
Ḥağarain, al- ○ Y 132-133 F 6
Ḥağar aš-Šarqī ▲ OM 132-133 L 2
Hagar Banga ○ SUD 206-207 F 3
Hagari ∼ IND 140-141 G 3
Ḥağda ○ Y 132-133 C 7
Hagemeister Island ⌒ USA 22-23 Q 3
Hagemeister Strait ≈ 22-23 Q 3
Hagen ○ CDN (SAS) 232-233 N 3
Hagen ○ D 92-93 J 3
Hagen, Mount ▲ PNG 183 C 3
Hagen Fjord ≈ 26-27 m 3
Hagensborg ○ CDN (BC) 228-229 H 4
Hägere Hiywet ○• ETH 208-209 C 4
Hägere Selam ○ ETH 208-209 D 5
Hagerman ○ USA (ID) 252-253 D 4
Hagerman ○ USA (NM) 256-257 L 5
Hagerman National Wildlife Refuge ⊥ USA (TX) 264-265 H 5
Hagerstown ○ USA (IN) 274-275 N 5
Hagerstown ○ USA (MD) 280-281 J 4
Ḥağğa ○• Y 132-133 C 6
Ḥāǧǧ 'Alī Qolī, Kavīr-e ○ IR 136-137 D 7
Ḥağğiābād ○ IR 134-135 F 4
Hagi ○ J 152-153 D 7
Hà Giang ☆ VN 156-157 D 5
Ḥağr, al- ○ KSA 130-131 K 5
Hague ○ CDN (SAS) 232-233 M 3
Hague, Cap de la ▲ F 90-91 G 7
Hague, Hasy < LAR 190-191 H 7
Haguenau ○• F 90-91 L 7
Hahan ∼ RUS 120-121 D 4
Hahčan ∼ RUS 110-111 N 6
Hahira ○ USA (GA) 284-285 G 6
Hahndorf ○ AUS 180-181 E 3
Hahnville ○ USA (LA) 268-269 K 7
Haho ○ BF 202-203 J 4
Haho ∼ RT 202-203 L 6
Haia ○ PNG 183 C 4
Hai'an ○ VRC (GDG) 156-157 G 6
Hai'an ○ VRC (JIA) 154-155 M 5
Haib ○ NAM 220-221 D 4
Haib ∼ NAM 220-221 C 4
Ḫaibar ○ KSA 130-131 F 5
Ḫaibar al-Ğanūb ○ KSA 132-133 C 4
Haicheng ○ VRC 150-151 D 7
Haida ○• CDN (BC) 228-229 B 2
Haida = Nový Bor ○ CZ 92-93 N 3
Haidra • TN 190-191 G 3
Hải Dương ☆ VN 156-157 E 6
Haifa = Hefa ☆• IL 130-131 D 1
Haifān ○ Y 132-133 D 7
Haifeng ○ VRC 156-157 J 5
Haig ○ AUS 176-177 J 5
Haigler ○ USA (NE) 262-263 E 4
Haikang ○ VRC 156-157 G 6
Haikou ☆• VRC 156-157 G 6
Ḥā'il ▫ KSA 130-131 G 4
Ḥā'il ☆• KSA (HAI) 130-131 G 4
Ḥā'il, Wādī ∼ KSA 130-131 G 4
Hailalua ○ SOL 184 I e 3
Hailar ○ VRC 150-151 B 3
Hailar He ∼ VRC 150-151 C 3
Hailey ○ USA (ID) 252-253 D 3
Haileybury ○ CDN (ONT) 236-237 J 5
Hailin ○ VRC 150-151 G 5
Hailino ○ RUS 112-113 O 6
Hailun ○ VRC 150-151 F 4
Hailuogou • VRC 156-157 B 2
Hailuoto (Karlö) ⌒ FIN 88-89 H 4
Ḫaima, Ra's al- ○ UAE 134-135 F 6
Haimen ○ VRC 154-155 M 6
Hainan ▫ VRC 156-157 F 7
Hainan Dao ⌒ VRC 156-157 G 7
Hainan Strait = Qiongzhou Haixia ≈ VRC 156-157 F 6
Hainault Tourist Mine • AUS 176-177 F 5
Haindi ○ LB 202-203 E 6
Haines ○ USA (AK) 20-21 X 7
Haines ○ USA (OR) 244-245 H 6
Haines City ○ USA (FL) 286-287 H 3
Haines Highway II CDN 20-21 W 6
Haines Junction ○ CDN 20-21 W 6
Haingsisi ○ RI 166-167 B 7
Hainin ○ Y 132-133 F 6
Haining ○ VRC 154-155 M 6
Hải Ninh ☆ VN 156-157 E 6
Hải Phong ☆• VN 156-157 E 6
Ḥair, Qaṣr al- • SYR 128-129 H 5
Ḥair al-Ġarbī, Qaṣr al- ∴• SYR 128-129 G 5
Hairé Lao ○ SN 196-197 C 6
Hairjuzova ∼ RUS 120-121 R 5
Hairy Hill ○ CDN (ALB) 232-233 G 2
Ḥais ○ Y 132-133 C 7
Ḥaiṣat an-Naum, Ra's ▲ Y 132-133 H 7
Haishiwan ○ VRC 154-155 C 3
Ḥā'iṭ, al- ○ KSA 130-131 G 5
Haitan Dao ⌒ VRC 156-157 L 4
Haiti = Haïti ■ RH 54-55 J 5
Haitou ○ VRC 156-157 F 7
Haiwee Reservoir ○ USA (CA) 248-249 G 3
Haiyan ○ VRC (QIN) 154-155 B 3
Haiyan ○ VRC (ZHE) 154-155 M 6
Haiyang ○ VRC 154-155 M 3
Haiyuan ○ VRC 154-155 D 3
Haizhou Wan ∼ VRC 154-155 L 4
Haja, Džebariki- ○ RUS 120-121 F 2
Haja, Jurjung- ○ RUS 110-111 J 3
Hajata, Suntar-hrebet ▲ RUS 110-111 V 7
Hajdarkan ○ KS 136-137 M 5
Hajeb El Ayoun ○ TN 190-191 G 3
Hajiki-saki ▲ J 152-153 H 5
Hajja, Ějě- ○ RUS 110-111 U 6
Hajjulja ∼ RUS 120-121 T 4
Hajnówka ○ PL 92-93 R 2
Hajo Do ⌒ ROK 150-151 F 10
Hajpudyrskaja, guba ○ RUS 108-109 H 7
Hajrjuzovo ○ RUS 120-121 R 5
Hajrjuzovo, Ust'- ○ RUS 120-121 R 5
Hajsyn ☆ UA 102-103 F 3
Hajyr ○ RUS 110-111 T 4
Hajysardah ○ RUS 118-119 O 5
Haka ○ MYA 142-143 H 4
Hakai Recreation Area ⊥ CDN (BC) 230-231 A 2
Hakalau ○ USA (HI) 288 K 5
Hakanča ∼ 108-109 T 7
Hakčan, Ust'- ○ RUS 120-121 M 2
Hakkari ☆ TR 128-129 K 4
Hakkâri Dağları ▲ TR 128-129 K 4
Hakken-san ▲ J 152-153 F 7
Hakkoda-san ▲ J 152-153 J 4
Hakkulabad ○ US 136-137 N 4
Hakodate ○ J 152-153 J 4
Hakoma ∼ RUS 116-117 J 2
Hakskeenpan ○ ZA 220-221 E 3
Hakui ○ J 152-153 G 6
Haku-san ▲ J 152-153 G 6
Hakusan National Park ⊥ J 152-153 G 6
Hāla ○• PK 138-139 B 7
Ḥalab (Aleppo) ☆••• SYR 128-129 G 4
Halaban ○ RI 162-163 B 3
Ḥalabğa ☆ IRQ 128-129 M 5
Halač ○ TM 136-137 J 5
Ḥalā'ib ○ ET 194-195 H 6
Halali ○ NAM 216-217 D 9
Halali Reservoir < IND 138-139 F 8
Ḥālat 'Ammār ○ KSA 130-131 E 3
Halawa ○ USA (HI) 288 J 3
Halberstadt ○•• D 92-93 L 3
Halbrite ○ CDN (SAS) 232-233 P 6
Halčaganahta, krjaž ▲ RUS 110-111 G 4
Halcon, Mount ▲ RP 160-161 D 6
Haldane River ∼ CDN 30-31 J 2
Halden ☆ N 86-87 E 7
Haldia ○ IND 142-143 F 4
Hal'džaj, Krest- ○ RUS 120-121 F 2
Hale, Mount ▲ AUS 176-177 D 3
Haleakala Crater ▲ USA (HI) 288 J 4
Haleakala National Park ⊥• USA (HI) 288 J 4
Halebid ○• IND 140-141 F 4
Hale Center ○ USA (TX) 264-265 C 4
Haleiwa ○ USA (HI) 288 G 3
Hale River ∼ AUS 178-179 C 2
Haley Dome ○ USA (UT) 254-255 F 4
Haleyville ○ USA (AL) 284-285 C 2
Ḥalfain, Wādī ∼ OM 132-133 K 2
Half Assini ○ GH 202-203 J 7
Ḥalfāyat al-Mulūk ○ SUD 200-201 F 5
Hal Flood Range ▲ ARK 16 F 23
Halfmoon Bay ○ CDN (BC) 230-231 F 4
Halfmoon Bay ○ NZ 182 B 7
Half Moon Bay ○ USA (CA) 248-249 B 2
Half Moon Lake ○ AUS 176-177 M 4
Halfway ○ USA (OR) 244-245 H 6
Half Way Hills ▲ CDN 30-31 V 3
Halfway Point ▲ CDN 34-35 Q 5
Halfway River ∼ CDN 32-33 J 3
Halgen ○ SP 208-209 G 6
Ḫalḫal ○ IR 128-129 N 4
Halhgol ○ MAU 148-149 O 4
Ḫalibān ○ KSA 130-131 J 6
Haliburton ○ CDN (ONT) 238-239 G 3
Haliburton Highlands ▲ CDN (ONT) 238-239 G 3
Ḫālid ○ IRQ 128-129 L 6
Ḫālida, Bi'r < ET 194-195 C 2
Halifax ○ AUS 174-175 J 6
Halifax ☆ CDN (NS) 240-241 M 6
Halifax ○ GB 90-91 G 5
Halifax ○ USA (NC) 282-283 K 4
Halifax, Mount ▲ AUS 174-175 J 6
Halifax Bay ≈ 174-175 J 6
Ḫalīğ-e Fārs • IR 134-135 C 4
Halikarnassos ∴• TR 128-129 B 4
Ḫalīl, al- = Hevron ☆ WB 130-131 D 2
Ḫalīlābād ○ IR 136-137 E 7
Ḫalīle, Ra's-e ▲ IR 134-135 D 4
Halilovo ○ RUS 96-97 L 8
Halīl Rūd ∼ IR 134-135 H 5
Halilulik ○ RI 166-167 C 6
Halin, Ruins of • MYA 142-143 J 4
Ḫālis, al- ○ IRQ 128-129 L 6
Haliyāl ○ IND 140-141 F 3
Haljala ○ EST 94-95 K 2
Haljango, ostrov ⌒ RUS 108-109 P 5
Halkanskij hrebet ▲ RUS 120-121 L 3
Halke Shan ▲ VRC 146-147 E 4
Halkett, Cape ▲ USA 20-21 O 1
Hálki ⌒ GR 100-101 L 6
Halkida ○ GR 100-101 J 5
Halkidiki ∴ GR 100-101 J 4
Halkirk ○ CDN (ALB) 232-233 F 3
Hallam Peak ▲ CDN (BC) 228-229 Q 4
Halland ∴ S 86-87 F 8
Hallandale ○ USA (FL) 286-287 J 6
Ḥallāniyāt, al- ⌒ Y 132-133 K 5
Hallasan ▲ ROK 150-151 F 11
Hallasan National Park ⊥• ROK 150-151 F 11
Hall Bassin ≈ 26-27 T 3
Hall Beach ○ CDN 24-25 f 6
Hallboro ○ CDN (MAN) 234-235 D 4
Hall Bredning ≈ 26-27 n 8
Hall Creek ∼ USA (UT) 254-255 D 6
Halle (Saale) ○• D 92-93 L 3
Hallebourg ○ CDN (ONT) 236-237 E 3
Halleck ○ USA (NV) 246-247 K 3
Hallein ○ A 92-93 M 5
Hallen ○ S 86-87 G 5
Hallersville ○ USA 22-23 S 3
Hallett ○ AUS 180-181 E 2
Hallettsville ○ USA (TX) 266-267 L 4
Halley Bay ○ ARK 16 F 34
Halliday ○ USA (ND) 258-259 E 4
Halliday Lake ○ CDN 30-31 P 5
Hall Indian Reservation, Fort ⊼ USA (ID) 252-253 F 3
Hallingdal ∪ N 86-87 D 6
Hallingdalselvi ∼ N 86-87 D 6
Hallingskarvet ▲ N 86-87 C 6
Hall in Tirol ○ A 92-93 L 5
Hall Island ⌒ FSM 13 G 2
Hall Island ⌒ USA 112-113 Y 6
Hall Lake ○ CDN 24-25 f 6
Hall Land ∴ GRØ 26-27 U 3
Hällnäs ○ S 86-87 J 4
Hallock ○ USA (MN) 270-271 B 2
Hallonquist ○ CDN (SAS) 232-233 N 5
Hallowell, Cape ▲ CDN 24-25 d 6
Hall Peninsula ⌒ CDN 36-37 Q 3
Hall Point ▲ AUS 174-175 B 2
Halls ○ USA (TN) 276-277 F 5
Halls Creek ○• AUS 172-173 H 5
Halls Crossroads ○ USA (TN) 282-283 D 4
Halls Gap ○• AUS 180-181 G 4
Hallson ○ USA (ND) 258-259 K 3
Hallsville ○ USA (TX) 264-265 K 6
Hallville ○ CDN (ONT) 238-239 K 3
Hallyŏ Haesang National Park ⊥• ROK 150-151 G 10
Halmahera, Pulau ⌒ RI 164-165 L 3
Halmahera Sea = Halmahera, Laut ≈ RI 166-167 E 1
Hal'mer"ju, ozero ○ RUS 108-109 N 7
Halmstad ○ S 86-87 F 8
Hālol ○ IND 138-139 D 8
Halong ○ RI 166-167 E 3
Hal'šany ○ BY 94-95 K 4
Halstad ○ USA (MN) 270-271 B 3
Halstead ○ USA (KS) 262-263 J 7
Haltom City ○ USA (TX) 264-265 G 6
Halturin ○ RUS 96-97 F 4
Halura, Pulau ⌒ RI 168 E 8
Halvad ○ IND 138-139 C 8
Halverson Ridge ▲ CDN 32-33 L 3
Halvmåneøya ⌒ N 84-85 N 4
Halvorgate ○ CDN (SAS) 232-233 M 5
Ḥalwān al-Ḫunfa ▲ KSA 130-131 F 3
Halyja ∼ RUS 120-121 H 2
Halzan Sogootyn davaa ▲ MAU 148-149 D 3
Ham ∼ NAM 220-221 D 4
Ham ○ TCH 206-207 B 3
Hamab ○ NAM 220-221 D 4
Ḥamād, al- ∴ KSA 130-131 F 2
Hamada ○ J 152-153 E 7
Hamadān ○• IR 134-135 C 1
Hamadān ▫ IR 134-135 C 1
Hamaguir ○ DZ 188-189 K 5
Hamāh ☆•• SYR 128-129 G 5
Hamakua Coast ∪ USA (HI) 288 K 4
Hamamah ○ LAR 192-193 J 1
Hamamasu ○ J 152-153 J 3
Hamamatsu ○ J 152-153 G 7
Haman ○ CAM 204-205 K 6
Hamar ☆• N 86-87 E 6
Hamar ○ USA (ND) 258-259 J 4
Ḥamar, al- ○ KSA 130-131 K 6
Hamar-Daban, hrebet ▲ RUS 116-117 L 10
Hamasaka ○ J 152-153 F 7
Ḥamāsīn, al- ○ KSA 132-133 D 3
Ḥamāṭa, Ğabal ▲ ET 194-195 G 5
Hama-Tombetsu ○ J 152-153 K 2
Hamba ○ COM 222-223 C 4
Hambantota ○ CL 140-141 J 7
Hambaroaing ○ RI 168 E 7
Hamberg ○ USA (ND) 258-259 H 4
Hamber Provincial Park ⊥ CDN (BC) 228-229 R 4
Hambidge Conservation Park ⊥ AUS 180-181 C 2
Hamborgerland ⌒ GRØ 28-29 O 4
Hamburg ☆•• D 92-93 L 2
Hamburg ○ SME 62-63 G 3
Hamburg ○ USA (AR) 276-277 D 7
Hamburg ○ USA (CA) 246-247 B 2
Hamburg ○ USA (IA) 274-275 C 4
Hamburg ○ USA (NY) 278-279 C 6
Hamburg ○ ZA 220-221 H 6
Hamchang ○ VRC 144-145 B 4
Hamḍ, Wādī al- ∼ KSA 130-131 E 5
Hämeenlinna ☆ FIN 88-89 H 6
Hamelin ○ AUS 176-177 C 3
Hamelin, Mount ▲ CDN 24-25 P 3
Hamelin Pool ≈ 176-177 B 3
Hameln ○• D 92-93 K 2
Hamen Wan ∼ VRC 156-157 K 5
Hamer ○ USA (ID) 252-253 F 3
Hamer Koke ○ ETH 208-209 C 6
Hamero Hadad ○ ETH 208-209 F 5
Hamersley ○ AUS 172-173 C 7
Hamersley Lakes ○ AUS 176-177 E 5
Hamersley Range ▲ AUS 172-173 C 6
Hamersley Range National Park ⊥•• AUS 172-173 C 7
Hamğa, al- ○ KSA 130-131 H 5
Hamhung ○ DVR 150-151 F 8
Hami ○ VRC 146-147 L 4
Ḥāmī, al- ○ Y 132-133 F 6
Hamid ○ SUD 200-201 E 2
Ḥamīdī, Qal'at ○ IRQ 128-129 L 6
Ḥamīdiya ○ SYR 128-129 F 5
Ḥamīdiye ○ IR 134-135 C 3
Hamill Creek ∼ CDN (BC) 230-231 N 3
Hamilton ○ AUS (TAS) 180-181 J 7
Hamilton ○• AUS (VIC) 180-181 G 4
Hamilton ○ CDN (ONT) 238-239 F 5
Hamilton ☆ GB 54-55 L 1
Hamilton ○ NZ 182 E 2
Hamilton ○ USA (AK) 20-21 J 5
Hamilton ○ USA (AL) 284-285 C 2
Hamilton ○ USA (CO) 254-255 H 3
Hamilton ○ USA (IL) 274-275 G 4
Hamilton ○ USA (IN) 274-275 O 3
Hamilton ○ USA (KS) 262-263 K 7
Hamilton ○ USA (MO) 274-275 D 5
Hamilton ○ USA (MT) 250-251 E 5

Hamilton ○ USA (OH) 280-281 B 4
Hamilton ○ USA (TX) 266-267 J 2
Hamilton ○ USA (WA) 244-245 D 2
Hamilton, Lake ○ AUS 180-181 C 6
Hamilton, Lake ~ USA (AR) 276-277 B 6
Hamilton, Mount ▲ USA (NV) 246-247 K 4
Hamilton Bank ≃ 6-7 D 3
Hamilton City ○ USA (CA) 246-247 C 4
Hamilton Creek ~ AUS 176-177 M 3
Hamilton Dome ○ USA (WY) 252-253 K 3
Hamilton Downs ○ AUS 176-177 M 1
Hamilton Hotel ○ AUS 178-179 F 2
Hamilton Island ⌒ AUS 174-175 K 7
Hamilton River ~ AUS 178-179 F 2
Hamim ○ UAE 132-133 J 2
Hamina ○ FIN 88-89 J 6
Hamiota ○ CDN (MAN) 234-235 C 4
Hami Pendi ⊥ VRC 146-147 L 4
Hamir ○• Y 132-133 C 6
Ḥāmir, Wādī ~ IRQ 128-129 J 7
Ḥāmir, Wādī ~ KSA 130-131 G 2
Ḥāmir, Wādī ~ Y 132-133 F 6
Hami Rotoki • SUD 200-201 B 6
Hamirpur ○ IND 142-143 B 3
Ḥamis al-Bahr ○ KSA 132-133 B 4
Ḥamis Mušaiṭ ○ KSA 132-133 C 4
Ḥamis Mutair ○ KSA 132-133 C 4
Hamlen Bay ≈ 36-37 Q 3
Hamlet ○ USA (NC) 282-283 H 6
Hamlet, Mount ▲ USA 20-21 H 2
Hamlin ○ CDN (ALB) 232-233 G 2
Hamlin ○ CDN (SAS) 232-233 K 3
Hamlin ○ USA (TX) 264-265 D 6
Hamlin Valley ○ USA (UT) 254-255 B 6
Hàm Luông ~ VN 158-159 J 5
Hamm ○ D 92-93 J 3
Ḥammām, al- ○ IRQ 128-129 L 7
Ḥammām 'Alī ○ Y 132-133 D 6
Hammamet ○ TN 190-191 H 2
Hammamet, Golfe de ≈ 190-191 H 2
Hammam-Lif ☆ TN 190-191 H 2
Hamman, Oued ~ DZ 190-191 C 3
Hammer, Kap ▲ GRØ 28-29 Z 2
Hammerdal ○ S 86-87 G 5
Hammerfest ○•• N 86-87 L 1
Hammern ⌒ GRØ 26-27 q 4
Hammilton Sound ≈ 38-39 R 4
Hammilton Sound ≈ CDN 242-243 O 3
Hammock, Kap ▲ GRØ 26-27 d 2
Hammon ○ USA (OK) 264-265 E 3
Hammond ○ USA (CA) 248-249 F 3
Hammond ○ USA (IN) 274-275 L 3
Hammond ○ USA (LA) 268-269 K 6
Hammond ○ USA (MT) 250-251 P 6
Hammond Bay ≈ USA 272-273 E 2
Hammond Island ⌒ AUS 183 B 6
Hammondvale ○ CDN (NB) 240-241 K 5
Hammonton ○ USA (NJ) 280-281 M 4
Hamna ~ RUS 120-121 F 3
Hamnej ~ RUS 116-117 L 10
Ham-Nord ○ CDN (QUE) 238-239 O 3
Hamoud ○ RIM 196-197 E 7
Hamoyet, Ğabal ▲ SUD 200-201 J 4
Hampa ○ RUS 118-119 L 4
Hampden ○ CDN (NFL) 242-243 M 3
Hampden ○ USA (ME) 278-279 N 4
Hampenanperak ○ RI 162-163 C 3
Hampi ○••• IND 140-141 G 3
Hampshire ○ USA (IL) 274-275 K 2
Hampton ○ CDN (NB) 240-241 K 5
Hampton ○ CDN (NS) 240-241 K 6
Hampton ○ USA (AR) 276-277 C 7
Hampton ○ USA (FL) 286-287 G 2
Hampton ○ USA (GA) 284-285 F 3
Hampton ○ USA (IA) 274-275 E 2
Hampton ○ USA (NH) 278-279 L 6
Hampton ○ USA (SC) 284-285 J 4
Hampton ○ USA (VA) 280-281 K 6
Hampton Butte ▲ USA (OR) 244-245 E 7
Hampton Roads ≈ USA 280-281 K 7
Hamra ~ RUS 118-119 F 5
Hamra ○ SUD 206-207 J 3
Ḥamrā', al- ○ OM 132-133 K 2
Ḥamrān, Bi'r < IRQ 128-129 K 5
Hamrånge ○ S 86-87 H 6
Hamrat al-Wuzz ○ SUD 200-201 E 5
Hamrat as-Shaykh ○ SUD 200-201 C 5
Hamrin, Ğabal ▲ IRQ 128-129 L 5
Hamsara ~ RUS 116-117 H 9
Hams Fork ~ USA (WY) 252-253 H 5
Hamstead ○ USA (NC) 282-283 K 6
Hàm Thuận ○ VN 158-159 K 5
Hamtown ○ CDN (NB) 240-241 J 4
Hamūd, 'Ain ○ IRQ 130-131 J 2
Hamuku ○ RI 166-167 H 3
Hāmūn-e Ğaz Mūrīān ○ IR 134-135 H 5
Hāmūn-i-Lora ○ PK 134-135 L 4
Hamyski ○ RUS 126-127 D 5
Hana ○ USA (HI) 288 K 4
Ḥānābād ○ AFG 136-137 L 6
Hanabanilla, Presa del <• C 54-55 E 3
Hanahan ○ PNG 184 I b 1
Hanahan ○ USA (SC) 284-285 L 4
Hanak ○ TR 128-129 K 2
Ḥanākīya, al- ○ KSA 130-131 G 5
Ḥanākīya, Wādī al- ~ KSA 130-131 G 5
Ḥān al-Baġdādī ○ IRQ 128-129 K 6
Hanalei ○ USA (HI) 288 F 2
Ḥān al-Mahāwīl ○ IRQ 128-129 L 6
Hà Nam ☆ VN 156-157 D 6
Hanamaki ○ J 152-153 J 5
Hanamaulu ○ USA (HI) 288 F 3
Hanapepe ○ USA (HI) 288 F 3
Ḥānaqīn ☆ IRQ 128-129 L 5
Hanarasalja, mys ▲ RUS 108-109 P 6
Ḥān ar-Raḥba ○ IRQ 128-129 L 7
Hanaša, al- ○ KSA 132-133 C 5
Ḥanāṣir ○ SYR 128-129 G 5
Hān Beben ○ IR 136-137 D 6
Hanbogd = Ihbulag ○ MAU 148-149 G 6
Hanbury Island ⌒ CDN 30-31 Y 4
Hanbury River ~ CDN 30-31 Q 4
Hanceville ○ CDN (BC) 230-231 G 2
Hancheng ○ VRC 154-155 G 4
Hanchuan ○ VRC 154-155 H 6
Hancock ○ USA (MD) 280-281 H 4
Hancock ○ USA (ME) 278-279 N 4
Hancock ○ USA (MI) 270-271 K 3
Hancock ○ USA (NY) 280-281 L 2
Hancock, Lake ~ AUS 176-177 H 2
Hancock, Lake ○ USA (FL) 286-287 H 4
Hancock Summit ▲ USA (NV) 248-249 J 2
Handa ○ J 152-153 G 7
Handa ~ RUS 116-117 N 8
Handa ~ RUS 120-121 F 3
Handa ○ SP 208-209 K 3
Handagajty ☆ RUS 116-117 F 10
Handan ○ VRC 154-155 J 3
Handel ○ CDN (SAS) 232-233 K 3
Handeni ○ EAT (TAN) 212-213 G 6
Handöl ○ S 86-87 F 5
Handsworth ○ AUS 178-179 J 3
Handwara ○• IND 138-139 E 2
Handyga ☆ RUS 120-121 F 2
Handyga ~ RUS 120-121 F 2
Hāne Sor ○ IRQ 128-129 J 4
Hanestad ○ N 86-87 E 6
Ḥān-e Taḥtī ○ IR 128-129 L 3
Hanford ○ CDN (NB) 240-241 K 5
Hanford ○ USA (CA) 248-249 E 3
Hanford Site • USA (WA) 244-245 F 4
Hangajn Nuruu ▲ MAU 148-149 C 4
Hāngal ○ IND 140-141 F 3
Han Gang ~ ROK 150-151 F 9
Hanga Roa ○ RCH 78-79 B 2
Hanger Wenz ~ ETH 208-209 C 4
Hanggin Houqi ○ VRC 154-155 E 1
Hanggin Qi ○ VRC 154-155 F 2
Hanging Rock ▲ AUS 172-173 E 7
Hangingstone River ~ CDN 32-33 P 3
Hanging Trail ⊥ LB 202-203 F 7
Hanglong ○ VRC 156-157 E 4
Hangö ○•• FIN 88-89 G 7
Hangu ○ PK 138-139 C 3
Hangzhou ☆ •• VRC 154-155 M 6
Hangzhou Wan ≈ 154-155 M 6
Hanhöhij ○ MAU 148-149 L 4
Han Höhijn Nuruu ▲ MAU 116-117 F 11
Hani ○ RUS 118-119 J 7
Hani ~ RUS 118-119 K 7
Hani ☆ TR 128-129 J 3
Haniá ○ GR 100-101 K 7
Ḥanīḏ ○ KSA 130-131 L 4
Ḥanīšal al-Kabīr ⌒ Y 132-133 C 7
Hanja ~ ANG 216-217 B 6
Han Jiang ~ VRC 156-157 K 5
Hanka ☆ US 136-137 G 4
Hanka, ozero ○ RUS 122-123 E 6
Hankendi = Khankendi ☆ AZ 128-129 M 3
Hankey ○ ZA 220-221 G 6
Hankins ○ USA (NY) 280-281 L 2
Hankinson ○ USA (ND) 258-259 L 5
Hanko = Hangö ○•• FIN 88-89 G 7
Hanksville ○ USA (UT) 254-255 E 5
Hanlar = Xanlar ○ AZ 128-129 M 2
Hanley ○ CDN (SAS) 232-233 M 4
Hanmer Springs ○ NZ 182 D 5
Ḥān Muğidda ○ IRQ 128-129 K 6
Hann, Mount ▲ AUS 172-173 G 3
Hanna ○ CDN (ALB) 232-233 G 4
Hanna ○ USA (UT) 254-255 E 3
Hanna ○ USA (WY) 252-253 M 5
Hannaford ○ USA (ND) 258-259 J 4
Hannagan Meadow ○ USA (AZ) 256-257 F 5
Hannah ○ USA (ND) 258-259 J 3
Hannah Bay ≈ 38-39 E 3
Ḥān Nešin ○ AFG 134-135 K 3
Hannibal ○ USA (MO) 274-275 G 5
Hannik < SUD 200-201 F 3
Hannja ~ RUS 110-111 L 7
Hann Münden ○• D 92-93 K 3
Hannover ☆• D 92-93 K 2
Hann River ~ AUS 172-173 H 4
Hann River ~ AUS 174-175 G 4
Hanöbukten ≈ 86-87 G 9
Hà Nội ☆ •• VN 156-157 D 6
Hanoi = Hà Nội ☆ •• VN 156-157 D 6
Hanover ○ CDN (ONT) 238-239 D 4
Hanover ○ USA (IL) 274-275 H 2
Hanover ○ USA (IN) 274-275 N 6
Hanover ○ USA (NH) 278-279 J 5
Hanover ○ USA (PA) 280-281 K 4
Hanover ○ USA (VA) 280-281 J 6
Hanover ○ ZA 220-221 G 5
Hanover = Hannover ☆• D 92-93 L 2
Hanover, Isla ⌒ RCH 80 C 5
Hanover Road ○ ZA 220-221 G 5
Ḥān Šaiḫūn ○ SYR 128-129 G 5
Hansard ○ CDN (BC) 228-229 N 2
Hansboro ○ USA (ND) 258-259 H 3
Hānsdiha ○ IND 142-143 E 3
Hanse ○ IND 138-139 F 3
Hansen ○ USA (NE) 262-263 H 4
Hansenfjella ▲ ARK 16 G 6
Hanshou ○ VRC 156-157 G 2
Han Shui ~ VRC 154-155 H 6
Hānsi ○ IND 138-139 E 5
Hansine Lake ○ CDN 36-37 G 2
Hanskoe, ozero ○ RUS 102-103 L 4
Hans Meyer Range ▲ PNG 183 G 3
Hanson, Lake ○ AUS 178-179 D 6
Hanson River ~ AUS 174-175 B 7
Hänsot ○ IND 138-139 D 9
Hans Tavsens Iskappe ⊂ GRØ 26-27 f 2
Hanstholm ○ DK 86-87 D 8
Hanston ○ USA (KS) 262-263 G 6
Hantai ○ VRC 156-157 G 2
Hantajka ~ RUS 108-109 W 7
Hantajskoe vodohranilišče ○ RUS 108-109 X 7
Hantamsberg ▲ ZA 220-221 D 5
Hantengri Feng ▲ KA 146-147 E 4
Hantoukoura ○ BF 202-203 L 3
Hanty-Mansijsk ☆ RUS 114-115 K 4
Hantzsch River ~ CDN 28-29 F 2
Hanuj gol ~ MAU 148-149 E 3
Hanumana ○ IND 142-143 C 3
Hanumāngarh ○ IND 138-139 E 5
Hanyin ○ VRC 154-155 F 5
Hanyuan ○ VRC 156-157 C 2
Ḥān Yūnis ○ AUT 130-131 C 2
Hanzhong ○ VRC 154-155 E 5
Ḥān Zūr ○ IRQ 128-129 L 5
Haora ○ IND 142-143 F 4
Haotan ○ VRC 154-155 F 3
Haouach, Ouadi ~ TCH 198-199 K 4
Haoud El Hamra ○ DZ 190-191 E 5
Haouich ○ TCH 198-199 K 6
Haouza ○ MA 188-189 F 7
Hapai ○ SOL 184 I c 3
Hapakant ○ MYA 142-143 K 3
Haparanda ○ S 86-87 M 4
Hapčaganahta, krjaž ▲ RUS 110-111 G 4
Hapčeranga ○ RUS 118-119 F 11
Hapica, Bol'šaja ~ RUS 120-121 T 6
Hapo ○ RI 164-165 L 2
Hapolio ○ IND 142-143 H 2
Happy ○ USA (TX) 264-265 C 4
Happy Camp ○ USA (CA) 246-247 B 2
Happy Jack ○ USA (AZ) 256-257 D 4
Happy Valley ○ AUS 178-179 G 2
Hapsal = Haapsalu ☆ EST 94-95 H 2
Haptagaj ○ RUS 118-119 O 5
Hāpur ○ IND 138-139 F 5
Ḥaql, al- ○ KSA 130-131 D 3
Harabali ☆ RUS 96-97 E 10
Ḥarābe-ye Tarāqū ∴• AFG 134-135 K 1
Harabyl ~ RUS 110-111 J 3
Harad ○ KSA 130-131 L 5
Harad ○ Y 132-133 C 5
Ḥarad, Ğabal ▲ JOR 130-131 D 3
Harāda ○ KSA 130-131 K 6
Haradok ☆ BY 94-95 L 4
Haraǧa ○ KSA 132-133 C 5
Haragu ○ PNG 183 B 4
Harajaha ~ RUS 88-89 Y 3
Hara Lake ○ CDN 30-31 S 6
Harald Moltke, Kap ▲ GRØ 28-29 U 5
Haramachi ○ J 152-153 J 6
Harami, pereval ▲ RUS 126-127 G 6
Harampur ~ RUS 114-115 P 2
Ḥarānaq ○ IR 134-135 F 2
Ḥarānaq, Kūh-e ▲ IR 134-135 F 2
Haranor ○ RUS 118-119 H 10
Harapa ○ SOL 184 I b 2
Harappa ○•• PK 138-139 D 4
Harare ★•• ZW 218-219 F 3
Harasavèj ~ RUS 108-109 M 6
Harat ⌒ ER 200-201 J 4
Harāt ○ IR 134-135 F 3
Hara-Tas, krjaž ▲ RUS 108-109 e 6
Hara-Tumus, poluostrov ~ RUS 110-111 H 3
Harau Canyon • RI 162-163 D 5
Hara-Ulah ~ RUS 110-111 R 4
Haraulahskij hrebet ▲ RUS 110-111 Q 3
Harāvaǧān ○ IR 134-135 F 3
Harāz, Ğabal ▲ Y 132-133 C 6
Haraze-Djombo ○ TCH 198-199 J 6
Haraze Mangueigne ○ TCH 206-207 E 4
Harbalah ○ RUS 120-121 F 2
Harbel ○ LB 202-203 E 6
Harbin ☆ VRC 150-151 F 5
Harbor Beach ○ USA (MI) 272-273 G 4
Harbor Springs ○ USA (MI) 272-273 E 2
Harbour Breton ○ CDN (NFL) 242-243 N 5
Harbour Deep ○ CDN (NFL) 242-243 M 2
Harbour Grace ○ CDN (NFL) 242-243 P 5
Harbour View ○ JA 54-55 G 6
Harbourville ○ CDN (NS) 240-241 L 5
Harbutt Range ▲ AUS 172-173 F 7
Harcourt ○ AUS 180-181 H 4
Harcourt ○ CDN (NB) 240-241 K 4
Harda ○ IND 138-139 F 8
Hardali ○ IND 140-141 F 4
Hardangerfjorden ≈ 86-87 C 6
Hardangerjøkulen ⊂ N 86-87 C 6
Hardangervidda ▲ N 86-87 C 6
Hardangervidda nasjonalpark ⊥ N 86-87 C 6
Hard Bargin ○ BS 54-55 G 1
Hardeeville ○ USA (SC) 284-285 J 4
Harderwijk ○ NL 92-93 H 2
Hardey River ~ AUS 172-173 C 7
Hardin ○ USA (IL) 274-275 H 5
Hardin ○ USA (MT) 250-251 M 6
Harding ○ USA (KS) 262-263 M 7
Harding ○ ZA 220-221 J 5
Harding, Lake < USA (AL) 284-285 E 4
Hardinge Bay ≈ 24-25 K 2
Harding River ~ AUS 172-173 C 6
Hardinsburg ○ USA (KY) 276-277 J 3
Hardisty ○ CDN (ALB) 232-233 G 3
Hardisty Lake ○ CDN 30-31 K 3
Hardoi ○ IND 142-143 B 2
Hardtner ○ USA (KS) 262-263 H 7
Hardwick ○ USA (CA) 248-249 E 3
Hardwick ○ USA (GA) 284-285 G 3
Hardwick ○ USA (VT) 278-279 J 4
Hardwicke Bay ≈ 180-181 D 3
Hardwicke Island ⌒ CDN (BC) 230-231 D 3
Hardwick Ferndale ○ CDN (ONT) 238-239 D 4
Hardy ○ CDN (SAS) 232-233 O 6
Hardy ○ USA (AR) 276-277 D 4
Hardy, Península ~ RCH 80 F 7
Hardy Bay ≈ 24-25 O 3
Hardy Lake ○ CDN 30-31 P 3
Hardy Lake ○ USA (IN) 274-275 N 6
Hardyville ○ USA (KY) 276-277 K 3
Hare Bay ≈ 38-39 Q 3
Hare Bay ○ CDN (NFL) 242-243 O 4
Hare Bay ≈ CDN 242-243 M 1
Hare Fiord ≈ 26-27 G 3
Hareford Inlet ≈ USA 280-281 M 4
Hare Indian River ~ CDN 30-31 F 2
Hare Ø ⌒ GRØ 28-29 N 1
Hārer ☆ ETH 208-209 F 4
Hārergē □ ETH 208-209 E 4
Hārer Wildlife Sanctuary ⊥ ETH 208-209 F 4
Hāresābād ○ IR 136-137 E 6
Hareto ○ ETH 208-209 C 4
Harewa ○ ETH 208-209 E 4
Harf, al- ○ Y 132-133 D 5
Ḥarǧ, al- ○ KSA 130-131 K 5
Hargele ○ ETH 208-209 F 6
Hargeysa ☆ SP 208-209 G 4
Hargrave ○ CDN (MAN) 234-235 B 5
Hargrave River ~ CDN 34-35 G 3
Hargreaves ○ CDN (BC) 228-229 M 4
Har Hu ○ VRC 146-147 N 6
Hari ~ RI 162-163 E 5
Haría ○ E 188-189 E 6
Ḥarib ○ Y 132-133 D 6
Haribomo ○ RMM 196-197 J 6
Haribongo, Lac ○ RMM 196-197 J 6
Haridwar ○•• IND 138-139 G 5
Harihar ○ IND 140-141 F 3
Harihari ○ NZ 182 C 5
Hā Rikāt ~ OM 132-133 J 4
Harilek ~ RI 162-163 E 6
Hārim ☆ SYR 128-129 G 4
Harima-nada ≈ 152-153 F 7
Harimkotan, ostrov ⌒ RUS 122-123 Q 4
Haringhata ~ BD 142-143 F 4
Haripad ○ IND 140-141 G 6
Haripur ○ PK 138-139 D 2
Ḥarīrī, Tall • SYR 128-129 J 5
Hari Rūd ~ IR 136-137 G 6
Harīrūd, Daryā-ye ~ AFG 134-135 K 1
Harīrūd, Daryā-ye ~ AFG 136-137 G 7
Harisal ○ IND 138-139 F 9
Härjedalen ⊥ S 86-87 F 5
Ḥārk ○ IR 134-135 D 4
Ḥārk, Ğazīre-ye ⌒ IR 134-135 D 4
Harkány ○ H 92-93 P 6
Harker Heights ○ USA (TX) 266-267 K 2
Harkers Island ○ USA (NC) 282-283 L 6
Harkidum ○ IND 138-139 G 4
Harkin Bay ≈ 36-37 K 2
Har'kov = Charkiv ○ UA 102-103 K 3
Ḥārkū, Ğazīre-ye ⌒ IR 134-135 D 4
Harlan ○ USA (IA) 274-275 C 3
Harlan ○ USA (KY) 276-277 M 4
Harlan County Lake ○ USA (NE) 262-263 G 4
Harlem ○ USA (GA) 284-285 H 3
Harlem ○ USA (MT) 250-251 L 3
Harleston ○ USA (MS) 268-269 M 6
Harleton ○ USA (TX) 264-265 K 6
Harlin ○ AUS 178-179 M 4
Harlingen ○• NL 92-93 H 2
Harlingen ○ USA (TX) 266-267 K 7
Harlovka ○ RUS (MUR) 88-89 O 2
Harlovka ~ RUS 88-89 O 2
Harlow ○ USA (ND) 258-259 H 3
Harlowton ○ USA (MT) 250-251 K 5
Harman ○ USA (WV) 280-281 G 5
Härmänkylä ○ FIN 88-89 K 4
Harmanli ○ BG 102-103 D 7
Harmil ⌒ ER 200-201 K 4
Harmonia ○ BR 76-77 J 6
Harmony ○ USA (ME) 278-279 M 4
Harmony ○ USA (MN) 270-271 F 7
Harnāi ○ PK 134-135 M 3
Harney Basin ~ USA (OR) 244-245 F 7
Harney Lake ○ USA (OR) 244-245 F 7
Harney Peak ▲ USA (SD) 260-261 C 3
Härnösand ☆ S 86-87 H 5
Har nuur ○ MAU (HOV) 146-147 L 1
Har nuur ○ MAU (ZAV) 148-149 C 3
Haro ○ E 98-99 F 3
Haro ~ SP 212-213 H 3
Haro, Cabo ▲ MEX 50-51 D 4
Harobo ○ J 152-153 J 2
Harold Byrd Range ▲ ARK 16 E 0
Haroldswick ○ GB 90-91 G 1
Harovsk ○ RUS 94-95 R 2
Harovskaja grjada ▲ RUS 94-95 R 2
Harpanahalli ○ IND 140-141 F 3
Harper ○ USA (KS) 262-263 H 7
Harper ○ USA (OR) 244-245 H 7
Harper ○ USA (TX) 266-267 H 3
Harper, Mount ▲ USA 20-21 T 4
Harper Creek ~ CDN 30-31 M 6
Harpers Ferry National Historic Park • USA (WV) 280-281 J 4
Harpersville ○ USA (AL) 284-285 D 3
Harpin ~ RUS 122-123 G 3
Harpster ○ USA (ID) 250-251 D 5
Harqin Qi ○ VRC 148-149 O 7
Harqūs ⌒ KSA 130-131 L 4
Harrai ○ IND 138-139 G 8
Harran ☆ TR 128-129 H 4
Harrand ○ PK 138-139 C 5
Ḥarrat al-Buqūm ⊥ KSA 132-133 B 3
Ḥarrat al-'Uwairiḍ ⊥ KSA 130-131 E 4
Ḥarrat Ḥaḍan ⊥ KSA 132-133 B 3
Ḥarrat Ḥaibar ⊥ KSA 130-131 F 5
Ḥarrat Rahaṭ ⊥ KSA 130-131 G 6
Harrells ○ USA (NC) 282-283 J 6
Harricana, Rivière ~ CDN (QUE) 236-237 K 3
Harricana, Rivière ~ CDN (QUE) 236-237 J 2
Harrigan, Cape ▲ CDN 36-37 T 7
Harriman ○ USA (TN) 282-283 C 5
Harrington ○ USA (DE) 280-281 L 5
Harrington ○ USA (WA) 244-245 G 3
Harrington Harbour ○ CDN (QUE) 242-243 J 2
Harris ○ CDN (SAS) 232-233 L 4
Harris, Lake ○ AUS 178-179 C 6
Harris, Lake ○ USA (FL) 286-287 H 3
Harris, Mount ▲ AUS 176-177 K 2
Harrisburg ○ USA (AR) 276-277 E 5
Harrisburg ○ USA (IL) 276-277 G 3
Harrisburg ○ USA (NC) 282-283 G 5
Harrisburg ○ USA (NE) 262-263 C 3
Harrisburg ○ USA (OR) 244-245 B 6
Harrisburg ☆ USA (PA) 280-281 K 3
Harris Hill ○ CDN (ONT) 234-235 J 6
Harris Lake ○ AUS 176-177 G 5
Harrismith ○ ZA 220-221 J 4
Harrison ○ USA (AR) 276-277 B 4
Harrison ○ USA (ID) 250-251 C 4
Harrison ○ USA (MI) 272-273 E 3
Harrison ○ USA (MT) 250-251 H 6
Harrison ○ USA (NE) 262-263 C 2
Harrison ○ USA (OH) 280-281 B 4
Harrison, Cape ▲ CDN 36-37 V 7
Harrison Bay ≈ 20-21 O 1
Harrisonburg ○ USA (LA) 268-269 J 5
Harrisonburg ○ USA (VA) 280-281 H 5
Harrison Hot Springs ○ CDN (BC) 230-231 H 4
Harrison Islands ⌒ CDN 24-25 b 6
Harrison Lake ○ CDN (BC) 230-231 H 4
Harrison Mills ○ CDN (BC) 230-231 H 4
Harrison Pass ▲ USA (NV) 246-247 K 3
Harrisonville ○ USA (MO) 274-275 D 6
Harrisonville ○ USA (OH) 280-281 D 4
Harris Reservoir, R. L. < USA (AL) 284-285 E 3
Harriston ○ CDN (ONT) 238-239 E 5
Harrisville ○ USA (MI) 272-273 F 3
Harrisville ○ USA (WI) 270-271 J 7
Harrisville ○ USA (WV) 280-281 E 4
Harrodsburg ○ USA (KY) 276-277 L 3
Harrogate ○ CDN (BC) 230-231 N 3
Harrogate ○•• GB 90-91 G 5
Harrogate ○ USA (TN) 282-283 D 4
Harrold ○ USA (SD) 260-261 G 2
Harrold ○ USA (TX) 264-265 E 4
Harrop ○ CDN (BC) 230-231 M 4
Harrow ○ AUS 180-181 F 4
Harrowby ○ CDN (MAN) 234-235 B 4
Harrowby Bay ≈ 24-25 H 5
Harrow Kingsville ○ CDN (ONT) 238-239 C 6
Ḥar Rūd ~ IR 128-129 N 5
Harry's Harbour ○ CDN (NFL) 242-243 N 3
Harry S. Truman Reservoir < USA (MO) 274-275 E 6
Harry Strunk Lake ○ USA (NE) 262-263 F 4
Harsāni ○ IND 138-139 C 7
Harsē, mys ▲ RUS 108-109 P 6
Harsin ○• IR 134-135 B 1
Harşit Çayı ~ TR 128-129 H 2
Harstad ○ N 86-87 H 2
Harsūd ○ IND 138-139 F 8
Hart ○ USA (TX) 264-265 B 4
Hart, Cape ▲ AUS 180-181 D 3
Hart, Lake ○ AUS 178-179 D 6
Hart, Mount ▲ CDN 20-21 U 5
Har Tavor • IL 130-131 D 1
Hartbeesfontein ○ ZA 220-221 H 3
Hart Dyke, Monte ▲ RCH 80 C 6
Hartebeestrivier ~ ZA 220-221 E 4
Hårteigen ▲ N 86-87 C 6
Hartell ○ CDN (ALB) 232-233 D 5
Hartford ○ USA (AL) 284-285 E 5
Hartford ○ USA (AR) 276-277 A 5
Hartford ○ USA (KY) 276-277 J 3
Hartford ○ USA (SD) 260-261 K 3
Hartford ○ USA (WI) 274-275 K 1
Hartford ☆• USA (CT) 280-281 O 2
Hartford City ○ USA (IN) 274-275 N 4
Hartington ○ USA (NE) 262-263 J 2
Hartland ○ CDN (NB) 240-241 H 4
Hartland ○ USA (ME) 278-279 M 4
Hartland ○ USA (WV) 280-281 E 5
Hartlepool ○ GB 90-91 G 4
Hartley ○ USA (IA) 274-275 C 1
Hartley ○ USA (TX) 264-265 B 3
Hartley Bay ○ CDN (BC) 228-229 E 3
Hartley Safari Area ⊥ ZW 218-219 E 3
Hartline ○ USA (WA) 244-245 F 3
Hartmannberge ▲ NAM 216-217 B 8
Hart Mount ▲ CDN (MAN) 234-235 B 2
Hart Mountain ▲ USA (OR) 244-245 F 8
Hart Mountain National Antelope Refuge ⊥ • USA (OR) 244-245 F 8
Hartney ○ CDN (MAN) 234-235 C 5
Hartola ○ FIN 88-89 J 6
Hart River ~ CDN 20-21 W 4
Hartseer ○ NAM 216-217 D 10
Hartsel ○ USA (CO) 254-255 K 4
Hartselle ○ USA (AL) 284-285 D 2
Hartsfield ○ USA (GA) 284-285 G 5
Hartshorne ○ USA (OK) 264-265 J 4
Harts Range ○ AUS 178-179 C 2
Harts Range ▲ AUS 178-179 C 2
Hartsrivier ~ ZA 220-221 G 3
Hartsville ○ USA (SC) 284-285 K 2
Hartsville ○ USA (TN) 276-277 J 4
Hartūm, al- ★•• SUD 200-201 F 5
Hartville ○ USA (MO) 276-277 C 3
Hartwell ○ USA (GA) 284-285 H 2
Hartwell Lake < USA (SC) 284-285 H 2
Hartwood ○ USA (VA) 280-281 J 5
Harty ○ CDN (ONT) 236-237 F 3
Hartz Mountains ▲ CDN 24-25 e 4
Haruku ○ RI 166-167 E 3
Haruku, Pulau ⌒ RI 166-167 E 3
Hārūnābād ○ PK 138-139 D 5
Harur ○ IND 140-141 H 4
Har-Us ○ MAU 116-117 F 11
Har Us nuur ○ MAU 146-147 L 1
Harūt ○ Y 132-133 H 5
Hārūt Rūd ~ AFG 134-135 J 2
Harvard ○ USA (CA) 248-249 H 5
Harvard ○ USA (ID) 250-251 C 4
Harvard ○ USA (IL) 274-275 K 2
Harvard ○ USA (NE) 262-263 H 4
Harvest Home ○ AUS 174-175 J 7
Harvey ○ AUS 176-177 C 6
Harvey ○ USA (ND) 258-259 H 4
Harvey, Lake ○ AUS 176-177 D 5
Harvey Junction ○ CDN (QUE) 238-239 N 2
Harward Øer ⌒ GRØ 26-27 R 5
Harwich ○ GB 90-91 H 6
Harwill ○ CDN (MAN) 234-235 F 3
Harwood ○ USA (ND) 258-259 L 5
Harwood ○ USA (TX) 266-267 K 4
Haryana □ IND 138-139 E 5
Haryjalah ○ RUS 110-111 J 5
Haryn' ~ BY 94-95 K 5
Harz ▲ D 92-93 L 3
Hāš ○ IR 134-135 J 4
Ḥasā', al- ▲ KSA 130-131 L 4
Ḥasā', Ğabal al- ▲ Y 132-133 D 7
Ḥasā, Wādī l- ~ JOR 130-131 E 2
Hašaat ○ MAU 148-149 J 5
Ḥaṣab, al- ○ OM 134-135 G 5
Hasaka, al- ☆ SYR 128-129 J 4
Hasama ○ J 152-153 J 5
Hasan ○ RUS 122-123 D 7
Ḥasanābād ○ IR 134-135 E 3
Ḥasanābād ○ IR (ESF) 134-135 E 2
Ḥasanābād ○ IR (TEH) 136-137 B 7
Hasan al Halqim, Bi'r < LAR 192-193 J 1
Hasan Daǧı ▲ TR 128-129 F 3
Hasan Kale ∴• TR 128-129 J 2
Hasankeyf ○ TR 128-129 J 4
Hasān Langī, Rūdḫāne-ye ~ IR 134-135 G 5
Hasanparti ○ IND 138-139 G 10
Hasanpur ○ IND 138-139 G 5
Hasavjurt ○ RUS 126-127 G 6
Ḥasawiya Fauqāni ○ SYR 128-129 J 4
Hasenpoth = Aizpute ○•• LV 94-95 G 3
Hashab ○ SUD 200-201 B 6
Ḥasi, al- ○ Y 132-133 F 6
Ḥasib, Abū l- ☆ IRQ 130-131 K 2
Hasil, Pulau ⌒ RI 164-165 L 4
Hāsilpur ○ PK 138-139 D 5
Hāšimiya, al- ☆ IRQ 128-129 L 6
Haskanit ○ SUD 206-207 H 3
Haskell ○ USA (OK) 264-265 J 3
Haskell ○ USA (TX) 264-265 E 5
Haskovo ○ BG 102-103 D 7
Ḥašm ad-Dibi ▲ KSA 130-131 K 5
Ḥasmat 'Umar, Bi'r < SUD 200-201 G 2
Hasnābād ○ IND 142-143 F 4
Ḥasr, Ğazīrat ⌒ KSA 132-133 B 4
Hassa ☆ TR 128-129 G 4
Hassan ○ IND 140-141 G 4
Hassan-Addakhil, Barrage < MA 188-189 J 5
Hassane, Hassi < MA 188-189 K 5
Hassayampa River ~ USA (AZ) 256-257 C 5
Hassela ○ S 86-87 H 5
Hassel Highway II AUS 176-177 E 6
Hassel National Park ⊥ AUS 176-177 E 7
Hassel Sound ≈ 24-25 W 1
Hasselt ☆ B 92-93 H 3
Hassi Bahbah ○ DZ 190-191 D 3
Hassi Bel Guebbour ○ DZ 190-191 F 6
Hassi el Ghella ○ DZ 188-189 L 3
Hassi Messaoud ○ DZ 190-191 F 5
Hassi-Onuz ○ MA 188-189 F 6
Hassi R'Mel ○ DZ 190-191 D 4
Hässleholm ○ S 86-87 F 8
Hassman ○ USA (MN) 270-271 E 4
Hastah ~ RUS 110-111 X 6
Hastah ~ RUS 110-111 N 3
Hastings ○ AUS 180-181 H 5
Hastings ○ CDN (ONT) 238-239 H 4
Hastings ○ GB 90-91 H 6
Hastings ○ NZ 182 F 3
Hastings ○ USA (FL) 286-287 H 2
Hastings ○ USA (MI) 272-273 D 5
Hastings ○ USA (MN) 270-271 F 6
Hastings ○ USA (NE) 262-263 H 4
Hastings, Port ○ CDN (NS) 240-241 O 5
Hastings River ~ AUS 178-179 M 6
Haštpar ○ IR 128-129 N 4
Hastrūd ○ IR 128-129 M 4
Hasty ○ USA (CO) 254-255 N 5
Hašuri ○ GE 126-127 E 7
Hasvik ○ N 86-87 L 1
Haswell ○ USA (CO) 254-255 M 5
Hasyn ~ RUS 120-121 O 3
Ḥaṭab, Bi'r < SUD 200-201 F 2
Hat'ae Do ⌒ ROK 150-151 E 10
Hatanbulag = Ërgël ○ MAU 148-149 J 6
Hatanga ○ RUS 108-109 e 6
Hatanga ~ RUS 108-109 f 5
Hatangskij zaliv ≈ 110-111 F 3
Hatansuudal ○ MAU 148-149 E 5
Hatay (Antakya) ☆ TR 128-129 G 4
Hatch ○ USA (NM) 256-257 H 6
Hatch ○ USA (UT) 254-255 C 6
Hatchel ○ USA (TX) 266-267 H 2
Hatches Creek ○ AUS 174-175 C 7
Hatchet Lake ○ CDN 30-31 S 6
Hatchet Mountains ▲ USA (NM) 256-257 G 7
Hatchet Peak, Big ▲ USA (NM) 256-257 G 7
Hatchie River ~ USA (MS) 268-269 M 2
Hatchie River ~ USA (TN) 276-277 F 5
Hat Creek ○ USA (WY) 252-253 O 4
Hateg ○ RO 102-103 C 5
Hatfield ○ AUS 180-181 G 2
Hatfield ○ CDN (SAS) 232-233 O 4
Hatgal ○ MAU 148-149 E 2
Hathaway ○ USA (MT) 250-251 N 5
Hat Head National Park ⊥ AUS 178-179 M 6
Hathras ○ IND 138-139 G 6
Hatia ~ BD 142-143 G 4
Hatia Islands ⌒ BD 142-143 G 4
Hà Tiên ○• VN 158-159 H 5
Hatikali ○ IND 142-143 H 3
Hatilah ○ AUS 174-175 J 7
Hatillo, El ○ YV 60-61 J 2
Ḥātim, al- ○ UAE 134-135 F 6
Hatiman ○ J 152-153 G 7
Hà Tĩnh ☆ VN 156-157 D 7
Hatkamba ○ IND 140-141 E 2
Hat Nai Yang National Park ⊥ THA 158-159 E 6
Hato Corozal ○ CO 60-61 F 4
Hatohud ○ RI 166-167 C 6
Hatra ∴• IRQ 128-129 K 5
Hatscher, Cerro ▲ RA 80 D 4
Hatta ○ IND 138-139 G 7
Hattah ○ AUS 180-181 G 3
Hattah-Kulkyne National Park ⊥ AUS 180-181 G 3
Hatteras ○ USA (NC) 282-283 M 5
Hatteras, Cape ▲ USA (NC) 282-283 M 5
Hatteras Abyssal Plain ≃ 6-7 B 5
Hatteras Island ⌒ USA (NC) 282-283 M 5
Hatteras National Seashore, Cape ⊥ USA (NC) 282-283 M 5
Hattfjelldal ○ N 86-87 F 4
Hattiesburg ○ USA (MS) 268-269 L 5
Hattieville ○ BH 52-53 K 3
Hatton ○ CDN (SAS) 232-233 J 5
Hatton ○ USA (ND) 258-259 K 4
Hatton ○ USA (WA) 244-245 G 4
Hatton-Dikoya ○ CL 140-141 J 7
Hattusas ••• TR 128-129 F 3
Ḥatūnābād ○ IR 134-135 F 3
Ḥatūnīya ○ SYR 128-129 J 4
Hatvan ○ H 92-93 P 5
Haty ○ RUS 118-119 H 4
Hat Yai ○• THA 158-159 F 7
Hatygyn-Uèlete ~ RUS 110-111 L 3
Hatymy ~ RUS 118-119 M 7
Hatyng-Jurjah ~ RUS 118-119 M 4
Hatyngnah ○ RUS (MAG) 120-121 O 2
Hatyngnah ○ RUS (SAH) 110-111 d 6
Hatyngnah ○ RUS (SAH) 110-111 S 6
Hatynnah ~ RUS 110-111 Y 5
Hatyrka ○ RUS 112-113 S 5
Hatyrka ~ RUS 112-113 R 5
Hatystyr ○ RUS 118-119 M 6
Hatzfeldhafen ○ PNG 183 C 3
Ḥauba, al- ○ KSA 132-133 C 5
Haud ⊥ ETH 208-209 G 4
Haugesund ☆ N 86-87 B 7
Ḥauḥā, al- ○ Y 132-133 C 7
Hauhui ○ SOL 184 I e 3
Haukeligrend ○ N 86-87 C 7
Haukivesi ○ FIN 88-89 K 5
Haukivuori ○ FIN 88-89 J 5
Haultain River ~ CDN 34-35 C 2
Haumonía ○ RA 76-77 G 4
Ḥaur, al- ○ Q 134-135 D 6
Ḥaura, al- ○ Y 132-133 E 7
Ḥaura, Nahr al- ~ IRQ 128-129 M 7
Ḥaur 'Abdallāh ≈ 134-135 C 4
Hauraha ○ SOL 184 I e 4
Hauraki Gulf ≈ 182 E 2
Haur al-Habbānīya < IRQ 128-129 K 6
Haur al-Hammār ○ IRQ 130-131 K 2
Haur al-Hawīza ○ IRQ 128-129 M 7
Haurān, Wādī ~ IRQ 128-129 K 6
Haur as-Sa'dīya ○ IRQ 128-129 M 6
Haur aš-Šubaika ○ IRQ 128-129 L 6
Ḥaur Dayāt ~ SUD 200-201 H 2
Ḥaur Fakkān ○ UAE 134-135 G 6
Ḥaur Ğamūqa ○ IRQ 128-129 M 7
Hauser Lake ○ USA (MT) 250-251 H 5
Haut, Isle au ⌒ USA (ME) 278-279 N 4
Hautajärvi ○ FIN 88-89 L 3
Ḥautama, al- ⌒ Y 132-133 C 6
Hautat Bani Tamim ○ KSA 130-131 K 6
Hautavaara ○ RUS 88-89 M 5
Haute-Kotto □ RCA 206-207 E 5
Haute-Normandie □ F 90-91 H 7
Hauterive ○ CDN 38-39 K 4
Haut-Mbomou □ RCA 206-207 G 5
Hauts Plateaux de l'Ouest ▲ CAM 204-205 H 5
Haut-Zaïre □ ZRE 210-211 K 2
Hauz-Han ○ TM 136-137 G 6
Hauz-Hanskoe vodohranilišče < TM 136-137 G 6
Ḥāv ○ IR 128-129 M 5
Havana ○ USA (AR) 276-277 B 5
Havana ○ USA (FL) 286-287 E 1
Havana ○ USA (IL) 274-275 H 4
Havana ○ USA (ND) 258-259 K 6
Havana = La Habana ★••• C 54-55 D 3
Havast ○ US 136-137 L 4
Havasu, Lake ○ USA (CA) 248-249 K 5
Havasupai Indian Reservation ⅄ USA (AZ) 256-257 C 2
Havchināl ○ IND 140-141 F 3
Have Etoe ○ GH 202-203 L 6
Havel ~ D 92-93 M 2
Havelī ○ PK 138-139 D 4
Havelīān ○ PK 138-139 D 2
Haveli Baladur Shāh ○ PK 138-139 D 4
Havelock ○ CDN (ONT) 238-239 H 4
Havelock ○ CDN (QUE) 238-239 M 3
Havelock ○ NZ 182 D 4
Havelock ○ USA (NC) 282-283 L 6
Havelock Island ⌒ IND 140-141 L 4
Haven ○ USA (KS) 262-263 J 7
Haven, Cape ▲ CDN 36-37 R 3
Havensville ○ USA (KS) 262-263 K 5
Haverfordwest ○ GB 90-91 E 6
Haverhill ○ USA (NH) 278-279 K 5
Hāveri ○ IND 140-141 F 3
Haviland Bay ≈ 24-25 d 7
Havirga ○ MAU 148-149 L 5
Havlíčkův Brod ○ CZ 92-93 N 4
Havøysund ○ N 86-87 M 1
Havre ○ USA (MT) 250-251 K 3
Havre, Le ○ F 90-91 H 7
Havre-Aubert ○ CDN (QUE) 242-243 G 5
Havrylivka ○ UA 102-103 K 3
Havza ☆ TR 128-129 F 2
Hawaii □ USA (HI) 288 K 5
Hawaii ⌒ USA (HI) 288 K 5
Hawaiian Islands ⌒ USA (HI) 288 F 2
Hawaiian Ridge ≃ 48-49 B 6
Hawaii Volcanoes National Park ⊥• USA (HI) 288 K 5
Hawaii Volcanoes National Park ⊥••• USA (HI) 288 K 5
Hawal, River ~ WAN 204-205 K 3
Hawār, Ğazīrat ⌒ BRN 134-135 D 6
Hawarden ○ CDN (SAS) 232-233 M 4
Hawarden ○ USA (IA) 274-275 B 2
Hawea, Lake ○ NZ 182 B 6
Hawera ○ NZ 182 E 3
Hawesville ○ USA (KY) 276-277 J 3
Hawi ○ USA (HI) 288 K 4
Hawick ○ GB 90-91 F 4
Hawiǧat Arbān ○ IRQ 128-129 K 5
Hawke, Cape ▲ AUS 180-181 M 2
Hawke Bay ≈ 182 F 3
Hawke Island ⌒ CDN 38-39 R 2
Hawker ○ AUS 178-179 E 6
Hawke River ~ CDN 38-39 Q 2
Hawkes, Mount ▲ ARK 16 E 0
Hawke's Bay ○ CDN (NFL) 242-243 L 2
Hawkesbury ○ CDN (ONT) 238-239 L 3
Hawkesbury Island ⌒ CDN (BC) 228-229 E 3
Hawkesbury Point ▲ AUS 174-175 C 2
Hawk Hill Lake ○ CDN 30-31 U 5
Hawk Inlet ○ USA 32-33 C 2
Hawkins ○ USA (TX) 264-265 J 6

Hawkins o USA (WI) 270-271 H 5
Hawkins Island ⌒ USA 20-21 R 6
Hawkinsville o USA (GA) 284-285 G 4
Hawk Junction o CDN (ONT) 236-237 D 4
Hawk Lake o CDN (ONT) 234-235 K 5
Hawk Point o USA (MO) 274-275 G 6
Hawks o USA (MI) 272-273 F 2
Hawk's, Cape ▲ CDN 26-27 O 4
Hawksbill ▲ USA (VA) 280-281 H 5
Hawk Springs o USA (WY) 252-253 O 5
Hawley o USA (CO) 254-255 M 6
Hawley o USA (MN) 270-271 B 4
Hawley o USA (PA) 280-281 L 2
Hawley o USA (TX) 264-265 E 6
Haw River ~ USA (NC) 282-283 H 5
Hawston o ZA 220-221 D 7
Hawthorne o USA (FL) 286-287 G 2
Hawthorne o USA (NV) 246-247 G 5
Haxtun o USA (CO) 254-255 N 3
Hay o AUS 180-181 H 3
Hay, Cape ▲ CDN 24-25 g 4
Hay, Mount ▲ AUS 176-177 M 1
Hay, Mount ▲ CDN 20-21 W 7
Haya o RI 166-167 E 3
Haya o SUD 200-201 H 3
Haya, Tanjung ▲ RI 166-167 E 3
Haya'er o VRC 144-145 J 2
Haybān o SUD 206-207 K 3
Hayden o USA (CO) 254-255 H 3
Hayden o USA (ID) 250-251 C 4
Hayes o USA (LA) 268-269 H 6
Hayes o USA (SD) 260-261 E 2
Hayes, Mount ▲ USA 20-21 R 5
Hayes Center o USA (NE) 262-263 E 4
Hayes Creek o AUS 172-173 K 2
Hayes Fiord ≈ 26-27 M 4
Hayes Halvø ⌣ GRØ 26-27 Q 4
Hayes River ~ CDN 30-31 W 2
Hayes River ~ CDN 34-35 K 2
Hayfield o PNG 183 B 2
Hayfield o USA (MN) 270-271 F 7
Hayfield Lake o USA (CA) 248-249 J 6
Häyk' o ETH 208-209 D 3
Häyk' Häyk' o ETH 208-209 D 3
Haykota o ER 200-201 H 5
Hayla, Wādī ~ OM 132-133 H 5
Hay Lake Indian Reserve ✕ CDN 30-31 K 6
Hay Lakes o CDN (ALB) 232-233 E 2
Haylow o USA (GA) 284-285 H 6
Haymana ☆ TR 128-129 E 3
Hayman Island ⌒ AUS 174-175 K 7
Haymarket o USA (VA) 280-281 J 5
Haymond o USA (TX) 266-267 D 3
Haynesville o USA (LA) 268-269 G 4
Haynesville o USA (ME) 278-279 O 3
Hayneville o USA (AL) 284-285 D 4
Hayneville o USA (GA) 284-285 G 4
Hayrabolu ☆ TR 128-129 B 2
Hay River ~ AUS 178-179 D 2
Hay River o• CDN 30-31 M 5
Hay River ~ CDN 30-31 K 6
Hays o CDN (ALB) 232-233 G 5
Hays o USA (KS) 262-263 G 6
Hays o USA (MT) 250-251 L 4
Haysardah o RUS 110-111 U 6
Haysi o USA (VA) 280-281 D 6
Hayspor t o CDN (BC) 228-229 D 2
Hay Springs o USA (NE) 262-263 D 2
Haystack Mount ▲ USA 20-21 O 4
Haystack Peak ▲ USA (UT) 254-255 B 4
Haysville o USA (KS) 262-263 J 7
Hayti o USA (MO) 276-277 F 4
Hayti o USA (SD) 260-261 J 2
Hayward o USA (CA) 248-249 B 2
Hayward o USA (WI) 270-271 G 4
Haywood Channel ≈ 142-143 H 6
Hay al-Mahatta o KSA 130-131 K 5
Ḥaz'aliya an-Našwa o IRQ 130-131 K 2
Hazar, Wādī ~ Y 132-133 F 5
Ḥazarābād o IR 136-137 C 6
Hazard o USA (KY) 276-277 M 3
Hazard o USA (NE) 262-263 G 3
Hazārībāg o• IND 142-143 D 4
Hazāribāg National Park ⊥ IND 142-143 D 3
Hazāribāg Plateau ▲ IND 142-143 D 4
Hazārmani o AFG 136-137 K 7
Hazel o CDN (MAN) 234-235 G 5
Hazel o USA (KY) 276-277 G 4
Hazel Green o USA (KY) 276-277 M 3
Hazel Green o USA (WI) 274-275 H 2
Hazelton o CDN 32-33 G 4
Hazelton o USA (ND) 258-259 G 5
Hazelton Mountains ▲ CDN 32-33 F 4
Hazelview Summit ▲ USA (CA) 246-247 B 2
Hazen o USA (AR) 276-277 D 6
Hazen o USA (ND) 258-259 F 4
Hazen o USA (NV) 246-247 F 4
Hazen, Lake o CDN 26-27 P 3
Hazen Bay ≈ 20-21 H 6
Hazen Land ⊥ GRØ 26-27 e 2
Hazenmore o CDN (SAS) 232-233 L 6
Hazen Strait ≈ 24-25 Q 2
Hazeva, 'En o IL 130-131 D 2
Hazipur o IND 142-143 D 3
Hazlehurst o USA (GA) 284-285 H 5
Hazlehurst o USA (MS) 268-269 K 5
Hazlet o CDN (SAS) 232-233 K 5
Hazleton o USA (PA) 280-281 L 3
Hazlett, Lake o AUS 172-173 J 6
Ḥazm, al- o Y 132-133 D 5
Hazorasp ☆ US 136-137 G 4
Hazrat-e Soltān o AFG 136-137 K 6
Hazro o PK 138-139 D 3
Hažuu-Us o MAU 148-149 H 5
Ḥazzān Aswān <• ET 194-195 F 5
Headingley o CDN (MAN) 234-235 F 5
Headingly o AUS 178-179 E 1
Headland o USA (AL) 284-285 E 5
Headlands o ZW 218-219 G 4
Head of Bay d'Espoir o CDN (NFL) 242-243 N 5
Head of Bight ≈ 176-177 L 5
Headquarters o USA (ID) 250-251 D 5
Headquarters o USA (NM) 256-257 J 6
Head Smashed-in Bison Jump ••• CDN (ALB) 232-233 E 6
Heafford Junction o USA (WI) 270-271 J 5
Healesville o AUS 180-181 H 4
Healey Lake o CDN 30-31 Q 3
Healton o USA (OK) 264-265 G 4
Healy o USA 20-21 Q 5
Healy o USA (KS) 262-263 F 6
Heany Junction o ZW 218-219 E 5
Heard Island ⌒ AUS 12 F 10
Hearne o CDN (SAS) 232-233 N 5
Hearne o USA (TX) 266-267 L 3
Hearst o CDN (ONT) 236-237 E 3
Hearst Island ⌒ ARK 16 G 30
Hearst San Simeon State Historic Monument • USA (CA) 248-249 C 4
Heart Butte o USA (MT) 250-251 G 3
Heart River ~ USA (ND) 258-259 F 5
Heart's Content o CDN (NFL) 242-243 P 5
Heath, Río ~ BOL 70-71 C 3
Heathcote o AUS 180-181 H 4
Heatherdown o CDN (ALB) 232-233 D 2
Heath Steele o CDN (NB) 240-241 J 3
Heavener o USA (OK) 264-265 K 4
H. E. Bailey Turnpike II USA (OK) 264-265 F 4
Hebbale o IND 140-141 F 4
Hebbronville o USA (TX) 266-267 J 6
Hebburli o IND 140-141 F 4
Hebei ▫ VRC 154-155 J 2
Hebel o AUS 178-179 J 5
Heber o USA (AZ) 256-257 E 4
Hebera o RI 166-167 E 2
Heber City o USA (UT) 254-255 D 3
Heber Springs o USA (AR) 276-277 C 5
Hebert o USA (LA) 268-269 J 4
Hébertville o CDN (QUE) 240-241 D 2
Hebgen Lake o USA (MT) 250-251 H 7
Hebi o VRC 154-155 J 4
Hebo o USA (OR) 244-245 B 5
Hebri o IND 140-141 F 4
Hebrides, Sea of the ≈ 90-91 D 3
Hebron o CDN 36-37 S 5
Hebron o USA (IN) 274-275 L 3
Hebron o USA (MS) 268-269 L 5
Hebron o USA (ND) 258-259 E 5
Hebron o USA (NE) 262-263 J 4
Hebron = Hevron ☆ IL 130-131 D 2
Hebron, Mount o USA (CA) 246-247 C 2
Hebron Fiord ≈ 36-37 S 5
Heby ☆ S 86-87 H 7
Hecate o CDN (BC) 230-231 C 4
Hecate Strait ≈ 32-33 E 5
Hecate Strait ≈ CDN 228-229 C 2
Hecelchakán o• MEX 52-53 J 1
Heceta Island ⌒ USA 32-33 D 4
Hechevarria o C 54-55 H 4
Hechi o VRC 156-157 F 4
Hechuan o VRC 154-155 E 6
Hechun o VRC 156-157 G 6
Heckford Bank ≈ 158-159 D 5
Hecla o CDN (MAN) 234-235 G 3
Hecla o USA (SD) 260-261 H 1
Hecla and Griper Bay ≈ 24-25 P 2
Hecla Island ⌒ CDN (MAN) 234-235 G 3
Hecla Provincial Park ⊥ CDN (MAN) 234-235 G 3
Hectanooga o CDN (NS) 240-241 J 6
Hector o USA (AR) 276-277 C 5
Hector o USA (MN) 270-271 D 6
Hector, Mount ▲ CDN (ALB) 232-233 B 4
Hectorspruit o ZA 220-221 K 2
Hector Tejada o PE 70-71 B 4
Hedaru o EAT 212-213 F 6
Heddal stavkirke •• N 86-87 D 7
Hede o S 86-87 F 5
Hedenäset o S 86-87 L 3
Hedgesville o USA (WV) 280-281 J 4
Hediondas, Las o RCH 76-77 C 5
Hedi SK ~ VRC 156-157 G 6
Hedley o CDN (BC) 230-231 J 4
Hedley o USA (TX) 264-265 D 4
Heerenveen o NL 92-93 H 2
Heer Land ⊥ N 84-85 K 4
Heerlen o NL 92-93 H 3
Heezen Fracture Zone ≃ 14-15 Q 13
Hefa ☆• IL 130-131 D 1
Hefar Qesari ∴• IL 130-131 D 1
Hefei ☆ VRC 154-155 K 6
Hefeng o VRC 156-157 G 2
Heffley Creek o CDN (BC) 230-231 J 3
Heflin o USA (AL) 284-285 E 3
Hegang o VRC 150-151 H 4
Heggadadevankote o IND 140-141 G 4
Hegigio River ~ PNG 183 B 4
Heguri-shima ⌒ J 152-153 G 6
Hehua o VRC 154-155 G 6
Heiau o Kalalea o USA (HI) 288 K 6
Heide o D 92-93 K 1
Heidelberg o•• D 92-93 K 4
Heidelberg o USA (MS) 268-269 M 5
Heidelberg o ZA (CAP) 220-221 E 7
Heidelberg o ZA (TRA) 220-221 J 3
Heiden, Port ≈ 22-23 R 4
Heidenheim an der Brenz o D 92-93 L 4
Hei-gawa ~ J 152-153 J 5
Height of Land ▲ USA (ON) 278-279 K 3
Heihe o VRC 150-151 F 2
Hei He ~ VRC 154-155 A 2
Heilbron o ZA 220-221 H 3
Heilbronn o• D 92-93 K 4
Heilongjiang ▫ VRC 150-151 E 4
Heilong Jiang ~ VRC 150-151 F 3
Heilprin Gletscher ⊂ GRØ 26-27 S 5
Heilprin Land ⊥ GRØ 26-27 h 3
Heilsberg = Lidzbark Warmiński o• PL 92-93 Q 1
Heimaey ⌒ IS 86-87 c 3
Heimahe o VRC 144-145 M 2
Heinola o FIN 88-89 J 6
Heinsburg o CDN (ALB) 232-233 H 2
Heinze Chaung ≈ 158-159 D 3
Ḥeirābād o AFG 136-137 K 6
Heirane < DZ 188-189 L 7
Heishan SK ~ VRC 154-155 J 6
Heisler o CDN (ALB) 232-233 F 3
Heist, Knokke- o• B 92-93 G 3
Heitoraí o BR 72-73 F 3
Heitske o RI 166-167 K 5
Hejaz = Hiğāz, al- ▲ KSA 130-131 E 4
Hejdžanskij hrebet ▲ RUS 120-121 L 4
Hejgijaha ~ RUS 114-115 L 2
Hejian o VRC 154-155 K 2
Hejiang o VRC (GDG) 156-157 G 6
Hejiang o VRC (SIC) 156-157 D 2
Hejin o VRC 154-155 G 4
Hejing o VRC 146-147 H 4
Hějjaha ~ RUS 108-109 K 7
Hejsa, ostrov ⌒ RUS 84-85 e 2
Hěkčekit-Sene ~ RUS 108-109 d 7
Hekimhan ☆ TR 128-129 G 3
Hekla ▲ IS 86-87 d 2
Hekou o VRC (GAN) 154-155 C 3
Hekou o VRC (HUB) 154-155 H 6
Hekou o VRC (YUN) 156-157 C 5
Helagsfjället ▲ S 86-87 F 5
Helaliturku, ozero o RUS 108-109 X 5
Hel-Amkanni, gora ▲ RUS 110-111 c 5
Helan o VRC 154-155 E 2
Helan Shan ▲ VRC 154-155 D 2
Helanshan Z.B. • VRC 154-155 D 2
Helder, Den o NL 92-93 H 2
Helen o USA (GA) 284-285 G 2
Helena o USA (AR) 276-277 E 6
Helena ☆ USA (MT) 250-251 G 5
Helena Island ⌒ USA (SC) 284-285 K 4
Helendale o USA (CA) 248-249 G 5
Helen Springs o AUS 174-175 B 6
Helensville o NZ 182 E 2
Helgoland ⌒ D 92-93 J 1
Helgoländer Bucht ≈ D 92-93 J 1
Helgum o S 86-87 H 5
Helheimfjord ≈ 28-29 V 3
Heliopolis ∴• ET 194-195 E 2
Helleland o N 86-87 C 7
Helleristninger ••• N 86-87 L 2
Hellesvik o N 86-87 D 5
Hellier o USA (KY) 276-277 N 3
Hellin o E 98-99 G 5
Hells Canyon • USA (OR) 244-245 J 5
Hells Canyon National Recreation Area • USA (OR) 244-245 J 5
Hells Canyon Wilderness Area ⊥ USA (OR) 244-245 J 5
Hells Gate Airtram • CDN (BC) 230-231 H 4
Hells Gate Roadhouse o AUS 174-175 E 5
Hellshire Beach ⊥• JA 54-55 G 6
Hell Ville = Andoany o RM 222-223 F 4
Helmand ▫ AFG 134-135 K 3
Helmand, Rūd-e ~ AFG 134-135 M 1
Helmcken Falls ~ CDN (BC) 230-231 J 2
Helmeringhausen o NAM 220-221 C 2
Helmond o NL 92-93 H 3
Helmsdale o GB 90-91 F 2
Helmstedt o• D 92-93 L 2
Heloise o USA (TN) 276-277 F 4
Helong o VRC 150-151 G 6
Helotes o USA (TX) 266-267 J 4
Helper o USA (UT) 254-255 E 4
Helsingborg o•• S 86-87 F 8
Helsingfors = Helsinki ★••• FIN 88-89 H 6
Helsingør o•• DK 86-87 F 8
Helsinki ★••• FIN 88-89 H 6
Helska, Mierzeja ⌣ PL 92-93 P 1
Heltonville o USA (IN) 274-275 M 6
Helvecia o RA 76-77 G 6
Helvetia o USA (WV) 280-281 F 5
Hemando o RA 78-79 H 2
Hemaruka o CDN (ALB) 232-233 G 4
Hemčik ~ RUS 116-117 E 10
Hemčik ~ RUS 124-125 Q 3
Hemet o USA (CA) 248-249 H 6
Hemingford o USA (NE) 262-263 C 2
Heming Lake o CDN 34-35 F 3
Hemingway o USA (SC) 284-285 L 3
Hemlo o CDN (ONT) 236-237 C 4
Hemlock o USA (OR) 244-245 B 5
Hemlock Grove o USA (PA) 280-281 L 2
Hemmingford o CDN (QUE) 238-239 M 3
Hemnesberget o N 86-87 F 3
Hemphill o USA (TX) 268-269 G 5
Hemphill, Cape ▲ CDN 24-25 O 2
Hempstead o USA (NY) 280-281 N 3
Hempstead o USA (TX) 266-267 L 3
Hemse o S 86-87 J 8
Hemsö o S 86-87 J 5
Hemudu Wenhua Yizhi ∴ VRC 156-157 M 2
Henan ▫ VRC 154-155 H 5
Hen and Chicken Islands ⌒ NZ 182 E 1
Henares, Río ~ E 98-99 F 4
Henasi-saki ▲ J 152-153 H 4
Henbury o AUS 176-177 M 2
Henbury Meteorite Craters • AUS 176-177 M 2
Hendek ☆ TR 128-129 D 2
Henderson o RA 78-79 J 4
Henderson o USA (IL) 274-275 H 3
Henderson o USA (KY) 276-277 H 3
Henderson o USA (LA) 268-269 J 6
Henderson o USA (MN) 270-271 E 6
Henderson o USA (NC) 282-283 J 4
Henderson o USA (NE) 262-263 J 4
Henderson o USA (NV) 248-249 K 3
Henderson o USA (NY) 278-279 E 5
Henderson o USA (TN) 276-277 G 5
Henderson o USA (TX) 264-265 K 6
Hendersonville o USA (NC) 282-283 E 5
Hendersonville o USA (TN) 276-277 J 4
Hendiğān o IR 134-135 C 3
Hendiğān, Rūdhāne-ye ~ IR 134-135 C 3
Hendon o CDN (SAS) 232-233 P 3
Hendorābi o IR 134-135 E 5
Hendorābi, Ǧazire-ye ⌒ IR 134-135 E 5
Hendricks o USA (KY) 276-277 M 3
Hendrik Ø ⌒ GRØ 26-27 Y 2
Hendriksen Strait ≈ 24-25 X 2
Hendrik Verwoerddam < ZA 220-221 G 5
Hendrik Verwoerd Dam Nature Reserve ⊥ ZA 220-221 G 5
Hendrina o ZA 220-221 J 3
Hendrix Lake o CDN (BC) 228-229 O 4
Hengām, Ǧazire-ye ⌒ IR 134-135 F 5
Ḥengān o AFG 136-137 L 7
Henganofi o PNG 183 C 4
Hengchun o RC 156-157 M 5
Hengduan Shan ▲ VRC 144-145 M 7
Hengelo o NL 92-93 J 2
Hengshan o VRC (HUN) 156-157 H 3
Hengshan ▲ VRC (HUN) 156-157 H 3
Hengshan • VRC (HUN) 156-157 H 3
Hengshan • VRC (SHA) 154-155 H 2
Hengshui o VRC 154-155 J 3
Heng Xian o VRC 156-157 F 5
Hengyang o VRC 156-157 H 3
Heničes'k o UA 102-103 J 4
Henley Falls o USA (MN) 270-271 C 6
Henlopen, Cape ▲ USA (DE) 280-281 L 5
Hennaya o DZ 188-189 L 3
Hennebont o F 90-91 F 8
Hennenman o ZA 220-221 H 3
Hennessey o USA (OK) 264-265 G 2
Hennigsdorf o D 92-93 M 2
Henning o USA (MN) 270-271 C 4
Henribourg o CDN (SAS) 232-233 N 2
Henrietta o USA (TX) 264-265 F 5
Henrietta Maria, Cape ▲ CDN 34-35 P 3
Henriette o USA (MN) 270-271 E 5
Henri Pittier, Parque Nacional ⊥ YV 60-61 H 2
Henry o USA (ID) 252-253 G 4
Henry o USA (IL) 274-275 J 3
Henry o USA (NE) 262-263 B 3
Henry o USA (SD) 260-261 J 2
Henry, Cape ▲ CDN (BC) 228-229 B 4
Henry, Cape ▲ USA (NC) 282-283 M 4
Henryetta o USA (OK) 264-265 J 3
Henry Horton State Park ⊥ USA (TN) 276-277 J 5
Henry House o CDN (ALB) 228-229 Q 4
Henry Kater, Cape ▲ CDN 28-29 G 2
Henry Kater Peninsula ⌣ CDN 28-29 F 2
Henry Lawrence Island ⌒ IND 140-141 L 3
Henry Mountains ▲ USA (UT) 254-255 E 5
Henry River ~ AUS 176-177 C 1
Henry's Fork ~ USA (ID) 252-253 G 3
Henryville o USA (IN) 274-275 N 6
Henshaw, Lake ⌣ USA (CA) 248-249 H 6
Hěntějn nuruu ▲ MAU 148-149 H 3
Hentiesbaai o NAM 216-217 C 11
Hěntij ▫ MAU 148-149 J 3
Henvey Inlet Indian Reserve ✕ CDN (ONT) 238-239 E 3
Henzada o MYA 158-159 C 2
Hepburn o CDN (SAS) 232-233 M 3
Hepburn Lake o CDN 30-31 M 2
Hephzibah o USA (GA) 284-285 H 3
Heping o VRC 156-157 J 4
Heppner o USA (OR) 244-245 F 5
Hepu o VRC 156-157 F 6
Hepworth o CDN (ONT) 238-239 D 4
Heqing o VRC 142-143 M 2
Heraclea •• MK 100-101 H 4
Heraðsvötn ~ IS 86-87 d 2
Heraion ∴••• TR 128-129 B 4
Ḥerāme o IR 134-135 E 4
Heras, Las o RA 80 F 3
Herāt ▫ AFG 134-135 J 1
Herāt ☆• AFG (HE) 134-135 K 1
Heraz, Rūdḫāne-ye ~ IR 136-137 B 6
Herbagat o SUD 200-201 H 3
Herbang o BD 142-143 H 5
Herbert o CDN (SAS) 232-233 L 5
Herbert o NZ 182 C 6
Herbert, Mount ▲ AUS 172-173 G 4
Herbert Hoover National Historic Site • USA (IA) 274-275 G 3
Herbert Island ⌒ USA 22-23 L 6
Herbert Lake o CDN 30-31 R 6
Herbert Ø ⌒ GRØ 26-27 P 5
Herberton o AUS 174-175 H 5
Herbertpur o IND 138-139 F 4
Herbert River ~ AUS 174-175 H 6
Herbert River Falls • AUS 174-175 H 6
Herbertsdale o ZA 220-221 E 7
Herbert Vale o AUS 174-175 E 6
Herbert Wash o AUS 176-177 H 2
Herbiers, les o F 90-91 G 8
Herceg-Novi o• YU 100-101 G 3
Herchmer o CDN 34-35 J 2
Hercílio Luz o BR 74-75 F 7
Herciliópolis o BR 74-75 E 6
Hercules Bay ≈ 183 D 4
Hercules Gemstone Deposit • AUS 176-177 D 3
Herdlak ⌒ GRØ 28-29 Q 5
Herðubreið ▲ IS 86-87 e 2
Hereda, Punta ▲ PE 64-65 B 4
Heredia ☆ CR 52-53 B 6
Hereford • GB 90-91 F 5
Hereford o USA (CO) 254-255 L 3
Hereford o USA (OR) 244-245 G 6
Hereford o USA (SD) 260-261 D 2
Hereford o USA (TX) 264-265 B 4
Hereke ☆ TR 128-129 C 2
Herene, In < LAR 190-191 G 7
Hereroland ⊥ NAM 216-217 E 10
Herford o• D 92-93 K 2
Hergu ~ RUS 122-123 E 2
Herington o USA (KS) 262-263 K 6
Heriot Bay o CDN (BC) 230-231 D 3
Heris o IR 128-129 M 3
Heritage Range ▲ ARK 16 F 28
Herkimer o USA (NY) 278-279 F 5
Hěrlěn o MAU 148-149 J 4
Hěrlěn gol ~ MAU 148-149 M 3
Herlen He ~ VRC 148-149 N 3
Herluf Trolles Land ⊥ GRØ 26-27 l 2
Herman o USA (MN) 270-271 B 5
Hermanas o USA (NM) 256-257 H 7
Hermanas, Las o YV 60-61 L 3
Herma Ness ▲ GB 90-91 G 1
Hermann o USA (MO) 274-275 G 6
Hermannsburg ✕ AUS 176-177 M 1
Hermannsburg Aboriginal Land ✕ AUS 176-177 M 1
Hermanos, Cerro ▲ RCH 80 D 3
Hermanos, Islas Los ⌒ YV 60-61 J 2
Hermansville o USA (MI) 270-271 L 5
Hermantown o USA (MN) 270-271 F 4
Hermanusdorings o ZA 220-221 H 2
Hermidale o AUS 178-179 J 6
Hermiston o USA (OR) 244-245 F 5
Hermitage o USA (AR) 276-277 C 7
Hermitage o USA (MO) 276-277 B 3
Hermitage Bay ≈ 38-39 Q 5
Hermitage Bay ≈ CDN 242-243 M 5
Hermleigh o USA (TX) 264-265 D 6
Hermon o ZA 220-221 D 6
Hermopolis ∴• ET 194-195 E 4
Hermosa o USA (SD) 260-261 C 3
Hermosa, La o CO 60-61 F 5
Hermosas, Parque Nacional las ⊥ CO 60-61 D 6
Hermosillo ☆ MEX 50-51 D 3
Hernandarias o RA 76-77 H 6
Hernando o USA (MS) 268-269 L 2
Hernán Mejía Miraval o RA 76-77 F 4
Herndon o USA (VA) 280-281 J 5
Herning o DK 86-87 D 8
Hérodier, Lac o CDN 36-37 P 6
Heroica Zitácuaro o MEX 52-53 D 2
Herold o ZA 220-221 F 6
Heroldsbaai o ZA 220-221 F 7
Heron o USA (MT) 250-251 D 3
Heron Bay o CDN (ONT) 236-237 B 4
Heron Bay ≈ CDN 236-237 B 4
Heron Island ⌒ AUS 178-179 L 2
Heron Lake o USA (MN) 270-271 C 7
Heron Lake o USA (MN) 270-271 C 7
Herøy o N 86-87 F 4
Herradura o MEX 50-51 J 6
Herradura o RA 76-77 H 4
Herreid o USA (SD) 260-261 F 1
Herrera del Duque o• E 98-99 E 5
Herrera de Pisuerga o E 98-99 E 3
Herreras, Las o MEX 50-51 G 5
Herreras, Los o MEX 50-51 K 5
Herrero, Punta ▲ MEX 52-53 L 2
Herrick Center o USA (PA) 280-281 L 2
Herrick Creek ~ CDN (BC) 228-229 N 2
Herries Range ▲ AUS 178-179 L 5
Herrin o USA (IL) 276-277 F 3
Herring Cove o CDN (NS) 240-241 M 6
Herrington Lake o USA (KY) 276-277 L 3
Herschel o CDN 20-21 W 2
Herschel o CDN (SAS) 232-233 K 4
Herschel o ZA 220-221 H 5
Herschel Island ⌒ CDN 20-21 W 2
Hersfeld, Bad o• D 92-93 K 3
Hershey o USA (PA) 280-281 K 3
Herson = Cherson ☆• UA 102-103 H 4
Hertford o USA (NC) 282-283 L 4
Hertogenbosch, 's- ☆• NL 92-93 H 3
Hertugen of Orleans Land ⊥ GRØ 26-27 o 5
Hertzogville o ZA 220-221 G 4
Heruff Trolle, Kap ▲ GRØ 28-29 T 6
Herval o BR 76-77 K 2
Hervey Bay ≈ 178-179 M 3
Hervey Bay o AUS 178-179 M 3
Hervey Junction o CDN (QUE) 238-239 N 2
Herveys Range ▲ AUS 180-181 K 2
Herzliyya o IL 130-131 D 1
Herzog-Ernst-Bucht ≈ 16 F 33
Hesādi o IND 142-143 D 4
Hesārak o AFG 138-139 B 2
Heshan o VRC 156-157 H 5
Heshun o VRC 154-155 H 3
Hesperia o USA (CA) 248-249 G 5
Hesperia o USA (MI) 272-273 C 4
Hesperus Mountain ▲ USA (CO) 254-255 G 6
Hessel o USA (MI) 270-271 O 4
Hessen ▫ D 92-93 K 3
Hessfjord o N 86-87 J 2
Hess Mountains ▲ CDN 20-21 Z 5
Hess River ~ CDN 20-21 Y 5
Hester, Peak ▲ AUS 172-173 D 7
Hestkjølen ▲ N 86-87 F 4
Heta o RUS 108-109 c 6
Heta ~ RUS 108-109 c 6
Heta, Bol'šaja ~ RUS 108-109 V 8
Hetagčan ~ RUS 112-113 H 5
Hetagima o RI 166-167 K 4
Hetauda o NEP 144-145 E 7
Hetch Hetchy Aqueduct < USA (CA) 248-249 C 2
Het Kruis o ZA 220-221 D 6
Hetovo o RUS 88-89 R 5
Hettinger o USA (ND) 258-259 E 5
Hětylky ~ RUS 114-115 R 2
Heuru o SOL 184 I e 4
Heva ☆••• US 136-137 G 4
Héva, Rivière- o CDN (QUE) 236-237 K 4
Hevelândia o BR 66-67 G 5
Hevi o GH 202-203 L 6
Hevron ☆ WB 130-131 D 2
Heward o CDN (SAS) 232-233 P 6
Hewitt o USA (MN) 270-271 C 4
Hewitt o USA (TX) 266-267 K 2
Hewitt, Kap ▲ GRØ 26-27 p 8
Hexham o• GB 90-91 F 4
He Xian o VRC (ANH) 154-155 L 6
He Xian o VRC (GXI) 156-157 G 4
Hexigten Qi o VRC 148-149 N 6
Hex River Pass ▲ ZA 220-221 D 6
Hexrivierberge ▲ ZA 220-221 D 6
Hext o USA (TX) 266-267 H 3
Heyang o VRC 154-155 G 4
Heyburn o USA (ID) 252-253 E 4
Heyburn Lake o USA (OK) 264-265 H 3
Heyden o CDN (ONT) 236-237 D 6
Heydon o ZA 220-221 G 5
Heyfield o AUS 180-181 J 4
Heyu o VRC 156-157 G 5
Heyuan o VRC 156-157 J 5
Heywood o AUS 180-181 F 5
Heywood Islands ⌒ AUS 172-173 G 3
Heywood Shoal ⌒ AUS 172-173 G 2
Heyworth o USA (IL) 274-275 K 4
Hezār, Kūh-e ▲ IR 134-135 G 4
Heze o VRC 154-155 J 4
Hezhang o VRC 156-157 D 3
Hezri o IR 134-135 H 1
Hezuozhen o VRC 154-155 C 4
Hhohho o SD 220-221 K 2
Hiagtin Gol ~ VRC 144-145 L 2
Hialeah o USA (FL) 286-287 J 6
Hian o GH 202-203 J 4
Hiawatha o USA (CO) 254-255 G 3
Hiawatha o USA (KS) 262-263 L 5
Hiawatha o USA (UT) 254-255 D 4
Hibāk, al- ⊥ KSA 132-133 H 3
Hibarba ~ RUS 108-109 b 7
Hibberdene o ZA 220-221 K 5
Hibbing o USA (MN) 270-271 F 3
Hibbs, Point ▲ AUS 180-181 H 7
Hibernia Reef ⌒ AUS 172-173 F 1
Hibiny ▲ RUS 88-89 M 3
Hibis, Temple of ∴• ET 194-195 E 5
Hickiwan o USA (AZ) 256-257 C 6
Hickman o USA (KY) 276-277 F 4
Hickman o USA (NM) 256-257 H 4
Hickman, Mount ▲ CDN 32-33 E 3
Hickmann o RA 76-77 F 2
Hickory o USA (NC) 282-283 F 5
Hickory, Lake o USA (NC) 282-283 F 5
Hickory Flat o USA (MS) 268-269 L 2
Hickory Plains o USA (AR) 276-277 D 5
Hickory Ridge o USA (AR) 276-277 E 5
Hicks, Point ▲ AUS 180-181 K 4
Hicks Cays ⌒ BH 52-53 K 3
Hicks Lake o CDN 30-31 T 5
Hickson o CDN (ONT) 238-239 E 5
Hickson Lake o CDN 34-35 D 2
Hicksville o USA (OH) 280-281 B 2
Hico o USA (TX) 266-267 J 2
Hico o USA (WV) 280-281 E 5
Hida-gawa ~ J 152-153 G 7
Hidaka o J 152-153 K 3
Hidaka-sanmyaku ▲ J 152-153 K 3
Hidaldo o MEX 50-51 K 5
Hidalgo o MEX (DGO) 50-51 G 5
Hidalgo o MEX (NL) 50-51 J 5
Hidalgo ▫ MEX 52-53 E 1
Hidalgo del Parral o• MEX 50-51 G 4
Hida-sanmyaku ▲ J 152-153 G 6
Hidden Peak = Gasherbrum I ▲ PK 138-139 F 2
Hiddensee ⌒ D 92-93 M 1
Hidden Timber o USA (SD) 260-261 F 3
Hidden Valley o AUS (NT) 172-173 L 4
Hidden Valley o AUS (QLD) 174-175 J 6
Hidden Valley o AUS (QLD) 174-175 J 7
Hidden Valley National Park ⊥ AUS 172-173 J 3
Hidrelétrica Curuá-Una o BR 66-67 K 4
Hidrolândia o BR 68-69 H 4
Hierapolis ••• TR 128-129 C 4
Hierro ⌒ E 188-189 B 7
Higashi-Hiroshima o J 152-153 E 7
Higashikagura o J 152-153 K 3
Higashi-Ōsaka o J 152-153 F 7
Higashi Shina Kai = Dong Hai ≈ 154-155 N 6
Higashi-suidō ≈ 152-153 C 8
Hiğāz, al- ▲ KSA 130-131 E 4
Higgins o USA (TX) 264-265 D 2
Higginson o USA (AR) 276-277 D 5
Higginsville o AUS 176-177 F 5
High Atlas = Haut Atlas ▲ MA 9 C 2
High Bank o CDN (NS) 240-241 N 5
High Bluff o CDN (MAN) 234-235 E 4
Highbourn Cay ⌒ BS 54-55 G 2
Highbury o AUS (QLD) 174-175 G 5
Highbury o AUS (QLD) 178-179 H 2
Highbury o GUY 62-63 F 2
Highflats o ZA 220-221 K 5
Highgate o CDN (SAS) 232-233 K 3
High Hill River ~ CDN 32-33 P 3
High Island o USA (TX) 268-269 F 7
High Island ⌒ USA 22-23 Q 3
High Island ⌒ USA (MI) 272-273 D 2
Highland o USA (CA) 248-249 G 5
Highland o USA (IL) 274-275 J 6
Highland Home o USA (AL) 284-285 D 5
Highland Park o USA (IL) 274-275 L 2
Highland Peak ▲ USA (NV) 248-249 K 2
Highland Plains o AUS 174-175 D 6
Highlands o CDN (NFL) 242-243 K 4
Highlands o USA (NC) 282-283 D 5
Highlands o USA (NJ) 280-281 M 3
Highlands o USA (TX) 268-269 E 7
Highlands Hammock State Park ⊥• USA (FL) 286-287 H 4
Highland Springs o USA (VA) 280-281 J 6
High Level o CDN 30-31 L 6
Highmore o USA (SD) 260-261 G 2
High Peak ▲ GB 90-91 G 5
High Peak ▲ USA (NC) 282-283 F 5
High Plateaus = Hauts Plateaux ▲ DZ 190-191 B 4
High Point o USA (NC) 282-283 G 5
High Prairie o CDN 32-33 M 4
High River o CDN (ALB) 232-233 E 5
High Rock o BS 54-55 F 1
Highrock Indian Reserve ✕ CDN 34-35 F 3
Highrock Lake o CDN (MAN) 34-35 F 3
Highrock Lake < CDN (SAS) 34-35 D 2
High Rock Lake < USA (NC) 282-283 G 5
High Rolling Mountains ▲ RP 160-161 D 6
High Rolls o USA (NM) 256-257 K 6
High Springs o USA (FL) 286-287 G 2
Hightowers o USA (NC) 282-283 H 4
High Uintas Wilderness Area ⊥ USA (UT) 254-255 E 3
Highwood o USA (MT) 250-251 J 4
Highwood Peak ▲ USA (MT) 250-251 J 4
Highwood River ~ CDN (ALB) 232-233 D 5
Higirio, El o RCH 76-77 B 5
Hiğla o KSA 132-133 C 4
Hiğr, al- o• KSA 130-131 E 4
Higuera, La o RCH 76-77 B 5
Higüero, Punta ▲ USA (PR) 286-287 O 2
Higuerote o• YV 60-61 H 2
Higüey ☆ DOM 54-55 L 5
Hiiraan ▫ SP 208-209 G 6
Hiiumaa saar ⊥ EST 94-95 H 2
Hijar o E 98-99 G 4
Hikone o J 152-153 G 7
Hikurangi o NZ 182 E 1
Hikurangi ▲ NZ 182 G 2
Hikurangi Trench ≃ 182 F 4
Hila o RI (MAL) 166-167 E 3
Hila o RI (MAL) 166-167 D 5
Hilakondji o DY 202-203 L 6
Hilāl, Ǧabal ▲ ET 194-195 F 2
Hiland Park o USA (FL) 286-287 D 1
Hilda o CDN (ALB) 232-233 H 5
Hildale o USA (UT) 254-255 C 6
Hildesheim o•• D 92-93 K 2
Hilger o USA (MT) 250-251 K 4
Hilham o USA (TN) 276-277 K 4
Hili o UAE 134-135 F 6
Hiliardton o CDN (ONT) 236-237 J 5
Hiliomódi o GR 100-101 J 6
Hilismaetano o• RI 162-163 B 4
Hill o USA (LA) 268-269 H 4
Hill, Fort A.P. • USA (VA) 280-281 J 5
Hilla, al- ☆ IRQ 128-129 L 6
Hillabee Creek ~ USA (AL) 284-285 E 3
Hill Air Force Base ✕✕ USA (UT) 254-255 B 2
Hill City o USA (ID) 252-253 C 3
Hill City o USA (KS) 262-263 G 5
Hill City o USA (MN) 270-271 E 4
Hill City o USA (SD) 260-261 C 3
Hill Creek Extension Uintah and Ouray Indian Reservation ✕ USA (UT) 254-255 F 4
Hilléket o TCH 198-199 K 6
Hill End o• AUS 180-181 K 2
Hillerød o• DK 86-87 F 9
Hilli o IND 142-143 F 3
Hilliard o USA (FL) 286-287 H 1
Hill Island ⌒ CDN 36-37 P 3
Hill Island Lake o CDN 30-31 P 5
Hillman o USA (MI) 272-273 F 2
Hillman, Lake o AUS 176-177 D 5
Hillmond o CDN (SAS) 232-233 J 2
Hills o CDN (BC) 230-231 M 3
Hillsboro o USA (GA) 284-285 G 3
Hillsboro o USA (IL) 274-275 J 5
Hillsboro o USA (KS) 262-263 J 6
Hillsboro o USA (MO) 274-275 H 6
Hillsboro o USA (ND) 258-259 K 4
Hillsboro o USA (NM) 256-257 H 6
Hillsboro o USA (OH) 280-281 C 4
Hillsboro o USA (OR) 244-245 C 5
Hillsboro o USA (TX) 264-265 G 6
Hillsboro o USA (WI) 270-271 H 7
Hillsboro Canal < USA (FL) 286-287 J 5
Hillsborough o USA (NC) 282-283 H 4
Hillsborough o USA (NH) 278-279 K 5
Hillsborough o WG 56 E 5
Hillsborough Bay ≈ 38-39 N 5
Hillsborough Bay ≈ CDN 240-241 M 4
Hillsdale o USA (MI) 272-273 E 6
Hillsdale Lake o USA (KS) 262-263 M 6
Hillside o AUS 172-173 D 6
Hillside o USA (AZ) 256-257 C 4
Hillside National Wildlife Refuge ⊥ USA (MS) 268-269 K 3
Hillsport o CDN (ONT) 236-237 C 3
Hill Spring o CDN (ALB) 232-233 E 6
Hillston o AUS 180-181 H 2
Hillsville o USA (VA) 280-281 F 7
Hillswick o GB 90-91 G 1
Hilltop o USA (WI) 274-275 H 1
Hilo o• USA (HI) 288 K 5
Hilo Bay ≈ USA 288 K 5
Hilok ☆ RUS (CTN) 118-119 E 10
Hilok ~ RUS 116-117 O 10
Hilok ~ RUS 118-119 F 10
Hilt o USA (CA) 246-247 C 2
Hiltaba, Mount ▲ AUS 180-181 C 2
Hilton o AUS 174-175 E 7
Hilton o USA (NY) 278-279 D 5
Hilton Beach o CDN (ONT) 238-239 B 2
Hilton Head Island o USA (SC) 284-285 K 4
Hilton Head Island ⌒ USA (SC) 284-285 K 4
Hilvan ☆ TR 128-129 H 4
Hilversum o NL 92-93 H 2
Himachal Pradesh ▫ IND 138-139 F 3
Himālaya ▲ IND 144-145 C 5
Himalaya = Himalaya Shan ▲ 10-11 G 5
Himalaya = Himalaya Shan ▲ VRC 144-145 B 4
Himalaya Shan ▲ VRC 144-145 G 6
Himal Chuli ▲ NEP 144-145 E 6
Himana, Hassi < DZ 188-189 K 6
Himanka o FIN 88-89 G 4
Himarë o• AL 100-101 G 4
Himatnagar o IND 138-139 D 8
Himbirti o ER 200-201 J 5
Himeji o J 152-153 F 7
Himeji-jo Castle ••• J 152-153 F 7
Himi o J 152-153 G 6
Himki ☆ RUS 94-95 P 4
Himora o ETH 200-201 H 5
Ḥimṣ ☆ SYR 128-129 G 5
Hinatuan Passage ≈ 160-161 F 8
Hîncești ☆ MD 102-103 F 4
Hinche ☆ RH 54-55 J 5
Hinchinbrook, Cape ▲ USA 20-21 R 6
Hinchinbrook Entrance ≈ 20-21 R 6
Hinchinbrook Island ⌒ AUS 174-175 J 6
Hinchinbrook Island ⌒ USA 20-21 R 6
Hinchinbrook Island National Park ⊥ AUS 174-175 J 6
Hinckley o USA (IL) 274-275 K 3
Hinckley o USA (MN) 270-271 F 5
Hinckley o USA (MN) 270-271 F 4
Hinckley o USA (UT) 254-255 C 4
Hinckley, Mount ▲ AUS 176-177 K 3
Hincks Conservation Park ⊥ AUS 180-181 C 2
Hinda o RCB 210-211 D 6
Hindan ~ IND 138-139 F 5
Hindes o USA (TX) 266-267 J 5

Hindiktig-Hol', ozero ⊖ RUS 124-125 Q 3
Hindiya, al- ☆ IRQ 128-129 L 6
Hindmarsh, Lake ⊖ AUS 180-181 F 4
Hinds Lake ⊖ CDN (NFL) 242-243 M 4
Hindubāgh o PK 134-135 M 3
Hindukusch ▲ 138-139 B 2
Hindu Kush = Hendūkoš ▲ 10-11 G 5
Hindupur o IND 140-141 G 4
Hindustan ∪ IND 142-143 B 2
Hines o USA (FL) 286-287 F 2
Hines o USA (OR) 244-245 F 7
Hines Creek o CDN 32-33 L 3
Hinesville o USA (GA) 284-285 J 5
Hinganghāt o IND 138-139 G 9
Hinganskij zapovednik ⊥ RUS 122-123 C 4
Hingham o USA (MT) 250-251 J 3
Hinglaj o PK (BEL) 134-135 L 6
Hinglaj o • PK (BEL) 138-139 E 7
Hingol ~ PK 134-135 L 6
Hingoli o IND 138-139 F 10
Hingoraja o PK 138-139 B 6
Hinidān o PK 134-135 M 6
Hinike ~ RUS 120-121 L 2
Hinis ☆ TR 128-129 J 3
Hink Land ⊥ GRØ 26-27 l 8
Hinkleville o USA (KY) 276-277 G 3
Hinlopenrenna ≃ 84-85 J 2
Hinlopenstretet ≈ 84-85 K 2
Hinnøya ⌒ N 86-87 G 2
Hinoba-an o RP 160-161 E 8
Hino-gawa ~ J 152-153 E 7
Hinogyaung o MYA 158-159 C 2
Hinojo o RA 78-79 J 4
Hinojosa del Duque o •• E 98-99 E 5
Hinomi-saki ▲ J 152-153 E 7
Hinsdale o USA (MT) 250-251 M 3
Hinsdale o USA (NY) 278-279 C 6
Hinton o CDN (ALB) 228-229 R 3
Hinton o USA (OK) 264-265 F 3
Hinton o USA (WV) 280-281 F 6
Híos o GR 100-101 L 5
Híos ⌒ GR 100-101 L 5
Hipólito o MEX 50-51 J 5
Hipuapua Falls ~ • USA (HI) 288 J 3
Hīr o IR 136-137 B 6
Hira o IND 140-141 G 2
Hirado o • J 152-153 C 8
Hirado-shima ⌒ J 152-153 C 8
Hirafok o DZ 190-191 E 9
Hīrākūd Reservoir < IND 142-143 C 5
Hiram o USA (ME) 278-279 L 5
Hiraman ~ EAK 212-213 G 4
Hiranai o J 152-153 J 4
Hiratsuka o J 152-153 H 7
Ḫirbat al-Umbāšī ∴ • SYR 128-129 G 6
Ḫirbat Isrīya o SYR 128-129 G 5
Hirehadagalli o IND 140-141 F 3
Hiré-Watta o CI 202-203 H 6
Hirfanlı Barajı < TR 128-129 E 3
Hiripitiya o CL 140-141 J 7
Hiriyur o IND 140-141 G 4
Hirmās, Bi'r Ibn o KSA 130-131 E 3
Hirmil, al- ☆ RL 128-129 G 5
Hirna o ETH 208-209 E 4
Hiroo o J 152-153 K 3
Hirosaki o • J 152-153 J 4
Hiroshima o J (HOK) 152-153 J 3
Hiroshima ☆ • J (HIR) 152-153 E 7
Ḫirr, Wādī l- ~ IRQ 128-129 K 7
hirs'ka miscevisc' • UA 102-103 G 3
Hirs'kyj Tikyč ~ UA 102-103 F 3
Hirson o F 90-91 K 7
Hîrșova o • RO 102-103 F 5
Hirtshals o DK 86-87 D 8
Hisaka-shima ⌒ J 152-153 C 8
Hisāna, al- o KSA 132-133 B 3
Hisār o IND 138-139 E 5
Ḥisb, Ša'īb ~ IRQ 128-129 K 7
Hišig-Öndör = Maan't o MAU 148-149 F 3
Hisiu o PNG 183 D 5
Hislaviči o RUS 94-95 N 4
Hisle o USA (SD) 260-261 E 3
Ḥisn, Qal'at al- •• SYR 128-129 G 5
Ḥiṣn aṣ Šahābī o LAR 192-193 J 2
Hispaniola ⌒ 54-55 K 6
Historic Fort Delaware • USA (NY) 280-281 M 2
Historic Remains ∴ • RI 164-165 K 3
Historic Remains, Forts ∴ • RI 164-165 K 3
Historyland ∴ • USA (WI) 270-271 G 5
Ḥisw, al- o KSA 130-131 G 5
Hīt o IRQ 128-129 K 6
Hitachi o J 152-153 J 6
Hitia Sand Hills o GUY 62-63 F 3
Hitoyoshi o J 152-153 D 8
Hitra ~ N 86-87 D 5
Hiu = Île Hiu ⌒ VAN 184 II a 1
Hiu, Île = Hiu ⌒ VAN 184 II a 1
Hiuchi-nada ≈ 152-153 E 7
Hiva-Oa ⌒ F 13 O 3
Hivaro o PNG 183 B 4
Hiw o ET 194-195 F 4
Hiwarkhed o IND 138-139 F 9
Hiwassee Lake < USA (NC) 282-283 C 5
Hiwassee River ~ USA (TN) 282-283 C 5
Hixon o CDN (BC) 228-229 M 3
Hiyoshi o J 152-153 E 8
Hiyyon, Nāal ~ IL 130-131 D 2
Hizan ☆ TR 128-129 K 3
Hjälmaren ⊖ S 86-87 G 7
Hjalmar Lake ⊖ CDN 30-31 P 5
Hjargas nuur ⊖ MAU 116-117 F 11
Hjellset o N 86-87 C 5
Hjerkinn o N 86-87 D 5
Hjørring o DK 86-87 E 8
Hkākabo Rāzi ▲ MYA 142-143 K 1
Hkqingzi o MYA 142-143 H 5
Hkyenhpa o MYA 142-143 K 2
Hlabisa o ZA 220-221 K 4
Hlebarovo = Car Kalojan o BG 102-103 E 6
Hlegu o MYA 158-159 D 2
Hlobyne o UA 102-103 H 3
Hlotse o LS 220-221 J 4
Hluchiv o UA 102-103 H 2
Hluhluwe o ZA 220-221 L 4
Hluhluwe Game Reserve ⊥ ZA 220-221 L 4
Hluthi o SD 220-221 K 3
Hlybokae o BY 94-95 K 4
Hmel'nickij = Chmel'nyc'kyj ☆ UA 102-103 E 3
Hmitevskogo, poluostrov ∪ RUS 120-121 N 4
Hnalān o IND 142-143 H 4
H. N. Andersen, Kap ▲ GRØ 26-27 r 3
Hnausa o CDN (MAN) 234-235 G 4
Hnilij Tikič ~ UA 102-103 G 3
Ho ☆ GH 202-203 L 6
Hòa Bình o VN 158-159 J 2
Hòa Bình ☆ VN 156-157 D 6
Hoadley o CDN (ALB) 232-233 D 3
Hoài Nho'n o VN 158-159 K 3
Hoanib ~ NAM 216-217 B 9
Hoar, Lake ⊖ AUS 176-177 G 2
Hoare Bay ≈ 36-37 S 2
Hoarusib ~ NAM 216-217 B 9
Hoback Junction o USA (WY) 252-253 H 3
Hoba Meteorite •• NAM 216-217 D 9
Hoban o DVR 150-151 F 7
Hobart ☆ • AUS 180-181 J 7
Hobart o USA (IN) 274-275 L 3
Hobart o USA (OK) 264-265 E 3
Hobart Island ⌒ CDN 36-37 N 2
Hobbema o CDN (ALB) 232-233 E 3
Hobbs o USA (NM) 256-257 M 6
Hobbs Coast ∪ ARK 16 F 23
Hobetsu o J 152-153 K 3
Hobhouse o ZA 220-221 H 4
Hobo o CO 60-61 D 6
Hoboken o USA (GA) 284-285 H 5
Hoboksar o VRC 146-147 G 2
Hobol ~ RUS 110-111 R 6
Hobro o DK 86-87 D 8
Hobson, Cape ▲ CDN 24-25 X 5
Hobson Lake ⊖ CDN (BC) 228-229 O 4
Hobucken o USA (NC) 282-283 L 5
Hobyo o SP 208-209 J 6
Hoceima, Al ☆ MA 188-189 K 3
Hochalmspitze ▲ A 92-93 M 5
Hochberry Draw ~ USA (TX) 266-267 D 2
Hochfeld o NAM 216-217 D 10
Hochfield o CDN (MAN) 234-235 F 5
Hochheim o USA (TX) 266-267 K 4
Hồ Chí Minh, Thành Phố = Thành Phố Hồ Chí Minh ☆ •• VN 158-159 J 5
Hochstetterbugten ≈ 26-27 q 6
Hochstetter Forland ⊥ GRØ 26-27 p 6
Hockin o CDN 34-35 H 3
Hocking River ~ USA (OH) 280-281 D 4
Hockley o USA (TX) 268-269 E 6
Hóc Môn o VN 158-159 J 5
Hočo o RUS 120-121 D 3
Hočo, Ystannah- o RUS 110-111 N 3
Hoctún o MEX 52-53 K 1
Ḥodā Āfarīn o IR 128-129 M 3
Hodal o IND 138-139 F 6
Hodar, utes • RUS 122-123 H 3
Hodgenville o USA (KY) 276-277 K 3
Hodges Gardens ∴ • USA (LA) 268-269 G 5
Hodges Hill ▲ CDN (NFL) 242-243 N 3
Hodgeville o CDN (SAS) 232-233 M 5
Hodgkins Ridge ≃ 32-33 B 5
Hodgson o CDN (MAN) 234-235 F 3
Hodgson Downs o AUS 174-175 C 4
Hodgson River o AUS 174-175 C 4
Hodh ⊥ RIM 196-197 F 6
Hodh ech-Chargui ◘ RIM 196-197 G 5
Hodh el-Gharbi ◘ RIM 196-197 E 6
Hodigere o IND 140-141 G 4
Hodma ~ SP 208-209 H 3
Hódmezővásárhely o H 92-93 Q 5
Hodna, Plaine du ⊥ DZ 190-191 E 3
Hodo Dan ▲ DVR 150-151 F 8
Hồ Đo'n Du'o'ng ⊖ VN 158-159 K 5
Hodonín o CZ 92-93 O 4
Hodq Shamo ⊥ VRC 154-155 E 1
Hodutka, gora ▲ RUS 122-123 R 2
Hodžambas o TM 136-137 J 5
Hodzana River ~ USA 20-21 Q 3
Hodža-Obigarm o TJ 136-137 L 5
Hodžejli = Hūdžajli ☆ • US 136-137 F 3
Hoè o RUS 122-123 K 3
Hoedspruit o ZA 220-221 K 2
Hoehne o USA (CO) 254-255 L 6
Hoë Karoo = Upper Karoo ⊥ ZA 220-221 D 5
Hoek van Holland o NL 92-93 H 3
Hoeryong o DVR 150-151 G 6
Hoëveld ⊥ ZA 220-221 J 3
Hoey o CDN (SAS) 232-233 N 3
Hoeyang o DVR 150-151 F 8
Hof o D 92-93 L 3
Höfðakaupstaður = Skagaströnd o IS 86-87 c 2
Hoffmans Cay ⌒ BS 54-55 G 2
Hofmarkt = Odorheiu Secuiesc o RO 102-103 D 4
Hofmeyr o ZA 220-221 G 5
Höfn o IS 86-87 f 2
Hofsjökull ⊂ IS 86-87 d 2
Hofsós o IS 86-87 d 2
Hōfu o J 152-153 D 7
Hōğalāk, Kūh-e ▲ IR 128-129 M 5
Höganäs o S 86-87 F 8
Hogan Group ⌒ AUS 180-181 J 5
Hogansville o USA (GA) 284-285 F 3
Hogart, Mount ▲ AUS 178-179 D 1
Hogatza River ~ USA 20-21 N 3
Hogback Mountain ▲ USA (NE) 262-263 C 3
Hog Cay ⌒ BS 54-55 H 3
Hogeland o USA (MT) 250-251 K 3
Høgeloft ▲ N 86-87 D 6
Hogem Range ▲ CDN 32-33 G 3
Hogem Ranges ▲ CDN 32-33 G 4
Hoggar ▲ DZ 190-191 E 9
Hoggar, Tassili du ▲ DZ 190-191 E 10
Høggia ▲ N 86-87 E 5
Hog Harbor o VAN 184 II a 2
Hog Island ⌒ USA (MI) 272-273 D 2
Hog Island ⌒ USA (VA) 280-281 L 6
Hog Landing o USA 20-21 N 4
Hogsback o ZA 220-221 H 6
Högsby ☆ S 86-87 H 8
Høgtuvbreen ▲ N 86-87 F 3
Hohenstein = Olsztynek o PL 92-93 Q 2
Hohenwald o USA (TN) 276-277 H 5
Hohe Tatra = Tatry ▲ SK 92-93 P 4
Hohe Tauern ▲ A 92-93 M 5
Hohhot ☆ VRC 154-155 G 1
Hoh Indian Reservation ✗ USA (WA) 244-245 A 3
Hohoe o GH 202-203 L 6
Hoholitna River ~ USA 20-21 M 6
Hoh Sai Hu ⊖ VRC 144-145 J 3
Höhuku o J 152-153 D 7
Hoh Xil Hu ⊖ VRC 144-145 H 3
Hoh Xil Shan ▲ VRC 144-145 F 3
Hội An o •• VN 158-159 K 3
Hoima o EAU 212-213 C 3
Hoisington o USA (KS) 262-263 H 6
Hoj, vozvyšennost' ▲ RUS 108-109 O 7
Hoja Wajeer o SP 212-213 H 4
Hojd Tamir gol ~ MAU 148-149 E 4
Hoka o RI 166-167 E 5
Hokitika o NZ 182 C 5
Hokkaidō ⌒ J 152-153 K 3
Hokksund ☆ N 86-87 D 7
Ḥokmābād o IR 136-137 E 6
Hokua o VAN 184 II a 2
Hola o EAK 212-213 H 4
Holalagondi o IND 140-141 G 3
Holanda Rous, Reserva Florestal ⊥ RCH 80 F 7
Hola Prystan' o UA 102-103 H 4
Holbæk o DK 86-87 E 9
Holbein o CDN (SAS) 232-233 M 2
Holberg o CDN (BC) 230-231 A 3
Holberg Inlet ≈ CDN 230-231 A 3
Holbox, Isla ⌒ MEX 52-53 L 1
Holbrook o AUS 180-181 J 3
Holbrook o USA (AZ) 256-257 E 4
Holbrook o USA (ID) 252-253 F 4
Holchit, Punta ▲ MEX 52-53 K 1
Holcomb o USA (MS) 268-269 L 3
Holden o CDN (ALB) 232-233 F 2
Holden o USA (MO) 274-275 E 6
Holden o USA (UT) 254-255 C 4
Holdenville o USA (OK) 264-265 H 3
Holdfast o CDN (SAS) 232-233 N 5
Holdingford o USA (MN) 270-271 D 5
Holdman o USA (OR) 244-245 G 5
Holdrege o USA (NE) 262-263 G 4
Hold with Hope Halvø ∪ GRØ 26-27 p 7
Hole in the Wall ∴ • BS 54-55 G 2
Holejaha ~ RUS 108-109 O 5
Holešov o CZ 92-93 O 4
Holger Danskes Tinde ▲ GRØ 26-27 n 6
Holguín ☆ C 54-55 G 4
Holhol o DJI 208-209 F 3
Holiday o USA (FL) 286-287 G 3
Holiday Resort • AUS 176-177 E 7
Holitna River ~ USA 20-21 M 6
Hollabrunn o A 92-93 O 4
Holland o CDN (MAN) 234-235 E 5
Holland o • USA (MI) 272-273 C 5
Hollandale o USA (MS) 268-269 K 3
Hollandale o USA (WI) 274-275 J 2
Holland Bay ≈ 54-55 G 6
Hollat o RI 166-167 G 4
Holleschau = Holešov o CZ 92-93 O 4
Hollick-Kenyon Plateau ▲ ARK 16 F 26
Holliday o USA (TX) 264-265 F 5
Hollidaysburg o USA (PA) 280-281 H 3
Hollis o USA (AK) 32-33 D 4
Hollis o USA (AR) 276-277 B 6
Hollis o USA (OK) 264-265 E 4
Hollister o USA (CA) 248-249 C 3
Hollister o USA (ID) 252-253 D 4
Hollister o USA (MO) 276-277 B 4
Hollister o USA (OK) 264-265 F 4
Hollister, Mount ▲ AUS 172-173 B 7
Hollókő o ••• H 92-93 P 4
Hollow Water o CDN (MAN) 234-235 G 3
Hollow Water Indian Reserve ✗ CDN (MAN) 234-235 G 3
Holly o USA (CO) 254-255 N 5
Holly Beach o USA (LA) 268-269 G 7
Holly Bluff o USA (MS) 268-269 K 4
Holly Hill o USA (SC) 284-285 K 3
Holly Hrove o USA (AR) 276-277 D 6
Holly Ridge o USA (NC) 282-283 K 6
Holly Springs o USA (AR) 276-277 C 7
Holly Springs o USA (MS) 268-269 L 2
Hollywood o USA (AR) 276-277 B 6
Hollywood o USA (FL) 286-287 J 5
Hollywood, Los Angeles •• USA (CA) 248-249 F 5
Holm ☆ RUS 94-95 M 3
Holma o WAN 204-205 K 4
Holman Island o CDN 24-25 N 5
Hólmavík ☆ IS 86-87 c 2
Holme Park o ZA 220-221 J 2
Holmes Creek ~ USA (FL) 286-287 D 1
Holmes Reef ⌒ AUS 174-175 J 5
Holmes River ~ CDN (BC) 228-229 P 3
Holmfield o CDN (MAN) 234-235 D 5
Holmia o GUY 62-63 E 3
Holm Land ⊥ GRØ 26-27 q 3
Holmogorskaja o RUS 88-89 Q 5
Holmogory o RUS 88-89 Q 4
Holmsk o RUS 122-123 K 5
Holmskij o RUS 126-127 C 5
Holms Ø ⌒ GRØ 26-27 W 6
Holmsund o S 86-87 K 5
Holm-Žirkovskij o RUS 94-95 N 4
Holnicote Bay ≈ 183 E 5
Holohovčan ~ RUS 112-113 N 5
Holoj ~ RUS 118-119 F 9
Holokit ~ RUS 108-109 a 7
Holomolch-Jurjah ~ RUS 118-119 G 4
Holoog o NAM 220-221 C 3
Holroyd River ~ AUS 174-175 F 4
Holstebro o •• DK 86-87 D 8
Holstein o USA (IA) 274-275 C 2
Holsteinsborg = Sisimiut o GRØ 28-29 O 3
Holston Lake ⊖ USA (TN) 282-283 E 4
Holston River ~ USA (TN) 282-283 D 4
Holston River ~ USA (VA) 280-281 D 7
Holt o USA (AL) 284-285 C 3
Holt o USA (FL) 286-287 C 1
Holt o USA (MI) 272-273 E 5
Holter Lake ⊖ USA (MT) 250-251 H 5
Holt Lake < USA (AL) 284-285 C 3
Holton o CDN 36-37 V 7
Holton o USA (KS) 262-263 L 5
Holt Rock o AUS 176-177 E 6
Holtville o USA (CA) 248-249 J 7
Holualoa o USA (HI) 288 K 5
Holub o USA (AR) 276-277 E 6
Holuwon o RI 166-167 K 4
Holyhead o GB 90-91 E 5
Holy Island o GB 90-91 G 4
Holyoke o USA (CO) 254-255 N 3
Holyoke o USA (MA) 278-279 J 6
Holyrood o CDN (NFL) 242-243 P 5
Holyrood o USA (KS) 262-263 H 6
Holy Trinity o USA (AL) 284-285 E 4
Hom ~ NAM 220-221 D 4
Homa Bay o EAK 212-213 E 4
Ḥomām o IR 128-129 N 4
Homand o IR 134-135 H 2
Hománe o MOC 218-219 H 6
Homathko Icefield ⊂ CDN (BC) 230-231 E 2
Homathko River ~ CDN (BC) 230-231 E 2
Hombetsu o J 152-153 K 3
Hombori o RMM 202-203 K 2
Hombori, Monts du ▲ RMM 202-203 J 2
Hombre Muerto, Salar del ⊖ RA 76-77 D 3
Home Bay ≈ 28-29 G 2
Homedale o USA (ID) 252-253 B 3
Homefield o CDN (SAS) 232-233 P 4
Home Hill o AUS 174-175 J 6
Ḥomein o IR 134-135 D 2
Homel' ☆ BY 94-95 M 5
Home of Bullion Mine • AUS 178-179 C 1
Homer o USA (AK) 22-23 V 3
Homer o USA (IA) 274-275 E 2
Homer o USA (IL) 274-275 L 4
Homer o USA (LA) 268-269 G 4
Homer Tunnel ▲ NZ 182 A 6
Homerville o USA (GA) 284-285 H 5
Homestead o AUS 174-175 H 7
Homestead o USA (FL) 286-287 J 6
Homestead National Monument ∴ USA (NE) 262-263 K 4
Homewood o USA (AL) 284-285 D 3
Homi, hrebet ▲ RUS 122-123 H 3
Hominy o USA (OK) 264-265 H 2
Homnābād o IND 140-141 G 2
Homo, Cerro el ▲ HN 52-53 L 4
Homochitto River ~ USA (MS) 268-269 J 5
Homodji < RN 198-199 F 4
Homolha o RUS 118-119 G 6
Homolho ~ RUS 118-119 H 6
Homonhon Island ⌒ RP 160-161 F 7
Homosassa Springs o USA (FL) 286-287 G 3
Homot Tohadar, Ğabal ▲ SUD 200-201 H 3
Homustah o RUS 118-119 P 4
Homyel' = Homel' ☆ BY 94-95 M 5
Honaunau o USA (HI) 288 K 5
Honāvar o IND 140-141 F 3
Honaz Dağ ▲ TR 128-129 C 4
Honda o CO 60-61 D 5
Honda, Chott El ⊖ DZ 190-191 E 3
Honda, Monts du ▲ DZ 190-191 E 3
Honda Bay ≈ 160-161 C 8
Hòn Đất o VN 158-159 H 5
Hondeklipbaai o ZA 220-221 C 5
Hondo ~ C 54-55 D 3
Hondo o J 152-153 D 8
Hondo o USA (NM) 256-257 K 5
Hondo o USA (TX) 266-267 H 4
Hondo, Río ~ USA (NM) 256-257 K 5
Hondo Creek ~ USA (TX) 266-267 H 4
Hondo River ~ BH 52-53 K 3
Honduras ■ HN 52-53 A 4
Honduras, Cabo de ▲ HN 52-53 L 3
Hone o CDN 34-35 F 2
Honea Path o USA (SC) 284-285 H 2
Hønefoss ☆ N 86-87 E 6
Hone River ~ CDN 36-37 O 2
Honesdale o USA (PA) 280-281 L 2
Honey Grove o USA (TX) 264-265 J 5
Honey Lake ⊖ USA (CA) 246-247 E 3
Honeymoon Bay o CDN (BC) 230-231 E 5
Hong o IR 134-135 E 5
Hong'an o VRC 154-155 J 6
Hongch'ŏn o ROK 150-151 F 9
Hongde o VRC 154-155 E 3
Hong Do ⌒ ROK 150-151 E 10
Hongdong o VRC 154-155 G 3
Hongfeng Hu ⊖ VRC 156-157 E 3
Hông Gai ☆ VN 156-157 E 6
Honggun-ri o DVR 150-151 G 7
Hongguqu o VRC 154-155 C 3
Honghu o VRC 156-157 H 2
Hong Hu ⊖ VRC 156-157 H 2
Hongjiang o VRC 156-157 F 3
Hong Kong = Xianggang ◘ HK 156-157 J 5
Hongliuyuan o VRC (GAN) 146-147 M 5
Hongliuyuan o VRC (GAN) 154-155 B 2
Hongmen o VRC 154-155 L 6
Hongmenhe o VRC 154-155 F 5
Hông Ngu' o VN 158-159 H 5
Hòn Gốm, B. D. ⌒ VN 158-159 K 4
Hongor o MAU (DOG) 148-149 K 5
Hongor o MAU (SUH) 148-149 L 5
Hongshan o VRC 154-155 H 6
Hongshishan o VRC 148-149 C 6
Hongshui He ~ VRC 156-157 E 4
Hongū o J 152-153 F 8
Honguedo, Détroit d' ≈ CDN 242-243 D 3
Hongwei o VRC 156-157 K 2
Hongwon o DVR 150-151 F 7
Hongya o VRC 156-157 C 2
Hongyuan o VRC 154-155 C 5
Hongze o VRC 154-155 L 5
Hongze Hu ⊖ VRC 154-155 L 5
Hongzhi Liang ▲ VRC 154-155 F 4
Honi o GE 126-127 E 6
Honiara ★ • SOL 184 I d 3
Honiton o GB 90-91 F 6
Honjō o J 152-153 J 5
Honkawane o J 152-153 H 7
Hon Minh Hoa ⌒ VN 158-159 J 5
Honnali o IND 140-141 F 3
Honningsvåg o N 86-87 M 1
Honobia o USA (OK) 264-265 K 4
Honohina o USA (HI) 288 K 5
Honokaa o USA (HI) 288 K 4
Honokahua o USA (HI) 288 J 4
Honolulu ☆ • USA (HI) 288 H 3
Honoria o PE 64-65 E 6
Hon Rái ⌒ VN 158-159 H 6
Honshū ⌒ J 152-153 E 7
Hòn Thị, Mũi ▲ VN 158-159 K 4
Hontorbé o SN 202-203 D 2
Honuu ☆ RUS 110-111 Y 6
Hood, Fort ✕✕ USA (TX) 266-267 K 2
Hood, Mount ▲ USA 244-245 D 5
Hood Bay ≈ 183 D 6
Hood Canal ~ USA (WA) 244-245 B 3
Hood Point ▲ AUS 176-177 E 7
Hood River ~ CDN 30-31 P 2
Hood River o USA (OR) 244-245 D 5
Hoodsport o USA (WA) 244-245 B 3
Hoogeveen o NL 92-93 J 2
Hooker o USA (OK) 264-265 C 2
Hooker Creek Aboriginal Land ✗ AUS 172-173 K 5
Hook Island ⌒ AUS 174-175 K 7
Hook Point ▲ CDN 34-35 P 3
Hool o MEX 52-53 J 2
Hoonah o USA 32-33 C 2
Hoopa o USA (CA) 246-247 B 2
Hoopa Valley Indian Reservation ✗ USA (CA) 246-247 B 2
Hooper o USA (CO) 254-255 K 6
Hooper o USA (NE) 262-263 K 3
Hooper o USA (WA) 244-245 G 4
Hooper, Cape ▲ CDN 28-29 G 2
Hooper Bay ≈ 20-21 G 6
Hooper Bay o USA 20-21 G 6
Hooper Inlet ≈ 24-25 f 6
Hooper Point ▲ CDN (BC) 228-229 D 2
Hooper Strait ≈ USA 280-281 K 5
Hoopeston o USA (IL) 274-275 L 4
Hooping Harbour o CDN (NFL) 242-243 M 2
Hoople o USA (ND) 258-259 K 3
Hoop Nature Reserve, De ⊥ ZA 220-221 E 7
Hoopstad o ZA 220-221 G 3
Hoosick Falls o USA (NY) 278-279 H 6
Hoosier o CDN (SAS) 232-233 J 4
Hoover o USA (TX) 264-265 D 3
Hoover Dam < • USA (NV) 248-249 K 3
Hoover Reservoir ⊖ USA (OH) 280-281 D 3
Hopa ☆ TR 128-129 J 2
Ho-pong o MYA 142-143 L 4
Hope o CDN (BC) 230-231 H 4
Hope < NAM 220-221 C 3
Hope o USA (AK) 20-21 Q 6
Hope o USA (AR) 276-277 B 7
Hope o USA (ID) 250-251 C 3
Hope o USA (IN) 274-275 N 5
Hope o USA (ND) 258-259 K 4
Hope o USA (NM) 256-257 L 6
Hope, Cape ▲ CDN 24-25 O 6
Hope, Kap = Ittaajimmiit o GRØ 26-27 o 8
Hope, Lake ⊖ AUS 176-177 F 6
Hope, Mount o AUS 180-181 H 2
Hope Campbell Lake ⊖ AUS 176-177 G 4
Hopefield o ZA 220-221 D 6
Hopeful o USA (GA) 284-285 F 5
Hope Island ⌒ CDN (ONT) 238-239 E 4
Hopelchén o • MEX 52-53 K 2
Hopeless, Mount ▲ AUS 178-179 E 5
Hope Mills o USA (NC) 282-283 J 6
Hopen o N (ROM) 86-87 D 5
Hopen ⌒ N (SVA) 84-85 O 4
Hopenbanken ≃ 84-85 O 4
Hopen Radio o N 84-85 O 4
Hope or Panda, Lake ⊖ AUS 178-179 E 5
Hoper ~ RUS 94-95 S 5
Hoper ~ RUS 102-103 N 2
Hope River ~ AUS 176-177 E 3
Hopes Advance Bay ≈ 36-37 P 5
Hopeton o USA (OK) 264-265 F 2
Hopetoun o AUS (VIC) 180-181 G 3
Hopetoun o AUS (WA) 176-177 F 6
Hopetown o CDN (ONT) 238-239 J 3
Hopetown o ZA 220-221 G 4
Hope Vale ✗ AUS 174-175 H 4
Hope Vale Aboriginal Land ✗ AUS 174-175 H 4
Hopewell o USA (VA) 280-281 J 6
Hopewell Cape o CDN (NB) 240-241 L 5
Hopewell Islands ⌒ CDN 36-37 K 5
Hồ Phú Ninh ⊖ VN 158-159 K 3
Hopi Buttes ▲ USA (AZ) 256-257 E 3
Hopi Indian Reservation ✗ USA (AZ) 256-257 E 2
Hopin o MYA 142-143 K 3
Hopkins o USA (MO) 274-275 D 4
Hopkins, Lake ⊖ AUS 176-177 K 2
Hopkinsville o USA (KY) 276-277 H 4
Hopland o USA (CA) 246-247 B 5
Ho-pong o MYA 142-143 K 5
Hoppner Inlet ≈ 24-25 e 7
Hopton Lake ⊖ CDN 30-31 V 5
Hoque o ANG 216-217 B 7
Hoquiam o USA (WA) 244-245 B 4
Hor ~ RUS 122-123 F 5
Horace Mount ▲ USA 20-21 Q 3
Horana o CL 140-141 J 7
Ḥorāsān ◘ IR 134-135 G 2
Horasan ☆ TR 128-129 K 2
Horatio o USA (AR) 276-277 A 7
Horbusuonka ~ RUS 110-111 P 4
Hörby o S 86-87 F 9
Horcajo de los Montes o E 98-99 E 5
Horcones, Río ~ RA 76-77 E 3
Horden, Lac ⊖ CDN (ONT) 236-237 L 2
Horden River ~ PNG 183 A 2
Hor'dil Sar'dag ▲ MAU 148-149 D 2
Hordogoj o RUS 118-119 G 4
Horej-Ver o RUS 88-89 Y 3
Horezmskaja oblast' ◘ US 136-137 G 4
Horezu • RO 102-103 C 5
Horgo o MAU 148-149 D 3
Horgoččuma ~ RUS 110-111 N 7
Horicon o USA (WI) 274-275 K 1
Horicon National Wildlife Refuge ⊥ USA (WI) 274-275 K 1
Horincy o RUS 118-119 K 5
Horinger o VRC 154-155 G 1
Horinsk ☆ RUS 118-119 D 9
Horizontina o BR 76-77 K 4
Horki ☆ BY 94-95 M 4
Horlick Mountains ▲ ARK 16 E 0
Horlivka o UA 102-103 L 3
Horlog Hu ~ VRC 144-145 L 2
Hormigas, Las o PE 70-71 C 3
Hormoz o IR 134-135 F 5
Hormoz, Ğazīre-ye ⌒ IR 134-135 G 5
Hormoz, Kūh-e ▲ IR 134-135 F 5
Hormozgān ◘ IR 134-135 F 5
Hormūd o IR 134-135 F 5
Hormuz, Strait of = Hormoz, Tange-ye ≈ 134-135 G 5
Horn, The ▲ AUS 180-181 J 4
Horn, Van o USA (TX) 266-267 C 2
Horna o RI 166-167 G 2
Hornachos o E 98-99 D 5
Hornaday River ~ CDN 24-25 K 6
Hornavan ⊖ S 86-87 H 3
Hornbjarg ▲ IS 86-87 b 1
Hornby Bay ⊖ CDN 30-31 L 2
Hornby Island o CDN (BC) 230-231 E 4
Hornconcitos o PA 52-53 C 7
Horndal o S 86-87 H 6
Horndean o CDN (MAN) 234-235 F 5
Hornell o USA (NY) 278-279 D 6
Hornell Lake ⊖ CDN 30-31 K 4
Hornepayne o CDN (ONT) 236-237 D 3
Hornillos, Punta ▲ PE 70-71 A 5
Horn Island ⌒ AUS 174-175 G 2
Horn Island ⌒ USA (MS) 268-269 M 6
Horn Mountains ▲ USA 20-21 L 6
Horno Islands ⌒ PNG 183 D 2
Hornos, Caleta los ≈ 76-77 B 5
Horn Plateau ▲ CDN 30-31 J 4
Horn River ~ CDN 30-31 K 4
Hornsby o AUS 180-181 L 2
Hornslandet ⊥ S 86-87 H 6
Hornsund ≈ 84-85 J 4
Hornsundtind ▲ N 84-85 K 4
Horodnja o UA 102-103 G 2
Horodok ☆ UA 102-103 C 3
Horog ☆ TJ 136-137 M 6
Horol' o RUS 122-123 E 6
Horombe ▲ RM 222-223 D 9
Horošee ozero ⊖ RUS 124-125 J 2
Horoshiri-dake ▲ J 152-153 K 3
Horowupotana o CL 140-141 J 6
Horqin Youyi Zhongqi o VRC 150-151 C 5
Horqin Zuoyi Houqi o VRC 150-151 D 6
Horqueta o PY 76-77 J 2
Horqueta, La o YV (BOL) 62-63 D 2
Horqueta, La o YV (DAM) 60-61 K 3
Horquetas, Las o CR 52-53 C 6
Ḥorramābād ☆ • IR 134-135 C 2
Ḥorram Darre o IR 128-129 N 4
Ḥorramšahr o • IR 134-135 C 3
Horrocks o AUS 176-177 C 4
Horru o VRC 144-145 H 5
Horsburgh Atoll ⌒ MV 140-141 B 5
Horse (Saint Barbe) Islands ⌒ CDN (NFL) 242-243 N 2
Horse Creek o USA (WY) 252-253 N 5
Horse Creek ~ USA (CO) 254-255 M 5
Horse Creek ~ USA (FL) 286-287 H 4
Horse Creek ~ USA (GA) 284-285 G 5
Horse Creek ~ USA (MO) 276-277 A 3
Horse Creek ~ USA (WY) 252-253 O 5
Horsefly o CDN (BC) 228-229 N 4
Horsefly Lake ⊖ CDN (BC) 228-229 N 4
Horsefly River ~ CDN (BC) 228-229 N 4
Horse Gap ▲ USA (NC) 282-283 F 4
Horsens o DK 86-87 D 9
Horse River ~ CDN 32-33 P 3
Horseshoe Bay o CDN (ALB) 32-33 P 4
Horseshoe Bay o CDN (BC) 230-231 F 4
Horseshoe Bay ≈ USA 286-287 F 2
Horseshoe Beach o USA (FL) 286-287 F 2
Horseshoe Bend o USA (ID) 252-253 B 3
Horseshoe Bend National Military Park • USA (AL) 284-285 E 4
Horsham o • AUS 180-181 G 4
Horsham o CDN (SAS) 232-233 J 5
Horten ☆ N 86-87 E 7
Hortense o USA (GA) 284-285 J 5
Hortensias, Las o RCH 78-79 C 5
Horti o IND 140-141 F 2
Hortobágy o H 92-93 Q 5
Hortobágyi Nemzeti Park ⊥ H 92-93 Q 5
Horton o USA (KS) 262-263 L 5
Horton Bay o USA (MI) 272-273 D 2
Horton Lake ⊖ CDN 30-31 H 2
Horton River ~ CDN 24-25 H 6
Horumnug-Tajga, hrebet ▲ RUS 116-117 G 10
Horuongka ~ RUS 110-111 O 6
Horus, Temple of ∴ •• ET 194-195 F 5
Horwood Lake ⊖ CDN (ONT) 236-237 F 5
Horyn' ~ UA 102-103 D 3
Horyn' ~ UA 102-103 E 2
Horyuji ••• J 152-153 F 7
Hosab Kalesi •• TR 128-129 K 3
Hoşab Kalesi • TR 128-129 K 3
Hosahalli o IND 140-141 F 4
Hosa'ina o ETH 208-209 C 5
Hosakote o IND 140-141 G 3
Hos-Alas o RUS 110-111 S 6
Ḥošāmand o AFG 138-139 B 3
Hosanagara o IND 140-141 F 4
Hosato, ozero ⊖ RUS 108-109 T 6
Hosdrug o IND 140-141 F 4
Hosdurga o IND 140-141 G 4
Hose, Pegunungan ▲ MAL 162-163 K 3
Hosedaju ~ RUS 108-109 H 8
Ḥoseinābād o IR 128-129 M 5
Ḥoseinābād o IR 134-135 J 3
Ḥoseinābād, Rūdḫāne-ye ~ IR 134-135 J 3
Ḥoseiniye-ye Ḥoda Dād o IR 134-135 C 2
Hoselaw o CDN 32-33 P 4
Hoševtovo o RUS 96-97 E 10
Hosford o USA (FL) 286-287 E 1
Hoshāb o PK 134-135 K 5
Hoshangābād o IND 138-139 F 8
Hoshiārpur o IND 138-139 E 4
Hoshib ~ SUD 200-201 G 3
Ḥōsī o AFG 138-139 B 2
Hoska ~ RUS 110-111 c 6
Hoskins o PNG 183 F 3
Hoskins o USA (NE) 262-263 J 2
Hoskote o IND 140-141 G 4
Hosmer o CDN (BC) 230-231 P 4
Hösööt o MAU 146-147 J 1
Hospah o USA (NM) 256-257 H 3
Ḥospās Rūd ~ AFG 134-135 K 3
Hospet o IND 140-141 G 3
Hospicia o PE 70-71 B 6
Hospicio o PE 70-71 B 5
Hospital, Cuchilla del ▲ ROU 78-79 M 2
Ḥosrovī o IR 134-135 A 1
Hosrovskij zapovednik ⊥ AR 128-129 L 2
Ḥōst o AFG 138-139 B 3
Hoste, Isla ⌒ RCH 80 F 7
Hostomel' o UA 102-103 G 2
Hosūr o IND 140-141 G 4
Ḥōš Yeilāg o IR 136-137 D 6
Hot o THA 142-143 L 6
Hotaka-dake ▲ J 152-153 G 6
Hotamış Gölü ⊖ TR 128-129 E 4
Hotan o VRC 144-145 B 2
Hotan He ~ VRC 146-147 E 6
Hotazel o ZA 220-221 F 3
Ḥotbe Sarā o IR 128-129 N 3
Hotchkiss o CDN 32-33 M 3
Hotchkiss o USA (CO) 254-255 H 5
Hotchkiss River ~ CDN 32-33 L 3
Hotel dos Manantiales o RA 80 F 4
Hotel el Cerrito o RA 80 E 5
Hotel las Horquetas o RA 80 E 4
Hotel Río Negro o PY 76-77 H 3
Hotevilla o USA (AZ) 256-257 E 3
Hồ Thác Bà < VN 156-157 D 6
Hotham, Cape ▲ AUS 172-173 K 2
Hotham, Cape ▲ CDN 24-25 Z 3
Hotham Inlet ≈ 20-21 J 3
Hotham River ~ AUS 176-177 D 6
Hotmin Mission o PNG 183 A 3
Hotoho ~ RUS 118-119 F 5
Hotpaas o RI 166-167 D 5
Hot Springs o USA (NC) 282-283 E 5
Hot Springs o USA (SD) 260-261 C 3
Hot Springs o • USA (AR) 276-277 B 6
Hot Springs • USA (AR) 256-257 B 6
Hot Springs • USA (OR) 244-245 E 8
Hot Springs o ZW 218-219 G 4
Hot Springs, Cove • USA (OR) 244-245 H 5
Hot Springs Cove o CDN (BC) 230-231 C 4
Hot Springs National Park ⊥ USA (AR) 276-277 B 6
Hot Springs Village o USA (AR) 276-277 B 6
Hotspur Seamount ≃ 72-73 M 4
Hot Sulphur Springs o USA (CO) 254-255 J 3
Hottah Lake ⊖ CDN 30-31 K 3
Hottentotsbaai ≈ 220-221 B 3
Hottentotskloof o ZA 220-221 D 6
Hot Water Beach • NZ 182 E 2
Hot Wells o USA (TX) 266-267 C 3
Houègbo o DY 204-205 E 5
Houeïriye o RIM 196-197 G 6
Houghton o USA (NY) 278-279 C 6
Houghton o USA (WI) 270-271 K 3
Houghton Lake ⊖ USA (MI) 272-273 E 3
Houghton Lake o USA (MI) 272-273 E 3
Houhai ⊖ VRC 156-157 G 6
Houhora o NZ 182 D 1
Houhu o VRC 156-157 G 6
Houlton o USA (ME) 278-279 O 2
Houma o TON 184 IV a 2
Houma o USA (LA) 268-269 K 7
Houma o VRC 154-155 G 4
Houmt Souk o TN 190-191 H 4
Houndé o • BF 202-203 J 4
Hounien, Zouan- o CI 202-203 F 6
Hourtin et de Carcans, Lac d' ⊖ F 90-91 G 9
Housatonic River ~ USA (CT) 280-281 N 2
House o USA (NM) 256-257 M 4
Householder Pass ▲ USA (AZ) 256-257 A 3
Houshui Wan ≈ 156-157 F 7
Houston o CDN (BC) 228-229 H 2
Houston o USA (AK) 20-21 Q 6
Houston o USA (MN) 270-271 G 7
Houston o USA (MO) 276-277 D 3
Houston o USA (MS) 268-269 M 3
Houston o • USA (TX) 268-269 E 7
Houston, Lake < USA (TX) 268-269 E 6
Houston Co. Lake < USA (TX) 268-269 E 5
Houston Point ▲ CDN 34-35 Q 4
Houston River ~ USA (LA) 268-269 G 6
Houtman Abrolhos ⌒ AUS 176-177 B 4
Houton Island ⌒ CDN (NS) 240-241 L 7
Houxia o VRC 146-147 H 4
Houz-e Soltān o IR 134-135 D 1
Hova o S 86-87 G 7
Hovd o MAU (ÖVÖ) 148-149 F 5
Hovd ◘ MAU 146-147 L 2

Hovd ☆ MAU 146-147 K 1
Hovden o N 86-87 C 7
Hovd gol ~ MAU 146-147 K 1
Hoveize o IR 134-135 C 3
Hoven o USA (SD) 260-261 G 1
Hovenweep National Monument ∴ USA (UT) 254-255 F 6
Hoverla, hora ▲ UA 102-103 D 3
Hovgaards Ø ⩥ GRØ 26-27 q 4
Hovland o USA (MN) 270-271 H 3
Hovoro o SOL 184 I c 3
Hövsgöl ◘ MAU 148-149 D 3
Hövsgöl nuur ⊂ MAU 148-149 E 2
Hovu-Aksy o RUS 116-117 F 10
Howakil ⌒ ER 200-201 K 5
Howakil Bay ≈ 200-201 K 5
Howard o USA (KS) 262-263 K 7
Howard o USA (SD) 260-261 J 2
Howard o USA (WI) 270-271 K 6
Howard City o USA (MI) 272-273 D 4
Howard Island ⌒ AUS 174-175 C 3
Howard Junction o NZ 182 D 4
Howard Lake o CDN 30-31 Q 4
Howard Lake o USA (MN) 270-271 D 5
Howards Creek ~ USA (TX) 266-267 F 3
Howard Springs o • AUS 172-173 K 2
Howe o USA (ID) 252-253 F 3
Howe, Cape ▲ AUS 180-181 K 4
Howell o USA (MI) 272-273 F 5
Howell o USA (UT) 254-255 C 2
Howells o USA (NE) 262-263 K 3
Howes o USA (SD) 260-261 D 2
Howe Sound ≈ 32-33 J 7
Howe Sound ≈ CDN 230-231 F 4
Howick o ZA 220-221 K 4
Howick Group ⌒ AUS 174-175 H 4
Howitt, Lake ⊂ AUS 178-179 E 4
Howland o USA (ME) 278-279 N 3
Howley o CDN (NFL) 242-243 L 3
Howlong o AUS 180-181 J 3
Howser o CDN (BC) 230-231 N 3
Howship, Mount ▲ AUS 174-175 B 3
Hoxie o USA (AR) 276-277 E 4
Hoxie o USA (KS) 262-263 F 5
Hoxtolgay o VRC 146-147 H 2
Hoxud o VRC 146-147 H 4
Höy o • IR 128-129 L 3
Høyanger ☆ N 86-87 C 6
Hoyé, Bin- o CI 202-203 F 6
Hoyerswerda o D 92-93 N 3
Høylandet o N 86-87 F 4
Hoyo, Mont ▲ ZRE 212-213 C 3
Hoyt o USA (CO) 254-255 L 4
Hoyt Lakes o USA (MN) 270-271 F 3
Hozier Islands ⌒ CDN 36-37 R 2
Hpangpai o MYA 142-143 L 4
Hpawngtut o MYA 142-143 K 3
Hradec Králové o CZ 92-93 N 3
Hradyz'k o UA 102-103 H 3
Hrami ~ GE 126-127 F 7
Hrebinka o UA 102-103 H 2
Hrebtovaja gora ▲ RUS 122-123 R 2
Hristais o BR 68-69 J 4
Hrodna ☆ BY 94-95 H 5
Hroma ~ RUS 110-111 Z 4
Hromskaja guba ≈ 110-111 Z 4
Hromtau ☆ KA 126-127 N 2
Hron ~ SK 92-93 P 4
Hrubieszów o PL 92-93 R 3
Hsenwi o MYA 142-143 K 4
Hsinchu o RC 156-157 M 4
Hsingying o RC 156-157 M 5
Hsipaw o MYA 142-143 K 4
Hsuen Shan ▲ RC 156-157 M 4
Htingu o MYA 142-143 K 3
Hua'an o VRC 156-157 K 4
Huab ~ NAM 216-217 C 9
Huabuzhen o VRC 156-157 L 2
Huaca o EC 64-65 D 1
Huacalera o RA 76-77 E 2
Huacaña o PE 64-65 E 9
Huacas, Las ∴ • CR 52-53 B 6
Huacaya o BOL 70-71 F 7
Huacaya, Río ~ BOL 76-77 F 1
Huacaybamba o PE 64-65 D 6
Huachacalla o BOL 70-71 C 6
Huachi o VRC 154-155 E 3
Huachi, Lago o BOL 70-71 F 4
Huacho o PE 64-65 D 7
Huachos o PE 64-65 E 8
Huachuca City o USA (AZ) 256-257 E 7
Huacrachuco o PE 64-65 D 6
Huacullani o PE 70-71 C 5
Huade o VRC 148-149 M 7
Huadian o VRC 150-151 F 6
Huaguang Jiao ⌒ VRC 158-159 L 2
Huahaizi o VRC 146-147 M 6
Hua Hin o THA 158-159 E 4
Huahua, Río = Río Wawa ~ NIC 52-53 B 4
Huaiá-Miçu, Rio ~ BR 68-69 B 7
Huai'an o VRC (HEB) 154-155 J 1
Huai'an o VRC (JIA) 154-155 L 5
Huaibei o VRC 154-155 K 5
Huaibin o VRC 154-155 J 5
Huai He ~ VRC 154-155 K 5
Huaihua o VRC 156-157 F 3
Huaiji o VRC 156-157 H 5
Huailai o VRC 154-155 J 1
Huaillas, Cerro ▲ BOL 70-71 D 5
Huai Na o THA 158-159 F 2
Huainan o VRC 154-155 K 5
Huairen o VRC 154-155 H 2
Huaiyang o VRC 154-155 J 5
Huaiyin o VRC 154-155 L 5
Huai Yot o THA 158-159 E 7
Huaiyuan o VRC 154-155 K 5
Huajialing o VRC 154-155 D 4
Huajianzi o VRC 150-151 E 7
Huajuapan o MEX 50-51 G 5
Huajuapan de León o • MEX 52-53 F 3
Huaki o • RI 166-167 D 5
Hualalai ▲ USA (HI) 288 K 5
Hualapai Indian Reservation ✗ USA (AZ) 256-257 B 3
Hualapai Mountain Park ⊥ • USA (AZ) 256-257 B 3
Hualapai Mountains ▲ USA (AZ) 256-257 B 4
Hualiangting SK ~ VRC 154-155 J 6
Hualien o RC 156-157 M 5
Huallaga, Río ~ PE 64-65 D 6
Huallanca o PE 64-65 D 6
Hualong o VRC 154-155 C 3
Huamachuco o PE 64-65 C 5
Huamali o PE 64-65 E 7
Huamani o PE 64-65 E 8
Huamantla o MEX 52-53 F 2
Huambo ◘ ANG 216-217 C 6
Huambo ☆ ANG (HBO) 216-217 C 6
Huambo o PE 64-65 F 9
Humboya o EC 64-65 C 2
Huampami o PE 64-65 C 4
Huamuxtitlán o MEX 52-53 E 3
Huañamarca o PE 70-71 A 5
Huanan o VRC 150-151 H 4
Huancabamba o PE 64-65 C 4
Huancabamba, Río ~ PE 64-65 C 4
Huancacho, Sierra ▲ RA 78-79 D 7
Huancane o PE 70-71 C 4
Huancano o PE 64-65 E 8
Huancapallac o PE 64-65 D 6
Huanca Sancos o PE 64-65 E 8
Huancavelica ☆ PE 64-65 E 8
Huancayo ☆ • PE 64-65 E 8
Huanchaca, Cerro ▲ BOL 70-71 D 7
Huanchaca, Parque Nacional ⊥ BOL 70-71 G 4
Huanchon o PE 64-65 E 7
Huangcangyu • VRC 154-155 K 5
Huangchuan o VRC 154-155 J 5
Huangda Yang ~ VRC 154-155 N 6
Huangdi Ling • VRC 154-155 F 4
Huanggang o VRC 154-155 J 6
Huangganglang ▲ VRC 148-149 N 6
Huanggang Shan ▲ VRC 156-157 K 3
Huangguoshu Pubu • VRC 156-157 D 3
Huang He ~ VRC 154-155 G 3
Huanghe Kou ≈ 154-155 L 3
Huanghua o VRC 154-155 K 2
Huanglianyu ▲ VRC 156-157 K 4
Huangling o VRC 154-155 F 4
Huanglong o VRC 154-155 F 4
Huanglonggong ••• VRC 154-155 M 6
Huanglong Si • VRC 154-155 C 5
Huangmei o VRC 154-155 J 6
Huangpi o VRC 154-155 J 6
Huangping o VRC 156-157 E 3
Huangqi Hai ⊂ VRC 154-155 H 1
Huangsha o VRC 156-157 L 3
Huangshan o • VRC (ANH) 156-157 L 2
Huangshan ••• VRC (ANH) 154-155 L 6
Huangshi o VRC 154-155 J 6
Huang Shui ~ VRC 154-155 C 3
Huangtu Gaoyuan ⩥ VRC 154-155 E 3
Huangyaguan • VRC 154-155 K 1
Huangyan o VRC 156-157 M 2
Huangyuan o VRC 154-155 B 3
Huangzhong o VRC 154-155 B 3
Huaninaoyuan o VRC 156-157 G 3
Huaning o VRC 156-157 C 4
Huaniqueo o MEX 52-53 D 2
Huanquelén o RA 78-79 J 4
Huanquer o RA 76-77 G 6
Huanren o VRC 150-151 E 7
Huanta o PE 64-65 E 8
Huantacareo o MEX 52-53 D 2
Huantraico, Sierra del ▲ RA 78-79 E 4
Huanuco ☆ PE 64-65 D 6
Huanuni o BOL 70-71 D 6
Huanusco o MEX 50-51 H 7
Huan Xian o VRC 154-155 E 3
Huanza o PE 64-65 D 7
Huanzo, Cordillera de ▲ PE 64-65 F 9
Huapí, Serranías ▲ NIC 52-53 B 5
Huaping o VRC 156-157 B 3
Huaping Yü ⌒ RC 156-157 M 4
Huaping Z.B. ⊥ • VRC 156-157 F 4
Huaqiao o VRC 154-155 E 6
Huaqingchi • VRC 154-155 F 4
Huaquén o RCH 78-79 D 2
Huaquillas o EC 64-65 B 3
Huara o RCH 70-71 C 7
Huaral o PE 64-65 D 7
Huaraz ☆ PE 64-65 D 6
Huari o PE 64-65 D 6
Huarina o BOL 70-71 C 5
Huarmey o PE 64-65 C 7
Huarochirí o PE 64-65 D 8
Huarocondo o PE 64-65 F 8
Huarong o VRC 156-157 H 2
Huarquehue, Parque Nacional ⊥ RCH 78-79 D 5
Huasabas o MEX 50-51 E 3
Huasaga o EC 64-65 D 3
Huasago, Río ~ PE 64-65 D 3
Hua Sai o THA 158-159 F 6
Huascarán, Parque Nacional ⊥ ••• PE 64-65 D 6
Huasco o RCH 76-77 B 5
Huasco, Río ~ RCH 76-77 B 5
Huasco, Salar de ⊂ RCH 70-71 C 7
Huashan o VRC (GXI) 156-157 F 4
Huashan • VRC (SXI) 154-155 G 4
Huashan-Yabihua • VRC 156-157 E 6
Huashaoying o VRC 154-155 J 1
Huashixia o VRC 144-145 M 3
Huata, Península de ⌣ BOL 70-71 C 5
Huatabampo o MEX 50-51 E 4
Huatugou o VRC 146-147 K 6
Huatunas, Lago ⊂ BOL 70-71 E 3
Huatusco de Chicuellar o MEX 52-53 F 2
Huaura, Río ~ PE 64-65 D 7
Hautla o MEX 50-51 K 7
Hautla de Jiménez o MEX 52-53 F 2
Huaxi • VRC 156-157 E 3
Hua Xian o VRC (GDG) 156-157 H 5
Hua Xian o VRC (HEN) 154-155 J 4
Huayabamba, Río ~ PE 64-65 D 5
Huayacocotla o MEX 52-53 E 1
Huaying o VRC (SIC) 154-155 E 6
Huaying o VRC (SXI) 154-155 F 4
Huayllacayan o PE 64-65 D 7
Huayllay o PE 64-65 D 7
Huaynamota, Río ~ MEX 50-51 G 6
Huaytiquina o RA 76-77 D 2
Huayuan o VRC 156-157 F 2
Huayucachi o PE 64-65 E 8
Huayuri, Pampa de ⩥ PE 64-65 E 9
Huazhou o VRC 156-157 G 6
Hubar, al- o KSA 134-135 D 5
Hubayah, Bi'r < LAR 192-193 K 2
Hubbard o CDN (SAS) 232-233 P 4
Hubbard o USA (IA) 274-275 E 2
Hubbard o USA (TX) 266-267 L 2
Hubbard, Mount ▲ CDN 20-21 V 6
Hubbard, Pointe ▲ CDN 36-37 Q 5
Hubbard Creek Reservoir ⊂ USA (TX) 264-265 E 6
Hubbard Glacier ⊂ CDN 20-21 V 6
Hubbard Lake o USA (MI) 272-273 F 3
Hubbard Lake ⊂ USA (MI) 272-273 F 3
Hubbards o CDN (NS) 240-241 L 6
Hub Chauki o PK 134-135 M 6
Hub City o USA (WI) 274-275 H 1
Hubei ◘ VRC 154-155 G 6
Hubli o IND 140-141 F 3
Hubynycha o UA 102-103 J 3
Hucal o RA 78-79 G 4
Hucal, Valle de ⌣ RA 78-79 G 4
Hučeto, ozero ⊂ RUS 108-109 S 6
Huckitta o AUS 178-179 C 2
Huckitta Creek ~ AUS 178-179 C 2
Huckitta Out Station o AUS 178-179 C 2
Hudaida, al- o Y 132-133 C 6
Hudain, Wādī ~ ET 194-195 G 6
Hudan ~ RUS 118-119 E 10
Hudat = Xudat o AZ 128-129 N 2
Huddersfield o GB 90-91 G 5
Hudgin Creek ~ USA (AR) 276-277 D 7
Hüdi o SUD 200-201 G 4
Hudie Quan • VRC 142-143 M 2
Hudiksvall o S 86-87 H 6
Hud Mount ▲ USA 20-21 T 3
Hudosej ~ RUS 114-115 S 2
Hudra, Wādī ~ Y 132-133 F 5
Hudson o CDN (ONT) 234-235 L 4
Hudson o USA (CO) 254-255 L 3
Hudson o USA (FL) 286-287 G 3
Hudson o USA (IA) 274-275 F 2
Hudson o USA (MD) 280-281 K 5
Hudson o USA (MI) 272-273 E 6
Hudson o USA (NY) 278-279 H 6
Hudson o USA (TX) 268-269 F 5
Hudson o USA (WI) 270-271 F 6
Hudson, Cerro ▲ RCH 80 D 3
Hudson, Lake ⊂ USA (OK) 264-265 J 2
Hudson Bay ≈ 34-35 N 2
Hudson Bay o CDN (SAS) 232-233 Q 3
Hudson Canyon ≃ 46-47 M 6
Hudson Falls o USA (NY) 278-279 H 5
Hudson Land ⩥ GRØ 26-27 o 7
Hudson Mountains ▲ ARK 16 F 27
Hudson River ~ USA (GA) 284-285 G 2
Hudson's Hope o CDN 32-33 K 3
Hudson Strait ≈ CDN 36-37 M 3
Huduk, Naryn- o RUS 126-127 G 5
Hudwin Lake ⊂ CDN 34-35 J 4
Hudžah ~ RUS 120-121 M 2
Hüdžaji ☆ • US 136-137 F 3
Hué ☆ ••• VN 158-159 J 2
Huechulafquén, Lago ⊂ RA 78-79 D 5
Hueco o USA (TX) 266-267 B 2
Huecu, El o RA 78-79 D 4
Huedin o RO 102-103 C 4
Huehuetenango ☆ GCA 52-53 J 4
Huehuetla o MEX 52-53 E 1
Huejotzingo o MEX 52-53 E 2
Huejúcar o MEX 50-51 H 6
Huejuquilla El Alto o MEX 50-51 H 6
Huejutla de Reyes o MEX 50-51 K 7
Huelma o E 98-99 F 6
Huelva o • E 98-99 D 6
Huenquecho Sur o RCH 78-79 D 3
Huéneja o E 98-99 F 6
Huenque, Río ~ PE 70-71 C 5
Huepil o RCH 78-79 D 4
Hueque, Río ~ YV 60-61 G 2
Huequi, Península ⌣ RCH 78-79 C 7
Huequi, Volcán ▲ RCH 78-79 C 7
Huércal-Overa o E 98-99 G 6
Huerfano River ~ USA (CO) 254-255 L 6
Huerfano Trading Post o USA (NM) 256-257 H 2
Huerta, La o MEX 52-53 B 2
Huerta, La o RCH 78-79 D 3
Huerta, Sierra de la ▲ RA 76-77 D 6
Huertecillas o MEX 50-51 J 5
Huesca o • E 98-99 G 3
Huéscar o E 98-99 F 6
Huesos, Arroyo de los ~ RA 78-79 K 4
Huetamo de Nuñez o MEX 52-53 D 2
Huey Yang Waterfall ⊥ • THA 158-159 E 5
Hufayyira, al- o KSA 130-131 J 5
Hufra, al- ⩥ KSA 130-131 F 3
Huftarøy ⌒ N 86-87 B 6
Hufūf, al- o KSA 130-131 L 5
Hufuma o RI 166-167 G 2
Hugand ☆ TJ 136-137 L 4
Hugdjakit ~ RUS 108-109 b 7
Hugdjungda, hrebet ▲ RUS 116-117 H 2
Huger o USA (SC) 284-285 L 3
Hugh Butler Lake ⊂ USA (NE) 262-263 F 4
Hughenden o AUS 174-175 H 7
Hughenden o CDN (ALB) 232-233 H 3
Hughes o RA 78-79 J 2
Hughes o USA 20-21 N 3
Hughes o USA (AR) 276-277 E 6
Hughes Springs o USA (TX) 264-265 K 6
Hughesville o USA (MD) 280-281 K 5
Hughesville o USA (PA) 280-281 K 2
Hugh Glass Monument • USA (SD) 260-261 D 1
Hugh River ~ AUS 176-177 M 2
Hugh White State Recreational Park • USA (MS) 268-269 L 3
Hugli ~ IND 142-143 E 5
Hugo o USA (CO) 254-255 M 4
Hugo o USA (OK) 264-265 J 4
Hugo Reservoir ⊂ USA (OK) 264-265 J 4
Hugoton o USA (KS) 262-263 E 7
Huguangyan • VRC 156-157 G 6
Huguenot Memorial • ZA 220-221 D 6
Huguo o VRC 156-157 D 2
Huia o NZ 182 E 2
Hui'an o VRC 156-157 L 4
Hui'anpu o VRC 154-155 E 3
Huib-Hochplato ⩥ NAM 220-221 C 3
Huichang o VRC 156-157 J 4
Huichapan o MEX 52-53 E 1
Huichon o DVR 150-151 F 7
Huichuan o VRC 154-155 C 4
Huidong o VRC (GDG) 156-157 J 5
Huidong o VRC (SIC) 156-157 C 3
Huila ◘ ANG 216-217 C 7
Huilai o VRC 156-157 K 5
Huila Plateau ▲ ANG 216-217 C 7
Huili o VRC 156-157 C 3
Huillapima o RA 76-77 E 5
Huilong o VRC 156-157 G 3
Huimbayoc o PE 64-65 E 5
Huimilpan o MEX 52-53 D 1
Huimin o VRC 154-155 K 3
Huiñaimarca, Lago ⊂ PE 70-71 C 5
Huinan o VRC 150-151 F 6
Huinca Renancó o RA 78-79 G 3
Huining o VRC 154-155 D 4
Huishui o VRC 156-157 E 3
Huisne ~ F 90-91 H 7
Huitimbo o GH 202-203 J 7
Huitong o VRC 156-157 F 3
Huitoto, Raudal ~ CO 64-65 F 1
Huitoyacu, Río ~ PE 64-65 D 3
Huittinen o FIN 88-89 G 6
Huitzo o MEX 52-53 F 3
Huivulai o MEX 50-51 E 4
Huixtepec o MEX 52-53 F 3
Huixtla o MEX 52-53 H 4
Huiyang o VRC 156-157 J 5
Huize o VRC 156-157 C 3
Huizhou o VRC 156-157 J 5
Huji o VRC 154-155 H 6
Hujra Shāh Meqeem o PK 138-139 D 4
Hukeri o IND 140-141 F 2
Hukou o VRC 156-157 K 2
Hukou Pubu • VRC 154-155 G 4
Hukovo o UA 102-103 L 3
Hukuntsi o RB 220-221 E 1
Hula o PNG 183 D 6
Hulah Lake ⊂ USA (OK) 264-265 H 2
Hulaiba o KWT 130-131 K 2
Hulaifa as-Sufla, al- o KSA 130-131 G 5
Hulais o KSA 130-131 F 6
Hul'ajpole o UA 102-103 K 4
Hulan o VRC 150-151 F 5
Hulane o RI 166-167 D 3
Hulekal o IND 140-141 F 3
Hulett o USA (WY) 252-253 O 2
Hulga ~ RUS 114-115 G 2
Hulhuta o RUS 96-97 E 10
Hulin o VRC 150-151 J 5
Huliyar o IND 140-141 G 4
Hull o CDN (QUE) 238-239 K 3
Hull o USA (IA) 274-275 B 1
Hull o USA (IL) 274-275 G 5
Hull o USA (TX) 268-269 F 6
Hullehgush o IND 138-139 E 1
Hulm o • AFG 136-137 K 6
Hulo o GE 126-127 E 7
Hultsfred ☆ S 86-87 G 8
Hulun Nur ~ VRC (NMZ) 148-149 N 3
Hulun Nur • VRC (NMZ) 148-149 N 3
Hulwa, al- o KSA 130-131 K 6
Hulwān o • ET 194-195 E 3
Huma o VRC 150-151 F 2
Humā' aš-Šimālīya, al- o KSA 130-131 J 5
Humacao o USA (PR) 286-287 Q 2
Humahuaca o RA 76-77 E 2
Humaid, al- o KSA 132-133 B 4
Humaitá o BOL 70-71 D 2
Humaitá o BR 66-67 F 6
Humansdorp o ZA 220-221 G 7
Humari o SUD 200-201 G 4
Humay o PE 64-65 E 8
Humbe o ANG 216-217 C 8
Humber ≈ 90-91 G 5
Humberto 1 o RA 76-77 G 6
Humberto de Campas o BR 68-69 G 3
Humbert River o AUS 172-173 K 4
Humble o USA (TX) 268-269 E 7
Humble City o USA (NM) 256-257 M 6
Humboldt o CDN (SAS) 232-233 N 3
Humboldt o USA (IA) 274-275 D 2
Humboldt o USA (KS) 262-263 L 7
Humboldt o USA (NE) 262-263 L 4
Humboldt o USA (NV) 246-247 G 3
Humboldt o USA (SD) 260-261 J 3
Humboldt o USA (TN) 276-277 G 5
Humboldt Bay ≈ 40-41 B 5
Humboldt Bay o CDN (ONT) 234-235 P 5
Humboldt Bay ≈ USA 246-247 A 3
Humboldt Gletscher ⊂ GRØ 26-27 S 4
Humboldt Redwoods State Park ⊥ USA (CA) 246-247 B 3
Humboldt River ~ USA (NV) 246-247 G 3
Humboldt Salt Marsh ⊂ USA (NV) 246-247 H 4
Hume, Lake < AUS 180-181 J 4
Hume Highway II AUS 180-181 J 3
Humeida, al- o KSA 130-131 D 3
Humenné o SK 92-93 Q 4
Hume River ~ CDN 30-31 E 3
Humeston o USA (IA) 274-275 E 4
Hummi, ozero ⊂ RUS 122-123 G 3
Humocaro Bajo o YV 60-61 G 3
Humos, Cabo ▲ RCH 78-79 C 3
Humos, Isla ⌒ RCH 80 C 2
Humpata o ANG 216-217 B 7
Humphrey o USA (AR) 276-277 D 6
Humphrey o USA (ID) 252-253 F 2
Humphrey o USA (NE) 262-263 J 3
Humphreys Peak ▲ USA (AZ) 256-257 D 3
Humpolec o CZ 92-93 N 4
Humptulips o USA (WA) 244-245 B 3
Humpty Doo o AUS 172-173 K 2
Humuula o USA (HI) 288 K 5
Hün ☆ • LAR 192-193 F 3
Húnaflói ≈ 86-87 c 2
Hunan ◘ VRC 156-157 G 3
Hunchun o VRC 150-151 H 6
Hundested o DK 86-87 E 9
Hundred and Two River ~ USA (MO) 274-275 D 4
Hundred Islands National Park • RP 160-161 D 4
Hunedoara o • RO 102-103 C 5
Hunga ⌒ TON 184 IV a 1
Hunga Ha'apai ⌒ TON 184 IV a 2
Hungary = Magyarország ■ H 92-93 O 5
Hunga Tonga ⌒ TON 184 IV a 2
Hungerford o AUS 178-179 H 5
Hungij o MAU 146-147 M 1
Hungnam o DVR 150-151 F 8
Hungry Horse o USA (MT) 250-251 F 3
Hungry Horse Reservoir ⊂ USA (MT) 250-251 F 3
Hunguj gol ~ MAU 146-147 L 1
Hungund o IND 140-141 G 2
Hu'ng Yên ☆ VN 156-157 E 6
Hunhada ~ RUS 110-111 U 7
Hünik o IR 134-135 J 3
Huni Valley o GH 202-203 K 7
Hunjiang o VRC 150-151 F 7
Hunkurāb, Ra's ▲ ET 194-195 G 5
Hunkuyi o WAN 204-205 G 3
Hünsār o • IR 134-135 D 2
Hunsberge ▲ NAM 220-221 C 3
Hunsrück ▲ D 92-93 J 4
Hunstein Range ▲ PNG 183 B 3
Hunsür o IND 140-141 G 4
Hunt o USA (AZ) 256-257 F 4
Hunte ~ D 92-93 K 2
Hunter o USA (AR) 276-277 D 5
Hunter o USA (KS) 262-263 H 5
Hunter o USA (ND) 258-259 K 4
Hunter Island ⌒ AUS 180-181 H 6
Hunter Island ⌒ CDN (BC) 230-231 A 2
Hunter Liggett Military Reservation, Fort xx USA (CA) 248-249 C 4
Hunter River ~ AUS 180-181 L 2
Hunter River o CDN (PEI) 240-241 M 4
Hunters o USA (WA) 244-245 G 2
Hunter's Lodge o EAK 212-213 F 5
Huntingburg o USA (IN) 274-275 M 6
Huntingdon o CDN (QUE) 238-239 L 3
Huntingdon o USA (TN) 276-277 G 5
Hunting Island ⌒ USA (SC) 284-285 K 4
Huntington o USA (IN) 274-275 N 4
Huntington o USA (MA) 278-279 J 6
Huntington o USA (NY) 280-281 N 3
Huntington o USA (OR) 244-245 H 6
Huntington o USA (PA) 280-281 J 3
Huntington o USA (TX) 268-269 F 5
Huntington o USA (UT) 254-255 E 4
Huntington o USA (WV) 280-281 D 5
Huntington Beach o USA (CA) 248-249 G 6
Huntland o USA (TN) 276-277 J 5
Huntly o GB 90-91 F 3
Huntly o NZ 182 E 2
Huntoon o CDN (SAS) 232-233 P 6
Hunts Inlet o CDN (BC) 228-229 D 2
Huntsville o CDN (ONT) 238-239 F 3
Huntsville o USA (AR) 276-277 B 4
Huntsville o USA (MO) 274-275 F 5
Huntsville o USA (TX) 268-269 E 6
Huntsville o USA (UT) 254-255 D 2
Huntsville o • USA (AL) 284-285 D 2
Hunucma o MEX 52-53 K 1
Hunyuan o VRC 154-155 H 2
Hunza ~ PK 138-139 E 1
Huocheng o VRC 146-147 E 3
Huolingol o VRC 148-149 O 5
Huonfels o NAM 216-217 G 6
Hu'o'ng Diên o VN 158-159 J 2
Hu'o'ng Khê ☆ VN 156-157 D 7
Hu'o'ng So'n ☆ VN 156-157 D 7
Huon Gulf ≈ 183 D 4
Huon Peninsula ⌣ PNG 183 D 4
Hüon Rāi ⌒ VN 158-159 H 6
Huonville-Ranelagh o AUS 180-181 J 7
Huoqiu o VRC 154-155 K 5
Huoshan o VRC 154-155 K 6
Huoshou o VRC 154-155 G 3
Hupel o CDN (BC) 230-231 L 3
Huqf, al- ⩥ OM 132-133 K 4
Huqna, Tall o IRQ 128-129 K 4
Huqui, Ilha do ⌒ BR 66-67 K 4
Hür o IR (ESF) 134-135 F 2
Hür o IR (HOR) 134-135 H 2
Huraba o RI 162-163 C 4
Huraiba,al- o Y 132-133 F 6
Huraimilā o KSA 130-131 K 5
Hurais o KSA (EPR) 130-131 L 5
Hurais o KSA (EPR) 130-131 K 5
Hüran ≈ 134-135 F 5
Hurd, Cape ▲ CDN (ONT) 238-239 D 3
Hurdiyo o SP 208-209 K 3
Hurdsfield o USA (ND) 258-259 H 4
Huren ~ RUS 120-121 M 3
Hure Qi o VRC 150-151 C 6
Hurghada = al-Gurdaqa ☆ • ET 194-195 F 4
Huri Hills ▲ EAK 212-213 F 2
Huringda ~ RUS 114-115 U 2
Huringda ~ RUS 116-117 F 2
Huriyā Muriyā, Ġazā'ir ⌒ Y 132-133 J 5
Hurki o BY 94-95 M 4
Hurley o USA (NM) 256-257 G 6
Hurley o USA (WI) 270-271 H 4
Hurma, al- o KSA 132-133 C 3
Hurman Çayı ~ TR 128-129 G 3
Hurmuli o RUS 122-123 G 3
Huron o USA (CA) 248-249 D 3
Huron o USA (SD) 260-261 H 2
Huron, Lake ⊂ 46-47 G 3
Huron, Lake ⊂ 272-273 F 2
Huron Islands ⌒ USA (MI) 270-271 L 4
Hurr, Wādī al- ~ KSA 130-131 H 2
Hurricane o USA (AK) 20-21 Q 5
Hurricane o USA (UT) 254-255 B 6
Hurricane o USA (WV) 280-281 D 5
Hurricane Creek ~ USA (GA) 284-285 H 5
Hurry Fjord ≈ 26-27 o 8
Hurso o ETH 208-209 E 4
Hurstown o USA (TX) 268-269 F 5
Hurtado o RCH 76-77 B 6
Hurtado, Río ~ RCH 76-77 B 6
Hurtsboro o USA (AL) 284-285 E 4
Hurwitz Lake ⊂ CDN 30-31 V 5
Husa, al- o KSA 132-133 C 5
Husaibi, al- o KSA 130-131 H 5
Husainābād o IND 142-143 D 3
Husain al-Ġāfūs o IRQ 128-129 L 6
Husana ~ RUS 108-109 b 7
Húsavík ☆ IS 86-87 e 1
Húsf o IR 134-135 H 2
Husheib o SUD 200-201 G 5
Huși o RO 102-103 F 4
Hūš Isā o ET 194-195 E 2
Huskisson o AUS 180-181 L 3
Huskvarna o S 86-87 G 8
Huslia o USA 20-21 M 4
Huslia River ~ USA 20-21 M 4
Husmund ~ RUS 116-117 K 2
Hussar o CDN (ALB) 232-233 F 4
Hustisford o USA (WI) 274-275 K 1
Hustonville o USA (KY) 276-277 L 3
Husum o D 92-93 K 1
Husum o USA (WA) 244-245 D 5
Hūt o Y 132-133 C 5
Hutag o MAU 148-149 F 3
Hutan Melintang o MAL 162-163 D 3
Hutchinson o USA (KS) 262-263 J 6
Hutchinson o USA (MN) 270-271 D 6
Hutchinson o ZA 220-221 F 5
Hutchinson Island ⌒ USA (FL) 286-287 J 4
Hutch Mountain ▲ USA (AZ) 256-257 D 4
Hutjena o PNG 184 I b 1
Hutou o VRC 150-151 J 5
Hutta, al- o KSA 130-131 G 3
Hutton Range ▲ AUS 176-177 G 2
Huttonsville o USA (WV) 280-281 G 5
Hutubi o VRC 146-147 H 3
Hutudabiga ~ RUS 108-109 W 4
Huu o RI 168 D 7
Hữu Lũng ☆ VN 156-157 E 6
Huvin Hippargi o IND 140-141 G 2
Huwair, al- o KSA 130-131 H 4
Huwairah, Wādī ~ Y 132-133 F 6
Huwār, Wādī ~ SUD 200-201 B 4
Huwaymi, al- o Y 132-133 H 5
Huwayt, Wādī ~ SUD 200-201 F 2
Huxi Xincun o VRC 148-149 E 7
Huxley o CDN (ALB) 232-233 E 4
Huxley, Mount ▲ USA 20-21 U 6
Huyuyun He ~ VRC 144-145 M 2
Hüzestān ◘ IR 134-135 C 3
Huzhong Z.B. II VRC (HEI) 150-151 D 2
Huzhong Z.B. ⊥ • VRC (HEI) 150-151 D 2
Huzhou o VRC 154-155 M 6
Huzhu Tuzu Zizhixian o VRC 154-155 B 3
Hužir o RUS 116-117 N 9
Hužirt o MAU 148-149 F 4
Huzūrābād o IND 138-139 G 10
Hvåge o IR 128-129 M 3
Hvåge Mohammad, Kūh-e ▲ AFG 136-137 M 7
Hvalynsk ☆ RUS 96-97 F 7
Hvammstangi o IS 86-87 c 2
Hvar o • HR 100-101 F 3
Hvar ⌒ HR 100-101 F 3
Hvitfeldt, Kap ▲ GRØ 28-29 T 6
Hvojnaja o RUS 94-95 O 2
Hvolsvöllur ☆ IS 86-87 c 3
Hvormūǵ o IR 134-135 D 4
Hvorostjanka ☆ RUS 96-97 F 7
Hvostovo o RUS 122-123 K 5
Hwali o ZW 218-219 E 5
Hwange o ZW 218-219 D 4
Hwange National Park ⊥ ZW 218-219 D 4
Hwedza o ZW 218-219 F 4
Hyades, Cerro ▲ RCH 80 D 3
Hyak o USA (WA) 244-245 D 3
Hyannis o USA (MA) 278-279 L 7
Hyannis o USA (NE) 262-263 E 3
Hyas o CDN (SAS) 232-233 Q 4
Hyattsville o USA (MD) 280-281 K 5
Hyattville o USA (WY) 252-253 L 2
Hybart o USA (AL) 284-285 C 5
Hyco Reservoir ⊂ USA (NC) 282-283 H 4
Hyco River ~ USA (VA) 280-281 G 7
Hydaburg o USA 32-33 D 4
Hyde Inlet ≈ 24-25 g 3
Hyde Lake ⊂ CDN 30-31 W 5
Hyden o AUS 176-177 E 6
Hyden o USA (KY) 276-277 M 3
Hyde Park o GUY 62-63 E 2
Hyder o USA (AK) 32-33 E 4
Hyder o USA (AZ) 256-257 B 5
Hyderābād ☆ •• IND 140-141 H 2
Hyderābād ☆ •• PK 138-139 B 7
Hydraulic o CDN (BC) 228-229 N 4
Hyen o N 86-87 B 6
Hyères o F 90-91 L 10
Hyères, Îles d' ⌒ • F 90-91 L 10
Hyesan ☆ DVR 150-151 G 7
Hyland Bay ≈ 172-173 J 2
Hyland Plateau ▲ CDN 30-31 E 5
Hyland River ~ CDN 30-31 E 5
Hyľčuju ~ RUS 88-89 X 2
Hylly o AZ 128-129 N 3
Hymera o USA (IN) 274-275 L 5
Hynčešť = Hînceşti ☆ MD 102-103 F 4
Hyndman Peak ▲ USA (ID) 252-253 D 3
Hyono-sen ▲ J 152-153 F 7
Hyrax Hill ∴ • EAK 212-213 F 4
Hyrdalan = Xırdalan o AZ 128-129 N 2
Hyrynsalmi o FIN 88-89 K 4
Hysham o USA (MT) 250-251 M 5
Hythe o CDN 32-33 L 4
Hyūga o J 152-153 D 8
Hyūga-nada ≈ 152-153 D 8

I

Iá, Rio ~ BR 66-67 D 3
Iabes, Erg ⩥ DZ 188-189 K 7
Iaciara o BR 72-73 G 3
Iaco, Rio ~ BR 66-67 C 7
Iaco, Río ~ PE 70-71 B 2
Iaçu o BR 72-73 K 2
Iakora o RM 222-223 E 9
Ia Krăng Po' Cô ~ VN 158-159 J 3
Ialibu o PNG 183 B 4
Ialomița ~ RO 102-103 E 5
Ialpug ~ MD 102-103 F 4
Iamara o PNG 183 B 5
Iamonia, Lake ⊂ USA (FL) 286-287 E 1
Ianabinda o RM 222-223 D 9
Ianca o RO 102-103 E 5
Ian Lake ⊂ CDN (BC) 228-229 B 3
Iao Valley ⌣ • USA (HI) 288 J 4
Iaripo o BR 62-63 G 5
Iași ☆ • RO 102-103 E 4
Iauaretê o BR 66-67 C 2
Iauaretê, Cachoeira ~ BR 66-67 D 3
Iauiari, Igarapé ~ BR 66-67 C 2
Iba ☆ RP 160-161 C 5
Ibadan ☆ WAN 204-205 E 5
Ibague ☆ CO 60-61 D 5
Ibaiti o BR 72-73 E 7
Ibanabuiú o BR 68-69 J 4
Ibanda o EAU 212-213 C 4
Ibáñez, Río ~ RCH 80 D 3
Ibanga o ZRE 212-213 A 5
Ibapah o USA (UT) 254-255 B 3
Ibar ~ YU 100-101 H 3
Ibarej, Río ~ BOL 70-71 E 4
Ibarra ☆ EC 64-65 C 1
Ibb o • Y 132-133 D 6
Ibba o SUD (SR) 206-207 J 6
Ibba ~ SUD 206-207 J 5
Ibembo o ZRE 210-211 J 2
Ibenga ~ RCB 210-211 F 2
Iberá, Esteros del ~ RA 76-77 J 5
Iberá, Laguna ⊂ RA 76-77 J 5
Iberia o PE (LOR) 64-65 E 4
Iberia o PE (MDI) 70-71 C 2
Iberia o USA (MO) 274-275 F 6
Iberville, Lac d' ⊂ CDN 36-37 N 7
Ibestad o N 86-87 H 2
Ibeto o WAN 204-205 F 3
Ibex Pass ▲ USA (CA) 248-249 H 4
Ibi o E 98-99 G 5
Ibi o WAN 204-205 H 4
Ibiá o BR 72-73 G 5
Ibiaí o BR 72-73 H 4
Ibiapaba, Serra da ▲ BR 68-69 H 3
Ibiapina o BR 68-69 H 3
Ibiara o BR 68-69 J 5
Ibib, Wādī ~ ET 194-195 G 6
Ibibobo o BOL 76-77 F 1
Ibicaraí o BR 72-73 L 3
Ibicuí, Rio ~ BR 76-77 J 5
Ibicuitinga o BR 68-69 J 4
Ibimirim o BR 68-69 K 6
Ibina ~ ZRE 212-213 B 3
Ibindy ▲ RM 222-223 E 8
Ibipeba o BR 68-69 G 7
Ibipira o BR 68-69 F 5
Ibipitanga o BR 72-73 J 2
Ibiporã o BR 72-73 E 7
Ibiquera o BR 72-73 K 2
Ibiraba o BR 68-69 G 7
Ibiraci o BR 72-73 G 6
Ibirama o BR 74-75 F 6
Ibirocaí, Rio ~ BR 76-77 J 5
Ibiruba o BR 74-75 D 7
Ibitiara o BR 72-73 J 2
Ibitinga o BR 72-73 F 6
Ibitinga, Represa < BR 72-73 F 6
Ibitira o BR 72-73 J 3
Ibitirama o BR 72-73 K 6
Ibó o BR 68-69 J 6
Ibo o MOC 214-215 L 7
Ibobobo, Serranía de ▲ BOL 76-77 F 1
Ibohamane o RN 198-199 C 5
Iboko o ZRE 210-211 G 4
Ibondo o ZRE 212-213 B 4
Ibonma o RI 166-167 G 3
Iboro o WAN 204-205 E 5
Ibotirama o BR 72-73 J 2
Iboundji, Mont ▲ G 210-211 C 4
Ibra o OM 132-133 L 2
Ibra o RI 166-167 G 4
Ibra, Wādī ~ SUD 206-207 G 3
'Ibri o OM 132-133 K 2
Ibsawāy o ET 194-195 E 3
Ibstone o CDN (SAS) 232-233 K 3
Ibuaçu o BR 68-69 J 4
Ibuguaçu o BR 68-69 H 3
Ibusuki o • J 152-153 D 9
Ica o PE 64-65 E 9
Iča ~ RUS 114-115 P 6
Iča ~ RUS 120-121 R 6
Içá, Rio ~ BR 66-67 C 4
Ica, Río de ~ PE 64-65 E 9
Icabarú o YV 62-63 D 3
Icalma, Paso de ▲ RA 78-79 D 5
Içana o BR 66-67 D 2
Içana, Rio ~ BR 66-67 D 2
Icaño o RA 76-77 E 5
Icapuí o BR 68-69 K 4
Icaraí o BR 68-69 J 3
Icaraíma o BR 72-73 D 7
Icatu o BR 68-69 F 3
Iceberg Point ▲ CDN 26-27 G 3
Ice Caves ∴ USA (WA) 244-245 D 5
Icefields Parkway o CDN (ALB) 228-229 R 4
Iceland = Ísland ■ IS 86-87 c 2
Iceland Basin ≃ 6-7 G 3
Iceland-Faroe Rise ≃ 6-7 H 2
Icelandic Plateau ≃ 6-7 H 2
Icém o BR 72-73 F 6
Ice Mountain ▲ CDN (BC) 228-229 N 2
Ičera ~ RUS 118-119 D 6
Ichalkaranji o IND 140-141 F 2
Iche o MA 188-189 L 4
Icheu o WAN 204-205 G 5
Ichi-gawa ~ J 152-153 F 7
Ichilo, Río ~ BOL 70-71 E 5
Ichinomiya o J 152-153 G 7
Ichinoseki o J 152-153 J 5
Ichkeul, Parc national de l' ⊥ ••• TN 190-191 G 2
Ichmul o MEX 52-53 K 1

Ichoa, Río ~ **BOL** 70-71 E 4
Ichocan o **PE** 64-65 C 5
Ich'ŏn o **ROK** 150-151 F 9
Ichuña o **PE** 70-71 B 5
Ičigemskij hrebet ▲ **RUS** 112-113 L 5
Ičinskaja Sopka, vulkan ▲ **RUS** 120-121 R 6
Ičinskij o **RUS** 120-121 Q 6
Icó o **BR** 68-69 J 5
Icoca o **ANG** 216-217 D 3
Ičoda ~ **RUS** 118-119 E 5
Ičuveem ~ **RUS** 112-113 Q 2
Icy Bay ≈ 20-21 U 7
Icy Cape ▲ **USA** 20-21 J 1
Icy Cape ▲ **USA** 20-21 T 7
Icy Reef ⌒ **USA** 20-21 U 2
Icy Strait ≈ 32-33 C 2
Ida ~ **RUS** 116-117 M 9
Ida o **USA** (LA) 268-269 G 4
Idabato o **CAM** 204-205 H 6
Idabel o **USA** (OK) 264-265 K 5
Idabo o **ETH** 208-209 E 5
Idaga Hamus o **ETH** 200-201 J 5
Ida Grove o **USA** (IA) 274-275 C 2
Idah o **WAN** 204-205 G 5
Idaho □ **USA** (ID) 252-253 B 2
Idaho Army National Guard Artillery Range xx **USA** (ID) 252-253 B 3
Idaho Falls o **USA** (ID) 252-253 F 3
Idaho National Engineering Laboratory • **USA** (ID) 252-253 F 3
Idaiatuba o **BR** 72-73 G 7
Idak, Cape ▲ **USA** 22-23 N 6
Idalia o **USA** (CO) 254-255 N 4
Idalia National Park ⊥ **AUS** 178-179 H 3
Idalina, Cachoeira ~ **BR** 70-71 G 2
Idalou o **USA** (TX) 264-265 C 5
Idanre o• **WAN** 204-205 F 5
Ida-Oumarkt o **MA** 188-189 G 6
Idāppādi o **IND** 140-141 G 5
Idar o **IND** 138-139 D 8
Idar-Oberstein o **D** 92-93 J 4
Ida Valley o **AUS** 176-177 F 4
'Idd al-Ghanam o **SUD** 206-207 G 3
Iddesleigh o **CDN** (ALB) 232-233 G 5
Ideal, El o **MEX** 52-53 L 1
Ideles o **DZ** 190-191 E 9
Idenao o **CAM** 204-205 H 6
Idèr gol ~ **MAU** 148-149 D 3
Idfū o• **ET** 194-195 F 5
Idhan' Awbārī ∸ **LAR** 192-193 D 4
Idi o **RI** 162-163 B 2
Idi-Iroko o **WAN** 204-205 E 5
İdil ☆ **TR** 128-129 J 4
Idini o **RIM** 196-197 C 6
Idiofa o **ZRE** 210-211 G 6
Idiriya o **MA** 188-189 F 7
Idjiwi o **ZRE** 212-213 B 5
Idjiwi, Ile ⌒ **ZRE** 212-213 B 5
Idjum ~ **RUS** 120-121 D 6
Idkū o **ET** 194-195 E 2
Idlib ☆ **SYR** 128-129 G 5
Idoani o **WAN** 204-205 F 5
Idodi o **EAT** 214-215 H 4
Idogo o **WAN** 204-205 E 5
Idoho < **WAN** 204-205 G 6
Idolo, Isla del ⌒ **MEX** 50-51 L 7
Idongo o **RCA** 206-207 E 5
Ídra ⌒ **GR** 100-101 J 6
Idre o **S** 86-87 F 6
Idrigill o **GB** 90-91 D 3
Idrija o **SLO** 100-101 D 2
Idrinskoe ☆ **RUS** 116-117 F 8
Idriss 1., Barrage < **MA** 188-189 J 3
Idumbe o **ZRE** 210-211 H 5
Idutywa o **ZA** 220-221 J 6
Idwa, al- o **KSA** 130-131 H 4
Idževan o **AR** 128-129 L 2
Iecava o **LV** 94-95 J 3
Iengra ~ **RUS** 118-119 M 7
Iepê o **BR** 72-73 E 7
Ieper o·· **B** 92-93 G 3
Ierápetra o **GR** 100-101 K 7
Ie-shima ⌒ **J** 152-153 B 11
Ievlevo o **RUS** 114-115 J 6
Ifakara o **EAT** 214-215 J 5
Ifaki o **WAN** 204-205 F 5
'Ifāl, Wādī ~ **KSA** 130-131 D 3
Ifanadiana o **RM** 222-223 E 8
Ifanirea o **RM** 222-223 E 9
Ifaty o **RM** 222-223 C 9
Ife o• **WAN** 204-205 F 5
Ifenat o **TCH** 198-199 J 6
Iferouâne o **RN** 198-199 D 3
Ifertas, Hassi < **LAR** 190-191 H 6
Ifetedo o **WAN** 204-205 F 5
Ifetesene ▲ **DZ** 190-191 E 8
Iffley o **AUS** 174-175 F 6
Iffley o **CDN** (SAS) 232-233 K 2
Ifjord o **N** 86-87 N 1
Ifon o **WAN** 204-205 F 5
Iforhas, Adrar des ▲ **RMM** 196-197 L 4
Ifould Lake ⬭ **AUS** 176-177 M 5
Ifrane ☆ **MA** 188-189 J 4
Ifri, Imi-n- • **MA** 188-189 H 5
Ifunda o **EAT** 214-215 H 4
Iga ~ **RUS** 116-117 N 7
Iga ~ **RUS** 122-123 D 2
Igabi o **WAN** 204-205 G 3
Igaliku o **GRØ** 28-29 S 6
Igaliku Fjord ≈ 28-29 S 6
Igalula o **EAT** 212-213 D 6
Iganga o **EAU** 212-213 D 3
Igangan o **WAN** 204-205 E 5
Igapó o **BR** 68-69 K 6
Igapora o **BR** 72-73 J 2
Igara Paraná, Río ~ **CO** 64-65 F 2
Igarapava o **BR** 72-73 G 6
Igarapé-Açu o **BR** 68-69 E 2
Igarapé Grande o **BR** 68-69 F 4
Igarapé Lage, Area Indígena X **BR** 70-71 E 2
Igarapé Lourdes, Área Indígena X **BR** 70-71 G 2
Igarapé Mirim o **BR** 62-63 K 6
Igarite o **BR** 68-69 G 7
Igarka o **RUS** 108-109 W 8
Igarka-Lybangajaha ~ **RUS** 108-109 R 7
Igarra o **WAN** 204-205 G 5
Igawa o **EAT** 214-215 H 5
Igbeti o **WAN** 204-205 F 4
Igbogor o **WAN** 204-205 F 5
Igboho o **WAN** 204-205 E 4
Igbo-Ora o **WAN** 204-205 E 5
Igbor o **WAN** 204-205 H 5
Iğdır ☆ **TR** 128-129 L 3
Igdlorssuit Sund ≈ 26-27 Y 8
Igdlulik o **GRØ** 26-27 W 6
Igèl'veem ~ **RUS** 112-113 Y 4
Igichuk Hills ▲ **USA** 20-21 J 3
Igirma o **RUS** 116-117 L 7
Igiugig o **USA** 22-23 T 3
Iglau = Jihlava o **CZ** 92-93 N 4
Igle, Cerro ▲ **RA** 80 D 5
Iglesia, Arroyo de la ~ **RA** 76-77 C 6
Iglesias o **I** 100-101 B 5
Iglesias, Cerro ▲ **RA** 80 G 3
Igli o **DZ** 188-189 K 5
Iglino ☆ **RUS** 96-97 K 6
Igloolik o **CDN** 24-25 f 6
Igloolik Island ⌒ **CDN** 24-25 f 6
Iglusuaktalialuk Island ⌒ **CDN** 36-37 T 6
Ignace o **CDN** (ONT) 234-235 M 5
Ignacio o **USA** (CO) 254-255 H 6
Ignalina o **LT** 94-95 K 4
Ignašino o **RUS** 118-119 L 9
Ignatovo o **RUS** 94-95 P 1
İğneada o **TR** 128-129 B 2
Ignit Fiord ≈ 36-37 T 2
Igolo o **DY** 204-205 E 5
Igom o **RI** 166-167 F 2
Igoma o **EAT** 214-215 G 4
Igombe ~ **EAT** 212-213 D 6
Igombe ~ **EAT** (TAB) 212-213 C 6
Igornachoix Bay ≈ 38-39 Q 3
Igornachoix Bay ≈ **CDN** 242-243 L 2
Igoumenítsa o **GR** 100-101 H 5
Igporin o **WAN** 204-205 F 4
Igra ☆ **RUS** 96-97 H 5
Igreja o **CV** 202-203 B 6
Igrim o **RUS** 114-115 H 3
Igrita o **WAN** 204-205 G 6
Iguache, Mesas de ∸ **CO** 64-65 F 1
Iguaçu, Parque Nacional do ⊥··· **BR** 74-75 D 5
Iguaçu, Rio ~ **BR** 74-75 D 5
Iguaí o **BR** 72-73 K 3
Iguala de la Independencia o **MEX** 52-53 E 2
Iguape o **BR** 74-75 G 5
Iguará, Rio ~ **BR** 68-69 G 3
Iguatemi o **BR** 76-77 K 2
Iguatemi, Rio ~ **BR** 76-77 K 2
Iguatu o **BR** 68-69 J 5
Iguazú, Cataratas del ~·· **RA** 76-77 K 3
Iguazú, Parque Nacional del ⊥··· **RA** 76-77 K 3
Iguéla o **G** 210-211 B 4
Iguetti < **RIM** 196-197 F 2
Iguetti, Sebkhet ⬭ **RIM** 196-197 F 2
Iguguno o **EAT** 212-213 E 6
Iguîdi, Erg ∸ **DZ** 196-197 G 2
Iguidi Ouan Kasa ∸ **LAR** 190-191 H 8
Iguitu o **BR** 68-69 G 7
Igumnovskaja o **RUS** 94-95 S 1
Igunga o **EAT** 212-213 D 6
Igurubi o **EAT** (TAB) 212-213 D 5
Igžej o **RUS** 116-117 L 8
Iharana o **RM** 222-223 G 4
Ihavandiffulu Atoll ⌒ **MV** 140-141 B 4
Ihbulag o **MAU** 148-149 G 6
Ihema, Lac ⬭ **RWA** 212-213 C 4
Iherir o• **DZ** 190-191 G 8
Iheya o **J** 152-153 B 11
Iheya-shima ⌒ **J** 152-153 B 11
Ihhairhan o **MAU** 148-149 H 4
Ihiala o **WAN** 204-205 G 6
Ihitsa < **LAR** 192-193 E 5
Ihosy o **RM** 222-223 E 9
Ihotry, Fahiry ⬭ **RM** 222-223 C 8
Ih suuž o **MAU** 148-149 H 3
Ihtiman o **BG** 102-103 C 6
İhtiyarşahap Dağları ▲ **TR** 128-129 K 3
Ihu o **PNG** 183 C 4
Ihuari o **PE** 64-65 D 7
Ihugh o **WAN** 204-205 H 5
Ihumri Tilaiya o **IND** 142-143 D 3
Ihuo o **WAN** 204-205 G 6
Ih-Uul = Selenge o **MAU** 148-149 E 3
Iida o **J** 152-153 G 7
Iidaan o **SP** 208-209 J 5
Iide-san ▲ **J** 152-153 H 6
Iijoki ~ **FIN** 88-89 J 4
Iisaku o **EST** 94-95 K 2
Iisalmi o **FIN** 88-89 J 5
Iiyama o **J** 152-153 H 6
Iizuka o **J** 152-153 D 8
Ij o **IND** 140-141 G 2
Ija ~ **RUS** 116-117 K 8
Ijâfene ∸ **RIM** 196-197 F 4
Ijaji o **ETH** 208-209 C 4
Ijebu-Igbo o **WAN** 204-205 F 5
Ijebu-Ode o **WAN** 204-205 E 5
Ijero o **WAN** 204-205 F 5
Ijkharrah o **LAR** 192-193 J 3
Ijoubban ∸ **RIM** 196-197 G 4
Ijoukak o **MA** 188-189 G 5
IJsselmeer ≈ **NL** 92-93 H 2
Ijuí o **BR** 74-75 D 7
Ik ~ **RUS** 96-97 H 7
Ik, ozero ⬭ **RUS** 114-115 L 6
Ika o **RUS** 116-117 N 6
Ikahavo ▲ **RM** 222-223 D 6
Ikalamavony o **RM** 222-223 E 8
Ikamiut o **GRØ** 28-29 O 4
Ikamiut = Qeersorfik o **GRØ** 28-29 P 2
Ikanbujmal o **VRC** 146-147 J 6
Ikanda o **ZRE** 210-211 H 5
Ikang o **WAN** 204-205 H 6
Ikanga o **EAK** 212-213 G 4
Ikare o **WAN** 204-205 F 5
Ikaría ⌒ **GR** 100-101 L 6
Ikatskij, hrebet ▲ **RUS** 118-119 E 9
Ikauna o **IND** 142-143 B 2
Ikebe o **WAN** 204-205 G 5
Ikeda o **J** 152-153 K 3
Ikej o **RUS** 116-117 K 8
Ikej ~ **RUS** 116-117 J 8
Ikeja ☆ **WAN** 204-205 E 5
Ikela o **ZRE** 210-211 J 4
Ikelemba ~ **ZRE** 210-211 H 3
Ikelenge o **Z** 214-215 C 6
Ikem o **WAN** 204-205 G 5
Ikèn ~ **RUS** 108-109 X 6
Ikèngué o **G** 210-211 B 4
Ikeq Sund ≈ 28-29 T 6
Ikerasârssuk o **GRØ** 26-27 X 7
Ikere o **WAN** 204-205 F 5
Ikermiut ⌒ **GRØ** 28-29 U 5
Ikerssuaq ≈ 28-29 V 4
Ikertivaq ≈ 28-29 X 3
Iki ⌒ **J** 152-153 C 8
Ikimba Kamachumu, Lake ⬭ **EAT** (KAG) 212-213 C 4
Ikire o **WAN** 204-205 F 5
Ikirun o **WAN** 204-205 F 5
Iki-Tsushima Quasi National Park ⊥ **J** 152-153 C 7
Ikkatteq o **GRØ** 28-29 W 4
Ikobé o **G** 210-211 C 4
Ikohahoene, Adrar ▲ **DZ** 190-191 G 8
Ikola o **EAT** 214-215 F 4
Ikole o **WAN** 204-205 F 5
Ikolik, Cape ▲ **USA** 22-23 T 4
Ikom o **WAN** 204-205 H 6
Ikomu o **WAN** 204-205 E 4
Ikongo o **RM** 222-223 E 8
Ikonongo o **ZRE** 210-211 G 3
Ikoo o **EAK** 212-213 G 4
Ikopa ~ **RM** 222-223 E 7
Ikorodu o **WAN** 204-205 E 5
Ikot Ekpene o **WAN** 204-205 G 6
Ikoto o **SUD** 208-209 A 6
Ikoy ~ **G** 210-211 C 4
Ikpik Bay ≈ 24-25 j 6
Ikpikpuk River ~ **USA** 20-21 N 1
Ikrjanoe ☆ **RUS** 96-97 E 10
Iksa ~ **RUS** 114-115 R 6
Ikutha o **EAK** 212-213 G 5
Ila o **USA** (GA) 284-285 G 2
Ilafergh, Oued ~ **DZ** 196-197 L 4
Ilaga o **RI** 166-167 J 4
Ilagan ☆ **RP** 160-161 D 4
Ilaiyānkudi o **IND** 140-141 H 6
Ilaji o **WAN** 204-205 E 5
Ilaka Atsinanana o **RM** 222-223 F 7
Ilakaka o **RM** 222-223 D 9
Ilakana Patatpe o **F** 62-63 G 4
Īlām □ **IR** 134-135 B 2
Īlām ☆• **IR** 134-135 B 2
Ilan o **RC** 156-157 M 4
Ilanskil ☆ **RUS** 116-117 H 7
Ila-Orangun o **WAN** 204-205 F 4
Ilara o **WAN** 204-205 F 5
Ilaro o **WAN** 204-205 E 5
Ilaura o **PNG** 183 D 4
Ilave o **PE** 70-71 C 5
Ilave, Río ~ **PE** 70-71 C 5
Ilawe o **WAN** 204-205 F 5
Ilbenge o **RUS** 118-119 M 4
Ilbilbie o **AUS** 178-179 K 1
Île à la Crosse, Lac ⬭ **CDN** 34-35 C 3
Ilebgâne, Adrar ▲ **RMM** 196-197 L 5
Ilebo o **ZRE** 210-211 H 6
Ileck, Sol'- ☆ **RUS** 96-97 J 8
Île-de-France □ **F** 90-91 J 7
Île-d'Entrée o **CDN** (QUE) 242-243 G 5
Ileg o **PNG** 183 C 3
Ilek ~ **KA** 126-127 M 3
Ilek ☆ **RUS** (ORB) 96-97 H 8
Ilek ~ **RUS** 96-97 H 8
Ileksa ~ **RUS** 88-89 O 5
Ileret o **EAK** 212-213 F 1
Île-Rousse, L' o **F** 98-99 M 3
Iles, Lac des ⬭ **CDN** (QUE) 238-239 H 2
Ileša ~ **RUS** 88-89 T 5
Ilesa o **WAN** (KWA) 204-205 E 4
Ilesa o **WAN** (OYO) 204-205 F 5
Ilford o **CDN** 34-35 J 2
Ilfracombe o **AUS** 178-179 H 2
Ilfracombe o• **GB** 90-91 E 6
Ilga ~ **RUS** 116-117 M 9
Ilgaz ☆ **TR** 128-129 E 2
Ilgaz Dağları ▲ **TR** 128-129 E 2
Ilgın ☆ **TR** 128-129 D 3
Ilha Grande, Baía da ≈ 72-73 H 7
Ilha Solteira o **BR** 72-73 E 6
Ilhéus o• **BR** 72-73 L 3
Ilhota da Maloca Arori o **BR** 62-63 F 5
Ili ~ **KA** 146-147 D 4
Ilia o **RO** 102-103 C 5
Ilia o **USA** (WA) 244-245 H 4
Iliamna Lake ⬭ **USA** 22-23 T 3
Iliamna Volcano ▲ **USA** 20-21 O 6
Il'ič o **KA** 136-137 L 4
Ilıca o **TR** 128-129 B 3
Ilıca ☆ **TR** 128-129 J 3
Ilicínia o **BR** 72-73 H 6
Ilidža o **BIH** 100-101 G 3
Ilig, Raas ▲ **SP** 208-209 J 5
Iligan ☆ **RP** 160-161 F 8
Iligan ~ **RP** 160-161 D 4
Iligan Bay ≈ 160-161 E 8
Iligan Point ▲ **RP** 160-161 E 3
Ili He ~ **VRC** 146-147 E 4
Ilikok Island ⌒ **CDN** 36-37 S 2
Ilim ~ **RUS** 116-117 L 8
Ilimanaq = Claushavn o **GRØ** 28-29 P 2
Ilimo o **PNG** 183 D 5
Ilimpeja ~ **RUS** 116-117 M 4
Ilimsk o **RUS** 116-117 L 7
Ilin-Dželi ~ **RUS** 118-119 H 4
Ilingelyo, Tanjung ▲ **RI** 166-167 E 2
Ilin Island ⌒ **RP** 160-161 D 6
Ilin-Jurjah ~ **RUS** 110-111 c 5
Il'inka o **RUS** 96-97 K 8
Il'ino o **RUS** 94-95 M 4
Il'inovka o **RUS** 122-123 C 4
Il'inskaja Sopka, vulkan ▲ **RUS** 122-123 R 3
Il'inskij o **RUS** 96-97 J 4
Il'inskij o **RUS** 122-123 K 5
Iliomar o **RI** 166-167 D 6
Ilio Point ▲ **USA** (HI) 288 H 3
Ilir o **RUS** 116-117 K 8
Ilir ~ **RUS** 116-117 K 8
Ilirgytgyn, ozero ⬭ **RUS** 112-113 K 1
Ilirnej o **RUS** 112-113 P 3
Ilirnej, ozero ⬭ **RUS** 112-113 P 3
Ilirnejskij krjaž ▲ **RUS** 112-113 P 3
Ilistaja ~ **RUS** 122-123 E 6
Ilısu Barajı < **TR** 128-129 J 4
Il'ja ~ **RUS** 110-111 F 4
Ilja ~ **RUS** 118-119 F 10
Il'jak ~ **RUS** 114-115 O 4
Il'jali ☆ **TM** 136-137 F 4
Iljalinskij kanal < **TM** 136-137 E 4
Iljara o **EAK** 212-213 H 4
Ilktugitak, Cape ▲ **USA** 22-23 T 3
Ill ~ **F** 90-91 L 7
Illampu, Nevado ▲ **BOL** 70-71 C 4
Illapel o **RCH** 76-77 B 6
Illapel, Río ~ **RCH** 76-77 B 6
Illara Creek ~ **AUS** 176-177 M 2
Illawarra, Lake ⬭ **AUS** 180-181 L 3
Illawong o **AUS** 176-177 C 4
Illbillee, Mount ▲ **AUS** 176-177 M 3
Illecillewaet Névé ~ **CDN** (BC) 230-231 M 2
Illéla o **RN** 198-199 B 5
Illela o **WAN** 198-199 B 6
Iller ~ **D** 92-93 L 4
Illes Balears ⌒ **E** 98-99 H 5
Illesca, Cerro ▲ **PE** 64-65 B 4
Illescas o **MEX** 50-51 H 6
Illgen City o **USA** (MN) 270-271 G 3
Illimo o **PE** 64-65 C 5
Illingworth o **CDN** (ALB) 232-233 G 5
Illiniza, Volcán ▲ **EC** 64-65 C 2
Illinois □ **USA** (IL) 274-275 H 4
Illinois City o **USA** (IL) 274-275 H 3
Illinois Point ▲ **USA** (MT) 250-251 D 4
Illinois River ~ **USA** (AR) 276-277 B 5
Illinois River ~ **USA** (IL) 274-275 H 5
Illinois River ~ **USA** (OK) 264-265 K 2
Illinois River ~ **USA** (OR) 244-245 B 8
Illiopolis o **USA** (IL) 274-275 J 5
Illiwa ~ **GUY** 62-63 E 4
Illizi o **DZ** 190-191 G 7
Illmo o **USA** (MO) 276-277 F 3
Illorsuit o **GRØ** 26-27 Y 8
Illueca o **E** 98-99 G 4
Illusion Lake ⬭ **USA** (TX) 264-265 B 5
Ilma, Lake ⬭ **AUS** 176-177 J 4
Ilmalianuk, Cape ▲ **USA** 22-23 M 6
Il'men', ozero ⬭ **RUS** 94-95 M 2
Il'menskij zapovednik ⊥ **RUS** 96-97 M 6
Ilnik o **USA** 22-23 R 4
Ilo o **PE** 70-71 B 5
Ilobasco o• **ES** 52-53 K 5
Ilobi ~ **RCB** 210-211 F 2
Ilobu o **WAN** 204-205 F 5
Iloca o **RCH** 78-79 C 3
Ilofa o **WAN** 204-205 F 4
Ilog ~ **RP** 160-161 E 8
Iloilo City ☆·· **RP** 160-161 E 7
Ilomantsi o **FIN** 88-89 L 5
Ilonga o **EAT** 214-215 J 5
Ilorin ☆ **WAN** 204-205 F 4
Ilovlja ~ **RUS** 96-97 D 8
Il'pinskij, mys ▲ **RUS** 120-121 V 4
Il'pinskij, poluostrov ᴗ **RUS** 120-121 V 4
Il'pyr, poluostrov ᴗ **RUS** 120-121 V 4
Il'pyrskij o **RUS** 120-121 V 4
Ilua Fjord ≈ 28-29 S 6
Ilubabor □ **ETH** 208-209 B 5
Ilugwa o **RI** 166-167 K 3
Iluileq ⌒ **GRØ** 28-29 T 6
Ilūkste o **LV** 94-95 K 4
Ilula o **EAT** 212-213 D 5
Ilulissat = Jakobshavn o **GRØ** 28-29 P 2
Ilur o **RI** 166-167 F 4
Ilushi o **WAN** 204-205 G 5
Ilwaco o **USA** (WA) 244-245 B 4
Ilwendo o **Z** 218-219 C 3
Ilyč ~ **RUS** 114-115 D 3
Im ~ **RUS** 122-123 H 2
Imabari o **J** 152-153 E 7
Imabetsu o **J** 152-153 J 4
Imaichi o **J** 152-153 H 6
Imajō o **J** 152-153 G 7
Imakane o **J** 152-153 H 3
Imala o **MOC** 218-219 K 2
Imām Ānas o **IRQ** 130-131 K 2
İmamoğlu ☆ **TR** 128-129 F 4
Imanbūlak ~ **KA** 124-125 E 2
Imandi o **RI** 164-165 H 3
Imandra, ozero ⬭ **RUS** 88-89 M 3
Imangra ~ **RUS** 118-119 K 7
Imanombo o **RM** 222-223 D 10
Imantau, köli ⬭ **KA** 124-125 F 2
Imari o **J** 152-153 C 8
Imasa o **SUD** 200-201 H 3
Imassogo o **BF** 202-203 J 3
Imata o **PE** 70-71 B 4
Imata, Serrania de ▲ **YV** 62-63 D 2
Imataca, Reserva Forestal ⊥ **YV** 60-61 L 3
Imataca, Reserva Forestal ⊥ **YV** 62-63 D 2
Imatong Mountains ▲ **SUD** 206-207 L 6
Imatra o **FIN** 88-89 K 6
Imbāba o **ET** 194-195 E 2
Imbituba o **BR** 74-75 F 7
Imbituba, Ponta de ▲ **BR** 74-75 F 7
Imbituva o **BR** 74-75 E 5
Imbler o **USA** (OR) 244-245 H 5
Imboden o **USA** (AR) 276-277 D 4
Imborditure Creek ~ **AUS** 178-179 D 2
Imbrinis o **PNG** 183 A 2
Imbwae o **Z** 218-219 C 3
Iménas < **RMM** 196-197 L 6
Imerimandroso o **RM** 222-223 F 6
Imerina Imady o **RM** 222-223 E 8
Imerintsiatesika o **RM** 222-223 E 7
Imese o **ZRE** 210-211 G 2
Imessouane, Pointe ▲ **MA** 188-189 G 5
Imgyt ~ **RUS** 114-115 M 5
Imgytskoe, boloto ∸ **RUS** 114-115 L 5
Īmī o **ETH** 208-209 F 5
Imi-n-Tanoute o **MA** 188-189 G 5
Imišly = İmişli o **AZ** 128-129 N 3
Imja Do ⌒ **ROK** 150-151 F 10
Imjin Gang ~ **DVR** 150-151 F 8
Imlan ~ **RUS** 112-113 P 5
Imlay o **USA** (NV) 246-247 G 3
Imlay City o **USA** (MI) 272-273 F 4
Imlily o **MA** 196-197 C 3
Immokalee o **USA** (FL) 286-287 H 5
Immouzzer-des-Ida-Outanane o **MA** 188-189 G 5
Imnaha o **USA** (OR) 244-245 J 5
Imnaha River ~ **USA** (OR) 244-245 J 5
Imnlor, ozero ⬭ **RUS** 114-115 N 4
Imo □ **WAN** 204-205 G 6
Imofossen ~ **N** 86-87 K 2
Ímola o **I** 100-101 C 2
Imonda o **PNG** 183 A 2
Imo River ~ **WAN** 204-205 G 6
Imotski o **HR** 100-101 F 3
Imoulaye, Hassi < **DZ** 190-191 G 6
Imouzèr-du-Kandar o **MA** 188-189 J 4
Impenvèem ~ **RUS** 112-113 P 5
Imperatriz o **BR** 68-69 E 4
Imperia o **I** 100-101 B 3
Imperial o **CDN** (SAS) 232-233 N 4
Imperial o **USA** (CA) 248-249 J 7
Imperial o **USA** (NE) 262-263 E 4
Imperial o **USA** (TX) 266-267 E 2
Imperial, Río ~ **RCH** 78-79 C 5
Imperial Mills o **CDN** 32-33 P 4
Imperieuse Reef ⌒ **AUS** 172-173 D 4
Impfondo ☆ **RCB** 210-211 G 3
Imphāl ☆• **IND** 142-143 H 3
Imposible, Parque Nacional El ⊥ **GCA** 52-53 J 5
Impulo o **ANG** (HUA) 216-217 B 6
Impulo ~ **ANG** 216-217 B 6
İmranlı ☆ **TR** 128-129 H 3
İmroz o **TR** 128-129 A 2
Imtān o **SYR** 128-129 G 6
Imuris o **MEX** 50-51 D 2
Imuruan Bay ≈ 160-161 C 7
Imuruk Basin ⬭ **USA** 20-21 H 4
Imuruk Lake ⬭ **USA** 20-21 J 4
Imusho o **Z** 218-219 B 3
Ina ~ **PL** 92-93 N 2
Ina ~ **RUS** 118-119 E 9
Inaafmadow o **SP** 208-209 G 4
Inabu o **J** 152-153 G 7
Inácio Dias, Ponta ▲ **BR** 74-75 F 5
Inácio Martins o **BR** 74-75 E 5
Inadale o **USA** (TX) 264-265 D 6
I-n-Adiattafene o **RMM** 202-203 J 2
Inaja o **BR** 66-67 H 5
Inajá o **BR** 68-69 K 6
Inaja, Rio ~ **BR** 68-69 C 6
Inâl o **RIM** 196-197 C 4
Inalik o **USA** 20-21 F 4
Inambari o **PE** 70-71 C 3
Inambari, Río ~ **PE** 70-71 B 3
In Amenas o **DZ** 190-191 G 6
In Amguel o **DZ** 190-191 E 9
Inangahua o **NZ** 182 C 4
Inan'ja ~ **RUS** 120-121 N 2
Inanudak Bay ≈ 22-23 M 6
Inanwatan o **RI** 166-167 G 3
Iñapari o **PE** 70-71 C 2
Inari o• **FIN** 88-89 J 2
Inarigda o **RUS** 116-117 N 4
Inarijärvi ⬭·· **FIN** 88-89 J 2
Inaru River ~ **USA** 20-21 M 1
Inarwa o **NEP** 144-145 F 7
Inauini, Rio ~ **BR** 66-67 C 7
Inawashiro-ko ⬭ **J** 152-153 J 6
in-Azaoua o **RN** 198-199 C 2
In Azzene, Djebel ▲ **DZ** 190-191 C 7
In Belbel o **DZ** 190-191 C 7
Inca o **E** 98-99 J 5
Inca, Cerro del ▲ **RCH** 76-77 C 1
Inca, Río del ~ **RA** 76-77 C 5
Inca de Oro o **RCH** 76-77 C 4
Incahuasi o **PE** 64-65 C 5
Incahuasi o **RA** 76-77 D 3
Īnč e Borūn o **IR** 136-137 D 6
İnce Burnu ▲ **TR** 128-129 F 2
İncesu ☆• **TR** 128-129 F 3
Inchbonnie o **NZ** 182 C 5
Inchiri □ **RIM** 196-197 C 4
Inch'ŏn o **ROK** 150-151 F 9
Inchope o **MOC** 218-219 G 4
Inchul ~ **UA** 102-103 H 3
Inchulec' ~ **UA** 102-103 H 3
Incisioni Rupestri, Parco Nazionale ⊥··· **I** 100-101 C 1
Incomappleaux River ~ **CDN** (BC) 230-231 M 3
Incomati, Rio ~ **MOC** 220-221 L 2
Inčoun o **RUS** 112-113 Z 3
Increase o **USA** (MS) 268-269 M 4
Incudine, Monte ▲ **F** 98-99 M 4
Incuyo o **PE** 64-65 F 9
Indaial o **BR** 74-75 F 6
Indalsälven ~ **S** 86-87 H 5
Inda Medhanī o **ETH** 200-201 J 6
Indapur o **IND** 138-139 E 10
Indara Point o **IND** 140-141 L 6
Indara Point ▲ **IND** 140-141 L 6
Indargarh o **IND** 138-139 F 7
Inda Silasē o **ETH** 200-201 J 5
Indaugyi Aing ⬭ **MYA** 142-143 K 2
Indaw o **MYA** 142-143 K 5
Indé o **MEX** 50-51 G 5
Independence o **USA** (CA) 248-249 F 3
Independence o **USA** (IA) 274-275 G 2
Independence o **USA** (KS) 262-263 L 7
Independence o **USA** (KY) 276-277 L 2
Independence o **USA** (LA) 268-269 K 6
Independence o **USA** (MN) 270-271 F 4
Independence o **USA** (MN) 270-271 E 5
Independence o **USA** (MO) 274-275 D 5
Independence o **USA** (OR) 244-245 B 6
Independence o **USA** (VA) 280-281 E 7
Independence Creek ~ **USA** (TX) 266-267 E 3
Independence Fjord ≈ 26-27 k 3
Independence Hall ··· **USA** (PA) 280-281 M 4
Independence Mine • **USA** 20-21 Q 6
Independence Rock State Historic Site ∴ **USA** (WY) 252-253 L 4
Independencia o **BOL** (COC) 70-71 D 5
Independencia o **BOL** (PAN) 70-71 D 2
Independência o **BR** 68-69 H 4
Independencia o **YV** 60-61 E 4
Independencia, Isla de la ⌒ **PE** 64-65 D 9
Independența o **RO** 102-103 F 5
Inder, köl ⬭ **KA** 96-97 H 9
Inderaba o **SUD** 200-201 F 6
Inderbor ☆ **KA** 96-97 H 9
Index o **USA** (WA) 244-245 D 3
Indi o **IND** 140-141 F 2
India ■ **IND** 138-139 D 7
Indiana o **AUS** 178-179 C 2
Indiana o **USA** (PA) 280-281 G 3
Indiana □ **USA** (IN) 274-275 M 5
Indiana Dunes • **USA** (IN) 274-275 L 3
Indianapolis ☆ **USA** (IN) 274-275 M 5
Indiana Trail Caverns • **USA** (OH) 280-281 C 3
Indian Bay o **CDN** (NFL) 242-243 P 3
Indian Bayou ~ **USA** (AR) 276-277 D 6
Indian Brook ~ **CDN** (NS) 240-241 P 4
Indian Cabins o **CDN** 30-31 L 6
Indian Community ∴• **BS** 54-55 J 3
Indian Creek ~ **USA** (UT) 254-255 F 5
Indian Falls o **USA** (CA) 246-247 E 3
Indian Gardens o **CDN** (NS) 240-241 K 6
Indian Grave Mount ▲ **USA** 20-21 U 4
Indian Harbour o **CDN** (NS) 240-241 M 6
Indian Head o **CDN** (SAS) 232-233 P 5
Indian Head o **USA** (MD) 280-281 J 5
Indian Heaven Wilderness ⊥ **USA** (WA) 244-245 D 4
Indian Lake o **USA** (NY) 278-279 G 5
Indian Lake ⬭ **USA** (MI) 270-271 M 4
Indian Lake ⬭ **USA** (OH) 280-281 C 3
Indian Lake Estates o **USA** (FL) 286-287 H 4
Indian Nation Turnpike II **USA** (OK) 264-265 J 4
Indian Ocean ≈ 12 F 6
Indianola o **USA** (IA) 274-275 E 3
Indianola o **USA** (MS) 268-269 K 3
Indianola o **USA** (NE) 262-263 F 4
Indianola o **USA** (OK) 264-265 J 3
Indianópolis o **BR** 72-73 G 5
Indian-Pacific II **AUS** 176-177 H 5
Indian Passage ≈ **USA** 286-287 D 2
Indian Pine o **USA** (AZ) 256-257 F 4
Indian Point ▲ **USA** (UT) 254-255 B 5
Indian Reservation X **CDN** (MAN) 234-235 G 5
Indian Reservation X **CDN** (MAN) 234-235 C 5
Indian Reservation X **CDN** (QUE) 236-237 P 2
Indian Reserve X **CDN** (MAN) 234-235 H 3
Indian Reserve X **CDN** (MAN) 234-235 C 5
Indian Reserve X **CDN** (ONT) 234-235 L 4
Indian Reserve X **CDN** (ONT) 234-235 J 4
Indian Reserve X **CDN** (ONT) 234-235 O 3
Indian Reserve X **CDN** (SAS) 232-233 K 3
Indian Reserve X **CDN** (SAS) 232-233 P 4
Indian Reserve X **CDN** (SAS) 232-233 R 4
Indian Reserve X• **CDN** (ONT) 236-237 D 3
Indian Reserve 3 X **CDN** (MAN) 234-235 G 4
Indian Reserve 13 X **CDN** (MAN) 234-235 G 2
Indian Reserve 33 X **CDN** 34-35 G 4
Indian Reserve 159 X **CDN** (SAS) 232-233 K 2
Indian Reserve 194 X **CDN** 32-33 Q 4
Indian Reserve Birds Hill X **CDN** (MAN) 234-235 G 5
Indian Reserve Fort Albany X **CDN** 34-35 Q 4
Indian Reserve Nineteen X **CDN** 34-35 H 3
Indian Reserves X **CDN** (SAS) 232-233 Q 5
Indian Reserves 81-84 X **CDN** (SAS) 232-233 P 5
Indian Reserve Seventeen X **CDN** 34-35 H 3
Indian River ≈ 48-49 H 5
Indian River ~ **CDN** (NFL) 242-243 M 3
Indian River ~ **CDN** (ONT) 238-239 H 3
Indian River o **USA** (MI) 272-273 E 2
Indian River ≈ **USA** 286-287 J 3
Indian River Bay < **USA** (DE) 280-281 L 5
Indian Springs o **USA** (NV) 248-249 J 3
Indiantown o **USA** (FL) 286-287 J 4
Indian Township o **USA** (ME) 278-279 O 3
Indian Trail Caverns ∴ **USA** (OH) 280-281 C 2
Indian Wells o **USA** (AZ) 256-257 E 3
Indiara o **BR** 72-73 E 4
Indiaroba o **BR** 68-69 K 7
Indibir o **ETH** 208-209 C 4
Indiga o **RUS** 88-89 U 3
Indiga ~ **RUS** 88-89 U 3
Indigenas de Quilmes, Ruinas • **RA** 76-77 D 4
Indigirka ~ **RUS** 110-111 Y 6
Indigirka ~ **RUS** 120-121 K 2
Indik"jaha ~ **RUS** 108-109 S 7
Indin Lake ⬭ **CDN** 30-31 M 3
Indio o **USA** (CA) 248-249 H 6
Indio, El o **USA** (TX) 266-267 G 5
Indio, Río ~ **NIC** 52-53 B 6
Indio Rico o **RA** 78-79 J 5
Indio Rico, Arroyo ~ **RA** 78-79 J 5
Índios, Cachoeira dos ~ **BR** 66-67 F 2
Indios, Cayos los ⌒ **C** 54-55 D 4
Indios, Los o **C** 54-55 H 4
Indios, Rio dos ~ **BR** 72-73 D 7
Indiskaja guba ≈ 88-89 U 3
Indispensable Strait ≈ 184 I e 3
Indombo o **G** 210-211 D 3
Indonesia ■ **RI** 168 B 2
Indooroopilly Outstation o **AUS** 176-177 M 4
Indore o• **IND** 138-139 E 8
Indragiri ~ **RI** 162-163 E 5
Indralaya o **RI** 162-163 F 6
Indramayu o **RI** 168 C 3
Indrapura o **RI** 162-163 C 3
Indravati ~ **IND** 142-143 C 6
Indre ~ **F** 90-91 H 8
Indulkana X **AUS** 176-177 M 3
Indus = Sind ~ **IND** 138-139 F 7
Indus Fan ≃ 12 E 2
Industry o **USA** (IL) 274-275 H 4
Industry o **USA** (TX) 266-267 L 4
Indwe o **ZA** 220-221 H 5
Ine Abeg < **RMM** 196-197 K 4
İnebolu ☆ **TR** 128-129 E 2
İnegöl ☆ **TR** 128-129 C 2
Ineguha o **ETH** 208-209 G 4
Inékar o **RMM** 196-197 M 7
Inés, Monte ▲ **RA** 80 F 4
Inewari o **ETH** 208-209 D 4
Inez o **USA** (KY) 276-277 N 3
Inezgane o **MA** 188-189 G 5
Infanta o **RP** 160-161 D 5
I-n-Farba o **RIM** 196-197 E 7
Inferior, Laguna ≈ 52-53 G 3
Inferno, Cachoeira ~ **BR** 66-67 K 4
Inferno, Cachoeira do ~ **BR** 66-67 H 7
Infiernillo o **MEX** 52-53 D 2
Infiernillo, Presa del < **MEX** 52-53 D 2
Ingá o **BR** 68-69 L 5
Inga • **ZRE** 210-211 D 6
Ingaí, Rio ~ **BR** 72-73 H 6
Ingal o **RN** 198-199 C 4
Ingaliston o **USA** (MI) 270-271 L 5
Ingallan Creek ~ **AUS** 172-173 L 6
Ingalls Lake ⬭ **CDN** 30-31 R 5
Ingaly o **RUS** 114-115 N 7
Inğāna o **IRQ** 128-129 L 5
Inganda o **ZRE** 210-211 H 4
Ingapirca • **EC** 64-65 C 3
Ingavi o **BOL** 70-71 D 2
Ingawa o **WAN** 198-199 D 6
Ingende o **ZRE** 210-211 G 4
Ingeniero Chanourdie o **RA** 76-77 H 5
Ingeniero Giagnoni o **RA** 78-79 E 2
Ingeniero G. N. Juárez o **RA** 76-77 G 2
Ingeniero Jacobacci o **RA** 78-79 E 6
Ingeniero Moneta o **RA** 78-79 K 2
Ingenika River ~ **CDN** 32-33 H 3
Ingenio Mora o **BOL** 70-71 F 6
Ingenstrem Rocks ⌒ **USA** 22-23 D 6
Inğeqare, Kūh-e ▲ **IR** 128-129 N 5
Ingersoll o **CDN** (ONT) 238-239 E 5
Ingham o **AUS** 174-175 J 6
Ingia Fjord ≈ 26-27 Y 8
Ingile < **EAK** 212-213 G 4
Ingili ~ **RUS** 120-121 F 4
Inginiyagala o **CL** 140-141 J 7
Inglefield, Kap ▲ **GRØ** 26-27 O 4
Inglefield Bredning ≈ 26-27 Q 5
Inglefield Land ∸ **GRØ** 26-27 P 4
Inglefield Mountains ▲ **CDN** 24-25 g 2
Inglesa, Bahía ≈ 76-77 B 4
Ingleses do Rio Vermelho o **BR** 74-75 F 6
Ingleside o **CDN** (ONT) 238-239 L 3
Ingleside o **USA** (TX) 266-267 K 6
Inglewood o **AUS** (QLD) 178-179 L 5
Inglewood o **AUS** (VIC) 180-181 G 4
Inglewood o **USA** (CA) 248-249 F 6
Inglewood o **USA** (NE) 262-263 K 3
Inglis o **CDN** (MAN) 234-235 B 4
Inglis o **USA** (FL) 286-287 G 2
Inglis, Mount ▲ **AUS** 178-179 K 3
Inglutalik River ~ **USA** 20-21 K 4
Ingneril ≈ 26-27 Z 8
Ingnerit ⌒ **GRØ** 26-27 X 8
Ingoda ~ **RUS** 118-119 E 10
Ingo holiday resort • **RI** 164-165 G 5
Ingolf Fjord ≈ 26-27 q 3
Ingólfhöfði ▲ **IS** 86-87 e 3
Ingolo o **RCB** 210-211 D 5
Ingolstadt o **D** 92-93 L 4
Ingomar o **USA** (MT) 250-251 M 5
Ingonish o **CDN** (NS) 240-241 P 4
Ingonish Beach o **CDN** (NS) 240-241 P 4
Ingoré o **GNB** 202-203 C 3
Ingrāj Bazār o **IND** 142-143 F 3
Ingray Lake ⬭ **CDN** 30-31 L 3
Ingrid Christensen land ∸ **ARK** 16 F 8
Ingujagun ~ **RUS** 114-115 N 3
Inguri ~ **GE** 126-127 E 6
Ingushetia = Galgaj Respublika □ **RUS** 126-127 F 6
Ingušskaja Respublika □ **RUS** 126-127 F 6
Ingwe o **Z** 218-219 D 1
Ingwempisi ~ **ZA** 220-221 K 3
Inhaca o **MOC** 220-221 L 3
Inhaca, Ilha da ⌒ **MOC** 220-221 L 2
Inhafenga o **MOC** 218-219 G 5
Inhagapi o **BR** 68-69 E 2
Inhaí o **BR** 72-73 J 4
Inhambane □ **MOC** 218-219 G 6
Inhambane ☆ **MOC** (INH) 218-219 H 6
Inhambane, Baía de ≈ 218-219 H 6
Inhambupe o **BR** 68-69 J 7
Inhambupe, Rio ~ **BR** 68-69 J 7
Inhaminga o **MOC** 218-219 H 4
Inhamissiba, Rio ~ **MOC** 218-219 G 6
Inhamitanga o **MOC** 218-219 H 4
Inharrime o **MOC** 218-219 H 7
Inharrime, Rio ~ **MOC** 220-221 M 2
Inhassoro o **MOC** 218-219 H 5
Inhaúmas o **BR** 72-73 H 2
In Hihaou, Adrar ▲ **DZ** 190-191 D 9
In Hihaou, Oued ~ **DZ** 190-191 C 9
Inhuçu o **BR** 68-69 H 4
Inhul ~ **UA** 102-103 H 4
Inhulec' ~ **UA** 102-103 H 4
Inhúma o **BR** 68-69 H 5
Inhumas o **BR** 72-73 F 4
Inhuporanga o **BR** 68-69 J 4
Inifel, Hassi < **DZ** 190-191 D 6
Inin < **WAN** 204-205 G 6
Inírida, Río ~ **CO** 60-61 G 6
Inis = Ennis ☆• **IRL** 90-91 C 5

Inis Ceithleann = Enniskillen ☆• GB 90-91 D 4
Inis Córthaidh = Enniscorthy ○ IRL 90-91 D 5
Iniu ○ SOL 184 I c 3
Inja ○ RUS 124-125 P 3
Inja ~ RUS 114-115 S 7
Inja ~ RUS 120-121 L 3
In'jali ~ RUS 110-111 Y 7
Inje ○ ROK 150-151 G 8
Injibara ○ ETH 208-209 C 3
I-n-Jitane ○ RN 198-199 C 4
Injune ○ AUS 178-179 K 3
Inkanwaya • BOL 70-71 C 4
Inkerman ○ AUS 174-175 F 5
Inkisi ~ ZRE 210-211 E 6
Inklin River ~ CDN 32-33 D 2
Inkom ○ USA (ID) 252-253 F 4
Inkouèle ○ RCB 210-211 E 4
Inkster ○ USA (ND) 258-259 K 3
Inlander II AUS 174-175 G 7
Inland Kaikoura Range ▲ NZ 182 D 5
Inland Lake ○ USA 20-21 L 3
Inman ○ USA (KS) 262-263 J 6
Inman ○ USA (NE) 262-263 H 2
Inman ○ USA (SC) 284-285 H 1
Inman River ~ CDN 24-25 N 6
Inn ~ D 92-93 M 4
Innahas Chebbi ○ DZ 190-191 D 7
Innalik ○ GRØ 28-29 O 2
Innamincka ○ AUS 178-179 F 4
Innamincka Regional Reserve ⊥ AUS 178-179 F 4
Inndyr ○ N 86-87 G 3
Inner Mongolia = Nei Mongol Zizhiqu ▫ VRC 154-155 D 2
Innes National Park ⊥ AUS 180-181 D 3
Inneston ○ AUS 180-181 D 3
Innesvale ○ AUS 172-173 K 3
Innetalling Island ⌒ CDN 36-37 K 7
Innisfail ○• AUS 174-175 J 5
Innisfail ○ CDN (ALB) 232-233 E 4
Innisfree ○ CDN (ALB) 232-233 G 2
Innjah ○ RUS 118-119 J 6
Innokent'evka ○ RUS 122-123 C 4
Innoko River ~ USA 20-21 L 5
Innsbruck ☆ A 92-93 L 5
Innuksuac, Rivière ~ CDN 36-37 L 5
Inobonto ○ RI 164-165 J 3
Inoca ○ BOL 70-71 C 5
Inocência ○ BR 72-73 E 5
Inocentes, Los ○ MEX 50-51 D 6
Inongo ○ ZRE 210-211 G 4
Inoni ○ RCB 210-211 E 5
Inostranceva, zaliv ○ RUS 108-109 L 3
Inowrocław ○• PL 92-93 P 2
Inpyněkuľ ~ RUS 112-113 T 4
I-n-Quezzam ○ DZ 198-199 B 3
Inquisivi ○ BOL 70-71 D 5
In Rhar ○ DZ 190-191 C 7
Inriville ○ RA 78-79 H 2
I-n-Sâkâne, Erg ⊥ RMM 196-197 K 4
In Salah ○• DZ 190-191 D 7
Insar ○ RUS 96-97 D 7
Inscription, Cape ▲ AUS 176-177 B 2
Insculas ○ PE 64-65 C 4
Insein ○ MYA 158-159 D 2
Inskip Point ▲ AUS 178-179 M 3
In Sokki, Oued ~ DZ 190-191 D 6
Inster ○ USA (ND) 258-259 K 3
Instow ○ CDN (SAS) 232-233 K 6
Însurăţei ○ RO 102-103 E 5
Inta ○ RUS 108-109 J 8
Intakareyen < RN 198-199 C 5
In Talak ○ RMM 196-197 M 6
I-n-Tebezas ○ RMM 196-197 L 6
Intendente Alvear ○ RA 78-79 H 3
Intercoastal Waterway ~ USA (VA) 280-281 K 7
Interior ○ USA (SD) 260-261 E 3
Interlachen ○ USA (FL) 286-287 H 2
Interlaken ○ CDN (ONT) 238-239 G 3
Interlaken ○• CH 92-93 J 5
Interlochen ○ USA (MI) 272-273 D 3
International Amistad Reservoir < USA (TX) 266-267 F 4
International Falcon Reservoir < USA (TX) 266-267 H 7
International Falls ○ USA (MN) 270-271 E 2
Intervew Island ⌒ IND 140-141 L 3
Intich'o ○ ETH 200-201 J 5
Intihuasi, Gruta de • RA 78-79 G 2
I-n-Tillit ○ RMM 202-203 K 2
Intracoastal Waterway < USA (FL) 286-287 H 1
Intracoastal Waterway < USA (LA) 268-269 K 7
Intracoastal Waterway < USA (SC) 284-285 M 3
Intracoastal Waterway < USA (TX) 268-269 F 7
Intrepid Inlet ≈ 24-25 M 2
Intutu ○ PE 64-65 E 3
Inuartigssuaq ○ GRØ 26-27 Q 4
Inúbia ○ BR 72-73 K 2
Inubō-saki ▲ J 152-153 J 7
Inugsuin Fiord ≈ 28-29 F 2
Inukjuak ○ CDN 36-37 K 5
Inulik Lake ○ CDN 30-31 N 2
Inulterg Sø ○ GRØ 26-27 h 3
Inuo ○ PNG 183 B 4
Inuria, Lago ○ PE 64-65 E 6
Inutil, Bahía ≈ 80 E 6
Inuvik ○• CDN 20-21 Y 2
Inuya, Río ~ PE 64-65 F 7
In'va ~ RUS 96-97 J 4
Inveraray ○• GB 90-91 E 3
Invercargill ○ NZ 182 B 7
Inverell ○ AUS 178-179 L 5
Inverhuron ○ CDN (ONT) 238-239 D 4
Inverleigh ○ AUS (QLD) 174-175 F 6
Inverleigh ○ AUS (VIC) 180-181 H 5
Inverloch ○ AUS 180-181 H 5
Invermay ○ CDN (SAS) 232-233 P 4
Invermere ○ CDN (BC) 230-231 N 3
Inverness ○ AUS 178-179 H 2
Inverness ○ CDN (NS) 240-241 O 4
Inverness ○ CDN (QUE) 238-239 O 2
Inverness ○• GB 90-91 E 3
Inverness ○ USA (FL) 286-287 G 3
Inverurie ○ GB 90-91 F 3
Inverway ○ AUS 172-173 J 4
Investigator Channel ≈ 158-159 E 5
Investigator Group ⌒ AUS 180-181 C 2
Investigator Passage ≈ 158-159 D 4
Investigator Ridge ≃ 12 H 5
Investigator Strait ≈ 180-181 D 3
Inwood ○ CDN (MAN) 234-235 F 4
Inwood ○ USA (IA) 274-275 B 1
Inyangani ▲ ZW 218-219 G 4
Inyarinyi (Kenmore Park) ✗ AUS 176-177 M 3
Inyathi ○ ZW 218-219 E 4
Inyokern ○ USA (CA) 248-249 G 4
Inyo Mountains ▲ USA (CA) 248-249 F 2
Inyonga ○ EAT (RUK) 214-215 G 4
Inza ○ RUS (ULN) 96-97 E 7
Inza ~ RUS 96-97 D 7
Inzana Lake ○ CDN (BC) 228-229 K 2
Inžavino ○ RUS 94-95 S 5
Inzia ~ ZRE 210-211 F 6
Ioánnina ○• GR 100-101 H 5
Iokanga ~ RUS 88-89 O 3
Iola ○ USA (KS) 262-263 L 7
Iola ○ USA (WI) 270-271 J 6
Iolgo, hrebet ▲ RUS 124-125 P 3
Iolotan ○ TM 136-137 H 6
Iomi, ozero ○ RUS 112-113 Y 4
Iona ○ ANG 216-217 B 8
Iona, Parque Nacional do ⊥ ANG 216-217 B 8
Ionava ☆ LT 94-95 J 4
Ione ○ USA (CA) 246-247 H 5
Ione ○ USA (CA) 246-247 E 5
Iones, Cap ▲ CDN 36-37 K 7
Ionesport ○ USA (ME) 278-279 O 4
Iongo ○ ANG 216-217 D 4
Ionia ○ USA (MI) 272-273 D 4
Ionian Islands = Iónioi Nísoi ⌒ GR 100-101 G 5
Ionian Sea ≈ 100-101 F 6
Ionian Sea = Iónio, Mare ≈ 100-101 F 6
Iónioi Nísoi ▫ GR 100-101 H 5
Iónio Pélagos ≈ 100-101 F 6
Ioniveem ~ RUS 112-113 Y 4
Ión Nisoi ≈ 100-101 G 5
Iony, ostrov ⌒ RUS 120-121 K 5
Iori ~ GE 126-127 F 6
Iori ○ PNG 183 C 4
Ios ⌒ GR 100-101 K 6
Iō-shima ⌒ J 152-153 D 9
Iota ○ USA (LA) 268-269 H 6
Ioué Juruena, Estação Ecológica ⊥ BR 70-71 H 3
Iouigharacène, Ibel ▲ MA 188-189 J 4
Iouik ○ RIM 196-197 B 5
Iowa ○ USA (LA) 268-269 H 6
Iowa ▫ USA (IA) 274-275 D 2
Iowa City ○ USA (IA) 274-275 G 3
Iowa Falls ○ USA (IA) 274-275 E 2
Iowa Park ○ USA (TX) 264-265 F 5
Iowa River ~ USA (IA) 274-275 G 3
Iowa River ~ USA (IA) 274-275 E 1
Iowa Sac and Fox Indian Reservation ✗ USA (KS) 262-263 L 5
Ipadu, Cachoeira ~ BR 66-67 D 2
Ipala ○ GCA 52-53 K 4
Ipameri ○ BR 72-73 F 4
Ipanema ○ BR 72-73 K 5
Ipao ○ VAN 184 II c 4
Iparia ○ PE 64-65 E 6
Ipatinga ○ BR 72-73 J 5
Ipatovo ○ RUS 102-103 N 5
Ipauçu ○ BR 72-73 F 7
Ipaumirim ○ BR 68-69 J 5
İpek Geçidi ▲ TR 128-129 K 3
Iperu ○ WAN 204-205 E 5
Ipetu-Ijesha ○ WAN 204-205 F 5
Ipewik River ~ USA 20-21 H 2
Iphigenia Bay ≈ 32-33 C 4
Ipiaçava, Rio ~ BR 68-69 B 4
Ipiaçu ○ BR 72-73 F 5
Ipiales ○ CO 64-65 D 1
Ipiaú ○ BR 72-73 L 3
Ipil ○ RP 160-161 E 9
Ipira ○ BR 72-73 L 2
Ipiranga, Rio ~ BR 66-67 K 7
Ípiros ▫ GR 100-101 H 5
Ipita ○ BOL 70-71 F 6
Ipitinga, Rio ~ BR 62-63 H 5
Ipixuma, Igarapé ~ BR 66-67 D 5
Ipixuma, Rio ~ BR 64-65 F 5
Ipixun ○ BR 62-63 J 6
Ipixuna ○ BR 66-67 B 6
Ipixuna, Área Indígena ✗ BR 66-67 F 5
Ipixuna, Igarapé ~ BR 68-69 B 4
Ipixuna, Ilha ⌒ BR 66-67 F 4
Ipixuna, Rio ~ BR 66-67 F 6
Ipixuna ou Paraná Pixuna, Rio ~ BR 66-67 F 6
i pobutu • UA 102-103 G 2
Ipoh ☆• MAL 162-163 D 2
Iporá ○ BR 72-73 E 4
Iporanga ○ BR 74-75 F 5
Ipota ○ VAN 184 II b 4
Ippy ○ RCA 206-207 E 5
Ipsári ▲ GR 100-101 K 4
Ipswich ○ AUS 178-179 M 4
Ipswich ○ GB 90-91 H 5
Ipswich ○ USA (MA) 278-279 L 6
Ipswich ○ USA (SD) 260-261 G 1
Ipu ○ BR 68-69 H 4
Ipumirim ○ BR 74-75 D 6
Ipun, Isla ⌒ RCH 80 C 2
Ipupuruto, Río ~ BOL 70-71 E 4
Iqe ○ VRC 146-147 M 6
Iqlit ○ ET 194-195 F 5
Iquipi ○ PE 64-65 F 9
Iquique ☆ RCH 70-71 B 7
Iquitos ☆• PE 64-65 F 3
Ira ○ USA (TX) 264-265 D 6
Irá, Igarapé ~ BR 66-67 C 3
Iraan ○ USA (TX) 266-267 F 3
Ira Banda ○ RCA 206-207 F 6
Iracaja, Cachoeira do ~ BR 70-71 E 2
Iracema ○ BR 68-69 J 4
Iracoubo ○ F 62-63 H 3
Iraël' ○ RUS 88-89 X 4
Iraí de Minas ○ BR 72-73 G 5
Iraffia < MA 196-197 C 2
Irajuba ○ BR 72-73 K 2
Iraka ○ WAN 204-205 H 3
Iráklio ○ GR 100-101 K 7
Iramaia ○ BR 72-73 K 2
Iran = Īrān ■ IR 134-135 D 2
Iranduba ○ BR 66-67 G 4
Īrānšahr ○ IR 134-135 J 5
Irantxé, Área Indígena ✗ BR 70-71 H 3
Irapuato ○ MEX 52-53 D 1
Iraq = 'Irāq ■ IRQ 128-129 J 6
Iraquara ○ BR 72-73 K 2
Irará ○ BR 72-73 L 2
Irarraren ⊥ DZ 190-191 E 7
Irasville ○ USA (VT) 278-279 J 4
Irati ○ BR 74-75 E 5
Irau, Gunung ▲ RI 166-167 G 2
Irauçuba ○ BR 68-69 J 3
Irawan, Wādī < LAR 192-193 D 4
Irbejskoe ☆ RUS 116-117 G 8
Irbeni väin ≈ 94-95 G 3
Irbes Šaurums ≈ 94-95 G 3
Irbid ☆ JOR 130-131 D 1
Irbit ☆ RUS 114-115 G 6
Irebue ○ ZRE 210-211 F 4
Irecê ○ BR 68-69 H 7
Irech, I-n- < RMM 196-197 K 5
Iredell ○ USA (TX) 264-265 G 6
Ireland = Éire ■ IRL 90-91 C 5
Ireland = Éire ⊥ IRL 90-91 C 5
Irendyk hrebet ▲ RUS 96-97 L 7
Irène ○ F 62-63 H 3
Irene ○ RA 78-79 J 5
Irene ○ USA (SD) 260-261 J 3
Iretama ○ BR 74-75 D 5
Iretskij, mys ▲ RUS 120-121 Q 4
Iretskij liman ○ RUS 120-121 Q 3
Ireupuow ○ VAN 184 II b 4
Irgakly ○ RUS 126-127 F 5
Irgičan ~ RUS 110-111 W 5
Irgičanskij hrebet ▲ RUS 110-111 V 5
Irharhar, Oued ~ DZ 190-191 E 8
Irharhar, Oued ~ DZ 198-199 C 2
Irherm ○ MA 188-189 G 5
Irhil M'Goun ▲ MA 188-189 H 5
Iri ○ ROK 150-151 F 10
Iriaki ○ RI 166-167 H 3
Irian Jaya ▫ RI 166-167 H 4
Iriba ○ TCH 198-199 L 5
Irié ○ RG 202-203 F 5
Iriji < RIM 196-197 D 5
Iriki ○ MA 188-189 H 6
Iriklinskoe vodohranilišče < RUS 96-97 L 8
Irimi ○ RI 166-167 G 2
Iringa ▫ EAT 214-215 H 4
Iringa ☆ EAT 214-215 H 4
Iriona ○ HN 54-55 C 7
Iriri, Rio ~ BR 68-69 B 5
Iririmirim, Baía ≈ 68-69 F 2
Iriri Nôvo, Rio ~ BR 68-69 B 6
Iritka ~ RUS 116-117 M 4
Irituia ○ BR 68-69 E 2
Irkeštam ○ KS 136-137 N 5
Irkineeva ~ RUS 116-117 J 6
Irkineevo ○ RUS 116-117 H 6
Irkut ~ RUS 116-117 L 10
Irkutsk ☆• RUS 116-117 M 9
Irkutsko-Čeremhovskaja ravnina ⌣ RUS 116-117 K 8
Irlir, togi ▲ US 136-137 H 3
Irma ○ CDN (ALB) 232-233 G 3
Irminger Basin ≃ 6-7 E 3
Irminger Sea ≈ 6-7 F 2
Irmo ○ USA (SC) 284-285 J 2
Irnogou ~ CI 202-203 J 5
Iro, Lac ○ TCH 206-207 D 3
Irobo ○ CI 202-203 H 7
Iroise ≈ 90-91 E 7
Ironasiteri ○ YV 66-67 E 2
Iron Bridge ○ CDN (ONT) 238-239 B 2
Iron-Bridge ○ GB 90-91 F 5
Ironbridge ••• GB 90-91 F 5
Iron Creek ~ CDN (ALB) 232-233 G 3
Iron Creek ○ USA 20-21 H 4
Irondequoit ○ USA (NY) 278-279 D 5
Irondo ○ EAT 214-215 J 4
Irondro ○ RM 222-223 E 8
Irong, Gunung ▲ MAL (PAH) 162-163 E 2
Iron Knob ○ AUS 180-181 D 2
Iron Mountain ○ USA (MI) 270-271 K 5
Iron Mountain ○ USA (WY) 252-253 N 5
Iron Mountains ▲ USA (TN) 282-283 E 4
Iron Range National Park ⊥ AUS 174-175 G 3
Iron River ○ USA (MI) 270-271 K 4
Iron River ○ USA (WI) 270-271 G 4
Ironside ○ USA (OR) 244-245 H 6
Iron Springs ○ USA (UT) 254-255 B 6
Ironton ○ USA (MO) 276-277 E 3
Ironton ○ USA (OH) 280-281 D 5
Ironwood ○ USA (MI) 270-271 H 4
Iroquois ○ CDN (ONT) 238-239 K 4
Iroquois ○ USA (SD) 260-261 J 2
Iroquois Falls ○ CDN (ONT) 236-237 H 4
Iroquois River ~ CDN 30-31 E 2
Irō-saki ▲ J 152-153 H 7
'Irqa, al- ○ Y 132-133 E 7
Irrawaddy ~ MYA 142-143 J 6
Irrua ○ WAN 204-205 G 5
'Irsāl ○ RL 128-129 G 5
Irsina ○ I 100-101 F 4
Irtjaš, ozero ○ RUS 96-97 M 6
Irtyš ~ RUS 114-115 K 4
Irtyš ~ RUS 124-125 J 1
Irtyš = Ertis ~ KA 124-125 K 3
Irtyšsk ☆ KA 124-125 J 2
Irumu ○ ZRE 212-213 B 3
Irún ○ E 98-99 G 3
Irupana ○ BOL 70-71 D 5
Irurita ○ E 98-99 G 3
Irurzun ○ E 98-99 G 3
Iruya, Río ~ RA 76-77 E 2
Irva ~ RUS 88-89 U 5
Irvine ○ CDN (ALB) 232-233 H 6
Irvine ○ USA (CA) 248-249 G 6
Irvine ○ USA (KY) 276-277 M 3
Irvine Inlet ≈ 36-37 Q 2
Irvines Landing ○ CDN (BC) 230-231 F 4
Irving ○ USA (IA) 274-275 F 3
Irving ○ USA (TX) 264-265 H 6
Irvington ○ USA (KY) 276-277 J 3
Irwin ○ USA (IA) 274-275 C 3
Irwin ○ USA (ID) 252-253 G 3
Irwin Military Reservation, Fort • USA (CA) 248-249 H 4
Irwin River ~ AUS 176-177 C 4
Irwinton ○ USA (GA) 284-285 G 4
Iryguarenda ○ BOL 76-77 F 1
'Is, al- ○ KSA 130-131 F 5
Is, Ğabal ▲ ET 194-195 G 6
Isa ○ RUS 122-123 D 3
Isa ○ WAN 198-199 C 6
'Īsā, 'Ain ○ SYR 128-129 H 4
Isaac River ~ AUS 178-179 K 2
Isaaq Jilible ~ SP 212-213 H 3
Isabel ○ USA (SD) 260-261 E 1
Isabel, Bahía ≈ 64-65 B 10
Isabela ○ RP 160-161 D 9
Isabela ○ USA (PR) 286-287 O 2
Isabela, Cabo ▲ DOM 54-55 K 5
Isabela, Canal ≈ 64-65 B 10
Isabela, Isla ⌒ EC 64-65 B 10
Isabela, La ○ C 54-55 E 3
Isabela, La ○ DOM 54-55 K 5
Isabela, Ruinas de la ∴• DOM 54-55 K 5
Isabela de Sagua ○ C 54-55 E 3
Isabel II ○ USA (PR) 286-287 O 2
Isabella ○ CDN (MAN) 234-235 C 4
Isabella ○ USA (MN) 270-271 G 3
Isabella, Bahía de la ≈ 54-55 K 5
Isabella, Cape ▲ CDN 26-27 N 4
Isabella, Cordillera ▲ NIC 52-53 B 5
Isabella Bay ≈ 28-29 G 2
Isabella Indian Reservation ✗ USA (MI) 272-273 E 4
Isabella Reservoir ○ USA (CA) 248-249 F 4
Isabelle Range ▲ AUS 172-173 E 6
Isabel Pass ▲ USA 20-21 S 5
Isabel Rubio ○ C 54-55 C 3
Isabis ○ NAM 220-221 C 1
Isaccea ○ RO 102-103 F 5
Isačenko, ostrov ⌒ RUS 108-109 Y 3
Isachsen ○ CDN 24-25 T 1
Isachsen, Cape ▲ CDN 24-25 T 1
Isachsen Peninsula ⌣ CDN 24-25 T 1
Ísafjörður ☆ IS 86-87 b 1
Isahaya ○ J 152-153 D 8
Isaka ○ ZRE 210-211 F 5
Isa Khel ○ PK 138-139 C 3
Isakly ☆ RUS 96-97 G 6
Isalo ▲ RM 222-223 D 9
'Isalo Parc National de l' ⊥ RM 222-223 D 9
Isambe ○ ZRE 210-211 L 4
Isandja ○ ZRE (EQU) 210-211 H 4
Isandja ○ ZRE (KOC) 210-211 H 5
Isanga ○ ZRE (Ban) 210-211 G 4
Isanga ○ ZRE (EQU) 210-211 J 4
Isangano National Park ⊥ Z 214-215 F 6
Isangi ○ ZRE 210-211 K 3
Isango ○ ZRE 212-213 B 4
Isanlu ○ WAN 204-205 F 4
Isanlu-Esa ○ WAN 204-205 F 4
Išan Şalib ○ IRQ 128-129 L 7
Isar ~ D (BAY) 92-93 M 4
Isas ○ CDN (ONT) 236-237 F 4
'Išāš, al- ○ KSA 130-131 F 4
Isasa ○ ZRE 212-213 B 5
'Isāwiya, al- ○ KSA 130-131 F 2
Isbil, Ğabal ▲ Y 132-133 D 6
Isbjorn Strait ≈ 26-27 O 8
Iscayachi ○ BOL 76-77 E 1
Iscehisar ☆ TR 128-129 D 3
Ischia ○ I 100-101 C 1
Ischia ○ I 100-101 D 4
Ìschia, Ìsola d' ⌒ I 100-101 D 4
Ischigualasto y, Parque Natural Provincial ⊥•• RA 76-77 C 5
Iscuande, Río ~ CO 60-61 C 6
Isdell River ~ AUS 172-173 G 4
Ise ○ J 152-153 G 7
Iševka ☆ RUS 96-97 F 6
Iseke ○ EAT 214-215 H 4
Iseo, Lago d' ○ I 100-101 C 2
Isérnia ☆ I 100-101 E 4
Ise-shima National Park ⊥ J 152-153 G 7
Iset' ~ RUS 96-97 M 5
Iset' ~ RUS 114-115 J 6
Isetskoe ☆ RUS 114-115 H 6
Ise-wan ≈ 152-153 G 7
Iseyin ○ WAN 204-205 E 5
Isfahan = Eşfahān ☆•• IR 134-135 D 2
Isfahan = Eşfahān ☆••• IR 134-135 D 2
Isfara ○ TJ 136-137 M 4
Isfjordbanken ≃ 84-85 H 4
Isfjorden ≈ 84-85 J 3
Isfjord Radio ○ N 84-85 H 3
Isfjordrenna ≃ 84-85 G 3
Isha ○ PK 138-139 C 3
Ishak Paşa Sarayı •• TR 128-129 L 3
Isham ○ CDN (SAS) 232-233 K 4
Ishasha ○ EAU 212-213 B 4
Isherton ○ GUY 62-63 E 4
Ishiara ○ EAK 212-213 F 4
Ishikari ○ J 152-153 J 3
Ishikari-wan ≈ 152-153 J 3
Ishikawa ○ J 152-153 B 11
Ishimskaja Step' = Išimskaja ravnina ⌣ RUS 114-115 J 6
Ishinomaki ○ J 152-153 J 5
Ishioka ○ J 152-153 J 6
Ishizuchi-san ▲ J 152-153 E 8
Ishpeming ○ USA (MI) 270-271 L 4
Ishurdi ○ BD 142-143 F 3
Isiboro Securé, Parque Nacional ⊥ BOL 70-71 D 5
Isikari-santi ▲ J 152-153 K 3
Isil'kul' ☆ RUS 124-125 G 1
Išim ○ RUS 114-115 K 6
Išim ~ RUS 114-115 L 6
Išim = Esim ~ KA 124-125 E 2
Išim, Ust'- ○ RUS 114-115 L 6
Isimala • EAT 214-215 H 4
Išimbaj ☆ RUS 96-97 K 7
Isimbira ○ EAT 214-215 G 4
Išimskaja ravnina ⌣ RUS 114-115 J 6
Išimskaja ravnina ⌣ RUS 114-115 J 6
Isinga ○ RUS 118-119 E 9
Isiolo ○ EAK 212-213 F 3
Isiolo, Lagh ~ EAK 212-213 F 3
Isiovo, Río ~ BOL 70-71 E 5
Isipingo ○ ZA 220-221 K 5
Isiro ○ ZRE 212-213 A 2
Isisford ○ AUS 178-179 H 3
Isit ○ RUS 118-119 M 5
Isjangulovo ☆ RUS 96-97 K 7
Iska ○ RUS 114-115 H 6
Iskanawatu, Tanjung ▲ RI 166-167 D 5
Iskandariya, al- = Alexandria ☆•• ET 194-195 D 2
Iskăr ~ BG 102-103 C 6
Iškašim ○ TJ 136-137 M 6
Iskaten', hrebet ▲ RUS 112-113 V 3
İskenderun ☆ TR 128-129 G 4
İskenderun Körfezi ≈ 128-129 F 4
İskilip ☆ TR 128-129 F 2
Iskitim ☆ RUS 124-125 N 1
Iskushuban ○ SP 208-209 K 3
Iskut River ~ CDN 32-33 E 3
Isla ○ MEX 52-53 G 2
Isla, Salar de la ○ RCH 76-77 C 3
Isla Angel de la Guarda, Parque Natural ⊥ MEX 50-51 C 3
Isla de Aguada ○ MEX 52-53 J 2
Isla de Salamanca, Parque Nacional ⊥•• CO 60-61 D 2
Isla de Taiamã, Estação Ecológica ⊥ BR 70-71 J 5
Isla Guamblin, Parque Nacional ⊥ RCH 80 C 2
İslahiye ☆ TR 128-129 G 4
Islamabad ★• PK 138-139 D 3
Isla Magdalena, Parque Nacional ⊥ RCH 80 D 2
Islāmgarh ○ PK 138-139 C 6
Isla Mona ⌒ USA (PR) 286-287 O 2
Islamorada ○ USA (FL) 286-287 J 7
Islāmpur ○ BD 142-143 F 3
Islāmpur ○ IND 142-143 F 2
Islāmpur ○ IND 142-143 D 3
Island Bay ≈ 160-161 C 8
Island City ○ USA (OR) 244-245 G 5
Island Falls ○ CDN (ONT) 236-237 G 3
Island Falls ○ USA (ME) 278-279 N 2
Island Lagoon ○ AUS 178-179 D 6
Island Lake ○ CDN (ONT) 236-237 F 5
Island Lake ○ CDN 34-35 K 4
Island Lake ○ USA (MN) 270-271 F 3
Island Lake Indian Reserve ✗ CDN 34-35 J 4
Island Park Reservoir ~ USA (ID) 252-253 G 2
Island Pond ○ CDN (NFL) 242-243 M 4
Island Pond ○ USA (VT) 278-279 K 4
Island River ~ CDN 30-31 J 5
Islands, Bay of ≈ 36-37 U 7
Islands, Bay of ≈ 38-39 P 4
Islands, Bay of ≈ 182 E 1
Islands, Bay of ≈ CDN 242-243 K 3
Isla Riesco, Reserva Florestal ⊥ RCH 80 D 6
Islas Columbretes ⌒ E 98-99 H 5
Isla Umbú ○ PY 76-77 H 4
Islay ○ CDN (ALB) 232-233 H 2
Islay ⌒ GB 90-91 D 4
Islay ○ PE 70-71 A 5
Islaz ○ RO 102-103 D 6
Isle ○ USA (MN) 270-271 E 4
Isle aux Morts ○ CDN (NFL) 242-243 K 5
Isle Historic Site, Fort de L' • CDN (ALB) 232-233 G 2
Isle of Man ▫ GBM 90-91 E 4
Isle of Wight ⌒ GB 90-91 G 6
Isle Pierre ○ CDN (BC) 228-229 L 3
Isle Royale National Park ⊥ USA (MI) 270-271 K 2
Isles of Scilly ⌒•• GB 90-91 D 7
Isleta ○ CO 60-61 H 6
Isleta ○ USA (NM) 256-257 J 4
Isleta Indian Reservation ✗ USA (NM) 256-257 J 4
Isle Woodah ⌒ AUS 174-175 D 3
Islington ○ CDN (NFL) 242-243 P 5
Isluga, Parque Nacional ⊥ RCH 70-71 C 6
Isly, Oued ~ MA 188-189 K 3
Ismael Cortinas ○ ROU 78-79 L 2
Isma'īliya, al- ☆ ET 194-195 F 2
Ismailly = İsmayıllı ○ AZ 128-129 N 2
Ismaning ○ D 92-93 L 4
Isnā ○• ET 194-195 F 5
Isoanala ○ RM 222-223 D 9
Isoka ○ Z 214-215 G 6
Isola ○ USA (MS) 268-269 K 3
Ìsola di Capo Rizzuto ○ I 100-101 F 5
Isom ○ USA (KY) 276-277 N 3
Isonga ○ PNG 183 F 3
Isopa ○ EAT 214-215 F 5
Isorana ○ RM 222-223 E 8
Isororo ○ GUY 62-63 E 1
Isortoq ○ GRØ (ØGR) 28-29 V 4
Isortoq ○ GRØ (VGR) 28-29 O 3
Iso-Vietonen ○ FIN 88-89 H 3
Isparta ☆ TR 128-129 D 4
Isperih ○ BG 102-103 E 6
Ìspica ○ I 100-101 E 6
Ispir ☆ TR 128-129 J 2
Isquiliac, Isla ⌒ RCH 80 C 2
Israel = Yiśrā'el ■ IL 130-131 D 2
Israelite Bay ≈ 176-177 G 6
Israelite Bay ○ AUS 176-177 G 6
Isra-tu ⌒ ER 200-201 J 4
Issa ○ RUS 96-97 D 7
Issaba ○ DY 204-205 E 5
Issangele ○ CAM 204-205 H 6
Issano ○ GUY 62-63 E 3
Issaouane, Erg ⊥ DZ 190-191 F 7
Issaquah ○ USA (WA) 244-245 C 3
Isseke ○ EAT 214-215 H 4
Issia ☆ CI 202-203 G 6
Issimu ○ RI 164-165 H 3
Issinga ○ G 210-211 B 4
Issoire ○ F 90-91 J 9
Issoro ○ SUD 212-213 D 2
Issoudun ○ F 90-91 H 8
Issoulane Erarenine ⊥ DZ 190-191 D 9
Issyk = Esik ○ KA 146-147 C 4
Issyk-Kul', ozero ○ KS 146-147 C 4
Issyk-Kul' = Ysyk-Köl ○ KS 146-147 C 4
İstanbul ☆••• TR 128-129 C 2
İstanbul Boğazi ≈ 128-129 C 2
Istgāh-e Nāin ○ IR 134-135 E 2
Isthmus of Kra ⌒ THA 158-159 E 5
Istiéa ○ GR 100-101 J 5
Istisu ○• AZ 128-129 L 3
Istmina ○ CO 60-61 C 5
Istmo de Ofqui ○ RCH 80 C 3
Istmo Malagua ⌒ CO 60-61 C 5
Istokpoga, Lake ○ USA (FL) 286-287 H 4
Istra ☆• RUS 94-95 P 4
Istra ⊥ SLO 100-101 D 1
Istunmäki ○ FIN 88-89 J 5
Isumrud Strait ≈ 183 C 3
Isuna ○ EAT (SIN) 212-213 E 6
Iswepe ○ ZA 220-221 K 3
Itabaiana ○ BR (PA) 68-69 L 5
Itabaiana ○ BR (SER) 68-69 K 7
Itabaianinha ○ BR 68-69 K 7
Itabaliza ○ BR 68-69 E 7
Itabapoana ○ BR 72-73 K 6
Itabapoana, Rio ~ BR 72-73 K 6
Itaberá ○ BR 72-73 F 7
Itaberaba ○ BR 72-73 K 2
Itaberaí ○ BR 72-73 F 4
Itabira ○ BR 72-73 J 5
Itabirinha de Mantena ○ BR 72-73 K 5
Itabirito ○ BR 72-73 J 6
Itaboca ○ BR 66-67 F 5
Itaboraí ○ BR 72-73 J 7
Itabuna ○ BR 72-73 L 3
Itacaiuna ○ BR 68-69 C 4
Itacaiúna, Rio ~ BR 68-69 D 4
Itacaja ○ BR 68-69 E 6
Itacambira ○ BR 72-73 J 4
Itacarambi ○ BR 72-73 H 3
Itacaré ○ BR 72-73 L 3
Itacaruaré ○ RA 76-77 K 4
Itacolomi, Ilha ⌒ BR 74-75 E 5
Itaeté ○ BR 72-73 K 2
Itaguaí ○ BR 72-73 J 7
Itaguajé ○ BR 72-73 E 7
Itaguara ○ BR 72-73 H 6
Itaguari, Rio ~ BR 72-73 H 3
Itagüí ○ CO 60-61 D 4
Itah Lake ○ AUS 180-181 H 3
Ita Ibaté ○ RA 76-77 J 4
Itaim, Rio ~ BR 68-69 H 5
Itainópolis ○ BR 68-69 H 5
Itainzinho, Rio ~ BR 68-69 H 5
Itaiópolis ○ BR 74-75 F 6
Itaipu • BR 76-77 K 3
Itaipu, Represa de < BR 76-77 K 3
Itäisen Suomenlahden kansallispuisto ⊥ FIN 88-89 J 6
Itaitu ○ BR 68-69 H 7
Itaituba ○ BR (AMA) 66-67 F 5
Itaituba ○ BR (P) 66-67 K 5
Itajá ○ BR 72-73 E 5
Itajaí ○ BR 74-75 F 6
Itají ○ BR 72-73 K 3
Itajubá ○ BR 72-73 H 7
Itajubaquara ○ BR 68-69 G 7
Itaju do Colônia ○ BR 72-73 L 3
Itakhola ○ BD 142-143 G 3
Itala Nature Reserve ⊥ ZA 220-221 K 3
Italy ○ USA (TX) 264-265 H 6
Italy = Italia ■ I 100-101 C 4
Itamaraju ○ BR 72-73 L 4
Itamarandiba ○ BR 72-73 J 4
Itamarati ○ BR 66-67 C 6
Itamataré ○ BR 68-69 E 3
Itambacuri ○ BR 72-73 K 5
Itambé ○ BR 72-73 K 3
Itamirim ○ BR 72-73 J 3
Itampolo ○ RM 222-223 D 10
Itanagar ☆• IND 142-143 H 2
Itanagra ○ BR 72-73 L 2
Itanajé ○ BR 72-73 J 2
Itanari ○ NEP 144-145 F 7
Itang ○ ETH 208-209 B 4
Itangua ○ BR 68-69 H 3
Itanhaém ○ BR 74-75 G 5
Itanhauã, Rio ~ BR 66-67 E 5
Itanhém ○ BR 72-73 K 4
Itanhém, Rio ~ BR 72-73 L 4
Itanhoma ○ BR 72-73 K 5
Itaobim ○ BR 72-73 K 4
Itaocara ○ BR 72-73 J 6
Itapaci ○ BR 72-73 E 3
Itapacurá, Rio ~ BR 66-67 K 5
Itapaiúna ○ BR 70-71 J 2
Itapajé ○ BR 68-69 J 3
Itaparaná, Rio ~ BR 66-67 F 6
Itaparica ○ BR 72-73 L 2
Itaparica, Ilha ⌒•• BR 72-73 L 2
Itapebi ○ BR 72-73 L 3
Itapecerica ○ BR 72-73 H 6
Itapecerica da Serra ○ BR 72-73 G 7
Itapecurumirim ○ BR 68-69 F 3
Itapeipu ○ BR 68-69 H 7
Itapejara d'Oeste ○ BR 74-75 D 5
Itapemirim ○ BR 72-73 K 6
Itapemirim, Rio ~ BR 72-73 K 6
Itapera ○ BR 68-69 G 3
Itapera, Lagoa ○ BR 74-75 F 7
Itaperuna ○ BR 72-73 K 6
Itapetinga ○ BR 72-73 K 3
Itapetininga ○ BR 72-73 F 7
Itapetininga, Rio ~ BR 72-73 F 7
Itapeva ○ BR 72-73 F 7
Itapeví ○ BR 72-73 G 7
Itapicuru, Rio ~ BR 68-69 J 7
Itapicuru, Rio ~ BR 68-69 G 4
Itapicuru-Açu, Rio ~ BR 68-69 H 7
Itapicuru-Mirim, Rio ~ BR 68-69 H 7
Itapipoca ○ BR 68-69 J 3
Itapira ○ BR 72-73 G 7
Itapiranga ○ BR (AMA) 66-67 H 4
Itapiranga ○ BR (CAT) 74-75 D 6
Itapirapuã ○ BR 72-73 E 3
Itapirapuã, Pico ▲ BR 74-75 F 5
Itapiúna ○ BR 68-69 J 4
Itápolis ○ BR 72-73 F 6
Itapora ○ BR 76-77 K 2
Itaporanga ○ BR (PA) 68-69 J 5
Itaporanga ○ BR (PAU) 72-73 F 7
Itapuã ○ BR 74-75 E 8
Itapuã do Oeste ○ BR 66-67 F 7
Itapuranga ○ BR 72-73 F 3
Itaquai, Rio ~ BR 66-67 B 5
Itaquaquecetuba ○ BR 72-73 G 7
Itaquatiara ○ BR 66-67 H 4
Itaqui ○ BR 76-77 J 5
Itaquyry ○ PY 76-77 K 3
Itarana ○ BR 72-73 K 6
Itarana, Ilha ⌒ BR 68-69 E 2
Itarare ○ BR 74-75 F 5
Itararé, Rio ~ BR 72-73 F 7
Itarema ○ BR 68-69 J 3
Itārsi ○ IND 138-139 F 8
Itasca ○ USA (TX) 264-265 G 6
Itasca State Park ⊥ USA (MN) 270-271 C 3
Itasy, Farihy ○ RM 222-223 E 7
Itata, Río ~ RCH 78-79 C 4
Itati ○• RA 76-77 H 4
Itatiaia, Parque Nacional do ⊥ BR 72-73 H 7
Itatiba ○ BR 72-73 G 7
Itatinga ○ BR 72-73 F 7
Itatingui ○ BR 72-73 L 3
Itatira ○ BR 68-69 J 4
Itatupã ○ BR 62-63 J 6
Itaú ○ BR 68-69 K 4
Itaú, Río ~ BOL 76-77 E 2
Itauba ○ BR 70-71 K 2
Itauçu ○ BR 72-73 F 4
Itaueira ○ BR 68-69 G 5
Itaueira, Rio ~ BR 68-69 G 5
Itaum ○ BR 76-77 K 2
Itauna ○ BR 68-69 F 3
Itaúna ○ BR 72-73 H 6
Itaúnas ○ BR 72-73 L 5
Itaunja ○ IND 142-143 B 2
Itbayat Island ⌒ RP 160-161 D 2
Itbu Point ▲ RP 160-161 D 6
Itche Lake ○ CDN 30-31 N 3
Ite ○ PE 70-71 B 5
Itéa ○ GR 100-101 J 5
Itemgen, köli ○ KA 124-125 G 2
Iten ○ EAK 212-213 E 3
Itenecito, Río ~ BOL 70-71 E 3
Itenes o Guaporé, Río ~ BOL 70-71 F 3
Iterh, Oued ~ DZ 196-197 M 4
Itete ○ EAT 214-215 J 5
Itezhi-Tezhi Dam ○ Z 218-219 D 2
Ithaca ○ USA (MI) 272-273 E 4
Ithaca ○ USA (NY) 278-279 E 6
Ithaca ○ USA (OH) 280-281 B 4
Itháki ○ GR 100-101 H 5
Itigi ○ EAT 212-213 E 6
Itiki ○ IND 140-141 G 3
Itilleq ○ GRØ 28-29 O 3
Itimbiri ~ ZRE 210-211 J 2
Itinga, Rio ~ BR 68-69 E 4
Itipo ○ ZRE 210-211 G 4
Itiquira ○ BR 70-71 K 5
Itiquira, Rio ~ BR 70-71 K 5
Itiquira ou Piquiri ~ BR 70-71 J 5
Itirapuão ○ BR 72-73 G 6
Itirr Plain ⊥ EAK 212-213 G 2
Itiúba ○ BR 68-69 J 7
Itiyuro, Arroyo ~ RA 76-77 F 2
Itkillik River ~ USA 20-21 P 2
Itō ○ J 152-153 H 7
Ito, Paysage d' • MA 188-189 J 4
Itobe ○ WAN 204-205 G 5
Itobo ○ EAT 212-213 D 6
Itoculo ○ MOC 218-219 L 2
Itoigawa ○ J 152-153 G 6
Itoko ○ ZRE 210-211 H 4
Itomampy ~ RM 222-223 E 9
Itonamas, Río ~ BOL 70-71 E 3
Itoquois River ~ USA (IL) 274-275 L 4
Itquiy ○ MA 188-189 E 7
Ittaajimmiit = Kap Hope ○ GRØ 26-27 o 8
Ittel, Oued ~ DZ 190-191 E 3
Ittoqqortoormiit = Scoresbysund ○ GRØ 26-27 p 8
Itu ○ BR 72-73 G 7
Itu ○ WAN 204-205 G 6
Ituaçu ○ BR 72-73 K 2
Ituango ○ CO 60-61 D 4
Ituberá ○ BR 72-73 L 2
Itui, Rio ~ BR 66-67 B 5
Ituiutaba ○ BR 72-73 F 5
Itula ○ ZRE 212-213 A 5
Itumba ○ EAT (MBE) 214-215 G 5
Itumba ○ EAT (SIN) 214-215 G 4
Itumbiara ○ BR 72-73 F 5
Ituna ○ CDN (SAS) 232-233 P 4
Itungi ○ EAT 214-215 G 5
Ituni ○ GUY 62-63 E 3
Ituporanga ○ BR 74-75 F 6
Iturama ○ BR 72-73 E 5
Iturbide ○ MEX (CAM) 52-53 K 2
Iturbide ○ MEX (NL) 50-51 K 5
Ituri ~ ZRE 212-213 B 3
Iturup, ostrov ⌒ RUS 122-123 N 6
Itutinga ○ BR 72-73 H 6
Itutinga, Represa < BR 72-73 H 6
Ituverava ○ BR 72-73 G 6
Ituxi, Rio ~ BR 66-67 E 6
Ituzaingo ○ RA 76-77 J 4
Itwangi ○ EAT 212-213 D 5
Itzamna ∴• MEX 52-53 K 1
Itztapa ○ GCA 52-53 J 5
Iuka ○ USA (KS) 262-263 H 7
Iuka ○ USA (MS) 268-269 M 2
Iul'tin ○ RUS 112-113 V 3
Iuiú ○ MOC 218-219 K 2
Iva ○ USA (SC) 284-285 H 2
Ivacevičy ○ BY 94-95 J 5
Ivaí ○ BR 74-75 E 5
Ivaí, Rio ~ BR 72-73 D 7
Ivaiporã ○ BR 74-75 E 5
Ivakoany ▲ RM 222-223 E 9
Ivalo ○ FIN 88-89 J 2

Ivalojoki ○ FIN 88-89 J 2
Ivan ○ USA (FL) 286-287 E 1
Ivan ∼ USA (LA) 268-269 G 4
Ivangorod ○ RUS 94-95 L 2
Ivangrad ○ YU 100-101 G 3
Ivanhoe ○ AUS 180-181 H 2
Ivanhoe ○ USA (MN) 270-271 B 6
Ivanhoe River ∼ CDN (ONT) 236-237 F 4
Ivanivka ○ UA 102-103 C 3
Ivanjica ○• YU 100-101 H 3
Ivankiv ○ UA 102-103 F 2
Ivano-Frankivs'k ☆ UA 102-103 D 3
Ivano-Frankovsk = Ivano-Frankivs'k ☆ UA 102-103 D 3
Ivanovka ○ RUS (AMR) 122-123 B 3
Ivanovka ○ RUS (CTN) 118-119 J 10
Ivanovka ○ RUS (ORB) 96-97 H 7
Ivanovka ∼ RUS 122-123 C 3
Ivanovo ○••• BG 102-103 D 6
Ivanovo ○ RUS (PSK) 94-95 M 3
Ivanovo ☆ RUS (IVN) 94-95 R 3
Ivanovsk, Katav- ○ RUS 96-97 L 6
Ivanteevka ☆ RUS 96-97 F 7
Ivaška ○ RUS 120-121 U 4
Ivato ○ RM 222-223 E 8
Ivdel' ○ RUS 114-115 F 4
Iveetok Camp ○ USA 20-21 E 5
Ivindo ∼ RCB 210-211 D 3
Ivinheima, Rio ∼ BR 76-77 K 1
Ivinhema ○ BR 72-73 D 7
Ivisan ○ RP 160-161 E 7
Ivisaruk River ∼ USA 20-21 K 2
Ivittuut ○ GRØ 28-29 Q 6
Ivnanganek ○ GRØ 26-27 R 6
Ivnarssuit ○ GRØ 26-27 W 7
Ivohibe ○ RM 222-223 E 9
Ivolginsk ☆ RUS 116-117 N 10
Ivon, Río ∼ BOL 70-71 D 2
Ivondro ∼ RM 222-223 F 6
Ivongo, Soanierana- ○ RM 222-223 F 6
Ivori River ∼ PNG 183 C 4
Ivorogbo ○ WAN 204-205 G 6
Ivory Coast ∪ CI 202-203 H 7
Ivrea ○ I 100-101 A 2
Ivrindi ☆ TR 128-129 B 3
Ivujivik ○ CDN 36-37 L 3
Ivuna ○ EAT 214-215 G 5
Iwa Island ⌒ PNG 183 F 5
Iwaizumi ○ J 152-153 J 5
Iwaki ○ J 152-153 J 6
Iwaki-san ▲ J 152-153 J 4
Iwakuni ○ J 152-153 E 7
Iwala ○ ZRE 210-211 J 5
Iwamizawa ○ J 152-153 J 3
Iwanai ○ J 152-153 J 3
Iwanuma ○ J 152-153 J 5
Iwatebu ○ PNG 183 B 4
Iwate-san ▲ J 152-153 J 5
Iwe ○ ZRE 210-211 K 5
Iwo ○ WAN 204-205 F 5
Iwopin ○ WAN 204-205 F 5
Iwungu ○ ZRE 210-211 G 6
Iwupataka X AUS 176-177 M 1
Ixcún ∴• GCA 52-53 K 4
Ixiamas ○ BOL 70-71 C 3
Ixmiquilpan ○• MEX 52-53 E 1
Ixopo ○ ZA 220-221 K 5
Ixtapa ○ MEX (GRO) 52-53 D 3
Ixtapa ○ MEX (OAX) 52-53 F 3
Ixtapan de la Sal ○ MEX 52-53 E 2
Ixtlahuaca ○ MEX 52-53 F 2
Ixtlahuacan ○ MEX 52-53 C 2
Ixtlahuacan del Río ○ MEX 52-53 C 1
Ixtlán ∴• MEX 52-53 B 1
Ixtlán de Juárez ○• MEX 52-53 F 3
Ixtlán del Río ○ MEX 50-51 G 7
Ixu ○ BR 70-71 J 5
'Iyāl Bakhīt ○ SUD 200-201 D 6
Iyapa ○ WAN 204-205 F 5
Iyayi ○ EAT 214-215 H 5
Iyo ○ J 152-153 E 8
Iyo-nada ≈ 152-153 D 8
Iž ∼ RUS 96-97 H 5
Izabal, Lago de ○ GCA 52-53 K 4
Izadhvāst ○ IR 134-135 E 3
Izaguène < RIM 196-197 C 6
Izamal ○ MEX 52-53 K 1
Izapa ∴• MEX 52-53 H 4
'Izbat al-Ǧāǧa ○ ET 194-195 E 5
Izberbaš ○ RUS 126-127 G 6
Izborsk ○•• RUS 94-95 K 3
Iże ○ IR 134-135 C 3
Izena-shima ⌒ J 152-153 B 11
Iževsk ☆ RUS 96-97 H 5
Izhevsk = Iževsk ☆ RUS 96-97 H 5
Izhma = Ižma ∼ RUS 88-89 X 5
Izium ○ UA 102-103 K 3
Izki ○ OM 132-133 K 2
Izlistan = Žižah ☆• US 136-137 K 4
Ižma ○ RUS 88-89 W 4
Ižma ∼ RUS 88-89 W 4
Izmail = Izmajil ☆ UA 102-103 F 5
Izmajil ☆ UA 102-103 F 5
İzmir ☆•• TR 128-129 B 3
İzmit=Kocaeli ○ TR 128-129 C 2
Ižmorskij ☆ RUS 114-115 T 6
İznik ☆ TR 128-129 C 2
İznik Gölü ○ TR 128-129 C 2
Izobil'noe ○ KA 124-125 H 2
Izobil'nyj ○ RUS 102-103 M 5
Izozog ○ BOL 70-71 F 6
Izozog, Bañados de ○ BOL 70-71 F 6
Izra' ☆ SYR 128-129 G 6
Izúcar de Matamoros ○ MEX 52-53 E 2
Izu-hantō ∪ J 152-153 H 7
Izuhara ○ J 152-153 C 7
Izumi ○ J 152-153 J 5
Izumo ○ J 152-153 E 7
Izu-shotō ⌒ J 152-153 H 7
Izvestij CIK, ostrova ⌒ RUS 108-109 T 4
Izyestkovyj ○ RUS 122-123 D 4

J

Jaab Lake ○ CDN 34-35 P 5
Jaala ○ FIN 88-89 J 6
Jaba ○ PK 138-139 D 3
Jabali, Isla ⌒ RA 78-79 H 6
Jabalón, Río ∼ E 98-99 F 5
Jabalpur ○ IND 138-139 G 8
Jabarona < SUD 200-201 C 4
Jabillo ○ CR 52-53 C 7
Jabiru ○ AUS 172-173 L 2
Jabitaca ○ BR 68-69 K 5
Jablanica ○ BG 102-103 D 6
Jablanica ○ BIH 100-101 F 3
Jablon ∼ RUS 112-113 P 4
Jablonevyj ○ RUS 120-121 O 3
Jablonovyj hrebet ▲ RUS 118-119 D 10
Jabo ○ WAN 198-199 B 6
Jabon ○ RI 168 E 3
Jaboncillos Creek ∼ USA (TX) 266-267 J 6
Jabotá, Rio ∼ BR 70-71 K 3
Jabung, Tanjung ▲ RI 162-163 F 5
Jaburu, Rio ∼ BR 68-69 C 7
Jabuticabal ○ BR 72-73 F 6
Jabuticatubas ○ BR 72-73 J 5
Jaca ○ E 98-99 G 3
Jacaf, Canal ≈ 80 D 2
Jacaí ○ SP 208-209 H 6
Jacala ○ MEX 50-51 K 7
Jacana ○ BR 68-69 K 5
Jacaraí, Rio ∼ BR 68-69 H 3
Jacaraú Estradas ○ BR 68-69 L 5
Jacaré ○ BR 66-67 C 6
Jacaré, Ilha ⌒ BR 66-67 H 5
Jacaré, Rio ∼ BR 66-67 F 6
Jacaré, Rio ∼ BR 72-73 H 6
Jacareacanga ○ BR 66-67 J 6
Jacaré Grande ○ BR 72-73 J 3
Jacaré Guaçu, Rio ∼ BR 72-73 F 6
Jacareí ○ BR 72-73 H 7
Jacaré Pepira, Rio ∼ BR 72-73 F 6
Jacaretinga ○ BR 66-67 F 7
Jacas Grande ○ PE 64-65 D 6
Jacaúna ○ BR 68-69 J 3
Jaceel, togga ∼ SP 208-209 K 3
Jaceyl ∼ SP 208-209 K 3
Jáchal, Río ∼ RA 76-77 C 6
Jáchymov ○ CZ 92-93 M 3
Jaciara ○ BR 70-71 K 4
Jacinto ○ BR 72-73 K 4
Jacinto, San ○ USA (CA) 248-249 H 6
Jaci Paraná ○ BR 66-67 E 7
Jaciparaná, Rio ∼ BR 66-67 E 7
Jacitara ○ BR 66-67 E 4
Jack ○ USA (AL) 284-285 D 5
Jack Creek ○ USA (NV) 246-247 J 2
Jack Daniels Distillery • USA (TN) 276-277 J 5
Jackfish Creek ∼ CDN 30-31 N 6
Jackfork Mountain ▲ USA (OK) 264-265 J 4
Jackhead Harbour ○ CDN (MAN) 234-235 F 3
Jack Lee, Lake < USA (AR) 276-277 C 7
Jackman ○ USA (ME) 278-279 L 3
Jackpint River ∼ CDN (ALB) 228-229 P 3
Jackpot ○ USA (NV) 246-247 L 2
Jacksboro ○ USA (TX) 264-265 F 5
Jacks Fork ∼ USA (MO) 276-277 D 3
Jackson ○ AUS 178-179 K 4
Jackson ○ CDN (NS) 240-241 M 5
Jackson ○ USA (AL) 284-285 C 5
Jackson ○ USA (CA) 246-247 E 5
Jackson ○ USA (GA) 284-285 G 3
Jackson ○ USA (KY) 276-277 M 3
Jackson ○ USA (LA) 268-269 J 6
Jackson ○ USA (MN) 272-273 E 5
Jackson ○ USA (MN) 270-271 D 7
Jackson ○ USA (MO) 276-277 F 3
Jackson ○ USA (MT) 250-251 F 6
Jackson ○ USA (NC) 282-283 K 4
Jackson ○ USA (OH) 280-281 D 4
Jackson ○ USA (TN) 276-277 G 5
Jackson ○ USA (WY) 252-253 H 3
Jackson ☆• USA (MS) 268-269 K 4
Jackson, Fort ✕✕ USA (LA) 268-269 L 7
Jackson, Kap ▲ GRØ 26-27 R 3
Jackson, Lake ○ USA (FL) 286-287 E 1
Jackson, Mount ▲ AUS 176-177 E 5
Jackson Arm ○ CDN (NFL) 242-243 M 3
Jackson Bay ○ CDN (BC) 230-231 D 3
Jacksonboro ○ USA (SC) 284-285 K 4
Jackson Junction ○ USA (IA) 274-275 F 1
Jackson Lake ○ USA (OH) 280-281 D 5
Jackson Lake ○ USA (WY) 252-253 H 3
Jackson Lake < USA (GA) 284-285 G 3
Jackson Lake Lodge ○ USA (WY) 252-253 H 3
Jackson River ∼ USA (VA) 280-281 G 6
Jacksonville ○ C 54-55 D 4
Jacksonville ○ USA (AL) 284-285 E 3
Jacksonville ○ USA (AR) 276-277 C 6
Jacksonville ○ USA (FL) 286-287 H 1
Jacksonville ○ USA (GA) 284-285 H 5
Jacksonville ○ USA (IL) 274-275 H 5
Jacksonville ○ USA (NC) 282-283 K 6
Jacksonville ○ USA (TX) 268-269 E 5
Jacksonville Beach ○ USA (FL) 286-287 H 1
Jacktown ○ USA (KY) 276-277 K 3
Jack Wade ○ USA 20-21 U 4
Jacmel ☆• RH 54-55 J 5
Jacó ○ CR 52-53 B 7
Jacobābād ○• PK 138-139 B 5
Jacob Island ⌒ USA 22-23 R 5
Jacob Lake ○ USA (AZ) 256-257 C 2
Jacobsdal ○ ZA 220-221 G 4
Jacobson ○ USA (MN) 270-271 E 4
Jacobsville ○ USA (MI) 270-271 K 4
Jacona ○ MEX 52-53 C 2
Jacques, Lac ○ CDN (QUE) 240-241 D 3
Jacques, Lac à ○ CDN 30-31 F 2
Jacques Cartier, Mont ▲ CDN (QUE) 240-241 K 2
Jacques Cartier, Parc de la ⊥ CDN (QUE) 240-241 D 3
Jacques Cartier, Rivière ∼ CDN (QUE) 240-241 D 3
Jacqueville ○• CI 202-203 H 7
Jacquinot Bay ≈ 183 F 3
Jacu ○ BR 68-69 F 6
Jacuba, Rio ∼ BR 72-73 D 5
Jacuí ○ BR 72-73 G 6
Jacuí, Rio ∼ BR 74-75 D 7
Jacuípe ○ BR 72-73 L 2
Jacuípe, Rio ∼ BR 68-69 J 7
Jacuizinho ○ BR 74-75 D 7
Jacumba ○ USA (CA) 248-249 H 7
Jacundá ○ BR 66-67 F 7
Jacundá, Rio ∼ BR 66-67 F 7
Jacunda, Rio ∼ BR 68-69 C 3
Jacup ○ AUS 176-177 E 6
Jacupiranga ○ BR 74-75 F 5
Jacurici, Açude < BR 68-69 J 7
Jacurici, Rio ∼ BR 68-69 J 7
Jada ○ WAN 204-205 K 4
Jadajahodyjaha ∼ RUS 108-109 O 8
Jaddi, Rās ▲ PK 134-135 K 6
Jadebusen ≈ D 92-93 K 2
Jadkal ○ IND 140-141 F 4
Jadranska magistrala II HR 100-101 F 3
Jadransko more ≈ 100-101 D 2
Jādū ○• LAR 192-193 E 2
Jaén ○ E 98-99 F 6
Jaen ○ PE 64-65 C 4
Jafarābād ○ IND 138-139 F 9
Jāfarābād ○ IND 138-139 C 9
Jāfarah ⩦ TN 190-191 H 4
Jaffa, Cape ▲ AUS 180-181 E 4
Jaffa, Cirque de • MA 188-189 J 4
Jaffna ○•• CL 140-141 J 6
Jagalūr ○ IND 140-141 G 3
Jagbahun ○ WAL 202-203 D 5
Jagdagi ○ VRC 150-151 E 2
Jagdalpur ○ IND 142-143 C 6
Jagdispur ○ IND 142-143 B 2
Jagdyg ○ RUS 118-119 E 8
Jagel'urta, gora ▲ RUS 88-89 P 3
Jagenetta ∼ RUS 114-115 O 2
Jagersfontein ○ ZA 220-221 G 4
Jaggayyapeta ○ IND 140-141 J 2
Jagodnoe ☆ RUS 120-121 N 2
Jago River ∼ USA 20-21 T 2
Jagtial ○ IND 138-139 G 10
Jagua ○• C 54-55 E 3
Jagua, La ○ C 54-55 F 4
Jaguapitã ○ BR 72-73 E 7
Jaguaquara ○ BR 72-73 L 2
Jaguarão ○ BR 74-75 D 9
Jaguarão, Rio ∼ BR 74-75 D 9
Jaguarari ○ BR 68-69 H 7
Jaguaré ○ BR 72-73 K 5
Jaguarembé ○ BR 72-73 J 6
Jaguaretama ○ BR 68-69 J 4
Jaguari ○ BR 76-77 K 5
Jaguari, Rio ∼ BR 72-73 G 7
Jaguariaíva ○ BR 74-75 F 5
Jaguaribe ○ BR 68-69 J 4
Jaguaribe, Rio ∼ BR 68-69 J 5
Jaguaruana ○ BR 68-69 K 4
Jaguaruna ○ BR 74-75 F 7
Jagüé, Río ∼ RA 76-77 C 5
Jagüey Grande ○ C 54-55 E 3
Jagvi ○ IND 140-141 F 3
Jagyl'ja ∼ RUS 114-115 N 5
Jah, Pyt'- ○ RUS 114-115 M 4
Jahadyjaha ∼ RUS 108-109 O 5
Jahānābād ○ IND 142-143 D 3
Jahangiraba ○ IND 138-139 G 5
Jahleel, Point ▲ AUS 172-173 K 1
Jahorina ▲ BIH 100-101 G 3
Jahuey Creek ∼ USA (TX) 266-267 H 5
Jaicós ○ BR 68-69 H 5
Jailleu, Bourgoin- ○ F 90-91 K 9
Jailolo ○ RI 164-165 K 3
Jailolo, Selat ≈ 166-167 E 2
Jainagar ○ IND 142-143 C 4
Jainpur ○ IND 142-143 B 4
Jaintiapur ○ BD 142-143 H 3
Jainu ○ BR 66-67 C 6
Jaipur ○ IND (ASS) 142-143 J 2
Jaipur ☆•• IND (RAJ) 138-139 E 6
Jaisalmer ○• IND 138-139 C 6
Jaisinghnagar ○ IND 142-143 B 4
Jaj ∼ RUS 122-123 H 3
Jaja ☆ RUS 114-115 T 6
Jaja ∼ RUS 114-115 T 6
Jājapur ○ IND 142-143 E 5
Jājapur Road ○ IND 142-143 E 5
Jajarkot ○ NEP 144-145 D 6
Jajce ○ BIH 100-101 F 2
Jajpan ○ US 136-137 M 4
Jajva ○ RUS 114-115 D 5
Jakar ○ BHT 142-143 G 2
Jakarta ★ RI 168 B 3
Jakarta, Teluk ≈ 168 B 3
Jaken ○ RI 168 D 3
Jakes Corner ○ USA (AZ) 256-257 D 4
Jakiri ○ CAM 204-205 J 5
Jäkkvik ○ S 86-87 H 3
Jako, Pulau ⌒ RI 166-167 D 6
Jakob Kjode Bjerg ▲ GRØ 26-27 m 6
Jakobshavn = Ilulissat ○ GRØ 28-29 P 2
Jakobshavns Isfjord ≈ 28-29 P 2
Jakob's Ladder Great Falls ∼ GUY 62-63 E 4
Jakobstad ○ FIN 88-89 G 5
Jakokit ○ RUS 118-119 M 6
Jakokut ○ RUS 118-119 M 6
Jakovleva ∼ RUS 108-109 U 6
Jakpa ○ WAN 204-205 F 6
Jakšino ○ RUS 88-89 W 3
Jaktali ∼ RUS 116-117 H 2
Jaktali, plato ⩦ RUS 116-117 H 2
Jakutsk ☆•• RUS 118-119 O 4
Jal ○ USA (NM) 256-257 M 6
Jalaid Qi ○ VRC 150-151 D 4
Jalal-Abad ○ KS 136-137 N 4
Jalālpur ○ IND 142-143 C 2
Jalālpur ○ PK 138-139 E 3
Jalālpur Pīrwāla ○ PK 138-139 C 5
Ja'lān ⩦ OM 132-133 L 2
Jalán, Río ∼ HN 52-53 L 4
Jalang ○ RI 164-165 G 6
Jalapa ☆ GCA 52-53 K 4
Jalapa ○ MEX (TAB) 52-53 H 3
Jalapa ☆ MEX (VER) 52-53 F 2
Jalapa de Díaz ○ MEX 52-53 F 2
Jalapa Enríquez = Jalapa ☆• MEX 52-53 F 2
Jalasjärvi ○ FIN 88-89 G 5
Jalaté, Río ∼ MEX 52-53 J 3
Jalaud ∼ RP 160-161 E 7
Jalbyn'ja ∼ RUS 114-115 G 3
Jales ○ BR 72-73 E 6
Jaleshwar ○ NEP 144-145 E 7
Jaleswar ○ IND 142-143 E 5
Jalgaon ○ IND 138-139 E 10
Jālgaon ○ IND (MAH) 138-139 F 9
Jālgaon ○•• IND (MAH) 138-139 E 9
Jalingo ○ WAN 204-205 J 4
Jalisco ◘ MEX 52-53 B 2
Jālna ○ IND 138-139 E 10
Jālor ○ IND 138-139 D 7
Jalostotitlan ○ MEX 50-51 H 7
Jalpa ○ MEX 50-51 H 7
Jalpa de Méndez ○ MEX 52-53 H 2
Jalpāiguri ○ IND 142-143 F 2
Jalpan ○ MEX 50-51 K 7
Jalpuh, ozero ○ UA 102-103 F 5
Jalta ☆•• UA 102-103 J 5
Jáltipan de Morelos ○ MEX 52-53 G 3
Jalu ○ LAR 192-193 J 3
Jalutorovsk ☆ RUS 114-115 J 6
Jama ○ EC 64-65 B 2
Jama ∼ RUS 120-121 P 3
Jama, Paso de ▲ RA 76-77 D 2
Jamaame ○ SP 212-213 J 3
Jāmai ○ IND 138-139 G 8
Jamaica ■ JA 54-55 F 6
Jamaica ⌒ JA 54-55 G 5
Jamaica Channel ≈ 54-55 H 6
Jamal ○ C 54-55 H 4
Jamal, poluostrov ∪ RUS 108-109 N 7
Jamalin', hrebet ▲ RUS 122-123 F 2
Jamalpur ○ BD 142-143 F 3
Jamalwal ○ PK 138-139 B 4
Jamantau, gora ▲ RUS 96-97 L 6
Jamanxim, Rio ∼ BR 66-67 K 6
Jamari ○ WAN 204-205 J 3
Jamari, Rio ∼ BR 66-67 F 7
Jamarovka ○ RUS 118-119 E 10
Jamb ○ IND 138-139 G 9
Jamba ○ ANG (HUA) 216-217 D 7
Jamba ∼ ANG 216-217 E 4
Jambeli, Canal de ≈ 64-65 B 3
Jambi ◘ RI 162-163 E 5
Jambi ☆ RI 162-163 E 5
Jambi = Telanaipura ☆ RI 162-163 E 5
Jamboeye ∼ RI 162-163 B 2
Jambol ○ BG 102-103 E 6
Jambon, Pointe ▲ CDN (QUE) 240-241 J 2
Jambongan, Pulau ⌒ MAL 160-161 B 9
Jambuair, Tanjung ▲ RI 162-163 B 2
Jambu Bongkok, Kampung ○ MAL 162-163 E 2
Jambukan ∼ RUS 116-117 J 3
Jambusar ○ IND 138-139 D 8
Jambuto, ozero ○ RUS (JAN) 108-109 S 6
Jambuto, ozero ○ RUS (JAN) 108-109 O 6
Jambuto, ozero ○ RUS (JAN) 108-109 N 7
James ○ USA (MS) 268-269 J 3
James, Isla ⌒ RCH 80 C 2
James, Lake < USA (NC) 282-283 F 5
Jamesābād ○ PK 138-139 B 7
James A. Reed Memorial Wildlife Refuge ⊥ USA (MO) 274-275 D 6
James Bay ≈ 34-35 Q 4
James Beach, Fort • AG 56 E 3
James Cook Monument • AUS 174-175 H 4
James Creek ∼ CDN 30-31 L 6
James Dalton Highway II USA 20-21 P 3
James Island ○ USA (SC) 284-285 L 4
Jameson, Cape ▲ CDN 24-25 j 4
Jameson Islands ⌒ CDN 24-25 R 6
Jameson Land ⩦ GRØ 26-27 o 8
James Ranges ▲ AUS 176-177 M 2
James River ∼ CDN 30-31 P 2
James River ∼ CDN (ALB) 232-233 C 4
James River ∼ USA (MO) 276-277 B 4
James River ∼ USA (ND) 258-259 H 4
James River ∼ USA (SD) 260-261 J 3
James River ∼ USA (VA) 280-281 H 6
James Ross, Cape ▲ CDN 24-25 O 3
James Ross Strait ≈ 24-25 Y 6
James Smith Indian Reservation X CDN (SAS) 232-233 O 2
Jamestown ○ AUS 180-181 E 2
Jamestown ☆ GB 202-203 C 7
Jamestown ○ USA (MO) 274-275 F 6
Jamestown ○ USA (NY) 278-279 B 6
Jamestown ○ USA (PA) 280-281 F 2
Jamestown ○ USA (SC) 284-285 L 3
Jamestown ○ USA (TN) 282-283 C 4
Jamestown ○• USA (ND) 258-259 J 5
Jamestown ○ ZA 220-221 H 5
Jamestown Reservoir ○ USA (ND) 258-259 J 4
Jamesville ○ USA (NC) 282-283 L 5
Jamieson ○• AUS 180-181 J 4
Jaminawá, Área Indígena X BR 64-65 F 6
Jaminawá Arara, Área Indígena X BR 64-65 F 6
Jämjö ○ S 86-87 G 8
Jam Jodhpur ○ IND 138-139 C 9
Jamkhandi ○ IND 140-141 F 2
Jāmkhed ○ IND 138-139 E 10
Jamkie, Verchnie ○ RUS 112-113 L 2
Jamliyah, al- ○ Q 134-135 D 6
Jamm ○ RUS 94-95 L 2
Jammalamadugu ○ IND 140-141 H 3
Jammerbugten ≈ 86-87 D 8
Jammersdrif ○ ZA 220-221 H 4
Jammu ○• IND 138-139 E 3
Jammu and Kashmir ◘ IND 138-139 E 2
Jāmnagar ○• IND 138-139 C 8
Jämner ○ IND 138-139 E 9
Jamozero ○ RUS 88-89 V 4
Jampangkulon ○ RI 168 B 3
Jampil' ☆ UA 102-103 F 3
Jampue ○ RI 164-165 F 5
Jämpur ○ PK 138-139 C 5
Jämsä ○ FIN 88-89 H 6
Jamsavèj ∼ RUS 114-115 O 2
Jamshedpur ○•• IND 142-143 E 4
Jamsk ○ RUS 120-121 Q 4
Jamskaja, guba ○ RUS 120-121 Q 4
Jamskaja nizmenost' ∪ RUS 120-121 P 3
Jamskie, ostrova ⌒ RUS 120-121 Q 4
Jamskoe lesničestvo ⊥ RUS 120-121 O 4
Jamtari ○ WAN 204-205 J 5
Jämtland ⩦ S 86-87 F 5
Jamu ○ ETH 208-209 B 5
Jamūi ○ IND 142-143 E 3
Jamul ○ USA (CA) 248-249 H 7
Jamuna ∼ BD 142-143 F 3
Jamundi ○ CO 60-61 C 6
Jamutarida ∼ RUS 108-109 e 4
Jana ○ RUS (MAG) 120-121 N 3
Jana ∼ RUS 110-111 V 4
Janakpur ○• NEP 144-145 E 7
Janauacá, Lago ○ BR 66-67 G 4
Janaúba ○ BR 72-73 J 3
Janauçu, Ilha ⌒ BR 62-63 J 5
Janaul ☆ RUS 96-97 J 5
Jand ○ PK 138-139 D 3
Jandaia do Sul ○ BR 72-73 E 7
Jandaíra ○ BR 68-69 K 4
Jandía Playa ○ E 188-189 D 6
Jandiatuba, Rio ∼ BR 66-67 C 5
Jandola ○ PK 138-139 C 3
Jandowae ○ AUS 178-179 L 4
Janeiro, 31 de ○ ANG 216-217 C 3
Janeiro, Área Indígena 9 de X BR 66-67 F 6
Janeiro, Rio de ∼ BR 68-69 F 7
Janesville ○ USA (MN) 270-271 E 6
Janesville ○ USA (WI) 274-275 J 2
Janeville ○ CDN (NB) 240-241 K 3
Jang ○ GH 202-203 J 5
Jang ○ IND 142-143 G 2
Jang, plato ⩦ RUS 108-109 b 7
Jangada ○ BR 70-71 J 4
Jangamo ○ MOC 218-219 H 7
Jangaon ○ IND 140-141 H 2
Jangeto ∼ RUS 116-117 G 3
Jangiabad ○ US 136-137 M 4
Jangier ○ US 136-137 L 4
Jangijūl ○ US 136-137 L 4
Jangikišlok ○ US 136-137 K 4
Jangikurgan ○ US 136-137 M 4
Jangil', hrebet ▲ RUS 116-117 K 4
Jangipur ○ IND 142-143 F 3
Jangirabad ○ US 136-137 J 4
Jangngai Shan ▲ VRC 144-145 F 4
Jangoda ∼ RUS 108-109 X 6
Jangozero, ozero ○ RUS 88-89 M 5
Janice ○ USA (MS) 268-269 L 5
Jāni Khel ○ PK 138-139 C 3
Janiopolis ○ BR 74-75 D 5
Janiševo ○ RUS 88-89 O 6
Janiuay ○ RP 160-161 E 7
Jankan, hrebet ▲ RUS 118-119 H 8
Jan Kempdorp ○ ZA 220-221 G 3
Jan Lake ○ CDN (SAS) 34-35 E 3
Jan Lake ○ CDN (SAS) 34-35 E 3
Jan Mayen ⌒ N 6-7 J 1
Jan Mayen Fracture Zone ≃ 6-7 J 1
Jannaye, Lac la ○ CDN 38-39 L 2
Jano-Indigirskaja nizmennost ∪ RUS 110-111 U 4
Janos ○ MEX 50-51 E 2
Janów Lubelski ○ PL 92-93 R 3
Janrakynnot ○ RUS 112-113 Y 4
Janranaj ○ RUS 112-113 Q 2
Jansen ○ CDN (SAS) 232-233 O 4
Jansen ○ USA (CO) 254-255 L 6
Jansenville ○ ZA 220-221 G 6
Jansk, Ust'- ○ RUS 110-111 V 4
Janskie porogi ∼ RUS 110-111 T 5
Janskij zaliv ≈ 110-111 U 4
Janskoe ploskogor'e ▲ RUS 110-111 T 6
Jantan ○ RI 166-167 H 3
Jantetelco ○ MEX 52-53 E 2
Janthoe ○ RI 162-163 A 2
Jantingue ○ MOC 220-221 L 2
Januária ○ BR 72-73 H 3
Janúario Cicco ○ BR 68-69 L 5
Janus Ø ⌒ GRØ 26-27 p 8
Janykurgan ○ KA 136-137 K 3
Jaora ○ IND 138-139 E 8
Japan = Nippon ■ J 152-153 J 6
Japan, Sea of ≈ 10-11 N 4
Japan, Sea of = Nippon Kai = Sea of Japan = Japonskoe more ≈ 10-11 N 4
Japan Basin ≃ 10-11 N 4
Japanese War Cemetery • AUS 180-181 K 2
Japanese World War II Bunker ∴• RI 166-167 G 4
Japan Trench ≃ 152-153 K 7
Japaratinga ○ BR 68-69 L 6
Japaratuba ○ BR 68-69 K 7
Japerica ○ BR 68-69 E 2
Japerica, Baía do ≈ 68-69 E 2
Japim ○ BR 64-65 F 5
Japon, mys ▲ RUS 120-121 Q 4
Japtiksale ○ RUS 108-109 O 7
Japuíra, Área Indígena X BR 70-71 H 2
Japurá ○ BR 66-67 D 3
Japurá, Rio ∼ BR 66-67 D 3
Jaqué ○ PA 52-53 E 8
Jaques-Cartier, Détroit de ≈ CDN 242-243 E 2
Jar ○ RUS 114-115 H 6
Jar ☆ RUS (UDM) 96-97 H 4
Jar, Krasnyj ○ RUS 114-115 T 7
Jara ∼ RUS 108-109 T 7
Jara, La ○ USA (CO) 254-255 K 6
Jarabacoa ○• DOM 54-55 K 5
Jaraguá ○ BR 72-73 F 3
Jaraguá ○ BR 74-75 F 6
Jaraguá do Sul ○ BR 74-75 F 6
Jaraguari ○ BR (GSU) 70-71 K 7
Jaraguari ○ BR (GSU) 70-71 K 6
Jarahueca ○ C 54-55 F 3
Jaram, La ⩦ MA 188-189 F 7
Jaraniyo ○ ETH 208-209 D 3
Jaransk ○ RUS 96-97 E 5
Jarānwāla ○ PK 138-139 D 4
Jarato, ozero ○ RUS 108-109 Q 6
Jarauçu, Rio ∼ BR 68-69 B 3
Jarawara, Área Indígena X BR 66-67 E 6
Jarbidge ○ USA (NV) 246-247 K 2
Jarbo Pass ▲ USA (CA) 246-247 D 4
Jarcevo ○ RUS 116-117 E 5
Jarcevo ☆ RUS (SML) 94-95 N 4
Jarclas al Abid ○ LAR 192-193 J 1
Jardim ○ BR (CEA) 68-69 J 5
Jardim ○ BR (GSU) 76-77 J 1
Jardim do Serido ○ BR 68-69 K 5
Jardín, Sierra del ▲ RCH 76-77 C 3
Jardín América ○ RA 76-77 K 4
Jardine River ∼ AUS 174-175 G 2
Jardine River National Park ⊥ AUS 174-175 G 2
Jardines de la Reina, Archipiélago de los ⌒ C 54-55 F 4
Jardymly = Yardımlı ○ AZ 128-129 N 3
Jaredi ○ WAN 198-199 B 6
Jarega ○ RUS 88-89 W 5
Jarenga ○ RUS (ARH) 88-89 U 5
Jarenga ∼ RUS 88-89 U 5
Jarensk ○ RUS 88-89 U 5
Jari ○ BR 76-77 K 5
Jari, Estação Ecológica do ⊥ BR 62-63 H 5
Jari, Lago ○ BR 66-67 F 5
Jari, Rio ∼ BR 62-63 H 5
Jari, Rio ∼ BR 66-67 F 5
Jaria-Jhanjail ○ BD 142-143 G 3
Jarif, Wādī ∼ LAR 192-193 G 2
Jarina ou Juruna, Rio ∼ BR 68-69 B 7
Jarkovo ☆ RUS 114-115 J 6
Jarnema ○ RUS 88-89 P 5
Jarny ○ F 90-91 K 7
Jarocin ○• PL 92-93 O 3
Jarok, ostrov ⌒ RUS 110-111 V 4
Jaroslavl' ☆•• RUS 94-95 Q 3
Jaroslavskij ○ RUS 118-119 F 5
Jarosław ○• PL 92-93 R 3
Jaroto pervoe, ozero ○ RUS 108-109 O 8
Jaroto vtoroe, ozero ○ RUS 108-109 O 7
Jarotschin = Jarocin ○• PL 92-93 O 3
Jarovaja ∼ RUS 112-113 L 3
Jarovoe ○ RUS 124-125 L 2
Järpen ○ S 86-87 F 5
Jarqurghon ○ US 136-137 K 6
Jarrahdale ○ AUS 176-177 D 6
Jarrow ○ CDN (ALB) 232-233 G 3
Jar-Sale ○ RUS 108-109 O 8
Jarso ○ ETH 208-209 B 4
Jartai ○ VRC 154-155 D 2
Jartai Yanchi ○ VRC 154-155 D 2
Jaru ○ BR 70-71 F 2
Jaru, Reserva Biológica do ⊥ BR 66-67 G 7
Jaru, Rio ∼ BR 70-71 F 2
Jarudej ∼ RUS 114-115 L 2
Jarud Qi ○ VRC 150-151 C 5
Jaruma ○ BOL 70-71 C 6
Järva-Jaani ○ EST 94-95 J 2
Järvakandi ○ EST 94-95 J 2
Järvenpää ○ FIN 88-89 H 6
Jarvis ○ CDN (ONT) 238-239 E 6
Jarvis Island ⌒ USA 13 L 3
Järvsö ○ S 86-87 H 6
Jārwāli ○ IND 138-139 D 5
Jary ○ RUS 108-109 M 7
Jasaan ○ RP 160-161 F 8
Jasačnaja ∼ RUS 110-111 c 7
Jasačnaja ∼ RUS 120-121 Q 2
Jasavèjjaha ∼ RUS 108-109 O 6
Jasavèjto, ozero ○ RUS 108-109 N 7
Jaseľda ∼ BY 94-95 J 5
Jashpurnagar ○ IND 142-143 D 4
Jasiira ○ SP 212-213 K 3
Jasikan ○ GH 202-203 L 6
Jašil'kul', ozero ○ TJ 136-137 N 6
Jašiūnai ○•• LT 94-95 J 4
Jaškino ☆ RUS 114-115 S 7
Jaškuľ ○ RUS 96-97 D 10
Jaškur-Bodja ☆ RUS 96-97 H 5
Jasło ○• PL 92-93 Q 4
Jasmin ○ CDN (SAS) 232-233 P 4
Jasnaja ○ RUS 118-119 G 10
Jasnoe ○ RUS 94-95 G 4
Jasnogorsk ☆• RUS 94-95 P 4
Jasnomorskij ○ RUS 122-123 J 5
Jasnyj ○ RUS (AMR) 122-123 C 2
Jasnyj ☆ RUS (ORB) 126-127 N 2
Jasonhalvöy ∪ ARK 16 G 30
Jason Islands ⌒ GB 78-79 K 6
Jasper ○ CDN (ALB) 228-229 Q 4
Jasper ○ USA (AL) 284-285 C 3
Jasper ○ USA (AR) 276-277 B 4
Jasper ○ USA (FL) 286-287 G 1
Jasper ○ USA (GA) 284-285 F 2
Jasper ○ USA (IN) 274-275 M 6
Jasper ○ USA (MN) 270-271 B 7
Jasper ○ USA (NY) 278-279 D 6
Jasper ○ USA (TN) 276-277 K 5
Jasper ○ USA (TX) 268-269 G 6
Jasper Lake ○ CDN (ALB) 228-229 R 3
Jasper National Park ⊥••• CDN (ALB) 228-229 Q 3
Jasrāna ○ IND 138-139 G 6
Jastrow = Jastrowie ○ PL 92-93 O 2
Jastrowie ○ PL 92-93 O 2
Jasubibeteri ○ YV 60-61 J 6
Jataí ○ BR 72-73 E 4
Jatapu, Rio ∼ BR 66-67 H 4
Jatapu, Serra do ▲ BR 62-63 E 6
Jatapuzinho, Rio ∼ BR 62-63 E 5
Jatei ○ BR 76-77 K 2
Jath ○ IND 140-141 F 2
Jati ○ BR 68-69 J 5
Jati ○ PK 138-139 B 7
Jati ○ RI 168 D 3
Jatibarang ○ RI 168 C 3
Jatibonico ○ C 54-55 F 4
Jatiluhur, Danau ○ RI 168 B 3
Jatirogo ○ RI 168 D 3
Jatiwangi ○ RI 168 C 3
Jatobá ○ BR (MAT) 70-71 K 3
Jatobá ○ BR (P) 68-69 B 4
Jaú ○ BR 72-73 F 7
Jaú, Parque Nacional do ⊥ BR 66-67 F 4
Jaú, Rio ∼ BR 66-67 F 4
Jauaperi, Rio ∼ BR 62-63 E 5
Jauarauá ○ BR 66-67 E 4
Jaucha, Arroyo de ∼ RA 78-79 E 3
Jauharābād ○ PK 138-139 D 3
Jauja ○• PE 64-65 E 7
Jaumave ○ MEX 50-51 K 6
Jaunpiebalga ○•• LV 94-95 K 3
Jaunpur ○ IND 142-143 C 3
Jaupaci ○ BR 72-73 E 4
Jauquara, Rio ∼ BR 70-71 J 4
Jaurdi ○ AUS 176-177 F 5
Jaurin ∼ RUS 122-123 D 4
Jauru ○ BR (GSU) 70-71 K 6
Jauru ○ BR (MAT) 70-71 H 4
Jauru, Rio ∼ BR 70-71 H 5
Java Barat ◘ RI 168 B 3
Java Center ○ USA (NY) 278-279 C 6
Javaj, poluostrov ∪ RUS 108-109 Q 5
Javan ○ TJ 136-137 L 5
Javari, Rio ∼ BR 62-63 H 6
Javari, Rio ∼ BR 64-65 F 4
Java Sea = Jawa, Laut ≈ 13 C 3
Java Tengah ◘ RI 168 C 3
Java Timur ◘ RI 168 D 4
Java Trench ≃ 168 C 8
Javier, Isla ⌒ RCH 80 C 3
Javier de Viana ○ ROU 76-77 J 6
Javlenka ☆ KA 124-125 F 1
Jawa ⌒ RI 168 B 3
Jawad ○ IND 138-139 E 7
Jawi ○ RI 162-163 H 5
Jawor ○• PL 92-93 O 3
Jaworzno ○ PL 92-93 P 3
Jay ○ USA (OK) 264-265 K 2
Jayamkondacholapuram ○ IND 140-141 H 5
Jayanca ○ PE 64-65 C 5
Jayapura ☆ RI 166-167 L 3
Jayawijaya, Pegunungan ▲ RI 166-167 K 4
Jay Em ○ USA (WY) 252-253 O 4
Jayton ○ USA (TX) 264-265 D 5
Jazā'ir, Al ★••• DZ 190-191 D 2
Jaželbicy ○ RUS 94-95 N 2
Jazevec ○ RUS 88-89 T 4
Jazira Tarut ○ KSA 134-135 D 5
Jazykovo ○ RUS (ULN) 96-97 E 6
Jazykovo ☆ RUS (BAS) 96-97 J 6
J. C. Jacobsen, Kap ▲ GRØ 28-29 Z 2
Jconha ○ BR 72-73 K 6
Jean ○ USA (NV) 248-249 J 4
Jean ○ USA (TX) 264-265 F 5
Jean de Baie ○ CDN (NFL) 242-243 N 5
Jeanerette ○ USA (LA) 268-269 J 7
Jeanette Bay ≈ 36-37 V 7
Jean Rabel ○ RH 54-55 J 5
Jeavons, Lake ○ AUS 172-173 G 4
Jebala ⩦ MA 188-189 J 3
Jebba ○ WAN 204-205 F 4
Jeberos ○ PE 64-65 D 4
Jebiniana ○ TN 190-191 H 3
Jebri ○ PK 134-135 L 5
Jedburgh ○ CDN (SAS) 232-233 P 4
Jeddah = Ǧidda ○ KSA 132-133 A 3
Jeddore Cape ▲ CDN (NS) 240-241 M 6
Jędrzejów ○• PL 92-93 Q 3
Jeedamya ○ AUS 176-177 F 4
Jefawa ○ SUD 206-207 F 3
Jefe, Cerro ▲ PA 52-53 E 7
Jeffara ⩦ TN 190-191 H 4
Jeffers ○ USA (MN) 270-271 C 6
Jefferson ○ USA (AR) 276-277 C 6
Jefferson ○ USA (CO) 254-255 K 4
Jefferson ○ USA (GA) 284-285 G 2
Jefferson ○ USA (IA) 274-275 D 2
Jefferson ○ USA (NC) 282-283 F 4
Jefferson ○ USA (OR) 244-245 B 6
Jefferson ○ USA (SC) 284-285 K 2
Jefferson ○ USA (SD) 260-261 K 4
Jefferson ○ USA (TX) 264-265 K 6
Jefferson, Fort • USA (OH) 280-281 B 4
Jefferson, Mount ▲ USA (NV) 246-247 J 5
Jefferson, Mount ▲ USA (OR) 244-245 D 6
Jefferson City ○ USA (MO) 274-275 F 6
Jefferson City ○ USA (MT) 250-251 G 5
Jefferson City ○ USA (TN) 282-283 D 4
Jefferson National Memorial, Fort ∴• USA (FL) 286-287 G 7
Jefferson Proving Ground ✕✕ USA (IN) 274-275 N 6
Jefferson State Memorial, Fort • USA (OH) 280-281 B 3
Jeffersontown ○ USA (KY) 276-277 K 2
Jeffersonville ○ USA (GA) 284-285 G 4
Jeffersonville ○ USA (IN) 274-275 N 6
Jeffersonville ○ USA (OH) 280-281 C 4
Jeffersonville ○ USA (VT) 278-279 J 4
Jeffrey City ○ USA (WY) 252-253 L 4
Jeffries, Lake ○ AUS 176-177 G 3
Jef-Jef el Kébir ⩦ TCH 198-199 K 2
Jega ○ WAN 198-199 B 6
Jege ○ WAN 204-205 F 4
Jeinemeni, Cerro ▲ RCH 80 D 3
Jejekangphu Kang ▲ BHT 142-143 F 1
Jejevo ○ SOL 184 I d 3
Jejuí-Guazú, Río ∼ PY 76-77 J 3
Jēkabpils ○•• LV 94-95 K 3
Jekyll Island ⌒ USA (GA) 284-285 J 5
Jelai ∼ RI 162-163 J 6
Jelap La ▲ BHT 142-143 F 2
Jelenia Góra ☆• PL 92-93 N 3
Jelgava ○•• LV 94-95 H 3
Jeli ○ MAL 162-163 D 2
Jellico ○ USA (TN) 282-283 C 4
Jellicoe ○ CDN (BC) 230-231 J 4
Jellicoe ○ CDN (ONT) 234-235 Q 5
Jelly Bean Crystals • AUS 178-179 L 5
Jelmusibak ○ RI 164-165 D 4
Jelsa ○ HR 100-101 F 3
Jema ○ GH 202-203 K 6
Jemâa-Ida-Oussemlat ○ MA 188-189 G 6
Jemaluang ○ MAL 162-163 E 3
Jema Shet' ∼ ETH 208-209 D 4
Jembawan, Danau ○ RI 162-163 F 6
Jember ○ RI 168 E 4

Jemberam o GNB 202-203 C 4
Jemez Indian Reservation X USA (NM) 256-257 J 3
Jemez Pueblo o USA (NM) 256-257 J 3
Jemez Springs o USA (NM) 256-257 J 3
Jemil'čyne o UA 102-103 E 2
Jeminay o VRC 146-147 G 2
Jemison o USA (AL) 284-285 D 4
Jemma o WAN (BAU) 204-205 H 3
Jemma o WAN (KAD) 204-205 H 4
Jempang, Danau ⊂ RI 164-165 D 4
Jemseg o CDN (NB) 240-241 J 5
Jen o WAN 204-205 J 4
Jena o D 92-93 L 3
Jena o USA (LA) 268-269 H 5
Jenakijeve o UA 102-103 L 3
Jenda o MW 214-215 G 7
Jendouba ☆ TN 190-191 G 2
Jeneien, Oued ~ TN 190-191 G 5
Jenerhodar o UA 102-103 J 4
Jeneshuaya, Arroyo ~ BOL 70-71 D 3
Jenin o•• WB 130-131 D 1
Jenipapo o BR (AMA) 66-67 G 5
Jenipapo o BR (P) 62-63 K 6
Jenipapo o BR (TOC) 68-69 D 5
Jenipapo, Ribeiro ~ BR 68-69 D 5
Jenipapo, Rio ~ BR 68-69 G 4
Jenissej = Enisej ⌒ 10-11 H 2
Jenissej = Enisej ~ RUS 10-11 H 2
Jenkins o USA (KY) 276-277 N 3
Jenkins o USA (NJ) 280-281 M 4
Jenner o CDN (ALB) 232-233 G 5
Jenner o USA (CA) 246-247 B 5
Jennings ~ CDN 20-21 Z 7
Jennings o USA (LA) 268-269 H 6
Jennings Randolph Lake ⊂ USA (MD) 280-281 G 4
Jenny o SME 62-63 G 3
Jenny Lind Island ⌒ CDN 24-25 V 6
Jenolan Caves • AUS 180-181 L 2
Jensen o USA (UT) 254-255 F 3
Jensen, Cape ▲ CDN 24-25 h 6
Jens Munk Island ⌒ CDN 24-25 g 6
Jens Munk Ø ⌒ GRØ 28-29 U 4
Jepara o RI 168 D 3
Jeparit o AUS 180-181 F 4
Jequié o BR 72-73 K 2
Jequitinhonha, Rio ~ BR 72-73 L 3
Jequiriçá o BR 72-73 L 2
Jequitaí o BR 72-73 H 4
Jequitaí, Rio ~ BR 72-73 H 4
Jequitiba o BR 72-73 J 5
Jequitinhonha o BR 72-73 K 4
Jequitinhonha, Rio ~ BR 72-73 J 4
Jerada o MA 188-189 K 3
Jerangau, Kampung o MAL 162-163 E 2
Jerangle o AUS 180-181 K 3
Jerantut o MAL 162-163 E 3
Jerba, Île de ⌒ TN 190-191 G 4
Jerbar o SUD 206-207 K 6
Jerdera o RI 166-167 H 5
Jere o RI 164-165 K 4
Jerecuaro o MEX 52-53 D 1
Jérémie ☆•• RH 54-55 H 5
Jeremoabo o BR 68-69 J 7
Jerer Shet' ~ ETH 208-209 F 4
Jerez, Río ~ MEX 50-51 H 6
Jerez de García Salinas o• MEX 50-51 H 6
Jerez de la Frontera o E 98-99 D 6
Jerez de los Caballeros o•• E 98-99 D 5
Jericho o AUS 178-179 J 2
Jericho o SOL 184 I c 3
Jericho = Arīḥā ☆•• AUT 130-131 D 2
Jericho Dam < ZA 220-221 K 3
Jericoacoara o BR 68-69 H 3
Jericoacoara, Ponta ▲ BR 68-69 H 3
Jerigu o GH 202-203 K 5
Jerilderie o AUS 180-181 H 3
Jerko La ▲ VRC 144-145 C 5
Jerome o USA (AZ) 256-257 C 4
Jerome o USA (FL) 286-287 H 6
Jerome o USA (ID) 252-253 D 4
Jerori o BOL 70-71 E 4
Jerramungup o AUS 176-177 E 6
Jersey ⌒ GBJ 90-91 F 7
Jersey City o USA (NJ) 280-281 M 3
Jersey Cove o CDN (QUE) 240-241 L 2
Jersey Shore o USA (PA) 280-281 J 2
Jerseyville o USA (IL) 274-275 H 5
Jertih o MAL 162-163 E 2
Jerumenha o BR 68-69 G 5
Jerusalem = Yĕrūshalayim ★••• IL 130-131 D 2
Jervis, Monte ▲ RCH 80 C 4
Jervis Bay • AUS 180-181 L 3
Jervis Inlet ≈ 32-33 J 7
Jervis Inlet ≈ CDN 230-231 F 4
Jervois o AUS 178-179 D 2
Jesenice o SLO 100-101 E 1
Jeseník o CZ 92-93 O 3
Jesi o I 100-101 D 3
Jesi, Monte ▲ MOC 214-215 H 7
Jesmond o CDN (BC) 230-231 H 2
Jessama o USA (NC) 282-283 L 5
Jessamine Creek ~ AUS 178-179 G 2
Jesseltown = Kota Kinabalu ☆• MAL 160-161 B 10
Jessheim ☆ N 86-87 E 6
Jessore o BD 142-143 F 4
Jester o USA (OK) 264-265 E 3
Jesup o USA (GA) 284-285 J 5
Jesup o USA (IA) 274-275 F 2
Jesus, Mount ▲ USA (KS) 262-263 G 7
Jesús Carranza o MEX 52-53 G 3
Jesus María o RA 76-77 E 6
Jesús Menéndez o C 54-55 G 4
Jet o USA (OK) 264-265 F 2
Jeta, Ilha de ⌒ GNB 202-203 B 4
Jetmore o USA (KS) 262-263 G 6
Jetpur o IND 138-139 C 9
Jeudin, Pulau ⌒ RI 166-167 H 5
Jevargi o IND 140-141 G 2
Jevnaker ☆ N 86-87 E 6
Jevpatorija ☆• UA 102-103 H 5
Jewel Cave National Monument ∴ USA (SD) 260-261 C 3
Jewell o USA (IA) 274-275 E 2
Jewell o USA (KS) 262-263 H 5
Jewell o USA (OR) 244-245 B 5
Jewett o USA (TX) 266-267 L 2
Jewish Autonomous Region = Evrejskaja avtonomnaja oblast' □ RUS 122-123 D 4
Jeypore o IND 142-143 C 6
Jezercës, maja e ▲ AL 100-101 G 3
Jgarassu o• BR 68-69 L 5
Jhābua o IND 138-139 E 8
Jhajjar o IND 138-139 F 5
Jhal o PK 134-135 M 4
Jhālawār o IND 138-139 F 7
Jhālāwār ⊥ IND 138-139 C 8
Jhamat o PK 138-139 C 3
Jhang o PK 138-139 D 4
Jhang Branch < PK 138-139 D 4
Jhānsi o IND 138-139 G 7
Jharol o IND 138-139 D 7
Jhārsuguda o IND 142-143 D 5
Jhatpat o PK 138-139 B 5
Jheeruk o PK 138-139 B 7
Jhelum ~ IND 138-139 E 3
Jhelum o PK (PU) 138-139 D 3
Jhelum ~ PK 138-139 D 4
Jhenida o BD 142-143 F 4
Jhimpir o PK 138-139 B 7
Jhudo o PK 138-139 B 7
Jhunjhunūn o IND 138-139 E 5
Jiading o VRC 154-155 M 6
Jiahe o VRC 156-157 H 4
Jiajiang o VRC 156-157 C 2
Jialing Jiang ~ VRC 154-155 E 6
Jiamusi o VRC 150-151 H 4
Ji'an o VRC (JIL) 150-151 F 7
Ji'an o VRC (JXI) 156-157 J 3
Jianchang o VRC 154-155 L 1
Jianchuan o VRC 142-143 L 2
Jiande o VRC 156-157 L 2
Jiangaoshan ▲ MYA 142-143 L 3
Jiangbai o VRC 156-157 K 2
Jiangcheng o VRC 156-157 B 5
Jiangcheng Hanizu Yizu Zizhixian o VRC 156-157 B 5
Jiange o VRC 154-155 D 5
Jianghong o VRC 156-157 F 6
Jianghua o VRC 156-157 G 4
Jiangjin o VRC 156-157 E 2
Jiangjunmiao o VRC 146-147 J 3
Jiangkou o VRC (GZH) 156-157 F 3
Jiangkou o VRC (SIC) 154-155 F 6
Jiangle o VRC 156-157 K 3
Jiangling o VRC 154-155 H 6
Jiangluo o VRC 154-155 D 5
Jiangmen o VRC 156-157 H 5
Jiangshan o VRC 156-157 L 2
Jiang Shan ⛰ VRC 154-155 G 6
Jiangsu □ VRC 154-155 L 5
Jiangxi □ VRC 156-157 J 3
Jiangyin o VRC 154-155 M 6
Jiangyong o VRC 156-157 G 4
Jiangyou o VRC 154-155 D 6
Jianhe o VRC 156-157 F 3
Jianhu o VRC 154-155 L 5
Jianli o VRC 156-157 H 2
Jianmen G. • VRC 154-155 D 5
Jianning o VRC 156-157 K 3
Jian'ou o VRC 156-157 L 3
Jianping o VRC 154-155 L 1
Jianshi o VRC 154-155 F 6
Jianshui o VRC 156-157 C 5
Jianyang o VRC (FUJ) 156-157 L 3
Jianyang o VRC (SIC) 154-155 D 6
Jiaohe o VRC 150-151 F 6
Jiaohe Gucheng ∴• VRC 146-147 J 4
Jiaojiang o VRC 156-157 M 2
Jiaokou o VRC 154-155 G 3
Jiaoling o VRC 156-157 K 4
Jiaonan o VRC 154-155 L 4
Jiaotelo o VRC 144-145 F 6
Jiaozhou o VRC 154-155 L 3
Jiaozuo o VRC 154-155 H 4
Jiashan o VRC 154-155 K 5
Jiashi o VRC 146-147 C 6
Jia Tsuo La ▲ VRC 144-145 F 6
Jia Xian o VRC (HEN) 154-155 H 5
Jia Xian o VRC (SHA) 154-155 G 2
Jiaxing o VRC 154-155 M 6
Jiayin o VRC 150-151 H 3
Jiayu o VRC 156-157 H 2
Jiayu G. • VRC 146-147 O 6
Jiayuguan o VRC 146-147 O 6
Jibaro, El o C 54-55 F 4
Jiberu o WAN 204-205 K 4
Jibisa ▲ EAK 212-213 F 1
Jibiya o WAN 198-199 C 6
Jibóia o BR 66-67 C 2
Jibou o RO 102-103 C 4
Jicarilla Apache Indian Reservation X USA (NM) 256-257 H 2
Jicaro Galán o HN 52-53 L 5
Jichang o VRC 156-157 D 3
Jičín o CZ 92-93 N 3
Jidali, togga ~ SP 208-209 H 3
Jiddah = Ğidda o• KSA 132-133 A 3
Jidhi o SP 208-209 F 3
Jiekkevarrebreen ▲ N 86-87 J 2
Jieshi o VRC 156-157 J 5
Jieshi Wan ≈ VRC 156-157 J 5
Jieshou o VRC 154-155 J 5
Jiexi o VRC 156-157 J 5
Jiexiu o VRC 154-155 G 3
Jieyang o VRC 156-157 K 5
Jieznas o LT 94-95 J 4
Jiga o ETH 208-209 C 3
Jiggalong X AUS 176-177 F 1
Jiggalong Aboriginal Land X AUS 176-177 F 1
Jiggs o USA (NV) 246-247 K 3
Jigongshan • VRC 154-155 J 6
Jiguaní o C 54-55 G 4
Jigzhi o VRC 154-155 B 5
Jihlava o CZ 92-93 N 4
Jihlava ~ CZ 92-93 N 4
Jihur o ETH 208-209 D 4
Jiiqley o SP 208-209 G 6
Jijel ☆ DZ 190-191 E 2
Jijie o VRC 156-157 C 5
Jijiga o ETH 208-209 F 4
Jijona = Xixona o E 98-99 G 5
Jilakin Lake ⊂ AUS 176-177 E 6
Jilamo o HN 52-53 L 4
Jilib ☆ SP 212-213 J 3
Jilin o VRC (JIL) 150-151 F 6
Jilin □ VRC 150-151 E 6
Jilin Hada Ling ⛰ VRC 150-151 E 6
Jilotlán de los Dolores o MEX 52-53 C 2
Jima ☆ ETH 208-209 C 5
Jimani ☆ DOM 54-55 K 5
Jimata o ETH 208-209 C 4
Jimbe o ANG 214-215 B 6
Jimei o VRC 156-157 L 4
Jiménez o MEX (CHA) 50-51 G 4
Jiménez o MEX (COA) 50-51 J 3
Jimenez o RP 160-161 E 8
Jiménez de Teul o MEX 50-51 H 6
Jimeta o WAN 204-205 K 4
Jimi River ~ PNG 183 C 3
Jimkar o BHT 142-143 G 2
Jimna Range ⛰ AUS 178-179 M 4
Jimo o VRC 154-155 M 3
Jimsar o VRC 146-147 J 4
Jimulco o MEX 50-51 H 5
Jin, Kepulauan ⌒ RI 166-167 H 5
Jinan ☆• VRC 154-155 K 3
Jinchang o VRC 154-155 C 2
Jincheng o VRC (SHA) 154-155 H 4
Jincheng o VRC (YUN) 156-157 C 4
Jinchuan o VRC 154-155 C 6
Jin Ci • VRC 154-155 H 3
Jind o IND 138-139 F 5
Jindabyne o AUS 180-181 K 4
Jindare o AUS 172-173 K 3
Jin Dian • VRC 156-157 C 4
Jindřichův Hradec o CZ 92-93 N 4
Jinfo Shan ▲ VRC 156-157 E 2
Jingbian o VRC 154-155 F 3
Jingchuan o VRC 154-155 E 4
Jingde o VRC 154-155 L 6
Jingdezhen o• VRC 156-157 K 2
Jingdong o VRC 142-143 M 3
Jingellic o AUS 180-181 J 3
Jingemarra o AUS 176-177 D 3
Jinggangshan o VRC (JXI) 156-157 J 3
Jinggangshan • VRC (JXI) 156-157 J 3
Jinggu o VRC 142-143 M 4
Jinghe o VRC 146-147 F 3
Jing He ~ VRC 154-155 F 4
Jinghong o VRC 142-143 M 5
Jingjiang o VRC 154-155 M 5
Jingle o VRC 154-155 G 2
Jingmen o VRC 154-155 H 6
Jingning o VRC 154-155 D 4
Jingpo o VRC 150-151 G 6
Jingpo Hu • VRC 150-151 G 6
Jingshan o VRC 154-155 H 6
Jingtai o VRC 154-155 D 3
Jingtieshan o VRC (GAN) 146-147 N 6
Jingtieshan o VRC (XUZ) 146-147 O 6
Jingtie Shan ⛰ VRC 146-147 N 6
Jingxi o VRC 156-157 E 5
Jing Xian o VRC 154-155 L 6
Jingxing o VRC 154-155 J 3
Jingyan o VRC 156-157 D 2
Jingyu o VRC 150-151 F 6
Jingyuan o VRC 154-155 D 3
Jingyu Hu ~ VRC 144-145 G 2
Jingyu Nao ▲ VRC 154-155 F 5
Jingzhou o VRC 156-157 F 3
Jinhe o VRC 150-151 C 2
Jinhua o VRC 156-157 L 2
Jining o VRC (NMZ) 148-149 L 7
Jining o VRC (SHD) 154-155 K 4
Jinja ☆ EAU 212-213 D 3
Jinka o AUS 178-179 C 2
Jinka o ETH 208-209 C 6
Jinkou o VRC 154-155 J 6
Jinning o VRC 156-157 C 4
Jinniu o VRC 154-155 K 6
Jinotega ☆ NIC 52-53 B 5
Jinotepe ☆ NIC 52-53 L 6
Jinping o VRC (GZH) 156-157 F 3
Jinping o VRC (YUN) 156-157 C 5
Jinqian He ~ VRC 154-155 F 5
Jinsha o VRC 156-157 E 3
Jinsha Jiang ~ VRC 142-143 L 2
Jinsha Jiang ~ VRC 144-145 M 4
Jinsha Jiang ~ VRC 156-157 C 3
Jinshanlin • VRC 154-155 K 1
Jinshatan o VRC 154-155 H 2
Jinshi ☆ VRC 156-157 G 2
Jinshiqiao o VRC 156-157 G 3
Jinta o VRC 146-147 O 6
Jintan o VRC 154-155 L 6
Jintang o VRC 154-155 D 6
Jintotolo Channel ≈ 160-161 E 7
Jintur o IND 138-139 F 10
Jinxi o VRC (JXI) 156-157 K 3
Jinxi o VRC (LIA) 150-151 C 7
Jinxian o VRC 156-157 K 2
Jinxiang o VRC 154-155 K 4
Jinyin Dao ⌒ VRC 158-159 L 2
Jinyun o VRC 156-157 M 2
Jinyunshan • VRC 156-157 E 2
Jinzhai o VRC 154-155 J 6
Jinzhong Shan ▲ VRC 156-157 D 4
Jinzhou o VRC (LIA) 150-151 C 8
Jinzhou o VRC (LIA) 150-151 C 7
Jinzū-gawa ~ J 152-153 G 6
Ji-Paraná o BR 70-71 G 2
Jipe, Lake ⊂ EAK 212-213 F 5
Jipijapa o EC 64-65 B 2
Jiquí o C 54-55 F 4
Jiquilpan o MEX 52-53 C 1
Jiquiriçá, Rio ~ BR 72-73 L 2
Jirau, Salto do ~ BR 66-67 E 7
Jiri o NEP 144-145 F 7
Jirriiban o SP 208-209 J 5
Jishan o VRC 154-155 G 4
Jishou o VRC 156-157 F 2
Jishu o VRC 150-151 F 5
Jitang Gulou • VRC 156-157 F 3
Jitarning o AUS 176-177 E 6
Jitaúna o BR 72-73 L 3
Jitra o MAL 162-163 D 2
Jitschin = Jičín o CZ 92-93 N 3
Jiu ~ RO 102-103 C 6
Jiucai Ling ▲ VRC 156-157 G 4
Jiuchang o VRC 156-157 E 3
Jiuhuashan • VRC 154-155 K 6
Jiujiang o VRC 156-157 K 2
Jiulihu • VRC 156-157 L 4
Jiuling Shan ⛰ VRC 156-157 J 2
Jiulong = Kowloon o HK 156-157 J 5
Jiulongpo o VRC 156-157 E 2
Jiulongshibatan • VRC 156-157 H 4
Jiuquan o VRC 146-147 O 6
Jiurongcheng o VRC 154-155 N 3
Jiusuo o VRC 156-157 F 7
Jiutai o VRC 150-151 E 5
Jiuxu o VRC 156-157 E 4
Jiuyishan • VRC 156-157 H 4
Jiuzhaigou ••• VRC 154-155 C 5
Jivundu o Z 218-219 C 1
Jiwā', al- ⊥ UAE 132-133 H 2
Jiwani o PK 134-135 J 6
Jiwani, Rās ▲ PK 134-135 J 6
Jixi o VRC (ANH) 154-155 L 6
Jixi o VRC (HEI) 150-151 H 5
Jixian o VRC 150-151 H 4
Ji Xian o VRC (SXI) 154-155 G 3
Ji Xian o VRC (TIA) 154-155 K 1
Jiyang o VRC 154-155 K 3
Jiyuan o VRC 154-155 H 4
Jīzān = Ğīzān ☆ KSA 132-133 C 5
Jlam o NEP 144-145 F 7
Jī ~ KA 124-125 K 6
Joaçaba o BR 74-75 E 6
Joachín o MEX 52-53 F 2
Joaíma o BR 72-73 K 4
Joal-Fadiout o• SN 202-203 B 2
Joana o YV 60-61 J 3
Joana Coeli o BR 62-63 K 6
Joanna o USA (SC) 284-285 J 2
João, Rio ~ BR 72-73 J 7
João Arregui o BR 76-77 J 5
João Câmara o BR 68-69 L 4
João Chagas o ANG 214-215 B 6
João Fagundes o BR 76-77 J 6
João Farias o BR 62-63 E 6
João Lisboa o BR 68-69 E 4
João Monlevade o BR 72-73 J 5
João Neiva o BR 72-73 K 5
João Pessoa ☆• BR 68-69 L 5
João Pinheiro o BR 72-73 G 4
João Vaz o BR 72-73 K 2
Joaquim o BR 68-69 G 5
Joaquim Gomes o BR 68-69 L 6
Joaquim Rios, Salto ~ BR 70-71 H 3
Joaquin o USA (TX) 268-269 F 5
Jobabo o C 54-55 G 4
Jobele o WAN 204-205 E 5
Jobillos, Los o DOM 54-55 K 5
Jobos, Playa ⊥ USA (PR) 286-287 O 2
Jócar o E 98-99 F 6
Jocoli o RA 78-79 E 2
Jocotepec o MEX 52-53 C 1
Jodensavanna o SME 62-63 G 3
Jodhpur o• IND 138-139 D 6
Joe Batts Arm o CDN (NFL) 242-243 O 3
Joensuu ☆ FIN 88-89 K 5
Joerg Plateau ⛰ ARK 16 F 30
Jōetsu o J 152-153 H 6
Joe Wheeler State Park ⊥ USA (AL) 284-285 C 2
Jof o TN 190-191 H 4
Jofane o MOC 218-219 H 5
Joffre o CDN (ALB) 232-233 E 3
Joffre, Mount ▲ CDN (BC) 230-231 O 3
Jogana o WAN 198-199 D 6
Jogbani o IND 142-143 E 2
Jõgeva o EST 94-95 K 2
Jogg Falls ~• IND 140-141 F 3
Jogighopa o IND 142-143 G 2
Jogindarnagar o IND 138-139 F 4
Jogipet o IND 140-141 H 2
Jog Lake ⊂ CDN (ONT) 236-237 C 2
Jogues o CDN (ONT) 236-237 E 3
Johán o PK 134-135 M 4
Johan en Margeretha o SME 62-63 G 3
Johannesburg o•• ZA 220-221 J 3
Johan Peninsula ⌄ CDN 26-27 N 4
Johi o GUY 62-63 E 5
Johi o PK 134-135 M 5
John Day o USA (OR) 244-245 G 6
John Day Fossil Beds National Monument ∴ USA (OR) 244-245 F 6
John Day Fossil Beds National Monument • USA (OR) 244-245 E 6
John Day River ~ USA (OR) 244-245 F 6
John D'Or Prairie o CDN 30-31 M 6
John D'Or Prairie Indian Reserve X CDN 30-31 M 6
John D. Rockefeller Junior Memorial Parkway ⊥ USA (WY) 252-253 H 2
John Dyer, Cape ▲ CDN 24-25 V 4
John Eyre Motel o AUS 176-177 H 6
John Eyre Telegraph Station ∴ AUS 176-177 J 6
John Flagler, Kap ▲ GRØ 26-27 n 2
John Flynn Memorial • AUS 174-175 C 6
John H. Kerr Reservoir ⊂ USA (NC) 282-283 J 4
John Martin Reservoir ⊂ USA (CO) 254-255 M 5
John Murray Ø ⌒ GRØ 26-27 a 2
Johnny Hoe River ~ CDN 30-31 J 3
John Redmond Reservoir ⊂ USA (KS) 262-263 L 6
John River ~ USA 20-21 O 3
John's Corner o EAT (IRI) 214-215 H 5
Johnson, Mount ▲ AUS 176-177 H 2
Johnson, Pico de ▲ MEX 50-51 C 3
Johnson City o USA (KS) 262-263 E 7
Johnson City o USA (TN) 282-283 E 4
Johnson City o USA (TX) 266-267 J 3
Johnson Dam, Daniel ⊥• CDN 38-39 K 3
Johnson Draw ~ USA (TX) 266-267 F 3
Johnson Island ⌒ CDN 36-37 K 6
Johnson National Historic Park, Lyndon Baines ∴ USA (TX) 266-267 J 3
Johnson Pass ▲ USA (UT) 254-255 C 3
Johnson River ~ CDN 30-31 G 4
Johnsons o USA (CA) 246-247 B 2
Johnsons Crossing o CDN 20-21 Y 6
Johnsons Landing o CDN (BC) 230-231 N 3
Johnson Space Center, Lyndon Baines ∴ USA (TX) 268-269 E 7
Johnsonville o USA (SC) 284-285 L 3
Johnston o USA (SC) 284-285 J 3
Johnston, Chute ~• ZRE 214-215 E 6
Johnstone Hill ▲ AUS 176-177 L 1
Johnstone South o• AUS 174-175 J 5
Johnstone Strait ≈ 32-33 G 6
Johnstone Strait ≈ CDN 230-231 C 3
Johnston Islands ⌒ PNG 183 D 2
Johnston Lakes, The ⊂ AUS 176-177 F 6
Johnstown o CDN (NS) 240-241 P 5
Johnstown o USA (NE) 262-263 F 2
Johnstown o USA (OH) 280-281 D 3
Johnstown o USA (PA) 280-281 H 3
Johnstown Flood National Monument • USA (PA) 280-281 H 3
Johnsville o USA (AR) 276-277 C 7
Johntown o USA (GA) 284-285 F 2
John W. Kyle State Park ⊥• USA (MS) 268-269 L 2
Johor □ MAL 162-163 E 3
Johor Bahru ☆•• MAL 162-163 E 4
Jõhvi-Ahtme o EST 94-95 K 2
Joigny o F 90-91 J 8
Joinville o BR 74-75 F 6
Joinville, Île ⌒ ARK 16 G 31
Jojutla de Juárez o MEX 52-53 E 2
Jokau o SUD 208-209 A 4
Jokau ~ SUD 208-209 A 4
Jøkel-bugten ≈ 26-27 p 4
Jokkmokk o• S 86-87 J 3
Jökulsá á Brú ~ IS 86-87 f 2
Jökulsá á Fjöllum ~ IS 86-87 e 2
Joli, Mont- o CDN (QUE) 240-241 G 2
Joliet o USA (IL) 274-275 K 3
Joliette o CDN (QUE) 238-239 M 2
Jolly Lake ⊂ CDN 30-31 N 3
Jolo ☆ RP 160-161 D 9
Jolo o USA (WV) 280-281 E 6
Jolo Island ⌒ RP 160-161 D 9
Jomala o FIN 88-89 F 6
Jomalig Island ⌒ RP 160-161 E 5
Jombang o RI 168 E 3
Jombo ~ ANG 216-217 E 5
Jombo o GH 202-203 L 5
Jomda o VRC 144-145 M 5
Jommon o RI 166-167 H 5
Jomo Lhari ▲ BHT 142-143 F 2
Jomonkum kumligi ⊥ US 136-137 H 4
Jomsom o NEP 144-145 D 6
Jomu o EAT 212-213 D 5
Jona o USA (SD) 260-261 G 3
Jonathan Dickinson State Park ⊥ USA (FL) 286-287 J 4
Jonava = Ionava ☆ LT 94-95 J 4
Jonê o VRC 154-155 C 4
Jones o CDN (ONT) 234-235 J 5
Jones, Cape ▲ CDN 30-31 Y 4
Jones, Kap ▲ GRØ 26-27 p 8
Jones, Lake ⊂ AUS (WA) 172-173 H 5
Jones, Lake ⊂ AUS (WA) 176-177 G 2
Jonesboro o USA (AR) 276-277 E 5
Jonesboro o USA (GA) 284-285 F 3
Jonesboro o USA (LA) 268-269 H 4
Jonesboro o USA (TX) 266-267 K 2
Jonesborough o USA (TN) 282-283 E 4
Jones Islands ⌒ USA 20-21 Q 1
Jones Sound ≈ 24-25 c 2
Jones Swamp ⊂ USA (SC) 284-285 K 4
Jonesville o USA (LA) 268-269 J 5
Jonesville o USA (SC) 284-285 J 2
Jonesville o USA (TN) 282-283 C 4
Jonesville o USA (VA) 280-281 C 7
Jonggol o RI 168 B 3
Jonglei Canal = Junqoley Canal < SUD 206-207 K 4
Joniškis ☆ LT 94-95 H 3
Jönköping ☆ S 86-87 G 8
Jonquière o CDN (QUE) 240-241 D 2
Jonuta o MEX 52-53 H 2
Joowhar ☆ SP 212-213 K 2
Jopalayo, Cerro ▲ RA 76-77 D 3
Joplin o USA (MO) 276-277 A 3
Joplin o USA (MT) 250-251 J 3
Jorgucat o• AL 100-101 H 5
Jorhāt o IND 142-143 J 2
Joriapani o NEP 144-145 C 6
Jörn o S 86-87 K 4
Jornada del Muerto ⊥ USA (NM) 256-257 J 6
Jorong o RI 164-165 D 5
Joronga = Pulau Hasil ⌒ RI 164-165 L 4
Jorskoe ploskogor'e ⛰ GE 126-127 F 7
Joru o WAL 202-203 E 6
Jos ☆• WAN 204-205 H 4
Jose Abad Santos o RP 160-161 F 10
José Batlley Ordoñez o ROU 78-79 M 2
José Cardel o MEX 52-53 F 2
José de la Costa o YV 60-61 G 2
José del Carmen Ramirez, Parque Nacional ⊥ DOM 54-55 K 5
José de San Martín o RA 80 E 2
José Díaz, Ponta ▲ BR 74-75 F 6
José E. Rodo o ROU 78-79 L 2
Josefa Ortiz de Dominguez Estacione, Presa < MEX 50-51 E 4
Josegun River ~ CDN 32-33 M 4
Joselândia o BR 70-71 J 5
José Pedro Varela o ROU 78-79 M 2
Joseph o USA (OR) 244-245 H 5
Joseph, Lake ⊂ CDN (NFL) 38-39 M 2
Joseph, Lake ⊂ CDN (ONT) 238-239 F 3
Joseph Bonaparte Gulf ≈ 172-173 J 3
Josephburg o CDN (ALB) 232-233 E 2
Joseph City o USA (AZ) 256-257 E 4
Joseph Henry, Cape ▲ CDN 26-27 T 2
Josephine River ~ CDN 30-31 Y 4
Josephstaal o PNG 183 C 3
José Rodrigues o BR 68-69 C 4
Joshimath o IND 138-139 G 4
Jōshin Etsu Kōgen National Park ⊥ J 152-153 G 6
Joshkar Ola = Joškar-Ola ☆ RUS 96-97 E 5
Joshua o USA (TX) 264-265 G 6
Joshua Tree o USA (CA) 248-249 H 5
Joshua Tree National Monument ⊥ USA (CA) 248-249 J 6
Joškar-Ola ☆ RUS 96-97 E 5
Jos Plateau ⛰ WAN 204-205 H 3
Jostedalsbreen ⊂ N 86-87 C 6
Jost van Dyke ⌒ GB (VI) 286-287 R 2
Jotajana o YV 60-61 L 3
Jotunheimen ⛰ N 86-87 D 6
Jotunheimen nasjonalpark ⊥ N 86-87 D 6
Joubertberge ⛰ NAM 216-217 B 9
Joubertina o ZA 220-221 F 6
Joulter Cays ⌒ BS 54-55 F 2
Jourdanton o USA (TX) 266-267 J 5
Joutel o CDN (QUE) 236-237 K 3
Joutsa o FIN 88-89 J 6
Joutsijärvi o FIN 88-89 J 3
Jovellanos o C 54-55 E 3
Joviânia o BR 72-73 F 4
Joy o USA (KY) 276-277 G 3
Joy, Mount ▲ CDN 20-21 Y 5
Joya de Ceren ∴••• ES 52-53 K 5
Joya de los Sachas, La o EC 64-65 D 2
Joy Bay ≈ 36-37 O 4
Joyce o USA (WA) 244-245 B 2
Jreïda o RIM 196-197 B 5
Jreïf < RIM 196-197 D 6
J. Richardson Bay ≈ 26-27 P 3
Juaben o GH 202-203 K 6
Juami, Rio ~ BR 66-67 D 3
Juami-Japura, Reserva Ecológica ⊥ BR 66-67 C 4
Juanacatlán o MEX 52-53 C 1
Juan Aldamo o MEX 50-51 H 5
Juan Antonio o YV 60-61 K 2
Juan B. Alberdi o RA 76-77 E 4
Juan Bautista Tuxtepec o• MEX 52-53 F 2
Juan de Fuca Strait ≈ 40-41 B 1
Juan de Fuca Strait ≈ USA 244-245 A 2
Juan de Guia, Cabo San ▲ CO 60-61 D 2
Juân de Nova, Île ⌒ F 222-223 C 6
Juan E. Barra o RA 78-79 J 4
Juan Fernández, Islas ⌒ RCH 78-79 B 1
Juangchen o VRC 154-155 J 4
Juangon o RP 160-161 F 7
Juan Guerra o PE 64-65 D 5
Juani Island ⌒ EAT 214-215 K 4
Juanita o USA (CO) 254-255 H 6
Juan Jorba o RA 78-79 G 2
Juán José Perez o BOL 70-71 C 4
Juanjuí o PE 64-65 D 5
Juankoski o FIN 88-89 K 5
Juan L. Lacaze o ROU 78-79 L 3
Juan Perez Sound ≈ CDN 228-229 C 4
Juan R. Cháve o PY 76-77 J 3
Juan Sola o RA 76-77 F 2
Juan Stuben, Isla ⌒ RCH 80 C 3
Juan Vicente o C 54-55 H 4
Juan W. Gez o RA 78-79 F 2
Juapon o GH 202-203 L 6
Juara o BR 70-71 J 2
Juárez o MEX (CHA) 50-51 E 2
Juárez o MEX (CHI) 52-53 H 3
Juárez o MEX (COA) 50-51 J 4
Juárez, Ciudad o• MEX 50-51 F 2
Juarez, Sierra de ⛰ MEX 50-51 B 1
Juari, Rio ~ BR 68-69 C 5
Juatinga, Ponta da ▲ BR 72-73 H 7
Juazeiro o• BR 68-69 H 6
Juázeiro, Riachão ~ BR 72-73 J 2
Juazeiro do Norte o• BR 68-69 J 5
Juazohn o LB 202-203 F 7
Jūbā ☆ SUD 206-207 K 6
Juba, Rio ~ BR 70-71 H 4
Jubaylah, al- ⌒ Y 132-133 K 5
Jubba, Webi ~ SP 212-213 J 2
Jubbada Dhexe □ SP 212-213 J 3
Jubbada Hoose □ SP 212-213 H 3
Juberina o YV 60-61 L 3
Jubilee Island ⌒ CDN 36-37 N 2
Jubilee Lake ⊂ AUS 176-177 J 4
Jubilee Lake ⊂ CDN (NFL) 242-243 N 4
Jubilee Pass ▲ USA (CA) 248-249 H 4
Jubni, Bi'r < LAR 192-193 L 2
Jucá, Rio ~ BR 68-69 H 5
Júcar, Río ~ E 98-99 G 5
Juçara o BR (BAH) 68-69 H 7
Juçara o BR (GOI) 72-73 E 3
Jucás o BR 68-69 J 5
Juchipila o MEX 50-51 H 7
Juchitán o MEX 52-53 G 3
Juchitán de Zaragoza o• MEX 52-53 G 3
Juchusujahuira, Río ~ BOL 70-71 D 5
Juciape o BR 72-73 K 2
Jučjugej o RUS 120-121 K 2
Jucuí o PE 64-65 D 7
Jucumarini, Lago ⊂ PE 70-71 B 5
Jucuri o BR 68-69 K 4
Jucuruçu, Rio ~ BR 72-73 L 4
Jucurutu o BR 68-69 K 5
Judenburg o A 92-93 N 5
Judëto, ozero ⊂ RUS 108-109 O 8
Judge Daly Promontory ⊥ CDN 26-27 Q 3
Judith Gap o USA (MT) 250-251 K 5
Judith River ~ USA (MT) 250-251 K 4
Judoma ~ RUS 120-121 J 2
Judoma ~ RUS 120-121 E 4
Judomskij, hrebet ⛰ RUS 120-121 J 3
Judybaevo o RUS 96-97 K 7
Juelsminde o DK 86-87 E 9
Jufrah, Al □ LAR 192-193 G 3
Jug ~ RUS 96-97 D 4
Juganskij, zapovednik ⊥ RUS 114-115 N 5
Jugarskaja Ob' ~ RUS 114-115 M 4
Jugiong o AUS 180-181 K 3
Jugo-Kamskij o RUS 96-97 J 5
Jugorënok o RUS 120-121 G 4
Jugorskij poluostrov ⌄ RUS 108-109 J 7
Jugorskij Šar, proliv ≈ RUS 108-109 H 7
Juh o VRC 154-155 F 3
Juhnov o RUS 94-95 O 4
Juhoviči o RUS 94-95 L 3
Juhua Dao • VRC 150-151 C 7
Jui ~ RO 102-103 C 5
Juigalpa ☆ NIC 52-53 B 5
Juína o BR 70-71 H 2
Juinamirim, Rio ~ BR 70-71 H 2
Juiná ou Zui-Uina, Rio ~ BR 70-71 H 3
Juist ⌒ D 92-93 J 2
Juiz de Fora o BR 72-73 J 6
Juizhou o VRC 156-157 D 4
Jujun o RI 162-163 D 6
Jujuy □ RA 76-77 D 2
Jukagirskoe ploskogor'e ⛰ RUS 110-111 d 6
Jukamenskoe ☆ RUS 96-97 H 5
Jukkasjärvi o• S 86-87 K 3
Jukonda ~ RUS 114-115 J 4
Juksa, Bol'šaja ~ RUS 114-115 S 6
Jukseevo o RUS 96-97 J 4
Jukta o RUS 116-117 M 4
Juktali ~ RUS 116-117 O 5
Jula ~ RUS 88-89 S 5
Jula, Jasiira ⌒ SP 212-213 J 4
Julaca o BOL 70-71 D 7
Juldessa ▲ ETH 208-209 D 7
Julesburg o USA (CO) 254-255 N 3
Juli o PE 70-71 C 5
Júlia o BR 66-67 C 3
Juliaca o PE 70-71 B 4
Julia Creek o AUS 174-175 F 7
Julia-Mabay o C 54-55 G 4
Julian o USA (CA) 248-249 H 6
Julian o USA (NC) 282-283 H 5
Julian, Lac ⊂ CDN 36-37 L 7
Julianatop ▲ SME 62-63 F 4
Julianehab = Qaqortoq o GRØ 28-29 R 6
Julianehabsfjord ≈ 28-29 R 6
Juliasdale o ZW 218-219 G 4
Julijske Alpe ⛰ SLO 100-101 D 1
Julio, 9 de o RA 78-79 J 3
Julio, 16 de o RA 78-79 J 4
Julio de Castilhos o BR 74-75 D 7
Jullundur o IND 138-139 E 4
Julong Shan ⛰ VRC 154-155 G 6
Julpa, Río ~ BOL 70-71 E 6
Julwānia o IND 138-139 E 9
Juma o RUS 88-89 M 4
Juma, Rio ~ BR 66-67 G 4
Juma, Rio ~ BR 66-67 E 5
Jumandi, Cuevas de • EC 64-65 D 2
Jumbe Salim's o EAT 214-215 J 6
Jumbilla o PE 64-65 D 4
Jumboo o SP 212-213 J 4
Jumelles, Longué- o F 90-91 G 8
Jumentos Cays ⌒ BS 54-55 H 3
Jumilla o E 98-99 G 5
Jumi Pozo o RA 76-77 E 5
Jumla o NEP 144-145 D 6
Jummayza o SUD (SR) 206-207 J 5
Jummayza o SUD (SR) 206-207 K 6
Jumper Uajv, gora ▲ RUS 88-89 O 3
Jump River o USA (WI) 270-271 H 5
Jump River ~ USA (WI) 270-271 H 5
Jumurčen ~ RUS 118-119 G 9
Jun', Allah- o RUS 120-121 H 3
Juna o BR 72-73 K 6
Juna Downs o AUS 172-173 D 7
Jūnāgadh o• IND 138-139 C 9
Junāgarh o IND 142-143 C 6
Junan o VRC 154-155 L 4
Junari ~ RUS 116-117 J 4
Juncal, Quebrada ~ RCH 76-77 C 3
Juncos o USA (PR) 286-287 Q 2
Junction o USA (TX) 266-267 H 3
Junction o USA (UT) 254-255 C 5
Junction, Mount ▲ AUS 172-173 J 5
Junction Bay ≈ 36-37 J 3
Junction Bay ≈ 174-175 B 2
Junction City o USA (AR) 276-277 C 7
Junction City o USA (KS) 262-263 K 5
Junction City o USA (OR) 244-245 B 6
Junction City o USA (SD) 260-261 K 4
Jundah o AUS 178-179 G 3
Jundiaí o BR 72-73 G 7
Juneau ☆ USA 32-33 C 2
Junee o AUS (NSW) 180-181 J 3
Junee o AUS (QLD) 178-179 K 2
June in Winter, Lake ⊂ USA (FL) 286-287 H 4
Junekèn ~ RUS 116-117 M 3
June Lake o USA (CA) 248-249 E 2
Jungar Qi o VRC 154-155 G 2
Jungbunzlau = Mladá Boleslav o•• CZ 92-93 N 3
Jungfrau ▲ CH 92-93 J 5
Junge o ANG 216-217 C 5
Juniata o CDN (SAS) 232-233 L 3
Juniata River ~ USA (PA) 280-281 J 3
Junin o CO 64-65 C 1
Junin o EC 64-65 B 2
Junin o PE 64-65 E 7
Junin o RA 78-79 J 3
Junin o RCH 70-71 B 6
Junin, Lago de ⊂ PE 64-65 D 7
Junín, Parque Nacional ⊥ PE 64-65 E 7
Junín de los Andes o RA 78-79 D 5
Juniper o CDN (NB) 240-241 H 4
Juniper Dunes Wilderness ⊥ USA (WA) 244-245 G 4
Juniper Springs ∴• USA (FL) 286-287 H 2
Jun'jaga ~ RUS 108-109 K 8
Junkjur o RUS 110-111 T 6
Junleri o WAN 204-205 J 4
Junlian o VRC 156-157 D 2
Junnar o IND 138-139 D 10
Juno o USA (TX) 266-267 F 3
Juno, El ▲ BOL 70-71 E 5
Junosuando o S 86-87 K 3
Junqoley o SUD 206-207 K 5

Junqoley Canal = Jonglei Canal < SUD 206-207 K 4
Junsele ○ S 86-87 H 5
Junta, La ○ BOL 70-71 G 4
Junta, La ○ MEX 50-51 F 3
Junta, La ○ USA (CO) 254-255 M 6
Juntas ○ CR 52-53 B 6
Juntas ○ RCH 76-77 C 5
Juntura ○ USA (OR) 244-245 G 7
Juntusranta ○ FIN 88-89 K 4
Junyi, proliv ≈ 108-109 Y 1
Jupati, Rio ~ BR 62-63 J 5
Jupiter ○ USA (FL) 286-287 J 5
Jupiter, Rivière ~ CDN (QUE) 242-243 E 3
Juquiá ○ BR 74-75 G 5
Jur ~ SUD 206-207 J 4
Jura ⌒ GB 90-91 E 4
Jurackaja guba ≈ RUS 108-109 R 5
Juradó ○ CO 60-61 C 4
Juramento ○ BR 72-73 J 4
Juranda Roadhouse ○ AUS 176-177 G 6
Jurbarkas ☆·· LT 94-95 H 4
Juredejjaha ~ RUS 108-109 S 8
Jurege, Rio ~ MOC 214-215 K 6
Jurema, Termas de • BR 74-75 D 5
Juremal ○ BR 68-69 H 6
Jur'evec ○ RUS 94-95 S 3
Jur'ev-Pol'skij ○· RUS 94-95 Q 3
Jurga ○ RUS 114-115 S 7
Jurgamyš ☆ RUS 114-115 H 7
Juribej ~ RUS 108-109 O 7
Juribejskaja grjada ▲ RUS 108-109 Q 7
Jurien ○ AUS 176-177 C 5
Jurien Bay ≈ 176-177 C 5
Juriepe, Río ~ YV 60-61 G 4
Juries, Los ○ RA 76-77 F 5
Jurilovca ○ RO 102-103 F 5
Juring ○ RI 166-167 H 5
Jurique, Serra ▲ BR 70-71 K 5
Jur'ja ○ RUS 96-97 F 4
Jurjaga ~ RUS 88-89 X 3
Jurjah, Tas ○ RUS 118-119 F 5
Jurjung-Haja ○ RUS 110-111 J 3
Jurjuzan' ○ RUS (CEL) 96-97 L 6
Jurjuzan' ~ RUS 96-97 L 6
Jurla ☆ RUS 96-97 J 4
Jūrmala ☆·· LV 94-95 H 3
Jurong ○ VRC 154-155 L 6
Juruá ○ BR 66-67 D 4
Juruá, Área Indígena ✕ BR 66-67 D 5
Juruá, Rio ~ BR 66-67 D 5
Juruazinho, Rio ~ BR 66-67 F 7
Juruena ○ BR 70-71 H 2
Juruena, Rio ~ BR 66-67 H 7
Juruena ou Ananiná, Rio ~ BR 70-71 H 3
Jurumirim, Represa de < BR 72-73 F 7
Jurumkuveem ~ RUS 112-113 R 3
Jurupari, Rio ~ BR 66-67 C 7
Juruti ○ BR 66-67 J 4
Juscimeira ○ BR 70-71 K 5
Jušino ○ RUS 88-89 X 2
Juskatia ○ CDN (BC) 228-229 B 3
Juškozero ○ RUS 88-89 M 4
Jušno-Kuril'skij proliv ≈ RUS 122-123 L 7
Justa, Quebrada de la ~ RCH 76-77 B 4
Justice ○ CDN (MAN) 234-235 D 4
Justiceburg ○ USA (TX) 264-265 C 5
Justiniano Posse ○ RA 78-79 H 2
Justo Daract ○ RA 78-79 G 2
Justozero ○ RUS 88-89 M 5
Jus'va ☆ RUS 96-97 J 4
Jutaí ○ BR 66-67 D 4
Jutaí, Cachoeira ~ BR 66-67 G 6
Jutaí, Rio ~ BR 66-67 D 4
Jutaí, Rio ~ BR 66-67 D 4
Jutaí Grande ○ BR 66-67 E 3
Jutaí-Solimões, Reserva Ecológica ⊥ BR 66-67 D 4
Jüterbog ○· D 92-93 M 3
Juti ○ BR 76-77 K 2
Jutiapa ☆ GCA 52-53 K 4
Jutiapa ○ HN 52-53 L 4
Juticalpa ☆ HN 52-53 L 4
Jutuarana ○ BR 66-67 H 4
Juuka ○· FIN 88-89 K 5
Juva ○ FIN 88-89 J 6
Juvenilia ○ BR 72-73 H 3
Juventud, Isla de la ⌒·· C 54-55 D 4
Juwana ○ RI 168 D 3
Ju Xian ○ VRC 154-155 L 4
Juxtlahuaca ○ MEX 52-53 F 3
Juye ○ VRC 154-155 K 4
Juža ○ RUS 94-95 S 3
Južkuduk ○ US 136-137 H 3
Južnaja Čunja ~ RUS 116-117 L 5
Južnaja Tajmura ~ RUS 116-117 L 4
Južna Morava ~ YU 100-101 H 3
Južno-Aleksandrovka ○ RUS 116-117 H 8
Južno-Aličurskij hrebet ▲ TJ 136-137 N 6
Juzno-Golodnostepskij kanal < US 136-137 L 4
Južno-Kamyšovyj hrebet ▲ RUS 122-123 K 5
Južno-Kuril'sk ○ RUS 122-123 L 6
Južno-Majnskij hrebet ▲ RUS 112-113 Q 5
Južno-Sahalinsk ☆ RUS 122-123 K 5
Južnoukrains'k ○ UA 102-103 K 3
Južnoural'sk ○ RUS 96-97 M 6
Južnyj ○ KA 126-127 N 4
Južnyj ○ RUS 112-113 Q 2
Južnyj, mys ▲ RUS (KMC) 120-121 X 6
Južnyj, mys ▲ RUS (KOR) 120-121 U 5
Južnyj, mys ▲ RUS (KOR) 120-121 R 5
Južnyj, ostrov ⌒ RUS 108-109 k 3
Južnyj Ergalah ~ RUS 108-109 W 7
Južnyj Ural ▲ RUS 96-97 K 8
Juzzak ○ PK 134-135 J 4
Jwaneng ○ RB 220-221 G 2
Jyväskylä ☆ FIN 88-89 H 5
Jzaviknek River ~ USA 20-21 J 6

K

K2 ▲ PK 138-139 F 2
Kaabong ○ EAU 212-213 E 2
Kaabougou ○ BF 204-205 E 3
Kaahka ○ TM 136-137 F 6
Kaala ▲ USA (HI) 288 G 3
Kaalualu ○ USA (HI) 288 K 6
Kaamanen ○ FIN 88-89 J 2
Kaap die Goeie Hoop = Cape of Good Hope ▲· ZA 220-221 D 7
Kaapmuiden ○ ZA 220-221 K 2
Kaapstad = Cape Town ☆·· ZA 220-221 D 6
Kaaresuvanto ○ FIN 88-89 G 2
Kaart ∸ RMM 202-203 F 3
Kaavi ○ FIN 88-89 K 5
Kabacan ○ RP 160-161 F 9
Kabaena, Pulau ⌒ RI 164-165 G 6
Kabaena, Selat ≈ 164-165 G 6
Kabah ∴· MEX 52-53 K 1
Kabaklyoba ○ TM 136-137 H 5
Kabala ○ WAL 202-203 E 5
Kabale ○ EAU 212-213 B 4
Kabalo ○ ZRE 214-215 D 5
Kabamba, Lac ○ ZRE 214-215 D 4
Kabambare ○ ZRE 212-213 A 6
Kabanga ○ ZRE 216-217 E 3
Kabango ○ ZRE 214-215 D 4
Kabangu ○ ZRE 214-215 B 6
Kabania Lake ○ CDN (ONT) 234-235 P 2
Kabanjahe ○ RI 162-163 C 3
Kabankalan ○ RP 160-161 E 8
Kabara ⌒ FJI 184 III c 3
Kabara ○ RMM 196-197 J 6
Kabara, Lac ○ RMM 202-203 H 2
Kabarai ○ RI 166-167 F 2
Kabardino-Balkaria = Kèbèrdej-Balkèr Respublikèm ◻ RUS 126-127 E 6
Kabardino-Balkarskaja Respublika ◻ RUS 126-127 E 6
Kabare ○ ZRE 212-213 B 5
Kabarnet ○ EAK 212-213 E 3
Kabasalan ○ RP 160-161 E 9
Kabau ○ RI 164-165 J 5
Kābāw ○ LAR 192-193 D 2
Kabba ○ WAN 204-205 G 5
Kabe ○ WAN 204-205 F 3
Kaberamaido ○ EAU 212-213 D 3
Kabetogama Lake ○ USA (MN) 270-271 F 2
Kabeya ○ ZRE 214-215 B 4
Kabi ○ ETH 208-209 D 3
Kabia ~ TCH 206-207 B 4
Kabika River ~ CDN (ONT) 236-237 J 3
Kabinakagami Lake ○ CDN (ONT) 236-237 D 4
Kabinakagami River ~ CDN (ONT) 236-237 D 4
Kabinakagami River ~ CDN (ONT) 236-237 D 2
Kabin Buri ○ THA 158-159 F 3
Kabinda ○ ZRE 214-215 C 4
Kabir ○ RI 166-167 C 6
Kabīr, Kūh-e ▲ IR 134-135 B 2
Kabir, Nahr az-Zāb al ~ IRQ 128-129 K 4
Kabīrwāla ○ PK 138-139 C 4
Kabkābīyah ○ SUD 200-201 B 6
Kablebet ○ RI 166-167 E 2
Kabna ○ SUD 200-201 F 3
Kabo ○ RCA 206-207 D 5
Kabolaa ○ RI 166-167 F 2
Kabombo ~ Z 218-219 C 1
Kabompo ○ Z 218-219 C 1
Kabompo ~ Z 218-219 C 1
Kabondo-Dianda ○ ZRE 214-215 C 5
Kabongo ○ ZRE (SHA) 214-215 C 4
Kabongo ○ ZRE (SHA) 214-215 E 5
Kabou ○ RCA 206-207 E 6
Kabou ○ RT 202-203 L 5
Kaboudia, Rass ▲ TN 190-191 H 3
Kabrousse ○ SN 202-203 B 3
Kabš, Ra's al- ▲ OM 132-133 L 3
Kabšān ○ KSA 130-131 H 5
Kabūd Rāhang ○ IR 128-129 N 5
Kābul ◻ AFG 138-139 B 2
Kābul ☆ AFG 138-139 B 2
Kābul, Daryā-ye ~ AFG 138-139 B 2
Kabul = Kābul ★ AFG 138-139 B 2
Kabulamwanda ○ Z 218-219 D 2
Kabumbu ○ ZRE 210-211 L 6
Kabunda ○ ZRE 214-215 E 7
Kabunduk ○ RI 168 D 7
Kabur ○ SUD 200-201 E 6
Kaburuang ○ RI 164-165 K 2
Kaburuang, Pulau ⌒ RI 164-165 K 2
Kabūshiya ○ SUD 200-201 F 4
Kabūtārhan ○ IR 134-135 G 3
Kabuzal Island ⌒ MYA 158-159 D 4
Kabwe ☆ Z 218-219 E 2
Kabwum ○ PNG 183 D 4
Kabyé, Monts ▲ RT 202-203 L 5
Kabyrga ~ KA 126-127 P 2
Kačanik ○· YU 100-101 H 3
Kacepi ○ RI 166-167 E 2
Kačerikova ○ RUS 116-117 N 9
Kach ○ PK 134-135 M 3
Kachako ○ WAN 204-205 H 3
Kachalola ○ Z 218-219 F 2
Kachchh, Gulf of ≈ 138-139 B 8
Kacheh Kūh ▲ PK 134-135 J 4
Kachekabwe ○ RB 218-219 C 4
Kachemak Bay ≈ 22-23 V 3
Kachia ○ WAN 204-205 G 4
Kachikani Pass ▲ PK 138-139 D 2
Kachisi ○ ETH 208-209 C 4
Kachovka ○ UA (HER) 102-103 H 4
Kachovs'ke vodoschovyšče < UA 102-103 H 4
Kachovs'kyj kanal < UA 102-103 J 4
Kachulu ○ MW 218-219 H 2
Kachung ○ EAU 212-213 D 3
Kačikatcy ○ RUS 118-119 O 5
Kačiry ☆ KA 124-125 K 2
Kačkanar ○ RUS 96-97 L 4
Kaçkar Dağı ▲ TR 128-129 J 2
Kačug ☆ RUS 116-117 M 9
Kačul = Cahul ☆ MD 102-103 F 5
Kaczawa ~ PL 92-93 N 3
Kada ○ AFG 134-135 K 3
Ka Dake Station ○ SD 220-221 K 3
Kadaly, Ust'e ○ RUS 118-119 E 6
Kadambūr ○ IND 140-141 G 6
Kadaney Rūd ~ AFG 134-135 M 3
Kadan Kyun ⌒ MYA 158-159 E 4
Kadavu ⌒ FJI 184 III b 3
Kadavu Passage ≈ 184 III b 3
Kaddam ○ IND 138-139 G 10
Kaddam Dam < IND 138-139 G 10
Kade ○ GH 202-203 K 6
Kadéï ~ RCA 210-211 E 2
Kadepur ○ IND 140-141 F 2
Kadi, ozero ○ RUS 122-123 J 3
Kadiana ○ RMM 202-203 G 4
Kadiaso ○ CI 202-203 G 5
Kadijivka ○ UA 102-103 L 3
Kadina ○ AUS 180-181 D 2
Kadınhanı ○ TR 128-129 E 3
Kadioha ○ CI 202-203 H 5
Kadiolo ○ RMM 202-203 H 4
Kadiondola ▲ RG 202-203 E 4
Kadipaten ○ RI 168 C 3
Kadiri ○ IND 140-141 H 3
Kadirli ☆ TR 128-129 G 4
Kadiwéu, Reserva Indígena ✕ BR 70-71 J 7
Kadjebi ○ GH 202-203 L 6
Kadji ○ TCH 206-207 E 3
Kadkan ○ IR 136-137 F 7
Kado ○ WAN 204-205 H 5
Kadoka ○ USA (SD) 260-261 E 3
Kadoma ○ ZW 218-219 E 4
Kadovar Island ⌒ PNG 183 C 2
Kadu ○ RI 168 D 7
Kadugli ○ SUD 206-207 J 3
Kaduj ○ RUS 94-95 P 2
Kaduna ◻ WAN 204-205 G 3
Kaduna ☆· WAN (KAD) 204-205 G 3
Kaduna, River ~ WAN 204-205 F 4
Kadung Ga ○ MYA 142-143 K 2
Kadupendak ○ RI 168 A 3
Kadūr ○ IND 140-141 G 4
Kadyj ○ RUS 94-95 S 3
Kadykčan ○ RUS 120-121 M 2
Kadžaran ○ AR 128-129 M 3
Kadžerom ○ RUS 88-89 X 4
Kadži-Saj ○ KS 146-147 C 4
Kaechon ○ DVR 150-151 E 8
Kaédi ☆ RIM 196-197 D 6
Kaélé ○ CAM 206-207 B 3
Kaena Point ▲· USA (HI) 288 G 3
Kaeng Khlo ○ THA 158-159 G 2
Kaeo ○ NZ 182 D 1
Kaesŏng ○ ROK 150-151 F 9
Kaevanga ○ SOL 184 I d 3
Kafakumba ○ ZRE 214-215 B 5
Kafan ○ AR 128-129 M 3
Kafanchan ○ WAN 204-205 H 4
Kafferrivier ~ ZA 220-221 G 4
Kaffin-Saru ○ WAN 204-205 G 4
Kaffrine ○ SN 202-203 C 2
Kafia Kingi ○ SUD 206-207 G 4
Kafiau, Pulau ⌒ RI 166-167 E 2
Kafin ○ WAN 204-205 G 4
Kafindibei ○ SUD 206-207 G 4
Kafin Hausa ○ WAN 198-199 D 6
Kafirnigan ~ TJ 136-137 L 6
Kåfjord ○ N 86-87 M 1
Kafolo ○ CI 202-203 H 5
Kafountine ○ SN 202-203 B 3
Kafr ad-Dawwār ○ ET 194-195 E 2
Kafr as-Šaiḫ ☆ ET 194-195 E 2
Kafu ~ EAU 212-213 C 3
Kafubu ~ ZRE 214-215 E 6
Kafue ○ Z (Lus) 218-219 E 2
Kafue ~ Z 218-219 D 2
Kafue Flats ∸ Z 218-219 D 2
Kafue National Park ⊥ Z 218-219 C 2
Kafukule ○ MW 214-215 G 6
Kafulwe ○ Z 214-215 E 5
Kafuya ~ ZRE 210-211 L 6
Kafwata Rest Camp ○ Z 218-219 D 2
Kaga ○ J 152-153 G 6
Kaga Bandoro ☆ RCA 206-207 D 5
Kagadi ○ EAU 212-213 C 3
Kağaki ○ AFG 134-135 L 2
Kağaki, Band-e ○·· AFG 134-135 L 2
Kagalaska Island ⌒ USA 22-23 H 7
Kagal'nik ~ RUS 102-103 L 4
Kagal'nik ~ RUS 102-103 M 4
Kagamil Island ⌒ USA 22-23 L 6
Kagamil Pass ≈ 22-23 M 6
Kagan ○ PK 138-139 D 2
Kagan ☆ US 136-137 J 5
Kagangan, Pulau ⌒ RI 164-165 F 6
Kagaré ○ BF 202-203 K 3
Kagarko ○ WAN 204-205 G 4
Kagegawa ○ J 152-153 H 7
Kagera ◻ EAT 212-213 C 4
Kagera ~ EAT 212-213 C 4
Kaggi ○ IND 140-141 F 4
Kagianagami Lake ○ CDN (ONT) 234-235 Q 4
Kağızman ☆ TR 128-129 K 2
Kaglik Lake ○ CDN 20-21 a 2
Kaglorvuak River ~ CDN 24-25 Q 5
Kagmadi ○ SUD 200-201 E 5
Kagnel ○ TCH 206-207 D 4
Kagologolo ○ RI 162-163 C 5
Kagombo ○ ZRE 214-215 D 6
Kagopal ○ TCH 206-207 C 4
Kagora, Mount ▲ WAN 204-205 H 4
Kagoshima ☆ J 152-153 D 9
Kagoshima-wan ≈ 152-153 D 9
Kağrān ○ AFG 134-135 L 2
Kāğū, Rūdḫāne-ye ~ IR 134-135 J 6
Kagua ○ PNG 183 B 4
Kāğūğ ○ ET 194-195 F 5
Kahakuloa ○ USA (HI) 288 J 4
Kahal Tabelbala ▲ DZ 188-189 K 6
Kahama ○ EAT 212-213 D 5
Kahān ○ PK 138-139 B 5
Kahana ○ USA (HI) 288 H 3
Kahatola, Pulau ⌒ RI 164-165 K 3
Kahayan ~ RI 162-163 K 5
Kahayan ~ RI 164-165 D 5
Kahemba ○ ZRE 216-217 E 3
Kahfa, al- ○ KSA 130-131 H 4
Kahir ○ IR 134-135 L 6
Kahiri ○ IR 134-135 J 5
Kahlotus ○ USA (WA) 244-245 G 4
Kahmard ○ AFG 136-137 K 7
Kähna Nau ○ PK 138-139 E 4
Kahnple ○ LB 202-203 F 6
Kahnūg ○ IR 134-135 G 5
Kahnwia ○ LB 202-203 F 7
Kahoka ○ USA (MO) 274-275 G 4
Kahokunui ○ USA (HI) 288 J 4
Kahone ○ SN 202-203 C 2
Kahoolawe ⌒ USA (HI) 288 J 4
Kahramanmaraş ☆· TR 128-129 G 4
Kahrizak ○ IR 136-137 B 7
Kahror Pakka ○ PK 138-139 C 5
Kāhta ☆ TR 128-129 H 4
Kahtana ~ RUS 120-121 T 4
Kahuku ○ USA (HI) 288 H 3
Kahuku Point ▲ USA (HI) 288 H 3
Kahul = Cahul ☆ MD 102-103 F 5
Kahului ○· USA (HI) 288 J 4
Kahului Bay ≈ USA 288 J 4
Kahunge ○ EAU 212-213 C 3
Kahūta ○ PK 138-139 D 3
Kahuzi-Biega, Parc National du ⊥··· ZRE 212-213 A 4
Kai, Kepulauan ⌒ RI 166-167 G 4
Kaiam ○ PNG 183 B 4
Kaiama ○ WAN 204-205 E 4
Kaiapit ○ PNG 183 D 4
Kaiapoi ○ NZ 182 D 5
Kaiashk Bay ≈ CDN 234-235 O 5
Kaibab Indian Reservation ✕ USA (AZ) 256-257 C 2
Kaibab Plateau ▲ USA (AZ) 256-257 C 2
Kai Beab ○ RI 166-167 K 5
Kai Besar, Pulau ⌒ RI 166-167 G 4
Kaibito ○ USA (AZ) 256-257 D 2
Kaibito Plateau ▲ USA (AZ) 256-257 D 2
Kaibola ○ PNG 183 F 5
Kaibus, Teluk ≈ 166-167 F 2
Kaidu He ~ VRC 146-147 G 4
Kai Dulah, Pulau ⌒ RI 166-167 G 4
Kaiemothia ○ SUD 208-209 B 6
Kaieteur Fall ~·· GUY 62-63 E 3
Kaieteur National Park ⊥ GUY 62-63 E 3
Kaifeng ○· VRC 154-155 J 4
Kaigani ○ USA 32-33 D 4
Kaihu ○ NZ 182 D 1
Kaihua ○ VRC 156-157 L 2
Kai Ketjil, Pulau ⌒ RI 166-167 G 4
Kaikohe ○ NZ 182 D 1
Kaikoura ○ NZ 182 D 5
Kailahun ○ WAL 202-203 E 5
Kailash = Kangrinboqê Feng ▲ VRC 144-145 C 5
Kailashahar ○ IND 142-143 H 3
Kaileuna Island ⌒ PNG 183 F 5
Kaili ○ VRC 156-157 E 3
Kailu ○ VRC 150-151 C 6
Kailua ○ USA (HI) 288 H 3
Kailua Kona ○· USA (HI) 288 K 5
Kaima ○ RI 166-167 K 4
Kaimana ○ RI 166-167 G 3
Kaimeer, Pulau ⌒ RI 166-167 G 4
Kaimur Hills ▲ IND 142-143 B 3
Käina ○·· EST 94-95 H 2
Kainab ~ NAM 220-221 D 3
Kainan ○ J 152-153 F 8
Kainantu ○ PNG 183 C 4
Kaindu ○ Z 218-219 D 2
Kaindy ○ KS 136-137 N 3
Kainji Dam < WAN 204-205 F 4
Kainji Lake National Park ⊥ WAN 204-205 E 3
Kainji Reservoir < WAN 204-205 F 3
Kaipara Harbour ≈ 182 E 2
Kaiparowits Plateau ▲ USA (UT) 254-255 D 6
Kaiping ○ VRC 156-157 H 5
Kaipotok Bay ≈ 36-37 U 7
Kaipuri, Pulau ⌒ RI 166-167 J 2
Kairāna ○ IND 138-139 F 5
Kairiru Island ⌒ PNG 183 B 2
Kairoi ○ RI 166-167 G 2
Kairouan ☆·· TN 190-191 H 3
Kais ~ RI 166-167 G 2
Kaiserslautern ○ D 92-93 J 4
Kaiserstuhl ▲ D 92-93 J 4
Kaiser Wilhelm II-Land ∸ ARK 16 G 9
Kaisho ○ EAT 212-213 C 4
Kaišiadorys ☆ LT 94-95 J 4
Kaisu ○ EAU 212-213 C 3
Kaisut Desert ∸ EAK 212-213 F 3
Kait ○ PNG 183 G 3
Kait, Tanjung ▲ RI 162-163 G 6
Kaita ○ EAU 212-213 D 3
Kaitaia ○ NZ 182 D 1
Kaitangata ○ NZ 182 B 7
Kaitanimbar, Pulau ⌒ RI 166-167 G 5
Kaiteriteri ○ NZ 182 D 4
Kaithal ○ IND 138-139 F 5
Kaititja-Warlpiri Aboriginal Land ✕ AUS 174-175 B 6
Kaitum ○ S 86-87 K 3
Kaitumälven ~ S 86-87 J 3
Kaiwatu ○ RI 166-167 D 6
Kaiwi Channel ≈ 48-49 D 7
Kaiwi Channel ≈ USA 288 H 3
Kai Xian ○ VRC 154-155 F 6
Kaiyang ○ VRC 156-157 E 3
Kaiyuan ○ VRC (LIA) 150-151 E 6
Kaiyuan ○ VRC (YUN) 156-157 C 5
Kaiyuh Mountains ▲ USA 20-21 L 5
Kaja, Wādī ~ SUD 198-199 L 6
Kajaani ○ FIN 88-89 J 4
Kajabbi ○ AUS 174-175 F 7
Kajak ○ RUS 108-109 e 6
Kajang ○ MAL 162-163 D 3
Kajang (Typical Amatowa Village) ○·· RI 164-165 G 6
Kajasan National Park ⊥· ROK 150-151 G 10
Kajdak, sor ∸ KA 126-127 K 5
Kajdak, Šor ○ KA 126-127 K 5
Kajerkan ○ RUS 108-109 W 7
Kajiado ○ EAK (RIF) 212-213 F 4
Kajlastuj ○ RUS 118-119 J 11
Kajmonovo ○ RUS 116-117 M 7
Kajnar ○ KA 124-125 K 4
Kajo Kaji ○ SUD 212-213 C 2
Kajola ○ WAN 204-205 F 5
Kajpil'gakuj, ozero ○ RUS 112-113 T 5
Kajrakkum ○ TJ 136-137 L 4
Kajrakkumskoe vodohranilišče < TJ 136-137 M 4
Kajrakty ~ KA 126-127 N 3
Kajser Franz Joseph Fjord ≈ 26-27 m 7
Kajuru ○ WAN 204-205 G 3
Kak, köli ○ KA 124-125 E 2
Käkä ○ SUD 206-207 L 3
Kaka ○ USA (AZ) 256-257 C 6
Kakaban, Pulau ⌒ RI 164-165 F 2
Kakabeka Falls ○· CDN (ONT) 234-235 O 6
Kakabia, Pulau ⌒ RI 166-167 B 5
Kakachischuan, Pointe ▲ CDN 36-37 K 7
Kakadu Holiday Village · AUS 172-173 L 2
Kakadu National Park ⊥··· AUS 172-173 L 2
Kakagi Lake ○ CDN (ONT) 234-235 K 5
Kakali ○ RI 164-165 F 4
Kakamas ○ ZA 220-221 E 4
Kakamega ☆ EAK 212-213 E 3
Kakamenga Forest Reserve ⊥ EAK 212-213 E 3
Kaka Mundi Section ⊥ AUS 178-179 J 3
Kākān ○ AFG 136-137 M 6
Kakanda ○ ZRE 214-215 D 6
Kakat, Ujung ▲ RI 162-163 B 3
Kakata ○ LB 202-203 E 6
Kakavi Theollogu ○ GR 100-101 H 5
Kakching ○ MYA 142-143 J 3
Kakdwip ○ IND 142-143 F 5
Kake ○ J 152-153 E 7
Kake ○ USA 32-33 D 3
Kakenge ○ ZRE 210-211 H 6
Kakeroma-shima ⌒ J 152-153 C 10
Käki ○ IR 134-135 D 4
Kakielo ○ ZRE 214-215 E 7
Kakimba ○ ZRE 212-213 B 6
Kakināda ○ IND 140-141 K 2
Kakisa River ~ CDN 30-31 K 5
Kakkar ○ PK 134-135 M 5
Kakobola ○ ZRE 210-211 G 6
Kakogawa ○ J 152-153 F 7
Kakonko ○ EAT 212-213 C 5
Kakoro ○ PNG 183 D 4
Kakpin ○ CI 202-203 J 5
Kakrima ~ RG 202-203 D 4
Kakšaal-Too', hrebet ▲ KS 146-147 C 5
Kaktovik ○ USA 20-21 T 1
Kakuma ○ EAK 212-213 E 2
Kakumbi ○ Z 218-219 F 1
Kakumi ○ WAN 204-205 G 3
Kakumiro ○ EAU 212-213 C 3
Kakunodate ○ J 152-153 J 5
Kakwa Provincial Recreation Area ⊥ CDN (BC) 228-229 O 2
Kakwa River ~ CDN (ALB) 228-229 P 2
Kakya ○ EAK 212-213 G 4
Kakyl, tau ▲ KA 124-125 F 4
Kala ○ EAT 214-215 F 5
Kala ○ WAN 198-199 G 6
Kalaallit Nunaat ◻ GRØ 26-27 P 6
Kalaallit Nunaat = Grønland ◻ GRØ 26-27 c 8
Kalaat Khasba ○ TN 190-191 G 3
Kālābāgh ○ PK 138-139 C 3
Kalabahi ○ RI 166-167 C 6
Kalabakan ○ MAL 160-161 B 10
Kalabi ○ EAU 212-213 D 2
Kalabo ○ Z 218-219 B 2
Kalabsha ∴· ET 194-195 F 6
Kalabua ○ ZRE 214-215 B 4
Kalač ○ RUS 102-103 M 2
Kalāčāy ○ IR 136-137 B 6
Kalačinsk ☆ RUS 114-115 N 7
Kalač-na-Donu ○ RUS 102-103 N 3
Kaladan ○ IND 142-143 H 4
Kaladan ~ IND 142-143 H 4
Kaladar ○ CDN (ONT) 238-239 H 4
Ka Lae ▲ USA (HI) 288 K 6
Kalafgān ○ AFG 136-137 L 6
Kalafilia ○ RG 202-203 F 5
Kalahari Desert ∸ RB 220-221 E 1
Kalahari Gemsbok National Park ⊥ ZA 220-221 E 2
Kalaheo ○ USA (HI) 288 F 3
Kalaigaon ○ IND 142-143 G 2
Kalaihum ○ TJ 136-137 M 5
Kalaji ○ WAG 202-203 C 3
Kalajoki ○ FIN 88-89 G 4
Kalakala · BOL 70-71 D 6
Kalakan ○ RUS (CTN) 118-119 H 8
Kalakan ~ RUS 118-119 J 8
Kalalé ○ DY 204-205 E 3
Kalāle ○ IR 136-137 D 6
Kala-I-Mor ○ TM 136-137 H 7
Kalaloch ○ USA (WA) 244-245 A 3
Kalām ○ PK 138-139 D 2
Kalama < EAK 212-213 F 2
Kalama ○ USA (WA) 244-245 C 4
Kalamaloué, Parc National de ⊥ CAM 198-199 G 6
Kalamariá ○ GR 100-101 J 4
Kalamáta ○ GR 100-101 J 6
Kalamazoo ○ USA (MI) 272-273 D 5
Kalamazoo River ~ USA (MI) 272-273 D 5
Kalambáka ○· GR 100-101 H 5
Kalambo ~ EAT 214-215 F 5
Kalambo Falls ~ EAT 214-215 F 5
Kalamits'ka zatoka ≈ 102-103 H 5
Kalana ○ EST 94-95 H 2
Kalana ○ RMM 202-203 F 4
Kalangali ○ EAT 214-215 G 4
Kalanguj ○ RUS 118-119 H 10
Kalanshiyū, Sarīr ∸ LAR 192-193 J 4
Kalao, Pulau ⌒ RI 168 E 6
Kalaotoa, Pulau ⌒ RI 168 E 6
Kala Oya ~ CL 140-141 J 6
Kalapana ○ USA (HI) 288 L 5
Kalar ~ RUS 118-119 J 7
Kalār, Kūh-e ▲ IR 134-135 D 3
Kalar, Srednij ○ RUS 118-119 H 8
Kalaraš = Călăraşi ☆ MD 102-103 F 4
Kälarne ○ S 86-87 H 5
Kalarskij hrebet ▲ RUS 118-119 H 8
Kalasin ○ THA 158-159 G 2
Kalāt ○· PK 134-135 M 4
Kalāte ○ IR 136-137 D 6
Kalāte-ye Siyāh ○ IR 134-135 J 4
Kalatungan Mountains ▲ RP 160-161 F 9
Kalaupapa ○ USA (HI) 288 J 3
Kalaupapa National Historical Park ⊥· USA (HI) 288 J 3
Kalaus ~ RUS 102-103 N 5
Kalaus ~ RUS 126-127 E 5
Kalaw ○ MYA 142-143 K 5
Kalb, De ○ USA (IL) 274-275 K 3
Kalb, De ○ USA (MS) 268-269 M 4
Kalb, De ○ USA (TX) 264-265 K 5
Kalb, Ra's al- ▲ Y 132-133 F 6
Kalbā ○ UAE 134-135 G 6
Kalbān, al- ○ OM 132-133 L 3
Kalbarri ○· AUS 176-177 C 3
Kalbarri National Park ⊥ AUS 176-177 C 3
Kalbinskij toglari ▲ KA 124-125 M 4
Kaldakvistl ~ IS 86-87 d 2
Kaldykajty ~ KA 96-97 H 9
Kaldyköl ○ KA 136-137 L 3
Kaldykol', ozero ○ KA 136-137 L 3
Kalé ○ RMM 202-203 E 3
Kale ☆ TR 128-129 D 4
Kale ☆ TR 128-129 C 4
Kalecik ☆· TR 128-129 E 2
Kaledon ○ CDN (BC) 230-231 K 4
Kaledougou ○ RMM 202-203 H 3
Kaledupa, Pulau ⌒ RI 164-165 H 6
Kalegauk ⌒ MYA 158-159 D 3
Kalegosilik River ~ USA 20-21 Q 2
Kalehe ○ ZRE 212-213 B 5
Kaleibar ○ IR 128-129 M 3
Kaleida ○ CDN (MAN) 234-235 E 5
Kalema ○ ZRE 210-211 K 6
Kalemie ○ ZRE 212-213 B 6
Kalemyo ○ MYA 142-143 J 4
Kalengwa ○ Z 218-219 C 1
Kalěnoe ○ KA 96-97 G 9
Kaleo ○ GH 202-203 J 4
Kaleste ○ EST 94-95 H 2
Kāl-e Šūr ~ IR 134-135 G 1
Kāl-e Šūr, Rūd-e ~ IR 136-137 F 6
Kaleva ○ USA (MI) 272-273 C 3
Kalevala ○ RUS 88-89 L 4
Kale Valley ~· WAN 204-205 J 3
Kalewa ○ MYA 142-143 J 4
Kalf ~ NAM 220-221 C 2
Kálfafell ○ IS 86-87 e 3
Kálfafellsstaður ○ IS 86-87 f 2
Kalfou ○ CAM 206-207 B 3
Kalfou, Réserve de ⊥ CAM 206-207 B 3
Kalga ☆ RUS 118-119 J 10
Kalgalakša, guba ≈ 88-89 N 4
Kalgary ○ USA (TX) 264-265 C 5
Kalghatgi ○ IND 140-141 F 3
Kalginčevajam ~ RUS 120-121 T 5
Kalgin Island ⌒ USA 20-21 O 6
Kalgo ○ WAN 198-199 B 6
Kali ~ NEP 144-145 C 6
Kali ○ RMM 202-203 E 3
Kal'i ○ RUS 88-89 R 5
Kalia ~ CAM 206-207 B 3
Kaliakair ○ BD 142-143 G 3
Kaliakra, Nos ▲ BG 102-103 F 6
Kalian ○ RP 160-161 F 9
Kalianda ○ RI 162-163 F 7
Kalianget ○ RI 168 E 3
Kaliānpur ○ IND 138-139 B 8
Kalibo ☆ RP 160-161 E 7
Kaliet ○ RI 162-163 C 6
Kali Gandaki ~ NEP 144-145 D 6
Kaliganj ○ BD 142-143 F 4
Kaligondang ○ RI 168 C 3
Kalima ○ ZRE 210-211 L 5
Kalimantan ⌒ 162-163 J 5
Kalimantan Barat ◻ RI 162-163 J 4
Kalimantan Selatan ◻ RI 164-165 D 5
Kalimantan Tengah ◻ RI 162-163 K 5
Kalimantan Timur ◻ RI 164-165 D 2
Kálimnos ○· GR 100-101 L 6
Kálimnos ⌒ GR 100-101 L 6
Kalimpong ○ IND 142-143 F 2
Kalinga ○ AUS 174-175 G 4
Kalinga ○ IND 142-143 D 5
Kalingupatti ○ IND 140-141 H 6
Kalinin ☆ TM 136-137 F 3
Kalinin = Tver' ☆ RUS 94-95 O 3
Kalinina ○ RUS 116-117 O 8
Kalinina, zaliv ○ RUS 108-109 Y 2
Kalininabad ○ TJ 136-137 L 6
Kaliningrad ☆·· RUS 94-95 G 4
Kalinino ○ RUS 122-123 C 4
Kalinino = Tašir ○ AR 128-129 L 2
Kalininsk ○ RUS 96-97 D 8
Kalinkavičy ○ BY 94-95 L 5
Kalinko ○ RG 202-203 E 4
Kalip ○ PNG 183 F 3
Kalipagan ○ RP 160-161 F 10
Kalipucang ○ RI 168 C 3
Kaliro ○ EAU 212-213 D 3
Kalis ○ SP 208-209 J 4
Kalisat ○ RI 168 E 4
Kāli Sindh ○ IND 138-139 F 8
Kalisizo ○ EAU 212-213 C 4
Kalispel Indian Reservation ✕ USA (WA) 244-245 H 2
Kalispell ○ USA (MT) 250-251 E 3
Kalisz ☆·· PL 92-93 P 3
Kalitidu ○ RI 168 D 3
Kalitva ~ RUS 102-103 M 3
Kaliua ○ EAT (TAB) 212-213 C 6
Kalivia ○ GR 100-101 J 6
Kalitva ~ RUS 102-103 M 3
Kaliwiro ○ RI 168 C 3
Kaliwungu ○ RI 168 D 3
Kalix ○ S 86-87 L 4
Kalixälven ~ S 86-87 L 3
Kaljazin ☆·· RUS 94-95 P 3
Kalkaman ○ KA 124-125 K 3
Kalkan ○ TR 128-129 C 4
Kalkaringi ○ AUS 172-173 K 4
Kalkaska ○ USA (MI) 272-273 D 3
Kalkbank ○ ZA 218-219 E 6
Kalkfeld ○ NAM 216-217 D 10
Kalkfontein = Tshootsha ○ RB 216-217 F 11
Kalkrand ○ NAM 220-221 C 2
Kalkuni ○ GUY 62-63 F 3
Kallakkurichchi ○ IND 140-141 H 5
Kallam ○ IND 138-139 F 10
Kallambella ○ IND 140-141 G 4
Källandsö ⌒ S 86-87 F 7
Kallar ○ IND 140-141 F 4
Kallār ○ IRQ 128-129 L 5
Kallar Kahār ○ PK 138-139 D 3
Kalli ○ AUS 176-177 D 3
Kalli ○ EST 94-95 J 2
Kallidaikurichchi ○ IND 140-141 G 6
Kallislahti ○ FIN 88-89 K 6
Kallsjön ○ S 86-87 F 5
Kalmakkol, köli ○ KA 124-125 E 2
Kalmakkyrgan ~ KA 124-125 D 5
Kalmali ○ IND 140-141 G 2
Kalmanka ☆ RUS 124-125 N 2
Kalmar ☆ S 86-87 H 8
Kalmard ○ IR 134-135 G 2
Kalmard, Godār-e ▲ IR 134-135 G 2
Kalmarsund ≈ 86-87 H 8
Kalmeta ○ AUS 174-175 F 6
Kalmiopsis Wilderness Area ⊥ USA (OR) 244-245 B 8
Kal'mius ~ UA 102-103 K 4
Kalmunai ○ CL 140-141 J 7
Kalmykia = Hal'mg-Tangč ◻ RUS 126-127 F 4
Kalmykovo ☆ KA 96-97 G 9
Kālna ○ IND 142-143 F 4
Kalnciems ○ LV 94-95 H 3
Kalni ~ BD 142-143 G 3
Kalocsa ○ H 92-93 P 5
Kalohi Channel ≈ USA 288 H 4
Kalo Kalo ○ PNG 183 F 5
Kaloke ○ LB 202-203 G 7
Kalokitting ○ SUD 200-201 B 6
Kaloko ○ ZRE 214-215 C 4
Kalokol ○ EAK 212-213 E 2
Kālol ○ IND 138-139 D 8
Kalole ○ ZRE 212-213 A 5
Kalomo ○ Z 218-219 D 3
Kalomo ~ Z 218-219 D 3
Kalona ○ USA (IA) 274-275 G 3
Kalone Peak ▲ CDN (BC) 228-229 H 4
Kalonje ○ Z 214-215 F 7
Kalosi ○ RI 164-165 F 5
Kalossia ○ EAK 212-213 E 3
Kalounka ○ RG 202-203 C 4
Kalourat, Mount ▲ SOL 184 I e 3
Kalpáki ○ GR 100-101 H 5
Kalpeni Island ⌒ IND 140-141 B 3
Kalpitiya ○ CL 140-141 H 6
Kalskag ○ USA 20-21 K 6
Kaltag ○ USA 20-21 L 4
Kaltamy ~ RUS 108-109 Z 7
Kaltasy ☆ RUS 96-97 J 5
Kaltinėnai ○ LT 94-95 H 4
Kaltuk ○ RUS 116-117 K 8
Kaltungo ○ WAN 204-205 J 4
Kaluga ☆·· RUS 94-95 P 4
Kalugumalai ○ IND 140-141 G 6
Kalu hrebet ▲ RUS 96-97 K 7
Kālu Khuhar ○ PK 134-135 M 6
Kaluluma ○ MW 214-215 G 7
Kalulushi ○ Z 214-215 E 7
Kaluma-Kanda ○ BD 142-143 G 3
Kalumbu, Mwadi- ○ ZRE 216-217 E 3
Kalumburu ✕ AUS 172-173 H 3
Kalumburu Aboriginal Land ✕ AUS 172-173 H 3
Kalumengongo ~ ZRE 214-215 D 5
Kalumpang ○ RI 164-165 F 5
Kalundborg ○· DK 86-87 E 9
Kalundu ○ ZRE 212-213 B 5
Kalundwe ○ ZRE 214-215 C 4
Kalungu ~ Z 214-215 G 5
Kalungwishi ~ Z 214-215 E 5
Kalūr Kot ○ PK 138-139 C 3
Kaluš ☆ UA 102-103 D 3
Kalvakurti ○ IND 140-141 H 2
Kalvarija ○·· LT 94-95 H 4
Kalvesta ○ USA (KS) 262-263 F 6
Kalyān ○ IND 138-139 D 10
Kalyandrug ○ IND 140-141 G 3
Kalybaj ○ KA 126-127 O 3
Kalybek, köli ○ KA 124-125 G 2
Kalygir', buhta ≈ RUS 120-121 S 7
Kalynivka ☆ UA 102-103 F 3
Kam ~ NAM 220-221 C 2
Kam, River ~ WAN 204-205 J 4
Kama ○ RMM 202-203 E 3
Kama ~ RUS 96-97 H 4
Kama ~ RUS 96-97 G 6
Kama ~ RUS 96-97 H 5
Kama ~ RUS 114-115 J 4
Kama ~ RUS 114-115 D 5
Kamada < TCH 198-199 G 4
Kamaday ○ TCH 206-207 E 3
Kamaishi ○ J 152-153 J 5
Kamakawalar, Danau ○ RI 166-167 H 3
Kamakwie ○ WAL 202-203 D 5
Kamal ○ RI 168 E 3
Kamal ○ TCH 198-199 H 2
Kamāl, Abū ☆ SYR 128-129 J 5
Kamale Mountain ▲ WAN 204-205 K 3
Kamālia ○ PK 138-139 D 4
Kamalo ○ USA (HI) 288 J 3
Kamalpur ○ IND 142-143 G 3
Kaman ☆ TR 128-129 E 3
Kamanga ○ EAT 212-213 D 5
Kamangu ○ Z 214-215 D 6
Kamanyola ○ ZRE 212-213 B 5
Kamāraj ○ IR 134-135 D 4
Kamarān ○ Y 132-133 C 6
Kamarān ⌒ Y 132-133 C 6
Kamarang ○ GUY 62-63 D 3
Kāmāreddi ○ IND 138-139 G 10
Kamaron ○ WAL 202-203 E 5
Kamarsuk ○ CDN 36-37 T 6
Kamas ○ USA (UT) 254-255 D 3

Kamaši o US 136-137 K 5
Kamativi o ZW 218-219 D 4
Kamba o WAN 204-205 E 3
Kamba Kota o RCA 206-207 C 5
Kambal o SUD 208-209 B 3
Kambalda o • AUS 176-177 F 5
Kambal'naja Sopka, vulkan ▲ RUS 122-123 R 3
Kambal'nickie Koški, ostrova ⌒ RUS 88-89 T 2
Kambal'nyj, mys ▲ RUS 122-123 R 3
Kambang o RI 162-163 D 5
Kambarka ☆ RUS 96-97 J 5
Kamberatoro o PNG 183 A 2
Kambia o WAL 202-203 D 5
Kambing, Gunung ▲ MAL 162-163 E 2
Kambolé o RT 202-203 L 5
Kambot o PNG 183 C 3
Kambove o ZRE 214-215 D 6
Kambuku o PNG 183 G 3
Kambüt o LAR 192-193 L 2
Kamčatka ~ RUS 120-121 R 6
Kamčatskij, mys ▲ RUS 120-121 U 5
Kamčatskij poluostrov ⌣ RUS 120-121 U 5
Kamčatsk, Ust'- ☆ RUS 120-121 U 5
Kamčatskij, Petropavlovsk- ☆ • RUS 120-121 S 7
Kamčatskij proliv ≈ 120-121 U 6
Kamčatskij zaliv ≈ 120-121 T 6
Kamchatka Peninsula = Kamčatka, poluostrov ⌣ RUS 120-121 Q 5
Kămděš o • AFG 136-137 M 7
Kameasi o RI 164-165 G 4
Kameel o ZA 220-221 G 3
Kamélé o CI 202-203 J 5
Kamelik ~ RUS 96-97 F 8
Kamen' o BY 94-95 L 4
Kamen', Serdce-mys ▲ RUS 112-113 Z 3
Kamende o ZRE 214-215 C 4
Kamenec-Podol'skij = Kam'janec'-Podil's'kyj ☆ UA 102-103 E 3
Kamenğ o AFG 134-135 L 1
Kameng ~ IND 142-143 H 2
Kamenica o BIH 100-101 G 3
Kamenka ☆ KA 96-97 G 8
Kamenka o RUS (ARH) 88-89 S 4
Kamenka o RUS (HBR) 122-123 G 2
Kamenka o RUS (KRN) 116-117 G 6
Kamenka o RUS (PEN) 96-97 D 7
Kamenka o RUS (SML) 94-95 N 4
Kamenka ~ RUS 108-109 d 2
Kamenka ~ RUS 110-111 d 6
Kamenka ~ RUS 116-117 G 6
Kamenka ~ RUS 124-125 O 2
Kamennaja, kosa ∸ RUS 108-109 P 7
Kamennaja tundra ∸ RUS 108-109 a 7
Kamen'-na-Obi ☆ RUS 124-125 M 2
Kamennik, gora ▲ RUS 88-89 N 3
Kamennogorsk o RUS 94-95 L 1
Kamennyj, Mys- o RUS 108-109 P 7
Kamennyj, mys ▲ RUS 110-111 c 2
Kamennyj Dubčes ~ RUS 114-115 T 4
Kamennyj Stolb, mys ▲ RUS 110-111 S 4
Kameno o BG 102-103 E 6
Kamen'-Rybolov o RUS 122-123 E 6
Kamenskoe ☆ RUS 112-113 O 5
Kamensk-Šahtinskij o RUS 102-103 M 3
Kamensk-Ural'skij ☆ RUS 96-97 M 5
Kamensk Ural'skiy = Kamensk-Ural'skij ☆ RUS 96-97 M 5
Kamenz o D 92-93 N 3
Kameshia o ZRE 214-215 D 5
Kameškova ~ RUS 112-113 M 3
Kameškovo ☆ RUS 94-95 R 3
Kāmet ▲ IND 138-139 G 4
Kameur, Bahr ~ RCA 206-207 E 4
Kamiah o USA (ID) 250-251 C 5
Kamienna, Skarżysko- o PL 92-93 Q 3
Kamiesberge ▲ ZA 220-221 C 5
Kamieskroon o ZA 220-221 C 5
Kami-Furano o J 152-153 K 3
Kamiiso o J 152-153 J 4
Kamiji o ZRE 214-215 B 4
Kamikawa o J 152-153 K 3
Kami-koshiki-shima ⌒ J 152-153 C 9
Kāmil, al- o KSA 130-131 F 6
Kāmil, al- o OM 132-133 L 2
Kamileroi o AUS 174-175 F 6
Kamilukuak Lake ○ CDN 30-31 T 4
Kamilukuak River ~ CDN 30-31 S 5
Kamimbi Fuka, Chute ~ ZRE 214-215 C 5
Kamina o PNG 183 C 4
Kamina o RT 202-203 L 5
Kamina o ZRE (SHA) 210-211 L 6
Kamina o ZRE (SHA) 214-215 C 5
Kamina Base o ZRE 214-215 C 5
Kaminak Lake ○ CDN 30-31 W 4
Kamin'-Kašyrs'kyj o UA 102-103 D 2
Kaminokuni o J 152-153 J 4
Kamino-shima ⌒ J 152-153 C 7
Kaminuriak Lake ○ CDN 30-31 W 4
Kamioka o J 152-153 G 6
Kamishak Bay ≈ 22-23 T 3
Kamishak River ~ USA 22-23 T 3
Kami-Shihoro o J 152-153 K 3
Kami-shima ⌒ J 152-153 D 8
Kamitsushima o J 152-153 C 7
Kamituga o ZRE 212-213 B 5
Kami-Yaku o J 152-153 D 9
Kamjana mohyla • UA 102-103 J 4
Kam'janec'-Podil's'kyj ☆ UA 102-103 E 3
Kamjani Mohyly • UA 102-103 K 4
Kam'janka o UA 102-103 H 3
Kam'janka o UA 102-103 G 4
Kam'janske o UA 102-103 C 3
Kamjong o IND 142-143 J 3
Kamkaly o KA 124-125 G 6
Kamloops o CDN (BC) 230-231 J 3
Kamloops Indian Reserve ⊼ CDN (BC) 230-231 J 3
Kamloops Plateau ▲ CDN (BC) 230-231 J 3
Kammanassieberge ▲ ZA 220-221 F 6
Kamo o AR 128-129 L 2
Kamo ~ RUS 116-117 G 6
Kămoke o PK 138-139 E 4
Kamola o ZRE 214-215 D 4
Kamoro ▲ RM 222-223 E 6
Kamoro ~ RM 222-223 E 6
Kamoro, Tampoketsan'i ▲ RM 222-223 E 6
Kamoto o Z 218-219 G 1
Kamp 52 o SME 62-63 F 3
Kampa, Teluk ≈ 162-163 F 5
Kampa do Rio Amônea, Área Indígena ⊼ BR 64-65 F 6
Kampala ★ EAU 212-213 D 3
Kampala o SUD 206-207 G 4
Kampar o MAL 162-163 D 2
Kampar ~ RI 162-163 E 4
Kamparkanan ~ RI 162-163 D 4
Kamparkiri ~ RI 162-163 D 4
Kampene o ZRE 210-211 L 5
Kamphaeng Phet o THA 158-159 E 2
Kamphambale o MW 214-215 G 7
Kampi Katoto o EAT 214-215 G 4
Kampi Ya Moto o EAK 212-213 E 4
Kampli o IND 140-141 G 3
Kampolombo, Lake ○ Z 214-215 E 6
Kâmpóng Cham o K 158-159 H 4
Kâmpóng Chhnăng o K 158-159 H 4
Kâmpóng Saôm ≈ 158-159 G 5
Kâmpóng Saôm o K 158-159 G 5
Kâmpóng Spoe o K 158-159 H 5
Kâmpóng Trach o K 158-159 H 5
Kâmpôt o K 158-159 H 5
Kampsville o USA (IL) 274-275 H 5
Kampti o BF 202-203 J 4
Kampumbu o Z 214-215 G 6
Kampung ~ RI 166-167 K 4
Kampung Ayer Puteh o MAL 162-163 E 2
Kampung Balok o MAL 162-163 E 3
Kampung Berawan o MAL 164-165 D 1
Kampung Buloh o MAL 162-163 E 2
Kampung Chenereh o MAL 162-163 E 2
Kampung Cherating o MAL 162-163 E 2
Kampung Gajah o MAL 162-163 D 2
Kampung Jambu Bongkok o MAL 162-163 E 2
Kampung Jerangau o MAL 162-163 E 2
Kampung Kemara o MAL 162-163 E 2
Kampung Koh o MAL 162-163 D 2
Kampung Lamir o MAL 162-163 E 3
Kampung Laut o MAL 162-163 F 4
Kampung Leban Condong o MAL 162-163 E 3
Kampung Merang o MAL 162-163 E 2
Kampung Merting o MAL 162-163 E 2
Kampung Nibong o MAL 162-163 D 2
Kampung Penarik o MAL 162-163 E 2
Kampung Relok o MAL 162-163 E 2
Kampung Sekinchan o MAL 162-163 D 3
Kampung Sepat o MAL 162-163 E 3
Kampung Sook o MAL 160-161 B 10
Kampung Sungai Ayer Deras o MAL 162-163 E 2
Kampung Sungai Rengit o MAL 162-163 F 4
Kampung Tebingtinggi o RI 162-163 H 3
Kampung Tekek o • MAL 162-163 F 3
Kampung Tengah o MAL 162-163 F 4
Kampung Terolak o MAL 162-163 D 2
Kamrau, Teluk ≈ 166-167 G 3
Kamsack o CDN (SAS) 232-233 R 4
Kamsar o RG 202-203 C 4
Kamskoe Ust'e ☆ RUS 96-97 F 6
Kamskoe vodohranilišče < RUS 96-97 K 4
Kamskoye Vodokhranilishche = Kamskoe vodohranilišče < RUS 96-97 K 4
Kamsuuma o SP 212-213 J 3
Kāmthi o IND 138-139 G 9
Kamtsha ~ ZRE 210-211 G 6
Kamuchawi Lake ○ CDN 34-35 E 2
Kamudi o IND 140-141 H 6
Kamuela o USA (HI) 288 K 4
Kamuj, gora ▲ RUS 122-123 N 6
Kâmuk, Cerro ▲ CR 52-53 C 7
Kamuli o EAU 212-213 D 3
Kamušnyj ☆ KA 124-125 B 2
Kamutambai ~ ZRE 214-215 B 4
Kam'yanets'-Podil's'ky = Kam'janec'-Podil's'kyj ☆ UA 102-103 E 3
Kāmyārān o IR 134-135 B 1
Kamyšanovka o KS 146-147 B 4
Kamyšet o RUS 116-117 J 8
Kamyševatskaja o RUS 102-103 K 4
Kamyševka o RUS 114-115 H 6
Kamyshin = Kamyšin o RUS 96-97 D 8
Kamyšin o RUS 96-97 D 8
Kamyškol o KA 96-97 H 10
Kamyšlov ☆ RUS 114-115 G 6
Kamyšovyj, Južno-, hrebet ▲ RUS 122-123 K 5
Kamyšovyj hrebet ▲ RUS 122-123 K 3
Kamys-Samarkölinin küjmasy o KA 96-97 G 9
Kamysty-Ajat ~ KA 124-125 B 2
Kamystybas, köl ○ KA 126-127 O 4
Kamyzjak ☆ RUS (AST) 96-97 F 10
Kamyzjak ~ RUS 126-127 H 5
Kan ~ RUS 116-117 G 8
Kan o US 136-137 K 5
Kanaaupscow, Rivière ~ CDN 36-37 M 7
Kanab o USA (UT) 254-255 C 6
Kanab Creek ~ USA (AZ) 256-257 C 2
Kanacea ⌒ FJI 184 III c 2
Kanadej o RUS 96-97 E 7
Kanaga Pass ≈ 22-23 H 7
Kanagi o J 152-153 J 4
Kanaima Fall ~ GUY 62-63 D 2
Kanairiktok River ~ CDN 36-37 S 7
Kanaka o RI 166-167 G 3
Kanakakee River ~ USA (IN) 274-275 L 3
Kanakapura o IND 140-141 G 4
Kanakatte o IND 140-141 G 4
Kanakoro o BF 202-203 G 4
Kanaktok Mount ▲ USA 20-21 L 3
Kanamari do Rio Juruá, Área Indígena ⊼ BR 66-67 C 6
Kananaskis River ~ CDN (ALB) 232-233 C 5
Kananga ☆ ZRE (KOC) 210-211 J 6
Kananggar o RI 168 E 8
Kanangio, Mount ▲ PNG 183 C 3
Kanangra Boyd National Park ⊥ AUS 180-181 L 2
Kananto o GH 202-203 K 5
Kananyga ~ RUS 120-121 Q 3
Kanaraville o USA (UT) 254-255 B 6
Kanas o IND 138-139 E 8
Kanaš o RUS 96-97 E 6
Kanatak o USA 22-23 S 4
Kanawha o USA (IA) 274-275 E 2
Kanawha River ~ USA (WV) 280-281 D 5
Kanawi, Pulau ⌒ MAL 160-161 B 10
Kanazawa ☆ • J 152-153 G 6
Kanazi o EAT 212-213 C 4
Kanbalu o MYA 142-143 J 4
Kanbe o MYA 158-159 D 2
Kanbi ~ BF 202-203 K 3
Kančalan o RUS 112-113 T 4
Kančalan ~ RUS 112-113 T 4
Kanchana Buri o THA 158-159 E 3
Kanchanadit o THA 158-159 E 6
Kanchanpur o NEP 144-145 F 7
Kanchenjunga ▲ NEP 144-145 G 7
Kanchibya ~ Z 214-215 F 6
Kānchipuram o • • IND 140-141 H 4
Kanci o RI 168 C 3
Kandahar o CDN (SAS) 232-233 O 4
Kandāhār o IND 138-139 F 10
Kandahar = Qandahār ☆ • • AFG 134-135 L 3
Kandahār = Qandahār ☆ • • AFG 134-135 L 3
Kandalakša o RUS 88-89 M 3
Kandalakshskaya Guba = Kandalakšskaja guba ≈ RUS 88-89 M 3
Kandalakšskaja guba ≈ 88-89 M 3
Kandalakšskij bereg ⌣ RUS 88-89 M 3
Kandang o RI 162-163 B 3
Kandangan o RI 164-165 D 5
Kandanghaur o RI 168 C 3
Kandar o RI 166-167 F 6
Kandare o WAN 204-205 H 4
Kandarisa o PNG 183 A 5
Kandé o RT 202-203 L 5
Kandéko ~ RCB 210-211 F 3
Kandep o PNG 183 B 3
Kandero o DY 204-205 E 3
Kandi o DY 204-205 E 3
Kāndi o IND 142-143 F 4
Kandi, Tanjung ▲ RI 164-165 G 3
Kandiadiou o SN 202-203 B 3
Kandiāro o PK 138-139 B 6
Kandika o RG 202-203 D 3
Kandik River ~ USA 20-21 T 4
Kandil Bouzou < RN 198-199 E 5
Kandıra ☆ TR 128-129 D 2
Kandjia o RCA 206-207 E 6
Kandkhot o PK 138-139 B 5
Kāndla o IND 138-139 C 8
Kando ~ ZRE 214-215 D 6
Kandos o AUS 180-181 K 2
Kandreho o RM 222-223 E 6
Kandrian o PNG 183 E 4
Kandry ☆ RUS 96-97 J 6
Kanduanam o PNG 183 B 3
Kandukür o IND 140-141 H 3
Kandy o • • • CL 140-141 J 7
Kane o CDN (MAN) 234-235 F 5
Kane, Kap ▲ GRØ 26-27 e 2
Kane Basin ≃ 26-27 P 4
Kane Bassin ≃ 26-27 P 4
Kane Fracture Zone ≃ 6-7 D 6
Kanektok River ~ USA 22-23 Q 3
Kanel o SN 202-203 D 2
Kanem □ TCH 198-199 G 5
Kaneohe o USA (HI) 288 H 3
Kaneohe Bay ☆ USA 288 H 3
Kanevka o RUS 88-89 P 3
Kanevskaja o RUS 102-103 L 4
Kanferandé o RG 202-203 C 4
Kang o AFG 134-135 J 3
Kang o RB 218-219 B 6
Kangaamiut = Gammel Sukkertoppen o GRØ 28-29 O 4
Kangaatsiaq o GRØ 28-29 O 2
Kangahun o WAL 202-203 D 5
Kangal ☆ TR 128-129 G 3
Kangalassy o RUS 118-119 O 4
Kangalas-Uële ~ RUS 110-111 L 3
Kangān o IR 134-135 E 5
Kangān Čam ~ IR 134-135 B 2
Kangar o MAL 162-163 D 2
Kangara o RMM 202-203 F 4
Kangaré o RMM 202-203 F 4
Kangaroo Island ⌒ AUS 180-181 D 3
Kangaroo Valley ⌣ AUS 180-181 L 3
Kangasniemi o FIN 88-89 J 6
Kangāvar o • IR 134-135 B 1
Kangding o VRC 154-155 B 6
Kangdong o DVR 150-151 F 8
Kangean, Kepulauan ⌒ RI 168 B 6
Kangean, Pulau ⌒ RI 168 B 6
Kangeak Point ▲ CDN 28-29 H 3
Kangen ~ SUD 208-209 A 5
Kangeq ⌒ GRØ 26-27 X 7
Kangerdluarssuk ≈ 26-27 Z 8
Kangerdlugssuaq ≈ 26-27 Z 8
Kangerdluluk Fjord ≈ 28-29 T 6
Kangerluarsoruseq = Færingehavn o GRØ 28-29 P 5
Kangerluarsuk o GRØ 28-29 O 4
Kangerluk = Diskofjord o GRØ 28-29 N 2
Kangerlussuaq ≈ 26-27 Z 8
Kangerlussuaq ≈ 28-29 Y 2
Kangerlussuaq ≈ 28-29 O 3
Kangerlussuaq = Søndrestrømfjord o GRØ 28-29 P 3
Kangersuneq ≈ 28-29 P 4
Kangertittivaq ≈ 26-27 X 3
Kangertittivag = Scoresby Sund ≈ 26-27 o 8
Kanghwa o ROK 150-151 F 9
Kanghwa Do ⌒ ROK 150-151 F 9
Kangi o SUD 206-207 H 4
Kangik o USA 20-21 L 1
Kangikajip Appalia = Brewster, Kap ▲ GRØ 26-27 p 8
Kangilinnguit = Grønnedal o GRØ 28-29 Q 6
Kangilo Fiord ≈ 28-29 G 3
Kangiqsujuak o CDN 36-37 O 4
Kangiwa o WAN 204-205 E 2
Kangkir o VRC 144-145 B 2
Kang Kra Chan National Park ⊥ • THA 158-159 E 4
Kangmar o VRC 144-145 G 6
Kangnŭng o ROK 150-151 G 9
Kango o G 210-211 C 3
Kangole o EAU 212-213 E 2
Kangonde o EAK 212-213 F 4
Kangounadéni o BF 202-203 H 4
Kangping o VRC 150-151 D 6
Kangrinboqê Feng ▲ VRC 144-145 C 5
Kangro o VRC 144-145 E 4
Kangsar, Kuala o • MAL 162-163 D 2
Kangto ▲ IND 142-143 H 2
Kangye ☆ DVR 150-151 F 7
Kangz'gyai ▲ VRC 146-147 N 6
Kanha National Park ⊥ • IND 142-143 B 4
Kanhar ~ IND 142-143 C 4
Kani o • CI 202-203 G 5
Kani o J 152-153 G 7
Kani o MYA 142-143 J 4
Kaniama o ZRE 214-215 C 4
Kaniasso o CI 202-203 G 5
Kanibadam o TJ 136-137 M 4
Kanibes ~ NAM 220-221 C 2
Kanigiri o IND 140-141 H 3
Kanimeh o US 136-137 J 4
Kanin, poluostrov ⌣ RUS 88-89 S 3
Kanin Kamen' ▲ RUS 88-89 R 2
Kanin Nos o RUS 88-89 R 2
Kanin Nos, mys ▲ RUS 88-89 R 2
Kaninskaja tundra ∸ RUS 88-89 S 3
Kanioumé o RMM 202-203 J 2
Kanisa o SUD 200-201 E 3
Kanita o J 152-153 J 4
Kaniva o AUS 180-181 F 4
Kanivs'ke vodoschovyšče < UA 102-103 G 2
Kaniya o PNG 183 B 4
Kanji-dong o DVR 150-151 G 7
Kanjirapalli o IND 140-141 G 6
Kanjiroba ▲ NEP 144-145 D 6
Kankaanpää o FIN 88-89 G 6
Kankai ~ IND 142-143 E 2
Kankakee o USA (IL) 274-275 L 3
Kankakee River ~ USA (IL) 274-275 K 3
Kankalabé o RG 202-203 E 4
Kankan □ RG 202-203 E 4
Kankan ☆ RG 202-203 F 4
Kankara o WAN 204-205 G 3
Kankelaba ~ RMM 202-203 G 4
Kankesanturai o CL 140-141 J 6
Kankiya o WAN 198-199 C 6
Kankossa o RIM 196-197 E 7
Kankunskij o RUS 118-119 N 7
Kanmaw Kyun ⌒ MYA 158-159 E 5
Kann o IR 136-137 B 7
Kanna o MYA 142-143 K 6
Kannad o IND 138-139 E 9
Kannapolis o USA (NC) 282-283 G 5
Kannata Valley o CDN (SAS) 232-233 O 5
Kannavam o IND 140-141 F 5
Kannoka = Sillamäe o EST 94-95 K 2
Kannonkoski o FIN 88-89 H 5
Kannonsaha o FIN 88-89 H 5
Kannus o FIN 88-89 G 5
Kano o J 152-153 D 7
Kano o RMM 202-203 F 3
Kano □ WAN 204-205 H 3
Kano ☆ • • WAN 198-199 D 6
Kano, River ~ WAN 204-205 H 3
Kanobe, Pulau ⌒ RI 166-167 F 1
Kanona o Z 218-219 F 1
Kano Nak o VN 158-159 K 3
Kanoni o ZRE 214-215 D 6
Kanono o NAM 218-219 C 3
Kanopolis Lake ○ USA (KS) 262-263 H 6
Kanorado o USA (KS) 262-263 D 5
Kanoroba o CI 202-203 G 5
Kanosh o USA (UT) 254-255 C 5
Kanouri ∸ RN 198-199 F 5
Kanovlei o NAM 216-217 E 9
Kanowit o MAL 162-163 K 3
Kanowna ∴ AUS 176-177 F 5
Kanoya o J 152-153 D 9
Kanozero o RUS 88-89 N 3
Kanpur o IND 142-143 B 2
Kansanshi o Z 214-215 D 7
Kansas o USA (IL) 274-275 L 5
Kansas o USA (OK) 264-265 K 2
Kansas □ USA (KS) 262-263 F 6
Kansas City o USA (KS) 262-263 M 5
Kansas City o USA (MO) 274-275 D 5
Kansas River ~ USA (KS) 262-263 K 5
Kanšengeľ o KA 124-125 J 6
Kansenia o ZRE 214-215 D 6
Kansk ☆ RUS 116-117 G 7
Kant o KS 146-147 B 4
Kantah o CDN 30-31 J 6
Kantah River ~ CDN 32-33 K 3
Kantalai o CL 140-141 J 6
Kantang o THA 158-159 E 7
Kantchari o BF 202-203 L 3
Kantche o RN 198-199 D 6
Kantegir ~ RUS 116-117 E 9
Kantemirovka o KA 136-137 M 3
Kantemirovka o RUS 102-103 L 3
Kantharalak o THA 158-159 H 3
Kānthi o IND 142-143 E 5
Kantishna o USA 20-21 P 5
Kantishna River ~ USA 20-21 P 4
Kanto-sanchi ▲ J 152-153 H 6
Kantunil o MEX 52-53 K 1
Kanuku Mountains ▲ GUY 62-63 E 4
Kanur o IND 140-141 G 3
Kanus o NAM 220-221 D 3
Kanu Woralaksaburi o THA 158-159 E 2
Kanye ☆ RB 220-221 G 2
Kanyemba o ZW 218-219 F 2
Kanyilombi o Z 214-215 C 7
Kanym Boľšoj, gora ▲ RUS 114-115 U 7
Kanyš-Kija o KS 136-137 M 4
Kanyu o RB 218-219 C 5
Kao o RN 198-199 B 5
Kaôh Kŏng ⌒ K 158-159 G 5
Kaôh Rŭng ⌒ K 158-159 G 5
Kaôh Rŭng Sâmlŏem ⌒ K 158-159 G 5
Kaohsiung o RC 156-157 M 5
Kaôh Tang ⌒ K 158-159 G 5
Kaôh Thmei ⌒ K 158-159 G 5
Kaoka o SOL 184 I e 3
Kaokaona ☆ SOL 184 I e 4
Kaokoveld ∸ NAM 216-217 B 8
Kaolack ☆ SN 202-203 B 2
Kaolak River ~ USA 20-21 K 2
Kaolé < RIM 196-197 F 6
Kaoleni o EAK 212-213 G 5
Kaole Ruins • EAT 214-215 K 4
Kaolinovo o BG 102-103 E 6
Kaolo o SOL 184 I d 3
Kaoma o Z 218-219 C 2
Kaouadja o RCA (Kot) 206-207 F 5
Kaouadja ~ RCA 206-207 E 4
Kaouadja ~ RCA 206-207 G 5
Kap o IND 138-139 G 10
Kap o PK 134-135 K 5
Kapa o MYA 158-159 E 4
Kapaa o USA (HI) 288 F 2
Kapaahu o USA (HI) 288 K 5
Kapaau o USA (HI) 288 K 4
Kapadokya ∸ TR 128-129 F 4
Kapadvanj o IND 138-139 D 8
Kapaimeri o PNG 183 B 3
Kapalabuaya o RI 164-165 K 4
Kapalala o Z 214-215 E 7
Kapandae o GH 202-203 K 5
Kapande ~ ZRE 214-215 D 6
Kapanga o ZRE 214-215 B 5
Kapangan o RP 160-161 D 4
Kapapa o ZRE 214-215 E 5
Kapasia o BD 142-143 G 4
Kapatu ~ EAT 212-213 E 6
Kapatu o Z 214-215 F 5
Kapau River ~ PNG 183 D 4
Kapčagaj = Kapšagaj o KA 146-147 C 4
Kapchorwa o EAU 212-213 E 3
Kapčiamiestis o LT 94-95 H 4
Kapedo o EAK 212-213 F 3
Kapema o ZRE 214-215 E 6
Kapenguria o EAK 212-213 E 3
Kapia o ZRE 210-211 G 6
Kapichira Falls ~ MW 218-219 H 2
Kapini o LV 94-95 K 3
Kapip o PK 138-139 B 4
Kapiri Mposhi o Z 218-219 E 1
Kāpīsa □ AFG 138-139 B 2
Kapisillit o GRØ 28-29 P 4
Kapiskau River ~ CDN 34-35 O 4
Kapiskau River ~ CDN (ONT) 234-235 R 3
Kapiskong Lake ○ CDN (ONT) 236-237 G 5
Kapit o MAL 162-163 K 3
Kapiti Island ⌒ NZ 182 E 4
Kapiura River ~ PNG 183 F 3
Kapka, Massif du ▲ TCH 198-199 K 5
Kaplamada, Gunung ▲ RI 166-167 D 3
Kaplan o USA (LA) 268-269 H 7
Kaplankyr, plato ▲ US 136-137 E 4
Kaplankyrskij zapovednik ⊥ TM 136-137 E 4
Kapoe o THA 158-159 E 6
Kapoeta o SUD 208-209 A 6
Ka Poh National Park ⊥ • THA 158-159 E 5
Kapoke o Z 214-215 F 5
Kapona o ZRE 214-215 E 4
Kapondai, Tanjung ▲ RI 166-167 B 6
Kaponde o ZRE 214-215 B 4
Kapong o THA 158-159 E 6
Kapoposang, Pulau ⌒ RI 164-165 F 6
Kaporo o MW 214-215 G 5
Kaposvár o H 92-93 O 5
Kapotakshi ~ BD 142-143 F 4
Kap-Kudzur o RUS 116-117 J 9
Kappar o PK 134-135 K 6
Kappelshkär o S 86-87 J 7
Kappelshamn o S 86-87 J 8
Kapp Platen ▲ N 84-85 N 2
Kapps o NAM 216-217 D 11
Kapsabet o EAK 212-213 E 3
Kapšagaj o KA 146-147 C 4
Kapšagaj su kojmasy < KA 146-147 C 4
Kapsan o DVR 150-151 G 7
Kapsaouis, Rivière ~ CDN 36-37 K 7
Kāpsi o IND 140-141 F 2
Kaptai o BD 142-143 H 4
Kaptai Lake ○ BD 142-143 H 4
Kaptiau o RI 166-167 K 3
Kapuas ~ RI 162-163 H 5
Kapuas ~ RI 162-163 J 4
Kapuas ~ RI 164-165 D 4
Kapuas Hulu, Banjaran ▲ MAL 162-163 K 4
Kapur Utara, Pegunungan ▲ RI 168 D 3
Kapuskasing o CDN (ONT) 236-237 F 3
Kapuskasing River ~ CDN (ONT) 236-237 F 4
Kapuskasing River ~ CDN (ONT) 236-237 F 3
Kapustin Jar o RUS 96-97 D 9
Kaputa o Z 214-215 E 5
Kaputir o EAK 212-213 E 2
Kap Walløe Banke ≃ 28-29 T 6
Kapydžik, gora ▲ AZ 128-129 L 3
Kapyl'uši, ozero ○ RUS 118-119 F 8
Kara o RI 166-167 C 5
Kara ☆ RT (DLK) 202-203 L 5
Kara ~ RT 202-203 L 5
Kara ~ RUS 108-109 L 8
Kara, Ust'- o RUS 108-109 L 7
Karaba, Ra's ▲ KSA 130-131 E 5
Kara-Balta ☆ Kara-Balty o KS 136-137 N 3
Kara-Balty o KS 136-137 N 3
Karabaš ☆ RUS 96-97 M 6
Karabastau o KA 136-137 M 3
Karabau o KA 96-97 H 9
Karabaur, pastiligi ▲ KA 126-127 L 6
Karabekaul o TM 136-137 J 5
Karabil', vozvyšennosť ▲ TM 136-137 H 6
Karabinka o RUS 124-125 P 2
Kara-Bogaz-Gol = Garabogazköl ≈ TM (KRS) 136-137 C 4
Karabogazköl, zaliv ≈ 136-137 C 4
Karabuget o KA 124-125 H 6
Karabük ☆ TR 128-129 E 2
Karabula o RUS 116-117 H 6
Karabula ~ RUS 116-117 H 7
Karabulak o KA 136-137 L 3
Karaburun ☆ TR 128-129 B 3
Karabütak ☆ KA 126-127 O 3
Karaca Dağ ▲ TR 128-129 H 4
Karačaevsk o RUS 126-127 D 6
Karacaköy o TR 128-129 C 2
Karacasu ☆ TR 128-129 C 4
Karacek, köl ○ KA 126-127 L 6
Karačev o RUS 94-95 O 5
Karachay-Cherkessia = Karačaj-Čerkes Respublika □ RUS 126-127 D 6
Karāchi ☆ • PK 134-135 M 6
Karaçoban ☆ TR 128-129 K 3
Karād o IND 140-141 F 2
Kara Deniz ≈ 128-129 D 1
Karadeniz Boğazi = Bosporus ≈ 128-129 C 2
Karaespe ~ KA 124-125 E 5
Karağ o IR 136-137 B 7
Karaga o GH 202-203 K 5
Karaga ~ RUS 120-121 U 4
Karaga, buhta ○ RUS 120-121 U 4
Karagaj ☆ RUS 96-97 J 4
Karagajly o KA 124-125 J 4
Karagajly o KA 124-125 J 4
Karagajly-Ajat ~ RUS 124-125 B 2
Karaganda = Karaghandy o KA 124-125 H 4
Karagandysay o KA 126-127 L 2
Karagaz, hrebet ▲ TM 136-137 D 5
Karaghandy ☆ KA 124-125 H 4
Karagije, vpadina ⌣ KA 126-127 J 6
Karaginskij, ostrov ⌒ RUS 120-121 V 4
Karaginskij zaliv ≈ 120-121 U 4
Karagoš, gora ▲ RUS 124-125 Q 3
Karagüney Dağı ▲ TR 128-129 E 2
Karahalı ☆ TR 128-129 C 3
Kara Hobda ~ KA 126-127 M 2
Karaiai o PNG 183 E 3
Karaideľ ☆ RUS 96-97 K 6
Karaisalı ☆ TR 128-129 F 4
Karaitem o PNG 183 B 2
Karajagi o IND 140-141 F 2
Karaja Masef'ga o RUS 88-89 N 5
Karak, al- ☆ • JOR 130-131 D 2
Karak o MAL 162-163 E 3
Kara-Kabak o KS 136-137 N 5
Kara-Kala o TM 136-137 E 5
Karakamys o KA 96-97 H 10
Karakax He ~ VRC 138-139 F 1
Karakax He ~ VRC 144-145 B 2
Karakaya Barajı < TR 128-129 H 3
Karakeçi o TR 128-129 H 4
Karakeču ∸ KA 126-127 K 5
Karakelong, Kepulauan ⌒ RI 164-165 K 1
Kara-Kengir ~ KA 124-125 E 4
Karaketang, Pulau ⌒ RI 164-165 J 2
Karaklis o AR 128-129 L 2
Karakoçan ☆ TR 128-129 J 3
Karakojyn, köl ○ KA 124-125 F 5
Karaköl o KA (GUR) 96-97 H 9
Karaköl o KA (KZL) 126-127 O 5
Karaköl o KA (KZL) 124-125 D 6
Karakol o KS 146-147 C 5
Karaköl, köl ~ KA 126-127 N 3
Karakoram ▲ IND 138-139 E 1
Karakoro o ETH 208-209 D 3
Karakoro ~ RMM 202-203 E 2
Karakorum Highway II PK 138-139 E 1
Karakovaja ~ RUS 120-121 S 6
Karaktau, gory ▲ KA 136-137 K 3
Kara-Kudžur ~ KS 146-147 C 5
Kara-Kul' o KS 136-137 N 4
Karakul' o TJ 136-137 N 5
Karakul' o US 136-137 H 5
Karakul', ozero ○ TJ 136-137 N 5
Kara-Kul'dža o KS 136-137 N 4
Karakulino o RUS 96-97 H 5
Karaküm ∸ KA 96-97 H 10
Karaküm ∸ KA 96-97 H 10
Karakum ∸ KA 124-125 E 5
Kara Kum = Garagum ∸ TM 136-137 E 4
Karakumskij kanal < TM (ASH) 136-137 E 5
Karakumskij kanal < TM (MAR) 136-137 H 6
Karal o TCH 198-199 G 6
Karaľka ~ RUS 114-115 R 3
Karalundi Mission o AUS 176-177 E 3
Karam o RUS 116-117 N 8
Karama ~ RI 164-165 F 5
Karamadai o IND 140-141 G 5
Karaman ☆ TR 128-129 E 4
Karamanbeyli Geçidi ▲ TR 128-129 D 4
Karamay o VRC 146-147 G 3
Karambu o RI 164-165 E 5
Karamea o NZ 182 D 4
Karamea Bight ≈ 182 C 4
Karamet-Nijaz o TM 136-137 J 6
Karami, River ~ WAN 204-205 H 3
Karamian, Pulau ⌒ RI 164-165 D 6
Karamiran o VRC 144-145 E 2
Karamiran He ~ VRC 144-145 E 2
Karamken o RUS 120-121 O 3
Karamoja □ EAU 208-209 B 6
Karamor, Pegunungan ▲ RI 166-167 K 3
Karamyk o KS 136-137 M 5
Karamyševo o RUS 116-117 K 7
Karān ⌒ KSA 130-131 L 4
Karang o SN 202-203 B 3
Karangampel o RI 168 C 3
Karanganyar o RI 168 D 3
Karangasem o • RI 168 B 7
Karangbotolo, Tanjung ▲ RI 168 C 3
Karanggede o RI 168 D 3
Karangjati o RI 168 D 3
Karangnunggal o RI 168 C 3
Karangoua ~ RCB 210-211 D 3
Karangpandan o RI 168 D 3
Karangua o Z 214-215 D 7
Karanguana o RMM 202-203 H 3
Karanji o IND 138-139 G 9
Karanpur o IND 138-139 D 5
Karaoba o KA 126-127 M 4
Karaoj o KA 124-125 J 6
Karap o PNG 183 C 3
Karapınar ☆ TR 128-129 E 4
Karapuz ~ RUS 114-115 P 7
Karara o AUS 178-179 L 5
Kararaô, Área Indígena ⊼ BR 68-69 B 4
Karas, Pulau ⌒ RI 166-167 G 3
Kara-Saj o KS 146-147 C 5
Kara-Saľ ~ RUS 102-103 N 4
Karasavvon o FIN 88-89 G 2
Karasburg ☆ NAM 220-221 D 4
Karas'e, ozero Bol'šoe ○ RUS 114-115 J 5
Kara Sea = Karskoe more ≈ RUS 10-11 F 1
Karašek, Ozero = köl Karacek ○ KA 126-127 L 6
Karasjok o N 86-87 M 2
Karašjokka ~ N 86-87 M 2
Karasoľ, köli ○ KA 124-125 K 3
Karasoľ, ozero = Köli Karasor ○ KA 124-125 K 3
Karasor, köli ○ KA 124-125 J 4
Karasor, köli ○ KA 124-125 J 4
Karasor, ozero = köli Karasor ○ KA 124-125 J 4
Karasu ☆ TR 128-129 D 2
Karasu ~ TR 128-129 K 3
Karasu-Aras Dağları ▲ TR 128-129 J 3
Karasu Çayı ~ TR 128-129 G 4
Karasuk ☆ RUS 124-125 L 2
Karasuk Hills ▲ EAK 212-213 E 2
Kara-Suu o KS 136-137 N 4
Karāt o IR 134-135 J 1
Karatajka o RUS 108-109 J 7
Karatal ~ KA 124-125 K 6
Karatas o KA 136-137 L 4
Karatas o KA 136-137 L 4
Karataş ☆ TR 128-129 F 4
Karataš, gora ▲ RUS 96-97 L 7
Karatau o KA 136-137 L 3
Karatau o KA (DZM) 136-137 M 3
Karatau ▲ KA 126-127 J 5
Karatau, hrebet ▲ KA 124-125 E 6
Karatau, žota ▲ KA 124-125 E 6
Karatau hrebet ▲ RUS 96-97 K 6
Karatina o EAK 212-213 F 4
Karatöbe ☆ KA 96-97 H 9
Karatogaj o KA 124-125 O 4
Karaton o KA 96-97 H 10
Kara-Torgaj ~ KA 124-125 E 4
Karats o S 86-87 J 3
Karatsu o J 152-153 C 8
Karatu o EAT 212-213 E 5
Karatulej, sor ∸ KA 126-127 L 5
Karatung, Pulau ⌒ RI 164-165 K 1
Karaudanawa o GUY 62-63 E 4
Karaul o KA 124-125 L 4
Karaul o RUS 108-109 U 6
Karaulbazar o US 136-137 J 5
Karauli o IND 138-139 F 6
Karaungir ∸ KA 124-125 J 5
Karauwi o PNG 183 C 4
Karavan o KS 136-137 M 4
Karavānsarāy-ye Šams o IR 134-135 F 3
Karavás o GR 100-101 J 6
Karawa o ZRE 210-211 H 2
Karawanella o CL 140-141 J 7
Karawang o RI 168 B 3
Karawang, Tanjung ▲ RI 168 B 2
Karawanken ▲ A 92-93 M 5
Karawari River ~ PNG 183 B 3
Karayazı ☆ TR 128-129 K 3
Karaye o WAN 204-205 H 3
Karayulgun o VRC 146-147 E 5
Karažal o KA 124-125 G 5
Karažal o KA 124-125 G 4
Karbalā' ☆ IRQ 128-129 J 6
Karbalā' ☆ IRQ (KAR) 128-129 L 6
Karböle o S 86-87 G 6
Karbulik o RUS 116-117 O 9
Karchat o PK 134-135 M 6
Karda o RUS 116-117 L 8
Kardakāta o GR 100-101 H 5
Kardeljevo = Ploče o HR 100-101 F 3
Karditsa o GR 100-101 H 5
Kardiva Channel ≈ 140-141 B 5
Kärdla ☆ EST 94-95 H 2
Kărdžali o BG 102-103 D 7
Kărdžali o BG 102-103 D 7
Karé, Monts ▲ RCA 206-207 C 5
Kareeberge ▲ ZA 220-221 F 5
Kareebospoort ▲ ZA 220-221 F 5
Karegari o PNG 183 B 3
Karelia = Karelija ∸ 94-95 L 1
Karelia = Karelija, Respublika □ RUS 88-89 M 5
Karelka ~ RUS 108-109 E 5
Karel'skij bereg ⌣ RUS 88-89 M 3
Karema o EAT 214-215 F 4
Karema o PNG 183 D 5
Karenga ~ RUS 118-119 H 8
Karenga, Ust'- o RUS 118-119 H 8
Karengi o WAN 204-205 E 3
Karera o IND 138-139 G 7
Karesuando o S 86-87 L 2
Kārevāndar o IR 134-135 J 5
Kargal o IND 140-141 F 3
Kargala o RUS 114-115 R 6
Kargala o RUS (ORB) 96-97 H 8
Kargalinskaja o RUS 126-127 G 6
Kargalytau ▲ KA 126-127 P 2
Kargapol'e ☆ RUS 114-115 H 6
Kargasok ☆ RUS 114-115 Q 5
Kargat ☆ RUS 114-115 Q 7
Kargat ~ RUS 114-115 Q 7
Kargat, Forpost- o RUS 114-115 Q 7
Kargı ☆ TR 128-129 F 2
Kargil o IND 138-139 F 2
Kargopol' ☆ RUS 88-89 P 6

Karguéri o RN 198-199 E 6
Karhe, Rūd-e ~ IR 134-135 C 3
Karhe, Rūdḫāne-ye ~ IR 134-135 D 3
Kari o WAN 204-205 J 3
Karia o PNG 183 F 2
Karianga o RM 222-223 E 9
Kariba o ZW 218-219 E 3
Kariba, Lake < Z 218-219 D 3
Kariba-yama ▲ J 152-153 H 3
Karibib ☆ NAM 216-217 C 10
Karie o SOL 184 I f 4
Kariega ~ ZA 220-221 F 6
Kariés o GR 100-101 K 4
Karigasniemi o FIN 88-89 H 2
Karikachi-tōge ▲ J 152-153 K 3
Kārikāl o IND 140-141 H 5
Karikari, Cape ▲ NZ 182 D 1
Karilatsi o EST 94-95 K 2
Karima o SUD 200-201 E 3
Karimabad o• IND 138-139 E 1
Karimama o DY 204-205 E 2
Karimata, Pulau ⌒ RI 162-163 H 5
Karimata Kepulauan ⌒ RI 162-163 H 5
Karimata Strait = Karimata, Selat ≈ 162-163 G 5
Karimbola ⊥ RM 222-223 D 10
Karimganj o IND 142-143 H 3
Karimnagar o IND 138-139 G 10
Karimui o PNG 183 C 4
Karimui, Mount ▲ PNG 183 C 4
Karimun, Pulau ⌒ RI 162-163 E 4
Karimunjawa, Kepulauan ⌒ RI 168 D 2
Karin o SP 208-209 G 3
Karina o WAL 202-203 E 5
Karipuna, Área Indígena ✕ BR 66-67 E 7
Karisimbi, Mount ▲ RWA 212-213 B 4
Káristos o GR 100-101 K 5
Karitiana, Área Indígena ✕ BR 66-67 E 7
Kariya o J 152-153 G 7
Kāriyāpatti o IND 140-141 H 6
Karjala ⊥ FIN 88-89 K 6
Karjat o IND 138-139 E 10
Karkabane, Hâssi < RMM 196-197 K 6
Kārkal o IND 140-141 F 4
Karkar o PNG 183 C 3
Karkaralinsk = Qarqaraly o KA 124-125 J 4
Karkaraly o KA 124-125 J 4
Karkar Island ⌒ PNG 183 D 3
Karkas, Kūh-e ▲ IR 134-135 D 2
Karkh o PK 134-135 M 5
Karkinits'ka zatoka ≈ 102-103 H 5
Karkonosze ▲ PL 92-93 N 3
Karksi-Nuia o•• EST 94-95 J 2
Karla-Aleksandra, ostrov ⌒ RUS 84-85 e 2
Karlaralong, Kepulauan ⌒ RI 164-165 J 1
Karleby = Kokkola o FIN 88-89 G 5
Karlik ▲ VRC 146-147 L 4
Karlıova ☆ TR 128-129 J 3
Karlivka o UA 102-103 J 3
Karl-Marx-Stadt = Chemnitz o D 92-93 M 3
Karlobag o HR 100-101 E 2
Karlo-Libknehtovsk = Soledar o UA 102-103 L 3
Karlovac o HR 100-101 E 2
Karlovássi o GR 100-101 L 6
Karlovo o BG 102-103 D 6
Karlovy Vary o CZ 92-93 M 3
Karlsbad = Karlovy Vary o CZ 92-93 M 3
Karlsborg ☆ S 86-87 G 7
Karlsena, mys ▲ RUS 108-109 M 3
Karlshamn ☆ S 86-87 G 8
Karlskoga ☆ S 86-87 G 7
Karlskrona ☆• S 86-87 G 8
Karlsruhe o• D 92-93 K 4
Karlsruhe o USA (ND) 258-259 G 3
Karlstad ☆•• S 86-87 F 7
Karlstad o USA (MN) 270-271 B 2
Karlstadt o• D 92-93 K 4
Karlštejn • CZ 92-93 O 4
Karluk o USA 22-23 T 4
Karma o RN 202-203 L 3
Karma ~ TCH 206-207 C 3
Karmah o• SUD 200-201 E 3
Karmāla o• IND 138-139 E 10
Karmaskaly ☆ RUS 96-97 K 6
Karmé o TCH 198-199 G 6
Karmelitskyj monastyr • UA 102-103 E 3
Karmina ☆ US 136-137 J 4
Karmøy ⌒ N 86-87 B 7
Karnak, al- o•• ET 194-195 F 5
Karnāl o IND 138-139 F 5
Karnali ~ NEP 144-145 C 6
Karnaou ▲ TCH 198-199 H 2
Karnaphuli ~ BD 142-143 G 4
Karnataka □ IND 140-141 F 3
Karnataka Plateau ▲ IND 140-141 F 2
Karnes City o USA (TX) 266-267 K 5
Karnobat o BG 102-103 E 6
Karnprayāg o IND 138-139 G 4
Kärnten □ A 92-93 M 5
Karo Batak House • RI 162-163 C 3
Karoi o ZW 218-219 E 3
Karo La ▲ VRC 144-145 H 6
Karolinen ⌒ FSM 13 F 2
Karoma, Mount ▲ PNG 183 B 3
Karonga o MW 214-215 G 5
Karoni, Gunung ▲ RI 164-165 G 5
Karonie o AUS 176-177 G 5
Karoo National Park ⊥ ZA 220-221 F 6
Karoonda o AUS 180-181 E 3
Karor o PK 138-139 C 4
Karora o SUD 200-201 J 4
Karosa o RI 164-165 F 4
Karoso, Tanjung ▲ RI 168 D 7
Karpathio Pélagos ≈ 100-101 L 6
Kárpathos o GR 100-101 L 7
Kárpathos ⌒ GR 100-101 L 7
Karpenissi o GR 100-101 H 5
Karpinsk o RUS 114-115 F 5
Karpinskogo, vulkan ▲ RUS 122-123 Q 3
Karpogory o RUS 88-89 S 4
Karpuzlu ☆ TR 128-129 B 4
Karpysak o RUS 114-115 R 7
Karratha o AUS 172-173 C 6
Karratha Roadhouse o AUS 172-173 C 6
Karrats Fjord ≈ 26-27 Y 8
Karredouw o ZA 220-221 G 6
Karridale o AUS 176-177 C 7
Kars ☆• TR 128-129 K 2
Karsakbaj o KA 124-125 E 5
Kärsämäki o FIN 88-89 H 5
Kārsava o LV 94-95 K 3
Karshi o WAN 204-205 G 4
Karši ☆ US 136-137 J 5
Karšinskaja step' ⊥ US 136-137 J 5
Karsk, Ust'- o RUS 118-119 J 9
Karskie Vorota, proliv ≈ 108-109 G 6
Karskiye Vorota, Proliv = Karskie Vorota, proliv ≈ RUS 108-109 G 6
Karsrivierviei o ZA 220-221 E 7
Kartabu o GUY 62-63 E 2
Kartabyz, ozero o RUS 114-115 G 7
Kartaěľ o RUS 88-89 W 4
Kartaly ☆ RUS 124-125 B 2
Karte Conservation Park ⊥ AUS 180-181 F 3
Karthala ▲ COM 222-223 C 3
Karti o IR 134-135 H 6
Kartosuro o RI 168 D 3
Kartuzy o• PL 92-93 P 1
Karu o PNG 183 G 2
Karubaga o RI 166-167 K 3
Karubeamsberge ▲ NAM 220-221 C 1
Karufa o RI 166-167 G 3
Karuḥ o• AFG 134-135 K 1
Karumba o AUS 174-175 F 5
Kārumbhar Island ⌒ IND 138-139 B 8
Karumei o J 152-153 J 4
Karumwa o EAT 212-213 D 5
Kārūn, Kūh-e ▲ IR 134-135 D 3
Kārūn, Rūd-e ~ IR 134-135 C 3
Karungu o EAK 212-213 E 4
Karūr o IND 140-141 H 5
Karuzi o BU 212-213 C 5
Karval o USA (CO) 254-255 M 5
Karviná o CZ 92-93 P 4
Karwai o RI 166-167 H 4
Kārwār o IND 140-141 F 3
Karwin = Karviná o CZ 92-93 P 4
Karymskoe ☆ RUS 118-119 G 10
Karyngürly ⊥ KA 126-127 L 6
Karynžaryk ⊥ KA 126-127 K 6
Kas ~ RUS 116-117 E 6
Kas o SUD 200-201 B 6
Kaş ☆•• TR 128-129 C 4
Kasa o RP 160-161 D 3
Kasa o VRC 154-155 B 6
Kasa o ZRE 210-211 G 4
Kasaan Bay ≈ 32-33 D 4
Kasaba o Z 214-215 E 6
Kasabi o ZRE 214-215 E 5
Kasabonika o CDN 34-35 M 4
Kasaf Rūd ~ IR 136-137 G 6
Kasah ~ AR 128-129 L 2
Kasai o J 152-153 F 7
Kasai ~ ZRE 210-211 G 5
Kasai-Occidental □ ZRE 210-211 H 6
Kasai-Oriental □ ZRE 210-211 J 5
Kasaji o ZRE 214-215 B 6
Kāsa Khurd o IND 138-139 D 10
Kasāl o IND 140-141 E 2
Kasalu o Z 218-219 D 2
Kasama ☆ Z 214-215 F 6
Kāsān o• IR 134-135 D 2
Kašan ~ TM 136-137 H 7
Kasan o US 136-137 J 5
Kasane ☆ RB 218-219 C 3
Kasanga o EAT 214-215 F 5
Kasangulu o ZRE 210-211 E 6
Kasanka National Park ⊥ Z 214-215 F 7
Kasansaj o US 136-137 M 4
Kasanza o ZRE 214-215 B 4
Kāsaragod o IND 140-141 F 4
Kasari o J 152-153 C 10
Kasaro ~ SUD 200-201 F 6
Kasasi o WAL 202-203 E 5
Kasatochi Island ⌒ USA 22-23 J 6
Kasbahs, Route des • MA 188-189 H 5
Kasba Lake o CDN 30-31 S 5
Kasba-Tadla o MA 188-189 H 4
Kascjukovičy o BY 94-95 N 5
Kasdir < DZ 188-189 L 4
Kaseda o J 152-153 D 9
Kasegaluk Lagoon ≈ 20-21 J 2
Kasei ~ ZRE 216-217 F 3
Kasempa o Z 218-219 C 1
Kasenga o ZRE (SHA) 214-215 B 6
Kasenga o ZRE (SHA) 214-215 E 6
Kasenge o ZRE 210-211 G 4
Kasengo o ZRE 212-213 C 2
Kasenye o ZRE 212-213 C 3
Kasese o EAU 212-213 C 3
Kasese o ZRE 212-213 A 4
Kaset Wisai o THA 158-159 G 3
Kaseyville o USA (MO) 274-275 F 5
Kashabowie o CDN (ONT) 234-235 N 6
Kashechewan o CDN 34-35 Q 4
Kashega o USA 22-23 N 6
Kashi o• VRC 146-147 C 6
Kashileshi ~ ZRE 214-215 B 6
Kashima o J 152-153 J 7
Kashima-nada ≈ 152-153 J 6
Kashinatpur o BD 142-143 F 4
Kāshipur o IND 138-139 G 5
Kashiwa o J 152-153 H 7
Kashiwazaki o J 152-153 H 6
Kāshmor o PK 138-139 B 5
Kashnuk River ~ USA 20-21 H 6
Kashwal o SUD 206-207 J 5
Kasi ~ RI 166-167 G 2
Kasidishi ~ ZRE 214-215 B 6
Kasigau ▲ EAK 212-213 G 5
Kasigluk o USA 20-21 J 6
Kasimbar o RI 164-165 G 4
Kasimov o RUS 94-95 R 4
Kašin ☆• RUS 94-95 P 3
Kasindi o ZRE 212-213 B 3
Kasingie o MW 218-219 H 2
Kašira ☆• RUS 94-95 Q 4
Kasiruta, Pulau ⌒ RI 164-165 K 4
Kasiui, Pulau ⌒ RI 166-167 F 4
Kaskabulak o KA 124-125 L 4
Kaškadar'inskaja oblast' □ US 136-137 J 5
Kaškadar'ja ~ US 136-137 J 5
Kaškān, Rūdḫāne-ye ~ IR 134-135 B 2
Kaškarancy o RUS 88-89 O 3
Kaskas o SN 196-197 C 6
Kaskaskia River ~ USA (IL) 274-275 J 6
Kaskaskia River State Fish and Wildlife Area ⊥ USA (IL) 274-275 J 6
Kaskaskia State Historic Site, Fort • USA (IL) 274-275 J 6
Kaškasu o KS 146-147 B 5
Kaskattama River ~ CDN 34-35 L 2
Ķaskelen o KA 146-147 C 4
Ķaskelen ~ KA 146-147 C 4
Kaskelen = Ķaskelen o KA 146-147 C 4
Kaskelen = Ķaskelen ~ KA 146-147 C 4
Kaskinen o FIN 88-89 F 5
Kaskö = Kaskinen o FIN 88-89 F 5
Kasli ☆ RUS 96-97 M 6
Kaslo o CDN (BC) 230-231 N 4
Kāšmar o IR 136-137 F 7
Kasmere Lake o CDN 30-31 T 6
Kasompe o Z 218-219 C 1
Kasongo o ZRE 210-211 L 6
Kasongo-Lunda o ZRE 216-217 D 3
Kasongo-Lunda, Chutes ~ ZRE 216-217 D 3
Kasouga o ZA 220-221 H 6
Kaspi o GE 126-127 F 7
Kaspij many sineklizasy = Prikaspijskaja nizmennost' ⊥ RUS 126-127 F 5
Kaspijsk o RUS 126-127 G 6
Kaspijskij = Lagan' ☆ RUS 126-127 G 5
Kasr, Ra's ▲ SUD 200-201 J 3
Kassa o DY 204-205 E 3
Kassalā ☆• SUD 200-201 H 5
Kassama o RMM 202-203 E 3
Kassándra ~ GR 100-101 J 5
Kassándras, Kólpos ≈ 100-101 J 4
Kassándria o GR 100-101 J 4
Kassel o• D 92-93 K 3
Kasséré o CI 202-203 G 5
Kasserine ☆ TN 190-191 G 3
Kassipute o RI 164-165 H 6
Kassler o USA (CO) 254-255 K 4
Kássos ⌒ GR 100-101 L 7
Kassoum o BF 202-203 J 3
Kastamonu ☆• TR 128-129 E 2
Kastéli o GR 100-101 J 7
Kastoriá o GR 100-101 H 4
Kasuga o J (FKA) 152-153 D 8
Kasuga o J (HYO) 152-153 F 7
Kasuku ~ ZRE 210-211 K 4
Kasuku, Lac o ZRE 210-211 K 5
Kasulu o EAT 212-213 C 6
Kasumba o ZRE 214-215 D 7
Kasumi o J 152-153 F 7
Kasumiga-ura-ura o J 152-153 J 6
Kasumkent o RUS 126-127 H 7
Kasumpti o IND 138-139 F 4
Kasungu o MW 218-219 G 1
Kasungu National Park ⊥ MW 214-215 G 7
Kasūr o PK 138-139 E 4
Kat o IR 134-135 C 3
Kata ~ RUS 116-117 L 6
Kataba o Z 218-219 C 3
Katabaie o ZRE 214-215 B 4
Katagum o WAN 198-199 E 6
Katagum, River ~ WAN 204-205 H 3
Katahdin, Mount ▲ USA (ME) 278-279 N 3
Katajsk ☆ RUS 114-115 G 6
Kataka o IND 142-143 D 5
Katakakishi o ZRE 214-215 B 5
Katako-Kombe o ZRE 210-211 K 5
Katako o RI 168 D 7
Katakwi o EAU 212-213 D 3
Katalah o RUS 118-119 N 6
Katamatite o AUS 180-181 H 4
Katana o RI 164-165 L 3
Katana o ZRE 212-213 B 5
Katanda o ZRE 214-215 B 4
Katanga ~ RUS 116-117 L 6
Katangi o IND 138-139 G 8
Katangi o IND 138-139 G 9
Katanning o AUS 176-177 D 6
Kataouâne o RIM 196-197 G 6
Kataramba ~ RUS 116-117 H 4
Katavi National Park ⊥ EAT 214-215 F 4
Katav-Ivanovsk ☆ RUS 96-97 L 6
Katcha o WAN 204-205 G 4
Katchall Island ⌒ IND 140-141 L 6
Katchamba o RT 202-203 L 5
Katchirga o BF 202-203 L 2
Kateel River ~ USA 20-21 L 4
Kateman, Pulau ⌒ RI 162-163 E 4
Katemcy o USA (TX) 266-267 H 3
Katende o ZRE 214-215 B 4
Katende, Chutes de ~ ZRE 214-215 B 4
Katenge o ZRE 214-215 B 4
Katenge o ZRE 212-213 B 6
Katepwa Beach o CDN (SAS) 232-233 P 5
Katere o NAM 216-217 F 9
Katerini o GR 100-101 J 4
Katesh o EAT 212-213 E 6
Katete o Z 218-219 G 2
Katha o MYA 142-143 K 3
Kathang o IND 142-143 K 2
Kathangor, Ǧabal ▲ SUD 208-209 A 6
Kathawachaga Lake o CDN 30-31 O 2
Katherine o AUS 172-173 L 3
Katherine River ~ AUS 172-173 K 3
Kāthiāwār Peninsula ⌒ IND 138-139 B 8
Kathleen Lake o CDN (ONT) 236-237 E 5
Kathmandu ☆••• NEP 144-145 E 7
Kathu o ZA 220-221 F 3
Kathua o IND 138-139 E 3
Kati ~ NEP 144-145 C 6
Kati o RMM 202-203 F 3
Katiali o CI 202-203 G 5
Katiati o PNG 183 C 3
Katīb, Ra's al- ▲ Y 132-133 C 6
Katiéna o RMM 202-203 H 3
Katihar o IND 142-143 E 3
Katima Mulilo ☆ NAM 218-219 C 3
Katimik Lake o CDN (MAN) 234-235 D 2
Katini o ZRE 216-217 E 3
Katiola ☆ CI 202-203 H 5
Katios, Parque Nacional los ⊥ CO 60-61 C 4
Katiti Aboriginal Land ✕ AUS 176-177 L 2
Katla o SUD 206-207 J 3
Katlanovo o MK 100-101 H 4
Katmai, Mount ▲ USA 22-23 T 3
Katmai National Park and Preserve ⊥ USA 22-23 T 3
Katmay Bay ≈ 22-23 T 4
Kato o GUY 62-63 E 3
Katoa o TCH 206-207 B 3
Kátoda o IND 138-139 E 7
Káto Glikóvrisi o GR 100-101 J 6
Kátol o IND 138-139 G 9
Katombe o ZRE 210-211 H 6
Katompi o ZRE 214-215 D 4
Katonga ~ EAU 212-213 C 3
Katon-Karagaj o KA 124-125 O 4
Katoomba-Wentworth Falls o AUS 180-181 L 2
Katoposo, Gunung ▲ RI 164-165 G 4
Káto Soúnio o GR 100-101 K 6
Katoto o EAT 212-213 C 6
Katowice ☆•• PL 92-93 P 3
Katoya o IND 142-143 F 4
Katrancık Dağı ▲ TR 128-129 D 4
Katrina, Ǧabal ▲ ET 194-195 F 3
Katrineholm ☆ S 86-87 H 7
Katse o EAK 212-213 G 4
Katséna ~ CAM 204-205 J 5
Katsepy o RM 222-223 E 5
Katsina o WAN 198-199 C 6
Katsina □ WAN 198-199 C 6
Katsina-Ala o WAN 204-205 H 5
Katsina-Ala, River ~ WAN 204-205 H 5
Katsumoto o J 152-153 C 8
Katsuta o J 152-153 J 6
Katsuura o J (CHI) 152-153 J 7
Katsuura o J (WAK) 152-153 F 8
Kattakišlok o US 136-137 K 5
Kattakurgan = Kattaķūrgon o US 136-137 K 5
Kattaķūrgon o US 136-137 K 5
Kattankudi o CL 140-141 J 7
Kattarakara o IND 140-141 G 6
Kattavia o GR 100-101 L 7
Kattawagami Lake o CDN (ONT) 236-237 H 3
Kattawagami River ~ CDN (ONT) 236-237 H 2
Kattegat ≈ 86-87 E 8
Katterjåkk o S 86-87 J 2
Kättupputtūr o IND 140-141 H 5
Katumbi o MW 214-215 G 6
Katun' ~ RUS 124-125 P 3
Katundu o Z 218-219 C 3
Katunguru o EAU 212-213 C 4
Katunskij hrebet ▲ RUS 124-125 O 3
Katupa o RI 168 D 7
Kātūria o IND 142-143 E 3
Katwe o EAU 212-213 B 4
Katwe o ZRE 214-215 B 5
Katy o USA (TX) 268-269 E 7
Katym ~ RUS 114-115 K 5
Kau o RI 164-165 K 3
Kau, Teluk ≈ 164-165 K 3
Kauai ⌒ USA (HI) 288 F 2
Kauai Channel ≈ 48-49 C 7
Kauai Channel ≈ USA 288 G 3
Kauara o CI 202-203 H 4
Kaubi o PNG 183 F 3
Kaudom o NAM 216-217 F 9
Kaudom ~ NAM 216-217 F 9
Kaudom Game Park ⊥ NAM 216-217 F 9
Kaufbeuren o• D 92-93 L 5
Kaufman o USA (TX) 264-265 H 6
Kaugel River ~ PNG 183 C 4
Kauhajoki o FIN 88-89 G 5
Kauhava o FIN 88-89 G 5
Kaukas o RI 164-165 H 4
Kaukauna o USA (WI) 270-271 K 6
Kaukauveld ⊥ NAM 216-217 F 9
Kauksi o• EST 94-95 K 2
Kaula ⌒ USA (HI) 288 E 3
Kaulakahi Channel ≈ 48-49 B 6
Kaulakahi Channel ≈ USA 288 E 2
Kaulžur ~ KA 126-127 N 3
Kaumalapau Harbor o USA (HI) 288 J 4
Kauman o RI 168 E 3
Kaunakakai o• USA (HI) 288 H 3
Kauna Point ▲ USA (HI) 288 K 5
Kaunas ☆•• LT 94-95 H 4
Kaundy, vpadina ⊥ KA 126-127 K 6
Kaunolu o• USA (HI) 288 J 4
Kaup o PNG 183 B 2
Kaupanger o N 86-87 C 6
Kaupena o PNG 183 C 4
Kaupo o USA (HI) 288 J 4
Kaurai o PNG 183 G 5
Kauro ~ EAK 212-213 F 3
Kaušany = Căușeni ☆ MD 102-103 F 4
Kaustinen o FIN 88-89 G 5
Kautokeino o N 86-87 L 2
Kauur o WAG 202-203 C 3
Kauwa o WAN 198-199 F 6
Kau-Ye Kyun ⌒ MYA 158-159 E 5
Kava ~ RUS 120-121 M 4
Kavadarci o MK 100-101 J 4
Kavak ☆ TR 128-129 G 2
Kavála o GR 100-101 K 4
Kavalerovo o RUS 122-123 F 6
Kavalga Island ⌒ USA 22-23 G 7
Kāvali o IND 140-141 J 3
Kavār o IR 134-135 E 4
Kavaratti o IND 140-141 E 5
Kavendu ▲ RG 202-203 D 4
Kavi o IND 138-139 D 8
Kavieng ☆ PNG 183 F 2
Kavigyalik Lake o USA 20-21 J 6
Kavik River ~ USA 20-21 R 2
Kavinga o Z 214-215 G 7
Kavīr, Dašt-e ⊥ IR 134-135 E 1
Kavkazskij zapovednik ⊥ RUS 126-127 D 6
Kávos o GR 100-101 H 5
Kavrizhka, Cape ▲ USA 22-23 N 6
Kavuu ~ EAT 214-215 F 4
Kawa o CDN (ONT) 234-235 O 4
Kawa o RI 166-167 E 3
Kawa ~ RI 166-167 E 3
Kawa, Temple of • SUD 200-201 E 3
Kawagit o RI 166-167 L 4
Kawagoe o J 152-153 H 7
Kawaguchi o J 152-153 H 7
Kawaihae o• USA (HI) 288 K 4
Kawaihae Bay ≈ USA 288 L 4
Kawaihoa Point ▲ USA (HI) 288 E 3
Kawaikini ▲ USA (HI) 288 F 2
Kawajena o SUD 206-207 J 5
Kawakawa o NZ 182 E 1
Kawala o MYA 142-143 J 2
Kawali o RI 168 C 3
Kawambwa o Z 214-215 E 5
Kawana o Z 218-219 C 1
Kawanee o USA (MO) 276-277 F 4
Kawangko o RI 168 D 7
Kawangkoan o RI 164-165 J 3
Kawanoe o J 152-153 E 7
Kawant o IND 138-139 E 8
Kawardha o IND 142-143 B 4
Kawarga ~ RI 166-167 K 5
Kawartha Lakes o CDN (ONT) 238-239 G 4
Kawasa o ZRE 214-215 E 5
Kawasaki o J 152-153 H 7
Kawatipoli o MYA 142-143 K 6
Kawauchi o J 152-153 J 4
Kawau Island ⌒ NZ 182 E 2
Kawaya o ZRE 214-215 E 5
Kawayan o RP 160-161 F 7
Kawayu o J 152-153 L 3
Kawe, Pulau ⌒ RI 166-167 F 2
Kaweah, Lake o USA (CA) 248-249 F 3
Kaweka ▲ NZ 182 F 3
Kawembwe o Z 214-215 F 6
Kawene o CDN (ONT) 234-235 M 6
Kawentinkim o RI 166-167 L 4
Kawe Rapids ~ Z 218-219 F 2
Kawhia o NZ 182 E 3
Kawich Peak ▲ USA (NV) 246-247 J 5
Kawich Peak ▲ USA (NV) 248-249 H 2
Kawinaw Lake o CDN (MAN) 234-235 D 2
Kawkawlin o USA (MI) 272-273 F 4
Kawkpalut o MYA 158-159 E 2
Kawkwareik o MYA 158-159 E 2
Kawlin o MYA 142-143 J 4
Kawltang o MYA 142-143 J 3
Kaw Reservoir o USA (OK) 264-265 H 2
Kaxarari, Área Indígena ✕ BR 66-67 D 7
Kaxgar He ~ VRC 146-147 C 6
Kax He ~ VRC 146-147 F 4
Kaxian D. ∴• VRC 150-151 D 2
Kaxinawá Nova Olinda, Área Indígena ✕ BR 66-67 B 7
Kaxinawá do Rio Humaitá, Área Indígena ✕ BR 66-67 B 7
Kaxinawá do Rio Jordão, Área Indígena ✕ BR 64-65 F 6
Kaya ☆ BF 202-203 K 3
Kayaapu o RI 162-163 F 7
Kayabi, Área Indígena ✕ BR 70-71 J 2
Kayak Island ⌒ USA 20-21 S 7
Kayambi o Z 214-215 G 5
Kayan ~ RI 164-165 E 3
Kayanga ~ SN 202-203 C 3
Kāyankulam o IND 140-141 G 6
Kayanza o BU 212-213 B 5
Kayapó, Área Indígena ✕ BR 68-69 B 5
Kayar o SN 202-203 B 2
Kayasa o RI 164-165 K 3
Kayattār o IND 140-141 G 6
Kaycee o USA (WY) 252-253 M 3
Kaye, Mount ▲ AUS 180-181 K 4
Kayedon Lake o CDN (ONT) 236-237 B 2
Kayeli o RI 166-167 D 3
Kayembe-Mukulu o ZRE 214-215 B 5
Kayenta o USA (AZ) 256-257 E 2
Kayenzi o EAT 212-213 D 5
Kayes □ RMM 202-203 E 3
Kayes ☆ RMM 202-203 E 2
Kayima o WAL 202-203 E 5
Kaymor o SN 202-203 C 3
Kaynabayongo o ZRE 212-213 B 4
Kayoa, Pulau ⌒ RI 164-165 K 3
Kayokwe o BU 212-213 B 5
Kayonza o RWA 212-213 C 4
Kay Point ▲ CDN 20-21 W 2
Kayrunnera o AUS 178-179 G 6
Kayseri ☆•• TR 128-129 F 3
Kayuadi, Pulau ⌒ RI 168 E 6
Kayuagung o RI 162-163 F 6
Kayuku o RI 164-165 G 4
Kayupangang, Pulau ⌒ RI 168 D 6
Kayuyu o ZRE 210-211 L 5
Kayville o CDN (SAS) 232-233 N 6
Kazabazua o CDN (QUE) 238-239 J 3
Kazača Lopan' o UA 102-103 K 2
Kazač'e o RUS 110-111 V 4
Kazačinskoe ☆ RUS 116-117 F 7
Kazah o• AZ 128-129 L 2
Kazahdar'ja o US 136-137 F 3
Kazahskij zaliv ≈ 126-127 K 6
Kazakhstan = Ķazaķstan ■ KA 126-127 K 3
Kazakh Uplands = Saryarķa ⊥ KA 124-125 G 4
Kazak'jaha ~ RUS 108-109 V 6
Kazamabika o G 210-211 C 4
Kazan' ☆• RUS 96-97 F 6
Kazandžik = Gazanǧyk o TM 136-137 D 5
Kazanlăk o••• BG 102-103 D 6
Kazan River ~ CDN 30-31 V 4
Kazanskoe ☆ RUS 114-115 K 7
Kazantips'ka zatoka ≈ 102-103 J 5
Kazarman o KS 146-147 B 5
Kazas ~ RUS 116-117 H 9
Kazaure o WAN 198-199 D 6
Kazbegi o GE 126-127 F 6
Kazbek, gora ▲ GE 126-127 F 6
Kaz Dağı ▲ TR 128-129 B 3
Kazer • TCH 198-199 J 3
Kazer, Pico ▲ RCH 80 G 7
Kāzerūn o IR 134-135 D 4
Kāzi Ahmad o PK 138-139 B 6
Kazibacna ~ BD 142-143 F 4
Kazıklı Çayı ~ TR 128-129 G 3
Kazil'skoe ☆ RUS 96-97 L 7
Kazi-Magomed o AZ 128-129 N 2
Kāzimiya, al- o IRQ 128-129 L 6
Kâzımkarabekir ☆• TR 128-129 E 4
Kaziranga National Park ⊥••• IND 142-143 H 2
Kaziza o ZRE 214-215 B 6
Kaznakovka o KA 124-125 N 4
Ķaztalovka ☆ KA 96-97 F 9
Kažukas = Marijampole ☆•• LT 94-95 H 4
Kazuma Pan National Park ⊥ ZW 218-219 C 4
Kazumba o ZRE 214-215 B 4
Kazungula o Z 218-219 C 3
Kazuno o J 152-153 J 4
Kazym ~ RUS 114-115 L 3
Kazyr ~ RUS 116-117 G 9
Kbombole o SN 202-203 B 2
Kbor Roumia • DZ 190-191 D 2
Ké o G 210-211 C 3
Ké, Enneri ~ TCH 198-199 H 3
Kéa ⌒ GR 100-101 K 6
Keaau o USA (HI) 288 K 5
Keahole Point ▲ USA (HI) 288 J 5
Kealaikahiki Channel ≈ USA 288 H 4
Kealakekua o USA (HI) 288 K 5
Kealia o USA (HI) 288 K 5
Keanae o USA (HI) 288 J 4
Keansburg o USA (NJ) 280-281 M 3
Kearney o USA (NE) 262-263 G 4
Kearns o USA (UT) 254-255 C 3
Kearny o USA (AZ) 256-257 E 5
Kearsarge Pass ▲ USA (CA) 248-249 F 3
Keating Point ▲ IND 140-141 L 5
Kébaly o RCB 202-203 D 4
Keban ☆ TR 128-129 H 3
Keban Barajı < TR 128-129 H 3
Kebaowek Indian Reservation ✕ CDN (QUE) 238-239 G 2
Kébara o RCB 210-211 E 5
Kebasen o RI 168 C 3
Kebbe o WAN 198-199 B 6
Kebbi, Mayo ~ TCH 206-207 B 4
Kébémer o SN 202-203 B 2
Kébi, Mayo ~ CAM 204-205 K 4
Kébila o RMM 202-203 G 4
Kebili ☆ TN 190-191 G 4
Kebnekaise ▲•• S 86-87 J 3
K'ebri Dehar o ETH 208-209 G 5
Kebumen o RI 168 C 3
Kech ~ PK 134-135 K 5
K'ech'a Terara ▲ ETH 208-209 D 5
Kéché o RCA 206-207 E 3
Kechika Ranges ▲ CDN 30-31 F 6
Kechika River ~ CDN 30-31 F 6
Kecskemét o H 92-93 P 5
Keda o GE 126-127 D 7
Kedah □ MAL 162-163 D 2
Kėdainiai ☆• LT 94-95 H 4
Kedawung o RI 168 C 3
Keddie o USA (CA) 246-247 E 3
Kédédéssé o TCH 206-207 C 3
Kedgwick o CDN (NB) 240-241 H 3
Kedgwick River ~ CDN (NB) 240-241 H 3
Kedgwick River ~ CDN (NB) 240-241 H 3
Kedi o IND 138-139 F 4
Kedi o RI 164-165 K 3
Kedir o RI 166-167 K 3
Kediri o RI 168 E 3
Kedon o RUS 112-113 K 4
Kedon ~ RUS 112-113 K 4
Kedonskij hrebet ▲ RUS 112-113 K 4
Kédougou o SN 202-203 D 3
Kedrovaja, gora ▲ RUS 122-123 D 6
Kedrovyj o RUS 114-115 P 6
Kedungwuni o RI 168 C 3
Kedva ~ RUS 88-89 W 4
Kędzierzyn-Koźle o• PL 92-93 P 3
Keefton o USA (OK) 264-265 J 3
Keekorok Lodge o EAK 212-213 E 4
Keel = An Caol o IRL 90-91 B 5
Keele Peak ▲ CDN 30-31 E 4
Keeler o USA (CA) 248-249 G 3
Keele River ~ CDN 30-31 F 3
Keeley Lake o CDN 32-33 Q 4
Keelinawi o USA (HI) 288 E 3
Keelung o• RC 156-157 M 4
Keene o USA (CA) 248-249 F 4
Keene o USA (NH) 278-279 J 6
Keene, Lake o AUS 176-177 G 2
Keenjhar Lake o•• PK 138-139 B 7
Keepit, Lake < AUS 178-179 L 6
Keep River < AUS 172-173 J 3
Keep River National Park ⊥ AUS 172-173 J 3
Keerweer, Cape ▲ AUS 174-175 F 3
Keeseville o USA (NY) 278-279 H 4
Keetmannshoop ☆ NAM 220-221 D 3
Keewatin o CDN (ONT) 234-235 J 5
Keewatin River ~ CDN 34-35 F 2
Keezhik Lake o CDN (ONT) 234-235 P 3
Kefa □ ETH 208-209 B 5
Kefaloniá ⌒ GR 100-101 H 5
Kefamenanu o RI 166-167 C 6
Keffi o WAN 204-205 G 4
Keflavík o IS 86-87 b 2
K'eftya o ETH 200-201 H 6
Kegajli ☆ US 136-137 F 3
Kegali ~ RUS 112-113 L 4
Kēgart o KS 136-137 N 4
Kegaska o CDN (QUE) 242-243 G 2
Kegdal o IND 140-141 F 3
Kegen o KA 146-147 D 4
Kegworth o CDN (SAS) 232-233 P 5
Kehiwin Indian Reserve ✕ CDN 32-33 P 4
Kehl o D 92-93 J 4
Keibul-Lamjoa National Park ⊥ IND 142-143 H 3
Keikakolo o RI 168 E 7
Keila o•• EST 94-95 J 2
Keila ⌒ SOL 184 I d 1
Keimoes o ZA 220-221 E 4
Kei Mouth o ZA 220-221 J 6
Keipene o LV 94-95 J 3
Kei Road o ZA 220-221 H 6
Keiskammarivier ~ ZA 220-221 H 6
Keita o RN 198-199 B 5
Keita ou Douka, Bahr ~ TCH 206-207 D 4
Keitele o FIN (KPN) 88-89 J 5
Keitele o FIN (KSS) 88-89 H 5
Keith o AUS 180-181 F 4
Keith, Cape ▲ AUS 172-173 K 1
Keith Arm o CDN 30-31 J 3
Keithley Creek o CDN (BC) 228-229 N 4
Keith Sebelius Lake o USA (KS) 262-263 G 5
Keithville o USA (LA) 268-269 G 4
Keiyasi o FJI 184 III a 2
Keizer o USA (OR) 244-245 C 5
Kejaman o MAL 162-163 K 3
Kejimkujik National Park ⊥ CDN (NS) 240-241 K 6
Kėjngypil'gyn, laguna o RUS 112-113 U 5
Kejobon o RI 168 C 3
Kejvy ▲ RUS 88-89 O 3
Kekaha o USA (HI) 288 F 3
Kėkėjgyr o KS 146-147 B 5
Kėk-Art o KS 146-147 B 5
Keke o PNG 183 D 5
Kékem o CAM 204-205 J 6
Kekertuk o CDN 28-29 J 3
Kekesu o PNG 184 I b 1
Kekirawa o CL 140-141 J 6
Kekneno, Gunung ▲ RI 166-167 C 6
Kekova Adası ⌒ TR 128-129 C 4
Kekovandasi ⌒ TR 128-129 C 4
Kekri o IND 138-139 E 7
Kekurnoi, Cape ▲ USA 22-23 T 4
Kekurnyj, zaliv o RUS 120-121 Q 4
Keku Strait ≈ 32-33 D 3
Kelabo o PNG 183 B 3
K'elafo o ETH 208-209 G 6
Kelag o VRC 154-155 B 6
Kelagay o AFG 136-137 L 7
Kelai ~ RI 164-165 E 3
Kélakam o RN 198-199 E 6
Kelambakkam o IND 140-141 J 4
Kelan o VRC 154-155 G 2
Kelandic Plateau ≃ 86-87 g 1
Kelang, Pulau ⌒ RI 166-167 D 3
Kelankyla o FIN 88-89 J 4
Kelanoa o PNG 183 D 4
Kelantan □ MAL 162-163 D 2
Kelapa o RI 162-163 F 5
Kélbo o BF 202-203 K 3
Këlcyrë o• AL 100-101 H 4
Keľda ~ RUS 88-89 R 4
Kele ~ RUS 118-119 P 4
Keleft o AFG 136-137 K 6
Kelem o ETH 208-209 B 6
Kelema o EAT 212-213 E 6
Kelèraš' = Călărași ☆ MD 102-103 F 4
Keles ☆ US 136-137 L 4
Kéléya o RMM 202-203 G 4
Kelež ~ RUS 116-117 F 9
Kelfield o CDN (SAS) 232-233 K 4
Kelford o USA (NC) 282-283 K 4
Kelgo Bay ≈ 36-37 R 5
Kelibia o TN 190-191 H 2
Kelifskij Uzboj ⊥ TM 136-137 H 6
Kelifvun, gora ▲ RUS 112-113 O 2
Kelimjar ~ RUS 110-111 P 4
Keling o RI 168 D 3
Kelkit ☆ TR 128-129 H 2
Kelkit Çayı ~ TR 128-129 G 2
Kelkit Çayı ~ TR 128-129 H 2
Kéllé o RCB 210-211 E 4
Kellé o RN 198-199 E 5
Keller o USA (WA) 244-245 G 2
Kellerberrin o AUS 176-177 D 5
Keller Lake o CDN 30-31 J 3
Kellerville o USA (TX) 264-265 D 3
Kellet, Canal de ≈ 50-51 B 4
Kellet, Cape ▲ CDN 24-25 H 5
Kellet River ~ CDN 24-25 b 6
Kellett River ~ CDN 24-25 K 5
Kellett River ~ CDN 24-25 K 5
Kellett Strait ≈ 24-25 M 3
Kelliher o CDN (SAS) 232-233 P 4
Kelliher o USA (MN) 270-271 D 3
Kelloe o CDN (MAN) 234-235 C 4
Kellog o RUS 114-115 T 3
Kellog ~ RUS 114-115 S 3
Kellogg o USA (ID) 250-251 C 4
Kellogg o USA (MN) 270-271 F 6
Kelloselkä o FIN 88-89 K 3
Kelly, Mount ▲ USA 20-21 J 2
Kelly Lake o CDN (BC) 230-231 H 2
Kelly Lake o CDN 30-31 G 3
Kelly Range ▲ AUS 176-177 F 2
Kelly River ~ USA 20-21 J 2
Keľma ~ RUS 114-115 U 5
Kelmė ☆ LT 94-95 H 4
Kelmet o ER 200-201 J 4
Kelo o TCH 206-207 B 4
Kelongwa o Z 218-219 D 1
Kelowna o CDN (BC) 230-231 K 4
Kelsey o CDN 34-35 H 2
Kelsey Bay o CDN (BC) 230-231 C 3
Kelso o CDN (SAS) 232-233 R 6
Kelso o• GB 90-91 F 4
Kelso o USA (CA) 248-249 J 4
Kelso o USA (WA) 244-245 C 4
Kelstern o CDN (SAS) 232-233 M 5
Keltie Bugt ≈ 26-27 Z 2
Kelton o USA (TX) 264-265 D 3
Kelton o USA (UT) 254-255 B 2
Kelu o VRC 156-157 G 6
Kelua o RI 164-165 D 5
Keluang, Tanjung ▲ RI 162-163 H 5
Kelume o RI 162-163 F 5
Keľvat ~ RUS 114-115 N 5
Kelvin o USA (AZ) 256-257 E 5
Kelvington o CDN (SAS) 232-233 P 3
Kem' o RUS (KAR) 88-89 N 4

Kem' ~ RUS 88-89 M 4
Kem' ~ RUS 116-117 E 6
Kemah ☆ • TR 128-129 H 3
Kemal, Gunung ▲ RI 164-165 E 3
Kemâliye ☆ TR 128-129 H 3
Kemano o CDN (BC) 228-229 G 3
Kemano River ~ CDN (BC) 228-229 G 3
Kemara, Kampung o MAL 162-163 E 2
Kemasik o MAL 162-163 E 2
Kemata I o TCH 206-207 D 4
Kemba o RCA 206-207 F 6
Kembani o RI 164-165 H 4
Kembapi o RI 166-167 L 6
Kembé o RCA 206-207 E 6
Kembé, Chutes de ~ RCA 206-207 E 6
Kembéra o RG 202-203 D 4
Kembolcha o ETH (Wel) 208-209 C 4
Kembolcha o ETH (Weo) 208-209 D 3
Kemčug ~ RUS 116-117 E 7
Kémédé o TCH 206-207 D 4
Kemenagi, Mount ▲ PNG 183 B 4
Kemer o TR 128-129 C 4
Kemer ☆ TR 128-129 D 4
Kemerhisar o TR 128-129 F 4
Kemerovo ☆ RUS 114-115 T 7
Kemi o FIN 88-89 H 4
Kemijärvi o FIN (LAP) 88-89 J 3
Kemijärvi ~ FIN (LAP) 88-89 J 3
Kemijoki ~ FIN 88-89 H 3
Kemkara o RUS 120-121 H 5
Kemlja o RUS 96-97 D 6
Kemmerer o USA (WY) 252-253 H 5
Kemnay o CDN (MAN) 234-235 C 5
Kémo ◘ RCA 206-207 D 6
Kemp o USA (TX) 264-265 H 6
Kemp, Lake < USA (TX) 264-265 E 5
Kempaž ~ RUS 114-115 F 2
Kempe Fjord ≈ 26-27 m 7
Kempele o FIN 88-89 H 4
Kempendjaj o RUS 118-119 J 4
Kempendjaj ~ RUS 118-119 J 4
Kemp Land ⊥ ARK 16 G 6
Kemp Peninsula ⌣ ARK 16 F 30
Kemps Bay o BS 54-55 G 2
Kempsey o AUS 178-179 M 6
Kempt, Lac o CDN (QUE) 236-237 O 5
Kempten (Allgäu) o • D 92-93 L 5
Kempton o AUS 180-181 J 7
Kempton Park o ZA 220-221 J 2
Kemptown o CDN (NS) 240-241 M 5
Kemptville o CDN (NS) 240-241 K 6
Kemptville o CDN (ONT) 238-239 K 3
Kemubu o MAL 162-163 E 2
Ken ~ IND 142-143 B 3
Kenadsa o DZ 188-189 K 5
Kenai o • USA 20-21 P 6
Kenai Fjords National Park ⊥ USA 22-23 V 3
Kenai Mountains ▲ USA 20-21 P 7
Kenai National Wildlife Refuge ⊥ USA 20-21 P 6
Kenai Peninsula ⌣ USA 20-21 P 6
Kenalia o PNG 183 B 5
Kenam o NEP 144-145 D 6
Kenamuke Swamp ⊖ SUD 208-209 A 5
Kenamu River ~ CDN 38-39 P 2
Kenamu River ~ CDN 38-39 O 2
Kenansville o USA (FL) 286-287 J 4
Kenapuru Head o NZ 182 E 4
Kenār Daryā o IR 136-137 B 6
Kenari o RI 168 D 7
Kenaston o CDN (SAS) 232-233 M 4
Kenawa o PNG 183 B 5
Kenbridge o USA (VA) 280-281 H 7
Kencong o RI 168 E 4
Kendal o CDN (SAS) 232-233 P 5
Kendal o • GB 90-91 F 4
Kendal o RI 168 D 3
Kendall o USA (FL) 286-287 J 6
Kendall o USA (KS) 262-263 E 7
Kendall o USA (WA) 244-245 C 2
Kendall, Cape ▲ CDN (NWT) 24-25 O 6
Kendall, Cape ▲ CDN (NWT) 36-37 F 3
Kendall, Mount ▲ NZ 182 D 4
Kendall, Point ▲ CDN 24-25 d 6
Kendall River ~ AUS 174-175 F 4
Kendallville o USA (IN) 274-275 N 3
Kendari ☆ RI 164-165 H 5
Kendawangan o RI 162-163 J 6
Kendégué o TCH 206-207 D 3
Kendeng, Pegunungan ▲ RI 168 D 3
Kendenup o • AUS 176-177 D 7
Kendleton o USA (TX) 266-267 L 4
Kendrāpāra o IND 142-143 E 5
Kendrick o USA (ID) 250-251 C 5
Kendu Bay o EAK 212-213 E 4
Kendujhargarh o IND 142-143 D 5
Kendujhar Plateau ▲ IND 142-143 D 5
Kendyrli-Kajasanskoe plato ▲ KA 126-127 K 6
Kenedy o USA (TX) 266-267 K 5
Kenel o USA (SD) 260-261 F 1
Kenema ☆ WAL 202-203 E 6
Kenenikjan ~ RUS 118-119 J 5
Kenenkou o RMM 202-203 G 3
Kenevi, Mount ▲ PNG 183 D 5
Kënga ~ RUS 114-115 Q 6
Këngdaj ~ RUS 110-111 Q 4
Kenge o ZRE 210-211 F 6
Kengirli sukojmasy < KA 124-125 E 5
Kengjade ~ RUS 110-111 H 5
Kengkeme ~ RUS 118-119 O 4
Keng Tung o MYA 142-143 L 5
Kengué o RCB 210-211 D 5
Kenhardt o ZA 220-221 E 4
Kéniéba o RMM 202-203 E 3
Kénié'bandi o RMM 202-203 E 3
Kéniébaoulé, Reserve de ⊥ RMM 202-203 F 3
Keningau o MAL 160-161 B 10
Kénitra = Al-Q'nitra ☆ MA 188-189 H 3
Kénitra = al-Q'nitra ☆ MA 188-189 H 3
Kenli o VRC 154-155 L 3
Kenly o USA (NC) 282-283 J 5
Kenmare o USA (ND) 258-259 E 3
Kenmare = Neidín o IRL 90-91 C 6
Kenmare River ≈ 90-91 C 6
Kenna o USA (NM) 256-257 M 5
Kenna o USA (WV) 280-281 E 5
Kennard o USA (TX) 268-269 E 5
Kennebec o USA (SD) 260-261 G 3
Kennebecasis River ~ CDN (NB) 240-241 K 5
Kennebec River ~ USA (ME) 278-279 M 3
Kennebunk o USA (ME) 278-279 L 5
Kennedy o AUS 174-175 H 6
Kennedy o CDN (SAS) 232-233 Q 5
Kennedy o USA (NE) 262-263 F 2
Kennedy o USA (NY) 278-279 B 6
Kennedy o ZW 218-219 D 4
Kennedy Channel ≈ 26-27 Q 3
Kennedy Development Road II AUS 174-175 H 6
Kennedy Hill ▲ AUS 174-175 G 3
Kennedy Kanal ≈ 26-27 R 3
Kennedy Peak ▲ MYA 142-143 H 4
Kennedy Range ▲ AUS 176-177 C 2
Kennedy River ~ AUS 174-175 H 4
Kennedy Space Center, John Fitzgerald xx USA (FL) 286-287 J 3
Kennedy's Vale o ZA 220-221 K 2
Kenner o USA (LA) 268-269 K 6
Kennesaw Mountain National Battlefield Park • USA (GA) 284-285 F 3
Kennetcook o CDN (NS) 240-241 M 5
Kenneth Range ▲ AUS 176-177 D 1
Kennett o USA (MO) 276-277 E 4
Kennewick o USA (WA) 244-245 F 4
Kenney Dam • CDN (BC) 228-229 K 3
Kennisis Lake o CDN (ONT) 238-239 G 3
Keno o USA (OR) 244-245 D 8
Keno City o CDN 20-21 X 5
Kenogami Lake o CDN (ONT) 236-237 H 4
Kenogami River ~ CDN (ONT) 236-237 D 2
Kenogami River ~ CDN (ONT) 236-237 C 2
Kenogamissi Lake ⊖ CDN (ONT) 236-237 G 5
Kenora o CDN (ONT) 234-235 J 5
Kenosee Park o CDN (SAS) 232-233 Q 6
Kenosha o USA (WI) 274-275 L 2
Kensal o USA (ND) 258-259 J 4
Kenscoff o •• RH 54-55 J 5
Kensett o USA (AR) 276-277 D 5
Kensington o CDN (PEI) 240-241 M 4
Kensington o USA (KS) 262-263 G 5
Kensington Downs o AUS 178-179 H 2
Kent o USA (MN) 270-271 B 4
Kent o USA (OH) 280-281 E 2
Kent o USA (OR) 244-245 E 5
Kent o USA (TX) 266-267 C 2
Kent o USA (WA) 244-245 C 3
Kentau o KA 136-137 L 3
Kentau o KA 136-137 L 3
Kent City o USA (MI) 272-273 D 4
Kent Group ⌒ AUS 180-181 J 5
Ken Thao o LAO 158-159 F 2
Kenting National Park ⊥ • RC 156-157 M 5
Kent Island ⌒ USA (MD) 280-281 K 5
Kent Junction o CDN (NB) 240-241 K 4
Kentland o USA (IN) 274-275 L 4
Kenton o CDN (MAN) 234-235 C 5
Kenton o USA (MI) 270-271 K 4
Kenton o USA (OH) 280-281 C 3
Kenton o USA (OK) 264-265 B 2
Kenton o USA (TN) 276-277 F 4
Kent Peninsula ⌣ CDN 24-25 S 6
Kentrikí Macedonía ◘ GR 100-101 J 4
Kentucky ◘ USA (KY) 276-277 H 3
Kentucky Lake < USA (KY) 276-277 G 4
Kentucky River ~ USA (KY) 276-277 L 3
Kentville o CDN (NS) 240-241 L 5
Kentwood o USA (LA) 268-269 K 6
Kenya ■ EAK 212-213 E 3
Kenya, Mount ▲ •• EAK 212-213 F 4
Kenya National Park, Mount ⊥ EAK 212-213 F 4
Kenyon o USA (MN) 270-271 E 6
Kenzou o CAM 206-207 B 6
Keokuk o USA (IA) 274-275 G 4
Keoladeo National Park ⊥ ••• IND 138-139 F 6
Keoma o CDN (ALB) 232-233 E 4
Keosauqua o USA (IA) 274-275 G 4
Keota o USA (IA) 274-275 G 3
Keowee, Lake ⊖ USA (SC) 284-285 H 2
Kepa o RUS 88-89 M 4
Kepahiang o RI 162-163 E 6
Kepanjen o RI 168 E 4
Kepelekese ~ ZRE 216-217 F 3
Keperveem o RUS 112-113 N 3
Kepi o RI 166-167 K 5
Kepina ~ RUS 88-89 Q 4
Kepino o RUS 88-89 Q 4
Kepno o PL 92-93 O 3
Keppe o RI 164-165 G 5
Keppel Bay ≈ 178-179 L 2
Keppel Island ⌒ GB 78-79 L 6
Kepsut ☆ TR 128-129 C 3
Kepteni o RUS 118-119 P 4
Keptin o RUS 118-119 M 4
Kepudori o RI 166-167 H 2
Kepuhi o USA (HI) 288 H 3
Kerai, Kuala o MAL 162-163 E 2
Kerala ◘ IND 140-141 F 5
Kerama-rettō ⌒ J 152-153 B 11
Keram River ~ PNG 183 C 3
Keran o IND 138-139 D 2
Kéran ~ RT 202-203 L 4
Kéran, Gorges du ⌣ • RT 202-203 L 5
Kéran, Parc National de la ⊥ RT 202-203 L 4
Kerang o AUS 180-181 G 3
Kerang o RI 164-165 E 5
Keranirhat o BD 142-143 H 4
Keraudren, Cape ▲ AUS 172-173 D 5
Keravat o PNG 183 G 3
Kerawa o CAM 204-205 K 3
Kerba, Col de ▲ DZ 190-191 D 3
Kerbau, Tanjung ▲ RI 162-163 E 6
Kerbi ~ RUS 122-123 F 2
Kerby o USA (OR) 244-245 B 8
Kerč o UA 102-103 K 5
Kerčens'ka Protoka ≈ 102-103 K 5
Kerch = Kerč o • UA 102-103 K 5
Kerchouel < RMM 196-197 L 6
Kerdëm o • RUS 118-119 O 5
Kéré o RCA 206-207 G 6
Kéré ~ RCA 206-207 H 6
Kerec, mys ▲ RUS 88-89 P 4
Kerein Hills o AUS 180-181 J 2
Kerej, köli o KA 124-125 F 3
Kerema ☆ PNG 183 C 4
Keremeos o CDN (BC) 230-231 K 4
Keremeos Ranche Indian Reserve ✗ CDN (BC) 230-231 K 4
Keremesit ~ RUS 110-111 b 4
Kérémou o DY 204-205 E 3
Kerempe Burnu ▲ TR 128-129 E 1
Keren o ER 200-201 J 5
Kerend o IR 134-135 B 1
Kerens o USA (TX) 264-265 H 6
Kereru Range ▲ PNG 183 C 4
Keret' o RUS 88-89 M 3
Keret', ozero o RUS 88-89 M 4
Kerewan ☆ WAG 202-203 B 3
Kerguélen, Îles ⌒ F 12 E 9
Kerguélen Plateau ≃ 12 F 10
Keria Landing o GUY 62-63 F 2
Kericho o • EAK 212-213 E 4
Keri Kera o SUD 200-201 F 6
Kerikeri o NZ 182 D 1
Kerimgaon o IND 142-143 J 2
Kerinci, Danau o RI 162-163 D 6
Kerinci, Gunung ▲ RI 162-163 D 5
Kerio ~ EAK 212-213 F 2
Keriya He ~ VRC 144-145 C 2
Kerkenah, Îles de ⌒ TN 190-191 H 3
Kerkertaluk Island ⌒ CDN 28-29 G 2
Kerki o TM 136-137 J 6
Kerkiči o TM 136-137 J 6
Kérkira o •• GR 100-101 G 5
Kérkira ⌒ GR 100-101 G 5
Kerkouane ∴ ••• TN 190-191 H 2
Kermadec Islands ⌒ NZ 13 K 5
Kermadec Trench ≃ 14-15 L 11
Kermān ◘ IR 134-135 F 4
Kermān ☆ • IR 134-135 G 3
Kermānšāhan o IR 134-135 F 3
Kermāšāh o IR 134-135 D 3
Kermit o USA (TX) 266-267 D 2
Kërmjukej, gora ▲ AZ 128-129 N 3
Kermū, Kōtal-e ▲ AFG 134-135 M 1
Kernay ⊥ TM 136-137 F 3
Kernersville o USA (NC) 282-283 G 4
Kernertut, Cap ▲ CDN 36-37 Q 5
Kern National Wildlife Refuge ⊥ • USA (CA) 248-249 E 4
Kern River ~ USA (CA) 248-249 F 3
Kernville o USA (CA) 248-249 F 4
Kernville o USA (OR) 244-245 B 6
Kérou o DY 204-205 E 3
Kérouané o RG 202-203 F 5
Kerrick o USA (TX) 264-265 B 2
Kerriya Shankou ▲ VRC 144-145 C 3
Kerr Lake, Robert S. ⊖ USA (OK) 264-265 J 3
Kerrobert o CDN (SAS) 232-233 J 4
Kerr Scott Reservoir, W. ⊖ USA (NC) 282-283 F 4
Kerrville o USA (TX) 266-267 H 3
K'ersa o ETH 208-209 E 4
Kersa Dek o ETH 208-209 D 6
Kershaw o USA (SC) 284-285 K 2
Kersinyané o RMM 202-203 E 2
Kersley o CDN (BC) 228-229 M 4
Kertamulia o RI 162-163 H 5
Kerteh o MAL 162-163 E 2
Kerteminde o • DK 86-87 E 9
Kertosono o RI 168 E 3
Keruak o RI 168 C 7
Kerugoya o EAK 212-213 F 4
Kervansaray ∴ •• TR 128-129 E 3
Keryneia o • TR 128-129 E 5
Kerzaz o DZ 188-189 L 6
Kesagami Lake ⊖ CDN (ONT) 236-237 H 2
Kesagami Lake Provincial Park ⊥ CDN (ONT) 236-237 H 2
Kesagami River ~ CDN (ONT) 236-237 H 2
Keşan ☆ TR 128-129 B 2
Kešem o AFG 136-137 M 6
Kesem Wenz ~ ETH 208-209 D 4
Kesennuma o J 152-153 J 5
Keshena o USA (WI) 270-271 K 6
Keshod o IND 138-139 C 9
Kesiman o RI 168 B 7
Keskin o TR 128-129 E 3
Kestell o ZA 220-221 J 4
Kestenga o RUS 88-89 L 4
Keswick o GB 90-91 F 4
Keszthely o H 92-93 O 5
Ket' ~ RUS 114-115 R 5
Ket' ~ RUS 116-117 E 6
Keta o GH 202-203 L 7
Keta, gory ▲ RUS 108-109 Y 7
Ketahun o RI 162-163 D 6
Keta Lagoon ⊖ GH 202-203 L 7
Ketama o MA 188-189 J 3
Ketanda o RUS 120-121 J 3
Ketanda ~ RUS 120-121 J 3
Ketanggungan o RI 168 C 3
Ketapang o RI (JTI) 168 E 3
Ketapang o RI (KBA) 162-163 H 5
Ketčenery o RUS 96-97 D 10
Ketchen o CDN (SAS) 232-233 Q 4
Ketchikan o USA 32-33 E 4
Ketchum o USA (ID) 252-253 D 3
Kete-Krachi o GH 202-203 K 6
Ketesso o CI 202-203 J 7
Keti Bandar o PK 134-135 M 6
Ketlica, ostrov ⌒ RUS 84-85 c 2
Ketlik River ~ USA 20-21 L 2
Ketoj, ostrov ⌒ RUS 122-123 P 5
Ketok Mountain ▲ USA 22-23 S 3
Ketomoknai o PNG 183 A 3
Ketoria, Cape ▲ CDN 36-37 M 2
Kétou o • DY 204-205 E 5
Ketovo ☆ RUS 114-115 H 7
Ke Town o LB 202-203 F 6
Kętrzyn o PL 92-93 Q 1
Ketsko-Tymskaja, ravnina ⌣ RUS 114-115 S 4
Ketta o RCB 210-211 E 3
Kétté o CAM 206-207 B 6
Kettering o USA (OH) 280-281 B 4
Kettle Falls o USA (WA) 244-245 G 2
Kettleman City o USA (CA) 248-249 E 3
Kettleman Hills ▲ USA (CA) 248-249 D 3
Kettle Point ▲ CDN (ONT) 238-239 C 5
Kettle Range ▲ USA (WA) 244-245 G 2
Kettle River ~ CDN 34-35 M 2
Kettle River ~ CDN 230-231 L 4
Kettle River ~ USA (MN) 270-271 F 4
Kettle River ~ USA (WA) 244-245 G 2
Kettle Valley o CDN (BC) 230-231 L 4
Keudeuteunom o RI 162-163 A 2
Keuka Lake ⊖ USA (NY) 278-279 D 6
Keul' o RUS 116-117 L 6
Keum ~ RUS 114-115 L 5
Keur Madiabel o SN 202-203 B 3
Keur Massène o RIM 196-197 B 6
Keur Momar Sar o SN 196-197 C 7
Keuruu o FIN 88-89 H 5
Kėušen' = Căuseni ☆ MD 102-103 F 4
Kévé o RT 202-203 L 6
Kėveem ~ RUS 112-113 R 2
Kewanee o USA (IL) 274-275 J 3
Kewapante o RI 166-167 B 6
Kewasasap o PNG 183 E 5
Kewaskum o USA (WI) 274-275 K 1
Kewaunee o USA (WI) 270-271 L 6
Keweenaw Bay o USA (MI) 270-271 K 4
Keweenaw Bay o USA (MI) 270-271 K 4
Keweenaw Bay Indian Reservation ✗ USA (MI) 270-271 K 4
Keweenaw Peninsula ⌣ USA 270-271 K 3
Keweenaw Point ▲ USA (MI) 270-271 L 3
Key o USA (TX) 264-265 C 6
K'ey Āfer o ETH 208-209 C 6
Keyaluvik o USA 20-21 H 6
Keyapaha o USA (SD) 260-261 F 3
Keya Paha River ~ USA (SD) 260-261 F 3
Keyes o CDN (MAN) 234-235 D 4
Keyes o USA (OK) 264-265 B 2
Keyhole Reservoir ⊖ USA (WY) 252-253 O 2
Keyihe o VRC 150-151 D 2
Key Largo o USA (FL) 286-287 J 6
Key Largo ⌒ USA (FL) 286-287 J 6
Key Lake Mine o CDN 34-35 D 2
Keyling Inlet ≈ 172-173 J 3
Keyser o USA (WV) 280-281 H 4
Keystone o USA (CA) 248-249 D 2
Keystone o USA (NE) 262-263 E 3
Keystone o USA (SD) 260-261 C 3
Keystone o USA (WA) 244-245 C 2
Keystone Heights o USA (FL) 286-287 G 2
Keystone Lake ⊖ USA (OK) 264-265 H 2
Keysville o USA (VA) 280-281 H 6
Keytesville o USA (MO) 274-275 F 5
Key West o • USA (FL) 286-287 H 7
Kez ☆ RUS 96-97 H 5
Kezar Falls o USA (ME) 278-279 L 5
Kezi o ZW 218-219 E 5
Kežma o RUS 116-117 K 6
Kežmarok o SK 92-93 Q 4
Kgalagadi ◘ RB 220-221 E 2
Kgatleng ◘ RB 220-221 H 2
Kgokgole ~ ZA 220-221 F 3
Kgun Lake ⊖ USA 20-21 H 6
Khabou o RIM 202-203 D 2
Khadki o IND 138-139 D 10
Khadwa o IND 138-139 F 9
Khagaria o IND 142-143 E 3
Khagia Sumna o VRC 144-145 C 5
Khairāgarh o IND 142-143 B 5
Khairapa o IND 138-139 D 6
Khairpur o PK (PU) 138-139 D 5
Khairpur o • PK (SIN) 138-139 B 6
Khairpur Nāthan Shāh o PK 134-135 M 5
Khajuraho o ••• IND 138-139 G 7
Khajuri Kach o PK 138-139 B 3
Khakassia = Hakasija, Respublika ◘ RUS 116-117 D 9
Khakhea o RB 220-221 F 2
Khakurdi o IND 138-139 E 9
Khalaf Allāh, Bi'r < LAR 192-193 G 4
Khalaf Allāh, Qārat ▲ LAR 192-193 G 4
Khalfallah o DZ 190-191 C 3
Khalij al-Bahrain ≈ 134-135 D 6
Khalij al Bumbah ≈ 192-193 K 1
Khambhāliya o IND 138-139 B 8
Khambhat o IND 138-139 D 8
Khambhāt, Gulf of ≈ 138-139 C 9
Khāmgaon o IND 138-139 F 9
Khami Ruins ∴ ••• ZW 218-219 E 5
Khamis Mushayt = Ḫamis Mušaiṭ o KSA 132-133 C 4
Kham Khuan Kaeo o THA 158-159 H 3
Khammam o IND 142-143 B 7
Khampat o MYA 142-143 J 4
Kham Ta Kla o THA 158-159 G 2
Khan ~ NAM 216-217 C 11
Khānāpur o IND 140-141 F 3
Khandala o IND 138-139 F 10
Khānewāl o PK 138-139 C 4
Khāngāh Dogrān o PK 138-139 D 4
Khāngarh o PK 138-139 C 5
Khangar Sidi Nadji o DZ 190-191 F 3
Khanka, Ozero = Hanka, ozero o RUS 122-123 E 6
Khankendi = Xankandi ☆ AZ (NAG) 128-129 M 3
Khanna o IND 138-139 F 4
Khannfoussa, Gara ▲ DZ 190-191 F 7
Khanom o THA 158-159 E 6
Khānpur o PK (PU) 138-139 C 5
Khānpur o PK (SIN) 138-139 B 6
Khansiir, Raas ▲ SP 208-209 G 3
Khanty-Mansi Autonomous District=Hanty-Mans.avt.okrug ◘ RUS 114-115 G 3
Khao Chmao National Park ⊥ • THA 158-159 F 4
Khao Kha Khaeng ▲ THA 158-159 E 2
Khao Kheaw National Park ⊥ • THA 158-159 F 3
Khao Khieo Open Zoo • THA 158-159 F 4
Khao Laem Reservoir < THA 158-159 E 3
Khao Sok National Park ⊥ THA 158-159 E 6
Khapalu o IND 138-139 F 2
Khaptada National Park ⊥ NEP 144-145 C 6
Kharagpur o IND 142-143 E 4
Khārān o PK 134-135 L 4
Kharar o IND 138-139 F 4
Khardung La ▲ IND 138-139 F 2
Kharepātan o IND 140-141 E 2
Khārga, El = Ḫāriğa, al- ☆ • ET 194-195 E 5
Khargon o IND 138-139 E 9
Khāriān o PK 138-139 D 3
Khariār o IND 142-143 C 5
Kharikhola o NEP 144-145 F 7
Kharj, al = Ḫarğ, al o KSA 130-131 K 5
Khârroûb, Oued ~ RIM 196-197 F 3
Kharsia o IND 142-143 C 5
Khartaksho o IND 138-139 F 2
Khartoum = al-Ḫarṭūm ★ •• SUD 200-201 F 5
Khartoum North = al-Ḫarṭūm Baḥrī o SUD 200-201 F 5
Khartoum North = Ḫarṭūm Baḥrī, al- o SUD 200-201 F 5
Khashm al-Qirbah o SUD 200-201 G 5
Khasi Hills ▲ IND 142-143 G 3
Khāsi-Jaintia Hills ▲ IND 142-143 G 3
Khasm Elmi o SUD 200-201 C 6
Khatauli o IND 138-139 F 5
Khātegaon o IND 138-139 F 8
Khatima o IND 138-139 G 5
Khatoli o IND 138-139 F 7
Khatt Atoui ~ RIM 196-197 C 4
Khaur o PK 138-139 D 3
Khāvda o IND 138-139 B 8
Khazzān ar-Ruṣayri < SUD 208-209 B 3
Khed o IND 140-141 E 2
Kheda o IND 138-139 D 8
Khèmis-des-Zèmamra o MA 188-189 G 4
Khemis Miliana o DZ 190-191 D 2
Khemissa ∴ • DZ 190-191 F 2
Khemisset ☆ MA 188-189 H 4
Khemmarat o THA 158-159 H 2
Khenchela ☆ DZ 190-191 F 3
Khenifra ☆ MA 188-189 J 4
Kherālu o IND 138-139 D 8
Kherba o DZ 190-191 C 2
Kheri o IND 138-139 F 9
Kherir, Oued ~ RIM 196-197 F 2
Kherrata o DZ 190-191 E 2
Kherson = Cherson ☆ • UA 102-103 H 4
Khewra o IND 138-139 D 8
Khe Sanh ☆ • VN 158-159 J 2
Khe Ve o VN 158-159 H 2
Khewra o PK 138-139 D 3
Khezmir < RIM 196-197 E 5
Khimki = Himki ☆ RUS 94-95 P 4
Khipro o PK 138-139 B 7
Khiran, al- o KWT 130-131 L 3
Khiu o PK 138-139 C 4
Khlong Ngae o THA 158-159 F 7
Khlong Thom o THA 158-159 E 7
Khmel'nyts'kyy = Chmel'nyc'kyj ☆ UA 102-103 E 3
Khodzhavend = Xocavand o AZ (NAG) 128-129 M 3
Khogué Tobène o SN 202-203 C 2
Khojak Pass ▲ PK 134-135 M 3
Khokarmoho o IND 138-139 E 10
Khok Chang o THA 158-159 G 2
Khok Kloi o THA 158-159 E 6
Khok Phek o THA 158-159 G 3
Khok Pho o THA 158-159 F 7
Khok Samrong o THA 158-159 F 3
Khomas Hochland ▲ NAM 216-217 D 11
Khomeynišahr o IR 134-135 D 2
Khon o THA 158-159 E 2
Khondmāl Hills ▲ IND 142-143 C 5
Khong Chiam o THA 158-159 H 3
Khong Khi Sua o THA 158-159 F 3
Khon Kaen o THA 158-159 G 2
Khôr Anyâr o DJI 200-201 L 6
Khorāsān ◘ IR 134-135 G 1
Khorasgān o IR 134-135 D 2
Khordha o IND 142-143 D 5
Khor Fakkan = Ḫaur Fakkān o UAE 134-135 G 6
Khor Gamdze o VRC 144-145 M 5
Khorixas ☆ NAM 216-217 C 10
Khor Khor o IR 128-129 L 4
Khorlak o NEP 144-145 E 6
Khossanto o SN 202-203 E 3
Khost o PK 134-135 M 3
Khotol Mount ▲ USA 20-21 M 4
Khouribga ☆ MA 188-189 H 4
Khreum o MYA 142-143 H 5
Khswan Mountain ▲ CDN 32-33 F 4
Khuang Nai o THA 158-159 H 3
Khubus o ZA 220-221 C 4
Khuchinarai o THA 158-159 H 2
Khudabad o IND 138-139 E 1
Khudābād o PK 134-135 M 5
Khudiān o PK 138-139 E 4
Khudzhand = Ḫuǧand ☆ TJ 136-137 L 4
Khukhan o THA 158-159 H 3
Khulna o BD 142-143 F 4
Khums, Al ◘ LAR 192-193 F 1
Khums, Al ☆ LAR (AKM) 192-193 F 1
Khunaniwāla o PK 138-139 C 4
Khunjerab Pass ▲ PK 138-139 E 1
Khun Yuam o THA 142-143 K 6
Khuraburi o THA 158-159 E 6
Khurai o IND 138-139 G 7
Khurayt o SUD 200-201 B 6
Khurībgah = Khouribga ☆ MA 188-189 H 4
Khurja o IND 138-139 F 5
Khushāb o PK 138-139 D 3
Khutzeymateen Inlet ≈ CDN 228-229 D 2
Khuzdār o PK 134-135 M 5
Khwai River Lodge o RB 218-219 B 4
Khwane o MYA 158-159 E 3
Khwazakhela o PK 138-139 D 2
Khwebe Hills ▲ RB 218-219 B 5
Khyber Pass ▲ PK 138-139 C 2
Kia ⌒ FJI 184 III b 2
Kia o SOL 184 I d 2
Kiakalamu o ZRE 214-215 E 5
Ķiaķty, köli ⊖ KA 124-125 F 3
Kiama o AUS 180-181 L 3
Kiamba o RP 160-161 F 9
Kiambere Reservoir < EAK 212-213 F 4
Kiambi o ZRE 214-215 E 4
Kiambu o EAK 212-213 F 4
Kiamichi Mountain ▲ USA (OK) 264-265 J 4
Kiamichi River ~ USA (OK) 264-265 J 4
Kiampanjang o RI 164-165 E 2
Kiana o AUS 174-175 D 5
Kiana o USA 20-21 K 3
Kiandarat o RI 166-167 F 3
Kiandra o AUS 180-181 K 3
Kiangara o RM 222-223 E 6
Kiangarow, Mount ▲ AUS 178-179 L 4
Kiangdom o IND 138-139 G 3
Kiangwe ~ ZRE 210-211 L 6
Kiantajärvi ⊖ FIN 88-89 K 4
Kia Ora o AUS 180-181 E 2
Kiasko River ~ CDN (ONT) 236-237 H 2
Kiatai o VRC 146-147 E 4
Kiáto o GR 100-101 J 5
Kiau, Bi'r < SUD 200-201 G 2
Kiawah Island ⌒ USA (SC) 284-285 K 4
Kibakwe o EAT 214-215 J 4
Kibale o EAU 212-213 C 3
Kibali ~ ZRE 212-213 C 2
Kibangou o RCB 210-211 D 5
Kibau o EAT 214-215 H 5
Kibawe o RP 160-161 F 9
Kibaya o EAT 212-213 F 6
Kibbanahalli o IND 140-141 G 4
Kibeni o PNG 183 B 4
Kiberege o EAT 214-215 J 4
Kibi o GH 202-203 K 6
Kibira, Parc National de la ⊥ BU 212-213 B 5
Kibiti o EAT 214-215 K 4
Kibiya o WAN 204-205 H 3
Kibo ▲ EAT 212-213 F 5
Kiboga o EAU 212-213 C 3
Kiboko ~ EAK 212-213 F 5
Kibombo o ZRE 210-211 K 5
Kibondo o EAT 212-213 C 5
Ķibraj ☆ US 136-137 L 4
Kibre Mengist o ETH 208-209 D 6
Kıbrıscık ☆ TR 128-129 D 2
Kibungo o RWA 212-213 C 5
Kibunzi o ZRE 210-211 D 6
Kibuye o RWA 212-213 B 5
Kibwesa o EAT 214-215 E 4
Kibwezi o EAK 212-213 F 5
Kičevo o MK 100-101 H 4
Kichha o IND 138-139 G 5
Kichi-Kichi < TCH 198-199 H 4
Kichimiloo Claypan ⊖ AUS 178-179 H 5
Kichwamba o EAU 212-213 B 4
Kici Borsyk, kùm ⊥ KA 126-127 O 4
Kickapoo, Lake < USA (TX) 264-265 F 5
Kickapoo Indian Caverns ∴ USA (WI) 274-275 H 1
Kickapoo Indian Reservation ✗ USA (KS) 262-263 L 5
Kickene Özen ~ KA 96-97 F 9
Kicking Horse Pass ▲ CDN (ALB) 232-233 B 4
Kičmengskij Gorodok ☆ RUS 96-97 D 4
Kidal o RMM 196-197 L 5
Kidan, al- ⊥ KSA 132-133 H 2
Kidapawan ☆ RP 160-161 F 9
Kidatu o EAT 214-215 J 4
Kidd's Beach o ZA 220-221 H 6
Kidekša o ••• RUS 94-95 R 3
Kidepo ~ SUD 208-209 A 6
Kidepo National Park ⊥ EAU 212-213 D 2
Kidete o EAT 214-215 J 4
Kidira o SN 202-203 D 2
Kidnappers, Cape ▲ NZ 182 F 3
Kidney Island ⌒ CDN 36-37 J 6
Kidston o AUS 174-175 H 6
Kiekinkoski o FIN 88-89 L 4
Kiel ☆ • D 92-93 L 1
Kiel o USA (WI) 270-271 K 7
Kielce ☆ • PL 92-93 Q 3
Kieler Bucht ≈ D 92-93 L 1
Kiembara o BF 202-203 J 3
Kienge o ZRE 214-215 D 6
Kieng-Kjuel', ozero ⊖ RUS 110-111 G 3
Kiên Lu'o'ng o VN 158-159 H 5
Kiester o USA (MN) 270-271 E 7
Kieta o PNG 184 I b 2
Kiev = Kyjiv ★ ••• UA 102-103 G 2
Kiev = Kyjiv ★ ••• UA 102-103 G 2
Kievka o KA 124-125 G 3
Kievka ~ RUS 122-123 E 7
Kievskij Egan ~ RUS 114-115 Q 4
Kifaya o RG 202-203 D 3
Kiffa ☆ RIM 196-197 E 6
Kifinga o ZRE 214-215 D 5
Kifissiá o GR 100-101 J 5
Kifri ☆ IRQ 128-129 L 5
Kifunankese o ZRE 210-211 K 6
Kifusa o ZRE 214-215 C 4
Kigač ~ RUS 96-97 F 10
Kigali ★ RWA 212-213 C 4
Kigalik River ~ USA 20-21 N 2
Kigataq ⌒ GRØ 26-27 X 7
Kiği ☆ TR 128-129 J 3
Kigiljah o RUS 110-111 W 3
Kigiljah, mys ▲ RUS 110-111 W 3
Kigiljah, poluostrov ⌣ RUS 110-111 W 3
Kigluaik Mountains ▲ USA 20-21 H 4
Kignan o RMM 202-203 H 4
Kigoma ◘ EAT 212-213 C 6
Kigoma ☆ EAT 212-213 B 6
Kigomasha, Ras ▲ EAT 212-213 G 6
Kigosi ~ EAT 212-213 C 5
Kigumo o EAK 212-213 F 4
Kihčik ~ RUS 120-121 R 7
Kihei o USA (HI) 288 J 4
Kihelkona o EST 94-95 H 2
Kihnu saar ⌒ EST 94-95 J 2
Kiholo o USA (HI) 288 K 5
Kihurio o EAT 212-213 G 6
Kii-hantō ⌣ J 152-153 G 8
Kii-Nagashima o J 152-153 G 7
Kii-sanchi ▲ J 152-153 F 8
Kii-suidō ≈ 152-153 F 8
Kija ~ RUS 114-115 U 7
Kija ~ RUS 116-117 E 6
Kija ~ RUS 118-119 G 10
Ķijaly-Būrta ~ KA 126-127 M 2
Kijanebalola, Lake ⊖ EAU 212-213 C 4
Kijasovo o RUS 96-97 H 5
Kiji, Île ⌒ RIM 196-197 B 5
Kijungu o EAT 212-213 F 6
Kika o DY 204-205 E 4
Kikagati o EAU 212-213 C 4
Kikai-shima ⌒ J 152-153 C 10
Kikale o EAT 214-215 K 4
Kikamba o ZRE 210-211 L 5
Kikambala o EAK 212-213 G 5
Kikegtek Island ⌒ USA 22-23 O 3
Kikert Lake ⊖ CDN 30-31 N 2
Kikiakrovak River ~ USA 20-21 O 2
Kikinda o • YU 100-101 H 2
Kikiongolo o ZRE 210-211 E 6
Kikkertavak Island ⌒ CDN 36-37 T 6
Kikombo o EAT 214-215 H 4
Kikonai o J 152-153 J 4
Kikondja o ZRE 214-215 D 5
Kikori o PNG 183 C 4
Kikori River ~ PNG 183 B 4
Kikwit o ZRE 210-211 G 6
Kil ☆ S 86-87 F 7
Kilaguni Lodge o EAK 212-213 G 5
Kilakkarai o IND 140-141 H 6
Kilala o EAK 212-213 F 4
Kilauea o USA (HI) 288 F 2
Kilauea Crater ⊥ USA (HI) 288 K 5
Kilauea Lighthouse (Largest Lighthouse in the World) II • USA (HI) 288 F 2
Kilbeggan = Cill Bheagáin o IRL 90-91 D 5
Kilbella River ~ CDN (BC) 230-231 B 2
Kilbogharn o N 86-87 F 3
Kilbuck Mountains ▲ USA 20-21 K 6
Kilcoy o AUS 178-179 M 4
Kildala River ~ CDN (BC) 228-229 F 3
Kildare = Cill Dara o IRL 90-91 D 5
Kil'din, ostrov ⌒ RUS 88-89 M 2
Kildonan o CDN (BC) 230-231 E 5
Kildonan o ZW 218-219 F 3
Kildurk o AUS 172-173 J 4
Kilekale Lake ⊖ CDN 30-31 H 2
Kilembe o ZRE (BAN) 210-211 G 6
Kilembe o ZRE (SHA) 214-215 D 4
Kilembi o ZRE 210-211 L 6
Kileo o ZRE 210-211 K 6
Kilgana ~ RUS 120-121 P 3
Kilganskij massiv ▲ RUS 120-121 P 3
Kilgore o USA (NE) 262-263 F 2
Kilgore o USA (TX) 264-265 K 6
Kilgoris o EAK 212-213 E 4
Kili ~ US 136-137 K 4
Kilia o PNG 183 F 5
Kilian, Erg ⊥ DZ 190-191 G 9
Kilibo o DY 204-205 E 4
Kili Bulak o VRC 144-145 J 4
Kilifarevo o BG 102-103 D 6
Kilifas o PNG 183 A 2
Kilifi o EAK 212-213 G 5
Kiligwa River ~ USA 20-21 L 2
Kilija ☆ UA 102-103 F 5
Kilikkollūr o IND 140-141 G 6
Kilim o TCH 206-207 D 3
Kilimanjaro ◘ EAT 212-213 F 5
Kilimanjaro ▲ •• EAT 212-213 F 5
Kilimanjaro Buffalo Lodge o EAK 212-213 F 5
Kilimanjaro National Park ⊥ ••• EAT 212-213 F 5
Kilimatinde o EAT 212-213 E 6
Kilimbangara ⌒ SOL 184 I c 2
Kilindoni o EAT 214-215 K 4
Kilingi-Nõmme o EST 94-95 J 2
Kilini o • GR 100-101 H 6
Kilinochchi o CL 140-141 J 6
Kilipsjärvi o FIN 88-89 F 2
Kilis ☆ TR 128-129 G 4
Kiliuda Bay ≈ 22-23 U 4
Kiljanki o RUS 120-121 E 2
Kilju o DVR 150-151 G 7
Kilkee = Cill Chaoi o IRL 90-91 C 5
Kilkenny = Cill Chainnigh ☆ • IRL 90-91 D 5
Kilkís o GR 100-101 J 4
Killaloe Station o CDN (ONT) 238-239 H 3
Killalo Lake ⊖ CDN (ONT) 236-237 B 3
Killaly o CDN (SAS) 232-233 Q 5
Killam o CDN (ALB) 232-233 G 3
Killarney o AUS (NT) 172-173 K 4
Killarney o AUS (QLD) 178-179 H 2
Killarney o CDN (MAN) 234-235 D 5
Killarney o CDN (ONT) 238-239 D 3
Killarney = Cill Airne o • IRL 90-91 C 5
Killarney Provincial Park ⊥ CDN (ONT) 238-239 D 3
Killdeer o CDN (SAS) 232-233 M 6
Killdeer o USA (ND) 258-259 E 4
Kill Devil Hills o USA (NC) 282-283 M 4
Killé, I-n- < RMM 196-197 K 6
Killeen o USA (TX) 266-267 K 2
Killik River ~ USA 20-21 N 2
Killiney Beach o CDN (BC) 230-231 K 3
Killington Peak ▲ USA (VT) 278-279 J 5
Killorglin = Cill Orglan o IRL 90-91 C 5
Kilmarnock o GB 90-91 E 4
Kilmarnock o USA (VA) 280-281 K 6
Kil'mez' ☆ RUS (KIR) 96-97 G 5
Kil'mez' ~ RUS 96-97 H 5
Kilmichael o USA (MS) 268-269 L 3

Kilmore o AUS 180-181 H 4
Kiln o USA (MS) 268-269 L 6
Kilogbe o WAN 204-205 E 3
Kilombero ~ EAT 214-215 J 5
Kilómetro 133 o YV 60-61 J 3
Kilosa o EAT 214-215 J 4
Kilrush = Cill Rois o IRL 90-91 C 5
Kilto o AUS 172-173 F 4
Kilu o PNG 183 F 3
Kiluan o RI 162-163 F 7
Kilubi o ZRE 210-211 L 6
Kilubi ~ ZRE 214-215 C 5
Kilunguye ~ ZRE 212-213 A 6
Kilwa o ZRE 214-215 E 5
Kilwa Kisiwani ∴ ••• EAT 214-215 K 5
Kilwa Kivinje o EAT 214-215 K 5
Kilwa Masoko o EAT 214-215 K 5
Kilwat o RI 166-167 G 4
Kilwinning o CDN (SAS) 232-233 M 2
Kim ~ CAM 204-205 J 6
Kim o TCH 206-207 B 4
Kim o USA (CO) 254-255 M 6
Kima ☆ KA 124-125 E 3
Kimaan o RI 166-167 K 5
Kimamba o EAT 214-215 J 4
Kimana o EAK 212-213 F 5
Kimân al-Matâ'ina o ET 194-195 F 5
Kimanis, Teluk ≈ 160-161 A 10
Kimano II o ZRE 212-213 B 6
Kimba o AUS (QLD) 174-175 G 4
Kimba o AUS (SA) 180-181 D 2
Kimba o RCB 210-211 E 5
Kimball o USA (MN) 270-271 D 5
Kimball o USA (NE) 262-263 C 3
Kimball o USA (SD) 260-261 H 3
Kimball, Mount ▲ USA 20-21 S 5
Kimbao o ZRE 210-211 F 6
Kimbe ☆ PNG 183 F 3
Kimbe Bay ≈ 183 F 3
Kimberley ∴ AUS 172-173 G 4
Kimberley o CDN (BC) 230-231 O 4
Kimberley o ZA 220-221 G 4
Kimberley Aboriginal Land X AUS 172-173 H 3
Kimberley Downs o AUS 172-173 G 4
Kimberley Plateau ∴ AUS 172-173 G 4
Kimberley Research Station o AUS 172-173 J 3
Kimberly o USA (OR) 244-245 F 6
Kimbirila Sud o CI 202-203 G 5
Kimchaek o DVR 150-151 G 7
Kimču ~ RUS 116-117 K 5
Kimenga ~ RCB 210-211 D 5
Kimi o GR 100-101 K 5
Kimilili o EAK 212-213 E 3
Kimirekkum, peski ∴ US 136-137 H 5
Kimjongsuk-up o DVR 150-151 F 7
Kimobetsu o J 152-153 J 3
Kimongo o RCB 210-211 D 6
Kimovsk ☆ RUS 94-95 Q 5
Kimowin River ~ CDN 32-33 Q 3
Kimpanga o ZRE 214-215 C 4
Kimparana o RMM 202-203 H 3
Kimpata-Eku o ZRE 210-211 G 6
Kimpelo o RCB 210-211 E 5
Kimpese o ZRE 210-211 E 6
Kimry ☆ RUS 94-95 P 3
Kimsambi o EAT 212-213 C 4
Kimsi o EAT 212-213 C 5
Kim So'n ☆ • VN 156-157 E 6
Kimsquit o CDN (BC) 228-229 H 4
Kimsquit River ~ CDN (BC) 228-229 G 3
Kimvula o ZRE 210-211 E 6
Kimža ~ RUS 88-89 S 4
Kin o J 152-153 B 11
Kinabalu, Gunung ▲ • MAL 160-161 B 9
Kinabalu National Park ⊥ MAL 160-161 B 9
Kinak Bay ≈ 22-23 O 3
Kinangaly ▲ RM 222-223 D 7
Kinango o EAK 212-213 G 6
Kinara o RI 166-167 G 3
Kinard o USA (FL) 286-287 D 1
Kinbasket Lake ⊂ CDN (BC) 228-229 Q 4
Kincaid o CDN (SAS) 232-233 M 6
Kincaid o USA (KS) 262-263 L 6
Kincardine o CDN (ONT) 238-239 D 4
Kinchafoonee Creek ~ USA (GA) 284-285 F 5
Kinchega National Park ⊥ AUS 180-181 G 2
Kinchil o MEX 52-53 K 1
Kincolith o CDN 32-33 F 4
Kinda o ZRE 214-215 C 5
Kindakun Point ▲ CDN (BC) 228-229 B 3
Kindamba o RCB 210-211 E 5
Kinder o USA (LA) 268-269 H 6
Kindersley o CDN (SAS) 232-233 J 4
Kindi o BF 202-203 J 3
Kindi o ZRE 210-211 F 6
Kindia ◘ RG 202-203 D 4
Kindia ☆ RG 202-203 D 4
Kindikti, kõli ⊂ KA 124-125 C 3
Kindu o ZRE 210-211 K 5
Kinel' ☆ RUS 96-97 G 7
Kinel'-Čerkasy ☆ RUS 96-97 G 7
Kinel'skie jary ▲ RUS 96-97 G 7
Kinešma = Kinešma ☆ RUS 94-95 S 3
Kinesi o EAT 212-213 D 4
Kinešma ☆ RUS 94-95 S 3
King o USA (TX) 266-267 K 2
King, Cayo ⌒ NIC 52-53 C 5
King, Lake ⊂ AUS (WA) 176-177 F 2
King, Lake ⊂ AUS (WA) 176-177 E 6
King, Mount ▲ AUS 178-179 J 3
Kinga o ZRE 214-215 B 6
Kinganga o ZRE 210-211 D 6
Kingaroy o AUS 178-179 L 4
King Charles Cape ▲ CDN 36-37 K 2
King Christian Island ⌒ CDN 24-25 U 2
King Christian IX Land = Kong Christian IX Land ∴ GRØ 28-29 V 3
King Christian X Land = Kong Christian X Land ∴ GRØ 26-27 k 7
King City o USA (CA) 248-249 C 3
King City o USA (MO) 274-275 D 4
Kingcome Inlet o CDN (BC) 230-231 C 3
Kingcome Inlet ≈ CDN 230-231 C 3
King Cove o USA 22-23 P 5
King Edward River ~ AUS 172-173 H 3
King Edward VIIth Gulf ≈ 16 G 6
Kingfisher o USA (OK) 264-265 G 3
Kingfisher Lake o CDN (ONT) 234-235 O 2
King Frederik IX Land = Kong Frederik IX Land ∴ GRØ 28-29 P 3
King Frederik VI Coast = Kong Frederik VI Kyst ∴ GRØ 28-29 T 5
King Frederik VIII Land = Kong Frederik VIII Land ∴ GRØ 26-27 m 5
King George Bay ≈ 78-79 K 6
King George Island ⌒ ARK 16 G 31
King George Islands ⌒ CDN 36-37 K 6
King George Sound ≈ 36-37 N 4
King George Sound ≈ 176-177 E 7
King George Vth Sound ≈ 16 F 30
King George Vth Land ∴ ARK 16 F 16
King Haakon Bay ≈ 78-79 O 7
Kingisepp ☆ • RUS 94-95 L 2
Kingisepp = Kuressaare o •• EST 94-95 H 2
King Island ⌒ AUS 180-181 H 5
King Island ⌒ CDN (BC) 228-229 G 4
King Island ⌒ USA 20-21 F 4
King Junction o AUS 174-175 G 4
King Lear ▲ USA (NV) 246-247 G 2
King Leopold Ranges ▲ AUS 172-173 G 4
Kingman o CDN (ALB) 232-233 F 2
Kingman o USA (AZ) 256-257 A 3
Kingman o USA (KS) 262-263 H 7
King Mountain ▲ USA (OR) 244-245 G 7
King Mountain ▲ USA (TX) 266-267 E 2
Kingnait Fiord ≈ 36-37 R 2
Kingnait Range ▲ CDN 36-37 L 2
Kingombe o ZRE 210-211 L 5
Kingoonya o AUS 178-179 C 6
Kingora River ~ CDN 24-25 e 6
Kingoué o RCB 210-211 E 5
Kingri o PK 138-139 B 4
King River ~ AUS 172-173 L 3
King River ~ AUS 180-181 J 4
King Salmon o USA 22-23 S 3
King Salmon River ~ USA 22-23 S 3
King Salmon River ~ USA 22-23 S 4
King's-Bay-Fall • TT 60-61 L 2
Kings Bay Naval Submarine Base xx USA (GA) 284-285 J 6
Kingsburg o CDN (NS) 240-241 L 6
Kingsburg o USA (CA) 248-249 E 3
Kingsburg o USA (SC) 284-285 L 3
Kingsburg o ZA 220-221 K 5
Kings Canyon • AUS 176-177 L 2
Kings Canyon National Park ⊥ USA (CA) 248-249 F 3
Kings Canyon National Park ⊥ USA (CA) 248-249 F 2
Kingscote o AUS 180-181 D 3
Kings Cove o CDN (NFL) 242-243 P 4
Kingsfield o USA (ME) 278-279 L 4
Kingsford o USA (WI) 270-271 K 5
Kingsgate o CDN (BC) 230-231 N 4
Kings Hill Pass ▲ USA (MT) 250-251 J 5
Kingslake National Park ⊥ AUS 180-181 H 4
Kingsland o USA (GA) 284-285 J 6
Kingsland o USA (TX) 266-267 J 3
Kings Landing Historical Settlement • CDN (NB) 240-241 H 5
Kingsley o USA (IA) 274-275 C 2
Kingsley o ZA 220-221 K 3
King's Lynn o • GB 90-91 H 5
Kings Mountain o USA (NC) 282-283 F 5
Kings Mountain National Military Park • USA (SC) 284-285 J 1
King Sound ≈ 172-173 F 4
Kings Peak ▲ USA (UT) 254-255 E 3
King's Point o CDN (NFL) 242-243 M 3
Kingsport o USA (TN) 282-283 E 4
Kings River ~ USA (AR) 276-277 B 4
Kingston o AUS 180-181 J 7
Kingston o CDN (NB) 240-241 K 5
Kingston o CDN (ONT) 238-239 J 4
Kingston ★ • JA 54-55 G 5
Kingston o USA (IL) 274-275 G 5
Kingston o USA (MO) 274-275 D 5
Kingston o USA (NM) 256-257 H 6
Kingston o USA (NV) 246-247 H 4
Kingston o USA (NY) 280-281 N 2
Kingston o USA (OK) 264-265 H 5
Kingston o USA (PA) 280-281 L 2
Kingston o USA (TN) 282-283 C 5
Kingston-on-Murray o AUS 180-181 F 3
Kingston Peak ▲ USA (CA) 248-249 J 4
Kingston S.E. o AUS 180-181 E 4
Kingston upon Hull o • GB 90-91 G 5
Kingstown ★ WV 56 E 5
Kingstree o USA (SC) 284-285 L 3
Kings Trough ≃ 6-7 G 4
Kings Valley o USA (OR) 244-245 B 6
Kingsville o USA (TX) 266-267 K 6
Kingswood o ZA 220-221 G 3
Kingulube o ZRE 212-213 B 5
Kingungi o ZRE 210-211 F 6
Kingurutik Lake ⊂ CDN 36-37 S 6
Kingurutik River ~ CDN 36-37 S 6
Kingussie o GB 90-91 E 3
Kingwaya o ZRE 210-211 G 6
King William Island ⌒ CDN 24-25 X 6
King Williams Town o LB 202-203 F 7
King William's Town o • ZA 220-221 H 6
Kingwood o USA (WV) 280-281 G 4
Kiniama o ZRE 214-215 E 6
Kinik ☆ TR 128-129 B 3
Kinipaghulghat Mountains ▲ USA 20-21 F 5
Kiniraport o ZA 220-221 J 5
Kinistino o CDN (SAS) 232-233 N 3
Kinkala ☆ RCB 210-211 E 6
Kinkasan-shima ⌒ J 152-153 J 5
Kinkon, Chutes de ~ RG 202-203 D 4
Kinkony, Farihy ⊂ RM 222-223 D 6
Kinkosi o ZRE 210-211 E 6
Kinley o CDN (SAS) 232-233 L 3
Kinley Point ▲ CDN 26-27 L 3
Kinmundy o USA (IL) 274-275 K 6
Kinna o EAK 212-213 G 3
Kinna ☆ S 86-87 F 8
Kinnaird Head ▲ GB 90-91 G 3
Kinnear o USA (WY) 252-253 K 3
Kinnegad o IRL 90-91 D 5
Kinnekulle ▲ • S 86-87 F 7
Kinniconick o USA (KY) 276-277 M 2
Kinniya o CL 140-141 J 6
Kino, Bahía ≈ 50-51 C 3
Kino-gawa ~ J 152-153 F 7
Kinoje River ~ CDN 34-35 Q 5
Kinomoto o J 152-153 G 7
Kinoosao o CDN 34-35 F 2
Kinrara o AUS 174-175 H 6
Kinross o ZA 220-221 J 3
Kinsarvik ☆ N 86-87 C 6
Kinsella o CDN (ALB) 232-233 G 3
Kinsey o USA (MT) 250-251 O 5
Kinshasa ◘ ZRE 210-211 E 6
Kinshasa ★ • ZRE (Kin) 210-211 E 6
Kinsley o USA (KS) 262-263 G 7
Kinston o USA (NC) 282-283 K 5
Kinta o USA (OK) 264-265 J 3
Kintampo o GH 202-203 K 5
Kintinnian o RG 202-203 F 4
Kintom o RI 164-165 H 4
Kintop o RI 164-165 D 5
Kintore, Mount ▲ AUS 176-177 L 3
Kintore Range ▲ AUS 176-177 K 1
Kintyre ∴ GB 90-91 E 4
Kinu-gawa ~ J 152-153 H 6
Kinushseo River ~ CDN 34-35 P 3
Kinuso o CDN 32-33 N 4
Kinwat o IND 138-139 G 10
Kinyéran o RG 202-203 F 4
Kinyeti ▲ SUD 212-213 D 2
Kinyinya o BU 212-213 C 5
Kioa ⌒ FJI 184 III b 2
Kiokluk Mountains ▲ USA 20-21 L 6
Kiona o USA (WA) 244-245 F 4
Kiosk o CDN (ONT) 238-239 G 2
Kiowa o USA (CO) 254-255 L 4
Kiowa o USA (KS) 262-263 H 7
Kiowa o USA (MT) 250-251 F 3
Kiowa o USA (OK) 264-265 J 4
Kiowa, Fort • USA (SD) 260-261 G 3
Kiowa Creek ~ USA (CO) 254-255 L 4
Kiowa Creek ~ USA (TX) 264-265 D 2
Kipahulu o USA (HI) 288 J 4
Kipaila o ZRE 214-215 E 4
Kipaka o ZRE 210-211 L 6
Kiparissia o GR 100-101 H 6
Kipawa, Lac ⊂ CDN (QUE) 238-239 G 2
Kipemba o ZRE 210-211 E 6
Kipembawe o EAT 214-215 G 4
Kipengere Range ▲ EAT 214-215 G 5
Kipievo o RUS 88-89 X 4
Kipili o EAT 214-215 F 4
Kipini o EAK 212-213 H 5
Kipisa o ZRE 210-211 G 6
Kipkelion o EAK 212-213 E 4
Kipling o CDN (SAS) 232-233 Q 5
Kipnuk o USA 22-23 O 3
Kipti o UA 102-103 G 2
Kipushi o ZRE 214-215 D 6
Kipushia o ZRE (KOR) 214-215 C 4
Kipushia o ZRE (SHA) 214-215 E 7
Kiran ~ RUS 120-121 F 6
Kirana, Tanjung ▲ RI 166-167 G 3
Kirandul o IND 142-143 B 6
Kirané o RMM 202-203 E 2
Kiranomena o RM 222-223 E 7
Kiranūr o IND 140-141 H 5
Kiranur o IND 140-141 H 5
Kiraz ☆ TR 128-129 C 3
Kirbej o RUS 110-111 H 5
Kirbikân, Wâdi ~ SUD 200-201 F 3
Kirby o USA (AR) 276-277 B 6
Kirbyville o USA (TX) 268-269 G 6
Kirchhoffer River ~ CDN 36-37 G 2
Kireevsk ☆ RUS 94-95 P 5
Kirej ~ RUS 116-117 K 9
Kirenga ~ RUS 116-117 N 8
Kirensk ☆ RUS 116-117 O 7
Kirevna ~ RUS 120-121 T 5
Kirganik o RUS 120-121 S 6
Kirganik ~ RUS 120-121 S 6
Kirgiz-Mijaki ☆ RUS 96-97 J 7
Kirgizskij hrebet ▲ KA 136-137 N 3
Kiri o ZRE 210-211 G 4
Kiriab o RI 166-167 J 2
Kiriaini o EAK 212-213 F 4
Kinkhan ☆ TR 128-129 G 4
Kinkkale ☆ TR 128-129 E 3
Kirillov ☆ RUS 94-95 Q 2
Kirillovo o RUS 122-123 K 5
Kirinda o CL 140-141 J 7
Kirishima-Yaku National Park ⊥ J 152-153 D 9
Kirishima-yama ▲ J 152-153 D 9
Kiriši o RUS 94-95 N 2
Kirit o SP 208-209 H 4
Kiritappu o J 152-153 L 3
Kiritimati Island ⌒ KIB 13 M 2
Kirititi o EAK 212-213 F 4
Kiriwa o PNG 183 A 5
Kiriwina Island ⌒ PNG 183 F 5
Kirjaka-Tas, grjada ▲ RUS 108-109 f 4
Kirk o USA (OR) 244-245 D 8
Kirkalocka o AUS 176-177 D 4
Kirkcaldy o GB 90-91 F 3
Kirkella o CDN (MAN) 234-235 B 4
Kirkenes o N 86-87 P 2
Kirkensville o USA (OH) 280-281 D 4
Kirkfield o CDN (ONT) 238-239 G 4
Kirkgeçit o TR 128-129 K 3
Kirk Gemstone Deposit, Mount • AUS 176-177 F 6
Kirkimbie o AUS 172-173 J 4
Kirk Lake ⊂ CDN 30-31 P 4
Kirkland o USA (AZ) 256-257 C 4
Kirkland o USA (IL) 274-275 K 3
Kirkland o USA (TX) 264-265 D 4
Kirkland o USA (WA) 244-245 C 3
Kirkland Lake o • CDN (ONT) 236-237 J 4
Kirklareli ☆ TR 128-129 B 2
Kirklin o USA (IN) 274-275 M 4
Kirkpatrick Lake ⊂ CDN (ALB) 232-233 G 4
Kirksville o USA (MO) 274-275 F 4
Kirkük ☆ IRQ 128-129 L 5
Kirkun ~ RUS 118-119 E 11
Kirkwall o • GB 90-91 F 2
Kirkwood o USA (IL) 274-275 H 4
Kirkwood o USA (MO) 274-275 H 6
Kirkwood o ZA 220-221 G 6
Kirobasi o TR 128-129 E 4
Kirov o RUS 94-95 O 4
Kirov o RUS (KIR) 96-97 F 4
Kirova, ostrov ⌒ RUS 108-109 Z 3
Kirovabad = Ganža o • AZ 128-129 M 2
Kirovakan = Karaklis o AR 128-129 L 2
Kirovo o RUS 118-119 L 3
Kirovo-Čepeck ☆ RUS 96-97 G 4
Kirovograd = Kirovohrad ☆ UA 102-103 H 3
Kirovohrad ☆ UA 102-103 H 3
Kirovsk o RUS (LEN) 94-95 M 2
Kirovsk o RUS (MUR) 88-89 M 3
Kirovsk = Babadayhan o TM 136-137 G 6
Kirovs'ke o UA 102-103 J 5
Kirovskij o RUS 122-123 E 6
Kirovskij o RUS (AMR) 118-119 N 8
Kirovskij o RUS (AST) 126-127 H 5
Kirovskij o RUS (KMC) 120-121 Q 6
Kirovskij o RUS (KRN) 116-117 G 6
Kirovskij o TJ 136-137 L 6
Kirovskoe o KS 136-137 M 3
Kirov su kojmasy < KA 96-97 G 8
Kirpili ~ RUS 102-103 L 5
Kirs ☆ RUS 96-97 H 4
Kirsanov o RUS 94-95 S 5
Kırşehir ☆ TR 128-129 F 3
Kirtachi o RN 204-205 E 2
Kirtāka o AFG 134-135 L 3
Kirtāka ∴ • PK 134-135 J 4
Kirthar National Park ⊥ PK 134-135 M 6
Kirthar Range ▲ PK 134-135 M 5
Kirtland o USA (NM) 256-257 G 2
Kirtland o USA (OH) 280-281 E 2
Kiru o WAN 204-205 H 3
Kiruna o • S 86-87 K 3
Kirundo o BU 212-213 C 5
Kirundu o ZRE 210-211 K 4
Kirwin National Wildlife Refuge ⊥ USA (KS) 262-263 G 5
Kirwin Reservoir ⊂ USA (KS) 262-263 G 5
Kiryandongo o EAU 212-213 D 3
Kiryū o J 152-153 H 6
Kiržač ☆ RUS 94-95 Q 3
Kiš o IR 134-135 E 5
Kiš, Ğazīre-ye ⌒ IR 134-135 E 5
Kisa ☆ S 86-87 G 8
Kisaki o EAT 214-215 J 4
Kisanga o EAT 214-215 J 4
Kisangani ☆ ZRE (HAU) 210-211 K 3
Kisangire o EAT 214-215 K 4
Kisantete o ZRE 210-211 F 6
Kisantu o • ZRE 210-211 E 6
Kisar, Pulau ⌒ RI 166-167 D 6
Kisaralik River ~ USA 20-21 K 6
Kisaran o RI 162-163 C 3
Kisarawe o EAT 214-215 K 4
Kisarazu o J 152-153 H 7
Kisasi o EAT 212-213 G 6
Kisatchie o USA (LA) 268-269 G 5
Kisbey o CDN (SAS) 232-233 Q 6
Kiselevka o RUS 122-123 H 3
Kiselëvsk o RUS 124-125 P 1
Kiselevsk = Kiselëvsk o RUS 124-125 P 1
Kisengi o EAT 212-213 D 6
Kisengwa o ZRE (KOR) 210-211 L 6
Kisengwa o ZRE (KOR) 214-215 C 4
Kishanganj o IND 142-143 E 2
Kishangar o IND 138-139 C 6
Kishangarh o IND (MAP) 138-139 G 7
Kishangarh o IND (RAJ) 138-139 E 6
Kishari o PK 134-135 M 5
Kishiwada o J 152-153 F 7
Kishtwar o • IND 138-139 E 3
Kisi o EAT 214-215 F 4
Kisi o WAN 204-205 E 4
Kisigo ~ EAT 214-215 H 4
Kisigo Game Reserve ⊥ EAT 214-215 H 4
Kisii o EAK 212-213 E 4
Kisiju o EAT 214-215 K 4
Kisima o EAK 212-213 F 3
Kišinev = Chişinău ★ MD 102-103 F 4
Kisiwani o EAT 212-213 F 6
Kisiwani, Kilwa •• EAT 214-215 K 5
Kiska Island ⌒ USA 22-23 E 7
Kiskatinaw River ~ CDN 32-33 K 4
Kiska Volcan ▲ USA 22-23 E 6
Kiskittogisu Lake ⊂ CDN 34-35 G 3
Kiskitto Lake ⊂ CDN 34-35 G 3
Kiskőrös o H 92-93 P 5
Kiskunfélegyháza o H 92-93 P 5
Kiskunhalas o H 92-93 P 5
Kislovodsk o RUS 126-127 E 6
Kismaanyo ☆ SP 212-213 J 4
Kismet o USA (KS) 262-263 F 7
Kiso-gawa ~ J 152-153 G 7
Kisogwa o EAT 212-213 C 5
Kisomoro o EAU 212-213 C 3
Kisoro o EAU 212-213 B 4
Kiso-sanmyaku ▲ J 152-153 G 7
Kisose o ZRE 214-215 C 4
Kisoshi o ZRE 212-213 B 6
Kispiox River ~ CDN 32-33 F 4
Kissen ~ RG 202-203 D 4
Kissidougou o RG 202-203 E 5
Kissimmee o USA (FL) 286-287 H 3
Kissimmee, Lake ⊂ USA (FL) 286-287 H 4
Kissimmee River ~ USA (FL) 286-287 H 4
Kissingen, Bad o D 92-93 L 3
Kississing Lake ⊂ CDN 34-35 F 3
Kistanje o HR 100-101 E 3
Kistigan Lake ⊂ CDN 34-35 K 3
Kisuki o J 152-153 E 7
Kisumu ☆ EAK 212-213 E 4
Kisvárda o H 92-93 R 4
Kit, mys ▲ RUS 108-109 d 3
Kita o RMM 202-203 F 3
Kitaa = Vestgrønland ◘ GRØ 26-27 Z 6
Kita-Daitō-shima ⌒ J 152-153 D 12
Kitāf o Y 132-133 D 5
Kitahiyama o J 152-153 H 3
Kitaibaraki o J 152-153 J 6
Kitakami o J 152-153 J 5
Kitakami-gawa ~ J 152-153 J 5
Kitakami-kōti ▲ J 152-153 J 5
Kitakata o J 152-153 H 6
Kitakyūshū o J 152-153 D 8
Kitale o EAK 212-213 E 3
Kitamaat Village o CDN (BC) 228-229 F 3
Kitami o J 152-153 K 3
Kitami-santi ▲ J 152-153 K 2
Kitami-tōge ▲ J 152-153 K 3
Kitami-Yamato-tai ≃ 152-153 L 2
Kita-Nagato Quasi National Park ⊥ J 152-153 D 7
Kitanda o ZRE 214-215 D 4
Kitangari o EAT 214-215 K 6
Kitangiri, Lake ⊂ EAT 212-213 E 6
Kitani Safari Camp o EAK 212-213 F 5
Kitava Island ⌒ PNG 183 F 5
Kitaya o EAT 214-215 L 6
Kit Carson o USA (CO) 254-255 N 5
Kitchener o AUS 176-177 H 5
Kitchener o CDN (BC) 230-231 N 4
Kitchener o CDN (ONT) 238-239 E 5
Kitchigama, Rivière ~ CDN (QUE) 236-237 K 2
Kitchings Mill o USA (SC) 284-285 J 3
Kite o USA (GA) 284-285 H 4
Kite o USA (KY) 276-277 N 3
Kiteba o ZRE 214-215 C 4
Kitee o FIN 88-89 L 5
Kitendwe o ZRE 214-215 E 4
Kitenga o ZRE 210-211 F 6
Kitengo o ZRE 214-215 C 4
Kiterput qorno ≈ 28-29 R 6
Kitgum o EAU 212-213 D 2
Kithira o GR 100-101 J 6
Kithira ⌒ GR 100-101 J 6
Kíthnos ⌒ GR 100-101 K 6
Kitika o RCA 206-207 F 6
Kitimat o CDN (BC) 228-229 F 2
Kitimat Ranges ▲ CDN (BC) 228-229 E 2
Kitimat River ~ CDN (BC) 228-229 F 2
Kitinen ~ FIN 88-89 J 3
Kitiwaka ~ EAT (IRI) 214-215 H 6
Kitkatla o CDN (BC) 228-229 D 3
Kitilä o FIN 88-89 H 3
Kitlope River ~ CDN (BC) 228-229 G 3
Kitob ☆ US 136-137 K 5
Kitobojnyj o RUS 122-123 O 5
Kitoj ~ RUS 116-117 K 9
Kitou o J 152-153 F 8
Kitsamby ~ RM 222-223 E 7
Kitscoty o CDN (ALB) 232-233 H 2
Kitsuki o J 152-153 D 8
Kitsumkalum Lake ⊂ CDN (BC) 228-229 F 2
Kitsumkalum River ~ CDN (BC) 228-229 E 2
Kittakittaooloo, Lake ⊂ AUS 178-179 E 5
Kittanning o USA (PA) 280-281 G 3
Kittery o USA (ME) 278-279 L 5
Kitt Peak National Observatory • USA (AZ) 256-257 D 7
Kitty Hawk o USA (NC) 282-283 M 4
Kitui o EAK 212-213 G 4
Kitumbeine o EAT 212-213 F 5
Kitumbini o EAT 214-215 K 5
Kitunda o EAT 214-215 G 4
Kitunga o ZRE 214-215 C 5
Kitutu o ZRE 212-213 B 5
Kitwanga o CDN 32-33 F 4
Kitwe o Z 214-215 E 7
Kitzbühel o • A 92-93 M 5
Kitzingen o D 92-93 L 4
Kiu o EAK 212-213 F 4
Kiubo, Chute ~ ZRE 214-215 D 5
Kiuga Marine National Reserve ⊥ EAK 212-213 H 4
Kiu Lom Reservoir ⊂ THA 142-143 L 6
Kiumbila o ZRE 210-211 L 6
Kiunga o EAK 212-213 H 4
Kiunga o PNG 183 A 4
Kiuruvesi o FIN 88-89 J 5
Kivalina o USA 20-21 H 3
Kivalina River ~ USA 20-21 H 3
Kivi o IR 128-129 N 4
Kivijärvi o FIN 88-89 H 5
Kiviõli o EST 94-95 K 2
Kivori-Kui o PNG 183 D 5
Kivu ◘ ZRE 210-211 L 5
Kivu, Lac o ZRE 212-213 B 4
Kiwai Island ⌒ PNG 183 B 5
Kiwalik o USA 20-21 K 4
Kiwatama o EAT 214-215 K 5
Kiwayuu Bay ≈ 212-213 H 5
Kiwi House • NZ 182 E 3
Kiworo o RI 166-167 K 5
Kiyāmaki Dāğ ▲ IR 128-129 L 3
Kiyāsar o IR 136-137 C 6
Kiyāt o KSA 132-133 B 4
Kiyawa o WAN 204-205 H 3
Kiyiu Lake ⊂ CDN (SAS) 232-233 K 4
Kiyl ~ KA 96-97 J 9
Kizel o RUS 114-115 D 5
Kizema o RUS 88-89 S 6
Kizhake Chalakudi o IND 140-141 G 5
Kiziba-Baluba ⊥ ZRE 214-215 D 6
Kiži-Hem ~ RUS 116-117 H 9
Kızılağaç o TR 128-129 J 3
Kızılcahamam ☆ TR 128-129 E 2
Kızılırmak ~ TR 128-129 G 3
Kızılırmak ~ TR 128-129 F 3
Kızılırmak ~ TR 128-129 F 2
Kizil'jurt o RUS 126-127 G 6
Kızılkum ∴ US 136-137 G 3
Kızılören o TR 128-129 E 4
Kizil Qianfodonga ◘ VRC 146-147 E 5
Kizil'tašskij liman ≈ 102-103 K 5
Kızıltepe ☆ TR 128-129 J 4
Kizimkazi o EAT 214-215 K 4
Kižinga ☆ RUS 118-119 D 10
Kižinga ~ RUS 118-119 D 10
Kiži Pogost ••• RUS 88-89 N 5
Kizir ~ RUS 116-117 G 8
Kızkalesi •• TR 128-129 F 4
Kizljar o RUS 126-127 G 6
Kizner ☆ RUS 96-97 G 5
Kizyl Arvat o TM 136-137 E 5
Kizyl Atrek = Gyzyletrek o TM 136-137 D 6
Kizyl Baudak o TM 136-137 F 3
Kizyl-Kaja o TM 136-137 D 4
Kjahta ☆ RUS 116-117 N 10
Kjalvaz o AZ 128-129 N 3
Kjël', Ytyk ☆ • RUS 120-121 E 2
Kjøllefjord o N 86-87 N 1
Kjøpsvik o N 86-87 H 2
Kjubjainde o RUS 118-119 K 3
Kjubjume ~ RUS 120-121 H 2
Kjuël', Aleko- o RUS 110-111 c 5
Kjuël', Bjas'- o RUS 118-119 J 6
Kjuël', Bjas' o RUS 118-119 N 4
Kjuël', Kudu- o RUS 118-119 K 6
Kjuël', Sebjan- o RUS 110-111 R 7
Kjuël', Segjan- o RUS 118-119 P 4
Kjuël', Ulahan- o RUS 110-111 V 6
Kjuël', Us- o RUS 118-119 P 4
Kjuël', Usun- o RUS 118-119 H 4
Kjuènelëkjan ~ RUS 110-111 G 5
Kjuente ~ RUS 120-121 J 2
Kjuëreljah o RUS 118-119 N 4
Kjulekjan' o RUS 118-119 K 3
Kjulenke ~ RUS 110-111 O 6
Kjundjae ~ RUS 118-119 J 4
Kjundjudej ~ RUS 110-111 P 7
Kjungej Ala-Too', hrebet ▲ KS 146-147 C 4
Kjunkju ~ RUS 118-119 N 5
Kjunkjuj-Rassoha ~ RUS 110-111 G 4
Kjupcy o RUS 120-121 F 3
Kjurdamir = Kürdamir o AZ 128-129 N 2
Kjurjungnekjan ~ RUS 116-117 O 3
Kjusjur o RUS 110-111 Q 4
Kjustendil o • BG 102-103 C 6
Klaarstrom o ZA 220-221 F 6
Klabat, Teluk ≈ 162-163 F 5
Kladanj o BIH 100-101 G 2
Kladar o RI 166-167 J 6
Kladno o CZ 92-93 N 3
Klaeng o THA 158-159 F 4
Klagenfurt ☆ A 92-93 N 5
Klaipėda ☆ •• LT 94-95 G 4
Klakah o RI 168 E 3
Klamath o USA (CA) 246-247 A 2
Klamath Falls o USA (OR) 244-245 D 8
Klamath Mountains ▲ USA (CA) 246-247 B 2
Klamath River ~ USA (CA) 246-247 B 2
Klamath River Lodge o USA (CA) 246-247 C 2
Klamono o RI 166-167 F 2
Klang o MAL 162-163 D 3
Klappen River ~ CDN 32-33 F 3
Klarälven ~ S 86-87 F 6
Klark ~ RUS 112-113 V 1
Klaserie Nature Reserve ⊥ ZA 220-221 K 2
Klaten o RI 168 D 3
Klatovy o CZ 92-93 M 4
Klattau = Klatovy o CZ 92-93 M 4
Klawer o ZA 220-221 D 5
Klawock o USA 32-33 D 4
Kle o LB 202-203 E 6
Kleena Kleene o CDN (BC) 230-231 E 2
Klein Aub o NAM 220-221 C 1
Kleinbegin o ZA 220-221 E 4
Klein Doringrivier ~ ZA 220-221 D 5
Kleiner Khingan ▲ VRC 150-151 F 2
Klein Karas o NAM 220-221 D 3
Klein Karoo = Little Karoo ∴ ZA 220-221 E 6
Klein Letaba ~ ZA 218-219 F 6
Kleinpoort o ZA 220-221 G 6
Klein Rietrivier ~ ZA 220-221 E 5
Klein's Camp o EAT 212-213 E 4
Kleinsee o ZA 220-221 C 4
Klein Swartberge ▲ ZA 220-221 E 6
Klekovača ▲ BIH 100-101 F 2
Kléla o RMM 202-203 H 4
Klemtu o CDN (BC) 228-229 F 4
Klerksdorp o ZA 220-221 H 3
Klerkskraal o ZA 220-221 H 3
Klery Creek o USA 20-21 K 3
Klésso o BF 202-203 J 4
Kletnja o RUS 94-95 N 5
Kleve o D 92-93 J 3
Klička o RUS 118-119 J 10
Kličkinskij, hrebet ▲ RUS 118-119 H 10
Klickitat o USA (WA) 244-245 D 5
Klickitat River ~ USA (WA) 244-245 D 4
Klimino o RUS 116-117 J 6
Klimpfjäll o S 86-87 G 4
Klin ☆ • RUS 94-95 P 3
Klina o YU 100-101 H 3
Klinaklini Glacier ⊂ CDN (BC) 230-231 C 2
Klinaklini River ~ CDN (BC) 230-231 D 2
Klincy o RUS 94-95 N 5
Klinovec ▲ CZ 92-93 M 3
Klinsko-Dmitrovskaja grjada ▲ RUS 94-95 O 3
Klintehamn o S 86-87 J 8
Klipfontein o ZA 220-221 G 6
Klipplaat o ZA 220-221 G 6
Kliprand o ZA 220-221 D 5
Kliprivier ~ ZA 220-221 J 3
Klipskool o ZA 220-221 K 2
Klis o RI 166-167 D 6
Klisurski Prohod ▲ BG 102-103 C 6
Kljavino ☆ RUS 96-97 H 6
Kljaz'ma ~ RUS 94-95 Q 4
Ključ o BIH 100-101 F 2
Ključ, Tëplyj o RUS 120-121 G 2
Ključevskaja Sopka, vulkan ▲ RUS 120-121 T 5
Ključi o RUS (KMC) 120-121 T 5
Ključi ☆ RUS (ALT) 124-125 L 2
Kljuevka ~ RUS 108-109 h 3
Kłodzko o •• PL 92-93 O 3
Klotz, Lac ⊂ CDN 36-37 N 4
Klondike Highway II CDN 20-21 W 5
Klondike Plateau ▲ CDN 20-21 U 5
Klondike River ~ CDN 20-21 V 4
Klos o • AL 100-101 H 4
Klosterneuburg o A 92-93 O 4
Klotz, Mount ▲ CDN 20-21 U 4
Kluane Lake ⊂ CDN 20-21 V 6
Kluang o MAL 162-163 E 3
Kluczbork o PL 92-93 P 3
Kludang o BRU 164-165 D 1
Kluhorskij, pereval ▲ RUS 126-127 D 6
Klunda o IND 138-139 F 2
Klungkung o • RI 168 B 7
Klutlan Glacier ⊂ USA 20-21 U 6
Klymovo o RUS 94-95 N 5
Km. 60 o PY 76-77 H 2
Km. 100 o RA 76-77 H 4
Km. 145 o PY 76-77 H 2
Kmpóng Thum o K 158-159 H 4
Knarvik o N 86-87 B 6
Kneehills Creek ~ CDN (ALB) 232-233 E 4
Knee Lake ⊂ CDN (MAN) 34-35 J 3
Knee Lake ⊂ CDN (SAS) 34-35 C 3
Knewstubb Lake ⊂ CDN (BC) 228-229 K 3
Kneža o BG 102-103 D 6
Knickerbocker o USA (TX) 266-267 G 2
Knidos • TR 128-129 B 4
Knifeblade Ridge ▲ USA 20-21 L 2
Knife Delta ≈ 30-31 W 6
Knife River ~ USA (ND) 258-259 E 4
Knife River Indian Village National Historic Site ∴ USA (ND) 258-259 F 4
Knight Inlet ≈ 32-33 H 6
Knight Inlet ≈ CDN 230-231 D 3
Knight Island ⌒ USA 20-21 R 6
Knight Islands ⌒ CDN 36-37 R 4
Knights Landing o USA (CA) 246-247 D 5
Knightstown o USA (IN) 274-275 N 5
Knin o HR 100-101 F 2
Knippa o USA (TX) 266-267 H 4
Knivskjelodden ▲ N 86-87 M 1
Knjaginino o RUS 96-97 D 6
Knjaze-Bolkonskoe o RUS 122-123 F 4
Knjaževac o YU 100-101 J 3
Knjaževo o RUS 94-95 S 2
Knjazevo o RUS 122-123 H 2
Knob, Cape ▲ AUS 176-177 E 7
Knobby Head ▲ AUS 176-177 C 4
Knobel o USA (AR) 276-277 E 4
Knob Noster o USA (MO) 274-275 E 6
Knokke-Heist o • B 92-93 G 3
Knolls o USA (UT) 254-255 B 3
Knorr, Cape ▲ CDN 26-27 P 4
Knossós o •• GR 100-101 K 7
Knott o USA (TX) 264-265 C 6
Knotts Island o USA (NC) 282-283 M 4
Knowles, Cape ▲ ARK 16 F 30
Knowles Lake ⊂ CDN 30-31 R 5
Knox o USA (IN) 274-275 M 3
Knox, Cape ▲ CDN (BC) 228-229 A 2
Knox City o USA (TX) 264-265 E 5
Knox Land ∴ ARK 16 G 11
Knoxville o USA (IA) 274-275 E 3
Knoxville o USA (IL) 274-275 H 4
Knoxville o USA (PA) 280-281 J 2
Knoxville o USA (TN) 282-283 D 5
Knuckles ▲ CL 140-141 J 7
Knud Rasmussen Land ∴ GRØ 26-27 V 4
Knud Rasmussen Land ∴ GRØ 26-27 m 8
Knysna o ZA 220-221 F 7
Knysna National Lake Area ⊥ ZA 220-221 F 7
Ko, gora ▲ RUS 122-123 G 5
Koaba o DY 202-203 L 4
Koagas o RI 166-167 G 3
Koalla o BF 202-203 K 3
Koamb o CAM 210-211 D 2
Koaties se Pan ⊂ ZA 220-221 D 5
Kob' o RUS 116-117 K 8
Koba o RG 202-203 D 4
Koba o RI (MAL) 166-167 H 5
Koba o RI (SUS) 162-163 G 6
Kobadie o RN 202-203 L 3
Kobadja o RCA 206-207 D 6
Kobayashi o J 152-153 D 9
Kobbermineburgt ≈ 28-29 Q 6
Kobe ☆ J 152-153 F 7
Kobe o RI 164-165 K 3
Kobédaigouré o CI 202-203 H 7
Kobeľaky o UA 102-103 J 3
Kobenni o RIM 196-197 F 7
Kobi o CAM 206-207 B 6
Kobi o RI 166-167 E 3
Kobi o WAN 204-205 K 4
Kobjaj o RUS 118-119 N 4
Koblagué o TCH 206-207 C 4
Koblenz o • D 92-93 J 3
Kobleve o UA 102-103 G 4
Kobli o DY 202-203 L 4
K'obo o ETH 200-201 J 6
Koboko o EAU 212-213 C 2
Kobona o RUS 94-95 M 1
Kobou o RMM 202-203 K 2
Kobroor, Pulau ⌒ RI 166-167 H 5
Kobryn o BY 94-95 J 5
Kobuk o USA 20-21 M 3
Kobuk River ~ USA 20-21 N 3
Kobuk Valley National Park ⊥ USA 20-21 L 3
Kobuleti o • GE 126-127 D 7
Koca Deresi ~ TR 128-129 C 2
Kocaeli (İzmit) ☆ TR 128-129 C 2
Kocaeli Yarımadası ∼ TR 128-129 C 2
Kocaköy o TR 128-129 J 3
Kočani o MK 100-101 J 4
Koçarlı ☆ TR 128-129 B 4
Kočečum ~ RUS 116-117 H 2
Kočegarovo o RUS 118-119 J 6
Kočenevo ☆ RUS 114-115 R 7
Kočenga ~ RUS 116-117 M 8
Kočerinovo o BG 102-103 C 6
Kočetovka o RUS 94-95 R 5
Kočevje o YU 100-101 E 2
Kočevo ☆ RUS 96-97 J 4

Kŏch'ang o ROK 150-151 F 10
Ko Chang ⌒ THA 158-159 E 6
Ko Chang ⌒ THA 158-159 G 4
Ko Chang National Park ⊥ • THA 158-159 G 4
Kochchikade o CL 140-141 H 7
Koch Creek ~ CDN (BC) 230-231 M 4
Kōchi ☆ • J 152-153 E 8
Koch Island ⌒ CDN 24-25 h 6
Koch Peak ▲ USA (MT) 250-251 H 6
Kochtel = Kohtla o EST 94-95 K 2
Kocjubyns'ke o UA 102-103 G 2
Kock o PL 102-103 C 2
Kočki ☆ RUS 124-125 M 1
Kočkoma o RUS 88-89 N 4
Kočkor-Ata o KS 136-137 N 4
Kočkorka o KS 146-147 B 4
Kočubeevskoe o RUS 126-127 D 5
Kočubej o RUS 126-127 G 5
Kočumdek ~ RUS 116-117 F 3
Koda ~ RUS 116-117 J 6
Kodār o IND 140-141 H 2
Kodari o NEP 144-145 E 7
Kodarma o IND 142-143 D 3
Kodiak o USA 22-23 U 4
Kodiak Island ⌒ USA 22-23 U 4
Kodina ~ RUS 88-89 P 5
Kodinār o IND 138-139 C 9
Kodino o RUS 88-89 P 5
Kodiyakkarai o IND 140-141 H 5
Kodjari o BF 202-203 L 4
Kodmo, togga ~ SP 208-209 J 4
Kodok o SUD 206-207 L 4
Kodumuru o IND 140-141 G 3
Kodyma ~ UA 102-103 F 4
Koébonou o CI 202-203 J 5
Koës o NAM 220-221 D 2
Koettlitz Glacier ⊂ ARK 16 F 16
Kofa Game Range ⊥ USA (AZ) 256-257 A 5
Kofa Mountains ▲ USA (AZ) 256-257 A 5
Kofarnihon o TJ 136-137 L 5
Kofelē o ETH 208-209 D 5
Koffiefontein o ZA 220-221 G 4
Kofoed-Hansen Bræ ⊂ GRØ 26-27 o 5
Koforidua ☆ GH 202-203 K 6
Kōfu o J (TOT) 152-153 E 7
Kōfu ☆ J (YMN) 152-153 H 7
Koga o J 152-153 H 6
Kogaluc, Lac o CDN 36-37 L 5
Kogaluc, Rivière ~ CDN 36-37 L 5
Kogaluk Bay ≈ 36-37 K 5
Kogaluk River ~ CDN 36-37 S 6
Kogalym o RUS 114-115 N 3
Køge o • DK 86-87 F 9
Køge Bugt ≈ 86-87 F 9
Køge Bugt = Pikiutdleq ≈ 28-29 U 4
Kogel' ~ RUS 114-115 D 3
Kogmanskloof ▲ ZA 220-221 E 6
Kognak River ~ CDN 30-31 U 5
Kogoluktuk River ~ USA 20-21 M 3
Kogon ~ RG 202-203 C 4
Kogrukluk River ~ USA 20-21 L 6
Kogtok River ~ CDN 30-31 V 4
Koğūr o IR 136-137 B 6
Kogyae Strict Nature Reserve ⊥ GH 202-203 K 6
Kohala Mountains ▲ USA (HI) 288 K 4
Kohan o PK 134-135 M 5
Kohāt o • PK 138-139 C 3
Kohāt Pass ▲ PK 138-139 C 3
Kohila o EST 94-95 J 2
Kohil'nik ~ UA 102-103 F 5
Kohima ☆ •• IND 142-143 J 3
Kohinggo = Arundel ⌒ SOL 184 I c 3
Ko Hinh o LAO 156-157 C 6
Koh-i-Patandar ▲ PK 134-135 L 5
Kohler Range ▲ ARK 16 F 25
Kohlu o PK 138-139 B 5
Kohol o RI 166-167 D 3
Kohtla-Järve o •• EST 94-95 K 2
Kohŭng o ROK 150-151 F 10
Kohunlich ∴ • MEX 52-53 K 2
Koiama, Jasiira ⌒ SP 212-213 J 4
Koichab ~ NAM 220-221 C 3
Koichab Pan o NAM 220-221 B 3
Koidern o CDN 20-21 U 6
Koidu o WAL 202-203 E 5
Koihoa o IND 140-141 L 5
Koila Kabé ~ SN 202-203 E 3
Koil Island ⌒ PNG 183 C 2
Koilkuntla o IND 140-141 H 3
Koimbani o COM 222-223 C 3
Koimekeah o IND 140-141 L 6
Koin ~ RUS 88-89 V 5
Koindu o WAL 202-203 E 5
Koito o EAK 212-213 G 5
Kojbagar, köli o KA 124-125 D 2
Kojda o RUS 88-89 R 3
Kojda ~ RUS 88-89 R 3
Kōje Do ⌒ ROK 150-151 G 10
Kojgorodok ☆ RUS 96-97 G 3
Kōjin o ROK 150-151 G 8
Kojmatdag ▲ TM 136-137 D 4
Kojnathun, ozero o RUS 112-113 V 4
Kojonup o AUS 176-177 D 6
Kojtoš o US 136-137 K 4
Kojvèrelan ~ RUS 112-113 R 5
Kojvèrelanskij krjaž ▲ RUS 112-113 R 5
K'ok'a o ETH 208-209 D 4
K'ok'a Gidib < ETH 208-209 D 4
K'ok'a Hāyk' o ETH 208-209 D 4
Kokand o US 136-137 M 4
Kokanee Glacier Provincial Park ⊥ CDN (BC) 230-231 M 4
Kokani ~ EAK 212-213 G 5
Kōkaral o KA 126-127 O 4
Kōkaral, tubegi ᴗ KA 126-127 O 4
Kokas o RI 166-167 G 3
Kokatha o AUS 178-179 C 6
Kokča o US 136-137 J 4
Kōkcengirsor, köli o KA 124-125 G 2
Kokcetau Üstirti ▲ KA 124-125 F 2
Kokenau o RI 166-167 J 4
Kokeragi Point ▲ CDN 30-31 H 3
Kokerboomwoud • NAM 220-221 D 3
Kokerit o GUY 62-63 E 2
Ko Kho Khao ⌒ THA 158-159 E 6
Kokish o CDN (BC) 230-231 C 3
Kok-Jangak o KS 136-137 N 4
Kokkola o FIN 88-89 G 5
Koklapperne ⌒ GRØ 28-29 V 4
Koknese o •• LV 94-95 J 3
Koko o WAN (BEL) 204-205 F 5
Koko o WAN (SOK) 204-205 F 3
Kokoda o PNG 183 D 5
Kokoda Trail • PNG 183 D 5
Kokola o PNG 183 G 2
Kokolik River ~ USA 20-21 K 2
Kokologo o BF 202-203 K 3
Kokomo o USA (IN) 274-275 M 4
Kokonselkä o FIN 88-89 H 5
Kokopo o PNG 183 G 3
Kokora, ozero o RUS 108-109 d 5
Kokoro ~ RG 202-203 F 3
Kokosa o ETH 208-209 D 5
Kokoso o GH 202-203 K 7
Kokoti Kouamékro o CI 202-203 H 6
Kokoula ~ RG 202-203 D 4
Kokpek o KA 146-147 D 4
Kokpekty o KA 124-125 N 4
Kokrajhar o IND 142-143 G 2
Kokrines Hills ▲ USA 20-21 N 4
Kokruagarok o USA 20-21 O 1
Koksa ~ RUS 124-125 O 3
Koksan o DVR 150-151 F 8
Kōksaraj o KA 136-137 L 3
Kōksengir, tau ▲ KA (AKT) 126-127 M 5
Kōksengir, tau ▲ KA (KZL) 124-125 D 6
Koksoak, Rivière ~ CDN 36-37 P 6
Kokstad o ZA 220-221 J 5
Kōksu o KA 136-137 L 4
Kōksu ~ KA 124-125 L 6
Koktac, Rivière ~ CDN 36-37 L 5
Koktal o KA 124-125 L 6
Kōktas ~ KA 124-125 G 5
Kōktōbe, tau ▲ KA 124-125 E 5
Koktokay o VRC 146-147 J 2
Kōktyrnak, tubegi ᴗ KA 126-127 O 4
Koku, Tanjung ▲ RI 164-165 G 6
Kokubo o J 152-153 D 9
Kokumbo o CI 202-203 H 6
Kŏkŭm Do ⌒ ROK 150-151 F 10
Ko Kut ⌒ THA 158-159 G 5
Kol o PNG 183 C 3
Kola o CDN (MAN) 234-235 B 5
Kola o RI 166-167 H 4
Kola o RUS 88-89 M 2
Kola, Gorges de ᴗ • CAM 204-205 K 4
Kola, Pulau ⌒ RI 166-167 H 4
Kolachel o IND 140-141 G 6
Kolāchi ~ PK 134-135 M 5
Kolahun o LB 202-203 E 5
Kolaka o RI 164-165 G 6
Kolan River ~ AUS 178-179 L 3
Ko Lanta ⌒ THA 158-159 E 7
Kola Peninsula = Kol'skij poluostrov ᴗ RUS 88-89 N 2
Kolār o • IND 140-141 H 4
Kolar Gold Fields o IND 140-141 H 4
Kolari o FIN 88-89 G 3
Kolåsen o S 86-87 F 5
Kolasib o IND 142-143 H 3
Kolašin o • YU 100-101 G 3
Kola Town o LB 202-203 G 6
Kolattupuzha o IND 140-141 G 6
Kolāyat o IND 138-139 D 6
Kōlbaj, tau ▲ KA 126-127 K 6
Kolbeinsstaðir o IS 86-87 b 2
Kolbio o EAK 212-213 H 4
Kol'covoe, ozero o RUS 122-123 Q 4
Kol'čugino ☆ RUS 94-95 Q 3
Kol'čum ~ RUS 114-115 U 4
Kolda ☆ SN 202-203 C 3
Koldaga o TCH 206-207 C 4
Kōldenen-Temir ~ KA 126-127 M 3
Kolding o • DK 86-87 D 9
Kole o ZRE (HAU) 210-211 K 2
Kole o ZRE (KOR) 210-211 J 5
Kolebira o IND 142-143 D 4
Kolek"egan ~ RUS 114-115 Q 3
Kolendo o RUS 122-123 K 2
Kolendo, Mount ▲ AUS 180-181 D 2
Kolenovskij, Elan'- o RUS 102-103 M 2
Kolenté o RG 202-203 D 4
Kolente ~ RG 202-203 D 5
Koležma o RUS 88-89 N 4
Kolgarin o AUS 176-177 E 6
Kolguev, ostrov ⌒ RUS 88-89 U 2
Kolhāpur o IND (ANP) 140-141 H 2
Kolhāpur o •• IND (MAH) 140-141 F 2
Kolhida ☆ GE 126-127 D 6
Kolhozabad o TJ 136-137 L 6
Koli ▲ FIN 88-89 K 5
Kolia o CI 202-203 G 5
Koliba ~ RG 202-203 D 4
Ko Libong ⌒ THA 158-159 E 7
Koliganek o USA 22-23 S 3
Kolín o •• CZ 92-93 N 3
Kolin o USA (MT) 250-251 K 4
Kolinbiné ~ RMM 202-203 E 2
K'olito o ETH 208-209 D 5
Koljučaja, gora ▲ RUS 112-113 S 3
Koljučin, ostrov ⌒ RUS 112-113 X 3
Koljučinskaja guba ≈ 112-113 X 3
Kolka o •• LV 94-95 H 3
Kolky o UA 102-103 D 2
Kollegal o IND 140-141 G 4
Kolleru Lake o IND 140-141 J 2
Kollipara o IND 140-141 J 2
Kollo o RN 204-205 E 2
Kolmackij, porog ~ RUS 88-89 P 3
Kolmakovo o RUS 114-115 P 7
Kolmanskop o NAM 220-221 B 3
Kolmar = Chodzież o • PL 92-93 O 2
Köln o •• D 92-93 J 3
Kolno o PL 92-93 Q 2
Kolo o EAT 212-213 E 6
Koło o PL 92-93 P 2
Koloa o USA (HI) 288 F 3
Kolobane o SN 202-203 C 2
Kolobeke o ZRE 210-211 G 4
Kolobrzeg o PL 92-93 N 1
Kolofata o CAM 206-207 B 3
Ko-lok, Sungai o THA 158-159 F 7
Kolokani o RMM 202-203 F 3
Koloko o BF 202-203 H 4
Kolokol, vulkan ▲ RUS 122-123 O 5
Kolokolkova guba ≈ 88-89 W 2
Kolokondé o DY 202-203 L 5
Kolomak o UA 102-103 J 3
Kolomino o RUS 114-115 R 6
Kolomna ☆ •• RUS 94-95 Q 4
Kolomoki Mounds • USA (GA) 284-285 F 5
Kolomonyi o ZRE 210-211 J 6
Kolomyja ☆ UA 102-103 D 3
Kolondieba o RMM 202-203 G 4
Kolondiéba o RMM 202-203 G 4
Kolongotomo o RMM 202-203 H 3
Kolonia ★ FSM 13 G 2
Kolono o RI 164-165 H 6
Kolonodale o RI 164-165 G 4
Kolosovyh, ostrov ⌒ RUS 108-109 W 4
Kolossa ~ RMM 202-203 G 3
Kolotambu = Avu Avu o SOL 184 I e 3
Kolowana-Watobo, Teluk ≈ 164-165 H 6
Kolozero o RUS 88-89 M 2
Kolp' ~ RUS 94-95 O 2
Kolpakova ~ RUS 120-121 R 6
Kolpaševo ☆ RUS 114-115 R 5
Kolpino o RUS 94-95 M 2
Kolpny o RUS 94-95 P 5
Kólpos Hanión ≈ 100-101 J 7
Kólpos Kissámou ≈ 100-101 J 7
Kolpur o PK 134-135 M 4
Kol'skij zaliv ≈ 88-89 M 2
Kolumadulu Atoll ⌒ MV 140-141 B 6
Koluton ~ KA 124-125 F 3
Kolva ~ RUS 88-89 Y 3
Kolva ~ RUS 108-109 H 8
Kolva ~ RUS 114-115 E 4
Kolvavis ~ RUS 108-109 H 8
Kolvereid o N 86-87 E 4
Kolvica o RUS 88-89 M 3
Kolvickoe, ozero o RUS 88-89 M 3
Kolwa o PK 134-135 L 5
Kolwezi o ZRE (SHA) 214-215 C 6
Kolyma ~ RUS 110-111 d 6
Kolyma ~ RUS 110-111 d 7
Kolyma ~ RUS 112-113 H 3
Kolyma ~ RUS 112-113 L 2
Kolyma ~ RUS 120-121 R 6
Kolyma ~ RUS 120-121 M 2
Kolymak ~ RUS 112-113 M 5
Kolymskaja guba ≈ 110-111 d 4
Kolymskaja nizmennost' o RUS 110-111 c 5
Kolymskoe o RUS 112-113 K 2
Kolymskoe, vodohranilišče < RUS 120-121 N 3
Kolymskoe nagor'e ▲ RUS 120-121 Q 3
Kolymskoye Nagor'ye = Kolymskoe nagor'e ▲ RUS 120-121 Q 3
Kolyšlej o RUS 96-97 D 7
Kolyvan' ☆ RUS 114-115 R 7
Kol'žat o KA 146-147 E 4
Kom ▲ BG 102-103 C 6
Kom o EAK 212-213 G 3
Kom ~ G 210-211 C 2
Koma o ETH 208-209 C 4
Komagasberge ▲ ZA 220-221 C 4
Komaio o PNG 183 B 4
Komako o PNG 183 C 4
Komanda o ZRE 212-213 B 3
Komandnaja, gora ▲ RUS 122-123 H 3
Komandorskaja kotlovina ⩦ RUS 120-121 V 5
Komandorskaya Basin ≃ RUS 120-121 V 5
Komandorskie ostrova ⌒ RUS 120-121 W 6
Komarno o CDN (MAN) 234-235 F 4
Komárno o SK 92-93 P 5
Komárom o H 92-93 P 5
Komarovka o RUS 116-117 E 7
Komatipoort o ZA 220-221 K 2
Komatirivier ~ ZA 220-221 K 2
Komatsu o J 152-153 G 6
Kommunizma, pik ▲ TJ 136-137 N 5
Komo ~ G 210-211 C 3
Komo o PNG 183 B 4
Komodimini o RMM 202-203 G 3
Komodo o RI 168 D 7
Komodo, Pulau ⌒ RI 168 D 7
Komodo National Park ⊥ •• RI 168 D 7
Komono o RCB 210-211 D 5
Komoran, Pulau ⌒ RI 166-167 K 6
Komorane o YU 100-101 H 3
Komoro o J 152-153 H 6
Komosi o ZRE 206-207 D 6
Komotiní o GR 100-101 K 4
Kompa o DY 204-205 E 2
Kompiam o PNG 183 B 3
Komponaone, Pulau ⌒ RI 164-165 H 6
Kompot o RI 164-165 J 3
Komrat = Comrat o MD 102-103 F 4
Komsberge ▲ ZA 220-221 E 6
Komsomol o KA (AKT) 126-127 O 2
Komsomol o KA (KST) 124-125 B 3
Komsomolabad o TJ 136-137 M 5
Komsomol cyganaky ≈ 126-127 K 5
Komsomolec, ostrov ⌒ RUS 108-109 Z 1
Komsomol'sk ☆ • RUS 94-95 R 3
Komsomol'sk, Ustjurtdagi o US 136-137 F 2
Komsomol'skij o RUS (CUK) 112-113 R 2
Komsomol'skij o RUS (HMN) 114-115 G 4
Komsomol'skij o RUS (KAR) 88-89 M 4
Komsomol'skij o RUS (KLM) 126-127 G 5
Komsomol'skij o RUS (KOM) 108-109 K 8
Komsomol'skij o RUS (MOR) 96-97 D 6
Komsomol'skij zapovednik ⊥ RUS 122-123 G 3
Komsomol'sk-na-Amure ☆ RUS 122-123 G 3
Komsomol'sk na Amure = Komsomol'sk-na-Amure ☆ RUS 122-123 G 3
Komsomol'sk-na-Pečore o RUS 114-115 D 3
Komsomol'skoj Pravdy, ostrova ⌒ RUS 108-109 g 3
Kŏmun Do ⌒ ROK 150-151 F 11
Kon o CAM 204-205 J 6
Kön ~ KA 124-125 F 4
Kona o RMM 202-203 J 2
Kona o RN 198-199 D 6
Kona o WAN 204-205 J 4
Kona = Kailua o USA (HI) 288 K 5
Kona Coast ᴗ USA (HI) 288 K 5
Konakovo ☆ RUS 94-95 P 3
Konanmoukro o CI 202-203 H 6
Konar ⌒ AFG 136-137 M 7
Konar, Daryā-ye ~ AFG 138-139 C 2
Konārak o ••• IND 142-143 E 6
Konārak o IR 134-135 J 6
Konar-e Ḫāṣṣ o AFG 138-139 C 2
Konār Tahte o IR 134-135 D 4
Konawa o USA (OK) 264-265 H 4
Konaweha ~ RI 164-165 G 5
Konda o RI 166-167 F 2
Konda ~ RUS 114-115 H 4
Konda ~ RUS 114-115 K 5
Konda ~ RUS 118-119 F 9
Kondagaon o IND 142-143 B 6
Kondakovskaja vozvyšennost' ▲ RUS 110-111 b 4
Kondan, ozero o RUS 114-115 K 6
Konde o EAT 212-213 G 6
Kondembaia o WAL 202-203 E 5
Kondinin o AUS 176-177 E 6
Kondinskaja nizmennost' ᴗ RUS 114-115 H 4
Kondinskoe ☆ RUS 114-115 K 5
Kondio = Kombongou o BF 204-205 E 3
Kondoa o EAT 212-213 E 6
Kondoma ~ RUS 124-125 Q 2
Kondopoga ☆ RUS 88-89 N 5
Kondostrov ⌒ RUS 88-89 O 4
Kondratovskaja o RUS 88-89 R 5
Kondromo ~ RUS 116-117 G 4
Kondrovo ☆ RUS 94-95 O 4
Kondue o ZRE 210-211 J 6
Konduga o WAN 204-205 K 3
Konduj-Muhor o RUS 118-119 F 9
Kondyreva ~ RUS 112-113 O 5
Konecbor o RUS 114-115 D 2
Konecbor o RUS (KOM) 88-89 Y 4
Koneng o RI 162-163 B 2
Konènmyveem ~ RUS 112-113 V 3
Konergino o RUS 112-113 V 4
Köneürgenč ☆ TM 136-137 F 3
Konevaam ~ RUS 112-113 P 2
Konevo o RUS 88-89 P 5
Kong o CAM 204-205 K 6
Kong o • CI 202-203 H 5
Kông ~ K 158-159 J 4
Kong, Bandar-e o IR 134-135 F 5
Kongakut River ~ USA 20-21 U 2
Kongasso o CI 202-203 G 6
Kongbeng Caves • RI 164-165 E 3
Kongbo o RCA 206-207 E 6
Kong Christian IX Land ⩦ GRØ 28-29 V 3
Kong Christian X Land ⩦ GRØ 26-27 k 7
Kong Dans Halvø ᴗ GRØ 28-29 U 5
Kongelai o EAK 212-213 E 3
Kong Frederik IX Land ⩦ GRØ 28-29 P 3
Kong Frederik VIII Land ⩦ GRØ 26-27 m 5
Kong Frederik VI Kyst ⩦ GRØ 28-29 T 6
Kong Fu • VRC 154-155 K 4
Konginskij hrebet ▲ RUS 112-113 K 4
Kong Karls Land ⌒ N 84-85 P 3
Kong Leopold og Dronning Astrid land ⩦ ARK 16 F 9
Kongola o NAM 218-219 B 3
Kongolo o ZRE 210-211 L 6
Kongor o LB 202-203 E 6
Kongor o SUD 206-207 K 5
Kong Oscar Fjord ≈ 26-27 n 7
Kongoussi o BF 202-203 K 3
Kongsberg ☆ N 86-87 D 7
Kongsfjorden ≈ 84-85 G 3
Kongsøya ⌒ N 84-85 Q 3
Kongsvinger ☆ • N 86-87 F 6
Kongtongshan • VRC 154-155 E 4
Kongur Shan ▲ VRC 146-147 B 6
Kongwa o EAT 214-215 J 4
Kong Wilhelm Land ⩦ GRØ 26-27 o 6
Koni o ZRE 214-215 D 6
Koni, poluostrov ᴗ RUS 120-121 O 4
Konig, Cape ▲ CDN 24-25 g 6
Königgrätz = Hradec Králové o CZ 92-93 N 3
Konimeh o US 136-137 J 4
Konin ☆ • PL 92-93 P 2
Konin ~ RUS 122-123 G 2
Konina o RMM 202-203 G 3
Konjed Jān o IR 134-135 D 2
Konka ~ UA 102-103 K 4
Kōnkämäälven ~ S 86-87 K 2
Kōnkämäeno ~ FIN 88-89 F 2
Konkan ~ IND 138-139 D 9
Konkče, Daryā-ye ~ AFG 136-137 L 6
Konkiep ~ NAM 220-221 D 3
Konko o ZRE 214-215 D 6
Konkoma o ETH 208-209 D 6
Konkouré o RG (KIN) 202-203 D 4
Konkouré ~ RG 202-203 D 4
Kon'kovaja ~ RUS 112-113 K 2
Kon'kovaja, Bol'šaja ~ RUS 112-113 J 2
Konkudera o RUS 118-119 F 7
Konkwesso o WAN 204-205 F 3
Konnūr o IND 140-141 F 2
Konobougou o RMM 202-203 G 3
Konogogo o PNG 183 G 2
Konololo o ZRE 210-211 K 3
Konomerume = Donderkamp o SME 62-63 F 3
Konončan ~ RUS 118-119 H 3
Kononda ~ RUS 116-117 M 3
Konongo o GH 202-203 K 6
Konos o PNG 183 F 2
Konoša o RUS 94-95 R 1
Kōnosu o J 152-153 H 6
Konotop o UA 102-103 H 2
Kon Plong o VN 158-159 K 3
Konqi He ~ VRC 146-147 G 5
Konsankoro o RG 202-203 F 5
Konséguéla o RMM 202-203 H 3
Końskie o • PL 92-93 Q 3
Konso o ETH 208-209 C 6
Konstantina, mys ▲ RUS 108-109 N 3
Konstantinopel = İstanbul ☆ ••• TR 128-129 C 2
Konstantinovka ☆ RUS 122-123 B 4
Konstantinovsk o RUS 102-103 M 4
Konstanz o • D 92-93 K 5
Konta o IND 142-143 B 7
Kontagora o WAN 204-205 F 3
Kontagora, River ~ WAN 204-205 F 3
Kontcha o CAM 204-205 K 5
Kontinemo, Área Indígena ⚔ BR 68-69 B 4
Kontiolahti o FIN 88-89 K 5
Kontiomäki o FIN 88-89 K 4
Kontovskoe o US 136-137 F 2
Kon Tum o VN 158-159 K 3
Konus, gora ▲ RUS (CUK) 112-113 U 3
Konus, gora ▲ RUS (HBR) 120-121 D 5
Konus, ostrov ⌒ RUS 120-121 U 3
Konušin, mys ▲ RUS 88-89 R 3
Konya ☆ •• TR 128-129 E 4
Konza o EAK 212-213 F 4
Konžakovskij Kamen', gora ▲ RUS 114-115 E 5
Konzanso o RMM 202-203 H 4
Konzi ~ ZRE 210-211 F 6
Koobi Fora ∴ • EAK 212-213 F 1
Koocanusa, Lake o USA (MT) 250-251 D 3
Koodnanie, Lake o AUS 178-179 E 4
Kookooligit Mountains ▲ USA 20-21 E 5
Kookynie o AUS 176-177 F 4
Koolatah o AUS 174-175 G 4
Koolau Range ▲ USA (HI) 288 G 3
Koolen', ozero o RUS 112-113 Z 4
Kooline o AUS 172-173 C 7
Koolkootinnie, Lake o AUS 178-179 D 4
Koolpinyah o AUS 172-173 K 2
Koolyanobbing o • AUS 176-177 E 5
Koombooloomba o AUS 174-175 H 5
Koonalda Cave • AUS 176-177 K 5
Koondoo o AUS 178-179 H 3
Koongie Park o AUS 172-173 H 5
Koopmansfontein o ZA 220-221 G 4
Koor o RI 166-167 G 2
Koorawatha o AUS 180-181 K 3
Koorda o AUS 176-177 D 5
Koordarrie o AUS 172-173 B 7
Koosharem o USA (UT) 254-255 D 5
Kooskia o USA (ID) 250-251 D 5
Kootenai Indian Reservation ⚔ USA (ID) 250-251 C 3
Kootenai River ~ USA (MT) 250-251 D 3
Kootenay Bay o CDN (BC) 230-231 N 4
Kootenay Indian Reserve ⚔ CDN (BC) 230-231 O 4
Kootenay Lake o CDN (BC) 230-231 N 4
Kootenay National Park ⊥ CDN (BC) 230-231 N 2
Kootenay River ~ CDN (BC) 230-231 O 3
Koo Wee Rup o AUS 180-181 H 5
Koozata Lagoon ≈ 20-21 E 5
Kopa o KA 146-147 B 4
Kopa o Z 214-215 F 6
Kopang o RI 168 C 7
Kopanzu o LB 202-203 F 6
Kopaonik ▲ YU 100-101 G 3
Kopargo o DY 202-203 L 5
Kópasker o IS 86-87 e 1
Kopasor, köl o KA 126-127 N 4
Kópavogur o IS 86-87 c 2
Ko Payang ⌒ THA 158-159 D 6
Kopbirlik o KA 124-125 K 5
Kopé, Mont ▲ CI 202-203 G 7
Kopejsk o RUS 96-97 M 6
Kopeng o RI 168 D 3
Koper o SLO 100-101 D 2
Kopervik o N 86-87 B 7
Kop'evo ☆ RUS 114-115 U 7
Kop Geçidi ▲ TR 128-129 J 2
Ko Phangan ⌒ THA 158-159 E 6
Ko Phangan ⌒ THA 158-159 F 6
Ko Phi ⌒ THA 158-159 E 7
Ko Phra Thong ⌒ MYA 158-159 E 6
Ko Phuket ⌒ •• THA 158-159 E 7
Kopi, Ugol'nye o RUS 112-113 T 4
Kopiago o PNG 183 B 3
Köping ☆ • S 86-87 G 7
Kopinguè o CI 202-203 J 5
Koporokendié-Na o RMM 202-203 J 2
Koppa o IND 140-141 F 4
Koppal o IND 140-141 G 3
Koppang ☆ N 86-87 E 6
Kopparberg o S 86-87 G 7
Koppe Dāġ ▲ IR 136-137 E 5
Kopperamanna Bore o AUS 178-179 E 5
Koppi o RUS 122-123 J 4
Koppies o ZA 220-221 H 3
Koppieskraalpan o ZA 220-221 E 3
Koprivnica o HR 100-101 F 1
Köprüçay ~ TR 128-129 D 4
Kor, Rūd-e ~ IR 134-135 E 4
Ko Ra ⌒ THA 158-159 E 6
Korab ▲ AL 100-101 H 4
Korabavur pastligi ⩦ US 136-137 E 3
Korača o RUS 102-103 K 2
Ko Racha Noi ⌒ THA 158-159 E 7
Ko Racha Yai ⌒ THA 158-159 E 7
K'orahē o ETH 208-209 G 5
Korakata cukurligi ⩦ US 136-137 J 4
Korakŭlka ⩦ US 136-137 E 3
Kora National Park ⊥ EAK 212-213 G 4
Korangal o IND 140-141 G 2
Korannaberg ▲ ZA 220-221 F 3
Korān-o-Monğān o AFG 136-137 M 6
Koraon o IND 142-143 C 3
Koraput o IND 142-143 C 6
Korasa o SOL 184 I c 2
Koratagere o IND 140-141 G 4
Ko Rawi ⌒ THA 158-159 E 7
Korbėndja, hrebet ▲ RUS 112-113 K 5
Korbenič o RUS 94-95 O 1
Korbol o TCH 206-207 C 4
Korbol, Bahr ~ TCH 206-207 C 3
Korbu, Gunung ▲ MAL 162-163 D 2
Korbunčana ~ RUS 116-117 L 3
Korçë ☆ •• AL 100-101 H 4
Korčula o • HR 100-101 F 3
Korčula ⌒ HR 100-101 F 3
Korda o IND 138-139 C 8
Kordestān ▫ IR 128-129 M 5
Kordié o BF 202-203 J 3
Kord-Kuy o IR 136-137 D 6
Kord Myriem, Hassi < DZ 188-189 K 6
Kordofan = Kurdufān ⩦ SUD 200-201 D 6
Kore o RI 168 D 7
Korea Bay ≈ 150-151 D 8
Korean Folk Village • ROK 150-151 F 9
Koreare o RI 166-167 F 5
Korea Strait ≈ 152-153 C 8
Korec' o UA 102-103 E 2
Korem o ETH 200-201 J 6
Korémairwa o RN 204-205 E 2
Korenevo o RUS 102-103 J 2
Korenovsk o RUS 102-103 L 5
Korepino o RUS 114-115 D 4
Korf o RUS 120-121 V 3
Korfa, zaliv o RUS 120-121 V 3
Korgalžyn ☆ KA 124-125 G 3
Korgas o VRC 146-147 E 3
Korgen o N 86-87 F 3
Korgom o RN 198-199 D 6
Korhogo ☆ • CI 202-203 H 5
Koribundu o WAL 202-203 E 6
Korientze o RMM 202-203 J 2
Korim o RI 166-167 J 2
Korinthiakós Kólpos ≈ 100-101 J 5
Kórinthos o GR 100-101 J 6
Korioume o RMM 196-197 J 6
Koripobi o PNG 184 I b 2
Kōris-hegy ▲ • H 92-93 O 5
Korissía o GR 100-101 K 6
Kōriyama o J 152-153 J 6
Korizo, Passe de ▲ TCH 192-193 F 6
Korjaki o RUS 120-121 S 7
Korjakskaja Sopka, vulkan ▲ RUS 120-121 S 7
Korjažma ☆ RUS 88-89 T 6
Korkodon o RUS (MAG) 112-113 H 4
Korkodon ~ RUS 112-113 J 5
Korkodonskij hrebet ▲ RUS 112-113 J 4
Korkut ☆ TR 128-129 J 3
Korkuteli ☆ TR 128-129 D 4
Korla o VRC 146-147 H 5
Korliki o RUS 114-115 R 4
Kormak o CDN (ONT) 236-237 F 5
Kormakitis, Cape ▲ TR 128-129 E 5
Kornake o RN 198-199 C 5
Kornati ⌒ HR 100-101 E 3
Korneevka o KA 124-125 J 3
Kórnik o • PL 92-93 O 2
Koro o CI 202-203 G 5
Koro ⌒ FJI 184 III b 2
Koro o RMM 202-203 J 2
Koroba o PNG 183 B 3
Koroc, Rivière ~ CDN 36-37 R 5
Korodiga o EAT 212-213 F 6
Korodziba o RB 218-219 D 4
Köroğlu Dağları ▲ TR 128-129 D 2
Köroğlu Tepe ▲ TR 128-129 D 2
Korogwe o EAT 212-213 G 6
Korohane o RN 198-199 C 5
Koroit o AUS 180-181 G 5
Korolevu o FJI 184 III a 3
Korom, Bahr ~ TCH 206-207 D 3
Koronadal o RP 160-161 F 9
Korondougou o CI 202-203 G 5
Koronga o RMM 202-203 G 2
Koronga, Mont ▲ RT 202-203 L 5
Koróni o GR 100-101 H 6
Korónia, Límni o GR 100-101 J 4
Korontière o DY 202-203 L 4
Koror ☆ PAL (CRO) 13 E 2
Körös ~ H 92-93 Q 5
Koro Sea ≈ 184 III b 2
Korosten' o UA 102-103 F 2
Korostyšiv o UA 102-103 F 2
Korotaiha ~ RUS 108-109 K 7
Korotčaevo o RUS 114-115 P 2
Koro Toro o TCH 198-199 J 4
Korovin Island ⌒ USA 22-23 Q 5
Korovin Volcan ▲ USA 22-23 J 6
Korovou o FJI 184 III b 2
Korovou o SOL 184 I b 2
Korpilahti o FIN 88-89 H 5
Korpun o PNG 183 G 3
Korsakow o RUS 122-123 K 5
Korsimoro o BF 202-203 K 3
Korskrogen o S 86-87 G 6
Korsnäs o FIN 88-89 F 5
Korsør o DK 86-87 E 9
Koršunovo o RUS 118-119 E 6
Kortala o SUD 200-201 E 6
Kortkeros o RUS 96-97 G 3
Kortrijk o B 92-93 G 3
Korumburra o • AUS 180-181 H 5
Korup, Park National de ⊥ CAM 204-205 H 6
korvonsaroj Raboti Malik • US 136-137 J 4
Korwai o IND 138-139 G 7
Koryak Autonomous District = Korjakskij avtonomnyi okrug ▫ RUS 112-113 N 5
Koryl'ky ~ RUS 108-109 T 8
Kós o •• GR 100-101 L 6
Kós ⌒ GR 100-101 L 6
Kosa o ETH 208-209 C 5
Kosa ☆ RUS 96-97 J 4
kosa Arabats'ka Strilka ᴗ UA 102-103 J 4
kosa Byr'učyj Ostriv ᴗ UA 102-103 J 4
Koš-Agač o RUS 124-125 Q 3
Koš-Agač ☆ RUS (GOR) 124-125 Q 4
Kosaja Gora o • RUS 94-95 P 4
Kosa Mèèčkyn, ostrov ⌒ RUS 112-113 V 4
Ko Samet National Park • THA 158-159 F 4
Ko Samui ⌒ •• THA 158-159 F 6
Kosbūlak sor ⩦ KA 126-127 M 5
Kościan o • PL 92-93 O 2
Kościerzyna o • PL 92-93 O 1
Kosciusko o USA (MS) 268-269 L 3
Kosciusko, Mount ▲ AUS 180-181 K 4
Kosciusko Island ⌒ USA 32-33 D 3
Kosciusko National Park ⊥ AUS 180-181 K 4
Kosdāulet, kum ⩦ KA 96-97 F 10
Koš-Dèbè o KS 146-147 B 5
Kose o •• EST 94-95 J 2
Köse ☆ TR 128-129 H 2
Köse Dağları ▲ TR 128-129 G 2
Koses ~ RUS 114-115 R 4
Kosha o SUD 200-201 E 2
Kōshetau = Kōkšetau ☆ KA 124-125 F 2
Koshi o ZRE 210-211 G 6
Koshikishima-rettō ⌒ J 152-153 C 9
Kosibaai-natuurreservaat ⊥ ZA 220-221 L 3
Kosi Bay ≈ 220-221 L 3
Ko Si Boya ⌒ THA 158-159 E 7
Košice o SK 92-93 Q 4
Kōšim ~ KA 96-97 G 9
Kosimeer o ZA 220-221 L 3
Ko Similan ⌒ THA 158-159 D 6
Kosi Reservoir < NEP 144-145 F 7
Kosistyj o RUS 110-111 G 3
Kosjerić o YU 100-101 G 2
Kos'ju ~ RUS 108-109 H 8
Koskaecodde Lake o CDN (NFL) 242-243 N 5
Koškarkōl', kōli o KA 124-125 M 5
Koškê Kohne o AFG 134-135 K 1
Koški ☆ RUS 96-97 G 6
Koskol o KA 124-125 E 4
Koslan o RUS 88-89 U 5
Kosma ~ RUS 88-89 U 4
Kosma ~ RUS 88-89 U 3
Kosminskij Kamen' ▲ RUS 88-89 U 3
Kosminskoe, ozero o RUS 88-89 U 3
Košoba o TM 136-137 D 4
Kosong o DVR 150-151 G 8
Kosovo Polje ⩦ YU 100-101 H 3
Kosovska Mitrovica o • YU 100-101 H 3
Kosse o USA (TX) 266-267 L 2
Kossi ~ BF 202-203 J 3
Kossou, Lac de < CI 202-203 H 6
Kossuth o USA (MS) 268-269 M 2
Kósta o GR 100-101 J 6
Kostanaj ☆ KA 124-125 C 2
Koster o ZA 220-221 H 2
Kostinbrod o BG 102-103 C 6
Kostin Nos, mys ▲ RUS 108-109 E 6
Kostin Šar, proliv o RUS 108-109 E 6
Kostomukša o RUS 88-89 L 4
Kostopil' o UA 102-103 E 2
Kostroma o RUS 120-121 U 4
Kostroma o • RUS (KOS) 94-95 R 3
Kostroma ~ RUS 94-95 R 2
Kostrzyn o • PL 92-93 N 2
Kostyantynivka = Južnoukrains'k o UA 102-103 K 3
Kosubosu o WAN 204-205 E 4
Kosubuke o ZRE 210-211 J 6
Ko Surin Nua ⌒ THA 158-159 D 6
Ko Surin Tai ⌒ THA 158-159 D 6
Kos'va ~ RUS 96-97 K 4
Kos'va ~ RUS 114-115 E 5
Kos'va, Bol'šaja ~ RUS 114-115 E 5
Kosvinskij Kamen', gora ▲ RUS 114-115 E 4
Koszalin ☆ • PL 92-93 O 1
Kőszeg o •• H 92-93 O 5
Kota o IND (MAP) 142-143 C 4
Kota o IND (RAJ) 138-139 E 7
Kota, Cascades de la ~ • DY 202-203 L 4
Kotaagung o RI 162-163 F 7
Kotabangun o RI 164-165 E 4
Kotabaru o RI (KSE) 164-165 E 5
Kotabaru o RI (RIA) 162-163 D 5
Kota Belud o MAL 160-161 B 9
Kota Bharu o • MAL 162-163 E 2
Kotabumi o RI 162-163 F 7
Kot Addu o PK 138-139 C 4
Kotagayah o RI 162-163 F 7
Kotagede o RI 168 D 3
Kota Kinabalu ☆ • MAL 160-161 B 10
Kōtal-e Mollā Yā'qūb ▲ AFG 134-135 M 1
Kota Lenggong o MAL 162-163 D 2
Kotamangalam o IND 140-141 G 5
Kota Marudu o MAL 160-161 B 9
Kotamobagu o RI 164-165 J 3
Kotanopan o RI 162-163 C 4
Ko Tao ⌒ THA 158-159 E 5
Kotapinang o RI 162-163 D 4
Ko Tarutao ⌒ THA 158-159 E 7
Kota Tinggi o • MAL 162-163 E 4
Kotawaringin Teluk ≈ 162-163 J 6
Kotcho Lake o CDN 30-31 J 6
Kotcho River ~ CDN 30-31 J 6
Kot Chutta o PK 138-139 C 5
Kot Diji o • PK 138-139 B 6
Koteľnič o RUS 96-97 F 4
Koteľnikovo o RUS 102-103 N 4
Koteľnyj, ostrov ⌒ RUS 110-111 V 2
Koteľva o UA 102-103 J 2
Kotenko o RUS 110-111 a 4
Kotera ~ RUS 118-119 F 8

Kotiari ○ SN 202-203 D 3
Kotido ○ EAU 212-213 E 2
Kotira ○ PK 134-135 M 5
Kotjukan ∼ RUS 108-109 f 6
Kotjukan ∼ RUS 110-111 G 4
Kotka ★ FIN 88-89 J 6
Kot Kapūra ○ IND 138-139 E 4
Kotla Branch ∼ IND 138-139 E 4
Kotlas ★ RUS 88-89 T 6
Kotlik ○ USA 20-21 J 5
Kot Mūmin ○ PK 138-139 D 3
Koto ○ CAM 204-205 H 6
Kotobi ○ CI 202-203 H 6
Kotongoro II ○ TCH 206-207 D 4
Koton-Karifi ○ WAN 204-205 G 4
Koton-Koro ○ WAN 204-205 F 3
Kotopounga ○ DY 202-203 L 4
Kotor ○ YU 100-101 G 3
Kotor Varoš ○ BIH 100-101 F 2
Kotouba ○ CI 202-203 J 5
Kotoula ○ BF 202-203 G 4
Kotovo ○ RUS 96-97 D 8
Kotovsk ○ RUS 94-95 R 5
Kotovs'k ★ UA 102-103 F 4
Kotovsk = Hînceşti ★ MD 102-103 F 4
Kot Pūtli ○ IND 138-139 F 6
Kotri ∼ IND 142-143 B 6
Kotri ○ PK 138-139 B 7
Kot Shākir ○ PK 138-139 D 4
Kottagūdem ○ IND 142-143 B 7
Kottakota ○ IND 140-141 H 4
Kottayam ○• IND 140-141 G 6
Kotto ∼ RCA 206-207 F 5
Kottūru ○ IND 140-141 G 3
Kotu ⌒ TON 184 IV a 1
Kotu Group ⌒ TON 184 IV a 1
Kotuj ∼ RUS 108-109 e 6
Kotuj ∼ RUS 108-109 a 7
Kotuj ∼ RUS 116-117 L 2
Kotujkan ∼ RUS 116-117 J 2
Koturdepe ○ TM 136-137 C 5
Kotwa ○ ZW 218-219 G 3
Kotzebue ○ USA 20-21 J 3
Kotzebue Sound ≈ 20-21 J 3
Kouadiokro, Ananda- ○ CI 202-203 H 6
Kouadio-Prikro ○ CI 202-203 H 6
Kouaga ∼ RMM 202-203 E 2
Kouakourou ○ RMM 202-203 H 2
Kouandé ○ DY 202-203 L 4
Kouandikro ○ CI 202-203 H 6
Kouango ○ RCA 206-207 D 6
Kouankan ○ RG 202-203 F 5
Kouassikro ○ CI 202-203 J 6
Kouba Olanga ○ TCH 198-199 J 5
Koubia ○ RG 202-203 E 4
Koubo Abou Azraq ○ TCH 206-207 E 3
Kouchibouguac National Park ⊥ CDN (NB) 240-241 L 4
Koudou, Cascades de ∼• DY 204-205 E 3
Koudougou ★ BF 202-203 J 3
Kouéré ○ BF 202-203 J 4
Koufey < RN 198-199 F 5
Kouffo ∼ DY 202-203 L 6
Kouga ∼ ZA 220-221 F 6
Kougaberge ▲ ZA 220-221 F 6
Kougnohou ○ RT 202-203 L 6
Kougouleu ○ G 210-211 B 3
Kouibli ○ CI 202-203 G 6
Kouif, El ○ TN 190-191 G 3
Kouilou ▫ RCB 210-211 C 5
Kouilou ∼ RCB 210-211 C 6
Kouka ○ BF 202-203 H 4
Koukdjuak, Great Plain of the ⩡ CDN 28-29 D 3
Koukdjuak River ∼ CDN 28-29 D 3
Kouki ○ RCA 206-207 C 5
Koukla ○ CY 128-129 E 5
Koukou ○ TCH 206-207 F 3
Koukourou ○ RCA 206-207 E 5
Koukourou ∼ RCA 206-207 E 5
Koukourou-Bamingui, Réserve de faune du ⊥ RCA 206-207 D 5
Koula ○ RMM 202-203 G 3
Koulamoutou ★ G 210-211 D 4
Koulbo ○ TCH 198-199 K 6
Koulbous ○ SUD 198-199 L 5
Koulé ○ RG 202-203 F 5
Koulé Ekou ▲ DY 204-205 E 4
Koulikoro ○ RMM 202-203 G 3
Koulou ○ RN 204-205 E 2
Kouloughidi ○ RMM 202-203 E 3
Koulountou ∼ SN 202-203 D 3
Koulouoko ∼ BF 202-203 K 3
Koum ○ CAM 206-207 B 4
Kouma ○ RCA 206-207 D 5
Kouma ∼ RCA 206-207 D 6
Koumamevong ○ G 210-211 C 3
Koumantou ○ RMM 202-203 G 4
Koumba ∼ RG 202-203 D 4
Koumbal ○ RCA 206-207 F 4
Koumbala ○ RCA (Bam) 206-207 E 4
Koumbala ∼ RCA 206-207 E 4
Koumbia ○ BF 202-203 J 4
Koumbia ○ RG 202-203 D 4
Koumbi Saleh ∴• RIM 196-197 G 7
Koumbo ○ BF 202-203 K 4
Koumbri ○ BF 202-203 J 3
Koumia ○ RMM 202-203 H 3
Koumogo ○ TCH 206-207 D 4
Koumongou ○ RT 202-203 L 4
Koumongou ∼ RT 202-203 L 4
Koumou ∼ RCA 206-207 F 4
Koumpentoum ○ SN 202-203 C 2
Koumra ○ TCH 206-207 C 4
Kounahiri ○ CI 202-203 H 6
Koundara ○ RG 202-203 D 3
Koundé ○ RCA 206-207 B 5
Koundessong ○ CAM 210-211 D 2
Koundian ○ RMM 202-203 E 3
Koundian ○ RN 202-203 F 4
Koundjourou ○ TCH 198-199 J 6
Koundou ○ RG 202-203 E 5
Koundougou ○ BF 202-203 H 4
Koun-Fao ○ CI 202-203 J 6
Koungheul ○ SN 202-203 C 3
Koungouri ○ TCH 206-207 D 3
Kouniana ○ RMM 202-203 H 3
Kounkané ○ SN 202-203 C 3
Kounradskij ○ KA 124-125 J 5
Kountouata ○ SN 202-203 C 3
Kountze ○ USA (TX) 268-269 F 6
Kouoro ○ RMM 202-203 H 3
Koup ○ ZA 220-221 E 6
Koupé, Mont ▲ CAM 204-205 H 6
Koupéla ○ BF 202-203 K 3
Kouraï ∼ RG 202-203 F 5
Kouraqué ○ RMM 202-203 E 3
Kourémalé ○ RMM 202-203 F 4
Kourgou ○ TCH 206-207 C 3
Kourgui ○ CAM 206-207 B 3
Kouri ○ RMM 202-203 H 3
Kouri Kouri ○ TCH 198-199 H 6
Kourion • CY 128-129 E 5
Kourkéto ○ RMM 202-203 E 2
Kourou ○ F 62-63 H 3
Kourouba ▲ CI 202-203 G 5
Kourouba ○ RMM 202-203 F 3
Kouroudjél ○ RIM 196-197 E 6
Kourougui ∼ BF 202-203 J 3
Kouroukoto ○ RMM 202-203 E 3
Kourouma ○ BF 202-203 H 4
Kourouninkoto ○ RMM 202-203 F 3
Kouroussa ○ RG 202-203 F 4
Kourtiagou, Réserve de la ⊥ BF 202-203 L 4
Kous ○ NAM 220-221 C 1
Koussa Arma < RN 198-199 F 4
Koussanar ○ SN (SO) 202-203 C 3
Koussanar ∼ SN 202-203 D 2
Koussané ○ RMM 202-203 E 2
Koussane ○ SN 202-203 D 2
Kousseri ○ CAM 198-199 G 6
Koussi, Emi ▲ TCH 198-199 J 3
Koussountou ○ RT 202-203 L 5
Koutaba ○ CAM 204-205 J 6
Koutia Gaïdi ○ SN 202-203 D 2
Koutiala ○ RMM 202-203 H 3
Kouto ○ CI 202-203 G 5
Kouts ○ USA (IN) 274-275 L 3
Kouvola ○ FIN 88-89 J 6
Kouyou ∼ RCB 210-211 F 4
Kova ∼ RUS 116-117 K 6
Kovalam ○•• IND 140-141 G 6
Kovalevka ○ KA 124-125 K 2
Kovancılar ★ TR 128-129 H 3
Kovarzino ○ RUS 94-95 Q 1
Kovdor ○ RUS 88-89 L 3
Kovdozero ○ RUS 88-89 M 3
Kovel' ○ UA 102-103 D 2
Kovenskaja ∼ RUS 114-115 J 4
Kovernino ○ RUS 94-95 S 3
Kovero ○ FIN 88-89 L 5
Kovic, Rivière ∼ CDN 36-37 L 4
Kovik Bay ≈ 36-37 L 4
Kovillur ○ IND 140-141 G 6
Kovilpatti ○ IND 140-141 G 6
Kovin ○ YU 100-101 H 2
Kovkula ○ RUS 88-89 P 5
Kovran ○ RUS 120-121 R 5
Kovriga, gora ▲ RUS 88-89 U 3
Kovrov ★ RUS 94-95 R 3
Kovūr ○ IND 140-141 H 3
Kovylkino ○ RUS 94-95 S 4
Kowanyama ▲ AUS 174-175 F 4
Kowares ○ NAM 216-217 C 9
Kowloon = Jiulong ○ HK 156-157 J 5
Kowyn's Pass ▲ ZA 220-221 K 2
Koya ○ WAN 198-199 C 6
Koyama ○ RG 202-203 F 6
Koyan, Tanjung ▲ RI 162-163 F 6
Ko Yao Yai ⌒ THA 158-159 E 7
Köyceğiz ★ TR 128-129 C 4
Koyna Reservoir ○ IND 140-141 E 2
Koyuk ○ USA 20-21 K 4
Koyuk River ∼ USA 20-21 K 4
Koyukuk ○ USA 20-21 M 4
Koyukuk National Wildlife Refuge ⊥ USA 20-21 M 4
Koyukuk River ∼ USA 20-21 M 4
Koyvel'vèègryn ∼ RUS 112-113 V 2
Koza ○ CAM 204-205 K 3
Kožaköl ○ KA 124-125 F 3
Kozan ★ TR 128-129 F 4
Kozáni ★• GR 100-101 H 4
Kozel'sk ★• RUS 94-95 O 4
Koževina, mys ▲ RUS 110-111 Z 2
Koževnikova, buhta ≈ 110-111 G 3
Koževnikovo ○ RUS 114-115 S 6
Kozhikode = Calicut ○• IND 140-141 F 5
Kozienice ○ PL 92-93 Q 3
Kožima ∼ RUS 116-117 G 6
Koźle, Kędzierzyn- ○• PL 92-93 P 3
Kozloduj ○ BG 102-103 C 6
Kozlova ○ RUS 116-117 M 8
Kozlova, mys ▲ RUS 120-121 T 6
Kozlovka ○ RUS 96-97 F 6
Kozluk ★ TR 128-129 J 3
Koz'modem'jansk ○ RUS 96-97 E 5
Kozok darë ○ US 136-137 F 3
Kožozero ○ RUS 88-89 P 5
Kožuf ▲ MK 100-101 J 4
Kōzu-shima ⌒ J 152-153 H 7
Kožva ○ RUS 88-89 Y 4
Kožva ∼ RUS 88-89 X 4
Kožym ○ RUS 108-109 H 9
Kozyrevsk ○ RUS 120-121 S 5
Kozyrevskij hrebet ▲ RUS 120-121 S 6
Kpako ∼ DY 204-205 E 3
Kpakto ○ GH 202-203 K 5
Kpalbusi ○ GH 202-203 K 5
Kpalimé ○• RT 202-203 L 6
Kpandu ○ GH 202-203 L 6
Kpassa ∼ GH 202-203 L 5
Kpatinga ○ GH 202-203 K 5
Kpedze ○ GH 202-203 L 6
Kpèssi ○ RT 202-203 L 5
Kpèssi, Réserve de ⊥ RT 202-203 L 5
Kpété Béna ○ RT 202-203 L 6
Kpetoe ○ GH 202-203 L 6
Kpimé, Cascade de ∼ RT 202-203 L 6
Kpong ○ GH 202-203 L 6
Kpungan Pass ▲ MYA 142-143 K 2
Kraaifontein ○ ZA 220-221 D 6
Kraairivier ∼ ZA 220-221 H 5
Kraankuil ○ ZA 220-221 G 4
Krabbé ○ RA 78-79 J 4
Krabi ○ THA 158-159 E 6
Krâchéh ○ K 158-159 J 4
Krachi, Kete- ○ GH 202-203 K 6
Kracnooskil's'k vodoschovyšče < UA 102-103 K 3
Kragerø ★ N 86-87 D 7
Kragujevac ○• YU 100-101 H 2
Krainij ○ RUS 110-111 X 4
Kraj Gorbatka ○ RUS 94-95 R 4
Krajište ▲ YU 100-101 J 3
Krajnij, ostrov ∼ RUS 120-121 U 3
Krajnovka ○ RUS 126-127 G 6
Kraka hrebet ▲ RUS 96-97 K 7
Kraké ○ DY 204-205 E 5
Kraków ★••• PL 92-93 P 3
Krakurom ○ GH 202-203 J 6
Krâlanh ○ K 158-159 G 4
Kralendijk ○ NL 60-61 G 1
Kraljevo ○ YU 100-101 H 3
Kramators'k ○ UA 102-103 K 3
Kramatorsk = Kramators'k ○ UA 102-103 K 3
Kramfors ○ S 86-87 H 5
Kranéa ○ GR 100-101 H 5
Kranídi ○ GR 100-101 J 6
Kranj ○ SLO 100-101 E 1
Kransfontein ○ ZA 220-221 J 4
Kranskop ○ ZA 220-221 K 4
Kranuan ○ THA 158-159 G 2
Kranzberg ○ NAM 216-217 C 10
Krãolandia, Área Indígena ⨯ BR 68-69 E 6
Krapina ○ HR 100-101 E 1
Krapivinskij ★ RUS 114-115 T 7
Krapivnaja ○ RUS 120-121 S 6
Krašeninnikova, mys ▲ RUS 120-121 U 4
Krasin, ostrov ⌒ RUS 108-109 a 3
Krasin, zaliv ≈ 112-113 U 1
Krasinka ○ RUS 114-115 U 6
Krasino ○ RUS 108-109 F 6
Kraskino ○ RUS 122-123 D 7
Krāslava ★•• LV 94-95 K 4
Krasnaja Gorka ★ RUS 96-97 K 6
Krasnaja Jaruga ○ RUS 102-103 J 2
Krasnaja Poljana ○ RUS 126-127 D 6
Krasnapollė ○ BY 94-95 M 5
Krasneno ○ RUS 112-113 S 4
Krasnij Luč = Krasnyj Luč ○ UA 102-103 L 3
Kraśnik ○ PL 92-93 R 3
Krasni Okny ★ UA 102-103 F 4
Krasnoarmejsk ★ KA 124-125 F 2
Krasnoarmejsk ★ RUS (SAR) 96-97 D 8
Krasnoarmejsk ★ RUS (MOS) 94-95 Q 4
Krasnoarmejsk = Krasnoarmijs'k ○ UA 102-103 K 3
Krasnoarmejskaja ○ RUS 102-103 L 5
Krasnoarmejskij ○ RUS 112-113 Q 2
Krasnoarmejskoe ★ RUS 96-97 G 7
Krasnoarmijs'k ○ UA 102-103 K 3
Krasnoborsk ○ RUS 88-89 S 6
Krasnodar ★• RUS 102-103 L 5
Krasnodarskij kraj ▫ RUS 126-127 C 5
Krasnodon ○ UA 102-103 L 3
Krasnoe, ozero ○ RUS 112-113 S 4
Krasnoe Selo ○ RUS 94-95 M 2
Krasnoe Znamja ○ TM 136-137 H 6
Krasnoflotskie, ostrova ⌒ RUS 108-109 c 2
Krasnogorsk ○ RUS 122-123 K 4
Krasnogorskij ○ RUS (CEL) 96-97 M 6
Krasnogorskij ○ RUS (MAR) 96-97 F 5
Krasnogorskoe ★ RUS 96-97 H 5
Krasnogvardejski ○ US 136-137 K 5
Krasnoholm ○ RUS 96-97 J 8
Krasnohorivka ○ UA 102-103 K 3
Krasnohrad ○ UA 102-103 J 3
Krasnohvardijs'ke ★ UA 102-103 J 5
Krasnoj Armii, proliv ≈ 108-109 Z 2
Krasnojarovo ○ RUS 122-123 C 3
Krasnojarsk ★• RUS 116-117 F 7
Krasnojarskoe, vodohranilišče ○ RUS 116-117 E 8
Krasnokamensk ★ RUS 118-119 J 10
Krasnokamsk ○ RUS 96-97 J 4
Krasnokutsk ★ KA 124-125 J 2
Krasnomajskij ○ RUS 94-95 O 3
Krasnoperekops'k ★• UA 102-103 H 5
Krasnopil'la ○ UA 102-103 J 2
Krasnopol'e ○ RUS 122-123 K 4
Krasnošćel'e ○ RUS 88-89 O 3
Krasnosel'kup ○ RUS 114-115 R 2
Krasnoslobodsk ○ RUS (MOR) 94-95 S 4
Krasnoslobodsk ○ RUS (VLG) 96-97 D 9
Krasnotur'insk ○ RUS 114-115 F 5
Krasnoufimsk ★ RUS 96-97 K 5
Krasnousol'skij ★ RUS 96-97 K 7
Krasnova, gora ▲ RUS 122-123 K 4
Krasnovišersk ★ RUS 114-115 D 4
Krasnovodsk = Türkmenbaši ★ TM 136-137 C 4
Krasnovodskij zaliv ≈ 136-137 C 5
Krasnovodskij zapovednik ⊥ TM 136-137 C 5
Krasnovodskoe plato ▲ TM 136-137 C 4
Krasnoyarsk = Krasnojarsk ★• RUS 116-117 F 7
Krasnoznamjans'kyj kanal < UA 102-103 H 4
Krasnye Barrikady ○ RUS 96-97 E 10
Krasnyj, liman ≈ 102-103 K 5
Krasnyj Aul ○ KA 124-125 M 3
Krasnyj Holm ○ RUS 94-95 P 2
Krasnyj Jar ○ RUS (KMR) 114-115 T 7
Krasnyj Jar ○ RUS (OMS) 114-115 M 7
Krasnyj Jar ○ RUS (VLG) 96-97 D 8
Krasnyj Jar ★ RUS (AST) 96-97 F 10
Krasnyj Jar ★ RUS (SAM) 96-97 G 7
Krasnyj Kut ★ RUS 96-97 E 8
Krasnyj Luč ○ UA 102-103 L 3
Krasnystaw ○ PL 92-93 R 3
Krasnyy Luch = Krasnyj Luč ○ UA 102-103 L 3
Krasuha ○ RUS 94-95 O 2
Kratke Range ▲ PNG 183 C 4
Kratovo ○• MK 100-101 J 3
Krau ○ RI 166-167 L 3
Krebs ○ USA (OK) 264-265 J 4
Krečetovo ○ RUS 94-95 Q 1
Krefeld ○ D 92-93 J 3
Kregbé ○ CI 202-203 J 6
Krekatok Island ⌒ USA 20-21 G 5
Kremenchuk = Kremenčuk ○ UA 102-103 H 3
Kremenčuc'ke vodoschovyšče < UA 102-103 H 3
Kremenčug = Kremenčuk ○ UA 102-103 H 3
Kremenčuk ○ UA 102-103 H 3
Kremenec' ○ UA 102-103 D 2
Kremenec'ki hory • UA 102-103 D 2
Kreminci ○ UA 102-103 D 3
Kreminna ○ UA 102-103 L 3
Kreml' • RUS 96-97 F 10
Kremlin ○ USA (MT) 250-251 J 3
Kremmling ○ USA (CO) 254-255 J 3
Krems an der Donau ○ A 92-93 N 4
Kremsier = Kroměříž ○ CZ 92-93 O 4
Krenicyna, vulkan ▲ RUS 122-123 Q 4
Krenitzin Islands ⌒ USA 22-23 O 6
Krešćenskoe ○ RUS 114-115 Q 7
Kresik Luway • RI 164-165 D 4
Kress ○ USA (TX) 264-265 C 4
Kresta, zaliv ≈ 112-113 V 4
Krestcy ★ RUS 94-95 N 2
Krest-Hal'džaj ○ RUS 120-121 F 2
Krestjah ○ RUS 118-119 H 4
Krest'janskij ○ US 136-137 L 4
Krestovaja ○ RUS 118-119 F 6
Krestovaja, guba ○ RUS 108-109 F 4
Krestovaja Guba ○ RUS 108-109 F 4
Krestovka ○ RUS 88-89 W 3
Krestovoe ○ RUS 112-113 N 2
Krestovskij, mys ▲ RUS 112-113 L 1
Krestovskij, ostrov ⌒ RUS 112-113 L 1
Krestovyj, pereval ▲ GE 126-127 F 6
Krestovyj, mys ▲ RUS 122-123 S 3
Krestovyj, ostrov ⌒ RUS 110-111 c 4
Kresty ○ RUS 108-109 e 6
Kresty ○ RUS (KIR) 96-97 E 5
Kresty ○ RUS (Mos) 94-95 P 4
Kretinga ○ LT 94-95 G 4
Kreuzburg (Oberschlesien) = Kluczbork ○ PL 92-93 P 3
Kreuznach, Bad ○ D 92-93 J 4
Krėva ○ BY 94-95 K 4
Kriam ○ RI 168 E 3
Kribi ○• CAM 210-211 B 2
Kričal'skaja ∼ RUS 112-113 L 3
Krieger Mountains ▲ CDN 26-27 J 3
Kriel ○ ZA 220-221 J 3
Krigujgun, mys ▲ RUS 112-113 Z 4
Kril'on, mys ▲ RUS 122-123 K 6
Krim-Krim ○ TCH 206-207 B 4
Krishna ∼ IND 140-141 H 2
Krishnagiri ○ IND 140-141 H 4
Krishnarājānagara ○ IND 140-141 G 4
Krishnarajpet ○ IND 140-141 G 4
Kristiansand ★ N 86-87 C 7
Kristianstad ○ S 86-87 G 8
Kristiansund ★ N 86-87 C 5
Kristiinankaupunki = Kristinestad ○•• FIN 88-89 F 5
Kristinehamn ★ S 86-87 G 7
Kristinestad ○•• FIN 88-89 F 5
Kristoffer Bay ≈ 24-25 U 1
Kriti ▫ GR 100-101 K 7
Kriti ⌒ GR 100-101 K 7
Kritiko Pelagos ≈ 100-101 K 6
Kriuša ○ RUS 96-97 F 5
Kriva Palanka ○ MK 100-101 J 3
Krivodol ○ BG 102-103 C 6
Krivoj Rog = Kryvyj Rih ○ UA 102-103 H 4
Krivošeino ★ RUS 114-115 R 6
Krivyj Rih ○ UA 102-103 H 4
Križevci ○ HR 100-101 F 1
Krjučkovka ○ RUS 96-97 J 8
Krk ⌒ YU 100-101 E 2
Krk ∼ HR 100-101 F 2
Krkonoše ▲ CZ 92-93 N 3
Krkonošský národní park ⊥ CZ 92-93 N 3
Krohnwodoke ○ LB 202-203 G 7
Krokek ○ S 86-87 H 7
Krokodilrivier ∼ ZA 220-221 H 2
Krokom ○ S 86-87 G 5
Krokosua National Park ⊥ GH 202-203 J 6
Króksfjarðarnes ○ IS 86-87 c 2
Krolevec' ○ UA 102-103 H 2
Kroměříž ○ CZ 92-93 O 4
Kronau ○ CDN (SAS) 232-233 O 5
Kronborg Gletscher ⊂ GRØ 28-29 a 2
Krông Buk ○ VN 158-159 K 4
Krông Kaôh Kông ○ K 158-159 G 5
Krông Pa ○ VN 158-159 K 4
Kronkel ∼ RI 166-167 K 5
Kronockaja ∼ RUS 120-121 T 6
Kronockij, mys ▲ RUS 120-121 U 6
Kronockij, zaliv ≈ 120-121 T 6
Kronockij poluostrov ⌣ RUS 120-121 U 6
Kronockij zapovednik ⊥ RUS 120-121 T 6
Kronockoe, ozero ○ RUS 120-121 T 6
Kronprins Christian Land ⩡ GRØ 26-27 q 4
Kronprinsesse Mærtha land ⩡ ARK 16 F 35
Kronprins Olav land ⩡ ARK 16 G 5
Kronshtadt = Kronštadt ○ RUS 94-95 L 2
Kronštadt ○ RUS 94-95 L 2
Kroonstad ○ ZA 220-221 H 3
Kropačevo ○ RUS 96-97 K 6
Kropotkin ○ RUS 102-103 M 5
Krośniewice ○ PL 92-93 P 2
Krosno ★• PL 92-93 Q 4
Krosno Odrzańskie ○ PL 92-93 N 2
Krotoschin = Krotoszyn ○ PL 92-93 O 3
Krotoszyn ○ PL 92-93 O 3
Krotz Springs ○ USA (LA) 268-269 J 6
Kroya ○ RI 168 C 3
Krško ○ SLO 100-101 E 2
Kručina ∼ RUS 118-119 G 10
Kruet ∼ RI 162-163 B 3
Kruger National Park ⊥ ZA 218-219 F 6
Krugersdorp ○ ZA 220-221 H 3
Kruglyj, ostrov ⌒ RUS 108-109 V 4
Krui ○ RI 162-163 E 7
Kruidfontein ○ ZA 220-221 E 6
Kruis, Kaap = Cape Cross ▲ NAM 216-217 B 10
Krujë ★•• AL 100-101 G 4
Krumau = Český Krumlov ○ CZ 92-93 N 4
Krumaye ○ RI 166-167 G 2
Krumë ○•• AL 100-101 H 3
Krumovgrad ○ BG 102-103 D 7
Krung Thep = Bangkok ○ THA 158-159 F 4
Krupanj ○ YU 100-101 G 2
Krusenstern, Cape ▲ USA 20-21 H 3
Kruševac ○• YU 100-101 H 3
Kruševo ○ MK 100-101 H 4
Krušné hory ▲ CZ 92-93 M 3
Krutoвene ○ BG 102-103 D 6
Krutec ∼ RUS 96-97 D 7
Krutinka ★ RUS 114-115 L 7
Krutiška ★ RUS 124-125 M 2
Krutoberegovo ○ RUS 120-121 U 5
Krutogorova ∼ RUS 120-121 R 6
Krutoj ○ RUS 112-113 N 2
Kruzenšterna, proliv ○ RUS 122-123 P 4
Kruzof Island ⌒ USA 32-33 B 3
Kryčav ★ BY 94-95 M 5
Krydor ○ CDN (SAS) 232-233 L 3
Kryktytau hrebet ▲ RUS 96-97 L 7
Krylovo ○ RUS 94-95 G 4
Kryms'ki hory ▲ UA 102-103 H 5
Krynica ○•• PL 92-93 Q 4
Kryve Ozero ★ UA 102-103 G 4
Kryvyy Rih = Krivyj Rih ○ UA 102-103 H 4
'Ksan Indian Village •• CDN 32-33 G 4
Ksar Chellala ○ DZ 190-191 D 3
Ksar El Boukhari ○ DZ 190-191 D 3
Ksar El Hirane ○ DZ 190-191 D 4
Ksar Ghilane ○ TN 190-191 G 4
Ksel, Djebel ▲ DZ 190-191 C 4
Kšenskij ○ RUS 102-103 K 2
Kshwan Mountain ▲ CDN 32-33 F 4
Ksour, Monts des ▲ DZ 190-191 C 4
Ksour Essaf ○ TN 190-191 H 3
Ksour Jelidat ○ TN 190-191 H 4
Kstovo ○ RUS 96-97 D 5
Ktesiphon ∴•• IRQ 128-129 L 6
Kuah ○ MAL 162-163 C 2
Kuala ∼ RI 162-163 C 3
Kuala Baram ○ MAL 162-163 K 2
Kuala Belait ○ BRU 164-165 D 1
Kuala Berang ○ MAL 162-163 E 2
Kuala Dungun ○• MAL 162-163 E 2
Kuala Kangsar ○• MAL 162-163 D 2
Kualakapus ○ RI 164-165 D 5
Kuala Kerau ○ MAL 162-163 E 3
Kualakeriau ○ RI 162-163 K 4
Kuala Krai ○ MAL 162-163 E 2
Kuala Kubu Baharu ○ MAL 162-163 D 3
Kualalangsa ○ RI 162-163 C 2
Kuala Lipis ○• MAL 162-163 E 2
Kuala Lumpur ★•• MAL 162-163 D 3
Kualapembuang ○ RI 162-163 K 6
Kuala Penyu ○ MAL 160-161 A 10
Kuala Pilah ○ MAL 162-163 E 3
Kualapuu ○ USA (HI) 288 H 3
Kuala Selangor ○ MAL 162-163 D 3
Kualasimpang ○ RI 162-163 C 2
Kuala Tahan ○ MAL 162-163 E 2
Kualatanjung ○ RI 162-163 C 3
Kuala Tatau ○ MAL 162-163 K 3
Kuala Terengganu ★• MAL 162-163 E 2
Kualatungkal ○ RI 162-163 E 5
Kuamut ○ MAL 160-161 B 10
Kuamut ∼ MAL 160-161 B 10
Kuancheng ○ VRC 154-155 L 1
Kuanda ∼ RUS 118-119 H 7
Kuandang ○ RI 164-165 H 3
Kuandian ○ VRC 150-151 E 7
Kuangfu ○ RC 156-157 M 5
Kuantan ★•• MAL 162-163 E 3
Kuba, zaliv ○ RUS 110-111 O 3
Kuba-Aryta, ostrova ⌒ RUS 110-111 Q 3
Kubalah ∼ RUS 108-109 c 5
Kuban' ∼ RUS 102-103 M 5
Kuban' ∼ RUS 126-127 E 6
Kuban ∼ RUS 126-127 D 5
Kubārā ○ OM 132-133 K 2
Kubari, Mount ▲ PNG 183 C 3
Kubbi ○ SUD 206-207 G 3
Kubbum ○ SUD 206-207 F 3
Kubena ∼ RUS 94-95 R 1
Kubenskoe, ozero ○ RUS 94-95 Q 2
Kuberganja ○ RUS 110-111 Z 6
Kubkain ○ PNG 183 B 3
Kubli ○ WAN 204-205 F 3
Kubli Hill ▲ WAN 204-205 F 3
Kubokawa ○ J 152-153 E 8
Kūbonān ○ IR 134-135 G 3
Kubor Range ▲ PNG 183 C 4
Kubumesaai ○ RI 164-165 D 3
Kubuna ○ PNG 183 D 5
Kubupenelokan ○ RI 168 B 7
Kubutambahan ○ RI 168 B 7
Kūček, Rūd-e Zāb-e ∼ IRQ 128-129 L 4
Kūčesfahān ○ IR 128-129 N 4
Kučevo ○ YU 100-101 H 2
Kuchaiburi ○ IND 142-143 E 4
Kuchi ○ IND 140-141 F 2
Kuching ★• MAL 162-163 J 4
Kuchino-Erabu-shima ⌒ J 152-153 D 9
Kuchino-shima ⌒ J 152-153 C 10
Kučukskoe, ozero ○ RUS 124-125 L 2
Kučurhan ∼ UA 102-103 F 4
Kuda ○ RI 162-163 K 4
Kuda ∼ RUS 116-117 M 9
Kudāl ○ IND 140-141 E 3
Kudan ○ WAN 204-205 G 3
Kudang ○ WAG 202-203 C 3
Kudani ○ GH 202-203 L 4
Kudat ○ MAL 160-161 B 9
Kudatini ○ IND 140-141 G 3
Kudayn ○ SUD 200-201 E 3
Kudene ○ RI 166-167 H 5
Kūderu ○ IND 140-141 G 3
Kudever' ○ RUS 94-95 L 3
Kudiakof Islands ⌒ USA 22-23 P 5
Kudiaičaj ∼ AZ 128-129 N 2
Kudi-Boma ○ ZRE 210-211 D 6
Kudirkos Naumiestis ○•• LT 94-95 H 4
Kudjip ○ PNG 183 C 3
Kudligi ○ IND 140-141 G 3
Kudu ○ WAN 204-205 F 4
Kudu-Kjuël' ○ RUS 118-119 K 6
Kudus ○• RI 168 D 3
Kudymkar ★ RUS 96-97 J 4
Kueda ★ RUS 96-97 J 5
Kuedemane ○ RI 162-163 B 2
Kuee ○ USA (HI) 288 K 5
Kuènga ∼ RUS 118-119 H 9
Kūfa, al- ★ IRQ 128-129 L 6
Kufrah, Al ▫ LAR 192-193 J 5
Kufstein ○• A 92-93 M 5
Kugaluk River ∼ CDN 20-21 Z 2
Kugaluk River ∼ CDN 24-25 O 6
Kugaly ○ KA 124-125 L 6
Kuganavolok ○ RUS 88-89 O 5
Kugmallit Bay ≈ 20-21 Y 2
Kugong Island ⌒ CDN 36-37 K 6
Kugrua River ∼ USA 20-21 L 1
Kugruk River ∼ USA 20-21 J 4
Kugururok River ∼ USA 20-21 K 2
Kūhak ○ IR (SIS) 134-135 K 5
Kūhak ○ IR (SIS) 134-135 J 3
Kūhdašt ○ IR 134-135 B 2
Kūh-e Bahūn ▲ IR 134-135 G 5
Kūh-e Binālūd ▲ IR 136-137 F 6
Kūh-e Hūrān ▲ IR 134-135 H 5
Kūh-e Madvār ▲ IR 134-135 F 3
Kūh-e Šāfi ○ AFG 138-139 B 2
Kūh-e Šāh-e Gūlak ▲ IR 128-129 N 5
Kūh-e Šāhū ▲ IR 128-129 M 5
Kūh-e Vāhān ▲ AFG 136-137 N 6
Kūhgilūye, Būyer Aḥmad-o- ▫ IR 134-135 D 3
Kūhīn ○ IR 128-129 N 4
Kuhmo ○ FIN 88-89 K 4
Kuhmuh ○ RUS 126-127 G 6
Kuhn Ø ⌒ GRØ 26-27 p 6
Kūhpāye ○ IR 134-135 E 2
Kūhpāye, Kūhhā-ye ▲ IR 134-135 G 3
Kuhterin Lug ○ RUS 122-123 C 2
Kuhtuj ∼ RUS 120-121 K 4
Kuhtujskij hrebet ▲ RUS 120-121 K 3
Kui ○ PNG 183 D 4
Kui, Kivori- ○ PNG 183 D 5
Kui Buri ○ THA 158-159 E 4
Kuilsrivier ○ ZA 220-221 D 6
Kuiseb ∼ NAM 220-221 B 1
Kuiseb Canyon ⩡•• NAM 220-221 B 1
Kuito ★ ANG 216-217 D 6
Kuiu Island ⌒ USA 32-33 C 3
Kuiukta Bay ≈ 22-23 R 4
Kuixingyan • VRC 156-157 L 4
Kuiyang ○ VRC 156-157 D 3
Kuja ∼ RUS 88-89 W 3
Kujama ○ WAN 204-205 G 3
Kujat, Gunung ▲ RI 164-165 E 2
Kujbyšev ★• RUS 114-115 P 7
Kujbyšev = Bulgar ★ RUS 96-97 F 6
Kujbyšev = Samara ★ RUS 96-97 G 7
Kujbyševa, mys ▲ RUS 108-109 Y 1
Kujbyševskij ★ KA 124-125 E 2
Kujbyševskoe < RUS 96-97 D 5
Kujdusun ○ RUS 120-121 K 2
Kujdusun ∼ RUS 120-121 K 2
Kujgan ○ KA 124-125 J 6
Kujginskij kraž ▲ RUS 110-111 V 4
Kuji ○ J 152-153 J 4
Kujōri ○ ROK 150-151 G 9
Kujši kumlar • US 136-137 H 4
Kujtun ★ RUS 116-117 K 8
Kujūkuri-nada ≈ 152-153 J 7
Kujul ∼ RUS 120-121 V 3
Kujumba ○ RUS 116-117 H 5
Kujū-san ▲ J 152-153 D 8
Kujviveem ∼ RUS 112-113 R 3
Kujwa ○ ROK 150-151 F 11
Kukaklek Lake ○ USA 22-23 T 3
Kukaragi ○ WAN 204-205 G 4
Kukawa ○ WAN 198-199 F 6
Kükdarjo ∼ US 136-137 G 3
Kuke ○ RB 218-219 B 5
Kukës ★• AL 100-101 H 3
Kukipi ○ PNG 183 D 5
Kukmor ★ RUS 96-97 G 5
Kukpowruk River ∼ USA 20-21 J 2
Kukpuk River ∼ USA 20-21 H 2
Kukshi ○ IND 138-139 E 8
Kukuihaele ○ USA (HI) 288 K 4
Kukulbej, hrebet ▲ RUS 118-119 H 10
Kukuna ○ WAL 202-203 D 5
Kukup ○• MAL 162-163 E 4
Kukur ○ SUD 208-209 A 3
Kukusunda ∼ RUS 110-111 G 5
Kūl, Rūd-e ∼ IR 134-135 F 5
Kula ○ BG 102-103 C 6
Kula ★ TR 128-129 C 3
Kula ○ WAN 204-205 G 6
Kulāchi ○ PK 138-139 C 4
Kulagin ○ KA 96-97 G 9
Kulai ○ MAL 162-163 E 4
Kula Kangri ▲ BHT 142-143 G 1
Kulakovo ○ RUS 116-117 F 6
Kulal, Mount ▲ EAK 212-213 F 2
Kulaly, ostrov ⌒ KA 126-127 H 5
Kula Mawe ○ EAK 212-213 G 3
Kulampanga ○ ZRE 210-211 J 4
Kulandag ▲ TM 136-137 D 4
Kulandy, aral ⌒ KA 126-127 J 5
Kulandy, tubegi ⌣ KA 126-127 N 5
Kulankhor ○ VRC 144-145 K 4
Kūlanötpes ∼ KA 124-125 G 4
Kulanutpes ∼ KA 124-125 G 4
Kular ○ RUS 110-111 U 4
Kular, hrebet ▲ RUS 110-111 S 5
Kulasekarappattinam ○ IND 140-141 H 6
Kulassein Island ⌒ RP 160-161 D 9
Kūlatau ○ US 136-137 G 4
Kulawi ○ RI 164-165 F 4
Kulaykili ○ SUD 198-199 L 5
Kulaykili ○ SUD 206-207 G 3
Kul'či ○ RUS 122-123 H 2
Kuldiga ★•• LV 94-95 G 3
Kul'dino ○ RUS 112-113 H 3
Kul'dur ○ RUS 122-123 D 4
Kule ○ RB 220-221 E 1
Kulebaki ○ RUS 94-95 S 4
Kul'egan ∼ RUS 114-115 N 4
Kulen ○ K 158-159 H 4
Kulenga ∼ RUS 116-117 M 9
Kulgahtah gora ▲ RUS 108-109 X 7
Kulgera ○ AUS 176-177 M 2
Kulgeri ○ IND 140-141 F 3
Kulibi ○ ETH 208-209 E 4
Kulim ○ MAL 162-163 D 2
Kulin ○ AUS 176-177 E 6
Kulina do Médio Juruá, Área Indígena ⨯ BR 66-67 B 6
Kulioúou ○ USA (HI) 288 H 3
Kulittalai ○ IND 140-141 H 5
Kuljab ★ TJ 136-137 L 6
Kuljumbe ∼ RUS 108-109 X 8
Kūlkuduk ○ US 136-137 H 3
Kulkyne Creek ∼ AUS 178-179 H 6
Kullen ▲ S 86-87 F 8
Kulliparu Conservation Park ⊥ AUS 180-181 C 2
Kullorsuaq ○ GRØ 26-27 W 6
Kulm ○ USA (ND) 258-259 J 5
Kulmaç Dağlan ▲ TR 128-129 G 3
Kulmbach ○ D 92-93 L 3
Kulo ○ RI 164-165 K 3
Kuloj ∼ RUS 88-89 R 4
Kulom, Ust'- ○ RUS 96-97 H 3
Kulp ★ TR 128-129 J 3
Kulpara ○ AUS 180-181 E 3
Kulpawan ∼ GH 202-203 K 4
Kul'sary ★ KA 96-97 J 10
Kulu ○•• IND 138-139 F 4
Kulu ○ RUS (MAG) 120-121 M 3
Kulu ∼ RUS 120-121 L 3
Kulu ★ TR 128-129 E 3
Kulumadau ○ PNG 183 G 5
Kulunda ★ RUS 124-125 L 2
Kulundinskaja ravnina ⩡ RUS 124-125 L 3
Kulundinskoe, ozero ○ RUS 124-125 L 2
Kulun-Elbjut ○ RUS 110-111 Y 6
Kulungu ○ ZRE 210-211 F 6
Kulu River ∼ PNG 183 E 3
Kulusuk ⌒ GRØ 28-29 W 4
Kulusuk Kap Dan ○ GRØ 28-29 W 4
Kulykkol ○ KA 124-125 E 3
Külyndy Žazygy ⌣ KA 124-125 K 3
Kulynigol ∼ RUS 114-115 R 3
Kulžuktov toglari ▲ US 136-137 H 4
Kum, Kūh-e ▲ IR 134-135 E 3
Kuma ○ RI 164-165 F 4
Kuma ∼ RUS 114-115 J 5
Kuma ∼ RUS 114-115 H 5
Kuma ∼ RUS 126-127 F 5
Kumafa, Pegunungan ▲ RI 166-167 G 3
Kumagaya ○ J 152-153 H 6
Kumahy ∼ RUS 118-119 O 6
Kumai ○ RI 162-163 J 6
Kumait, al- ○ IRQ 128-129 M 6
Kumai Teluk ≈ 162-163 J 6
Kumajri = Gjumri ○ AR 128-129 K 2
Kumak ∼ RUS 96-97 L 8
Kumamba, Kepulauan ⌒ RI 166-167 K 2
Kumamoto ★• J 152-153 D 8
Kumana ○ CL 140-141 J 7
Kumandan ∼ RI 166-167 G 2
Kumano ○ J 152-153 G 8
Kumano-gawa ∼ J 152-153 F 8
Kumano-nada ≈ 152-153 G 7
Kumanovo ○• MK 100-101 H 3
Kumara ○ NZ 182 C 5
Kumarina Roadhouse ○ AUS 176-177 E 2
Kumarl B Fossicking Area • AUS 176-177 F 6
Kumashi ○ J 152-153 H 3
Kumasi ★••• GH 202-203 K 6
Kumattur ○ IND 140-141 J 4
Kumayri = Gjumri ○ AR 128-129 K 2
Kumba ○ CAM 204-205 H 6
Kumba ○ ZRE 214-215 C 4
Kumbakonam ○ IND 140-141 H 5
Kumbanikesa ○ SOL 184 I c 2
Kumbarilla ○ AUS 178-179 L 4
Kumbe ○ RI 166-167 L 6
Kumbe ∼ RI 166-167 L 6
Kumbia ○ AUS 178-179 L 4
Kumbla ○ IND 140-141 F 4
Kumbo ○ CAM 204-205 J 5
Kumbwareta ○ PNG 183 C 3
Kum-Dag = Gumdag ○ TM 136-137 D 5
Kūmeğan ○ IR 134-135 C 1
Kumeny ★ RUS 96-97 F 4
Kumertau ★ RUS 96-97 J 7
Kume-shima ⌒ J 152-153 B 11
Küm Gang ∼ ROK 150-151 F 9
Kümhwa ○ ROK 150-151 F 8
Kumi ○ EAU 212-213 D 3
Kumi ○ ROK 150-151 G 9
Kumiva Peak ▲ USA (NV) 246-247 F 3
Kumkurgan ○ US 136-137 K 6
Kumla ★ S 86-87 G 7
Kumlein Fiord ≈ 36-37 S 2
Kumliun, Cape ▲ USA 22-23 S 4
Kumluca ★ TR 128-129 D 4
Kumo ○ WAN 204-205 J 3
Kumola ∼ KA 124-125 E 5
Kumo-Manyčskij kanal < RUS 126-127 F 5
Kumon Taungdan ▲ MYA 142-143 K 2
Kumroč, hrebet ▲ RUS 120-121 T 6
Kumrovec ○ HR 100-101 E 1
Kumru ★ TR 128-129 G 2
Kums ○ NAM 220-221 D 4
Kūmsaj ○ KA 126-127 N 3
Kumshe ○ WAN 206-207 B 3
Kūmsŏng ○ ROK 150-151 F 10
Kumta ○ IND 140-141 F 3
Kumu ∼ RI 162-163 D 4
Kumu ○ ZRE 210-211 K 2
Kumuchuru < RB 218-219 B 6
Kumukaki, Cape ▲ USA (HI) 288 L 5
Küm Umbū ○• ET 194-195 F 5
Kumusi River ∼ PNG 183 E 5
Kumya ○ DVR 150-151 F 8
Kumzār ○ OM 134-135 G 5
Kuna ○ USA (ID) 252-253 B 3
Kuna Cave ∴ USA (ID) 252-253 B 3

Kunak ○ MAL 160-161 C 10
Kuna River ~ USA 20-21 M 2
Kunašak ☆ RUS 96-97 M 6
Kunašir, ostrov ⌒ RUS 122-123 L 6
Kunašírskij proliv = Nemuro-kaikyō ≈ 152-153 L 3
Kunatata Hill ▲ WAN 204-205 J 5
Kunayr, Wādī ~ LAR 192-193 F 4
Kunda ○·· EST 94-95 K 2
Kunda ○ ZRE 210-211 L 5
Kunda ~ ZRE 210-211 L 5
Kundalila Falls ~ Z 218-219 F 1
Kundam ○ IND 142-143 B 4
Kundamtumu ○ Z 214-215 E 6
Kundar ~ PK 138-139 B 4
Kundar, Pulau ⌒ RI 162-163 E 4
Kundara ○ IND 140-141 G 6
Kundelungu ▲ ZRE 214-215 D 6
Kundelungu, Parc National de ⊥ ZRE 214-215 D 6
Kundelungu ouest, Parc National de ⊥ ZRE 214-215 D 5
Kundiān ○ PK 138-139 C 3
Kundiawa ☆ PNG 183 C 4
Kundichi ○ EAT 214-215 K 4
Kundil Bazar ○ IND 142-143 J 2
Kundla ○ IND 138-139 C 9
Kundurpi ○ IND 140-141 G 3
Kundūz ◘ AFG 136-137 L 6
Kundūz ☆· AFG (KU) 136-137 L 6
Kundūz, Daryā-ye ~ AFG 136-137 L 6
Kunene ~ NAM 216-217 B 8
Künes He ~ VRC 146-147 F 4
Kungälv ☆· S 86-87 E 8
Kungasalah, ozero ⌓ RUS 110-111 F 2
Kunghit Island ⌒ CDN (BC) 228-229 D 4
Kungila ○ SUD 208-209 A 3
Kungirod ○ US 136-137 F 3
Kungirod-Mūjnok kanal < US 136-137 F 3
Kungsbacka ☆· S 86-87 F 8
Kungu ○ ZRE 210-211 G 2
Kungur ☆ RUS 96-97 K 5
Kungurtug ○ RUS 116-117 H 10
Kungus ~ RUS 116-117 G 8
Kungyangon ○ MYA 158-159 D 2
Kunhan ~ IND 138-139 G 9
Kunhār ~ PK 138-139 D 2
Kunhing ○ MYA 142-143 L 5
Kunigal ○ IND 140-141 G 4
Kunimaipa River ~ PNG 183 D 4
Kuningan ○ RI 168 C 3
Kun'ja ☆ RUS 94-95 M 3
Kunjingini ○ PNG 183 B 2
Kunjirap Daban = Khunjerab Pass ▲ VRC 138-139 E 1
Kunjirop Daban ▲ KA 138-139 E 1
Kunka, Bol'šaja ~ RUS 120-121 Q 3
Kunlun Shan ▲ VRC 144-145 A 1
Kunlun Shankou ▲ VRC 144-145 K 3
Kun-Man'ë ~ RUS 120-121 E 6
Kunmik, Cape ▲ USA 22-23 S 4
Kunming ☆· VRC 156-157 C 4
Kunmunya Aboriginal Land ⊼ AUS 172-173 G 3
Kunnui ○ J 152-153 J 3
Kunovat ~ RUS 114-115 J 2
Kunsan ○ ROK 150-151 F 10
Kunshan ○ VRC 154-155 M 6
Kuntanase ○ GH 202-203 K 6
Kun-Tas, hrebet ▲ RUS 110-111 W 4
Kunthi Kyun ⌒ MYA 158-159 D 5
Kuntykahy ~ RUS 108-109 c 7
Kunua ○ PNG 184 I b 1
Kununurra ○ AUS 172-173 J 3
Kunwak River ~ CDN 30-31 V 4
Kunya ○ WAN 198-199 D 6
Kunyao ○ EAK 212-213 E 3
K'unzila ○ ETH 208-209 C 3
Kuocang Shan ▲ VRC 156-157 M 2
Kuoi ○ LB 202-203 F 7
Kuojka ~ RUS 110-111 M 4
Kuokunu ○ RUS 118-119 H 4
Kuolaj ~ RUS 110-111 S 4
Kuoluma ~ RUS 120-121 F 3
Kuonamka, Bol'šaja ~ RUS 110-111 J 4
Kuonara ○ RUS 110-111 N 6
Kuopio ☆ FIN 88-89 J 5
Kuortane ○ FIN 88-89 G 5
Kupa ~ RUS 116-117 M 7
Kūpāl ○ IR 134-135 C 3
Kupang ☆ RI 166-167 B 7
Kupangnunding ○ RI 164-165 D 4
Kup'ians'k ○ UA 102-103 K 3
Kuparuk River ~ USA 20-21 Q 2
Kuper Island ○ CDN (BC) 230-231 F 5
Kupfer Range ▲ PNG 183 D 4
Kupiano ○ PNG 183 E 6
Kupino ☆ RUS 124-125 K 1
Kupiškis ○·· LT 94-95 J 4
Kupk ○ USA (AZ) 256-257 C 7
Kuppagallu ○ IND 140-141 G 3
Kuppam ○ IND 140-141 H 4
Kupreanof Island ⌒ USA 32-33 D 3
Kupreanof Point ▲ USA 22-23 R 5
Kupreanof Strait ≈ 22-23 U 3
Kupulima ○ GH 202-203 J 4
Kupuri ~ RUS 120-121 D 6
Kuputusan ○ RI 164-165 K 4
Kupwara ○ IND 138-139 E 2
Kuqa ○ VRC 146-147 F 5
Kur ~ RUS 122-123 F 3
Kur, Pulau ⌒ RI 166-167 F 4
Kura ~ AZ 128-129 L 2
Kura ○ WAN 204-205 H 3
Kura = Kür ~ AZ 128-129 M 2
Kurabalakota ○ IND 140-141 H 4
Kuragaty ○ KA 136-137 N 3
Kuragino ☆ RUS 116-117 F 9
Kuragwi ○ WAN 204-205 H 4
Kurahachi-shima ⌒ J 152-153 E 7
Kurajlysaj ○ KA 96-97 G 8
Kura Kurk ≈ 94-95 G 3
Kurali ○ IND 138-139 F 4
Kuraminskij hrebet ▲ TJ 136-137 L 4
Kuranah-Jurjah ~ RUS 110-111 S 5
Kuranda ○· AUS 174-175 H 5
Kura Nehri ~ TR 128-129 K 2
Kurashiki ○· J 152-153 E 7
Kurayn ⌒ KSA 130-131 L 4
Kurayoshi ○ J 152-153 E 7
Kurba ~ RUS 116-117 O 9
Kurbatovo ○ RUS 116-117 E 8
Kurcum ○ KA 124-125 N 4
Kurcum ~ KA 124-125 O 4
Kurdistan ⩧ 128-129 J 4
Kurduvādi ○ IND 138-139 E 10
Kūrdym, köl ⌓ KA 126-127 P 4
Kure ○ J 152-153 E 7
Küre Dağları ▲ TR 128-129 E 2
Kurejka ○ RUS (KRN) 108-109 W 8
Kurejka ~ RUS 108-109 a 7
Kurejka ~ RUS 116-117 H 2
Kurejskoe vodohranilišče ⌓ RUS 108-109 X 8
Kurenalus = Pudasjärvi ○ FIN 88-89 J 4
Kuressaare ○·· EST 94-95 H 2
Kurfi ○ WAN 198-199 C 6
Kurgan ☆ RUS 114-115 H 7
Kurganinsk ○ RUS 126-127 D 5
Kurgan-Tjube ☆ TJ 136-137 L 6
Kuri ~ RI 166-167 H 3
Kūri ○ SUD 200-201 E 3
Kuri Bay ○ AUS 172-173 G 3
Kurichedu ○ IND 140-141 H 3
Kūrīğān ○ IR 128-129 N 5
Kurigram ○ BD 142-143 F 3
Kurik ○ RI 166-167 K 6
Kurikka ○ FIN 88-89 G 5
Kurikoma Quasi National Park ⊥ J 152-153 J 5
Kuril Basin ⩧ 10-11 O 4
Kuril Islands = Kuril'skie ostrova ⌒ RUS 122-123 M 6
Kurilo-Kamčatskij želob ⩧ 120-121 T 7
Kuril'sk ○ RUS 122-123 M 6
Kuril'sk, Severo- ○ RUS 122-123 R 3
Kuril'skaja kotlovina ⩧ 122-123 M 6
Kuril'skoe, ozero ⌓ RUS 122-123 R 3
Kuril Trench ⩧ 10-11 P 4
Kurima ○ RI 166-167 K 4
Kurinelli Out Station ○ AUS 174-175 C 7
Ku-Ring-Gai Chase National Park ⊥ AUS 180-181 L 2
Kur'inskij krjaž ▲ RUS 112-113 K 3
Kurinwás, Río ~ NIC 52-53 B 5
Kuripapango ○ NZ 182 F 3
Kuriyama ○ J 152-153 J 3
Kur'ja ○ RUS 124-125 N 3
Kur'ja ○ RUS (KOM) 114-115 D 4
Kur'ja ~ RUS 112-113 L 3
Kurkhera ○ IND 142-143 B 5
Kurkino ○ RUS 94-95 Q 5
Kurkur ○ ET 194-195 F 6
Kurleja ○ RUS 118-119 J 9
Kurlek ○ RUS 114-115 S 6
Kurlin ○ RUS 96-97 G 8
Kurmanaevka ☆ RUS 96-97 G 7
Kurmuk ○ ETH 208-209 B 3
Kurmuk ○ SUD 208-209 B 3
Kurnool ○ IND 140-141 H 3
Kuroishi ○ J 152-153 J 4
Kuroiso ○ J 152-153 J 6
Kuroki ○ CDN (SAS) 232-233 P 4
Kuromatsunai ○ J 152-153 J 3
Kurong, Cape ▲ RI 166-167 B 7
Kuror, Gabal ▲ SUD 200-201 E 2
Kuro-shima ⌒ J 152-153 C 9
Kurovskoe ○ RUS 94-95 Q 4
Kurovyči ○ UA 102-103 D 3
Kurow ○ NZ 182 C 6
Kurów ○ PL 92-93 R 3
Kurram ~ PK 138-139 C 3
Kuršab ~ KS 136-137 N 4
Kursavka ○ RUS 126-127 E 5
Kuršėnai ○ LT 94-95 H 3
Kursk ○ RUS 102-103 K 2
Kuršskaja kosa ⩧ RUS 94-95 G 4
Kurškij zaliv ○ RUS 94-95 G 4
Kurşunlu ☆ TR 128-129 E 2
Kurtak ○ RUS 116-117 E 8
Kurtamyš ☆ RUS 114-115 H 7
Kurten ○ USA (TX) 266-267 L 3
Kürti ○ SUD 200-201 E 3
Kurtistown ○ USA (HI) 288 K 5
Kurty ~ KA 124-125 K 6
Kuru ~ BHT 142-143 G 2
Kuru ○ FIN 88-89 G 6
Kuru ○ IND 142-143 D 4
Kuru ~ SUD 206-207 H 5
Kurubonla ○ WAL 202-203 E 5
Kuruksaj ○ TJ 136-137 L 4
Kuruktag ▲ VRC 146-147 H 5
Kuruman ○ ZA (CAP) 220-221 F 3
Kuruman ~ ZA 220-221 F 3
Kuruman Hills ▲ ZA 220-221 F 3
Kurume ○ J 152-153 D 8
Kurumkan ☆ RUS 118-119 E 8
Kurundi ○ AUS 174-175 C 7
Kurundja, hrebet ▲ RUS 110-111 V 5
Kurunegala ○ CL 140-141 J 7
Kurun-Urjah ○ RUS 120-121 G 4
Kurupa Lake ⌓ USA 20-21 N 2
Kurupa River ~ USA 20-21 N 2
Kurupkan ~ RUS 112-113 X 4
Kurupukari ○ GUY 62-63 E 3
Kuryk ○ KA 126-127 J 6
Kuržina ~ RUS 114-115 R 5
Kuša ○ RUS 88-89 O 5
Kusa ☆ RUS 96-97 L 6
Kuşadası ☆· TR 128-129 B 4
Kuşadası Körfezi ≈ 128-129 B 4
Kusagaki-guntō ⌒ J 152-153 C 9
Kusak ~ KA 124-125 K 4
Kušalino ○ RUS 94-95 P 3
Kusawa Lake ⌓ CDN 20-21 W 6
Kuščevskaja ○ RUS 102-103 L 4
Kus'e-Aleksandrovskij ○ RUS 96-97 L 4
Kuş Gölü ⌓ TR 128-129 B 2
Kushālgarh ○ PK 138-139 C 3
Kusheriki ○ WAN 204-205 G 3
Kushikino ○ J 152-153 D 9
Kushimoto ○ J 152-153 F 8
Kushiro ○ J 152-153 L 3
Kushiro-chō ○ J 152-153 L 3
Kushiro-gawa ~ J 152-153 L 3
Kushtagi ○ IND 140-141 G 3
Kushtia ○ BD 142-143 F 4
Kūšik, Tall ○ SYR 128-129 K 4
Kusiwigasi, Mount ▲ PNG 183 A 3
Kūšk ○ AFG 134-135 K 1
Kuskanax Creek ~ CDN (BC) 230-231 M 3
Kuskokwim Bay ≈ 22-23 P 3
Kuskokwim Mountains ▲ USA 20-21 L 6
Kuskokwim River ~ USA 20-21 J 6
Kušmurun = Kūsmūryn ○ KA 124-125 D 2
Kušmurun, ozero = Kūsmūryn kölí ⌓ KA 124-125 D 2
Kūsmūryn ○ KA 124-125 D 2
Kūsmūryn kölí ⌓ KA 124-125 D 2
Kušnarenkovo ☆ RUS 96-97 J 6
Kusong ○ DVR 150-151 E 8
Kusova, ostrov ⌒ RUS 120-121 H 6
Kustatan ○ USA 20-21 P 6
Kūšti ☆ SUD 200-201 F 6
Kustur ○ RUS 110-111 S 5
Kusu ○ RI 164-165 K 3
Kusumkasa ○ IND 142-143 B 5
Kusuri ○ RI 164-165 K 3
Kušva ○ RUS 96-97 L 4
Kus'veem ~ RUS 112-113 S 2
Kūt, al- ☆ IRQ 128-129 L 6
Kuta ○ RI 168 C 7
Kuta ~ RUS 116-117 M 7
Kuta ○ WAN 204-205 G 4
Kutabagok ○ RI 162-163 B 2
Kutacane ○ RI 162-163 B 3
Kütahya ☆ TR 128-129 C 3
Kutainang ○ RI 162-163 A 3
Kutai National Park ⊥ RI 164-165 E 3
Kutaisi ○· GE 126-127 E 6
K'ut'aisi = Kutaisi ○··· GE 126-127 E 6
Kūt al-Hayy ☆ IRQ 128-129 M 6
Kutana ○ RUS 120-121 D 4
Kutanibong ○ RI 162-163 B 3
Kutaramakan ~ RUS 108-109 Z 7
Kutchan ○ J 152-153 J 3
Kutcharo-ko ⌓ J 152-153 L 3
Kutchi Hill ▲ WAN 204-205 H 4
Kute ○ GH 202-203 L 6
Kūt-e Gāpū ∴· IR 134-135 C 2
Kuti ○ RUS 118-119 J 10
Kutilax ○ WAN 206-207 B 3
Kutima ○ RUS 116-117 O 7
Kutima ~ RUS 118-119 E 7
Kutina ○ HR 100-101 F 2
Kutiwenji ○ WAN 204-205 F 4
Kutiyāna ○ IND 138-139 B 9
Kutná Hora ○·· CZ 92-93 N 4
Kutno ○ PL 92-93 P 2
Kutoarjo ○ RI 168 C 3
Kutop'jugan ○ RUS 108-109 O 8
Kutse Game Reserve ⊥ RB 218-219 C 6
Kutse Pan < RB 218-219 C 6
Kutshu ○ ZRE 210-211 G 2
Kuttenberg = Kutná Hora ○·· CZ 92-93 N 4
Kutu ○ ZRE 210-211 G 5
Kutubdia ⌒ BD 142-143 G 5
Kutubu, Lake ⌓ PNG 183 B 4
Kutulo, Lagh ~ EAK 212-213 H 2
Kutum ○ SUD 200-201 B 5
Kutu River ~ PNG 183 E 6
Kuujjuaq ○ CDN 36-37 P 5
Kuujjua River ~ CDN 24-25 O 5
Kuuli Majak ○ TM 136-137 C 4
Kuumiit ○ GRØ 28-29 W 4
Kuusalu ○ EST 94-95 J 2
Kuusamo ○ FIN 88-89 K 4
Kuusankoski ○ FIN 88-89 J 6
Kuvandyk ☆ RUS 96-97 K 8
Kuvasaj ○ US 136-137 N 4
Kuvet ~ RUS 112-113 S 2
Kuvšinovo ○ RUS 94-95 O 3
Kuvykta ○ RUS 118-119 M 8
Kuwait ○ IRQ 128-129 M 6
Kuwait ■ KWT 130-131 K 3
Kuwait, al- ○ KWT 130-131 K 3
Kuwait, al- ★ KWT (KUW) 130-131 K 3
Kuwait, Ḫalīğ al- ≈ 130-131 K 3
Kuwait = Kuwait, al- ◘ KWT 128-129 M 6
Kuwana ○ J 152-153 G 7
Kuwāra ○ SUD 206-207 J 3
Kuwawin ○ RI 166-167 G 2
Kuwethluk River ~ USA 20-21 K 6
Kuybyshevskoye Vodokhranilishche = Samarskoe vodohran. < RUS 96-97 F 7
Kūysanğaq ☆ IRQ 128-129 L 4
Kuytun ○ VRC 146-147 G 3
Kuyuwini ~ GUY 62-63 F 4
Kuyuwini Landing ○ GUY 62-63 E 4
Kužai ○ LT 94-95 H 4
Kūzarān ○ IR 134-135 B 1
Kuzedeevo ○ RUS 124-125 P 2
Kuzema ○ RUS (KAR) 88-89 N 4
Kuzema ~ RUS 88-89 M 4
Kuzitrin River ~ USA 20-21 H 4
Kužka ○ TM 136-137 H 7
Kužka = Gushgy ○ TM 136-137 H 7
Kūz Konar ○ AFG 138-139 C 2
Kuzkwa River ~ CDN (BC) 228-229 K 2
Kuzneck ○ RUS 96-97 E 7
Kuzneckaja guba ≈ 88-89 W 2
Kuzneckij, Leninsk ☆ RUS 114-115 T 7
Kuzneckij Alatau ▲ RUS 114-115 T 7
Kuznezovo ○ RUS 122-123 J 5
Kuzomen' ○ RUS 88-89 O 3
Kuzomen ○ RUS 88-89 R 4
Kuzovatovo ☆ RUS 96-97 E 7
Kuzumaki ○ J 152-153 J 4
Kvačina, buhta ○ RUS 120-121 R 5
Kvænangen ≈ N 86-87 K 1
Kværndrup ○ DK 86-87 E 9
Kvaløy ⌒ N 86-87 J 2
Kvaløya ⌒ N 86-87 L 1
Kvalsund ○ N 86-87 L 1
Kvareli ○ GE 126-127 F 6
Kvarkeno ☆ RUS 96-97 L 8
Kvarkuš, hrebet ▲ RUS 114-115 E 5
Kvarner ≈ 100-101 E 2
Kvarnerić ≈ 100-101 E 2
Kvemo-Ažara ○ GE 126-127 D 6
Kvichak Bay ≈ 22-23 S 3
Kvichak River ~ USA 22-23 S 3
Kvikkjokk ○ S 86-87 H 3
Kvina ~ N 86-87 C 7
Kvinesdal ☆ N 86-87 C 7
Kvirila ~ GE 126-127 E 6
Kviteseid ☆ N 86-87 D 7
Kvitøya ⌒ N 84-85 R 2
Kwa ~ ZRE 210-211 F 5
Kwadacha Wilderness Provincial Park ⊥ CDN 32-33 H 3
Kwadwokurom ○ GH 202-203 K 6
Kwahu Tafo ○ GH 202-203 K 6
Kwaiawata Island ⌒ PNG 183 F 5
Kwa-Ibo ○ WAN 204-205 G 6
Kwailibesi ○ SOL 184 I e 3
Kwajok ○ SUD 206-207 H 4
Kwakwani ○ GUY 62-63 F 3
Kwale ○ EAK 212-213 G 6
Kwale ○ WAN 204-205 G 6
Kwale Game Reserve ⊥ WAN 204-205 G 6
Kwamalasamutu ○ SME 62-63 F 4
Kwa-Mashu ○ ZA 220-221 K 4
Kwamedwamenokurom ○ GH 202-203 K 6
Kwamera ○ VAN 184 II b 4
Kwamor-Besar ○ RI 166-167 F 3
Kwamouth ○ ZRE 210-211 F 5
Kwa Mtoro ○ EAT 212-213 E 6
Kwandar Rūd ~ AFG 138-139 B 4
Kwando ~ RB 218-219 B 4
Kwanga ○ PNG 183 C 3
Kwanga ○ ZRE 210-211 K 6
Kwangch'ŏn ○ ROK 150-151 F 9
Kwangju ○ ROK 150-151 F 10
Kwango ~ ZRE 216-217 D 3
Kwanhio ○ MYA 142-143 L 4
Kwania, Lake ⌓ EAU 212-213 D 3
Kwanmo Bong ▲ DVR 150-151 G 7
Kwapsanek ○ PNG 183 D 4
Kwara ◘ WAN 204-205 E 4
Kwaraga ○ RB 218-219 C 5
Kware ○ WAN 198-199 B 6
Kwashebawa ○ WAN 198-199 C 6
Kwatisore ○ RI 166-167 H 3
Kwa Zulu (former Homeland, now part of Kwa Zulu/ Natal) ◘ ZA 220-221 K 3
Kwa Zulu/ Natal Province ◘ ZA 220-221 K 3
Kwekwe ○ ZW 218-219 E 4
Kwelkan ○ AUS 176-177 E 5
Kwendihn ○ LB 202-203 F 6
Kweneng ◘ RB 218-219 C 6
Kwenge ~ ZRE 210-211 G 6
Kwiambana Game Reserve ⊥ WAN 204-205 G 3
Kwidzyn ○· PL 92-93 P 2
Kwieftim ○ PNG 183 A 2
Kwigillingok ○ USA 22-23 P 3
Kwigluk Island ⌒ USA 22-23 O 3
Kwiguk ○ USA 20-21 H 5
Kwihā ○ ETH 200-201 J 6
Kwikila ○ PNG 183 D 5
Kwikpak ○ USA 20-21 H 5
Kwilu ~ ZRE 210-211 E 6
Kwilu ~ ZRE 210-211 G 6
Kwilu-Ngongo ○ ZRE 210-211 E 6
Kwinana ○ AUS 176-177 C 6
Kwinella ○ WAG 202-203 C 3
Kwinitsa ○ CDN (BC) 228-229 E 2
Kwisa ~ PL 92-93 N 3
Kwoka, Gunung ▲ RI 166-167 G 2
Kwolla ○ WAN 204-205 H 4
Kyabé ○ TCH 206-207 D 4
Kyabra ○ AUS 178-179 G 4
Kyaikkami (Amherst) ○ MYA 158-159 D 2
Kyaiklat ○ MYA 158-159 C 2
Kyaikto ○ MYA 158-159 D 2
Kyaka ○ EAT 212-213 C 4
Kyancutta ○ AUS 180-181 C 2
Kyangin ○ MYA 142-143 J 6
Ky Anh ☆ VN 158-159 J 1
Kyataw ○ MYA 158-159 E 4
Kyaukme ○ MYA 142-143 K 4
Kyaukpyu ○ MYA 142-143 H 6
Kyauksat ○ MYA 158-159 E 3
Kyaukse ○ MYA 142-143 K 5
Kyaukt ○ MYA 142-143 K 5
Kyauktaw ○ MYA 142-143 H 5
Kyaunggon ○ MYA 158-159 C 2
Kyawkku ○ MYA 142-143 K 5
Kybartai ○ LT 94-95 H 4
Kybeyan Range ▲ AUS 180-181 K 4
Kydžimit ~ RUS 118-119 E 9
Kyé ~ G 210-211 C 2
Kyeburn ○ NZ 182 C 6
Kyegegwa ○ EAU 212-213 C 3
Kyeintali ○ MYA 158-159 C 2
Kyela ○ EAT 214-215 G 5
Kyenjojo ○ EAU 212-213 C 3
Kyeryongsan National Park ⊥· ROK 150-151 F 9
Kyidaunggan ○ MYA 142-143 K 6
Kyjam, gora ▲ RUS 110-111 a 5
Kyjiv ★··· UA 102-103 G 2
Kyjivs'ke vodoschovyšče < UA 102-103 G 2
Kyjy ○ RUS 120-121 E 2
Kykotsmovi ○ USA (AZ) 256-257 E 3
Kyk-over-al · GUY 62-63 E 2
Kylajy ○ RUS 120-121 E 2
Kylás ▲ IND 142-143 G 3
Kyle ○ CDN (SAS) 232-233 K 5
Kyle, Lake ⌓ ZW 218-219 F 5
Kylemore ○ CDN (SAS) 232-233 P 4
Kyles Ford ○ USA (TN) 282-283 D 4
Kyll ~ D 92-93 J 3
Kyllah ~ RUS 110-111 c 6
Kylvynejveem ~ RUS 112-113 Q 5
Kyma ~ RUS 88-89 T 4
Kyneton ○ AUS 180-181 H 4
Kyngyldyözek ~ KA 126-127 P 4
Kynquot ○ CDN (BC) 230-231 B 3
Kynuna ○ AUS 178-179 F 1
Kyoga, Lake ⌓ EAU 212-213 D 3
Kyogami-saki ▲ J 152-153 F 7
Kyogche La ▲ VRC 144-145 H 5
Kyogle ○ AUS 178-179 M 5
Kyona, Plage ⩧· RH 54-55 J 5
Kyŏnggi Man ≈ 150-151 E 9
Kyŏngju ○ ROK 150-151 G 10
Kyŏngju National Park ⊥· ROK 150-151 G 10
Kyonkadun ○ MYA 158-159 C 2
Kyōto ☆·· J 152-153 F 7
Kyōwa ○ J 152-153 J 3
Kypcak, köli ⌓ KA 124-125 F 3
Kyra ☆ RUS (CTN) 118-119 E 11
Kyra ○ RUS 118-119 E 10
Kyra ~ RUS 118-119 E 11
Kyren ☆ RUS 116-117 L 10
Kyrgyz ○ KA 124-125 J 4
Kyrgyzstan ■ KS 136-137 M 4
Kyritz ○· D 92-93 M 2
Kyrnyčky ○ UA 102-103 F 5
Kyrönjoki ~ FIN 88-89 G 5
Kyrykkeles ~ KA 136-137 L 4
Kys"egan ~ RUS 114-115 R 4
Ký So'n ○ VN 156-157 D 7
Kystatayam ○ RUS 110-111 O 6
Kyštovka ○ RUS 114-115 O 6
Kystyk, plato ▲ RUS 110-111 O 4
Kystyktah ~ RUS 108-109 Y 6
Kyštym ○ RUS 96-97 M 6
Kysyl-Syr ○ RUS 118-119 L 4
Kytaj, ozero ⌓ UA 102-103 F 5
Kytėpana, gora ▲ RUS 120-121 S 5
Kytepkaj, grjada ▲ RUS 112-113 S 2
Kyttyk, poluostrov ⌒ RUS 112-113 O 2
Kytyl, Čumpu ○ RUS 110-111 Y 7
Kytyl-Djura ○ RUS 118-119 M 5
Kyungon ○ MYA 142-143 K 6
Kyunhla ○ MYA 142-143 J 4
Kyuquot Sound ≈ 32-33 G 6
Kyuquot Sound ≈ CDN 230-231 B 3
Kyuroku-shima ⌒ J 152-153 H 4
Kyūshū ⌒ J 152-153 C 8
Kyushu-Palau Ridge ⩧ 152-153 E 10
Kyūshū-sanchi ▲ J 152-153 D 9
Kyvėkvyn ~ RUS 112-113 U 2
Kyvrak ○ AZ 128-129 L 3
Kywebwe ○ MYA 142-143 K 6
Kywedatkon ○ MYA 142-143 K 6
Kyyjärvi ○ FIN 88-89 H 5
Kyzart ○ KS 146-147 B 5
Kyzyl ☆ RUS 116-117 G 10
Kyzylagadžskij zapovednik ⊥ AZ 128-129 N 3
Kyzylagaš ○ KA 124-125 L 6
Kyzyl-Art, pereval ▲ TJ 136-137 N 5
Kyzylbalyk ○ KA 96-97 G 10
Kyzyl-Hem ~ RUS 116-117 H 10
Kyzylkajyn ~ KA 126-127 N 2
Kyzylkak, köli ⌓ KA 124-125 H 2
Kyzyl-Kija ○ KS 136-137 N 4
Kyzylmazar ○ US 136-137 L 5
Kyzyl-Oj ○ KS 146-147 B 5
Kyzyloktjabr ○ KA 124-125 K 3
Kyzylorda ☆ KA 124-125 D 6
Kyzyl-Özgėrjuš ○ KS 136-137 N 4
Kyzylsu ~ TJ 136-137 L 5
Kyzyl-Suu ~ KS 136-137 N 5
Kyžyltepa ○ US 136-137 J 4
Kyzyl-Tuu ○ KS 146-147 C 4
Kyzylžar ○ KA 124-125 F 4
Kyzltu ☆ KA 124-125 H 2

L

Laa an der Thaya ○ A 92-93 O 4
Laag, Pulau ⌒ RI 166-167 J 4
Laamoro, Danau ⌓ RI 166-167 H 3
Laas Aano ○ SP 208-209 J 5
Laascaanood ○ SP 208-209 H 4
Laaso Dawaco ○ SP 208-209 J 3
Laasqoray ○ SP 208-209 J 3
Laau Point ▲ USA (HI) 288 H 3
Laâyoune = Al-'Ayun ☆ MA 188-189 E 7
Laayoune = Al-'Ayun ☆ WSA 188-189 E 7
Laba ○ BF 202-203 J 4
Laba ○ RN 198-199 B 5
Laba ~ RUS 126-127 D 5
Labadie, Plage ⩧· RH 54-55 J 5
Labahe Niuling Reserves ⊥ VRC 154-155 C 6
Labakkang ○ RI 164-165 F 6
Labala ○ RI 166-167 B 6
Labalama ○ PNG 183 B 3
Labardén ○ RA 78-79 K 4
La Barge ○ USA (WY) 252-253 H 4
La Barge Creek ~ USA (WY) 252-253 H 4
Labasa ○ FJI 184 III b 2
Labason ○ RP 160-161 E 8
Labaz, ozero ⌓ RUS 108-109 c 5
Labba ○ GUY 62-63 E 3
Labbal, al- ⩧ KSA 130-131 G 3
Labbezzanga ○ RMM 202-203 L 2
Labdah ∴··· LAR 192-193 F 1
Labe ~ CZ 92-93 N 3
Labé ◘ RG 202-203 D 4
Labé ☆ RG 202-203 D 4
Labelle ○ CDN (QUE) 238-239 L 2
Labengke, Pulau ⌒ RI 164-165 H 5
Laberge, Lake ⌓ CDN 20-21 X 6
Laberinto ○ CO 60-61 D 6
Laberinto, El ○ YV 60-61 E 2
Labḥa ○ KSA 130-131 J 5
Labi ○ BRU 164-165 D 1
Labin ○ HR 100-101 E 2
Labinsk ○ RUS 126-127 D 5
Labinsk, Ust'- ○ RUS 102-103 L 5
Labis ○ MAL 162-163 E 3
Lab Lab ○ PNG 183 E 3
Labná ∴· MEX 52-53 K 1
Labo ○ RP 160-161 E 5
Labo, Mount ▲ RP 160-161 E 5
Labobo, Pulau ⌒ RI 164-165 H 4
Labolatounka ○ RG 202-203 E 4
La Bolt ○ USA (SD) 260-261 K 1
Laboulaye ○ RA 78-79 H 3
Labozhi ○ WAN 204-205 F 4
Labrador, Cape ▲ CDN 36-37 R 4
Labrador = Labrador Péninsule ⌣ CDN 6-7 B 3
Labrador Basin ⩧ 6-7 D 3
Labrador City ○ CDN 38-39 L 2
Labrador Sea ≈ 6-7 D 3
Labrang Si · VRC 154-155 C 4
Labranza Grande ○ CO 60-61 E 5
Lábrea ○ BR 66-67 E 6
Labrieville ○ CDN 38-39 K 4
La Broquerie ○ CDN (MAN) 234-235 G 5
Labuan ○ MAL 160-161 A 10
Labuan ○ RI 168 A 3
Labuan, Pulau ⌒ MAL 160-161 A 10
Labuha ○ RI 164-165 K 4
Labuhanbilik ○ RI 162-163 D 3
Labuhanhaji ○ RI (ACE) 162-163 B 3
Labuhanhaji ○ RI (NBA) 168 C 7
Labuhan Kananga ○ RI 168 C 7
Labuhanmeringgai ○ RI 162-163 F 7
Labuhanpandan ○ RI 168 C 7
Labuhanruku ○ RI 162-163 C 3
Labuk, Teluk ≈ 160-161 B 9
Labutta ○ MYA 158-159 C 2
Labynkyr, ozero ⌓ RUS 120-121 K 2
Labyntangi ○ RUS 108-109 N 8
Labyrinth, Lake ⌓ AUS 178-179 C 6
Labyrinth Lake ⌓ CDN 30-31 Q 5
Laç ○·· AL 100-101 G 4
Lac ◘ TCH 198-199 G 6
Lắc ○ VN 158-159 K 4
Laća, ozero ⌓ RUS 88-89 P 6
Lacadena ○ CDN (SAS) 232-233 K 5
Lacajahuira, Río ~ BOL 70-71 D 6
Lac-Allard ○ CDN (QUE) 242-243 E 2
Lacanau ○ F 90-91 G 9
Lacanau-Océan ○ F 90-91 G 9
Lacandón, Sierra del ▲ MEX 52-53 J 3
Lacanja ○ MEX (CHI) 52-53 J 3
Lacanja ∴· MEX (CHI) 52-53 J 3
Lacantún, Río ~ MEX 52-53 J 3
Lacassine National Wildlife Refuge ⊥ USA (LA) 268-269 H 7
La Castellana ○ RP 160-161 E 7
Lacaune ○ F 90-91 J 10
Lac-au-Saumon ○ CDN (QUE) 240-241 H 2
Laccadive Islands ⌒ IND 140-141 E 6
Lac Cardinal ○ CDN 32-33 M 3
Lac-Cayamant ○ CDN (QUE) 238-239 J 2
Lac Courte Oreilles Indian Reservation ⊼ USA (WI) 270-271 G 4
Lac-des-Commissaires ○ CDN (QUE) 240-241 C 2
Lac du Bonnet ○ CDN (MAN) 234-235 G 4
Lac du Flambeau ○ USA (WI) 270-271 J 5
Lac du Flambeau Indian Reservation ⊼ USA (WI) 270-271 J 5
Lacepede Bay ≈ 180-181 E 4
Lacepede Islands ⌒ AUS 172-173 F 4
Lac-Etchemin ○ CDN (QUE) 240-241 E 4
Lacey ○ USA (WA) 244-245 C 3
Lac-Frontière ○ CDN (QUE) 240-241 E 4
Lachay, Reserva Nacional ⊥ PE 64-65 D 7
Lāchi ○ PK 138-139 C 3
Lachlan Range ▲ AUS 180-181 H 2
Lachlan River ~ AUS 180-181 H 3
Lach Truong ≈ 156-157 E 7
Lac Humqui ○ CDN (QUE) 240-241 H 2
Lachute ○ CDN (QUE) 238-239 L 3
Laçin ○ AZ 128-129 M 3
Läckö ○· S 86-87 F 7
Lac la Biche ○ CDN 32-33 O 4
Lac la Hache ○ CDN (BC) 230-231 H 2
Lac la Martre ○ CDN 30-31 L 4
Lac la Ronge Provincial Park ⊥ CDN 34-35 D 3
Laclede ○ USA (ID) 250-251 C 3
Lac Le Jeune ○ CDN (BC) 230-231 J 3
Lac-Mégantic ○ CDN (QUE) 240-241 E 5
Lacolle ○ CDN (QUE) 238-239 M 3
Lacombe ○ CDN (ALB) 232-233 E 3
Lacon ○ USA (IL) 274-275 J 3
Laconia ○ USA (NH) 278-279 K 5
La Corne ○ CDN (QUE) 236-237 L 4
La Crosse ○ USA (KS) 262-263 G 6
Lacrosse ○ USA (WA) 244-245 H 4
La Crosse ○ USA (WI) 270-271 G 7
Lac Seul ○ CDN (ONT) 234-235 L 4
Lac-Ste-Therese ○ CDN (ONT) 236-237 E 3
La Cueva ○ USA (NM) 256-257 J 3
Lac Vert ○ CDN (SAS) 232-233 O 3
Lacy, Mount ▲ AUS 172-173 G 4
La Cygne ○ USA (KS) 262-263 M 6
La Cygnes Lake ⌓ USA (KS) 262-263 M 6
Ladakh ⩧ IND 138-139 F 2
Ladakh Range ▲ IND 138-139 F 2
Ladar ○ RI 168 E 7
Ladário ○ BR 70-71 J 6
Ladder Creek ~ USA (KS) 262-263 E 6
Laddonia ○ USA (MO) 274-275 G 5
Ladd Reef ⩧ 158-159 L 6
Lade ○ WAN 204-205 F 4
Ládi ○ GR 100-101 L 4
Lādiqiya, al- ☆ SYR 128-129 F 5
Ladismith ○ ZA 220-221 E 6
Lādīz ○ IR 134-135 J 4
Ladner ○ USA (SD) 260-261 C 1
Ladoga ○ USA (IN) 274-275 M 5
Ladongi, Tanjung ▲ RI 164-165 G 5
Ladonia ○ USA (TX) 264-265 J 5
La Doré ○ CDN (QUE) 240-241 C 2
Ladožskoe ozero ⌓ RUS 88-89 L 6
Ladrillero, Monte ▲ RCH 80 D 6
Ladrones, Islas ⌒ PA 52-53 C 8
Ladron Peak ▲ USA (NM) 256-257 H 4
Ladue River ~ CDN 20-21 U 5
Laduškin ○ RUS 94-95 G 4
Lady Ann Strait ≈ 24-25 f 3
Ladybrand ○ ZA 220-221 H 4
Lady Elliot Island ⌒ AUS 178-179 M 3
Lady Evelyn Lake ⌓ CDN (ONT) 236-237 H 5
Lady Evelyn Smoothwater Provincial Park ⊥ CDN (ONT) 236-237 H 5
Lady Franklin Point ▲ CDN 24-25 P 6
Lady Frere ○ ZA 220-221 H 5
Lady Grey ○ ZA 220-221 H 5
Lady Grey Lake ⌓ CDN 30-31 O 5
Lady Lake ○ CDN (SAS) 232-233 Q 3
Lady Melville Lake ⌓ CDN 24-25 a 6
Lady Newnes Ice Shelf ⊂ ARK 16 F 18
Ladysmith ○ CDN (BC) 230-231 F 5
Ladysmith ○ USA (WI) 270-271 G 5
Ladysmith ○ ZA 220-221 J 4
Ladyženka ○ KA 124-125 F 3
Lae ☆ PNG 183 D 4
Laefu ○ PNG 183 F 2
Lægervallen ▲ GRØ 26-27 q 4
Laela ○ EAT 214-215 G 5
Laem Ngop ○ THA 158-159 G 4
Lærdalsøyri ☆· N 86-87 C 6
Læsø ⌒ DK 86-87 E 8
Lævvajokgiedde ○ N 86-87 N 2
Lafayette ○ USA (AL) 284-285 E 4
Lafayette ○ USA (CO) 254-255 K 4
Lafayette ○ USA (IN) 274-275 M 4
Lafayette ○ USA (LA) 268-269 J 6
Lafayette ○ USA (OR) 244-245 B 5
Lafayette ○ USA (TN) 276-277 J 4
Lafayette, Mount ▲ USA (NH) 278-279 K 4
Laferte River ~ CDN 30-31 K 5
Lafia ○ WAN 204-205 H 4
Lafiagi ○ WAN 204-205 F 4
Lafitte ○ USA (LA) 268-269 K 7
Laflamme, Rivière ~ CDN (QUE) 236-237 L 4
Lafleche ○ CDN (SAS) 232-233 M 6
Lafoi, Chute de la ~·· ZRE 214-215 D 6
Laforce ○ CDN (QUE) 236-237 K 5
La Forest ○ CDN (ONT) 236-237 G 5
Lafourche, Bayou ~ USA (LA) 268-269 K 7
Lāft-e Nou ○ IR 134-135 F 5
Lagaip River ~ PNG 183 B 3
Lagamar ○ BR 72-73 G 5
Lagan' ☆ RUS 126-127 G 5
Lagan ~ S 86-87 F 8
La Gan, Mũi ▲ VN 158-159 K 5
Lagartero ∴· MEX 52-53 J 4
Lagarto ○ BR 68-69 K 7
Lagarto, Serra do ▲ BR 72-73 D 7
Lagbar ○ SN 196-197 C 7
Lagdo ○ CAM 204-205 K 4
Lagdo, Lac de < CAM 204-205 K 4
Lågen ~ N 86-87 E 6
Lagernoe ○ RUS 108-109 F 5
Lages ○ BR 74-75 E 6
Lage's ○ USA (NV) 246-247 L 3
Lageuen ○ RI 162-163 A 2
Laǧǧ, Umm ○ KSA 130-131 E 5
Laghdaria ○ DZ 190-191 D 2
Laghouat ☆· DZ 190-191 D 4
La Gi ○ VN 158-159 J 5
l-'Aǧiğ, Wādī ~ IRQ 128-129 J 5
Laglan ○ AUS 178-179 J 2
Laǧmān ◘ AFG 136-137 M 7
Lågneset ▲ N 84-85 H 4
Lagoa da Canoa ○ BR 68-69 K 6
Lagoa da Prata ○ BR 72-73 H 5
Lagoa do Capim ○ BR 68-69 K 6
Lagoa do Mato ○ BR 68-69 J 4
Lagoa Dourada ○ BR 72-73 H 6
Lagoa Feia ⌓ BR 68-69 J 4
Lagoa Grande ○ BR 68-69 H 6
Lago Agrio ○ EC 64-65 D 1
Lagoa Nova ○ MOC 218-219 G 6
Lagoa Preta ○ BR 72-73 K 3
Lagoa Vermelho ○ BR 74-75 E 7
Lago Buenos Aires, Meseta del ⩧ RA 80 E 3
Lago das Pedras ○ BR 66-67 K 4
Lago de São Antônio ○ BR 66-67 F 6
Lago Dilolo ○ ANG 214-215 B 6
Lago Dorado, El ○ CO 66-67 B 2
Lago Fontana ○ RA 80 E 2
Lago Las Torres, Parque Nacional ⊥ RCH 80 D 2
La Gomera ⌒ E 188-189 C 6
Lagong, Pulau ⌒ RI 162-163 H 3
Lagonoy Gulf ≈ 160-161 E 6
Lagoon Point ▲ USA 22-23 Q 4
Lago Pasadas ○ RA 80 E 3
Lago Piratuba, Parque Natural do ⊥ BR 62-63 J 5
Lago Puelo, Parque Nacional ⊥ RA 78-79 D 7
Lago Ranco ○ RCH 78-79 C 6
Lagos ○ P 98-99 C 6
Lagos ○ WAN (LAG) 204-205 E 5
Lagos ◘ WAN 204-205 E 5
Lagos, Los ○ RCH 78-79 C 5
Lagos de Moreno ○· MEX 50-51 J 7
Lagos Lagoon ⌓ WAN 204-205 E 5
Lagossa ○ EAT 212-213 B 6
Lago Verde ○ BR 68-69 F 3
Lago Verde ○ RCH 80 E 2
Lago Viedma ○ RA 80 D 4
Lago Vintter ○ RA 78-79 D 7
Lågøya ⌒ N 84-85 L 2
La Grange ⊼ AUS 172-173 E 5
La Grange ○ USA (CA) 248-249 D 2
Lagrange ○ USA (IN) 274-275 N 3
La Grange ○ USA (WY) 252-253 O 5
La Grange Bay ≈ 172-173 E 5
Laguani, Salar del ○ BOL 70-71 C 7
Lagudri ○ RI 162-163 B 4
Laguna ○· BR 74-75 F 7
Laguna ○ USA (NM) 256-257 H 3
Laguna ○ USA (TX) 266-267 H 4
Laguna, Ilha da ⌒ BR 62-63 J 6
Laguna, La ○ RA 78-79 H 2
Laguna, La = San Cristóbal de la Laguna ○ E 188-189 C 6
Laguna, Parque Nacionale ⊥ YV 60-61 K 2
Laguna, Río de la ~ RCH 76-77 B 6
Laguna Beach ○ USA (CA) 248-249 G 6
Laguna Blanca ○ RA 78-79 E 6
Laguna Blanca, Parque Nacional ⊥ RA 78-79 D 5
Laguna Blanca, Sierra ▲ RA 76-77 D 4
Laguna de Bay ○ RP 160-161 D 5
Laguna de Chacahua, Parque Natural ⊥ MEX 52-53 F 5
Laguna del Laja, Parque Nacional ⊥ RCH 78-79 D 4

Laguna del Rey o MEX 50-51 H 4
Laguna Grande, Playa ∴ • DOM 54-55 L 5
Laguna Grande, Río ~ RCH 76-77 B 5
Laguna Indian Reservation ✗ USA (NM) 256-257 H 4
Laguna Južnaja o RUS 112-113 U 5
Laguna Lamar o C 54-55 F 4
Laguna Larga o USA (TX) 266-267 K 6
Laguna Limpia o RA 76-77 H 4
Laguna Paiva o RA 76-77 G 6
Laguna Parillar, Reserva Faunistica ⊥ RCH 80 E 6
Lagunas o PE (LAM) 64-65 C 5
Lagunas o PE (LOR) 64-65 E 4
Lagunas o RCH 70-71 C 7
Laguna Salada o DOM 54-55 K 5
Laguna San Rafael, Parque Nacional ⊥ RCH 80 D 3
Laguna Verde o YV 60-61 H 4
Laguna Verde, Salina de o RA 76-77 C 4
Laguna Yema o RA 76-77 G 3
Lagundi = Lagudri o RI 162-163 B 4
Lagundu, Tanjung ▲ RI 168 D 7
Lagunes de Montebello, Parque Nacional ⊥ MEX 52-53 J 3
Lagunillas o BOL 70-71 F 6
Lagunillas, Lago o PE 70-71 B 4
Lagunita Salada o RA 78-79 E 7
Laha o RI 166-167 E 3
La Habana ★ ··· C 54-55 D 3
Lahad Datu o MAL 160-161 C 10
La Hai o VN 158-159 K 4
Lahaina o • USA (HI) 288 J 4
Lahār o IND 138-139 G 6
Laharčana ~ RUS 118-119 D 3
Lahat o RI 162-163 E 6
La Have o CDN (NS) 240-241 L 6
La Have Island ∩ CDN (NS) 240-241 L 6
Lahemaa Rahvuspark ⊥ • EST 94-95 J 2
Lahewa o RI 162-163 B 4
Lahiğ o Y 132-133 D 7
Lāhīğān o • IR 128-129 N 4
Lahlangubo o ZA 220-221 J 5
Laḥm, Tall al- o IRQ 130-131 K 2
Lahn ~ D 92-93 K 3
Laholmsbukten ≈ 86-87 F 8
Lahontan Reservoir o USA (NV) 246-247 F 4
Lahore ☆ ··· PK 138-139 E 4
Lahri o PK 138-139 B 5
Lahti o FIN 88-89 H 6
Lahuarpia o PE 64-65 D 5
Laï ☆ TCH 206-207 C 4
Laiagam o PNG 183 B 3
Laiama o PNG 183 E 4
Lai'an o VRC 154-155 L 5
Laibin o VRC 156-157 F 5
Lai Châu ☆ VN 156-157 C 5
Laidlaw o CDN (BC) 230-231 H 4
Laifeng o VRC 156-157 F 2
Laihia o FIN 88-89 G 5
Lai-hka o MYA 142-143 K 5
Lailā o KSA 130-131 K 6
Laila, Umm ∴ • Y 132-133 C 5
Lailaba o WAN 198-199 B 6
Laimu o RI 166-167 E 3
Laingsburg o ZA 220-221 E 6
Laingsnek ▲ ZA 220-221 J 3
Laininir o RI 166-167 H 5
Lainioälven ~ S 86-87 L 3
Laird o CDN (SAS) 232-233 M 3
Lairg o GB 90-91 E 2
Lai River ~ PNG 183 B 3
Lais o RI (BEN) 162-163 E 6
Lais o RI (SLT) 164-165 G 3
Laisälven ~ S 86-87 H 4
Laisamis o EAK 212-213 F 3
Laitila o FIN 88-89 F 6
Laiwu o VRC 154-155 K 3
Laiwui o RI 164-165 K 4
Laixi o VRC 154-155 M 3
Laiyang o VRC 154-155 M 3
Laiyuan o VRC 154-155 J 2
Laizhou o VRC 154-155 L 3
Laizhou Wan ≈ 154-155 L 3
Laja o BOL 70-71 C 5
Laja ~ RUS 88-89 X 3
Laja, El Salto del ~ ··· RCH 78-79 C 4
Laja, La o MEX 50-51 L 7
Laja, La o RCH (BIO) 78-79 C 4
Laja, La o RCH (COQ) 76-77 B 5
Laja, Laguna de la o RCH 78-79 D 4
Laja, Le o YV 62-63 D 3
Laja, Río ~ RCH 78-79 C 4
Laja, Laguna o YV 60-61 H 4
Lajamanu ✗ AUS 172-173 K 5
Lajas o PE 64-65 C 5
Lajas, Las o RA 78-79 D 5
Lajas, Río las ~ RA 76-77 D 4
Laje o BR (BAH) 72-73 L 2
Laje o BR (MAR) 68-69 F 3
Laje, Cachoeira da ~ BR 70-71 E 2
Lajeado o BR (MAR) 68-69 E 5
Lajeado o BR (RSU) 74-75 E 7
Lajeado, Serra do ▲ BR 68-69 D 7
Lajeado Grande o BR 74-75 E 7
Lajedão o BR 72-73 K 4
Lajedao, Cachoeira ~ BR 70-71 H 2
Lajedo o BR 68-69 K 6
Lajedo, Cachoeira de ~ BR 68-69 E 6
Lajes o BR 68-69 K 4
Lajes, Cachoeira das ~ BR 68-69 D 5
Lajinha o BR 72-73 K 6
Lajitas o USA (TX) 266-267 D 4
Lajitas, Las o RA 76-77 E 3
Lajla, gora ▲ GE 126-127 E 6
Lajma ~ RUS 114-115 J 5
La Jolla Indian Reservation ✗ USA (CA) 248-249 G 6
Lajord o CDN (SAS) 232-233 O 5
Lajoya o USA (NM) 256-257 J 4
La Joya o USA (TX) 266-267 J 7
Laka ~ RUS 88-89 R 4
Lakamané o RMM 202-203 F 2
Lake o USA (MS) 268-269 L 4
Lake o USA (MT) 250-251 H 7
Lake o USA (WY) 252-253 H 2
Lake Alma o CDN (SAS) 232-233 O 6
Lake Andes o USA (SD) 260-261 H 3
Lake Argyle Tourist Village o AUS 172-173 J 4
Lake Arthur o USA (LA) 268-269 H 6
Lake Arthur o USA (NM) 256-257 L 6
Lake Benton o USA (MN) 270-271 B 6
Lake Biddy o AUS 176-177 E 6
Lake Boga o AUS 180-181 G 3
Lake Bolac o AUS 180-181 G 4
Lake Bronson o USA (MN) 270-271 B 2
Lake Butler o USA (FL) 286-287 G 1
Lake Cargelligo o AUS 180-181 J 2
Lake Charles o USA (LA) 268-269 G 6
Lake Chelan National Recreation Area ⊥ USA (WA) 244-245 E 2
Lake City o USA (AR) 276-277 E 5
Lake City o USA (CO) 254-255 H 5
Lake City o USA (FL) 286-287 G 1
Lake City o USA (IA) 274-275 D 2
Lake City o USA (MI) 272-273 D 3
Lake City o USA (MN) 270-271 F 6
Lake City o USA (SC) 284-285 L 3
Lake City o USA (SD) 260-261 J 1
Lake City o USA (TN) 282-283 C 4
Lake Clark National Park and Preserve ⊥ USA 20-21 O 6
Lake Cormorant o USA (MS) 268-269 K 2
Lake Cowichan o CDN (BC) 230-231 E 5
Lake Crystal o USA (MN) 270-271 D 6
Lake District National Park ⊥ GB 90-91 F 4
Lake Errock o CDN (BC) 230-231 G 4
Lake Eyre Basin ⌄ AUS 178-179 C 4
Lake Eyre National Park ⊥ AUS 178-179 D 5
Lakefield o AUS 174-175 H 4
Lakefield o CDN (ONT) 238-239 G 4
Lakefield o USA (MN) 270-271 C 7
Lakefield National Park ⊥ AUS 174-175 H 4
Lake Francis o CDN (MAN) 234-235 F 4
Lake Frome Regional Reserve ⊥ AUS 178-179 F 6
Lake Gairdner National Park ⊥ AUS 178-179 C 6
Lake Geneva o USA (WI) 274-275 K 2
Lake George o USA (CO) 254-255 K 5
Lake George o USA (MN) 270-271 C 3
Lake George o USA (NY) 278-279 H 5
Lake Gilles Conservation Park ⊥ AUS 180-181 D 2
Lake Grace o AUS 176-177 E 6
Lakehamu River ~ PNG 183 D 5
Lake Harbor o USA (FL) 286-287 J 5
Lake Harbour o CDN 36-37 P 3
Lake Havasu City o USA (AZ) 256-257 A 4
Lake Hawea o NZ 182 B 6
Lakehead o USA (CA) 246-247 C 3
Lake Helen o USA (FL) 286-287 H 3
Lake Henry o USA (MN) 270-271 D 5
Lake Hughes o USA (CA) 248-249 F 5
Lakehurst o USA (NJ) 280-281 M 4
Lake Isabella o USA (CA) 248-249 F 4
Lake Itasca o USA (MN) 270-271 C 3
Lake Jackson o USA (TX) 268-269 E 7
Lake Jipe Lodge o EAK 212-213 F 5
Lake King o AUS 176-177 E 6
Lakeland o CDN (MAN) 234-235 E 4
Lakeland o USA (FL) 286-287 H 3
Lakeland o USA (GA) 284-285 G 5
Lakeland Downs o AUS 174-175 H 4
Lake Lenore o CDN (SAS) 232-233 O 3
Lake Linden o USA (MI) 270-271 K 3
Lake Louise o CDN (ALB) 232-233 B 4
Lakelse Lake o CDN (BC) 228-229 F 2
Lake Mackay Aboriginal Land ✗ AUS 172-173 J 6
Lake Malawi National Park ⊥ ··· MW 218-219 H 1
Lake Mason o AUS 176-177 E 3
Lake Mattamuskeet National Wildlife Refuge ⊥ USA (NC) 282-283 L 5
Lake Mburo National Park ⊥ EAU 212-213 C 4
Lake McDonald o USA (MT) 250-251 F 3
Lake Mead City o USA (AZ) 256-257 A 3
Lake Mead National Recreation Area • USA (AZ) 256-257 B 2
Lake Mead National Recreation Area • USA (NV) 248-249 K 3
Lake Metigoshe International Peace Garden • USA (ND) 258-259 G 3
Lake Michigan Beach o USA (MI) 272-273 C 5
Lake Michigan Provincial Park ⊥ CDN (ONT) 234-235 P 5
Lake Mills o USA (IA) 274-275 E 1
Lake Mills o USA (WI) 274-275 K 1
Lake Minchumina o USA 20-21 O 5
Lake Murray o PNG 183 A 4
Lake Nash o AUS 178-179 D 1
Lakenheath o CDN (SAS) 232-233 M 6
Lake O'Brien o CDN (NFL) 242-243 O 3
Lake of the Ozarks State Park ⊥ USA (MO) 274-275 F 6
Lake of the Prairies o CDN (MAN) 234-235 B 3
Lake Oswego o USA (OR) 244-245 C 5
Lake Paringa o NZ 182 B 5
Lake Park o USA (FL) 286-287 J 5
Lake Park o USA (GA) 284-285 G 6
Lake Placid o USA (FL) 286-287 H 4
Lake Placid o USA (NY) 278-279 H 4
Lakeport o USA (NY) 278-279 F 5
Lake Preston o USA (SD) 260-261 J 2
Lake Providence o USA (LA) 268-269 J 4
Lake Rara National Park ⊥ NEP 144-145 C 6
Lake Seminole State Park ⊥ • USA (GA) 284-285 F 6
Lake Shasta Caverns ⊥ USA (CA) 246-247 C 3
Lakeshore o USA (CA) 248-249 E 2
Lakeside o USA (NY) 278-279 C 5
Lakeside o USA (OR) 244-245 A 7
Lakeside o USA (UT) 254-255 C 2
Lakeside o USA (VA) 280-281 J 6
Lakes National Park, The ⊥ AUS 180-181 J 4
Lake Stevens o USA (WA) 244-245 C 2
Lake Superieur Provincial Park ⊥ CDN (ONT) 236-237 D 5
Lake Tekapo o NZ 182 C 6
Lake Torrens National Park ⊥ AUS 178-179 D 6
Lake Valley o CDN (SAS) 232-233 M 5
Lake Valley o USA (NM) 256-257 H 6
Lake Victor o USA (TX) 266-267 J 3
Lakeview o USA (ID) 250-251 C 4
Lakeview o USA (MI) 272-273 D 4
Lakeview o USA (OH) 280-281 C 3
Lakeview o USA (OR) 244-245 E 8
Lake View o USA (SC) 284-285 L 2
Lake Village o USA (AR) 276-277 D 7
Lakeville o USA (MN) 270-271 E 6
Lake Wales o USA (FL) 286-287 H 4
Lake Way o AUS 176-177 F 3
Lake Wilson o USA (MN) 270-271 C 6
Lakewood o USA (CO) 254-255 K 4
Lakewood o USA (MI) 272-273 F 6
Lakewood o USA (NJ) 280-281 M 3
Lakewood o USA (NM) 256-257 L 6
Lake Woodruff National Wildlife Refuge ⊥ USA (FL) 286-287 H 2
Lake Worth o USA (FL) 286-287 J 5
Lake Zurich o USA (IL) 274-275 K 2
Lākheri o IND 138-139 F 7
Lakhimpur o IND 142-143 B 2
Lakhipur o IND 142-143 H 3
Lakhnādon o IND 138-139 G 8
Lakhpat o IND 138-139 B 8
Lākhra o PK 134-135 M 6
Lakin o USA (KS) 262-263 E 7
Lakinsk o RUS 94-95 Q 3
Lakitsuaki River ~ CDN 34-35 P 3
Lakki o PK 138-139 C 3
Lákkoma o GR 100-101 K 4
Laklo ~ RI 166-167 C 6
Laklubar o RI 166-167 C 6
Lakohembi o RI 168 E 7
Lakonikós Kólpos ≈ 100-101 J 6
Lakor, Pulau ∩ RI 166-167 E 6
Lakota ☆ CI 202-203 H 7
Lakota o USA (IA) 274-275 D 1
Lakota o USA (ND) 258-259 J 3
Laksefjorden ≈ 86-87 N 1
Lakselv o N 86-87 M 1
Laksfossen ~ ·· N 86-87 F 4
Lakshadweep ▫ IND 140-141 E 5
Lakshadweep Sea ≈ 140-141 F 6
Lakshimpur o BD 142-143 G 4
Lakshmipur o IND 140-141 L 3
Laktaši o BIH 100-101 F 2
Lakuan o RI 164-165 G 3
Lakuramau o PNG 183 F 2
Lalafuta ~ Z 218-219 C 2
Lalago o EAT 212-213 D 5
Lāla Mūsa o PK 138-139 D 3
Lalandai o RI 164-165 H 4
Lalapansi o ZW 218-219 F 4
Lalapaşa ☆ TR 128-129 B 2
Lalara o G 210-211 C 3
Lalaua o MOC 218-219 K 2
Lalaua, Rio ~ MOC 218-219 K 2
Lalbert o AUS 180-181 G 3
Lalbiti o NEP 144-145 E 7
Laleham o AUS 178-179 K 2
Laleia o RI 166-167 D 6
Lalete, Tanjung ▲ RI 166-167 C 6
Lālezār, Kūh-e ▲ IR 134-135 G 4
Lālezār, Rūd-e ~ IR 134-135 G 3
Lālganj o IND 142-143 B 2
Lāli o IR 134-135 C 2
Lalibela o ··· ETH 200-201 J 6
Laliki o RI 166-167 D 5
Lalik River ~ PNG 183 F 3
Lalin o E 98-99 C 3
Lalin o VRC 150-151 F 5
Lalindu ~ RI 164-165 G 5
Lalitpur o IND 138-139 G 7
Lalitpur o ·· NEP 144-145 E 7
Lalla Outka ▲ MA 188-189 J 3
l-'Allāqī, Wādī ~ ET 194-195 F 6
Lalla Rookh o AUS 172-173 D 6
LaHo o RP 160-161 D 3
Lalo o DY 202-203 L 6
La'l-ō-Sarğangal o AFG 134-135 M 1
La'l Pūra o AFG 138-139 C 2
Laluangon o RI 164-165 G 4
Lalung La ▲ VRC 144-145 F 6
Lalyo o SUD 206-207 K 6
Lam o CAM 204-205 J 5
Lama o BD 142-143 H 5
Lama, ozero o RUS 108-109 Y 7
Lamadongzhao o VRC 154-155 G 2
Lamainong o RI 162-163 B 3
Lamakera o RI 166-167 B 6
Lamalaga ∴ MA 196-197 B 3
Lamaline o CDN (NFL) 242-243 N 6
Lamanai ∴ • BH 52-53 K 3
Lamanche Valley Provincial Park ⊥ CDN (NFL) 242-243 Q 5
Lamanuna o RI 166-167 B 6
Lamap ☆ VAN 184 II a 3
Lamar o USA (CO) 254-255 N 5
Lamar o USA (LA) 268-269 J 4
Lamar o USA (MO) 276-277 A 3
Lamar o USA (OK) 264-265 H 3
Lamar o USA (SC) 284-285 K 2
Lāmard o IR 134-135 E 5
Lamari River ~ PNG 183 C 4
La Martre o CDN (QUE) 242-243 B 3
Lamas o PE (LOR) 64-65 F 3
Lamas o PE (MAR) 64-65 D 5
Lamassa o PNG 183 G 3
La Mauricie National Park ⊥ CDN (QUE) 240-241 C 3
Lambako o RI 164-165 H 4
Lambale o RI 164-165 H 6
Lamballe o F 90-91 F 7
Lambarene ☆ • G 210-211 C 4
Lambari o BR 72-73 H 6
Lambari, Rio ~ BR 72-73 H 5
Lambaro Angan o RI 162-163 A 2
Lambatu o RI 164-165 G 5
Lambayeque o PE 64-65 C 5
Lambell, Mount ▲ AUS 172-173 L 2
Lambert o USA (MS) 268-269 K 2
Lambert, Cape ▲ AUS 172-173 C 6
Lambert, Cape ▲ PNG 183 F 3
Lambert Glacier ⊂ ARK 16 F 8
Lambert Land ∴ GRØ 26-27 p 4
Lambertsbaai o ZA 220-221 D 6
Lamberts Bay = Lambertsbaai o ZA 220-221 D 6
Lambeth o CDN (ONT) 238-239 D 6
Lambi o SOL 184 I d 3
Lamborn o S 86-87 G 6
Lambrama o PE 64-65 F 8
Lambton, Cape ▲ CDN 24-25 K 5
Lambu o PNG 183 F 2
Lambubalano o RI 164-165 H 6
Lambumbu Bay ≈ 184 II a 3
Lambunao o RP 160-161 E 7
Lambuya o RI 164-165 H 5
Lamdesar o RI 166-167 F 5
Lamé o TCH 206-207 B 4
Lame Burra Game Reserve ⊥ WAN 204-205 H 3
Lame Deer o USA (MT) 250-251 N 6
Lamego o • 98-99 D 4
Lameguapi o RCH 78-79 C 6
Lameirão, Área Indígena ✗ BR 66-67 B 5
Lamen Bay o VAN 184 II b 3
Lamentin, Le o F 56 E 4
Lameroo o AUS 180-181 F 3
Lamesa o USA (TX) 264-265 C 6
Lami o FJI 184 III b 3
Lamia o GR 100-101 J 5
Lamie River ~ USA (MO) 274-275 E 6
Lamindo o SUD 206-207 K 6
Lamington, Mount ▲ PNG 183 E 5
Lamington National Park ⊥ AUS 178-179 M 5
Lamir, Kampung o MAL 162-163 E 3
Lamison o USA (AL) 284-285 C 4
Lamitan o RP 160-161 E 9
Lam Kachuan o THA 158-159 F 3
Lamkin o USA (TX) 266-267 J 2
Lammerkop o ZA 220-221 J 2
Lammeulo o RI 162-163 A 2
Lamming Mills o CDN (BC) 228-229 O 3
La Moille o USA (IL) 274-275 J 3
Lamoille o USA (NV) 246-247 K 3
Lamoille River ~ USA (VT) 278-279 H 4
La Moine River ~ USA (IL) 274-275 H 4
Lamon Bay ≈ 160-161 D 5
Lamongan o RI 168 E 3
Lamoni o USA (IA) 274-275 E 4
Lamont o CDN (ALB) 232-233 F 2
Lamont o USA (CA) 248-249 F 4
Lamont o USA (FL) 286-287 F 1
Lamont o USA (ID) 252-253 G 3
Lamont o USA (OK) 264-265 G 2
Lamont o USA (WY) 252-253 L 4
La Motte, Lac o CDN (QUE) 236-237 K 4
La Moure o USA (ND) 258-259 J 5
Lampa o PE 70-71 B 4
Lampa, Rio ~ PE 64-65 F 9
Lampanaih o RI 162-163 A 2
Lampang o THA 142-143 L 6
Lam Pao Reservoir o THA 158-159 G 2
Lampasas o USA (TX) 266-267 J 2
Lampasas River ~ USA (TX) 266-267 K 3
Lampazos de Naranjo o MEX 50-51 J 4
Lampedusa o I 100-101 D 7
Lampedusa, Ísola di ∩ I 100-101 D 7
Lamper o RI 164-165 E 4
Lamphun o THA 142-143 L 6
Lampione, Ísola di ∩ I 100-101 D 7
Lam Plaimat o THA 158-159 G 3
Lampman o CDN (SAS) 232-233 Q 6
Lamprey o CDN 30-31 W 6
Lampung ▫ RI 162-163 F 7
Lampung, Teluk ≈ 162-163 F 7
Lamsa, Ksar • TN 190-191 G 2
Lamu o • EAK (COA) 212-213 H 5
Lamud o PE 64-65 D 5
Lamu Island ∩ EAK 212-213 H 5
Lamutskaja ~ RUS 112-113 R 4
Lamutskoe o RUS 112-113 P 4
Lamy o USA (NM) 256-257 K 3
Lan' ~ BY 94-95 K 5
Lana, Río de la ~ MEX 52-53 G 3
Lanagan, Lake o AUS 172-173 H 5
Lanai ∩ USA (HI) 288 J 4
Lanai City o USA (HI) 288 J 4
Lanaihale ▲ USA (HI) 288 J 4
Lanalhué, Lago o RCH 78-79 C 4
Lanao, Lake o RP 160-161 F 9
Lanark o GB 90-91 F 4
Lanark o USA (NM) 256-257 J 7
Lanas o MAL 160-161 B 10
Lanbi Kyun ∩ MYA 158-159 E 5
Lancang o VRC 142-143 M 4
Lancang Jiang ~ VRC 142-143 M 4
Lancang Jiang ~ VRC 144-145 L 5
Lancaster o CDN (ONT) 238-239 L 3
Lancaster o • GB 90-91 F 4
Lancaster o USA (CA) 248-249 F 5
Lancaster o USA (IL) 274-275 L 6
Lancaster o USA (MN) 270-271 B 2
Lancaster o USA (MO) 274-275 F 4
Lancaster o USA (NH) 278-279 K 4
Lancaster o USA (OH) 280-281 D 4
Lancaster o USA (PA) 280-281 K 3
Lancaster o USA (SC) 284-285 K 2
Lancaster o USA (TX) 264-265 H 6
Lancaster o USA (WI) 274-275 H 2
Lancaster Sound ≈ 24-25 c 3
Lancaster State Historic Site, Fort ∴ USA (TX) 266-267 F 3
Lance Creek o USA (WY) 252-253 O 3
Lancelin o AUS 176-177 C 5
Lancer o CDN (SAS) 232-233 K 5
Lancester o USA (KY) 276-277 L 3
Lanciano o I 100-101 E 3
Lanco o RCH 78-79 C 5
Lancones o PE 64-65 B 4
Lancrenon, Chutes de ~ • CAM 206-207 B 5
Land, De o USA (FL) 286-287 H 2
Landa o USA (ND) 258-259 G 3
Landak ~ RI 162-163 H 4
Landana o ANG 210-211 D 6
Land Between The Lakes ⊥ USA (KY) 276-277 G 4
Landeck o A 92-93 L 5
Landegode ∩ N 86-87 G 3
Lander o USA (WY) 252-253 K 4
Lander River ~ AUS 172-173 K 6
Lander River ~ AUS 172-173 L 6
Landers o USA (CA) 248-249 H 5
Landete o E 98-99 G 5
Landfall Island ∩ IND 140-141 L 3
Landi o RG 202-203 E 4
Landi Kotal o PK 138-139 C 2
Landing Lake o CDN 34-35 H 3
Landis o CDN (SAS) 232-233 K 3
Land O'Lakes o USA (FL) 286-287 G 3
Landor o AUS 176-177 D 2
Landri Sales o BR 68-69 G 5
Landrum o USA (SC) 284-285 H 1
Landry, Lac o CDN (QUE) 242-243 G 2
Landšaftnyj park "Sofijivka" • UA 102-103 G 3
Land's End ▲ ·· GB 90-91 E 6
Landshut o D 92-93 M 4
Landskrona o ·· S 86-87 F 9
Landštejn • CZ 92-93 N 4
Lane City o USA (TX) 266-267 L 4
Lanett o USA (AL) 284-285 E 4
Lanfiéra o BF 202-203 J 3
Lang o CDN (SAS) 232-233 O 6
Langa o PE 64-65 D 8
Langabou o RT 202-203 L 5
Lan'ga Co o VRC 144-145 C 5
La'nga Co o VRC 144-145 C 5
Langadás o GR 100-101 J 4
Langa-Langa o ZRE 210-211 E 5
Langano Häyk' o ETH 208-209 D 5
Langar o US 136-137 J 4
Lángara, Bahía ≈ 80 G 3
Langara Island ∩ CDN 32-33 D 4
Langara Island ∩ CDN (BC) 228-229 A 2
Langarūd o IR 136-137 B 6
Langatabiki o SME 62-63 G 3
Langbank o CDN (SAS) 232-233 Q 5
Lang Bay o CDN (BC) 230-231 E 4
Langberg o ZA (CAP) 220-221 E 6
Langberg ▲ ZA 220-221 F 4
Langberge ▲ ZA 220-221 D 6
Langbinsi o GH 202-203 K 4
Langdale o CDN (BC) 230-231 F 4
Lang Dinh o VN 156-157 D 7
Langdon o CDN (ALB) 232-233 E 5
Langdon o USA (ND) 258-259 J 3
Langeac o F 90-91 J 9
Langeb, Wādi ~ SUD 200-201 H 4
Langeb, Wādi ~ SUD 200-201 H 3
Langebaan o ZA 220-221 D 6
Langeberg ▲ ZA 220-221 E 6
Langeland ∩ DK 86-87 E 9
Langell Valley o USA (OR) 244-245 D 8
Langenburg o CDN (SAS) 232-233 R 5
Langeoog ∩ D 92-93 J 2
Langepas o RUS 114-115 N 4
Langeri o RUS 122-123 K 3
Langfang o VRC 154-155 K 2
Langford o CDN (BC) 230-231 F 5
Langford o USA (SD) 260-261 J 1
Langgam o RI 162-163 D 4
Langgapayung o RI 162-163 C 4
Langgur o RI 166-167 G 4
Langham o CDN (SAS) 232-233 M 3
Langjökull ⊂ IS 86-87 c 2
Langka o RI 162-163 B 2
Langkahan o RI 162-163 B 2
Langkawi, Pulau ∩ MAL 162-163 C 2
Lang Kê o VN 156-157 D 6
Langkesi, Kepulauan ∩ RI 164-165 J 6
Langkobale o RI 164-165 G 5
Langkon o MAL 160-161 B 9
Langlade o USA (WI) 270-271 K 5
Langlade, Isthme de ∴ F (975) 242-243 M 6
Langlade ou Petit Miquelon ∩ F 38-39 Q 5
Langlade ou Petit Miquelon ∩ F (975) 242-243 M 6
Langley o CDN (BC) 230-231 G 4
Langley o USA (OK) 264-265 J 2
Langley Island ∩ CDN 20-21 X 2
Langlo Crossing P.O. o AUS 178-179 H 4
Langlois o USA (OR) 244-245 A 8
Langlo River ~ AUS 178-179 H 3
Langmusi o VRC 154-155 C 4
Langnes o N 86-87 O 1
Lango o G 210-211 E 3
Lango, Tarso ▲ TCH 198-199 J 2
Langogne o F 90-91 J 9
Langon o F 90-91 G 9
Langøya ∩ N 86-87 G 2
Langqên Zangbo ~ VRC 144-145 C 5
Langres o • F 90-91 K 8
Langruth o CDN (MAN) 234-235 E 4
Langry ~ RUS 122-123 K 2
Langsa o RI 162-163 B 2
Långseleån ~ S 86-87 G 4
Lang Shan ▲ VRC 148-149 H 7
Lang So'n ☆ VN 156-157 E 6
Lang Suan o THA 158-159 E 6
Langtang o NEP 144-145 E 6
Langtang o WAN 204-205 H 4
Langtang National Park ⊥ • NEP 144-145 E 6
Längtans udde ▲ ARK 16 G 31
Langtao o MYA 142-143 K 2
Langton o CDN (ONT) 238-239 E 6
Langton Bay ≈ 24-25 J 6
Långträsk o S 86-87 K 4
Langtry o USA (TX) 266-267 F 4
Langu o THA 158-159 E 7
Langudi Rassa National Park ⊥ ETH 208-209 E 3
Languedoc ∴ F 90-91 J 10
Languedoc-Roussillon ▫ F 90-91 J 10
Langueyú, Arroyo ~ RA 78-79 K 4
Langui Layo, Lago o PE 70-71 B 4
L'Anguille River ~ USA (AR) 276-277 E 5
Languiñeo o RA 78-79 D 7
Langxi o VRC 154-155 L 6
Langxiang o VRC 150-151 G 4
Langzhong o VRC 154-155 D 6
Laniel o CDN (QUE) 236-237 J 5
Lanigan o CDN (SAS) 232-233 N 4
Lanigan Creek ~ CDN (SAS) 232-233 N 4
Lanín, Parque Nacional ⊥ RA 78-79 D 5
Lanín, Volcán ▲ RA 78-79 D 5
Lanjut o RI 162-163 F 5
Lankao o VRC 154-155 J 4
Lankapatti o IND 142-143 H 3
Lankovaja ~ RUS 120-121 O 4
Lanlacuni Bajo o PE 70-71 B 3
Lannemezan o F 90-91 H 10
Lannes, Cape ▲ AUS 180-181 E 4
Lannion o F 90-91 F 7
L'Annonciation o CDN (QUE) 238-239 L 2
Lanquín o • GCA 52-53 K 4
Lansdale o USA (PA) 280-281 L 3
Lansdowne o AUS 172-173 H 4
Lansdowne o ·· IND 138-139 G 5
Lansdowne House o CDN (ONT) 234-235 Q 2
L'Anse o USA (MI) 270-271 K 4
L'Anse-au-Griffon o CDN (QUE) 240-241 L 2
L'Anse-au-Loup o CDN (NFL) 242-243 M 1
L'Anse-aux-Gascons o CDN (QUE) 240-241 L 2
L'Anse aux Meadows National Historic Park ⊥ ··· CDN (NFL) 242-243 N 1
L'Anse-à-Valleau o CDN (QUE) 242-243 D 3
Lansford o USA (ND) 258-259 F 3
Lansing o USA (IA) 274-275 G 1
Lansing ☆ USA (MI) 272-273 E 5
Lansjärv o S 86-87 L 3
Lantewa o WAN 198-199 E 6
Lanthenay, Romorantin- o F 90-91 H 8
Lantian o VRC 154-155 F 4
Lantigiang, Pulau ∩ RI 168 E 6
Lantz Corners o USA (PA) 280-281 H 2
Lantzville o CDN (BC) 230-231 E 4
Lanu o RI 164-165 G 3
Lanusei o I 100-101 B 5
Lanxi o VRC (HEI) 150-151 F 4
Lanxi o VRC (ZHE) 156-157 L 2
Lan Xian o VRC 154-155 G 2
Lanya o GH 202-203 L 5
Lanyu o RC 156-157 M 5
Lanyu ∩ RC 156-157 M 5
Lanza o BOL 70-71 D 2
Lanza, Río ~ PE 70-71 C 4
Lanzai o WAN 204-205 J 3
Lanzarote ∩ E 188-189 E 6
Lanzhou ☆ VRC 154-155 C 3
Laoag ☆ RP 160-161 D 3
Lào Cai ☆ VN 156-157 C 5
Laoguié o CI 202-203 H 7
Laohekou o VRC 154-155 G 5
Laokas o TCH 206-207 B 4
Laon ☆ • F 90-91 J 7
Laona o USA (WI) 270-271 K 5
Laoong o RP 160-161 F 6
Laora o RI 164-165 H 6
Laos = Lao ■ LAO 156-157 C 7
Laoshan • VRC 154-155 M 3
Laotieshan Shedao Z.B. ⊥ • VRC 150-151 C 8
Laouda o CI 202-203 H 6
Laoudi-Ba o CI 202-203 J 5
La'oueissi o RIM 196-197 D 6
Laouni, Oued ~ DZ 198-199 B 2
Laouridou o CI 202-203 H 7
Lao Xanh, Cù ∩ VN 158-159 K 4
Laoye Ling ▲ VRC 150-151 G 6
Lapa o BR 74-75 F 5
Lapachito o RA 76-77 H 4
Lapac Island ∩ RP 160-161 D 10
Lapai o WAN 204-205 G 4
Lapalisse o F 90-91 J 8
La Palma ∩ E 188-189 C 6
La Palma o USA (AZ) 256-257 D 6
La Panza Range ▲ USA (CA) 248-249 D 4
Laparan Island ∩ RP 160-161 D 10
Lapata o RA 80 F 7
La Patrie o CDN (QUE) 238-239 O 3
Lapau o PNG 183 F 3
La Paz ★ • BOL 70-71 C 5
Lape o RI 168 C 7
Lapeer o USA (MI) 272-273 F 4
Lapie River ~ CDN 20-21 Y 6
Lapihungkanan o RI 164-165 D 5
La Pine o USA (OR) 244-245 D 7
Lapining Island ∩ RP 160-161 F 7
Lapinlahti o FIN 88-89 J 5
La Plata ☆ • RA 78-79 L 3
La Plata o USA (MD) 280-281 K 5
La Plata River ~ USA (CO) 254-255 G 6
La Poile River ~ CDN (NFL) 242-243 K 5
Laporte o CDN (SAS) 232-233 J 4
La Porte o USA (CA) 246-247 D 4
Laporte o USA (PA) 280-281 K 2
La Porte City o USA (IA) 274-275 F 2
Lappa o RUS 120-121 D 4
Lappajärvi ~ FIN 88-89 G 5
Lappe o CDN (ONT) 234-235 O 6
Lappeenranta o • FIN 88-89 K 6
Lappland ∴ 86-87 H 3
Lappy ~ RUS 120-121 D 4
Lapri o RUS 118-119 M 8
Laprida o RA 78-79 J 4
Lapseki ☆ TR 128-129 B 2
Lapševo ☆ RUS 96-97 F 6
Laptev Sea = Laptevyh, more ≈ RUS 110-111 M 2
Lapua o FIN 88-89 G 5
Lapuko o RI 164-165 H 6
La Puntilla ▲ EC 64-65 B 3
La Purisima Mission State History Park • USA (CA) 248-249 D 5
Lapus, Munții ▲ RO 102-103 C 4
La Push o USA (WA) 244-245 A 3
Lapwai o USA (ID) 250-251 C 5
Laqiyat Arba'in < SUD 200-201 D 2
Laqiyat 'Umran < SUD 200-201 D 3
L'Aquila ☆ ·· I 100-101 D 3
Lār o IR 134-135 F 5
Lara o AUS 180-181 H 5
Lara ~ G 210-211 C 3
Larabanga o GH 202-203 K 5
Larache = El-Araïch o MA 188-189 H 3
Larache = El-Araïch o MA 188-189 H 3
Laragh = An Láithreach o • IRL 90-91 D 5
Lārak, Ğazīre-ye ∩ IR 134-135 G 5
Laramanay o TCH 206-207 B 4
Laramate o PE 64-65 E 9
Laramie o USA (WY) 252-253 N 5
Laramie Mountains ▲ USA (WY) 252-253 M 4
Laramie National Historic Site, Fort ∴ USA (WY) 252-253 O 4
Laramie Peak ▲ USA (WY) 252-253 N 4
Laramie River ~ USA (WY) 252-253 N 5
Laranjal o BR (AMA) 66-67 E 3
Laranjal o BR (RSU) 74-75 E 7
Laranjeiras do Sul o BR 74-75 D 5
Laranjinha, Rio ~ BR 72-73 E 7
Larantuka o RI 166-167 B 6
Larat o RI 166-167 F 5
Larat, Pulau ∩ RI 166-167 F 5
Larba o DZ 190-191 D 2
Larba o RUS 118-119 L 8
Lärbro o S 86-87 J 8
Larchwood o USA (IA) 274-275 B 1
Larde o MOC 218-219 K 3
Lardeau River ~ CDN (BC) 230-231 M 3
Larder Lake o CDN (ONT) 236-237 J 4
Larder River Provincial Park ⊥ CDN (ONT) 236-237 J 5
Lare o EAK 212-213 F 3
Laredo o E 98-99 F 3
Laredo o USA (TX) 266-267 H 6
Laredo Sound ≈ 32-33 F 5
Laredo Sound ≈ CDN 228-229 F 4
Lar'egan ~ RUS 114-115 O 4
Lār-e Polūr o IR 136-137 C 7
Lares o PE 64-65 F 8
Lares o • USA (PR) 286-287 P 2
La Réunion ▫ F 224 C 7
Larga, Laguna o RA 76-77 F 6
Largeau ☆ TCH 198-199 J 4
Largest Lighthouse in the World (Kilauea Lighthouse) II • USA (HI) 288 F 2
Largo o BR 68-69 H 7
Largo o USA (FL) 286-287 G 4
Largo, Cayo ∩ C 54-55 E 4
Lariang o RI 164-165 F 4
Lariang ~ RI 164-165 F 4
Lariat o USA (TX) 264-265 B 4
Larimore o USA (ND) 258-259 K 4
Larino o RUS 96-97 L 6
Lario = Lago di Como o I 100-101 B 2
La Rioja ▫ RA 76-77 C 5
l-Ariš, Wādī ~ ET 194-195 F 3
Lárissa o GR 100-101 J 5
La Rivière o CDN (MAN) 234-235 E 5
Lar'jak o RUS 114-115 Q 4
Lark o USA (TX) 264-265 C 3
Lārkāna o • PK 138-139 B 6
Lark Harbour o CDN (NFL) 242-243 K 3
Larkspur o USA (CO) 254-255 L 4
Larnaka o • CY 128-129 E 5
Larne o • GB 90-91 E 4
Larned o USA (KS) 262-263 G 6
Larned National Historic Site, Fort ∴ USA (KS) 262-263 G 6
Laro o CAM 204-205 K 4
La Ronser, ostrov ∩ RUS 84-85 g 2
Laropi o EAU 212-213 C 2
Larose o USA (LA) 268-269 K 7
Larrainzar o MEX 52-53 H 3
Larrey Point ▲ AUS 172-173 D 5
Larrimah o AUS 174-175 B 4
Larroque o RA 78-79 K 2
Larry's River o CDN (NS) 240-241 O 5
Lars Christensen land ∴ ARK 16 G 7
Larsen is-shelf ⊂ ARK 16 G 30
Larson o CDN (ONT) 234-235 N 5
Laru Mat, Tanjung ▲ RI 166-167 F 5
Larvik ☆ N 86-87 E 7
Larwill o USA (IN) 274-275 N 3
Lasahata o RI 166-167 E 3
Lasahau o RI 164-165 H 6
La Sal o USA (UT) 254-255 F 5
Lasalimu o RI 164-165 H 6
La Sal Mountains ▲ USA (UT) 254-255 F 5
Lasam o RP 160-161 D 3
Lasanga Island ∩ PNG 183 D 4
Las Animas o USA (CO) 254-255 M 5
Lasara o USA (TX) 266-267 K 7
Lasarat o ETH 208-209 F 3
Lascan, Volcán ▲ RCH 76-77 D 2
Lascano o EC 64-65 B 2
Lascano o ROU 78-79 M 2
Lascaux, Grotte de ··· F 90-91 H 9
Lascelles o AUS 180-181 G 3
L'Ascension o CDN (QUE) 240-241 D 2
L'Ascension-de-Patapédia o CDN (QUE) 240-241 H 3
Lasem o RI 168 D 3
Lashburn o CDN (SAS) 232-233 J 2
Lashio o MYA 142-143 K 4
Łask o PL 92-93 P 3
Laškargāh ☆ • AFG 134-135 L 3
Laskeek Bay ≈ CDN 228-229 C 4
Lāš-ō-Ğovein o AFG 134-135 J 3
Lasolo ~ RI 164-165 G 5
Lasoni, Tanjung ▲ RI 164-165 H 5
La Spézia o ·· I 100-101 B 2
Laspur o PK 138-139 D 1
Lassance o BR 72-73 H 4
Lassen Peak ▲ USA (CA) 246-247 D 3
Lassen Volcanic National Park ⊥ USA (CA) 246-247 D 3
Lasseter Highway II AUS 176-177 M 2

Lassio ~ G 210-211 D 4
Lassul o PNG 183 F 3
Last Chance o USA (CO) 254-255 M 4
Last Chance Creek ~ USA (UT) 254-255 D 6
Last Mountain Lake ⊙ CDN (SAS) 232-233 N 4
Lastoursville o G 210-211 D 4
Lastovo o HR 100-101 F 3
Lastovo ⌒ HR 100-101 F 3
Lasu o PNG 183 G 3
Las Vegas o USA (NM) 256-257 K 3
Las Vegas o•• USA (NV) 248-249 J 3
Las Vegas Valley ⌣ USA (NV) 248-249 J 3
Latacunga ☆ EC 64-65 C 2
Latady Island ⌒ ARK 16 F 29
Latah Creek ~ USA (WA) 244-245 H 3
Latakia = al-Lādiqīya ☆ SYR 128-129 F 5
Latakia = Lāḏiqīya, al- ☆ SYR 128-129 F 5
Latalata, Pulau ⌒ RI 164-165 K 4
Lata Papalang, Bukit ▲ MAL 162-163 D 2
Lataro ⌒ VAN 184 II a 2
Latas o RCH 76-77 C 2
Lätäseno ~ FIN 88-89 G 2
Latchford o CDN (ONT) 236-237 J 5
Late ⌒ TON 184 IV a 1
Lateriquique, Río ~ PY 70-71 H 6
Laterriere o CDN (QUE) 240-241 D 2
Latham o AUS 176-177 D 4
Latham o USA (AL) 284-285 C 5
Lathan o IND 142-143 J 2
Lathi = Île Sakao ⌒ VAN 184 II a 2
Lathom o CDN (ALB) 232-233 F 5
Lathu = Île Eléphant ⌒ VAN 184 II a 2
Latifiya, al- o IRQ 128-129 L 6
Latik < RIM 196-197 G 6
Latimojong Mountains Reserve ⊥ • RI 164-165 F 5
Latina ☆ I 100-101 D 4
Latinos, Ponta dos ▲ BR 74-75 D 9
Lat'juga o RUS 88-89 U 4
Latodo o RI 168 E 6
Latoma o RI 164-165 G 5
Latornell River ~ CDN (ALB) 228-229 Q 2
Latorre o RCH 76-77 B 5
Latou o RI 164-165 G 5
Latouche o USA 20-21 R 6
Latouche Island ⌒ USA 20-21 R 6
Latouche Treville, Cape ▲ AUS 172-173 E 5
Latour o CDN (QUE) 240-241 G 2
Látrar o IS 86-87 b 1
Latrobe o AUS 180-181 J 6
Latrobe o USA (PA) 280-281 G 3
Latta o USA (SC) 284-285 L 2
Latu o RI 166-167 E 3
Latulipe o CDN (QUE) 236-237 J 5
Lātūr o IND 138-139 F 10
Latura Vati, Tanjung ▲ RI 166-167 D 6
Latvia = Latvija ■ LV 94-95 J 3
Lau o PNG 183 F 3
Lau o WAN 204-205 J 4
Lauca, Parque Nacional ⊥ RCH 70-71 C 6
Laucala ⌒ FJI 184 III c 2
Laudar o Y 132-133 D 7
Lauder o CDN (MAN) 234-235 C 5
Lauderdale o USA (MS) 268-269 M 4
Lauenburg/ Elbe o D 92-93 L 2
Lauge Koch Kyst ⩦ GRØ 26-27 U 5
Laughing Fish Point ▲ USA (MI) 270-271 M 4
Laughland Lake ⊙ CDN 30-31 X 2
Laughlen, Mount ▲ AUS 178-179 C 2
Laughlin o USA (NV) 248-249 K 4
Laughlin Peak ▲ USA (NM) 256-257 L 2
Lauhkaung o MYA 142-143 L 3
Lauiya Nandangarh o IND 142-143 D 2
Launceston o AUS 180-181 J 6
Launceston o GB 90-91 E 6
Launglen o MYA 158-159 E 4
Laungmasu o IND 142-143 H 4
Launlonbok Islands ⌒ MYA 158-159 D 4
Laupahoehoe o USA (HI) 288 K 5
Lauqa o KSA 130-131 H 3
Laura o AUS (QLD) 174-175 H 4
Laura o AUS (SA) 180-181 E 2
Laura o CDN (SAS) 232-233 L 4
Laura o USA (IL) 274-275 J 4
Laura, Kapp ▲ N 84-85 P 2
Laurel o USA (DE) 280-281 L 5
Laurel o USA (FL) 286-287 G 4
Laurel o USA (IA) 274-275 F 3
Laurel o USA (MD) 280-281 K 4
Laurel o USA (MS) 268-269 L 5
Laurel o USA (MT) 250-251 L 6
Laurel o USA (NE) 262-263 J 2
Laurel o USA (VA) 280-281 J 6
Laurel, Cerro ▲ MEX 52-53 C 2
Laureles o ROU 76-77 K 6
Laureles Grande, Arroyo ~ ROU 76-77 J 6
Laurel Hill o USA (FL) 286-287 C 1
Laurel River ~ USA (KY) 276-277 L 3
Laurel River Lake < USA (KY) 276-277 L 3
Laurel Springs o USA (NC) 282-283 F 4
Laurelville o USA (OH) 280-281 D 4
Laurenceton o CDN (NFL) 242-243 N 3
Laurens o USA (IA) 274-275 D 2
Laurens o USA (SC) 284-285 H 2
Laurentians ⩦ CDN (QUE) 238-239 H 2
Laurentides o CDN (QUE) 238-239 M 3
Laurentides ⩦ CDN (QUE) 238-239 M 2
Lauri o MYA 142-143 J 3
Laurie, Mount ▲ AUS 176-177 G 3
Laurie Island ⌒ ARK 16 G 32
Laurie Lake ⊙ CDN 34-35 E 2
Laurier o CDN (MAN) 234-235 D 4
Laurier o USA (WA) 244-245 G 2
Laurier, Mont- o CDN (QUE) 238-239 K 2
Laurie River o CDN 34-35 F 2
Laurinburg o USA (NC) 282-283 H 6
Laurium o USA (WI) 270-271 K 3
Lauro de Freitas o BR 72-73 L 2
Lauro Sodré o BR 66-67 F 4
Lausanne ☆ • CH 92-93 J 5
Laut, Kampung o MAL 162-163 F 4
Laut, Pulau ⌒ RI 162-163 H 3
Laut, Pulau ⌒ RI 162-163 G 2
Laut, Pulau ⌒ RI (KSE) 164-165 E 5
Laut, Selat ≈ 164-165 E 5
Lautaret, Col du ▲ • F 90-91 L 9
Lautaro o RCH 78-79 C 5
Lautem o RI 166-167 D 6
Laut Kecil, Kepulauan ⌒ RI 164-165 D 6
Lautoka o FJI 184 III a 2
Lauttawar, Danau ⊙ RI 162-163 B 2
Lauz, Ǧabal al- ▲ KSA 130-131 D 3
Lauzon o CDN (QUE) 238-239 O 2
Lava Beds ⩦ USA (NM) 256-257 J 5
Lava Beds ⩦ USA (NM) 256-257 H 6
Lava Beds National Monument ∴ USA (CA) 246-247 D 2
Lavaca o USA (AR) 276-277 A 5
Lavaca, Port o USA (TX) 266-267 L 5
Lavaca Bay ≈ USA 266-267 L 5
Lavacicle Creek ∴ USA (OR) 244-245 E 7
Lava Flow ⩦ USA (NM) 256-257 H 4
Lava Hot Springs o USA (ID) 252-253 F 4
Laval o CDN (QUE) 238-239 M 3
Laval ☆ • F 90-91 G 7
Lavalle o RA 76-77 E 5
La Valle o USA (WI) 270-271 H 7
Lāvān, Ǧazire-ye ⌒ IR 134-135 E 5
Lavapié, Punta ▲ RCH 78-79 C 4
Lavaur o F 90-91 H 10
Lavenham o CDN (MAN) 234-235 E 5
La Vérendrye Provincial Réserve ⊥ CDN (QUE) 236-237 L 5
Laverlochère o CDN (QUE) 236-237 J 5
Laverne o USA (OK) 264-265 E 2
Laverton o AUS 176-177 G 4
Lavieille, Lake ⊙ CDN (ONT) 238-239 G 3
Laviera < EAT 212-213 F 6
Lavigne o CDN (ONT) 238-239 E 2
Lavik o N 86-87 B 6
Lavillette o CDN (NB) 240-241 K 3
Lavina o USA (MT) 250-251 L 5
Lavon o USA (TX) 264-265 H 5
Lavon, Lake ⊙ USA (TX) 264-265 H 5
Lavonia o USA (GA) 284-285 G 2
Lavoy o CDN (ALB) 232-233 G 2
Lavrador, Ribeiro do ~ BR 70-71 J 3
Lavras o BR 72-73 H 6
Lavrentija o RUS 112-113 Z 4
Lavrio o GR 100-101 K 6
Lavrova, buhta ≈ RUS 112-113 O 6
Lavrova, proliv ≈ 84-85 f 2
Lavumisa o SD 220-221 K 3
Lawang o RI 168 E 3
Lawan Gopeng o MAL 162-163 D 2
Lawas o MAL 164-165 D 1
Lawashi River ~ CDN 34-35 P 4
Lawatu o RI 164-165 G 5
Lawford Islands ⌒ CDN 30-31 N 2
Lawit, Gunung ▲ RI 162-163 K 4
Lawksawk o MYA 142-143 K 5
Lawn o USA (TX) 264-265 E 6
Lawn Bay ≈ 38-39 R 5
Lawn Bay ≈ CDN 242-243 N 6
Lawngngaw o MYA 142-143 J 2
Lawngtlai o IND 142-143 H 4
Lawn Hill o AUS 174-175 E 6
Lawnhill o CDN (BC) 228-229 C 3
Lawn Hill National Park ⊥ AUS 174-175 E 6
Lawowa o RI 164-165 H 6
Lawra o GH 202-203 J 4
Lawrence o NZ 182 B 6
Lawrence o USA (KS) 262-263 L 6
Lawrence o USA (MA) 278-279 K 6
Lawrence o USA (NC) 282-283 K 4
Lawrence o USA (NE) 262-263 H 4
Lawrenceburg o USA (KY) 276-277 L 2
Lawrenceburg o USA (TN) 276-277 H 5
Lawrence Station o CDN (NB) 240-241 H 5
Lawrenceville o USA (GA) 284-285 G 3
Lawrenceville o USA (IL) 274-275 L 6
Lawrenceville o USA (VA) 280-281 J 7
Lawrence Wells, Mount ▲ AUS 176-177 F 3
Lawtha o MYA 142-143 J 4
Lawton o USA (ND) 258-259 J 3
Lawton o USA (PA) 280-281 K 2
Lawton o USA (OK) 264-265 F 4
Lawushi Manda National Park ⊥ Z 214-215 F 7
Lay o BF 202-203 K 3
Lay o USA (CO) 254-255 H 3
Laya o RG 202-203 D 5
Laya Dula o RG 202-203 E 5
Layang Layang o MAL 160-161 A 10
Layar, Tanjung ▲ RI 164-165 E 6
Layarat • MA 188-189 F 7
Layawng Ga o MYA 142-143 K 3
Lay Lake < USA (AL) 284-285 D 3
Layo o PE 70-71 B 4
Layton o USA (FL) 286-287 J 7
Laytonville o USA (CA) 246-247 B 4
Lazarev o RUS 122-123 J 2
Lazarevac o YU 100-101 H 2
Lazarevskoe o RUS 126-127 C 6
Lázaro Cárdenas o MEX (BCN) 50-51 B 2
Lázaro Cárdenas o MEX (MIC) 52-53 C 3
Lazdijai o LT 94-95 H 4
Lāze o IR 134-135 E 5
Lazio ◻ I 100-101 D 3
Lazo o RUS 110-111 V 6
Lazo o RUS 122-123 E 7
L. Bistrups Bræ ⊂ GRØ 26-27 o 5
Lea o USA (NM) 256-257 M 6
Léach o K 158-159 G 4
Leach Island ⌒ CDN (ONT) 236-237 D 5
Leachville o USA (AR) 276-277 E 5
Leacross o CDN (SAS) 232-233 P 3
Lead o USA (SD) 260-261 C 2
Leader o CDN (SAS) 232-233 J 5
Lead Hill o USA (AR) 276-277 C 4
Leading Tickles o CDN (NFL) 242-243 N 3
Leadore o USA (ID) 252-253 E 2
Leadpoint o USA (WA) 244-245 H 2
Leadville o USA (CO) 254-255 J 4
Leaf Bay ≈ 36-37 P 5
Leaf Rapids o CDN 34-35 G 2
Leaf River ~ USA (MS) 268-269 L 5
League City o USA (TX) 268-269 E 7
Leahy o USA (WA) 244-245 F 3
Leakesville o USA (MS) 268-269 M 5
Leakey o USA (TX) 266-267 H 4
Lea Lea o PNG 183 D 5
Leamington o CDN (ONT) 238-239 C 6
Leamington o USA (UT) 254-255 C 4
Leander o USA (TX) 266-267 K 3
Leander Point ▲ AUS 176-177 C 4
Leandra o ZA 220-221 J 3
Leandro o BR 68-69 F 5
Leandro N. Alem o RA 76-77 K 4
Lea Park o CDN (ALB) 232-233 H 2
Learmonth o AUS 172-173 B 7
Leary o USA (GA) 284-285 F 5
Leasi, Kepulauan ⌒ RI 166-167 E 3
Leask o CDN (SAS) 232-233 M 3
Leatherwood o USA (KY) 276-277 M 3
Leaton State Historic Site, Fort ∴ USA (TX) 266-267 C 4
Leavenworth o USA (KS) 262-263 M 5
Leavenworth o USA (WA) 244-245 E 3
Leavenworth, Fort • USA (KS) 262-263 L 5
Leavitt o CDN (ALB) 232-233 E 6
Łeba o • PL 92-93 O 1
Lebak o RP 160-161 F 9
Lebam o USA (WA) 244-245 B 4
Lebamba o G 210-211 C 5
Leban Condong, Kampung o MAL 162-163 E 3
Lébango o RCB 210-211 E 3
Lébango ~ RCB 210-211 E 3
Lebanon o USA (IN) 274-275 M 4
Lebanon o USA (KS) 262-263 H 5
Lebanon o USA (KY) 276-277 K 3
Lebanon o USA (MO) 276-277 C 3
Lebanon o USA (NE) 262-263 F 4
Lebanon o USA (NH) 278-279 J 5
Lebanon o USA (OH) 280-281 B 4
Lebanon o USA (OR) 244-245 C 6
Lebanon o USA (PA) 280-281 K 3
Lebanon o USA (SD) 260-261 G 1
Lebanon o USA (TN) 276-277 J 4
Lebanon o USA (VA) 280-281 D 7
Lebanon = Lubnān, al- ■ RL 128-129 F 5
Lebanon Station o USA (FL) 286-287 G 3
Lebap o TM 136-137 G 4
Lebbeke o B 92-93 H 3
Lebeau o USA (LA) 268-269 J 6
Lebec o USA (CA) 248-249 F 5
Lebed' ~ RUS 124-125 P 2
Lebedjan' o RUS 94-95 Q 5
Lebedyn o UA 102-103 J 2
Lebel-sur-Quévillon o CDN (QUE) 236-237 L 3
Lebida o ZRE 210-211 F 5
Lebiolali < ETH 208-209 H 5
Lébiri ~ G 210-211 D 4
Lebjaže ☆ KA 124-125 K 3
Lebjaže ☆ RUS 96-97 F 5
Lebjažja ~ RUS 114-115 S 7
Lebo o USA (KS) 262-263 L 6
Lebo o ZRE 206-207 F 6
Leboma ~ ZRE 210-211 F 5
Lébombi ~ G 210-211 D 5
Lebombo ▲ SD 220-221 K 2
Lebongtandai o RI 162-163 D 6
Leboni o RI 164-165 G 5
Lebon Régis o BR 74-75 E 6
Lębork o • PL 92-93 O 1
Lebowa o ZA 218-219 E 6
Lebowa (former Homeland, now part of North-Transvaal) ◻ ZA 218-219 D 6
Lebowakgomo ☆ ZA 220-221 J 2
Lebret o CDN (SAS) 232-233 P 5
Lebrija o E 98-99 D 6
Lebu o RCH 78-79 C 4
Lebuhanbini, Tanjung ▲ RI 164-165 F 3
Lecce ☆ • I 100-101 G 4
Lecco ☆ • I 100-101 B 2
Lech ~ D 92-93 L 4
Lechang o VRC 156-157 H 4
Leche, Laguna de La ⊙ MEX 50-51 H 4
Lechiguanas, Islas de las ⌒ RA 78-79 K 2
Lechuguilla, Bahía ≈ 50-51 E 5
Lěči o LV 94-95 G 3
Le Claire o USA (IA) 274-275 H 3
Lecompte o USA (LA) 268-269 H 5
Łęczyca o • PL 92-93 P 2
Ledang, Gunung ▲ MAL (JOH) 162-163 E 3
Ledesma o E 98-99 D 4
Ledge o USA (MT) 250-251 H 3
Ledge Point o AUS 176-177 C 5
Ledjanaja ~ RUS 108-109 b 6
Ledjanaja gora ▲ RUS 112-113 Q 6
Ledmozero o RUS 88-89 M 4
Ledo o IND 142-143 J 2
Ledong o VRC 156-157 F 7
Ledu o VRC 154-155 C 3
Leduc o CDN (ALB) 232-233 E 2
Lee o USA (NV) 246-247 K 3
Leeburn o CDN (ONT) 238-239 B 2
Leech Lake o USA (MN) 270-271 D 3
Leech Lake ⊙ USA (MN) 270-271 D 3
Leech Lake Indian Reservation ✗ USA (MN) 270-271 D 3
Leedale o CDN (ALB) 232-233 D 3
Leeds o • GB 90-91 G 5
Leeds o GUY 62-63 F 2
Leeds o USA (AL) 284-285 D 3
Leeds o USA (ND) 258-259 H 3
Leeds, Mount ▲ CDN 26-27 M 4
Leek o GB 90-91 F 5
Leeman o AUS 176-177 C 4
Leeman o USA (WI) 270-271 K 6
Leer (Ostfriesland) o D 92-93 J 2
Leer, Pulau ⌒ RI 166-167 H 5
Lees o USA (TX) 264-265 C 6
Leesburg o USA (FL) 286-287 H 3
Leesburg o USA (GA) 284-285 F 5
Leesburg o USA (OH) 280-281 C 4
Leesburg o USA (VA) 280-281 J 4
Lees Camp o USA (OR) 244-245 B 5
Leeston o NZ 182 D 5
Leesville o USA (LA) 268-269 G 5
Leesville o USA (SC) 284-285 J 3
Leesville o USA (TX) 266-267 K 4
Leeton o AUS 180-181 J 3
Leeudoringstad o ZA 220-221 H 3
Leeu-Gamka o ZA 220-221 E 6
Leeupoort o ZA 220-221 H 2
Leeuwarden ☆ • NL 92-93 H 2
Leeuwin, Cape ▲ AUS 176-177 C 7
Leeuwin-Naturaliste National Park ⊥ AUS 176-177 C 6
Leeuwrivier ~ ZA 220-221 F 6
Lee Vining o USA (CA) 248-249 E 2
Leeward Islands ⌒ 56 E 2
Leffellier o CDN (MAN) 234-235 F 5
Léfini ~ RCB 210-211 E 5
Léfini, Réserve de chasse de la ⊥ RCB 210-211 E 5
Lefkáda o GR 100-101 H 5
Lefkáda ⌒ GR 100-101 H 5
Lefkónas o GR 100-101 J 4
Lefkosia ★ CY 128-129 E 5
Lefo, Mont ▲ CAM 204-205 J 6
Lefor o USA (ND) 258-259 E 5
Lefors o USA (TX) 264-265 D 3
Lefroy, Lake ⊙ AUS (WA) 176-177 G 5
Lefroy, Lake ⊙ AUS (WA) 176-177 F 5
Legal o CDN (ALB) 232-233 E 2
Legape o RB 220-221 G 2
Legazpi ☆ RP 160-161 E 6
Legend o CDN (ALB) 232-233 G 6
Legendre Island ⌒ AUS 172-173 C 6
Leggett o USA (CA) 246-247 B 4
Leggett o USA (TX) 268-269 F 6
Legion Mine o ZW 218-219 E 5
Legionnaire, Tunnel du • MA 188-189 J 4
Legionowo o PL 92-93 Q 2
Legkraal o ZA 218-219 E 6
Legnica ☆ • PL 92-93 O 3
Legokjawa o RI 168 C 3
Le Grand, Mount ▲ AUS 176-177 G 6
Leguan Island ⌒ GUY 62-63 E 2
Legunditua, Pulau ⌒ RI 162-163 F 7
Legune o AUS 172-173 J 3
Leh o • IND 138-139 F 2
Le Havre o F 90-91 H 7
Lehena o GR 100-101 H 6
Lehi o USA (UT) 254-255 D 3
Lehigh Acres o USA (FL) 286-287 H 5
Lehighton o USA (PA) 280-281 L 3
Lehman Caves ∴ USA (NV) 246-247 L 5
Lehmann o USA (TX) 264-265 B 5
Lehr o USA (MS) 268-269 K 5
Lehr o USA (ND) 258-259 H 5
Lehua Island ⌒ USA (HI) 288 E 2
Lehua Landing o USA (HI) 288 E 3
Lehututu o RB 220-221 E 1
Leiah o PK 138-139 C 4
Leibnitz o A 92-93 N 5
Leicester o GB 90-91 G 5
Leichhardt, Mount ▲ AUS 172-173 L 6
Leichhardt Range ▲ AUS 174-175 J 7
Leichhardt River ~ AUS 174-175 E 5
Leiden o • NL 92-93 H 2
Leifs Ø ⌒ GRØ 28-29 W 4
Leigh o USA (NE) 262-263 J 3
Leigh Creek o AUS 178-179 E 6
Leigh Creek South o AUS 178-179 E 6
Leighton o USA (AL) 284-285 C 2
Leigong Shan ▲ VRC 156-157 F 3
Leimebamba o PE 64-65 D 5
Leimus o HN 52-53 B 4
Leinan o CDN (SAS) 232-233 L 5
Leine ~ D 92-93 K 2
Leinster o AUS 176-177 F 3
Leiper, Kap ▲ GRØ 26-27 P 4
Leipzig o CDN (SAS) 232-233 K 3
Leipzig o • D 92-93 M 3
Leira ☆ N (OPP) 86-87 D 6
Leira ☆ N (ROM) 86-87 D 5
Leiria ☆ • P 98-99 C 5
Leirvik ☆ N 86-87 B 7
Leishan o VRC 156-157 F 3
Leisi o EST 94-95 H 2
Leisler, Mount ▲ AUS 176-177 K 1
Leitchfield o USA (KY) 276-277 J 3
Leite, Igarapé do ~ BR 66-67 K 5
Leiter o USA (WY) 252-253 M 2
Leith o CDN (ONT) 238-239 E 4
Leith, Point ▲ CDN 30-31 K 3
Leith Harbour o GB 78-79 O 7
Leith Peninsula ⌣ CDN 30-31 K 3
Leitmeritz = Litoměřice o CZ 92-93 N 3
Leitomischl = Litomyšl o CZ 92-93 O 4
Leitre o PNG 183 A 2
Leiva, Cerro ▲ CO 60-61 D 6
Leiyang o VRC 156-157 H 3
Leizhou Bandao ⌣ VRC 156-157 G 6
Leizhou Wan ≈ 156-157 G 6
Lejac o CDN (BC) 228-229 K 2
Lejeune o CDN (QUE) 240-241 G 3
Lejeune Marine Corps Base, Camp ✗✗ USA (NC) 282-283 K 6
Lejone o LS 220-221 J 4
Lek ~ NL 92-93 H 3
Leka ⌒ N 86-87 E 4
Lékana o RCB 210-211 E 5
Lekatero o ZRE 210-211 J 4
Lekeleka ⌒ TON 184 IV a 2
Lékéti ~ RCB 210-211 E 5
Lekhcheb o RIM 196-197 E 5
Lékila o G 210-211 D 4
Lekitobi o RI 164-165 J 4
Lekki Lagoon ⊙ WAN 204-205 F 5
Leknes o N 86-87 F 2
Lekona ~ RCB 210-211 E 4
Lékoni o G (Hau) 210-211 E 4
Lékoni ~ G 210-211 D 4
Lekos ~ RUS 114-115 R 3
Lekoumou ◻ RCB 210-211 D 5
Leksand o S 86-87 G 6
Leksozero o RUS 88-89 L 5
Lekst, Jbel ▲ MA 188-189 G 6
Leksula o RI 166-167 D 3
Leku o ETH 208-209 D 5
Lela o RI 166-167 B 6
Lelai, Tanjung ▲ RI 164-165 L 3
Lélali ~ RCB 210-211 D 5
Leland o USA (MS) 268-269 K 3
Lel'čycy o BY 94-95 L 6
Lelehudi o PNG 183 F 6
Lelepa = Île Leleppa ⌒ VAN 184 II b 3
Leleppa, Île = Lelepa ⌒ VAN 184 II b 3
Leleque o RA 78-79 D 7
Leling o VRC 154-155 K 3
Lelingluang o RI 166-167 F 5
Lelinta o RI 166-167 F 3
Leljuveem ~ RUS 112-113 Q 2
Lelogama o RI 166-167 B 6
Lélouma o RG 202-203 D 4
Lel'vergyrgyn ~ RUS 112-113 M 2
Lelydorp ☆ SME 62-63 G 3
Lelystad o NL 92-93 H 2
Léman, Lac ⊙ CH 92-93 J 5
Lemang o RI 162-163 E 4
Le Mans o • F 90-91 H 8
Lema Shilindi o ETH 208-209 F 6
Lematang ~ RI 162-163 E 6
Lembar o RI 168 C 7
Lembé o CAM 204-205 K 6
Lembeh, Pulau ⌒ RI 164-165 J 3
Lembeni o EAT 212-213 F 5
Lemberg o CDN (SAS) 232-233 P 5
Lemberg = L'viv ☆ • UA 102-103 D 3
Lembing, Sungai o MAL 162-163 E 3
Lembo o RI 164-165 H 5
Lemery o RP 160-161 D 6
Lemesos o • CY 128-129 E 5
Lemfu o ZRE 210-211 E 6
Lemhi, Fort ∴ USA (ID) 252-253 E 2
Lemhi Pass ▲ USA (MT) 250-251 F 7
Lemhi Range ▲ USA (ID) 252-253 E 2
Lemhi River ~ USA (ID) 250-251 F 6
Lemieux o CDN 20-21 Y 7
Lemieux Islands ⌒ CDN 36-37 R 2
Lemin o VRC 156-157 F 5
Leming o USA (TX) 266-267 J 4
Leming o USA (TX) 266-267 J 5
Lemitar o USA (NM) 256-257 J 4
Lem'ju ~ RUS 88-89 X 4
Lem"junskaja vozvyšennost' ▲ RUS 88-89 X 4
Lemmenjoen kansallispuisto ⊥ FIN 88-89 H 2
Lemmon o USA (SD) 260-261 D 1
Lemmon, Mount ▲ USA (AZ) 256-257 E 6
Lemoenshoek o ZA 220-221 E 6
Lemolemo o RI 164-165 L 4
Lemon, Lake ⊙ USA (IN) 274-275 M 5
Lemon Creek o CDN (BC) 230-231 M 4
Lemon Grove o USA 248-249 G 7
le Mont Saint-Michel o••• F 90-91 G 7
Lemoore o USA (CA) 248-249 E 3
Lemoore Naval Air Station ✗✗ USA (CA) 248-249 E 3
Lemoyne o USA (NE) 262-263 E 3
Lempa, Río ~ ES 52-53 K 5
Lempäälä o FIN 88-89 G 6
Lempriere o CDN (BC) 228-229 P 4
Lemsford o CDN (SAS) 232-233 J 5
Lemsid o MA 188-189 E 7
Lemtybož o RUS 114-115 D 3
Lemu o WAN 204-205 G 4
Lemukutan, Pulau ⌒ RI 162-163 H 4
Lemva ~ RUS 108-109 J 8
Lemvig o DK 86-87 D 8
Lemyethna o MYA 158-159 C 2
Lena o CDN (MAN) 234-235 D 5
Lena ~ RUS 10-11 M 2
Lena o USA (AR) 276-277 B 6
Lena o USA (LA) 268-269 H 5
Lena o USA (MS) 268-269 L 4
Lenakel ☆ VAN 184 II b 4
Lenangguar o RI 168 C 7
Lenapah o USA (OK) 264-265 J 2
Lena River Delta = Lena Delta ≈ RUS 110-111 P 2
Leñas, Paso de las ▲ RA 78-79 D 3
Lençóis o BR 72-73 K 2
Lençóis, Baía dos ≈ 68-69 F 2
Lençóis Maranhenses, Parque Nacional dos ⊥ BR 68-69 G 3
Lençóis Paulista o BR 72-73 F 7
Lenda ~ ZRE 212-213 B 3
Lendaha ~ RUS 116-117 F 6
Lendava o SLO 100-101 F 1
Lende o IR 134-135 D 3
Lendepas o NAM 220-221 D 2
Lendery o RUS 88-89 L 5
Lenexa o USA (KS) 262-263 M 6
Leney o CDN (SAS) 232-233 L 3
Lenge, Bandar-e o • IR 134-135 F 5
Lenger ☆ KA 136-137 L 3
Lengguru ~ RI 166-167 H 3
Lenghu o VRC 146-147 L 6
Lenglong Ling ▲ VRC 154-155 B 3
Lenglong Ling ▲ VRC 154-155 C 3
Lengo o RCA 206-207 E 6
Lengoué ~ RCB 210-211 E 3
Lengshuijiang o VRC 156-157 G 3
Lengshuitan o VRC 156-157 G 3
Leng Su Sin o VN 156-157 C 5
Lengua de Vaca, Punta ▲ RCH 76-77 B 6
Lengulu o ZRE 210-211 L 2
Lengwe National Park ⊥ MW 218-219 H 3
Lenhovda o S 86-87 G 8
Lenin ☆ TM 136-137 F 3
Lenina, kanal imeni < RUS 126-127 F 6
Lenina, pik ▲ KS 136-137 N 5
Lenina, proliv ≈ 108-109 b 3
Leninabad = Hudžand ☆ TJ 136-137 L 4
Leninabadskaja oblast' ◻ TJ 136-137 L 4
Leninakan = Gjumri o AR 128-129 K 2
Lenine o UA 102-103 J 5
Leningrad = Sankt-Peterburg ☆ ••• RUS 94-95 M 2
Leningradskaja o RUS (KRD) 102-103 L 4
Leningradskaja ~ RUS 108-109 d 3
Leningradskij o RUS 112-113 U 2
Leningradskij o TJ 136-137 M 5
Leningradskij, lednik ⊂ RUS 108-109 d 2
Leninogorsk o KA 124-125 N 3
Leninogorsk ☆ RUS 96-97 H 6
Leninsk o KA 126-127 P 5
Leninsk o RUS 96-97 D 9
Leninsk o US 136-137 N 4
Leninskij o KA 124-125 K 2
Leninskij o TJ 136-137 L 5
Leninsk-Kuzneckij ☆ RUS 114-115 T 7
Leninsk Kuznetskiy = Leninsk-Kuzneckij ☆ RUS 114-115 T 7
Leninskoe o KA (AKT) 126-127 M 2
Leninskoe ☆ KA (KST) 124-125 D 2
Leninskoe o KS 136-137 N 4
Leninskoe o RUS 96-97 E 4
Lenivaja ~ RUS 108-109 X 4
Lenkau o PNG 183 D 2
Lenkivci o UA 102-103 E 2
Lenkoran' = Lankaran o • AZ 128-129 N 3
Lenmalu o RI 166-167 F 2
Lennox o USA (SD) 260-261 K 3
Lennox, Isla ⌒ RCH 80 G 7
Leno-Angarskoe, plato ⩦ RUS 116-117 L 8
Leno-Angarskoe plato ⩦ RUS 116-117 L 8
Lenoir o USA (NC) 282-283 F 5
Lenoir City o USA (TN) 282-283 C 5
Lenora o USA (KS) 262-263 G 5
Lenore o CDN (MAN) 234-235 C 5
Lenore Lake ~ CDN (SAS) 232-233 O 3
Lenox o USA (GA) 284-285 G 5
Lenox o USA (IA) 274-275 D 4
Lens o F 90-91 J 6
Lensk ☆ • RUS 118-119 G 5
Lenskie stolby • RUS 118-119 N 5
Lenswood o CDN (MAN) 234-235 C 2
Lent'evo o RUS 94-95 P 2
Lentiira o FIN 88-89 K 4
Lentini o I 100-101 E 6
Lenwood o USA (CA) 248-249 G 5
Lenya o MYA 158-159 E 5
Léo o BF 202-203 J 4
Leoben o A 92-93 N 5
Leofnard o CDN (SAS) 232-233 N 3
Léogâne o RH 54-55 J 5
Leok o RI 164-165 G 3
Leola o USA (AR) 276-277 C 6
Leola o USA (SD) 260-261 H 1
Leominster o • GB 90-91 F 5
Leominster o USA (MA) 278-279 K 6
León o • E 98-99 E 3
León o F 90-91 G 10
León o • MEX 50-51 J 7
León ☆ ••• NIC 52-53 L 5
Leon o USA (IA) 274-275 E 4
Leon o USA (OK) 264-265 G 5
León, Cerro ▲ MEX 52-53 F 3
León, Cerro ▲ PY 70-71 F 7
Leon, De o USA (TX) 264-265 F 6
León, Montes de ▲ E 98-99 D 3
Leona, La o YV 60-61 K 3
Leona, Punta la ▲ EC 64-65 B 2
Leonard o USA (MN) 270-271 C 3
Leonard o USA (ND) 258-259 K 5
Leonard o USA (TX) 264-265 H 5
Leonards o USA (TX) 264-265 H 5
Leonardtown o USA (MD) 280-281 K 5
Leonardville o NAM 220-221 D 1
Leonard Wood, Fort ✗✗ USA (MO) 276-277 C 3
Leona River ~ USA (TX) 266-267 H 5
Leoncio Prado o PE 64-65 E 3
Leonia o USA (ID) 250-251 C 3
Leonidas o USA (MI) 272-273 D 5
Leonidio o GR 100-101 J 6
Leonidovka ~ RUS 122-123 K 4
Leonidovo o RUS 122-123 K 4
Leonora o AUS 176-177 F 4
Leon River ~ USA (TX) 264-265 G 6
Leon River ~ USA (TX) 266-267 K 2
Leont'evka, ostrov ⌒ RUS 112-113 L 1
León Viejo ∴ • NIC 52-53 L 5
Leopold Downs o AUS 172-173 G 4
Leopold II, Lac = Lac Mai-Ndombe ⊙ ZRE 210-211 G 5
Leopoldina o BR 72-73 J 6
Leopold Island ⌒ CDN 36-37 S 2
Leopold M'Clintock, Cape ▲ CDN 24-25 N 2
Leopoldo de Bulhões o BR 72-73 F 4
Leopoldsburg o B 92-93 H 3
Léopoldville = Kinshasa ★ • ZRE 210-211 E 6
Leoti o USA (KS) 262-263 E 6
Léoua o RCA 206-207 E 6
Léoura o BF 202-203 L 3
Leova ☆ MD 102-103 F 4
Leoville o CDN (SAS) 232-233 L 2
Leovo = Leova ☆ MD 102-103 F 4
Lepanto o USA (AR) 276-277 E 5
Lepar, Pulau ⌒ RI 162-163 G 6
Lepaterique o HN 52-53 L 4
Lepel' ☆ BY 94-95 L 4
Lepellé, Rivière ~ CDN 36-37 N 4
Lephephe o RB 218-219 C 6
Lepine o CDN (SAS) 232-233 N 3
Leping o VRC 156-157 K 2
Leplja ~ RUS 114-115 F 4
Lépoura o GR 100-101 K 5
Lepreau o CDN (NB) 240-241 J 5
Lepsy o KA 124-125 L 5
Lepsy ~ KA 124-125 M 6
Leptis Magna = Labdah ∴ ••• LAR 192-193 F 1
Leptokariá o GR 100-101 J 4
Leqceiba o RIM (BRA) 196-197 C 6
Leqceiba o RIM (GOR) 196-197 D 6
Lequena o RCH 76-77 C 1
Léraba ~ CI 202-203 H 5
Léraba Occidentale ~ CI 202-203 H 4
Lérabe o SN 196-197 C 6
Lercara Friddi o I 100-101 D 6
Lerdo de Tejada o MEX 52-53 G 2
Léré o RMM 202-203 H 2
Léré o TCH 206-207 B 4
Lere o WAN (BAU) 204-205 H 4
Lere o WAN (KAD) 204-205 H 3
Léré, Lac de ⊙ TCH 206-207 B 4
Lérez, Río ~ E 98-99 C 3
Lérida = Lleida o •• E 98-99 H 4
Lerma o E 98-99 F 3
Lerma o MEX 52-53 J 2
Lermá, Valle de ⩦ RA 76-77 E 3
Lerneb o RMM 196-197 H 6
Leron Plains o PNG 183 D 4
Leros ⌒ GR 100-101 L 6
Leross o CDN (SAS) 232-233 P 4
Leroy o CDN (SAS) 232-233 O 3
Le Roy o USA (MN) 270-271 F 7
Lerum ☆ S 86-87 F 8
Lerwick o GB 90-91 G 1
Ler Zerai < SUD 206-207 H 3
Lescoff o F 90-91 E 7
Lesdiguières, Lac ⊙ CDN 36-37 M 4
Leshan o VRC 156-157 C 2
Leshan Dafo • VRC 156-157 C 2
Les-Islets-Caribou o CDN (QUE) 242-243 A 3
Lesjaskog o N 86-87 D 5
Lesjöfors o S 86-87 G 7
Leskino o RUS 108-109 S 5
Lesko o • PL 92-93 R 4
Leskovac o • YU 100-101 H 3
Leskovik o • AL 100-101 H 4
Leslie o CDN (SAS) 232-233 P 4
Leslie o USA (AR) 276-277 C 5
Leslie o USA (GA) 284-285 F 5
Leslie o USA (ID) 252-253 E 3
Leslie o USA (MI) 272-273 E 5
Leslie, Kap ▲ GRØ 26-27 n 8
Leslieville o CDN (ALB) 232-233 D 3
Lesmiegan ~ RUS 114-115 G 2
Lesnaja o RUS 120-121 T 4
Lesnoj Gorodok o RUS 118-119 F 10
Lesnoj Voronež ~ RUS 94-95 R 5
Lesogorsk o RUS 122-123 K 4
Lesosibirsk o RUS 116-117 F 6
Lesotho ■ LS 220-221 H 4
Lesozavodsk o RUS 122-123 E 6
Lesozavodskij o RUS 122-123 M 6
Lesperon o F 90-91 G 10
Lessau o PNG 183 D 2
Léssé ~ RCA 206-207 D 6
Lesser Antilles ⌒ 56 B 5
Lesser Hinggan Range = Xiao Hinggan Ling ▲ VRC 150-151 F 2
Lesser Slave Lake ⊙ CDN 32-33 N 4
Lesser Slave Lake Provincial Park ⊥ CDN 32-33 N 4
Lesser Slave River ~ CDN 32-33 N 4
Lesser Sunda, Kepulauan ⌒ RI 168 C 7
Lesser Sunda Islands = Sunda Kecil, Kepulauan ⌒ RI 168 C 6
Lester Prairie o USA (MN) 270-271 D 6
Lestijärvi o FIN 88-89 H 5
Lestock o CDN (SAS) 232-233 O 4
Lesueur, Mount ▲ AUS 176-177 C 5
Lesung, Tanjung ▲ RI 168 A 3
Lesvos ⌒ GR 100-101 L 5
Leszno ☆ • PL 92-93 O 3
Letaba o ZA 218-219 F 6
Letas, Lac = Tes, Lake ⊙ VAN 184 II a 2
Letchworth State Park ⊥ USA (NY) 278-279 D 6
Letellier o CDN (MAN) 234-235 F 5
Letete o CDN (NB) 240-241 J 5
Letfata o RIM 196-197 D 6
Lethbridge o CDN (NFL) 242-243 P 4
Lethbridge o CDN (ALB) 232-233 F 6
Lethem ☆ GUY 62-63 E 4
Leti, Kepulauan ⌒ RI 166-167 D 6
Leti, Pulau ⌒ RI 166-167 D 6
Letiahau ~ RB 218-219 B 5
Leticia o CO 66-67 C 5
Leting o VRC 154-155 L 2
Letka o RUS 96-97 F 4
Letkhokpin o MYA 142-143 K 4
Letlhakeng o RB 220-221 G 2
Letnica o BG 102-103 D 6
Letnij bereg ⌣ RUS 88-89 O 4
Letniy Bereg = Letnij bereg ⌣ RUS 88-89 O 4
Letnjaja ~ RUS 112-113 H 3
Letnjaja Zolotica o RUS 88-89 O 4
Letoda o RI 166-167 E 6
Letohatchee o USA (AL) 284-285 D 4
Letoon ∴ ••• TR 128-129 C 4
Letpadan o MYA 158-159 C 2
Letpan o MYA 142-143 J 6
Letsitele o ZA 218-219 F 6
Letsok-Aw Kyun ⌒ MYA 158-159 E 5
Letta o CAM 204-205 K 6
Letterkenny o IRL 90-91 D 4
Letts o USA (IN) 274-275 N 5
Letwurung o RI 166-167 F 5
Léuá o ANG 216-217 F 5
Leuaniua ⌒ SOL 184 I d 1
Leucadia o USA (CA) 248-249 G 6
Leupp o USA (AZ) 256-257 E 3
Leura o AUS 178-179 K 2
Leuser, Gunung ▲ RI 162-163 B 3
Leušinskij Tuman, ozero ⊙ RUS 114-115 H 5
Leuven o •• B 92-93 H 3
Levack o CDN (ONT) 238-239 D 2
Levaja Avača ~ RUS 120-121 S 7
Levaja Bojarka ~ RUS 108-109 b 6
Levaja Bureja ~ RUS 122-123 F 3
Levaja Hetta ~ RUS 114-115 L 2
Levaja Kamenka ~ RUS 110-111 d 6
Levaja Lesnaja ~ RUS 120-121 T 4
Levaja Mama ~ RUS 118-119 E 7
Levaja Šapina ~ RUS 120-121 T 6
Levaja Vetv', kanal < RUS 102-103 N 5
Levaja Županova ~ RUS 120-121 S 6
Levan o USA (UT) 254-255 D 4
Levanger o N 86-87 E 5
Levante, Riviera di ⌣ I 100-101 B 2
Levantine Basin ≃ 128-129 B 6
Levasi o RUS 126-127 G 6
Levdiev, ostrov ⌒ RUS 108-109 M 7
Level, Isla ⌒ RCH 80 C 2

Levelland ○ USA (TX) 264-265 B 5
Leven ○ GB 90-91 F 3
Leven ~ GB 90-91 F 3
Leven Bank ≃ 222-223 E 4
Leveque, Cape ▲ AUS 172-173 F 4
Lever, Rio ~ BR 68-69 C 7
Leverett Glacier ⊂ ARK 16 E 0
Leverkusen ○ D 92-93 J 3
Levick, Mount ▲ ARK 16 F 17
Levídi ○ GR 100-101 J 6
Levin ○ NZ 182 E 4
Levinópolis ○ BR 72-73 H 3
Levis ○ CDN (QUE) 238-239 O 2
Levis, Lac ⊂ CDN 30-31 L 4
Levisa Fork ~ USA (KY) 276-277 N 3
Levittown ○ USA (PA) 280-281 M 3
Levkadíti ○ GR 100-101 J 5
Levkinskaja ○ RUS 88-89 V 4
Levroux ○ F 90-91 H 8
Levski ○ BG 102-103 D 6
Levuka ○ FJI 184 III b 2
Levyj Hetagčan ~ RUS 112-113 J 5
Levyj Kedon ~ RUS 112-113 K 4
Levyj Mamakan ~ RUS 118-119 F 7
Léwa ○ CAM 204-205 K 5
Lewa ○ RI 168 D 7
Le Ward ○ USA (TX) 266-267 L 5
Lewe ○ MYA 142-143 K 6
Lewellen ○ USA (NE) 262-263 D 3
Lewes ○ USA (DE) 280-281 L 5
Lewes Plateau ▲ CDN 20-21 W 5
Lewin's Cove ○ CDN (NFL) 242-243 N 5
Lewis ○ USA (CO) 254-255 G 6
Lewis and Clark Lake ⊂ USA (NE) 262-263 J 2
Lewisburg ○ USA (KY) 276-277 J 4
Lewisburg ○ USA (OH) 280-281 B 4
Lewisburg ○ USA (OR) 244-245 B 6
Lewisburg ○ USA (PA) 280-281 K 3
Lewisburg ○ USA (TN) 276-277 J 5
Lewisburg ○ USA (WV) 280-281 F 6
Lewis Creek ~ CDN (SAS) 232-233 N 4
Lewis Hills ▲ CDN (NFL) 242-243 K 4
Lewis Pass ▲ NZ 182 D 5
Lewis Point ○ USA 22-23 R 3
Lewisporte ○ CDN (NFL) 242-243 N 3
Lewis Range ▲ AUS 172-173 J 6
Lewis Range ▲ USA (MT) 250-251 F 3
Lewis River ~ USA (WA) 244-245 C 4
Lewis Smith Lake ⊂ USA (AL) 284-285 C 3
Lewiston ○ USA (ID) 250-251 C 5
Lewiston ○ USA (IN) 274-275 L 3
Lewiston ○ USA (ME) 278-279 L 4
Lewiston ○ USA (MI) 272-273 E 3
Lewiston ○ USA (MN) 270-271 G 7
Lewiston ○ USA (UT) 254-255 D 2
Lewistown ○ USA (IL) 274-275 H 4
Lewistown ○ USA (MT) 250-251 K 4
Lewistown ○ USA (PA) 280-281 J 3
Lewisville ○ USA (AR) 276-277 B 7
Lewisville ○ USA (TX) 264-265 H 5
Lewisville, Lake ⊂ USA (TX) 264-265 H 5
Lewoleba ○ RI 166-167 B 6
Lewvan ○ CDN (SAS) 232-233 O 5
Lexa ○ USA (AR) 276-277 E 6
Lexington ○ USA (GA) 284-285 G 3
Lexington ○ USA (KY) 276-277 L 2
Lexington ○ USA (MI) 272-273 G 4
Lexington ○ USA (MO) 274-275 E 5
Lexington ○ USA (MS) 268-269 K 3
Lexington ○ USA (NC) 282-283 G 5
Lexington ○ USA (NE) 262-263 G 4
Lexington ○ USA (OR) 244-245 F 5
Lexington ○ USA (SC) 284-285 J 2
Lexington ○ USA (TN) 276-277 G 5
Lexington ○ USA (TX) 266-267 K 3
Lexington ○ USA (VA) 280-281 G 6
Lexington Park ○ USA (MD) 280-281 K 5
Leybourne Islands ⌒ CDN 36-37 R 2
Leyburn ○ AUS 178-179 L 5
Leye ○ VRC 156-157 E 4
Leyland ○ CDN (ALB) 228-229 R 3
Leyson Point ▲ CDN 36-37 J 3
Leyte ⌒ RP 160-161 F 7
Leyte Gulf ≈ 160-161 F 7
Lezama ○ YV 60-61 H 3
Lezhë ☆·· AL 100-101 G 4
Lezhi ○ VRC 154-155 D 6
l-Ġadaf, Wādī ~ IRQ 128-129 J 6
l-Ġaut, Wādī ~ SYR 128-129 J 5
LG Deux, Réservoir < CDN 38-39 F 2
L'gotny, mys ▲ RUS 120-121 H 5
L'gov ○ RUS 102-103 J 2
L'govski, Dmitriev ○ RUS 94-95 O 5
LG Trois, Réservoir de < CDN 38-39 G 2
l-Ḥail, Wādī ~ SYR 128-129 H 5
Lhari ○ VRC 144-145 J 5
L'Haridon Bight ≈ 176-177 B 3
l-Ḥarīt, Wādī ~ ET 194-195 F 5
Lhasa ○·· VRC 144-145 H 6
Lhasa He ~ VRC 144-145 H 6
Lhazê ○· VRC 144-145 F 6
Lhokseumawe ○ RI 162-163 B 2
Lhoksukon ○ RI 162-163 B 2
Lhorong ○ VRC 144-145 K 5
Lhotse ▲ NEP 144-145 F 7
Lhuntsi ○ BHT 142-143 G 2
Lhünzê ○ VRC 144-145 J 6
Li ○ THA 158-159 E 2
Lia, Tanjung ▲ RI 166-167 D 3
Liambezi, Lake ⊂ NAM 218-219 C 3
Liang ○ RI 164-165 H 4
Liangcheng ○ VRC (NMZ) 154-155 H 1
Liangcheng ○ VRC (SHD) 154-155 L 4
Lianghe ○ VRC (SIC) 156-157 F 2
Lianghe ○ VRC (YUN) 142-143 L 3
Lianghekou ○ VRC 154-155 D 5
Liangping ○ VRC 154-155 E 6
Liangpran, Gunung ▲ RI 164-165 D 3
Liangshan ○ VRC 154-155 K 4
Lianhua ○ VRC 156-157 H 3
Lianhua Shan ▲ VRC 156-157 J 5
Lianjiang ○ VRC (FUJ) 156-157 L 3
Lianjiang ○ VRC (GDG) 156-157 G 6
Lianping ○ VRC 156-157 J 4
Lianshan ○ VRC (GDG) 156-157 H 4
Lianshan ○ VRC (SHD) 154-155 K 4
Lianshan ○ VRC (SIC) 154-155 D 6
Lianshui ○ VRC 154-155 L 5
Liantang ○ VRC 156-157 G 4
Lian Xian ○ VRC 156-157 H 4
Lianyuan ○ VRC 156-157 G 3
Lianyungang ○ VRC 154-155 L 4
Lianyungang (Xinpu) ○ VRC 154-155 L 4
Liaocheng ○ VRC 154-155 J 3
Liao Dao · VRC 144-145 M 2
Liaodong Bandao ⌣ VRC 150-151 D 8
Liaodong Wan ≈ 150-151 C 7
Liaodun ○ VRC 146-147 L 4
Liao He ~ VRC 150-151 D 6
Liaoning ▫ VRC 150-151 C 6
Liao Shangjingcheng Yizhi ∴· VRC 148-149 O 6
Liaotung, Gulf of = Liaodong Wan ≈ VRC 150-151 C 7
Liaoyang ○ VRC 150-151 D 7
Liaoyuan ○ VRC 150-151 E 6
Liaozhong ○ VRC 150-151 D 7
Liao Zhongjingcheng Yizhi · VRC 148-149 O 7
Liāquatpur ○ PK 138-139 C 5
Liard Highway II CDN 30-31 H 5
Liard Plateau ▲ CDN 30-31 F 5
Liard River ~ CDN 30-31 H 5
Liat, Pulau ⌒ RI 162-163 G 6
Libano ○ CO 60-61 D 5
Libano ○ RA 78-79 J 4
Libanos Gedam, Debre · ETH 208-209 D 4
Libao ○ VRC 154-155 M 5
Libatemo ○ RI 164-165 H 5
Libau ○ CDN (MAN) 234-235 G 4
Libba ○ WAN 204-205 F 3
Libby ○ USA (MN) 270-271 E 4
Libby ○ USA (MT) 250-251 D 3
Libenge ○ ZRE 210-211 G 2
Liberal ○ USA (KS) 262-263 F 7
Liberator Lake ⊂ USA 20-21 L 2
Liberdade, Rio ~ BR 68-69 B 6
Liberec ○· CZ 92-93 N 3
Liberia ☆ CR 52-53 B 6
Liberia ■ LB 202-203 E 6
Libertad ○ RA 76-77 J 6
Libertad ○ ROU 78-79 L 3
Libertad ○ YV 60-61 G 3
Libertad, La ○ ES 52-53 K 5
Libertad, La ○ HN 52-53 L 4
Libertador General San Martín ○ RA (JU) 76-77 E 2
Libertador General San Martín ○ RA (SLU) 78-79 G 2
Liberty ○ CDN (SAS) 232-233 N 4
Liberty ○ USA (IN) 274-275 O 5
Liberty ○ USA (KY) 276-277 L 3
Liberty ○ USA (ME) 278-279 M 4
Liberty ○ USA (MS) 268-269 K 5
Liberty ○ USA (NY) 280-281 M 2
Liberty ○ USA (SC) 284-285 H 2
Liberty ○ USA (TN) 276-277 K 4
Liberty ○ USA (TX) 268-269 F 6
Liberty ○ USA (UT) 254-255 D 2
Liberty Hill ○ USA (SC) 284-285 K 2
Liberty Lake ○ USA (WA) 244-245 H 3
Libertytown ○ USA (MD) 280-281 J 4
Libjo ○ RP 160-161 F 7
Libmanan ○ RP 160-161 E 6
Libobo, Tanjung ▲ RI 164-165 L 4
Libode ○ ZA 220-221 J 5
Liboi ○ EAK 212-213 H 3
Liboko ○ ZRE 210-211 H 2
Libono ○ LS 220-221 J 4
Liboumba ~ G 210-211 D 3
Libourne ○ F 90-91 G 9
Librazhd ☆· AL 100-101 H 4
Libreville ★· G 210-211 B 3
Librija ○ CO 60-61 E 4
Libro Point ▲ RP 160-161 C 7
Libuganon ~ RP 160-161 F 9
Libya = Lībiyā ■ LAR 192-193 D 4
Libyan Desert = as-Ṣaḥrā' al-Lībiyā ⚍ LAR 192-193 K 3
Licancabur, Volcán ▲ RCH 76-77 D 2
Licata ○ I 100-101 D 6
Lice ☆ TR 128-129 J 3
Licenciado Matienzo ○ RA 78-79 K 4
Lichang ○ VRC 154-155 H 6
Licheng ○ VRC 154-155 H 3
Lichinga ☆ MOC 218-219 H 1
Lichinga, Planalto de ▲ MOC 218-219 H 1
Lichtenburg ○ ZA 220-221 H 3
Lichteneger, Lac ⊂ CDN 38-39 G 2
Licínio de Almeida ○ BR 72-73 J 3
Liciro ○ MOC 218-219 J 3
Licking ○ USA (MO) 276-277 D 3
Licking River ~ USA (KY) 276-277 L 2
Licuare, Rio ~ MOC 218-219 J 3
Licungo, Rio ~ MOC 218-219 J 3
Lida ☆ BY 94-95 J 5
Lidan ~ S 86-87 F 7
Lida Summit ▲ USA (NV) 248-249 G 2
Liddon Gulf ≈ 24-25 P 3
Liden ○ S 86-87 H 5
Lidgerwood ○ USA (ND) 258-259 K 5
Lidi, Mayo ~ CAM 206-207 B 4
Lidia, Rio ~ PE 70-71 B 2
Lidji ~ ZRE 210-211 F 5
Lidjombo ○ RCA 210-211 F 2
Lidköping ☆ S 86-87 F 7
Lido ○ RN 204-205 E 2
Lido di Ostia ○ I 100-101 D 4
Lidskaja ravnina ▲ 94-95 J 5
Lidzbark Warmiński ○· PL 92-93 Q 1
Liebenthal ○ CDN (SAS) 232-233 J 5
Liebenthal ○ USA (KS) 262-263 G 6
Liebig, Mount ▲ AUS 176-177 L 1
Liechtenstein ■ FL 92-93 K 5
Liège ☆· B 92-93 H 3
Lieksa ○ FIN 88-89 L 5
Liemianzheng ○ VRC 154-155 E 6
Lienz ○ A 92-93 M 5
Liepāja ☆·· LV 94-95 G 3
Lier ○· B 92-93 H 3
Lierre = Lier ○· B 92-93 H 3
Lietnik ○ USA 20-21 F 5
Lièvre, Rivière du ~ CDN (QUE) 238-239 K 2
Liezen ○ A 92-93 N 5
Lifamatola, Pulau ⌒ RI 164-165 K 4
Lifford ☆ IRL 90-91 D 4
Lifjell ▲ N 86-87 D 7
Lifuka ⌒ TON 184 IV a 1
Lifune ~ ANG 216-217 C 4
Lifupa Lodge ○ MW 218-219 G 1
Ligao ○ RP 160-161 E 6
Ligar ○ TCH 206-207 C 4
Lighfoot Lake ⊂ AUS 176-177 G 4
Light ○ RP 160-161 F 7
Light, Cape ▲ ARK 16 F 30
Lighthouse Beach ⚍· BS 54-55 G 2
Lighthouse Cove ○ CDN (ONT) 238-239 C 6
Lighthouse Point ▲ USA (FL) 286-287 E 2
Lighthouse Reef ⌒ BH 52-53 L 3
Lightning Creek ~ USA (WY) 252-253 O 3
Lightning Ridge ○ AUS 178-179 J 5
Lignite ○ USA (ND) 258-259 E 3
Ligonha, Rio ~ MOC 218-219 K 2
Ligonier ○ USA (IN) 274-275 N 3
Ligonier ○ USA (PA) 280-281 G 3
Ligowola ○ EAT 214-215 J 6
Ligua, Caleta la ≈ 78-79 D 2
Ligua, La ○ RCH (COQ) 76-77 B 6
Ligua, La ○ RCH (VAL) 78-79 D 2
Ligua, Río la ~ RCH 78-79 D 2
Ligunga ○ EAT 214-215 J 6
Ligúria ▫ I 100-101 B 2
Ligurian Sea = Ligure, Mar ≈ 100-101 B 3
Ligurta ○ USA (AZ) 256-257 A 6
Lihás ○ GR 100-101 J 5
Lihin, al- ○ KSA 130-131 F 5
Lihir Group ⌒ PNG 183 G 2
Lihir Island ⌒ PNG 183 G 2
Lihoslavl' ☆ RUS 94-95 O 3
Lihou Reefs and Cays ⌒ AUS 174-175 M 5
Lihovskoj ○ RUS 102-103 M 3
Lihue ○· USA (HI) 288 F 3
Lihuel Calel, Parque Nacional ⊥ RA 78-79 G 4
Lihula ○ EST 94-95 H 2
Liivi Laht ≈ 94-95 H 2
Lijiang ○· VRC (YUN) 142-143 M 2
Lijiang ·· VRC (GXI) 156-157 G 4
Lik ~ LAO 156-157 C 7
Lik, Pulau ⌒ RI 166-167 K 2
Likala ○ ZRE 210-211 G 3
Likame ~ ZRE 210-211 H 2
Likasi ○ ZRE 214-215 D 6
Likati ○ ZRE (Hau) 210-211 J 2
Likati ~ ZRE 210-211 J 2
Likely ○ CDN (BC) 228-229 N 4
Likely ○ USA (CA) 246-247 E 2
Likete ○ ZRE 210-211 H 4
Likisia ○ RI 166-167 C 6
Likoma Islands ⌒ MW 214-215 H 7
Likoto ○ ZRE 210-211 K 4
Likouala ▫ RCB 210-211 E 2
Likouala ~ RCB 210-211 E 3
Likouala aux Herbes ~ RCB 210-211 F 3
Likum ○ PNG 183 D 2
Likuyu ○ EAT 214-215 J 6
Lilarea ○ AUS 178-179 H 2
Lilbourn ○ USA (MO) 276-277 F 4
Liliāni ○ PK 138-139 D 3
Lilikse ○ GH 202-203 J 4
Liling ○ VRC 156-157 H 3
Lilla ○ PK 138-139 D 3
Lille ☆· F 90-91 J 6
Lille Bælt ≈ DK 86-87 D 9
Lillehammer ☆ N 86-87 E 6
Lille Hellefiskebanke ≃ 28-29 N 4
Lilles, Punta ▲ RCH 78-79 D 2
Lillesand ☆· N 86-87 D 7
Lillestrom ○ CDN (SAS) 232-233 N 5
Lillestrøm ☆ N 86-87 E 7
Lillico Point ▲ CDN 36-37 K 6
Lillie ○ USA (LA) 268-269 H 4
Lillington ○ USA (NC) 282-283 J 5
Lilliwaup ○ USA (WA) 244-245 B 3
Lillooet ○ CDN (BC) 230-231 H 3
Lillooet Lake ⊂ CDN (BC) 230-231 G 3
Lillooet Range ▲ CDN (BC) 230-231 G 3
Lillooet River ~ CDN (BC) 230-231 F 3
Lilo ~ ZRE 210-211 K 4
Lilongwe ★· MW 218-219 G 1
Lilo Viego ○ RA 76-77 F 4
Liloy ○ RP 160-161 E 8
Lily ○ USA (SD) 260-261 J 1
Lily ○ USA (WI) 270-271 K 5
Lilydale ○ AUS 180-181 J 6
Lim ~ RCA 206-207 B 5
Lim ~ YU 100-101 G 3
Lima ○ OM 134-135 G 6
Lima ★··· PE 64-65 D 8
Lima ○ PY 76-77 J 2
Lima ○ USA (MT) 250-251 G 7
Lima ○ USA (OH) 280-281 B 3
Lima, La ○· HN 52-53 L 4
Limache ○ RA 76-77 F 5
Limache ○ RCH 78-79 D 2
Limal ○ BOL 76-77 E 2
Liman ☆ RUS 126-127 G 5
Limão, Igarapé do ~ BR 66-67 K 6
Limão do Curuá ○ BR 62-63 J 5
Limapuluh ○ RI 162-163 C 3
Limar ○ RI 166-167 D 5
Limari, Rio ~ RCH 76-77 B 6
Limasawa Island ⌒ RP 160-161 F 8
Limassa ○ RCA 206-207 F 6
Limaubungkuk, Tanjung ▲ RI 162-163 F 6
Limavady ○ GB 90-91 D 4
Limay, Rio ~ RA 78-79 E 5
Limba Limba ~ EAT 214-215 G 4
Limbang ○ MAL 164-165 D 1
Limbani ○ PE 70-71 C 4
Limbasa ○ ZRE 206-207 F 6
Limbaži ☆·· LV 94-95 J 3
Limbdi ○ IND 138-139 C 8
Limbe ○ MW 218-219 H 2
Limbé ○ RH 54-55 J 5
Limbé = Victoria ○· CAM 204-205 H 6
Limbla ○ AUS 178-179 C 2
Limbo, Pulau ⌒ RI 164-165 J 4
Limboto ○ RI 164-165 H 3
Limbunan ○ RP 160-161 E 9
Limbung ○ RI 164-165 F 5
Limbunya ○ AUS 172-173 J 4
Limburg an der Lahn ○·· D 92-93 K 3
Lime ○ USA (OR) 244-245 H 6
Lime Acres ○ ZA 220-221 F 4
Limeira ○ BR (MIN) 72-73 H 4
Limeira ○ BR (PAU) 72-73 G 7
Limerick ○ CDN (SAS) 232-233 M 6
Limerick ○ USA (ME) 278-279 L 5
Limerick = Luimneach ○ IRL 90-91 C 5
Limestone ○ CDN (NB) 240-241 H 4
Limestone ○ USA (ME) 278-279 O 2
Limestone ○ USA (MT) 250-251 K 6
Limestone, Lake < USA (TX) 266-267 L 2
Limestone Lake ⊂ CDN 34-35 J 2
Limestone Peak ▲ USA (AZ) 256-257 F 7
Limestone Point ▲ CDN 34-35 G 4
Limestone Rapids ~ CDN 34-35 M 3
Limestone River ~ CDN 34-35 J 2
Limfjorden ≈ 86-87 D 8
Limgytynot ~ RUS 112-113 W 4
Limia, Río ~ E 98-99 D 3
Limingen ⊂ N 86-87 F 4
Liminka ○ FIN 88-89 H 4
Limmen Bight ≈ 174-175 C 4
Limmen Bight Aboriginal Land ⚔ AUS 174-175 C 4
Limmen Bight River ~ AUS 174-175 C 4
Límnos ⌒ GR 100-101 K 5
Limnu ~ RUS 120-121 E 6
Limoeiro ○ BR 68-69 L 5
Limoeiro do Ajurú ○ BR 62-63 K 6
Limoeiro do Norte ○ BR 68-69 J 4
Limoges ☆· F 90-91 H 9
Limon ○ USA (CO) 254-255 M 4
Limonar ○ C 54-55 H 4
Limousin ▫ F 90-91 H 9
Limoux ○ F 90-91 J 10
Limpio ○ PY 76-77 J 3
Limpopo ○ MOC 218-219 G 6
Limpopo ~ ZA 218-219 E 6
Limpopo, Rio ~ MOC 220-221 L 2
Limppityřky ~ RUS 114-115 R 2
Limptèkan ~ RUS 116-117 M 4
Limuri ~ RUS 122-123 H 3
Limuru ○ EAK 212-213 F 4
Lina ○ KSA 130-131 H 3
Linaälven ~ S 86-87 K 3
Linahamari ○ RUS 88-89 L 2
Lin'an ○ VRC 154-155 L 6
Linao ○ RP 160-161 D 3
Linao Point ▲ RP 160-161 E 9
Linapacan Island ⌒ RP 160-161 C 7
Linapacan Strait ≈ 160-161 C 7
Linares ○ E 98-99 F 5
Linares ○ MEX 50-51 K 5
Linares ○ RCH 78-79 D 3
Linas, Monte ▲ I 100-101 B 5
Lincang ○ VRC 142-143 M 4
Linchang ○ VRC 154-155 F 5
Linchuan ○ VRC 156-157 K 3
Lincoln ☆· GB 90-91 G 5
Lincoln ○ NZ 182 D 5
Lincoln ○ RA 78-79 J 3
Lincoln ○ USA (AL) 284-285 D 3
Lincoln ○ USA (AR) 276-277 A 5
Lincoln ○ USA (CA) 246-247 D 5
Lincoln ○ USA (IL) 274-275 J 4
Lincoln ○ USA (KS) 262-263 H 5
Lincoln ○ USA (ME) 278-279 N 3
Lincoln ○ USA (MT) 250-251 G 5
Lincoln ○ USA (NH) 278-279 K 4
Lincoln ○ USA (NM) 256-257 K 5
Lincoln ☆ USA (NE) 262-263 K 4
Lincoln Birthplace National Historic Site, Abraham ∴ USA (KY) 276-277 K 3
Lincoln Boyhood National Memorial · USA (IN) 274-275 M 6
Lincoln Caverns ∴ USA (PA) 280-281 H 3
Lincoln City ○ USA (OR) 244-245 B 6
Lincoln City ○ USA (OR) 244-245 A 6
Lincoln Highway II AUS 180-181 D 2
Lincoln National Park ⊥ AUS 180-181 C 3
Lincoln Sea ≈ 26-27 U 2
Lincoln's New Salem · USA (IL) 274-275 J 5
Lincolnton ○ USA (GA) 284-285 H 3
Lincolnton ○ USA (NC) 282-283 F 5
Lind ○ USA (WA) 244-245 G 4
Linda ○ USA (CA) 246-247 D 5
Lindagadaw ○ MYA 142-143 J 5
Lindale ○ USA (GA) 284-285 E 2
Lindale ○ USA (TX) 264-265 J 6
Lindau (Bodensee) ○·· D 92-93 K 5
Lindbergh ○ CDN (ALB) 232-233 H 2
Lindbrook ○ CDN (ALB) 232-233 F 2
Linde ~ RUS 110-111 N 7
Linde ~ RUS 110-111 M 6
Linde ~ RUS 118-119 M 3
Lindela ○ MOC 218-219 H 7
Lindeman Group ⌒ AUS 174-175 K 7
Linden ○ CDN (ALB) 232-233 E 4
Linden ○ USA (AL) 284-285 C 4
Linden ○ USA (CA) 246-247 D 5
Linden ○ USA (IN) 274-275 M 4
Linden ○ USA (NJ) 280-281 M 3
Linden ○ USA (TN) 276-277 H 5
Linden ○ USA (TX) 264-265 K 5
Lindenows Fjord ≈ 28-29 T 6
Lindesnes ▲ N 86-87 C 8
Lindhard Ø ⌒ GRØ 26-27 o 5
Lindi ▫ EAT 214-215 J 5
Lindi ☆· EAT (LIN) 214-215 K 5
Lindi ~ ZRE 210-211 K 3
Lindian ○ VRC 150-151 E 4
Lindi Bay ≈ 214-215 K 5
Lindis Pass ▲ NZ 182 B 6
Lindley ○ ZA 220-221 H 3
Lindleyspoort ○ ZA 220-221 H 2
Líndos ○·· GR 100-101 M 6
Lindsay ○ CDN (ONT) 238-239 G 4
Lindsay ○ USA (CA) 248-249 E 3
Lindsay ○ USA (MT) 250-251 O 4
Lindsay ○ USA (OK) 264-265 G 4
Lindsay, Mount ▲ AUS 176-177 K 3
Lindsborg ○ USA (KS) 262-263 J 6
Lindstrom ○ USA (MN) 270-271 F 5
Lindström Peninsula ⌣ CDN 24-25 e 2
Lindu, Danau ⊂ RI 164-165 G 4
Linduri ○ VAN 184 II a 2
Línea de la Concepción, La ○ E 98-99 E 6
Line Islands ⌒ KIB 14-15 N 7
Linejnoe ○ RUS 96-97 E 10
Linek ○ RP 160-161 F 9
Lineville ○ USA (AL) 284-285 E 3
Lineville ○ USA (IA) 274-275 E 4
Linfen ○ VRC 154-155 G 3
Linganamakki Reservoir ⊂ IND 140-141 F 3
Lingayen Gulf ≈ 160-161 D 4
Lingbao ○ VRC 154-155 G 4
Lingbi ○ VRC 154-155 K 5
Lingbim ○ CAM 206-207 B 6
Lingen (Ems) ○ D 92-93 J 2
Lingga ○ MAL 162-163 J 4
Lingga, Kepulauan ⌒ RI 162-163 F 5
Lingga, Pulau ⌒ RI 162-163 F 5
Lingkeh ○ RI 164-165 G 5
Lingkobu, Tanjung ▲ RI 164-165 G 5
Lingle ○ USA (WY) 252-253 O 4
Linglingjuym, buhta ⊂ RUS 112-113 R 6
Lingo ○ USA (NM) 256-257 M 5
Lingomo ○ ZRE (EQU) 210-211 J 3
Lingomo ○ ZRE (EQU) 210-211 J 4
Lingqi D. · VRC 156-157 L 2
Lingqiu ○ VRC 154-155 J 2
Lingshan ○ VRC 156-157 F 6
Lingshan Dao ⌒ VRC 154-155 M 4
Lingshi ○ VRC 154-155 G 3
Lingshui ○ VRC 156-157 G 7
Lingsugūr ○ IND 140-141 G 2
Lingtai ○ VRC 154-155 E 4
Lingtou ○ VRC 156-157 F 7
Linguère ○ SN 202-203 C 2
Lingui ○ VRC 156-157 G 4
Lingwu ○ VRC 154-155 E 2
Ling Xian ○ VRC 156-157 H 3
Lingxiaoyan · VRC 156-157 G 5
Lingyuan ○ VRC 148-149 O 7
Linh, Ngoc ▲ VN 158-159 J 3
Linhai ○ VRC (HEI) 150-151 E 2
Linhai ○ VRC (ZHE) 156-157 M 2
Linhares ○ BR 72-73 K 5
Linhe ○ VRC 154-155 E 1
Linhemo ○ ANG 216-217 D 6
Linjiang ○ VRC 150-151 F 7
Linke Lakes ⊂ AUS 176-177 G 2
Linkiring ○ SN 202-203 D 3
Linköping ☆· S 86-87 G 7
Linkou ○ VRC 150-151 H 5
Linli ○ VRC 156-157 G 2
Linlithgow ○ GB 90-91 F 4
Linn ○ USA (KS) 262-263 J 5
Linn ○ USA (MO) 274-275 G 6
Linn ○ USA (TX) 266-267 J 7
Linn ○ USA (WV) 280-281 F 4
Linneus ○ USA (MO) 274-275 E 5
Linpeng ○ VRC 156-157 E 5
Linqing ○ VRC 154-155 J 3
Linqu ○ VRC 154-155 L 3
Linquan ○ VRC 154-155 J 5
Lins ○ BR 72-73 F 6
Linsan ○ RG 202-203 D 4
Linsell ○ S 86-87 F 5
Linshu ○ VRC 154-155 L 4
Linshui ○ VRC 154-155 E 6
Linstead ○ JA 54-55 G 5
Linta ~ RM 222-223 D 10
Lintao ○ VRC 154-155 C 4
Linté ○ CAM 204-205 J 6
Lintea Tiwolu, Pulau ⌒ RI 164-165 H 6
Linthipe ○ MW 218-219 H 2
Lintlaw ○ CDN (SAS) 232-233 P 3
Linton ○ USA (IN) 274-275 L 5
Linton ○ USA (KY) 276-277 H 4
Linton ○ USA (ND) 258-259 G 5
Lintong ○ VRC 154-155 F 4
Linville ○ USA (NC) 282-283 F 4
Linville Caverns ∴ USA (NC) 282-283 F 5
Linxi ○ VRC 148-149 O 6
Linxia ○ VRC 154-155 C 4
Lin Xian ○ VRC (HEN) 154-155 H 3
Lin Xian ○ VRC (SHA) 154-155 G 3
Linxiang ○ VRC 156-157 H 2
Linyanti ~ RB 218-219 B 4
Linyanti Swamp ⊂ NAM 218-219 B 4
Linyi ○ VRC (SHD) 154-155 K 3
Linyi ○ VRC (SHD) 154-155 L 4
Linz ☆ A 92-93 N 4
Linze ○ VRC 154-155 B 2
Linzhen ○ VRC 154-155 F 3
Linzor ○ RCH 76-77 D 2
Lioana ○ RP 160-161 D 4
Lioma ○ MOC 218-219 J 2
Lion, Golfe du ≈ 90-91 J 10
Lion Camp ○ Z 218-219 F 1
Liongsong, Tanjung ▲ RI 168 C 7
Lioni, Caño ~ CO 60-61 G 5
Lion Park ⊥ ZA 220-221 H 2
Lions Den ○ ZW 218-219 F 3
Lioppa ○ RI 166-167 C 5
Lios Tuathail = Listowel ○ IRL 90-91 C 5
Lioto ○ RCA 206-207 E 6
Lioua ○ TCH 198-199 G 6
Liouesso ○ RCB 210-211 E 3
Lipa ○ RP 160-161 D 6
Lipale ○ MOC 218-219 J 3
Lipari ○ I 100-101 E 5
Lipari, Ìsola ⌒ I 100-101 E 5
Lipcani ○ MD 102-103 E 3
Lipeck ○ RUS 94-95 Q 5
Lipeo, Rio ~ RA 76-77 E 2
Liperi ○ FIN 88-89 K 5
Lipetrén, Sierra ▲ RA 78-79 E 6
Lipetsk = Lipeck ○ RUS 94-95 Q 5
Lipin Bor ○ RUS 94-95 Q 1
Liping ○ VRC 156-157 F 3
Lipis, Kuala ○· MAL 162-163 E 2
Lipkany = Lipcani ○ MD 102-103 E 3
Lipki ○ RUS 94-95 P 5
Lipljan ○· YU 100-101 H 3
Lipno ○ PL 92-93 P 2
Lipno, údolní nádrž ⊂ CZ 92-93 N 4
Lipobane, Ponta ▲ MOC 218-219 K 3
Lipova ○ RO 102-103 B 4
Lippe ~ D 92-93 K 3
Lippstadt ○· D 92-93 K 3
Lipscomb ○ USA (TX) 264-265 D 2
Lipton ○ CDN (SAS) 232-233 P 5
Liptougou ○ BF 202-203 L 3
Liptrap, Cape ▲ AUS 180-181 H 5
Lipu ○ VRC 156-157 G 4
Liquica = Likisia ○ RI 166-167 C 6
Lira ○ EAU 212-213 D 2
Liran, Pulau ⌒ RI 166-167 C 6
Liranga ○ RCB 210-211 F 4
Lircay ○ PE 64-65 E 8
Lirung ○ RI 164-165 K 2
Lisakovsk ☆ KA 124-125 C 2
Lisala ○ ZRE 210-211 H 2
Lisboa ★··· P 98-99 C 5
Lisbon ○ USA (IL) 274-275 K 3
Lisbon ○ USA (ND) 258-259 K 5
Lisbon ○ USA (OH) 280-281 F 3
Lisbon = Lisboa ★··· P 98-99 C 5
Lisbon Falls ○ USA (ME) 278-279 L 4
Lisburn, Cape = Cape Mata'Avea ▲ VAN 184 II a 2
Lisburne, Cape ▲ USA 20-21 G 2
Liscomb ○ CDN (NS) 240-241 N 5
Liscomb Game Sanction ⊥ CDN (NS) 240-241 N 5
Liscomb Island ⌒ CDN (NS) 240-241 O 5
Liscomb Mills ○ CDN (NS) 240-241 N 5
Lishan ○ VRC 154-155 E 6
Lishan Z.B. ⊥· VRC 154-155 G 4
Lishi ○ VRC (SHA) 154-155 G 3
Lishi ○ VRC (SIC) 156-157 D 2
Lishu ○ VRC 154-155 L 6
Lishui ○ VRC 156-157 L 2
Lisianski Island ⌒ USA 14-15 L 5
Lisica ~ RUS 114-115 S 5
Lisičansk = Lysyčans'k ○ UA 102-103 L 3
Lisica-Pass ▲ YU 100-101 H 3
Lisieux ○· F 90-91 H 7
Lisinskaja buhta ⊂ RUS 120-121 W 6
Lisja ~ RUS 112-113 K 3
Lisjanskogo, poluostrov ⌣ RUS 120-121 M 4
Liski ○ RUS 102-103 L 2
L'Islet ○ CDN (QUE) 240-241 E 3
L'Isle-Verte ○ CDN (QUE) 240-241 F 2
Li-Smita, ostrov ⌒ RUS 84-85 d 2
Lismore ○ AUS (NSW) 178-179 M 5
Lismore ○ AUS (VIC) 180-181 G 4
Lismore ○ CDN (NS) 240-241 N 5
Lismore ○ USA (MN) 270-271 C 7
Lisnaskea ○· GB 90-91 D 4
Lisomu, Tanjung ▲ RI 166-167 C 6
Lissadell ○ AUS 172-173 J 4
Lister ○ CDN (BC) 230-231 N 4
Lister, Mount ▲ ARK 16 F 17
Lištica = Široki Brijeg ○ BIH 100-101 F 3
Listowel ○ CDN (ONT) 238-239 E 5
Listowel = Lios Tuathail ○ IRL 90-91 C 5
Listvjanka ○· RUS 116-117 M 10
Lit, al- ○ KSA 132-133 B 3
Lita ○ EC 64-65 C 1
Litang ○ MAL 160-161 C 10
Litang ○ VRC (GXI) 156-157 F 5
Litang ○ VRC (SIC) 154-155 B 6
Līṭānī ~ RL 128-129 F 6
Litanirivier ~ BR 62-63 G 4
Litchfield ○ USA (CA) 246-247 E 3
Litchfield ○ USA (IL) 274-275 J 5
Litchfield ○ USA (MN) 270-271 D 5
Litchfield ○ USA (NE) 262-263 G 3
Litchfield Beach ○ USA (SC) 284-285 L 3
Litchfield Out Station ○ AUS 172-173 K 2
Litchfield Park ⊥ AUS 172-173 K 2
Litchfield Park ○ USA (AZ) 256-257 C 5
Litchville ○ USA (ND) 258-259 J 5
Lithgow ○ AUS 180-181 L 2
Lithuania = Lietuva ■ LT 94-95 G 4
Litipāra ○ IND 142-143 E 3
Litke ○ RUS (ARH) 108-109 F 5
Litke ○ RUS (HBR) 122-123 J 2
Litke, mys ▲ RUS 112-113 W 1
Litke, poluostrov ⌣ RUS 108-109 J 3
Litke, proliv ≈ 120-121 U 4
Litoměřice ○ CZ 92-93 N 3
Litomyšl ○ CZ 92-93 O 4
Litovko ○ RUS 122-123 F 4
Littell ○ USA (WA) 244-245 B 4
Little Abaco Island ⌒ BS 54-55 G 1
Little Abitibi Lake ⊂ CDN (ONT) 236-237 H 3
Little Abitibi River ~ CDN (ONT) 236-237 G 2
Little Aden ○ Y 132-133 D 7
Little America ○ USA (WY) 252-253 J 5
Little Andaman ⌒ IND 140-141 L 4
Little Arkansas River ~ USA (KS) 262-263 J 6
Little Barrier Island ⌒ NZ 182 E 2
Little Bay ○ CDN (NFL) 242-243 N 3
Little Bay Beach ⚍ GB 56 D 3
Little Bay de Noc ≈ USA 270-271 L 5
Little Belt Mountains ▲ USA (MT) 250-251 H 4
Little Bitterroot River ~ USA (MT) 250-251 E 4
Little Black River ~ USA 20-21 T 3
Little Blue River ~ USA (KS) 262-263 K 5
Little Blue River ~ USA (NE) 262-263 H 4
Little Bow River ~ CDN (ALB) 232-233 E 5
Little Buffalo River ~ CDN 30-31 N 5
Little Burnt Bay ○ CDN (NFL) 242-243 N 3
Little Cadotte River ~ CDN 32-33 M 3
Little Cayman ⌒ GB 54-55 E 5
Little Chicago ○ CDN 30-31 E 2
Little Churchill River ~ CDN 34-35 J 2
Little Colorado River ~ USA (AZ) 256-257 F 4
Little Corwallis Island ⌒ CDN 24-25 Y 3
Littlecote Channel ≈ 36-37 R 2
Little Creek ○ USA (DE) 280-281 L 4
Little Creek Peak ▲ USA (UT) 254-255 C 6
Little Current ○ CDN (ONT) 238-239 D 3
Little Current River ~ CDN (ONT) 236-237 C 2
Little Current River ~ CDN (ONT) 236-237 B 2
Little Cypress Boyau ~ USA (TX) 264-265 K 6
Little Delta River ~ USA 20-21 R 5
Little Desert ⚍ AUS 180-181 F 4
Little Desert National Park ⊥ AUS 180-181 F 4
Little Diomede Island ⌒ USA 20-21 F 4
Little Exuma Island ⌒ BS 54-55 H 3
Little Falls ○ USA (MN) 270-271 D 5
Little Falls ○ USA (NY) 278-279 G 5
Littlefield ○ USA (AZ) 256-257 B 2
Littlefield ○ USA (TX) 264-265 B 5
Little Fork ○ USA (MN) 270-271 E 2
Little Fork River ~ USA (MN) 270-271 E 2
Little Fort ○ CDN (BC) 230-231 J 2
Little Gold River ~ AUS 172-173 H 4
Little Grand Rapids ○ CDN (MAN) 234-235 H 2
Little Harbour ○ BS 54-55 G 2
Little Harbour ○ CDN (NFL) 242-243 L 3
Little Hocking ○ USA (OH) 280-281 E 4
Little Humboldt River ~ USA (NV) 246-247 H 2
Little Inagua Island ⌒ BS 54-55 J 4
Little Kanawha River ~ USA (WV) 280-281 E 4
Little Karoo = Klein Karoo ⚍ ZA 220-221 E 6
Little Koniuji Island ⌒ USA 22-23 R 5
Little Lake ○ USA (CA) 248-249 G 4
Little Lake ○ USA (MI) 270-271 L 4
Little Lost River ~ USA (ID) 252-253 E 2
Little Lynches River ~ USA (SC) 284-285 K 2
Little Malad River ~ USA (ID) 252-253 F 4
Little Mecatina River ~ CDN 38-39 N 2
Little Miami River ~ USA (OH) 280-281 B 4
Little Missouri River ~ USA (AR) 276-277 B 7
Little Missouri River ~ USA (MT) 250-251 P 6
Little Missouri River ~ USA (ND) 258-259 E 4
Little Moose Island ⌒ CDN (MAN) 234-235 F 3
Little Muddy Creek ~ USA (WY) 252-253 H 5
Little Mud River ~ USA 20-21 O 4
Little Mulberry Creek ~ USA (AL) 284-285 D 4
Little Nemaha River ~ USA (NE) 262-263 L 4
Little Nicobar Island ⌒ IND 140-141 L 6
Little Norway ○ USA (CA) 246-247 E 5
Little Osage River ~ USA (MO) 274-275 D 6
Little Pee Dee River ~ USA (SC) 284-285 L 2
Little Pic ~ CDN (ONT) 236-237 B 3
Little Powder River ~ USA (WY) 252-253 N 3
Little Quill Lake ⊂ CDN (SAS) 232-233 O 4
Little Ragged Island ⌒ BS 54-55 H 3
Little Rancheria River ~ CDN 20-21 Z 7
Little Rapid Creek ~ CDN 30-31 L 6
Little Red Deer River ~ CDN (ALB) 232-233 D 4
Little Red River ~ USA (AR) 276-277 D 5
Little Ridge ○ CDN (MAN) 234-235 E 4
Little River ○ CDN (BC) 230-231 E 4
Little River ~ USA (AR) 276-277 E 5
Little River ~ USA (AR) 276-277 A 7
Little River ~ USA (GA) 284-285 G 5
Little River ~ USA (GA) 284-285 H 3
Little River ~ USA (KY) 276-277 H 4
Little River ~ USA (LA) 268-269 H 5
Little River ~ USA (NC) 282-283 J 5
Little River ~ USA (OK) 264-265 J 4
Little River ~ USA (SC) 284-285 H 2
Little River ~ USA (SC) 284-285 J 2
Little River ~ USA (TX) 266-267 K 3
Little River ~ USA (VA) 280-281 F 6
Littlerock ○ USA (CA) 248-249 G 5
Littlerock ○ USA (WA) 244-245 B 4
Little Rock ☆ USA (AR) 276-277 C 6
Little Ruaha ~ EAT 214-215 H 5
Little Sable Point ▲ USA (MI) 272-273 C 4
Little Sachigo Lake ⊂ CDN 34-35 K 3
Little Sahara Recreation Area ⊥ USA (UT) 254-255 C 4
Little Saint Lawrence ○ CDN (NFL) 242-243 N 6
Little Saint Simons Island ⌒ USA (GA) 284-285 J 5
Little Salkehatchie River ~ USA (SC) 284-285 J 3
Little Salmon Lake ⊂ CDN 20-21 X 5
Little Salt Lake ⊂ USA (UT) 254-255 C 6
Little Sandy River ~ USA (KY) 276-277 M 2
Little San Salvador Island ⌒ BS 54-55 H 2
Little Sauk ○ USA (MN) 270-271 D 5
Little Scarcies of Kaba ~ WAL 202-203 D 5
Little Seal River ~ CDN 30-31 W 6
Little Sevier River ~ USA (UT) 254-255 C 6

Little Sioux River ∼ USA (IA) 274-275 C 2
Little Sitkin Island ⌒ USA 22-23 F 7
Little Smoky o CDN (ALB) 228-229 R 2
Little Smoky River ∼ CDN 32-33 M 4
Little Snake River ∼ USA (CO) 254-255 G 3
Little Tallahatchie ∼ USA (MS) 268-269 L 2
Little Tallapoosa River ∼ USA (AL) 284-285 E 3
Little Tanaga Island ⌒ USA 22-23 H 7
Little Tennessee River ∼ USA (NC) 282-283 D 5
Littleton o USA (CO) 254-255 K 4
Littleton o USA (NC) 282-283 K 4
Littleton o USA (NH) 278-279 K 4
Little Traverse Bay ≈ USA 272-273 D 2
Little Valley o USA (CA) 246-247 D 3
Little Valley o USA (NY) 278-279 C 6
Little Wabash River ∼ USA (IL) 274-275 K 6
Little White River ∼ CDN (ONT) 238-239 B 2
Little Wichita River ∼ USA (TX) 264-265 F 5
Little Yellowstone Park ∴ USA (ND) 258-259 K 5
Littoral ◘ CAM 204-205 H 6
Lituhi o EAT 214-215 H 6
Litunde o MOC 218-219 H 1
Litvinova, mys ▲ RUS 108-109 Y 1
Litvinovo o RUS 96-97 F 3
Liu o RI 164-165 G 5
Liuba o VRC 154-155 E 5
Liuchiu Yü ⌒ RC 156-157 M 5
Liucura o RCH 78-79 D 5
Liuhe o VRC 150-151 E 6
Liuheng Dao ⌒ VRC 156-157 N 2
Liujiachang o VRC 154-155 G 6
Liujiang o VRC 156-157 F 4
Liujiaxia Sk. o VRC 154-155 C 4
Liujing o VRC 156-157 G 5
Liukanglu, Pulau ⌒ RI 164-165 G 6
Liuli o EAT 214-215 H 6
Liulin o VRC 154-155 G 3
Liupan Shan ▲ VRC 154-155 D 3
Liupanshan Z.B. ⊥ • VRC 154-155 E 4
Liupanshui o VRC 156-157 D 3
Liúpo o MOC 218-219 K 2
Liushai o VRC 156-157 E 4
Liushipu o VRC 154-155 J 5
Liuwa Plain National Park ⊥ Z 218-219 B 2
Liuxu o VRC 156-157 E 5
Liuyang o VRC 156-157 H 2
Liuzhao Shan ▲ VRC 156-157 D 5
Liuzhi o VRC 156-157 D 3
Liuzhou o • VRC 156-157 F 4
Liuzhuang o VRC 154-155 M 5
Liváði o GR 100-101 K 6
Livadiá o • GR 100-101 J 5
Livani o •• LV 94-95 K 3
Livanovka o KA 124-125 C 2
Livelong o CDN (SAS) 232-233 K 2
Lively o USA (VA) 280-281 K 6
Lively Island ⌒ GB 78-79 L 7
Livengood o USA 20-21 Q 4
Live Oak o USA (CA) 248-249 H 7
Live Oak o USA (FL) 286-287 G 1
Livermore o USA (CA) 248-249 C 2
Livermore o USA (KY) 276-277 H 3
Livermore, Mount ▲ USA (TX) 266-267 C 3
Livermore Falls o USA (ME) 278-279 L 4
Liverpool o AUS 180-181 L 2
Liverpool o CDN (NS) 240-241 L 6
Liverpool o • GB 90-91 F 5
Liverpool, Cape ▲ CDN 24-25 h 4
Liverpool Bay ≈ 20-21 Z 2
Liverpool Range ▲ AUS 178-179 K 6
Liviko Pélagos ≈ 100-101 J 7
Livingston o USA (AL) 284-285 B 4
Livingston o USA (KY) 276-277 L 3
Livingston o USA (LA) 268-269 K 6
Livingston o USA (MT) 250-251 J 6
Livingston o USA (TN) 276-277 K 4
Livingston o USA (TX) 268-269 F 6
Livingston, Lake < USA (TX) 268-269 E 6
Livingstone ☆ Z 218-219 C 3
Livingstone Memorial • Z 214-215 F 7
Livingstonia o • MW 214-215 H 6
Livingston Island ⌒ ARK 16 G 30
Livinstone's Cave • RB 220-221 G 2
Livno o BIH 100-101 F 3
Livny o RUS 94-95 P 5
Livonia o USA (MI) 272-273 F 5
Livorno o I 100-101 C 3
Livradois-Forez, Parc Naturel Régional ⊥ F 90-91 J 9
Livramento do Brumado o BR 72-73 K 2
Liwa o RI 162-163 F 7
Liwā', al- o OM 132-133 K 1
Liwale o EAT 214-215 J 5
Liwonde o MW 218-219 H 2
Liwonde National Park ⊥ MW 218-219 H 2
Li Xian o VRC (GAN) 154-155 D 4
Li Xian o VRC (SIC) 154-155 C 6
Lixin o VRC 154-155 K 5
Lixoúri o GR 100-101 H 5
Lixus ∴ • MA 188-189 H 3
Liyang o VRC 154-155 L 6
Li Yubu o SUD 206-207 H 6
Lizarda o BR 68-69 E 6
Lizard Head Peak ▲ USA (WY) 252-253 J 4
Lizard Island ⌒ AUS 174-175 H 4
Lizard Point ▲ GB 90-91 E 7
Lizard Point Indian Reserve ✗ CDN (MAN) 234-235 C 4
Lizella o USA (GA) 284-285 G 4
Lizotte o CDN (QUE) 240-241 C 2
Lizton o USA (IN) 274-275 M 5
Lizums o LV 94-95 K 3
Ljadova ∼ UA 102-103 E 3
Ljady o RUS 94-95 L 2
Ljahovskie ostrova ⌒ RUS 110-111 U 2
Ljaki o AZ 128-129 M 2
Ljamca o RUS 88-89 O 4
Ljamin ∼ RUS 114-115 L 4
Ljamin, pervyj ∼ RUS 114-115 K 3
Ljamin, vtoroj ∼ RUS 114-115 K 3
Ljamskie gory ▲ RUS 108-109 Y 7
Ljangar o TJ 136-137 N 6
Ljangasovo o RUS 96-97 F 4
Ljantorskij o RUS 114-115 M 4
Ljapin ∼ RUS 114-115 F 3
Ljapiske ∼ RUS 118-119 N 3
Ljig o • YU 100-101 H 2
Ljuban' o BY 94-95 L 5
Ljuban' o RUS 94-95 M 2
Ljubanskae vadashovišča < BY 94-95 L 5
Ljubar o UA 102-103 E 3
Ljubercy ☆ RUS 94-95 P 4
Ljubertsy = Ljubercy ☆ RUS 94-95 P 4
Ljubešiv o UA 102-103 D 2
Ljubinskij ☆ RUS 114-115 M 7
Ljubljana ★ SLO 100-101 E 1
Ljuboml' o UA 102-103 D 2
Ljubovija o YU 100-101 G 2
Ljubytino o RUS 94-95 N 2
Ljudinovo o RUS 94-95 O 5
Ljugarn o S 86-87 J 8
Ljukkum ⊥ KA 124-125 K 5
Ljungan ∼ S 86-87 H 5
Ljungby ☆ S 86-87 F 8
Ljungdalen o S 86-87 F 5
Ljusdal o S 86-87 H 6
Ljusnan ∼ S 86-87 G 6
Ljutoga ∼ RUS 122-123 K 5
Lk. Kambera ∼ RI 168 E 7
Llaima, Volcán ▲ RCH 78-79 D 5
Llallagua o BOL 70-71 D 6
Llalli o PE 70-71 B 4
Llamara, Salar de o RCH 76-77 C 1
Llançà o E 98-99 J 3
Llancañelo, Laguna y Salina ⊂ RA 78-79 E 3
Llanddovery o GB 90-91 F 6
Llandrindod Wells o GB 90-91 F 5
Llanes o • E 98-99 E 3
Llano o USA (TX) 266-267 J 3
Llano, El o PA 52-53 E 7
Llanobajo o CO 60-61 C 6
Llano Estacado ∪ USA (TX) 264-265 A 5
Llano Mariato o PA 52-53 D 8
Llano River ∼ USA (TX) 266-267 J 3
Llano River, North ∼ USA (TX) 266-267 G 3
Llano River, South ∼ USA (TX) 266-267 G 3
Llanos, Sierra de los ▲ RA 76-77 D 6
Llanos de Aridane, Los o E 188-189 C 6
Llanquihué o RCH 78-79 C 6
Llanquihué, Lago ⊂ RCH 78-79 C 6
Llao Llao o RA 78-79 D 6
Llaylla o PE 64-65 E 7
Llay-Llay o RCH 78-79 D 2
Lleida o •• E 98-99 H 4
Llera de Canales o MEX 50-51 K 6
Llerena o E 98-99 D 5
Llewellyn Glacier ⊂ CDN 20-21 X 7
Lleyn Peninsula ∪ GB 90-91 E 5
Llica o BOL 70-71 C 6
Llico o RCH 78-79 C 4
Lliria o E 98-99 G 5
Lliscaya, Cerro ▲ BOL 70-71 C 6
Lloyd o USA (MT) 250-251 K 3
Lloyd Bay ≈ 174-175 G 3
Lloyd Lake ⊂ CDN 32-33 Q 3
Lloydminster o CDN (ALB) 232-233 H 2
Lloyd Rock = The Brothers ⌒ BS 54-55 H 3
Lloyd's Camp o RB 218-219 C 4
Llullaillaco, Volcán ▲ RCH 76-77 C 3
Lluta o PE 70-71 A 5
Lluta, Río ∼ RCH 70-71 C 6
l-Miyāh, Wādī ∼ SYR 128-129 H 5
l-Murra, al-Buhaira < ET 194-195 F 2
Lo, Île = Loh ⌒ VAN 184 II a 1
Loa o USA (UT) 254-255 D 5
Loa, Caleta ≈ 76-77 B 1
Loa, Río ∼ RCH 76-77 C 1
Loanda ∼ ANG 216-217 D 4
Loandji ∼ ZRE 210-211 G 6
Loange ∼ ZRE 210-211 H 6
Loango o ZRE 210-211 D 6
Loanja ∼ Z 218-219 C 3
Loara o RI 164-165 G 5
Loay o RP 160-161 F 8
Loban o RUS 88-89 S 4
Lobatse ☆ RB 220-221 G 2
Lobaye ◘ RCA 206-207 C 6
Lobaye ∼ RCA 210-211 G 2
Lobaye ∼ ZRE 210-211 K 3
Lobé ∼ CAM 210-211 C 2
Lobé, Chutes de la = Lobé Falls ∼ CAM 210-211 B 2
Lobecks Pass ▲ USA (CA) 248-249 K 5
Lobé Falls = Chutes de la Lobé ∼ CAM 210-211 B 2
Lobeke ∼ CAM 210-211 F 2
Lobería o RA 78-79 K 5
Łobez o PL 92-93 N 2
Lobi o MW 218-219 H 2
Lobira o SUD 208-209 A 6
Lobito o ANG (BGU) 216-217 B 6
Lobitos o PE 64-65 B 4
Lobo ∼ CAM 210-211 D 2
Lobo o RI 166-167 H 3
Loboko o RCB 210-211 F 4
Lobo Lodge o EAT 212-213 E 4
Lobos o RA 78-79 K 3
Lobos, Caño los ∼ CO 64-65 E 1
Lobos, Cay ⌒ BS 54-55 G 3
Lobos, Cayo ⌒ MEX 52-53 L 2
Lobos, Isla ⌒ MEX 50-51 D 4
Lobos, Islas de ⌒ MEX 50-51 L 7
Lobos, Punta ▲ RA 78-79 J 5
Lobos, Punta ▲ RCH (ATA) 76-77 B 5
Lobos, Punta ▲ RCH (LIB) 78-79 C 3
Lobos, Punta ▲ RCH (TAR) 70-71 B 6
Lobos, Punta ▲ RCH (TAR) 76-77 B 1
Lobos, Río Los ∼ MEX 50-51 F 5
Lobos de Afuera, Islas ⌒ PE 64-65 B 5
Lobos de Tierra, Isla ⌒ PE 64-65 B 5
Lobotito ▲ RT 202-203 L 6
Lobu o RI 164-165 H 4
Lobuja o RUS 112-113 H 3
Lobutcha Creeks ∼ USA (MS) 268-269 L 4
Lobva o RUS 114-115 F 5
Locas de Cahuinari o CO 66-67 B 3
Locate o USA (MT) 250-251 O 5
Loceret o RI 168 D 3
Lochboisdale o GB 90-91 D 3
Loche, La o CDN 32-33 Q 3
Loche, Lac la ⊂ CDN 32-33 Q 3
Loches o • F 90-91 H 8
Loch Fyne ≈ 26-27 p 7
Loch Fyne ≈ 90-91 E 4
Loch Garman = Wexford ☆ IRL 90-91 D 5
Lochgilphead o GB 90-91 E 3
Lochiel o USA (AZ) 256-257 E 7
Lochiel o ZA 220-221 K 3
Lochinvar National Park ⊥ Z 218-219 D 2
Lochinver o GB 90-91 E 2
Loch Linnhe ≈ 90-91 E 3
Loch Lomond ⊂ GB 90-91 E 3
Lochloosa o USA (FL) 286-287 G 2
Lochmaddy o GB 90-91 D 3
Lochnagar ▲ GB 90-91 F 3
Loch Ness ⊂ GB 90-91 E 3
Łochów o PL 92-93 Q 2
Lochsa River ∼ USA (ID) 250-251 D 5
Loch Sport o AUS 180-181 J 5
Lock o AUS 180-181 C 2
Lockart o AUS 180-181 J 3
Locke o USA (WA) 244-245 H 2
Lockeport o CDN (NS) 240-241 K 7
Locker Point ▲ CDN 24-25 P 6
Lockesburg o USA (AR) 276-277 A 7
Lockhart o USA (SC) 284-285 J 2
Lockhart o USA (TX) 266-267 K 4
Lockhart, Lake ⊂ AUS 176-177 E 6
Lockhart River ✗ AUS 174-175 G 3
Lockhart River ∼ CDN 30-31 P 4
Lockhart River Aboriginal Land ✗ AUS 174-175 G 3
Lock Haven o USA (PA) 280-281 J 2
Lockney o USA (TX) 264-265 C 4
Lockport o CDN (MAN) 234-235 G 4
Lockport o USA (LA) 268-269 K 7
Lockport o USA (NY) 278-279 C 5
Lockwood o USA (CA) 248-249 C 4
Lockwood o USA (MO) 276-277 B 3
Lockwood Hills ▲ USA 20-21 M 3
Lọc Ninh o VN 158-159 J 5
Loco o USA (OK) 264-265 G 4
Loco Hills o USA (NM) 256-257 M 6
Locri o I 100-101 F 5
Locumba, Río ∼ PE 70-71 B 5
Locust o USA (IA) 274-275 G 1
Locust o USA (NC) 282-283 G 5
Locust Creek ∼ USA (MO) 274-275 E 4
Locust Fork ∼ USA (AL) 284-285 D 3
Lod ☆ IL 130-131 D 2
Loddon River ∼ AUS 180-181 G 3
Lodejnoe Pole ☆ RUS 94-95 N 1
Lodève o F 90-91 J 10
Lodge Creek ∼ CDN (ALB) 232-233 H 6
Lodge Grass o USA (MT) 250-251 M 6
Lodgepole o CDN (ALB) 232-233 C 2
Lodgepole o USA (NE) 262-263 D 3
Lodgepole o USA (SD) 260-261 D 1
Lodgepole Creek ∼ USA (WY) 252-253 O 5
Lodhrān o PK 138-139 C 5
Lodi o • I 100-101 B 2
Lodi o USA (CA) 246-247 D 5
Lodi o USA (OH) 280-281 D 2
Lodi o ZRE 210-211 H 6
Lodié ∼ G 210-211 D 3
Løding o N 86-87 G 3
Lødingen o N 86-87 G 2
Lodja o ZRE 210-211 J 5
Lod'ma ∼ RUS 88-89 Q 4
Lodmalasin ▲ EAT 212-213 F 5
Lodočnikova, plato ▲ RUS 108-109 e 3
Lodoga o USA (CA) 246-247 C 4
Lodoyo o RI 168 E 4
Lodrani o IND 138-139 C 8
Lodungokwe o EAK 212-213 F 3
Lodwar o EAK 212-213 E 2
Łódź ☆ •• PL 92-93 P 3
Loei o THA 158-159 F 2
Loeka ∼ ZRE 210-211 J 2
Loémé ∼ RCB 210-211 D 6
Loeng Nok Tha o THA 158-159 H 2
Loeriesfontein o ZA 220-221 D 5
Lofa River ∼ LB 202-203 E 6
Lofé o SN 202-203 C 2
Lofoten ⌒ • N 86-87 F 2
Loftahammar o S 86-87 H 8
Lofty Range ▲ AUS 176-177 E 2
Log o RUS 102-103 N 3
Loga o RN 204-205 E 2
Logba o SUD 206-207 K 6
Logan o USA (IA) 274-275 C 3
Logan o USA (KS) 262-263 G 5
Logan o USA (NM) 256-257 M 3
Logan o USA (OH) 280-281 D 4
Logan o USA (UT) 254-255 D 2
Logan o USA (WV) 280-281 D 6
Logan, Mount ▲ •• CDN 20-21 U 6
Logandale o USA (NV) 248-249 K 3
Logan Glacier ⊂ USA 20-21 U 6
Logan Island ⌒ CDN 234-235 P 4
Logan Lake o CDN (BC) 230-231 J 3
Logan Martin Lake < USA (AL) 284-285 D 3
Logan Mountains ▲ CDN 30-31 E 5
Logan Pass ▲ USA (MT) 250-251 F 3
Logan River ∼ USA (UT) 254-255 D 2
Logansport o USA (IN) 274-275 M 4
Logansport o USA (LA) 268-269 G 5
Loganton o USA (PA) 280-281 J 2
Loganville o USA (GA) 284-285 G 3
Lōgar ◘ AFG 138-139 B 3
Logas'egan ∼ RUS 114-115 J 2
Logaškino o RUS 110-111 d 4
Logatau ∼ RUS 108-109 c 5
Logdealven ∼ S 86-87 J 5
Loge ∼ ANG 216-217 C 3
Logeloge o EAT 214-215 K 4
Loggieville o CDN (NB) 240-241 K 3
Logobou o BF 202-203 L 4
Logoforok o SUD 212-213 D 2
Logone ∼ TCH 206-207 B 3
Logone Birni o CAM 206-207 B 3
Logone Gana o TCH 206-207 B 3
Logone Occidental ◘ TCH 206-207 B 4
Logone Occidental ∼ TCH 206-207 B 4
Logone Oriental ◘ TCH 206-207 B 4
Logone Oriental ∼ TCH 206-207 C 4
Logozone o DY 204-205 E 5
Logroño o E 98-99 F 3
Løgstør o DK 86-87 D 8
Loh = Île Lo ⌒ VAN 184 II a 1
Lohagara o BD 142-143 F 4
Lohāghāt o IND 144-145 C 6
Lohardaga o IND 142-143 D 4
Lohārghat o IND 142-143 G 3
Lohéac o F 90-91 G 8
Lohiniva o FIN 88-89 H 3
Lohja o FIN 88-89 H 6
Lohjanan o RI 164-165 E 4
Loh Liang o RI 168 D 7
Loi o PNG 183 D 2
Loiborsoit o EAT 212-213 F 5
Loi-kaw ☆ MYA 142-143 K 6
Loile ∼ ZRE 210-211 H 4
Loilo ∼ ZRE 210-211 J 3
Loimaa o FIN 88-89 G 6
Loima Hills ▲ EAK 212-213 E 2
Loir ∼ F 90-91 H 8
Loire ∼ F 90-91 H 8
Loiro Poco o BR 66-67 C 2
Lois ∼ RI 166-167 C 6
Loiš o US 136-137 K 5
Loita Hills ▲ EAK 212-213 E 4
Loita Plains ∪ EAK 212-213 E 4
Loja ☆ EC 64-65 C 3
Lojiš ☆ US 136-137 K 5
Lojmola o RUS 88-89 L 6
Lojno o RUS 96-97 H 4
Lokalema o ZRE 210-211 J 3
Lokandu o ZRE 210-211 K 5
Lokan tekojärvi ⊂ FIN 88-89 J 3
Lokata o RI 166-167 F 2
Lokbatan o AZ 128-129 N 2
Lokeli o ZRE 210-211 K 5
Lokichar o EAK 212-213 E 2
Lokichar ∼ EAK 212-213 E 2
Lokichogio o EAK 212-213 E 1
Lokila o ZRE 210-211 K 5
Lokitaung o EAK 212-213 E 1
Loknja ☆ RUS 94-95 M 3
Loko o WAN 204-205 G 4
Lokoja o WAN 204-205 G 5
Lokolama o ZRE 210-211 G 5
Lokolia o ZRE 210-211 H 4
Lokolo ∼ ZRE 210-211 H 4
Lokomby o RM 222-223 E 9
Lokomo o CAM (Est) 210-211 E 2
Lokomo ∼ CAM 210-211 E 2
Lokono o PNG 183 F 2
Lokori o EAK 212-213 F 3
Lokoro ∼ ZRE 210-211 H 5
Lokossa ☆ DY 202-203 L 6
Lokot o RUS 94-95 O 5
Lokoti o CAM 206-207 B 5
Lokoundjé ∼ CAM 210-211 C 2
Loksiati o SME 62-63 G 3
Loks Land ⌒ CDN 36-37 R 3
Lokutu o ZRE 210-211 J 3
Lokwa Kangole o EAK 212-213 E 2
Loky ∼ RM 222-223 F 4
Lol o SUD (SR) 206-207 J 5
Lol ∼ SUD 206-207 H 4
Lola o ANG 216-217 B 7
Lola o RG 202-203 F 6
Lold o RCH 78-79 D 3
Lole ∼ ZRE 210-211 G 5
Lolengi o ZRE 210-211 H 3
Loleta o USA (CA) 246-247 A 3
Lolgorien o EAK 212-213 E 4
Lolland ⌒ DK 86-87 E 9
Lol Lanok < EAT 212-213 F 6
Lolo o USA (MT) 250-251 E 5
Lolobata o RI 164-165 L 3
Lolobau Island ⌒ PNG 183 F 3
Lolobo o CI 202-203 H 6
Loloda Utara, Kepulauan ⌒ RI 164-165 K 2
Lolodorf o CAM 210-211 C 2
Lolo Hot Springs o USA (MT) 250-251 E 5
Lolo Pass ▲ USA (MT) 250-251 E 5
Lolui Island ⌒ EAU 212-213 D 4
Lolvavana ou Patteson, Passage ≈ 184 II b 2
Lolwane o ZA 220-221 F 3
Lolworth o AUS 174-175 H 7
Lolworth Range ▲ AUS 174-175 H 7
Lom o BG 102-103 C 6
Lom ∼ CAM 204-205 K 6
Lom ☆ N 86-87 D 6
Loma o ETH 208-209 C 5
Loma o USA (MT) 250-251 J 4
Loma o USA (ND) 258-259 J 3
Loma Alta o USA (TX) 266-267 G 4
Loma Arena o CO 60-61 D 2
Loma Bonita o MEX 52-53 G 2
Loma de Cabrera o DOM 54-55 K 5
Lomako ∼ ZRE 210-211 H 3
Lomaloma o FJI 184 III c 2
Lomami o ZRE 210-211 J 4
Lomami ∼ ZRE 210-211 K 5
Loma Mountains ▲ WAL 202-203 E 5
Lomas, Las o PE 64-65 B 4
Lomas, Río de ∼ PE 64-65 E 9
Loma San Martín ▲ RA 78-79 E 5
Lomas de Arena o USA (TX) 266-267 C 3
Lomas de Vallejos o RA 76-77 J 4
Lomas de Zamora o RA 78-79 K 3
Lomaum o ANG 216-217 C 6
Lomba ∼ ANG 216-217 E 7
Lombadina ✗ AUS 172-173 F 4
Lombang o RI 164-165 F 5
Lombarda, Serra ▲ BR 62-63 J 4
Lombardia ◘ I 100-101 B 2
Lombe o ANG 216-217 D 4
Lombe o RI 164-165 H 6
Lomblen (Kawela), Pulau ⌒ RI 166-167 B 6
Lombok o RI (NBA) 168 C 7
Lombok ⌒ RI (NBA) 168 C 7
Lombok, Selat ≈ 168 B 7
Lomé ★ • RT 202-203 L 6
Lomela o ZRE (KOR) 210-211 J 5
Lomela ∼ ZRE 210-211 H 4
Lometa o USA (TX) 266-267 J 2
Lomfjorden ≈ 84-85 K 3
Lomié o CAM 210-211 D 2
Loming o SUD 206-207 L 6
Lomitas, Las o RA 76-77 G 3
Lomond o CDN (ALB) 232-233 F 5
Lomonosov Ridge ≃ 16 A 25
Lomovoe o RUS 88-89 Q 4
Lomphāt o K 158-159 J 4
Lompobatang, Gunung ▲ RI 164-165 F 6
Lompoc o USA (CA) 248-249 D 5
Lompopana, Gunung ▲ RI 164-165 F 4
Lompoul o SN 202-203 B 2
Lom Sak o THA 158-159 F 2
Łomża ☆ PL 92-93 R 2
Lô'n ⌒ VN 158-159 K 4
Lona Bay ≈ 36-37 L 2
Lonambo o EC 64-65 D 2
Lonand o IND 138-139 E 10
Lonāvale o • IND 138-139 D 10
Lončakovo o RUS 122-123 F 5
Loncoche o RCH 78-79 C 5
Loncopangue o RCH 78-79 D 4
Loncopue o RA 78-79 D 5
Londa o IND 140-141 F 3
Londéla-Kayes o RCB 210-211 D 6
Londengo o ANG 216-217 D 6
Londiani o EAK 212-213 E 4
Londolovit o PNG 183 G 2
London o • CDN (ONT) 238-239 D 6
London ★ ••• GB 90-91 G 6
London o USA (KY) 276-277 L 3
London o USA (MN) 270-271 E 7
London o USA (OH) 280-281 C 4
London o USA (TX) 266-267 H 3
Londonderry o GB 90-91 D 4
Londonderry, Cape ▲ AUS 172-173 H 2
Londonderry, Isla ⌒ RCH 80 E 7
Londrina o BR 72-73 E 7
Lone Butte o CDN (BC) 230-231 H 2
Lonely Mine o ZW 218-219 E 4
Lone Oak o USA (TX) 264-265 J 6
Lone Pine o USA (CA) 248-249 F 3
Lonepine o USA (MT) 250-251 E 4
Lone Pine Indian Reservation ✗ USA (CA) 248-249 F 3
Lone Rock o CDN (SAS) 232-233 J 2
Lone Rock o USA (WI) 274-275 H 1
Lone Star o USA (TX) 264-265 K 6
Lonetree o USA (WY) 252-253 H 5
Long o THA 142-143 L 6
Long o USA (SC) 284-285 M 3
Longa o ANG (CUA) 216-217 E 7
Longa ∼ ANG 216-217 C 5
Longa ∼ ANG 216-217 E 8
Longa, proliv ≈ 112-113 T 1
Longá, Rio ∼ BR 68-69 H 3
Longa-Mavinga, Coutada Pública do ⊥ ANG 216-217 E 8
Long'an o VRC 154-155 E 3
Longana o VAN 184 II a 2
Long Arroyo ∼ USA (NM) 256-257 L 5
Longaví, Río ∼ RCH 78-79 D 4
Longbao Z.B. ⊥ VRC 144-145 L 4
Long Barn o USA (CA) 246-247 E 5
Long Bay ≈ 48-49 J 3
Long Bay ≈ 54-55 G 6
Long Bay ≈ USA 284-285 M 3
Long Bay Beach ⊥ • GB 56 C 2
Long Bay Beach ⊥ • JA 54-55 G 5
Longbeach o CDN (BC) 230-231 M 4
Long Beach o CDN (NFL) 242-243 P 6
Long Beach o USA (CA) 248-249 F 6
Long Beach o USA (NY) 280-281 N 3
Long Beach o USA (SC) 284-285 M 3
Long Beach o USA (WA) 244-245 A 4
Long Beach ⊥ • USA (NJ) 280-281 M 4
Long Beach, Playa de ⊥ • DOM 54-55 K 5
Longboat Key ⌒ USA (FL) 286-287 G 4
Longbow Lake o CDN (ONT) 234-235 J 5
Long Branch o USA (NJ) 280-281 M 3
Long Branch Lake o USA (MO) 274-275 F 5
Long Canes Creek ∼ USA (SC) 284-285 H 2
Long Cay ⌒ BH 52-53 L 3
Long Cay ⌒ BS 54-55 H 3
Longchang o VRC 156-157 D 2
Longchuan o VRC 156-157 J 4
Long Cove o CDN (NFL) 242-243 P 5
Long Creek o CDN (NB) 240-241 J 5
Long Creek o USA (OR) 244-245 F 6
Long Creek ∼ USA (NC) 282-283 G 5
Longe ∼ ANG 216-217 C 3
Longfengyan • VRC 156-157 K 3
Long Fjord, De ≈ 26-27 d 2
Longford o AUS 180-181 J 6
Longford = An Longfort ☆ IRL 90-91 D 5
Longgang Shan ▲ VRC 150-151 E 6
Longgang Z.B. ⊥ • VRC 156-157 E 5
Longgong • VRC 156-157 D 3
Longgong D. • VRC 156-157 K 2
Long Harbour o CDN (NFL) 242-243 P 5
Longhua o VRC 148-149 N 7
Longhui o VRC 156-157 G 3
Longhushan • VRC 156-157 K 2
Longido o EAT 212-213 F 5
Longikis o RI 164-165 E 4
Longiram o RI 164-165 D 4
Long Island ⌒ AUS 178-179 K 2
Long Island ⌒ BS 54-55 H 3
Long Island ⌒ CDN (NFL) 242-243 N 3
Long Island ⌒ CDN (NFL) 242-243 O 5
Long Island ⌒ CDN (NS) 240-241 J 6
Long Island ⌒ CDN (NWT) 36-37 K 7
Long Island ⌒ PNG 183 D 3
Long Island o USA (KS) 262-263 G 5
Long Island ⌒ USA (NY) 280-281 N 3
Long Island Sound ≈ 36-37 K 7
Long Island Sound ≈ 46-47 M 5
Long Island Sound ≈ USA 280-281 O 2
Longitudinal, Valle ⊥ RCH 78-79 C 4
Longjing o VRC 150-151 G 6
Longkay o RI 164-165 D 3
Long Key ⌒ USA (FL) 286-287 J 7
Longkou o VRC 154-155 M 3
Longlac o CDN (ONT) 236-237 B 3
Long Lake o CDN (ONT) 236-237 B 3
Long Lake o USA (NY) 278-279 G 5
Long Lake o USA (SD) 260-261 G 1
Long Lake o USA (WA) 244-245 H 3
Long Lake ⊂ USA (ND) 258-259 G 5
Long Lake, Indian Reserve ✗ CDN (ONT) 236-237 B 3
Long Lama o MAL 164-165 D 2
Long Lellang o MAL 164-165 D 2
Longlin o VRC 156-157 D 4
Longling o VRC 142-143 L 3
Long Malinau o RI 164-165 E 2
Longmen o VRC 156-157 J 5
Longmen o VRC 156-157 G 6
Longmen Shiku • VRC 154-155 H 4
Longmont o USA (CO) 254-255 K 3
Long Mountains, De ▲ USA 20-21 J 2
Long My o VN 158-159 H 6
Longnan o VRC 156-157 J 4
Longnawan o RI 164-165 D 3
Longo o G 210-211 D 4
Longonjo o ANG 216-217 C 6
Longonot ▲ EAK 212-213 F 4
Longotea o PE 64-65 D 5
Longot'egan ∼ RUS 108-109 M 8
Longozabe o RM 222-223 F 7
Long Palai o MAL 164-165 D 2
Long Pine o USA (NE) 262-263 G 2
Long Plain Indian Reserve ✗ CDN (MAN) 234-235 E 5
Long Point o CDN (ONT) 238-239 E 6
Long Point ▲ CDN (MAN) 34-35 G 4
Long Point ▲ CDN (NFL) 242-243 K 4
Long Point ▲ CDN (ONT) 238-239 E 6
Long Point ▲ RP 160-161 C 8
Long Point Bay ⊂ CDN (ONT) 238-239 E 6
Long Prairie o USA (MN) 270-271 D 5
Longquan o VRC 156-157 L 2
Long Range Mountains ▲ CDN (NFL) 242-243 K 5
Longreach o AUS 178-179 H 2
Long Seridan o MAL 164-165 D 1
Longshan o VRC (GDG) 156-157 H 5
Longshan o VRC (HUN) 156-157 F 2
Longsheng o VRC 156-157 F 4
Longshou Shan ▲ VRC 154-155 B 2
Longs Peak ▲ USA (CO) 254-255 K 3
Long Thành o VN 158-159 J 5
Longton o AUS 174-175 H 7
Longue, Pointe ▲ CDN 38-39 E 2
Longueuil o CDN (QUE) 238-239 M 3
Longvale o USA (CA) 246-247 B 4
Long Valley o USA (AZ) 256-257 D 4
Long Valley o USA (SD) 260-261 E 3
Long Valley Junction o USA (UT) 254-255 C 6
Longview o CDN (ALB) 232-233 D 5
Longview o USA (MS) 268-269 M 3
Longview o USA (TX) 264-265 K 6
Longview o USA (WA) 244-245 C 4
Longville o USA (LA) 268-269 G 6
Longwood o USA (FL) 286-287 H 3
Longworth o CDN (BC) 228-229 N 3
Longxi o VRC 154-155 D 4
Long Xian o VRC 154-155 E 4
Long Xuyên ☆ VN 158-159 H 5
Longyan o VRC 156-157 K 4
Longyao o VRC 154-155 J 3
Longyarbyen o N 84-85 J 3
Longyou o VRC 156-157 L 2
Longzhou o VRC 156-157 E 5
Loni Kand o IND 138-139 E 10
Lonkintsy o RM 222-223 F 6
Lonkonia ∼ ZRE 210-211 J 5
Lono o USA (AR) 276-277 C 6
Lonoke o USA (AR) 276-277 D 6
Lonquimay o RCH 78-79 D 5
Lonsdale o USA (MN) 270-271 E 6
Lons-le-Saunier o F 90-91 K 8
Lontar o RI 166-167 E 4
Lontar, Pulau ⌒ RI 166-167 E 4
Lontou o RMM 202-203 E 2
Lontra o BR 68-69 C 4
Lontra, Ribeirão ∼ BR 72-73 D 6
Lontra, Rio ∼ BR 68-69 D 5
Lontué, Río ∼ RCH 78-79 D 3
Lonua ∼ ZRE 210-211 J 3
Looc o RP (BOH) 160-161 E 8
Looc o RP (ROM) 160-161 D 6
Loogootee o USA (IN) 274-275 M 6
Lookout o USA (CA) 246-247 D 2
Lookout o USA (ME) 278-279 N 4
Lookout, Cape ▲ CDN 34-35 P 3
Lookout, Cape ▲ USA 244-245 B 5
Lookout, Cape ▲ USA (NC) 282-283 L 6
Lookout, Mount ▲ AUS 174-175 H 6
Lookout Mount ▲ USA 20-21 P 3
Lookout Pass ▲ USA (ID) 250-251 D 4
Lookout Point ▲ AUS 174-175 H 4
Lookout Ridge ▲ USA 20-21 L 2
Look Sembuang o MAL 160-161 C 10
Looma o AUS 172-173 G 5
Looma o CDN (ALB) 232-233 E 2
Loomis o CDN (SAS) 232-233 K 6
Loomis o USA (WA) 244-245 F 2
Loongana o AUS 176-177 J 5
Loon Lake o CDN 32-33 Q 4
Loon Lake o USA (WA) 244-245 H 2
Loon Point ▲ CDN 38-39 E 2
Loon River ∼ CDN 32-33 N 3
Loop o USA (TX) 264-265 B 6
Loos o CDN (BC) 228-229 O 3
Loosahatchie River ∼ USA (TN) 276-277 F 5
Loose Creek o USA (MO) 274-275 G 6
Lost River o USA 20-21 G 4
Lootsberg Pass ▲ ZA 220-221 G 5
Lop o VRC 144-145 C 2
Lopary o RM 222-223 E 9
Lopatina, gora ▲ RUS 122-123 K 3
Lopatino o RUS 96-97 D 7
Lopatka, mys ▲ RUS 122-123 R 3
Lopatka, poluostrov ∪ RUS 110-111 d 4
Lopburi o THA 158-159 F 3
Lopča ∼ RUS 118-119 L 8
Lopeno o USA (TX) 266-267 H 7
Lopevi = Ulveah ⌒ VAN 184 II b 3
Lopez o CO 60-61 C 6
Lopez o RP 160-161 E 6
Lopez, Cap ▲ G 210-211 B 4
López Mateos, Ciudad o MEX 52-53 E 2
Lop Nur ⊂ VRC 146-147 K 5
Lopori ∼ ZRE 210-211 H 3
Lopphavet ≈ 86-87 K 1
Lopp Lagoon ≈ 20-21 G 4
Loptjuga ∼ RUS 88-89 U 5
Loquilocon o RP 160-161 F 7
Lora, Punta ▲ RCH 78-79 C 3
Lora, Río ∼ YV 60-61 E 3
Lora Creek ∼ AUS 178-179 C 5
Lorain o USA (OH) 280-281 D 2
Loraine o USA (CA) 248-249 F 4
Loraine o USA (TX) 264-265 D 6
Loralai o PK 138-139 B 4
Loralai ∼ PK 138-139 B 4
Lorane o USA (OR) 244-245 B 7
Loranstation = Angisoq o GRØ 28-29 S 7
Lordegān o IR 134-135 D 3
Lord Howe Island ⌒ ••• AUS 180-181 N 7
Lord Howe Rise ≃ 13 H 6
Lord Howe Seamounts ≃ 13 H 5
Lord Lindsay River ∼ CDN 24-25 Z 5
Lord Loughborough Island ⌒ MYA 158-159 D 5
Lord Mayor Bay ≈ 24-25 a 6
Lordsburg o USA (NM) 256-257 G 6
Lord's Cove o CDN (NFL) 242-243 N 6
Lore o RI 166-167 D 6
Lore Lindu National Park ⊥ • RI 164-165 G 4
Lorella o USA (OR) 244-245 D 8
Loren, Pulau ⌒ RI 168 E 7
Lorena o BR (AMA) 66-67 B 6
Lorena o BR (PAU) 72-73 H 7
Lorena o USA (MS) 268-269 L 4
Lorengau ☆ PNG 183 D 2
Lorentz ∼ RI 166-167 K 4
Lorentz Reserve ⊥ • RI 166-167 J 4
Lorenzo o USA (TX) 264-265 C 5
Lōre Rūd ∼ AFG 134-135 M 2
Lorestān ◘ IR 134-135 B 2
Loreto o BOL 70-71 E 4
Loreto o BR (MAR) 68-69 F 5
Loreto o BR (MAT) 70-71 H 2
Loreto o CO 66-67 B 4
Loreto o • I 100-101 D 3
Loreto o MEX (ZAC) 50-51 J 6
Loreto o • MEX (BCS) 50-51 D 4
Loreto o RP 160-161 F 7
Loreto, Isla ⌒ PE 66-67 B 4
Loretta o USA (WI) 270-271 H 5
Lorette o CDN (MAN) 234-235 G 5
Loretteville o CDN (QUE) 238-239 O 2
Loretto o USA (TN) 276-277 H 5
Lorian Swamp ⊂ EAK 212-213 G 3
Lorica o CO 60-61 D 3
Lorida o USA (FL) 286-287 H 4
Lorient o F 90-91 F 8
Lorillard River ∼ CDN 30-31 Y 3
Loring o USA (MT) 250-251 M 3
Loring, Port o CDN (ONT) 238-239 F 3
Lorino o RUS 112-113 Z 4
Loris o USA (SC) 284-285 M 2
Loriscota, Lago ⊂ PE 70-71 B 5
Lorlie o CDN (SAS) 232-233 P 5
Lormes o F 90-91 J 8
Lorn, Firth of ≈ 90-91 E 3
Lorna Downs o AUS 178-179 F 2
Lorne o AUS (QLD) 178-179 J 3
Lorne o AUS (VIC) 180-181 G 5
Lorne o CDN (NS) 240-241 N 5
Lorneville o CDN (NB) 240-241 J 5
Loronyo o SUD 206-207 L 6
Loropéni o BF 202-203 J 4
Loros, Los o RCH 76-77 B 4
Lörrach o D 92-93 J 5
Lorraine o AUS 174-175 E 6
Lorraine ◘ F 90-91 K 7
Lorsch o ••• D (HES) 92-93 K 4
Lort, Cabo ▲ RCH 80 C 2
Lorton o USA (NE) 262-263 K 4
Loruk o EAK 212-213 F 3
Lorukumu o EAK 212-213 E 2
Lorzot o TN 190-191 H 5
Los o S 86-87 G 6
Los, Iles de ⌒ RG 202-203 D 5
Losai National Reserve ⊥ EAK 212-213 F 3
Los Angeles o • USA (CA) 248-249 F 5
Los Angeles Aqueduct < USA (CA) 248-249 F 4
Losantville o USA (IN) 274-275 N 4
Losari o RI 168 C 3
Los Cerrillos o USA (NM) 256-257 J 3
Los Coyotes Indian Reservation ✗ USA (CA) 248-249 H 6
Loseya < EAT 212-213 F 6
Los Fresnos o USA (TX) 266-267 K 7
Los Haitises, Parque Nacional ⊥ DOM 54-55 L 5
Losier Canyon ∼ USA (TX) 266-267 F 3
Losier Settlement o CDN (NB) 240-241 L 3
Lošinj ⌒ HR 100-101 E 2
Los Mochis o MEX 50-51 E 5
Loso ∼ ZRE 210-211 G 4
Losoni o RI 164-165 H 5
Lospalos o RI 166-167 D 6
Los Pinos River ∼ USA (NM) 256-257 H 2
Los Reyes Islands ⌒ PNG 183 E 1
Lossiemouth o GB 90-91 F 3
Lossogonoi Plateau ▲ EAT 212-213 F 5
Lost Creek ∼ USA (AL) 284-285 C 3
Lost Hills o USA (CA) 248-249 D 4
Lost Maples State Natural Area ⊥ • USA (TX) 266-267 H 4

Lost River ~ USA (WV) 280-281 H 4
Lost River Range ~ USA (ID) 252-253 E 2
Lost Springs o USA (WY) 252-253 O 4
Lost Trail Pass ▲ USA (ID) 250-251 F 6
Lostwood o USA (ND) 258-259 E 3
Lostwood National Wildlife Refuge ⊥ USA (ND) 258-259 E 3
Losuia o PNG 183 F 5
Lot ~ F 90-91 H 9
Lote 15, Cerro ▲ RA 80 E 2
Lotfābād o IR 136-137 F 6
Lothair o USA (MT) 250-251 H 3
Lothal o IND 138-139 D 8
Lotikipi Plain ⌣ EAK 212-213 E 1
Loto o ZRE (KOR) 210-211 J 5
Loto ~ ZRE 210-211 J 5
Lotoi ~ ZRE 210-211 G 4
Lotsane ~ RB 218-219 D 6
Lotsohina o RM 222-223 F 5
Lott o USA (TX) 266-267 K 2
Lotta ~ RUS 88-89 K 2
Lotuke ▲ SUD 208-209 A 6
Lötzen = Giżycko o• PL 92-93 Q 1
Louangphrabang ☆ LAO 156-157 C 7
Loubetsi o RCB 210-211 D 5
Loubomo ☆ RCB 210-211 D 6
Loudéac o F 90-91 F 7
Loudi o VRC 156-157 G 3
Loudima o RCB 210-211 D 6
Loudima ~ RCB 210-211 D 6
Loudonville o USA (OH) 280-281 D 3
Loudun o F 90-91 H 8
Louéssé ~ RCB 210-211 D 5
Louétsi ~ G 210-211 C 5
Louga ☆ SN 196-197 B 7
Lougheed Island ⌒ CDN 24-25 T 2
Loughrea = Baile Locha Riach o IRL 90-91 C 5
Lougou o DY 204-205 E 3
Louhi o RUS 88-89 M 3
Louingui o RCB 210-211 E 6
Louisa o USA (KY) 276-277 N 2
Louisa Downs o AUS 172-173 H 5
Louisbourg o CDN (NS) 240-241 P 5
Louisburg o USA (KS) 262-263 M 6
Louisburg o USA (NC) 282-283 J 4
Louis Creek o CDN (BC) 230-231 J 2
Louisdale o CDN (NS) 240-241 O 5
Louise o USA (TX) 266-267 L 4
Louise, Lake o USA 20-21 R 5
Louise Island ⌒ CDN (BC) 228-229 C 4
Louiseville o CDN (QUE) 238-239 N 2
Louisiade Archipelago ⌒ PNG 183 G 6
Louisiana o USA (MO) 274-275 G 5
Louisiana ◘ USA (LA) 268-269 G 5
Lou Island ⌒ PNG 183 D 2
Louis Trichardt o ZA 218-219 E 6
Louisville o CDN (QUE) 238-239 N 2
Louisville o USA (CO) 254-255 K 4
Louisville o USA (GA) 284-285 H 3
Louisville o USA (IL) 274-275 K 6
Louisville o USA (KY) 276-277 K 2
Louisville o USA (MS) 268-269 L 3
Louisville o USA (NE) 262-263 K 4
Louisville Ridge ≃ 14-15 L 10
Louis-XIV, Pointe ▲ CDN 36-37 K 7
Loukoléla o RCB 210-211 F 4
Loukouo o RCB 210-211 E 5
Loukout Mountain ▲ USA (AL) 284-285 E 2
Loulan Gucheng ∴• VRC 146-147 J 5
Loulé o P 98-99 C 6
Loulouni o RMM 202-203 H 4
Lou Lou Park o AUS 178-179 J 2
Loum o CAM 204-205 H 6
Loumbi o SN 196-197 D 7
Loumbol, Vallée du ~ SN 202-203 D 2
Loumo, Gati- o RMM 202-203 H 2
Loumou o RCB 210-211 E 6
Loungou o RCB 210-211 D 5
Loup, Rivière-du- o CDN (QUE) 240-241 F 3
Loup City o USA (NE) 262-263 H 3
Loup River ~ USA (NE) 262-263 H 3
Loups Marins, Lacs des o CDN 36-37 M 6
Lourdes o CDN (NFL) 242-243 K 4
Lourdes o• F 90-91 G 10
Lourenço o BR 62-63 J 4
Lour-Escale o SN 202-203 C 2
Lousana o CDN (ALB) 232-233 E 3
Lousserie o RIM 196-197 E 6
Louta o BF 202-203 J 3
Louth o AUS 178-179 H 6
Louth o GB 90-91 G 5
Louth < RIM 196-197 D 6
Louti, Mayo ~ CAM 204-205 K 3
Loutrá o GR 100-101 K 6
Louvain = Leuven o•• B 92-93 H 3
Louvakou o RCB 210-211 D 5
Louvicourt o CDN (QUE) 236-237 L 4
Louviers o F 90-91 H 7
Louwsburg o ZA 220-221 K 3
Lou Yaeger, Lake o USA (IL) 274-275 J 5
Lövånger o• S 86-87 K 4
Lovcova, mys ▲ RUS 122-123 M 6
Love o CDN (SAS) 232-233 O 2
Love Beach ⊥• BS 54-55 G 2
Lovech ☆• BG 102-103 D 6
Lovelady o USA (TX) 268-269 E 5
Loveland o USA (CO) 254-255 K 3
Loveland o USA (OH) 280-281 B 4
Lovell o USA (WY) 252-253 K 2
Lovells o USA (MI) 272-273 E 3
Lovelock o USA (NV) 246-247 G 3
Løvenørn, Kap ▲ GRØ 28-29 U 4
Lóvere o I 100-101 C 2
Loverna o CDN (SAS) 232-233 J 4
Lovewell Reservoir o USA (KS) 262-263 H 5
Loviisa = Lovisa o FIN 88-89 J 6
Loving o USA (NM) 256-257 L 6
Loving o USA (TX) 264-265 F 5
Lovington o USA (IL) 274-275 K 5
Lovington o USA (NM) 256-257 M 6
Lovisa o FIN 88-89 J 6
Lovoi ~ ZRE 214-215 C 5
Lovozero o RUS (MUR) 88-89 N 2
Lovozero o RUS (MUR) 88-89 N 3
Lóvua o ANG (LUN) 216-217 F 3
Lóvua o ANG (MOX) 214-215 B 6
Lovua ~ ZRE 216-217 F 3
Lovuški, ostrova ⌒ RUS 122-123 P 4
Low o CDN (QUE) 238-239 K 3
Low, Cape ▲ CDN 36-37 G 3
Low, Lac o CDN 38-39 F 2
Lowa ~ ZRE 210-211 L 4
Lowakamistik River ~ CDN (ONT) 236-237 J 2
Lowbanks o CDN (ONT) 238-239 F 6
Low Bay ≈ 78-79 L 7
Low Cape ▲ USA 22-23 T 4
Lowe Farm o CDN (MAN) 234-235 F 5
Lowell o USA (ID) 250-251 D 5
Lowell o USA (IN) 274-275 L 3
Lowell o USA (MA) 278-279 K 6
Lowell o USA (VT) 278-279 J 4
Lowelli o SUD 208-209 A 6
Löwen ~ NAM 220-221 D 3
Lower Arrow Lake o CDN (BC) 230-231 L 4
Lower Brule o USA (SD) 260-261 G 2
Lower Brule Indian Reservation ⨯ USA (SD) 260-261 G 2
Lower Forster Lake o CDN 34-35 D 2
Lower Glenelg National Park ⊥ AUS 180-181 F 5
Lower Gwelo o ZW 218-219 E 4
Lower Hutt o NZ 182 E 4
Lower Klamath National Wildlife Refuge ⊥ USA (CA) 246-247 D 2
Lower Lake o USA (CA) 246-247 C 5
Lower Lake o USA (CA) 246-247 E 2
Lower Loteni o ZA 220-221 J 4
Lower Lough Erne o GB 90-91 D 4
Lower Matecumbe Key ⌒ USA (FL) 286-287 J 7
Lower Nicola o CDN (BC) 230-231 J 3
Lower Otay Reservoir < USA (CA) 248-249 H 7
Lower Peach Tree o USA (AL) 284-285 C 5
Lower Peninsula ⌣ USA (MI) 272-273 D 3
Lower Post o CDN 30-31 E 6
Lower Red Lake o USA (MN) 270-271 C 3
Lower Sabie o ZA 220-221 K 2
Lower Savage Islands ⌒ CDN 36-37 Q 4
Lower Ship Harbour o CDN (NS) 240-241 N 6
Lower Sioux Indian Reservation ⨯ USA (MN) 270-271 D 6
Lower Souris National Wildlife Refuge ⊥ USA (ND) 258-259 G 3
Lower Valley of the Awash ••• ETH 208-209 E 3
Lower Zambezi National Park ⊥ Z 218-219 E 2
Lowestoft o GB 90-91 H 5
Lowest Point in United States ∴• USA (CA) 248-249 H 3
Łowicz o• PL 92-93 P 2
Lowman o USA (ID) 252-253 C 2
Lowrie Channel ≈ 174-175 C 4
Low Rocky Point ▲ AUS 180-181 H 7
Lowry o USA (MN) 270-271 C 5
Lowry Indian Ruins • USA (CO) 254-255 G 6
Lowther Island ⌒ CDN 24-25 X 3
Lowty, Pico ▲ MEX 50-51 B 4
Lowville o USA (NY) 278-279 F 5
Loxahatchee National Wildlife Refuge ⊥ USA (FL) 286-287 J 5
Lò Xo, Đèo ▲ VN 158-159 J 3
Loxton o AUS 180-181 F 3
Loxton o ZA 220-221 F 5
Loya ~ ZRE 212-213 A 4
Loyada o DJI 208-209 F 3
Loyalsock Creek ~ USA (PA) 280-281 K 2
Loyalton o USA (CA) 246-247 E 4
Loyangalani o EAK 212-213 F 2
Loyauté, Îles ⌒ F 13 H 5
Loyds River ~ CDN (NFL) 242-243 L 4
Loyengo o SD 220-221 K 3
Loyoro o EAU 212-213 E 2
Loysville o USA (PA) 280-281 J 3
Loza ~ RM 222-223 E 5
Lozère, Mont ▲ F 90-91 J 9
Loznica o YU 100-101 G 2
Ložnikovo o RUS 118-119 H 10
Lozova o UA 102-103 K 3
Loz'va ~ RUS 114-115 F 5
L. P. Kochs Fjord ≈ 26-27 c 2
Lua ~ ZRE 210-211 G 2
Luabo o MOC 218-219 J 4
Luabo o ZRE 214-215 C 5
Luabu ~ ZRE 210-211 G 5
Luacano o ANG 216-217 F 5
Luachimo o ANG 216-217 F 3
Luachimo ~ ANG 216-217 F 5
Luaco o ANG 216-217 F 3
Lua-Dekere ~ ZRE 206-207 D 6
Luadi, Wamba- o ZRE 216-217 D 3
Luagungu o ZRE 212-213 A 5
Luahula ~ ZRE 214-215 B 5
Luala, Rio ~ MOC 218-219 H 3
Lualaba ~ ZRE 210-211 K 4
Luali o ZRE 210-211 D 6
Luama ~ ZRE 212-213 A 6
Luambala, Rio ~ MOC 218-219 H 1
Luambe National Park ⊥ Z 214-215 G 7
Luampa o Z 218-219 C 2
Luampa ~ Z 218-219 C 2
Luampa Kuta o Z 218-219 C 2
Lu'an o VRC 154-155 K 6
Luanchuan o VRC 154-155 G 5
Luanco (Lluanco) o E 98-99 E 3
Luancundo ~ ANG 216-217 F 8
Luanda ◘ ANG 216-217 B 4
Luanda ★• ANG (LDA) 216-217 B 4
Luanda o BR (PAR) 72-73 D 7
Luanda o BR (PER) 68-69 J 5
Luanda Norte ◘ ANG 216-217 E 4
Luanda Sul ◘ ANG 216-217 E 5
Luando o ANG (BIE) 216-217 E 5
Luando ~ ANG 216-217 D 5
Luando, Reserva Natural Integral do ⊥ ANG 216-217 D 5
Luanginga ~ Z 218-219 B 2
Luang Namtha o LAO 156-157 B 6
Luango ~ ANG 210-211 D 6
Luangue o ANG (LUN) 216-217 E 4
Luangue ~ ANG 216-217 E 4
Luanguinga ~ ANG 216-217 F 6
Luangwa o Z (Lus) 218-219 F 2
Luangwa ~ Z 214-215 F 5
Luangwa ~ Z 218-219 F 2
Luan He ~ VRC 148-149 N 7
Luanheca o ANG 216-217 D 7
Luanjing o VRC 154-155 D 3
Lua Nova o BR 66-67 D 7
Luanping o VRC 154-155 K 1
Luanshya o Z 218-219 E 1
Luan Xian o VRC 154-155 L 2
Luanza o ZRE 214-215 E 5
Luapula ◘ Z 214-215 E 6
Luapula ~ ZRE 214-215 E 6
Luar, Danau o RI 162-163 K 4
Luarca o E 98-99 D 3
Luashi o ZRE 214-215 B 6
Luashi ~ ZRE 214-215 B 6
Luassingua ~ ANG 216-217 E 7
Luatamba o ANG 216-217 F 6
Luatize, Rio ~ MOC 218-219 J 1
Luatize, Rio ~ MOC 218-219 F 2
Luau o ANG 214-215 B 6
Lua-Vindu ~ ZRE 210-211 G 2
Luba o GQ 210-211 B 2
Lubaantun ∴• BH 52-53 K 3
Lubaczów o• PL 102-103 C 2
Lubahanbajo o RI 168 D 7
Lubalo ~ ANG 216-217 E 4
Lubamba o ZRE 210-211 L 6
Lubań o PL 92-93 N 3
Lubāna ezers o LV 94-95 K 3
Lubang o RP 160-161 D 6
Lubang Island ⌒ RP 160-161 D 6
Lubango ☆ ANG 216-217 B 7
Lubansenshi ~ Z 214-215 F 6
Lubanza o ZRE 210-211 H 6
Lubao o RP 160-161 D 5
Lubao o ZRE 210-211 K 6
Lubartów o PL 92-93 R 3
Lubbock o USA (TX) 264-265 C 5
Lubbub Creek ~ USA (AL) 284-285 B 3
Lubec o USA (ME) 278-279 O 4
Lübeck o••• D 92-93 L 2
Lubefu o ZRE (KOR) 210-211 K 6
Lubefu ~ ZRE 210-211 K 6
Lubembe ~ ZRE 216-217 F 3
Lüben = Lubin o• PL 92-93 O 3
Lubero o ZRE (KIV) 212-213 B 4
Lubero ~ ZRE 212-213 B 4
Lubi ~ ZRE 214-215 B 3
Lubilandji ~ ZRE 214-215 B 4
Lubilanji ~ ZRE 214-215 B 5
Lubile o ZRE 210-211 L 5
Lubile ~ ZRE 214-215 E 4
Lubimbi o ZW 218-219 D 4
Lubin o• PL 92-93 O 3
Lubishi ~ ZRE 214-215 C 4
Lublin ☆ PL 92-93 R 3
Lubliniec o PL 92-93 P 3
Lubnān al-Ġarbiya, Ǧabal ▲ RL 128-129 F 6
Lubnān aš-Šarqiya, Ǧabal ▲ RL 128-129 F 6
Lubny o UA 102-103 H 3
Lubok Antu o MAL 162-163 J 4
Lubu ~ Z 214-215 F 6
Lubudi o ZRE (SHA) 214-215 C 5
Lubudi ~ ZRE 210-211 J 6
Lubudi ~ ZRE 214-215 C 5
Lubue ~ ZRE 210-211 G 6
Lubukalung o RI 162-163 D 5
Lubukbargalung o RI 162-163 D 5
Lubuklinggau o RI 162-163 E 6
Lubukpakan o RI 162-163 C 3
Lubuksikaping o RI 162-163 D 4
Lubule ~ ZRE 214-215 D 5
Lubumbashi ☆• ZRE 214-215 D 6
Lubundji ~ ZRE 210-211 H 6
Lubungu o Z 218-219 D 2
Lubushi o Z 214-215 F 6
Lubutu o ZRE 210-211 L 4
Lubutu ~ ZRE 210-211 L 4
Lubwe o Z 214-215 E 6
Lucala o ANG 216-217 C 4
Lucala ~ ANG 216-217 C 4
Lucan o CDN (ONT) 238-239 D 5
Lucanas o PE 64-65 E 9
Lucapa ☆ ANG 216-217 F 4
Lucas o USA (IA) 274-275 E 3
Lucas, Arroyo ~ RA 76-77 H 6
Lucas, Lake o AUS 172-173 J 6
Lucca o I 100-101 C 3
Lucea o JA 54-55 F 5
Lucedale o USA (MS) 268-269 M 6
Lučegorsk o RUS 122-123 F 5
Lucena ☆ RP 160-161 D 6
Lučenec o SK 92-93 P 4
Lucera o I 100-101 E 4
Lucerna o HN 52-53 K 4
Lucerna o PE 70-71 C 3
Lucerne o USA (CA) 246-247 C 4
Lucerne o USA (MO) 274-275 E 4
Lucerne = Luzern ☆• CH 92-93 K 5
Lucerne Valley o USA (CA) 248-249 H 5
Lucero o MEX 50-51 F 2
Lucero, Lake o USA (NM) 256-257 J 6
Luceville o CDN (QUE) 240-241 G 2
Lucheng o VRC (GXI) 156-157 E 4
Lucheng o VRC (SHA) 154-155 H 3
Luchenza o MW 218-219 H 2
Luchering, Rio ~ MOC 214-215 H 7
Luchimva, Rio ~ MOC 218-219 H 2
Luchuan o VRC 156-157 G 5
Lüchun o VRC 156-157 C 5
Lucia o USA (CA) 248-249 C 3
Lucie, Lac o CDN (ONT) 236-237 K 2
Lucien o USA (MS) 268-269 K 5
Lucierivier ~ SME 62-63 F 4
Lucile o USA (ID) 250-251 C 6
Lucin o USA (UT) 254-255 B 2
Lucindale o AUS 180-181 F 4
Lucio V. Mansilla o RA 76-77 E 5
Lucipara, Kepulauan ⌒ RI 166-167 D 4
Lucira o ANG 216-217 B 6
Luc'k o UA 102-103 D 2
Luck o USA (WI) 270-271 F 5
Luck = Luc'k o UA 102-103 D 2
Luckau o• D 92-93 M 3
Luckeesarai o IND 142-143 E 3
Luckhoff o ZA 220-221 G 4
Luck Lake o CDN (SAS) 232-233 L 4
Lucknow o AUS 178-179 F 2
Lucknow o CDN (ONT) 238-239 D 5
Lucknow ☆•• IND 142-143 B 2
Lucky o USA (LA) 268-269 H 4
Lucky Bay o AUS 180-181 D 2
Lucky Boy Pass ▲ USA (NV) 246-247 G 5
Lucky Lake o CDN (SAS) 232-233 L 5
Lucma o PE (CUZ) 64-65 F 8
Lucma o PE (LIB) 64-65 C 5
Luçon o F 90-91 G 8
Lücongpo o VRC 154-155 G 6
Lucossa o ANG 216-217 C 2
Lucre o PE 70-71 B 3
Lucrecia, Cabo ▲ C 54-55 H 4
Lucunde o ANG 216-217 C 6
Lucunga o ANG 216-217 C 3
Lucunga ~ ANG 216-217 C 3
Lucusse o ANG 216-217 F 6
Lucy, Mount ▲ AUS 178-179 B 2
Lucy Creek o AUS 178-179 D 2
Lūdāb o IR 134-135 D 3
Ludden o USA (ND) 258-259 J 5
Lude o USA (MN) 270-271 D 2
Lüderitz ☆• NAM 220-221 B 3
Lüderitzbaai ≈ 220-221 B 3
Ludhiana o IND 138-139 E 4
Ludian o VRC 156-157 C 3
Ludimbi ~ ZRE 210-211 K 6
Luding o VRC 156-157 C 2
Ludington o USA (MI) 272-273 C 4
Ludlow o USA (CA) 248-249 H 5
Ludlow o USA (CO) 254-255 L 6
Ludlow o USA (SD) 260-261 C 1
Ludlow o USA (VT) 278-279 J 5
Ludlow Rieh, Cape ▲ CDN 24-25 O 2
Ludogorie ⊥ BG 102-103 E 6
Ludowici o USA (GA) 284-285 J 5
Luduș o RO 102-103 D 4
Ludwigsburg o• D 92-93 K 4
Ludwigshafen am Rhein o D 92-93 K 4
Ludwigslust o• D 92-93 L 2
Ludza ☆•• LV 94-95 K 3
Luebo o ZRE 210-211 H 6
Luebo ~ ZRE 210-211 H 6
Lueders o USA (TX) 264-265 E 6
Lueki o ZRE 210-211 K 5
Lueki ~ ZRE 210-211 K 6
Luele ~ ANG 216-217 F 4
Luemba o ZRE 212-213 B 5
Luembe ~ ANG 216-217 F 4
Luembe ~ ZRE 214-215 C 4
Luena ☆ ANG 216-217 E 5
Luena ~ ANG 216-217 F 5
Luena o Z 214-215 F 6
Luena ~ Z 218-219 C 2
Luena o ZRE 214-215 C 5
Luena Flats ⌣ Z 218-219 B 2
Luengué o ANG (CUA) 216-217 F 8
Luengué ~ ANG 216-217 E 8
Luengué, Coutada Pública do ⊥ ANG 216-217 E 8
Luenha ~ MOC 218-219 G 3
Lueo ~ ZRE 214-215 B 6
Lueta o ZRE 214-215 B 4
Lueta ~ ZRE 214-215 B 5
Lueti ~ ANG 216-217 F 7
Lüeyang o VRC 154-155 E 5
Lufeng o VRC (GDG) 156-157 J 5
Lufeng o VRC (YUN) 156-157 C 4
Lufico o ANG 216-217 B 3
Lufige ~ ANG 216-217 F 5
Lufimi ~ ZRE 210-211 F 6
Lufira ~ ZRE 214-215 D 5
Lufira, Lac de retenue de la < ZRE 214-215 D 6
Lufkin o USA (TX) 268-269 F 5
Lufu o ZRE 210-211 D 6
Lufu ~ ZRE 210-211 D 6
Lufuba ~ Z 214-215 F 5
Lufubu o Z 214-215 E 5
Lufuige ~ ANG 214-215 B 7
Lufukwe ~ ZRE 214-215 D 5
Lufupa ~ Z 218-219 C 2
Lufupa ~ ZRE 214-215 C 6
Lufupa Rest Camp o Z 218-219 D 2
Lufwa ~ ZRE 214-215 D 5
Lufwango ~ ZRE 210-211 L 6
Luga ☆ RUS (LNG) 94-95 L 2
Luga ~ RUS 94-95 L 2
Lugait o RP 160-161 F 8
Luganga o EAT 214-215 H 4
Lugano o• CH 92-93 K 5
Lugansk = Luhans'k ☆ UA 102-103 L 3
Luganville ☆• VAN 184 II a 2
Lugard's Falls ~ EAK 212-213 G 5
Lugazi o EAU 212-213 D 3
Lugela o MOC 218-219 J 3
Lugenda ~ MOC 214-215 J 7
Luggate o NZ 182 B 6
Lugmes Ridge ≃ 166-167 D 4
Lugo o E 98-99 D 3
Lugo o I 100-101 C 2
Lugoff o USA (SC) 284-285 K 2
Lugogo ~ EAU 212-213 D 3
Lugoj o• RO 102-103 B 5
Lugovoe o KA 136-137 N 3
Lugovskij o RUS 118-119 F 6
Lugu ▲ IND 142-143 D 4
Lugu o VRC (SIC) 156-157 C 2
Lugu o VRC (XIZ) 144-145 E 4
Lugulu ~ ZRE 212-213 A 5
Luguruka o EAT 214-215 J 5
Lugus Island ⌒ RP 160-161 D 10
Luhan Shan ▲ VRC 156-157 C 3
Luhans'k ☆ UA 102-103 L 3
Luhans'ke, Stanyčno- o UA 102-103 L 3
Luhayya, al- o Y 132-133 C 6
Luhe o VRC (GDG) 156-157 J 5
Luhe o VRC (JIA) 154-155 L 5
Luhira ~ EAT 214-215 J 5
Luhit ~ IND 142-143 K 2
Luhoho ~ ZRE 212-213 B 4
Luhombero ~ EAT 214-215 J 5
Luhovicy ☆ RUS 94-95 Q 4
Luhu o RI 166-167 D 3
Luhulu ~ ZRE 212-213 B 4
Luhuo o VRC 154-155 B 6
Lui ~ ANG 216-217 D 4
Lui ~ Z 218-219 B 3
Luia o ANG 216-217 F 4
Luia ~ ANG 216-217 F 4
Luia, Rio ~ MOC 218-219 G 2
Luia, Rio ~ MOC 218-219 G 3
Luiana o ANG (CUA) 218-219 B 3
Luiana ~ ANG 218-219 B 3
Luiana, Coutada Pública do ⊥ ANG 216-217 F 8
Luidži, ostrov ⌒ RUS 84-85 d 2
Luie ~ ZRE 210-211 F 6
Luik = Liège ☆• B 92-93 H 3
Luika ~ ZRE 210-211 L 6
Luiko ~ ZRE 212-213 B 6
Luilaka ~ ZRE 210-211 H 5
Luile ~ ZRE 210-211 J 4
Luilu ~ ZRE 214-215 B 4
Luimbale o ANG 216-217 C 6
Luimneach = Limerick o IRL 90-91 C 5
Luinga o ANG 216-217 C 4
Luio ~ ANG 216-217 F 6
Luís Correia o BR 68-69 H 3
Luís Domingues o BR 68-69 F 2
Luishia o ZRE 214-215 D 6
Luis L. León, Presa < MEX 50-51 G 3
Luis Moya o MEX 50-51 H 6
Luis Tamayo o EC 64-65 B 3
Luís Viana o BR 68-69 H 6
Luiza o ZRE 214-215 B 4
Luiza ~ ZRE 214-215 B 5
Luizavo ~ ANG 214-215 B 6
Luizi ~ ZRE 214-215 D 4
Lujan o RA 76-77 E 4
Luján o RA (SLU) 78-79 G 2
Luján o• RA (BUA) 78-79 K 3
Lujan, Río ~ RA 78-79 K 3
Lujan de Cuyo o RA 78-79 E 2
Luji o VRC 154-155 J 5
Lujiang o VRC 154-155 K 6
Luka ~ ZRE 212-213 B 5
Lukachukai o USA (AZ) 256-257 F 2
Lukafu o ZRE 214-215 D 6
Lukala o ZRE 210-211 E 6
Lukashi ~ ZRE 210-211 K 6
Lukasu o ZRE 214-215 C 5
Luke, Mount ▲ AUS 176-177 D 3
Luke Air Force Range xx USA (CA) 248-249 K 7
Lukedi ~ ZRE 210-211 J 5
Lukenga o ZRE 212-213 B 6
Lukenie ~ ZRE 210-211 H 5
Lukeville o USA (AZ) 256-257 C 7
Lukimwa ~ EAT 214-215 H 6
Lukojanov o RUS 96-97 D 6
Lukolela o ZRE (BAN) 210-211 F 4
Lukolela o ZRE (KOR) 210-211 K 6
Lukolini o EAT 214-215 G 4
Lukonzolwa o ZRE 214-215 E 5
Lukosi ~ ZW 218-219 D 4
Lukoshi ~ ZRE 214-215 B 6
Lukosi ~ EAT 214-215 J 4
Lukovit o BG 102-103 D 6
Lukovnikovo o RUS 94-95 O 3
Łuków o PL 92-93 R 3
Lukpenenteng o RI 164-165 H 4
Luksagu o RI 164-165 H 4
Luktah ~ RUS 108-109 Z 5
Lukufo ~ ZRE 214-215 E 4
Lukuga ~ ZRE 212-213 B 6
Lukula o ZRE (Bas) 210-211 D 6
Lukula o ZRE (SHA) 214-215 D 4
Lukula ~ ZRE 210-211 F 6
Lukula ~ ZRE 210-211 D 6
Lukula ~ ZRE 214-215 B 4
Lukulu o Z (WES) 218-219 B 2
Lukulu ~ Z 214-215 F 7
Lukulu ~ Z 214-215 F 6
Lukulu ~ ZRE 214-215 E 4
Lukumbi ~ ZRE 214-215 E 4
Lukumburu o EAT 214-215 H 5
Lukunga Swamp ⌣ Z 218-219 D 2
Lukuni o ZRE 210-211 F 6
Lukusashi ~ Z 218-219 F 2
Lukushi ~ ZRE 214-215 D 4
Lukusuzi ~ Z 218-219 G 1
Lukusuzi National Park ⊥ Z 214-215 G 7
Lukuswa ~ ZRE 214-215 D 4
Lukuzye ~ Z 218-219 G 1
Lukwaso o IND 138-139 F 7
Lukwila, Gouffre de • ZRE 216-217 E 3
Lula o USA (MS) 268-269 K 2
Lula ~ ZRE 210-211 H 5
Luleå o• S 86-87 L 4
Luleälven ~ S 86-87 K 3
Lüleburgaz ☆ TR 128-129 B 2
Luliang o VRC 156-157 C 4
Lüliang Shan ▲ VRC 154-155 G 3
Lüliāni o PK 138-139 E 4
Lulimba o ZRE 212-213 B 6
Lulindi ~ ZRE 210-211 L 6
Luling o USA (TX) 266-267 K 4
Lulo ~ ANG 216-217 E 4
Lulonga o ZRE (EQU) 210-211 G 3
Lulonga ~ ZRE 210-211 G 3
Lulu ~ ZRE 210-211 K 3
Lulu, Emi ▲ RN 190-191 H 9
Lulua ~ ZRE 210-211 H 6
Lulung o VRC 144-145 D 5
Lulworth, Mount ▲ AUS 176-177 D 3
Luma o WAN 204-205 F 3
Luma Cassai o ANG 216-217 E 5
Lumaco o RCH 78-79 C 5
Lumajang o RI 168 E 4
Lumajangdong Co o VRC 144-145 C 3
Lumana o ZRE 210-211 L 5
Lumangwe Falls ~ Z 214-215 E 5
Lūmār o IR 134-135 B 2
Lumata o Z 214-215 D 7
Lumba o ZRE 206-207 D 6
Lumbala o ANG 214-215 B 7
Lumbala ~ ANG 216-217 F 6
Lumbala N'guimbo o ANG 216-217 F 7
Lumbe ~ Z 218-219 B 3
Lumber City o USA (GA) 284-285 H 5
Lumbermen's Monument • USA (MI) 272-273 F 3
Lumber River ~ USA (NC) 282-283 H 6
Lumberton o CDN (BC) 230-231 O 4
Lumberton o USA (MS) 268-269 L 5
Lumberton o USA (NC) 282-283 H 6
Lumberton o USA (TX) 268-269 F 6
Lumbo o MOC 218-219 L 2
Lumbovskij zaliv ≈ 88-89 Q 3
Lumbrera o RA 76-77 E 3
Lumby o CDN (BC) 230-231 L 3
Lumding o IND 142-143 H 3
Lumege ~ ANG 216-217 F 5
Lumeje o ANG 216-217 F 5
Lumene ~ ZRE 210-211 F 6
Lumeta o ANG 216-217 F 8
Lumholtz National Park ⊥ AUS 174-175 H 6
Lumi o PNG 183 B 2
Lumimba o Z 214-215 G 7
Luminárias o BR 72-73 H 6
Lumoli o RI 166-167 E 3
Lumpkin o USA (GA) 284-285 F 4
Lumpur ~ RI 162-163 F 6
Lumsden o CDN (NFL) 242-243 P 3
Lumsden o CDN (SAS) 232-233 O 5
Lumsden o NZ 182 B 6
Lumuna ~ ANG 216-217 F 8
Lumut o BRU 164-165 D 1
Lumut, Gunung ▲ RI (KTI) 164-165 E 4
Lumut, Gunung ▲ RI (SLT) 164-165 G 4
Lumut, Tanjung ▲ RI 162-163 F 6
Lumwana o Z 214-215 C 6
Lun o MAU 148-149 G 4
Luna o USA (NM) 256-257 G 5
Luna, Laguna de o RA 76-77 J 5
Luna, Rio ~ BR 66-67 G 5
Lunahuana o PE 64-65 D 8
Lunan o VRC 156-157 C 4
Lunan Lake o CDN 30-31 X 3
Lunan Shilin • VRC 156-157 C 4
Lunar Crater • USA (NV) 246-247 J 5
Lunas, Los o USA (NM) 256-257 J 4
Lūnāvāda o IND 138-139 D 8
Lunca o RO 102-103 D 6
Lund o CDN (BC) 230-231 E 4
Lund o•• S 86-87 F 9
Lund o USA (NV) 246-247 K 5
Lund o USA (NV) 246-247 L 5
Lund o USA (UT) 254-255 B 5
Lunda, Kasongo- o ZRE 216-217 D 3
Lundamilumba o EAT (RUK) 214-215 F 4
Lundar o CDN (MAN) 234-235 E 4
Lundazi o Z 214-215 G 7
Lundazi ~ Z 214-215 G 7
Lundbreck o CDN (ALB) 232-233 D 6
Lundu o MAL 162-163 H 4
Lundu o Z 214-215 G 6
Lüneburg o• D 92-93 L 2
Lüneburger Heide ⊥ D 92-93 K 2
Lunenburg o CDN (NS) 240-241 L 6
Lunéville o• F 90-91 L 7
Lunga o MOC 218-219 L 2
Lunga ~ SOL 184 I d 3
Lunga ~ Z 218-219 D 2
Lunga Lunga o EAK 212-213 G 6
Lungar Shan ▲ VRC 144-145 D 5
Lunge o ANG 216-217 D 6
Lung"egan ~ RUS 114-115 P 4
Lunggar o VRC 144-145 D 5
Lungha ~ RUS 118-119 N 4
Lungharigi o VAN 184 II a 1
Lungi o WAL 202-203 D 5
Lunglei o IND 142-143 H 4
Lungué-Bungo ~ ANG 216-217 E 6
Lunguto o RI 164-165 G 3
Lungwebungu ~ Z 218-219 B 1
Luni ~ IND 138-139 D 7
Lunin o BY 94-95 K 5
Lunínec o BY 94-95 K 5
Luning o USA (NV) 246-247 G 5
Lūnkaransa o IND 138-139 D 5
Lunnyj o RUS 112-113 H 5
Lunsar o WAL 202-203 D 5
Lunsemfwa ~ Z 218-219 E 2
Lun'skij, zaliv ≈ RUS 122-123 K 3
Luntai o VRC 146-147 G 5
Lunyere ~ EAT 214-215 H 6
Lunyuk o RI 168 C 7
Lunzi ~ Z 214-215 G 6
Luo o RI 164-165 G 4
Luo, Rio ~ MOC 218-219 J 3
Luobei o VRC 150-151 H 4
Luobuzhuang o VRC 146-147 J 6
Luochuan o VRC 154-155 F 4
Luodian o VRC 156-157 E 4
Luoding o VRC 156-157 G 5
Luofushan • VRC 156-157 H 5
Luohe o VRC 154-155 J 5
Luo He ~ VRC 154-155 G 4
Luojishan • VRC 156-157 C 3
Luonan o VRC 154-155 G 4
Luongo ~ Z 214-215 E 6
Luoning o VRC 154-155 G 4
Luoping o VRC 156-157 D 4
Luoshan o VRC 154-155 J 5
Luotian o VRC 154-155 J 6
Luotuoquanzi o VRC 146-147 M 4
Luoxiao Shan ▲ VRC 156-157 H 3
Luoxu o VRC 156-157 F 5
Luoyang o• VRC 154-155 H 4
Luoyuan o VRC 156-157 L 3
Luozi o ZRE 210-211 E 6
Lupa ~ EAT 214-215 G 5
Lupa Market o EAT 214-215 G 5
Lupande ~ Z 218-219 F 1
Lupane o ZW 218-219 D 4
Lupar ~ MAL 162-163 J 4
Luperón o DOM 54-55 K 5
Lupiliche o MOC 214-215 H 6
Lupiro o EAT 214-215 J 5
Lupton Channel ≈ 36-37 R 3
Lupuka o Z 218-219 B 3
Lupula o ANG 216-217 D 7
Luputa o ZRE 214-215 B 4
Lupweji ~ ZRE 214-215 C 5
Luqu o VRC 154-155 C 4
Luque o PY 76-77 J 3
Luquembo o ANG 216-217 D 5
Luquillo o USA (PR) 286-287 Q 2
Lurahgung o RI 168 C 3
Luray o USA (KS) 262-263 H 5
Luray o USA (VA) 280-281 H 5
Lureco, Rio ~ MOC 218-219 J 1
Lurgan o• GB 90-91 D 4
Luribay o BOL 70-71 D 5
Lurín, Río ~ PE 64-65 D 8
Lúrio o MOC 218-219 L 1
Lúrio ~ MOC 218-219 J 2
Lurton o USA (AR) 276-277 B 5
Luruaco o CO 60-61 D 2
Lusahunga o EAT (KAG) 212-213 C 5
Lusaka ◘ Z 218-219 E 2
Lusaka ★• Z 218-219 E 2
Lusaka o ZRE 214-215 C 4
Lusako o ZRE 212-213 A 6
Lusamba o ZRE 210-211 K 6
Lusambo o ZRE 210-211 J 6
Lusancay Islands ⌒ PNG 183 F 5
Lusanga o ZRE 210-211 G 6
Lusangi o ZRE 212-213 A 6
Luscar o CDN (ALB) 228-229 R 3
Luseland o CDN (SAS) 232-233 J 3
Lusemfwa ~ Z 218-219 E 2
Lusemfwa Falls ~ Z 218-219 E 2
Lusenga Plain National Park ⊥ Z 214-215 E 5
Lushan o VRC (HEN) 154-155 H 5
Lushan ▲ VRC (SHD) 154-155 L 3
Lushan • VRC (JXI) 156-157 J 2
Lushi o VRC 154-155 G 4
Lushipuka ~ ZRE 214-215 E 6
Lushnjë ☆• AL 100-101 G 4
Lushoto o EAT 212-213 G 6
Lushui o VRC (YUN) 142-143 L 3
Lushui • VRC (HUB) 156-157 H 2
Lüshun o VRC 150-151 C 8
Lusibi o Z 218-219 C 3
Lusikisiki o ZA 220-221 J 5
Lusinga o ZRE 214-215 D 5
Lusitania o CO 60-61 D 6
Lusitu o EAT (IRI) 214-215 H 5
Lusk o USA (TN) 276-277 K 5
Lusk o USA (WY) 252-253 O 4
Lussanhando, Rio ~ MOC 218-219 J 1
Lussenga o ANG 216-217 B 3
Lussusso o ANG 216-217 C 5
Lustre o USA (MT) 250-251 O 3
Lusutfu ~ MOC 220-221 L 3
Luswaka o ZRE 214-215 D 5
Lūt, Dašt-e ⊥ IR 134-135 G 2
Lutao ⌒ RC 156-157 M 5
Lutcher o USA (LA) 268-269 K 6
Lutembo o ANG 216-217 F 6
Luth o SUD 206-207 K 5
Luther o USA (OK) 264-265 G 3
Luther Pass ▲ USA (CA) 246-247 F 5
Luthersburg o USA (PA) 280-281 H 2
Lutherstadt Wittenberg o• D 92-93 M 3
Luti o SOL 184 I c 2
Luti, River ~ WAN 204-205 K 4
Lutiba o ZRE 212-213 B 4
Lutie o USA (TX) 264-265 D 3
Lutlut o MYA 158-159 E 4
Luton o GB 90-91 G 6
Lutong o MAL 164-165 D 1
Lutope ~ ZW 218-219 E 4
Lutsen o USA (MN) 270-271 H 3
Lutshima o ZRE 210-211 G 6
Lutshima ~ ZRE 216-217 E 3
Lutshuadi ~ ZRE 210-211 H 6
Luts'k = Luc'k o UA 102-103 D 2
Lüttich = Liège ☆• B 92-93 H 3
Lutuai o ANG 216-217 F 6
Lutuhyne o UA 102-103 L 3
Lutunguru o ZRE 212-213 B 4
Lützow-Holm bukt ≈ 16 G 4
Lutzputs o ZA 220-221 E 4
Lutzville o ZA 220-221 D 5
Luuq o SP 212-213 J 2
Luveira ~ ZRE 214-215 C 6
Luverne o USA (AL) 284-285 D 5
Luverne o USA (MN) 270-271 B 7
Luvidjo ~ ZRE 214-215 D 4
Luvilombo ~ ZRE 214-215 D 5
Luvo o ANG 216-217 C 2
Luvua ~ ANG 214-215 B 6
Luvua ~ ZRE 214-215 E 4
Luvuei o ANG 216-217 F 6
Luvunzo ~ ZRE 214-215 E 4
Luwawa o MW 214-215 G 7
Luwe ~ ZRE 214-215 D 5
Luwego ~ EAT 214-215 J 6
Luwegu ~ EAT 214-215 J 5
Luwembe o Z 218-219 F 2
Luwingu o Z 214-215 E 6
Luwishi ~ Z 218-219 D 1
Luwombwa ~ Z 218-219 E 1
Luwuk o RI 164-165 H 4
Luwumbu ~ Z 214-215 G 6
Luxapallila Creek ~ USA (AL) 284-285 B 3
Luxembourg ■ L 92-93 J 4
Luxembourg ★••• L 92-93 J 4
Luxemburg o USA (IA) 274-275 G 2
Luxemburg o USA (WI) 270-271 L 6
Luxi o VRC (HUN) 156-157 F 2
Luxi o VRC (YUN) 142-143 L 3
Luxi o VRC (YUN) 156-157 C 4
Luxor = al-Uqsur o•• ET 194-195 F 5
Luxor = Uqsur, al- o•• ET 194-195 F 5
Luxora o USA (AR) 276-277 F 5
Luyamba o ZRE 210-211 L 5
Luyando o PE 64-65 E 6
Luz o BR 72-73 H 5
Luza o RUS (KIR) 96-97 E 3
Luza ~ RUS 96-97 E 3
Luza ~ RUS 96-97 F 4
Luzern ☆• CH 92-93 K 5
Luzhai o VRC 156-157 F 4

Luzhi o VRC 156-157 D 3
Luzhou o VRC 156-157 D 2
Luzi o ANG 216-217 F 6
Luzi o ZRE 210-211 G 6
Luziania o BR 72-73 G 4
Lužica o RUS 94-95 L 2
Luzilândia o BR 68-69 G 3
Lužina, proliv ⊂ RUS 122-123 Q 3
Luziwazi ∼ Z 218-219 F 1
Lužnice ∼ CZ 92-93 N 4
Luzon ⌒ RP 160-161 D 5
Luzon Sea ≈ 160-161 C 5
Luzon Strait ≈ 156-157 M 6
Luzy o F 90-91 J 8
L'vin = L'viv ☆• UA 102-103 D 3
L'viv ☆• UA 102-103 D 3
L'vov = L'viv ☆• UA 102-103 D 3
Lwakhaka o EAK 212-213 E 3
Lwela o Z (LUP) 214-215 E 6
Lwela ∼ Z 214-215 E 6
Lyallpur = Faisalābād o PK 138-139 D 4
Lyantonde o EAU 212-213 C 4
Lybangajaha, Igarka- ∼ RUS 108-109 R 7
Lycan o USA (CO) 254-255 N 6
Lyck = Ełk o PL 92-93 R 2
Lycksele o S 86-87 J 4
Lyddal o CDN 34-35 G 3
Lydenburg o ZA 220-221 K 2
Lydia o USA (KS) 262-263 E 6
Lyeffion o USA (AL) 284-285 D 5
Lyell, Mount ▲ AUS 172-173 G 3
Lyell Brown Bluff ▲ AUS 176-177 G 3
Lyell Icefield ⊂ CDN (BC) 230-231 M 2
Lyell Island ⌒ CDN (BC) 228-229 C 4
Lyell Land ⊥ GRØ 26-27 n 7
Lyford o USA (TX) 266-267 K 7
Lyhn ∼ RUS 114-115 J 3
Ly Hòa ☆ VN 158-159 J 2
Lykso o ZA 220-221 G 3
Lyle o USA (WA) 244-245 D 5
Lyles o USA (TN) 276-277 H 5
Lyleton o CDN (MAN) 234-235 B 5
Lyman o USA (MS) 268-269 L 6
Lymbel'ka ∼ RUS 114-115 R 4
Lyme Bay ≈ 90-91 F 6
Lymva ∼ RUS 88-89 W 5
Lynch o USA (NE) 262-263 H 2
Lynchburg o USA (TN) 276-277 J 5
Lynchburg o USA (VA) 280-281 G 6
Lynches River ∼ USA (SC) 284-285 K 2
Lynden o USA (WA) 244-245 C 2
Lyndhurst o AUS (QLD) 174-175 H 6
Lyndhurst o AUS (SA) 178-179 E 6
Lynd Junction, The o AUS 174-175 H 6
Lyndon o AUS 176-177 C 1
Lyndon o USA (KS) 262-263 L 6
Lyndon B. Johnson, Lake < USA (TX) 266-267 J 3
Lyndon River ∼ AUS 176-177 C 1
Lyndonville o USA (NY) 278-279 C 5
Lyndonville o USA (VT) 278-279 K 4
Lynd River ∼ AUS 174-175 G 5
Lynedock Bank ≃ 166-167 F 7
Lyness o GB 90-91 F 2
Lyngatgyrgovaam ∼ RUS 112-113 W 3
Lyngdal o N 86-87 D 7
Lyngen ≈• 86-87 K 2
Lyngseidet o N 86-87 K 2
Lynher Reef ⌒ AUS 172-173 E 3
Lynn o USA (IN) 274-275 O 4
Lynn o USA (MA) 278-279 L 6
Lynn o USA (UT) 254-255 B 2
Lynn, Mount ▲ USA (CA) 246-247 C 3
Lynnaj, gora ▲ RUS 112-113 M 5
Lynn Canal ≈ 32-33 C 2
Lynndyl o USA (UT) 254-255 C 4
Lynn Haven o USA (FL) 286-287 D 1
Lynn Lake o CDN 34-35 F 2
Lynns Ø ⌒ GRØ 26-27 q 3
Lynnwood o USA (WA) 244-245 C 3
Lynton o AUS 176-177 C 4
Lynx Lake ⊂ CDN 30-31 Q 4
Lyobahika o EAT (KAG) 212-213 C 5
Lyon, Cape ▲ CDN 24-25 K 6
Lyon Inlet ≈ 24-25 e 7
Lyons o USA (CO) 254-255 K 3
Lyons o USA (GA) 284-285 H 4
Lyons o USA (KS) 262-263 H 6
Lyons o USA (TX) 266-267 L 3
Lyons Falls o USA (NY) 278-279 F 5
Lyons River ∼ AUS 176-177 C 2
Lyons River ∼ AUS 176-177 D 2
Lyons River North ∼ AUS 176-177 D 2
Lypci o UA 102-103 K 2
Lyra Reef ⌒ PNG 183 G 1
Lysaja, gora ▲ RUS 116-117 F 6
Lysekil ☆ S 86-87 E 7
Lysite o USA (WY) 252-253 L 3
Lyskovo o RUS 96-97 D 5
Lysova, ostrov ⌒ RUS 112-113 L 1
Lys'va ☆ RUS 96-97 K 4
Lysyčans'k o UA 102-103 L 3
Lysychans'k = Lysyčans'k o UA 102-103 L 3
Lysye Gory o RUS 96-97 D 8
Lytle o USA (TX) 266-267 J 4
Lyttelton o NZ 182 D 5
Lytton o CDN (BC) 230-231 H 3
Lyža ∼ RUS 88-89 Y 4
Lyža, Ust'- o RUS 88-89 Y 4

M

Ma o CAM 204-205 J 5
Maadid, Djebel ▲ DZ 190-191 E 3
Maalaea o USA (HI) 288 J 4
Maalamba o MOC 218-219 G 6
Maamba o Z 218-219 D 3
Ma'an o CAM 210-211 C 2
Ma'ān ☆ JOR 130-131 D 2
Maana'oba = Ngwalulu ⌒ SOL 184 I e 3
Maaninkavaara o FIN 88-89 K 3
Ma'āniya, al- o IRQ 130-131 H 2
Maanselkä ⊥ FIN 88-89 K 3
Ma'anshan o VRC 154-155 L 6
Maan't o MAU (BUL) 148-149 F 3
Maan't o MAU (TÖV) 148-149 H 4
Maardu o EST 94-95 J 2
Maarianhamina = Mariehamn ☆ FIN 88-89 E 6
Maarmorilik o GRØ 26-27 Z 8
Ma'arrat an-Nu'mān o• SYR 128-129 G 5
Maas ∼ NL 92-93 J 3
Maasim o RP 160-161 F 10
Maasin ☆ RP 160-161 F 7
Maasstroom o ZA 218-219 E 6
Maastricht ☆•• NL 92-93 H 3
Maasupa o SOL 184 I e 3
Maatsuyker Group ⌒ AUS 180-181 J 7
Maba o RI 164-165 L 3
Mababe Depression ⊥ RB 218-219 C 4
Ma'bad o IR 136-137 D 7
Mabaduam o PNG 183 A 4
Mabaia o ANG 216-217 C 3
Mabana o ZRE 212-213 B 3
Mabanda o BU 212-213 B 6
Mabanda o G 210-211 C 5
Mabanda, Mont ▲ G 210-211 C 5
Mabank o USA (TX) 264-265 H 6
Ma'bar o Y 132-133 D 6
Mabé ∼ CAM 204-205 J 5
Mabein o MYA 142-143 K 4
Mabel o USA (MN) 270-271 G 7
Mabel Creek o AUS 178-179 C 5
Mabel Downs o AUS 172-173 J 4
Mabélé o CAM 204-205 K 5
Mabeleapudi o RB 218-219 D 6
Mabel Lake o CDN (BC) 230-231 L 3
Mabel Lake ⊂ CDN (BC) 230-231 L 3
Mabelle o USA (TX) 264-265 E 5
Mabel Range ▲ AUS 178-179 C 4
Mabenge o ZRE 206-207 G 6
Mabest, Lake ⊂ WAL 202-203 E 6
Mabeta o CAM 210-211 B 2
Mabitac o RP 160-161 D 5
Mabo o SN 202-203 C 3
Mabole ∼ WAL 202-203 D 5
Mabopane o ZA 220-221 J 2
Mabote o MOC 218-219 H 6
Mabou o CDN (NS) 240-241 O 4
Mabraz, al- o Y 132-133 C 6
Mabrouk < RMM 196-197 K 5
Mabrous o RN 198-199 F 2
Mabrūk < LAR 192-193 G 2
Mabton o USA (WA) 244-245 F 4
Mabu, Monte ▲ MOC 218-219 J 3
Mabuasehube Game Reserve ⊥ RB 220-221 E 2
Mabuiag Island ⌒ AUS 174-175 G 1
Mabuki o EAT 212-213 D 5
Mabula o ZA 220-221 J 2
Mabur ≈ 166-167 K 5
Mabura o GUY 62-63 E 3
Mabuto o WAN 204-205 F 3
Maća o RUS 118-119 H 6
Macá, Monte ▲ RCH 80 D 2
Macabi, Isla de ⌒ PE 64-65 C 5
Maçacara o BR 68-69 J 7
Macachin o RA 78-79 H 4
Macaco, Cachoeira do ∼ BR 68-69 E 6
Macacos, Ilha dos ⌒ BR 62-63 J 6
Macaé o BR 72-73 K 7
Macaene o MOC 220-221 L 2
Mačah o RUS 110-111 T 6
Macaíba o BR 68-69 L 4
Macajalar Bay ≈ 160-161 F 8
Macajuba o BR 72-73 K 2
Macalister o AUS 174-175 F 6
MacAlpine Lake ⊂ CDN 30-31 S 2
Maçambará o BR 76-77 J 5
Macamic o CDN (QUE) 236-237 J 4
Macan, Kepulauan ⌒ RI 168 E 6
Macanao = Boca de Pozo o YV 60-61 J 2
Macandze o MOC 218-219 G 6
Maçangana, Rio ∼ BR 66-67 F 7
Macanillal o YV 60-61 G 4
Macao ◘ P 156-157 H 5
Macao = Aomen ☆•• P 156-157 H 5
Macao, El o DOM 54-55 L 5
Macapá ☆ BR 62-63 J 5
Maçaparana o BR 68-69 L 5
Macapillo o RA 76-77 F 3
Macará o EC 64-65 C 4
Macaracas o PA 52-53 D 8
Maçaranduba, Cachoeira ∼ BR 62-63 H 6
Macarani o BR 72-73 K 3
Macarena, La o CO 60-61 E 6
Macarena, Parque Nacional La ⊥ CO 60-61 E 6
Macarena, Serranía de la ▲ CO 60-61 E 6
Macareo, Caño ∼ YV 60-61 L 3
Macari o PE 70-71 B 4
Maçarico, Cachoeira ∼ BR 66-67 D 7
Macaroni o AUS 174-175 F 5
Macarretane o MOC 220-221 L 2
Macarthur o AUS 180-181 G 5
Macas o EC 64-65 C 3
Macatanja o MOC 218-219 J 3
Macaú o BR 68-69 K 4
Macau = Macao ☆•• P 156-157 H 5
Macauã, Rio ∼ BR 70-71 C 2
Macauari o BR 62-63 E 6
Macaúbas o BR 72-73 J 2
Macaza, Rivière ∼ CDN (QUE) 238-239 L 2
Macbar, Raas ▲ SP 208-209 K 4
Maccles Lake ⊂ CDN (NFL) 242-243 O 4
Mac Cluer Gulf = Teluk Berau ≈ 166-167 G 3
Macculloch, Cape ▲ CDN 24-25 j 4
Mac Cullochs Range ▲ AUS 178-179 G 6
Macdiarmid o CDN (ONT) 234-235 P 5
MacDonald o CDN (MAN) 234-235 E 4
MacDonald, Lake ⊂ AUS 176-177 K 1
Macdonald, Mount ▲ VAN 184 II b 3
Mac Donald Downs o AUS 178-179 C 2
MacDonald Island ⌒ CDN 36-37 N 3
Mac Donnell, Port o AUS 180-181 F 5
Macdonnell Peninsula ⌣ AUS 180-181 E 3
Macdonnell Ranges ▲ AUS 176-177 M 1
Macdougall Lake ⊂ CDN 30-31 U 2
MacDowall o CDN (SAS) 232-233 N 2
MacDowell Lake ⊂ CDN (ONT) 234-235 L 2
Macedo de Cavaleiros o P 98-99 D 4
Macedonia = Makedonija ■ MK 100-101 H 4
Maceió ☆ BR 68-69 L 6
Macenta o RG 202-203 F 5
Macerata ☆ I 100-101 D 3
Mačevna, buhta ⊂ RUS 112-113 Q 6
Macfarlane, Lake ⊂ AUS 178-179 D 6
Macgillycuddy's Reeks ▲ IRL 90-91 C 6
MacGregor o CDN (MAN) 234-235 E 5
MacGregor o USA (TX) 266-267 K 2
Mach o PK 134-135 M 4
Machacamarca o BOL 70-71 D 6
Machachi o EC 64-65 C 2
Machadinho o BR 66-67 F 7
Machadinho, Rio ∼ BR 66-67 F 7
Machadinho, Rio ∼ BR 66-67 G 7
Machado o BR 72-73 H 6
Machado, Rio ∼ BR 70-71 G 2
Machadodorp o ZA 220-221 K 2
Machado ou Ji-Paraná, Rio ∼ BR 66-67 F 7
Machagai o RA 76-77 G 4
Machaila o MOC 218-219 G 6
Machakos o EAK 212-213 F 4
Machala ☆ EC 64-65 C 3
Machalilla, Parque Nacional ⊥ EC 64-65 B 2
Machaneng o RB 218-219 D 6
Machang o MAL 162-163 E 2
Machang o VRC 156-157 E 3
Machanga o MOC 218-219 H 5
Machaquilá ∴• GCA 52-53 K 3
Machaquilá, Río ∼ GCA 52-53 K 3
Machatti, Lake ⊂ AUS 178-179 E 3
Machawaian Lake ⊂ CDN (ONT) 234-235 P 3
Machecoul o F 90-91 G 8
Macheke o ZW 218-219 F 4
Machemma Ruins ∴• ZA 218-219 E 6
Macheng o VRC 154-155 J 6
Mācherla o IND 140-141 H 2
Machesse o MOC 218-219 H 4
Machhlishahr o IND 142-143 C 3
Machias o USA (ME) 278-279 O 4
Machias River ∼ USA (ME) 278-279 O 4
Machichaco, Cabo ▲ E 98-99 F 3
Machichi River ∼ CDN 34-35 L 2
Machile ∼ Z 218-219 C 3
Machilipatnam o IND 140-141 J 2
Machina o WAN 198-199 E 6
Machinga o MW 218-219 H 2
Machiques o YV 60-61 E 2
Machmell River ∼ CDN (BC) 230-231 C 2
Macho, Cerro del ∼ USA (NM) 256-257 L 5
Macho, El o C 54-55 G 5
Machu Picchu ••• PE 64-65 F 8
Machupo, Río ∼ BOL 70-71 E 3
Macia o MOC 220-221 L 2
Maciel o PY 76-77 J 4
Măcin o RO 102-103 F 5
Macintyre River ∼ AUS 178-179 K 5
Mack o USA (CO) 254-255 G 4
Maçka ☆ TR 128-129 H 2
Mackay o AUS 178-179 K 1
MacKay o CDN (ALB) 232-233 C 2
Mackay o USA (ID) 252-253 E 3
Mackay, Lake ⊂ AUS 172-173 J 7
Mackay Island National Wildlife Refuge ⊥ USA (NC) 282-283 M 4
MacKay Lake ⊂ CDN 30-31 O 4
Mackay River ∼ CDN 32-33 O 3
Mackenzie o CDN 32-33 J 4
Mackenzie o GUY 62-63 E 2
Mackenzie, Kap ▲ GRØ 26-27 p 7
Mackenzie Bay ≈ 20-21 W 2
Mackenzie Bison Sanctvary • CDN 30-31 L 5
Mackenzie Delta ⊥•• CDN 20-21 X 2
Mackenzie Highway II CDN (ALB) 32-33 M 3
Mackenzie Highway II CDN (NWT) 30-31 H 4
Mackenzie King Island ⌒ CDN 24-25 P 2
Mackenzie Mountains ▲ CDN 30-31 C 3
Mackenzie River ∼ AUS 178-179 K 2
Mackenzie River ∼ CDN 30-31 K 5
Mackinac Bridge II• USA (MI) 272-273 E 2
Mackinac Island ⌒ USA (MI) 272-273 E 2
Mackinac Island State Park • USA (MI) 272-273 E 2
Mackinaw o USA (IL) 274-275 J 4
Mackinaw City o USA (MI) 272-273 E 2
Mackinaw River ∼ USA (IL) 274-275 J 4
Mackinaw River ∼ USA (IL) 274-275 K 4
Mackinnon Road o EAK 212-213 G 5
Mackeys o USA (NC) 282-283 L 5
Macklin o CDN (SAS) 232-233 J 3
Macksburg o USA (IA) 274-275 D 3
Macks Inn o USA (ID) 252-253 G 2
Macksville o AUS 178-179 M 6
Maclaren River ∼ USA 20-21 R 5
Maclean o AUS 178-179 M 5
Maclean Strait ≈ 24-25 T 2
Macleantown o ZA 220-221 H 6
Maclear o ZA 220-221 J 5
Maclear, Cape ▲•• MW 218-219 H 1
Macleay River ∼ AUS 178-179 M 6
Macleod, Fort o CDN (ALB) 232-233 E 6
MacLeod, Lake ⊂ AUS 176-177 B 2
Macmillan Pass ▲ CDN 30-31 E 4
Macmillan Plateau ▲ CDN 20-21 Y 5
Macmillan River ∼ CDN 20-21 X 5
MacNutt o CDN (SAS) 232-233 R 4
Maco o RP 160-161 F 9
Maco, Cerro ▲ CO 60-61 D 3
Maçobere o MOC 218-219 G 5
Macocha ▲ CZ 92-93 O 4
Macocola o ANG 216-217 D 3
Macolla, La o YV 60-61 F 1
Macomb o USA (IL) 274-275 H 4
Macomber o USA (WV) 280-281 G 4
Macomér o I 100-101 B 4
Macomia o MOC 214-215 L 7
Mâcon ☆• F 90-91 K 8
Macon o USA (GA) 284-285 G 4
Macon o USA (MO) 274-275 F 5
Macon o USA (MS) 268-269 M 3
Macon o USA (OH) 280-281 C 5
Macondo o ANG 214-215 B 7
Macondo ∼ ANG 218-219 B 1
Macoppe o RI 164-165 G 6
Macossa o MOC 218-219 G 3
Macoun o CDN (SAS) 232-233 P 6
Macoun Lake ⊂ CDN 34-35 E 2
Macoupin River ∼ USA (IL) 274-275 H 5
Macouria = Tonate o F 62-63 H 3
Macovane o MOC 218-219 H 5
Macoya o BOL 70-71 C 6
Macpès o CDN (QUE) 240-241 G 2
Macquarie, Lake ⊂ AUS 180-181 L 2
Macquarie Harbour ≈ 180-181 H 7
Macquarie Ridge ≃ 14-15 H 13
Macquarie River ∼ AUS 178-179 J 6
MacQuoid Lake ⊂ CDN 30-31 W 4
Macroom = Maigh Chromtha o IRL 90-91 C 6
Macrorie o CDN (SAS) 232-233 L 4
Mac's Corner o USA (SD) 260-261 G 2
Mactan Island ⌒ RP 160-161 E 7
Macucocha, Lago ⊂ PE 64-65 F 9
Macuma o EC 64-65 D 3
Macumba River ∼ AUS 178-179 D 4
Macuna, Raudal ∼ CO 66-67 B 3
Macururé o BR 68-69 J 6
Macururé, Rio ∼ BR 68-69 J 6
Macusani o PE 70-71 B 4
Macuto o YV 60-61 H 2
Macúzari, Presa ⊂ MEX 50-51 E 4
Macuze o MOC 218-219 J 3
Macwahoc o USA (ME) 278-279 N 3
Mada, River ∼ WAN 204-205 H 4
Madabazouma o RCA 206-207 F 6
Madadeni o ZA 220-221 K 3
Madagascar, Arrecife ⌒ MEX 52-53 J 1
Madagascar = Madagasikara ■ RM 222-223 E 8
Madagascar = Madagasikara ⌒ RM 222-223 E 8
Madagascar Basin ≃ 12 D 7
Madagascar Ridge ≃ RM 9 H 9
Madagli o WAN 204-205 K 3
Madagoi ∼ SP 212-213 J 3
Ma Đa Gui o VN 158-159 J 5
Mada'in Salih •• KSA 130-131 E 4
Madakasira o IND 140-141 G 4
Madalena o BR 68-69 J 4
Madama o RN 198-199 F 2
Madamba o RP 160-161 F 9
Madana o TCH 206-207 C 4
Madanapalle o IND 140-141 H 4
Madang ☆• PNG 183 C 3
Madanganj o BD 142-143 G 4
Madaniqa, al- o KSA 132-133 C 5
Madaoua o RN 198-199 B 5
Madara o••• BG 102-103 E 6
Madara Canal < USA (CA) 248-249 E 2
Madarounfa o RN 198-199 C 6
Madau o TM 136-137 D 5
Madau Island ⌒ PNG 183 G 5
Madaun o RUS 120-121 O 3
Madavaram o IND 140-141 J 2
Madawaska o CDN (ONT) 238-239 G 3
Madawaska o USA (ME) 278-279 N 1
Madawaska River ∼ CDN (ONT) 238-239 H 3
Madaya o MYA 142-143 K 4
Madbar o SUD 206-207 K 5
Maddalena, Ísola ⌒ I 100-101 B 4
Maddalena, la o I 100-101 B 4
Madden o CDN (ALB) 232-233 D 4
Maddock o USA (ND) 258-259 H 4
Maddūr o IND 140-141 G 4
Madeir o SUD 206-207 J 5
Madeira ⌒ P 188-189 C 4
Madeira o USA (OH) 280-281 B 4
Madeira, Arquipélago da ⌒ P 188-189 C 4
Madeira, Rio ∼ BOL 70-71 E 2
Madeira, Rio ∼ BR 66-67 H 5
Madeira Park o CDN (BC) 230-231 F 4
Madeira Rise ≃ 6-7 H 5
Madeirinha, Rio ∼ BR 66-67 G 7
Madelaine, Îles de la ⌒ CDN (QUE) 242-243 G 5
Madeleine, Cap-de-la- o CDN (QUE) 238-239 N 2
Madeleine-Centre o CDN (QUE) 242-243 C 3
Madelia o USA (MN) 270-271 D 6
Madeline o USA (CA) 246-247 E 2
Madeline Island ⌒ USA (WI) 270-271 H 4
Maden ☆ TR 128-129 H 3
Madera o MEX 50-51 E 3
Madera o USA (CA) 248-249 D 3
Madera, La o YV 60-61 K 3
Madero o SP 212-213 H 4
Mādhavaram o IND 140-141 G 3
Madhira o IND 140-141 J 2
Madhu o CL 140-141 J 6
Madhuban o IND 142-143 D 2
Madhubani o• IND 142-143 E 2
Madhugiri o IND 140-141 G 4
Madhumati ∼ BD 142-143 F 4
Madhupur o BD 142-143 G 3
Madhupur o IND 142-143 E 3
Madhya Pradesh ◘ IND 138-139 E 8
Madī, Wādī ∼ OM 132-133 H 5
Madiany o EAK 212-213 E 4
Madibira o EAT 214-215 H 5
Madibogo o ZA 220-221 G 3
Madidi, Río ∼ BOL 70-71 D 3
Madigan Gulf ⊂ AUS 178-179 D 5
Madihui o VRC 154-155 G 3
Madikeri o• IND 140-141 F 4
Madill o USA (OK) 264-265 H 4
Madimba o ANG 216-217 C 3
Madimba o ZRE 210-211 E 6
Ma'din o SYR 128-129 H 5
Madina o RMM (KAY) 202-203 F 3
Madina o RMM (SIK) 202-203 G 4
Madīna, al- ◘ KSA 130-131 F 5
Madīna, al- ☆•• KSA (MAD) 130-131 F 5
Madīna, al- o Y 132-133 E 6
Madina de Baixo o GNB 202-203 C 4
Madina Junction o WAL 202-203 D 5
Madinani o CI 202-203 G 5
Madina-Oula o RG 202-203 D 5
Madina-Salambandé o RG 202-203 E 4
Madīnat al Abyar o LAR 192-193 J 1
Madīnat as-Ša'b o Y 132-133 D 7
Madīnat as-Sādāt o ET 194-195 E 2
Madīnat aš-Širq o Y 132-133 C 6
Madīnat aṭ-Ṭaura o SYR 128-129 H 5
Madīnat Nāṣir o ET 194-195 F 5
Madīnat Ṣahrā' o ET 194-195 F 6
Madingo-Kayes o RCB 210-211 C 6
Madingou ☆ RCB 210-211 D 6
Madingrin o CAM 206-207 B 4
Madi Opei o EAU 212-213 D 2
Madirovalo o RM 222-223 E 6
Madison o CDN (SAS) 232-233 K 4
Madison o USA (AL) 284-285 D 2
Madison o USA (FL) 286-287 F 1
Madison o USA (GA) 284-285 G 3
Madison o USA (IN) 274-275 N 6
Madison o USA (KS) 262-263 K 6
Madison o USA (ME) 278-279 M 4
Madison o USA (MN) 270-271 B 5
Madison o USA (NC) 282-283 H 4
Madison o USA (NE) 262-263 J 3
Madison o USA (SD) 260-261 J 2
Madison o USA (VA) 280-281 H 5
Madison o USA (WV) 280-281 E 5
Madison o USA (WY) 252-253 H 2
Madison ☆• USA (WI) 274-275 J 1
Madison Bird Refuge ⊥ USA (MT) 250-251 G 7
Madison Canyon Earthquake Area (1959) ∴ USA (MT) 250-251 H 7
Madison River ∼ USA (MT) 250-251 H 6
Madisonville o USA (KY) 276-277 H 3
Madisonville o USA (LA) 268-269 K 6
Madisonville o USA (TN) 282-283 C 5
Madisonville o USA (TX) 268-269 E 6
Madita, Pr. o RI 168 E 8
Madiun o RI 168 D 3
Madja o RCA 206-207 F 3
Madjingo o G 210-211 E 3
Madley, Mount ▲ AUS 176-177 G 2
Madley Rapids ∼ CDN 30-31 Q 3
Mado Derdetu < EAK 212-213 G 3
Mado Gashi o EAK 212-213 G 3
Madoi o VRC 144-145 M 3
Madona ☆•• LV 94-95 K 3
Madooile o SP 212-213 H 2
Madoville o SP 212-213 J 2
Madra Dağı ▲ TR 128-129 B 3
Madraka o KSA 130-131 G 6
Madraka, Ra's ▲ OM 132-133 K 4
Madras ☆•• IND 140-141 J 4
Madras o USA (OR) 244-245 D 6
Madre, Laguna ≈ 44-45 J 6
Madre, Laguna ≈ 50-51 L 5
Madre, Laguna ≈ USA 266-267 K 7
Madre de Chiapas, Sierra ▲ MEX 52-53 H 3
Madre de Deus de Minas o BR 72-73 H 6
Madre de Dios o PE 70-71 B 3
Madre de Dios, Isla ⌒ RCH 80 C 5
Madre de Dios, Río ∼ BOL 70-71 D 2
Madre de Dios, Río ∼ PE 70-71 C 3
Madre del Sur, Sierra ▲ MEX 52-53 D 3
Madre Occidental, Sierra ▲ MEX 50-51 E 2
Madre Oriental, Sierra ▲ MEX 50-51 H 3
Madrid ☆•• E 98-99 F 4
Madrid o RP 160-161 F 8
Madrid o USA (IA) 274-275 E 3
Madrid o USA (KY) 276-277 J 3
Madrid o USA (NE) 262-263 E 4
Madrid, La o RA 76-77 E 4
Madridejos o E 98-99 F 5
Madrigal o PE 70-71 B 4
Mad River ∼ USA (CA) 246-247 B 3
Madrona, Sierra ▲ E 98-99 E 5
Madruga o C 54-55 E 3
Madrugada, La o RA 80 G 3
Madsen o CDN (ONT) 234-235 K 3
Madu < SUD 200-201 C 5
Madu, Pulau ⌒ RI 168 E 6
Maduda o ZRE 210-211 D 6
Madula o ZRE 210-211 K 3
Madura, Pulau ⌒ RI 168 E 3
Madura, Selat ≈ 168 E 3
Madurai o••• IND 140-141 H 6
Madura Motel o AUS 176-177 J 5
Madurankuli o CL 140-141 H 7
Madurāntakam o IND 140-141 H 4
Madura Pass • AUS 176-177 J 5
Madyan o PK 138-139 D 2
Madyl-Tasa, gora ▲ RUS 110-111 U 4
Madžarovo o BG 102-103 D 7
Madzilobge o RB 218-219 D 5
Madziwadzido o ZW 218-219 E 3
Madziwa Mine o ZW 218-219 F 3
Maebashi ☆ J 152-153 H 6
Mae Chaem o THA 142-143 L 6
Mae Charim o THA 142-143 M 6
Mae Hong Son o THA 142-143 K 6
Mae Khajan o THA 142-143 L 6
Maelang o RI 164-165 H 3
Maele o MOC 220-221 L 2
Mae Nam Khwae Noi ∼ THA 158-159 E 3
Maengsan o DVR 150-151 F 8
Mae Pok o THA 158-159 E 2
Mae Sai o THA 142-143 L 5
Mae Sariang o THA 142-143 K 6
Maeser Creek ∼ USA (UT) 254-255 F 3
Mae Sot o THA 158-159 E 2
Maestra, Sierra ▲ C 54-55 G 4
Maestre de Campo Island ⌒ RP 160-161 D 6
Mae Su o THA 142-143 K 6
Mae Suai o THA 142-143 L 6
Mae Suya o THA 142-143 L 6
Mae Taeng o THA 142-143 L 6
Mae Tub Reservoir ⊂ THA 158-159 E 2
Maevarano ∼ RM 222-223 F 5
Maevatanana o RM 222-223 E 6
Maevo o RUS 94-95 L 3
Maewo = Île Aurora ⌒ VAN 184 II b 2
Mafa o RI 164-165 K 3
Mafeking o CDN (MAN) 234-235 B 2
Maféré o CI 202-203 J 7
Mafeteng o LS 220-221 H 4
Maffin o RI 166-167 K 2
Mafia Channel ≈ 214-215 K 4
Mafia Island ⌒ EAT 214-215 K 4
Mafikeng o ZA 220-221 G 2
Māfil o RCH 78-79 C 5
Mafou ∼ RG 202-203 E 4
Mafra o BR 74-75 F 6
Mafraq o JOR 130-131 E 1
Mafraq o Y 132-133 C 7
Mafraq, al ☆ JOR 130-131 E 1
Maga o CAM 206-207 B 3
Magadan ☆•• RUS 120-121 O 4
Magadanskij Kava-Čelomdžinskoe lesničestvo, zapovednik ⊥ RUS 120-121 M 3
Magadanskij Ol'skoe lesničestvo, zapovednik ⊥ RUS 120-121 O 4
Magadanskij Sejmčanskoe lesničestvo, zapovednik ⊥ RUS 120-121 P 2
Magadi o EAK 212-213 F 4
Magadi, Lake ⊂ EAK 212-213 F 4
Magāga o ET 194-195 E 3
Magaguadaric River ∼ CDN (NB) 240-241 J 5
Magalakwin ∼ ZA 218-219 E 6
Magalhães Barata o BR 68-69 E 2
Magaliesberg Natural Area ⊥ ZA 220-221 H 2
Magallanes, Estrecho de ≈ 80 E 6
Magamba o RCA 206-207 F 6
Magan o RUS (SAH) 118-119 O 4
Magan ∼ RUS 108-109 f 7
Magana, River ∼ WAN 204-205 H 4
Magandene o MOC 218-219 G 6
Magangue o CO 60-61 D 3
Maganoy ∼ RP 160-161 F 9
Magan-Tas, gora ▲ RUS 110-111 d 5
Magao o TCH 206-207 B 3
Magara o BU 212-213 B 5
Magāra, Ǧabal ▲ ET 194-195 F 2
Magaras o RUS 118-119 O 4
Maǧardal, al- o KSA 132-133 B 4
Magaria o RN 198-199 D 6
Magarida o PNG 183 E 6
Maǧārim, al- o Y 132-133 E 6
Magat ∼ RP 160-161 D 4
Magaubo o PNG 183 E 6
Magazine Mountain ▲ USA (AR) 276-277 B 5
Magba o CAM 204-205 J 6
Magbakele o ZRE 210-211 J 2
Magbuntoso o WAL 202-203 D 5
Magburaka o WAL 202-203 E 5
Magdad o SP 212-213 K 2
Magdagači ☆ RUS 118-119 M 9
Magdagači ∼ RUS 118-119 M 9
Maǧdal 'Anǧar o••• RL 128-129 F 6
Magdalena o BOL 70-71 E 3
Magdalena o MEX 52-53 C 1
Magdalena o RA 78-79 L 3
Magdalena o USA (NM) 256-257 H 4
Magdalena, Bahía ≈ 50-51 C 5
Magdalena, Gunung ▲ MAL 160-161 B 10
Magdalena, Isla ⌒ MEX 50-51 C 5
Magdalena, Isla ⌒ RCH 80 D 2
Magdalena, Punta ▲ CO 60-61 C 6
Magdalena, Río ∼ CO 60-61 D 5
Magdalena, Río ∼ MEX 50-51 D 2
Magdalena de Kino o MEX 50-51 D 2
Magdalena Tequisistlán o MEX 52-53 G 3
Magda Plateau ▲ CDN 24-25 f 4
Magdeburg ☆• D 92-93 L 2
Magedi o IND 140-141 G 4
Magee o USA (MS) 268-269 L 5
Magej ∼ RUS 120-121 F 5
Magelang o RI 168 D 3
Magellan Seamounts ≃ 14-15 H 6
Magens Bay Beach ⊥ USA (VI) 286-287 R 2
Magenta, Lake ⊂ AUS 176-177 E 6
Magerøya ⌒ N 86-87 M 1
Magetan o RI 168 D 3
Magga Range ▲ ARK 16 F 35
Maggieville o AUS 174-175 F 5
Maggiore, Lago ⊂ I 100-101 B 2
Maghama o RIM 196-197 D 7
Maghnia o DZ 188-189 L 3
Magic City o USA (ID) 252-253 D 3
Magic Hot Springs ∴ USA (ID) 252-253 D 4
Magic Reservoir < USA (ID) 252-253 D 3
Magill, Islas ⌒ RCH 80 D 7
Magindrano o RM 222-223 F 5
Magingo o EAT 214-215 H 6
Magistral'nyj o RUS 116-117 N 7
Máglie o I 100-101 G 4
Maǧma'a, al- o KSA 130-131 J 5
Magna o USA (UT) 254-255 C 3
Magna Bay o CDN (BC) 230-231 K 3
Magnet o CDN (MAN) 234-235 D 3
Magnet o USA (NE) 262-263 J 2
Magnetawar o CDN (ONT) 238-239 F 3
Magnetawan River ∼ CDN (ONT) 238-239 E 3
Magnetic Island ⌒ AUS 174-175 J 6
Magnetic Point ▲ CDN 28-29 E 3
Magnetity o RUS 88-89 M 2
Magnitogorsk o RUS 96-97 L 7
Magnolia o USA (AR) 276-277 B 7
Magnolia o USA (MS) 268-269 K 5
Magnolia Springs State Park ⊥ USA (GA) 284-285 J 4
Mago ⌒ FJI 184 III c 2
Mago o RUS 122-123 J 2
Magoé o MOC 218-219 F 2
Magog o CDN (QUE) 238-239 N 3
Magou ∼ DY 202-203 L 4
Magoura o DZ 188-189 L 3
Magoye o Z 218-219 D 3
Magpie o CDN (QUE) 242-243 D 2
Magpie, Lac ⊂ CDN 38-39 M 3
Magpie, Rivière ∼ CDN (QUE) 242-243 D 2
Magra ∼ BD 142-143 G 3
Magra o DZ 190-191 E 3
Magrath o CDN (ALB) 232-233 F 6
Magtá Lahjat o RIM 196-197 D 6
Magu, Rio ∼ BR 68-69 G 3
Maguan o VRC 156-157 D 5
Maguari o BR 66-67 E 3
Maguari, Cabo ▲ BR 62-63 K 6
Magude o MOC 220-221 L 2
Magui, Lac ⊂ RMM 202-203 E 2
Magumeri o WAN 198-199 F 6
Magunge o ZW 218-219 E 3
Magura o BD 142-143 F 4
Maguse Lake ⊂ CDN 30-31 W 5
Maguse Point ▲ CDN 30-31 X 5
Maguse River o CDN (MWT) 30-31 W 5
Maguse River ∼ CDN 30-31 W 5
Magushan • VRC 156-157 K 3
Magusheni o ZA 220-221 J 5
Magus River ∼ CDN (ONT) 236-237 J 4
Magwe ☆ MYA 142-143 J 5
Magwe o SUD 206-207 L 6
Magyichaung o MYA 142-143 H 5
Maǧz o Y 132-133 C 5
Mahābād o• IR 128-129 L 4
Mahābaleshwar o• IND 140-141 E 2
Mahabe o RM 222-223 E 6
Mahabharat Lekh ▲ NEP 144-145 E 7
Mahābharet Lekh ▲ NEP 144-145 C 6
Mahābiša, al- o Y 132-133 C 6
Mahabo o RM 222-223 E 9
Mahačkala ☆ RUS 126-127 G 6
Mahād o IND 138-139 D 10
Mahadday Weeyne o SP 212-213 K 2
Mahādeo Hills ▲ IND 138-139 G 8
Mahafalu, Tombeau • RM 222-223 D 10
Mahafaly ⊥ RM 222-223 E 9
Mahafasa o RM 222-223 E 9
Mahagi o ZRE 212-213 C 2
Mahagi Port o ZRE 212-213 C 2
Mahaicony o GUY 62-63 F 2
Mahā'il o KSA 132-133 C 4
Mahajamba ∼ RM 222-223 E 6
Mahajamba, Helodrano ≈ RM 222-223 E 5
Mahajanga ◘ RM 222-223 D 7
Mahajanga ☆ RM 222-223 E 5
Mahajilo ∼ RM 222-223 D 7
Mahakam ∼ RI 164-165 D 3
Mahākik, al- ⊥ KSA 132-133 G 3
Mahal o IND 140-141 H 4
Mahālānī, al- o KSA 130-131 H 4
Mahalapye o RB 218-219 D 6
Mahalchari o BD 142-143 H 4
Mahalevona o RM 222-223 F 5
Mahali Mountains ▲ EAT 214-215 E 4
Mahalla al-Kubrā, al- o ET 194-195 E 2
Mahallāt o IR 134-135 D 2
Mahalona o RI 164-165 G 5
Mahalona, Danau ⊂ RI 164-165 G 5
Mahambet ☆ KA 96-97 G 10
Mahambo o RM 222-223 F 6
Mahameru, Gunung ▲ RI 168 E 4
Mahamūd-e'Erāqi ☆ AFG 136-137 L 7
Mahān o IR 134-135 G 3
Mahānadi ∼ IND 142-143 C 5
Mahānadi Delta ⊥ IND 142-143 E 5
Mahananda ∼ IND 142-143 F 3
Mahananda ∼ IND 142-143 E 2
Mahanay Island ⌒ RP 160-161 F 7
Mahango Game Park ⊥ NAM 216-217 F 9
Mahanoro o RM 222-223 F 7
Maha Oya o CL 140-141 J 7
Mahārājganj o IND 142-143 C 2
Maharashtra ◘ IND 138-139 D 10
Mahari ∼ BD 142-143 G 3
Mahārlū, Daryāče-ye ⊂ IR 134-135 E 4
Mahāsamund o IND 142-143 C 5
Maha Sarakham o THA 158-159 G 2
Mahaska o USA (KS) 262-263 J 5
Mahasolo o RM 222-223 E 7
Mahatalaky o RM 222-223 E 10
Mahatsaratsara o RM 222-223 E 8
Mahaṭṭat 1 o SUD 200-201 E 2
Mahaṭṭat 2 o SUD 200-201 E 2
Mahaṭṭat 3 o SUD 200-201 E 2
Mahaṭṭat 4 o SUD 200-201 E 2
Mahaṭṭat 5 o SUD 200-201 E 2
Mahaṭṭat 6 o SUD 200-201 F 2
Mahaṭṭat 7 o SUD 200-201 F 2
Mahaṭṭat 8 o SUD 200-201 F 2
Mahaṭṭat 9 o SUD 200-201 F 3
Mahaṭṭat 10 o SUD 200-201 G 3
Mahaṭṭat Ṭalāṭa o ET 194-195 F 2
Mahavanona o RM 222-223 F 4
Mahavavy ∼ RM 222-223 E 6
Mahavelona o RM 222-223 E 7
Mahaweli Ganga ∼ CL 140-141 J 7
Mahaweli Ganga ∼ CL 140-141 J 7
Mahaxai o LAO 158-159 H 2
Mahayag o RP 160-161 F 8
Mahazoma o RM 222-223 E 6
Mahbūb o SUD 200-201 D 6
Mahbūbābād o IND 142-143 B 7
Mahbūbnagar o IND 140-141 G 2
Mahḍa o OM 134-135 F 6
Mahd aḍ-Ḍahab o KSA 130-131 G 6
Mahdia o GUY 62-63 E 3
Mahdia ☆ TN 190-191 H 3
Mahdīšahr o IR 136-137 C 7
Mahe o• IND 140-141 F 5
Mahébourg o• MS 224 C 7
Mahé Island ⌒ SY 224 D 2
Mahendragarh o IND 138-139 F 5
Mahendra Giri ▲ IND 142-143 D 6
Mahenge o EAT 214-215 J 5
Mahesāna o IND 138-139 D 8
Maheshkhali ⌒ BD 142-143 G 5
Maheshpur o IND 142-143 E 3
Maḥfar al-Ḥammām o SYR 128-129 H 5
Maḥǧil, al- o Y 132-133 D 5
Mahi ∼ IND 138-139 E 8

Mahia Peninsula ⌄ NZ 182 F 3
Māhīdašt o IR 134-135 B 1
Mahila o ZRE 212-213 B 6
Mahilëv o• BY 94-95 M 5
Mahilyow = Mahilëv o• BY 94-95 M 5
Mahimba Kanikolo ▲ SOL 184 I c 3
Mahin o WAN 204-205 F 5
Mahina o RMM 202-203 E 3
Mahitsy o RM 222-223 E 7
Mahkyetkawng o MYA 142-143 K 3
Mahlabatini o ZA 220-221 K 4
Mahlaing o MYA 142-143 J 5
Mahlake o IR 134-135 E 5
Mahmiya o SUD 200-201 F 4
Mahmoud, Bir < TN 190-191 G 4
Mahmūdābād o IR 136-137 C 6
Mahmūdiya, al- ☆ IRQ 128-129 L 6
Mahmud Jig o IR 128-129 M 4
Maḥmūr o IRQ 128-129 K 5
Mahne o IR 134-135 H 1
Māhnešān o IR 128-129 M 4
Mahnja ~ RUS 114-115 O 5
Mahnomen o USA (MN) 270-271 C 3
Maho o CL 140-141 J 7
Mahoba o IND 138-139 G 7
Maho Bay ⩦ NA 56 D 2
Mahomet o USA (IL) 274-275 K 4
Mahone Bay ≈ 38-39 M 6
Mahone Bay o CDN (NS) 240-241 L 6
Mahone Bay ≈ CDN 240-241 L 6
Mahony Lake ⊙ CDN 30-31 G 3
Mahood Falls o CDN (BC) 230-231 J 2
Mahood Lake ⊙ CDN (BC) 230-231 J 2
Mahora o E 98-99 G 5
Mahoua o TCH 206-207 D 3
Mahra, al- ⩦ Y 132-133 G 5
Mahrauni o IND 138-139 G 7
Mahres o TN 190-191 H 3
Mährisch Schönberg = Šumperk o CZ 92-93 O 4
Māhšahr, Bandar-e o IR 134-135 C 3
Mahtowa o USA (MN) 270-271 F 4
Mahūd Budrukh o IND 140-141 F 2
Mahukona o USA (HI) 288 K 4
Mahulu o ZRE 212-213 A 4
Mahuneni o RI 164-165 J 2
Mahur Island ⌒ PNG 183 G 2
Mahuta o WAN 204-205 F 3
Mahuva o IND 138-139 C 9
Maḥwa, al- o KSA 132-133 B 4
Mahwah o IND 138-139 F 6
Maḥwit, al- o Y 132-133 C 6
Maḥya, Wādī ~ Y 132-133 F 5
Mahzez, Hassi < DZ 188-189 J 6
Mai, Île = Emae ⌒ VAN 184 II b 3
Maiama o PNG 183 D 4
Maiauatá o BR 62-63 K 6
Maibo o TCH 206-207 D 4
Maica, Rivière ~ CDN (QUE) 236-237 M 3
Maicao o CO 60-61 E 2
Maici, Rio ~ BR 66-67 G 6
Maicillar o YV 60-61 G 2
Maicimirim, Rio ~ BR 66-67 F 6
Maicuru, Rio ~ BR 62-63 G 5
Maiden o USA (NC) 282-283 F 5
Maiden, Mount ▲ AUS 176-177 G 3
Maiden Rock o USA (WI) 270-271 F 6
Maidens o USA (VA) 280-281 H 6
Maidens o USA (VA) 280-281 J 6
Maidi o RI 164-165 K 3
Maidi o Y 132-133 C 5
Maidstone o CDN (SAS) 232-233 J 2
Maidstone o GB 90-91 H 6
Maiduguri ☆ WAN 204-205 K 3
Maidūm ∴• ET 194-195 E 3
Maie o ZRE 212-213 C 2
Maiella, la ▲ I 100-101 E 3
Maifa'a o• Y 132-133 E 6
Maigach Mada o SP 212-213 J 2
Maigatari o WAN 198-199 D 6
Maigh Chromtha = Macroom o IRL 90-91 C 6
Maigh Nuad = Maynooth o IRL 90-91 D 5
Maigualida, Sierra de ▲ YV 60-61 J 5
Mai Gudo ▲ ETH 208-209 C 5
Maihar o IND 142-143 B 3
Maiinchi o WAN 198-199 C 6
Maijdi o BD 142-143 G 4
Maijia o YV 60-61 K 5
Maijishan Shiku • VRC 154-155 E 4
Maika ~ ZRE 212-213 B 2
Maikala Range ▲ IND 142-143 B 4
Maiko ~ ZRE 210-211 L 4
Maiko, Parc National de la ⊥ ZRE 212-213 A 4
Maikonkele o WAN 204-205 G 4
Maikoor, Pulau ⌒ RI 166-167 H 5
Maikoro o TCH 206-207 C 4
Mailāni o IND 144-145 C 6
Mailepalli o IND 140-141 H 2
Mailin, Rio de ~ RA 76-77 F 5
Mailsi o PK 138-139 D 5
Maimana ☆• AFG 136-137 J 7
Maimará o RA 76-77 E 2
Maimlja ~ RUS 120-121 T 5
Maimón o DOM 54-55 K 5
Maimoon Palace • RI 162-163 C 3
Main ~ D 92-93 L 3
Main à Dieu o CDN (NS) 240-241 Q 4
Mainau ⌒• D 92-93 K 5
Main Brook o CDN (NFL) 242-243 M 1
Main Camp o ZW 218-219 D 4
Main Centre o CDN (SAS) 232-233 L 5
Main Channel ⊙ CDN (ONT) 238-239 D 3
Mai-Ndombe, Lac o ZRE 210-211 G 5
Main-Donau-Kanal < D 92-93 L 4
Main Duck Island ⌒ CDN (ONT) 238-239 J 5
Maine ▫ USA (ME) 278-279 L 4
Maine, Gulf of ≈ 46-47 P 4
Maine, Gulf of ≈ USA 278-279 O 5
Mainé-Soroa o RN 198-199 F 6
Maine TPK II USA (ME) 278-279 L 5
Maing Kwan o MYA 142-143 K 2
Mainistir Fhear Maí = Fermoy o IRL 90-91 C 5
Mainistir na Búille = Boyle o IRL 90-91 C 5
Mainistir na Féile = Abbeyfeale o IRL 90-91 C 5
Mainit o RP 160-161 E 8
Mainit o RP (SUN) 160-161 F 8
Mainit, Lake ⊙ RP 160-161 F 8
Mainland o CDN (NFL) 242-243 J 4
Mainland ⌒ GB 90-91 F 2
Mainling o VRC 144-145 K 6
Mainoru o AUS 174-175 C 4
Main Point o CDN (NFL) 242-243 O 3
Mainpuri o IND 138-139 G 6
Main River ~ CDN (NFL) 242-243 L 3
Maintirano o RM 222-223 D 7
Mainz ☆• D 92-93 K 4
Maio, Ilha de ⌒ CV 202-203 C 6
Maiparu o YV 62-63 D 2
Maipo, Río ~ RCH 78-79 D 2
Maipo, Volcán ▲ RA 78-79 E 3
Maipú o RA 78-79 L 4
Maiquetía o YV 60-61 H 2
Maiquinique o BR 72-73 K 3
Mairana o BOL 70-71 F 6
Maire, Estrecho de le ≈ 80 H 7
Mairi o BR 68-69 H 7
Mairinque o BR 72-73 G 7
Mairipotaba o BR 72-73 F 4
Maisān ▫ IRQ 128-129 M 7
Maisí o C 54-55 H 4
Maišiagala o LT 94-95 J 4
Maisonnette o CDN (NB) 240-241 K 3
Maitabi, Mount ▲ SOL 184 I c 2
Maitembge o RB 218-219 D 5
Maitén, El o RA 78-79 D 7
Maitioukoulou o RCA 206-207 C 5
Maitland o AUS (NSW) 180-181 L 2
Maitland o AUS (SA) 180-181 D 3
Maitland o CDN (NS) 240-241 M 5
Maitland, Lake ⊙ AUS 176-177 F 3
Maitland Range ▲ AUS 172-173 H 3
Maitland River ~ AUS 172-173 C 6
Maitland River ~ CDN (ONT) 238-239 D 5
Maitum o RP 160-161 F 9
Maituru o ZRE 212-213 B 2
Maiurno o• SUD 200-201 F 6
Maiwa o RI 164-165 F 5
Maíz, Islas del ⌒ NIC 52-53 C 5
Maíz Grande, Isla de ⌒ NIC 52-53 C 5
Maizho Kunggar o VRC 144-145 H 6
Maíz Pequeña, Isla de ⌒ NIC 52-53 C 5
Maizuru o J 152-153 F 7
Maja ~ RUS 120-121 H 4
Maja ~ RUS 120-121 E 6
Maja, Ust'- o• RUS 120-121 F 3
Majačnyj o RUS 96-97 J 7
Majačnyj, mys ▲ RUS 120-121 S 7
Majada, La o RA 76-77 E 5
Majadas, Las o YV 60-61 J 4
Majagua o C 54-55 F 4
Majahual o MEX 52-53 L 2
Majak o RUS 122-123 G 4
Majalaja o RI 168 B 3
Majalengka o RI 168 C 3
Majda o RUS 88-89 Q 3
Majdanpek o YU 100-101 H 2
Maje o BR 72-73 J 7
Majeicodoteri o YV 60-61 J 6
Majenang o RI 168 C 3
Majene o RI 164-165 F 5
Majes, Río de ~ PE 70-71 A 5
Majes-Colca, Cañon del • PE 64-65 F 9
Majestic o CDN (ALB) 232-233 H 5
Majete Game Reserve ⊥ MW 218-219 H 2
Majetú o BOL 70-71 E 3
Majgaon o IND 142-143 C 4
Majgungna ~ RUS 116-117 F 4
Majholi o IND 142-143 B 3
Maji o ETH 208-209 B 5
Majiahewan o VRC 154-155 D 3
Majiang o VRC 156-157 E 3
Majid o RI 164-165 K 3
Majie o VRC 156-157 D 5
Maji Moto o EAT 212-213 E 4
Majja ☆• RUS 120-121 D 3
Majkapcigaj o KA 124-125 O 5
Majkop ☆ RUS 126-127 D 5
Majli-Saj o KS 136-137 N 4
Majmaga o RUS 118-119 O 4
Majmakan ~ RUS 120-121 F 6
Majmeča ~ RUS 108-109 d 6
Majn ~ RUS 112-113 R 4
Majna ~ RUS 96-97 F 6
Majnefvegyrgyn ~ RUS 112-113 T 5
Majnic, ozero ⊙ RUS 112-113 T 5
Majnskoe ploskogor'e ▲ RUS 112-113 R 4
Major o CDN (SAS) 232-233 J 4
Major Gercino o BR 74-75 F 6
Major Isidoro o BR 68-69 K 6
Major Peak ▲ USA (TX) 266-267 D 3
Majrūr, Wādī ~ SUD 200-201 C 4
Majsejevščyna o BY 94-95 L 4
Majskij o RUS (AMR) 122-123 C 2
Majskij o RUS (CUK) 112-113 R 2
Majskij o RUS (KAB) 126-127 F 6
Majskij hrebet ▲ RUS 120-121 E 6
Majunga = Mahajanga ☆ RM 222-223 E 5
Majunga = Mahajanga = Mahajanga ☆ RM 222-223 E 5
Majuro ⌒ MAI 13 J 2
Maka o LB 202-203 E 6
Maka o SN (FLE) 196-197 B 6
Maka o SN (SO) 202-203 C 3
Maka o SOL 184 I e 3
Makabana o RCB 210-211 D 5
Makacanangano, Pulau ⌒ RI 168 D 6
Makado o ZW 218-219 E 5
Maka Gouye o SN 202-203 C 3
Makaha o• USA (HI) 288 G 3
Makah Indian Reservation ⊥ USA (WA) 244-245 A 2
Makak o CAM 210-211 C 2
Makaka o RCB 210-211 D 5
Makalamabedi o RB 218-219 B 5
Makale o RI 164-165 F 5
Makalondi o RN 202-203 L 3
Makalu ▲ NEP 144-145 F 7
Makamba o BU 212-213 B 6
Makambako o EAT (IRI) 214-215 H 5
Makanci o KA 124-125 N 5
Makanda o RCB 210-211 D 5
Makanjila o MW 218-219 H 1
Makanruši, ostrov ⌒ RUS 122-123 Q 4
Makanya o EAT 212-213 F 6
Makapala o USA (HI) 288 K 4
Makapuu Point ▲ USA (HI) 288 H 3
Makar, ostrov ⌒ RUS 110-111 W 4
Makarakombu = Mount Popomanaseu ▲ SOL 184 I e 3
Makar'ev o RUS 94-95 S 3
Makarfi o WAN 204-205 G 3
Makari o CAM 198-199 G 6
Makariki o RI 166-167 E 3
Makaroff o CDN (MAN) 234-235 B 3
Makarora o NZ 182 B 6
Makarov o RUS 122-123 K 4
Makarova, ostrov ⌒ RUS 108-109 Z 3
Makarov Basin ≃ 16 A 35
Makarov Dvor o RUS 88-89 Q 6
Makarovka o RUS 122-123 Q 4
Makarovo o RUS 116-117 N 7
Makarska o HR 100-101 F 3
Makasa o Z 214-215 F 5
Makasar = Ujung Pandang ☆ RI 164-165 F 6
Makassar = Ujung Pandang ☆ RI 164-165 F 6
Makassar Strait = Makasar, Selat ≈ RI 164-165 E 5
Makasse < SP 212-213 J 3
Makat ☆ KA 96-97 H 10
Makawao o USA (HI) 288 J 4
Makay ▲ RM 222-223 D 8
Makedonia ⩦ GR 100-101 H 4
Makeevka = Makijivka o UA 102-103 L 3
Makekeda o ZRE 212-213 A 2
Makena o USA (HI) 288 J 4
Makeni ☆ WAL 202-203 D 5
Makere o EAT 212-213 C 6
Makgadikgadi ⩦ RB 218-219 C 5
Makgadikgadi Pans Game Park ⊥ RB 218-219 C 5
Makha o THA 158-159 E 3
Makhaleng ~ LS 220-221 H 5
Makhdumnagar o IND 142-143 C 2
Makhtal o IND 140-141 G 2
Makhu o IND 138-139 E 4
Maki o RI 166-167 H 3
Makian, Pulau ⌒ RI 164-165 K 3
Makijivka o UA 102-103 L 3
Makilimbo o ZRE 212-213 B 5
Makina o SOL 184 I e 3
Makinak o CDN (MAN) 234-235 D 4
Maki National Park ⊥ ETH 208-209 C 6
Makinat Šihan o OM 132-133 H 5
Makinda o EAT 212-213 G 6
Makindu o EAK 212-213 F 5
Makinsk ☆ KA 124-125 G 2
Makinson Inlet ≈ 24-25 f 2
Makira, Lembalemban'i ▲ RM 222-223 F 5
Makiri, Danau ⊙ RI 166-167 G 2
Makiyivka = Makijivka o UA 102-103 L 3
Makka ▫ KSA 132-133 B 3
Makka ☆•• KSA 132-133 A 3
Makkah = Makka ☆ KSA 132-133 A 3
Mak-Klintoka, ostrov ⌒ RUS 84-85 e 2
Makkovik o CDN 36-37 U 7
Makkovik Bay ≈ 36-37 U 7
Makmin, al- o IRQ 128-129 K 7
Makó o H 92-93 Q 5
Mako o SN 202-203 D 3
Makogai ⌒ FJI 184 III b 2
Makokibatan Lake ⊙ CDN (ONT) 234-235 Q 3
Makokou ☆ G 210-211 D 3
Makonde Plateau ▲ EAT 214-215 K 6
Makongo o GH 202-203 K 5
Makongolosi o EAT 214-215 G 5
Makoop Lake ⊙ CDN 34-35 L 4
Makor o CAM 204-205 K 5
Makoro o ZRE 212-213 B 2
Makosa o ZRE 214-215 E 6
Makotipoko o RCB 210-211 F 4
Makoua o RCB 210-211 E 3
Makoua o TCH 206-207 E 4
Makoubi o RCB 210-211 D 5
Makovo o RUS 96-97 F 10
Makovskaja ~ RUS 108-109 V 8
Makovskoe, ozero ⊙ RUS 108-109 V 8
Makrān Coast Range ▲ PK 134-135 K 6
Maks al-Qiblī, 'Izbat o ET 194-195 E 5
Maksatiha ☆ RUS 94-95 O 3
Maksimova o RUS 116-117 M 7
Maksimovka o RUS 118-119 E 4
Maksudangarh o IND 138-139 F 7
Maktau o EAK 212-213 G 5
Makthar o• TN 190-191 G 3
Mākū o• IR 128-129 L 3
Makuende o ZRE 214-215 E 4
Makulakubu o ZRE 214-215 C 5
Makunduchi o EAT 214-215 K 4
Makung o RC 156-157 L 5
Makungo o SP 212-213 J 3
Makungu o EAT 214-215 H 5
Makunguwiro o EAT (LIN) 214-215 J 5
Makunudu Atoll ⌒ MV 140-141 B 4
Makurazaki o J 152-153 D 9
Makurdi ☆ WAN 204-205 H 5
Makuru ⌒ VAN 184 II b 3
Makushin Bay ≈ 22-23 N 6
Makushin Volcano ▲ USA 22-23 N 6
Makušino ☆ RUS 114-115 J 7
Makutano o EAK (EAS) 212-213 F 4
Makutano o EAK (RIF) 212-213 F 5
Makuti o ZW 218-219 E 3
Makuyuni o EAT 212-213 F 5
Makwate o RB 218-219 D 6
Makwiro o ZW 218-219 F 3
Mal o IND 142-143 F 2
Māl o RIM 196-197 D 6
Mala o PE 64-65 D 8
Mala o RI 166-167 F 2
Mala = Mallow o IRL 90-91 C 5
Mala, Río de ~ PE 64-65 D 8
Malaba o EAK 212-213 E 3
Malabang o RP 160-161 F 9
Malabar ⌒ SY 222-223 E 2
Malabar Coast ~ IND 140-141 E 3
Malabo ★ GQ 210-211 B 2
Malabo o RI 164-165 F 5
Malabrigo, Punta ▲ PE 64-65 C 5
Malabungan o RP 160-161 B 8
Malabwe o Z 218-219 C 3
Malaca Beach, Playa ⩦• DOM 54-55 L 5
Malacacheta o BR 72-73 J 4
Malacca o IND 140-141 L 5
Malacca, Strait of ≈ 162-163 D 3
Malachi o CDN (ONT) 234-235 J 5
Malacky o SK 92-93 O 4
Malacura o AUS 174-175 G 6
Malad ▲ ER 200-201 J 4
Malad City o USA (ID) 252-253 F 4
Maladzečna ☆ BY 94-95 K 4
Málaga o CO 60-61 E 4
Málaga o E 98-99 E 6
Malaga o USA (NJ) 280-281 L 4
Malaga o USA (NM) 256-257 L 6
Malagarasi o EAT (KIG) 212-213 C 6
Malagarasi ~ EAT 212-213 C 6
Malagueta, Bahía de ≈ 54-55 G 4
Malāha, al- o KSA 132-133 C 5
Malahajtari ~ RUS 108-109 g 4
Malahar o RI 168 E 7
Malahat o CDN (BC) 230-231 F 5
Malāhit, al- o Y 132-133 C 5
Malaimbandy o RM 222-223 D 8
Malaita ⌒ SOL 184 I e 3
Malaita o ZA 220-221 J 2
Malaja Anga ~ RUS 116-117 N 8
Malaja Balahnja ~ RUS 108-109 e 5
Malaja Belaja ~ RUS 116-117 L 9
Malaja Birjusa ~ RUS 116-117 J 8
Malaja Bykovka o RUS 96-97 E 8
Malaja Čažma ~ RUS 120-121 T 6
Malaja Čuja ~ RUS 118-119 E 6
Malaja Erëma ~ RUS 116-117 N 5
Malaja Heta o RUS 108-109 V 7
Malaja Heta ~ RUS 108-109 V 7
Malaja Ket' ~ RUS 116-117 E 7
Malaja Kon'kovaja ~ RUS 112-113 J 2
Malaja Kuonamka ~ RUS 110-111 J 4
Malaja Kuril'skaja grjada ⌒ RUS 122-123 L 7
Malaja Ob' ~ RUS 114-115 H 3
Malaja Pera ~ RUS 122-123 B 3
Malaja Pura ~ RUS 108-109 V 5
Malaja Purga ☆ RUS 96-97 H 5
Malaja Sos'va ~ RUS 114-115 G 3
Malaja Sos'va ~ RUS 114-115 H 3
Malaja Sos'va, zapovednik ⊥ RUS 114-115 H 4
Malaja Tira ~ RUS 116-117 N 7
Malaja Usa ~ RUS 108-109 L 8
Malaja Višera ☆ RUS 94-95 N 2
Malakāl ☆ SUD 206-207 K 4
Malakanagiri o IND 142-143 B 6
Malākand o• PK 138-139 C 2
Mālākand Pass ▲ PK 138-139 C 2
Malaka Ob' ~ RUS 108-109 M 8
Malakatyn-Tas, gora ▲ RUS 110-111 W 2
Malakoff o USA (TX) 264-265 H 6
Malakula ▫ VAN 184 II a 3
Malakula = Île Mallicolo ⌒ VAN 184 II a 3
Malakwa o CDN (BC) 230-231 L 3
Malakwāl o PK 138-139 D 3
Malala o PNG (MAD) 183 C 3
Malala o PNG (MAD) 183 D 3
Malalamai o PNG 183 D 3
Malalaua o PNG 183 D 5
Malam o PNG 183 B 5
Malamala o RI 164-165 G 5
Malambo o EAT 212-213 E 5
Malammaduri o WAN 198-199 D 6
Malampaka o EAT 212-213 D 5
Malān, Rās ▲ PK 134-135 L 6
Malanda o AUS 174-175 H 5
Malandji o ZRE 210-211 J 6
Malandy Hill ▲ AUS 176-177 D 4
Malang o• RI 168 E 3
Malanga o MOC 218-219 J 1
Malangani o EAT 214-215 H 5
Malangbong o RI 168 C 3
Malangke o RI 164-165 G 5
Malanje ▫ ANG 216-217 C 4
Malanje ☆ ANG (MAL) 216-217 D 4
Malantouen o CAM 204-205 J 6
Malanut Bay ≈ 160-161 B 8
Malanville o DY 204-205 E 3
Malanzan o RA 76-77 D 6
Malanzán, Sierra de ▲ RA 76-77 D 6
Malapatan o RP 160-161 F 10
Malapati Safari Area ⊥ ZW 218-219 F 5
Malappuram o IND 140-141 G 5
Malār o PK 134-135 L 5
Malarba o CAM 204-205 K 5
Mälaren ⊙ S 86-87 H 7
Malargüe o RA 78-79 E 3
Malargüe, Río ~ RA 78-79 E 3
Malartic o CDN (QUE) 236-237 K 4
Malartic, Lac ⊙ CDN (QUE) 236-237 L 4
Malasait o PNG 183 F 3
Malaso ~ RI 164-165 F 5
Malaspina Glacier ⊂ USA 20-21 U 7
Malata, Lake ⊙ AUS 180-181 C 3
Malatayur, Tanjung ▲ RI 162-163 K 6
Malatya ☆ TR 128-129 H 3
Malaulalo Island ⌒ SOL 184 I e 4
Malaut o IND 138-139 E 4
Malavalli o IND 140-141 G 4
Malāvi o IR 134-135 B 2
Malawali, Pulau ⌒ MAL 160-161 B 9
Malawi, Lake ⊙ MW 214-215 H 6
Malawi = Malawi ■ MW 218-219 G 1
Malay o RP 160-161 D 7
Malayagiri ▲ IND 142-143 D 5
Malay Balay ☆ RP 160-161 F 8
Malāyer o• IR 134-135 C 1
Malāyer, Rūdḫāne-ye ~ IR 134-135 C 1
Malay Peninsula = Semenanjung Malaysia ⌒ MAL 162-163 E 2
Malaysia ■ MAL 162-163 E 2
Malazgirt ☆• TR 128-129 K 3
Malbaie, La o CDN (QUE) 240-241 E 3
Malbazza o RN 198-199 B 6
Malbhanguwa o NEP 144-145 C 6
Malbon o AUS 178-179 F 1
Malbon Vale o AUS 178-179 E 1
Malbooma o AUS 178-179 C 6
Malbork o•• PL 92-93 P 1
Malbrán o RA 76-77 F 5
Malcolm o AUS 176-177 F 4
Malcolm o USA (NE) 262-263 K 4
Malcolm River ~ CDN 20-21 V 2
Malcom, Point ▲ AUS 176-177 G 6
Malden o USA (MO) 276-277 F 4
Maldives ■ MV 140-141 B 7
Maldives = Maldive Islands ⌒ MV 140-141 B 7
Maldon o• AUS 180-181 H 4
Maldonado o EC 64-65 C 1
Maldonado ☆ ROU 78-79 M 3
Maldonado, Punta ▲ MEX 52-53 E 3
Male ★ MV 140-141 B 5
Male, Lac du ⊙ CDN (QUE) 236-237 N 4
Malea, Gunung ▲ RI 162-163 C 4
Maleb o CDN (ALB) 232-233 G 6
Mālegaon o IND (MAH) 138-139 F 9
Mālegaon o IND (MAH) 138-139 E 9
Malei o MOC 218-219 J 3
Maleit o SUD 206-207 J 5
Malek o SUD 206-207 K 5
Malekkandi o IR 128-129 M 4
Malélé o RCB 210-211 D 6
Malema o MOC 218-219 J 2
Malé Malé o RN 198-199 D 6
Malemba-Nkulu o ZRE 214-215 D 5
Malème-Hodar o SN 202-203 C 2
Malena o RA 78-79 G 2
Malendo, River ~ WAN 204-205 F 3
Malendok Island ⌒ PNG 183 G 2
Malen'ga o RUS 88-89 O 5
Male polissja ⩦ UA 102-103 C 2
Mālestān o AFG 134-135 M 2
Maleta o RUS 116-117 O 10
Malewāra o IND 142-143 B 5
Malfa o I 100-101 E 5
Malgis ~ EAK 212-213 F 3
Malgobek o RUS 126-127 F 6
Malgrat de Mar o E 98-99 J 4
Malha o SUD 200-201 C 5
Malhada o BR 72-73 J 3
Malheur Lake ⊙ USA (OR) 244-245 G 7
Malheur National Wildlife Refuge ⊥ USA (OR) 244-245 G 7
Malheur River ~ USA (OR) 244-245 H 7
Mali ⌒ FJI 184 III b 2
Mali o LB 202-203 F 6
Mali o RG 202-203 D 3
Mali ■ RMM 202-203 G 2
Mali o ZRE 210-211 L 5
Maliana o RI 166-167 C 6
Maliça o BR 68-69 F 6
Malifut o RI 164-165 K 3
Maligayo o RP 160-161 D 5
Malignant Cove o CDN (NS) 240-241 N 5
Maligne River ~ CDN (ALB) 228-229 R 4
Mali K. ⌒ MYA 158-159 E 4
Malili o RI 164-165 G 5
Målilla o S 86-87 G 8
Mali Lošinj o HR 100-101 E 2
Malima ⌒ FJI 184 III c 2
Malimán de Abajo o RA 76-77 C 5
Malimasindi o ZW 218-219 E 4
Malinalco ∴• MEX 52-53 E 2
Malinche, Volcán La ▲ MEX 52-53 E 2
Malindang, Mount ▲ RP 160-161 E 8
Malindi o•• EAK 212-213 H 5
Malindi Marine National Park ⊥ EAK 212-213 H 5
Malines = Mechelen o• B 92-93 H 3
Malinga o RCB 210-211 D 5
Malingping o RI 168 B 3
Malin Head ▲ IRL 90-91 D 4
Malinke ⩦ SN 202-203 C 3
Malino o RI (SLT) 164-165 G 4
Malino o• RI (SSE) 164-165 F 6
Malino, Gunung ▲ RI 164-165 G 3
Malinovka o RUS (KMR) 124-125 P 2
Malinovka ~ RUS 122-123 F 6
Malinyi o EAT 214-215 J 5
Maliom o PNG 183 G 3
Malipo o VRC 156-157 D 5
Maliq o•• AL 100-101 H 4
Mali Rajinac ▲ HR 100-101 E 2
Malita o RP 160-161 F 9
Malitbog o RP 160-161 F 7
Maliva o IND 138-139 C 8
Māliya o IND 138-139 C 8
Maljamar o USA (NM) 256-257 M 6
Malka ~ RUS 126-127 E 6
Malkaaray o SP 212-213 H 2
Malka Mari o EAK 212-213 H 2
Malka Mari National Park ⊥ EAK 212-213 H 1
Malkāpur o IND (MAH) 138-139 F 9
Malkāpur o IND (MAH) 140-141 E 2
Malkara ☆ TR 128-129 B 2
Malki o RUS 120-121 R 7
Malkinskij hrebet ▲ RUS 120-121 R 7
Malko Tărnovo o BG 102-103 E 7
Malko Tărnovo o BG 102-103 E 7
Malla o IND 140-141 G 2
Mallacoota o AUS 180-181 K 4
Mallacoota Inlet • AUS 180-181 K 4
Mallaig o GB 90-91 E 3
Mallaoua o RN 198-199 D 6
Mallapunyah o AUS 174-175 C 5
Mallawi o ET 194-195 E 4
Mallawiya o SUD 200-201 H 5
Malleco, Río ~ RCH 78-79 C 5
Mallee Cliffs National Park ⊥ AUS 180-181 G 3
Mallen, laguna o RUS 112-113 S 6
Malleo, Río ~ RA 78-79 D 5
Mallery Lake ⊙ CDN 30-31 U 3
Mallet o BR 74-75 E 5
Mallicolo, Île = Malakula ⌒ VAN 184 II a 3
Mallig o RP 160-161 D 4
Mallina o AUS 172-173 D 6
Mallin Grande, Cerro ▲ RA 78-79 D 6
Malloch, Cape ▲ CDN 24-25 Q 1
Mallorca ⌒ E 98-99 J 5
Mallorytown o CDN (ONT) 238-239 K 4
Mallow = Mala o IRL 90-91 C 5
Malm o N 86-87 E 4
Malmal o PNG 183 F 3
Mālmand, Kūh-e ▲ AFG 134-135 K 2
Malmberget o•• S 86-87 K 3
Malmédy o B 92-93 J 3
Malmesbury o ZA 220-221 D 6
Malmö o•• S 86-87 F 9
Malmo o USA (MN) 270-271 E 4
Malmyž ☆ RUS 96-97 G 5
Malo ⌒ VAN 184 II a 2
Malo, Arroyo ~ ROU 78-79 M 2
Maloaini o SOL 184 I b 2
Maloarhangel'sk o RUS 116-117 O 10
Maloca o BR 62-63 G 5
Maloca do Gonçalo o BR 66-67 J 6
Maloca Velha o BR 62-63 G 4
Maloconan o RP 160-161 E 8
Malocu Macu o BR 60-61 K 6
Maloe Hantajskoe, ozero ⊙ RUS 108-109 X 7
Maloe Jarovoe ozero ⊙ RUS 124-125 L 2
Malojaz ☆ RUS 96-97 L 6
Malokuril'skoe o RUS 122-123 M 7
Malole o Z 214-215 F 6
Malolo ⌒ FJI 184 III a 2
Malolo o RI 166-167 F 2
Malolotja Nature Reserve ⊥ SD 220-221 K 3
Malom o PNG 183 F 2
Malombe < Z 218-219 B 3
Malombe, Lake ⊙ MW 218-219 H 2
Malonda o ZRE 214-215 C 5
Malone o USA (NY) 278-279 G 4
Malone o USA (TX) 266-267 L 2
Malone, Lake ⊙ USA (KY) 276-277 H 3
Malonga o ZRE 214-215 B 6
Malott o USA (WA) 244-245 F 2
Måløy ☆ N 86-87 B 6
Malozemel'skaja tundra ⩦ RUS 88-89 U 3
Maložujka o RUS (ARH) 88-89 O 5
Maložujka ~ RUS 88-89 O 5
Malpas Hut o AUS 174-175 G 6
Malpelo, Isla de ⌒ CO 5 C 4
Malpelo, Punta ▲ PE 64-65 B 3
Malpeque o CDN (PEI) 240-241 M 4
Malpeque Bay ≈ 38-39 N 5
Malpeque Bay ≈ CDN 240-241 M 4
Malpica (Malpica de Bergantiños) o E 98-99 C 3
Malprabha ~ IND 140-141 F 2
Mālpur o IND 138-139 D 8
Mālpura o IND 138-139 E 6
Malsūniyah, al- ~ KSA 130-131 L 5
Malta o BR 68-69 K 5
Malta o LV 94-95 K 3
Malta ■ M 100-101 E 7
Malta ⌒ M 100-101 E 7
Malta o USA (ID) 252-253 E 4
Malta o USA (MT) 250-251 M 3
Maltahöhe ☆ NAM 220-221 C 2
Maltais o CDN (NB) 240-241 J 3
Maltam o CAM 198-199 G 6
Maltan ~ RUS 120-121 O 3
Maltee o AUS 176-177 M 6
Malton o GB 90-91 G 4
Maluera o MOC 218-219 F 2
Maluku ▫ RI 164-165 J 5
Maluku o• ZRE 210-211 E 6
Malúli, Rio ~ MOC 218-219 K 2
Malumfashi o WAN 204-205 G 3
Malunda o RI 164-165 F 5
Malung o S 86-87 F 6
Malungwishi o ZRE 214-215 D 6
Malur o IND 140-141 G 4
Malūt o SUD 206-207 L 3
Maluti Mountains ▲ LS 220-221 J 4
Maluu o SOL 184 I e 3
Mālvan o IND 140-141 E 2
Malvas o PE 64-65 D 6
Malverick o USA (TX) 266-267 G 2
Malvern o USA (AR) 276-277 C 6
Malvern o USA (IA) 274-275 C 3
Malvern o USA (TX) 268-269 E 5
Malvinas, Islas ⌒ GB 78-79 L 6
Malwa ☆ IND 138-139 F 7
Malwal o SUD 206-207 K 4
Malya o EAT 212-213 D 5
Malye Čany ozero ⊙ RUS 124-125 K 1
Malye Donki ozero ⊙ RUS 114-115 H 7
Malygina, mys ▲ RUS 108-109 O 5
Malygina, proliv ≈ 108-109 O 5
Malyj Abakan ~ RUS 124-125 Q 3
Malyj Aim ~ RUS 120-121 E 4
Malyj Amalat ~ RUS 118-119 F 8
Malyj Anjuj ~ RUS 112-113 P 3
Malyj Ases"egan ~ RUS 114-115 S 4
Malyj Begičev, ostrov ⌒ RUS 110-111 H 2
Malyj Čaun ~ RUS 112-113 Q 2
Malyj Čaunskyj, proliv ⊙ RUS 112-113 O 2
Malyj Enisej ~ RUS 116-117 H 10
Malyj Hamar-Daban, hrebet ▲ RUS 116-117 L 10
Malyj Jugan ~ RUS 114-115 N 5
Malyj Karmakuly o RUS 108-109 E 5
Malyj Kas ~ RUS 114-115 U 5
Malyj Kavkaz ▲ GE (ADZ) 126-127 D 7
Malyj Kemčug ~ RUS 116-117 F 7
Malyj Kemčug ~ RUS 116-117 F 7
Malyj Ljahovskij, ostrov ⌒ RUS 110-111 W 2
Malyj Majn ~ RUS 112-113 Q 4
Malyj Megtyg"egan ~ RUS 114-115 Q 4
Malyj Naryn ~ KS 146-147 C 5
Malyj Nimnyr o RUS 118-119 M 7
Malyj Nimnyr ~ RUS 118-119 M 7
Malyj Oľdoj ~ RUS 118-119 L 8
Malyj Olër, ozero ⊙ RUS 112-113 J 2
Malyj Salym ~ RUS 114-115 L 4
Malyj Šantar, ostrov ⌒ RUS 120-121 G 6
Malyj Sarykul' ozero ⊙ RUS 96-97 M 6
Malyj Semljačik, vulkan ▲ RUS 120-121 S 6
Malyj Tagul ~ RUS 116-117 H 8
Malyj Turtas ~ RUS 114-115 L 5
Malyj Urkan ~ RUS 118-119 M 8
Malyj Uzen' o RUS (SAR) 96-97 E 8
Malyj Uzen' ~ RUS 96-97 E 8
Malyj Van'kin, mys ▲ RUS 110-111 Y 3
Malyjžemčužnyj, ostrov ⌒ RUS 126-127 H 5
Malyk, ozero ⊙ RUS 120-121 M 2
Malyn o UA 102-103 F 2
Malyy Kavkaz = Malyj Kavkaz ▲ GE 126-127 D 7
Mama o RUS (IRK) 118-119 F 6
Mama ~ RUS 118-119 F 7
Mamad o RP 160-161 E 9
Mamadyš ☆ RUS 96-97 G 6
Mamãe Ana o BR 66-67 J 5
Mamaj, kōli ⊙ KA 124-125 G 2
Mamakan o RUS 118-119 G 7
Mamakan ~ RUS 118-119 F 7
Mamallapuram o•• IND 140-141 J 4
Maman o PE 64-65 D 6
Mamana Island = Rum Cay ⌒ BS 54-55 H 3
Mamanguape o BR 68-69 L 5
Mamanuka Group ⌒ FJI 184 III a 2
Mamári o SN 202-203 D 2
Mamasa o RI 164-165 F 5
Mamasiware o RI 166-167 H 3
Mamawi Lake ⊙ CDN 30-31 O 6
Mamba o ZRE 214-215 D 5
Mambai o BR 72-73 G 3
Mambajao o RP 160-161 F 8
Mambal o CAM 204-205 K 5
Mambali o EAT 212-213 D 6
Mambare River ~ PNG 183 D 5
Mambasa o ZRE 212-213 B 3
Mambeco o MOC 218-219 G 6
Mambenga o ZRE 210-211 G 5
Mamberamo ~ RI 166-167 K 3
Mamberamo-Foja Mountains-Rouffaer Reserves ⊥• RI 166-167 J 2
Mamberano ~ RI 166-167 J 2
Mambéré ~ RCA 206-207 B 6
Mambéré-Kadéï ▫ RCA 206-207 B 6
Mambi o RI 164-165 F 5
Mambia o RG 202-203 D 5
Mambila Mountains ▲ WAN 204-205 J 5
Mambili ~ RCB 210-211 E 3
Mambilima Falls ~• Z 214-215 E 6
Mambonde ~ ANG 216-217 C 7
Mamboor, Kepulauan ⌒ RI 166-167 H 3
Mamborê o BR 74-75 D 5
Mambova Rapids ~ Z 218-219 C 3
Mambrui o EAK 212-213 H 5
Mamburao ☆ RP 160-161 D 6
Mambusao o RP 160-161 E 7
Mambwe o Z 214-215 F 5
Mamcai o RI 166-167 H 2
Mamčergyrgyn ~ RUS 112-113 U 4
Mamdapur o IND 140-141 F 2
Mameigwess Lake ⊙ CDN (ONT) 234-235 Q 2
Mameigwess Lake ⊙ CDN (ONT) 234-235 P 2
Mamelodi o ZA 220-221 J 2
Ma-Me-O-Beach o CDN (ALB) 232-233 E 3
Mametčinskij, poluostrov ⌄ RUS 120-121 U 3
Mametčinskij, zaliv ⊙ RUS 120-121 U 3
Mamfé o CAM 204-205 H 6
Māmi, Ra's ▲ Y 132-133 J 7
Mamiá, Lago ⊙ BR 66-67 F 5
Mamiña o RCH 70-71 C 7
Mamisi o RI 166-167 H 3
Mamisonski, pereval ▲ GE 126-127 E 6
Mamljutka ☆ KA 124-125 F 1
Mammama Hawa o CDN (ONT) 236-237 D 4
Mammoth o USA (AZ) 256-257 E 6
Mammoth Cave National Park ⊥•• USA (KY) 276-277 J 3
Mammoth Hot Sprimgs o USA (WY) 252-253 H 2
Mammoth Spring o USA (AR) 276-277 D 4
Mamoadate, Áreas Indígenas ⚔ BR 70-71 B 2
Mamoeiro o BR 66-67 C 7
Mamonovo ~ RUS 94-95 F 4
Mamonta ~ RUS 108-109 a 4
Mamonta, poluostrov ⌄ RUS 108-109 R 6
Mamontova gora • RUS 120-121 F 2
Mamontovaja ~ RUS 112-113 U 1
Mamontovo o RUS 114-115 M 4
Mamoré, Río ~ BOL 70-71 E 3
Mamori, Lago ⊙ BR 66-67 G 4
Mamori, Paraná do ~ BR 66-67 H 4
Mamoriá o BR 66-67 D 6
Mamoriazinho, Rio ~ BR 66-67 D 6
Mamou o RG 202-203 D 4
Mamou o USA (LA) 268-269 H 6
Mamoun, Lac ⊙ RCA 206-207 F 3
Mampikony o RM 222-223 E 6
Mampong o GH 202-203 K 6
Ma M'rê o VN 158-159 J 5
Mamry, Jezioro ⊙ PL 92-93 Q 1
Mamu o RI 164-165 F 4
Mamu o WAN 204-205 E 5
Mamuil Mulal, Paso ▲ RA 78-79 D 5
Mamuju o RI 164-165 F 5
Ma'mūniye o IR 136-137 B 7
Mamuno o RB 216-217 F 11
Mamure Kalesi • TR 128-129 E 4
Mamuru, Rio ~ BR 66-67 J 4
Mamutzu o COM 222-223 D 4
Man ☆•• CI 202-203 G 6
Man o RCA 206-207 B 5
Man ~ RI 168 C 3
Man, Río ~ PE 64-65 F 7
Mana o F 62-63 H 3
Mana ~ F 62-63 H 3
Mana ⌒ FJI 184 III a 2

Mana ∼ RUS 116-117 F 8
Mana ○ USA (HI) 288 F 2
Manacacias, Río ∼ CO 60-61 E 6
Manacapurú ○ BR 66-67 G 4
Manacapuru, Rio ∼ BR 66-67 G 4
Manacas ○ C 54-55 E 3
Manacor ○ E 98-99 J 5
Manādir, al- ∸ UAE 132-133 J 2
Manado ☆ RI 164-165 J 3
Manaffey ○ USA (PA) 280-281 H 3
Managua ★ NIC 52-53 L 5
Managua, Lago de ⊖ NIC 52-53 L 5
Manāḥa ○• Y 132-133 C 6
Manaira ○ BR 68-69 J 5
Manajuare ○ CO 60-61 F 5
Manakana ○ RM 222-223 E 6
Manakara ○ RM 222-223 E 9
Manalalondo ○ RM 222-223 E 7
Manali ○• IND 138-139 F 3
Manama ○ UAE 134-135 G 6
Manama ○ ZW 218-219 E 5
Manāma, al- ★• BRN 134-135 D 5
Mānāmadurai ○ IND 140-141 H 6
Manambaho ∼ RM 222-223 D 6
Manambaro ○ RM 222-223 E 10
Manambolo ∼ RM 222-223 D 7
Manambolosy ○ RM 222-223 F 6
Manambondro ○ RM 222-223 E 9
Manambovo ∼ RM 222-223 D 10
Manamgoora ○ AUS 174-175 D 5
Manami ○ RI 166-167 H 3
Manam Island ⌒ PNG 183 C 3
Manamo, Caño ∼ YV 60-61 K 3
Manampanihy ∼ RM 222-223 E 10
Manampatrana ∼ RM 222-223 E 9
Mananá, Cachoeira ∼ BR 62-63 H 4
Manantantanana ∼ RM 222-223 D 8
Mananara ∼ RM 222-223 F 6
Mananara Avaratra ○ RM 222-223 F 6
Manandona ○ RM 222-223 E 8
Manangatang ○ AUS 180-181 G 3
Mananjary ○ RM (FNS) 222-223 F 8
Mananjary ∼ RM 222-223 E 8
Manankoro ○ RMM 202-203 G 4
Manantali, Lac de < RMM 202-203 E 3
Manantenina ○ RM 222-223 E 10
Mānantoddy ○ IND 140-141 G 5
Mana Pass ▲ VRC 144-145 B 5
Mana Pools National Park ⊥··· ZW 218-219 E 2
Manapouri, Lake ⊖ NZ 182 A 6
Manappārai ○ IND 140-141 H 5
Manaquiri ○ BR 66-67 G 4
Manaquiri, Lago ⊖ BR 66-67 G 4
Manari ○ PNG 183 D 5
Manariā ○ BR 66-67 D 5
Manas ∼ BHT 142-143 G 2
Manas ○ PE 64-65 D 7
Manas ○ VRC 146-147 H 3
Manas, gora ▲ KS 136-137 M 3
Manasarowar = Mapam Yumco ⊖ VRC 144-145 C 5
Manas He ∼ VRC 146-147 G 3
Manas Hu ⊖ VRC 146-147 H 3
Manaslu ▲ NEP 144-145 E 6
Manassa ○ USA (CO) 254-255 K 6
Manassas ○ USA (VA) 280-281 J 5
Manassas National Battlefield Park • USA (VA) 280-281 J 5
Mănăstire Horezu ••• RO 102-103 C 5
Manastir Morača • YU 100-101 G 3
Manastir Ostrog • YU 100-101 G 3
Manas Wildlife Sanctuary ⊥··· IND 142-143 G 2
Manatee, Lake < USA (FL) 286-287 G 4
Manatee River ∼ USA (FL) 286-287 G 4
Manati ○ C 54-55 F 4
Manatí ○ C 54-55 G 4
Manati ○ USA (PR) 286-287 P 2
Manatlán ○ MEX 52-53 B 2
Manatuto ○ RI 166-167 C 6
Manau ○ PNG 183 D 5
Man'aung ○ MYA 142-143 H 6
Man'aung Kyûn ⌒ MYA 142-143 H 6
Manaure ○ CO 60-61 E 2
Manaus ○ BR (MAR) 68-69 E 2
Manaus ☆ BR (AMA) 66-67 G 4
Manavgat ☆ TR 128-129 D 4
Manawoka, Pulau ⌒ RI 166-167 F 4
Mañazo ○ PE 70-71 B 4
Mānbazār ○ IND 142-143 E 4
Manbij ☆ SYR 128-129 G 4
Manbiri ○ RMM 202-203 F 3
Mancelona ○ USA (MI) 272-273 D 3
Mancha, La ∸ E 98-99 F 5
Manchao, Sierra de ⛰ RA 76-77 D 5
Manchar ○ IND 138-139 D 10
Manche = English Channel ≈ 90-91 F 6
Mancheng Hanmu ∴• VRC 154-155 J 2
Mancherāl ○ IND 138-139 G 10
Manchester ○• GB 90-91 F 5
Manchester ○ USA (CT) 280-281 O 2
Manchester ○ USA (GA) 284-285 F 4
Manchester ○ USA (IA) 274-275 G 2
Manchester ○ USA (KY) 276-277 M 3
Manchester ○ USA (NH) 278-279 K 6
Manchester ○ USA (OH) 280-281 C 5
Manchester ○ USA (TN) 276-277 J 5
Manchester ○ USA (VT) 278-279 H 5
Manchester ○ USA (WI) 270-271 J 7
Manchester Lake ⊖ CDN 30-31 Q 5
Manchhar Lake ⊖ PK 134-135 M 5
Manchioneal ○ JA 54-55 G 5
Manchok ○ WAN 204-205 H 4
Manchuria = Dongbei ∸ VRC 150-151 E 6
Manciano ○ I 100-101 C 3
Máncora ○ PE 64-65 B 4
Mancos ○ USA (CO) 254-255 G 6
Mancos River ∼ USA (CO) 254-255 G 6
Mand ○ PK 134-135 K 5
Mand, Rūd-e ∼ IR 134-135 D 4
Manda ○ EAT (IRI) 214-215 H 6
Manda ○ EAT (MBE) 214-215 G 4
Manda ○ ETH 200-201 L 6
Manda ○ TCH 206-207 D 4
Manda, Parc National de ⊥ TCH 206-207 C 4
Mandabe ○ RM 222-223 D 8
Mandacaru ○ BR 68-69 G 3
Mandaguari ○ BR 72-73 E 7
Mandah = Töhöm ○ MAU 148-149 J 5
Manda Island ⌒ EAK 212-213 H 5
Mandal ☆ N 86-87 C 7
Mandalay ☆•• MYA 142-143 K 4
Mandalgov' ☆ MAU 148-149 H 5
Mandali ☆ IRQ 128-129 L 6
Mandal-Ovoo = Šarhulsan ○ MAU 148-149 G 5
Mandalselva ∼ N 86-87 C 7
Mandan ○• USA (ND) 258-259 G 5
Mandaon ○ RP 160-161 E 6
Mandar, Teluk ≈ 164-165 F 5
Mandara Mountains ⛰ WAN 204-205 K 3
Mandarin ○ USA (FL) 286-287 H 1
Mándas ○ I 100-101 B 5
Mandasor ○ IND 138-139 E 7
Mandaue ○ RP 160-161 E 7
Mandélia ○ TCH 206-207 B 3
Mandera ○ EAK 212-213 H 2
Manderson ○ USA (WY) 252-253 L 2
Mandeville ○• JA 54-55 G 5
Mandeville ○ USA (LA) 268-269 K 6
Mandheera ○ SP 208-209 G 4
Mandi ○• IND 138-139 F 4
Mandi, Raudal ∼ CO 66-67 B 2
Mandiakui ○ RMM 202-203 H 3
Mandiana ○ RG 202-203 F 4
Mandiangin ○ RI 162-163 C 5
Mandi Bahāuddin ○ PK 138-139 D 3
Mandi Burewāla ○ PK 138-139 D 4
Mandié ○ MOC 218-219 G 3
Mandi Langwé ▲ CAM 204-205 J 6
Mandimba ○ MOC 218-219 H 2
Mandingues, Monts ⛰ RMM 202-203 F 3
Mandioli, Pulau ⌒ RI 164-165 K 4
Mandioré, Lago ⊖ BOL 70-71 J 6
Mandirituba ○ BR 74-75 F 5
Mandji ○ G 210-211 C 4
Mandla ○ IND 142-143 B 4
Mandleshwar ○ IND 138-139 E 8
Mando ○ WAN 204-205 G 3
Mandōl ○ AFG 136-137 M 7
Mandon ○ RI 166-167 J 2
Mandor ○ RI 162-163 H 4
Mandora ○ AUS 172-173 E 5
Mandori ○ RI 166-167 H 2
Mandoro ○ ZRE 206-207 J 6
Mandoto ○ RM 222-223 E 7
Mandoul ∼ TCH 206-207 C 4
Mandouri ○ RT 202-203 L 4
Mandra ○ PK 138-139 D 3
Mandrare ∼ RM 222-223 E 10
Mandrikovo ○ RUS 112-113 K 3
Mandritsara ○ RM 222-223 F 5
Mandronarivo ○ RM 222-223 D 8
Mandrosonoro ○ RM 222-223 E 8
Mandu ○ IND 142-143 D 4
Mandul, Pulau ⌒ RI 164-165 E 2
Mandumbua ○ ANG 216-217 F 7
Mandurah ○• AUS 176-177 C 6
Mandúria ○ I 100-101 F 4
Mandūzai ○ AFG 138-139 B 3
Māndvi ○ IND (GUJ) 138-139 D 9
Māndvi ○ IND (GUJ) 138-139 B 8
Mandya ○ IND 140-141 G 4
Mané ○ BF 202-203 K 3
Maneadero ○ C 54-55 E 3
Maneadero ○ MEX 50-51 A 2
Mané Kondjo ∼ TCH 206-207 D 3
Manengouba, Massif du ▲ CAM 204-205 H 6
Maneromango ○ EAT 214-215 K 4
Manes ○ USA (MO) 276-277 C 3
Manevyči ○ UA 102-103 D 2
Manfalūt ○ ET 194-195 E 4
Manflas, Río ∼ RCH 76-77 C 5
Manfran ○ RG 202-203 F 5
Manfred Downs ○ AUS 174-175 F 7
Manfredónia ○ I 100-101 E 4
Manfredónia, Golfo di ≈ 100-101 F 4
Manga ○ BF 202-203 K 4
Manga ○ BR 72-73 J 3
Manga ▲ CAM 204-205 K 5
Manga ○ PNG 183 G 3
Manga ∸ RN 198-199 F 6
Mangabeiras, Chapada das ⛰ BR 68-69 E 6
Mangada ○ ZRE 212-213 A 2
Manga Grande ○ ANG 216-217 B 3
Mangai ○ PNG 183 F 2
Mangaizé ○ RN 202-203 L 2
Mangalia ○• RO 102-103 F 6
Mangalmé ○ TCH 198-199 J 6
Mangalore ○ AUS 178-179 J 4
Mangalore ○• IND 140-141 F 4
Mangalwedha ○ IND 140-141 F 2
Mangango ○ Z 218-219 C 2
Māngaon ○ IND 138-139 D 10
Mangas ○ USA (NM) 256-257 J 4
Mangatupopo ○ NZ 182 E 3
Mangawan ○ IND 142-143 B 3
Mangaweka ▲ NZ 182 F 3
Mangbwalu ○ ZRE 212-213 C 3
Mangdangshan • VRC 154-155 K 4
Măng Đen, Đèo ▲ VN 158-159 K 3
Mange ○ PNG 183 D 4
Mange ○ WAL 202-203 D 5
Mangeni, Hamada ∸ RN 192-193 E 6
Manggar ○ RI 162-163 H 6
Manggasi ○ RI 166-167 J 3
Manggawitu ○ RI 166-167 G 4
Manggar, Tanjung ▲ RI 166-167 H 3
Mangham ○ USA (LA) 268-269 J 4
Mangisor, kŏli ⊖ KA 124-125 F 1
Mangistau, gory ⛰ KA 126-127 J 5
Mangit ☆ US 136-137 G 3
Mangkalihat, Tanjung ▲ RI 164-165 F 3
Mangkok, Tanjung ▲ RI 164-165 E 5
Mangkutana ○ RI 164-165 G 5
Manglares ○ CO 60-61 C 5
Manglares, Cabo ▲ CO 64-65 C 1
Manglares, Punta ▲ CO 60-61 C 5
Manglares Churute, Reservat E. ⊥ EC 64-65 C 3
Mangla Reservoir < PK 138-139 D 3
Mangnai ○ VRC 144-145 H 2
Mangnai Zhen ○ VRC 146-147 K 6
Mangnuc, Lac ⊖ CDN 36-37 L 5
Mango ⌒ TON 184 IV a 2
Mangoaka ○ RM 222-223 F 4
Mangochi ○• MW 218-219 H 2
Mango Creek ○ BH 52-53 K 3
Mangodara ○ BF 202-203 H 5
Mangoky ∼ RM 222-223 D 9
Mangole, Pulau ⌒ RI 164-165 J 4
Mangole, Selat ≈ 164-165 J 4
Mangom ○ CAM 204-205 K 5
Mangombe ○ ZRE 210-211 L 4
Mangonui ○ NZ 182 D 1
Mangoro ∼ RM 222-223 F 7
Mangowra ○ AUS 174-175 F 5
Māngrol ○ IND 138-139 C 9
Mangrullo, Cuchilla de ⛰ ROU 74-75 D 9
Mangrūl Pīr ○ IND 138-139 F 9
Mangshan • VRC 154-155 H 4
Mangu ○ EAK 212-213 F 4
Manguaurcu ○ EC 64-65 B 4
Mangúchar ○ PK 134-135 M 4
Mangue ○ BR 68-69 F 2
Mangueigne ○ TCH 206-207 E 3
Mangueira, Lagoa ⊖ BR 74-75 D 9
Mangueirinha ○ BR 74-75 D 5
Manguel Creek ○ AUS 172-173 F 4
Mangues, Rio dos ∼ BR 68-69 D 7
Mangue Seco ○ BR 68-69 K 7
Mangues Secos, Ponta dos ▲ BR 68-69 G 3
Mangui ○ VRC 150-151 D 1
Manguito ○ C 54-55 E 3
Mangum ○ USA (OK) 264-265 E 4
Mangunça ○ BR 68-69 F 2
Mangunca, Ilha ⌒ BR 68-69 F 2
Mangungu ○ ZRE 210-211 F 6
Mangunza ○ Z 218-219 D 3
Manguohe ○ VRC 156-157 C 4
Mangurdejipa ○ ZRE 212-213 B 3
Mangut ○ RUS 118-119 F 11
Mangutiha ∼ RUS 114-115 T 3
Mangutiri, Igarapé ∼ BR 66-67 D 7
Mang Yang ○ VN 158-159 K 4
Măng Yang, Đèo ▲ VN 158-159 K 3
Mangyčlak ☆ KA 126-127 J 6
Mangyšlak ○ KA 126-127 J 6
Mangyšlak, plato ⛰ KA 126-127 K 6
Mangyšlakskij zaliv ≈ 126-127 J 5
Mangystau, taulary ⛰ KA 126-127 J 5
Manhan = Tögrög ○ MAU 146-147 L 2
Manhattan ○ USA (KS) 262-263 K 5
Manhattan ○ USA (MT) 250-251 H 6
Manhattan ○ USA (NV) 246-247 H 5
Manhica ○ MOC 220-221 L 2
Manhuaçu ○ BR 72-73 J 6
Manhumirim ○ BR 72-73 K 6
Mani ○ CO 60-61 E 5
Mani ○ TCH 198-199 G 6
Mani ○ WAN 198-199 C 6
Mani ○ ZRE 214-215 C 4
Mani, Quebrada de ∼ RCH 76-77 C 1
Mania ∼ RM 222-223 E 8
Maniaçu ○ BR 72-73 J 2
Maniamba ○ MOC 214-215 H 7
Mania-Muna ○ ZRE 214-215 B 5
Manica ○ MOC 218-219 G 4
Manica ■ MOC 218-219 G 5
Manicaland ■ ZW 218-219 F 4
Manicani Island ⌒ RP 160-161 F 7
Manicaragua ○ C 54-55 F 3
Maniche ○ RH 54-55 J 5
Manico Point ▲ CDN 36-37 F 3
Manicoré ○ BR 66-67 G 5
Manicoré, Rio ∼ BR 66-67 G 6
Manicorézinho, Rio ∼ BR 66-67 G 6
Manicouagan ○ CDN 38-39 K 3
Manicouagan, Réservoir <·· CDN 38-39 K 3
Manicouagan, Rivière ∼ CDN 38-39 K 4
Manicrois, Réservoir < CDN 38-39 K 3
Manifold, Cape ▲ AUS 178-179 L 2
Maniganggo ○ VRC 144-145 M 5
Manigotagan ○ CDN (MAN) 234-235 G 3
Maniitsoq ⌒ GRØ 28-29 O 4
Maniitsoq = Sukkertoppen ○ GRØ 28-29 O 4
Manika ○ ZRE 214-215 C 6
Manila ★•• RP 160-161 D 5
Manila ○ USA (AR) 276-277 E 5
Manila ○ USA (UT) 254-255 F 3
Manila Bay ≈ 160-161 D 5
Manilla ○ AUS 178-179 L 6
Manily ○ RUS 112-113 N 5
Manimbaya, Tanjung ▲ RI 164-165 F 4
Maningory ∼ RM 222-223 F 6
Maningoza ∼ RM 222-223 D 6
Maningrida X AUS 174-175 C 3
Maninjau ○ RI 162-163 D 5
Maninjau, Danau ⊖ RI 162-163 D 5
Manipa, Pulau ⌒ RI 166-167 D 3
Manipa, Selat ≈ 166-167 D 3
Manipur ■ IND 142-143 H 3
Manipur ∼ IND 142-143 H 3
Maniqui, Río ∼ BOL 70-71 D 4
Manisa ☆• TR 128-129 B 3
Manisaj ∼ KA 126-127 M 4
Manissauá-Miçu, Rio ∼ BR 70-71 K 3
Manistee ○ USA (MI) 272-273 C 3
Manistee River ∼ USA (MI) 272-273 D 3
Manistique ○ USA (MI) 270-271 M 5
Manistique Lake ⊖ USA (MI) 270-271 N 4
Manistique River ∼ USA (MI) 270-271 M 4
Manita pećina •• HR 100-101 E 2
Manito ○ USA (IL) 274-275 J 4
Manitoba ■ CDN 34-35 F 3
Manitoba, Lake ⊖ CDN (MAN) 234-235 D 3
Manito Lake ⊖ CDN (SAS) 232-233 J 3
Manitou ○ CDN (MAN) 234-235 E 5
Manitou ○ CDN (QUE) 242-243 C 2
Manitou, Lac ⊖ CDN (QUE) 242-243 E 2
Manitou, Rivière ∼ CDN (QUE) 242-243 C 2
Manitou Beach ○ CDN (SAS) 232-233 N 4
Manitou Falls ○ CDN (ONT) 234-235 K 4
Manitou Island ⌒ USA (MI) 270-271 L 3
Manitou Islands ⌒ USA (MI) 270-271 M 5
Manitou Lake ⊖ CDN (ONT) 238-239 D 3
Manitou Lakes ⊖ CDN (ONT) 234-235 L 5
Manitoulin Island ⌒ CDN (ONT) 238-239 C 3
Manitounuk Sound ≈ 36-37 L 7
Manitou Springs ○ USA (CO) 254-255 L 5
Manitouwadge ○ CDN (ONT) 236-237 C 3
Manitowaning ○ CDN (ONT) 238-239 D 3
Manitowoc ○ USA (WI) 270-271 L 6
Manitsoq ⌒ GRØ 26-27 X 7
Maniwaki ○ CDN (QUE) 238-239 K 2
Maniwaki Indian Reservation X CDN (QUE) 238-239 K 2
Maniwaki Indian Reserve X CDN (QUE) 238-239 J 2
Maniwori ○ RI 166-167 H 3
Maniyāchchi ○ IND 140-141 G 6
Manizales ☆ CO 60-61 D 5
Manja ○ RM 222-223 D 8
Manjacaze ○ MOC 220-221 L 2
Manjakandriana ○ RM 222-223 E 7
Manjakot ○ PK 138-139 D 2
Manjeri ○ IND 140-141 G 5
Mānjhand ○ PK 138-139 B 7
Manjimup ○ AUS 176-177 D 7
Manjo ○ CAM 204-205 H 6
Manjou ○ CAM 204-205 K 6
Manjra ∼ IND 138-139 F 10
Mānjra ∼ IND 138-139 F 10
Mankanza ○ ZRE 210-211 G 3
Mankarigu ○ GH 202-203 K 4
Man Kat ○ MYA 142-143 L 4
Mankato ○ USA (KS) 262-263 H 5
Mankato ○ USA (MN) 270-271 E 6
Mankayane ○ SD 220-221 K 3
Mankera ○ PK 138-139 C 4
Mankessim ○ GH 202-203 K 7
Manki II ○ CAM 204-205 J 6
Mankim ○ CAM 204-205 K 6
Mankins ○ USA (TX) 264-265 F 5
Mankono ☆ CI 202-203 G 5
Mankota ○ CDN (SAS) 232-233 L 6
Mankpan ○ GH 202-203 K 5
Mankranso ○ GH 202-203 K 6
Mankyclaks, cyganak ≈ 126-127 J 5
Manley Hot Springs ○ USA 20-21 P 4
Manlius ○ USA (NY) 278-279 F 6
Manly ○ USA (IA) 274-275 E 1
Man Na ○ MYA 142-143 K 4
Manna ○ RI 162-163 E 7
Mannahill ○ AUS 180-181 E 2
Manna Hill Gold Field • AUS 180-181 E 2
Mannampitiya ○ CL 140-141 J 7
Mannar, Gulf of ≈ 140-141 H 6
Mannārgudi ○ IND 140-141 H 5
Mannar Island ⌒ CL 140-141 H 6
Mannarkkad ○ IND 140-141 G 5
Manners Creek ○ AUS 178-179 D 2
Mannheim ○• D 92-93 K 4
Manni ○ VRC 144-145 F 3
Manning ○ USA (IA) 274-275 C 3
Manning ○ USA (ND) 258-259 E 4
Manning ○ USA (SC) 284-285 K 3
Manning, Cape ▲ CDN 24-25 K 3
Manning Park ○ CDN (BC) 230-231 J 4
Manning Provincial Park ⊥ CDN (BC) 230-231 J 4
Manning Range, Mount ⛰ AUS 176-177 E 4
Manning River ∼ AUS 178-179 M 6
Manning Strait ≈ 184 I c 2
Mannington ○ USA (WV) 280-281 F 4
Mann Ranges ⛰ AUS 176-177 K 3
Mann River ∼ AUS 174-175 C 3
Manns Harbor ○ USA (NC) 282-283 M 5
Mannville ○ CDN (ALB) 232-233 G 2
Mano ○ WAL 202-203 D 5
Manoá Pium, Área Indígena X BR 62-63 D 4
Mano Junction ○ WAL 202-203 E 5
Manokwari ○ RI (IRJ) 166-167 H 2
Manokwari ○ RI (IRJ) 166-167 H 3
Manolo Fortich ○ RP 160-161 F 8
Manoma ∼ RUS 122-123 G 4
Manombo Atsimo ○ RM 222-223 C 9
Manometimay ○ RM 222-223 D 8
Manompana ○ RM 222-223 F 6
Manonga ∼ EAT 212-213 D 5
Manono ○ ZRE 214-215 D 4
Manonwa ○ ZRE 210-211 K 6
Manor ○ CDN (SAS) 232-233 Q 6
Manor ○ USA (GA) 284-285 H 5
Manor ○ USA (TX) 266-267 K 3
Mano River ○ LB 202-203 E 6
Mano River ∼ LB 202-203 E 6
Manos, Cueva de las • RA 80 E 3
Manosque ○ F 90-91 K 10
Manou ○ RCA 206-207 E 4
Manouane ○ CDN (QUE) 236-237 O 5
Manouane, Lac ⊖ CDN (QUE) 38-39 J 3
Manouane, Lac ⊖ CDN (QUE) 236-237 O 5
Manouanis, Lac ⊖ CDN 38-39 J 3
Manovo = Tété ∼ RCA 206-207 E 4
Manpo ○ DVR 150-151 F 7
Manresa ○ E 98-99 H 4
Mānsa ○ IND 138-139 E 5
Mansa ☆ Z 214-215 E 6
Mansabá ○ GNB 202-203 C 3
Mansa Konko ☆• WAG 202-203 C 3
Mansalean ○ RI 164-165 H 4
Mansavillagra, Arroyo ∼ ROU 78-79 M 2
Mānsehra ○ PK 138-139 D 2
Mansel Island ⌒ CDN 36-37 K 3
Mansfield ○ AUS 180-181 J 4
Mansfield ○ GB 90-91 G 5
Mansfield ○ USA (AR) 276-277 A 5
Mansfield ○ USA (IN) 274-275 L 5
Mansfield ○ USA (LA) 268-269 G 4
Mansfield ○ USA (MA) 278-279 K 6
Mansfield ○ USA (MO) 276-277 C 3
Mansfield ○ USA (OH) 280-281 D 3
Mansfield ○ USA (PA) 280-281 J 2
Mansfield ○ USA (TX) 264-265 G 6
Mansfield ○ USA (WA) 244-245 F 3
Mansfield, Mount ▲ USA (VT) 278-279 J 4
Mansfield, Port ○ USA (TX) 266-267 K 7
Mansha ∼ Z 214-215 F 6
Mansi ○ MYA 142-143 J 3
Mansiari ○ IND 144-145 C 5
Mansidão ○ BR 68-69 F 7
Mansijsk, Hanty- ☆ RUS 114-115 K 4
Mansilla ○ E 98-99 F 3
Mansinam, Pulau ⌒ RI 166-167 H 2
Mansle ○ F 90-91 H 9
Manso, Rio ∼ BR 70-71 K 4
Mansôa ○ GNB 202-203 C 3
Mansôa, Rio ∼ GNB 202-203 C 3
Manso ou das Mortes, Rio ∼ BR 70-71 K 4
Manson ○ CDN (MAN) 234-235 B 4
Manson ○ USA (IA) 274-275 D 2
Manson ○ USA (WA) 244-245 E 3
Manson Creek ○ CDN 32-33 H 4
Manso-Nkwanta ○ GH 202-203 K 6
Mansons Landing ○ CDN (BC) 230-231 D 3
Mansoura ○ DZ 190-191 E 2
Mansourah • DZ 188-189 L 3
Mansuar, Pulau ⌒ RI 166-167 F 2
Mansuela ○ RI 166-167 E 3
Mansuela Reserve ⊥• RI 166-167 E 3
Mansura ○ USA (LA) 268-269 H 5
Manşūra, al- ☆ ET 194-195 E 2
Manşūriya, al- ○ Y 132-133 C 6
Mansurlu ○ TR 128-129 F 4
Manta ○ DY 202-203 L 4
Manta ○ EC 64-65 B 2
Manta, Bahía de ≈ 64-65 B 2
Manta, La ○ CO 60-61 D 3
Mantaba ∼ ZRE 210-211 F 5
Mantador ○ USA (ND) 258-259 L 5
Mantagao Lake ⊖ CDN (MAN) 234-235 F 3
Mantagao River ∼ CDN (MAN) 234-235 F 3
Mantalinga ○ RI 164-165 G 5
Mantalingajan, Mount ▲ RP 160-161 B 8
Mantanzilla, Quebrada ∼ RCH 76-77 B 3
Mantario ○ CDN (SAS) 232-233 J 4
Mantaro, Rio ∼ PE 64-65 E 8
Manteca ○ USA (CA) 248-249 C 2
Mantecal ○ YV (APU) 60-61 G 4
Mantecal ○ YV (BOL) 60-61 J 4
Manteco, El ○ YV 60-61 K 4
Mantehage, Pulau ⌒ RI 164-165 J 3
Mantena ○ BR 72-73 K 5
Mantenga Falls ∼• SD 220-221 K 3
Manteo ○ USA (NC) 282-283 M 5
Manthani ○ IND 138-139 G 10
Manti ○ USA (AL) 284-285 D 5
Manti ○ USA (UT) 254-255 D 4
Mantiqueira, Serra da ⛰ BR 72-73 G 7
Manto ○ HN 52-53 L 4
Manton ○ USA (MI) 272-273 D 3
Manton Knob ▲ AUS 176-177 J 3
Mantova ○• I 100-101 C 2
Mantralayam ○ IND 140-141 G 3
Mäntsälä ○ FIN 88-89 H 6
Mant's Harbour ○ CDN (NFL) 242-243 P 4
Mantua ○ C 54-55 C 3
Mantua ∼ C 54-55 C 3
Mantuan Downs P.O. ○ AUS 178-179 J 3
Manturovo ○ RUS 96-97 D 4
Manú ○ PE 70-71 B 3
Manu ○ WAN 198-199 B 6
Manú, Parque Nacional ⊥··· PE 70-71 B 2
Manu'a Islands ⌒ USA 184 V c 2
Manubepium ○ RI 166-167 H 2
Manuel ○ MEX 50-51 K 6
Manuela, La ○ RA 78-79 H 4
Manuel Alves, Rio ∼ BR 68-69 D 7
Manuel Alves Grande, Rio ∼ BR 68-69 E 5
Manuel Alves Pequena, Rio ∼ BR 68-69 E 6
Manuel Benavides ○ MEX 50-51 H 3
Manuel Emidio ○ BR 68-69 G 5
Manuel Lake ⊖ CDN 30-31 F 2
Manuel Ribas ○ BR 74-75 E 5
Manuel Rodríguez, Isla ⌒ RCH 80 D 6
Manuel Tames ○ C 54-55 H 4
Manuel Urbano ○ BR 66-67 C 7
Manuel Viana ○ BR 76-77 K 5
Manuel Vitorino ○ BR 72-73 K 3
Manūğān ○ IR 134-135 G 5
Manui, Pulau ⌒ RI 164-165 H 5
Manuk ∼ RI 168 C 3
Manuk, Pulau ⌒ RI 166-167 F 4
Manukan ○ RP 160-161 E 8
Manuk Mankaw ⌒ RP 160-161 C 10
Manundi, Tanjung ▲ RI 166-167 H 2
Manupampi, Pulau ⌒ RI 166-167 H 2
Manuran, Pulau ⌒ RI 166-167 F 1
Manurimi, Rio ∼ BOL 70-71 D 2
Manuripe, Rio ∼ PE 70-71 C 2
Manuripi, Rio ∼ BOL 70-71 D 2
Manuripi Heath, Natural Reserve ⊥ BOL 70-71 C 2
Manus Island ⌒ PNG 183 D 1
Manvel ○ USA (ND) 258-259 K 3
Mānvi ○ IND 140-141 G 2
Manville ○ USA (WY) 252-253 O 4
Many ○ USA (LA) 268-269 G 5
Manyame ∼ ZW 218-219 F 3
Manyani ○ EAK 212-213 G 5
Manyara, Lake ⊖ EAT 212-213 E 5
Manyara National Park ⊥ EAT 212-213 E 5
Manyas ☆ TR 128-129 B 2
Manyberries ○ CDN (ALB) 232-233 H 6
Manyč ∼ RUS 102-103 N 5
Manych Depression = Kumo-Manyčskaja vpadina ⌣ RUS 102-103 M 4
Manyémen ○ CAM 204-205 H 6
Manyinga ○ Z 218-219 C 1
Many Island Lake ⊖ CDN (ALB) 232-233 H 5
Manyo ○ EAT 214-215 F 4
Manyoni ○ EAT 212-213 E 6
Mānzai ○ PK 138-139 B 4
Manzai ○ PK 138-139 C 3
Manzanares ○ CO 60-61 D 5
Manzanares ○• E 98-99 F 5
Manzanillo ○ C 54-55 G 4
Manzanillo ○• MEX 52-53 B 2
Manzanillo, Punta ▲ YV 60-61 G 2
Manzanita ○ USA (OR) 244-245 B 5
Manzanita Indian Reservation X USA (CA) 248-249 H 7
Manzano ○ USA (NM) 256-257 J 4
Manzano, El ○ RCH 78-79 D 3
Manzengele ○ ZRE 216-217 D 3
Manzhouli ○ VRC 148-149 N 3
Manzini ○ SD 220-221 K 3
Manzurka ○ RUS 116-117 N 9
Manzurka ∼ RUS 116-117 N 9
Mao ☆ DOM 54-55 K 5
Mao ☆ TCH 198-199 G 5
Maogong ○ VRC 156-157 F 3
Maojing ○ VRC 154-155 E 3
Maoke, Pegunungan ⛰ RI 166-167 J 4
Maolan Z.B. ⊥• VRC 156-157 E 4
Mao Ling • VRC 154-155 F 4
Maoming ○ VRC 156-157 G 6
Maonanzu ○ VRC 156-157 F 4
Maopora, Pulau ⌒ RI 166-167 D 5
Maospati ○ RI 168 D 3
Maotou Shan ▲ VRC 142-143 M 3
Mao Xian ○ VRC 154-155 C 6
Mapaga ○ RI 164-165 F 4
Mapai ○ MOC 218-219 G 6
Mapamoiwa ○ PNG 183 F 5
Mapam Yumco • VRC 144-145 C 5
Mapane ○ RI 164-165 G 4
Mapangu ○ ZRE 210-211 H 6
Mapari, Rio ∼ BR 66-67 D 4
Mapastepec ○ MEX 52-53 H 4
Mapat, Pulau ⌒ RI 164-165 E 2
Mapes ○ CDN (BC) 228-229 L 3
Maphisa ○ ZW 218-219 E 5
Mapi ○ RI 166-167 K 5
Mapi ∼ RI 166-167 K 5
Mapia, Kepulauan Indonesia ⌒ RI 166-167 H 1
Mapiá, Rio ∼ BR 66-67 H 5
Mapichi, Serranía de ⛰ YV 60-61 H 5
Mapili ○ RI 164-165 F 5
Mapinhane ○ MOC 218-219 H 6
Mapire ○ YV 60-61 J 4
Mapiri ○ BOL 70-71 C 4
Mapiri, Rio ∼ BOL 70-71 C 4
Mapiri, Rio ∼ BOL 70-71 D 2
Mapiripán ○ CO 60-61 E 6
Maple Bluff ○ USA (WI) 274-275 J 1
Maple City ○ USA (MI) 272-273 D 3
Maple Creek ○ CDN (SAS) 232-233 J 6
Maple Creek ∼ CDN (SAS) 232-233 J 5
Maple Ridge ○ CDN (BC) 230-231 G 4
Maple Ridge ○ USA (MI) 272-273 F 3
Mapleshville ○ USA (AL) 284-285 D 4
Mapleton ○ USA (IA) 274-275 C 2
Mapleton ○ USA (MI) 272-273 D 3
Mapleton ○ USA (MN) 270-271 E 7
Mapleton ○ USA (OR) 244-245 B 6
Maple Valley ○ USA (WA) 244-245 C 3
Mapmakers Seamount ≃ 14-15 J 5
Mapoon X AUS 174-175 F 3
Mapoon Aboriginal Land X AUS 174-175 G 2
Mappsville ○ USA (VA) 280-281 L 6
Maprik ○ PNG 183 B 2
Mápuca ○• IND 140-141 E 3
Mapuera, Rio ∼ BR 62-63 E 6
Mapulanguene ○ MOC 220-221 L 2
Mapunda ○ ZRE 214-215 C 5
Mapunga ○ Z 218-219 D 1
Maputi, Pulau ⌒ RI 164-165 F 3
Maputo ■ MOC 220-221 L 2
Maputo ★ MOC (MAP) 220-221 L 2
Maputo ∸ MOC (MAP) 220-221 L 3
Maputo, Baía do ≈ 220-221 L 3
Maputo, Reserva de Elefantes do ⊥ MOC 220-221 L 3
Maputo, Rio ∼ MOC 220-221 L 3
Maputsoe ○ LS 220-221 H 4
Maqāriyūs, Dair ⌒• ET 194-195 E 2
Maqên ○ VRC 154-155 B 4
Maqên Gangri ▲ VRC 144-145 M 3
Maqrat ○ Y 132-133 G 6
Maqteïr ∸ RIM 196-197 E 4
Maqu ○ VRC 154-155 B 4
Maquan He (Damqog Zangbo) ∼ VRC 144-145 D 5
Maquatua, Rivière ∼ CDN 38-39 E 2
Maqueda Channel ≈ 160-161 E 6
Maquela do Zombo ○ ANG 216-217 C 3
Maqueze ○ MOC 220-221 L 2
Maquia, Rio ∼ PE 64-65 E 5
Máquina, La ○ C 54-55 H 4
Maquinchao ○ RA 78-79 E 6
Maquinista ○ BOL 70-71 D 2
Maquinista Levet ○ RA 78-79 F 2
Maquoketa ○ USA (IA) 274-275 H 2
Maquoketa River ∼ USA (IA) 274-275 G 2
Mar, La ∴• MEX 52-53 J 3
Mar, Serra do ⛰ BR 72-73 H 7
Mar, Serra do ⛰ BR 74-75 F 6
Mara ■ EAT 212-213 E 4
Mara ∼ EAT 212-213 E 4
Mara ○ GUY 62-63 F 2
Mara ○ ZA 218-219 E 6
Maraã ○ BR 66-67 E 3
Marabá ○ BR 68-69 D 4
Marabadiassa ○ CI 202-203 H 5
Marabahan ○ RI 164-165 D 5
Marabatua, Pulau ⌒ RI 164-165 D 6
Marabi, al- ○ KSA 132-133 C 5
Marabitanas ○ BR 66-67 D 2
Maracá ⌒ BR 62-63 J 4
Maracá, Ilha de ⌒ BR 62-63 J 4
Maracaçumé ○ BR 68-69 F 3
Maracaçumé, Baía de ≈ 68-69 F 2
Maracaçumé, Rio ∼ BR 68-69 F 2
Maracaí ○ BR 72-73 E 7
Maracaibo ☆ YV 60-61 F 2
Maracaibo, Lago de ≈ 60-61 F 2
Maracá-Jipioca, Estação Ecológica ⊥ BR 62-63 J 4
Maracaju ○ BR 76-77 K 1
Maracajú, Serra de ⛰ BR 76-77 K 1
Maracanã ○ BR 68-69 E 2
Maracanã, Baía de ≈ 68-69 E 2
Maracanã, Rio ∼ BR 66-67 H 7
Maracanai, Cachoeira ∼ BR 62-63 H 6
Maracanaquará, Planalto ∸ BR 62-63 H 5
Maracás ○ BR 72-73 K 2
Maracas Bay Village ○ TT 60-61 L 2
Maracay ☆ YV 60-61 H 2
Maracoa ○ CO 60-61 G 6
Maracó Grande, Valle ⌣ RA 78-79 G 4
Maracuni, Rio ∼ YV 60-61 J 6
Marādah ○ LAR 192-193 H 3
Maradankadawala ○ CL 140-141 J 6
Maradi ■ RN 198-199 C 5
Maradi ☆ RN (MAR) 198-199 C 6
Maradun ○ WAN 198-199 C 6
Maraetai ○ NZ 182 E 2
Marafa ○ EAK 212-213 G 5
Marag ○ BR 72-73 L 2
Maragahawewa ○ CL 140-141 J 6
Marāģe ○• IR 128-129 M 4
Maraguay, Punta ▲ YV 60-61 F 2
Marāhayy ○ Y 132-133 G 6
Mārahra ○ IND 138-139 G 6
Marahuaca, Cerro ▲ YV 60-61 J 6
Marais des Cygnes River ∼ USA (MO) 274-275 D 6
Marajó, Baía de ≈ 62-63 K 6
Marajó, Ilha de ⌒ BR 62-63 J 6
Marakabei ○ LS 220-221 J 4
Marakalalo Hills ⛰ RB 218-219 D 6
Marakesa ○ ZRE 210-211 L 3
Maraku ○ WAN 204-205 H 3
Mara Lake ○ CDN (BC) 230-231 L 3
Mara Lake ⊖ CDN (BC) 230-231 K 3
Maralal ○ EAK 212-213 F 3
Maralal National Sanctuary ⊥ EAK 212-213 F 3
Maraldy, kŏli ⊖ KA 124-125 K 2
Marale ○ HN 52-53 L 4
Maraleda ≈ 80 D 2
Maraleda, Canal ≈ 80 D 2
Marali ○ RCA 206-207 D 5
Maralinga ○ AUS 176-177 L 5
Maralinga -Tjarutja Aboriginal Lands X AUS 176-177 L 4
Maramag ○ RP 160-161 F 9
Maramasike = Small Malaita ⌒ SOL 184 I e 3
Maramec ○ USA (OK) 264-265 H 2
Marāmiya, al- ○ KSA 130-131 E 5
Maramuni ○ PNG 183 B 3
Maramuni River ∼ PNG 183 B 3
Maran ○ MAL 162-163 E 3
Mārān, Kōh-i- ▲ PK 134-135 M 4
Marana ○ USA (AZ) 256-257 D 6
Maranchón, Puerto de ▲ E 98-99 F 4
Marand ○• IR 128-129 L 3
Marangu ○ EAT (KIL) 212-213 F 5
Maranguape ○ BR 68-69 J 3
Maranhão ○ BR 66-67 J 4
Maranhão ■ BR 68-69 E 5
Maranhão, Rio ∼ BR 72-73 F 3
Maranhoto ○ BR 66-67 F 4
Maranoa River ∼ AUS 178-179 K 4
Marañón, Río ∼ PE 64-65 C 4
Maransabadi, Pulau ⌒ RI 166-167 H 3
Marantale ○ RI 164-165 G 4
Marantao ○ RP 160-161 F 9
Maranura ○ PE 64-65 F 8
Marão ○ MOC 220-221 M 2
Maraoué ∼ CI 202-203 G 6
Maraoué, Parc National de la ⊥ CI 202-203 G 6
Marapa Island ⌒ SOL 184 I e 3
Marapi, Gunung ▲ RI 162-163 D 5
Marapi, Rio ∼ BR 62-63 F 5
Marapinim ○ BR 68-69 E 2
Marapinim, Rio ∼ BR 68-69 E 2
Marapiti, Ilha do ⌒ BR 66-67 G 5
Marari, Rio ∼ BR 66-67 E 2
Mara River ∼ CDN 30-31 P 2
Mara Rosa ○ BR 72-73 F 2
Mărăşeşti ○ RO 102-103 E 5
Marāši, al- ○ Y 132-133 D 5
Marasimsim ○ MAL 160-161 B 9
Marassu ∼ RUS 124-125 Q 2
Marat ○ US 136-137 J 3
Marat, Ğabal ▲ Y 132-133 G 5
Marata, Ford ○ RUS 108-109 c 2
Marateca ○ P 98-99 C 5
Marathon ○ AUS 174-175 G 7
Marathon ○ CDN (ONT) 236-237 B 4
Marathon ○ USA (FL) 286-287 H 7
Marathon ○ USA (TX) 266-267 D 3
Maratua, Pulau ⌒ RI 164-165 F 2
Marau ○ BR 74-75 D 7
Marauiá, Rio ∼ BR 66-67 E 2
Marau Island ⌒ SOL 184 I e 4
Maravaam ∼ RUS 112-113 U 3
Maravade ○ IND 140-141 F 2
Maravatio ○ MEX 52-53 D 2
Marāve Tappe ○ IR 136-137 D 6
Maravilha ○ BR 66-67 G 4
Maravilhas ○ BR 72-73 H 5
Maravilla ○ BOL 70-71 D 2
Maravillas ○ MEX 50-51 G 4
Maravillas Creek ∼ USA (TX) 266-267 D 4
Marāwah ○ LAR 192-193 J 1
Marawaka ○ PNG 183 C 4
Marawi ☆ RP 160-161 F 9
Marawi = Merowe ○ SUD 200-201 E 3
Marāwi'a, al- ○ Y 132-133 C 6
Marawih ⌒ UAE 134-135 E 6
Maraxo Patá ○ BR 62-63 F 5
Marayes ○ RA 76-77 D 6
Marbella ○ E 98-99 E 6
Marble ○ USA (WA) 244-245 H 2
Marble Bar ○ AUS 172-173 D 6
Marble Canyon ○ USA (AZ) 256-257 D 2

Marble Canyon ⌄ USA (AZ) 256-257 D 2
Marble City ○ USA (OK) 264-265 K 3
Marble Falls ○ USA (TX) 266-267 J 3
Marble Hall ○ ZA 220-221 J 2
Marblehead ○ USA (OH) 280-281 D 2
Marble Hill ○ USA (MO) 276-277 F 3
Marble Island ⌒ CDN 30-31 Y 4
Marblethorpe ○ GB 90-91 H 5
Marbleton ○ USA (GA) 284-285 F 3
Marble Valley ○ USA (AL) 284-285 D 3
Marburg (Lahn) ○• D 92-93 K 3
Marcabeli ○ EC 64-65 C 3
Marcala ○ HN 52-53 K 4
Marcali ○ H 92-93 O 5
Marcapata ○ PE 70-71 B 3
Marcapomacocha ○ PE 64-65 D 7
Marceau, Lac ○ CDN 38-39 L 3
Marcel, Lac ○ CDN 36-37 Q 6
Marcelândia ○ BR 70-71 K 2
Marcelino ○ BR (AMA) 66-67 D 2
Marcelino ○ BR (AMA) 66-67 D 3
Marcelino Ramos ○ BR 74-75 E 6
Marcell ○ USA (MN) 270-271 E 3
Marcellus ○ USA (MI) 272-273 D 6
Marcelo ○ BR 68-69 C 3
Marchajanovskij, ostrov ⌒ RUS 112-113 L 2
Marchand ○ CDN (MAN) 234-235 G 5
Marche ∸ F 90-91 H 8
Marche ▫ I 100-101 D 3
Marche-en-Famenne ○ B 92-93 H 3
Marchena ○ E 98-99 E 6
Marchena, Isla ⌒ EC 64-65 B 9
Marches Point ○ CDN (NFL) 242-243 J 4
Marchinbar Island ⌒ AUS 174-175 D 2
Mar Chiquita, Laguna ○ RA (BUA) 78-79 L 4
Mar Chiquita, Laguna ○ RA (BUA) 78-79 J 3
Mar Chiquita, Laguna ○ RA (COD) 76-77 F 6
Marchwell ○ CDN (SAS) 232-233 R 5
Marcionílio Sousa ○ BR 72-73 K 2
Marco ○ BR 68-69 H 3
Marco ○ USA (FL) 286-287 H 6
Marcoing, gory ▲ RUS 112-113 Q 2
Marcona ○ PE 64-65 E 9
Marco Rondon ○ BR 70-71 G 3
Marcos Juárez ○ RA 78-79 H 2
Marcoux ○ USA (MN) 270-271 B 3
Marcus ○ USA (IA) 274-275 C 2
Marcus Baker, Mount ▲ USA 20-21 R 6
Marcy, Mount ▲ USA (NY) 278-279 H 4
Mard, al- ○ IRQ 128-129 K 6
Mardakan = Mardakan ○• AZ 128-129 O 2
Mardān ○ PK 138-139 D 2
Mar de Ajó ○ RA 78-79 L 4
Mar de Espanha ○ BR 72-73 J 6
Mar del Plata ○• RA 78-79 L 4
Mardiān ○ AFG 136-137 K 6
Mardie ○ AUS 172-173 B 6
Mardie Island ⌒ AUS 172-173 B 6
Mardin ☆ TR 128-129 J 4
Mardin Dağları ▲ TR 128-129 J 4
Marea del Portillo ○• C 54-55 G 5
Marechal Deodoro ○• BR 68-69 L 6
Mareeba ○ AUS 174-175 H 5
Mareeq ○ SP 208-209 H 7
Marek ○ RI 164-165 G 6
Maremma ∸ I 100-101 C 3
Maréna ○ RMM 202-203 E 2
Marendet ○ RN 198-199 C 4
Marenğāb ○ IR 134-135 D 1
Marenge ○ ZRE 212-213 B 6
Marengo ○ CDN (SAS) 232-233 J 4
Marengo ○ USA (IA) 274-275 F 3
Marengo ○ USA (IL) 274-275 K 2
Marenisco ○ USA (MI) 270-271 J 4
Marennes ○ F 90-91 G 9
Marerano ○ RM 222-223 D 8
Mareth ○ TN 190-191 H 4
Mareton's Harbour ○ CDN (NFL) 242-243 O 3
Mar'evka ○ RUS 96-97 F 7
Marevyj ○ RUS 118-119 M 8
Marfa ○ USA (TX) 266-267 C 3
Marfā', al- ○ UAE 134-135 E 6
Marganec = Marhanec' ○ UA 102-103 J 4
Margaree Forks ○ CDN (NS) 240-241 O 4
Margaree Harbour ○ CDN (NS) 240-241 O 4
Margaree Valley ○ CDN (NS) 240-241 P 4
Margaret, Cape ▲ CDN 24-25 a 5
Margaret, Mount ▲ AUS (SA) 178-179 D 5
Margaret, Mount ▲ AUS (WA) 172-173 C 6
Margaret Creek ~ AUS 178-179 D 5
Margaret Lake ○ CDN (ALB) 30-31 M 6
Margaret Lake ○ CDN (NWT) 30-31 L 3
Margaret Lake ○ CDN (NWT) 30-31 P 4
Margaret River ○ AUS (WA) 176-177 C 6
Margaret River ~ AUS 172-173 H 5
Margaretsville ○ CDN (NS) 240-241 K 5
Margarida, Monte ▲ BR 76-77 J 2
Margarima ○ PNG 183 B 3
Margarita, Isla ⌒ CO 60-61 D 3
Margarita, Isla de ⌒•• YV 60-61 J 2
Margarita, La ○ YV 60-61 L 3
Margaritas, Las ○ MEX 52-53 J 3
Margate ○ USA (FL) 286-287 J 5
Marğa'yūn ☆ RL 128-129 F 6
Margeride, Monts de la ▲ F 90-91 J 9
Margeta, Tanjung ▲ RI 166-167 C 6
Marghita ○ RO 102-103 C 4
Margie ○ CDN 32-33 P 4
Margie ○ USA (MN) 270-271 E 2
Margilan ○ US 136-137 M 4
Margo ○ CDN (SAS) 232-233 P 4
Mārgō, Dašt-e ∸ AFG 134-135 K 3
Margos ○ PE 64-65 D 7
Margosatubig ○ RP 160-161 E 9
Margua, Río ~ CO 60-61 E 4
Marguerite ○ CDN (BC) 228-229 M 4
Marguerite, Baie ≈ 16 G 30
Marguerite River ~ CDN 32-33 P 3
Margyang ○ VRC 144-145 G 6
Marha ○ RUS (SAH) 118-119 L 5
Marha ~ RUS 110-111 K 7
Marha ~ RUS 110-111 H 7
Marha ~ RUS 118-119 J 4
Marhačan ~ RUS 118-119 L 5
Marhamat ○ US 136-137 N 4
Marhāna • AFG 134-135 M 1
Marhanec' ○ UA 102-103 J 4
Marhara ~ RUS 110-111 J 7
Marhoum ○ DZ 188-189 L 3
Mari ○ BR 68-69 L 5
Mari ○ PNG 183 A 5
Maria ○ BR 62-63 K 6
Maria ○ CDN (QUE) 240-241 K 2
Maria ○ PE 64-65 D 5
María, El ○ PA 52-53 D 7
María Cleofas, Isla ⌒ MEX 50-51 F 7
Maria da Fé ○ BR 72-73 H 7
María Elena ○ RCH 76-77 C 2
María Eugenia ○ RA 76-77 G 6
María Grande, Arroyo ~ RA 76-77 H 5
María Ignacia ○ RA 78-79 K 4
Maria Island ⌒ AUS (NT) 174-175 C 4
Maria Island ⌒ AUS (TAS) 180-181 J 7
Mariakani ○ EAK 212-213 G 5
Marial ○ USA (OR) 244-245 B 8
María Linda, Río ~ GCA 52-53 J 4
Mariālva ○• P 98-99 D 4
María Madre, Isla ⌒ MEX 50-51 F 7
María Magdalena, Isla ⌒ MEX 50-51 F 7
Marian ○ AUS 178-179 K 1
Mariana ○• BR 72-73 J 6
Mariana, Ilha ⌒ MOC 220-221 L 2
Marianao ○ C 54-55 D 3
Mariana Trench ≃ 14-15 G 6
Mariani ○ IND 142-143 J 2
Marian Lake ○ CDN 30-31 L 4
Marianna ○ USA (AR) 276-277 E 6
Marianna ○ USA (FL) 286-287 D 1
Marianne Nunatakker ▲ GRØ 26-27 o 6
Marianno I. Loza ○ RA 76-77 H 5
Mariánópolis ○ BR 68-69 F 4
Marian River ~ CDN 30-31 L 4
Mariánské Lázně ○ CZ 92-93 M 4
Mariaou, Adrar ▲ DZ 190-191 G 9
Mariapolis ○ CDN (MAN) 234-235 D 5
Mariaqua, Rio ~ BR 66-67 J 4
Mariarano ○ RM 222-223 E 5
Marías, Islas ⌒ MEX 50-51 F 7
Marias Pass ▲ USA (MT) 250-251 F 3
Marias River ~ USA (MT) 250-251 J 3
Maria Teresa ○ ANG 216-217 C 4
Maria Teresa ○ RA 78-79 J 3
Mariaú, Porta de ▲ BR 68-69 E 2
Maria van Diemen, Cape ▲ NZ 182 D 1
Mariazell ○ A 92-93 N 5
Ma'rib ○• Y 132-133 D 6
Maribo ○• DK 86-87 E 9
Maribor ○• SLO 100-101 E 1
Marica ~ BG 102-103 E 7
Maricá ○ BR 72-73 J 7
Māri Čāg ○ AFG 136-137 H 7
Maricao ○•• USA (PR) 286-287 P 2
Maricas ~ RB 220-221 H 2
Maricopa ○ USA (AZ) 256-257 C 5
Maricopa ○ USA (CA) 248-249 E 4
Maricopa Akchin Indian Reservation ✗ USA (AZ) 256-257 C 6
Maricunga, Salar de ○ RCH 76-77 C 4
Maridi ○ SUD (SR) 206-207 J 6
Maridi ~ SUD 206-207 J 6
Marie ○ USA (AR) 276-277 E 5
Marié, Rio ~ BR 66-67 D 3
Marie-Galante ⌒ F 56 E 4
Mariehamn ☆ FIN 88-89 E 6
Mariel ○ C 54-55 D 3
Mari-Èl = Marij Èl, Respublika ▫ RUS 96-97 E 5
Marie Louise Island ⌒ SY 224 C 3
Marie Louise Bank ≃ 160-161 B 7
Marienbad = Mariánské Lázně ○ CZ 92-93 M 4
Marienberg ○ PNG 183 C 2
Mariental ☆ NAM 220-221 C 2
Marienthal ○ CDN (SAS) 232-233 P 6
Mariepauá, Rio ~ BR 66-67 G 5
Marie Shoal ≃ 166-167 E 7
Marie Sophie Gletscher ⊂ GRØ 26-27 g 3
Mariestad ☆ S 86-87 F 7
Marieta ○ YV 60-61 H 5
Marietta ○ USA (GA) 284-285 F 3
Marietta ○ USA (OH) 280-281 E 4
Marietta ○ USA (OK) 264-265 G 5
Marie Valdemar, Kap ▲ GRØ 26-27 q 5
Mariga ○ WAN 204-205 F 3
Mariga, River ~ WAN 204-205 G 3
Marigat ○ EAK 212-213 E 3
Marignane ○ F 90-91 K 10
Marigot ☆ F 56 D 2
Marigot ○ RH 54-55 J 5
Marigot ○ WD 56 E 4
Marii, mys ▲ RUS 120-121 K 6
Mariinsk ☆ RUS 114-115 T 6
Mariinskoe ○ RUS 122-123 J 3
Marii Prončiščevoj, buhta ≈ 108-109 k 4
Marijampolė ☆• LT 94-95 H 4
Marikal ○ IND 140-141 G 2
Marilândia do Sul ○ BR 72-73 E 7
Marília ○ BR 72-73 F 7
Marilla ○ CDN (BC) 228-229 J 3
Marimari, Rio ~ BR 66-67 H 5
Marimba ○ ANG 216-217 D 4
Marimbona ~ RM 222-223 F 6
Marimbondo ○ BR 68-69 K 6
Marín ○ E 98-99 C 3
Marín ○ MEX 50-51 J 5
Marin, Le ○ F 56 E 4
Marina ○ USA (AZ) 256-257 A 2
Marina ○ USA (CA) 248-249 C 3
Marina di Léuca ○• I 100-101 G 5
Mar'ina Horka ☆ BY 94-95 L 5
Marina Plains ○ AUS 174-175 G 4
Marinduque Island ⌒ RP 160-161 D 6
Marineland ○ USA (FL) 286-287 H 2
Marineland of Florida ∴ USA (FL) 286-287 H 2
Marine Museum Bath • USA (ME) 278-279 M 5
Marine National Park ⊥ ER 200-201 K 5
Marine National Reserve ⊥ EAK 212-213 H 5
Marine Reserve ⊥• RI (SSE) 168 E 6
Marine Reserve ⊥• RI (STG) 164-165 H 6
Marinette ○ USA (WI) 270-271 L 5
Maringá ○ BR 72-73 E 7
Maringa ~ ZRE 210-211 H 3
Maringouin ○ USA (LA) 268-269 J 6
Maringuè ○ MOC 218-219 H 3
Marinheiros, Ilha dos ⌒ BR 74-75 D 8
Marino Barbareta, Parque Nacional ⊥ HN 52-53 L 3
Marino Guanaja, Parque Nacional ⊥ HN 54-55 C 6
Marino Punta Sal, Parque Nacional ⊥ HN 52-53 L 4
Marinovka ☆ KA 124-125 F 3
Marion ○ USA (AL) 284-285 C 4
Marion ○ USA (AR) 276-277 E 5
Marion ○ USA (IA) 274-275 G 2
Marion ○ USA (IL) 276-277 G 3
Marion ○ USA (IN) 274-275 N 4
Marion ○ USA (KS) 262-263 J 6
Marion ○ USA (LA) 268-269 H 4
Marion ○ USA (MI) 272-273 D 3
Marion ○ USA (MT) 250-251 E 3
Marion ○ USA (NC) 282-283 E 5
Marion ○ USA (OH) 280-281 C 3
Marion ○ USA (SC) 284-285 L 2
Marion ○ USA (VA) 280-281 E 7
Marion, Lake ○ USA (SC) 284-285 K 3
Marion Downs ○ AUS 178-179 E 2
Marion Forks ○ USA (OR) 244-245 D 6
Marion Junction ○ USA (AL) 284-285 C 4
Marion Lake ○ USA (KS) 262-263 J 6
Marion Reef ⌒ AUS 174-175 M 6
Maripa ○ GUY 62-63 E 2
Maripasoula ○ F 62-63 G 4
Mariposa ○ USA (CA) 248-249 E 2
Mariposa, Sierra ▲ RCH 76-77 C 2
Mariquita ○ BR 72-73 H 2
Mariquita ○ CO 60-61 D 5
Marisa ○ RI 164-165 G 3
Mariscal Cáceres ○ PE 64-65 E 8
Mariscal de Juárez ○ MEX 52-53 E 3
Mariscal Estigarribia ○ PY 76-77 G 1
Marismas, Las ∸ E 98-99 D 6
Marissa ○ USA (IL) 274-275 J 6
Marita Downs ○ AUS 178-179 G 2
Marite ○ ZA 220-221 K 2
Mariupol' = Maryupol' ○ UA 102-103 K 4
Mariván ○ IR 128-129 M 5
Mariveles ○ RP 160-161 D 5
Marj, Al ☆•• LAR 192-193 J 1
Märjamaa ○•• EST 94-95 J 2
Mar'janovka ☆ RUS 124-125 H 1
Marjorie Hills ▲ CDN 30-31 J 3
Marjorie Lake ○ CDN 30-31 U 3
Marka ☆ SP 212-213 K 3
Markakol', köli ○ KA 124-125 O 4
Markala ○ RMM 202-203 G 3
Markam ○ VRC 144-145 M 6
Markama, proliv ≈ 84-85 d 2
Mārkāpur ○ IND 140-141 H 3
Markara ○ AR 128-129 L 2
Markazi ▫ IR 134-135 C 1
Markdale ○ CDN (ONT) 238-239 E 4
Marked Tree ○ USA (AR) 276-277 E 5
Marken ○ ZA 218-219 E 6
Markey ○ USA (MI) 272-273 E 3
Markham ○ CDN (ONT) 238-239 F 5
Markham ○ USA (MN) 270-271 F 3
Markham ○ USA (WA) 244-245 B 4
Markham, Mount ▲ ARK 16 E 0
Markham Bay ≈ 36-37 N 3
Markham Bay ≈ 183 D 4
Markham Lake ○ CDN 30-31 S 4
Markham River ~ PNG 183 D 4
Markinch ○ CDN (SAS) 232-233 O 5
Markit ○ VRC 146-147 C 6
Markivka ○ UA 102-103 L 3
Markle ○ USA (IN) 274-275 N 4
Markleeville ○ USA (CA) 246-247 F 5
Markley, Fort ∴ USA (KS) 262-263 K 5
Markleysburg ○ USA (PA) 280-281 G 4
Markos Paz ○ RA 78-79 K 3
Markounda ○ RCA 206-207 C 5
Markovac ○ YU 100-101 H 2
Markovo ○ RUS (CUK) 112-113 Q 4
Markovo ○ RUS (IRK) 116-117 N 7
Markoye ○ BF 202-203 L 2
Marks ○ RUS 96-97 E 8
Marks ○ USA (MS) 268-269 K 2
Marksville ○ USA (LA) 268-269 H 5
Marktredwitz ○ D 92-93 M 3
Marktredwitz ○ D (BAY) 92-93 M 4
Mark Twain Boyhood Home and Museum • USA (MO) 274-275 G 5
Mark Twain Lake ○ USA (MO) 274-275 G 5
Mark Twain National Wildlife Refuge ⊥ USA (IL) 274-275 G 5
Markundi ○ SUD 206-207 F 3
Markūz, al- ○ KSA 130-131 H 2
Markwassie ○ ZA 220-221 H 3
Marla ○ AUS 176-177 M 3
Marlboro ○ CDN (ALB) 232-233 B 2
Marlborough ○ AUS 178-179 K 2
Marlborough ○ GB 90-91 G 6
Marlborough ○ GUY 62-63 E 2
Marlborough ○ USA (MA) 278-279 K 6
Marlborough Sounds ∸ NZ 182 D 4
Marlette ○ USA (MI) 272-273 F 4
Marlin ○ USA (TX) 266-267 L 2
Marlin Coast ∸ AUS 174-175 H 5
Marlinton ○ USA (WV) 280-281 F 5
Marlo ○ AUS 180-181 K 4
Marloth Nature Reserve ⊥ ZA 220-221 E 6
Marlow ○ USA (NH) 278-279 J 5
Marlow ○ USA (OK) 264-265 F 4
Marmagao ○ IND 140-141 E 3
Marmande ○ F 90-91 H 9
Marmara Adası ⌒ TR 128-129 B 2
Marmara Denizi ≈ 128-129 B 2
Marmara Ereğlisi ☆ TR 128-129 B 2
Marmaris ☆•• TR 128-129 C 4
Marmarth ○ USA (ND) 258-259 D 5
Marmelo, Rio ~ BR 66-67 D 7
Marmelos, Rio dos ~ BR 66-67 G 6
Mar Menor ○ E 98-99 G 6
Marmion, Lake ○ AUS 176-177 F 4
Marmion Lake ○ CDN (ONT) 234-235 M 6
Marmites des géants • RM 222-223 E 9
Marmolada ▲ I 100-101 C 1
Marmoles, Parque Nacional Los ⊥ MEX 50-51 K 7
Marmora ○ CDN (ONT) 238-239 H 4
Marmot Bay ≈ 22-23 U 3
Marmot Island ⌒ USA 22-23 V 3
Marmul ○ OM 132-133 J 4
Marne ~ F 90-91 K 7
Marne-au-Rhin, Canal de la < F 90-91 L 7
Marneuli ○ GE 126-127 F 7
Marnoo ○ AUS 180-181 G 4
Maro ○ TCH 206-207 D 4
Maroa ○ YV 60-61 H 6
Maroala ○ RM 222-223 E 5
Maroambihy ○ RM 222-223 F 5
Maroantsetra ○ RM 222-223 F 5
Marofandilia ○ RM 222-223 D 8
Maroharatra ○ RM 222-223 E 8
Marojezy ▲ RM 222-223 F 5
Maroktua ○ RI 162-163 F 5
Marolambo ○ RM 222-223 E 8
Marolinta ○ RM 222-223 D 10
Maromandia ○ RM 222-223 G 5
Maromokotro ▲ RM 222-223 F 5
Marondera ○ ZW 218-219 F 4
Marongora ○ ZW 218-219 E 3
Maroni ~ SME 62-63 G 3
Maroochydore -Mooloolaba ○ AUS 178-179 M 4
Maroon-Village ∴• JA 54-55 G 5
Maropaika ○ RM 222-223 E 9
Maros ~ H 92-93 Q 5
Maros ○ RI 164-165 F 6
Maroseranana ○ RM 222-223 F 7
Marotandrano ○ RM 222-223 F 6
Marotolana ○ RM 222-223 F 5
Marova ○ BR 66-67 F 3
Marovato ○ RM 222-223 D 10
Marovoalavo, Lembalemban'i ▲ RM 222-223 F 6
Marovoay ○ RM 222-223 F 7
Marovoay Atsimo ○ RM 222-223 D 6
Marowijnerivier ~ SME 62-63 G 3
Marowinir ~ F 62-63 G 4
Marple Hill ○ USA (NC) 282-283 K 6
Marqab, al- •• IRQ 128-129 F 5
Marqadā ○ SYR 128-129 J 5
Marqua ○ AUS 178-179 D 2
Marquard ○ ZA 220-221 H 4
Marque, La ○ USA (TX) 268-269 F 7
Marquesas Fracture Zone ≃ 14-15 P 8
Marquesas Islands = Marquises, Îles ⌒ F 13 N 3
Marquesas Keys ⌒ USA (FL) 286-287 G 7
Marquette ○ CDN (MAN) 234-235 F 4
Marquette ○ USA (IA) 274-275 G 1
Marquette ○ USA (MI) 270-271 L 4
Marquette ○ USA (NE) 262-263 H 4
Marquez ○ USA (NM) 256-257 H 3
Marquez ○ USA (TX) 266-267 L 2
Marquis ○ CDN (SAS) 232-233 N 5
Marqūq ○ SUD 206-207 K 4
Marracua ○ MOC 218-219 J 3
Marracuene ○ MOC 220-221 L 2
Marrah, Ğabal ▲•• SUD 200-201 B 6
Marrakech = Marrākush ☆••• MA 188-189 H 5
Marraket, Hassi < DZ 190-191 D 5
Marrākush ☆••• MA 188-189 H 5
Marrān ○ KSA 130-131 G 6
Marrangua, Lagoa ○ MOC 220-221 M 2
Marrāt ○ KSA 130-131 J 5
Marrawah ○ AUS 180-181 H 6
Marrecão ○ BR 66-67 D 6
Marree ○ AUS 178-179 E 5
Marrero ○ USA (LA) 268-269 K 7
Marresal'skie koški ⌒ RUS 108-109 M 7
Marreteis, Ilha ⌒ BR 66-67 F 7
Marromeu ○ MOC 218-219 H 4
Marromeu, Reserva de ⊥ MOC 218-219 H 4
Marroonah ○ AUS 176-177 C 1
Marroquí o de Tarifa, Punta ▲ E 98-99 E 7
Marruás ○ BR 68-69 J 5
Marrupa ○ MOC 218-219 J 1
Mars, Le ○ USA (IA) 274-275 B 2
Marsa, La ○ TN 190-191 H 2
Marsá al Burayqah ○ LAR 192-193 H 2
Marsa-Ben-Mehidi ○ DZ 188-189 K 3
Marsabit ○ EAK 212-213 F 2
Marsabit National Reserve ⊥ EAK 212-213 F 2
Marsala ○ I 100-101 D 6
Marsá l-'Alam ○ ET 194-195 G 5
Marsá Maṭrūḥ ○ ET 194-195 C 2
Marsá Maṭrūḥ ○• ET 194-195 C 2
Marsá Mubārak ○ ET 194-195 G 5
Marsassoum ○ SN 202-203 C 3
Marsden ○ AUS 180-181 J 2
Marsden ○ CDN (SAS) 232-233 J 3
Marsden, Point ▲ AUS 180-181 D 3
Marseille ☆• F 90-91 K 10
Marseilles ○ USA (OH) 280-281 C 3
Marsella ○ CO 60-61 D 5
Māršenān, Kūh-e ▲ IR 134-135 E 2
Marsfjällen ▲ S 86-87 G 4
Marsh, Mount ▲ AUS 172-173 D 7
Marshall ○ CDN (SAS) 232-233 J 2
Marshall ○ LB 202-203 E 6
Marshall ○ USA (AK) 20-21 J 6
Marshall ○ USA (AR) 276-277 C 5
Marshall ○ USA (IL) 274-275 L 5
Marshall ○ USA (MI) 272-273 E 5
Marshall ○ USA (MN) 270-271 C 6
Marshall ○ USA (MO) 274-275 E 5
Marshall ○ USA (ND) 258-259 E 4
Marshall ○ USA (TX) 264-265 K 6
Marshall Islands ⌒ MAI 14-15 J 6
Marshall Lake ○ CDN (ONT) 234-235 Q 4
Marshall River ~ AUS 178-179 D 2
Marshall Seamounts ≃ 14-15 J 6
Marshalltown ○ USA (IA) 274-275 E 3
Marshallville ○ USA (GA) 284-285 G 4
Marshburg ○ USA (PA) 280-281 H 2
Marshfield ○ USA (MO) 276-277 C 3
Marshfield ○ USA (WI) 270-271 H 6
Marsh Fork ~ USA 20-21 R 2
Marsh Harbour ○ BS 54-55 G 1
Mars Hill ○ USA (ME) 278-279 O 2
Mars Hill ○ USA (NC) 282-283 E 5
Marsh Island ⌒ USA (LA) 268-269 J 7
Marsh Lake ○ CDN 20-21 X 6
Marsh Pass ▲ USA (AZ) 256-257 E 2
Marsh Point ▲ CDN 34-35 K 2
Marshville ○ USA (NC) 282-283 G 6
Marsing ○ USA (ID) 252-253 B 3
Marsiwang ~ RI 166-167 F 3
Marsiwang, Tanjung ▲ RI (MAL) 166-167 F 3
Marsoui ○ CDN (QUE) 242-243 B 3
Märsta ○ S 86-87 H 7
Mart ○ USA (TX) 266-267 L 2
Martaban ○ MYA 158-159 D 2
Martaban, Gulf of ≈ 158-159 D 2
Martadi ○ NEP 144-145 C 6
Martand ○• IND 138-139 E 3
Martap ○ CAM 204-205 K 5
Martapura ○ RI (KSE) 164-165 D 5
Martapura ○ RI (SUS) 162-163 F 7
Marte ○ WAN 198-199 F 6
Marte, Rivière à la ~ CDN 38-39 G 3
Martel ○ CDN (BC) 230-231 H 3
Martell ○ USA (WI) 270-271 F 6
Marten River ○ CDN (ONT) 238-239 F 2
Marten River ~ CDN 30-31 P 5
Martens Falls Indian Reserve ✗ CDN 34-35 O 5
Martensøya ⌒ N 84-85 M 2
Martensville ○ CDN (SAS) 232-233 M 3
Marthaguy River ~ AUS 178-179 J 6
Martha's Vineyard ⌒ USA (MA) 278-279 L 7
Marti ○ C 54-55 E 3
Martigny ○ CH 92-93 J 5
Martigues ○ F 90-91 K 10
Martil ○ MA 188-189 J 3
Martin ○ SK 92-93 P 4
Martin ○ USA (SC) 284-285 J 3
Martin ○ USA (SD) 260-261 E 3
Martin ○ USA (TN) 276-277 G 4
Martin, Lake < USA (AL) 284-285 E 4
Martinas, Las ○ C 54-55 C 4
Martinborough ○ NZ 182 E 4
Martindale ○ USA (TX) 266-267 K 4
Martineau, Cape ▲ CDN 24-25 e 7
Martineau River ~ CDN 32-33 Q 4
Martinez ○ USA (GA) 284-285 H 3
Martínez de la Torre ○ MEX 52-53 F 1
Martinez Lake ○ USA (AZ) 256-257 A 6
Martinho Campos ○ BR 72-73 H 5
Martin House ○ CDN 20-21 Y 3
Martinique ▫ F 56 E 4
Martinique = Oiapoque ○ BR 62-63 J 4
Martinique Passage ≈ 56 E 4
Martin National Wildlife Refuge ✗ USA (MD) 280-281 K 5
Martinópolis ○ BR 72-73 E 7
Martin Peninsula ⌄ ARK 16 F 25
Martin River ~ CDN 30-31 J 5
Martinsburg ○ USA (IA) 274-275 F 3
Martinsburg ○ USA (WV) 280-281 J 4
Martins Drift ○ RB 218-219 D 6
Martins Ferry ○ USA (OH) 280-281 F 3
Martinsville ○ USA (IN) 274-275 M 5
Martinsville ○ USA (TX) 268-269 F 5
Martinsville ○ USA (VA) 280-281 G 7
Martin Vaz Fracture Zone ≃ 6-7 H 10
Martok ☆ KA 126-127 M 2
Marton ○ NZ 182 E 4
Martos ○ E 98-99 F 6
Martre, Lac la ○ CDN 30-31 K 4
Martti ○ FIN 88-89 K 3
Martuni ○ AR 128-129 L 2
Martynovo ○ KA 96-97 G 8
Martynovo ○ RUS 124-125 O 2
Maru ○ RI 168 E 7
Maru ○ WAN 198-199 C 6
Maru, Pulau ⌒ RI 166-167 F 5
Maruanum ○ BR 62-63 J 5
Maruchin ∴• MEX 52-53 K 2
Maruda ○ BR 68-69 E 2
Marudi ○ MAL 164-165 D 1
Marudu, Teluk ≈ 160-161 B 9
Ma'rūf ○ AFG 134-135 M 3
Maruhskij, pereval ▲ RUS 126-127 D 6
Marum, Mount ▲ VAN 184 II b 3
Marumbi, Pico ▲ BR 74-75 F 5
Marungu ▲ ZRE 214-215 E 4
Marupa ○ PNG 183 G 3
Marupa, Rio ~ BR 66-67 J 6
Marusthali ∸ IND 138-139 C 7
Māruteru ○ IND 140-141 J 2
Maru'ura ○ SOL 184 I e 3
Marvão ○ P 98-99 D 5
Marvast ○ IR 134-135 F 3
Marv Dašt ○ IR 134-135 E 4
Marve ○ AFG 134-135 K 1
Marvel ○ USA (CO) 254-255 G 6
Marvell ○ USA (AR) 276-277 E 6
Marvine, Mount ▲ USA (UT) 254-255 D 5
Marvyn ○ USA (AL) 284-285 E 4
Marwān ○ KSA 130-131 K 6
Marwayne ○ CDN (ALB) 232-233 H 2
Mary ☆• TM 136-137 G 6
Maryal Bai ○ SUD 206-207 H 4
Mary Anne Group ⌒ AUS 172-173 B 6
Mary Anne Passage ≈ 172-173 B 6
Mary Ann Point ▲ AUS 176-177 F 6
Maryborough ○ AUS (QLD) 178-179 M 3
Maryborough ○ AUS (VIC) 180-181 G 4
Marydale ○ ZA 220-221 F 4
Marydell ○ USA (MS) 268-269 L 4
Maryfield ○ AUS 174-175 B 4
Mary Frances Lake ○ CDN 30-31 Q 4
Maryhill ○ USA (WA) 244-245 E 5
Mary Kathleen ∴ AUS 174-175 E 7
Mary Lake ○ CDN 30-31 S 4
Maryland ▫ USA (MD) 280-281 J 4
Maryneal ○ USA (TX) 264-265 D 6
Mary River ~ AUS 172-173 K 2
Mary River ~ AUS 172-173 H 5
Mary River ~ AUS 178-179 M 3
Marysburg ○ CDN (SAS) 232-233 N 3
Marys Corner ○ USA (WA) 244-245 C 4
Marystown ○ CDN (NFL) 242-243 N 5
Marysvale ○ USA (UT) 254-255 C 5
Marysville ○ CDN (BC) 230-231 N 4
Marysville ○ CDN (ONT) 238-239 J 4
Marysville ○ USA (AR) 276-277 C 7
Marysville ○ USA (CA) 246-247 D 4
Marysville ○ USA (IN) 274-275 N 6
Marysville ○ USA (KS) 262-263 K 5
Marysville ○ USA (OH) 280-281 C 3
Marysville ○ USA (WA) 244-245 C 2
Maryupol' ○ UA 102-103 K 4
Maryvale ○ AUS 174-175 H 6
Maryville ○ USA (MO) 274-275 D 4
Maryville ○ USA (TN) 282-283 D 5
Marzagão ○ BR 72-73 F 4
Marzanābād ○ IR 136-137 B 6
Marzo, 1 de ○ PY 76-77 J 3
Marzo, Punta ▲ CO 60-61 C 4
Marzūq ▫ LAR 192-193 E 5
Marzūq ☆ LAR 192-193 E 5
Marzūq, Hamādat ∸ LAR 192-193 E 4
Marzūq, ṣSaḥrā' ∸ LAR 192-193 E 5
Mas, Tanjung ▲ RI 166-167 B 6
Masagaweyn ○ SP 208-209 H 7
Masagua ○ GCA 52-53 J 4
Masaguara ○ HN 52-53 L 4
Masāhim, Kūh-e ▲ IR 134-135 F 3
Masahunga ○ EAT 212-213 D 5
Masai Mara National Reservat ⊥ EAK 212-213 E 4
Masā'iqa, al- ○ OM 132-133 K 2
Masai Steppe ∸ EAT 214-215 J 3
Masaka ☆ EAU 212-213 C 4
Ma'sal ○• KSA 130-131 J 5
Masalembobesar, Pulau ⌒ RI 164-165 D 6
Masalina, Kepulauan ⌒ RI 164-165 E 6
Masally = Masallı ○• AZ 128-129 N 3
Masamba ○ RI 164-165 G 5
Masan ○ ROK 150-151 G 10
Masanga ○ ZRE 210-211 J 4
Masānī', al- ○ Y 132-133 D 7
Masapun ○ RI 166-167 D 5
Masār, Ğabal ▲ Y 132-133 C 6
Masasi ○ EAT 214-215 K 6
Masatepe ○ NIC 52-53 L 6
Más a Tierra, Isla ⌒ RCH 78-79 C 1
Masavi ○ BOL 70-71 F 6
Masawa ○ RI 164-165 F 5
Masaya ☆• NIC 52-53 L 6
Masbagik ○ RI 168 C 7
Masbate ⌒ RP (MAS) 160-161 E 6
Masbate ☆ RP (MAS) 160-161 E 6
Mascara ☆• DZ 190-191 C 3
Mascarene Basin ≃ 12 D 6
Mascarene Islands ⌒ 224 C 6
Mascarene Plain ≃ 12 D 7
Mascarene Plateau ≃ 12 E 6
Mascasín, Salinas de ○ RA 76-77 D 6
Mascota ○ MEX 52-53 B 1
Mascouche ○ CDN (QUE) 238-239 M 3
Masefield ○ CDN (SAS) 232-233 L 6
Masela, Pulau ⌒ RI 166-167 E 6
Masel'gskaja ○ RUS 88-89 N 5
Måselvfossen ~• N 86-87 J 2
Maseru ☆ LS 220-221 H 4
Masetleng Pan < RB 220-221 E 1
Mašğed-e Abolfażl ○ IR 134-135 H 4
Mašğed-e Soleimān ○• IR 134-135 C 3
Masha ○ ETH 208-209 B 5
Mašhad ☆•• IR 136-137 F 6
Mashala ○ ZRE 210-211 J 6
Mashan ○ VRC 156-157 F 5
Mashansha, Rio ~ PE 64-65 F 7
Mashar ○ SUD 206-207 H 4
Mashava ○ ZW 218-219 F 5
Mashhad = Mašhad ☆•• IR 136-137 F 6
Mashi ○ VRC 156-157 G 2
Mashike ○ J 152-153 J 3
Māshkai ~ PK 134-135 L 5
Māshkel ~ PK 134-135 K 5
Māshkel, Hāmūn-i ○ PK 134-135 K 4
Mashki Chāh ○ PK 134-135 K 4
Mashkode ○ CDN (ONT) 236-237 D 5
Mashonaland Central ▫ ZW 218-219 F 3
Mashonaland East ▫ ZW 218-219 F 4
Mashonaland West ▫ ZW 218-219 E 3
Mashowingrivier ~ ZA 220-221 F 3
Mashra' ar-Raqq ○ SUD 206-207 J 4
Masi ○ N 86-87 L 2
Masi-Mbia ○ ZRE 210-211 F 5
Masian ○ RI 166-167 H 5
Masica, La ○ HN 52-53 L 4
Mašigina, guba ○ RUS 108-109 G 4
Masila, al- ~ Y 132-133 G 6
Masim, gora ▲ RUS 96-97 K 7
Masi-Manimba ○ ZRE 210-211 F 6
Masi-Masi, Pulau ⌒ RI 166-167 K 3
Masindi ○ EAU 212-213 C 3
Masindi Port ○ EAU 212-213 D 3
Masinga Reservoir < EAK 212-213 F 4
Masingbi ○ WAL 202-203 E 5
Masinloc ○ RP 160-161 C 5
Masira, Ğazirat ⌒ OM 132-133 L 3
Masira, Gulf of ≈ 132-133 L 3
Masira Channel ≈ 132-133 L 3
Masis ○ AR 128-129 L 2
Masisea ○ PE 64-65 E 6
Masisi ○ ZRE 212-213 B 4
Maskanah ○ SYR 128-129 H 4
Maskarenen Plateau ≃ 12 E 6
Maškel, Rūd-e ~ IR 134-135 K 5
Maskelyne Islands ⌒ VAN 184 II a 3
Maskinongé ○ CDN (QUE) 238-239 M 2
Masliya ○ KSA 132-133 C 5
Masljanino ○ RUS 114-115 S 7
Maṣna'a, al- ○ OM 132-133 K 2
Masoala, Saikanosy ⌄ RM 222-223 G 5
Masoala, Tanjona ▲ RM 222-223 G 6
Masohi ○ RI 166-167 E 3
Masoko ○ EAT (MBE) 214-215 G 5
Masoller ○ ROU 76-77 J 6
Masomeloka ○ RM 222-223 F 8
Mason ○ USA (MI) 272-273 E 5
Mason ○ USA (NV) 246-247 F 5
Mason ○ USA (OK) 264-265 H 3
Mason ○ USA (TX) 266-267 H 3
Mason, Lake ○ AUS 176-177 E 3
Mason Bay ≈ 182 A 7
Mason City ○ USA (IA) 274-275 E 1
Mason City ○ USA (IL) 274-275 J 4
Masoni, Pulau ⌒ RI 164-165 J 4
Mason River ~ CDN 24-25 H 6
Masontown ○ USA (PA) 280-281 G 4
Maspalomas ○ E 188-189 D 7
Masqa, al- ○ KSA 132-133 C 4
Masqat ☆•• OM 132-133 L 2
Massa ○ IND 138-139 E 10
Massa, Oued ~ MA 188-189 G 6
Massaango ○ ANG 216-217 D 4
Massachusetts ▫ USA (MA) 278-279 J 6
Massachusetts, Old Fort ∴ USA (MS) 268-269 M 6
Massachusetts Bay ≈ 46-47 N 4
Massachusetts Bay ≈ USA 278-279 L 6
Massacre Canyon Monument • USA (NE) 262-263 F 4
Massadona ○ USA (CO) 254-255 G 3
Massafra ○• I 100-101 F 4
Massaguet ○ TCH 198-199 G 6
Massajid Cali Guduud ○ SP 208-209 H 7
Massakory ○ TCH 198-199 G 6
Massalassef ○ TCH 206-207 C 3
Massama ○ WAN 198-199 C 6
Massa Marittima ○• I 100-101 C 3
Massangam ○ CAM 204-205 J 6
Massangano ○ ANG 216-217 C 4
Massangena ○ MOC 218-219 G 5
Massangulo ○ MOC 218-219 H 1
Massantola ○ RMM 202-203 G 3
Massapê ○ BR 68-69 H 3
Massaranduba ○ BR 74-75 F 6
Massarole < SP 212-213 K 2
Massau ○ ANG 216-217 D 3
Mass City ○ USA (MI) 270-271 J 4
Massena ○ USA (NY) 278-279 G 4
Massenya ○ TCH 206-207 C 3
Masset ○ CDN (BC) 228-229 B 2
Masset Inlet ≈ 32-33 D 5
Masset Inlet ≈ CDN 228-229 B 3
Massey ○ CDN (ONT) 238-239 C 2
Massey Island ⌒ CDN 24-25 U 3
Massey Sound ≈ 26-27 C 4
Massiac ○ F 90-91 J 9
Massibi ○ ANG 214-215 B 6
Massif Central ▲ F 90-91 J 9
Massif Tabulaire ▲ F 62-63 H 4
Massigui ○ RMM 202-203 G 4
Massili ~ BF 202-203 K 3
Massillon ○ USA (OH) 280-281 E 3
Massina ○ RMM 202-203 H 3
Massine, Oued ~ DZ 190-191 D 7
Massinga ○ MOC 218-219 H 6
Massingir ○ MOC 218-219 G 6
Massingir, Barragem de < MOC 218-219 F 6
Masson Island ⌒ ARK 16 G 10
Massosse ○ ANG 216-217 D 7
Maštaga ○ AZ 128-129 O 2
Mastah, ozero ○ RUS 118-119 L 3
Mastermans Range ▲ AUS 178-179 L 5
Masterton ○ NZ 182 E 4
Mastic Beach ○ USA (NY) 280-281 O 3
Mastic Point ○ BS 54-55 G 2
Mastodonte, Cerro ▲ RCH 76-77 C 2
Mastūj ~ PK 138-139 D 1
Mastung ○• PK 134-135 M 4
Mastūra ○ KSA 130-131 F 6
Mas'ūd ○ IRQ 128-129 K 4
Masuda ○ J 152-153 D 7
Masuguru ○ EAT 214-215 K 6
Masuika ○ ZRE 214-215 B 4
Mašuk, gora ▲ RUS 112-113 O 4
Masur ○ IR 134-135 C 2
Masurai, Gunung ▲ RI 162-163 D 6
Masvingo ▫ ZW 218-219 F 5
Masvingo ☆ ZW 218-219 F 5
Maswaar, Pulau ⌒ RI 166-167 H 3
Maswa Game Reservat ⊥ EAT 212-213 E 5
Masyaf ○ SYR 128-129 G 5
Mata ○ ZRE 216-217 F 3
Mata'Avea, Cape = Cape Lisburn ▲ VAN 184 II a 2
Matabeleland North ▫ ZW 218-219 D 4
Matabeleland South ▫ ZW 218-219 E 5
Mata Bia, Gunung ▲ RI 166-167 D 6
Matacawa Levu ⌒ FJI 184 III a 2
Matachel, Río ~ E 98-99 D 5
Matachewan ○ CDN (ONT) 236-237 H 5
Matachic ○ MEX 50-51 F 3
Matacú ○ BOL 70-71 F 5
Matad = Zuunbulag ○ MAU 148-149 M 4
Mata da Corda, Serra da ▲ BR 72-73 G 5
Matadi ☆• ZRE 210-211 D 6
Matador ○ USA (TX) 264-265 D 4
Matagalpa ☆ NIC 52-53 B 5
Matagalpa, Río Grande de ~ NIC 52-53 B 5
Matagami ○ CDN (QUE) 236-237 L 3
Matagami, Lac ○ CDN (QUE) 236-237 L 3
Matagamon Lake ○ USA (ME) 278-279 N 2
Matagorda ○ USA (TX) 266-267 M 5
Matagorda Bay ≈ 44-45 J 5
Matagorda Bay ≈ USA 266-267 L 5
Matagorda Island ⌒ USA (TX) 266-267 L 5
Matagorda Peninsula ⌄ USA (TX) 266-267 L 5
Mataj ~ RUS 122-123 F 5

Matak, Pulau ⌒ RI 162-163 G 3
Matakali o RI 164-165 F 5
Matakana Island ⌒ NZ 182 F 2
Matakaoa Point ▲ NZ 182 G 2
Matakawau o NZ 182 E 2
Matakil, Chutes de ~•• RCA 206-207 E 4
Matala o ANG 216-217 C 7
Matala o GR 100-101 K 7
Matāla o IND 140-141 G 2
Matala o ZRE 210-211 L 5
Matalaque o PE 70-71 B 5
Matale o CL 140-141 J 7
Matale o ZRE 212-213 B 5
Matam o SN 202-203 D 2
Maṭamah, al- o Y 132-133 D 5
Mata Mata o ZA 220-221 E 2
Matamatá, Cachoeira ~ BR 66-67 G 6
Matamec o CDN (QUE) 242-243 B 2
Matamey o RN 198-199 D 6
Matamoros o MEX (COA) 50-51 H 5
Matamoros o MEX (TAM) 50-51 L 5
Matana o BU 212-213 B 5
Matana o RI 164-165 G 5
Matana, Danau ⊂ RI 164-165 G 5
Matanal Point ▲ RP 160-161 E 9
Ma'tan as Sarah o LAR 198-199 K 2
Ma'tan Bisciara < LAR 192-193 K 6
Matanda o Z 214-215 E 6
Matandu ~ EAT 214-215 K 5
Matane o CDN (QUE) 240-241 H 2
Matane, Parc Provincial de ⊥ CDN (QUE) 240-241 H 2
Matanga o RI 164-165 H 4
Matanga o RM 222-223 E 9
Matankari o RN 198-199 B 6
Matantas o VAN 184 II a 2
Matanuska River ~ USA 20-21 Q 6
Matanzas ☆ C 54-55 E 3
Matanzas o MEX 50-51 J 7
Matanzas o YV 60-61 K 3
Matanzilla, Pampa de la ≐ RA 78-79 E 4
Matão o BR 72-73 F 6
Mataojo o ROU 76-77 J 6
Mataoleo o RI 164-165 H 6
Mata Ortiz o MEX 50-51 E 2
Matapédia o CDN (QUE) 240-241 J 3
Matapédia, Rivière ~ CDN (QUE) 240-241 H 2
Matapi, Cachoeira ~ BR 66-67 F 2
Matapi, Rio ~ BR 62-63 J 5
Mataquito, Río ~ RCH 78-79 C 3
Matara o CL 140-141 J 8
Matara o• ER 200-201 J 5
Matara o PE 64-65 C 5
Matará o RA 76-77 F 5
Mataraca o BR 68-69 L 5
Mataram ☆ RI 168 C 7
Mataranka o AUS 174-175 B 4
Mataró o E 98-99 J 4
Mataso ⌒ VAN 184 II b 3
Matatiele o ZA 220-221 J 5
Matatindoe Point ▲ RP 160-161 E 8
Mataupa o PNG 183 F 5
Matauná, Rio ~ BR 66-67 G 5
Matausu o RI 164-165 G 6
Matawai o NZ 182 F 3
Matawin, Rivière ~ CDN (QUE) 238-239 M 2
Matawin Reservoir ⊂ CDN (QUE) 238-239 M 2
Matay o ET 194-195 E 3
Matayaya o DOM 54-55 K 5
Matechai o ANG 216-217 F 5
Matecumbe Key, Lower ⌒ USA (FL) 286-287 J 7
Mategua o BOL 70-71 F 3
Matehuala o MEX 50-51 J 6
Mateiros o BR 68-69 E 7
Matekwe o EAT 214-215 K 6
Matela o LS 220-221 H 4
Matelot o TT 60-61 L 2
Matema o EAT 214-215 H 5
Matema o MOC 218-219 G 2
Matemo o MOC 218-219 G 2
Matera ☆• I 100-101 F 4
Matéri o DY 202-203 L 4
Matemillos, Punta ▲ C 54-55 G 4
Mátészalka o H 92-93 R 5
Matete o ZRE 212-213 A 3
Matetsi o ZW 218-219 C 4
Matetsi ~ ZW 218-219 D 4
Mateur o TN 190-191 G 2
Matewar o RI 166-167 K 2
Mather o CDN (MAN) 234-235 D 5
Matherān o• IND 138-139 D 10
Matheson o CDN (ONT) 236-237 H 4
Matheson Island o CDN (MAN) 234-235 G 3
Matheson Point ▲ CDN 24-25 Y 6
Mathews, Lake ⊂ USA (CA) 248-249 G 6
Mathiassen Brook ~ CDN 36-37 H 2
Mathis o USA (TX) 266-267 K 5
Mathiston o USA (MS) 268-269 L 3
Mathoura o AUS 180-181 H 3
Mathura o•• IND 138-139 F 6
Mati ~ RUS 120-121 H 4
Matia ~ EAK 212-213 G 4
Matiacoali o BF 202-203 L 3
Matiāri o PK 138-139 B 7
Matias Cardoso o BR 72-73 J 3
Matias Olimpio o BR 68-69 G 3
Matías Romero o MEX 52-53 G 3
Matibane o MOC 218-219 L 2
Maticora, Río ~ YV 60-61 F 2
Matiguás o NIC 52-53 B 5
Matiide o RA 76-77 G 6
Matilla o RCH 70-71 C 7
Matima o RB 218-219 C 5
Matina o BR 72-73 J 2
Matinenda Lake ⊂ CDN (ONT) 238-239 C 2
Matinha o BR 74-75 F 5
Matiši o LV 94-95 J 3
Matjiesfontein o ZA 220-221 E 6
Matlahaw Point ▲ CDN (BC) 230-231 C 4
Mātli o PK 138-139 B 7
Matlock o USA (WA) 244-245 B 3
Matmata o• TN 190-191 G 4
Matnog o RP 160-161 F 6
Mato, El o YV 60-61 J 4
Matochkin Shar, Proliv = Matočkin Šar, proliv ≈ RUS 108-109 F 5
Matočkin Šar o RUS 108-109 G 5
Matočkin Šar, proliv ≈ RUS 108-109 F 5
Matões o BR 68-69 G 4
Matogrossense, Pantanal ~• BR 70-71 J 5
Mato Grosso □ BR 70-71 J 3
Mato Grosso, Planalto do ≐ BR 70-71 K 4
Mato Grosso do Sul □ BR 70-71 J 6
Mato Guarrojo o CO 60-61 F 5
Matola o MOC 220-221 L 2
Matondo o MOC 218-219 H 3
Matong o PNG 183 F 3
Matope o MW 218-219 H 2
Matopo o ZW 218-219 E 5
Matos, Río ~ BOL 70-71 D 4
Matos Costa o BR 74-75 E 6
Matoury o F 62-63 H 3
Mato Verde o BR 72-73 J 3
Matraca o CO 60-61 G 6
Matrah o• OM 132-133 L 2
Matras Beach • RI 162-163 G 5
Matroosberg o ZA 220-221 D 6
Matru o WAL 202-203 D 6
Matrūbah o LAR 192-193 K 1
Matsalu Riiklik Looduskaitseala ⊥ EST 94-95 H 2
Matsanga o RCB 210-211 D 4
Matsari o CAM 204-205 K 6
Matshumbi o ZRE 212-213 B 4
Matsiatra ~ RM 222-223 E 8
Matsoandakana o RM 222-223 F 5
Matsue o J 152-153 E 7
Matsuka o G 210-211 B 4
Matsu Liehtao ⌒ RC 156-157 L 3
Matsumae o J 152-153 J 4
Matsumoto o J 152-153 G 6
Matsu Temple • RC 156-157 M 5
Matsuyama ☆ J 152-153 E 8
Matsuzaka o J 152-153 G 7
Mattagami Lake ⊂ CDN (ONT) 236-237 G 5
Mattagami River ~ CDN (ONT) 236-237 G 3
Mattagami River ~ CDN (ONT) 236-237 F 2
Mattamuskeet Lake ⊂ USA (NC) 282-283 L 5
Mattaponi River ~ USA (VA) 280-281 J 6
Mattawa o CDN (ONT) 238-239 G 2
Mattawa o USA (WA) 244-245 F 4
Mattawamkeag o USA (ME) 278-279 N 3
Mattawa River Provincial Park ⊥ CDN (ONT) 238-239 F 2
Mattawishkwia River ~ CDN (ONT) 236-237 E 3
Mattawitchewan River ~ CDN (ONT) 236-237 D 3
Matterhorn ▲•• CH 92-93 J 5
Matterhorn ▲ USA (NV) 246-247 K 2
Mattesalja, mys ▲ RUS 108-109 Q 5
Matthews o USA (NC) 282-283 G 5
Matthews Ridge o GUY 62-63 D 2
Matthew Town o BS 54-55 J 4
Mattice o CDN (ONT) 236-237 E 3
Mattili o IND 142-143 C 6
Mattō o J 152-153 G 6
Mattoon o USA (IL) 274-275 K 5
Matty Island ⌒ CDN 24-25 Y 6
Matu o MAL 162-163 J 3
Matua, ostrov ⌒ RUS 122-123 P 4
Matucana o PE 64-65 D 7
Matuda, ozero ⊂ RUS 108-109 b 5
Matugama o CL 140-141 J 7
Matukar o PNG 183 C 3
Matuku ⌒ FJI 184 III b 3
Matundu o ZRE 206-207 F 6
Matupi, Igarapé ~ BR 66-67 G 6
Ma'tuq o SUD 200-201 F 5
Maturín ☆ YV 60-61 K 3
Matusadona National Park ⊥ ZW 218-219 E 3
Matuseviča, fiord ≈ 108-109 b 2
Matveev, ostrov ⌒ RUS 108-109 H 7
Matveevka o RUS (ULN) 96-97 F 6
Matveevka ☆ RUS (ORB) 96-97 H 7
Matveev Kurgan o RUS 102-103 L 4
Maty-Centre o RCB 210-211 E 5
Matykil', ostrov ⌒ RUS 120-121 Q 4
Mau o IND (UTP) 142-143 C 3
Mau o IND (UTP) 142-143 B 3
Mau, Île = Emao ⌒ VAN 184 II b 3
Mauá o BR 72-73 G 7
Maua o EAK 212-213 F 3
Maúa o MOC 218-219 J 1
Mauba, Wādī ~ Y 132-133 G 5
Mauban o RP 160-161 D 5
Maubin o MYA 158-159 C 2
Maubisse o RI 166-167 C 6
Maud o USA (OK) 264-265 H 3
Maud o USA (TX) 264-265 K 5
Maude o AUS 180-181 H 3
Maué o ANG 216-217 E 8
Maués o BR 66-67 J 4
Maués, Rio ~ BR 66-67 J 4
Maués-Mirim, Rio ~ BR 66-67 J 4
Maugris < RIM 196-197 C 5
Maui ⌒ USA (HI) 288 J 4
Mauk o RI 168 B 3
Maukeli o RI 168 E 7
Maulamyaing o MYA 158-159 D 2
Maulbronn o••• D 92-93 K 4
Mauldin o USA (SC) 284-285 H 2
Maule, Laguna del ⊂ RCH 78-79 D 4
Maule, Río ~ RCH 78-79 C 3
Maule o Pehuenche, Paso ▲ RA 78-79 D 4
Maullín o RCH 78-79 C 6
Maullín, Bahía ≈ 78-79 C 6
Maumee o USA (OH) 280-281 C 2
Maumee River ~ USA (OH) 280-281 B 2
Maumela o RI 166-167 C 6
Maumelle, Lake < USA (AR) 276-277 C 6
Maumere o RI 166-167 B 6
Maun ☆ RB 218-219 B 4
Mauna Kea ▲ USA (HI) 288 K 5
Maunaloa o USA (HI) 288 H 3
Mauna Loa ▲ USA (HI) 288 K 5
Mauneluk River ~ USA 20-21 N 3
Maungmagan Islands ⌒ MYA 158-159 D 3
Maungu o EAK 212-213 G 5
Maunoir, Lac ⊂ CDN 30-31 G 2
Maupertuis, Lac ⊂ CDN 38-39 J 3
Maupin o USA (OR) 244-245 D 5
Mauqaq o KSA 130-131 G 4
Maur, Wādī ~ Y 132-133 C 6
Mau Rānipur o IND 138-139 G 7
Maure, Col de ▲ F 90-91 L 9
Maurelle Islands Wilderness ⊥ USA 32-33 C 4
Maurepas, Lake ⊂ USA (LA) 268-269 K 6
Maurepas, Point ▲ CDN (ONT) 236-237 C 5
Mauri, Río ~ PE 70-71 C 5
Maurice, Lac ⊂ CDN (ONT) 236-237 L 2
Maurice, Lake ⊂ AUS 176-177 L 4
Maurice Ewing Bank ≃ 6-7 E 14
Mauriceville o USA (TX) 268-269 G 6
Mauricio Batista o BR 76-77 K 5
Maurine o USA (SD) 260-261 D 1
Mauritania = Mawritaniyah ■ RIM 196-197 C 4
Mauritius ■ MS 224 C 7
Maury Channel ≈ 24-25 Y 3
Mausolée • RCA 206-207 D 6
Mauston o USA (WI) 270-271 H 7
Mauterndorf o A 92-93 M 5
Mauyama o WAN 204-205 E 2
Mavaca, Río ~ YV 66-67 E 2
Māvelikara o IND 140-141 G 6
Mavengue o ANG 216-217 E 8
Mavila o PE 70-71 C 2
Mavillette o CDN (NS) 240-241 J 6
Mavinga o ANG 216-217 F 7
Mavis Reef ⌒ AUS 172-173 F 3
Mavita o MOC 218-219 G 4
Mavua o Z 218-219 B 2
Mavuè o MOC 218-219 G 5
Mavuji ~ EAT 214-215 K 5
Mavunga ~ ANG 216-217 F 6
Mavuradonha o ZW 218-219 F 3
Mawa o ZRE 210-211 L 2
Mawa-Geti o ZRE 210-211 L 2
Mawai o MAL 162-163 E 4
Mawanella o CL 140-141 J 7
Mawang o VRC 156-157 F 2
Mawanga o ZRE 216-217 D 3
Mawangdui Hanmu ∴ VRC 156-157 H 2
Mawara Island ⌒ PNG 184 I b 2
Mawasangka o RI 164-165 H 6
Mawat o IRQ 128-129 L 5
Mawdin o MYA 158-159 C 3
Mawefan o RI 166-167 H 3
Mawhun o MYA 142-143 K 3
Mawlaik o MYA 142-143 J 4
Maw Point ▲ USA (NC) 282-283 L 5
Mawson o ARK 16 G 7
Maxaans o SP 208-209 H 6
Maxanguape o BR 68-69 L 4
Maxbass o USA (ND) 258-259 F 3
Maxcanú o MEX 52-53 J 1
Maxesibeni o ZA 220-221 J 5
Maxeys o USA (GA) 284-285 G 3
Maxim o CDN (SAS) 232-233 O 6
Maximeville o CDN (PEI) 240-241 L 4
Máximo Gómez o C 54-55 E 3
Maxixe o MOC 218-219 H 6
Maxstone o CDN (SAS) 232-233 N 6
Maxville o USA (FL) 286-287 G 1
Maxville o USA (MT) 250-251 F 5
Maxwell o USA (CA) 246-247 C 4
Maxwell o USA (NE) 262-263 F 3
Maxwell o USA (NM) 256-257 L 2
Maxwell o USA (TN) 276-277 J 5
Maxwell Bay ≈ 24-25 b 3
Maxwell Fracture Zone ≃ 6-7 F 4
Maxwelton o AUS 174-175 G 7
May o PNG 183 A 3
May o USA (OK) 264-265 E 2
May o USA (TX) 266-267 J 2
May, Kap ▲ GRØ 26-27 Z 2
Maya o• SUD 200-201 F 6
Maya, La o C 54-55 H 4
Maya, Pulau ⌒ RI 162-163 H 5
Mayabander o IND 140-141 L 3
Mayādin, al- o SYR 128-129 J 5
Mayaguana Island ⌒ BS 54-55 J 3
Mayaguana Passage ≈ 54-55 J 3
Mayagüez o USA (PR) 286-287 O 2
Mayahi o RN 198-199 C 6
Mayala o ZRE 216-217 D 3
Mayama o RCB 210-211 E 5
Mayamaya o EAT (DOD) 212-213 E 6
Mayamba o ZRE 210-211 F 6
Maya Mountains ▲ BH 52-53 K 3
Mayang o VRC 156-157 F 3
Mayanja ~ EAU 212-213 C 3
Mayankwa o Z 218-219 B 2
Mayapan ∴• MEX 52-53 K 1
Mayari o C 54-55 H 4
Mayarí Arriba o C 54-55 H 4
Mayata < RN 198-199 C 5
Maybee o USA (MI) 272-273 F 6
Maybell o USA (CO) 254-255 G 3
Maybelle River ~ CDN 30-31 O 6
Maych'ew o ETH 200-201 J 6
May City o USA (IA) 274-275 C 1
May Dara Shet' ~ ETH 208-209 C 3
Maydena o AUS 180-181 J 7
Maydh o SP (San) 208-209 H 3
Maydh ⌒ SP (San) 208-209 H 3
May Downs o AUS 178-179 K 2
Mayel-Samou ~ SN 202-203 D 3
Mayenne o F 90-91 G 7
Mayenne ~ F 90-91 G 7
Mayer o USA (AZ) 256-257 C 4
Mayerthorpe o CDN (ALB) 232-233 C 2
Mayetta o USA (KS) 262-263 L 5
Mayfair o CDN (SAS) 232-233 L 3
Mayfield o CDN (SAS) 232-233 R 6
Mayfield o USA (ID) 252-253 C 3
Mayfield o USA (KY) 276-277 G 4
Mayfield o USA (UT) 254-255 D 4
Mayflower o USA (AR) 276-277 C 6
Mayhew Lake ⊂ USA (MN) 270-271 E 5
Mayhill o USA (NM) 256-257 K 6
Mayi, Mbuji- ☆ ZRE 214-215 B 4
May Inlet ≈ 24-25 V 2
May-Jirgui o RN 198-199 D 6
Maymont o CDN (SAS) 232-233 L 3
Maymūn, Wādī ~ LAR 190-191 H 5
Maymyo o MYA 142-143 K 4
Maynard o USA (AR) 276-277 E 4
Maynas ≐ PE 64-65 D 3
Mayne River ~ AUS 178-179 F 2
Mayneside o AUS 178-179 G 2
Māyni o IND 140-141 F 2
Maynooth o CDN (ONT) 238-239 H 3
Maynooth = Maigh Nuad o IRL 90-91 D 5
Mayo o USA (FL) 286-287 F 1
Mayo, 25 de o RA (BUA) 78-79 J 3
Mayo, 25 de o RA (MEN) 78-79 E 3
Mayo, 25 de o ROU 78-79 L 3
Mayo, Río ~ MEX 50-51 E 4
Mayo, Río ~ PE 64-65 D 5
Mayo, Río ~ RA 80 E 2
Mayo Belwa o WAN 204-205 K 4
Mayo Butale o WAN 204-205 K 4
Mayo Chehu o WAN 204-205 J 4
Mayo Darle o CAM 204-205 J 5
Mayo Djoi o CAM 206-207 B 4
Mayo Faran o WAN 204-205 K 4
Mayo Jarandi o WAN 204-205 J 5
Mayo-Kebbi □ TCH 206-207 B 3
Mayoko o RCB 210-211 D 5
Mayo Lake ⊂ CDN 20-21 X 5
Mayombé ▲ G 210-211 C 5
Mayo Ndaga o WAN 204-205 J 5
Mayon Vulcano ▲ RP 160-161 E 6
Mayo Oulo o CAM 204-205 K 4
Mayor Buratovich o RA 78-79 H 5
Mayorga o RP 160-161 F 7
Mayor Island ⌒ NZ 182 F 2
Mayor Otano o PY 76-77 K 4
Mayototo o WAL 202-203 E 5
Mayotte ⌒ COM 222-223 D 4
Mayoworth o USA (WY) 252-253 M 3
May Pen o JA 54-55 G 6
May Point, Cape ▲ USA (DE) 280-281 M 5
Mayqū' o KSA 130-131 F 3
Mayraira Point ▲ RP 160-161 D 3
Mayran, Desierto de ≐ MEX 50-51 H 5
May River ~ AUS 172-173 G 4
Maysel o USA (WV) 280-281 E 5
Mayson Lake ⊂ CDN 34-35 C 2
Maysville o USA (KY) 276-277 M 2
Maysville o USA (MO) 274-275 D 5
Maysville o USA (NC) 282-283 K 6
Maysville o USA (OK) 264-265 G 4
Maytown ∴ AUS 174-175 H 5
Mayu ≈ 166-167 K 5
Mayu, Pulau ⌒ RI 164-165 K 3
Mayumba o G 210-211 C 5
Mayumba o ZRE 214-215 E 4
Mayum La ▲ VRC 144-145 D 5
Māyūram o IND 140-141 H 5
May Valley o USA (CO) 254-255 N 5
Mayville o USA (MI) 272-273 F 4
Mayville o USA (ND) 258-259 K 4
Mayville o USA (NY) 278-279 B 6
Maywood o USA (NE) 262-263 F 4
Maza o RA 78-79 H 4
Maza o WAN 204-205 K 3
Mazabuka o Z 218-219 D 2
Mazagão o BR 62-63 J 6
Mazagão Velho o BR 62-63 J 6
Mazagón o E 98-99 D 6
Mazama o USA (WA) 244-245 E 2
Mazamari o PE 64-65 E 7
Mazamet o F 90-91 J 10
Mazán o PE 64-65 F 3
Mazandarān □ IR 136-137 B 6
Mazar o VRC 138-139 F 1
Mazār, Kūh-e ▲ AFG 134-135 L 2
Mazara del Vallo o I 100-101 D 6
Mazār-e Adschaeb •• AFG 136-137 K 6
Mazār-e Šarīf ☆ AFG 136-137 K 6
Mazargão o BR 70-71 K 4
mazar Karasopy • KA 136-137 K 3
Mazarredo o RA 80 G 3
Mazartag o VRC 146-147 E 6
Mazar Tag ▲ VRC 146-147 D 6
Mazaruni River ~ GUY 62-63 E 3
Mazarwala o VRC 138-139 F 1
Mazatán o MEX (CHI) 52-53 H 4
Mazatán o MEX (SON) 50-51 D 3
Mazatenango ☆ GCA 52-53 J 4
Mazatlán o• MEX 50-51 F 6
Mazatzal Peak ▲ USA (AZ) 256-257 D 4
Mazdaqān, Rūdḫane-ye ~ IR 128-129 N 5
Mažeikiai ☆• LT 94-95 H 3
Mazéla o BF 202-203 G 4
Maze Lake ⊂ CDN 30-31 R 4
Mazenod o CDN (SAS) 232-233 M 6
Mazeppa Bay o ZA 220-221 J 6
Mazıdağı ☆ TR 128-129 J 4
Mazimechopes, Rio ~ MOC 220-221 L 2
Mazinān o IR 136-137 E 6
Mazocahui o MEX 50-51 D 3
Mazoco o MOC 214-215 H 6
Mazo-Cruz o PE 70-71 C 5
Mazoe, Rio ~ MOC 218-219 G 3
Mazomeno o ZRE 212-213 A 6
Mazomora o EAT 214-215 K 4
Mazon o USA (IL) 274-275 K 3
Mazong Shan ▲ VRC 148-149 C 7
Mazorca, Isla ⌒ PE 64-65 D 7
Mazoula o DZ 190-191 F 6
Mazowe o ZW (Mlc) 218-219 F 3
Mazowe ~ ZW 218-219 F 3
Maz'ra'a, al- o JOR 130-131 D 2
Mazra'eh Akhund o IR 134-135 E 3
Mazrūb o SUD 200-201 D 6
Mazsalaca o•• LV 94-95 J 3
Mazu Miao • VRC 156-157 L 4
Mazunga o ZW 218-219 E 5
Mazyr o BY 94-95 L 5
Mazzamitla o MEX 52-53 C 2
Mba o CAM 204-205 J 5
Mbabala o Z 218-219 D 3
Mbabane ★ SD 220-221 K 3
Mbacha o WAN 204-205 H 5
Mbadduna o SOL 184 I c 3
Mbadi o G 210-211 C 5
Mbadjé Akpa o RCA 206-207 E 5
Mbaéré ~ RCA 206-207 C 6
Mbagne o RIM 196-197 D 6
Mbahiakro o CI 202-203 H 6
Mbaïki ☆ RCA 210-211 F 2
Mbakaou o CAM 204-205 K 5
Mbakaou, Barrage de < CAM 204-205 K 5
Mbakaou, Lac de < CAM 204-205 K 5
Mbaké o SN 202-203 C 2
Mbako o RCA 206-207 B 6
Mbala o• Z 214-215 F 5
Mbalabala o ZW 218-219 E 5
Mbalageti ~ EAT 212-213 E 5
Mbalam o CAM 210-211 D 2
Mbalambala o EAK 212-213 G 4
Mbale ☆• EAU 212-213 E 3
Mbali ~ RCA 206-207 C 6
Mbali-Iboma o ZRE 210-211 F 5
Mbalmayo o CAM 210-211 C 2
Mbam ~ CAM 204-205 J 6
Mbam, Massif du ▲ CAM 204-205 J 6
Mbama o CAM 210-211 D 2
Mbama o RCB 210-211 E 4
Mbamba Bay o EAT 214-215 H 6
Mbambanakira o SOL 184 I d 3
Mbam Minkom ▲ CAM 210-211 C 2
Mbandaka ☆ ZRE 210-211 G 3
Mbandjok o CAM 204-205 J 6
Mbandza o G 210-211 E 3
Mbandza-Ndounga o RCB 210-211 E 6
Mbane o SN 196-197 C 6
Mbang o CAM 210-211 E 2
Mbanga o CAM 204-205 H 6
Mbanga o SOL 184 I c 3
Mbangala ~ EAT 214-215 K 6
Mbanika Island ⌒ SOL 184 I d 3
M'banza Congo ☆ ANG 216-217 C 3
Mbanza-Ngungu = Thysville o ZRE 210-211 E 6
Mbar o SN 202-203 C 2
Mbarang'andu o EAT 214-215 J 6
Mbarangandu ~ EAT 214-215 J 6
Mbarara ☆ EAU 212-213 C 4
Mbārek, Hāssei < RIM 196-197 E 6
Mbargué o CAM 204-205 K 6
Mbari ~ RCA 206-207 F 6
Mbarizunga Game Reserve ⊥ SUD 206-207 J 6
Mbaswana o ZA 220-221 L 3
Mbata o RCA 210-211 G 2
Mbati o Z 214-215 F 6
Mbava ⌒ SOL 184 I c 2
Mbé o CAM 204-205 K 5
Mbé ~ G 210-211 C 3
Mbé o RCB 210-211 E 5
Mbeiporo o SOL 184 I c 3
Mbéloba o RCA 206-207 E 6
Mbemkuru ~ EAT 214-215 K 5
Mbéna o RCB 210-211 C 6
Mbengué o CI 202-203 H 4
Mbengwi o CAM 204-205 J 5
M'Beni o COM 222-223 C 3
Mbéré ~ CAM 206-207 B 5
Mberengwa o ZW 218-219 E 5
Mbet o CAM 204-205 K 6
Mbéti = Alayo o RCA 206-207 F 6
Mbéwé o CAM 204-205 K 5
Mbeya □ EAT 214-215 G 5
Mbeya ☆ EAT (MBE) 214-215 G 5
Mbeya o Z 214-215 G 6
Mbi ~ RCA 206-207 C 6
Mbiama o WAN 204-205 G 6
Mbié o RCB 210-211 E 4
Mbigou o G 210-211 C 4
Mbinda o RCB 210-211 D 5
Mbinga o EAT 214-215 H 6
Mbini o GQ 210-211 B 3
Mbita o EAK 212-213 E 4
Mbitao o CAM 206-207 B 5
Mbitom o CAM 204-205 K 6
Mbiyi o RCA 206-207 F 6
Mbizi o ZW 218-219 F 5
Mbizi Mountains ▲ EAT 214-215 F 4
Mbo o RCA 206-207 D 4
Mboké o CAM 204-205 K 6
Mboki o RCA 206-207 G 6
Mboko o ZRE 212-213 B 5
Mbokonimbeti Island = Sandfly Island ⌒ SOL 184 I d 3
Mbokou ~ RCA 206-207 H 6
Mbolo Island ⌒ SOL 184 I d 3
Mbomo o G 210-211 E 3
Mbomou □ RCA 206-207 F 6
Mbomou ~ RCA 206-207 F 6
Mbon o RCB 210-211 E 5
Mbonge o CAM 204-205 H 6
Mborokua Island ⌒ SOL 184 I d 3
Mboroma o Z 218-219 E 2
Mborong o RI 168 E 7
Mboro-sur-Mer o SN 202-203 B 2
Mbot o CAM 204-205 J 5
Mbouda o CAM 204-205 J 6
Mboula o CAM 204-205 K 5
Mboula o RCA 206-207 C 6
Mbouma o CAM 210-211 E 2
Mboune o SN 202-203 D 2
Mboungou Badouma o G 210-211 D 4
Mbour o SN 202-203 B 2
Mbout o RIM 196-197 D 6
Mboutou ~ RCA 206-207 G 6
Mbozi o EAT 214-215 G 5
Mbozi Meteorit • EAT 214-215 G 5
Mbrés o• RCA 206-207 D 5
Mbu ~ CAM 204-205 H 6
Mbudi o ZRE 210-211 F 6
Mbugwe o EAT 212-213 F 5
Mbuji-Mayi ☆ ZRE (KOR) 214-215 B 4
Mbuji-Mayi ~ ZRE 214-215 B 4
Mbuke Islands ⌒ PNG 183 D 2
Mbulu o EAT 212-213 E 5
Mbuma o SOL 184 I e 3
Mburucuyá o RA 76-77 H 5
Mbuyuni o EAT (KIL) 212-213 F 6
Mbuyuni o EAT (MOR) 214-215 J 4
Mbwamaji o EAT 214-215 K 4
Mbwewe o EAT 214-215 K 4
McAdam National Park ⊥ PNG 183 D 4
McAdoo o USA (TX) 264-265 C 5
McAleese Lake ⊂ CDN 30-31 U 5
McAlester o USA (OK) 264-265 J 4
McAlester Army Ammunition Plant ✕✕ USA (OK) 264-265 J 4
McAllen o USA (TX) 266-267 J 7
McAllister State Historic Site, Fort • USA (GA) 284-285 J 5
McArthur o USA (OH) 280-281 D 4
McArthur Falls o CDN (MAN) 234-235 G 4
Mc Arthur River ~ AUS 174-175 D 5
McBee o USA (SC) 284-285 K 2
McBeth Fiord ≈ 28-29 F 2
McBeth River ~ CDN 28-29 E 2
McBride o CDN (BC) 228-229 O 3
McCall o USA (ID) 252-253 B 2
McCall Seamount ≃ 288 J 6
McCallum o CDN (NFL) 242-243 M 5
McCamey o USA (TX) 266-267 E 2
McCammon o USA (ID) 252-253 F 4
McCann Lake ⊂ CDN 30-31 Q 5
McCarthy o USA 20-21 T 6
McCauley Island ⌒ CDN (BC) 228-229 D 3
McCauley Islands ⌒ CDN (BC) 228-229 D 3
McCaulley o USA (TX) 264-265 D 6
McCleary o USA (WA) 244-245 B 3
McClellan Creek ~ USA (TX) 264-265 D 3
McClellanville o USA (SC) 284-285 L 3
Mcclenny o USA (FL) 286-287 G 1
McClintock Channel ≈ 24-25 U 4
McClintock Point ▲ CDN 24-25 W 6
McClintock Range ▲ AUS 172-173 H 5
McCloud o USA (CA) 246-247 C 2
McCluer Island ⌒ AUS 172-173 L 1
McClure o USA (OH) 280-281 C 2
McClure Strait ≈ 24-25 M 3
McClusky o USA (ND) 258-259 G 4
McClusky Pass ▲ USA (NV) 246-247 J 4
McColl o USA (SC) 284-285 L 2
McComb o USA (MS) 268-269 K 5
McConaughy, Lake C.W. ⊂ USA (NE) 262-263 E 3
McCondy o USA (MS) 268-269 M 3
McConkey Hill ▲ AUS 176-177 F 2
McConnells o USA (SC) 284-285 J 2
McConnellsburg o USA (PA) 280-281 H 4
McConnel Range ▲ CDN 30-31 G 3
McConnel River ~ CDN 30-31 W 5
McConnelsville o USA (OH) 280-281 E 4
McCook o USA (NE) 262-263 F 4
McCool o USA (MS) 268-269 L 3
McCool Junction o USA (NE) 262-263 J 4
McCormick o USA (SC) 284-285 H 3
McCoy Creek ~ CDN (SAS) 232-233 J 6
McCoy Mountains ▲ USA (CA) 248-249 K 6
McCracken o USA (KS) 262-263 G 6
McCreary o CDN (MAN) 234-235 D 4
McCredie Springs o USA (OR) 244-245 C 7
McCrory o USA (AR) 276-277 D 5
McCulloch o CDN (BC) 230-231 K 4
McCullough Range ▲ USA (NV) 248-249 J 4
McCusker River ~ CDN 32-33 Q 4
McDavid o USA (FL) 286-287 B 1
McDermitt o USA (NV) 246-247 H 2
McDonald o USA (KS) 262-263 E 5
McDonald Peak ▲ USA (MT) 250-251 F 4
McDonnel, Cape ▲ CDN 30-31 J 2
McDonough o USA (GA) 284-285 F 3
Mc Douall Peak o AUS 178-179 C 5
McDougal, Lake ⊂ ZW 218-219 F 5
McDougal Creek ~ CDN 34-35 D 3
McDougall Sound ≈ 24-25 X 3
McDowell o USA (AZ) 256-257 D 5
McDowell o USA (VA) 280-281 G 5
McDowell Indian Reservation, Fort ✗ USA (AZ) 256-257 D 5
McDowell River ~ CDN (ONT) 234-235 L 2
Mcensk o RUS 94-95 P 5
McEwen o USA (TN) 276-277 H 4
McFaddin o USA (TX) 266-267 K 5
McFarland o USA (CA) 248-249 E 4
McFarlane River ~ CDN 30-31 P 6
McGee o CDN (SAS) 232-233 K 4
McGehee o USA (AR) 276-277 D 7
McGill o USA (NV) 246-247 L 4
McGillivray Bay ≈ 24-25 X 6
McGivney o CDN (NB) 240-241 J 4
McGrath o USA (AK) 20-21 N 5
McGrath o USA (MN) 270-271 E 4
McGregor o USA (MN) 270-271 E 4
McGregor o USA (ND) 258-259 E 3
McGregor, Lake ⊂ CDN (ALB) 232-233 F 5
Mc Gregor Range ▲ AUS 178-179 G 4
McGregor River ~ CDN (BC) 228-229 N 2
McGuire, Mount ▲ USA (ID) 250-251 E 6
McHenry River ~ AUS 174-175 G 2
Mcherrah ≐ DZ 188-189 J 7
Mcheta o GE 126-127 F 7
Mchinga o EAT 214-215 K 5
Mchinji o MW 218-219 G 1
M'Chouneche o DZ 190-191 F 3
Mcllwraith Range ▲ AUS 174-175 G 3
McInnes Lake ⊂ CDN (ONT) 234-235 K 2
McIntosh o USA (SD) 260-261 E 1
McIntosh Lake ⊂ CDN 34-35 D 3
McIntyre Bay ≈ CDN 228-229 B 2
McIntyre Bay ⊂ CDN (ONT) 234-235 P 5
McIver's o CDN (NFL) 242-243 K 3
McIvor River ~ CDN 30-31 N 6
McKague o CDN (SAS) 232-233 P 3
McKay, Mount ▲ AUS 172-173 E 7
McKay Lake ⊂ CDN (NFL) 38-39 M 2
McKay Lake ⊂ CDN (ONT) 236-237 B 3
McKay Range ▲ AUS 176-177 F 7
McKeand River ~ CDN 36-37 P 2
McKellar o CDN (ONT) 238-239 F 3
McKeller o CDN (ONT) 238-239 F 3
McKenna o USA (WA) 244-245 C 4
McKenzie o USA (AL) 284-285 D 5
McKenzie o USA (TN) 276-277 G 4
McKenzie Bridge o USA (OR) 244-245 C 6
McKenzie Draw ~ USA (TX) 264-265 B 6
McKenzie River ~ USA (OR) 244-245 C 6
McKinlay o AUS 178-179 F 1
McKinlay River ~ AUS 178-179 F 1
McKinley, Mount ▲•• USA 20-21 P 5
McKinney o USA (TX) 264-265 H 5
McKinney Mountain ▲ USA (TX) 266-267 D 4
McKinnon o USA (WY) 252-253 J 5
McKittrick o USA (CA) 248-249 E 4
McLain o USA (MS) 268-269 M 5
McLaren Creek o AUS 174-175 C 7
Mc Laren Vale o AUS 180-181 E 3
McLaughlin o USA (SD) 260-261 F 1
McLean o CDN (SAS) 232-233 O 5
McLean o USA (IL) 274-275 J 4
McLean o USA (TX) 264-265 D 3
McLeansboro o USA (IL) 274-275 K 6
McLeese Lake o CDN (BC) 228-229 M 4
McLeod o USA (MT) 250-251 J 6
McLeod o USA (ND) 258-259 K 5
McLeod Bay ⊂ CDN 30-31 O 4
McLeod Lake o CDN 32-33 J 4
McLeod River ~ CDN (ALB) 232-233 B 2
McLeod River ~ CDN (ALB) 228-229 R 3
McLeod River ~ CDN (ALB) 232-233 C 2
McLeods Corner o USA (MI) 270-271 N 4
McLeod Valley o CDN (ALB) 232-233 C 2
McLemon, Lake ⊂ AUS 172-173 H 5
M'Clintock o CDN 34-35 J 2
M'Clintock Inlet ≈ 26-27 M 2
McLoughlin, Mount ▲ USA (OR) 244-245 C 8
McLoughlin Bay ≈ 30-31 U 2
McLure o CDN (BC) 230-231 J 2
McMahon o CDN (SAS) 232-233 L 5
McManaman Lake ⊂ CDN 30-31 X 4
McMasterville o CDN (QUE) 238-239 M 3
McMillan o USA (MI) 270-271 N 4
McMillan, Lake ⊂ USA (NM) 256-257 L 6
McMinnville o USA (OR) 244-245 B 5
McMinnville o USA (TN) 276-277 K 5
McMorran o CDN (SAS) 232-233 K 4
McMurdo o ARK 16 F 17
McMurdo o CDN (BC) 230-231 N 2
Mc Murdo Sound ≈ 16 F 17
McMurray o USA (WA) 244-245 C 2
McMurtry, Lake ⊂ USA (OK) 264-265 G 2
McNab Cove o CDN (NS) 240-241 P 5
McNary o USA (AZ) 256-257 F 4
McNary o USA (TX) 266-267 B 2
McNaughton Lake ⊂ CDN 30-31 U 2
McNeal o USA (AZ) 256-257 F 7
McNeill o USA (MS) 268-269 L 6
McNeill, Port o CDN (BC) 230-231 B 3
McParlon Lake ⊂ CDN (ONT) 236-237 H 2
McPhee Reservoir < USA (CO) 254-255 G 6
Mc Pherson ▲ AUS 178-179 M 5
McPherson o USA (KS) 262-263 J 6
McPhersons Pillar ▲ AUS 176-177 H 2
McQuesten River ~ CDN 20-21 W 5
McRae o USA (GA) 284-285 H 4
McRobertson Land ≐ ARK 16 G 7
McTaggart o CDN (SAS) 232-233 O 6
McTavish o CDN (MAN) 234-235 F 5
McTavish Arm ⊂ CDN 30-31 K 2
McVicar Arm ⊂ CDN 30-31 J 3
McVille o USA (ND) 258-259 J 4
Mdandu o EAT 214-215 H 5
Mdantsane o ZA 220-221 H 6
Mdina o M 100-101 E 7
M'Doukal o DZ 190-191 E 3
M'Drac o VN 158-159 K 4
Meacham o CDN (SAS) 232-233 N 3
Mead o CDN (ONT) 236-237 E 3
Mead o USA (NE) 262-263 K 3
Mead, Lake ⊂ USA (NV) 248-249 K 3
Meade o USA (KS) 262-263 F 7
Meade Peak ▲ USA (ID) 252-253 G 4
Meade River ~ USA 20-21 M 2
Meadow o USA (TX) 264-265 B 5
Meadow o USA (UT) 254-255 C 5
Meadowbank o AUS 174-175 H 6
Meadowbank River ~ CDN 30-31 V 3
Meadow Brook Pass ▲ USA (OR) 244-245 G 6
Meadow Creek o CDN (BC) 230-231 M 3
Meadow Creek o USA (ID) 250-251 C 3
Meadow Lake o CDN 32-33 Q 4
Meadow Lake Provincial Park ⊥ CDN 32-33 Q 4
Meadowlands o USA (MN) 270-271 F 3
Meadow Portage o CDN (MAN) 234-235 D 3
Meadows o CDN (MAN) 234-235 F 4
Meadow Valley Range ▲ USA (NV) 248-249 J 2
Meadow Valley Wash ~ USA (NV) 248-249 K 3
Meadville o USA (PA) 280-281 F 2
Meaford o CDN (ONT) 238-239 E 4

Meakan-dake ▲ J 152-153 L 3
Mealhada ○ P 98-99 C 4
Méana ○ RN 202-203 L 2
Meana ○ TM 136-137 G 6
Meander River ○ CDN 30-31 L 6
Mearim, Rio ~ BR 68-69 F 4
Meath Park ○ CDN (SAS) 232-233 N 2
Meaux ○ F 90-91 J 7
Mebali ○ RI 164-165 F 5
Mebane ○ USA (NC) 282-283 H 4
Mebo, Gunung ▲ RI 166-167 G 2
Mebougou ○ RMM 202-203 G 4
Mebridege ~ ANG 216-217 B 3
Mecanhelas ○ MOC 218-219 H 2
Mecatan ○ MEX 50-51 G 7
Mécatina, Cap ▲ CDN (QUE) 242-243 J 2
Mecaya, Rio ~ CO 64-65 E 1
Mecca ○ USA (CA) 248-249 J 6
Mecca = Makka ✫•• KSA 132-133 A 3
Mecequesse, Rio ~ MOC 218-219 J 2
Mecham, Cape ▲ CDN 24-25 L 3
Mechanicsburg ○ USA (OH) 280-281 C 3
Mechanicville ○ USA (NY) 278-279 H 6
Mechára ○ ETH 208-209 E 4
Mechelen ○• B 92-93 H 3
Méchiméré ○ TCH 198-199 G 6
Méchins, Les ○ CDN (QUE) 240-241 J 2
Mechra-Bel-Ksiri ○ MA 188-189 J 3
Mechra-Benâbbou ○ MA 188-189 H 4
Mechroha ○ DZ 190-191 F 2
Mečigmenskij zaliv ≈ 112-113 Y 4
Mecitözü ✫ TR 128-129 F 2
Meckel ○ USA (KY) 276-277 M 4
Mečkereva ~ RUS 112-113 P 3
Mecklenburger Bucht ≈ D 92-93 L 1
Mecklenburg-Vorpommern ◘ D 92-93 M 2
Meconta ○ MOC 218-219 K 2
Mecubúri ○ MOC 218-219 K 2
Mecubúri, Rio ~ MOC 218-219 K 2
Mecúfi ○ MOC 218-219 L 1
Mecula ○ MOC 214-215 J 7
Medak ○• IND 138-139 G 10
Medan ✫ RI 162-163 C 3
Medan Fair • RI 162-163 C 3
Medang, Pulau ⌒ RI 168 C 7
Medang, Tanjung ▲ RI 162-163 D 3
Medanosa, Punta ▲ RA 80 H 4
Médanos de Coro, Parque Nacional ⊥ YV 60-61 G 2
Medart ○ USA (FL) 286-287 E 1
Medawachchiya ○ CL 140-141 J 6
Medd Allah ○ RMM 202-203 H 2
Médéa ✫ DZ 190-191 D 2
Medeiros ○ BR 72-73 G 5
Medellín ✫ CO 60-61 D 4
Medelpad ∸ S 86-87 H 5
Medenine ✫ TN 190-191 H 4
Méderdra ○ RIM 196-197 C 6
Medford ○ USA (NJ) 280-281 M 4
Medford ○ USA (OK) 264-265 G 2
Medford ○ USA (WI) 270-271 H 5
Medford ○• USA (OR) 244-245 C 8
Medgidia ○ RO 102-103 F 5
Medha ○ IND 140-141 E 2
Medi ○ SUD 206-207 K 6
Media Luna ○ RA 78-79 F 3
Media Luna, Cañada de ~ RA 76-77 F 2
Medianeira ○ BR 76-77 K 3
Mediapolis ○ USA (IA) 274-275 G 3
Mediaş ○• RO 102-103 D 4
Medical Lake ○ USA (WA) 244-245 H 3
Medical Springs ○ USA (OR) 244-245 H 5
Medicine Bow ○ USA (WY) 252-253 M 5
Medicine Bow Mountains ⛰ USA (WY) 252-253 M 5
Medicine Bow Peak ▲ USA (WY) 252-253 M 5
Medicine Creek ~ USA (MO) 274-275 E 5
Medicine Creek ~ USA (NE) 262-263 F 4
Medicine Hat ○ CDN (ALB) 232-233 H 5
Medicine Lake ○ USA (MT) 250-251 P 3
Medicine Lake ⊖ USA (MT) 250-251 P 3
Medicine Lodge ○ CDN (ALB) 232-233 B 2
Medicine Lodge ○ USA (KS) 262-263 H 7
Medicine Lodge River ~ USA (KS) 262-263 G 7
Medicine River ~ CDN (ALB) 232-233 D 3
Medina ○ BR 72-73 K 4
Medina ○ CDN (ONT) 238-239 D 5
Medina ○ USA (ND) 258-259 H 5
Medina ○ USA (NY) 278-279 C 5
Medina ○ USA (OH) 280-281 E 2
Medina ○ USA (TX) 266-267 H 4
Medina = Madina, al- ✫•• KSA 130-131 F 5
Medina, Rio ~ RA 76-77 E 4
Medina Azahara • E 98-99 E 6
Medina del Campo ○ E 98-99 E 4
Medina de Rioseco ○ E 98-99 E 4
Médina Gounas ○ SN 202-203 D 3
Medina Lake ⊖ USA (TX) 266-267 J 4
Medina River ~ USA (TX) 266-267 H 4
Medina-Sidonia ○ E 98-99 E 6
Médina-Yorofoula ○ SN 202-203 C 3
Médine • TN 190-191 G 3
Medininkai ○•• LT 94-95 J 4
Medinipur ○ IND 142-143 E 4
Medio, Arroyo del ~ RA 78-79 J 2
Medio Creek ~ USA (TX) 266-267 K 5
Mediouna ○ MA 188-189 H 4
Mediterranean Sea ≈ 8 D 5
Medjedel ○ DZ 190-191 D 3
Medjerda, Monts de la ⛰ DZ 190-191 F 2
Medley ○ CDN 32-33 P 4
Medley River ~ CDN 32-33 P 4
Mednogorsk ○ RUS 96-97 K 8
Mednyj, mys ▲ RUS 108-109 a 2
Mednyj, ostrov ⌒ RUS 120-121 W 6
Médoc ∸ F 90-91 G 9
Mêdog Z.B. ⊥ • VRC 144-145 K 6
Medora ○ CDN (MAN) 234-235 C 5
Medora ○ USA (IN) 274-275 M 6
Medora ○ USA (ND) 258-259 D 5
Medouneu ○ GQ 210-211 C 3
Medracen, Le • DZ 190-191 F 3
Medrissa ○ DZ 190-191 C 3
Medstead ○ CDN (SAS) 232-233 K 2
Medvedica ~ RUS 96-97 D 8
Medvež'e, ozero ⊖ RUS 114-115 K 7
Medvež'egorsk ✫ RUS 88-89 N 5
Medvežij, mys ▲ RUS (SAH) 110-111 W 2
Medvežij, mys ▲ RUS (SAH) 110-111 J 2
Medvežij, mys ▲ RUS (SAH) 112-113 M 2
Medvežij, ostrov ⌒ RUS 120-121 G 6
Medvežij, zaliv ⊖ RUS 108-109 G 5
Medveži ostrova ⌒ RUS 112-113 L 1
Medvež'ja ~ RUS 108-109 e 6
Medvežka ~ RUS 112-113 M 2
Medyn' ○ RUS 94-95 O 4
Medynskij Zavorot, mys ▲ RUS 108-109 H 7
Medze ○ LV 94-95 G 3
Medzilaborce ○ SK 92-93 Q 4
Mèèčkyn, Kosa-ostrov ⌒ RUS 112-113 V 4
Meekatharra ○ AUS 176-177 E 3
Meeker ○ USA (CO) 254-255 H 3
Meek Point ▲ CDN 24-25 J 4
Meeladeen ○ SP 208-209 J 3
Meeline ○ AUS 176-177 E 4
Meelpaeg Lake ⊖ CDN (NFL) 242-243 M 4
Meerut ○ IND 138-139 F 5
Meerzorg ○ SME 62-63 G 3
Meeteetse ○ USA (WY) 252-253 K 2
Meeting Creek ○ CDN (ALB) 232-233 F 3
Mēga ○ ETH 208-209 D 6
Mega ○ RI 166-167 F 2
Megalo ○ ETH 208-209 E 5
Megalópoli ○ GR 100-101 J 6
Megamo ○ RI 166-167 F 2
Megantic, Mont ▲ CDN (QUE) 238-239 O 3
Megara ○ GR 100-101 J 6
Megargel ○ USA (TX) 264-265 F 5
Megaruma, Rio ~ MOC 218-219 K 1
Megeitia < SUD 200-201 E 5
Megezez ▲ ETH 208-209 D 4
Meghālaya ◘ IND 142-143 G 3
Meghna ~ BD 142-143 G 4
Megion ○ RUS 114-115 O 4
Mégiscane, Lac ⊖ CDN (QUE) 236-237 N 4
Mégiscane, Rivière ~ CDN (QUE) 236-237 M 4
Megra ~ RUS 88-89 Q 4
Megri ○ AR 128-129 M 3
Méguet ○ BF 202-203 K 3
Meguidene ∸ DZ 190-191 C 6
Mehaïguene, Oued ~ DZ 190-191 D 4
Mehāl Mēda ○ ETH 208-209 D 3
Mehama ○ USA (OR) 244-245 C 6
Mehamn ○ N 86-87 N 1
Mehar ○ PK 134-135 M 5
Meharry, Mount ▲ AUS 172-173 D 7
Mehdia ○ DZ 190-191 C 3
Mehe, Kūh-e ▲ IR 134-135 H 5
Mehedjibat, Erg ∸ DZ 190-191 D 8
Mehekar ○ IND 138-139 F 9
Meherpur ○ BD 142-143 F 4
Meherrin River ~ USA (VA) 280-281 J 7
Mehmani ○ IR 134-135 G 5
Mehrābpur ○ PK 138-139 B 5
Mehrān ○ IR 134-135 B 2
Mehrān, Rūd-e ~ IR 134-135 E 5
Mehrān, Rūdhāne-ye ~ IR 134-135 F 5
Mehren'ga ~ RUS 88-89 Q 5
Mehrgarh ∴•• PK 134-135 M 4
Mehriz ○ IR 134-135 F 3
Mehtarlām ✫ • AFG 138-139 C 2
Meia Ponte, Rio ~ BR 72-73 F 5
Meibod ○ IR 134-135 E 2
Meidāni, Ra's-e ▲ IR 134-135 H 6
Meidānšahr ✫ • AFG 138-139 B 2
Meidougou ○ CAM 206-207 B 5
Meiganga ○ CAM 206-207 B 5
Meigs ○ USA (GA) 284-285 F 5
Meigu ○ VRC 156-157 C 2
Meihekou ○ VRC 150-151 E 6
Meiktila ○ MYA 142-143 J 5
Meili Xue Shan ▲ VRC 144-145 M 6
Meilleur River ~ CDN 30-31 G 5
Meimand ○ IR 134-135 D 3
Meime ○ IR 134-135 D 2
Meiningen ○• D 92-93 L 3
Meinmagwe ○ MYA 142-143 H 6
Meio, Ilhéu do ⌒ GNB 202-203 C 4
Meio, Rio da ~ BR 72-73 H 2
Meio, Rio do ~ BR 68-69 K 5
Meio, Rio do ~ BR 68-69 C 4
Meishan ○ VRC 154-155 C 6
Meißen ○•• D 92-93 M 3
Meister River ~ CDN 20-21 Z 6
Meitan ○ VRC 156-157 E 3
Mei Xian ○ VRC 154-155 E 4
Meizhou ○ VRC 156-157 K 4
Meizhou Dao ⌒ VRC 156-157 L 4
Mejerda, Oued ~ TN 190-191 G 2
Mejez el Bab ○ TN 190-191 G 2
Mejia ○ PE 70-71 B 5
Mejicana, La ○ RA 76-77 D 5
Mejillones ○ RCH 76-77 B 2
Mejillones, Quebrada de ~ RCH 76-77 B 2
Mejillones del Sur, Bahía de ≈ 76-77 B 2
Mejnypil'gyno ○ RUS 112-113 T 5
Mejnypil'gynskij hrebet ⛰ RUS 112-113 S 5
Mejo, El ○ YV 60-61 H 3
Meka ○ AUS 176-177 D 3
Mékambo ○ G 210-211 D 3
Mekane Selam ○ ETH 208-209 D 3
Mékel ○ CAM 210-211 E 2
Mek'elē ✫ • ETH 200-201 J 6
Mekerrhane, Sebkha ⊖ DZ 190-191 C 7
Mékhé ○ SN 202-203 B 2
Mekhtar ○ PK 138-139 B 4
Meki ○ ETH 208-209 D 4
Mékié ~ CAM 204-205 K 6
Me-kin ○ MYA 142-143 L 5
Mekinac, Lac ⊖ CDN (QUE) 240-241 C 3
Mekka = Makka ✫•• KSA 132-133 A 3
Mekmene Ben Amar ○ DZ 188-189 L 4
Meknassy ○ TN 190-191 G 3
Meknès = Miknās ✫ MA 188-189 J 4
Meknès = Miknās ✫ MA 188-189 J 4
Meko ○ WAN 204-205 E 5
Mekomo ○ CAM 210-211 C 2
Mekong ~ K 158-159 H 4
Mekongga, Pegunungan ⛰ RI 164-165 G 5
Mekoryuk ○ USA 20-21 G 6
Mékrou ~ DY 204-205 E 3
Mel, Ilha do ⌒ BR 74-75 F 5
Melá, Mont ▲ RCA 206-207 F 4
Melado, Río ~ RCH 78-79 D 4
Melak ○ RI 164-165 D 4
Melaka ◘ MAL 162-163 E 3
Melaka ✫ • MAL 162-163 E 3
Melaka, Selat ≈ 162-163 D 3
Melalih ○ RI 166-167 F 2
Melanesia ⌒ 13 E 2
Melanesian Basin ≃ 13 G 2
Melanguane ○ RI 164-165 K 1
Melanieskop ▲ ZA 220-221 J 4
Melati ○ RI 168 D 3
Melawi ~ RI 162-163 J 4
Melbourne ✫•• AUS 180-181 H 4
Melbourne ○ USA (AR) 276-277 D 4
Melbourne ○ USA (FL) 286-287 J 3
Melbourne ○ USA (IA) 274-275 E 3
Melbourne ○ USA (WA) 244-245 B 4
Melbourne Island ⌒ CDN 24-25 T 6
Melchett Lake ⊖ CDN (ONT) 234-235 Q 4
Melchor, Isla ⌒ RCH 80 C 2
Melchor Múzquiz ○ MEX 50-51 J 4
Meldal ✫ N 86-87 D 5
Meldrum Bay ○ CDN (ONT) 238-239 B 3
Meldrum Creek ○ CDN (BC) 228-229 N 4
Meldrum Creek ~ CDN (BC) 228-229 M 4
Mélé ○ RCA 206-207 E 4
Meleb ○ CDN (MAN) 234-235 F 4
Mele Bay ≈ 184 II b 3
Meleck ○ RUS 116-117 E 7
Melehova, proliv ≈ 112-113 L 1
Meleiro ○ BR 74-75 F 7
Melela ~ MOC 218-219 J 3
Melela, Rio ~ MOC 218-219 J 3
Melenki ○ RUS 94-95 R 4
Melet Irmağı ~ TR 128-129 G 2
Meleuz ✫ RUS 96-97 J 7
Mélèzes, Rivière aux ~ CDN 36-37 N 6
Melfi ○ • I 100-101 E 4
Melfi ○ TCH 206-207 C 3
Melford ○ CDN (NS) 240-241 O 5
Melfort ○ CDN (SAS) 232-233 O 3
Melgaço ○ BR 62-63 J 6
Melhus ✫ N 86-87 E 5
Meliandine Lake ⊖ CDN 30-31 X 4
Meliane, Oued ~ TN 190-191 G 2
Melide ○ E 98-99 C 3
Melides ○ P 98-99 C 5
Melilla = Melilla ○ E 98-99 F 7
Melilis, Pulau ⌒ RI 164-165 H 4
Melilla ○ E 98-99 F 7
Melimoyu, Monte ▲ RCH 78-79 C 7
Melincué ○ RA 78-79 J 2
Melincué, Laguna ⊖ RA 78-79 J 2
Melinka ○ RCH 78-79 C 7
Melintang, Danau ⊖ RI 164-165 E 4
Melipeuco ○ RCH 78-79 D 5
Melipilla ○ RCH 78-79 D 2
Melita ○ CDN (MAN) 234-235 C 5
Mélito di Porto Salvo ○ I 100-101 E 6
Melitopol' ○ UA 102-103 J 4
Melivia ○ GR 100-101 J 5
Melk ○ A 92-93 N 4
Melka Deka ○ ETH 208-209 F 5
Melka Guba ○ ETH 208-209 D 6
Melka Kunture • ETH 208-209 D 4
Melka Meri ○ ETH 208-209 E 6
Melkasa ○ ETH 208-209 D 4
Melkbosstrand ○ ZA 220-221 D 6
Melkoe, ozero ⊖ RUS 108-109 X 7
Melkovodnyj, zaliv ⊖ RUS 120-121 U 3
Melkrivier ○ ZA 220-221 J 2
Mella ○ C 54-55 H 4
Mellal, Oued ~ MA 188-189 H 4
Mellam ○ SUD 200-201 B 6
Mellegue, Oued ~ TN 190-191 F 2
Mellemfjord ≈ 28-29 N 2
Mellen ○ USA (WI) 270-271 H 4
Mellene, Anou < RMM 198-199 B 3
Mellene, Assouf ~ DZ 190-191 C 8
Mellerud ✫ S 86-87 F 7
Mellette ○ USA (SD) 260-261 H 1
Mellit ○ SUD 200-201 B 5
Mellizos ○ RCH 76-77 C 2
Mellizo Sur, Cerro ▲ RCH 80 D 4
Mellon ○ CDN (BC) 230-231 F 4
Mellouiou, Oued ~ MA 188-189 K 4
Mellwood ○ USA (AR) 276-277 E 6
Melmoth ○ ZA 220-221 K 4
Mel'ničnoe ○ RUS 122-123 F 6
Mel'ničnye, porogi ~ RUS 88-89 O 5
Mělník ○ CZ 92-93 N 3
Melo ○ G 210-211 C 2
Melo ✫ ROU 78-79 M 2
Melo, Río ~ PY 76-77 H 1
Meloco ○ MOC 218-219 K 1
Melolo ○ RI 168 E 7
Mélong ○ CAM 204-205 H 6
Melovoj, mys ▲ KA 126-127 J 6
Melovoj mujisi ▲ KA 126-127 J 6
Melozitna River ~ USA 20-21 N 4
Melrhir, Chott ⊖ DZ 190-191 F 3
Melrose ○ AUS (WA) 176-177 F 3
Melrose ○• AUS (SA) 180-181 E 2
Melrose ○ CDN (NS) 240-241 N 5
Melrose ○ USA (MN) 270-271 D 5
Melrose ○ USA (MT) 250-251 G 6
Melrose ○ USA (NM) 256-257 M 4
Melrose ○ USA (OR) 244-245 B 7
Melrose ○ USA (WI) 270-271 H 6
Melstone ○ USA (MT) 250-251 M 5
Melstrand ○ USA (MI) 270-271 M 4
Meltaus ○ FIN 88-89 H 3
Melton ○ AUS 180-181 H 4
Meluco ○ MOC 214-215 K 7
Melukua ○ RI 166-167 E 5
Melume ○ ZRE 210-211 K 2
Melun ✫ F 90-91 J 7
Melun ○ MYA 142-143 H 5
Melung Tse Jobo Garu ▲ NEP 144-145 F 6
Melur ○ IND 140-141 H 5
Melvern Lake ⊖ USA (KS) 262-263 L 6
Melville ○ CDN (SAS) 232-233 Q 5
Melville ○ USA (LA) 268-269 J 6
Melville ○ USA (MT) 250-251 K 5
Melville, Cape ▲ AUS 174-175 H 4
Melville, Cape ▲ RP 160-161 B 9
Melville, Kap ▲ GRØ 26-27 T 5
Melville, Lake ⊖ CDN 38-39 P 2
Melville Bay ≈ 174-175 D 3
Melville Bugt ≈ 26-27 S 6
Melville Hills ⛰ CDN 24-25 J 6
Melville Island ⌒ AUS 172-173 K 1
Melville Island ⌒ CDN 24-25 P 3
Melville Land ∸ GRØ 26-27 k 2
Melville Peninsula ⌣ CDN 24-25 d 6
Melville Sound ≈ 24-25 S 6
Melville Trough ≃ 24-25 Q 3
Melvin River ~ CDN 30-31 L 6
Melvis, La ○ C 54-55 D 4
Memala ○ RI 162-163 K 5
Memári ○ IND 142-143 F 4
Memba ○ CO 60-61 C 5
Memba ○ MOC 218-219 L 2
Membalong ○ RI 162-163 G 6
Membeca, Rio ~ BR 70-71 J 3
Memboro ○ RI 168 D 7
Membrillo, El ○ RCH 78-79 D 2
Memel ○ ZA 220-221 J 3
Memel = Klaipėda ✫•• LT 94-95 G 4
Memmingen ○• D 92-93 L 5
Memo ○ YV 60-61 H 3
Memori, Tanjung ▲ RI 166-167 H 2
Mempawah ○ RI 162-163 H 4
Memphis ∴••• ET 194-195 E 3
Memphis ○ USA (MO) 274-275 F 4
Memphis ○ USA (TX) 264-265 D 4
Memphis ○• USA (TN) 276-277 E 5
Memphremagog, Lac ⊖ CDN (QUE) 238-239 N 3
Memramcook ○ CDN (NB) 240-241 L 4
Ména ○ RMM 202-203 G 3
Mena ○ UA 102-103 H 2
Mena ○ USA (AR) 276-277 A 6
Mena, Wabē ~ ETH 208-209 E 6
Menaa ○ DZ 190-191 F 3
Menabe ∸ RM 222-223 D 8
Menahga ○ USA (MN) 270-271 C 4
Menai ⌒ SY 222-223 E 2
Ménaka ○ RMM 196-197 M 7
Mènam Khong (Mekong) ~ LAO 156-157 B 7
Menan ○ USA (ID) 252-253 G 3
Menanga ○ RI 164-165 J 4
Menangina ○ AUS 176-177 F 4
Menarandra ~ RM 222-223 D 10
Menarbu ○ RI 166-167 H 3
Menard ○ USA (TX) 266-267 H 3
Menard Fracture Zone ≃ 14-15 R 12
Menaskwagama, Lac ⊖ CDN 38-39 N 3
Menawashei ○ SUD 200-201 B 6
Menchia ○ TN 190-191 H 4
Menda ~ RUS 118-119 O 5
Mendale ○ USA (OH) 280-281 B 2
Mendaña Fracture Zone = Mendana Fracture Zone ≃ 5 B 6
Mendanau, Pulau ⌒ RI 162-163 G 6
Mendawai ~ RI 162-163 K 5
Mendaya ○ RI 168 B 7
Mende ○• F 90-91 J 9
Mendebo ⛰ ETH 208-209 D 5
Mendel' ~ RUS 116-117 E 7
Mendeleeva, gory ⛰ RUS 108-109 J 3
Mendeleevsk ✫ RUS 96-97 H 6
Mendenhall ○ USA (MS) 268-269 L 5
Mendenhall, Cape ▲ USA 22-23 N 3
Mendenhall Glacier ⊂ USA 32-33 C 2
Mendes ○ DZ 190-191 C 3
Méndez ○ EC 64-65 C 3
Méndez ○ MEX 50-51 K 5
Mendham ○ CDN (SAS) 232-233 J 5
Mendi ○ ETH 208-209 B 4
Mendi ✫ PNG 183 B 4
Mendiköl ○ KA 126-127 O 3
Mendiya-Plage ○ MA 188-189 H 3
Mendocino ○ USA (CA) 246-247 B 4
Mendocino, Cape ▲ USA (CA) 246-247 A 3
Mendocino Fracture Zone ≃ 14-15 M 4
Mendocino Pass ▲ USA (CA) 246-247 C 4
Mendol, Pulau ⌒ RI 162-163 E 4
Mendon ○ USA (IL) 274-275 G 4
Mendon ○ USA (MO) 274-275 E 5
Mendooran ○ AUS 178-179 K 6
Mendopolo ○ SUD 206-207 K 6
Mendota ○ USA (CA) 248-249 D 3
Mendota ○ USA (IL) 274-275 J 3
Mendoza ○ PE 64-65 D 5
Mendoza ◘ RA 78-79 E 3
Mendoza ✫ • RA 78-79 E 2
Mene de Mauroa ○ YV 60-61 F 2
Menegers Dam ○ USA (AZ) 256-257 C 7
Mene Grande ○ YV 60-61 F 3
Menemen ✫ TR 128-129 B 3
Menen ○ B 92-93 G 3
Menéndez, Lago ⊖ RA 78-79 D 7
Menéndez, Paso de ▲ RCH 78-79 C 7
Menengai Crater • EAK 212-213 F 4
Menesjärvi ○ FIN 88-89 J 2
Meng ~ CAM 204-205 K 5
Menga ○ ANG 216-217 C 5
Menga, Puerto de ▲ E 98-99 E 4
Mengam, Mount ▲ PNG 183 C 3
Mengcheng ○ VRC 154-155 K 5
Menggala ○ RI 162-163 F 7
Menggari ○ RI 166-167 H 2
Menghai ○ VRC 142-143 M 5
Mengkatip ○ RI 164-165 D 5
Mengkoka, Gunung ▲ RI 164-165 G 5
Mengla ○ VRC 156-157 B 6
Menglian ○ VRC 142-143 L 4
Mengong ○ CAM 210-211 C 2
Mengshan ○ VRC 156-157 G 4
Ménguémé ○ CAM 210-211 C 2
Meng Xian ○ VRC 154-155 H 4
Mengxing ○ VRC 156-157 B 6
Mengyan ○ VRC 156-157 F 3
Mengyin ○ VRC 154-155 K 4
Mengzi ○ VRC 156-157 C 5
Menidi ○ GR 100-101 H 5
Menier, Port ○ CDN (QUE) 242-243 D 3
Menihek Lakes ⊖ CDN 36-37 Q 7
Menindee ○ AUS 180-181 G 2
Menindee Lake ⊖ AUS 180-181 G 2
Meningie ○ AUS 180-181 E 3
Mènkèrè ~ RUS 110-111 O 6
Menkerja ~ RUS 110-111 O 6
Menkjule ~ RUS 120-121 G 2
Menneval ○ CDN (QUE) 240-241 H 3
Menno ○ USA (SD) 260-261 J 3
Menoken ○ USA (ND) 258-259 G 5
Menominee ○ USA (MI) 270-271 L 5
Menominee Indian Reservation X USA (WI) 270-271 K 5
Menominee River ~ USA (WI) 270-271 L 5
Menomonee Falls ○ USA (WI) 274-275 K 1
Menomonie ○ USA (WI) 270-271 G 6
Menongue ✫ ANG 216-217 D 7
Menorca ⌒ E 98-99 J 4
Men'šikova, mys ▲ RUS 108-109 G 6
Men'šikova, ostrov ⌒ RUS 120-121 H 6
Mentasta Pass ▲ USA 20-21 T 5
Mentawai, Kepulauan ⌒ RI 162-163 C 5
Mentawai Strait = Mentawai, Selat ≈ RI 162-163 C 5
Menteke, kum ∸ KA 96-97 F 10
Mentmore ○ USA (NM) 256-257 G 3
Menton ○ F 90-91 L 10
Mentone ○ USA (TX) 266-267 D 2
Mentor ○ USA (OH) 280-281 E 2
Menucos, Bajo de los ∸ RA 78-79 F 5
Menucos, Los ○ RA 78-79 E 6
Menukung ○ RI 162-163 K 5
Menyamya ○ PNG 183 D 4
Menyapa, Gunung ▲ RI 164-165 E 3
Menyuan ○ VRC 154-155 B 3
Menza ○ RUS (CTN) 116-117 O 11
Menza ~ RUS 116-117 O 10
Menza ~ RUS 116-117 O 11
Menzel Bourguiba ○ TN 190-191 G 2
Menzel Chaker ○ TN 190-191 H 3
Menzelinsk ✫ RUS 96-97 H 6
Menzel Temime ○ TN 190-191 H 2
Menzie ○ CDN (MAN) 234-235 C 4
Menzies ○ AUS 176-177 F 4
Menzies, Mount ▲ ARK 16 F 7
Meoqui ○ MEX 50-51 G 3
Meota ○ CDN (SAS) 232-233 K 2
Mepala ○ ANG 216-217 B 3
Mepica ○ MOC 218-219 J 2
Mepiskaro, gora ▲ GE 126-127 E 7
Meponda ○ MOC 218-219 H 1
Mepozo ~ ANG 216-217 B 3
Meppadi ○ IND 140-141 G 5
Meppel ○ NL 92-93 J 2
Meppen ○ D 92-93 J 2
Mepuse, Rio ~ MOC 218-219 H 3
Mequens, Rio ~ BR 70-71 F 3
Mequinenza, Embalse de < E 98-99 H 4
Mequon ○ USA (WI) 274-275 L 1
Mera ○ EC 64-65 C 2
Merai ○ PNG 183 G 3
Merak ○ RI 168 B 2
Meråker ○ N 86-87 E 5
Meralaba, Île = Mere Lava ⌒ VAN 184 II b 2
Merama Hill ○ EAU 212-213 C 4
Meramangye, Lake ⊖ AUS 176-177 M 4
Meramec River ~ USA (MO) 274-275 G 6
Meramec State Park ⊥ USA (MO) 274-275 G 6
Merampi, Pulau ⌒ RI 164-165 K 1
Meran = Merano ○ I 100-101 C 1
Merangin ~ RI 162-163 D 6
Merano = Meran ○ I 100-101 C 1
Merapah ○ AUS 174-175 G 3
Merapi, Gunung ▲ RI 168 D 3
Merasheen Island ⌒ CDN (NFL) 242-243 O 5
Meratswe ~ RB 218-219 C 6
Merauke ○ RI 166-167 L 6
Merauke ~ RI 166-167 L 6
Mercaderes ○ CO 60-61 C 7
Mercan Dağları ⛰ TR 128-129 H 3
Mercantour, Parc National du ⊥ • F 90-91 L 9
Merced ○ USA (CA) 248-249 D 2
Mercedario, Cerro ▲ RA 78-79 D 2
Mercedes ○ RA (BUA) 78-79 K 3
Mercedes ○ RA (CO) 76-77 H 5
Mercedes ○ RA (SLU) 78-79 G 2
Mercedes ✫ ROU 78-79 K 2
Mercedes ○ USA (TX) 266-267 K 7
Mercedes, Ilha das ⌒ BR 70-71 E 2
Mercedes, Las ○ YV (AMA) 60-61 H 5
Mercedes, Las ○ YV (GUA) 60-61 H 3
Mercedes, Las ○ YV (PSA) 60-61 G 3
Merced River ~ USA (CA) 248-249 D 2
Mercer ○ USA (ND) 258-259 G 4
Mercer ○ USA (PA) 280-281 F 2
Mercer ○ USA (TN) 276-277 F 5
Mercer ○ USA (WI) 270-271 H 4
Mercers Bottom ○ USA (WV) 280-281 D 5
Merchants Bay ≈ 28-29 J 3
Merčimden ~ RUS 110-111 M 5
Mercoal ○ CDN (ALB) 228-229 R 3
Mercoya ○ RMM 202-203 E 3
Mercury ○ USA (NV) 248-249 J 3
Mercy, Cape ▲ CDN 36-37 S 2
Mercy Bay ≈ 24-25 N 3
Merdani, Hassi < MA 188-189 K 5
Mereb Wenz ~ ETH 200-201 J 5
Merecure ○ YV 60-61 G 4
Meredith ○ AUS 180-181 H 4
Meredith ○ USA (CO) 254-255 J 4
Meredith ○ USA (NH) 278-279 K 5
Meredith, Cape ▲ GB 78-79 K 7
Meredosia ○ USA (IL) 274-275 H 5
Meredosia Lake ⊖ USA (IL) 274-275 H 5
Meredoua ○ DZ 190-191 C 8
Merefa ○ UA 102-103 K 3
Mereksen ○ DZ 190-191 G 6
Mere Lava = Île Meralaba ⌒ VAN 184 II b 2
Merenga ○ RUS 120-121 R 3
Meresichic ○ MEX 50-51 D 2
Merewa ○ ETH 208-209 C 5
Merga = Nukhaylah < SUD 200-201 C 3
Mergui ○ MYA 158-159 E 4
Mergui Archipelago = Myeik Kyûnzu ⌒ MYA 158-159 D 4
Mergui Archipelago = Myeik Kyûnzu ⌒ MYA 158-159 E 4
Merhder Lefâa < MA 188-189 K 4
Méri ○ CAM 206-207 B 3
Méri ○ SN 196-197 C 6
Meriç Nehri ~ TR 128-129 B 2
Mérida ○•• E 98-99 D 5
Mérida ✫•• MEX 52-53 K 1
Mérida ✫ • YV 60-61 F 3
Mérida, Cordillera de ⛰ YV 60-61 F 3
Meriden ○ USA (CT) 280-281 O 2
Meriden ○ USA (WY) 252-253 O 5
Meridian ○ USA (ID) 252-253 B 3
Meridian ○ USA (MS) 268-269 M 4
Meridian ○ USA (TX) 266-267 K 2
Meridian Island ⌒ CDN 30-31 K 5
Meridianville ○ USA (AL) 284-285 D 2
Meridith, Lake ⊖ USA (TX) 264-265 C 3
Meridja ○ DZ 188-189 K 5
Merig = Île Merigi ⌒ VAN 184 II a 2
Merigi, Île = Merig ⌒ VAN 184 II a 2
Merigur ○ AUS 180-181 F 3
Méri Harmsourt, mys ▲ RUS 84-85 Y 2
Merikarvia ○ FIN 88-89 F 6
Merimbula ○ AUS 180-181 K 4
Merin, Laguna ⊖ ROU 74-75 D 9
Meringa ○ WAN 204-205 K 3
Merino Downs ○ AUS 178-179 H 2
Merino Jarpa, Isla ⌒ RCH 80 C 3
Merit ○ MAL 162-163 K 3
Merite Stigbøjlen, Kap ▲ GRØ 26-27 q 4
Merivale ○ AUS 178-179 K 3
Merkánam ○ IND 140-141 H 4
Merkel ○ USA (TX) 264-265 D 6
Merkušina Strelka, poluostrov ⌣ RUS 110-111 Z 3
Merlin ○ USA (OR) 244-245 B 8
Merluna ○ AUS 174-175 G 3
Mermaid Reef ⌒ AUS 172-173 D 4
Merna ○ USA (NE) 262-263 G 3
Merna ○ USA (WY) 252-253 H 4
Mernoo Bank ≃ 182 E 5
Meroe •• SUD 200-201 F 4
Merolia ○ AUS 176-177 G 4
Meropoh ○ MAL 162-163 D 2
Meros, Ponta dos ▲ BR 72-73 H 7
Merouana ○ DZ 190-191 E 3
Merouane, Chott ⊖ DZ 190-191 F 3
Merowe = Marawi ○ SUD 200-201 E 3
Merredin ○ AUS 176-177 E 5
Merrick ▲ GB 90-91 E 4
Merrickville ○ CDN (ONT) 238-239 K 4
Merridale ○ CDN (MAN) 234-235 B 3
Merrie Range ⛰ AUS 176-177 F 2
Merrifield Bay ≈ 36-37 T 7
Merrill ○ USA (MI) 272-273 E 4
Merrill ○ USA (MS) 268-269 M 6
Merrill ○ USA (OR) 244-245 D 8
Merrill ○ USA (WI) 270-271 J 5
Merrillan ○ USA (WI) 270-271 H 6
Merrillville ○ USA (CA) 246-247 E 3
Merrillville ○ USA (NY) 278-279 H 4
Merrimack River ~ USA (NH) 278-279 K 5
Merriman ○ USA (NE) 262-263 E 2
Merriman ○ ZA 220-221 F 5
Merrimerriwa, Mount ▲ AUS 180-181 H 2
Merritt Island ⌒ USA (FL) 286-287 J 3
Merritt ○ CDN (BC) 230-231 J 3
Merritt Island ○ USA (FL) 286-287 J 3
Merritt Reservoire ⊖ USA (NE) 262-263 F 2
Merriwa ○ AUS 180-181 L 2
Mer Rouge ○ USA (LA) 268-269 J 4
Merry Island ⌒ CDN 36-37 L 7
Merryville ○ USA (LA) 268-269 G 6
Mersa Fatma ○ ER 200-201 K 5
Mersa Gulbub ○ ER 200-201 J 4
Merseburg ○• D 92-93 L 3
Mersey ~ GB 90-91 F 5
Mersey River ~ AUS 180-181 J 6
Mersin = İçel ○ TR 128-129 F 4
Mersing ○• MAL 162-163 E 3
Mērsrags ○ LV 94-95 H 3
Merta ○ IND 138-139 E 6
Merthyr Tydfil ○ GB 90-91 F 6
Merti ○ EAK 212-213 G 3
Merting, Kampung ○ MAL 162-163 E 2
Merti Plateau ⛰ EAK 212-213 G 3
Mértola ○• P 98-99 D 6
Merton ○ AUS 180-181 H 4
Mertoutek ○ DZ 190-191 E 8
Mertule Maryam ○ ETH 208-209 D 3
Merty Merty ○ AUS 178-179 F 5
Mertz Glacier ⊂ ARK 16 G 15
Mertzon ○ USA (TX) 266-267 G 2
Meru ○ EAK 212-213 F 3
Meru ▲•• EAT 212-213 F 5
Merume Mountains ⛰ GUY 62-63 D 3
Meru Mulika Lodge ○ EAK 212-213 G 3
Meru National Park ⊥ EAK 212-213 G 3
Meruóco ○ BR 68-69 H 3
Merure, Área Indígena X BR 72-73 D 3
Merville ○ CDN (BC) 230-231 D 4
Mervin ○ CDN (SAS) 232-233 K 2
Merweville ○ ZA 220-221 E 6
Měry ✫ BY 94-95 K 4
Meryemana ∴•• TR 128-129 B 4
Merzifon ✫ TR 128-129 F 2
Mesa ○ MOC 218-219 K 1
Mesa ○ RI 164-165 L 3
Mesa ○ USA (AZ) 256-257 D 5
Mesa ○ USA (CO) 254-255 G 4
Mesa ○ USA (ID) 252-253 B 2
Mesa ○ USA (NM) 256-257 L 5
Mesa ○ USA (WA) 244-245 G 4
Mesa, Cerro ▲ RA 78-79 E 5
Mesa, La ○ CO 60-61 D 5
Mesa, La ○ USA (CA) 248-249 G 7
Mesa, La ○ USA (NM) 256-257 J 6
Mesa, La ○ YV 60-61 F 2
Mesabi Range ▲ USA (MN) 270-271 F 3
Mesa de las Tablas ○ MEX 50-51 J 5
Mesagrós ○ GR 100-101 J 6
Mesai, Rio ~ CO 64-65 F 1
Mešakli ○ US 136-137 G 4
Mesanak, Pulau ⌒ RI 162-163 F 4
Mesaraba ○ ZRE 210-211 L 5
Mesa Verde National Park ⊥••• USA (CO) 254-255 G 6
Mescalero ○ USA (NM) 256-257 K 5
Mescalero Apache Indian Reservation X USA (NM) 256-257 K 5
Meščerskaja nizmenost' ⛰ RUS 94-95 Q 4
Meschetti ○ SP 212-213 H 3
Meschkakur ▲ MA 188-189 K 4
Mescit Dağları ⛰ TR 128-129 J 2
Meseta Baya ▲ RA 78-79 E 5
Meseta de Jaua ⛰ YV 60-61 J 5
Meseta de Somuncurá ∸ RA 78-79 F 6
Meseta el Pedrero ∸ RA 80 F 3
Mesfinto ○ ETH 200-201 H 6
Meşginšahr ○ IR 128-129 M 3
Mesgouez, Lac ⊖ CDN 38-39 G 3
Meshik River ~ USA 22-23 R 4
Mesick ○ USA (MI) 272-273 D 3
Mesilinka River ~ CDN 32-33 H 3
Mesilla ○ USA (NM) 256-257 J 6
Mesilla, La ○ GCA 52-53 J 4
Mésima ~ I 100-101 F 5
Mesjagutovo ✫ RUS 96-97 L 6
Mesjid Raya • RI 162-163 C 3
Meškān ○ IR 136-137 F 6
Meskanaw ○ CDN (SAS) 232-233 N 3
Meski, Source bleue de • MA 188-189 J 5
Meskiana, Oued ~ DZ 190-191 F 3
Mesklip ○ ZA 220-221 C 4
Meslo ○ ETH 208-209 D 5
Mesna ~ RUS 88-89 S 2
Mesudiye ○ TR 128-129 G 2
Mesogi ○ CY 128-129 E 5
Mesopotamia ∸ IRQ 128-129 J 5
Mesopotamia ∸ RA 76-77 H 6
Mesquaie Indian Settlement X USA (IA) 274-275 F 3
Mesquita ○ BR 72-73 J 5
Mesquite ○ USA (NV) 248-249 K 3
Mesquite ○ USA (TX) 264-265 H 6
Messaad ○ DZ 190-191 D 3
Messalo ~ MOC 214-215 K 7
Messaména ○ CAM 210-211 D 2
Messaoud, Oued ~ DZ 188-189 L 6
Mess Creek ~ CDN 32-33 E 3
Messeied ○ MA 188-189 F 6
Messejana ○ BR 68-69 J 3
Messelesek ○ RI 164-165 H 4
Messent Conservation Park ⊥ AUS 180-181 E 4
Messier, Canal ≈ 80 C 3
Messina ○ I 100-101 E 5
Messina ○ ZA 218-219 F 6
Messina, Stretto di ≈ 100-101 E 5
Messinge, Rio ~ MOC 214-215 H 7
Messiniakos Kólpos ≈ 100-101 J 6
Messojaha ~ RUS 108-109 T 7
Messolóngi ○ GR 100-101 H 5
Messondo ○ CAM 210-211 C 2
Messum Crater • NAM 216-217 C 10
Mesters Vig ○ GRØ 26-27 n 7
Mestia ○ GE 126-127 E 6
mesto padenija Tungusskogo meteorita • RUS 116-117 L 5
Mesuji ~ RI 162-163 F 7
Mesurado, Cape ▲ LB 202-203 E 6
Meta, Rio ~ CO 60-61 E 5
Métabetchouan ○ CDN (QUE) 240-241 D 2
Metaca ○ MOC 214-215 J 7
Metagama ○ CDN (ONT) 236-237 G 5
Meta Incognita Peninsula ⌣ CDN 36-37 O 3
Metairie ○ USA (LA) 268-269 K 7
Métal, Mont du ▲ DZ 198-199 D 2
Meta Lake ⊖ CDN (ONT) 234-235 Q 4
Metaliferi, Munții ⛰ RO 102-103 C 4
Metaline Falls ○ USA (WA) 244-245 H 2
Metán ○ RA 76-77 E 3
Metangobalame ○ MOC 218-219 H 2
Metangula ○ MOC 214-215 H 7
Metapán ○ ES 52-53 K 4
Metaponto ○• I 100-101 F 4
Metarica ○ MOC 218-219 J 2
Metchosin ○ CDN (BC) 230-231 F 5
Metchum ~ CAM 204-205 H 5
Metea ○ USA (IN) 274-275 M 4
Meteghan ○ CDN (NS) 240-241 J 6
Metema ○ ETH 200-201 H 6
Meteóra ••• GR 100-101 H 5
Meteor Crater • USA (AZ) 256-257 D 3
Meteor Creek ~ AUS 178-179 K 3
Meteorit Ø ⌒ GRØ 26-27 S 5
Meteorologist Peninsula ⌣ CDN 24-25 V 1
Metepec ○ MEX (HGO) 52-53 E 1
Metepec ○ MEX (PUE) 52-53 E 2
Meteran ○ PNG 183 F 2
Métet ○ CAM 210-211 C 2
Meteti ○ PA 52-53 F 7
Methy River ~ CDN 32-33 Q 3
Metil ○ MOC 218-219 K 3
Metionga Lake ⊖ CDN (ONT) 234-235 N 5
Metiskow ○ CDN (ALB) 232-233 H 3
Metković ○ HR 100-101 F 3

Metlakatla ○ CDN (BC) 228-229 D 2
Metlakatla ○ USA 32-33 E 4
Metlaoui ○ TN 190-191 G 3
Metlili, Oued ~ DZ 190-191 D 4
Metlili Chaamba ○ DZ 190-191 D 4
Meto, Bayou ~ USA (AR) 276-277 D 6
Metohija ∸ YU 100-101 H 3
Metro ○ RI 162-163 F 7
Metoro ○ MOC 218-219 K 1
Metropolis ○ USA (IL) 276-277 G 3
Metsera ○ ZRE 210-211 L 5
Métsovo • GR 100-101 H 5
Mettenpherg Creek ~ USA 20-21 O 3
Metter ○ USA (GA) 284-285 H 4
Mettuppālaiyam ○ IND 140-141 G 5
Mettur ○ IND 140-141 G 5
Metu ☆ ETH 208-209 B 4
Metuge ○ MOC 214-215 L 7
Metz ☆• F 90-91 L 7
Metztitlán ○ MEX 52-53 E 1
Meulaboh ○ RI 162-163 B 2
Meureudu ○ RI 162-163 B 2
Meuse ~ B 92-93 H 3
Meuse ~ F 90-91 K 7
Meuse, Côtes de ∸ F 90-91 K 7
Mēwār ∸ IND 138-139 D 7
Mexcaltitán ○ MEX 50-51 G 7
Mexia ○ USA (TX) 266-267 L 2
Mexia, Lake < USA (TX) 266-267 L 2
Mexiana, Ilha ⌒ BR 62-63 K 6
Mexicali ☆ MEX 50-51 B 1
Mexican Hat ○ USA (UT) 254-255 F 6
Mexicanos, Laguna Los ⊝ MEX 50-51 F 3
Mexican Plateau = Altiplanicie Mexicana ▲ MEX 50-51 G 4
Mexican Water ○ USA (AZ) 256-257 F 2
México ◘ MEX 52-53 D 2
Mexico ○ USA (ME) 278-279 L 4
Mexico ○ USA (MO) 274-275 G 5
México, Ciudad de = México ★··· MEX 52-53 E 2
México, Golfo de = Gulf of Mexico ≈ 4 E 6
Mexico, Gulf of = México, Golfo de ≈ 4 E 6
Mexico = México ■ MEX 52-53 C 1
Mexico Bay ≈ USA 278-279 E 5
Mexico Beach ○ USA (FL) 286-287 D 2
Mexico City = México, Ciudad de ★··· MEX 52-53 E 2
Mexiko ○ USA (NY) 278-279 E 5
Meyāmei ○ IR 136-137 D 6
Meyanodas ○ RI 166-167 F 5
Meydancık ○ TR 128-129 K 2
Meyers Canyon ~ USA (TX) 266-267 E 3
Meyersdale ○ USA (PA) 280-281 G 4
Méyo Centre ○ CAM 210-211 C 2
Mezada ∴• IL 130-131 D 2
Mezaligon ○ MYA 158-159 C 2
Mezcalapa, Río ~ MEX 52-53 H 3
Mezdra ○ BG 102-103 C 6
Meždurečensk ○ RUS 124-125 Q 2
Meždurečenskij ○ RUS 114-115 H 5
Meždušarskij, ostrov ⌒ RUS 108-109 F 6
Mezen' ○ RUS 88-89 S 4
Mezen' ~ RUS 88-89 T 4
Mézenc, Mont ▲• F 90-91 K 9
Mezenskaja guba ≈ 88-89 R 3
Mezens'kaja Pižma ~ RUS 88-89 U 4
Mézessé ○ CAM 210-211 D 2
Mézessé, Rocher du = Mézessé Rock • CAM 210-211 D 2
Mézessé Rock = Rocher du Mézessé • CAM 210-211 D 2
Mežgornoe, ozero ⊝ RUS 112-113 W 4
Mézier, Charleville ☆ F 90-91 K 7
Mezón ○ BOL 76-77 E 2
Mežozernyj ○ RUS 96-97 L 6
Mezquita Catedral •• E 98-99 E 6
Mezquital ○ MEX (DGO) 50-51 G 6
Mezquital ○ MEX (TAM) 50-51 L 5
Mezquital, Río ~ MEX 50-51 G 6
Mfou ○ CAM 210-211 C 2
Mfouati ○ RCB 210-211 D 6
Mfum ○ WAN 204-205 H 6
Mgači ○ RUS 122-123 K 3
Mgangerabeli Plains ∸ EAK 212-213 H 4
Mgbidi ○ WAN 204-205 G 6
Mgende ○ EAT 212-213 C 6
Mgeta ~ EAT 214-215 K 4
Mg.Mu'o'n ○ VN 156-157 C 6
Mgneta, Hassi < MA 188-189 K 4
Mgunga ○ EAT 214-215 J 4
Mhamid ○ MA 188-189 J 6
Mhangura ○ ZW 218-219 F 3
Mhasvād ○ IND 140-141 F 2
Mhlatuze ~ ZA 220-221 K 4
Mi, Enneri ~ TCH 198-199 G 2
Miagao ○ RP 160-161 E 7
Miahuatlán ○ MEX 52-53 F 3
Miahuatlán, Sierra de ▲ MEX 52-53 F 3
Miajadas ○ E 98-99 E 5
Miājlār ○ IND 138-139 C 6
Mial, Oued ~ DZ 190-191 D 6
Miamére ○ RCA 206-207 D 4
Miami ○ USA (AZ) 256-257 E 5
Miami ○ USA (OK) 264-265 K 2
Miami ○ USA (TX) 264-265 D 3
Miami ○• USA (FL) 286-287 J 6
Miami, North ○ USA (FL) 286-287 J 6
Miami Beach ○• USA (FL) 286-287 J 6
Miami Canal < USA (FL) 286-287 J 5
Miami River ~ USA (OH) 280-281 B 4
Miami River ~ USA (OH) 280-281 B 3
Miamo, El ○ YV 62-63 D 2
Miān Channūn ○ PK 138-139 D 4
Miandrivazo ○ RM 222-223 D 7
Miangas, Pulau ⌒ RI 164-165 K 1
Miani ○ PK 138-139 D 3
Miani Hor ≈ 134-135 M 6
Mianmian Shan ▲ VRC 156-157 B 2
Mianmin ○ PNG 183 A 3
Mianning ○ VRC 156-157 C 2
Miānwāli ○ PK 138-139 C 3
Mian Xian ○ VRC 154-155 E 5
Mianyang ○ VRC 154-155 D 6
Mianzhu ○ VRC 154-155 D 6
Miao ~ ZRE 214-215 B 4
Miaodao Qundao ⌒ VRC 150-151 C 8
Miaoergou ○ VRC 146-147 F 3
Miao Li ○ RC 156-157 M 4
Miao Ling ▲ VRC 156-157 E 3
Miaozu ○ VRC 156-157 E 4
Miarinarivo ○ RM 222-223 E 7
Miaru ○ PNG 183 D 5
Miass ☆ RUS (CEL) 96-97 M 6
Miass ~ RUS 96-97 L 6
Miass ~ RUS 114-115 H 7
Miasskoe ☆ RUS 96-97 M 6
Miastko ○ PL 92-93 O 1
Miāti ○ IND 138-139 E 8
Mibalaie ○ ZRE 210-211 H 6
Mibenge ○ Z 214-215 E 6
Mibu Island ⌒ PNG 183 B 5
Mica ○ ZA 220-221 K 2
Mica Creek ○ CDN (BC) 228-229 Q 4
Micaúne ○ MOC 218-219 J 4
Miccosukee, Lake ⊝ USA (FL) 286-287 F 1
Miccosukee Indian Reservation X USA (FL) 286-287 J 5
Michael, Lake ⊝ CDN 36-37 U 7
Michael, Mount ▲ PNG 183 C 4
Michalovce ○ SK 92-93 Q 4
Michel ○ CDN 32-33 Q 3
Michel, Lake ⊝ CDN (NFL) 242-243 L 2
Michel, Pointe à ▲ CDN (QUE) 240-241 G 2
Michelago ○ AUS 180-181 K 3
Michel Peak ▲ CDN (BC) 228-229 H 3
Michelsen, Cape ▲ CDN 24-25 U 5
Michelson, Mount ▲ USA 20-21 S 2
Miches ○ DOM 54-55 L 5
Michichi ○ CDN (ALB) 232-233 F 4
Michie, Lake ⊝ USA (NC) 282-283 J 4
Michigamme River ~ USA (MI) 270-271 K 4
Michigan ◘ USA (MI) 270-271 M 6
Michigan, Lake ⊝ USA (MI) 272-273 B 5
Michigan Bar ○ USA (CA) 246-247 D 5
Michigan Center ○ USA (MI) 272-273 E 5
Michigan City ○ USA (IN) 274-275 M 3
Michigan City ○ USA (ND) 258-259 J 3
Michigan Potawatomi Indian Reservation X USA (MI) 270-271 L 5
Michilla ○ RCH 76-77 B 2
Michipicoten Bay ⊝ CDN (ONT) 236-237 C 5
Michipicoten Island ⌒ CDN (ONT) 236-237 C 5
Michoacan ◘ MEX 52-53 C 2
Michurinsk = Mičurinsk ○ RUS 94-95 R 5
Mico, Río ~ NIC 52-53 B 5
Micronesia ⌒ 14-15 G 6
Microondas ○ MEX 50-51 C 2
Mičurinsk ○ RUS 94-95 R 5
Midal < RN 198-199 B 4
Midale ○ CDN (SAS) 232-233 P 6
Midar ○ MA 188-189 K 3
Midas ○ USA (NV) 246-247 J 2
Midas Şehri ∴• TR 128-129 D 3
Mid-Atlantic Ridge ≃ 6-7 E 5
Midau, Pulau ⌒ RI 162-163 G 3
Mid Baffin ○ CDN 28-29 E 2
Middelburg ☆ NL 92-93 G 3
Middelburg ○ ZA (CAP) 220-221 G 5
Middelburg ○ ZA (TRA) 220-221 J 2
Middelpos ○ ZA 220-221 E 5
Middelveld ∸ ZA 220-221 G 3
Middelveld ∸ ZA 220-221 F 4
Middelwit ○ ZA 220-221 H 2
Middendorfa, zaliv ⊝ RUS 108-109 Y 4
Middle Alkali Lake ⊝ USA (CA) 246-247 E 2
Middle America Trench ≃ 52-53 F 4
Middle Andaman ⌒ IND 140-141 L 3
Middleboro ○ USA (MA) 278-279 L 7
Middlebro ○ CDN (MAN) 234-235 H 5
Middleburg ○ USA (PA) 280-281 J 3
Middleburgh ○ USA (NY) 278-279 G 6
Middlebury ○ USA (VT) 278-279 H 4
Middlecamp ○ AUS 180-181 F 2
Middle Cay ⌒ JA 54-55 G 6
Middle Channel ~ CDN 20-21 X 2
Middle Creek ~ USA (NC) 282-283 J 5
Middle Fabius River ~ USA (MO) 274-275 F 4
Middle Fiord ≈ 26-27 C 4
Middle Fork ○ USA (IN) 274-275 M 4
Middle Fork ~ USA 20-21 T 4
Middle Fork ~ USA (KY) 276-277 M 3
Middle Fork ~ USA (TN) 276-277 G 5
Middle Fork Chandalar ~ USA 20-21 R 2
Middle Fork John Day River ~ USA (OR) 244-245 F 6
Middle Fork Koyukuk ~ USA 20-21 P 3
Middle Fork Kuskokwim River ~ USA 20-21 N 5
Middle Fork River ~ USA 22-23 Q 3
Middle Fork Salmon River ~ USA (ID) 252-253 C 2
Middle Fork Salt River ~ USA (MO) 274-275 F 5
Middle Gate ○ USA (NV) 246-247 G 4
Middle Ground ≈ 54-55 G 2
Middle Hart River ~ CDN 20-21 W 4
Middle Island ⌒ AUS 176-177 G 7
Middle Lake ○ CDN (SAS) 232-233 N 3
Middle Loup River ~ USA (NE) 262-263 G 3
Middlemount ○ AUS 178-179 K 2
Middle Musquodoboit ○ CDN (NS) 240-241 M 5
Middle Ohio ○ CDN (NS) 240-241 K 7
Middle Park ○ AUS 174-175 G 6
Middle Pease River ~ USA (TX) 264-265 D 4
Middle Rapids ~ CDN 32-33 O 3
Middle Ridge ▲ CDN (NFL) 242-243 N 4
Middle River ~ CDN (BC) 228-229 J 2
Middle River ~ USA (MN) 270-271 B 2
Middle Sackville ○ CDN (NS) 240-241 M 6
Middle Sand Hills ▲ CDN (ALB) 232-233 H 5
Middlesboro ○ USA (KY) 276-277 M 4
Middlesbrough ○ GB 90-91 G 4
Middleton ○ AUS 178-179 F 2
Middleton ○ CDN (NS) 240-241 K 6
Middleton ○ USA (MI) 272-273 E 4
Middleton ○ USA (TN) 276-277 G 5
Middleton ○ USA (WI) 274-275 J 1
Middleton ○ ZA 220-221 G 6
Middleton, Mount ▲ CDN (QUE) 236-237 M 2
Middleton Island ⌒ USA 20-21 R 7
Middletown ○ USA (CA) 246-247 C 5
Middletown ○ USA (CT) 280-281 O 2
Middletown ○ USA (DE) 280-281 L 4
Middletown ○ USA (IA) 274-275 G 4
Middletown ○ USA (NY) 280-281 M 2
Middletown ○ USA (OH) 280-281 C 3
Middletown ○ USA (OH) 280-281 B 4
Middletown ○ USA (PA) 280-281 K 3
Middleville ○ USA (MI) 272-273 D 5
Middleville ○ USA (NY) 278-279 G 5
Middlewood ○ CDN (NS) 240-241 L 6
Midfield ○ USA (TX) 266-267 L 5
Midi, Canal du < F 90-91 J 10
Mid-Indian Basin ≃ 12 F 5
Mid-Indian Ridge ≃ 12 E 5
Midi-Pyrénées ◘ F 90-91 H 10
Midkiff ○ USA (TX) 266-267 F 2
Midland ○ AUS 176-177 C 5
Midland ○ CDN (ONT) 238-239 F 4
Midland ○ USA (CA) 248-249 K 6
Midland ○ USA (MI) 272-273 E 4
Midland ○ USA (SD) 260-261 E 2
Midland ○ USA (TX) 266-267 E 2
Midlander II AUS 178-179 H 2
Midlands ◘ ZW 218-219 E 4
Midlothian ○ USA (TX) 264-265 G 6
Midnab, al- ○ KSA 130-131 J 5
Midongy ∸ RM 222-223 E 9
Midongy Atsimo ○ RM 222-223 E 9
Midouze ~ F 90-91 G 10
Mid-Pacific-Seamounts ≃ 14-15 H 5
Midpines ○ USA (CA) 248-249 E 2
Midsandur ○ IS 86-87 c 2
Midsayap ○ RP 160-161 F 9
Midsommersø ⊝ GRØ 26-27 g 2
Midu ○ VRC 142-143 M 3
Midvale Summit ▲ USA (ID) 252-253 B 2
Midville ○ USA (GA) 284-285 H 4
Midway ○ USA (AL) 284-285 E 4
Midway ○ USA (AL) 284-285 C 5
Midway ○ USA (MS) 268-269 K 4
Midway ○ USA (TX) 268-269 E 5
Midway Corner ○ USA (AR) 276-277 E 5
Midway Island ⌒ USA 14-15 L 5
Midway Islands ⌒ USA 20-21 Q 1
Midway Range ▲ CDN (BC) 230-231 L 4
Midway Stores ○ USA (SD) 260-261 J 3
Midway Well ○ USA (CA) 248-249 K 6
Midwest ○ USA (WY) 252-253 M 3
Midwest City ○ USA (OK) 264-265 G 3
Midwestern Highway II AUS 180-181 H 3
Midyat ☆• TR 128-129 J 4
Midyobo ○ GQ 210-211 C 3
Midžor ▲•• YU 100-101 J 3
Miechów ○• PL 92-93 Q 3
Międzyrzec Podlaski ○ PL 92-93 R 3
Międzyrzecz ○• PL 92-93 N 2
Mielec ○• PL 92-93 Q 3
Miélékouka ○ RCB 210-211 E 3
Miembwe ○ EAT 214-215 J 5
Mier ○ MEX 50-51 K 4
Miera ○ USA (NM) 256-257 J 4
Miercurea-Ciuc ☆• RO 102-103 D 4
Mieres ○ E 98-99 E 3
Mier y Noriega ○ MEX 50-51 J 6
Mierzeja Wiślana ∪ PL 92-93 P 1
Mi'ēso ○ ETH 208-209 E 4
Miette Hot Springs ∴• CDN (ALB) 228-229 R 3
Mifflin ○ USA (TN) 276-277 G 5
Migdol ○ ZA 220-221 G 3
Migliónico ○• I 100-101 F 4
Migole ○ EAT 214-215 H 4
Migoli ○ EAT (SIN) 212-213 E 6
Migori ○ EAK 212-213 E 4
Migration Lake ⊝ CDN 30-31 P 3
Miguasha, Parc Provencial de ⊥ CDN (QUE) 240-241 J 2
Miguel Alemán, Presa < MEX 52-53 F 2
Miguel Alves ○ BR 68-69 G 4
Miguel Auza ○ MEX 50-51 H 5
Miguel Calmon ○ BR 68-69 H 7
Miguel Hidalgo, Presa < MEX 50-51 E 4
Miguel Leão ○ BR 68-69 G 4
Miguelópolis ○ BR 72-73 F 6
Miguel Pereira ○ BR 72-73 J 7
Miguel y Alex Tejada, Meteorite craters: • BOL 70-71 D 6
Migues ○ ROU 78-79 M 3
Mihajlov ☆• RUS 94-95 Q 4
Mihajlovgrad = Monatana ☆ BG 102-103 C 6
Mihajlovka ○ KA 136-137 M 3
Mihajlovka ○ RUS 116-117 M 10
Mihajlovka ○ RUS 122-123 D 7
Mihajlovka ○ RUS (SAH) 120-121 E 3
Mihajlovka ○ RUS (VLG) 102-103 N 2
Mihajlovka, Podyem- ○ RUS 96-97 G 7
Mihajlovo ○ BG 102-103 C 6
Mihajlovsk ○ RUS 96-97 L 5
Mihajlovskij ☆ RUS 124-125 L 3
Mihalıççık ○ TR 128-129 D 3
Mihalkino ○ RUS 112-113 L 2
Mihama ○ J 152-153 G 7
Mihintale ○ CL 140-141 J 6
Mihnevo ○ RUS 94-95 P 4
Miho-wan ≈ 152-153 E 7
Mihrād, al- ∸ KSA 132-133 H 3
Mihuanoyacu ○ EC 64-65 D 2
Mihumo Chini ○ EAT 214-215 K 5
Mijaki, Kirgiz- ☆ RUS 96-97 J 7
Mijaly ☆ KA 96-97 H 9
Mijek ○ MA 196-197 D 3
Mikado ○ CDN (SAS) 232-233 Q 4
Mikasa ○ J 152-153 J 3
Mikaševičy ○ BY 94-95 K 5
Mikawa-wan ≈ 152-153 G 7
Mikčangda ~ RUS 108-109 Y 7
Mikese ○ EAT 214-215 J 4
Miki ○ ZRE 212-213 B 5
Mikindani ○ EAT 214-215 L 6
Mikkeli ☆ FIN 88-89 J 6
Mikkwa River ~ CDN 32-33 N 3
Mikkâs ☆ MA 188-189 J 4
Mikojana, zaliv ⊝ RUS 108-109 e 2
Mikonos ⌒ GR 100-101 K 6
Mikulkin, mys ▲ RUS 88-89 T 3
Mikumi ○ EAT 214-215 J 4
Mikumi Lodge ○ EAT 214-215 J 4
Mikumi National Park ⊥ EAT 214-215 J 4
Mikumi-sanmyaku ▲ J 152-153 H 6
Mikun' ○ RUS 88-89 V 5
Mikuni ○ J 152-153 G 6
Mikwam River ~ CDN (ONT) 236-237 H 3
Mil' ~ RUS 120-121 E 3
Mil', Ust'- ○ RUS 120-121 E 4
Mila ☆ DZ 190-191 F 2
Milaca ○ USA (MN) 270-271 E 5
Milach, In- < RMM 196-197 K 6
Miladummadulu Atoll ⌒ MV 140-141 B 4
Milagres ○ BR (BAH) 72-73 L 2
Milagres ○ BR (CEA) 68-69 J 5
Milagro ○ EC 64-65 C 3
Milagro ○ USA (NM) 256-257 K 4
Milagro, El ○ MEX 50-51 H 3
Milagros ○ RP 160-161 E 6
Milait ⌒ GRØ 28-29 Y 3
Milam ○ USA (TX) 268-269 G 5
Milan ○ USA (GA) 284-285 G 4
Milan ○ USA (IN) 274-275 N 5
Milan ○ USA (KS) 262-263 J 7
Milan ○ USA (MI) 272-273 F 5
Milan ○ USA (MN) 270-271 C 5
Milan ○ USA (MO) 274-275 E 4
Milan ○ USA (NM) 256-257 H 3
Milan ○ USA (TN) 276-277 G 5
Milan = Milano ☆··· I 100-101 B 2
Milando ○ ANG 216-217 D 4
Milando, Reserva Especial do ⊥ ANG 216-217 D 4
Milang ○ AUS 180-181 E 3
Milange ○ MOC 218-219 H 3
Milange ○ ZRE 212-213 A 5
Milango ~ RI 164-165 G 3
Milano ☆··· I 100-101 B 2
Milano ○ USA (TX) 266-267 L 3
Milanoa ○ RM 222-223 F 4
Milas ☆• TR 128-129 B 4
Milazzo ○ I 100-101 E 5
Milbank ○ USA (SD) 260-261 K 1
Milbanke Sound ≈ 32-33 F 5
Milbanke Sound ≈ CDN 228-229 F 4
Milbridge ○ USA (ME) 278-279 O 4
Milburn ○ USA (NE) 262-263 G 3
Milden ○ CDN (SAS) 232-233 L 4
Mildet ○ MA 188-189 J 4
Mildred ○ CDN (SAS) 232-233 L 2
Mildred ○ USA (MT) 250-251 P 5
Mildura ○ AUS 180-181 G 3
Mildura Gemstone Deposit • AUS 176-177 F 6
Milë ○ ETH 208-209 E 3
Mile ○ VRC 156-157 C 4
Milepa ○ EAT 214-215 F 5
Miles ○ AUS 178-179 L 4
Miles ○ USA (TX) 266-267 G 2
Miles ○ USA (WA) 244-245 G 3
Miles, Cape ▲ CDN 24-25 d 6
Miles City ○ USA (FL) 286-287 H 5
Miles City ○ USA (MT) 250-251 O 5
Milestone ○ CDN (SAS) 232-233 O 6
Milesville ○ USA (SD) 260-261 E 2
Milet ∴•• TR 128-129 B 4
Mileura ○ AUS 176-177 D 3
Milē Wenz ~ ETH 208-209 E 3
Milford ○ USA (CA) 246-247 E 3
Milford ○ USA (CT) 280-281 N 2
Milford ○ USA (DE) 280-281 L 5
Milford ○ USA (IA) 274-275 C 1
Milford ○ USA (IL) 274-275 L 4
Milford ○ USA (MA) 278-279 K 6
Milford ○ USA (MI) 272-273 F 5
Milford ○ USA (NE) 262-263 J 4
Milford ○ USA (PA) 280-281 M 2
Milford ○ USA (UT) 254-255 B 5
Milford Lake ⊝ USA (KS) 262-263 J 5
Milford Sound ≈ 182 A 6
Milford Sound ○ NZ 182 A 6
Milgarra ○ AUS 174-175 F 6
Milgun ○ AUS 176-177 E 2
Mil'guveem ~ RUS 112-113 R 2
Milhana ○ MOC 218-219 K 2
Milhāt ○ IRQ 128-129 K 5
Miliana ○ DZ 190-191 D 2
Milikapiti X AUS 172-173 K 1
Milim ○ PNG 183 F 3
Milingimbi X AUS 174-175 C 3
Milijutkējveem ~ RUS 112-113 W 3
Milkengay Lake ⊝ AUS 180-181 F 2
Mil'kovo ☆ RUS 120-121 S 6
Milk River ~ 32-33 P 7
Milk River ○ CDN (ALB) 232-233 F 6
Milk River ~ USA (MT) 250-251 J 3
Milk River ~ USA (MT) 250-251 F 3
Milk River Ridge ▲ CDN (ALB) 232-233 F 6
Mill ○ USA (OK) 264-265 H 4
Millaa Millaa ○• AUS 174-175 H 5
Millaroo ○ AUS 174-175 J 7
Millarville ○ CDN (ALB) 232-233 D 5
Millas ○ F 90-91 J 10
Millau ○ F 90-91 J 9
Millboro ○ USA (VA) 280-281 G 5
Millbrook ○ CDN (ONT) 238-239 G 4
Millburne ○ USA (WY) 252-253 H 5
Mill City ○ USA (OR) 244-245 C 6
Milledgeville ○ USA (GA) 284-285 G 3
Milledgeville ○ USA (IL) 274-275 J 3
Mille Lacs, Lac des ⊝ CDN (ONT) 234-235 N 6
Mille Lacs Lake ⊝ USA (MN) 270-271 E 4
Millen ○ USA (GA) 284-285 J 4
Millenbeck ○ USA (VA) 280-281 K 6
Miller ○ USA (NE) 262-263 G 4
Miller ○ USA (OK) 264-265 J 4
Miller ○ USA (SD) 260-261 H 2
Miller ○ ZA 220-221 F 6
Miller, Mount ▲ USA 20-21 T 6
Millerdale ○ CDN (SAS) 232-233 K 4
Millerovo ○ RUS 102-103 M 3
Millersburg ○ USA (OH) 280-281 E 3
Millersburg ○ USA (PA) 280-281 K 3
Millers Corners ○ USA (PA) 280-281 H 4
Millers Creek ~ AUS 178-179 C 5
Millers Creek Reservoir < USA (TX) 264-265 E 5
Millersview ○ USA (TX) 266-267 H 2
Millerton ○ BS 54-55 H 3
Millerton ○ CDN (NB) 240-241 K 4
Millerton ○ USA (NY) 280-281 N 2
Millertown ○ CDN (NFL) 242-243 M 4
Millertown Junction ○ CDN (NFL) 242-243 M 3
Millett ○ CDN (ALB) 232-233 E 2
Millett ○ USA (TX) 266-267 H 5
Millevaches, Plateau de ▲ F 90-91 H 9
Millican ○ USA (OR) 244-245 E 7
Millicent ○ AUS 180-181 F 4
Millie ○ AUS 178-179 K 5
Milligan College ○ USA (TN) 282-283 E 4
Milligan Hills ▲ CDN 32-33 K 3
Millington ○ USA (TN) 276-277 F 5
Millinocket ○ USA (ME) 278-279 N 3
Millinocket Lake ⊝ USA (ME) 278-279 N 3
Mill Iron ○ USA (MT) 250-251 P 6
Mill Island ⌒ ARK 16 G 11
Millmerran ○ AUS 178-179 L 4
Millport ○ USA (AL) 284-285 B 3
Millrose ○ AUS 176-177 E 2
Millry ○ USA (AL) 284-285 B 5
Millsboro ○ USA (DE) 280-281 L 5
Mills Lake ⊝ CDN 30-31 K 5
Millston ○ USA (WI) 270-271 H 6
Millstream ○ AUS 172-173 C 6
Millstream Chichester National Park ⊥ AUS 172-173 C 6
Milltown ○ CDN (NFL) 242-243 N 5
Milltown ○ USA (IN) 274-275 M 6
Millungera ○ AUS 174-175 F 6
Mill Village ○ CDN (NS) 240-241 L 6
Millville ○ CDN (NB) 240-241 H 4
Millville ○ USA (NJ) 280-281 M 4
Millville ○ USA (PA) 280-281 K 2
Millwood ○ CDN (MAN) 234-235 B 4
Millwood ○ USA (GA) 284-285 H 5
Millwood ○ USA (OH) 280-281 D 3
Millwood ○ USA (WA) 244-245 H 3
Millwood Lake ⊝ USA (AR) 276-277 A 7
Millyeewilpa Lake ⊝ AUS 178-179 D 4
Milly Milly ○ AUS 176-177 D 3
Milne Bay ≈ 183 F 6
Milne Inlet ≈ 24-25 g 4
Milne Land ∸ GRØ 26-27 m 8
Milner Lake ⊝ CDN 38-39 L 2
Milnesand ○ USA (NM) 256-257 M 5
Milnor ○ USA (ND) 258-259 K 5
Milo ○ CDN (ALB) 232-233 F 5
Milo ○ ETH 208-209 F 3
Milo ~ RG 202-203 F 4
Milo ○ USA (ME) 278-279 N 3
Milo ○ USA (OK) 264-265 G 4
Milodon, Cueva del • RCH 80 D 5
Milogradovo ○ RUS 122-123 F 7
Miloli'i ○ USA (HI) 288 K 5
Milos ○ GR 100-101 K 6
Milos ⌒ GR 100-101 K 6
Milot ○ RH 54-55 J 5
Milparinka ○ AUS 178-179 F 5
Milpitas ○ USA (CA) 248-249 C 2
Milpitas Wash ~ USA (CA) 248-249 J 6
Milroy ○ USA (MN) 270-271 C 6
Mil'skaja ravnina ∪ AZ 128-129 M 3
Milton ○ CDN (NFL) 242-243 P 4
Milton ○ CDN (NS) 240-241 L 6
Milton ○ NZ 182 B 7
Milton ○ USA (DE) 280-281 L 5
Milton ○ USA (FL) 286-287 B 1
Milton ○ USA (IA) 274-275 F 4
Milton ○ USA (ND) 258-259 J 3
Milton ○ USA (OK) 264-265 K 3
Milton ○ USA (PA) 280-281 K 2
Milton ○ USA (WV) 280-281 D 5
Miltona ○ USA (MN) 270-271 C 4
Milton-Freewater ○ USA (OR) 244-245 G 5
Milton Lake ⊝ CDN 30-31 S 6
Miltonvale ○ USA (KS) 262-263 J 5
Miltou ○ TCH 206-207 C 3
Miluo ○ VRC 156-157 H 2
Milverton ○ CDN (ONT) 238-239 E 5
Milwaukee ○• USA (WI) 274-275 L 1
Milwaukie ○ USA (OR) 244-245 C 5
Mimbelly ○ RCB 210-211 F 2
Mimbres River ~ USA (NM) 256-257 H 6
Mimili (Everard Park) X AUS 176-177 M 3
Miminiska Lake ⊝ CDN (ONT) 234-235 P 3
Mi Mi Rocks ▲ AUS 176-177 H 3
Mimizan ○ F 90-91 G 9
Mimongo ○ G 210-211 C 4
Mimouna, Kef ▲ DZ 190-191 D 4
Mimpoutou ○ RCB 210-211 F 2
Mims ○ USA (FL) 286-287 J 3
Mina ~ RI 166-167 C 7
Mina ○ USA (NV) 246-247 G 5
Mina ○ USA (SD) 260-261 H 1
Mina', al- ○ RL 128-129 F 5
Mina, Oued ~ DZ 190-191 C 3
Mina, Salar de la ⊝ RA 76-77 D 4
Minā' 'Abdallāh ○ KWT 130-131 L 3
Mināb ○• IR 134-135 G 5
Mina Clavero ○ RA 76-77 E 6
Minaçu ○ BR 72-73 F 2
Mina Exploradora ○ RCH 76-77 C 3
Minahasa Semenao djung ∪ RI 164-165 G 3
Mina Jebel Ali ○ UAE 134-135 F 6
Minaki ○ CDN (ONT) 234-235 J 5
Mina la Casualidad ○ RA 76-77 C 3
Mina la Juanita ○ RCH 78-79 D 3
Minam ○ USA (OR) 244-245 H 5
Minami-Alps National Park ⊥ J 152-153 H 7
Minami-Daitō ○ J 152-153 D 12
Minamikayabe ○ J 152-153 J 4
Minami-Tane ○ J 152-153 D 9
Minas ○ C 54-55 G 4
Minas ○ RI 162-163 D 4
Minas ☆ ROU 78-79 M 3
Minas, Cerro las ▲ HN 52-53 K 4
Minas, Sierra de las ▲ GCA 52-53 J 4
Minas Basin ≈ 38-39 M 6
Minas Basin ≈ CDN 240-241 L 5
Minas Channel ≈ CDN 240-241 L 5
Minas de Barroterán ○ MEX 50-51 J 4
Minas de Corrales ○ ROU 76-77 K 6
Minas del Oro • CO 60-61 E 4
Minas de Matahambre ○ C 54-55 D 3
Minas do Mimoso ○ BR 68-69 H 7
Minas Gerais ◘ BR 72-73 H 4
Minas Novas ○ BR 72-73 J 4
Minā' Su'ud ○ KWT 130-131 L 3
Minatina Batoche National Historic Park • CDN (SAS) 232-233 M 3
Minatitlán ○ MEX (COL) 52-53 B 2
Minatitlán ○• MEX (VER) 52-53 G 3
Minbu ○ MYA 142-143 J 5
Min Buri ○ THA 158-159 F 4
Minburn ○ CDN (ALB) 232-233 G 2
Minch, The ≈ 90-91 E 3
Minch, The Little ≈ 90-91 D 3
Minchika ○ WAN 204-205 K 3
Minchinābād ○ PK 138-139 D 4
Minchinmávida, Volcán ▲ RCH 78-79 C 7
Minchumina, Lake ⊝ USA 20-21 O 5
Minco ○ USA (OK) 264-265 G 3
Mindanao ⌒ RP 160-161 G 8
Mindanao Sea ≈ 160-161 E 10
Mindelo ○• CV 202-203 B 5
Minden ○ CDN (ONT) 238-239 G 4
Minden ○• D 92-93 K 2
Minden ○ USA (IA) 274-275 C 3
Minden ○ USA (LA) 268-269 G 4
Minden ○ USA (NE) 262-263 H 4
Minderla ○ RUS 116-117 F 7
Mindif ○• CAM 206-207 B 3
Mindif, Dent de ▲• CAM 206-207 B 3
Mindik ○ PNG 183 D 4
Mindiptana ○ RI 166-167 L 4
Mindjik ○ TCH 206-207 E 3
Mindo ○ EC 64-65 C 2
Mindon ○ MYA 142-143 J 6
Mindona Lake ⊝ AUS 180-181 G 2
Mindoro ⌒ RP 160-161 D 6
Mindoro Strait ≈ 160-161 D 6
Mindouli ○ RCB 210-211 E 6
Mindourou ○ CAM 210-211 D 2
Minduri ○ BR 72-73 H 6
Mindživan ○ AZ 128-129 M 3
Mine ○ J (NAG) 152-153 C 7
Mine ○ J (YMG) 152-153 D 7
Mine ○ USA (AZ) 256-257 A 5
Mine Centre ○ CDN (ONT) 234-235 L 6
Minehead ○ GB 90-91 F 6
Mineiros ○ BR 72-73 D 4
Mine New Hosco ○ CDN (QUE) 236-237 L 3
Mineola ○ USA (TX) 264-265 J 6
Mineral ○ USA (CA) 246-247 D 3
Mineral, Cerro ▲ RCH 80 E 2
Mineral Hot Springs ○ USA (CO) 254-255 K 5
Mineral'nye Vody ○ RUS 126-127 E 5
Mineral Point ○ USA (WI) 274-275 H 2
Mineral Springs ○ USA (AR) 276-277 B 7
Mineral Wells ○ USA (TX) 264-265 F 6
Miner River ~ CDN 20-21 Z 2
Miners Bird Sanctuary • CDN (ONT) 238-239 C 6
Miners Point ▲ USA 22-23 U 4
Minersville ○ USA (UT) 254-255 C 5
Minerva ○ USA (NY) 278-279 H 5
Minerva ○ USA (OH) 280-281 E 3
Minerva, Presa < C 54-55 F 3
Minette, Bay ○ USA (AL) 284-285 C 6
Minfeng ○ VRC 144-145 D 2
Minford ○ USA (OH) 280-281 D 5
Minga ○ Z 218-219 F 2
Minga ○ ZRE 214-215 D 6
Mingala ○ RCA 206-207 E 6
Mingan ○ CDN (QUE) 242-243 D 2
Mingan, Îles de ⌒ CDN (QUE) 242-243 E 2
Mingan, Rivière ~ CDN (QUE) 242-243 E 2
Minganja ○ ANG 216-217 F 6
Mingao ○ CO 60-61 H 6
Mingary ○ AUS 180-181 F 2
Mingbuloķ ○ US 136-137 H 3
Mingbuloķ cukurligi ∸ US 136-137 H 3
Mingechevir = Mingaçevir ○• AZ 128-129 M 2
Mingechevirskoe vodohranilišče < AZ 128-129 M 2
Mingela ○ AUS 174-175 J 6
Mingenew ○ AUS 176-177 C 4
Minggang ○ VRC 154-155 J 5
Minghoshan = Dunhuang ○• VRC 146-147 M 5
Mingin ○ MYA 142-143 J 4
Ming Ming ○ PNG 183 D 3
Mingo Lake ⊝ CDN 36-37 N 2
Mingo National Wildlife Refuge ⊥ USA (MO) 276-277 E 3
Mingora ○• PK 138-139 D 2
Mingoyo ○ EAT 214-215 K 6
Ming's Bight ○ CDN (NFL) 242-243 M 3
Mingshui ○ VRC 150-151 E 4
Mingue ○ CAM 204-205 K 6
Mingun ○•• MYA 142-143 J 4
Minguri ○ MOC 218-219 L 2
Mingxi ○ VRC 156-157 K 3
Minhe Huizu Tuzu Zizhixian ○ VRC 154-155 C 3
Minh Hải ☆ VN 158-159 H 6
Minh Hòa, Hòn ⌒ VN 158-159 H 5
Minhla ○ MYA 142-143 J 4
Minhla ○ MYA 158-159 C 2
Minho, Rio ~ P 98-99 C 4
Minichinas Hills ▲ CDN (SAS) 232-233 M 3
Minicoy Island ⌒ IND 140-141 E 6
Minidoka ○ USA (ID) 252-253 E 4
Minier ○ USA (IL) 274-275 J 4
Minigwal, Lake ⊝ AUS 176-177 G 4
Minilya Bridge Roadhouse ○ AUS 176-177 B 1
Minilya River ~ AUS 176-177 C 1
Mininian ○ CI 202-203 G 4
Miniota ○ CDN (MAN) 234-235 B 4
Minipi Lake ⊝ CDN 38-39 O 2
Minisiare, Caño ~ CO 60-61 G 6
Minissa ○ BF 202-203 J 3
Miniss Lake ⊝ CDN (ONT) 234-235 N 4
Ministro Ramos Mexía ○ RA 78-79 F 6
Minitas, Playa ∸• DOM 54-55 L 5
Minja ~ RUS 118-119 D 7
Min'jar ○ RUS 96-97 K 6
Min Jiang ~ VRC 154-155 C 5
Min Jiang ~ VRC 156-157 L 3
Min Jiang ~ VRC 156-157 D 2
Minjilang X AUS 172-173 L 1
Minjip ○ PNG 183 B 3
Minlaton ○ AUS 180-181 D 3
Minle ○ VRC 154-155 B 2
Minna ☆ WAN 204-205 G 4
Minneapolis ○ USA (KS) 262-263 J 5
Minneapolis ○• USA (MN) 270-271 E 6
Minnedosa ○ CDN (MAN) 234-235 D 4
Minneola ○ USA (KS) 262-263 F 7
Minneota ○ USA (MN) 270-271 C 6
Minnesota ◘ USA (MN) 270-271 B 4
Minnesota River ~ USA (MN) 270-271 C 6
Minnesott Beach ○ USA (NC) 282-283 L 5
Minnewanka, Lake ⊝ CDN (ALB) 232-233 C 4
Minnewaukan ○ USA (ND) 258-259 H 3
Minnie Creek ○ AUS 176-177 C 2
Minnies Out Station ○ AUS 174-175 G 5
Minnipa ○ AUS 180-181 C 2
Minnitaki Lake ⊝ CDN (ONT) 234-235 M 4
Minnkri ○ RMM 196-197 J 6
Miño, Río ~ E 98-99 D 3
Miñoes ○ RA 76-77 H 6
Minong ○ USA (WI) 270-271 G 4
Minonk ○ USA (IL) 274-275 J 4
Minor Hill ○ USA (TN) 276-277 H 5
Minot ○ USA (ND) 258-259 F 3
Minqin ○ VRC 154-155 C 2
Minqing ○ VRC 156-157 L 3
Minquan ○ VRC 154-155 J 4
Min Shan ▲ VRC 154-155 C 5
Minsk ★ BY 94-95 K 5
Mińsk Mazowiecki ○ PL 92-93 Q 2
Minster ○ USA (OH) 280-281 B 3
Minstrel Island ○ CDN (BC) 230-231 C 3
Minta ○ CAM 204-205 K 6
Mintabie ○ AUS 176-177 M 3
Mintaqat ash Shu'bah ∸ LAR 192-193 L 2
Mintaqat Umm Khuwayt ∸ LAR 192-193 K 2
Mint Hill ○ USA (NC) 282-283 G 5
Mintirib, al- ○ OM 132-133 L 2
Minto ○ CDN (MAN) 234-235 D 5
Minto ○ CDN (NB) 240-241 J 4
Minto ○ CDN (YT) 20-21 W 5
Minto ○ USA (ND) 258-259 K 3
Minto, Lac ⊝ CDN 36-37 M 6
Minto Inlet ≈ 24-25 N 5
Mintom II ○ CAM 210-211 D 2
Minton ○ CDN (SAS) 232-233 O 6
Mintonas ○ CDN (MAN) 234-235 B 2
Mintonsville ○ USA (NC) 282-283 L 4
Minturn ○ USA (CO) 254-255 J 4
Minūdašt ○ IR 136-137 D 6
Minusinsk ☆ RUS 116-117 E 9
Minvoul ○ G 210-211 D 2
Min Xian ○ VRC 154-155 D 4
Minyā, al- ☆ ET 194-195 E 3
Minzawi, Wādī al- ~ OM 132-133 H 5
Minž gol ~ MAU 148-149 H 3
Mio ○ USA (MI) 272-273 E 3
Miocene ○ CDN (BC) 228-229 N 4
Miosnum, Pulau ⌒ RI 166-167 H 2
Mipia, Lake ⊝ AUS 178-179 E 3
Miqdādīya, al- ☆ IRQ 128-129 L 6
Miquelon ○ CDN (QUE) 236-237 M 3
Miquelon, Cap ▲ CDN (F) 242-243 M 5
Miquihuana ○ MEX 50-51 K 6
Mira ○ EC 64-65 C 1
Mira ○ P 98-99 C 4
Mira, buhta ≈ 110-111 a 2
Mira, Río ~ EC 64-65 C 1
Mirabel ○ CDN (QUE) 238-239 L 3
Mirabela ○ BR 72-73 H 4
Miracema ○ BR 72-73 J 6
Miracema de Tocantins ○ BR 68-69 D 6
Miracosta ○ PE 64-65 C 5
Mirador ○ BR (AMA) 64-65 F 4
Mirador ○ BR (MAR) 68-69 F 5
Mirador, El ∴• GCA 52-53 K 3
Mirador, Parque Nacional de ⊥ BR 68-69 F 5
Mirador-Dos Lagunas-Río Azul, Parque Nacional ⊥•• GCA 52-53 K 3
Miradouro ○ BR 72-73 J 6
Miraflores ○ BR 66-67 E 4
Miraflores ○ CO (BOY) 60-61 E 5
Miraflores ○ CO (VAU) 66-67 B 2
Mirage Bay ⊝ CDN 28-29 E 3
Mirāglia, Portella della ▲ I 100-101 E 6
Miragoâne ○ RH 54-55 J 5
Miraj ○ IND 140-141 F 2
Mira Loma ○ USA (CA) 248-249 G 5
Miramar ○ BR 66-67 G 5
Miramar ○ RA 78-79 L 5
Miramichi Bay ≈ 38-39 M 5
Miramichi Bay ≈ CDN 240-241 K 3
Miramichi River ~ CDN (NB) 240-241 J 4
Miram Shāh ○ PK 138-139 C 3
Miran ○ PK 138-139 C 4
Miran ○ VRC 146-147 J 6
Miranda ○ BR (GSU) 70-71 J 7

Miranda o BR (MAR) 68-69 F 3
Miranda o YV 60-61 G 2
Miranda, Lake o AUS 176-177 F 3
Miranda, Rio ∼ BR 70-71 J 7
Miranda de Ebro o E 98-99 F 3
Miranda do Douro o P 98-99 D 4
Miranda Downs o AUS 174-175 F 5
Mirandela o BR 68-69 J 7
Mirandela o P 98-99 D 4
Mirandiba o BR 68-69 J 6
Mirando City o USA (TX) 266-267 H 6
Mirandópolis o BR 72-73 E 6
Mirani o AUS 178-179 K 1
Miranle da Sura o BR 70-71 F 2
Miranorte o BR 68-69 D 6
Mirante o BR 72-73 K 3
Mirante do Paranapanema o BR 72-73 E 7
Mira por vos Cays ∩ BS 54-55 H 3
Mira por vos Passage ≈ 54-55 H 3
Mirassol o BR 72-73 F 6
Mirassol d'Oeste o BR 70-71 H 4
Miratu, Área Indígena ⩇ BR 66-67 E 4
Miratuba, Lago ○ BR 66-67 H 4
Miravalles ▲ E 98-99 D 3
Miravalles, Volcán ▲ CR 52-53 B 6
Mir Bačče Kūt o AFG 138-139 B 2
Mir-Bašir = Terter o AZ 128-129 M 2
Mirbāṭ o OM 132-133 J 5
Mirebalais o RH 54-55 J 5
Mirǧāve o IR 134-135 J 4
Mirhleft o MA 188-189 G 6
Miri o MAL 162-163 K 2
Miria o RN 198-199 D 6
Miriālgūda o IND 140-141 H 2
Miriam Vale o AUS 178-179 L 3
Mirim, Lagoa ○ BR 74-75 D 9
Mirim, Lagoa do ○ BR 74-75 F 7
Mirim do Abufari, Paraná ∼ BR 66-67 F 5
Mirimire o YV 60-61 G 2
Mirina o GR 100-101 K 5
Miriñay, Esteros ○ RA 76-77 J 5
Miriñay, Río ∼ RA 76-77 J 5
Mirinzal o BR 68-69 F 3
Miritiparaná, Río ∼ CO 66-67 B 3
Miriye, togga ∼ SP 208-209 G 3
Mirjan o IND 140-141 F 3
Mirnoe, ozero ○ RUS 114-115 P 6
Mirnyj o ARK 16 G 10
Mirnyj ☆• RUS 118-119 F 4
Mirobia o RI 166-167 G 3
Mirogi o EAK 212-213 E 4
Miroki o US 136-137 K 5
Mirond Lake ○ CDN 34-35 E 3
Mirong o VRC 156-157 C 5
Mirosławiec o PL 92-93 O 2
Mirowāl o PK 138-139 E 4
Mirpur Batoro o PK 138-139 B 7
Mirpur Khās o• PK 138-139 B 7
Mirpur Mathelo o• PK 138-139 B 5
Mirpur Sakro o PK 134-135 M 6
Mirra Mitta Bore o AUS 178-179 E 4
Mirrngadja Village ⩇ AUS 174-175 C 3
Mirror o CDN (ALB) 232-233 E 3
Mirror River ∼ CDN 32-33 Q 3
Mirrote o MOC 218-219 K 1
Mirsale o SP 208-209 H 6
Mirtna o AUS 178-179 J 1
Mirtóo Pélagos ≈ 100-101 J 6
Miruro o MOC 218-219 F 2
Mirwāh o PK 138-139 B 7
Mirzā 'Arab, Kūh-e ▲ IR 134-135 J 2
Mirzapur o IND 142-143 C 3
Misāha, Bi'r < ET 194-195 C 6
Misaine Bank ≃ 38-39 P 6
Misaki o EAT 212-213 E 6
Misaki o J (EHI) 152-153 E 8
Misaki o J (OSA) 152-153 F 7
Misantla o MEX (VER) 52-53 F 2
Misantla ∴• MEX (VER) 52-53 F 2
Misau o WAN 204-205 J 3
Misawa o J 152-153 J 4
Misaw Lake ○ CDN 30-31 S 6
Miscou Centre o CDN (NB) 240-241 L 3
Miscou Island ∩ CDN (NB) 240-241 L 3
Miscou Point ▲ CDN (NB) 240-241 L 2
Misehkov River ∼ CDN (ONT) 234-235 O 3
Misekumaw Lake ○ CDN 30-31 S 6
Misele o ZRE 210-211 F 6
Misgund o ZA 220-221 F 6
Mishagomish, Lac ○ CDN (QUE) 236-237 M 2
Mishagua, Río ∼ PE 64-65 F 7
Mishamo o EAT 212-213 C 6
Mishan o VRC 150-151 H 5
Mishanattawa River ∼ CDN 34-35 N 3
Mishibishu Lake ○ CDN (ONT) 236-237 C 4
Mishicot o USA (WI) 270-271 L 6
Mi-shima ∩ J 152-153 D 7
Misi o FIN 88-89 J 3
Misiki o PNG 183 B 4
Misión, La o MEX 50-51 A 1
Mision de San Fernando o MEX 50-51 B 2
Misiones ◘ RA 76-77 K 4
Misiones, Sierra de ▲ RA 76-77 K 4
Miski o SUD 200-201 B 5
Miškino ☆ RUS 114-115 G 7
Miškino ☆ RUS (BAS) 96-97 J 6
Miskitos, Cayos ∩ NIC 52-53 C 4
Miskolc o H 92-93 Q 4
Mismār o SUD 200-201 G 3
Mismya, al- o SYR 128-129 G 6
Misol-Ha Waterfall ∼• MEX 52-53 H 3
Misool, Pulau ∩ RI 166-167 F 2
Misouminien o CI 202-203 J 6
Miśrāfa, al- o Y 132-133 C 6
Misrātah ◘ LAR 192-193 F 1
Miṣrātah ☆ LAR 192-193 F 1
Misrikh o IND 142-143 B 2
Missanabie o CDN (ONT) 236-237 D 4
Misseni o RMM 202-203 G 4
Missi Falls ∼ CDN 34-35 G 2
Missinaibi Lake ○ CDN (ONT) 236-237 E 4
Missinaibi Lake Provincial Park ⊥ CDN (ONT) 236-237 E 4
Missinaibi River ∼ CDN (ONT) 236-237 F 2
Missinipe o CDN 34-35 D 3
Mission o CDN (BC) 230-231 G 4
Mission o USA (SD) 260-261 F 3
Mission o USA (TX) 266-267 J 7
Mission Beach o AUS 174-175 J 5
Misión de San Borja o MEX 50-51 C 3
Mission Indian Reservation ⩇ USA (CA) 248-249 G 6
Mission Mountains Wilderness Area ⊥ USA (MT) 250-251 F 4
Mission Ridge o USA (SD) 260-261 F 2
Mission Valley o USA (TX) 266-267 K 5
Mission Viejo o USA (CA) 248-249 G 6
Missira o SN (SO) 202-203 E 3
Missira o SN (SO) 202-203 D 3
Missisagi River ∼ CDN (ONT) 238-239 B 2
Missisa Lake ○ CDN 34-35 O 4
Mississicabi, Rivière ∼ CDN 38-39 E 3
Mississicabi, Rivière ∼ CDN (QUE) 236-237 K 2
Mississagi Provincial Park ⊥ CDN (ONT) 238-239 C 2
Mississagi River Provincial Park ⊥ CDN (ONT) 236-237 F 5
Mississauga o CDN (ONT) 238-239 F 5
Mississinewa River ∼ USA (IN) 274-275 N 4
Mississippi ◘ USA (MS) 268-269 L 5
Mississippi River ∼ USA 4 E 5
Mississippi River Delta ∪ USA (LA) 268-269 L 7
Mississippi Sound ≈ 48-49 D 4
Mississippi Sound ≈ USA 268-269 L 6
Missoula o USA (MT) 250-251 F 5
Missour o MA 188-189 K 4
Missouri ◘ USA (MO) 274-275 E 6
Missouri Breaks Wild and Scenic River ⊥ USA (MT) 250-251 K 4
Missouri City o USA (TX) 268-269 E 7
Missouri Coteau ⊥ CDN (SAS) 232-233 M 5
Missouri River ∼ USA 4 D 4
Missouri Valley o USA (IA) 274-275 C 3
Mist o USA (OR) 244-245 B 5
Mistake Creek ∼ AUS 178-179 G 2
Mistassibi, Rivière ∼ CDN (QUE) 236-237 Q 2
Mistassini o CDN (QUE) 236-237 P 2
Mistassini o CDN (QUE) 240-241 C 2
Mistassini, Lac ○ CDN (QUE) 236-237 P 2
Mistassini, Rivière ∼ CDN (QUE) 236-237 Q 3
Mistatim o CDN (SAS) 232-233 P 3
Mistawak, Lac ○ CDN (ONT) 236-237 K 3
Mistawak, Rivière ∼ CDN (QUE) 236-237 K 3
Mistawasis Indian Reserve ⩇ CDN (SAS) 232-233 M 2
Mistelbach an der Zaya o A 92-93 O 4
Misterei o SUD 198-199 L 6
Misti, Volcán ▲ PE 70-71 B 5
Mistinibi Lake ○ CDN 36-37 R 7
Mistoles, Laguna los ○ RA 76-77 F 6
Mistra ∴ GR 100-101 J 6
Mistuskwia River ∼ CDN (ONT) 236-237 F 2
Misty Fiords National Monument ⊥• USA 32-33 E 4
Misty Fiords National Monument Wilderness ⊥• USA 32-33 E 4
Misty Lake ○ CDN 30-31 T 6
Misumba o ZRE 210-211 H 6
Misumi o J 152-153 D 8
Misvær o N 86-87 G 3
Mišwara o Y 132-133 D 6
Mita, Punta ▲ MEX 52-53 B 1
Mita Hills Dam < Z 218-219 E 2
Mitaho • RM 222-223 C 10
Mita-Mirim o BR 66-67 E 3
Mitande o MOC 218-219 J 2
Mitare o YV 60-61 F 2
Mitau = Jelgava o• LV 94-95 H 3
Mitchell o AUS 178-179 J 4
Mitchell o CDN (ONT) 238-239 D 5
Mitchell o USA (GA) 284-285 H 3
Mitchell o USA (IN) 274-275 M 6
Mitchell o USA (NE) 262-263 C 3
Mitchell o USA (OR) 244-245 E 6
Mitchell o USA (SD) 260-261 H 3
Mitchell, Mount ▲ USA (NC) 282-283 E 5
Mitchell and Alice Rivers National Park ⊥ AUS 174-175 G 4
Mitchell Highway II AUS 178-179 J 6
Mitchell Lake ○ CDN (BC) 228-229 O 4
Mitchell Lake < USA (AL) 284-285 D 4
Mitchell River ∼ AUS 172-173 G 3
Mitchell River ∼ AUS 172-173 G 3
Mitchell River ∼ AUS 174-175 G 4
Mitchell River National Park ⊥ AUS 180-181 J 4
Mitchell's Bay o CDN (ONT) 238-239 C 6
Mitchells Brook o CDN (NFL) 242-243 P 5
Mitchelstown = Baile Mhistéala o IRL 90-91 C 5
Mitchinamécus, Lac ○ CDN (QUE) 236-237 N 5
Mitchinamecus, Rivière ∼ CDN (QUE) 236-237 O 5
Mitémele, Río ∼ GQ 210-211 C 3
Mit Ġamr o ET 194-195 E 2
Mithankot o PK 138-139 C 5
Mitha Tiwāna o PK 138-139 D 3
Mithi o PK 138-139 B 7
Mithimna o GR 100-101 L 5
Miti, Pulau ∩ RI 164-165 L 3
Mitiamo o AUS 180-181 H 4
Mitiaro ∩ NZ 13 M 4
Mitilini ☆• GR 100-101 L 5
Mitji ∼ SN 202-203 D 3
Mitjušiha, guba ○ RUS 108-109 F 5
Mitla ∴• MEX 52-53 F 3
Mitla, Laguna ≈ 52-53 D 3
Mitliktavik o USA 20-21 K 1
Mito ☆ J 152-153 J 6
Mitoko o ZRE 210-211 H 2
Mitole o EAT 214-215 K 5
Mitomoni o EAT 214-215 H 6
Mitre, Peninsula ∪ RA 80 H 7
Mitrofania Island ∩ USA 22-23 R 5
Mitsamiouli o COM 222-223 C 3
Mitsinjo o RM 222-223 D 5
Mitsio, Nosy ∩ RM 222-223 F 4
Mits'iwa o• ER 200-201 J 5
Mits'iwa Channel ≈ 200-201 J 5
Mitsuishi o J 152-153 K 3
Mitsushima o J 152-153 C 7
Mittagong o AUS 174-175 G 6
Mitta Mitta o AUS 180-181 J 4
Mittiebah o AUS 174-175 D 6
Mittlintown o USA (PA) 280-281 J 3
Mitu ☆ CO 66-67 B 2
Mitumba, Monts ▲ ZRE 212-213 B 5
Mitunguu o EAK 212-213 F 4
Mitwaba o ZRE 214-215 D 5
Mityana o EAU 212-213 D 3
Mitzic o G 210-211 C 3
Miura-hanto ∪ J 152-153 H 7
Mius ∼ RUS 102-103 L 4
Mivo River ∼ PNG 184 I b 2
Mixco o• GCA 52-53 J 4
Mixquiahuala o MEX 52-53 E 1
Mixteco, Río ∼ MEX 52-53 E 2
Mixtlán o MEX 52-53 B 1
Miya o WAN 204-205 H 3
Miya-gawa ∼ J 152-153 G 7
Miyāh, Wādī l- ∼ ET 194-195 F 5
Miyake-shima ∩ J 152-153 H 7
Miyako o J 152-153 J 5
Miyakonojō o J 152-153 D 9
Miyāndōab o• IR 128-129 M 4
Miyāne o• IR 128-129 M 4
Miyanoura-dake ▲ J 152-153 D 9
Miya-shima ∩• J 152-153 E 7
Miyazaki ☆ J 152-153 D 9
Miyazu o J 152-153 F 7
Miyi o VRC 156-157 C 3
Miyoshi o J 152-153 E 7
Miyun o VRC (BEI) 154-155 K 1
Miyun • VRC (BEI) 154-155 K 1
Mizāni o AFG 134-135 M 2
Mizan Teferi o ETH 208-209 B 5
Mizdah o LAR 192-193 E 2
Mizen Head ▲ IRL 90-91 C 6
Mizhi o VRC 154-155 G 3
Mizil o RO 102-103 E 5
Mizo Hills ▲ IND 142-143 H 4
Mizoram ◘ IND 142-143 H 4
Mizpah o USA (MT) 250-251 O 5
Mizpah Creek ∼ USA (MT) 250-251 O 5
Mizque o BOL 70-71 E 5
Mizque, Río ∼ BOL 70-71 E 5
Mizur o RUS 126-127 F 6
Mizusawa o J 152-153 J 5
Mjadzel ☆ BY 94-95 K 4
Mjagostrov ∩ RUS 88-89 N 4
Mjakit o RUS 120-121 P 3
Mjangad = Bajanhošuu o MAU 146-147 K 1
Mjanji o EAU 212-213 E 3
Mjatis' ∼ RUS 110-111 Z 6
Mjölby ☆ S 86-87 G 7
Mjonga ∼ EAT (MOR) 214-215 J 4
Mjörn ○ S 86-87 F 8
Mjøsa ○ N 86-87 E 6
Mjurjule ∼ RUS 110-111 X 7
Mkambati Nature Reserve ⊥ ZA 220-221 J 5
Mkanga o EAT 214-215 H 4
Mkata o EAT 212-213 G 6
Mkata ∼ EAT 214-215 J 4
Mkoani o EAT 212-213 G 6
Mkokotoni o EAT 214-215 K 3
Mkomazi Game Reserve ⊥ EAT 212-213 G 6
Mkondoa ∼ EAT 214-215 J 4
Mkondowe o MW 214-215 H 6
Mkonjowano o EAT 214-215 K 6
Mkowe o EAK 212-213 H 5
Mkowela o EAT 214-215 K 6
Mkujani o EAT 212-213 G 6
Mkunumbi o EAK 212-213 H 5
Mkuranga o EAT 214-215 K 4
Mkushi o Z 218-219 E 1
Mkushi ∼ Z 218-219 E 2
Mkushi River o Z 218-219 E 1
Mkuze o ZA (NTL) 220-221 L 3
Mkuze ∼ ZA 220-221 K 3
Mkuzi Game Reserve ⊥ ZA 220-221 L 3
Mkwaja o EAT 212-213 G 6
Mladá Boleslav o• CZ 92-93 N 3
Mladenovac o• YU 100-101 H 2
Mlalo o EAT 212-213 G 6
Mlandizi o EAT 214-215 K 4
M'lang o RP 160-161 F 9
Mława o PL 92-93 Q 2
Mlelin ∼ RUS 112-113 Q 2
Mlenganapas ▲ ZA 220-221 J 5
Mligasi ∼ EAT 212-213 G 6
Mljet ∩ HR 100-101 F 3
Mmabatho ☆ ZA 220-221 G 2
Mmadinare o RB 218-219 D 5
Mmamabula o RB 218-219 D 6
Mmashoro o RB 218-219 D 5
Mmathethe o RB 220-221 G 2
Mmatshumo o RB 218-219 C 5
Mnamuk o RI 166-167 D 3
Mnanzi o EAT 212-213 G 6
Mnarani ∴• EAK 212-213 G 5
Mnjoli Dam < SD 220-221 K 3
Mnogoveršinnyj o RUS 122-123 H 2
Mo ∼ CAM 204-205 H 6
Mo ∼ GH 202-203 L 5
Mô ∼ RT 202-203 L 5
Moa o C 54-55 H 4
Moa ∼ WAL 202-203 E 6
Moa, Pulau ∩ RI 166-167 E 6
Moa, Rio ∼ BR 64-65 F 5
Moab o USA (UT) 254-255 F 5
Moabi o G 210-211 C 5
Moaco, Rio ∼ BR 66-67 C 6
Moai •• RCH 78-79 B 2
Moa Island ∩ AUS 174-175 G 2
Moala ∩ FJI 184 III b 3
Mo'allemān o IR 136-137 D 7
Mo'allem Kalāyeh o IR 136-137 B 6
Moamba o MOC 220-221 L 2
Moanda o G 210-211 D 4
Moanda ∼ ZRE 210-211 G 2
Moapa o USA (NV) 248-249 K 3
Moapa River Indian Reservation ⩇ USA (NV) 248-249 K 3
Móar Bay ≈ 38-39 E 2
Moatize o MOC 218-219 G 3
Moba o ZRE 214-215 E 4
Mobara o J 152-153 J 7
Mobārak, Kūh o IR 134-135 G 6
Mobārake o IR 134-135 D 2
Mobaye ☆• RCA 206-207 E 6
Mobayi-Mbongo o ZRE 206-207 E 6
Mobdoua < RIM 196-197 G 7
Mobeetie o USA (TX) 264-265 D 3
Mobena o ZRE 210-211 G 3
Moberly o USA (MO) 274-275 F 5
Mobert o CDN (ONT) 236-237 C 4
Mobile o USA (AZ) 256-257 C 5
Mobile o• USA (AL) 284-285 B 6
Mobile Bay ≈ 48-49 D 4
Mobile Bay ≈ USA 284-285 B 6
Mobile River ∼ USA (AL) 284-285 B 6
Mobridge o USA (SD) 260-261 F 1
Moca ☆ DOM 54-55 K 5
Moca o GQ 210-211 B 2
Mocajuba o BR 68-69 D 3
Moçambicana ⊥ MOC 218-219 H 5
Moçambique o MOC 218-219 L 2
Moçambique, Ilha de ∩•• MOC 218-219 L 2
Moccasin o USA (AZ) 256-257 C 2
Moccasin o USA (MT) 250-251 K 4
Mộc Châu ☆ VN 156-157 D 6
Mocha, Isla ∩ RCH 78-79 C 5
Mocha = Muḫā, al- o•• Y 132-133 C 7
Mochara, Cordillera de ▲ BOL 76-77 E 1
Moche Pyramids • PE 64-65 C 6
Mochirma, Parque Nacionale ⊥ YV 60-61 J 2
Mochis, Los o MEX 50-51 E 5
Mộc Hóa o VN 158-159 H 5
Mochudi ☆ RB 220-221 H 2
Mochumi o PE 64-65 C 5
Mocimboa da Praia o MOC 214-215 L 6
Mocimboa do Rovuma o MOC 214-215 K 6
Mockonema o USA (WA) 244-245 H 4
Mocksville o USA (NC) 282-283 G 5
Môco ▲ ANG 216-217 C 6
Mocoa ☆ CO 64-65 D 1
Mocoduene o MOC 218-219 H 6
Moções, Rio ∼ BR 62-63 K 6
Mocomoco o BOL 70-71 C 4
Mocorito o MEX 50-51 F 5
Mocotó o BR 68-69 E 3
Moctezuma o MEX (CHA) 50-51 F 2
Moctezuma o MEX (SLP) 50-51 J 6
Moctezuma o MEX (SON) 50-51 E 3
Moctezuma, Río ∼ MEX 50-51 K 7
Mocuba o MOC 218-219 J 3
Mocupe o PE 64-65 C 5
Modan o RI 166-167 G 3
Modane o F 90-91 L 9
Modāsa o IND 138-139 D 8
Modderrivier ∼ ZA 220-221 G 4
Model o USA (CO) 254-255 L 6
Modena o I 100-101 C 2
Modena o USA (UT) 254-255 B 6
Modesto o USA (CA) 248-249 C 2
Modesto Méndez o GCA 52-53 K 4
Modjamboli o ZRE 210-211 H 2
Modjigo ⊥ RN 198-199 F 4
Modoc Point o USA (OR) 244-245 D 8
Modoguhe o CI 202-203 G 6
Modot o MAU 148-149 J 4
Modriča o BIH 100-101 G 2
Moebase o MOC 218-219 K 3
Moeilijk, Pulau ∩ RI 164-165 L 4
Moeko ∼ ZRE 210-211 G 2
Moen o N 86-87 J 2
Moenkopi o USA (AZ) 256-257 D 2
Moenkopi Wash ∼ USA (AZ) 256-257 D 2
Moeraki Boulders • NZ 182 C 6
Moerkesung o VRC 144-145 E 5
Moero, Lac ○ ZRE 214-215 E 5
Moers o D 92-93 J 3
Moe-Yallourn o AUS 180-181 J 5
Moffat o GB 90-91 F 4
Moffat Creek ∼ CDN (BC) 228-229 N 4
Moffat Secton, Mount ⊥ AUS 178-179 J 3
Moffet, Mount ▲ USA 22-23 H 7
Moffet Point ▲ USA 22-23 P 5
Moffit o USA (ND) 258-259 G 5
Mofu o Z 214-215 F 6
Moga ∼ RUS 116-117 O 5
Moga o ZRE 210-211 L 5
Mogadishu = Mugdiisho ★ SP 212-213 K 2
Mogadouro o P 98-99 D 4
Mogalu o ZRE 210-211 G 2
Mogami-gawa ∼ J 152-153 J 5
Moganshan • VRC 154-155 L 6
Mogao Ku •• VRC 146-147 M 5
Mogapinyana o RB 218-219 D 6
Mogaung o MYA 142-143 K 3
Mogdy o RUS (HBR) 122-123 E 3
Mogdy ∼ RUS 116-117 N 3
Mogen o IR 136-137 D 6
Mogens Heinesens Fjord ≈ 28-29 T 5
Mogi Cruzes o BR 72-73 G 7
Mogila ▲ EAK 212-213 E 1
Mogilev = Mahilëv o• BY 94-95 M 5
Mogilno o• PL 92-93 O 2
Mogiľnyj Mys o RUS 114-115 R 5
Mogi-Mirim o BR 72-73 G 7
Mogincual o MOC 218-219 L 2
Mogna o RA 76-77 C 6
Mogna, Sierra de ▲ RA 76-77 C 6
Mogoča ☆ RUS 118-119 J 9
Mogoi o RI 166-167 G 2
Mogojtuj ☆ RUS 118-119 G 10
Mogok o MYA 142-143 K 4
Mogollon Mountains ▲ USA (NM) 256-257 G 5
Mogollon Rim ▲ USA (AZ) 256-257 D 4
Mogotes, Punta ▲ RA 78-79 L 5
Mogotoevo, ozero ○ RUS 110-111 b 3
Mogotón, Cerro ▲ NIC 52-53 L 5
Mogou o RT 202-203 L 4
Mogroum o TCH 206-207 B 3
Mogui Cheng • VRC 146-147 G 2
Mogüye, Bandar-e o IR 134-135 F 5
Mogwase o ZA 220-221 H 2
Mogzon o RUS 118-119 E 10
Mohács o H 92-93 P 5
Mohale's Hoek o LS 220-221 H 5
Mohall o USA (ND) 258-259 F 3
Mohamed 5., Barrage < MA 188-189 K 3
Mohammadābād o IR (ESF) 134-135 E 2
Mohammadābād o IR (KER) 134-135 G 4
Mohammadābād o IR (SIS) 134-135 J 3
Mohammadābād o IR (YAZ) 134-135 F 3
Mohammad Āġā o AFG 138-139 B 2
Mohammadia o DZ 190-191 C 3
Mohammedia o MA 188-189 H 4
Mohana o IND 142-143 D 6
Mohanganj o BD 142-143 G 3
Mohania o IND 142-143 C 3
Mohanpur o NEP 144-145 F 7
Mohave, Lake ○ USA (NV) 248-249 K 4
Mohawk o USA (AZ) 256-257 B 6
Mohawk o USA (WI) 270-271 K 3
Mohawk River ∼ USA (NY) 278-279 G 6
Mohe o VRC 150-151 D 1
Mohej ∼ RUS 118-119 H 7
Mohenjo Daro ∴•• PK 138-139 B 6
Mohican, Cape ▲ USA 20-21 G 6
Moho o PE 70-71 C 4
Mohol o IND 140-141 F 2
Mohon Peak ▲ USA (AZ) 256-257 B 4
Mohoro o EAT 214-215 K 5
Mohovaja ∼ RUS 108-109 V 6
Mohovaja, gora ▲ RUS 88-89 S 2
Mohrungen = Morąg o PL 92-93 P 2
Mohyliv-Podil's'kyj ☆ UA 102-103 E 3
Moiben o EAK 212-213 E 3
Moila Point ▲ PNG 184 I b 2
Moili ∩ COM 222-223 C 4
Moimba o ANG 216-217 B 8
Moin o CR 52-53 C 7
Moincêr o VRC 144-145 C 5
Moinerie, Lac la ○ CDN 36-37 Q 6
Moines, Des o USA (NM) 256-257 M 2
Moines River, Des ∼ USA (IA) 274-275 D 2
Moira o USA (NY) 278-279 G 4
Mo i Rana o N 86-87 G 3
Moirang o IND 142-143 H 3
Mõisaküla o EST 94-95 J 2
Moiseevskaja o RUS 94-95 R 1
Moisie o CDN (QUE) 242-243 B 2
Moisie, Rivière ∼ CDN 38-39 L 3
Moisie, Rivière ∼ CDN (QUE) 242-243 B 2
Moison Lake ○ CDN 34-35 H 3
Moissac o F 90-91 H 9
Moissala o TCH 206-207 C 4
Moitaco o YV 60-61 J 3
Moján, El = San Rafael o YV 60-61 F 2
Mojave o USA (CA) 248-249 F 4
Mojave Desert ⊥ USA (CA) 248-249 G 4
Mojave River ∼ USA (CA) 248-249 G 5
Mojero ∼ RUS 108-109 f 7
Mojero ∼ RUS 116-117 L 2
Mojerokan ∼ RUS 116-117 M 2
Mojiang o VRC 156-157 B 5
Moji Guaçu, Rio ∼ BR 72-73 G 6
Mojiquiçaba o BR 72-73 L 4
Mojkovac o YU 100-101 G 3
Mojo o ETH 208-209 D 4
Mojoagung o RI 168 E 3
Mojokerto o RI 168 E 3
Mojos, Llanos de ⊥ BOL 70-71 D 4
Mojosari o RI 168 E 3
Moju, Rio ∼ BR 68-69 D 3
Mojuí dos Campos o BR 66-67 K 4
Moj-Urusta o RUS 120-121 N 3
Mojyldy o KA 124-125 D 3
Mojynkūm ⊥ KA 124-125 E 5
Mojynty o KA 124-125 H 5
Mōka o J 152-153 J 6
Mokāma o IND 142-143 D 3
Mokambo o ZRE 214-215 E 7
Mokau o NZ 182 E 3
Mokelumne Aqueduct < USA (CA) 246-247 D 5
Mokelumne Hill o USA (CA) 246-247 E 5
Mokgomane o RB 220-221 G 2
Mokhotlong o LS 220-221 J 4
Mokka = al-Muḫā o•• Y 132-133 C 7
Mokla ∼ RUS 118-119 K 8
Moknine o TN 190-191 H 3
Mokoan, Lake ○ AUS 180-181 J 4
Mokobela Pan < RB 218-219 D 5
Mokokchung o IND 142-143 J 2
Mokolo o CAM 204-205 K 3
Mokolo ∼ ZA 220-221 H 2
Mokombe ∼ ZRE 210-211 J 4
Mokoreta o NZ 182 B 7
Mokoto, Lacs ○ ZRE 212-213 B 4
Mokp'o o ROK 150-151 F 10
Mokrous o RUS 96-97 E 8
Mokša ∼ RUS 94-95 T 5
Mōktama Kwe ≈ 158-159 D 2
Mokwa o WAN 204-205 F 4
Mola ∼ GH 202-203 K 5
Moladjakit, gora ▲ RUS 116-117 L 3
Molakalmuru o IND 140-141 G 3
Molalatau o RB 218-219 E 6
Molalē o ETH 208-209 D 3
Molalla o USA (OR) 244-245 C 5
Molas del Norte, Punta ▲ MEX 52-53 L 1
Molat ⊥ HR 100-101 E 2
Moldary o KA 124-125 L 3
Molde ☆ N 86-87 C 5
Moldotau, hrebet ▲ KS 146-147 B 5
Moldova ■ MD 102-103 F 4
Moldova Nouă o RO 102-103 B 5
Molegbe o ZRE 206-207 E 6
Mole Island ∩ PNG 183 D 2
Mole Lake Indian Reservation ⩇ USA (WI) 270-271 K 5
Mole National Park ⊥ GH 202-203 K 5
Molepolole ☆ RB 220-221 G 2
Moleque, Morro do ▲ BR 74-75 F 7
Mole River ∼ AUS 178-179 L 5
Molėtai o LT 94-95 J 4
Molfetta o I 100-101 F 4
Molibagu o RI 164-165 H 3
Molina o E 98-99 G 4
Molina o RCH 78-79 D 3
Molina de Segura o E 98-99 G 5
Moline o USA (IL) 274-275 H 3
Moline o USA (KS) 262-263 K 7
Moline Mine ∴ AUS 172-173 L 2
Molinggapoto o RI 164-165 H 3
Molinillo, Puerto El ▲ E 98-99 F 6
Molino o USA (FL) 286-287 B 1
Molinos, Embalse los < RA 76-77 E 6
Molinos, Los o USA (CA) 246-247 C 3
Moliro o ZRE 214-215 F 5
Molise ◘ I 100-101 E 4
Mol'katy, hrebet ▲ RUS 112-113 J 4
Mollendo o PE 70-71 A 5
Mollepata o PE 64-65 F 8
Moller, Port ≈ 22-23 Q 5
Mollera, zaliv ○ RUS 108-109 E 5
Mollerussa = Mollerussa o E 98-99 H 4
Mollerussa o E 98-99 H 4
Molles, Punta ▲ RCH 78-79 D 2
Molo o EAK (RIF) 212-213 E 4
Molo ∼ EAK 212-213 E 3
Molo o MYA 142-143 K 4
Moločna ∼ UA 102-103 J 4
Moločnyj lyman ≈ 102-103 J 4
Molocopote o BR 62-63 G 5
Molócuè ∼ MOC 218-219 J 2
Molocué, Rio ∼ MOC 218-219 J 2
Molodečno = Maladzečna ☆ BY 94-95 K 4
Molodežnaja o ARK 16 G 5
Molodežnyj ☆ KA 124-125 H 3
Molodëžnyj o RUS 120-121 N 2
Molodo o RMM 202-203 G 2
Molodo ∼ RUS 110-111 N 5
Mologa ∼ RUS 94-95 O 2
Molokai ∩ USA (HI) 288 H 3
Molokai Fracture Zone ≃ 14-15 O 5
Moloma ∼ RUS 96-97 E 4
Molona o RI 164-165 H 6
Molong o AUS 180-181 K 2
Molongda ∼ RUS 112-113 L 4
Molongdinskij hrebet ▲ RUS 112-113 L 4
Molopo ∼ RB 220-221 E 3
Moloporivier ○ ZA 220-221 G 2
Moloskovicy o RUS 94-95 L 2
Moloundou o CAM 210-211 E 2
Molsheim o• F 90-91 L 7
Molt o USA (MT) 250-251 L 6
Molteno o ZA 220-221 H 5
Moltenopas ▲ ZA 220-221 F 6
Moltke Nunatak ▲ GRØ 26-27 o 4
Moltyrkan ∼ RUS 110-111 V 7
Molu, Pulau ∩ RI 166-167 F 5
Molucca, Laut ≈ 164-165 J 3
Moluccas = Maluku ◘ RI 166-167 D 4
Moluccas = Maluku, Kepulauan ∩ RI 166-167 J 2
Molucca Sea = Maluku, Laut ≈ RI 164-165 J 4
Molūki o AFG 136-137 G 7
Molumbo o MOC 218-219 J 2
Molume o GH 202-203 J 5
Molus River o CDN (NB) 240-241 K 4
Molvo ∼ RUS 118-119 H 6
Molwe o ZRE 214-215 C 6
Moma o MOC 218-219 K 3
Moma ∼ RUS 110-111 Y 6
Moma o ZRE 214-215 B 4
Moma, Ilha de ∩ MOC 218-219 K 3
Momaligi o WAL 202-203 D 6
Momats ∼ RI 166-167 K 4
Momba o Z 218-219 E 2
Mombaca o BR 68-69 J 4
Mombasa ☆•• EAK 212-213 G 6
Mombasa Marine National Reserve ⊥ EAK 212-213 G 6
Mombenzélé o RCB 210-211 F 3
Mombetsu o J (HOK) 152-153 K 2
Mombetsu o J (HOK) 152-153 K 3
Mombo ∼ ANG 216-217 F 5
Mombo o EAT 212-213 G 6
Mombongo o ZRE (HAU) 210-211 J 3
Mombongo o ZRE (HAU) 210-211 K 3
Momboyo ∼ ZRE 210-211 G 4
Momburn o RI 166-167 K 6
Momfafa, Tanjung ▲ RI 166-167 F 2
Mommon, Tanjung ▲ RI 166-167 G 3
Momo o RI 164-165 G 4
Momo-Selennjahskaja vpadina ∪ RUS 110-111 W 5
Momote o PNG 183 D 2
Momotombo, Volcán ▲ NIC 52-53 L 5
Mompiche, Ensenada de ≈ 64-65 B 1
Mompog Pass ≈ 160-161 E 6
Mompono o ZRE 210-211 H 3
Mompós o CO 60-61 D 3
Momskij hrebet ▲ RUS 110-111 Y 6
Momskij Khrebet = Momskij hrebet ▲ RUS 110-111 Y 6
Møn ∩ DK 86-87 F 9
Mona o USA (UT) 254-255 D 4
Mona, Isla ∩ USA (PR) 286-287 O 2
Monaco ■ MC 90-91 L 10
Monaco ★• MC 90-91 L 10
Monaco Deep ≃ 6-7 G 5
Monadotua, Pulau ∩ 164-165 J 3
Monadyr o KA 124-125 G 4
Monaghan = Muineachán ☆ IRL 90-91 D 4
Monahans o USA (TX) 266-267 E 2
Monana o G 210-211 D 4
Monango o USA (ND) 258-259 J 5
Mona Passage ≈ 56 A 2
Monapo o MOC 218-219 L 2
Mona Quimbundo o ANG 216-217 E 4
Monarch o CDN (ALB) 232-233 E 6
Monarch o USA (CO) 254-255 J 5
Monarch o USA (MT) 250-251 J 4
Monarch Icefield ⊂ CDN (BC) 228-229 H 4
Monarch Mountain ▲ CDN (BC) 230-231 D 2
Monashee Mountains ▲ CDN (BC) 228-229 P 4
Monashee Provincial Park ⊥ CDN (BC) 230-231 L 3
Monaši o UA 102-103 G 4
Monasterace Marina o I 100-101 F 5
Monastery o CDN (NS) 240-241 O 5
Monastir ☆ TN 190-191 H 3
Monastyrščina ☆ RUS 94-95 M 4
Monatélé o CAM 204-205 J 6
Monati, mys ▲ RUS 120-121 W 6
Monboré o CAM 206-207 B 4
Monção o BR 68-69 F 3
Mončegorsk o RUS 88-89 M 3
Mönchengladbach o D 92-93 J 3
Monchy o CDN (SAS) 232-233 L 6
Moncks Corner o USA (SC) 284-285 K 3
Monclova o MEX 50-51 J 4
Monco Bünnyi o VRC 144-145 F 5
Moncton o CDN (NB) 240-241 L 4
Mondaí o BR 74-75 D 6
Mondamin o USA (IA) 274-275 B 3
Mondego, Cabo ▲ P 98-99 C 4
Mondego, Rio ∼ P 98-99 C 4
Mondjamboli o ZRE 210-211 J 2
Mondjuku o ZRE 210-211 H 4
Mondo o TCH 198-199 G 6
Mondombe o ZRE 210-211 J 4
Mondómo o CO 60-61 C 6
Mondoñedo o• E 98-99 D 3
Mondono o RI 164-165 H 4
Mondovi o• I 100-101 A 2
Mondovi o USA (WI) 270-271 G 6
Mondragone o I 100-101 D 4
Mondrague, Enneri ∼ TCH 198-199 H 2
Mondrain Island ∩ AUS 176-177 G 7
Mondubi, Ponta ▲ BR 74-75 G 5
Monduli o EAT 212-213 F 5
Monduran Reservoir < AUS 178-179 L 3
Mondy o RUS 116-117 K 10
Moné ∼ CAM 204-205 H 6
Moneague o JA 54-55 G 5
Monemvassía o GR 100-101 J 6
Moneragala o CL 140-141 J 7
Moneron, ostrov ∩ RUS 122-123 J 5
Moneta o USA (WY) 252-253 L 3
Monett o USA (MO) 276-277 B 4
Monette o USA (AR) 276-277 E 5
Money Island = Jinyin Dao ∩ VRC 158-159 L 2
Monfalcone o I 100-101 D 2
Monforte o P 98-99 D 5
Monforte (Monforte de Lemos) o• E 98-99 D 3
Monga o ZRE 206-207 F 6
Mongala ∼ ZRE 210-211 H 2
Mongalla o SUD 206-207 K 6
Mongar o BHT 142-143 G 2
Monge o EC 64-65 D 3
Mongemputu o ZRE 210-211 H 5
Monger, Île ∩ CDN 38-39 P 3
Mongeri o WAL 202-203 E 5
Mongers Lake ○ AUS 176-177 D 4
Mongge o RI 166-167 G 2
Monggui o RI 166-167 H 2
Möng Hpayak o MYA 142-143 L 5
Mong Hsan o MYA 142-143 K 5
Möng Hsat o MYA 142-143 L 5
Möng Hsu o MYA 142-143 L 5
Möng Küng o MYA 142-143 K 5
Mongla o BD 142-143 F 4
Möng Mit o MYA 142-143 K 4
Möng Nai o MYA 142-143 K 5
Mongo ☆ TCH 198-199 J 6
Mongočejaha ∼ RUS 108-109 S 5
Mongoj ∼ RUS 118-119 F 9
Mongol Altajn Nuruu ▲ MAU 146-147 J 1
Mongol Els ⊥ MAU 146-147 L 2
Mongolia = Mongol Ard Uls ■ MAU 148-149 E 5
Mongomo o GQ 210-211 C 3
Möngönmort = Bulag o MAU 148-149 J 3
Mongonu o WAN 198-199 F 6
Mongororo o TCH 198-199 L 6
Mongoumba o RCA 210-211 G 2
Möng Ping o MYA 142-143 L 5
Möng Ton o MYA 142-143 L 5
Mongu ☆ Z 218-219 B 2
Mongua o ANG 216-217 C 8
Mongubal, Cachoeira do ∼ BR 66-67 J 5
Mongubal Grande, Cachoeira ∼ BR 66-67 J 5
Mönguel o RIM 196-197 D 6
Möng Yai o MYA 142-143 L 4
Möng Yang o MYA 142-143 L 5
Möng Yawng o MYA 142-143 M 5
Möngyu o MYA 142-143 K 4
Mönhbulag o MAU 148-149 F 4
Monheagan Island ∩ USA (ME) 278-279 M 5
Mönhhaan = Bajasgalant o MAU 148-149 L 4
Mönh Hajrhan ▲ MAU 146-147 K 2
Moni o• RI 168 E 7
Monico o USA (WI) 270-271 J 5
Monida o USA (MT) 250-251 G 7
Monida Pass ▲ USA (ID) 252-253 F 2
Monimpébougou o RMM 202-203 H 2
Moni River ∼ PNG 183 E 5
Monito, Isla ∩ USA (PR) 286-287 O 2
Monitor o CDN (ALB) 232-233 H 4
Monitor Pass ▲ USA (CA) 246-247 F 5
Monitor Range ▲ USA (NV) 246-247 J 5
Monitos o CO 60-61 C 3
Monje o RA 78-79 J 2
Monjes, Islas los ∩ YV 60-61 F 1
Monjolos o BR 72-73 H 5
Monkey Bay o MW 218-219 H 2
Monkey Mia o AUS 176-177 B 2

Mońki o PL 92-93 R 2
Monkira o AUS 178-179 F 3
Monkman Provincial Park ⊥ CDN (BC) 228-229 N 2
Monkoto o ZRE 210-211 H 4
Monkstown o CDN (NFL) 242-243 O 5
Monkstown o USA (TX) 264-265 J 5
Monmouth o USA (IL) 274-275 H 4
Monmouth o USA (OR) 244-245 B 6
Monmouth Mountain ▲ CDN (BC) 230-231 F 3
Mono ~ DY 202-203 L 6
Mono, Caño ~ CO 60-61 G 5
Mono, Punta del ▲ NIC 52-53 C 6
Monobamba o PE 64-65 E 7
Mono Island ⌒ SOL 184 I b 2
Mono Lake ⊖ USA (CA) 246-247 G 5
Monólithos o GR 100-101 L 6
Monolon o AUS 178-179 G 6
Monomoy Point ▲ USA (MA) 278-279 M 7
Monon o USA (IN) 274-275 M 4
Monona o USA (IA) 274-275 G 1
Monopamba o CO 64-65 D 1
Mono Pass ▲ USA (CA) 248-249 F 2
Monos, Los o RA 80 F 3
Monou o TCH 198-199 L 4
Monowai o NZ 182 A 6
Monreal del Campo o E 98-99 G 4
Monroe o CDN (NFL) 242-243 P 4
Monroe o USA (GA) 284-285 G 3
Monroe o USA (IA) 274-275 E 3
Monroe o USA (MI) 272-273 F 6
Monroe o USA (NC) 282-283 G 6
Monroe o USA (NY) 280-281 M 2
Monroe o USA (OH) 280-281 B 4
Monroe o USA (OR) 244-245 B 6
Monroe o USA (UT) 254-255 C 5
Monroe o USA (WA) 244-245 D 3
Monroe o USA (WI) 274-275 J 2
Monroe o• USA (LA) 268-269 H 4
Monroe, Lake ⊖ USA (FL) 286-287 H 3
Monroe City o USA (MO) 274-275 G 5
Monroe Lake ~ USA (IN) 274-275 M 5
Monroeville o USA (AL) 284-285 C 5
Monroeville o USA (PA) 280-281 G 3
Monrovia ★• LB 202-203 E 6
Mons ☆• B 92-93 G 3
Monsenhor Gil o BR 68-69 G 4
Monsenhor Hipolito o BR 68-69 H 5
Monserat, Isla ⌒ MEX 50-51 D 5
Møns Klint ⌣·· DK 86-87 F 9
Monsombougou o RMM 202-203 E 2
Montagne d'Ambre, Parc National de la ⊥ RM 222-223 F 4
Montagne du Pin, Lac de la ⊖ CDN 38-39 G 2
Montagnes Françaises ▲ F 62-63 G 3
Montagu o ZA 220-221 E 6
Montague o CDN (PEI) 240-241 N 4
Montague o USA (TX) 264-265 G 5
Montague Island ⌒ AUS 180-181 L 4
Montague Island ⌒ USA 20-21 R 6
Montague Sound ≈ 172-173 G 3
Montague Strait ≈ 20-21 Q 7
Montaigu o F 90-91 G 8
Montajtas o KA 136-137 L 3
Montalbán o E 98-99 G 4
Montalbo o E 98-99 F 5
Montalegre o ANG 216-217 D 4
Montalegre o P 98-99 D 4
Montalto (Monte Cocuzza) ▲ I 100-101 E 5
Montalvânia o BR 72-73 H 3
Montalvo o EC 64-65 D 3
Montana ☆ BG 102-103 C 6
Montana ◘ USA (MT) 250-251 H 5
Montaña, La ⊥ PE 64-65 E 5
Montana City o USA (MT) 250-251 H 5
Montaña de Yoro, Parque Nacional ⊥ HN 52-53 L 4
Montañas de Onzole ▲ EC 64-65 C 1
Montandón o RCH 76-77 C 4
Mont-Apica o CDN (QUE) 240-241 D 3
Montargis o F 90-91 J 8
Montauban ☆• F 90-91 H 9
Montauk o USA (NY) 280-281 P 2
Montauk Point ▲ USA (NY) 280-281 P 2
Montbard o F 90-91 K 8
Mont Bata o RCA 206-207 B 6
Montbéliard o• F 90-91 L 8
Mont Blanc ▲·· F 90-91 L 9
Montceau-les-Mines o F 90-91 K 8
Montcerf o CDN (QUE) 238-239 J 2
Mont Darwin o ZW 218-219 F 3
Mont-de-Marsan ☆ F 90-91 G 10
Mont-Dore, le o F 90-91 J 9
Monte, Laguna del ⊖ RA 78-79 H 4
Monteagle o AUS 178-179 J 2
Monteagle o USA (TN) 276-277 K 5
Monteagudo o BOL 70-71 F 6
Monteagudo o RA 76-77 K 4
Monte Alban ∴··· MEX 52-53 F 3
Monte Alegre o BR 62-63 G 6
Monte Alegre de Goiás o BR 72-73 G 2
Monte Alegre de Minas o BR 72-73 F 5
Monte Alegre de Sergipe o BR 68-69 K 7
Monte Aprazível o BR 72-73 F 6
Monte Azul o BR 72-73 J 3
Montebello o CDN (QUE) 238-239 L 3
Montebello Islands ⌒ AUS 172-173 B 6
Monte Belo o ANG 216-217 C 6
Monte Bianco = Mont Blanc ▲·· I 100-101 A 2
Monte-Carlo o MC 90-91 L 10
Monte Carmelo o BR 72-73 G 5
Monte Caseros o RA 76-77 J 6
Monte Castelo o BR 74-75 E 6
Montecito o USA (CA) 248-249 E 5
Monte Comán o RA 78-79 F 3
Monte Creek o CDN (BC) 230-231 K 3
Monte Cristi ☆ DOM 54-55 K 5
Montecristi o EC 64-65 B 2
Monte Cristi, Parque Nacional ⊥ DOM 54-55 K 5
Monte Cristo o BR 66-67 D 5
Monte Cristo o USA (WA) 244-245 D 3
Montecristo, Cerro ▲ ES 52-53 K 4
Montecristo, Ísola di ⌒ I 100-101 C 3
Monte Dourado o BR 62-63 H 6
Monte Escobedo o MEX 50-51 H 6
Montego Bay o• JA 54-55 G 5
Monte Grande ⊥ BOL 70-71 F 5
Monte Grande o NIC 52-53 B 5
Monte Hermoso o RA 78-79 J 5
Monteiro o BR 68-69 K 5
Monteiro Lobato o BR 72-73 H 7
Monte Lake o CDN (BC) 230-231 K 3
Monte León, Cerro ▲ RA 80 F 5
Montélimar o F 90-91 K 9
Monte Limar o NIC 52-53 L 6
Monte Lindo, Arroyo ~ RA 76-77 H 3
Monte Lindo, Río ~ PY 76-77 J 2
Monte Lindo Grande, Riacho ~ RA 76-77 H 3
Montello o USA (NV) 246-247 L 2
Montello o USA (WI) 270-271 J 7
Montemayor, Meseta de ⊥ RA 80 G 2
Montemorelos o MEX 50-51 K 5
Montemor-o-Novo o P 98-99 C 5
Montenegro o BR 74-75 E 7
Montenegro = Crna gora ◘ YU 100-101 G 3
Monte Negro, Quedas de ~ ANG 216-217 B 8
Monte Pascoal, Parque Nacional de ⊥ BR 72-73 L 4
Monte Patria o RCH 76-77 B 6
Monte Peruvia • PE 64-65 D 4
Montepescali o I 100-101 C 3
Montepío o MEX 52-53 G 2
Monte Plata ☆ DOM 54-55 L 5
Montepuez o MOC 218-219 K 1
Montepuez, Rio ~ MOC 218-219 K 1
Montepulciano o• I 100-101 C 3
Monte Quemado o RA 76-77 F 3
Monterey o USA (TN) 276-277 K 4
Monterey o USA (VA) 280-281 G 5
Monterey o• USA (CA) 248-249 C 3
Montería ☆ CO 60-61 D 3
Montero o BOL 70-71 F 5
Monteros o RA 76-77 E 4
Monte Rosa ▲ CH 92-93 J 6
Monte Rosa ▲ I 100-101 A 2
Monterrey ☆• MEX 50-51 J 5
Monterrey, Parque Nacional de ⊥ MEX 50-51 J 5
Monterrey Bay ≈ 40-41 D 7
Monterrey Bay ≈ USA 248-249 C 3
Monterrico o GCA 52-53 J 5
Monterrubio o CO 60-61 D 2
Montes, Punta ▲ RA 80 F 5
Montes Altos o BR 68-69 E 4
Montesano o USA (WA) 244-245 B 3
Montesano sulla Marcellana o I 100-101 E 4
Monte Sant'Ángelo o I 100-101 E 4
Monte Santo o BR 68-69 J 7
Monte Santo de Minas o BR 72-73 G 6
Montes Claros o BR 72-73 J 4
Montes de Oca o RA 78-79 H 5
Montesquieu Islands ⌒ AUS 172-173 G 3
Montevallo o USA (AL) 284-285 D 3
Montevideo ★• ROU 78-79 L 3
Montevideo o USA (MN) 270-271 C 6
Monte Vista o USA (CO) 254-255 J 6
Monte Vista National Wildlife Refuge • USA (CO) 254-255 J 6
Montezuma o BR 72-73 J 3
Montezuma o USA (GA) 284-285 F 4
Montezuma o USA (IA) 274-275 F 3
Montezuma o USA (IN) 274-275 L 5
Montezuma Castle National Monument ∴ USA (AZ) 256-257 D 4
Montezuma Creek o USA (UT) 254-255 F 6
Montezuma Creek ~ USA (UT) 254-255 F 6
Montfort o USA (WI) 274-275 H 2
Montgomery o USA (LA) 268-269 H 5
Montgomery o USA (MN) 270-271 E 6
Montgomery o USA (WV) 280-281 E 5
Montgomery ☆• USA (AL) 284-285 D 4
Montgomery = Sāhīwāl o PK 138-139 D 4
Montgomery City o USA (MO) 274-275 G 6
Montgomery Islands ⌒ AUS 172-173 G 3
Monticello o USA (AR) 276-277 D 7
Monticello o USA (FL) 286-287 F 1
Monticello o USA (GA) 284-285 G 3
Monticello o USA (IA) 274-275 G 2
Monticello o USA (IL) 274-275 K 4
Monticello o USA (KY) 276-277 L 4
Monticello o USA (MN) 270-271 E 5
Monticello o USA (MO) 274-275 G 4
Monticello o USA (MS) 268-269 K 5
Monticello o USA (NM) 256-257 H 5
Monticello o USA (NY) 280-281 M 2
Monticello o USA (SC) 284-285 J 2
Monticello o USA (UT) 254-255 F 6
Monticello ··· USA (VA) 280-281 H 6
Montijo o E 98-99 D 5
Montijo, Golfo de ≈ 52-53 D 8
Montilla o E 98-99 E 6
Montima ~ ZRE 210-211 H 2
Montipa o ANG 216-217 B 7
Montividiu o BR 72-73 E 4
Mont-Louis o F 90-91 J 10
Montluçon o F 90-91 J 8
Montmagny o CDN (QUE) 240-241 E 4
Montmarault o F 90-91 J 8
Montmartre o CDN (SAS) 232-233 P 5
Mont Nebo o CDN (SAS) 232-233 M 2
Monto o AUS 178-179 L 3
Montoro o• E 98-99 E 5
Montoya o USA (NM) 256-257 L 3
Montpelier o JA 54-55 G 5
Montpelier o USA (ID) 252-253 G 4
Montpelier o USA (IN) 274-275 N 4
Montpelier o USA (ND) 258-259 J 5
Montpelier o USA (VA) 280-281 J 6
Montpelier ☆ USA (VT) 278-279 J 4
Montpellier ☆• F 90-91 J 10
Montpensier, Kap ▲ GRØ 26-27 r 5
Montréal o• CDN (QUE) 238-239 M 3
Montreal Falls ~ CDN (ONT) 236-237 D 5
Montreal Lake o CDN (SAS) 34-35 D 3
Montreal Lake ⊖ CDN (SAS) 34-35 D 3
Montreal Lake Indian Reserve ⅹ CDN (SAS) 232-233 N 2
Montreal River o CDN (ONT) 236-237 D 5
Montreal River ~ CDN (ONT) 236-237 E 5
Montreal River ~ CDN (ONT) 236-237 H 5
Montreux o• CH 92-93 J 5
Montrose o CDN (BC) 230-231 M 4
Montrose o GB 90-91 F 3
Montrose o USA (AR) 276-277 D 7
Montrose o USA (CO) 254-255 H 5
Montrose o USA (IA) 274-275 G 4
Montrose o USA (IL) 274-275 K 5
Montrose o USA (PA) 280-281 L 2
Montrose Wildlife Area ⊥ USA (MO) 274-275 D 6
Montrouis o RH 54-55 J 5
Monts, Pointe des ▲ CDN (QUE) 242-243 A 3
Mont Saint-Michel, le o··· F 90-91 G 7
Mont Sangbé, Parc National du ⊥ CI 202-203 G 5
Mont Selinda o ZW 218-219 G 5
Montserrat Island ⌒ GB 56 D 3
Monturaqui o RCH 76-77 C 3
Monument o USA (CO) 254-255 L 4
Monument o USA (NM) 256-257 M 6
Monument o USA (OR) 244-245 F 6
Monument, The o AUS 178-179 E 1
Monument Draw ~ USA (TX) 264-265 B 6
Monument Hill State Historic Site ∴ USA (TX) 266-267 L 4
Monument Pass ▲ USA (AZ) 256-257 E 2
Monument Rocks ∴ USA (KS) 262-263 F 6
Monument Valley ⌣ USA (UT) 254-255 E 6
Monument Valley Navajo Tribal Park ⊥• USA (AZ) 256-257 E 2
Monywa o MYA 142-143 J 4
Monza o• I 100-101 B 2
Monza o VRC 144-145 J 4
Monze o Z 218-219 D 3
Monzón o• E 98-99 H 4
Monzon o PE 64-65 D 6
Mooat, Danau ⊖ RI 164-165 J 3
Moodiarrup o AUS 176-177 D 6
Moody o USA (TX) 266-267 K 2
Mooirivier ~ ZA 220-221 H 3
Mooirivier ~ ZA 220-221 K 4
Mooketsi o ZA 218-219 F 6
Mooki River ~ AUS 178-179 L 6
Moola, Rio ~ MOC 214-215 H 6
Mooloo Downs o AUS 176-177 D 2
Mooloogool o AUS 176-177 E 3
Mooloolo Out Station o AUS 172-173 K 4
Moomaw, Lake ⊖ USA (VA) 280-281 G 5
Moomba o AUS 178-179 F 4
Moomin Creek ~ AUS 178-179 K 5
Moonan Flat o AUS 178-179 L 6
Moonaree o AUS 178-179 C 6
Moonbeam o CDN (ONT) 236-237 F 3
Moonbi Range ▲ AUS 178-179 L 6
Moonda Lake ⊖ AUS 178-179 F 3
Moondarra, Lake ⊖ AUS 174-175 E 7
Moonie o AUS 178-179 L 4
Moonie Highway II AUS 178-179 L 4
Moonie River ~ AUS 178-179 K 4
Moonie River ~ AUS 178-179 K 5
Moonlight Head ▲ AUS 180-181 G 5
Moonta Bay o AUS 180-181 D 3
Moonya o AUS 178-179 H 2
Moor, Kepulauan ⌒ RI 166-167 H 3
Moora o AUS 176-177 D 5
Mooraberree o AUS 178-179 F 3
Moorarie o AUS 176-177 D 2
Moorcroft o USA (WY) 252-253 O 2
Moordkuil o ZA 220-221 D 6
Moore o USA (ID) 252-253 E 3
Moore o USA (MT) 250-251 K 5
Moore o USA (OK) 264-265 G 3
Moore o USA (TX) 266-267 H 4
Moore, Lake ⊖ AUS 176-177 D 4
Moore, Mount ▲ AUS 176-177 G 2
Moore Bay ≈ 24-25 N 2
Moorefield o USA (WV) 280-281 H 4
Moorefield River ~ USA (WV) 280-281 G 5
Moore Haven o USA (FL) 286-287 H 5
Moore Home State Historic Site • USA (IL) 274-275 K 5
Mooreland o USA (OK) 264-265 E 2
Moore Mountain ▲ USA (ID) 252-253 B 3
Moore Park o AUS 178-179 M 3
Moore Park o CDN (MAN) 234-235 D 4
Moore River ~ AUS 176-177 C 5
Moore River National Park ⊥ AUS 176-177 C 5
Moores Bridge o USA (AL) 284-285 C 3
Moores Creek National Battlefield • USA (NC) 282-283 J 6
Moore's Island ⌒ BS 54-55 G 1
Moorestown o USA (MI) 272-273 E 3
Mooresville o USA (NC) 282-283 G 5
Mooreton o USA (ND) 258-259 L 5
Moorhead o USA (MN) 270-271 B 4
Moorhead o USA (MS) 268-269 K 3
Mooirivier o ZA 220-221 K 4
Moornanyah Lake ⊖ AUS 180-181 G 2
Moorpark o USA (CA) 248-249 F 5
Moose o USA (WY) 252-253 H 3
Moosehead Lake ⊖ USA (ME) 278-279 M 3
Moose Heights o CDN (BC) 228-229 M 3
Moose Hill o CDN (ONT) 234-235 O 6
Moosehorn o CDN (MAN) 234-235 E 3
Moose Island ⌒ CDN (MAN) 234-235 F 3
Moose Jaw o CDN (SAS) 232-233 N 5
Moose Jaw Creek ~ CDN (SAS) 232-233 O 5
Moose Lake o CDN (MAN) 34-35 F 4
Moose Lake ⊖ CDN (MAN) 34-35 G 4
Moose Lake o USA (MN) 270-271 F 4
Mooselookmeguntic Lake ⊖ USA (ME) 278-279 L 4
Moose Mount ▲ CDN (SAS) 232-233 Q 6
Moose Mountain Creek ~ CDN (SAS) 232-233 P 5
Moose Mount Provincial Park ⊥ CDN (SAS) 232-233 Q 6
Moose Pass o USA 20-21 Q 6
Moose River o CDN (ONT) 236-237 G 2
Moose River ~ CDN 34-35 Q 5
Moosomin o CDN (SAS) 232-233 R 5
Moosonee o CDN 34-35 Q 5
Mootwingee Historic Site • AUS 178-179 G 6
Mootwingee National Park ⊥ AUS 178-179 G 6
Mopádu o IND 140-141 H 3
Mopán, Río ~ GCA 52-53 K 3
Mopane o ZA 218-219 E 6
Mopeia o MOC 218-219 H 3
Mopipi o RB 218-219 C 5
Mopti ◘ RMM 202-203 H 2
Mopti ☆ RMM (MOP) 202-203 H 2
Moqām, Bandar-e o IR 134-135 E 5
Moquegua ☆ PE 70-71 B 5
Moquegua, Río ~ PE 70-71 B 5
Moquehuá o RA 78-79 K 3
Mór o H 92-93 P 5
Mora o CAM 206-207 B 3
Mora o E 98-99 F 5
Mora o P 98-99 C 5
Mora o S 86-87 G 6
Mora o USA (MN) 270-271 E 5
Mora o USA (NM) 256-257 K 3
Mora, La o RA 78-79 F 3
Morab o IND 140-141 F 3
Morača ~ YU 100-101 G 3
Moradabad o IND 138-139 G 5
Morada Nova o BR 68-69 J 4
Morada Nova de Minas o BR 72-73 H 5
Morado, Quebrada del ~ RCH 76-77 B 4
Morado I, Cerro ▲ RA 76-77 E 2
Moraes o BR 74-75 D 8
Morafeno o RM 222-223 E 6
Morafenobe o RM 222-223 D 6
Morag o PL 92-93 P 2
Morai o RI 166-167 H 5
Moraine State Park ⊥ USA (PA) 280-281 F 3
Morais de Almeida o BR 66-67 K 6
Morajuana o GUY 62-63 E 1
Moralana Creek ~ AUS 178-179 E 6
Moraleja o E 98-99 D 4
Moramanga o RM 222-223 F 7
Moran o USA (KS) 262-263 L 7
Moran o USA (MI) 272-273 E 2
Moran o USA (TX) 264-265 E 6
Moran o USA (WY) 252-253 H 3
Morán, Laguna ⊖ RA 78-79 K 2
Moranbah o AUS 178-179 K 2
Moran River ~ AUS 172-173 G 3
Morant Bay o JA 54-55 G 6
Morant Cays ⌒ JA 54-55 H 6
Morappur o IND 140-141 H 4
Morarano o RM 222-223 E 8
Morarano-Chrome o RM 222-223 F 6
Mora River ~ USA (NM) 256-257 L 3
Moratalla o E 98-99 G 5
Moratuwa o CL 140-141 H 7
Moraújo o BR 68-69 H 3
Morava ⊥ CZ 92-93 O 4
Morava ~ CZ 92-93 O 4
Moravia o USA (IA) 274-275 F 4
Moravia o USA (NY) 278-279 E 6
Morávia, Planalto de ▲ MOC 218-219 F 2
Moravian Falls o USA (NC) 282-283 F 4
Morawa o AUS 176-177 C 4
Moray Downs o AUS 178-179 J 1
Moray Firth ≈ 90-91 E 3
Morazán o HN 52-53 L 4
Morbanipari, Mount ▲ PNG 183 B 3
Morbi o IND 138-139 C 8
Mörbylånga ☆ S 86-87 H 8
Morcego o BR 66-67 F 4
Morden o CDN (MAN) 234-235 E 5
Mordovo o RUS 94-95 R 5
Mordovskij zopovednik ⊥ RUS 94-95 S 4
Mordvinia = Mordovskaja Respublika ◘ RUS 94-95 S 4
Mordvinof, Cape ▲ USA 22-23 O 5
Mordvinova, zaliv ⊖ RUS 122-123 K 5
Mordyjaha ~ RUS 108-109 N 6
Mor'e o RUS 94-95 M 1
Moreau River ~ USA (SD) 260-261 F 1
Morecambe o CDN (ALB) 232-233 G 2
Morecambe o GB 90-91 F 4
Moree o AUS 178-179 K 5
Moreh o IND 142-143 J 3
Morehead o PNG 183 A 5
Morehead o USA (KY) 276-277 M 2
Morehead City o USA (NC) 282-283 L 6
Morehead River ~ PNG 183 A 5
Moreira, Arroyo ~ RA 76-77 H 6
More-Ju ~ RUS 108-109 H 8
Morela, Ponta ▲ CV 202-203 C 6
Morelia o CO 64-65 E 1
Morelia ☆··· MEX 52-53 D 2
Morell o CDN (PEI) 240-241 N 4
Morella o AUS 178-179 G 2
Morella o E 98-99 G 4
Morelos o MEX (COA) 50-51 H 3
Morelos o MEX (COA) 50-51 J 3
Morelos ◘ MEX 52-53 E 2
Morembe o RM 222-223 C 8
Moremi Wildlife Reserve ⊥ RB 218-219 B 4
Morena o IND 138-139 F 6
Morena, Cachoeira ~ BR 66-67 H 4
Morena, Salto da ~ BR 66-67 H 6
Morena, Sierra ▲ E 98-99 E 5
Morenci o USA (AZ) 256-257 F 5
Morenci o USA (MI) 272-273 E 6
Morenero o YV 60-61 K 3
Moreno o BR 68-69 L 6
Moreno o RA 78-79 K 3
Moreno, Bahía ≈ 76-77 B 2
Moreno, Sierra de ▲ RCH 76-77 C 1
Moreno Chillanes o EC 64-65 C 2
Moreno Valley o USA (CA) 248-249 G 6
Moresby Camp o CDN (BC) 228-229 B 3
Moresby Island ⌒ CDN (BC) 228-229 C 4
Mores Creek Summit ▲ USA (ID) 252-253 C 3
Moreton, Cape ▲ AUS 178-179 M 4
Moreton Bay ≈ 178-179 M 4
Moreton Island ⌒ AUS 178-179 M 4
Moreton Post Office o AUS 174-175 G 3
Morewood o CDN (ONT) 238-239 K 3
Morfou o TR 128-129 E 5
Morgāb o AFG 136-137 H 7
Morgāb, Daryā-ye ~ AFG 136-137 H 7
Morgābrūd, Daryā-ye ~ AFG 136-137 J 7
Morgan o AUS 180-181 E 3
Morgan o USA (MN) 270-271 D 6
Morgan o USA (TX) 264-265 G 6
Morgan o USA (UT) 254-255 D 2
Morgana, proliv ≈ 84-85 h 2
Morgan City o USA (AL) 284-285 D 2
Morgan City o USA (LA) 268-269 J 7
Morgan Creek ~ USA (MT) 250-251 N 3
Morganfield o USA (KY) 276-277 H 3
Morgan Hill o USA (CA) 248-249 C 2
Morgan Mill o USA (TX) 264-265 F 6
Morgan's Corner o USA (NC) 282-283 L 4
Morganton o USA (NC) 282-283 F 5
Morgantown o USA (IN) 274-275 M 5
Morgantown o USA (KY) 276-277 J 3
Morgantown o USA (WV) 280-281 G 4
Morgan Vale o AUS 180-181 F 2
Morgenzon o ZA 220-221 J 3
Morgim o IND 140-141 E 3
Morhaja ~ RUS 118-119 D 4
Morhiban, Lac de ⊖ CDN 38-39 N 2
Mori o J 152-153 J 3
Mori o VRC 146-147 K 4
Moriah, Mount ▲ USA (NV) 246-247 L 4
Moriarty o USA (NM) 256-257 J 3
Moribaya o RG 202-203 F 5
Morice Lake ⊖ CDN (BC) 228-229 G 2
Morice River ~ CDN (BC) 228-229 G 2
Moricetown o CDN 32-33 G 4
Morichal Largo, Río ~ YV 60-61 K 3
Morichal Viejo o CO 60-61 F 6
Morigbadougou o RG 202-203 F 5
Morigim o IND 140-141 E 3
Morigio Island ⌒ PNG 183 B 4
Morija o LS 220-221 H 4
Morijo o EAK 212-213 E 4
Moriki o WAN 198-199 C 6
Morin Dawa o VRC 150-151 E 3
Morin Heights o CDN (QUE) 238-239 L 3
Morinville o CDN (ALB) 232-233 E 2
Morioka ☆• J 152-153 J 5
Morire o MOC 218-219 H 3
Mori River ~ PNG 183 E 5
Moristyj, ostrov ⌒ RUS 126-127 G 5
Morita, La o MEX 50-51 G 3
Moriyama o J 152-153 F 7
Morjakovskij Zaton o RUS 114-115 S 6
Morjen ~ PK 134-135 K 4
Morki ☆ RUS 96-97 F 5
Morkill River ~ CDN (BC) 228-229 O 3
Morkoka ~ RUS 116-117 O 2
Morkoka ~ RUS 118-119 G 3
Morlaix o F 90-91 F 7
Morland o USA (KS) 262-263 F 5
Morley o CDN (ALB) 232-233 D 4
Mormanno o I 100-101 E 5
Mormon Lake o USA (AZ) 256-257 D 4
Mormon Lake ⊖ USA (AZ) 256-257 D 4
Mormon Print Shop • USA (MI) 272-273 D 2
Mormon Range ▲ USA (NV) 248-249 K 3
Morne-à-L'eau o F 56 E 3
Morne Seychellois National Park ⊥ SY 224 D 2
Morney o AUS 178-179 F 3
Morningside o CDN (ALB) 232-233 E 3
Morning Star o USA (MS) 268-269 K 4
Mornington, Isla ⌒ RCH 80 C 4
Mornington Abyssal Plain ≈ 5 C 1
Mornington Island ⌒ AUS 174-175 E 5
Mornington Island Aboriginal Land Trust ⅹ AUS 174-175 E 5
Moro o PE 64-65 C 6
Moro o PK 138-139 B 6
Moro o USA (OR) 244-245 E 5
Moro, Arroyo el ~ RA 78-79 K 5
Moroak o AUS 174-175 B 4
Moro Bay o USA (AR) 276-277 C 7
Morobe o PNG 183 D 4
Morobo o SUD 212-213 C 2
Morocco o USA (IN) 274-275 L 4
Morocco = al-Maghrib ◘ MA 188-189 H 4
Morococala, Cerro ▲ BOL 70-71 D 6
Moro Creek ~ USA (AR) 276-277 C 7
Morodougou o RN 202-203 F 4
Morogari < SP 208-209 F 6
Morogoro ◘ EAT 214-215 J 5
Morogoro ☆ EAT 214-215 J 4
Moro Gulf ≈ 160-161 E 9
Moroiemu o RI 166-167 K 5
Morokweng o ZA 220-221 F 3
Moromaho, Pulau ⌒ RI 166-167 C 5
Morón o C 54-55 F 3
Mörön ☆ MAU 148-149 E 3
Morón o RA 78-79 K 3
Moron o USA (UT) 254-255 D 4
Morón o YV 60-61 G 2
Morona, Río ~ PE 64-65 D 4
Morondava o RM 222-223 D 8
Morón de la Frontera o E 98-99 E 6
Morondo o CI 202-203 G 5
Morongo Indian Reservation ⅹ USA (CA) 248-249 H 5
Moroni ★• COM 222-223 C 3
Moronou o CI 202-203 H 6
Morošečnaja ~ RUS 120-121 R 5
Morotai, Pulau ⌒ RI 164-165 L 2
Morotai, Selat ≈ 164-165 K 2
Moroto ☆ EAU 212-213 E 2
Moroto, Mount ▲ EAU 212-213 E 2
Morouba o RCA 206-207 E 5
Morowali o RI 164-165 G 4
Morowali Reserve ⊥• RI 164-165 G 4
Morozova, mys ▲ RUS 108-109 f 2
Morozovsk o RUS 102-103 M 3
Morpará o BR 68-69 G 7
Morpeth o GB 90-91 G 4
Morrasale o RUS 108-109 M 7
Morreesburg o ZA 220-221 D 6
Morretes o BR 74-75 F 5
Morrillito, Isla ⌒ USA (PR) 286-287 P 3
Morrilton o USA (AR) 276-277 C 5
Morrin o CDN (ALB) 232-233 F 4
Morrinhos o BR (CEA) 68-69 H 3
Morrinhos o BR (GOI) 72-73 F 4
Morrinhos o BR (MAR) 68-69 E 6
Morrinhos, Cachoeira ~ BR 66-67 E 7
Morrinsville o NZ 182 E 2
Morrión, El o MEX 50-51 G 3
Morris o CDN (MAN) 234-235 F 5
Morris o USA (IL) 274-275 K 3
Morris o USA (MN) 270-271 C 5
Morris o USA (NY) 278-279 F 6
Morris o USA (OK) 264-265 J 3
Morris o USA (PA) 280-281 J 2
Morris, Mount ▲ AUS 178-179 H 3
Morrisburg o CDN (ONT) 238-239 K 4
Morris Jesup, Kap ▲ GRØ 26-27 j 2
Morris Jesup Gletscher ⊂ GRØ 26-27 P 5
Morrison Bay ≈ 158-159 E 5
Morriston o USA (FL) 286-287 G 2
Morristown o USA (AZ) 256-257 C 5
Morristown o USA (NJ) 280-281 M 3
Morristown o USA (NY) 278-279 F 4
Morristown o USA (SD) 260-261 E 1
Morristown o USA (TN) 282-283 D 4
Morrisville o USA (NY) 278-279 F 6
Morrisville o USA (VT) 278-279 J 4
Morro o EC 64-65 B 3
Morro, Canal de ≈ 64-65 B 3
Morro, Punta ▲ MEX 52-53 J 2
Morro, Punta ▲ RCH 76-77 B 4
Morro, Sierra del ▲ RA 78-79 G 2
Morro Agudo o BR 72-73 F 6
Morro Bay o USA (CA) 248-249 D 4
Morro Chico o RCH 80 E 6
Morrocoy, Parque Nacional ⊥ YV 60-61 G 2
Morro de Coco o BR 72-73 K 6
Morro do Alvarenga o BR 66-67 D 6
Morro do Chapéu o BR 68-69 H 7
Morro do Pilar o BR 72-73 J 5
Morropón o PE 64-65 C 4
Morro River ~ WAL 202-203 E 6
Morros o BR 68-69 F 3
Morrosquillo, Golfo de ≈ 60-61 D 3
Morrowville o USA (KS) 262-263 K 5
Morrumbala o MOC 218-219 H 3
Morrumbene o MOC 218-219 H 6
Moršank o RUS 94-95 R 5
Morse o CDN (SAS) 232-233 L 5
Morse o USA (TX) 264-265 C 2
Morse Reservoir ⊖ USA (IN) 274-275 M 4
Morsi o IND 138-139 G 9
Morskoj, aral ⌒ KA 126-127 J 5
Morskoj, ostrov ⌒ KA 126-127 J 5
Morskoj Birjučok, ostrov ⌒ RUS 126-127 G 5
Morsø ⌒ DK 86-87 D 8
Morson o CDN (ONT) 234-235 J 5
Morstone o AUS 174-175 E 6
Mørsvikbotn o N 86-87 G 3
Mort, Chutes de la ~ RM 222-223 F 7
Mortandade, Cachoeira ~ BR 68-69 E 5
Mortara o I 100-101 B 2
Morteros o RA 76-77 F 6
Mortes, Rio das ~ BR 72-73 E 3
Mortesoro o SUD 208-209 B 3
Mortimers o• BS 54-55 H 3
Mortlach o CDN (SAS) 232-233 M 5
Mortlake o AUS 180-181 G 5
Morton o USA (IL) 274-275 J 4
Morton o USA (MN) 270-271 D 6
Morton o USA (MS) 268-269 L 4
Morton o USA (TX) 264-265 B 5
Morton o USA (WA) 244-245 C 4
Morton National Park ⊥ AUS 180-181 L 3
Mort River ~ AUS 178-179 F 1
Mortugaba o BR 72-73 J 3
Moruga o TT 60-61 L 2
Moruita o EAU 212-213 E 3
Morundah o AUS 180-181 J 3
Moruppatti o IND 140-141 H 5
Moruya o AUS 180-181 L 3
Morven o AUS 178-179 J 4
Morven o USA (GA) 284-285 G 6
Morven o USA (NC) 282-283 G 6
Morvongole ▲ EAU 212-213 E 2
Morweena o CDN (MAN) 234-235 F 4
Morwell o AUS 180-181 J 5
Morzhovoi Bay ≈ 22-23 P 5
Moržovec, ostrov ⌒ RUS 88-89 R 3
Mosa o PNG 183 F 3
Moša ~ RUS 88-89 Q 5
Mosby o USA (MT) 250-251 M 5
Mosca o USA (CO) 254-255 K 6
Moscas, Las o RA 78-79 K 2
Mosconi o RA 78-79 J 3
Moscow o USA (ID) 250-251 C 5
Moscow o USA (KS) 262-263 E 7
Moscow o USA (TN) 276-277 G 5
Moscow = Moskva ★··· RUS 94-95 P 4
Mosel ~ D 92-93 J 4
Moselebe ~ RB 220-221 F 2
Moselle ~ F 90-91 L 7
Moselle o USA (MS) 268-269 L 5
Moselle Swamp ⊖ USA (SC) 284-285 K 3
Mošens'ka dubrava • UA 102-103 G 3
Moser River o CDN (NS) 240-241 N 6
Mosers River o CDN (NS) 240-241 N 6
Moses o USA (NM) 256-257 M 2
Moses, Mount ▲ USA (NV) 246-247 H 3
Moses Lake o• USA (WA) 244-245 F 3
Moses Point ▲ USA 20-21 J 4
Mosetse o RB 218-219 D 5
Mošgān o IR 134-135 F 4
Mosgiel o NZ 182 C 6
Mosher o CDN (ONT) 236-237 D 4
Moshesh's Ford o ZA 220-221 H 5
Moshi ☆ EAT 212-213 F 5
Moshi, River ~ WAN 204-205 F 4
Moshi Rest Camp o Z 218-219 D 2
Mosi o WAN 204-205 E 4
Mosigo o PNG 184 I b 2
Mosi-Oa-Tunya National Park ⊥ Z 218-219 C 3
Mosite o ZRE 210-211 J 3
Mosjøen o N 86-87 F 4
Moskalenki ☆ RUS 124-125 G 1
Moskal'vo o RUS 122-123 K 2
Moskenesøya ⌒ N 86-87 F 3
Moskosel o S 86-87 J 4
Moškovo ☆ RUS 114-115 R 7
Moskovskij o TJ 136-137 L 6
Moskva ★··· RUS (Mos) 94-95 P 4
Moskva ~ RUS 94-95 O 4
Mosley Creek ~ CDN (BC) 230-231 D 2
Moso, Île = Verao ⌒ VAN 184 II b 3
Mošok o RUS 94-95 R 4
Mosomane o RB 220-221 H 2
Mosonmagyaróvár o H 92-93 O 5
Mosopa o RB 220-221 G 2
Mosque o• RI 164-165 G 6
Mosque (Gantarang) • RI 168 E 6
Mosqueiro o BR (P) 62-63 K 6
Mosqueiro o BR (SER) 68-69 K 7
Mosquera o CO 60-61 B 6
Mosquero o USA (NM) 256-257 M 3
Mosquitia ⊥ HN 54-55 C 7
Mosquito, Río ~ PY 76-77 H 2
Mosquito Bay ≈ 36-37 K 4
Mosquito Creek Reservoir ⊖ USA (OH) 280-281 F 2
Mosquito Fork River ~ USA 20-21 T 5
Mosquito Lagoon ≈ 48-49 H 5
Mosquito Lagoon ≈ USA 286-287 J 3
Mosquito Lake ⊖ CDN 30-31 S 4
Mosquitos, Costa de ⌣ NIC 52-53 C 5
Mosquitos, Golfo de los ≈ 52-53 D 7
Moss ☆ N 86-87 E 7
Mossaka o RCB 210-211 F 4
Mossbank o CDN (SAS) 232-233 N 6
Mossburn o NZ 182 B 6
Mosselbaai = Mossel Bay o ZA 220-221 F 7
Mossel Bay = Mosselbaai o ZA 220-221 F 7
Mossendjo o RCB (Nia) 210-211 D 5
Mosses Hill o USA (TX) 268-269 F 6
Mossgiel o AUS 180-181 H 2
Mossleigh o CDN (ALB) 232-233 E 5
Mossman o AUS 174-175 H 5
Mossoró o BR 68-69 K 4
Mossoró, Rio ~ BR 68-69 K 4
Moss Point o USA (MS) 268-269 M 6
Moss Town o BS 54-55 H 2
Mossuril o MOC 218-219 L 2
Moss Vale o AUS 180-181 L 3
Mossy River ~ CDN 34-35 E 3
Mossyrock o USA (WA) 244-245 C 4
Most o CZ 92-93 M 3
Mostaganem ☆ DZ 190-191 C 3
Mostar o• BIH 100-101 F 3
Mostardas o BR 74-75 E 8
Mosteiro de Batalha ··· P 98-99 C 5
Moșteni, Trivalea- o RO 102-103 D 5
Mostling Tvillingøen, Kap ▲ GRØ 28-29 U 5
Móstoles o E 98-99 F 4
Mostovskoj o RUS 126-127 D 5
Mosul = al-Mauṣil ☆ IRQ 128-129 K 4
Mosul = Al Mauṣil ☆ IRQ 128-129 K 4
Møsvatnet ⊖ N 86-87 D 7
Mot'a o ETH 208-209 C 3
Mota ⌒ VAN 184 II a 1
Motaba ~ RCB 210-211 F 2
Motagua, Río ~ GCA 52-53 K 4
Motaha o RI 164-165 H 6
Motala ☆• S 86-87 G 7
Mota Lava ⌒ VAN 184 II a 1
Motengpas ▲ LS 220-221 J 4
Motherwell o GB 90-91 F 4
Moti, Pulau ⌒ RI 164-165 K 3
Motigu o GH 202-203 J 5
Motihari o IND 142-143 D 2
Motilla del Palancar o E 98-99 G 5
Motiti Island ⌒ NZ 182 F 2
Motley o USA (MN) 270-271 D 4
Motloutse ~ RB 218-219 E 6
Motloutse Ruins ∴• RB 218-219 E 6
Motobu o J 152-153 B 11
Motorčuna ~ RUS 110-111 N 5
Motor Speedway • USA (IN) 274-275 M 5
Motozintla de Mendoza o MEX 52-53 H 4
Motril o E 98-99 F 6
Motru o RO 102-103 C 4
Mott o USA (ND) 258-259 E 5
Motueka o NZ 182 D 4
Motul o MEX 52-53 K 1
Motupe o PE 64-65 C 5
Motupena Point ▲ PNG 184 I b 2
Moturiki ⌒ FJI 184 III b 2
Motygino ☆ RUS 116-117 G 6
Motykleį o RUS 120-121 N 4
Mouali Gbangba o RCB 210-211 F 2
Mouat, Cape ▲ CDN 24-25 h 2
Moubolo, Mont ▲ RN 198-199 E 3
Moubotsi o RCB 210-211 D 6
Moucha, Île ⌒ DJI 208-209 F 3
Mouchalagane, Rivière ~ CDN 38-39 K 2
Mouchchene, Ibel ▲ MA 188-189 H 4
Mouchoir Passage ≈ 54-55 K 4

Moudjéria ○ **RIM** 196-197 D 6
Moúdros ○ **GR** 100-101 K 5
Mouenda ○ **G** 210-211 C 5
Mougalaba, Reserve de la ⊥ **G** 210-211 C 5
Mougamou ○ **G** 210-211 D 4
Mouila ☆ **G** 210-211 C 4
Moujia ○ **RN** 198-199 B 5
Mouka ○ **RCA** 206-207 E 5
Moukoumbi ○ **G** 210-211 D 4
Moul < **RN** 198-199 F 5
Moula ~ **TCH** 206-207 D 4
Moulamein ○ **AUS** 180-181 H 3
Moulares ○ **TN** 190-191 G 3
Moulay Bouâzza ○ **MA** 188-189 H 4
Moulay-Bousselham ○ **MA** 188-189 H 3
Moulay-Idriss ○·· **MA** 188-189 J 3
Mould Bay ○ **CDN** 24-25 M 2
Moulèngui Binza ○ **G** 210-211 C 5
Moulins ☆· **F** 90-91 J 8
Mouli Pouli ○ **G** 210-211 D 4
Moulmein = Maulamayaing ○ **MYA** 158-159 D 2
Moulmein = Maulamyaing ○ **MYA** 158-159 D 2
Moulmeingyun ○ **MYA** 158-159 C 2
Mouloud ○ **DJI** 208-209 F 3
Moulouya, Oued ~ **MA** 188-189 K 3
Moulton ○ **USA** (AL) 284-285 C 2
Moulton ○ **USA** (IA) 274-275 F 4
Moulton ○ **USA** (TX) 266-267 K 4
Moultrie ○ **USA** (GA) 284-285 G 5
Moultrie, Lake ○ **USA** (SC) 284-285 K 3
Moulvi Bazar ○ **BD** 142-143 G 3
Moulvouday ○ **CAM** 206-207 B 3
Mounanko ○ **CAM** 210-211 B 2
Mound City ○ **USA** (IL) 276-277 F 3
Mound City ○ **USA** (KS) 262-263 M 6
Mound City ○ **USA** (MO) 274-275 C 4
Mound City ○ **USA** (SD) 260-261 F 1
Mound City Group National Monument ∴ **USA** (OH) 280-281 D 4
Moundhill Point ▲ **USA** 22-23 K 6
Moundou ☆ **TCH** 206-207 C 4
Moundridge ○ **USA** (KS) 262-263 J 6
Mounds ○ **USA** (IL) 276-277 F 3
Mound State Monument · **USA** (AL) 284-285 C 4
Moundsville ○ **USA** (WV) 280-281 F 4
Moundville ○ **USA** (AL) 284-285 C 4
Moundville ○ **USA** (AL) 284-285 C 3
Moungoun-dou-sud ○ **RCB** 210-211 D 5
Moŭng Roessei ○ **K** 158-159 G 4
Mounguel ○ **CAM** 204-205 K 5
Mount Adams Wilderness ⊥ **USA** (WA) 244-245 D 4
Mountain ○ **USA** (WI) 270-271 K 5
Mountainair ○ **USA** (NM) 256-257 J 4
Mountain Brook ○ **USA** (AL) 284-285 D 3
Mountainburg ○ **USA** (AR) 276-277 A 5
Mountain City ○ **USA** (NV) 246-247 K 2
Mountain City ○ **USA** (TN) 282-283 F 4
Mountain Creek ~ **USA** (GA) 284-285 E 4
Mountain Gate ○ **USA** (CA) 246-247 C 3
Mountain Grove ○ **USA** (MO) 276-277 C 3
Mountain Home ○ **USA** (AR) 276-277 C 4
Mountain Home ○ **USA** (ID) 252-253 C 3
Mountain Home ○ **USA** (TX) 266-267 H 3
Mountain Lake ○ **CDN** 30-31 U 5
Mountain Lake ○ **USA** (MN) 270-271 D 7
Mountain Lodge ○ **EAK** 212-213 F 4
Mountain Park ○ **CDN** (ALB) 228-229 R 4
Mountain Pass ▲ **USA** (CA) 248-249 J 4
Mountain Pine ○ **USA** (AR) 276-277 B 6
Mountain Point ○ **USA** 32-33 E 4
Mountain River ~ **CDN** 30-31 E 3
Mountain Road ○ **CDN** (MAN) 234-235 D 4
Mountainside ○ **CDN** (MAN) 234-235 C 5
Mountain Springs ○ **USA** (NV) 248-249 J 3
Mountain Valley ○ **AUS** 174-175 B 4
Mountain View ○ **CDN** (ALB) 232-233 E 6
Mountain View ○ **USA** (AR) 276-277 C 5
Mountain View ○ **USA** (AZ) 256-257 E 6
Mountain View ○ **USA** (HI) 288 K 5
Mountain View ○ **USA** (MO) 276-277 D 4
Mountain View ○ **USA** (WV) 280-281 E 6
Mountain View ○ **USA** (WY) 252-253 H 5
Mountain Village ○ **USA** 20-21 J 5
Mount Airy ○ **USA** (MD) 280-281 J 4
Mount Airy ○ **USA** (NC) 282-283 G 4
Mount Airy ○ **USA** (VA) 280-281 G 7
Mount Airy Mesa ▲ **USA** (NV) 246-247 H 4
Mount Allan ○ **AUS** 172-173 L 7
Mount Alto ○ **USA** (WV) 280-281 E 5
Mount Amhurst ○ **AUS** 172-173 H 5
Mount Aspiring National Park ⊥ **NZ** 182 B 6
Mount Assiniboine Provincial Park ⊥ **CDN** (ALB) 232-233 C 4
Mount Augustus ○ **AUS** 176-177 D 2
Mount Augustus National Park ⊥ **AUS** 176-177 D 2
Mount Ayliff ○ **ZA** 220-221 J 5
Mount Ayr ○ **USA** (IA) 274-275 D 4
Mount Barker ○ **AUS** (SA) 180-181 E 3
Mount Barker ○ **AUS** (WA) 176-177 D 7
Mount Barnett ○ **AUS** 172-173 H 4
Mountbatten Indian Reserve ⚔ **CDN** (ONT) 236-237 F 5
Mount Baw Baw ○ **AUS** 180-181 J 4
Mount Bayou ○ **USA** (MS) 268-269 K 3
Mount Beauty ○ **AUS** 180-181 J 4
Mount Belvieu ○ **USA** (TX) 268-269 F 7
Mount Brockman ○ **AUS** 172-173 C 7
Mount Buffalo National Park ⊥ **AUS** 180-181 J 4
Mount Bullion ○ **USA** (CA) 248-249 D 2
Mount Carleton Provincial Park ⊥ **CDN** (NB) 240-241 J 3
Mount Carmel ○ **USA** (IL) 274-275 L 6
Mount Carmel ○ **USA** (ND) 258-259 J 3
Mount Carmel Junction ○ **USA** (UT) 254-255 C 6
Mount Carrol ○ **USA** (IL) 274-275 J 2
Mount Celia ○ **AUS** 176-177 G 4
Mount Charleston ○ **USA** (NV) 248-249 J 3
Mount Clemens ○ **USA** (MI) 272-273 G 5
Mount Clere ○ **AUS** 176-177 D 2
Mount Cook ○ **NZ** 182 C 5
Mount Cook National Park ⊥··· **NZ** 182 C 5
Mount Coolon ○ **AUS** 178-179 J 1
Mount Croghan ○ **USA** (SC) 284-285 K 2
Mount Denison ○ **AUS** 172-173 L 7
Mount Desert Island ⌒ **USA** (ME) 278-279 N 4
Mount Divide ○ **AUS** 172-173 E 7
Mount Dora ○ **USA** (FL) 286-287 H 3
Mount Dora ○ **USA** (NM) 256-257 M 2
Mount Doreen ○ **AUS** 172-173 K 7
Mount Douglas ○ **AUS** 178-179 J 1
Mount Eba ○ **AUS** 178-179 C 6
Mount Ebenezer ○ **AUS** 176-177 M 2
Mount Eccles National Park ⊥ **AUS** 180-181 F 5
Mount Edgar ○ **AUS** 172-173 E 6
Mount Edziza Provincial Park ⊥ **CDN** 32-33 E 3
Mount Elizabeth ○ **AUS** 172-173 H 4
Mount Enterprise ○ **USA** (TX) 268-269 F 5
Mount Everest ▲ **NEP** 144-145 F 7
Mount Field National Park ⊥ **AUS** 180-181 J 7
Mount Fletcher ○ **ZA** 220-221 J 5
Mount Florance ○ **AUS** 172-173 C 6
Mount Forest ○ **CDN** (ONT) 238-239 E 5
Mount Frere ○ **ZA** 220-221 J 5
Mount Gambier ○ **AUS** 180-181 F 4
Mount Garnet ○ **AUS** 174-175 H 5
Mount Gilead ○ **USA** (NC) 282-283 H 5
Mount Gilead ○ **USA** (OH) 280-281 D 3
Mount Hagen ☆·· **PNG** 183 C 3
Mount Harris Tine Mine Area ○ **AUS** 172-173 K 2
Mount Holly ○ **USA** (NJ) 280-281 M 3
Mount Holly Springs ○ **USA** (PA) 280-281 J 3
Mount Hood ○ **USA** (OR) 244-245 D 5
Mount Hope ○ **AUS** 180-181 C 3
Mount Horeb ○ **USA** (WI) 274-275 J 1
Mount House ○ **AUS** 172-173 G 4
Mount Hutt ○ **NZ** 182 C 5
Mount Ida ○ **AUS** 176-177 F 4
Mount Ida ○ **USA** (AR) 276-277 B 6
Mountin Zebra National Park ⊥ **ZA** 220-221 G 6
Mount Isa ○·· **AUS** 174-175 E 7
Mount Jackson ○ **AUS** 176-177 E 5
Mount Kaichui ▲ **SOL** 184 I e 3
Mount Kalourat ▲ **SOL** 184 I e 3
Mount Kaputar National Park ⊥ **AUS** 178-179 L 6
Mount Keith ○ **AUS** 176-177 F 3
Mount Lakes Wilderness Area ⊥ **USA** (OR) 244-245 C 8
Mount Larcom ○ **AUS** 178-179 L 2
Mount Lofty Range ▲ **AUS** 180-181 E 3
Mount Madden Wheat Bin ○ **AUS** 176-177 E 6
Mount Magnet ○ **AUS** 176-177 D 4
Mount Maitabi ▲ **SOL** 184 I c 2
Mount Mary ○ **AUS** 180-181 E 3
Mount Meigs ○ **USA** (AL) 284-285 D 4
Mount Molloy ○ **AUS** 174-175 H 5
Mount Montgomery ○ **USA** (NV) 248-249 F 2
Mount Morgan ○· **AUS** 178-179 L 2
Mount Morris ○ **USA** (MI) 272-273 F 4
Mount Morris ○ **USA** (WI) 270-271 J 6
Mount Mulgrave ○ **AUS** 174-175 G 5
Mount Mulligan ○ **AUS** 174-175 H 5
Mount Narryer ○ **AUS** 176-177 C 3
Mountnorris Bay ≈ 172-173 L 1
Mount Olive ○ **USA** (NC) 282-283 J 5
Mount Padbury ○ **AUS** 176-177 E 2
Mount Paget ▲ **GB** 78-79 O 7
Mount Pearl ○ **CDN** (NFL) 242-243 Q 5
Mount Perry ○ **AUS** 178-179 L 3
Mount Pleasant ○ **USA** (IA) 274-275 G 4
Mount Pleasant ○ **USA** (MI) 272-273 E 4
Mount Pleasant ○ **USA** (OH) 280-281 D 4
Mount Pleasant ○ **USA** (PA) 280-281 G 3
Mount Pleasant ○ **USA** (SC) 284-285 L 4
Mount Pleasant ○ **USA** (TN) 276-277 H 5
Mount Pleasant ○ **USA** (TX) 264-265 K 5
Mount Pleasant ○ **USA** (UT) 254-255 D 4
Mount Pocono ○ **USA** (PA) 280-281 L 2
Mount Pulaski ○ **USA** (IL) 274-275 J 5
Mount Rainier National Park ⊥ **USA** (WA) 244-245 D 4
Mount Remarkable National Park ⊥ **AUS** 180-181 D 2
Mount Revelstoke National Park ⊥ **CDN** (BC) 230-231 L 2
Mount Richmond National Park ⊥ **AUS** 180-181 F 5
Mount Robson ○ **CDN** (BC) 228-229 P 3
Mount Robson Provincial Park ⊥ **CDN** (BC) 228-229 Q 4
Mount Rogers National Recreation Area ⊥ **USA** (VA) 280-281 E 7
Mount Rupert ○ **ZA** 220-221 G 4
Mount Rushmore National Memorial ∴ **USA** (SD) 260-261 C 3
Mount Sage National Park ⊥ **GB** (VI) 286-287 R 2
Mount Saint Helens National Volcanic Monument ∴ **USA** (WA) 244-245 D 4
Mount -Sandiman ○ **AUS** 176-177 C 2
Mount Sanford ○ **AUS** 172-173 K 4
Mount Sasan ▲ **SOL** 184 I d 3
Mount Seymour Provincial Park ⊥ **CDN** (BC) 230-231 G 4
Mount Skinner ○ **AUS** 178-179 C 2
Mount Somers ○ **NZ** 182 C 5
Mount Spokane State Park ⊥ **USA** (WA) 244-245 H 3
Mount Sterling ○ **USA** (IL) 274-275 H 5
Mount Sterling ○ **USA** (KY) 276-277 M 2
Mount Sterling ○ **USA** (OH) 280-281 C 4
Mount Sterling ○ **USA** (WI) 274-275 H 1
Mount Storm Lake ○ **USA** (WV) 280-281 G 4
Mount Strzelecki National Park ⊥ **AUS** 180-181 K 6
Mount Surprise ○ **AUS** 174-175 H 6
Mount Swan ○ **AUS** 178-179 C 2
Mount Trumbull ○ **USA** (AZ) 256-257 B 2
Mount Union ○ **USA** (PA) 280-281 J 3
Mount Vernon ○ **AUS** 176-177 E 2
Mount Vernon ○ **USA** (AL) 284-285 B 5
Mount Vernon ○ **USA** (GA) 284-285 H 4
Mount Vernon ○ **USA** (IA) 274-275 G 3
Mount Vernon ○ **USA** (IL) 274-275 K 6
Mount Vernon ○ **USA** (IN) 274-275 L 7
Mount Vernon ○ **USA** (KY) 276-277 L 3
Mount Vernon ○ **USA** (MO) 276-277 B 3
Mount Vernon ○ **USA** (OH) 280-281 D 3
Mount Vernon ○ **USA** (OR) 244-245 F 6
Mount Vernon ○ **USA** (SD) 260-261 H 3
Mount Vernon ○ **USA** (TX) 264-265 J 5
Mount Vernon ○ **USA** (WA) 244-245 C 2
Mount Vetters ○ **AUS** 176-177 F 5
Mount Walker ○ **AUS** 176-177 E 6
Mount Washington ○ **USA** (KY) 276-277 K 2
Mount Wedge ○ **AUS** (NT) 172-173 L 7
Mount Wedge ○ **AUS** (SA) 180-181 C 2
Mount William National Park ⊥ **AUS** 180-181 K 6
Mount Zion ○ **USA** (IL) 274-275 K 5
Mount Zion ○ **USA** (MD) 280-281 K 5
Mouping ○ **VRC** 154-155 M 3
Moura ○ **AUS** 178-179 K 3
Moura ○ **BR** 62-63 D 6
Moura ○·· **P** 98-99 D 5
Moura, Cachoeira ~ **BR** 66-67 H 5
Mourão ○ **P** 98-99 D 5
Mouray ○ **TCH** 206-207 E 3
Mourdi, Dépression du ⩦ **TCH** 198-199 K 3
Mourdiah ○ **RMM** 202-203 G 2
Mouri Mountains ▲ **WAN** 204-205 J 4
Mourindi ○ **G** 210-211 C 5
Mouroubra ○ **AUS** 176-177 D 4
Mouroungoulay ○ **TCH** 206-207 C 4
Mouscron ○ **B** 92-93 G 3
Mousgougou ○ **TCH** 206-207 C 3
Mousôayah ○ **RG** 202-203 D 5
Moussa, Hassi < **DZ** 190-191 C 6
Moussadey ○ **RN** 204-205 E 2
Moussafoyo ○ **TCH** 206-207 D 4
Moussaya ○ **RG** 202-203 E 4
Moussoro ○ **TCH** 198-199 H 6
Moustiers-Sainte-Marie ○ **F** 90-91 L 10
Moutamba ○ **RCB** 210-211 D 5
Mouth of the Mekong = Cửa Sông Cửu Long ⩦ **VN** 158-159 J 6
Mouth of Wilson ○ **USA** (VA) 280-281 E 7
Mouths of the Indus ~ **PK** 134-135 M 6
Moûtiers ○ **F** 90-91 L 9
Moutong ○ **RI** 164-165 G 3
Moutouroua ○ **CAM** 206-207 B 3
Mouydir, Monts du ▲ **DZ** 190-191 E 8
Mouyonndzi ○ **RCB** 210-211 D 5
Mouzarak ○ **TCH** 198-199 G 6
Movila Miresii ○ **RO** 102-103 E 5
Moville ○ **USA** (IA) 274-275 B 2
Mowanjum ⚔ **AUS** 172-173 F 4
Mowasi ○ **GUY** 62-63 E 3
Moweaqua ○ **USA** (IL) 274-275 J 5
Mowewe ○ **RI** 164-165 G 5
Moxey Town ○ **BS** 54-55 G 2
Moxico ◘ **ANG** 216-217 E 6
Moxotó, Rio ~ **BR** 68-69 K 6
Moyagee Gemstone Deposit · **AUS** 176-177 D 3
Moyahua ○ **MEX** 50-51 H 7
Moyale ○ **EAK** 212-213 G 2
Moyalé ○ **ETH** 208-209 D 7
Moyamba ○ **WAL** 202-203 D 5
Moyen Atlas ▲ **MA** 188-189 H 4
Moyen-Chari ◘ **TCH** 206-207 C 4
Moyeni ○ **LS** 220-221 H 5
Moyenne Sido ○ **RCA** 206-207 D 4
Moyie ○ **CDN** (BC) 230-231 O 4
Moyie River ~ **CDN** (BC) 230-231 N 4
Moyie Springs ○ **USA** (ID) 250-251 C 3
Moyne, Lac le ○ **CDN** 36-37 P 6
Moyo ○ **EAU** 212-213 C 2
Moyo ~ **RI** 168 C 7
Moyo, Pulau ⌒ **RI** 168 C 7
Moyobamba ☆ **PE** 64-65 D 5
Moyock ○ **USA** (NC) 282-283 L 4
Moyogalpa ○ **NIC** 52-53 B 6
Moyo Pulau Reserve ⊥· **RI** 168 C 7
Moyowosi ~ **EAT** 212-213 C 5
Møysalen ▲ **N** 86-87 G 2
Moyto ○ **TCH** 198-199 H 6
Moyu ○ **VRC** 144-145 B 2
Możaffarābād-e Masileh ○ **IR** 134-135 D 1
Možaisk ☆·· **RUS** 94-95 P 4
Mozambique = Moçambique ■ **MOC** 218-219 G 6
Mozambique Basin ⩦ 9 G 8
Mozambique Channel ≈ 222-223 A 7
Mozambique Plateau ⩦ 9 G 9
Mozambique Plateau = Natal Ridge ⩦ 220-221 M 6
Mozdok ○ **RUS** 126-127 F 6
Mozdūrān ○ **IR** 136-137 G 6
Možga ☆ **RUS** 96-97 H 5
Mozyr' = Mazyr ○ **BY** 94-95 L 5
Mpaem ○ **GH** 202-203 K 6
Mpaka Station ○ **SD** 220-221 K 3
Mpala ○ **ZRE** 214-215 E 4
Mpama ~ **RCB** 210-211 E 5
Mpana ○ **GH** 202-203 K 5
Mpanda ○ **EAT** 214-215 F 4
Mpandamatenga ○ **RB** 218-219 C 4
Mpanga ○ **EAT** 214-215 K 4
Mpase ○ **ZRE** 210-211 H 4
Mpataba ○ **GH** 202-203 J 7
Mpatora ○ **EAT** 214-215 K 5
Mpem ~ **CAM** 204-205 J 6
Mpepayi ○ **EAT** (RUV) 214-215 H 6
Mpessoba ○ **RMM** 202-203 H 3
Mphaki ○ **LS** 220-221 J 5
Mphoengs ○ **ZW** 218-219 D 5
Mpiéla ○ **RMM** 202-203 G 3
Mpigi ○ **EAU** 212-213 D 3
Mpika ○ **Z** 214-215 F 6
Mpitimbi ○ **EAT** (RUV) 214-215 H 6
Mpo ○ **ZRE** 210-211 G 6
Mpoko ~ **RCA** 206-207 D 6
Mpoko ○ **ZRE** 210-211 G 5
Mponde ~ **EAT** 212-213 E 6
Mponela ○ **MW** 218-219 G 1
Mpongwe ○ **Z** 218-219 E 1
Mporokoso ○ **Z** 214-215 F 5
Mpoukou ~ **RCB** 210-211 D 5
Mpoumé, Chute ~· **CAM** 210-211 C 2
Mpouop ~ **CAM** 210-211 D 2
Mpouya ○ **RCB** 210-211 F 5
Mpraeso ○ **GH** 202-203 K 6
Mpui ○ **EAT** 214-215 F 5
Mpulungu ○ **Z** 214-215 F 5
Mpumalanga ○ **ZA** 220-221 K 4
Mpume ○ **ZRE** 210-211 G 6
M'Pupa, Rápidos ~ **ANG** 216-217 F 8
Mpwapwa ○ **EAT** 214-215 J 4
Mrakovo ☆ **RUS** 96-97 K 7
Mrara ○ **DZ** 190-191 E 4
Mrassu ~ **RUS** 124-125 Q 2
Mrčajevci ○ **YU** 100-101 H 3
Mrezzig < **RMM** 196-197 K 5
M'saken ○ **TN** 190-191 H 3
Msak Millet ▲ **LAR** 192-193 D 5
Msandile ~ **Z** 218-219 G 1
Msangasi ~ **EAT** 212-213 G 6
Msanzara ~ **Z** 218-219 F 1
Msata ○ **EAT** 214-215 K 4
Msembe ○ **EAT** 214-215 H 4
M'Sila ☆ **DZ** 190-191 E 3
Msima ~ **EAT** 214-215 F 4
Mšinskaja ○ **RUS** 94-95 L 2
Msoro ○ **Z** 218-219 F 1
Msta ~ **RUS** 94-95 O 3
Msuna ○ **ZW** 218-219 D 4
Mszczonów ○ **PL** 92-93 Q 3
Mtakuja ○ **EAT** 214-215 F 4
Mtama ○ **EAT** 214-215 K 6
Mtambo ~ **EAT** 214-215 F 4
Mtandikeni ○ **EAT** 212-213 G 6
Mtangano Island ⌒ **EAT** 212-213 D 5
Mtarazi Falls ~ **ZW** 218-219 G 4
Mtera Dam < **EAT** 214-215 H 4
Mtina ○ **EAT** 214-215 J 6
Mtito Andei ○ **EAK** 212-213 G 5
Mto Wa Mbu ○ **EAT** 212-213 E 5
Mtubatuba ○ **ZA** 220-221 L 4
Mtwara ◘ **EAT** 214-215 K 6
Mtwara ☆ **EAT** (MTW) 214-215 L 6
Muadiala ○ **ZRE** 216-217 F 3
Muaguide ○ **MOC** 214-215 L 7
Mualádzi ○ **MOC** 218-219 G 2
Mualama ○ **MOC** 218-219 K 3
Muaná ○ **BR** 62-63 K 6
Muanda ○ **ZRE** 210-211 D 6
Muangai ○ **ANG** 216-217 E 6
Muang Gnômmarat ○ **LAO** 158-159 H 2
Muang Hiam ○ **LAO** 156-157 C 6
Muang Hôngsa ○ **LAO** 156-157 B 7
Muang Houn ○ **LAO** 156-157 B 6
Muang Huang ○ **LAO** 156-157 C 7
Muang Khammouan ○ **LAO** 158-159 H 2
Muang Không ○ **LAO** 158-159 H 3
Muang Khôngxédôn ○ **LAO** 158-159 H 3
Muang Khoua ○ **LAO** 156-157 C 6
Muang May ○ **LAO** 158-159 J 3
Muang Namo ○ **LAO** 156-157 B 6
Muang Nan ○ **LAO** 156-157 B 7
Muang Ou Thai ○ **LAO** 156-157 B 5
Muang Pa ○ **LAO** 156-157 B 7
Muang Pakbèng ○ **LAO** 156-157 B 7
Muang Pak-Cay ○ **LAO** 156-157 B 7
Muang Pakxan ○ **LAO** 156-157 C 7
Muang Phalan ○ **LAO** 158-159 H 2
Muang Phin ○ **LAO** 158-159 J 2
Muang Phôn -Hông ○ **LAO** 156-157 C 7
Muang Samsip ○ **THA** 158-159 H 3
Muang Souy ○ **LAO** 156-157 C 7
Muang Xaigna-bouri ○ **LAO** 156-157 B 7
Muang Xay ○ **LAO** 156-157 B 6
Muang Xépôn ○ **LAO** 158-159 J 2
Muanza ○ **MOC** 218-219 H 4
Muanzanza ○ **ZRE** 216-217 F 3
Muar ○· **MAL** 162-163 E 3
Muara ○ **BRU** 164-165 D 1
Muara ○ **RI** 162-163 D 5
Muaraaman ○ **RI** 162-163 E 6
Muaraatap ○ **RI** 164-165 E 3
Muarabeliti ○ **RI** 162-163 E 6
Muarabengkal ○ **RI** 164-165 E 3
Muarabinuangeun ○ **RI** 168 A 3
Muarabulian ○ **RI** 162-163 E 5
Muarabungo ○ **RI** 162-163 E 5
Muaradua ○ **RI** 162-163 E 7
Muaraenim ○ **RI** 162-163 E 6
Muarahalung ○ **RI** 164-165 D 5
Muarajawa ○ **RI** 164-165 E 4
Muara Koman ○ **RI** 164-165 D 4
Muaranayan ○ **RI** 164-165 E 4
Muarapayang ○ **RI** 164-165 D 4
Muararupit ○ **RI** 162-163 E 6
Muarasiberut ○ **RI** 162-163 C 5
Muarasimatalu ○ **RI** 162-163 C 5
Muarasoma ○ **RI** 162-163 C 4
Muaratalang ○ **RI** 162-163 E 6
Muaratebo ○ **RI** 162-163 E 5
Muaratembesi ○ **RI** 162-163 E 5
Muarateweh ○ **RI** 164-165 D 4
Muara Tuang ○ **MAL** 162-163 J 4
Muarawahau ○ **RI** 164-165 E 3
Muari, Pulau ⌒ **RI** 164-165 K 4
Muāri, Rās ▲ **PK** 134-135 M 6
Muaro Takus Ruins · **RI** 162-163 D 4
Muatua ○ **MOC** 218-219 K 2
Mubambe ○ **ZRE** 214-215 D 6
Mubārak, Ğabal ▲ **JOR** 130-131 D 2
Mubarek ○ **US** 136-137 J 5
Mubarraz ○ **KSA** 130-131 L 5
Mubayira ○ **ZW** 218-219 F 4
Mubende ○ **EAU** 212-213 C 3
Mubi ○ **WAN** 204-205 K 3
Mubo ○ **VRC** 154-155 E 3
Mubrani ○ **RI** 166-167 G 2
Mucajá ○ **BR** 62-63 D 4
Mucajaí ○ **BR** 62-63 D 4
Mucajaí, Reserva Biológica de ⊥ **BR** 60-61 K 6
Mucajaí, Rio ~ **BR** 62-63 D 4
Mucajaí, Serra ▲ **BR** 60-61 K 6
Mucalic, Rivière ~ **CDN** 36-37 Q 5
Mucanha ~ **MOC** 218-219 F 2
Mucari ○ **ANG** 216-217 D 4
Muccan ○ **AUS** 172-173 E 7
Muchalat Inlet ≈ **CDN** 230-231 C 4
Muchea ○ **AUS** 176-177 C 5
Muchena ○ **MOC** 218-219 G 2
Muchinga Escarpment ⩦ **Z** 218-219 E 2
Muchinga Mountains ▲ **Z** 214-215 F 7
Muchinka ○ **Z** 214-215 F 7
Muchuan ○ **VRC** 156-157 C 2
Muchuchu Ruins ∴· **ZW** 218-219 F 4
Mucianyu · **VRC** 154-155 K 1
Muckadilla ○ **AUS** 178-179 K 4
Muckaty ○ **AUS** 174-175 B 6
Mučnoj, poluostrov ~ **RUS** 108-109 E 6
Muco, Río ~ **CO** 60-61 F 5
Mucojo ○ **MOC** 214-215 L 7
Muconda ○ **ANG** 216-217 F 5
Mucondo ○ **ANG** 216-217 C 4
Mucope ○ **ANG** 216-217 C 8
Mucubela ○ **MOC** 218-219 J 3
Mucucuaú, Rio ~ **BR** 62-63 D 5
Mucuim, Rio ~ **BR** 66-67 E 6
Mucujê ○ **BR** 72-73 K 2
Mucum ○ **BR** 74-75 E 7
Mucumbura ○ **MOC** 218-219 F 3
Mucumbura ○ **ZW** 218-219 F 3
Mucupia ○ **MOC** 218-219 J 4
Mucur ☆ **TR** 128-129 F 3
Múcura ○ **YV** 60-61 J 3
Mucura, Cachoeira da ~ **BR** 68-69 B 5
Mucuri ○ **BR** 72-73 L 5
Mucuri, Rio ~ **BR** 72-73 L 5
Mucurici ○ **BR** 72-73 K 5
Mucuripe, Ponta de ▲ **BR** 68-69 J 3
Mucuru, Cachoeira ~ **BR** 62-63 H 5
Mucusso ○ **ANG** 216-217 F 8
Mucusso, Coutada Pública do ⊥ **ANG** 216-217 F 8
Mucussueje ○ **ANG** 216-217 F 5
Mūd ○ **IR** 134-135 H 2
Muḍailif, al- ○ **KSA** 132-133 B 4
Muḍairib, al- ○· **OM** 132-133 L 2
Mudaisis ○ **OM** 132-133 J 2
Mudākim, Bi'r < **LAR** 192-193 E 1
Mudanjiang ○ **VRC** 150-151 G 5
Mudan Jiang ~ **VRC** 150-151 G 5
Mudanya ☆ **TR** 128-129 C 2
Mudarraq ○ **KSA** 130-131 H 4
Mudawwa ○ **JOR** 130-131 E 3
Muḍayy ○ **OM** 132-133 H 5
Mūdbidri ○· **IND** 140-141 F 4
Mud Butte ○ **USA** (SD) 260-261 D 2
Mud Creek ~ **USA** (OK) 264-265 G 4
Muddebihāl ○ **IND** 140-141 G 2
Mudderbugten ≈ 28-29 P 2
Muddus nationalpark ⊥· **S** 86-87 K 3
Muddy Boggy Creek ~ **USA** (OK) 264-265 J 4
Muddy Creek ~ **USA** (UT) 254-255 D 5
Muddy Creek ~ **USA** (WY) 252-253 L 5
Muddy Gap ○ **USA** (WY) 252-253 L 4
Muddy Gap ▲ **USA** (WY) 252-253 L 4
Muddy Pass ▲ **USA** (CO) 254-255 J 3
Mudgal ○ **IND** 140-141 G 2
Mudgee ○· **AUS** 180-181 K 2
Mudgeeraba ○· **AUS** 178-179 M 5
Mudhol ○ **IND** 140-141 F 2
Mudigere ○ **IND** 140-141 F 4
Mudigubba ○ **IND** 140-141 G 3
Mudimbi ○ **ZRE** 210-211 K 5
Mud Island ⌒ **CDN** (NS) 240-241 J 7
Mudjatik River ~ **CDN** 34-35 C 2
Mud Lake ○ **USA** (ID) 252-253 F 3
Mud Lake ○ **USA** (MN) 270-271 C 2
Mudon ○ **MYA** 158-159 D 2
Mud River ○ **CDN** (ONT) 234-235 P 4
Mud River ~ **USA** (KY) 276-277 J 3
Mudug ◘ **SP** 208-209 J 5
Mudujjaha ~ **RUS** 108-109 S 7
Mudukulattūr ○ **IND** 140-141 H 6
Muecate ○ **MOC** 218-219 K 2
Mueda ○ **MOC** 214-215 K 6
Muelle de los Bueyes ○ **NIC** 52-53 B 5
Mueller Range ▲ **AUS** 172-173 H 5
Muembe ○ **MOC** 218-219 H 1
Muende ○ **MOC** 218-219 G 2
Muermos, Los ○ **RCH** 78-79 C 6
Muerte, Meseta de la ⩦ **RA** 80 D 4
Muerto, Mar ≈ 52-53 G 3
Muerto, Río ~ **RA** 76-77 F 2
Muertos Trough ⩦ 56 A 3
Muezerskij ○ **RUS** 88-89 M 5
Mufulira ○ **Z** 214-215 E 7
Mufu Shan ▲ **VRC** 156-157 H 2
Mufu Shan ▲ **VRC** 156-157 H 2
Muğahhar, Dār ○ **Y** 132-133 D 7
Muğaira ○ **KSA** 130-131 F 4
Mugal, Wādī ~ **SUD** 200-201 G 3
Mugang ○ **VRC** 156-157 D 5
Mugango ○ **EAT** 212-213 D 4
Muganskaja ravnina ⩦ **AZ** 128-129 N 3
Mūgār ○ **IR** 134-135 E 2
Mugdiisho ☆ **SP** 212-213 K 2
Muger ○ **ETH** 208-209 D 4
Muger Falls ~ **ETH** 208-209 D 4
Muger Wenz ~ **ETH** 208-209 D 4
Muggar Kangri ▲ **VRC** 144-145 F 4
Muggon ○ **AUS** 176-177 C 3
Mughal Sarai ○ **IND** 142-143 C 3
Mughsail ○ **OM** 132-133 H 5
Muğib, Wādī l- ~ **JOR** 130-131 D 2
Mugila, Monts ▲ **ZRE** 214-215 E 4
Mugina ○ **EAT** 212-213 B 6
Mugla ☆ **TR** 128-129 C 4
Mügodžor, tau ▲ **KA** 126-127 N 3
Mugur Aksy ☆ **RUS** 116-117 E 10
Muḥā, al- ○·· **Y** 132-133 C 7
Muhabura ▲ **EAU** 212-213 B 4
Muhāgiria ○ **SUD** 206-207 G 3
Muhaiwir ○ **IRQ** 128-129 J 6
Muhala ○ **ZRE** 212-213 B 6
Muhammad, Ra's ▲ **ET** 194-195 G 4
Muhammadābād ○ **IND** 142-143 C 2
Muhammadiya ○ **IRQ** 128-129 K 6
Muhammad Qol ○ **SUD** 200-201 H 2
Muharraq, al- ○ **BRN** 134-135 D 5
Muhāt ○ **KSA** 132-133 C 5
Muhazi, Lac ○ **RWA** 212-213 C 4
Muheit, Wādī ~ **SUD** 200-201 F 4
Muheza ○ **EAT** 212-213 G 6
Muhino ○ **RUS** 118-119 N 9
Mühldorf am Inn ○ **D** 92-93 M 4
Mühlhausen/ Thüringen ○· **D** 92-93 L 3
Mühlig-Hofmann Mountains = Mühlig-Hofmann-fjella ▲ **ARK** 16 F 1
Muhorini ○ **EAK** 212-213 E 4
Muhor-Konduj ○ **RUS** 118-119 F 9
Muhoro ○ **EAK** 212-213 E 4
Muhoršibir' ☆ **RUS** 116-117 N 10
Muhos ○ **FIN** 88-89 J 4
Muhu saar ⌒ **EST** 94-95 H 2
Muhutwe ○ **EAT** 212-213 C 4
Muhuwesi ~ **EAT** (RUV) 214-215 J 6
Mui ○ **ETH** 208-209 B 5
Mũi Cà Mau ▲ **VN** 158-159 H 6
Mũi Chân Mây ▲ **VN** 158-159 K 2
Muico ○ **MOC** 218-219 K 1
Mũi Dinh ▲ **VN** 158-159 K 5
Mũi Độc ▲ **VN** 158-159 J 2
Muidumbe ○ **MOC** 214-215 K 6
Muié ○ **ANG** 216-217 F 7
Mũi Én ▲ **VN** 158-159 K 4
Mũi Gành ▲ **VN** 158-159 K 4
Mũi Kê Gà ▲ **VN** 158-159 K 5
Mũi Ky Vân ▲ **VN** 158-159 J 5
Mũi Lach Quèn ▲ **VN** 156-157 D 7
Mũi La Gân ▲ **VN** 158-159 K 5
Mũi Lai ▲ **VN** 158-159 J 2
Mũi Nai ▲ **VN** 158-159 H 5
Mũi Nam Trâm ▲ **VN** 158-159 K 3
Mũi Nay ▲ **VN** 158-159 K 4
Muine ○ **ANG** 216-217 F 8
Muineachán = Monaghan ☆ **IRL** 90-91 D 4
Muira, Rio ~ **MOC** 200-201 F 3
Muir Glacier ⊂ **USA** 20-21 W 7
Muiron Islands ⌒ **AUS** 172-173 B 6
Muisma ~ **RUS** 116-117 E 3
Muisne ○ **EC** 64-65 B 1
Muite ○ **MOC** 218-219 K 2
Muitos Capões ○ **BR** 74-75 E 7
Muiuçu ou Puiuçu, Igarapé ~ **BR** 66-67 H 6
Muizenberg ○ **ZA** 220-221 D 7
Muja ~ **RUS** 118-119 G 7
Mujakan ~ **RUS** 118-119 F 7
Mujazzam, Sabkhat ○ **LAR** 190-191 G 5
Mujeres, Isla ⌒·· **MEX** 52-53 L 1
Mujnak ☆ **US** 136-137 F 3
Mujšin ~ **RUS** 118-119 G 9
Muju ○ **ROK** 150-151 F 9
Mujunkum ⩦ **KA** 124-125 H 6
Mukačeve ☆ **UA** 102-103 C 3
Mukačevo = Mukačeve ☆ **UA** 102-103 C 3
Mukah ○ **MAL** 162-163 K 3
Muka Head ▲ **MAL** 162-163 D 2
Mukala ○ **ZRE** 210-211 F 6
Mukana ○ **ZRE** 214-215 D 5
Mukanga ○ **ZRE** 216-217 F 3
Mukarylian ~ **RUS** 112-113 Q 5
Mukawa ○ **PNG** 183 E 5
Mukawa-gawa ~ **J** 152-153 K 3
Mukawwa', Ğazirat ⌒ **SUD** 200-201 H 2
Mukdahan ○ **THA** 158-159 H 2
Mukden = Shenyang ○ **VRC** 150-151 D 7
Mukebo ○ **ZRE** 214-215 E 4
Mukeriān ○ **IND** 138-139 E 4
Muketei River ~ **CDN** (ONT) 234-235 R 2
Muke T'uri ○ **ETH** 208-209 D 4
Mukilteo ○ **USA** (WA) 244-245 C 3
Mukinbudin ○ **AUS** 176-177 E 5
Mukomuko ○ **RI** 162-163 E 6
Mukongo ○ **EAU** 212-213 D 3
Mukry ○ **TM** 136-137 J 6
Muksu ~ **TJ** 136-137 M 5
Muksuniha ~ **RUS** 108-109 V 6
Muksunuoha-Tas, gora ▲ **RUS** 110-111 X 4
Muktsar ○ **IND** 138-139 E 4
Mukuku ○ **Z** 214-215 E 7
Mukulu, Kayembe- ○ **ZRE** 214-215 B 5
Mukulu, Mutombo- ○ **ZRE** 214-215 C 5
Mukulushi ~ **ZRE** 214-215 C 6
Mukunsa ○ **Z** 214-215 E 5
Mukupa Kaoma ○ **Z** 214-215 F 5
Mukurob · **NAM** 220-221 D 2
Mukutawa River ~ **CDN** 34-35 H 4
Mūl ○ **IND** 138-139 G 9
Mula ○ **E** 98-99 G 5
Mula ~ **PK** 134-135 M 4
Mula, la ▲ **I** 100-101 E 5
Mulaiih, al- ○ **KSA** 130-131 F 5
Mulaku Atoll ⌒ **MV** 140-141 B 6
Mūlali cukurligi ⩦ **US** 136-137 J 4
Mulam ~ **RUS** 120-121 D 5
Mulamba Gungu, Chute ~ **ZRE** 214-215 B 5
Mulan ○ **VRC** 150-151 G 5
Mulanay ○ **RP** 160-161 E 6
Mulanje ○ **MW** 218-219 H 2
Mulanje Mountains ▲ **MW** 218-219 H 2
Mulanweichang · **VRC** 148-149 N 6
Mulatos ○ **CO** 60-61 C 3
Mulawa ○ **PK** 138-139 D 3
Mulbāgal ○ **IND** 140-141 H 4
Mulberry ○ **USA** (AR) 276-277 A 5
Mulberry ○ **USA** (FL) 286-287 H 4
Mulberry Creek ~ **USA** (AL) 284-285 C 4
Mulberry Creek ~ **USA** (TX) 264-265 C 4
Mulberry Fork ~ **USA** (AL) 284-285 D 3
Mulberry River ~ **USA** (AR) 276-277 B 5
Mulchatna River ~ **USA** 20-21 N 6
Mulchen ○ **RCH** 78-79 C 4
Mulchole ○ **IND** 140-141 G 5
Mulde ~ **D** 92-93 M 3
Muldrow ○ **USA** (OK) 264-265 K 3
Muleba ○ **EAT** 212-213 C 4
Mule Creek Junction ○ **USA** (WY) 252-253 O 3
Mulegé ○· **MEX** 50-51 D 4
Mulembe ○ **ZRE** 212-213 B 5
Muleshoe ○ **USA** (TX) 264-265 B 4
Muleta ▲ **ETH** 208-209 E 4
Muleta ~ **RP** 160-161 F 9
Mulevala ○ **MOC** 218-219 J 3
Mulga Creek ~ **AUS** 178-179 J 6
Mulgildie ○ **AUS** 178-179 L 3
Mulgrave ○ **CDN** (NS) 240-241 O 5
Mulgrave Hills ▲ **USA** 20-21 J 3
Mulgul ○ **AUS** 176-177 E 2
Mulhacén ▲ **E** 98-99 F 6
Mulhouse ○ **F** 90-91 L 8
Mulhurst Bay ○ **CDN** (ALB) 232-233 E 2
Muli ≈ 166-167 K 5
Mulia ○ **RI** 166-167 J 3
Muli Channel ≈ 166-167 K 5
Mulilansolo ○ **Z** 214-215 G 6
Muling ○ **VRC** 150-151 H 5
Mulis'ma ~ **RUS** 118-119 D 6
Mūlki ○ **IND** 140-141 F 4
Mull ⌒ **GB** 90-91 D 3
Mullaittivu ○ **CL** 140-141 J 6
Mullaley ○ **AUS** 178-179 K 6
Mullan ○ **USA** (MT) 250-251 D 4
Mullen ○ **USA** (NE) 262-263 E 2
Mullens ○ **USA** (WV) 280-281 E 6
Müller, Pegunungan ▲ **RI** 162-163 K 4
Muller Range ▲ **PNG** 183 B 3
Mullet Key ⌒ **USA** (FL) 286-287 G 4
Mullett Lake ○ **USA** (MI) 272-273 E 2
Mullewa ○ **AUS** 176-177 C 4
Mulligan River ~ **AUS** 178-179 E 3
Mullingar ○ **CDN** (SAS) 232-233 L 2
Mullingar = An Muileann -gCearr ○ **IRL** 90-91 D 5
Mullins ○ **USA** (SC) 284-285 L 2
Mul'muga ~ **RUS** 118-119 O 8
Mulobezi ○ **Z** 218-219 C 3
Mulondo ○ **ANG** 216-217 C 7
Mulonga Plain ⩦ **Z** 218-219 B 3
Mulongo ○ **ZRE** 214-215 D 4
Mulongoie ~ **ZRE** 210-211 L 6
Multai ○ **IND** 138-139 G 9
Multān ○·· **PK** 138-139 C 4
Mulu ○ **ETH** 208-209 E 4
Mulu, Gunung ▲ **MAL** 164-165 D 1
Mulungu ~ **ZRE** 214-215 B 5
Mulungushi ○ **Z** 218-219 E 2
Mulungushi Dam < **Z** 218-219 E 2
Mulūr ○ **IND** 140-141 F 4
Mulurulu Lake ○ **AUS** 180-181 G 2
Mulvihill ○ **CDN** (MAN) 234-235 E 4
Mulym'ja ~ **RUS** 114-115 H 4
Mulyungarie ○ **AUS** 178-179 F 6
Muma ○ **ZRE** 210-211 J 2
Mumallah ○ **SUD** 206-207 G 3
Mumbai = Bombay ☆ **IND** 138-139 D 10
Mumballup ○ **AUS** 176-177 D 6
Mumbeji ○ **Z** 218-219 B 1
Mumbleberry Lake ○ **AUS** 178-179 E 3
Mumbondo ○ **ANG** 216-217 C 5
Mumbué ○ **ANG** 216-217 D 6
Mumbwa ○ **Z** 218-219 D 2
Mume, Swana- ○ **ZRE** 214-215 D 6
Mumena ○ **ZRE** 214-215 D 6
Mumeng ○ **PNG** 183 D 4
Mumias ○ **EAK** 212-213 E 3
Mumoma ○ **ZRE** 214-215 B 4
Mumulusan ○ **RI** 164-165 H 4
Mun ○ **RI** 166-167 G 4
Muna ○ **MEX** 52-53 K 1
Muna ~ **RUS** 110-111 K 5
Muna ~ **RUS** 110-111 N 5
Muna, Pulau ⌒ **RI** 164-165 H 6
Muna, Selat ≈ 164-165 H 6
Münajšy ○ **KA** 126-127 K 6
Munakan ~ **RUS** 110-111 M 6
Munarra ○ **AUS** 176-177 E 3
Munaya ~ **CAM** 204-205 H 6
Muncakabau ○ **RI** 162-163 F 7
München ☆ **D** 92-93 L 4
Munchique, Parque Nacional ⊥ **CO** 60-61 C 6
Muncho Lake ○ **CDN** 30-31 G 6
Muncho Lake Provincial Park ⊥ **CDN** 30-31 G 6
Muncie ○ **USA** (IN) 274-275 N 4
Muncoonie Lake West ○ **AUS** 178-179 E 3
Munda ○ **PK** 138-139 C 4
Munda ○ **SOL** 184 I c 3
Mundabullangana ○ **AUS** 172-173 D 6
Mundare ○ **CDN** (ALB) 232-233 F 2
Mundaring ○ **AUS** 176-177 D 5
Munday ○ **USA** (TX) 264-265 E 5
Mundemba ○ **CAM** 204-205 H 6
Mundgod ○ **IND** 140-141 F 3
Mundico Coelho ○ **BR** 66-67 J 6
Mundijong ○ **AUS** 176-177 C 6
Mundiwindi ○ **AUS** 176-177 F 1
Mundo Novo ○ **BR** (BAH) 68-69 H 7
Mundo Novo ○ **BR** (GSU) 76-77 K 2
Mundo Nuevo ○ **YV** 60-61 J 3
Mundra ○ **IND** 138-139 B 8
Mundrabilla ○ **AUS** 176-177 J 5
Mundrabilla Motel ○ **AUS** 176-177 K 5
Mundubbera ○ **AUS** 178-179 L 3
Mundujskoe, ozero ○ **RUS** 108-109 X 8
Mundurucânia, Reserva Florestal ⊥ **BR** (P) 66-67 J 6
Mundurucânia, Reserva Florestal ⊥ **BR** (P) 66-67 H 6

Munduručču ~ RUS 118-119 O 5
Mundurucu, Área Indígena ✕ BR 66-67 J 6
Mūndwa o IND 138-139 D 6
Munenga o ANG 216-217 C 5
Munera o E 98-99 F 5
Munford o USA (TN) 276-277 F 5
Munfordville o USA (KY) 276-277 K 3
Mungabroom o AUS 174-175 C 5
Mungallala o AUS 178-179 J 4
Mungallala Creek ~ AUS 178-179 J 5
Mungaoli o IND 138-139 G 7
Mungári o MOC 218-219 G 3
Mungbere o ZRE 212-213 B 2
Munger o IND 142-143 E 3
Mungeranie o AUS 178-179 E 5
Mungguresak, Tanjung ▲ RI 162-163 H 4
Mungindi o AUS 178-179 K 5
Munglinup o AUS 176-177 F 6
Mungo o ANG (HBO) 216-217 D 5
Mungo o ANG (LUN) 216-217 E 3
Mungo o SME 62-63 G 3
Mungo National Park ⊥ AUS 180-181 G 2
Mungra Badshahpur o IND 142-143 C 3
Munhango o ANG 216-217 E 6
Munhoz o BR 72-73 G 7
Munich = München ☆ D 92-93 L 4
Muniengashi ~ ZRE 218-219 E 1
Muniesa o E 98-99 G 4
Munikan ~ RUS 122-123 F 2
Munim, Rio ~ BR 68-69 G 3
Munimadugu o IND 140-141 G 3
Munising o USA (MI) 270-271 M 4
Muniungu o ZRE 210-211 F 6
Muniz Freire o BR 72-73 K 6
Munkamba ~ RUS 116-117 N 4
Munkumpu o Z 218-219 D 1
Mūnly, tau ▲ KA 124-125 G 5
Munmarlary o AUS 172-173 L 2
Munn, Cape ▲ CDN 36-37 G 2
Munnat o IND 140-141 G 5
Munnikspoort ▲ ZA 220-221 G 6
Muñoz Gamero, Península ⌣ RCH 80 D 6
Munqaṭiʿ, al- o Y 132-133 D 6
Munro, Mount ▲ AUS 180-181 K 6
Munsan o ROK 150-151 F 9
Munse o RI 164-165 H 6
Munson o CDN (ALB) 232-233 F 4
Munson o USA (FL) 286-287 C 1
Münster o·· D 92-93 J 3
Münster = Müstair o·· CH 92-93 L 5
Munte o RI 164-165 F 3
Munteme o EAU 212-213 C 3
Muntgatsi o EAK 212-213 E 3
Muntilan o RI 168 D 3
Muntok o RI 162-163 F 6
Muntu o EAU 212-213 D 3
Muntu o ZRE 210-211 G 5
Munukata o J 152-153 D 8
Munyamadzi ~ Z 218-219 F 1
Munyaroo Conservation Park ⊥ AUS 180-181 D 2
Munyati ~ ZW 218-219 E 3
Munzur Vadisi Milli Parkı ⊥ TR 128-129 H 3
Muoco o MOC 218-219 J 1
Muodoslompolo o S 86-87 L 3
Muohyang San ▲ DVR 150-151 F 7
Mu'ò'ng Cha o VN 156-157 B 6
Muong Het o LAO 156-157 D 6
Mu'ò'ng Kim o VN 156-157 C 6
Mu'ò'ng Lạm o VN 156-157 D 7
Mu'ò'ng Loi o VN 156-157 C 6
Mu'ò'ng Mu'o'n o VN 156-157 C 6
Mu'ò'ng Pôn o VN 156-157 C 6
Mu'ò'ng Tè ☆ VN 156-157 C 5
Muonio o FIN 88-89 G 3
Muonioälven ~ S 86-87 L 3
Muonionjoki ~· FIN 88-89 G 3
Muor, Pulau ⌒ RI 164-165 L 3
Muostah, mys ▲ RUS 110-111 R 4
Muostah, ostrov ⌒ RUS 110-111 S 4
Mupa o ANG 216-217 C 8
Mupa ~ MOC 218-219 H 4
Mupa, Parque Nacional da ⊥ ANG 216-217 C 7
Mupamadzi ~ Z 218-219 F 1
Mupele, Chute ~ ZRE 210-211 K 3
Mupfure ~ ZW 218-219 E 3
Muqaddam, Wādī ~ SUD 200-201 E 5
Muqakoori o SP 208-209 H 6
Muqsim, Ğabal ▲ ET 194-195 G 6
Muqšin o OM 132-133 J 4
Muqui o BR 72-73 K 6
Muqui, Rio ~ BR 70-71 F 2
Muqur o AFG 134-135 M 2
Mura o BR 66-67 H 4
Mura ~ RUS 116-117 J 7
Muradiye o TR 128-129 K 3
Muraduagar o IND 138-139 F 5
Murafa ~ UA 102-103 F 3
Murair, Ğazīrat ⌒ ET 194-195 G 6
Murakami o J 152-153 H 5
Muralgarra o AUS 176-177 D 4
Murallón, Cerro ▲ RCH 80 D 4
Muramgaon o IND 142-143 B 5
Muramvya o BU 212-213 B 5
Muranga o EAK 212-213 F 4
Murangering o EAK 212-213 E 2
Muraré, Rio ~ BR 62-63 H 5
Murași o RUS 96-97 F 4
Murat, Château · F 56 E 4
Murat Çayı ~ TR 128-129 K 3
Murat Dağı ▲ TR 128-129 C 3
Murat Nehri ~ TR 128-129 J 3
Muratus, Pegunungan ▲ RI 164-165 D 5
Muravera o I 100-101 B 5
Murbād o IND 138-139 D 10
Murça o P 98-99 D 4
Mūrče Ḫūrt o IR 134-135 D 2
Murchinson Range ▲ AUS 174-175 C 7
Murchison o AUS 180-181 H 4
Murchison o NZ 182 D 4
Murchison, Cape ▲ CDN 36-37 R 3
Murchison, Mount ▲ AUS 176-177 D 3
Murchison Falls ~ EAU 212-213 C 2
Murchison Falls National Park ⊥ EAU 212-213 C 2
Murchison Island ⌒ CDN (ONT) 234-235 P 4
Murchison River ~ AUS 176-177 C 3
Murchison River ~ CDN 24-25 a 6
Murchison Settlement Roadhouse o AUS 176-177 C 3
Murchison Sund ≈ 26-27 P 5
Murchisson, Mount ▲ WAN 204-205 H 4
Murcia o E 98-99 G 6
Murcia ▫ E 98-99 G 6
Murder Creek ~ USA (AL) 284-285 D 5
Murdo o USA (SD) 260-261 F 3
Murdochville o CDN (QUE) 240-241 K 2
Murdock o USA (MN) 270-271 C 5
Murdock o USA (NE) 262-263 K 4
Murehwa o ZW 218-219 F 3
Mureji o WAN 204-205 F 4
Murèn, Zun ~ RUS 116-117 L 10
Mureș ~ RO 102-103 D 4
Muret o F 90-91 H 10
Murfreesboro o USA (AR) 276-277 B 6
Murfreesboro o USA (NC) 282-283 K 4
Murfreesboro o USA (TN) 276-277 J 5
Murgab o TJ (GOR) 146-147 B 6
Murgab ~ TJ 136-137 N 5
Murgab o TM 136-137 H 6
Murgab ~ TM 136-137 H 7
Murgal' ~ RUS 112-113 O 4
Murgenella ✕ AUS 172-173 L 1
Murgenella Wildlife Sanctuary ⊥ AUS 172-173 L 1
Murgha Kibzai o PK 138-139 B 4
Murgho, Hāmūn-i- o PK 134-135 L 5
Murgon o AUS 178-179 L 4
Murgoo o AUS 176-177 D 3
Murgud o IND 140-141 F 2
Muri o VRC 154-155 B 3
Muriaê o BR 72-73 J 6
Muriaé, Rio ~ BR 72-73 K 6
Murici, Ponta do ▲ BR 68-69 F 3
Muricilândia o BR 68-69 D 5
Muricizal, Rio ~ BR 68-69 D 5
Muridke o PK 138-139 E 4
Muriege o ANG 216-217 F 4
Muriel Lake o CDN 32-33 P 4
Murighiol = Indenpența o· RO 102-103 F 5
Murillo o CDN (ONT) 234-235 O 6
Murinja o RUS 116-117 N 8
Muritiba o BR 72-73 L 2
Müritz o D 92-93 M 2
Müritz-National-Park ⊥ D 92-93 M 2
Muriwai o NZ 182 F 3
Murizidié Pass ▲ LAR 192-193 F 6
Murman, zaliv o RUS 108-109 G 4
Murmanca, buhta o RUS 108-109 N 3
Murmansk ☆ RUS 88-89 M 2
Murmanskiy Bereg = Murmanskij bereg ⌣ RUS 88-89 M 2
Murmanskoye Rise ≃ 10-11 C 1
Murmaši o RUS 88-89 M 2
Muro Lucano o I 100-101 E 4
Murom ☆ RUS 94-95 S 4
Muroran o J 152-153 J 3
Muros o E 98-99 C 3
Muroto o J 152-153 F 8
Muroto-saki ▲ J 152-153 F 8
Murphy o USA (ID) 252-253 B 3
Murphy o USA (NC) 282-283 C 5
Murphy o USA (OR) 244-245 B 8
Murphy Head ▲ CDN 36-37 S 5
Murphy Hot Springs · USA (ID) 252-253 C 4
Murphysboro o USA (IL) 276-277 F 3
Mūrqūm, Kūh-e ▲ IR 134-135 G 2
Murra Murra o AUS 178-179 J 5
Murray o USA (IA) 274-275 E 3
Murray o USA (KY) 276-277 G 4
Murray o USA (UT) 254-255 D 3
Murray, Cape ▲ CDN 24-25 O 2
Murray, Lake o PNG 183 A 4
Murray, Lake < USA (OK) 264-265 G 4
Murray, Lake < USA (SC) 284-285 J 2
Murray Bridge o· AUS 180-181 E 3
Murray Downs o AUS 178-179 C 1
Murray Fracture Zone ≃ 14-15 N 4
Murray Harbour o CDN (NS) 240-241 N 4
Murray Inlet ≈ 24-25 P 3
Murray Islands ⌒ AUS 183 C 5
Murray Maxwell Bay ≈ 24-25 f 5
Murray Range ▲ PNG 183 B 4
Murray River ~ AUS 180-181 E 3
Murray River ~ CDN (BC) 228-229 N 2
Murray River Basin ∸ AUS 180-181 F 2
Murraysburg o ZA 220-221 F 5
Murray-Sunset National Park ⊥ AUS 180-181 F 3
Murray Town o AUS 180-181 E 2
Murrayville o AUS 180-181 F 3
Murree o PK 138-139 D 3
Murrej, mys ▲ RUS 84-85 b 2
Murri, Río ~ CO 60-61 C 4
Murroa o MOC 218-219 J 3
Murroe Lake o CDN 30-31 U 6
Murrumbidgee River ~ AUS 180-181 H 3
Murrumburrah o AUS 180-181 K 3
Murrupula o MOC 218-219 K 2
Murrurundi o AUS 178-179 L 6
Murrysville o USA (PA) 280-281 G 3
Murshidābād o· IND 142-143 F 3
Murtajāpur o IND 138-139 F 9
Murtaugh o USA (ID) 252-253 D 4
Murtle Lake o CDN (BC) 228-229 P 4
Murtle River ~ CDN (BC) 228-229 P 4
Murtoa o AUS 180-181 G 4
Murtovaara o FIN 88-89 K 4
Muru, Rio ~ BR 66-67 B 7
Murua o PNG 183 C 4
Murua Island = Woodlark Island ⌒ PNG 183 G 5
Muruaul, Lake < USA (TX) 264-265 K 6
Muruchachi o YV 60-61 F 3
Murud o· IND 138-139 D 10
Murud, Gunung ▲ MAL 164-165 D 2
Muruken o PNG 183 C 3
Murun, gora ▲ RUS 118-119 J 6
Murupara o NZ 182 F 3
Muruptumatari ~ RUS 108-109 h 4
Murupu o BR 62-63 D 4
Mururé, Igarapé ~ BR 68-69 C 6
Mururoa Atoll ⌒ F 13 O 5
Murwāra o IND 142-143 B 4
Murwillumbah o AUS 178-179 M 5
Murygino o RUS 96-97 F 4
Mürzzuschlag o A 92-93 N 5
Muş ☆ TR 128-129 J 3
Mūsa, 'Ain · ET 194-195 F 3
Mūsa, Ğabal ▲ ET 194-195 F 3
Mūsā, Ḫōr-e ≈ 134-135 C 3
Mūsa, Wādī o JOR 130-131 D 2
Musa Ālī Terara ▲ DJI 200-201 L 6
Musadi o ZRE 210-211 J 5
Mūsā Ḫēl o AFG 138-139 B 3
Musaia o WAL 202-203 E 5
Musai'id o Q 134-135 D 6
Musaimir o Y 132-133 D 7
Mušairib, Ra's ▲ UAE 134-135 D 6
Mušairifa, al- o SYR 128-129 H 4
Mūsa Khel o PK 138-139 C 3
Mūsa Khel Bāzār o PK 138-139 B 4
Musala ▲ BG 102-103 C 6
Musala, Pulau ⌒ RI 162-163 C 4
Muṣallā, al- o OM 132-133 L 2
Musan o DVR 150-151 G 6
Musandam, Ra's ▲ OM 134-135 G 5
Mūsā Qal'e o AFG 134-135 L 2
Mūsā Qal'e, Rūd-e ~ AFG 134-135 L 2
Musa River ~ PNG 183 E 5
Musashi o J 152-153 D 8
Mušattā, Qaṣr al- ∴· JOR 130-131 E 2
Musawa o WAN 198-199 C 6
Musawwarat, Temples of · SUD 200-201 F 4
Musayyib, al- ☆ IRQ 128-129 L 6
Mušbih, Ğabal ▲ ET 194-195 G 6
Muscat = Masqaṭ ★·· OM 132-133 L 2
Muscatatuck River ~ USA (IN) 274-275 M 6
Muscatine o USA (IA) 274-275 G 3
Muscoda o USA (WI) 274-275 H 1
Muse o USA (OK) 264-265 K 4
Musenge o ZRE (KIV) 212-213 B 4
Musenge o ZRE (SHA) 214-215 B 5
Musengezi ~ ZW 218-219 F 3
Museum o· RI 164-165 G 6
Musgrave o AUS 174-175 G 4
Musgrave o CDN (BC) 230-231 F 5
Musgrave, Port ≈ 174-175 F 3
Musgrave Harbour o CDN (NFL) 242-243 P 3
Musgrave Ranges ▲ AUS 176-177 L 3
Mus-Haja, gora ▲ RUS 120-121 J 2
Mushandike Sanctuary ⊥ ZW 218-219 F 5
Mushayfāt o SUD 206-207 K 3
Mushenge o ZRE 210-211 H 6
Mushie o ZRE 210-211 F 5
Mushima o Z 218-219 C 2
Mushipashi o Z 214-215 F 6
Mushota o Z 214-215 E 5
Mushu Island ⌒ PNG 183 B 2
Mūsi ~ IND 140-141 H 2
Musi ~ RI 162-163 F 6
Musidora o CDN (ALB) 232-233 G 2
Musin o WAN 204-205 E 5
Musiri o IND 140-141 H 5
Mūsiyan o IR 134-135 B 2
Muskeg Lake Indian Reservation ✕ CDN (SAS) 232-233 M 3
Muskego o USA (WI) 274-275 K 2
Muskegon o USA (MI) 272-273 C 4
Muskegon Heights o USA (MI) 272-273 C 4
Muskegon River ~ USA (MI) 272-273 D 4
Muskeg River o CDN (ALB) 228-229 Q 3
Muskeg River ~ CDN 30-31 H 5
Muskingum River ~ USA (OH) 280-281 E 4
Muskira o IND 138-139 G 7
Muskoday Indian Reservation ✕ CDN (SAS) 232-233 N 2
Muskogee o USA (OK) 264-265 J 3
Muskox Lake o CDN 30-31 P 3
Muskratdam Lake o CDN 34-35 L 4
Muskwa o CDN 30-31 H 6
Muskwa River ~ CDN 30-31 H 6
Muskwa River ~ CDN 32-33 N 3
Muslimiya o SYR 128-129 G 4
Musljumovo ☆ RUS 96-97 H 6
Musoma ☆ EAT 212-213 D 4
Musondweji ~ Z 218-219 C 1
Musongoie o ZRE 214-215 C 5
Mus-Onnjue ~ RUS 118-119 O 7
Musoro o Z 218-219 F 1
Musoshi o ZRE 214-215 D 6
Musquaro, Lac o CDN (QUE) 242-243 G 2
Musquash o CDN (NB) 240-241 J 5
Musquodoboit Harbour o CDN (NS) 240-241 M 6
Mussel Fork ~ USA (MO) 274-275 F 5
Musselshell o USA (MT) 250-251 L 5
Musselshell River ~ USA (MT) 250-251 L 5
Mussende o ANG 216-217 D 5
Musserra o ANG 216-217 B 3
Mussolo o ANG 216-217 D 4
Mussuma o ANG (MOX) 216-217 F 7
Mussuma ~ ANG 216-217 F 7
Mustāfābād o PK 138-139 D 4
Mustafakemalpaşa ☆ TR 128-129 C 2
Mustahil o ETH 208-209 G 6
Müstair = Münster o·· CH 92-93 L 5
Mustang o NEP 144-145 D 6
Mustang ~ USA (TX) 264-265 B 6
Mustang Himal ▲ NEP 144-145 D 6
Mustang Island ⌒ USA (TX) 266-267 K 6
Musters, Lago o RA 80 F 2
Mustique Island ⌒ WV 56 E 5
Mustjala o EST 94-95 H 2
Mustvee o EST 94-95 K 2
Musu Dan ▲ DVR 150-151 G 7
Musún, Cerro ▲ NIC 52-53 B 5
Muswellbrook o· AUS 180-181 L 2
Mūṭ o ET 194-195 D 5
Mut ☆ TR 128-129 E 4
Mutá, Ponta do ▲ BR 72-73 L 2
Mutale ~ ZA 218-219 F 6
Mutanda o Z 214-215 D 7
Muṯannā, al ▫ IRQ 130-131 J 2
Mutarara o MOC 218-219 H 3
Mutare ☆· ZW 218-219 G 4
Mutarnee o AUS 174-175 J 6
Muteba, Xá- o ANG 216-217 D 4
Mutenge o Z 218-219 E 1
Mutha o EAK (EAS) 212-213 G 4
Mutha ▲ EAK (EAS) 212-213 G 4
Mutici o BR 68-69 L 6
Mutiene o ZRE 210-211 E 6
Muting o RI 166-167 L 5
Mutinglupa o RP 160-161 D 5
Mutir o EAU 212-213 C 2
Mutis, Gunung ▲ RI 166-167 C 6
Mutki ☆ TR 128-129 J 3
Mutnaja, buhta o RUS 120-121 S 7
Mutni ~ PK 134-135 M 6
Mutnyj Materik o RUS 88-89 X 4
Mutoko o ZW 218-219 G 3
Mutombo, Bwana- o ZRE 216-217 E 3
Mutombo-Mukulu o ZRE 214-215 C 5
Mutomo o EAK 212-213 G 4
Mutoraj o RUS 116-117 K 5
Mutorashanga o ZW 218-219 F 3
Mutoto o ZRE (KOC) 210-211 J 6
Mutoto o ZRE (SHA) 214-215 E 4
Mutsamudu o· COM 222-223 D 4
Mutshatsha o ZRE 214-215 C 6
Mutsu o J 152-153 J 4
Muttaburra o AUS 178-179 H 2
Mutton Bay o CDN (QUE) 242-243 J 2
Mutúali o MOC 218-219 J 2
Mutukula o EAU 212-213 C 4
Mutum o BR (AMA) 66-67 G 6
Mutum o BR (MIN) 72-73 K 5
Mutum, Cachoeira ~ BR 66-67 J 5
Mutum, Ilha do ⌒ BR 66-67 F 7
Mutum, Rio ~ BR 66-67 C 5
Mutumbi o ZRE 214-215 E 4
Mutum Biyu o WAN 204-205 J 4
Mutumbu o ANG 216-217 D 6
Mutum Daya o WAN 204-205 J 4
Mutum ou Madeira, Rio ~ BR 70-71 K 5
Mutum Paraná o BR 66-67 E 7
Mutungu-Tari o ZRE 216-217 D 3
Mutuoca, Ilha da ⌒ BR 68-69 F 2
Mutur o CL 140-141 J 6
Mututi, Ilha ⌒ BR 62-63 J 6
Mutu-wan ≈ 152-153 J 4
Mutwanga o ZRE 212-213 B 3
Muurola o FIN 88-89 H 3
Mu Us Shamo ∸ VRC 154-155 E 2
Mūvattupula o IND 140-141 G 6
Muwaih, al- o KSA 130-131 G 6
Muwaiḥa, Ğabal ▲ UAE 134-135 F 6
Muwailiḥ, al- o KSA 130-131 D 4
Muwassam o KSA 132-133 C 5
Muwo Island ⌒ PNG 183 F 5
Muxima o ANG 216-217 B 4
Muyinga o BU 212-213 C 5
Muy Muy o NIC 52-53 B 5
Muyombe o Z 214-215 G 6
Muyuka o CAM 204-205 H 6
Muyumba o ZRE 214-215 D 4
Muzaffarabad o IND 138-139 D 2
Muzaffargarh o PK 138-139 C 4
Muzaffarnagar o IND 138-139 F 5
Muzaffarpur o IND 142-143 D 2
Muzāḥimiya, al- o KSA 130-131 K 5
Muzambinho o BR 72-73 G 6
Muze o MOC 218-219 F 2
Muzej narodnoji architektury i pobutu · UA 102-103 G 2
muzej-usad'ba "Tarhany" · RUS 94-95 S 5
Muzhen o VRC 154-155 K 6
Muži o RUS 114-115 H 2
Muzizi ~ EAU 212-213 C 3
Muzkol, hrebet ▲ TJ 136-137 N 5
Muzo o CO 60-61 D 5
Muzon, Cape ▲ USA 32-33 D 4
Muztag ▲ VRC 144-145 C 2
Muztag ▲ VRC 144-145 F 2
Muztagata ▲ VRC 146-147 B 6
Mvangan o CAM 210-211 C 2
Mveng o CAM 210-211 D 2
Mvengué o CAM 210-211 C 2
Mvera o MW 218-219 H 1
Mvolo o SUD 206-207 J 5
Mvomero o EAT 214-215 J 4
Mvoung ~ G 210-211 D 3
Mvouti o RCB 210-211 D 6
Mvuha o EAT 214-215 J 4
Mvuma o ZW 218-219 F 4
Mvurwi o ZW 218-219 F 3
Mvuvye ~ Z 218-219 F 2
Mwabungu o EAK 212-213 G 6
Mwadi-Kalumbu o ZRE 216-217 E 3
Mwadingusha o ZRE 214-215 D 6
Mwafwe ~ Z 218-219 C 1
Mwaga o EAT 214-215 J 5
Mwala o MW 218-219 H 3
Mwaleshi ~ Z 214-215 F 6
Mwambo o EAT 214-215 L 6
Mwambwa ~ Z 214-215 G 6
Mwami o ZW 218-219 E 3
Mwana-Ndeke o ZRE 210-211 L 6
Mwangalala o ZRE 214-215 D 6
Mwangia, Pania- o ZRE 214-215 E 4
Mwango o ZRE 214-215 C 4
Mwanibwaghosu o SOL 184 I f 4
Mwanisenga o EAT 212-213 D 6
Mwanza ▫ EAT 212-213 D 5
Mwanza ☆· EAT 212-213 D 5
Mwanza o MW 218-219 H 2
Mwanza o ZRE 214-215 D 4
Mwanza Gulf o EAT 212-213 D 5
Mwanzangoma ~ ZRE 210-211 J 6
Mwaru ~ EAT 212-213 E 6
Mwatasi o EAT (IRI) 214-215 J 4
Mwatate o EAK 212-213 G 5
Mwatate ~ EAK 212-213 G 5
Mwea National Reserve ⊥ EAK 212-213 F 4
Mweka o ZRE 210-211 H 6
Mwembeshi o Z 218-219 D 2
Mwenda o Z 214-215 E 6
Mwene-Biji o ZRE 214-215 B 5
Mwene-Ditu o ZRE 214-215 B 4
Mwenezi o ZW (Mvi) 218-219 F 5
Mwenezi ~ ZW 218-219 F 5
Mwenga o ZRE 212-213 B 5
Mweru, Lake o Z 214-215 E 5
Mweru Wantipa, Lake o Z 214-215 E 5
Mweru Wantipa National Park ⊥ Z 214-215 E 5
Mwilambwe o ZRE 214-215 C 5
Mwimbwi o EAT (RUK) 214-215 F 5
Mwingi o EAK 212-213 G 4
Mwinilunga o Z 214-215 C 6
Mwitika o EAK 212-213 G 4
Mwitikira o EAT (DOD) 214-215 H 4
Mwogo ~ RWA 212-213 B 5
Mwombezhi ~ Z 218-219 C 1
My ~ RUS 122-123 J 2
Mya, Oued ~ DZ 190-191 D 6
Myaing o MYA 142-143 J 5
Myakka City o USA (FL) 286-287 G 4
Myakka Head o USA (FL) 286-287 G 4
Myakka River ~ USA (FL) 286-287 G 4
Myakka River State Park ⊥ USA (FL) 286-287 G 4
Myall Lakes National Park ⊥ AUS 180-181 M 2
Myanaung o MYA 142-143 J 6
Myanmar ■ MYA 142-143 J 5
Mychajlivka o UA 102-103 J 4
Mychla o MYA 142-143 K 6
Mye, Mount ▲ CDN 20-21 Y 5
Myerstown o USA (PA) 280-281 K 3
Myingyan o MYA 142-143 J 5
Myinmoletkat Taung ▲ MYA 158-159 E 4
Myitkyina o MYA 142-143 K 3
Myitnge ~ MYA 142-143 K 5
Myittha o MYA 142-143 K 5
Mykenai ·· GR 100-101 J 6
Mykolajiv o UA 102-103 G 4
Mykolajivs'ka cerkva · UA 102-103 C 3
Mykolayiv = Mykolajiv o UA 102-103 G 4
Myky, Área Indígena ✕ BR 70-71 H 3
Myla o RUS 88-89 V 4
Myla ~ RUS 88-89 V 4
Mylga ~ RUS 120-121 N 2
Mylius Erichsen Land ∸ GRØ 26-27 m 3
Mylo o USA (ND) 258-259 H 3
Mymensingh o BD 142-143 G 3
Mynämäki o FIN 88-89 F 6
Myndagaj o RUS 120-121 E 3
Mynfontein o ZA 220-221 F 5
Mynsualmas ▲ KA 126-127 L 5
Myohaung o MYA 142-143 H 5
Myoko-san ▲ J 152-153 H 6
Myola o AUS 174-175 F 6
Myola o PNG 183 D 5
Myotha o MYA 142-143 J 5
Myra ∴·· TR 128-129 D 4
Myre o N 86-87 G 2
Myrhorod o UA 102-103 H 3
Mýri o IS 86-87 e 2
Myrnam o CDN (ALB) 232-233 G 2
Myronivka ☆ UA 102-103 G 3
Myrtle o CDN (ONT) 238-239 G 4
Myrtle Beach o· USA (SC) 284-285 M 3
Myrtle Creek o USA (OR) 244-245 B 7
Myrtleford o· AUS 180-181 J 4
Myrtle Grove o USA (LA) 268-269 L 7
Myrtle Point o USA (OR) 244-245 A 7
Mysen ☆ N 86-87 E 7
Mys-Kamennyj o RUS 108-109 P 7
Myski o RUS 124-125 P 2
Myškin ☆ RUS 94-95 Q 3
Myškino = Myškin ☆ RUS 94-95 Q 3
Myślenice o· PL 92-93 P 4
My So'n · VN 158-159 K 3
Mysore o·· IND 140-141 G 4
Mystery Caves ∴ USA (MN) 270-271 F 7
Mys Želanija o RUS 108-109 N 3
Myszyniec o PL 92-93 Q 2
My Tho ☆· VN 158-159 J 5
Mytišči ☆ RUS 94-95 P 4
Mytishchi = Mytišči ☆ RUS 94-95 P 4
Myton o USA (UT) 254-255 E 3
Mývatn · IS 86-87 e 2
Myzeqe ⌣ AL 100-101 G 4
M'Zab ∸··· DZ 190-191 D 4
M'Zab, Oued ~ DZ 190-191 E 4
Mže ~ CZ 92-93 M 4
Mzenga o EAT 214-215 K 4
Mziha o EAT 212-213 F 6
Mzimba o MW 214-215 G 6
Mzimkulwana Nature Reserve ⊥ ZA 220-221 J 4
Mzuzu ☆ MW 214-215 H 6

N

Naab ~ D 92-93 M 4
Naala o TCH 198-199 G 6
Naalehu o USA (HI) 288 K 5
Na'am o SUD 206-207 J 4
Na'ām ~ SUD 206-207 J 6
Na'ama o ET 194-195 G 4
Na'ān, an- o KSA 130-131 K 6
Naantali o· FIN 88-89 G 6
Naas = An Nás ☆ IRL 90-91 D 5
Nababeep o ZA 220-221 C 4
Naban SK ~ VRC 156-157 F 5
Nabar < TCH 198-199 K 3
Nabarlek o AUS 174-175 B 3
Nabas o RP 160-161 E 7
Nabaṭiya t-Taḥtā ☆ RL 128-129 F 6
Nabavatu o FJI 184 III b 2
Nabawa o AUS 176-177 C 4
Nabawan o MAL 160-161 B 10
Nabberu, Lake o AUS 176-177 F 2
Nabéré, Réserve Partielle de ⊥ BF 202-203 J 4
Naberera o EAT 212-213 F 6
Naberezhnyye Chelny = Naberežnye Čelny ☆ RUS 96-97 H 6
Naberežnye Čelny ☆ RUS 96-97 H 6
Nabesna River ~ USA 20-21 T 5
Nabeul ☆ TN 190-191 H 2
Nabǧa o UAE 134-135 F 6
Nabhāniya, an- o KSA 130-131 H 5
Nabī, Wādī ~ SUD 200-201 F 2
Nabil' ~ RUS 122-123 K 3
Nabilatuk o EAU 212-213 E 2
Nabileque, Pantanal de o BR 70-71 J 7
Nabileque, Rio ~ BR 70-71 J 7
Nabil'skij, zaliv o RUS 122-123 K 3
Nabingora o EAU 212-213 C 3
Nabire o RI 166-167 H 3
Nabisar o PK 138-139 B 7
Nabī Šu'aib, Ğabal an- ▲ Y 132-133 C 6
Nabk, an- o KSA 130-131 F 2
Nabljudenij, mys ▲ RUS 120-121 T 3
Naboga o GH 202-203 K 5
Naboomspruit o ZA 220-221 J 2
Nabou o BF 202-203 J 4
Naboulgou o RT 202-203 L 4
Nabouwalu o FJI 184 III b 2
Nabq o ET 194-195 G 3
Nabukjuak Bay ≈ 36-37 L 2
Nābulus = Shekhem ☆ WB 130-131 D 1
Nabuquen, Caño ~ CO 60-61 G 6
Nabusamke o EAU 212-213 D 3
Nabwān o KSA 130-131 G 4
Nacala o MOC 218-219 L 2
Načalovo ☆ RUS 96-97 F 10
Nacaome ☆ HN 52-53 L 5
Nacaroa o MOC 218-219 K 2
Nacebe o BOL 70-71 D 2
Naches o USA (WA) 244-245 E 4
Naches River ~ USA (WA) 244-245 D 4
Nachicapau, Lac o CDN 36-37 Q 6
Nachingwea o EAT 214-215 K 6
Nāchna o IND 138-139 C 6
Nachtigal, Cap ▲ CAM 210-211 B 2
Nachtigal, Chutes de ~ CAM 204-205 J 6
Nachuge o IND 140-141 L 4
Nachvak Fiord ≈ 36-37 S 5
Načikinskij, mys ▲ RUS 120-121 U 5
Nacimiento Reservoir o USA (CA) 248-249 D 4
Nacionalni park Brioni ⊥ HR 100-101 D 2
Nacionalni park Kornati ⊥ HR 100-101 E 3
Nacionalni park Kozara ⊥ BIH 100-101 F 2
Nacionalni park Mljet ⊥ HR 100-101 F 3
Nacionalni park Orjen ⊥ YU 100-101 G 3
Nacionalni park Paklenica ⊥· HR 100-101 E 2
Nacionalni park Plitvička Jezera ⊥··· HR 100-101 E 2
Nacional'nyj park "Losinyj ostrov" ⊥ RUS 94-95 P 4
Nackara o AUS 180-181 E 2
Nackawic o CDN (NB) 240-241 H 4
Nacmine o CDN (ALB) 232-233 F 4
Naco o CDN (ALB) 232-233 H 4
Naco ∴ HN 52-53 K 4
Nacogdoches o USA (TX) 268-269 F 5
Nacori Chico o MEX 50-51 E 3
Nacozari de García o MEX 50-51 E 2
Nacula ⌒ FJI 184 III a 2
Ñacuñán o RA 78-79 F 3
Ñacuñán, Reserva Ecológica ⊥ RA 78-79 E 2
Nacyjanal'ny park Belavežskaja pušča ⊥··· BY 94-95 J 5
Nada o USA (TX) 266-267 L 4
Nadawli o GH 202-203 J 4
Nād-e 'Alī o AFG 134-135 L 3
Nāder Šāh Kūt o AFG 138-139 C 2
Nadëžnyj, mys ▲ RUS 110-111 c 2
Nadi o FJI 184 III a 2
Nadi o SUD 200-201 F 3
Nadiād o IND 138-139 D 8
Nadina River o CDN (BC) 228-229 H 3
Nadina River ~ CDN (BC) 228-229 H 3
Nadoba o RT 202-203 L 4
Nadojaha ~ RUS 108-109 N 6
Nador o MA 188-189 K 3
Nadudoturku ozero o RUS 108-109 U 5
Nadura, Temple of ∴· ET 194-195 E 5
Naduri o FJI 184 III b 2
Nadvirna ☆ UA 102-103 D 3
Nadym o RUS 114-115 M 2
Nadym ~ RUS 114-115 L 3
Nadymskaja Ob' ≈ 108-109 N 8
Nadzab o PNG 183 D 4
Nā'ebābād o AFG 136-137 K 6
Naejangsan National Park ⊥· ROK 150-151 F 10
Nærøyfjorden ∸· N 86-87 C 6
Næstved o· DK 86-87 E 9
Nafada o WAN 204-205 J 3
Nafadj, Baté- o RG 202-203 F 4
Nafadji o SN 202-203 E 3
Nafaq Aḥmad Ḥamdī II ET 194-195 F 2
Nafi o KSA 130-131 H 5
Nafiša o ET 194-195 F 2
Náfpaktos o GR 100-101 H 5
Nafplio o· GR 100-101 J 6
Naft-e Šāh o IR 134-135 A 1
Nafūd ad-Daḥī ∸ KSA 132-133 D 3
Nafūd al-Kubrā, an- ∸ KSA 130-131 G 3
Nafūd al-'Uraik ∸ KSA 130-131 H 5
Nafūd as-Sirr ∸ KSA 130-131 J 5
Nafūsah, Jabal ▲ LAR 192-193 D 2
Nāg o PK 134-135 L 5
Naga o RP (CAS) 160-161 E 6
Naga o RP (CEB) 160-161 E 7
Nağaf, an- ▫ IRQ 128-129 K 7
Nağaf, an- ☆ IRQ (NAG) 128-129 L 7
Nağafābād o IR 134-135 D 2
Nagagami Lake o CDN (ONT) 236-237 C 3
Nagagami River ~ CDN (ONT) 236-237 D 3
Nagai Island ⌒ USA 22-23 Q 5
Nagaj o IND 140-141 F 2
Nāgāland ▫ IND 142-143 J 2
Nağ' al-Ma'mariya o ET 194-195 F 5
Nagamangala o IND 140-141 G 4
Nagambie o AUS 180-181 H 4
Nagamisis Provincial Park ⊥ CDN (ONT) 236-237 D 3
Nagam River Mission o PNG 183 B 2
Nagandana o CI 202-203 H 4
Nagano o J 152-153 H 6
Naganuma o J 152-153 J 3
Nagaoka o J 152-153 H 6
Nagaon o IND 142-143 H 2
Nagappattinam o IND 140-141 H 5
Nagara o RMM 202-203 E 2
Nagare Augū ▲ MYA 158-159 C 2
Nagarhole National Park ⊥ IND 140-141 G 4
Nagari o IND 140-141 H 4
Nagarjuna Sāgar o IND 140-141 H 2
Nagar Karnūl o IND 140-141 H 2
Nagarote o NIC 52-53 L 5
Nagar Pārkar o PK 138-139 C 7
Nagarzê o VRC 144-145 H 6
Nagasaki ☆·· J 152-153 C 8
Naga-shima ⌒ J 152-153 D 8
Nāgaur o IND 138-139 D 6
Nagayaman Point ▲ RP 160-161 E 3
Nāgbhīr o IND 138-139 G 9
Nagbo o GH 202-203 K 4
Nağd ∸ KSA 130-131 G 4
Nage o RI 168 E 7
Nageezi o USA (NM) 256-257 H 2
Nagercoil o IND 140-141 G 6
Nageriwāla o PK 138-139 C 4
Nağ 'Hammādī o ET 194-195 F 4
Nagichot o SUD 208-209 A 6
Nagina o IND 138-139 G 5
Naglějngynvaam ~ RUS 112-113 O 2
Naglějnyn, gora ▲ RUS 112-113 P 2
Naglějnyn, mys ▲ RUS 112-113 P 2
Nago o J 152-153 B 11
Nāgod o IND 142-143 B 3
Nagor'e o RUS 94-95 Q 3
Nagorno-Karabakh = Dağliq Qarabağ Muxtar Vilayati ▫ AZ 128-129 M 2
Nagornyj o RUS (SAH) 118-119 M 8
Nagornyj ☆ RUS (KOR) 112-113 U 5
Nagorsk ☆ RUS 96-97 G 4
Nagoya ☆· J 152-153 G 7
Nāgpur o IND 138-139 G 9
Nagqu o VRC 144-145 J 5
Nāgrāl o IND 140-141 H 2
Nağrān ▫ KSA 132-133 D 4
Nağrān ☆· KSA (NAG) 132-133 D 5
Nağrān, Wādī ~ Y 132-133 D 5
Nagslaran o RP 160-161 D 5
Nagua ☆ DOM 54-55 L 5
Naguabo o USA (PR) 286-287 Q 2
Nagvaraaluk, Lac o CDN 36-37 O 4
Nagykanizsa o H 92-93 O 5
Naha o J 152-153 B 11
Na Haeo o THA 158-159 F 2
Nāhan o IND 138-139 F 4
Na Hang ☆ VN 156-157 D 5
Nahang, Rūd-e ~ IR 134-135 K 5
Nahanni Butte o CDN 30-31 H 5
Nahanni National Park ⊥··· CDN 30-31 G 5
Nahara, Orto- o RUS 118-119 G 5
Nahatlatch River ~ CDN (BC) 230-231 G 3
Nahatta ~ RUS 110-111 X 6
Naheleg ⌒ ER 200-201 K 4
Nahīa Lọ ☆ VN 156-157 D 6
Nāhid, Bi'r < ET 194-195 D 2
Naḥl, Rūd-e ~ IR 134-135 H 3
Nahlin o CDN 32-33 E 2
Nahlin Plateau ▲ CDN 32-33 D 2
Nahma Junction o USA (MI) 270-271 M 5
Nahmint o CDN (BC) 230-231 E 4
Naho o SOL 184 I e 3
Nahodka o RUS 108-109 R 8
Nahodka o RUS 122-123 E 7
Nahodka, buhta ≈ 108-109 P 8
Nahodka, ostrov ⌒ RUS 112-113 V 1
Nahoi, Cape = Cape Cumberland ▲ VAN 184 II a 2
Nahrīn o AFG 136-137 L 6
Nahr Ouessel ~ DZ 190-191 C 3
Nahualate, Río ~ GCA 52-53 J 4
Nahuatzen o MEX 52-53 D 2
Nahuélbuta, Cordillera de ▲ RCH 78-79 C 5
Nahuelbuta, Parque Nacional ⊥ RCH 78-79 C 4
Nahuel Huapi o RA 78-79 D 6
Nahuel Huapi, Lago o RA 78-79 D 6
Nahuel Huapi, Parque Nacional ⊥ RA 78-79 D 6
Nahuel Mapá o RA 78-79 F 3
Nahum, Hefar ∴· IL 130-131 D 1
Nahunta o USA (GA) 284-285 J 5
Nahuo o VRC 156-157 G 6
Nahwitti o CDN (BC) 230-231 A 3
Nā'ī, an- o KSA 130-131 H 4
Naiams Fort · NAM 220-221 C 3
Naica o MEX 50-51 G 4
Naicam o CDN (SAS) 232-233 O 3
Nā'id Abār o KSA 132-133 C 5
Naidi o FJI 184 III b 2
Nā'if al-'Āğil o IRQ 128-129 L 7
Naihbawi o IND 142-143 H 4
Naij Tal o VRC 144-145 K 3
Naikliu o RI 166-167 B 6
Naikoon Provincial Park ⊥ CDN (BC) 228-229 C 3
Naila o D 92-93 L 3
Nailaga o FJI 184 III a 2
Naiman Qi o VRC 150-151 C 6
Nain o CDN 36-37 T 6
Nāīn o· IR 134-135 E 2
Naini Tāl o· IND 138-139 G 5
Nainpur o IND 142-143 B 4
Naiopue o MOC 218-219 J 2
Nairai ⌒ FJI 184 III b 2
Nairn o GB 90-91 F 3
Nairobi ▫ EAK 212-213 F 4
Nairobi ★ EAK 212-213 F 4
Nairobi National Park ⊥·· EAK 212-213 F 4
Nairoto o MOC 214-215 K 7

Naitaba ⌒ FJI 184 III c 2
Naivasha o EAK 212-213 F 4
Naivasha, Lake ⇔ EAK 212-213 F 4
Naiwangaa o EAT 214-215 K 5
Najahan ~ RUS 112-113 K 5
Najahanskaja guba ⇔ RUS 120-121 S 3
Najahanskij hrebet ▲ RUS 112-113 K 5
Najasa ~ C 54-55 G 4
Najba o RUS 110-111 S 4
Najba ~ RUS 122-123 K 5
Nājera o•• E 98-99 F 3
Najībābād o IND 138-139 G 5
Najtingejl, proliv ≈ 84-85 a 2
Najverga ~ RUS 118-119 G 6
Najzataš, pereval ▲ TJ 136-137 N 6
Nakadori-shima ⌒ J 152-153 C 8
Na Kae o THA 158-159 H 2
Nakagawa o J 152-153 K 2
Naka-gawa ~ J 152-153 J 6
Nakamoéka o RCB 210-211 D 6
Nakamura o J 152-153 E 8
Nakanai Mountains ▲ PNG 183 F 3
Nakanno o RUS 116-117 O 4
Nakano-shima ⌒ J (KGA) 152-153 C 10
Nakano-shima ⌒ J (SHM) 152-153 E 6
Nakasato o J 152-153 J 4
Naka-Shibetsu o J 152-153 L 3
Nakasongola o EAU 212-213 D 3
Naka-Tane o J 152-153 D 9
Nakatsu o J 152-153 D 8
Nakatsugawa o J 152-153 G 7
Nakchamik Island ⌒ USA 22-23 S 4
Naked Island ⌒ USA 20-21 R 6
Nakel = Nakło nad Notecią o PL 92-93 O 2
Nak'fa o ER 200-201 J 4
Nakhchyvan = Naxçıvan ☆ AZ 128-129 L 3
Nakhichevan = Naxçıvan Muxtar Respublikası ◘ AZ 128-129 L 3
Nakhon Nayok o THA 158-159 F 3
Nakhon Pathom o THA 158-159 F 4
Nakhonphanom o THA 158-159 H 2
Nakhon Ratchasima o THA 158-159 G 3
Nakhon Sawan o THA 158-159 F 3
Nakhon Si Thammarat o•• THA 158-159 E 6
Nakhon Thai o THA 158-159 F 2
Nakhtarāna o IND 138-139 B 8
Naki-Est o RT 202-203 L 4
Nakina o CDN (ONT) 236-237 B 2
Nakina o USA (NC) 282-283 J 6
Nakitoma o EAU 212-213 D 3
Nakivali, Lake ⇔ EAU 212-213 C 4
Nakkala o CL 140-141 J 7
Naknek o USA 22-23 S 3
Naknek Lake ⇔ USA 22-23 S 3
Nako o BF 202-203 J 4
Nakonde o Z 214-215 G 5
Nakong-Atinia o GH 202-203 K 4
Nakop o NAM 220-221 D 4
Nako-Tombetsu o J 152-153 K 2
Nakpanduri o GH 202-203 K 4
Nakpayili o GH 202-203 L 5
Nakskov o DK 86-87 E 9
Nakson, gora ▲ RUS 116-117 G 3
Naktong Gang ~ ROK 150-151 G 10
Nakum ∴• GCA 52-53 K 3
Nakuru ☆ EAK 212-213 F 4
Nakuru, Lake ⇔ EAK 212-213 F 4
Nakusp o CDN (BC) 230-231 M 3
Nāl ~ PK 134-135 L 5
Nalagāmula o IND 140-141 J 4
Nālāgarh o IND 138-139 F 4
Nalajh o MAU 148-149 H 4
Nalatale Ruins ∴• ZW 218-219 E 4
Nālatvād o IND 140-141 G 2
Nalázi o MOC 220-221 L 2
Nalbarra o AUS 176-177 D 4
Nalcayec, Isla ⌒ RCH 80 D 3
Nal'čik ☆ RUS 126-127 E 6
Naldrug o IND 140-141 G 2
Nalgonda o IND 140-141 H 2
Nali o VRC 156-157 F 6
Nalim'e, ozero ⇔ RUS 108-109 V 8
Nalim-Rassoha ~ RUS 110-111 G 4
Nalimsk o RUS 110-111 d 6
Naliya o IND 138-139 B 8
Näljänkä o FIN 88-89 K 4
Nalkhera o IND 138-139 F 8
Nallıhan ☆ TR 128-129 D 2
Nalong o MYA 142-143 K 3
Nalusuku Pool < Z 218-219 B 3
Nālūt o LAR 190-191 H 5
Nama ~ NAM 216-217 F 9
Nama o RI 166-167 E 4
Namaa, Tanjung ▲ RI 166-167 E 3
Namaacha o MOC 220-221 L 2
Namacunde o ANG 216-217 C 8
Namacurra o MOC 218-219 J 3
Namadgi National Park ⊥ AUS 180-181 K 3
Namadi, Dag-e ⇔ AFG 134-135 J 2
Namak, Daryā-ye ⇔ IR 134-135 D 1
Namak, Kavir-e ⇔ IR 134-135 G 1
Namak, Kūh-e ▲ IR 134-135 D 4
Namakan ~ RUS 108-109 a 6
Namak-e Sirğān, Kavir-e ⇔ IR 134-135 F 4
Namakia o RM 222-223 D 5
Nāmakkal o IND 140-141 H 5
Namaksār ⇔ AFG 134-135 J 2
Namaksar, Kāl-e ⇔ IR 134-135 J 1
Namakwaland ∸ ZA 220-221 C 4
Namaland ∸ NAM 220-221 C 3
Namana ~ RUS 118-119 K 5
Namanga o EAK 212-213 F 5
Namangan o US 136-137 M 4
Namanganskaja oblast' ◘ US 136-137 M 4
Namanyere o EAT (RUA) 214-215 F 4
Namao o CDN (ALB) 232-233 E 2
Namapa o MOC 218-219 K 1
Namaponda o MOC 218-219 K 2
Namarrói o MOC 218-219 J 2
Namas o RI 166-167 L 4
Namasagali o EAU 212-213 D 3
Namasale o EAU 212-213 D 3
Namassi o CI 202-203 J 6
Namatanai o PNG 183 G 2
Namatote, Pulau ⌒ RI 166-167 G 3
Namba o ANG 216-217 C 5
Nambazo o MW 218-219 H 2
Nambe Indian Reservation ✗ USA (NM) 256-257 K 3
Namber o RI 166-167 H 2
Nambi o AUS 176-177 F 4
Nambikwara, Área Indígena ✗ BR 70-71 H 3
Nambima, Tanjung ▲ RI 166-167 H 4
Nambolaki, Pulau ⌒ RI 168 E 6
Namboukaha o CI 202-203 H 5
Nambour o AUS 178-179 M 4
Nambuangongo o ANG 216-217 C 4
Nambucca Heads o AUS 178-179 M 6
Nambung National Park ⊥ AUS 176-177 C 5
Namche Bazar o NEP 144-145 F 7
Namchi o IND 142-143 F 2
Nam Chon Reservoir < THA 158-159 E 3
Nam Co ⇔ VRC (XIZ) 144-145 H 5
Nam Co • VRC (XIZ) 144-145 H 5
Namcy ☆• RUS 118-119 O 4
Nam Du, Quần Đảo ⌒ VN 158-159 H 6
Namen = Namur ☆• B 92-93 H 3
Namenalala ⌒ FJI 184 III b 2
Nà Mèo o VN 156-157 D 6
Nametil o MOC 218-219 K 2
Namew Lake ⇔ CDN 34-35 F 3
Namgorab ▲ NAM 220-221 C 2
Namhae Do ⌒ ROK 150-151 F 10
Namhan Gang ~ ROK 150-151 F 9
Nami o MAL 162-163 D 2
Namialo o MOC 218-219 K 2
Namibe ◘ ANG 216-217 B 7
Namibe ☆• ANG 216-217 B 7
Namibe, Deserto de ∸ ANG 216-217 A 8
Namibe, Reserva de ⊥ ANG 216-217 B 7
Namibia ■ NAM 216-217 C 10
Namib-Naukluft Park ⊥ NAM 220-221 B 2
Namibwoestyn = Namib Desert ∸ NAM 216-217 B 9
Namidobe o MOC 218-219 J 3
Namie o J 152-153 J 6
Namies o ZA 220-221 D 4
Namin o IR 128-129 N 3
Namina o MOC 218-219 K 2
Namioka o J 152-153 J 4
Namiquipa o MEX 50-51 F 3
Namiroe, Rio ~ MOC 218-219 K 2
Namitete o MW 218-219 G 2
Namjagbarwa Feng ▲ VRC 144-145 K 6
Namlan o MYA 142-143 K 4
Namlea o RI 166-167 D 3
Nam Léa, Mount ▲ K 158-159 J 4
Namling o VRC 144-145 G 6
Nam-mawng o MYA 142-143 L 5
Nam Ngum Reservoir ⇔ LAO 156-157 C 7
Namo o RI 164-165 F 4
Namoda, Kaura- o WAN 198-199 C 6
Namoi River ~ AUS 178-179 K 6
Namon o RT 202-203 L 5
Namor o BR 66-67 F 6
Namorona o RM 222-223 F 8
Nam Ou ~ LAO 156-157 C 6
Namounou o BF 202-203 L 4
Namous, Oued ~ DZ 190-191 D 3
Nampa o USA (ID) 252-253 B 3
Nampagan o MYA 142-143 J 3
Nampala o RMM 202-203 H 2
Nam Pat o THA 158-159 F 2
Nampevo o MOC 218-219 J 3
Nampo o DVR 150-151 E 8
Nam Poon o THA 142-143 M 6
Nampuecha o MOC 218-219 L 1
Nampula ◘ MOC 218-219 K 2
Nampula ☆ MOC (Nam) 218-219 K 2
Namrole o RI 166-167 D 3
Namru o VRC 144-145 C 5
Namslau = Namysłów o• PL 92-93 O 3
Namsos o N 86-87 E 4
Namsskogan o N 86-87 F 4
Namtabung o RI 166-167 F 6
Namtha o MYA 142-143 J 3
Nam Theun o LAO 158-159 H 2
Nam Tok Chat Trakan National Park ⊥ THA 158-159 F 2
Namtu o MYA 142-143 K 4
Namtumbo o EAT 214-215 J 6
Namu o CDN (BC) 230-231 B 2
Namudi o PNG 183 E 5
Namuiranga o MOC 214-215 L 6
Namukumbo o Z 218-219 D 2
Namuli, Monte ▲ MOC 218-219 J 3
Namuno o MOC 218-219 K 1
Nam Un Reservoir ⇔ THA 158-159 G 2
Namur ☆• B 92-93 H 3
Namur o CDN (QUE) 238-239 L 3
Namur Lake ⇔ CDN 32-33 O 3
Namur Lake Indian Reserve ✗ CDN 32-33 O 3
Namutoni o NAM 216-217 D 9
Namwaan, Pulau ⌒ RI 166-167 F 5
Namwala o Z 218-219 D 2
Namwera o MW 218-219 H 2
Namwŏn o ROK 150-151 F 10
Namy o RUS 110-111 T 5
Namyłdżylah ~ RUS 118-119 K 5
Namyndykan ~ RUS 112-113 K 4
Namysłów o• PL 92-93 O 3
Nan o THA 142-143 M 6
Nan, Sa o THA 142-143 M 6
Nana o CAM 206-207 B 5
Nana ~ RCA 206-207 B 6
Nana Bakassa o RCA (OUH) 206-207 C 5
Nana Bakassa ~ RCA 206-207 C 5
Nana Barya ~ TCH 206-207 C 5
Nana Barya, Réserve de la ⊥ RCA 206-207 C 5
Nana Candundo o ANG 214-215 B 6
Nanae o J 152-153 J 4
Nanafalia o USA (AL) 284-285 C 4
Nana-Grébizi ◘ RCA 206-207 D 5
Nanaimo o CDN (BC) 230-231 F 4
Nanakuli o USA (HI) 288 G 3
Nana-Mambéré ◘ RCA 206-207 B 6
Nanambinia o AUS 176-177 G 6
Nana Museum of the Arctic • USA 20-21 J 3
Nanango o AUS 178-179 L 4
Nananu-i-ra ⌒ FJI 184 III b 2
Nanao o J 152-153 G 6
Nan'ao Dao ⌒ VRC 156-157 K 5
Nanase o PNG 183 B 4
Nanay, Río ~ PE 64-65 F 3
Nanbu o VRC 154-155 E 6
Nancay, Arroyo ~ RA 78-79 K 4
Nance Creek ~ USA (AL) 284-285 C 2
Nancha o VRC 150-151 G 4
Nanchang ☆• VRC 156-157 J 2
Nancheng o VRC 156-157 K 3
Nanchititla, Parque Natural ⊥ MEX 52-53 D 2
Nanchong o VRC 154-155 E 6
Nanchuan o VRC 156-157 E 2
Nancowry Island ⌒ IND 140-141 L 6
Nancy ☆••• F 90-91 L 7
Nanda Devi ▲••• IND 144-145 C 5
Nandaime o NIC 52-53 L 6
Nandalūr o IND 140-141 H 3
Nandaly o AUS 180-181 G 3
Nandan o VRC 156-157 E 4
Nanded o IND 138-139 F 10
Nandewar Range ▲ AUS 178-179 L 6
Nandgāōt o IND 142-143 B 5
Nandi o ZW 218-219 F 5
Nandigāma o IND 140-141 J 2
Nandigram o BD 142-143 F 3
Nandi Hills o• IND 140-141 G 4
Nandikotkūr o IND 140-141 H 3
Nanding Hé ~ VRC 142-143 L 4
Nandipadu o IND 140-141 H 3
Nandom o GH 202-203 J 4
Nandouta o RT 202-203 L 5
Nandowrie P.O. o AUS 178-179 J 3
Nāndūra o IND 138-139 F 9
Nandurbār o IND 138-139 E 9
Nandyal o IND 140-141 H 3
Nanfeng o VRC 156-157 K 3
Nangade o MOC 214-215 K 6
Nanga Eboko o CAM 204-205 K 6
Nangah Ketungau o RI 162-163 J 4
Nangah Pinoh o RI 162-163 J 5
Nangah Sokan o RI 162-163 J 5
Nangalala ✗ AUS 174-175 C 3
Nanganga o EAT 214-215 K 6
Nanga Parbat ▲ PK 138-139 E 2
Nangarhār ◘ AFG 138-139 C 2
Nangaroro o RI 168 E 7
Nanga Tamin o MAL 162-163 K 3
Nanga Tayap o RI 162-163 J 5
Nangbéto o RT 202-203 L 6
Nangbéto, Retenue de < RT 202-203 L 6
Nang'egan ~ RUS 114-115 L 3
Nangin o MYA 158-159 E 5
Nango o J 152-153 D 8
Nangolet o SUD 208-209 A 6
Nangomba o EAT 214-215 K 6
Nangong o VRC 154-155 J 3
Nangqên o VRC 144-145 L 4
Nang Rong o THA 158-159 G 3
Nānguneri o IND 140-141 G 6
Nangunhe Z.B. ⊥• VRC 142-143 L 4
Nangurukuru o EAT 214-215 K 5
Nanguruwe o EAT 214-215 L 6
Nang Xian o VRC 144-145 J 6
Nan Hai ≈ 156-157 J 6
Nanhua o RC 156-157 M 5
Nanhua o VRC 156-157 B 4
Nanhui o VRC 154-155 M 6
Nanika Lake ⇔ CDN (BC) 228-229 G 3
Nanjangud o• IND 140-141 G 4
Nanjian o VRC 142-143 M 3
Nanjiang o VRC 154-155 E 5
Nanjing ☆• VRC 154-155 L 5
Nanjirinji o EAT 214-215 K 5
Nankāna Sāhib o PK 138-139 D 4
Nankang o VRC (GXI) 156-157 F 6
Nankang o VRC (JXI) 156-157 J 4
Nanking = Nanjing ☆• VRC 154-155 L 5
Nankoku o J 152-153 E 8
Nankova o ANG 216-217 E 8
Nankunshan • VRC 156-157 H 5
Nanle o VRC 154-155 J 3
Nanling o VRC 154-155 L 6
Nan Ling ▲ VRC 156-157 G 4
Nanlixa o MOC 218-219 J 1
Nannine o AUS 176-177 E 3
Nanning ☆ VRC 156-157 F 5
Nannup o AUS 176-177 C 6
Nano ~ DY 204-205 E 4
Nanoose Bay o CDN (BC) 230-231 E 4
Nanoro o BF 202-203 J 3
Nanortalik o GRØ 28-29 S 6
Nanortalik Banke ≈ 28-29 R 6
Nanosnyj, ostrov ⌒ RUS 110-111 X 1
Nanpan Jiang ~ VRC 156-157 D 4
Nanpara o IND 142-143 B 2
Nanpeng Liedao ⌒ VRC 156-157 K 5
Nanping o VRC (FUJ) 156-157 L 3
Nanping o VRC (HUN) 156-157 H 2
Nansebo o ETH 208-209 D 5
Nansei-shotō ⌒ J 152-153 B 11
Nansen, Kap ▲ GRØ (ØGR) 26-27 r 4
Nansen, Kap ▲ GRØ (ØGR) 28-29 a 2
Nansen, Mount ▲ CDN 20-21 W 5
Nansena, ostrov ⌒ RUS 108-109 Z 3
Nansena, ostrov ⌒ RUS (ARH) 84-85 d 2
Nansen Fjord ≈ 28-29 a 2
Nansen Gletscher ⊂ GRØ 26-27 V 6
Nansen Land ∸ GRØ 26-27 c 2
Nansen Sound ≈ 26-27 E 3
Nanshui SK ~ VRC 156-157 H 4
Nansio o EAT 212-213 D 5
Nantahala Mountains ▲ USA (NC) 282-283 D 5
Nantais, Lac ⇔ CDN 36-37 M 4
Nantamba o PNG 183 F 3
Nantes ☆• F 90-91 G 8
Nanticoke River ~ USA (MD) 280-281 L 5
Nanton o CDN (ALB) 232-233 E 5
Nanton o GH 202-203 K 5
Nantong o VRC 154-155 M 5
Nantong (Jinsha) o VRC 154-155 M 5
Nantou o RC 156-157 M 5
Nantucket o USA (MA) 278-279 L 7
Nantucket Island ⌒ USA (MA) 278-279 L 7
Nantucket Shoals ≈ 46-47 N 5
Nantucket Shoals ≈ USA 278-279 L 7
Nantulo o MOC 214-215 K 7
Nanuku Passage ≈ 184 III c 2
Nanumea ⌒ TUV 13 J 3
Nanuque o BR 72-73 K 4
Nanūr o IR 128-129 M 5
Nanusa, Kepulauan ⌒ RI 164-165 K 1
Nanutarra Roadhouse o AUS 172-173 B 7
Nan Xian o VRC 156-157 H 2
Nanxiao o VRC 156-157 F 5
Nanxijiang • VRC 156-157 M 2
Nanxiong o VRC 156-157 J 4
Nanxu o VRC 156-157 G 4
Nanyamba o EAT 214-215 K 6
Nanyang o VRC 154-155 H 5
Nanyang Hu ~ VRC 154-155 K 4
Nanyi Hu o VRC 154-155 L 6
Nan-yō o J 152-153 J 5
Nanyuki o EAK 212-213 F 3
Nanzhai o VRC 156-157 F 3
Nanzhang o VRC 154-155 G 6
Nanzhao o VRC 154-155 H 5
Nanzhila o Z (SOU) 218-219 C 3
Nanzhila ~ Z 218-219 D 3
Nao, Cabo de la ▲ E 98-99 H 5
Naococane, Lac ⇔ CDN 38-39 J 2
Naogaon o BD 142-143 F 3
Não-me-Toque o BR 74-75 D 7
Náoussa o GR 100-101 J 4
Naozhou Dao ⌒ VRC 156-157 G 6
Napa o USA (CA) 246-247 C 5
Napabale Lagoon ∸•• RI 164-165 H 6
Napacao Point ▲ RP 160-161 F 8
Napadogan o CDN (NB) 240-241 J 4
Napaha o MOC 218-219 K 1
Napaiskak o USA 20-21 K 6
Napaleofú, Arroyo ~ RA 78-79 K 4
Napanee o CDN (ONT) 238-239 J 4
Napanwainami o RI 166-167 H 3
Napan-yaur o RI 166-167 H 3
Napas o RUS 114-115 R 5
Napassorssuaq Fjord ≈ 28-29 T 6
Napatok Bay ≈ 36-37 S 6
Napavine o USA (WA) 244-245 B 4
Napeitom o EAK 212-213 F 3
Naper o USA (NE) 262-263 G 2
Napido o RI 166-167 H 2
Napier o NZ 182 F 3
Napier o ZA 220-221 D 7
Napier, Mount ▲ AUS 172-173 J 4
Napier Broome Bay ≈ 172-173 H 3
Napier Downs o AUS 172-173 G 4
Napier Mountains ▲ ARK 16 G 6
Napier Peninsula ⌣ AUS 174-175 C 3
Napier Range ▲ AUS 172-173 G 4
Napierville o CDN (QUE) 238-239 M 3
Napinka o CDN (MAN) 234-235 C 5
Naples o USA (FL) 286-287 H 5
Naples o USA (ID) 250-251 C 3
Naples o USA (NY) 278-279 D 6
Naples o USA (SD) 260-261 J 2
Naples o USA (TX) 264-265 K 5
Naples = Nápoli ☆•• I 100-101 E 4
Napo o VRC 156-157 D 5
Napo, Río ~ EC 64-65 E 2
Napoca, Cluj- ☆• RO 102-103 C 4
Napoleon o USA (IN) 274-275 N 5
Napoleon o USA (ND) 258-259 H 5
Napoleon o USA (OH) 280-281 B 2
Napoleonville o USA (LA) 268-269 J 7
Nápoli ☆•• I 100-101 E 4
Nápoli, Golfo di ≈ 100-101 E 4
Napoopoo o USA (HI) 288 K 5
Nappa Merrie o AUS 178-179 F 4
Napperby o AUS 172-173 L 7
Nappernee o USA (IN) 274-275 M 3
Naqa, Temples of •• SUD 200-201 F 4
Naqāda o ET 194-195 F 5
Naqade o• IR 128-129 L 4
Naqb, Ra's an- o JOR 130-131 D 2
Naquen, Serranía de ▲ CO 60-61 G 6
Nār, Umm an- o UAE 134-135 F 6
Nara o AUS 174-175 G 6
Nara ☆•• J 152-153 F 7
Nara o RMM 202-203 G 2
Narač o BY 94-95 K 4
Nāra Canal < PK 138-139 B 7
Naracoorte o AUS 180-181 F 4
Naracoorte Caves Conservation Park ⊥ AUS 180-181 F 4
Naradhan o AUS 180-181 J 2
Naraini o IND 142-143 B 3
Nārāinpur o IND 142-143 B 6
Nārājankher o IND 138-139 F 10
Naramata o CDN (BC) 230-231 K 4
Naran o PK 138-139 D 2
Naran = Hongor o MAU 148-149 L 5
Narandiba o BR 72-73 E 7
Naranjal o EC 64-65 C 3
Naranjas, Punta ▲ PA 52-53 D 8
Naranjito o EC 64-65 C 3
Naranjo ∴• GCA 52-53 K 3
Naranjo o MEX 50-51 E 5
Naranjos o MEX 50-51 L 7
Narao o J 152-153 C 8
Narasannapeta o IND 142-143 D 6
Narasapuram o IND 140-141 J 2
Narasaraopet o IND 140-141 J 2
Narasimharajapura o IND 140-141 F 4
Narataj o RUS 116-117 K 8
Narathiwat ☆ THA 158-159 F 7
Nara Visa o USA (NM) 256-257 M 3
Naravuka o FJI 184 III b 2
Narayangadh o NEP 144-145 E 7
Narāyangaon o IND 138-139 D 10
Narbonne o F 90-91 J 10
Narcisse o CDN (MAN) 234-235 F 4
Narcondan Island ⌒ IND 158-159 C 4
Narcosli Creek ~ CDN (BC) 228-229 M 4
Narding River ~ CDN 24-25 N 6
Naré o RA 76-77 G 6
Nareči, ostrov ⌒ RUS 108-109 O 8
Narega Island ⌒ PNG 183 E 3
Naregal o IND 140-141 F 3
Narembeen o AUS 176-177 E 6
Naréna o RMM 202-203 F 3
Nares Abyssal Plain ≃ 6-7 F 1
Nares Land ∸ GRØ 26-27 b 2
Nares Stræde ≈ 26-27 O 4
Nares Strait ≈ 26-27 N 4
Narew o PL 92-93 R 2
Narew ~ PL 92-93 Q 2
Nargund o IND 140-141 F 3
Nāri ~ PK 134-135 M 4
Nari ~ PK 134-135 M 4
Narib o NAM 220-221 C 2
Narijn gol ~ MAU 116-117 F 10
Narijntèèl = Čagaan-Ovoo o MAU 148-149 E 5
Narimanov ☆ RUS 96-97 E 10
Narinda, Helodrano ≈ 222-223 E 5
Narin Nur o VRC 154-155 F 2
Narita o• J 152-153 J 7
Nar'jan-Mar ☆ RUS 88-89 W 3
Narkatiāganj o IND 142-143 D 2
Narmada ~ IND 138-139 D 9
Narmada ~ IND 138-139 E 8
Narmajaha ~ RUS 108-109 L 7
Nārnaul o IND 138-139 F 5
Narndee o AUS 176-177 E 4
Narob ~ NAM 220-221 C 2
Naroda ~ RUS 114-115 F 2
Narodnaja, gora ▲ RUS 114-115 F 2
Národní park Šumava ⊥ CZ 92-93 M 4
Naro-Fominsk ☆• RUS 94-95 P 4
Naro Island ⌒ RP 160-161 E 7
Narok o EAK 212-213 E 4
Naro Moru o EAK 212-213 F 4
Narooma o AUS 180-181 L 4
Nārowāl o PK 138-139 E 3
Narrabri o AUS 178-179 K 6
Narracoota o AUS 176-177 E 2
Narragansett Bay ≈ 46-47 N 5
Narragansett Bay ≈ USA 278-279 K 7
Narrandera o AUS 180-181 J 3
Narran Lake ⇔ AUS 178-179 J 5
Narran River ~ AUS 178-179 J 5
Narraway River ~ CDN (BC) 228-229 O 2
Narrien Range ▲ AUS 178-179 J 2
Narrogin o AUS 176-177 D 6
Narromine o AUS 180-181 K 2
Narrow Cape ▲ USA 22-23 U 4
Narrows o USA (VA) 280-281 F 6
Narrowsburg o USA (NY) 280-281 L 2
Narrows Indian Reserve, The ✗ CDN (MAN) 234-235 E 3
Narryer, Mount ▲ AUS 176-177 D 3
Narsalik o GRØ 28-29 Q 6
Narsampet o IND 140-141 H 2
Narsaq Kujalleg = Frederiksdal o GRØ 28-29 S 6
Narsarsuaq o GRØ 28-29 S 6
Narsimhapur o IND 138-139 G 8
Narsinghgarh o IND 138-139 F 8
Narsipatnam o IND 142-143 C 7
Nart o VRC 148-149 M 6
Narubis o NAM 220-221 D 3
Naru-shima ⌒ J 152-153 C 8
Naruto o J 152-153 F 7
Narva o• EST 94-95 L 2
Narva o RUS 116-117 F 8
Narva laht ≈ 94-95 K 2
Narvik o• N 86-87 H 2
Narvskoe vodohranilišče < RUS 94-95 L 2
Narwietooma o AUS 176-177 M 1
Nary hrebet ▲ RUS 96-97 K 6
Naryilco o AUS 178-179 F 5
Naryn ~ KA 124-125 J 6
Naryn o KS 146-147 B 5
Naryn ~ KS 136-137 N 4
Naryn o RUS 116-117 G 10
Naryn ~ RUS 116-117 G 10
Naryn-Huduk o RUS 126-127 G 5
Narynkol o KA 146-147 D 4
Naryntau, hrebet ▲ KS 146-147 C 5
Nasa, Gara ▲ ETH 208-209 B 4
Na'sān, Umm ⌒ BRN 134-135 D 5
Nasanabad o IND 138-139 G 10
Nasarawa o WAN 198-199 B 6
Nasa Test Site xx USA (MS) 268-269 L 6
Näsåud o RO 102-103 D 4
Naschitti o USA (NM) 256-257 G 2
Naselle o USA (WA) 244-245 B 4
Nashan Island ⌒ 160-161 A 7
Nash Harbor o USA 20-21 G 6
Nāshik o IND 138-139 D 10
Nashino, Río ~ EC 64-65 D 2
Nashū', Wādi an ~ LAR 192-193 E 4
Nashua o USA (IA) 274-275 F 2
Nashua o USA (MT) 250-251 N 3
Nashua o USA (NH) 278-279 K 6
Nashville o USA (AR) 276-277 B 7
Nashville o USA (GA) 284-285 G 5
Nashville o USA (IL) 274-275 J 6
Nashville o USA (IN) 274-275 M 5
Nashville o USA (KS) 262-263 H 7
Nashville o USA (MI) 272-273 D 5
Nashville o USA (NC) 282-283 K 5
Nashville ☆• USA (TN) 276-277 J 4
Nashville Basin ⌣ USA (TN) 276-277 J 4
Nashwaak o CDN (NB) 240-241 J 4
Nashwaak Bridge o CDN (NB) 240-241 J 4
Nashwaak River ~ CDN (NB) 240-241 J 4
Nashwauk o USA (MN) 270-271 E 3
Nasia o GH 202-203 K 4
Nasia ~ GH 202-203 K 4
Našice o HR 100-101 G 2
Näsijärvi ⇔ FIN 88-89 G 6
Nasikonis, Tanjung ▲ RI 166-167 B 6
Nasipit o RP 160-161 F 8
Nāşir o SUD 208-209 A 4
Nāşir, Buhairat < ET 194-195 F 6
Nasīrābād o IR 136-137 G 7
Nasīrābād o PK 134-135 K 5
Nasīrābād o PK 138-139 B 5
Nāşirah, Bi'r < LAR 192-193 D 2
Nāşiriya, an- ☆ IRQ 128-129 M 7
Nasiya, Ğabal ▲ ET 194-195 F 6
Naskaupi River ~ CDN 36-37 T 7
Nasmah o LAR 192-193 E 2
Nasolot National Reservoir ⊥ EAK 212-213 E 3
Nasondoye o ZRE 214-215 C 6
Nasorolevu ▲ FJI 184 III b 2
Nāsriganj o IND 142-143 D 3
Nasriyān o IR 134-135 B 2
Nassarawa o WAN 204-205 G 4
Nassau ☆•• BS 54-55 G 2
Nassau, Bahía ≈ 80 G 7
Nassau, Fort • GUY 62-63 F 3
Nassau River ~ AUS 174-175 F 4
Nassau River ~ USA (FL) 286-287 H 1
Nassau Sound ≈ USA 286-287 H 1
Nass Basin ∸ CDN 32-33 F 3
Nasser, Lake = Nāşir, Buhairat < ET 194-195 F 6
Nassian o CI (BOA) 202-203 J 5
Nassian o CI (FER) 202-203 H 5
Nassoukou o DY 202-203 L 4
Nass River ~ CDN 32-33 F 4
Nastapoka, Rivière ~ CDN 36-37 L 6
Nastapoka Islands ⌒ CDN 36-37 L 6
Nastapoka Sound ≈ 36-37 L 6
Nasugbu o RP 160-161 D 5
Nasuraghena o SOL 184 I f 4
Nasva o RUS 94-95 M 3
Nata o•• PA 52-53 D 7
Nata o RB (CEN) 218-219 D 5
Nata ~ RB 218-219 D 5
Nataboti o RI 166-167 D 3
Natal o BR (TOC) 68-69 D 4
Natal ☆ BR (RNO) 68-69 L 4
Natal o CDN (BC) 230-231 P 4
Natal o RI 162-163 C 4
Natalia o USA (TX) 266-267 J 4
Natalii, buhta ⇔ RUS 112-113 R 6
Natalschwelle ≃ 220-221 M 6
Natal Valley ≃ 9 G 9
Natanz o• IR 134-135 D 2
Natar o RI 162-163 F 7
Natara ~ RUS 110-111 P 5
Nataš, Wādi ~ ET 194-195 F 5
Natashquan o CDN (QUE) 242-243 G 2
Natashquan, Pointe de ▲ CDN (QUE) 242-243 G 2
Natashquan, Rivière ~ CDN 38-39 O 3
Natashquan River ~ CDN 38-39 N 2
Natchamba o RT 202-203 L 5
Natchez o USA (MS) 268-269 J 5
Natchez Trace Parkway • USA (MS) 268-269 K 4
Natchez Trace Parkway • USA (TN) 276-277 H 5
Natchez Trace State Park ⊥ USA (TN) 276-277 G 5
Natchitoches o USA (LA) 268-269 G 5
Nate o IND 140-141 E 2
Natewa Bay ≈ 184 III b 2
Nathahu o MYA 158-159 C 2
Nathalia o AUS 180-181 H 4
Nathan o USA (AR) 276-277 B 6
Nathan River o AUS 174-175 C 4
Na Thawi o THA 158-159 F 7
Nāthdwāra o IND 138-139 D 7
Nathenje o MW 218-219 G 2
Nathia Gali o PK 138-139 D 2
Nathon o THA 158-159 E 6
Nathorst Land ∸ GRØ 26-27 m 7
Nathorst Land ∸ N 84-85 J 4
Nathrop o USA (CO) 254-255 J 5
Natiaboani o BF 202-203 L 4
Natingui o BR 74-75 E 5
Nation o USA 20-21 U 4
National Bison Range ⊥ USA (MT) 250-251 E 4
National City o USA (CA) 248-249 G 7
National Parachute Test Range • USA (CA) 248-249 J 7
National Park ⊥ CDN (ONT) 238-239 J 4
National Park o NZ 182 E 3
National Park ⊥ PNG 183 B 4
Nationalpark Bayerischer Wald ⊥ D 92-93 M 4
Nationalpark Berchtesgaden ⊥ D 92-93 M 5
Nationalpark Hochharz ⊥ D 92-93 L 3
Nationalpark i Nordgrønland og Østgrønland ⊥ GRØ 26-27 e 5
Nationalpark Niedersächsisches Wattenmeer ⊥ D 92-93 J 2
Nationalpark Sächsische Schweiz ⊥ D 92-93 N 3
Nationalpark Schleswig-Holsteinisches Wattenmeer ⊥ D 92-93 K 1
Nationalpark Vorpommersche Boddenlandschaft ⊥ D 92-93 M 1
National Reactor Testing Station xx USA (ID) 252-253 F 3
National Wildlife Refuge ⊥ USA (ID) 252-253 G 3
National Wildlife Refuge ⊥ USA (ID) 252-253 F 3
National Wildlife Refuge ⊥ USA (MN) 270-271 E 5
National Wildlife Refuge ⊥ USA (MN) 270-271 E 4
National Wildlife Refuge ⊥ USA (MT) 250-251 H 4
National Wildlife Refuge ⊥ USA (MT) 250-251 P 3
National Wildlife Refuge ⊥ USA (MT) 250-251 M 3
National Wildlife Refuge ⊥ USA (MT) 250-251 L 5
National Wildlife Refuge ⊥ USA (MT) 250-251 K 5
National Wildlife Refuge ⊥ USA (ND) 258-259 J 4
National Wildlife Refuge ⊥ USA (ND) 258-259 G 5
National Wildlife Refuge ⊥ USA (SD) 260-261 C 2
National Wildlife Refuge ⊥ USA (SD) 260-261 H 1
National Wildlife Refuge ⊥ USA (UT) 254-255 B 4
National Wildlife Refuge ⊥ USA (UT) 254-255 C 2
National Wildlife Refuge ⊥ USA (UT) 254-255 F 3
National Wildlife Refuge ⊥ USA (WI) 270-271 H 6
National Wildlife Refuge ⊥ USA (WY) 252-253 M 4
National Wildlife Refuge and Wilderness Area ⊥ USA (MT) 250-251 H 7
Nation River ~ CDN 32-33 H 4
Natitingou ☆ DY 202-203 L 4
Natityay, Ğabal ▲ ET 194-195 G 6
Native Bay ≈ 36-37 H 3
Native Point ▲ CDN 36-37 H 3
Natividade o BR 68-69 E 7
Natkusiak Peninsula ⌣ CDN 24-25 R 4
Natla River ~ CDN 30-31 E 4
Natmauk o MYA 142-143 J 5
Natong Kuangqu o VRC 156-157 E 2
Nator o BD 142-143 F 3
Natovi o FJI 184 III b 2
Nat River ~ CDN (ONT) 236-237 F 4
Natron, Lake ⇔ EAT 212-213 F 5
Natron, Trou du • TCH 198-199 H 2
Natrona o USA (WY) 252-253 M 3
Nattam o IND 140-141 H 5
Nattavaara station o S 86-87 K 3
Natukanaoka Pan ⇔ NAM 216-217 C 9
Natuna Besar, Pulau ⌒ RI 162-163 H 2
Natural Arch ∴ USA (KY) 276-277 L 4
Natural Bridge o USA (AL) 284-285 C 2
Natural Bridge ∴ USA (AL) 284-285 C 2
Natural Bridge • USA (FL) 286-287 E 1
Natural Bridges ∴ USA (TN) 276-277 H 5
Natural Bridges National Monument ∴ USA (UT) 254-255 F 6
Natural Bridge State Monument • USA (MT) 250-251 J 6
Natural Dam Salt Lake ⇔ USA (TX) 264-265 C 6
Naturaliste, Cape ▲ AUS (TAS) 180-181 K 6
Naturaliste, Cape ▲ AUS (WA) 176-177 C 6
Naturaliste Plateau ≃ 176-177 B 6
Naturita o USA (CO) 254-255 G 5
Nau o TJ 136-137 L 4
Nauabu o PNG 183 F 6
Nauarai, Bi'r < SUD 200-201 G 2
Nauari o BR 62-63 G 5
Naubise o NEP 144-145 E 7
Nauchas o NAM 220-221 C 1
Naudesberg Pass ▲ ZA 220-221 G 5
Naudesnek ▲ ZA 220-221 J 5
Nauela o MOC 218-219 J 2
Naufal le-Chateau o IR 134-135 D 1
Naufrage o CDN (NS) 240-241 N 4
Naugarh o IND 142-143 C 2
Naujan o RP 160-161 D 6
Naujan Lake ⇔ RP 160-161 D 6
Naukot o PK 138-139 B 7
Naulila o ANG 216-217 C 8
Nauľjaha ~ RUS 108-109 H 7
Naumatang o RI 166-167 D 5
Naumburg (Saale) o• D 92-93 L 3
Nauna Island ⌒ PNG 183 E 2
Naungmo o MYA 142-143 J 3
Nauru ⌒ NAU 13 H 3
Naushahro Firoz o PK 138-139 B 6
Nausori o FJI 184 III b 3
Nauta o PE 64-65 F 4
Nautanwa o IND 142-143 C 2
Nautilus, Selat ≈ 166-167 G 4
Nautimuk o AUS 180-181 F 4
Nautla o MEX 52-53 F 1
Nautsi o RUS 88-89 K 2
Nauvoo o USA (AL) 284-285 C 3
Näv o IR 128-129 N 4
Nava o MEX 50-51 J 3
Nava ~ ZRE 212-213 A 2
Nava de Ricomalillo, La o E 98-99 E 5
Navahrudak ☆ BY 94-95 J 5
Navahrudskae uzvyšša ▲ BY 94-95 J 5
Navajo o USA (AZ) 256-257 F 3
Navajo o USA (NM) 256-257 G 3
Navajo (^ry o USA (NM) 256-257 H 2
Navajo Indian Reservation ✗ USA (AZ) 256-257 D 2
Navajo Mountain ▲ USA (UT) 254-255 E 6
Navajo National Monument ∴ USA (AZ) 256-257 E 2
Navajo Reservoir < USA (NM) 256-257 H 2
Naval o RP 160-161 F 7
Navalmoral de la Mata o E 98-99 E 5
Navalmorales, Los o E 98-99 E 5
Navan = An Uaimh o IRL 90-91 D 5
Navapara o BD 142-143 F 4
Navapolack ☆•• BY 94-95 L 4
Navapur o IND 138-139 D 9
Navarin, mys ▲ RUS 112-113 U 5
Navarino, Isla ⌒ RCH 80 G 7
Navarino, Pico ▲ RCH 80 G 7
Navarra ◘ E 98-99 F 3
Navarre o AUS 180-181 G 4
Navarre o CDN (ALB) 232-233 E 3
Navarre o USA (FL) 286-287 C 1
Navarro o RA 78-79 K 3
Navarro o USA (CA) 246-247 B 4
Navarro Mills Lake < USA (TX) 266-267 L 2
Navas, Las o RP 160-161 F 6
Navašino o RUS 94-95 S 4
Navasota o USA (TX) 266-267 L 3
Navasota River ~ USA (TX) 266-267 L 3
Navassa Island ⌒ USA 54-55 H 5
Nāve o AFG 134-135 M 2
Navere o RI 166-167 K 3
Navia o E 98-99 D 3
Navidad Bank ≃ 54-55 L 4
Navidad River ~ USA (TX) 266-267 L 4
Naviraí o BR 76-77 K 2

Naviti ⌒ FJI 184 III a 2
Naviu Island ⌒ PNG 183 B 5
Navlakhi o IND 138-139 C 8
Navlja o RUS 94-95 O 5
Năvodari o RO 102-103 F 5
Navoi = Navoij ☆ US 136-137 J 4
Navoij ☆ US 136-137 J 4
Navojoa o MEX 50-51 E 4
Na Vong o LAO 156-157 C 6
Nāvor o AFG (ĠA) 134-135 M 2
Nāvor ⬭ AFG (ĠA) 134-135 M 2
Nāvor, Kōtal-e ▲ AFG 134-135 M 1
Navrongo o GH 202-203 K 4
Navsāri o IND 138-139 D 9
Navua o FJI 184 III b 3
Navua River ~ FJI 184 III a 3
Navy Board Inlet ≈ 24-25 f 4
Nāwa o IND 138-139 E 6
Nawābshāh o PK 138-139 B 6
Nawāda o IND 142-143 D 3
Na Wai o THA 142-143 L 6
Nawa Kot o PK 138-139 C 5
Nawākshūt = Nouakchott ★• RIM 196-197 C 5
Nāwalkal o IND 140-141 G 2
Nawalpur o NEP 144-145 E 7
Nawāpāra o IND 142-143 C 5
Nawar o RT 202-203 L 5
Nawinda Kuta o Z 218-219 C 3
Nawnghkio o MYA 142-143 K 4
Nawngleng o MYA 142-143 L 4
Nawuni o GH 202-203 K 5
Náxos o•• GR 100-101 K 6
Náxos ⌒ GR 100-101 K 6
Naya Chor o PK 138-139 B 7
Nāyakanhatti o IND 140-141 G 3
Nayar o MEX 50-51 G 6
Nayarit □ MEX 50-51 G 6
Nayau ⌒ FJI 184 III c 2
Nāyband o IR 134-135 G 2
Nāyband, Kūh-e ▲ IR 134-135 G 2
Nayé o SN 202-203 D 2
Nayoro o J 152-153 K 2
Nayorunun River ~ USA 22-23 Q 3
Nayouri o BF 202-203 L 3
Nayuchi o MW 218-219 H 2
Nāyudupeta o IND 140-141 H 4
Nazaré o BR (APA) 62-63 J 4
Nazaré o BR (BAH) 72-73 L 2
Nazaré o BR (P) 62-63 K 6
Nazaré o BR (TOC) 68-69 E 5
Nazaré o• P 98-99 C 5
Nazaré, Cachoeira ~ BR 70-71 G 2
Nazaré da Mata o BR 68-69 L 5
Nazaré do Piauí o BR 68-69 G 5
Nazareth o BOL 70-71 E 4
Nazareth o CO 60-61 D 5
Nazareth o USA (TX) 264-265 B 4
Nazareth = Nazerat ☆ IL 130-131 D 1
Nazarovo ☆ RUS 116-117 E 7
Nazas, Río ~ MEX 50-51 G 5
Nazca o• PE 64-65 E 9
Nazca Linea • PE 64-65 E 9
Nazca Ridge ≃ 5 C 7
Naze o J 152-153 C 10
Nazerat ☆ IL 130-131 D 1
Nazilli ☆ TR 128-129 C 4
Nazinskaja ~ RUS 114-115 P 4
Nazirhat o BD 142-143 G 4
Nazko o CDN (BC) 228-229 L 4
Nazko River ~ CDN (BC) 228-229 L 4
Nazombe o MOC 214-215 K 6
Nazran ☆ RUS 126-127 F 6
Nazrēt o ETH 208-209 D 4
Nazwā o• OM 132-133 K 2
Nazym ~ RUS 114-115 K 4
Nazyvaevsk ☆ RUS 114-115 L 7
Nbâk o RIM 196-197 C 6
Nbeïket Dlim < RIM 196-197 G 6
Nbeïket el Ahouâch < RIM 196-197 H 6
Ncamasere ~ RB 216-217 F 9
Ncanaha o ZA 220-221 G 6
Nchalo o MW 218-219 H 3
Nchelenge o Z 214-215 E 5
Ncojane o RB 220-221 E 1
Ncojane Ranches ∸ RB 216-217 F 11
Ncora Dam < ZA 220-221 H 5
Ncue o GQ 210-211 C 2
Ndaki o RMM 202-203 K 2
Ndala o EAT 212-213 D 6
Ndalambo o EAT 214-215 G 5
N'Dalatando ☆ ANG 216-217 C 4
Ndali o DY 204-205 E 4
Ndanda o EAT 214-215 K 6
Ndanda o RCA 206-207 F 6
Ndande o SN 202-203 B 2
Ndangane o SN 202-203 B 2
Ndao, Pulau ⌒ RI 166-167 B 7
Ndarapo Swamp ⬭ EAK 212-213 G 5
Ndarassa o RCA 206-207 F 5
Ndedu o ZRE 212-213 B 2
Ndeji o WAN 204-205 F 4
Ndekesha o ZRE 214-215 B 4
Ndéko ~ RCB 210-211 F 4
Ndélé ☆• RCA 206-207 E 4
Ndélélé o CAM 206-207 B 6
Ndemba o CAM 204-205 K 6
Ndembera ~ EAT 214-215 H 5
Ndendé o G 210-211 C 5
Ndeyini < EAK 212-213 G 4
Ndia o SN 202-203 D 2
Ndian ~ CAM 204-205 H 6
Ndiékro o CI 202-203 H 6
Ndiguina o CAM 206-207 B 3
Ndikiniméki o CAM 204-205 J 6
Ndikoko o CAM 204-205 J 6
Ndim o RCA 206-207 B 5
Ndindi o G 210-211 C 5
Ndindi o SN 202-203 B 2
Ndioum o SN 196-197 C 6
Ndioum Guènt o SN 202-203 C 2
Nditam o CAM 204-205 J 6
Ndiya o WAN 204-205 G 6
N'djaména ★• TCH 198-199 G 6
Ndji ~ RCA 206-207 F 5
Ndjim ~ CAM 204-205 J 6
Ndjolé o CAM 204-205 J 6
Ndjolé o G 210-211 C 4
Ndjoundou o RCB 210-211 F 4
Ndjwé ~ CAM 210-211 E 2
Ndofane o SN 202-203 C 3
Ndogo, Lagune ⬭ G 210-211 B 5
Ndok o CAM 206-207 B 5
Ndokama o CAM 204-205 J 6
Ndokayo o CAM 206-207 B 6
Ndoki ~ RCB 210-211 F 3
Ndola ☆ Z 214-215 E 7
Ndom o CAM 204-205 J 6
Ndondo o SOL 184 I e 3
Ndonga o NAM 216-217 F 8
Ndongolo o G 210-211 C 3
Ndop o CAM 204-205 J 6
Ndora Mountains ▲ WAN 204-205 J 5
Ndorola o BF 202-203 H 4
Ndoto Mountains ▲▲ EAK 212-213 F 3
Ndouci o CI 202-203 H 7
Ndoukou o RCA 206-207 E 6
Ndoumbou o RCA 206-207 C 5
Ndrhamcha, Sebkha ⬭ RIM 196-197 C 5
Ndu o CAM 204-205 J 5
Ndu o ZRE 206-207 F 6
Nduluku o EAK 212-213 F 4
Ndumbwe o EAT 214-215 K 6
Ndumo o ZA 220-221 L 3
Ndumo Game Reserve ⊥ ZA 220-221 L 3
Ndurumo ~ EAT 212-213 E 6
Ndzouani ⌒ COM 222-223 D 4
Neabul Creek ~ AUS 178-179 J 4
Neagh, Lough ⬭ GB 90-91 D 4
Neah Bay o USA (WA) 244-245 A 2
Neakongut Bay ≈ 36-37 K 4
Neale, Lake ⬭ AUS 176-177 K 2
Neale Junction o AUS 176-177 H 4
Neales Creek ~ AUS 178-179 C 4
Neales River ~ AUS 178-179 D 5
Néá Moni ••• GR 100-101 L 5
Néa Moudania o GR 100-101 J 4
Neamț, Piatra- ☆• RO 102-103 E 4
Neápoli o GR 100-101 J 6
Neápoli o GR 100-101 H 4
Nearchuss Passage ≈ 158-159 D 5
Near Islands ⌒ USA 22-23 C 6
Nebbou o BF 202-203 K 4
Nebe o RI 166-167 B 6
Nebelat el Hagana o SUD 200-201 D 6
Nebine Creek ~ AUS 178-179 J 5
Nebitdag o TM 136-137 D 5
Neblina, Cerro de la ▲ YV 66-67 E 2
Neblina, Sierra de la ▲▲ YV 66-67 E 2
Nebo o AUS 178-179 K 1
Nebraska □ USA (NE) 262-263 D 3
Nebraska City o USA (NE) 262-263 L 4
Nebrodi, Monti ▲ I 100-101 E 6
Necanicum Junction o USA (OR) 244-245 B 5
Necedah o USA (WI) 270-271 H 6
Nečera ~ RUS 118-119 H 6
Nechako Plateau ▲▲ CDN (BC) 228-229 G 2
Nechako Reservoir ⬭ CDN (BC) 228-229 J 3
Nechako River ~ CDN (BC) 228-229 K 3
Neche o USA (ND) 258-259 K 3
Neches o USA (TX) 268-269 E 5
Neches, Port o USA (TX) 268-269 G 7
Neches River ~ USA (TX) 268-269 F 6
Nechi o CO 60-61 D 3
Nechi, Río ~ CO 60-61 D 4
Nechisar National Park ⊥ ETH 208-209 C 5
Neckarboo Range ▲▲ AUS 180-181 H 2
Necker Island ⌒ USA 14-15 M 5
Necker Island ⌒ USA (HI) 288 A 1
Necochea o RA 78-79 K 5
Necocli o CO 60-61 C 3
Necungas o MOC 218-219 H 3
Nédéley o TCH 198-199 J 5
Nederland o USA (CO) 254-255 K 4
Nederland o USA (TX) 268-269 G 7
Nedlouc, Lac ⬭ CDN 36-37 N 6
Nedrata o ETH 208-209 D 3
Nedroma o DZ 188-189 L 3
Nedryhajliv o UA 102-103 H 2
Nedumangad o IND 140-141 G 6
Nedunkeni o CL 140-141 J 6
N. Edwards o USA (CA) 248-249 G 4
Needham, Mount ▲ CDN (BC) 228-229 B 3
Needles o CDN (BC) 230-231 L 4
Needles o USA (CA) 248-249 K 5
Needmore o USA (TX) 264-265 B 4
Needville o USA (TX) 268-269 E 7
Neel o USA (AL) 284-285 C 2
Neelin o CDN (MAN) 234-235 D 5
Neelyville o USA (MO) 276-277 E 4
Neenah o USA (WI) 270-271 K 6
Neepawa o CDN (MAN) 234-235 D 4
Neergaard Lake ⬭ CDN 24-25 g 5
Neerim South o AUS 180-181 H 5
Neeses o USA (SC) 284-285 J 3
Nefasīt o ER 200-201 J 5
Nefas Mewch'a o ETH 208-209 D 3
Neffatia o TN 190-191 H 4
Nefhi Shet' ~ ER 200-201 J 5
Nefta o TN 190-191 F 4
Neftchala = Neftçala o AZ 128-129 N 3
Neftegorsk o RUS 122-123 K 2
Neftegorsk ☆ RUS (SAM) 96-97 G 7
Neftejugansk ☆ RUS 114-115 M 4
Neftekamsk ☆ RUS 96-97 J 5
Neftekumsk ☆ RUS 126-127 F 5
Nefza o TN 190-191 G 2
Negage o ANG 216-217 C 3
Négala o RMM 202-203 F 3
Negampaha o CL 140-141 J 7
Nega Nega o Z 218-219 E 2
Négansi o DY 204-205 E 3
Negār o IR 134-135 G 4
Negara ~ RI 164-165 D 5
Negele o ETH 208-209 D 5
Negēlē o ETH 208-209 D 6
Negerilama o RI 164-165 H 3
Negeri Sembilan □ MAL 162-163 E 3
Negev, ha- ∸ IL 130-131 D 2
Negiralama o RI 162-163 D 3
Nëgjučej ~ RUS 118-119 M 6
Negley o USA (TX) 264-265 J 5
Negola o ANG 216-217 C 7
Negomane o MOC 214-215 K 6
Negombo o• CL 140-141 H 7
Negotin o• YU 100-101 J 2
Negotino o MK 100-101 J 4
Negra, Cordillera ▲▲ PE 64-65 C 6
Negra, La o RA 78-79 K 4
Negra, La o RCH 76-77 B 2
Negra, Ponta ▲ BR 68-69 L 4
Negra, Punta ▲ PE 64-65 B 4
Negra, Punta ▲ RA 78-79 K 5
Negril o JA 54-55 F 5
Negril Beach ∸• JA 54-55 F 5
Negrine o DZ 190-191 F 3
Negri River ~ AUS 172-173 J 4
Negrito, El o HN 52-53 L 4
Negro, Arroyo ~ ROU 78-79 L 2
Negro, Cerro ▲ PA 52-53 D 7
Negro, Cerro ▲ RA (CHU) 80 F 2
Negro, Cerro ▲ RA (NEU) 78-79 E 5
Negro, Cerro ▲ RCH 76-77 B 4
Negro, Laguna ⬭ ROU 74-75 D 10
Negro, Riacho ~ RA 76-77 H 3
Negro, Río ~ BOL 70-71 E 2
Negro, Río ~ BOL 70-71 F 4
Negro, Río ~ BOL 70-71 D 3
Negro, Rio ~ BR 66-67 F 3
Negro, Rio ~ BR 70-71 J 6
Negro, Río ~ CO 66-67 D 2
Negro, Río ~ HN 52-53 L 5
Negro, Río ~ PY 76-77 J 3
Negro, Río ~ PY 76-77 J 2
Negro, Río ~ RA 76-77 H 4
Negro, Río ~ RA 78-79 G 5
Negro, Río ~ ROU 78-79 L 2
Negro, Río ~ YV 60-61 E 3
Negros ⌒ RP 160-161 E 8
Negro Urco o PE 64-65 F 3
Negru Vodă o RO 102-103 F 6
Neguac o CDN (NB) 240-241 K 3
Nëgus"jah ~ RUS 114-115 N 5
Nehaevskij o RUS 102-103 M 2
Nehalem o USA (OR) 244-245 B 5
Nehalen River ~ USA (OR) 244-245 B 5
Nehāvand o• IR 134-135 C 1
Nehbandān o IR 134-135 J 3
Nehe o VRC 150-151 E 3
Nehoiu o RO 102-103 E 5
Nehone o ANG 216-217 D 8
Nehuentue o RCH 78-79 C 5
Neiafu o TON 184 IV b 1
Neiba ☆ DOM 54-55 K 5
Neiba, Bahía de ≈ 54-55 K 5
Neiba, Sierra de ▲▲ DOM 54-55 K 5
Neiden o N 86-87 O 2
Neidenburg = Nidzica o• PL 92-93 Q 2
Neidín = Kenmare o IRL 90-91 C 6
Neidpath o CDN (SAS) 232-233 L 5
Neiges, Piton des ▲ F 224 B 7
Neihart o USA (MT) 250-251 J 5
Neijiang o VRC 156-157 D 2
Neil Armstrong Air & Space Museum • USA (OH) 280-281 B 3
Neilburg o CDN (SAS) 232-233 J 3
Neilersdrif o ZA 220-221 E 4
Neils Harbour o CDN (NS) 240-241 P 4
Neilton o USA (WA) 244-245 B 3
Nei Mongol Gaoyuan ∸ VRC 148-149 G 7
Neinsberg ▲ NAM 216-217 D 9
Neirīz o• IR 134-135 F 4
Neis Beach o CDN (SAS) 232-233 N 2
Neiße ~ D 92-93 N 3
Neiva ☆ CO 60-61 D 6
Neixiang o VRC 154-155 G 5
Neizār o IR 134-135 D 1
Neizvestnaja ~ RUS 112-113 V 1
Neja o RUS 94-95 S 2
Nejanilin Lake ⬭ CDN 30-31 V 6
Nejime o J 152-153 D 9
Nejo o ETH 208-209 B 4
Nëjtajaha ~ RUS 108-109 Q 6
Nëjto, ozero ⬭ RUS 108-109 O 6
Nëjto pervoe, ozero ⬭ RUS 108-109 O 6
Nejva ~ RUS 96-97 M 5
Nekā o IR 136-137 C 6
Nekèkum ~ RUS 110-111 L 4
Nek'emte ☆ ETH 208-209 C 4
Nekljudovo o RUS 94-95 S 3
Nekob o MA 188-189 J 5
Nekongdakon, ozero ⬭ RUS 116-117 L 3
Nekongdokon ~ RUS 116-117 E 3
Nekoosa o USA (WI) 270-271 J 6
Neksø o DK 86-87 G 9
Neladero, Sierra del ▲▲ RA 76-77 C 5
Nelamangala o IND 140-141 G 4
Nelemnoe o RUS 110-111 c 7
Nel'gese ~ RUS 110-111 T 7
Nel'gjuu ~ RUS 118-119 N 7
Nelia o AUS 174-175 G 7
Nelidovo ☆ RUS 94-95 N 3
Neligh o USA (NE) 262-263 H 2
Neligh Mills ∴ USA (NE) 262-263 H 2
Neljaty o RUS 118-119 G 7
Nel'kan o RUS (HBR) 120-121 G 5
Nel'kan o RUS (SAH) 110-111 Y 7
Nel'koba o RUS 120-121 N 3
Nellie, Mount ▲ AUS 172-173 G 4
Nellikkuppam o IND 140-141 H 5
Nellimö o FIN 88-89 K 2
Nellipaka o IND 142-143 B 7
Nellis Air Force Range xx USA (NV) 248-249 H 2
Nelliyālam o IND 140-141 F 5
Nellore o IND 140-141 H 3
Nel'ma o RUS 122-123 H 5
Nelma o USA (WI) 270-271 K 4
Nëlon ~ RUS 110-111 Q 5
Nelshoogte ▲ ZA 220-221 K 2
Nelson o CDN (BC) 230-231 M 4
Nelson o NZ 182 D 4
Nelson o RA 76-77 G 6
Nelson o USA (NE) 262-263 H 4
Nelson o USA (NV) 248-249 K 4
Nelson o USA (WI) 270-271 G 6
Nelson, Cape ▲ AUS 180-181 F 5
Nelson, Cape ▲ PNG 183 E 5
Nelson, Estrecho ≈ 80 C 5
Nelson, Mount ▲ PNG 183 D 5
Nelson, Port ≈ 34-35 K 2
Nelson House o CDN 34-35 G 3
Nelson Island ⌒ USA 20-21 H 6
Nelson Lakes National Park ⊥ NZ 182 D 5
Nelson-Miramichi o CDN (NB) 240-241 K 4
Nelson Museum • KAN 56 D 3
Nelson River ~ CDN 34-35 J 2
Nelsonville o USA (OH) 280-281 D 4
Nelspoort o ZA 220-221 F 6
Nelspruit o• ZA 220-221 K 2
Nelway o CDN (BC) 230-231 M 4
Nem ~ RUS 114-115 D 4
Nem, Ust'- o RUS 96-97 J 3
Néma ☆ RIM 196-197 G 6
Nema ☆ RUS 96-97 G 5
Nemah o USA (WA) 244-245 B 4
Nemaiah Valley o CDN (BC) 230-231 B 2
Nëman ~ BY 94-95 K 5
Neman ☆ RUS 94-95 H 4
Nembe o WAN 204-205 G 6
Nembrala o RI 166-167 B 7
Nemenčinė o LT 94-95 J 4
Nementcha, Monts des ▲▲ DZ 190-191 F 3
Némiscau, Lac ⬭ CDN 38-39 F 3
Némiscau, Rivière ~ CDN 38-39 F 3
Nemkučenskij hrebet ▲▲ RUS 110-111 W 4
Nemnjuga ~ RUS 88-89 S 4
Nemo, vulkan ▲ RUS 122-123 Q 4
Nemours o F 90-91 J 7
Nemrut Dağı ••• TR 128-129 H 4
Nemuj o RUS 120-121 G 6
Nemunas ~ LT 94-95 H 4
Nemuro o J 152-153 L 3
Nemuro-hanto ᴗ J 152-153 L 3
Nemuro-kaikyō = Kunaširskij proliv ≈ 152-153 L 3
Nemuro-wan ≈ 152-153 L 3
Nemyriv ☆ UA 102-103 F 3
Nenagh = An tAonach o IRL 90-91 C 5
Nenana o USA 20-21 Q 4
Nenasi o MAL 162-163 E 3
Nendel'ginskij, hrebet ▲▲ RUS 110-111 V 6
Nenets Autonomous District = Neneckij avtonomnyj okrug □ RUS 88-89 T 3
Nenggiri ~ MAL 162-163 D 2
Nengo ~ ANG 216-217 F 7
Nenjiang o VRC 150-151 E 3
Nen Jiang ~ VRC 150-151 D 4
Nenoksa o RUS 88-89 P 4
Nens"egan ~ RUS 114-115 K 3
Neo o J 152-153 G 7
Neodesha o USA (KS) 262-263 L 7
Neola o USA (UT) 254-255 E 3
Néo Petrítsi o GR 100-101 J 4
Neopit o USA (WI) 270-271 K 6
Neópolis o BR 68-69 K 7
Neosho o USA (MO) 276-277 A 4
Neosho River ~ USA (KS) 262-263 L 6
Nepa o RUS (IRK) 116-117 O 6
Nepa ~ RUS 116-117 N 6
Nepa ~ RUS 116-117 M 6
Nepal ■ NEP 144-145 C 6
Nepalganj o NEP 144-145 C 6
Nepara o NAM 216-217 E 8
Nepean o CDN (ONT) 238-239 K 3
Nepean Mine • AUS 176-177 F 5
Nepean Sound ≈ CDN 228-229 E 3
Nepeña o PE 64-65 C 6
Nephi o USA (UT) 254-255 D 4
Nephin Beg Range ▲▲ IRL 90-91 C 4
Nepisiguit Bay ≈ 38-39 M 5
Nepisiguit Bay ≈ CDN 240-241 K 3
Nepisiguit River ~ CDN (NB) 240-241 J 3
Nepoko ~ ZRE 212-213 A 2
Nepomuceno o BR 72-73 J 6
Neponjatnaja ~ RUS 108-109 Y 4
Nèptènnè ~ RUS 116-117 K 4
Neptune Bay ≈ 36-37 R 2
Neptune Beach o USA (FL) 286-287 H 1
Neptune Islands ⌒ AUS 180-181 D 3
Nera ~ RUS 110-111 Z 7
Nera, Ust'- ☆• RUS 110-111 Y 7
Nérac o F 90-91 H 9
Neragon Island ⌒ USA 20-21 G 6
Nërangda, ozero ~ RUS 108-109 c 7
Nerča ~ RUS 118-119 H 8
Nerčinsk ☆ RUS 118-119 H 10
Nerčugan ~ RUS 118-119 H 9
Nerehta ☆• RUS 94-95 R 3
Nereta o•• LV 94-95 J 3
Neretva ~ HR 100-101 F 3
Neria ≈ 28-29 Q 6
Neria o GRØ (VGR) 28-29 Q 6
Neria ⌒ GRØ (VGR) 28-29 Q 6
Nerica ~ RUS 88-89 W 4
Neriquinha o ANG 216-217 F 7
Neris (Vilija) ~ LT 94-95 J 4
Nerja o E 98-99 F 6
Nerjuktjajinsk (Pervyj) o RUS 118-119 J 5
Nerjungri ☆• RUS 118-119 M 7
Nerka, Lake ⬭ USA 22-23 R 3
Nerl' ~ RUS 94-95 P 3
Nerla o IND 140-141 F 2
Nero, ozero ⬭ RUS 94-95 Q 3
Nerohi o RUS 114-115 F 3
Nerojka, gora ▲ RUS 114-115 E 2
Nerong, Selat ≈ 166-167 G 4
Nerópolis o BR 72-73 F 4
Nerpič'e o RUS 122-123 L 4
Nerpič'e, ozero ⬭ RUS (KMC) 120-121 U 5
Nerpič'e, ozero ⬭ RUS (SAH) 112-113 L 2
Nerpičij, mys ▲ RUS 110-111 Y 2
Nerpo o RUS 118-119 G 7
Nerren Nerren o AUS 176-177 C 3
Nerrima o AUS 172-173 G 5
Nerskoe ploskogor'e ▲▲ RUS 110-111 Z 7
Neruta ~ RUS 88-89 X 3
Nerutajaha ~ RUS 108-109 N 7
Nes o N 86-87 D 6
Nes' o RUS 88-89 S 3
Nes' ~ RUS 88-89 S 3
Nēšāpūr o• IR 136-137 F 6
Nesbitt o CDN (MAN) 234-235 D 5
Nesebăr o••• BG 102-103 E 6
Nes'egan ~ RUS 114-115 G 2
Nesgo o PNG 183 F 2
Neškan o RUS 112-113 Y 3
Neskaupstaður o IS 86-87 g 2
Nèskènpil'gyn, laguna ≈ 112-113 Y 3
Nesna o N 86-87 F 3
Nesøya ⌒ N 86-87 F 3
Nespelem o USA (WA) 244-245 G 2
Ness City o USA (KS) 262-263 G 6
Nessona o MOC 218-219 H 4
Nestaocano, Rivière ~ CDN (QUE) 236-237 P 2
Nesterov = Žovkva ☆ UA 102-103 C 2
Nesterovo o RUS 116-117 N 9
Nestiary o RUS 96-97 D 5
Nestorville o USA (WV) 280-281 G 4
Nët ~ RUS 120-121 H 4
Netaar o RI 166-167 L 3
Netanya ☆ IL 130-131 D 1
Netap o BHT 142-143 F 2
Netarhāt o IND 142-143 D 4
Netarts o USA (OR) 244-245 B 5
Netawaka o USA (KS) 262-263 L 5
Netcong o USA (NJ) 280-281 M 3
Netherhill o CDN (SAS) 232-233 K 4
Netherlands = Nederland ■ NL 92-93 G 2
Netherlands Antilles = Nederlandse Antillen ■ NA 60-61 G 1
Netia o MOC 218-219 K 2
Neto ~ I 100-101 F 5
Netrakona o BD 142-143 G 3
Netsilik Lake ⬭ CDN 24-25 a 6
Nettilling Lake ⬭ CDN 28-29 E 3
Nett Lake o USA (MN) 270-271 E 2
Nett Lake ⬭ USA (MN) 270-271 E 2
Nett Lake Indian Reservation X USA 270-271 E 2
Nettleton o USA (MS) 268-269 M 2
Nettling Fjord ≈ 28-29 F 3
Nettogami Lake ⬭ CDN (ONT) 236-237 H 2
Nettogami River ~ CDN (ONT) 236-237 H 2
Neubrandenburg o D 92-93 M 2
Neuchâtel ☆• CH 92-93 J 5
Neuchâtel, Lac de ⬭ CH 92-93 J 5
Neudač, buhta ⬭ RUS 108-109 f 2
Neudorf o CDN (SAS) 232-233 P 5
Neuenahr-Ahrweiler, Bad o• D 92-93 J 3
Neuenburg = Neuchâtel ☆• CH 92-93 J 5
Neuenburger See = Lac de Neuchâtel ⬭ CH 92-93 J 5
Neufchâteau o B 92-93 H 4
Neufchâteau o F 90-91 K 7
Neufchâtel-en-Bray o F 90-91 H 7
Neuhaus = Jindřichův Hradec o CZ 92-93 N 4
Neukaledonien ⌒ F 13 H 5
Neumarkt in der Oberpfalz o D 92-93 L 4
Neumünster o D 92-93 K 1
Neunkirchen o A 92-93 O 5
Neunkirchen o D 92-93 J 4
Neupokoeva, mys ▲ RUS 108-109 c 3
Neupokoeva, ostrov ⌒ RUS 108-109 R 5
Neuquén □ RA 78-79 D 5
Neuquén ☆ RA (NEU) 78-79 E 5
Neuquén, Río ~ RA 78-79 E 4
Neuruppin o• D 92-93 M 2
Neu Sandez = Nowy Sącz ☆• PL 92-93 Q 4
Neuschwabenland ∸ ARK 16 F 36
Neuschwanstein •• D 92-93 L 5
Neuse River ~ USA (NC) 282-283 L 6
Neuse River ~ USA (NC) 282-283 K 5
Neusiedler See ⬭ A 92-93 O 5
Neusohl = Banská Bystrica o SK 92-93 P 4
Neustadt (Orla) o D 92-93 L 3
Neustadt an der Aisch o D 92-93 L 4
Neustrelitz o• D 92-93 M 2
Neutenskij hrebet ▲▲ RUS 112-113 N 4
Neu-Titschein = Nový Jičín o CZ 92-93 P 4
Neutral Hills o CDN (ALB) 232-233 H 3
Neutral Junction o AUS 178-179 C 1
Neuwied o D 92-93 J 3
Neva ~ RUS 94-95 M 2
Nevada o USA (IA) 274-275 E 2
Nevada o USA (MO) 276-277 A 3
Nevada □ USA (NV) 246-247 G 4
Nevada, Sierra ▲▲ RA 78-79 E 7
Nevada, Sierra ▲▲ USA 40-41 D 6
Nevada de Lagunas Bravas, Sierra ▲ RCH 76-77 C 4
Nevada de Santa Marta, Sierra ▲▲ CO 60-61 E 2
Nevada Scheelite Mine o USA (NV) 246-247 G 4
Nevada Test Site xx USA (NV) 248-249 H 2
Nevadita, La o CO 60-61 E 2
Nevado, Cerro ▲ RCH 78-79 C 7
Nevado, Cerro el ▲ RA 78-79 E 3
Nevado, Sierra del ▲▲ RA 78-79 E 3
Nevado Ampato ▲ PE 70-71 B 4
Nevado Ancohuma ▲ BOL 70-71 C 4
Nevado Cololo Keasani ▲ BOL 70-71 C 4
Nevado Cóndor ▲ RCH 80 D 2
Nevado Coropuna ▲ PE 64-65 F 9
Nevado de Acay ▲ RA 76-77 D 3
Nevado de Cachí ▲ RA 76-77 D 3
Nevado de Chañi ▲ RA 76-77 E 3
Nevado de Colima ▲ MEX 52-53 C 2
Nevado de Cumbal ▲ CO 64-65 D 1
Nevado de Incahuasi ▲ RA 76-77 C 4
Nevado del Huila ▲ CO 60-61 D 6
Nevado del Huila, Parque Nacional ⊥ CO 60-61 D 6
Nevado del Illimani ▲ BOL 70-71 D 5
Nevado de Longaví ▲ RCH 78-79 D 4
Nevado de los Palos ▲ RCH 80 D 2
Nevado del Ruiz ▲ CO 60-61 D 5
Nevado del Tolima ▲ CO 60-61 D 5
Nevado de Putre ▲ RCH 70-71 C 6
Nevado de Sajama ▲ BOL 70-71 C 6
Nevado de Toluca, Parque Nacional ⊥ MEX 52-53 E 2
Nevado Huayasa ▲ PE 70-71 B 5
Nevado Huayna Potosi ▲ BOL 70-71 C 5
Nevado Ojos del Salado ▲•• RCH 76-77 C 4
Nevado Queva ▲ RA 76-77 D 3
Nevados, Parque Nacional los ⊥ CO 60-61 D 5
Nevado Salcantay ▲ PE 64-65 F 8
Neve, Serra do ▲▲ ANG 216-217 B 6
Nevel' ☆ RUS 94-95 L 3
Nevel'sk o RUS 122-123 J 5
Nevel'skogo, proliv ⬭ RUS 122-123 J 3
Never o RUS 118-119 M 8
Nevers ☆• F 90-91 J 8
Neversink River ~ USA (NY) 280-281 M 2
Nevertire o AUS 178-179 J 6
Neves, Rio ~ BR 68-69 F 5
Nevesinje o BIH 100-101 G 3
Neville o CDN (SAS) 232-233 L 6
Nevinnomyssk o RUS 126-127 D 5
Nevis o CDN (ALB) 232-233 E 3
Nevis Island ⌒ KAN 56 D 3
Nev'jansk ☆ RUS 96-97 M 5
Nevşehir ☆• TR 128-129 F 3
Nevskoe, ozero ⬭ RUS 122-123 K 4
New Aiyansh o CDN 32-33 F 4
Newala o EAT 214-215 K 6
New Albany o USA (IN) 274-275 N 6
New Albany o USA (MS) 268-269 L 2
New Albin o USA (IA) 274-275 G 1
New Alton Downs o AUS 178-179 E 4
New Amsterdam o GUY 62-63 F 2
Newark o USA (AR) 276-277 D 5
Newark o USA (DE) 280-281 L 4
Newark o USA (NJ) 280-281 M 3
Newark o USA (NY) 278-279 D 5
Newark o USA (OH) 280-281 D 3
Newark on Trent o• GB 90-91 G 5
New Athens o USA (IL) 274-275 J 6
New Athens o USA (OH) 280-281 E 3
New Augusta o USA (MS) 268-269 L 5
Newaygo o USA (MI) 272-273 D 4
New Baltimore o USA (MI) 272-273 G 5
New Bedford o USA (MA) 278-279 L 7
New Bercthal o CDN (MAN) 234-235 F 5
Newberg o USA (OR) 244-245 C 5
New Berlin o USA (NY) 278-279 F 6
New Bern o USA (NC) 282-283 K 5
Newbern o USA (TN) 276-277 F 4
Newberry o USA (FL) 286-287 G 2
Newberry o USA (MI) 270-271 N 4
Newberry o USA (SC) 284-285 J 2
New Bethlehem o USA (PA) 280-281 G 2
New Bight o BS 54-55 H 2
New Bonaventure o CDN (NFL) 242-243 P 4
New Boston o USA (IL) 274-275 H 3
New Boston o USA (IN) 274-275 M 6
New Boston o USA (MO) 274-275 F 5
New Boston o USA (OH) 280-281 D 5
New Boston o USA (TX) 264-265 K 5
New Bothwell o CDN (MAN) 234-235 G 5
New Braunfels o USA (TX) 266-267 J 4
New Brigden o CDN (ALB) 232-233 H 4
New Britain ⌒ PNG 183 E 4
New Britain o USA (CT) 280-281 O 2
New Britain Trench ≃ 183 E 4
New Brockton o USA (AL) 284-285 E 5
Newbrook o CDN 32-33 O 4
New Brunswick □ CDN (NB) 240-241 J 3
New Brunswick o USA (NJ) 280-281 M 3
New Buffalo o USA (MI) 272-273 C 6
Newburgh o USA (NY) 280-281 M 2
New Burnside o USA (IL) 276-277 G 3
Newbury o GB 90-91 G 6
Newburyport o USA (MA) 278-279 L 6
New Bussa o WAN 204-205 F 4
Newby River ~ CDN 32-33 P 3
New Caledonia = Nouvelle-Calédonie, Île ⌒ F 13 H 5
New Caledonia Basin ≃ 13 H 5
New Caledonian Basin ≃ 182 B 2
New Canaan o CDN (NB) 240-241 K 4
New Carlisle o CDN (QUE) 240-241 K 2
New Carlisle o USA (OH) 280-281 B 4
Newcastle o AUS 180-181 L 2
Newcastle o CDN (NB) 240-241 K 3
Newcastle o CDN (ONT) 238-239 G 5
Newcastle o GB 90-91 E 4
Newcastle o USA (CA) 246-247 D 5
New Castle o USA (IN) 274-275 N 5
Newcastle o USA (NE) 262-263 K 2
New Castle o USA (PA) 280-281 F 2
Newcastle o USA (TX) 264-265 F 5
Newcastle o USA (UT) 254-255 B 6
New Castle o USA (VA) 280-281 F 6
Newcastle o USA (WY) 252-253 O 3
Newcastle o ZA 220-221 J 3
Newcastle Creek ~ AUS 174-175 C 5
Newcastle upon Tyne ☆ GB 90-91 G 4
Newcastle Waters o AUS 174-175 B 5
Newcastle West = An Caisleán Nua o IRL 90-91 C 5
New Centreville o USA (PA) 280-281 G 4
New Cholossa o PNG 183 A 2
New Cleeves o CDN (SAS) 232-233 J 2
New Cornwall o CDN (NS) 240-241 L 6
New Cumberland o USA (PA) 280-281 K 3
Newdale o CDN (MAN) 234-235 C 4
Newdale o USA (ID) 252-253 G 3
New Dayton o CDN (ALB) 232-233 F 6
New Deal o USA (TX) 264-265 C 5
New Delamere o AUS 172-173 K 3
New Delhi ★• IND 138-139 F 5
New Denver o CDN (BC) 230-231 M 4
New Dixie o AUS 174-175 G 4
Newell o USA (SD) 260-261 C 2
Newell, Lake ⬭ AUS 176-177 J 2
Newell, Lake ⬭ CDN (ALB) 232-233 G 5
New Ellenton o USA (SC) 284-285 J 3
Newell Highway II AUS 178-179 K 6
Newellton o USA (LA) 268-269 J 4
New England o USA (ND) 258-259 E 5
New England Highway II AUS 178-179 L 6
New England National Park ⊥ AUS 178-179 M 6
New England Range ▲▲ AUS 178-179 L 6
New England Seamounts ≃ 6-7 E 1
Newenham, Cape ▲ USA 22-23 P 3
New Era o USA (MI) 272-273 C 4
New Featherstone o ZW 218-219 F 4
Newfolden o USA (MN) 270-271 B 2
Newfound Gap ▲ USA (NC) 282-283 D 5
Newfoundland □ CDN 38-39 N 2
Newfoundland, Grand Banks of ≃ 6-7 D 4
Newfoundland, Island of ⌒ CDN (NFL) 242-243 L 4
Newfoundland Evaporation Basin ∸ USA (UT) 254-255 B 2
New Gabloi o LB 202-203 F 6
New Galloway o GB 90-91 E 4
Newgate o CDN (BC) 230-231 O 4
New Georgia ⌒ SOL 184 I c 3
New Georgia Group ⌒ SOL 184 I c 3
New Georgia Sound = The Slot ≈ 184 I c 2
New Germany o CDN (NS) 240-241 L 6
New Glarus o USA (WI) 274-275 J 2
New Glasgow o CDN (NS) 240-241 N 5
New Grand Chain o USA (IL) 276-277 F 3
New Greenleaf o USA (MI) 272-273 F 4
New Guinea ⌒ RI 166-167 J 3
New Guinea Trench ≃ 166-167 J 2
Newgulf o USA (TX) 268-269 E 7
Newhalem o USA (WA) 244-245 D 2
Newhalen o USA 22-23 T 3
Newhalen River ~ USA 22-23 T 3
New Halfa o SUD 200-201 G 5
Newhall o USA (CA) 248-249 F 5
New Hamilton o USA 20-21 J 5
New Hampshire □ USA (NH) 278-279 K 5
New Hampton o USA (IA) 274-275 F 1
New Hanover ⌒ PNG 183 F 2
New Hanover o ZA 220-221 K 4
New Harbor o USA (ME) 278-279 M 5
New Harmony o USA (IN) 274-275 L 6
Newhaven o AUS 172-173 K 7
Newhaven o GB 90-91 H 6
New Haven o USA (IN) 274-275 N 3
New Haven o USA (KY) 276-277 K 3
New Haven o• USA (CT) 280-281 O 2
New Hazelton o CDN 32-33 G 4
New Hebrides ⌒ VAN 184 II a 1
New Hope o USA (AL) 284-285 D 2
New Hope o USA (PA) 280-281 M 3
New Iberia o USA (LA) 268-269 J 6
New Ireland ⌒ PNG 183 F 2
New Jersey □ USA (NJ) 280-281 M 4
New Jersey Turnpike o USA (NJ) 280-281 M 3
Newkirk o USA (NM) 256-257 L 3
Newkirk o USA (OK) 264-265 G 2
New Knockhock o USA 20-21 H 5
Newlands o CDN (BC) 228-229 M 2
New Lebanon o USA (NY) 278-279 H 6
New Leipzig o USA (ND) 258-259 F 5
New Lexington o USA (AL) 284-285 C 3
New Lexington o USA (OH) 280-281 D 4
Newlin o USA (TX) 264-265 D 4
New Lisbon o USA (WI) 270-271 H 7
New Liskeard o CDN (ONT) 236-237 J 5
New London o CDN (PEI) 240-241 M 4
New London o USA (IA) 274-275 G 4
New London o USA (MN) 270-271 D 5
New London o USA (MO) 274-275 G 5
New London o USA (WA) 244-245 B 3
New London o USA (WI) 270-271 K 6
New London o• USA (CT) 280-281 O 2
New Madrid o USA (MO) 276-277 F 4
Newman o AUS 176-177 E 1
Newman o USA (CA) 248-249 C 2
Newman o USA (IL) 274-275 L 5
Newman o USA (NM) 256-257 J 6
Newman Bugt ≈ 26-27 V 3
Newmarket o CDN (ONT) 238-239 F 4
Newmarket o• GB 90-91 H 5
New Market o USA (TN) 282-283 D 4
New Market o USA (VA) 280-281 H 5
New Martinsville o USA (WV) 280-281 F 4
New Matamoras o USA (OH) 280-281 E 4
New Meadows o USA (ID) 252-253 B 2
New Mexico □ USA (NM) 256-257 J 4
New Milford o USA (CT) 280-281 N 2
New Milford o USA (PA) 280-281 L 2
New Mirpur o IND 138-139 D 3
New Moore o USA (TX) 264-265 B 5
Newnan o USA (GA) 284-285 F 3
Newnes ∴ AUS 180-181 L 2
New Norfolk o AUS 180-181 J 7
New Norway o CDN (ALB) 232-233 F 3
New Orleans o USA (LA) 268-269 K 7
New Osgoode o CDN (SAS) 232-233 P 2
New Osnaburgh o CDN (ONT) 234-235 N 3
New Paltz o USA (NY) 280-281 M 2
New Pekin o USA (IN) 274-275 M 6
New Perlican o CDN (NFL) 242-243 P 5
New Philadelphia o USA (OH) 280-281 E 3
New Pine Creek o USA (OR) 244-245 E 8
New Plymouth o NZ 182 E 3
New Plymouth o USA (ID) 252-253 B 3
Newport o CDN (NS) 240-241 L 6
Newport o CDN (QUE) 240-241 L 2
Newport o GB (ENG) 90-91 G 6
Newport o GB (WAL) 90-91 F 6
Newport o USA (AR) 276-277 D 5
Newport o USA (FL) 286-287 E 1
Newport o USA (KY) 276-277 L 1

Newport o USA (NC) 282-283 L 6
Newport o USA (NE) 262-263 G 2
Newport o USA (NH) 278-279 J 5
Newport o USA (OH) 280-281 B 3
Newport o USA (OR) 244-245 A 6
Newport o USA (TN) 282-283 D 5
Newport o USA (TX) 264-265 F 5
Newport o USA (VA) 280-281 F 6
Newport o USA (VT) 278-279 J 4
Newport o USA (WA) 244-245 H 2
Newport o• USA (RI) 278-279 K 7
Newport Beach o USA (CA) 248-249 G 6
Newport News o USA (VA) 280-281 K 7
New Port Richey o USA (FL) 286-287 G 3
New Prague o USA (MN) 270-271 E 6
New Princeton o USA (OR) 244-245 G 7
New Providence ⌒ BS 54-55 G 2
Newquay o• GB 90-91 E 6
New Raymer o USA (CO) 254-255 M 3
New Richland o USA (MN) 270-271 E 7
New Richmond o CDN (QUE) 240-241 K 2
New Richmond o USA (WI) 270-271 F 5
New Ringold o USA (OK) 264-265 J 4
New River ~ GUY 62-63 F 4
New River o USA (AZ) 256-257 C 5
New River ~ USA (FL) 286-287 E 1
New River ~ USA (GA) 284-285 G 5
New River ~ USA (NC) 282-283 F 4
New River ~ USA (NC) 282-283 K 6
New River ~ USA (WV) 280-281 F 7
New Roads o USA (LA) 268-269 J 6
New Rochelle o USA (NY) 280-281 N 3
New Rockford o USA (ND) 258-259 H 4
New Ross o CDN (NS) 240-241 L 6
New Ross = Ros Mhic Thriúin o IRL 90-91 D 5
Newry o AUS 172-173 J 4
Newry o USA (ME) 278-279 L 4
Newry Island ⌒ AUS 174-175 K 7
New Salem o USA (ND) 258-259 F 5
New Schwabenland ∴ ARK 16 F 36
New Sharon o USA (IA) 274-275 F 3
New Siberian Islands = Novosibirskie ostrova ⌒ RUS 110-111 Z 3
New Site o USA (AL) 284-285 E 3
New Smyrna Beach o USA (FL) 286-287 J 2
Newsome o USA (TX) 264-265 J 6
New South Wales ◻ AUS 180-181 G 2
New Springs o AUS 176-177 F 2
New Stanton o USA (PA) 280-281 G 3
Newstead o CDN (NFL) 242-243 O 3
New Stuyahok o USA 22-23 S 3
New Summerfield o USA (TX) 268-269 E 5
Newton o USA (GA) 284-285 F 5
Newton o USA (IA) 274-275 E 3
Newton o USA (IL) 274-275 K 6
Newton o USA (KS) 262-263 J 6
Newton o USA (MS) 268-269 L 4
Newton o USA (NC) 282-283 F 5
Newton o USA (NJ) 280-281 M 2
Newton o USA (TX) 268-269 G 6
Newton Grove o USA (NC) 282-283 J 5
Newton Lake < USA (IL) 274-275 K 6
Newton Mills o CDN (NS) 240-241 N 5
Newtontoppen ▲ N 84-85 K 3
Newtown o CDN (NFL) 242-243 P 3
New Town o USA (ND) 258-259 E 4
Newtownabbey o GB 90-91 E 4
Newtown Steward o GB 90-91 D 4
New Ulm o USA (MN) 270-271 D 6
New Vienna o USA (OH) 280-281 C 4
New Waterford o CDN (NS) 240-241 P 4
New Waverly o USA (TX) 268-269 E 6
New Westminster o CDN (BC) 230-231 G 4
New World Island ⌒ CDN (NFL) 242-243 O 3
New York o•• USA (NY) 280-281 N 3
New York ◻ USA (NY) 278-279 C 6
New York Mountains ▲ USA (CA) 248-249 J 4
New York State Thruway II USA (NY) 278-279 F 5
New York State Thruway II USA (NY) 280-281 M 2
New Zealand ■ NZ 182 E 4
New Zealand ⌒ NZ 182 E 4
Nexapa, Río ~ MEX 52-53 E 2
Nexpa, Río ~ MEX 52-53 C 2
Neyyāttinkara o IND 140-141 G 6
Nezahualcóyotl, Ciudad o MEX 52-53 E 2
Nezahualcóyotl, Presa < MEX 52-53 H 3
Neždaninskoe o RUS 120-121 H 2
Nežin = Nižyn o UA 102-103 G 2
Neznaemyj, zaliv o RUS 108-109 G 5
Neznanovo o RUS 94-95 R 4
Nezperce o USA (ID) 250-251 C 5
Nez Perce Indian Reservation X USA (ID) 250-251 C 5
Nez Perce National Historic Park • USA (ID) 250-251 C 5
Nez Perce Pass ▲ USA (ID) 250-251 E 6
Nezpique, Bayou ~ USA (LA) 268-269 H 6
Nfiss, Oued ~ MA 188-189 G 5
Ngabang o RI 162-163 H 4
Ngabe o RCB 210-211 F 5
Ngabordamlu, Tanjung ▲ RI 166-167 H 5
Ngabu o MW 218-219 H 3
Ngabwe o Z 218-219 D 1
Ngadda, River ~ WAN 204-205 K 3
Ngadiluwih o RI 168 E 3
Ngadza o RCA 206-207 E 6
Ngajira o EAT 214-215 H 4
Ngala o WAN 198-199 G 6
Ngali o ZRE 210-211 G 5
Ngalo o ZRE 206-207 F 6
Ngalu o• RI 168 E 8
Ngam o CAM 206-207 B 5
Ngam o TCH 206-207 C 3
Ngama o TCH 206-207 C 3
Ngamakwe o ZA 220-221 H 6
Ngambé o CAM 204-205 J 6
Ngambé Tikar o CAM 204-205 J 6
Ngamdu o WAN 204-205 K 3
Ngami, Lake o RB 218-219 B 5
Ngamiland ◻ RB 216-217 F 9
Ngamo o ZW 218-219 D 4
Ngamring o VRC 144-145 F 6
Nganda o RCA 206-207 F 6
Nganda o SN 202-203 C 3
Ngangala o SUD 206-207 K 6
Ngangla Ringco o VRC 144-145 D 5
Nganglong Kangri ▲ VRC 144-145 C 4
Nganglong Kangri ▲ VRC 144-145 C 4
Ngangzê Co o VRC 144-145 F 5
Nganha, Montagne de ▲ CAM 206-207 B 5
Nganji o ZRE 212-213 A 5
Nganjuk o RI 168 D 3
Ngantru o RI 168 D 3
Nganzi o ANG 210-211 D 6
Ngao o THA 142-143 L 6
Ngaoui, Mont ▲ CAM 206-207 B 5
Ngaoundal o CAM 204-205 K 5
Ngaoundéré ☆ CAM 204-205 K 5
Ngara o EAT 212-213 C 5
Ngara o MW 214-215 H 6
Ngarama o RWA 212-213 C 4
Ngarangou o TCH 198-199 G 6
Ngaras o RI 162-163 F 7
Ngarimbi o EAT 214-215 K 5
Ngarka-Pyrjajaha ~ RUS 114-115 L 2
Ngarkat Conservation Park ⊥ AUS 180-181 F 3
Ngaso Plain ∴ EAK 212-213 F 2
Ngassao Noum ▲ CAM 206-207 B 4
Ngasumet o EAT 212-213 F 6
Ngathainggyaung o MYA 158-159 C 2
Ngato o CAM 210-211 E 2
Ngawi o RI 168 D 3
Ngawihi o NZ 182 E 4
Ngayu ~ ZRE 212-213 B 3
Ngazidja ⌒ COM 222-223 C 3
Ngazun o MYA 142-143 J 5
Ngbala o RCB 210-211 E 3
Ngerengere o EAT 214-215 K 4
Ngezi ~ ZW 218-219 E 4
Nggatokae ⌒ SOL 184 I d 3
Nggela Pile ⌒ SOL 184 I e 3
Nggela Sule ⌒ SOL 184 I d 3
Nghi Lôc ☆ VN 156-157 D 7
Ngilikomba o SOL 184 I e 3
Ngina o ZRE (Ban) 210-211 F 5
Ngina o ZRE (HAU) 212-213 A 2
N'Giva ☆ ANG 216-217 C 8
Ngo o RCB 210-211 E 5
Ngoa o ZRE 212-213 B 2
Ngoassé o CAM 210-211 D 2
Ngọc Hiền o VN 158-159 H 6
Ngofakiaha o RI 164-165 K 3
Ngog Mapubi o CAM 210-211 C 2
Ngoila o CAM 210-211 E 2
Ngoko ~ CAM 210-211 E 3
Ngoko o RCB 210-211 E 4
Ngoko ~ RCB 210-211 E 4
Ngola o CAM 210-211 E 2
Ngol Kedju ▲ CAM 204-205 H 5
Ngolo o Z 214-215 F 5
Ngolo o ZRE 210-211 G 3
Ngolo, Chutes de ~ RCA 206-207 F 6
Ngolopopo, Tanjung ▲ RI 164-165 L 3
Ngoma o NAM 218-219 C 3
Ngoma o Z 218-219 C 2
Ngoma Bridge o RB 218-219 C 3
Ngoma Tsé-Tsé o RCB 210-211 E 6
Ngomba o EAT 214-215 G 5
Ngomedzap o CAM 210-211 C 2
Ngomeni, Ras ▲ EAK 212-213 H 5
Ngomo o G 210-211 B 4
Ngom Qu ~ VRC 144-145 K 4
Ngong o CAM 204-205 K 4
Ngong o EAK 212-213 F 4
Ngonga o CAM 204-205 J 6
Ngoni, Tanjung ▲ RI 166-167 H 5
Ngonye Falls ~• Z 218-219 B 3
Ngora o EAU 212-213 D 3
Ngorengore o EAK 212-213 E 4
Ngoring Hu o VRC 144-145 L 3
Ngoro o CAM 204-205 J 6
Ngorongoro Conservation Area ⊥ EAT (ARV) 212-213 E 5
Ngorongoro Crater ▲••• EAT 212-213 E 5
Ngorongoro Crater Lodge o EAT 212-213 E 5
Ngororero o RWA 212-213 B 4
Ngoso o ZRE 210-211 G 6
Ngoto o RCA 206-207 C 6
Ngotwane ~ RB 220-221 H 2
Ngouanga ~ RCA 206-207 G 5
Ngoui o SN 196-197 D 6
Ngoulemakong o CAM 210-211 C 2
Ngoulonkila o RCB 210-211 E 5
Ngouma o RMM 202-203 J 2
Ngouni o G 210-211 D 4
Ngounié ~ G 210-211 C 4
Ngoura o CAM 206-207 B 6
Ngoura o TCH 198-199 H 6
Ngouri o TCH 198-199 G 6
Ngourti o RN 198-199 F 5
Ngoussa o DZ 190-191 E 4
Ngoutchéy < TCH 198-199 H 4
Ngouyo o RCA 206-207 G 6
Ngovayang ▲ CAM 210-211 C 2
Ngové-Ndogo, Domaine de chasse de ⊥ G 210-211 B 5
Ngoyeboma o RCB 210-211 E 3
Ngozi o BU 212-213 B 5
Ngudu o EAT 212-213 D 5
Nguélémendouka o CAM 204-205 K 6
Nguema o ZRE 214-215 B 4
Ngui o RCA 206-207 F 5
Nguia Bouar o RCA 206-207 B 6
Nguigmi o RN 198-199 F 5
Nguila o CAM 204-205 J 6
Nguini < RN 198-199 D 5
Nguiu X AUS 172-173 K 1
Ngukurr X AUS 174-175 C 4
Ngula o ZW 218-219 D 5
Nguling o RI 168 E 3
Nguna ⌒ VAN 184 II b 3
Ngundu o ZW 218-219 F 5
Nguni o EAK 212-213 G 4
Ngunju, Tanjung ▲ RI 168 E 8
Ngunut o RI 168 E 4
Nguroje o WAN 204-205 J 5
Ngurore o WAN 204-205 K 4
Nguru o WAN 198-199 E 6
Nguti o CAM 204-205 H 6
Nguyakro o CI 202-203 H 6
Nguyên Binh ☆ VN 156-157 D 5
Ngwale o EAT 214-215 J 6
Ngwalulu = Maana'oba ⌒ SOL 184 I e 3
Ngwedaung o MYA 142-143 K 6
Ngweze ~ Z 218-219 C 3
Ngwo o CAM 204-205 H 5
Ngynesëjaha ~ RUS 108-109 R 6
Nhabe ~ RB 218-219 B 5
Nhachengue o MOC 218-219 H 6
Nhacra o GNB 202-203 C 4
Nhamalábue o MOC 218-219 H 3
Nhamatanda o MOC 218-219 H 4
Nhamunda o BR 66-67 J 4
Nhamunda, Rio ~ BR 62-63 F 6
Nhamundá Mapuera, Área Indígena X BR 62-63 E 6
Nhandeara o BR 72-73 E 6
Nhandu, Rio ~ BR 66-67 K 7
Nharêa o ANG 216-217 D 5
Nha Trang ☆• VN 158-159 K 4
Nhecolândia o BR 70-71 J 6
Nhia ~ ANG 216-217 C 5
Nhill o AUS 180-181 F 4
Nhlangano o SD 220-221 K 3
Nho Quan ☆ VN 156-157 D 6
Nhoquim, Igarapé ~ BR 68-69 C 6
Nhu' Kuân ☆ VN 156-157 D 7
Nhulunbuy (Gove) o AUS 174-175 D 3
Niabayo o CI 202-203 G 7
Niablé o CI 202-203 J 6
Niada o RCA 206-207 E 6
Niafounké o RMM 202-203 H 2
Niagara o USA (ND) 258-259 K 4
Niagara Creek ~ CDN (BC) 228-229 O 4
Niagara Escarpment ▲ CDN (ONT) 238-239 D 3
Niagara Falls o CDN (ONT) 238-239 F 5
Niagara Falls •• CDN (ONT) 238-239 F 5
Niagara Falls o USA (NY) 278-279 C 5
Niagara River ~ 46-47 J 4
Niague o CI 202-203 G 7
Niah o MAL 162-163 K 3
Niah Caves • MAL 162-163 K 3
Niah National Park ⊥ MAL 162-163 K 3
Niakaramandougou o CI 202-203 H 5
Niakhar o SN 202-203 B 2
Niaklan o LB 202-203 F 7
Nialaha'u Point = Cape Zele'e ▲ SOL 184 I e 3
Niambézaria o CI 202-203 H 7
Niamey ◻ RN 204-205 D 1
Niamey ★• RN (NIA) 204-205 E 2
Niamina o RMM 202-203 G 3
Niampak o RI 164-165 K 3
Niamtougou o RT 202-203 L 5
Niamvoudou o CAM 204-205 K 6
Niandakoro o RG 202-203 F 4
Niandan ~ RG 202-203 F 5
Nianfasa o CI 202-203 G 5
Nianforando o RG 202-203 E 5
Niangandu o EAT 214-215 J 4
Niangara o ZRE 212-213 A 2
Niangay, Lac o RMM 202-203 J 2
Niangoloko o BF 202-203 H 4
Niangua River ~ USA (MO) 276-277 C 3
Niangyuan o VRC 156-157 G 4
Nia-Nia o ZRE 212-213 A 3
Nianing o SN 202-203 B 2
Niantan ~ RG 202-203 E 4
Niantanina o RN 202-203 F 4
Nianyushan SK ~ VRC 154-155 J 6
Niaoshu Shan ▲ VRC 154-155 D 4
Niapidou o CI 202-203 G 7
Niapu o ZRE 210-211 L 2
Niaqornaarsuk o GRØ 28-29 O 2
Niaqornat o GRØ 26-27 Y 8
Niara o RG 202-203 E 4
Niari ◻ RCB 210-211 D 5
Niari ~ RCB 210-211 D 5
Niaro o SUD 206-207 K 3
Nias, Pulau ⌒ RI 162-163 B 4
Niassa ◻ MOC 218-219 J 1
Niassa, Lago o MOC 214-215 H 7
Niassa, Reserva do ⊥ MOC 214-215 J 7
Niáta o GR 100-101 J 6
Niau ⌒ F 13 N 4
Nibinamik Lake o CDN (ONT) 234-235 P 2
Nibong, Kampung o MAL 162-163 D 2
Nibong Tebal o MAL 162-163 D 2
Nica ~ RUS 114-115 G 6
Nicabau o CDN (QUE) 236-237 P 3
Nicaragua ■ NIC 52-53 A 5
Nicaragua, Lago de o NIC 52-53 B 6
Nicasio o PE 70-71 B 4
Nicastro o I 100-101 F 5
Ničatka, ozero o RUS 118-119 H 7
Nicatous Lake o USA (ME) 278-279 N 3
Nice ☆• F 90-91 L 10
Niceville o USA (FL) 286-287 C 1
Nichicun, Lac o CDN 38-39 J 2
Nichinan o J 152-153 D 9
Nichlaul o IND 142-143 C 2
Nicholas Channel ≈ 54-55 E 3
Nicholasville o USA (KY) 276-277 L 3
Nichol Island ⌒ CDN (NS) 240-241 N 6
Nicholls o USA (GA) 284-285 H 5
Nicholls Warm Springs o USA (CA) 248-249 K 6
Nicholson o AUS 172-173 J 5
Nicholson, Mount ▲ AUS 178-179 K 3
Nicholson Lake o CDN (ONT) 236-237 E 5
Nicholson Lake o CDN 30-31 S 4
Nicholson Peninsula ⌣ CDN 24-25 G 6
Nicholson Range ▲ AUS 176-177 D 3
Nicholson River ~ AUS 174-175 E 5
Nichols Town o BS 54-55 F 2
Nicholsville o CDN (NFL) 242-243 L 3
Nicholville o USA (NY) 278-279 G 4
Nička o TM 136-137 H 6
Nickel Center o CDN (ONT) 238-239 E 2
Nickerieriver ~ SME 62-63 F 3
Nickerson o USA (KS) 262-263 H 6
Nickerson o USA (MN) 270-271 F 4
Nickol Bay ≈ 172-173 C 6
Nicktown o USA (PA) 280-281 H 3
Nicman o CDN (QUE) 242-243 B 2
Ničnij Pjandž o TJ 136-137 L 6
Nicola o CDN (BC) 230-231 J 3
Nicola Mameet Indian Reserve X CDN (BC) 230-231 J 3
Nicola River ~ CDN (BC) 230-231 J 3
Nicolás Bruzzone o RA 78-79 G 3
Nicolás Levalle o RA 78-79 H 5
Nicolet o CDN (QUE) 238-239 N 2
Nicolet, Rivière ~ CDN (QUE) 238-239 N 2
Nicollet o USA (MN) 270-271 D 6
Nicondocho, Rio ~ MOC 218-219 K 1
Nicosia o I 100-101 E 6
Nicosia = Lefkosia ★ CY 128-129 E 5
Nicoya o CR 52-53 B 6
Nicoya, Golfo de ≈ 52-53 B 7
Nicoya, Península de ⌣ CR 52-53 B 7
Nictau o CDN (NB) 240-241 H 3
Nicuadala o MOC 218-219 J 3
Nicupa o MOC 218-219 K 2
Nida o•• LT 94-95 G 4
Nida o USA (OK) 264-265 H 4
Nidadavole o IND 140-141 J 2
Nidelva ~ N 86-87 D 7
Nidili, ozero o RUS 118-119 M 4
Nido, El o RP 160-161 C 7
Nidpalli o IND 140-141 F 4
Nidri o GR 100-101 H 5
Nidym ~ RUS 116-117 K 4
Nidymkan ~ RUS 116-117 J 4
Nidzica o• PL 92-93 Q 2
Niéboré o RG 202-203 E 4
Niebüll o D 92-93 K 1
Niechorze o PL 92-93 N 1
Niedere Tauern ▲ A 92-93 M 5
Niederösterreich ◻ A 92-93 N 4
Niedersachsen ◻ D 92-93 J 2
Niefang o GQ 210-211 C 3
Niega o BF 202-203 K 3
Niekerkshoop o ZA 220-221 F 4
Niellé o CI 202-203 H 4
Niellim o TCH 206-207 C 4
Niem o RCA 206-207 B 5
Niemba o ZRE 212-213 B 6
Niemba ~ ZRE 214-215 E 4
Niemelane < RIM 196-197 E 5
Niemisel o S 86-87 L 3
Niéna o RMM 202-203 G 4
Nienburg (Weser) o D 92-93 K 2
Niénokue, Mont ▲ CI 202-203 G 7
Niéri Ko ~ SN 202-203 D 3
Nieu Bethesda o ZA 220-221 G 5
Nieuw Amsterdam ☆ SME 62-63 G 3
Nieuw Nickerie ☆ SME 62-63 F 3
Nieuwoudtville o ZA 220-221 D 5
Nieuwpoort o NL 60-61 G 1
Nieva, Río ~ PE 64-65 D 4
Nieves, Las o MEX 50-51 G 4
Niğde ☆• TR 128-129 F 3
Nigei Island ⌒ CDN (BC) 230-231 B 3
Nigel o ZA 220-221 J 3
Niger ~ 9 D 4
Niger ■ RN 198-199 B 4
Niger ◻ WAN 204-205 F 4
Niger Delta ⌣ WAN 204-205 F 6
Niger Fan ≃ 9 D 5
Nigeria ■ WAN 204-205 F 4
Night Hawk Lake o CDN (ONT) 236-237 H 4
Nightmote o USA 20-21 H 6
Nigisaktuvik River ~ USA 20-21 L 1
Nigu River ~ USA 20-21 M 2
Niha Settlements • RI 162-163 B 4
Nihing o PK 134-135 L 4
Nihing ~ PK 134-135 K 5
Nihoa ⌒ USA (HI) 288 D 1
Nihonmatsu o J 152-153 J 6
Nihuil, El o RA 78-79 E 3
Nihuil, Embalse del < RA 78-79 E 3
Nihuil, Salto ~ RA 78-79 E 3
Niigata ☆ J 152-153 H 6
Niihau ⌒ USA (HI) 288 E 3
Niijima ⌒ J 152-153 H 7
Niimi o J 152-153 E 7
Niitsu o J 152-153 H 6
Nijadluk Bay ≈ 36-37 R 2
Nijgarh o NEP 144-145 E 7
Nijmegen o• NL 92-93 H 3
Nikeľ o RUS 88-89 L 2
Nikiniki o RI 166-167 C 6
Nikitinka o KA 124-125 N 4
Nikkaluokta o S 86-87 J 3
Nikki o DY 204-205 E 4
Nikkō o•• J 152-153 H 6
Nikko National Park ⊥ J 152-153 H 6
Nikoemvon o CAM 210-211 C 2
Nikolaev = Mykolajiv o UA 102-103 G 4
Nikolaevka o KA 124-125 E 1
Nikolaevo o RUS 94-95 L 2
Nikolaevsk o RUS 96-97 D 8
Nikolaevsk-na-Amure ☆• RUS 122-123 J 2
Nikolaja, mys ▲ RUS 108-109 F 4
Nikolaja, zaliv o RUS 122-123 H 2
Nikolka, gora ▲ RUS 120-121 T 6
Nikolo-L'vovskoe o RUS 122-123 D 7
Nikoľsk o RUS 96-97 D 4
Nikoľsk o RUS (PNZ) 96-97 E 7
Nikoľskij = Satpaev ☆ KA 124-125 E 5
Nikoľskoe o RUS (AST) 96-97 E 10
Nikoľskoe ☆ RUS 120-121 V 6
Nikonga ~ EAT 212-213 C 5
Nikopol o BG 102-103 D 6
Nikopoľ o UA 102-103 J 4
Nikopolis •• GR 100-101 H 5
Nikšahr o IR 134-135 J 5
Nikšahr, Rūdḫāne-ye ~ IR 134-135 J 5
Niksar ☆• TR 128-129 G 2
Nikšić o YU 100-101 G 3
Nil, an- ~ ET 194-195 E 3
Nila o RI 168 E 7
Nila, Pulau ⌒ RI 166-167 E 5
Nilahué, Estrecho de ~ RCH 78-79 D 3
Nilakkottai o IND 140-141 G 5
Nilan ~ RUS 122-123 F 3
Niland o USA (CA) 248-249 J 6
Nilanga o IND 138-139 F 10
Nile ◻ EAU 212-213 C 2
Nile = an-Nil ~ ET 194-195 E 3
Nile = Nil, an- ~ SUD 194-195 E 3
Niles o USA (MI) 272-273 C 6
Niles o USA (OH) 280-281 F 2
Nilgysy ~ RUS 120-121 L 3
Nilka o VRC 146-147 F 4
Nil Kōtal, Kōtal-e ▲ AFG 134-135 M 1
Nilópolis o BR 72-73 J 7
Nilsiä o FIN 88-89 K 5
Nilt o PK 138-139 E 1
Nimach o IND 138-139 E 7
Niman ~ RUS 122-123 E 3
Nimar ∴ IND 138-139 E 9
Nimba, Monts ▲•• RG 202-203 F 6
Nimbāhera o IND 138-139 E 7
Nimba Range ∴ LB 202-203 F 6
Nimbin o AUS 178-179 M 5
Nimbotong o RI 166-167 L 3
Nimburg = Nymburk o• CZ 92-93 N 3
Nimčan ~ RUS 112-113 H 3
Nimdė ~ RUS 116-117 E 3
Nimelen ~ RUS 122-123 G 2
Nîmes ☆• F 90-91 K 10
Nimi ~ RUS 120-121 F 6
Nimingdė ~ RUS 110-111 Q 6
Nimiuktuk River ~ USA 20-21 L 2
Nimjat o RIM 196-197 C 6
Nim Ka Thāna o IND 138-139 E 6
Nim Li Punit ∴• BH 52-53 K 3
Nimmitabel o AUS 180-181 K 4
Nimpkish River ~ CDN (BC) 230-231 C 3
Nimpo Lake o CDN (BC) 228-229 J 4
Nimrod o USA (MN) 270-271 D 4
Nimrod Lake o USA (AR) 276-277 B 6
Nimrūd ∴•• IRQ 128-129 K 4
Nimule o SUD 212-213 D 2
Nimule National Park ⊥ SUD 212-213 D 2
Nimún, Punta ▲ MEX 52-53 J 1
Nina o NAM 216-217 E 11
Nina, Île = Aniwa Island ⌒ VAN 184 II b 4
Ninā, Wādī ~ LAR 192-193 F 3
Nina Bang Lake o CDN 24-25 g 5
Nina Lake o CDN 30-31 X 2
Ninami-Daitō-shima ⌒ J 152-153 D 12
Ninawā ∴•• IRQ 128-129 K 4
Ninawia ◻ IRQ 128-129 J 5
Nindo o ANG 216-217 F 7
Nindigully o AUS 178-179 K 5
Nine Degree Channel ≈ 140-141 E 6
Nine Mile Falls o USA (WA) 244-245 H 3
Ninette o CDN (MAN) 234-235 D 5
Ninette o NAM 216-217 E 11
Ninetyeast Ridge ≃ 12 G 7
Ninety Mile Beach ∴ AUS 180-181 J 5
Ninety Six o USA (SC) 284-285 H 2
Ninety Six National Historic Site ∴• USA (SC) 284-285 H 2
Ninfas, Punta ▲ RA 78-79 G 7
Ninga o CDN (MAN) 234-235 D 5
Ningaloo o AUS 172-173 A 7
Ning'an o VRC 150-151 G 5
Ningan o VRC 156-157 C 3
Ningari o RMM 202-203 J 2
Ningau Island ⌒ PNG 183 E 3
Ningbo o• VRC 156-157 M 2
Ningcheng o VRC 148-149 O 7
Ningde o VRC 156-157 L 3
Ningdu o VRC 156-157 J 3
Ningeehak o USA 20-21 E 5
Ningera o PNG 183 A 2
Ningerum o PNG 183 A 3
Ningguo o VRC 154-155 L 6
Ninghai o VRC 156-157 M 2
Ninghe o VRC 154-155 K 2
Ninghua o VRC 156-157 K 3
Ningi o WAN 204-205 H 3
Ningjin o VRC 154-155 K 3
Ningjing Shan ▲ VRC 144-145 L 5
Ningming o VRC 156-157 E 5
Ningqiang o VRC 154-155 E 5
Ningshan o VRC 154-155 F 5
Ningwu o VRC 154-155 H 2
Ningxia Huizu Zizhiqu ◻ VRC 154-155 D 3
Ning Xian o VRC (GAN) 154-155 E 4
Ning Xian o VRC (SXI) 154-155 F 4
Ningxiang o VRC 156-157 H 2
Ninh Binh ☆ VN 156-157 D 6
Ninh Hòa o VN 158-159 K 4
Ninh So'n o VN 158-159 K 5
Ninia o RI 166-167 K 4
Ninilchik o USA 20-21 P 6
Niniva ⌒ TON 184 IV a 1
Ninive = Ninawā ∴•• IRQ 128-129 K 4
Ninnescah River ~ USA (KS) 262-263 J 7
Ninnis Glacier ⊂ ARK 16 G 15
Ninocminda o GE 126-127 E 7
Ninohe o J 152-153 J 4
Nioaque o BR 76-77 K 1
Niobrara o USA (NE) 262-263 H 2
Niobrara River ~ USA (NE) 262-263 E 2
Niodior o SN 202-203 B 3
Niofouin o CI 202-203 G 5
Nioghalvfjerdsfjorden ⊂ GRØ 26-27 o 4
Nioka o ZRE (HAU) 212-213 C 2
Nioka o ZRE (KOR) 214-215 B 4
Niokolo-Koba o SN 202-203 D 3
Niokolo-Koba, Parc National du ⊥••• SN 202-203 D 3
Niono o RMM 202-203 H 2
Nionsamoridu o RG 202-203 F 5
Niorenge, Rio ~ MOC 218-219 J 1
Nioro du Rip o SN 202-203 C 3
Nioro du Sahel o RMM 202-203 F 2
Niort ☆• F 90-91 G 8
Nioût o RIM 196-197 G 6
Nipa o PNG 183 B 4
Nipāni o IND 140-141 F 2
Nipanipa, Tanjung ▲ RI 164-165 H 5
Nipawin o CDN (SAS) 232-233 O 2
Nipawin Provincial Park ⊥ CDN 34-35 D 3
Nipe, Bahía de ≈ 54-55 H 4
Nipekamew River ~ CDN 34-35 D 3
Nipele ~ NAM 216-217 D 9
Nipgen o USA (OH) 280-281 C 4
Niphad o IND 138-139 E 9
Nipigon o CDN (ONT) 234-235 P 5
Nipigon, Lake o CDN (ONT) 234-235 P 5
Nipigon Bay o CDN (ONT) 234-235 P 6
Nipigon River ~ CDN (ONT) 234-235 P 5
Nipin River ~ CDN 32-33 Q 4
Nipiodi o MOC 218-219 J 3
Nipishish Lake o CDN 36-37 T 7
Nipisi River ~ CDN 32-33 N 4
Nipissing, Lake o CDN (ONT) 238-239 F 2
Nipissing River ~ CDN (ONT) 238-239 G 3
Nipisso o CDN (QUE) 242-243 C 2
Nipisso, Lac o CDN (QUE) 242-243 C 2
Nipomo o USA (CA) 248-249 D 4
Nippers Harbour o CDN (NFL) 242-243 N 3
Nipton o USA (CA) 248-249 J 4
Niquelândia o BR 72-73 F 3
Nir o IR (AZS) 128-129 M 3
Nir o IR (YAZ) 134-135 F 3
Nira o IND 138-139 E 10
Ñire-Có o RA 78-79 E 4
Ñireguao o RCH 80 E 2
Nirgua o YV 60-61 G 2
Nirmal o IND 138-139 G 10
Nirumoar, Pulau ⌒ RI 166-167 K 2
Niš o AFG 134-135 L 2
Niš o• YU 100-101 H 3
Nisa o P 98-99 D 5
Nisāb o KSA 130-131 J 3
Nisāb o Y 132-133 E 6
Nišan o US 136-137 J 5
Niseko Shakotan Otaru-kaigan Quasi National Park ⊥ J 152-153 J 3
Nishi o VRC 156-157 G 2
Nishibetsu-gawa ~ J 152-153 L 3
Nishi-Chugoku-sanchi Quasi National Park ⊥ J 152-153 E 7
Nishi-no-Omote o J 152-153 D 9
Nishino-shima ⌒ J 152-153 E 6
Nishi-Okoppe o J 152-153 K 2
Nishi-Sonogi-hantō ⌣ J 152-153 C 8
Nishi-suidō ≈ 152-153 C 7
Nishnabotna River ~ USA (IA) 274-275 C 4
Nisi-no-shima ⌒ J 152-153 D 11
Niskibi River ~ CDN 34-35 M 2
Nisko o PL 92-93 R 3
Nisland o USA (SD) 260-261 C 2
Nisling River ~ CDN 20-21 V 5
Nisqually River ~ USA (WA) 244-245 C 4
Nissan ~ S 86-87 F 8
Nisséko o BF 202-203 J 4
Nisser o N 86-87 D 7
Nissiros ⌒ GR 100-101 L 6
Nissum Bredning ≈ 86-87 D 8
Nistru ~ MD 102-103 F 4
Nistru ~ MD 102-103 G 4
Ništūn o Y 132-133 H 6
Nisutlin Plateau ▲ CDN 20-21 Z 6
Nisutlin River ~ CDN 20-21 Y 6
Nita Downs o AUS 172-173 E 5
Nitchequon o CDN 38-39 J 2
Niterói o BR 72-73 J 7
Nith ~ GB 90-91 F 4
Nitija, gora ▲ RUS 120-121 G 4
Nitinat o CDN (BC) 230-231 E 5
Nitinat River ~ CDN (BC) 230-231 E 5
Niti Pass ▲ VRC 144-145 B 5
Nitmiluk (Katherine Gorge) National Park ⊥•• AUS 172-173 L 3
Nitra o•• SK 92-93 P 4
Nitro o USA (WV) 280-281 E 5
Nituj ~ RUS 122-123 K 4
Niu' Aunofo Point ▲ TON 184 IV a 2
Niuchang o VRC 156-157 D 4
Niut, Gunung ▲ RI 162-163 H 4
Niutaca, Corrego ~ BR 70-71 J 7
Niutoushan o VRC 154-155 L 6
Niuwudu, Tanjung ▲ RI 168 E 8
Nivala o FIN 88-89 H 5
Niváno o PK 134-135 K 5
Nive River ~ AUS 178-179 J 3
Niverville o CDN (MAN) 234-235 F 5
Niviarsiat ▲ GRØ 28-29 T 6
Nivšera ~ RUS 88-89 W 5
Niwai o IND 138-139 E 6
Niwelin Lake o CDN 30-31 G 2
Nixon o USA (NV) 246-247 F 4
Nixon o USA (TX) 266-267 K 4
Niyrakpak Lagoon ≈ 20-21 E 5
Nizāmābād o IND 138-139 G 10
Nizām Sāgar o IND 138-139 F 10
Nizgan, Rūd-e ~ AFG 134-135 L 2
Nižnekamsk = Nižnekamsk ☆ RUS 96-97 G 6
Nizhnekamskoye Vodohranilishche = Nižnekamskoe vodohr. < RUS 96-97 H 6
Nizhnevartovsk = Nižnevartovsk ☆ RUS 114-115 O 4
Nizhniy Novgorod = Nižnij Novgorod ☆•• RUS 94-95 S 3
Nizhniy Tagil = Nižnij Tagil ☆ RUS 96-97 L 5
Nizhnyaya Tunguska = Nižnjaja Tunguska ~ RUS 116-117 D 3
Nizi o ZRE 212-213 C 3
Nizina Sępolska ⌣ PL 92-93 Q 1
Nizip ☆ TR 128-129 G 4
Nizke Tatry ▲ SK 92-93 P 4
Nizkī Island ⌒ USA 22-23 D 6
Nizkij, mys ▲ RUS (CUK) 112-113 U 4
Nizkij, mys ▲ RUS (KOR) 112-113 R 6
Niz'ma ~ RUS 88-89 T 4
Nižneangarsk o RUS 118-119 D 8
Nižnejansk o RUS 110-111 V 4
Nižnekamsk ☆ RUS 96-97 G 6
Nižnekamskoe vodohranilišče < RUS 96-97 H 6
Nižnekolymsk o RUS 112-113 L 2
Nižnetambovskoe o RUS 122-123 H 3
Nižneudinsk ☆ RUS 116-117 J 8
Nižnevartovsk ☆ RUS 114-115 O 4
Nižnie Sergi ☆ RUS 96-97 L 5
Nižnij Bestjah o RUS 118-119 O 5
Nižnij Casučej ☆ RUS 118-119 G 10
Nižnij Dvojnik ~ RUS 88-89 W 4
Nižnij Imbak ~ RUS 114-115 T 3
Nižnij Ingaš ☆ RUS 116-117 H 7
Nižnij Lomov o RUS 94-95 S 5
Nižnij Novgorod ☆•• RUS 94-95 S 3
Nižnij Odes o RUS 88-89 X 5
Nižnij Suzun ~ RUS 124-125 N 1
Nižnij Tagil ☆ RUS 96-97 L 5
Nižnij Viljujkan ~ RUS 116-117 N 3
Nižnjaja ~ RUS 108-109 f 5
Nižnjaja Agapa ~ RUS 108-109 W 6
Nižnjaja Baiha ~ RUS 114-115 T 2
Nižnjaja Buotankaga ~ RUS 108-109 W 5
Nižnjaja Cipa ~ RUS 118-119 F 8
Nižnjaja Čunku ~ RUS 116-117 H 4
Nižnjaja Kočoma ~ RUS 116-117 N 4
Nižnjaja Larba ~ RUS 118-119 L 8
Nižnjaja Peša o RUS 88-89 T 3
Nižnjaja Pojma o RUS 116-117 H 7
Nižnjaja Suetka o RUS 124-125 L 2
Nižnjaja Tajmyra ~ RUS 108-109 c 4
Nižnjaja Talovaja ~ RUS 108-109 X 6
Nižnjaja Tavda ☆ RUS 114-115 J 6
Nižnjaja Tunguska ~ RUS 114-115 U 2
Nižnjaja Tunguska ~ RUS 116-117 M 4
Nižnjaja Tunguska ~ RUS 116-117 H 4
Nižnjaja Tunguska ~ RUS 116-117 N 7
Nižnjaja Tura o RUS 96-97 L 4
Nižn Pronge o RUS 122-123 J 2
Nižyn o UA 102-103 G 2
Nizzana o IL 130-131 D 2
Njadajaha ~ RUS 108-109 T 7
Njagamja, ozero o RUS 108-109 X 5
Njagan' o RUS 114-115 H 3
Njaiama-Sewafe o WAL 202-203 E 5
Njajs ~ RUS 114-115 F 3
Njakšingda, ozero o RUS 116-117 F 2
Njalinskoe o RUS 114-115 K 4
Njamakit, gora ▲ RUS 108-109 f 6
Njandoma o RUS 88-89 Q 6
Njangus'jaha ~ RUS 108-109 T 7
Njanneli ~ RUS 110-111 V 5
Njarðvík o IS 86-87 b 3
Njarga ~ RUS 114-115 S 5
Njasviž ☆ BY 94-95 K 5
Njatlongajagun ~ RUS 114-115 M 3
Njau o WAG 202-203 C 3
Njazepetrovsk ☆ RUS 96-97 L 5
Njenje ~ EAT 214-215 J 5
Njiapanda o EAT (MBE) 214-215 G 5
Njinjo o EAT 214-215 K 5
Njoko ~ Z 218-219 C 3
Njombe o EAT (IRI) 214-215 H 5
Njombe ~ EAT 214-215 H 4
Njoro o EAK 212-213 E 4
Njuhča o RUS (ARH) 88-89 T 5
Njuhča ~ RUS 88-89 O 5
Njuja o RUS (SAH) 118-119 H 5
Njuja ~ RUS 118-119 G 5
Njuja ~ RUS 118-119 F 5
Njuja ~ RUS 118-119 D 5
Njuja ~ RUS 118-119 E 5
Njuk, ozero o RUS 88-89 L 4
Njukčorok ~ RUS 116-117 L 3
Njukža ~ RUS 118-119 L 8
Njukža, Ust'- o RUS 118-119 K 7
Njun'karakutari ~ RUS 108-109 f 4
Njun Pelgrimkondre o SME 62-63 G 3
Njurba ☆• RUS 118-119 J 4
Njuroľka ~ RUS 114-115 O 5
Nkalagu o WAN 204-205 G 5
Nkam ~ CAM 204-205 J 6
Nkamba Lodge o Z 214-215 F 5
Nkambe o CAM 204-205 J 5
Nkaw o ZRE 210-211 G 5
Nkawie o GH 202-203 K 6
Nkayi o RCB 210-211 D 6
Nkayi o ZW 218-219 E 4
Nkeni ~ RCB 210-211 E 4
Nkhata Bay o• MW 214-215 H 6
Nkhilé < RIM 196-197 G 6
Nkhotakota o MW 214-215 H 7
Nkhotakota Game Reserve ⊥ MW 214-215 G 7
Nkoambang o CAM 204-205 K 6
Nkolabona o G 210-211 C 3
Nkole o Z 214-215 F 6
Nkolmengboua o G 210-211 C 2
Nkomfap o WAN 204-205 H 5
Nkomi ~ G 210-211 B 4
Nkomi, Lagune = Fernan Vaz o G 210-211 B 4
Nkondwe o EAT 212-213 C 6
Nkongjok o CAM 204-205 J 6
Nkongsamba o CAM 204-205 H 6
Nkon Ngok o CAM 204-205 J 6
Nkoranza o GH 202-203 K 6
Nkoteng o CAM 204-205 K 6
Nkoué o RCB 210-211 E 5
Nkourala o RMM 202-203 G 4
Nkula Falls ~ MW 218-219 H 2
Nkulu, Malemba- o ZRE 214-215 D 5
Nkundi o EAT 214-215 F 4
Nkurenkuru o NAM 216-217 E 8
Nkuruman Escarpment ▲ EAK 212-213 F 5
Nkwalini o ZA 220-221 K 4
Nkwanta o GH (VTA) 202-203 L 5
Nkwanta o GH (WTN) 202-203 J 7
Nkwanta, Atasi o GH 202-203 K 7
Nkwanta, Manso- o GH 202-203 K 6
Nmai Hka ~ MYA 142-143 L 2
n-Natrūn, Wādī ~• ET 194-195 E 2
Nnewi o WAN 204-205 G 5
No.1, Canal < RA 78-79 L 4
No.2, Canal < RA 78-79 L 4
No.5, Canal < RA 78-79 L 4
No.9, Canal < RA 78-79 K 4
No.11, Canal < RA 78-79 K 4

No.12, Canal < RA 78-79 K 4
No.16, Canal < RA 78-79 K 3
Noabanki ○ BD 142-143 F 4
Noakhali ○ BD 142-143 G 4
Noanama ○ CO 60-61 C 5
Noatak ○ USA 20-21 J 3
Noatak National Preserve ⊥ USA 20-21 K 2
Noatak River ~ USA 20-21 M 3
Nobel ○ CDN (ONT) 238-239 E 3
Nobeoka ○ J 152-153 D 8
Nobéré ○ BF 202-203 K 4
Nobleboro ○ USA (NY) 278-279 G 5
Nobleford ○ CDN (ALB) 232-233 E 6
Nobles Nob Mine • AUS 174-175 C 6
Noble's Trail Monument ∴ USA (SD) 260-261 H 2
Noblesville ○ USA (IN) 274-275 M 4
Nobokwe ○ ZA 220-221 H 5
Noboribetsu ○ J 152-153 J 3
Nobres ○ BR 70-71 J 4
Nocina ○ E 98-99 F 3
Nockatunga ○ AUS 178-179 G 4
Nocona ○ USA (TX) 264-265 G 5
Nocuchich ∴• MEX 52-53 K 2
Noda ○ J 152-153 J 4
Nodaway River ~ USA (MO) 274-275 C 4
Noe ○ CI 202-203 J 7
Noefs, Île des ⌒ SY 224 C 3
Noel ○ CDN (NS) 240-241 M 5
Noel ○ USA (MO) 276-277 A 4
Noell Lake ⊖ CDN 20-21 Y 2
Noelville ○ CDN (ONT) 238-239 E 2
Noenieput ○ ZA 220-221 E 3
Noépé ○ RT 202-203 L 6
Noetinger ○ RA 78-79 H 2
Nogajskaja step ∴ RUS 126-127 F 5
Nogal ○ USA (NM) 256-257 K 5
Nogales ○ MEX (CHA) 50-51 E 2
Nogales ○ MEX (VER) 52-53 F 2
Nogales ○• MEX (SON) 50-51 D 2
Nogales ○ RCH 78-79 D 2
Nogales ○ USA (AZ) 256-257 E 7
Nogamut ○ USA 20-21 M 6
Nogara ○ ETH 200-201 H 6
Nōgata ○ J 152-153 D 8
Nogent-le-Rotrou ○ F 90-91 H 7
Nogent-sur-Seine ○ F 90-91 J 7
Noginsk ☆ RUS 94-95 Q 4
Nogiri Point ▲ SOL 184 I c 2
Nogliki ☆ RUS 122-123 K 3
Nogoyá ○ RA 78-79 K 2
Nogoyá, Arroyo ~ RA 78-79 K 2
Noguira, Riacho ~ RA 76-77 G 4
Nohar ○ IND 138-139 E 5
Noheji ○ J 152-153 J 4
Nohili Point ▲ USA (HI) 288 F 2
Noḥonč, Kūh-e ▲ IR 134-135 J 5
Noia ○ E 98-99 C 3
Noice Peninsula ⌣ CDN 24-25 T 1
Noire, Rivière ~ CDN (QUE) 238-239 H 2
Noires, Montagnes ▲ RH 54-55 J 5
Noirmoutier, Île de ⌒ F 90-91 F 8
Noirmoutier-en-l'Île ○ F 90-91 F 8
Nojabr'sk ○ RUS 114-115 N 3
Nojack ○ CDN (ALB) 232-233 C 2
Nojima-saki ▲ J 152-153 H 7
Nokaneng ○ RB 218-219 B 4
Nokha ○ IND 138-139 D 6
Nokia ○ FIN 88-89 G 6
Nokomis ○ CDN (SAS) 232-233 O 4
Nokomis ○ USA (IL) 274-275 J 5
Nokou ○ TCH 198-199 G 5
Nokoué, Lac ⊖ DY 204-205 E 5
Nokuku ○ VAN 184 II a 2
Nola ○ I 100-101 E 4
Nola ☆• RCA 210-211 F 2
Nolalu ○ CDN (ONT) 234-235 O 6
Nolan ○ USA (TX) 264-265 D 6
Nol'de guba ⊂ RUS 112-113 R 1
Noling ~ RI 164-165 G 5
Nolinsk ☆ RUS 96-97 G 5
Noll ○ ZA 220-221 F 6
Nom ○ VRC 146-147 M 4
Nomad ○ PNG 183 B 4
Nomad River ~ PNG 183 B 4
Noma misaki ▲ J 152-153 D 9
Nomane ○ PNG 183 C 4
Nomansland Point ▲ CDN 34-35 Q 4
Nombre de Dios ○ MEX 50-51 G 6
Nombre de Dios, Cordillera ▲ HN 52-53 L 4
Nome ○ USA 20-21 H 4
Nome, Cape ▲ USA 20-21 H 4
Nome-Council-Highway II USA 20-21 H 4
Nome-Taylor-Highway II USA 20-21 H 4
Nomhon ○ VRC 144-145 L 2
Nomtsas ○ NAM 220-221 C 2
Nomuka ⌒ TON 184 IV a 2
Nomuka Group ⌒ TON 184 IV a 2
Nona, La ○ MEX 50-51 F 6
Nonacho Lake ⊖ CDN 30-31 P 5
Nonagama ○ CL 140-141 J 7
Non Champa ○ THA 158-159 G 2
Nondalton ○ USA 20-21 N 6
Nondo ○ Z 214-215 F 5
Nong'an ○ VRC 150-151 E 5
Nong Bua ○ THA 158-159 F 3
Nong Bua Daeng ○ THA 158-159 F 2
Nong Bua Khok ○ THA 158-159 F 3
Nong Bua Lamphu ○ THA 158-159 G 2
Nongchang ○ VRC 154-155 F 3
Nong Khae ○ THA 158-159 F 3
Nong Khai ○ THA 158-159 G 2
Nongoma ☆ ZA 220-221 K 3
Nong Phai ○ THA 158-159 F 2
Nong Phok ○ THA 158-159 H 2
Nong Phu ○ THA 158-159 H 3
Nongra Lake ⊖ AUS 172-173 J 5
Nong Rua ○ THA 158-159 G 2
Nongsa ○ RI 162-163 F 4
Nonoava ○ MEX 50-51 F 4
Nonogasta ○ RA 76-77 D 5
Non Thai ○ THA 158-159 G 3
Nooleeye ○ SP 208-209 H 6
Noolyeana Lake ⊖ AUS 178-179 D 4
Noonan ○ USA (ND) 258-259 D 3
Noonday ○ USA (TX) 264-265 J 6
Noondoonia ○ AUS 176-177 G 6
Noonkanbah ○ AUS 172-173 G 5
Noonthorangee Range ▲ AUS 178-179 G 6
Noonyereena Hill ▲ AUS 176-177 E 2
Noordoewer ○ NAM 220-221 C 4
Noordzeekanaal < NL 92-93 H 2
Noorvik ○ USA 20-21 K 3
Noosa Heads ○ AUS 178-179 M 4
Nootka ○ CDN (BC) 230-231 C 4
Nootka Island ⌒ CDN (BC) 230-231 C 4
Nootka Sound ≈ 32-33 G 7
Nootka Sound ≈ CDN 230-231 C 4
Nopoló ○ MEX 50-51 D 5
Nopoming Provincial Park ⊥ CDN (MAN) 234-235 H 4
Nóqui ○ ANG 216-217 B 2
Nora ○ CDN (SAS) 232-233 P 3
Nora ~ RUS 122-123 D 2
Norah ⌒ ER 200-201 K 4
Norala ○ RP 160-161 F 9
Noranside ○ AUS 178-179 E 2
Nora Springs ○ USA (IA) 274-275 F 1
Norassoba ○ RG 202-203 F 4
Norberg ○ N 86-87 D 6
Norberto de la Riesta ○ RA 78-79 K 3
Norcatur ○ USA (KS) 262-263 F 5
Norcross ○ USA (GA) 284-285 F 3
Nord, Île du ⌒ SY 224 B 5
Nord = North ◻ CAM 204-205 K 4
Nord, ostrov ⌒ RUS 108-109 b 3
Nordaustlandet ⌒ N 84-85 L 3
Nordaust-Svalbard naturreservat ⊥ N 84-85 M 3
Nordbruk, ostrov ⌒ RUS 84-85 b 3
Nordby ○ DK 86-87 E 9
Nordegg ○ CDN (ALB) 232-233 B 3
Nordegg River ~ CDN (ALB) 232-233 C 3
Norden ○ D 92-93 J 2
Nordenšel'da, arhipelag ⌒ RUS 108-109 Z 3
Nordenšel'da, zaliv ≈ RUS 108-109 G 4
Nordenskiöld Islands ⌒ CDN 24-25 W 6
Nordenskiöld Land ∴ N 84-85 J 4
Nordenskiöld River ~ CDN 20-21 W 6
Nordenskiöld Gletscher ⊂ GRØ 28-29 P 2
Nordenskjöld Fjord ≈ 26-27 b 2
Norderney ⌒ D 92-93 J 2
Norderstedt ○ D 92-93 K 2
Nordeste ○ ANG 216-217 F 3
Nordfjordeid ☆ N 86-87 B 6
Nordfjorden ≈ 84-85 J 3
Nordfjorden ≈ 86-87 B 6
Nordfold ○ N 86-87 G 3
Nordfriesische Inseln ∴ D 92-93 K 1
Nordgrønland = Avannaarsua ◻ GRØ 26-27 V 4
Nordhausen ○• D 92-93 L 3
Nordhorn ○ D 92-93 J 2
Nordkapp ▲ N 26-27 w 8
Nordkapp ▲ N (SVA) 84-85 L 2
Nordkapp ▲•• N (FIN) 86-87 M 1
Nordkinnhalvøya ⌣ N 86-87 N 1
Nordkvaløy ⌒ N 86-87 J 1
Nordli ○ N 86-87 F 4
Nördlingen ○•• D 92-93 L 4
Nordmaling ○ S 86-87 J 5
Nordman ○ USA (ID) 250-251 C 3
Nordostrundingen ▲ GRØ 26-27 t 3
Nord-Ostsee-Kanal < D 92-93 K 1
Nord-Ouest = North-West ◻ CAM 204-205 J 5
Nord-Pas-de-Calais ◻ F 90-91 J 6
Nordreisa ○ N 86-87 K 2
Nordre Isortoq ≈ 28-29 O 3
Nordre Strømfjord ≈ 28-29 O 3
Nordrhein-Westfalen ◻ D 92-93 J 3
Nordvestfjord ≈ 26-27 m 8
Nordvestinskij, aral ⌒ KA 96-97 G 10
Nordvest-spitsbergen nasjonalpark ⊥ N 84-85 G 3
Nordvik ○ RUS 110-111 H 3
Nordvik, buhta ≈ RUS 110-111 H 3
Norembega ○ CDN (ONT) 236-237 H 4
Norfolk ○ USA (NE) 262-263 J 2
Norfolk ○ USA (VA) 280-281 K 7
Norfolk, Mount ▲ AUS 180-181 H 6
Norfolk Island ⌒ AUS 13 H 5
Norfolk Lake ⊖ USA (AR) 276-277 C 4
Norfolk Ridge ≃ 182 B 1
Norgate ○ CDN (MAN) 234-235 D 4
Nor Harberd ○ AR 128-129 L 2
Norias ○ MEX 50-51 H 5
Norias ○ USA (TX) 266-267 K 7
Norilka ~ RUS 108-109 X 7
Noril'sk ○ RUS 108-109 X 7
Noring, Gunung ▲ MAL 162-163 D 2
Noring, Gunung ▲ MAL 162-163 D 2
Norland ○ CDN (ONT) 238-239 G 4
Norlina ○ USA (NC) 282-283 J 4
Normal ○ USA (IL) 274-275 J 4
Norman ○ USA (AR) 276-277 B 6
Norman ○ USA (OK) 264-265 G 3
Norman, Lake < USA (NC) 282-283 G 5
Normanby Island ⌒ PNG 183 F 5
Normanby River ~ AUS 174-175 H 4
Normandia ○ BR 62-63 E 4
Normandie ∴ F 90-91 G 7
Normandin ○ CDN (QUE) 240-241 C 2
Normandy ○ USA (TX) 266-267 G 5
Norman Park ○ USA (GA) 284-285 G 5
Norman Range ▲ CDN 30-31 F 3
Norman River ~ AUS 174-175 F 6
Norman's Cay ⌒ BS 54-55 G 2
Normanton ○ AUS 174-175 F 5
Normantown ○ USA (WV) 280-281 F 5
Normanville ○ AUS 180-181 E 3
Norman Wells ○ CDN 30-31 G 3
Normetal ○ CDN (QUE) 236-237 J 4
Normétal ○ CDN (QUE) 236-237 J 4
Norna, Mount ▲ AUS 174-175 F 7
Norquay ○ CDN (SAS) 232-233 Q 4
Norquinco ○ RA 78-79 D 6
Norråker ○ S 86-87 G 4
Norra Ny ○ S 86-87 F 6
Norra Storfjället ▲ S 86-87 G 4
Norrbotten ∴ S 86-87 K 4
Norris ○ USA (MT) 250-251 H 6
Norris ○ USA (SD) 260-261 E 3
Norris ○ USA (WY) 252-253 H 2
Norris Arm ○ CDN (NFL) 242-243 N 3
Norris Lake ⊖ USA (TN) 282-283 D 4
Norris Point ○ CDN (NFL) 242-243 L 3
Norristown ○ USA (PA) 280-281 L 3
Norrköping ☆• S 86-87 H 7
Norrtälje ○ S 86-87 J 7
Norseman ○ AUS 176-177 F 6
Norsjö ○ S 86-87 J 4
Norsk ○ RUS 122-123 C 2
Norskebanken ≃ 84-85 H 2
Norskehavet ≈ 86-87 E 3
Norske Øer ⌒ GRØ 26-27 r 4
Norsup ○ VAN 184 II a 3
Norte, Cabo ▲ EC 64-65 C 10
Norte, Cabo do ▲ BR 62-63 K 5
Norte, Canal do ~ BR 62-63 J 5
Norte, Cayo ⌒ MEX 52-53 L 2
Norte, Cerro ▲ RA 80 D 4
Norte, Ponta ▲ CV 202-203 C 5
Norte, Punta ▲ MEX 50-51 E 5
Norte, Serra do ▲ BR 70-71 H 2
Norte de Chiapas, Montañe del ▲ MEX 52-53 H 3
Norte del Cabo San Antonio, Punta ▲ RA 78-79 L 4
Nortelândia ○ BR 70-71 J 4
North ○ USA (SC) 284-285 J 3
North, Cape ▲ CDN (NS) 240-241 P 3
North = Nord ◻ CAM 204-205 K 4
North Adams ○ USA (MA) 278-279 H 6
North Albany ○ USA (OR) 244-245 B 6
Northam ○ AUS 176-177 D 5
Northam ○ ZA 220-221 H 2
Northampton ○ AUS 176-177 C 4
Northampton ☆ GB 90-91 G 5
Northampton ○ USA (MA) 278-279 J 6
North Andaman ⌒ IND 140-141 L 3
North Arm ≈ 24-25 j 5
North Arm ○ CDN 30-31 M 4
North Arm ○ GB 78-79 L 7
North Aspy River ~ CDN (NS) 240-241 P 4
North Atlantic Ocean ≈ 6-7 D 6
North Augusta ○ CDN (ONT) 238-239 K 4
North Augusta ○ USA (SC) 284-285 J 3
North Aulatsivik Island ⌒ CDN 36-37 S 5
North Australia Basin ≃ 13 C 4
North Balabac Strait ≈ 160-161 B 8
North Baldy ▲ USA (WA) 244-245 H 2
North Banda Basin ≃ 166-167 B 3
North Bannister ○ AUS 176-177 D 6
North Battleford ○ CDN (SAS) 232-233 K 3
North Bay ≈ 36-37 P 3
North Bay ≈ 140-141 L 5
North Bay ○ CDN (ONT) 238-239 F 2
North Bay ○ CDN (NWT) 36-37 O 2
North Bay ○ CDN (ONT) 234-235 P 4
North Belcher Islands ⌒ CDN 36-37 K 6
North Belmont ○ USA (NC) 282-283 F 5
North Bend ○ USA (NE) 262-263 K 3
North Bend ○ USA (OR) 244-245 A 7
North Bend ○ USA (WA) 244-245 D 3
North Berwick ○ USA (ME) 278-279 L 5
North Bimini ⌒ BS 54-55 F 2
North Bluff ▲ CDN 36-37 O 3
North Bonaparte ○ CDN (BC) 230-231 J 2
North Bonneville ○ USA (WA) 244-245 D 5
North Bosque River ~ USA (TX) 266-265 G 6
North Branch ○ CDN (NFL) 242-243 K 4
North Branch < PK 138-139 D 3
North Branch ○ USA (MN) 270-271 F 5
North Bridge ○ CDN (ONT) 234-235 J 6
North Caicos ⌒ GB 54-55 K 4
North Canadian River ~ USA (OK) 264-265 F 3
North Cape ○ CDN (PEI) 240-241 M 3
North Cape ▲ CDN (PEI) 240-241 M 3
North Cape ▲ NZ 182 D 1
North Cape ▲ PNG 183 F 2
North Cape May ○ USA (NJ) 280-281 M 4
North-Cape Province ◻ ZA 220-221 D 4
North Caribou Lake ⊖ CDN (ONT) 234-235 N 2
North Carolina ◻ USA (NC) 282-283 E 5
North Cascades National Park ⊥• USA (WA) 244-245 D 2
North Channel ≈ 90-91 E 4
North Channel ⊖ CDN (ONT) 238-239 B 2
North Charleston ○ USA (SC) 284-285 K 4
North China Plain = Huabei ⌣ VRC 154-155 J 3
North Clymer ○ USA (NY) 278-279 B 6
North Cowden ○ USA (TX) 264-265 B 6
North Cowichan ○ CDN (BC) 230-231 F 5
North Creek ~ AUS 178-179 C 5
North Dakota ◻ USA (ND) 258-259 E 4
North East ○ RB 218-219 D 6
North East ○ USA (PA) 280-281 G 1
Northeast Cape ▲ USA 20-21 F 5
Northeast Cape Fear River ~ USA (NC) 282-283 K 6
North East Carry ○ USA (ME) 278-279 M 3
Northeast Coast National Scenic Area • RC 156-157 M 4
North Eastern ◻ EAK 212-213 G 3
Northeast Point ▲ BS 54-55 J 3
Northeast Point ▲ BS 54-55 J 4
Northeast Point ▲ BS 54-55 H 2
Northeast Point ▲ CDN (NFL) 38-39 R 2
Northeast Point ▲ CDN (NWT) 24-25 Z 2
Northeast Point ▲ USA 22-23 L 4
Northeast Providence Channel ≈ 54-55 G 2
Northeim ○• D 92-93 K 3
Northern ◻ EAU 212-213 C 2
Northern ◻ MW 214-215 H 6
Northern ◻ Z 214-215 F 6
Northern Arm ○ CDN (NFL) 242-243 N 3
Northern Cay ⌒ BZ 52-53 L 3
Northern Cheyenne Indian Reservation ✕ USA (MT) 250-251 N 6
Northern Frontier ◻ KSA 130-131 H 3
Northern Indian Lake ⊖ CDN 34-35 H 2
Northern Lau Group ⌒ FJI 184 III c 2
Northern Light Lake ⊖ CDN (ONT) 234-235 N 6
Northern Mariana Islands = Mariana Islands ⌒ USA 14-15 G 6
Northern Perimeter Highway = Rodovia Perimetral Norte II BR 62-63 F 5
Northern Region ◻ GH 202-203 K 5
Northern Region ◻ SUD 200-201 B 5
Northern Salwati Pulau Reserve ⊥• RI 166-167 F 2
Northern Territory ◻ AUS 174-175 B 6
Northern Yukon National Park ⊥ CDN 20-21 U 2
North Etomi River ~ CDN (MAN) 234-235 G 2
North Fabius River ~ USA (MO) 274-275 F 4
Northfield ○ USA (MN) 270-271 E 6
Northfield ○ USA (TX) 264-265 D 4
North Fiji Basin ≃ 13 J 4
North Fond du Lac ○ USA (WI) 270-271 K 7
North Fork ○ USA (ID) 250-251 F 6
North Fork ○ USA (NV) 246-247 K 2
North Fork ~ USA (ID) 250-251 C 4
North Fork ~ USA (KY) 276-277 M 3
North Fork ~ USA (MO) 274-275 F 4
North Fork ~ USA (MO) 274-275 G 5
North Fork ~ USA (NE) 262-263 K 4
North Fork ~ USA (TN) 276-277 G 4
North Fork ~ USA (TX) 266-267 K 3
North Fork Chandalar ~ USA 20-21 Q 3
North Fork Cimarron River ~ USA (CO) 254-255 N 6
North Fork Clearwater River ~ USA (ID) 250-251 D 5
North Fork Counkee Creek ~ USA (AL) 284-285 E 4
North Fork Holston River ~ USA (VA) 280-281 D 7
North Fork John Day River ~ USA (OR) 244-245 F 5
North Fork Kuskokwim ~ USA 20-21 N 5
North Fork Pavette River ~ USA (ID) 252-253 B 2
North Fork Red River ~ USA (OK) 264-265 E 4
North Fork River ~ USA (WV) 280-281 E 4
North Fork Shenandoah River ~ USA (VA) 280-281 H 5
North Fork Smoky Hill River ~ USA (CO) 254-255 N 4
North Fork Solomon River ~ USA (KS) 262-263 F 5
North French River ~ CDN (ONT) 236-237 G 2
North Frisian Islands = Nordfriesische Inseln ∴ D 92-93 J 1
Northgate ○ CDN (SAS) 232-233 Q 6
Northgate ○ USA (ND) 258-259 E 3
North Head ▲ AUS 176-177 C 5
North Head ○ CDN (NB) 240-241 J 6
North Head ▲ CDN (NFL) 38-39 Q 2
North Head ▲ NZ 182 E 2
North Heart River ~ CDN 32-33 M 3
North Hendon, Cape ▲ CDN 24-25 a 5
North Henik Lake ⊖ CDN 30-31 V 5
Northhome ○ USA (MN) 270-271 D 3
North Horr ○ EAK 212-213 F 2
North Island ⌒ AUS (NT) 174-175 D 4
North Island ⌒ AUS (WA) 176-177 B 4
North Island ⌒ EAK 212-213 F 1
North Island ⌒ NZ 182 D 2
North Island ⌒ USA (SC) 284-285 L 3
North Jadito Wash ~ USA (AZ) 256-257 E 3
North Judson ○ USA (IN) 274-275 M 3
North Kamloops ○ CDN (BC) 230-231 J 3
North Kitui National Reserve ⊥ EAK 212-213 G 4
North Knife Lake ⊖ CDN 30-31 V 6
North Knife River ~ CDN 30-31 V 6
North Komelik ○ USA (AZ) 256-257 C 6
North Korea = Choson M.I.K. ■ DVR 150-151 G 7
North Lake ○ CDN (NB) 240-241 H 5
North Lakhimpur ○ IND 142-143 J 2
Northland ○ USA (MI) 270-271 L 4
North Land = Severnaja Zemlja ⌒ RUS 108-109 c 1
North Las Vegas ○ USA (NV) 248-249 J 3
North Liberty ○ USA (IA) 274-275 G 3
North Limington ○ USA (ME) 278-279 L 5
North Lincoln Land ∴ CDN 24-25 f 2
North Little Rock ○ USA (AR) 276-277 C 6
North Lochaber ○ CDN (NS) 240-241 N 5
North Loup River ~ USA (NE) 262-263 F 2
North Luangwa National Park ⊥ Z 214-215 G 6
North Luconia Shoals ≃ 162-163 K 2
North Lucy ○ USA (NM) 256-257 K 4
North Magnetic Pole = Magnetic Pole Area ARK 24-25 V 3
North Magnetic Pole Area II CDN 24-25 V 3
North Male Atoll ⌒ MV 140-141 B 5
North Malosmadulu Atoll ⌒ MV 140-141 B 5
North Manchester ○ USA (IN) 274-275 N 3
North Mankato ○ USA (MN) 270-271 D 6
North Milk River ~ CDN (ALB) 232-233 F 6
North Minch ≈ 90-91 E 2
North Moose Lake ⊖ CDN 34-35 F 3
North Muskegon ○ USA (MI) 272-273 C 4
North Myrtle Beach ○ USA (SC) 284-285 M 3
North Nahanni River ~ CDN 30-31 G 4
North Nilandu Atoll ⌒ MV 140-141 B 6
North Ossetia = Cægat Irystony Respublikæ ◻ RUS 126-127 F 6
North Palisade ▲ USA (CA) 248-249 F 2
North Palm Beach ○ USA (FL) 286-287 J 5
North Pangnirtung Fiord ≈ 28-29 H 3
North Pease River ~ USA (TX) 264-265 D 4
North Peninsula ⌣ CDN (ONT) 234-235 P 4
North Peron Island ⌒ AUS 172-173 K 2
North Platte ○ USA (NE) 262-263 F 3
North Platte River ~ USA (WY) 252-253 M 4
North Point ▲ USA (MI) 272-273 F 2
North Point ▲ WAN 204-205 F 6
North Pole ∴ 16 A 28
Northport ○ USA (AL) 284-285 C 3
North Port ○ USA (FL) 286-287 G 4
Northport ○ USA (MI) 272-273 D 2
Northport ○ USA (WA) 244-245 H 2
North Portal ○ CDN (SAS) 232-233 Q 6
North Powder ○ USA (OR) 244-245 H 5
North Racoon River ~ USA (IA) 274-275 D 2
North Redstone River ~ CDN 30-31 F 4
North Reef = Bei Jiao ⌒ VRC 158-159 L 2
North Richmond ○ USA (OH) 280-281 F 2
North Rim ○ USA (AZ) 256-257 C 2
North River ○ CDN 30-31 X 6
North River ~ USA (AL) 284-285 C 3
North River ~ USA (MO) 274-275 F 5
North River ~ USA (VA) 280-281 G 6
North Saanich ○ CDN (BC) 230-231 F 5
North Sandwich ○ USA (NH) 278-279 K 5
North Santiam River ~ USA (OR) 244-245 C 6
North Saskatchewan River ~ CDN (ALB) 232-233 F 2
North Scotia Ridge ≃ 6-7 E 14
North Sea ≈ 90-91 D 3
North Seal River ~ CDN 30-31 T 6
North Sentinel Island ⌒ IND 140-141 L 4
North Siberian Lowland = Severo-Sibirskaja nizmennost' ⌣ RUS 108-109 W 5
Northside ○ CDN (SAS) 232-233 N 2
North Slope ∴ USA 20-21 K 2
North Solitary Island ⌒ AUS 178-179 M 5
North Spicer Island ⌒ CDN 24-25 h 6
North Spirit Lake ○ CDN (ONT) 234-235 K 2
North Star ○ AUS 178-179 L 5
North Star ○ CDN 32-33 M 3
North Stradbroke Island ⌒ AUS 178-179 M 4
North Stratford ○ USA (NH) 278-279 K 4
North Sulphur River ~ USA (TX) 264-265 J 5
North Sydney ○ CDN (NS) 240-241 P 4
North Thames River ~ CDN (ONT) 238-239 D 5
North Thompson River ~ CDN (BC) 228-229 P 4
North Thompson River ~ CDN (BC) 230-231 J 3
North Tonawanda ○ USA (NY) 278-279 C 5
North Truchas Peak ▲ USA (NM) 256-257 K 3
North Tweedsmuir Island ⌒ CDN 28-29 C 2
North Twin Island ⌒ CDN 34-35 Q 4
North Twin Lake ⊖ CDN (NFL) 242-243 M 3
North Uist ⌒ GB 90-91 D 3
Northumberland Isles ⌒ AUS 178-179 K 1
Northumberland National Park ⊥ GB 90-91 F 4
Northumberland Ø ⌒ GRØ 26-27 O 5
Northumberland Strait ≈ 38-39 M 5
Northumberland Strait ≈ CDN 240-241 L 4
North Umpqua River ~ USA (OR) 244-245 C 7
North Vancouver ○ CDN (BC) 230-231 F 4
North Vernon ○ USA (IN) 274-275 N 6
Northville ○ USA (NY) 278-279 G 5
Northville ○ USA (SD) 260-261 H 1
North Wabasca Lake ⊖ CDN 32-33 O 3
North Washagami Lake ⊖ CDN 34-35 O 3
North Waterford ○ USA (ME) 278-279 L 4
North-West = Nord-Ouest ◻ CAM 204-205 J 5
Northwest Angle Forest Reserve ⊥ CDN (MAN) 234-235 H 5
North West Basin ∴ AUS 176-177 C 2
Northwest Bay ○ CDN (ONT) 234-235 K 6
North West Brooke ○ CDN (NFL) 242-243 P 4
North West Cape ▲ AUS 172-173 B 6
Northwest Cape ▲ USA 20-21 E 5
Northwest Cay ⌒ BS 54-55 J 4
North West Coastal Highway II AUS 176-177 C 3
North Western ◻ Z 218-219 C 1
Northwest Feeder ~ CDN 38-39 Q 2
North West Frontier Province ◻ PK 138-139 D 2
Northwest Gander River ~ CDN (NFL) 242-243 N 4
Northwest Highlands ▲ GB 90-91 E 3
North West Island ⌒ AUS 178-179 L 2
Northwest Pacific Basin ≃ 14-15 G 4
Northwest Point ▲ BS 54-55 J 4
Northwest Providence Channel ≈ 54-55 F 1
North-West Province ◻ ZA 220-221 F 3
North West River ○ CDN 38-39 O 2
North West River ~ CDN (NFL) 242-243 O 4
Northwest Territories ◻ CDN 30-31 D 2
North Wilkesboro ○ USA (NC) 282-283 F 4
North Wind Lake ⊖ CDN (ONT) 234-235 Q 5
Northwood ○ USA (IA) 274-275 E 1
Northwood ○ USA (ND) 258-259 K 4
North Woodstock ○ USA (NH) 278-279 K 4
North York Moors National Park ⊥ GB 90-91 G 4
North Zulch ○ USA (TX) 266-267 L 3
Norton ○ CDN (NB) 240-241 K 5
Norton ○ USA (KS) 262-263 G 5
Norton ○ USA (VA) 280-281 D 7
Norton ○ USA (VT) 278-279 K 4
Norton ○ ZW 218-219 F 3
Norton, Cape ▲ CDN 24-25 Y 6
Norton Bay ≈ 20-21 K 4
Norton Shaw, Cape ▲ CDN 24-25 g 2
Norton Shores ○ USA (MI) 272-273 C 4
Norton Sound ≈ 20-21 H 5
Nortonville ○ USA (KY) 276-277 H 3
Nortonville ○ USA (ND) 258-259 J 5
Norutak Lake ⊖ USA 20-21 N 3
Norwalk ○ USA (CA) 248-249 F 6
Norwalk ○ USA (CT) 280-281 N 2
Norwalk ○ USA (IA) 274-275 E 3
Norwalk ○ USA (OH) 280-281 D 2
Norway ○ USA (KS) 262-263 J 5
Norway ○ USA (MI) 270-271 L 5
Norway = Norge ■ N 86-87 D 7
Norway House ○ CDN 34-35 H 4
Norwegia, Kapp ▲ ARK 16 F 35
Norwegian Basin ≃ 6-7 J 2
Norwegian Bay ≈ 24-25 Z 2
Norwegian Sea ≈ 8 C 1
Norwegian Trench = Norskerenna ∴ N 86-87 B 7
Norwich ○ CDN (ONT) 238-239 E 6
Norwich ○•• GB 90-91 H 5
Norwich ○ USA (CT) 280-281 O 2
Norwich ○ USA (NY) 278-279 F 6
Norwood ○ CDN (ONT) 238-239 H 4
Norwood ○ USA (CO) 254-255 G 5
Norwood ○ USA (LA) 268-269 J 6
Norwood ○ USA (MN) 270-271 E 6
Norwood ○ USA (NC) 282-283 G 5
Nosappu-misaki ▲ J 152-153 L 3
Nosara ○ CR 52-53 B 7
Nose Creek ~ CDN (ALB) 228-229 P 2
Nosehill Creek ~ CDN (ALB) 232-233 B 2
Nose Lake ⊖ CDN 30-31 P 3
Noshiro ○ J 152-153 H 4
Nosive, Farihy ⊖ RM 222-223 F 7
Nosivolo ~ RM 222-223 E 8
Noska ~ RUS 114-115 J 5
Noso ~ RI 166-167 D 3
Nosong, Tanjung ▲ MAL 160-161 A 10
Nosop ~ RB 220-221 E 2
Nosratābād ○• IR 134-135 H 4
Nossa Senhora das Dores ○ BR 68-69 K 7
Nossa Senhora do Livramento ○ BR 70-71 J 4
Nossa Senhora do Socorro ○ BR 68-69 K 7
Nossob ~ NAM 220-221 D 1
Nossob Camp ○ ZA 220-221 E 2
Nossombougou ○ RMM 202-203 G 3
Nosy Varika ○ RM 222-223 F 8
Notakwanon River ~ CDN 36-37 S 7
Notasulga ○ USA (AL) 284-285 E 4
Noteć ~ PL 92-93 N 2
Nothaburi ○ THA 158-159 F 4
Nothern Biak Reserve ⊥• RI 166-167 H 2
Notintsila ○ ZA 220-221 J 5
Nótio Egéo ◻ GR 100-101 L 6
Noto ○ I 100-101 E 6
Notocote ○ MOC 218-219 K 3
Notodden ☆ N 86-87 D 7
Noto-hantō ⌣ J 152-153 G 6
Notora ~ RUS 120-121 F 3
Noto-shima ⌒ J 152-153 G 6
Notre-Dame, Monts ▲ CDN (QUE) 240-241 D 5
Notre Dame Bay ≈ 38-39 R 4
Notre Dame Bay ≈ CDN 242-243 N 3
Notre-Dame-de-Lorette ○ CDN (QUE) 236-237 Q 3
Notre-Dame-du-Lac ○ CDN (QUE) 240-241 G 3
Notre-Dame-du-Laus ○ CDN (QUE) 238-239 K 2
Notre-Dame-du-Nord ○ CDN (QUE) 236-237 J 5
Notre-Dame-du-Rosaire ○ CDN (QUE) 240-241 D 2
Notre Dame Junction ○ CDN (NFL) 242-243 N 3
Notrees ○ USA (TX) 266-267 E 2
Notsé ○ RT 202-203 L 6
Nott, Mount ▲ AUS 180-181 C 2
Nottawasaga Bay ⊖ CDN (ONT) 238-239 E 4
Nottaway, Rivière ~ CDN 38-39 E 3
Nottaway Rivière ~ CDN (ONT) 236-237 K 1
Nottely Lake < USA (GA) 284-285 F 2
Nottely River ~ USA (GA) 284-285 G 2
Nottingham ○ GB 90-91 G 5
Nottingham Downs ○ AUS 178-179 G 1
Nottingham Island ⌒ CDN 36-37 K 3
Nottingham Road ○ ZA 220-221 J 4
Nottoway River ~ USA (VA) 280-281 J 7
Notuken Creek ~ CDN (SAS) 232-233 M 6
Nouâdhibou ☆ RIM 196-197 B 4
Nouâdhibou, Râs ▲ RIM 196-197 B 4
Nouakchott = Nawākshūt ★• RIM 196-197 C 5
Nouâmghâr ○ RIM 196-197 B 5
Nouazereg < RIM 196-197 D 5
Noubandegān ○ IR 134-135 E 4
Noubarān ○ IR 128-129 N 5
Nouhao ~ BF 202-203 K 4
Nouméa ☆• F 13 H 5
Noumoukiédougou ○ BF 202-203 H 5
Noun ~ CAM 204-205 J 6
Nouna ○ BF 202-203 J 3
Nouna ~ G 210-211 D 3
Noupoort ○ ZA 220-221 G 5
Nourlangie Rock • AUS 172-173 L 2
Noušahr ○• IR 136-137 B 6
Noušūd ○ IR 128-129 M 5
Nouveau-Québec, Cratère du ▲ CDN 36-37 N 4
Nouvelle ○ CDN (QUE) 240-241 J 2
Nouvelle-France, Cap de ▲ CDN 36-37 N 3
Nouvelles Hebrides = Vanuatu ⌒ VAN 184 II a 1
Nouzād ○ AFG 134-135 L 2
Nova Alegria ○ BR 72-73 L 4
Nova Aliança ○ BR 72-73 F 6
Nova Almada ○ MOC 218-219 H 4
Nova Almeida ○ BR 72-73 K 6
Nova Alvorada ○ BR 76-77 K 1
Nova Andradina ○ BR 72-73 D 7
Nova Aurora ○ BR 72-73 D 5
Nova Brasilândia ○ BR (MAT) 70-71 K 4
Nova Brasilândia ○ BR (RON) 70-71 F 2
Nova Caipemba ○ ANG 216-217 C 3
Nova Canaã do Norte ○ BR 70-71 K 2
Nova Coimbra ○ MOC 214-215 H 7
Nova Cruz ○ BR 68-69 L 5
Nova Esperança ○ ANG 216-217 C 3
Nova Esperança ○ BR 72-73 D 7
Nova Floresta ○ BR 68-69 K 5
Nova Friburgo ○ BR 72-73 J 7
Nova Gaia ○ ANG 216-217 D 5
Nova Golegã ○ MOC 218-219 G 5
Nova Gradiška ○ HR 100-101 F 2
Nova Granada ○ BR 72-73 F 6
Nova Iguaçu ○ BR 72-73 J 7
Nova Independência ○ BR 72-73 E 6
Nova Itaipe ○ BR 72-73 K 2
Novaja ○ RUS (TMR) 108-109 d 6
Novaja ~ RUS 108-109 e 5
Novaja ~ RUS 110-111 G 2
Novaja Igirma ○ RUS 116-117 L 7
Novaja Inja ○ RUS 120-121 L 4
Novaja Kahovka = Nova Kachovka ○ UA 102-103 H 4
Novaja Ladoga ○ RUS 94-95 N 1
Novaja Ljalja ☆ RUS 114-115 F 5
Novaja Sibir', ostrov ⌒ RUS 110-111 a 2
Nova Jorque ○ BR 68-69 F 5
Nova Kachovka ○ UA (HER) 102-103 H 4
Novales, Punta ▲ RA 80 G 2
Nova Lima ○ BR 72-73 J 5
Novalukomľ ○ BY 94-95 L 4
Nova Macajuba ○ BR 68-69 E 2
Nova Mambone ○ MOC 218-219 H 5
Nova Módica ○ BR 72-73 K 5
Nova Nabúri ○ MOC 218-219 K 3
Nova Olímpia ○ BR 72-73 D 7
Nova Olinda ○ BR 66-67 K 4
Nova Olinda, Riachão ~ BR 68-69 G 6
Nova Olinda do Norte ○ BR 66-67 H 4
Nova Prata ○ BR 74-75 E 7
Novara ☆ I 100-101 B 2
Nova Resende ○ BR 72-73 G 6
Nova Roma ○ BR 72-73 G 2
Nova Russas ○ BR 68-69 H 4
Nova Santarém ○ MOC 218-219 H 1
Nova Scotia ◻ CDN (NS) 240-241 K 6
Nova Serrana ○ BR 72-73 H 5
Nova Soure ○ BR 68-69 J 7
Nova Timboteua ○ BR 68-69 E 2
Novato ○ USA (CA) 246-247 C 5
Nova Vandúzi ○ MOC 218-219 G 4
Nova Venécia ○ BR 72-73 K 5
Nova Viçosa ○ BR 72-73 L 4
Nova Vida ○ BR 66-67 C 5
Nova Viseu ○ MOC 214-215 J 7
Nova Vodolaha ○ UA 102-103 J 3
Nova Xavantina ○ BR 72-73 D 3
Novaya Zemlya = Novaja Zemlja ⌒ RUS 108-109 E 6
Nova Zagora ○ BG 102-103 E 6
Nova Zembla Island ⌒ CDN 26-27 N 7
Nove de Abril, Cachoeira ~ BR 70-71 G 2
Novembro, Cachoeira 15. de ~ BR 70-71 G 3
Nové Zámky ○ SK 92-93 P 5
Novgorod ☆••• RUS 94-95 M 2
Novgorodka ○ RUS 94-95 L 3
Novhorodka ○ UA 102-103 H 3
Novi ○ USA (MI) 272-273 F 5
Novi Iskăr ○ BG 102-103 C 6
Novikbož ○ RUS 88-89 Y 3
Novikovo ○ RUS 122-123 K 5
Novillero ○ MEX 50-51 G 6
Novi Pazar ○ BG 102-103 E 6
Novi Pazar ○• YU 100-101 H 3
Novi Sad ○• YU 100-101 G 2
Novi Sanžary ○ UA 102-103 J 3
Nóvita ○ CO 60-61 C 5
Novo, Lago ○ BR 62-63 J 5
Novo, Rio ~ BR 66-67 J 6
Novo, Rio ~ BR 68-69 B 4
Novo, Rio ~ BR 70-71 E 2
Novo Acordo ○ BR (P) 68-69 B 3
Novo Acordo ○ BR (TOC) 68-69 E 6
Novo Acre ○ BR 72-73 K 2
Novoagansk ○ RUS 114-115 O 4
Novo Airão ○ BR 66-67 G 4
Novoaleksandrovka ○ RUS 116-117 K 8
Novoaleksandrovsk ○ RUS 102-103 M 5
Novoalekseevka = Karagandysay ☆ KA 126-127 L 2
Novoaltajsk ☆ RUS 124-125 N 2
Novoanninskij ○ RUS 102-103 N 2
Novo Areal ○ BR 66-67 E 6
Novo Aripuanã ○ BR 66-67 G 5
Novoazovs'k ○ UA 102-103 L 4

Novobelokataj ☆ RUS 96-97 L 6
Novobogat o KA 96-97 G 10
Novoburejskij ☆ RUS 122-123 C 4
Novočeboksarsk o RUS 96-97 E 5
Novočerkassk ☆• RUS 102-103 M 4
Novočerkasskoe o KA 124-125 F 3
Novočernoreč'enskij o RUS 116-117 E 7
Novocheboksarsk = Novočeboksarsk o RUS 96-97 E 5
Novocherkassk = Novočerkassk ☆• RUS 102-103 M 4
Novo Cruzeiro o BR 72-73 K 4
Novočuguevka o RUS 122-123 E 6
Novodvinsk o RUS 88-89 Q 4
Novoe o RUS 122-123 E 5
Novoe Čaplino o RUS 112-113 Y 4
Novoe Mašozero o RUS 88-89 M 4
Novofedorivka o UA 102-103 H 4
Novograd-Volynskij = Novohrad-Volyns'kyj o UA 102-103 E 2
Novo Hamburgo o BR 74-75 E 7
Novohoperskij o RUS 102-103 M 2
Novo Horizonte o BR 72-73 F 6
Novohrad-Volyns'kyj o UA 102-103 E 2
Novokačalinsk o RUS 122-123 E 6
Novokašpirskij o RUS 96-97 F 7
Novokazaly ☆ KA 126-127 P 5
Novokievskij Uval ☆ RUS 122-123 C 3
Novokubansk o RUS 102-103 M 5
Novokujbyševsk o RUS 96-97 F 7
Novokuybyshevsk = Novokujbyševsk o RUS 96-97 F 7
Novokuzneck ☆ RUS 124-125 P 2
Novokuznetsk = Novokuzneck ☆ RUS 124-125 P 2
Novolazarevskaja o ARK 16 F 1
Novo Mesto o SLO 100-101 E 2
Novomičurinsk o RUS 94-95 Q 4
Novomihajlovskij o RUS 126-127 C 5
Novomoskovsk ☆ RUS 94-95 Q 4
Novomoskovs'k o UA 102-103 J 3
Novomoskovsk = Novomoskovs'k o UA 102-103 J 3
Novo Mundo o BR 72-73 E 2
Novo Mundo, Igarapé ∼ BR 70-71 F 2
Novomuraptalovo o RUS 96-97 J 7
Novonadeždinka o KA 96-97 J 8
Novonikolaevskij o RUS 102-103 N 2
Novooleksiïvka o UA 102-103 J 4
Novo Oriente o BR (CEA) 68-69 H 4
Novo Oriente o BR (RON) 66-67 F 7
Novoorsk ☆ RUS 96-97 L 8
Novo Paraíso o BR 74-75 D 7
Novo Paraná o BR 70-71 J 2
Novopavlovsk o RUS 126-127 E 6
Novo Pensamento o BR 66-67 F 3
Novopetrovskoe o RUS 94-95 P 4
Novopokrovka o RUS 122-123 F 6
Novopokrovskaja o RUS 102-103 M 5
Novopolock = Navapolack ☆•• BY 94-95 L 4
Nôvo Pôrto o BR 66-67 B 7
Novopskov o UA 102-103 L 3
Novorossijskoe o KA 126-127 N 2
Novorybnaja o RUS 110-111 F 3
Novoržev ☆ RUS 94-95 L 3
Novošahtinsk o RUS 102-103 L 4
Novo São Joaquim o BR 72-73 D 3
Novosel'e o RUS 94-95 L 2
Novoselickoe o RUS 126-127 E 5
Novoselivs'ke o UA 102-103 H 5
Novoselycja ☆ UA 102-103 E 3
Novosemejkino o RUS 96-97 G 7
Novosergievka ☆ RUS 96-97 H 7
Novošešminsk o RUS 96-97 G 6
Novoshakhtinsk = Novošahtinsk o RUS 102-103 L 4
Novosibirsk ☆• RUS 114-115 R 7
Novosibirskoe vodohranilišče < RUS 124-125 M 1
Novosokol'niki ☆ RUS 94-95 M 3
Novotroick o RUS 96-97 L 8
Novotroickoe o RUS 122-123 B 3
Novotroickoe o RUS 122-123 D 4
Novotroitsk = Novotroick o RUS 96-97 L 8
Novotroïc'ke o UA 102-103 J 4
Novoukrajinka o UA 102-103 G 3
Novoul'janovsk o RUS 96-97 F 6
Novouzensk ☆ RUS 96-97 F 8
Novovjatsk o RUS 96-97 F 4
Novovolyns'k o UA 102-103 D 2
Novovolynsk = Novovolyns'k o UA 102-103 D 2
Novovoskresenovka o RUS 118-119 N 9
Novozavidovskij o RUS 94-95 P 3
Novozemel'skaja vpadina ≃ 108-109 G 6
Novozybkov o BY 94-95 M 5
Novra o CDN (MAN) 234-235 B 2
Novska o HR 100-101 F 2
Nový Bor o CZ 92-93 N 3
Novye Ljady o RUS 96-97 K 4
Novye Zjatcy o RUS 96-97 H 5
Novyj Bor o RUS 88-89 W 3
Novyj Buh o UA 102-103 H 4
Nový Jičín o CZ 92-93 P 4
Novyj Port o RUS 108-109 P 8
Novyj Tartas o RUS 114-115 O 7
Novyj Uojan o RUS 118-119 E 7
Novyj Urengoj o RUS 114-115 O 1
Novyj Uzen' o KA 126-127 K 6
Nowashe Lake o CDN 34-35 P 4
Nowa Sól o PL 92-93 N 3
Nowata o USA (OK) 264-265 J 2
Nowe o• PL 92-93 P 2
Nowendoc o AUS 178-179 L 6
Nowgong o IND 138-139 G 7
Nowitna River ∼ USA 20-21 N 4
Nowleye Lake o CDN 30-31 T 4
Nowogard o PL 92-93 N 2
Nowood Creek ∼ USA (WY) 252-253 L 2
Nowra-Bomaderry o AUS 180-181 L 3
Nowshehrvirkhan o PK 138-139 D 4
Nowshera o PK 138-139 C 3
Nowy Sącz ☆• PL 92-93 Q 4
Noxon o USA (MT) 250-251 D 4
Noxubee National Wildlife Refuge ⊥ USA (MS) 268-269 M 3
Noxubee River ∼ USA (MS) 268-269 M 4
Noya ∼ G 210-211 B 3
Noyabr'sk = Nojabr'sk o RUS 114-115 N 3
Noyes Island ∩ USA 32-33 D 4
Noyo o USA (CA) 246-247 B 4
Noyon o F 90-91 J 7
Nqadubolu o RI 168 D 7
Nritu Ga o MYA 142-143 K 2
Nsa o RCB 210-211 E 5
Nsadzu o Z 218-219 G 2
Nsakaluba o Z 214-215 E 6
Nsama o Z 214-215 E 5
Nsambi o ZRE 210-211 F 4
Nsanje o MW 218-219 H 3
Nsawam o GH 202-203 K 7
Nsawkaw o GH 202-203 J 6
Nsele ∼ ZRE 210-211 E 6
Nsem o CAM 204-205 K 6
Nsiza o ZW 218-219 E 4
Nsog o GQ 210-211 C 3
Nsoko o SD 220-221 K 3
Nsombo o Z 214-215 E 6
Nsontin o ZRE 210-211 G 5
Nsukka o WAN 204-205 G 5
Ntambu o Z 214-215 C 7
Ntandembele o ZRE 210-211 F 5
Ntatrat < RIM 196-197 C 6
Ntcheu o MW 218-219 H 2
Ntchisi o MW 218-219 G 1
Nteko o Z 214-215 G 5
Ntem ∼ CAM 210-211 C 2
Ntemwa o Z 218-219 D 2
Nterguent o RIM 196-197 D 5
Nthalire o MW 214-215 G 6
Nthunga o MW 214-215 H 7
Ntibane o ZA 220-221 J 5
Ntimaru o EAK 212-213 E 4
Ntiona o TCH 198-199 G 5
Ntlenyana, Thabana ▲ LS 220-221 J 4
Ntokou o G 210-211 E 3
Ntomba, Lac o• ZRE 210-211 G 4
Ntoum o G 210-211 B 3
Ntsel, Hassi < DZ 190-191 F 7
Ntsou o RCB 210-211 E 4
Ntui o CAM 204-205 J 6
Ntungamo o EAU 212-213 C 4
Ntusi o EAU 212-213 C 3
Ntwetwe Pan o RB 218-219 C 5
Ntyébougou o RMM 202-203 G 2
Nu'airiya, an- o KSA 130-131 L 4
Nuakata Island ∩ PNG 183 F 6
Nuaneteze, Rio ∼ MOC 218-219 F 6
Nuangan o RI 164-165 J 3
Nuangola o USA (PA) 280-281 L 2
Nūba, Buḥairat o SUD 200-201 E 2
Nubarašen o AR 128-129 L 2
Nubeena o AUS 180-181 J 7
Nubia = Nūba, an- ⩦ SUD 200-201 D 3
Nubian Desert = Nūba, Şaḥrā' an- ⩦ SUD 200-201 E 2
Nubieber o USA (CA) 246-247 D 2
Ñuble, Río ∼ RCH 78-79 C 4
Nuboai o RI 166-167 J 3
Nučča ∼ RUS 110-111 W 4
Nucla o USA (CO) 254-255 G 5
Nucuray, Río ∼ PE 64-65 D 4
Nudlung Fiord ≈ 28-29 G 2
Nudo Allincapac ▲ PE 70-71 B 3
Nudo Aricoma ▲ PE 70-71 B 4
Nudo Ausangate ▲ PE 70-71 B 3
Nudo Chicllaraza ▲ PE 64-65 E 8
Nudo de Apolobamba ▲ PE 70-71 C 4
Nudo de Paramillo ▲ CO 60-61 D 4
Nudo de Sunipani ▲ PE 70-71 B 4
Nudymi ∼ RUS 120-121 H 4
Nueces River ∼ USA (TX) 266-267 H 5
Nueces River, East ∼ USA (TX) 266-267 G 4
Nueces River, West ∼ USA (TX) 266-267 G 4
Nueltin Lake o CDN 30-31 U 5
Nuestra Señora del Rosario de Caá Catí o RA 76-77 J 4
Nueva, Isla ∩ RCH 80 G 7
Nueva, La o EC 64-65 D 1
Nueva Alejandría o PE 64-65 F 4
Nueva Arcadia o HN 52-53 K 4
Nueva Ciudad Guerrero o MEX 50-51 K 4
Nueva Coahuila o MEX 52-53 J 3
Nueva Constitución o RA 78-79 F 3
Nueva Era o RP 160-161 D 4
Nueva Esperanza o RA (SAE) 76-77 E 4
Nueva Esperanza o RA (SAE) 76-77 F 4
Nueva Florida o YV 60-61 G 3
Nueva Galia o RA 78-79 G 3
Nueva Gerona ☆ C 54-55 D 4
Nueva Granada o CO 60-61 D 3
Nueva Guinea o NIC 52-53 B 6
Nueva Imperial o RCH 78-79 C 5
Nueva Italia o PY 76-77 J 3
Nueva Italia o RA 76-77 G 5
Nueva Italia de Ruíz o MEX 52-53 C 2
Nueva Lubecka o RA 80 E 2
Nueva Ocotepeque ☆ HN 52-53 K 4
Nueva Palmira o ROU 78-79 K 2
Nueva Pompeya o RA 76-77 G 3
Nueva Rosita o MEX 50-51 J 4
Nueva San Salvador ☆ ES 52-53 K 5
Nuevitas o C 54-55 G 4
Nuevo, Cayo ∩ MEX 52-53 H 1
Nuevo Andoas o PE 64-65 D 3
Nuevo Campechito o MEX 52-53 H 2
Nuevo Casas Grandes o MEX 50-51 F 2
Nuevo Esperanza o PE 64-65 E 2
Nuevo Laredo o MEX 50-51 K 4
Nuevo Leon □ MEX 50-51 J 4
Nuevo Mundo o BOL 70-71 E 3
Nuevo Mundo o CO 60-61 F 5
Nuevo Mundo, Cerro ▲ BOL 76-77 D 1
Nuevo Padilla o MEX 50-51 K 5
Nuevo Riaño o E 98-99 E 3
Nuevo Rocafuerte o EC 64-65 E 2
Nuevo Turino o RA 76-77 G 6
Nugaal □ SP 208-209 H 4
Nugaal, togga ∼ SP 208-209 J 4
Nuga Nuga, Lake o AUS 178-179 K 3
Nugents Corner o USA (WA) 244-245 C 2
Nugong, Mount ▲ AUS 180-181 J 4
Nugtat Būlis al Habilīyah o LAR 192-193 D 1
Nuguaçu o BR 68-69 H 7
Nuguškoe vodohranilišče < RUS 96-97 K 7
Nuḥaib o IRQ 128-129 K 6
Nuhaida o OM 132-133 K 2
Nuhaka o NZ 182 F 3
Nui Lang Bian ▲ VN 158-159 K 4
Nuiqsut o USA 20-21 P 1
Nui Thành o VN 158-159 K 3
Nuja = Karksi-Nuja o•• EST 94-95 J 2
Nüjiang o VRC 144-145 B 4
Nu Jiang ∼ VRC 142-143 L 3
Nu Jiang ∼ VRC 144-145 L 6
Nūkābād o IR 134-135 J 4
Nuka Bay ≈ 22-23 V 3
Nuka Island ∩ USA 22-23 V 3
Nuka River ∼ USA 20-21 L 2
Nukhaylah < SUD 200-201 C 3
Nukiki o SOL 184 I c 2
Nukko Lake o CDN (BC) 228-229 L 2
Nukshak, Cape ▲ USA 22-23 U 3
Nuku o PNG 183 B 2
Nuku'alofa ★• TON 184 IV a 2
Nukubasaga ∩ FJI 184 III c 2
Nuku-Hiva ∩ F 13 N 3
Nukuhu o PNG 183 E 3
Nukulaelae Atoll ∩ TUV 13 J 3
Nukus ☆ US 136-137 F 3
Nula, El o YV 60-61 F 4
Nulato o USA 20-21 L 4
Nulato River ∼ USA 20-21 L 4
Nuli o ZW 218-219 F 6
Nullagine o AUS 172-173 E 6
Nullagine River ∼ AUS 172-173 E 6
Nullarbor o AUS 174-175 H 6
Nullarbor National Park ⊥ AUS 176-177 L 5
Nullarbor Plain ⩦ AUS 176-177 J 5
Nullarbor Regional Reserve ⊥ AUS 176-177 K 5
Nullarbor Roadhouse o AUS 176-177 L 5
Nuluk River ∼ USA 20-21 G 4
Num o NEP 144-145 F 7
Num, Pulau ∩ RI 166-167 H 2
Numalla, Lake o AUS 178-179 H 5
Numan o WAN 204-205 K 4
Nu'mān, Ğazīrat an- ∩ KSA 130-131 D 4
Nū'mān, Ma'arrat an- o• SYR 128-129 G 5
Numancia (Ruinas celtibércas y romanas) ∴• E 98-99 F 4
Nu'māniya, an- ☆ IRQ 128-129 L 6
Numata o J (GUM) 152-153 H 6
Numata o J (HOK) 152-153 J 3
Numatinna ∼ SUD 206-207 H 5
Numazu o J 152-153 H 7
Number 24 Well o AUS 172-173 F 7
Number 35 Well < AUS 172-173 G 7
Numbi o ZRE 212-213 B 4
Numbulwar ⅄ AUS 174-175 C 4
Numedal ⩦ N 86-87 D 6
Numfor, Pulau ∩ RI 166-167 H 2
Numil Downs o AUS 174-175 F 6
Numto o RUS 114-115 L 3
Numto, ozero o RUS 114-115 L 3
Numto, uval ▲ RUS 114-115 K 3
Numurkah o AUS 180-181 H 4
Nunalla (abandoned) o CDN 30-31 W 6
Nunarsuaq ∩ GRØ 28-29 U 5
Nunarsuit ∩ GRØ 28-29 Q 6
Nunavakanuk Lake o USA 20-21 H 5
Nunavakpak Lake o USA 20-21 J 6
Nunavaugaluk, Lake o USA 22-23 R 3
Nunavik ∼ GRØ 26-27 X 8
Nunda o USA (NY) 278-279 D 6
Nunda o USA (SD) 260-261 J 2
Nundle o AUS 178-179 L 6
Nundroo o AUS 176-177 M 5
Nunea o USA (MI) 272-273 C 4
Ñúñez, Isla ∩ RCH 80 D 6
Nungesser Lake o CDN (ONT) 234-235 K 3
Nungo o MOC 218-219 J 1
Nungwaia o PNG 183 B 2
Nungwe Bay o EAT 212-213 D 5
Nunim Lake o CDN 30-31 S 6
Nunivak Island ∩ USA 20-21 G 6
Nunjamo o RUS 112-113 Z 4
Nunjamovaam ∼ RUS 112-113 X 4
Nunligran o RUS (CUK) 112-113 T 3
Nunligran o RUS (CUK) 112-113 X 4
Nunn o USA (CO) 254-255 L 3
Ñuñoa o PE 70-71 B 4
Nun River ∼ WAN 204-205 G 6
Nunukan Timur, Pulau ∩ RI 164-165 E 1
Nuora ∼ RUS 118-119 O 3
Nuoraldžyma ∼ RUS 118-119 M 4
Nuoro o I 100-101 B 4
Nuporanga o BR 72-73 G 6
Nuqay, Jabal ▲ LAR 192-193 H 6
Nuqra, Ğabal ▲ ET 194-195 G 5
Nuqūb o Y 132-133 D 6
Nuqum, Ğabal ▲ Y 132-133 D 6
Nūr o IR 136-137 B 6
Nura o KA (AKT) 126-127 P 3
Nūra ∼ KA 124-125 J 4
Nūra ∼ KA 124-125 G 3
Nūra ∼ KA 124-125 H 4
Nūra ∼ KA 124-125 F 3
Nūra ∼ KA 124-125 H 4
Nūrābād o• IR (FAR) 134-135 D 3
Nūrābād o• IR (LOR) 134-135 B 1
Nurata ☆ US 136-137 J 4
Nurataldy o KA 124-125 H 4
Nuratau tog tizmasi ▲ US 136-137 J 4
Nur Dağları ▲ TR 128-129 G 4
Nurei o SUD 198-199 L 6
Nurek o TJ 136-137 L 5
Nuremberg = Nürnberg o D 92-93 L 4
Nūrestān o• AFG 138-139 C 2
Nūr Gāma o PK 134-135 M 4
Nurhak ☆ TR 128-129 G 4
Nurhak Dağı ▲ TR 128-129 G 3
Nurí o MEX 50-51 E 3
Nuri •• SUD 200-201 E 3
Nuri, Teluk ≈ 162-163 H 5
Nuriootpa o AUS 180-181 E 3
Nurkaat o RI 166-167 F 5
Nurlat ☆ RUS 96-97 G 6
Nurmes o FIN 88-89 K 5
Nurmijärvi o FIN 88-89 K 5
Nürnberg o D 92-93 L 4
Nurobod ☆ US 136-137 K 5
Nurota sovhozi o US 136-137 K 4
Nürpur o PK 138-139 D 4
Nursery o USA (TX) 266-267 K 5
Nusa Barung, Pulau ∩ RI 168 E 4
Nusa Dua o RI 168 B 7
Nusa Kambangan ∩ RI 168 C 3
Nusa Laut, Pulau ∩ RI 166-167 E 3
Nusa Tenggara Timur □ RI 166-167 B 6
Nusawulan o RI 166-167 G 4
Nusaybin ☆ TR 128-129 J 4
Nusela, Kepulauan ∩ RI 166-167 F 2
Nushagak Bay ≈ 22-23 R 3
Nushagak Peninsula ⌣ USA 22-23 R 3
Nushagak River ∼ USA 22-23 S 3
Nu Shan ▲ VRC 142-143 L 2
Nushki o PK 134-135 L 4
Nutaarmiut ∩ GRØ 26-27 X 7
Nutak o CDN 36-37 T 6
Nutaugè, laguna ≈ 112-113 W 3
Nut Mountain o CDN (SAS) 232-233 P 3
Nutrias, Las o RA 78-79 K 5
Nutrioso o USA (AZ) 256-257 F 5
Nuttal o PK 138-139 B 5
Nutuvukti Lake o USA 20-21 N 3
Nutwood Downs o AUS 174-175 C 4
Nuu o EAK 212-213 G 4
Nuugaatsiaq o GRØ 26-27 Y 8
Nuuk = Godthåb ☆ GRØ 28-29 P 4
Nuuk Kangerluaq ≈ 28-29 P 4
Nuurst o MAU 148-149 J 4
Nuussuaq Halvø ⌣ GRØ 28-29 O 1
Nuvuk Point ▲ CDN 36-37 R 2
Nuwaibi' al-Muzayyina o ET 194-195 G 3
Nuwaisib, al- o KWT 130-131 L 3
Nuwara Eliya o•• CL 140-141 J 7
Nuwefontein o NAM 220-221 D 3
Nuweh o RI 166-167 K 5
Nuwekloof ▲ ZA 220-221 J 6
Nuwerus o ZA 220-221 D 5
Nuweveldberge ▲ ZA 220-221 E 6
Nuy o ZA 220-221 D 6
Nuyakuk Lake o USA 22-23 R 3
Nuyts Archipelago ∩ AUS 176-177 M 6
Nuyts Reefs ∩ AUS 176-177 M 6
Nūzvīd o IND 140-141 J 2
Nwa o CAM 204-205 J 5
Nwanetsi o ZA 220-221 L 2
N.W. Crocodile Island ∩ AUS 174-175 C 2
Nxai Pan o RB 218-219 C 4
Nxai Pan National Park ⊥ RB 218-219 C 4
Nya ∼ TCH 206-207 B 4
Nyabarongo ∼ RWA 212-213 B 4
Nyabisindu o RWA 212-213 B 5
Nyadire ∼ ZW 218-219 G 3
Nyagassola o RG 202-203 F 3
Nya-Ghezi o ZRE 212-213 B 5
Nyahanga o EAT 212-213 D 5
Nyahua ∼ EAT 212-213 D 6
Nyahururu o EAK 212-213 F 3
Nyah West o AUS 180-181 G 3
Nyainqêntanglha Feng ▲ VRC 144-145 H 5
Nyainqêntanglha Shan ▲ VRC 144-145 G 6
Nyainrong o VRC 144-145 J 4
Nyakahura o EAT 212-213 C 5
Nyakanazi o EAT 212-213 C 5
Nyak Co o VRC 144-145 B 4
Nyalā o SUD 200-201 B 6
Nyalam o VRC 144-145 E 6
Ny Ålesund o N 84-85 G 3
Nyali o G 210-211 C 5
Nyalikungu o EAT 212-213 D 5
Nyamandhlovu o ZW 218-219 E 4
Nyamapanda o ZW 218-219 G 3
Nyamassila o RT 202-203 L 6
Nyāmati o IND 140-141 F 3
Nyamirembe o EAT 212-213 C 5
Nyamlell o SUD 206-207 H 4
Nyamoko o CAM 204-205 J 6
Nyamuswa o EAT (Ma) 212-213 E 4
Nyanding, Khor ∼ SUD 206-207 L 4
Nyanga ∼ G 210-211 C 5
Nyanga o RCB 210-211 C 5
Nyanga o ZW 218-219 G 4
Nyangamara o EAT 214-215 K 6
Nyang Qu o VRC 144-145 G 6
Nyanza □ EAK 212-213 E 4
Nyanza-Lac o BU 212-213 B 6
Nyarling River ∼ CDN 30-31 M 5
Nyaru o EAK 212-213 E 3
Nyasa o ZRE 210-211 L 6
Nyassar o CAM 206-207 B 5
Nyaungbintho o MYA 142-143 K 4
Nyaungkhashe o MYA 158-159 D 2
Nyaunglebin o MYA 158-159 D 2
Nyaung U o MYA 142-143 J 5
Nyazura o ZW 218-219 G 4
Nyazwidzi ∼ ZW 218-219 F 4
Nybergsund o N 86-87 F 6
Nybor o RUS 114-115 D 4
Nyborg o•• DK 86-87 E 9
Nybro ☆ S 86-87 G 8
Nyčalah o RUS 110-111 a 5
Nyda o RUS 108-109 P 8
Nyda ∼ RUS 108-109 Q 8
Nyé ∼ G 210-211 C 2
Nye o USA (OR) 244-245 G 5
Nyeboe Land ⩦ GRØ 26-27 W 3
Nyegezi o EAT 212-213 D 5
Nyěmo o VRC 144-145 G 6
Nyenase o GH 202-203 K 7
Nyensung o GH 202-203 K 5
Nyeri ☆ EAK 212-213 F 4
Nyeri ▲ EAU 212-213 C 2
Ny-Friesland ⌣ N 84-85 K 3
Nygčekveem ∼ RUS 112-113 T 5
Nygčigen, mys ▲ RUS 112-113 Y 4
Nyibiam o WAN 204-205 H 4
Nyiel o SUD 206-207 K 5
Nyika o ZW 218-219 F 4
Nyikine o SN 202-203 B 3
Nyima o VRC 144-145 F 5
Nyimba o Z 218-219 F 2
Nyiminiama o RMM 202-203 J 2
Nyingchi o VRC 144-145 K 6
Nyiragongo ▲ ZRE 212-213 B 4
Nyírbátor o H 92-93 R 5
Nyíregyháza o H 92-93 Q 5
Nyiri Desert ⩦ EAK 212-213 F 5
Nyiru Range ▲ EAK 212-213 F 2
Nyjskij, zaliv o RUS 122-123 K 3
Nykarleby o FIN 88-89 G 5
Nykia National Park ⊥ MW 214-215 G 6
Nykia Plateau ▲•• MW 214-215 G 6
Nykøbing Falster o DK 86-87 E 9
Nykøbing Mors o DK 86-87 D 8
Nyköping o S 86-87 H 7
Nyland = Uusima ⩦ FIN 88-89 H 6
Nylrivier ∼ ZA 220-221 J 2
Nylstroom o ZA 220-221 J 2
Nymagee o AUS 180-181 J 2
Nymburk o• CZ 92-93 N 3
Nymphe Bank ≈ 90-91 D 6
Nynäshamn ☆ S 86-87 H 7
Nyngan o AUS 178-179 J 6
Nyoma Rap o IND 138-139 G 3
Nyong ∼ CAM 204-205 K 6
Nyons o F 90-91 K 9
Nyos, Lac o CAM 204-205 J 5
Nyrud o RUS 88-89 K 2
Nyš o RUS 122-123 K 3
Nyš ∼ RUS 122-123 K 3
Nysa o• PL 92-93 O 3
Nysa Kłodzka ∼ PL 92-93 O 3
Nysa Łużycka ∼ PL 92-93 N 3
Nyssa o USA (OR) 244-245 H 7
Nytva ☆ RUS 96-97 J 5
Nyudō-saki ▲ J 152-153 H 4
Nyumba ya Mungu Reservoir < EAT (ARU) 212-213 F 5
Nyunzu o ZRE 212-213 B 6
Nyvrovo o RUS 120-121 K 6
Nyžni Sirohozy o UA 102-103 J 4
Nyžni Torhaji o UA 102-103 J 4
Nyžn'ohirs'kyj ☆ UA 102-103 J 5
Nzako o RCA 206-207 F 5
Nzako ∼ RCA 206-207 F 5
Nzambi o RCB 210-211 C 5
Nzara o SUD 206-207 J 6
Nzassi o RCB 210-211 D 6
Nzébéla o RG 202-203 F 5
Nzega o EAT 212-213 D 6
Nzérékoré □ RG 202-203 F 5
Nzérékoré ☆ RG 202-203 F 6
N'Zeto o ANG 216-217 B 3
Nzi ∼ CI 202-203 H 6
Nzilo, Bahr ∼ RCA 206-207 F 3
Nzilo, Lac < ZRE 214-215 C 6
Nzima o EAT 212-213 D 5
Nzo ∼ CI 202-203 G 6
Nzo o RG 202-203 F 6
N'zo, Réserve de faune du ⊥ CI 202-203 G 6
Nzoia ∼ EAK 212-213 E 3
Nzoro o RCA 206-207 E 5
Nzoro ∼ ZRE 212-213 C 2

O

Oā', Wādī al- ∼ KSA 130-131 F 4
Oahe, Lake o USA (SD) 260-261 F 2
Oahu ∩ USA (HI) 288 H 3
Oakbank o AUS 180-181 F 2
Oak Bay o CDN (BC) 230-231 F 5
Oak Bluff o CDN (MAN) 234-235 F 5
Oak Bluffs o USA (MA) 278-279 L 7
Oakburn o CDN (MAN) 234-235 C 4
Oak City o USA (NC) 282-283 K 5
Oak City o USA (UT) 254-255 C 4
Oak Creek o USA (CO) 254-255 J 3
Oak Creek o USA (WI) 274-275 L 2
Oakdale o USA (CA) 248-249 D 2
Oakdale o USA (LA) 268-269 H 6
Oakes o USA (ND) 258-259 J 5
Oakey o AUS 178-179 L 4
Oakey Creek ∼ AUS 178-179 L 4
Oak Grove o USA (LA) 268-269 J 4
Oak Harbor o USA (OH) 280-281 C 2
Oak Harbor o USA (WA) 244-245 C 2
Oak Hill o USA (AL) 284-285 C 5
Oak Hill o USA (FL) 286-287 J 3
Oak Hill o USA (OH) 280-281 D 5
Oak Hill o USA (WV) 280-281 E 6
Oak Hills o AUS 174-175 H 6
Oakhurst o USA (CA) 248-249 E 2
Oak Lake o CDN (MAN) 234-235 C 5
Oak Lake o CDN (MAN) 234-235 C 5
Oakland o CDN (MAN) 234-235 E 4
Oakland o USA (CA) 248-249 B 2
Oakland o USA (IA) 274-275 C 3
Oakland o USA (IL) 274-275 K 5
Oakland o USA (MD) 280-281 G 4
Oakland o USA (MS) 268-269 L 2
Oakland o USA (NE) 262-263 K 3
Oakland City o USA (IN) 274-275 L 6
Oakland Park o USA (FL) 286-287 J 5
Oaklands o AUS 180-181 J 3
Oak Lawn o USA (IL) 274-275 L 3
Oak Level o USA (AL) 284-285 E 3
Oakley o USA (ID) 252-253 E 4
Oakley o USA (KS) 262-263 F 5
Oakover River ∼ AUS 172-173 E 6
Oak Park o USA (GA) 284-285 H 4
Oak Point o CDN (MAN) 234-235 F 4
Oak Ridge o USA (LA) 268-269 J 4
Oakridge o USA (OR) 244-245 C 7
Oak Ridge o USA (TN) 282-283 C 4
Oak Ridge o USA (TN) 282-283 C 4
Oak River o CDN (MAN) 234-235 C 4
Oakshela o CDN (SAS) 232-233 Q 5
Oakview o CDN (MAN) 234-235 E 3
Oak View o USA (CA) 248-249 E 5
Oakville o CDN (MAN) 234-235 E 5
Oakville o CDN (ONT) 238-239 F 5
Oakville o USA (TX) 266-267 J 5
Oakville o USA (WA) 244-245 B 4
Oakwood o USA (IL) 274-275 L 4
Oakwood o USA (OK) 264-265 F 3
Oakwood o USA (TN) 276-277 H 4
Oakwood o USA (TX) 268-269 E 5
Oaky Creek o AUS 178-179 K 2
Oamaru o NZ 182 C 6
Oan o RI 164-165 G 3
Oasis o USA (CA) 248-249 G 2
Oasis o USA (NM) 256-257 L 5
Oasis o USA (NV) 246-247 L 2
Oates Land ⩦ ARK 16 F 17
Oatlands o AUS 180-181 J 7
Oatman o USA (AZ) 256-257 A 3
Oaxaca □ MEX 52-53 F 3
Oaxaca de Juárez ☆••• MEX 52-53 F 3
Ob' o RUS 114-115 R 7
Ob' ∼ RUS 10-11 G 2
Oba o CDN (ONT) 236-237 D 3
Oba o WAN 204-205 F 5
Obaa o RI 166-167 K 5
Obaba o RCB 210-211 F 4
Obaha o PNG 183 B 5
Obakamiga Lake o CDN (ONT) 236-237 C 3
Obala o CAM 204-205 J 6
Obalapuram o IND 140-141 G 3
Obama o J 152-153 F 7
Oban o AUS 178-179 E 1
Oban o CDN (SAS) 232-233 K 3
Oban o GB 90-91 E 3
Oban o RCB 210-211 E 4
Oban o WAN 204-205 H 6
Obanazawa o J 152-153 J 5
Oban Hills ▲ WAN 204-205 H 6
Obanska, Rivière ∼ CDN (QUE) 236-237 K 2
Obatanga Provincial Park ⊥ CDN (ONT) 236-237 C 4
Obe o• AFG 134-135 K 1
Obe = Île Aoba ∩ VAN 184 II a 2
Obed o CDN (ALB) 228-229 R 3
Obed River ∼ USA (TN) 282-283 C 4
Obehie o WAN 204-205 G 6
Obeiz, hrebet ▲ RUS 108-109 H 9
Obele o WAN 204-205 G 5
Obeliai o LT 94-95 J 4
Obelisco, Monumento el • YV 60-61 G 2
Obel-prolaz ▲ MK 100-101 J 4
Obera o• RA 76-77 K 4
Oberlin o USA (KS) 262-263 F 5
Oberlin o USA (LA) 268-269 H 6
Oberon o AUS 180-181 K 2
Oberon o CDN (MAN) 234-235 D 4
Oberösterreich □ A 92-93 M 4
Oberpfälzer Wald ⩦ D 92-93 M 4
Oberstdorf o• D 92-93 L 5
Oberstein, Idar- o D 92-93 J 4
Obhur o KSA 132-133 A 3
Obi o WAN 204-205 H 5
Obi, Pulau ∩ RI 164-165 K 4
Obi, Selat ≈ 164-165 K 4
Obiaruku o WAN 204-205 G 6
Óbidos o BR 62-63 G 6
Óbidos o•• P 98-99 C 5
Obigarm o TJ 136-137 L 5
Obihingou ∼ TJ 136-137 M 5
Obihiro o J 152-153 K 3
Obilatu, Pulau ∩ RI 164-165 K 4
Obilebit, Riacho ∼ PY 76-77 H 1
Obion o USA (TN) 276-277 F 4
Obispo Trejo o RA 76-77 F 6
Obitočna kosa ⌣ UA 102-103 K 4
Oblačnaja, gora ▲ RUS 122-123 F 7
Oblačnyj Golec, gora ▲ RUS 120-121 F 5
Oblong o USA (IL) 274-275 L 6
Obluč'e o RUS 122-123 D 4
Oblukovina ∼ RUS 120-121 R 6
Obninsk o RUS 94-95 P 4
Obo ☆ RCA 206-207 H 6
Obo o VRC 154-155 B 3
Oboa ▲ EAU 212-213 E 3
Obock o DJI 200-201 L 6
Obogu o GH 202-203 K 6
Obojan o RUS 102-103 K 2
Obokote o ZRE 210-211 L 4
Oboli o RCB 210-211 E 4
Obolo o WAN 204-205 G 5
Obonga Lake o CDN (ONT) 234-235 O 4
Obout o CAM 210-211 C 2
Obouya o RCB 210-211 E 4
Obozerskij o RUS 88-89 Q 5
Obra ∼ PL 92-93 N 2
Obregón, Ciudad o MEX 50-51 E 4
Obrenovac o YU 100-101 H 2
O'Brien o USA (OR) 244-245 B 8
O'Brien Creek ∼ USA (MT) 250-251 J 3
Obrovac o HR 100-101 E 2
Obručeva, vozvyšennost' ▲ RUS 120-121 V 7
Obruchev Rise ≃ 14-15 J 2
Obruk Yaylâsı ▲ TR 128-129 E 3
Obryvistaja, gora ▲ RUS 112-113 S 3
Obryvistyj, mys ▲ RUS 108-109 c 2
Obryvistyj, mys ▲ RUS 112-113 M 5
Obščij syrt ▲ RUS 96-97 F 8
Observatory Hill ▲ AUS 176-177 M 4
Observatory Inlet ≈ 32-33 E 4
Obskaja guba ≈ 108-109 P 8
Obskaya Guba = Obskaja guba ≈ RUS 108-109 P 8
Obuasi o CI 202-203 K 6
Obubra o WAN 204-205 H 5
Obuchiv o UA 102-103 G 2
Obudu o WAN 204-205 H 5
Obudu Cattle Ranch o• WAN 204-205 H 5
Obusa o RUS 116-117 L 9
Obusa ∼ RUS 116-117 M 9
Obytočna zatoka ≈ 102-103 J 4
Očakiv o UA 102-103 G 4
Ocala o USA (FL) 286-287 G 2
Ocalli o PE 64-65 C 5
Očamčira o GE 126-127 D 6
Ocampo o MEX (COA) 50-51 H 4
Ocampo o MEX (TAM) 50-51 K 6
Ocaña o CO 60-61 E 3
Ocaña o E 98-99 F 5
Ocaso o CO 64-65 F 1
Ocate o USA (NM) 256-257 K 2
Occidental, Cordillera ▲ RCH 64-65 C 5
Occidente o CO 64-65 F 2
Ocean Cape ▲ USA 20-21 U 7
Ocean City o USA (MD) 280-281 L 5
Ocean City o USA (NJ) 280-281 M 4
Ocean City o USA (WA) 244-245 A 3
Ocean Falls o CDN (BC) 228-229 G 4
Ocean Grove-Barwon Heads o AUS 180-181 H 5
Oceanographer Fracture Zone ≃ 6-7 E 5
Ocean Shores o USA (WA) 244-245 A 4
Oceanside o USA (CA) 248-249 G 6
Ocean Springs o USA (MS) 268-269 M 6
Ocean View o USA (NJ) 280-281 M 4
Očenyrd, gora ▲ RUS 108-109 L 7
Očer ☆ RUS 96-97 J 5
Ochiai o J 152-153 E 7
O'Chiese Indian Reserve ⅄ CDN (ALB) 232-233 C 3
Ochito ∼ PK 134-135 M 6
Ochlockonee River ∼ USA (FL) 286-287 E 1
Ochoa, La o MEX 50-51 H 5
Ochobo o WAN 204-205 G 5
Ochopee o USA (FL) 286-287 H 6
Ocho Rios o• JA 54-55 G 5
Ochre River o CDN (MAN) 234-235 D 3
Ochtyrka o UA 102-103 J 2
Ocilla o USA (GA) 284-285 G 5
Ockelbo o S 86-87 H 6
Ocmulgee National Monument • USA (GA) 284-285 G 4
Ocmulgee River ∼ USA (GA) 284-285 H 5
Ocmulgee River ∼ USA (GA) 284-285 G 3
Ocmulgee River ∼ USA (GA) 284-285 G 4
Ocoa, Bahía de ≈ 54-55 K 5
Ocoa, Sierra de ▲ DOM 54-55 K 5
Ocoee o USA (TN) 282-283 C 5
Ocoee, Lake o USA (TN) 282-283 C 5
Ocoña o PE 70-71 A 5
Ocoña, Río de ∼ PE 70-71 A 5
Oconee, Lake < USA (GA) 284-285 G 3
Oconee River ∼ USA (GA) 284-285 H 4
Oconee River, North ∼ USA (GA) 284-285 G 2
Ocongate o PE 70-71 B 3
O'Connor, Port o USA (TX) 266-267 L 5
Oconomowoc o USA (WI) 274-275 K 1
Oconto o USA (NE) 262-263 G 3
Oconto o USA (WI) 270-271 L 6
Oconto River ∼ USA (WI) 270-271 K 6
Ocoruro o PE 70-71 B 4
Ocós o GCA 52-53 H 4
Ocosingo o MEX 52-53 H 3
Ocotal ☆ NIC 52-53 L 5
Ocotillo Wells o USA (CA) 248-249 H 6
Ocotito, El o MEX 52-53 E 3
Ocotlán o MEX (JAL) 52-53 C 1
Ocotlán o• MEX (OAX) 52-53 F 3
Ocozocoautla o MEX 52-53 H 3
Ocracoka Island ∩ USA (NC) 282-283 M 5
Ocracoke o USA (NC) 282-283 M 5
Ocreza, Ribeiro do ∼ P 98-99 D 5
Ocros o PE (ANC) 64-65 D 7
Ocros o PE (AYA) 64-65 F 8
Octavia o USA (NE) 262-263 J 3
Ocotillo o USA (CA) 248-249 H 7
Octy, Mount ▲ AUS 178-179 C 1
Ocú o• PA 52-53 D 8
Ocua o MOC 218-219 K 1
Očuguj-Botuobuja ∼ RUS 118-119 G 4
Ocujal o C 54-55 G 5
Ocumare del Tuy o YV 60-61 H 2
Ocuri o BOL 70-71 E 6
Oda o GH 202-203 K 7
Ódáðahraun ▲ IS 86-87 e 2
Odaejin o DVR 150-151 G 7
Odaesan National Park ⊥• ROK 150-151 G 9
Odammun ∼ RI 166-167 K 5
Ódate o J 152-153 J 4
Odawara o J 152-153 H 7
Odde, Oke- o WAN 204-205 F 4
Odebolt o USA (IA) 274-275 C 2
Odei River ∼ CDN 34-35 G 2
Odell o USA (IN) 274-275 L 4
Odell o USA (NE) 262-263 K 4
Odell o USA (TX) 264-265 E 4
Odem o USA (TX) 266-267 K 6
Odemira o P 98-99 C 6
Ödemiş ☆ TR 128-129 B 3
Odendaalsrus o ZA 220-221 H 3
Odense o• DK 86-87 E 9
Odenton o USA (MD) 280-281 K 4
Oder ∼ D 92-93 N 2
Oderbruch ⩦ D 92-93 N 2
Odesa ☆•• UA 102-103 G 4
Odesa o USA (NJ) 280-281 L 4
Odessa o CDN (SAS) 232-233 P 5
Odessa o USA (MO) 274-275 E 6
Odessa o USA (TX) 266-267 E 2
Odessa o USA (WA) 244-245 G 3
Odessa = Odesa ☆•• UA (ODS) 102-103 G 4
Odienné ☆• CI 202-203 G 5
Odighi o WAN 204-205 F 5
Odincovo ☆ RUS 94-95 P 4
Odiongan o RP 160-161 D 6
Odjala o G 210-211 D 4
Odjan, zaliv o RUS 120-121 O 4
Odoev ☆ RUS 94-95 P 5
Odomlja ☆ RUS 94-95 O 3
Odon o USA (IN) 274-275 M 6
Ödöngk o K 158-159 H 5
Odonkawkrom o GH 202-203 K 6
O'Donnell o USA (TX) 264-265 C 6
O'Donnell River ∼ AUS 172-173 H 5
Odorheiu Secuiesc o RO 102-103 D 4
Odra ∼ PL 92-93 N 2
Odrus ∼ SUD 200-201 H 3

Odum o USA (GA) 284-285 H 5
Oduponkpehe o GH 202-203 K 7
Odžaci o YU 100-101 G 2
Odzala, Parc National d' ⊥ RCB 210-211 E 3
Odzema o RCB 210-211 F 4
Odzi o ZW 218-219 G 4
Odzi ~ ZW 218-219 G 4
Odziba o RCB 210-211 E 5
Oeiras o BR 68-69 G 5
Oeiras do Pará o BR 62-63 K 6
Oekussi o RI 166-167 C 6
Oelrichs o USA (SD) 260-261 C 3
Oelwein o USA (IA) 274-275 G 2
Oenpelli ✗ AUS 174-175 B 3
Oesilo o RI 166-167 C 6
Oever, Den o NL 92-93 H 2
Of ☆ TR 128-129 J 2
Ofa o WAN 204-205 F 4
Ófærufoss ·· IS 86-87 d 3
O'Fallon Creek ~ USA (MT) 250-251 O 5
Ofanto ~ I 100-101 E 4
Ofaqin o JOR 130-131 D 2
Ofcolaco o ZA 220-221 K 2
Ofe, River ~ WAN 204-205 F 4
Ofelia, La o RA 78-79 D 5
Ofere o WAN 204-205 G 4
Offenbach am Main o D 92-93 K 3
Offenburg o D 92-93 J 4
Offerle o USA (KS) 262-263 G 7
Officer Creek ~ AUS 176-177 M 3
Offoué ~ G 210-211 C 4
Offoue, Réserve de l' ⊥ G 210-211 C 4
Offumpo o CI 202-203 H 7
Ofhidro, Isla ⌒ RCH 80 C 4
Ofhidro, Lago ○ RCH 80 F 6
Oficina Victoria o RCH 70-71 C 7
Ofinso o GH 202-203 K 6
Ofizina Alemania o RCH 76-77 C 3
Ofjord ≈ 26-27 m 8
Ofoase o GH 202-203 K 6
Ofolanga ⌒ TON 184 IV a 1
Ofotfjorden ≈ 86-87 H 2
Ofu o USA 184 V c 2
Ofugo o WAN 204-205 G 5
Ofu Island ⌒ USA 184 V c 2
Ōfunato o J 152-153 J 5
Oga o J 152-153 H 5
Oga, zaliv ○ RUS 108-109 H 4
Ogaden ∴ ETH 208-209 F 5
Oga-hantō ⌄ J 152-153 H 5
Ōgaki o J 152-153 G 7
Ogaki-Hachim-Shrinj • J 152-153 J 5
Ogallala o USA (NE) 262-263 E 3
Ogan ~ RI 162-163 F 6
Oganda, Parc National de l' ⊥ G 210-211 C 4
Oganda, Portes de l' • G 210-211 C 4
Ogani o WAN 204-205 G 6
Ogar, Pulau ⌒ RI 166-167 G 3
Ogascana, Lac ○ CDN (QUE) 236-237 K 5
Ogba o WAN 204-205 F 5
Ogbia o WAN 204-205 G 6
Ogbomoso o WAN 204-205 F 4
Ogden o CDN (NS) 240-241 O 5
Ogden o USA (AR) 276-277 A 7
Ogden o USA (IA) 274-275 D 2
Ogden o USA (UT) 254-255 D 2
Ogden Center o USA (MI) 272-273 F 6
Ogdensburg o USA (NY) 278-279 F 4
Ogeechee River ~ USA (GA) 284-285 J 4
Ogeechee River ~ USA (GA) 284-285 H 3
Ogema o CDN (SAS) 232-233 O 6
Ogema o USA (MN) 270-271 C 3
Ogema o USA (WI) 270-271 H 5
Ogembo o EAK 212-213 E 4
Oger = Ogre ☆ ·· LV 94-95 J 3
Ogi o J 152-153 H 6
Ogies o ZA 220-221 J 3
Ogiinuur = Zögstėj o MAU 148-149 F 4
Ogilvie o AUS 176-177 C 4
Ogilvie o CDN 20-21 V 4
Ogilvie Mountains ▲ CDN 20-21 U 3
Ogilvie River ~ CDN 20-21 V 4
Oglala o USA (SD) 260-261 D 3
Oglala Pass ≈ 22-23 F 7
Oglanly o TM 136-137 D 5
Oglat Beraber < MA 188-189 K 5
Oglat el Faci o DZ (TIN) 188-189 L 7
Oglat el Faci < DZ (TIN) 188-189 J 7
Oglat el Khnâchîch < RMM 196-197 J 4
Oglat Marhboura < DZ 188-189 L 4
Ogle Point ▲ CDN 24-25 Y 6
Oglethorpe o USA (GA) 284-285 F 4
Oglinga Island ⌒ USA 22-23 G 7
Ogmore o AUS 178-179 K 2
Ognon ~ F 90-91 L 8
Ogodža o RUS 122-123 E 2
Ogoja o WAN 204-205 H 5
Ogoki o CDN 34-35 O 5
Ogoki Lake ○ CDN (ONT) 234-235 Q 4
Ogoki Reservoir ○ CDN (ONT) 234-235 P 4
Ogoki River ~ CDN (ONT) 234-235 P 4
Ogoki River ~ CDN (ONT) 234-235 R 3
Ogooué ~ G 210-211 C 4
Ogorodtah o RUS 118-119 P 4
Ogoron o RUS 118-119 O 8
Ogou ~ RT 202-203 L 5
Ogoulou ~ G 210-211 C 4
Ogr o SUD 200-201 C 6
Ogre ☆ • LV 94-95 J 3
Ogulin o HR 100-101 E 2
Ogun o WAN 204-205 F 4
Ogun ◻ WAN 204-205 E 5
Ogun, River ~ WAN 204-205 E 5
Ogurčinskij, ostrov = Ogurğaly a. ⌒ TM 136-137 C 5
Ogurugu o WAN 204-205 G 5
Oguta o WAN 204-205 G 6
Ogwashi-Uku o WAN 204-205 G 5
Oha ☆ • RUS 122-123 K 2
Ohafia o WAN 204-205 G 6
Ohai o NZ 182 A 6
Ohanapecosh o USA (WA) 244-245 D 4
Ohansk ☆ RUS 96-97 J 5
Ohanskaja vozvyšennosť ▲ RUS 96-97 J 5
Ōhata o J 152-153 J 4
Ohaton o CDN (ALB) 232-233 F 3
Ohau, Lake o NZ 182 B 6
Ōhi ▲ GR 100-101 K 5
O'Higgins, Lago ○ RCH 80 D 4
Ohinskij perešeek ⌄ RUS 122-123 K 2
Ohio ◻ USA (OH) 280-281 C 3
Ohiopyle o USA (PA) 280-281 G 4
Ohiopyle State Park ⊥ USA (PA) 280-281 G 4
Ohio River ~ USA (IN) 274-275 N 6
Ohio River ~ USA (KY) 276-277 J 2
Ohio River ~ USA (OH) 280-281 F 3
Ohogamuit o USA 20-21 K 6
Ohogrigol ~ RUS 114-115 P 3
Ohonua o TON 184 IV a 2
Ohoopee River ~ USA (GA) 284-285 H 4
Ohota ~ RUS 120-121 K 3
Ohotsk ☆ • RUS 120-121 K 4
Ohotskij Perevoz o RUS 120-121 F 3
Ohotskoe o RUS 122-123 K 5
Ohře ~ CZ 92-93 M 3
Ohrid o ··· MK 100-101 H 4
Ohridsko Ezero ○ MK 100-101 H 4
Ohrigstad o ZA 220-221 K 2
Ohrit, Liqueni i ○ AL 100-101 H 4
Ohura o NZ 182 E 3
Oiapoque o BR (APA) 62-63 J 4
Oiapoque ~ BR 62-63 H 4
Oiapoque, Reserva Biológica de ⊥ BR 62-63 H 4
Oies, Île aux ⌒ CDN (QUE) 240-241 E 3
Ōi-gawa ~ J 152-153 H 7
Oijärvi o FIN 88-89 H 4
Oil City o USA (LA) 268-269 G 4
Oil City o USA (PA) 280-281 G 2
Oil Creek State Park ⊥ USA (PA) 280-281 G 2
Oildale o USA (CA) 248-249 E 4
Oil Gathering Station < LAR 192-193 G 3
Oilmont o USA (MT) 250-251 H 3
Oil Springs o CDN (ONT) 238-239 C 6
Oil Through o USA (AR) 276-277 D 5
Oilton o USA (TX) 266-267 J 6
Oise ~ F 90-91 J 7
Ōita ☆ J 152-153 D 8
Oiyug o VRC 144-145 G 6
Oja ~ RUS 116-117 F 9
Ojai o USA (CA) 248-249 E 5
Ojašinskij, Stancionno- o RUS 114-115 R 7
Oje o WAN 204-205 G 5
Ojibwa o USA (WI) 270-271 G 5
Ojinaga o MEX 50-51 G 3
Ojiya o J 152-153 H 6
Ojmauyt o KA 126-127 L 4
Ojmjakon o RUS 120-121 K 2
Ojmjakonskoe nagor'e ▲ RUS 120-121 J 2
Ojmur o RUS 116-117 N 9
Ojnaa o RUS 116-117 H 10
Ojobo o WAN 204-205 F 6
Ojo Caliente o MEX 50-51 H 6
Ojo Caliente o USA (NM) 256-257 J 2
Ojo de Carrizo o MEX 50-51 G 3
Ojo de Liebre, Laguna ≈ 50-51 B 4
Ojo Feliz o USA (NM) 256-257 K 2
Ojokkuduk o US 136-137 J 4
Ojos Negros o MEX 50-51 A 2
Ojotung o RUS 110-111 b 4
Ojsylkara ~ KA 126-127 N 3
Ojtal o KA 136-137 N 3
Oj-Tal o KS (OSS) 146-147 B 5
Oj-Tal ~ KS 136-137 N 4
Oju o WAN 204-205 H 5
Ojuelos de Jalisco o MEX 50-51 J 7
Ojusardah o RUS 112-113 H 2
Ojusut o RUS 118-119 G 4
Oka o CDN (QUE) 238-239 L 3
Oka o RCB 210-211 E 5
Oka ~ RUS 94-95 P 4
Oka ~ RUS 116-117 K 9
Oka o WAN 204-205 F 5
Okaba o RI 166-167 K 6
Okahandja ☆ NAM 216-217 D 10
Okakarara o NAM 216-217 D 10
Okak Island ⌒ CDN 36-37 T 6
Okali o RCB 210-211 E 4
Okaliktok Islands ⌒ CDN 36-37 U 7
Okanagan Centre o CDN (BC) 230-231 K 3
Okanagan Falls o CDN (BC) 230-231 K 4
Okanagan Indian Reserve ✗ CDN (BC) 230-231 K 3
Okanagan Lake ○ CDN (BC) 230-231 K 4
Okanagan Landing o CDN (BC) 230-231 K 3
Okanagan Range ▲ CDN (BC) 230-231 J 4
Okanagan Valley ⌄ CDN (BC) 230-231 K 4
Okangoho o NAM 216-217 D 10
Okankolo o NAM 216-217 D 8
Okano ~ G 210-211 C 3
Okanogan o USA (WA) 244-245 F 2
Okanogan Range ▲ 244-245 E 1
Okanogan River ~ USA (WA) 244-245 F 2
Okanono o NAM 216-217 C 10
Okapa o PNG 183 C 4
Okapi, Parc National de la ⊥ ZRE 210-211 L 3
Okapilco Creek ~ USA (GA) 284-285 G 5
Okāra o PK 138-139 D 4
Okarche o USA (OK) 264-265 G 3
Okarem = Ekerem o TM 136-137 C 5
Okata o WAN 204-205 E 4
Okatibbee Lake < USA (MS) 268-269 M 4
Okatjoruu o NAM 216-217 E 9
Okatjuru o NAM 216-217 C 9
Okato o NZ 182 D 3
Okatoma Creek ~ USA (MS) 268-269 L 5
Okaukuejo o NAM 216-217 C 9
Okavango ~ NAM 216-217 F 8
Okavangobecken ∸ RB 218-219 B 4
Okavango Delta ∸ RB 218-219 B 4
Okavango River Lodge o RB 218-219 B 4
Okave o NAM 216-217 D 10
Okaya o J 152-153 H 6
Okayama o J 152-153 E 7
Okazaki o J 152-153 G 7
Okazize o NAM 216-217 D 10
Okdarjo ~ US 136-137 K 5
Okeechobee o USA (FL) 286-287 J 4
Okeechobee, Lake ○ USA (FL) 286-287 J 5
Okeene o USA (OK) 264-265 F 2
Okefenokee National Wildlife Refuge ⊥ USA (GA) 284-285 H 6
Okefenokee Swamp ○ USA (GA) 284-285 H 6
Oke-Iho o WAN 204-205 E 4
Okélataka o RCB 210-211 E 4
Okemah o USA (OK) 264-265 H 3
Okemasis Indian Reservation ✗ CDN (SAS) 232-233 M 3
Okene o WAN 204-205 G 5
Oke-Odde o WAN 204-205 F 4
Oké Owo o DY 204-205 E 4
Oketsew o GH 202-203 K 7
Okha o IND 138-139 B 8
Okha Māthi o IND 138-139 B 8
Okhotsk, Sea of = Ohotskoe more ≈ RUS 10-11 O 3
Oki o RI 166-167 D 3
Okiep o ZA 220-221 C 4
Okigwe o WAN 204-205 G 6
Oki-kaikyō ≈ J 152-153 E 7
Okinawa ☆ J 152-153 B 11
Okinawa-shima ⌒ J 152-153 C 11
Okinawa-shotō ⌒ J 152-153 B 11
Okinoerabu-shima ⌒ J 152-153 C 11
Okino-shima ⌒ J 152-153 E 8
Oki-shoto ⌒ J 152-153 E 6
Oki-tai ≃ 152-153 F 6
Okitipupa o WAN 204-205 F 5
Okkan o MYA 158-159 C 2
Okkurgan ☆ US 136-137 L 4
Okkyn"egan ~ RUS 114-115 R 3
Okla o CDN (SAS) 232-233 P 3
Oklahoma ◻ USA (OK) 264-265 F 3
Oklahoma City ☆ USA (OK) 264-265 G 3
Oklan o RUS 112-113 O 5
Oklan ~ RUS 112-113 N 5
Oklanskoe plato ▲ RUS 112-113 N 5
Oklawaha, Lake < USA (FL) 286-287 H 2
Oklawaha River ~ USA (FL) 286-287 H 2
Okmulgee o USA (OK) 264-265 J 3
Oko o WAN 204-205 F 5
Oko, Wādī ~ SUD 200-201 G 2
Okoboji o USA (IA) 274-275 C 1
Ok Ohm River ~ PNG 183 B 3
Okok ~ EAU 212-213 D 2
Okokmilaga River ~ USA 20-21 O 2
Okola o CAM 204-205 J 6
Okolli Island ⌒ CDN 36-37 L 2
Okollo o EAU 212-213 C 2
Okolona o USA (MS) 268-269 M 2
Okondja o G 210-211 D 4
Okondjatu o NAM 216-217 E 10
Okongo o NAM 216-217 D 8
Okongomba o NAM 216-217 B 9
Okoppe o J 152-153 K 2
Okoppe, Nishi- o J 152-153 K 2
Okora, Mount ▲ WAN 204-205 G 5
Okoruro o BOL 70-71 C 5
Okotoks o CDN (ALB) 232-233 E 5
Okotusu < NAM 216-217 A 8
Okoyo o RCB 210-211 E 4
Okpala-Ngwa o WAN 204-205 G 6
Okpara ~ DY 204-205 E 4
Okpo o MYA 142-143 J 6
Okrika o WAN 204-205 G 6
Okrouyo o CI 202-203 G 7
Oksaj, gory ▲ TJ 146-147 B 7
Oksapmin o PNG 183 B 3
Øksfjord o N 86-87 L 1
Øksfjordjøkelen ▲ ·· N 86-87 L 1
Oksibil o RI 166-167 L 4
Oksino o RUS 88-89 W 3
Okskij Gosudarstvennyj zapovednik ⊥ RUS 94-95 R 4
Oksovskij o RUS 88-89 P 5
Okstindan ▲ N 86-87 G 4
Okstindane ▲ N 84-85 J 3
Oksu ~ TJ 146-147 B 6
Oksym ~ RUS 114-115 U 4
Oktemberjan o AR 128-129 L 2
Oktjabrina o RUS 112-113 J 5
Oktjabr'sk ☆ KA 126-127 M 3
Oktjabr'sk o RUS 96-97 F 7
Oktjabr'skaja, gora ▲ RUS 108-109 f 3
Oktjabr'skij o RUS (AMR) 122-123 C 2
Oktjabr'skij o RUS (ARH) 88-89 R 6
Oktjabr'skij o RUS (BAS) 96-97 H 6
Oktjabr'skij o RUS (IRK) 116-117 J 7
Oktjabr'skij o RUS (KMC) 122-123 R 2
Oktjabr'skij o RUS (MUR) 88-89 N 3
Oktjabr'skij o RUS (ULN) 96-97 F 6
Oktjabr'skij o RUS (VOL) 88-89 O 6
Oktjabr'skij ☆ RUS (PRM) 96-97 K 5
Oktjabr'skoe o RUS 96-97 J 7
Oktjabr'skoje ☆ RUS 114-115 G 4
Oktjabr'skoj Revoljucii, ostrov ⌒ RUS 108-109 a 2
Oktoš ☆ US 136-137 J 5
Oktumkum ∸ TM 136-137 C 4
Oktwin o MYA 142-143 K 6
Oktyabr'skiy = Oktjabr'skij o RUS 96-97 H 6
Oku o CAM 204-205 J 5
Oku o J 152-153 C 11
Oku ~ ZRE 210-211 L 4
Oku, Mont ▲ CAM 204-205 J 5
Okubie o WAN 204-205 F 6
Okubie < WAN 204-205 F 6
Ōkuchi o J 152-153 D 8
Okulovka ☆ RUS 94-95 N 2
Okunajka ~ RUS 118-119 D 7
Okundi o WAN 204-205 H 5
Okushiri o J 152-153 H 3
Okushiri-tō ⌄ J 152-153 H 3
Okuta o WAN 204-205 E 4
Okwa ~ RB 216-217 F 11
Okwa, River ~ WAN 204-205 G 4
Olá o PA 52-53 D 7
Ola ☆ • RUS 120-121 O 4
Ola ~ RUS 120-121 O 4
Ola o USA (AR) 276-277 B 5
Ola o USA (ID) 252-253 B 2
Ola, Joškar- o RUS 96-97 E 5
Ola, Zapadnyj Tannu, hrebet ▲ RUS 116-117 E 10
Olaf Prydz bukt ≈ 16 G 8
Ólafsfjörður o IS 86-87 d 1
Ólafsvík o IS 86-87 b 2
Olancha o USA (CA) 248-249 G 3
Olanchito o HN 52-53 L 4
Öland ⌒ • S 86-87 H 8
Olanga ~ RUS 88-89 L 3
Olanta o USA (SC) 284-285 L 3
Olary o AUS 180-181 F 2
Olathe o USA (CO) 254-255 H 5
Olathe o USA (KS) 262-263 M 6
Olavarría o RA 78-79 J 4
Olav V Land ∸ N 84-85 L 3
Olbernhau o D 92-93 M 3
Ólbia o I 100-101 B 4
Ol'čan o RUS 110-111 Y 7
Olcott o USA (NY) 278-279 C 5
Old Andado ∴ AUS 178-179 C 3
Old Bahama Channel ≈ 54-55 F 3
Old Bohemia Church • USA (MD) 280-281 L 4
Old Brahmaputra ~ BD 142-143 G 3
Old Coralie (Ruins) o AUS 174-175 F 6
Old Cork o AUS 178-179 F 2
Old Crow o CDN 20-21 V 3
Old Crow Mount ▲ CDN 20-21 U 3
Old Crow River ~ CDN 20-21 V 3
Old Delamere o AUS 172-173 K 3
Old Dime o USA (TX) 266-267 L 3
Old Dongola • SUD 200-201 E 3
Old Dutch Capital of Biak ⊥ • RI 166-167 J 2
Oldē ~ RUS 110-111 V 5
Oldeani o EAT (ARV) 212-213 E 5
Oldeani ▲ EAT (ARU) 212-213 E 5
Olden o USA (MO) 276-277 D 4
Oldenburg o D 92-93 K 2
Oldenburg (Holstein) o D 92-93 L 1
Olderdalen o N 86-87 K 2
Olderfjord o N 86-87 M 1
Oldest Christian Mission Site • CDN (QUE) 240-241 F 2
Old Factory Bay ≈ 38-39 E 2
Old Faithful o USA (WY) 252-253 H 2
Old Faithful Geyser ∴ USA (WY) 252-253 H 2
Oldfield River ~ AUS 176-177 F 6
Old Ford o USA (NC) 282-283 K 5
Old Forge o USA (NY) 278-279 G 5
Old Fort Benton • USA (MT) 250-251 J 4
Old Fort Dodge ∴ USA (KS) 262-263 G 7
Old Fort Hays • USA (KS) 262-263 G 6
Old Fort Henry • CDN (ONT) 238-239 J 4
Old Fort Massachusetts • USA (MS) 268-269 M 6
Old Fort Parker State Historic Site ∴ USA (TX) 266-267 L 2
Old Fort River ~ CDN 30-31 O 6
Old Ghan Route, The II • AUS 178-179 C 3
Old Glory o USA (TX) 264-265 D 5
Oldham o GB 90-91 F 5
Oldham o USA (SD) 260-261 J 2
Old Harbor o USA 22-23 U 4
Old Harbour o JA 54-55 G 6
Old Herbert Vale o AUS 174-175 E 6
Old Hickory Reservoir < USA (TN) 276-277 J 4
Old Horse Springs o USA (NM) 256-257 G 5
Old Houlka o USA (MS) 268-269 M 2
Old Irontown Ruins • USA (UT) 254-255 B 6
Old Ivy Mine o AUS 178-179 B 1
Old Limbunya o AUS 172-173 J 4
Oldman Creek ~ CDN (ALB) 228-229 R 3
Oldman River ~ CDN (ALB) 232-233 D 6
Old Minto o USA 20-21 Q 4
Old Mkushi o Z 218-219 E 2
Old Numery o AUS 178-179 C 2
Oldoiniyo Orok ▲ EAK 212-213 F 5
Ol Doinyo Lengai ▲ EAT 212-213 E 5
Ol Doinyo Lenkiyio ▲ EAK 212-213 F 3
Ol-Doinyo Sabuk National Park ⊥ EAK 212-213 F 4
Ol'doj ~ RUS 118-119 L 9
Oldon ~ RUS 118-119 F 5
Old Orchard Beach o USA (ME) 278-279 L 5
Old Oyo Game Reserve ⊥ WAN 204-205 F 4
Old Parakylia o AUS 178-179 D 6
Old Perlican o CDN (NFL) 242-243 Q 4
Old Rampart o USA 20-21 U 3
Old River o USA (CA) 248-249 E 4
Old River Lake ○ USA (MS) 268-269 J 5
Öldsijt gol ~ MAU 148-149 D 4
Old Sitka o USA 32-33 C 3
Old Station o USA (CA) 246-247 D 3
Old Stock Exchange • ZA 220-221 K 2
Old Town o USA (FL) 286-287 G 2
Old Town o USA (ME) 278-279 N 4
Old Trap o USA (NC) 282-283 L 4
Olduvai Gorge • EAT 212-213 E 5
Old Village o USA 20-21 N 6
Old Wives Lake ○ CDN (SAS) 232-233 M 5
Old Woman Mountains ▲ USA (CA) 248-249 J 5
Old Woman River ~ USA 20-21 L 5
Olean o USA (NY) 278-279 C 6
O'Leary o CDN (PEI) 240-241 L 4
Oleb o SUD 200-201 H 4
Olecko o PL 92-93 R 1
Oleiros o P 98-99 D 5
Olëkma o RUS (AMR) 118-119 K 7
Olëkma ~ RUS 118-119 K 7
Olëkma ~ RUS 118-119 J 8
Olëkma ~ RUS 118-119 K 8
Olëkma ~ RUS 118-119 H 9
Olëkma ~ RUS 118-119 K 5
Olëkminsk ☆ • RUS 118-119 K 5
Olëkminskij stanovik ▲ RUS 118-119 H 9
Olëkminskij zapovednik ⊥ RUS 118-119 L 6
Olëkmo-Čarskoe nagor'e ▲ RUS 118-119 J 6
Oleksandrivka o UA (KRV) 102-103 H 3
Olendi ~ KA 96-97 H 8
Olenegorsk o RUS 110-111 a 5
Olenëk o RUS (SAH) 110-111 J 5
Olenëk ~ RUS 110-111 M 5
Olenëk ~ RUS 110-111 J 6
Olenëk ~ RUS 110-111 O 3
Olenëk ~ RUS 116-117 N 2
Olenëk, Ust'- o RUS 110-111 M 3
Olenëkskaja, protoka ~ RUS 110-111 O 3
Olenëkskij zaliv ≈ 110-111 M 3
Olenguj ~ RUS 118-119 F 10
Olenguruone o EAK 212-213 E 4
Olenica o RUS 88-89 N 3
Olenij, mys ▲ RUS 108-109 R 5
Olenij, ostrov ⌒ RUS (JAN) 108-109 R 5
Olenij, ostrov ⌒ RUS (KAR) 88-89 N 4
Olenij, ostrov ⌒ RUS (TMR) 108-109 V 4
Olenij, proliv ○ RUS 108-109 S 5
Olenino o RUS 94-95 N 3
Olen'ja ~ RUS 122-123 K 4
Olenogorsk o RUS 88-89 M 2
Olentangy River ~ USA (OH) 280-281 C 3
Ölenti ~ KA 124-125 H 3
Olër ~ RUS 112-113 J 2
Ole Rømer Land ∸ GRØ 26-27 n 6
Oléron, Île d' ⌒ F 90-91 G 9
Olesskyj zamok • UA 102-103 D 2
Oletha o USA (TX) 266-267 L 2
Olevs'k o UA 102-103 E 2
Olex o USA (OR) 244-245 E 5
Ølfjellet ▲ N 86-87 G 3
Ol'ga o RUS 122-123 F 7
Ol'ga ~ RUS 118-119 M 9
Olga(Kata Tjuta), Mount ▲ AUS 176-177 L 2
Ol'ga, mys ▲ RUS 120-121 T 6
Olgastretet ≈ 84-85 N 3
Ölgij ☆ MAU 146-147 J 1
Ölgij = Har-Us o MAU 116-117 F 11
Ol'ginsk o RUS 122-123 E 2
Olgujdah o RUS 118-119 F 4
Olgujdah ~ RUS 118-119 F 3
Olha o CDN (MAN) 234-235 C 4
Olhão o P 98-99 D 6
Olho d'Água do Casado o BR 68-69 K 6
Olhon, ostrov ⌒ RUS 116-117 N 9
Olhovka o RUS 96-97 D 9
Oli ~ DY 204-205 E 3
Oli o WAN 204-205 F 4
Olib ∸ HR 100-101 E 2
Olifants ~ NAM 220-221 D 1
Olifants ~ ZA 218-219 F 6
Olifantshoek o ZA 220-221 F 3
Olifantsrivier ~ ZA 220-221 E 6
Olifantsrivier ~ ZA 220-221 D 6
Olifantsrivier ~ ZA 220-221 J 2
Oliktok Point ▲ USA 20-21 Q 1
Oli Kŭltyk, sor ∸ KA 126-127 K 5
Olimarao ⌒ FSM 13 F 2
Olimar Chico, Río ~ ROU 78-79 M 2
Olimbia o GR 100-101 H 6
Olímpia o BR 72-73 F 6
Ólimpos ▲ GR 100-101 J 4
Olin o USA (TX) 266-267 J 2
Olinalá o MEX 52-53 E 3
Olinda o ··· BR 68-69 L 5
Olindina o BR 68-69 J 7
Olinga o MOC 218-219 J 3
Olio o AUS 178-179 G 1
Oliva o E 98-99 G 5
Oliva o RA 78-79 H 2
Oliva de la Frontera o E 98-99 D 5
Olivares, Cordillera de ▲ RA 76-77 C 6
Olive o USA (MT) 250-251 O 6
Olive Branch o USA (MS) 268-269 L 2
Olivedos o BR 68-69 K 5
Olive Hill o USA (KY) 276-277 M 2
Olivehill o USA (TN) 276-277 G 5
Oliveira o BR 72-73 H 6
Oliveira dos Brejinhos o BR 72-73 J 2
Olivença-a-Nova o ANG 216-217 B 7
Olivenza o E 98-99 D 5
Oliver o CDN (BC) 230-231 K 4
Oliver o USA (GA) 284-285 J 4
Oliver Creek ~ CDN (BC) 230-231 K 2
Oliver Lake ○ CDN 34-35 E 2
Oliver Sound ≈ 24-25 h 4
Oliver Springs o USA (TN) 282-283 C 4
Olivet o USA (SD) 260-261 J 3
Olivia o USA (MN) 270-271 D 6
Olivier Islands ⌒ CDN 20-21 X 2
Ol Joro Orok o EAK 212-213 F 4
Oljoro Wells < EAT 212-213 F 6
Oljutorskij, mys ▲ RUS 112-113 Q 7
Oljutorskij, zaliv ≈ 112-113 O 6
Oljutorskij hrebet ▲ RUS 112-113 Q 6
Oljutorskij poluostrov ⌄ RUS 112-113 Q 6
Ol Keju Ado ~ EAK 212-213 F 5
Olla o USA (LA) 268-269 H 5
Ollagüe o RCH 76-77 C 1
Ollagüe, Volcán ▲ BOL 76-77 C 1
Ollita, Cordillera de ▲ RA 76-77 B 6
Ollita, Paso de la ▲ RCH 76-77 C 5
Olmazor o US 136-137 L 4
Olmedo o E 98-99 E 4
Olmesutye o EAK 212-213 E 4
Olmito o USA (TX) 266-267 K 7
Olmos o PE 64-65 C 4
Olmos Creek, Los ~ USA (TX) 266-267 J 6
Olmütz = Olomouc o CZ 92-93 O 4
Olney o USA (IL) 274-275 K 6
Olney o USA (MD) 280-281 J 4
Olney o USA (MT) 250-251 E 3
Olney o USA (TX) 264-265 F 5
Oloči o RUS 118-119 J 10
Olodio o CI 202-203 G 7
Olofström ☆ S 86-87 G 8
Ologbo Game Reserve ⊥ WAN 204-205 F 5
Ologo, Čapo- o RUS 118-119 J 7
Oloibiri o WAN 204-205 G 6
Oloiserri o EAK 212-213 F 5
Oloitokitok o EAK 212-213 F 5
Oloj ~ RUS 112-113 L 4
Olojčan ~ RUS 112-113 L 3
Olojskij hrebet ▲ RUS 112-113 K 3
Ololdou o SN 202-203 D 2
Olom o RUS 118-119 J 5
Olomane, Rivière ~ CDN (QUE) 242-243 H 2
Olomburi o SOL 184 I e 3
Olomouc o CZ 92-93 O 4
Olonec o RUS 94-95 N 1
Olongapo o RP 160-161 D 5
Olonki o RUS 116-117 L 9
Olorgasailie National Monument • EAK 212-213 F 4
Oloron-Sainte-Marie o • F 90-91 G 10
Olosega Island ⌒ USA 184 V c 2
Olov, gora ▲ RUS 88-89 O 5
Olovjannaja ☆ RUS 118-119 G 10
Olowalu o USA (HI) 288 J 4
Olrik Fjord ≈ 26-27 Q 5
Ol'ša o RUS 94-95 M 4
Olsztyn ☆ • PL 92-93 Q 2
Olsztynek o PL 92-93 Q 2
Olt ~ RO 102-103 D 6
Olt, Drăgănești o RO 102-103 D 5
Olta o RA 76-77 D 6
Olten o CH 92-93 J 5
Oltenița o • RO 102-103 E 5
Oltepesi o EAK 212-213 F 4
Oltinkŭl o US 136-137 F 3
Oltjan ~ RUS 112-113 R 4
Olton o USA (TX) 264-265 B 4
Oltu ☆ TR 128-129 K 2
Oltu Çayı ~ TR 128-129 J 2
Ol Tukai o EAK 212-213 F 5
Oluanpi o RC 156-157 M 6
Oluanpi ▲ RC 156-157 M 6
Oluku o WAN 204-205 F 5
Olu Malua = Three Sisters Islands ⌒ SOL 184 I f 4
Olur ☆ TR 128-129 K 2
Olustee o USA (OK) 264-265 E 4
Olustee Creek ~ USA (FL) 286-287 G 1
Olutange o RP 160-161 E 9
Olutange Island ⌒ RP 160-161 E 9
Olvido, El o CO 60-61 F 6
Ol'vinskij Kamen', gora ▲ RUS 114-115 E 5
Olympia = Ólimpos ▲ GR 100-101 J 4
Olympia ··· GR 100-101 H 6
Olympia ☆ USA (WA) 244-245 C 3
Olympic Dam o AUS 178-179 D 6
Olympic Mountains ▲ USA (WA) 244-245 B 3
Olympic National Park ⊥ ··· USA (WA) 244-245 B 3
Olympic National Park ⊥ ··· USA (WA) 244-245 A 2
Olympos ▲ CY 128-129 E 5
Olympus, Mount ▲ USA (WA) 244-245 B 3
Olynthos • GR 100-101 J 4
Ölzijt o MAU 148-149 E 3
Om' ~ RUS 114-115 N 7
Om' ~ RUS 114-115 Q 6
Ōma o J 152-153 J 4
Oma o RUS (NAO) 88-89 T 3
Oma ~ RUS 88-89 T 3
Oma o USA (MS) 268-269 K 5
Oma o VRC 144-145 D 4
Ōmachi o J 152-153 G 6
Omae-saki ▲ J 152-153 H 7
Ōmagari o J 152-153 J 5
Omagh ☆ • GB 90-91 D 4
Omaha o USA (AL) 284-285 E 4
Omaha o USA (AL) 284-285 E 3
Omaha o USA (AR) 276-277 B 4
Omaha o USA (NE) 262-263 L 3
Omaha Indian Reservation ✗ USA (NE) 262-263 K 2
Omak o USA (WA) 244-245 F 2
Omakau o NZ 182 B 6
Omakwia o GUY 62-63 E 3
Omal ~ RUS 122-123 G 2
Oman, Gulf of ≈ IR 10-11 E 6
Oman = Salṭanat 'Umān ◼ OM 132-133 J 4
Oman Lake ○ CDN (NWT) 30-31 S 4
Oman Lake ○ CDN (SAS) 30-31 Q 6
Omapere o NZ 182 D 1
Omarama o NZ 182 B 6
Omar Combon o SP 212-213 K 2
Omarolluk Sound ≈ 36-37 K 7
Omaruru ☆ NAM 216-217 C 10
Omaruru ~ NAM 216-217 D 10
Omas o PE 64-65 D 8
Ōma-saki ▲ J 152-153 J 4
Omatako ▲ NAM (OKA) 216-217 D 10
Omatako ~ NAM 216-217 F 9
Omate o PE 70-71 B 5
Omati o PNG 183 B 4
Omati River ~ PNG 183 B 4
Omawewozonyanda o NAM 216-217 E 10
Ombabika Bay ○ CDN (ONT) 234-235 P 4
Ombai = Pulau Alor ⌒ RI 166-167 C 6
Ombai, Selat ≈ 166-167 C 6
Ombalantu o NAM 216-217 C 8
Ombella ~ RCA 206-207 D 6
Ombella-Mpoko ◻ RCA 206-207 C 6
Ombos • ET 194-195 F 5
Ombotozu ▲ NAM 216-217 D 10
Omboué o G 210-211 B 4
Ombrone ~ I 100-101 C 3
Ombu o RA 76-77 G 6
Ombues de Lavalle o ROU 78-79 L 2
Ombuku ~ NAM 216-217 B 8
Omčak o RUS 120-121 M 3
Omchi o TCH 198-199 H 2
Omčikandja o RUS 110-111 X 5
Omčug, Ust'- ☆ RUS 120-121 N 3
Omdurman = Umm Durmān o ·· SUD 200-201 F 5
Ōme o J 152-153 H 7
Omega o USA (NM) 256-257 G 4
Omeľdinskij hrebet ▲ RUS 122-123 G 2
Omelič ~ RUS 114-115 Q 5
Omeo o AUS 180-181 J 4
Omer o USA (MI) 272-273 F 3
Ometepe, Isla de ⌒ NIC 52-53 B 6
Ometepec o • MEX 52-53 E 3
Omgon, mys ▲ RUS 120-121 R 5
Omi, Río ~ BOL 70-71 E 3
Ōmi-Hachiman o J 152-153 G 7
Omineca Mountains ▲ CDN 32-33 G 3
Omineca River ~ CDN 32-33 H 4
Ominzatov toglari ▲ US 136-137 H 4
Omiš o • HR 100-101 F 3
Ōmi-shima ⌒ J 152-153 E 7
Omitara o NAM 216-217 E 11
Ōmiya o J 152-153 H 7
Ommaney, Cape ▲ USA 32-33 C 3
Ommanney Bay ≈ 24-25 V 4
Omnial o RI 166-167 E 2
Omnja ~ RUS 120-121 F 4
Ömnögov' ◻ MAU 148-149 F 6
Omoa o • HN 52-53 K 4
Omoku o WAN 204-205 G 6
Omoloj ~ RUS 110-111 S 5
Omolon ~ RUS 112-113 L 4
Omolon ~ RUS 112-113 K 2
Omo National Park ⊥ ETH 208-209 B 5
Omono-gawa ~ J 152-153 J 5
Omoto-gawa ~ J 152-153 J 5
Omo Wenz ~ ETH 208-209 C 5
Ompah o CDN (ONT) 238-239 J 3
Ompupa o ANG 216-217 B 8
Omreľkaj ~ RUS 112-113 Q 2
Omsk ☆ • RUS 124-125 H 1
Omskij o RUS 116-117 L 8
Omsukčan ☆ RUS 112-113 H 5
Omsukčanskij hrebet ▲ RUS 112-113 H 4
Ōmu o J 152-153 K 2
Omu-Aran o WAN 204-205 F 4
Omulevka ~ RUS 110-111 c 7
Omulevka ~ RUS 120-121 M 2
Omulljahskaja guba ≈ 110-111 Z 3
Omuo o WAN 204-205 F 5
Omuramba Ovambo ~ NAM 216-217 D 9
Ōmura-wan ≈ 152-153 C 8
Omurtag o BG 102-103 E 6
Ōmuta o J 152-153 D 8
Omutinskij ☆ RUS 114-115 J 6
Omutninsk ☆ RUS 96-97 H 4
Oña o E 98-99 F 3
Oña o EC 64-65 C 3
Ona ~ RUS 118-119 E 9
Ona ~ RUS 124-125 Q 3
Ona = Birjusa ~ RUS 116-117 G 7
Ona Basin ≃ 6-7 O 9
Onakawana o CDN (ONT) 236-237 G 2
Onakawana River ~ CDN (ONT) 236-237 G 2
Onaman Lake ○ CDN (ONT) 234-235 Q 4
Onamia o USA (MN) 270-271 E 4
Onancock o USA (VA) 280-281 L 6
Onandaga Cave State Park ⊥ USA (MO) 274-275 G 6
Onang o RI 164-165 F 5
Onanga o USA (IL) 274-275 K 4
Onanganjang o RI 162-163 C 3
Onangué, Lac ○ G 210-211 C 4
Onanhasang o RI 162-163 C 4
Onaping Lake ○ CDN (ONT) 238-239 D 2
Onawa o USA (IA) 274-275 B 2
Onaway o USA (MI) 272-273 E 2
Onça, Cachoeira da ~ BR 62-63 G 6
Onça, Corredeira ~ BR 66-67 H 6
Onça, Travessia da ~ BR 68-69 B 4
Onças, Lago das ○ BR 70-71 J 5
Oncativo o RA 76-77 F 6
Oncócua o ANG 216-217 B 8
Onda o E 98-99 G 5
Onda ~ RUS 88-89 M 5
Ondangwa ☆ NAM 216-217 C 8
Ondas, Rio das ~ BR 72-73 H 2
Ondaw o MYA 142-143 J 4
Ondo o WAN 204-205 F 5
Ondo ◻ WAN 204-205 F 5
Ondores o PE 64-65 D 7
Öndörhaan ☆ MAU 148-149 K 4
Ondozero o RUS (KAR) 88-89 M 5
Ondozero ○ RUS (KAR) 88-89 M 5
Onega o RUS 88-89 P 5
Onega ~ RUS 88-89 P 5
Önege o KA 96-97 F 9
One Hundred and Fifty Mile House o CDN (BC) 228-229 N 4
One Hundred Mile House o CDN (BC) 230-231 H 2
Oneida o USA (NY) 278-279 F 5
Oneida o USA (TN) 282-283 C 4
Oneida Indian Reservation ✗ CDN (ONT) 238-239 D 6
Oneida Indian Reservation ✗ USA (WI) 270-271 K 6
Oneida Lake ○ USA (NY) 278-279 F 5
O'Neill o USA (NE) 262-263 H 2
Oneko, ozero ○ RUS 116-117 E 3
Onekotan, ostrov ⌒ RUS 122-123 Q 4
Onema-Okolo o ZRE 210-211 J 5
Onema Ututu o ZRE 210-211 J 5
Onemen, zaliv ≈ 112-113 T 4
Oneonta o USA (AL) 284-285 D 3
Oneonta o USA (NY) 278-279 F 6
Onești o RO 102-103 E 4
Onezhskaya Guba = Onežskaja guba ≈ RUS 88-89 N 4
Onežskaja guba ≈ 88-89 N 4
Onežskij poluostrov ⌄ RUS 88-89 O 4
Onga o G 210-211 E 4

Ongandjera o NAM 216-217 C 8
Ông Cô, Đèo ▲ VN 158-159 K 5
Ongeri o ZRE 210-211 K 6
Ongersrivier ~ ZA 220-221 F 5
Ongi o MAU 148-149 F 5
Ongi gol ~ MAU 148-149 F 4
Ongjin o DVR 150-151 E 9
Ongka o RI 164-165 G 3
Ongkaw o RI 164-165 J 3
Ongkharak o THA 158-159 F 3
Ongniud Qi o VRC 148-149 O 6
Ongoka o ZRE 210-211 L 4
Ongole o IND 140-141 J 3
Ongon o PE 64-65 D 6
Ongon = Havirga o MAU 148-149 L 5
Ongongoro o NAM 216-217 E 10
Ongonyi o RCB 210-211 F 4
Ongoro Gotjari o NAM 216-217 D 11
Onhne o MYA 158-159 D 2
Oni o GE 126-127 E 6
Oni, River ~ WAN 204-205 F 5
Onibe ~ RM 222-223 F 6
Onida o USA (SD) 260-261 F 2
Onie ú Olin, Río ~ RA 80 E 3
Onilahy ~ RM 222-223 G 9
Onin (Fakfak) Peninsula ᴗ RI 166-167 F 3
Onioni o PNG 183 E 6
Onion Lake o CDN (SAS) 232-233 J 2
Onitsha ☆ WAN 204-205 G 5
Onive ~ RM 222-223 E 7
Onkamo o FIN 88-89 L 5
Onkivesi ⊂ FIN 88-89 J 5
Onnekon ~ RUS 118-119 O 6
Onnës o RUS 120-121 D 3
Onnë-Siligir ~ RUS 110-111 J 6
Ono ⌒ FJI 184 III b 3
Ōno o J 152-153 G 7
Onoko o TCH 206-207 B 3
Onomichi o J 152-153 E 7
Onon ~ RUS 118-119 G 10
Onon gol ~ MAU 148-149 K 3
Onor o RUS 122-123 K 3
Onor ~ RUS 122-123 K 3
Onor, gora ▲ RUS 122-123 K 3
Onot ~ RUS 116-117 K 9
Onoto o YV 60-61 J 3
Onoway o CDN (ALB) 232-233 D 2
Onseepkans o ZA 220-221 D 4
Onslow o AUS 172-173 B 6
Onslow Bay ≈ 48-49 K 2
Onslow Bay ≈ USA 282-283 K 6
Ontake-san ▲ J 152-153 G 7
Ontar o VAN 184 II a 2
Ontaratue River ~ CDN 20-21 Z 3
Ontario □ CDN (ONT) 234-235 K 4
Ontario o USA (CA) 248-249 G 5
Ontario o USA (OR) 244-245 H 6
Ontario o USA (WI) 270-271 H 7
Ontario, Lake ⊂ 46-47 J 4
Ontario, Lake ⊂ 278-279 C 5
Ontario Peninsula ᴗ CDN (ONT) 238-239 D 5
Ontmoeting o ZA 220-221 E 3
Ontonagon o USA (MI) 270-271 J 4
Ontonagon River ~ USA (MI) 270-271 J 4
Ontong Java ⌒ SOL 184 I d 1
Ōnuma Quasi National Park ⊥ J 152-153 J 4
Onverwacht ☆ SME 62-63 G 3
Onwul River ~ WAN 204-205 H 5
Onyx o USA (CA) 248-249 F 4
Onyx Cave ∴ USA (AR) 276-277 B 4
Oobagooma o AUS 172-173 G 4
Oodnadatta o AUS 178-179 C 4
Oodnadatta Track II AUS 178-179 C 5
Oodongo o RI 168 D 7
Oodweyne o SP 208-209 G 4
Ookala o USA (HI) 288 K 4
Ooldea Range ▲ AUS 176-177 L 5
Oolloo o AUS 172-173 K 2
Oologah Lake ⊂ USA (OK) 264-265 J 2
Oona River o CDN (BC) 228-229 D 3
Ooratippra o AUS 178-179 D 1
Oorindi o AUS 174-175 F 7
Oos-Londen = East London o• ZA 220-221 H 6
Ooste Lake o CDN (BC) 228-229 H 3
Oostende o• B 92-93 G 3
Oostermoed o ZA 220-221 H 2
Oosterschelde ≈ 92-93 G 3
Ootsa Lake ⊂ CDN (BC) 228-229 J 3
Opachuanau Lake ⊂ CDN 34-35 G 2
Opaka o BG 102-103 E 6
Opal o CDN (ALB) 232-233 E 2
Opal o USA (WY) 252-253 H 5
Opala ~ RUS 122-123 R 2
Opala o ZRE 210-211 K 4
Opalocka o USA (FL) 286-287 J 6
Opang o RI 164-165 K 4
Opari o SUD 212-213 D 2
Oparino o RUS 96-97 F 4
Opasatika o CDN (ONT) 236-237 F 3
Opasatika Lake ⊂ CDN (ONT) 236-237 E 3
Opasatika River ~ CDN (ONT) 236-237 F 2
Opasnyj, mys ▲ RUS (KMC) 120-121 S 7
Opasnyj, mys ▲ RUS (KOR) 120-121 U 3
Opataca, Lac ⊂ CDN (QUE) 236-237 O 2
Opatija o HR 100-101 E 2
Opava o CZ 92-93 O 4
Opawica, Lac ⊂ CDN (QUE) 236-237 N 3
Opelika o USA (AL) 284-285 E 4
Opelousas o USA (LA) 268-269 H 6
Opémisca, Lac ⊂ CDN (QUE) 236-237 O 3
Opémiska, Mount ▲ CDN (QUE) 236-237 O 3
Open Bay ≈ 183 F 3
Open Bay o PNG 183 F 3
Openshaw o CDN (SAS) 232-233 Q 6
Opeongo Lake ⊂ CDN (ONT) 238-239 G 3
Opeta, Lake ⊂ EAU 212-213 E 3
Opheim o USA (MT) 250-251 N 3
Ophir o CDN (ONT) 238-239 B 2
Ophir o USA 20-21 M 5
Ophir, Gunung ▲ RI 162-163 C 4
Ophthalmia Range ▲ AUS 172-173 D 7
Opi o WAN 204-205 G 5
Opichén o MEX 52-53 K 1
Opienge o ZRE 212-213 A 3
Opihikao o USA (HI) 288 L 5
Opikeigen Lake ⊂ CDN (ONT) 234-235 P 3
Opilija ▲ UA 102-103 D 3
Opinaca, Réservoir < CDN 38-39 F 2
Opinaca, Rivière ~ CDN 38-39 G 2
Opinnagau Lake ⊂ CDN 34-35 O 4
Opinnagau River ~ CDN 34-35 P 3
Opiscotéo, Lac ⊂ CDN 38-39 K 2
Opiscotiche, Lac ⊂ CDN 38-39 L 2
Opišn'a o UA 102-103 J 3
Opitsat o CDN (BC) 230-231 D 4
Opobo o WAN 204-205 G 6
Opočka ☆ RUS 94-95 L 3
Opocopa, Lac ⊂ CDN 38-39 L 2
Opoczno o PL 92-93 Q 3
Opole ☆• PL 92-93 O 3
Opopeo o MEX 52-53 D 2
Opornyj o KA 96-97 J 10
Opotiki o NZ 182 F 3
Opp o USA (AL) 284-285 D 5
Oppa-wan ≈ 152-153 J 5
Oppdal ☆ N 86-87 D 5
Opportunity o USA (MT) 250-251 G 5
Opportunity o USA (WA) 244-245 H 3
Opposite Island ⌒ CDN 36-37 H 2
Oppstryn o N 86-87 C 6
Optic Lake o CDN 34-35 F 3
Optima o USA (OK) 264-265 C 2
Optima National Wildlife Refuge ⊥ USA (OK) 264-265 C 2
Optima Reservoir ⊂ USA (OK) 264-265 C 2
Opuka ~ RUS 112-113 R 5
Opuka, laguna ⊂ RUS 112-113 S 6
Opunake o NZ 182 D 3
Opuntia Lake ⊂ CDN (SAS) 232-233 K 4
Opuwo ☆ NAM 216-217 B 9
Oquawka o USA (IL) 274-275 H 4
Oquossoc o USA (ME) 278-279 L 4
Or ~ KA 126-127 N 3
Or' ~ RUS 96-97 L 8
Or, Cape d' ▲ CDN (NS) 240-241 L 5
Ora o PNG 183 F 3
Ora ~ VAN 184 II a 2
Oraba o EAU 212-213 C 2
Oracle o USA (AZ) 256-257 E 6
Oracle Junction o USA (AZ) 256-257 E 6
Oradea ☆• RO 102-103 B 4
Öræfajökull ▲ IS 86-87 e 2
Orah o WAN 204-205 F 5
Orai o IND 138-139 G 7
Oraibi Wash ~ USA (AZ) 256-257 E 3
Oral ☆ KA 96-97 G 8
Oral ~ KA 96-97 G 9
Ora Loma o USA (CA) 248-249 D 3
Orami o PNG 184 I b 2
Oran = Wahrān ☆•• DZ 188-189 L 3
Oranapai o GUY 62-63 E 2
Orange o AUS 180-181 K 2
Orange o• F 90-91 K 9
Orange o USA (TX) 268-269 G 6
Orange o USA (VA) 280-281 H 5
Orange ~ ZA 220-221 D 4
Orange, Cap ▲ F 62-63 J 3
Orange, Port o USA (FL) 286-287 J 2
Orange Bay ≈ CDN 242-243 M 2
Orangeburg o USA (SC) 284-285 K 3
Orange Cay ⌒ BS 54-55 F 2
Orange Cove o USA (CA) 248-249 E 3
Orangedale o CDN (NS) 240-241 O 5
Orange Fan ≃ 9 E 9
Orange Free State = Oranje-Vrystaat □ ZA 220-221 G 4
Orange Grove o USA (TX) 266-267 K 6
Orange Lake ⊂ USA (FL) 286-287 G 2
Orange Park o USA (FL) 286-287 H 1
Orangerie Bay ≈ 183 E 6
Orangeville o CDN (ONT) 238-239 E 5
Orangeville o USA (IL) 274-275 J 2
Orangeville o USA (MI) 272-273 D 5
Orange Walk o BH 52-53 K 2
Orangi ~ EAT 212-213 E 5
Orango, Ilha de ⌒ GNB 202-203 B 4
Orangozinho, Ilha de ⌒ GNB 202-203 C 4
Orangutang, mys ▲ RUS 112-113 R 6
Orania o ZA 220-221 G 4
Oranjefontein o ZA 218-219 D 6
Oranjemund o NAM 220-221 C 4
Oranjerivier ~ ZA 220-221 F 4
Oranjestad ☆ ARU 60-61 F 1
Oranjestad ☆•• NA (NA) 56 D 3
Oranjeville o ZA 220-221 J 3
Oranje Vrystaat □ ZA 220-221 G 4
Oransbari o RI 166-167 H 2
Oranžeri o RUS 126-127 G 5
Orapa o RB 218-219 C 5
Oras o RP 160-161 F 6
Oratia, Mount ▲ USA 22-23 Q 3
Oratorio o RA 76-77 D 2
Orattanādu o IND 140-141 H 5
Orava o PNG 184 I b 2
Oravita o RO 102-103 B 5
Orb ~ F 90-91 J 10
Orbata, Jebel ▲ TN 190-191 G 3
Orbetello o I 100-101 C 3
Órbigo, Río ~ E 98-99 E 3
Orbost o AUS 180-181 K 4
Orcadas o ARK 16 G 32
Orchard o USA (NE) 262-263 H 2
Orchard City o USA (CO) 254-255 H 5
Orchards o USA (WA) 244-245 C 5
Orchard Valley o USA (WY) 252-253 O 5
Orchardville o USA (IL) 274-275 K 6
Orchila, Isla ⌒ YV 60-61 H 2
Orco ~ I 100-101 A 2
Orcococha, Lago ⊂ PE 64-65 E 8
Orcopampa o PE 64-65 F 9
Ord o USA (NE) 262-263 H 3
Ord, Mount ▲ AUS 172-173 G 4
Orda ☆ RUS 96-97 K 5
Orda < TCH 198-199 H 2
Ordale o CDN (SAS) 232-233 M 2
Orderville o USA (UT) 254-255 C 6
Ordes o•• E 98-99 C 3
Ord Mountain ▲ USA (CA) 248-249 H 5
Ordoqui o RA 78-79 J 3
Ordos = Mu Us Shamo ∸ VRC 154-155 E 2
Ord Regeneration Depot o AUS 172-173 J 4
Ord River ~ AUS 172-173 J 4
Ordu ☆ TR 128-129 G 2
Ordubad o AZ 128-129 M 3
Ordway o USA (CO) 254-255 M 5
Ordynskoe ☆ RUS 124-125 M 1
Ordženikidze ☆ KA 124-125 B 2
Ordžonikidze o UA 102-103 J 4
Ordžonikidzeabad = Kofarnihon o TJ 136-137 L 5
Ore o WAN 204-205 F 5
Örebro ☆• S 86-87 G 7
Ore City o USA (TX) 264-265 K 6
Oredež o RUS 94-95 M 2
Oregon o USA (MO) 274-275 C 5
Oregon o USA (OH) 280-281 C 2
Oregon o USA (WI) 274-275 J 2
Oregon □ USA (OR) 244-245 B 7
Oregon Caves National Monument ∴ USA (OR) 244-245 B 8
Oregon City o USA (OR) 244-245 C 5
Oregon Dunes ⊥ USA (OR) 244-245 A 7
Oregon Inlet ≈ USA 282-283 M 5
Orehovo-Zuevo ☆ RUS 94-95 Q 4
Orekhovo-Zuyevo = Orehovo-Zuevo ☆ RUS 94-95 Q 4
Orel o RUS 94-95 P 5
Orel' ~ UA 102-103 J 3
Orel', ozero ⊂ RUS 122-123 H 2
Orellana o PE (AMA) 64-65 C 4
Orellana o PE (LOR) 64-65 E 5
Orellana la Vieja o E 98-99 E 5
Orem o USA (UT) 254-255 D 3
Ören o TR 128-129 B 4
Orenburg ☆ RUS 96-97 J 8
Oreng o RI 162-163 B 2
Orense = Ourense o E 98-99 D 3
Orerokpe o WAN 204-205 F 6
Øresund ≈ 86-87 F 9
Oretown o USA (OR) 244-245 B 5
Orewa o NZ 182 E 2
Orford, Port o USA (OR) 244-245 A 8
Organ o USA (NM) 256-257 J 6
Organabo o F 62-63 H 3
Organ Pipe Cactus National Monument ∴ USA (AZ) 256-257 C 6
Orgeev = Orhei ☆ MD 102-103 F 4
Orgūn o AFG 138-139 B 3
Orhaneli ☆ TR 128-129 C 3
Orhangazi o TR 128-129 C 2
Orhei ☆ MD 102-103 F 4
Orhej = Orhei ☆ MD 102-103 F 4
Orhon o MAU 148-149 G 3
Orhon gol ~ MAU 148-149 F 3
Ori ~ RT 202-203 L 5
Orianda, laguna ⊂ RUS 112-113 U 5
Orica o HN 52-53 L 4
Orichiv o UA 102-103 J 4
Orick o USA (CA) 246-247 A 2
Orient o USA (SD) 260-261 G 2
Orient o USA (WA) 244-245 G 2
Oriental, Cordillera ▲ DOM 54-55 L 5
Oriental, Cordillera ▲ PE 64-65 D 4
Oriental, Llanura ▲ DOM 54-55 L 5
Orient Bay o CDN (ONT) 234-235 P 5
Oriente o RA 78-79 J 5
Oriente, Cachoeira do ~ BR 66-67 E 7
Orient Point o USA (NY) 280-281 O 2
Orihuela o E 98-99 G 5
Orillia o CDN (ONT) 238-239 F 4
Orin o USA (WY) 252-253 N 4
Orinduik o GUY 62-63 D 3
Orinoca o BOL 70-71 D 6
Orinoco, Delta del ≈ 60-61 L 3
Orinoco, Llanos del ∸ 60-61 F 5
Orinoco, Río ~ YV 60-61 J 6
Oriomo o PNG 183 B 5
Orion o CDN (ALB) 232-233 H 6
Orion o USA (AL) 284-285 E 5
Orion o USA (AR) 276-277 C 6
Oriska o USA (ND) 258-259 K 5
Orissa □ IND 142-143 C 5
Orissaare o EST 94-95 H 2
Oristano o• I 100-101 B 5
Orito o CO 64-65 D 1
Orituco o YV 60-61 H 3
Orituco, Río ~ YV 60-61 H 3
Oritupano, Río ~ YV 60-61 K 3
Orivesi o FIN 88-89 H 6
Oriximiná o BR 62-63 G 6
Orizaba o MEX 52-53 F 2
Orizaba, Pico de ▲ MEX 52-53 F 2
Orjahovo o BG 102-103 C 6
Orjen ▲ YU 100-101 G 3
Orjus-Miele ~ RUS 118-119 K 7
Orkadiéré o SN 202-203 D 2
Orkanger o N 86-87 D 5
Örkelljunga o S 86-87 F 8
Orkjule, mys ▲ RUS 110-111 S 4
Orkla ~ N 86-87 D 5
Orkney o CDN (SAS) 232-233 L 6
Orkney o ZA 220-221 H 3
Orkney Islands ⌒ GB 90-91 F 2
Orla o USA (TX) 266-267 D 2
Orlameš o AFG 136-137 K 6
Orland o USA (CA) 246-247 C 4
Orlândia o BR 72-73 G 6
Orlando o• USA (FL) 286-287 H 3
Orleães o BR 74-75 F 7
Orléanais ⌒ F 90-91 H 8
Orléans o F 90-91 H 8
Orleans o USA (IN) 274-275 M 6
Orleans o USA (MA) 278-279 M 7
Orleans o USA (NE) 262-263 G 4
Orléans, Île d' ⌒ CDN (QUE) 240-241 E 4
Orleans Farms o AUS 176-177 G 6
Orle River Game Reserve ⊥ WAN 204-205 G 5
Orlik ☆ RUS 116-117 J 9
Orlinaja gora ▲ RUS 112-113 U 5
Orlinga o RUS 116-117 M 7
Orlinga ~ RUS 116-117 N 8
Orlov Gaj o RUS 96-97 F 8
Orlovka o RUS (NVS) 114-115 O 6
Orlovka ~ RUS 112-113 N 3
Orlovka ~ RUS 112-113 P 4
Orlovka ~ RUS 114-115 T 5
Orlovka ~ RUS 122-123 C 2
Orlovskij o RUS 102-103 N 4
Orlovskij, mys ▲ RUS 88-89 Q 3
Orlovskij hrebet ▲ RUS 112-113 N 3
Orlovskij zaliv ≈ 88-89 Q 3
Orlu o WAN 204-205 G 6
Ormachea, Bosque Petrificado J. • RA 80 F 2
Ormāra o PK 134-135 L 6
Ormāra, Rās ▲ PK 134-135 L 6
Ormea o•• I 100-101 A 2
Ormiston o CDN (SAS) 232-233 N 6
Ormiston Gorge National Park ⊥ AUS 176-177 M 1
Ormoc o RP 160-161 F 7
Ormond Beach o USA (FL) 286-287 H 2
Ormonde Island ⌒ CDN 24-25 e 6
Ormos Almirou ≈ 100-101 K 7
Ormsby o USA (MN) 270-271 D 7
Ormstown o CDN (QUE) 238-239 M 3
Ormtjørn nasjonalpark ⊥ N 86-87 D 6
Orne ~ F 90-91 G 7
Ørnes o N 86-87 F 3
Örnsköldsvik o S 86-87 J 5
Oro, Lac ⊂ RMM 196-197 J 6
Oro, Mesa del ▲ USA (NM) 256-257 H 4
Oro, Museo del • CO 60-61 D 5
Oro, Río de ~ RA 76-77 H 4
Oro, Río del ~ MEX 50-51 G 5
Orobayaya o BOL 70-71 F 3
Oro Blanco o USA (AZ) 256-257 D 7
Orocó o BR 68-69 J 6
Orocue o CO 60-61 F 5
Orodara o BF 202-203 H 4
Orodel o• RO 102-103 C 5
Oroek o RUS 110-111 d 7
Orofino o USA (ID) 250-251 C 5
Orog nuur ⊂ MAU 148-149 E 5
Orogrande o USA (NM) 256-257 J 6
Orol dengizi = Aral teңizi ⊂ 126-127 N 5
Orom o EAU 212-213 D 2
Oromocto o CDN (NB) 240-241 J 5
Oromocto Lake ⊂ CDN (NB) 240-241 J 5
Oron o RUS 118-119 H 7
Oron o WAN 204-205 H 6
Orondo o USA (WA) 244-245 E 3
Oroners Out Station o AUS 174-175 G 4
Oronga o PNG 183 C 3
Orono o USA (ME) 278-279 N 4
Orono o USA (MN) 270-271 E 6
Oronoquerivier ~ GUY 62-63 F 4
Orope o YV 60-61 E 3
Oropesa o• E 98-99 E 5
Oropesa, Río ~ PE 64-65 F 8
Oroqen Zizhiqi o VRC 150-151 D 2
Oroquieta ☆ RP 160-161 E 8
Orós o BR 68-69 J 5
Orós, Açude < BR 68-69 J 5
Orosei o I 100-101 B 4
Orosháza o H 92-93 Q 5
Orosi o USA (CA) 248-249 E 3
Orosmayo, Río de ~ RA 76-77 D 2
Orotina o CR 52-53 B 7
Orotko, ozero ⊂ RUS 110-111 W 4
Orotuk o RUS 120-121 N 2
Orotukan o RUS 120-121 O 2
Orotukan ~ RUS 120-121 O 2
Orovada o USA (NV) 246-247 H 2
Oro Valley o USA (AZ) 256-257 E 6
Oroville o USA (WA) 244-245 F 2
Oroville o• USA (CA) 246-247 D 4
Oroville Reservoir < USA (CA) 246-247 D 4
Oroya, La o PE 64-65 E 7
Orpheus Lake ⊂ CDN 30-31 Q 5
Orquídeas, Parque Nacional las ⊥ CO 60-61 C 4
Orr o USA (MN) 270-271 F 2
Orroroo o AUS 180-181 E 2
Orrville o USA (AL) 284-285 C 4
Orša ☆ BY 94-95 M 4
Orsa o S 86-87 F 6
Orsha = Orša ☆ BY 94-95 M 4
Orsk o RUS 96-97 L 8
Ørstavik ☆ N 86-87 C 5
Ortaca ☆ TR 128-129 C 4
Ortaköy o TR 128-129 F 3
Ortasu ~ KA 124-125 J 5
Orte o I 100-101 D 3
Ortega o CO 60-61 D 6
Ortegal, Cabo ▲ E 98-99 D 3
Orteguaza, Río ~ CO 64-65 E 1
Orthez o F 90-91 G 10
Ortho, Río ~ BOL 70-71 D 2
Ortigueira o BR 74-75 E 5
Ortigueira o E 98-99 D 3
Orting o USA (WA) 244-245 C 3
Ortit o GRØ 28-29 V 4
Ortiz o MEX 50-51 D 3
Ort"jagun ~ RUS 114-115 N 4
Ortler = Örtles ▲ I 100-101 C 1
Ortona o I 100-101 E 3
Orto-Nahara o RUS 118-119 G 5
Ortonville o USA (MI) 272-273 F 5
Ortonville o USA (MN) 270-271 B 5
Orto-Surt o RUS 118-119 M 4
Orto-Tokoj o KS 146-147 C 4
Oru o CO 60-61 E 3
Oruhito o NAM 216-217 B 9
Orulgan, hrebet ▲ RUS 110-111 R 5
Orūmīye ☆• IR 128-129 L 4
Orūmīye, Daryāče-ye ⊂ IR 128-129 L 3
Oruro ☆ BOL 70-71 D 5
Orust ⌒ S 86-87 E 7
Orūzgān o AFG (OR) 134-135 M 2
Orūzgān □ AFG 134-135 L 2
Orvieto o• I 100-101 D 3
Orville Escarpment ▲ ARK 16 F 30
Orwell o USA (OH) 280-281 F 2
Orzūiye o IR 134-135 G 4
Oržycja ~ UA 102-103 H 3
Orzysz o• PL 92-93 Q 2
Oš ☆ KS 136-137 N 4
Os ☆ N 86-87 E 5
Osa ☆ RUS 116-117 L 9
Osa ☆ RUS (PRM) 96-97 J 5
Oša ~ RUS 114-115 M 6
Osa ~ RUS 116-117 M 9
Osa, Peninsula de ᴗ CR 52-53 C 7
Osage o CDN (SAS) 232-233 P 6
Osage o USA (AR) 276-277 B 4
Osage o USA (IA) 274-275 F 1
Osage Beach o USA (MO) 274-275 F 6
Osage City o USA (KS) 262-263 L 6
Osage Fork ~ USA (MO) 276-277 C 3
Osage River ~ USA (MO) 274-275 F 6
Osage River ~ USA (MO) 276-277 A 3
Ōsaka ☆• J 152-153 F 7
Osakarovka o KA 124-125 H 3
Osakarovka = Askarly ☆ KA 124-125 H 3
Ōsaka-wan ≈ 152-153 F 7
Osakis o USA (MN) 270-271 C 5
Osasco o BR 72-73 G 7
Osawatomie o USA (KS) 262-263 M 6
Osborne o CDN (MAN) 234-235 F 5
Osborne o USA (KS) 262-263 H 5
Osburn o USA (ID) 250-251 C 4
Osby o S 86-87 F 8
Osca, Río ~ BOL 70-71 E 5
Oscar o F 62-63 H 4
Oscar II land ∸ N 84-85 H 3
Oscar Soto Máynes o MEX 50-51 F 3
Osceola o USA (AR) 276-277 F 5
Osceola o USA (IA) 274-275 E 3
Osceola o USA (MO) 274-275 E 6
Osceola o USA (NE) 262-263 J 3
Osceola o USA (SD) 260-261 J 2
Osceola o USA (WI) 270-271 F 5
Óschiri o I 100-101 B 4
Oscoda o USA (MI) 272-273 F 3
Oscura o USA (NM) 256-257 J 5
Oscura, Punta ▲ GQ 210-211 B 2
Oscura Peak ▲ USA (NM) 256-257 J 5
Osetr ~ RUS 94-95 Q 4
Osgood o USA (IN) 274-275 N 5
Osh = Oš ☆ KS 136-137 N 4
Oshakati o NAM 216-217 C 8
Oshamambe o J 152-153 J 3
Oshawa o CDN (ONT) 238-239 G 5
Oshetna River ~ USA 20-21 R 5
Oshika-hanto ᴗ J 152-153 J 5
Oshikango o NAM 216-217 C 8
Oshikuku o NAM 216-217 C 8
Ōshima o J (TOK) 152-153 H 7
Ō-shima ⌒ J (KGA) 152-153 C 10
Ōshima ⌒ J (TOK) 152-153 H 7
Ō-shima ⌒ J (YMG) 152-153 E 8
Oshima-hantō ᴗ J 152-153 J 3
Oshivelo o NAM 216-217 D 9
Oshkosh o USA (NE) 262-263 D 3
Oshkosh o USA (WI) 270-271 K 6
Oshun, River ~ WAN 204-205 F 5
Oshwe o ZRE 210-211 G 5
Osiān o IND 138-139 D 6
Osijek ☆• HR 100-101 G 2
Osilinka River ~ CDN 32-33 H 3
Osinniki ☆ RUS 124-125 P 2
Osinovaja, Bol'šaja ~ RUS 112-113 T 3
Osinovka o RUS 116-117 K 7
Osinovo o RUS 88-89 R 5
Osinovoe Pleso o RUS 114-115 T 7
Osinovskij hrebet ▲ RUS 112-113 S 3
Osinovskij porog •• RUS 114-115 U 4
Oskaloosa o USA (IA) 274-275 F 3
Oskaloosa o USA (KS) 262-263 L 5
Oskarshamn ☆ S 86-87 H 8
Oskélanéo o CDN (QUE) 236-237 N 4
Öskemen o KA 124-125 N 4
Os'kino o RUS 102-103 L 2
Os'kino o RUS 116-117 N 5
Oskoba ~ RUS 116-117 K 6
Os'koto, ozero ⊂ RUS 88-89 Y 3
Oskū o IR 128-129 M 4
Osland o CDN (BC) 228-229 D 2
Osler o CDN (SAS) 232-233 M 3
Osljanka, gora ▲ RUS 114-115 E 5
Oslo ★•• N 86-87 E 7
Oslo o USA (MN) 270-271 A 2
Oslofjorden ≈ 86-87 E 7
Osmānābād o IND 138-139 F 10
Osmancık ☆ TR 128-129 F 2
Osmaneli ☆ TR 128-129 D 2
Osmaniye ☆ TR 128-129 G 4
Osmānnagar o IND 138-139 G 10
Os'mino o RUS 94-95 L 2
Ösmo o S 86-87 H 7
Osnabrück o• D 92-93 K 2
Osnaburgh House o CDN (ONT) 234-235 N 3
Ošnūye o• IR 128-129 L 4
Oso o USA (WA) 244-245 D 2
Oso ~ ZRE 212-213 A 4
Oso, El o YV 60-61 J 5
Osogbo o• WAN 204-205 F 5
Osogovski pl. ▲ MK 100-101 J 3
Osório o BR 74-75 E 7
Osório da Fonseca o BR 66-67 H 4
Osorno o E 98-99 E 3
Osorno o RCH 78-79 C 6
Osorno, Volcán ▲ RCH 78-79 C 6
Ososo o WAN 204-205 G 5
Osoyoos o CDN (BC) 230-231 K 4
Osoyoos Indian Reserve ⅄ CDN (BC) 230-231 K 4
Osøyra o N 86-87 B 6
Ospasquia Provincial Park ⊥ CDN 34-35 K 4
Ospika River ~ CDN 32-33 H 3
Ospino o YV 60-61 G 3
Osprey o USA (FL) 286-287 G 4
Osprey Reef ⌒ AUS 174-175 J 3
Ossa ▲ P 98-99 D 5
Ossa, Mount ▲ AUS 180-181 J 6
Ossabaw Island ⌒ USA (GA) 284-285 J 5
Ossabaw Sound ≈ USA 284-285 J 5
Ossa de Montiel o E 98-99 F 5
Ossalinskij krjaž ▲ RUS 110-111 c 7
Osse, River ~ WAN 204-205 F 5
Osséle o RCB 210-211 E 4
Osseo o USA (MN) 270-271 E 5
Osseo o USA (WI) 270-271 G 6
Ossima o PNG 183 A 2
Ossineke o USA (MI) 272-273 F 3
Ossining o USA (NY) 280-281 N 2
Ossokmanuan Lake ⊂ CDN 38-39 M 2
Ossora ☆ RUS 120-121 U 4
Ossora, buhta ⊂ RUS 120-121 U 4
Ostapazifisches Südpolarbecken ≈ 16 G 27
Ostaškin, kamen' • RUS 114-115 T 7
Ostaškov ☆ RUS 94-95 N 3
Östavall o S 86-87 G 5
Østby o N 86-87 E 5
Oste ~ D 92-93 K 2
Ostenfeld o CDN (MAN) 234-235 G 5
Oster ~ RUS 94-95 N 4
Österbotten = Pohjanmaa ∸ FIN 88-89 G 5
Österbybruk o S 86-87 H 6
Østerdalen ᴗ N 86-87 E 6
Östergötland ∸ S 86-87 G 7
Østerø = Eysturoy ⌒ FR 90-91 D 1
Östersund ☆• S 86-87 G 5
Osterwick o CDN (MAN) 234-235 E 5
Ostfriesische Inseln ∸ D 92-93 J 2
Østgrønland = Tunu □ GRØ 26-27 d 8
Östhammar o S 86-87 J 6
Oštinskij Pogost o RUS 94-95 O 1
Ostorinān o IR 134-135 C 1
Ostraja, gora ▲ RUS 112-113 P 5
Ostraja, gora ▲ RUS 122-123 E 6
Ostraja, gora ▲ RUS (KOR) 120-121 T 4
Ostrau = Ostrava o CZ 92-93 P 4
Ostrau = Ostrov nad Oslavou o CZ 92-93 N 4
Ostrava o CZ 92-93 P 4
Ostrjak, gora ▲ RUS 112-113 Q 4
Ostróda o• PL 92-93 P 2
Ostrogožsk o RUS 102-103 L 2
Ostrołęka ☆• PL 92-93 Q 2
Ostrov o RO 102-103 E 5
Ostrov ☆ RUS 94-95 L 3
Ostroveršinnyj hrebet ▲ RUS 112-113 N 4
Ostrovnoe o RUS 112-113 N 2
Ostrovnoe o RUS (ORB) 96-97 K 8
Ostrovnoj, mys ▲ RUS 114-115 M 2
Ostrovnoj, zaliv ⊂ RUS 120-121 Q 3
Ostrovskoe o RUS 94-95 S 3
ostrov Vozroždenija ⌒ US 136-137 F 2
Ostrowiec Świętokrzyski o PL 92-93 Q 3
Ostrów Mazowiecka o PL 92-93 Q 2
Ostrów Wielkopolski ☆• PL 92-93 O 3
Osttirol □ A 92-93 M 5
Ostuni o I 100-101 F 4
Ošturān, Kūh-e ▲ IR 134-135 C 2
Ōst Vank • TR 128-129 J 2
O'Sullivan Lake ⊂ CDN (ONT) 234-235 Q 4
Ōsumi-hantō ᴗ J 152-153 D 9
Ōsumi-kaikyō ≈ 152-153 D 9
Ōsumi-shotō ⌒ J 152-153 D 9
Osuna o E 98-99 E 6
Oswegatchie River ~ USA (NY) 278-279 F 4
Oswego o USA (KS) 262-263 L 7
Oswego o USA (NY) 278-279 E 5
Oswego River ~ USA (NY) 278-279 E 5
Oświęcim o••• PL 92-93 P 3
Ōta o J 152-153 E 7
Otacílio Costa o BR 74-75 E 6
Ōta-gawa ~ J 152-153 E 7
Otago Peninsula ᴗ•• NZ 182 C 6
Otajkačanskij hrebet ▲ RUS 112-113 J 5
Otaki o NZ 182 E 4
Otakwa o RI 166-167 J 4
Otakwa ~ RI 166-167 J 4
Otaru o J 152-153 J 3
Otasawian River ~ CDN (ONT) 236-237 D 2
Otatal, Cerro ▲ MEX 50-51 D 3
Otavalo o• EC 64-65 C 1
Otavi o NAM 216-217 D 9
Otchinjau o ANG 216-217 B 8
OTC International Satellite Earth Station • AUS 176-177 M 5
O.T.Downs o AUS 174-175 C 5
Otelnuk, Lac ⊂ CDN 36-37 P 6
Oterkpolu o GH 202-203 L 6
Otgon Tėngėr ▲ MAU 148-149 C 4
Otha o IND 138-139 C 9
O'the Cherokees, Lake ⊂ USA (OK) 264-265 K 2
Othello o USA (WA) 244-245 F 4
O'the Pines, Lake ⊂ USA (TX) 264-265 K 6
Otherside River ~ CDN 30-31 Q 6
Oti ~ GH 202-203 L 5
Oti o RI 164-165 F 4
Oti, Réserve de l' ⊥ RT 202-203 L 4
Otinolândia o BR 72-73 J 3
Otis o USA (NM) 256-257 L 6
Otish, Monts ▲ CDN 38-39 J 2
Otjikondo o NAM 216-217 C 9
Otjikoto Lake • NAM 216-217 D 9
Otjimbingwe o• NAM 216-217 D 11
Otjinene o NAM 216-217 E 10
Otjinhungwa o NAM 216-217 B 8
Otjisemba o NAM 216-217 D 10
Otjitanda o NAM 216-217 B 8
Otjiwarongo ☆ NAM 216-217 D 10
Otjosondjou ~ NAM 216-217 E 10
Otjosondu o NAM 216-217 D 10
Otmėk, pereval ▲ KS 136-137 N 3
Otoca o PE 64-65 E 9
Otog Qi o VRC 154-155 E 2
Otog Qian Qi o VRC 154-155 E 2
Otoineppu o J 152-153 K 2
Otola o DY 202-203 L 6
Otorohanga o NZ 182 E 3
Otoskwin River ~ CDN (ONT) 234-235 O 3
Otosquen o CDN (SAS) 232-233 R 2
Ōtoyo o J 152-153 E 8
Otra ~ N 86-87 C 7
Otradnaja o RUS 126-127 D 5
Otradnyj o RUS 96-97 G 7
Otranto o I 100-101 G 4
Otranto, Canale d' ≈ 100-101 G 4
Otrožnyj o RUS 112-113 R 4
Otsego o USA (OH) 280-281 E 3
Otsego Lake ⊂ USA (NY) 278-279 G 6
Otselic o USA (NY) 278-279 F 6
Ōtsu ☆ J 152-153 F 7
Ōtsuki o J 152-153 H 7
Otta ~ N 86-87 C 5
Ottappidāram o IND 140-141 H 6
Ottawa ★• CDN (ONT) 238-239 K 3
Ottawa o USA (IL) 274-275 K 3
Ottawa o USA (KS) 262-263 L 6
Ottawa o USA (OH) 280-281 B 2
Ottawa Islands ⌒ CDN 36-37 J 5
Ottawa River ~ CDN (ONT) 238-239 F 2
Otte Krupens Fjord ≈ 28-29 U 5
Ottenby o S 86-87 H 8
Otter o CDN (QUE) 242-243 E 3
Otter o USA (MT) 250-251 N 6
Otter, Peaks of ▲ USA (VA) 280-281 G 6
Otterburne o CDN (MAN) 234-235 G 5
Otter Creek o USA (FL) 286-287 G 2
Otter Creek ~ USA (UT) 254-255 D 5
Otter Creek ~ USA (VT) 278-279 H 5
Otter Creek Reserve ⊂ USA (UT) 254-255 D 5
Otter Head ▲ CDN (ONT) 236-237 B 4
Otter Island ⌒ CDN (ONT) 236-237 B 4
Otter Island ⌒ USA 22-23 L 4
Otter Lake o CDN (QUE) 238-239 J 3
Otter Lake o USA (MI) 272-273 F 4
Otter Lake ⊂ USA (IL) 274-275 J 5
Otterøyane, Von ⌒ N 84-85 M 3
Otter Point ▲ USA 22-23 P 5
Otter Rapids o CDN (ONT) 236-237 G 2
Otter River ~ CDN 34-35 M 4
Otter Rock o USA (OR) 244-245 A 6
Ottertail o USA (MN) 270-271 C 4
Otthon o CDN (SAS) 232-233 Q 4
Otto Fiord ≈ 26-27 F 3
Otto-Sala ~ RUS 110-111 S 7
Ottosdal o ZA 220-221 G 3
Ottoshoop o ZA 220-221 G 2
Ottuk o KS 146-147 C 4
Ottumwa o USA (IA) 274-275 F 3
Otu o CAM 204-205 H 6
Otukamamoan Lake ⊂ CDN (ONT) 234-235 L 6
Otukpa o WAN 204-205 G 5
Otumpa o RA 76-77 F 4
Otuquis, Bañados de ⊂ BOL 70-71 H 6
Otuquis, Río ~ BOL 70-71 H 6
Oturkpo o WAN 204-205 H 5
Otu Tolu Group ⌒ TON 184 IV a 2
Otuzco o PE 64-65 C 5
Otway o USA (OH) 280-281 C 5
Otway, Cape ▲ AUS 180-181 G 5
Otway, Seno ≈ 80 E 6
Otway National Park ⊥ AUS 180-181 G 5
Otwell o USA (AR) 276-277 E 5
Oua ~ G 210-211 D 3
Ouachita, Lake ⊂ USA (AR) 276-277 B 6
Ouachita Mountains ▲ USA (OK) 264-265 J 4
Ouachita River ~ USA (AR) 276-277 C 7
Ouachita River ~ USA (LA) 268-269 J 4
Ouadda o RCA 206-207 F 4
Ouaddaï ⊓ TCH 198-199 K 6
Ouâd Nâga o RIM 196-197 C 6
Ouadou ~ RIM 196-197 E 7
Ouagadougou ★ BF 202-203 K 3
Ouagar, I-n- o RN 198-199 C 4
Ouahabou o BF 202-203 J 4
Ouahigouya ☆ BF 202-203 J 3
Ouaka □ RCA 206-207 E 5
Ouaka ~ RCA 206-207 E 6
Ouaké o DY 202-203 L 5
Oualâta o RIM 196-197 G 6
Oualâta, Dahr ∸ RIM 196-197 G 6
Oualia o RMM 202-203 E 3
Oualla ▲ RG 202-203 E 4
Ouallam o RN 204-205 E 1
Ouana ~ G 210-211 D 4
Ouanary o F 62-63 J 3
Ouanazein < TCH 198-199 H 4
Ouanda Djallé o• RCA 206-207 F 4
Ouandago o RCA 206-207 D 5
Ouandja o RCA (Kot) 206-207 F 4
Ouandja ~ RCA 206-207 F 4
Ouandja-Vakaga, Réserve de faune de la ⊥ RCA 206-207 F 4
Ouando o RCA 206-207 G 6
Ouango o RCA 206-207 E 6
Ouangolodougou o CI 202-203 H 5
Ouaninou o• CI 202-203 G 5
Ouara ~ RCA 206-207 G 6
Ouarak o SN 202-203 B 2
Ouareau, Rivière ~ CDN (QUE) 238-239 M 2
Ouargaye o BF 202-203 L 4
Ouargla ☆• DZ 190-191 E 5
Ouarititoufoulout < RMM 196-197 M 6
Ouarkla o CAM 206-207 B 4
Ouarkziz, Jbel ∸ MA 188-189 F 6
Ouarsenis, Massif de l' ▲ DZ 190-191 C 3
Ouarzazate ☆ MA 188-189 H 5
Ouassa Bamvélé o CAM 204-205 K 6
Ouatagouna o RMM 202-203 L 2
Ouatcha o RN 198-199 D 6
Ouatéré Galafondo o RCA 206-207 D 6
Oubangui ~ RCA 210-211 G 1
Ouchi o VRC 156-157 H 2
Oudâne o• RIM 196-197 E 4
Ouday ~ RIM 196-197 C 4
Oudenaarde o• B 92-93 G 3
Oudjilla o• CAM 206-207 B 3
Oudna • TN 190-191 H 2
Oudtshoorn o ZA 220-221 F 6
Oued el Abiod ~ RIM 196-197 D 6
Oued el Hajar < RMM 196-197 J 5
Oueden Nsa ~ DZ 190-191 D 4
Oued Mimoun ☆ DZ 188-189 L 3
Oued Rhiou o DZ 190-191 C 3
Oued Rhir ∸ DZ 190-191 F 4
Oued Tlelat o DZ 188-189 L 3
Oued-Zem o MA 188-189 H 4
Oued Zenati o DZ 190-191 F 2
Ouéléssébougou o RMM 202-203 G 4
Ouéllé o CI 202-203 H 6

Ouémé ∼ DY 204-205 E 5
Ouémé = Affon ∼ DY 202-203 L 5
Ouenkoro o RMM 202-203 J 3
Ouénou o DY 204-205 E 4
Ouenza o DZ 190-191 G 3
Oué-Oué o DY 204-205 E 4
Ouerrha, Oued ∼ MA 188-189 J 3
Ouessa o BF 202-203 J 4
Ouessant ⌒ F 90-91 E 7
Ouèssè o DY 204-205 E 4
Ouest, Pointe de l' ▲ CDN (QUE) 242-243 D 3
Ouest = West ▫ CAM 204-205 J 6
Ouezzane o MA 188-189 J 3
Oufrane o DZ 190-191 C 6
Ougarou o BF 202-203 L 3
Oughterard = Uachtar Ard o IRL 90-91 C 5
Ougooué ∼ RCB 210-211 D 5
Ouham ▫ RCA 206-207 C 5
Ouham ∼ RCA 206-207 D 5
Ouham-Pendé ▫ RCA 206-207 B 5
Ouidah o• DY 204-205 E 5
Ouidi o RN 198-199 F 5
Ouinardène o RMM 196-197 K 6
Ouinhi o DY 204-205 E 5
Oujâf < RIM 196-197 G 6
Oujda = Ujdah ☆ MA 188-189 L 3
Oujeft o RIM 196-197 D 4
Ou Jiang ∼ VRC 156-157 M 2
Ouka ∼ RCA 206-207 E 5
Oukaimeden o MA 188-189 H 5
Oukal o AFG 134-135 J 2
Oukraal o ZA 220-221 D 7
Oukré < RIM 196-197 E 6
Oula, Madina- o RG 202-203 D 5
Oulad-Teïma o MA 188-189 G 5
Oulainen o FIN 88-89 H 4
Ould Yenjé o RIM 196-197 E 7
Ouled Allenda o DZ 190-191 F 4
Ouled Djellal o DZ 190-191 E 3
Ouled Naïl, Monts de ▲ DZ 190-191 D 3
Ouli o CAM 206-207 B 6
Oulmes o MA 188-189 J 4
Oulnina Hill ▲ AUS 180-181 E 2
Oulo, Mayo ∼ CAM 204-205 K 4
Oulu ☆ FIN 88-89 H 4
Oulu, Bahr ∼ RCA 206-207 F 3
Oulujärvi ∼ FIN 88-89 J 4
Oulujoki ∼ FIN 88-89 H 4
Oum, Bir < TN 190-191 F 4
Oumache o DZ 190-191 E 3
Oumba ∼ G 210-211 C 4
Oum-Chalouba o TCH 198-199 K 5
Oumcheggag < MA 188-189 E 7
Oum Djerane o DZ 190-191 C 3
Oumé ☆ CI 202-203 H 6
Oum el Achar < DZ 188-189 G 6
Oum el Bouaghi ☆ DZ 190-191 F 3
Oum er Rbia, Oued ∼ MA 188-189 J 4
Oum-Hadjer o TCH 198-199 J 6
Oumm Debua, Sebkha ⊂ MA 188-189 E 7
Oumm ed Droûs Guebli, Sebkhet ⊂ RIM 196-197 E 3
Oumm ed Droûs Telli, Sebkhet ⊂ RIM 196-197 E 2
Oumm el Khezz o RIM 196-197 E 6
Ounâne, Bir < RMM 196-197 J 4
Ounane, Djebel ▲ DZ 190-191 F 8
Ounara o MA 188-189 G 5
Ounasjoki ∼ FIN 88-89 H 3
Ounay, Kôtal-e ▲ AFG 138-139 B 2
Oundou ∼ RG 202-203 E 4
Oungre o CDN (SAS) 232-233 P 6
Ounianga Kébir o TCH 198-199 K 3
Ounianga Sérir o TCH 198-199 K 3
Ountivou o RT 202-203 L 6
Ouo o RMM 202-203 J 2
Ouogo o RCA 206-207 C 5
Ouray o USA (CO) 254-255 H 5
Ouray o USA (UT) 254-255 F 3
Oureï < RIM 196-197 G 6
Ouré-Kaba o RG 202-203 E 4
Ourém o BR 68-69 E 2
Ourense (Orense) o E 98-99 D 3
Ouret, Oued ∼ DZ 190-191 G 8
Ouricana, Serra do ▲ BR 72-73 K 3
Ouricuri o BR 68-69 H 5
Ourikéla o RMM 202-203 H 3
Ourilândia o BR 68-69 C 5
Ourinhos o BR 72-73 F 7
Ourini o TCH 198-199 L 4
Ourique o P 98-99 C 6
Ourlal o DZ 190-191 E 3
Ouro, Rio do ∼ BR 72-73 F 2
Ouro Amat o SN 202-203 D 2
Ouro Branco o BR 68-69 H 7
Ourofane o RN 198-199 D 5
Ouro Fino o BR 72-73 G 7
Ouro Prêto o••• BR 72-73 J 6
Ouro Preto, Rio ∼ BR 70-71 E 2
Ouro Preto d'Oeste o BR 70-71 F 2
Ouro Sawabé o RN 202-203 L 3
Ouro Sogui o SN 202-203 D 2
Ourou Rapids ∼ WAN 204-205 F 4
Ouro Velho o BR 68-69 K 5
Oursi o BF 202-203 K 2
Oursi, Mare de ⊂ BF 202-203 K 2
Ous o RUS 114-115 F 4
Ōu-sanmyaku ▲ J 152-153 J 5
Ouse ∼ GB 90-91 G 5
Oushutou o VRC 154-155 L 4
Oussouye o SN 202-203 B 3
Oust, Djebel ▲ DZ 188-189 L 4
Outamba-Kilimbi National Park ⊥ WAL 202-203 D 5
Outaouais ▲ CDN (ONT) 238-239 H 2
Outaouais, River ∼ CDN (ONT) 238-239 K 3
Outaouais, Rivière des ∼ CDN (QUE) 236-237 K 5
Outaouais, Rivière des ∼ CDN (QUE) 236-237 M 5
Outaouais, Rivière des ∼ CDN (QUE) 238-239 G 2
Outardes, Rivière ∼ CDN 38-39 K 4
Outardes, Rivière aux ∼ CDN 38-39 K 3
Outardes Quatre, Réservoir < CDN 38-39 K 3
Outat-Oulad-El-Haj o MA 188-189 K 4
Outeid Arkass < RMM 196-197 H 6
Outeniekwaberge ▲ ZA 220-221 E 6
Outer Bill Bailey Bank = Outer Bailey Bank ≃ 90-91 A 1
Outer Hebrides ⌒ GB 90-91 D 2
Outer Island ⌒ USA (WI) 270-271 H 3
Outfene < RIM 196-197 F 6
Outing o USA (MN) 270-271 E 4
Outjo ☆ NAM 216-217 D 10
Outlet Bay ⊂ CDN 30-31 T 4
Outlook o CDN (SAS) 232-233 L 4
Outlook o USA (MT) 250-251 P 3
Outokumpu o FIN 88-89 K 5
Outoul o DZ 190-191 E 9
Ouzibi ∼ G 210-211 C 5
Ouzoud, Cascades d' ∼•• MA 188-189 H 4
Ouzzeine, Adrar- ⩦ RMM 196-197 L 5
Ovalau ⌒ FJI 184 III b 2
Ovalle o RCH 76-77 B 6
Ovamboland ⩦ NAM 216-217 C 9
Ovan o G 210-211 D 3
Ovana, Cerro ▲ YV 60-61 H 5
Ovando o USA (MT) 250-251 F 4
Ovar o P 98-99 C 4
Ovau Island ⌒ SOL 184 I c 2
Ovcyna, proliv ⊂ RUS 108-109 S 5
Ovejas, Cerro de las ▲ RA 78-79 G 2
Ovejería o RA 78-79 F 3
Oveng o CAM 210-211 D 2
Ovens, The ∴ CDN (NS) 240-241 L 6
Ovens Natural Park ⊥ CDN (NS) 240-241 L 6
Ovens River ∼ AUS 180-181 J 4
Overflowing River o CDN 34-35 F 4
Overflowing River ∼ CDN (SAS) 232-233 R 2
Overgaard o USA (AZ) 256-257 E 4
Øvergård o N 86-87 J 2
Överkalix o S 86-87 L 3
Overlander Roadhouse o AUS 176-177 C 3
Overland Park o USA (KS) 262-263 M 6
Overton o USA (NV) 248-249 K 3
Overton o USA (TX) 264-265 K 6
Övertorneå o• S 86-87 L 3
Överum o S 86-87 H 8
Ovett o USA (MS) 268-269 L 5
Ovgog ∼ RUS 116-117 K 3
Ovid o USA (ID) 252-253 G 4
Ovid o USA (MI) 272-273 E 5
Ovid o USA (NY) 278-279 E 6
Oviedo o DOM 54-55 K 6
Oviedo = Uviéu ☆••• E 98-99 E 3
Övögdij o MAU 148-149 C 3
Övör-Hangaj ▫ MAU 148-149 F 5
Ovražnaja, gora ▲ RUS 108-109 j 3
Øvre Anarjokka nasjonalpark ⊥ N 86-87 M 2
Øvre Dividal nasjonalpark ⊥ N 86-87 J 2
Øvre Pasvik Nasjonalpark ⊥ N 86-87 O 2
Övre Soppero o S 86-87 K 2
Ovruč o UA 102-103 F 2
Ovsjanka o RUS 118-119 N 9
Owaka o NZ 182 B 7
Owalama Range ▲ PNG 183 E 5
Owando ☆ RCB 210-211 E 4
Owa Rafa = Santa Ana Island ⌒ SOL 184 I f 4
Owa Riki = Santa Catalina Island ⌒ SOL 184 I f 4
Owase o J 152-153 G 7
Owatonna o USA (MN) 270-271 E 6
Owdoms o USA (SC) 284-285 J 3
Oweenee, Mount ▲ AUS 174-175 H 6
Owego o USA (NY) 278-279 E 6
Owen o USA (WI) 270-271 H 6
Owen, Islas ⌒ RCH 80 C 5
Owen, River ∼ WAN 204-205 F 5
Owena o WAN 204-205 F 5
Owen Bay o CDN (BC) 230-231 D 3
Owen Channel ≈ CDN 238-239 D 3
Owen Falls Dam < EAU 212-213 D 3
Owen Fracture Zone ≃ 12 D 4
Owens o USA (VA) 280-281 J 5
Owensboro o USA (KY) 276-277 H 3
Owens Lake ⊂ USA (CA) 248-249 G 3
Owen Sound o• CDN (ONT) 238-239 E 4
Owen Sound ≈ CDN 238-239 E 4
Owen Springs o AUS 176-177 M 1
Owens River ∼ USA (CA) 248-249 F 2
Owen Stanley Range ▲ PNG 183 D 5
Owensville o USA (IN) 274-275 L 6
Owensville o USA (MO) 274-275 G 6
Owenton o USA (KY) 276-277 L 2
Owerri ☆ WAN 204-205 G 6
Owikeno Lake ⊂ CDN (BC) 230-231 B 2
Owl Creek o USA (WY) 252-253 K 3
Owl Creek Mountains ▲ USA (WY) 252-253 K 3
Owl River ∼ CDN 32-33 P 4
Owl River ∼ CDN 34-35 K 2
Owo o WAN 204-205 F 5
Owode o WAN 204-205 E 5
Owosso o USA (MI) 272-273 E 4
Owutu o WAN 204-205 G 6
Owyhee o USA (NV) 246-247 J 2
Owyhee, Lake ⊂ USA (OR) 244-245 H 7
Owyhee Ridge ▲ USA (OR) 244-245 H 8
Owyhee River ∼ USA (OR) 244-245 H 7
Oxapampa o PE 64-65 E 7
Oxberry o USA (MS) 268-269 K 3
Oxbow o CDN (SAS) 232-233 Q 6
Oxbow o LS 220-221 J 4
Oxdrift o CDN (ONT) 234-235 L 5
Oxelösund ☆ S 86-87 H 7
Oxenhope Out Station o AUS 178-179 H 1
Oxford o CDN (NS) 240-241 M 5
Oxford o•• GB 90-91 G 6
Oxford o NZ 182 D 5
Oxford o USA (AL) 284-285 E 3
Oxford o USA (AR) 276-277 D 4
Oxford o USA (IN) 274-275 L 4
Oxford o USA (KS) 262-263 J 7
Oxford o USA (MI) 272-273 F 5
Oxford o USA (MS) 268-269 L 2
Oxford o USA (NC) 282-283 J 4
Oxford o USA (NE) 262-263 G 4
Oxford o USA (OH) 280-281 B 4
Oxford o USA (PA) 280-281 L 4
Oxford, Mount ▲ CDN 26-27 O 2
Oxford House o CDN 34-35 J 3
Oxford House Indian Reserve ⚔ CDN 34-35 J 3
Oxford Junction o USA (IA) 274-275 H 3
Oxford Lake ⊂ CDN 34-35 H 3
Oxford Peak ▲ USA (ID) 252-253 F 4
Oxkutzcab o• MEX 52-53 K 1
Oxley o AUS 180-181 H 3
Oxley Highway II AUS 178-179 L 6
Oxnard o USA (CA) 248-249 E 5
Oxville o USA (IL) 274-275 H 5
Oya o MAL 162-163 J 3
Oyabi o RCB 210-211 E 4
Oya-Kannon • J 152-153 H 6
Oyama o CDN (BC) 230-231 K 3
Oyama o J 152-153 H 6
Oyan o G 210-211 C 4
Oyan, River ∼ WAN 204-205 E 4
Oyapok ∼ F 62-63 H 4
Oyarbide, Cerro ▲ RCH 70-71 B 7
Oyem ☆ G 210-211 C 3
Oyen o CDN (ALB) 232-233 H 4
Øyeren ⊂ N 86-87 E 7
Oyé Yeska < TCH 198-199 J 3
Oyo o RCB 210-211 E 4
Oyo o WAN (OYO) 204-205 E 5
Oyo ▫ WAN 204-205 E 5
Oyou Bezzé Denga < RN 198-199 F 4
Oyoué o G 210-211 E 3
Øyrlandsodden ▲ N 84-85 K 4
Oyster Island ⌒ MYA 142-143 H 6
Oysterville o USA (WA) 244-245 A 4
Özalp ☆ TR 128-129 K 3
Ozamiz o RP 160-161 E 8
Ozark o USA (AL) 284-285 E 5
Ozark o USA (AR) 276-277 B 5
Ozark o USA (MO) 276-277 B 3
Ozark National Scenic Riverways ⊥ USA (MO) 276-277 D 3
Ozark Plateau ▲ USA (MO) 276-277 A 4
Ozarks, Lake of the ⊂ USA (MO) 274-275 F 6
Ozark Wonder Cave ∴ USA (MO) 276-277 A 4
Ożarów o PL 92-93 Q 3
Ożen o KA 126-127 K 6
Ozerki o RUS 96-97 E 5
Ozernaja ∼ RUS 108-109 b 2
Ozernaja ∼ RUS 120-121 T 5
Ozërnoe o RUS 120-121 M 2
Ozernoj, mys ▲ RUS 120-121 U 5
Ozernoj, poluostrov ∼ RUS 120-121 U 5
Ozernoj, zaliv ⊂ RUS 120-121 U 5
Ozernovskij o RUS 122-123 R 3
Ozërnyj o RUS 112-113 V 3
Ozerskij o RUS 122-123 K 5
Ozërskoe, Sosnovo ☆ RUS 118-119 E 9
Ozery ☆ RUS 94-95 Q 4
Ozette Indian Reservation ⚔ USA (WA) 244-245 A 3
Ozhiski Lake ⊂ CDN (ONT) 234-235 P 3
Ožidaevo o RUS 122-123 K 5
Ozieri o I 100-101 B 4
Ozimek o PL 92-93 P 3
Ozinki ☆ RUS 96-97 F 8
Ožogina ∼ RUS 110-111 X 6
Ožogino, ozero ⊂ RUS 110-111 a 5
Ozona o USA (TX) 266-267 F 3
Ozondati o NAM 216-217 C 10
Ozone o USA (AR) 276-277 B 5
Ozori o G 210-211 B 4
Ozorków o PL 92-93 P 3
Ozoro o WAN 204-205 G 6
Ōzu o J 152-153 E 8
Ozuluama o MEX 50-51 L 7
Ozurgeti o GE 126-127 E 7

P

Pa o BF 202-203 J 4
Paakitsup Nunaa ⌣ GRØ 28-29 P 2
Paama ▫ VAN 184 II b 3
Paama = Île Pau Uma ⌒ VAN 184 II b 3
Paamiut = Frederikshåb o GRØ 28-29 Q 5
Pa-an o MYA 158-159 D 2
Paanto o RI 164-165 G 4
Paarl o ZA 220-221 D 6
Paauilo o USA (HI) 288 K 4
Pabal o IND 138-139 E 10
Pabbiring, Kepulauan ⌒ RI 164-165 F 6
Pabean o RI 168 B 6
Pabedanâ o• IR 134-135 G 3
Pabellón, El ∴• MEX 52-53 J 3
Pabianice o PL 92-93 P 3
Pablo o USA (MT) 250-251 E 4
Pabna o BD 142-143 F 4
Pabradė o LT 94-95 J 4
Pab Range ▲ PK 134-135 M 5
Pacaás Novos, Parque Nacional de ⊥ BR 70-71 F 2
Pacaás Novos, Rio ∼ BR 70-71 E 2
Pacaás Novos, Serra dos ▲ BR 70-71 E 2
Pacacocha, Rio ∼ PE 64-65 F 8
Pacaembu o BR 72-73 E 6
Pacahuaras, Rio ∼ BOL 70-71 D 2
Pacajá, Rio ∼ BR 68-69 C 3
Pacajás, Rio ∼ BR 68-69 C 3
Pacajazinho, Rio ∼ BR 68-69 C 4
Pacajus o BR 68-69 J 4
Pacapausa o PE 64-65 F 9
Pacaraima, Sierra ▲ YV 60-61 K 5
Pacaraos o PE 64-65 D 7
Pacasmayo o PE 64-65 C 5
Pacatuba o BR 68-69 J 3
Pacaya-Samiria, Reserva Nacional ⊥ PE 64-65 E 4
Pắc Bo o VN 156-157 D 5
Pắc Bó o VN 156-157 D 5
Paccha o EC 64-65 C 3
Pacchani o PE 70-71 C 3
Pacet o RI 168 B 3
Pachacámac o PE (LIM) 64-65 D 8
Pachacámac • PE (LIM) 64-65 D 8
Pachaconas o PE 64-65 F 9
Pachia o PE 70-71 B 5
Pachino o I 100-101 E 6
Pachitea, Río ∼ PE 64-65 E 6
Pacho o CO 60-61 D 5
Pachon, El o RA 76-77 B 6
Pachuca de Soto ☆ MEX 52-53 E 1
Pachuta o USA (MS) 268-269 M 4
Paciá o BR 66-67 E 6
Paciá, Rio ∼ BR 66-67 E 6
Paciencia, Llano de la ⩦ RCH 76-77 C 2
Pacific o CDN (BC) 228-229 F 2
Pacific o USA (MO) 274-275 H 6
Pacifica o USA (CA) 248-249 B 2
Pacific Beach o USA (WA) 244-245 A 3
Pacific Grove o USA (CA) 248-249 C 3
Pacific Highway II AUS 178-179 M 6
Pacific House o USA (CA) 246-247 E 5
Pacific Ocean ≈ 14-15 H 4
Pacific Ranges ▲ CDN (BC) 230-231 B 2
Pacific Rim National Park ⊥ CDN (BC) 230-231 D 5
Pacijan Island ⌒ RP 160-161 F 7
Paciran o RI 168 E 3
Pacitan o RI 168 D 4
Packington o CDN (QUE) 240-241 G 3
Packsaddle o AUS 178-179 F 6
Pack Trail II USA 20-21 K 6
Packwood o USA (WA) 244-245 D 4
Pắc Ma o VN 156-157 C 5
Pacolet o USA (SC) 284-285 J 2
Pacolet River ∼ USA (SC) 284-285 J 2
Pacora o PA 52-53 E 7
Pacoval o BR 66-67 K 4
Pacquet o CDN (NFL) 242-243 N 3
Pac Seng o LAO 156-157 C 6
Pacuária da Barra do Longa o ANG 216-217 B 5
Pacuativa o CO 66-67 B 2
Pacucha, Lago ⊂ PE 64-65 F 8
Pacuí, Rio ∼ BR 72-73 H 4
Pacujá o BR 66-67 B 7
Pacuneiro, Rio ∼ BR 72-73 D 2
Pacutinga, Igarapé ∼ BR 66-67 H 7
Padag o PK 134-135 L 4
Padako o CI 202-203 H 7
Padalere o RI 164-165 H 5
Padam o IND 138-139 F 3
Padamarang, Pulau ⌒ RI 164-165 G 6
Padang ☆ RI 162-163 D 5
Padang, Pulau ⌒ RI 162-163 E 4
Padang, Selat ≈ 162-163 E 4
Padanganget o RI 162-163 E 7
Padangcermin o RI 162-163 F 7
Padangguci o RI 162-163 E 7
Padangpanjang o RI 162-163 D 5
Padang Sidempuan o RI 162-163 C 4
Padang Tikar, Tanjung ▲ RI 162-163 H 5
Padany o RUS 88-89 M 5
Padar, Pulau ⌒ RI 168 D 7
Padas ∼ MAL 160-161 A 10
Padauiri, Rio ∼ BR 66-67 E 2
Padawan o MAL 162-163 J 4
Padawiya o CL 140-141 J 6
Padcaya o BOL (HUQ) 70-71 E 7
Padcaya o BOL (TAR) 76-77 E 1
Paddig o RP 160-161 D 3
Paddington o AUS 180-181 H 2
Paddle River ∼ CDN 32-33 N 4
Paddockwood o CDN (SAS) 232-233 N 2
Padeabesar, Pulau ⌒ RI 164-165 H 5
Paden City o USA (WV) 280-281 F 4
Padeniya o CL 140-141 J 7
Paderborn o•• D 92-93 K 3
Pāderu o IND 142-143 C 6
Padibe o EAU 212-213 D 2
Padilla o BOL 70-71 E 6
Padillas, Los o USA (NM) 256-257 J 4
Padjelanta nationalpark ⊥ S 86-87 H 3
Padlei (abandoned) o CDN 30-31 V 5
Padloping Island ⌒ CDN 28-29 J 3
Padma ∼ BD 142-143 F 4
Padmanābhapuram o IND 140-141 G 6
Padova ☆• I 100-101 C 2
Padrauna o IND 142-143 C 2
Padre, Morro do ▲ BR 72-73 G 4
Padre Angel Buodo o RA 78-79 G 4
Padre Bernardo o BR 72-73 F 3
Padre Isla ⌒ PE 64-65 F 3
Padre Island ⌒ USA (TX) 266-267 K 6
Padre Island National Seashore ⊥ USA (TX) 266-267 K 7
Padre Paraiso o BR 72-73 K 4
Padriya o NEP 144-145 E 7
Padrón o• E 98-99 C 3
Padrone, Cape ▲ ZA 220-221 H 6
Paducah o USA (KY) 276-277 G 3
Paducah o USA (TX) 264-265 D 4
Padun ☆ RUS 114-115 J 6
Padun, Vodopad ∼ RUS 88-89 O 3
Paegam o DVR 150-151 G 7
Paegnyŏngdo ⌒ DVR 150-151 E 9
Paekdu San ▲ DVR 150-151 G 6
Paëlavajaha ∼ RUS 108-109 T 6
Paeroa o NZ 182 E 2
Paestum •• I 100-101 E 4
Paete o RP 160-161 D 5
Paet Point ▲ RP 160-161 F 9
Pafos o••• CY 128-129 E 5
Pafúri o MOC 218-219 F 6
Pafuri ∼ ZA 218-219 F 6
Pafuri Gate o ZA 218-219 F 6
Pag o HR 100-101 E 2
Paga o RI 166-167 B 6
Pagadenbaru o RI 168 B 3
Pagadian ☆ RP 160-161 E 9
Pagadian Bay ≈ 160-161 E 9
Pagai, Kepulauan ⌒ RI 162-163 C 6
Pagai Selatan, Pulau ⌒ RI 162-163 D 6
Pagai Utara, Pulau ⌒ RI 162-163 C 6
Pagalu, Isla de = Annobón ⌒ GQ 210-211 a 3
Pagan o•• MYA 142-143 J 5
Pagani Bay ≈ 212-213 G 6
Paganzo o RA 76-77 D 6
Pagaralam o RI 162-163 E 7
Pagas Divisas o BR 62-63 H 6
Pagassitikós Kólpos ≈ 100-101 J 5
Pagatan o RI 164-165 D 5
Pagawyun o MYA 158-159 E 3
Page o USA (AZ) 256-257 D 2
Page o USA (ND) 258-259 K 4
Page o USA (OK) 264-265 K 4
Pagėgiai o LT 94-95 G 4
Pageland o USA (SC) 284-285 K 2
Pagergunung o RI 162-163 F 6
Pagimana o RI 164-165 H 4
Pagmān o• AFG 138-139 B 2
Pagoh o MAL 162-163 E 3
Pago Pago o USA 184 V b 2
Pagosa Springs o USA (CO) 254-255 H 6
Pagou o BF 202-203 L 3
Pagouda o RT 202-203 L 5
Pagri o VRC 144-145 G 7
Pagutan o RI 168 C 7
Paguyaman o RI 164-165 H 3
Paguyaman ∼ RI 164-165 H 3
Pagwachuan Lake ⊂ CDN (ONT) 236-237 B 3
Pagwachuan River ∼ CDN (ONT) 236-237 C 2
Pagwa River o CDN (ONT) 236-237 C 2
Pagwi o PNG 183 B 3
Pahača ∼ RUS 112-113 P 6
Pahači o RUS 112-113 P 6
Pahačinskij hrebet ▲ RUS 112-113 P 6
Pahala o USA (HI) 288 K 5
Pahang ▫ MAL 162-163 E 3
Pahang ∼ MAL 162-163 E 3
Paharpur ••• BD 142-143 F 3
Pahārpur o PK 138-139 C 3
Pahaska Tepee o USA (WY) 252-253 J 2
Pahiatua o NZ 182 E 4
Pahn Wroal o LB 202-203 F 7
Pahoa o USA (HI) 288 L 5
Pahokee o USA (FL) 286-287 J 5
Pahoturi River ∼ PNG 183 B 5
Pah River ∼ USA 20-21 N 3
Pahrump o USA (NV) 248-249 J 3
Pahsien Cave • RC 156-157 M 5
Pahtaabad o US 136-137 N 4
Pahur o IND 138-139 E 9
Pahute Peak ▲ USA (NV) 246-247 F 2
Pai o THA 142-143 L 6
Pai, River ∼ WAN 204-205 J 4
Paia o USA (HI) 288 J 4
Paicuru, Rio ∼ BR 62-63 H 6
Paide ☆ EST 94-95 J 2
Paiela o PNG 183 B 3
Paige o USA (TX) 266-267 K 3
Paijan o PE 64-65 C 5
Päijänne ⊂ FIN 88-89 H 6
Päijärvi ⊂ FIN 88-89 J 6
Paiko o WAN 204-205 G 4
Pail o PK 138-139 D 3
Paila o MEX 50-51 H 5
Paila, Río ∼ BOL 70-71 F 5
Pailin o K 158-159 G 4
Paillaco o RCH 78-79 C 6
Pailolo Channel ≈ USA 288 J 3
Pailon o BOL 70-71 F 5
Pailou o VRC 148-149 N 7
Paimbu ∼ RUS 116-117 J 5
Paim Filho o BR 74-75 E 6
Paimpol o F 90-91 F 7
Painan o RI 162-163 D 5
Painan, Teluk ≈ 162-163 D 5
Paine o RCH 78-79 D 2
Paineiras o BR 72-73 H 5
Painel o BR 74-75 E 6
Painesville o USA (OH) 280-281 E 2
Paint Creek ∼ USA (OH) 280-281 C 4
Paint Creek Lake < USA (OH) 280-281 C 4
Painted Desert ⩦ USA (AZ) 256-257 D 2
Painted Rock Ranch o USA (CA) 248-249 E 4
Paint Lake ⊂ CDN 34-35 G 3
Paint Lake Provincial Park ⊥ CDN 34-35 H 3
Paint Rock o USA (TX) 266-267 H 2
Paint Rock River ∼ USA (AL) 284-285 D 2
Paintsville o USA (KY) 276-277 N 3
Paipa o CO 60-61 E 5
Paipote o RCH 76-77 B 4
Paipote, Quebrada ∼ RCH 76-77 B 4
Paisano o USA (TX) 266-267 D 3
Paisha o RC 156-157 L 5
Paisley o CDN (ONT) 238-239 D 4
Paisley o GB 90-91 E 4
Paisley o USA (OR) 244-245 E 8
Paita o PE 64-65 B 4
Paita, Bahía de ≈ 64-65 B 4
Paitan, Teluk ≈ 160-161 B 9
Paiton o RI 168 E 3
Pajala o S 86-87 L 3
Pajalele o RI 164-165 F 5
Pajapita o GCA 52-53 H 4
Pajarito o CO 60-61 E 5
Pajaro o CO 60-61 E 2
Pajaros, Islas ⌒ RCH 76-77 B 5
Pajdugina ∼ RUS 114-115 S 5
Pajer, gora ▲ RUS 108-109 L 8
Pajera, ostrov ⌒ RUS 84-85 e 2
Pajeú, Rio ∼ BR 68-69 J 6
Pajonal, Cerro ▲ RCH 76-77 C 1
Pajonales, Salar de ⊂ RCH 76-77 C 3
Pajtug o US 136-137 N 4
Pajule o EAU 212-213 D 2
Pakaá-Nova, Área Indígena ⚔ BR 70-71 E 2
Pakabong o PNG 183 G 2
Pakan o MAL 162-163 J 4
Pakapaka o SME 62-63 G 3
Pakar, Tanjung ▲ RI 164-165 G 6
Pakaraima Mountains ▲ GUY 62-63 D 3
Pakari o NEP 144-145 F 7
Pakashkan Lake ⊂ CDN (ONT) 234-235 N 5
Pak Charang o THA 158-159 G 3
Pakenham o AUS 180-181 H 5
Paki o WAN 204-205 H 3
Pakijangan, Tanjung ▲ RI 168 C 7
Pak Island ⌒ PNG 183 D 2
Pakistan = Pākistān ■ PK 134-135 K 4
Pakokku o MYA 142-143 J 5
Pakowki Lake ⊂ CDN (ALB) 232-233 G 6
Pākpattan o• PK 138-139 D 4
Pākpattan Canal < PK 138-139 D 4
Pak Phanang o THA 158-159 F 6
Pakrac o HR 100-101 F 2
Pakri o NEP 144-145 D 7
Pakruojis ☆•• LT 94-95 H 4
Paksa, mys ▲ RUS 110-111 J 2
Paksa Dinh o LAO 156-157 D 7
Pak Tho o THA 158-159 E 4
Pak Thong Chai o THA 158-159 G 3
Paktikā ▫ AFG 138-139 B 3
Paktyā ▫ AFG 138-139 B 3
Pakuli o RI 164-165 G 4
Pakuliha ∼ RUS 114-115 T 2
Pakwach o EAU 212-213 C 2
Pakwash Lake ⊂ CDN (ONT) 234-235 K 4
Pakxé o•• LAO 158-159 H 3
Pal o SN 196-197 B 7
Pala o TCH 206-207 B 4
Pala o USA (CA) 248-249 G 6
Palabaka o RCB 210-211 E 4
Palace Museum Dalem Loka o• RI 168 C 7
Palace Wolio, Fort ∴• RI 164-165 H 6
Palacio, Gruta del • ROU 78-79 L 2
Palacios o BOL (BEN) 70-71 D 3
Palacios o BOL (BEN) 70-71 E 3
Palacios o RA 76-77 G 6
Palacios o USA (TX) 266-267 L 5
Palacios o YV 60-61 H 3
Palacios, Los o C 54-55 D 3
Palacode o IND 140-141 H 4
palac Perení • UA 102-103 C 3
Palaes o RI 164-165 J 3
Palafoy Ruins ∴• USA (TX) 266-267 H 6
Palafrugell o• E 98-99 J 4
Palagruža ⌒ HR 100-101 F 3
Palahana o IND 142-143 B 3
Pālai o IND 140-141 G 6
Palais, le o F 90-91 F 8
Palaiyam o IND 140-141 H 5
Palala o LB 202-203 F 6
Palala o ZA 220-221 J 2
Palālak o AFG 134-135 K 3
Palamau National Park ⊥ IND 142-143 D 4
Palame o BR 72-73 M 2
Palamea o RI 164-165 K 4
Palamós o E 98-99 J 4
Palana o AUS 180-181 J 5
Palana ☆ RUS 120-121 S 4
Palana ∼ RUS 120-121 T 4
Palanan Bay ≈ 160-161 E 4
Palanga o•• LT 94-95 G 4
Palangān, Kūh-e ▲ IR 134-135 J 3
Palangkaraya ☆ RI 162-163 K 6
Palani o IND 140-141 G 5
Pālanpur o IND 138-139 D 7
Palanro o RI 164-165 F 6
Palanskoe, ozero ⊂ RUS 120-121 T 4
Palantak o PK 134-135 L 5
Palapye o RB 218-219 D 6
Palasa o RI 164-165 G 3
Palasamudram o IND 140-141 G 4
Palasan Island ⌒ RP 160-161 E 5
Palasbari o BD 142-143 F 3
Palašt o IR 136-137 B 7
Palatae o RI 164-165 G 6
Palatka ☆ RUS 120-121 O 3
Palatka o USA (FL) 286-287 H 2
Palau o MEX 50-51 J 4
Palau ⌒ PAL (CRO) 13 E 2
Palauco, Sierra de ▲ RA 78-79 E 3
Palaui Island ⌒ RP 160-161 E 3
Palauk o MYA 158-159 E 4
Palavaamskij hrebet ▲ RUS 112-113 T 2
Palaw o MYA 158-159 E 4
Palawan ⌒ RP 160-161 C 8
Palawan Passage ≈ 160-161 B 8
Palāyankottai o IND 140-141 G 6
Palazzo Farnese • I 100-101 D 3
Palazzolo Acreide o I 100-101 E 6
Palca o PE 64-65 E 7
Palca o RCH 70-71 C 6
Palca, Rio de la ∼ RA 76-77 C 5
Palcamayo o PE 64-65 E 7
Palcazú, Rio ∼ PE 64-65 E 7
Paleisheuwel o ZA 220-221 D 6
Paleleh o RI 164-165 G 3
Paleleh, Pegunungan ▲ RI 164-165 G 3
Palelon o RI 164-165 J 3
Palembang ☆ RI 162-163 F 6
Palena o RCH 78-79 D 7
Palena, Rio ∼ RCH 78-79 C 7
Palencia o• E 98-99 E 3
Palen Lake o USA (CA) 248-249 J 6
Palen Mountains ▲ USA (CA) 248-249 J 6
Palenque o MEX (CHI) 52-53 J 3
Palenque ••• MEX (CHI) 52-53 H 3
Palenque o PA 52-53 E 7
Palenque o YV 60-61 H 3
Palenque, Punta ▲ DOM 54-55 K 5
Paleohóra o GR 100-101 J 7
Paleokastritsa o GR 100-101 G 5
Palermo o CO 60-61 D 5
Palermo o I 100-101 D 5
Palermo o USA (ND) 258-259 E 3
Palesskij radyjacyjna-èkalagičny zapavednik ⚔ BY 94-95 L 6
Palesse ⌣ BY 94-95 J 5
Palestina o BR 72-73 E 6
Palestina o CO 60-61 C 5
Palestina o EC 64-65 C 2
Palestina o RCH 76-77 C 2
Palestina, Cerro ▲ RCH 76-77 C 2
Palestine o USA (AR) 276-277 E 6
Palestine o USA (TX) 268-269 E 5
Palestine, Lake ⊂ USA (TX) 264-265 J 6
Paletwa o MYA 142-143 H 5
Palevo o RUS 122-123 K 3
Pālghar o IND 138-139 D 10
Palghāt o IND 140-141 G 5
Palgrave, Mount ▲ AUS 176-177 C 1
Palha, Rio ∼ BR 70-71 G 2
Palhano, Rio ∼ BR 68-69 J 4
Palheta o BR 66-67 E 4
Pāli o IND 138-139 D 7
Paliaike, Parque Nacional ⊥ RCH 80 F 6
Palian o THA 158-159 E 7
Paliat, Pulau ⌒ RI 168 B 6
Palimbang o RP 160-161 F 9
Palindi o RI 168 E 8
Palisade o USA (CO) 254-255 G 4
Palisade o USA (NE) 262-263 E 4
Palisades Reservoir < USA (ID) 252-253 G 3
Palit o RI 168 E 7
Pālitāna o•• IND 138-139 C 9
Palito, El o YV 60-61 G 2
Palito, Raudal ∼ CO 66-67 B 2
Palizada o MEX 52-53 H 2
Paljavaam ∼ RUS 112-113 T 2
Palk Bay ≈ 140-141 H 6
Pālkonda o IND 142-143 C 6
Palk Strait ≈ 140-141 H 6
Palkül Co ⊂ VRC 144-145 E 6
Palladam o IND 140-141 G 5
Pāl Lahara o IND 142-143 D 5
Pallasa, vulkan ▲ RUS 122-123 P 5
Pallasca o PE 64-65 D 6
Pallas-ja Ounastunturin kansallispuisto ⊥ FIN 88-89 G 2
Pallastunturi ▲•• FIN 88-89 H 2
Pallegama o CL 140-141 J 7
Pallina, Rio ∼ BOL 70-71 C 5
Palling o CDN (BC) 228-229 J 2
Pallisa o EAU 212-213 D 3
Palliser, Cape ▲ NZ 182 E 4
Palliser Bay ≈ 182 E 4
Palliser River ∼ CDN (BC) 230-231 O 3
Palm o USA (AR) 276-277 B 7
Palma o MOC 214-215 L 6
Palma, La o C 54-55 D 3
Palma, La o CO 60-61 D 5
Palma, La ⌒ E 188-189 C 6
Palma, La o MEX (NAY) 50-51 G 6
Palma, La o MEX (TAB) 52-53 J 3
Palma, La ☆ PA 52-53 E 7
Palma, Rio ∼ BR 72-73 G 2
Palmácia o BR 68-69 J 4
Palma del Condado, La o E 98-99 D 6
Palma del Río o E 98-99 E 6
Palma de Mallorca ☆ E 98-99 J 5
Palmales o EC 64-65 B 3
Palmaner o IND 140-141 H 4
Palmar o EC 64-65 B 3
Palmar, El o YV 60-61 L 3
Palmar, Laguna del ⊂ RA 76-77 G 5
Palmar, Parque Nacional el ⊥ RA 76-77 H 6
Palmar, Península El ⌣ MEX 52-53 J 2
Palmar, Represa de < ROU 78-79 L 2
Palmar, Río ∼ YV 60-61 E 2
Palmar, Salto ∼ PY 76-77 H 3
Palmarejo o YV 60-61 F 2
Palmares o BR (BAH) 72-73 L 3
Palmares o BR (PER) 68-69 L 6
Palmar Grande o RA 76-77 J 4
Palmarin o SN 202-203 B 3
Palmarito, La o C 54-55 F 4
Palmarito o YV 60-61 F 4
Palmar Norte o CR 52-53 C 7
Palmarolle o CDN (QUE) 236-237 J 4
Palmas o BR (PAR) 74-75 D 6
Palmas o BR (TOC) 68-69 D 7
Palmas, Barra de ≃ 52-53 F 1
Palmas, Cap ▲ CI 202-203 G 7
Palmas, Las o PE 64-65 E 6
Palmas de Gran Canaria, Las ☆ E 188-189 D 6
Palmas de Monte Alto o BR 72-73 J 3
Palma Sola o RA 76-77 E 2
Palma Soriano o C 54-55 G 4
Pal'matkina ∼ RUS 112-113 P 5
Palm Bay o USA (FL) 286-287 J 3
Palm Cove o AUS 174-175 H 5
Palmdale o USA (CA) 248-249 F 5
Palmdale o USA (FL) 286-287 H 5
Palm Desert o USA (CA) 248-249 H 6
Palmeira o BR 74-75 F 5
Palmeira o CV 202-203 C 5
Palmeira das Missões o BR 74-75 D 6
Palmeira dos Índios o BR 68-69 K 6
Palmeirândia o BR 68-69 F 3
Palmeirante o BR 68-69 E 5
Palmeiras o BR (MIN) 72-73 G 4
Palmeiras o BR (PIA) 68-69 G 5
Palmeiras, Cachoeira ∼ BR 66-67 G 6
Palmeiras, Rio ∼ BR 68-69 E 7
Palmeiras, Rio ∼ BR 72-73 E 3
Palmeiras de Goiás o BR 72-73 F 4
Palmeiras do Javari o BR 64-65 F 4
Palmeirinhas, Ponta das ▲ ANG 216-217 B 4
Palmeirópolis o BR 72-73 F 2
Palmer o ARK 16 G 30
Palmer o CDN (SAS) 232-233 M 6
Palmer o USA 20-21 Q 6
Palmer o USA (TX) 264-265 H 6
Palmer Lake o USA (CO) 254-255 L 4
Palmer River ∼ AUS 174-175 H 5
Palmer River ∼ AUS 176-177 M 2
Palmer River ∼ PNG 183 A 3
Palmers o USA (MN) 270-271 G 4
Palmerston o CDN (ONT) 238-239 E 5
Palmerston o NZ 182 C 6
Palmerston ⌒ NZ 13 L 4
Palmerston, Cape ▲ AUS 178-179 K 1
Palmerston North o NZ 182 E 4
Palmerston Point ▲ CDN 24-25 X 3
Palmerton o USA (PA) 280-281 L 3
Palmerville P.O. o AUS 174-175 H 4
Palmeta, Riacho ∼ RA 76-77 H 4

Palmetto ○ USA (FL) 286-287 G 4
Palmetto ○ USA (GA) 284-285 F 3
Palmetto Point ▲ AG 56 E 3
Palmgrove National Park ⊥ AUS 178-179 K 3
Palm Harbor ○ USA (FL) 286-287 G 3
Palmietfontein ○ ZA 220-221 H 5
Palmillas ○ MEX 50-51 K 6
Palmira ○ CO 60-61 C 6
Palmira ○ EC 64-65 C 3
Palmira ○ RA 78-79 E 2
Palmira ○ YV 60-61 E 3
Palm Islands ⌒ AUS 174-175 J 6
Palmiste ○ RH 54-55 J 4
Palmita, La ○ CO 60-61 D 6
Palmital ○ BR (PAR) 74-75 D 5
Palmital ○ BR (PAU) 72-73 E 7
Palmito, El ○ MEX 50-51 G 5
Palm Springs ○ USA (FL) 286-287 J 5
Palm Springs ○• USA (CA) 248-249 H 6
Palm Tree Creek ~ AUS 178-179 K 3
Palmyra ○ USA (IN) 274-275 M 6
Palmyra ○ USA (MO) 274-275 G 5
Palmyra ○ USA (NY) 278-279 D 5
Palmyra ○ USA (VA) 280-281 H 6
Palmyra = Tadmur ✩••• SYR 128-129 H 5
Palmyra Island ⌒ USA 13 L 2
Palnosiai ○ LT 94-95 H 3
Palo ○ CDN (SAS) 232-233 K 3
Palo ○ RP 160-161 F 7
Palo ○ USA (IA) 274-275 G 2
Palo Alto ○ USA (CA) 248-249 B 2
Palo Alto ○ USA (PA) 280-281 H 4
Palo Blanco ○ RA 76-77 D 4
Palo Duro Canyon ⌵ USA (TX) 264-265 C 4
Palo Duro Canyon State Park ⊥• USA (TX) 264-265 C 4
Palo Duro Creek ~ USA (TX) 264-265 C 2
Palo Flores ○ YV 60-61 F 3
Paloh ○ MAL 162-163 E 3
Paloh ○ RI 162-163 H 4
Paloich ○ SUD 206-207 L 3
Paloma, La ○ ROU 78-79 M 3
Palomares ○ MEX 52-53 G 3
Palomar Mountain ▲ USA (CA) 248-249 H 6
Palomas ○ ROU 76-77 J 6
Palomas, Laguna de ⊖ MEX 50-51 H 4
Palomas, Las ○ USA (NM) 256-257 H 5
Palometillas, Río ~ BOL 70-71 E 5
Palomitas ○ RA 76-77 E 3
Palompon ○ RP 160-161 F 7
Palo Pinto ○ USA (TX) 264-265 F 6
Palo Pinto Creek ~ USA (TX) 264-265 F 6
Palopo ○ RI 164-165 G 5
Palora ○ EC 64-65 D 2
Palos ○ C 54-55 E 3
Palos, Cabo de ▲ E 98-99 G 6
Palos, Los ○ RH 54-55 K 5
Palos Blancos ○ BOL 76-77 F 1
Pološčeľe ○ RUS 88-89 T 4
Palos Verdes ○ USA (CA) 248-249 F 6
Palotina ○ BR 74-75 D 5
Palouse ○ USA (WA) 244-245 H 4
Palouse River ~ USA (WA) 244-245 H 3
Palo Verde ○ USA (CA) 248-249 K 6
Palpa ○ PE 64-65 E 9
Palpalá ○ RA 76-77 E 3
Palparara ○ AUS 178-179 F 3
Palpetu, Tanjung ▲ RI 166-167 D 3
Palpite ○ C 54-55 E 3
Paltamo ○ FIN 88-89 J 4
Paltauto, ozero ⊖ RUS 108-109 O 7
Pältsan ▲ S 86-87 K 2
Palu ✩ RI 164-165 F 4
Palu ✩ TR 128-129 H 3
Palu, Pulau ⌒ RI 168 E 7
Palu, Teluk ≈ 164-165 F 4
Paluan ○ RP 160-161 D 6
Paluga ○ RUS 88-89 S 4
Palumeu ○ SME 62-63 G 4
Palumeu ~ SME 62-63 G 4
Palursoq ≈ 28-29 T 6
Palwal ○ IND 138-139 F 5
Pama ○ BF 202-203 L 4
Pama ~ RCA 206-207 C 6
Pama, Réserve de ⊥ BF 202-203 L 4
Pamamaroo Lake ⊖ AUS 180-181 G 2
Pamana, Pulau ⌒ RI 166-167 B 7
Pamana Besar, Pulau ⌒ RI 166-167 B 6
Pamanukan ○ RI 168 B 3
Pamanukan, Ujung pulau ▲ RI 168 B 3
Pamanzi-Bé ⌒ COM 222-223 D 4
Pamatata ○ RI 164-165 G 6
Pāmban Island ⌒ IND 140-141 H 6
Pambarra ○ MOC 218-219 H 5
Pambauang ○ RI 164-165 F 5
Pambeguwa ○ WAN 204-205 H 3
Pambrun ○ CDN (SAS) 232-233 L 6
Pamdai ○ RI 166-167 J 2
Pamekasan ○ RI 168 E 3
Pameue ○ RI 162-163 B 2
Pameungpeuk ○ RI 168 B 3
Pāmidi ○ IND 140-141 G 3
Pamiers ○ F 90-91 H 10
Pamir ~ TJ 136-137 N 6
Pamirs = Pāmir ⛰ TJ 136-137 M 5
Pamlico River ~ USA (NC) 282-283 L 5
Pamlico Sound ≈ 48-49 K 2
Pamlico Sound ≈ USA 282-283 L 5
Pamolaa Mine • RI 164-165 G 6
Pamoni ○ YV 60-61 J 6
Pampa ○ USA (TX) 264-265 D 3
Pampa, Cerro ▲ RA 76-77 D 4
Pampa, La ○ PE 64-65 D 6
Pampa, La ▫ RA 78-79 F 4
Pampā, Rio ~ BR 72-73 K 4
Pampa Aullagas ○ BOL 70-71 D 6
Pampa Blanca ○ RA 76-77 E 3
Pampachiri ○ PE 64-65 F 9
Pampa de Agnia ○ RA 78-79 E 7
Pampa del Castillo ○ RA 80 F 2
Pampa del Indio ○ RA 76-77 H 4
Pampa del Infierno ○ RA 76-77 G 4
Pampa de los Guanacos ○ RA 76-77 G 4
Pampa de Talagapa ∸ RA 78-79 E 7
Pampa El Toro ○ PE 64-65 B 3
Pampa Galeras, Reserva Nacional ⊥ PE 64-65 E 9
Pampa Grande ○ BOL 70-71 E 6
Pampa Grande ○ RA 76-77 E 3
Pampa Hermosa ○ PE 64-65 E 5
Pampa Húmeda ∸ RA 78-79 H 3
Pampamarca, Río ~ PE 64-65 E 9
Pampanga ~ RP 160-161 D 5
Pampanua ○ RI 164-165 G 6
Pampas ○ PE (ANC) 64-65 D 6
Pampas ○ PE (HUA) 64-65 E 8
Pampas, Río ~ BOL 70-71 F 6
Pampas, Río ~ PE 64-65 F 8
Pampatar ○ YV 60-61 K 2
Pampeiro ○ BR 76-77 K 6
Pampita, La ○ RCH 76-77 B 5
Pamplico ○ USA (SC) 284-285 L 3
Pamplin City ○ USA (VA) 280-281 H 6
Pamplona ○• CO 60-61 E 4
Pamplona ○ RP 160-161 D 3
Pamplona (Iruña) ○•• E 98-99 G 3
Pampoenpoort ○ ZA 220-221 F 5
Pamukkale ••• TR 128-129 C 4
Pamuru ○ IND 140-141 H 3
Pana ○ G 210-211 D 4
Pana ~ RUS 88-89 N 3
Pana ○ USA (IL) 274-275 J 5
Panabá ○ MEX 52-53 K 1
Panabo ○ RP 160-161 F 9
Panaca ○ USA (NV) 248-249 K 2
Panaca Summit ▲ USA (NV) 248-249 K 2
Panache, Lake ⊖ CDN (ONT) 238-239 D 2
Pañacocha ○ EC 64-65 D 2
Panadero ○ PY 76-77 K 2
Panadura ○ CL 140-141 H 7
Panagjurište ○ BG 102-103 D 6
Panagtaran Point ▲ RP 160-161 C 8
Panahaikó ⛰ GR 100-101 H 5
Panaitan, Pulau ⌒ RI 168 A 3
Panaitan, Selat ≈ 168 A 3
Panaji ✩• IND 140-141 E 3
Panakudi ○ IND 140-141 G 6
Panal, Air ≈ RI 162-163 D 3
Panamá ★•• PA 52-53 E 7
Panamá, Bahía de ≈ 52-53 E 7
Panamá, Golfo de ≈ 52-53 E 8
Panama = Panamá ■ PA 52-53 E 7
Panama Canal <•• PA 52-53 E 7
Panama City ○ USA (FL) 286-287 D 1
Panama City Beach ○ USA (FL) 286-287 D 1
Panambi ○ BR 74-75 D 7
Panamericana II•• PE 64-65 B 5
Panamin, Ilha ⌒ BR 66-67 E 4
Panamint Range ⛰ USA (CA) 248-249 G 3
Panamint Springs ○ USA (CA) 248-249 G 3
Panamint Valley ⌵ USA (CA) 248-249 G 3
Panamo ○ YV 60-61 K 4
Pan'an ○ VRC 156-157 M 2
Panao ○ PE 64-65 E 6
Panaon Island ⌒ RP 160-161 F 7
Panarea, Ísola ⌒ I 100-101 E 5
Panarik ○ RI 162-163 H 3
Panaro ~ I 100-101 C 2
Panarukan ○ RI 168 E 3
Panay ⌒ RP 160-161 D 7
Panay ~ RP 160-161 E 7
Panay Gulf ≈ 160-161 E 7
Panban ○ AUS 180-181 G 2
Pancada, Cachoeira ~ BR 66-67 K 6
Pancake Rocks and Blowholes •• NZ 182 C 5
Pancas, Rio ~ BR 72-73 K 5
Pančevo ○• YU 100-101 H 2
Panchane ○ MOC 220-221 L 2
Panchari Bazar ○ BD 142-143 G 4
Pancho Negro ○ EC 64-65 C 3
Pančičev vrh ▲ YU 100-101 H 3
Pançudo ○ BR 62-63 J 6
Pancungapang, Gunung ▲ RI 164-165 D 3
Panda ○ MOC 218-219 H 7
Pandaidori, Kepulauan ⌒ RI 166-167 J 2
Pandale ○ USA (TX) 266-267 F 3
Pandalkudi ○ IND 140-141 H 6
Pandan ○ RP (ANT) 160-161 E 7
Pandan ○ RP (CAT) 160-161 F 5
Pandanan Island ⌒ RP 160-161 B 8
Pandan Bay ≈ 160-161 D 7
Pandang Endau ○ MAL 162-163 E 3
Pandanus ○ AUS 174-175 H 6
Pandattarippu ○ CL 140-141 H 6
Pandaubyin ○ MYA 142-143 J 5
Pāndavapura ○ IND 140-141 G 4
Pan de Azúcar, Cerro ▲ RA 80 F 4
Pan de Azúcar, Parque Nacional ⊥ RCH 76-77 B 4
Pan de Azúcar, Quebrada ~ RCH 76-77 B 4
Pandegelang ○ RI 168 B 3
Pandeiros, Riachão ~ BR 72-73 H 3
Pandėlys ○•• LT 94-95 J 3
Pandhāna ○ IND 138-139 F 9
Pandharpur ○• IND 140-141 F 2
Pandi ○ CO 60-61 D 5
Pandiri ○ RI 164-165 G 4
Pandivalasai ○ IND 140-141 H 6
Pando ○ ROU 78-79 M 3
Pandogari ○ WAN 204-205 G 3
Pandu ○ ZRE 206-207 D 6
Pañe, Lago ⊖ PE 70-71 B 4
Panelão, Paraná do ~ BR 66-67 F 5
Panelas ○ BR (MAT) 66-67 G 7
Panelas ○ BR (PER) 68-69 K 6
Panevėžys ○•• LT 94-95 J 4
Panfilov = Žarkent ○ KA 124-125 M 6
Panfilovcev, zaliv ⊖ RUS 108-109 Z 2
Pang, Daryā-ye ~ AFG 136-137 M 6
Panga ○ ZRE 210-211 L 3
Pangāb ○ AFG 134-135 M 1
Pangai ○ TON 184 IV a 1
Pangaimotu ⌒ TON 184 IV b 1
Pangala ○ RCB 210-211 E 5
Pangandaran ○ RI 168 C 3
Pangani ○ EAT (TAN) 212-213 G 6
Pangani ~ EAT 212-213 F 5
Pangar ~ CAM 204-205 K 6
Pangar Djerem, Réserve ⊥ CAM 204-205 K 5
Pangburn ○ USA (AR) 276-277 D 5
Pangelah ○ RI 164-165 D 5
Pangeo ○ RI 164-165 L 2
Pangertot Peninsula ⌵ CDN 30-31 X 4
Pangga, Tanjung ▲ RI 168 C 7
Panggoe ○ SOL 184 I c 2
Panggul ○ RI 168 D 4
Pangi ○ ZRE 210-211 L 5
Pangia ○ PNG 183 C 4
Pangian ○ RI 164-165 F 4
Pangin ○ IND 142-143 J 1
Pang Kae ○ THA 158-159 F 3
Pangkah, Tanjung ▲ RI 168 E 3
Pangkajene ○ RI (SSE) 164-165 F 5
Pangkajene ○ RI (SSE) 164-165 F 6
Pangkalanbrandan ○ RI 162-163 C 2
Pangkalanduran ○ RI 162-163 E 5
Pangkalanpanduk ○ RI 162-163 E 4
Pangkalansusu ○ RI 162-163 C 2
Pangkalaseang ○ RI 164-165 H 4
Pangkalpinang ○ RI 162-163 G 6
Pangkor, Pulau ⌒ MAL 162-163 D 2
Pang La ○ THA 142-143 L 6
Panglao ○ RP 160-161 E 8
Panglao Island ⌒ RP 160-161 E 8
Pangman ○ CDN (SAS) 232-233 O 6
Pangnirtung ○ CDN 28-29 H 3
Pango ○ PNG 183 G 2
Pangoa ○ PNG 183 A 4
Pango Aluquem ○ ANG 216-217 C 4
Pangonda ○ RCA 206-207 E 5
Pangong Tso ⊖ IND 138-139 G 3
Pangquangou Z.B. ⊥• VRC 154-155 G 3
Pangthang ○ BHT 142-143 G 2
Pangu ○ VRC 150-151 D 1
Pangu, Chutes ~ ZRE 210-211 L 2
Panguipulli ○ RCH 78-79 C 5
Panguipulli, Lago ⊖ RCH 78-79 C 5
Panguitch ○ USA (UT) 254-255 C 6
Panguma ○ WAL 202-203 E 5
Pangururan ○ RI 162-163 C 3
Pangutaran Group ⌒ RP 160-161 D 9
Pangutaran Island ⌒ RP 160-161 D 9
Panhame, Rio ~ MOC 218-219 F 2
Panhandle ○ USA (TX) 264-265 C 3
Paniai, Danau ⊖ RI 166-167 J 3
Pania-Mwanga ○ ZRE 214-215 E 4
Panio Mutombo ○ ZRE 210-211 J 6
Panipat ○ IND 138-139 F 5
Panitan ○ RP 160-161 C 8
Panja ~ RUS 114-115 P 5
Panjang ○ RI 162-163 F 7
Panjang, Pulau ⌒ RI (JBA) 168 B 2
Panjang, Pulau ⌒ RI (MAL) 166-167 F 4
Panjang, Selat ≈ 162-163 E 4
Panjang, Tanjung ▲ RI 164-165 G 3
Panjgūr ○ PK 134-135 L 5
Panjin ○ VRC 150-151 D 7
Panjnad ~ PK 138-139 C 5
Panjpāi ○ PK 134-135 M 4
Pankof, Cape ▲ USA 22-23 P 5
Pankrat'eva, ostrov ⌒ RUS 108-109 H 3
Pankshin ○ WAN 204-205 H 4
Panlong ○ VRC 154-155 E 6
P'anmunjŏm ○ DVR 150-151 F 9
Panna ○ IND 142-143 B 3
Panna Hills ⛰ IND 142-143 B 3
Pannawonica ○ AUS 172-173 C 6
Panne, De ○ B 92-93 G 3
Panngi ○ VAN 184 II b 2
Panny River ~ CDN 32-33 N 3
Panora ○ USA (IA) 274-275 D 3
Panorama ○ BR 72-73 E 6
Panshan • VRC 154-155 L 1
Panshanu-Pass ▲ WAN 204-205 H 3
Panshi ○ VRC 150-151 F 6
Panshi Ju ⌒ VRC 158-159 L 2
Pansian ○ RP 160-161 D 3
Pānskura ○ IND 142-143 E 4
Pantai ○ RI 164-165 E 5
Pantai Remis ○ MAL 162-163 D 2
Pantanal, Igarapé ~ BR 66-67 J 6
Pantanal Matogrossense ⌵• BR 70-71 J 5
Pantanal Matogrossense, Parque Nacional do ⊥ BR 70-71 J 5
Pântano do Sul ○ BR 74-75 F 6
Pântano Grande ○ BR 74-75 D 8
Pantasma ○ NIC 52-53 B 5
Pantekra ○ RI 162-163 B 2
Pantelleria ○ I 100-101 C 6
Pantelleria, Ísola di ⌒ I 100-101 D 6
Pantemakassar ○ RI 166-167 C 6
Panteraja ○ RI 162-163 B 2
Pantha ○ MYA 142-143 J 4
Panti ○ RI (SUB) 162-163 D 4
Panti ⊥• RI (MAL) 166-167 E 4
Pantoja ○ PE 64-65 E 2
Pantonbili ○ RI 162-163 B 2
Pantu ○ MAL 162-163 J 4
Pantukan ○ RP 160-161 F 9
Panu ○ ZRE 210-211 G 5
Pánuco ○• MEX 50-51 K 6
Pánuco, Río ~ MEX 50-51 K 7
Pan Xian ○ VRC 156-157 D 4
Panyabungan ○ RI 162-163 C 4
Panyam ○ WAN 204-205 H 4
Panyčevo ○ RUS 114-115 Q 6
Panyikleang, Pulau ⌒ RI 164-165 F 5
Panzakent ✩• TJ 136-137 K 5
Panzarani ○ CI 202-203 J 5
Panzhihua ○ VRC 156-157 B 3
Panzi ○ ZRE 216-217 D 3
Panzós ○ GCA 52-53 K 4
Pao, El ○ YV 60-61 K 3
Pao, Río ~ YV 60-61 G 3
Pão de Açucar ○ BR 68-69 K 6
Pao de La Fortuna, El ○ YV 60-61 K 4
Páola ○ I 100-101 F 5
Paola ○ USA (KS) 262-263 M 6
Paoli ○ USA (IN) 274-275 M 6
Paoli ○ USA (OK) 264-265 G 4
Paoni ○ RI 166-167 E 3
Paonia ○ USA (CO) 254-255 H 5
Paoua ○ RCA 206-207 C 5
Paouignan ○ DY 204-205 E 5
Pap ○ US 136-137 M 4
Pápa ○ H 92-93 O 5
Papa ○ USA (HI) 288 K 5
Papadiánika ○ GR 100-101 J 6
Papagaio ○ BR 68-69 F 5
Papagaio, Rio ~ BR 66-67 F 4
Papagaios ○ BR 72-73 H 5
Papagayo, Golfo de ≈ 52-53 B 6
Papagayo, Río ~ MEX 52-53 E 3
Pāpāgni ~ IND 140-141 G 4
Papagni ~ IND 140-141 H 3
Papago Indian Reservation ⚔ USA (AZ) 256-257 C 6
Papaikou ○ USA (HI) 288 K 5
Papakura ○ NZ 182 E 2
Papalote ○ USA (TX) 266-267 K 5
Papantla de Olarte ○ MEX 52-53 F 1
Papar ○ MAL 160-161 A 10
Paparoa National Park ⊥ NZ 182 C 5
Papeete ✩ F 13 N 4
Papel, Embalse < RCH 78-79 D 2
Papela ○ RI 166-167 B 7
Papera ○ BR 66-67 E 3
Papey ⌒ IS 86-87 f 2
Papialou Island ⌒ PNG 183 D 2
Papigochic, Río ~ MEX 50-51 E 3
Papillion ○ USA (NE) 262-263 K 3
Papisoi, Tanjung ▲ RI 166-167 G 4
Paporotno ○ RUS 94-95 M 2
Paposa ○ RCH 76-77 B 3
Papua, Gulf of ≈ 183 C 5
Papua New Guinea ■ PNG 183 B 4
Papuk ▲ HR 100-101 F 2
Papun ○ MYA 142-143 K 6
Papunáua, Río ~ CO 60-61 F 7
Papunya ⚔ AUS 176-177 L 1
Papurí ○ CO 66-67 C 2
Paqiu ○ SUD 206-207 K 5
Paquera ○ CR 52-53 B 7
Paquetville ○ CDN (NB) 240-241 K 3
Paquica, Cabo ▲ RCH 76-77 B 1
Paquiçama ○ BR 68-69 C 3
Paquisha ○ EC 64-65 C 3
Pará ▫ BR 68-69 B 3
Pará, Ilha do ⌒ BR 62-63 J 6
Pará, Rio ~ BR 62-63 K 6
Para, Rio ~ BR 72-73 H 5
Para, Rio ~ BR 72-73 H 6
Parabel' ○ RUS 114-115 Q 5
Parabel' ~ RUS 114-115 Q 5
Parabubure, Área Indígena ⚔ BR 72-73 D 3
Paraburdoo ○ AUS 176-177 D 1
Paracale ○ RP 160-161 E 5
Paracambi ○ BR 72-73 J 7
Paracanã, Área Indígena ⚔ BR 68-69 C 4
Paracas ○ PE 64-65 D 8
Paracas, Bahía de ≈ 64-65 D 8
Paracas, Península de ⌵ PE 64-65 D 8
Paracas, Punta ▲ PE 64-65 D 8
Paracas, Reserva Nacional ⊥ PE 64-65 D 9
Paracatu ○ BR 72-73 G 4
Paracatu, Rio ~ BR 72-73 G 4
Paracauti, Rio ~ BR 62-63 K 6
Parachilna ○ AUS 178-179 E 6
Pārachinār ○ PK 138-139 C 3
Parachute ○ USA (CO) 254-255 G 4
Paraćin ○ YU 100-101 H 3
Paraconi, Rio ~ BR 66-67 H 4
Paracuaro ○ MEX 52-53 C 2
Paracuru ○ BR 68-69 J 3
Parada ○ BR 68-69 C 3
Parade ○ USA (SD) 260-261 E 1
Pará de Minas ○ BR 72-73 H 5
Paradero ○ YV (ANZ) 60-61 J 3
Paradero ○ YV (SUC) 60-61 K 2
Paradise ○ CDN (NFL) 242-243 P 4
Paradise ○ USA (CA) 246-247 D 4
Paradise ○ USA (KS) 262-263 H 5
Paradise ○ USA (MI) 270-271 N 4
Paradise ○ USA (NV) 248-249 J 3
Paradise ○ USA (UT) 254-255 D 2
Paradise Hill ○ CDN (SAS) 232-233 J 2
Paradise Hill Pass ▲ USA (NV) 246-247 H 2
Paradise Island ⌒ BS 54-55 G 2
Paradise Valley ○ USA (NV) 246-247 H 2
Parado ○ RI 168 D 7
Parado, Rio ~ BR 70-71 K 2
Pará do Uruará ~ BR 68-69 B 3
Paradox ○ USA (CO) 254-255 G 5
Paradwip ○ IND 142-143 E 5
Paragominas ○ BR 68-69 E 3
Paragould ○ USA (AR) 276-277 E 4
Paragua, La ○ YV 60-61 K 4
Paragua, Reserva Forestal La ⊥ YV 60-61 K 4
Paraguá, Río ~ BOL 70-71 G 4
Paragua, Río ~ YV 60-61 K 5
Paraguaçu, Rio ~ BR 72-73 K 2
Paraguaçu Paulista ○ BR 72-73 E 7
Paraguai, Rio ~ BR 70-71 J 5
Paraguaipoa ○ YV 60-61 F 2
Paraguana, Península de ⌵ YV 60-61 F 1
Paraguarí ○ PY 76-77 J 3
Paraguassú, Área Indígena ⚔ BR 72-73 L 3
Paraguay ■ PY 76-77 G 2
Paraguay, Riacho ~ PY 76-77 H 2
Paraguay, Río ~ PY 76-77 J 3
Paraíba ▫ BR 68-69 J 5
Paraíba, Rio ~ BR 68-69 L 5
Paraibuna ○ BR 72-73 H 7
Paraibuna, Represa < BR 72-73 H 7
Parainen ○ FIN 88-89 G 6
Paraíso ○ BR (AMA) 66-67 B 5
Paraíso ○ BR (AMA) 66-67 H 6
Paraíso ○ BR (GSU) 72-73 D 5
Paraíso ○ BR (RSU) 76-77 K 6
Paraíso ○ CR 52-53 C 7
Paraíso ○• MEX 52-53 H 2
Paraíso, El ○ BOL 70-71 G 4
Paraíso, El ○ CO 60-61 E 3
Paraíso, El ○ HN 52-53 L 5
Paraíso, Ilhas do ⌒ MOC 218-219 H 5
Paraíso, Río ~ BOL 70-71 G 4
Paraíso do Leste ○ BR 70-71 K 5
Paraíso do Norte ○ BR 72-73 D 7
Paraíso do Tocantins ○ BR 68-69 D 7
Paraisópolis ○ BR 72-73 H 7
Pārak ○ IR 134-135 J 6
Parakan ○ RI 168 D 3
Parakao ○ NZ 182 D 1
Parakou ✩ DY 204-205 E 4
Paralia ○ GR 100-101 J 6
Paraltinga, Rio ~ BR 72-73 H 7
Parama Island ⌒ PNG 183 B 5
Paramakkudi ○ IND 140-141 H 6
Paramaribo ★ SME 62-63 G 3
Parambu ○ BR 68-69 H 5
Parambul ○ IND 140-141 F 4
Paramé, Lac ⊖ CDN 38-39 P 3
Paramillo, Parque Nacional ⊥ CO 60-61 C 4
Paramirim ○ BR 72-73 J 2
Parámirim, Rio ~ BR 68-69 G 7
Páramo Frontino ▲ CO 60-61 C 4
Paramonga • PE 64-65 D 7
Paramušir, ostrov ⌒ RUS 122-123 Q 3
Paran ○ RI 164-165 D 5
Paran, Nāal ~ IL 130-131 D 2
Paraná ○ BR 72-73 G 2
Paraná ▫ BR 74-75 D 5
Paraná ✩• RA 76-77 G 6
Paraná, Delta del ~ RA 78-79 K 3
Paraná, Rio ~ BR 68-69 F 3
Paraná, Rio ~ BR 72-73 G 2
Paraná, Rio ~ BR 72-73 D 7
Paraná, Río ~ RA 76-77 H 4
Paraná Bravo, Río ~ RA 78-79 K 2
Paranacito, Río ~ RA 78-79 K 2
Paraná de Jacumpa ~ BR 66-67 C 4
Paraná do Ouro ~ BR 66-67 B 7
Paraná do Ramos ~ BR 66-67 J 4
Paranaguá ○ BR 74-75 F 5
Paranaguá, Baía de ≈ 74-75 F 5
Paraná Guazu, Río ~ RA 78-79 K 2
Paranaíba ○ BR 72-73 E 5
Paranaíba, Rio ~ BR 68-69 B 7
Paranaíba, Rio ~ BR 72-73 E 5
Paraná Ibicuy, Río ~ RA 78-79 K 2
Paranaiguara ○ BR 72-73 E 5
Paranaita ○ BR 66-67 J 7
Paraná Juca ○ BR 66-67 C 2
Paranal ○ RCH 76-77 B 3
Paranam ○ SME 62-63 G 3
Paraná Mini, Río ~ RA 76-77 H 5
Paraná Panapuã ~ BR 66-67 E 4
Paranapanema, Rio ~ BR 72-73 D 7
Paranapebas ○ BR 68-69 D 5
Paraná Piacaba, Serra ⛰ BR 74-75 F 5
Paranaquara, Serra ⛰ BR 62-63 H 6
Paranatinga ○ BR 70-71 K 4
Paranatinga, Rio ~ BR 70-71 K 4
Paranavaí ○ BR 72-73 D 7
Parandak ○ IR 136-137 B 7
Parang ○ RP (MAG) 160-161 F 9
Parang ○ RP (SUL) 160-161 D 10
Parang, Pulau ⌒ RI 166-167 F 3
Paranga ○ EAU 212-213 D 2
Paran'ga ○ RUS 96-97 F 5
Parangaíba, Rio ~ BR 72-73 G 5
Parantan ○ CL 140-141 J 6
Parao, Arroyo del ~ ROU 78-79 M 2
Paraopeba ○ BR 72-73 H 5
Paraopeba, Rio ~ BR 72-73 H 5
Paraparaumu ○ NZ 182 E 4
Parapetí, Río ~ BOL 70-71 F 6
Parapol'skij Dol, ravnina ⌵ RUS 120-121 U 3
Parapuã ○ BR 72-73 E 6
Parara = Vonavona ⌒ SOL 184 I c 3
Pará Ridge ≃ 62-63 K 3
Parás ○ MEX 50-51 K 4
Paras ○ PE 64-65 E 8
Parasi ○ NEP 144-145 D 7
Paraso ○ SOL 184 I c 2
Parata, Pointe de la ▲ F 98-99 M 4
Paratebueno ○ CO 60-61 E 5
Parateca ○ BR 72-73 J 2
Parati ○•• BR 72-73 H 7
Paratinga ○ BR 72-73 J 2
Paratoo ○ AUS 180-181 E 2
Paratunka ○ RUS 120-121 S 7
Parauapebas, Rio ~ BR 68-69 C 5
Parauari, Rio ~ BR 66-67 J 5
Paraúna ○ BR 72-73 E 4
Paravur ○ IND 140-141 G 6
Paray-le-Monial ○• F 90-91 K 8
Paray Tepuy ○ YV 62-63 D 3
Parazinho ○ BR 68-69 L 4
Pārbati ~ IND 138-139 F 7
Parbatipur ○ BD 142-143 F 3
Parbhani ○ IND 138-139 F 10
Parbig ~ RUS 114-115 Q 6
Parc du Mont Tremblant ⊥ CDN (QUE) 238-239 L 2
Parc Gatineau ⊥ CDN (QUE) 238-239 J 3
Parc National de la Mauricie ⊥ CDN (QUE) 238-239 M 2
Parc Naturel Régional d'Armorique ⊥ F 90-91 F 7
Parc Naturel Régional de Brière ⊥ F 90-91 F 8
Parc Naturel Régional de Brotonne ⊥ F 90-91 H 7
Parc Naturel Régional de Camargue ⊥• F 90-91 K 10
Parc Naturel Régional de la Corse ⊥ F 98-99 M 3
Parc Naturel Régional du Marais Potevin Val de Sèvre et ⊥ F 90-91 G 8
Parcoy ○ PE 64-65 D 5
Parc Provincial de Forestville ⊥ CDN 38-39 K 4
Parc Provincial de Mistassini ⊥ CDN 38-39 H 3
Parc Provincial de Port Cartier Sept-Îles ⊥ CDN (QUE) 242-243 B 2
Parc Provincial des Laurentides ⊥ CDN (QUE) 240-241 D 3
Parc Provincial du Frontenac ⊥ CDN (QUE) 238-239 O 3
Parc Régional des Landes de Gascogne ⊥ F 90-91 G 9
Parc Régional des Volcans d'Auvergne ⊥ F 90-91 J 9
Parc Régional du Luberon ⊥ F 90-91 K 10
Parc Régional du Morvan ⊥ F 90-91 J 8
Parc Régional du Vercors ⊥ F 90-91 K 9
Parczew ○ PL 92-93 R 3
Pardi ○ IND 138-139 D 9
Pardillal ○ YV (ANZ) 60-61 J 3
Pardillal ○ YV (ARA) 60-61 H 3
Pardo, Rio ~ BR 64-65 F 4
Pardo, Rio ~ BR 68-69 B 4
Pardo, Rio ~ BR 70-71 F 2
Pardo, Rio ~ BR 72-73 K 3
Pardo, Rio ~ BR 72-73 D 6
Pardo, Rio ~ BR 72-73 F 6
Pardoo Roadhouse ○ AUS 172-173 D 6
Pardubice ○ CZ 92-93 N 3
Pardubitz = Pardubice ○•• CZ 92-93 N 3
Pare ○ RI 168 E 3
Parece Vela Basin ≃ 14-15 F 6
Parecis ○ BR 70-71 J 4
Parecis, Chapada dos ⛰ BR 70-71 F 2
Parecis, Rio ~ BR 70-71 J 3
Paredão de Minas ○ BR 72-73 H 4
Pareditas ○ RA 78-79 E 2
Paredón ○• MEX 52-53 H 3
Paren' ○ RUS (KOR) 112-113 M 5
Paren' ~ RUS 112-113 M 5
Paren' ~ RUS 112-113 L 5
Paren', Verhnij ○ RUS 112-113 M 5
Parenda ○ IND 138-139 E 10
Pareng ○ IND 142-143 J 1
Paren'skoe, ozero ⊖ RUS 112-113 M 5
Parent ○ CDN (QUE) 236-237 O 5
Parent, Lac ⊖ CDN (QUE) 236-237 L 4
Parepare ○ RI 164-165 F 6
Paresi, Área Indígena ⚔ BR 70-71 H 4
Paresi do Rio Formoso, Área Indígena ⚔ BR 70-71 H 4
Párga ○ GR 100-101 H 5
Pargaon Sudrik ○ IND 138-139 E 10
Pargas = Parainen ○ FIN 88-89 G 6
Pargua ○ RCH 78-79 C 6
Parguaza, Río ~ YV 60-61 H 5
Parguera ∸ USA (PR) 286-287 O 3
Parhar ○ TJ 136-137 L 6
Paria ○ BOL 70-71 D 5
Paria, Golfo de ≈ 60-61 K 2
Paria, Península de ⌵ YV 60-61 K 2
Pariacoto ○ PE 64-65 D 6
Pariaguán ○ YV 60-61 J 3
Pariaman ○ RI 162-163 D 5
Paria River ~ USA (UT) 254-255 D 6
Paricatuba ○ BR 66-67 G 5
Paricutín, Volcán ▲ MEX 52-53 C 2
Parika ○ GUY 62-63 E 2
Parima, Reserva Florestal ⊥ BR 60-61 K 6
Parima, Serra ⛰ BR 60-61 J 6
Parinacochas, Lago ⊖ PE 64-65 F 9
Parinari ○ PE 64-65 E 4
Pariñas, Punta ▲ PE 64-65 B 4
Parintins ○ BR 66-67 J 4
Paripiranga ○ BR 68-69 K 7
Paririque Grande ○ RA 76-77 D 2
Paris ○ CDN (ONT) 238-239 E 5
Paris ★••• F 90-91 J 7
Paris ○ USA (AR) 276-277 B 5
Paris ○ USA (ID) 252-253 G 4
Paris ○ USA (IL) 274-275 L 5
Paris ○ USA (KY) 276-277 L 2
Paris ○ USA (MO) 274-275 G 5
Paris ○ USA (TN) 276-277 G 4
Paris ○ USA (TX) 264-265 J 5
Pariserøne ⌒ GRØ 26-27 q 4
Parish Glacier ⊂ CDN 26-27 M 4
Paris Mountain State Park ⊥ USA (SC) 284-285 H 2
Pārispea ○ EST 94-95 J 2
Parit ○ MAL 162-163 D 2
Parit ○ RI 162-163 D 4
Parita ○ PA 52-53 D 7
Parita, Golfo de ≈ 52-53 D 7
Parittanjungmelayu ○ RI 162-163 E 5
Pāriz ○ IR 134-135 F 4
Parkāl ○ IND 138-139 G 10
Parkano ○ FIN 88-89 G 5
Parkbeg ○ CDN (SAS) 232-233 M 5
Park City ○ USA (KY) 276-277 J 3
Park City ○ USA (UT) 254-255 D 3
Parkent ○ US 136-137 L 4
Parker ○ USA (AZ) 256-257 A 4
Parker ○ USA (SD) 260-261 J 3
Parker, Mount ▲ AUS 172-173 J 4
Parker Dam ○ USA (CA) 248-249 K 5
Parker Lake ⊖ CDN 30-31 W 4
Parkersburg ○ USA (IA) 274-275 F 2
Parkersburg ○ USA (WV) 280-281 E 4
Parkers Prairie ○ USA (MN) 270-271 C 4
Parkerview ○ CDN (SAS) 232-233 P 4
Parkes ○ AUS 180-181 K 2
Park Falls ○ USA (WI) 270-271 H 5
Parkfield ○ USA (CA) 248-249 D 4
Parkhill ○ CDN (ONT) 238-239 D 5
Parkin ○ USA (AR) 276-277 E 5
Parkman ○ CDN (SAS) 232-233 R 6
Parkman ○ USA (OH) 280-281 E 2
Parkman ○ USA (WY) 252-253 L 2
Park Range ⛰ USA (CO) 254-255 J 3
Park Rapids ○ USA (MN) 270-271 C 4
Park Rapids ○ USA (WA) 244-245 H 2
Park River ○ USA (ND) 258-259 K 3
Park River ~ USA (ND) 258-259 K 3
Park Rynie ○ ZA 220-221 K 5
Parkside ○ CDN (SAS) 232-233 M 2
Parkston ○ USA (SD) 260-261 J 3
Parksville ○ CDN (BC) 230-231 E 4
Parlākimidi ○ IND 142-143 D 6
Parli ○ IND 138-139 F 10
Parma ○•• I 100-101 C 2
Parma ○ USA (ID) 252-253 B 3
Parma ○ USA (OH) 280-281 E 2
Parmana ○ YV 60-61 J 4
Parnagua ○ BR 68-69 F 7
Parnaíba ○ BR 68-69 H 3
Parnaíba, Rio ~ BR 68-69 G 3
Parnaíba, Serra do ⛰ BR 68-69 E 6
Parnamirim ○ BR 68-69 J 6
Parnarama ○ BR 68-69 G 4
Parnassus ○ NZ 182 D 5
Parndana ○ AUS 180-181 D 3
Pärnu ✩•• EST 94-95 J 2
Pärnu-Jaagupi ○•• EST 94-95 J 2
Paro ○ BHT 142-143 F 2
Paromang ○ RI 168 E 6
Paron ○ USA (AR) 276-277 C 6
Paroo ○ AUS 176-177 E 3
Paroo River ~ AUS 178-179 H 4
Páros ○ GR 100-101 K 6
Páros ⌒ GR 100-101 K 6
Parou, Kūh-e ▲ IR 134-135 B 1
Parow ○ ZA 220-221 D 6
Parowan ○ USA (UT) 254-255 C 6
Par Pond < USA (SC) 284-285 J 3
Parraburdu Mining Area • AUS 176-177 D 1
Parral ○ RCH 78-79 D 4
Parramatta ○ AUS 180-181 L 2
Parramore Island ⌒ USA (VA) 280-281 L 6
Parras de la Fuente ○ MEX 50-51 H 5
Parrish ○ USA (WI) 270-271 J 5
Parrita ○ CR 52-53 B 7
Parrott ○ USA (GA) 284-285 F 5
Parrsboro ○ CDN (NS) 240-241 L 5
Parrs Halt ○ ZA 218-219 D 6
Parry ○ CDN (SAS) 232-233 O 6
Parry, Cape ▲ CDN 24-25 K 5
Parry, Kap ▲ GRØ (NGR) 26-27 P 5
Parry, Kap ▲ GRØ (ØGR) 26-27 p 7
Parry, Lac ⊖ CDN 36-37 M 5
Parry Bay ≈ 24-25 f 6
Parry Beach ○ AUS 176-177 D 7
Parry Falls ~ CDN 30-31 P 4
Parry Island ⌒ CDN (ONT) 238-239 E 3
Parry Island Indian Reservation ⚔ CDN (ONT) 238-239 E 3
Parry Islands ⌒ CDN 24-25 P 3
Parryøya ⌒ N 84-85 M 2
Parry Peninsula ⌵ CDN 24-25 K 6
Parry Sound ○ CDN (ONT) 238-239 E 3
Pārsābād ○ IR 128-129 M 3
Parseierspitze ▲ A 92-93 L 5
Parshall ○ USA (ND) 258-259 E 4
Parsnip River ~ CDN (BC) 228-229 N 2
Parsnip River ~ CDN (BC) 228-229 M 2
Parsoburan ○ RI 162-163 C 3
Parsons ○ USA (KS) 262-263 L 7
Parsons ○ USA (TN) 276-277 G 5
Parsons, Mount ▲ AUS 174-175 C 3
Parsons Lake ⊖ CDN 20-21 Y 2
Parson's Pond ○ CDN (NFL) 242-243 L 2
Parson's Pond ⊖ CDN (NFL) 242-243 L 3
Parsons Range ⛰ AUS 174-175 C 3
Partābpur ○ IND 142-143 C 4
Partago ○ DY 202-203 L 5
Partāwal ○ IND 142-143 C 2
Pårtefjällen ⛰ S 86-87 H 3
Partenkirchen, Garmisch- ○• D 92-93 L 5
Parthenay ○ F 90-91 G 8
Pārtibanūr ○ IND 140-141 H 6
Partizanka ○ KA 124-125 G 2
Partizansk ○ RUS 116-117 G 6
Partizansk ○ RUS 122-123 E 7
Partoun ○ USA (UT) 254-255 B 4
Partridge Island ⌒ CDN 34-35 N 2
Partūr ○ IND 138-139 F 10
Paru, Ilha ⌒ BR 62-63 G 6
Paru, Rio ~ BR 62-63 H 5
Paru, Río ~ YV 60-61 J 5
Paruá ○ BR 68-69 F 3
Paru de Este, Área Indígena ⚔ BR 62-63 G 5
Paru de Este, Rio ~ BR 62-63 G 5
Paruna ○ AUS 180-181 F 3
Parur ○ IND 140-141 G 5
Paruro ○ PE 70-71 B 3
Parusovaja ~ RUS 108-109 U 8
Parvān ▫ AFG 138-139 B 2
Pārvatipuram ○ IND 142-143 C 6
Parwan ~ IND 138-139 F 7
Paryang ○ VRC 144-145 D 5
Parys ○ ZA 220-221 H 3
Pas, Rivière de ~ CDN 36-37 R 7
Pas, The ○ CDN 34-35 F 4
Paša ○ RUS 94-95 N 1
Pasāband ○ AFG 134-135 L 2
Pasadena ○ CDN (NFL) 242-243 L 3
Pasadena ○ USA (CA) 248-249 F 5
Pasadena ○ USA (TX) 268-269 E 7
Pasaje ○ EC 64-65 C 3
Pasaje o Juramento, Río ~ RA 76-77 E 3
Pasān ○ IND 142-143 C 4
Pasangkayu ○ RI 164-165 F 4
Pasapuat ○ RI 162-163 D 6
Pasaquina ○ ES 52-53 L 5
Pasarae ○ SOL 184 I c 2
Pasarbantal ○ RI 162-163 D 6
Pasarbembah ○ RI 162-163 E 6
Pasārgād ○•• IR 134-135 E 3
Pasarsibuhuan ○ RI 162-163 C 4
Pasarsorkam = Sorkam ○ RI 162-163 C 4
Pasartalo ○ RI 162-163 E 7
Pasarwajo ○ RI 164-165 H 6
Pasawng ○ MYA 142-143 K 6
Pasayten Wilderness ⊥ USA (WA) 244-245 E 2
Pascagoula ○ USA (MS) 268-269 M 6
Pascagoula River ~ USA (MS) 268-269 M 6
Pascal ○ CDN (SAS) 232-233 L 2
Paşcani ○ RO 102-103 E 4
Pasco ○ USA (WA) 244-245 F 4
Pascoe, Mount ▲ AUS 176-177 F 3
Pasco Island ⌒ AUS 172-173 B 6
Pasewalk ○• D 92-93 M 2
Pasfield Lake ⊖ CDN 30-31 R 6
Pasi, Pulau ⌒ RI 168 E 6
Pasiene ○•• LV 94-95 L 3
Pasig ✩ RP 160-161 D 5
Pa'sina ○ RUS 116-117 J 6

Pasinler ☆ TR 128-129 J 3
Pašino o RUS 114-115 R 7
Pasión, Río de la ~ GCA 52-53 J 3
Pasir, Tanjung ▲ MAL 162-163 J 3
Pasir, Tanjung ▲ RI 162-163 H 5
Pasir Panjang o MAL 162-163 D 3
Pasirpengarayan o RI 162-163 D 4
Pasir Puteh o MAL 162-163 E 2
Pasirputih o RI 166-167 C 6
Pasitelu, Kepulauan ⌒ RI 168 E 6
Påskallavik o S 86-87 H 8
Paskenta o USA (CA) 246-247 C 4
Pasłęk o• PL 92-93 P 1
Pasley, Cape ▲ AUS 176-177 G 6
Pasley Bay ≈ 24-25 Y 5
Pašman ⌒ HR 100-101 E 3
Pasmore River ~ AUS 178-179 E 6
Pasni o PK 134-135 K 6
Paso o RI 166-167 E 3
Paso, El o USA (IL) 274-275 J 4
Paso, El o• USA (TX) 266-267 A 2
Paso de Indios o RA 78-79 E 7
Paso de la Laguna o RA 76-77 H 6
Paso de las Piedras, Embalse < RA 78-79 J 5
Paso de Lesca o C 54-55 G 4
Paso del Indio ≈ 80 C 4
Paso de los Algarrobos o RA 78-79 F 4
Paso de los Indios o RA 78-79 E 5
Paso de los Libres o RA 76-77 J 5
Paso de los Toros o ROU 78-79 L 2
Paso del Rey o RA 78-79 F 2
Paso del Sapo o RA 78-79 E 7
Paso del Toro o MEX 52-53 F 2
Paso de Ovejas o MEX 52-53 F 2
Paso de Patria o PY 76-77 H 4
Paso Flores o RA 78-79 D 6
Paso Nacional o MEX 50-51 H 5
Paso Nuevo o YV 60-61 K 3
Paso Real de Macaira o YV 60-61 H 3
Paso Real de San Diego o C 54-55 D 3
Paso Robles o USA (CA) 248-249 D 4
Paso Rodolfo Raballos o RA 80 E 3
Paspébiac o CDN (QUE) 240-241 K 2
Pasqua o CDN (SAS) 232-233 N 5
Pasquatchai River ~ CDN 34-35 L 3
Pasquia Hills ▲ CDN (SAS) 232-233 P 3
Pasrur o PK 138-139 E 3
Passa ~ G 210-211 E 4
Passa e Fica o BR 68-69 L 5
Passagem o BR 68-69 L 5
Passagem Franca o BR 68-69 G 5
Passage Point ▲ CDN 24-25 O 4
Passamaquoddy Bay ≈ 38-39 L 6
Passamaquoddy Bay ≈ CDN 240-241 H 5
Passau o D 92-93 M 4
Passayten Wilderness Area ⊥ USA (WA) 244-245 E 2
Passayten Wilderness Area • USA (WA) 244-245 E 2
Pass Christian o USA (MS) 268-269 L 6
Passi o RP 160-161 E 7
Passi o SN 202-203 B 3
Passira o BR 68-69 L 5
Pass Island o CDN (NFL) 242-243 M 5
Pass Lake o CDN (ONT) 234-235 P 6
Passmore o CDN (BC) 230-231 M 4
Passo da Guarda o BR 76-77 J 6
Passo Fundo o BR 74-75 D 7
Passo Fundo, Represa de < BR 74-75 D 6
Passo Real, Represa de < BR 74-75 D 7
Passos o BR 72-73 G 6
Passu Keah = Panshi Ju ⌒ VRC 158-159 L 2
Pastaza, Río ~ PE 64-65 D 3
Pasteur o RA 78-79 H 3
Pasto ☆ CO 64-65 D 1
Pastol Bay ≈ 20-21 J 5
Pastor, El o MEX 50-51 G 3
Pastos Bons o BR 68-69 F 5
Pastos Chicos, Río ~ RA 76-77 D 2
Pastos Grandes, Sierra de los ▲ RA 76-77 D 3
Pastrana o E 98-99 F 4
Pastura o USA (NM) 256-257 L 4
Pasuruan o RI 168 E 3
Pasvalys ☆ LT 94-95 J 3
Pasvikelva ~ N 86-87 O 2
Pata o BOL 70-71 C 4
Pata o CO 66-67 B 3
Pata o RCA 206-207 E 4
Pata o SN 202-203 C 3
Patacamaya o BOL 70-71 D 5
Patache, Punta ▲ RCH 70-71 B 7
Patadkal o••• IND 140-141 F 3
Patagonia ∸ 80 E 5
Patagônia ∸ RA 80 E 5
Patagonia o USA (AZ) 256-257 E 7
Patagónica, Cordillera ▲ RCH 80 D 5
Pata Island ⌒ RP 160-161 D 10
Pataiya o IND 140-141 G 5
Patalasang o RI 164-165 F 6
Patambalu o ZRE 210-211 G 5
Patambuco o PE 70-71 C 4
Patamuté o BR 68-69 J 6
Pātan o IND (GUJ) 138-139 D 8
Pātan o IND (MAH) 140-141 E 2
Patani o RI 164-165 L 3
Patani o WAN 204-205 G 6
Patas o IND 138-139 E 10
Patauá, Cachoeira do ~ BR 66-67 G 7
Pataula Creek ~ USA (GA) 284-285 F 5
Patay Rondos o PE 64-65 D 6
Patchepawapoko River ~ CDN 34-35 P 4
Patchogue o USA (NY) 280-281 N 3
Patea o NZ 182 E 3
Pategi o WAN 204-205 F 4
Pate Island ⌒ EAK 212-213 H 5
Patelão, Rio ~ BR 70-71 J 2
Patensie o ZA 220-221 G 6
Paternó o I 100-101 E 6
Paternoster o ZA 220-221 C 6
Pateros o USA (WA) 244-245 F 2
Paterson o USA (NJ) 280-281 M 3
Paterson o USA (WA) 244-245 F 5
Paterson o ZA 220-221 G 6
Paterson Inlet ≈ 182 B 7
Paterson Range ▲ AUS 172-173 F 6
Pathalaia o NEP 144-145 E 7
Pathalgaon o IND 142-143 C 4
Pathānkot o IND 138-139 E 3
Patharkot o NEP 144-145 E 7
Pathfinder Reservoir ⊂ USA (WY) 252-253 M 4
Pathin o THA 158-159 E 5
Pathlow o CDN (SAS) 232-233 O 3
Pāthrud o IND 138-139 E 10
Pathum Thanni o THA 158-159 F 3
Pati o RI 168 D 3
Patia = El Bordo o CO 60-61 C 6
Patía, Río ~ CO 60-61 B 7
Patiala o IND 138-139 F 4
Patillas o•• USA (PR) 286-287 P 2
Patinti, Selat ≈ 164-165 K 4
Patio Chiquito o CO 60-61 F 5
Patiroriolo o RI 164-165 G 6
Pativilca o PE 64-65 D 7
Pātkai Bum ▲ IND 142-143 J 2
Patlahara o NEP 144-145 D 7
Patman, Lake ⊂ USA (TX) 264-265 K 5
Pat Mayse Lake < USA (TX) 264-265 J 5
Pátmos ⌒ GR 100-101 L 6
Patna ☆•• IND 142-143 D 3
Patnanungan Island ⌒ RP 160-161 E 5
Patnitola o BD 142-143 F 3
Patnos ☆ TR 128-129 K 3
Pato, Cachoeira do ~ BR 62-63 E 6
Pato Branco o BR 74-75 D 6
Patoka o USA (IL) 274-275 J 6
Patoka Lake ⊂ USA (IN) 274-275 M 6
Patoka River ~ USA (IN) 274-275 L 6
Patomskoe, nagor'e ∸ RUS 118-119 F 6
Patonga o AUS 172-173 L 2
Patonga o EAU 212-213 D 2
Patopsco Reservoir ⊂ USA (MD) 280-281 K 4
Patos o BR (CEA) 68-69 H 3
Patos o BR (PA) 68-69 K 5
Patos, Cachoeira dos ~ BR 70-71 H 2
Patos, Lagoa dos ⊂ BR 74-75 E 8
Patos, Río de los ~ RA 78-79 E 2
Patos de Minas o BR 72-73 G 5
Patos ou São José, Rio dos ~ BR 70-71 J 3
Patquia o RA 76-77 D 6
Pátra o• GR 100-101 H 5
Patraikos Kólpos ≈ 100-101 H 5
Patrakeevka o RUS 88-89 Q 4
Patreksfjörður ☆ IS 86-87 b 2
Patricia o CDN (ALB) 232-233 G 5
Patricia o USA (TX) 264-265 B 6
Patricios, Los o CO 66-67 B 3
Patrick o USA (SC) 284-285 K 2
Patrimonio o BR 72-73 F 5
Patrocinio o BR 72-73 G 5
Pattamada o IND 140-141 G 6
Pattani ☆ THA 158-159 F 7
Pattaya o•• THA 158-159 F 4
Patten River ~ CDN (ONT) 236-237 J 3
Patterson ≈ 172-173 K 2
Patterson o USA (CA) 248-249 C 2
Patterson o USA (GA) 284-285 H 5
Patterson o USA (ID) 252-253 E 2
Patterson o USA (LA) 268-269 J 7
Patterson, Mount ▲ AUS 176-177 F 2
Patterson, Mount ▲ CDN 20-21 X 4
Patterson Pass ▲ USA (NV) 246-247 L 5
Patti o I 100-101 E 5
Pattison o USA (MS) 268-269 K 5
Pattoki o PK 138-139 D 4
Patton o USA (MO) 276-277 E 3
Pattonsburg o USA (MO) 274-275 D 4
Pattukkottai o IND 140-141 H 5
Patu o BR 68-69 K 5
Patuakhali o BD 142-143 G 4
Patuanak o CDN 34-35 C 3
Patuca, Punta ▲ HN 54-55 C 7
Patuca, Río ~ HN 54-55 C 7
Patugu o RI 168 E 6
Patullo, Mount ▲ CDN 32-33 F 3
Patungan o RP 160-161 D 5
Paturau River o NZ 182 D 4
Patuxent River ~ USA (MD) 280-281 K 5
Patvinsuom kansallispuisto ⊥ FIN 88-89 L 5
Pátzcuaro o•• MEX 52-53 D 2
Patzimaro o MEX 52-53 C 1
Pau ☆• F 90-91 G 10
Pau, Tanjung ▲ RI 166-167 B 6
Pau Alto, Rio ~ BR 72-73 L 4
Paucarbamba o PE 64-65 E 8
Paucarcolla o PE 70-71 B 4
Paucartambo o PE 70-71 B 3
Paucartambo, Río ~ PE 64-65 E 7
Pau d'Arco, Rio ~ BR 68-69 C 5
Pau de Ferros o BR 68-69 J 5
Pauh o RI 162-163 E 6
Pauini o BR 66-67 D 6
Pauini, Rio ~ BR 66-67 F 3
Pauk o MYA 142-143 J 5
Paukkaung o MYA 142-143 J 6
Pauksa Taung ▲ MYA 142-143 J 6
Paulatuk o CDN 24-25 K 6
Paulaya, Río ~ HN 54-55 C 7
Paul B. Johnson State Park ⊥ USA (MS) 268-269 L 5
Paul Bunyan & Blue Ox Statue • USA (MN) 270-271 D 3
Paulden o USA (AZ) 256-257 C 4
Paulding o USA (OH) 280-281 B 2
Paulina o USA (OR) 244-245 F 6
Paulina Peak ▲ USA (OR) 244-245 D 7
Pauline o USA (ID) 252-253 F 4
Paul Island ⌒ CDN 36-37 T 6
Paul Island ⌒ USA 22-23 R 5
Paulista o BR 68-69 L 5
Paulistana o BR 68-69 H 6
Paullina o USA (IA) 274-275 C 2
Paulo Afonso o• BR 68-69 J 6
Paulo Afonso, Parque Nacional ⊥ BR 68-69 J 6
Paulo de Faria o BR 72-73 F 6
Paulo Ramos o BR 68-69 F 4
Paulpietersburg o ZA 220-221 K 3
Paul Roux o ZA 220-221 H 4
Paul Sauer Dam < ZA 220-221 G 6
Paul Spur o USA (AZ) 256-257 F 7
Pauls Valley o USA (OK) 264-265 G 4
Paungdawthi o MYA 158-159 D 2
Paungde o MYA 142-143 J 6
Pauni o IND 138-139 G 9
Paup o PNG 183 B 2
Pauri o IND 138-139 F 7
Pausa o PE 64-65 F 9
Paute o EC 64-65 C 3
Pauto, Río ~ CO 60-61 F 5
Pau Uma, Île = Paama ⌒ VAN 184 II b 3
Pauwasi ~ RI 166-167 L 3
Pauwela o USA (HI) 288 J 4
Pāvagada o IND 140-141 G 3
Pavant Range ▲ USA (UT) 254-255 C 5
Pavão o BR 72-73 K 4
Pāve o IR 128-129 M 5
Pavia ☆• I 100-101 B 2
Pavilion o CDN (BC) 230-231 H 3
Pavilion o USA (NY) 278-279 C 6
Pavillion o USA (WY) 252-253 K 3
Pāvilosta o LV 94-95 G 3
Pavlikeni o BG 102-103 D 6
Pavlodar ☆• KA 124-125 K 2
Pavlof Bay ≈ 22-23 Q 5
Pavlof Islands ⌒ USA 22-23 Q 5
Pavlof Volcano ▲ USA 22-23 Q 5
Pavlograd = Pavlohrad o UA 102-103 J 3
Pavlogradka ☆ RUS 124-125 H 1
Pavlohrad o UA 102-103 J 3
Pavlovac o HR 100-101 F 2
Pavlović, Erofej o RUS 118-119 L 8
Pavlovka o RUS 96-97 E 7
Pavlovo ☆ RUS 94-95 S 4
Pavlovsk o RUS 102-103 M 2
Pavlovsk o•• RUS (LEN) 94-95 M 2
Pavlovsk ☆ RUS 124-125 N 2
Pavlovskij Posad ☆ RUS 94-95 Q 4
Pavlovskoe vodohranilišče < RUS 96-97 K 6
Pavlyš o UA 102-103 H 3
Pavo o USA (GA) 284-285 G 6
Pavon, Arroyo ~ RA 78-79 J 2
Pavullo nel Frignano o I 100-101 C 2
Pavylon, ozero ⊂ RUS 110-111 d 5
Pawanoa o PNG 183 C 4
Pawan ~ RI 162-163 J 5
Pawāyan o IND 144-145 C 6
Pawé ▲ CAM 204-205 J 6
Pawhuska o USA (OK) 264-265 H 2
Pawleys Island o USA (SC) 284-285 L 3
Pawnee o USA (OK) 264-265 H 2
Pawnee Bill Museum • USA (OK) 264-265 H 2
Pawnee City o USA (NE) 262-263 K 4
Pawnee Indian Village ∴ USA (KS) 262-263 J 5
Pawnee River ~ USA (KS) 262-263 G 6
Pawnee Rock o USA (KS) 262-263 H 6
Pawnee Rock State Monument • USA (KS) 262-263 H 6
Paw Paw o USA (MI) 272-273 D 5
Pawtucket o USA (RI) 278-279 K 7
Pawut o MYA 158-159 E 4
Paxí ⌒ GR 100-101 H 5
Paxiúba, Rio ~ BR 66-67 G 7
Paxson o USA 20-21 S 5
Paxton o USA (IL) 274-275 K 4
Paxton o USA (NE) 262-263 E 3
Paxville o USA (SC) 284-285 K 3
Paya, Parque Nacional la ⊥ CO 64-65 E 1
Payagyi o MYA 158-159 D 2
Payahe o RI 164-165 K 3
Payakumbuh o RI 162-163 D 5
Payang, Gunung ▲ RI 164-165 D 3
Payar o SN 202-203 C 2
Payas, Cerro ▲ HN 54-55 C 7
Payer, Kap ▲ GRØ 26-27 b 2
Payer Land ∸ GRØ 26-27 o 6
Payero, Río ~ CO 60-61 E 5
Payette o USA (ID) 252-253 B 2
Payette River ~ USA (ID) 252-253 B 3
Payne, Lac ⊂ CDN 36-37 M 5
Payne Bay ≈ 36-37 P 4
Paynes Creek o USA (CA) 246-247 D 3
Paynes Find o AUS 176-177 D 4
Paynesville o AUS 180-181 J 4
Paynesville o USA (MN) 270-271 D 5
Paynton o CDN (SAS) 232-233 K 2
Payogasta o RA 76-77 D 3
Payong, Tanjung ▲ MAL 162-163 K 3
Paysandú ☆ ROU 78-79 K 2
Pays de la Loire ◻ F 90-91 G 8
Payson o USA (AZ) 256-257 D 4
Payson o USA (UT) 254-255 D 3
Payún, Cerro ▲ RA 78-79 E 4
Payung o RI 162-163 G 6
Pa Yup o THA 158-159 F 4
Payyannūr o IND 140-141 F 4
Paz, Corredeira da ~ BR 68-69 B 6
Paz, Gruta • EC 64-65 D 1
Paz, La ★• BOL 70-71 C 5
Paz, La o CO 60-61 E 2
Paz, La ☆ HN 52-53 L 4
Paz, La ☆• MEX 50-51 D 5
Paz, La o RA (COD) 78-79 G 2
Paz, La o RA (ERI) 76-77 H 6
Paz, La o RA (MEN) 78-79 F 2
Paz, La o ROU 78-79 L 3
Paz, Ribeiro da ~ BR 68-69 C 6
Paz, Rio de la ~ BOL 70-71 D 5
Pazar ☆ TR 128-129 J 2
Pazarbaşı Burnu ▲ TR 128-129 D 2
Pazarcık o TR 128-129 G 4
Pazardžik o BG 102-103 D 6
Pazardžik o BG 102-103 D 6
Paz Centro, La o NIC 52-53 L 5
Paz del Río o CO 60-61 E 4
Pazha o PK 138-139 B 3
Pazos Kanki o RA 78-79 H 3
Pčič ~ BY 94-95 K 5
Pčinja ~ MK 100-101 H 4
Pe o MYA 158-159 E 4
Peabody o USA (KS) 262-263 J 6
Peabody Bugt ≈ 26-27 R 4
Peace Point o CDN 30-31 N 6
Peace River o CDN (ALB) 32-33 M 3
Peace River ~ CDN 30-31 L 6
Peace River ~ CDN 32-33 J 3
Peace River ~ USA (FL) 286-287 H 4
Peach Creek ~ USA (TX) 266-267 K 4
Peachland o CDN (BC) 230-231 K 4
Peach Springs o USA (AZ) 256-257 B 3
Peachtree City o USA (GA) 284-285 F 3
Peacock Bay ≈ 16 F 26
Peacock Hills ▲ CDN 30-31 O 3
Pea Island National Wildlife Refuge ⊥ USA (NC) 282-283 M 5
Peak Charles National Park ⊥ AUS 176-177 F 6
Peak District National Park ⊥ GB 90-91 G 5
Peak Downs Mine • AUS 178-179 K 2
Peake o AUS 180-181 E 3
Peake Creek ~ AUS 178-179 C 5
Peaked Point ▲ RP 160-161 C 7
Peak Hill o AUS (NSW) 180-181 K 2
Peak Hill o AUS (WA) 176-177 E 2
Peak Mountain ▲ USA (CA) 248-249 E 5
Peale, Mount ▲ USA (UT) 254-255 F 5
Pearblossom o USA (CA) 248-249 G 5
Pearce o CDN (ALB) 232-233 E 6
Pearce o USA (AZ) 256-257 F 7
Pearce Point ▲ AUS 172-173 J 3
Pearcy o USA (AR) 276-277 B 6
Peard Bay ≈ 20-21 L 1
Pea Ridge National Military Park • USA (AR) 276-277 A 4
Pearisburg o USA (VA) 280-281 F 6
Pea River ~ USA (AL) 284-285 E 5
Pea River ~ USA (AL) 284-285 D 5
Pearl o USA (MS) 268-269 K 4
Pearland o USA (TX) 268-269 E 7
Pearl City o USA (HI) 288 H 3
Pearl Harbor ≈• USA 288 G 3
Pearl River o USA (LA) 268-269 L 6
Pearl River ~ USA (MS) 268-269 L 5
Pearsall o USA (TX) 266-267 H 5
Pearse Island ⌒ CDN (BC) 228-229 D 2
Pearson o USA (AL) 284-285 C 3
Pearson o USA (GA) 284-285 H 5
Pearston o ZA 220-221 G 6
Peary Channel ≈ 24-25 U 1
Peary Gletscher ⊂ GRØ 26-27 U 5
Peary Land ∸ GRØ 26-27 f 2
Pease River ~ USA (TX) 264-265 E 4
Peawanuck o CDN 34-35 O 3
Peba, Rio ~ BR 68-69 D 5
Pebane o MOC 218-219 K 3
Pebas o PE 66-67 B 4
Pebble Island ⌒ GB 78-79 L 6
Péč o AFG 138-139 C 2
Peč o• YU 100-101 H 3
Pečalky ~ RUS 114-115 R 2
Pecangakan o RI 168 D 3
Peçanha o BR 72-73 J 5
Pecan Island o USA (LA) 268-269 H 7
Peças, Ilha das ⌒ BR 74-75 F 5
Pecatonica River ~ USA (IL) 274-275 J 2
Pečeněžske vodoschovyšče < UA 102-103 K 2
Pečenga o RUS 88-89 L 2
Pechanga Indian Reservation X USA (CA) 248-249 G 6
Peche-Merle, Grotte du • F 90-91 H 9
Pechora = Pečora ~ RUS 88-89 W 3
Pechorskaya Guba = Pečorskaja guba ≈ RUS 88-89 W 2
Pechorskoye More = Pečorskoe more ≈ RUS 88-89 V 2
Pecixe, Ilha de ⌒ GNB 202-203 B 4
Peckerwood Lake < USA (AR) 276-277 D 6
Peck Lake, Fort ⊂ USA (MT) 250-251 N 4
Pecnoj tubek ∸ KA 96-97 G 10
Pečora ☆ RUS (KOM) 88-89 Y 4
Pečora ~ RUS 88-89 W 3
Pečora ~ RUS 114-115 E 4
Pečora ~ RUS 114-115 D 2
Pečoro-Ilyčskij, zapovednik ⊥ RUS 114-115 E 3
Pečoro-Ilyčskij zapovednik ⊥ RUS 114-115 D 4
Pečorsk, Troicko- ☆ RUS 114-115 D 3
Pečorskaja grjada ▲ RUS 88-89 X 3
Pečorskaja guba ≈ 88-89 X 2
Pečorskoe More ≈ 88-89 V 2
Pecos o USA (NM) 256-257 K 3
Pecos o USA (TX) 266-267 D 2
Pecos National Historic Park ∴ USA (NM) 256-257 K 3
Pecos Plains ∸ USA (NM) 256-257 L 5
Pecos River ~ USA (NM) 256-257 L 4
Pecos River ~ USA (TX) 266-267 F 3
Pécs o• H 92-93 P 5
Pedasi o PA 52-53 D 8
Pedda Ahobilam o IND 140-141 H 3
Pedda Arikatla o IND 140-141 H 3
Peddapalli o IND 138-139 G 10
Pedder, Lake ⊂ AUS 180-181 J 7
Peddie o ZA 220-221 H 6
Pedergosa Mountains ▲ USA (AZ) 256-257 F 7
Pedernales ☆ DOM 54-55 K 6
Pedernales o RCH 76-77 C 4
Pedernales o YV 60-61 K 3
Pedernales, Punta ▲ EC 64-65 B 1
Pedernales, Salar de ⊂ RCH 76-77 C 4
Pedernales River ~ USA (TX) 266-267 J 3
Pederneira, Cachoeira ~ BR 66-67 E 7
Pederneiras o BR 72-73 F 7
Pé de Serra o BR 68-69 J 7
Pedirka o AUS 178-179 C 4
Pediwang o RI 164-165 K 3
Pedra Alta, Cachoeira ~ BR 68-69 C 3
Pedra Azul o BR 72-73 K 3
Pedra Azul, Pico ▲ BR 72-73 K 6
Pedra Badejo o CV 202-203 C 6
Pedra Branca o BR 68-69 J 4
Pedra Corrida o BR 72-73 J 5
Pedra de Amolar, Rio ~ BR 68-69 E 6
Pedra do Feitiço o ANG 216-217 B 2
Pedra-Furada, Riachão ~ BR 68-69 E 6
Pedra Grande o BR 72-73 L 5
Pedra Lavrada o BR 68-69 K 5
Pedra Lume o CV 202-203 C 5
Pedra Preta o BR 70-71 K 5
Pedra Preta, Corredeira da ~ BR 68-69 C 5
Pedras, Cachoeira, ~ BR 68-69 D 7
Pedras Descobertas ~ BR 70-71 J 3
Pedras Grandes o BR 74-75 F 7
Pedras Negras • ANG 216-217 C 4
Pedras Negras o BR 70-71 F 3
Pedras Tinhosas ⌒ STP 210-211 b 2
Pedregal o BR 76-77 K 6
Pedregal o YV 60-61 F 2
Pedregal, Río ~ MEX 52-53 H 3
Pedregulho o BR 72-73 G 6
Pedreira, Rio ~ BR 62-63 J 5
Pedreiras o BR (MAR) 68-69 F 4
Pedreiras o BR (P) 66-67 K 5
Pedreiras o BR (RSU) 74-75 D 9
Pedrera, La o CO 66-67 C 3
Pedrero, Cerro el ▲ RA 80 E 2
Pedriceña o MEX 50-51 H 5
Pedrinhas o BR 68-69 K 7
Pedro Alexandre o BR 68-69 K 6
Pedro Alonso o BR 68-69 D 6
Pedro Antunes o BR 74-75 D 8
Pedro Avelino o BR 68-69 K 4
Pedro Barros o BR 74-75 G 5
Pedro Betancourt o C 54-55 E 3
Pedro Canário o BR 72-73 L 5
Pedro Carbo o EC 64-65 B 2
Pedro Cays ⌒ JA 54-55 F 6
Pedro de Valdivia o RCH 76-77 C 2
Pedro Gomes o BR 70-71 K 6
Pedro II o BR 68-69 H 4
Pedro J. Montero o EC 64-65 C 3
Pedro Juan Caballero ☆ PY 76-77 K 2
Pedro Luro o RA 78-79 H 5
Pedro Montoya o MEX 50-51 K 7
Pedroñeras, Las o E 98-99 F 5
Pedro Osório o BR 74-75 D 8
Pedro Vega ∴• MEX 52-53 J 3
Peebinga o AUS 180-181 F 3
Peebles o CDN (SAS) 232-233 Q 5
Peebles o GB 90-91 F 4
Peebles o USA (OH) 280-281 C 5
Peedamulla o AUS 172-173 B 6
Pee Dee National Wildlife Refuge ⊥ USA (NC) 282-283 G 5
Pee Dee River ~ USA (SC) 284-285 L 2
Peekskill o USA (NY) 280-281 N 2
Peel o• GBM 90-91 E 4
Peel Channel ~ CDN 20-21 X 2
Pe Ell o USA (WA) 244-245 B 4
Peel Plateau ▲ CDN 20-21 Y 3
Peel Point ▲ CDN 24-25 P 4
Peel River ~ AUS 178-179 L 6
Peel River ~ CDN 20-21 W 4
Peel River Game Reserve ⊥ CDN 20-21 Y 3
Peel Sound ≈ 24-25 Y 4
Peene ~ D 92-93 M 2
Peeples Valley o USA (AZ) 256-257 C 4
Peeramudlayeppa Lake ⊂ AUS 178-179 D 4
Peera Peera Poolanna Lake ⊂ AUS 178-179 D 4
Peerless o CDN 32-33 Q 4
Peerless o USA (MT) 250-251 O 3
Peerless Lake ⊂ CDN 32-33 N 3
Peers o CDN (ALB) 232-233 C 2
Peesane o CDN (SAS) 232-233 P 3
Peetz o USA (CO) 254-255 M 3
Pegasus Bay ≈ 182 D 5
Pegatan o RI 162-163 K 6
Peggys Cove o• CDN (NS) 240-241 M 6
Peg. Müller ▲ RI 162-163 K 4
Pego o E 98-99 G 5
Pego o P 98-99 C 5
Pegram o USA (TN) 276-277 H 4
Pegtymel' ~ RUS 112-113 T 2
Pegtymel'skij hrebet ▲ RUS 112-113 S 2
Pegu o MYA 158-159 D 2
Peguis Indian Reserve X CDN (MAN) 234-235 F 3
Pegunungan, Barisan ▲ RI 162-163 E 6
Pegyš o RUS 88-89 V 5
Pehonko o DY 202-203 L 4
Pehuajó o RA 78-79 J 3
Pehuén-Co o RA 78-79 J 5
Peigan Indian Reserve X CDN (ALB) 232-233 E 6
Peili o SUD 206-207 H 5
Peinata, Cerro ▲ RA 80 D 5
Peipsi Järv o EST 94-95 K 2
Peipus, Lake = Peipsi Järv ⊂ EST 94-95 K 2
Peixe o BR 72-73 F 2
Peixe, Lagoa do ⊂ BR 74-75 E 8
Peixe, Rio ~ BR 72-73 D 4
Peixe, Rio do ~ BR 72-73 F 4
Peixe, Rio do ~ BR 72-73 F 3
Peixe, Rio do ~ BR 72-73 E 3
Peixeboi o BR 68-69 E 2
Peixe Couro ou Aquinabo, Rio ~ BR 70-71 K 5
Peixes ou de São Francisco, Rio dos ~ BR 70-71 J 2
Pei Xian o VRC 154-155 K 4
Peixoto, Represa < BR 72-73 G 6
Peixoto de Azevedo o BR 70-71 K 2
Peixoto de Azevedo, Rio ~ BR 70-71 K 2
Pejantan, Pulau ⌒ RI 162-163 G 4
Pekabata o RI 164-165 F 5
Pekalongan o RI 168 C 3
Pekan o• MAL 162-163 E 3
Pekanbaru ☆ RI 162-163 D 4
Pekin o USA (IL) 274-275 J 4
Pekin o USA (ND) 258-259 J 4
Pekin, Pulau ⌒ RI 164-165 E 2
Peking = Beijing ★••• VRC 154-155 K 2
Pekinga o DY 204-205 E 2
Peklino o RUS 94-95 N 5
Peko, Mont ▲ CI 202-203 G 6
Peko, Parc National du Mont ⊥ CI 202-203 G 6
Peko Mine • AUS 174-175 C 6
Pekul'nej, hrebet ▲ RUS 112-113 S 4
Pekyl'nejskoe, ozero ⊂ RUS 112-113 T 5
Péla o RG 202-203 F 6
Pelabuhanratu o RI 168 B 3
Pelabuhan Ratu, Teluk ≈ 168 B 3
Pelada, Pampa ∸ RA 80 F 2
Pelagie, Isole = Pelagie, Isole ⌒ I 100-101 D 7
Pelahatchie o USA (MS) 268-269 L 4
Pelaihari o RI 164-165 D 5
Pelau ⌒ SOL 184 I d 1
Pelé, Mont ▲ G 210-211 C 5
Pélébina o DY 202-203 L 5
Pelechuco o BOL 70-71 C 4
Peleduj ~ RUS 118-119 F 6
Pelée, Mont ▲ F 56 E 4
Pelee, Point ▲ CDN (ONT) 238-239 C 7
Pelee Island ⌒ CDN (ONT) 238-239 C 7
Pelei o RI 164-165 H 4
Pelejo o PE 64-65 E 5
Pelekech ▲ EAK 212-213 E 2
Pelencho o YV 60-61 L 3
Peleng, Pulau ⌒ RI 164-165 H 4
Peleng, Selat ≈ 164-165 H 4
Pelézi o CI 202-203 G 6
Pelham o AUS 174-175 G 6
Pelham o USA (AL) 284-285 D 3
Pelhřimov o CZ 92-93 N 4
Pelican o USA 32-33 B 3
Pelican, Lac ⊂ CDN 36-37 N 5
Pelican Lake ⊂ CDN (MAN) 234-235 C 2
Pelicano, Quebrada del ~ RCH 76-77 B 5
Pelican Point (Beach) • AUS 176-177 B 2
Pelican Rapids o CDN (MAN) 234-235 C 2
Pelican River ~ CDN 32-33 O 4
Pelikan Lake ⊂ USA (MN) 270-271 F 2
Pelikan Narrows o CDN 34-35 E 3
Pelikan Rapids o USA (MN) 270-271 B 4
Pelileo o EC 64-65 C 2
Pelindã, Ponta ▲ GNB 202-203 B 4
Pelion o USA (SC) 284-285 J 3
Pelkie o USA (MI) 270-271 K 4
Pelkosenniemi o FIN 88-89 J 3
Pella o USA (IA) 274-275 F 3
Pelland o USA (MN) 270-271 E 2
Pellatt Lake ⊂ CDN 30-31 P 3
Pell City o USA (AL) 284-285 D 3
Pellegrini o RA 78-79 H 4
Pellegrini, Lago ⊂ RA 78-79 F 5
Pelletier o CDN (QUE) 240-241 F 3
Pell Inlet ≈ 24-25 U 3
Pello o FIN 88-89 G 3
Pellston o USA (MI) 272-273 E 2
Pellworm ⌒ D 92-93 K 1
Pelly o CDN (SAS) 232-233 R 4
Pelly Bay ≈ 24-25 b 6
Pelly Bay o CDN 24-25 a 6
Pelly Island ⌒ CDN 20-21 X 2
Pelly Lake ⊂ CDN 30-31 T 3
Pelly Mountains ▲ CDN 20-21 Y 6
Pelly Plateau ▲ CDN 20-21 Z 5
Pelly Point ▲ CDN 24-25 W 5
Pelly River ~ CDN 20-21 W 5
Pelmadulla o CL 140-141 J 7
Pelokang, Pulau ⌒ RI 168 D 6
Pelona Mountain ▲ USA (NM) 256-257 G 5
Pelopónissos ◻ GR 100-101 J 6
Pelopónnissos ⌒ GR 100-101 H 6
Peloritani, Monti ▲ I 100-101 E 5
Pelotas o BR 74-75 D 8
Pelotas, Rio ~ BR 74-75 E 7
Pelsart Group ⌒ AUS 176-177 C 4
Peluitepu o SME 62-63 G 4
Pelus ~ MAL 162-163 D 2
Pelusium ∴• ET 194-195 F 2
Pelym ~ RUS 114-115 F 4
Pelymskij Tuman, ozero ⊂ RUS 114-115 G 4
Pemadumcook Lake ⊂ USA (ME) 278-279 M 3
Pemalang o RI 168 C 3
Pemali, Tanjung ▲ RI (SLT) 164-165 H 4
Pemali, Tanjung ▲ RI (STG) 164-165 H 6
Pemangil, Pulau ⌒ MAL (KED) 162-163 F 3
Pemangkat o RI 162-163 H 4
Pemarung, Tanjung ▲ RI 164-165 E 4
Pematang Purba o RI 162-163 C 3
Pematangsiantar o RI 162-163 C 3
Pematangtanabjawa o RI 162-163 C 3
Pemba ☆ MOC 214-215 L 7
Pemba o Z 218-219 D 3
Pemba Channel ≈ 212-213 G 6
Pemba Island ⌒ EAT 212-213 G 6
Pembe o MOC 218-219 H 6
Pemberton o• AUS 176-177 D 7
Pemberton o CDN (BC) 230-231 G 3
Pemberton o USA (MN) 270-271 E 6
Pemberton Icefield ⊂ CDN (BC) 230-231 F 3
Pemberton Meadows o CDN (BC) 230-231 F 3
Pembina River ~ CDN (ALB) 232-233 B 2
Pembina River ~ CDN (MAN) 234-235 D 5
Pembine o USA (WI) 270-271 K 5
Pembre o RI 166-167 J 5
Pembridge o CDN (ALB) 232-233 D 2
Pembroke o CDN (ONT) 238-239 H 3
Pembroke o• GB 90-91 E 6
Pembroke o USA (GA) 284-285 J 4
Pembroke o USA (NC) 282-283 H 6
Pembroke, Cape ▲ CDN 36-37 J 3
Pembroke Castle •• GB 90-91 E 6
Pembrokeshire Coast National Park ⊥ GB 90-91 E 6
Pemuco o RCH 78-79 C 4
Pen o IND 138-139 D 10
Peña Blanco o RCH 76-77 B 4
Penadoto, ozero ⊂ RUS 108-109 P 7
Peñafiel o E 98-99 E 4
Penafiel o P 98-99 C 4
Peñaflor o RCH 78-79 D 2
Penalva o BR 68-69 F 3
Penambuan o RI 164-165 K 4
Penambulai, Pulau ⌒ RI 166-167 H 5
Penampang o MAL 160-161 B 10
Peña Nevada, Cerro ▲ MEX 50-51 K 6
Penang, Pulau ⌒ MAL 162-163 D 2
Penanjung Game Park ⊥ RI 168 C 3
Penápolis o BR 72-73 E 6
Penarak, Kampung o MAL 162-163 E 2
Peñaranda de Bracamonte o E 98-99 E 4
Peñarroya ▲ E 98-99 G 4
Peñarroya-Pueblonueva o E 98-99 E 5
Peñas, Cabo ▲ RA 80 G 6
Peñas, Golfo de ≈ 80 C 3
Peñas, Las o RA 76-77 D 5
Peñas, Sierra de las ▲ RA 78-79 G 2
Peñas Blancas o NIC 52-53 B 6
Peñasco, Rio ~ USA (NM) 256-257 L 6
Peñas Negras o YV 60-61 J 4
Pench National Park ⊥ IND 138-139 G 9
Penck, Cape ▲ ARK 16 G 9
Pendarves o NZ 182 C 5
Pendé o RCA 206-207 C 5
Pendé ~ RCA 206-207 B 5
Pendelton Bay o CDN (BC) 228-229 J 2
Pendembu o WAL (EAS) 202-203 E 5
Pendembu o WAL (NOR) 202-203 D 5
Pendeng o RI 162-163 B 2
Pender o USA (NE) 262-263 K 2
Pender Bay ≈ 172-173 F 4
Pender Island o CDN (BC) 230-231 F 5
Pendjari ~ DY 202-203 L 4
Pendjari, Parc National de la ⊥ DY 202-203 L 4
Pendjari, Zone Cynégétique de la ⊥ DY 202-203 L 4
Pendjua o ZRE 210-211 G 4
Pendleton o USA (IN) 274-275 N 5
Pendleton o USA (OR) 244-245 G 5
Pendopo o RI 162-163 E 6
Pend Oreille, Mount ▲ USA (ID) 250-251 C 3
Pend Oreille Lake ⊂ USA (ID) 250-251 C 3
Pend Oreille River ~ USA (WA) 244-245 H 2
Pendroy o USA (MT) 250-251 G 3
Pendryl o CDN (ALB) 232-233 D 3
Pendulum Øer ⌒ GRØ 26-27 q 6
Penebangan, Pulau ⌒ RI 162-163 H 5
Penebel o RI 168 B 7
Peneda ▲ P 98-99 C 4
Penedo o BR 68-69 K 7
Pene-Katamba o ZRE 210-211 K 4
Penela o P 98-99 C 4
Pene-Mende o ZRE 212-213 B 6
Pénessoulou o DY 202-203 L 5
Penet, Tanjung ▲ RI 162-163 F 7
Penetanguishene o CDN (ONT) 238-239 F 4
Penfro = Pembroke o GB 90-91 E 6
Pengalengan o RI 168 B 3
Peng'an o VRC 154-155 E 6
Penganga ~ IND 138-139 G 10
Pengastulan o RI 168 B 7
Pengchia Yü ⌒ RC 156-157 N 4
Penge o ZRE (HAU) 212-213 A 2
Penge o ZRE (KOR) 210-211 K 6
Penge, Chute ~ ZRE 212-213 B 3
Penghu Islands ⌒ RC 156-157 L 5
Pengjie o VRC 154-155 F 6
Pengkalan Kubor, Kampung o MAL 162-163 E 2
Pengkou o VRC 156-157 K 4
Penglai o VRC 154-155 M 3
Penglai o VRC 156-157 G 7
Penglai Ge • VRC 154-155 M 3
Pengshan o VRC 154-155 C 6
Pengshui o VRC 156-157 F 2
Penguin o AUS 180-181 H 6
Penguin Bank ≃ 288 H 4
Penguin Island ⌒ CDN (NFL) 242-243 M 5
Penguin Shoal ~ AUS 172-173 G 2
Pengxi o VRC 154-155 D 6
Penhalonga o ZW 218-219 G 4
Penhoek Pass ▲ ZA 220-221 H 5
Péni o BF 202-203 H 4
Peniche o• P 98-99 C 5
Penida, Nusa ⌒ RI 168 B 7
Peninga o RUS 88-89 M 5
Peninton o USA (AL) 284-285 B 4
Peninsular Development Road II AUS 174-175 G 4
Peninsular Lake ⊂ CDN (ONT) 234-235 P 3
Penitente, Serra do ▲ BR 68-69 E 6
Pénjamo o MEX 52-53 D 1
Penmarc'h o• F 90-91 E 8
Penmarc'h, Pointe de ▲• F 90-91 E 8
Pennādam o IND 140-141 H 5
Pennant o CDN (SAS) 232-233 K 5
Pennant Point ▲ CDN (NS) 240-241 M 6
Penner ~ IND 140-141 H 3
Penneshaw o AUS 180-181 D 3
Penn Hills o USA (PA) 280-281 G 3
Pennines, The ▲ GB 90-91 F 4
Pennsboro o USA (WV) 280-281 F 4
Pennsville o USA (NJ) 280-281 L 4
Pennsylvania ◻ USA (PA) 280-281 G 2
Pennsylvania TPK II USA (PA) 280-281 K 3
Penny o CDN (BC) 228-229 N 3
Penn Yan o USA (NY) 278-279 D 6
Penny Farms o USA (FL) 286-287 H 2
Penny Highlands ▲ CDN 28-29 G 3
Penny Ice Cap ⊂ CDN 28-29 G 3
Pennyroyal Plateau ▲ USA (TN) 276-277 J 4
Penny Strait ≈ 24-25 X 2
Peno ☆ RUS 94-95 N 3
Penobscot Bay ≈ USA 278-279 N 4
Penobscot River ~ USA (ME) 278-279 N 3
Penoka o LB 202-203 G 7
Penola o AUS 180-181 F 4
Peñón Blanco o MEX 50-51 H 5
Peñón del Rosario, Cerro ▲ MEX 52-53 E 2
Penong o AUS 176-177 M 5
Peñón Nevado del Falso Azufre ▲ RCH 76-77 C 4
Peñón Nevado del Falso Azufre ▲ RA 76-77 C 4

Penonomé ☆•• PA 52-53 D 7
Penot, Mount ▲ VAN 184 II a 3
Penrhyn, Cape ▲ CDN 24-25 I 7
Penrhyn Basin ≃ 13 M 3
Penrith o GB 90-91 F 4
Penrose o USA (CO) 254-255 K 5
Pensa o BF 202-203 K 3
Pensacola o USA (FL) 286-287 B 1
Pensacola Bay ≈ 48-49 E 4
Pensacola Bay ≈ USA 286-287 B 1
Pensacola Mountains ▲ ARK 16 E 0
Pensamiento, El o BOL 70-71 G 4
Pense o CDN (SAS) 232-233 O 5
Pensepeľ, mys ▲ RUS 120-121 T 4
Penshurst o AUS 180-181 G 4
Pensilvania o CO 60-61 D 5
Pentálofos o GR 100-101 H 4
Pentecost ◘ VAN 184 II b 2
Pentecost Downs o AUS 172-173 H 4
Pentecostes o BR 68-69 J 3
Pentecost Island = Île Pentecôte ⌒ VAN 184 II b 2
Pentecost Range ▲ AUS 172-173 H 3
Pentecost River ~ AUS 172-173 H 3
Pentecôte, Île = Pentecost Island ⌒ VAN 184 II b 2
Pentecôte, Rivière o CDN (QUE) 242-243 A 3
Pentenga o BF 202-203 L 4
Penticton o CDN (BC) 230-231 K 4
Penticton Indian Reserve X CDN (BC) 230-231 K 4
Pentland o AUS 174-175 H 7
Pentland Firth ≈ 90-91 F 2
Pentwater o USA (MI) 272-273 C 4
Penu o RI 164-165 J 4
Penuin, Fiordo ≈ 80 C 4
Penukonda o• IND 140-141 G 3
Penwegon o MYA 142-143 K 6
Penwell o USA (TX) 266-267 E 2
Penylan Lake ⌒ CDN 30-31 Q 5
Penyu, Kepulauan ⌒ RI 166-167 D 4
Penyu, Teluk ≈ 168 C 3
Penza ☆ RUS 96-97 D 7
Penzance o GB 90-91 E 6
Penzance Lake ⌒ CDN 30-31 Q 5
Penze o VRC 156-157 J 2
Penzele o ZRE 210-211 G 4
Penžina ~ RUS 112-113 M 4
Penžinskaja guba ≈ 120-121 T 3
Penžinskij hrebet ▲ RUS 120-121 V 3
Peoria o USA (AZ) 256-257 C 5
Peoria o USA (IL) 274-275 J 4
Pep o USA (NM) 256-257 M 5
Pepa o ZRE 214-215 E 4
Pepacton Reservoir ⌒ USA (NY) 278-279 G 6
Pepani ~ ZA 220-221 F 3
Pepeekeo o USA (HI) 288 K 5
Pepita ou Porte Alegre, Rio ~ BR 68-69 B 6
Peque o CO 60-61 D 4
Pequena, Cachoeira ~ BR 68-69 C 3
Pequeri, Rio ~ BR 70-71 K 5
Pequop Summit ▲ USA (NV) 246-247 L 2
Pequot Lakes o USA (MN) 270-271 D 4
Perabumulih o RI 162-163 F 6
Pérade, La o CDN (QUE) 238-239 N 2
Peraguaizinho, Rio ~ BR 70-71 J 4
Peraiyur o IND 140-141 G 6
Perak ◘ MAL 162-163 D 2
Perak o RI 168 E 3
Perambalūr o IND 140-141 H 5
Perämeri ≈ 88-89 G 4
Perapat, Tanjung ▲ MAL 164-165 D 1
Peras-2 ▲ MEX 50-51 G 5
Perbaugan o RI 162-163 C 3
Perbulan o RI 162-163 C 3
Percé o CDN (QUE) 240-241 L 2
Percival o CDN (SAS) 232-233 Q 5
Percival Lakes ⌒ AUS 172-173 G 6
Percy, Mount ▲ AUS 172-173 G 4
Percy Isles ⌒ AUS 178-179 L 1
Percy Priest Lake, J. ⌒ USA (TN) 276-277 J 4
Percy Quin State Park ⊥ USA (MS) 268-269 K 5
Perdekop o ZA 220-221 J 3
Perdida, Rio ~ BR 68-69 E 6
Perdido, Arroyo ~ RA 78-79 F 7
Perdido Bay ≈ USA 286-287 B 1
Perdido River ~ USA (FL) 286-287 B 1
Perdidos, Cachoeira dos ~ BR 70-71 H 2
Perdizes o BR 72-73 G 5
Perdões o BR 72-73 H 6
Perdón, Puerto del ▲ E 98-99 G 3
Perdue o CDN (SAS) 232-233 L 3
Perehins'ke o UA 102-103 D 3
Pereira ☆ CO 60-61 D 5
Pereira, Cachoeira ~ BR 66-67 J 5
Pereira Barreto o BR 72-73 E 6
Pereirinha o BR 66-67 J 7
Perejaslav-Chmel'nyc'kyj o UA 102-103 G 2
Perejastavka o RUS 122-123 F 5
Pereljub ☆ RUS 96-97 G 8
Pereljubovka o KA 126-127 M 3
Peremetnoe ☆ KA 96-97 G 8
Peremul Par ⊥ IND 140-141 B 2
Perené, Rio ~ PE 64-65 E 7
Perenjori o AUS 176-177 D 4
Pérèrè o DY 204-205 E 4
Pereščepyne o UA 102-103 J 3
Pereslavľ-Zalesskij o• RUS 94-95 Q 3
pereval Kajtezek ▲ TJ 136-137 N 6
Perevolockij ☆ RUS 96-97 J 8
Perevoz o RUS 118-119 H 6
Perevoz o RUS (GOR) 96-97 D 6
Perevoznaja, guba ⌒ RUS 108-109 H 7
Perez o RA 78-79 J 2
Perez o USA (CA) 246-247 D 2
Pergamino o RA 78-79 J 2
Pergamon ∴•• TR 128-129 B 3
Perge ∴•• TR 128-129 D 4
Pérgola o I 100-101 D 3
Perham o USA (MN) 270-271 C 4
Perhentian Besar, Pulau ⌒ MAL (TER) 162-163 E 2
Perho o FIN 88-89 H 5
Perhonjoki ~ FIN 88-89 G 5
Periá, Rio ~ BR 68-69 G 3
Peribán de Ramos o MEX 52-53 C 2
Péribonca, Lac ⌒ CDN 38-39 J 3
Péribonca, Rivière ~ CDN 38-39 J 3
Peribonka o CDN (QUE) 240-241 C 2
Péribonka o CDN (QUE) 240-241 C 2
Perico o C 54-55 E 3
Perico o USA (TX) 264-265 B 2
Perico Creek ~ USA (TX) 264-265 B 2
Pericos o MEX 50-51 F 5
Peridot o USA (AZ) 256-257 E 5
Périgban o BF 202-203 J 4
Perigord o CDN (SAS) 232-233 P 3
Perigosa, Cachoeira ~ BR 70-71 H 2
Perigoso, Canal ~ BR 62-63 K 6
Périgueux ☆•• F 90-91 H 9
Perijá, Parque Nacional ⊥ YV 60-61 E 3
Perijá, Sierra de ▲ YV 60-61 E 3
Peri Lake ⌒ AUS 178-179 G 6
Peril Strait ≈ 32-33 C 3
Perim = Barim, Ğazirat ⌒ Y 132-133 C 7
Peringat o MAL 162-163 E 2
Periptaveto, ozero ~ RUS 108-109 S 6
Periquen o YV 62-63 D 3
Periquito, Cachoeira ~ BR 66-67 K 6
Periquito, Cachoeira do ~ BR 66-67 G 6
Peristrema • TR 128-129 F 3
Peri Suyu ~ TR 128-129 H 3
Perito Moreno o RA 80 E 3
Peritoro o BR 68-69 F 4
Periyar Lake ⌒ IND 140-141 G 6
Perkat, Tanjung ▲ RI 162-163 F 5
Perkins o USA (MI) 270-271 L 5
Perkins o USA (OK) 264-265 G 3
Perkinstown o USA (WI) 270-271 H 5
Perkiston o USA (MS) 268-269 L 6
Perla, La o MEX 50-51 G 3
Perlah ▲ MAL 162-163 E 3
Perlas, Archipiélago de las ⌒ PA 52-53 E 7
Perlas, Cayos de ⌒ NIC 52-53 C 5
Perlas, Laguna de ⌒ NIC 52-53 C 5
Perlas, Punta de ▲ NIC 52-53 C 5
Perleporten o N 84-85 L 5
Perley o USA (MN) 270-271 B 3
Perley Island ⌒ CDN 36-37 J 5
Perlis ◘ MAL 162-163 D 2
Perlis, Kuala o MAL 162-163 D 2
Perm' ☆ RUS 96-97 K 4
Perma o DY 202-203 L 4
Perma o USA (MT) 250-251 E 4
Përmet ☆ AL 100-101 H 4
Permin Land ⊥ GRØ 26-27 Z 3
Pernambuco ◘ BR 68-69 J 6
Pernambuco Abyssal Plain ≃ 6-7 G 9
Pernambut o IND 140-141 H 4
Pernatty Lagoon ⌒ AUS 178-179 D 6
Pernehué, Cordillera de ▲ RCH 78-79 D 4
Pernik o BG 102-103 C 6
Perniö o FIN 88-89 G 6
Pernštejn • CZ 92-93 O 4
Perola o BR 72-73 D 7
Peron North, Cape ▲ AUS 176-177 B 2
Peron Peninsula ⌒ AUS 176-177 B 2
Perote o MEX 52-53 F 2
Perote o USA (AL) 284-285 E 5
Peroto o BOL 70-71 E 4
Perouse Strait, La = Laperuza, proliv ≈ 122-123 J 6
Perow o CDN (BC) 228-229 H 2
Perpignan ☆• F 90-91 J 10
Perquilauquén, Río ~ RCH 78-79 D 4
Perrault Falls o CDN (ONT) 234-235 K 4
Perret, Punta ▲ YV 60-61 F 2
Perrin o USA (TX) 264-265 F 5
Perrine o USA (FL) 286-287 J 6
Perrin Vale o AUS 176-177 F 4
Perris o USA (CA) 248-249 G 6
Perrivale o AUS 174-175 G 6
Perro, Laguna del ⌒ USA (NM) 256-257 K 4
Perry o CDN (ONT) 236-237 D 5
Perry o USA (FL) 286-287 F 1
Perry o USA (GA) 284-285 G 4
Perry o USA (IA) 274-275 D 3
Perry o USA (MI) 272-273 E 5
Perry o USA (MO) 274-275 G 5
Perry o USA (OK) 264-265 G 2
Perry o USA (TX) 266-267 L 2
Perry Island ⌒ USA 20-21 R 6
Perry Lake ⌒ USA (KS) 262-263 L 5
Perry River ~ CDN 30-31 T 2
Perry River ~ CDN (BC) 230-231 L 2
Perryton o USA (TX) 264-265 D 2
Perryville o USA (AK) 22-23 R 5
Perryville o USA (AR) 276-277 C 5
Perryville o USA (MO) 276-277 F 3
Persepolis ∴••• IR 134-135 E 4
Perseverança o BR 66-67 E 3
Perseverancia o BOL 70-71 F 4
Perseverancia o BR 68-69 E 2
Persian Gulf ≈ 10-11 E 6
Pertek ☆ TR 128-129 H 3
Perth o AUS (TAS) 180-181 J 6
Perth ☆• AUS (WA) 176-177 C 5
Perth o CDN (ONT) 238-239 J 4
Perth o GB 90-91 F 3
Perth Amboy o USA (NJ) 280-281 M 3
Perth-Andover o CDN (NB) 240-241 H 4
Perth Basin ≃ 176-177 A 5
Perth Road o CDN (ONT) 238-239 J 4
Pertominsk o RUS 88-89 P 4
Pertuis Breton ≈ 90-91 G 8
Pertuis d'Antioche ≈ 90-91 G 8
Pertusato, Capo ▲ F 98-99 M 4
Perú o BOL 70-71 D 3
Peru ■ PE 64-65 D 4
Peru o USA (IL) 274-275 J 3
Peru o USA (IN) 274-275 M 4
Peru o USA (NE) 262-263 L 4
Peru, El o YV 62-63 D 2
Peru Basin ≃ 5 C 6
Peru-Chile Trench ≃ 5 C 5
Perugia ☆• I 100-101 D 3
Perugorria o RA 76-77 H 5
Peruhumpenai Mountains Reserve ⊥• RI 164-165 G 5
Peruíbe o BR 74-75 G 5
Peruípe, Rio ~ BR 72-73 L 4
Perumpāvūr o IND 140-141 G 5
Perundurai o IND 140-141 G 5
Perung o RI 168 C 7
Perupuk, Tanjung ▲ RI 164-165 F 3
Pervari ☆ TR 128-129 K 4
Perves, Alt de ▲ E 98-99 H 3
Pervomaevka o RUS 116-117 O 9
Pervomaiskyj o UA 102-103 K 3
Pervomajs'k o UA (LUG) 102-103 L 3
Pervomajs'k ☆ UA (NIK) 102-103 G 3
Pervomajsk = Pervomajs'k ☆ UA 102-103 G 3
Pervomajs'ke ☆ UA 102-103 H 5
Pervomajskij o KA 124-125 N 3
Pervomajskij o RUS 94-95 R 5
Pervomajskij o RUS 118-119 G 10
Pervomajskij o RUS (CEL) 96-97 M 6
Pervomajskij ☆ RUS (ORB) 96-97 G 8
Pervomajskoe o RUS 122-123 K 4
Pervomajskoe o RUS (LEN) 94-95 L 1
Pervosovetsk ☆ KA 96-97 G 8
Pervoural'sk ☆ RUS 96-97 L 5
Pervyj Kuril'skij proliv ⌒ RUS 122-123 R 3
Pervyj Mindej o RUS 116-117 L 7
Peša ~ RUS 88-89 T 3
Pesalai o CL 140-141 H 6
Pésaro o I 100-101 D 3
Pesca, La o MEX 50-51 L 6
Pesca, Punta ▲ RCH 78-79 C 4
Pescada, Ponta da ▲ BR 62-63 J 4
Pescadero o USA (CA) 248-249 B 2
Pescado Castigado, Arroyo el ~ RA 78-79 K 4
Pescadores = Penghu Islands ⌒ RC 156-157 L 5
Pescanaja ~ RUS 124-125 O 2
Pesčanaja ~ RUS 124-125 O 2
Pesčanka ~ RUS 88-89 U 2
Pesčanoe o RUS 88-89 N 5
Pesčanoe, ozero ⌒ RUS 88-89 W 2
Pesčanoe ozero ⌒ RUS 124-125 L 2
Pesčanokopskoe o RUS 102-103 M 4
Pesčany, mys ▲ KA 126-127 J 6
Pesčanyj, mys ▲ RUS 108-109 e 2
Pescara ☆• I 100-101 E 3
Pescara Cassiano o MOC 218-219 H 2
Peščera Kristaličeska •• UA 102-103 E 3
Pescodo, Rio ~ RA 76-77 E 2
Pescovaja, buhta ≈ 112-113 U 1
Peshāwar ☆•• PK 138-139 C 3
Peshkopi ☆•• AL 100-101 H 4
Peshtigo o USA (WI) 270-271 L 5
Peshtigo River ~ USA (WI) 270-271 K 5
Pesjakov, ostrov ⌒ RUS 88-89 Y 2
peski Séjunagsak ⊥ TM 136-137 D 5
Peškovka ☆ KA 124-125 C 2
Pesqueira o BR 68-69 K 6
Pesquería, Rio ~ MEX 50-51 J 4
Peštera o BG 102-103 D 6
Pestovo o RUS 94-95 O 2
Pestravka ☆ RUS 96-97 F 7
Petah Tiqwa ☆ IL 130-131 D 1
Petäjävesi o FIN 88-89 H 5
Petak, Tanjung ▲ RI 164-165 L 3
Petal o USA (MS) 268-269 L 5
Petaling Jaya o MAL 162-163 D 3
Petaluma o USA (CA) 246-247 C 5
Petani, Sungai ~ MAL 162-163 D 2
Petaquillas o MEX 52-53 E 3
Petarbar o IND 142-143 D 4
Petare o YV 60-61 H 2
Petas, Rio Las ~ BOL 70-71 H 5
Petatlán o MEX 52-53 D 3
Petatlán, Rio ~ MEX 50-51 F 4
Petauke o Z 218-219 F 2
Petawanga Lake ⌒ CDN (ONT) 234-235 P 3
Petawawa o CDN (ONT) 238-239 H 3
Petcacab o MEX 52-53 K 2
Petchaburi o THA 158-159 E 4
Pété o CAM 206-207 B 3
Pétel, Djoutou- o RG 202-203 D 4
Petén Itzá, Lago ⌒ GCA 52-53 K 3
Petenwell Lake < USA (WI) 270-271 J 6
Peterbell o CDN (ONT) 236-237 E 4
Peterborough o AUS (SA) 180-181 E 2
Peterborough o AUS (VIC) 180-181 G 5
Peter Borough o• CDN (ONT) 238-239 G 4
Peterborough o• CDN (ONT) 238-239 G 4
Peterborough o• GB 90-91 G 5
Peterborough o USA (NH) 278-279 K 6
Peterhead o GB 90-91 G 3
Peter Island ⌒ GB (VI) 286-287 R 2
Peter Lake ⌒ CDN 30-31 X 4
Peter Lougheed Provincial Park ⊥ CDN (ALB) 232-233 C 5
Petermann Aboriginal Land X AUS 176-177 K 2
Petermann Bjerg ▲ GRØ 26-27 I 7
Petermann Fjord ≈ 26-27 U 3
Petermann Gletscher ⊂ GRØ 26-27 U 3
Petermann Ranges ▲ AUS 176-177 K 2
Peteroa, Volcán ▲ RA 78-79 D 3
Peter Pond Lake ⌒ CDN 32-33 Q 3
Peter Pond Lake Indian Reserve X CDN 32-33 Q 4
Peter Richards, Cape ▲ CDN 24-25 M 5
Petersburg o USA (AK) 32-33 D 3
Petersburg o USA (IL) 274-275 J 4
Petersburg o USA (IN) 274-275 L 6
Petersburg o USA (ND) 258-259 K 3
Petersburg o USA (NE) 262-263 H 3
Petersburg o USA (NY) 278-279 H 6
Petersburg o USA (OK) 264-265 G 4
Petersburg o USA (TN) 276-277 J 5
Petersburg o USA (TX) 264-265 C 5
Petersburg o USA (VA) 280-281 J 6
Petersburg o USA (WV) 280-281 G 4
Petersburg Creek-Duncan Salt Chuck Wilderness ⊥ USA 32-33 D 3
Petersburg National Battlefield • USA (VA) 280-281 J 6
Peter's Mine o GUY 62-63 E 2
Peterson o CDN (SAS) 232-233 N 3
Peterson o USA (IA) 274-275 C 2
Peterson, ostrov ⌒ RUS 108-109 b 3
Peterstown o USA (WV) 280-281 F 6
Petersville o USA 20-21 P 5
Pethel Peninsula ⌒ CDN 30-31 O 4
Petifu Junction o WAL 202-203 D 5
Petín o E 98-99 D 3
Pétionville o• RH 54-55 J 5
Petit-Bourg o F 56 E 3
Petit-Cap o CDN (QUE) 242-243 D 3
Petitcodiac o CDN (NB) 240-241 K 5
Petitcodiac River ~ CDN (NB) 240-241 K 5
Petite Bois Island ⌒ USA (MS) 268-269 M 6
Petite Forte o CDN (NFL) 242-243 O 5
Petite Kabylie ⊥ DZ 190-191 E 2
Petite-Rivière-de-l'Ile o CDN (NB) 240-241 L 3
Petite Rivière de la Baleine ~ CDN 36-37 L 7
Petite Rivière de Povungnituk ~ CDN 36-37 M 4
Petites-Bergeronnes o CDN (QUE) 240-241 F 2
Petit Étang o CDN (NS) 240-241 P 4
Petite-Vallée o CDN (QUE) 242-243 C 3
Petit Goâve o RH 54-55 J 5
Petit Jardin o CDN (NFL) 242-243 J 4
Petit Jean Mountain ▲ USA (AR) 276-277 B 6
Petit Jean State Park ⊥ USA (AR) 276-277 C 5
Petit Lac des Loups Marins ⌒ CDN 36-37 N 6
Petit Lac Manicouagan ⌒ CDN 38-39 L 3
Petit Lac Opinaca ⌒ CDN 38-39 F 2
Petit Loango, Parc National du ⊥ G 210-211 B 5
Petit Mécatina, Île du ⌒ CDN (QUE) 242-243 J 2
Petit Mécatina, Rivière du ~ CDN 38-39 O 3
Petit Mont Cameroun ▲ CAM 204-205 H 6
Petitot River ~ CDN 30-31 J 6
Petit Point ▲ AUS 176-177 B 2
Petit-Rocher o CDN (NB) 240-241 K 3
Petit-Saguenay o CDN (QUE) 240-241 E 2
Petits-Escoumins o CDN (QUE) 240-241 F 2
Petitsikapau Lake ⌒ CDN 36-37 Q 7
Petlād o IND 138-139 D 8
Peto o MEX 52-53 K 1
Petoh o MAL 162-163 E 3
Petorca, Rio ~ RCH 78-79 D 2
Petoskey o USA (MI) 272-273 E 2
Petra ∴••• JOR 130-131 D 2
Petra, ostrova ⌒ RUS 108-109 k 3
Petra I, ostrov ⌒ ARK 16 G 27
Petra Velikogo, zaliv ≈ 122-123 D 7
Petrel Bank ≃ 22-23 F 6
Petrič o BG 102-103 C 7
Petrified Forest • USA (MS) 268-269 K 4
Petrified Forest National Park ∴ USA (AZ) 256-257 F 4
Petrified Wood Park ∴ USA (SD) 260-261 D 1
Petrinja o HR 100-101 F 2
Petriščevo o RUS 94-95 N 4
Petrivs'ka fortec'a • UA 102-103 K 4
Petro o PK 138-139 C 6
Petrodvorec o RUS 94-95 L 2
Petroglyphs • USA (HI) 288 J 4
Petroglyphs National Park • CDN (ONT) 238-239 G 4
Petrohué o RCH 78-79 C 6
Petrokrepost' = Šlissel'burg o RUS 94-95 M 2
Petrolândia o BR 68-69 J 6
Petrolia o USA (CA) 246-247 A 3
Petrolia o USA (TX) 264-265 F 5
Petrolina o BR 68-69 H 6
Petrolina de Goiás o BR 72-73 F 4
Petropavl ☆• KA 124-125 F 1
Petropavlivka o UA 102-103 K 3
Petropavlovka o KA 126-127 M 2
Petropavlovka o RUS (IRK) 116-117 J 7
Petropavlovka ☆ RUS (BUR) 116-117 M 10
Petropavlovsk o RUS 116-117 O 6
Petropavlovsk-Kamčatskij ☆• RUS 120-121 S 7
Petropavlovsk Kamchatskiy = Petropavlovsk-Kamčatskij ☆• RUS 120-121 S 7
Petropavlovskoe, ozero ⌒ RUS 122-123 F 4
Petrópolis o BR 72-73 J 7
Petroquímica o RA 80 G 2
Petroșani o RO 102-103 C 5
Petrovac o YU 100-101 H 2
Petrovka o RUS 124-125 O 2
Petrovsk o RUS 96-97 D 7
Petrovsk-Zabajkal'skij ☆ RUS 116-117 O 10
Petrov Val o RUS 96-97 D 8
Petrozavodsk ☆ RUS 88-89 N 6
Petrusburg o ZA 220-221 G 4
Petrusdal o NAM 220-221 C 1
Petrus Steyn o ZA 220-221 J 3
Petrusville o ZA 220-221 G 5
Petrykav o BY 94-95 L 5
Pettigrew o USA (AR) 276-277 B 5
Pettus o USA (TX) 266-267 K 5
Petty Harbour o CDN (NFL) 242-243 Q 5
Petucalco, Bahía de ≈ 52-53 C 3
Petuhovo ☆ RUS 114-115 J 7
Petuški o RUS 112-113 L 2
Petuški ☆ RUS (VL) 94-95 Q 4
Peulik, Mount ▲ USA 22-23 S 4
Peulla o RCH 78-79 C 6
Peumo o RCH 78-79 D 3
Peunto, ozero ⌒ RUS 108-109 O 7
Peureula o RI 162-163 B 2
Peureula, Tanjung ▲ RI 162-163 B 2
Peureulak o RI 162-163 B 2
Peusangan ~ RI 162-163 B 2
Pevek o RUS 112-113 Q 2
Peyuami, Sierra ▲ YV 60-61 K 5
Peza ~ RUS 88-89 S 4
Pezas o RUS 114-115 T 7
Pézenas o F 90-91 J 10
Peženka ~ RUS 112-113 M 3
Pežostrov ⌒ RUS 88-89 M 3
Pezu o PK 138-139 C 3
Pfarmigan, Cape ▲ CDN 24-25 M 5
Pfarrkirchen o D 92-93 M 4
Pfizner, Mount ▲ AUS 178-179 C 2
Pforzheim o D 92-93 K 4
Phaileng o IND 142-143 H 4
Phalaborwa o ZA 218-219 F 6
Phà Lai o VN 156-157 E 6
Phalodi o IND 138-139 D 6
Phalombe o MW 218-219 H 2
Phāltan o IND 140-141 F 2
Phan o THA 142-143 L 6
Phang Khon o THA 158-159 G 2
Phangnga o THA 158-159 E 6
Phanom o THA 158-159 E 6
Phanom Dong Rak ▲ THA 158-159 G 3
Phanom Sarakham o THA 158-159 F 4
Phan Rang Tháp Chàm o VN 158-159 K 5
Phan Rí, Vũng ~ VN 158-159 K 5
Phan Thiết ☆ VN 158-159 K 5
Phantoms Cave = Trou des Fantomes • CAM 210-211 C 2
Pharenda o IND 142-143 C 2
Pharphing o NEP 144-145 E 7
Pharr o USA (TX) 266-267 J 7
Phaselis ∴•• TR 128-129 D 4
Phatthalung o THA 158-159 F 7
Phayakhapun Phiasi o THA 158-159 G 3
Phayao o THA 142-143 L 6
Phayuha Khiri o THA 158-159 F 3
Phedra o SME 62-63 G 3
Phelp River ~ AUS 174-175 C 3
Phelps Lake ⌒ CDN 30-31 S 6
Phelps Lake ⌒ USA (NC) 282-283 L 5
Phen o THA 158-159 G 2
Phenix City o USA (AL) 284-285 E 4
Phetchabun o THA 158-159 F 2
Phibun Mangsahan o THA 158-159 H 3
Phichit o THA 158-159 F 2
Phikwe, Selebi- o RB 218-219 D 6
Philadelphia o USA (MS) 268-269 L 4
Philadelphia o• USA (PA) 280-281 L 4
Philae ∴••• ET 194-195 F 5
Phil Campbell o USA (AL) 284-285 C 2
Phil Campbell o USA (AL) 284-285 B 2
Philip o USA (SD) 260-261 E 2
Philip Broke, Kap ▲ GRØ 26-27 r 6
Philipp o USA (MS) 268-269 K 3
Philippeville o B 92-93 H 3
Philippi o USA (WV) 280-281 F 4
Philippi, Lake ⌒ AUS 178-179 E 3
Philippi, Monte ▲ RA 80 E 5
Philippine Basin ≃ 14-15 E 6
Philippines = Pilipinas ■ RP 160-161 D 5
Philippines = Pilipinas ⌒ RP 160-161 D 5
Philippine Trench ≃ 160-161 G 6
Philippolis o ZA 220-221 G 5
Philipsburg o NA 56 D 2
Philipsburg o USA (MT) 250-251 F 5
Philipsburg o USA (PA) 280-281 H 3
Philip Smith Mountains ▲ USA 20-21 Q 2
Philipstown o ZA 220-221 G 5
Phil Kearny, Fort • USA (WY) 252-253 M 2
Phillip Bay, Port ≈ 180-181 H 5
Phillip Creek o AUS 174-175 C 6
Phillip Creek Station o AUS 174-175 C 6
Phillip Gap ▲ USA (NC) 282-283 F 4
Phillip Island ⌒ AUS 180-181 H 5
Phillips o USA (ME) 278-279 L 4
Phillips o USA (WI) 270-271 H 5
Phillips Arm o CDN (BC) 230-231 D 3
Phillipsburg o USA (KS) 262-263 G 5
Phillipsburg o USA (MO) 276-277 C 3
Phillipsburg o USA (NJ) 280-281 L 3
Phillips Inlet ≈ 26-27 G 2
Phillips Mountains ▲ ARK 16 F 23
Phillips Point ▲ CDN 24-25 h 2
Phillips Range ▲ AUS 172-173 G 4
Philo o USA (CA) 246-247 B 4
Philomath o USA (OR) 244-245 B 6
Philpots Island ⌒ CDN 24-25 g 3
Philpott Lake ⌒ USA (VA) 280-281 F 7
Phippen o CDN (SAS) 232-233 K 3
Phippsøya ⌒ N 84-85 M 2
Phitsanulok o THA 158-159 F 2
Phitshane o RB 220-221 G 2
Phnom Penh = Phnum Pénh ★• K 158-159 H 5
Phnum Pénh ★• K 158-159 H 5
Phoenix o USA (MI) 270-271 K 3
Phoenix ☆• USA (AZ) 256-257 C 5
Phoenixville o USA (CT) 278-279 J 7
Phoenixville o USA (PA) 280-281 L 3
Phon o THA 158-159 H 2
Phon o THA 158-159 G 3
Phoncharoen o THA 158-159 G 2
Phonda o IND 140-141 E 2
Phongota o IND 138-139 E 3
Phôngsali o LAO 156-157 C 6
Phong Thổ ☆ VN 156-157 C 5
Phong Thong o THA 158-159 G 2
Phôn Sa Van o LAO 156-157 E 7
Phoque, Rivière au ~ CDN 36-37 K 7
Phou Khoun o LAO 156-157 C 7
Phrae o THA 142-143 M 6
Phranakhon Si Ayutthaya o••• THA 158-159 F 3
Phran Kratai o THA 158-159 E 2
Phra Pathom Chedi •• THA 158-159 E 4
Phù Bài o VN 158-159 J 2
Phù Cát o VN 158-159 K 3
Phu Đen Đin ▲ VN 156-157 C 5
Phú Hung o VN 158-159 J 5
Phuket o• THA 158-159 E 7
Phukradung o THA 158-159 F 2
Phulbari o BD 142-143 F 3
Phulchari o BD 142-143 F 3
Phuldu o IND 142-143 H 4
Phú Lộc ☆ VN 158-159 J 2
Phu Luông ▲ VN 156-157 D 6
Phumĭ Ântoăt o K 158-159 G 5
Phumĭ Bahm o K 158-159 H 4
Phumĭ Banam o K 158-159 H 5
Phumĭ Chhlong o K 158-159 H 4
Phumĭ Chŏâm Sla o K 158-159 G 5
Phumĭ Chŭb Krau o K 158-159 H 5
Phumĭ Kâmpóng Trâbêk o K 158-159 H 4
Phumĭ Kdŏl Kraŏm o K 158-159 G 4
Phumĭ Khley o K 158-159 H 4
Phumĭ Khna o K 158-159 H 5
Phumĭ Krêk o K 158-159 H 5
Phumĭ Labang Siĕk o K 158-159 J 4
Phumĭ Mlu Prey o K 158-159 H 4
Phumĭ o Snguŏt o K 158-159 G 4
Phumiphon Reservoir ⌒ THA 158-159 E 2
Phumĭ Phsa Rômèas o K 158-159 H 4
Phumĭ Prek Sândêk o K 158-159 H 5
Phumĭ Pring o K 158-159 H 4
Phumĭ Sala Vichey o K 158-159 H 4
Phumĭ Sâmraông o K 158-159 G 3
Phumĭ Spoe Tbong o K 158-159 H 4
Phumĭ Taek Sŏk o K 158-159 G 4
Phumĭ Thmâ Pŏk o K 158-159 G 3
Phumĭ Véal Rénh o K 158-159 G 5
Phú Mỹ o VN 158-159 J 5
Phù Mỹ o VN 158-159 K 3
Phú Nhon o VN 158-159 K 3
Phunphin o THA 158-159 E 6
Phuntsholing o BHT 142-143 F 2
Phu'ó'c Long o VN 158-159 H 6
Phu'ó'c So'n o VN 158-159 J 3
Phú Quốc, Đảo ⌒ VN 158-159 H 5
Phù Qủy ⌒ VN 158-159 K 5
Phurkia o IND 138-139 G 4
Phu Sa Phin ▲ VN 156-157 D 6
Phu Thọ ☆ VN 156-157 D 6
Phutnaditjhaba o ZA 220-221 J 4
Phutthaisong o THA 158-159 G 3
Phu Yen ▲ THA 158-159 F 2
Piaçabuçu o BR 68-69 K 7
Piaca dos Mineiros o BR 72-73 D 5
Piacenza ☆• I 100-101 B 2
Piamonte o CO 60-61 D 4
Pianag o RP 160-161 D 6
Pianco o BR 68-69 K 5
Piancó, Rio ~ BR 68-69 J 5
Pian Creek ~ AUS 178-179 K 5
Piandang, Tanjung o MAL 162-163 D 2
Piangil o AUS 180-181 G 3
Pianguan o VRC 154-155 G 2
Piankana o ZRE 210-211 G 5
Pianosa, Ísola ⌒ I 100-101 C 3
Piapot o CDN (SAS) 232-233 J 5
Piapot Indian Reservation X CDN (SAS) 232-233 O 5
Piaseczno o PL 92-93 Q 2
Piaski o PL 92-93 R 3
Piatra-Neamț ☆• RO 102-103 E 4
Piauí ◘ BR 68-69 F 6
Piauí, Rio ~ BR 68-69 G 5
Piaui, Rio ~ BR 68-69 G 6
Piauí, Rio ~ BR 68-69 K 7
Piave ~ I 100-101 D 1
Piaxtla, Punta ▲ MEX 50-51 F 6
Piaxtla, Rio ~ MEX 50-51 F 6
Pibor ~ SUD 208-209 A 5
Pibor Post o SUD 208-209 A 5
Píbrans = Příbram o CZ 92-93 N 4
Pica o RCH 70-71 C 7
Pica, La o YV 60-61 J 3
Picacho o USA (AZ) 256-257 D 6
Picacho o USA (CA) 248-249 K 6
Picacho o USA (NM) 256-257 K 5
Picacho de la Laguna ▲ MEX 50-51 E 6
Picada o BR 70-71 G 3
Pičaevo o RUS 94-95 S 5
Picão, Ponta do ▲ BR 72-73 J 7
Pica-Pau, Cachoeira ~ BR 62-63 E 6
Picard ⌒ SY 222-223 E 2
Picardie ◘ F 90-91 H 6
Picayune o USA (MS) 268-269 L 6
Picentini, Monti ▲ I 100-101 E 4
Pich o MEX 52-53 J 2
Pichalo, Punta ▲ RCH 70-71 B 6
Pichaman o RCH 78-79 C 3
Pichana, Río ~ RA 76-77 E 6
Pichanal o RA 76-77 E 2
Picher o USA (OK) 264-265 K 2
Pichereguas, Paso ▲ RA 76-77 C 6
Pichilemu o RCH 78-79 D 3
Pichileufu, Cerro ▲ RA 78-79 D 6
Pichilingue o MEX 50-51 D 5
Pichi Mahuida o RA 78-79 G 5
Pichincha, Volcán ▲ EC 64-65 C 2
Pichi Richi Railway • AUS 180-181 E 2
Pichis, Río ~ PE 64-65 E 7
Pichor o IND 138-139 G 7
Pichucalco o MEX 52-53 H 3
Pichupichu, Volcán ▲ PE 70-71 B 5
Pic Island ⌒ CDN (ONT) 236-237 B 4
Pickens o USA (MS) 268-269 L 4
Pickens o USA (OK) 264-265 J 4
Pickens o USA (SC) 284-285 H 2
Pickens, Fort • USA (FL) 286-287 B 1
Pickerel Lake ⌒ CDN (ONT) 234-235 M 6
Pickerel River ~ CDN (ONT) 238-239 E 3
Pickering o USA (LA) 268-269 G 5
Pickertaramoor X AUS 172-173 K 1
Pickford o USA (MI) 270-271 O 4
Pickneyville o USA (IL) 274-275 J 6
Pickstown o USA (SD) 260-261 H 3
Pickwick Landing State Park ⊥ USA (TN) 276-277 G 5
Pico ⌒ P 6-7 E 6
Pico da Neblina, Parque Nacional do ⊥ BR 66-67 D 2
Pico de Orizaba, Parque Nacional ⊥ MEX 52-53 F 2
Pico de Salamanca o RA 80 G 2
Pico Fracture Zone ≃ 6-7 E 5
Pico Negro, Cerro ▲ RCH 70-71 C 6
Picos o BR 68-69 H 5
Picos, Los o MEX 50-51 H 3
Picota o PE 64-65 D 5
Pico Truncado o RA 80 G 3
Pic River ~ CDN (ONT) 236-237 B 3
Picton o• AUS 180-181 L 3
Picton o CDN (ONT) 238-239 H 4
Picton o NZ 182 E 4
Picton, Isla ⌒ RCH 80 G 7
Pictou o CDN (NS) 240-241 N 5
Pictou Island o CDN (NS) 240-241 N 5
Pictou Island ⌒ CDN (NS) 240-241 N 5
Picture Butte o CDN (ALB) 232-233 F 6
Pictured Rocks National Lakeshore ⊥ USA (MI) 270-271 M 4
Picturesque Site ∴• RI 166-167 H 2
Picudo, Cerro ▲ RA 80 F 3
Picuí o BR 68-69 K 5
Picunda o• GE 126-127 D 6
Picunda, mys ▲ GE 126-127 D 6
Picún Leufú o RA 78-79 E 5
Picún Leufú, Arroyo ~ RA 78-79 E 5
Picúnleufú, Cerro ▲ RA 78-79 D 5
Picuris Indian Reservation X USA (NM) 256-257 K 2
Pidando ⌒ DVR 150-151 E 8
Pidarak o PK 134-135 K 6
Pidie, Ujung ▲ RI 162-163 A 2
Pidurutalagala ▲ CL 140-141 J 7
Piebli o CI 202-203 G 6
Piedad de Cavadas, La o MEX 52-53 C 1
Piedade o BR 72-73 G 7
Pié de Palo, Sierra ▲ RA 76-77 C 6
Piedmont o USA (AL) 284-285 E 3
Piedmont o USA (MO) 276-277 E 3
Piedmont o USA (SD) 260-261 C 2
Piedmont Lake < USA (OH) 280-281 E 3
Piedmont National Wildlife Refuge ⊥ USA (GA) 284-285 G 3
Piedra, Cerro ▲ RCH 78-79 C 4
Piedrabuena o E 98-99 E 5
Piedra del Águila o RA 78-79 D 6
Piedra de la Virgen • YV 62-63 D 3
Piedra de Olla, Cerro ▲ MEX 52-53 F 3
Piedra Echada o RA 78-79 H 5
Piedrahita o E 98-99 E 4
Piedra River ~ USA (CO) 254-255 H 6
Piedras, Las o PE 70-71 C 3
Piedras, Las o ROU 78-79 L 3
Piedras, Punta ▲ RA 78-79 L 3
Piedras, Río de las ~ PE 70-71 B 2
Piedras Altas o BR 74-75 D 8
Piedras Blancas o CR 52-53 C 7
Piedras Negras ∴• GCA 52-53 J 3
Piedras Negras o MEX 50-51 J 3
Piedra Sola o ROU 78-79 L 2
Piedras Point ▲ RP 160-161 C 7
Piedritas o MEX 50-51 H 3
Piedritas o RA 78-79 H 3
Pie Island ⌒ CDN (ONT) 234-235 O 6
Piekenaarskloof ▲ ZA 220-221 D 6
Pieksämäki o FIN 88-89 J 5
Piéla o BF 202-203 K 3
Pielavesi o FIN 88-89 J 5
Pielinen ⌒ FIN 88-89 K 5
Pieljekaise nationalpark ⊥ S 86-87 H 3
Pieman River ~ AUS 180-181 H 6
Piemonte ◘ I 100-101 A 2
Pienaarsrivier o ZA 220-221 J 2
Piendamo o CO 60-61 C 6
Pieniężno o• PL 92-93 Q 1
Pienza o• I 100-101 C 3
Pierce o USA (ID) 250-251 D 5
Pierce o USA (NE) 262-263 J 2
Pierce Inlet, Fort ≈ USA 286-287 J 4
Pierce Lake ⌒ CDN 34-35 K 3
Pierceland o CDN 32-33 Q 4
Pierceville o USA (KS) 262-263 F 7
Pieres o RA 78-79 K 5
Pierowall o GB 90-91 F 2
Pierre ☆ USA (SD) 260-261 F 2
Pierre Hoho o F 62-63 H 4
Pierre Lake ⌒ CDN (ONT) 236-237 H 3
Pierrette o F 62-63 H 3
Pierre Verendrye Monument, Fort • USA (SD) 260-261 F 2
Pierreville o CDN (QUE) 238-239 N 2
Pierreville o TT 60-61 L 2
Pierson o CDN (MAN) 234-235 B 5
Pierson o USA (FL) 286-287 H 2
Pierz o USA (MN) 270-271 D 5
Piešt'any o SK 92-93 O 4
Pietarsaari = Jakobstad o FIN 88-89 G 5
Pietermaritzburg ☆•• ZA 220-221 K 4
Pietersburg o ZA 218-219 E 6
Pietlo o LB 202-203 F 7
Pie Town o USA (NM) 256-257 G 4
Piet Plessis o ZA 220-221 G 3
Piet Retief o• ZA 220-221 K 3
Pietroșani o RO 102-103 D 6
Pifo o EC 64-65 C 2
Pigeon Creek ~ USA (AL) 284-285 D 5
Pigeon Forge o USA (NC) 282-283 D 5
Pigeon Hill o CDN (NB) 240-241 L 3
Pigeon Hole o AUS 172-173 K 4
Pigeon Lake ⌒ CDN (ALB) 232-233 D 2
Pigeon River ~ USA (IN) 274-275 N 3
Piggott o USA (AR) 276-277 E 4
Piggs Peak o SD 220-221 K 2
Pignon o RH 54-55 J 5
Pigu o GH 202-203 K 5
Pigüé o RA 78-79 H 4
Pigüé, Arroyo ~ RA 78-79 H 4
Pigüm Do ⌒ ROK 150-151 E 10
Pihtipudas o FIN 88-89 H 5
Pihtovyj greben', gora ▲ RUS 114-115 S 7
Pijijiapan o• MEX 52-53 H 4
Pikalevo o RUS 94-95 O 2
Pikangikum o CDN (ONT) 234-235 K 3
Pikangikum Lake ⌒ CDN (ONT) 234-235 J 3
Pikas', hrebet ▲ RUS 112-113 Q 5
Pikasilla o EST 94-95 K 2
Pikas'vajat ~ RUS 112-113 R 5
Pike o USA (NY) 278-279 C 6
Pike Island ⌒ CDN 36-37 P 3
Pike Lake o CDN (SAS) 232-233 M 4
Pikes Peak ▲ USA (CO) 254-255 K 5
Piketberg o ZA 220-221 D 6
Piketon o USA (OH) 280-281 C 4

Pikeville ○ USA (KY) 276-277 N 3
Pikeville ○ USA (TN) 276-277 K 5
Pikin Rio ~ SME 62-63 G 4
Pikiutdleq = Køge Bugt ≈ 28-29 U 4
Pikmiktalik ○ USA 20-21 J 5
Pikounda ○ RCB 210-211 F 3
Pikovka, Bol'šaja ~ RUS 114-115 R 5
Pila ★• PL 92-93 O 2
Pila ○ RA 78-79 K 4
Pila, La ○ MEX 50-51 J 6
Pilaga, Riacho ~ RA 76-77 H 3
Pilah, Kuala ○ MAL 162-163 E 3
Pila Kyun ⌒ MYA 158-159 D 5
Pilane ○ RB 220-221 H 2
Pilanesberg ▲ ZA (TRA) 220-221 H 2
Pilanesberg ⊥ ZA (TRA) 220-221 H 2
Pilang ○ RI 164-165 D 5
Pilani ○ IND 138-139 E 5
Pilão Arcado ○ BR 68-69 G 6
Pilar ○• IND 140-141 E 3
Pilar ★ PY 76-77 H 4
Pilar ○ RA (BUA) 78-79 K 3
Pilar ○ RA (COD) 76-77 F 6
Pilar, El ○ YV 60-61 K 2
Pilar de Goiás ○ BR 72-73 F 3
Pilas Group ⌒ RP 160-161 D 9
Pilas Island ⌒ RP 160-161 D 9
Pilaya, Río ~ BOL 76-77 E 1
Pilbara ⩩ AUS 172-173 C 7
Pilcaniyeu ○ RA 78-79 D 6
Pilcomayo, Río ~ PY 76-77 G 2
Pilcopata ○ PE 70-71 B 3
Pil'da ~ RUS 122-123 H 3
Pile Bay Village ○ USA 22-23 U 3
Pileru ○ IND 140-141 H 4
Pilger ○ CDN (SAS) 232-233 N 3
Pilgrams = Pelhřimov ○ CZ 92-93 N 4
Pilgrim Springs ○ USA 20-21 H 4
Pilgrim's Rest ○• ZA 220-221 K 2
Pilibhit ★ IND 138-139 G 5
Piling Lake ⊂ CDN 28-29 C 2
Pilka ~ RUS 118-119 F 6
Pilliga ○ AUS 178-179 K 6
Pillinger ○ AUS 180-181 H 7
Pillo, Isla del ⌒ RA 78-79 J 2
Pillsbury ○ USA (ND) 258-259 K 4
Pilluana ○ PE 64-65 D 5
Pil'nja, ozero ⊂ RUS 108-109 H 7
Pilões ○ BR (MIN) 72-73 H 3
Pilões ○ BR (PA) 68-69 L 5
Pilões, Cachoeira do ~ BR 68-69 D 6
Pilón ○ C 54-55 G 5
Pilón, El ○ PA 52-53 D 8
Pilón, Río ~ MEX 50-51 J 5
Pilos ○ GR 100-101 H 6
Pilot, The ▲ AUS 180-181 K 4
Pilota Mohotkina, ostrov ⌒ RUS 108-109 b 3
Pilot Knob ▲ USA (ID) 250-251 D 6
Pilot Mound ○ CDN (MAN) 234-235 E 5
Pilot Mountain ○ USA (NC) 282-283 G 4
Pilot Peak ▲ USA (NV) 246-247 H 5
Pilot Point ○ USA 22-23 S 4
Pilot Point ○ USA (TX) 264-265 H 5
Pilot Rock ○ USA (OR) 244-245 G 5
Pilot Santa ○ USA 20-21 J 6
Pilowo ○ RI 164-165 L 2
Pilquen, Cerro ▲ RCH 78-79 C 4
Pilsen = Plzeň ○ CZ 92-93 M 4
Pil'tanlor, ozero ⊂ RUS 114-115 M 4
Pil'tun, zaliv ⊂ RUS 122-123 K 2
Pil'vo ○ RUS 122-123 K 3
Pim ~ RUS 114-115 L 4
Pima ○ USA (AZ) 256-257 F 6
Pimba ○ AUS 178-179 D 6
Pimbee ○ AUS 176-177 C 2
Pimenta Bueno ○ BR 70-71 G 2
Pimenteiras ○ BR (PIA) 68-69 H 5
Pimenteiras ○ BR (RON) 70-71 G 3
Pimentel ○ PE 64-65 C 5
Pimentel Barbosa, Área Indígena ⚔ BR 72-73 E 2
Pim Island ⌒ CDN 26-27 N 4
Pimpalgaon Basvant ○ IND 138-139 E 9
Pina ○ GH 202-203 K 4
Piña ○ PA 52-53 D 7
Piña, Cerro ▲ PA 52-53 E 8
Pinabasan, Pulau ⌒ RI 164-165 E 2
Pinacate, Cerro del ▲ MEX 50-51 C 2
Pináculo, Cerro ▲ RA 80 D 5
Pinagsabangan ○ RP 160-161 D 6
Pinal, Caño el ~ CO 60-61 F 5
Piñal, El ○ CO 60-61 D 3
Pinaleno Mountains ▲ USA (AZ) 256-257 E 6
Piñalito ○ CO 60-61 E 6
Pinamalayan ○ RP 160-161 D 6
Pinamar ○ RA 78-79 L 4
Pinamula ○ RI 164-165 G 3
Pinang ○ RI 162-163 F 4
Pinanga ○ ZRE 210-211 G 5
Pinangah ○ MAL 160-161 B 10
Pinantan ○ CDN (BC) 230-231 J 3
Pınarbaşı ★ TR 128-129 G 3
Pinar del Río ★ C 54-55 D 3
Pinaré ○ BR 74-75 E 5
Pınarhisar ★ TR 128-129 B 2
Pinatubo, Mount ▲ RP 160-161 D 5
Pinawa ○ CDN (MAN) 234-235 H 4
Pincher ○ CDN (ALB) 232-233 E 6
Pincher Creek ○ CDN (ALB) 232-233 E 6
Pinchi ○ CDN (BC) 228-229 K 2
Pinçon, Mont ▲ F 90-91 G 7
Pincón de Boygorri, Represa < ROU 78-79 L 2
Pinconning ○ USA (MI) 272-273 F 4
Pińczów ○• PL 92-93 Q 3
Pinda ○ MOC 218-219 H 3
Pindaí ○ BR 72-73 J 3
Pindaíba, Rio ~ BR 72-73 D 3
Pindal ○ EC 64-65 B 4
Pindar ○ AUS 176-177 C 4
Pindarama do Tocantins ○ BR 68-69 E 7
Pindare, Rio ~ BR 68-69 F 3
Pindaré, Rio ~ BR 68-69 E 4
Pind Dādan Khān ○ PK 138-139 D 3
Pindi Bhattiān ○ PK 138-139 D 4
Pindi Gheb ○ PK 138-139 D 3
Pindiu ○ PNG 183 D 4
Pindolo ○ RI 164-165 G 5
Píndos Oros ▲ GR 100-101 H 5
Pinduši ○ RUS 88-89 N 5
Pine ○ USA (AZ) 256-257 D 4
Pine Apple ○ USA (AL) 284-285 D 5
Pine Barren Creek ~ USA (AL) 284-285 D 5
Pine Bluff ○ USA (AR) 276-277 C 6
Pine Bluffs ○ USA (WY) 252-253 O 5
Pine City ○ USA (MN) 270-271 F 5
Pine City ○ USA (OR) 244-245 F 5
Pine Creek ○• AUS 172-173 K 2
Pine Creek ~ CDN 30-31 K 4
Pine Creek ~ CDN 32-33 O 4
Pinecreek ○ USA (MN) 270-271 C 2
Pine Creek ○ USA (MT) 250-251 J 6
Pine Creek ~ USA (PA) 280-281 J 2
Pine Creek Gorge ∴ USA (PA) 280-281 J 2
Pine Creek Indian Reserve ⚔ CDN (MAN) 234-235 C 2
Pine Creek Lake < USA (OK) 264-265 J 4
Pinedale ○ USA (WY) 252-253 J 4
Pine Dock ○ CDN (MAN) 234-235 G 3
Pine Falls ○ CDN (MAN) 234-235 G 4
Pinefield ○ BS 54-55 J 3
Pine Flat ○ USA (CA) 248-249 F 4
Pine Flat Reservoir ⊂ USA (CA) 248-249 E 3
Pinega ○ RUS 88-89 R 4
Pinega ~ RUS 88-89 S 5
Pinegrove ○ AUS 176-177 C 3
Pine Grove ○ USA (OR) 244-245 D 5
Pine Hill ○ AUS 178-179 B 2
Pine Hill ○ CDN (QUE) 238-239 L 3
Pine Hill ○ USA (AL) 284-285 C 5
Pinehouse Lake ⊂ CDN 34-35 C 3
Pinehurst ○ USA (CA) 248-249 E 3
Pinehurst ○ USA (NC) 282-283 H 5
Pineimuta River ~ CDN (ONT) 234-235 O 2
Pine Island ○ USA (LA) 268-269 H 6
Pine Island ○ USA (MN) 270-271 F 6
Pine Island ⌒ USA (FL) 286-287 G 5
Pine Island Bay ≈ 16 F 26
Pine Island Bayou ~ USA (TX) 268-269 F 6
Pine Islands ⌒ USA (FL) 286-287 H 7
Pine Island Sound ≈ USA 286-287 G 5
Pine Lake ○ CDN (ALB) 232-233 E 3
Pineland ○ USA (SC) 284-285 J 4
Pineland ○ USA (TX) 268-269 G 5
Pine Level ○ USA (AL) 284-285 D 4
Pinellas Park ○ USA (FL) 286-287 G 4
Pine Lodge ○ USA (NM) 256-257 K 5
Pine Mountain ○ USA (GA) 284-285 F 4
Pine Mountain ▲ USA (GA) 284-285 F 4
Pine Mountain Summit ▲ USA (CA) 248-249 E 5
Pinemuta River ~ CDN (ONT) 234-235 N 2
Pine Point ○ CDN (NWT) 30-31 M 5
Pine Point ▲ CDN (NWT) 30-31 M 5
Pine Portage ○ CDN (ONT) 234-235 P 5
Piñera ○ ROU 78-79 L 2
Pine Ridge ○ USA (CA) 248-249 E 2
Pine Ridge ○ USA (SD) 260-261 D 3
Pine Ridge Indian Reservation ⚔ USA (SD) 260-261 D 3
Pine River ○ CDN (MAN) 234-235 C 3
Pine River ~ CDN 30-31 Q 6
Pine River ~ CDN 32-33 J 4
Pine River ○ USA (MN) 270-271 D 4
Pinerolo ○ I 100-101 A 2
Pines, Point of ○ USA (AZ) 256-257 F 5
Pine Springs ○ USA (TX) 266-267 C 2
Pineto ○ I 100-101 E 3
Pinetop-Lakeside ○ USA (AZ) 256-257 F 4
Pinetops ○ USA (NC) 282-283 K 5
Pinetown ○ ZA 220-221 K 4
Pinetta ○ USA (FL) 286-287 F 1
Pine Valley ○ USA (UT) 254-255 B 6
Pineview ○ USA (GA) 284-285 G 4
Pineview ○ USA (UT) 254-255 D 3
Pine Village ○ USA (IN) 274-275 L 4
Pineville ○ USA (KY) 276-277 M 4
Pineville ○ USA (LA) 268-269 H 5
Pineville ○ USA (MO) 276-277 A 4
Pineville ○ USA (WV) 280-281 E 6
Pine Woods ○ USA (MS) 268-269 L 4
Piney ○ CDN (MAN) 234-235 H 5
Piney Buttes ⩩ USA (MT) 250-251 M 4
Piney Creek ~ USA (AR) 276-277 B 5
Piney Island ⌒ USA (FL) 286-287 E 1
Pingal ○ IND 138-139 D 1
Ping'an ○ VRC 154-155 C 3
Pingaring ○ AUS 176-177 E 6
Pingba ○ VRC 156-157 E 3
Pingchang ○ VRC 154-155 E 6
Pingdingshan ○ VRC 154-155 H 5
Pingding Shan ▲ VRC 150-151 G 4
Pingdu ○ VRC 154-155 L 3
Pingelly ○ AUS 176-177 D 6
Pinger Point ▲ CDN 24-25 f 6
Pingguo ○ VRC 156-157 E 5
Pinghe ○ VRC 156-157 K 4
Pinghu ○ VRC 154-155 M 6
Pingjiang ○ VRC (GZH) 156-157 F 4
Pingjiang ○ VRC (HUN) 156-157 H 2
Pingle ○ VRC 156-157 G 4
Pingli ○ VRC 154-155 F 5
Pingliang ○ VRC 154-155 E 4
Pingling ○ VRC 156-157 J 5
Pinglu ○ VRC 154-155 H 2
Pinglu ○ VRC 156-157 F 5
Pingluo ○ VRC 154-155 E 2
Pingnan ○ VRC (FUJ) 156-157 L 3
Pingnan ○ VRC (GXI) 156-157 G 5
Pingo, El ○ RA 76-77 H 6
Pingo Pingo, Cerro ▲ RCH 76-77 C 2
Pingquan ○ VRC 148-149 O 7
Pingree ○ USA (ND) 258-259 J 4
Pingrup ○ AUS 176-177 E 6
Pingshan ○ VRC (HEB) 154-155 J 2
Pingshan ○ VRC (HEI) 150-151 F 5
Pingshi ○ VRC 156-157 H 4
Pingtang ○ VRC 156-157 E 4
Pingtung ○ RC 156-157 M 5
Pingua Hills ▲ CDN 28-29 D 3
Pingüicas, Cerro ▲ MEX 50-51 K 7
Pingüinos, Reserva Faunística los ⊥ RCH 80 E 6
Pingurbek Island ⌒ USA 22-23 O 3
Þingvallavatn ⊂ IS 86-87 c 2
Þingvellir ○• IS 86-87 c 2
Pingwang ○ VRC 154-155 M 6
Pingwu ○ VRC 154-155 D 5
Pingxiang ○ VRC (GXI) 156-157 E 5
Pingxiang ○ VRC (JXI) 156-157 H 3
Pingyang ○ VRC 156-157 M 3
Pingyao ○ VRC 154-155 H 3
Pingyi ○ VRC 154-155 K 4
Pingyin ○ VRC 154-155 K 3
Pingyu ○ VRC 154-155 J 5
Pingyuan ○ VRC 156-157 J 4
Pingyuanjie ○ VRC 156-157 C 5
Pinhal ○ BR 74-75 E 8
Pinhalzinho ○ BR 74-75 D 6
Pinhão ○ BR 74-75 E 5
Pinheiro ○ BR 68-69 F 3
Pinheiro Machado ○ BR 74-75 D 8
Pinheiros ○ BR 72-73 K 5
Pinhél ○ BR 66-67 K 4
Pinhuã, Rio ~ BR 66-67 E 6
Pini, Pulau ⌒ RI 162-163 C 4
Pinillos ○ CO 60-61 D 3
Pinjarra ○• AUS 176-177 C 6
Pinjug ○ RUS 96-97 E 3
Pinkan ○ MYA 142-143 K 4
Pinkawillinie Conservation Park ⊥ AUS 180-181 C 2
Pinkha ○ MYA 142-143 J 3
Pink Hill ○ USA (NC) 282-283 K 5
Pink Mountain ○ CDN 32-33 J 3
Pink River ~ CDN 34-35 D 2
Pinland ○ USA (FL) 286-287 F 2
Pinlebu ○ MYA 142-143 J 3
Pinnacles ○ AUS 176-177 F 4
Pinnacles, The ⊥•• AUS 176-177 C 5
Pinnacles National Monument ∴ USA (CA) 248-249 C 3
Pinnaroo ○ AUS 180-181 F 3
Pinney's Beach ⩩ KAN 56 D 3
Pinogu ○ RI 164-165 H 3
Pinoh ~ RI 162-163 J 5
Pino Hachado, Paso de ▲ RA 78-79 D 5
Pinola ○ USA (MS) 268-269 L 5
Piñon ○ CO 60-61 E 2
Pinon ○ USA (NM) 256-257 K 6
Pinon Canyon ○ USA (CO) 254-255 M 6
Piñon Hills ○ USA (CA) 248-249 G 5
Pinos ○ MEX 50-51 J 6
Pinos, Mount ▲ USA (CA) 248-249 E 5
Pinos Altos ○ USA (NM) 256-257 G 6
Pinotepa Nacional ○• MEX 52-53 E 3
Pinrang ○ RI 164-165 F 5
Pins, Pointe aux ▲ CDN (ONT) 238-239 D 6
Pinsk ○ BY 94-95 K 5
Pinski bolota ⩩ UA 102-103 D 2
Pinta, Isla ⌒ EC 64-65 B 9
Pintada, La ○ PA 52-53 D 7
Pintada, Sierra ▲ MEX 50-51 B 4
Pintadas ○ BR 68-69 J 7
Pintado ○ BR 68-69 G 6
Pintado, Cerro ▲ RA 80 D 4
Pintado, Rio ~ BR 72-73 E 2
Pintados ○ RCH 70-71 C 7
Pintados, Salar de ⊂ RCH 70-71 C 7
Pintatu ○ RI 164-165 K 3
Pinto ○ RA 76-77 F 5
Pinto Creek ~ CDN (ALB) 228-229 R 3
Pinto Creek ~ CDN (ALB) 228-229 P 2
Pinto Creek ~ CDN (SAS) 232-233 L 6
Pinto Summit ▲ USA (NV) 246-247 K 4
Pintoyacu, Rio ~ EC 64-65 D 2
Pinturas, Río ~ RA 80 E 3
Pintuyan ○ RP 160-161 F 8
Pintwater Range ▲ USA (NV) 248-249 J 3
Piñuelas ○ CO 60-61 D 2
Piñuña Negra ○ CO 64-65 D 1
Pinware ○ CDN (NFL) 242-243 M 1
Pinware River ~ CDN 38-39 Q 2
Pinware River Provincial Park ⊥ CDN (NFL) 242-243 M 1
Pinzon, Canal de ≈ 64-65 B 10
Pinzon, Isla ⌒ EC 64-65 B 10
Pioche ○ USA (NV) 248-249 K 2
Piodi ○ ZRE 214-215 C 4
Pio IX ○ BR 68-69 H 5
Pioka ○ ZRE 210-211 E 6
Piombino ○ I 100-101 C 3
Pioneer ○ USA (AZ) 256-257 B 5
Pioneer ○ USA (CA) 246-247 E 5
Pioneer Fracture Zone ≃ 14-15 O 4
Pioneer Huron City • USA (MI) 272-273 G 3
Pioneer Mountains ▲ USA (ID) 252-253 D 3
Pioneer Mountains ▲ USA (MT) 250-251 F 6
Pioneer Woman Monument ∴ USA (OK) 264-265 G 2
Pioneiros d'Oeste ○ BR 72-73 D 3
Pioner ○ RUS 122-123 M 6
Pioner, ostrov ⌒ RUS 108-109 Y 2
Piore River ~ PNG 183 A 2
Piorini ○ BR 66-67 F 4
Piorini, Lago ⊂ BR 66-67 F 4
Piotrków Trybunalski ★ PL 92-93 P 3
Pio XII. ○ BR 68-69 F 3
Pipa, Cerro ▲ RA 78-79 E 6
Pipalyatjara ○ AUS 176-177 K 3
Pipanaco, Salar de ⊂ RA 76-77 D 5
Piparia ○ IND 138-139 G 8
Pipe Spring National Monument • USA (AZ) 256-257 C 2
Pipestone ○ CDN (ALB) 232-233 E 2
Pipestone ○ CDN (MAN) 234-235 C 5
Pipestone ○ USA (MN) 270-271 B 7
Pipestone Creek ~ CDN (SAS) 232-233 Q 5
Pipestone National Monument ∴• USA (MN) 270-271 B 6
Pipestone Pass ▲ USA (MT) 250-251 G 6
Pipestone River ~ CDN 30-31 Q 6
Pipestone River ~ CDN (ONT) 234-235 N 2
Pipi ~ RCA 206-207 F 4
Pipi, Gorges de la •• RCA 206-207 F 4
Pipili ○ IND 142-143 D 5
Pipinas ○ RA 78-79 L 3
Pipiriki ○ NZ 182 E 3
Piplān ○ PK 138-139 C 3
Piplod ○ IND 138-139 D 8
Pipmuacan, Réservoir < CDN 38-39 J 4
Pipon Island ⌒ AUS 174-175 H 4
Pipri ○ IND 142-143 C 3
Piprod ○ IND 142-143 B 4
Piqua ○ USA (OH) 280-281 B 3
Piqua Historic Area • USA (OH) 280-281 B 3
Piquenes, Paso de los ▲ RA 78-79 E 2
Piqueras, Puerto de ▲ E 98-99 F 3
Piquet Carneiro ○ BR 68-69 J 4
Piquete ○ BR 72-73 H 7
Piqui ○ BR 76-77 K 1
Piquiri, Rio ~ BR 74-75 D 5
Pir ○ IR 134-135 B 2
Pira ○ DY 202-203 L 5
Pirabeiraba ○ BR 74-75 F 6
Piraca, Rio ~ BR 72-73 F 4
Piracaia ○ BR 72-73 G 7
Piracanjuba ○ BR 72-73 F 4
Piracanjuba, Rio ~ BR 72-73 F 4
Piracicaba ○ BR 72-73 G 7
Piracuruca ○ BR 68-69 H 3
Piracuruca, Rio ~ BR 68-69 H 4
Pirada ○ GNB 202-203 C 3
Pirada Km. 101 ○ RA 76-77 E 5
Pirahã, Área Indígena ⚔ BR 66-67 F 6
Piraí ○ BR 66-67 J 4
Piraí do Sul ○ BR 74-75 F 5
Pirajiba ○ BR 72-73 J 2
Piraju ○ BR 72-73 F 7
Pirajuí ○ BR 72-73 F 7
Pirambu ○ BR 68-69 K 7
Piramidal'nyj, pik ▲ KS 136-137 M 5
Pirámide, Cerro ▲ RCH 80 D 4
Pirané ○ RA 76-77 H 3
Piranga ○ BR 72-73 J 6
Piranga, Rio ~ BR 72-73 J 6
Pirangi, Rio ~ BR 68-69 J 4
Piranguinho ○ BR 72-73 H 7
Piranha, Rio ~ BR 66-67 D 6
Piranhaquara, Igarapé ~ BR 68-69 B 4
Piranhas ○ BR (ALA) 68-69 K 6
Piranhas ○ BR (GOI) 72-73 E 4
Piranhas, Rio ~ BR 66-67 J 6
Piranhas, Rio ~ BR 68-69 D 6
Piranhas, Rio ~ BR 68-69 K 5
Piranhas, Rio ~ BR 72-73 E 4
Pīrānšahr ○ IR 128-129 L 4
Piranteira, Cachoeira ~ BR 66-67 F 2
Pira Paraná, Río ~ CO 66-67 B 3
Pirapemas ○ BR 68-69 F 3
Pirapó, Rio ~ BR 72-73 D 7
Pirapó, Rio ~ PY 76-77 J 4
Pirapó, Serra do ▲ BR 76-77 K 5
Pirapora ○ BR 72-73 H 4
Pirapozinho ○ BR 72-73 E 7
Piraquara ○ BR 74-75 F 5
Pirarajá ○ ROU 78-79 M 2
Pirassununga ○ BR 72-73 G 6
Piratinga, Rio ~ BR 72-73 G 3
Piray, Río ~ BOL 70-71 F 6
Pircas, Cerro ▲ RA 76-77 C 6
Pirda ~ RUS 116-117 M 3
Pireás ○ GR 100-101 J 6
Pirehueico, Lago ⊂ RCH 78-79 D 5
Pirenópolis ○ BR 72-73 F 3
Pires do Rio ○ BR 72-73 F 4
Pirgí ○ GR 100-101 K 5
Pírgos ○ GR 100-101 H 6
Pírgos ○ GR 100-101 K 7
Piriá, Rio ~ BR 68-69 E 2
Piriápolis ○ ROU 78-79 M 3
Pirica, Río ~ RA 76-77 D 4
Pirie, Lac ⊂ CDN (ONT) 236-237 L 2
Piri Grande ○ BR 62-63 J 5
Pirin, Naroden Park ⊥•• BG 102-103 C 7
Pirinem ○ RUS 88-89 S 4
Pirineos ▲ E 98-99 G 3
Piripá ○ BR 72-73 K 3
Piripiri ○ BR 68-69 H 4
Piritiba ○ BR 68-69 H 7
Piriyāpatna ○ IND 140-141 F 4
Pirjo Goth ○ PK 138-139 B 6
Pir Mangho ○• PK 134-135 M 6
Pirmasens ○ D 92-93 J 4
Pirna ○• D 92-93 M 3
Piro ○ MOC 218-219 H 4
Pirojpur ○ BD 142-143 G 4
Piros, Cerro los ▲ RCH 78-79 C 4
Pirot ○• YU 100-101 J 3
Pirovac ○ HR 100-101 E 3
Pirožnikova ~ RUS 120-121 S 5
Pirpainti ○ IND 142-143 E 3
Pir Panchal Range ▲ IND 138-139 E 2
Pirré, Cerro ▲ PA 52-53 F 8
Pirsagat ~ AZ 128-129 N 2
Pirtleville ○ USA (AZ) 256-257 F 7
Pirttikoski ○ FIN 88-89 J 3
Piru ○ RI 166-167 E 3
Piru ○ USA (CA) 248-249 F 5
Piru, Teluk ≈ 166-167 E 3
Piruru ○ GUY 62-63 F 3
Pisa ○•• I 100-101 C 3
Pisac ○ PE 70-71 B 3
Pisacoma ○ PE 70-71 C 5
Pisagua ○ RCH 70-71 B 6
Pisanda ○ CO 64-65 D 1
Pisandaungsaung ○ MYA 158-159 E 5
Pisang, Kepulauan ⌒ RI 166-167 F 3
Pisau, Tanjung ▲ MAL 160-161 C 9
Pisba, Parque Nacional ⊥ CO 60-61 E 5
Piščа ○ UA 102-103 C 2
Pisco ○ PE 64-65 D 8
Pisco Elqui ○ RCH 76-77 B 6
Piscovo ○• RUS 94-95 R 3
Písek ○ CZ 92-93 N 4
Pisek ○ USA (ND) 258-259 K 3
Písek = Písek ○ CZ 92-93 N 4
Pisgah ○ USA (IA) 274-275 C 3
Pisgah ○ USA (NC) 282-283 H 5
Pisgah Crater • USA (CA) 248-249 H 5
Pishan ○ VRC 144-145 B 2
Pishin ○ PK 134-135 M 3
Pishin Lora ~ PK 134-135 M 3
Pishin Lora ~ PK 134-135 L 4
Pišin ○ IR 134-135 J 5
Pisinimo ○ USA (AZ) 256-257 C 6
Pismo Beach ○ USA (CA) 248-249 D 4
Pismo Beach • USA (CA) 248-249 D 4
Piso, Lake ⊂ LB 202-203 E 6
Piso Firme ○ BOL 70-71 G 3
Pisqui, Río ~ PE 64-65 E 5
Pissila ○ BF 202-203 K 3
Piste ○ MEX 52-53 K 1
Pisticci ○ I 100-101 F 4
Pistóia ○ I 100-101 C 3
Pistolet Bay ≈ 38-39 R 3
Pistolet Bay ≈ CDN 242-243 N 1
Pistol River ○ USA (OR) 244-245 A 8
Pisuerga, Río ~ E 98-99 E 3
Pisz ○• PL 92-93 Q 2
Pit ○ RI 166-167 K 3
Pita ○ RG 202-203 D 4
Pita, La ∴ PA 52-53 D 7
Pitaga ○ CDN 38-39 M 2
Pital ○ CO 60-61 D 6
Pitalito ○ CO 60-61 C 7
Pitanga ○ BR 74-75 E 5
Pitangui ○ BR 72-73 H 5
Pitarpunga Lake ⊂ AUS 180-181 G 3
Pitas ○ MAL 160-161 B 9
Pitäv ○ AFG 136-137 M 6
Pitcairn Island ⌒ GB 13 O 5
Pitche ○ GNB 202-203 D 3
Pitch Lake • TT 60-61 L 2
Piteå ○ S 86-87 K 4
Piteälven ~ S 86-87 J 4
Pitești ★• RO 102-103 D 5
Pit-Gorodok ○ RUS 116-117 F 6
Pithāpuram ○ IND 142-143 C 7
Pithara ○ AUS 176-177 D 5
Pithiviers ○ F 90-91 J 7
Piti ~ EAT 214-215 G 4
Piti, Lagoa ⊂ MOC 220-221 L 3
Pitigala ○ CL 140-141 J 7
Pitinga, Rio ~ BR 62-63 E 6
Pitjantjatjara Aboriginal Land ⚔ AUS 176-177 L 3
Pitkas Point ○ USA 20-21 J 5
Pitkin ○ USA (CO) 254-255 J 5
Pitkin ○ USA (LA) 268-269 H 6
Pitkjaranta ★ RUS 88-89 L 6
Pitljar ~ RUS 114-115 J 2
Pitman ○ CDN (SAS) 232-233 N 5
Pitmegea River ~ USA 20-21 H 2
Pitoa ○ CAM 204-205 K 4
Pitok River ~ CDN 30-31 T 2
Pit River ~ USA (CA) 246-247 D 2
Pitrufquen ○ RCH 78-79 C 5
Pit Siding ○ CDN 34-35 H 3
Pitt, Canal ≈ 80 C 5
Pitt Island ⌒ CDN (BC) 228-229 D 3
Pitt Lake ⊂ CDN (BC) 230-231 G 4
Pitt Meadows ○ CDN (BC) 230-231 G 4
Pittsboro ○ USA (NC) 282-283 H 5
Pittsboro ○ USA (KS) 262-263 M 7
Pittsburg ○ USA (KY) 276-277 L 3
Pittsburg ○ USA (TX) 264-265 K 5
Pittsburgh ○ USA (CA) 246-247 D 5
Pittsburgh ○ USA (PA) 280-281 G 3
Pittsfield ○ USA (IL) 274-275 H 5
Pittsfield ○ USA (MA) 278-279 H 6
Pittsfield ○ USA (ME) 278-279 M 4
Pittsfield ○ USA (PA) 280-281 G 2
Pittston ○ USA (PA) 280-281 L 2
Pittston Farm ○ USA (ME) 278-279 M 3
Pitts Town ○ BS 54-55 H 3
Pittsview ○ USA (AL) 284-285 E 4
Pittsville ○ USA (MD) 280-281 L 5
Pittsville ○ USA (WI) 270-271 H 6
Pittsworth ○ AUS 178-179 L 4
Pitu ~ EAT 214-215 H 5
Pituffik Gletscher ⊂ GRØ 26-27 Q 5
Pituil ○ RA 76-77 D 5
Pituil, Río ~ RA 76-77 D 5
Pituri Creek ~ AUS 178-179 E 2
Pitz Lake ⊂ CDN 30-31 V 4
Piu ○ PNG 183 D 4
Piúí ○ BR 72-73 H 6
Piulip Nunaa ⩩ GRØ 26-27 Q 5
Pium ○ BR 68-69 D 7
Pium, Rio ~ BR 68-69 D 7
Piúma ○ BR 72-73 K 6
Piuna ○ BOL 70-71 C 4
Piura ★ PE 64-65 B 4
Piura, Río ~ PE 64-65 B 4
Piva ~ YU 100-101 G 3
Pivabiska Lake ⊂ CDN (ONT) 236-237 E 3
Pivdennyj Buh ~ UA 102-103 F 3
Pivdennyj Buh ~ UA 102-103 G 4
Pivdennyj Buh ~ UA 102-103 E 3
Pivnično-Kpyms'kyj, kanal < UA 102-103 J 5
Pivot ○ CDN (ALB) 232-233 H 5
Pivski manastir • YU 100-101 G 3
Pixa ○ VRC 144-145 B 2
Pi Xian ○ VRC (JIA) 154-155 K 4
Pi Xian ○ VRC (SIC) 154-155 C 6
Pixley ○ USA (CA) 248-249 E 4
Pixley National Wildlife Refuge ⊥• USA (CA) 248-249 E 4
Pixoyal ○ MEX 52-53 J 2
Pixtun ○ MEX 52-53 J 2
Piž ~ RUS 96-97 J 5
Pizhi ○ WAN 204-205 F 4
Pižma ~ RUS 88-89 V 4
Pizzo ○ I 100-101 F 5
Pjadungina ~ RUS 114-115 Q 5
Pjagina, poluostrov ⌒ RUS 120-121 Q 4
Pjakupur ~ RUS 114-115 Q 2
Pjakuto, ozero ⊂ RUS 114-115 M 3
Pjandž ○ TJ 136-137 L 6
Pjandž ~ TJ 136-137 M 5
Pjaozero ○ RUS 88-89 L 3
Pjasedajaha ~ RUS 108-109 N 6
Pjasina ~ RUS 108-109 X 6
Pjasino, ozero ⊂ RUS 108-109 W 7
Pjasinskij, zaliv ⊂ RUS 108-109 V 5
Pjatibratskij, mys ▲ RUS 120-121 S 4
Pjatigorsk ○ RUS 126-127 E 5
Pjat'-Jah ○ RUS 114-115 M 4
Pjatychatky ○ UA 102-103 H 3
Þjóðgarður Skaftafell ⊥ IS 86-87 e 2
Þjórsá ~ IS 86-87 c 3
Þjórsá ~ IS 86-87 d 2
Pjuťky ~ RUS 114-115 Q 3
Plá ○ RA 78-79 J 3
Place, La ○ USA (LA) 268-269 K 6
Placentia ○ CDN (NFL) 242-243 P 5
Placentia Bay ≈ 38-39 R 5
Placentia Bay ≈ CDN 242-243 O 5
Placer ○ RP 160-161 E 7
Placerville ○ USA (CA) 246-247 E 5
Placerville ○ USA (CO) 254-255 G 5
Placetas ○ C 54-55 F 3
Placeton, Cerro del ▲ RCH 76-77 B 5
Placid, Lake ⊂ USA (FL) 286-287 H 4
Placido de Castro ○ BR 70-71 D 2
Placita ○ USA (NM) 256-257 H 5
Placitas ○ USA (NM) 256-257 K 2
Placongo ○ RCB 210-211 D 5
Plain ○ USA (WA) 244-245 E 3
Plain City ○ USA (OH) 280-281 C 3
Plain City ○ USA (UT) 254-255 C 2
Plain Dealing ○ USA (LA) 268-269 G 4
Plainfield ○ USA (IA) 274-275 F 2
Plainfield ○ USA (WI) 270-271 J 6
Plains ○ USA (GA) 284-285 F 4
Plains ○ USA (KS) 262-263 F 7
Plains ○ USA (MT) 250-251 E 4
Plains ○ USA (TX) 264-265 B 5
Plains, Des ○ USA (IL) 274-275 L 2
Plainview ○ USA (MN) 270-271 F 6
Plainview ○ USA (NE) 262-263 J 2
Plainview ○ USA (TX) 264-265 C 4
Plainville ○ USA (KS) 262-263 G 5
Plainwell ○ USA (MI) 272-273 D 5
Plaju ○ RI 162-163 F 6
Plampang ○ RI 168 C 7
Plana Cays ⌒ BS 54-55 J 3
Planada ○ USA (CA) 248-249 D 2
Planadas ○ CO 60-61 D 6
Planaltina ○ BR (FED) 72-73 G 3
Planaltina ○• BR (GOI) 72-73 G 3
Planaltina do Paraná ○ BR 72-73 D 7
Planalto ○ BR (BAH) 72-73 K 3
Planalto ○ BR (PAR) 74-75 D 5
Planalto ○ BR (RSU) 74-75 D 6
Planas, Río ~ CO 60-61 F 5
Planchón, El ∴• MEX 52-53 J 3
Planchon, Paso del ▲ RCH 78-79 D 3
Plandi ▲ BF 202-203 H 4
Planeta Rica ○ CO 60-61 D 3
Planet Creek ~ AUS 178-179 K 3
Planet Downs ○ AUS 174-175 E 6
Plankinton ○ USA (SD) 260-261 H 3
Plano ○ USA (TX) 264-265 H 5
Plano Alto ○ BR 76-77 K 5
Plant, La ○ USA (SD) 260-261 F 1
Planta de Azufre ○ RA 78-79 E 3
Planta Esmeralda ○ RCH 76-77 B 3
Plantation Key ⌒ USA (FL) 286-287 J 7
Plant City ○ USA (FL) 286-287 G 3
Planura ○ BR 72-73 F 6
Plaquemine ○ USA (LA) 268-269 J 6
Plaridel ○ RP 160-161 E 8
Plasë ○ AL 100-101 H 4
Plasencia ○ E 98-99 D 4
Plast ○ RUS 96-97 M 6
Plaster City ○ USA (CA) 248-249 J 7
Plaster Rock ○ CDN (NB) 240-241 H 4
Plastun ○ RUS 122-123 G 6
Plata, Isla de la ⌒ EC 64-65 B 2
Plata, La ○ CO 60-61 D 6
Plata, La ★• RA 78-79 L 3
Plata, La ○ USA (MO) 274-275 F 4
Plata, Lago la ⊂ RA 80 E 2
Plata, Minas de ○•• MEX 50-51 H 6
Plata, Río de la ~ RA 78-79 K 3
Plata, Río de la ○ USA (PR) 286-287 P 2
Platanal = Majeicodoteri ○ YV 60-61 J 6
Platbakkies ○ ZA 220-221 D 5
Plate, Île ⌒ SY 224 C 6
Plateau ◘ WAN 204-205 G 4
Plateaux ◘ RCB 210-211 E 5
Plateforme, La ○ RH 54-55 J 5
Platen, Kapp ▲ N 84-85 N 2
Plateros ○ MEX 50-51 H 6
Platina ○ USA (CA) 246-247 C 3
Platinum ○ USA 22-23 Q 3
Plato ○ CDN (SAS) 232-233 K 4
Plato ○ CO 60-61 D 3
Plato de Sopa ○ RCH 76-77 C 3
Platón Sánchez ○ MEX 50-51 K 7
Platoro ○ USA (CO) 254-255 J 6
Platt Bank ≃ 278-279 M 5
Platte ○ USA (SD) 260-261 H 3
Platte City ○ USA (MO) 274-275 D 5
Platten ○ USA (ME) 278-279 N 2
Platte River ~ USA (IA) 274-275 D 4
Platteville ○ USA (CO) 254-255 L 3
Platteville ○ USA (WI) 274-275 H 2
Plattsburg ○ USA (MO) 274-275 D 5
Plattsburgh ○ USA (NY) 278-279 H 4
Plattsmouth ○ USA (NE) 262-263 L 4
Platveld ○ NAM 216-217 D 9
Plauen ○ D 92-93 M 3
Plavinas ○ LV 94-95 J 3
Plavnikovye, ostrova ⌒ RUS 108-109 V 4
Plavsk ★• RUS 94-95 P 5
Playa Azul ○ MEX 52-53 C 3
Playa Blanca ○ E 188-189 E 6
Playa Bonita ○ YV 60-61 E 2
Playa Dayaniguas ○ C 54-55 D 3
Playa de Florida ○ C 54-55 F 4
Playa del Carmen ○• MEX 52-53 L 1
Playa Lauro Villar ○ MEX 50-51 L 5
Playa Los Corchos ○ MEX 50-51 G 7
Playa Noriega, Laguna ⊂ MEX 50-51 D 3
Playa Rosario ○• C 54-55 D 3
Playas ○ EC 64-65 B 3
Playa Vicente ○ MEX 52-53 G 3
Playgreen Lake ⊂ CDN 34-35 G 3
Plây Ku ★ VN 158-159 K 4
Plaza ○ USA (ND) 258-259 F 3
Plaza Huincul ○ RA 78-79 E 5
Pleasant ○ USA (IN) 274-275 N 6
Pleasant, Lake ⊂ USA (AZ) 256-257 C 5
Pleasant Bay ○ CDN (NS) 240-241 P 4
Pleasant Grove ○ USA (AL) 284-285 D 3
Pleasant Grove ○ USA (AL) 284-285 C 3
Pleasant Grove ○ USA (NC) 282-283 L 5
Pleasant Hill ○ USA (IL) 274-275 H 5
Pleasant Hill ○ USA (LA) 268-269 G 5
Pleasant Hill ○ USA (MO) 274-275 D 6
Pleasant Hill ○ USA (SC) 284-285 K 2
Pleasant Lake ○ USA (ND) 258-259 H 3
Pleasanton ○ USA (KS) 262-263 M 6
Pleasant Plains ○ USA (AR) 276-277 C 5
Pleasant Valley ○ USA (OR) 244-245 H 6
Pleasant View ○ USA (CO) 254-255 G 6
Pleasonton ○ USA (TX) 266-267 J 4
Pledger Lake ⊂ CDN (ONT) 236-237 E 2
Plenty ○ CDN (SAS) 232-233 K 4
Plenty, Bay of ≈ 182 F 2
Plenty Downs ∴ AUS 178-179 D 2
Plenty Highway II AUS 178-179 D 2
Plenty River ~ AUS 178-179 C 2
Plentywood ○ USA (MT) 250-251 P 3
Plered ○ RI 168 B 3
Plešanovo ★ RUS 96-97 H 7
Plesant, Mount ▲ USA (VA) 280-281 G 6
Pleščanicy ○ BY 94-95 K 4
Pleseck ★•• RUS 88-89 Q 5
Pleskau = Pskov ★•• RUS 94-95 L 3
Pleskauer See = Pskovskoe ozero ⊂ RUS 94-95 K 2
Pleso, Osinovoe ○ RUS 114-115 T 7
Plessisville ○ CDN (QUE) 238-239 O 2
Pleszew ○ PL 92-93 O 3
Plétipi, Lac ⊂ CDN 38-39 J 3
Plettenberg Bay ○ ZA 220-221 F 7
Plettenberg Bay = Plettenbergbaai ○• ZA 220-221 F 7
Pleven ○ BG 102-103 D 6
Plevna ○ USA (MT) 250-251 P 5
Plevna Downs ○ AUS 178-179 G 4
Pliny ○ USA (MN) 270-271 E 4
Plitvica ○ HR 100-101 E 2
Plitvička Jezera, Nacionalni park ⊥••• HR 100-101 E 2
Pljevlja ○• YU 100-101 G 3
Ploaghe ○ I 100-101 B 4
Ploče ○ HR 100-101 F 3
Płock ★• PL 92-93 P 2
Ploërmel ○ F 90-91 F 8
Ploiești ★• RO 102-103 E 5
Plonge, Lac la ⊂ CDN 34-35 C 3
Płońsk ○ PL 92-93 Q 2
Ploskij, mys ▲ RUS 110-111 b 2
Ploskoš' ○ RUS 94-95 M 3
Ploso ○ RI 168 E 3
Plotava ○ RUS 124-125 M 2
Plotnikova ~ RUS 122-123 R 2
Plotnikovo ○ RUS 114-115 R 6
Plouëzec ○ F 90-91 F 7
Plouguer, Carhaix- ○ F 90-91 F 7
Plovdiv ★ BG 102-103 D 6
Plover ○ USA (WI) 270-271 J 6
Plover Islands ⌒ USA 20-21 N 1
Plumas ○ CDN (MAN) 234-235 D 4
Plumas, Las ○ RA 78-79 F 7
Plum Coulee ○ CDN (MAN) 234-235 F 5
Plum Creek ~ USA (TX) 266-267 K 4
Plummer ○ USA (ID) 250-251 C 4
Plummer ○ USA (MN) 270-271 B 3
Plummer, Mount ▲ USA 20-21 L 6
Plumridge Lakes ⊂ AUS 176-177 H 4
Plumtree ○ ZW 218-219 D 5
Plungė ★•• LT 94-95 G 4
Plunkett ○ CDN (SAS) 232-233 N 4
Plush ○ USA (OR) 244-245 F 8
Plutarco Elías Calles, Presa < MEX 50-51 E 3
Plymouth ○ GB (ENG) 90-91 E 6
Plymouth ★• GB 56 D 3
Plymouth ○ TT 60-61 L 2
Plymouth ○ USA (CA) 246-247 E 5
Plymouth ○ USA (IN) 274-275 M 3
Plymouth ○ USA (MI) 272-273 F 5
Plymouth ○ USA (NC) 282-283 L 5
Plymouth ○ USA (NE) 262-263 K 4
Plymouth ○ USA (NH) 278-279 K 5
Plymouth ○ USA (PA) 280-281 L 2
Plymouth ○ USA (RI) 278-279 L 7
Plymouth ○ USA (WA) 244-245 F 5
Plymouth ○ USA (WI) 270-271 K 1
Plzeň ○ CZ 92-93 M 4
Pniewy ○ PL 92-93 O 2
Pô ○ BF 202-203 K 4
Po ~ I 100-101 C 2
Pô, Parc Nationale de ⊥ BF 202-203 K 4
Poan High Knob ▲ USA (NC) 282-283 E 4
Poano ○ CI 202-203 K 6
Poat, Pulau ⌒ RI 164-165 H 3
Poatina ○ AUS 180-181 J 6
Pobè ○ DY 204-205 E 5
Pobeda ○ TM (ASH) 136-137 G 6
Pobeda ○ TM (MAR) 136-137 H 6
Pobeda, gora ▲ RUS 110-111 a 7
Pobedy, pik ▲ KS 146-147 E 4
Pobé Mengao ○ BF 202-203 K 3
Población ○ RCH 78-79 D 3
Pobla de Segur, la ○ E 98-99 H 3
Poblet, Reial Monestir de ••• E 98-99 H 4
Poča ○ RUS 88-89 P 5
Pocahontas ○ CDN (ALB) 228-229 R 3
Pocahontas ○ USA (AR) 276-277 E 4
Pocahontas ○ USA (IA) 274-275 D 2
Pocahontas ○ USA (IL) 274-275 J 6
Pocatello ○ USA (ID) 252-253 F 4
Pocatière, La ○ CDN (QUE) 240-241 E 3
Poccha, Río ~ PE 64-65 D 6
Počep ○ RUS 94-95 N 5
Pocetas ○ YV 60-61 F 4
Pochotitán ○ MEX 50-51 G 7
Pocinhos ○ BR 68-69 K 5
Počinok ★ RUS 94-95 N 4
Počitelj • BIH 100-101 F 3
Pocito, El ○ BOL 70-71 F 4

Pocitos, Salar ○ RA 76-77 D 3
Pocoata ○ BOL 70-71 D 6
Poço de Fora ○ BR 68-69 J 6
Poçõe ○ BR 72-73 K 3
Poções ○ BR 68-69 H 3
Pocomoke City ○ USA (MD) 280-281 L 5
Pocomoke River ~ USA (MD) 280-281 L 5
Pocomoke Sound ≈ 46-47 K 7
Pocomoke Sound ≈ USA 280-281 L 6
Pocone ○ BR 70-71 J 5
Poço Redondo ○ BR 68-69 K 6
Poços de Caldas ○ BR 72-73 G 6
Poço Verde ○ BR 68-69 J 7
Pocrane ○ BR 72-73 K 5
Podberez'e ○ RUS (NVG) 94-95 M 2
Podberez'e ○ RUS (PSK) 94-95 M 3
Podbořany ○ CZ 92-93 M 3
Podborov'e ○ RUS 94-95 L 3
Podčer'e ○ RUS 114-115 D 3
Podčer'e ~ RUS 114-115 E 3
Poddor'e ○ RUS 94-95 M 3
Podelga ~ RUS 114-115 R 4
Podena, Kepulauan ⌒ RI 166-167 K 3
Podgorenski ○ RUS 102-103 L 2
Podgorica ✩ YU 100-101 G 3
Podgornyj, aral ⌒ KA 126-127 J 5
Podile ○ IND 140-141 H 3
Podil's'ka vysočyna ▲ UA 102-103 D 3
Podkagernaja, buhta ○ RUS 120-121 T 3
Podkamennaja ~ RUS 110-111 G 2
Podkamennaja Tunguska ~ RUS 116-117 E 5
Podkamennaja Tunguska = Podkamennaja Tunguska ~ RUS 116-117 E 5
Podkova ○ BG 102-103 D 7
Podkova, ostrov ⌒ RUS 108-109 V 4
Podlomka ~ RUS 88-89 O 5
Podocarpus, Parque Nacional ⊥ EC 64-65 C 4
Podol'sk ✩ • RUS 94-95 P 4
Podor ○ SN 196-197 C 6
Podora ○ RUS 88-89 X 5
Podporože ○ RUS 94-95 O 1
Podravska Slatina ○ HR 100-101 F 2
Podupalskij Ūstirti ▲ KA 126-127 M 3
Podyem-Mihajlovka ○ RUS 96-97 G 7
Poe Bank ≃ 158-159 D 6
Poechos, Embalse < PE 64-65 B 4
Poelela, Lagoa ○ MOC 218-219 H 7
Poeppel Corner • AUS 178-179 D 3
Pofadder ○ ZA 220-221 D 4
Pogge II, Chute ~ • ZRE 216-217 F 3
Poggibonsi ○ I 100-101 C 3
Pogibi ○ RUS 122-123 J 2
Pognoa ○ BF 202-203 L 4
Pogo ○ CI 202-203 H 4
Pogoanele ○ RO 102-103 E 5
Pogorelec ○ RUS 88-89 S 4
Pogost ○ RUS 88-89 Q 5
Pogradec ✩ •• AL 100-101 H 4
Pograničnyi ○ BY 94-95 J 5
Pograničnyj ○ RUS 122-123 D 6
Pogromni Volcano ▲ USA 22-23 O 5
Poguba, Rio ~ BR 70-71 K 5
Pogynden ~ RUS 112-113 M 2
Pogyndino ○ RUS 112-113 N 2
Poh ○ RI 164-165 H 4
Pohang ○ ROK 150-151 G 9
Pohénégamook ○ CDN (QUE) 240-241 F 3
Pohiois-li ○ FIN 88-89 H 4
Pohjanlahti ≈ 86-87 K 5
Pohjanmaa ⊥ FIN 88-89 G 5
Pohodsk ○ RUS 112-113 L 2
Pohvistnevo ✩ RUS 96-97 H 7
Poie ○ ZRE 210-211 J 5
Poi Island ⌒ SOL 184 I e 4
Poile, La ○ CDN (NFL) 242-243 K 5
Poinsett, Lake ○ USA (SD) 260-261 J 2
Point, Cap ▲ WL 56 E 4
Point "A" Lake < USA (AL) 284-285 D 5
Point au Fer ▲ USA (LA) 268-269 J 7
Point au Mal ○ CDN (NFL) 242-243 K 4
Point Baker ○ USA 32-33 D 3
Point Bickerton ○ CDN (NS) 240-241 O 5
Pointblank ○ USA (TX) 268-269 E 6
Point Bridget State Park ⊥ USA 32-33 C 2
Point Dume Beach • USA (CA) 248-249 F 5
Pointe-à-la-Garde ○ CDN (QUE) 240-241 J 2
Pointe-à-Pitre ○ F 56 E 3
Pointe-au-Père ○ CDN (QUE) 240-241 G 2
Pointe-aux-Anglais ○ CDN (QUE) 242-243 A 3
Pointe-Carleton ○ CDN (QUE) 242-243 E 3
Pointe des Lataniers ○ RH 54-55 J 5
Pointe du Bois ○ CDN (MAN) 234-235 H 4
Pointe-Mistassini ○ CDN (QUE) 242-243 A 3
Pointe Noire ○ F 56 E 3
Pointe-Noire ✩ RCB 210-211 C 6
Pointe Ouest ▲ RH 54-55 J 4
Pointe Parent ○ CDN (QUE) 242-243 G 2
Pointe Rivière de l'Artibonite ○ RH 54-55 J 5
Point Gamble ○ USA (WA) 244-245 C 3
Point Grondine Indian Reservation X CDN (ONT) 238-239 D 3
Point Harbor ○ USA (NC) 282-283 M 4
Point Hope ○ USA 20-21 G 2
Point Judith ○ USA (RI) 278-279 K 7
Point Lake ○ CDN 30-31 N 3
Point Lay ○ USA 20-21 J 2
Point Leamington ○ CDN (NFL) 242-243 N 3
Point Lookout ○ USA (MD) 280-281 K 5
Point Lookout ▲ USA (MD) 280-281 K 5
Point Marion ○ USA (PA) 280-281 G 4
Point May ○ CDN (NFL) 242-243 N 6
Point Mc Leay ○ AUS 180-181 E 3
Point Michaud ○ CDN (NS) 240-241 P 5
Point of Rocks ○ USA (MD) 280-281 J 4
Point of Rocks ○ USA (WY) 252-253 K 5
Point Pedro ○ CL 140-141 J 6
Point Pelee National Park ⊥ CDN (ONT) 238-239 C 7
Point Pleasant ○ USA (NJ) 280-281 M 3
Point Pleasant ○ USA (WV) 280-281 D 5
Point Pleasant State Historic Monument • USA (WV) 280-281 D 5
Point Renfrew ○ CDN (BC) 230-231 E 5
Point Reyes National Seashore ⊥ USA (CA) 246-247 B 5
Point Salvation Aboriginal Land X AUS 176-177 H 4
Point Samson ○ AUS 172-173 C 6
Point Stuart ∴ AUS 172-173 K 2
Point Washington ○ USA (FL) 286-287 C 1
Poisson-Blanc ○ CDN (QUE) 236-237 P 3
Poissonnier Point ▲ AUS 172-173 D 5
Poitiers ✩ • F 90-91 H 8
Poitou ⊥ F 90-91 G 8
Poitou-Charentes □ F 90-91 G 8
Poivre Atoll ⌒ SY 224 C 2
Poix-de-Picardie ○ F 90-91 H 7
Pojarkovo ✩ RUS 122-123 C 4
Pojasovyj kamen' hrebet ▲ RUS 114-115 E 4
Pojezierze Mazurskie ⊥ PL 92-93 P 2
Pojezierze Pomorskie ⊥ PL 92-93 O 2
Pojkovskij ○ RUS 114-115 L 4
Pojlovajaha ~ RUS 108-109 R 7
Pojlovajaha, Arka- ~ RUS 108-109 Q 8
Pojlu ○ AZ 128-129 M 2
Pojma ~ RUS 116-117 H 7
Pojmyga ~ RUS 116-117 N 6
Pojo, Rio de ~ BOL 70-71 E 5
Pojuca ○ BR 72-73 L 2
Pojuca, Rio ~ BR 72-73 L 2
Pojuščie peski •• RUS 118-119 D 9
Pokanaevka ○ RUS 116-117 H 7
Pokaran ○ IND 138-139 C 6
Pokataroo ○ AUS 178-179 K 5
Pokemouche ○ CDN (NB) 240-241 L 3
Pokhara ○ • NEP 144-145 E 6
Pokigron ○ SME 62-63 G 3
Po-kil Do ⌒ ROK 150-151 F 10
Pokka ○ FIN 88-89 H 2
Poko ○ ZRE 210-211 L 2
Pokojnickaja ~ RUS 108-109 U 8
Pokok Sena ○ MAL 162-163 D 2
Pokoľka ~ RUS 114-115 R 3
Pokrovka ○ KA 126-127 M 3
Pokrovka ○ KS 146-147 C 4
Pokrovka ○ RUS 114-115 O 7
Pokrovsk ○ RUS (IRK) 116-117 H 8
Pokrovsk ✩ RUS (SAH) 118-119 O 5
Pokrovs'ke ○ UA 102-103 K 4
Pokšen'ga ~ RUS 88-89 R 5
Pokuma ○ Z 218-219 D 3
Pokur ○ RUS 114-115 N 4
Pola ○ RP 160-161 D 6
Pola, La ○ ••• E 98-99 E 3
Polacca ○ USA (AZ) 256-257 E 3
Polacca Wash ~ USA (AZ) 256-257 E 3
Polače ○ • HR 100-101 F 3
Polack ✩ •• BY 94-95 L 4
Pola de Laviana ○ E 98-99 E 3
Pola de Lena ○ E 98-99 E 3
Poladpur ○ IND 140-141 E 2
Polán ○ IR 134-135 J 6
Polanco ○ ROU 78-79 M 2
Polanco ○ RP 160-161 E 8
Poland = Polska ■ PL 92-93 O 3
Polar Bear Provincial Park ⊥ CDN 34-35 N 3
Polaris ○ USA (MT) 250-251 F 6
Polaris Forland ⊥ GRØ 26-27 U 3
Polar Plateau ▲ ARK 16 E 0
Polatlı ○ TR 128-129 E 3
Polavaram ○ IND 142-143 B 7
Polazna ○ RUS 96-97 K 4
Polcura, Rio ~ RCH 78-79 D 4
Pol-e 'Alam ✩ AFG 138-139 B 2
Poleang ~ RI 164-165 G 6
Polebridge ○ USA (MT) 250-251 E 3
Pol-e Fasā ○ IR 134-135 E 4
Pol-e Ḥomri ○ AFG 136-137 L 7
Pol-e Ḥomri, Darrya-ye ~ AFG 136-137 L 7
Pol-e Loušān ○ IR 128-129 N 4
Pol-e Safid ○ IR 136-137 C 6
Polessk ✩ RUS 94-95 G 4
Polevskoj ✩ RUS 96-97 M 5
Polewali ○ RI 164-165 F 5
Polgahawela ○ CL 140-141 J 7
Poli ○ CAM 204-205 K 4
Poli ○ CY 128-129 E 5
Policastro, Golfo di ≈ 100-101 E 5
Police, Pointe ▲ SY 224 D 2
Policemans Point ○ AUS 180-181 E 4
Policoro ○ I 100-101 F 4
Poligiros ○ GR 100-101 J 4
Polihnitos ○ GR 100-101 L 5
Polikastro ○ GR 100-101 J 4
Poliny Osipenko, imeni ✩ RUS 122-123 G 2
Polis'ke ○ UA 102-103 F 2
Politovo ○ RUS 88-89 U 4
Poliva ~ RUS 116-117 L 6
Polja ~ RUS 94-95 Q 4
Poljakovskij ○ RUS 118-119 N 9
Poljana ○ UA 102-103 C 3
Poljarnoe ○ RUS 110-111 b 4
Poljarnyj ○ RUS (CUK) 112-113 U 2
Poljarnyj ○ RUS (MUR) 88-89 M 2
Poljarnyj ○ RUS (SAH) 110-111 H 6
Poljarnyj hrebet ▲ RUS 120-121 O 2
Poljarnyj Ural ▲ RUS 114-115 E 2
Polk ○ USA (AL) 284-285 D 4
Polk, Fort xx USA (LA) 268-269 G 5
Pollāchi ○ IND 140-141 G 5
Pollença ○ E 98-99 J 5
Pollilo ○ RP 160-161 D 5
Pollilo Island ⌒ RP 160-161 D 5
Pollilo Islands ⌒ RP 160-161 E 5
Pollilo Strait ≈ 160-161 D 5
Pollino, Parco del ⊥ I 100-101 F 5
Pollock ○ USA (ID) 250-251 C 6
Pollock ○ USA (LA) 268-269 H 5
Pollock Hills ▲ AUS 172-173 H 7
Pollockville ○ CDN (ALB) 232-233 G 4
Pol'noj Voronež ~ RUS 94-95 R 5
Polo ○ USA (IL) 274-275 J 3
Polobaya Grande ○ PE 70-71 B 5
Polochic, Río ~ GCA 52-53 K 4
Polock = Polack ✩ •• BY 94-95 L 4
Pologij-Sergeeva, ostrov ⌒ RUS 108-109 T 4
Pologoe Zajmišče ○ RUS 96-97 E 9
Polohy ○ UA 102-103 K 4
Polom ○ RUS 96-97 G 4
Polomolok ○ RP 160-161 F 9
Polonina-Runa hora ▲ UA 102-103 C 3
Polonnaruwa ○ ••• CL 140-141 J 7
Polonoje ○ PNG 183 D 3
Poloňské ○ RI 164-165 G 5
Polousnyj krjaž ▲ RUS 110-111 X 5
Polovinnoe, ozero ○ RUS 108-109 W 6
Polson ○ USA (MT) 250-251 E 4
Poltava ✩ UA 102-103 J 3
Poltavka ✩ RUS 124-125 G 1
Põltsamaa ○ •• EST 94-95 J 2
Poluj ~ RUS 108-109 M 8
Poluj ~ RUS 114-115 K 2
Polujskaja vozvyšennost' ▲ RUS 114-115 J 2
Polūr ○ IND 140-141 H 4
Põlva ✩ EST 94-95 K 2
Polvadera Peak ▲ USA (NM) 256-257 J 2
Polvār, Rūd-e ~ IR 134-135 E 3
Polvaredas ○ RA 78-79 K 3
Polvora ○ PE 64-65 D 5
Polwarth ○ CDN (SAS) 232-233 M 2
Põlwe = Põlva ✩ EST 94-95 K 2
Polyarnyy Ural = Poljarnyj Ural ▲ RUS 114-115 E 2
Polynesia ⌒ 14-15 M 7
Polyuc ○ MEX 52-53 K 2
Poma ○ ZRE 210-211 K 4
Pomabamba ○ PE 64-65 D 6
Pomacanchi ○ PE 70-71 B 3
Pomahuaca ○ PE 64-65 C 4
Pomarkku ○ FIN 88-89 F 6
Pomasi, Cerro de ▲ PE 70-71 B 4
Pombal ○ BR (PA) 68-69 K 5
Pombal ○ BR (RON) 70-71 F 2
Pombal ○ P 98-99 C 5
Pombal, Igarapé do ~ BR 68-69 B 5
Pombangi ○ RI 164-165 G 5
Pombas ○ BR 66-67 F 3
Pombas, Rio das ~ BR 66-67 G 6
Pombuige ~ ANG 216-217 C 5
Pomene ○ MOC 218-219 H 6
Pomerene ○ USA (AZ) 256-257 E 6
Pomeroy ○ USA (OH) 280-281 D 4
Pomeroy ○ USA (WA) 244-245 H 4
Pomeroy ○ ZA 220-221 K 4
Pomfret ○ ZA 220-221 F 2
Pomio ○ PNG 183 F 3
Pomme de Terre Lake ○ USA (MO) 276-277 B 3
Pomona ○ RA 78-79 G 5
Pomona ○ USA (CA) 248-249 G 5
Pomona ○ USA (KS) 262-263 L 6
Pomona Lake ○ USA (KS) 262-263 L 6
Pomorska, Zatoka ≈ 92-93 N 1
Pomorskij proliv ≈ 88-89 U 2
Pomorskoe ○ RUS 108-109 E 5
Pomos ○ CY 128-129 E 5
Pompano Beach ○ USA (FL) 286-287 J 5
Pompei •• I 100-101 E 4
Pompéia ○ BR 72-73 E 7
Pompeu ○ BR 72-73 H 5
Pompeys Pillar ○ USA (MT) 250-251 M 6
Pompeys Pillar • USA (MT) 250-251 M 5
Pom Phra Chunlachomkiao ○ THA 158-159 F 4
Pompton Lakes ○ USA (NJ) 280-281 M 3
Pompué, Rio ~ MOC 200-201 F 3
Pomr', zaliv ○ RUS 122-123 K 2
Pomut ~ RUS 114-115 K 3
Ponape ⌒ FSM 13 G 2
Ponass Lake ○ CDN (SAS) 232-233 O 3
Ponazyrevo ○ RUS 96-97 E 4
Ponca ○ USA (NE) 262-263 K 2
Ponca City ○ USA (OK) 264-265 G 2
Ponce ○ USA (PR) 286-287 P 2
Ponce de Leon ○ USA (FL) 286-287 D 1
Poncha Springs ○ USA (CO) 254-255 J 5
Ponchatoula ○ USA (LA) 268-269 K 6
Poncheville, Lac ○ CDN (QUE) 236-237 M 2
Pond ○ USA (CA) 248-249 E 4
Pond Creek ○ USA (OK) 264-265 G 2
Pondera Coulee ~ USA (MT) 250-251 H 3
Ponderosa ○ USA (CA) 248-249 F 3
Pond Fork ~ USA (WV) 280-281 E 6
Pondicherry □ IND 140-141 H 5
Pondicherry ✩ •• IND 140-141 H 5
Pond Inlet ≈ 24-25 h 4
Pond Inlet ○ CDN 24-25 h 4
Pondosa ○ USA (CA) 246-247 D 2
Pond River ~ USA (KY) 276-277 H 3
Ponds, Isle of ⌒ CDN 38-39 R 2
Ponds Lake, River of ○ CDN (NFL) 242-243 L 2
Pondung Lamanggang ○ RI 162-163 D 6
Poneloya ○ NIC 52-53 L 5
Ponente, Riviera di ~ I 100-101 A 3
Ponerečnyj Algan ~ RUS 112-113 R 4
Ponferrada ○ • E 98-99 D 3
Põnfi ~ MOC 218-219 G 2
Pongai ○ BR 72-73 F 6
Pongara, Pointe ▲ G 210-211 B 3
Pong Chi ○ THA 158-159 F 2
Pong Nam Ron ○ THA 158-159 G 4
Pongo ~ SUD 206-207 H 5
Pongo de Cumbinama ~ PE 64-65 C 4
Pongo de Paquipachango ~ PE 64-65 E 7
Pongola ○ ZA 220-221 K 3
Pongola ~ ZA 220-221 K 3
Pongolapoortdam < ZA 220-221 L 3
Pongore ○ ZW 218-219 D 4
Poni ~ BF 202-203 J 4
Ponindilisa, Tanjung ▲ RI 164-165 G 4
Ponio ○ RT 202-203 L 4
Ponio, Río ~ RCH 76-77 B 6
Ponna ○ MYA 142-143 J 5
Ponnaiyar ~ IND 140-141 H 4
Ponnāni ○ IND 140-141 F 5
Ponneri ○ IND 140-141 J 4
Ponnūru Nidubrolu ○ IND 140-141 J 2
Ponoj ○ RUS (MUR) 88-89 Q 3
Ponoj ~ RUS 88-89 N 3
Ponoka ○ CDN (ALB) 232-233 E 3
Ponomarevka ○ RUS 114-115 R 6
Ponomarevka ✩ RUS (ORB) 96-97 J 7
Ponondougou ○ CI 202-203 G 5
Ponorogo ○ RI 168 D 3
Ponrang ○ RI 164-165 G 5
Ponson Island ⌒ RP 160-161 F 7
Ponta ○ BR 66-67 E 3
Ponta Delgada ⌒ P 6-7 E 6
Ponta de Mata ○ YV 60-61 K 3
Ponta de Pedras ○ BR 62-63 K 6
Ponta dos Indios ○ BR 62-63 J 3
Ponta do Sol ○ CV 202-203 B 5
Ponta do Zumbi ○ BR 68-69 F 2
Ponta Freitas Morna ○ ANG 216-217 B 3
Ponta Grande ▲ BR 72-73 L 4
Ponta Grossa ○ BR 74-75 E 5
Pontal ○ BR 72-73 F 6
Pontal, Rio do ~ BR 68-69 H 6
Pontalina ○ BR 72-73 F 4
Pontan River ~ CDN 30-31 L 6
Ponta Porã ○ BR 76-77 K 2
Pontarlier ○ • F 90-91 L 8
Pontas de Pedras ○ BR 68-69 L 5
Pont-Audemer ○ F 90-91 H 7
Pontchartrain, Lake ○ USA (LA) 268-269 K 6
Pontchâteau ○ F 90-91 F 8
Pont de Suert, el ○ E 98-99 H 3
Pont du Gard ••• F 90-91 K 10
Ponte Alta, Rio ~ BR 68-69 E 7
Ponte Alta do Tocantins ○ BR 68-69 E 7
Ponteareas ○ E 98-99 C 3
Ponte Branca ○ BR 72-73 D 4
Ponte da Barca ○ P 98-99 C 4
Ponte de Itabapoana ○ BR 72-73 K 6
Ponte de Sor ○ P 98-99 C 5
Ponte Firme ○ BR 72-73 G 5
Ponteix ○ CDN (SAS) 232-233 L 6
Ponte Nova ○ BR 72-73 J 6
Ponte Ribeiro, Lago ○ BR 70-71 H 4
Pontes e Lacerda ○ BR 70-71 H 4
Ponte Serrada ○ BR 74-75 D 6
Pontevedra ○ E 98-99 C 3
Pontiac ○ USA (IL) 274-275 K 4
Pontiac ○ USA (MI) 272-273 F 5
Pontianak ✩ RI 162-163 H 5
Pontian Kecil ○ MAL 162-163 E 4
Pontic Mountains = Kuzey Anadolu Dağları ▲ TR 10-11 C 4
Pontivy ○ F 90-91 F 7
Ponto Arari ○ BR 62-63 J 5
Ponto Busch ○ BOL 70-71 J 6
Pontoise ✩ F 90-91 J 7
Pontokerasia ○ GR 100-101 J 4
Ponton ○ CDN 34-35 G 3
Ponton Creek ~ AUS 176-177 G 5
Pontorson ○ F 90-91 G 7
Pontotoc ○ USA (MS) 268-269 L 2
Pontotoc ○ USA (TX) 266-267 J 3
Pontrémoli ○ • I 100-101 B 2
Pontrilas ○ CDN (SAS) 232-233 O 2
Pont-Rouge ○ CDN (QUE) 238-239 O 2
Ponts ○ E 98-99 H 4
Pontypool ○ CDN (ONT) 238-239 G 4
Ponuga ○ PA 52-53 D 8
Pony Express Station ∴ USA (KS) 262-263 K 5
Ponza ○ I 100-101 D 4
Ponziane, Isole ⌒ I 100-101 D 4
Poochera ○ AUS 180-181 C 2
Pool □ RCB 210-211 E 5
Poole ○ GB 90-91 G 6
Poole's Monument • AUS 178-179 F 5
Poolesville ○ USA (MD) 280-281 J 4
Pooley Island ⌒ CDN (BC) 228-229 F 4
Pool Malebo ○ ZRE 210-211 E 6
Poolowanna Lake ○ AUS 178-179 D 4
Pools Cove ○ CDN (NFL) 242-243 N 5
Poolville ○ USA (TX) 264-265 G 6
Poonamallee ○ IND 140-141 J 4
Pooncarie ○ AUS 180-181 G 2
Pooneryn ○ CL 140-141 J 6
Poopó ○ BOL 70-71 D 6
Poopó, Lago de ○ BOL 70-71 D 6
Pooppelloe Lake ○ AUS 178-179 G 6
Poorman ○ USA 20-21 N 4
Poor Man Indian Reserve X CDN (SAS) 232-233 O 4
Popa Falls ~ • NAM 216-217 F 9
Popayán ✩ •• CO 60-61 C 6
Popča ○ RUS 88-89 W 5
Pope ○ • LV 94-95 G 3
Popenguine ○ • SN 202-203 B 2
Poperechnoi Island ⌒ USA 22-23 Q 5
Poperinge ○ B 92-93 G 3
Popham Bay ≈ 36-37 R 2
Popham Beach ○ USA (ME) 278-279 M 5
Popigaj ○ RUS (TMR) 110-111 H 4
Popigaj ~ RUS 110-111 F 3
Popigaj ~ RUS 110-111 H 4
Popilta Lake ○ AUS 180-181 F 2
Poplar ○ USA (CA) 248-249 E 3
Poplar ○ USA (MN) 270-271 D 4
Poplar ○ USA (MT) 250-251 O 3
Poplar ○ USA (WI) 270-271 G 4
Poplar Bay ○ CDN (ALB) 232-233 D 2
Poplar Bluff ○ USA (MO) 276-277 E 4
Poplarfield ○ CDN (MAN) 234-235 F 4
Poplar Hill ○ CDN (ONT) 234-235 J 2
Poplar Hill ○ USA (VA) 280-281 F 6
Poplar Point ○ CDN (MAN) 234-235 F 4
Poplar Rapids River ~ CDN (ONT) 236-237 G 3
Poplar River ~ CDN 30-31 J 5
Poplar River ~ CDN (MAN) 234-235 G 2
Poplar River ~ CDN (MAN) 234-235 F 2
Poplar River ~ CDN (SAS) 232-233 N 6
Poplarville ○ USA (MS) 268-269 L 6
Popocatepetl, Volcán ▲ •• MEX 52-53 E 2
Popof Island ⌒ USA 22-23 Q 5
Popoh ○ RI 168 D 4
Popokabaka ○ ZRE 210-211 F 6
Pópoli ○ I 100-101 D 3
Popomanaseu, Mount = Makarakombu ▲ SOL 184 I e 3
Popondetta ✩ PNG 183 E 5
Popovka ○ RUS (ROS) 102-103 M 3
Popovka ~ RUS 110-111 c 7
Popovka ~ RUS 120-121 P 2
Popovo ○ BG 102-103 E 6
Popov Porog ○ RUS 88-89 N 5
Poprad ○ SK 92-93 Q 4
Poptún ○ GCA 52-53 K 3
Poquoson ○ USA (VA) 280-281 K 6
Porāli ~ PK 134-135 M 5
Porangatu ○ BR 72-73 F 2
Porbandar ○ • IND 138-139 B 9
Porčaman ○ AFG 134-135 K 2
Porção, Cachoeira do ~ BR 68-69 B 3
Porcher Island ⌒ CDN (BC) 228-229 D 3
Porciúngula ○ BR 72-73 J 6
Porcos, Riacho dos ~ BR 68-69 J 5
Porcos, Rio dos ~ BR 72-73 H 2
Porcupine ○ USA 20-21 W 7
Porcupine, Cape ▲ CDN 38-39 Q 2
Porcupine Abyssal Plain ≃ 6-7 H 3
Porcupine Forest Reserve ⊥ CDN (MAN) 234-235 B 2
Porcupine Gorge National Park ⊥ AUS 174-175 H 7
Porcupine Plain ○ CDN (SAS) 232-233 P 3
Porcupine Plain ⊥ CDN 20-21 V 2
Porcupine Plateau ▲ CDN 20-21 U 3
Porcupine River ~ CDN 30-31 R 6
Porcupine River ~ USA 20-21 U 3
Porcupine State Park ⊥ USA (MI) 270-271 J 4
Pordenone ✩ • I 100-101 D 2
Pore ○ CO 60-61 F 5
Porebada ○ PNG 183 D 5
Porecatu ○ BR 72-73 E 7
Poreckoe ○ RUS 96-97 E 6
Porédaka ○ RG 202-203 D 4
Porekautimbu, Gunung ▲ RI 164-165 G 4
Porga ○ DY 202-203 L 4
Porgera ○ PNG 183 B 3
Porhov ✩ RUS 94-95 L 3
Pori ○ FIN 88-89 F 6
Porirua ○ NZ 182 E 4
Þórisvatn ○ IS 86-87 d 2
Porjus ○ S 86-87 J 3
Pork Peninsula ⌣ CDN 30-31 X 4
Porlákshöfn ○ IS 86-87 c 3
Porlamar ○ YV 60-61 K 2
Porog ○ RUS 88-89 P 5
Poro Island ⌒ RP 160-161 F 7
Poro Island ⌒ SOL 184 I c 2
Poroma ○ PNG 183 B 4
Poronaj ~ RUS 122-123 K 4
Poronajsk ○ RUS 122-123 K 4
Porong ○ RI 168 E 3
Póros ○ GR 100-101 H 5
Porosozero ○ RUS 88-89 M 5
Porotos, Punta ▲ RCH 76-77 B 5
Porožsk ○ RUS 88-89 W 5
Porpoise Bay ≈ 16 G 13
Porquis Junction ○ CDN (ONT) 236-237 H 4
Porsangen ≈ 86-87 M 1
Porsangerhalvøya ⌣ N 86-87 M 1
Porsea ○ RI 162-163 C 3
Porsgrunn ✩ N 86-87 D 7
Þórshöfn ○ IS 86-87 f 1
Porsild Mountains ▲ CDN 36-37 H 2
Porsuk Çayı ~ TR 128-129 D 3
Port, Le ○ F 224 B 7
Porta, Rio da ~ BR 68-69 C 5
Porta Ascotan ó del Jardin ▲ BOL 76-77 C 1
Port Adelaide ○ AUS 180-181 E 3
Portage ○ CDN (PEI) 240-241 L 4
Portage ○ USA (AK) 20-21 Q 6
Portage ○ USA (UT) 254-255 C 2
Portage ○ USA (WI) 270-271 J 7
Portage Bay ≈ 22-23 T 4
Portage Bay ○ CDN (MAN) 234-235 E 3
Portage la Prairie ○ CDN (MAN) 234-235 E 5
Portageville ○ USA (MO) 276-277 F 4
Portal ○ USA (ND) 258-259 E 3
Port Alberni ○ CDN (BC) 230-231 E 4
Port Albion ○ CDN (BC) 230-231 D 5
Portalegre ○ •• P 98-99 D 5
Portales ○ USA (NM) 256-257 M 4
Port Alexander ○ USA 32-33 C 3
Port Alfred ○ ZA 220-221 H 6
Port Alice ○ CDN (BC) 230-231 B 3
Port Allegany ○ USA (PA) 280-281 H 2
Port Allen ○ USA (HI) 288 F 3
Port Allen ○ USA (LA) 268-269 J 6
Port Alma ○ AUS 178-179 L 2
Port Andrew ○ USA (WI) 274-275 H 1
Port Antonio ○ • JA 54-55 G 5
Portão de Baixo, Cachoeira ~ BR 66-67 K 5
Port Arthur ○ USA (TX) 268-269 G 7
Port Arthur = Lüshun ○ VRC 150-151 C 8
Port Askaig ○ GB 90-91 D 4
Port au Choix ○ CDN (NFL) 242-243 L 2
Port Augusta ○ • AUS 180-181 D 2
Port au Port Bay ≈ CDN 242-243 K 4
Port au Port Peninsula ⌣ CDN (NFL) 242-243 J 4
Port-au-Prince ★ • RH 54-55 J 5
Port Austin ○ USA (MI) 272-273 G 3
Port aux Choix National Historic Park • CDN (NFL) 242-243 L 2
Port Bay, Port au ≈ 38-39 P 4
Port Bell ○ EAU 212-213 D 3
Port-Bergé = Boriziny ○ RM 222-223 E 5
Port Blair ✩ IND 140-141 L 4
Port Blandford ○ CDN (NFL) 242-243 O 4
Port Bolivar ○ USA (TX) 268-269 F 7
Port Broughton ○ AUS 180-181 D 2
Port Bruce ○ CDN (ONT) 238-239 D 6
Port Burwell ○ CDN (ONT) 238-239 E 6
Port Campbell ○ AUS 180-181 G 5
Port Campbell National Park ⊥ AUS 180-181 G 5
Port Charlotte ○ USA (FL) 286-287 G 4
Port Chester ○ USA (NY) 280-281 N 3
Port Chilkoot ○ USA 20-21 X 7
Port Clements ○ CDN (BC) 228-229 B 3
Port Clinton ○ USA (OH) 280-281 D 2
Port Clyde ○ USA (ME) 278-279 M 5
Port Coquitlam ○ CDN (BC) 230-231 G 4
Port-Daniel ○ CDN (QUE) 240-241 L 2
Port-Daniel, Réserve faunique de ⊥ CDN (QUE) 240-241 L 2
Port-de-Paix ✩ RH 54-55 J 5
Port Dickson ○ • MAL 162-163 D 3
Port Douglas ○ • AUS 174-175 H 5
Port Dover ○ CDN (ONT) 238-239 E 6
Port Dufferin ○ CDN (NS) 240-241 N 6
Porte, La ○ USA (IN) 274-275 M 3
Porte, La ○ USA (TX) 268-269 E 7
Port Edward ○ CDN (BC) 228-229 D 2
Port Edward ○ ZA 220-221 K 5
Porteira, Cachoeira da ~ BR 66-67 H 7
Porteiras ○ BR 62-63 F 6
Porteirinha ○ BR 72-73 J 3
Portél ○ BR 62-63 J 6
Portel ○ P 98-99 D 5
Portelândia ○ BR 72-73 D 4
Port Elgin ○ CDN (NB) 240-241 L 4
Port Elgin ○ CDN (ONT) 238-239 D 4
Port Elizabeth ○ ZA 220-221 G 6
Port Ellen ○ GB 90-91 D 4
Porteno, Rio ~ RA 76-77 H 3
Porter ○ CDN (SAS) 232-233 K 3
Porter ○ USA (WA) 244-245 B 4
Porters Corner ○ USA (MT) 250-251 F 5
Porterville ○ USA (CA) 248-249 E 3
Porterville ○ ZA 220-221 D 6
Port Essington ○ CDN (BC) 228-229 E 2
Portezuela ▲ BOL 76-77 C 1
Portezuela del Huaytiquina ▲ RCH 76-77 D 2
Portezuela Llullaillaco Norte ▲ RCH 76-77 C 3
Portezuela Pasto Ventura ▲ RA 76-77 D 4
Portezuelo ○ RCH 78-79 C 4
Portezuelo, El ○ RA 76-77 E 5
Port Fitzroy ○ NZ 182 E 2
Port Fourchon ○ USA (LA) 268-269 K 7
Port Gentil ✩ G 210-211 B 4
Port Germein ○ AUS 180-181 D 2
Port Gibson ○ USA (MS) 268-269 J 5
Port Grosvenor ○ ZA 220-221 J 5
Port-Harcourt ✩ WAN 204-205 G 6
Port Hardy ○ CDN (BC) 230-231 B 3
Port Harrison = Inukjuak ○ CDN 36-37 K 5
Port Hawkesbury ○ CDN (NS) 240-241 O 5
Port Hedland ○ AUS 172-173 D 6
Port Heiden ○ USA 22-23 R 4
Port Henry ○ USA (NY) 278-279 H 4
Porthill ○ USA (ID) 250-251 C 3
Port Hillford ○ CDN (NS) 240-241 O 5
Port Hood ○ CDN (NS) 240-241 O 4
Port Hope ○ CDN (ONT) 238-239 G 5
Port Hope ○ USA (MI) 272-273 G 4
Port Hope Simpson ○ CDN 38-39 Q 2
Port Howard ○ GB 78-79 L 6
Port Howe ○ BS 54-55 H 2
Port Hueneme ○ USA (CA) 248-249 E 5
Port Huron ○ USA (MI) 272-273 G 5
Portillo, Paso del ▲ RA 76-77 B 6
Portimão ○ P 98-99 C 6
Portimo ○ FIN 88-89 J 3
Portis ○ USA (KS) 262-263 H 5
Port Isabel ○ USA (TX) 266-267 K 7
Port Isabel Lighthouse State Historic Site ∴ USA (TX) 266-267 K 7
Port Jackson ≈ 180-181 L 2
Port Jackson ○ NZ 182 E 2
Port Jefferson ○ USA (NY) 280-281 N 3
Port Jervis ○ USA (NY) 280-281 M 2
Port Kenny ○ AUS 180-181 C 2
Port Kent ○ USA (NY) 278-279 H 4
Port Láirge = Waterford ○ • IRL 90-91 D 5
Portland ○ AUS 180-181 F 5
Portland ○ USA (IN) 274-275 O 4
Portland ○ USA (ME) 278-279 L 5
Portland ○ USA (MI) 272-273 E 5
Portland ○ USA (OR) 244-245 C 5
Portland ○ USA (TN) 276-277 J 4
Portland ○ USA (TX) 266-267 K 6
Portland, Cape ▲ AUS 180-181 J 6
Portland Bay ≈ 180-181 F 5
Portland Bight ≈ 54-55 G 6
Portland Canal ≈ 32-33 E 4
Portland Creek ○ CDN (NFL) 242-243 L 2
Portland Creek Pond ○ CDN (NFL) 242-243 L 2
Portland Inlet ≈ 32-33 E 4
Portland Inlet ≈ CDN 228-229 D 2
Portland Island ⌒ NZ 182 F 3
Portland Point ▲ JA 54-55 G 6
Port Langdon ≈ 174-175 D 3
Port Laoise ○ IRL 90-91 D 5
Port Lincoln ○ •• AUS 180-181 C 3
Port Lions ○ USA 22-23 U 4
Portlock Reefs ⌒ PNG 183 C 5
Port Loko ○ WAL 202-203 D 5
Port-Louis ○ F 56 E 3
Port Louis ★ • MS 224 C 7
Port Mac Donnell ○ AUS 180-181 F 5
Port Macquarie ○ • AUS 178-179 M 6
Port Maitland ○ CDN (NS) 240-241 J 7
Port Mansfield ○ USA (TX) 266-267 K 7
Port Maria ○ JA 54-55 G 5
Port Mathurin ○ MS 224 F 6
Port Maurant ○ GUY 62-63 F 2
Port Mayaca ○ USA (FL) 286-287 J 5
Port Mc Arthur ≈ 174-175 D 4
Port Mellon ○ CDN (BC) 230-231 F 4
Port Menier ○ CDN (QUE) 242-243 D 3
Port Moller ○ USA 22-23 Q 5
Port Moody ○ CDN (BC) 230-231 G 4
Portmore ○ JA 54-55 G 6
Port Moresby ★ PNG 183 D 5
Port Morien ○ CDN (NS) 240-241 Q 4
Port Neill ○ AUS 180-181 D 3
Port Nelson ○ BS 54-55 H 3
Port Nelson (abandoned) ○ CDN 34-35 K 2
Portneuf, Rivière ~ CDN (QUE) 240-241 F 2
Port Neville ○ CDN (BC) 230-231 C 3
Portnjagino, ozero ○ RUS 110-111 F 2
Port Nolloth ○ ZA 220-221 C 4
Port Norris ○ USA (NJ) 280-281 L 4
Port-Nouveau-Québec ○ CDN 36-37 R 5
Porto ○ BR 68-69 G 3
Porto ○ F 98-99 M 3
Porto ✩ •• P 98-99 C 4
Pôrto Acre ○ BR 66-67 D 7
Pôrto Alegre ○ BR 70-71 J 5
Porto Alegre ○ BR (BAH) 72-73 K 2
Porto Alegre ○ BR (P) 66-67 J 5
Porto Alegre ✩ BR (RSU) 74-75 E 8
Porto-Alegre ○ STP 210-211 b 2
Porto Alegre do Norte ○ BR 68-69 C 7
Porto Amazonas ○ BR 74-75 F 5
Porto Amboim ○ ANG 216-217 B 5
Porto Antunes ○ BR 66-67 D 4
Porto Azzurro ○ I 100-101 C 3
Portobelo ○ ••• PA 52-53 E 7
Porto Belo, Baía de ≈ 74-75 F 6
Porto Belo, Ponta do ▲ BR 74-75 F 6
Porto Bicentenário ○ BR 70-71 F 2
Porto Braga ○ BR (AMA) 66-67 E 4
Porto Braga ○ BR (GSU) 70-71 J 7
Porto Cabello ○ YV 60-61 G 2
Porto Camargo ○ BR 72-73 D 7
Porto Cristo ○ E 98-99 J 5
Porto da Soledade ○ BR 72-73 G 4
Pôrto de Fora ○ BR 70-71 K 5
Porto de Pedras ○ BR 68-69 L 6
Porto do Caititu ○ BR 68-69 F 4
Porto do Mangue ○ BR 68-69 K 4
Porto do Moz ○ BR 62-63 H 6
Porto dos Gaúchos ○ BR 70-71 J 2
Porto dos Mosteiros ○ CV 202-203 B 6
Porto Esperanza ○ RA 76-77 K 4
Porto Esperidião ○ BR 70-71 H 4
Porto Estrela ○ BR 70-71 J 4
Porto Euchdes da Cunha ○ BR 72-73 D 7
Portoferráio ○ I 100-101 C 3
Porto Ferreira ○ BR 72-73 G 6
Port of Ness ○ GB 90-91 D 2
Porto Franco ○ BR 68-69 E 5
Port of Spain ✩ TT 60-61 L 2
Porto Gen. Nac. el Portillo ▲ RA 78-79 E 2
Porto Grande ○ BR 62-63 J 5
Portogruaro ○ • I 100-101 D 2
Porto Henrique ○ MOC 220-221 L 3
Pôrto Jofre ○ BR 70-71 J 5
Portola ○ USA (CA) 246-247 E 4
Porto Levante ○ I 100-101 E 5
Port-Olry ○ VAN 184 II a 2
Porto Lucena ○ BR 76-77 K 4
Port Omna = Portumna ○ IRL 90-91 C 5
Porto Moniz ○ P 188-189 C 4
Porto Mosquito ○ CV 202-203 C 6
Pôrto Murtinho ○ BR 76-77 J 1
Porto Nacional ○ BR 68-69 D 7
Porto Novo ○ BR 72-73 J 2
Porto-Novo ★ • DY 204-205 E 5
Portonovo ○ IND 140-141 H 5
Porto Novo, Vila de ○ CV 202-203 B 5
Porto Quebra ○ BR 66-67 F 4
Port Orchard ○ USA (WA) 244-245 C 3
Porto Reis ○ BR 66-67 E 4
Porto Rico ○ BR 70-71 D 2
Porto Rolha ○ BR 70-71 E 2
Porto Santo ⌒ P 188-189 C 4
Porto São José ○ BR 72-73 D 7
Portoscuso ○ I 100-101 B 5
Porto Seguro ○ • BR 72-73 L 4
Porto Seguro, Corredeira ~ BR 68-69 B 5
Porto Tolle ○ I 100-101 D 2
Porto Tórres ○ I 100-101 B 4
Porto União ○ BR 74-75 E 6
Porto Valter ○ BR 64-65 F 6
Porto-Vecchio ○ F 98-99 M 4
Porto Velho ✩ BR 66-67 F 7
Portovelo ○ EC 64-65 C 3
Portoviejo ✩ EC 64-65 B 2
Portpatrick ○ GB 90-91 E 4
Port Perry ○ CDN (ONT) 238-239 G 4
Port Philip ○ CDN (NS) 240-241 M 5
Port Pirie ○ AUS 180-181 D 2
Port Radium ○ CDN 30-31 L 2
Portree ○ GB 90-91 D 3
Port Rowan ○ CDN (ONT) 238-239 E 6
Port Royal ○ USA (VA) 280-281 J 5
Port Royal National Historic Park • CDN (NS) 240-241 K 6
Port Royal Sound ≈ USA 284-285 K 4
Port Said = Būr Sa'īd ✩ ET 194-195 F 2
Port Saint Joe ○ USA (FL) 286-287 D 2
Port Saint Johns ○ ZA 220-221 J 5
Port-Saint-Louis-du-Rhône ○ F 90-91 K 10
Port Saint Lucie ○ USA (FL) 286-287 J 4
Portsalon ○ IRL 90-91 D 4
Port Salut ○ RH 54-55 J 5
Port Salut, Plage ⊥ • RH 54-55 H 5
Port Sanilac ○ USA (MI) 272-273 G 4
Port Saunders ○ CDN (NFL) 242-243 L 2
Port Shepstone ○ ZA 220-221 K 5
Port Simpson ○ CDN (BC) 228-229 D 2
Portsmouth ○ GB 90-91 G 6
Portsmouth ○ USA (IA) 274-275 C 3
Portsmouth ○ USA (NH) 278-279 L 5
Portsmouth ○ USA (OH) 280-281 D 5
Portsmouth ○ USA (VA) 280-281 K 7
Portsmouth ○ WD 56 E 4
Portsmouth Island ⌒ USA (NC) 282-283 L 5
Port Stephens ○ GB 78-79 K 7

Port Sudan = Būr Sūdān ☆• SUD 200-201 H 3
Port Sulphur ○ USA (LA) 268-269 L 7
Port Talbot ○ CDN (ONT) 238-239 D 6
Porttipahdan tekojärvi ⊂ FIN 88-89 J 2
Port Townsend ○• USA (WA) 244-245 C 2
Portugais, Grotte des = Tenika • RM 222-223 D 9
Portugal ■ P 98-99 B 4
Portugal, Cachoeira ∼ BR 66-67 E 7
Portugal Cove ○ CDN (NFL) 242-243 Q 5
Portugal Cove South ○ CDN (NFL) 242-243 P 6
Portuguesa, Río ∼ YV 60-61 H 3
Portuguese Cove ○ CDN (NS) 240-241 M 6
Portumna = Port Omna ○ IRL 90-91 C 5
Port-Vato ○ VAN 184 II b 3
Port-Vendres ○ F 90-91 J 10
Port Victoria ○ AUS 180-181 D 3
Port Victoria ○ EAK 212-213 D 3
Port-Vila ★• VAN 184 II b 3
Port Vincent ○ AUS 180-181 D 3
Port Wakefield ○ AUS 180-181 E 3
Port Washington ○ USA (WI) 274-275 L 1
Port Wing ○ USA (WI) 270-271 G 4
Poruj, mys ▲ RUS 108-109 P 6
Poruk Çayı ∼ TR 128-129 D 3
Porumamilla ○ IND 140-141 H 3
Porvenir ○ 64-65 B 10
Porvenir ○ BOL 70-71 C 2
Porvenir ○ PE 64-65 D 3
Porvenir ○ RCH 80 E 6
Porvenir, El ○ MEX 50-51 G 2
Porvenir, El ☆ PA 52-53 E 7
Porvenir, El ○ YV (APU) 60-61 G 4
Porvenir, El ○ YV (BAR) 60-61 F 4
Posadas ☆ RA 76-77 K 4
Pošegda ○ RUS 88-89 R 5
Pošehon'e ○ RUS 94-95 Q 2
Pošehon'e-Volodarsk = Pošehon'e ○ RUS 94-95 Q 2
Poseidon, Temple of ∴ GR 100-101 K 6
Posen ○ USA (MI) 272-273 F 2
Posesión, Bahía ≈ 80 F 6
Posevnaja ○ RUS 124-125 N 1
Poshkokagan River ∼ CDN (ONT) 234-235 O 5
Posik, Pulau ⌒ RI 162-163 F 5
Posio ○ FIN 88-89 K 3
Posiposi ○ RI 164-165 L 2
Posito, El ∴• BH 52-53 K 3
Poso ○ RI 164-165 G 4
Poso, Danau ⊂ RI 164-165 G 4
Posof ☆ TR 128-129 K 2
Posŏng ○ ROK 150-151 F 10
Posorja ○ EC 64-65 B 3
Pospeliha ○ RUS 124-125 M 3
Posse ○ BR 72-73 G 3
Possel ○ RCA 206-207 D 6
Possession, Point ▲ USA 20-21 P 6
Possessioneiland ⌒ NAM 220-221 B 3
Possoš' ○ RUS 102-103 L 2
Possum Kingdom Lake ⊂ USA (TX) 264-265 F 6
Post ○ USA (OR) 244-245 E 6
Post ○ USA (TX) 264-265 C 5
Posta Cambio a Zalazar ○ RA 76-77 G 3
Posta Km. 45 ○ RA 76-77 G 3
Posta Lencina ○ RA 76-77 G 3
Posta Arinda ○ GUY 62-63 E 3
Poste-de-la-Baleine ○ CDN 36-37 L 7
Post Falls ○ USA (ID) 250-251 C 4
Postmasburg ○ ZA 220-221 F 4
Posto Ajuricaba ○ BR 66-67 F 2
Postoak ○ USA (MO) 274-275 E 6
Posto Cocraimore ○ BR 68-69 B 5
Post Office Tree • ZA 220-221 F 7
Posto Funai ○ BR (AMA) 62-63 E 6
Posto Funai ○ BR (AMA) 62-63 D 6
Posto Funai ○ BR (AMA) 64-65 F 4
Posto Funai ○ BR (APA) 62-63 J 4
Postojna ○ SLO 100-101 E 2
Postojnska jama ∴• SLO 100-101 E 2
Posto Uaçá ○ BR 62-63 J 4
Postrervalle ○ BOL 70-71 F 6
Postville ○ USA (IA) 274-275 G 1
Pota ○ RI 168 E 7
Potato Creek ∼ USA (GA) 284-285 F 4
Potawatomi Indian Reservation X USA (KS) 262-263 L 5
Potchefstroom ○ ZA 220-221 H 3
Potčurk, gora ▲ RUS 88-89 W 5
Poté ○ BR 72-73 K 4
Poteau ○ USA (OK) 264-265 K 3
Poteau Mountain ▲ USA (AR) 276-277 A 6
Poteau River ∼ USA (OK) 264-265 K 3
Poteet ○ USA (TX) 266-267 J 4
Potengi ○ BR 68-69 H 5
Potenji, Rio ∼ BR 68-69 K 4
Potenza ☆• I 100-101 E 4
Potfontein ○ ZA 220-221 G 5
Potgietersrus ○ ZA 220-221 J 2
Poth ○ USA (TX) 266-267 J 4
Potherie, Lac la ⊂ CDN 36-37 N 5
Potholes Reservoir ⊂ USA (WA) 244-245 F 3
Poti ○• GE 126-127 D 6
Poti, Rio ∼ BR 68-69 G 4
Potidaia • GR 100-101 J 4
Potiguara, Área Indígena X BR 68-69 L 5
Potimalal, Río ∼ RA 78-79 D 4
Potin ○ IND 142-143 H 2
Potiragua ○ BR 72-73 L 3
Potiskum ○ WAN 204-205 J 3
Pot Jostler Creek ∼ AUS 178-179 F 2
Potlatch ○ USA (ID) 250-251 C 5
Pot Mountain ▲ USA (ID) 250-251 D 5
Potol Point ▲ RP 160-161 D 7
Potomac River ∼ USA (VA) 280-281 K 5
Potomac River ∼ USA (VA) 280-281 J 4
Potoru ○ WAL 202-203 E 6
Potosí ☆∴ BOL 70-71 E 6
Potosí ○ NIC 52-53 L 5
Potosi ○ USA (MO) 276-277 E 3
Potosí, Río ∼ MEX 50-51 K 5
Pototan ○ RP 160-161 E 7
Potrerillos ○ RA 78-79 E 2
Potrerillos, Río ∼ RCH 76-77 B 5
Potrero ○ USA (CA) 248-249 H 7
Potrero de Gallegos ○ MEX 50-51 H 6
Potrero del Llano ○ MEX 50-51 G 3
Potrero Grande ○ CR 52-53 C 7
Potrero Quemado ○ BOL 70-71 H 6
Potrero Seco ○ RCH 76-77 B 4
Potro, Cerro del ▲ RCH 76-77 C 5
Potro, Río ∼ PE 64-65 D 4
Potrorillos Abajo ○ PA 52-53 C 7
Potsdam ☆∴ D 92-93 M 2
Potsdam ○ USA (NY) 278-279 G 4
Potter ○ USA (NE) 262-263 C 3
Potter Island ⌒ CDN 36-37 R 3
Potters Mills ○ USA (PA) 280-281 J 3
Potts Mountain ▲ USA (VA) 280-281 F 6
Pottstown ○ USA (PA) 280-281 L 3
Pottsville ○ USA (PA) 280-281 K 3
Pottuvil ○ CL 140-141 J 7
Pötürge ☆ TR 128-129 H 3
Pouch Cove ○ CDN (NFL) 242-243 Q 5
Pouéré ○ RCB 210-211 E 4
Poughkeepsie ○ USA (NY) 280-281 N 2
Pougol ○ RCA 206-207 C 5
Poularies ○ CDN (QUE) 236-237 K 4
Poulsbo ○ USA (WA) 244-245 C 3
Poultney ○ USA (VT) 278-279 H 5
Pouma ○ CAM 210-211 C 2
Poumalé ○ RCA 206-207 D 6
Pound ○ USA (WI) 270-271 K 5
Pound Maker Indian Reserve X CDN (SAS) 232-233 J 3
Poura ○ BF 202-203 J 4
Pourerere ○ NZ 182 F 4
Pourtage Lake ⊂ USA (MI) 270-271 K 3
Pouso Alegre ○ BR 72-73 H 7
Pouso Grande ○ BR 66-67 J 5
Pouss ○• CAM 206-207 B 3
Poŭthisăt ○ K 158-159 G 4
Pouto ○ NZ 182 E 2
Pouytenga ○ BF 202-203 K 3
Poveneckij zaliv ≈ 88-89 N 5
Poverty Bay ≈ 182 F 3
Póvoa de Varzim ○ P 98-99 C 4
Povorot ○ RUS 116-117 N 10
Povorotnyj, mys ▲ RUS (CUK) 112-113 V 4
Povorotnyj, mys ▲ RUS (MAG) 120-121 T 3
Povorotnyj, mys ▲ RUS (SAH) 110-111 V 3
Povorotnyj, mys ▲ RUS (TMR) 108-109 X 4
Povungnituk ○ CDN 36-37 L 4
Povungnituk, Lac de ⊂ CDN 36-37 L 4
Povungnituk, Monts de ▲ CDN 36-37 M 4
Povungnituk, Rivière de ∼ CDN 36-37 M 4
Povungnituk Bay ≈ 36-37 L 5
Powassan ○ CDN (ONT) 238-239 F 2
Powder River ∼ USA (WY) 252-253 M 3
Powder River ∼ USA (MT) 250-251 O 6
Powder River ∼ USA (OR) 244-245 H 6
Powder River ∼ USA (WY) 252-253 M 3
Powder River Pass ▲ USA (WY) 252-253 L 2
Powderville ○ USA (MT) 250-251 O 6
Powell ○ USA (WY) 252-253 K 2
Powell, Lake ⊂ USA (UT) 254-255 D 6
Powell, Mount ▲ USA (CO) 254-255 J 4
Powell Creek ∼ AUS 178-179 G 3
Powell Point ▲ BS 54-55 G 2
Powell River ○ CDN (BC) 230-231 E 4
Powellsville ○ USA (NC) 282-283 L 4
Power ○ USA (MT) 250-251 H 4
Powers ○ USA (MI) 270-271 L 5
Powers Lake ○ USA (ND) 258-259 E 3
Powhatan ○ USA (LA) 268-269 G 5
Powhatan Point ○ USA (OH) 280-281 F 4
Powlathanga ○ AUS 174-175 H 7
Powlett, Kap ▲ GRØ 26-27 P 5
Powoollak Camp ○ USA 20-21 E 5
Poxoréo ○ BR 70-71 K 4
Poyang Hu ⊂ VRC 156-157 K 2
Poyanghu Z.B. ⊥• VRC 156-157 K 2
Poyata, La ○ CO 60-61 E 5
Poyen ○ USA (AR) 276-277 C 6
Poygan, Lake ⊂ USA (WI) 270-271 K 6
Pozantı ☆ TR 128-129 F 4
Požarevac ○• YU 100-101 H 2
Poza Rica ○ MEX 52-53 F 1
Poza Rica de Hidalgo = Poza Rica ○ MEX 52-53 F 1
Pozas de Santa Ana ○ MEX 50-51 J 6
Pozdeevka ○ RUS 122-123 C 3
Požeg ○ RUS 96-97 J 3
Požega ○ YU 100-101 H 3
Poznań ☆∴ PL 92-93 O 2
Pozo ○ USA (CA) 248-249 D 4
Pozo, Río del ∼ RA 76-77 D 4
Pozo Alcón ○ E 98-99 F 6
Pozo Almonte ○ RCH 70-71 C 7
Pozo Colorado ☆ PY 76-77 H 2
Pozo del Molle ○ RA 76-77 F 6
Pozo del Tigre ○ BOL 70-71 G 5
Pozo del Tigre ○ RA 76-77 G 3
Pozo del Zorro ○ RA 76-77 F 2
Pozo de Maza ○ RA 76-77 G 2
Pozo Dulce ○ RA 76-77 F 5
Pozo Herrera ○ RA 76-77 F 5
Pozo Hondo ○ RA 76-77 E 4
Pozón ○ YV 60-61 H 4
Pozos, Los ○ PA 52-53 D 8
Pozos, Punta ▲ RA 80 H 3
Pozo Summit ▲ USA (CA) 248-249 D 4
Pozuelos ○ YV 60-61 J 2
Pozuelos, Laguna de ⊂∴ RA 76-77 D 2
Pozuzo ○ PE 64-65 E 7
Pozuzo, Río ∼ PE 64-65 E 6
Pozzuoli ○• I 100-101 E 4
P. Pelapis, Pulau ⌒ RI 162-163 H 5
Pra ∼ GH 202-203 K 7
Prachin Buri ○ THA 158-159 F 3
Prachuap Khirikhan ○ THA 158-159 E 5
Pracupi, Rio ∼ BR 68-69 C 3
Praděd ▲ CZ 92-93 O 3
Prado ○ BR 72-73 L 4
Pradópolis ○ BR 72-73 F 6
Prague ○ USA (NE) 262-263 K 3
Prague ○ USA (OK) 264-265 H 3
Prague = Praha ★∴ CZ 92-93 N 3
Praha ★∴ CZ 92-93 N 3
Praia ○ BR 66-67 K 5
Praia ★ CV 202-203 C 6
Praia da Barata ○ BR 66-67 D 3
Praia de Vaca ○ BR 66-67 C 7
Praia do Bilene ○ MOC 220-221 L 2
Praia do Maçarico ○ BR 66-67 D 3
Praia do Tofo ○ MOC 218-219 H 6
Praia do Xai-Xai ○ MOC 220-221 L 2
Praia Grande ○ BR (CAT) 74-75 F 7
Praia Grande ○ BR (PAU) 74-75 G 5
Praikalogu ○ RI 168 D 7
Prailiu ○• RI 168 E 7
Prainha ○ BR 66-67 D 6
Prainha ○ BR (P) 62-63 H 6
Prainha ○ BR (P) 68-69 C 3
Prainha Nova ○ BR 66-67 G 6
Prairie ○ AUS 174-175 H 7
Prairie ○ USA (MN) 270-271 E 6
Prairie City ○ USA (OR) 244-245 G 6
Prairie Creek ∼ CDN (ALB) 228-229 P 2
Prairie Creek ∼ USA (IN) 274-275 L 5
Prairie Creek ∼ USA (FL) 286-287 H 4
Prairie Creek Reservoir ⊂ USA (IN) 274-275 N 4
Prairie Dell ○ USA (TX) 266-267 K 3
Prairie Dog Creek ∼ USA (KS) 262-263 F 5
Prairie Dog Town Fork of the Red River ∼ USA 264-265 C 4
Prairie Downs ○ AUS 176-177 E 1
Prairie du Chien ○ USA (WI) 274-275 G 1
Prairie Grove ○ USA (AR) 276-277 A 5
Prairie River ○ CDN (SAS) 232-233 Q 3
Prairie View ○ USA (TX) 268-269 E 6
Prairie Village ∴ USA (SD) 260-261 J 3
Praiyawang ○• RI 168 E 7
Prakhon Chai ○ THA 158-159 G 3
Prambanan ○∴ RI 168 D 3
Prampram ○ GH 202-203 L 7
Pran Buri ○ THA 158-159 E 4
Pran Buri Reservoir < THA 158-159 E 4
Prándarjökull ⊂ IS 86-87 f 2
Prāntij ○ IND 138-139 D 8
Prapat ○ RI 162-163 C 3
Prasat ○ THA 158-159 G 3
Praslin Island ⌒ SY 224 D 2
Prasokuma ○ GH 202-203 K 6
Prat ○ RCH 76-77 B 2
Prat, Cerro ▲ RCH 80 F 6
Prat, Isla ⌒ RCH 80 C 4
Prata ○ BR 68-69 H 3
Prata, Igarapé ∼ BR 66-67 J 5
Prata, Rio ∼ BR 72-73 F 5
Prata, Rio da ∼ BR 72-73 G 4
Prathai ○ THA 158-159 G 3
Prato ○ I 100-101 C 3
Prats-de-Mollo-la-Preste ○ F 90-91 J 10
Pratt ○ USA (KS) 262-263 H 7
Prattville ○ USA (AL) 284-285 D 4
Pratudão, Rio ∼ BR 72-73 H 2
Pravaja Bojarka ∼ RUS 108-109 b 6
Pravaja Bureja ∼ RUS 122-123 F 3
Pravaja Hetta ∼ RUS 114-115 M 2
Pravaja Hodutka ∼ RUS 122-123 R 3
Pravaja Kamenka ∼ RUS 110-111 d 6
Pravaja Mama ∼ RUS 118-119 E 7
Pravaja Šapina ∼ RUS 120-121 S 6
Pravdinsk ○∴ RUS 94-95 G 4
Pravyj Kihčik ∼ RUS 120-121 R 7
Pravyj Mamakan ∼ RUS 118-119 G 7
Prawda ○ CDN (MAN) 234-235 H 5
Prawn Fishing Base • AUS 174-175 C 4
Praya ○ RI 168 C 7
Prazaroki ○ BY 94-95 L 4
Preacher Creek ∼ USA 20-21 S 4
Preăh Vihéar ○ K 158-159 H 3
Precipice National Park ⊥ AUS 178-179 L 3
Prečistoe ○ RUS 94-95 N 4
Precordillera ▲ RA 76-77 C 6
Predaltajskaja ravnina ⊥ RUS 124-125 M 3
Predbajkal'skaja vpadina ⊥ RUS 116-117 M 9
Predporožnyj ○ RUS 110-111 Y 7
Preeceville ○ CDN (SAS) 232-233 Q 4
Preemption ○ USA (IL) 274-275 H 3
Preguiça ○ CV 202-203 B 5
Prehistoric Mounds ∴• CDN (MAN) 234-235 C 5
Preissac, Lac ⊂ CDN (QUE) 236-237 K 4
Prekestolen ∴ N 86-87 C 7
Prekonosta pećina ∴ YU 100-101 J 3
Prelate ○ CDN (SAS) 232-233 J 5
Prele Ranger Station, La ○ USA (WY) 252-253 N 4
Premier Diamond Mine • ZA 220-221 J 2
Premier Downs ○ AUS 176-177 H 5
Premio ○ CDN 38-39 M 3
Premont ○ USA (TX) 266-267 J 6
Prend Town ○ LB 202-203 F 7
Prentice ○ USA (WI) 270-271 H 5
Prentiss ○ USA (MS) 268-269 L 5
Prenzlau ○• D 92-93 M 2
Preobraženija, ostrov ⌒ RUS 110-111 J 2
Preobraženija, zaliv ○ RUS 108-109 P 5
Prescott ○ USA (AR) 276-277 B 7
Prescott ○ USA (AZ) 256-257 C 4
Prescott ○ USA (WA) 244-245 G 4
Prescott ○ USA (WI) 270-271 F 6
Prescott Island ⌒ CDN 24-25 Y 4
Prescott Lakes ○ AUS 172-173 G 6
Prescott Valley ○ USA (AZ) 256-257 C 4
Preseka ▲ MK 100-101 H 4
Preservation Inlet ≈ 182 A 7
Presho ○ USA (SD) 260-261 F 3
Presidencia de la Plaza ○ RA 76-77 H 4
Presidencia Roque Sáenz Peña ○ RA 76-77 G 4
Presidente Barros Dutra ○ BR 68-69 F 4
Presidente Bernardes ○ BR 72-73 E 7
Presidente Epitácio ○ BR 72-73 D 6
Presidente Figueiredo ○ BR 66-67 G 4
Presidente Jânio Quadros ○ BR 72-73 K 3
Presidente Juscelino ○ BR (MAR) 68-69 F 3
Presidente Juscelino ○ BR (MIN) 72-73 H 5
Presidente Kennedy ○ BR 68-69 D 6
Presidente Medici ○ BR 70-71 G 2
Presidente Olegário ○ BR 72-73 G 5
Presidente Prudente ○ BR 72-73 E 7
Presidente Ríos, Lago ○ RCH 80 C 3
Presidente Vargas ○ BR 68-69 F 3
Presidente Venceslau ○ BR 72-73 E 6
Presidio ○ USA (TX) 266-267 C 4
Presidio, Río ∼ MEX 50-51 F 6
Preslav = Veliki Preslav ○• BG 102-103 E 6
Presnovka ☆ KA 124-125 E 1
Prešov ○ SK 92-93 Q 4
Prespansko Ezero ⊂∴ MK 100-101 H 4
Presque Isle ○ USA (ME) 278-279 O 2
Presque Isle ○ USA (MI) 272-273 F 2
Presque Isle ○ USA (WI) 270-271 J 4
Presque Isle State Park ⊥ USA (PA) 280-281 F 1
Preßburg = Bratislava ★∴ SK 92-93 O 4
Press Lake ⊂ CDN (ONT) 234-235 M 5
Preston ○ GB 90-91 F 5
Preston ○ USA (ID) 252-253 G 4
Preston ○ USA (MN) 270-271 F 7
Preston ○ USA (MO) 276-277 B 3
Preston ○ USA (MS) 268-269 M 4
Preston ○ USA (NV) 246-247 K 5
Preston, Cape ▲ AUS 172-173 C 6
Prestonsburg ○ USA (KY) 276-277 N 3
Prêto, Rio ∼ BR 66-67 E 2
Preto, Rio ∼ BR 66-67 E 3
Preto, Rio ∼ BR 66-67 F 3
Preto, Rio ∼ BR 66-67 F 7
Prêto, Rio ∼ BR 68-69 G 3
Preto, Rio ∼ BR 68-69 F 7
Prêto, Rio ∼ BR 72-73 G 4
Prêto, Rio ∼ BR 72-73 L 2
Prêto, Rio ∼ BR 72-73 F 2
Prêto, Rio ∼ BR 72-73 F 6
Preto da Eva, Rio ∼ BR 66-67 H 4
Preto do Candeias, Rio ∼ BR 66-67 F 7
Preto do Crespo, Rio ∼ BR 66-67 F 7
Prêto do Igapó-Açu, Rio ∼ BR 66-67 G 5
Preto ou Grande do Piau, Igarapé ∼ BR 66-67 J 7
Pretoria ★• ZA 220-221 J 2
Pretoria Witwatersrand Vereeniging □ ZA 220-221 J 2
Preußisch Holland = Pasłęk ○• PL 92-93 P 1
Préveza ○ GR 100-101 H 5
Prevost River ∼ CDN 20-21 Z 5
Prey Khmêr ○ K 158-159 H 4
Prey Vêng ○ K 158-159 H 5
Priangarskoe plato ⊥ RUS 116-117 G 6
Priargunsk ☆ RUS 118-119 J 10
Pribilof Islands ⌒ USA 22-23 L 4
Pribojnyj ○ RUS 116-117 L 8
Příbram ○ CZ 92-93 N 4
Pribrežnyj hrebet ▲ RUS 120-121 F 6
Price ○ CDN (QUE) 240-241 G 2
Price ○ USA (MD) 280-281 L 4
Price ○ USA (NC) 282-283 H 4
Price ○ USA (UT) 254-255 E 4
Price Island ⌒ CDN (BC) 228-229 F 4
Price River ∼ USA 20-21 O 2
Price River ∼ USA (UT) 254-255 E 4
Prichard ○ USA (AL) 284-285 B 6
Prichard ○ USA (ID) 250-251 D 4
Priddis ○ CDN (ALB) 232-233 D 5
Priddy ○ USA (TX) 266-267 J 2
Pridnjaprovskaja nizina ∪ BY 94-95 M 5
Priego de Córdoba ○ E 98-99 E 6
Priekule ○ LT 94-95 G 4
Priekule ☆ LV 94-95 G 3
Prienai ○∴ LT 94-95 H 4
Priene • TR 128-129 B 4
Prieska ○ ZA 220-221 F 4
Priest Lake ○ USA (ID) 250-251 C 3
Priest River ○ USA (ID) 250-251 C 3
Prieto, Cerro ▲ PE 64-65 B 4
Prievidza ○ SK 92-93 P 4
Prijedor ○ BIH 100-101 F 2
Prijepolje ○ YU 100-101 G 3
Prijutovo ○ RUS 96-97 H 7
Prikro ○ CI 202-203 H 6
Prikro, Kouadio- ○ CI 202-203 H 6
Prilenskoe, plato ⊥ RUS 118-119 E 5
Prilep ○ MK 100-101 H 4
Priluki = Pryluky ○ UA 102-103 H 2
Primate ○ CDN (SAS) 232-233 J 3
Primavera ○ BR 68-69 E 2
Primavera do Leste ○ BR 70-71 K 4
Primeira Cruz ○ BR 68-69 G 3
Primeiro, Salto ∼ BR 70-71 K 3
Primeiro de Abril, Salto ∼ BR 70-71 G 2
Primeiro de Maio ○ BR 72-73 E 7
Primeiró de Março, Cachoeira ∼ BR 70-71 G 2
Primero, Cabo ▲ RCH 80 C 4
Primero, Río ∼ RA 76-77 F 6
Primero de Mayo ○ MEX 50-51 J 4
Primero Salto, Cachoeira ∼ BR 66-67 H 6
Primorsk ○ RUS 94-95 G 4
Primorsk ○ RUS (LEN) 94-95 L 1
Primorsk ○ RUS (VLG) 96-97 D 9
Primorsk = Danızkanarı ○ AZ 128-129 N 2
Primorskij hrebet ▲ RUS 116-117 M 9
Primorsko-Ahtarsk ○ RUS 102-103 L 4
Primošten ○• HR 100-101 E 3
Primrose Lake ⊂ CDN 32-33 Q 4
Prince ○ CDN (SAS) 232-233 K 3
Prince Albert ○ CDN (SAS) 232-233 N 2
Prince Albert ○ ZA 220-221 F 6
Prince Albert Mountains ▲ ARK 16 F 17
Prince Albert National Park ⊥ CDN 34-35 C 3
Prince Albert Peninsula ∪ CDN 24-25 N 4
Prince Albert Road ○ ZA 220-221 E 6
Prince Albert Sound ≈ 24-25 O 5
Prince Alexander Mountains ▲ PNG 183 B 2
Prince Alfred, Cape ▲ CDN 24-25 J 3
Prince Alfred Bay ≈ 24-25 Z 2
Prince Charles Island ⌒ CDN 24-25 h 6
Prince Charles Range ▲ ARK 16 F 7
Prince Edward Bay ≈ CDN 238-239 J 4
Prince Edward Island □ CDN (PEI) 240-241 M 4
Prince Edward Island ⌒∴ CDN (PEI) 240-241 M 4
Prince Edward Island National Park ⊥ CDN (PEI) 240-241 M 4
Prince Edward Islands ⌒ ZA 9 G 10
Prince Edward Peninsula ∪ CDN (ONT) 238-239 H 4
Prince Frederick ○ USA (MD) 280-281 K 5
Prince George ○• CDN (BC) 228-229 M 3
Prince George ○ USA (VA) 280-281 J 6
Prince Gustav Adolf Sea ≈ 24-25 R 1
Prince Leopold Island ⌒ CDN 24-25 a 3
Prince of Wales, Cape ▲ USA 20-21 F 4
Prince of Wales Bank ≃ 158-159 L 6
Prince of Wales Island ⌒ AUS 174-175 G 2
Prince of Wales Island ⌒ AUS 183 B 6
Prince of Wales Island ⌒ CDN 24-25 W 4
Prince of Wales Island ⌒ USA 32-33 D 4
Prince of Wales Strait ≈ 24-25 M 4
Prince Patrick Island ⌒ CDN 24-25 L 2
Prince Regent Inlet ≈ 24-25 a 4
Prince Regent Nature Reserve ⊥ AUS 172-173 G 3
Prince Regent River ∼ AUS 172-173 G 3
Prince Rupert ○• CDN (BC) 228-229 D 2
Princesa Isabel ○ BR 68-69 J 5
Princess Anne ○ USA (MD) 280-281 L 5
Princess Anne ○ USA (VA) 280-281 K 7
Princess Charlotte Bay ≈ 174-175 G 4
Princess Elizabeth Land ⌒ ARK 16 F 8
Princess Harbour ○ CDN (MAN) 234-235 G 3
Princess Highway II AUS 180-181 K 4
Princess Margaret Range ▲ CDN 26-27 D 3
Princess Marie-Bay ≈ 26-27 M 4
Princess Mary Lake ⊂ CDN 30-31 V 3
Princess Ranges ▲ AUS 176-177 F 3
Princess Royal Channel < CDN (BC) 228-229 F 3
Princess Royal Island ⌒ CDN (BC) 228-229 F 3
Princess Royal Island ⌒ CDN (BCL) 228-229 F 4
Prince's Town ○ GH 202-203 J 7
Princeton ○ CDN (BC) 230-231 J 4
Princeton ○ USA (AL) 284-285 D 2
Princeton ○ USA (AR) 276-277 C 7
Princeton ○ USA (CA) 246-247 C 4
Princeton ○ USA (FL) 286-287 J 6
Princeton ○ USA (IL) 274-275 J 3
Princeton ○ USA (IN) 274-275 L 6
Princeton ○ USA (KY) 276-277 H 3
Princeton ○ USA (MN) 270-271 E 5
Princeton ○ USA (MO) 274-275 E 4
Princeton ○ USA (NJ) 280-281 M 3
Princeton ○ USA (SC) 284-285 H 2
Princeton ○ USA (WI) 270-271 J 7
Princeton ○ USA (WV) 280-281 E 6
Princetown ○ AUS 180-181 G 5
Princeville ○ USA (IL) 274-275 J 4
Prince William Sound ≈ 20-21 R 6
Príncipe ⌒ STP 210-211 b 2
Principe Channel ≈ 32-33 E 5
Principe Channel ≈ CDN 228-229 D 3
Príncipe da Beira ○ BR 70-71 E 3
Prindle ○ USA (WA) 244-245 C 5
Prineville ○ USA (OR) 244-245 E 6
Pringamosa ○ CO 60-61 D 5
Pringle ○ USA (SD) 260-261 C 3
Pringle Bay ○ ZA 220-221 D 7
Pringsewu ○ RI 162-163 F 7
Prins Bernhardpolder ○ SME 62-63 F 3
Prins Christian Sund ≈ 28-29 T 6
Prinsesse Astrid land ⊥ ARK 16 F 2
Prinsesse Dagmar Ø ⌒ GRØ 26-27 q 3
Prinsesse Margrethe Ø ⌒ GRØ 26-27 q 2
Prinsesse Ragnhild land ⊥ ARK 16 F 3
Prinsesse Thyra Ø ⌒ GRØ 26-27 p 2
Prins Frederik Øer ⌒ GRØ 26-27 p 3
Prins Harald land ⊥ ARK 16 F 4
Prins Karls Forland ⌒ N 84-85 G 3
Prins Oscars Land ∪ N 84-85 N 2
Prinzapolka, Río ∼ NIC 52-53 B 5
Prinzregent-Luitpold-Land ⊥ ARK 16 F 33
Priob'e ○ RUS 114-115 H 3
Prior, Cabo ▲ E 98-99 C 3
Priozernyj ○ KA 124-125 O 5
Priozërsk ☆ RUS 88-89 L 6
Prip'jat' ∼ UA 102-103 G 2
Pripoljarnyj Ural ▲ RUS 114-115 E 2
Prirečnyj ○ RUS 88-89 L 2
Prirodnyj nacional'nyj park "Pereslavl'" ⊥ RUS 94-95 Q 3
Prišib ○ AZ 128-129 N 3
Pristan'-Prževal'sk ○ KS 146-147 D 4
Priština ○∴ YU 100-101 H 3
Pritchard ○ CDN (BC) 230-231 K 3
Pritchards Island ⌒ USA (SC) 284-285 K 4
Pritchett ○ USA (CO) 254-255 N 6
Pritzwalk ○ D 92-93 M 2
Priverno ○ I 100-101 D 4
Privolž'e ☆ RUS 96-97 F 7
Privolžskaya Vozvyshennost' = Privolžskaja vozvyšennosť ▲ RUS 96-97 D 9
Privolžsk ○ RUS 94-95 R 3
Privolžskaja vozvyšennosť ▲ RUS 96-97 D 9
Priwitz = Prievidza ○ SK 92-93 P 4
Prizren ○∴ YU 100-101 H 3
Prjadčino ○ RUS 122-123 B 3
Prjaža ☆ RUS 88-89 M 6
Probolinggo ○ RI 168 E 3
Procter ○ CDN (BC) 230-231 N 4
Proctor ○ USA (MN) 270-271 F 4
Proctor ○ USA (TX) 266-267 J 2
Proctor Lake ⊂ USA (TX) 264-265 F 6
Proctorville ○ USA (OH) 280-281 D 5
Proddatūr ○ IND 140-141 H 3
Produjevo ○ YU 100-101 H 3
Proebstel ○ USA (WA) 244-245 C 5
Profeta, Quebrada de ∼ RCH 76-77 C 3
Progreso ○ MEX (COA) 50-51 J 4
Progreso ○• MEX (YUC) 52-53 K 1
Progreso ○ PE 64-65 F 9
Progreso ○ USA (TX) 266-267 B 2
Progreso, El ☆ GCA 52-53 J 4
Progreso, El ○ HN 52-53 L 4
Progress ○ RUS 122-123 C 4
Progresso ○ BR 64-65 F 6
Prohladyj ○ RUS 126-127 F 6
Prokof'eva, ostrov ⌒ RUS 120-121 H 6
Prokop'evsk ☆ RUS 124-125 P 2
Prokop'yevsk = Prokop'evsk ☆ RUS 124-125 P 2
Prokuplje ○• YU 100-101 H 3
Proletarsk ○ RUS 102-103 M 4
Proletarskoe vodohranilišče < RUS 102-103 M 4
Prome ○ MYA 142-143 J 6
Promežutočnyj ○ RUS 112-113 R 2
Promise ○ USA (OR) 244-245 H 5
Promissão ○ BR (GSU) 70-71 K 6
Promissão ○ BR (PAU) 72-73 F 6
Promissão, Represa < BR 72-73 F 6
Promontory ○ USA (UT) 254-255 C 2
Promontory Point ○ USA (UT) 254-255 C 2
Promyšlennaja ☆ RUS 114-115 S 7
Promyšlennyj ○ RUS 118-119 N 3
Promyslovka ○ RUS 126-127 G 5
Prončiščeva, krjaž ▲ RUS 110-111 K 3
Prončiščeva, mys ▲ RUS 108-109 g 3
Prončiščeva, ozero ⊂ RUS 108-109 k 4
Pronin ○ RUS 102-103 N 3
Pronja ∼ BY 94-95 M 4
Pronja ∼ RUS 94-95 R 4
Prophet River ∼ CDN 30-31 H 6
Prophetstown ○ USA (IL) 274-275 J 3
Proposed National Park ⊥ PNG 183 B 4
Propriá ○ BR 68-69 K 7
Propriano ○ F 98-99 M 4
Proserpine ○ AUS 174-175 K 7
Prospect ○ AUS 174-175 G 6
Prospect ○ USA (OR) 244-245 C 8
Prospector ○ CDN 34-35 F 4
Prospect Plantation Tour • JA 54-55 G 5
Prosperança ○ BR 62-63 D 6
Prosperidad ☆ RP 160-161 F 8
Prosperity ○ USA (PA) 280-281 F 3
Prosser ○ USA (WA) 244-245 F 4
Proßnitz = Prostějov ○ CZ 92-93 O 4
Prostějov ○ CZ 92-93 O 4
Prostor, zaliv ○ RUS 122-123 N 6
Prostornoe ○ KA 124-125 H 4
Protection ○ USA (KS) 262-263 G 7
Protem ○ ZA 220-221 E 7
Protivin ○ USA (IA) 274-275 F 1
Protoka ∼ RUS 102-103 L 5
Protoka Kalymskaja ∼ RUS 110-111 b 4
Protva ∼ RUS 94-95 P 4
Proussós ○ GR 100-101 H 5
Provadija ○ BG 102-103 E 6
Provence ⊥ F 90-91 K 10
Provence-Alpes-Côtes d'Azur □ F 90-91 K 10
Providence ○ USA (KY) 276-277 H 3
Providence ☆ USA (RI) 278-279 K 7
Providence, Cape ▲ USA 22-23 S 4
Providence, Lake ⊂ CDN 30-31 N 3
Providence Atoll ⌒ SY 224 B 4
Providence Bay ○ CDN (ONT) 238-239 C 3
Providence Island ⌒ SY 224 B 4
Providence Mountains ▲ USA (CA) 248-249 J 5
Providencia, Isla de ⌒ CO 52-53 D 5
Providenciales Island ⌒ GB 54-55 J 4
Providenija ○• RUS 112-113 Y 4
Providenija, buhta ≈ 112-113 Y 4
Provincetown ○ USA (MA) 278-279 L 6
Provins ○• F 90-91 J 7
Provo ○ USA (SD) 260-261 C 3
Provo ○ USA (UT) 254-255 D 3
Provost ○ CDN (ALB) 232-233 H 3
Prozor ○ BIH 100-101 F 3
Prozorovo ○ RUS 96-97 F 5
Prudhoe Bay ≈ 20-21 Q 1
Prudhoe Bay ○ USA 20-21 Q 1
Prudhoe Island ⌒ AUS 178-179 K 1
Prudhoe Land ⊥ GRØ 26-27 Q 5
Prud'homme ○ CDN (SAS) 232-233 N 3
Prüm ○ D 92-93 J 3
Prundu ○ RO 102-103 E 5
Prungle ○ AUS 180-181 G 3
Prupuk ○ RI 168 C 3
Prut ∼ MD 102-103 E 4
Prut ∼ RO 102-103 E 5
Prut ∼ UA 102-103 D 3
Prut ∼ UA 102-103 E 4
Pružany ○ BY 94-95 J 5
Pryazovs'ka vysočyna ▲ UA 102-103 J 4
Pryčornomors'ka Nyzovyna ⊥ UA 102-103 F 5
Prydniprovs'ka vysočyna ▲ UA 102-103 F 3
Pryluky ○ UA 102-103 H 2
Prymors'k ○ UA 102-103 K 4
Pryor ○ USA (MT) 250-251 L 6
Pryor, La ○ USA (TX) 266-267 H 5
Pryor Creek ○ USA (OK) 264-265 J 2
Pryor Creek ∼ USA (MT) 250-251 L 6
Prypjac' ∼ BY 94-95 L 5
Prypjackì dzjaržavny zapavednik ⊥ BY 94-95 K 6
Pryp'jat' ∼ UA 102-103 C 2
Przasnysz ○ PL 92-93 Q 2
Przemyśl ☆∴ PL 92-93 R 4
Prževal'sk ☆ KS 146-147 D 4
Prževal'skogo, gory ▲ RUS 122-123 E 7
Przeworsk ○• PL 102-103 C 2
Psará ⌒ GR 100-101 K 5
Psári ○ GR 100-101 J 6
Psebaj ○ RUS 126-127 D 5
Psël ∼ RUS 102-103 K 2
Pskem ∼ US 136-137 M 4
Pskent ○ US 136-137 L 4
Pskov ☆∴ RUS 94-95 L 3
Pskovskij ○ KA 126-127 O 2
Pskovskoe ozero ⊂ RUS 94-95 K 2
Pskovskoye Ozero = Pskovskoe ozero ⊂ RUS 94-95 K 2
Ps'ol ∼ UA 102-103 H 3
Ptarmigan Fiord ≈ 36-37 Q 2
Ptarmigan Lake ⊂ CDN 30-31 Q 4
Ptarmigan Mountain ▲ CDN 20-21 W 5
Pt. Calimere ▲ IND 140-141 H 5
Pteri ▲ GR 100-101 H 5
Ptičij, ostrov ⌒ RUS 120-121 R 5
Ptolemaïda ○ GR 100-101 H 4
Ptuj ○ SLO 100-101 E 1
Puako ○ USA (HI) 288 K 5
Puán ○ RA 78-79 H 4
Pu'an ○ VRC 156-157 D 4
Puas ○ PNG 183 F 2
Pubei ○ VRC 156-157 F 5
Public Landing ○ USA (MD) 280-281 L 5
Pubnico ○ CDN (NS) 240-241 K 7
Pucallpa ☆ PE 64-65 E 6
Pucara ○ PE (CAJ) 64-65 C 5
Pucara ○ PE (PUN) 70-71 B 4
Pucara, Río ∼ PE 70-71 B 4
Pucaurco ○ PE 64-65 E 3
Pucauro ○ PE 66-67 B 4
Puč'èveem ∼ RUS 112-113 Q 2
Pučež ○ RUS 94-95 S 3
Puchapucha ○ EAT 214-215 J 6
Pucheng ○ VRC (FUJ) 156-157 L 3
Pucheng ○ VRC (HUN) 156-157 H 4
Pucheng ○ VRC (SXI) 154-155 F 4
Puchini ○ BOL 70-71 D 5
Puch'ŏn ○ ROK 150-151 F 9
Pucioasa ○• RO 102-103 D 5
Pucio Point ▲ RP 160-161 D 7
Puckett ○ USA (MS) 268-269 L 4
Pucon ○ RCH 78-79 D 5
Pucté ○ MEX 52-53 K 2
Pucuro ○ PA 52-53 F 7
Pucuruí, Rio ∼ BR 68-69 C 4
Pudasjärvi ○ FIN 88-89 J 4
Pudimoe ○ ZA 220-221 G 3
Pudož ☆ RUS 88-89 O 6
Pudu Chattram ○ IND 140-141 G 5
Pudu He ∼ VRC 156-157 C 4
Pudukkottai ○• IND 140-141 H 5
Pudur ○ IND 140-141 G 5
Pue ○ RI 166-167 L 3
Puebla ■ MEX 52-53 E 2
Puebla ☆∴ MEX 52-53 E 2
Puebla de Alcocer ○ E 98-99 E 5
Puebla de Don Rodrigo ○ E 98-99 E 5
Puebla de Montalbán ○ E 98-99 E 5
Puebla de Sanabria ○ E 98-99 D 3
Puebla de Valverde, La ○ E 98-99 G 4
Pueblito, El • CO 60-61 D 2
Pueblo ○ USA (CO) 254-255 L 5
Pueblo Bello ○ CO 60-61 E 2
Pueblo del Carmen ○ ROU 78-79 L 2
Pueblo Hundido ○ RCH 78-79 D 2
Pueblo Ledesma ○ RA 76-77 E 2
Pueblo Mountain Park ○ USA (CO) 254-255 K 5
Pueblo Nueva Tiquisate ○ GCA 52-53 J 4
Pueblo Nuevo ○ CO 60-61 G 6
Pueblo Nuevo ○ YV (APU) 60-61 F 4
Pueblo Nuevo ○ YV (FAL) 60-61 E 2
Pueblo Nuevo Huesital ○ PA 52-53 D 7
Pueblo Pintado ○ USA (NM) 256-257 H 3
Puebloviejo ○ EC 64-65 C 2
Pueblo Viejo ○ HN 52-53 L 4
Pueblo Viejo, Laguna ○ MEX 50-51 L 6
Puelches ○ RA 78-79 G 5
Puelén ○ RA 78-79 F 4
Puéllaro ○ EC 64-65 C 1
Puelo, Río ∼ RCH 78-79 C 6
Puente, El ○ BOL (SAC) 70-71 F 5
Puente, El ○ BOL (TAR) 76-77 E 1
Puente Alto ○ RCH 78-79 D 2
Puente de Boyacá • CO 60-61 E 5
Puente de Ixtla ○ MEX 52-53 E 2
Puente del Inca ○• RA 78-79 E 2
Puente de Plate ○ RA 76-77 E 3
Puente-Genil ○ E 98-99 E 6
Puentes, Los ○ MEX 50-51 F 5
Pu'er ○ VRC 156-157 B 5
Puerca, Punta ▲ USA (PR) 286-287 Q 2
Puerco, Rio ∼ USA (NM) 256-257 H 3
Puerco River ∼ USA (AZ) 256-257 F 3
Puerta, La ○ RA 76-77 F 6
Puerta Tastil ○ RA 76-77 E 3
Puertecitos ○ MEX 50-51 B 2
Puerto Acosta ○ BOL 70-71 C 4
Puerto Adolfo López Mateos ○ MEX 50-51 C 5
Puerto Aisén ○ RCH 80 D 2
Puerto Alegre ○ RA 76-77 E 3
Puerto Alegria ○ CO 64-65 E 3
Puerto Angel ○• MEX 52-53 F 4
Puerto Argentina ○ CO 64-65 E 1
Puerto Arica ○ PE 64-65 E 2
Puerto Arista ○• MEX 52-53 H 4
Puerto Armuelles ○• PA 52-53 C 7
Puerto Arquia ○ CO 60-61 C 4
Puerto Arturo ○ PE 64-65 E 2
Puerto Arturo ○ RCH 80 E 7
Puerto Asis ○ CO 64-65 D 1
Puerto Ayacucho ☆ YV 60-61 H 5
Puerto Ayora ○ EC 64-65 B 10
Puerto Bahía Negra ○ PY 70-71 H 7
Puerto Banegas ○ BOL 70-71 F 5
Puerto Baquerizo Moreno ☆ EC 64-65 C 10
Puerto Barrios ☆ GCA 52-53 K 4
Puerto Belén ○ EC 64-65 F 3
Puerto Bélgica ○ CO 60-61 D 7
Puerto Bermúdez ○ PE 64-65 E 7
Puerto Berrío ○ CO 60-61 D 4

Puerto Bolívar o EC 64-65 C 3
Puerto Boy o CO 64-65 E 1
Puerto Boyacá o CO 60-61 D 5
Puerto Busch o BOL 70-71 J 7
Puerto Cabezas o NIC 52-53 C 4
Puerto Caituma o GUY 62-63 E 2
Puerto Calvimontes o BOL 70-71 E 4
Puerto Canoa o BOL 70-71 D 4
Puerto Carabuco o BOL 70-71 C 4
Puerto Carare o CO 60-61 D 4
Puerto Cardenas o PE 64-65 E 2
Puerto Cárdenas o RCH 78-79 C 7
Puerto Carreño ☆ CO 60-61 H 4
Puerto Castilla o HN 54-55 C 6
Puerto Chacabuco o RCH 80 D 2
Puerto Chama o YV 60-61 F 3
Puerto Chicama o PE 64-65 C 5
Puerto Chicxulub o MEX 52-53 K 1
Puerto Cisnes o RCH 80 D 2
Puerto Claver o CO 60-61 D 4
Puerto Coig o RA 80 F 5
Puerto Colombia o CO 64-65 E 2
Puerto Colón o PY 76-77 J 2
Puerto Constanza o RA 78-79 K 2
Puerto Cortés o HN 52-53 L 4
Puerto Cumarebo o YV 60-61 G 2
Puerto Cunambo o PE 64-65 D 3
Puerto de Aseses o NIC 52-53 B 6
Puerto de Cayo o EC 64-65 B 2
Puerto de la Cruz o E 188-189 C 6
Puerto de la Estaca o E 188-189 C 7
Puerto de los Angeles, Parque Nacional del ⊥ MEX 50-51 G 6
Puerto del Rosario o E 188-189 E 6
Puerto de Luna o USA (NM) 256-257 L 4
Puerto de San José o GCA 52-53 J 5
Puerto Deseado o RA 80 H 3
Puerto Eden o RCH 80 C 4
Puerto Ele o CO 60-61 F 4
Puerto Escondido o MEX (BCS) 50-51 D 5
Puerto Escondido o • MEX (OAX) 52-53 F 4
Puerto Flores o EC 64-65 B 10
Puerto Francisco de Orellana o EC 64-65 D 2
Puerto Fuy o RCH 78-79 D 5
Puerto Gaitan o CO 60-61 E 5
Puerto Galilea o PE 64-65 D 3
Puerto Grande ▲ E 98-99 E 5
Puerto Grande o EC 64-65 B 3
Puerto Gutierrez o CO 60-61 D 5
Puerto Heath o BOL 70-71 C 3
Puerto Humbria o CO 64-65 D 1
Puerto Inca o PE 64-65 E 6
Puerto Ingeniero Ibáñez o RCH 80 E 3
Puerto Inírida ☆ CO 60-61 H 6
Puerto Itambey o PY 76-77 K 3
Puerto Izozog o BOL 70-71 F 6
Puerto Japones o BOL 70-71 C 5
Puerto Juárez o • MEX 52-53 L 1
Puerto La Cruz o YV 60-61 J 2
Puerto la Esperanza o PY 76-77 J 2
Puerto la Victoria o PY 76-77 J 2
Puerto Leguía o PE 70-71 B 3
Puerto Leguízamo o CO 64-65 E 2
Puerto Leitón o BOL 70-71 G 3
Puerto Lempira ☆ HN 54-55 D 7
Puerto Libertad o MEX 50-51 C 3
Puerto Libertador o CO 60-61 D 4
Puerto Limón o CO 64-65 D 1
Puerto Limón ☆ •• CR 52-53 C 7
Puertollano o E 98-99 E 5
Puerto Llifén o RCH 78-79 C 6
Puerto Lobos o RA 78-79 G 7
Puerto Lodo o CO 60-61 F 1
Puerto Lopez o CO 60-61 F 2
Puerto López o EC 64-65 B 2
Puerto Lumbreras o E 98-99 G 6
Puerto Madero o MEX (CHI) 52-53 H 4
Puerto Madero o MEX (QR) 52-53 L 2
Puerto Madryn o RA 78-79 G 7
Puerto Magdalena o MEX 50-51 C 5
Puerto Maldonado ☆ PE 70-71 C 3
Puerto María o PY 76-77 J 1
Puerto Masachapa o NIC 52-53 L 6
Puerto Montt ☆ RCH 78-79 C 6
Puerto Morazán o NIC 52-53 L 5
Puerto Napo o EC 64-65 D 2
Puerto Nare o CO 60-61 D 4
Puerto Natales o RCH 80 D 5
Puerto Navarino o RCH 80 F 7
Puerto Ninfas o RA 78-79 G 7
Puerto Nuevo o CO 60-61 G 5
Puerto Obaldía o PA 52-53 F 7
Puerto Octay o RCH 78-79 C 6
Puerto Olaya o CO 60-61 D 4
Puerto Ospina o CO 64-65 E 1
Puerto Padre o C 54-55 G 4
Puerto Palomas o MEX 52-53 G 3
Puerto Paranay o RA 76-77 K 4
Puerto Pardo o PE 64-65 D 3
Puerto Patiño o BOL 70-71 E 5
Puerto Peñasco o MEX 50-51 C 2
Puerto Piedras o RCH 78-79 C 7
Puerto Piña o PA 52-53 E 8
Puerto Pinasco o PY 76-77 J 2
Puerto Pipa o PE 66-67 B 4
Puerto Pirámides o RA 78-79 G 7
Puerto Pizarro o CO (CA) 64-65 F 2
Puerto Pizarro o CO (CHO) 60-61 C 5
Puerto Plata ☆ • DOM 54-55 K 5
Puerto Porfía o CO 60-61 E 5
Puerto Portillo o PE 64-65 F 6
Puerto Prado o PE 64-65 E 7
Puerto Princesa ☆ RP 160-161 C 8
Puerto Proano o EC 64-65 D 3
Puerto Pupuña o EC 66-67 B 4
Puerto Puyuguapi o RCH 80 D 2
Puerto Quijarro o BOL 70-71 J 5
Puerto Quimba o PA 52-53 E 7
Puerto Ramírez o RCH 78-79 C 7
Puerto Raúl Marín Balmaceda o RCH 78-79 C 7
Puerto Rico o BOL 70-71 D 2
Puerto Rico o PE 64-65 E 7
Puerto Rico ◘ USA (PR) 286-287 P 2
Puerto Rico ⌒ USA 56 B 2
Puerto Rico Trench ≃ 4 H 6
Puerto Rondón o CO 60-61 F 4
Puerto San Antonio o RA 78-79 G 6
Puerto San Carlos o PE 70-71 B 3
Puerto Sandino o NIC 52-53 L 5
Puerto San Julián o RA 80 G 4
Puerto San Martín o PE 64-65 D 8
Puerto Santa Cruz o RA 80 F 5
Puerto Saucedo o BOL 70-71 F 3
Puerto Siles o BOL 70-71 E 3
Puerto Silvania o CO 66-67 B 2
Puerto Suarez o BOL 70-71 J 6
Puerto Tacurú Pytá o PY 76-77 J 2
Puerto Tamborapa o PE 64-65 C 4
Puerto Tejada o CO 60-61 C 6
Puerto Tumaco = Sabaloyaco o EC 64-65 F 3
Puerto Turumbán o GUY 62-63 D 2
Puerto Valencia o CO 60-61 G 6
Puerto Vallarta o • MEX 52-53 B 1
Puerto Varas o RCH 78-79 C 6
Puerto Victoria o PE 64-65 E 6
Puerto Viejo o CR (Car) 52-53 C 7
Puerto Viejo o CR (HER) 52-53 B 6
Puerto Villamil o EC 64-65 B 10
Puerto Visser o RA 80 G 2
Puerto Weber o RCH 80 D 5
Puerto Williams o RCH 80 G 7
Puerto Yahape o RA 76-77 J 4
Puerto Yungay o RCH 80 D 3
Puesto Avanzado o PE 64-65 D 3
Puesto Esperanza o PY 76-77 H 2
Pueyrredón, Lago o RA 80 E 3
Pugačev ☆ RUS 96-97 F 7
Pugačevo o RUS 122-123 K 4
Pugačev muzej uji • KA 96-97 G 8
Puge o VRC 156-157 C 3
Puger o RI 168 E 4
Puget Sound ≈ 40-41 C 2
Puget Sound ≈ USA 244-245 C 3
Pugima o RI 166-167 K 4
Puglia ◘ I 100-101 E 4
Pugwash o CDN (NS) 240-241 M 5
Puhal-e Ḫamīr, Kūh-e ▲ IR 134-135 F 5
Puhos o FIN 88-89 K 5
Puiatoq ≈ 28-29 T 6
Puig o SUD 206-207 J 4
Puig Major ▲ E 98-99 J 5
Puinahua, Canal de < PE 64-65 E 4
Puir o RUS 122-123 J 2
Puissortoq Gletscher ⊂ GRØ 28-29 T 5
Pujehun o WAL 202-203 E 6
Pujiang o VRC (SIC) 154-155 C 6
Pujiang o VRC (ZHE) 156-157 L 2
Pujonryong Sanmaek ▲ DVR 150-151 F 7
Pukaki, Lake o NZ 182 C 5
Pukalani o USA (HI) 288 J 4
Puk'ansan National Park ⊥ • DVR 150-151 F 9
Pukaskwa National Park ⊥ • CDN (ONT) 236-237 B 4
Pukatawagan o CDN 34-35 F 3
Pukchong o DVR 150-151 G 7
Pukë ☆ • AL 100-101 G 3
Pukekohe o NZ 182 E 2
Pukota o Z 218-219 E 1
Pukšen'ga ~ RUS 88-89 Q 5
Puksubaek San ▲ DVR 150-151 F 7
Pukuanratu o RI 162-163 F 7
Pukuatu, Tanjung ▲ RI 166-167 B 7
Pula o HR 100-101 D 2
Pula o I 100-101 B 5
Pula, Goi- o ZRE 214-215 D 4
Pulai o RI 164-165 F 3
Pulaksama o RI 162-163 B 3
Pulanduta Point ▲ RP 160-161 E 7
Pulangi ~ RP 160-161 F 9
Pulangpisau o RI 164-165 D 5
Pular, Cerro ▲ RCH 76-77 C 3
Pularumpi ⚓ AUS 172-173 K 1
Pulasi, Pulau ⌒ RI 168 E 6
Pulaski o USA (NY) 278-279 E 5
Pulaski o USA (TN) 276-277 H 5
Pulaski o USA (VA) 280-281 F 6
Pulaski National Monument, Fort • USA (GA) 284-285 K 4
Pulau o RI (BEN) 162-163 D 6
Pulau ~ RI 166-167 K 4
Pulau Banding o MAL 162-163 D 2
Pulauberingin o RI 162-163 E 7
Pulau Penang ◘ MAL 162-163 D 2
Pulausekopong, Tanjung ▲ RI 162-163 F 7
Pulau Tiga Park ⊥ MAL 160-161 A 10
Pulau Tioman ⌒ •• MAL 162-163 F 3
Puławy o • PL 92-93 Q 3
Puleowine o SME 62-63 G 4
Pulguk Sa • ROK 150-151 G 10
Pulicat o IND 140-141 J 4
Pulicat Lake ○ IND 140-141 J 4
Pulie River ~ PNG 183 E 3
Pulingom o IND 140-141 F 4
Pulisan, Tanjung ▲ RI 164-165 J 3
Pulivendla o IND 140-141 H 3
Puliyangudi o IND 140-141 G 6
Pulkkila o FIN 88-89 H 4
Pullman o USA (WA) 244-245 H 4
Pullo o PE 64-65 F 9
Pulmoddai o CL 140-141 J 6
Pulo Buda ⌒ MYA 158-159 E 5
Pulog, Mount ▲ RP 160-161 D 4
Pulozero o RUS 88-89 M 2
Pulpit Harbor o USA (ME) 278-279 N 4
Pulp River o CDN (MAN) 234-235 C 3
Pulpul o PNG 183 F 3
Pułtusk o • PL 92-93 Q 2
Pulu o VRC 144-145 C 2
Pülümür ☆ TR 128-129 H 3
Pulupanda o RI 164-165 H 5
Puluqui, Isla ⌒ RCH 78-79 C 6
Pulwama o IND 138-139 E 3
Puma o EAT 212-213 E 6
Puma Yumco ○ VRC 144-145 H 6
Pumpville o USA (TX) 266-267 F 4
Puna o EC 64-65 C 3
Puna, Isla ⌒ EC 64-65 B 3
Punakaiki o NZ 182 C 5
Punakha o BHT 142-143 F 2
Punalūr o IND 140-141 G 6
Punang o MAL 164-165 D 1
Punarupka o PNG 183 F 3
Punása o IND 138-139 F 8
Punata o BOL 70-71 E 5
Puncak Jaya ▲ RI 166-167 J 4
Puncak Mandala ▲ RI 166-167 L 4
Puncak Trikora ▲ RI 166-167 K 4
Puncak Yamin ▲ RI 166-167 K 4
Punch o IND 138-139 E 3
Punchaw o CDN (BC) 228-229 L 3
Punda Hamlets o PNG 183 A 2
Punda Maria o ZA 218-219 F 6
Pundanhar o MOC 214-215 L 6
Pune o • IND 138-139 D 10
Punei, Tanjung ▲ RI 162-163 F 6
Pungai, Kampung o MAL 162-163 F 4
Pungali ~ RUS 112-113 H 4
Pungalina o AUS 174-175 D 5
Punganuru o IND 140-141 H 4
Punggaluku o RI 164-165 H 6
Pungo Andongo o ANG 216-217 C 4
Púngoè, Rio ~ MOC 218-219 G 4
Púngoè, Rio ~ MOC 218-219 G 4
Pungo National Wildlife Refuge ⊥ USA (NC) 282-283 L 5
Pungo River ~ USA (NC) 282-283 L 5
Pungwe Falls ~ • ZW 218-219 G 4
Punia o ZRE 210-211 L 4
Punilla, La o RCH 78-79 D 4
Punilla, Sierra de la ▲ RA 76-77 C 5
Puning o VRC 156-157 K 5
Punja o RUS 116-117 J 6
Punjab ◘ IND 138-139 E 4
Punjab ◘ PK 138-139 C 4
Punkaharju o FIN 88-89 K 6
Punkalaidun o FIN 88-89 G 6
Punkasalmi = Punkaharju o FIN 88-89 K 6
Punkin Center o USA (CO) 254-255 M 5
Puno ☆ • PE 70-71 B 4
Punos o PE 64-65 D 6
Punrun, Lago ○ PE 64-65 D 7
Punta Alegre o C 54-55 F 3
Punta Allen o MEX 52-53 L 2
Punta Alta o RA 78-79 H 5
Punta Arenas ☆ RCH 80 E 6
Punta Arenas, Caleta ≈ 76-77 B 1
Punta Cana o DOM 54-55 L 5
Punta Cardón o YV 60-61 F 2
Punta Chame o PA 52-53 E 7
Punta Corral o RA 76-77 F 5
Punta de Balosto o RA 76-77 D 4
Punta de Bombon o PE 70-71 B 5
Punta de Díaz o RCH 76-77 B 5
Punta del Agua o RA 78-79 E 3
Punta del Este o C 54-55 D 4
Punta Delgada o RCH 80 F 6
Punta Delgado o RA 78-79 H 7
Punta de los Llanos o RA 76-77 D 6
Punta del Viento o RCH 76-77 B 5
Punta Eugenia o MEX 50-51 B 4
Punta Gorda o BH 52-53 K 3
Punta Gorda o USA (FL) 286-287 G 5
Punta Gorda, Playa ⌒ • DOM 54-55 L 5
Punta Mala ▲ PA 52-53 D 8
Punta Negra, Salar ○ RCH 76-77 C 3
Punta Norte o RA 78-79 H 7
Punta Nueva o YV 60-61 K 4
Punta Piaroa o YV 60-61 H 5
Puntarenas ☆ • CR 52-53 B 7
Puntawolana, Lake ○ AUS 178-179 E 5
Punto Alegre o BR 62-63 J 6
Punto Catatumbo o YV 60-61 E 3
Punto da Barca o BR 62-63 K 6
Punto Fijo o YV 60-61 F 2
Punto M.O.P. o YV 60-61 K 6
Punxsutawney o USA (PA) 280-281 H 3
Puolanka o FIN 88-89 J 4
Puponga o NZ 182 D 4
Pupri o IND 142-143 D 2
Pupuan o RI 168 B 7
Pupunhas, Ilha ⌒ BR 66-67 F 6
Pupū Pu'e National Parc ⊥ WS 184 V b 1
Pupyr, mys ▲ RUS 112-113 M 5
Puqi o VRC 156-157 H 2
Puquina o PE 70-71 B 5
Puquio o PE 64-65 E 9
Pur ~ RUS 108-109 S 8
Pur ~ RUS 114-115 O 2
Pura ~ RUS 108-109 X 6
Pura, Cachoeira da ~ BR 66-67 H 6
Puracé, Parque Nacional ⊥ CO 60-61 C 6
Puracé, Volcán ▲ CO 60-61 C 6
Purándiro o MEX 52-53 D 1
Purangarh o IND 140-141 E 2
Puranpur o IND 144-145 C 6
Puraquê Ponta o BR 66-67 C 2
Purari River ~ PNG 183 C 4
Purbalingga o RI 168 C 3
Purcell o USA (OK) 264-265 G 3
Purcell Mountains ▲ CDN (BC) 230-231 M 2
Purcell Wilderness Conservancy ⊥ • CDN (BC) 230-231 N 3
Purchase Bay ≈ 24-25 N 3
Purchena o E 98-99 F 6
Purdum o USA (NE) 262-263 F 2
Purdy Islands ⌒ PNG 183 D 2
Pure, Rio ~ EC 66-67 C 4
Pureba Conservation Reserve ⊥ AUS 180-181 C 2
Pureh o RUS 94-95 S 3
Purepero o MEX 52-53 C 2
Puretê ou Purata, Rio ~ BR 66-67 C 4
Purgatoire River ~ USA (CO) 254-255 M 6
Purgatorio o YV 62-63 D 2
Puri o ANG 216-217 C 3
Puri o •• IND 142-143 D 6
Puricaure o YV 60-61 F 2
Purificacion o CO 60-61 D 6
Purificación o MEX 52-53 B 2
Purificacion, Río ~ MEX 52-53 B 2
Puring o RI 168 C 3
Purinskoe vtoroe, ozero ○ RUS 108-109 X 6
Purísima, La o MEX 50-51 C 4
Purma o EC 64-65 F 3
Purmamarca o RA 76-77 E 2
Pūrna o IND (MAH) 138-139 F 10
Pūrna ~ IND 138-139 F 9
Pūrna ~ IND 138-139 E 9
Purnač ~ RUS 88-89 P 3
Pūrnia o IND 142-143 E 3
Purnong o AUS 180-181 E 3
Purpe o RUS 114-115 O 2
Purpe ~ RUS 114-115 N 2
Purple Springs o CDN (ALB) 232-233 G 6
Purranque o RCH 78-79 C 6
Purros o NAM 216-217 B 9
Puruarán o MEX 52-53 D 2
Puruí, Rio ~ BR 66-67 C 3
Purukcahu o RI 164-165 D 4
Puruliya o IND 142-143 E 4
Purureche o YV 60-61 F 2
Purus, Rio ~ BR 66-67 E 5
Purutu Island ⌒ PNG 183 B 5
Purvachal ⌒ IND 142-143 H 4
Pūrvāchal ⌒ IND 142-143 H 4
Purvis o USA (MS) 268-269 L 5
Purwakarta o RI 168 B 3
Purwo, Tanjung ▲ RI 168 B 7
Purwodadi o RI 168 D 3
Purwodadi o RI 168 C 3
Purwokerto o RI 168 C 3
Purworejo o RI 168 D 3
Puryong o DVR 150-151 G 6
Purzell Mount ▲ USA 20-21 M 3
Pusa o MAL 162-163 J 4
Pusad o IND 138-139 F 10
Pusan o ROK 150-151 G 10
Pusat Gajo, Pegunungan ▲ RI 162-163 B 2
Pusegaon o IND 140-141 F 2
Pusesāvli o IND 140-141 F 2
Pushkar o IND 138-139 E 6
Pusisama o SOL 184 I c 2
Puškarëva, ostrov ⌒ RUS 112-113 L 1
Puškin o •• RUS 94-95 M 2
Puškino o RUS 96-97 E 8
Puškino = Biljasuvar o AZ 128-129 N 3
Puskwaskau River ~ CDN 32-33 M 4
Puš́lahta o RUS 88-89 O 4
Pušma ☆ RUS 114-115 G 6
Pušnoj o RUS 88-89 N 4
Pusok Sa • ROK 150-151 G 9
Püspökladány o H 92-93 Q 5
Pustaja ~ RUS 120-121 U 3
Pusticamicca, Lac ○ CDN (QUE) 236-237 M 3
Pustoška ☆ RUS 94-95 L 3
Pustunich o MEX (CAM) 52-53 J 2
Pustunich ∴ • MEX (CAM) 52-53 J 2
Pusuga o GH 202-203 K 5
Putahow Lake ○ CDN 30-31 T 6
Putahow River ~ CDN 30-31 T 5
Putai o RC 156-157 M 5
Putao o MYA 142-143 K 2
Puteran, Pulau ⌒ RI 168 B 6
Puthein (Bassein) o MYA 158-159 C 2
Puthukkudiyiruppu o CL 140-141 J 6
Putia o RI 166-167 D 3
Putian o VRC 156-157 L 4
Putina o PE 70-71 C 4
Putina, Río ~ PE 70-71 C 4
Putineiu o RO 102-103 D 6
Puting, Tanjung ▲ RI 162-163 J 6
Putnam o USA (CT) 278-279 K 7
Putnam o USA (OK) 264-265 F 3
Putnam o USA (TX) 264-265 E 6
Putončany o RUS 116-117 F 3
Putorana, plato ▲ RUS 108-109 Z 7
Putoranskij zapovednik ⊥ RUS 108-109 a 7
Putre o RCH 70-71 C 6
Putsonderwater o ZA 220-221 E 4
Puttalam o CL 140-141 H 6
Puttalam Lagoon ≈ 140-141 H 6
Puttgarden o D 92-93 L 1
Puttur o IND (ANP) 140-141 H 4
Puttur o IND (KAR) 140-141 F 4
Putty o AUS 180-181 L 2
Putumayo, Río ~ PE 66-67 B 4
Putuoshan • VRC 154-155 N 6
Putus, Tanjung ▲ RI 162-163 H 5
Putyvl' o UA 102-103 H 2
Puuanahulu o USA (HI) 288 K 5
Puuhonua o Honaunau National Historical Park ⊥ • USA (HI) 288 K 5
Puukohola Heiau National Historical Park ⊥ • USA (HI) 288 K 5
Puula ○ FIN 88-89 J 6
Puumala o FIN 88-89 K 6
Puu Ulaula ▲ USA (HI) 288 J 4
Puuwai o USA (HI) 288 E 3
Pu Xian o VRC 154-155 G 3
Puxico o USA (MO) 276-277 E 4
Puyallup o USA (WA) 244-245 C 3
Puyang o VRC 154-155 J 4
Puyca o PE 64-65 F 9
Puyehue, Lago ○ RCH 78-79 C 6
Puyehue, Parque Nacional ⊥ RCH 78-79 C 6
Puyehue, Volcán ▲ RCH 78-79 C 6
Puy-en-Velay, le ☆ •• F 90-91 J 9
Puymorens, Col de ▲ F 90-91 H 10
Puyo ☆ EC 64-65 D 2
Puyuguapi, Canal ≈ 80 D 2
Pūzak, Hāmūn-e ○ AFG 134-135 J 3
Puzino o RUS 122-123 D 5
Pwalugu o GH 202-203 K 4
Pwani ◘ EAT 214-215 K 4
Pweto o ZRE 214-215 E 5
Pwllheli o GB 90-91 E 5
PWV = Pretoria Witwatersrand Vereeniging ◘ ZA 220-221 H 2
Pyachnung o MYA 142-143 H 5
Pyanangazu o MYA 142-143 K 5
Pyawbwe o MYA 142-143 K 5
Pyechin o MYA 142-143 H 5
Pye Islands ⌒ USA 20-21 V 3
Pyhäjärvi o FIN 88-89 H 5
Pyhäjoki o FIN 88-89 H 4
Pyhäjoki ~ FIN 88-89 H 4
Pyhäntä o FIN 88-89 J 4
Pyhäselkä ○ FIN 88-89 K 5
Pyhätunturi ▲ FIN 88-89 J 3
Pyingaing o MYA 142-143 J 4
Pyinmana o MYA 142-143 K 6
Pyjakojajaha ~ RUS 108-109 N 6
Pylema o RUS 88-89 S 4
Pylginskij hrebet ▲ RUS 112-113 O 7
Pylgovajam ~ RUS 112-113 O 6
Pymatuning Reservoir ○ USA (PA) 280-281 F 2
Pymatuning State Park ⊥ USA (PA) 280-281 F 2
Pyngan o US 136-137 M 4
Pyonggang o DVR 150-151 F 8
Pyongsan o DVR 150-151 F 8
Pyongsong o DVR 150-151 E 8
Pyŏngt'aek o ROK 150-151 F 9
Pyongyang ★ DVR 150-151 E 8
Pyote o USA (TX) 266-267 D 2
Pyramid o RI 166-167 K 3
Pyramiden o N 84-85 K 3
Pyramid Hill o AUS 180-181 H 4
Pyramid Lake ○ AUS 176-177 F 6
Pyramid Lake ○ USA (NV) 246-247 F 3
Pyramid Lake Indian Reservation ⚓ USA (NV) 246-247 F 3
Pyramids Mountains ▲ USA (NM) 256-257 G 6
Pyrénées, Parc National des ⊥ • F 90-91 G 10
Pyrenees = Pyrénées ▲ F 90-91 G 10
Pyre Peak ▲ USA 22-23 K 6
Pyrjatyn o UA 102-103 H 2
Pyrkanaj ▲ RUS 112-113 N 2
Pyrzyce o • PL 92-93 N 2
Pyščug o RUS 96-97 D 4
Pyšma ~ RUS 96-97 M 5
Pyšma ~ RUS 114-115 J 6
Pyssa ~ RUS 88-89 U 4
Pytalovo = Abrene ☆ RUS 94-95 K 3
Pythonga, Lac ○ CDN (QUE) 238-239 J 2
Pyt'-Jah = Pjat'-Jah o RUS 114-115 M 4
Pyttegga ▲ N 86-87 C 5
Pyu o MYA 142-143 K 6
Pyuthan o NEP 144-145 D 6
Pyžina ~ RUS 114-115 R 5

Q

Qa'āmiyāt, al- ⌒ KSA 132-133 E 5
Qaanaaq = Thule ☆ GRØ 26-27 Q 5
Qaarsut o GRØ 28-29 O 1
Qab o VRC 154-155 E 2
Qabane o LS 220-221 J 4
Qabr Hūd o Y 132-133 F 5
Qacha's Nek o LS 220-221 J 5
Qadam o SUD 200-201 D 6
Qadamgāh o IR 136-137 F 6
Qaḍarif, al- o SUD 200-201 G 5
Qādes o AFG 134-135 K 1
Qadir Purrān o PK 138-139 C 4
Qādisīya, al- ◘ IRQ 128-129 L 7
Qādisīya, al- ∴ • IRQ 128-129 K 5
Qafa o OM 132-133 H 5
Qaffāy, al- ⌒ UAE 134-135 D 6
Qagan Nur ○ VRC (NMZ) 154-155 F 2
Qagan Nur ○ VRC (JIL) 150-151 E 5
Qagan Nur ○ VRC (NMZ) 148-149 M 6
Qagcaka o VRC 144-145 C 4
Qagdlumiut o GRØ 28-29 S 6
Qahar Youyi Houqi o VRC 148-149 L 7
Qahar Youyi Zhongqi o VRC 148-149 L 7
Qahāvand o IR 134-135 C 1
Qahb, Ǧabal al- ▲ KSA 130-131 J 5
Qāhira, al- ★ ••• ET 194-195 E 2
Qahmah, al- o KSA 132-133 B 4
Qā'id, Abū al- o KSA 132-133 C 5
Qaidam He ~ VRC 144-145 L 2
Qaidam Pendi ⌒ VRC 146-147 L 6
Qāimšahr o IR 136-137 C 6
Qaisār o AFG 136-137 J 7
Qaiwain, Umm al- o UAE 134-135 F 6
Qā'iya, al- o KSA 130-131 H 5
Qala'an-Nahl o SUD 200-201 G 6
Qalamat Nadqān o KSA 132-133 G 2
Qalana o Y 132-133 G 6
Qalansiya o Y 132-133 H 7
Qalāt o AFG 134-135 M 2
Qalat al-Hafirah • KSA 130-131 F 5
Qal'at al-Ḥiṣn ☆ SYR 128-129 G 5
Qal'at al-Mu'azzam o KSA 130-131 E 4
Qal'at ar-Rabaḍ ∴ • JOR 130-131 D 1
Qalat az Zubaidiyah • KSA 130-131 F 5
Qal'at Ǧābir • SYR 128-129 H 5
Qal'at Hamidi o IRQ 128-129 L 6
Qal'at Ṣalāḥaddīn ∴ •• SYR 128-129 G 5
Qal'at Ṣāliḥ ☆ IRQ 128-129 M 7
Qal'at Sam'ān •• SYR 128-129 G 4
Qal'at Sukkar ☆ IRQ 128-129 M 7
Qal'a-ye Nau ☆ AFG 136-137 H 7
Qal'e Dize ☆ IRQ 128-129 L 4
Qal'e Ra'isi o IR 134-135 D 3
Qal'e-ye Kāh o AFG 134-135 J 2
Qal'e-ye Mīr Dāvūd o AFG 134-135 K 1
Qal'e-ye Panğe o AFG 136-137 N 6
Qalhāt o OM 132-133 L 2
Qaliba, al- o KSA 130-131 E 3
Qalluviartuuq, Lac ○ CDN 36-37 M 5
Qalti al-Adusa < SUD 200-201 C 4
Qalti al-Khudairā < SUD 200-201 C 4
Qalti Immaseri < SUD 200-201 B 5
Qalyūb o ET 194-195 E 2
Qambar o PK 134-135 M 5
Qamdo o VRC 144-145 L 5
Qamea ⌒ FJI 184 III c 2
Qaminis o •• LAR 192-193 J 2
Qāmišli, al- ☆ SYR 128-129 J 4
Qamşar o IR 134-135 D 2
Qanā o KSA 130-131 G 4
Qandahār ◘ AFG 134-135 L 3
Qandahār ☆ •• AFG 134-135 L 3
Qandala o SP 208-209 J 3
Qaqortoq = Julianehab o GRØ 28-29 R 6
Qāra o ET 192-193 L 3
Qāra o KSA 130-131 G 3
Qarā', Ǧabal al- ▲ OM 132-133 H 5
Qara Āǧaǧ, Rūdḫāne-ye ~ IR 134-135 E 4
Qarabāġ o AFG (ĠA) 138-139 B 3
Qarabāġ o AFG (HE) 134-135 J 1
Qarabāġ o AFG (KB) 138-139 B 2
Qara Čāy ~ IR 128-129 N 5
Qara Dāġ ▲ IR 128-129 M 3
Qara Dāġ ▲ IRQ 128-129 L 5
Qara Ertis ~ KA 124-125 O 5
Qaraghandy = Karaǧandy ☆ KA 124-125 H 4
Qaraghandy = Karaghandy o KA 124-125 H 4
Qarah Dāġ ▲ IRQ 128-129 K 4
Qarajaqs Isfjord ≈ 28-29 P 1
Qaramqol o AFG 136-137 J 6
Qarānqū, Rūd-e ~ IR 128-129 M 4
Qara Qash ~ IND 138-139 G 2
Qara Sū ~ IR 134-135 B 1
Qar'āt ad Dibah, Bi'r < LAR 190-191 G 6
Qardho o SP 208-209 J 4
Qardlilt Ikerat ≈ 28-29 V 4
Qare Āġāǧ o IR 128-129 M 4
Qare Sū ~ IR 136-137 E 6
Qare Ziyā'od-Din o IR 128-129 L 3
Qarhan o VRC 144-145 K 2
Qārloq o IR 136-137 E 6
Qarqāi o AFG 138-139 C 2
Qarqan He ~ VRC 146-147 H 6
Qarqaraut, Wādī ~ Y 132-133 G 6
Qārūn, Birkat ○ ET 194-195 E 3
Qaryah ash Sharqiyah, Al o LAR 192-193 E 2
Qaryās, Bi'r < LAR 192-193 G 3
Qaryat Abū Nujaym o LAR 192-193 F 2
Qaryat Abū Qurays o LAR 192-193 F 2
Qaryatain, al- o SYR 128-129 G 5
Qaryat al Fā'idiyah o LAR 192-193 J 1
Qaryat al-'Ulyā o KSA 130-131 K 4
Qaryat az Zuwaytīnah o LAR 192-193 J 2
Qaryat Shumaykh o LAR 192-193 E 2
Qarzah, Wādī ~ LAR 192-193 E 2
Qaṣab, Wādī l- ~ IRQ 128-129 K 5
Qaṣabe ▲ IR 128-129 M 3
Qasi bu Hadi o LAR 192-193 G 2
Qasigiannguit = Christianshåb o GRØ 28-29 P 2
Qasir, Sabhat al- ○ SYR 128-129 J 5
Qaṣr, Umm o IRQ 130-131 K 2
Qaṣr al-Farāfira o ET 194-195 C 4
Qaṣr al-Hair • SYR 128-129 H 5
Qaṣr al-Hair al-Ġarbi ∴ • SYR 128-129 G 5
Qaṣr al-Harāna ∴ • JOR 130-131 E 2
Qaṣr al Jady o LAR 192-193 L 2
Qaṣr al Kharrūbah o LAR 192-193 J 1
Qaṣr al-Mušattā ∴ • JOR 130-131 E 2
Qaṣr al Qarn o LAR 192-193 L 2
Qaṣr 'Amīq o IRQ 128-129 J 6
Qaṣr ash Shaqqah o LAR 192-193 L 2
Qaṣr aṭ-Ṭūbā ∴ • JOR 130-131 E 2
Qaṣr-e Qand o IR 134-135 J 5
Qaṣr-e Širīn o • IR 134-135 A 1
Qasr Ibn Rashid Palace • KSA 130-131 G 4
Qaṣrīk o IR 128-129 L 3
Qaṣr Khulayf o LAR 192-193 E 4
Qaṣr Larocu o LAR 192-193 E 4
Qaṣr Šaqra ∴ • IRQ 130-131 K 2
Qassiarsuk o GRØ 28-29 S 6
Qassim, al- ◘ KSA 130-131 H 5
Qa'taba o Y 132-133 D 7
Qaṭanā o SYR 128-129 G 6
Qatar = Qatar ■ Q 134-135 D 6
Qaṭīf, al- o KSA 134-135 D 5
Qatlīš o IR 136-137 E 6
Qaṭn, al- o KSA 130-131 K 6
Qaṭn, al- o Y 132-133 F 6
Qaṭrāna, al- o JOR 130-131 E 2
Qaṭrānī, Ǧabal ▲ ET 194-195 E 3
Qaṭrūye o IR 134-135 F 4
Qaṭṭār, Ǧabal ▲ ET 194-195 F 4
Qattara Depression ⌒ ET 194-195 C 3
Qattara Depression = Qattāra, Munhafad al ⌒ ET 194-195 C 3
Qawām al-Hamza o IRQ 128-129 L 7
Qawz Ragab o SUD 200-201 G 4
Qāyen o • IR 134-135 H 2
Qaysan o SUD 208-209 B 3
Qayyāra o IRQ 128-129 K 5
Qazvin o • IR 128-129 N 4
Qeersorfik = Ikamiut o GRØ 28-29 P 2
Qelelevu ⌒ FJI 184 III c 2
Qeqertaq o GRØ (VGR) 28-29 P 1
Qeqertaq ⌒ GRØ (VGR) 26-27 X 8
Qeqertarssuaq ⌒ GRØ 28-29 O 2
Qeqertarssuaq ⌒ GRØ (VGR) 26-27 X 7
Qeqertarssuaq ⌒ GRØ (VGR) 26-27 Y 8
Qeqertarsuaq = Godhavn o GRØ 28-29 O 2
Qeqertarsuatsiaat = Fiskenæsset o GRØ 28-29 P 5
Qeqertat o GRØ 26-27 R 5
Qerri o SUD 200-201 F 4
Qešm o • IR 134-135 G 5
Qešm, Ǧazīre-ye ⌒ IR 134-135 G 5
Qezaltepeque o ES 52-53 K 5
Qezel o AFG 134-135 M 1
Qezel Ūzan, Rūd-e ~ IR 128-129 M 4
Qezel Ūzan Qoli, Čam-e ~ IR 128-129 M 5
Qian'an o VRC 150-151 E 5
Qianarteq ⌒ GRØ 28-29 W 4
Qiandaohu • VRC 156-157 L 2
Qianfoshan • VRC 154-155 K 3
Qianfo Yan • VRC 154-155 D 5
Qianheshangyuan o VRC 154-155 F 3
Qianjiang o VRC (HUB) 154-155 H 6
Qianjiang o VRC (SIC) 156-157 F 2
Qianjin o VRC 150-151 J 4
Qian Ling ∴ • VRC 154-155 F 4
Qianshan o • VRC (ANH) 154-155 K 6
Qianshan o VRC (GDG) 156-157 G 6
Qian Shan ▲ VRC 150-151 D 7
Qianshan • VRC (LIA) 150-151 D 7
Qianwei o VRC 156-157 C 2
Qianxi o VRC 156-157 E 3
Qian Xian o VRC 154-155 F 4
Qianyang o VRC (HUN) 156-157 G 3
Qianyang o VRC (SXI) 154-155 E 4
Qiaochuan o VRC 154-155 E 3
Qiaojdang o VRC 156-157 E 5
Qiaojia o VRC 156-157 C 3
Qiaojian o VRC 156-157 E 5
Qiaowan o VRC 148-149 C 7
Qiaozhen o VRC 154-155 F 3
Qichoi o VRC 156-157 F 6
Qichun o VRC 154-155 J 6
Qidong o VRC 154-155 M 6
Qidugou o VRC 144-145 K 3
Qiemo o VRC 146-147 G 6
Qift o ET 194-195 F 5
Qijiang o VRC 156-157 E 2
Qijiaojing o VRC 146-147 K 4
Qila Didār Singh o PK 138-139 E 3
Qila Lādgasht o PK 134-135 K 5
Qilaotu Shan ▲ VRC 148-149 O 6
Qila Saifullāh o PK 138-139 B 4
Qilian o VRC 154-155 B 2
Qilian Shan ▲ VRC 146-147 N 6
Qilian Shan ▲ VRC 146-147 O 6
Qilwa o KSA 132-133 B 4
Qimen o VRC 156-157 K 2
Qinā ☆ ET 194-195 F 4
Qinā, Wādī ~ ET 194-195 F 4
Qin'an o VRC 154-155 D 4
Qin Binmayong ∴ ••• VRC 154-155 F 4
Qing'an o VRC 150-151 F 4
Qingchengshan • VRC 154-155 C 6
Qingdao ☆ VRC 154-155 M 3
Qing Donling • VRC 154-155 K 1
Qinggang o VRC 150-151 F 4
Qinghai ◘ VRC 144-145 J 4
Qinghai Hu ○ VRC 144-145 M 2
Qinghai Nanshan ▲ VRC 144-145 M 2
Qinghe o VRC (HEB) 154-155 J 3
Qinghe o VRC (XUZ) 146-147 K 2
Qingjian o VRC 154-155 G 3
Qing Jiang ~ VRC 154-155 G 6
Qingkou o VRC 156-157 E 3
Qinglan • VRC 156-157 G 7
Qinglong o VRC 154-155 L 1
Qinglong D. • VRC 156-157 F 3
Qingping o VRC 156-157 F 6
Qingpu o VRC 154-155 M 6
Qingshan o VRC 154-155 J 6
Qingshizoi o VRC 154-155 B 3
Qingshui o VRC 154-155 A 2
Qingshuihe o VRC (NMZ) 154-155 G 2
Qingshuihe o VRC (QIN) 144-145 L 4
Qingshui He ~ VRC 154-155 E 3
Qingtang o VRC 156-157 H 4
Qingtian o VRC 156-157 M 2
Qingtongxia o VRC 154-155 E 2
Qing Xiling • VRC 154-155 J 2
Qingxu o VRC 154-155 H 3
Qingyang o VRC (ANH) 154-155 K 6
Qingyang o VRC (GAN) 154-155 E 3
Qingyuan o VRC (GDG) 156-157 H 5
Qingyuan o VRC (LIA) 150-151 E 6
Qingyuanshan • VRC 156-157 J 3
Qingyun Huaxuechang • VRC 150-151 G 5
Qingzhang Gaoyuan ⌒ VRC 144-145 D 4
Qingzhen o VRC 156-157 E 3
Qingzhou o VRC 154-155 L 3
Qinhuangdao o VRC 154-155 L 2
Qin Ling ▲ VRC 154-155 E 5
Qintang o VRC 156-157 F 5
Qinwangdao Shan ▲ VRC 156-157 E 4
Qin Xian o VRC 154-155 H 3
Qinyang o VRC 154-155 H 4
Qinzhou o VRC 156-157 F 6
Qinzhou Wan ≈ 156-157 F 6
Qionghai o VRC 156-157 G 7
Qionglai o VRC 154-155 C 6
Qionglai Shan ▲ VRC 154-155 C 6
Qiongzhong o VRC 156-157 F 7
Qiongzhou Haixia ≈ 156-157 F 6
Qiqian o VRC 150-151 C 1
Qiqihar o VRC 150-151 D 4
Qiqushan Damiao • VRC 154-155 D 6
Qir o IR 134-135 E 4
Qira o VRC 144-145 C 2
Qisba, Ra's ▲ KSA 130-131 D 3
Qisha o VRC 156-157 F 6
Qishu o VRC 154-155 F 6
Qišla, al- o IRQ 130-131 L 3
Qišn o Y 132-133 G 6
Qitai o VRC 146-147 J 4
Qitaihe o VRC 150-151 H 5
Qitbīt, Wādī ~ OM 132-133 J 4
Qitian Ling ▲ VRC 156-157 H 4
Qiubei o VRC 156-157 D 5
Qiujin o VRC 156-157 J 2
Qixia o VRC 154-155 M 3
Qiyang o VRC 156-157 G 3
Qiyuanshan • VRC 156-157 L 2
Qizhou Liedao ⌒ VRC 156-157 G 7
Qogir Feng = K2 ▲ VRC 138-139 F 2
Qoǧūr o IR 128-129 M 4
Qohrūd, Kūhhā-ye ▲ IR 134-135 D 1
Qoltag ▲ VRC 146-147 J 4
Qom o •• IR 134-135 D 1
Qom, Rūd-e ~ IR 134-135 D 1
Qomolangma Feng = Mount Everest ▲ VRC 144-145 F 7
Qomše o • IR 134-135 D 2
Qonggyai o VRC 144-145 H 6
Qongkol o VRC 146-147 H 5
Qooriga Neegro ≈ 208-209 J 5
Qorqi o IR 136-137 F 6
Qôrsungnitsoq ⌒ GRØ 28-29 P 2
Qorve o IR (HAM) 128-129 N 5
Qorve o IR (KOR) 128-129 M 5
Qoryooley o SP 212-213 K 3
Qostanay = Kostanaj ☆ KA 124-125 C 2
Qoṭābād o IR 134-135 E 4
Qoṭūr o IR 128-129 L 3
Qoṭūr Čāy ~ IR 128-129 L 3
QiPuáng Ngãi o •• VN 158-159 K 3
Quabbin Reservoir ○ USA (MA) 278-279 J 6
Quadeville o CDN (ONT) 238-239 H 3
Quadra Island ⌒ CDN (BC) 230-231 D 3
Quadros, Lagoa dos ○ BR 74-75 E 7
Quaidabad o PK 138-139 C 3

Quail ○ USA (TX) 264-265 D 4
Quairading ○ AUS 176-177 D 6
Quakertown ○ USA (PA) 280-281 L 3
Qualicum Beach ○ CDN (BC) 230-231 E 4
Quallene ○ DZ 190-191 C 8
Quambone ○ AUS 178-179 J 6
Quamby ○ AUS 174-175 F 7
Quanah ○ USA (TX) 264-265 E 4
Quân Dao Nam Du ⌒ VN 158-159 H 6
Quảng Trị ☆ VN 158-159 J 2
Quan Hóa ○ VN 156-157 D 6
Quantico Marine Corps ✕✕ USA (VA) 280-281 J 5
Quanzerbé ○ RN 202-203 L 2
Quanzhou ○ VRC (GXI) 156-157 G 4
Quanzhou ○• VRC (FUJ) 156-157 L 4
Quapaw ○ USA (OK) 264-265 K 2
Qu'Appelle ○ CDN (SAS) 232-233 P 5
Qu'Appelle River ∼ CDN (SAS) 232-233 N 5
Quaqtaq ○ CDN 36-37 P 4
Quaraí ○ BR 76-77 J 6
Quarkoye ○ BF 202-203 J 3
Quarryville ○ USA (PA) 280-281 K 4
Quartier Militaire ○ MS 224 C 7
Quartu Sant'Elena ○ I 100-101 B 5
Quartzite Lake ⊖ CDN 30-31 W 4
Quartzite Mountain ▲ USA (NV) 248-249 H 2
Quartz Lake ⊖ CDN (NWT) 24-25 f 5
Quartz Lake ⊖ CDN (ONT) 34-35 O 5
Quartz Mountain ○ USA (OR) 244-245 E 8
Quartz Mountain State Park ⊥• USA (OK) 264-265 E 4
Quartzsite ○ USA (AZ) 256-257 A 5
Quathiaski Cove ○ CDN (BC) 230-231 D 3
Quatipuru, Ponta de ▲ BR 68-69 E 2
Quatorze de Abril, Cachoeira ∼ BR 62-63 G 5
Quatorze de Abril, Rio ∼ BR 70-71 G 2
Quatre Cantons, Lac de = Vierwaldstädtersee ⊖ CH 92-93 K 5
Quatsino Sound ≈ 32-33 F 6
Quatsino Sound ≈ CDN 230-231 A 3
Quay ○ USA (NM) 256-257 M 4
Qubayyat, al- ○ RL 128-129 G 5
Qūčān ○• IR 136-137 F 6
Qudaiḥ ○ KSA 134-135 D 5
Qué ∼ ANG 216-217 C 7
Queanbeyan, Canberra- ○ AUS 180-181 K 3
Québec ◘ CDN 38-39 F 3
Québec ☆••• CDN (QUE) 238-239 O 2
Quebo ○ GNB 202-203 C 4
Quebra-Anzol, Rio ∼ BR 72-73 G 5
Quebracho ○ ROU 76-77 J 6
Quebrada Arriba ○ YV 60-61 F 2
Quebrada de los Cueervos • ROU 78-79 M 2
Quebrada Honda ○ CR 52-53 B 6
Quedas ○ MOC 218-219 G 4
Quedas do Iguaçu ○ BR 74-75 D 5
Quedas do Lúrio ∼• MOC 218-219 L 1
Quedlinburg ○•• D 92-93 L 3
Queen, De ○ USA (AR) 276-277 A 6
Queen Alexandra Range ▲ ARK 16 E 0
Queen Bess, Mount ▲ CDN (BC) 230-231 E 2
Queen Charlotte Bay ≈ 78-79 K 6
Queen Charlotte City ○ CDN (BC) 228-229 B 3
Queen Charlotte Islands ⌒ CDN (BC) 228-229 A 3
Queen Charlotte Islands ⌒ CDN (BC) 228-229 C 4
Queen Charlotte Islands Museum • CDN (BC) 228-229 C 3
Queen Charlotte Mountains ▲ CDN (BC) 228-229 B 4
Queen Charlotte Sound ≈ 32-33 F 6
Queen Charlotte Sound ≈ CDN 228-229 D 5
Queen Charlotte Strait ≈ 32-33 G 6
Queen Charlotte Strait ≈ CDN 230-231 B 2
Queen City ○ USA (MO) 274-275 F 4
Queen Elizabeth Islands ⌒ CDN 16 B 30
Queen Elizabeth National Park ⊥ EAU 212-213 B 4
Queen Lake, De ∼ USA (AR) 276-277 A 6
Queen Mary Land ⚍ ARK 16 G 10
Queen Maud Gulf ≈ 24-25 U 6
Queens Bay ○ CDN (BC) 230-231 N 4
Queens Cape ▲ CDN 36-37 R 2
Queens Channel ≈ 24-25 X 2
Queenscliff ○ AUS 180-181 H 5
Queensferry ○• GB 90-91 F 4
Queensland ◘ AUS 174-175 E 6
Queenslander II AUS 174-175 K 7
Queensland Plateau ≃ 174-175 K 5
Queensport ○ CDN (NS) 240-241 O 5
Queens Sound ≈ 32-33 F 6
Queens Sound ≈ CDN 230-231 A 2
Queenstown ○ AUS 180-181 H 7
Queenstown ○ CDN (ALB) 232-233 F 5
Queenstown ○•• NZ 182 B 6
Queenstown ○ ZA 220-221 H 5
Queen Victoria Rock ▲ AUS 176-177 F 5
Que'ergou ○ VRC 146-147 H 4
Queets ○ USA (WA) 244-245 A 3
Queguay Grande, Río ∼ ROU 78-79 L 2
Quehue ○ PE 70-71 B 4
Quehué ○ RA 78-79 G 4
Quehué, Valle de ⌣ RA 78-79 G 4
Queidār ○ IR 128-129 N 4
Queilén ○ RCH 78-79 C 7
Queimadas ○ BR (BAH) 68-69 J 7
Queimadas ○ BR (PA) 68-69 L 5
Queirós ○ BR 72-73 E 6
Queiros, Cape ▲ VAN 184 II a 2
Quela ○ ANG 216-217 D 4
Quélé ○ CI 202-203 G 4
Quelele ○ ANG 216-217 E 4
Quelimane ☆ MOC 218-219 J 3
Quellón ○ RCH 78-79 C 7
Quellouno ○ PE 64-65 F 8
Quelo ○ ANG 216-217 B 3
Queluz ○ BR 72-73 H 7
Quemado ○ USA (NM) 256-257 G 4
Quemado ○ USA (TX) 266-267 G 5
Quemado, Cerro ▲ CO 60-61 D 2
Quemado de Güines ○ C 54-55 E 3
Quemados, Punta de ▲ C 54-55 H 4
Quembo ∼ ANG 216-217 E 7
Quemchi ○ RCH 78-79 C 7
Quemu Quemu ○ RA 78-79 H 4
Quenco, Cerro ▲ BOL 76-77 E 1
Queñoal, Río ∼ BOL 76-77 D 2
Quénomisca, Lac ⊖ CDN (ONT) 236-237 M 2
Quepe, Río ∼ RCH 78-79 C 5
Quế Phong ☆ VN 156-157 D 7
Quepos ○ CR 52-53 B 7
Quepos, Punta ▲ CR 52-53 B 7
Quequén ○ RA 78-79 K 5
Quequén Grande, Río ∼ RA 78-79 K 5
Quequén Salado, Río ∼ RA 78-79 J 5
Querari ○ CO 66-67 C 2
Querari, Río ∼ CO 66-67 B 2
Querco ○ PE 64-65 E 8
Querência do Norte ○ BR 72-73 D 7
Querendaro ○ MEX 52-53 D 2
Querétaro ◘ MEX 52-53 D 1
Querétaro ☆•• MEX (QRO) 52-53 D 1
Quero ○ EC 64-65 C 2
Querobamba ○ PE 64-65 F 8
Querocotillo ○ PE 64-65 C 5
Quesnel ○ CDN (BC) 228-229 M 4
Quesnel Lake ⊖ CDN (BC) 228-229 N 4
Quesnel River ∼ CDN (BC) 228-229 M 4
Quesso ☆ RCB (San) 210-211 F 3
Questa ○ USA (NM) 256-257 K 2
Questro, El ○ AUS 172-173 H 4
Quetico ○ CDN (ONT) 234-235 N 6
Quetico Lake ⊖ CDN (ONT) 234-235 M 6
Quetico Provincial Park ⊥ CDN (ONT) 234-235 M 6
Quetico Provincial Park ⊥ USA (MN) 270-271 G 2
Quetta ☆• PK 134-135 M 3
Queue de Turtue, Bayou ∼ USA (LA) 268-269 H 6
Queulat, Parque Nacional ⊥ RCH 80 D 2
Queve ∼ ANG 216-217 C 5
Quevedo ○ EC 64-65 C 2
Quevedo, Río ∼ EC 64-65 C 2
Quévillon, Lac ⊖ CDN (QUE) 236-237 M 3
Quezaltenango ☆• GCA 52-53 J 4
Quezon ○ RP 160-161 C 8
Quezon City ○ RP 160-161 D 5
Qufu ○• VRC 154-155 K 4
Quiabaya ○ BOL 70-71 C 4
Quiaca, La ○ RA 76-77 E 2
Quiahniztlan • MEX 52-53 F 2
Quiba ○ ZA 220-221 H 5
Quibala ○ ANG (CZS) 216-217 C 5
Quibala ○ ANG (ZAI) 216-217 B 3
Quibaxe ○ ANG 216-217 C 4
Quibdó ☆ CO 60-61 C 5
Quibell ○ CDN (ONT) 234-235 K 5
Quiberon ○ F 90-91 F 8
Quibor ○ YV 60-61 G 3
Quicabo ○ ANG 216-217 B 4
Quicacha ○ PE 64-65 F 9
Quicama, Parque Nacional do ⊥ ANG 216-217 B 4
Quichaura, Cerro ▲ RA 78-79 D 7
Quicksand ○ USA (KY) 276-277 M 3
Quiculungo ○ ANG 216-217 C 4
Quidico ○ RCH 78-79 C 5
Quidong ○ VRC 156-157 H 3
Quiet Lake ⊖ CDN 20-21 Y 6
Quijadas, Sierra las ▲ RA 78-79 F 2
Quijingue ○ BR 68-69 J 7
Quijotoa ○ USA (AZ) 256-257 C 6
Quijoux, Col ▲ RCA 206-207 F 4
Quila ○ MEX 50-51 F 5
Quilán, Cabo ▲ RCH 78-79 B 7
Quilandi ○ IND 140-141 F 5
Quilca ○ PE (ARE) 70-71 A 5
Quilca ○ PE (LIM) 64-65 D 7
Quilcene ○ USA (WA) 244-245 C 3
Quilchena ○ CDN (BC) 230-231 J 3
Quilempa ○ ANG 216-217 B 7
Quilenda ○ ANG 216-217 C 5
Quilengues ○ ANG 216-217 C 7
Quillabamba ○ PE 64-65 F 8
Quillacollo ○ BOL 70-71 D 5
Quillagua ○ RCH 76-77 C 1
Quillan ○ F 90-91 J 10
Quillayute Indian Reservation ✕ USA (WA) 244-245 A 3
Quillen, Río ∼ RCH 78-79 C 5
Quill Lake ○ CDN (SAS) 232-233 O 3
Quill Lakes ⊖ CDN (SAS) 232-233 O 4
Quilmes ○ RA 78-79 K 3
Quilombo dos Dembos ○ ANG 216-217 C 4
Quilon ○• IND 140-141 G 6
Quilpie ○ AUS 178-179 H 4
Quilpue ○ RCH 78-79 D 2
Quilua ○ MOC 218-219 K 3
Quilu Hu ∼ VRC 156-157 C 4
Quimal, Llano del ⚍ RCH 76-77 C 2
Quimantag ▲ VRC 144-145 H 2
Quimbala ○ ANG 216-217 C 2
Quimbaya ○ CO 60-61 D 5
Quimbele ○ ANG 216-217 D 3
Quimet ○ CDN (ONT) 234-235 P 6
Quimili ○ RA 76-77 F 4
Quimome, Río ∼ BOL 70-71 G 6
Quimper ☆• F 90-91 E 8
Quinabucasan Point ▲ RP 160-161 E 5
Quinapondan ○ RP 160-161 F 7
Quinault ○ USA (WA) 244-245 B 3
Quinault Indian Reservation ✕ USA (WA) 244-245 A 3
Quinault River ∼ USA (WA) 244-245 B 3
Quince Mil ○ PE 70-71 B 3
Quinchao, Isla ⌒ RCH 78-79 C 7
Quinché, Raudal ∼ CO 66-67 B 3
Quincy ○ USA (FL) 286-287 E 1
Quincy ○ USA (IL) 274-275 G 5
Quincy ○ USA (MA) 278-279 L 6
Quincy ○ USA (WA) 244-245 F 3
Quincy, De ○ USA (LA) 268-269 G 6
Quincy Hills ▲ USA (IL) 274-275 G 5
Quines ○ RA 78-79 G 2
Quinga ○ MOC 218-219 L 2
Quingenge ○ ANG 216-217 C 6
Quinhagak ○ USA 22-23 Q 3
Quinhámel ○ GNB 202-203 C 4
Quiniluban Group ⌒ RP 160-161 D 7
Quinjalca ○ PE 64-65 D 5
Quinkan Nature Reserve ⊥ AUS 174-175 H 4
Quinlan ○ USA (TX) 264-265 H 6
Quinn River ∼ USA (NV) 246-247 G 2
Quinns Rocks ○ AUS 176-177 C 5
Quinota ○ PE 64-65 F 9
Quintana de la Serena ○ E 98-99 E 5
Quintana Roo ◘ MEX 52-53 K 2
Quintana Roo, Parque Nacional de ⊥ MEX 52-53 L 1
Quinter ○ USA (KS) 262-263 F 5
Quintero ○ RCH 78-79 D 2
Quintero, Bahía ≈ 78-79 D 2
Quintín Banderas ○ C 54-55 E 3
Quinto, Río ∼ RA 78-79 G 2
Quinton ○ CDN (SAS) 232-233 O 4
Quinton ○ USA (OK) 264-265 J 3
Quinzala ○ ANG 216-217 C 3
Quinzau ○ ANG 216-217 B 3
Quionga ○ MOC 214-215 L 6
Quiongua ○ ANG 216-217 C 4
Quiotepec ○ MEX 52-53 F 3
Quipapa ○ BR 68-69 K 6
Quipeio ○ ANG 216-217 C 6
Quipungo ○ ANG 216-217 C 7
Quirigua ∴••• GCA 52-53 K 4
Quirihué ○ RCH 78-79 C 4
Quirima ○ ANG 216-217 E 5
Quirindi ○ AUS 178-179 L 6
Quiriñeo, Cerro ▲ RCH 78-79 D 3
Quirinópolis ○ BR 72-73 E 5
Quiriquire ○ YV 60-61 K 3
Quiroga ○ BOL 70-71 E 6
Quiroga ○ MEX 52-53 D 2
Quiroga ○ RA 78-79 J 3
Quiroga, Punta ▲ RA 78-79 G 7
Quiros ○ YV 60-61 F 2
Quirpon ○ CDN (NFL) 242-243 N 1
Quiruvilca ○ PE 64-65 C 5
Quisquiro, Salar de ⊖ RCH 76-77 D 2
Quissanga ○ MOC 214-215 L 7
Quissico ○ MOC 220-221 M 2
Quitandinha ○ BR 74-75 F 5
Quitapa ○ ANG 216-217 E 5
Quitaque ○ USA (TX) 264-265 C 4
Quiterajo ○ MOC 214-215 L 6
Quitéria, Rio ∼ BR 72-73 E 5
Quiteve ○ ANG 216-217 C 8
Quitexe ○ ANG 216-217 C 3
Quitilipi ○ RA 76-77 G 4
Quitman ○ USA (AR) 276-277 C 5
Quitman ○ USA (GA) 284-285 G 6
Quitman ○ USA (LA) 268-269 H 4
Quitman ○ USA (MS) 268-269 M 4
Quitman ○ USA (TX) 264-265 J 6
Quitman Ruins, Fort • USA (TX) 266-267 B 2
Quito ★••• EC 64-65 C 2
Quivira National Wildlife Refuge ⊥ USA (KS) 262-263 H 6
Quivolgo ○ RCH 78-79 C 3
Quixadá ○ BR 66-67 D 7
Quixada ○ BR 68-69 J 4
Quixaxe ○ MOC 218-219 L 2
Quixeramobim ○ BR 68-69 J 4
Quizenga ○ ANG 216-217 C 4
Qujiang ○ VRC 156-157 H 4
Qujing ○ VRC 156-157 C 4
Qulaita, Umm ○ Y 132-133 E 7
Qulin ○ USA (MO) 276-277 E 4
Qumar He ∼ VRC 144-145 J 3
Qumar Heyan ○ VRC 144-145 J 3
Qumarlêb ○ VRC 144-145 K 3
Qummāh, Ǧazīrat ⌒ KSA 132-133 B 5
Qunaiṭira, al- ☆ SYR 128-129 F 6
Qunfuḏa, al- ○ KSA 132-133 B 4
Quobba ○ AUS 176-177 B 2
Quobba, Point ▲ AUS 176-177 B 2
Quoich River ∼ CDN 30-31 W 2
Quoin, Du ○ USA (IL) 274-275 J 6
Quoin Head ▲ AUS 176-177 B 2
Quoin Island ⌒ AUS 172-173 J 3
Quoy, Pulau ⌒ RI 166-167 F 1
Qurayd ○ SUD 206-207 K 3
Qurayyāt ○• OM 132-133 L 2
Qurayyāt, al- ◘ KSA 130-131 E 3
Qurayyāt, al- ☆• KSA 130-131 E 2
Qurdūd ○ SUD 206-207 J 3
Qureida ○ SUD 206-207 G 3
Qurna, al- ☆ IRQ 128-129 M 7
Qurnat as-Saudā' ▲ RL 128-129 G 5
Qurrāṣah ○ SUD 200-201 F 5
Qūs ○ ET 194-195 F 5
Quṣaiba ○ IRQ 128-129 J 5
Quṣair, al- ○ IRQ 130-131 J 2
Quṣair, al- ☆ SYR 128-129 G 5
Quṣair 'Amra ∴••• JOR 130-131 E 2
Quṣay'ir ○ Y 132-133 G 6
Qusum ○ VRC 144-145 J 6
Quṭaifa, al- ☆ SYR 128-129 G 6
Qutau ▲ KA 124-125 K 4
Qutdligssat ○ GRØ 28-29 O 1
Qutdlikorssuit ⌒ GRØ 26-27 W 7
Quthing = Moyeni ○ LS 220-221 H 5
Qutsigsormiut ⌒ GRØ 28-29 U 5
Quṭū', Ǧazīrat ⌒ KSA 132-133 B 4
Qutūf ○ UAE 132-133 H 2
Quwair, al- ○ IRQ 128-129 K 4
Quwāra, al- ○ KSA 130-131 H 4
Quwu Shan ▲ VRC 154-155 D 3
Qu Xian ○ VRC 154-155 E 6
Qüxü ○ VRC 144-145 H 6
Quyāğū ○ IRQ 128-129 L 5
Quyang ○ VRC 154-155 J 2
Quyanghai SK ∼ VRC 156-157 H 3
Quyen ○ AUS 180-181 G 3
Quynh Lu'u ○ VN 156-157 D 7
Quy Nho'n ☆• VN 158-159 K 4
Qūz, al- ○ KSA 132-133 B 4
Qūz, al- ○ Y 132-133 G 6
Quza, al- ○ Y 132-133 F 6
Quzhou ○ VRC 156-157 L 2
Qwa Qwa (former homeland) now part of Oranje Vrystaat ◘ ZA 220-221 J 4
Qyzylorda = Ķyzylorda ☆ KA 124-125 D 6

R

Raab ∼ A 92-93 N 5
Raadoľnaja ∼ RUS 122-123 D 6
Raahe ○ FIN 88-89 H 4
Raanes Peninsula ⌒ CDN 26-27 G 4
Raanujärvi ○ FIN 88-89 H 3
Raas, Pulau ⌒ RI 168 B 6
Raattama ○ FIN 88-89 H 2
Rab ○• HR 100-101 E 2
Rab ⚍•• HR 100-101 E 2
Raba ○• RI 168 D 7
Rabaable ○ SP 208-209 J 4
Rabaḍ, Qal'at ar- ∴• JOR 130-131 D 1
Rabah ○ WAN 198-199 B 6
Rabak ○ SUD 200-201 F 6
Rabal ○ RI 166-167 H 5
Rabang ○ VRC 144-145 C 4
Rabaraba ○ PNG 183 E 5
Rabārika ○ IND 138-139 C 9
Rabat ○ M 100-101 E 7
Rabat = Ar-Ribāt ★•• MA 188-189 K 4
Rabat = Victoria ○ M 100-101 E 6
Rabaul ☆• PNG 183 G 3
Rabba ○ WAN 204-205 F 4
Rabbāḍ, ar- ⚍ UAE 132-133 J 2
Rabbit Ears Pass ▲ USA (CO) 254-255 J 3
Rabbit Flat Store ○ AUS 172-173 K 6
Rabbit Lake ○ CDN (SAS) 232-233 L 2
Rabbit River ∼ CDN 30-31 F 6
Rabbitskin River ∼ CDN 30-31 J 5
Raber ○ USA (MI) 270-271 O 4
Rabi ⌒ FJI 184 III c 2
Rabi'a ○ IRQ 128-129 K 4
Rabia ○ RI 166-167 F 2
Rabida, Isla ⌒ EC 64-65 B 10
Rābiġ ○ KSA 130-131 F 6
Rabka ○ PL 92-93 P 4
Rabkavi Banhatti ○ IND 140-141 F 2
Rabočeostrovsk ○ RUS 88-89 N 4
Rabo da Onça ○ BR 66-67 E 3
Rābor ○ IR 134-135 G 4
Raboti Malik, korvonsaroj • US 136-137 J 5
Rabt Sbayta ⚍ MA 196-197 C 3
Rabun Bald ▲ USA (GA) 284-285 G 2
Rabwah ○ PK 138-139 D 4
Rabyanah ○ LAR 192-193 K 5
Raccon Cay ⌒ BS 54-55 H 3
Raccoon Creek ∼ USA (OH) 280-281 D 5
Raccoon Creek State Park ⊥ USA (PA) 280-281 F 3
Raceland ○ USA (LA) 268-269 K 7
Race Pond ○ USA (GA) 284-285 H 6
Rachal ○ USA (TX) 266-267 J 7
Rachel ○ USA (NV) 248-249 J 2
Rạch Gía ☆• VN 158-159 H 5
Rachid ○ RIM 196-197 E 5
Rachiv ☆ UA 102-103 D 3
Racibórz ○ PL 92-93 P 3
Racine ○ USA (OH) 280-281 E 5
Racine ○ USA (WI) 274-275 L 2
Racing River ∼ CDN 30-31 G 6
Rackham ○ CDN (MAN) 234-235 C 4
Rackla Range ▲ CDN 20-21 X 4
Radā' ○ Y 132-133 D 6
Radama, Nosy ⌒ RM 222-223 E 4
Rădăuți ○ RO 102-103 D 4
Radcliff ○ USA (KY) 276-277 K 3
Radde ○ RUS 122-123 D 4
Radechiv ○ UA 102-103 D 2
Radford ○ USA (AL) 284-285 C 4
Radford ○ USA (VA) 280-281 F 6
Radford Lake ⊖ CDN 30-31 R 4
Radford River ∼ CDN 30-31 R 4
Rādhan ○ PK 134-135 M 5
Rādhānagari ○• IND 140-141 E 2
Rādhanpur ○ IND 138-139 C 8
Radial'naja, gora ▲ RUS 112-113 Q 3
Radimlja • BIH 100-101 F 3
Radio Australia • AUS 172-173 K 2
Radio Australia Station • AUS 176-177 B 2
Radio Telescope • AUS 180-181 K 2
Radioville ○ USA (IN) 274-275 M 3
Radisson ○ CDN (QUE) 38-39 F 2
Radisson ○ CDN (SAS) 232-233 L 3
Radisson, Pointe ▲ CDN 36-37 N 3
Radium Hot Springs ○ CDN (BC) 230-231 O 3
Radium Springs ○ USA (NM) 256-257 J 6
Rādkān ○ IR 136-137 F 6
Radom ☆ PL 92-93 Q 3
Radom ○ SUD 206-207 G 4
Radomsko ○ PL 92-93 P 3
Radoviš ○ MK 100-101 J 4
Radstadt ○• A 92-93 M 5
Radužnyj ○ RUS 114-115 O 3
Radviliškis ☆•• LT 94-95 H 4
Radville ○ CDN (SAS) 232-233 O 6
Radwan ○ KSA 130-131 G 6
Radzyń Podlaski ○ PL 92-93 R 3
Rae ○ CDN 30-31 L 4
Rāe Bareli ○ IND 142-143 B 2
Raeford ○ USA (NC) 282-283 H 6
Rae Isthmus ⌣ CDN 24-25 c 7
Rae Lake ⊖ CDN 30-31 L 3
Rae River ∼ CDN 24-25 M 6
Raeside, Lake ⊖ AUS 176-177 F 4
Raes Junction ○ NZ 182 B 6
Rae Strait ≈ 24-25 Y 6
Raetihi ○ NZ 182 E 3
Raevskij ☆ RUS 96-97 J 6
Rafaela ○ RA 76-77 G 6
Rafael Freyre ○ C 54-55 G 4
Rafaḥ ○ AUT 130-131 C 2
Rafaï ○ RCA 206-207 F 6
Raffingora ○ ZW 218-219 F 3
Raffin-Kada ○ WAN 204-205 H 5
Rafḥā' ○ KSA 130-131 H 3
Rafin-Cabas ○ WAN 204-205 H 4
Rāfit, Ǧabal ▲ SUD 200-201 F 2
Rafsaï ○ MA 188-189 J 3
Raft River ∼ CDN (BC) 230-231 K 2
Raft River ∼ USA (ID) 252-253 E 4
Raft River Mountains ▲ USA (UT) 254-255 B 2
Raga ○ SUD 206-207 G 4
Raga ∼ SUD 206-207 G 4
Ragaing Yōma ▲ MYA 142-143 J 6
Ragama ○ CL 140-141 H 7
Ragang, Mount ▲ RP 160-161 F 9
Ragay Gulf ≈ 160-161 E 6
Ragged Island ⌒ CDN 36-37 U 7
Ragged Island ⌒ USA (ME) 278-279 N 5
Ragged Island Range ⌒ BS 54-55 H 3
Raghwan ○ KSA 132-133 A 3
Raglan ○ NZ 182 E 2
Ragland ○ USA (NM) 256-257 M 4
Ragley ○ USA (LA) 268-269 G 6
Rago ○ USA (KS) 262-263 H 7
Rago nasjonalpark ⊥ N 86-87 G 3
Ragozina, mys ▲ RUS 108-109 N 5
Ragueneau ○ CDN 38-39 K 4
Ragusa ○ I 100-101 E 6
Raha ○ RI 164-165 H 6
Rahad ∼ ETH 200-201 H 6
Rahad al-Bardī ○ SUD 206-207 F 3
Rahama ○ WAN 204-205 H 3
Rāhatgarh ○ IND 138-139 G 8
Raḥḥālīya, ar- ○ IRQ 128-129 K 6
Rahib < SUD 200-201 C 4
Rāhida, ar- ○ Y 132-133 D 7
Rahim ki Bāzār ○ PK 138-139 B 7
Rahīmyār Khān ○ PK 138-139 C 5
Rahmanovka ○ RUS 96-97 F 8
Rahmanovskie Kljuci ○ KA 124-125 P 4
Rahmat, Ra's ▲ ER 200-201 L 6
Rahmet ○ KA 124-125 D 4
Rahole National Reserve ⊥ EAK 212-213 G 3
Råholt ○ N 86-87 E 6
Rahouia ○ DZ 190-191 C 3
Rahué ○ RA 78-79 D 5
Rahue, Río ∼ RCH 78-79 C 6
Raiatéa ⌒ F 13 M 4
Rāichūr ○• IND 140-141 G 2
Raida ○ Y 132-133 D 6
Raidāk ∼ IND 142-143 F 2
Raiford ○ USA (FL) 286-287 G 1
Raiganj ○ IND 142-143 F 3
Raigarh ○ IND 142-143 C 5
Raijua, Pulau ⌒ RI 168 E 8
Raikal ○ IND 138-139 G 10
Railroad Pass ▲ USA (NV) 246-247 H 4
Railroad Valley ⌣ USA (NV) 246-247 K 5
Raima, Wādī ∼ Y 132-133 C 6
Rain, ar- ○ KSA 130-131 J 6
Rainbow ○ USA 20-21 Q 6
Rainbow ○ USA (OR) 244-245 C 6
Rainbow Beach ○ AUS 178-179 M 3
Rainbow Bridge National Monument ∴ USA (UT) 254-255 E 6
Rainbow City ○ USA (AL) 284-285 D 3
Rainbow Falls ∼• USA (HI) 288 K 5
Rainbow Lake ○ CDN 30-31 K 6
Rainier ○ CDN (ALB) 232-233 F 5
Rainier ○ USA (OR) 244-245 C 4
Rainier, Mount ▲ USA (WA) 244-245 D 4
Rainpura ○ IND 140-141 G 3
Rainsville ○ USA (AL) 284-285 E 2
Rainy Lake ⊖ CDN (ONT) 234-235 K 6
Rainy River ○ CDN (ONT) 234-235 J 6
Rainy River ∼ USA (MN) 270-271 E 2
Raipur ○ IND (MAP) 142-143 B 3
Raipur ○ IND (MAP) 142-143 B 5
Raisūt ○ OM 132-133 J 5
Raith ○ CDN (ONT) 234-235 O 6
Rai Valley ○ NZ 182 D 4
Rāiwind ○ PK 138-139 E 4
Raja, Pulau ⌒ RI 168 E 3
Raja Ampat, Kepulauan ⌒ RI 166-167 E 2
Rajada ○ BR 68-69 H 6
Rajagangapur ○ IND 142-143 D 4
Rājahmundry ○ IND 142-143 B 7
Rājākhera ○ IND 138-139 G 6
Rajampet ○ IND 140-141 H 3
Rajang ○ MAL (SAR) 162-163 J 3
Rajang ∼ MAL 162-163 K 3
Rājanpur ○ PK 138-139 C 5
Rājāpalaiyam ○ IND 140-141 G 6
Rājapur ○ IND 140-141 E 2
Rajasthan ◘ IND 138-139 C 6
Rajčihinsk ○ RUS 122-123 C 4
Rajga ∼ RUS 114-115 S 5
Rājgarh ○ IND (MAP) 138-139 F 8
Rājgarh ○ IND (RAJ) 138-139 F 6
Rājgarh ○ IND (RAJ) 138-139 E 5
Rajgarhat ○ NEP 144-145 F 7
Rajin ○ DVR 150-151 H 6
Rajkoke, ostrov ⌒ RUS 122-123 P 4
Rājkot ○ IND 138-139 C 8
Rājmahāl ○ IND 142-143 E 3
Rajmahal Hills ▲ IND 142-143 E 3
Rāj-Nāndgaon ○ IND 142-143 B 5
Rajnera, ostrov ⌒ RUS 84-85 f 2
Rājpiipla ○ IND 138-139 D 9
Raj Samund ○ IND 138-139 D 7
Rajshahi ☆• BD 142-143 F 3
Raka ○ VRC 144-145 E 6
Rakan, Ra's ▲ Q 134-135 D 5
Rakata, Pulau ⌒ RI 168 A 3
Rakaye ○ BF 202-203 K 4
Raka Zangpo ∼ VRC 144-145 F 6
Rakhni ○ PK 138-139 B 4
Rakhni ∼ PK 138-139 B 5
Rakhshān ∼ PK 134-135 K 5
Rakiraki ○ FJI 184 III b 2
Rakit, Pulau ⌒ RI 168 C 2
Rakitnoe ○ RUS 122-123 F 6
Rakom ○ THA 158-159 G 4
Rakonitz = Rakovník ○ CZ 92-93 M 3
Rakops ○ RB 218-219 C 5
Rakovník ○ CZ 92-93 M 3
Rakovskaja ○ RUS 88-89 Q 5
Rakušečnyj, mys ▲ KA 126-127 J 6
Rakvere ☆•• EST 94-95 K 2
Rakwa ○ RI 166-167 H 3
Ralco ○ RCH 78-79 D 4
Rālegaon ○ IND 138-139 G 9
Raleigh ○ CDN (NFL) 242-243 N 1
Raleigh ○ USA (MS) 268-269 L 4
Raleigh ☆ USA (NC) 282-283 J 5
Raleigh Bay ≈ 48-49 K 2
Raleigh Bay ≈ USA 282-283 L 6
Raleigh National Historic Site, Fort • USA (NC) 282-283 M 5
Raleighvallen ∼ SME 62-63 F 3
Raleighvallen Voltzberg, National Reservaat ⊥ SME 62-63 F 3
Raley ○ CDN (ALB) 232-233 E 6
Ralls ○ USA (TX) 264-265 C 5
Ralph ○ CDN (SAS) 232-233 P 6
Ralston ○ USA (NE) 262-263 K 3
Ralston ○ USA (WA) 244-245 G 4
Ralston ○ USA (WY) 252-253 K 2
Rama ○ CDN (SAS) 232-233 P 4
Rama ○ NIC 52-53 B 5
Rāmabhadrapuram ○ IND 142-143 C 6
Rama Caída ○ RA 78-79 E 3
Rāmachandraparam ○ IND 140-141 K 2
Ramad, Hassi < DZ 190-191 F 6
Ramada, La ○ RA 76-77 E 4
Ramadas, Las ○ RCH 76-77 B 6
Ramādī, ar- ☆ IRQ 128-129 K 6
Ramadillas ○ RCH 76-77 C 1
Ramagiri ○ IND 140-141 G 3
Ramah ○ USA (NM) 256-257 G 3
Ramah Navajo Indian Reservation ✕ USA (NM) 256-257 G 4
Rāmak ○ AFG 138-139 B 3
Ramalho, Serra do ▲ BR 72-73 H 2
Rāmallāh ☆ WB 130-131 D 2
Ramallo ○ RA 78-79 J 2
Rāmanāthapuram ○ IND 140-141 H 6
Rāman Mandi ○ IND 138-139 E 5
Rāmānuj Ganj ○ IND 142-143 C 4
Ramardori ○ RI 166-167 H 2
Ramas, Las = Salitre ○ EC 64-65 C 2
Rāmasamudram ○ IND 140-141 G 5
Ramatlabama ○ ZA 220-221 G 2
Ramayampet ○ IND 138-139 G 10
Rāmāypatnam ○ IND 140-141 J 3
Rambipuji ○ RI 168 E 4
Rambouillet ○ F 90-91 H 7
Rambrè ○ MYA 142-143 H 6
Rambrè ⌒ MYA 142-143 H 6
Rambutyo Island ⌒ PNG 183 D 2
Ramea ○ CDN (NFL) 242-243 L 5
Ramea Island ⌒ CDN (NFL) 242-243 L 5
Rameau ○ CDN (QUE) 240-241 L 2
Ramechhap ○ NEP 144-145 F 7
Rame Head ▲ AUS 180-181 K 4
Ramena ○ RM 222-223 F 4
Rameški ☆ RUS 94-95 P 3
Rāmeswaram ○•• IND 140-141 H 6
Ramey ○ USA (MN) 270-271 E 5
Ramezān Kalak ○ IR 134-135 J 5
Ramganga ∼ IND 138-139 G 6
Rāmganj Mandi ○ IND 138-139 E 7
Ramgarh ○ BD 142-143 G 4
Rāmgarh ○ IND 138-139 C 6
Ramgarh ○ IND (BIH) 142-143 D 4
Ramgarh ○ IND (MAP) 142-143 C 4
Rāmgarh Tāl ⊖ IND 142-143 C 2
Rāmhormoz ○ IR 134-135 C 3
Ramhurst ○ USA (GA) 284-285 F 2
Ramingining ✕ AUS 174-175 C 3
Ramis Shet' ∼ ETH 208-209 E 4
Ramkan ○• IR 134-135 G 5
Ramkhamhaeng National Park ⊥ THA 158-159 E 2
Raml ○ IRQ 128-129 K 5
Ramla ☆ IL 130-131 D 2
Ramlat al-Ĝāfa ⚍ OM 132-133 J 3
Ramlat al-Wahība ⚍ OM 132-133 L 2
Ramlat as-Sab'atain ⚍ Y 132-133 D 6
Ramlat Rabyanah ⚍ LAR 192-193 J 5
Ramlat Zallāf ⚍ LAR 192-193 E 4
Ramlu ▲ ER 200-201 K 6
Ramnaga ○ IND 142-143 B 2
Rāmnagar ○ IND 138-139 G 5
Ramnagar ○ IND 138-139 E 3
Rāmnagor ○ IND 142-143 B 3
Ramo ○ ETH 208-209 E 5
Ramon ○ USA (NM) 256-257 L 4
Ramon, Mitzpé ○ IL 130-131 D 2
Ramona ○ USA (CA) 248-249 H 6
Ramonal ∴• MEX 52-53 K 2
Ramones, Los ○ MEX 50-51 K 5
Ramon Grande, Laguna ⊖ PE 64-65 B 4
Ramore ○ CDN (ONT) 236-237 H 4
Ramos ○ BR 62-63 H 6
Ramos, Cachoeira ∼ BR 70-71 G 2
Ramos, Río de ∼ MEX 50-51 G 5
Ramos Arizpe ○ MEX 50-51 J 5
Ramos Island ⌒ RP 160-161 B 8
Ramos Otero ○ RA 78-79 K 4
Ramotswa ○ RB 220-221 G 2
Rampa ○ ANG 216-217 C 4
Rampart ○ USA 20-21 P 4
Ramparts River ∼ CDN 30-31 D 3
Rāmpur ○ IND (GUJ) 138-139 D 8
Rāmpur ○ IND (HIP) 138-139 F 4
Rampur ○ IND (MAP) 142-143 B 4
Rāmpur ○ IND (ORI) 142-143 D 5
Rampur ○ IND (UTP) 138-139 G 5
Rāmpura ○ IND 138-139 E 7
Rampur Hāt ○ IND 142-143 E 3
Ramree = Rambrè ○ MYA 142-143 H 6
Ramree Island = Rambrè ⌒ MYA 142-143 H 6
Ram River ∼ CDN 30-31 H 5
Ram River ∼ CDN (ALB) 232-233 C 3
Rams ○ UAE 134-135 F 6
Rāmsar ○• IR 136-137 B 6
Ramsay, Mount ▲ AUS 172-173 H 5
Ramsay Lake ⊖ CDN (ONT) 236-237 F 5
Rāmše ○ IR 134-135 E 3
Ramsele ○ S 86-87 H 5
Ramseur ○ USA (NC) 282-283 H 5
Ramsey ○ CDN (ONT) 236-237 F 5
Ramsey ○ USA (IL) 274-275 J 5
Ramsey ○ USA (NC) 282-283 F 5
Ramsgate ○• GB 90-91 H 6
Ramsgate ○ ZA 220-221 K 5
Ramsing ○ IND 142-143 J 1
Rāmšir ○ IR 134-135 C 3
Ramsjö ○ S 86-87 G 5
Ramta, ar ☆ JOR 130-131 E 1
Rāmtek ○ IND 138-139 G 9
Ramu ○ BD 142-143 H 5
Ramu ○ EAK 212-213 H 2
Ramu ○ NEP 144-145 C 6
Ramu National Park ⊥ PNG 183 C 3
Ramundberget ○ S 86-87 F 5
Ramu River ∼ PNG 183 C 3
Ramusio, Lac ⊖ CDN 36-37 S 7
Ramvik ○ S 86-87 H 5
Ramygala ○•• LT 94-95 J 4
Ran ○ WAN 198-199 G 6
Rana, Danau ⊖ RI 166-167 D 3
Rana, La ○ C 54-55 F 3
Rānahu ○ PK 138-139 B 7
Ranai ○ RI 162-163 H 3
Ranakah, Gunung ▲ RI 168 E 7
Rana Pratap Sāgar ⊖ IND 138-139 E 7
Ranarmoye ∼ RI 166-167 F 5
Ranau ○ MAL 160-161 B 10
Ranau, Danau ⊖ RI 162-163 E 7
Ranbausawa, Tanjung ▲ RI 166-167 J 3
Ranburne ○ USA (AL) 284-285 E 3
Rancagua ☆ RCH 78-79 D 3
Rancahué, Cerro ▲ RA 78-79 D 5
Rancharia ○ BR 72-73 E 7
Rancheria, Río ∼ CO 60-61 E 2
Rancheria River ∼ CDN 30-31 E 5
Ranchester ○ USA (WY) 252-253 L 2
Ranchi ○•• IND 142-143 D 4
Rānchi ○•• IND 142-143 D 4
Rānchi Plateau ▲ IND 142-143 D 4
Rancho California ○ USA (CA) 248-249 G 6
Rancho Cordova ○ USA (CA) 246-247 D 5
Rancho Queimado ○ BR 74-75 F 6
Ranchos ○ RA 78-79 K 3
Rancho Velho ○ BR 74-75 E 8
Rancho Viejo ○ MEX 52-53 E 3
Ranchuelo ○ C 54-55 E 3
Ranco, Lago ⊖ RCH 78-79 C 6
Rand ○ USA (CO) 254-255 J 3
Randa ○ DJI 208-209 F 3
Randado ○ USA (TX) 266-267 J 6
Randale ∼ DJI 200-201 L 6
Randall Dam, Fort • USA (SD) 260-261 H 3
Randangan-Panua Reserves ⊥• RI 164-165 G 3
Randazzo ○ I 100-101 E 6
Randberge ▲ ZA 220-221 K 3
Randeggi ○ WAN 204-205 G 3
Randers ○ DK 86-87 E 8
Randfontein ○ ZA 220-221 H 3
Randijaure ⊖ S 86-87 J 3
Randle ○ USA (WA) 244-245 D 4
Randlett ○ USA (OK) 264-265 F 4
Randolph ○ USA (KS) 262-263 K 5
Randolph ○ USA (NE) 262-263 J 2
Randolph ○ USA (TN) 276-277 F 5
Randolph ○ USA (UT) 254-255 D 2
Randolph ○ USA (VT) 278-279 J 5
Random Island ⌒ CDN (NFL) 242-243 P 4
Randowaya ○ RI 166-167 J 2
Randsburg ○ USA (CA) 248-249 G 4
Randsfjorden ⊖ N 86-87 E 6
Randudongkal ○ RI 168 C 3
Råneälven ∼ S 86-87 K 3
Ranemsletta ○ N 86-87 E 4
Ranérou ○ SN 202-203 D 2
Ranfurly ○ CDN (ALB) 232-233 G 2
Rangaranga ○ RI 164-165 H 4
Rangasa, Tanjung ▲ RI 164-165 F 5
Range ○ USA (AL) 284-285 C 5
Rangeley ○ USA (ME) 278-279 L 4
Rangely ○ USA (CO) 254-255 G 3
Ranger ○ CDN (SAS) 232-233 L 2
Ranger ○ USA (TX) 264-265 F 6
Ranger Brook ∼ CDN 36-37 G 3
Rangers Valley ○ AUS 178-179 H 2
Ranger Uranium Mine • AUS 172-173 L 2
Ranges Valley ○ AUS 178-179 F 1
Rangia ○ IND 142-143 G 2
Rangiora ○ NZ 182 D 5
Rangkaspitung ○ RI 168 B 3
Rangkul' ○ TJ 146-147 B 6
Rangnim ○ DVR 150-151 F 7
Rangnim Sanmaek ▲ DVR 150-151 F 7
Rangoon = Yangon ★ MYA 158-159 D 2
Rangoon = Yangon ★•• MYA 158-159 D 2
Rangpo ○ IND 142-143 F 2
Rangpur ○ BD 142-143 F 3
Rangpur Canal < PK 138-139 C 4
Rangsang, Pulau ⌒ RI 162-163 E 4
Ranguana Cay ⌒ BH 52-53 K 3
Ranhal ○ PK 138-139 C 5
Rānībennur ○ IND 140-141 F 3
Raniganj ○ IND 142-143 E 4
Rāniganj ○ IND 142-143 E 2
Rānīkhet ○• IND 138-139 G 5
Ranikot ∴• PK 138-139 B 7
Rānipettai ○ IND 140-141 H 4
Rānipur ○ PK 138-139 B 6
Rāniya ☆ IRQ 128-129 L 4
Ranken Store ○ AUS 174-175 D 6
Rankin ○ USA (IL) 274-275 L 4
Rankin ○ USA (OK) 264-265 E 3
Rankin ○ USA (TX) 266-267 F 2
Rankin Inlet ≈ 30-31 X 4
Rankin Inlet ○ CDN 30-31 X 4
Rankin's Pass ▲ ZA 220-221 H 2
Rankins Springs ○ AUS 180-181 J 2
Rankoshi ○ J 152-153 J 3
Rannee ○ RUS 96-97 H 8
Rannes ○ AUS 178-179 L 3
Rann of Kachchh ⚍ IND 138-139 B 7

Rano o WAN 204-205 H 3
Ranobe ~ RM 222-223 D 6
Ranohira o RM 222-223 D 9
Ranoke o CDN (ONT) 236-237 G 2
Ranoketang o RI 164-165 J 3
Ranomaeto o RI 164-165 H 6
Ranomafana o RM 222-223 E 10
Ranomena o RM 222-223 E 9
Ranong o THA 158-159 E 6
Ranongga ⌒ SOL 184 I c 3
Ranopiso o RM 222-223 E 10
Ranot o THA 158-159 F 7
Ranotsara Avaratra o RM 222-223 E 9
Ranquil, Caleta ≈ 78-79 C 4
Ranquil-Có o RA 78-79 E 4
Ranquil Norte o RA 78-79 E 4
Ransiki o RI 166-167 H 2
Ransom o USA (KS) 262-263 G 6
Ransom o USA (MI) 272-273 E 6
Rantabe o RM (TMA) 222-223 F 5
Rantabe ~ RM 222-223 F 5
Rantau o RI 164-165 D 5
Rantau (Tebingtinggi), Pulau ⌒ RI 162-163 E 4
Rantaubalai o RI 164-165 D 5
Rantaupanjang o RI 162-163 E 5
Rantauparangin o RI 162-163 D 4
Rantauprapat o RI 162-163 C 3
Rantaupulut o RI 162-163 K 5
Rantberge ▲ NAM 220-221 C 1
Rantemario, Gunung ▲ RI 164-165 G 5
Rantepao o RI 164-165 F 5
Rantoul o USA (IL) 274-275 K 4
Rantyirrity Point ▲ AUS 174-175 C 4
Ranua o FIN 88-89 J 4
Ranya o KSA 132-133 C 3
Ranya, Wādī ~ KSA 132-133 C 3
Rao o SN 196-197 B 7
Raohe o VRC 150-151 J 4
Raoping o VRC 156-157 K 5
Rapa ⌒ F 13 N 5
Rapa, Ponta do ▲ BR 74-75 F 6
Rapallo o I 100-101 B 2
Rāpar o IND 138-139 C 8
Rapel, Río ~ RCH 78-79 D 2
Rapelje o USA (MT) 250-251 K 6
Raper, Cabo ▲ RCH 80 C 3
Raper, Cape ▲ CDN 28-29 G 2
Rapidan River ~ USA (VA) 280-281 H 5
Rapid City o CDN (MAN) 234-235 C 4
Rapid City o USA (MI) 272-273 D 3
Rapid City o USA (SD) 260-261 C 2
Rapide-Blanc o CDN (QUE) 236-237 P 5
Rapide-Deux o CDN (QUE) 236-237 K 5
Rapide-Sept o CDN (QUE) 236-237 K 5
Rapid of the Drowned ~ CDN 30-31 G 6
Rapidos Coemani ~ CO 64-65 F 2
Rapid River ~ CDN 30-31 E 6
Rapid River o USA (MI) 270-271 M 5
Rapid River ~ USA (MN) 270-271 D 2
Rapids o USA 20-21 S 5
Rapids City o USA (IL) 274-275 H 3
Rāpina o EST 94-95 K 2
Rapla o·· EST 94-95 J 2
Raposa o BR 68-69 F 3
Raposa Serra do Sol, Área Indígena X BR 62-63 D 3
Rappang o RI 164-165 F 5
Rapti ~ IND 142-143 C 2
Rapulo, Río ~ BOL 70-71 D 4
Rapur o IND 140-141 H 3
Rapu-Rapu Island ⌒ RP 160-161 F 6
Raqdalin o LAR 192-193 D 1
Raqqa, ar- ☆ SYR 128-129 H 5
Raquette River ~ USA (NY) 278-279 G 4
Raragala Island ⌒ AUS 174-175 D 2
Rare ~ EAK 212-213 G 5
Rarotonga ⌒ NZ 13 M 5
Rasa, Punta ▲ RA 78-79 H 6
Rašaant o MAU 146-147 K 2
Rašaant = Ulaanšivèèt o MAU 148-149 F 4
Rasa Island ⌒ RP 160-161 C 8
Rasakān o IR 128-129 L 4
Ra's al-'Ain ☆ SYR 128-129 J 4
Ra's al-Barr o ET 194-195 E 2
Ra's al Hilāl o LAR 192-193 K 1
Rasāťin, ar- ▲ JOR 130-131 F 1
Ras Attabil o LAR 192-193 E 2
Rasawi o RI 166-167 H 3
Rasčënënnyj hrebet ▲ RUS 112-113 S 5
Raseiniai ☆·· LT 94-95 H 4
Ras el Erg, Hassi < DZ 190-191 D 6
Rās el Mā o RMM 196-197 H 6
Rasgado o BR 66-67 D 5
Ra's Gārib o ET 194-195 F 3
Rasha o VRC 144-145 M 5
Rashād o SUD 206-207 K 3
Rāsib, Ra's ▲ KSA 132-133 B 5
Ra's Ibn Hānī' ▲ SYR 128-129 F 5
Rašid o· ET 194-195 E 2
Rašid, Ğabal ▲ SYR 128-129 G 5
Rašid, Maşabb ~ ET 194-195 E 2
Rašidiya o SYR 128-129 J 4
Rāsipuram o IND 140-141 H 5
Rasirik o PNG 183 G 2
Rasi Salai o THA 158-159 H 3
Rāsk o IR 134-135 J 5
Raška o YU 100-101 H 3
Rās Kōh ▲ PK 134-135 L 4
Raskovoj, imeni o RUS 120-121 M 2
Ras Lanuf o LAR 192-193 H 2
Ra's Madhar, Ğabal ▲ KSA 130-131 E 5
Rasm al-Arwām, Sabhat o SYR 128-129 G 5
Ra's Muhammad National Park ⊥ ET 194-195 G 4
Rasmussen Basin ≈ 24-25 Y 6
Raso, Ilhéu ⌒ CV 202-203 B 5
Rasoabe, Farihy o RM 222-223 F 7
Raso da Caterina ▲ BR 68-69 J 6
Rason Lake o AUS 176-177 H 4
Ra's oš-Šatt ▲ IR 134-135 D 4
Raspberry Island ⌒ USA 22-23 U 3
Rasra o IND 142-143 C 3
Rass, ar- o KSA 130-131 H 5
Rašša o Y 132-133 E 6
Rass Ajdir o TN 192-193 D 1
Rasskazovo o RUS 94-95 R 5
Rassoha ~ RUS 108-109 b 6
Rassoha ~ RUS 110-111 d 5
Rassoha ~ RUS 110-111 b 7
Rassoha ~ RUS 110-111 G 4
Rassošina ~ RUS 120-121 S 5
Rasšua, ostrov ⌒ RUS 122-123 P 5
Rašt ☆· IR 128-129 N 4
Rastān, ar- ☆ SYR 128-129 G 5
Rastatt o· D 92-93 K 4
Raštḥvār o IR 134-135 H 1
Rāstoci o RO 102-103 C 4
Rastorgueva, ostrov ⌒ RUS 108-109 V 4
Rastro ▲ MEX 50-51 K 5
Rasu, Monte ▲ I 100-101 B 4
Rasūlnagar o PK 138-139 D 3
Ratangarh o IND 138-139 E 5
Rätansbyn o S 86-87 G 5
Ratcatchers Lake o AUS 180-181 G 2
Ratcha Buri o THA 158-159 E 4
Ratchford Creek ~ CDN (BC) 230-231 L 2
Ratcliff o USA (TX) 268-269 E 5
Ratcliff City o USA (OK) 264-265 G 4
Rat Creek ~ CDN (ALB) 232-233 C 2
Ratewo, Pulau ⌒ RI 166-167 H 3
Rāth o IND 138-139 G 7
Rathbon Ø ⌒ GRØ 26-27 p 8
Rathbun Lake o USA (IA) 274-275 E 4
Rathdrum o USA (ID) 250-251 C 4
Rathedaung o MYA 142-143 H 5
Rathenow o D 92-93 M 2
Rathtrevor Beach ∴· CDN (BC) 230-231 E 4
Rathwell o CDN (MAN) 234-235 E 5
Ratibor = Racibórz o PL 92-93 P 3
Rätische Alpen ▲ CH 92-93 K 5
Rat Island ⌒ USA 22-23 F 7
Rat Islands ⌒ USA 22-23 D 6
Rat Lake o CDN 34-35 G 2
Ratlām o IND 138-139 E 8
Ratmanova, ostrov ⌒ RUS 112-113 Q 4
Ratnachuli ▲ NEP 144-145 E 6
Ratnapura o CL 140-141 J 7
Ratne o UA 102-103 D 2
Rato, Igarapé do ~ BR 66-67 J 5
Ratodero o PK 138-139 B 6
Raton o USA (NM) 256-257 L 2
Raton Pass ▲ USA (CO) 254-255 L 6
Rat River ~ CDN 20-21 W 3
Ratta o RUS 114-115 R 3
Ratta ~ RUS 114-115 S 3
Rattan o USA (OK) 264-265 J 4
Rattaphum o THA 158-159 F 7
Rattlesnake Creek ~ USA (KS) 262-263 G 7
Rattling Brook o CDN (NFL) 242-243 M 3
Rättvik o S 86-87 G 6
Ratz, Mount ▲ CDN 32-33 D 3
Ratzeburg o· D 92-93 L 2
Rau o RI 162-163 C 4
Rau, Pulau ⌒ RI 164-165 L 2
Raub o MAL 162-163 D 3
Rauch o RA 78-79 K 4
Raučua ~ RUS 112-113 P 2
Raučuanskij hrebet ▲ RUS 112-113 O 2
Rauḍa, ar- o KSA 130-131 J 5
Rauḍa, ar- o Y 132-133 D 6
Rauḍa, ar- o Y 132-133 E 6
Raudales de Malpaso o MEX 52-53 H 3
Rauḍatain, ar- o KWT 130-131 K 3
Rauḍat Habbās o KSA 130-131 J 3
Raufarhöfn o IS 86-87 f 1
Raukumara Plain ≃ 182 F 1
Raukumara Range ▲ NZ 182 F 3
Raul, ar- o UAE 134-135 G 6
Raul Pialo o BR 76-77 K 6
Raul Soares o BR 72-73 J 6
Rauma o··· FIN 88-89 F 6
Rauma ~ N 86-87 C 5
Raung, Gunung ▲ RI 168 B 7
Raunsepna o PNG 183 F 3
Raurkela o· IND 142-143 D 4
Rausu o J 152-153 L 2
Rausu-d. ▲ J 152-153 L 2
Rāut ~ MD 102-103 E 3
Rāut ~ MD 102-103 F 4
Rautavaara o FIN 88-89 K 5
Ravalli o USA (MT) 250-251 E 4
Rāvand o IR 134-135 D 1
Rāvand, Čam-e ~ IR 134-135 B 1
Ravanel o USA (SC) 284-285 K 4
Ravānsar o IR 134-135 B 1
Rāvar o IR 134-135 G 3
Rava-Rus'ka o UA 102-103 C 2
Ravat o KS 136-137 M 5
Ravavaé Inseln ⌒ F 13 N 5
Ravendale o CDN (SAS) 232-233 P 2
Ravendale o USA (CA) 246-247 E 3
Ravenna ☆·· I 100-101 D 2
Ravenna o USA (NE) 262-263 H 3
Ravenna o USA (OH) 280-281 E 2
Ravensborne Creek ~ AUS 178-179 H 3
Ravensburg o· D 92-93 K 5
Ravenscrag o CDN (SAS) 232-233 J 6
Ravenshoe o AUS 174-175 H 5
Ravensthorpe o AUS 176-177 F 6
Ravenswood ∴ AUS 174-175 J 7
Ravenswood o USA (WV) 280-281 E 5
Rāvi ~ IND 138-139 F 3
Rāvi ~ IND 138-139 E 3
Rāvi ~ PK 138-139 E 4
Rāvi ~ PK 138-139 D 4
Ravn, Kap ▲ GRØ 28-29 a 2
Ravnina o TM 136-137 H 6
Ravo ~ SOL 184 I e 4
Rāvulādiki o IND 140-141 G 3
Rāwa o IRQ 128-129 J 5
Rawa Aopa-Watumohae National Park ⊥· RI 164-165 H 6
Rawalak o PK 138-139 D 3
Rāwalpindi o PK 138-139 D 3
Rawalpind Lake o CDN 30-31 M 3
Rawa Mazowiecka o PL 92-93 Q 3
Rāwandūz ☆ IRQ 128-129 L 4
Rawang o MAL 162-163 D 3
Rawarra ~ RI 166-167 G 2
Rawas o RI (IRJ) 166-167 G 2
Rawas ~ RI 162-163 E 6
Rawāwais, Wādī ~ LAR 192-193 F 2
Rawicz o· PL 92-93 O 3
Rawlinna o AUS 176-177 H 5
Rawlins o USA (WY) 252-253 L 5
Rawlinson, Mount ▲ AUS 176-177 J 2
Rawlinson Range ▲ AUS 176-177 J 2
Rawson ☆ RA 78-79 G 7
Rawu o VRC 144-145 L 6
Rawua o RI 164-165 H 5
Rāwuk, ar- o Y 132-133 F 6
Ray o USA (MN) 270-271 E 2
Ray o USA (ND) 258-259 D 3
Ray, Cape ▲ CDN (NFL) 242-243 J 5
Raya, Gunung ▲ RI 162-163 K 5
Raya, Tanjung ▲ RI (ACE) 162-163 B 3
Raya, Tanjung ▲ RI (SUS) 162-163 G 5
Rayachoti o IND 140-141 H 3
Rāyadrug o IND 140-141 G 3
Rāyagada o IND 142-143 C 6
Rayakottai o IND 140-141 H 4
Rayao, Raudal de ~ CO 60-61 G 6
Rāyāt o IRQ 128-129 L 4
Raybiraj o NEP 144-145 F 7
Rayborn o USA (TX) 268-269 F 6
Rāyin o IR 134-135 G 4
Raymond o CDN (ALB) 232-233 F 6
Raymond o USA (IL) 274-275 J 5
Raymond o USA (ME) 278-279 L 5
Raymond o USA (MS) 268-269 K 4
Raymond o USA (MT) 250-251 P 3
Raymond o USA (WA) 244-245 B 4
Raymond Terrace o AUS 180-181 L 2
Raymondville o USA (TX) 266-267 K 7
Raymore o CDN (SAS) 232-233 O 4
Ray Mountains ▲ USA 20-21 O 4
Rayne o USA (LA) 268-269 H 6
Raynesford o USA (MT) 250-251 J 4
Rayo ▲ MEX 50-51 G 5
Rayo Cortado o RA 76-77 F 6
Rayón o MEX (CHI) 52-53 H 3
Rayón o MEX (SLP) 50-51 K 7
Rayón o MEX (SON) 50-51 D 3
Rayong o THA 158-159 F 4
Raypatan o IND 140-141 E 2
Ray Roberts, Lake o USA (TX) 264-265 G 5
Raytown o USA (MO) 274-275 D 6
Rayville o USA (LA) 268-269 J 4
Rayyān, ar- o Q 134-135 D 6
Rāz o IR 136-137 E 6
Raz, Pointe du ⌣ F 90-91 E 7
Razan o IR 128-129 N 5
Razdan o AR 128-129 L 2
Razdol'noe o RUS 122-123 D 7
Rāzeqān o IR 128-129 N 5
Razgort o RUS 88-89 U 5
Razgrad ☆ BG 102-103 E 6
Razi o· IR 136-137 D 6
Razim, Lacul o RO 102-103 F 5
Razlog o BG 102-103 C 7
Razmak o PK 138-139 B 3
Ré, Île de ⌒ F 90-91 G 8
Reading o GB 90-91 G 6
Reading o USA (IL) 274-275 K 3
Reading o USA (OH) 280-281 B 4
Reading o· USA (PA) 280-281 L 3
Readstown o USA (WI) 274-275 H 1
Reagan o USA (TX) 266-267 L 2
Real, Cordillera ▲ BOL 70-71 C 4
Real, Cordillera ▲ EC 64-65 C 3
Real, Estero ~ NIC 52-53 L 5
Real, Río ~ BR 68-69 K 7
Real de Santa María, El o PA 52-53 F 7
Realeza o BR 72-73 J 6
Realico o RA 78-79 G 3
Realitos o USA (TX) 266-267 J 6
Reardan o USA (WA) 244-245 H 3
Rebalse, El o MEX 50-51 G 3
Rebbenesøy ⌒ N 86-87 J 1
Rebecca, Lake o AUS 176-177 G 5
Rebecca, Mount ▲ AUS 176-177 C 3
Reboly o RUS 88-89 L 5
Rebordelo, Ponta ▲ BR 62-63 K 5
Rebro, mys ▲ RUS 120-121 U 3
Rebun o J 152-153 J 2
Rebun-suido ≈ 152-153 J 2
Rebun-tō ⌒ J 152-153 J 2
Recalde o RA 78-79 J 4
Rečane o RUS 94-95 M 3
Recheáchic o MEX 50-51 F 4
Rečica = Rèčyca o BY 94-95 M 5
Recife ☆ BR (AMA) 66-67 B 6
Recife ☆ BR (PER) 68-69 L 6
Recife, Kaap ▲ ZA 220-221 G 7
Recife do Silva ⌒ BR 68-69 F 2
Recife Grande, Cachoeira ~ BR 70-71 H 2
Recife Manuel Luís ⌒ BR 68-69 F 2
Récifs, Îles = Reef Islands ⌒ VAN 184 II a 1
Rečka, Bofšaja ~ RUS 124-125 O 2
Recknitz ~ D 92-93 M 1
Reco o CDN (ALB) 232-233 B 2
Reconquista o RA 76-77 H 5
Recreio o BR 72-73 J 6
Recreo o RA 76-77 E 5
Rector o USA (AR) 276-277 E 4
Recuay o PE 64-65 D 6
Rèčyca o BY 94-95 M 5
Recz o PL 92-93 N 2
Redang, Pulau ⌒ MAL (TER) 162-163 E 2
Redbank o AUS 180-181 G 4
Red Bank o CDN (NB) 240-241 K 4
Red Bank o USA (NJ) 280-281 M 3
Red Bank o USA (TN) 276-277 K 5
Red Bank 4 Indian Reserve X· CDN (NB) 240-241 K 4
Red Basin = Sichuan Pendi ∸ VRC 156-157 D 2
Red Bay o CDN 38-39 Q 3
Red Bay o CDN (NFL) 242-243 M 1
Red Bay o USA (AL) 284-285 B 2
Redberry Lake o CDN (SAS) 232-233 L 3
Red Bird o USA (WY) 252-253 O 3
Red Bluff o USA (CA) 246-247 C 3
Red Bluff Lake < USA (TX) 266-267 D 2
Red Boiling Springs o USA (TN) 276-277 K 4
Redbridge o CDN (ONT) 238-239 F 2
Red Bud o USA (IL) 274-275 J 6
Redbush o USA (KY) 276-277 N 3
Red Butte ▲ USA (AZ) 256-257 C 3
Redby o USA (MN) 270-271 D 3
Red Cliff ▲ AUS 178-179 C 2
Redcliff o CDN (ALB) 232-233 H 5
Redcliff o ZW 218-219 E 4
Redcliffe, Mount ▲ AUS 176-177 F 4
Red Cliff Indian Reservation X USA (WI) 270-271 G 4
Red Cliffs o AUS 180-181 G 3
Red Cloud o USA (NE) 262-263 H 4
Red Creek ~ USA (MS) 268-269 L 6
Red Deer o CDN (ALB) 232-233 E 3
Red Deer Creek ~ CDN (BC) 228-229 O 2
Red Deer Hill o CDN (SAS) 232-233 N 2
Red Deer Lake o CDN 34-35 F 4
Red Deer River ~ CDN (ALB) 232-233 E 3
Red Deer River ~ CDN (SAS) 232-233 Q 3
Red Deer Valley Badlands ∸ CDN (ALB) 232-233 F 4
Reddersburg o ZA 220-221 H 4
Reddick o USA (IL) 274-275 K 3
Redding o USA (CA) 246-247 C 3
Redding Creek ~ CDN (BC) 230-231 N 4
Reddit o CDN (ONT) 234-235 J 5
Redditch o GB 90-91 G 5
Redditt o CDN (ONT) 234-235 J 5
Red Earth o CDN (SAS) 232-233 P 2
Redearth Creek ~ CDN 32-33 N 3
Redenção o BR (CEA) 68-69 J 4
Redenção o BR (P) 68-69 D 5
Redenção do Gurguéira o BR 68-69 F 6
Redentora o BR 74-75 D 6
Redeyef o TN 190-191 G 3
Red Feather Lakes o USA (CO) 254-255 K 3
Redfield o CDN (SAS) 232-233 L 3
Redfield o USA (AR) 276-277 C 6
Redfield o USA (NY) 278-279 F 5
Redfield o USA (SD) 260-261 H 2
Redford o USA (TX) 266-267 C 4
Red Harbour o CDN (NFL) 242-243 N 5
Red Hill o AUS 172-173 C 7
Red Hills ▲ USA (KS) 262-263 G 7
Red Hook o USA (NY) 280-281 N 2
Red House o USA (VA) 280-281 H 6
Rédics o H 92-93 O 5
Redig o USA (SD) 260-261 C 1
Red Indian Lake ~ CDN (NFL) 242-243 L 4
Redington o USA (AZ) 256-257 E 6
Red Jacket o CDN (SAS) 232-233 R 5
Redkey o USA (IN) 274-275 N 4
Redkino o RUS 94-95 P 3
Redknife River ~ CDN 30-31 K 5
Red Lake o CDN (BC) 230-231 J 3
Red Lake o CDN (ONT) 234-235 K 3
Red Lake o CDN (ONT) 234-235 J 3
Red Lake o USA (AZ) 256-257 C 3
Red Lake o USA (AZ) 256-257 E 2
Red Lake o USA (AZ) 256-257 A 3
Red Lake Falls o USA (MN) 270-271 B 3
Red Lake Indian Reservation X USA (MN) 270-271 C 1
Red Lake River ~ USA (MN) 270-271 C 2
Red Lake Road o CDN (ONT) 234-235 K 5
Red Lake State Management Area ⊥ USA (MN) 270-271 C 2
Redlands o USA (CA) 248-249 G 5
Red Lion o USA (PA) 280-281 K 4
Red Lodge o USA (MT) 250-251 K 6
Redmond o AUS 176-177 D 7
Redmond o USA (OR) 244-245 D 6
Redmond o USA (WA) 244-245 C 3
Red Mountain o USA (CA) 248-249 G 4
Red Mountain ▲ USA (MT) 250-251 G 4
Red Mountain Pass ▲ USA (CO) 254-255 H 6
Red Oak o USA (IA) 274-275 C 3
Redoak o USA (OH) 280-281 C 5
Redon o F 90-91 F 8
Redonda ⌒ AG 56 D 3
Redonda, Isla ⌒ YV 60-61 L 3
Redonda Bay o CDN (BC) 230-231 E 3
Redonda Island ⌒ CDN (BC) 230-231 E 3
Redondela, La o E 98-99 C 3
Redondo o P 98-99 D 5
Redoupt Volcano ▲ USA 20-21 O 6
Redoute Flatters · RN 198-199 C 2
Red Owl o USA (SD) 260-261 D 2
Red Pass o CDN (BC) 228-229 Q 3
Red Pheasant o CDN (SAS) 232-233 K 3
Red River ~ AUS 174-175 G 5
Red River ~ CDN 30-31 E 4
Red River ~ USA (KY) 276-277 M 3
Red River ~ USA (LA) 268-269 H 5
Red River ~ USA (OK) 264-265 F 4
Red River ~ USA (TN) 276-277 H 4
Red River ~ USA (TX) 264-265 G 5
Red River of the North ~ USA (MN) 270-271 A 2
Red Rock o CDN (ONT) 234-235 P 6
Red Rock o USA (AZ) 256-257 D 6
Red Rock o USA (AZ) 256-257 F 2
Red Rock o USA (OK) 264-265 G 2
Red Rock o USA (PA) 280-281 K 2
Red Rock o USA (TX) 266-267 K 4
Redrock Coulee ~ USA (MT) 250-251 K 3
Red Rock Creek ~ USA (OK) 264-265 G 2
Redrock Lake o CDN 30-31 M 3
Red Rock Pass ▲ USA (ID) 252-253 G 2
Red Rock Pass ▲ USA (NV) 246-247 K 4
Red Rock Reservoir < USA (IA) 274-275 E 3
Red Rock River ~ USA (MT) 250-251 G 7
Red Rose o CDN (MAN) 234-235 F 3
Redscar Bay ≈ 183 D 5
Red Sea ≈ 9 G 3
Red Shirt o USA (SD) 260-261 D 3
Red Spring o USA (MO) 276-277 B 4
Red Springs o USA (NC) 282-283 H 6
Redstone o CDN (BC) 228-229 L 4
Redstone o USA (MI) 272-273 E 4
Redstone Arsenal xx USA (AL) 284-285 D 2
Redstone River ~ CDN 30-31 F 4
Red Sucker Lake o CDN 34-35 K 3
Red Sucker River ~ CDN 34-35 K 3
Redsucker River ~ CDN (ONT) 236-237 G 3
Redut o KA 96-97 H 10
Redvers o CDN (SAS) 232-233 R 6
Redwater o CDN (ALB) 232-233 E 2
Redwater Creek ~ USA (MT) 250-251 O 4
Red Willow o CDN (ALB) 232-233 F 3
Red Willow Creek ~ USA (NE) 262-263 F 4
Redwillow Rapids ~ CDN 30-31 S 6
Redwillow River ~ CDN 32-33 L 4
Red Wing o USA (MN) 270-271 F 6
Redwood o USA (MS) 268-269 K 4
Redwood City o USA (CA) 248-249 B 2
Redwood Empire ∸ USA (CA) 246-247 B 2
Redwood Falls o USA (MN) 270-271 C 6
Redwood National Park ⊥··· USA (CA) 246-247 A 2
Redwood Valley o USA (CA) 246-247 B 4
Ree, Lough o IRL 90-91 D 5
Reed o USA (OK) 264-265 E 4
Reed Bank ≃ 160-161 B 7
Reed City o USA (MI) 272-273 D 4
Reeder o USA (ND) 258-259 E 5
Reed Lake o CDN 34-35 F 3
Reedley o USA (CA) 248-249 E 3
Reedpoint o USA (MT) 250-251 K 6
Reedsburg o USA (WI) 274-275 H 1
Reedsport o USA (OR) 244-245 A 7
Reedville o USA (VA) 280-281 K 6
Reedy Creek ~ AUS 180-181 F 4
Reedy Creek ~ USA (FL) 286-287 H 3
Reedy River ~ USA (SC) 284-285 H 2
Reedy Springs o AUS 174-175 H 6
Reef Icefield ⊂ CDN (BC) 228-229 Q 3
Reef Islands = Îles Récifs ⌒ VAN 184 II a 1
Reefton o NZ 182 C 5
Reelfoot Lake o USA (TN) 276-277 F 4
Reese o USA (MI) 272-273 F 4
Reese River ~ USA (NV) 246-247 H 4
Reeves o USA (LA) 268-269 G 6
Refahiye ☆ TR 128-129 H 3
Reform o USA (AL) 284-285 B 3
Reforma, La o C 54-55 D 4
Reforma, La o RA 78-79 K 3
Reforma, La o YV 62-63 D 2
Reforma, Río ~ MEX 50-51 E 4
Reftinskij o RUS 96-97 M 5
Refuge Cove o CDN (BC) 230-231 E 3
Refuge Headquarters o USA (OR) 244-245 F 8
Refugio o RCH 78-79 D 5
Refugio o USA (TX) 266-267 K 5
Refugio, El o MEX 50-51 D 5
Refugio, Isla ⌒ RCH 78-79 C 7
Refugio, Punta ▲ MEX 50-51 C 3
Refugio Beach · USA (CA) 248-249 D 5
Refugio la Faja o RA 78-79 E 3
Rega ~ PL 92-93 N 2
Regaia o MA 188-189 J 3
Regalo o BR 68-69 F 6
Regalo, El o YV 60-61 G 3
Regen o D (BAY) 92-93 M 4
Regen ~ D 92-93 M 4
Regência o BR 72-73 L 5
Regência, Pontal de ▲ BR 72-73 L 5
Regeneração o BR 68-69 G 5
Regensburg o D 92-93 M 4
Regent o CDN (MAN) 234-235 C 5
Regent o USA (ND) 258-259 E 5
Regente Feijó o BR 72-73 E 7
Régestān ∸ AFG 134-135 L 3
Reggane o DZ 190-191 C 7
Reggio o USA (LA) 268-269 L 7
Réggio di Calábria o I 100-101 E 5
Réggio nell'Emília ☆ I 100-101 C 2
Reggou o MA 188-189 K 4
Reghin o RO 102-103 D 4
Regina ☆ CDN (SAS) 232-233 O 5
Regina o F 62-63 H 3
Regina Beach o CDN (SAS) 232-233 O 5
Registro o BR 74-75 G 5
Regocijo o MEX 50-51 G 6
Regola o RI 166-167 E 6
Regone o MOC 218-219 K 3
Regresso, Cachoeira do ~ BR 62-63 G 6
Reguengos de Monsaraz o P 98-99 D 5
Regway o CDN (SAS) 232-233 O 6
Rehli o IND 138-139 G 8
Rehoboth o NAM 220-221 C 1
Rehoboth Bay ≈ USA 280-281 L 5
Rehovot ☆ IL 130-131 D 2
Reichenberg = Liberec o· CZ 92-93 N 3
Reid Lake o CDN (BC) 228-229 L 3
Reidsville o USA (GA) 284-285 H 4
Reidsville o USA (NC) 282-283 H 4
Reigate o GB 90-91 G 6
Reims ☆··· F 90-91 K 7
Reina Adelaida, Archipiélago ⌒ RCH 80 C 6
Reindeer Depot o CDN 20-21 Y 2
Reindeer Island ⌒ CDN (MAN) 234-235 E 2
Reindeer Lake o CDN 34-35 E 2
Reindeer River ~ CDN 34-35 E 3
Reindeer Station o USA 20-21 K 3
Reine o N 86-87 F 3
Reine, La o CDN (QUE) 236-237 J 4
Reinga, Cape ▲ NZ 182 D 1
Reinosa o· E 98-99 E 3
Reinsdyrflya ⌣ N 84-85 H 3
Reisaelva ~ N 86-87 K 2
Reisa nasjonalpark ⊥ N 86-87 K 2
Reisjärvi o FIN 88-89 H 5
Reisterstown o USA (MD) 280-281 K 4
Reitoca o HN 52-53 L 5
Reitz o ZA 220-221 J 3
Reivilo o ZA 220-221 G 3
Rejaf o SUD 206-207 K 6
Rejdovo o RUS 122-123 N 6
Rekinniskaja guba ≈ RUS 120-121 U 3
Rekkam, Plateau du ▲ MA 188-189 K 4
Relem, Cerro ▲ RA 78-79 D 5
Reliance o CDN 30-31 P 4
Reliance o USA (SD) 260-261 G 3
Reliance o USA (WY) 252-253 J 5
Relizane ☆ DZ 190-191 C 3
Rellano o MEX 50-51 G 4
Relógio o BR 74-75 E 5
Relok, Kampung o MAL 162-163 E 2
Reloncaví, Seno de ≈ 78-79 C 6
Remada o TN 190-191 H 4
Remanso o BR (AMA) 66-67 C 6
Remanso o BR (BAH) 68-69 G 6
Remarkable, Mount ▲ AUS (QLD) 174-175 E 7
Remarkable, Mount ▲ AUS (SA) 180-181 E 2
Remarkable, Mount ▲ AUS (WA) 172-173 H 4
Rembang o RI 168 D 3
Rembang, Teluk ≈ 168 D 3
Remboken o· RI 164-165 J 3
Remedios o C 54-55 F 3
Remedios o PA 52-53 D 7
Remedios, Río Los ~ MEX 50-51 F 5
Remel El Abiod ▲ TN 190-191 G 5
Remennikovo o RUS 94-95 L 3
Remer o USA (MN) 270-271 E 3
Remešk o IR 134-135 H 5
Remígio o BR 68-69 L 5
Remington o USA (IN) 274-275 L 4
Remire o F 62-63 H 3
Remiremont o F 90-91 L 7
Remolino, El o MEX 50-51 J 3
Remolino, Puerto o RA 80 G 7
Rena ☆ N 86-87 E 6
Renaico, Río ~ RCH 78-79 C 4
Renard, Rivière-au- o CDN (QUE) 240-241 L 2
Renata o CDN (BC) 230-231 L 4
Renca o RA 78-79 G 2
Renceni o LV 94-95 J 3
Renčin humbe = Zöölön o MAU 148-149 E 2
Rencontre East o CDN (NFL) 242-243 N 5
Rencoret o RCH 76-77 C 2
Rende o· RI 168 E 7
Rend Lake o USA (IL) 274-275 J 6
Rendova ⌒ SOL 184 I c 3
Rendsburg o· D 92-93 K 1
René Brunell Provincial Park ⊥ CDN (ONT) 236-237 F 3
Renews o CDN (NFL) 242-243 Q 6
Renfrew o CDN (ONT) 238-239 J 3
Rengas, Tanjung ▲ RI 164-165 F 5
Rengat o RI 162-163 E 5
Rengel o RI 168 E 3
Rengleng River ~ CDN 20-21 Y 3
Rengo o RCH 78-79 D 3
Renhe o VRC 154-155 E 6
Renhua o VRC 156-157 H 4
Renhuai o VRC 156-157 E 3
Reni ☆ UA 102-103 F 5
Reni, Pulau ⌒ RI 166-167 F 1
Renigunta o IND 140-141 H 4
Reñihue, Fiordo ≈ 78-79 C 7
Reninjauan o RI 162-163 D 4
Renland ∸ GRØ 26-27 m 8
Renmark o AUS 180-181 F 3
Renmei o VRC 154-155 B 6
Rennell, Islas ⌒ RCH 80 C 5
Rennell Sound ≈ CDN 228-229 B 3
Renner Springs o AUS 174-175 B 6
Rennes ☆· F 90-91 G 7
Rennick Glacier ⊂ ARK 16 F 17
Rennie o CDN (MAN) 234-235 H 5
Rennie Lake o CDN 30-31 R 5
Reno o USA (MN) 270-271 G 7
Reno o USA (NV) 246-247 F 4
Reno, El o USA (OK) 264-265 G 3
Renosterrivier ~ ZA 220-221 H 3
Renosterrivier ~ ZA 220-221 E 5
Renous o CDN (NB) 240-241 K 4
Renovo o USA (PA) 280-281 J 2
Renqiu o VRC 154-155 K 2
Rens Fiord ≈ 26-27 C 3
Renshi o VRC 154-155 E 6
Rensselaer o USA (IN) 274-275 L 4
Renton o USA (WA) 244-245 C 3
Rentoul River ~ PNG 183 B 4
Renville o USA (MN) 270-271 C 6
Renwick o USA (IA) 274-275 E 2
Réo o· BF 202-203 J 3
Reo o RI 168 E 7
Reodhar o IND 138-139 D 7
Réole, la o F 90-91 G 9
Repalle o IND 140-141 J 2
Repartimento o BR (AMA) 66-67 G 4
Repartimento o BR (AMA) 66-67 J 4
Repartimento, Corredeira do ~ BR 68-69 C 5
Repentigny o CDN (QUE) 238-239 M 3
Repetekskij zapovednik ⊥ TM 136-137 H 5
Represa da Boa Esperança < BR 68-69 F 5
Represa de São Simão < BR 72-73 E 5
Republic o USA (MI) 270-271 L 4
Republic o USA (MO) 276-277 B 3
Republic o USA (WA) 244-245 G 2
Republican River ~ USA (NE) 262-263 H 4
Repulse Bay ≈ 24-25 c 7
Repulse Bay o CDN 24-25 c 7
Repununi River ~ GUY 62-63 E 4
Reque o PE 64-65 C 5
Requena o· E 98-99 G 5
Requena o PE 64-65 F 4
Requena o YV 60-61 J 3
Rera o BR 62-63 D 3
Reriutaba o BR 68-69 H 4
Reşadiye o TR 128-129 B 4
Reşadiye ☆ TR 128-129 G 2
Reşadiye Yarımadası ⌣ TR 128-129 B 4
Reschenpass = Passo di Rèsia ▲ I 100-101 C 1
Reseida, Wādī ~ SUD 200-201 F 2
Resen o MK 100-101 H 4
Resende o BR 72-73 H 7
Reserva o BR 74-75 E 5
Reserva o CO 64-65 F 2
Reserva Natural de Ría Formosa ⊥ P 98-99 D 6
Reserva Natural do Estuário do Sado ⊥ P 98-99 C 5
Reserve o CDN (SAS) 232-233 Q 3
Reserve o USA (KS) 262-263 L 5
Reserve o USA (MT) 250-251 P 3
Reserve o USA (NM) 256-257 G 5
Réserve d'Ashuapmushuan ⊥ CDN (QUE) 236-237 P 3
Réserve Faunique de Pipineau Labelle ⊥ CDN (QUE) 238-239 K 2
Réserve Faunique Mastigouche ⊥ CDN (QUE) 238-239 M 2
Réserve Faunique Rouge-Matawin ⊥ CDN (QUE) 238-239 L 2
Reserve Mines o CDN (NS) 240-241 P 4
Réservoir Baskatong < CDN (QUE) 238-239 K 2
Réservoir Manicouagan ⊥·· CDN 38-39 K 3
Rèsia, Passo di = Reschenpass ▲ I 100-101 C 1
Resistencia ☆ RA 76-77 H 4
Reşiţa ☆ RO 102-103 B 5
Resolute o CDN 24-25 Y 3
Resolution Island o CDN (NWT) 36-37 R 4
Resolution Island ⌒ CDN (NWT) 36-37 R 4
Resolution Island ⌒ NZ 182 A 6
Resource o CDN (SAS) 232-233 O 3
Respiro, El o YV 60-61 G 4
Resplendor o BR 72-73 K 5
Restauração o BR 62-63 D 5
Restauración o DOM 54-55 K 5
Resthaven Icefield ⊂ CDN (ALB) 228-229 P 3
Restigouche o CDN (QUE) 240-241 J 2
Restigouche Indian Reserve X· CDN (QUE) 240-241 H 2
Restigouche River ~ CDN (NB) 240-241 H 3
Restin, Punta ▲ PE 64-65 B 4
Restinga de Marambaia ⌣ BR 72-73 J 7
Restinga Seca o BR 74-75 D 7
Reston o CDN (MAN) 234-235 B 5
Restored Village · USA (IA) 274-275 G 4
Restoule o CDN (ONT) 238-239 F 2
Resurrection, Cape ▲ USA 20-21 Q 7
Retalhuleu ☆ GCA 52-53 J 4
Retallack o CDN (BC) 230-231 M 3
Retamo, El o RA 78-79 F 2
Retchel Head ▲ CDN 36-37 S 5
Retem, Oued ~ DZ 190-191 E 4
Retén Atalaya o RCH 78-79 D 2
Reten Laguna o RA 78-79 D 3
Rethel o F 90-91 K 7
Réthimno o GR 100-101 K 7
Reting · VRC 144-145 H 5
Retiro o BR (AMA) 66-67 D 4
Retiro o BR (MAT) 72-73 D 3
Retiro, El o YV 60-61 H 3
Retiro Baia Grande o BR 70-71 K 5
Retiro São Benedito o BR 70-71 J 5
Retlaw o CDN (ALB) 232-233 F 5
Retra o PK 138-139 C 4
Retreat o AUS 178-179 G 3
Return Islands ⌒ USA 20-21 Q 1
Réunion ⌒ F 224 B 7
Réunion, La ◘ F 224 C 7
Reus o E 98-99 H 4
Reutlingen o· D 92-93 K 4
Reva o USA (SD) 260-261 C 1
Reval = Tallinn ☆·· EST 94-95 J 2
Revda ☆ RUS 96-97 L 5
Reveca o RCH 76-77 B 2
Reveille Peak ▲ USA (NV) 248-249 H 2
Revello Channel ≈ 140-141 L 6
Revelstoke o CDN (BC) 230-231 L 3
Revelstoke, Lake o CDN (BC) 230-231 L 2
Reventon, El o MEX 50-51 J 6
Revenue o CDN (SAS) 232-233 K 3
Revés, El o MEX 50-51 H 4
Révia o MOC 218-219 J 1
Revilla Gigedo, Islas ⌒ MEX 50-51 A 7
Revillagigedo Channel ≈ 32-33 E 4
Revillagigedo Island ⌒ USA 32-33 E 4
Revillo o USA (SD) 260-261 K 1
Revoljucii, pik ▲ TJ 136-137 N 5
Revué ~ MOC 218-219 G 4
Rewa o IND 142-143 B 3
Reward o CDN (SAS) 232-233 J 3
Rewari o IND 138-139 F 5
Rewa River ~ FJI 184 III b 2
Rex, Mount ▲ ARK 16 F 29
Rexburg o USA (ID) 252-253 G 3
Rexford o USA (KS) 262-263 F 5
Rexford o USA (MT) 250-251 D 3
Rexton o CDN (NB) 240-241 L 4
Rey, Arroyo del ~ RA 76-77 H 5
Rey, El o RA 76-77 E 3
Rey, Isla de ⌒ PA 52-53 E 7
Rey, Laguna del o MEX 50-51 H 4
Rey, Mayo ~ CAM 206-207 B 4
Rey, Parque Nacional el ⊥ RA 76-77 E 3
Reyābād o IR 136-137 D 6
Rey Bouba o CAM 206-207 B 4
Reydon o USA (OK) 264-265 E 3
Reyes o BOL 70-71 D 4
Reyes, Point ▲ USA (CA) 246-247 B 5
Reyes, Point ▲ USA (CA) 248-249 A 2
Reyes, Punta ▲ CO 60-61 B 6
Reyes, Punta das ▲ RCH 76-77 B 3

Reyes Creek ▲ USA (CA) 248-249 E 5
Reyes Salgado, Los ○ MEX 52-53 C 2
Reyhanlı ☆ TR 128-129 G 4
Reykjanes Ridge ≃ 6-7 F 3
Reykjanestá ▲ IS 86-87 b 3
Reykjavík ○ CDN (MAN) 234-235 E 3
Reykjavík ★ • IS 86-87 c 2
Reynaud ○ CDN (SAS) 232-233 N 3
Reynolds ○ USA (GA) 284-285 F 4
Reynolds ○ USA (ID) 252-253 B 3
Reynolds ○ USA (IN) 274-275 L 4
Reynolds ○ USA (ND) 258-259 K 4
Reynoldsburg ○ USA (OH) 280-281 D 4
Reynolds Range ▲ AUS 172-173 L 7
Reynosa ○ MEX 50-51 K 4
Reyy ○ • IR 136-137 B 7
Rež ☆ RUS 96-97 M 5
Reza, gora ▲ TM 136-137 F 6
Rēzekne ☆ •• LV 94-95 K 3
Rezina ☆ MD 102-103 F 4
Rēznas ezers ○ • LV 94-95 K 3
Rezovo ○ BG 102-103 E 6
Režván Šahr ○ IR 128-129 N 4
Rhame ○ USA (ND) 258-259 D 5
Rharb ⊥ MA 188-189 H 3
Rharous ☆ RMM 196-197 L 5
Rhea ○ USA (OK) 264-265 E 3
Rhein ○ CDN (SAS) 232-233 Q 4
Rhein ～ D 92-93 J 3
Rheine ○ D 92-93 J 2
Rheinfall ～ •• CH 92-93 K 5
Rheinland-Pfalz ■ D 92-93 J 3
Rheinwaldhorn ▲ CH 92-93 K 5
Rhemilès ☾ DZ 188-189 J 6
Rhems ○ USA (SC) 284-285 L 3
Rheris, Oued ～ MA 188-189 J 5
Rhine ○ USA (GA) 284-285 G 5
Rhine = Rhein ～ D 92-93 K 4
Rhinelander ○ USA (WI) 270-271 J 5
Rhino Camp ○ EAU 212-213 C 2
Rhiou, Oued ～ DZ 190-191 C 3
Rhir, Cap ▲ MA 188-189 G 5
Rhode Island ■ USA (RI) 278-279 K 7
Rhode Island ⌒ USA (RI) 278-279 K 7
Rhodes Inyangani National Park ⊥ ZW 218-219 G 4
Rhodes Matopos National Park ⊥ ZW 218-219 E 5
Rhododendron ○ USA (OR) 244-245 D 5
Rhodope Mountains = Rodopi ▲ BG 102-103 C 7
Rhome ○ USA (TX) 264-265 G 5
Rhön ▲ D 92-93 K 3
Rhondda ○ GB 90-91 F 6
Rhône ～ CH 92-93 J 5
Rhône ～ F 90-91 K 10
Rhône-Alpes ■ F 90-91 K 9
Rhoraffa, Bir ☾ DZ 190-191 G 5
Rhoufi ○ DZ 190-191 F 3
Rhourd El Baguel ○ DZ 190-191 F 5
Rhum ⌒ GB 90-91 D 3
Rhumel, Oued ～ DZ 190-191 F 2
Rhyolite Ghost Town ∴ • USA (NV) 248-249 H 3
Riaba ○ GQ 210-211 B 2
Ría Celestún Parque Natural ⊥ MEX 52-53 J 1
Riachão ○ BR 68-69 E 5
Riachão, Rio ～ BR 68-69 G 5
Riachão das Neves ○ BR 68-69 F 7
Riachão do Banabuiú ○ BR 68-69 J 4
Riachão do Jacuípe ○ BR 68-69 J 7
Riacho de Santana ○ BR 72-73 J 2
Riacho do Sal ○ BR 68-69 J 6
Riacho dos Machados ○ BR 72-73 J 3
Riacho de los, Isla de los ⌒ RA 78-79 H 6
Riacho Seco ○ BR 68-69 J 6
Riákia ○ GR 100-101 J 4
Riamkanan, Danau ○ RI 164-165 D 5
Rianápolis ○ BR 72-73 F 3
Riangnom ○ SUD 206-207 K 4
Riaño, Embalse de ☾ E 98-99 E 3
Riau ■ RI 162-163 D 5
Riau, Kepulauan ⌒ RI 162-163 F 4
Ribadavia ○ • E 98-99 C 3
Ribadeo ○ E 98-99 D 3
Ribadesella ○ E 98-99 E 3
Ribah ○ WAN 204-205 F 3
Riban'i Manamby ▲ RM 222-223 D 9
Ribariće ○ YU 100-101 H 3
Ribas do Rio Pardo ○ BR 72-73 D 6
Ribāṭ, ar- ○ IRQ 128-129 J 5
Ribatejo ⊥ P 98-99 C 5
Ribāt Qila ○ PK 134-135 J 4
Ribáuè ○ MOC 218-219 K 2
Ribe ○ • DK 86-87 D 9
Ribeira Brava, Vila de ○ CV 202-203 B 5
Ribeira de Cruz ○ CV 202-203 B 5
Ribeira do Pombal ○ BR 68-69 J 7
Ribeira do Pombal, Rio ～ BR 68-69 J 7
Ribeirão ○ BR 68-69 L 6
Ribeirão, Área Indígena ✗ BR 70-71 E 2
Ribeirão, Rio ～ BR 70-71 E 2
Ribeirão das Neves ○ BR 72-73 H 5
Ribeirão do Pinhal ○ BR 72-73 E 7
Ribeirão Preto ○ BR 72-73 G 6
Ribeiro Gonçalves ○ BR 68-69 F 5
Ribera ○ I 100-101 D 6
Ribera ○ USA (NM) 256-257 K 3
Ribérac ○ F 90-91 H 9
Riberalta ○ BOL 70-71 D 2
Ribnița ☆ MD 102-103 F 4
Ribnitz-Damgarten ○ D 92-93 M 1
Ribo Escale ○ SN 202-203 C 2
Ribstone ○ CDN (ALB) 232-233 H 3
Ribstone Creek ～ CDN (ALB) 232-233 G 3
Rica, Cañada ～ RA 76-77 F 2
Ricardo ○ USA (TX) 266-267 K 6
Ricardo Flores Magón ○ MEX 50-51 F 3
Ricaute ○ CO 60-61 D 6
Rice ○ USA (CA) 248-249 K 5
Rice ○ USA (TX) 264-265 H 6
Rice ○ USA (WA) 244-245 G 2
Riceboro ○ USA (GA) 284-285 J 5
Rice Hill ○ USA (OR) 244-245 B 7
Rice Historic Site, Fort • USA (ND) 258-259 G 5
Rice Lake ○ CDN (ONT) 238-239 G 4
Rice Lake ○ USA (WI) 270-271 G 5
Rice Terraces •• RP 160-161 D 4
Riceton ○ CDN (SAS) 232-233 O 5
Riceville ○ USA (PA) 280-281 G 2
Rich ○ MA 188-189 J 4
Richan ○ CDN (ONT) 234-235 L 5
Richão do Dantas ○ BR 68-69 K 7
Richão dos Paulos ○ BR 68-69 F 6
Richard Collinson Inlet ≈ 24-25 P 4
Richardsbaai = Richards Bay ○ ZA 220-221 L 4
Richards Bay = Richardsbaai ○ ZA 220-221 L 4
Richards Island ⌒ CDN 20-21 Y 2
Richardson ○ USA (OR) 244-245 B 7
Richardson ○ USA (TX) 264-265 H 6
Richardson, Cape ▲ CDN 24-25 d 6
Richardson Bay ≈ 30-31 M 2
Richardson Island ⌒ CDN 30-31 L 3
Richardson Islands ⌒ CDN 24-25 R 6
Richardson Lake ○ CDN 30-31 O 6
Richardson Mountains ▲ CDN 20-21 W 2
Richardson Point ▲ AUS 180-181 H 6
Richardson River ～ CDN 30-31 L 2
Richardson River ～ CDN 32-33 P 3
Richards Trench ≃ 76-77 B 4
Richard Toll ○ SN 196-197 C 6
Richardton ○ USA (ND) 258-259 E 5
Richburg ○ USA (SC) 284-285 J 2
Riche, Cape ▲ AUS 176-177 E 7
Richelieu, Rivière ～ CDN (QUE) 238-239 M 3
Richer ○ CDN (MAN) 234-235 G 5
Richey ○ USA (MT) 250-251 O 4
Richfield ○ USA (ID) 252-253 D 3
Richfield ○ USA (KS) 262-263 E 7
Richfield ○ USA (NC) 282-283 G 5
Richfield ○ USA (UT) 254-255 C 5
Richfield Springs ○ USA (NY) 278-279 G 6
Richford ○ USA (NY) 278-279 E 6
Richford ○ USA (VT) 278-279 J 4
Richgrove ○ USA (CA) 248-249 E 4
Rich Hill ○ USA (MO) 274-275 D 6
Richibucto ○ CDN (NB) 240-241 L 4
Richibucto 15 Indian Reserve ✗ • CDN (NB) 240-241 L 4
Richibucto-Village ○ CDN (NB) 240-241 L 4
Richland ○ USA (GA) 284-285 F 4
Richland ○ USA (MO) 276-277 C 3
Richland ○ USA (OR) 244-245 H 6
Richland ○ USA (TX) 266-267 L 2
Richland ○ USA (WA) 244-245 F 4
Richland Balsam ▲ USA (NC) 282-283 E 5
Richland Center ○ USA (WI) 274-275 H 1
Richland Creek ～ USA (TX) 266-267 L 2
Richland Creek Reservoir ○ USA (TX) 264-265 H 6
Richlands ○ USA (VA) 280-281 E 6
Richlands Springs ○ USA (TX) 266-267 J 2
Richmond ○ USA (MI) 272-273 G 5
Richmond ○ AUS 174-175 G 7
Richmond ○ CDN (BC) 230-231 F 4
Richmond ○ CDN (ONT) 238-239 K 3
Richmond ○ CDN (QUE) 238-239 N 3
Richmond ○ NZ 182 D 4
Richmond ○ USA (CA) 248-249 B 2
Richmond ○ USA (IL) 274-275 K 2
Richmond ○ USA (IN) 274-275 O 5
Richmond ○ USA (KS) 262-263 L 6
Richmond ○ USA (KY) 276-277 L 3
Richmond ○ USA (MO) 274-275 E 5
Richmond ○ USA (OH) 280-281 F 3
Richmond ○ USA (TX) 268-269 E 7
Richmond ☆ USA (VA) 280-281 J 6
Richmond ○ ZA (CAP) 220-221 F 5
Richmond ○ ZA (NTL) 220-221 K 4
Richmond Dale ○ USA (OH) 280-281 D 4
Richmond Hill ○ CDN (ONT) 238-239 F 5
Richmond Hill ○ USA (GA) 284-285 J 5
Richmond Hills ○ AUS 178-179 H 2
Richmond River ～ AUS 178-179 M 5
Richmound ○ CDN (SAS) 232-233 J 5
Rich Mountain ▲ USA (AR) 276-277 A 6
Rich Square ○ USA (NC) 282-283 K 4
Richtersveld National Park ⊥ ZA 220-221 C 4
Richthofen, Mount ▲ AUS 172-173 C 6
Richton ○ USA (MS) 268-269 M 5
Rich Valley ○ CDN (ALB) 232-233 D 2
Richwood ○ USA (WV) 280-281 F 5
Ricinus ○ CDN (ALB) 232-233 D 3
Ricketts, Cape ▲ CDN 24-25 a 3
Rickman ○ USA (TN) 276-277 K 4
Rickwood Caverns • USA (AL) 284-285 D 3
Rico ○ USA (CO) 254-255 G 6
Ricrah ○ PE 64-65 E 7
Ridder, De ○ USA (LA) 268-269 G 6
Ridderspranget • N 86-87 D 6
Riddle ○ USA (ID) 252-253 B 4
Riddle ○ USA (OR) 244-245 B 8
Rideau Hills ▲ CDN (ONT) 238-239 H 4
Rideau Lake ○ CDN (ONT) 238-239 J 4
Ridge ○ USA (TX) 266-267 L 2
Ridgecrest ○ USA (CA) 248-249 G 4
Ridgedale ○ CDN (SAS) 232-233 O 2
Ridgefield ○ USA (WA) 244-245 C 5
Ridgeland ○ USA (MS) 268-269 K 4
Ridgeland ○ USA (SC) 284-285 K 4
Ridgely ○ USA (TN) 276-277 F 4
Ridge River ～ CDN (ONT) 236-237 D 2
Ridgetown ○ CDN (ONT) 238-239 D 6
Ridgeville ○ CDN (MAN) 234-235 F 5
Ridgeville ○ USA (IN) 274-275 N 4
Ridgeway ○ USA (SC) 284-285 K 2
Ridgewood Summit ▲ USA (CA) 246-247 B 4
Ridgway ○ USA (CO) 254-255 H 5
Ridgway ○ USA (PA) 280-281 H 2
Riding Mountain ▲ CDN (MAN) 234-235 C 4
Riding Mountain National Park ⊥ CDN (MAN) 234-235 C 4
Riding Rock Point ▲ BS 54-55 H 2
Riebeck Bay ≈ 183 E 3
Riebeek Kasteel ○ ZA 220-221 D 6
Riebeek-Oos ○ ZA 220-221 H 6
Riebeekstaad ○ ZA 220-221 H 3
Riecito ○ YV 60-61 G 2
Riecito, Río ～ YV 60-61 G 4
Rieppe ▲ N 86-87 K 2
Riesa ○ D 92-93 M 3
Riesco, Isla ⌒ RCH 80 D 6
Rietavas ○ LT 94-95 G 4
Rietbron ○ ZA 220-221 F 6
Rietfontein ○ NAM 216-217 F 10
Rietfontein ～ NAM 216-217 F 10
Rietfontein ○ ZA 220-221 E 3
Rieti ☆ I 100-101 D 3
Rietrivier ～ ZA 220-221 G 4
Rietse Vloer ○ ZA 220-221 E 5
Rietvlei ○ ZA 220-221 K 4
Rievaulx Abbey •• GB 90-91 G 4
Rifā'ī, ar- ☆ IRQ 128-129 M 7
Rifaina ○ BR 72-73 G 6
Riffe Lake ○ USA (WA) 244-245 C 4
Rifle ○ USA (CO) 254-255 H 4
Rifleman Bank ≃ 158-159 L 7
Rift Valley ■ EAK 212-213 F 2
Rift Valley ⊥ •• EAK 212-213 F 4
Rift Valley National Park ⊥ ETH 208-209 D 5
Rig, Bandar-e ○ IR 134-135 D 4
Riga, Gulf of = Rīgas Jūras Līcis ≈ LV 94-95 H 3
Rīga = Riga ★ •• LV 94-95 J 3
Riğā', Umm ○ Y 132-133 D 7
Rigacikun ○ WAN 204-205 G 3
Riğal Alma' ○ KSA 132-133 C 4
Rīgas Jūras Līcis ≈ 94-95 H 3
Rigaud ○ CDN (QUE) 238-239 L 3
Rigby ○ USA (ID) 252-253 G 3
Riggins ○ USA (ID) 250-251 C 6
Rigolet ○ CDN 36-37 U 7
Rig Rig ○ TCH 198-199 G 5
Rigsdagen, Kap ▲ GRØ 26-27 o 2
Riguldi ○ EST 94-95 H 2
Rihab, ar- ⊥ IRQ 128-129 L 7
Riihimäki ○ FIN 88-89 H 6
Riiser-Larsen halvøy ⊥ ARK 16 G 4
Riisitunturin kansallispuisto ⊥ FIN 88-89 K 3
Riistina ○ FIN 88-89 J 6
Rijau ○ WAN 204-205 F 3
Rijeka ○ HR 100-101 E 2
Rijpfjorden ≈ 84-85 N 2
Rikām Panchū, Gardaneh-ye ▲ IR 134-135 J 5
Rikbaktsa, Área Indígena ✗ BR 70-71 H 2
Rikorda, mys ▲ RUS 122-123 M 6
Rikorda, proliv ○ RUS 122-123 P 5
Rikuchū-Kaigan National Park ⊥ J 152-153 K 5
Rikumbetsu ○ J 152-153 K 3
Rila ○ • BG 102-103 C 6
Rila ▲ BG 102-103 C 6
Riley ○ USA (KS) 262-263 K 5
Riley ○ USA (OR) 244-245 F 7
Riley, Fort • USA (KS) 262-263 K 5
Rileyville ○ USA (PA) 280-281 L 2
Rillito ○ USA (AZ) 256-257 D 6
Rilski Manastir ••• BG 102-103 C 6
Rima ～ WAN 198-199 B 6
Rima, Wādī ar- ～ KSA 130-131 H 5
Rimac, Río ～ PE 64-65 D 8
Rimbey ○ CDN (ALB) 232-233 D 3
Rime ～ TCH 198-199 J 5
Rimé, Ouadi ～ TCH 198-199 J 6
Rimel ○ USA (WV) 280-281 F 5
Rimini ○ I 100-101 D 2
Rîmnicu Sărat ○ RO 102-103 E 5
Rîmnicu Vîlcea ☆ • RO 102-103 D 5
Rimouski ○ CDN (QUE) 240-241 G 2
Rimouski, Réserve de ⊥ CDN (QUE) 240-241 G 2
Rimrock ○ USA (WA) 244-245 D 4
Rimsko-Korsakovka ○ RUS 96-97 F 8
Rim Village ○ USA (OR) 244-245 C 8
Rinaré ○ BR 68-69 J 4
Rinbung ○ VRC 144-145 G 6
Rinca, Pulau ⌒ RI 168 D 7
Rincão ○ BR 72-73 F 6
Rincón ○ CR 52-53 C 7
Rincón ○ DOM 54-55 K 5
Rincon ○ USA (NM) 256-257 H 6
Rincón ○ • USA (PR) 286-287 O 2
Rincon, Cerro ▲ RA 76-77 D 3
Rincón, Salina del ○ RA 76-77 D 3
Rinconada ○ RA 76-77 D 2
Rinconada ○ USA (NM) 256-257 K 2
Rincón de la Vieja, Parque Nacional ⊥ CR 52-53 B 6
Rincón de la Vieja, Volcán ⩕ CR 52-53 B 6
Rincón del Guanal ○ C 54-55 D 4
Rincón de Palometas ○ BOL 70-71 F 5
Rincos de Romos ○ MEX 50-51 H 6
Rind ～ IND 142-143 B 2
Rindal ☆ N 86-87 D 5
Ringba ○ VRC 154-155 H 6
Ringgi ○ SOL 184 I c 3
Ringgold ○ USA (LA) 268-269 G 4
Ringgold ○ USA (TX) 264-265 G 5
Ringgold Isles ⌒ FJI 184 III c 2
Ringim ○ WAN 198-199 D 6
Ringkøbing ○ DK 86-87 D 8
Ringkøbing Fjord ○ DK 86-87 D 8
Ringling ○ USA (MT) 250-251 J 5
Ringling ○ USA (OK) 264-265 G 4
Ring of Kerry • IRL 90-91 B 6
Ringoma ○ ANG 216-217 D 6
Ringvassøy ⌒ N 86-87 J 2
Ringwood ○ AUS 178-179 C 2
Ringwood ○ USA (OK) 264-265 F 2
Riñihue, Lago ○ RCH 78-79 C 5
Riñinahue ○ RCH 78-79 C 6
Riniquiari ○ CO 60-61 F 6
Rinjani, Gunung ▲ RI 168 C 7
Rintala ○ RUS 88-89 K 6
Rio ○ GR 100-101 H 5
Río, El ○ DOM 54-55 K 5
Río Abiseo, Parque Nacional ⊥ ••• PE 64-65 D 5
Rio Acre, Estação Ecologica ⊥ BR 70-71 B 2
Rio Amazonas, Estuário do ～ BR 62-63 K 5
Río Ariapo ○ BR 66-67 E 2
Río Ariguaisa ○ YV 60-61 E 3
Río Azul ∴ • GCA 52-53 K 3
Riobamba ○ EC 64-65 C 2
Rio Bananal ○ BR 72-73 K 5
Río Bermejo, Valle del ⌣ RA 76-77 C 6
Rio-Biá, Áreas Indígenas ✗ BR 66-67 D 5
Río Blanco ○ CO 60-61 C 6
Rioblanco ○ CO 60-61 D 6
Rio Blanco ○ USA (CO) 254-255 H 4
Rio Bonito ○ BR (PAR) 74-75 E 5
Rio Bonito ○ BR (RIO) 72-73 J 7
Rio Branco ○ BR (ACR) 64-65 F 6
Rio Branco ○ BR (MAT) 70-71 H 4
Río Branco ○ ROU 74-75 D 9
Rio Branco, Área Indígena ✗ BR 70-71 F 3
Rio Branco, Parque Nacional do ⊥ BR 66-67 F 2
Rio Branco do Sul ○ BR 74-75 F 5
Rio Bravo ○ GCA 52-53 J 4
Río Bravo ○ MEX 50-51 K 5
Río Bravo, Parque Internacional del ⊥ MEX 50-51 H 3
Rio Brilhante ○ BR 76-77 K 1
Río Bueno ○ JA 54-55 G 5
Río Bueno ○ RCH 78-79 C 6
Río Caribe ○ YV 60-61 K 2
Rio Casca ○ BR 72-73 J 6
Río Cauto ○ C 54-55 G 4
Río Ceballos ○ RA 76-77 E 6
Río Chico ○ YV 60-61 J 2
Río Chiquito ○ HN 54-55 C 7
Río Clarillo, Parque Nacional ⊥ RCH 78-79 D 2
Rio Claro ○ BR 72-73 G 7
Rio Claro ○ TT 60-61 L 2
Río Colorado ○ RA 78-79 G 5
Rio Conchas ○ BR (MAT) 70-71 K 3
Rio Conchas ○ BR (MAT) 70-71 K 4
Rio Cuarto ○ RA 78-79 G 2
Rio das Pedras ○ MOC 218-219 H 6
Rio de Janeiro ■ BR 72-73 J 7
Rio de Janeiro ☆ • BR 72-73 J 7
Rio de Janeiro, Serra do ▲ BR 72-73 H 4
Río de la Plata ≈ 78-79 L 3
Río Dell ○ USA (CA) 246-247 A 3
Río Deseado, Valle del ⊥ RA 80 F 3
Rio do Pires ○ BR 72-73 J 2
Rio do Prado ○ BR 72-73 K 4
Rio do Sul ○ BR 74-75 F 6
Río Dulce, Parque Nacional ⊥ GCA 52-53 K 4
Río Gallegos ☆ RA 80 F 5
Río Grande ○ BOL 70-71 D 7
Rio Grande ○ BR 74-75 D 9
Río Grande ○ MEX 50-51 H 6
Río Grande ○ RA 80 G 6
Rio Grande ○ USA (NJ) 280-281 M 4
Rio Grande ～ USA (CO) 254-255 J 6
Rio Grande ～ USA (NM) 256-257 J 4
Rio Grande ～ USA (TX) 266-267 G 5
Río Grande, Ciudad de = Río Grande ○ MEX 50-51 H 6
Río Grande, Salar de ○ RA 76-77 C 3
Rio Grande City ○ USA (TX) 266-267 J 7
Rio Grande do Norte ■ BR 68-69 K 4
Rio Grande do Sul ■ BR 76-77 K 5
Rio Grande Fracture Zone ≃ 6-7 H 11
Rio Grande Plateau ≃ 6-7 F 12
Río Gregorio, Área Indígena ✗ BR 66-67 B 7
Río Guaporé, Área Indígena ✗ BR 70-71 E 2
Río Guengue ○ RA 80 E 2
Riohacha ☆ CO 60-61 E 2
Río Hato ○ PA 52-53 D 7
Río Hondo ○ GCA 52-53 K 4
Río Hondo, Embalse ☾ RA 76-77 E 4
Río Hondo, Termas de ○ • RA 76-77 E 4
Rio Ichilo ○ BOL 70-71 E 5
Rioja ○ PE 64-65 D 5
Rioja, La ■ E 98-99 F 3
Rioja, La ■ RA 76-77 C 5
Rioja, La ☆ • RA (LAR) 76-77 D 5
Rioja, Llanos de la ⊥ RA 76-77 D 5
Rio Lagartos ○ • MEX 52-53 K 1
Río Lagartos, Parque Natural ⊥ MEX 52-53 L 1
Rio Largo ○ BR 68-69 L 6
Riom ○ F 90-91 J 9
Rio Maior ○ P 98-99 C 5
Río Malo ○ RCH 78-79 D 3
Rio Mayo ○ RA 80 E 2
Rio Mequens, Área Indígena ✗ BR 70-71 G 3
Río Mulatos ○ BOL 70-71 D 6
Riondel ○ CDN (BC) 230-231 N 4
Rio Negrinho ○ BR 74-75 F 6
Rio Negro ○ BR (GSU) 70-71 K 6
Rio Negro ○ BR (GSU) 70-71 J 6
Rio Negro ○ BR (PAR) 74-75 F 6
Rionegro ○ CO 60-61 E 4
Río Negro ■ RA 78-79 E 6
Río Negro ○ RCH 78-79 C 6
Rio Negro, Pantanal do ○ BR 70-71 J 6
Río Negro, Represa del ☾ ROU 78-79 L 2
Rio Negro, Reserva Florestal do ⊥ BR 66-67 C 2
Rio Negro Ocaiai, Área Indígena ✗ BR 70-71 E 2
Rioni ～ GE 126-127 E 5
Rio Pardo ○ BR 74-75 D 7
Rio Pardo de Minas ○ BR 72-73 J 3
Rio Pilcomayo, Parque Nacional ⊥ RA 76-77 H 3
Río Plátano, Parque Nacional ⊥ ••• HN 54-55 C 7
Rio Pomba ○ BR 72-73 J 6
Rio Preto ○ BR 72-73 J 7
Rio Prêto, Serra do ▲ BR 72-73 G 4
Rio Preto da Eva ○ BR 66-67 H 4
Río Primero ○ RA 76-77 F 6
Río Queguay, Cascadas del ～ ROU 78-79 K 2
Rio Quente • BR 72-73 F 4
Río San Juan ○ DOM 54-55 K 5
Río Seco ○ RA 76-77 E 2
Río Seco ○ YV 60-61 F 2
Río Segundo ○ RA 76-77 F 6
Río Simpson, Parque Nacional ⊥ RCH 80 D 2
Rio Sono ○ BR 68-69 E 6
Ríosucio ○ CO 60-61 D 5
Río Sucio ○ CO 60-61 D 4
Ríosucio ○ CO 60-61 C 4
Rio Telha ○ BR 74-75 E 7
Río Tercero, Embalse del ☾ RA 78-79 G 2
Rio Tinto ○ BR 68-69 L 5
Río Tocuyo ○ YV 60-61 G 2
Río Trombetas, Reserva Biológica do ⊥ BR 62-63 F 6
Riou, Point ▲ USA 20-21 U 7
Rioug ☾ RIM 196-197 E 6
Riou Lake ○ CDN 30-31 Q 6
Rio Verde ○ BR 72-73 E 4
Río Verde ○ MEX 50-51 K 7
Río Verde ○ YV 60-61 H 3
Rio Verde de Mato Grosso ○ BR 70-71 K 6
Rio Verde Grande ～ BR 72-73 J 3
Rio Vermelho ○ BR 72-73 J 5
Río Villegas ○ RA 78-79 D 6
Rio Vista ○ USA (CA) 246-247 D 5
Rio Vista ○ USA (TX) 264-265 G 6
Riozinho ～ BR 66-67 D 6
Riozinho ～ BR 68-69 F 6
Riozinho, Rio ～ BR 66-67 G 4
Riozinho, Rio ～ BR 68-69 B 5
Riozinho do Anfrísio ～ BR 66-67 K 5
Riozinho ou Rio Verde, Rio ～ BR 72-73 E 2
Ripky ○ UA 102-103 G 2
Ripley ○ USA (CA) 248-249 K 6
Ripley ○ USA (KY) 276-277 M 2
Ripley ○ USA (MS) 268-269 M 2
Ripley ○ USA (TN) 276-277 F 5
Ripley ○ USA (WV) 280-281 E 5
Ripoll ○ • E 98-99 Q 4
Ripon ○ USA (WI) 270-271 K 7
Ririe ○ USA (ID) 252-253 G 3
Rišā', Wādī ar- ～ KSA 130-131 H 5
Risālpur ○ PK 138-139 D 2
Risasa ○ ZRE 210-211 K 4
Rishikesh ○ IND 138-139 G 4
Rishiri ○ J 152-153 J 2
Rishiri-fuji ○ J 152-153 J 2
Rishiri-Rebun National Park ⊥ J 152-153 J 2
Rishiri-suidō ≈ 152-153 J 2
Rishiri-tō ⌒ J 152-153 J 2
Rishon le Ẕiyyon ☆ IL 130-131 D 2
Rising Star ○ USA (TX) 264-265 F 6
Rising Sun ○ USA (IN) 274-275 O 6
Rison ○ USA (AR) 276-277 C 7
Risør ☆ • N 86-87 D 7
Risøyhamn ○ N 86-87 G 2
Rissa ○ N 86-87 E 5
Rissani ○ MA 188-189 J 5
Rištan ○ US 136-137 M 4
Risti ○ EST 94-95 J 2
Ritchie ○ ZA 220-221 G 4
Ritch Island ⌒ CDN 30-31 K 2
Rithi ○ IND 142-143 B 4
Rito ○ ANG 216-217 E 8
Rito, El ○ USA (NM) 256-257 J 2
Ritta Island ⌒ USA (FL) 286-287 J 5
Ritter ○ USA (OR) 244-245 F 6
Ritter, Mount ▲ USA (CA) 248-249 E 2
Ritzville ○ USA (WA) 244-245 G 3
Riv ～ UA 102-103 F 3
Rivadavia ○ RA (BUA) 78-79 J 3
Rivadavia ○ RA (MEN) 78-79 E 2
Rivadavia ○ RA (SAJ) 76-77 C 6
Rivadavia ○ RA (SAL) 76-77 F 3
Rivadavia ○ RCH 76-77 B 5
Riva del Garda ○ I 100-101 C 2
Rivalensundet ≈ 84-85 P 3
Rivaš ○ IR 136-137 F 7
Rivas ☆ NIC 52-53 B 6
Rivera ○ EC 64-65 C 3
Rivera ○ RA 78-79 H 4
Rivera ☆ ROU 76-77 K 6
Riverbank ○ USA (CA) 248-249 D 2
Riverboat Cruise • AUS 180-181 H 4
River Cess ○ LB 202-203 F 7
Rivercourse ○ CDN (ALB) 232-233 H 2
Riverdale ○ USA (CA) 248-249 E 3
Riverdale ○ USA (ND) 258-259 F 4
River Falls ○ USA (WI) 270-271 F 6
Riverhead ○ USA (NY) 280-281 O 3
River Hebert ○ CDN (NS) 240-241 L 5
River Hills ○ CDN (MAN) 234-235 H 4
Riverhurst ○ CDN (SAS) 232-233 M 5
Riverina ～ AUS 180-181 H 3
River John ○ CDN (NS) 240-241 M 5
Rivero, Isla ⌒ RCH 80 C 2
River of No Return Wilderness ⊥ USA (ID) 250-251 D 6
River of Ponds ○ CDN (NFL) 242-243 L 2
Rivers ○ CDN (MAN) 234-235 C 4
Rivers ■ WAN 204-205 G 6
Rivers, Lake of the ○ CDN (SAS) 232-233 N 6
Riversdal = Riversdale ○ ZA 220-221 E 7
Riversdale ○ BH 52-53 K 3
Riversdale ○ CDN (ONT) 238-239 D 4
Riversdale = Riversdal ○ ZA 220-221 E 7
Riversdale Beach ○ NZ 182 F 4
Riverside ○ AUS 178-179 K 1
Riverside ○ USA (CA) 248-249 G 6
Riverside ○ USA (IA) 274-275 G 3
Riverside ○ USA (ID) 252-253 F 3
Riverside ○ USA (MD) 280-281 J 5
Riverside ○ USA (OR) 244-245 G 7
Riverside ○ USA (WA) 244-245 F 2
Riverside ○ USA (WY) 252-253 M 5
Rivers Inlet ≈ 32-33 G 6
Rivers Inlet ≈ CDN 230-231 B 2
Riversleigh ○ AUS 174-175 E 6
Riverton ○ CDN (MAN) 234-235 G 4
Riverton ○ NZ 182 B 7
Riverton ○ USA (IL) 274-275 J 5
Riverton ○ USA (WY) 252-253 K 3
River Valley ○ CDN (ONT) 238-239 E 2
Riverview ○ CDN (NB) 240-241 L 4
Rivesaltes ○ F 90-91 J 10
Riviera ○ USA (TX) 266-267 K 6
Riviera Beach ○ USA (FL) 286-287 J 5
Riviera Beach ○ USA (TX) 266-267 K 6
Rivière, George ～ CDN 36-37 Q 5
Rivière-à-Pierre ○ CDN (QUE) 238-239 N 2
Rivière-au-Tonnere ○ CDN (QUE) 242-243 D 2
Rivière-aux-Saumons ○ CDN (QUE) 242-243 F 3
Rivière-Bleue ○ CDN (QUE) 240-241 F 3
Rivière-Boisvert ○ CDN (QUE) 236-237 O 3
Rivière-de-la-Chaloupe ○ CDN (QUE) 242-243 F 3
Rivière-Éperlan ○ CDN (QUE) 240-241 F 2
Rivière-Éternité ○ CDN (QUE) 240-241 E 2
Rivière-Pigou ○ CDN (QUE) 242-243 C 2
Rivière Qui Barre ○ CDN (ALB) 232-233 E 2
Rivière Veuve ○ CDN (ONT) 238-239 E 2
Riviersonderend ○ ZA 220-221 D 7
Rivne ○ UA 102-103 E 2
Rivoli ○ I 100-101 A 2
Rivungo ○ ANG 218-219 B 3
Riwat ○ PK 138-139 D 3
Riwoqê ○ VRC 144-145 L 5
Riyāḍ, ar- ■ KSA 130-131 J 6
Riyāḍ, ar- ★ •• KSA 130-131 K 5
Riyāḍ al-Ḫabra ○ KSA 130-131 H 4
Riyadh = Riyāḍ, ar- ★ •• KSA 130-131 K 5
Rize ☆ TR 128-129 J 2
Rizhao ○ VRC 154-155 L 4
Rizokarpaso ○ TR 128-129 F 5
Rizzuto, Capo ▲ I 100-101 F 5
Rjabovskij ○ RUS 102-103 M 2
Rjazan' ☆ • RUS 94-95 Q 4
Rjažsk ☆ • RUS 94-95 R 5
Rjukan ☆ N 86-87 D 7
Rkîz ○ RIM 196-197 C 6
Rkîz, Lac ○ RIM 196-197 C 6
Roadhouse ○ AUS 174-175 B 5
Road River ～ CDN 20-21 X 3
Road Town ☆ •• GB 56 C 2
Road Town ☆ •• GB (VI) 286-287 R 2
Roan Cliffs ▲ USA (UT) 254-255 F 4
Roan Mountain ○ USA (TN) 282-283 E 4
Roanne ○ F 90-91 K 8
Roanoke ○ USA (AL) 284-285 E 3
Roanoke ○ USA (TX) 264-265 G 5
Roanoke ○ USA (VA) 280-281 G 6
Roanoke Island ⌒ USA (NC) 282-283 M 5
Roanoke Rapids ○ USA (NC) 282-283 K 4
Roanoke Rapids Lake ○ USA (NC) 282-283 K 4
Roanoke River ～ USA (NC) 282-283 K 4
Roanoke River ～ USA (VA) 280-281 G 6
Roaring Springs ○ USA (TX) 264-265 D 5
Roaring Springs Ranch ○ USA (OR) 244-245 G 8
Roatán ☆ HN 52-53 L 3
Roatán, Isla de ⌒ HN 52-53 L 3
Robalo, Cachoeira do ～ BR 70-71 K 6
Roban ○ MAL 162-163 J 4
Robanda ○ EAT 212-213 E 5
Robāṭak ○ AFG 136-137 L 6
Robāṭ-e Ğa'lī ○ AFG 134-135 J 4
Robāṭ-e Ḫān ○ IR 134-135 G 2
Robāṭe Ḥoṣāb ○ IR 134-135 G 2
Robāṭ-e Ḫoṣk ○ AFG 134-135 K 2
Robāṭ-e-Mīrzā, Kōtal-e ▲ AFG 134-135 K 1
Robāṭ-e Pošt Badām ○ IR 134-135 F 2
Robāṭ-e Sang ○ IR 136-137 F 7
Robāṭ-e Sang-e Pāin ○ AFG 134-135 K 1
Robāṭkarīm ○ IR 136-137 B 7
Robb ○ CDN (ALB) 232-233 B 2
Robbeneiland ⌒ ZA 220-221 D 6
Robbies Pass ▲ NAM 216-217 B 9
Robbins ○ USA (NC) 282-283 H 5
Robbins Island ⌒ AUS 180-181 H 6
Robbinsville ○ USA (NC) 282-283 D 5
Robe ○ AUS 180-181 E 4
Robē ○ ETH (Ars) 208-209 D 5
Robē ○ ETH (Bal) 208-209 E 5
Robe, Mount ▲ AUS 178-179 F 6
Robeline ○ USA (LA) 268-269 G 5
Robe River ～ AUS 172-173 B 6
Robersonville ○ USA (NC) 282-283 K 5
Robert, Le ○ F 56 E 4
Roberta ○ USA (GA) 284-285 F 4
Robert Lee ○ USA (TX) 266-267 G 2
Roberts ○ USA (IL) 274-275 K 4
Robert's Arm ○ CDN (NFL) 242-243 N 3
Roberts Creek ○ CDN (BC) 230-231 F 4
Roberts Creek Montain ▲ USA (NV) 246-247 J 4
Robertsdale ○ USA (AL) 284-285 C 6
Robertsganj ○ IND 142-143 C 3
Robertson ○ USA (WY) 252-253 H 5
Robertson ○ ZA 220-221 D 6
Robertson, Kap ▲ GRØ 26-27 O 5
Robertson, Lac ○ CDN (QUE) 242-243 J 2
Robertson, Lake ☾ ZW 218-219 F 3
Robertson Bay ≈ 16 F 18
Robertson Bay ≈ 36-37 K 7
Robertson Fjord ≈ 26-27 P 5
Robertson Range ▲ AUS 172-173 E 7
Robertson River ～ CDN 24-25 e 5
Robertsons Øy ⌒ ARK 16 G 31
Roberts Port ☆ LB 202-203 E 6
Robertville ○ CDN (NB) 240-241 K 3
Roberval ○ CDN (QUE) 240-241 C 2
Robi ○ ETH 208-209 D 4
Robin Falls • AUS 172-173 K 2
Robinhood ○ CDN (SAS) 232-233 J 2
Robins Camp ○ ZW 218-219 C 4
Robinson ○ USA (IL) 274-275 L 5
Robinson ○ USA (ND) 258-259 H 4
Robinson ○ USA (TX) 266-267 K 2
Robinson, Mount ▲ AUS 172-173 D 7
Robinson Island ⌒ ARK 16 G 30
Robinson Pass ▲ ZA 220-221 F 6
Robinson Range ▲ AUS 176-177 E 2
Robinson River ○ AUS 174-175 D 5
Robinson River ～ AUS 174-175 D 5
Robinson River ○ PNG 183 E 6
Robinson Sound ≈ 36-37 R 3
Robinsons River ～ CDN (NFL) 242-243 K 4
Robinson Summit ▲ USA (NV) 246-247 K 4
Robinsonville ○ CDN (NB) 240-241 H 3
Robinvale ○ AUS 180-181 G 3
Robious ○ USA (VA) 280-281 J 6
Robla, La ○ E 98-99 E 3
Roble Alto, Cerro ▲ RCH 78-79 D 2
Robles Junction ○ USA (AZ) 256-257 D 6
Roblin ○ CDN (MAN) 234-235 B 3
Roblin ○ CDN (ONT) 238-239 H 4
Robooksibia ○ RI 166-167 H 2
Rob Roy Island ⌒ SOL 184 I c 2
Robsart ○ CDN (SAS) 232-233 J 6
Robson ○ CDN (BC) 230-231 M 4
Robson, Mount ▲ CDN (BC) 228-229 P 3
Robstown ○ USA (TX) 266-267 K 6
Roby ○ USA (MO) 276-277 C 3
Roby ○ USA (TX) 264-265 D 6
Roca, Cabo da ▲ •• P 98-99 C 5
Roca, Península ⌒ RCH 80 D 5
Roça de Bruno ○ BR 68-69 E 2
Roca de la Sierra, La ○ E 98-99 D 5
Rocafuerte ○ EC 64-65 B 2
Rocanville ○ CDN (SAS) 232-233 R 5
Roca Partida, Isla ⌒ MEX 50-51 B 7
Roca Redonda ⌒ EC 64-65 B 9
Rocas, Atol das ⌒ BR 68-69 L 1
Rocas Alijos ⌒ MEX 50-51 B 5
Roça Tapirapé ○ BR 68-69 C 6
Rocha ☆ ROU 78-79 M 3
Rocha, Laguna de ○ ROU 78-79 M 3
Rochebaucourt ○ CDN (QUE) 236-237 L 4
Roche Cabrit ○ F 62-63 H 3
Rochedo ○ BR 70-71 K 6
Rochefort ○ F 90-91 G 9
Rochelle ○ USA (GA) 284-285 G 5
Rochelle ○ USA (IL) 274-275 J 3
Rochelle ○ USA (TX) 266-267 H 2
Rochelle, la ○ CDN (MAN) 234-235 G 5
Rochelle, la ☆ • F 90-91 G 8
Roche River, La ～ CDN 30-31 O 5
Rocher River ○ CDN 30-31 N 5
Roches Point ○ CDN (ONT) 238-239 F 4
Rochester ○ USA (IN) 274-275 M 3
Rochester ○ USA (KY) 276-277 J 3
Rochester ○ USA (MI) 272-273 F 5
Rochester ○ USA (NH) 278-279 L 5
Rochester ○ USA (NY) 278-279 D 5
Rochester ○ USA (TX) 264-265 E 5
Rochester ○ USA (VT) 278-279 J 5
Rochester ○ USA (WA) 244-245 B 4
Rochester ○ • USA (MN) 270-271 F 6
Roche-sur-Yon, la ☆ • F 90-91 G 8
Rochon Sands ○ CDN (ALB) 232-233 F 3
Rock ○ USA (MI) 270-271 L 4
Rock, The ○ AUS 180-181 J 3
Rockall Plateau ≃ 6-7 H 3
Rockall Trough ≃ 6-7 H 3
Rock Bay ○ CDN (BC) 230-231 D 3
Rock Camp ○ USA (WV) 280-281 F 6
Rock Cave ○ USA (WV) 280-281 F 5
Rock Creek ○ CDN (BC) 230-231 K 4
Rock Creek ～ USA (UT) 254-255 E 3
Rockdale ○ USA (TX) 266-267 L 3
Rockefeller National Wildlife Refuge ⊥ USA (LA) 268-269 H 7
Rockefeller Plateau ▲ ARK 16 F 24
Rock Engravings Music Stones • NAM 220-221 C 3
Rock Falls ○ USA (IL) 274-275 J 3
Rockford ○ USA (AL) 284-285 D 4
Rockford ○ USA (IL) 274-275 J 2
Rockford ○ USA (OH) 280-281 B 3
Rockford ○ USA (WA) 244-245 H 3
Rockglen ○ CDN (SAS) 232-233 N 6
Rock Hall ○ USA (MD) 280-281 K 4
Rockhampton ○ • AUS 178-179 L 2
Rockhampton Downs ○ AUS 174-175 C 6
Rockhaven ○ CDN (SAS) 232-233 K 3
Rock Hill ○ USA (SC) 284-285 J 2
Rockhouse Island ⌒ CDN 30-31 Y 4
Rockingham ○ USA (NC) 282-283 H 6
Rockingham Bay ≈ 174-175 J 6
Rock Island ○ CDN (QUE) 238-239 N 3
Rock Island ⌒ USA (WI) 270-271 M 5
Rocklake ○ USA (ND) 258-259 H 3
Rock Lake ○ USA (WA) 244-245 H 3
Rockland ○ CDN (ONT) 238-239 K 3
Rockland ○ USA (ID) 252-253 F 4
Rockland ○ USA (ME) 278-279 M 4
Rocklands Reservoir ☾ AUS 180-181 G 4
Rocklea ○ AUS 172-173 C 7
Rockledge ○ USA (FL) 286-287 J 3
Rockmart ○ USA (GA) 284-285 E 2
Rock of Cashel •• IRL 90-91 D 5
Rock Point ○ USA (MD) 280-281 K 5
Rockport ○ USA (IN) 274-275 L 7
Rock Port ○ USA (MO) 274-275 C 4
Rockport ○ USA (TX) 266-267 K 6
Rockport ○ USA (WA) 244-245 D 2
Rock Rapids ○ USA (IA) 274-275 B 1
Rock River ～ CDN 20-21 X 3
Rock River ～ CDN 30-31 F 5
Rock River ○ USA (WY) 252-253 N 5
Rock River ～ USA (IL) 274-275 J 3
Rock River ～ USA (MN) 270-271 B 7

Rock Sound ○• BS 54-55 G 2
Rock Springs ○ USA (AZ) 256-257 C 4
Rock Springs ○ USA (MT) 250-251 N 5
Rocksprings ○ USA (TX) 266-267 G 3
Rock Springs ○ USA (WY) 252-253 J 5
Rockstone ○ GUY 62-63 E 2
Rockton ○ AUS 180-181 K 4
Rockville ○ USA (IN) 274-275 L 5
Rockville ○ USA (MD) 280-281 J 4
Rockville ○ USA (NE) 262-263 H 3
Rockville ○ USA (UT) 254-255 B 6
Rockwall ○ USA (TX) 264-265 H 6
Rockwell City ○ USA (IA) 274-275 D 2
Rockwood ○ USA (ME) 278-279 M 3
Rockwood ○ USA (TN) 282-283 C 5
Rockwood ○ USA (TX) 266-267 H 2
Rocky ○ USA (OK) 264-265 E 3
Rocky Arroyo ∼ USA (NM) 256-257 L 6
Rocky Boy ○ USA (MT) 250-251 K 3
Rocky Boys Indian Reservation ⨯ USA (MT) 250-251 K 3
Rocky Ford ○ USA (CO) 254-255 M 5
Rocky Fork Lake < USA (OH) 280-281 C 4
Rocky Gap ○ USA (VA) 280-281 E 6
Rocky Gully ○ AUS 176-177 D 7
Rocky Harbour ○ CDN (NFL) 242-243 L 3
Rocky Island Lake ⊖ CDN (ONT) 238-239 C 2
Rocky Lake ⊖ CDN 34-35 F 3
Rocky Mount ○ USA (NC) 282-283 K 5
Rocky Mount ○ USA (VA) 280-281 G 6
Rocky Mountain House ○ CDN (ALB) 232-233 D 3
Rocky Mountain House National Historic Park • CDN (ALB) 232-233 D 3
Rocky Mountain National Park ⊥ USA (CO) 254-255 K 3
Rocky Mountains ▲ 4 B 3
Rocky Mountains Forest Reserve ⊥ CDN (ALB) 232-233 D 6
Rocky Mountains Forest Reserve ⊥ CDN (ALB) 232-233 B 3
Rocky Point ○ CDN (PEI) 240-241 M 4
Rocky Point ▲ NAM 216-217 B 9
Rockypoint ○ USA (WY) 252-253 N 2
Rocky Point ▲ USA 20-21 J 4
Rocky Rapids ○ CDN (ALB) 232-233 D 2
Rocky River ∼ CDN (ALB) 228-229 R 3
Rocky River ∼ USA (NC) 282-283 H 5
Rocky River ∼ USA (NC) 282-283 G 5
Roda, La ○ E 98-99 F 5
Roda Velha ○ BR 72-73 H 2
Rödbär ○ AFG 134-135 K 3
Rødberg ○ N 86-87 D 6
Rødbyhavn ○ DK 86-87 E 9
Roddickton ○ CDN (NFL) 242-243 M 2
Rodds Bay ≈ 178-179 L 2
Røde Fjord ≈ 26-27 I 8
Rodel ○ GB 90-91 D 3
Rodelas ○ BR 68-69 J 6
Rodeo ○ USA (NM) 256-257 G 7
Rodeo Viejo ○ PA 52-53 D 7
Roderick Island ⌒ CDN (BC) 228-229 F 4
Rodez ☆• F 90-91 J 9
Rodgers Bank ≃ 72-73 M 4
Rodi, Tanjung ▲ RI 166-167 B 7
Rodino ☆ RUS 124-125 M 2
Rodnei, Munții ▲ RO 102-103 D 4
Rodney ○ USA (MS) 268-269 J 5
Rodney, Cape ▲ NZ 182 E 2
Rodniki ○ RUS 94-95 R 3
Rodnikovskoe ○ KA 124-125 H 3
Rododero-Playa, El • CO 60-61 D 2
Ródos ☆•• GR 100-101 M 6
Ródos ⌒ GR 100-101 M 6
Rodovia Perimetral Norte II BR 62-63 F 5
Rodrigo Arenas Betancourt, Monumento • CO 60-61 E 5
Rodrigues ⌒ MS 12 E 6
Rodrigues ⌒ MS 224 F 6
Rodrigues Ridge ≃ 224 E 6
Rodríguez, Los ○ MEX 50-51 J 4
Rodžers, buhta ≈ 112-113 V 1
Roe, Lake ⊖ AUS 176-177 G 5
Roebourne ○ AUS 172-173 C 6
Roebuck Bay ≈ 172-173 F 5
Roebuck Roadhouse ○ AUS 172-173 F 4
Roedtan ○ ZA 220-221 J 2
Roe River ∼ AUS 172-173 G 3
Roermond ○ NL 92-93 J 3
Roeselare ○ B 92-93 G 3
Roes Welcome Sound ≈ 36-37 F 3
Roff ○ USA (OK) 264-265 H 4
Rofia ○ WAN 204-205 F 3
Rogačeva ∼ RUS 108-109 E 6
Rogačevka ○ RUS 102-103 L 2
Rogačevo ○ RUS 94-95 P 3
Rogagua, Lago ⊖ BOL 70-71 D 3
Rogaguado ⊖ BOL 70-71 E 3
Rogasen = Rogoźno ○ PL 92-93 O 2
Rogatica ○ BIH 100-101 G 3
Rogberi ○ WAL 202-203 D 5
Rogeia Island ⌒ PNG 183 F 6
Rogers ○ USA (AR) 276-277 A 4
Rogers ○ USA (ND) 258-259 J 4
Rogers ○ USA (TX) 266-267 K 3
Rogers, Mount ▲ USA (VA) 280-281 E 7
Rogers City ○ USA (MI) 272-273 F 2
Rogers Lake ⊖ USA (CA) 248-249 G 5
Rogerson ○ USA (ID) 252-253 D 4
Rogers Pass ○ CDN (BC) 230-231 M 2
Rogers Pass ▲ CDN (BC) 230-231 M 2
Rogers Pass ▲ USA (MT) 250-251 G 4
Rogersville ○ CDN (NB) 240-241 K 4
Rogersville ○ USA (AL) 284-285 C 2
Rogersville ○ USA (TN) 282-283 D 4
Roggeveen Basin ≃ 5 B 8
Roggeveldberge ▲ ZA 220-221 E 5
Rognan ○ N 86-87 G 3
Rogo ○ WAN 204-205 G 3
Rogoaguado, Lago ⊖ BOL 70-71 E 3
Rogovaja, Bol'šaja ∼ RUS 108-109 J 8
Rogoźno ○ PL 92-93 O 2
Rogue River ∼ USA (OR) 244-245 A 8
Rogun ○ WAN 204-205 F 4
Roha ○ IND 138-139 D 10
Rohat ○ IND 138-139 D 7
Rohatyn ☆ UA 102-103 D 3
Rohault, Lac ⊖ CDN (QUE) 236-237 O 3
Rohmojva, gora ▲ RUS 88-89 K 3
Rohri ○ PK 138-139 B 6
Rohri Canal < PK 138-139 B 6
Rohru ○ IND 138-139 F 4
Rohtak ○ IND 138-139 F 5
Rohtak, Rūdḫāne-ye ∼ IR 134-135 K 5
Rohtas Fort • PK 138-139 D 3
Rohuküla ○ EST 94-95 H 2
Rohwer ○ USA (AR) 276-277 D 7
Roi Et ○ THA 158-159 G 2
Roja ○•• LV 94-95 H 3
Roja, Punta ▲ RA 80 H 2
Rojas ○ RA 78-79 J 3
Rojhān ○ PK 138-139 B 5
Rojo, Cabo ▲ MEX 50-51 L 7
Rojo, Cabo ▲ USA (PR) 286-287 O 3
Rokan ○ RI 162-163 D 4
Rokan-Kanan ∼ RI 162-163 D 4
Rokan-Kiri ∼ RI 162-163 D 4
Rokeby ○ AUS 174-175 G 3
Rokeby ○ CDN (SAS) 232-233 Q 4
Rokeby-Croll Creek National Park ⊥ AUS 174-175 G 3
Rokiškis ☆•• LT 94-95 J 4
Rokkasho ○ J 152-153 J 4
Rokom ○ SUD 206-207 K 6
Rokskij, pereval ▲ RUS 126-127 F 6
Roland ○ CDN (MAN) 234-235 F 5
Rolândia ○ BR 72-73 E 7
Røldal ○ N 86-87 C 7
Roldán ○ RA 78-79 J 2
Rolette ○ USA (ND) 258-259 H 3
Rolim de Moura ○ BR (RON) 70-71 F 3
Rolim de Moura ○ BR (RON) 70-71 G 2
Roll ○ USA (AZ) 256-257 B 6
Roll ○ USA (OK) 264-265 E 3
Rolla ⌒ N 86-87 H 2
Rolla ○ USA (KS) 262-263 E 7
Rolla ○ USA (MO) 276-277 D 3
Rolla ○ USA (ND) 258-259 H 3
Rollapenta ○ IND 140-141 H 3
Rolleston ○ AUS 178-179 K 3
Rolleston ○ NZ 182 D 5
Rollet ○ CDN (QUE) 236-237 J 5
Rolleville ○• BS 54-55 H 3
Rolling Fork ○ USA (MS) 268-269 K 4
Rolling Fork ∼ USA (KY) 276-277 K 3
Rolling Hills ○ CDN (ALB) 232-233 G 5
Rolling River Indian Reserve ⨯ CDN (MAN) 234-235 D 4
Rollins ○ USA (MN) 270-271 G 3
Rollins ○ USA (MT) 250-251 E 4
Rolvsøya ⌒ N 86-87 M 1
Roma ○ AUS 178-179 K 4
Roma ★••• I 100-101 D 4
Roma ○ LS 220-221 H 4
Roma ○ S 86-87 J 8
Roma ○ USA (TX) 266-267 J 7
Roma, Pulau ⌒ RI 166-167 D 5
Romain, Cape ▲ USA (SC) 284-285 L 4
Romaine ○ CDN (QUE) 242-243 H 2
Romaine, Rivière ∼ CDN 38-39 N 3
Roman ○ BG 102-103 C 6
Roman ○• RO 102-103 E 4
Romana, La ☆ DOM 54-55 L 5
Romanche Fracture Zone ≃ 6-7 G 9
Romancoke ○ USA (MD) 280-281 K 5
Romanek, Lac ⊖ CDN 36-37 Q 6
Romang, Selat ≈ 166-167 D 5
Romania = România ■ RO 102-103 C 5
Romanina, Bol'šaja ∼ RUS 108-109 c 6
Roman-Koš, hora ▲ UA 102-103 J 5
Romano, Cape ▲ USA (FL) 286-287 H 6
Romano, Cayo ⌒ C 54-55 F 3
Romanovka ○ RUS 118-119 F 9
Romans-sur-Isère ○ F 90-91 K 9
Romanzof, Cape ▲ USA 20-21 G 6
Romanzof Mountains ▲ USA 20-21 S 2
Romblon ☆ RP 160-161 E 6
Romblon Island ⌒ RP 160-161 E 6
Romblon Strait ≈ 160-161 E 6
Rome ○ USA (AL) 284-285 D 5
Rome ○ USA (GA) 284-285 E 2
Rome ○ USA (NY) 278-279 F 5
Rome ○ USA (OH) 280-281 F 2
Rome ○ USA (OR) 244-245 H 8
Rome ○ USA (TN) 276-277 J 4
Rome = Roma ★••• I 100-101 D 4
Romeo ○ USA (MI) 272-273 F 5
Romeoville ○ USA (IL) 274-275 K 3
Romero ○ USA (TX) 264-265 B 3
Romero, Isla ⌒ RCH 80 C 2
Romer Sø ⊖ GRØ 26-27 q 3
Romita ○ MEX 52-53 D 1
Rommani ○ MA 188-189 H 4
Romney ○ USA (IN) 274-275 M 4
Romney ○ USA (WV) 280-281 H 4
Romny ○ RUS 122-123 C 3
Romny ○ UA 102-103 H 2
Rømø ⌒ DK 86-87 D 9
Romodan ○ UA 102-103 H 2
Romorantin-Lanthenay ○ F 90-91 H 8
Rompía ○ YV 60-61 H 4
Rompin ∼ MAL 162-163 E 3
Romsdalen ⌣ N 86-87 C 5
Ronan ○ USA (MT) 250-251 E 4
Roncador ○ BR 74-75 D 5
Roncador, Serra do ▲ BR 72-73 E 2
Roncador Reef ⌒ SOL 184 I d 2
Roncesvalles ○• E 98-99 G 3
Roncière Falls, La ∼ CDN 24-25 L 6
Ronda ○ E 98-99 E 6
Ronda, Serranía de ▲ E 98-99 E 6
Rønde ○ DK 86-87 E 8
Ronde, Rivière la ∼ CDN 38-39 L 2
Ronde Island ⌒ WG 56 E 5
Rondon ○ BR 72-73 D 7
Rondon, Pico ▲ BR 66-67 F 2
Rondon Dopara ○ BR 68-69 D 4
Rondônia ■ BR 70-71 F 2
Rondonópolis ○ BR 70-71 K 5
Rond-Point de Gaulle ▲ TCH 198-199 H 3
Rondslottet ▲ N 86-87 D 6
Rondu ○ IND 138-139 E 2
Rong'an ○ VRC 156-157 F 4
Rongbuk ○ VRC 144-145 F 6
Rongchang ○ VRC 156-157 D 2
Rongcheng ○ VRC 154-155 N 3
Ronge, La ○ CDN 34-35 D 3
Ronge, Lac la ⊖ CDN 34-35 D 3
Rongjiang ○ VRC 156-157 F 4
Rongkong ∼ RI 164-165 G 5
Rong Kwang ○ THA 142-143 M 6
Rongo ○ EAK 212-213 E 4
Rongshui ○ VRC 156-157 F 4
Rõngu ○ EST 94-95 K 2
Rongxar ○ VRC 144-145 F 6
Rong Xian ○ VRC (GXI) 156-157 G 5
Rong Xian ○ VRC (SIC) 156-157 D 2
Rønne ○ DK 86-87 G 9
Ronne Bay ≈ 16 F 29
Ronneby ☆ S 86-87 G 8
Rönnöfors ○ S 86-87 F 5
Ron Phibun ○ THA 158-159 E 6
Ronsard, Cape ▲ AUS 176-177 B 2
Ronuro, Rio ∼ BR 70-71 K 3
Roodepoort ○ ZA 220-221 H 3
Roof Butte ▲ USA (AZ) 256-257 F 2
Rooiberge ▲ ZA 220-221 J 4
Rooibokkraal ○ ZA 220-221 H 2
Rooikloof ▲ ZA 220-221 D 6
Rooikop ○ NAM 216-217 C 11
Rooikraal ○ ZA 220-221 J 2
Rooirand ▲ NAM 220-221 C 2
Room, Pulau ⌒ RI 166-167 H 3
Rooney Point ▲ AUS 178-179 M 3
Roopville ○ USA (GA) 284-285 E 3
Roosendaal ○ NL 92-93 H 3
Roosevelt ○ USA (AZ) 256-257 D 5
Roosevelt ○ USA (OK) 264-265 E 4
Roosevelt ○ USA (TX) 266-267 G 3
Roosevelt ○ USA (UT) 254-255 E 3
Roosevelt ○ USA (WA) 244-245 E 5
Roosevelt, Área Indígena ⨯ BR 70-71 G 2
Roosevelt, Mount ▲ CDN 30-31 G 6
Roosevelt, Rio ∼ BR 66-67 G 7
Roosevelt Beach ○ USA (OR) 244-245 A 6
Roosevelt Campobello International Park ∴ CDN (NB) 240-241 J 6
Roosevelt Fjelde ▲ GRØ 26-27 g 2
Roosevelt Island ⌒ ARK 16 F 21
Roossenekal ○ ZA 220-221 J 2
Roosville ○ CDN (BC) 230-231 O 4
Rootok Island ⌒ USA 22-23 O 5
Root River ∼ CDN 30-31 G 4
Root River ∼ USA (MN) 270-271 G 7
Roper Bar ○ AUS 174-175 C 4
Roper River ∼ AUS 174-175 C 4
Roper Valley ○ AUS 174-175 C 4
Ropesville ○ USA (TX) 264-265 B 6
Roquefort ○ F 90-91 G 9
Roques, Islas los ⌒ YV 60-61 H 2
Roques, Los ○ YV 60-61 H 2
Roquetas de Mar ○ E 98-99 F 6
Roraima ■ BR 62-63 D 5
Roraima, Mount ▲ GUY 62-63 D 3
Roraya ∼ RI 164-165 H 6
Rorey Lake ⊖ CDN 30-31 F 2
Rori ○ RI 166-167 J 2
Rorketon ○ CDN (MAN) 234-235 D 3
Røros ☆••• N 86-87 E 5
Rørvik ○ N 86-87 E 4
Ros' ∼ UA 102-103 G 3
Rosa ○ CDN (MAN) 234-235 G 5
Rosa, La ○ YV 60-61 G 3
Rosa, Lake ⊖ BS 54-55 J 4
Rosa, Rio Santa ∼ BOL 70-71 D 5
Rosal ○ BR 72-73 K 6
Rošal' ○ RUS 94-95 Q 4
Rosal, El ○ CO 60-61 D 5
Rosal de la Frontera ○ E 98-99 D 6
Rosalia ○ USA (WA) 244-245 H 3
Rosalind ○ CDN (ALB) 232-233 F 3
Rosamond ○ USA (CA) 248-249 F 5
Rosamoraga ○ MEX 50-51 G 6
Rosana ○ BR 72-73 D 7
Rosário ○ BR 68-69 F 3
Rosario ○ DOM 54-55 K 5
Rosario ○ MEX 50-51 E 4
Rosario ○ PE 70-71 B 4
Rosario ○ PY 76-77 J 3
Rosario ○ RA (BUA) 78-79 J 2
Rosario ○ RA (JU) 76-77 D 2
Rosario ○ RA (COD) 78-79 J 2
Rosario ○ RCH 76-77 B 4
Rosario ○ RP (BTG) 160-161 D 6
Rosario ○ RP (LUN) 160-161 D 4
Rosario, Cayo del ⌒ C 54-55 E 4
Rosario, El ○ MEX (BCN) 50-51 B 2
Rosario, El ○ MEX (SIN) 50-51 G 6
Rosario, El ○ YV (BOL) 60-61 J 4
Rosario, El ○ YV (MON) 60-61 K 3
Rosario, Río ∼ RA 76-77 E 3
Rosario, Río ∼ RA 76-77 D 2
Rosario de la Frontera ○• RA 76-77 E 3
Rosario de Lerma ○ RA 76-77 D 3
Rosario del Ingre ○ BOL 70-71 F 7
Rosario del Tala ○ RA 78-79 K 2
Rosário do Catete ○ BR 68-69 K 7
Rosário do Sul ○ BR 76-77 K 6
Rosário Oeste ○ BR 70-71 J 4
Rosario Strait ≈ USA 244-245 C 2
Rosarito ○ MEX (BCN) 50-51 B 3
Rosarito ○ MEX (BCS) 50-51 D 4
Rosarito ○ MEX (BCN) 50-51 A 1
Rosas ○ CO 60-61 C 6
Rosas, Las ○ MEX 52-53 H 3
Rosas, Las ○ RA 78-79 J 2
Rosaspata ○ PE 70-71 C 4
Rosa Zárate ○ EC 64-65 C 1
Rosburg ○ USA (WA) 244-245 B 4
Roscoe ○ USA (NY) 280-281 M 2
Roscoe ○ USA (SD) 260-261 G 1
Roscoe ○ USA (TX) 264-265 D 6
Roscoe River ∼ CDN 24-25 M 6
Roscoff ○ F 90-91 F 7
Ros Comáin = Roscommon ☆ IRL 90-91 C 5
Roscommon ○ USA (MI) 272-273 E 3
Roscommon = Ros Comáin ☆ IRL 90-91 C 5
Ros Cré = Roscrea ○ IRL 90-91 D 5
Roscrea = Ros Cré ○ IRL 90-91 D 5
Roseau ○ USA (MN) 270-271 C 2
Roseau ★ WD 56 E 4
Roseau River ∼ USA (MN) 270-271 B 2
Roseau River Wildlife Refuge ⊥ USA (MN) 270-271 B 2
Roseaux ○ RH 54-55 H 5
Rosebank ○ CDN (MAN) 234-235 E 5
Rose Belle ○ MS 224 C 7
Rosebery ○ AUS 180-181 H 6
Roseblade Lake ⊖ CDN 30-31 V 5
Rose Blanche ○ CDN (NFL) 242-243 K 5
Roseboro ○ USA (NC) 282-283 J 6
Rosebud ○ CDN (ALB) 232-233 F 4
Rose Bud ○ USA (AR) 276-277 C 5
Rosebud ○ USA (SD) 260-261 F 3
Rosebud ○ USA (TX) 266-267 L 2
Rosebud Creek ∼ USA (MT) 250-251 N 6
Rosebud Indian Reservation ⨯ USA (SD) 260-261 F 3
Rosebud River ∼ CDN (ALB) 232-233 E 4
Roseburg ○ USA (OR) 244-245 B 7
Rose City ○ USA (MI) 272-273 E 3
Rose Creek ∼ CDN (ALB) 232-233 D 3
Rosedale ○ AUS 178-179 J 2
Rosedale ○ CDN (ALB) 232-233 F 4
Rosedale ○ CDN (BC) 230-231 H 4
Rosedale ○ USA (IN) 274-275 L 5
Rosedale ○ USA (MS) 268-269 J 3
Rosefield ○ USA (LA) 268-269 H 5
Roseglen ○ USA (ND) 258-259 F 4
Rose Harbour ○ CDN (BC) 228-229 C 4
Rose Hill ○ MS 224 C 7
Rose Hill ○ USA (MS) 268-269 L 4
Rose Hill ○ USA (NC) 282-283 J 6
Rose Island ⌒ BS 54-55 G 2
Roseisle ○ CDN (MAN) 234-235 E 5
Rose Lake ○ CDN (BC) 228-229 H 2
Rose Lake ○ USA (ID) 250-251 C 4
Roseland ○ USA (LA) 268-269 K 6
Roselle ○ USA (IL) 274-275 K 3
Rosemount ○ USA (MN) 270-271 E 6
Rosenberg ○ USA (TX) 268-269 E 7
Rosenberg = Ružomberok ○ SK 92-93 P 4
Rosenberg, Sulzbach- ○ D 92-93 L 4
Rosenburg ○ CDN (MAN) 234-235 F 3
Rosendal ☆ N 86-87 C 7
Rosendal ○ ZA 220-221 H 4
Rosenfeld ○ USA (TX) 266-267 E 3
Rosenheim ○ D 92-93 M 5
Rosenort ○ CDN (MAN) 234-235 F 5
Rose Point ▲ CDN (BC) 228-229 C 2
Rose Prairie ○ CDN 32-33 K 3
Rose River ∼ AUS 174-175 C 3
Roses ○ USA (PA) 280-281 G 2
Rosetitla ○ MEX 50-51 G 3
Rosetown ○ CDN (SAS) 232-233 L 4
Rosetta = Rašīd ○• ET 194-195 E 2
Rosette ○ USA (UT) 254-255 B 2
Rose Valley ○ CDN (SAS) 232-233 P 3
Rosevear ○ CDN (ALB) 232-233 B 2
Roseveltpiek ▲ SME 62-63 G 4
Roseville ○ USA (IL) 274-275 H 4
Roseville Rio ○ USA (CA) 246-247 D 5
Rosewood ○ AUS 172-173 J 4
Rosharon ○ USA (TX) 268-269 E 7
Rosh Pinah ○ NAM 220-221 C 3
Rosi ∼ IND 138-139 G 5
Rosie Creek ○ AUS 174-175 C 4
Rosiers, Cap-des- ○ CDN (QUE) 240-241 L 2
Rosignano Marittima ○ I 100-101 C 3
Rosignol ○ GUY 62-63 F 2
Rosillo, Cañada el ∼ RA 76-77 F 2
Roșiori de Vede ○ RO 102-103 D 5
Rosita, La ○ CO 60-61 F 5
Rosita, La ○ NIC 52-53 B 5
Roskilde ○•• DK 86-87 F 9
Roslavl' ○ RUS 94-95 N 5
Roslin ○ CDN (ONT) 238-239 H 4
Roslyn Lake ⊖ CDN (ONT) 234-235 Q 5
Rosman ○ USA (NC) 282-283 E 5
Rosmead ○ ZA 220-221 G 5
Ros Mhic Thriúin = New Ross ○ IRL 90-91 D 5
Ross, Cape ▲ RP 160-161 C 7
Rossano ○ I 100-101 F 5
Ross Barnett Reservoir < USA (MS) 268-269 L 4
Ross Bay ≈ 24-25 d 7
Ross Bay Junction ○ CDN 38-39 L 2
Ross-Béthio ○ SN 196-197 B 6
Rossburn ○ CDN (MAN) 234-235 C 4
Ross City ○ USA (TX) 264-265 C 6
Rosseau ○ CDN (ONT) 238-239 F 3
Rosseau, Lake ⊖ CDN (ONT) 238-239 F 3
Rosser ○ CDN (MAN) 234-235 F 4
Ross Ice Shelf ⊂ ARK 16 E 0
Rossignol, Lac ⊖ CDN 38-39 H 2
Rossignol, Lake ⊖ CDN (NS) 240-241 K 6
Rössing ○ NAM 216-217 C 11
Ross Inlet ≈ 24-25 c 7
Ross Island ⌒ ARK 16 G 31
Ross Island ⌒ ARK 16 F 17
Ross Island ⌒ CDN 34-35 H 3
Ross Lake ⊖ USA (WA) 244-245 E 2
Rossland ○ CDN (BC) 230-231 M 4
Rosslare = Ros Láir ○ IRL 90-91 D 5
Rosso ☆ RIM 196-197 C 6
Rossomaha ∼ RUS 114-115 T 5
Rossošino ○ RUS 118-119 G 8
Rossouw ○ ZA 220-221 H 5
Rossport ○ CDN (ONT) 234-235 Q 6
Ross River ○ AUS 178-179 C 2
Ross River ○ CDN (NWT) 20-21 Y 6
Ross River ∼ CDN 20-21 Z 5
Ross Sea ≈ 16 F 19
Rosston ○ USA (AR) 276-277 B 7
Rosston ○ USA (OK) 264-265 E 2
Røssvatnet ⊖ N 86-87 F 4
Rossville ○ AUS 174-175 H 4
Rossville Mission • CDN 34-35 H 4
Rosswood ○ CDN (BC) 228-229 F 2
Røst ○ N 86-87 F 3
Rostāq ○ AFG 136-137 L 6
Rostāq ○ IR 134-135 E 5
Rosthern ○ CDN (SAS) 232-233 M 3
Rostock ○•• D 92-93 M 1
Rostov ☆•• RUS 94-95 Q 3
Rostov-na-Donu ☆ RUS 102-103 L 4
Rostraver ○ USA (PA) 280-281 G 3
Rostrenen ○ F 90-91 F 7
Roswell ○ USA (GA) 284-285 F 2
Roswell ○ USA (NM) 256-257 L 5
Roswell ○ USA (SD) 260-261 J 2
Rosyth ○ CDN (ALB) 232-233 G 3
Rotan ○ USA (TX) 264-265 D 6
Rote = Pulau Roti ⌒ RI 166-167 B 7
Rothenburg ob der Tauber ○•• D 92-93 L 4
Rotherham ○ GB 90-91 G 5
Rothesay ○• GB 90-91 E 4
Rothsay ○ USA (MN) 270-271 B 4
Rothschild ○ USA (WI) 270-271 J 6
Roti ○ RI 166-167 B 7
Roti, Pulau ⌒ RI 166-167 B 7
Roti, Selat ≈ 166-167 B 7
Rotifunk ○ WAL 202-203 D 5
Roto ○ AUS 180-181 H 2
Rotonda West ○ USA (FL) 286-287 G 5
Rotondo, Monte ▲ F 98-99 M 3
Rotorua ○•• NZ 182 F 3
Rotterdam ○• NL 92-93 H 3
Rottnest Island ○• AUS (WA) 176-177 C 6
Rottnest Island ⌒ AUS (WA) 176-177 C 6
Rottweil ○• D 92-93 K 4
Roualist Bank ≃ 158-159 H 6
Roubaix ○ F 90-91 J 6
Rouen ☆• F 90-91 H 7
Rouge, P.K. ○ RCB 210-211 E 5
Rouge, Rivière ∼ CDN (QUE) 238-239 L 3
Rouge, Rivière ∼ CDN (QUE) 238-239 L 2
Rough River ∼ USA (KY) 276-277 J 3
Rough River Reservoir < USA (KY) 276-277 J 3
Rough Rock ○ USA (AZ) 256-257 F 2
Rouhia ○ TN 190-191 G 3
Rouleau ○ CDN (SAS) 232-233 O 5
Roumsiki ○• CAM 204-205 K 3
Roundeyed, Lac ⊖ CDN 38-39 J 2
Roundhead ○ USA (OH) 280-281 C 3
Round Hill ○ CDN (ALB) 232-233 F 2
Round Hill ○ USA (KY) 276-277 J 3
Round House ▲ USA (KS) 262-263 G 6
Round Lake ○ CDN (ONT) 238-239 H 3
Round Mountain ▲ AUS 178-179 M 6
Round Mountain ○ USA (CA) 246-247 D 3
Round Mountain ○ USA (NV) 246-247 H 5
Round Pond ⊖ CDN (NFL) 242-243 N 4
Round Rock ○ USA (AZ) 256-257 F 2
Round Rock ○ USA (TX) 266-267 K 3
Round Spring ○ USA (MO) 276-277 D 3
Round Spring Cave • USA (MO) 276-277 D 3
Round Top ○ USA (TX) 266-267 L 3
Roundup ○ USA (MT) 250-251 L 5
Round Valley Indian Reservation ⨯ USA (CA) 246-247 B 4
Rounthwaite ○ CDN (MAN) 234-235 D 5
Roura ○ F 62-63 H 3
Rourkela = Raurkela ○• IND 142-143 D 4
Rouses Point ○ USA (NY) 278-279 H 4
Routhierville ○ CDN (QUE) 240-241 H 2
Rouxdam, P.K. le < ZA 220-221 G 5
Rouxville ○ ZA 220-221 H 5
Rouyn-Noranda ○ CDN (QUE) 236-237 J 4
Rovdino ○ RUS 88-89 R 6
Roven'ky ○ UA 102-103 L 3
Rover ○ USA (AR) 276-277 B 6
Rover, Mount ▲ CDN 20-21 U 3
Rovereto ○• I 100-101 C 2
Roversi ○ RA 76-77 G 4
Rovigo ☆ I 100-101 C 2
Rovinari ○ RO 102-103 C 5
Rovinj ○• HR 100-101 D 2
Rovno = Rivne ○ UA 102-103 E 2
Rovnoe ○ RUS 96-97 E 8
Rovnyj, mys ▲ RUS 120-121 V 4
Rovnyj, ostrov ⌒ RUS 120-121 U 3
Rovubo ∼ EAT (KAG) 212-213 C 5
Rovuma ∼ MOC 214-215 K 6
Rowala Kot ○ IND 138-139 D 3
Rowan, Port ○ CDN (ONT) 238-239 E 6
Rowatt ○ CDN (SAS) 232-233 O 5
Rowden ○ USA (TX) 264-265 E 6
Rowdy ○ USA (KY) 276-277 M 3
Rowena ○ USA (TX) 266-267 G 2
Rowland ○ USA (NC) 282-283 H 6
Rowletta ○ CDN (SAS) 232-233 N 5
Rowley ○ CDN 24-25 g 6
Rowley Island ⌒ CDN 24-25 h 6
Rowley Lake ⊖ CDN 30-31 R 5
Rowley River ∼ CDN 24-25 j 5
Rowley Shelf ≃ 172-173 C 5
Rowley Shoals ⌒ AUS 172-173 D 4
Roxa, Ilha ⌒ GNB 202-203 C 4
Roxas ○ RP (ISA) 160-161 D 4
Roxas ○ RP (MIO) 160-161 D 6
Roxas ○ RP (PAL) 160-161 C 7
Roxas ☆ RP (CAP) 160-161 E 7
Roxboro ○ USA (NC) 282-283 J 4
Roxborough Downs ○ AUS 178-179 E 2
Roxby Downs ○ AUS 178-179 D 6
Roxie ○ USA (MS) 268-269 J 5
Roxo, Cap ▲ GNB 202-203 B 3
Roxton ○ USA (TX) 264-265 J 5
Roxton Falls ○ CDN (QUE) 238-239 N 3
Roy ○ USA (MT) 250-251 L 4
Roy ○ USA (NM) 256-257 L 3
Roy ○ USA (TX) 264-265 B 4
Roy ○ USA (UT) 254-255 C 2
Roy, Lac le ⊖ CDN 36-37 M 5
Royal, Mount ▲ CDN (ONT) 234-235 P 5
Royal Center ○ USA (IN) 274-275 M 4
Royal Charlotte, Bank ≃ 72-73 L 4
Royal Chitawan National Park ⊥••• NEP 144-145 E 7
Royal City ○ USA (WA) 244-245 F 4
Royale, Isle ⌒ USA (MI) 270-271 J 3
Royal Geographical Society Islands ⌒ CDN 24-25 W 6
Royal Gorge • USA (CO) 254-255 K 5
Royal Island ⌒ BS 54-55 G 2
Royal Natal National Park ⊥ ZA 220-221 J 4
Royal National Park ⊥ AUS 180-181 L 3
Royal Palace ○• RI 168 D 7
Royal Palm Hammock ○ USA (FL) 286-287 H 6
Royal Park ○ CDN (ALB) 232-233 F 2
Royal Society Range ▲ ARK 16 F 16
Royal Soud, Port ≈ 48-49 H 3
Royalties ○ CDN (ALB) 232-233 D 5
Royalton ○ USA (MN) 270-271 D 5
Royalton ○ USA (VT) 278-279 J 5
Royan ○• F 90-91 G 9
Roye ○ F 90-91 J 7
Roy Hill ○ AUS (WA) 172-173 D 7
Roy Hill ▲ AUS (WA) 172-173 D 7
Røyrvik ○ N 86-87 F 4
Royston ○ USA (GA) 284-285 G 2
Rožaje ○• YU 100-101 H 3
Różan ○ PL 92-93 Q 2
Rozdol'ne ☆ UA 102-103 H 5
Rozel ○ USA (KS) 262-263 G 6
Rozet ○ USA (WY) 252-253 N 2
Rozivka ○ UA 102-103 K 4
Rožňava ○ SK 92-93 Q 4
Rozy Ljuksemburga, mys ▲ RUS 108-109 c 1
r-Raṭqa, Wādi ∼ IRQ 128-129 J 6
Rtiščevo ○ RUS 94-95 S 5
Ruacana ○ NAM 216-217 C 8
Ruacaná, Quedas do ∼•• ANG 216-217 C 8
Ruacana Falls ∼•• NAM 216-217 C 8
Ruaha National Park ⊥ EAT 214-215 H 4
Ruahine Range ▲ NZ 182 F 3
Ru'ais ○ UAE 134-135 E 6
Ruangwa ○ EAT 214-215 K 6
Ruapehu, Mount ▲ NZ 182 E 3
Ruapuke Island ⌒ NZ 182 B 7
Ruarwe ○ MW 214-215 H 6
Ruatahuna ○ NZ 182 F 3
Ruatoria ○ NZ 182 G 2
Ruawai ○ NZ 182 E 2
Rubafu ○ EAT 212-213 C 4
Rubai'iya, ar- ○ KSA 130-131 J 4
Rub' al-Ḫālī, ar- ⁂ KSA 132-133 D 4
Rubcovsk ○ RUS 124-125 M 3
Rubeho Mountains ▲ EAT 214-215 J 4
Rubens, Rio ∼ RCH 80 D 6
Ruberong ▲ IND 138-139 F 3
Rubeshibe ○ J 152-153 K 3
Rubi ○ ZRE 210-211 K 2
Rubi ∼ ZRE 210-211 K 2
Rubiataba ○ BR 72-73 F 3
Rubicon River ∼ USA (CA) 246-247 E 5
Rubikon, mys ▲ RUS 112-113 S 6
Rubim ○ BR 72-73 K 4
Rubinéia ○ BR 72-73 E 6
Rubio ○ YV 60-61 E 4
Ruble ○ USA (IA) 274-275 B 2
Rubondo Island ⌒ EAT 212-213 C 5
Rubondo National Park ⊥ EAT 212-213 C 5
Ruby ○ USA 20-21 N 4
Ruby ○ USA (AZ) 256-257 D 7
Ruby Dome ▲ USA (NV) 246-247 K 3
Ruby Lake ○ CDN (SAS) 232-233 Q 2
Ruby Lake ⊖ USA (NV) 246-247 K 3
Ruby Mountains ▲ USA (NV) 246-247 K 3
Ruby Plains ○ AUS 172-173 H 5
Ruby Range ▲ CDN 20-21 V 6
Ruby River ∼ USA (MT) 250-251 G 6
Rubys Inn ○ USA (UT) 254-255 C 6
Rubyvale ○ AUS 178-179 J 2
Ruby Valley ○ USA (NV) 246-247 K 3
Rucachoroi, Cerro ▲ RA 78-79 D 5
Rucava ○ LV 94-95 G 3
Ruch ○ USA (OR) 244-245 B 8
Ruči ○ RUS 88-89 O 3
Rucio, El ○ MEX 50-51 H 6
Ruckersville ○ USA (VA) 280-281 H 5
Rūd ○ IR 134-135 J 1
Rudal ○ AUS 180-181 D 2
Rudall River National Park ⊥ AUS 172-173 E 7
Rūdbar ○• IR 128-129 N 4
Ruddell ○ CDN (SAS) 232-233 L 3
Ruddera, buhta ≈ 112-113 W 4
Rūd-e Čalūs ∼ IR 136-137 B 6
Rūd-e Helle ∼ IR 134-135 D 4
Rūdehen ○ IR 136-137 B 7
Rūd-e Mārūn ∼ IR 134-135 C 3
Rūd-e Šindand ∼ AFG 134-135 K 2
Rudewa ○ EAT 214-215 H 6
Rūdḫāne-ye 'Alīābād ∼ IR 134-135 J 3
Rūdḫāne-ye Ġarrāhī ∼ IR 134-135 C 3
Rūdḫāne-ye Nekā ∼ IR 136-137 C 6
Rudkøbing ○• DK 86-87 E 9
Rudnaja Pristan' ○ RUS 122-123 G 6
Rudnik ▲• YU 100-101 H 2
Rudnja ☆ RUS 94-95 M 4
Rudnyj ○ KA 124-125 C 2
Rudnyy = Rudnyj ○ KA 124-125 C 2
Rud Ø ⌒ GRØ 28-29 T 5
Rudolf, Lake = Turkana, Lake ⊖ EAK 212-213 F 2
Rudolf'a ○ RUS 84-85 e 2
Rudolf'a, ostrov ⌒ RUS 84-85 f 2
Rudong ○ VRC 154-155 M 5
Rūdsar ○ IR 136-137 B 6
Rudyard ○ USA (MI) 270-271 O 4
Rudyard ○ USA (MT) 250-251 J 3
Rue, La ○ USA (TX) 264-265 J 6
Ruente Nacional ○ CO 60-61 E 5
Ruenya ∼ ZW 218-219 G 3
Rufā'ah ○ SUD 200-201 F 5
Ruff Creek ○ USA (PA) 280-281 F 4
Ruffin ○ USA (SC) 284-285 K 3
Rufiji ∼ EAT 214-215 J 5
Rufino ○ BR 62-63 F 6
Rufino ○ RA 78-79 H 3
Rufisque ○ SN 202-203 B 2
Rufrufua ○ RI 166-167 G 3
Rufunsa ○ Z 218-219 E 2
Rufunsa ∼ Z 218-219 E 2
Rufus ○ USA (OR) 244-245 E 5
Rufus Lake ⊖ CDN 20-21 Z 2
Rugāji ○ LV 94-95 K 3
Rugao ○ VRC 154-155 M 5
Rugby ○ USA (ND) 258-259 G 3
Rügen ⌒ D 92-93 M 1
Rügenwalde = Darłowo ○• PL 92-93 O 1
Rugged Island ⌒ USA 20-21 Q 7
Rugheiwa < SUD 200-201 E 4
Rugufu ∼ EAT 212-213 C 6
Ruḥaimiya, ar- ○ IRQ 130-131 J 3
Ruḥayyah, Ġabal ar- ▲ KSA 130-131 L 4
Ruhengeri ○ RWA 212-213 B 4
Ruhnu saar ⌒• EST 94-95 H 3
Ruhudji ∼ EAT 214-215 H 5
Ruhuhu ∼ EAT 214-215 H 6
Rui'an ○ VRC 156-157 M 3
Rui Barbosa ○ BR 72-73 K 2
Ruichang ○ VRC 156-157 J 2
Ruicheng ○ VRC 154-155 G 4
Ruidosa ○ USA (TX) 266-267 C 3
Ruidoso ○ USA (NM) 256-257 K 5
Ruidoso Downs ○ USA (NM) 256-257 K 5
Ruijin ○ VRC 156-157 J 4
Ruiki ∼ ZRE 210-211 K 4
Ruili ○ VRC 142-143 K 3
Ruimte ○ NAM 220-221 B 1
Ruin Point ▲ CDN 36-37 H 3
Ruins ∴ AUS 176-177 L 5
Ruins of Sambor • K 158-159 H 4
Ruipa ○ EAT (MOR) 214-215 J 5
Ruiru ○ EAK 212-213 F 4
Ruisseau-à-Rebours ○ CDN (QUE) 242-243 C 3
Ruitersbos ○ ZA 220-221 F 6
Rūjiena ○•• LV 94-95 J 3
Ruka ○ FIN 88-89 K 3
Rukanga ○ EAK 212-213 G 5
Rukarara ∼ RWA 212-213 B 5
Ruki ∼ ZRE 210-211 G 4
Rukua ○ RI 164-165 J 6
Rukubji ○ BHT 142-143 G 2
Rukutama ∼ RUS 122-123 K 4
Rukwa ■ EAT 214-215 F 4
Rukwa, Lake ⊖ EAT 214-215 F 4
Rule ○ USA (TX) 264-265 E 5
Rulenge ○ EAT 212-213 C 5
Ruleville ○ USA (MS) 268-269 K 3
Ruma ○ WAN 198-199 C 6
Ruma ○ YU 100-101 G 2
Rumāḥ ○ KSA 130-131 K 5
Rumahbaru ○ RI 162-163 B 2
Rumahkai ○ RI 166-167 E 3
Rumah Kulit ○ MAL 164-165 D 2
Rumahtinggih ○ RI 166-167 L 5
Rumaila ○ IRQ 130-131 K 2
Ruma National Park ⊥ EAK 212-213 E 4
Rumbek ○ SUD 206-207 J 5
Rumberpon, Pulau ⌒ RI 166-167 H 2
Rumble Beach ○ CDN (BC) 230-231 B 3
Rum Cay = Mamana Island ⌒ BS 54-55 H 3
Rum Jungle ○ AUS 172-173 K 2
Rummāna ○ ET 194-195 F 2
Rumo ○ BR 68-69 F 2
Rumoi ○ J 152-153 J 3
Rumonge ○ BU 212-213 B 5
Rumorosa, La ○• MEX 50-51 A 1
Rumphi ○ MW 214-215 G 6
Rumpi Hills ▲ CAM 204-205 H 6
Rum River ∼ USA (MN) 270-271 E 5
Rumsey ○ CDN (ALB) 232-233 F 4
Rumuruti ○ EAK 212-213 F 3
Run, Pulau ⌒ RI 166-167 E 4
Runan ○ VRC 154-155 J 5
Runaway, Cape ▲ NZ 182 F 2
Runaway Bay ○ JA 54-55 G 5
Runazi ○ EAT 212-213 C 5
Runde ∼ ZW 218-219 F 5
Rundeng ○ RI 162-163 B 3
Rundu ☆ NAM (KV1) 216-217 E 8
Runduma, Pulau ⌒ RI 164-165 J 6
Runge ○ USA (TX) 266-267 K 5
Rungu ○ ZRE 212-213 A 2
Rungwa ○ EAT (RUK) 214-215 F 4
Rungwa ○ EAT (SIN) 214-215 G 4
Rungwa ∼ EAT 214-215 G 4
Rungwa Game Reserve ⊥ EAT 214-215 G 4
Runmarö ⌒ S 86-87 J 7
Running Springs ○ USA (CA) 248-249 G 5
Running Water Draw ∼ USA (TX) 264-265 B 4
Runnymede ○ AUS 174-175 G 7
Runnymede ○ CDN (SAS) 232-233 R 4
Runton Range ▲ AUS 176-177 G 1
Ruokolahti ○ FIN 88-89 K 6
Ruoqiang ○ VRC 146-147 J 6
Ruo Shui ∼ VRC 148-149 D 7
Ruo Shui ∼ VRC 154-155 B 2
Ruovesi ○ FIN 88-89 H 6
Rupanco, Lago ⊖ RCH 78-79 C 6
Rupanyup ○ AUS 180-181 G 4
Rupat, Pulau ⌒ RI 162-163 D 4
Rupat, Selat ≈ 162-163 D 4
Rupert ○ USA (AR) 276-277 C 5
Rupert ○ USA (ID) 252-253 E 4
Rupert ○ USA (WV) 280-281 F 6
Rupert, Baie de ⊖ CDN 38-39 E 3
Rupert, Fort ○ CDN 38-39 E 3
Rupert, Rivière ∼ CDN 38-39 F 3
Rupert, Rivière ∼ CDN 38-39 E 3
Rupisi ○ ZW 218-219 G 5
Ruponda ○ EAT 214-215 K 6
Ruppert Coast ⌣ ARK 16 F 22
Ruqai', ar- ○ KSA 130-131 K 3
Ruqayba ○ SUD 200-201 E 5
Rural Hall ○ USA (NC) 282-283 G 4
Rurópolis Presidente Médici ○ BR 66-67 K 5
Rurutu Island ⌒ F 13 M 5
Ruṣāfa, ar- ○•• SYR 128-129 H 5

Rušan o TJ 136-137 M 6
Rusanova, lednik ⊂ RUS 108-109 b 2
Rusanova, zaliv ⊂ RUS 108-109 J 4
Rusanovo o RUS 108-109 G 6
Rusape o ZW 218-219 G 4
Rusayriş Dam < SUD 208-209 B 3
Ruse o BG 102-103 D 6
Rushan o VRC 154-155 M 3
Rush Center o USA (KS) 262-263 G 6
Rush City o USA (MN) 270-271 F 5
Rush Creek ~ USA (CO) 254-255 M 5
Rush Creek ~ USA (OK) 264-265 G 4
Rushfort o USA (MN) 270-271 G 7
Rush Lake o CDN (SAS) 232-233 L 5
Rush Springs o USA (OK) 264-265 G 4
Rushville o USA (IL) 274-275 H 4
Rushville o USA (IN) 274-275 N 5
Rushville o USA (NE) 262-263 D 2
Rushworth o AUS 180-181 H 4
Rusizi ~ BU 212-213 B 5
Rusk o USA (TX) 268-269 E 5
Rus'ka o UA 102-103 D 4
Rus'ka, Rava- o UA 102-103 C 2
Ruskin o USA (FL) 286-287 G 4
Ruskin o USA (NE) 262-263 J 4
Rusksele o S 86-87 J 4
Rusné o•· LT 94-95 G 4
Ruso o USA (ND) 258-259 G 4
Rus Rus o HN 52-53 B 4
Russas o BR 68-69 K 4
Russel o CDN (MAN) 234-235 B 4
Russel o USA (MN) 270-271 C 6
Russell o USA (KS) 262-263 H 6
Russell o USA (ND) 258-259 G 3
Russell o USA (NY) 278-279 F 4
Russell, Cape ▲ CDN 24-25 N 3
Russell, Kap ▲ GRØ 26-27 Q 4
Russell, Mount ▲ AUS 176-177 L 1
Russell, Mount ▲ USA 20-21 P 5
Russel Lake ⊂ CDN 30-31 M 4
Russell Fiord ≈ 20-21 V 7
Russell Fiord Wilderness ⊥ USA 20-21 V 7
Russell Gletscher ⊂ GRØ 28-29 P 3
Russell Inlet ≈ 20-21 Z 2
Russell Island ⌒ CDN 24-25 W 4
Russell Islands ⌒ SOL 184 I d 3
Russell Lake ⊂ CDN 34-35 F 2
Russell Lake < USA (GA) 284-285 H 2
Russellville o USA (AL) 284-285 C 2
Russellville o USA (AR) 276-277 B 5
Russellville o USA (KY) 276-277 J 4
Russel Springs o USA (KS) 262-263 E 6
Russia = Rossija ■ RUS 114-115 H 4
Russian River ~ USA (CA) 246-247 B 4
Russiaville o USA (IN) 274-275 M 4
Russkaja Gavan, zaliv ⊂ RUS 108-109 K 3
Russkaja Lučajaha ~ RUS 108-109 T 8
Russkaja Rečka o RUS 118-119 K 5
Russkaja Tavra o RUS 96-97 K 5
Russkie gory ▲ RUS 112-113 P 4
Russkij, ostrov ⌒ RUS 108-109 b 3
Russkij Zavorot, poluostrov ⌣ RUS 88-89 W 2
Rust, De o ZA 220-221 F 6
Rustāq, ar- o OM 132-133 K 2
Rustavi o GE 126-127 F 7
Rustburg o USA (VA) 280-281 G 6
Rust de Winter o ZA 220-221 J 2
Rust de Winterdam < ZA 220-221 J 2
Rustefjelbma o N 86-87 O 1
Rustenburg o ZA 220-221 H 2
Rustfontein Dam < ZA 220-221 H 4
Rustic o USA (CO) 254-255 K 3
Ruston o USA (LA) 268-269 H 4
Rusumo Falls ~• EAT (KAG) 212-213 C 5
Ruta o RI 164-165 K 4
Rutaimi, ar- o IRQ 128-129 J 5
Rutan o CDN (SAS) 232-233 N 3
Rutana o BU 212-213 C 5
Rutba, ar- o IRQ 128-129 J 6
Ruten ▲ N (OPP) 86-87 D 6
Ruten ▲ N (STR) 86-87 D 5
Ruteng o• RI 168 E 7
Rutenga o ZW 218-219 F 5
Ruth o USA (NC) 282-283 F 5
Ruth o USA (NV) 246-247 L 4
Rutherford Fork ~ USA (TN) 276-277 G 4
Rutherglen o AUS 180-181 J 4
Ruthilda o CDN (SAS) 232-233 K 4
Ruthville o USA (ND) 258-259 F 3
Ruti o PNG 183 C 3
Rutland o CDN (BC) 230-231 K 4
Rutland o CDN (SAS) 232-233 J 3
Rutland o USA (VT) 278-279 J 5
Rutland Island ⌒ IND 140-141 L 4
Rutland Plains o AUS 174-175 F 4
Rutledge o USA (TN) 282-283 D 4
Rutledge Lake ⊂ CDN 30-31 O 5
Rutledge River ~ CDN 30-31 O 5
Rutog o VRC 144-145 B 4
Rutshuru o ZRE 212-213 B 4
Rutukira ~ EAT 214-215 H 6
Rutul o RUS 126-127 G 7
Ruvu ~ EAT 214-215 K 4
Ruvubu, Parc National de la ⊥ BU 212-213 C 5
Ruvuma ◘ EAT 214-215 H 6
Ruvuma ~ EAT 214-215 K 6
Ruwaida, ar- o KSA (RIY) 130-131 J 5
Ruwaida, ar- o KSA (RIY) 130-131 J 6
Ruwais, ar- o Q 134-135 D 5
Ruwaišid, Wādī r- ~ JOR 130-131 F 1
Ruwāq, Ǧabal ar- ▲ SYR 128-129 G 5
Ruwenzori ▲ ZRE 212-213 B 3
Ruwi o OM 132-133 L 2
Ruya ~ ZW 218-219 F 3
Ruyang o VRC 154-155 H 4
Rū-ye Dōāb o AFG 136-137 K 7
Ruyigi o BU 212-213 C 5
Ruyuan o VRC 156-157 H 4
Ruza ☆ RUS 94-95 P 4
Ruzaevka o RUS 96-97 D 6
Ružany o BY 94-95 J 5
Ruzhou o VRC 154-155 H 4
Ružomberok o SK 92-93 P 4
Rwamagana o RWA 212-213 C 4
Rwanda ■ RWA 212-213 B 5
Rwashamaire o EAU 212-213 C 4
Rweru, Lac ⊂ BU 212-213 C 5
Ryan o USA (OK) 264-265 G 4
Ryan, Mount ▲ AUS (NSW) 180-181 K 2
Ryan, Mount ▲ AUS (QLD) 174-175 G 4
Ryazan' = Rjazan' ☆·· RUS 94-95 Q 4
Rybač'e = Ysyk-Köl o KS 146-147 C 4
Rybacij, aral ⌒ KA 126-127 J 5
Rybačij, poluostrov ⌣ RUS 88-89 M 2
Ryberg Fjord ≈ 28-29 Z 2
Rybinsk ☆ RUS 94-95 Q 2
Rybinskoe vodohranilišče < RUS 94-95 Q 2
Rybinskoye Vodokhranilishche = Rybinskoe vodohranilišče < RUS 94-95 Q 2
Rybnaja ~ RUS 108-109 h 3
Rybnaja ~ RUS 116-117 G 8
Rybnaja ~ RUS 116-117 E 5
Rybnaja Sloboda ☆ RUS 96-97 G 6
Rybnica = Rîbnița ☆ MD 102-103 F 4
Rybnik o• PL 92-93 P 3
Rybnoe o RUS 116-117 G 8
Rybnoe o RUS (RZN) 94-95 Q 4
Rybnovsk o RUS 122-123 J 2
Ryčkovo o RUS 96-97 M 4
Rycroft o CDN 32-33 L 4
Ryder o USA (ND) 258-259 F 4
Ryder Gletscher ⊂ GRØ 26-27 a 3
Ryder Øer ⌒ GRØ 26-27 V 6
Ryderwood o USA (WA) 244-245 B 4
Ryegate o USA (MT) 250-251 K 5
Rye Patch Reservoir ⊂ USA (NV) 246-247 G 3
Ryerson o CDN (SAS) 232-233 R 6
Ryjanranot, ostrov ⌒ RUS 112-113 P 1
Rykerts o CDN (BC) 230-231 N 4
Ryki o PL 92-93 Q 3
Ryley o CDN (ALB) 232-233 F 2
Ryl'sk o RUS 102-103 J 2
Rylstone o AUS 180-181 K 2
Rynda ~ RUS 88-89 O 2
Ryn-kum ∴ KA 96-97 E 9
Ryohaku-sanchi ▲ J 152-153 G 6
Ryōhū-kaizan ≃ 152-153 L 5
Ryōtsu o J 152-153 H 5
Rypin o PL 92-93 P 2
Rys'ja o RUS 118-119 E 6
Rytkuči o RUS 112-113 Q 2
Ryukyu Islands = Nansei-shotō ⌒ J 152-153 B 1
Ryūkyū-shotō ⌒ J 152-153 C 12
Ryukyu Trench = Ryūkyū Trench ≃ 152-153 C 12
Rzeszów ☆ PL 92-93 R 3
Ržev ☆ RUS 94-95 O 3

S

Sa o PNG 183 C 3
Saa o CAM 204-205 J 6
Sa'a o SOL 184 I e 3
Sa'ādatābād o IR 134-135 E 3
Sa'ādatābād o IR 134-135 F 4
Saale ~ D 92-93 L 3
Saalfeld o• D 92-93 L 3
Saanich o CDN (BC) 230-231 F 5
Saarbrücken ☆• D 92-93 J 4
Sääre o EST 94-95 H 3
Saaremaa ⌒ EST 94-95 G 2
Saarijärvi o FIN 88-89 H 5
Saariselkä o FIN 88-89 J 2
Saaristomeren kansallispuisto =Skärgårdshavets nationalpar ⊥ FIN 88-89 F 7
Saarland ◘ D 92-93 J 4
Saarloq o GRØ (VGR) 28-29 P 4
Saarloq o GRØ (VGR) 28-29 S 6
Saarlouis o D 92-93 J 4
Šaartuz o TJ 136-137 L 6
Saatly = Saatlı o AZ 128-129 N 3
Saattut o GRØ 26-27 Z 8
Saaz = Žatec o CZ 92-93 M 3
Saba ⌒ NA 56 D 3
Sa'ba, Wādī aš- ~ KSA 130-131 G 4
Sababa o BR 68-69 F 2
Sab 'Ābār o SYR 128-129 G 6
Šabac o• YU 100-101 G 2
Sabah ◘ MAL 160-161 B 10
Sabaiya o SUD 206-207 H 5
Sabak, Cape ▲ USA 22-23 C 6
Sabaki ~ EAK 212-213 G 5
Sabalān, Kūhhā-ye ▲ IR 128-129 M 3
Sabalana, Kepulauan ⌒ RI 168 D 6
Sabalana, Pulau ⌒ RI 168 D 6
Sabalgarh o IND 138-139 F 6
Sabalito o CR 52-53 C 7
Sabaloyaco = Puerto Tumaco o EC 64-65 F 3
Sabana o C 54-55 H 4
Sabana o SME 62-63 G 3
Sabana, Archipiélago de ⌒ C 54-55 E 3
Sabana, La o MEX 52-53 E 3
Sabana, La o YV 60-61 H 2
Sabana Creek ~ USA (TX) 264-265 F 6
Sabana de Cardona o YV 60-61 H 4
Sabana de la Mar o DOM 54-55 L 5
Sabana de Mendoza o YV 60-61 F 3
Sabanagrande o HN 52-53 L 5
Sabana Grande de Palenque o DOM 54-55 K 5
Sabanalarga o CO (ANT) 60-61 D 4
Sabanalarga o CO (ATL) 60-61 D 2
Sabanalarga o CO (BOY) 60-61 E 5
Sabancuy o MEX 52-53 J 2
Sabaneta ☆ DOM 54-55 K 5
Sabaneta o YV 60-61 G 3
Sabang o RI 166-167 K 4
Sabangan o RP 160-161 D 4
Sabanilla o EC 64-65 C 3
Şabanözü ☆ TR 128-129 E 2
Sabara o BR 72-73 J 5
Sabarei o EAK 212-213 F 1
Sabari o GH 202-203 L 5
Sābarmati ~ IND 138-139 D 8
Sabaru, Pulau ⌒ RI 168 D 6
Sabatai o RI 164-165 L 2
Sabatino = Lago di Bracciano ⊂ I 100-101 D 3
Sabáudia o I 100-101 D 4
Sabaya o BOL 70-71 C 6
Şabāyā, Ǧazīrat aş- ⌒ KSA 132-133 B 4
Sabbāǧ, Ǧabal ▲ ET 194-195 G 3
Sabben Islands ⌒ PNG 183 D 2
Sabbioneta o I 100-101 C 2
Sabeila o NEP 144-145 F 7
Sabena Desert ∴ EAK 212-213 G 3
Saberania o RI 166-167 K 3
Sāberi, Hāmūn-e ⊂ AFG 134-135 J 3
Sabestar o IR 128-129 L 3
Sabetha o USA (KS) 262-263 L 5
Sabettajaha ~ RUS 108-109 O 6
Sabeugukgung o RI 162-163 D 6
Şabha o KSA 130-131 G 6
Sabhā ◘ LAR 192-193 F 4
Sabhā ☆ LAR (SAB) 192-193 F 4
Sabha, as- o SYR 128-129 H 5
Sabhat al-'Urūq al-Mu'tarida ∴ KSA 132-133 H 3
Sabhat Maṭṭī ∴ UAE 132-133 G 2
Sabidana, Ǧabal ▲ SUD 200-201 H 3
Sabiè o MOC 220-221 L 2
Sabie o ZA 220-221 K 2
Sabie Lower o ZA 220-221 K 2
Sabierivier ~ ZA 220-221 K 2
Sabiles o•· LV 94-95 H 3
Sabinal o USA (TX) 266-267 H 4
Sabinal, Cayo ⌒ C 54-55 G 4
Sabiñánigo o E 98-99 G 3
Sabinas o MEX 50-51 J 4
Sabinas, Río ~ MEX 50-51 J 4
Sabinas Hidalgo o MEX 50-51 J 4
Sabine Bay ≈ 24-25 R 3
Sabine Lake o USA (TX) 268-269 G 7
Sabine Land ∴ N 84-85 L 3
Sabine National Wildlife Refuge ⊥ USA (LA) 268-269 G 7
Sabine Ø ⌒ GRØ 26-27 q 6
Sabine Pass o USA (TX) 268-269 G 7
Sabine Peninsula ⌒ CDN 24-25 R 2
Sabine River ~ USA (LA) 268-269 G 6
Sabine River ~ USA (TX) 264-265 K 6
Sabini, Monti ▲ I 100-101 D 3
Sabino o BR 72-73 F 6
Sabinópolis o BR 72-73 J 5
Sabīr, Ǧabal ▲ Y 132-133 D 7
Sabirabad o AZ 128-129 N 2
Sabi Sand Game Reserve ⊥ ZA 220-221 K 2
Šabla o BG 102-103 F 6
Sablayan o RP 160-161 D 6
Sable, Cape ▲ CDN (NS) 240-241 K 7
Sable, Cape ▲ USA (FL) 286-287 H 6
Sable Island ⌒ CDN (NS) 240-241 Q 7
Sable Island Bank ≃ 38-39 O 6
Sable River o CDN (NS) 240-241 K 7
Sables, River aux ~ CDN (ONT) 238-239 C 2
Sables, Rivière aux ~ CDN 38-39 J 4
Sables-d'Olonne, les o F 90-91 G 8
Sablé-sur-Sarthe o F 90-91 G 8
Šablš, ozero ⊂ RUS 96-97 M 5
Saboba o GH 202-203 L 5
Saborni o WAN 204-205 F 5
Sabonagri o RN 204-205 E 2
Sabon Birni o RN 204-205 E 3
Sabon Birnin Gwari o WAN 204-205 G 3
Sabongari o CAM 204-205 J 5
Sabongida o WAN 204-205 F 5
Sabonkafi o RN 198-199 D 5
Sabór, Rio ~ P 98-99 D 4
Sabou o BF 202-203 J 3
Sabourin, Lac ⊂ CDN (QUE) 236-237 L 5
Sabra o DZ 188-189 L 3
Sabra, Tanjung ▲ RI 166-167 G 3
Şabrātah ··· LAR 192-193 E 1
Sabratha = Şabrātah ··· LAR 192-193 E 1
Sabres o F 90-91 G 9
Sabrina Land ∴ ARK 16 G 12
Şabrūm, aš- o IRQ 130-131 H 2
Sabt al-Ǧarāh o KSA 132-133 B 4
Sabt al-'Ulyā o KSA 132-133 B 4
Sabtang Island ⌒ RP 160-161 D 2
Sabuda, Pulau ⌒ RI 166-167 F 3
Sabugal o P 98-99 D 4
Sabulubek o RI 162-163 C 5
Sabun ~ RUS 114-115 Q 4
Sabunči o AZ 128-129 N 2
Sabunten, Pulau ⌒ RI 168 B 6
Şabwa o• Y 132-133 E 6
Şabyā o KSA (GIZ) 132-133 C 5
Şabyā o KSA (MAK) 132-133 B 4
Sabyda ~ RUS 108-109 d 6
Sabyndy o KA 124-125 G 3
Sabzak, Kōtal-e ▲ AFG 134-135 K 1
Sabzak, Kotal-e ▲ AFG 136-137 K 7
Sabzevār o• IR 136-137 E 6
Sabzvārān o IR 134-135 G 4
Sacabaya o BOL 70-71 C 6
Sacaca o BOL 70-71 D 6
Sacacama o ANG 216-217 F 6
Sacado do Humaitá o BR 66-67 C 6
Sacambanda o ANG 216-217 F 8
Sacambunge o ANG 214-215 B 6
Sacanche o PE 64-65 D 5
Sac and Fox Indian Reservation ✗ USA (IA) 274-275 F 2
Sacandica o ANG 216-217 C 2
Sacanta o RA 76-77 F 6
Sacapulas o• GCA 52-53 J 4
Sacaton o USA (AZ) 256-257 D 5
Sac City o USA (IA) 274-275 D 2
Sacco Uein o SP 212-213 J 3
Sacedón o E 98-99 F 4
Săcele o RO 102-103 D 5
Sachayo o RA 76-77 G 4
Sachigo Lake ⊂ CDN 34-35 K 4
Sachigo River ~ CDN 34-35 L 3
Sachojere o BOL 70-71 E 4
Sachsen ◘ D 92-93 M 3
Sachsen-Anhalt ◘ D 92-93 L 3
Sachs Harbour o CDN 24-25 J 5
Šachtars'k o UA 102-103 L 3
Sachula o ANG 216-217 F 5
Sack o RUS 94-95 R 4
Sackville o CDN (NB) 240-241 L 5
Saco o USA (ME) 278-279 L 5
Saco o USA (MT) 250-251 M 3
Sacol Island ⌒ RP 160-161 E 9
Saco River ~ USA (ME) 278-279 L 5
Sacramento o MEX 50-51 J 4
Sacramento o USA (KY) 276-277 H 3
Sacramento ☆• USA (CA) 246-247 D 5
Sacramento, Pampas de ∴ PE 64-65 E 5
Sacramento Mountains ▲ USA (NM) 256-257 K 5
Sacramento River ~ USA (CA) 246-247 D 5
Sacramento Valley ⌣ USA (CA) 246-247 C 4
Sacré-Coeur o CDN (QUE) 240-241 F 2
Sacred Falls ~• USA (HI) 288 H 3
Sacree Indian Reserve ✗ CDN (ALB) 232-233 D 5
Sacre ou Timalacia, Rio ~ BR 70-71 H 4
Sac River ~ USA (MO) 276-277 B 3
Sacta, Rio ~ BOL 70-71 E 5
Sacuriuina ou Ponte de Pedra, Rio ~ BR 70-71 J 3
Sacuunda o ANG 214-215 B 6
Sada o COM 222-223 D 4
Sa'da o•· Y 132-133 C 5
Sada o ZA 220-221 H 6
Sa'dābād o IR 134-135 D 4
Sadam o OM 132-133 L 2
Sada-misaki ▲ J 152-153 E 8
Sadang ~ RI 164-165 F 5
Sadani o EAT 214-215 K 4
Şadāra, aş- o Y 132-133 F 6
Sadaseopet o IND 140-141 G 2
Sad-as-Sultāni o JOR 130-131 D 2
Sadau o RI 162-163 J 6
Sadawi, as- o KSA 130-131 K 3
Šaddādī o SYR 128-129 J 4
Sadd-e Eskandar (Qezel Alān) • IR 136-137 D 6
Saddleback Pass ▲ ZA 220-221 K 2
Saddle Lake o CDN (ALB) 232-233 G 2
Saddle Lake Indian Reserve ✗ CDN 32-33 P 4
Saddle Mount ▲ USA (ID) 252-253 E 3
Saddle Peak ▲ IND 140-141 L 3
Sa Đéc o VN 158-159 H 5
Šādegān o IR 134-135 C 3
Sādeqābād o IR 134-135 F 3
Šadh o OM 132-133 J 5
Sadi o ETH (Sid) 208-209 E 6
Sadi o ETH (Wel) 208-209 B 4
Sadio o SN 202-203 C 2
Sadiola o RMM 202-203 E 3
Sādiqābād o PK 138-139 C 5
Sa'diyāt ⌒ UAE 134-135 F 6
Sado, Rio ~ P 98-99 C 5
Sado-shima ⌒ J 152-153 H 6
Sadova o• RO 102-103 C 6
Sadovoe o RUS 96-97 D 10
Sado Yahiko Quasi National Park ⊥ J 152-153 H 6
Sadramento o BR 72-73 G 5
Sadrinsk ☆ RUS 114-115 G 6
Sadus • KSA 130-131 K 5
Šadwān, Ǧazīrat ⌒ ET 194-195 F 4
Saebyol o DVR 150-151 H 6
Saelsøen ⊂ GRØ 26-27 p 5
Şafa, aš- o KSA 132-133 B 3
Safad ▲ ETH 200-201 H 6
Şafāğa ▲ KSA 130-131 F 4
Safāğa, Ǧazīrat ⌒ ET 194-195 F 4
Şafāha o SUD 206-207 H 4
Safakulevo ☆ RUS 114-115 G 7
Šafallahiya, aš- o KSA 130-131 L 4
Safané o BF 202-203 J 3
Safapur o IND 138-139 E 2
Šafār o AFG 134-135 L 3
Säffle ☆ S 86-87 F 7
Safford o USA (AZ) 256-257 F 6
Safi < TCH 198-199 H 5
Safi = Asfi ☆ MA 188-189 G 4
Safi = Asfi ☆ MA 188-189 G 4
Safia o PNG 183 E 5
Safīdār, Kūh-e ▲ IR 134-135 E 4
Safīd Ḫers, Kūh-e ▲ AFG 136-137 M 6
Safīd Kūh, Selsele-ye ▲ AFG 136-137 G 7
Safiet Iniguel, Hassi < DZ 190-191 D 5
Şāfīṯā, aš- o SYR 128-129 J 4
Safira, as- o• SYR 128-129 G 4
Şāfīṯā ☆ SYR 128-129 G 5
Safonovo o RUS (ARH) 88-89 T 4
Safonovo ☆ RUS (SML) 94-95 N 4
Safotu o WS 184 V a 1
Şafrā' o IRQ 128-129 J 5
Safranbolu ☆• TR 128-129 E 2
Safsaf, Oued ~ DZ 190-191 E 5
Sag o SN 196-197 B 7
Saga ☆ J 152-153 D 8
Saga o RI 166-167 G 3
Saga o VRC 144-145 E 6
Sagabari o RMM 202-203 F 3
Sagai o PK 134-135 M 3
Sagaing ☆ MYA 142-143 J 5
Sagami-gawa ~ J 152-153 H 7
Sagami-wan ≈ 152-153 H 7
Sagamu o WAN 204-205 E 5
Sagan o KA 124-125 H 4
Sagan ~ KA 124-125 L 3
Sagan ~ KA 124-125 L 4
Sagan ~ KA 126-127 N 4
Sagan o VRC 144-145 B 2
Sagana o EAK 212-213 F 4
Saganak ~ US 136-137 K 4
Saganash River ~ CDN (ONT) 236-237 F 3
Sağand o IR 134-135 F 2
Sagandža ~ RUS 110-111 Q 7
Sagar o IND (KAR) 140-141 F 3
Sagar o IND (MAP) 138-139 G 8
Sagara, Lake o EAT 212-213 C 6
Sagard o CDN (QUE) 240-241 E 2
Sagaredžo o GE 126-127 F 7
Sagarmatha = Mount Everest ▲ NEP 144-145 F 7
Sagarmatha National Park ⊥··· NEP 144-145 F 7
Sagaryč'e, ozero ⊂ RUS 110-111 a 4
Sagastyr o RUS 110-111 Q 3
Sagata o SN 202-203 B 2
Sagauli Bāzār o IND 142-143 D 2
Sagavanirktok River ~ USA 20-21 Q 2
Sagay o RP 160-161 E 7
Saǧd, Ǧazīrat ⌒ KSA 132-133 B 5
Sage o USA (WY) 252-253 H 5
Sage Creek ~ CDN (ALB) 232-233 H 6
Sage Creek ~ USA (MT) 250-251 J 3
Sage Creek Junction o USA (UT) 254-255 D 2
Sage Hen Summit ▲ USA (CA) 246-247 E 2
Sagehen Summit ▲ USA (OR) 244-245 F 7
Sage Mesa o CDN (BC) 230-231 K 4
Sageo o EC 64-65 C 3
Sageurin, Selat ≈ 166-167 F 2
Saggi ··· I 100-101 C 2
Sagiāda o GR 100-101 H 5
Saginaw o USA (MI) 272-273 F 4
Saginaw Bay o USA (MI) 272-273 F 4
Sāğir o KSA 130-131 J 5
Sāğir, Ra's ▲ OM 132-133 H 5
Šāgir Bāzār, Tall o• SYR 128-129 J 4
Sagleipie o LB 202-203 F 6
Saglek Bank ≃ 6-7 C 3
Saglek Bay ≈ 36-37 S 5
Sagne o RIM 196-197 D 7
Sago, Pulau ⌒ RI 164-165 H 5
Sagola o USA (MI) 270-271 K 4
Sagonar ☆ RUS 116-117 F 10
Sagra ▲ E 98-99 F 6
Sagres o P 98-99 C 6
Sag Sag o PNG 183 E 3
Sagu o MYA 142-143 J 5
Sagu o RI 166-167 B 6
Sagua-Baracoa, Grupo ▲ C 54-55 H 4
Saguache o USA (CO) 254-255 J 5
Saguache Creek ~ USA (CO) 254-255 J 5
Sagua de Tánamo o C 54-55 H 4
Sagua la Grande o C 54-55 E 3
Sagua la Grande ~ C 54-55 E 3
Sagua National Monument • USA (AZ) 256-257 D 6
Saguaro National Monument ⊥ USA (AZ) 256-257 E 6
Saguay, Lac- o CDN (QUE) 238-239 K 2
Saguenay, Parc de Conservation du ⊥ CDN (QUE) 240-241 E 2
Saguenay, Rivière ~ CDN (QUE) 240-241 E 2
Saguia el Hamra ~ MA 188-189 F 7
Sagunt o E 98-99 G 5
Sagunto = Sagunt o E 98-99 G 5
Sagure o ETH 208-209 D 5
Sagya o• VRC 144-145 G 6
Sagyz o KA (ZPK) 96-97 J 9
Sagyz ~ KA 96-97 H 9
Sagyz ~ KA 126-127 M 3
Sah o RMM 202-203 H 2
Sāh o UAE 132-133 H 2
Šāh, Kūh-e ▲ IR 134-135 H 3
Sahaba o SUD 200-201 E 3
Sāhābād o IND 138-139 G 5
Sahagún o CO 60-61 D 3
Sahagún o E 98-99 E 3
Sahalinsk, Juženo- ☆ RUS 122-123 K 5
Sahalinskij zaliv ≈ 122-123 J 2
Sahami, Ǧabal as- ▲ KSA 130-131 L 4
Sahana, Ambodītetezana- o RM 222-223 G 5
Sahand, Kūh-e ▲ IR 128-129 M 4
Sahanina, guba ⊂ RUS 108-109 F 6
Sahanina, mys ▲ RUS 108-109 F 6
Sahara ∴ 9 C 3
Sahara ~ RUS 120-121 G 3
Sahāra o• Y 132-133 C 5
Saharan Atlas = Atlas Saharien ▲ DZ 190-191 C 4
Saharanpur o IND 138-139 F 5
Saharsa o IND 142-143 E 3
Sahaswan o IND 138-139 G 5
Šahbā ☆ SYR 128-129 G 6
Šāh Bodāğ o IR 134-135 B 2
Šahbuz o AZ 128-129 L 3
Šāhdād o IR 134-135 G 3
Šahdād, Namakzār-e ⊂ IR 134-135 G 3
Šahdag, gora ▲ AZ 128-129 L 2
Saheib o SUD 206-207 G 3
Sahel ∴ 9 D 4
Sahel ∴ TN 190-191 H 3
Sahel, Canal du < RMM 202-203 G 3
Šāh Ǧahān, Kūh-e ▲ IR 136-137 F 6
Šāh Güy o AFG 134-135 M 2
Sahibganj o IND 142-143 E 3
Sahibi ~ IND 138-139 F 6
Sahijpur o IND 138-139 D 8
Šāhīliya o IRQ 128-129 K 6
Šāhin Dež o IR 128-129 M 4
Sāhiwāl o PK 138-139 D 4
Sāhiwāl o PK 138-139 D 4
Sahjurta o RUS 116-117 N 9
Šāh Kūh ▲ IR 136-137 D 6
Šahlābād o IR 134-135 H 2
Šahm o OM 132-133 K 1
Šahmirzād o IR 136-137 C 7
Şahne o• IR 134-135 B 1
Šahovskaja ☆ RUS 94-95 O 3
Šahpūr = Salmās o• IR 128-129 L 3
Šahrak o AFG 134-135 L 1
Šahrak o IR (FAR) 134-135 E 3
Šahrak o IR (TEH) 136-137 B 6
Şahrā' Surt ∴ LAR 192-193 G 2
Šahrazūr o IRQ 128-129 L 5
Šahr-e Bābak o IR 134-135 F 3
Šahr-e Kord ☆• IR 134-135 D 2
Šahr-e Nou o IR 134-135 J 1
Šahr-e Safā o AFG 134-135 M 3
Šahrestān o AFG 134-135 M 2
Šahreżā = Qomše o• IR 134-135 D 2
Šahrihan o US 136-137 N 4
Šahrisabz ☆• US 136-137 K 5
Šahristan o TJ 136-137 L 5
Šahrivar o IR 128-129 N 3
Šahriyar o IR 136-137 B 7
Šāhrūd o• IR 136-137 D 6
Šāh Rūd ~ IR 136-137 B 6
Sahsemen ∴• TM 136-137 F 4
Sahtaneh River ~ CDN 30-31 H 6
Šahtersk o RUS 122-123 K 4
Šahtërskij o RUS 112-113 T 4
Šahtinsk o KA 124-125 H 4
Šahtinsk o KA 124-125 H 4
Šahtinskij, Kamensk- o RUS 102-103 M 3
Šahty o RUS 102-103 M 4
Sahu o RI 164-165 K 3
Sahuaral o MEX 50-51 D 3
Sahuaripa o MEX 50-51 E 3
Sahuarita o USA (AZ) 256-257 E 7
Sahuaro, El o MEX 50-51 C 2
Sahuayo o MEX 52-53 C 1
Sahul Bank ≃ 166-167 C 7
Sahul Banks ≃ 172-173 F 2
Sahul Shelf ≃ 172-173 G 2
Šahun'ja o RUS 96-97 E 5
Sāhūq, Wādī ~ KSA 130-131 G 5
Šahy o SK 92-93 P 4
Sai ~ IND 142-143 B 2
Sai o J 152-153 J 4
Sai ~ RI 162-163 J 4
Ša'īb ad-Dāt ~ KSA 130-131 H 5
Saibai Island ⌒ AUS 174-175 G 1
Ša'īb al-Banāt, Ǧabal ▲ ET 194-195 F 4
Šaibāra, Ǧazīrat ⌒ KSA 130-131 E 5
Sai Buri o THA 158-159 F 7
Saïda ☆ DZ 190-191 C 3
Şaidā ☆·· RL 128-129 F 6
Sa'īd Bin Sarān o OM 132-133 K 2
Saïdia o MA 188-189 K 3
Saidor o PNG 183 D 3
Saidpur o BD 142-143 F 3
Saidpur o IND 142-143 C 3
Saidu (Mingora) o• PK 138-139 D 2
Saiedābād o IR 134-135 J 5
Saigo o J 152-153 E 6
Sài Gòn, Sông ~ VN 158-159 J 5
Saigon = Thành Phô Hô Chí Minh ☆• VN 158-159 J 5
Šaiḫ o IRQ 128-129 K 5
Saiha o IND 142-143 H 4
Šaiḫ 'Abid o IRQ 128-129 M 6
Šaiḫ Ahmad o IRQ 128-129 M 6
Saihan Toroi o VRC 148-149 E 7
Šaiḫ Fāris o IRQ 128-129 M 6
Šaiḫ Humaid, aš- o KSA 130-131 D 3
Šaiḫ Miskin o SYR 128-129 G 6
Šaiḫ Sa'd o IRQ 128-129 M 6
Saihūt o Y 132-133 G 6
Šaiḫ 'Uṯmān, aš- o Y 132-133 D 7
Saikanosy Ampasindava ⌣ RM 222-223 E 4
Saikhoa Ghāt o IND 142-143 J 2
Saiki o J 152-153 D 8
Sail al-Kabir, as- o KSA 132-133 B 3
Sailāna o IND 138-139 E 8
Sailolof o RI 166-167 F 2
Sailusbesar, Pulau ⌒ RI 168 C 6
Saimaa o FIN 88-89 K 6
Sain Alto, Río ~ MEX 50-51 H 6
Saindak o PK 134-135 J 4
Sainsbury Point ▲ CDN 36-37 K 7
Sainsoutou o SN 202-203 E 3
Saint-Adelme o CDN (QUE) 240-241 H 2
Saint Adolphe o CDN (MAN) 234-235 F 5
Saint Albans o CDN (NFL) 242-243 N 5
Saint Albans o• GB 90-91 G 6
Saint Albans o USA (VT) 278-279 H 4
Saint Albans o USA (WV) 280-281 E 5
Saint Albert o CDN (ALB) 232-233 E 2
Saint Albert Dome ▲ PNG 183 B 3
Saint-Alexandre o CDN (QUE) 240-241 F 3
Saint Alphonse o CDN (MAN) 234-235 D 5
Saint Ambroise o CDN (MAN) 234-235 E 4
Saint-Ambroise o CDN (QUE) 240-241 D 2
Saint-André o F 224 B 7
Saint André, Cap = Tanjona Vilanandro ▲ RM 222-223 D 6
Saint-André-de-Restigouche o CDN (QUE) 240-241 J 2
Saint-André-du-Lac-Saint-Jean o CDN (QUE) 240-241 D 2
Saint Andrew Bay ≈ 48-49 F 4
Saint Andrew Bay ≈ USA 286-287 D 1
Saint Andrews o CDN (NB) 240-241 H 5
Saint Andrew's o CDN (NFL) 242-243 J 5
Saint Andrews o•· GB 90-91 F 3
Saint Andrew Sound ≈ 48-49 H 4
Saint Andrew Sound ≈ USA 284-285 J 5
Saint Anne o USA (IL) 274-275 L 3
Saint Anne Island ⌒ SY 224 D 2
Saint Ann's Bay ≈ 38-39 O 5
Saint Ann's Bay o CDN 240-241 P 4
Saint Ann's Bay o JA 54-55 G 5
Saint Ansgar o USA (IA) 274-275 F 1
Saint Anthony o CDN (NFL) 242-243 N 1
Saint Anthony o USA (ID) 252-253 G 3
Saint Anthony, Monastery of • ET 194-195 F 3
Saint Arnaud o AUS 180-181 G 4
Saint Arnaud o NZ 182 D 4
Saint-Arsène o CDN (QUE) 240-241 F 3
Saint-Augustin o CDN 38-39 P 3
Saint-Augustin = Anantsono o RM 222-223 C 9
Saint-Augustin, Rivière ~ CDN 38-39 P 3
Saint-Augustine o CDN (QUE) 240-241 D 2
Saint Augustine o USA (IL) 274-275 H 4
Saint Augustine o•· USA (FL) 286-287 H 2
Saint Augustin Nord-Ouest, Rivière ~ CDN 38-39 P 3
Saint Barbe o CDN (NFL) 242-243 M 1
Saint-Barnabe o CDN (QUE) 238-239 N 2
Saint-Barthélemy ⌒ F 56 D 3
Saint-Basile o CDN (NB) 240-241 G 3
Saint-Basile-de-Tableau o CDN (QUE) 240-241 E 2
Saint Benedict o CDN (SAS) 232-233 N 3
Saint-Benoît o F 224 B 7
Saint Bernard's o CDN (NFL) 242-243 O 5
Saint Brendan's o CDN (NFL) 242-243 P 4
Saint Bride, Mount ▲ CDN (ALB) 232-233 C 4
Saint Bride's o CDN (NFL) 242-243 O 6
Saint-Brieuc ☆ F 90-91 F 7
Saint Brieux o CDN (SAS) 232-233 O 3
Saint-Bruno o CDN (QUE) 240-241 D 2
Saint-Calais o F 90-91 H 8
Saint Carols o CDN (NFL) 242-243 N 1
Saint Catharines o CDN (ONT) 238-239 F 5
Saint Catherine, Cape ▲ CDN 24-25 a 5
Saint Catherine, Monestery of ·· ET 194-195 F 3
Saint Catherines Island ⌒ USA (GA) 284-285 J 5
Saint Catherines Sound ≈ USA 284-285 J 5
Saint-Céré o F 90-91 H 9
Saint-Césaire o CDN (QUE) 238-239 N 3
Saint-Chamond o F 90-91 K 9
Saint Charles o USA (AR) 276-277 D 6
Saint Charles o USA (ID) 252-253 G 4
Saint Charles o USA (IL) 274-275 K 3
Saint Charles o USA (MI) 272-273 E 4
Saint Charles o USA (MN) 270-271 F 7
Saint Charles o USA (MO) 274-275 H 6
Saint-Charles-Garnier o CDN (QUE) 240-241 G 2
Saint Charles Rapids ~ CDN 30-31 H 3
Saint-Chély-d'Apcher o F 90-91 J 9
Saint-Chinian o F 90-91 J 10
Saint-Christophe = Île Juân de Nova ⌒ F 222-223 C 6
Saint Christopher = Saint Kitts ⌒ KAN 56 D 3
Saint Clair o USA (MI) 272-273 G 5
Saint Clair o USA (MO) 274-275 H 6
Saint Clair, Lake ⊂ 46-47 G 4
Saint Clair, Lake ⊂ 280-281 D 1
Saint Clairsville o USA (OH) 280-281 F 3
Saint Claude o CDN (MAN) 234-235 E 5
Saint-Clément o CDN (QUE) 240-241 F 3
Saint Cloud o USA (FL) 286-287 H 3
Saint Cloud o USA (MN) 270-271 D 5
Saint Cricq, Cape ▲ AUS 176-177 B 2
Saint Croix o CDN (NB) 240-241 H 5
Saint Croix ⌒ USA (VI) 286-287 R 3
Saint Croix Falls o USA (WI) 270-271 F 5
Saint Croix Island National Monument • CDN (NB) 240-241 H 5
Saint Croix River ~ USA (MN) 270-271 F 5
Saint Croix State Park ⊥ USA (MN) 270-271 F 5
Saint Cyr Range ▲ CDN 20-21 Y 5
Saint David o USA (AZ) 256-257 E 7
Saint-David-de-Falardeau o CDN (QUE) 240-241 D 2
Saint David's o CDN (NFL) 242-243 K 4
Saint David's o• GB 90-91 E 6
Saint-Denis o CDN (QUE) 238-239 M 3
Saint-Denis ☆ F 224 B 7
Saint Dennis o CDN (SAS) 232-233 M 3
Saint-Dié o• F 90-91 L 7
Saint-Dizier o F 90-91 K 7
Saint-Donat o CDN (QUE) 238-239 L 2
Sainte Agathe o CDN (MAN) 234-235 F 5
Sainte-Agathe-des-Monts o CDN (QUE) 238-239 L 2
Sainte Amélie o CDN (MAN) 234-235 D 4
Sainte-Angèle-de-Merici o CDN (QUE) 240-241 G 2
Sainte Anne o CDN (MAN) 234-235 G 5
Sainte-Anne o F 56 E 3
Sainte-Anne, Lac ⊂ CDN 38-39 L 3
Sainte-Anne-de-Beaupré o CDN (QUE) 240-241 E 3
Sainte-Anne-de-Portneuf o CDN (QUE) 240-241 F 2
Sainte-Anne-des-Monts o CDN (QUE) 242-243 B 3
Sainte-Anne-du-Lac o CDN (QUE) 238-239 K 2
Sainte Anne Marine National Park ⊥ SY 224 D 2
Sainte-Brigitte-de-Laval o CDN (QUE) 238-239 O 2
Sainte-Catherine o CDN (QUE) 238-239 O 2
Sainte-Croix o CDN (QUE) 238-239 O 2
Sainte Croix o USA (IN) 274-275 M 6
Sainte-Edgar o CDN (QUE) 240-241 K 2
Sainte Elisabeth o CDN (MAN) 234-235 F 5
Sainte-Émélie-de-l'Énergie o CDN (QUE) 238-239 M 2
Sainte-Eulalie o CDN (QUE) 238-239 N 2
Sainte-Félicité o CDN (QUE) 240-241 H 2
Sainte-Florence o CDN (QUE) 240-241 H 2
Sainte-Foy-la-Grande o F 90-91 H 9
Sainte Genevieve o USA (MO) 276-277 E 3
Sainte-Gertrude o CDN (QUE) 236-237 K 4
Sainte-Hedwige-de-Roberval o CDN (QUE) 240-241 C 2
Sainte-Justine o CDN (QUE) 240-241 E 4
Saint Eleanors o CDN (PEI) 240-241 M 4
Sainte-Éleuthère o CDN (QUE) 240-241 F 3
Saint Elias, Cape ▲ USA 20-21 S 7
Saint Elias Mountains ▲ CDN 20-21 V 6
Saint-Élie o F 62-63 H 3
Saint Elmo o USA (AL) 284-285 B 6
Saint-Elzéar o CDN (QUE) 240-241 F 3
Saint-Elzéar o CDN (QUE) 240-241 K 2

Sainte-Marguerite ○ CDN (QUE) 240-241 H 2
Sainte-Marguerite, Rivière ~ CDN (QUE) 242-243 B 2
Sainte-Marie ○ CDN (QUE) 238-239 O 2
Sainte-Marie ○ F 56 E 4
Sainte-Marie, Cap = Tanjona Vohimena ▲ RM 222-223 D 10
Sainte-Marie, Nosy ⌒ RM 222-223 F 6
Sainte-Marie Among the Hurons • CDN (ONT) 238-239 F 4
Sainte-Marie-de-Blandford ○ CDN (QUE) 238-239 N 2
Sainte-Marie-de-Kent ○ CDN (NB) 240-241 L 4
Sainte-Martine ○ CDN (QUE) 238-239 M 3
Sainte-Maure-de-Touraine ○ F 90-91 H 8
Sainte-Monique ○ CDN (QUE) 240-241 D 2
Sainte-Odile, Mont ▲• F 90-91 L 7
Sainte-Epiphane ○ CDN (QUE) 240-241 F 3
Sainte-Rita ○ CDN (QUE) 240-241 G 3
Sainte Rose du Lac ○ CDN (MAN) 234-235 D 3
Sainte-Rose-du-Nord ○ CDN (QUE) 240-241 E 2
Saintes ○ F 90-91 G 9
Saintes, Les ⌒ F 56 E 4
Saint-Esprit ○ CDN (QUE) 238-239 M 3
Sainte-Thérese ○ CDN (QUE) 238-239 K 2
Sainte-Thérèse, Lac ○ CDN 30-31 J 3
Sainte-Thérèse-de-Gaspé ○ CDN (QUE) 240-241 L 2
Saint-Étienne ☆ F 90-91 K 9
Saint-Eugène ○ CDN (QUE) 238-239 N 3
Saint-Fabien ○ CDN (QUE) 240-241 G 2
Saint-Fabien-sur-Mer ○ CDN (QUE) 240-241 G 2
Saint-Félicien ○ CDN (QUE) 240-241 C 2
Saint-Félix-de-Valois ○ CDN (QUE) 238-239 M 2
Saint-Félix-d'Otis ○ CDN (QUE) 240-241 E 2
Saint-Fidèle-de-Mont-Murray ○ CDN (QUE) 240-241 F 3
Saint-Florentin ○ F 90-91 J 8
Saint Floris, Parc National de ⊥ ⋯ RCA 206-207 E 4
Saint-Flour ○• F 90-91 J 9
Saint-Fond, Rivière ~ CDN 36-37 O 5
Saint Francis ○ CDN (ALB) 232-233 D 2
Saint Francis ○ USA (KS) 262-263 E 5
Saint Francis ○ USA (ME) 278-279 N 1
Saint Francis ○ USA (MN) 270-271 E 5
Saint Francis ○ USA (SD) 260-261 F 3
Saint Francis Bay ≈ 220-221 G 7
Saint Francis Isles ⌒ AUS 176-177 M 6
Saint Francis River ~ USA (AR) 276-277 E 5
Saint Francis River ~ USA (MO) 276-277 E 4
Saint Francisville ○ USA (LA) 268-269 J 6
Saint François ○ CDN (QUE) 240-241 E 3
Saint-François ○•• F 56 E 3
Saint-François, Lac ○ CDN (QUE) 238-239 O 3
Saint-Francois, Plage ≐ F 56 E 3
Saint-François, Rivière ~ CDN (QUE) 238-239 N 2
Saint François Island ⌒ SY 224 C 3
Saint Francois Mountains ▲▲ USA (MO) 276-277 E 3
Saint Front ○ CDN (SAS) 232-233 O 3
Saint-Fulgence ○ CDN (QUE) 240-241 E 2
Saint-Gabriel ○ CDN (QUE) 238-239 M 2
Saint-Gabriel ○ CDN (QUE) 240-241 G 2
Saint-Gaudens ○ F 90-91 H 10
Saint Gaudens National Historic Site • USA (VT) 278-279 J 5
Saint George ○ AUS 178-179 K 5
Saint George ○ CDN (MAN) 234-235 G 4
Saint George ○ CDN (NB) 240-241 J 5
Saint George ○ CDN (ONT) 238-239 E 5
Saint George ○ USA (SC) 284-285 K 3
Saint George ○ USA (UT) 254-255 B 6
Saint George, Cape ○ CDN (NFL) 242-243 J 4
Saint George, Cape ▲ CDN (NFL) 242-243 J 4
Saint George, Cape ▲ PNG 183 G 3
Saint George, Cape ▲ USA (FL) 286-287 D 2
Saint George, Point ▲ USA (CA) 246-247 A 2
Saint George Basin ≈ 172-173 G 3
Saint George Fjord ≈ 26-27 X 2
Saint George Island ○ USA (MD) 280-281 K 5
Saint George Island ⌒ USA (AK) 22-23 M 4
Saint George Island ⌒ USA (FL) 286-287 E 2
Saint George's ○ CDN (NFL) 242-243 K 4
Saint-Georges ○ CDN (QUE) 240-241 E 4
Saint-Georges ○ F 62-63 J 4
Saint George's ○ WG 56 E 5
Saint George's ★ WG 56 E 5
Saint George's Bay ≈ 38-39 O 6
Saint George's Bay ≈ 38-39 P 4
Saint George's Bay ≈ CDN 240-241 O 5
Saint George's Bay ≈ CDN 242-243 J 4
Saint George's Channel ≈ 90-91 D 6
Saint George's Channel ≈ 183 G 3
Saint-Georges-de-Malbaie ○ CDN (QUE) 240-241 L 2
Saint George Sound ≈ USA 286-287 E 2
Saint-Gérard ○ CDN (QUE) 236-237 K 4
Saint-Gérard ○ CDN (QUE) 238-239 O 3
Saint-Gilles ○ F 90-91 K 10
Saint-Girons ○ F 90-91 H 10
Saint Gregor ○ CDN (SAS) 232-233 O 3
Saint Gregory, Mount ▲ CDN (NFL) 242-243 K 3
Saint Helen ○ USA (MI) 272-273 E 3
Saint Helena ⌒ GB 202-203 C 7
Saint Helenabaai ≈ 220-221 D 6
Saint Helena Fracture Zone ≃ 6-7 H 10
Saint Helena Sound ≈ 48-49 H 3
Saint Helena Sound ≈ USA 284-285 K 4
Saint Helens ○ AUS 180-181 K 6
Saint Helens ○ USA (OR) 244-245 C 5
Saint Helens, Mount ▲ USA (WA) 244-245 C 4
Saint-Helier ○ GBJ 90-91 F 7
Saint-Henri ○ CDN (QUE) 238-239 O 2
Saint-Henri-de-Taillon ○ CDN (QUE) 240-241 D 2
Sainthiya ○ IND 142-143 E 4
Saint-Honoré ○ CDN (QUE) 240-241 D 2
Saint-Hubert ○ CDN (QUE) 240-241 F 3
Saint-Hyacinthe ○ CDN (QUE) 238-239 N 3
Saint-Ignace ○ CDN (NB) 240-241 K 4
Saint Ignace ○ USA (MI) 272-273 E 2
Saint-Ignaçe-du-Lac ○ CDN (QUE) 238-239 M 2
Saint Ignace Island ⌒ CDN (ONT) 234-235 Q 6
Saint Ignatius ○ USA (MT) 250-251 F 4
Saint-Isidore ○ CDN (NB) 240-241 K 3
Saint Ives ○ GB 90-91 E 6
Saint-Jacques ○ CDN (NB) 240-241 G 3
Saint James ○ USA (AR) 276-277 D 5
Saint James ○ USA (MI) 272-273 D 2
Saint James ○ USA (MN) 270-271 D 7
Saint James ○ USA (MO) 276-277 D 3
Saint James, Cape ▲ CDN (BC) 228-229 C 5
Saint-Jean, Lac ○•• CDN (QUE) 240-241 C 2
Saint Jean, Rivière- ○ CDN (QUE) 242-243 D 2
Saint-Jean, Rivière ~ CDN (QUE) 240-241 K 2
Saint-Jean, Rivière ~ CDN (QUE) 242-243 D 2
Saint Jean Baptiste ○ CDN (MAN) 234-235 F 5
Saint-Jean-d'Angély ○ F 90-91 G 9
Saint-Jean-de-Cherbourg ○ CDN (QUE) 240-241 H 2
Saint-Jean-de-Dieu ○ CDN (QUE) 240-241 F 2
Saint-Jean-de-Luz ○ F 90-91 G 10
Saint-Jean-Port-Joli ○ CDN (QUE) 240-241 E 3
Saint-Jean-sur-Richelieu ○ CDN (QUE) 238-239 M 3
Saint-Jérome ○ CDN (QUE) 238-239 L 3
Saint Jo ○ USA (TX) 264-265 G 5
Saint Joe ○ USA (AR) 276-277 C 4
Saint Joe ○ USA (ID) 250-251 C 4
Saint Joe Mountains ▲▲ USA (ID) 250-251 C 4
Saint Joe River ~ USA (ID) 250-251 C 4
Saint John ○ CDN (NB) 240-241 J 5
Saint John ○ USA (KS) 262-263 H 7
Saint John ○ USA (WA) 244-245 H 3
Saint John ⌒ USA (VI) 286-287 R 2
Saint John Bay ≈ 38-39 Q 3
Saint John Bay ≈ CDN 242-243 L 2
Saint John Harbour ≈ CDN 240-241 J 5
Saint John Island ⌒ CDN (NFL) 242-243 L 2
Saint John River ~ CDN (NB) 240-241 H 4
Saint John River ~ LB 202-203 F 6
Saint John River ~ USA (ME) 278-279 M 2
Saint John's ★ AG 56 E 3
Saint John's ☆ CDN (NFL) 242-243 Q 5
Saint Johns ○ USA (AZ) 256-257 F 4
Saint Johns ○ USA (MI) 272-273 E 4
Saint Johnsbury ○ USA (VT) 278-279 J 4
Saint Johns Marsh ≐ USA (FL) 286-287 J 4
Saint Johns River ~ USA (FL) 286-287 H 1
Saint John Station ○ USA (UT) 254-255 C 3
Saint Jonas Within ○ CDN (NFL) 242-243 P 4
Saint Joseph ○ CDN (NB) 240-241 L 5
Saint-Joseph ○ F 224 B 7
Saint Joseph ○ USA (LA) 268-269 J 5
Saint Joseph ○ USA (MI) 272-273 C 5
Saint Joseph ○ USA (MO) 274-275 D 5
Saint Joseph, Lake ○ CDN (ONT) 234-235 N 3
Saint Joseph Bay ≈ USA 286-287 D 2
Saint-Joseph-de-Clérícy ○ CDN (QUE) 236-237 K 4
Saint Joseph Island ⌒ SY 224 C 2
Saint Joseph Peninsula ⌒ USA (FL) 286-287 D 2
Saint Joseph Plateau ▲▲ CDN 24-25 c 4
Saint Joseph Point ▲ USA (FL) 286-287 D 2
Saint Joseph River ~ USA (IN) 274-275 O 3
Saint Joseph River ~ USA (MI) 272-273 C 5
Saint Joseph River ~ USA (MI) 272-273 D 5
Saint Josephs ○ CDN (NFL) 242-243 P 5
Saint Jovite ○ CDN (QUE) 238-239 L 2
Saint-Junien ○ F 90-91 H 9
Saint Kilda ⌒ ⋯ GB 90-91 C 3
Saint Kitts ⌒ KAN 56 D 3
Saint Kitts and Nevis ■ KAN 56 D 3
Saint Labre ○ CDN (MAN) 234-235 G 5
Saint-Lambert ○ CDN (QUE) 238-239 O 2
Saint Laurent ○ CDN (MAN) 234-235 F 4
Saint-Laurent, Fleuve = Saint Lawrence River ~ CDN (QUE) 240-241 F 2
Saint-Laurent-du-Maroni ☆ F 62-63 G 3
Saint Lawrence ○ AUS 178-179 K 2
Saint Lawrence ○ CDN (NFL) 242-243 N 6
Saint Lawrence, Cape ▲ CDN (NS) 240-241 P 3
Saint Lawrence, Gulf of ≈ 38-39 N 4
Saint Lawrence, Gulf of ≈ CDN 242-243 F 4
Saint Lawrence Island National Park ⊥ USA (NY) 278-279 F 4
Saint Lawrence River ~ CDN (QUE) 238-239 K 4
Saint Lawrence River = Fleuve Saint-Laurent ~ CDN (QUE) 240-241 F 2
Saint Lazare ○ CDN (MAN) 234-235 B 4
Saint-Leonard ○ CDN (NB) 240-241 H 3
Saint Lewis Inlet ≈ 38-39 Q 2
Saint Lewis River ~ CDN 38-39 Q 2
Saint Lewis Sound ≈ 38-39 R 2
Saint-Lô ☆ F 90-91 G 7
Saint-Louis ○ CDN (QUE) 238-239 N 3
Saint Louis ○ CDN (SAS) 232-233 N 3
Saint-Louis ○ F 224 B 7
Saint Louis ☆• SN 196-197 B 6
Saint Louis ○ USA (MI) 272-273 E 4
Saint Louis ○• USA (MO) 274-275 H 6
Saint Louis, Bay ○ USA (MS) 268-269 L 6
Saint-Louis-de-Kent ○ CDN (NB) 240-241 L 4
Saint Louis River ~ USA (MN) 270-271 F 3
Saint Lucia ■ WL 56 E 5
Saint Lucia ⌒ WL 56 E 5
Saint Lucia ○ ZA 220-221 L 4
Saint Lucia, Lake ○ ZA 220-221 L 4
Saint Lucia Channel ≈ 56 E 4
Saint Lucia Game Reserve ⊥ ZA 220-221 L 4
Saint Luciameer ○ ZA 220-221 L 4
Saint Lucia Park ⊥ ZA 220-221 L 4
Saint Lucie Canal < USA (FL) 286-287 J 4
Saint-Ludger ○ CDN (QUE) 240-241 E 5
Saint-Ludger-de-Milot ○ CDN (QUE) 240-241 D 2
Saint Luis ○ CDN (SAS) 232-233 N 3
Saint-Malachie ○ CDN (QUE) 240-241 E 4
Saint-Malo ○ CDN (QUE) 238-239 O 3
Saint-Malo ○ F 90-91 F 7
Saint Malo, Golfe de ≈ 90-91 F 7
Saint Marc ○ RH 54-55 J 5
Saint Marc, Canal de ≈ 54-55 J 5
Saint-Marc-des-Carrières ○ CDN (QUE) 238-239 N 2
Saint-Marcel ○ CDN (QUE) 240-241 E 4
Saint Margaret Bay ≈ 38-39 Q 3
Saint Margaret Bay ≈ CDN 242-243 M 1
Saint Margarets ○ CDN (NB) 240-241 K 4
Saint Margaret Village ○ CDN (NS) 240-241 P 4
Saint Maries ○ USA (ID) 250-251 C 4
Saint Marks ○ USA (FL) 286-287 E 1
Saint Marks ○ ZA 220-221 H 6
Saint Marks National Wildlife Refuge ⊥ USA (FL) 286-287 E 1
Saint Marks River ~ USA (FL) 286-287 E 1
Saint Martin ○ CDN (MAN) 234-235 E 3
Saint-Martin ○ CDN (QUE) 240-241 E 5
Saint-Martin ⌒ F 56 D 2
Saint Martin, Lake ○ CDN (SAS) 234-235 E 3
Saint Martin Bay ≈ USA 270-271 O 4
Saint Martin Island ⌒ USA (MI) 270-271 M 5
Saint Martins ○ CDN (NB) 240-241 K 5
Saint Martinville ○ USA (LA) 268-269 J 6
Saint Mary ○ USA (MT) 250-251 F 3
Saint Mary, Cape ▲ CDN (NS) 240-241 O 5
Saint-Mary Îles ⌒ CDN (QUE) 242-243 J 2
Saint Mary Reservoir ○ CDN (ALB) 232-233 E 6
Saint Mary River ~ CDN (BC) 230-231 N 4
Saint Marys ○ AUS 180-181 K 6
Saint Marys ○ CDN (ONT) 238-239 D 5
Saint Marys ○ USA (GA) 284-285 J 6
Saint Marys ○ USA (KS) 262-263 K 5
Saint Marys ○ USA (OH) 280-281 B 3
Saint Marys ○ USA (PA) 280-281 H 2
Saint Marys ○ USA (WV) 280-281 E 4
Saint Mary's ○ Z 214-215 D 7
Saint Mary's, Cape ▲ CDN (NFL) 242-243 O 6
Saint Mary's Alpine Provincial Park ⊥ CDN (BC) 230-231 N 4
Saint Mary's Bay ≈ 38-39 S 5
Saint Mary's Bay ≈ CDN 240-241 J 6
Saint Mary's Bay ≈ CDN 242-243 P 6
Saint Marys Peak ▲ AUS 178-179 E 6
Saint Marys River ~ CDN (NS) 240-241 N 5
Saint Marys River ~ USA (FL) 286-287 H 1
Saint-Mathieu ▲•• F 90-91 E 7
Saint Matthew Island ⌒ USA 112-113 Y 6
Saint Matthews ○ USA (SC) 284-285 K 3
Saint-Maurice, Réserve ⊥ CDN (QUE) 236-237 P 5
Saint Maurice, Rivière ~ CDN (QUE) 236-237 P 4
Saint-Maurice, Rivière ~ CDN (QUE) 236-237 P 4
Saint-Maurice, Rivière ~ CDN (QUE) 240-241 C 3
Saint-Médard ○ CDN (QUE) 240-241 G 2
Saint-Méthode ○ CDN (QUE) 240-241 C 2
Saint Michael ○ USA 20-21 J 5
Saint Michaels ○ USA (AZ) 256-257 F 3
Saint Michaels Bay ≈ 38-39 R 2
Saint-Michel, le Mont ○•• F 90-91 G 7
Saint Michel de l'Attalaye ○ RH 54-55 J 5
Saint-Michel-des-Saints ○ CDN (QUE) 238-239 M 2
Saint-Moise ○ CDN (QUE) 240-241 H 2
Saint-Nazaire ○ CDN (QUE) 240-241 D 2
Saint-Nazaire ○ F 90-91 F 8
Saint-Nicholas Abbey • BDS 56 F 5
Saint-Noël ○ CDN (QUE) 240-241 H 2
Saint Norbert ○ CDN (MAN) 234-235 F 5
Saint-Octave-de-l'Avenir ○ CDN (QUE) 242-243 B 3
Saintogne ≐ F 90-91 G 8
Saint-Omer ○• F 90-91 J 6
Saint-Pamphile ○ CDN (QUE) 240-241 F 4
Saint-Pascal ○ CDN (QUE) 240-241 F 3
Saint-Patrice, Lac ○ CDN (QUE) 238-239 H 2
Saint Paul ○ CDN 32-33 P 4
Saint-Paul ○ CDN 38-39 Q 3
Saint-Paul ○• F 224 B 7
Saint Paul ○ USA (AR) 276-277 B 5
Saint Paul ○ USA (NE) 262-263 H 3
Saint Paul ○ USA (VA) 280-281 D 7
Saint Paul ☆• USA (MN) 270-271 E 6
Saint-Paul, Baie- ○ CDN (QUE) 240-241 E 3
Saint Paul, Cape ▲ GH 202-203 L 7
Saint-Paul, Île ⌒ F 12 F 8
Saint Paul, Monastery of • ET 194-195 F 3
Saint-Paule ○ CDN (QUE) 240-241 H 2
Saint Paul Fracture Zone ≃ 6-7 G 8
Saint Paul Island ⌒ CDN (NS) 240-241 P 3
Saint Paul Island ⌒ USA 22-23 L 4
Saint Paul National Park ⊥ RP 160-161 C 7
Saint Paul River ~ CDN 38-39 Q 2
Saint Paul River ~ LB 202-203 E 6
Saint Pauls ○ CDN (NFL) 242-243 L 3
Saint Pauls ○ USA (NC) 282-283 J 6
Saint Pauls Inlet ≈ 38-39 P 4
Saint Pauls Inlet ≈ CDN 242-243 K 3
Saint Peter Bay ≈ 38-39 R 2
Saint Peter Island ⌒ AUS 176-177 M 6
Saint Peter Port ○ GBG 90-91 F 7
Saint Peters ○ CDN (NS) 240-241 P 5
Saint Peters ○ CDN (PEI) 240-241 N 4
Saint Petersburg ○ USA (FL) 286-287 G 4
Saint Petersburg ○ USA (PA) 280-281 G 2
Saint Petersburg = Sankt-Peterburg ☆ ⋯ RUS 94-95 M 2
Saint Petersburg Beach ○ USA (FL) 286-287 G 4
Saint-Philémon ○ CDN (QUE) 240-241 E 4
Saint-Philippe ○ F 224 B 7
Saint-Philippe-de-Neri ○ CDN (QUE) 240-241 F 3
Saint-Pierre ○ CDN (QUE) 238-239 K 3
Saint-Pierre ○ CDN (QUE) 238-239 O 2
Saint-Pierre ○ F 56 E 4
Saint-Pierre ○• F 224 B 7
Saint-Pierre ☆ F 38-39 Q 5
Saint-Pierre ☆ F (975) 242-243 M 6
Saint-Pierre, Fort ∴• SN 202-203 D 2
Saint-Pierre, Havre- ○ CDN (QUE) 242-243 E 2
Saint-Pierre, Île de ⌒ F 38-39 Q 5
Saint-Pierre, Île de ⌒ F (975) 242-243 M 6
Saint-Pierre, Lac ○ CDN (QUE) 238-239 N 2
Saint-Pierre and Miquelon = Saint-Pierre et Miquelon □ F 38-39 Q 5
Saint-Pierre Bank ≃ 38-39 Q 5
Saint-Pierre Bank ≃ 242-243 M 6
Saint-Pierre et Miquelon □ F (975) 242-243 M 6
Saint Pierre-Jolys ○ CDN (MAN) 234-235 G 5
Saint Pierre Jolys ○ CDN (MAN) 234-235 G 5
Saint-Pol-de-Léon ○ F 90-91 F 7
Saint-Pol-sur-Ternoise ○ F 90-91 J 6
Saint-Prime ○ CDN (QUE) 240-241 C 2
Saint-Quentin ○ CDN (NB) 240-241 H 3
Saint-Quentin ○ F 90-91 J 7
Saint-Raphaël ○ CDN (QUE) 240-241 E 4
Saint Raphaël ○ RH 54-55 J 5
Saint-Raymond ○ CDN (QUE) 238-239 O 2
Saint Regis ○ USA (MT) 250-251 D 4
Saint-Rémi ○ CDN (QUE) 238-239 M 3
Saint-René-de-Matane ○ CDN (QUE) 240-241 H 2
Saint Robert ○ USA (MO) 276-277 C 3
Saint-Roch ○ CDN (QUE) 236-237 K 4
Saint Roch Basin ≈ 24-25 Y 6
Saint-Savin ○•• F 90-91 H 8
Saint Sebastian Bay ≈ 220-221 E 7
Saint Shott's ○ CDN (NFL) 242-243 P 6
Saint-Siméon ○ CDN (QUE) 240-241 F 3
Saint Simeon, Monastery of • ET 194-195 F 5
Saint-Simon ○ CDN (QUE) 240-241 F 2
Saint Simons Island ○ USA (GA) 284-285 J 5
Saint Simons Island ⌒ USA (GA) 284-285 J 5
Saint Simons Sound ≈ USA 284-285 J 5
Saint-Stanislas ○ CDN (QUE) 238-239 N 2
Saint Stephen ○ CDN (NB) 240-241 H 5
Saint Stephen ○ USA (SC) 284-285 L 3
Saint Stephens Historic Site • USA (AL) 284-285 B 5
Saint Teresa ○ USA (FL) 286-287 E 2
Saint Theresa Point ○ CDN 34-35 J 4
Saint Thomas ○ CDN (ONT) 238-239 D 6
Saint Thomas ○ USA (ND) 258-259 K 3
Saint Thomas ⌒ USA (VI) 286-287 R 2
Saint-Thomas-Didyme ○ CDN (QUE) 240-241 C 2
Saint-Tite ○ CDN (QUE) 238-239 N 2
Saint-Tropez ○ F 90-91 L 10
Saint-Ulrie ○ CDN (QUE) 240-241 H 2
Saint-Urbain ○ CDN (QUE) 240-241 E 3
Saint-Vianney ○ CDN (QUE) 240-241 H 2
Saint Victor ○ CDN (SAS) 232-233 N 6
Saint Victor's Petroglyphs Historic Park • CDN (SAS) 232-233 N 6
Saint Vidgeon ○ AUS 174-175 C 4
Saint Vincent ○ USA (MN) 270-271 A 2
Saint Vincent ⌒ WV 56 E 5
Saint Vincent, Cap = Tanjona Ankaboa ▲ RM 222-223 C 8
Saint Vincent, Gulf ≈ 180-181 E 3
Saint Vincent and the Grenadines ■ WV 56 E 5
Saint Vincent Island ⌒ USA (FL) 286-287 D 2
Saint Vincent National Wildlife Refuge ⊥ USA (FL) 286-287 D 2
Saint Vincent Passage ≈ 56 E 5
Saint Vincent's ○ CDN (NFL) 242-243 P 6
Saint Walburg ○ CDN (SAS) 232-233 J 2
Saint Xavier ○ USA (MT) 250-251 M 6
Saint-Yrieix-la-Perche ○ F 90-91 H 9
Saint-Zénon ○ CDN (QUE) 238-239 M 2
Sainyinan-Daji ○ WAN 198-199 B 6
Saipal ▲ NEP 144-145 C 6
Saipina ○ BOL 70-71 E 6
Šā'ir ○ OM 132-133 J 5
Sairs, Lac ○ CDN (QUE) 238-239 G 2
Sais, Ğabal ∴• SYR 128-129 G 6
Saisal, Cachoeira ~ BR 66-67 H 7
Saito ○ J 152-153 D 8
Saiton ○ RP 160-161 E 8
Sai'ün ○• Y 132-133 F 6
Sajam ○ RI 166-167 G 2
Sajama ○ BOL 70-71 C 6
Sajama, Río ~ BOL 70-71 C 6
Šajan ○ KA 136-137 L 3
Šajan ~ KA 136-137 L 3
Sajanogorsk ○ RUS 116-117 E 9
Sajano-Šušenskoe, vodohranilišče ○ RUS 116-117 E 9
Sajansk ○ RUS 116-117 L 8
Sajat ○ TM 136-137 H 5
Šajboveem ~ RUS 112-113 N 4
Sajčik ~ RUS 120-121 R 6
Sajdy ○ RUS 110-111 U 5
Sajhan-Ovoo = Ongi ○ MAU 148-149 F 5
Sajkyn ☆ KA 96-97 E 9
Sajljugem, hrebet ▲▲ RUS 124-125 Q 4
Šajmak ○ TJ 146-147 B 7
Sajnšand ○ MAU (ÖMN) 148-149 F 6
Sajnšand ○ MAU (DOG) 148-149 K 5
Sajrab ○ US 136-137 K 5
Saj-Utjës ○ KA 126-127 J 5
Sajylyk ○ RUS (SAH) 110-111 W 5
Sajylyk ○ RUS (SAH) 118-119 J 4
Sajylyk ○ RUS (SAH) 118-119 L 4
Saka ○ ETH 208-209 C 4
Saka ○ MA 188-189 K 3
Sakabinda ○ ZRE 214-215 C 6
Sa Kaeo ○ THA 158-159 G 4
Sakai ○ GH 202-203 J 4
Sakai ○ J 152-153 F 7
Sakaide ○ J 152-153 E 7
Sakaiminato ○ J 152-153 E 7
Sakai National Park ⊥ J 152-153 C 8
Sakaka ☆• KSA 130-131 G 3
Sakakawea, Lake ○ USA (ND) 258-259 E 4
Sakala, Pulau ⌒ RI 168 C 6
Sakaleona ~ RM 222-223 F 8
Sakami, Lac ○ CDN 38-39 F 2
Sakami, Rivière ~ CDN 38-39 H 2
Sakania ○ ZRE 214-215 E 7
Sakania, Réserve partielle à éléphants de ⊥ ZRE 214-215 E 6
Sakao, Île = Lahti ⌒ VAN 184 II a 2
Sakapane ○ RB 218-219 B 4
Sakar, Pulau ⌒ MAL 160-161 C 10
Sakaraha ○ RM 222-223 D 9
Sakar Island ⌒ PNG 183 E 3
Sakarya ○ TR 128-129 D 2
Sakarya Nehri ~ TR 128-129 D 2
Sakassou ○ CI 202-203 H 6
Sakata ○ J 152-153 H 5
Sakata ○ RI 164-165 K 4
Sakbayémé ○ CAM 204-205 J 6
Sake ○ ZRE 212-213 B 4
Sakété ○ DY 204-205 E 5
Sakha = Yakutia = Respublika Saha □ RUS 118-119 G 4
Sakhalin = Sahalin, ostrov ⌒ RUS 122-123 K 3
Sakhonnakhon ○ THA 158-159 H 2
Saki ○ WAN 204-205 E 4
Šakiai ☆ LT 94-95 H 4
Sakiet Sidi Youssef ○ TN 190-191 G 2
Sakiramke ○ RI 166-167 L 6
Sak Lek ○ THA 158-159 F 2
Sakleshpur ○ IND 140-141 F 4
Sakmara ~ RUS 96-97 L 7
Sakoamadinika ○ RM 222-223 F 6
Sakongen Bay ≈ 36-37 H 2
Sakpiegu ○ GH 202-203 K 5
Sakrand ○ PK 138-139 B 6
Sakré Délèb ○ TCH 206-207 D 4
Sakri ○ IND 138-139 E 9
Sakrivier ○ ZA 220-221 E 5
Sakrivier ~ ZA 220-221 E 5
Saksauyl ○ KA 126-127 O 4
Šakšinskoe, ozero ○ RUS 118-119 F 9
Saku ○ J 152-153 H 6
Sakubo ○ RI 162-163 C 5
Sakura ○ J 152-153 J 7
Sakwatamau River ~ CDN 32-33 M 4
Saky ☆• UA 102-103 H 5
Sakyndyk mujisi ▲ KA 126-127 J 5
Sal ~ RUS 102-103 N 4
Sal, Cadena de Cerro de la ▲▲ PE 64-65 E 7
Sal, Cay ⌒ BS 54-55 E 3
Sal, Ilha do ⌒ CV 202-203 C 5
Sal, Raudal de la ~ CO 64-65 F 2
Sala ○ EAT 214-215 F 4
Sala ☆ S 86-87 H 7
Salabangka, Kepulauan ⌒ RI 164-165 H 5
Salaberry-de-Valleyfield ○ CDN (QUE) 238-239 L 3
Sālābih, as- ○ UAE 134-135 F 6
Salačgriva ○ LV 94-95 J 3
Sala Consilina ○ I 100-101 E 4
Salada, Estrecho ~ RCH 76-77 B 6
Saladas ○ RA 76-77 H 5
Saladas, Lagunas ○ RA 76-77 F 5
Saladillo ○ RA 78-79 K 3
Saladillo, Arroyo ~ RA 78-79 J 2
Saladillo, Arroyo del ~ RA 76-77 G 6
Saladillo, Río ~ RA 76-77 E 5
Saladillo, Río ~ RA 78-79 H 2
Saladillo Amargo, Arroyo ~ RA 76-77 G 6
Salado ○ RA 76-77 D 5
Salado, Arroyo ~ RA 78-79 J 4
Salado, Arroyo ~ RA 78-79 F 6
Salado, Arroyo ~ RA 78-79 G 6
Salado, El ○ RA 80 G 4
Salado, El ○ RCH 76-77 B 4
Salado, Riacho ~ RA 76-77 H 3
Salado, Río ~ MEX 50-51 K 4
Salado, Río ~ RA 76-77 H 4
Salado, Río ~ RA 76-77 F 5
Salado, Río ~ RA 78-79 D 5
Salado, Río ~ RA 78-79 E 3
Salado, Río ~ RA 78-79 F 3
Salado, Río ~ USA (NM) 256-257 H 4
Salado Creek ~ USA (NM) 256-257 L 4
Salado Creek ~ USA (TX) 266-267 J 6
Salado o Amblayo, Río ~ RA 76-77 E 3
Salado o Chadileuvu, Río ~ RA 78-79 F 4
Salado o Curacó, Río ~ RA 78-79 G 5
Saladougou ○ RG 202-203 F 4
Salado Viejo ~ RA 76-77 D 5
Salaga ○ GH 202-203 K 5
Salagle ○ SP 212-213 J 3
Salāhaddīn □ IRQ 128-129 K 5
Salahleh = Salahly ○ SP 208-209 G 4
Salahly = Salahleh ○ SP 208-209 G 4
Salairskij krjaž ≐ RUS 124-125 O 1
Salajwe ○ RB 218-219 C 6
Salal ○ TCH 198-199 H 5
Salāla ○•• OM 132-133 J 5
Salāla ○ SUD 200-201 H 2
Salamá ☆ GCA 52-53 J 4
Salamá ○ HN 52-53 L 4
Salamanca ○ ⋯ E 98-99 E 4
Salamanca ○ MEX 52-53 D 1
Salamanca ○ RCH 76-77 B 6
Salamanca ○ USA (NY) 278-279 C 6
Salamanie River ~ USA (IN) 274-275 N 4
Salamat □ TCH 206-207 E 3
Salamat, Bahr ~ TCH 206-207 D 3
Salamaua ○ PNG 183 D 4
Salamina ○ CO (CAL) 60-61 D 5
Salamina ○ CO (MAG) 60-61 D 2
Salamina ○ GR 100-101 J 6
Salamiya ○ SYR 128-129 G 5
Salamiya, as- ○ KSA 130-131 K 5
Salamo ○ PNG 183 F 5
Salamzār ○ IR 134-135 D 2
Salang, Kōtal-e ▲ AFG 136-137 L 7
Salangketo, Tanjung ▲ RI 164-165 G 6
Sa'lāniya, aš- ○ KSA 130-131 H 4
Salantai ○ LT 94-95 G 3
Salar de Pocitos ○ RA 76-77 D 3
Salas ○ PE 64-65 C 5
Salas de los Infantes ○ E 98-99 F 3
Salat ~ RUS 114-115 P 5
Šalatain, Bi'r < ET 194-195 G 6
Salatiga ○ RI 168 D 3
Salatine, Tchi-n- < RN 198-199 B 4
Šalaurova ○ RUS 110-111 Y 3
Šalaurova, mys ▲ RUS 110-111 Y 3
Salavat ○ RUS 96-97 J 7
Salavātābād ○ IR 128-129 M 5
Salawati, Pulau ⌒ RI 166-167 F 2
Salay ○ RP 160-161 F 8
Sala y Gomez Ridge ≃ 5 B 7
Salayie ○ LB 202-203 F 6
Salazar ○ RA 78-79 H 4
Salazie ○ F 224 B 7
Salbris ○ F 90-91 J 8
Salcabamba ○ PE 64-65 E 8
Salcedo ☆ DOM 54-55 K 5
Salcha River ~ USA 20-21 R 4
Saldaña ○ CO 60-61 D 6
Saldaña ○ E 98-99 E 3
Saldanha ○ ZA 220-221 C 6
Saldanhabaai ≈ 220-221 C 6
Saldé ○ SN 196-197 D 6
Saldus ○•• LV 94-95 H 3
Sale ○ AUS 180-181 J 5
Sale, Jar- ○ RUS 108-109 O 8
Salé, Lac ○• COM 222-223 C 3
Salé = Slā ○ MA 188-189 H 3
Sale, Tarko- ☆ RUS 114-115 O 2
Salea ○ RI 164-165 G 4
Salée < RIM 196-197 F 5
Saleh ~ RI 162-163 F 6
Saleh, Teluk ≈ 168 C 7
Şāleḥābād ○ IR (HAM) 134-135 C 1
Şāleḥābād ○ IR (HOR) 136-137 G 7
Salehard ☆ RUS 108-109 M 8
Sålekinna ▲ N 86-87 E 5
Salelologa ○ WS 184 V a 1
Salem ○ IND 140-141 H 5
Salem ○ USA (AR) 276-277 D 4
Salem ○ USA (FL) 286-287 F 2
Salem ○ USA (IL) 274-275 K 6
Salem ○ USA (IN) 274-275 M 6
Salem ○ USA (MO) 276-277 D 3
Salem ○ USA (NH) 278-279 K 6
Salem ○ USA (NJ) 280-281 L 4
Salem ○ USA (OH) 280-281 F 3
Salem ○ USA (SD) 260-261 J 3
Salem ○ USA (VA) 280-281 F 6
Salem ○ USA (WV) 280-281 F 4
Salem ☆ USA (OR) 244-245 C 6
Salem ○ ZA 220-221 H 6
Salemal ○ RUS 108-109 N 8
Salémata ○ SN 202-203 D 3
Salem Maritime National Historic Site • USA (MA) 278-279 L 6
Salem Plateau ▲▲ USA (MO) 276-277 D 3
Salentina, Penisola ∪ I 100-101 G 4
Salerno ☆• I 100-101 E 4
Salerno, Golfo di ≈ 100-101 E 4
Sales ○ BR 72-73 F 6
Sālesatele ○ WS 184 V b 2
Salesópolis ○ BR 72-73 H 7
Saleta ~ RUS 108-109 O 8
Saleye ○ CI 202-203 J 5
Salga ~ RUS 110-111 K 3
Salga Rede, Corredeira ~ BR 66-67 F 2
Salgótarján ○ H 92-93 P 4
Šalgovaara ○ RUS 88-89 M 5
Salgueiro ○ BR 68-69 J 6
Salḥad ○ SYR 128-129 G 6
Salhir ~ UA 102-103 J 5
Salhyr ~ UA 102-103 J 5
Sali ○ DZ 188-189 L 7
Šali ○ RUS 126-127 F 6
Sali ○ VRC (XIZ) 144-145 F 4
Sali ○ VRC (YUN) 142-143 L 2
Sali, Río ~ RA 76-77 E 4
Salibabu, Pulau ⌒ RI 164-165 K 2
Salida ○• USA (CO) 254-255 J 5
Saliente, Punta ▲ RCH 76-77 B 6
Şalif ○ Y 132-133 C 6
Şālih, Qal'at ☆ IRQ 128-129 M 7
Salihli ☆ TR 128-129 C 3
Salihorsk ○ BY 94-95 K 5
Salikénié ○ SN 202-203 C 3
Šalim ○ OM 132-133 J 4
Salima ○ MW 218-219 H 1
Salima ≐ SUD 200-201 D 2
Salima < SUD (Shi) 200-201 D 2
Salima, Wāhāt ≐• SUD 200-201 D 2
Salimo ○ MOC 214-215 J 7
Salin ○ MYA 142-143 J 5
Salina ○ USA (KS) 262-263 J 6
Salina ○ USA (OK) 264-265 J 2
Salina ○ USA (UT) 254-255 D 5
Salina, Isola ⌒ I 100-101 E 5
Salina, La ○ CO 60-61 E 4
Salina Colorada Grande ○ RA 78-79 H 5
Salina Cruz ○• MEX 52-53 G 3
Salina Grande ○ RA 78-79 F 4
Salina Point ▲ BS 54-55 H 3
Salinas ○ BOL 76-77 E 1
Salinas ○ BR 72-73 J 4
Salinas ○ EC 64-65 B 3
Salinas ○ PE 64-65 B 5
Salinas ○ RCH 76-77 C 2
Salinas ○ USA (CA) 248-249 C 3
Salinas, Bahía de ≈ 52-53 B 6
Salinas, Bahía de ≈ 64-65 D 7
Salinas, Pampa de las ≐ RA 76-77 D 6
Salinas, Punta ▲ PE 64-65 D 7
Salinas, Río ~ BOL 76-77 E 1
Salinas, Río ~ BR 68-69 G 5
Salinas, Río ~ BR 72-73 J 4
Salinas, Río ~ MEX 52-53 J 3
Salinas-Aguada Blanca, Reserva Nacional ⊥ PE 70-71 B 5
Salinas de Garci Mendoza ○ BOL 70-71 D 6
Salinas de Hidalgo ○ MEX 50-51 J 6
Salinas Peak ▲ USA (NM) 256-257 J 5
Salinas Pueblo Missions National Monument • USA (NM) 256-257 J 4
Salinas River ~ USA (CA) 248-249 C 3
Salinas Victoria ○ MEX 50-51 J 5
Saline ○ USA (LA) 268-269 H 4
Saline Lake < USA (LA) 268-269 H 5
Salineno ○ USA (TX) 266-267 H 7
Saline River ~ USA (AR) 276-277 C 7
Saline River ~ USA (IL) 274-275 K 6
Saline River ~ USA (KS) 262-263 J 6
Saline River ~ USA (LA) 268-269 H 4
Salines Royales ○•• F 90-91 K 8
Saline Valley ∪ USA (CA) 248-249 G 3
Salineville ○ USA (OH) 280-281 F 3
Salino ○ USA (MI) 272-273 F 5
Salinópolis ○ BR 68-69 E 2
Salis Bay, De ≈ 24-25 L 5
Salisbjuri, ostrov ⌒ RUS 84-85 d 2
Salisbury ○ CDN (NB) 240-241 K 4
Salisbury ○• GB 90-91 G 6
Salisbury ○ USA (MD) 280-281 L 5
Salisbury ○ USA (MO) 274-275 F 5
Salisbury ○ USA (NC) 282-283 G 5
Salisbury = Harare ★•• ZW 218-219 F 3
Salisbury, Mount ▲ USA 20-21 R 2
Salisbury Channel ≈ 212-213 D 4
Salisbury Island ⌒ AUS 176-177 G 7
Salisbury Island ⌒ CDN 36-37 L 3
Salish Mountains ▲▲ USA (MT) 250-251 E 3
Salitral ○ PE 64-65 C 4
Salitral ○ RA 78-79 H 5
Salitral de la Barrancas ○ RA 78-79 H 5
Salitral de la Perra ○ RA 78-79 F 4
Salitral Levalle ○ RA 78-79 G 4
Salitre ○ EC 64-65 C 2
Salitre, Río ~ BR 68-69 H 6
Salitrosa, Quebrada ~ RCH 76-77 B 4
Šalja ☆ RUS 96-97 L 5
Salka ○ WAN 204-205 F 3
Salkaj, ostrov ⌒ RUS 110-111 M 3
Šalkar ☆ KA 126-127 N 4
Šalkar-Egakara, ozero ○ RUS 126-127 O 2
Salkehatchie River ~ USA (SC) 284-285 J 3
Salkum ○ USA (WA) 244-245 C 4
Salla ○ FIN 88-89 K 3
Salle, La ○ USA (CO) 254-255 L 3
Salliaruseq ⌒ GRØ 28-29 P 1
Salliqueló ○ RA 78-79 H 4
Sallisaw ○ USA (OK) 264-265 K 3
Sallom ○ SUD 200-201 H 3
Salluit ○ CDN 36-37 M 3
Sallyan ○ NEP 144-145 C 6
Sally's Cove ○ CDN (NFL) 242-243 L 3
Sal'm, ostrov ⌒ RUS 84-85 f 2
Salmān, as- ○ IRQ 130-131 J 2
Salmās ○ IR 128-129 L 3
Salmi ○ RUS 88-89 L 6
Salmo ○ CDN (BC) 230-231 M 4
Salmon ○ USA (ID) 250-251 F 6
Salmon Arm ○ CDN (BC) 230-231 K 3
Salmon Cove ○ CDN (NFL) 242-243 P 5
Salmon Falls Creek ~ USA (NV) 246-247 L 2
Salmon Falls Creek Reservoir ○ USA (ID) 252-253 D 4
Salmon Fork ~ USA 20-21 U 3
Salmon Gums ○ AUS 176-177 F 6

Salmon River ∼ CDN 38-39 Q 3
Salmon River ∼ CDN (BC) 228-229 L 2
Salmon River ∼ CDN (NB) 240-241 K 4
Salmon River ∼ USA 20-21 L 3
Salmon River ∼ USA (ID) 250-251 D 6
Salmon River ∼ USA (ID) 252-253 D 2
Salmon River ∼ USA (NY) 278-279 F 5
Salmon River ∼ USA (NY) 278-279 G 4
Salmon River Mountains ▲ USA (ID) 252-253 B 1
Salmon Valley o CDN (BC) 228-229 M 2
Salmo-Priest Wilderness Area ⊥ USA (WA) 244-245 H 2
Salmossi o BF 202-203 K 2
Salo o FIN 88-89 G 6
Salo o RCA 210-211 F 2
Salobra, Ribeiro ∼ BR 70-71 J 7
Salomão, Ilha ⌒ BR 66-67 F 6
Salome o USA (AZ) 256-257 B 5
Salonga ∼ ZRE 210-211 H 4
Salonga Nord, Parc National de la ⊥ ••• ZRE 210-211 H 4
Salonga Sud, Parc National de la ⊥ ••• ZRE 210-211 H 4
Salonsa o RI 162-163 F 5
Salor, Río ∼ E 98-99 D 5
Salou, Cap de ▲ E 98-99 H 4
Saloum ∼ SN 202-203 C 2
Salpausselkä ⩦ FIN 88-89 H 6
Salsa, Paraná do ∼ BR 66-67 F 5
Salsacate o RA 76-77 E 6
Salsberry Pass ▲ USA (CA) 248-249 H 4
Salsipuedes, Canal de ≈ 50-51 C 3
Salsipuedes Grande, Arroyo ∼ ROU 78-79 L 2
Sal'sk o RUS 102-103 M 4
Sal'skij o RUS 88-89 O 6
Sal'sko-Manyčskaja grjada ▲ RUS 102-103 M 4
Salso ∼ I 100-101 D 6
Salt, as- ☆ JOR 130-131 D 1
Salta ▫ RA 76-77 D 3
Salta ☆ •• RA (SAL) 76-77 E 3
Saltaim, ozero o RUS 114-115 L 6
Salt Basin ⊙ USA (TX) 266-267 B 2
Salt Cay ⌒ GB 54-55 K 4
Saltcoats o CDN (SAS) 232-233 Q 4
Salt Creek ∼ AUS 178-179 F 6
Salt Creek ∼ USA (IL) 274-275 J 4
Salt Creek ∼ USA (NM) 256-257 L 5
Salt Desert = Kavir, Dašt-e ⩦ IR 134-135 E 1
Salt Draw ∼ USA (TX) 266-267 C 2
Salteelva ∼ N 86-87 G 3
Saltery Bay o CDN (BC) 230-231 E 4
Saltfjell-Svartisen nasjonalpark ⊥ N 86-87 G 3
Saltfjorden ≈ 86-87 F 3
Salt Flat o USA (TX) 266-267 B 2
Salt Fork ∼ USA (KS) 262-263 G 7
Salt Fork Brazos River ∼ USA (TX) 264-265 D 5
Salt Fork Lake ⊙ USA (OH) 280-281 E 3
Salt Fork Red River ∼ USA (TX) 264-265 D 4
Saltillo ☆ • MEX 50-51 J 5
Saltillo o USA (MS) 268-269 M 2
Salt Lake ⊙ USA (NM) 256-257 M 6
Salt Lake ⊙ USA (TX) 266-267 C 2
Salt Lake, The ⊙ AUS 178-179 G 6
Salt Lake City ☆ USA (UT) 254-255 D 3
Salt Lakes ⊙ AUS 176-177 E 4
Salt March ⊙ USA (KS) 262-263 H 6
Salto o RA 78-79 J 3
Salto ☆ ROU 76-77 J 6
Salto, El o MEX (DGO) 50-51 G 6
Salto, El o MEX (SLP) 50-51 K 6
Salto, El o RCH 78-79 D 3
Salto, El o YV 60-61 K 3
Salto, Río ∼ RA 78-79 J 3
Salto da Divisa o BR 72-73 L 4
Salto de Cavalo ∼ • ANG 216-217 C 4
Salto de las Rosas o RA 78-79 E 3
Salto del Guaira ☆ PY 76-77 K 3
Salto Grande, Embalse < ROU 76-77 J 6
Salton City o USA (CA) 248-249 J 6
Salton Sea ⊙ USA (CA) 248-249 J 6
Salto Osório, Represa < BR 74-75 D 5
Salto Santiago, Represa de < BR 74-75 D 5
Salt Pan ⊙ NAM 220-221 D 3
Salt Range ▲ PK 138-139 D 3
Salt River ∼ USA (AZ) 256-257 E 5
Salt River ∼ USA (KY) 276-277 K 3
Salt River ∼ USA (MO) 274-275 G 5
Saltsjöbaden o S 86-87 J 7
Salt Spring Island ⌒ CDN (BC) 230-231 F 5
Salt Springs o USA (FL) 286-287 H 2
Saltville o USA (VA) 280-281 E 7
Saluda o USA (SC) 284-285 J 2
Saluda River ∼ USA (SC) 284-285 H 2
Salue Besar, Pulau ⌒ RI 164-165 H 4
Salue Kecil, Pulau ⌒ RI 164-165 H 5
Salue Timpaus, Selat ≈ 164-165 H 4
Salugan o RI 164-165 G 3
Salumbar o IND 138-139 E 7
Salus o USA (AR) 276-277 B 5
Salut, Îles du ⌒ F 62-63 H 3
Saluta o RI 164-165 K 2
Saluzzo o I 100-101 A 2
Salvacion o RP 160-161 E 7
Salvación, Bahía ≈ 80 C 5
Salvador ☆ ••• BR 72-73 L 2
Salvador o CDN (SAS) 232-233 J 3
Salvador, El ■ ES 52-53 K 5
Salvador, Lake ⊙ USA (LA) 268-269 K 7
Salvador, Passe de ▲ RN 192-193 E 6
Salvador do Sul o BR 74-75 E 7
Salvage o CDN (NFL) 242-243 P 4
Salvaterra o BR 62-63 K 6
Salvaterra o E 98-99 C 3
Salvatierra o MEX 52-53 D 1
Salvation, Point ▲ AUS 176-177 G 4
Salvator Rosa Section ⊥ AUS 178-179 J 3
Salve Ø ⌒ GRØ 26-27 R 5
Salve River ∼ CDN 30-31 O 6
Salvo o USA (NC) 282-283 M 5
Salvus o CDN (BC) 228-229 E 2
Salwā, as- o KSA 134-135 D 6
Salwā Bahrī o ET 194-195 F 5
Salween ∼ MYA 142-143 K 6
Salyan o AZ 128-129 N 3
Salyersville o USA (KY) 276-277 M 3
Šalyhyne o UA 102-103 J 2
Salzberger Bay ≈ 16 F 22
Salzburg ▫ A 92-93 M 5
Salzburg ☆ •• A 92-93 M 5
Salzgitter o D 92-93 L 2
Salzwedel o • D 92-93 L 2
Sam o G 210-211 C 3
Ša'm, aš o UAE 134-135 G 5
Sam, kum ⩦ KA 126-127 L 5
Sama o PE 70-71 B 5
Sama, Río ∼ PE 70-71 B 5
Samachique o MEX 50-51 F 4
Samachvalavičy o BY 94-95 K 5
Samadābād o IR 134-135 H 2
Samagaltaj ☆ RUS 116-117 G 10
Samah ∼ MYA 142-143 K 5
Samā'il o OM 132-133 L 2
Samaipata • BOL 70-71 F 6
Samak, Tanjung ▲ RI 162-163 F 5
Samakona o CI 202-203 G 5
Samakoulou o RMM 202-203 F 3
Samal o RP 160-161 F 9
Samal, Tanjung ▲ RI 166-167 E 3
Samalá, Río ∼ GCA 52-53 J 4
Samalayuca o MEX 50-51 F 2
Samales Group ⌒ RP 160-161 D 9
Samalga Island ⌒ USA 22-23 M 6
Samalga Pass ≈ 22-23 M 6
Samal Island ⌒ RP 160-161 F 9
Sāmalkot o IND 142-143 C 7
Samalusi o LAR 192-193 J 1
Samālūṭ o ET 194-195 E 3
Šamalzāi o AFG 134-135 M 3
Samambaia, Rio ∼ BR 72-73 D 7
Šaman, gora • RUS 122-123 H 3
Sam'ān, Qal'at •• SYR 128-129 G 4
Samaná ☆ •• DOM 54-55 L 5
Samaná, Bahía de ≈ 54-55 L 5
Samaná, Cabo ▲ DOM 54-55 L 5
Samaná, Península ⌄ DOM 54-55 L 5
Samana Cay ⌒ BS 54-55 J 3
Samana Cays = Atwood Cays ⌒ BS 54-55 J 3
Samanco o PE 64-65 C 6
Samandağ ☆ TR 128-129 F 4
Samandré Lake ⊙ CDN 30-31 M 2
Samanga o EAT (KIL) 212-213 F 5
Samanga o EAT (LIN) 214-215 K 5
Samangán o AFG (SAM) 136-137 L 6
Samangān ▫ AFG 136-137 K 6
Samangan, Rūd-e ∼ AFG 136-137 K 7
Šamaniha ∼ RUS 110-111 d 7
Šamanij kamen' • RUS 116-117 M 8
Šamanka ∼ RUS 120-121 T 4
Samanturai o CL 140-141 J 7
Samaqua, Rivière ∼ CDN (QUE) 236-237 Q 3
Samar ⌒ RP 160-161 F 7
Samara ☆ RUS 96-97 G 7
Samara ∼ RUS 96-97 H 7
Samara ∼ UA 102-103 J 3
Samara ∼ UA 102-103 K 3
Samarai o PNG 183 F 6
Samarang, Tanjung ▲ MAL 160-161 B 9
Samarga o RUS 122-123 H 5
Samarga ∼ RUS 122-123 H 5
Samari o PNG 183 B 5
Samariapo o YV 60-61 H 5
Samarinda ☆ • RI 164-165 E 4
Samarkand ☆ •• US 136-137 K 5
Samarkand = Samarkand ☆ •• US 136-137 K 5
Samarkandskaja oblast' ▫ US 136-137 H 3
Samarqand = Samarkand ☆ •• US 136-137 K 5
Sāmarrā' ☆ • IRQ 128-129 K 5
Samar Sea ≈ 160-161 F 6
Samarskoe o KA 124-125 N 4
Samarskoe vodohranilišče < RUS 96-97 F 7
Samaru o WAN 204-205 G 3
Samastipur o IND 142-143 D 3
Samate o RI 166-167 F 2
Samatiguila o • CI 202-203 G 5
Sāmatra o IND 138-139 B 8
Samaúma o BR 66-67 F 3
Samāwa, as- ☆ IRQ 128-129 L 7
Samba o BF 202-203 J 3
Samba o IND 138-139 E 3
Samba o RCA 206-207 C 6
Samba ∼ RI 162-163 K 5
Samba o ZRE (EQU) 210-211 H 3
Samba o ZRE (KIV) 210-211 L 6
Samba Cajú o ANG 216-217 C 4
Sambailo o RG 202-203 D 3
Sambalgou o BF 202-203 L 3
Sambaliung Pegunungan ▲ RI 164-165 E 3
Sambalpur o IND 142-143 C 5
Sambao ∼ RM 222-223 D 6
Sambar, Tanjung ▲ RI 162-163 J 6
Sambas o RI 162-163 H 4
Sambas ∼ RI 162-163 H 4
Sambau o RI 162-163 F 5
Sambava o RM 222-223 G 5
Sambazô, Rio ∼ MOC 218-219 H 4
Samberi o RI 166-167 H 2
Sambhal o IND 138-139 G 5
Sāmbhar Salt Lake ⊙ IND 138-139 E 6
Sambialgou o BF 202-203 L 3
Sambir ☆ UA 102-103 C 3
Sambirano ∼ RM 222-223 F 4
Sambisumbi o SOL 184 I c 2
Sambito, Rio ∼ BR 68-69 H 5
Sambo o ANG 216-217 D 6
Sambo o RI 164-165 F 5
Samboja o RI 164-165 E 4
Samborombón, Bahía ≈ 78-79 L 3
Samborombón, Río ∼ RA 78-79 L 3
Samborondón o EC 64-65 C 2
Sāmbrāni o IND 140-141 F 3
Sambriāl o PK 138-139 E 3
Sambro o CDN (NS) 240-241 M 6
Samburg o RUS 108-109 S 8
Samburu o EAK 212-213 G 5
Samburu National Reserve ⊥ EAK 212-213 F 3
Sambusu o NAM 216-217 E 8
Samch'ŏk o ROK 150-151 G 9
Samch'ŏnp'o o ROK 150-151 G 10
Samdrup Jonkhar o BHT 142-143 G 2
Same o EAT 212-213 F 6
Samene, Oued ∼ DZ 190-191 F 7
Sam Ford Fiord ≈ 26-27 P 8
Samfya o Z 214-215 E 6
Samha ⌒ Y 132-133 H 7
Samha, al- o UAE 134-135 F 6
Šamhor = Šamkir o • AZ 128-129 L 2
Sámi o GR 100-101 H 5
Sami o IND 138-139 C 8
Samia o RN 198-199 D 5
Samia, Tanjung ▲ RI 164-165 H 3
Sāmi ji Veri o PK 138-139 C 7
Šāmili, aš- o KSA 130-131 G 4
Samim, Umm as- ⩦ OM 132-133 J 3
Samirā' o KSA 130-131 H 4
Samiria, Río ∼ PE 64-65 E 4
Samita o KSA 132-133 C 5
Šāmiya, aš- ⩦ IRQ 130-131 K 2
Samjiyon o DVR 150-151 G 7
Samka o MYA 142-143 K 5
Šamkir = Şamkir o • AZ 128-129 L 2
Šammar, Ǧabal ▲ KSA 130-131 F 4
Sām Nām o VN 156-157 C 6
Samnū o LAR 192-193 F 4
Samo o CI 202-203 J 7
Samo o PNG 183 G 2
Samoa o ANG 216-217 F 4
Samoa Basin ≃ 13 L 4
Sāmoa-i-Sisifo ⌒ WS 184 V b 1
Samoded o RUS 88-89 Q 5
Samoé o RG 202-203 F 6
Samoedskaja Rečka ∼ RUS 108-109 Y 6
Samojlovka o RUS 102-103 N 2
Samokov o BG 102-103 C 6
Samoleta, ostrov ⌒ RUS 110-111 N 3
Samorogouan o BF 202-203 H 4
Sámos ☆ • GR 100-101 L 6
Sámos ⌒ GR 100-101 L 6
Samosir, Pulau ⌒ RI 162-163 C 3
Samothráki o GR 100-101 K 4
Samothráki ⌒ GR 100-101 K 4
Samotlor, ozero o RUS 114-115 O 4
Sampa o GH 202-203 J 6
Sampacho o RA 78-79 G 2
Sampadi o MAL 162-163 H 4
Sampaga o RI 164-165 F 5
Sampaio o BR 68-69 E 4
Sampanago, Ruins of • MYA 142-143 K 3
Sampang o RI 168 E 3
Sampara ∼ RI 164-165 H 5
Sampelga o BF 202-203 L 3
Sampit o RI 162-163 K 6
Sampit ∼ RI 162-163 K 6
Sampit Teluk ≈ 162-163 K 6
Sampolawa o RI 164-165 H 6
Sampsel o USA (MO) 274-275 E 5
Sampun o PNG 183 G 3
Sampwe o ZRE 214-215 D 5
Sam Rayburn Lake < USA (TX) 268-269 F 5
Samrē o ETH 200-201 J 6
Samreboe o GH 202-203 J 7
Sams o USA (CO) 254-255 H 5
Samsang o VRC 144-145 D 5
Samsherpur o IND 138-139 D 10
Šamsiya, aš- o KSA 130-131 J 4
Samsø ⌒ DK 86-87 E 9
Samson o USA (AL) 284-285 D 5
Sām Sơn o VN 156-157 D 7
Samson Indian Reserve ⧗ CDN (ALB) 232-233 E 3
Samsudin Noor • RI 164-165 D 5
Samsun ☆ • TR 128-129 G 2
Samtredia o GE 126-127 E 6
Samucumbi o ANG 216-217 E 6
Samuel, Represa de < BR 66-67 F 7
Samuels o USA (ID) 250-251 C 3
Samuhú o RA 76-77 G 4
Samulondo o ZRE 214-215 B 5
Samundri o PK 138-139 D 4
Samur ∼ AZ 128-129 N 2
Samur-Apšeronskij kanal < AZ 128-129 N 2
Samuro, Raudal ∼ CO 60-61 G 6
Samut Prakan o THA 158-159 F 4
Samut Sakhon o THA 158-159 F 4
Samut Songkhram o THA 158-159 E 4
San ∼ K 158-159 J 3
San ∼ PL 92-93 R 4
San o RMM 202-203 H 3
Saña o PE 64-65 C 5
Sanā o Y 132-133 F 5
Ṣan'ā' ☆ ••• Y 132-133 D 6
Sanā, Wādī ∼ Y 132-133 F 5
Sanaa = Ṣan'ā' ☆ ••• Y 132-133 D 6
Sanaag ▫ SP 208-209 H 3
Sanaba o BF 202-203 J 3
Sanaba ∼ RMM 202-203 F 2
Sanabria o CO 60-61 C 6
Sanae o ARK 16 F 36
Sanāfir, Ǧazīrat ⌒ KSA 130-131 D 4
Sanaga ∼ CAM 204-205 K 6
San Agusin o YV 60-61 H 4
San Agustín, Arroyo ∼ BOL 70-71 D 3
San Agustín de Valle Fértil o RA 76-77 D 6
Sanak o USA 22-23 P 5
Sanak Island ⌒ USA 22-23 P 5
Sanak Islands ⌒ USA 22-23 P 5
San Alberto o CO 60-61 E 4
San Alejandro o PE 64-65 E 6
Sanām, as- ⩦ KSA 132-133 G 3
Sanamain, aš- o SYR 128-129 G 6
San Ana o BR 66-67 C 2
Sanana o RI 164-165 J 5
Sanana, Pulau ⌒ RI 164-165 J 5
Sanandağ ☆ • IR 128-129 M 5
Sanando o RMM 202-203 G 3
San Andreas o USA (CA) 246-247 E 5
San Andrés o C 54-55 G 4
San Andres o CO 60-61 D 4
San Andres o RP 160-161 F 6
San Andrés, Isla de ⌒ CO 52-53 D 5
San Andrés, Quebrada de ∼ RCH 76-77 C 4
San Andrés de Giles o RA 78-79 K 3
San Andres de Sotavento o CO 60-61 D 3
San Andres Mountains ▲ USA (NM) 256-257 J 6
San Andres National Wildlife Refuge • USA (NM) 256-257 J 6
San Andres Point ▲ RP 160-161 D 6
San Andrés y Sauces o E 188-189 C 6
San Andros o BS 54-55 F 2
Sananduva o BR 74-75 E 6
Sanane Besar, Pulau ⌒ RI 168 D 6
Sananferedougou o CI 202-203 G 4
San Angelo o USA (TX) 266-267 G 2
Sanankoroba o RMM 202-203 G 3
San Anselmo o USA (CA) 248-249 B 2
San Anton o PE 70-71 B 4
San Antonio o BH 52-53 K 3
San Antônio o BR 62-63 J 5
San Antonio o CO 60-61 B 7
San Antonio o MEX 50-51 D 6
San Antonio o RA 78-79 F 2
San Antonio o RCH 78-79 D 2
San Antonio o USA (NM) 256-257 J 5
San Antonio o • USA (TX) 266-267 J 4
San Antonio o YV 60-61 H 6
San Antonio, Cabo ∼ RA 78-79 L 4
San Antonio, Cabo de ▲ C 54-55 C 4
San Antônio, Cachoeira de o BR 62-63 H 6
San Antonio, Río ∼ BOL 76-77 D 1
San Antonio, Sierra ▲ MEX 50-51 D 2
San Antonio Bay ≈ 44-45 J 5
San Antonio Bay ≈ 160-161 B 8
San Antonio Bay ≈ USA 266-267 L 5
San Antonio de Tabasca o YV 60-61 K 3
San Antonio de Areco o RA 78-79 K 3
San Antonio de Esmoraca o BOL 76-77 D 1
San Antonio de Esquilache o PE 70-71 B 5
San Antonio de Getucha o CO 64-65 E 1
San Antonio de Golfo o YV 60-61 K 2
San Antonio de los Baños o C 54-55 D 3
San Antonio de los Cobres o RA 76-77 D 3
San Antonio del Sur o C 54-55 H 4
San Antonio de Tamanaco o YV 60-61 H 3
San Antonio El Grande o MEX 50-51 G 3
San Antonio Huitepec o MEX 52-53 F 3
San Antonio Mountain ▲ USA (NM) 256-257 K 6
San Antonio Oeste o RA 78-79 G 6
San Antonio River ∼ USA (TX) 266-267 K 5
San Antonio Villalongín o MEX 52-53 D 2
San Antonio y Torcuga, Canal < RA 78-79 H 2
San Ardo o USA (CA) 248-249 D 3
Sanaroa Island ⌒ PNG 183 F 5
San Augustin o CO 60-61 C 6
San Augustín o MEX 50-51 B 3
San Augustin o RP 160-161 E 6
San Augustín, Parque Arquelógico • CO 60-61 C 7
San Augustine o USA (TX) 268-269 F 5
Sanāw o Y 132-133 G 5
Sanāwad o IND 138-139 F 8
San Bartolo o BOL 70-71 D 4
San Bartolo o PE 64-65 D 8
San Bartolomé de Tirajana o E 188-189 D 7
Sanbei Yangchang o VRC 154-155 E 2
San Benedetto del Tronto o I 100-101 D 3
San Benedicto, Isla ⌒ MEX 50-51 C 7
San Benito o GCA 52-53 K 3
San Benito o NIC 52-53 L 5
San Benito o USA (TX) 266-267 K 7
San Benito Abad o CO 60-61 D 3
San Benito Mountain ▲ USA (CA) 248-249 D 3
San Bernardino o USA (CA) 248-249 G 5
San Bernardino Strait ≈ 160-161 F 6
San Bernard National Wildlife Refuge ⊥ USA (TX) 266-267 M 5
San Bernardo o RA (BUA) 78-79 J 4
San Bernardo o RA (SAF) 76-77 G 5
San Bernardo o RCH 78-79 D 2
San Bernardo, Islas de ⌒ CO 60-61 C 3
San Bernardo, Punta ▲ CO 60-61 C 3
San Bernardo del Viento o CO 60-61 D 3
San Bernhard River ∼ USA (TX) 268-269 E 7
San Blas o MEX (COA) 50-51 J 4
San Blas o MEX (SIN) 50-51 E 4
San Blas o • MEX (NAY) 50-51 G 7
San Blas, Archipiélago de ⌒ • PA 52-53 E 7
San Blas, Cape ▲ USA (FL) 286-287 D 2
San Blas, Cordillera de ▲ PA 52-53 E 7
San Borja o BOL 70-71 D 4
San Borja, Sierra de ▲ MEX 50-51 C 3
Sanborn o USA (MN) 270-271 C 6
Sanbornville o USA (NH) 278-279 K 5
San Buenaventura o BOL 70-71 C 4
San Buenaventura o MEX 50-51 J 4
San Buenaventura, Cordillera de ▲ RA 76-77 C 4
Sanca o CDN (BC) 230-231 N 4
Sança o MOC 218-219 H 3
San Carlos o MEX (BCS) 50-51 C 5
San Carlos o MEX (COA) 50-51 J 3
San Carlos o MEX (TAM) 50-51 K 5
San Carlos ☆ NIC 52-53 B 6
San Carlos o • PA 52-53 E 7
San Carlos o RA (MEN) 78-79 E 2
San Carlos o RA (SAE) 76-77 F 5
San Carlos o RCH 78-79 D 4
San Carlos o ROU 78-79 M 3
San Carlos o RP (NED) 160-161 E 7
San Carlos o RP (PAN) 160-161 D 5
San Carlos o USA (AZ) 256-257 E 5
San Carlos ☆ YV 60-61 G 3
San Carlos, Arroyo ∼ RA 78-79 E 3
San Carlos, Caldera de ▲ GQ 210-211 B 2
San Carlos = Ciudad Quesada o CR 52-53 B 6
San Carlos, Punta ▲ MEX 50-51 C 4
San Carlos, Río ∼ CR 52-53 B 6
San Carlos, Río ∼ PY 76-77 H 2
San Carlos Bay ≈ 48-49 G 6
San Carlos Bay ≈ USA 286-287 G 5
San Carlos de Bariloche o • RA 78-79 D 6
San Carlos de Bolívar o RA 78-79 J 4
San Carlos de Guaroa o CO 60-61 E 6
San Carlos del Meta o YV 60-61 H 4
San Carlos del Zulia o YV 60-61 F 3
San Carlos de Río Negro o YV 66-67 D 2
San Carlos Indian Reservation ⧗ USA (AZ) 256-257 E 5
San Carlos Lake ⊙ USA (AZ) 256-257 E 5
San Carlos Yautepec o MEX 52-53 F 3
San Cayetano o CO 60-61 D 5
San Cayetano o RA 78-79 K 5
Sancha o VRC (GXI) 156-157 F 4
Sancha o VRC (SHA) 154-155 G 2
Sanchakou o VRC 146-147 D 6
Sánchez o DOM 54-55 L 5
Sánchez, Cerro ▲ RA 80 F 5
Sánchez Magallanes o • MEX 52-53 H 2
Sanchi o ••• IND 138-139 F 8
Sanchi River ∼ PNG 183 B 2
Sancho, Corrego ∼ BR 68-69 D 6
Sānchor o IND 138-139 C 7
San Christóbal, Quebrada ∼ RCH 76-77 C 2
San Cirilo, Cerro ▲ PE 64-65 C 5
San Clara o CDN (MAN) 234-235 B 3
San Clemente o E 98-99 F 5
San Clemente o RCH 78-79 D 3
San Clemente o USA (CA) 248-249 G 6
San Clemente del Tuyú o RA 78-79 L 4
San Clemente Island ⌒ USA (CA) 248-249 F 7
San Clemente o San Valentín, Cerro ▲ RCH 80 D 3
Sanclerlândia o BR 72-73 E 4
Sanco o USA (TX) 264-265 D 6
Sancos o PE 64-65 F 9
San Cosme y Damián o ••• PY 76-77 J 4
San Cristóbal o BOL 76-77 D 1
San Cristóbal o C 54-55 D 3
San Cristóbal ☆ • DOM 54-55 K 5
San Cristóbal o PA 52-53 D 7
San Cristobal o RA 76-77 G 6
San Cristóbal o RCH 76-77 C 2
San Cristobal ⌒ SOL 184 I e 4
San Cristóbal ☆ YV 60-61 E 4
San Cristóbal, Isla ⌒ EC 64-65 C 10
San Cristóbal, Volcán ▲ NIC 52-53 L 5
San Cristóbal de la Laguna = La Laguna o E 188-189 C 6
San Cristóbal de las Casas o •• MEX 52-53 H 3
San Cristobal Trench ≃ 184 I e 4
San Cristobal Wash ∼ USA (AZ) 256-257 B 6
Sancti Spíritu o RA 78-79 H 3
Sancti Spíritus ☆ •• C 54-55 F 4
Sanctuaire des Addax, Réserve Naturelle Intégrale Dite ⊥ RN 198-199 D 3
Sanctuary o CDN (SAS) 232-233 K 5
Sančursk o RUS 96-97 E 5
Sancy, Puy de ▲ • F 90-91 J 9
Sand ☆ N 86-87 C 7
Sand ∼ ZA 218-219 E 6
Sandafa al-Far o ET 194-195 E 3
Sandakan o MAL 160-161 C 10
Sandakan, Teluk ≈ 160-161 B 10
Šāndak Bālā ∼ IR 134-135 H 4
Sandal, ozero o RUS 88-89 M 5
Sandama o RG 202-203 F 3
Sandando o ANG 216-217 F 5
Sandane ☆ N 86-87 C 6
Sandanski o BG 102-103 C 7
Sandaré o RMM 202-203 E 2
Sand Arroyo River ∼ USA (CO) 254-255 N 6
Sanday ⌒ GB 90-91 F 2
Sandbank Lake ⊙ CDN 34-35 P 5
Sandberg o ZA 220-221 D 6
Sandburg Home National Historic Site, Carl • USA (NC) 282-283 E 5
Sand Creek ∼ USA (CO) 254-255 M 4
Sandefjord ☆ N 86-87 E 7
Sandégué o CI 202-203 J 6
Sandema o GH 202-203 K 4
Sānderāo o IND 138-139 D 7
Sanders o USA (AZ) 256-257 F 3
Sanderson o USA (TX) 266-267 E 3
Sanderson Canyon ∼ USA (TX) 266-267 E 4
Sanderson Lake ⊙ CDN 30-31 R 5
Sandersville o USA (GA) 284-285 H 3
Sandfire Flat Roadhouse o AUS 172-173 E 5
Sandfloeggi ▲ N 86-87 C 7
Sandfly Island = Mbokonimbeti Island ⌒ SOL 184 I d 3
Sandford Lake ⊙ CDN (ONT) 234-235 M 5
Sandhill o CDN (ONT) 238-239 F 5
Sandhill o USA (MS) 268-269 L 4
Sand Hill o USA (MS) 268-269 M 5
Sand Hill River ∼ CDN 38-39 Q 2
Sand Hill River ∼ USA (MN) 270-271 B 3
Sand Hills ▲ USA (NE) 262-263 E 2
Sandhornøy ⌒ N 86-87 G 3
Sandi o SUD 200-201 F 4
Sandia o PE 70-71 C 4
Sandia Crest ▲ USA (NM) 256-257 J 3
Sandian He ∼ VRC 148-149 M 7
San Diego o USA (TX) 266-267 J 6
San Diego o • USA (CA) 248-249 G 7
San Diego, Cabo ▲ RA 80 H 7
San Diego de Alcala • USA (CA) 248-249 G 7
San Diego de la Unión o MEX 50-51 J 7
Sandies Creek ∼ USA (TX) 266-267 K 4
Sandıklı ☆ TR 128-129 D 3
Sandila o IND 142-143 B 2
Sandilands Forest Reserve ⊥ CDN (MAN) 234-235 G 5
Sanding, Pulau ⌒ RI 162-163 D 6
Sanding, Selat ≈ 162-163 D 6
Sandino o C 54-55 C 3
San Dionisio del Mar o MEX 52-53 G 3
Sand Islands ⌒ USA 20-21 G 5
Sand Lake o CDN (ONT) 236-237 D 5
Sand Lake o CDN (ONT) 238-239 F 3
Sand Lake ⊙ CDN (NWT) 30-31 U 3
Sand Lake ⊙ CDN (ONT) 234-235 J 4
Sandlake o USA (OR) 244-245 B 5
Sand Lake ⊙ USA (OK) 264-265 H 2
Sand Mountains ▲ USA (AL) 284-285 D 2
Sandnes ☆ N 86-87 B 7
Sandnessjøen o N 86-87 F 3
Sandoa o ZRE 214-215 B 5
Sandomierska, Kotlina ⌄ PL 92-93 Q 3
Sandomierz o •• PL 92-93 Q 3
Sandougou o CI 202-203 H 6
Sandougou ∼ SN 202-203 C 3
Sandoval o USA (IL) 274-275 J 6
Sandover Highway II AUS 178-179 D 1
Sandover River ∼ AUS 178-179 C 1
Sandovo o RUS 94-95 P 2
Sandoway o MYA 142-143 J 6
Sand Pass ▲ USA (UT) 254-255 B 4
Sand Point o CDN (NS) 240-241 O 5
Sand Point o USA 22-23 Q 5
Sandpoint o USA (ID) 250-251 C 3
Sandrakatsy o RM 222-223 F 6
Sandrakota ∼ RM 222-223 F 5
Sandratsino ∼ RM 222-223 F 6
Sandridge o CDN (MAN) 234-235 F 4
Šandrin ∼ RUS 110-111 c 4
Sand River ∼ CDN 32-33 P 4
Sandrivier ∼ ZA 220-221 H 4
Sandrun ∼ RUS 110-111 d 4
Sandspit o CDN (BC) 228-229 C 3
Sand Springs o USA (MT) 250-251 M 4
Sand Springs o USA (OK) 264-265 H 2
Sandstad o N 86-87 D 5
Sandstone o AUS 176-177 E 4
Sandstone o USA (MN) 270-271 F 4
Sandur o IND 140-141 G 3
Sandusky o USA (MI) 272-273 G 4
Sandusky o USA (OH) 280-281 D 2
Sandusky River ∼ USA (OH) 280-281 C 3
Sandveld Nature Reserve ⊥ ZA 220-221 G 3
Sandvig o DK 86-87 G 9
Sandvika o S 86-87 F 5
Sandviken ☆ S 86-87 H 6
Sandvisbaai ≈ 220-221 B 1
Sandwich o USA (IL) 274-275 K 3
Sandwich, Cape ▲ AUS 174-175 J 6
Sandwich Bay ⊙ CDN 38-39 Q 2
Sandwich Harbour o NAM 220-221 B 1
Sandwip o BD 142-143 G 4
Sandwip ⌒ BD 142-143 G 4
Sandwith o CDN (SAS) 232-233 K 2
Sandy o USA (OR) 244-245 C 5
Sandy o USA (UT) 254-255 D 3
Sandy Bar ⌒ CDN (MAN) 234-235 F 2
Sandy Bay o CDN 34-35 E 3
Sandy Bay Indian Reserve ⧗ CDN (MAN) 234-235 E 4
Sandy Beach o CDN (ALB) 232-233 D 2
Sandy Bight ≈ 176-177 G 6
Sandy Cape ▲ AUS 178-179 M 3
Sandy Cove o CDN (NS) 240-241 J 6
Sandy Creek ∼ AUS 178-179 J 2
Sandy Creek ∼ AUS 180-181 H 2
Sandy Creek ∼ USA (NE) 262-263 J 4
Sandy Creek ∼ USA (WY) 252-253 J 4
Sandy Desert ⩦ PK 134-135 K 4
Sandy Harbor Beach o USA (NY) 278-279 D 5
Sandy Hills ▲ USA (TX) 264-265 J 6
Sandy Hook o USA (KY) 276-277 M 2
Sandy Hook o USA (MS) 268-269 L 5
Sandykači o TM 136-137 H 6
Sandy Lake o CDN (ALB) 32-33 O 4
Sandy Lake o CDN (MAN) 234-235 C 4
Sandy Lake o CDN (ONT) 34-35 K 4
Sandy Lake ⊙ CDN (NFL) 242-243 M 3
Sandy Lake ⊙ CDN (NWT) 20-21 Z 3
Sandy Lake ⊙ CDN (ONT) 234-235 K 2
Sandy Lake o USA (PA) 280-281 F 2
Sandy Lake Indian Reserve ⧗ CDN 34-35 K 4
Sandy Point o BS 54-55 G 1
Sandy Point ▲ IND 140-141 L 4
Sandy Ridge o USA (NC) 282-283 G 4
Sandy River ∼ CDN 36-37 P 7
Sandy River ∼ USA (TN) 276-277 G 4
Sandy Springs o USA (OH) 280-281 C 5
San Estanislao o CO 60-61 D 2
San Estanislao o PY 76-77 J 3
San Esteban o HN 54-55 C 7
San Esteban o MEX 50-51 C 4
San Estéban, Golfo ≈ 80 C 3
San Esteban, Isla ⌒ MEX 50-51 C 3
San Felipe o MEX (GTO) 50-51 J 7
San Felipe o MEX (YUC) 52-53 K 1
San Felipe o • MEX (BCN) 50-51 B 2
San Felipe o RCH 78-79 D 2
San Felipe ☆ YV 60-61 G 2
San Felipe, Bahía ≈ 80 F 6
San Felipe, Castillo de • GCA 52-53 K 4
San Felipe, Cayos de ⌒ C 54-55 D 4
San Felipe, Parque Natural ⊥ MEX 52-53 K 1
San Felipe de Vichayal o PE 64-65 B 4
San Felipe Nuevo Mercurio o MEX 50-51 H 5
San Felipe Pueblo o USA (NM) 256-257 J 3
San Félix o YV 60-61 K 3
San Fernando o E 98-99 D 6
San Fernando o MEX 50-51 K 5
San Fernando o RA 76-77 D 4
San Fernando o RCH 78-79 D 3
San Fernando ☆ RP (LUN) 160-161 D 4
San Fernando ☆ RP (PAM) 160-161 D 5
San Fernando o TT 60-61 L 2
San Fernando o USA (CA) 248-249 F 5
San Fernando, Río ∼ BOL 70-71 H 5
San Fernando, Río ∼ MEX 50-51 K 5
San Fernando de Apure ☆ YV 60-61 H 4
San Fernando de Atabapo o YV 60-61 H 5
San Fernando del Valle de Catamarca ☆ • RA 76-77 E 5
Sånfjället nationalpark ⊥ S 86-87 F 5
Sanford o CDN (MAN) 234-235 F 5
Sanford o USA (FL) 286-287 H 3
Sanford o USA (ME) 278-279 L 5
Sanford o USA (NC) 282-283 H 5
Sanford, Mount ▲ USA 20-21 S 5
Sanford River ∼ AUS 176-177 D 3
San Francisco o BOL 70-71 E 5
San Francisco o BOL 70-71 E 4
San Francisco ☆ ES 52-53 K 5
San Francisco o PE 64-65 F 8
San Francisco o RA 76-77 F 6
San Francisco o RP 160-161 F 8
San Francisco o •• USA (CA) 248-249 B 2
San Francisco o YV 60-61 F 2
San Francisco, Cabo de ▲ EC 64-65 B 1
San Francisco, Igarapé ∼ BR 66-67 C 7
San Francisco, Paso de ▲ RA 76-77 C 4
San Francisco, Río ∼ RA 76-77 C 6
San Francisco, Sierra de ▲ ••• MEX 50-51 C 4
San Francisco Bay ≈ 40-41 C 7
San Francisco Bay ≈ USA 248-249 B 2
San Francisco Creek ∼ USA (TX) 266-267 E 4
San Francisco de Becerra o HN 52-53 L 4
San Francisco de Bellocq o RA 78-79 J 5
San Francisco de Borja o MEX 50-51 F 4
San Francisco de Horizonte o MEX 50-51 H 5
San Francisco de Laishi o RA 76-77 H 4
San Francisco de la Paz o HN 52-53 L 4
San Francisco del Chañar o RA 76-77 F 5
San Francisco del Oro o MEX 50-51 G 4
San Francisco del Rincón o MEX 52-53 D 1
San Francisco de Macoris ☆ DOM 54-55 K 5
San Francisco de Mostazal o RCH 78-79 D 2
San Francisco Ixhuatán o MEX 52-53 G 3
San Francisco River ∼ USA (AZ) 256-257 F 5
San Francisco River ∼ USA (NM) 256-257 G 5
San Francisco Wash ∼ USA (AZ) 256-257 D 3
San Francisquito o MEX 50-51 C 3
Sang o GH 202-203 K 5
Sanga o ANG 216-217 C 5
Sanga o BF 202-203 L 4
Sanga o EAU 212-213 C 4
Sanga o MOC 214-215 H 7
Sanga o • RMM 202-203 J 2
San Gabriel o EC 64-65 D 1
San Gabriel da Cachoeira o BR 66-67 D 3
San Gabriel Mixtepec o MEX 52-53 F 3
San Gabriel Mountains ▲ USA (CA) 248-249 F 5
San Gabriel River ∼ USA (TX) 266-267 K 3
Sangagüey, Volcán ▲ MEX 50-51 G 7
Sanga-Jurjah ∼ RUS 110-111 X 3
Sangala o RI 164-165 G 5
San Galgano • I 100-101 C 3
San Gallan, Isla ⌒ PE 64-65 D 8
Sangama o EAT 214-215 G 5
Sangameshwar o IND 140-141 E 2
Sangamner o IND 138-139 E 10
Sangamon River ∼ USA (IL) 274-275 J 4
Sangān o IR 134-135 J 1
Sanganer o IND 138-139 E 6
Sangar ☆ RUS 118-119 N 4
Sangardo o RG 202-203 E 5
Sangarh ∼ PK 138-139 C 4
Sangata, o RI 164-165 E 3
Sangau, Tanjung ▲ RI 162-163 F 5
Sangāv o IRQ 128-129 L 5
Sangay, Parque Nacional de ⊥ ••• EC 64-65 C 2
Sangay, Volcan ▲ EC 64-65 C 2
Sangayam o RI 164-165 D 5
Sangbast o IR 136-137 F 7
Sangbé o CAM 204-205 K 5
Sangbor o AFG 136-137 H 7
Sang Čārak o AFG 136-137 K 7
Sangchris Lake ⊙ USA (IL) 274-275 J 5
Sange o ZRE 214-215 E 4
Sangeang, Pulau ⌒ RI 168 D 7
San Genaro o RA 78-79 J 2
Sanger o USA (CA) 248-249 E 3
Sanger o USA (TX) 264-265 G 5
San Germán o • USA (PR) 286-287 O 2
Sanggan He ∼ VRC 154-155 J 1
Sanggau o RI 162-163 J 4
Sangha ▫ RCB 210-211 E 3
Sangha ∼ RCB 210-211 F 3
Sangha-Mbaéré ▫ RCA 210-211 E 3
Sānghar o PK 138-139 B 6
Sangiang, Pulau ⌒ RI 162-163 F 7
Sangihe, Kepulauan ⌒ RI 164-165 J 2
Sangijn Dalaj o MAU 148-149 G 4
Sangijn Dalaj nuur ⊙ MAU 148-149 D 3
San Gil o CO 60-61 E 4
Sangil'ka ∼ RUS 114-115 Q 4
San Gimignano o ••• I 100-101 C 3
Sangin o AFG 134-135 L 2
Šangina ∼ RUS 110-111 b 5
Sanginkylä o FIN 88-89 J 4
San Giovanni in Fiore o I 100-101 F 5

Sangir, Kepulauan ⌢ RI 164-165 J 2
Sangir, Pulau ⌢ RI 164-165 J 2
Sangkha Buri ○ THA 158-159 E 3
Sangkulirang ○ RI 164-165 E 3
Sāngla Hill ○ PK 138-139 D 4
Sāngli ○ • IND 140-141 F 2
Sanglia Dol (Traditional Village) ○ • RI 166-167 F 5
Sangmelima ○ • CAM 210-211 D 2
Sango ○ ZW 218-219 F 6
Sangola ○ IND 140-141 F 2
Sangolquí ○ EC 64-65 C 2
Sangonera, Río ∼ E 98-99 G 6
Sangoshe ○ RB 218-219 B 4
San Gottardo, Passo del ▲ CH 92-93 K 5
Sangouani ○ CI 202-203 G 5
Sangouiné ○ CI 202-203 G 6
Sangowo ○ RI 164-165 L 2
Sangradouro, Área Indígena ✗ BR 72-73 D 3
Sangradouro, Rio ∼ BR 70-71 J 5
Sangrafa ○ RIM 196-197 D 6
Sangre de Cristo Mountains ▲ USA (CO) 254-255 K 6
San Gregorio ○ MEX 52-53 J 4
San Gregorio ○ PE 64-65 F 6
San Gregorio ○ USA (CA) 248-249 B 2
San Gregorio Carrio ○ ROU 78-79 L 2
Sangre Grande ○ TT 60-61 L 2
Sangrūr ○ IND 138-139 E 4
Sangsang ○ VRC 144-145 F 6
Sangudo ○ CDN (ALB) 232-233 D 2
Sangue, Rio do ∼ BR 70-71 H 2
Sanguéya ○ RG 202-203 C 4
Sanguiana ○ RG 202-203 E 4
San Guillermo ○ RP 160-161 D 4
Sangutane, Rio ∼ MOC 218-219 G 6
Sangwali ○ NAM 218-219 B 4
Sangzhi ○ VRC 156-157 G 2
Sanhala ○ CI 202-203 G 4
Šanhar ○ RUS 116-117 K 9
San Hilario ○ RA 76-77 H 4
Sāni ○ RIM 196-197 E 6
Sanibel ○ USA (FL) 286-287 G 5
Sanibel Island ⌢ USA (FL) 286-287 G 5
San Ignacio ○ CR 52-53 B 7
San Ignacio ○ MEX (SIN) 50-51 F 6
San Ignacio ○ • MEX (BCS) 50-51 C 4
San Ignacio ○ PE 64-65 C 4
San Ignacio ○ PY 76-77 J 4
San Ignacio ○ YV 62-63 D 3
San Ignacio, Isla de ⌢ MEX 50-51 E 5
San Ignacio de Velasco ○ BOL 70-71 G 5
San Ignazio ○ BH 52-53 K 3
San Ildefonso, Cape ▲ RP 160-161 E 4
Sanipas ▲ LS 220-221 J 4
Sanire ○ PE 70-71 B 3
San Isidro ○ NIC 52-53 L 5
San Isidro ○ RA 78-79 K 3
San Isidro ○ USA (TX) 266-267 J 7
San Isidro ○ YV 62-63 D 2
San Isidro de El General ○ CR 52-53 C 7
San Jacinto ○ PE 64-65 B 4
San Jacinto ○ RP 160-161 E 6
San Jacinto, East Fork ∼ USA (TX) 268-269 E 6
San Jacinto, Mount ▲ USA (CA) 248-249 H 6
San Jacinto, West Fork ∼ USA (TX) 268-269 E 6
San Jaime ○ RA 76-77 H 6
San Janvier ○ E 98-99 G 6
San Javier ○ BOL 70-71 E 4
San Javier ○ MEX 50-51 D 5
San Javier ○ RA (COD) 78-79 G 2
San Javier ○ RA (SAF) 76-77 H 6
San Javier, Río ∼ RA 76-77 H 5
San Javier de Loncomilla ○ RCH 78-79 D 3
Sanje ○ EAU 212-213 C 4
San Jeronimo, Isla ⌢ RA 76-77 H 5
Sanjia ○ VRC 156-157 G 5
Sanjiang ○ VRC 156-157 F 4
Sanjiaotang ○ VRC 156-157 M 2
Sanjō ○ J 152-153 H 6
San Joaquim ○ BR 62-63 K 6
San Joaquín ○ MEX 52-53 E 1
San Joaquín ○ RA 78-79 H 3
San Joaquín ○ YV 60-61 H 2
San Joaquín ○ YV 60-61 J 3
San Joaquín, Cerro ▲ EC 64-65 C 10
San Joaquín, Río ∼ BOL 70-71 F 3
San Joaquin River ∼ USA (CA) 248-249 D 2
San Joaquin Valley ⌣ USA (CA) 248-249 C 2
San Jon ○ USA (NM) 256-257 M 3
San Jorge ○ CO 60-61 G 4
San Jorge ○ RA 76-77 G 6
San Jorge ○ ROU 78-79 M 2
San Jorge, Bahía ≈ 50-51 C 2
San Jorge, Golfo ≈ 80 G 2
San Jorge, Río ∼ CO 60-61 D 3
San Jorge Island ⌢ SOL 184 I d 3
San José ○ CO 64-65 D 1
San José ★ CR 52-53 B 7
San José ○ E 98-99 F 6
San José ○ HN 52-53 L 4
San José ○ MEX 50-51 D 4
San José ∼ MEX 50-51 E 6
San José ○ PY 76-77 J 3
San José ○ RA (CAT) 76-77 D 4
San José ○ RA (MIS) 76-77 K 4
San Jose ○ RP (MID) 160-161 D 6
San Jose ○ RP (NEC) 160-161 D 5
San Jose ☆ RP (ANT) 160-161 D 7
San Jose ○ USA (CA) 248-249 C 2
San Jose ○ USA (IL) 274-275 J 4
San José ○ YV 60-61 E 2
San José, Golfo ≈ 78-79 G 7
San José, Isla ⌢ MEX 50-51 D 5
San José, Isla ⌢ PA 52-53 E 7
San José, Río ∼ RCH 78-79 C 5
San Jose, Rio ∼ USA (NM) 256-257 H 4
San José, Volcán ▲ RA 78-79 E 2
San José de Amacuro ○ YV 60-61 L 3
San José de Buja ○ YV 60-61 K 3
San José de Chimbo ○ EC 64-65 C 2
San José de Chiquitos ○ ••• BOL 70-71 G 5
San José de Dimas ○ MEX 50-51 D 3
San José de Feliciano ○ RA 76-77 H 6
San José de Gracia ○ MEX 50-51 F 4
San José de Guanipa ○ YV 60-61 J 3
San José de Guaribe ○ YV 60-61 J 3
San José de Jáchal ○ RA 76-77 C 6
San José de la Dormida ○ RA 76-77 F 6
San José del Alto ○ PE 64-65 C 4
San José de la Mariquina ○ RCH 78-79 C 5
San José de las Lajas ○ C 54-55 D 3
San José del Cabo ○ • MEX 50-51 E 6
San José del Guaviare ○ CO 60-61 E 6
San José del Monte ○ RP 160-161 D 5
San José del Morro ○ RA 78-79 G 2
San José del Palmar ○ CO 60-61 C 5
San José del Progreso ○ MEX 52-53 F 3
San José de Maipo ○ RCH 78-79 D 2
San José de Mayo ☆ ROU 78-79 L 3
San José de Ocoa ○ DOM 54-55 K 5
San José de Quero ○ PE 64-65 E 8
San José de Raíces ○ MEX 50-51 J 5
San Jose Island ⌢ USA (TX) 266-267 L 6
San José Iturbide ○ MEX 50-51 J 7
San Jose River ∼ CDN (BC) 230-231 H 2
Sanju ○ VRC 144-145 B 2
San Juan ○ BOL 70-71 G 6
San Juán ○ BOL 70-71 D 7
San Juan ☆ DOM 54-55 K 5
San Juan ○ PE (ICA) 64-65 E 9
San Juan ○ PE (LOR) 66-67 B 5
San Juan ◘ RA 76-77 C 6
San Juan ☆ • RA (SAJ) 76-77 C 6
San Juan ○ RCH 76-77 C 2
San Juan ○ RP 160-161 F 7
San Juan ○ USA (AK) 20-21 Q 6
San Juan ☆ ••• USA (PR) 286-287 P 2
San Juan, Bahía ≈ 64-65 E 9
San Juan, Cabo ▲ GQ 210-211 B 3
San Juan, Cabo ▲ RA 80 J 7
San Juan, Punta ▲ PE 64-65 E 9
San Juan, Quebrada ∼ RCH 76-77 B 5
San Juan, Río ∼ BOL 70-71 D 6
San Juan, Río ∼ BOL 76-77 E 1
San Juan, Río ∼ CO 60-61 C 5
San Juan, Río ∼ DOM 54-55 K 5
San Juan, Río ∼ MEX 50-51 G 5
San Juan, Río ∼ NIC 52-53 B 6
San Juan, Río ∼ PY 76-77 H 2
San Juan, Río ∼ RA 76-77 C 6
San Juan, Río ∼ RA 78-79 F 2
San Juan, Río ∼ ROU 78-79 L 3
San Juan, Río ∼ YV 60-61 K 2
San Juan Bautista ☆ PY 76-77 J 4
San Juan Bautista ○ RCH 78-79 C 1
San Juan Bautista ○ YV 60-61 K 2
San Juan Capistrano ○ USA (CA) 248-249 G 6
San Juan Chiquihuitlán ○ MEX 52-53 F 3
San Juan de Alacant ○ E 98-99 G 5
San Juan de Alicante = San Juan de Alacant ○ E 98-99 G 5
San Juan de Arama ○ CO 60-61 E 6
San Juan de Colon ○ YV 60-61 E 3
San Juán de Flores ○ HN 52-53 L 4
San Juan de Guadalupe ○ MEX 50-51 H 5
San Juan de la Costa ○ MEX 50-51 D 5
San Juán del Caite ○ HN 52-53 K 4
San Juan del César ○ CO 60-61 E 2
San Juan de Lima, Punta ▲ MEX 52-53 C 2
San Juán de Limay ○ NIC 52-53 L 5
San Juán del Norte, Bahía de ≈ 52-53 C 6
San Juan de los Cayos ○ YV 60-61 G 2
San Juan de los Galdonas ○ YV 60-61 K 2
San Juan de los Lagos ○ MEX 50-51 H 7
San Juan de los Morros ☆ YV 60-61 H 3
San Juan de los Planes ○ • MEX 50-51 E 6
San Juan del Río ○ MEX (DGO) 50-51 G 5
San Juan del Río ○ MEX (QRO) 52-53 E 1
San Juán del Sur ○ NIC 52-53 B 6
San Juan de Manpiare ○ YV 60-61 H 5
San Juan de Pastocalle ○ EC 64-65 C 2
San Juan de Sabinas ○ MEX 50-51 J 4
San Juan de Tocoma ○ YV 60-61 K 4
San Juan de Yanac ○ PE 64-65 E 8
San Juan Evangelista ○ MEX 52-53 G 3
San Juan Indian Reservation ✗ USA (NM) 256-257 J 2
San Juan Islands ⌢ USA (WA) 244-245 C 2
San Juanito ○ MEX 50-51 F 4
San Juanito, Isla ⌢ MEX 50-51 F 7
San Juan Ixcaquixtla ○ MEX 52-53 F 2
San Juan Mountains ▲ USA (CO) 254-255 H 6
San Juan National Historic Park ⊥ USA 244-245 B 2
San Juan River ∼ USA (CA) 248-249 D 4
San Juan River ∼ USA (UT) 254-255 E 6
San Juan Seamount ≃ 248-249 D 6
San Juan y Martínez ○ C 54-55 D 3
San Just, Puerto de ▲ E 98-99 G 4
San Justo ○ RA 76-77 G 6
Sankadiakro ○ CI 202-203 J 6
Sankarani ∼ RG 202-203 F 4
Sankarankovil ○ IND 140-141 G 6
Sankari Drug ○ IND 140-141 G 5
Sankha ○ THA 158-159 G 3
Sankosh ○ BHT 142-143 G 2
Sankosh ∼ BHT 142-143 F 2
Sankra ○ IND 138-139 G 5
Sankt Gallen ☆ ••• CH 92-93 K 5
Sankt Gotthardpass = Passo del San Gottardo ▲ CH 92-93 K 5
Sankt Joachimsthal = Jáchymov ○ CZ 92-93 M 3
Sankt Moritz ○ • CH 92-93 K 5
Sankt-Peterburg ☆ ••• RUS 94-95 M 2
Sankt Peter-Ording ○ D 92-93 K 1
Sankt Pölten ☆ A 92-93 N 4
Sankulirang, Teluk ≈ 164-165 F 3
Sankuru ∼ ZRE 210-211 J 6
San Leonardo de Yagüe ○ E 98-99 F 4
Sanlifan ○ VRC 154-155 J 6
Şanlı Urfa ☆ • TR 128-129 H 4
San Lorenzo ○ BOL 70-71 H 5
San Lorenzo ○ CO 60-61 F 4
San Lorenzo ○ EC (ESM) 64-65 C 1
San Lorenzo ○ EC (MAN) 64-65 B 2
San Lorenzo ○ HN 52-53 L 5
San Lorenzo ○ PE 70-71 C 2
San Lorenzo ○ RA 76-77 H 5
San Lorenzo ○ RP 160-161 E 5
San Lorenzo ○ USA (NM) 256-257 H 6
San Lorenzo ○ USA (PR) 286-287 Q 2
San Lorenzo, Cabo ▲ EC 64-65 B 2
San Lorenzo, Cerro ▲ PE 64-65 C 5
San Lorenzo, Isla ⌢ MEX 50-51 C 3
San Lorenzo, Isla ⌢ PE 64-65 D 8
San Lorenzo, Río ∼ MEX 50-51 F 5
San Lorenzo, Río ∼ MEX 50-51 F 5
San Lorenzo, Sierra de ▲ E 98-99 F 3
San Louis Pass ≈ USA 268-269 E 7
San Lourdes ○ BOL 70-71 C 2
Sanlúcar de Barrameda ○ E 98-99 D 6
Sanlúcar la Mayor ○ E 98-99 D 6
San Lucas ○ USA (CA) 248-249 C 3
San Lucas, Cabo ▲ •• MEX 50-51 E 6
San Luís ○ C 54-55 H 4
San Luis ○ CO 60-61 D 4
San Luis ○ GCA 52-53 K 3
San Luis ○ MEX 50-51 B 3
San Luis ◘ RA 78-79 F 2
San Luis ☆ RA 78-79 F 2
San Luis ○ RCH 76-77 C 4
San Luis ○ ROU 74-75 D 9
San Luis ○ RP 160-161 F 7
San Luis ○ USA (AZ) 256-257 D 6
San Luis ○ USA (CO) 254-255 K 6
San Luis ○ YV 60-61 G 2
San Luis, Lago de ⊖ BOL 70-71 E 3
San Luis, Sierra de ▲ RA 78-79 F 2
San Luis Acatlán ○ MEX 52-53 E 3
San Luis Canal < USA (CA) 248-249 D 3
San Luis Creek ∼ USA (CO) 254-255 K 6
San Luis del Cordero ○ MEX 50-51 G 5
San Luis del Palmar ○ • RA 76-77 H 4
San Luis de Shuaro ○ PE 64-65 E 7
San Luis Obispo ○ USA (CA) 248-249 D 4
San Luis Potosí ◘ MEX 50-51 H 6
San Luis Potosí ☆ •• MEX (SLP) 50-51 J 6
San Luis Reservoir ⊖ USA (CA) 248-249 C 2
San Luis Rey de Francia • USA (CA) 248-249 G 6
San Luis Río Colorado ○ • MEX 50-51 B 1
San Luis San Pedro ○ MEX 52-53 D 3
San Luis Valley ⌣ USA (CO) 254-255 K 6
San Luiz de la Paz ○ MEX 50-51 J 7
Sanluri ○ I 100-101 B 5
San Manuel ○ C 54-55 G 4
San Manuel ○ USA (AZ) 256-257 E 6
San Marcial ○ USA (NM) 256-257 J 5
San Marco, Capo ▲ I 100-101 B 5
San Marco, Capo ▲ I 100-101 D 6
San Marcos ○ BR 62-63 K 6
San Marcos ☆ GCA 52-53 J 4
San Marcos ○ MEX 52-53 E 3
San Marcos ○ USA (TX) 266-267 K 4
San Marcos, Isla ⌢ MEX 50-51 C 4
San Marcos, Laguna ≈ 52-53 E 3
San Marcos de Colón ○ HN 52-53 L 5
San Marcos River ∼ USA (TX) 266-267 K 4
San Marcus Pass ▲ USA (CA) 248-249 E 5
San Mariano ○ RP 160-161 E 4
San Marino ○ AUS 178-179 C 5
San Marino ■ RSM 100-101 C 3
San Marino ☆ • RSM 100-101 D 3
San Martín ○ CO 60-61 E 6
San Martín ⌢ MEX 50-51 A 2
San Martín ○ RA 76-77 E 6
San Martín, Lago ⊖ RA 80 D 4
San Martín, Península ⌣ RCH 80 C 4
San Martín, Río ∼ BOL 70-71 F 3
San Martín Chalchicuautla ○ MEX 50-51 K 7
San Martín de los Andes ○ RA 78-79 D 6
San Mateo ○ USA (CA) 248-249 B 2
San Mateo ○ USA (NM) 256-257 H 3
San Mateo ○ YV 60-61 J 3
San Mateo Ixtatán ○ GCA 52-53 J 4
San Mateo Matengo ○ MEX 52-53 E 2
San Mateo Peak ▲ USA (NM) 256-257 H 5
San Matías ○ BOL 70-71 H 5
San Matías, Golfo ≈ 78-79 G 6
Sanmaur ○ CDN (QUE) 236-237 P 5
Sanmen ○ VRC 156-157 M 2
Sanmen Wan ≈ 156-157 M 2
Sanmenxia ○ • VRC 154-155 G 4
San Miguel ○ CO 66-67 B 2
San Miguel ○ EC (BOL) 64-65 C 2
San Miguel ○ EC (ESM) 64-65 C 1
San Miguel ☆ ES 52-53 K 5
San Miguel ○ PA (Pan) 52-53 E 7
San Miguel ○ PE 64-65 F 8
San Miguel ○ RA (BUA) 78-79 K 3
San Miguel ○ RA (COR) 76-77 J 4
San Miguel ○ RP 160-161 E 9
San Miguel ○ USA (AZ) 256-257 D 7
San Miguel ○ USA (CA) 248-249 D 4
San Miguel ∼ USA (CA) 248-249 D 5
San Miguel ○ YV 60-61 J 3
San Miguel, Cerro ▲ BOL 70-71 G 6
San Miguel, Fortaleza • ROU 74-75 D 9
San Miguel, Río ∼ BOL 70-71 G 5
San Miguel, Río ∼ CO 64-65 D 1
San Miguel, Río ∼ MEX 50-51 F 4
San Miguel, Río ∼ MEX 50-51 D 3
San Miguel, Sierra ▲ RCH 76-77 C 4
San Miguel, Volcán ▲ ES 52-53 K 5
San Miguel Aloapan ○ MEX 52-53 F 3
San Miguel Bay ≈ 160-161 E 6
San Miguel Creek ∼ USA (TX) 266-267 J 5
San Miguel de Allende ○ • MEX 52-53 D 1
San Miguel de Baga ○ C 54-55 G 4
San Miguel de Huachi ○ BOL 70-71 D 4
San Miguel del Monte ○ RA 78-79 K 3
San Miguel de Pallaques ○ PE 64-65 C 5
San Miguel de Salcedo ○ EC 64-65 C 2
San Miguel de Tucumán ☆ • RA 76-77 E 4
San Miguelito ○ BOL 70-71 C 2
San Miguelito ○ MEX 50-51 E 2
San Miguelito ○ NIC 52-53 B 6
San Miguel River ∼ USA (CO) 254-255 G 5
San Miguel Sola de Vega ○ MEX 52-53 F 3
San Miguel Suchixtepec ○ MEX 52-53 F 3
San Miguel Tulancingo ○ • MEX 52-53 F 3
Sanming ○ VRC 156-157 K 3
San Narcisco ○ RP 160-161 D 5
Sannaspos ○ ZA 220-221 H 4
San Nicolas ○ BOL 70-71 E 4
San Nicolás ○ MEX 50-51 E 3
San Nicolás, Bahía ≈ 64-65 E 9
San Nicolas de los Arroyos ○ RA 78-79 J 2
San Nicolas de los Garzas ○ MEX 50-51 J 5
San Nicolás de Tolentino ○ E 188-189 D 7
San Nicolas Island ⌢ USA (CA) 248-249 E 6
San Nicolás Tolentino ○ MEX 50-51 J 6
Sannieshof ○ ZA 220-221 G 3
Sannikovo ○ RUS 110-111 W 2
Sannikova, proliv ≈ 110-111 W 2
Sanniquellie ☆ LB 202-203 F 6
Sannohe ○ J 152-153 J 4
Sanogasta, Sierra de ▲ RA 76-77 D 5
Sanok ○ • PL 92-93 R 4
San Onofre ○ CO 60-61 D 3
Sanosti ○ USA (NM) 256-257 G 2
Sanoyie ○ LB 202-203 F 6
San Pablo ○ BOL 76-77 D 1
San Pablo ○ C 54-55 F 4
San Pablo ○ CO (BOL) 60-61 E 4
San Pablo ○ CO (NAR) 64-65 D 1
San Pablo ○ PE 64-65 C 5
San Pablo ○ RCH 78-79 C 6
San Pablo ○ RP 160-161 D 5
San Pablo ○ YV (ANZ) 60-61 J 3
San Pablo ○ YV (BOL) 60-61 H 4
San Pablo ○ YV (BOL) 60-61 K 4
San Pablo, Punta ▲ MEX 50-51 B 4
San Pablo, Río ∼ BOL 70-71 F 4
San Pablo, Río ∼ PE 64-65 C 4
San Pablo Balleza ○ MEX 50-51 F 4
San Pablo Bay ≈ 40-41 C 6
San Pablo Bay ≈ USA 246-247 C 5
San Pablo de Balzar, Cordillera de ▲ EC 64-65 B 2
Sanpaka ○ RMM 202-203 F 2
San Pascual ○ RP 160-161 E 6
San Pasqual Indian Reservation ✗ USA (CA) 248-249 H 6
San Pedro ○ BOL 70-71 F 5
San Pedro ∼ C 54-55 F 4
San Pédro ○ CI 202-203 G 7
San Pedro ○ CO 60-61 D 4
San Pedro ○ MEX (BCS) 50-51 D 6
San Pedro ○ MEX (CHA) 50-51 G 3
San Pedro ○ MEX (SON) 50-51 D 3
San Pedro ○ MEX (SON) 50-51 C 2
San Pedro ○ PE 70-71 B 2
San Pedro ☆ PY 76-77 J 3
San Pedro ○ RA (BUA) 78-79 K 2
San Pedro ○ RA (JU) 76-77 E 3
San Pedro ○ RA (MIS) 76-77 K 4
San Pedro ○ RA (SAE) 76-77 E 4
San Pedro ○ RCH (ANT) 76-77 C 1
San Pedro ○ RCH (BIO) 78-79 C 4
San Pedro ○ RP 160-161 E 6
San Pedro ○ YV 60-61 K 2
San Pedro, Isla ⌢ RCH 78-79 C 7
San Pedro, Observatorio de • MEX 50-51 B 2
San Pedro, Punta ▲ RCH 76-77 B 3
San Pedro, Río ∼ BOL 70-71 E 6
San Pedro, Río ∼ BOL 76-77 D 1
San Pedro, Río ∼ GCA 52-53 J 3
San Pedro, Río ∼ MEX 50-51 F 4
San Pedro, Río ∼ MEX 50-51 G 6
San Pedro, Río ∼ MEX 52-53 B 2
San Pedro, Río ∼ MEX 52-53 H 3
San Pedro, Río ∼ RCH 76-77 C 2
San Pedro, Sierra de ▲ E 98-99 D 5
San Pedro, Volcán ▲ RCH 76-77 C 1
San Pedro Channel ≈ USA 248-249 F 6
San Pedro de Atacama ○ • RCH 76-77 C 2
San Pedro de Buena Vista ○ BOL 70-71 E 6
San Pedro de Cachi ○ PE 64-65 E 8
San Pedro de Colalao ○ RA 76-77 E 4
San Pedro de Coris ○ PE 64-65 E 8
San Pedro de Curahuara ○ BOL 70-71 C 5
San Pedro de la Cueva ○ MEX 50-51 E 3
San Pedro de Las Bocas ○ YV 60-61 K 4
San Pedro de las Colonias ○ MEX 50-51 H 5
San Pedro de Lloc ○ PE 64-65 C 5
San Pedro del Norte ○ NIC 52-53 B 5
San Pedro del Paraná ○ PY 76-77 J 4
San Pedro de Macorís ☆ DOM 54-55 L 5
San Pedro de Quemes ○ BOL 70-71 C 7
San Pedro de Urabá ○ CO 60-61 C 3
San Pedro el Alto ○ MEX 52-53 F 3
San Pedro Huamelula ○ MEX 52-53 G 3
San Pedro Lagunillas ○ MEX 50-51 G 7
San Pedro Mártir, Sierra de ▲ MEX 50-51 B 2
San Pedro Nolasco, Isla ⌢ MEX 50-51 D 4
San Pedro Norte ○ RA 76-77 E 6
San Pedro Peak ▲ USA (NM) 256-257 J 2
San Pedro Pochutla ○ MEX 52-53 F 4
San Pedro River ∼ USA (AZ) 256-257 E 6
San Pedro Sacatepéquez ○ GCA 52-53 J 4
San Pedro Sula ☆ HN 52-53 K 4
San Pedro Tapanatepec ○ MEX 52-53 G 3
San Pietro, Ísola di ⌢ I 100-101 B 5
Sanpoil River ∼ USA (WA) 244-245 G 2
Sanpoku ○ J 152-153 H 5
Sanqingshan • VRC 156-157 L 2
Sanquianga, Parque Nacional ⊥ CO 60-61 B 6
San Quintín ○ MEX 50-51 B 2
San Quintín, Cabo ▲ MEX 50-51 B 2
San Rafael ○ BOL (COC) 70-71 E 5
San Rafael ○ BOL (PAZ) 70-71 C 4
San Rafael ○ BOL (SAC) 70-71 G 5
San Rafael ○ CO 66-67 D 2
San Rafael ○ CR 52-53 B 6
San Rafael ○ MEX (DGO) 50-51 G 5
San Rafael ○ MEX (NL) 50-51 J 5
San Rafael ○ PE 64-65 D 7
San Rafael ○ RA 78-79 E 3
San Rafael, Cabo ▲ DOM 54-55 L 5
San Rafael, Catarate de • EC 64-65 D 2
San Rafael = El Moján ○ YV 60-61 F 2
San Rafael, Glaciar ⊂ RCH 80 D 3
San Rafael, Río ∼ BOL 70-71 H 6
San Rafael, Río ∼ MEX 50-51 K 6
San Rafael de Curiapo ○ YV 60-61 L 3
San Rafael de Imataca ○ YV 62-63 D 2
San Rafael de Onoto ○ YV 60-61 G 3
San Rafael Knob ▲ USA (UT) 254-255 E 5
San Rafael Mountains ▲ USA (CA) 248-249 D 5
San Rafael River ∼ USA (UT) 254-255 E 4
San Ramon ○ BOL 70-71 F 5
San Ramon ○ BOL (BEN) 70-71 E 3
San Ramon ○ BOL (SAC) 70-71 F 4
San Ramón ○ C 54-55 G 4
San Ramón ○ CR 52-53 B 6
San Ramón ○ PE 64-65 D 4
San Ramon ○ PE 64-65 E 7
San Ramón ○ RA 76-77 D 6
San Ramón ○ RCH 76-77 B 4
San Ramon ○ ROU 78-79 M 3
San Ramon ○ RP 160-161 D 9
San Ramón, Río ∼ BOL 70-71 G 4
San Ramón de la Nueva Oran ○ RA 76-77 E 2
San Remo ○ I 100-101 A 3
San Roberto ○ MEX 50-51 J 5
San Roque ○ CO 60-61 E 3
San Roque ○ E 98-99 E 6
San Roque ○ MEX 50-51 B 4
San Roque ○ RP 160-161 D 5
San Roque ○ RP 160-161 F 7
San Roque ○ RP (NSA) 160-161 F 6
San Saba ○ USA (TX) 266-267 J 2
San Saba River ∼ USA (TX) 266-267 H 3
San Salvador ⌢ BS 54-55 H 2
San Salvador ○ P 98-99 C 4
San Salvador ★ • ES 52-53 K 5
San Salvador ○ PE 66-67 B 4
San Salvador ○ RA (CO) 76-77 J 5
San Salvador ○ RA (ERI) 76-77 H 6
San Salvador, Canal de ≈ 64-65 B 10
San Salvador = Guanahani Island ⌢ BS 54-55 H 2
San Salvador, Isla ⌢ EC 64-65 B 10
San Salvador, Río ∼ ROU 78-79 L 2
San Salvador de Jujuy ☆ RA 76-77 E 3
San Salvador el Seco ○ MEX 52-53 F 2
Sansanding ○ RMM 202-203 H 3
San Sandrés, Laguna de ⊖ MEX 50-51 L 6
Sansanné-Mango ○ RT 202-203 L 4
Sansārpur ○ IND 144-145 C 6
Sans Bois Creek ∼ USA (OK) 264-265 J 3
San Sebastian ○ MEX 52-53 B 1
San Sebastián ○ RA 80 F 6
San Sebastian ○ USA (PR) 286-287 P 2
San Sebastián, Bahía ≈ 80 F 6
San Sebastian de Buenavista ○ CO 60-61 D 3
San Sebastián de la Gomera ○ E 188-189 C 6
San Sebastián de los Reyes ○ E 98-99 F 4
San Sebastião do Uatuma ○ BR 66-67 J 4
Sansepolcro ○ I 100-101 D 3
San Severo ○ I 100-101 E 4
Sansha Wan ≈ 156-157 L 3
Sanshui ○ VRC 156-157 H 5
San Silvestre ○ BOL 70-71 C 2
San Silvestre ○ YV 60-61 F 3
San Simeon ○ USA (CA) 248-249 C 4
San Simon ○ USA (AZ) 256-257 F 6
San Simón, Río ∼ BOL 70-71 F 3
San Simon River ∼ USA (AZ) 256-257 F 6
Sanso ○ RMM 202-203 G 4
Sans Sault Rapids ∼ CDN 30-31 E 3
Sans-Souci ∴ • RH 54-55 J 5
Sans Souci ○ USA (MI) 272-273 G 5
Sansui ○ VRC 156-157 F 3
Sansundi ○ RI 166-167 H 2
Sansu-ri ○ DVR 150-151 F 7
Sansynakac žyrasy ∸ KA 126-127 O 2
Santa ○ PE 64-65 C 6
Santa ○ USA (ID) 250-251 C 4
Santa, Isla ⌢ PE 64-65 C 6
Santa, Río ∼ PE 64-65 D 6
Santa Ana ○ BOL (BEN) 70-71 E 3
Santa Ana ○ BOL (SAC) 70-71 H 6
Santa Ana ○ C 54-55 F 4
Santa Ana ○ CO 60-61 D 3
Santa Ana ○ EC 64-65 B 2
Santa Ana ☆ ES 52-53 K 5
Santa Ana ○ HN 52-53 L 5
Santa Ana ○ MEX (SON) 50-51 D 2
Santa Ana ○ MEX (TAB) 52-53 H 2
Santa Ana ○ PE 64-65 E 9
Santa Ana ○ RA 76-77 K 4
Santa Ana ○ RP 160-161 E 3
Santa Ana ○ USA (CA) 248-249 G 6
Santa Ana ○ YV 60-61 J 3
Santa Ana, Bahía ≈ 50-51 C 4
Santa Ana, Río ∼ YV 60-61 E 3
Santa Ana Island ⌢ SOL 184 I f 4
Santa Ana Maya ○ MEX 52-53 D 1
Santa Anna ○ USA (TX) 266-267 H 2
Santa Bárbara ○ BR 66-67 D 5
Santa Bárbara ○ BR 72-73 J 5
Santa Barbara ○ CO 60-61 D 5
Santa Bárbara ▲ E 98-99 F 6
Santa Bárbara ☆ HN 52-53 K 4
Santa Bárbara ○ MEX 50-51 G 4
Santa Bárbara ○ RCH 78-79 C 4
Santa Barbara ○ • USA (CA) 248-249 E 5
Santa Bárbara ○ YV 60-61 F 4
Santa Bárbara ○ YV (AMA) 60-61 H 6
Santa Bárbara ○ YV (ANZ) 60-61 K 3
Santa Bárbara ○ YV (BOL) 60-61 K 4
Santa Bárbara ○ YV (GUA) 60-61 J 3
Santa Bárbara, Parque Nacional ⊥ HN 52-53 K 4
Santa Barbara, Rio ∼ BOL 70-71 G 5
Santa Bárbara, Serra de ▲ BR 70-71 H 4
Santa Barbara, Sierra de ▲ RA 76-77 E 3
Santa Barbara Channel ≈ 40-41 D 8
Santa Barbara Channel ≈ USA 248-249 D 5
Santa Barbara do Sul ○ BR 74-75 D 7
Santa Barbara Island ⌢ USA (CA) 248-249 E 6
Santa Brígida ○ BR 68-69 J 6
Santa Casilda ○ MEX 52-53 D 2
Santa Catalina ○ RA 76-77 E 5
Santa Catalina ○ RP 160-161 E 8
Santa Catalina, Arroyo ∼ RA 78-79 G 2
Santa Catalina, Gulf of ≈ 40-41 E 9
Santa Catalina, Gulf of ≈ USA 248-249 F 6
Santa Catalina, Isla ⌢ MEX 50-51 D 5
Santa Catalina Island ⌢ USA (CA) 248-249 F 6
Santa Catalina Island = Owa Riki ⌢ SOL 184 I f 4
Santa Catarina ◘ BR 74-75 D 6
Santa Catarina ○ CV 202-203 C 6
Santa Catarina ○ MEX 50-51 J 5
Santa Catarina, Ilha de ⌢ BR 74-75 F 6
Santa Catarina, Río ∼ MEX 52-53 E 3
Santa Cecília ○ BR 74-75 E 6
Santa Clara ○ BR 62-63 J 6
Santa Clara ☆ •• C 54-55 F 3
Santa Clara ○ RA 76-77 E 3
Santa Clara ○ USA (UT) 254-255 B 6
Santa Clara ○ YV 60-61 J 3
Santa Clara, Bahía de ≈ 54-55 E 3
Santa Clara, Isla ⌢ RCH 78-79 C 1
Santa Clara, Río ∼ MEX 50-51 F 3
Santa Clara, Sierra de ▲ MEX 50-51 C 4
Santa Clara Indian Reservation ✗ USA (NM) 256-257 J 3
Santa Clotilde ○ PE 64-65 F 3
Santa Comba Dão ○ P 98-99 C 4
Santa Cruz ○ BOL 70-71 C 4
Santa Cruz ○ BR (BAH) 68-69 H 6
Santa Cruz ○ BR (GSU) 70-71 J 7
Santa Cruz ○ BR (P) 66-67 J 4
Santa Cruz ○ BR (P) 68-69 B 3
Santa Cruz ○ BR (PAU) 72-73 G 6
Santa Cruz ○ BR (RNO) 68-69 K 5
Santa Cruz ○ BR (RON) 66-67 F 7
Santa Cruz ○ CR 52-53 B 6
Santa Cruz ∼ MEX 50-51 D 5
Santa Cruz ○ PE (LIM) 64-65 D 7
Santa Cruz ○ PE (LOR) 64-65 E 4
Santa Cruz ◘ RA 80 E 3
Santa Cruz ○ RCH 78-79 D 3
Santa Cruz ○ RP (DAS) 160-161 F 9
Santa Cruz ○ RP (MAR) 160-161 E 6
Santa Cruz ○ RP (ZAM) 160-161 C 5
Santa Cruz ☆ RP (LAG) 160-161 D 5
Santa Cruz ○ USA (AZ) 256-257 C 7
Santa Cruz ○ • USA (CA) 248-249 B 3
Santa-Cruz ○ YV 62-63 D 2
Santa Cruz ○ YV (APU) 60-61 G 4
Santa Cruz ○ YV (BOL) 60-61 K 4
Santa Cruz, Isla ⌢ EC 64-65 B 10
Santa Cruz, Río ∼ RA 76-77 E 2
Santa Cruz, Río ∼ RA 80 F 5
Santa Cruz Cabrália ○ BR 72-73 L 4
Santa Cruz de Bucaral ○ YV 60-61 G 2
Santa Cruz de Campezo = Santi Kurutze Kanpezu ○ E 98-99 F 3
Santa Cruz de la Palma ○ E 188-189 C 6
Santa Cruz de la Sierra ☆ BOL 70-71 F 5
Santa Cruz del Norte ○ C 54-55 E 3
Santa Cruz del Quiché ☆ GCA 52-53 J 4
Santa Cruz del Sur ○ C 54-55 G 4
Santa Cruz de Mudela ○ E 98-99 F 5
Santa Cruz de Tenerife ☆ E 188-189 C 6
Santa Cruz do Arari ○ BR 62-63 K 6
Santa Cruz do Capibaribe ○ BR 68-69 K 5
Santa Cruz do Sul ○ BR 74-75 D 7
Santa Cruz Island ⌢ USA (CA) 248-249 E 5
Santa Cruz Verapaz ○ GCA 52-53 J 4
Santa de Ayes Laguna Colorada, Parque Nacional ⊥ BOL 76-77 D 2
Santa Doménica Taláo ○ I 100-101 E 5
Santa Elena ○ EC 64-65 B 3
Santa Elena ○ MEX 50-51 H 4
Santa Elena ○ RA 76-77 H 6
Santa Elena ○ YV 60-61 K 3
Santa Elena, Bahía de ≈ 52-53 B 6
Santa Elena, Bahía de ≈ 64-65 B 3
Santa Elena, Cabo ▲ CR 52-53 B 6
Santa Elena, Cerro ▲ RA 80 H 2
Santa Elena, Paso de ▲ RA 78-79 D 3
Santa Elena de Arenales ○ YV 60-61 F 3
Santa Elena de Uairén ○ YV 62-63 D 3
Santa Eleodora ○ RA 78-79 H 3
Santa Eugenia (Ribeira) ○ E 98-99 C 3
Santa Eulalia ○ MEX 50-51 J 3
Santa Eulària del Riu ○ E 98-99 H 5
Santa Fé ○ BR 68-69 J 5
Santa Fé ○ C 54-55 D 3
Santa Fe ○ CO 60-61 F 4
Santa Fé ○ E 98-99 F 6
Santa Fé ○ PA (Dar) 52-53 E 7
Santa Fé ○ PA (Ver) 52-53 D 7
Santa Fé ○ PE 64-65 F 4
Santa Fe ◘ RA 76-77 G 5
Santa Fe ☆ • RA (SAF) 76-77 G 6
Santa Fe ○ RP 160-161 D 6
Santa Fe ○ RP 160-161 E 9
Santa Fe ○ USA (TX) 268-269 E 7
Santa Fe ☆ • USA (NM) 256-257 K 3
Santa Fe, Isla ⌢ EC 64-65 B 10
Santa Fé de Minas ○ BR 72-73 H 4
Santa Fé do Sul ○ BR 72-73 E 6
Santa Fe River ∼ USA (FL) 286-287 G 2
Santa Filomena ○ BR 68-69 F 6
Santa Helena ○ BR (MAR) 68-69 F 3
Santa Helena ○ BR (PAR) 76-77 K 3
Santa Helena ○ CO 60-61 E 6
Santa Helena de Cusima ○ CO 60-61 F 5
Santa Helena de Goiás ○ BR 72-73 E 4
Santai ○ VRC 154-155 D 6
Santa Inês ○ BR (BAH) 72-73 L 2
Santa Inês ○ BR (MAR) 68-69 F 3
Santa Inés ○ YV 60-61 G 2
Santa Ines ○ YV 60-61 J 3
Santa Ines, Bahía ≈ 50-51 D 4
Santa Inés, Isla ⌢ RCH 80 D 6
Santa Isabel ○ BR 68-69 J 5
Santa Isabel ○ MEX 52-53 H 3
Santa Isabel ○ PA 52-53 E 7
Santa Isabel ○ PE 64-65 E 4
Santa Isabel ○ RA 78-79 F 4
Santa Isabel ⌢ SOL 184 I d 2
Santa Isabel ○ USA (PR) 286-287 P 3
Santa Isabel, Cachoeira ∼ BR 68-69 D 5
Santa Isabel, Río ∼ GCA 52-53 K 4
Santa Isabel do Araguaia ○ BR 68-69 D 5
Santa Isabel d'Oeste ○ BR 74-75 D 5
Santa Isabel do Pará ○ BR 62-63 K 6
Santa Isabel do Preto ○ BR 72-73 H 7
Santa Isabel do Rio Negro ○ BR 66-67 E 3
Santa Júlia ○ BR 66-67 G 6
Santa Lucía ○ C 54-55 D 3
Santa Lucía ○ EC 64-65 C 2
Santa Lucía ○ PE 70-71 B 4
Santa Lucía ○ RA (CO) 76-77 H 5
Santa Lucía ○ RA (SAJ) 76-77 C 6
Santa Lucía ○ ROU 78-79 L 3
Santa Lucía, Río ∼ RA 76-77 H 5
Santa Lucía, Río ∼ ROU 78-79 L 3
Santa Lucía, Sierra de ▲ MEX 50-51 C 4
Santa Lucia Bank ≃ 248-249 C 5
Santa Lucía Cotzumalguapa ○ GCA 52-53 J 4
Santa Lucia la Reforma ○ GCA 52-53 J 4
Santa Lucia Range ▲ USA (CA) 248-249 C 3
Santa Lugarda, Punta ▲ MEX 50-51 E 4
Santa Luisa ○ RCH 76-77 B 3
Santa Luz ○ BR (BAH) 68-69 J 7
Santa Luz ○ BR (PIA) 68-69 F 6
Santa Luzia ○ BR (BAH) 72-73 L 3
Santa Luzia ○ BR (MAR) 68-69 F 3
Santa Luzia ○ BR (MIN) 72-73 J 5
Santa Luzia ○ BR (PA) 68-69 K 5
Santa Luzia ○ BR (ROR) 62-63 D 5
Santa Luzia, Ilha de ⌢ CV 202-203 B 5
Santa Luzia do Pacuí ○ BR 62-63 J 5
Santa Magdalena ○ RA 78-79 H 3
Santa Margarita, Isla ⌢ MEX 50-51 D 5
Santa Maria ○ ANG 216-217 B 6
Santa Maria ○ BR (AMA) 66-67 H 5
Santa Maria ○ BR (P) 62-63 J 6
Santa Maria ○ BR (RSU) 74-75 D 7
Santa Maria ○ CO 60-61 E 5
Santa Maria ○ CR 52-53 C 7
Santa Maria ○ CV 202-203 C 5
Santa Maria ○ HN 52-53 L 4
Santa Maria ∼ PA 52-53 D 7
Santa Maria ○ RA 76-77 F 2
Santa Maria ○ RP 160-161 F 9
Santa Maria ○ USA (CA) 248-249 D 5
Santa Maria ○ YV 60-61 F 3
Santa Maria ○ YV (APU) 60-61 H 4
Santa Maria ○ YV (SUC) 60-61 K 2
Santa Maria, Bahía ≈ 50-51 B 2
Santa Maria, Boca ≈ 50-51 L 5
Santa Maria, Cabo de ▲ P 98-99 D 6
Santa Maria, Cape ▲ BS 54-55 H 3
Santa Maria, Corredeira ∼ BR 66-67 H 6
Santa Maria, Isla ⌢ EC 64-65 B 10
Santa Maria, Isla ⌢ RCH 78-79 C 4
Santa Maria, Laguna de ⊖ MEX 50-51 F 2
Santa Maria, Punta ▲ ROU 78-79 M 3
Santa Maria, Ribeiro ∼ BR 68-69 D 5
Santa Maria, Rio ∼ BR 72-73 G 3
Santa Maria, Río ∼ MEX 50-51 J 7
Santa Maria, Río ∼ MEX 50-51 F 2
Santa Maria, Río ∼ RA 76-77 E 4
Santa Maria da Vitória ○ BR 72-73 H 2
Santa Maria da Vitória, Mosteiro de •• P 98-99 C 5
Santa Maria de Ipire ○ YV 60-61 J 3
Santa Maria de Itabira ○ BR 72-73 J 5
Santa Maria de Jebitá ○ BR 72-73 K 6
Santa Maria del Camí ○ E 98-99 J 5
Santa Maria del Oro ○ MEX 50-51 G 5
Santa Maria de Los Guaicas ○ YV 60-61 J 6
Santa Maria del Río ○ MEX 50-51 J 7
Santa Maria del Valle ○ PE 64-65 D 6
Santa Maria de Nanay ○ PE 64-65 F 3
Santa Maria de Nieva ○ PE 64-65 D 4
Santa Maria di Léuca, Capo ▲ I 100-101 G 5
Santa Maria do Para ○ BR 68-69 E 2
Santa Maria do Suaçuí ○ BR 72-73 J 5
Santa Maria Ecatepec ○ MEX 52-53 G 3
Santa Maria Eterna ○ BR 72-73 L 3

Santa Maria Island = Île Gaua ⌒ VAN 184 II a 2
Santa María Zacatepec ○ MEX 52-53 F 3
Santa María Zoquitlán ○ MEX 52-53 F 3
Santa Marta ○ ANG 216-217 B 6
Santa Marta ○ C 54-55 E 3
Santa Marta ✩ • CO 60-61 D 2
Santa Marta, Cabo de ▲ BR 74-75 F 7
Santa Monica ○ USA (CA) 248-249 F 5
Santa Monica Mountains National Recreation Area • USA (CA) 248-249 E 5
Santan ○ RI 164-165 E 4
Santan, Tanjung ▲ RI 164-165 E 3
Santana ○ BR (AMA) 66-67 F 3
Santana ○ BR (APA) 62-63 J 6
Santana ○ BR (BAH) 72-73 H 2
Santana ○ BR (P) 68-69 E 3
Santana ○ CO (MET) 60-61 D 6
Santana ○ CO (SAN) 60-61 E 4
Santana ○ P 188-189 C 4
Santana, Área Indígena ✕ BR 70-71 K 4
Santana, Cachoeira ∼ BR 72-73 F 3
Santana, Caverna de • BR 74-75 F 5
Santana, Ilha ⌒ BR 68-69 G 3
Santana, Ribeiro ∼ BR 68-69 C 6
Santana, Rio ∼ BR 68-69 G 6
Santana da Boa Vista ○ BR 74-75 D 8
Santana da Vargem ○ BR 72-73 H 6
Santana de Pirapama ○ BR 72-73 H 5
Santana do Acaraú ○ BR 68-69 H 3
Santana do Araguaia ○ BR 68-69 C 6
Santana do Garambeu ○ BR 72-73 H 6
Santana do Ipanema ○ BR 68-69 K 6
Santana do Itarare ○ BR 72-73 F 7
Santana do Livramento ○ BR 76-77 K 6
Santana do Manhuaçu ○ BR 72-73 K 6
Santana do Matos ○ BR 68-69 K 4
Santander ○ • E 98-99 F 3
Santander ○ RP 160-161 E 8
Santander Jiménez ○ MEX 50-51 K 5
Santanilla, Islas = Islas del Cisne ⌒ HN 54-55 D 6
Sant'Antíoco ○ I 100-101 B 5
Sant'Antioco, Ísola di ⌒ I 100-101 B 5
Sant Antoni Abat ○ E 98-99 H 5
Santa Olalla del Cala ○ E 98-99 D 6
Santa Paula ○ USA (CA) 248-249 E 5
Santa Pola ○ E 98-99 G 5
Santaquin ○ USA (UT) 254-255 D 4
Santa Quitéria ○ BR 68-69 H 4
Santa Quitéria do Maranhão ○ BR 68-69 G 3
Sant'Arcángelo ○ I 100-101 F 4
Santarém ○ BR 66-67 K 4
Santarém ○ • P 98-99 C 5
Santarém, Ponta de ▲ BR 62-63 J 5
Santarém Novo ○ BR 68-69 E 2
Santaren Channel ≈ 54-55 F 2
Santa Rita ∴ • BH 52-53 K 2
Santa Rita ○ BR (AMA) 66-67 C 4
Santa Rita ○ BR (PA) 68-69 L 5
Santa Rita ○ CO (CA) 64-65 F 1
Santa Rita ○ CO (VIC) 60-61 G 5
Santa Rita ○ HN 52-53 L 4
Santa Rita ○ MEX 50-51 D 5
Santa Rita ○ PA 52-53 D 7
Santa Rita ○ YV (BOL) 60-61 K 3
Santa Rita ○ YV (GUA) 60-61 H 3
Santa Rita ○ YV (ZUL) 60-61 F 2
Santa Rita, Arroyo ∼ RA 76-77 E 2
Santa Rita, Ilha de ⌒ BR 62-63 F 6
Santa Rita de Caldas ○ BR 72-73 G 7
Santa Rita de Cássia ○ BR 68-69 F 7
Santa Rita do Araguaia ○ BR 72-73 D 4
Santa Rita do Sul ○ BR 74-75 E 8
Santa Rosa ○ BOL (BEN) 70-71 D 4
Santa Rosa ○ BOL (PAN) 70-71 D 2
Santa Rosa ○ BR (CAT) 74-75 F 7
Santa Rosa ○ BR (RON) 70-71 G 3
Santa Rosa ○ BR (ROR) 60-61 K 6
Santa Rosa ○ BR (RSU) 76-77 K 4
Santa Rosa ○ BR (TOC) 68-69 D 7
Santa Rosa ○ CO (CAU) 64-65 D 1
Santa Rosa ○ CO (GU) 60-61 G 6
Santa Rosa ○ CO (VAU) 66-67 B 2
Santa Rosa ○ EC (ELO) 64-65 C 3
Santa Rosa ○ EC (PAS) 64-65 D 3
Santa Rosa ○ MEX (BCS) 50-51 E 6
Santa Rosa ○ MEX (QR) 52-53 K 2
Santa Rosa ○ PE (LOR) 64-65 F 3
Santa Rosa ○ PE (PUN) 70-71 B 4
Santa Rosa ○ RA (CO) 76-77 H 5
Santa Rosa ✩ RA (LAP) 78-79 G 4
Santa Rosa ○ USA (CA) 246-247 C 5
Santa Rosa ○ USA (NM) 256-257 L 4
Santa Rosa ○ YV (ANZ) 60-61 J 3
Santa Rosa ○ YV (APU) 60-61 G 4
Santa Rosa ○ YV (BOL) 60-61 K 4
Santa Rosa, Baja de ≈ 62-63 K 5
Santa Rosa, Cordillera de ▲▲ RA 76-77 C 5
Santa Rosa, Isla ⌒ EC 64-65 C 1
Santa Rosa, Lago ○ BOL 70-71 H 6
Santa Rosa Aboriginal Land ✕ AUS 178-179 C 2
Santa Rosa de Amonadona ○ YV 66-67 D 2
Santa Rosa de Copán ✩ HN 52-53 K 4
Santa Rosa de Cusubamba ○ EC 64-65 C 2
Santa Rosa del Conlara ○ RA 78-79 G 2
Santa Rosa de los Pastos Grandes ○ RA 76-77 D 3
Santa Rosa de Ocopa • PE 64-65 E 7
Santa Rosa de Quijos ○ EC 64-65 D 2
Santa Rosa de Sucumbíos ○ EC 64-65 D 1
Santa Rosa de Viterbo ○ BR 72-73 G 6
Santa Rosa dos Dourados ○ BR 72-73 G 5
Santa Rosa Indian Reservation ✕ USA (CA) 248-249 H 6
Santa Rosa Island ⌒ USA (CA) 248-249 D 6
Santa Rosa Island ⌒ USA (FL) 286-287 C 1
Santa Rosa Lake < USA (NM) 256-257 L 3
Santa Rosalía ○ • MEX 50-51 C 4
Santa Rosalía ○ YV 60-61 J 4
Santa Rosa Range ▲▲ USA (NV) 246-247 H 2
Santa Rosa Wash ∼ USA (AZ) 256-257 D 6
Šantarskie, ostrova ⌒ RUS 120-121 G 6
Šantarskoe more ≈ 120-121 G 6
Santa Si • VRC 142-143 M 3
Santa Sylvina ○ RA 76-77 G 4
Santa Tecla = Nueva San Salvador ○ ES 52-53 K 5
Santa Teresa ✕ AUS 178-179 C 3
Santa Teresa ○ MEX 50-51 L 5
Santa Teresa ○ RA 78-79 J 2
Santa Teresa ○ YV 60-61 H 2
Santa Teresa, Forteleza • ROU 74-75 D 10
Santa Teresa, Parque Nacional de ⊥ ROU 74-75 D 10
Santa Teresa, Punta ▲ MEX 50-51 D 4
Santa Teresa, Rio ∼ BR 72-73 F 2
Santa Teresa de Goiás ○ BR 72-73 F 2
Santa Teresa di Gallura ○ I 100-101 B 4
Santa Teresinha de Goiás ○ BR 72-73 F 3
Santa Teresita ○ RA 78-79 L 4
Santa Terezinha ○ BR 68-69 C 7
Santa Ursula, Cachoeira ∼ BR 66-67 H 7
Sant' Auta ○ BR 74-75 E 8
Santa Victoria ○ RA 76-77 E 2
Santa Victoria, Río ∼ RA 76-77 E 2
Santa Victoria, Sierra ▲▲ RA 76-77 E 2
Santa Vitória do Palmar ○ BR 74-75 D 9
San-ta-Wani Safari Lodge ○ RB 218-219 B 4
Santa Ynez ○ USA (CA) 248-249 D 5
Santa Ynez Mountains ▲▲ USA (CA) 248-249 D 5
Santa Ysabel ○ USA (CA) 248-249 H 6
Sant Carles de la Ràpita ○ E 98-99 H 4
Sant Celoni ○ E 98-99 J 4
Santchou ○ CAM 204-205 H 6
Santee ○ USA (CA) 248-249 H 7
Santee ○ USA (NE) 262-263 J 2
Santee Indian Reservation ✕ USA (NE) 262-263 J 2
Santee National Wildlife Refuge ⊥ USA (SC) 284-285 K 3
Santee River ∼ USA (SC) 284-285 L 3
Sante Marie Among the Hurons Historic Park • CDN (ONT) 238-239 F 4
San Tempo, Sierra de ▲▲ BOL 76-77 E 2
Sant Feliu de Guíxols ○ E 98-99 J 4
Sant Francesc de Formentera ○ E 98-99 H 5
Santhe ○ MW 218-219 G 1
Santiago ○ BOL 70-71 H 6
Santiago ○ BR 76-77 K 5
Santiago ○ CO 60-61 E 4
Santiago ○ EC 64-65 C 3
Santiago ○ MEX (BCS) 50-51 E 6
Santiago ○ MEX (NL) 50-51 J 5
Santiago ✩ PA 52-53 D 7
Santiago ★ •• RCH 78-79 D 2
Santiago ○ RP 160-161 D 4
Santiago, Cabo ▲ RCH 80 C 5
Santiago, Cerro ▲ PA 52-53 D 7
Santiago, Ilha de ⌒ CV 202-203 C 6
Santiago, Punta ▲ GQ 210-211 B 2
Santiago, Rio ∼ PE 64-65 D 3
Santiago, Río de ∼ MEX 50-51 H 5
Santiago Atitlán ○ GCA 52-53 J 4
Santiago Chazumba ○ MEX 52-53 F 2
Santiago de Cao ○ PE 64-65 C 5
Santiago de Choeorvos ○ PE 64-65 E 8
Santiago de Chuco ○ PE 64-65 C 6
Santiago de Compostela ○ ••• E 98-99 C 3
Santiago de Cuba ✩ •• C 54-55 H 4
Santiago de Cuba, Bahía de ≈ 54-55 G 5
Santiago del Estero □ RA 76-77 E 4
Santiago del Estero ✩ RA (SAE) 76-77 E 4
Santiago de Los Caballeros ○ MEX 50-51 F 5
Santiago de los Cabelleros ✩ • DOM 54-55 K 5
Santiago de Machaca ○ BOL 70-71 C 5
Santiago de Pacaguaras ○ BOL 70-71 C 3
Santiago Ixcuintla ○ MEX 50-51 G 7
Santiago Jamiltepec ○ MEX 52-53 F 3
Santiago Maior ○ CV 202-203 C 6
Santiago Maravatío ○ MEX 52-53 D 1
Santiago Mountains ▲▲ USA (TX) 266-267 D 3
Santiago Papasquiaro, Río ∼ MEX 50-51 G 5
Santiago Peak ▲ USA (TX) 266-267 D 4
Santiago Tamazola ○ MEX 52-53 E 3
Santiago Tuxtla ○ • MEX 52-53 G 2
Santiago Yosondúa ○ MEX 52-53 F 3
Santiam Junction ○ USA (OR) 244-245 D 6
Santianna Point ▲ CDN 36-37 G 3
San Tiburcio ○ MEX 50-51 J 5
Santigi ○ RI 164-165 G 3
Santigi, Tanjung ▲ RI (SLT) 164-165 G 3
Santigi, Tanjung ▲ RI (SLT) 164-165 H 4
Santiguila ○ RMM 202-203 G 3
Santipur ○ IND 142-143 B 5
Säntis ▲ CH 92-93 K 5
Santissima Trinità di Saccàrgia • I 100-101 B 4
Sant Joan de Labritja ○ E 98-99 H 5
Sant Jordi, Golf de ≈ 98-99 H 4
Santo ○ USA (TX) 264-265 F 6
Santo/ Malo □ VAN 184 II a 2
Santo Agostinho ○ BR 72-73 K 5
Santo Amaro ○ BR 66-67 B 6
Santo Amore, Ilha de ⌒ BR 72-73 H 7
Santo André ○ ANG 216-217 C 6
Santo André ○ BR (P) 62-63 K 6
Santo André ○ BR (PAU) 72-73 G 7
Santo Ângelo ○ • BR 76-77 K 5
Santo Antão, Ilha de ⌒ • CV 202-203 B 5
Santo Antônio ○ BR 62-63 F 6
Santo Antonio ○ BR 66-67 G 4
Santo Antônio ○ BR 68-69 L 5
Santo Antônio ○ CV 202-203 C 6
Santo Antonio ○ STP 210-211 b 2
Santo Antônio, Ponta de ▲ BR 68-69 L 5
Santo Antônio, Rio ∼ BR 68-69 D 7
Santo Antônio da Patrulha ○ BR 74-75 E 7
Santo Antonio de Leverger ○ BR 70-71 J 4
Santo Antônio de Lisboa ○ BR 68-69 H 5
Santo Antônio Desejado ○ BR 66-67 D 7
Santo Antônio do Içá ○ BR 66-67 D 4
Santo Antônio do Monte ○ BR 72-73 H 6
Santo Antônio dos Lopes ○ BR 68-69 F 4
Santo Antônio do Sudoeste ○ BR 74-75 D 6
Santo Corazón ○ BOL 70-71 H 5
Santo Domingo ○ C 54-55 E 3
Santo Domingo ○ CO 60-61 D 4
Santo Domingo ★ ••• DOM 54-55 L 5
Santo Domingo ○ MEX (BCS) 50-51 D 5
Santo Domingo ○ MEX (JAL) 50-51 G 7
Santo Domingo ○ MEX (SLP) 50-51 J 6
Santo Domingo ○ NIC 52-53 B 5
Santo Domingo ○ RA 76-77 F 3
Santo Domingo, Cay ⌒ BS 54-55 H 4
Santo Domingo, Río ∼ MEX 52-53 F 3
Santo Domingo, Río ∼ MEX 52-53 J 3
Santo Domingo, Río ∼ MEX 52-53 H 3
Santo Domingo, Río ∼ YV 60-61 F 3
Santo Domingo de Acobamba ○ PE 64-65 E 7
Santo Domingo de los Colerados ○ EC 64-65 C 2
Santo Domingo Indian Reservation ✕ USA (NM) 256-257 J 3
Santo Domingo Pueblo ○ USA (NM) 256-257 J 3
Santo Domingo Tehuantepec ○ • MEX 52-53 G 3
Santo Inácio do Piauí ○ BR 68-69 H 5
San Tomé ○ YV 60-61 J 3
Santoméri ○ GR 100-101 H 6
Santoña ○ E 98-99 F 3
Santonia ○ F 62-63 G 3
Santop ▲ VAN 184 II b 4
Santópolis do Aguapeí ○ BR 72-73 E 6
Santorini = Thíra ⌒ •• GR 100-101 K 6
Santos ○ AUS 178-179 F 5
Santos ○ BR 72-73 G 7
Santos, Baía de ≈ 72-73 G 7
Santos, El ○ C 54-55 F 3
Santos, General ✩ RP 160-161 F 9
Santos, Los ○ •• PA 52-53 D 8
Santos Dumont ○ BR 72-73 J 6
Santos Lugares ○ RA 76-77 F 4
Santos Mercado ○ BOL 66-67 D 7
Santos Plateau ≃ 6-7 E 11
Santo Tirso ○ P 98-99 C 4
Santo Tomás ○ MEX 50-51 F 3
Santo Tomás ○ MEX 50-51 A 2
Santo Tomás ○ NIC 52-53 B 5
Santo Tomas ○ PA 52-53 C 7
Santo Tomas ○ RP 160-161 F 9
Santo Tomas, Río ∼ PE 64-65 F 9
Santo Tomás, Volcán ▲ GCA 52-53 J 4
Santo Tomé ○ RA (CO) 76-77 J 5
Santo Tomé ○ RA (SAF) 76-77 G 6
Santu Antine, Nuraghe • I 100-101 B 4
Santuaria Nacional de Ampay ⊥ PE 64-65 F 8
Santuario de Flora y Fauna Arauca ⊥ CO 60-61 F 4
Santuario de la Coromoto ○ • YV 60-61 G 3
Santuario Nacional Huayllay ⊥ PE 64-65 D 7
Santuario Nacional Pampas del Heath ⊥ BOL 70-71 C 3
Santubong ○ MAL 162-163 J 4
Santu Lussùrgiu ○ I 100-101 B 4
Sanup Plateau ▲▲ USA (AZ) 256-257 B 3
San Vicente ○ BOL 76-77 D 1
San Vicente ✩ ES 52-53 K 5
San Vicente ○ RA 76-77 K 4
San Vicente ○ YV (AMA) 60-61 H 5
San Vicente ○ YV (ANZ) 60-61 J 3
San Vicente ○ YV (SUC) 60-61 K 2
San Vicente, Bahía ≈ 78-79 C 4
San Vicente de Tagua Tagua ○ RCH 78-79 D 3
San Vicente Tancuayalab ○ MEX 50-51 K 7
San Victor ○ GUY 62-63 D 2
San Victor ○ RA 76-77 H 6
San Vincente de Caguan ○ CO 60-61 D 6
San Vincente de Cañete ○ PE 64-65 D 8
San Vito ○ CR 52-53 C 7
San Vito, Capo ▲ I 100-101 D 5
San Vito, Capo ▲ I 100-101 F 4
San Xavier Indian Reservation ✕ USA (AZ) 256-257 D 6
Sanya ○ • VRC 156-157 F 7
Sanya Juu ○ EAT 212-213 F 5
Sanyang ○ VRC 156-157 L 2
Sanyat ad Daffah < LAR 192-193 L 2
Sanyati ○ ZW (Mlw) 218-219 E 3
Sanyati ∼ ZW 218-219 E 3
Sanying ○ VRC 154-155 E 3
San Ysidro ○ USA (NM) 256-257 J 3
Sanyuan ○ VRC 154-155 F 4
Sanza Pombo ○ ANG 216-217 C 3
São Agostinho, Cabo de ▲ BR 68-69 L 6
Sao Amaro ○ • BR 72-73 L 2
São André, Ribeiro ∼ BR 72-73 G 4
São Antônia ○ BR 62-63 D 4
São Antônio ○ BR 66-67 K 6
São Antônio, Cachoeira ∼ BR 66-67 E 7
São Antônio, Rio ∼ BR 72-73 K 4
São Antônio, Rio ∼ BR 72-73 J 5
São Antônio da Abunari ○ BR 62-63 D 6
São Antônio da Platina ○ BR 72-73 E 7
São Antônio das Missões ○ BR 76-77 K 5
São Antônio de Jesus ○ BR 72-73 L 2
São Antônio de Pádua ○ BR 72-73 J 6
São Antônio de Posse ○ BR 72-73 G 7
São Antônio do Amparo ○ BR 72-73 H 6
São Antônio do Jacinto ○ BR 72-73 K 4
São Bartolomeu, Rio ∼ BR 72-73 G 4
São Benedito, Rio ∼ BR 66-67 J 7
São Bento ○ BR (GSU) 70-71 J 6
São Bento ○ BR (MAR) 68-69 F 3
São Bento ○ BR (P) 68-69 E 3
São Bento do Norte ○ BR 68-69 K 4
São Bento do Sul ○ BR 74-75 F 6
São Bento do Una ○ BR 68-69 K 6
São Bernardo ○ BR (MAR) 68-69 G 3
São Bernardo ○ BR (RSU) 76-77 K 5
São Borja ○ BR 76-77 K 5
São Caetano de Odivelas ○ BR 62-63 K 6
São Caitano ○ BR 68-69 K 6
São Canuto ○ BR 76-77 K 5
São Carlos ○ BR (CAT) 74-75 D 6
São Carlos ○ BR (PAU) 72-73 G 7
São Carlos ○ BR (RON) 70-71 E 2
São Cosme ○ BR 62-63 J 6
São Cristóvão ○ ANG 216-217 B 6
São Cristóvão ○ • BR 68-69 K 7
São Cruz, Ribeiro de ∼ BR 72-73 G 4
São Desidério ○ BR 72-73 H 2
São Domingos ○ BR 66-67 F 6
São Domingos ○ BR (GOI) 72-73 G 2
São Domingos ∼ BR 70-71 F 3
São Domingos ○ GNB 202-203 B 3
São Domingos, Rio ∼ BR 72-73 G 2
São Domingos, Serra de ▲▲ BR 72-73 G 3
São Domingos da Maranhão ○ BR 68-69 F 4
São Domingos da Prata ○ BR 72-73 J 5
São Domingos do Azeitão ○ BR 68-69 F 5
São Domingos do Capim ○ BR 68-69 E 2
São Efigênia de Minas ○ BR 72-73 J 5
São Estêvão ○ BR 72-73 L 2
São Felício ○ BR 62-63 H 5
São Felix de Balsas ○ BR 68-69 F 5
São Felix do Araguaia ○ BR 68-69 C 7
São Félix do Piauí ○ BR 68-69 G 4
São Felix do Xingu ○ BR 68-69 C 5
São Fidélis ○ BR 72-73 K 6
São Filipe ○ CV 202-203 B 6
São Florêncio, Cachoeira ∼ BR 66-67 H 7
São Francisco ○ BR (GSU) 70-71 J 6
São Francisco ○ BR (MIN) 72-73 H 3
São Francisco ○ BR (P) 68-69 E 3
São Francisco, Cachoeira ∼ BR 66-67 K 5
São Francisco, Ilha de ⌒ BR 74-75 F 6
São Francisco, Rio ∼ BR 66-67 E 7
São Francisco, Rio ∼ BR 68-69 H 6
São Francisco, Rio ∼ BR 72-73 K 3
São Francisco, Serra de ▲▲ BR 74-75 D 5
São Francisco das Chagas ○ BR 62-63 F 6
São Francisco de Assis ○ BR 76-77 K 5
São Francisco de Paula ○ BR 74-75 E 7
São Francisco do Maranhão ○ BR 68-69 G 5
São Francisco do Sul ○ BR 74-75 F 6
São Gabriel ○ BR (CAT) 74-75 F 6
São Gabriel ○ BR (RSU) 76-77 K 6
São Gabriel da Palha ○ BR 72-73 K 5
São Geraldo do Araguaia ○ BR 68-69 D 5
São Gonçalo ○ BR 72-73 J 7
São Gonçalo do Abaeté ○ BR 72-73 H 5
São Gonçalo do Amarante ○ BR 68-69 J 3
São Gonçalo do Para ○ BR 72-73 H 5
São Gonçalo do Rio ○ BR 72-73 J 5
São Gonçalo do Sapucaí ○ BR 72-73 H 6
São Gotardo ○ BR 72-73 G 5
Sao Hill ○ EAT 214-215 H 5
São Inácio ○ BR 72-73 E 7
São Jerônimo ○ BR 74-75 E 7
São Jerônimo, Serra de ▲▲ BR 70-71 K 5
São João ○ BR 66-67 G 5
São João, Ilha de ⌒ BR 68-69 F 2
São João, Ribeiro ∼ BR 72-73 K 4
São João, Rio ∼ BR 72-73 E 2
São João, Serra de ▲▲ BR 74-75 E 5
São João Batista ○ BR 68-69 F 3
São João Batista do Gloria ○ BR 72-73 G 6
São João da Aliança ○ BR 72-73 G 3
São João da Barra ○ BR 72-73 K 6
São João da Barra, Cachoeira ∼ BR 66-67 H 7
São João da Barra, Rio ∼ BR 66-67 H 7
São João da Ponte ○ BR 72-73 H 3
São João da Pracajuba ○ BR 62-63 J 6
São João de Cortes ○ BR 68-69 F 3
São João del Rei ○ • BR 72-73 H 6
São João de Meriti ○ BR 72-73 J 7
São João do Araguaia ○ BR 68-69 D 4
São João do Branco, Igarapé ∼ BR 70-71 F 2
São João do Caiuá ○ BR 72-73 D 7
São João do Paraíso ○ BR 72-73 J 3
São João do Paraná ○ BR 66-67 J 7
São João do Piauí ○ BR 68-69 G 6
São João do Sabuji ○ BR 68-69 K 5
São João do Tigre ○ BR 68-69 K 6
São João Evangelista ○ BR 72-73 J 5
São Joaquim ○ BR (AMA) 66-67 D 2
São Joaquim ○ BR (CAT) 74-75 F 7
São Joaquim, Parque Nacional de ⊥ BR 74-75 F 7
São Joaquim da Barra ○ BR 72-73 G 6
São Jorge, Ilha ⌒ BR 68-69 F 2
São Jorge do Ivaí ○ BR 72-73 D 7
São José ○ BR (ACR) 66-67 C 7
São José ○ BR (CAT) 74-75 F 6
São José ○ BR (P) 68-69 D 3
São Jóse, Baía ≈ 68-69 G 3
São José, Igarapé ∼ BR 68-69 B 4
São José de Piranhas ○ BR 68-69 J 5
São José de Ribamar ○ BR 68-69 F 3
São José di Mipibu ○ BR 68-69 L 5
São José do Anauá ○ BR 62-63 D 5
São José do Barreiro ○ BR 72-73 H 7
São José do Belmonte ○ BR 68-69 J 5
São José do Caciporé ○ BR 62-63 J 4
São José do Calcado ○ BR 72-73 K 6
São José do Cedro ○ BR 74-75 D 6
São José do Cerrito ○ BR 74-75 E 6
São José do Egito ○ BR 68-69 K 5
São José do Norte ○ BR 74-75 D 9
São José do Peixe ○ BR 68-69 G 5
São José do Prado ○ BR 72-73 L 4
São José do Rio Claro ○ BR 70-71 J 3
São José do Rio Preto ○ BR 72-73 F 6
São José dos Campos ○ BR 72-73 H 7
São José dos Cordeiros ○ BR 68-69 K 5
São José dos Dourados, Rio ∼ BR 72-73 E 6
São José dos Martírios ○ BR 68-69 D 5
São José dos Pinhais ○ BR 74-75 F 5
São José do Xingu ○ BR 68-69 B 7
São Julia do Jurupari ○ BR 62-63 J 5
São Juliana ○ BR 72-73 G 5
Saoleil Ashraf ○ SUD 200-201 G 6
São Lourenço, Pantanal do ∼ BR 70-71 J 5
São Lourenço, Riachão ∼ BR 68-69 G 6
São Lourenço, Rio ∼ BR 70-71 K 5
São Lourenço do Sul ○ BR 74-75 E 8
São Lucas ○ ANG 216-217 D 5
São Lucas, Cachoeira ∼ BR 66-67 H 7
São Luís ○ BR 66-67 G 4
São Luís ○ BR (AMA) 66-67 E 3
São Luís ✩ • BR (MAR) 68-69 F 3
São Luís, Cachoeira ∼ BR 66-67 H 7
São Luís, Ilha de ⌒ BR 68-69 F 3
São Luís de Montes Belos ○ BR 72-73 E 4
São Luís do Curu ○ BR 68-69 J 3
São Luís do Paraitinga ○ BR 72-73 H 7
São Luís do Puruná ○ BR 74-75 F 5
São Luís do Quitunde ○ BR 68-69 L 6
São Luís do Tapajós ○ BR 66-67 J 5
São Luis Gonzaga ○ BR 76-77 K 5
São Luis Gonzaga do Maranhão ○ BR 68-69 F 4
São Manuel ○ BR (MAT) 70-71 K 4
São Manuel ○ BR (PAU) 72-73 F 7
São Manuel ou Teles Pires, Rio ∼ BR 70-71 K 2
São Marcos, Área Indígena ✕ BR (MAT) 72-73 D 3
São Marcos, Área Indígena ✕ BR (ROR) 62-63 D 3
São Marcos, Baía de ≈ 68-69 F 3
São Marcos, Rio ∼ BR 72-73 G 4
São Martinho ○ BR 74-75 F 7
São Mateus ○ BR 72-73 L 5
São Mateus, Pico ▲ BR 72-73 K 6
São Mateus do Sul ○ BR 74-75 E 5
São Miguel ○ BR (APA) 62-63 J 5
São Miguel ○ BR (MAT) 72-73 D 2
São Miguel ○ BR (RNO) 68-69 J 5
São Miguel ⌒ P 6-7 E 6
São Miguel, Rio ∼ BR 70-71 F 3
São Miguel, Rio ∼ BR 70-71 J 3
São Miguel Arcanjo ○ BR 72-73 G 7
São Miguel das Missões ○ ••• BR 76-77 K 5
São Miguel do Araguaia ○ BR 72-73 E 2
São Miguel d'Oeste ○ BR 74-75 D 6
São Miguel do Guama ○ BR 68-69 E 2
São Miguel do Iguaçu ○ BR 76-77 K 3
São Miguel dos Campos ○ BR 68-69 K 6
São Miguel dos Macacos ○ BR 62-63 J 6
São Miguel do Tapuio ○ BR 68-69 H 4
Saona, Isla ⌒ DOM 54-55 L 5
Saône ∼ F 90-91 L 7
São Nicolau ○ ANG 216-217 B 7
São Nicolau ○ BR 76-77 K 5
São Nicolau, Ilha de ⌒ CV 202-203 B 5
São Nicolau, Rio ∼ BR 68-69 H 4
São Onofre, Rio ∼ BR 72-73 J 2
São Paulo □ BR 72-73 E 6
São Paulo ✩ • BR (PAU) 72-73 G 7
São Paulo de Olivença ○ BR 66-67 C 4
São Pedro ○ BR (AMA) 66-67 D 3
São Pedro ○ BR (MIN) 72-73 K 4
São Pedro ○ BR (P) 68-69 C 3
São Pedro ○ BR (PAU) 72-73 G 7
São Pedro ○ BR (RNO) 68-69 L 4
São Pedro ○ CV 202-203 B 5
São Pedro, Ribeiro ∼ BR 72-73 G 4
São Pedro, Rio ∼ BR 70-71 G 2
São Pedro, Rio de ∼ BR 68-69 H 5
São Pedro da Aldeia ○ BR 72-73 J 7
São Pedro da Garça ○ BR 72-73 J 4
São Pedro da Quilemba ○ ANG 216-217 C 4
São Pedro do Butiá ○ BR 76-77 K 5
São Pedro do Icó ○ BR 66-67 C 7
São Pedro do Paraná ○ BR 72-73 D 7
São Pedro do Piauí ○ BR 68-69 G 4
São Pedro dos Crentes ○ BR 68-69 E 5
São Pedro do Sul ○ BR 76-77 K 5
São Raimundo das Mangabeiras ○ BR 68-69 F 5
São Raimundo Nonato ○ BR 68-69 G 6
São Ramão ○ BR 72-73 H 4
São Romão ○ BR 66-67 D 5
São Roque, Cabo de ▲ BR 68-69 L 4
São Roque, Cachoeira ∼ BR 70-71 F 2
São Sebastião ○ BR 72-73 H 7
São Sebastião, Ilha de ⌒ BR 72-73 H 7
São Sebastião, Ponta ▲ MOC 218-219 H 6
São Sebastião da Amoreira ○ BR 72-73 E 7
São Sebastião da Boa Vista ○ BR 62-63 K 6
São Sebastião da Gama ○ BR 72-73 G 6
São Sebastião do Caí ○ BR 74-75 E 7
São Sebastião do Maranhão ○ BR 72-73 J 5
São Sebastião do Paraíso ○ BR 72-73 G 6
São Sebastião do Rio Verde ○ BR 72-73 H 7
São Sebastião dos Poções ○ BR 72-73 H 3
São Sebastião do Tocantins ○ BR 68-69 D 4
São Sepé ○ BR 74-75 D 8
São Simão, Cachoeira ∼ BR 66-67 H 7
São Simão, Ponta ▲ BR 74-75 E 8
São Simão ou Branco, Rio ∼ BR 70-71 F 3
São Teotónio ○ P 98-99 C 6
São Timóteo ○ BR 72-73 J 2
São Tomé ○ BR (APA) 62-63 J 6
São Tomé ○ BR (RIO) 72-73 K 7
São Tomé ★ STP 210-211 b 2
São Tomé ⌒ STP 210-211 b 2
São Tomé, Cabo de ▲ BR 72-73 K 6
São Tomé and Príncipe = São Tomé e Príncipe ■ STP 210-211 B 5
Saoura, Oued ∼ DZ 188-189 L 6
São Valentim ○ BR 74-75 D 6
São Vendelino ○ BR 74-75 E 7
São Vice ○ BR 76-77 K 5
São Vicente ○ BR (ACR) 66-67 B 6
São Vicente ○ BR (GOI) 72-73 G 2
São Vicente ○ BR (GSU) 70-71 J 6
São Vicente ○ BR (MAT) 70-71 K 4
São Vicente ○ BR (P) 62-63 J 6
São Vicente ○ BR (PAU) 72-73 G 7
São Vicente, Cabo de ▲ P 98-99 C 6
São Vicente, Ilha de ⌒ CV 202-203 B 5
São Vicente, Rio ∼ BR 68-69 G 5
São Vicente Ferrer ○ BR 68-69 F 3
Sapang ○ MAL 160-161 C 10
Sapão, Rio ∼ BR 68-69 F 7
Saparua ○ RI 166-167 E 3
Saparua, Pulau ⌒ RI 166-167 E 3
Sapé ○ BR 68-69 L 5
Sape ○ RI 168 D 7
Sape, Selat ≈ 168 D 7
Sapeaçu ○ BR 72-73 L 2
Sapele ○ WAN 204-205 F 6
Sapello ○ USA (NM) 256-257 K 3
Sapelo Island ⌒ USA (GA) 284-285 J 5
Sapelo Sound ≈ USA 284-285 J 5
Sapëmoe ○ RUS 94-95 L 1
Sápes ○ GR 100-101 K 4
Saphane Dağı ▲ TR 128-129 C 3
Šapina ∼ RUS 120-121 S 6
Sapinero ○ USA (CO) 254-255 H 5
Sapiranga ○ BR 74-75 E 7
Sapiranga do Sul ○ BR 74-75 E 7
Sapi Safari Area ⊥ ZW 218-219 E 2
Šapki ○ RUS 94-95 M 2
Šapkina ∼ RUS 88-89 X 3
Sap Malua ○ THA 158-159 G 3
Sapo, Serrania del ▲▲ PA 52-53 E 8
Sapoba ○ WAN 204-205 F 5
Sapočani ••• YU 100-101 H 3
Sapocoy, Mount ▲ RP 160-161 D 4
Sapodilla Cays ⌒ BH 52-53 K 3
Saponac ○ USA (ME) 278-279 N 3
Saponé ○ BF 202-203 K 3
Sapo Sapo ○ ZRE 210-211 J 6
Saposoa ○ PE 64-65 D 5
Sapouy ○ BF 202-203 K 4
Sappa Creek ∼ USA (KS) 262-263 F 5
Sapphire Mountains ▲▲ USA (MT) 250-251 F 5
Sapping ○ USA (WA) 244-245 A 2
Sapporo ✩ J 152-153 J 3
Sapri ○ I 100-101 E 4
Šapšal'skij hrebet ▲▲ RUS 124-125 Q 3
Sapucaí, Rio ∼ BR 72-73 F 6
Sapucaia ○ BR (AMA) 66-67 J 4
Sapucaia ○ BR (MIN) 72-73 J 6
Sapucaia ○ BR (RIO) 72-73 J 7
Sapudi, Pulau ⌒ RI 168 B 6
Sapuka-Besar, Pulau ⌒ RI 168 D 6
Sapulpa ○ USA (OK) 264-265 H 2
Sapulu ○ RI 168 E 3
Sapulut ○ MAL 160-161 B 10
Saputing Lake ○ CDN 24-25 d 5
Saqadi ○ SUD 200-201 F 6
Sāqain ○ Y 132-133 C 5
Sāqiya ○ IRQ 128-129 K 5
Šaqlāwa ✩ IRQ 128-129 L 4
Saqqaq ○ GRØ 28-29 P 1
Saqqāra ○ ET 194-195 E 3
Saqqara, Pyramids of ∴ ••• ET 194-195 E 3
Šaqqat al-Ḥarīta ⊥ KSA 132-133 D 5
Saqqez ○ IR 128-129 M 4
Šaqr ○ Y 132-133 G 6
Šaqrā' ○ KSA 130-131 J 5
Šaqrā' ○ Y 132-133 D 7
Saqū ○ IR 134-135 G 5
Ša'r, aš ○ KSA 130-131 J 4
Sara ○ BF 202-203 J 4
Sara ○ RI 166-167 G 3
Sara ○ RP 160-161 E 7
Ša'rā', aš- ○ KSA 132-133 B 3
Sara, Col de ▲ RN 198-199 F 2
Saraar, Bannaanka ⊥ SP 208-209 G 4
Sarāb ○ IR 128-129 M 4
Sarāb Dōre ○ IR 134-135 C 2
Saraburi ○ THA 158-159 F 3
Šaraf al-Ba'l ○ KSA 130-131 D 3
Sarafara ∼ SUD 206-207 K 3
Saraf Doungous ○ TCH 198-199 J 6
Sarafére ○ RMM 202-203 J 2
Sarafğegān ○ IR 134-135 D 1
Šarafhāne ○ IR 128-129 L 3
Šarafiya, aš- ○ KSA 132-133 B 3
Saragosa ○ USA (TX) 266-267 D 2
Saraguro ○ EC 64-65 C 3
Sarah Lake ○ CDN 30-31 L 4
Sarahs ○ IR 136-137 G 6
Sarahsville ○ USA (OH) 280-281 E 4
Sarai ○ RUS 94-95 R 5
Šarā'i', aš- ○ KSA 132-133 A 3
Sarai Gambila ○ PK 138-139 C 3
Saraipāli ○ IND 142-143 C 5
Sarajevo ★ • BIH 100-101 G 3
Saraj-Ordasy ansambli • KA 136-137 J 5
Sara-Kawa ○ RT 202-203 L 5
Saraktaš ✩ RUS 96-97 K 8
Sarala ○ CI 202-203 G 5
Saraland ○ USA (AL) 284-285 B 6
Saramaccarivier ∼ SME 62-63 G 3
Saramaguacán ∼ C 54-55 G 4
Saran' ○ KA 124-125 H 4
Šaran ✩ RUS 96-97 J 6
Saran, Gunung ▲ RI 162-163 J 5
Saranac Lake ○ USA (NY) 278-279 G 4
Saranac River ∼ USA (NY) 278-279 H 4
Saranda ○ EAT 212-213 E 6
Sarandë ✩ •• AL 100-101 H 5
Sarandi ○ BR 74-75 D 6
Sarandi, Arroyo ∼ RA 76-77 H 6
Sarandí del Yí ○ ROU 78-79 M 2
Sarandí de Navarro ○ ROU 78-79 L 2
Sarandi Grande ○ ROU 78-79 L 2
Šaranga ○ RUS 96-97 E 5
Sarangani Bay ≈ 160-161 F 10
Sarangani Island ⌒ RP 160-161 F 10
Saranglayang, Tanjung ▲ RI 162-163 G 6
Sārangpur ○ IND 138-139 F 8
Sarannoe, ozero ○ RUS 120-121 W 6
Saranpaul' ○ RUS 114-115 F 2
Saransk ○ RUS 96-97 D 6
Saranzal ○ BR 68-69 D 4
Šarapov Šar, zaliv ○ RUS 108-109 M 6
Šarapovy koški, ostrova ⌒ RUS 108-109 M 6
Sarapul ✩ RUS 96-97 H 5
Sarapul'skaja vozvyšennost' ▲▲ RUS 96-97 H 5
Šaraqraq ○ SYR 128-129 H 4
Sarār ○ Y 132-133 G 6
Sarare, Área Indígena ✕ BR 70-71 H 4
Sarare, Rio ∼ BR 70-71 H 4
Sarare, Río ∼ YV 60-61 F 4
Sarasota ○ USA (FL) 286-287 G 4
Sarasota Bay ≈ USA 286-287 G 4
Sarata ∼ UA 102-103 F 4
Saratoga ○ USA (AR) 276-277 B 7
Saratoga ○ USA (CA) 248-249 B 2
Saratoga ○ USA (NC) 282-283 K 5
Saratoga ○ USA (WY) 252-253 M 5
Saratoga Hot Springs ∴ USA (WY) 252-253 M 5
Saratoga National Historic Park • USA (NY) 278-279 H 5
Saratoga Springs ○ USA (NY) 278-279 H 5
Saratok ○ MAL 162-163 J 4
Saratov ✩ RUS 96-97 E 8
Saratovskoe vodohranilišče < RUS 96-97 F 7
Saratovskoye Vodokhranilishche = Saratovskoe vodohranil. < RUS 96-97 F 7
Šaraura, aš- ○ KSA 132-133 E 5
Sarāvān ○ IR 134-135 K 5
Saravan ○ LAO 158-159 J 3
Sarawak □ MAL 162-163 J 3
Saray ✩ TR 128-129 B 2
Saraya ○ SN 202-203 E 3
Sarāyān ○ IR 134-135 H 2
Sarayköy ✩ TR 128-129 C 4
Šarbakty ○ KA 124-125 L 3
Sar Bandar ○ IR 134-135 C 3
Sarbāz ○ IR (SIS) 134-135 J 5
Sarbāz ⊥ IR 134-135 J 5
Sarbāz, Rūdḫāne-ye ∼ IR 134-135 J 5
Sarbīše ○ IR 134-135 H 2
Šarbitāt ○ OM 132-133 K 5
Šarbitāt, Ra's ▲ OM 132-133 K 5
Sarbulak ○ VRC 146-147 J 2
Sarcee Indian Reservation ✕ CDN (ALB) 232-233 D 5
Sarco ○ RCH 76-77 B 5
Sarcoxie ○ USA (MO) 276-277 A 3
Sarda ∼ NEP 144-145 C 6
Sardanga ○ RUS 118-119 H 4
Šardara ✩ KA 136-137 L 4
Šardara, kŭm ⊥ KA 136-137 K 4
Šardara sukojmasy < KA 136-137 L 4
Sardārshahr ○ IND 138-139 E 5
Sardašt ○ IR (AZG) 128-129 L 4
Sardašt ○ IR (HUZ) 134-135 D 3
Sarde Band < AFG 138-139 B 3
Sardegna □ I 100-101 B 4
Sardegna, Mar di ≃ 98-99 L 4
Sardegna, Punta ⌒ I 100-101 B 4
Sardes ∴ •• TR 128-129 C 3
Sardinas ○ EC 64-65 D 2
Sardinata ○ CO 60-61 E 3
Sardinia ○ USA (IN) 274-275 N 5
Sardinia = Sardegna □ I 100-101 B 4
Sardinia = Sardegna ⌒ I 100-101 B 4
Sardis ○ CDN (BC) 230-231 H 4
Sardis ○ USA (GA) 284-285 J 4
Sardis ○ USA (MS) 268-269 L 2
Sardis Lake ○ USA (MS) 268-269 L 2
Sardis Lake ○ USA (OK) 264-265 J 4
Šardonem' ○ RUS 88-89 S 5
Sare, Rumah ○ MAL 164-165 D 1
Sarege, Pulau ⌒ RI 168 D 6
Sar-e'in ○ IR 128-129 N 3
Saré Kali ○ RG 202-203 D 4
Sareks nationalpark ⊥ S 86-87 H 3
Saré Ndiaye ○ SN 202-203 C 3
Sar-e Pol ○ AFG 136-137 J 6
Sar-e Pol, Daryā-ye ∼ AFG 136-137 J 6
Sar-e Pol-e Zahāb ○ • IR 134-135 A 1
Sarepta ○ USA (MS) 268-269 L 2
Saréyamou ○ RMM 196-197 J 6
Sarezckoe, ozero ○ TJ 136-137 N 5
Sarfannguaq ○ GRØ 28-29 O 3
Šarga ○ MAU (GAL) 146-147 M 2
Šarga ○ MAU (HÖG) 148-149 D 3
Šargalant ○ MAU 146-147 K 2
Sargapur ○ IND 140-141 G 2
Sargasso Sea ≈ 4 G 5
Sargent ○ USA (NE) 262-263 G 3
Sargent ○ USA (TX) 266-267 M 5
Sargent Icefield ⊂ USA 20-21 Q 6
Sargento, Bahía ≈ 50-51 C 3
Sargento Ayte Victor Sanabria ○ RA 76-77 G 3
Sargents ○ AUS 172-173 K 2
Sargodha ○ PK 138-139 D 3
Sargul', ozero ○ RUS 124-125 L 1
Sarh ✩ TCH 206-207 D 4
Sarhād ⊥ IR 134-135 J 4
Sarhro, Jbel ▲▲ MA 188-189 H 5
Šarhulsan ○ MAU 148-149 G 5
Sārī ✩ • IR 136-137 C 6
Šari ○ KSA 130-131 H 4
Šari, Buḥairat < IRQ 128-129 L 5
Saria ⌒ GR 100-101 L 7
Saria ○ IND 138-139 E 3
Sariā, Rio ∼ BR 66-67 E 6

Sariba Island ⌒ PNG 183 F 6
Saribi, Tanjung ▲ RI 166-167 H 2
Saric ○ MEX 50-51 D 2
Sarichef, Cape ▲ USA 22-23 O 5
Şārif ○ Y 132-133 G 5
Šarifa, Ğazirat ⌒ KSA 132-133 B 3
Sariga, Kepulauan ⌒ RI 166-167 G 3
Sarıgöl ☆ TR 128-129 C 3
Sarıkamış ☆ TR 128-129 K 2
Sarıkaya ☆ TR 128-129 F 3
Sarikei ○ MAL 162-163 J 3
Sarina ○ AUS 178-179 K 1
Sarina Beach ○ AUS 178-179 K 1
Sariñena ○ E 98-99 G 4
Saripai ○ RI 164-165 D 4
Sar-i-Parom ○ PK 134-135 K 5
Šāriqa, Aš- ○ UAE 134-135 F 6
Sariri ○ PNG 183 E 5
Sarita ○ CDN (BC) 230-231 D 5
Sarita ○ USA (TX) 266-267 K 6
Sariwon ○ DVR 150-151 E 8
Sar'ja ○ RUS 96-97 D 4
Sark ⌒ GBG 90-91 F 7
Şarkan ☆ RUS 96-97 H 5
Sarkand ○ KA 124-125 L 6
Sarkari Tala ○ IND 138-139 C 6
Šarkavščyna ☆ BY 94-95 K 4
Şarkîkaraağaç ☆ TR 128-129 D 3
Šarkin ○ KA 96-97 G 9
Sarkin Kudin ○ WAN 204-205 H 4
Şarkışla ☆ TR 128-129 G 3
Şarköy ☆ TR 128-129 B 2
Sarlat Ghar ▲ PK 134-135 M 4
Sarlat-la-Canéda ○ F 90-91 H 9
Šarlauk = Šarlavuk ○ TM 136-137 D 5
Šarlavuk = Šarlauk ○ TM 136-137 D 5
Sarles ○ USA (ND) 258-259 J 3
Šarlyk ☆ RUS 96-97 J 7
Šarma ○ KSA 130-131 D 3
Sarmanovo ☆ RUS 96-97 H 6
Sărmășel Gară ○ RO 102-103 D 4
Šarm aš-Šaiḫ ○• ET 194-195 G 4
Sarmette ○ VAN 184 II a 3
Sarmi ○ RI 166-167 K 2
Sarmiento ○ RA (CHU) 80 F 2
Sarmiento ○ RA (COD) 76-77 E 6
Sarmiento, Monte ▲ RCH 80 E 7
Šarmsabun ~ RUS 114-115 Q 3
Šarmuḫiya ○ IRQ 128-129 M 7
Särna ○ S 86-87 F 6
Sarnako ○ RI 164-165 G 5
Sarnia ○ CDN (ONT) 238-239 C 6
Sarny ○ UA 102-103 E 2
Sarōbi ○• AFG 138-139 B 2
Sarolangun ○ RI 162-163 E 6
Saroma ○ J 152-153 K 2
Saroma-ko ⊖ J 152-153 K 2
Šaromy ○ RUS 120-121 S 6
Sarona ○ USA (WI) 270-271 G 5
Saronikós Kólpos ≈ 100-101 J 6
Sarore ○ RI 166-167 L 6
Saros Körfezi ≈ 128-129 B 2
Šarovce ○ SK 92-93 P 4
Sarpinskie ozera ⊖ RUS 96-97 D 9
Sarpsborg ☆ N 86-87 E 7
Sarqardliit ⌒ GRØ 28-29 O 2
Šarrār, aš ○ KSA 130-131 L 4
Sarre ~ F 90-91 L 7
Sarre, La ○ CDN (QUE) 236-237 J 4
Sarrebourg ○ F 90-91 L 7
Sarria ○ E 98-99 D 3
Sarro ○ RMM 202-203 H 3
Sarstoon River ~ BH 52-53 K 4
Sartang ~ RUS 110-111 T 7
Sartang ~ RUS 110-111 T 6
Sartell ○ USA (MN) 270-271 D 5
Sartène ○• F 98-99 M 4
Sarthe ~ F 90-91 G 8
Sartinville ○ USA (MS) 268-269 K 5
Sartlan, ozero ⊖ RUS 114-115 P 7
Saru, Kaffin- ○ WAN 204-205 G 4
Sarubetsu ○ J 152-153 K 3
Sarufutsu ○ J 152-153 K 2
Saru-gawa ~ J 152-153 K 3
Sar-Us gol ~ MAU 148-149 C 4
Saruwaged Range ▲▲ PNG 183 D 4
Sárvár ○ H 92-93 O 5
Sarvestān ○• IR 134-135 E 4
Sarwain, Ra's ▲ Y 132-133 G 6
Saryagaš ☆ KA 136-137 L 4
Sary-Bulak ○ KS 146-147 B 5
Sarybylak ○ KA 136-137 M 3
Saryčevo ○ RUS 122-123 P 4
Sary-Džaz ~ KS 146-147 D 4
Saryesik-Atyrau ∴ KA 124-125 J 6
Saryg-Sep ☆ RUS 116-117 G 10
Sary Hobda ~ KA 126-127 M 3
Saryjazinskoe vodohranilišče < TM 136-137 H 6
Sarykamyšskaja kotlorina ∪ US 136-137 E 3
Sarykamyšskoe ozero ⊖ US 136-137 E 3
Sarykamyšskoe ozero = Sarygamyš köli ○ TM 136-137 E 4
Sarykol ○ KA 124-125 D 2
Sarykopa, köli ⊖ KA 124-125 D 3
Sarykūdyk ○ KA 96-97 F 9
Sarykul' ○ US 136-137 K 5
Sarylah ○ RUS 110-111 Y 7
Sarymojyn, köli ⊖ KA 124-125 D 3
Saryozek ○ KA 124-125 K 6
Saryozen ~ KA 124-125 D 3
Šarypovo ○ RUS 114-115 U 7
Saryšagan ○ KA 124-125 H 5
Sarysu ~ KA 124-125 F 4
Sary syganak köli ⊖ KA 96-97 F 9
Sary-Taš ○ KS 136-137 N 5
Sary-Torgaj ~ KA 124-125 E 4
Sarzal ○ KA 124-125 L 4
Saržo, kuduk ○ US 136-137 E 3
Sasa ○ PNG 183 G 2
Sasabe ○ USA (AZ) 256-257 D 7
Sasabeneh ○ ETH 208-209 F 4
Sasan, Mount ▲ SOL 184 I d 3
Sasar, Tanjung ▲ RI 168 D 7
Sasarām ○ IND 142-143 D 3
Sasebo ○ J 152-153 C 8
Šašgāv, Kōtal-e ▲ AFG 138-139 B 3
Saskal' ○ RUS 122-123 B 3
Saskatchewan □ CDN 32-33 Q 4
Saskatchewan, Fort ○ CDN (ALB) 232-233 E 2
Saskatchewan Landing Provincial Park ⊥ CDN (SAS) 232-233 L 5
Saskatchewan River ~ CDN (SAS) 232-233 N 2
Saskatchewan River Crossing ○ CDN (ALB) 232-233 B 4
Saskatoon ○• CDN (SAS) 232-233 M 3
Saskylah ○ RUS 110-111 K 4
Saslaya, Cerro ▲ NIC 52-53 B 5
Saslaya, Parque Nacional ⊥ NIC 52-53 B 5
Sasmik, Cape ▲ USA 22-23 H 7
Sasolburg ○ ZA 220-221 H 3
Sasoma ○ IND 138-139 F 2
Sasovo ○ RUS 94-95 R 4
Sassafras Mountain ▲ USA (NC) 282-283 E 5
Sassandra ☆• CI (SAS) 202-203 G 7
Sassandra ~ CI 202-203 G 7
Sàssari ☆• I 100-101 B 4
Sassélé ○ RCA 206-207 C 6
Sasser ○ USA (GA) 284-285 F 5
Sassi ○ I 100-101 C 2
Sassie Island ⌒ AUS 174-175 G 1
Sassnitz ○ D 92-93 M 1
Saßnitz = Sassnitz ○ D 92-93 M 1
Sassoumbouroum ○ RN 198-199 D 6
Sass River ~ CDN 30-31 N 5
Sass Town ○ LB 202-203 F 7
Sastre ○ RA 76-77 G 6
Sastyg-Hem ○ RUS 116-117 G 9
Sāsvad ○ IND 138-139 E 10
Sasykköl ⊖ KA 124-125 B 2
Sasykköl, köli ⊖ KA 124-125 M 5
Sasyk ozero ⊖ UA 102-103 H 5
Sasyr ○ RUS 110-111 a 7
Sata ○ J 152-153 D 9
Satadougou ○ RMM 202-203 E 3
Satagaj ○ RUS 118-119 L 3
Satama-Sokoro ○ CI 202-203 H 6
Satama-Sokoura ○ CI 202-203 H 6
Sata misaki ▲ J 152-153 D 9
Satāna ○ IND 138-139 E 9
Satanta ○ USA (KS) 262-263 F 7
Sātāra ○ IND 140-141 E 2
Satara ○ ZA 220-221 K 2
Satartia ○ USA (MS) 268-269 K 4
Satellite Bay ≈ 24-25 N 2
Satellite Beach ○ USA (FL) 286-287 J 3
Satéma ○ RCA 206-207 E 6
Satengar, Kepulauan ⌒ RI 168 C 6
Satengar, Pulau ⌒ RI 168 C 6
Sathing Phra ○ THA 158-159 F 7
Satilla River ~ USA (GA) 284-285 J 5
Satilla River ~ USA (GA) 284-285 H 5
Satilpa Creek ~ USA (AL) 284-285 C 5
Satipo ○ PE 64-65 E 7
Satiri ○ BF 202-203 H 4
Satiwāla ○ PK 138-139 D 4
Satka ☆ RUS 96-97 L 6
Satluj ~ IND 138-139 F 4
Satluj ~ IND 138-139 E 4
Satna ○ IND 142-143 B 3
Sato ○ J 152-153 C 9
Sátoraljaújhely ○ H 92-93 Q 4
Satpaev ☆ KA 124-125 E 5
Sātpura Range ▲▲ IND 138-139 E 9
Šaṭra, aš- ☆ IRQ 128-129 M 7
Šatrovo ☆ RUS 114-115 H 6
Satsuma-hantō ∪ J 152-153 D 9
Sattahip ○ THA 158-159 F 4
Šaṭṭ al-'Arab ~ IRQ 130-131 K 2
Šaṭṭ al-Ḥilla ~ IRQ 128-129 L 6
Sattenapalle ○ IND 140-141 J 2
Šaṭṭ-e Šūr ~ IR 134-135 E 1
Satti ○ IND 138-139 F 2
Šātū, Kōtal-e ▲ AFG 134-135 M 1
Sātuimalufilufi ○ WS 184 V a 1
Satuk ○ THA 158-159 G 3
Satu Mare ☆ RO 102-103 C 4
Satun ○ THA 158-159 F 7
Satunan-shotō ∴ J 152-153 C 11
Šatura ☆ RUS 94-95 Q 4
Saturna ○ CDN (BC) 230-231 F 5
Satus Pass ▲ USA (WA) 244-245 E 4
Saty ○ KA 146-147 D 4
Satyg-Hem ○ RUS 116-117 G 9
Satymangalam ○ IND 140-141 G 5
Šaubak ○• JOR 130-131 D 2
Sauble Falls ○ CDN (ONT) 238-239 D 4
Sauce ○ RA 76-77 H 6
Sauce, El ○ NIC 52-53 L 5
Sauce Blanco ○ RA 78-79 H 6
Sauce Chico, Río ~ RA 78-79 H 5
Sauce Corto, Arroyo ~ RA 78-79 J 4
Sauces, Los ○ RCH 78-79 C 4
Saucier ○ USA (MS) 268-269 L 6
Saucillo ○ MEX 50-51 G 3
Sauda ☆ N 86-87 C 7
Saudā', as- ⌒ Y 132-133 J 5
Saudade ○ BR 66-67 E 5
Saudade, Cachoeira de ~ BR 72-73 D 3
Saudade, Serra da ▲▲ BR 72-73 H 5
Sauðárkrkur ☆ IS 86-87 d 2
Saudavel ○ BR 72-73 J 2
Saúde ○ BR 68-69 H 7
Saudi Arabia = al-Mamlaka al-'Arabīya as-Sa'ūdīya ■ KSA 130-131 F 3
Saueninā, Rio ~ BR 70-71 H 3
Sauer ○ ZA 220-221 D 6
Sauēruinā ou Papagaio, Rio ~ BR 70-71 H 4
Saugatuck ○ USA (MI) 272-273 C 5
Saugeen River ~ CDN (ONT) 238-239 D 4
Saugstad, Mount ▲ CDN (BC) 228-229 H 4
Šauildir ☆ KA 136-137 L 3
Saujil ○ RA 76-77 D 5
Sauk Centre ○ USA (MN) 270-271 D 5
Sauk City ○ USA (WI) 274-275 J 1
Saukorem ○ RI 166-167 G 2
Sauk Rapids ○ USA (MN) 270-271 D 5
Saül ○ F 62-63 H 4
Sauldre ~ F 90-91 J 8
Saulieu ○ F 90-91 K 8
Saulkrasti ○ LV 94-95 J 3
Sault-au-Mouton ○ CDN (QUE) 240-241 F 2
Saulteaux Indian Reservation ✗ CDN (SAS) 232-233 K 2
Saulteaux River ~ CDN 32-33 N 4
Sault Sainte Marie ○ CDN (ONT) 236-237 D 6
Sault Sainte Marie ○ USA (MI) 270-271 O 4
Saum ○ USA (MN) 270-271 D 3
Saum, as- ○ Y 132-133 F 5
Saumarez Reef ⌒ AUS 178-179 M 1
Saumlakki ○• RI 166-167 F 5
Saumur ○• F 90-91 G 8
Saundatti ○ IND 140-141 F 3
Saunders ○ CDN (ALB) 232-233 C 3
Saunders Ø ⌒ GRØ 26-27 P 5
Saunders Point ▲ AUS 176-177 H 3
Saunemin ○ USA (IL) 274-275 K 4
Saunyi ~ EAT 212-213 F 6
Sauqira ○ OM 132-133 K 5
Sauqira Bay ≈ 132-133 K 4
Sauren ○ PNG 183 E 3
Sauri Hill ▲ WAN 204-205 G 3
Saurimo ☆ ANG 216-217 F 4
Sauriwaunawa ○ GUY 62-63 E 4
Sausalito ○• USA (CA) 248-249 B 2
Sausar ○ IND 138-139 G 9
Sausi ○ PNG 183 C 3
Sausu ○ RI 164-165 G 4
Sautar ○ ANG 216-217 E 5
Sautatá ○ CO 60-61 C 4
Saut Macague ~ F 62-63 H 4
Sauvage, Lac du ⊖ CDN 30-31 P 3
Sauvolles, Lac ⊖ CDN 38-39 H 2
Sauz, El ○ MEX 50-51 F 3
Sauzal ○ RCH 78-79 C 3
Sava ~ BIH 100-101 G 2
Savá ○ HN 52-53 L 4
Sava ~ HR 100-101 F 2
Sava ~ SLO 100-101 E 1
Savage ○ USA (MT) 250-251 P 4
Savage Cove ○ CDN (NFL) 242-243 M 1
Savage Islands ⌒ CDN 30-31 Z 3
Savage River ○ AUS 180-181 H 6
Savai'i Island ⌒ WS 184 V a 1
Savalou ○ DY 202-203 L 6
Savalou, Montagne de ▲ DY 202-203 L 5
Sävandvādi ○ IND 140-141 E 3
Savane ○ MOC 218-219 H 4
Savane Bissainthe ○ RH 54-55 J 5
Savane Zombi ○ RH 54-55 K 5
Savanna ○ USA (IL) 274-275 H 2
Savanna ○ USA (OK) 264-265 J 4
Savannah ○ USA (MO) 274-275 D 5
Savannah ○ USA (TN) 276-277 G 5
Savannah ○•• USA (GA) 284-285 J 4
Savannah Downs ○ AUS 174-175 F 6
Savannah River ~ USA (GA) 284-285 J 3
Savannah River ~ USA (SC) 284-285 H 2
Savannah River Plant ✗✗ USA (SC) 284-285 J 3
Savannakhet ○•• LAO 158-159 H 2
Savanna-la-Mar ○ JA 54-55 F 5
Savant Lake ○ CDN (ONT) 234-235 N 4
Savant Lake ⊖ CDN (ONT) 234-235 N 4
Savanūr ○ IND 140-141 F 3
Savaştepe ☆ TR 128-129 B 3
Savate ○ ANG 216-217 D 8
Savè ○ DY 204-205 E 4
Save ~ F 90-91 H 10
Sāve ○• IR 136-137 B 7
Save ○ MOC 218-219 H 5
Save ~ ZW 218-219 G 5
Săveni ○ RO 102-103 E 4
Savigliano ○ I 100-101 A 2
Savina ~ RUS 108-109 F 6
Savinobor ○ RUS 114-115 D 3
Savinskij ○ RUS 88-89 Q 5
Savitaipale ○ FIN 88-89 J 6
Šavnik ○ YU 100-101 G 3
Savoff ○ CDN (ONT) 236-237 D 3
Savoie ∴ F 90-91 L 9
Savo Island ⌒ SOL 184 I d 3
Savona ○ CDN (BC) 230-231 J 3
Savona ☆• I 100-101 B 2
Savonlinna ○•• FIN 88-89 K 6
Savoonga ○ USA 20-21 E 5
Savory River ~ AUS 176-177 F 1
Šavot ○ US 136-137 G 4
Savu = Pulau Sawu ⌒ RI 168 E 8
Savu = Sawu ○ RI 168 E 8
Savukoski ○ FIN 88-89 K 3
Savusavu ○ FJI 184 III b 2
Savusavu Bay ≈ 184 III b 2
Savu Sea = Sawu, Laut ≈ RI 166-167 A 6
Savute ~ RB 218-219 B 4
Saw ○ MYA 142-143 J 5
Sawādiya, as- ○ Y 132-133 D 6
Sawadori ○ RI 166-167 J 2
Sawahlunto ○ RI 162-163 D 5
Sawai ○ RI 166-167 E 3
Sawai Mādhopur ○ IND 138-139 F 7
Sawaleke ○ FJI 184 III b 2
Sawang Dan Din ○ THA 158-159 G 2
Sawāq ○ KSA 130-131 E 4
Sawara ○ J 152-153 J 7
Sawāri ○ IRQ 128-129 K 5
Sawatch Mountains ▲▲ USA (CO) 254-255 J 4
Sawbill Landing ○ USA (MN) 270-271 G 3
Sawfajjin ~ LAR 192-193 F 2
Sawfajjin, Wādī ~ LAR 192-193 F 2
Sawi ○ THA 158-159 E 5
Sawia ○ RI 166-167 L 3
Šāwiya, aš- ○ IRQ 130-131 J 2
Sawkanah ○ LAR 192-193 F 3
Sawla ○ GH 202-203 J 5
Sawmill ○ USA (AZ) 256-257 F 3
Sawmill Bay ○ CDN 30-31 L 3
Sawmills ○ ZW 218-219 E 4
Sawn, Laut ≈ 168 E 7
Sawtooth Mount ▲ USA 20-21 Q 4
Sawtooth Mountains ▲▲ USA (ID) 252-253 D 2
Sawtooth National Recreation Area ⊥ USA (ID) 252-253 D 3
Sawtooth Wilderness Area ⊥ USA (ID) 252-253 C 2
Sawu ○• RI 168 E 8
Sawu, Kepulauan ⌒ RI 168 E 8
Sawu, Pulau ⌒ RI 168 E 8
Sawyer ○ USA (KS) 262-263 H 7
Sawyer ○ USA (MI) 272-273 C 6
Sawyer ○ USA (MN) 270-271 F 4
Saxby Downs ○ AUS 174-175 G 7
Saxis ○ USA (VA) 280-281 L 6
Saxon ○ CDN (NS) 240-241 K 7
Saxon ○ USA (WI) 270-271 H 4
Say ○ RMM 202-203 H 3
Say ○ RN 204-205 E 2
Sayabec ○ CDN (QUE) 240-241 H 2
Sayafi, Pulau ⌒ RI 164-165 L 3
Sāyalkudi ○ IND 140-141 H 6
Sayan ○ PE 64-65 D 7
Sayang, Pulau ⌒ RI 166-167 E 1
Sayaxché ○ GCA 52-53 J 3
Sayengga ○ RI 166-167 G 3
Sayil ∴• MEX 52-53 K 1
Saylac ○ SP 208-209 F 3
Saylor Creek Aerial Gunnery Range ✗✗ USA (ID) 252-253 C 4
Sayner ○ USA (WI) 270-271 J 5
Sayram Hu ⊖ VRC 146-147 E 3
Sayre ○ USA (OK) 264-265 E 3
Sayre ○ USA (PA) 280-281 K 2
Say Tha Ni ○ LAO 156-157 C 7
Sayula ○ MEX 52-53 C 2
Sayula de Alemán ○ MEX 52-53 G 3
Sayward ○ CDN (BC) 230-231 D 3
Sayyāni, as- ○ Y 132-133 D 7
Šāzand ○ IR 134-135 C 2
Sázava ~ CZ 92-93 N 4
Sazin ○ PK 138-139 D 2
Sazonovo ○ RUS 94-95 O 2
Saztöbe ○ KA 136-137 M 3
Sazykuľ, ozero ⊖ RUS 114-115 J 7
Sbaa ○ DZ 188-189 L 6
Sbeitla ○ TN 190-191 G 3
Scaër ○ F 90-91 F 7
Scafell Pike ▲ GB 90-91 F 4
Scales Mound ○ USA (IL) 274-275 H 2
Scammon Bay ≈ 20-21 G 6
Scammon Bay ○ USA 20-21 H 6
Scamp Hill ▲ AUS 176-177 J 2
Scandia ○ CDN (ALB) 232-233 F 5
Scandia ○ USA (KS) 262-263 J 5
Scandola, La ∪••• F 98-99 M 3
Scapa ○ CDN (ALB) 232-233 G 4
Scapegoat Wilderness Area ⊥ USA (MT) 250-251 G 4
Scappoose ○ USA (OR) 244-245 C 5
Ščara ~ BY 94-95 J 5
Scarborough ○• GB 90-91 G 4
Scarborough Shoal ⌒ 160-161 B 5
Scarth ○ CDN (MAN) 234-235 C 5
Ščast'ja, zaliv ⊖ RUS 122-123 J 2
Scawfell Bank ≃ 158-159 J 7
Scawfell Island ⌒ AUS 174-175 K 7
Sceccai Reba ▲ ER 200-201 H 4
Ščekino ☆• RUS 94-95 P 5
Ščeljabož ○ RUS 88-89 Y 3
Ščeljajur ○ RUS 88-89 W 4
Ščelkovo ☆ RUS 94-95 Q 4
Scenic ○ USA (SD) 260-261 D 3
Scenic Narrow Gauge Steam Railroad • USA (CO) 254-255 H 6
Ščerbakovo ○ KA 124-125 D 2
Schaffhausen ☆• CH 92-93 K 5
Schakalskuppe ○ NAM 220-221 C 3
Schefferville ○ CDN 36-37 Q 7
Schei Peninsula ∪ CDN 26-27 F 3
Schelde ~ B 92-93 G 3
Schell Creek Range ▲▲ USA (NV) 246-247 L 5
Schemnitz = Banská Štiavnica ○ SK 92-93 P 4
Schenectady ○ USA (NY) 278-279 H 6
Scheveningen ○• NL 92-93 H 2
Schidni Karpaty ▲▲ UA 102-103 C 3
Schiermonnikoog ⌒ NL 92-93 J 2
Schleinitz Ranch ▲▲ PNG 183 F 2
Schleinitz Range ▲▲ PNG 183 F 2
Schleswig ○• D 92-93 K 1
Schleswig-Holstein □ D 92-93 K 1
Schlüchtern ○ D 92-93 K 3
Schluderns = Sluderno ○ I 100-101 C 1
Schmidtsdrif ○ ZA 220-221 G 4
Schnauders Øer ⌒ GRØ 26-27 q 4
Schoen Lake Provincial Park ⊥ CDN (BC) 230-231 C 3
Schoharie Creek ~ USA (NY) 278-279 G 6
Schoodic Lake ⊖ USA (ME) 278-279 N 3
Schoodic Point ▲ USA (ME) 278-279 O 4
Schoolcraft ○ USA (MI) 272-273 D 5
Schoombee ○ ZA 220-221 G 5
Schouten Island ⌒ AUS 180-181 J 7
Schouten Islands ⌒ PNG 183 C 2
Schouwen ∴ NL 92-93 G 3
Schrader Range ▲▲ PNG 183 C 3
Schreiber ○ CDN (ONT) 234-235 Q 6
Schrobenhausen ○ D 92-93 L 4
Schroda = Środa Wielkopolska ○ PL 92-93 O 2
Schroeder ○ USA (MN) 270-271 H 3
Schroffenstein ▲ NAM 220-221 D 3
Schuchert Flod ≈ 26-27 n 8
Schuckmansburg ○ NAM 218-219 C 3
Schulenburg ○ USA (TX) 266-267 L 4
Schuler ○ CDN (ALB) 232-233 H 5
Schuls, Scuols/ ○ CH 92-93 L 5
Schultz Lake ⊖ CDN 30-31 V 3
Schurz ○ USA (NV) 246-247 G 5
Schuyler ○ USA (NE) 262-263 J 3
Schuylkill River ~ USA (PA) 280-281 L 3
Schwabach ○ D 92-93 L 4
Schwäbische Alb ▲▲ D 92-93 K 4
Schwäbisch Gmünd ○• D 92-93 K 4
Schwäbisch Hall ○• D 92-93 K 4
Schwandorf ○ D 92-93 M 4
Schwaner, Pegunungan ▲▲ RI 162-163 J 5
Schwarzrand ▲▲ NAM 220-221 C 2
Schwarzwald ▲▲ D 92-93 K 4
Schwatka Mountains ▲▲ USA 20-21 M 3
Schwedt ○ D 92-93 N 2
Schweinfurt ○ D 92-93 L 3
Schweitzergletscher ⊂ ARK 16 F 33
Schweizer Jura ▲▲ CH 92-93 J 5
Schweizerland ∴ GRØ 28-29 W 3
Schweizer Reneke ○ ZA 220-221 G 3
Schwerin ☆• D 92-93 L 2
Schwerin Mural Crescent ▲▲ AUS 176-177 K 2
Schwyz ☆ CH 92-93 K 5
Sciacca ○ I 100-101 D 6
Scie, La ○ CDN (NFL) 242-243 N 3
Scieri, La ○ G 210-211 D 3
Ščigry ○ RUS 102-103 K 2
Scioto River ~ USA (OH) 280-281 C 4
Scipio ○ USA (UT) 254-255 C 4
Ščit, gora ▲ RUS 112-113 R 3
Scituate ○ USA (MA) 278-279 L 6
Sclater ○ CDN (MAN) 234-235 C 3
Scobey ○ USA (MT) 250-251 O 3
Scone ○ AUS 180-181 L 2
Scoresby Land ∴ GRØ 26-27 n 8
Scoresbysund = Ittoqqortoormiit ○ GRØ 26-27 p 8
Scotch Creek ~ CDN (BC) 230-231 K 2
Scotfield ○ CDN (ALB) 232-233 G 4
Scotia ○ USA (CA) 246-247 A 3
Scotia ○ USA (NE) 262-263 H 3
Scotia Bay ○ CDN 20-21 Y 7
Scotia Sea ≈ 6-7 E 14
Scotland ○ CDN (ONT) 238-239 E 5
Scotland ○ USA (SD) 260-261 J 3
Scotland Neck ○ USA (NC) 282-283 K 4
Scotsburn ○ CDN (NS) 240-241 N 5
Scotsguard ○ CDN (SAS) 232-233 K 6
Scotstour Lake ⊖ CDN 30-31 M 3
Scotstown ○ CDN (QUE) 238-239 O 3
Scotsville ○ CDN (NS) 240-241 O 4
Scott ○ ARK 16 F 17
Scott ○ CDN (SAS) 232-233 K 3
Scott, Cape ▲ AUS 172-173 J 2
Scott, Cape ▲ CDN (BC) 230-231 A 3
Scott, Cape ▲ CDN (NWT) 24-25 O 2
Scott, Mount ▲ AUS 178-179 K 1
Scott Channel ≈ 32-33 F 6
Scott Channel ≈ CDN 230-231 A 3
Scott City ○ USA (KS) 262-263 F 6
Scott City ○ USA (MO) 276-277 F 3
Scott Glacier ⊂ ARK 16 E 0
Scott Glacier ⊂ ARK 16 G 11
Scott Inlet ≈ 26-27 P 8
Scott Islands ⌒ CDN (BC) 230-231 A 3
Scott Lake ⊖ CDN 30-31 Q 6
Scott National Historic Site, Fort ∴ USA (KS) 262-263 M 7
Scott Point ▲ AUS 174-175 D 3
Scott Range ▲▲ ARK 16 G 6
Scott Reef ⌒ AUS 172-173 F 2
Scotts Bay ○ CDN (NS) 240-241 L 5
Scottsbluff ○ USA (NE) 262-263 C 3
Scotts Bluff National Monument ∴ USA (NE) 262-263 C 3
Scottsboro ○ USA (AL) 284-285 D 2
Scottsburg ○ USA (IN) 274-275 N 6
Scottsdale ○ AUS 180-181 J 6
Scottsdale ○ USA (AZ) 256-257 D 5
Scottsville ○ USA (KY) 276-277 J 4
Scottsville ○ USA (VA) 280-281 H 6
Scottville ○ USA (MI) 272-273 C 4
Scotty's Castle • USA (CA) 248-249 G 2
Scotty's Junction ○ USA (NV) 248-249 G 2
Scout Lake ○ CDN (SAS) 232-233 N 6
Scraggy Lake ⊖ CDN (NS) 240-241 N 5
Scranton ○ USA (AR) 276-277 B 5
Scranton ○ USA (NC) 282-283 L 5
Scranton ○ USA (ND) 258-259 D 5
Scranton ○ USA (PA) 280-281 L 2
Screven ○ USA (GA) 284-285 H 5
Scribner ○ USA (NE) 262-263 K 3
Ščuč'e ○ RUS (JAN) 108-109 N 8
Ščuč'e ☆ RUS (KRG) 114-115 G 7
Ščuč'e, ozero ⊖ RUS 114-115 J 7
Ščuč'e Ozero ○ RUS 96-97 K 5
Ščučij hrebet ▲▲ RUS 112-113 P 4
Ščučinsk ☆ KA 124-125 G 2
Ščučja ~ RUS 108-109 M 8
Ščučyn ○ BY 94-95 J 5
Ščugor ~ RUS 114-115 E 3
Scuol/ Schuls ○ CH 92-93 L 5
Sea-Arama Marineworld • USA (TX) 268-269 F 7
Seabird Resting Pulau ⊥• RI 166-167 C 5
Seabra ○ BR 72-73 K 2
Seabrook ○ USA (TX) 268-269 E 7
Seabrook, Lake ⊖ AUS 176-177 E 5
Seadrift ○ USA (TX) 266-267 L 5
Seafoam ○ CDN (NS) 240-241 N 5
Seaford ○ USA (DE) 280-281 L 5
Seaforth ○ AUS 174-175 K 7
Seaforth ○ CDN (ONT) 238-239 D 5
Seagoville ○ USA (TX) 264-265 H 6
Seagraves ○ USA (TX) 264-265 B 6
Seahorse Island ⌒ USA 20-21 L 1
Seahorse Point ▲ CDN 36-37 J 3
Sea Islands ⌒ USA (GA) 284-285 K 5
Sea Isle City ○ USA (NJ) 280-281 M 4
Sea Lake ○ AUS 180-181 G 3
Seal Cape ▲ USA 22-23 R 5
Seal Cove ○ CDN (NB) 240-241 J 6
Seal Cove ○ CDN (NFL) 242-243 M 3
Seale ○ USA (AL) 284-285 E 4
Seal Harbour ○ CDN (NS) 240-241 O 5
Sealhole Lake ⊖ CDN 30-31 U 5
Seal Lion Islands ⌒ GB 78-79 L 7
Seal Island ⌒ CDN (NS) 240-241 J 7
Seal Islands ⌒ USA 22-23 R 4
Seal Reserve • NAM 216-217 B 10
Seal River ~ CDN 30-31 W 6
Seal Rock ○ USA (OR) 244-245 A 6
Sealy ○ USA (TX) 266-267 L 4
Seaman ○ USA (OH) 280-281 C 5
Sea Otter Sound ≈ 32-33 D 4
Sea Park ○ ZA 220-221 K 5
Seara ○ BR 74-75 D 6
Searchlight ○ USA (NV) 248-249 K 4
Searchmont ○ CDN (ONT) 236-237 D 6
Searcy ○ USA (AR) 276-277 D 5
Searles ○ USA (CA) 248-249 G 4
Searles Lake ⊖ USA (CA) 248-249 G 4
Searsport ○ USA (ME) 278-279 N 4
Seashore Shoal ≃ 162-163 K 2
Seaside ○ USA (OR) 244-245 B 5
Seaside Heights ○ USA (NJ) 280-281 M 4
Seaspray ○ AUS 180-181 J 5
Seattle ○• USA (WA) 244-245 C 3
Seaward Kaikoura Range ▲▲ NZ 182 D 5
Seba ○ RI 168 E 8
Sébaco ○ NIC 52-53 L 5
Sebago Lake ⊖ USA (ME) 278-279 L 5
Sebakor, Teluk ≈ 166-167 G 3
Šebalino ○ RUS 124-125 O 3
Sebamban ○ RI 164-165 D 5
Sebangan Teluk ≈ 162-163 K 6
Sebangka, Pulau ⌒ RI 162-163 F 4
Sebapala ○ LS 220-221 H 5
Sebarak ○ RI 166-167 G 3
Sebastian ○ USA (FL) 286-287 J 4
Sebastián Vizcaíno, Bahía de ≈ 50-51 B 3
Sebatik, Pulau ⌒ RI 164-165 E 1
Sebauh ○ MAL 162-163 K 3
Sebayan, Gunung ▲ RI 162-163 J 5
Sebba ○ BF 202-203 L 3
Sebderat ○ ER 200-201 H 5
Sebdou ○ DZ 188-189 L 3
Sébé ~ G 210-211 D 4
Sébé ○ TCH 206-207 D 4
Sebec Lake ○ USA (ME) 278-279 M 3
Sebec Lake ⊖ USA (ME) 278-279 M 3
Šebekino ○ RUS 102-103 K 2
Sébékoro ○ RG 202-203 F 3
Šeberğān ☆ AFG 136-137 J 6
Seberida ○ RI 162-163 E 5
Sebeş ○ RO 102-103 C 5
Sebesi, Pulau ⌒ RI 162-163 F 7
Sebeta ○ ETH 208-209 D 4
Sébété ○ RMM 202-203 G 2
Sebewaing ○ USA (MI) 272-273 F 4
Sebež ☆ RUS 94-95 L 3
Şebinkarahisar ☆ TR 128-129 H 2
Sebino = Lago d'Iseo ⊖ I 100-101 C 2
Sebiş ○ RO 102-103 C 4
Sebit ○ EAK 212-213 E 3
Sebjaki ~ RUS 108-109 b 7
Sebjan-Kjuëľ ○ RUS 110-111 R 7
Seblat, Gunung ▲ RI 162-163 E 6
Seboeis Lake ⊖ USA (ME) 278-279 N 3
Sebol ○ GCA 52-53 K 4
Sebonpopo ○ RI 164-165 L 3
Seboomook Lake ⊖ USA (ME) 278-279 M 3
Seboto Point ▲ RP 160-161 E 9
Sebou, Oued ~ MA 188-189 J 3
Seboyeta ○ USA (NM) 256-257 H 3
Sebree ○ USA (KY) 276-277 H 3
Sebring ○ USA (FL) 286-287 H 4
Sebta = Ceuta ○ E 98-99 E 7
Sebuku, Pulau ⌒ RI (KSE) 164-165 E 5
Sebuku, Pulau ⌒ RI (LAM) 162-163 F 7
Sebuku Teluk ≈ 164-165 E 2
Šebunino ○ RUS 122-123 J 5
Sebuyau ○ MAL 162-163 J 4
Sebyar ~ RI 166-167 G 2
Sëbys' ~ RUS 88-89 W 4
Seca, Cachoeira ~ BR 66-67 K 5
Seca, Pampa ∴ RA 78-79 F 3
Secang ○ RI 168 D 3
Secca Abū el-cosu ⌒ ER 200-201 K 5
Sechelt ○ CDN (BC) 230-231 F 4
Sechura ○ PE 64-65 B 4
Sechura, Bahía de ≈ 64-65 B 4
Sechura, Desierto de ∴ PE 64-65 B 4
Seco, Río ~ RA 76-77 E 4
Seco de las Peñas, Río ~ RA 78-79 E 3
Second Mesa ○ USA (AZ) 256-257 E 3
Seco ó Yaminué, Arroyo ~ RA 78-79 F 6
Secos ou do Rombo, Ilheus ⌒ CV 202-203 B 6
Secretary Island ⌒ NZ 182 A 6
Secunderābād ○ IND 140-141 H 2
Sécure, Río ~ BOL 70-71 E 4
Security-Widefield ○ USA (CO) 254-255 L 5
Seda ○ LT 94-95 H 3
Sedalia ○ USA (MO) 274-275 E 6
Sedan ○ AUS (QLD) 178-179 G 3
Sedan ○ AUS (SA) 180-181 E 3
Sedan ○ F 90-91 K 7
Sedan ○ USA (KS) 262-263 K 7
Sedan ○ USA (NM) 256-257 M 2
Sedanka ○ RUS 120-121 S 5
Sedanka ~ RUS 120-121 S 5
Sedanka Island ⌒ USA 22-23 N 6
Sedati ○ RI 168 E 3
Seddenga, Temple of • SUD 200-201 E 2
Seddon, Kap ▲ GRØ 26-27 V 6
Seddons Corner ○ CDN (MAN) 234-235 G 4
Seddonville ○ NZ 182 C 4
Sededema ~ RUS 110-111 b 6
Sedeh ○ IR 134-135 H 2
Sedeľnikovo ○ RUS 114-115 N 6
Sederberge ▲▲ ZA 220-221 D 6
Sedgefield ○ ZA 220-221 F 7
Sedgewick ○ CDN (ALB) 232-233 G 3
Sedgwick ○ USA (CO) 254-255 N 3
Sedgwick ○ USA (KS) 262-263 J 7
Sédhiou ○ SN 202-203 C 3
Sedič ○ IR 134-135 J 5
Sedič, Rūdḫāne-ye ~ IR 134-135 H 6
Sed"ju ~ RUS 88-89 W 5
Sedley ○ CDN (SAS) 232-233 O 5
Sedoa ○ RI 164-165 G 4
Sedom ○• IL 130-131 D 2
Sedona ○ USA (AZ) 256-257 D 4
Sedova, pik ▲ RUS 108-109 F 5
Sedova, zaliv ⊖ RUS 108-109 H 4
Sedrata ○ DZ 190-191 F 2
Sedro Woolley ○ USA (WA) 244-245 C 2
Šeduva ○•• LT 94-95 H 4
Seebe ○ CDN (ALB) 232-233 C 4
Seeber ○ RA 76-77 G 6
Seedskadee National Wildlife Refuge ⊥ USA (WY) 252-253 J 5
Seeheim ○ NAM 220-221 C 3
Seeis ○ NAM 216-217 D 11
Seeis ~ NAM 216-217 D 11
Seekaskootch Indian Reserve ✗ CDN (SAS) 232-233 J 2
Seekoegat ○ ZA 220-221 F 6
Seekoerivier ~ ZA 220-221 G 5
Seeley Lake ○ USA (MT) 250-251 F 4
Seely ○ USA (WY) 252-253 O 2
Seelyville ○ USA (IN) 274-275 L 5
Seemore Downs ○ AUS 176-177 H 5
Sèèr ○ MAU 146-147 L 1
Şefaatli ☆ TR 128-129 F 3
Seferihisar ☆ TR 128-129 B 3
Séféto ○ RMM 202-203 E 2
Sefidābe ○ IR 134-135 J 3
Sefidān, Rūdḫāne-ye ~ IR 134-135 F 3
Sefid Rūd ~ IR 128-129 N 4
Sefophe ○ RB 218-219 D 6
Sefrou ○ MA 188-189 J 4
Sefton, Mount ▲ AUS 176-177 G 4
Segaf, Kepulauan ⌒ RI 166-167 F 3
Segag ○ ETH 208-209 F 5
Segala ⌒ ER 200-201 K 5
Ségala ○ RMM 202-203 E 2
Segalaherang ○ RI 168 B 3
Segama ~ MAL 160-161 C 10
Segamat ○ MAL 162-163 E 3
Segara Anakan ≈ 168 C 3
Šegarka ~ RUS 114-115 R 6
Ségbana ○ DY 204-205 E 3
Segbwema ○ WAL 202-203 E 6
Segen Wenz ~ ETH 208-209 C 6
Segera ○ EAT 212-213 G 6
Segeri ○ RI 164-165 F 6
Seget ○ RI 166-167 F 2
Segeža ○ RUS 88-89 N 5
Seghe ○ SOL 184 I c 3
Segjan-Kjuëľ ○ RUS 118-119 P 4
Šegmas ○ RUS 88-89 U 4
Segnān ○ AFG 136-137 M 6
Segno ○ USA (TX) 268-269 F 6
Segoch, Kūh-e ▲ IR 134-135 G 3
Ségou □ RMM 202-203 G 2
Ségou ☆ RMM (SÉ) 202-203 G 3
Segovia ○ CO 60-61 D 4
Segovia ○••• E 98-99 E 4
Segozero ⊖ RUS 88-89 M 5
Segré ○ F 90-91 G 8
Segre, el ~ E 98-99 H 4
Seguam Island ⌒ USA 22-23 K 6
Seguam Pass ≈ 22-23 K 6
Ségué ○ RMM 202-203 J 3
Seguedine ○ RN 198-199 F 2
Séguéla ☆ CI 202-203 G 6
Séguéla ○ RMM 202-203 G 3
Seguéla ○ RMM 202-203 G 3
Séguénéga ○ BF 202-203 K 3
Seguin ○ USA (TX) 266-267 K 4
Seguin River ~ CDN (ONT) 238-239 F 3
Segula Island ⌒ USA 22-23 F 6
Segunda, Río ~ RA 76-77 F 6
Segura ○ P 98-99 D 5
Segura, Sierra de ▲▲ E 98-99 F 5
Seguro ○ BR 68-69 E 2
Sehān ~ PK 138-139 B 4
Sehesteds Fjord ≈ 28-29 T 5
Sehithwa ○ RB 218-219 B 5
Sehnkwehn River ~ LB 202-203 F 6
Seho, Pulau ⌒ RI 164-165 J 4
Sehonghong ○ LS 220-221 J 4
Sehore ○ IND 138-139 F 8
Sehulea ○ PNG 183 F 5
Sehwān ○•• PK 134-135 M 5
Seia ○ P 98-99 D 4
Seibert ○ USA (CO) 254-255 N 4
Seibo, El ☆ DOM 54-55 L 5
Seigals Creek ○ AUS 174-175 D 5
Seiḥ 'Ali ○ AFG 138-139 B 2
Seikan Tunnel •• J 152-153 J 4
Seikpyu ○ MYA 142-143 J 5
Seiland ⌒ N 86-87 L 1
Seiling ○ USA (OK) 264-265 F 2
Seille ~ F 90-91 K 8
Seinäjoki ○ FIN 88-89 G 5
Seine ~ F 90-91 H 7
Seine, Baie de la ≈ 90-91 G 7
Seine Bank ≃ 188-189 D 4
Seine River ~ CDN (ONT) 234-235 L 6
Seinma ○ RI 166-167 K 4
Seira, Pulau ⌒ RI 166-167 F 5
Seis de Julho, Cachoeira ~ BR 66-67 F 7
Seival ○ BR 74-75 D 8
Šeja ○ RUS 118-119 H 4
Sējaha ○ RUS (JAN) 108-109 P 6
Sējaha ~ RUS 108-109 N 6
Sējaha ~ RUS 108-109 O 7
Sejaka ○ RI 164-165 E 5
Sejenane ○ TN 190-191 G 2
Sejm ~ RUS 102-103 K 2
Sejm ~ UA 102-103 J 2
Sejm ~ UA 102-103 H 2
Sejmčan ☆• RUS 120-121 P 2
Sejmčan ~ RUS 120-121 O 2
Sejmčan ~ RUS 118-119 N 7
Sejmkan ~ RUS 120-121 N 3
Sejorong ○ RI 168 C 7
Seka ○ ETH 208-209 C 5
Seka Banza ○ ZRE 210-211 D 6
Sekak ○ RI 166-167 G 2
Sekampung ~ RI 162-163 F 7
Sekatak Teluk ≈ 164-165 E 2
Sekayu ○ RI 162-163 E 6
Sekenke ○ EAT 212-213 E 6
Seki ○ J 152-153 G 7
Šeki = Şəki ○• AZ 128-129 M 2
Sekigahara-Oro Quasi National Park ⊥ J 152-153 G 7
Sekinchan, Kampung ○ MAL 162-163 D 3
Sekoma ○ RB 220-221 F 2
Sekondi ☆• GH 202-203 J 7
Sek'ot'a ○ ETH 200-201 J 6

Šeksna ○ RUS 94-95 Q 2
Sela Dingay ○ ETH 208-209 D 4
Šelagskij, mys ▲ RUS 112-113 Q 1
Selah ○ USA (WA) 244-245 E 4
Şelâle • TR 128-129 D 4
Selama ○ MAL 162-163 D 2
Selangor □ MAL 162-163 D 3
Selangor, Kuala ○ MAL 162-163 D 3
Sela Nok ○ MYA 142-143 J 2
Selaphum ○ THA 158-159 G 2
Selapiu Island ⌒ PNG 183 F 2
Selaru, Pulau ⌒ RI 166-167 F 6
Šelaša ○ RUS 88-89 R 6
Selassi ○ RI 166-167 G 3
Selatan, Tanjung ▲ RI 164-165 D 6
Selatan Natuna Kepulauan ≈ 162-163 H 3
Selatpanjang ○ RI 162-163 E 4
Selawik ○ USA 20-21 K 3
Selawik Lake ⊂ USA 20-21 K 3
Selawik River ~ USA 20-21 L 3
Selayar = Benteng ○ RI 168 E 6
Selayar, Pulau ⌒ RI (JAM) 162-163 F 5
Selayar, Pulau ⌒ RI (SSE) 168 E 5
Selayar, Selat ≈ 164-165 G 6
Sélba ○ BF 202-203 K 2
Selbach ○ BR 74-75 D 7
Selbu ○ N 86-87 E 5
Selby ○ USA (SD) 260-261 F 1
Selbyville ○ USA (DE) 280-281 L 5
Selçuk ☆ • TR 128-129 B 4
Selden ○ USA (KS) 262-263 F 5
Seldja, Gorges du • TN 190-191 G 3
Seldovia ○ USA 22-23 V 3
Sele, Selat ≈ 166-167 F 2
Sele, Tanjung ▲ RI 166-167 F 2
Selebi-Phikwe ○ RB 218-219 D 6
Šelehov ○ RUS 116-117 L 9
Selemadeg ○ RI 168 B 7
Selemdža ~ RUS 122-123 F 2
Selemdža ~ RUS 122-123 C 3
Selemdžinskij, hrebet ▲ RUS 122-123 D 2
Selendi ☆ TR 128-129 C 3
Selenga ~ RUS 116-117 N 9
Sèlèngè ○ MAU 148-149 E 3
Sèlèngè □ MAU 148-149 G 3
Selengei ○ EAK 212-213 F 5
Sèlèngè mörön ~ MAU 148-149 G 3
Selenginsk ○ RUS 116-117 N 10
Selennahskij hrebet ▲ RUS 110-111 V 4
Selennjah ~ RUS 110-111 W 5
Sele Pele, Tanjung ▲ RI 166-167 F 2
Sélestat ○ • F 90-91 L 7
Séléti ○ SN 202-203 B 3
Selfoss ☆ IS 86-87 c 3
Selfridge ○ USA (ND) 258-259 G 5
Seľgi ○ RUS 88-89 M 5
Selib ○ RUS 88-89 U 5
Sélibaby ☆ RIM 202-203 D 2
Seliger, ozero ⊂ RUS 94-95 N 3
Seligman ○ USA (AZ) 256-257 C 3
Seligman ○ USA (MO) 276-277 B 4
Selihino ○ RUS 122-123 G 3
Šelihova, zaliv ≈ 120-121 R 3
Sélim ○ RCA 206-207 H 6
Seling ○ IND 142-143 H 4
Sélingue, Lac de < RMM 202-203 F 4
Sélinnkegni ○ RMM 202-203 E 2
Selinsgrove ○ USA (PA) 280-281 K 3
Selitkan ~ RUS 122-123 E 2
Seližarovo ☆ RUS 94-95 N 3
Seljanskaja guba ≈ 110-111 W 4
Seljelvnes ○ N 86-87 J 2
Selkämeri ≈ 88-89 E 6
Selkirk ○ CDN (MAN) 234-235 G 4
Selkirk ○ CDN (ONT) 238-239 F 6
Selkirk Island ⌒ CDN 34-35 G 4
Selkirk Mountains ▲ CDN (BC) 230-231 M 2
Selkirk Mountains ▲ USA (ID) 250-251 C 3
Selle, Massif de la ▲ RH 54-55 J 5
Selleck ○ USA (WA) 244-245 D 3
Sellers ○ USA (AL) 284-285 D 4
Sellers ○ USA (MS) 268-269 L 6
Sellersburg ○ USA (IN) 274-275 M 6
Selles-sur-Cher ○ F 90-91 H 8
Selljah ~ RUS 110-111 X 4
Sello, Lago del ○ RA 80 E 3
Sells ○ USA (AZ) 256-257 D 7
Selma ○ USA (AL) 284-285 C 4
Selma ○ USA (CA) 248-249 E 3
Selmer ○ USA (TN) 276-277 G 5
Selokan, Tanjung ▲ RI 162-163 F 6
Sélo Kouré ○ RG 202-203 E 4
Selong ○ RI 168 C 7
Šelonskie ostrova ⌒ RUS 110-111 W 4
Šelopugino ☆ RUS 118-119 H 10
Selouane ○ MA 188-189 K 3
Selous ○ ZW 218-219 F 4
Selous, Mount ▲ CDN 20-21 Y 5
Selous Game Reserve ⊥ ••• EAT 214-215 J 5
Selsele-ye Pir-e Šūrān ▲ IR 134-135 J 4
Selter Island ⌒ CDN (ONT) 234-235 Q 6
Šeľtinga ○ RUS 120-121 M 4
Šeľtinga, zaliv ⊂ RUS 120-121 N 4
Selty ☆ RUS 96-97 H 5
Selu ○ IND 138-139 F 10
Selu, Pulau ⌒ RI 166-167 F 5
Selva Alegre ○ EC 64-65 C 1
Selvagens, Ilhas ⌒ P 188-189 D 5
Selvas ∸ BR 66-67 D 5
Selvíria ○ BR 72-73 E 6
Selway-Bitterroot Wilderness ⊥ USA (ID) 250-251 D 5
Selway Falls ~ USA (ID) 250-251 D 5
Selway River ~ USA (ID) 250-251 D 5
Selwyn, Detroit de ≈ 184 II b 3
Selwyn Lake ⊂ CDN 30-31 R 5
Selwyn Mountains ▲ CDN 20-21 X 4
Selwyn Post Office ○ AUS 178-179 F 1
Selwyn Range ▲ AUS 178-179 F 1
Semajang, Danau ⊂ RI 164-165 E 4
Semamung ○ RI 168 C 7
Semangka ~ RI 162-163 F 7
Semangka, Teluk ≈ 162-163 F 7
Semans ○ CDN (SAS) 232-233 O 4
Semanu ○ RI 164-165 E 2
Semarang ☆ RI 168 D 3
Semaras ○ RI 164-165 E 5
Sematan ○ MAL 162-163 H 4
Semau, Pulau ⌒ RI 166-167 B 7
Sembabule ○ EAU 212-213 C 4
Sembakung ~ RI 164-165 E 2
Sembatti ○ IND 140-141 G 5
Sembe ○ LB 202-203 E 6
Sembé ○ RCB 210-211 E 3
Sembehon ○ WAL 202-203 E 6
Sembehun ○ WAL 202-203 D 6
Semberang ○ RI 164-165 F 3
Semberong ~ MAL 162-163 E 3
Sembilan, Negeri □ MAL 162-163 E 3
Sembilan, P. ▲ RI 162-163 D 2
Şemdinli ☆ TR 128-129 L 4
Sémé ○ CI 202-203 G 4
Semeih ○ SUD 200-201 E 6
Semejka, gora ▲ RUS 110-111 V 5
Sèmè-Kpodji ○ DY 204-205 E 5
Semenanjung Blambangan Game Park ⊥ RI 168 B 7
Semenov ○ RUS 96-97 D 5
Semenovka ○ KA 124-125 L 3
Semënovka ○ RUS 122-123 B 3
Semera ○ MAL 162-163 J 4
Semeteh ○ RI 162-163 E 6
Semey ○ KA 124-125 M 3
Semiahmoo Bay ≈ USA 244-245 C 2
Semiai, Pulau ⌒ RI 166-167 G 3
Semichi Islands ⌒ USA 22-23 C 6
Semi Desert ∸ AUS 174-175 C 7
Semidi Islands ⌒ USA 22-23 S 4
Sémien ○ CI 202-203 G 6
Semikarakorsk ○ RUS 102-103 M 4
Semillero ○ GCA 52-53 J 4
Semiluki ○ RUS 102-103 L 2
Seminoe Dam ○ USA (WY) 252-253 M 4
Seminoe Reservoir ⊂ USA (WY) 252-253 M 4
Seminole ○ USA (OK) 264-265 H 3
Seminole ○ USA (TX) 264-265 B 6
Seminole, Lake < USA (GA) 284-285 F 6
Seminole Draw ~ USA (TX) 264-265 B 6
Seminskij, pereval ▲ RUS 124-125 O 3
Semiozernoe ☆ KA 124-125 D 2
Semipalatinsk = Semey ○ KA 124-125 M 3
Semirara Island ⌒ RP 160-161 D 6
Semirom ○ IR 134-135 D 3
Semisopochnoi Island ⌒ USA 22-23 F 7
Semitau ○ RI 162-163 J 4
Semliki ~ ZRE 212-213 B 3
Semna ○ SUD 200-201 E 2
Semnān □ IR 136-137 C 6
Semnān ☆ • IR 136-137 C 7
Semolale ○ RB 218-219 E 5
Semonaiha ○ KA 124-125 M 3
Semongkat ○ RI 168 C 7
Sempang Mangayan, Tanjung ▲ MAL 160-161 B 9
Sempol ○ • RI 168 B 7
Semporna ○ MAL 160-161 C 10
Sempu, Pulau ⌒ RI 168 E 4
Šemšak ○ • IR 136-137 B 7
Sem-Tripa, Cachoeira ~ BR 66-67 K 5
Semu ~ EAT 212-213 E 5
Semuntai, Tanjung ▲ RI 164-165 F 3
Sěmža ○ RUS 88-89 S 3
Sen' ~ RUS 118-119 H 7
Sena ○ BOL 70-71 D 2
Sena, Rio ~ BOL 70-71 D 2
Senachwine Lake ⊂ USA (IL) 274-275 J 3
Senador ○ BR 68-69 H 3
Senador José Porfírio ○ BR 68-69 C 3
Senador Pompeu ○ BR 68-69 J 4
Sen'afē ○ ER 200-201 J 5
Senaki ○ • GE 126-127 E 6
Señal Canoas ▲ PE 64-65 D 7
Señal Huascarán ▲ PE 64-65 D 6
Señal Mongon ▲ PE 64-65 C 6
Señal Nevado Champará ▲ PE 64-65 D 6
Sena Madureira ○ BR 66-67 C 7
Senanga ○ Z 218-219 B 3
Senās, Ra's-e ▲ IR 134-135 F 5
Senate ○ CDN (SAS) 232-233 J 6
Senath ○ USA (MO) 276-277 E 4
Senatobia ○ USA (MS) 268-269 L 2
Senaton, Teluk ≈ 162-163 A 3
Sendafa ○ ETH 208-209 D 4
Sendai ○ J (KGA) 152-153 D 9
Sendai ☆ • J (MIY) 152-153 J 5
Sendai-wan ≈ 152-153 J 5
Sendān Dāg, Kūh-e ▲ IR 128-129 N 4
Sendelingsfontein ○ ZA 220-221 H 3
Sendhwa ○ IND 138-139 E 9
Senebui, Tanjung ▲ RI 162-163 D 3
Seneca ○ USA (AZ) 256-257 E 5
Seneca ○ USA (IL) 274-275 K 3
Seneca ○ USA (KS) 262-263 K 5
Seneca ○ USA (MO) 276-277 A 4
Seneca ○ USA (NE) 262-263 F 2
Seneca ○ USA (OR) 244-245 G 6
Seneca ○ USA (SC) 284-285 H 2
Seneca ○ USA (SD) 260-261 G 1
Seneca Caverns ∴ USA (WV) 280-281 G 5
Seneca Falls ○ USA (NY) 278-279 E 6
Seneca Lake ⊂ USA (NY) 278-279 E 6
Seneca Rocks ○ USA (WV) 280-281 G 5
Seneca Rocks National Recreation Area ⊥ USA (WV) 280-281 G 5
Senecaville Lake ⊂ USA (OH) 280-281 E 4
Sénégal ~ SN 196-197 C 6
Senegal = Sénégal ■ SN 202-203 C 2
Senekal ○ ZA 220-221 H 4
Senero, Rio ~ BOL 70-71 E 4
Seney ○ USA (MI) 270-271 N 4
Seney National Wildlife Refuge ⊥ USA (MI) 270-271 M 4
Senga ○ MW 218-219 H 1
Sengan ○ WAN 204-205 F 6
Sengana < WAN 204-205 F 6
Sengar ~ IND 138-139 G 6
Sengbo ○ RI 166-167 G 3
Senge ○ ZRE 212-213 B 5
Sengejskij, ostrov ⌒ RUS 88-89 V 2
Sênggê Zangbo ~ VRC 144-145 C 4
Senggigi ○ • RI 168 C 7
Sengilen, hrebet ▲ RUS 116-117 G 10
Sengkiju ~ RUS 110-111 J 5
Senguerr, Rio ~ RA 80 F 2
Sengwa ~ ZW 218-219 E 3
Senhora do Porto ○ BR 72-73 J 5
Senhor do Bonfim ○ BR 68-69 H 7
Senia, Bir < DZ 190-191 C 4
Senigállia ○ I 100-101 D 3
Senindara ○ RI 166-167 G 3
Senirkent ☆ TR 128-129 D 3
Senj ○ HR 100-101 E 2
Senja ⌒ N 86-87 H 2
Senjavina, proliv ≈ 112-113 Y 4
Senkanse ○ BF 202-203 L 4
Şenkaya ☆ TR 128-129 K 2
Senkobo ○ Z 218-219 C 3
Šenkursk ○ RUS 88-89 R 5
Senmonorom ○ K 158-159 J 4
Senmuto, ozero ⊂ RUS 114-115 P 2
Sennār ☆ • SUD 200-201 F 6
Sennār Dam < SUD 200-201 F 6
Senneterre ○ CDN (QUE) 236-237 L 4
Sennoj ○ RUS 96-97 E 7
Sénoba ○ SN 202-203 C 3
Senoia ○ USA (GA) 284-285 F 3
Senorbì ○ I 100-101 B 5
Sénoudébou ○ • SN 202-203 D 2
Senqunyana ~ LS 220-221 J 4
Sens ○ F 90-91 J 7
Senta ○ YU 100-101 H 2
Šentala ☆ RUS 96-97 G 6
Sentani, Danau ⊂ RI 166-167 L 3
Sentinel ○ USA (AZ) 256-257 B 6
Sentinel ○ USA (OK) 264-265 E 3
Sentinel Peak ▲ CDN (BC) 228-229 N 2
Sentinel Range ▲ ARK 16 F 28
Sentolo ○ RI 168 D 3
Sento Sé ○ BR 68-69 H 6
Sentrum ○ ZA 220-221 H 2
Senuda ○ RI 162-163 K 6
Senye ○ GQ 210-211 B 2
Senoath ~ IND 142-143 B 5
Seoni ○ IND 138-139 G 8
Seoni Mālwa ○ IND 138-139 F 8
Seorinārāyan ○ IND 142-143 C 5
Seoul = Sŏul ☆ ROK 150-151 F 9
Sepa ○ RI 166-167 E 3
Sepakat, Tanjung ▲ RI 164-165 E 2
Sepang ○ RI 168 E 7
Sepanjang, Pulau ⌒ RI 168 B 6
Separ ○ USA (NM) 256-257 G 6
Separation Point ○ CDN 38-39 Q 2
Separation Point ▲ NZ 182 D 4
Sepasu ○ RI 164-165 E 3
Sepat, Kampung ○ MAL 162-163 E 3
Sepatini, Rio ~ BR 66-67 E 6
Sepeteri ○ WAN 204-205 E 4
Šepetivka ☆ UA 102-103 E 2
Sepiddašt ○ IR 134-135 C 2
Sepik River ~ PNG 183 A 3
Sepilok Sancturay ⊥ MAL 160-161 B 10
Šepit ○ UA 102-103 D 4
Sepo ○ DVR 150-151 F 8
Sepo ○ RI 164-165 L 3
Sępólno Krajeńskie ○ PL 92-93 O 2
Sepon ○ IND 142-143 J 2
Sepoti, Rio ~ BR 66-67 G 6
Sepotuba, Rio ~ BR 70-71 J 4
Sept-des-Gzoula ○ MA 188-189 G 4
Septembre, Embalse de 15 < ES 52-53 K 5
Septentrional, Cordillera ▲ DOM 54-55 K 5
Sept-Îles ○ CDN (QUE) 242-243 B 2
Sept-Îles, Baie des ≈ 38-39 L 3
Sept-Îles, Baie des ≈ CDN 242-243 B 2
Sepupa ○ RB 218-219 B 4
Seputih ~ RI 162-163 F 7
Sequatchie River ~ USA (TN) 276-277 K 5
Sequim ○ USA (WA) 244-245 C 2
Sequoia National Park ⊥ USA (CA) 248-249 F 3
Sequoyah National Wildlife Refuge ⊥ USA (OK) 264-265 J 3
Sequoyah's Cabin ∴ USA (OK) 264-265 K 3
Šerabad ~ US 136-137 K 6
Şerafettin Dağları ▲ TR 128-129 J 3
Serafimovič ○ RUS 102-103 N 3
Serafina ○ USA (NM) 256-257 K 3
Šeragul ○ RUS 116-117 K 8
Serahs ○ TM 136-137 G 6
Serai ○ PNG 183 A 2
Seraij ○ RI 164-165 J 3
Seraja gora ▲ RUS 112-113 O 4
Serakhi ○ ETH 208-209 E 6
Seram ○ IND 140-141 G 2
Seram, Pulau ⌒ RI 166-167 E 3
Seram Laut, Pulau ⌒ RI 166-167 F 3
Serang ○ RI 168 B 3
Serang ~ RI 168 D 3
Seraran ○ RI 166-167 G 3
Sérarou ○ DY 204-205 E 4
Serasan, Pulau ⌒ RI 162-163 H 3
Serasan, Selat ≈ 162-163 H 3
Šerbakty ☆ KA 124-125 L 2
Serbewel ~ CAM 198-199 G 6
Serbia = Srbija □ YU 100-101 G 2
Serca ○ VRC 144-145 K 5
Serčejja ~ RUS 88-89 X 3
Serdce-Kamen', mys ▲ RUS 112-113 Z 3
Serdo ○ ETH 208-209 E 3
Serdobsk ○ RUS 96-97 D 7
Sérébou ○ CI 202-203 J 6
Serebrjansk ○ KA 124-125 N 4
Seredka ○ RUS 94-95 L 2
Sérédou ○ RG 202-203 F 5
Şereflikoçhisar ☆ TR 128-129 E 3
Serein ~ F 90-91 K 8
Serekunda ○ WAG 202-203 B 3
Seremban ☆ • MAL 162-163 D 3
Serena, La ☆ • RCH 76-77 B 5
Serengeti National Park ⊥ ••• EAT 212-213 E 5
Serengeti Plain ∸ EAT 212-213 E 5
Serengeti Plains ∸ EAK 212-213 F 5
Serenje ○ Z 218-219 F 1
Sereno, Rio ~ BR 68-69 E 5
Séres ○ GR 100-101 J 4
Seret ~ UA 102-103 D 3
Serež ~ RUS 114-115 U 7
Sergač ○ RUS 96-97 D 6
Sergeevka ○ RUS 122-123 E 7
Sergeevsk ☆ RUS 96-97 G 7
Sergeevskoe sukojmasy < KA 124-125 E 2
Sergeja Kirova, ostrova ⌒ RUS 108-109 X 3
Sèrgèlèn ○ MAU 148-149 K 4
Sergeljah ~ RUS 118-119 J 5
Sergeulangit, Pegunungan ▲ RI 162-163 B 3
Sergiev Posad ☆ ••• RUS 94-95 Q 3
Sergino ○ RUS 116-117 N 9
Sergipe □ BR 68-69 K 7
Sergipe, Rio ~ BR 68-69 K 7
Sergiyev Posad = Sergiev-Posad ☆ ••• RUS 94-95 Q 3
Sergozero ⊂ RUS 88-89 O 3
Seria ○ BRU 164-165 D 1
Serian ○ MAL 162-163 J 4
Sériba ○ RG 202-203 D 4
Seribu, Kepulauan ⌒ RI 168 B 2
Seribudolok ○ RI 162-163 C 3
Sericita ○ BR 72-73 J 6
Sérifos ⌒ GR 100-101 K 6
Serik ☆ TR 128-129 D 4
Serikkembelo ○ RI 166-167 D 3
Seringal Jaboti ○ BR 70-71 F 2
Seringal Santa Maria ○ BR 66-67 E 6
Seringal São Pedro ○ BR 70-71 F 2
Seringal Torrões ○ BR 66-67 D 6
Seringapatam Reef ⌒ AUS 172-173 F 2
Serinhisar ☆ TR 128-129 C 4
Serki ~ RUS 110-111 N 6
Serkout ▲ DZ 190-191 F 9
Šerlovaja Gora ○ RUS 118-119 H 10
Sermata, Kepulauan ⌒ RI 166-167 E 6
Sermata, Pulau ⌒ RI 166-167 E 6
Sermersooq ⌒ GRØ 28-29 S 6
Sermersôq ▲ GRØ 28-29 S 6
Sermiligaaq ≈ 28-29 W 3
Sermiligaarsuk ≈ 28-29 Q 6
Sermilik ≈ 28-29 W 3
Sermilik ≈ 28-29 Q 6
Sermilik ≈ 28-29 S 6
Sermowai ~ RI 166-167 L 3
Sernovodsk ○ RUS 122-123 L 7
Seroglazka ○ RUS 96-97 E 10
Seronera Lodge ○ EAT 212-213 E 5
Seronga ○ RB 218-219 B 4
Serou ○ IR 128-129 L 4
Serouenout, Hassi < DZ 190-191 F 8
Serov ☆ RUS 114-115 F 5
Serowe ☆ RB 218-219 D 6
Serpa ○ P 98-99 D 6
Serpentine Hot Springs ○ USA 20-21 H 4
Serpentine River ~ USA 20-21 H 3
Serpent Mound State Memorial • USA (OH) 280-281 C 4
Serpent River ○ CDN (ONT) 238-239 C 2
Serpents, Île aux ⌒ MS 224 C 6
Serpuhov ☆ • RUS 94-95 P 4
Serpukhov = Serpuhov ☆ • RUS 94-95 P 4
Serra ○ BR 72-73 K 6
Serra Bonita ○ BR 72-73 G 3
Serra Branca ○ BR 68-69 K 5
Serra da Bocaina, Parque Nacional da ⊥ BR 72-73 H 7
Serra da Canastra, Parque Nacional da ⊥ BR 72-73 G 6
Serra da Capivara, Parque Nacional da ⊥ ••• BR 68-69 G 6
Serra das Araras ○ BR 72-73 H 3
Serra das Araras, Estação Ecológica da ⊥ BR 70-71 J 4
Serra do Divisor, Parque Nacional da ⊥ BR 64-65 F 6
Serra do Moa ○ BR 64-65 F 5
Serra do Navio ○ BR 62-63 H 5
Serra do Salitre ○ BR 72-73 G 5
Serra Dourada ○ BR (BAH) 72-73 J 2
Serra Dourada ○ BR (MAT) 72-73 D 2
Serra Encantada, Igarapé ~ BR 68-69 B 5
Serra Hills ▲ PNG 183 A 2
Serra Mecula ▲ MOC 218-219 J 1
Serra Morena, Área Indígena ⅹ BR 70-71 H 2
Serrana ○ BR 72-73 G 6
Serra Negra, Reserva Biológica da ⊥ BR 68-69 J 6
Serrania, La ∸ CO 60-61 E 6
Serrania de la Neblina, Parque Nacional ⊥ YV 66-67 D 2
Serranilla, Banco de ≃ 54-55 F 7
Serrano, Isla ⌒ RCH 80 C 4
Serranópolis ○ BR 72-73 D 5
Serra Preta ○ BR 72-73 L 2
Serraria ○ BR 68-69 E 3
Serraria, Ilha da ⌒ BR 62-63 J 6
Serra San Bruno ○ I 100-101 F 5
Serrat, Cap ▲ TN 190-191 G 2
Serra Talhada ○ BR 68-69 J 5
Serres ○ F 90-91 K 9
Serrinha ○ BR 68-69 J 7
Serro ○ BR 72-73 J 5
Serrolândia ○ BR (BAH) 68-69 H 7
Serrolândia ○ BR (PER) 68-69 H 5
Sersou, Plateau du ▲ DZ 190-191 C 3
Sertã ○ P 98-99 C 5
Serta ~ RUS 114-115 U 7
Sertânia ○ BR 68-69 K 6
Sertanópolis ○ BR 72-73 E 7
Sertão ∸ BR 68-69 H 7
Sertão de Camapuã ∸ BR 72-73 D 5
Sertãozinho ○ BR 72-73 G 6
Sêrtar ○ VRC 154-155 B 5
Serti ○ WAN 204-205 J 5
Sertung, Pulau ⌒ RI 168 A 3
Sêru ○ ETH 208-209 E 5
Serua, Pulau ⌒ RI 166-167 F 5
Šerubaj-Nura ~ KA 124-125 H 4
Serui ○ RI 166-167 J 2
Serule ○ RB 218-219 D 5
Serutu, Pulau ⌒ RI 162-163 H 5
Seruyan ~ RI 162-163 K 6
Servi ○ TR 128-129 J 3
Sérvia ○ GR 100-101 J 4
Service Creek ○ USA (OR) 244-245 E 6
Sěnxü ○ VRC 144-145 M 4
Seryh Gusej, ostrova ⌒ RUS 112-113 X 3
Seryševo ○ RUS 122-123 C 3
Sesayap ○ RI 164-165 E 2
Sesayap ~ RI 164-165 E 2
Šeš Borğe ○ AFG 134-135 M 2
Sese ○ ZRE 210-211 K 2
Seseganaga Lake ⊂ CDN (ONT) 234-235 N 4
Sese Islands ⌒ EAU 212-213 D 4
Sesenta, El ○ CO 60-61 E 3
Sesepe ○ RI 164-165 K 4
Sesfontein ○ NAM 216-217 B 9
Seshego ○ ZA 218-219 E 6
Sesheke ○ Z 218-219 C 3
Sesibi, Temple of • SUD 200-201 E 2
Sesimbra ○ • P 98-99 C 5
Seskarö ○ S 86-87 L 4
Šešma ~ RUS 96-97 G 6
Sespamco ○ USA (TX) 266-267 J 4
Sesriem ○ NAM 220-221 B 2
Sessa ○ ANG 216-217 F 6
Sesser ○ USA (IL) 274-275 J 6
Šeštamad ○ IR 136-137 E 7
Sesuntepeque ☆ ES 52-53 K 5
Šet-Bakanas ~ KA 124-125 J 6
Sète ○ F 90-91 J 10
Sete de Setembro, Área Indígena ⅹ BR 70-71 G 2
Sete de Setembro, Rio ~ BR 72-73 D 2
Sete Lagoas ○ BR 72-73 H 5
Setenta, Pampa del ∸ RA 80 F 3
Sete Quedas, Ilha das ⌒ BR 72-73 D 7
Sete Quedas, Salto das ~ BR 66-67 J 7
Setermoen ○ N 86-87 J 2
Setesdal ⌣ N 86-87 C 7
Sethkokna River ~ USA 20-21 O 4
Seti ~ NEP 144-145 C 6
Sétif ☆ DZ 190-191 E 2
Setit ~ SUD 200-201 H 6
Setlagole ○ ZA 220-221 G 3
Seto-naikai ≈ 152-153 E 7
Seto-Nakai National Park ⊥ J 152-153 D 8
Setouchi ○ J 152-153 C 10
Šetre ☆ KA 126-127 K 5
Settaf, Djebel ▲ DZ 190-191 D 7
Settala, Hassi < DZ 190-191 D 4
Settat ☆ MA 188-189 H 4
Setté Cama ○ G 210-211 B 5
Sette-Daban, hrebet ▲ RUS 120-121 G 2
Setters ○ USA (ID) 250-251 C 4
Settiya ○ IND 140-141 H 5
Settlement, The ○ GB (VI) 286-287 R 2
Settlers ○ ZA 220-221 J 2
Setto ○ DY 204-205 E 5
Setúbal ○ P 98-99 C 5
Setúbal, Baía de ≈ 98-99 C 5
Setubinha ○ BR 72-73 J 4
Šet-Yrgyz ~ KA 126-127 N 3
Seu d'Urgell, la ○ • E 98-99 H 3
Seuf ~ RUS 114-115 J 4
Seul, Lac ⊂ CDN (ONT) 234-235 L 4
Seulimeum ○ RI 162-163 A 2
Seuté, Hosséré ▲ CAM 204-205 K 5
Sevan ○ AR 128-129 L 2
Sevan, ozero ⊂ AR 128-129 L 2
Sévaré ○ RMM 202-203 H 2
Sevaruyo ○ BOL 70-71 D 6
Sevastopol' ○ •• UA 102-103 H 5
Ševčenko = Aktau ☆ KA 126-127 J 6
Ševčenko, Fort- ○ KA 126-127 J 5
Seven Emu ○ AUS 174-175 D 5
Seven Islands Bay ≈ 36-37 S 5
Seven Lakes ○ USA (NM) 256-257 H 3
Seven Mile Beach ∸ AUS 176-177 C 4
Seven Persons ○ CDN (ALB) 232-233 H 6
Seven Persons Creek ~ CDN (ALB) 232-233 H 6
Seven Springs ○ USA (AZ) 256-257 D 5
Seventeen Mile Ranch ○ USA (AZ) 256-257 B 4
Seventy Five Mile Beach ∸ AUS 178-179 M 3
Seventy Mile House ○ CDN (BC) 230-231 H 2
Severgina, proliv ≈ RUS 122-123 Q 4
Severgino ○ RUS 122-123 Q 4
Severn ~ GB 90-91 F 6
Severn ○ ZA 220-221 F 3
Severnaja ~ RUS 108-109 j 4
Severnaja ~ RUS 108-109 X 8
Severnaja ~ RUS 110-111 M 6
Severnaja Čunja ~ RUS 116-117 M 5
Severnaja Dvina ~ RUS 88-89 Q 5
Severnaja grjada ▲ RUS 108-109 d 4
Severnaja Keľtma ~ RUS 96-97 J 3
Severnaja Mylva ~ RUS 114-115 D 3
Severnaja Sos'va ~ RUS 114-115 G 3
Severnaja Suľmeneva, guba ⊂ RUS 108-109 F 4
Severnaja Tajmura ~ RUS 116-117 L 4
Severnaja zemlja ⌒ RUS 108-109 c 1
Severnaya Dvina = Severnaja Dvina ~ RUS 88-89 Q 5
Severn Falls ○ CDN (ONT) 238-239 F 4
Severn Lake ⊂ CDN 34-35 L 4
Severnoe ○ RUS 114-115 P 6
Severnoe ☆ RUS (ORB) 96-97 H 6
Severnoe, ozero ⊂ RUS 116-117 F 2
Severn River ~ AUS 178-179 L 5
Severn River ~ CDN 34-35 M 3
Severn River ~ CDN (ONT) 234-235 L 2
Severnye uvaly ▲ RUS 96-97 D 4
Severnyj ○ RUS (KAR) 88-89 M 4
Severnyj ○ RUS (KOM) 108-109 L 8
Severnyj ○ RUS (SAH) 110-111 U 4
Severnyj, mys ▲ RUS 108-109 k 3
Severnyj, ostrov ⌒ RUS (TMR) 108-109 k 3
Severnyj, ostrov ⌒ RUS (TMR) 108-109 Y 3
Severnyj, proliv ≈ 110-111 H 2
Severnyj, zaliv ⊂ RUS 120-121 K 6
Severnyj Kamen' ∸ RUS 108-109 X 8
Severnyj liman ⊂ RUS 112-113 Q 6
Severnyj mys ~ RUS 108-109 S 5
Severnyj Pèkuľnejveem ~ RUS 112-113 R 4
Severnyj proliv ⊂ RUS 120-121 G 6
Severnyj Uj ~ RUS 120-121 H 5
Severnyj Ural ▲ RUS 114-115 E 5
Severnyy Ural = Severnyj Ural ▲ RUS 114-115 E 5
Severobajkaľsk ☆ RUS 118-119 D 8
Severo-Bajkaľskoe, nagor'e ▲ RUS 118-119 E 7
Severodonec'k ○ UA 102-103 L 3
Severodvinsk ○ RUS 88-89 P 4
Severo-Enisejsk ☆ RUS 116-117 F 5
Severo-Kuriľsk ○ RUS 122-123 R 3
Severomorsk ○ RUS 88-89 M 2
Severo-Sahalinskaja ravnina ⌣ RUS 122-123 J 3
Severo sos'vinskaja vozvyšennost' ▲ RUS 114-115 G 4
Severouraľsk ○ RUS 114-115 F 4
Severo-Vostočnyj, proliv ≈ 84-85 f 2
Severo-Vostočnyj proliv ⊂ RUS 120-121 G 6
Severo-Zadonsk ○ RUS 94-95 Q 4
Severo-Zapadnyj, mys ▲ RUS 120-121 V 6
Severskij Donec ~ RUS 102-103 M 3
Severskij Donec ~ RUS 102-103 L 3
Severy ○ USA (KS) 262-263 K 7
Sevettijärvi ○ FIN 88-89 K 2
Sevey ○ USA (NY) 278-279 G 4
Sevier ○ USA (UT) 254-255 C 5
Sevier Bridge Reservoir < USA (UT) 254-255 D 4
Sevier Desert ∸ USA (UT) 254-255 C 4
Sevier Lake ⊂ USA (UT) 254-255 B 5
Sevier River ~ USA (UT) 254-255 C 4
Sevierville ○ USA (TN) 282-283 D 5
Sevigny Point ▲ CDN 24-25 f 6
Sevilla ~ C 54-55 G 4
Sevilla ○ CO 60-61 D 5
Sevilla ○ ••• E 98-99 E 6
Seville ○ USA (FL) 286-287 H 2
Seville ○ USA (GA) 284-285 G 5
Ševli ~ RUS 122-123 E 2
Sevlievo ○ BG 102-103 D 6
Sèvrèj = Sajnšand ○ MAU 148-149 F 6
Sèvre Niortaise ~ F 90-91 G 8
Sevsk ○ RUS 94-95 O 5
Sevštari ○ •• BG 102-103 E 6
Sewa ~ WAL 202-203 E 5
Sewall ○ CDN (BC) 228-229 B 3
Sewanee ○ USA (TN) 276-277 K 5
Seward ○ USA (AK) 20-21 Q 6
Seward ○ USA (NE) 262-263 J 4
Seward Glacier ⊂ CDN 20-21 U 6
Seward Peninsula ⌣ USA 20-21 G 4
Sewell ○ RCH 78-79 D 3
Sewell Inlet ○ CDN (BC) 228-229 B 4
Sewerimabu ○ PNG 183 B 5
Sexsmith ○ CDN 32-33 L 4
Sey ○ RA 76-77 D 2
Seyāhū ○ IR 134-135 G 5
Seybouse, Oued ~ DZ 190-191 F 2
Seychelles ■ SY 224 A 5
Seychelles ⌒ SY 224 A 5
Seychelles Bank ≃ 224 D 2
Seydişehir ☆ TR 128-129 D 4
Seyðisfjörður ☆ IS 86-87 f 2
Seyhan Barajı < TR 128-129 F 4
Seyhan N. ~ TR 128-129 F 4
Seyhan Nehri ~ TR 128-129 F 4
Seyitgazi ☆ TR 128-129 D 3
Seymour ○ AUS 180-181 H 4
Seymour ○ USA (IA) 274-275 E 4
Seymour ○ USA (IN) 274-275 N 6
Seymour ○ USA (MO) 276-277 C 3
Seymour ○ USA (TX) 264-265 E 5
Seymour ○ ZA 220-221 H 6
Seymour Arm ○ CDN (BC) 230-231 K 2
Seymour Canal ≈ 32-33 C 3
Seymour Inlet ≈ CDN 230-231 B 2
Seymour River ~ CDN (BC) 230-231 L 2
Seymourville ○ CDN (MAN) 234-235 G 3
Seymourville ○ USA (LA) 268-269 J 6
Seyyedābād ○ AFG 138-139 B 2
Seyyedābād ○ IR (HOR) 136-137 F 6
Seyyedābād ○ IR (MAZ) 136-137 E 6
Seyyedān ○ IR 128-129 M 5
Seyyed Karam ○ AFG 138-139 B 3
SEZ = Special Economic Zone □ VRC 156-157 F 7
Sézanne ○ F 90-91 J 7
Sezela ○ ZA 220-221 K 5
Sezin ○ MYA 142-143 K 3
Sfakia ○ GR 100-101 K 7
Sfax ☆ TN 190-191 H 3
Sfinári ○ GR 100-101 J 7
Sfîntu Gheorghe ☆ • RO 102-103 D 5
's-Gravenhage = Den Haag ○ ••• NL 92-93 H 2
Sgurr Mór ▲ GB 90-91 E 3
Shaanxi □ VRC 154-155 F 5
Shaba □ ZRE 214-215 C 5
Shaba National Reserve ⊥ EAK 212-213 F 3
Shabaqua Corners ○ CDN (ONT) 234-235 O 6
Shabasha ○ SUD 200-201 F 5
Shabaskwia Lake ⊂ CDN (ONT) 234-235 O 3
Shabeellaha Dhexe □ SP 212-213 K 2
Shabeellaha Hoose □ SP 212-213 J 3
Shabeelle, Webi ~ SP 212-213 K 2
Shabogamo Lake ⊂ CDN 38-39 L 2
Shabqadar ○ PK 138-139 C 2
Shabunda ○ ZRE 212-213 A 5
Shabuskwia Lake ⊂ CDN (ONT) 234-235 P 3
Shache ○ VRC 146-147 C 6
Shackleton ○ CDN (SAS) 232-233 K 5
Shackleton Ice Shelf ⊂ ARK 16 G 10
Shackleton Inlet ≈ 16 E 0
Shackleton Range ▲ ARK 16 E 0
Shādan Lund ○ PK 138-139 C 4
Shadao ○ VRC 156-157 F 2
Shādara ○ PK 138-139 E 4
Shade Gap ○ USA (PA) 280-281 J 3
Shadehill ○ USA (SD) 260-261 D 1
Shadehill Reservoir ⊂ USA (SD) 260-261 D 1
Shadiwāl ○ PK 138-139 E 3
Shadon Downs ○ AUS 174-175 C 5
Shady Cove ○ USA (OR) 244-245 C 8
Shady Dale ○ USA (GA) 284-285 G 3
Shaerer Dale ○ CDN 32-33 K 3
Shafter ○ USA (CA) 248-249 E 4
Shafter ○ USA (NV) 246-247 L 3
Shafter ○ USA (TX) 266-267 C 4
Shafter Lake ⊂ USA (TX) 264-265 B 6
Shagamu River ~ CDN 34-35 N 3
Shagari ○ WAN 198-199 B 6
Shagein ▲ EAT 212-213 G 6
Shageluk ○ USA 20-21 L 5
Shag Harbour ○ CDN (NS) 240-241 K 7
Shagouije ○ VRC 154-155 F 5
Shagunnu ○ WAN 204-205 F 3
Shagwa ○ WAN 204-205 F 3
Shāhāda ○ IND 138-139 E 9
Shah Alam ○ MAL 162-163 D 3
Shāhāpur ○ IND 138-139 D 10
Shahar Sultān ○ PK 138-139 C 5
Shāhbandar ○ PK 134-135 M 6
Shāhbāz Kalāt ○ PK 134-135 K 5
Shahbazpur ~ BD 142-143 G 4
Shahda Bohotleh ○ SP 208-209 H 4
Shāhdādkot ○ PK 134-135 M 5
Shāhdādpur ○ PK 138-139 B 7
Shahdol ○ IND 142-143 B 4
Shahe ○ VRC (HEB) 154-155 J 3
Shahe ○ VRC (SHD) 154-155 L 3
Shāhganj ○ IND 142-143 C 2
Shāh Hasan ○ PK 134-135 M 5
Shahhāt ∴ ••• LAR 192-193 J 1
Shahistagani ○ BD 142-143 G 3
Shahjahānpur ○ IND 138-139 G 6
Shāh Kot ○ PK 138-139 D 4
Shāhpur ○ IND (KAR) 140-141 G 2
Shāhpur ○ IND (RAJ) 138-139 E 6
Shāhpur ○ PK 138-139 D 3
Shahpuri Island ○ BD 142-143 H 5
Shaighālū ○ PK 138-139 B 4
Shai Hills Game Reserve ⊥ GH 202-203 L 7
Shaikhpura ○ IND 142-143 D 3
Shaka, Ras ▲ EAK 212-213 H 5
Shakani ∴ • EAK 212-213 H 4
Shakargarh ○ PK 138-139 E 3
Shakaskraal ○ ZA 220-221 K 4
Shakawe ○ RB 216-217 F 9
Shakertown ∴ USA (KY) 276-277 L 3
Shakespeare Ghost Town • USA (NM) 256-257 G 6
Shakespeare Island ⌒ CDN 234-235 P 5
Shakiso ○ ETH 208-209 D 6
Shakleford Banks ≃ 282-283 L 6
Shakotan-misaki ▲ J 152-153 J 3
Shākshūk ○ LAR 192-193 D 1
Shaktoolik ○ USA 20-21 K 4
Shaktoolik River ~ USA 20-21 K 4
Shalaanbood ○ SP 212-213 K 2
Shala Hāyk' ⊂ ETH 208-209 D 5
Shalalth ○ CDN (BC) 230-231 G 3
Shaler Mountains ▲ CDN 24-25 Q 5
Shāli al-Fil ○ SUD 208-209 B 3
Shallotte ○ USA (NC) 282-283 J 7
Shallow Bay ≈ 20-21 X 2
Shallow Lake ⊂ AUS 178-179 F 3
Shallow Water ○ USA (KS) 262-263 F 6
Shaluli Shan ▲ VRC 144-145 M 5
Shama ~ EAT 214-215 G 4
Shamakhy = Šamaxı ☆ AZ 128-129 N 2
Shamattawa River ~ CDN 34-35 O 3
Shambe ○ SUD 206-207 K 5
Shamboyacu ○ PE 64-65 D 5
Shambu ○ ETH 208-209 C 4
Shames ○ CDN (BC) 228-229 F 2
Shamganj ○ BD 142-143 G 3
Shamli ○ IND 138-139 F 5
Shamokin ○ USA (PA) 280-281 K 3
Shamputa ○ Z 218-219 D 2
Shamrock ○ CDN (SAS) 232-233 M 5
Shamrock ○ USA (TX) 264-265 D 3
Shamsābād ○ IND 140-141 H 2
Shamshergani ○ NEP 144-145 C 6
Shamva ○ ZW 218-219 F 3
Shanbahe ○ VRC 154-155 J 6
Shandaken ○ USA (NY) 278-279 G 6
Shandan ○ VRC 154-155 B 2
Shandon ○ USA (CA) 248-249 D 4
Shandong □ VRC 154-155 K 4
Shandong Bandao ⌣ VRC 154-155 M 3
Shangani ○ ZW 218-219 E 4
Shangcai ○ VRC 154-155 J 5
Shangcheng ○ VRC 154-155 J 6
Shangchuan Dao ⌒ VRC 156-157 H 6
Shangdu ○ VRC 148-149 L 7
Shangev-Tiev ○ WAN 204-205 H 5
Shanggao ○ VRC 156-157 J 2
Shang Gongma ○ VRC 144-145 M 4
Shanghai ☆ ••• VRC 154-155 M 6
Shanghai Shi □ VRC 154-155 M 6
Shanghang ○ VRC 156-157 K 4
Shanghe ○ VRC 154-155 K 3
Shangla Pass ▲ PK 138-139 D 2
Shanglin ○ VRC 156-157 F 5
Shangman ○ VRC 154-155 G 5
Shangombo ○ Z 218-219 B 3
Shangqiu ○ VRC 154-155 J 4
Shangrao ○ VRC 156-157 K 2
Shangtu ○ VRC 156-157 J 2
Shangying ○ VRC 156-157 E 5
Shangyou Yichang ○ VRC 146-147 E 5
Shangyu ○ VRC 154-155 M 6
Shangzhi ○ VRC 150-151 F 5
Shangzhou ○ VRC 154-155 F 5
Shanhaiguan ○ VRC (HEB) 154-155 L 1
Shanhaiguan • VRC (HEB) 154-155 L 1
Shanhetun ○ VRC 150-151 F 5
Shani ○ WAN 204-205 K 3
Shaniko ○ USA (OR) 244-245 E 6
Shanjuan D. • VRC 154-155 L 6
Shankou ○ VRC (GXI) 156-157 F 6

Shankou ○ VRC (HUN) 156-157 G 2
Shanngaw Taungdan ▲ MYA 142-143 K 3
Shannon ○ AUS 176-177 D 7
Shannon ~ IRL 90-91 C 5
Shannon ○ USA (MS) 268-269 M 2
Shannon = Sionainn ○ IRL 90-91 C 5
Shannon Bay ○ CDN (BC) 228-229 B 3
Shannon Ø ⌒ GRØ 26-27 q 6
Shannon Sund ≈ 26-27 q 6
Shanshan ○ VRC 146-147 K 4
Shantarskiye Ostrova = Šantarskie, ostrova ⌒ RUS 120-121 G 6
Shantou ○ VRC 156-157 K 5
Shantung Peninsula = Shandong Bandao ⊻ VRC 154-155 K 3
Shanusi ○ PE 64-65 D 5
Shanwei ○ VRC 156-157 J 5
Shanxi □ VRC 154-155 G 2
Shan Xian ○ VRC 154-155 K 4
Shanyang ○ VRC 154-155 F 5
Shanyin ○ VRC 154-155 H 2
Shaodong ○ VRC 156-157 G 3
Shaoguan ○• VRC 156-157 H 4
Shaolin Si • VRC 154-155 H 4
Shaoshan ○ VRC 156-157 H 3
Shaowu ○ VRC 156-157 K 3
Shaoxing ○ VRC 154-155 M 6
Shaoyang ○ VRC 156-157 G 3
Shaoyang (Tangdukou) ○ VRC 156-157 G 3
Shapembe ○ ZRE 210-211 H 6
Shaping ○ VRC 156-157 F 5
Shapotou • VRC 154-155 D 3
Shāpur Chākar ○ PK 138-139 B 6
Shaquanzi ○ VRC 146-147 F 3
Sharan Jogizai ○ PK 138-139 B 4
Shara Tohay ○ VRC 144-145 L 2
Sharbot Lake ○ CDN (ONT) 238-239 J 4
Share ○ WAN 204-205 F 4
Shargalle ○ WAN 198-199 D 6
Shari ○ J 152-153 L 3
Shari ~ ZRE 212-213 C 2
Sharjah = aš-Šariqa ○ UAE 134-135 F 6
Shark Bank ≃ 100-101 C 6
Shark Bay ⊥••• AUS 176-177 B 2
Shark Bay ○ VAN 184 II a 2
Sharon ○ USA (PA) 280-281 F 2
Sharon Springs ○ USA (KS) 262-263 E 6
Sharpe, Lake ⊖ AUS 176-177 F 6
Sharpe Lake ⊖ CDN 34-35 K 3
Sharp Mount ▲ CDN 20-21 V 3
Sharpsburg ○ USA (KY) 276-277 M 2
Sharqpur ○ PK 138-139 E 4
Sharwangai ○ PK 138-139 C 3
Shasha ○ ETH 208-209 B 5
Shasha ○ WAN 204-205 F 5
Shashani ~ ZW 218-219 E 5
Shashe ○ RB 218-219 D 5
Shashe ~ ZW 218-219 E 5
Shashemenë ○ ETH 208-209 D 5
Shashi ○ VRC 154-155 H 6
Shasta, Mount ○ USA (CA) 246-247 C 2
Shasta, Mount ▲ USA (CA) 246-247 C 2
Shasta Caverns, Lake ∴ USA (CA) 246-247 C 3
Shasta Lake ○ USA (CA) 246-247 C 3
Shasta-Trinity Wilderness Area ⊥ USA (CA) 246-247 C 3
Shatahkung ○ MYA 142-143 L 2
Shatawi ○ SUD 200-201 F 5
Shāṭi, Wādī ash ~ LAR 192-193 E 4
Shattuck ○ USA (OK) 264-265 E 2
Shatui ○ VRC 154-155 B 6
Shaughnessy ○ CDN (ALB) 232-233 F 6
Shaunavon ○ CDN (SAS) 232-233 K 6
Shaviovik River ~ USA 20-21 R 2
Shaw ○ USA (LA) 268-269 J 5
Shaw ○ USA (MS) 268-269 K 3
Shawan ○ VRC 146-147 G 3
Shawanaga Island ⌒ CDN (ONT) 238-239 E 3
Shawano ○ USA (WI) 270-271 K 6
Shawinigan ○ CDN (QUE) 238-239 N 2
Shawmut ○ USA (MT) 250-251 K 5
Shawnee ○ USA (OK) 264-265 H 3
Shawneetown ○ USA (IL) 276-277 G 3
Shawneetown State Historic Site • USA (IL) 276-277 G 3
Shawo ○ VRC 154-155 J 6
Shaw River ~ AUS 172-173 D 6
Shawville ○ CDN (QUE) 238-239 J 3
Shayang ○ VRC 154-155 H 6
Shay Gap ○ AUS 172-173 E 6
Shaykh Gok ○ SUD 206-207 L 3
Shayngja ○ NEP 144-145 D 6
Shea ○ GUY 62-63 E 4
Sheahan ○ CDN (ONT) 238-239 D 2
Shebandowan ○ CDN (ONT) 234-235 N 6
Shebë ○ ETH 208-209 C 5
Shebelë Wenz, Wabë ~ ETH 208-209 D 5
Sheboygan ○ USA (WI) 270-271 L 7
Shebshi Mountains ▲ WAN 204-205 J 4
Shediac ○ CDN (NB) 240-241 L 4
Shedin Peak ▲ CDN 32-33 G 4
Sheemahant River ~ CDN (BC) 230-231 C 2
Sheenboro ○ CDN (QUE) 238-239 H 3
Sheenjek River ~ USA 20-21 T 2
Sheepmoor ○ ZA 220-221 K 3
Sheep River ~ CDN (ALB) 232-233 D 5
Sheep Springs ○ USA (NM) 256-257 G 2
Sheerness ○ CDN (ALB) 232-233 G 4
Sheerness ○ GB 90-91 H 6
Sheet Harbour ○ CDN (NS) 240-241 N 6
Sheffield ○ AUS 180-181 H 6
Sheffield ○ CDN (NB) 240-241 J 5
Sheffield ○ GB 90-91 G 5
Sheffield ○ NZ 182 D 5
Sheffield ○ USA (AL) 284-285 C 2
Sheffield ○ USA (IA) 274-275 E 2
Sheffield ○ USA (IL) 274-275 J 3
Sheffield ○ USA (PA) 280-281 G 2
Sheffield ○ USA (TX) 266-267 F 3
Sheffield Lake ○ CDN (NFL) 242-243 M 3
Shegamook Lake ⊖ CDN 36-37 T 7
Shēh Husēn ○ ETH 208-209 E 5
Sheho ○ CDN (SAS) 232-233 P 4
Shehong ○ VRC 154-155 D 6
Sheikh Hasan ○ ETH 200-201 G 6
Sheila Out Station ○ AUS 178-179 E 1
Shekak River ~ CDN (ONT) 236-237 D 3
Shekhem ☆ WB 130-131 D 1
Shekhupura ○ PK 138-139 D 4
Sheki ○ ETH 208-209 C 5
Sheklukshuk Range ▲ USA 20-21 M 3
Shelbina ○ USA (MO) 274-275 F 5
Shelburne ○ CDN (NS) 240-241 K 7
Shelburne ○ CDN (ONT) 238-239 E 4
Shelburne ○ USA (VT) 278-279 H 4
Shelburne Bay ≈ 174-175 G 2
Shelburne Museum • USA (VT) 278-279 H 4
Shelby ○ USA (MS) 268-269 K 3
Shelby ○ USA (MT) 250-251 H 3
Shelby ○ USA (NC) 282-283 F 5
Shelby ○ USA (OH) 280-281 D 3
Shelbyville ○ USA (IL) 274-275 K 5
Shelbyville ○ USA (IN) 274-275 N 5
Shelbyville ○ USA (KY) 276-277 K 2
Shelbyville ○ USA (MO) 274-275 F 5
Shelbyville ○ USA (TN) 276-277 J 5
Shelbyville, Lake ⊖ USA (IL) 274-275 K 5
Sheldon ○ USA (AZ) 256-257 F 6
Sheldon ○ USA (IA) 274-275 C 1
Sheldon ○ USA (IL) 274-275 L 4
Sheldon ○ USA (MO) 276-277 A 3
Sheldon ○ ZA 220-221 G 6
Sheldon Antelope Wildlife Refuge ⊥ USA (NV) 246-247 F 2
Sheldrake ○ CDN (QUE) 242-243 D 2
Shelekhova, Zaliv = Šelihova, zaliv ≈ RUS 120-121 R 3
Shelikof Strait ≈ 22-23 T 4
Shell ○ USA (WY) 252-253 L 2
Shell Bluff ○ USA (GA) 284-285 J 3
Shell Cemetery • THA 158-159 E 6
Shellen ○ WAN 204-205 K 4
Shelley ○ CDN (BC) 228-229 M 2
Shelley ○ USA (ID) 252-253 G 3
Shellharbour ○ AUS 180-181 L 3
Shell Lake ○ CDN (SAS) 232-233 L 2
Shell Lakes ⊖ AUS 176-177 J 4
Shellman ○ USA (GA) 284-285 F 5
Shellmouth ○ CDN (MAN) 234-235 B 4
Shell-Osage Wildlife Area ⊥ USA (MO) 276-277 A 3
Shell Rock River ~ USA (IA) 274-275 F 2
Shelter Bay ○ CDN (BC) 230-231 M 3
Shelter Cove ○ USA (CA) 246-247 A 3
Shelton ○ USA (WA) 244-245 B 3
Shemankar, River ~ WAN 204-205 H 4
Shemgang ○ BHT 142-143 G 2
Shemya Island ⌒ USA 22-23 D 6
Shenandoah ○ USA (IA) 274-275 C 4
Shenandoah ○ USA (PA) 280-281 K 3
Shenandoah Mountains ▲ USA (WV) 280-281 G 5
Shenandoah National Park ⊥ USA (VA) 280-281 H 5
Shenandoah River ~ USA (VA) 280-281 H 5
Shenandoah Tower ▲ USA (WV) 280-281 G 5
Shenandoah Valley ⊻ USA (VA) 280-281 H 5
Shenango River Lake ⊖ USA (PA) 280-281 F 2
Shendam ○ WAN 204-205 H 4
Shenge ○ WAL 202-203 D 6
Shengjing Guan ▲ VRC 156-157 D 4
Shengli ○ VRC 150-151 F 5
Shengsi ⌒ VRC 154-155 N 6
Shengsi Liedao ⌒ VRC 154-155 N 6
Sheng Xian ○ VRC 156-157 M 2
Shenjiamen ○ VRC 156-157 N 2
Shenmu ○ VRC 154-155 G 2
Shennijek River ~ USA 20-21 S 3
Shennongjia Z.B. ⊥ • VRC 154-155 G 6
Sheno ○ ETH 208-209 D 4
Shentang Shan ▲ VRC 156-157 G 5
Shenton, Mount ▲ AUS 176-177 G 3
Shen Xian ○ VRC (HEB) 154-155 J 2
Shen Xian ○ VRC (SHD) 154-155 J 3
Shenyang ☆ VRC 150-151 D 7
Shenzhen ○• VRC 156-157 J 5
Sheo ○ IND 138-139 C 6
Sheokhala ○ IND 142-143 F 4
Sheopur ○ IND 138-139 F 7
Shepahua ○ PE 64-65 F 7
Shepard ○ CDN (ALB) 232-233 E 5
Shepardville ○ USA (AL) 284-285 C 4
Shepherd ○ USA (TX) 268-269 F 6
Shepherd □ VAN 184 II b 3
Shepherd, Îles = Shepherd Islands ⌒ VAN 184 II b 3
Shepherd Bay ≈ 24-25 Z 6
Shepherd Islands = Îles Shepherd ⌒ VAN 184 II b 3
Shepherd of the Hills Farm • USA (MO) 276-277 B 4
Shepherdsville ○ USA (KY) 276-277 K 2
Shepparton-Mooroopna ○ AUS 180-181 H 4
Sherard ○ USA (MS) 268-269 K 2
Sherard, Cape ▲ CDN 24-25 g 3
Sherard Osborn Fjord ≈ 26-27 Y 2
Sheraton ○ CDN (BC) 228-229 J 2
Sherbo Island ⌒ WAL 202-203 D 6
Sherbo River ~ WAL 202-203 D 6
Sherborne ○ ZA 220-221 G 5
Sherbrooke ○ CDN (QUE) 238-239 O 3
Sherbrooke Lake ⊖ CDN (NS) 240-241 L 6
Sherburn ○ USA (MN) 270-271 D 7
Sherburne Reef ⌒ PNG 183 E 2
Sherda ○ TCH 198-199 H 2
Sherer, Mount ▲ CDN 24-25 b 4
Shergrove ○ CDN (MAN) 234-235 D 3
Sheridan ○ USA (AR) 276-277 C 6
Sheridan ○ USA (MT) 250-251 G 6
Sheridan ○ USA (TX) 266-267 L 4
Sheridan ○ USA (WY) 252-253 M 2
Sheridan, Fort • USA (IL) 274-275 L 2
Sheridan Lake ○ USA (CO) 254-255 N 5
Sheringa ○ AUS 180-181 C 2
Sheringham ○• GB 90-91 H 5
Sherlock ○ AUS 180-181 E 3
Sherlock River ~ AUS 172-173 C 6
Sherman ○ USA (ME) 278-279 N 3
Sherman ○ USA (MS) 268-269 M 2
Sherman ○ USA (TX) 264-265 H 5
Sherman Basin ≈ 30-31 V 2
Sherman Mills ○ USA (ME) 278-279 N 3
Sherman Mountain ▲ USA (NV) 246-247 K 3
Sherman Pass ▲ USA (WA) 244-245 G 2
Sherman Reservoir ⊖ USA (NE) 262-263 H 3
Sherpur ○ BD 142-143 F 3
Sherrick, Mont ▲ CDN 38-39 E 3
Sherridon ○ CDN 34-35 F 3
's-Hertogenbosch ☆• NL 92-93 H 3
Sherwood ○ RB 218-219 D 6
Sherwood ○ USA (AR) 276-277 C 6
Sherwood ○ USA (ND) 258-259 F 3
Sherwood Lake ⊖ CDN 30-31 S 5
Sherwood Park ○ CDN (ALB) 232-233 E 2
Sheshalik ○ USA 20-21 J 3
Shesheeb Bay ≈ CDN 234-235 P 6
Sheshegwaning Indian Reserve ⨯ CDN (ONT) 238-239 C 3
Sheslay River ~ CDN 32-33 D 2
Shethanei Lake ⊖ CDN 30-31 V 6
Shetland Islands ⌒ GB 90-91 G 1
Shevgaon ○ IND 138-139 E 10
She Xian ○ VRC (ANH) 156-157 L 2
She Xian ○ VRC (SHA) 154-155 H 3
Sheyang ○ VRC 154-155 M 5
Sheyenne ○ USA (ND) 258-259 H 4
Sheyenne National Grassland ⊥ USA (ND) 258-259 K 5
Sheyenne River ~ USA (ND) 258-259 J 4
Shia ○ GH 202-203 L 6
Shibata ○ J 152-153 H 6
Shibecha ○ J 152-153 L 3
Shibetsu ○ J (HOK) 152-153 K 2
Shibetsu ○ J (HOK) 152-153 L 3
Shibetsu, Nishi- ○ J 152-153 L 3
Shibinacocha, Lago ⊖ PE 70-71 B 3
Shibing ○ VRC 156-157 F 3
Shibogama Lake ⊖ CDN 34-35 M 4
Shibushi ○ J 152-153 D 9
Shibuyunje ○ Z 218-219 D 2
Shicheng ○ VRC 156-157 K 3
Shichinohe ○ J 152-153 J 4
Shidao ○ VRC 154-155 N 3
Shidler ○ USA (OK) 264-265 H 2
Shidler Lake ⊖ USA (OK) 264-265 H 2
Shield, Cape ▲ AUS 174-175 D 3
Shields ○ USA (ND) 258-259 F 5
Shifshawn = Chefschaouene ☆ MA 188-189 J 3
Shigons Temple ○ VRC 154-155 F 3
Shihaidongxiang • VRC 156-157 D 2
Shihezi ○ VRC 146-147 H 3
Shihua ○ VRC 154-155 G 5
Shiikh ○ SP 208-209 G 4
Shijiazhuang ○ VRC 154-155 J 2
Shikabe ○ J 152-153 J 3
Shikaoi ○ J 152-153 K 3
Shikārpur ○ IND 140-141 F 3
Shikārpur ○ PK 138-139 B 6
Shikengkong ▲ VRC 156-157 H 4
Shikine-shima ⌒ J 152-153 H 7
Shikohābād ○ IND 138-139 G 6
Shikoku ⌒ J 152-153 E 8
Shikoku Basin ≃ 152-153 E 9
Shikoku-sanchi ▲ J 152-153 E 8
Shikotsu-ko ⊖ J 152-153 J 3
Shikotsu Tōya National Park ⊥ J 152-153 J 3
Shikrapur ○ IND 138-139 E 10
Shilabo ○ ETH 208-209 G 5
Shiliburi ○ IND 142-143 F 2
Shiliguri ○ IND 142-143 F 2
Shilipu ○ VRC 154-155 H 6
Shilka = Šilka ~ RUS 118-119 J 9
Shillington ○ CDN (ONT) 236-237 H 4
Shillong ☆•• IND 142-143 G 3
Shilo ○ CDN (MAN) 234-235 D 5
Shiloango ~ ZRE 210-211 D 6
Shiloh National Military Park • USA (TN) 276-277 G 5
Shimabara ○• J 152-153 D 8
Shimba Hills National Park ⊥ EAK 212-213 G 6
Shimen ○• VRC 156-157 G 2
Shimian ○ VRC 156-157 C 2
Shimizu ○ J (HOK) 152-153 K 3
Shimizu ○ J (SHI) 152-153 H 7
Shimoda ○ J 152-153 H 7
Shimodate ○ J 152-153 H 6
Shimoga ○ IND 140-141 F 4
Shimokita hanto ⊻ J 152-153 J 4
Shimokita Quasi National Park ⊥ J 152-153 J 4
Shimo-Koshiki ○ J 152-153 C 9
Shimo-Koshiki-shima ⌒ J 152-153 C 9
Shimong ○ IND 142-143 J 1
Shimoni ○ EAK 212-213 G 6
Shimonoseki ○• J 152-153 D 8
Shimono-shima ⌒ J 152-153 C 7
Shimuwini ○ ZA 218-219 F 6
Shinan ○ VRC 156-157 F 5
Shinano-gawa ~ J 152-153 H 6
Shiner ○ USA (TX) 266-267 K 4
Shinga ○ ZRE 210-211 K 5
Shingbwiyang ○ MYA 142-143 K 2
Shingerdar Stupa ∴• PK 138-139 D 2
Shingleton ○ USA (MI) 270-271 M 4
Shingletown ○ USA (CA) 246-247 D 3
Shingū ○ J 152-153 F 8
Shingwedzi ○ ZA (Tra) 218-219 F 6
Shingwedzi ~ ZA 218-219 F 6
Shinjō ○ J 152-153 J 5
Shinkafe ○ WAN 198-199 C 6
Shinnston ○ USA (WV) 280-281 F 4
Shin Pond ○ USA (ME) 278-279 N 2
Shinyanga □ EAT 212-213 D 5
Shinyanga ☆ EAT (SHI) 212-213 D 5
Shiocton ○ USA (WI) 270-271 K 6
Shiogama ○ J 152-153 J 5
Shiojiri ○ J 152-153 G 6
Shiono-misaki ▲ J 152-153 F 8
Ship Bottom ○ USA (NJ) 280-281 M 4
Ship Harbour ○ CDN (NFL) 242-243 P 5
Ship Harbour ○ CDN (NS) 240-241 N 6
Shiping ○ VRC 156-157 C 5
Ship Island ⌒ USA (MS) 268-269 M 6
Shipki La ▲ VRC 144-145 B 5
Shipman ○ CDN (SAS) 232-233 O 2
Shippegan ○ CDN (NB) 240-241 L 3
Shippegan Island = Île Lameque ⌒ CDN (NB) 240-241 L 3
Shippensburg ○ USA (PA) 280-281 J 3
Shiprock ○ USA (NM) 256-257 G 2
Shipshaw, Rivière ~ CDN (QUE) 240-241 D 2
Shipu ○ VRC 156-157 M 2
Shipwreck • PNG (MIB) 183 F 5
Shipwreck • PNG (NIR) 183 E 2
Shiqian ○ VRC 156-157 F 3
Shiqiao ○ VRC 154-155 L 6
Shiquan ○ VRC 154-155 F 5
Shiquanhe ○ VRC 144-145 B 4
Shirahama ○ J 152-153 F 8
Shirakami-dake ▲••• J 152-153 J 4
Shirakawa ○ J 152-153 J 6
Shirane-san ▲ J 152-153 H 6
Shirane-san ▲ J 152-153 H 7
Shirang ○ MYA 142-143 J 3
Shiranuka ○ J 152-153 L 3
Shiraro ○ ETH 200-201 J 5
Shiraroi ○ J 152-153 J 3
Shirati ○ EAT 212-213 E 4
Shiratori ○ J 152-153 G 7
Shirazehyōga ▲ ARK 16 F 4
Shirdi ○ IND 138-139 E 10
Shire ~ MW 218-219 H 3
Shiretoko-hanto ⊻ J 152-153 L 2
Shiretoko-misaki ▲ J 152-153 L 2
Shiretoko National Park ⊥ J 152-153 L 2
Shiribetsu-gawa ~ J 152-153 J 3
Shirin Āb ~ PK 134-135 M 4
Shirinthorn Reservoir < THA 158-159 H 3
Shiripuno, Río ~ EC 64-65 D 2
Shirley ○ NAM 220-221 D 2
Shirley ○ USA (AR) 276-277 C 5
Shirley, Fort ∴ WD 56 E 4
Shirley Basin ○ USA (WY) 252-253 M 4
Shiro ○ USA (TX) 268-269 E 6
Shiroishi ○ J 152-153 J 6
Shirpur ○ IND 138-139 E 9
Shirya-saki ▲ J 152-153 J 4
Shisan Ling • VRC 154-155 K 1
Shishaldin Volcano ▲ USA 22-23 P 5
Shishi ○ VRC 156-157 L 4
Shishinda ○ ETH 208-209 B 5
Shishmaref ○ USA 20-21 G 3
Shishmaref Inlet ≈ 20-21 G 3
Shishou ○ VRC 156-157 H 2
Shiuji ○ BHT 142-143 F 2
Shiura ○ J 152-153 J 4
Shivel ○ USA (KY) 276-277 K 2
Shivgaon ○ IND 140-141 F 3
Shivpuri ○• IND 138-139 F 7
Shivpuri National Park ⊥ IND 138-139 F 7
Shivta • IL 130-131 D 2
Shivwits ○ USA (UT) 254-255 B 6
Shivwits Plateau ▲ USA (AZ) 256-257 B 2
Shiwan Dashan ▲ VRC 156-157 E 6
Shiwa Ngandu ○ Z 214-215 F 6
Shiwulidun ○ VRC 154-155 E 3
Shixing ○ VRC 156-157 J 4
Shiyan ○ VRC 154-155 G 5
Shizangsi ○ VRC 154-155 B 4
Shizhu ○ VRC (SIC) 156-157 F 2
Shizhu ○ VRC (ZHE) 156-157 M 2
Shizilu ○ VRC 156-157 F 6
Shizong ○ VRC 156-157 C 4
Shizuishan ○ VRC 154-155 E 2
Shizunai ○ J 152-153 K 3
Shizuoka ☆ J 152-153 H 7
Shkodër ☆•• AL 100-101 G 3
Shkumbin, Lumi ~ AL 100-101 H 4
Shoal Bay ○ IND 140-141 L 4
Shoal Bay Beach ≐ GB 56 D 2
Shoalhaven River ~ AUS 180-181 L 3
Shoal Lake ○ CDN (MAN) 234-235 C 4
Shoal River ~ CDN 32-33 N 3
Shoal River ~ USA (FL) 286-287 C 1
Shoals, Isles of ⌒ USA (NH) 278-279 L 6
Shoalwater Bay ≈ 178-179 L 2
Shōbara ○ J 152-153 E 7
Shōdo-shima ⌒ J 152-153 F 7
Shoe Cove ○ CDN (NFL) 242-243 N 3
Shoga ○ EAT 214-215 G 5
Shokambetsu-dake ▲ J 152-153 J 3
Sholinghur ○ IND 140-141 H 4
Sholl, Monte ▲ RA 80 G 4
Shona Ridge ≃ 6-7 K 14
Shongaloo ○ USA (LA) 268-269 G 4
Shonto ○ USA (AZ) 256-257 E 2
Shoran Bay ≈ 36-37 H 3
Shoranūr ○ IND 140-141 G 5
Shorap ○ PK 134-135 L 6
Shoreacres ○ CDN (BC) 230-231 M 4
Shorkot ○ PK 138-139 D 4
Shorobe ○ RB 218-219 B 4
Short, Lake ⊖ AUS 178-179 E 4
Shorter ○ USA (AL) 284-285 E 4
Shortland Islands ⌒ SOL 184 I b 2
Shoshone ○ USA (CA) 248-249 H 4
Shoshone ○ USA (ID) 252-253 D 4
Shoshone Falls ~ USA (ID) 252-253 D 4
Shoshone Ice Caves ∴• USA (ID) 252-253 D 3
Shoshone Indian Ice Caves • USA (ID) 252-253 D 3
Shoshone Mountains ▲ USA (NV) 246-247 H 5
Shoshone River ~ USA (WY) 252-253 K 2
Shoshong ○ RB 218-219 D 6
Shoshoni ○ USA (WY) 252-253 K 3
Shouchang ○ VRC 156-157 L 2
Shoup ○ USA (ID) 250-251 E 6
Shou Xian ○ VRC 154-155 K 5
Shouyang ○ VRC 154-155 H 3
Shōwa ○ J 152-153 K 3
Showil ~ SUD 200-201 E 5
Show Low ○ USA (AZ) 256-257 E 4
Shreveport ○• USA (LA) 268-269 G 4
Shrewsbury ○• GB 90-91 F 5
Shrewsbury ○ USA (PA) 280-281 K 4
Shrigonda ○ IND 138-139 E 10
Shrines of Ise •• J 152-153 G 7
Shuajingsi ○ VRC 154-155 C 5
Shuangcheng ○ VRC 150-151 F 5
Shuangfeng ○ VRC 156-157 H 3
Shuanghe ○ VRC 154-155 E 6
Shuangjiang ○ VRC 142-143 L 4
Shuangliao ○ VRC 150-151 D 6
Shuangling Si • VRC 154-155 H 3
Shuangou ○ VRC 154-155 H 5
Shuangpai ○ VRC 156-157 G 4
Shuangpaishan ○ VRC 156-157 H 3
Shuangpai SK ~ VRC 156-157 G 4
Shuangyang ○ VRC 150-151 E 6
Shuanyashan ○ VRC 150-151 H 4
Shubenacadie Indian Reserve ⨯ • CDN (NS) 240-241 M 5
Shubert ○ USA (NE) 262-263 L 4
Shubuta ○ USA (MS) 268-269 M 5
Shucheng ○ VRC 154-155 K 6
Shudanzhuang ○ VRC 144-145 E 2
Shufu ○ VRC 146-147 B 6
Shuganu ○ IND 142-143 H 3
Shuibo ○ VRC 156-157 F 2
Shuikou ○ VRC 156-157 F 4
Shujāābād ○ PK 138-139 C 5
Shukbuk Bay ≈ 36-37 M 2
Shulan ○ VRC 150-151 F 5
Shule ○ VRC 146-147 C 6
Shule He ~ VRC 146-147 M 5
Shullsburg ○ USA (WI) 274-275 H 2
Shumagin Bank ≃ 22-23 R 5
Shumagin Islands ⌒ USA 22-23 Q 5
Shumarina-ko ⊖ J 152-153 K 2
Shumen = Šumen ○ BG 102-103 E 6
Shunan Zhuhai • VRC 156-157 D 2
Shunayn, Sabkhat ⊖ LAR 192-193 J 2
Shunchang ○ VRC 156-157 K 3
Shunde ○ VRC 156-157 H 5
Shungnak ○ USA 20-21 M 3
Shuongtaihekou Z.B. ⊥ • VRC 150-151 C 7
Shuozhou ○ VRC 154-155 H 2
Shurshūt, Wādī ~ LAR 190-191 H 5
Shurugwi ○ ZW 218-219 F 4
Shushufindi Central ○ EC 64-65 D 2
Shuswap ○ CDN (BC) 230-231 K 3
Shuswap Lake ⊖ CDN (BC) 230-231 L 2
Shuswap River ~ CDN (BC) 230-231 L 3
Shute Harbour ○ AUS 174-175 K 7
Shuttleworth ○ AUS 178-179 J 2
Shuyak Island ⌒ USA 22-23 U 3
Shuyang ○ VRC 154-155 L 4
Shwebo ○ MYA 142-143 J 4
Shwedaung ○ MYA 142-143 K 5
Shwedaung ○ MYA 142-143 J 6
Shwegyin ○ MYA 158-159 D 2
Shwemyo ○ MYA 142-143 K 5
Shymkent = Šymkent ☆• KA 136-137 L 3
Shyok ○ IND 138-139 G 2
Shyok ~ IND 138-139 G 2
Shyok ~ PK 138-139 F 2
Si ○ RMM 202-203 H 3
Sia ○ RI 166-167 H 5
Siabu ○ RI 162-163 C 4
Siabuwa ○ ZW 218-219 E 3
Siaeb ○ G 210-211 D 5
Siagut, Tanjung ▲ MAL 160-161 B 9
Siāhān Range ▲ PK 134-135 K 5
Siak ~ RI 162-163 E 4
Sialivakou ○ RCB 210-211 C 6
Sialkot ○ NEP 144-145 C 6
Sialkot ○ PK 138-139 E 3
Siama ○ PNG 183 D 4
Siaman ○ PNG 183 G 3
Sian Ka'an Biosphere Reserve ⊥••• MEX 52-53 L 2
Siantan, Pulau ⌒ RI 162-163 G 3
Siapa ○ YV 60-61 H 6
Siapo o Matapire, Río ~ YV 66-67 D 2
Siara ○ PNG 184 I b 1
Siare, Río ~ CO 60-61 F 6
Siare Guajibos ○ CO 60-61 F 6
Siari, Isla ⌒ MEX 50-51 D 4
Siasi ○ RP 160-161 D 10
Siasi Island ⌒ RP 160-161 D 10
Siasikabole ○ Z 218-219 D 3
Siassi ○ PNG 183 D 3
Siatlai ○ MYA 142-143 H 4
Siaton Point ▲ RP 160-161 E 8
Siau, Pulau ⌒ RI 164-165 J 2
Šiauliai ○ LT 94-95 H 4
Šiauliai ☆•• LT 94-95 H 4
Siavonga ○ Z 218-219 E 3
Siayyira, as- ○ KSA 130-131 H 4
Siazan' = Siyazan ○ AZ 128-129 N 2
Sib, as- ○ OM 132-133 L 2
Siba ○ IR 134-135 C 3
Siba, as- ○ IRQ 130-131 J 3
Sibabli ○ CI 202-203 G 6
Sibaj ○ RUS 96-97 L 7
Sibalanga ○ RI 162-163 C 3
Sibalay Aricha ○ BD 142-143 F 4
Šibam ○••• Y 132-133 F 6
Sibanicú ○ C 54-55 G 4
Šibar, Kōtal-e ▲ AFG 138-139 B 2
Sibari ○ I 100-101 F 5
Sibaru, Cachoeira do ~ BR 68-69 B 5
Sibayameer ⊖ ZA 220-221 L 3
Sibayo ○ PE 70-71 B 4
Sibayu ○ RI 164-165 F 3
Sibbald ○ CDN (ALB) 232-233 H 4
Sibbeston Lake ⊖ CDN 30-31 H 5
Šibenik ○ HR 100-101 E 3
Siberia = Sibir' □ RUS 10-11 H 2
Siberimanua ○ RI 162-163 C 6
Siberut, Pulau ⌒ RI 162-163 C 5
Siberut, Selat ≈ 162-163 C 5
Sibi ○ PK 134-135 M 4
Sibi ○ RMM 202-203 F 3
Sibidiri ○ PNG 183 B 5
Sibie ○ LB 202-203 F 6
Sibigo ○ RI 162-163 A 3
Sibiloi National Park ⊥ EAK 212-213 F 1
Šibīn al-Kūm ☆ ET 194-195 E 2
Sibircevo ○ RUS 122-123 E 6
Sibirien ⫠ RUS 10-11 H 2
Sibirjakova, ostrov ⌒ RUS 108-109 S 5
Sibirskaja ravina ⫠ RUS 114-115 J 4
Sibirskie Uvaly ▲ RUS 114-115 J 3
Sibiti ~ EAT 212-213 E 5
Sibiti ☆ RCB 210-211 D 5
Sibiu ☆• RO 102-103 D 5
Sib Kūh ▲ IR 134-135 E 5
Sibley ○ USA (IA) 274-275 C 1
Sibley ○ USA (LA) 268-269 G 4
Sibley ○ USA (ND) 258-259 J 4
Siboa ○ RI 164-165 G 3
Sibolga ○ RI 162-163 C 4
Siboluton ○ RI 164-165 G 3
Siborongborong ○ RI 162-163 C 3
Sibr ○ OM 132-133 J 5
Sibsa ~ BD 142-143 F 4
Sibsagar ○ IND 142-143 J 2
Sibt, as- ○ KSA 132-133 C 5
Sibu ○ MAL 162-163 J 3
Sibu, Pulau ⌒ MAL 162-163 F 3
Sibuco ○ RP 160-161 E 9
Sibuguey ~ RP 160-161 E 9
Sibuguey Bay ≈ 160-161 E 9
Si Bun Ruang ○ THA 158-159 G 2
Siburan ○ MAL 162-163 J 4
Sibut ☆ RCA 206-207 D 6
Sibutu Island ⌒ RP 160-161 C 10
Sibutu Kepulauan ⌒ RP 160-161 C 10
Sibutu Passage ≈ RP 160-161 C 10
Sibuyan Island ⌒ RP 160-161 E 6
Sibuyan Sea ≈ 160-161 E 6
Sicamous ○ CDN (BC) 230-231 L 3
Sicapoo, Mount ▲ RP 160-161 D 3
Sicasica, Serranía de ▲ BOL 70-71 D 5
Siccus River ~ AUS 178-179 E 6
Si Chomphu ○ THA 158-159 G 2
Sichon ○ THA 158-159 E 6
Sichuan □ VRC 154-155 C 6
Sicilia □ I 100-101 D 6
Sicily = Sicilia ⌒ I 100-101 E 6
Sico, Paso ▲ RCH 76-77 D 2
Sico Tinto o Negro, Río ~ HN 54-55 C 7
Sicuani ○ PE 70-71 B 4
Šičuga ○ RUS 88-89 T 6
Sicunusa ○ SD 220-221 K 3
Sida ~ RUS 116-117 L 2
Sid Ahmed < RIM 196-197 F 6
Sidamo □ ETH 208-209 D 6
Sidangoli ○ RI 164-165 K 3
Sidareja ○ RI 168 C 3
Siddāpur ○ IND 140-141 F 3
Siddhapur ○ IND 138-139 D 8
Siddipet ○ IND 138-139 G 10
Side • TR 128-129 D 4
Sideia Island ⌒ PNG 183 F 6
Sidéradougou ○ BF 202-203 H 4
Sideros, Akra ▲ GR 100-101 L 7
Šiderti ○ KA 124-125 J 3
Šiderty ~ KA 124-125 H 3
Sidewood ○ CDN (SAS) 232-233 K 5
Sidhauli ○ IND 142-143 B 2
Sidhi ○ IND 142-143 B 3
Sidhnūr ○ IND 140-141 G 3
Sidi ○ RCA 206-207 D 6
Sidi 'Abdarrahmān ○ ET 194-195 D 2
Sidi Aïssa ○ DZ 190-191 D 3
Sidi Ali ○ DZ 190-191 C 2
Sidi-Allal-el-Babravi ○ MA 188-189 H 4
Sidi Amor Bou Hajla ○ TN 190-191 H 3
Sidi as Ṣayd ○ LAR 192-193 E 1
Sidi Barrāni ○ ET 192-193 L 2
Sidi-Bennour ○ MA 188-189 G 4
Sidi-Bettache ○ MA 188-189 H 4
Sidi Boubekeur ○ DZ 190-191 C 3
Sidi Bouzid ☆ TN 190-191 G 3
Sidi El Hani, Sebkhet ⊖ TN 190-191 H 3
Sidi-Hajjaj ○ MA 188-189 H 4
Sidi Hamadouche ○ DZ 188-189 L 3
Sidi-Harazem ○ MA 188-189 J 4
Sidi Hasseur, Oued ~ DZ 190-191 C 3
Sidi Ifni ○ MA 188-189 F 6
Sidi-Kacem ☆ MA 188-189 J 3
Sidikalang ○ RI 162-163 C 3
Sidi Khaled ○ DZ 190-191 E 3
Sidi Khalifah ○ LAR 192-193 J 1
Sidikidougou ○ RG 202-203 F 5
Sidikila ○ RG 202-203 F 4
Sidi Ladjel ○ DZ 190-191 D 3
Sidi Mohamed, Barrage < MA 188-189 H 4
Sidi-Mokhtar ○ MA 188-189 G 5
Sidi Mokhtâr < RMM 196-197 J 5
Sidi Moulay Lahsene • DZ 190-191 E 8
Sidi Moussa ~ DZ 190-191 E 7
Sidi-Moussa ○ MA 188-189 G 4
Siding Spring Observatory • AUS 178-179 K 6
Sidi-Slimane ○ MA 188-189 J 3
Sidi-Smaïl ○ MA 188-189 G 4
Sidi Youssef ○ TN 190-191 H 3
Sidlaghatta ○ IND 140-141 G 4
Sid Lake ⊖ CDN 30-31 R 4
Sidley, Mount ▲ ARK 16 F 24
Sidli ○ IND 142-143 G 2
Sidmouth, Cape ▲ AUS 174-175 G 3
Sidney ○ CDN (BC) 230-231 F 5
Sidney ○ CDN (MAN) 234-235 D 5
Sidney ○ USA (IA) 274-275 C 4
Sidney ○ USA (MT) 250-251 P 4
Sidney ○ USA (NE) 262-263 D 3
Sidney ○ USA (NY) 278-279 F 6
Sidney ○ USA (OH) 280-281 B 3
Sidney Lanier, Lake < USA (GA) 284-285 G 2
Sido ○ RMM 202-203 G 4
Sidoarjo ○ RI 168 E 3
Sidole, Gunung ▲ RI 164-165 F 4
Sidondo ○ RI 164-165 F 4
Sidra = Surt ○ LAR 192-193 G 2
Sidrolândia ○ BR 70-71 K 7
Siedge Island ⌒ USA 20-21 G 4
Siedlce ○ PL 92-93 R 2
Siegburg ○ D 92-93 J 3
Siegen ○ D 92-93 K 3
Siekobenkurom ○ GH 202-203 J 6
Siékorolé ○ RMM 202-203 F 4
Sielezavanga ○ SOL 184 I c 2
Siembra ○ RI 166-167 G 3
Siemiatycze ○ PL 92-93 R 2
Siĕmpang ○ K 158-159 J 3
Siĕmréap ○ K 158-159 G 4
Siena ○•• I 100-101 C 3
Sieradz ☆• PL 92-93 P 3
Sierpc ○ PL 92-93 P 2
Sierpe, La ○ C 54-55 F 4
Sierra, Punta ▲ RA 78-79 G 6
Sierra Blanca ○ USA (TX) 266-267 B 2
Sierra Chica ○ RA 78-79 J 4
Sierra Colorada ○ RA 78-79 F 6
Sierra de Lacandón, Parque Nacional ⊥ • GCA 52-53 J 3
Sierra de la Ventana ○ RA 78-79 J 5
Sierra de San Pedro Mártir, Parque Nacional ⊥ MEX 50-51 B 2
Sierra Gorda ○• RCH 76-77 C 2
Sierra Grande ○ RA 78-79 G 6
Sierra Leone ■ WAL 202-203 D 5
Sierra Leone Basin ≃ 6-7 H 8
Sierra Leone Rise ≃ 6-7 G 8
Sierra Madre ▲ RP 160-161 D 4
Sierra Mojada ○ MEX 50-51 H 4
Sierra Morena ▲ E 98-99 D 6
Sierra Nevada ▲ E 98-99 F 6
Sierra Nevada ▲ USA 40-41 D 6
Sierra Nevada, Parque Nacional ⊥ YV 60-61 F 3
Sierra Nevada de Santa Marta ▲ CO 60-61 E 2
Sierra Overa, Pampa ⫠ RCH 76-77 B 3
Sierra Pailemán ○ RA 78-79 G 6
Sierraville ○ USA (CA) 246-247 E 4
Sierra Vista ○ USA (AZ) 256-257 E 7
Siete Puntas, Río ~ PY 76-77 J 2
Siete Tazas, Parque Nacional ⊥ RCH 78-79 D 3
Sietindže ~ RUS 110-111 S 5
Šifā', Ğabal aš- ▲ KSA 130-131 E 4
Sifahandra ○ RI 162-163 B 4
Sifeni ○ ETH 200-201 K 6
Sif Fatima ○ DZ 190-191 G 5
Siffleur Wilderness ⊥ CDN (ALB) 232-233 B 4
Sifié ○ CI 202-203 G 6
Sifni, 'Ain ○ IRQ 128-129 K 4
Sifnos ⌒ GR 100-101 K 6
Sifton ○ CDN (MAN) 234-235 C 3
Sigaiéktap ~ RUS 120-121 U 4
Sigatoka ○ FJI 184 III a 3
Sigel ○ USA (PA) 280-281 G 2
Sigenti ○ RI 164-165 G 3
Sigfried, Monte ▲ RCH 80 C 4
Sighetu Marmaţiei ○• RO 102-103 C 4
Sighişoara ○• RO 102-103 D 4
Sigiriya ○••• CL 140-141 J 6
Sigiso Plain ⫠ EAK 212-213 G 2
Sigli ○ RI 162-163 A 2
Siglufjörður ○ IS 86-87 d 1
Signal Hill National Historic Park ⊥• CDN (NFL) 242-243 Q 5
Signal Mountain ○ USA (TN) 276-277 K 5
Signal Peak ▲ USA (AZ) 256-257 A 5
Signy ○ ARK 16 G 32
Sigoisooinan ○ RI 162-163 C 6
Šigony ☆ RUS 96-97 F 7
Sigor ○ EAK 212-213 E 3
Sigourney ○ USA (IA) 274-275 F 3
Sigovec, ostrov ⌒ RUS 88-89 N 5
Sigsbee Deep ≃ 4 E 6
Sigsig ○ EC 64-65 C 3
Siguanea ○ C 54-55 D 4
Siguatepeque ○ HN 52-53 L 4
Sigüenza ○ E 98-99 F 4
Sigüés ○ E 98-99 G 3
Siguiri ○ RG 202-203 F 4
Sigulda ○•• LV 94-95 J 3
Sigurd ○ USA (UT) 254-255 D 5
Siguri Falls ~ EAT 214-215 J 5
Sihabuhabu, Gunung ▲ RI 162-163 C 3
Šihām ○• Y 132-133 C 6
Šihan, Wādī ~ OM 132-133 H 4
Šihany ○ RUS 96-97 E 7
Sihāwā ○ IND 142-143 B 5
Sihong ○ VRC 154-155 L 5
Sihora ○ IND 142-143 B 4
Sihotè-Alin' ▲ RUS 122-123 E 7
Šihr, aš- ○• Y 132-133 F 6
Sihuas ○ PE 64-65 D 6
Sihuas, Pampas de ⫠ PE 70-71 A 5
Sihui ○ VRC 156-157 H 5
Siikajoki ~ FIN 88-89 H 4
Siilinjärvi ○ FIN 88-89 J 5
Siirt ☆• TR 128-129 J 4
Sijetindenskij hrebet ▲ RUS 110-111 R 5
Sik ○ MAL 162-163 D 2
Sika ○ IND 138-139 B 8
Sikaiana Island ⌒ SOL 184 I f 3
Sikakap, Selat ≈ 162-163 D 6
Sikandra Rao ○ IND 138-139 G 6
Sikanni Chief River ~ CDN 32-33 J 3
Sikar ○ IND 138-139 E 6
Sikasso □ RMM 202-203 F 4
Sikasso ☆ RMM (SIK) 202-203 H 4
Sikeli ○ RI 164-165 G 6
Sikensi ○ CI 202-203 H 7
Sikereti ○ NAM 216-217 F 9
Sikeston ○ USA (MO) 276-277 F 4
Sikhoraphum ○ THA 158-159 G 3
Sikía ○ GR 100-101 J 4
Sikinos ⌒ GR 100-101 K 6
Sikiré ○ BF 202-203 K 2
Sikkim □ IND 142-143 F 2
Sikonge ○ EAT 212-213 D 6
Sikongo ○ Z 218-219 B 2
Sikopo Island ⌒ SOL 184 I c 2
Sikoro ○ EAU 212-213 E 3
Šikotan, ostrov ⌒ RUS 122-123 M 7
Sikr, as- ○ IRQ 130-131 H 2
Siktjah ○ RUS 110-111 P 5

Sikutu o RI 164-165 G 3
Sil, Río ~ E 98-99 D 3
Sila o PNG 183 E 5
Sila o RI 168 D 7
Sila, La ▲ I 100-101 F 5
Silaer o RI 162-163 C 3
Šil Āġa o SYR 128-129 J 4
Silago o RP 160-161 F 7
Šilalė o•• LT 94-95 H 4
Silang o RI 164-165 K 4
Silango o PNG 183 F 3
Silao o MEX 52-53 D 1
Silas o USA (AL) 284-285 B 5
Silavatturai o CL 140-141 H 6
Silay o RP 160-161 E 7
Silchar o IND 142-143 H 3
Silcox o CDN 34-35 J 2
Silda o IND 142-143 E 4
Šifda o RUS 96-97 L 8
Şile ☆• TR 128-129 C 2
Sileia o SUD 198-199 L 5
Silencio, El o YV 60-61 K 3
Siler City o USA (NC) 282-283 H 5
Sileru ~ IND 142-143 B 7
Silesia o USA (MT) 250-251 L 6
Silet o DZ 190-191 E 9
Sileti ~ KA 124-125 G 3
Siletiteniz, köli o KA 124-125 H 2
Siletz o USA (OR) 244-245 B 6
Silhouette Island ⌒ SY 224 D 2
Šili ☆ KA 124-125 E 6
Siliana ☆ TN 190-191 G 2
Siliana, Oued ~ TN 190-191 G 2
Silifke o TR 128-129 E 4
Siligir ~ RUS 110-111 J 6
Šilik o KA 136-137 L 3
Šilikty o KA 124-125 O 5
Silil, togga ~ SP 208-209 F 3
Siling o VRC 144-145 E 6
Siling Co o VRC 144-145 G 5
Silisili, Mount ▲ WS 184 V a 1
Silivri ☆ TR 128-129 C 2
Siljan o S 86-87 G 6
Siljap ~ RUS 110-111 . 6
Šilka ~ RUS 118-119 G 10
Šilka ~ RUS 118-119 J 9
Silkeborg o DK 86-87 D 8
Silk Road -North Road II VRC 146-147 E 5
Silk Road -South Road II• VRC 144-145 D 2
Silk Weaving o• RI 164-165 G 6
Silkwood o AUS 174-175 J 5
Sill, Fort xx USA (OK) 264-265 F 4
Silla o E 98-99 G 5
Silla, La o CO 60-61 E 3
Sillānwāli o PK 138-139 D 4
Sillein = Žilina o SK 92-93 P 4
Silli o BF 202-203 J 4
Sillod o IND 138-139 E 9
Silmi o ETH 208-209 E 4
Šil'naja Balka o KA 96-97 F 8
Sil Nakya o USA (AZ) 256-257 D 6
Siloam Springs o USA (AR) 276-277 A 4
Silobela o ZW 218-219 E 4
Silom o PNG 183 G 2
Silong o VRC 156-157 F 5
Silopi ☆ TR 128-129 K 4
Silovajaha ~ RUS 108-109 K 7
Šilovo o RUS 94-95 R 4
Silowana Plains ⩡ Z 218-219 B 3
Silsand o N 86-87 H 2
Silsbee o USA (TX) 268-269 F 6
Silsby Lake o CDN 34-35 J 3
Silton o CDN (SAS) 232-233 O 5
Siltou < TCH 198-199 G 4
Siluas o RI 162-163 H 4
Siluko o WAN 204-205 F 5
Siluko, River ~ WAN 204-205 F 5
Silumiut, Cap ▲ CDN 30-31 Y 4
Šilutė ☆•• LT 94-95 G 4
Silutshana o ZA 220-221 K 4
Silva o USA (MO) 276-277 E 3
Silva, Ribeiro da ~ BR 72-73 E 2
Silvan ☆ TR 128-129 J 3
Silvan Baraji < TR 128-129 J 3
Silvāne o IR 128-129 L 4
Silvânia o BR 72-73 F 4
Silva Porto Gare o ANG 216-217 D 6
Silvassa ☆ IND 138-139 D 9
Silver o CDN (MAN) 234-235 F 4
Silver Bank ≃ 54-55 L 4
Silver Bank Passage ≈ 54-55 K 4
Silver Bay o USA (MN) 270-271 G 3
Silver Beach o USA (VA) 280-281 L 6
Silver City o USA (IA) 274-275 C 3
Silver City o USA (NM) 256-257 G 6
Silver City o USA (TX) 266-267 L 2
Silver City o USA (ID) 252-253 B 3
Silver City Highway II AUS 180-181 F 2
Silver Creek o USA (NE) 262-263 J 3
Silver Creek o USA (NY) 278-279 B 6
Silver Creek ~ USA (OR) 244-245 F 7
Silverdale o USA (MN) 270-271 E 3
Silverdale o USA (WA) 244-245 C 3
Silver Dollar o CDN (ONT) 234-235 M 5
Silver Gate o USA (MT) 250-251 K 6
Silver Islet o CDN (ONT) 234-235 P 6
Silver Lake o USA (OR) 244-245 D 7
Silver Lake o USA (WA) 244-245 C 4
Silver Lake o USA (CA) 248-249 H 4
Silver Park o CDN (SAS) 232-233 O 3
Silverpeak o USA (NV) 248-249 G 2
Silver Plains o AUS 174-175 G 4
Silversand o NAM 216-217 D 11
Silver Springs o USA (NV) 246-247 F 4
Silver Springs o• USA (FL) 286-287 G 2
Silver Star Mine o AUS 174-175 E 6
Silver Star Provincial Recreation Area ⊥ CDN (BC) 230-231 L 3
Silverthorne o USA (CO) 254-255 J 4
Silverthrone Glacier ⊂ CDN (BC) 230-231 C 2
Silverthrone Mountain ▲ CDN (BC) 230-231 C 2
Silverton o AUS 178-179 F 6
Silverton o CDN (MAN) 234-235 B 4
Silverton o USA (CO) 254-255 H 6
Silverton o USA (OR) 244-245 C 5
Silverton o USA (TX) 264-265 C 4
Silver Zone Pass ▲ USA (NV) 246-247 L 3
Silves o BR 66-67 H 4
Silves o• P 98-99 C 6
Silvia o CO 60-61 C 6
Silvies River ~ USA (OR) 244-245 F 7
Silvituc o MEX 52-53 J 2
Silvrettagruppe ▲ CH 92-93 K 5
Sim ☆ RUS 96-97 K 6
Sim ~ RUS 96-97 K 6
Sim, Cap ▲ MA 188-189 G 5
Sima o COM 222-223 D 4
Sima o USA (CO) 254-255 L 4
Simakalo o RI 162-163 D 6
Simamba o Z 218-219 C 3
Simanindo o• RI 162-163 C 3
Šimanovsk o RUS 122-123 B 3
Šimanovsk ☆ RUS 118-119 N 9
Simao o VRC 156-157 B 5
Simão Dias o BR 68-69 K 7
Simão Pereira o BR 72-73 J 6
Simara Island ⌒ RP 160-161 E 6
Simard, Lac o CDN (QUE) 236-237 K 5
Simatang, Pulau ⌒ RI 164-165 G 3
Simav ☆ TR 128-129 C 3
Simav Çayı ~ TR 128-129 C 3
Simba o ZRE 210-211 J 3
Simbai o PNG 183 C 3
Simberi Island ⌒ PNG 183 G 2
Simbi o RMM 202-203 F 2
Simbirsk ☆ RUS 96-97 F 6
Simbo o EAT 212-213 B 6
Simbo o MYA 142-143 K 3
Simbo ⌒ SOL 184 I c 3
Simcoe o CDN (ONT) 238-239 E 6
Simcoe, Lake o CDN (ONT) 238-239 F 4
Simdega o IND 142-143 D 4
Simēn ▲ ETH 200-201 J 6
Simēn National Park ⊥••• ETH 200-201 J 6
Simenti o SN 202-203 D 3
Simeonof Island ⌒ USA 22-23 R 5
Simeto ~ I 100-101 E 6
Simeulue, Pulau ⌒ RI 162-163 B 3
Simferopol' ☆•• UA 102-103 J 5
Simhadripuram o IND 140-141 H 3
Šimḥān, Ǧabal ▲ OM 132-133 J 5
Simi ⌒ GR 100-101 L 6
Simianona ~ RM 222-223 F 6
Simiegan ~ RUS 114-115 M 3
Simikot o NEP 144-145 C 6
Similigurha o IND 142-143 C 6
Similkameen River ~ CDN (BC) 230-231 J 4
Simindou o RCA 206-207 F 5
Simine Rūd ~ IR 128-129 L 4
Siminiout o F 62-63 H 4
Simiri o RN 204-205 E 1
Simiriundui o GUY 62-63 D 2
Šimiš, Rūd-e ~ IR 134-135 J 5
Simitli o BG 102-103 C 7
Simiutaq ⌒ GRØ 28-29 O 3
Simi Valley o USA (CA) 248-249 F 5
Simiyu ~ EAT 212-213 D 5
Simla ☆• IND 138-139 F 4
Simlipal Massif ▲ IND 142-143 E 5
Simlipal National Park ⊥ IND 142-143 E 5
Simmesport o USA (LA) 268-269 J 6
Simmie o CDN (SAS) 232-233 K 6
Simmler o USA (CA) 248-249 E 4
Simmons's Peninsula ⌣ CDN 24-25 b 2
Simms o BS 54-55 H 3
Simms o USA (MT) 250-251 H 4
Simo o FIN 88-89 H 4
Simões o BR 68-69 H 5
Simões Filho o BR 72-73 L 2
Simojärvi o FIN 88-89 J 3
Simojovel de Allende o MEX 52-53 H 3
Simon, Lac o CDN (QUE) 238-239 K 3
Simona o BOL 70-71 G 4
Simonette River ~ CDN (ALB) 228-229 R 2
Simonhouse o CDN 34-35 F 3
Simoni o Z 214-215 G 7
Simonstad = Simon's Town o ZA 220-221 D 7
Simon's Town = Simonstad o ZA 220-221 D 7
Simoon Harbour o CDN (BC) 230-231 C 3
Simoon Sound o CDN (BC) 230-231 C 3
Simpang o RI 162-163 F 5
Simpang Ampat Rungkup o MAL 162-163 D 3
Simpang-Kanan ~ RI 162-163 C 3
Simpangkawat o RI 162-163 C 3
Simpang Kiri ~ RI 162-163 B 3
Simpangsukarame o RI 162-163 F 7
Simpatia o BR 66-67 B 7
Simplício Mendes o BR 68-69 H 5
Simplonpass ▲ CH 92-93 K 5
Simpsom, Río ~ RCH 80 D 2
Simpson o CDN (SAS) 232-233 N 4
Simpson o USA (LA) 268-269 H 5
Simpson o USA (MT) 250-251 J 3
Simpson, Cape ▲ USA 20-21 N 1
Simpson, Mount ▲ PNG 183 E 6
Simpson, Port o CDN (BC) 228-229 D 2
Simpson Bay ≈ 24-25 P 6
Simpson Desert ⌣ AUS 178-179 D 3
Simpson Desert Conservation Park ⊥ AUS 178-179 D 4
Simpson Desert National Park ⊥ AUS 178-179 E 3
Simpson Island ⌒ CDN (ONT) 234-235 Q 6
Simpson Islands ⌒ CDN 30-31 N 5
Simpson Lake o CDN 24-25 J 6
Simpson Peninsula ⌣ CDN 24-25 b 6
Simpson Regional Reserve ⊥ AUS 178-179 D 4
Simpson River ~ CDN 30-31 U 2
Simpsons Gap National Park ⊥ AUS 176-177 M 1
Simpson Strait ≈ 24-25 X 6
Simpsonville o USA (SC) 284-285 H 2
Simrishamn o S 86-87 G 9
Šimsk o RUS 94-95 M 2
Sims Lake o CDN 36-37 Q 7
Simsom, Isla ⌒ RCH 80 D 2
Simtustus, Lake o USA (OR) 244-245 D 6
Simuk, Pulau ⌒ RI 162-163 B 5
Simunjan o MAL 162-163 J 4
Simunul Island ⌒ RP 160-161 C 10
Simušir, ostrov ⌒ RUS 122-123 P 5
Sina ~ IND 138-139 E 10
Sina o PE 70-71 C 4
Sinabang o RI 162-163 B 3
Sina Daqha o SP 208-209 H 6
Sinadipan o RP 160-161 D 4
Šināfiya, as- o IRQ 128-129 L 7
Sinagoga, Ponta da o CV 202-203 B 5
Sinai, Mount = Ǧabal Mūsa ▲ ET 194-195 F 3
Sinai = Sinā' ⌣ ET 194-195 F 3
Sinaia o• RO 102-103 D 5
Sinaloa ◘ MEX 50-51 E 4
Sinaloa, Río ~ MEX 50-51 E 5
Sinaloa de Leyva o MEX 50-51 E 5
Sinamaica o YV 60-61 F 2
Sinamatella Camp o ZW 218-219 D 4
Sinan o VRC 156-157 F 3
Sinanpaşa ☆ TR 128-129 D 3
Sināw o OM 132-133 K 1
Sinau o WAN 204-205 E 4
Sināwin o LAR 190-191 H 5
Sinawongourou o DY 204-205 E 3
Sinazongwe o Z 218-219 D 3
Sinbaungwe o MYA 142-143 J 6
Sinbyugyun o MYA 142-143 J 5
Sincan o TR 128-129 G 3
Since o CO 60-61 D 3
Sincelejo ☆ CO 60-61 D 3
Sincerin o CO 60-61 D 2
Sinchaingbyin o MYA 142-143 H 5
Sinclair o CDN (MAN) 234-235 B 5
Sinclair o USA (WY) 252-253 L 5
Sinclair, Lake < USA (GA) 284-285 G 3
Sinclair Mills o CDN (BC) 228-229 N 2
Sincorá, Serra do ▲ BR 72-73 K 2
Sincos o PE 64-65 E 7
Sind ◘ PK 134-135 M 5
Sinda o Z 218-219 F 2
Šindand o• AFG 134-135 K 2
Sindangan o RP 160-161 E 8
Sindangan Bay ≈ 160-161 E 8
Sindangbarang o RI 168 B 3
Sindanglaut o RI 168 C 3
Sindari o IND 138-139 C 7
Sindia o SN 202-203 B 2
Sindian o SN 202-203 B 3
Šindib, Ǧabal ▲ ET 194-195 H 6
Sindor o RUS 88-89 V 5
Sindou o BF 202-203 H 4
Sine ~ SN 202-203 B 2
Sinee morco cyganckaya ≈ 96-97 F 10
Sinegor'e o RUS 120-121 O 2
Sinegorsk o RUS 122-123 K 5
Sinegorskij o RUS 102-103 M 3
Sinendé o DY 204-205 E 3
Sines o P 98-99 C 6
Sines, Cabo de ▲ P 98-99 C 6
Siné-Saloum, Parc National du ⊥ SN 202-203 B 3
Sinettä o FIN 88-89 H 3
Šinėžinsk = Zalaa o MAU 148-149 D 5
Sinfra o CI 202-203 H 6
Singa o• SUD 200-201 F 6
Singa o ZRE 210-211 J 3
Singako o TCH 206-207 D 4
Singapore ■ SGP 162-163 E 4
Singapore ☆•• SGP 162-163 E 4
Singapore, Selat ≈ 162-163 E 4
Singār, Balad o IRQ 128-129 J 4
Singār, Ǧabal ▲ IRQ 128-129 J 4
Singaraja o RI 168 B 7
Sing Buri o THA 158-159 F 3
Singer o USA (LA) 268-269 G 6
Singhampton o CDN (ONT) 238-239 E 4
Singhamton o CDN (ONT) 238-239 E 4
Singida ◘ EAT 214-215 H 4
Singida ☆ EAT 212-213 E 6
Singilej ☆ RUS 96-97 F 7
Singiro ▲ EAU 212-213 C 4
Singkang o RI 164-165 G 6
Singkarak o RI 162-163 D 5
Singkarak, Danau o RI 162-163 D 5
Singkawang o RI 162-163 H 4
Singkep, Pulau ⌒ RI 162-163 F 5
Singkil = Singkilbaru o RI 162-163 B 3
Singkilbaru o RI 162-163 B 3
Singleton o AUS 180-181 L 2
Singleton, Mount ▲ AUS (NT) 172-173 K 7
Singleton, Mount ▲ AUS (WA) 176-177 D 4
Singorokai o PNG 183 D 3
Singosari o• RI 168 E 3
Singou ~ BF 202-203 L 4
Singou, Réserve du ⊥ BF 202-203 L 4
Singrobo o CI 202-203 H 6
Singuédeze, Rio ~ MOC 218-219 F 6
Singye o DVR 150-151 F 8
Sinharagama o CL 140-141 J 6
Sinharaja Forest Reserve ⊥••• CL 140-141 J 7
Sin Hồ o VN 156-157 C 5
Sinhung o DVR 150-151 F 7
Sinie Lipjagi o RUS 102-103 L 2
Sinij, hrebet ▲ RUS 122-123 E 6
Siniscóla o I 100-101 B 4
Sinj o HR 100-101 F 3
Sinjai o RI 164-165 G 6
Sinjaja ~ RUS 118-119 N 5
Sinjembela o Z 218-219 B 3
Sinjuga o RUS 118-119 G 7
Sinkāt o• SUD 200-201 H 3
Sinkiang = Xinjiang Uygur Zizhiqu ◘ VRC 146-147 D 5
Sinko o RG 202-203 F 5
Sinmido ⌒ DVR 150-151 E 8
Sinnamary o F 62-63 H 3
Sinnamary ~ F 62-63 H 3
Sinnar o IND 138-139 E 10
Sinnett o CDN (SAS) 232-233 O 4
Sînnicolau Mare o RO 102-103 B 4
Sin Nombre, Cerro ▲ RCH 80 D 3
Sinnūris o ET 194-195 E 3
Sinop o BR 70-71 K 2
Sinop ☆• TR 128-129 F 1
Sinque ~ LS 220-221 J 5
Šinšār o SYR 128-129 G 5
Sinsicap o PE 64-65 C 5
Sinsk o RUS 118-119 N 5
Sintaluta o CDN (SAS) 232-233 P 5
Sintang o RI 162-163 J 4
Sint Eustatius ⌒ NA 56 D 3
Sint Maarten ⌒ NA 56 D 2
Sint Nicolaas o ARU 60-61 G 1
Sint-Niklaas o B 92-93 H 3
Sinton o USA (TX) 266-267 K 5
Sintong o RI 162-163 D 4
Sintra o•• P 98-99 C 5
Sinú, Río ~ CO 60-61 C 3
Sinuiju ☆ DVR 150-151 E 7
Sinujiif o SP 208-209 J 4
Sinuk o USA 20-21 G 4
Sinuk River ~ USA 20-21 H 4
Sinungu o Z 218-219 B 2
Siodjuru o SOL 184 I e 3
Siófok o H 92-93 P 5
Sioma o Z 218-219 B 3
Sioma Ngwezi National Park ⊥ Z 218-219 B 3
Sion ☆• CH 92-93 J 5
Sionainn = Shannon o IRL 90-91 C 5
Siorapaluk o GRØ 26-27 P 5
Siorarsuk Peninsula ⌣ CDN 24-25 f 5
Siota o RI 166-167 D 6
Siota o SOL 184 I e 3
Sioux Center o USA (IA) 274-275 B 1
Sioux City o USA (IA) 274-275 B 2
Sioux Falls o• USA (SD) 260-261 K 3
Sioux Indian Museum • USA (SD) 260-261 F 3
Sioux Lookout o CDN (ONT) 234-235 M 4
Sioux Narrows o CDN (ONT) 234-235 J 5
Sioux Rapids o USA (IA) 274-275 C 2
Sioux Valley o USA (MN) 270-271 C 7
Sipacate o GCA 52-53 J 5
Sipahutar o RI 162-163 C 3
Sipai o PNG 184 I b 1
Sipalay o RP 160-161 E 8
Sipaliwini o SME 62-63 F 4
Sipán • PE 64-65 C 5
Sipang, Tanjung ▲ MAL 162-163 J 4
Sipao o YV 60-61 J 4
Sipapo, Reserva Florestal ⊥ YV 60-61 H 5
Šipčenski Prohod ▲ BG 102-103 D 6
Sipi o CO 60-61 C 5
Šipicyno o RUS 88-89 T 6
Sipilou o CI 202-203 F 6
Siping o VRC 150-151 E 6
Sipiongot o RI 162-163 C 4
Sipirok o RI 162-163 C 4
Sipitang o MAL 160-161 A 10
Sipiwesk o CDN 34-35 H 3
Sipiwesk Lake o CDN 34-35 H 3
Siple, Mount ▲ ARK 16 F 24
Sipora, Selat ≈ 162-163 C 6
Šipovlės • RUS 102-103 M 2
Sippar ∴• IRQ 128-129 L 6
Sipsey Fork ~ USA (AL) 284-285 C 2
Sipsey Fork ~ USA (AL) 284-285 C 3
Sipsey River ~ USA (AL) 284-285 C 3
Sipuca, Quebrada de ~ RCH 76-77 C 1
Šipunovo o RUS 124-125 N 2
Šipunskij, poluostrov ⌣ RUS 120-121 T 7
Sipura, Pulau ⌒ RI 162-163 C 6
Siquerres o CR 52-53 C 6
Siquia o NIC 52-53 B 5
Siquia, Río ~ NIC 52-53 B 5
Siquijor ☆ RP 160-161 E 8
Siquijor Island ⌒ RP 160-161 E 8
Siquisique o YV 60-61 G 2
Sira o YV 60-61 H 5
Sira o IND 140-141 G 4
Sira ~ N 86-87 C 7
Šira ☆ RUS 116-117 E 8
Šira, ozero o RUS 116-117 E 8
Sira, Reserva Nacional del ⊥ PE 64-65 E 6
Širaāz ☆•• IR 134-135 E 4
Sir Abu Nu'air ⌒ UAE 134-135 F 6
Sirač o HR 100-101 E 2
Sirač o IR 134-135 G 3
Siracha o THA 158-159 F 4
Siracusa o I 100-101 E 6
Siraguay o RP 160-161 E 9
Širā'īn o KSA 132-133 B 3
Sirajganj o BD 142-143 F 3
Sirakoro o RMM (KAY) 202-203 F 3
Sirakoro o RMM (SIK) 202-203 G 4
Sirakorola o RMM 202-203 G 3
Sir Alexander, Mount ▲ CDN (ALB) 228-229 O 3
Siramana o RG 202-203 F 4
Şiran ☆ TR 128-129 H 2
Sirana d'Odienne o CI 202-203 G 5
Sirasso o CI 202-203 G 5
Sirba ~ RN 202-203 L 3
Sir Bani Yās ⌒ UAE 134-135 E 6
Sirbin o ET 194-195 E 2
Sir Charles Todo Monument • AUS 174-175 B 5
Sirdān o IR 128-129 N 4
Sirdar o CDN (BC) 230-231 N 4
Sirdarē ☆ US 136-137 L 4
Sir Douglas, Mount ▲ CDN (ALB) 232-233 C 5
Sire o EAT 212-213 C 6
Sire o ETH (Ars) 208-209 D 4
Sirē o ETH (Wel) 208-209 C 4
Sirebi River ~ PNG 183 C 4
Sir Edward Pellew Group ⌒ AUS 174-175 D 4
Širēēt o MAU 148-149 L 5
Siref o TCH 198-199 K 6
Siren o USA (WI) 270-271 F 5
Sirena o CR 52-53 C 7
Sireniki o RUS 112-113 Y 4
Siret ~ RO 102-103 E 5
Siret ~ UA 102-103 D 3
Širgāh o IR 136-137 C 6
Širǧān o IR 134-135 F 4
Sirha o NEP 144-145 F 7
Šir Ḥān o AFG 136-137 L 6
Sirhān, Wādi as- ⩡ KSA 130-131 E 2
Sirheni o ZA 218-219 F 6
Sirik o IR 134-135 G 5
Sirik o MAL 162-163 J 3
Sirikit Reservoir < THA 142-143 M 6
Sirinhaém o BR 68-69 L 6
Sirin Rūd ~ IR 136-137 C 6
Širin Tagāb o AFG 136-137 J 6
Širin Tagāb, Daryā-ye ~ AFG 136-137 J 6
Sirinumu Lake < PNG 183 D 5
Siriri o BR 68-69 K 7
Sirius Seamount ≃ 22-23 Q 7
Siriwo ~ RI 166-167 H 3
Siriworra o RI 166-167 G 3
Sir James MacBrien, Mount ▲ CDN 30-31 F 4
Sir Joseph Banks Group ⌒ AUS 180-181 D 3
Sirkazhi o IND 140-141 H 5
Sirkka o FIN 88-89 H 3
Sir Kūh ▲ IR 134-135 F 3
Sirmaur o IND 142-143 B 3
Şırnak ☆ TR 128-129 K 4
Sirohi o IND 138-139 D 7
Širokaja gora ▲ RUS 96-97 L 5
Širokaja Pad' o RUS 122-123 K 3
Široki Brijeg o BIH 100-101 F 3
Širokij o RUS 120-121 N 2
Širokij, kanal < RUS 126-127 E 5
Širokostan, poluostrov ⌣ RUS 110-111 W 3
Širokovo o RUS 116-117 J 8
Sirombu o RI 162-163 B 4
Sironcha o IND 138-139 G 10
Sirong o RI 164-165 H 4
Sirong o VRC 156-157 F 4
Sironj o IND 138-139 F 7
Siros ⌒ GR 100-101 K 6
Siroua, Ibel ▲ MA 188-189 H 5
Sirri, Ǧazire-ye ⌒ IR 134-135 F 6
Sir Robert Campbell Island ⌒ MYA 158-159 E 5
Sir R. Squires Memorial Provincial Park ⊥ CDN (NFL) 242-243 L 3
Sirsa o IND 138-139 E 5
Sirsāla o IND 138-139 F 10
Sirsi o IND 140-141 F 3
Sirsilla o IND 138-139 G 10
Sirsiri o SUD 206-207 K 6
Širšjutjur, peski ⩡ TM 136-137 H 5
Širšova, hrebet ≃ 112-113 Q 7
Sirta, Bol'šaja ~ RUS 114-115 S 2
Sir Thomas, Mount ▲ AUS 176-177 K 3
Siruguppa o IND 140-141 G 3
Siru'iye o IR 134-135 G 3
Sirūr o IND 138-139 E 10
Sirusābād o IR 134-135 F 3
Širvān o IR 136-137 E 6
Sirvān, Āb-e ~ IR 128-129 M 5
Sirvān-e Māzin o IRQ 128-129 L 4
Širvankaja ∴• TM 136-137 F 3
Širvanskaja ravnina ⌣ AZ 128-129 M 2
Širvanskij zapovednik ⊥ AZ 128-129 N 3
Širvintos o LT 94-95 J 4
Sirwā o• Y 132-133 D 6
Siryābet ∴• KA 126-127 P 5
Sis o IR 128-129 L 3
Šiš ~ RUS 114-115 N 6
Sisa o PE 64-65 D 5
Sisa, Mount ▲ PNG 183 B 4
Sisak o HR 100-101 F 2
Si Sa Ket o THA 158-159 H 3
Sisal o MEX 52-53 J 1
Sisal, Arrecife ⌒ MEX 52-53 J 1
Si Samrong o THA 158-159 E 2
Si Satchanalai o THA 158-159 E 2
Si Satchanalai National Park ⊥ THA 158-159 E 2
Si Sawat o THA 158-159 E 3
Sisember o RI 166-167 H 2
Šišhėd gol ~ MAU 148-149 D 2
Sishen o ZA 220-221 F 3
Sishiliang o VRC 154-155 F 2
Sishui o VRC 154-155 K 4
Sisian o AR 128-129 L 3
Sisi Bargaon o IND 142-143 J 2
Sisim ~ RUS 116-117 F 8
Sisimiut = Holsteinsborg o GRØ 28-29 O 3
Sisipuk Lake o CDN 34-35 F 3
Siskiwit Bay ≈ USA 270-271 K 3
Siskiyou o USA (OR) 244-245 C 8
Siskiyou Mountains ▲ USA (CA) 246-247 B 2
Si Songkhram o THA 158-159 H 2
Sisŏphŏn o K 158-159 G 4
Sisquelan, Peninsula ⌣ RCH 80 D 3
Sisquoc o USA (CA) 248-249 D 5
Sisquoc River ~ USA (CA) 248-249 E 5
Sissano o PNG 183 B 2
Sisseton o USA (SD) 260-261 J 1
Sisseton Indian Reservation ✕ USA (SD) 260-261 J 1
Sissi o TCH 206-207 D 3
Sissili ~ BF 202-203 K 4
Sissonville o USA (WV) 280-281 E 5
Sistān ⩡ IR 134-135 J 3
Sistan, Daryace-ye o IR 134-135 J 3
Sistān -ō-Balūčestān ◘ IR 134-135 H 5
Sister Bay o USA (WI) 270-271 L 5
Sisterdale o USA (TX) 266-267 J 4
Sisteron o F 90-91 K 9
Sisters o USA (OR) 244-245 D 6
Sistonens Crs. o CDN (ONT) 234-235 O 6
Sitakili o RMM 202-203 E 3
Sitalike o EAT 214-215 F 4
Sitamarhi o IND 142-143 D 2
Sitampiky o RM 222-223 E 6
Sitang o VRC 154-155 B 3
Sitāpur o IND 142-143 B 2
Sitasjaure o S 86-87 H 2
Site of Jamestown Ashby Fort ∴ KAN 56 D 3
Sitgreaves Pass ▲ USA (AZ) 256-257 A 3
Si That o THA 158-159 G 2
Sithobela o SD 220-221 K 3
Sithoniá ⌣ GR 100-101 J 4
Sitiá o BR 68-69 J 4
Sitía o GR 100-101 L 7
Sitidgi Lake o CDN 20-21 Z 2
Sitiecito o C 54-55 E 3
Sitila o MOC 218-219 H 6
Sitio da Abadia o BR 72-73 G 3
Sitio do Mato o BR 72-73 J 2
Sitio Novo o BR 68-69 E 4
Sitio Nôvo de Tocantins o BR 68-69 E 4
Sitionuevo o CO 60-61 D 2
Sitka o USA (KS) 262-263 G 7
Sitka o• USA (AK) 32-33 C 3
Sitkalidak Island ⌒ USA 22-23 U 4
Sitka Sound ≈ 32-33 C 3
Sitkinak, Cape ▲ USA 22-23 U 4
Sitkinak Island ⌒ USA 22-23 U 4
Sitkinak Strait ≈ 22-23 T 4
Šitkino o RUS 116-117 J 7
Sitkum o USA (OR) 244-245 B 7
Sitnica ~ YU 100-101 H 3
Sitona o ER 200-201 H 5
Sitoti o Z 218-219 B 3
Sitte o RUS 118-119 O 4
Sitte ~ RUS 118-119 N 4
Sitten = Sion ☆• CH 92-93 J 5
Sitting Bull Burial Site • USA (ND) 258-259 G 5
Sitting Bull's Grave • USA (SD) 260-261 F 1
Sittwe ☆ MYA 142-143 H 5
Situbondo o RI 168 B 6
Sitwe o Z 214-215 G 6
Sit. Wilfrid, Mont ▲ CDN (QUE) 238-239 K 2
Si-u o MYA 142-143 K 4
Siulakderas o RI 162-163 D 5
Siumbatu o RI 164-165 H 5
Siumpu, Pulau ⌒ RI 164-165 H 6
Siuna o NIC 52-53 B 5
Siuna Kawalo o RI 164-165 H 4
Siuri o IND 142-143 E 4
Siva o RUS 96-97 J 4
Sivaganga o IND 140-141 H 6
Sivaki o RUS 118-119 N 9
Sivakka o FIN 88-89 K 5
Sivas ☆• TR 128-129 G 3
Sivé o RIM 196-197 D 7
Šiveluč, vulkan ▲ RUS 120-121 T 5
Siver ~ RUS 112-113 J 3
Siverek ☆ TR 128-129 H 4
Siverga, ozero o RUS 114-115 K 7
Siverskij hrebet ▲ RUS 112-113 K 3
Sivers'kyj Donec' ~ UA 102-103 K 3
Sivolândia o BR 70-71 K 6
Sivomaskinskij o RUS 108-109 K 8
Sivrice ☆ TR 128-129 H 3
Sivrihisar ☆• TR 128-129 D 3
Sivučij, mys ▲ RUS (KMC) 120-121 U 5
Sivučij, mys ▲ RUS (KMC) 122-123 R 3
Siwa o• ET 192-193 L 3
Siwa o RI 164-165 G 5
Siwa, al-Wāhāt ⩡ ET 192-193 L 3
Siwan o IND 142-143 D 2
Sixaola o CR 52-53 C 7
Sixaola ~ PA 52-53 C 7
Si Xian o VRC 154-155 K 5
Six Lakes o USA (MI) 272-273 D 4
Six Nations Indian Reservation ✕ CDN (ONT) 238-239 E 5
Siyabuswa o ZA 220-221 J 2
Siyāh, Kūh-e ▲ IR 134-135 D 4
Siyāh Kūh, Kavir-e o IR 134-135 E 2
Siyāh Kūh, Selsele-ye ▲ AFG 134-135 K 2
Siyāl, Ǧazā'ir ⌒ ET 194-195 H 6
Siyān Češme o IR 128-129 L 3
Siyang o VRC 154-155 L 5
Siyang o VRC 156-157 E 5
Siyeteb o SUD 200-201 G 3
Sizhuang Qi o VRC 148-149 K 7
Sizun o F 90-91 E 7
Sjælland ⩡ DK 86-87 E 9
Sjain o RUS 122-123 E 5
Sjakutjaha ~ RUS 108-109 R 6
Sjamža o RUS 94-95 R 1
Sjan ~ RUS 116-117 O 3
Sjanno ☆ BY 94-95 L 4
Sjapjakine ~ RUS 110-111 d 7
Sjarednelimanskaja nizina ⩡ 94-95 J 5
Sjas'stroj o RUS 94-95 N 1
Sjatavsē ~ RUS 108-109 O 7
Sjatvato, ozero o RUS 108-109 O 7
Sjenica o• YU 100-101 H 3
Sjöbo o S 86-87 F 9
Sjøholt ☆ N 86-87 C 5
Sjøvegan o N 86-87 H 2
Sjubrebanken ≃ 84-85 F 3
Sjugdžer, ozero o RUS 118-119 G 3
Sjul'ban ~ RUS 118-119 H 7
Sjul'djukar o RUS 118-119 F 4
Sjumsi ☆ RUS 96-97 G 5
Sjun' ~ RUS 96-97 H 6
Sjun'egan ~ RUS 114-115 K 3
Sjungjude ~ RUS 110-111 N 5
Sjuøyane ⌒ N 84-85 M 2
Sjurjah-Džangy, kriaž ▲ RUS 110-111 H 3
Sjurjuktjah ~ RUS 110-111 X 4
Sjurkum o RUS 122-123 J 3
Sjurkum, mys ▲ RUS 122-123 J 3
Skaap ~ NAM 220-221 C 1
Skadarsko jezero o YU 100-101 G 3
Skadovs'k o UA 102-103 H 4
Skærfjorden ≈ 26-27 q 5
Skagaströnd o IS 86-87 c 2
Skagaströnd = Höfðakaupstaður o IS 86-87 c 2
Skagen o DK 86-87 E 8
Skagern o S 86-87 G 7
Skagerrak ≈ 86-87 D 8
Skagit Provincial Park ⊥ CDN (BC) 230-231 H 4
Skagit River ~ USA (WA) 244-245 D 2
Skagshamn o S 86-87 J 5
Skagway o• USA 20-21 X 7
Skála o GR 100-101 J 6
Skälderviken ≈ 86-87 F 8
Skálholt o IS 86-87 c 2
Skalistaja, gora ▲ RUS 120-121 U 5
Skalistyj Golec, gora ▲ RUS 118-119 J 7
Skalistyj ⩡ RUS 126-127 D 5
Skalistyj, hrebet ▲ RUS 120-121 G 2
Skalistyj, mys ▲ RUS 110-111 U 2
Skalkaho Pass ▲ USA (MT) 250-251 F 5
Skanderborg o DK 86-87 D 8
Skane ⩡ S 86-87 F 9
Skånevik o N 86-87 B 7
Skara ☆ S 86-87 F 7
Skardu o IND 138-139 E 2
Skare o N 86-87 C 7
Skärgårdshavets nationalpark ⊥ FIN 88-89 F 7
Skarsvåg o N 86-87 M 1
Skarżysko-Kamienna o PL 92-93 Q 3
Skaudvilė o LT 94-95 H 4
Skaymat o MA 196-197 C 2
Skead o CDN (ONT) 238-239 E 2
Skeena o CDN (BC) 228-229 E 2
Skeena Mountains ▲ CDN 32-33 F 3
Skeena River ~ CDN (BC) 228-229 E 2
Skegness o• GB 90-91 H 5
Skeiðarársandur ⩡ IS 86-87 e 3
Skeldon o GUY 62-63 F 3
Skeleton Coast Park ⊥ NAM 216-217 B 9
Skellefteå o• S 86-87 K 4
Skellefteälven ~ S 86-87 J 4
Skelleftehamn o S 86-87 K 4
Skene Bay ≈ 24-25 S 3
Skerki Bank ≃ 100-101 C 6
Skhira o TN 190-191 H 3
Skhirat o MA 188-189 H 4
Skhour-des-Rehamna o MA 188-189 H 4
Ski ☆ N 86-87 E 7
Skíathos o GR 100-101 J 5
Skíathos ⌣ GR 100-101 J 5
Skiatook o USA (OK) 264-265 H 2
Skiatook Lake o USA (OK) 264-265 H 2
Skibotn o N 86-87 K 2
Skidegate o CDN (BC) 228-229 B 3
Skidegate Channel ≈ CDN 228-229 B 3
Skidegate Inlet ≈ 32-33 E 5
Skidegate Inlet ≈ CDN 228-229 C 3
Skidegate Inlet ≈ CDN 228-229 B 3
Skidmore o USA (TX) 266-267 K 5
Skien ☆ N 86-87 D 7
Skiff o CDN (ALB) 232-233 G 6
Skihist Mountain ▲ CDN (BC) 230-231 H 3
Skikda ☆ DZ 190-191 F 2
Skilak Lake o USA 20-21 P 6
Skiller Fork River ~ USA (IL) 274-275 K 6
Skipperville o USA (AL) 284-285 E 5
Skipskop o ZA 220-221 E 7
Skipton o AUS 180-181 G 4
Skipton o GB 90-91 F 5
Skiros ⌒ GR 100-101 K 5
Skirring, Cap ▲ SN 202-203 B 3
Skive o DK 86-87 D 8
Skjálfandafljót ~ IS 86-87 e 2
Skjern o DK 86-87 D 9
Skjervøy o N 86-87 K 1
Skjolden o N 86-87 C 6
Skjoldungen o GRØ 28-29 U 5
Skjoldungen Ø ⌒ GRØ 28-29 U 5
Sklad o RUS 110-111 O 4
Škov o BY 94-95 M 4
Škocjanske jame ••• SLO 100-101 D 2
Skógafoss ~• IS 86-87 d 3
Skokie o USA (IL) 274-275 L 2
Sköllersta o S 86-87 G 7
Skón o K 158-159 H 4
Skookumchuck o CDN (BC) 230-231 O 4
Skookumchuck Creek ~ CDN (BC) 230-231 N 4
Skópelos o GR 100-101 J 5
Skopin o RUS 94-95 Q 5
Skopje ★ MK 100-101 H 3
Skorodnoe o RUS 102-103 J 2
Skosai o RI 166-167 L 3
Skotterud o N 86-87 F 7
Skoura o MA 188-189 H 5
Skövde ☆ S 86-87 F 7
Skovorodino ☆ RUS 118-119 L 9
Skowhegan o USA (ME) 278-279 M 4
Skownan o CDN (MAN) 234-235 D 3
Skrimfjella ▲ N 86-87 D 7
Skriveri o•• LV 94-95 J 3
Skruis Point ▲ CDN 24-25 b 3
Skrunda o LV 94-95 H 3
Skudeneshavn o N 86-87 B 7
Skukuza o ZA 220-221 K 2
Skuljabiha o RUS 96-97 D 5
Skull Mountain ▲ USA (NV) 248-249 H 3
Skull Rock Pass ▲ USA (UT) 254-255 B 4
Skull Valley Indian Reservation ✕ USA (UT) 254-255 C 3
Skuna River ~ USA (MS) 268-269 L 3
Skunk River ~ USA (IA) 274-275 F 3
Skuodas ☆ LT 94-95 G 3
Skuratova, mys ▲ RUS 108-109 N 5
Skuratovskij o RUS 94-95 P 4
Skutvik o N 86-87 G 2
Skvyra ☆ UA 102-103 F 3
Skwentna River ~ USA 20-21 O 6
Skwierzyna o PL 92-93 N 2
Skye ⌒ GB 90-91 D 3
Skykomish o USA (WA) 244-245 D 3
Skykomish River ~ USA (WA) 244-245 D 3
Sky Lake Wilderness Area ⊥ USA (OR) 244-245 C 8
Skyline Caverns ∴ USA (VA) 280-281 H 5
Skyline Drive II USA (VA) 280-281 H 5
Skyring, Monte ▲ RCH 80 D 7
Skyring, Peninsula ⌣ RCH 80 C 2
Skyring, Seno ≈ 80 D 6

Slā o MA 188-189 H 3
Slade Point ▲ AUS 174-175 G 2
Slagelse o • DK 86-87 E 9
Slamet, Gunung ▲ RI 168 C 3
Slancy ☆ RUS 94-95 L 2
Slapout o USA (OK) 264-265 D 2
Śląska, Niżina ~ PL 92-93 N 3
Slate Islands ⌒ CDN (ONT) 236-237 B 4
Slater o USA (MO) 274-275 E 5
Slatina ☆ RO 102-103 D 5
Slaton o USA (TX) 264-265 C 5
Slaughterville o USA (OK) 264-265 G 3
Slautnoe o RUS 112-113 P 5
Slave Coast ∪ 202-203 L 7
Slave Lake o CDN 32-33 N 4
Slave Point ▲ CDN 30-31 M 5
Slave River ~ CDN 30-31 N 5
Slavgorod ☆ RUS 124-125 L 2
Slavharad ☆ BY 94-95 M 5
Slavjanka o RUS 122-123 G 4
Slavjanka o RUS 122-123 D 7
Slavjansk = Slovjans'k o UA 102-103 K 3
Slavjansk-na-Kubani o RUS 102-103 L 5
Slavkoviči o RUS 94-95 L 3
Slavkov u Brna o CZ 92-93 O 4
Slavnoe o RUS 122-123 N 6
Slavonice o CZ 92-93 N 4
Slawi o RI 168 C 3
Sławno o PL 92-93 O 1
Slayton o USA (MN) 270-271 C 7
Sled Lake o CDN 34-35 C 3
Sleeman o CDN (ONT) 234-235 J 6
Sleeper Islands ⌒ CDN 36-37 K 6
Sleeping Bear Dunes National Lakeshore • USA (MI) 272-273 C 2
Sleeping Giant Provincial Park ⊥ CDN (ONT) 234-235 P 6
Sleepy Eye o USA (MN) 270-271 D 6
Sleisbeck Mine ∴ AUS 172-173 L 2
Sletten = Ammassivik o GRØ 28-29 S 6
Slidell o USA (LA) 268-269 L 6
Slidell o USA (TX) 264-265 G 5
Slide Mountain ▲ USA (NY) 280-281 M 2
Slieve League ▲ IRL 90-91 C 4
Sligeach = Sligo ☆ • IRL 90-91 C 4
Sligo = Sligeach ☆ • IRL 90-91 C 4
Slim o DZ 190-191 D 3
Slim Creek ~ CDN (BC) 228-229 N 3
Slim River o MAL 162-163 D 3
Slipper Island ⌒ NZ 182 E 2
Šlisseľburg o RUS 94-95 M 2
Slite o S 86-87 J 8
Sliven o BG 102-103 E 6
Sljeme ▲ HR 100-101 E 2
Sljudjanka ☆ RUS 116-117 L 10
Šljupočnyj, mys ▲ RUS 112-113 Q 6
Sloan o USA (IA) 274-275 B 2
Sloan River ~ CDN 30-31 M 2
S'loboda Boľšaja Martynovka o RUS 102-103 M 4
Slobodskoj ☆ RUS 96-97 G 4
Slobozia ☆ RO 102-103 E 5
Slocan o CDN (BC) 230-231 M 4
Slocan Park o CDN (BC) 230-231 M 4
Slocan River ~ CDN (BC) 230-231 M 4
Slogen ▲ N 86-87 C 5
Slonim o BY 94-95 J 5
Sloping Point ▲ AUS 172-173 C 6
Slovak o USA (AR) 276-277 D 6
Slovakia = Slovenská Republika ■ SK 92-93 O 4
Slovenia = Slovenija ■ SLO 100-101 D 2
Slovenské rudohorie ▲ SK 92-93 P 4
Slovjans'k o UA 102-103 K 3
Slov'yans'k = Slovjans'k o UA 102-103 K 3
Słowiński Park Narodowy ⊥ PL 92-93 O 1
Složnyj, ostrov ⌒ RUS 108-109 X 3
Sluč ~ UA 102-103 E 3
Sluck o BY 94-95 K 5
Sluderno = Schluderns o I 100-101 C 1
Slunj o HR 100-101 E 2
Słupsk ☆ • PL 92-93 O 1
Slurry o ZA 220-221 G 2
Smackover o USA (AR) 276-277 C 7
Småland ∸ S 86-87 F 8
Smålandsstenar o S 86-87 F 8
Smaljany o BY 94-95 M 4
Small o USA (ID) 252-253 F 2
Small Malaita = Maramasike ⌒ SOL 184 I e 3
Small Point ▲ USA (ME) 278-279 M 5
Smalltree Lake o CDN 30-31 R 5
Smallwood Reservoir < CDN 36-37 R 7
Smara o MA 188-189 F 7
Smarhon' ☆ BY 94-95 K 4
Smart Syndicate Dam < ZA 220-221 F 5
Smeaton o CDN (SAS) 232-233 O 2
Smederevo o • YU 100-101 H 2
Smela = Smila o UA 102-103 G 3
Smet, De o USA (SD) 260-261 J 2
Smethport o USA (PA) 280-281 H 2
Smidovič o RUS 108-109 G 4
Smidovič o RUS 122-123 E 4
Šmidta, grjada ▲ RUS 110-111 W 1
Šmidta, Mys o RUS 112-113 V 2
Šmidta, mys ▲ RUS 112-113 V 2
Šmidta, poluostrov ∪ RUS 120-121 K 6
Smila o UA 102-103 G 3
Smiley o CDN (SAS) 232-233 J 4
Smiltene o • LV 94-95 J 3
Smirnenski o BG 102-103 E 6
Smirneuski o BG 102-103 C 6
Smirnyh o RUS 122-123 K 4
Smir-Restinga o MA 188-189 J 3
Smith o CDN 32-33 N 4
Smith, Cape ▲ CDN 36-37 K 4
Smith Arm o CDN 30-31 H 2
Smith Bay ≈ 20-21 N 1
Smith Bay ≈ 24-25 g 2
Smith Center o USA (KS) 262-263 H 5
Smithdale o USA (MS) 268-269 K 5
Smithers o CDN (BC) 228-229 G 2
Smithfield o USA (NC) 282-283 J 5
Smithfield o USA (UT) 254-255 D 2
Smithfield o USA (VA) 280-281 K 6
Smith Field o USA (WV) 280-281 F 4
Smithfield o ZA 220-221 H 5
Smith Inlet ≈ CDN 230-231 B 2
Smith Island ⌒ CDN (NWT) 24-25 f 2
Smith Island ⌒ CDN (NWT) 36-37 K 4
Smith Island ⌒ IND 140-141 L 3
Smith Island ⌒ USA (MD) 280-281 K 5
Smithland o USA (IA) 274-275 C 2
Smithland o USA (TX) 264-265 K 6
Smith Mountain Lake ○ USA (VA) 280-281 G 6
Smith Peak ▲ USA (ID) 250-251 C 3
Smith Point ▲ AUS 172-173 L 1
Smith Point o USA (TX) 268-269 F 7
Smith River o USA (CA) 246-247 A 2
Smith River ~ USA (MT) 250-251 H 4
Smiths Corner o CDN (NB) 240-241 K 4
Smiths Falls o CDN (ONT) 238-239 J 4
Smiths Ferry o USA (ID) 252-253 B 2
Smiths Grove o USA (KY) 276-277 J 3
Smithton o AUS 180-181 H 6
Smithville o CDN (ONT) 238-239 F 5
Smithville o USA (GA) 284-285 F 5
Smithville o USA (OK) 264-265 K 4
Smithville o USA (TN) 276-277 K 5
Smithville o USA (TX) 266-267 K 4
Smithville o USA (WV) 280-281 E 4
Smithville Reservoir ○ USA (MO) 274-275 D 5
Smjadovo o BG 102-103 E 6
S. M. Jørgensen, Kap ▲ GRØ 28-29 Y 3
Smoke Creek Desert ∸ USA (NV) 246-247 F 3
Smoke Hole Caverns • USA (WV) 280-281 G 4
Smoke River ~ CDN 20-21 a 2
Smokey Hill Air National Guard Range • USA (KS) 262-263 J 6
Smoking Tent o CDN (SAS) 232-233 Q 3
Smoky Bay o AUS 176-177 M 6
Smoky Cape ▲ AUS 178-179 M 6
Smoky Falls o CDN (ONT) 236-237 F 2
Smoky Falls ~ CDN (ONT) 236-237 F 2
Smoky Hill River ~ USA (CO) 254-255 N 5
Smoky Hill River ~ USA (KS) 262-263 F 6
Smoky Hills ▲ USA (KS) 262-263 G 5
Smoky Lake o CDN 32-33 O 4
Smoky Mountains ▲ USA (ID) 252-253 D 3
Smoky River ~ CDN (ALB) 228-229 P 3
Smøla ⌒ N 86-87 C 5
Smolensk ☆ • RUS 94-95 N 4
Smolensko-Moskovskaja vozvyšennosť ▲ RUS 94-95 N 4
Smolevičí o BY 94-95 L 4
Smólikas ▲ GR 100-101 H 4
Smoljan o BG 102-103 D 7
Smoljaninovo o RUS 122-123 E 7
Smoot o USA (WY) 252-253 H 4
Smooth Rock Falls o CDN (ONT) 236-237 G 3
Smoothrock Lake ○ CDN (ONT) 234-235 O 4
Smoothstone Lake ○ CDN 34-35 C 3
Smoothstone River ~ CDN 34-35 C 3
Smörfjöll ▲ IS 86-87 f 2
Smuts o CDN (SAS) 232-233 M 3
Smyer o USA (TX) 264-265 B 5
Smyrna o USA (DE) 280-281 L 4
Smyrna o USA (GA) 284-285 F 3
Smyrna o USA (OH) 280-281 E 3
Smyrna o USA (TN) 276-277 J 5
Smyšljaevsk o RUS 96-97 G 7
Smyth, Canal ≈ 80 C 5
Snabai o RI 166-167 H 2
Snaefell ▲ • GBM 90-91 E 4
Snake and Manjang Caverns • ROK 150-151 F 11
Snake Falls o CDN (ONT) 234-235 K 4
Snake Indian River ~ CDN (ALB) 228-229 Q 3
Snake Island ⌒ AUS 180-181 J 5
Snake River ~ CDN 20-21 Y 4
Snake River ~ USA (ID) 252-253 B 3
Snake River ~ USA (WA) 244-245 G 4
Snake River Canyon ∴ USA (WA) 244-245 H 4
Snake River Plains ~ USA (ID) 252-253 E 4
Snape, Pointe ▲ CDN 38-39 E 3
Snape Island ⌒ CDN 36-37 K 7
Snap Point ▲ BS 54-55 G 3
Snare Lake ○ CDN 30-31 M 3
Snare River ~ CDN 30-31 L 4
Snåsa o N 86-87 F 4
Snåsvatnet ○ N 86-87 E 4
Snead o USA (AL) 284-285 D 2
Sneedville o USA (TN) 282-283 D 4
Sneek o • NL 92-93 H 2
Sneeuberg ▲ ZA 220-221 G 5
Snelling o USA (CA) 248-249 D 2
Snellman o USA (MN) 270-271 C 4
Snellville o USA (GA) 284-285 F 3
Sněžka ▲ • CZ 92-93 N 3
Sneżnaja ~ RUS 116-117 L 10
Sneżnaja, gora ▲ KS 136-137 N 4
Sneżnaja gora ▲ RUS 112-113 N 4
Sneżnoe o RUS 112-113 R 4
Sneżnogorsk o RUS 108-109 W 7
Sneżnogorskij o RUS 118-119 O 8
Śniardwy, Jezioro ○ PL 92-93 Q 2
Śnieżka ▲ • PL 92-93 N 3
Snihurivka o UA 102-103 H 4
Snipe Lake o CDN (SAS) 232-233 K 4
Snipe Lake ○ CDN 32-33 M 4
Sniżne o UA 102-103 L 3
Snøhetta ▲ N 86-87 D 5
Snohomish o USA (WA) 244-245 C 3
Snønuten ▲ N 86-87 C 7
Snooks Arm o CDN (NFL) 242-243 N 3
Snopa ~ RUS 88-89 T 3
Snoqualmie Pass ▲ USA 244-245 D 3
Snota ▲ N 86-87 D 5
Snøtinden ▲ • N 86-87 F 3
Snøtoppen ▲ N 84-85 L 2
Snowbank River ~ CDN 24-25 c 7
Snowbird Lake ○ CDN 30-31 S 5
Snowbird Mountains ▲ USA (NC) 282-283 D 5
Snowcrest Mountain ▲ CDN (BC) 230-231 N 4
Snowden o CDN (SAS) 232-233 O 2
Snowdon ▲ GB 90-91 E 5
Snowdrift o CDN 30-31 O 4
Snowdrift River ~ CDN 30-31 P 4
Snowflake o CDN (MAN) 234-235 E 5
Snowflake o USA (AZ) 256-257 E 4
Snow Hill o USA (MD) 280-281 L 5
Snow Hill o USA (NC) 282-283 K 5
Snow Hill Island ⌒ ARK 16 G 31
Snow Lake o CDN 34-35 F 3
Snow Lake o USA (AR) 276-277 D 6
Snow Mount ▲ USA (CA) 246-247 C 4
Snowshoe Peak ▲ USA (MT) 250-251 D 3
Snowtown o AUS 180-181 E 2
Snowville o USA (UT) 254-255 C 2
Snow Water Lake ○ USA (NV) 246-247 L 3
Snowy Mountains ▲ AUS 180-181 K 4
Snowy River ~ AUS 180-181 K 4
Snowy River National Park ⊥ AUS 180-181 K 4
Snug Corner o BS 54-55 J 3
Snuöl o K 158-159 J 4
Snyde Bay ≈ 36-37 T 6
Snyder o USA (AR) 276-277 D 7
Snyder o USA (NE) 262-263 K 3
Snyder o USA (OK) 264-265 F 4
Soabuwe o RI 166-167 E 3
Soacha o CO 60-61 D 5
Soalala o RM 222-223 D 6
Soamanonga o RM 222-223 D 9
Soân ~ PK 138-139 C 3
Soanierana-Ivongo o RM 222-223 F 6
Soanindrariny o RM 222-223 E 7
Soan River ~ PNG 183 B 4
Soap Lake o USA (WA) 244-245 F 3
Soa-Siu o RI 166-167 K 3
Soata o CO 60-61 E 4
Soavina o RM 222-223 F 8
Soavinandriana o RM 222-223 E 7
Sob' o RUS 108-109 L 8
Sob' ~ RUS 108-109 L 8
Sob ~ UA 102-103 F 3
Soba o WAN 204-205 H 3
Sobaeksan National Park ⊥ • ROK 150-151 G 9
Sobaek Sanmaek ▲ ROK 150-151 F 10
Sobangouma o RMM 202-203 J 2
Sobāt ~ SUD 206-207 L 4
Soberbio, El o RA 76-77 K 4
Sober Island ⌒ CDN (NS) 240-241 N 6
Sobger ~ RI 166-167 L 3
Sobinka ☆ RUS 94-95 R 4
Sobni ▲ ETH 200-201 J 5
Sobo-Katamuki Quasi National Park ⊥ J 152-153 D 8
Sobolevka, Ust'- o RUS 122-123 H 5
Sobolevo ☆ RUS 120-121 Q 6
Soboloh o RUS 110-111 Y 6
Soboloh-Majan ~ RUS 110-111 P 6
Sobopol ~ RUS 110-111 R 6
Sobor, skala • RUS 122-123 D 3
Sobo-Sise, ostrov ⌒ RUS 110-111 R 3
Sobradinho o BR (FED) 72-73 G 3
Sobradinho o BR (MAR) 68-69 G 5
Sobradinho o BR (RSU) 74-75 D 7
Sobradinho, Represa de < BR 68-69 G 7
Sobrado, Rio ~ BR 72-73 G 2
Sobral o BR (ACR) 66-67 B 7
Sobral o BR (CEA) 68-69 H 3
Sobtyegan ~ RUS 114-115 J 2
Socavão o BR 74-75 F 5
Sochaczew o PL 92-93 Q 2
Sochora, Río ~ BOL 76-77 E 1
Soči o • RUS 126-127 C 6
Social Circle o USA (GA) 284-285 G 3
Society Hill o USA (SC) 284-285 L 2
Society Islands = Société, Îles de la ⌒ F 13 M 4
Socompa o RA 76-77 C 3
Socorra, Isla ⌒ MEX 50-51 C 7
Socorro o BR 72-73 G 7
Socorro o CO 60-61 E 4
Socorro o USA (NM) 256-257 J 4
Socorro o USA (TX) 266-267 A 2
Socorro, El o CO 60-61 F 4
Socorro, El o RA 78-79 J 2
Socorro do Piauí o BR 68-69 G 5
Socota o CO 60-61 E 4
Socota o PE 64-65 C 5
Socotra = Suquṭrā ⌒ Y 132-133 J 7
Sóc Trăng o VN 158-159 H 6
Sočur ~ RUS 114-115 U 5
Soda Creek o CDN (BC) 228-229 M 4
Soda Lake ○ USA (CA) 248-249 J 4
Soda Lake ○ USA (CA) 248-249 E 4
Sodankylä o FIN 88-89 J 3
Soda Springs o USA (ID) 252-253 G 4
Soddie Lake ○ CDN 30-31 L 4
Soddy-Daisy o USA (TN) 276-277 K 5
Soder, Mount ▲ AUS 176-177 M 1
Sodere o • ETH 208-209 D 4
Söderfors o S 86-87 H 6
Söderhamn o S 86-87 H 6
Söderköping o • S 86-87 H 7
Södertälje ☆ S 86-87 H 7
Sodiri o SUD 200-201 D 5
Sodium o ZA 220-221 F 5
Sodo o ETH 208-209 C 5
Södra Möckleby o S 86-87 H 8
Södra Vallgrund o FIN 88-89 F 5
Soe o RI 166-167 C 6
Soekmekaar o ZA 218-219 E 6
Soeng Sari o THA 158-159 G 3
Soetendalsvlei ○ ZA 220-221 D 7
Sofala o MOC (Sof) 218-219 H 5
Sofala ■ MOC 218-219 H 4
Sofara o RMM 202-203 H 2
Sofia ~ RM 222-223 E 5
Sofia = Sofija ☆ • • BG 102-103 C 6
Sofija ☆ • • BG 102-103 C 6
Sofijsk o RUS (HBR) 122-123 F 2
Sofijsk o RUS (HBR) 122-123 H 3
Sof Omar caves • ETH 208-209 D 5
Sofporog o RUS 88-89 L 4
Šoğā'ābād o IR 134-135 D 2
Sogakofe o GH 202-203 L 6
Sogamoso o CO 60-61 E 5
Sogamoso, Río ~ CO 60-61 E 4
Soğanlı Çayı ~ TR 128-129 E 2
Sogda o RUS 122-123 E 3
Sogeram River ~ PNG 183 C 3
Sogeri o PNG 183 D 5
Sogndal ☆ N 86-87 C 6
Søgne ☆ N 86-87 C 7
Sognefjorden ≈ 86-87 B 6
Sognesjøen ≈ 86-87 B 6
Sogod o RP 160-161 F 7
Sogolle < TCH 198-199 G 5
Sogolomik o PNG 183 A 3
Sogoot o MAU 148-149 D 3
Sogoubéni o RG 202-203 F 5
Sogra o RUS 88-89 T 5
Söğüip'o o ROK 150-151 F 11
Söğüt o TR 128-129 C 4
Söğütlü Çayı ~ TR 128-129 G 3
Sog Xian o VRC 144-145 J 5
Soh o US 136-137 M 5
Sohagi o IND 142-143 B 3
Soheil o IR 134-135 E 2
Sohela o IND 142-143 C 5
Sohonto, ozero ○ RUS 108-109 O 7
Sohor, gora ▲ RUS 116-117 M 10
Sohós o GR 100-101 J 4
Sohüksan Do ⌒ ROK 150-151 E 10
Soin o BF 202-203 J 3
Sointula o CDN (BC) 230-231 C 3
Soi Rap, Cửa ≈ 158-159 J 5
Sōja o J 152-153 E 7
Sojana o RUS 88-89 R 4
Sojat o IND 138-139 D 7
Sojda ~ RUS 88-89 O 6
Sojma ~ RUS 88-89 V 3
Šojna o RUS 88-89 S 3
Sŏjoŝon Man ≈ 150-151 E 8
Sojoton Point ▲ RP 160-161 E 8
Sojuznoe o KA 126-127 O 2
Sojva ~ RUS 88-89 X 5
Sok ~ RUS 96-97 G 7
Šokaj-Datka mazar • KA 136-137 L 3
Šokaľskogo, mys ▲ RUS 108-109 Q 5
Šokaľskogo, proliv ≈ 108-109 d 2
Sokch'o o ROK 150-151 G 8
Söke ☆ TR 128-129 B 4
Sokele o ZRE 214-215 C 5
Sokhumi = Suchumi ☆ GE 104 C 5
Soko o CI 202-203 J 6
Soko Banja o • YU 100-101 H 3
Sokodé ☆ RT 202-203 L 5
Sokode Etoe o GH 202-203 L 6
Sokol o RUS 94-95 R 2
Sokol o RUS (MAG) 120-121 O 4
Sokol o RUS (SHL) 122-123 K 5
Sokółka o PL 92-93 R 2
Sokolo o RMM 202-203 G 2
Sokołów Podlaski o PL 92-93 R 2
Sokone o SN 202-203 B 3
Søkongen Ø ⌒ GRØ 28-29 a 2
Sokoro, Satama- o CI 202-203 H 6
Sokosti ▲ FIN 88-89 K 2
Sokotindji o DY 204-205 E 3
Sokoto ■ WAN 204-205 F 3
Sokoto ☆ WAN 198-199 B 6
Sokoto, River ~ WAN 204-205 F 3
Sokoura o RMM 202-203 J 3
Sokoura, Satama- o CI 202-203 H 6
Šokša o RUS 88-89 N 6
Sol, Catedral de • CO 60-61 E 5
Sola o C 54-55 G 4
Sola o VAN 184 II a 1
Solan o IND 138-139 F 4
Solana Beach o USA (CA) 248-249 G 7
Solana del Pino o E 98-99 E 5
Solander Island ⌒ NZ 182 A 7
Solano o YV 66-67 D 2
Solano, Bahía ≈ 80 G 2
Solano, Punta S.F. ▲ CO 60-61 C 4
Solāpur o • IND 140-141 F 2
Solar Observatory • AUS 178-179 K 6
Solarte, Raudal ~ CO 66-67 B 3
Solat, Gunung ▲ RI 164-165 K 3
Solberg o S 86-87 H 5
Soldado Monge o EC 64-65 D 3
Soldado Pionero, Monumento al • YV 62-63 D 3
Soldatskaja Tašla o RUS 96-97 F 7
Soldau = Działdowo o • PL 92-93 Q 2
Sol de Julio o RA 76-77 F 5
Soldier Creek ~ USA (KS) 262-263 L 5
Soldier Point ▲ AUS 172-173 K 1
Soldier Summit o USA (UT) 254-255 D 4
Soldotna o USA 20-21 P 6
Soledad o CO 60-61 D 2
Soledad o USA (CA) 248-249 C 3
Soledad o YV 60-61 K 3
Soledad, Isla ⌒ CO 60-61 C 6
Soledad, La o CO 60-61 F 5
Soledad, La o MEX (COA) 50-51 J 4
Soledad, La o MEX (DGO) 50-51 G 5
Soledad de Doblado o MEX 52-53 F 2
Soledad Diéz Gutiérrez o MEX 50-51 J 6
Soledade o BR (PA) 68-69 K 5
Soledade o BR (RSU) 74-75 D 7
Soledade, Cachoeira ~ BR 68-69 B 4
Soledar o UA 102-103 L 3
Sølen ▲ N 86-87 E 6
Solënaja ~ RUS 108-109 V 7
Solenoe, ozero ○ RUS 114-115 L 7
Solentiname, Archipiélago de ⌒ NIC 52-53 B 6
Solënyj o RUS 96-97 E 10
Solenzara o F 98-99 M 4
Solenzo o BF 202-203 H 3
Soleure = Solothurn ☆ CH 92-93 J 5
Šolgara o AFG 136-137 K 6
Solgonskij krjaž ∸ RUS 116-117 E 8
Šolhābād o IR 136-137 E 7
Solhan ☆ TR 128-129 J 3
Soligalič o RUS 94-95 S 2
Soligorsk = Salihorsk o BY 94-95 K 5
Solikamsk ☆ RUS 114-115 D 5
Sol'-Ileck ☆ RUS 96-97 J 8
Solimões, Rio ~ BR 66-67 F 4
Solingen o D 92-93 J 3
Solita o CO 64-65 E 1
Solitaire o NAM 220-221 C 1
Soljanka ~ KA 96-97 G 8
Soljanka o RUS 118-119 K 5
Soljanka o RUS (SAR) 96-97 G 8
Solleftea o S 86-87 H 5
Sóller o E 98-99 J 5
Solna o BF 202-203 L 3
Solnečnogorsk ☆ RUS 94-95 P 3
Solnečnyj ☆ RUS 122-123 G 3
Solo o RI 164-165 G 6
Solodniki o RUS 96-97 D 9
Šolohovskij o RUS 102-103 M 3
Solok o • RI 162-163 D 5
Sololá ☆ GCA 52-53 J 4
Sololo o EAK 212-213 G 2
Soloma o GCA 52-53 J 4
Solomon o USA (AZ) 256-257 F 6
Solomon o USA (KS) 262-263 J 6
Solomon Islands ■ SOL 184 I d 2
Solomon Islands ⌒ SOL 184 I b 2
Solomon River ~ USA (KS) 262-263 H 5
Solomons o USA (MD) 280-281 K 5
Solomon Sea ≈ 13 G 3
Solon o VRC 150-151 C 4
Soloncy o RUS (HBR) 122-123 J 2
Soloncy o RUS (IRK) 116-117 J 8
Solonešnoe o RUS 124-125 O 3
Solongotyn davaa ▲ MAU 148-149 D 3
Solonópole o BR 68-69 J 4
Solon Springs o USA (WI) 270-271 G 4
Solor, Kepulauan ⌒ RI 166-167 B 6
Solor, Pulau ⌒ RI 166-167 B 6
Solothurn ☆ CH 92-93 J 5
Soloveckie o RUS 88-89 N 4
Soloveckie ostrova ⌒ • • • RUS 88-89 N 4
Solov'ëvsk o RUS (AMR) 118-119 M 8
Solov'ëvsk o RUS (CTN) 118-119 G 11
Solsgirth o CDN (MAN) 234-235 C 4
Solsona o • E 98-99 H 4
Solsona o RP 160-161 D 3
Solsqua o CDN (BC) 230-231 K 3
Soltānābād o IR 136-137 F 6
Soltān Bakvā o AFG 134-135 K 2
Soltane, Bir < TN 190-191 G 4
Soltāniye o • IR 128-129 N 4
Soltau o D 92-93 K 2
Soltau, tau ▲ KA 126-127 K 5
Soluntah, ozero ○ RUS 110-111 Y 4
Solusi o ZW 218-219 E 5
Solvang o • USA (CA) 248-249 D 5
Sölvesborg ☆ S 86-87 G 8
Solway o USA (MN) 270-271 C 3
Solway Firth ○ GB 90-91 F 4
Solwezi ☆ Z 214-215 D 7
Sol'zavod o RUS 116-117 K 5
Sōma o J 152-153 J 6
Soma ☆ TR 128-129 B 3
Somabhula o ZW 218-219 E 4
Somadougou o RMM 202-203 H 2
Somalia = Soomaaliya ■ SP 212-213 J 2
Somali Basin ▲ 12 D 4
Somalomo o CAM 210-211 D 2
Soma Zangpo ~ VRC 144-145 E 5
Sombo o ANG 216-217 F 4
Sombo ~ ANG 216-217 F 4
Sombor o • YU 100-101 G 2
Sombrerete o MEX 50-51 H 6
Sombrero ⌒ KAN 56 D 2
Sombrero ⌒ RCH 80 F 6
Sombrero, El o RA 80 F 2
Sombrero, El o YV 60-61 H 3
Sombrero Channel ≈ 140-141 L 6
Sombrio, Lagoa ○ BR 74-75 F 7
Som Det o THA 158-159 G 2
Somerdale o USA (NJ) 280-281 M 4
Somerdale o USA (NJ) 280-281 L 4
Somero o FIN 88-89 G 6
Somers o USA (MT) 250-251 E 3
Somerset ∴ AUS 174-175 G 2
Somerset o CDN (MAN) 234-235 E 5
Somerset o USA (CA) 246-247 E 5
Somerset o USA (CO) 254-255 H 5
Somerset o USA (KY) 276-277 L 3
Somerset o USA (MI) 272-273 E 5
Somerset o USA (OH) 280-281 D 4
Somerset o USA (PA) 280-281 G 3
Somerset Aboriginal Land ✗ AUS 174-175 G 2
Somerset East = Somerset-Oos o • ZA 220-221 G 6
Somerset Island ⌒ CDN 24-25 Z 4
Somerset-Oos o • ZA 220-221 G 6
Somersetwes o ZA 220-221 D 7
Somerville o USA (PA) 280-281 M 3
Somerville o USA (TN) 276-277 F 5
Somerville o USA (TX) 266-267 L 3
Somerville Lake < USA (TX) 266-267 L 3
Somes Bar o USA (CA) 246-247 B 2
Somil o ANG 216-217 F 7
Somme ~ F 90-91 H 6
Sommen ○ S 86-87 G 7
Sommerberry o CDN (SAS) 232-233 P 5
Sommerton o USA (AZ) 256-257 A 6
Sømna ⌒ N 86-87 F 4
Somnenija, buhta ○ RUS 112-113 O 6
Somnja ~ RUS 122-123 H 2
Somokoro o CI 202-203 H 5
Somosomo Strait ≈ 184 III b 2
Somotillo o NIC 52-53 L 5
Somoto ☆ NIC 52-53 L 5
Sompeta o IND 142-143 D 6
Som Poi o THA 158-159 G 3
Somra o MYA 142-143 J 3
Son ~ IND 142-143 D 3
Soná o PA 52-53 D 7
Sonaco o GNB 202-203 C 3
Sonaimur o BD 142-143 G 4
Sonanga o RMM 202-203 G 3
Sonapur o IND (ASS) 142-143 G 2
Sonapur o IND (ORI) 142-143 C 5
Sonār ~ IND 138-139 G 7
Sonbong o DVR 150-151 H 6
Sonchon o DVR 150-151 E 8
Soncillo o E 98-99 F 3
Sondagsrivier ~ ZA 220-221 G 6
Sønderborg o DK 86-87 D 9
Sondershausen o D 92-93 L 3
So'n Đọng ☆ VN 156-157 E 6
Sondre Isortoq ≈ 28-29 O 4
Søndre Strømfjord = Kangerlussuaq o GRØ 28-29 P 3
Søndre Upernavik = Upernavik Kujalleq o GRØ 26-27 X 7
Sondrio ☆ I 100-101 B 1
Sondu o EAK 212-213 E 4
Sonepat o IND 138-139 F 5
Song o MAL 162-163 K 3
Song o WAN 204-205 K 4
Songa o RI 164-165 K 4
Songa o ZRE 214-215 C 5
Songaw Lagoon ○ GH 202-203 L 7
Sông Ba ~ VN 158-159 K 4
Sông Câu o VN 158-159 K 4
Sông Cô Chiên ~ VN 158-159 J 5
Sông Cua Dai ~ VN 158-159 J 5
Sông Đa ~ VN 156-157 D 6
Sông Đông Nai ~ VN 158-159 J 5
Songea ☆ EAT 214-215 H 6
Songgato ~ RI 166-167 L 3
Sông Hâu ~ VN 158-159 H 5
Sông Hông ~ VN 156-157 D 5
Songhua Hu ○ VRC (JIL) 150-151 F 6
Songhua Hu • VRC (JIL) 150-151 F 6
Songhua Jiang ~ VRC 150-151 E 5
Songino = Cavdan o MAU 148-149 C 3
Songir o IND 138-139 E 9
Songjiang o VRC (JIL) 150-151 G 6
Songjiang o VRC (SGH) 154-155 M 6
Song-Kël', ozero ○ KS 146-147 B 5
Song-Kël', ozero ○ KS 146-147 B 5
Songkhla ☆ THA 158-159 F 7
Songkou o VRC 156-157 L 4
Song Ling ▲ VRC 154-155 L 1
Sông Lüy o VN 158-159 K 5
Songming o VRC 156-157 C 4
Songnam o ROK 150-151 F 9
Songnim o DVR 150-151 E 8
Songnisan National Park ⊥ • ROK 150-151 F 9
Songo o ANG 216-217 C 3
Songo o MOC 218-219 G 2
Songo o SUD 206-207 G 4
Songololo o ZRE 210-211 E 6
Songo Mnara ∴ • • • EAT 214-215 K 5
Songpan o VRC 154-155 C 5
Song Phinong o THA 158-159 F 3
Songsang o IND 142-143 H 3
Songsha o VRC 144-145 C 5
Song Shan ▲ VRC 154-155 H 4
Songshang • VRC 154-155 H 4
Songshan Z.B. ⊥ • VRC 154-155 J 1
Sông Tiên ~ VN 158-159 H 5
Songwe ~ EAT 214-215 G 5
Song Xian o VRC 154-155 H 4
Songyang o VRC 156-157 L 2
Songyu Cave • ROK 150-151 G 9
Songzi o VRC 154-155 G 6
So'n Hiệp o VN 158-159 K 5
Sonid Youqi o VRC 148-149 L 6
Sonid Zuoqi o VRC 148-149 L 6
Soniquera, Cerro ▲ BOL 76-77 D 2
Sonitë, Boľšaja ~ RUS 108-109 Z 6
Sonjo o EAT 212-213 E 5
Sonjol, Gunung ▲ RI 166-167 G 3
Sonkwale Mountains ▲ WAN 204-205 H 5
So'n La ☆ VN 156-157 C 6
Son Mbong o CAM 210-211 C 2
Sonmiāni Bay ≈ 134-135 M 6
Sonneberg o D 92-93 L 3
Sonningdale o CDN (SAS) 232-233 L 3
Sono, Rio do ~ BR 68-69 E 6
Sono, Rio do ~ BR 72-73 H 4
Sonoita o USA (AZ) 256-257 E 7
Sonoma o USA (CA) 246-247 C 5
Sonoma Range ▲ USA (NV) 246-247 H 3
Sonora o MEX 50-51 B 1
Sonora ■ MEX 50-51 D 3
Sonora o USA (CA) 248-249 D 2
Sonora o USA (TX) 266-267 G 3
Sonora, Río ~ MEX 50-51 D 3
Sonora Island ⌒ CDN (BC) 230-231 D 3
Sonora Junction o USA (CA) 246-247 F 5
Sonoran Desert ∸ USA (AZ) 248-249 K 6
Sonoumon o DY 204-205 E 4
Sonoyta o MEX 50-51 C 2
Sonqor o IR 134-135 B 1
Sonskij o RUS 116-117 E 8
Sonsón o CO 60-61 D 5
Sonsonate ☆ ES 52-53 K 5
Sonstraal o ZA 220-221 F 3
Sonta o ZRE 214-215 E 6
So'n Tây, Thi Xã ☆ VN 156-157 D 6
Sooke o CDN (BC) 230-231 F 5
Sooner Lake ○ USA (OK) 264-265 G 2
Soos, Tanjung ▲ RI 166-167 E 2
Sooyac o SP 212-213 J 3
Sopachuy o BOL 70-71 E 6
Sopas, Arroyo ~ ROU 76-77 J 6
Sopau o PNG 183 G 2
Sopčaju ~ RUS 108-109 K 7
Sopchoppi o USA (FL) 286-287 E 1
Soperton o USA (GA) 284-285 H 4
Soperton o USA (WI) 270-271 K 5
Sop Hao o LAO 156-157 D 6
Sop Huai o THA 142-143 L 6
Sopi o RI 164-165 L 2
Sopi, Tanjung ▲ RI 164-165 L 2
Sopinusa o RI 166-167 G 3
Sopo ~ SUD 206-207 H 4
Sopočnaja ~ RUS 120-121 Q 5
Sopore o IND 138-139 E 2
Sopot o • • PL 92-93 P 1
Sop Prap o THA 158-159 E 2
Sopron o • H 92-93 O 5
Sop's Arm o CDN (NFL) 242-243 M 3
Sopsoum o LAO 156-157 D 6
Soquee River ~ USA (GA) 284-285 G 2
Sõr, Ribeira de ~ P 98-99 D 5
Sora o I 100-101 D 4
Sora, Rio de ~ RA 76-77 E 2
Sorab o IND 140-141 F 3
Soracaba, Rio ~ BR 72-73 G 7
Sorāh o PK 138-139 B 6
Sōraksan ▲ ROK 150-151 G 8
Sōraksan National Park ⊥ • ROK 150-151 G 8
Sora Mboum o CAM 206-207 B 5
Sorapa o PE 70-71 C 5
Soras, Rio ~ PE 64-65 F 9
Sorata o BOL 70-71 C 4
Sorath ∪ IND 138-139 B 9
Sorati-gawa ~ J 152-153 K 3
Sorau o WAN 204-205 K 4
Søraust-spitsbergen nat-res ⊥ N 84-85 M 3
Sorbas o E 98-99 F 6
Sore o F 90-91 G 9
Sorel o CDN (QUE) 238-239 M 2
Sorell-Midway Point o AUS 180-181 J 7
Sorere o EAU 212-213 D 3
Sør-Flatanger o N 86-87 E 4
Sorfta o ETH 208-209 D 5
Sorgun ☆ TR 128-129 F 3
Sorḥ, Kōtal-e ▲ AFG 134-135 K 1
Sorḥ, Kūh-e ▲ IR 134-135 F 2
Sorḥ, Kūh-e ▲ IR 136-137 D 5
Sorḥ-Pārsā o AFG 138-139 B 2
Sori o DY 204-205 E 3
Soria o • E 98-99 F 4
Sorido o RI 166-167 J 2
Sorkam o RI 162-163 C 4
Sørkapp ▲ N 26-27 v 8
Sørkapp Land ∸ N 84-85 K 4
Sørkappøya ⌒ N 84-85 K 4
Sørli o N 86-87 F 4
Sormiento, Canal ≈ 80 C 5
Soro o IND 142-143 E 5
Soro o PK 134-135 M 3
Soro = Bahr el Ghazal ~ TCH 198-199 H 5
Sorobango o CI 202-203 J 5
Soroca ☆ MD 102-103 F 3
Sorocaba o BR 72-73 G 7
Soročinsk ☆ RUS 96-97 H 7
Soroki = Soroca ☆ MD 102-103 F 3
Sorokino o RUS 94-95 L 3
Sorokskaja guba ≈ 88-89 N 4
Sorombéo o CAM 206-207 B 4
Sorondideri o RI 166-167 H 2
Sorong o RI 166-167 F 2
Sororó, Rio ~ BR 68-69 D 4
Soroti o EAU 212-213 D 3
Sørøya ⌒ N 86-87 L 1
Sørøysundet ≈ N 86-87 L 1
Sorraia, Rio ~ P 98-99 C 5
Sorrento o CDN (BC) 230-231 K 3
Sorrento o • I 100-101 E 4
Sorrento o USA (LA) 268-269 K 6
Sorriso o BR 70-71 K 3
Sør-Rondane ▲ ARK 16 F 3
Sorsele o S 86-87 H 4
Sorsk o RUS 116-117 E 8
Sorsogon ☆ RP 160-161 E 6
Sørspitsbergen nasjonalpark ⊥ N 84-85 J 4
Sørstraumen o N 86-87 K 2
Sort o E 98-99 H 3
Šortandy ☆ KA 124-125 G 3
Sortavala o RUS 88-89 L 6
Sortebræ ⊂ GRØ 28-29 b 2
Sortehest ▲ GRØ 26-27 I 7
Sortija, La o RA 78-79 J 5
Sortland o N 86-87 G 2
Sorūbī o AFG 138-139 B 3
Sorūd, Rūdḫāne-ye ~ IR 136-137 B 7
Sorum ~ RUS 114-115 K 2
Sørværøy o N 86-87 F 3
Sørvågen o N 86-87 F 3
Sørvágur o FR 90-91 D 1
Sorvenok o KA 124-125 P 4
Sørvika o N 86-87 E 5
Sōsan o ROK 150-151 F 9
Sōsan Haean National Park ⊥ • ROK 150-151 E 9
Soscumica, Lac ○ CDN (QUE) 236-237 L 2
Soskie jary ▲ RUS 96-97 G 7
Sosneado, El o RA 78-79 E 3
Sosnogorsk o RUS 88-89 W 5
Sosnove o UA 102-103 E 2
Sosnovec, ostrov ⌒ RUS 88-89 Q 3
Sosnovka o KA 124-125 L 3
Sosnovka o RUS 118-119 D 8
Sosnovka o RUS (KIR) 96-97 G 5
Sosnovka o RUS (MUR) 88-89 Q 3
Sosnovo-Ozërskoe ☆ RUS 118-119 E 9
Sosnovyj o RUS 88-89 M 3
Sosnovyj Bor o RUS 114-115 Q 4
Sosnovyj Bor ☆ RUS (LEN) 94-95 L 2
Sosnowiec o PL 92-93 P 3
Soso Bay ≈ 184 III b 3
Sosogoh o MAL 160-161 B 10
Sosok o RI 162-163 J 4
Sosso o RCA 210-211 E 2
Sosso, Cascades de ~ • DY 204-205 E 3
Sossusvlei ○ • NAM 220-221 B 2
Šostka o UA 102-103 H 2
Sosúa o • DOM 54-55 K 5
Sos'va ☆ RUS (SVR) 114-115 F 5
Sos'va ~ RUS 114-115 G 5
Sot' ~ RUS 94-95 R 2
Sota ~ DY 204-205 E 3
Sotará, Volcán ▲ CO 60-61 C 6
Sotavento, Ilhas de ⌒ CV 202-203 B 6
Sotério, Rio ~ BR 70-71 E 2
Sotian o RMM 202-203 G 4
Sotik o EAK 212-213 E 4
Sotkamo o FIN 88-89 K 4
Soto o RA 76-77 E 6
Soto, De o USA (MO) 274-275 H 6
Soto, De o USA (WI) 274-275 G 1
Soto, Isla ⌒ PE 70-71 C 4
Soto la Marina o MEX 50-51 K 6
Sotomayo, Quebrada ~ BOL 76-77 D 1
Sotomayor o CO 64-65 D 1
Šotorhūn, Kōtal-e ▲ AFG 134-135 L 1
Sotouboua o RT 202-203 L 5
Sotuta o MEX 52-53 K 1
Souanké o RCB 210-211 E 2
Soubakaniédougou o BF 202-203 H 4

Soubakpérou ○ DY 204-205 E 4
Soubala ○ RMM 202-203 E 3
Soubané ○ RG 202-203 C 4
Soubéira ○ BF 202-203 K 3
Soubré ☆ CI 202-203 G 7
Soudan ○ AUS 174-175 D 7
Soudan Bank ≃ 224 D 6
Soudougui ○ BF 202-203 L 4
Souellaba, Pointe de ▲ CAM 210-211 B 2
Souf ⩲ DZ 190-191 F 4
Souf, Oued ~ DZ 190-191 D 7
Soufa, Passe de ▲ RIM 196-197 E 7
Soufflets River ~ CDN (NFL) 242-243 M 2
Soufrière ○ WL 56 E 5
Soufrière, La ▲ F 56 E 3
Sougueur ○ DZ 190-191 C 3
Souillac ○ MS 224 C 7
Souk Ahras ☆ DZ 190-191 F 2
Souk-el-Arab-des-Beni-Hassan ○ MA 188-189 J 3
Souk-el-Arab-du-Rharb ○ MA 188-189 H 3
Souk-el-Kella ○ MA 188-189 J 3
Souk-Jemaâ-des-Oulad-Abbou ○ MA 188-189 H 4
Soukoukoutane ○ RN 204-205 E 1
Souk-Tleta-des-Akhasass ○ MA 188-189 G 6
Sŏul ★ ROK 150-151 F 9
Soula, Djebel Adrar ▲ DZ 190-191 G 8
Soulabali ○ SN 202-203 C 3
Soulis Pond ○ CDN (NFL) 242-243 O 4
Souma'e Sarā ○ IR 128-129 N 4
Soummam, Oued ~ DZ 190-191 E 2
Sounders River ~ CDN 36-37 L 2
Sound Hill Cove ≈ 38-39 Q 2
Sounding Creek ~ CDN (ALB) 232-233 H 4
Sounding Lake ○ CDN (ALB) 232-233 H 3
Sounga ○ G 210-211 B 5
Soungrougrou ~ SN 202-203 C 3
Source du Nil • RWA 212-213 B 5
Sources, Mont aux ▲•• LS 220-221 J 4
Sources Sud du Nil • BU 212-213 B 5
Souris ○ CDN (MAN) 234-235 C 5
Souris ○ CDN (PEI) 240-241 N 4
Souris ○ USA (ND) 258-259 G 3
Souris River ~ CDN (MAN) 234-235 C 5
Souris River ~ CDN (SAS) 232-233 P 6
Souris River ~ USA (ND) 258-259 F 3
Sour Lake ○ USA (TX) 268-269 F 6
Sourou ~ RMM 202-203 J 3
Souroukaha ○ CI 202-203 H 5
Sous, Oued ~ MA 188-189 G 5
Sousa ○ BR 68-69 J 5
Sousel ○ P 98-99 D 5
Sousse ☆••• TN 190-191 H 3
Souterraine, la ○ F 90-91 H 8
South = Sud ■ CAM 210-211 C 2
South Africa ■ ZA 220-221 E 3
South Alligator River ~ AUS 172-173 L 2
Southampton ○ CDN (NS) 240-241 L 5
Southampton ○ CDN (ONT) 238-239 D 4
Southampton ○• GB 90-91 G 6
Southampton ○ USA (NY) 280-281 O 3
Southampton, Cape ▲ CDN 36-37 H 3
Southampton Island ⌒ CDN 36-37 G 2
South Andaman ⌒ IND 140-141 L 4
South Andros Island ⌒ BS 54-55 G 3
South Aulatsivik Island ⌒ CDN 36-37 T 6
South Australia ■ AUS 178-179 C 4
South Australian Basin ≃ 13 D 6
Southaven ○ USA (MS) 268-269 L 2
South Baldy ▲ USA (NM) 256-257 H 4
South Banda Basin ≃ RI 166-167 D 5
Southbank ○ CDN (BC) 228-229 J 2
South Baranof Island Wilderness ⊥ USA 32-33 C 3
South Bay ≈ 36-37 H 2
South Bay ○ CDN (ONT) 234-235 L 3
South Baymouth ○ CDN (ONT) 238-239 C 3
South Beloit ○ USA (IL) 274-275 J 2
South Bend ○ USA (IN) 274-275 M 3
South Bend ○ USA (TX) 264-265 F 5
South Bend ○ USA (WA) 244-245 B 4
South Bentinck Arm ~ CDN (BC) 228-229 H 4
South Bimini ⌒ BS 54-55 F 2
South-Bolton ○ CDN (QUE) 238-239 N 3
South Boston ○ USA (VA) 280-281 H 7
South Branch ○ CDN (NFL) 242-243 J 5
South Branch Potomac River ~ USA (WV) 280-281 H 4
South Brook ○ CDN (NFL) 242-243 M 3
South Brook ~ CDN (NFL) 242-243 M 3
South Brookfield ○ CDN (NS) 240-241 L 6
South Buganda ■ EAU 212-213 C 4
South Caicos ⌒ GB 54-55 K 4
South Cape ▲ CDN 24-25 d 2
South Cape ▲ USA 22-23 T 5
South Cape Seamount ≃ 288 K 6
South Carolina ■ USA (SC) 284-285 J 2
South Charleston ○ USA (OH) 280-281 C 4
South Charleston ○ USA (WV) 280-281 E 5
South China ○ USA (ME) 278-279 M 4
South China Basin ≃ 14-15 D 6
South China Sea ≈ 10-11 L 7
South Coast Range ▲ AUS 180-181 K 4
South Cooking Lake ○ CDN (ALB) 232-233 E 2
South Cove ○ USA (AZ) 256-257 A 2
South Dakota ■ USA (SD) 260-261 E 1
South East ■ RB 220-221 G 2
South East Aru Marine Reserve ⊥• RI 166-167 H 5
South East Bight ○ CDN (NFL) 242-243 O 5
South East Cape ▲ AUS 180-181 J 7
Southeast Cape ▲ USA 20-21 F 5
Southeast Indian Ridge ≃ 12 F 8
South East Islands ⌒ AUS 176-177 G 7
South East Point ▲ AUS 180-181 J 5
Southeast Point ▲ BS 54-55 J 3
Southeast Point ▲ BS 54-55 J 4
South End ▲ AUS 172-173 B 6
Southend ○ CDN 34-35 E 2
Southend-on-Sea ○ GB 90-91 H 6
Southern ■ EAU 212-213 C 4
Southern ■ MW 218-219 H 2
Southern ■ RB 220-221 F 2
Southern ■ Z 218-219 C 3
Southern Alps ▲ NZ 182 B 6
Southern Cross ○ AUS 176-177 E 5
Southern Cross Club ○ GB 54-55 E 5
Southern Harbour ○ CDN (NFL) 242-243 P 5
Southern Indian Lake ○ CDN 34-35 G 2
Southern Kashiji ~ Z 218-219 B 2
Southern Lau Group ⌒ FJI 184 III c 3
Southern Long Cays ⌒ BH 52-53 K 3
Southern Lueti ~ Z 218-219 B 2
Southern National Park ⊥ SUD 206-207 J 5
Southern Pines ○ USA (NC) 282-283 H 5
Southern Region ■ SUD 206-207 H 5
Southern Uplands ⩲ GB 90-91 E 4
Southern Ute Indian Reservation X USA (CO) 254-255 H 6
Southesk River ~ CDN (ALB) 228-229 R 4
Southesk Tablelands ⩲ AUS 172-173 H 6
Southey ○ CDN (SAS) 232-233 O 5
South Fabius River ~ USA (MO) 274-275 F 4
South Fiji Basin ≃ 13 J 5
South Fork ○ CDN (SAS) 232-233 K 6
South Fork ○ USA (CO) 254-255 J 6
South Fork ~ USA (TN) 276-277 G 4
South Fork ~ USA (TN) 276-277 F 5
South Fork ~ USA (VA) 280-281 E 7
South Fork Cumberland River ~ USA (TN) 282-283 C 4
South Fork John Day River ~ USA (OR) 244-245 F 6
South Fork Koyukuk ~ USA 20-21 P 3
South Fork Kuskokwim River ~ USA 20-21 N 5
South Fork Licking River ~ USA (KY) 276-277 L 2
South Fork Owyhee River ~ USA (ID) 252-253 B 4
South Fork Republican River ~ USA (CO) 254-255 N 4
South Fork River ~ USA (WV) 280-281 E 4
South Fork Salmon River ~ USA (ID) 252-253 C 2
South Fork Salt River ~ USA (MO) 274-275 G 5
South Fork Shenandoah River ~ USA (VA) 280-281 H 5
South Fork Solomon River ~ USA (KS) 262-263 F 5
South Fork Trinity River ~ USA (CA) 246-247 B 3
South Fork White River ~ USA (SD) 260-261 E 3
South Galway ○ AUS 178-179 G 3
Southgate River ~ CDN (BC) 230-231 E 3
South Grand River ~ USA (MO) 274-275 D 6
South Gut Saint Ann's ○ CDN (NS) 240-241 P 4
South Harbour ○ CDN (NS) 240-241 P 4
South Haven ○ USA (KS) 262-263 J 7
South Haven ○ USA (MI) 272-273 C 5
South Head ○ AUS 174-175 G 6
South Heart ○ USA (ND) 258-259 E 5
South Heart River ~ CDN 32-33 M 4
South Henik Lake ○ CDN 30-31 V 5
South Hill ○ USA (VA) 280-281 H 7
South Horr ○ EAK 212-213 F 2
South Indian Lake ○ CDN 34-35 G 2
South Island ⌒ EAK 212-213 F 2
South Island ⌒ NZ 182 B 5
South Junction ○ CDN (MAN) 234-235 H 5
South Junction ○ USA (OR) 244-245 D 6
South Kitui National Reserve ⊥ EAK 212-213 G 4
South Knife River ~ CDN 30-31 V 6
South Korea = Taehan-Min'guk ■ ROK 150-151 G 9
South Lake Tahoe ○ USA (CA) 246-247 E 5
Southland ○ USA (TX) 264-265 C 5
South Loup River ~ USA (NE) 262-263 G 3
South Luangwa National Park ⊥ Z 214-215 F 7
South Luconia Shoals ≃ 162-163 K 2
South Lyon ○ USA (MI) 272-273 F 5
South Magnetic Pole = Magnetic Pole Area II CDN 24-25 V 3
South Male Atoll ⌒ MV 140-141 B 6
South Malosmadulu Atoll ⌒ MV 140-141 B 5
South Milford ○ CDN (NS) 240-241 K 6
South Milwaukee ○ USA (WI) 274-275 L 2
South Moose Lake ○ CDN 34-35 G 4
South Moresby Gwaii Haanas National Park Reserve ⊥ CDN (BC) 228-229 C 4
South Moresby Gwaii Haanas National Provincial Reserve ⊥•• CDN (BC) 228-229 C 4
South Moresby National Park Reserve ⊥•• CDN (BC) 228-229 C 4
South Mountain ○ CDN (ONT) 238-239 K 4
South Mountain ▲ USA (ID) 252-253 B 4
South Nahanni River ~ CDN 30-31 E 4
South Nation River ~ CDN (ONT) 238-239 K 3
South Negril Point ▲ JA 54-55 F 5
South Nilandu Atoll ⌒ MV 140-141 B 6
South Ogden ○ USA (UT) 254-255 D 2
South Orkneys ⩲ GB 16 G 32
South Ossetia = Jugo-Osetinskaja Avtonomnaja Respublika ■ GE 126-127 F 6
South Pacific Ocean ≈ 14-15 N 11
South Pare Mountains ▲ EAT 212-213 F 6
South Paris ○ USA (ME) 278-279 L 4
South Pass ▲ USA (CA) 248-249 K 5
South Pass ▲ USA (WY) 252-253 K 4
South Pass City ○ USA (WY) 252-253 K 4
South Pease River ~ USA (TX) 264-265 D 5
South Pender ○ CDN (BC) 230-231 F 5
South Peron Island ⌒ AUS 172-173 K 2
South Pittsburg ○ USA (TN) 276-277 K 5
South Plains ○ USA (TX) 264-265 C 4
South Platte River ~ USA (CO) 254-255 M 3
South Point ▲ BS 54-55 H 3
South Pole ARK 16 E 28
South Porcupine ○ CDN (ONT) 236-237 G 4
Southport ○ AUS (QLD) 178-179 M 4
Southport ○ AUS (TAS) 180-181 J 7
Southport ○ CDN (NFL) 242-243 P 4
Southport ○• GB 90-91 F 5
Southport ○ USA (FL) 286-287 D 1
Southport ○ USA (NC) 282-283 J 7
South Prince of Wales Wilderness ⊥• USA 32-33 D 4
South Racoon River ~ USA (IA) 274-275 D 3
South Redstone River ~ CDN 30-31 F 4
South River ○ CDN (ONT) 238-239 F 3
South River ~ CDN (ONT) 238-239 F 3
South River ~ USA (NC) 282-283 J 6
South Rukuru ~ MW 214-215 G 6
South Sandwich Trench ≃ 6-7 G 14
South Saskatchewan River ~ CDN (SAS) 232-233 L 4
South Seal River ~ CDN 34-35 G 2
South Shetlands ⩲ GB 16 G 30
South Shields ○ GB 90-91 G 4
South Shore ○ USA (KY) 276-277 N 2
South Shore ○ USA (SD) 260-261 K 1
South Sioux City ○ USA (NE) 262-263 K 2
South Siox City ○ USA (IA) 274-275 B 2
South Slocan ○ CDN (BC) 230-231 M 4
South Solitary Island ⌒ AUS 178-179 M 6
South Spicer Island ⌒ CDN 24-25 h 6
South Stradbroke Island ⌒ AUS 178-179 M 4
South Sulphur River ~ USA (TX) 264-265 J 5
South Sunday Creek ~ USA (MT) 250-251 N 5
South Tasman Rise ≃ 13 F 7
South Tetagouche ○ CDN (NB) 240-241 K 3
South Teton Wilderness Area ⊥ USA (WY) 252-253 H 3
South Thompson River ~ CDN (BC) 230-231 K 3
South Tucson ○ USA (AZ) 256-257 E 6
South Turkana National Reservoir ⊥ EAK 212-213 E 3
South Tweedsmuir Island ⌒ CDN 28-29 C 2
South Twin Island ⌒ CDN 38-39 E 2
South Twin Lake ○ CDN (NFL) 242-243 N 3
South Uist ⌒ GB 90-91 D 3
South Wabasca Lake ○ CDN 32-33 O 4
South Wellesley Islands ⌒ AUS 174-175 E 5
South-West = Sud Ouest ■ CAM 204-205 H 6
South West Cape ▲ AUS 180-181 J 7
Southwest Cape ▲ NZ 182 A 7
South Western Highway II AUS 176-177 C 6
Southwest Gander River ~ CDN (NFL) 242-243 N 4
South West Harbor ○ USA (ME) 278-279 N 4
Southwest Indian Ridge ≃ 12 B 9
South West Island ⌒ AUS 174-175 K 5
Southwest Miramichi River ~ CDN (NB) 240-241 J 4
South West National Park ⊥ AUS 180-181 J 7
Southwest Pacific Basin ≃ 14-15 N 11
Southwest Passage ≈ USA 268-269 H 7
Southwest Point ▲ BS 54-55 H 3
Southwest Point ▲ BS 54-55 G 2
Southwest Point ▲ BS 54-55 J 4
South West Rocks ○ AUS 178-179 M 6
Southworth ○ USA (WA) 244-245 C 3
Souto Soares ○ BR 72-73 K 2
Soutpan ○ ZA 220-221 H 4
Soutpansberg ▲ ZA 218-219 E 6
Soutpansnek ▲ ZA 220-221 G 6
Soutrivier ~ ZA 220-221 D 5
Soutrivier ~ ZA 220-221 E 4
Soverato ○ I 100-101 F 5
Sovereign ○ CDN (SAS) 232-233 L 4
Sovetabad ○ US 136-137 N 4
Sovetašen = Nubarašen ○ AR 128-129 L 2
Sovetsk ○ RUS (KIR) 96-97 F 5
Sovetsk ○• RUS (RF) 94-95 G 4
Sovetskaja ○ RUS (KRA) 126-127 D 5
Sovetskaja ○ RUS (STA) 126-127 F 6
Sovetskaja gora ▲ RUS 112-113 V 1
Sovetskaja Gavan' ○ RUS 122-123 J 4
Sovetskij ○ RUS (MAR) 96-97 F 5
Sovetskij ☆ RUS 114-115 G 4
Sovetskoe, ozero ○ RUS 108-109 U 8
Sovhoz, Boľšereckij ○ RUS 122-123 R 2
Sovpoľe ○ RUS 88-89 S 4
Sowa Pan ○ RB 218-219 C 5
Soweto ○ ZA 220-221 H 3
Soy ○ EAK 212-213 E 3
Sōya-kaikyō ≈ 152-153 J 2
Soyaló ○ MEX 52-53 H 3
Sōya-misaki ▲ J 152-153 J 2
Soyo ○ ANG 216-217 B 3
Sož ~ BY 94-95 M 5
Sozak ○ KA 124-125 F 6
Sozva ~ RUS 88-89 W 3
Spa ○• B 92-93 H 3
Spade ○ USA (TX) 264-265 B 5
Spafar'eva, ostrov ⌒ RUS 120-121 N 4
Spain = España ■ E 98-99 D 4
Spalding ○ AUS 180-181 E 2
Spalding ○ CDN (SAS) 232-233 O 3
Spalding ○ USA (NE) 262-263 H 3
Spaldings ○ JA 54-55 G 5
Španberga, proliv ≈ RUS 122-123 M 7
Spanda, Akra ▲ GR 100-101 J 7
Spangle ○ USA (WA) 244-245 H 3
Spaniard's Bay ○ CDN (NFL) 242-243 P 5
Spanish ○ CDN (ONT) 238-239 C 2
Spanish Fork ○ USA (UT) 254-255 D 3
Spanish Peak ▲ USA (OR) 244-245 F 6
Spanish Point ▲ AG 56 E 3
Spanish River ~ CDN (ONT) 238-239 D 2
Spanish River Indian Reserve X CDN (ONT) 238-239 C 2
Spanish Town ○ GB (VI) 286-287 R 2
Spanish Town ○•• JA 54-55 G 6
Spanish Wells ○ BS 54-55 G 2
Sparbo, Cape ▲ CDN 24-25 e 3
Sparbu ○ N 86-87 E 5
Sparke Range ▲ AUS 172-173 H 5
Sparkman ○ USA (AR) 276-277 C 7
Sparks ○ USA (NV) 246-247 F 4
Sparrows Point ○ USA (MD) 280-281 K 4
Sparta ○ CDN (ONT) 238-239 D 6
Sparta ○ USA (GA) 284-285 H 3
Sparta ○ USA (NC) 282-283 F 4
Sparta ○ USA (TN) 276-277 K 5
Sparta ○ USA (WI) 270-271 H 7
Spartanburg ○ USA (SC) 284-285 J 2
Spartel, Cap ▲ MA 188-189 J 3
Spárti ○• GR 100-101 J 6
Sparwood ○ CDN (BC) 230-231 P 4
Spas-Demensk ○ RUS 94-95 O 4
Spas-Klepiki ☆ RUS 94-95 R 4
Spasskaja Guba ○ RUS 88-89 M 5
Spassk-Dal'nij ○ RUS 122-123 E 6
Spassk-Rjazanskij ○• RUS 94-95 R 4
Spath Plateau ▲ GRØ 26-27 p 7
Spatsizi Plateau ▲ CDN 32-33 F 3
Spatsizi River ~ CDN 32-33 F 3
Spavinaw Creek ~ USA (OK) 264-265 K 2
Speaks ○ USA (TX) 266-267 L 4
Spearfish ○ USA (SD) 260-261 C 2
Spearhole Creek ~ AUS 176-177 E 1
Spearman ○ USA (TX) 264-265 C 2
Special Economic Zone (SEZ) ■ VRC 156-157 F 7
Specimen Hill ▲ AUS 178-179 L 3
Speculator ○ USA (NY) 278-279 G 5
Speed ○ USA (WV) 280-281 E 5
Speedwell Island ⌒ GB 78-79 L 7
Speers ○ CDN (SAS) 232-233 L 3
Speery Island ⌒ GB 202-203 C 8
Speightstown ○ BDS 56 F 5
Speke Gulf ○ EAT 212-213 D 5
Spence Bay ≈ 24-25 Z 6
Spence Bay ○ CDN 24-25 Z 6
Spencer ○ USA (IA) 274-275 C 1
Spencer ○ USA (ID) 252-253 F 2
Spencer ○ USA (IN) 274-275 M 5
Spencer ○ USA (NE) 262-263 H 2
Spencer ○ USA (TN) 276-277 K 5
Spencer ○ USA (WV) 280-281 E 5
Spencer, Cape ▲ AUS 180-181 D 3
Spencer, Cape ▲ CDN (NB) 240-241 K 5
Spencer, Cape ▲ USA 32-33 B 2
Spencer, Point ▲ USA 20-21 G 4
Spencer Gulf ≈ 180-181 D 3
Spencerville ○ CDN (ONT) 238-239 K 4
Spencerville ○ USA (OH) 280-281 B 3
Spences Bridge ○ CDN (BC) 230-231 H 3
Spēra ○ AFG 138-139 B 3
Sperling ○ CDN (MAN) 234-235 F 5
Sperryville ○ USA (VA) 280-281 H 5
Spessart ▲ D 92-93 K 4
Spetch ○ CDN (BC) 230-231 G 3
Spey ~ GB 90-91 F 3
Speyer ○• D 92-93 K 4
Spezzano Albanese ○ I 100-101 F 5
Spicewood ○ USA (TX) 266-267 J 3
Spickard ○ USA (MO) 274-275 E 4
Spiekeroog ⌒ D 92-93 J 2
Spiller Channel ~ CDN (BC) 228-229 F 4
Spillimacheen ○ CDN (BC) 230-231 N 3
Špiľ-Tarbaganniah, gora ▲ RUS 120-121 H 3
Spinazzola ○ I 100-101 F 4
Spin Bōldak ○ AFG 134-135 M 3
Spin Gar ▲ AFG 138-139 B 2
Spink ○ USA (SD) 260-261 K 4
Spirit Falls ○ USA (WI) 270-271 J 5
Spirit Lake ○ USA (IA) 274-275 C 1
Spiritwood ○ CDN (SAS) 232-233 L 2
Spiritwood Lake ○ USA (ND) 258-259 J 4
Spirka ~ RUS 110-111 X 4
Spiro ○ USA (OK) 264-265 K 3
Spišský hrad ••• SK 92-93 Q 4
Spitak ○ AR 128-129 L 2
Spit Point ▲ AUS 172-173 D 6
Spitsbergen ⌒ N 84-85 H 3
Spitskopvlei ○ ZA 220-221 G 5
Spittal an der Drau ○ A 92-93 M 5
Spitzkoppe ▲•• NAM 216-217 C 10
Split ○••• HR 100-101 F 3
Split, Cape ▲ CDN (NS) 240-241 L 5
Split Island ⌒ CDN 36-37 K 6
Split Lake ○ CDN (MAN) 34-35 H 2
Split Lake ○ CDN (MAN) 34-35 J 2
Split Lake Indian Reserve X CDN 34-35 J 2
Split Rock Dam < AUS 178-179 L 6
Spofford ○ USA (TX) 266-267 G 4
Špogi ○ LV 94-95 K 3
Spokane ○ USA (MO) 276-277 B 4
Spokane ○• USA (WA) 244-245 H 3
Spokane House • USA (WA) 244-245 H 3
Spokane Indian Reservation X USA (WA) 244-245 H 3
Spokane River ~ USA (WA) 244-245 G 3
Špola ○ UA 102-103 G 3
Spoleto ○• I 100-101 D 3
Spondin ○ CDN (ALB) 232-233 G 4
Spooner ○ USA (WI) 270-271 G 5
Spoon River ~ USA (IL) 274-275 H 4
Sporades = Sporádes, Notioi ⌒ GR 100-101 K 6
Sporádes, Vóries ⌒ GR 100-101 J 5
Sporavskoe, vozero ○ BY 94-95 J 5
Spornoe ○ RUS 120-121 O 2
Sporyj Navolok, mys ▲ RUS 108-109 N 3
Spotted House ○ USA (WY) 252-253 N 2
Spotted Island ○ CDN (NFL) 38-39 R 2
Spotted Island ⌒ CDN (NFL) 38-39 R 2
Spotted Range ▲ USA (NV) 248-249 J 3
Sprague ○ CDN (MAN) 234-235 H 5
Sprague ○ USA (WA) 244-245 H 3
Sprague River ~ USA (OR) 244-245 D 8
Spray ○ USA (OR) 244-245 F 6
Spree ~ D 92-93 M 2
Sprenger, Lake ○ AUS 176-177 H 2
Sprengisandur ▲ IS 86-87 d 2
Spring Bay ≈ USA 254-255 C 2
Springbok ○ ZA 220-221 C 4
Springbrook ○ USA (WI) 270-271 G 5
Spring City ○ USA (TN) 282-283 C 5
Spring Coulee ○ CDN (ALB) 232-233 E 6
Spring Creek ○ AUS 174-175 H 6
Spring Creek ~ AUS 178-179 F 2
Spring Creek ~ USA (TX) 264-265 C 5
Spring Creek ~ USA (TX) 268-269 E 6
Springdale ○ CDN (NFL) 242-243 M 3
Springdale ○ USA (AR) 276-277 A 4
Springdale ○ USA (WA) 244-245 H 2
Springer ○ USA (NM) 256-257 L 2
Springer ○ USA (OK) 264-265 G 4
Springer Mountain ▲ USA (GA) 284-285 F 2
Springerville ○ USA (AZ) 256-257 F 4
Springfield ○ CDN (NB) 240-241 K 5
Springfield ○ USA (CO) 254-255 N 6
Springfield ○ USA (FL) 286-287 D 1
Springfield ○ USA (GA) 284-285 J 4
Springfield ○ USA (ID) 252-253 F 3
Springfield ○ USA (IL) 274-275 J 5
Springfield ○ USA (KY) 276-277 K 3
Springfield ○ USA (MA) 278-279 J 6
Springfield ○ USA (ME) 278-279 N 3
Springfield ○ USA (MN) 270-271 D 6
Springfield ○ USA (MO) 276-277 B 3
Springfield ○ USA (OH) 280-281 C 4
Springfield ○ USA (OR) 244-245 B 6
Springfield ○ USA (SD) 260-261 J 4
Springfield ○ USA (TN) 276-277 J 4
Springfield ○ USA (VA) 280-281 J 5
Springfield ○ USA (VT) 278-279 J 5
Springfield, Lake ○ USA (IL) 274-275 J 5
Springfield Plateau ▲ USA (MO) 276-277 B 3
Springfontein ○ ZA 220-221 G 5
Spring Garden ○ GUY 62-63 E 2
Spring Green ○ USA (WI) 274-275 H 1
Spring Grove ○ USA (VA) 280-281 K 6
Springhill ○ CDN (NS) 240-241 L 5
Spring Hill ○ USA (FL) 286-287 G 3
Spring Hill ○ USA (KS) 262-263 M 6
Springhill ○ USA (LA) 268-269 G 4
Spring Hill ○ USA (TN) 276-277 J 5
Springhouse ○ CDN (BC) 230-231 G 2
Spring Lake ○ USA (NC) 282-283 J 5
Springlake ○ USA (TX) 264-265 B 4
Spring Mill State Park • USA (IN) 274-275 M 6
Spring Mountain Ranch State Park ⊥• USA (NV) 248-249 J 3
Spring Mountains ▲ USA (NV) 248-249 J 3
Springrale ○ AUS 178-179 F 2
Spring River ~ USA (AR) 276-277 D 4
Spring River ~ USA (MO) 276-277 A 3
Spring River ~ USA (OK) 264-265 K 2
Springs ○ ZA 220-221 J 3
Springside ○ CDN (SAS) 232-233 Q 4
Springs Junction ○ NZ 182 D 5
Springsure ○ AUS 178-179 K 3
Springtown ○ USA (TX) 264-265 G 6
Springvale ○ AUS 172-173 H 4
Spring Vale ○ AUS 174-175 D 6
Springvale ○ USA (ME) 278-279 L 5
Springvale Homestead ○• AUS 172-173 L 3
Spring Valley ○ CDN (SAS) 232-233 N 6
Spring Valley ○ USA (CA) 248-249 G 7
Spring Valley ○ USA (IL) 274-275 J 3
Spring Valley ○ USA (MN) 270-271 F 7
Spring Valley ○ ZA 220-221 H 6
Springview ○ USA (NE) 262-263 G 2
Springville ○ USA (AL) 284-285 D 3
Springville ○ USA (CA) 248-249 F 3
Springville ○ USA (NY) 278-279 C 6
Springville ○ USA (UT) 254-255 D 3
Springwater ○ CDN (SAS) 232-233 K 4
Sproat Lake ○ CDN (BC) 230-231 E 4
Sprouses Corner ○ USA (VA) 280-281 H 6
Sprova ○ N 86-87 E 4
Spruce Brook ○ CDN (NFL) 242-243 K 4
Sprucedale ○ CDN (ONT) 238-239 F 3
Spruce Grove ○ CDN (ALB) 232-233 E 2
Spruce Home ○ CDN (SAS) 232-233 N 2
Spruce Island ⌒ USA 22-23 U 4
Spruce Knob ▲ USA (WV) 280-281 G 5
Spruce Knob National Recreation Area ⊥ USA (WV) 280-281 G 5
Spruce Lake ○ CDN (SAS) 232-233 K 2
Spruce Mountain ▲ USA (NV) 246-247 L 3
Spruce Pine ○ USA (NC) 282-283 E 5
Spruce River ~ CDN 30-31 V 6
Spruce View ○ CDN (ALB) 232-233 D 3
Spruce Woods Forest Reserve ⊥ CDN (MAN) 234-235 D 5
Spruce Woods Provincial Park ⊥ CDN (MAN) 234-235 D 5
Spur ○ USA (TX) 264-265 D 5
Spurger ○ USA (TX) 268-269 F 6
Spurn Head ▲ GB 90-91 H 5
Sputinow ○ CDN (ALB) 232-233 H 2
Squamish ○ CDN (BC) 230-231 F 4
Squapan Lake ○ USA (ME) 278-279 N 2
Square Hill ▲ AUS 176-177 H 3
Square Ilands ○ CDN 38-39 R 2
Square Lake ○ USA (ME) 278-279 N 1
Squamish River ~ CDN (BC) 230-231 F 3
Squatec ○ CDN (QUE) 240-241 G 3
Squaw Creek National Wildlife Refuge ⊥ USA (MO) 274-275 C 4
Squaw Lake ○ USA (MN) 270-271 D 3
Squaw River ~ CDN (ONT) 236-237 D 2
Squilax ○ CDN (BC) 230-231 K 3
Squillace, Golfo di ≈ 100-101 F 5
Squires, Mount ▲ AUS 176-177 J 3
Squirrel River ~ CDN (ONT) 236-237 D 2
Squirrel River ~ USA 20-21 K 3
Sragen ○ RI 168 D 3
Srbica ○ YU 100-101 H 3
Srbobran ○ YU 100-101 G 2
Srebărna, Naroden Park ⊥••• BG 102-103 E 5
Sredec ○ BG 102-103 E 6
Sredinnyj hrebet ▲ RUS 120-121 R 7
Srednebelaja ○ RUS 122-123 C 3
Srednee Kujto, ozero ○ RUS 88-89 L 4
Srednekan, Ust'- ○ RUS 120-121 P 3
Srednekolymsk ○ RUS 110-111 d 6
Sredneobskaja nizmennost' ⌣ RUS 114-115 L 3
Sredne russkaja vozvyšennost' ▲ RUS 94-95 Q 5
Srednij, ostrov ⌒ RUS 108-109 Y 3
Srednij, proliv ≈ 112-113 P 2
Srednij, zaliv ○ RUS 120-121 S 3
Srednij Ikorec ○ RUS 102-103 L 2
Srednij Kalar ○ RUS 118-119 H 8
Srednij Mamakan ~ RUS 118-119 G 7
Srednij Ural ▲ RUS 114-115 E 5
Srednij Viljujkan ~ RUS 116-117 N 3
Sredniy Ural = Srednij Ural ▲ RUS 114-115 E 5
Srednjaja ~ RUS 110-111 K 3
Srednjaja, gora ▲ RUS 108-109 a 4
Srednjaja Kočoma ~ RUS 116-117 N 4
Srednjaja Mokla ~ RUS 118-119 J 8
Srednjaja Olëkma ○ RUS 118-119 K 8
Srednogorie = Pirdop + Zlatica ○ BG 102-103 D 6
Šrenk ~ RUS 108-109 Z 4
Srê Noy ○ K 158-159 H 4
Srê Sbov ○ K 158-159 J 4
Sretensk ☆ RUS 118-119 H 9
Sribne ○ UA 102-103 H 2
Sribordi ○ BD 142-143 F 3
Sri Dungargarh ○ IND 138-139 E 5
Srikākulam ○ IND 142-143 C 6
Sri Kālahasti ○• IND 140-141 H 4
Sri Lanka ■ CL 140-141 J 6
Srinagar ☆• IND 138-139 E 2
Srinakarin National Park ⊥• THA 158-159 E 3
Srinakarin Reservoir < THA 158-159 E 3
Sringeri ○ IND 140-141 F 4
Srinivāspur ○ IND 140-141 H 4
Sriparumbudur ○ IND 140-141 H 4
Srirāmapura ○ IND 140-141 G 4
Srirāmpur ○ IND 138-139 E 10
Srirangam ○• IND 140-141 H 5
Srirangapatnam ○• IND 140-141 G 4
Srirangarājupuram ○ IND 140-141 H 3
Srisailam ○ IND 140-141 H 2
Sri Toi ○ PK 138-139 B 4
Srivaikuntam ○ IND 140-141 G 6
Srivardhan ○ IND 138-139 D 10
Srivilliputtūr ○• IND 140-141 G 6
Środa Wielkopolska ○ PL 92-93 O 2
Srostki ○ RUS 124-125 O 2
Srungavarapukota ○ IND 142-143 C 6
s-Sawāb, Wādī ~ SYR 128-129 J 5
s-Sibū', Wādī ∴• ET 194-195 F 6
Staaten River ~ AUS 174-175 G 5
Staaten River National Park ⊥ AUS 174-175 G 5
Stabbursdalen nasjonalpark ⊥ N 86-87 M 1
Stabkirche Urnes ••• N 86-87 C 6
Stackpool ○ CDN (ONT) 236-237 G 5
Stack Skerry ⌒ GB 90-91 E 2
Stacyville ○ USA (IA) 274-275 F 1
Stade ○• D 92-93 K 2
Stadukhino ○ RUS 112-113 O 3
Staffell ○ USA (AR) 276-277 D 5
Stafford ☆ GB 90-91 F 5
Stafford ○ USA (KS) 262-263 H 7
Stafford Springs ○ USA (CT) 280-281 O 2
Stahanov = Kadijivka ○ UA 102-103 L 3
Staines, Península ⌒ RCH 80 D 5
Staked Plain = Llano Estacado ⌣ USA (TX) 264-265 A 5
Stalingrad = Zarizyn ☆• RUS 96-97 D 9
Stalwart ○ CDN (SAS) 232-233 N 4
Stamberg, gora ▲ RUS 122-123 K 5
Stamford ○ AUS 178-179 G 1
Stamford ○ GB 90-91 G 5
Stamford ○ USA (CT) 280-281 N 3
Stamford ○ USA (NY) 278-279 G 6
Stamford ○ USA (TX) 264-265 E 6
Stamford, Lake < USA (TX) 264-265 E 5
Stamping Ground ○ USA (KY) 276-277 L 2
Stampriet ○ NAM 220-221 D 2
Stamps ○ USA (AR) 276-277 B 7
Stamsund ○ N 86-87 F 2
Stanberry ○ USA (MO) 274-275 D 4
Stancionno-Ojašinskij ○ RUS 114-115 R 7
Standard ○ CDN (ALB) 232-233 F 4
Standerton ○ ZA 220-221 J 3
Standing Rock Indian Reservation X USA (SD) 260-261 E 1
Standing Stone State Park ⊥ USA (TN) 276-277 K 4
Standish ○ USA (MI) 272-273 F 4
Stand Off ○ CDN (ALB) 232-233 E 6
Stand Rock • USA (WI) 270-271 J 7
Stanfield ○ USA (AZ) 256-257 D 6
Stanfield ○ USA (OR) 244-245 F 5
Stanford ○ USA (KY) 276-277 L 3
Stanford ○ USA (MT) 250-251 J 4
Stang, Cape ▲ CDN 24-25 U 5
Stanger ○ ZA 220-221 K 4
Stanhope ○ AUS 180-181 H 4
Stanhope ○ CDN (PEI) 240-241 M 4
Stanhope ○ GB 90-91 F 4
Staniard Creek ○ BS 54-55 G 2
stanica Bagaevskaja ○ RUS 102-103 M 4
Staniel Cay Beach ⩲• BS 54-55 G 2
Stanislaus River ~ USA (CA) 246-247 E 5
Stanke Dimitrov = Dupnica ○ BG 102-103 C 6
Stanley ○ AUS 180-181 H 6
Stanley ○ CDN (NB) 240-241 J 4
Stanley ☆ GB 78-79 M 6
Stanley ○ USA (ID) 252-253 D 2
Stanley ○ USA (ND) 258-259 E 3
Stanley ○ USA (NM) 256-257 K 3
Stanley, Mount ▲ ZRE 212-213 B 3
Stanley, Port ○ CDN (ONT) 238-239 D 6
Stanley Mission ○ CDN 34-35 D 3
Stanley Pool ○ ZRE 210-211 E 6
Stanley Reservoir ○ IND 140-141 G 5
Stanleyville = Kisangani ☆ ZRE 210-211 K 3
Stanmore ○ CDN (ALB) 232-233 G 4
Stanmore ○ ZW 218-219 E 5
Stannard Rock ~ USA (MI) 270-271 L 3
Stanovik, hrebet ▲ RUS 118-119 F 11
Stanovoe kōli ○ KA 124-125 F 1
Stanovoe nagor'e ▲ RUS 118-119 E 7
Stanovoj hrebet ▲ RUS 118-119 L 7
Stanovoye Nagor'ye = Stanovoe nagor'e ▲ RUS 118-119 E 7
Stanovoy Khrebet = Stanovoj hrebet ▲ RUS 118-119 L 7
Stansmore Range ▲ AUS 172-173 H 6
Stanthorpe ○ AUS 178-179 L 5
Stanton ○ USA (MI) 272-273 D 4
Stanton ○ USA (ND) 258-259 F 4
Stanton ○ USA (NE) 262-263 J 3
Stanton ○ USA (TN) 276-277 F 5
Stanton ○ USA (TX) 264-265 C 6
Stanwell ○ AUS 178-179 L 2
Stanwell Fletcher Lake ○ CDN 24-25 Y 4
Stanwix National Monument, Fort • USA (NY) 278-279 F 5
Stanwood ○ USA (MI) 272-273 D 4
Stanwood ○ USA (WA) 244-245 C 2
Stanyčno-Luhans'ke ○ UA 102-103 L 3
Stapleford ○ ZW 218-219 G 4
Staples ○ CDN (ONT) 238-239 C 6
Staples ○ USA (MN) 270-271 D 4
Stapleton ○ USA (NE) 262-263 F 3
Stapylton Bay ≈ 24-25 O 6
Star ○ CDN (ALB) 232-233 F 2
Star ○ USA (MS) 268-269 K 4
Staraja Kulatka ☆ RUS 96-97 E 7
Staraja Majna ☆ RUS 96-97 F 6
Staraja Poltavka ☆ RUS 96-97 E 8
Staraja Russa ☆ RUS 94-95 M 3
Staraja Toropa ○ RUS 94-95 M 3
Stará Ľubovňa ○ SK 92-93 Q 4
Staravina ○ MK 100-101 H 4
Stara Zagora ○ BG 102-103 D 6
Starboard ○ USA (ME) 278-279 O 4
Starbuck ○ CDN (MAN) 234-235 F 5
Starbuck ○ USA (MN) 270-271 C 5
Starbuck Island ⌒ 13 M 3
Star City ○ CDN (SAS) 232-233 O 3
Star City ○ USA (AR) 276-277 D 7
Starcke National Park ⊥ AUS 174-175 H 4
Stargard Szczeciński ○ PL 92-93 N 2
Starica ○ RUS (AST) 96-97 D 9
Starica ○ RUS (TVR) 94-95 O 3
Starigrad-Paklenica ○ HR 100-101 E 2
Stark ○ USA (KS) 262-263 L 7
Starke ○ USA (FL) 286-287 G 2
Stark Lake ○ CDN 30-31 O 4
Starks ○ USA (LA) 268-269 G 6
Starkville ○ USA (CO) 254-255 L 6
Starkville ○ USA (MS) 268-269 M 3
Starkweather ○ USA (ND) 258-259 J 3
Starnberg ○ D 92-93 L 4
Starnberger See ○ D 92-93 L 5
Starobaltačevo ☆ RUS 96-97 J 6
Starobeševe ○ UA 102-103 L 4
Starobil's'k ○ UA 102-103 L 3
Starokostjantyniv ☆ UA 102-103 E 3
Starominskaja ○ RUS 102-103 L 4
Staro Orjahovo ○ BG 102-103 E 6
Staroščerbinovskaja ○ RUS 102-103 L 4
Starosubhangulovo ○ RUS 96-97 K 7
Starting Point to Baliem Valley ⊥• RI 166-167 K 4
Start Point ▲ GB 90-91 F 6
Start Point to Torajaland ⊥•• RI 164-165 G 5
Startup ○ USA (WA) 244-245 D 3
Staryi Oskol ○ RUS 102-103 K 2
Staryja Darohi ○ BY 94-95 L 5
State Bridge ○ USA (CO) 254-255 J 4
State College ○ USA (PA) 280-281 J 3
State Line ○ USA (MS) 268-269 M 5
Stateline ○ USA (NV) 248-249 J 4
Staten Island ⌒ USA (NY) 280-281 M 3
Statenville ○ USA (GA) 284-285 G 6
Statesboro ○ USA (GA) 284-285 J 4
Statesville ○ USA (AL) 284-285 D 4
Statesville ○ USA (NC) 282-283 G 5
Statham ○ USA (GA) 284-285 G 3
Station Nord ○ GRØ 26-27 r 3
Statue of Liberty ••• USA (NY) 280-281 N 3
Stauffer ○ CDN (ALB) 232-233 D 3
Stauing Alper ▲ GRØ 26-27 n 7
Staunton ○ USA (IL) 274-275 J 6
Staunton ○ USA (VA) 280-281 G 5
Stavanger ☆• N 86-87 B 7

Stave Lake ⊖ CDN (BC) 230-231 G 4
Stavely ○ CDN (ALB) 232-233 E 5
Stavropol' ☆ RUS 102-103 M 5
Stavropol'skij kraj ◻ RUS 126-127 E 5
Stawell ○• AUS 180-181 G 4
Stayner ○ CDN (ONT) 238-239 E 4
Stayton ○ USA (OR) 244-245 C 6
Steady Brook ○ CDN (NFL) 242-243 L 4
Steamboat ○ USA (OR) 244-245 C 7
Steamboat Springs ○ USA (CO) 254-255 J 3
Steamboat Trading Post ○ USA (AZ) 256-257 F 3
Stebbins ○ USA 20-21 J 5
Stedman ○ USA (MO) 274-275 G 6
Steele ○ USA (AL) 284-285 D 3
Steele ○ USA (MO) 276-277 F 4
Steele ○ USA (ND) 258-259 H 5
Steele, Fort ○ CDN (BC) 230-231 O 4
Steele, Mount ▲ CDN 20-21 U 6
Steele Bayou ~ USA (MS) 268-269 J 4
Steele Island ⌒ ARK 16 F 30
Steelman ○ CDN (SAS) 232-233 Q 6
Steelpoortrivier ~ ZA 220-221 J 2
Steel River ~ CDN (ONT) 236-237 B 3
Steels Harbor Island ⌒ USA (ME) 278-279 O 4
Steelville ○ USA (MO) 276-277 D 3
Steenkampsberge ▲ ZA 220-221 J 2
Steen River ~ CDN 30-31 L 6
Steensby Gletscher ⊂ GRØ 26-27 Y 3
Steensby Inlet ≈ 24-25 h 5
Steensby Land ⊥ GRØ 26-27 P 5
Steensby Peninsula ⌣ CDN 24-25 d 4
Steens Mountain ▲ USA (OR) 244-245 G 8
Steenstrup Gletscher ⊂ GRØ 26-27 V 6
Steenwijk ○ NL 92-93 J 2
Steepbank River ~ CDN 32-33 P 3
Steep Cape ▲ USA 22-23 U 3
Steephill Lake ⊖ CDN 34-35 E 3
Steep Point ▲ AUS 176-177 B 3
Steep Rock ○ CDN (MAN) 234-235 E 3
Steeprock ○ CDN (MAN) 234-235 E 3
Steese Highway II USA 20-21 R 4
Stefansson Island ⌒ CDN 24-25 T 4
Steffen, Cerro ▲ RA 80 E 2
Ştei ○ RO 102-103 C 4
Steiermark ◻ A 92-93 N 5
Steilloopsbrug ○ ZA 218-219 E 6
Steilrand ○ ZA 220-221 K 3
Steilrandberge ▲ NAM 216-217 B 8
Stein am Rhein ○• CH 92-93 K 5
Steinbach ○ CDN (MAN) 234-235 G 5
Steine ○ N 86-87 G 2
Steinen, Rio ~ BR 70-71 K 3
Steinhagen Lake, B.A. < USA (TX) 268-269 F 6
Steinhatchee ○ USA (FL) 286-287 F 2
Steinhausen ○ NAM 216-217 E 10
Steinkjer ☆ N 86-87 E 4
Steinkopf ○ ZA 220-221 C 4
Steins ○ USA (NM) 256-257 G 6
Steins Ghost Town • USA (NM) 256-257 G 6
Steinsland ○ N 86-87 H 2
Stella ○ ZA 220-221 G 3
Stellarton ○ CDN (NS) 240-241 N 5
Stellenbosch ○• ZA 220-221 D 6
Stellera, gora ▲ RUS 120-121 W 6
Stèlvio, Parco Nazionale d. = Nationalpark Stilfser Joch ⊥ I 100-101 C 1
Stendal ○• D 92-93 L 2
Steneby ○ S 86-87 F 7
Stenen ○ CDN (SAS) 232-233 Q 4
Stenón Elafonissou ≈ 100-101 J 6
Stenón Kásu ≈ 100-101 L 7
Stenón Kimolou Sífnou ≈ 100-101 K 6
Stenón Kithéron ≈ 100-101 J 6
Stenón Kíthnou ≈ 100-101 K 6
Stenón Serifou ≈ 100-101 K 6
Stenón Sífnou ≈ 100-101 K 6
Stenungsund ☆ S 86-87 E 7
Stepanakert = Khankendi ☆ AZ 128-129 M 3
Stepanavan ○ AR 128-129 L 2
Stepan Razin ○ AZ 128-129 O 2
Stephanie Wildlife Reserve ⊥ ETH 208-209 C 6
Stephan Strait ≈ 183 C 3
Stephen ○ USA (MN) 270-271 B 2
Stephens ○ USA (AR) 276-277 B 7
Stephens, Cape ▲ NZ 182 D 4
Stephens City ○ USA (VA) 280-281 H 4
Stephens Creek ~ AUS 180-181 F 2
Stephens Island ⌒ CDN (BC) 228-229 C 2
Stephenson ○ USA (MI) 270-271 L 5
Stephenson Ø ⌒ GRØ 26-27 a 2
Stephens Passage ≈ 32-33 C 2
Stephenville ○ CDN (NFL) 242-243 K 4
Stephenville ○ USA (TX) 264-265 F 6
Stephenville Crossing ○ CDN (NFL) 242-243 K 4
Stepnoe ○ RUS (CEL) 96-97 M 6
Stepnoe ☆ RUS (SAR) 96-97 E 8
Stepovak Bay ≈ 22-23 R 5
Steppe, The = Kazahskij melkosopočnik ⊥ KA 124-125 F 3
Steptoe ○ USA (WA) 244-245 H 3
Sterkfonteindam < ZA 220-221 J 4
Sterkspruit ○ ZA 220-221 H 5
Sterkstroom ○ ZA 220-221 H 5
Sterlibaševo ☆ RUS 96-97 J 7
Sterling ○ USA (CO) 254-255 M 3
Sterling ○ USA (KS) 262-263 H 6
Sterling ○ USA (ND) 258-259 G 5
Sterling ○ USA (OK) 264-265 F 4
Sterling ○ ZA 220-221 E 5
Sterling City ○ USA (TX) 266-267 G 2
Sterling Heights ○ USA (MI) 272-273 F 5
Sterling Highway II USA 22-23 V 3
Sterling Landing ○ USA 20-21 N 5
Sterlington ○ USA (LA) 268-269 H 4
Sterlitamak ☆ RUS 96-97 J 7
Sternes ○ GR 100-101 K 7
Steroh ○ Y 132-133 H 7
Stettin Bay ≈ 183 F 3
Stettiner Haff ⊖ D 92-93 N 2
Stettler ○ CDN (ALB) 232-233 F 3
Steuben ○ USA (MI) 270-271 M 4
Steubenville ○ USA (OH) 280-281 F 3
Stevenage ○ GB 90-91 G 6
Stevenson ○ USA (AL) 284-285 E 2
Stevenson ○ USA (WA) 244-245 D 5
Stevenson, Mount ▲ CDN (BC) 228-229 N 4
Stevenson Creek ~ AUS 178-179 C 4
Stevenson Lake ⊖ CDN 34-35 J 4
Stevenson Mountain ▲ USA (OR) 244-245 E 6
Stevensons Peak ▲ AUS 176-177 L 2
Stevens Pass ▲ USA (WA) 244-245 D 3
Stevens Point ○ USA (WI) 270-271 J 6
Stevens Village ○ USA 20-21 Q 3
Stevensville ○ USA (MI) 272-273 C 5
Stevensville ○ USA (MT) 250-251 E 5
Stevinson ○ USA (CA) 248-249 D 2
Stewardson Inlet ○ CDN (BC) 230-231 C 4
Stewart ○ CDN 32-33 F 4
Stewart ○ USA (MN) 270-271 D 6
Stewart, Cape ▲ AUS 174-175 C 2
Stewart, Isla ⌒ RCH 80 E 7
Stewart, Monte ▲ RCH 80 E 7
Stewart, Mount ▲ AUS 174-175 H 7
Stewart, Mount ▲ CDN 20-21 V 5
Stewart Crossing ○ CDN 20-21 W 5
Stewart Island ⌒ NZ 182 A 7
Stewart Islands ⌒ SOL 184 I f 3
Stewart Lake ⊖ CDN 30-31 Z 2
Stewart Plateau ▲ CDN 20-21 W 4
Stewart River ~ CDN 20-21 V 5
Stewarts Point ○ USA (CA) 246-247 B 5
Stewartstown ○ USA (NH) 278-279 K 4
Stewart Valley ○ CDN (SAS) 232-233 L 5
Stewartville ○ USA (MN) 270-271 F 7
Stewiacke ○ CDN (NS) 240-241 M 5
Stewiacke River ~ CDN (NS) 240-241 M 5
Steynsburg ○ ZA 220-221 G 5
Steynsrus ○ ZA 220-221 H 3
Steyr ○• A 92-93 N 4
Steytlerville ○ ZA 220-221 G 6
Stickney ○ USA (SD) 260-261 H 3
Stickney Corner ○ USA (ME) 278-279 M 4
Stiegler's Gorge • EAT 214-215 K 4
Stigler ○ USA (OK) 264-265 J 3
Stikine-Lecconte Wilderness ⊥• USA 32-33 D 3
Stikine Plateau ▲ CDN 32-33 D 2
Stikine Ranges ▲ CDN 20-21 Z 7
Stikine River ~ CDN 32-33 F 3
Stikine Strait ≈ 32-33 D 3
Stilbaai-Wes ○ ZA 220-221 E 7
Stile ○ DZ 190-191 E 3
Stiles ○ USA (TX) 266-267 F 2
Stiles Junction ○ USA (WI) 270-271 K 6
Stilfontein ○ ZA 220-221 H 3
Stilfser Joch = Passo dello Stèlvio ▲ I 100-101 C 1
Stillhouse Hollow Lake < USA (TX) 266-267 K 3
Stillons ○ USA (AR) 276-277 C 7
Stillwater ○ USA (MN) 270-271 F 5
Stillwater ○ USA (NV) 246-247 G 4
Stillwater ○ USA (OK) 264-265 G 2
Stillwater Mountains ▲ USA (NV) 246-247 G 4
Stillwater River ~ USA (MT) 250-251 K 6
Stilo ○ I 100-101 F 5
Stilo, Punta ▲ I 100-101 F 5
Stilwell ○ USA (OK) 264-265 K 3
Stinear Nunataks ▲ ARK 16 F 7
Stinkingwater Pass ▲ USA (OR) 244-245 G 7
Stinnett ○ USA (TX) 264-265 C 3
Stintino ○ I 100-101 B 4
Štip ○ MK 100-101 J 4
Stirling ○ AUS (NT) 178-179 B 1
Stirling ○ AUS (QLD) 174-175 F 5
Stirling ○ CDN (ALB) 232-233 F 6
Stirling ○ CDN (ONT) 238-239 H 4
Stirling ○• GB 90-91 F 3
Stirling Creek ~ AUS 172-173 J 4
Stirling North ○ AUS 180-181 D 2
Stirling Range National Park ⊥ AUS 176-177 D 7
Stjørdalshalsen ○ N 86-87 E 5
St. Kitts = Saint Cristopher Island ⌒ KAN 56 D 3
Stockach ○ D 92-93 K 5
Stockbridge ○ USA (GA) 284-285 F 3
Stockbridge ○ USA (MI) 272-273 E 5
Stockbridge Indian Reservation Ẋ USA (WI) 270-271 J 6
Stockdale ○ USA (TX) 266-267 K 4
Stockerau ○ A 92-93 O 4
Stockers Hill ▲ CDN (NFL) 242-243 M 1
Stockett ○ USA (MT) 250-251 H 4
Stockholm ○ CDN (SAS) 232-233 Q 5
Stockholm ★•• S 86-87 J 7
Stockman's Hall of Fame • AUS 178-179 H 2
Stockport ○ AUS 178-179 E 2
Stockport ○ GB 90-91 F 5
Stockton ○ USA (CA) 248-249 C 2
Stockton ○ USA (FL) 286-287 G 1
Stockton ○ USA (IL) 274-275 H 2
Stockton ○ USA (KS) 262-263 G 5
Stockton ○ USA (MO) 276-277 B 3
Stockton Island ⌒ USA (WI) 270-271 H 4
Stockton Islands ⌒ USA 20-21 R 1
Stockton Lake ⊖ USA (MO) 276-277 B 3
Stockton Plateau ▲ USA (TX) 266-267 D 3
Stockville ○ USA (NE) 262-263 F 4
Stöde ○ S 86-87 H 5
Stŏng Trêng ○ K 158-159 H 4
Stoffberg ○ ZA 220-221 J 2
Stohid ~ UA 102-103 D 2
Stojba ○ RUS 122-123 D 2
Stokan, gora ▲ RUS 122-123 M 6
Stoke-on-Trent ○ GB 90-91 F 5
Stokes, Bahía ≈ 80 D 7
Stokesdale ○ USA (PA) 280-281 J 2
Stokes Point ▲ AUS 180-181 G 6
Stokes Range ▲ AUS 172-173 K 3
Stokkvågen ○ N 86-87 F 3
Stokmarknes ○ N 86-87 G 2
Stolac ○ BIH 100-101 F 3
Stolbovaja ~ RUS 116-117 E 4
Stolbovoe, ozero ⊖ RUS 120-121 U 5
Stolbovoj, mys ▲ RUS 120-121 U 5
Stolbovoj, ostrov ⌒ RUS 110-111 V 2
Stolby ○ RUS 110-111 U 6
Stolby, zapovednik ⊥ RUS 116-117 F 8
Stole, Mountain ▲ PNG 183 A 3
Stolin ○ BY 94-95 K 6
Stompneuspunt ▲ ZA 220-221 C 6
Ston ○ HR 100-101 F 3
Stonecliffe ○ CDN (ONT) 238-239 H 2
Stone Forest •• VRC 156-157 C 4
Stone Cabin ○ USA (AZ) 256-257 A 5
Stoneham ○ USA (CO) 254-255 M 3
Stone Harbor ○ USA (NJ) 280-281 M 4
Stonehaven ○ GB 90-91 F 3
Stonehenge ○ AUS 178-179 G 3
Stonehenge ••• GB 90-91 G 6
Stone House ○ USA (PA) 280-281 G 2
Stone Indian Reserve Ẋ CDN (BC) 230-231 F 2
Stone Lake ⊖ CDN (ONT) 234-235 Q 4
Stone Lake ○ USA (WI) 270-271 G 5
Stonepynten ▲ N 84-85 O 4
Stoner ○ CDN (BC) 228-229 M 3
Stone Rondavel • NAM 220-221 D 3
Stones River National Battlefield ∴• USA (TN) 276-277 J 5
Stonewall ○ CDN (MAN) 234-235 F 4
Stonewall ○ USA (MS) 268-269 M 4
Stonewall ○ USA (TX) 266-267 J 3
Stoney Point ▲ AUS 178-179 F 4
Stonington ○ ARK 16 G 30
Stonington ○ USA (ME) 278-279 N 4
Stony, Pointe ▲ CDN 36-37 P 5
Stony Beach ○ CDN (SAS) 232-233 N 5
Stony Creek ○ USA (VA) 280-281 J 7
Stony Creek Indian Reserve Ẋ CDN (BC) 228-229 K 3
Stonyford ○ USA (CA) 246-247 C 4
Stony Indian Reserve Ẋ CDN (ALB) 232-233 D 4
Stony Island ⌒ CDN 38-39 R 2
Stony Island ⌒ USA (NY) 278-279 E 5
Stony Lake ⊖ CDN 30-31 U 6
Stony Lake ⊖ CDN (ONT) 238-239 G 4
Stony Lake ○ USA (MI) 272-273 C 4
Stony Mountain ○ CDN (MAN) 234-235 F 4
Stony Plain ○ CDN (ALB) 232-233 D 2
Stony Point ▲ CDN (MAN) 234-235 F 3
Stony Point ▲ USA (NY) 278-279 E 5
Stony Rapids ○ CDN 30-31 R 6
Stonyridge ○ CDN (ONT) 238-239 G 4
Stony River ○ USA 20-21 M 6
Stony River ~ USA 20-21 N 6
Stooping River ~ CDN 34-35 P 5
Stopem Blockem Range ▲ AUS 174-175 H 6
Storå ~ DK 86-87 D 8
Stora Blåsjön ○ S 86-87 G 4
Stora Lulevatten ⊖ S 86-87 J 3
Stora Sjöfallets nationalpark ⊥•• S 86-87 H 3
Storavan ⊖ S 86-87 J 4
Storby ○ FIN 88-89 E 6
Stord ⌒ N 86-87 B 7
Store Bælt ≈ DK 86-87 E 9
Store Hellefiskebanke ≃ 28-29 N 3
Store Koldewey ⌒ GRØ 26-27 q 5
Støren ☆ N 86-87 E 5
Store Sotra ⌒ N 86-87 B 6
Storfjordbanken ≃ 84-85 M 4
Storfjorden ≈ 84-85 L 4
Storfjordrenna ≃ 84-85 K 4
Storfors ☆ S 86-87 G 7
Storforsen ~•• S 86-87 K 4
Storforshei ○ N 86-87 G 3
Storis Passage ≈ 24-25 W 6
Storjord ○ N 86-87 G 3
Storkerson, Cape ▲ CDN 24-25 T 4
Storkerson Bay ≈ 24-25 J 4
Storkerson Peninsula ⌣ CDN 24-25 S 4
Storlien ○ S 86-87 F 5
Storm Bay ≈ 180-181 J 7
Stormberg ○ ZA 220-221 H 5
Stormberg ▲ ZA 220-221 H 5
Storm Lake ○ USA (IA) 274-275 C 2
Stormrivier ○ ZA 220-221 F 6
Stormsvlei ○ ZA 220-221 E 7
Stornoway ○ CDN (QUE) 238-239 O 3
Stornoway ○ GB 90-91 D 2
Stor Ø ⌒ GRØ 26-27 m 8
Storø ⌒ GRØ 28-29 X 3
Storøen ⌒ GRØ 26-27 q 4
Storøya ⌒ N 84-85 Q 2
Storož ~ RUS 120-121 T 6
Storoževoj, mys ▲ RUS 120-121 S 3
Storoževsk ○ RUS 88-89 W 5
Storsätern ○ S 86-87 F 5
Storsjö ○ S 86-87 F 5
Storsjøen ~ N 86-87 E 6
Storsjön ⊖• S 86-87 G 5
Storsteinhalvøya ⌣ N 84-85 L 2
Storstrømmen ≈ 26-27 o 5
Storthoaks ○ CDN (SAS) 232-233 R 6
Stortoppen ▲ S 86-87 H 3
Storuman ○ S (AC) 86-87 H 4
Storuman ⊖ S (AC) 86-87 H 4
Storvik ○ S 86-87 H 6
Story ○ USA (WY) 252-253 M 2
Story City ○ USA (IA) 274-275 E 2
Stöttingfjället ▲ S 86-87 H 4
Stouffville ○ CDN (ONT) 238-239 F 5
Stoughton ○ CDN (SAS) 232-233 P 6
Stoughton ○ USA (WI) 274-275 J 2
Stoŭng ○ K 158-159 H 4
Stout Lake ⊖ CDN (ONT) 234-235 J 2
Stowe ○ USA (VT) 278-279 J 4
Strabane ○ GB 90-91 D 4
Strachan ○ CDN (ALB) 232-233 C 3
Strahan ○ AUS 180-181 H 7
Straight Lake ⊖ CDN 34-35 N 4
Strait of Malacca = Melaka, Selat ≈ RI 162-163 C 2
Straits of Mackinac ≈ USA 272-273 D 2
Strakonice ○ CZ 92-93 M 4
Strakonitz = Strakonice ○ CZ 92-93 M 4
Stralki ○ BY 94-95 L 4
Stralsund ○•• D 92-93 M 1
Strand ○ ZA 220-221 D 7
Strandfontein ○ ZA (CAP) 220-221 D 5
Strandfontein ○ ZA (CAP) 220-221 D 7
Strang ○ USA (NE) 262-263 J 4
Stranger River ~ USA (KS) 262-263 L 5
Strangford ○• GB 90-91 E 4
Stranraer ○ CDN (SAS) 232-233 K 4
Stranraer ○ GB 90-91 E 4
Strasbourg ○ CDN (SAS) 232-233 O 4
Strasbourg ☆••• F 90-91 L 7
Strasburg ○ USA (CO) 254-255 L 4
Strasburg ○ USA (ND) 258-259 G 5
Strasburg ○ USA (VA) 280-281 H 5
Stratford ○ CDN (ONT) 238-239 E 5
Stratford ○ NZ 182 E 3
Stratford ○ USA (CA) 248-249 E 3
Stratford ○ USA (OK) 264-265 H 4
Stratford ○ USA (TX) 264-265 B 2
Stratford ○ USA (WI) 270-271 H 6
Stratford-upon-Avon ○• GB 90-91 G 5
Strathburn ○ AUS 174-175 G 4
Strathclair ○ CDN (MAN) 234-235 C 4
Strathcona Provincial Park ⊥ CDN (BC) 230-231 D 4
Strathcona ○ USA (MN) 270-271 B 2
Strathcona Sound ≈ 24-25 d 4
Strathfillan ○ AUS 178-179 G 2
Strathgordon ○ AUS (QLD) 174-175 G 4
Strathgordon ○ AUS (TAS) 180-181 J 7
Strathhaven ○ AUS 174-175 G 4
Strathleven ○ AUS 174-175 G 4
Strathlorne ○ CDN (NS) 240-241 O 4
Strathmore ○ AUS (QLD) 174-175 G 5
Strathmore ○ AUS (QLD) 174-175 J 7
Strathmore ○ CDN (ALB) 232-233 E 4
Strathnaver ○ CDN (BC) 228-229 M 3
Strathroy ○ CDN (ONT) 238-239 D 6
Stratóni ○ GR 100-101 J 4
Stratton ○ CDN (ONT) 234-235 J 6
Stratton ○ USA (CO) 254-255 N 4
Stratton ○ USA (ME) 278-279 L 3
Stratton ○ USA (NE) 262-263 E 4
Stratton Mountain ▲ USA (VT) 278-279 J 5
Straubing ○ D 92-93 M 4
Straubville ○ USA (ND) 258-259 K 5
Straughn ○ USA (IN) 274-275 N 5
Stravropol'-na-Volgi ☆ RUS 96-97 F 7
Strawberry ○ USA (CA) 246-247 E 5
Strawberry, Cape ▲ CDN 36-37 U 7
Strawberry Point ○ USA (IA) 274-275 G 2
Strawberry Reservoir < USA (UT) 254-255 D 3
Strawberry River ~ USA 254-255 E 3
Strawberry River ~ USA (AR) 276-277 D 4
Strawn ○ USA (TX) 264-265 F 6
Streaky Bay ≈ 180-181 C 2
Streaky Bay ○ AUS 180-181 C 2
Streamstown ○ CDN (ALB) 232-233 H 2
Streatfield Lake ⊖ CDN 34-35 O 4
Streatham ○ AUS 180-181 G 4
Streator ○ USA (IL) 274-275 K 3
Street ○ GB 90-91 F 6
Streeter ○ USA (ND) 258-259 H 5
Streetman ○ USA (TX) 266-267 L 2
Strehaia ○ RO 102-103 C 5
Streich Mound ▲ AUS 176-177 G 5
Strelka ○ RUS (KRN) 116-117 F 6
Strelka ○ RUS (MAG) 120-121 P 3
Strelka-Čunja ○ RUS 116-117 L 5
Strelley ○ AUS 172-173 D 6
Strel'na ○ RUS (MUR) 88-89 P 3
Strel'na ~ RUS 88-89 P 3
Strenči ○ LV 94-95 J 3
Stresa ○• I 100-101 B 2
Stretch Range ▲ AUS 172-173 H 6
Strevell ○ USA (ID) 252-253 E 4
Streymoy ⌒ FR 90-91 D 1
Strezelecki Track • AUS 178-179 E 6
Streževoj ○ RUS 114-115 O 4
Strickland River ~ PNG 183 B 3
Strickler ○ USA (AR) 276-277 A 5
Striding River ~ CDN 30-31 S 5
Strindberg Land ⊥ GRØ 26-27 n 6
Stringtown ○ USA (OK) 264-265 H 4
Strizament, gora ▲ RUS 126-127 E 5
Strobel, Lago ⊖ RA 80 E 4
Stroeder ○ RA 78-79 H 6
Strofiliá ○ GR 100-101 J 5
Strogonof Point ▲ USA 22-23 R 4
Strokkurgeysir •• IS 86-87 c 2
Strómboli, Ísola ⌒•• I 100-101 E 5
Strome ○ CDN (ALB) 232-233 F 3
Stromness ○ GB 90-91 F 2
Strømø = Streymoy ⌒ FR 90-91 D 1
Stromsburg ○ USA (NE) 262-263 J 3
Strömstad ☆ S 86-87 E 7
Strömsund ○ S 86-87 G 5
Ströms vattudal ⊥ S 86-87 G 4
Strong ○ USA (AR) 276-277 C 7
Strong ○ USA (MS) 268-269 M 3
Strong, Mount ▲ PNG 183 D 4
Strong City ○ USA (KS) 262-263 K 6
Strongfield ○ CDN (SAS) 232-233 M 4
Stronghurst ○ USA (IL) 274-275 H 4
Strong River ~ USA (MS) 268-269 L 4
Strongsville ○ USA (OH) 280-281 E 2
Stronsay ⌒ GB 90-91 F 2
Stroud ○ AUS 180-181 L 2
Stroud ○ USA (OK) 264-265 H 3
Stroudsburg ○ USA (PA) 280-281 L 2
Struan ○ CDN (SAS) 232-233 L 3
Struer ○ DK 86-87 D 8
Struga ○• MK 100-101 H 4
Struisbaai ≈ 220-221 E 7
Strumešnica ~ MK 100-101 J 4
Strumica ○• MK 100-101 J 4
Strydenburg ○ ZA 220-221 F 4
Strydpoortberge ▲ ZA 220-221 J 2
Stryj ☆ UA 102-103 C 3
Stryj ~ UA 102-103 C 3
Stryker ○ USA (MT) 250-251 E 3
Strymón ~ GR 100-101 J 4
Strypa ~ UA 102-103 D 3
Strzelce Krajeńskie ○ PL 92-93 N 2
Strzelecki Creek ~ AUS 178-179 F 5
Strzelecki Regional Reserve ⊥ AUS 178-179 E 5
Stuart ○ USA (FL) 286-287 J 4
Stuart ○ USA (IA) 274-275 D 3
Stuart ○ USA (NE) 262-263 G 2
Stuart ○ USA (OK) 264-265 H 4
Stuart ○ USA (VA) 280-281 F 7
Stuart, Mount ○ AUS 172-173 C 7
Stuart Bluff Range ▲ AUS 172-173 L 7
Stuartburn ○ CDN (MAN) 234-235 G 5
Stuart Highway II AUS 178-179 C 5
Stuart Island ○ CDN (BC) 230-231 D 3
Stuart Island ⌒ USA 20-21 J 5
Stuart Lake ⊖ CDN (BC) 228-229 K 2
Stuart Memorial • AUS 174-175 C 6
Stuart Ranges ▲ AUS 178-179 C 5
Stuart River ~ CDN (BC) 228-229 L 2
Stubbenkammer ▲•• D 92-93 M 1
Studenčeskoe ○ KA 126-127 M 2
Studenica ○••• YU 100-101 H 3
Studina ○ RO 102-103 D 6
Stugun ○ S 86-87 G 5
Stuie ○ CDN (BC) 228-229 H 4
Stull Lake ⊖ CDN 34-35 K 3
Stump Lake ○ CDN (BC) 230-231 J 3
Stupino ☆ RUS 94-95 Q 4
Sturgeon ○ CDN (QUE) 236-237 N 5
Sturgeon Bay ⊖ CDN (MAN) 234-235 E 2
Sturgeon Bay ○ USA (WI) 270-271 L 6
Sturgeon Falls ○ CDN (ONT) 238-239 F 2
Sturgeon Lake ⊖ CDN (ALB) 32-33 M 4
Sturgeon Lake ⊖ CDN (ONT) 234-235 N 5
Sturgeon Lake ⊖ CDN (ONT) 238-239 G 4
Sturgeon Lake Indian Reserve Ẋ CDN 32-33 M 4
Sturgeon River ~ CDN 34-35 L 3
Sturgeon River ~ CDN (ONT) 236-237 H 5
Sturgeon River ~ CDN (SAS) 232-233 M 2
Sturgeon River ~ USA (MI) 270-271 K 4
Sturges Islands ⌒ CDN 24-25 e 7
Sturgis ○ CDN (SAS) 232-233 Q 4
Sturgis ○ USA (MI) 272-273 D 6
Sturgis ○ USA (MS) 268-269 L 3
Sturgis ○ USA (SD) 260-261 C 2
Šturmovoj ○ RUS 120-121 N 2
Štúrovo ○ SK 92-93 P 5
Sturt, Mount ▲ AUS 178-179 F 5
Sturt Bay ≈ 180-181 D 3
Sturt Creek ○ AUS (WA) 172-173 J 5
Sturt Creek ~ AUS 172-173 J 5
Sturt Highway II AUS 180-181 H 3
Sturt National Park ⊥ AUS 178-179 F 5
Sturt Stony Desert ⌣ AUS 178-179 E 4
Stutterheim ○ ZA 220-221 H 6
Stuttgart ☆• D 92-93 K 4
Stuttgart ○ USA (AR) 276-277 D 6
Stuyahok ○ USA 20-21 K 5
Styal ○ CDN (ALB) 232-233 C 2
Stygge Glacier ⊂ CDN 26-27 L 4
Stykkishólmsbær ☆ IS 86-87 b 2
Styr ~ UA 102-103 D 2
Styx River ○ USA (FL) 286-287 B 1
Šu ~ KA 124-125 F 6
Suai ○ MAL 162-163 K 3
Suai ○ RI 166-167 C 6
Šu'aiba, aš- ○ KSA 130-131 H 4
Suain ○ PNG 183 B 2
Suakin ○• SUD 200-201 H 3
Suakin Archipelago ⌒ SUD 200-201 J 3
Suakoko ○ LB 202-203 F 6
Suam ~ EAK 212-213 E 3
Suana ○ ZRE 216-217 F 3
Suao ○ RC 156-157 M 4
Sua Phung ○ THA 158-159 E 4
Suapi ○ BOL 70-71 D 4
Suapure, Río ~ YV 60-61 H 4
Suaruru, Cordillera de ▲ BOL 76-77 E 1
Suasúa ○ YV 62-63 D 2
Suavanao ○ SOL 184 I d 2
Suay Riêng ○ K 158-159 H 5
Šu'b, Ra's ▲ Y 132-133 H 7
Šu'ba, aš- ○ KSA 130-131 J 3
Šubaihi, aš- ⊥ Y 132-133 C 7
Šubaikiya, aš- ○ KSA 130-131 H 5
Subang ○ RI 168 B 3
Suban Point ▲ RP 160-161 E 6
Suban Siri ~ IND 142-143 H 2
Šubarkūdyk ☆ KA 126-127 M 3
Šubaršy ○ KA 126-127 M 3
Subate ○• LV 94-95 J 3
Subei ○ VRC 146-147 M 6
Šuberta, mys ▲ RUS 108-109 O 5
Šuberta, zaliv ⊖ RUS 108-109 F 5
Subi Besar, Pulau ⌒ RI 162-163 H 3
Subiya, al- ○ KWT 130-131 L 3
Sublett ○ USA (ID) 252-253 E 4
Sublette ○ USA (KS) 262-263 F 7
Subotica ☆• YU 100-101 G 1
Šubrā al-Ḫaima ○ ET 194-195 E 2
Subrahmanya ○ IND 140-141 F 4
Subway Caves ∴ USA (CA) 246-247 D 3
Sucatinga ○ BR 68-69 J 4
Success ○ CDN (SAS) 232-233 K 5
Suceava ☆••• RO 102-103 E 4
Suches ○ USA (GA) 284-285 F 2
Suches, Lago ⊖ PE 70-71 B 5
Suches, Río ~ PE 70-71 C 4
Suchiapa, Río ~ MEX 52-53 H 3
Suchil ○ MEX 50-51 H 6
Suchumi ☆ GE 126-127 D 6
Sucio, Río ~ CO 60-61 C 4
Suckling, Mount ▲ PNG 183 E 5
Sucre ☆••• BOL 70-71 E 6
Sucre ○ CO 60-61 D 3
Sucre ○ EC 64-65 B 2
Sucúa ○ EC 64-65 C 3
Suçuarana ○ BR 72-73 K 3
Suçuarana, Serra do ▲ BR 72-73 H 3
Sucunduri, Rio ~ BR 66-67 H 6
Sucupira do Norte ○ BR 68-69 F 5
Sucuriju ○ BR 62-63 K 5
Sucuriú, Cachoeira ~ BR 68-69 F 5
Sucuriú, Rio ~ BR 72-73 D 6
Sud, Île du ⌒ SY 224 B 5
Sud = South ◻ CAM 210-211 C 2
Suda ~ RUS 94-95 P 2
Sudaira, as- ○ KSA 132-133 B 3
Sudak ☆• UA 102-103 J 5
Sudan ⊥ 200-201 C 4
Sudan ○ USA (TX) 264-265 B 4
Sudan = As-Sūdān ■ SUD 200-201 D 4
Sudbury ○• CDN (ONT) 238-239 E 2
Sud-Camerounais, Plateau ▲ CAM 204-205 K 6
Sudd ⊥ SUD 206-207 K 4
Suddie ○ GUY 62-63 E 2
Sudeten = Sudety ⊥ CZ 92-93 N 3
Sudety ⊥ CZ 92-93 N 3
Süd Ğān ○ IR 134-135 D 2
Sudirman, Pegunungan ▲ RI 166-167 J 3
Sudislavl' ○ RUS 94-95 R 3
Sud ou de la Hotte, Massif du ▲ RH 54-55 H 5
Sud-Ouest = South-West ◻ CAM 204-205 H 6
Südpol ⊥ ARK 16 E 0
Sudskoe, Borisovo- ○ RUS 94-95 P 2
Suduci, kŭli ⊖ US 136-137 F 3
Suđureyri ○ IS 86-87 b 1
Sudwala Caves • ZA 220-221 K 2
Sudža ○ RUS 102-103 J 2
Sudženšk, Anžero- ○ RUS 114-115 T 6
Sue ~ SUD 206-207 J 5
Sueca ○ E 98-99 G 5
Sueco, El ○ MEX 50-51 F 3
Suehn, Big ○ LB 202-203 F 7
Suemez Island ⌒ USA 32-33 D 4
Suess Land ⊥ GRØ 26-27 m 7
Sueur, Le ○ USA (MN) 270-271 E 6
Suez, Gulf of = Suwais, Ḫalīğ as- ≈ ET 194-195 F 3
Suez = Suwais, as- ☆ ET 194-195 F 3
Suez Canal = Suwais, Qanāt as- < ET 194-195 F 2
Šūf, Darre-ye ~ AFG 136-137 K 7
Sufetula • TN 190-191 G 3
Suffern ○ USA (NY) 280-281 M 2
Suffield ○ CDN (ALB) 232-233 G 5
Suffolk ○ USA (VA) 280-281 K 7
Sūfijon mašiti • US 136-137 J 4
Šufiyān ○ IR 128-129 L 3
Šuga ~ RUS 108-109 O 8
Sugaing ○• MYA 142-143 J 5
Sugal ○ RP 160-161 F 10
Sūg al Khamis ○ LAR 192-193 E 1
Sugar Creek ~ USA (IN) 274-275 L 5
Sugar Grove ○ USA (VA) 280-281 E 7
Sugar Land ○ USA (TX) 268-269 E 7
Sugarloaf Mount ▲ USA (ME) 278-279 L 3
Sugarloaf Mountain ▲ AUS 180-181 K 2
Sugarloaf Mountain ▲ USA 22-23 S 3
Sugar Mill = Château Murat • F 56 E 4
Sugar River ~ USA (WI) 274-275 J 2
Sugar Town • AUS 174-175 J 5
Sugarville ○ USA (UT) 254-255 C 4
Sugbongkogon ○ RP 160-161 F 8
Suge La ▲ VRC 144-145 H 6
Suggan Buggan ○ AUS 180-181 K 4
Suggi Lake ⊖ CDN 34-35 E 3
Sugi, Pulau ⌒ RI 162-163 E 4
Sugihwaras ○ RI 162-163 E 7
Suğla Gölü ⊖ TR 128-129 E 4
Suglug Inlet ≈ 36-37 M 3
Sugmutun"egan ~ RUS 114-115 R 4
Sugoj ~ RUS 112-113 H 4
Sugu ○ WAN 204-205 K 4
Sugun ○ VRC 146-147 C 6
Šugur ○ RUS 114-115 J 4
Sugut, Tanjung ▲ MAL 160-161 B 9
Suguta ~ EAK 212-213 F 3
Sugža ~ RUS 120-121 G 2
Sūhāg ☆• ET 194-195 E 4
Šuhair, Abū ☆ IRQ 128-129 L 7
Šuhair, aš- ○ Y 132-133 F 6
Suhait ○ VRC 154-155 D 2
Suhaja Bahta ~ RUS 114-115 U 3
Suhaja Tunguska ~ RUS 114-115 U 2
Šuhār ○• OM 132-133 K 7
Suhariha ~ RUS 108-109 W 8
Suhamyj, ostrov ⌒ RUS 112-113 L 2
Suhbaatar ◻ MAU 148-149 L 4
Suheli Par ⊥ IND 140-141 E 5
Suhiniči ○ RUS 94-95 O 4
Suhl ○ D 92-93 L 3
Suhmiten"jah ~ RUS 114-115 M 5
Suḫna, as- ○ SYR 128-129 H 5
Suḫna, as- ○ Y 132-133 C 6
Suhodol ○ RUS 96-97 G 7
Suhoj Log ☆ RUS 96-97 M 5
Suhoj Nos, mys ▲ RUS 108-109 E 5
Suhoj Pit ~ RUS 116-117 F 6
Suhoj Poluj ~ RUS 114-115 K 2
Suhona ~ RUS 94-95 S 1
Suhum ○ GH 202-203 K 6
Šuhut ☆ TR 128-129 D 3
Sui ~ DY 204-205 E 4
Sui ○ PK 138-139 B 5
Sui ○ PNG 183 B 5
Suiá-Miçu, Rio ~ BR 68-69 B 7
Suiá Missu, Rio ~ BR 72-73 D 2
Suibin ○ VRC 150-151 H 4
Suichang ○ VRC 156-157 L 2
Suichuan ○ VRC 156-157 J 3
Suide ○ VRC 154-155 G 3
Suifenhe ○ VRC 150-151 H 5
Suigam ○ IND 138-139 C 7
Suihua ○ VRC 150-151 F 4
Suijiang ○ VRC 156-157 C 2
Suileng ○ VRC 150-151 F 4
Suining ○ VRC (HUN) 156-157 G 3
Suining ○ VRC (JIA) 154-155 K 5
Suining ○ VRC (SIC) 154-155 D 6
Suir ~ IRL 90-91 D 5
Suixi ○ VRC 156-157 G 6
Sui Xian ○ VRC 154-155 J 4
Suiyang ○ VRC (GZH) 156-157 E 3
Suiyang ○ VRC (HEI) 150-151 H 5
Suizhou ○ VRC 154-155 H 6
Šuja ☆ RUS 94-95 R 3
Šuja ~ RUS 88-89 M 6
Sujālpur ○ IND 138-139 F 8
Sujāwal ○ PK 138-139 B 7
Sujawal ○ PK 138-139 B 6
Šujostrov ⌒ RUS 88-89 N 4
Sujutkina Kosa, mys ▲ RUS 126-127 G 5
Šukābad ○ IR 134-135 C 2
Sukabumi ○ RI 168 B 3
Sukadana ○ RI (KBA) 162-163 H 5
Sukadana ○ RI (LAM) 162-163 F 7
Sukadana Teluk ≈ 162-163 H 5
Sukagawa ○ J 152-153 J 6
Sukamenang ○ RI 162-163 E 6
Sukaraja ○ RI (JTE) 168 C 3
Sukaraja ○ RI (KBA) 162-163 J 6
Sukaraegara ○ RI 168 B 3
Sukeva ○ FIN 88-89 J 5
Sukhothai ○••• THA 158-159 E 2
Suki ○ PNG 183 A 5
Sukkar,as- ○ SYR 128-129 J 5
Sukkar, Qal'at ☆ IRQ 128-129 M 7
Sukkertoppen = Maniitsoq ○ GRØ 28-29 O 4
Sukkertoppen Isflade ⊂ GRØ 28-29 O 3
Sukkozero ○ RUS 88-89 M 5
Sukkur ○• PK 138-139 B 6
Sukkwan Island ⌒ USA 32-33 D 4
Sukodadi ○ RI 168 E 3
Sukoharjo ○ RI 168 D 3
Sukopuro ○ RI 168 E 3
Sukorejo ○ RI 168 D 3
Sukpai ~ RUS 122-123 G 5
Sukri ~ IND 138-139 D 7
Sukses ○ NAM 216-217 D 10
Suksun ☆ RUS 96-97 K 5
Sukumo ○ J 152-153 E 8
Sukunka River ~ CDN 32-33 J 4
Sul, Canal do ~ BR 62-63 K 6
Sula ⌒ N 86-87 B 6
Sula ~ RUS 88-89 U 4
Sula ~ RUS 88-89 U 3
Sula ~ UA 102-103 H 3
Sula ○ USA 250-251 F 6
Sula, Kepulauan ⌒ RI 164-165 J 4
Sulagiri ○ IND 140-141 H 4
Sulaib aṭ-Ṭarfā' ⊥ KSA 130-131 G 3
Sulaimāniya, as- ◻ IRQ 128-129 L 5
Sulaimāniya, as- ☆ IRQ 128-129 L 5
Sulaiman Range ▲ PK 138-139 B 5
Sulak ~ RUS 126-127 G 6
Sulakkan ~ RUS 110-111 a 6
Sulakyurt ☆ TR 128-129 E 2
Sulamu ○ RI 166-167 B 7
Sulat ~ RP 160-161 F 7
Sulatna River ~ USA 20-21 N 4
Sulawesi ⌒ RI 164-165 F 5
Sulawesi Selatan ◻ RI 164-165 F 5
Sulawesi Tengah ◻ RI 164-165 F 4
Sulawesi Tenggara ◻ RI 164-165 G 5
Sulawesi Utara ◻ RI 164-165 J 3
Šulb, aş- ▲ KSA 130-131 K 4
Sulb, Temple of • SUD 200-201 E 2
Sulby Creek ~ CDN (SAS) 232-233 K 5
Sulechów ○• PL 92-93 N 2
Suleja ○ WAN 204-205 G 4
Sulejów ○• PL 92-93 P 3
Sulen, Mount ▲ PNG 183 B 2
Sule Skerry ⌒ GB 90-91 E 2
Šul'gan-Taš zapovednik ⊥ RUS 96-97 K 7
Šūlič ○ KA 136-137 K 7
Suliki ○ RI 162-163 D 5
Sulima ○ WAL 202-203 E 6
Sulina ○• RO 102-103 F 5
Sulina, Braţul ~ RO 102-103 F 5
Sulitelma ▲ S 86-87 H 3
Sulitjelma ○ N 86-87 H 3
Suljukta ○ KS 136-137 L 5
Sulkovskogo, mys ▲ RUS 120-121 W 6
Sullana ☆ PE 64-65 B 4
Sulligent ○ USA (AL) 284-285 B 3
Sullivan ○ USA (IL) 274-275 K 5
Sullivan ○ USA (IN) 274-275 L 5
Sullivan ○ USA (MO) 274-275 G 6
Sullivan Lake ○ CDN (ALB) 232-233 G 3
Sullivan Lake ⊖ CDN (ALB) 232-233 G 4
Sullivan River ~ CDN (BC) 230-231 M 2
Sullorsuaq Vaigat ≈ 28-29 N 1
Sully ○ USA (IA) 274-275 F 3
Sully-sur-Loire ○ F 90-91 J 8
Sulmona ○ I 100-101 D 3
Sulop ○ RP 160-161 F 9
Sulphur ○ USA (LA) 268-269 G 6
Sulphur ○ USA (NV) 246-247 G 3
Sulphur ○ USA (OK) 264-265 H 4
Sulphur Bank ≃ 72-73 M 4
Sulphur Bluff ○ USA (TX) 264-265 J 5
Sulphur River ~ USA (AR) 276-277 B 7
Sulphur River ~ USA (TX) 264-265 K 5
Sulphur Springs ○ USA (TX) 264-265 J 5
Sulphur Springs Draw ~ USA (TX) 264-265 B 5
Sultan ○ CDN (ONT) 236-237 F 5
Sultān ○ IRQ 128-129 L 6
Sultandağı ☆ TR 128-129 D 3
Sultan Dağları ▲ TR 128-129 D 3
Sultan Hamud ○ EAK 212-213 F 5
Sultanhanı ○ TR 128-129 E 3
Sultan Kudarat ○ RP 160-161 F 9
Sultānpur ○ IND 142-143 C 2
Sultānpur = Kulu ○•• IND 138-139 F 4
Sultan-Ubajs ▲ US 136-137 G 3
Sultepec, Río ~ MEX 52-53 D 2
Sulu ○ ZRE 210-211 K 6
Sulu, Laut ≈ 160-161 B 9
Suluan Island ⌒ RP 160-161 F 7
Sulu Archipelago ⌒ RP 160-161 D 10
Suluistyk ~ TJ 146-147 B 7
Suluk ~ RUS 122-123 F 3
Sulukaska, togi ▲ KA 136-137 G 3
Sülüklü ○ TR 128-129 E 3
Sululta ○ ETH 208-209 D 4
Sulumei River ~ PNG 183 B 3
Suluntah ○ LAR 192-193 J 1
Sulūq ○ LAR 192-193 J 2

Sūlūru ○ IND 140-141 H 4
Sulusaray ○ TR 128-129 G 2
Sulu Sea ≈ 160-161 C 8
Sülütöbe ○ KA 124-125 E 6
Sulzbach-Rosenberg ○ D 92-93 L 4
Sumaco ○ EC 64-65 D 2
Sumaco, Volcán ▲ EC 64-65 D 2
Sumahode ○ RI 164-165 K 3
Sumaianyar ○ RI 164-165 E 5
Sumair, Ğazirat ⌒ KSA 132-133 C 5
Šumanaj ○ US 136-137 F 3
Sümär ○ IR 134-135 A 2
Sumara, Naqil ▲ Y 132-133 D 6
Sumaroto ○ RI 168 D 3
Sumas ○ USA (WA) 244-245 C 2
Sumatera Barat ◘ RI 162-163 C 5
Sumatera Selatan ◘ RI 162-163 F 6
Sumatera Utara ◘ RI 162-163 C 3
Sumatra ○ USA (FL) 286-287 E 1
Sumatra ○ USA (MT) 250-251 M 5
Sumatra = Sumatera ⌒ RI 162-163 B 2
Sumaúma ○ BR 66-67 G 6
Šumava ▲ CZ 92-93 M 4
Sumba ○ ANG 216-217 B 3
Sumba ⌒ RI 168 E 7
Sumba, Ile ⌒ ZRE 210-211 G 3
Sumba, Selat ≈ 168 D 7
Šumbar ∼ TM 136-137 E 5
Sumbawa ⌒ RI 168 C 7
Sumbawa Besar ○ RI 168 C 7
Sumbawanga ☆ EAT 214-215 F 4
Sumbe ☆ ANG 216-217 B 5
Sumbe ○ KA 146-147 E 4
Sumbèr = Čojr ○ MAU 148-149 J 4
Sumbi ○ ZRE 210-211 D 6
Sumbu ○ Z 214-215 F 5
Sumbu National Park ⊥ Z 214-215 F 5
Sumburgh ○ GB 90-91 G 2
Sumbuya ○ WAL 202-203 E 6
Sumé ○ BR 68-69 K 5
Sumedang ○ RI 168 B 3
Sumelas • TR 128-129 H 2
Šumen ○ BG 102-103 E 6
Sumenep ○ RI 168 E 3
Šumerlja ○ RUS 96-97 E 6
Sumgayıt = Sumqayıt ○ • AZ 128-129 N 2
Sumidouro Grande, Rio ∼ BR 70-71 J 4
Šumiha ☆ RUS 114-115 G 7
Šumilina ☆ BY 94-95 L 4
Šummān, aš- ▲ KSA 130-131 J 4
Summer ○ USA (MS) 268-269 K 3
Summer Creek ∼ CDN (BC) 230-231 J 4
Summerdown ○ NAM 216-217 E 10
Summerfield ○ USA (KS) 262-263 K 5
Summerfield ○ USA (LA) 268-269 H 4
Summerfield ○ USA (NC) 282-283 H 4
Summerfield ○ USA (TX) 264-265 B 4
Summer Island ⌒ USA (MI) 270-271 M 5
Summer Lake ○ USA (OR) 244-245 E 8
Summer Lake ○ USA (OR) 244-245 E 8
Summerland ○ CDN (BC) 230-231 K 4
Summerland Key ○ USA (FL) 286-287 H 7
Summerside ○ CDN (NFL) 242-243 L 3
Summerside ○ CDN (PEI) 240-241 M 4
Summer Strait ≈ 32-33 C 4
Summerstrand ○ ZA 220-221 G 6
Summersville ○ USA (MO) 276-277 D 3
Summersville ○ USA (WV) 280-281 F 5
Summersville Lake ○ USA (WV) 280-281 F 5
Summerton ○ USA (SC) 284-285 K 3
Summerville ○ CDN (NFL) 242-243 P 5
Summerville ○ USA (GA) 284-285 E 2
Summerville ○ USA (SC) 284-285 K 3
Summerville ○ USA (TN) 276-277 H 5
Summit ○ SUD 200-201 H 3
Summit ○ USA (MS) 268-269 K 5
Summit ○ USA (RI) 278-279 K 7
Summit ○ USA (SD) 260-261 K 1
Summit ▲ USA (UT) 254-255 E 3
Summit ▲ USA (UT) 254-255 D 4
Summit Lake ○ CDN (BC) 30-31 G 6
Summit Lake ○ CDN (BC) 228-229 M 2
Summit Peak ▲ USA (CO) 254-255 J 6
Sumner ○ USA (IA) 274-275 F 2
Sumner ○ USA (IL) 274-275 L 6
Sumner ○ USA (MO) 274-275 E 5
Sumner ○ USA (OR) 244-245 A 7
Sumner ○ USA (WA) 244-245 C 3
Sumner, Fort ○ USA (NM) 256-257 L 4
Sumner, Lake ○ USA (NM) 256-257 L 4
Sumner State Memorial, Fort • USA (NM) 256-257 L 4
Sumoto ○ J 152-153 F 7
Sumozero ○ RUS 88-89 N 4
Sumpangbinangae ○ RI 164-165 F 6
Šumperk ○ CZ 92-93 O 4
Sumpiuh ○ RI 168 C 3
Sumpter ○ USA (OR) 244-245 G 6
Sumpul, Río ∼ HN 52-53 K 4
Sumqayıt ∼ AZ 128-129 N 2
Sumqayıt = Sumqayıt ○ • AZ 128-129 N 2
Sumrall ○ USA (MS) 268-269 L 5
Sumskij Posad ○ RUS 88-89 N 4
Šumšu, ostrov ⌒ RUS 122-123 R 3
Sumter ○ USA (SC) 284-285 K 3
Sumter National Monument, Fort • USA (SC) 284-285 L 4
Sumuna ○ PNG 183 F 2
Sumur ○ RI 168 A 3
Sumxi ○ VRC 144-145 C 3
Sumy ☆ UA 102-103 J 2
Šumysker ○ KA 96-97 G 10
Suna ☆ RUS 96-97 G 5
Sūna ○ Y 132-133 F 6
Sunaisila ○ IRQ 128-129 J 5
Sunamganj ○ BD 142-143 G 3
Sunan ○ DVR 150-151 E 8
Sunan ○ VRC 154-155 A 2
Sunão ○ IND 138-139 D 8
Sunbeam ○ USA (ID) 252-253 D 2
Sunburg ○ USA (MN) 270-271 C 5
Sunburst ○ USA (MT) 250-251 H 3
Sunbury ○ AUS 180-181 H 4
Sunbury ○ USA (NC) 282-283 L 4
Sunbury ○ USA (OH) 280-281 D 3
Sunbury ○ USA (PA) 280-281 K 3
Sunchales ○ RA 76-77 G 6
Suncho Corral ○ RA 76-77 F 4
Sunchon ○ DVR 150-151 E 8
Sunch'ŏn ○ ROK 150-151 F 10
Sun City ○ USA (AZ) 256-257 C 5
Sun City ○ USA (CA) 248-249 G 6
Sun City ○ • ZA 220-221 H 2
Suncook ○ USA (NH) 278-279 K 5
Suncun ○ VRC 154-155 K 4
Sunda, Kepulauan ⌒ RI 168 B 2
Sunda, Selat ≈ 168 A 3
Sundarbans ⊥ IND 142-143 F 5
Sundarbans National Park ⊥ ••• IND 142-143 F 4
Sundargarh ○ IND 142-143 D 4
Sunda Shelf ≃ 12 J 4
Sunda Trench ≃ 12 J 5
Sunday Strait ≈ 172-173 F 4
Sunderland ○ GB 90-91 G 4
Sündiken Dağları ▲ TR 128-129 D 3
Sundi-Lutete ○ ZRE 210-211 E 6
Sundown ○ CDN (MAN) 234-235 G 5
Sundown National Park ⊥ AUS 178-179 L 5
Sundozero, ozero ○ RUS 88-89 M 5
Sundre ○ CDN (ALB) 232-233 D 4
Sundsvall ○ S 86-87 H 5
Sundukli, peski ⊥ TM 136-137 H 5
Sunel ○ IND 138-139 E 7
Sunflower ○ USA (AZ) 256-257 D 5
Sunflower ○ USA (MS) 268-269 K 3
Sunflower, Mount ▲ USA (CO) 254-255 N 4
Sunflower River ∼ USA (MS) 268-269 K 3
Sungaibamban ○ RI 162-163 C 3
Sungaibelidah ○ RI 162-163 F 6
Sungaibenkal ○ RI 162-163 E 5
Sungai Buloh ○ MAL 162-163 D 3
Sungaibuluh ○ RI 164-165 D 5
Sungaidareh ○ RI 162-163 D 5
Sungaigerung ○ RI 162-163 F 6
Sungaiguntung ○ RI 162-163 E 4
Sungai Ko-lok ○ THA 158-159 F 7
Sungai Lembing ○ MAL 162-163 E 3
Sungailiat ○ RI 162-163 G 5
Sungai Penuh ○ RI 162-163 D 6
Sungai Petani ○ MAL 162-163 D 2
Sungai Pin ○ MAL 160-161 B 10
Sungairaya ○ RI 162-163 H 4
Sungai Rengit, Kampung ○ MAL 162-163 F 4
Sungaiselan ○ RI 162-163 F 6
Sunggai Siput ○ MAL 162-163 D 2
Sungguminasa ○ RI 164-165 F 6
Sungikai ○ SUD 200-201 D 6
Sung Noen ○ THA 158-159 F 3
Sungo ○ MOC 218-219 G 3
Sungsang ○ RI 162-163 F 6
Sungurlu ☆ TR 128-129 F 2
Suni ○ SUD 200-201 B 6
Sun Kosi ∼ NEP 144-145 E 7
Sunlander II AUS 174-175 K 7
Sun Moon Lake •• RC 156-157 M 5
Sunndalsøra ☆ N 86-87 D 5
Sunne ☆ S 86-87 F 7
Sunniland ○ USA (FL) 286-287 H 5
Sunnybrae ○ CDN (NS) 240-241 N 5
Sunnybrook ○ CDN (ALB) 232-233 D 2
Sunny Hills ○ USA (FL) 286-287 D 1
Sunnynook ○ CDN (ALB) 232-233 G 4
Sunnyside ○ CDN (NB) 240-241 J 3
Sunnyside ○ CDN (NFL) 242-243 P 5
Sunnyside ○ USA (WA) 244-245 F 4
Sunnyvale ○ USA (CA) 248-249 B 2
Sunny Valley ○ USA (OR) 244-245 B 8
Sun Pass ▲ USA (OR) 244-245 D 8
Sun Prairie ○ USA (WI) 274-275 J 1
Sunray ○ USA (TX) 264-265 C 2
Sunrise ○ USA (WY) 252-253 O 4
Sunriver ○ USA (OR) 244-245 D 7
Sun River ∼ USA (MT) 250-251 H 4
Sunset Country ⊥ AUS 180-181 F 3
Sunset Crater National Monument ∴ USA (AZ) 256-257 D 3
Sunshine Coast ⊥ AUS 178-179 M 4
Sunspot ○ USA (NM) 256-257 K 6
Sunstrum ○ CDN (ONT) 234-235 L 4
Suntai ○ WAN 204-205 J 5
Suntai, River ∼ WAN 204-205 J 5
Suntar ☆ RUS 118-119 H 4
Suntar ∼ RUS 120-121 J 2
Suntar-Hajata, hrebet ▲ RUS 110-111 V 7
Suntaži ○ •• LV 94-95 J 3
Suntsar ○ PK 134-135 K 6
Suntu ○ ETH 208-209 C 4
Sun Valley ○ USA (ID) 252-253 D 3
Sunwapta Pass ▲ CDN (ALB) 228-229 R 4
Sunwi Do ⌒ DVR 150-151 E 9
Sunwu ○ VRC 150-151 F 3
Sunyani ☆ GH 202-203 J 6
Sunža ∼ RUS 126-127 F 6
Sun Zhongshan Guju • VRC 156-157 H 5
Suði Rút ☆ VN 156-157 D 6
Suojarvi ○ RUS 88-89 M 5
Suojarvi, ozero ○ RUS 88-89 M 5
Suola ∼ RUS 120-121 D 3
Suolama ∼ RUS 110-111 H 3
Suomenlinna = Sveaborg ••• FIN 88-89 H 6
Suomenselkä ⊥ FIN 88-89 H 5
Suomi ○ CDN (ONT) 234-235 O 6
Suō-nada ≈ 152-153 D 8
Suonenjoki ○ FIN 88-89 J 5
Suon-Tit ○ RUS 118-119 L 6
Suot-Ujala, hrebet ▲ RUS 110-111 d 5
Suowenna Shan ▲ VRC 144-145 E 4
Supai ○ USA (AZ) 256-257 C 2
Supamo, Río ∼ YV 60-61 K 4
Sup'ē ○ ETH 208-209 D 4
Superagui, Parque Nacional do ⊥ BR 74-75 F 5
Superb ○ CDN (SAS) 232-233 J 4
Superior ○ USA (AZ) 256-257 D 5
Superior ○ USA (MT) 250-251 E 4
Superior ○ USA (NE) 262-263 H 4
Superior ○ USA (WI) 270-271 F 4
Superior ○ USA (WY) 252-253 K 5
Superior, Laguna ≈ 52-53 G 3
Superior, Lake ○ 46-47 C 2
Supetar ○ HR 100-101 F 3
Suphan Buri ○ THA 158-159 F 3
Süphan Dağı ▲ TR 128-129 K 3
Supia ○ CO 60-61 D 5
Supiori, Pulau ⌒ RI 166-167 H 2
Supiori Pulau Reserve ⊥ • RI 166-167 H 2
Suplee ○ USA (OR) 244-245 F 6
Supplejack Downs ○ AUS 172-173 K 5
Suppli ○ USA (SC) 284-285 M 3
Supri ∼ RUS 112-113 J 3
Suqailibiya ○ SYR 128-129 G 5
Šuqaiq, aš- ○ KSA 132-133 C 5
Sūq al-Ğarrāhi ○ Y 132-133 C 6
Sūq al-'Inān ○ Y 132-133 D 5
Sūq aš-Šuyūh ☆ IRQ 130-131 K 2
Suqian ○ VRC 154-155 L 5
Šuqqān, aš- ⊥ KSA 132-133 F 3
Sūq Suwaiq ○ KSA 130-131 F 5
Suqu ○ VRC 156-157 J 5
Šur ○ OM 132-133 L 2
Šūr ○ • OM 132-133 L 2
Šūr ☆ RL 128-129 F 6
Šūr, Kāl-e ∼ IR 136-137 F 7
Sur, Point ▲ USA (CA) 248-249 C 3
Šūr, Rūd-e ∼ IR 134-135 H 5
Šūr, Rūd-e ∼ IR 134-135 J 2
Šūr, Rūd-e ∼ IR 134-135 G 3
Šūr, Rūd-e ∼ IR 134-135 H 3
Šūr, Rūd-e ∼ IR 134-135 D 4
Šūr, Rūd-e ∼ IR 134-135 F 5
Šūr, Rūd-e ∼ IR 134-135 E 5
Šūr, Rūd-e ∼ IR 136-137 B 7
Šūr, Rūdhāne-ye ∼ IR 134-135 E 4
Šūr, Rūdhāne-ye ∼ IR 134-135 F 3
Šūr, Rūdhāne-ye ∼ IR 136-137 B 7
Sura ○ ETH 208-209 E 5
Sura ∼ RUS 88-89 S 5
Sura ∼ RUS 96-97 D 7
Šūrā, aš- ○ IRQ 128-129 K 5
Sūrāb ○ IR 134-135 D 1
Sūrāb ○ IR 134-135 D 2
Sūrāb ○ IR 134-135 D 2
Šūr Āb ∼ IR 136-137 C 7
Sūrāb ○ PK 134-135 M 4
Surabaya ○ RI (LAM) 162-163 F 7
Surabaya ☆ RI (JTI) 168 E 3
Surahany ○ AZ 128-129 O 2
Surakarta ○ RI 168 D 3
Suramana ○ RI 164-165 F 4
Suranadi ○ •• RI 168 C 7
Surat ○ AUS 178-179 K 4
Surat ○ • IND 138-139 D 9
Suratgarh ○ IND 138-139 D 5
Suratkal ○ IND 140-141 F 4
Suratthani ○ THA 158-159 E 6
Šūr Āv ○ AFG 134-135 M 3
Suraž ○ BY 94-95 M 4
Suraž ○ RUS 94-95 N 5
Šurči ○ US 136-137 K 6
Surcubamba ○ PE 64-65 E 8
Sur del Cabo San Antonio, Punta ▲ RA 78-79 L 4
Surdūd, Wādī ∼ Y 132-133 C 6
Surendranagar ○ IND 138-139 C 8
Šūr-e Sabzevār, Kāl-e ∼ IR 136-137 E 6
Surf ○ USA (CA) 248-249 D 5
Surfers Paradise ○ AUS 178-179 M 5
Surfing Beaches • AUS 180-181 H 5
Surf Inlet ○ CDN (BC) 228-229 F 3
Surfside Beach ○ USA (SC) 284-285 M 3
Sürgaz ○ IR 134-135 H 4
Šūrgaz, Rūd-e ∼ IR 134-135 H 4
Surge Narrows ○ CDN (BC) 230-231 D 3
Surghet ○ NEP 144-145 C 6
Surgidero de Batabanó ○ C 54-55 D 3
Surgut ☆ RUS 114-115 M 4
Surgutskaja nizina ⌣ RUS 114-115 L 4
Surhan ○ US 136-137 K 6
Surhandar'inskaja oblast' ◘ US 136-137 K 6
Surhandarja ∼ US 136-137 L 5
Surhob ∼ TJ 136-137 M 5
Suriago Strait ≈ 160-161 F 7
Suriāpet ○ IND 140-141 H 2
Surigao ☆ RP 160-161 F 8
Surikova ○ RUS 116-117 E 7
Surin ○ THA 158-159 G 3
Suriname ■ SME 62-63 F 3
Surinda ○ RUS 116-117 H 4
Suringda ∼ RUS 116-117 N 6
Suringdakon ∼ RUS 116-117 E 4
Suringdè, ozero ○ RUS 116-117 M 3
Suringdèurèn, ustup ⊥ RUS 116-117 L 3
Suripá ○ YV 60-61 G 4
Surire, Salar de ○ RCH 70-71 C 6
Šurmān ○ LAR 192-193 E 1
Šūrmaq ○ IR 134-135 E 3
Surovikino ○ RUS 102-103 N 3
Surovo ○ RUS 116-117 M 8
Surprise ○ USA (AZ) 256-257 C 5
Surprise, Lac de la ○ CDN (QUE) 236-237 O 3
Šurra, aš- ○ Y 132-133 E 7
Surray ○ CDN (BC) 230-231 G 4
Surrency ○ USA (GA) 284-285 H 5
Surrey ○ USA (ND) 258-259 F 3
Surry ○ USA (VA) 280-281 K 6
Surskoe ○ RUS 96-97 E 6
Surt ☆ LAR 192-193 G 2
Surt, Orto- ○ RUS 118-119 M 4
Surtsey ⌒ IS 86-87 c 3
Šurtugaj ○ TJ 136-137 L 6
Suru ○ ZRE 212-213 B 2
Surubim ○ BR 68-69 L 5
Surubim, Rio ∼ BR 66-67 J 6
Surubim, Rio ∼ BR 68-69 D 7
Surubim, Rio ∼ BR 68-69 D 3
Suruç ☆ TR 128-129 H 4
Suruga-wan ≈ 152-153 H 7
Surulangun ○ RI 162-163 E 6
Surumu, Rio ∼ BR 62-63 D 4
Sur Vajo, Salar ○ RCH 70-71 C 7
Surville, Cape ▲ SOL 184 I f 4
Šurygino ○ RUS 114-115 P 6
Šuryškarskij Sor, ozero ○ RUS 114-115 H 2
Šūš ○ •• IR 134-135 C 2
Susa ○ CO 60-61 E 5
Susa ○ I 100-101 A 2
Susa ○ J 152-153 D 7
Šuša = Şuşa ○ • AZ 128-129 M 3
Sūsah ○ •• LAR 192-193 J 1
Susaki ○ J 152-153 E 8
Susang ○ VRC 154-155 K 6
Süsangerd ○ IR 134-135 C 3
Susanino ○ RUS 122-123 J 2
Susanville ○ USA (CA) 246-247 E 3
Susapampa, Sierra de ▲ RA 76-77 E 6
Suşehri ☆ TR 128-129 H 2
Šušenskoe ☆ RUS 116-117 E 9
Šušenskoe-Sajano, vodohranilišče ○ RUS 116-117 E 9
Susie, Rivière ∼ CDN (QUE) 236-237 N 4
Šušin ○ IRQ 128-129 L 4
Susitna River ∼ USA 20-21 Q 5
Suspiro ○ BR 76-77 K 6
Susquehanna ○ USA (PA) 280-281 L 2
Susquehanna River ∼ USA (NY) 278-279 F 6
Susquehanna River ∼ USA (PA) 280-281 K 4
Sussex ○ CDN (NB) 240-241 K 5
Sussex ○ USA (WY) 252-253 M 3
Šuštar ○ IR 134-135 C 2
Sustut Peak ▲ CDN 32-33 G 3
Sustut River ∼ CDN 32-33 G 3
Susua ○ RI 164-165 G 5
Susuka ○ SOL 184 I c 2
Susulatna River ∼ USA 20-21 N 5
Susuman ☆ RUS 120-121 N 2
Susunu ○ RI 166-167 G 3
Susupu ○ RI 164-165 K 3
Susurluk ☆ TR 128-129 C 3
Suswe ○ ZW 218-219 G 3
Sutaj ▲ MAU 146-147 L 2
Sutam ∼ RUS 118-119 N 8
Sutamo-Gonamskij, hrebet ▲ RUS 118-119 N 7
Sutcliffe ○ USA (NV) 246-247 F 4
Sutherland ○ USA (NE) 262-263 E 3
Sutherland ○ ZA 220-221 E 6
Sutherland Range ▲ AUS 176-177 H 3
Sutherland River ∼ CDN (BC) 228-229 K 2
Sutherlin ○ USA (OR) 244-245 B 7
Sutti ○ WAN 198-199 B 6
Sutton ○ CDN (ONT) 238-239 F 4
Sutton ○ CDN (QUE) 238-239 N 3
Sutton ○ USA (NE) 262-263 J 4
Sutton ○ USA (WV) 280-281 F 5
Sutton Downs ○ AUS 178-179 H 1
Sutton Lake ○ CDN 34-35 O 3
Sutton Lake ○ USA (WV) 280-281 F 5
Sutton River ∼ CDN 34-35 P 3
Suttons Bay ○ USA (MI) 272-273 D 3
Suttons Corner ○ USA (GA) 284-285 F 5
Suttor River ∼ AUS 178-179 J 1
Suttsu ○ J 152-153 J 3
Sutukoba ○ WAG 202-203 C 3
Suturuoha ○ RUS 110-111 a 5
Suturuoha ∼ RUS 110-111 Z 5
Sutvik Island ⌒ USA 22-23 S 4
Sutyr' ∼ RUS 122-123 E 3
Suugaant ○ MAU 148-149 H 5
Suunaajik Ø ⌒ GRØ 28-29 V 4
Suuraho ○ FIN 88-89 K 5
Suuž ○ MAU 148-149 G 4
Suva ★ • FJI 184 III b 3
Suvadiva Atoll ⌒ MV 140-141 B 7
Suva Reka ○ YU 100-101 H 3
Suvorov ○ RUS 94-95 P 4
Suvorovskaja ○ RUS 126-127 E 5
Suvut ○ PNG 183 F 2
Suwaidā', as- ☆ SYR 128-129 G 6
Suwaidira, as- ○ KSA 130-131 H 5
Suwaihān ○ UAE 134-135 F 6
Suwaihitiya, aš ○ KSA 130-131 G 2
Suwailih ○ JOR 130-131 D 1
Suwaimiya, as- ○ OM 132-133 J 5
Suwaiqia, Haur as- ○ IRQ 128-129 L 6
Suwair, aš ○ KSA 130-131 G 2
Şuwaira, as- ☆ IRQ 128-129 L 6
Suwairiqiya, as- ○ KSA 130-131 G 6
Suwais, as- ☆ ET 194-195 F 3
Suwa-ko ○ J 152-153 H 6
Suwałki ☆ PL 92-93 R 1
Suwannaphum ○ THA 158-159 G 3
Suwannee ○ USA (FL) 286-287 F 2
Suwannee Canal ○ USA (GA) 284-285 H 6
Suwannee National Wildlife Refuge ⊥ USA (FL) 286-287 F 2
Suwannee River ∼ USA (FL) 286-287 G 1
Suwannee River ∼ USA (FL) 286-287 F 2
Suwannee Sound ≈ USA 286-287 F 2
Suwanoochee Creek ∼ USA (GA) 284-285 H 6
Suwanose-shima ⌒ J 152-153 C 10
Šuwār, aš- ○ • SYR 128-129 J 5
Šuwayyir, Abū ○ IRQ 130-131 K 2
Suwŏn ○ ROK 150-151 F 9
Suxianling • VRC 156-157 H 4
Suyckutambo ○ PE 70-71 B 4
Suyo ○ PE 64-65 C 4
Sūzā ○ IR 134-135 G 5
Suzak ○ KS 136-137 N 4
Suzaka ○ J 152-153 H 6
Suzdal' ☆ ••• RUS 94-95 R 3
Suzhou ○ VRC (ANH) 154-155 K 5
Suzhou ○ • VRC (JIA) 154-155 M 6
Suzu ○ J 152-153 G 6
Suzuka ○ J 152-153 G 7
Suzuka Quasi National Park ⊥ J 152-153 G 7
Suzu-misaki ▲ J 152-153 G 6
Suzun ☆ RUS 124-125 N 2
Svalbard ⌒ N 84-85 H 3
Svappavaara ○ S 86-87 K 3
Svärdsjö ○ S 86-87 G 6
Svartisen ▲ •• N 86-87 F 3
Svataj ○ RUS 110-111 d 5
Svatove ○ UA 102-103 L 3
Svatý Kopeček ▲ CZ 92-93 O 4
Sveagruva ○ N 84-85 K 4
Svealand ⊥ S 86-87 F 7
Sveg ○ S 86-87 G 5
Švenčionys ☆ •• LT 94-95 K 4
Svendborg ○ • DK 86-87 E 9
Svendsen Peninsula ⌣ CDN 24-25 d 2
Svenes ○ N 86-87 D 7
Sven Hedin Gletscher ⊂ GRØ 26-27 Z 2
Svensen ○ USA (OR) 244-245 B 4
Svenskij monastyr • RUS 94-95 O 5
Svenskøya ⌒ N 84-85 P 3
Svenstavik ○ S 86-87 G 5
Šventoji ○ LT 94-95 G 3
Sverdlova, mys ▲ RUS 108-109 b 2
Sverdlovs'k ○ UA 102-103 L 3
Sverdlovsk = Ekaterinburg ☆ RUS 96-97 M 5
Sverdlovsk = Sverdlovs'k ○ UA 102-103 L 3
Sverdrup, ostrov ⌒ RUS 108-109 S 4
Sverdrup Inlet ≈ 24-25 c 3
Sverdrup Islands ⌒ CDN 24-25 U 1
Sverdrup Ø ⌒ GRØ 26-27 a 2
Sverdrup Pass ▲ CDN 26-27 K 4
Sverre, Cape ▲ CDN 24-25 X 1
Sveštari ○ ••• BG 102-103 E 6
Sveti Nikole ○ MK 100-101 H 4
Sveti Stefan • YU 100-101 G 3
Svetlahorsk ○ BY 94-95 L 5
Svetlaja ○ RUS (HRB) 122-123 H 5
Svetlaja ∼ RUS 118-119 E 8
Svetlogorsk ○ RUS 108-109 X 8
Svetlogorsk ☆ • RUS 94-95 G 4
Svetlogorsk = Svetlahorsk ○ BY 94-95 L 5
Svetlograd ○ RUS 102-103 N 5
Svetlovodnaja ○ RUS 122-123 G 5
Svetlovodsk = Svitlovods'k ○ UA 102-103 H 3
Svetlyj ○ RUS (IRK) 118-119 G 6
Svetlyj ○ RUS (SAH) 118-119 F 4
Svetlyj ☆ RUS (ORB) 126-127 O 2
Svetlyj Jar ○ RUS 96-97 D 9
Svetogorsk ○ RUS 88-89 K 6
Sviča ∼ UA 102-103 C 3
Svidník ○ SK 92-93 Q 4
Sviibi ○ EST 94-95 H 2
Svijaga ∼ RUS 96-97 E 7
Svijaga ∼ RUS 96-97 F 6
Svilengrad ○ BG 102-103 E 7
Svincovyj Rudnik ○ TM 136-137 K 6
Svir ○ BY 94-95 K 4
Svir' ∼ RUS 94-95 N 1
Svirsk ○ RUS 116-117 L 9
Svislač ∼ BY 94-95 L 5
Svištov ○ BG 102-103 D 6
Svitlovods'k ○ UA 102-103 H 3
Svjataja Anna, Žolob ≈ 84-85 I 2
Svjatoj Nos, mys ▲ RUS 110-111 X 3
Svjatoj Nos, mys ▲ RUS (MUR) 88-89 P 2
Svjatoj Nos, mys ▲ RUS (NAO) 88-89 U 3
Svjatoj Nos, poluostrov ⌣ RUS 88-89 P 2
Svjatoj Nos, poluostrov ⌣ RUS 116-117 O 9
Svobodnyj ☆ RUS 122-123 C 3
Svoge ○ BG 102-103 C 6
Svolvær ○ N 86-87 G 2
Svyataya Anna Trough = Svjataja Anna, Žolob ≈ 84-85 I 2
Swābi ○ PK 138-139 D 2
Swaershoek ○ ZA 220-221 G 6
Swain Post ○ CDN (ONT) 234-235 L 3
Swain Reefs ⌒ AUS 178-179 L 1
Swain's Atoll ⌒ USA 13 K 4
Swainsboro ○ USA (GA) 284-285 H 4
Swakop ∼ NAM 216-217 C 11
Swakopmund ☆ • NAM 216-217 C 11
Swalwell ○ CDN (ALB) 232-233 E 4
Swamp Biru and Wasur Reserve ⊥ • RI 166-167 L 6
Swan, Mount ▲ AUS 178-179 C 2
Swana-Mume ○ ZRE 214-215 D 6
Swanburg ○ USA (MN) 270-271 D 4
Swan Hill ○ • AUS 180-181 G 3
Swan Hills ○ CDN (ALB) 32-33 N 4
Swan Hills ▲ CDN 32-33 M 4
Swan Lake ○ CDN (MAN) 234-235 C 2
Swanlake ○ USA (ID) 252-253 G 4
Swan Lake ○ USA (MT) 250-251 F 4
Swan Lake National Wildlife Refuge ⊥ USA (MO) 274-275 E 5
Swan Mountain ▲ USA (AR) 276-277 B 4
Swannell Ranges ▲ CDN 32-33 G 3
Swan Plain ○ CDN (SAS) 232-233 Q 3
Swanquarter ○ USA (NC) 282-283 L 5
Swanquarter National Wildlife Refuge ⊥ USA (NC) 282-283 L 5
Swan Reach ○ AUS 180-181 E 3
Swan River ○ CDN (MAN) 234-235 B 2
Swan River ∼ CDN 32-33 N 4
Swan River ∼ CDN 34-35 P 4
Swan River ∼ CDN (SAS) 232-233 Q 3
Swan River ∼ USA (MN) 270-271 E 3
Swansboro ○ USA (NC) 282-283 K 6
Swansea ○ AUS 180-181 K 7
Swansea ○ GB 90-91 F 6
Swansea ○ USA (SC) 284-285 J 3
Swans Island ⌒ USA (ME) 278-279 N 4
Swanson ○ CDN (SAS) 232-233 L 4
Swanson Reservoir ○ USA (NE) 262-263 E 4
Swanton ○ USA (VT) 278-279 H 4
Swan Valley ○ USA (ID) 252-253 G 3
Swartberg ○ ZA 220-221 J 5
Swart Kei ∼ ZA 220-221 H 6
Swartkolkvloer ○ ZA 220-221 E 5
Swartkops ○ ZA 220-221 G 6
Swartmodder ○ ZA 220-221 E 4
Swartplaas ○ ZA 220-221 H 3
Swartruggens ○ ZA 220-221 H 2
Swartruggens ▲ ZA 220-221 D 6
Swartz Bay ○ CDN (BC) 230-231 F 5
Swartz Creek ○ USA (MI) 272-273 F 5
Swastika ○ CDN (ONT) 236-237 H 4
Swāt ∼ PK 138-139 D 2
Swate ○ WAN 204-205 E 3
Swayan, Pointe ▲ CDN 38-39 E 3
Swayzee ○ USA (IN) 274-275 N 4
Swaziland ■ SD 220-221 K 3
Swearingen ○ USA (TX) 264-265 D 4
Swedehome ○ USA (NE) 262-263 J 3
Sweden = Sverige ■ S 86-87 G 7
Swedru ○ GH 202-203 K 7
Sweeny ○ USA (TX) 268-269 E 7
Sweers Island ⌒ AUS 174-175 E 5
Sweet ○ USA (ID) 252-253 B 3
Sweet Grass ○ CDN (SAS) 232-233 K 3
Sweetgrass ○ USA (MT) 250-251 H 3
Sweet Grass Indian Reserve ✕ CDN (SAS) 232-233 K 3
Sweet Home ○ USA (OR) 244-245 C 6
Sweetwater ○ USA (OK) 264-265 E 3
Sweetwater ○ USA (TN) 282-283 C 5
Sweetwater ○ USA (TX) 264-265 D 6
Sweetwater River ∼ USA (WY) 252-253 K 4
Sweetwater Station ○ USA (WY) 252-253 K 4
Swellendam ○ • ZA 220-221 E 7
Swenson ○ USA (TX) 264-265 D 5
Swett, Peninsula ⌣ RCH 80 C 4
Świdnica ○ • PL 92-93 O 3
Świebodzin ○ • PL 92-93 N 2
Swift Creek ∼ USA (NC) 282-283 K 5
Swift Current ○ CDN (NFL) 242-243 O 5
Swift Current ○ CDN (SAS) 232-233 L 5
Swift Current Creek ∼ CDN (SAS) 232-233 K 6
Swift Falls ○ USA (MN) 270-271 C 5
Swift Fork Kuskokwim River ∼ USA 20-21 O 5
Swifton ○ USA (MS) 268-269 K 3
Swift River ∼ CDN 20-21 Z 7
Swift River ∼ CDN (BC) 228-229 N 4
Swift River ∼ USA 20-21 N 6
Swift Run Gap ▲ USA (VA) 280-281 H 5
Swifts Creek ○ AUS 180-181 J 4
Swift Trail Junction ○ USA (AZ) 256-257 F 6
Swinburne, Cape ▲ CDN 24-25 X 5
Swindle Island ⌒ CDN (BC) 228-229 F 4
Swindon ○ GB 90-91 G 6
Świnoujście ○ PL 92-93 N 2
Swiss Historic Village • USA (WI) 274-275 J 2
Swisshome ○ USA (OR) 244-245 B 6
Switz City ○ USA (IN) 274-275 L 5
Switzerland = Schweiz ■ CH 92-93 J 5
Swords Range ▲ AUS 178-179 F 1
Syaburbensi ○ NEP 144-145 E 6
Syagannah ○ RUS 110-111 Y 5
Syakotan-hantō ⌣ J 152-153 J 3
Syalysardah ∼ RUS 118-119 L 6
Syari-dake ▲ J 152-153 L 3
Sycamore ○ USA (IL) 274-275 K 3
Sycamore ○ USA (OH) 280-281 C 3
Sycamore Creek ∼ USA (AZ) 256-257 C 4
Syčevka ○ RUS 94-95 O 4
Sydenham River ∼ CDN (ONT) 238-239 C 6
Sydero = Suðuroy ⌒ FR 90-91 D 1
Sydkap ▲ GRØ 26-27 n 8
Sydkap Fiord ≈ 24-25 d 2
Sydney ☆ •• AUS 180-181 L 2
Sydney ○ CDN (NS) 240-241 P 4
Sydney Lake ○ CDN (ONT) 234-235 J 4
Sydney Mines ○ CDN (NS) 240-241 P 4
Sydostbugten ≈ 28-29 P 2
Sydyjaha ∼ RUS 108-109 Q 7
Sydykta ∼ RUS 118-119 H 7
Syeri ○ RI 166-167 H 2
Sygynah ∼ RUS 110-111 c 6
Šyhli 2-e ○ AZ 128-129 L 2
Syhtymlor, ozero ○ RUS 114-115 M 4
Sykes Bluff ▲ AUS 176-177 J 3
Sykotu-gawa ∼ J 152-153 K 2
Syktyvkar ☆ RUS 96-97 G 3
Sylacauga ○ USA (AL) 284-285 D 3
Sylgy-Ytar ○ RUS 112-113 H 3
Sylhet ○ • BD 142-143 G 3
Sylvia Seamount ≃ 72-73 M 6
Syloga ○ RUS 88-89 R 5
Sylt ⌒ D 92-93 K 1
Sylva ∼ RUS 96-97 K 5
Sylva ∼ RUS 96-97 L 5
Sylva ○ USA (NC) 282-283 D 5
Sylvan ○ CDN (MAN) 234-235 F 4
Sylvan Grove ○ USA (KS) 262-263 H 6
Sylvania ○ AUS 176-177 F 1
Sylvania ○ CDN (SAS) 232-233 P 3
Sylvania ○ USA (GA) 284-285 J 4
Sylvania ○ USA (OH) 280-281 C 2
Sylvan Lake ○ CDN (ALB) 232-233 D 3
Sylvan Lake ○ CDN (ALB) 232-233 D 3
Sylvan Pass ▲ USA (WY) 252-253 H 2
Sylvester ○ USA (GA) 284-285 G 5
Sylvester ○ USA (TX) 264-265 D 6
Sylvia ○ USA (KS) 262-263 H 7
Sylvia Grinnell Lake ○ CDN 36-37 P 2
Sylvinskij krjaž ▲ RUS 96-97 K 5
Sym ∼ RUS 114-115 U 4
Symbōget ○ KA 124-125 D 6
Šymkent ☆ • KA 136-137 L 3
Synča ∼ RUS 110-111 Q 6
Syndassko ○ RUS 110-111 G 3
Synder ○ USA (TX) 264-265 D 6
Synel'nykove ○ UA 102-103 J 3
Šyngyrlau ○ KA 96-97 J 8
Synja ○ RUS (KOM) 88-89 Y 4
Synja ∼ RUS 114-115 H 2
Synja, Bol'šaja ∼ RUS 108-109 H 9
Syn'jaha ∼ RUS 114-115 K 4
Synnfjell ▲ N 86-87 D 6
Synnot Range ▲ AUS 172-173 G 4
Synnyr, hrebet ▲ RUS 118-119 E 7
Syō-gawa ∼ J 152-153 G 6
Syowa ○ ARK 16 G 4
Syparky ∼ RUS 114-115 R 2
Syr, Kysyl ○ RUS 118-119 L 4
Syracuse ○ USA (IN) 274-275 N 3
Syracuse ○ USA (KS) 262-263 E 7
Syracuse ○ USA (NE) 262-263 K 4
Syracuse ○ • USA (NY) 278-279 E 5
Syradasaj ∼ RUS 108-109 U 5
Syran ∼ RUS 122-123 G 2
Syrdarija ∼ KA 124-125 D 6
Syrdarija ∼ KA 126-127 O 4
Syrdarija ∼ KA 136-137 L 4
Syrdar'ja ∼ KA 136-137 K 3
Syre ○ USA (MN) 270-271 B 3
Šyreksor, köli ○ KA 124-125 J 2
Syria = Sūrīya ■ SYR 128-129 G 5
Syriam ○ • MYA 158-159 D 2
Syrian Desert = Bādiyat aš-Šām ⊥ SYR 128-129 H 6
Šyrjajeve ☆ UA 102-103 G 4
Šyrkala, tizbek ▲ KA 126-127 M 4
Syrkovo, ozero ○ RUS 114-115 H 4
Syroke ○ UA 102-103 H 4
Syruta, ozero ○ RUS 108-109 X 5
Šyščycy ○ BY 94-95 K 5
Sysert' ○ RUS 96-97 M 5
Syskonsyn"ja ∼ RUS 114-115 G 3
Sysmä ○ FIN 88-89 H 6
Sysola ∼ RUS 96-97 G 3
Sytygan-Syyiba • RUS 120-121 L 2
Syväjärvi ○ FIN 88-89 H 3
Syverma ⊥ RUS 116-117 G 3
Syvtuga ∼ RUS 88-89 P 5
Syža vtoroi ○ KA 96-97 E 8
Syzran' ☆ RUS 96-97 F 7
Szaga, Lake ○ PNG 183 A 4
Szamotuły ○ • PL 92-93 O 2
Szarvas ○ H 92-93 Q 5
Szczecin ☆ PL 92-93 N 2
Szczecinek ○ PL 92-93 O 2
Szczeciński, Zalew ○ PL 92-93 N 2
Szczekociny ○ PL 92-93 P 3
Szczytno ○ • PL 92-93 Q 2
Szechwan = Sichuan ◘ VRC 154-155 C 6
Szeged ○ H 92-93 Q 5
Székesfehérvár ○ H 92-93 P 5
Szekszárd ○ H 92-93 P 5
Szentes ○ H 92-93 Q 5
Szolnok ○ H 92-93 Q 5
Szombathely ○ H 92-93 O 5

T

T1 ○ IRQ 128-129 J 5
Ta, 108 • VRC 154-155 D 3
Taabo, Lac de < CI 202-203 H 6
Taal, Lake ○ RP 160-161 D 5
Taam, Pulau ⌒ RI 166-167 G 4
Tāba ○ KSA 130-131 H 4
Tabaco ○ RP 160-161 E 6
Tabaconas ○ PE 64-65 C 4
Tabağbuğ, 'Ain < ET 194-195 C 3
Tabahanyar ○ RI 162-163 E 6
Tabajara ○ BR 66-67 F 7
Tabakkentatyr ⊥ KA 124-125 J 5
Tabāla ○ KSA 132-133 C 3
Tabala ○ MEX 50-51 F 5
Tabalosos ○ PE 64-65 E 5
Tabanan ○ RI 168 B 7
Tabankort < RMM 196-197 L 6
Tabankort, Hassi < DZ 190-191 F 6
Tábanos, Los ○ RA 76-77 H 5
Tabaquén ○ CO 60-61 G 6
Tábara ○ E 98-99 E 4
Tabarano ○ RI 164-165 G 5
Tabar Island ⌒ PNG 183 G 2
Tabar Islands ⌒ PNG 183 G 2
Tabarka ○ TN 190-191 G 2
Tabas ○ • IR 134-135 G 2
Tabasco ◘ MEX 52-53 H 2
Tabaskwia Channel < CDN 34-35 N 4
Tabatinga ○ BR 66-67 C 5
Tabatinga, Pico ▲ BR 66-67 F 2
Tabatinga, Serra da ▲ BR 68-69 F 7
Tabayog, Mount ▲ RP 160-161 D 4
Tabbowa ○ CL 140-141 H 6
Tabelbala ○ DZ 188-189 K 6
Tabelbalet, Hassi < DZ 190-191 F 7
Taber ○ CDN (ALB) 232-233 F 6
Taberdga ○ DZ 190-191 F 3
Taberfane ○ RI 166-167 H 5
Tabernas ○ E 98-99 F 6
Tabibuga ○ PNG 183 C 3
Tabina ○ RP 160-161 E 9
Tabingbulang ○ RI 162-163 E 6
Tab"jaha ∼ RUS 108-109 R 8
Tab"ju ∼ RUS 108-109 L 7
Tabkin Kouka ○ RN 204-205 E 1
Tabla ○ RN 204-205 E 2
Tablas ○ BOL 70-71 D 5
Tablas, Cabo ▲ RCH 76-77 B 6
Tablas, Las ☆ • PA 52-53 D 8
Tablas Island ⌒ RP 160-161 D 6
Tablas Strait ≈ 160-161 D 6
Tablazo de Ica ⊥ PE 64-65 D 9
Table Bay ≈ 183 E 6
Table Cape ▲ NZ 182 F 3
Table Head ▲ CDN 38-39 R 2
Tableland ○ AUS 172-173 H 4
Tableland Highway II AUS 174-175 C 6
Table Mountain ▲ ZA 220-221 D 6
Table Rock Lake ○ USA (MO) 276-277 B 4
Tabletop ▲ AUS (WA) 172-173 F 7
Tabletop ▲ AUS (WA) 176-177 E 4
Tabletop, Mount ▲ AUS 178-179 J 2
Tabligbo ○ RT 202-203 L 6
Taboada ○ RA 76-77 F 5
Taboca ○ BR 66-67 G 4
Tabocal ○ BR (AMA) 66-67 E 3
Tabocal ○ BR (AMA) 66-67 F 3
Tabocal ○ BR (AMA) 66-67 D 7
Tabocal, Igarapé ∼ BR 66-67 F 6
Tabocas ○ BR 72-73 H 3
Taboco, Rio ∼ BR 70-71 K 7
Tabola ∼ RUS 96-97 F 10
Taboleiro ⌣ BR 68-69 H 6
Tabon Caves • RP 160-161 C 8
Tabone ○ RI 164-165 F 5
Tabong ○ MYA 142-143 K 2
Tábor ○ CZ 92-93 N 4

Tabor o USA (IA) 274-275 C 4
Tabor o USA (SD) 260-261 J 4
Tabor = Tábor o CZ 92-93 N 4
Tabora ◘ EAT 212-213 D 6
Tabora ☆ • EAT (TAB) 212-213 D 6
Tabor City o USA (NC) 282-283 J 6
Tabory ☆ RUS 114-115 H 5
Tabou o BF 202-203 J 4
Tabou o • CI 202-203 G 7
Tabrinkout < RIM 196-197 C 5
Tabriz ☆ •• IR 128-129 M 3
Tábua, Riachão ∼ BR 68-69 F 6
Tabuaeran ⌒ KIB 13 L 2
Tabuan, Pulau ⌒ RI 162-163 F 7
Tabubil o PNG 183 A 3
Tabudarat o RI 164-165 D 5
Tabūk ◘ KSA 130-131 E 4
Tabūk ☆ KSA 130-131 E 3
Tabuk ☆ RP 160-161 D 4
Tabuleirinho, Cachoeira do ∼ BR 62-63 F 6
Tabuleiro o BR 76-77 K 6
Tabulga o RUS 124-125 K 1
Tabulo o RI 164-165 H 3
Tabūr o SUD 206-207 F 3
Tabusintac o CDN (NB) 240-241 K 3
Tabusintac Indian Reserve ⊻ CDN (NB) 240-241 K 3
Tabwemasana ▲ VAN 184 II a 2
Tacabamba o PE 64-65 C 5
Tacajó o C 54-55 H 4
Tacalaya o PE 70-71 B 5
Tacana, Volcán ▲ GCA 52-53 H 4
Tacañitas o RA 76-77 F 5
Tacarembó, Río ∼ ROU 78-79 M 2
Tacarigua o YV 60-61 H 2
Tacarigua, Parque Nacional Laguna de ⊥ YV 60-61 J 2
Tacarutu o BR 68-69 J 6
Tacbolubu o RP 160-161 B 8
Tachakou o VRC 146-147 G 3
Tachdaït, Adrar ▲ RMM 196-197 L 5
Tachee o USA (AZ) 256-257 E 2
Tacheng o VRC 146-147 F 2
Tachibana-wan ≈ 152-153 D 8
Tachichilte, Isla de ⌒ MEX 50-51 E 5
Tachie o CDN (BC) 228-229 K 2
Tachie River ∼ CDN (BC) 228-229 K 2
Tachilek o MYA 142-143 L 5
Tachiumet < LAR 190-191 H 7
Tacima o BR 68-69 L 5
Tacinskij o RUS 102-103 M 3
Taciuã, Lago ⊂ BR 66-67 G 5
Tacloban ☆ RP 160-161 F 7
Tacna ☆ PE 70-71 B 6
Tacoma o USA (WA) 244-245 C 3
Taco Pozo o RA 76-77 F 3
Tacora, Volcán ▲ RCH 70-71 C 5
Taco Taco o C 54-55 D 3
Tacuane o MOC 218-219 J 3
Tacuaras o PY 76-77 J 4
Tacuarembo ☆ ROU 76-77 K 6
Tacuato o YV 60-61 G 2
Tácume • PE 64-65 C 5
Tacunara, Rio ∼ BR 68-69 C 7
Tacupare, Cachoeira ∼ BR 66-67 K 5
Tacurong o RP 160-161 F 9
Tacuru o BR 76-77 K 2
Tacutu, Rio ∼ BR 62-63 E 4
Tadahadi o SOL 184 I e 4
Tadami-gawa ∼ J 152-153 H 6
Tadant, Oued ∼ DZ 190-191 F 9
Tadao o RP 160-161 D 3
Taddert o MA 188-189 H 5
Taddert, Tizi-n- ▲ MA 188-189 J 5
Tadebjajaha o RUS 108-109 Q 6
Tadek Lake ⊂ CDN 30-31 F 2
Tadélako < RN 198-199 D 5
Tademaït, Plateau du ▲ DZ 190-191 C 6
Tadenet Lake ⊂ CDN 24-25 J 6
Tādepallegūdem o IND 140-141 J 2
Tadéra, In- < RN 198-199 D 2
Tadio, Lagune ≈ 202-203 H 7
Tadjemout o DZ 190-191 D 4
Tadjentourt ▲ DZ 190-191 G 7
Tadjetaret, Oued ∼ DZ 190-191 F 9
Tadjmout o DZ 190-191 D 8
Tadjoura o DJI 208-209 F 3
Tadjoura, Golfe de ≈ 208-209 F 3
Tadjrouna o DZ 190-191 D 4
Tadmore o CDN (SAS) 232-233 Q 4
Tadmur Palmyra ☆ •• SYR 128-129 H 5
Tadoba National Park ⊥ IND 138-139 G 9
Tadohae Haesang National Park ⊥ • ROK 150-151 F 10
Tadoule Lake ⊂ CDN 30-31 U 6
Tadoussac o • CDN (QUE) 240-241 F 2
Tadpatri o IND 140-141 H 3
Tadrart, Jabal ▲ DZ 190-191 H 8
Taduna o RI 166-167 C 5
Taduno o RI 164-165 H 4
Taech'ŏn o ROK 150-151 F 9
Taech'ŏngdo ⌒ DVR 150-151 E 9
Taedong Gang ∼ DVR 150-151 E 8
Taegu o ROK 150-151 G 10
Taehan Haehyŏp ≈ 150-151 F 11
Taehŭksan Do ⌒ ROK 150-151 E 10
Taejŏn o ROK 150-151 F 9
Taejŏng o ROK 150-151 F 11
Taejŏnpyŏngdo ⌒ ROK 150-151 E 9
T'aepaek o ROK 150-151 G 9
Ta'er Si • VRC 154-155 B 3
Taěžnyj o RUS 116-117 G 7
Tafalla o E 98-99 G 3
Tafarit, Râs ▲ RIM 196-197 B 4
Tafassasset ∼ RN 198-199 D 2
Tafassasset, Oued ∼ DZ 190-191 G 9
Tafea ◘ VAN 184 II b 4
Tafédek < RN 198-199 C 4
Tafelberg ▲ SME 62-63 F 4
Tafelberg, National Reservaat ⊥ SME 62-63 F 4
Tafermaar o RI 166-167 H 5
Tafí del Valle o • RA 76-77 E 4
Tafila, aṭ- ☆ JOR 130-131 D 2
Tafilalt ⊥ MA 188-189 J 5
Tafinkar < RMM 196-197 M 7
Tafiré o CI 202-203 H 5
Tafraoute o •• MA 188-189 G 6
Tafreš o IR 134-135 D 1
Taft o IR 134-135 F 3
Taft o USA (CA) 248-249 E 4
Taft o USA (TN) 276-277 J 5
Taft o USA (TX) 266-267 K 6
Taftān, Kūh-e ▲ IR 134-135 J 4
Tāga o WS 184 V a 1
Tagāb o AFG 138-139 B 2
Tagab o SUD 200-201 E 3
Tagagawik River ∼ USA 20-21 L 4
Tagalak Island ⌒ USA 22-23 J 7
Tagânet Keyna < RMM 196-197 J 5
Taganito o RP 160-161 F 8
Taganrog o • RUS 102-103 L 4
Taganrogskij zaliv ≈ 102-103 K 4
Tagant ◘ RIM 196-197 E 5
Tagant ▲ RIM 202-203 B 5
Tagapula Island ⌒ RP 160-161 F 6
Taǧarak o IR 128-129 N 5
Tagarev, gora ▲ TM 136-137 E 5
Tagari River ∼ PNG 183 B 3
Tagaung o MYA 142-143 K 4
Tagaytay o RP 160-161 D 5
Tagbalé o RCA 206-207 E 6
Tagbara o RCA 206-207 E 6
Tagbilaran ☆ RP 160-161 E 8
Tage, Danau ⊂ RI 166-167 J 3
Tagelajiabo o VRC 144-145 F 4
Taggert o USA (IN) 274-275 M 5
Taghit o DZ 188-189 K 5
Taghouaji, Massif de ▲ RN 198-199 D 4
Taghum o CDN (BC) 230-231 M 4
Tāǧiābād, Rūdḫāne-ye ∼ IR 134-135 H 4
Tagish Lake ⊂ CDN 20-21 X 6
Taglo Point ▲ RP 160-161 E 8
Tagna ∼ RUS 116-117 K 9
Tagopah, Tanjung ▲ RI 166-167 G 3
Tagou o BF 202-203 L 4
Tagoûrâret < RIM 196-197 G 6
Tagpait o RP 160-161 C 8
Tagrina, Oued ∼ DZ 198-199 C 2
Taǧris o IR 136-137 B 7
Taguá o BR 68-69 F 7
Tagua, Río ∼ CO 60-61 D 6
Taguaruçu, Ribeiro ∼ BR 70-71 K 7
Taguas, Río de las ∼ RA 76-77 C 5
Taguatinga o BR (FED) 72-73 F 3
Taguatinga o BR (TOC) 72-73 G 2
Taguay o YV 60-61 H 3
Tagum ☆ RP 160-161 F 9
Tah, Sebkha ⊂ MA 188-189 E 7
Tahafo o RI 164-165 K 3
Tahalra ⊥ DZ 190-191 E 9
Tahalupu o RI 166-167 D 3
Tahamiyam o SUD 200-201 H 3
Tahan, Gunung ▲ MAL 162-163 E 2
Tahan, Kuala o MAL 162-163 E 2
Taḫār ◘ AFG 136-137 L 6
Taharoa o NZ 182 E 3
Tahar-Souk o MA 188-189 J 3
Tahat ▲ DZ 190-191 E 9
Tahawus o USA (NY) 278-279 G 4
Tahe o VRC 150-151 E 1
Ṭaheri, Bandar-e o IR 134-135 E 5
Tahifet o DZ 190-191 F 9
Tahifet, Oued ∼ DZ 190-191 F 9
Tahilt o MAU 148-149 C 5
Tahiryuak Lake ⊂ CDN 24-25 Q 5
Tahiti ⌒ F 13 N 4
Tahlāb ∼ PK 134-135 K 4
Tahlāb, Dasht-i- ⊥ PK 134-135 J 4
Tahoe, Lake ⊂ USA (CA) 246-247 E 4
Tahoe City o USA (CA) 246-247 E 4
Tahoe Lake ⊂ CDN 24-25 R 5
Tahoka o USA (TX) 264-265 C 5
Taholah o USA (WA) 244-245 A 3
Tahomi o LB 202-203 F 7
Tahoua ◘ RN 198-199 B 5
Tahoua ☆ RN (TAH) 198-199 B 5
Tahquamenon Falls State Park ⊥ USA (MI) 270-271 N 4
Tahrami o LAR 192-193 F 5
Taḫt-e Ğamšīd o •• IR 134-135 E 4
Tahrou, Oued ∼ DZ 190-191 G 8
Tahsis o CDN (BC) 230-231 C 4
Tahṭa o ET 194-195 E 4
Tahta o RUS 122-123 H 2
Tahta o TM 136-137 F 4
Tahta-Bazar o TM 136-137 H 7
Tahtakūpir ☆ US 136-137 G 3
Tahtakupyr o US 136-137 G 3
Tahtalı Dağları ▲ TR 128-129 F 3
Tahtamygda o RUS 118-119 L 8
Taḫt-e Soleiman, Kūh-e ▲ IR 136-137 B 6
Taḫt-e Suleimān o • IR 128-129 M 4
Tahtojama ∼ RUS 120-121 Q 3
Tahtojamsk o RUS 120-121 Q 3
Tahtsa Lake ⊂ CDN (BC) 228-229 G 3
Tahuamanu, Río ∼ PE 70-71 B 2
Tahulandang o RI 164-165 J 2
Tahulandang, Pulau ⌒ RI 164-165 J 2
Tahuna o RI 164-165 J 2
Tai o CI 202-203 G 7
Taï, Parc National de ⊥ ••• CI 202-203 G 7
Taiama o WAL 202-203 D 5
Tai'an o VRC 154-155 K 3
Taibai o VRC 154-155 E 5
Taibai Shan ▲ VRC 154-155 E 5
Taibai Dao ▲ VRC 154-155 M 3
Taibashan Z.B. ⊥ • VRC 154-155 E 5
Taibet o DZ 190-191 F 4
Taibique o E 188-189 C 7
Taibus Qi o VRC 148-149 M 7
Taichung o RC 156-157 M 4
Taidalt o MA 188-189 G 6
Tā'if, at o • KSA 132-133 B 3
Taigetos ▲ GR 100-101 J 6
Taigu o VRC 154-155 H 3
Taihang Shan ▲ VRC 154-155 H 4
Taihape o NZ 182 E 3
Taihe o VRC (ANH) 154-155 J 5
Taihe o VRC (JXI) 156-157 J 3
Tai Hu o VRC (ANH) 154-155 L 6
Taihu o VRC (ANH) 154-155 K 6
Tai Hu ⊂ VRC (JIA) 154-155 M 6
Taihu • VRC (JIA) 154-155 M 6
Taijiang o VRC 156-157 F 3
Taikang o VRC 154-155 J 4
Taikkyi o MYA 158-159 C 2
Tailai o VRC 150-151 D 4
Tailako o RI 166-167 C 6
Tailem Bend o AUS 180-181 E 3
Tailing o GUY 62-63 D 2
Taim o BR 74-75 D 9
Taimā' o • KSA 130-131 F 4
Taïmana o RMM 202-203 G 3
Taimba o RUS 116-117 J 5
Taimushan • VRC 156-157 M 3
Tain o GB 90-91 E 3
Tainan o RC 156-157 M 5
Tainhas o BR 74-75 E 7
Taining o VRC 156-157 K 3
Taino, Plage ⊥ • RH 54-55 J 5
Taió o BR 74-75 E 6
Taiobeiras o BR 72-73 J 3
Taiof Island ⌒ PNG 184 I b 1
Taipei ☆ •• RC 156-157 M 4
Taiping o • MAL 162-163 D 2
Taiping o VRC (GXI) 156-157 G 5
Taiping o VRC (GXI) 156-157 E 5
Taipingchuan o VRC 150-151 D 5
Taiping L. ▲ VRC 150-151 C 4
Taipong o GUY 62-63 E 3
Taipur o IND 142-143 D 3
Ṭair, Ğabal aṭ- ⌒ Y 132-133 B 6
Tairhemt, Tizi-n ▲ MA 188-189 J 4
Taírona, Parque Nacional ⊥ •• CO 60-61 D 2
Tais o RI 162-163 E 7
Taisha o EC 64-65 D 3
Taisha o • J 152-153 E 7
Taishan o VRC (GDG) 156-157 H 5
Taishan ▲ ••• VRC (SHD) 154-155 K 3
Taishi o RC 156-157 M 5
Taishun o VRC 156-157 L 3
Taisiya ⊥ KSA 130-131 H 3
Taita Hills ▲ EAK 212-213 G 5
Taitaitanopo, Pulau ⌒ RI 162-163 D 6
Taitao, Peninsula de ⌣ RCH 80 C 3
Taititu o BR 66-67 D 5
Taitna Lake ⊂ CDN 30-31 S 5
Taitung o RC 156-157 M 5
Taivalkoski o FIN 88-89 K 4
Taiwan ■ RC 156-157 M 5
Taiwan Banks ▲ 156-157 L 5
Taiwan Strait ≈ 156-157 L 5
Tai Xian o VRC 154-155 M 5
Taixing o VRC 154-155 M 5
Taiyang Dao • VRC 150-151 F 5
Taiyuan ☆ • VRC 154-155 H 3
Taizhou o VRC 154-155 L 5
Taizhou Liedao ⌒ VRC 156-157 M 2
Taizhou Wan ∼ VRC 156-157 M 2
Ta'izz o Y 132-133 D 7
Tajdon ∼ RUS 114-115 T 7
Tajen o RC 156-157 M 5
Tajga o RUS 114-115 S 6
Tajga o RUS (SHL) 122-123 K 4
Tajga ∼ RUS 116-117 H 6
Tajgan o MAU 148-149 C 4
Tajgonos, mys ▲ RUS 120-121 T 3
Tajgonos, poluostrov ⌣ RUS 120-121 T 3
Tajicaringa o MEX 50-51 G 6
Tajikistan = Tāǧīkistān ■ TJ 136-137 L 5
Tajima o J 152-153 H 6
Tajimi o J 152-153 G 7
Tajín, El ∴ ••• MEX 52-53 F 1
Tajique o USA (NM) 256-257 J 4
Tajkanskij, hrebet ▲ RUS 122-123 F 2
Tajlan, köl ⊂ KA 96-97 G 10
Taj Mahal ••• IND 138-139 G 6
Tajmendra, Boľšaja ∼ RUS 118-119 H 6
Tajmura ∼ RUS 116-117 K 4
Tajmylyr o RUS 110-111 N 3
Tajmyr, ostrov ⌒ RUS 108-109 a 3
Tajmyr, ozero ⊂ RUS 108-109 d 4
Tajmyra, mys ▲ RUS 108-109 e 2
Tajmyrskij zaliv ≈ RUS 108-109 b 3
Tajnynotskij hrebet ▲ RUS 120-121 T 3
Tajo, Río ∼ E 98-99 F 4
Tajšet ☆ RUS 116-117 J 8
Tajumulco, Volcán ▲ GCA 52-53 J 4
Tajuña, Río ∼ E 98-99 F 4
Tājūra' o LAR 192-193 E 1
Tajura ∼ RUS 116-117 N 7
Tak o THA 158-159 E 2
Takāb o IR 128-129 M 4
Takaba o EAK 212-213 H 2
Takachiho o J 152-153 D 8
Takahashi o J 152-153 E 7
Takahashi-gawa ∼ J 152-153 E 7
Takahe, Mount ▲ ARK 16 F 26
Takaka o NZ 182 D 4
Takalala o RI 164-165 F 6
Takalar o RI 164-165 F 6
Takalou o TCH 206-207 D 3
Takalous, Oued ∼ DZ 190-191 F 9
Takamaka o SY 224 D 2
Takamatsu o J (EHI) 152-153 E 8
Takamatsu ☆ • J (KAG) 152-153 F 7
Takan, Gunung ▲ RI 168 C 7
Takanabe o J 152-153 D 8
Takanosu o J 152-153 J 4
Takaoka o J 152-153 G 6
Takapuna o NZ 182 E 2
Takara o RCA 206-207 E 4
Takara-shima ⌒ J 152-153 C 10
Takasaki o J 152-153 H 6
Takatokwane o RB 220-221 G 2
Takatsuki o J 152-153 F 7
Takatu hrebet ▲ RUS 96-97 K 7
Takaungu o EAK 212-213 G 5
Takayama o J 152-153 G 6
Takefu o J 152-153 G 7
Takengon (Takingeun) o RI 162-163 B 2
Takeo o J 152-153 C 8
Takeo o K 158-159 H 5
Takestān o • IR 128-129 N 4
Taketa o J 152-153 D 8
Tak Fa o THA 158-159 F 3
Takhini River ∼ CDN 20-21 W 6
Takhro o THA 158-159 G 3
Takht-i-Bahi ∴ ••• PK 138-139 C 2
Takht-i-Sulaiman ▲ PK 138-139 B 4
Takiéta o RN 198-199 D 6
Takikawa o J 152-153 J 3
Takinoue o J 152-153 K 2
Takis o PNG 183 F 3
Takisset, Oued ∼ DZ 190-191 H 8
Takiyok, Pointe ▲ CDN 36-37 P 5
Takiyuak Lake ⊂ CDN 30-31 O 2
Takla Lake ⊂ CDN 32-33 H 4
Takla Landing o CDN 32-33 H 4
Takla Makan Desert = Taklimakan Shamo ⊥ VRC 146-147 E 6
Tākli Dhokeshwar o IND 138-139 E 10
Taklimakan Shamo ⊥ VRC 146-147 E 6
Taknis o LAR 192-193 J 1
Takobanda o RCA 206-207 E 5
Takoma Park o USA (MD) 280-281 K 5
Takoradi o • GH 202-203 K 7
Takorka o RN 198-199 C 6
Takoutala o SN 202-203 D 2
Takpamba o RT 202-203 L 5
Takpoima o LB 202-203 E 6
Takrit ☆ IRQ 128-129 K 5
Taksagerbej, grjada ▲ RUS 108-109 a 5
Taksimo o RUS 118-119 G 7
Takslesluk Lake ⊂ USA 20-21 J 6
Takuapa o THA 158-159 E 6
Taku Arm ⊂ CDN 20-21 X 7
Takum o WAN 204-205 H 5
Takundi o ZRE 210-211 F 6
Taku Plateau ▲ CDN 20-21 Y 7
Taku River ∼ CDN 32-33 D 2
Takwa ∴ • EAK 212-213 H 5
Tāl o IND 138-139 E 8
Tala o EAK 212-213 F 4
Tāla o IND 142-143 B 4
Tala o MEX 52-53 C 1
Tala o ROU 78-79 M 3
Tala, Čubuka-gora ▲ RUS 110-111 a 7
Tala, El o RA 76-77 E 4
Tala, Río ∼ RA 76-77 E 4
Talacasto o RA 76-77 C 6
Talacasto, Sierra de ▲ RA 76-77 C 6
Talačyn ☆ BY 94-95 L 4
Talagang o PK 138-139 D 3
Talagante o RCH 78-79 D 2
Talahāt, Ša'ib aṭ- ∼ IRQ 128-129 L 7
Talahini o CI 202-203 J 5
Talahini-Tomora o CI 202-203 J 5
Talaimannar o CL 140-141 H 6
Talaivasal o IND 140-141 H 5
Talaja o RUS 116-117 H 8
Talaja o RUS (MAG) 120-121 P 3
Talaja ∼ RUS 116-117 H 8
Talakalla o IND 140-141 F 3
Talakan o RUS (AMR) 122-123 D 3
Talakan o RUS (HBR) 122-123 E 4
Talali o RUS 122-123 B 3
Talamanca, Cordillera de ▲ CR 52-53 C 7
Talamba o PK 138-139 D 4
Talanga o HN 52-53 L 4
Talangbetutu o RI 162-163 F 6
Talangjauh o RI 162-163 F 6
Talangpadung o RI 162-163 F 7
Talara o PE 64-65 B 4
Talaroo o AUS 174-175 G 6
Talas ∼ KA 124-125 F 6
Talas ∼ KA 124-125 G 6
Talas ☆ KS 136-137 N 3
Talas ∼ KS 136-137 N 3
Talasea o PNG 183 F 3
Talasskij Alatau, hrebet ▲ KA 136-137 M 3
Talata-Ampano o RM 222-223 E 8
Talatakoh, Pulau ⌒ RI 164-165 H 4
Talata Mafara o WAN 198-199 C 6
Talat at-Timiat o KSA 130-131 H 3
Tal' at Damya ⊥ MA 188-189 G 7
Talaud, Kepulauan ⌒ RI 164-165 K 1
Talavera, Ilha ⌒ PY 76-77 J 4
Talavera de la Reina o • E 98-99 E 5
Talawana o AUS 172-173 E 7
Talawanta o AUS 174-175 F 6
Talawdi o SUD 206-207 K 3
Talawe, Mount ▲ PNG 183 E 3
Talawi o RI 162-163 D 5
Talbot, Cape ▲ AUS 172-173 H 2
Talbot, Mount ▲ AUS 176-177 J 3
Talbot Glacier ⊂ CDN 24-25 g 2
Talbot Inlet ≈ 24-25 h 2
Talbot Islands ⌒ AUS 183 B 5
Talbot Lake ⊂ CDN 34-35 G 3
Talbotton o USA (GA) 284-285 F 4
Talbragar River ∼ AUS 180-181 K 2
Talca ☆ • RCH 78-79 D 3
Talcahuano o RCH 78-79 C 4
Talcan, Isla ⌒ RCH 78-79 C 7
Tālcher o IND 142-143 D 5
Talcho o RN 204-205 E 1
Talco o USA (TX) 264-265 J 5
Taľdaktokon, vozvyšennosť ▲ RUS 116-117 E 2
Taldan o RUS 118-119 M 9
Taldom ☆ RUS 94-95 P 3
Taldy ∼ KA 124-125 J 4
Taldy, Tasty- ☆ KA 124-125 E 3
Taldy-Bulak o KS 136-137 N 3
Taldyk, pereval ▲ KS 136-137 N 5
Taldykorgan o KA 124-125 L 6
Taldy'korgan o KA 124-125 L 6
Taldyqorghan = Taldykorgan ☆ KA 124-125 L 6
Taleb, Bir < RIM 196-197 F 6
Taleex o SP 208-209 J 4
Talegaon o IND 138-139 G 9
Tālem o IR 128-129 N 4
Talence o F 90-91 G 9
Ṭāleqān ☆ AFG 136-137 L 6
Ṭāleqān Rūd ∼ AFG 136-137 L 6
Taleš, Kūhhā-ye ▲ IR 128-129 N 4
Talequah o USA (OK) 264-265 K 3
Taley o RCA 206-207 C 5
Talgar o KA 146-147 C 4
Talgar, pik ▲ KA 146-147 C 4
Talguharai o SUD 200-201 G 3
Talḫāb, Kōtal-e ▲ AFG 134-135 L 1
Talhār o PK 138-139 B 7
Taliabu, Pulau ⌒ RI 164-165 J 4
Talibon o RP 160-161 F 7
Talibura o RI 166-167 B 6
Talica ☆ RUS 114-115 G 6
Talicherla o IND 140-141 H 3
Talihina o USA (OK) 264-265 J 4
Tālikota o IND 140-141 G 2
Talimã o BR 62-63 G 5
Talimardžan o US 136-137 J 5
Talina, Río ∼ BOL 76-77 E 1
Taling Chan o THA 158-159 F 4
Taliouine o MA 188-189 H 5
Taliparamba o IND 140-141 F 4
Talipaw o RP 160-161 D 10
Talipolo, Tanjung ▲ RI 164-165 F 5
Tali Post o SUD 206-207 K 6
Talisay o RP 160-161 D 6
Talisayan o RP 160-161 F 8
Talisei, Pulau ⌒ RI 164-165 J 3
Taliwang o RI 168 C 7
Taljain ∼ RUS 112-113 S 4
Taľjany o RUS 116-117 L 9
Talkeetna o USA 20-21 P 5
Talkeetna Mountains ▲ USA 20-21 Q 6
Talkeetna River ∼ USA 20-21 Q 5
Tall, at- o SYR 128-129 G 6
Talladega o USA (AL) 284-285 D 3
Talladega Super Speedway • USA (AL) 284-285 D 3
Tall 'Afar o IRQ 128-129 K 4
Tallahala Creek ∼ USA (MS) 268-269 L 5
Tallahassee ☆ USA (FL) 286-287 E 1
Tallahatchie River ∼ USA (MS) 268-269 K 3
Tall al-Abyaḍ ☆ SYR 128-129 H 4
Tallangatta o AUS 180-181 J 4
Tallapoosa o USA (GA) 284-285 E 3
Tallapoosa River ∼ USA (AL) 284-285 E 3
Tallapoosa River ∼ USA (AL) 284-285 D 4
Tallaringa Conservation Park ⊥ AUS 176-177 M 4
Tallassee o USA (AL) 284-285 E 4
Tall Birāk o SYR 128-129 J 4
Tallering Peak ▲ AUS 176-177 C 4
Talleysville o USA (VA) 280-281 J 6
Tall Ğudaida ∴ • IRQ 130-131 K 2
Tall Hariri • SYR 128-129 J 5
Tall Huqna o IRQ 128-129 K 4
Tallin = Tallinn ☆ •• EST 94-95 J 2
Tallinn ☆ •• EST 94-95 J 2
Tallkalā o AFG 134-135 K 3
Tall-Kalaḫ o SYR 128-129 G 5
Tall Kūšik o SYR 128-129 K 4
Tallorutit ⌒ GRØ 28-29 O 6
Tall Pines o CDN (SAS) 232-233 Q 3
Tall Šāğir Bāzār o • SYR 128-129 J 4
Tall Tamr o SYR 128-129 J 4
Tallulah o USA (LA) 268-269 J 4
Tall 'Uwaināt o IRQ 128-129 K 4
Talmage o CDN (SAS) 232-233 P 6
Talmage o USA (KS) 262-263 J 6
Taľmenka ☆ RUS 124-125 N 2
Talmest o MA 188-189 G 5
Talnah o RUS 108-109 X 7
Taloard o IR 134-135 D 3
Taloda o IND 138-139 E 9
Taloga o USA (OK) 264-265 F 2
Talon o RUS 120-121 N 4
Talotajaha ∼ RUS 108-109 J 7
Talovaja o RUS 102-103 M 2
Talovka o RUS 112-113 O 5
Talovka ∼ RUS 112-113 N 5
Talovskoe, ozero ⊂ RUS 120-121 V 3
Talpa o USA (TX) 266-267 H 2
Talquin, Lake ⊂ USA (FL) 286-287 E 1
Talras < RN 198-199 D 5
Talšand o MAU 148-149 C 5
Talsen = Talsi o •• LV 94-95 H 3
Talsi o •• LV 94-95 H 3
Talsinnt o MA 188-189 K 4
Taltal o RCH 76-77 B 3
Taltal, Quebrada de ∼ RCH 76-77 B 3
Taltson River ∼ CDN 30-31 N 5
Talu o RI 162-163 C 4
Taludaa o RI 164-165 H 3
Taluk o RI 162-163 D 5
Talvār, Rūdḫāne-ye ∼ IR 128-129 N 4
Talwood o AUS 178-179 K 5
Talyawalka Anabranch ∼ AUS 180-181 G 2
Tama o RN 198-199 B 5
Tama o USA (IA) 274-275 F 3
Tama, Parque Nacional el ⊥ YV 60-61 E 4
Tama Abu, Banjaran ▲ MAL 164-165 D 2
Tamacuari, Pico ▲ BR 66-67 E 2
Ṭamad, aṭ- o KSA 130-131 F 5
Tamadan o RI 166-167 G 4
Tamafupa < RB 218-219 D 4
Tama-gawa ∼ J 152-153 J 5
Tamako o RI 164-165 J 2
Tamala = Yopei o GH 202-203 K 5
Tamale ☆ GH 202-203 K 5
Taman o RI 168 C 3
Tamaná, Cerro ▲ CO 60-61 C 5
Tamanaco, Embalse < YV 60-61 J 3
Tamanar o MA 188-189 G 5
Tamanco o PE 64-65 E 4
Tamandourirt < RMM 196-197 K 5
Tamanduá o BR (AMA) 66-67 D 5
Tamanduá o BR (MIN) 72-73 J 4
Tamaneke o SOL 184 I c 3
Tamango, Parque Nacional ⊥ RCH 80 D 3
Tamanhint o LAR 192-193 F 4
Tamani o RMM 202-203 G 3
Tamaniquá o BR 66-67 E 4
Taman Negara National Park ⊥ •• MAL 162-163 E 2
Tamano o J 152-153 E 7
Tamanrasset ☆ •• DZ 190-191 E 9
Tamanrasset, Oued ∼ DZ 190-191 D 9
Tamanredjo o SME 62-63 G 3
Tamanskij zaliv ≈ 102-103 K 5
Tamaqua o USA (PA) 280-281 L 3
Tamaquillo o PE 64-65 D 6
Tamar, Alto de ▲ CO 60-61 D 4
Tamarac o USA (FL) 286-287 J 5
Tamarack o USA (MN) 270-271 E 4
Tamarack Island ⌒ CDN (MAN) 234-235 F 3
Tamarac National Wildlife Refuge ⊥ USA (MN) 270-271 C 3
Tamarana o BR 72-73 E 7
Tamarike o RI 166-167 L 6
Ṭamarit o OM 132-133 J 5
Tamarou o DY 204-205 E 4
Tamaruga, Pampa del ⊥ RCH 70-71 C 6
Tamarugal, Pampa del ⊥ RCH 76-77 C 1
Tamási o H 92-93 P 5
Tamaso o SUD 200-201 F 6
Tamassoumit o RIM 196-197 D 5
Tamat, Wādī ∼ LAR 192-193 G 2
Tamatama o YV 60-61 J 6
Tamatave = Toamasina ☆ RM 222-223 F 7
Tamaulipas ◘ MEX 50-51 K 6
Tama Wildlife Reserve ⊥ ETH 208-209 C 5
Tamaya, Río ∼ PE 64-65 F 6
Tamazula de Gordiano o MEX 52-53 C 2
Tamazulapán o MEX 52-53 F 3
Tamazunchale o • MEX 50-51 K 7
Tambach o EAK 212-213 E 3
Tambacounda ☆ SN 202-203 D 3
Tambakara o RMM 202-203 E 2
Tamba Kosi ∼ NEP 144-145 F 7
Tambalongang, Pulau ⌒ RI 168 E 6
Tamban o RP 160-161 E 6
Tambaqui o BR 66-67 F 5
Tambaqui, Cachoeira ∼ BOL 66-67 E 7
Tambara o MOC 218-219 H 3
Tāmbaram o IND 140-141 J 4
Tambarga o BF 202-203 L 4
Tambar Springs o AUS 178-179 K 6
Tambaur o IND 142-143 B 2
Tambawel o WAN 198-199 B 6
Tambe o ANG 216-217 C 6
També o BR 68-69 L 5
Tambea o RI 164-165 G 6
Tambea o • SOL 184 I d 3
Tāmbeibui o IND 140-141 L 4
Tambej o RUS 108-109 O 6
Tambelan Besar, Pulau ⌒ RI 162-163 G 4
Tambelan Kepulauau ⌒ RI 162-163 G 4
Tambellup o AUS 176-177 D 7
Tamberu o RI 168 E 3
Tambillo o EC 64-65 C 2
Tambillo, Quebrada ∼ RCH 76-77 C 1
Tambisan, Pulau ⌒ MAL 160-161 C 10
Tambo o AUS 178-179 J 3
Tambo o PE 64-65 F 8
Tambo, El o CO 60-61 C 6
Tambo, Río ∼ PE 64-65 F 7
Tambo, Río ∼ PE 70-71 B 5
Tambobamba o PE 64-65 F 8
Tambo Colorado • PE 64-65 E 8
Tambo Grande o PE 64-65 B 4
Tambohorano o RM 222-223 C 6
Tamboli o RI 164-165 G 5
Tambopata, Río ∼ PE 70-71 C 3
Tambo Ponciano o PE 66-67 B 4
Tambo Pucacuro o PE 64-65 E 3
Tambor o ANG 216-217 B 8
Tambor o BR 66-67 F 4
Tambora, Gunung ▲ RI 168 C 7
Tambores o ROU 76-77 J 6
Tamboril o BR 68-69 H 4
Tamboritha, Mount ▲ AUS 180-181 J 4
Tambo Tambillo o BOL 70-71 D 6
Tamboura o RCA 206-207 G 6
Tambov o RUS 94-95 R 5
Tambovka o RUS 122-123 B 3
Tambo Yacu, Río ∼ PE 64-65 E 2
Tambrey ∴ AUS 172-173 C 6
Tambu, Teluk ≈ 164-165 F 3
Tambugo o RP 160-161 D 4
Tambul o PNG 183 B 3
Tambunan o MAL 160-161 B 10
Tambura o SUD 206-207 H 6
Tambuttegama o CL 140-141 J 6
Tamc dabaa ▲ MAU 146-147 L 3
Tâmchakett o RIM 196-197 E 6
Tamdibulak ☆ US 136-137 J 4
Tam Điệp ☆ VN 156-157 D 6
Tamdy ∼ KA 124-125 E 4
Tamdytov, toglari ▲ US 136-137 J 4
Tame o CO 60-61 F 4
Tâmega, Rio ∼ P 98-99 C 4
Tamegroute o MA 188-189 J 5
Tamelelt o MA 188-189 H 5
Tamelhat o DZ 190-191 F 4
Tamenglong o IND 142-143 H 3
Tamesi, Río ∼ MEX 50-51 K 6
Tamesna ⊥ RN 198-199 B 3
Tamewali = Khairpur o PK 138-139 D 5
Tamezret o TN 190-191 G 4
Tamghas o NEP 144-145 D 6
Tamiahua o MEX 50-51 L 7
Tamiahua, Laguna de ⊂ MEX 50-51 L 7
Tamiang ⌒ RI 162-163 B 2
Tamiang, Ujung ▲ RI 162-163 C 2
Tamica o RUS 88-89 P 4
Tami Islands ⌒ PNG 183 D 4
Tamil Nādu ◘ IND 140-141 G 5
Ta'mīn, at- ◘ IRQ 128-129 L 5
Tamir gol ∼ MAU 148-149 F 4
Tamitatoala, Rio ∼ BR 72-73 D 2
Tāmiya o ET 194-195 E 3
Tam Ky o VN 158-159 K 3
Tamlelt, Plaine de ⊥ MA 188-189 K 4
Tamluk o IND 142-143 E 4
Tamma ∼ RUS 118-119 O 5
Tammisaari = Ekenäs o • FIN 88-89 G 7
Tammū, Jabal ▲ LAR 192-193 F 6
Tamnūn o Y 132-133 G 6
Tamou o RN 204-205 E 2
Tampa o ANG (NAM) 216-217 B 7
Tampa ∼ ANG 216-217 B 7
Tampa o USA (FL) 286-287 G 4
Tampaang, Pulau ⌒ RI 168 C 6
Tampa Bay ≈ 48-49 G 6
Tampa Bay ≈ USA 286-287 G 4
Tampang o RI 162-163 E 6
Tampasis o MAL 160-161 B 10
Tampéna o RN 202-203 L 3
Tampere o • FIN 88-89 G 6
Tampia Hill ▲ AUS 176-177 E 6
Tampico o • MEX 50-51 L 6
Tampin o MAL 162-163 E 3
Tamp Kŏh o PK 134-135 J 6
Tampo o RI 164-165 H 6
Tampoaga ▲ BF 202-203 L 4
Tampon, Le o F 224 B 7
Tamqué, Massif du ▲ RG 202-203 D 3
Tamr, Tall o SYR 128-129 J 4
Tamrau, Pegunungan ▲ RI 166-167 G 2
Tamri o MA 188-189 G 5
Tamshiyacu o PE 64-65 F 3
Tamu o MYA 142-143 J 3
Tamūd o Y 132-133 F 5
Tamuin o • MEX 50-51 K 6
Tamur ∼ NEP 144-145 F 7
Tamvatvaam ∼ RUS 112-113 S 5
Tamworth o AUS 178-179 L 6
Tamyš ∼ RUS 116-117 H 6
Tana ∼ EAK 212-213 G 4
Tana ∼ N 86-87 O 1
Tana = Île Tanna ⌒ VAN 184 II b 4
Tana, Lake = T'ana Hayk' ⊂ ETH 200-201 H 6
Tanabe o J 152-153 F 8
Tanaberu o • RI 164-165 G 6
Tanabi o BR 72-73 F 6
Tanabru o N 86-87 O 1
Tanaf o SN 202-203 C 3
Tanafjorden ≈ 86-87 O 1
Tanaga Island ⌒ USA 22-23 H 7
Tanaga Pass ≈ 22-23 G 7
Tanahbala, Pulau ⌒ RI 162-163 C 5
Tanahgoyang o RI 166-167 E 3
Tanahgrogot o RI 164-165 E 4
Tanahjampea, Pulau ⌒ RI 168 E 6
Tanahmasa, Pulau ⌒ RI 162-163 C 5
Tanahmerah o RI (IRJ) 166-167 G 3
Tanahmerah o RI (IRJ) 166-167 L 5
Tanahmerah o RI (KTI) 164-165 E 2
Tanahmolala, Pulau ⌒ RI 168 E 6
Tanah Rata o MAL 162-163 D 2
Tanahwangko o RI 164-165 J 3
Tānai o PK 138-139 B 3
Tanakeke o RI 164-165 F 6
Tanakeke, Pulau ⌒ RI 164-165 F 6
Tanakpur o IND 144-145 C 6
Tanal o RMM 202-203 J 2
Tanama o BF 202-203 K 3
Tanama ∼ RUS 108-109 S 7
Tanamalwila o CL 140-141 J 7
Tanami, Mount ▲ AUS 172-173 J 5
Tanami Desert ⊥ AUS 172-173 K 5
Tanami Desert Wildlife Sanctuary ⊥ AUS 172-173 K 6
Tanami Mine ∴ AUS 172-173 J 6
Tanami Road II AUS 172-173 J 6
Tân An ☆ VN 158-159 J 5
Tanana o USA 20-21 O 4
Tanana River ∼ USA 20-21 S 4
Tanandava o RM 222-223 C 8
Tanani o USA 20-21 X 7
Tanantou o RG 202-203 F 5
Tana ó Camiña, Quebrada de ∼ RCH 70-71 B 6
Tana River Primate National Reserve ⊥ EAK 212-213 H 4
Tanārut, Wādī ∼ LAR 190-191 H 6
Tanatar, ozera ⊂ RUS 124-125 L 3
Tanba-kochi ▲ J 152-153 F 7
Tanbaoura, Falaise de ▲ RMM 202-203 E 3
Tancheng o VRC 154-155 L 4
Tanchon o DVR 150-151 G 7
Tanchon Karang o MAL 162-163 D 3
Tancitaro, Cerro ▲ MEX 52-53 C 2
Tancitaro, Parque Nacional ⊥ MEX 52-53 C 2
Tancuime o MEX 50-51 K 7
Tanda o CI 202-203 J 6
Tanda o • RUS 118-119 P 4
Tanda ∼ RUS 120-121 E 2
Tanda, Lac ⊂ RMM 202-203 H 2
Tandako o RG 202-203 C 4
Tandalti o SUD 200-201 E 6
Tāndārei o RO 102-103 E 5
Tanderiouel ∼ RMM 202-203 K 2
Tandi o IND 138-139 F 3
Tandil o RA 78-79 K 4
Tandil, Sierra del ▲ RA 78-79 K 4
Tandin o MYA 142-143 H 6
Tandjilé ◘ TCH 206-207 C 4
Tandjilé ∼ TCH 206-207 B 4
Tandjouaré o RT 202-203 L 4
Tāndliānwāla o PK 138-139 D 4
Tando Ādam o PK 138-139 B 7
Tando Allāhyār o PK 138-139 B 7
Tando Bāgo o PK 138-139 B 7
Tando Ikram o PK 138-139 B 7
Tando Jam o PK 138-139 B 7
Tando Muhammad Khān o PK 138-139 B 7
Tandou Lake ⊂ AUS 180-181 G 2
Tandovo, ozero ⊂ RUS 114-115 O 7
Tando Zinze o ANG 210-211 D 6
Tandubatu Island ⌒ RP 160-161 D 10
Tandung o RI 164-165 F 5
Tāndūr o IND 140-141 G 2
Tanega-shima ⌒ J 152-153 D 9
Taneichi o J 152-153 J 4
Tan Emellel o DZ 190-191 G 7
Tanemot, Danau ⊂ RI 166-167 G 2
Tanete o RI 164-165 G 6
Taneti, Pulau ⌒ RI 164-165 K 4
Taneytown o USA (MD) 280-281 J 4
Tanezrouft ⊥ DZ 196-197 K 3
Tanezrouft-Tan-Ahenet ⊥ DZ 190-191 C 9
Tanezzruft, Wādī ∼ LAR 190-191 H 8
Tanf, aṭ- o SYR 128-129 H 6
Tanga ◘ EAT 212-213 G 6
Tanga ☆ EAT (TAN) 212-213 G 6
Tanga o RUS 118-119 E 10
Tanga < TCH 198-199 J 4
Tangadee o AUS 176-177 E 2
Tangail o BD 142-143 F 3
Tanga Islands ⌒ PNG 183 G 2
Tangale Peak ▲ WAN 204-205 J 4

Tangalle o CL 140-141 J 7
Tanganyika, Lac = Lake Tanganyika ⊖ ZRE 214-215 E 3
Tanganyika, Lake = Lac Tanganyika ⊖ BU 214-215 E 3
Tangara o BR 68-69 L 5
Tangará da Serra o BR 70-71 J 4
Tangarana, Río ~ PE 64-65 E 3
Tangarare o SOL 184 I d 3
Tangaye o BF 202-203 J 3
Tangent Point ▲ USA 20-21 N 1
Tanger = Tanjah ☆• MA 188-189 J 3
Tangerang o RI 168 B 3
Tangermünde o• D 92-93 L 2
Tanggu o VRC 154-155 K 2
Tangguantun o VRC 154-155 K 2
Tanggula (Dangla) Shan ▲ VRC 144-145 G 4
Tanggulangin o RI 168 E 3
Tanggula Shankou ▲ VRC 144-145 H 4
Tangha ~ RUS 120-121 D 3
Tanghe o VRC 154-155 H 5
Tangi o PK 138-139 C 2
Tangier o CDN (NS) 240-241 N 6
Tangier o USA (VA) 280-281 L 6
Tangier = Tanjah ☆• MA 188-189 J 3
Tangier Island ⌐ USA (VA) 280-281 L 6
Tangier Sound ≈ USA 280-281 L 5
Tangjiahe Z.B. ⊥• VRC 154-155 D 5
Tangkak o MAL 162-163 E 3
Tangkoto-Batuangus-Dua Saudara Reserves ⊥• RI 164-165 J 3
Tang La ▲ VRC 144-145 G 7
Tangmai o VRC 144-145 K 5
Tangnary ~ RUS 118-119 L 4
Tangorin o AUS 178-179 H 1
Tangoutranat = Ti-n-Aguelhaj o RMM 196-197 J 6
Tangra Yumco ⊖ VRC 144-145 F 5
Tangse o RI 162-163 A 2
Tangshan o VRC 154-155 L 2
Tangu o PNG 183 C 3
Tangua o CO 64-65 D 1
Tangue River Reservoir < USA (MT) 250-251 N 6
Tangueita o DY 202-203 L 4
Tanguin-Dassouri o BF 202-203 K 3
Tangulbei o EAK 212-213 F 3
Tangyuan o VRC 150-151 G 4
Tân Hiep o VN 158-159 H 5
Tánh Linh o VN 158-159 J 5
Tanhoj o RUS 116-117 M 10
Tanhuijo, Arrecife ⌐ MEX 50-51 L 7
Tani o AFG 138-139 B 3
Taniantaweng Shan ▲ VRC 144-145 M 5
Tanichuchí o EC 64-65 C 2
Tanimbar, Kepulauan ⌐ RI 166-167 F 6
Taninga o MOC 220-221 L 2
Tanintharí o MYA 158-159 E 4
Tanintharí ~ MYA 158-159 E 4
Tanipaddi o IND 140-141 H 4
Tanis ∴• ET 194-195 E 2
Tanisapata o RI 166-167 G 3
Tāniya, Ğabal aṭ- ▲ Y 132-133 E 6
Tanjah ☆• MA 188-189 J 3
Tanjay o RP 160-161 E 8
Tan'ju ~ RUS 108-109 L 8
Tanjung o RI (JTE) 168 C 3
Tanjung o RI (KSE) 164-165 D 5
Tanjung o RI (NBA) 168 C 7
Tanjung Api Reserve ⊥• RI 164-165 G 4
Tanjungbalai o RI 162-163 C 3
Tanjungbatu o RI 164-165 F 2
Tanjungbuaya, Pulau ⌐ RI 164-165 F 3
Tanjungenim o RI 162-163 E 6
Tanjungkarang = Bandar Lampung o RI 162-163 F 7
Tanjunglolo o RI 162-163 D 5
Tanjung Malim o MAL 162-163 D 3
Tanjungmangil o RI 162-163 F 6
Tanjungmarcang o RI 162-163 C 2
Tanjungniur o RI 162-163 F 6
Tanjungpandan o RI 162-163 G 6
Tanjung Panjang Reserve ⊥• RI 164-165 G 3
Tanjung Piandang o MAL 162-163 D 2
Tanjungpinang o RI 162-163 F 4
Tanjungpura o RI 162-163 C 3
Tanjungraja o RI 162-163 F 6
Tanjungraya o RI 162-163 E 7
Tanjungredeb o RI 164-165 E 2
Tanjungsaleh, Pulau ⌐ RI 162-163 H 5
Tanjungseloka o RI 164-165 E 5
Tanjungselor o RI 164-165 E 2
Tanjung Sepat o MAL 162-163 D 3
Tanjunguban o RI 162-163 F 4
Tanjungwaringin o RI 162-163 J 5
Tanjurer ~ RUS 112-113 S 4
Tank o PK 138-139 C 3
Tank o USA (TX) 266-267 D 3
Tankersley o USA (TX) 266-267 G 2
Tankse o IND 138-139 G 2
Tankses ~ RUS 114-115 T 4
Tankwa ~ ZA 220-221 D 6
Tankwa-Karoo National Park ⊥ ZA 220-221 D 6
Tân Ky ☆ VN 156-157 D 7
Tanlova ~ RUS 114-115 N 2
Tanlovajaha ~ RUS 108-109 N 8
Tân Minh o VN 158-159 J 5
Tanna, Île = Tana ⌐ VAN 184 II b 4
Tannakallu o IND 140-141 H 4
Tanner, Mount ▲ CDN (BC) 230-231 L 4
Tanner Bank ≃ 248-249 F 7
Tannin o CDN (ONT) 234-235 M 5
Tannum Sands o AUS 178-179 L 2
Tannūra, Ra's o KSA 134-135 D 5
Tano ~ GH 202-203 J 6
Tano, Tanjung ▲ RI 168 C 7
Tanon Strait ≈ 160-161 E 8
Tanot o IND 138-139 C 6
Tanougou o DY 202-203 L 4
Tanougou, Cascades de ~• DY 202-203 L 4
Tanout o RN 198-199 D 5
Tanouzkka, Sebkhet ⊖ MA 196-197 C 3
Tân Phú o VN 158-159 J 5
Tanquary Fiord ≈ 26-27 L 3
Tanque Novo o BR 72-73 J 2
Tanque Nuevo o MEX 50-51 H 4
Tanque Verde o USA (AZ) 256-257 E 6
Tanquinho o BR 68-69 J 7
Tansarga o BF 202-203 L 4
Tansen o NEP 144-145 D 7
Tanshui • RC 156-157 M 4
Tansilla o BF 202-203 H 3
Tanşulūkh o LAR 192-193 J 1
Tanṭā ☆ ET 194-195 E 2
Tantallon o CDN (SAS) 232-233 R 5
Tantamayo o PE 64-65 D 6
Tan-Tan ☆ MA 188-189 F 6
Tan-Tan-Plage o MA 188-189 F 6
Tân Thu'o'ng o VN 158-159 J 5
Tan Ti-n-Missaou, Tassili ▲ DZ 196-197 M 4
Tantoyuca o MEX 50-51 K 7
Tanūma o KSA 132-133 C 4
Tanumbirini o AUS 174-175 C 5
Tanumshede ☆ S 86-87 E 7
Tanxi o VRC 156-157 F 3
Tanyan o MYA 142-143 L 4
Tanzania ■ EAT 214-215 F 3
Tanzilla Plateau ▲ CDN 32-33 E 2
Tanzilla River ~ CDN 32-33 E 2
Taocun o VRC 154-155 M 3
Tao He ~ VRC 154-155 C 4
Taohua Dao ⌐ VRC 156-157 N 2
Taohuayuan • VRC 156-157 G 2
Taojiang o VRC 156-157 H 2
Taonan o VRC 150-151 D 5
Taopa o RI 164-165 G 3
Taora o SOL 184 I c 2
Taormina o I 100-101 E 6
Taos o••• USA (NM) 256-257 K 2
Taoshan Shouliechang • VRC 150-151 G 4
Taos Indian Reservation ⚔ USA (NM) 256-257 K 2
Taos Pueblo ••• USA (NM) 256-257 K 2
Taouârdeï < RMM 196-197 L 6
Taoudenni o RMM 196-197 J 3
Taounate ☆ MA 188-189 J 3
Taourirt o MA (Ojd) 188-189 K 3
Taourirt o MA (Orz) 188-189 H 5
Taouz o MA 188-189 J 5
Taoyuan o RC 156-157 M 4
Taoyuan o VRC 156-157 G 2
Taoyuan D. • VRC 156-157 K 4
Tapachula o MEX 52-53 H 4
Tapah o MAL 162-163 D 2
Tapah, Tanjung ▲ RI 162-163 F 6
Tapaiuna, Cachoeira ~ BR 66-67 K 6
Tapaiuna, Ribeiro ~ BR 70-71 J 2
Tapajós, Rio ~ BR 66-67 K 4
Tapajos, Rio ~ BR 66-67 K 5
Tapaktuan o RI 162-163 B 3
Tapalpa o• MEX 52-53 C 2
Tapalqué o RA 78-79 J 4
Tapalqué, Arroyo ~ RA 78-79 J 4
Tapan o RI 162-163 D 6
Tapanahonirivier ~ SME 62-63 G 4
Tapandulu o RI 164-165 F 5
Tapanuli, Teluk ≈ 162-163 C 4
Tapat, Pulau ⌐ RI 164-165 K 4
Tapauá o BR 66-67 F 5
Tapauá, Rio ~ BR 66-67 E 5
Tapauá, Rio ~ BR 66-67 D 5
Tapaulama, Tanjung ▲ RI 164-165 H 5
Tapawera o NZ 182 D 4
Tapebicuá o RA 76-77 J 5
Tapejara o BR 74-75 E 7
Tapena o BOL 70-71 C 5
Tapenaga, Río ~ RA 76-77 H 4
Tapera o BR 66-67 F 3
Tapera, La o RCH 80 E 2
Tapera, Rio ~ BR 62-63 D 5
Taperaba o BR 62-63 J 5
Taperoá o BR 68-69 K 5
Tapes o BR 74-75 E 8
Tapes, Ponta de ▲ BR 74-75 E 8
Tapeta o LB 202-203 F 6
Taphan Hin o THA 158-159 F 2
Tāpi ~ IND 138-139 E 9
Tapi ~ IND 138-139 F 9
Tapian o RI 164-165 E 4
Tapiantana Channel ≈ 160-161 D 9
Tapiantana Group ⌐ RP 160-161 D 9
Tapiche, Río ~ PE 64-65 E 5
Tapini o PNG 183 D 5
Tapiocanga, Chapada do ▲ BR 72-73 G 4
Tapira o BR 72-73 G 5
Tapiraípe o BR 72-73 K 2
Tapirapecó, Sierra ▲ YV 66-67 E 2
Tapirapé Karajá, Área Indígena ⚔ BR 68-69 C 7
Tapiratiba o BR 72-73 G 6
Tapiruçu, Cachoeira ~ BR 68-69 E 3
Tapis, Gunung ▲ MAL 162-163 E 2
Tapiú, Cachoeira do ~ BR 62-63 F 6
Tapkaluk Islands ⌐ USA 20-21 M 1
Taplejung o NEP 144-145 F 7
Tapoa, La o BF (DOS) 204-205 E 2
Tapoa, La ~ BF 202-203 L 3
Tapol o TCH 206-207 B 4
Tappahannock o USA (VA) 280-281 K 6
Tappalang o RI 164-165 F 5
Tappen o CDN (BC) 230-231 K 3
Tapsuj ~ RUS 114-115 F 3
Taptugary o RUS 118-119 K 9
Tapul o RP 160-161 D 10
Tapul Group ⌐ RP 160-161 D 10
Tapul Island ⌐ RP 160-161 D 10
Ṭāqa o OM 132-133 J 5
Taq-e Bostān o• IR 128-129 M 4
Taqtaq o IRQ 128-129 L 5
Taqtaqāna, at- o IRQ 128-129 K 6
Taquara o BR 74-75 E 7
Taquari o BR 74-75 E 7
Taquari, Pantanal do o BR 70-71 J 6
Taquari, Rio ~ BR 70-71 J 6
Taquari, Rio ~ BR 72-73 E 6
Taquaritinga o BR 72-73 F 6
Taquarituba o BR 72-73 F 7
Taques, Los o YV 60-61 F 2
Taquili, Isla ⌐ PE 70-71 C 4
Tara o AUS 178-179 L 4
Tará o BR 68-69 K 6
Tara ☆ RUS (OMS) 114-115 N 6
Tara ~ RUS 114-115 N 6
Tara ~ RUS 114-115 P 6
Tara ~ YU 100-101 G 3
Tara o Z 218-219 D 3
Ṭarā, Ğazīrat ⌐ KSA 132-133 B 4
Taraba, River ~ WAN 204-205 J 4
Tarabuco o BOL 70-71 E 6
Tarābulus ◘ LAR 192-193 E 1
Tarābulus ★ LAR 192-193 E 1
Ṭarābulus o• RL 128-129 F 5
Ṭarābulus ☆• RL 128-129 F 5
Taraca, Golfo de ⊖ BOL 70-71 C 5
Taraco o PE 70-71 C 4
Tarād al-Kahf o IRQ 128-129 L 7
Taraf, at- o KSA 130-131 L 5
Ṭarafīya, aṭ- o KSA 130-131 J 4
Tarafo, Ponta ▲ CV 202-203 C 6
Tarag o IND 140-141 F 2
Tarāghin o LAR 192-193 F 5
Tarahumara, Sierra ▲ MEX 50-51 E 3
Taraira, Río ~ CO 66-67 C 3
Taraire o BOL 76-77 F 1
Tarajim o WAN 204-205 J 3
Taraka, Mount ▲ PNG 184 I b 2
Tarakan o RI 164-165 E 2
Tarakan, Pulau ⌐ RI 164-165 E 2
Tarakbits o PNG 183 A 3
Taralga o AUS 180-181 K 3
Taramana o RI 166-167 C 6
Taranaki Bight, North ≈ 182 E 3
Taranaki Bight, South ≈ 182 E 4
Tarancón o E 98-99 F 4
Tarangara o TCH 206-207 D 4
Tarangire ~ EAT 212-213 F 6
Tarangire National Park ⊥ EAT 212-213 F 5
Tarangire Safari Camp o EAT (ARV) 212-213 F 5
Tarankōl, kōli ⊖ KA 124-125 F 1
Taranovskij ☆ KA 124-125 C 2
Táranto ☆• I 100-101 F 4
Táranto, Golfo di ≈ 100-101 F 4
Tarapacá o CO 66-67 C 4
Tarapacá o RCH 70-71 C 6
Tarapoa o EC 64-65 D 2
Tarapoto o PE 64-65 D 5
Tārāpur o IND 138-139 D 10
Taraquá o BR 66-67 E 3
Tarara o C 54-55 D 3
Tarara o PNG 184 I b 2
Tarare o F 90-91 K 9
Taras o BD 142-143 F 3
Tarasa Dwip Island ⌐ IND 140-141 L 5
Tarascon o• F 90-91 K 10
Tarasovo o RUS 116-117 N 8
Tarasovo o RUS (NAO) 88-89 T 3
Tarasovsk o RUS 116-117 L 8
Tarat o DZ 190-191 G 7
Tarata o PE 70-71 B 5
Tarauacá o BR 66-67 B 7
Tarauacá, Rio ~ BR 66-67 B 6
Tarawai Island ⌐ PNG 183 B 2
Tarazona o E 98-99 G 4
Tarbagataj o KA 124-125 M 5
Tarbagataj ☆ RUS 116-117 N 10
Tarbagatay Range = Tarbağatai žotasy ▲ KA 124-125 M 5
Tarbaj o EAK 212-213 H 2
Tarbela Reservoir < PK 138-139 D 2
Tarbes ☆ F 90-91 H 10
Tarboro o USA (NC) 282-283 K 5
Tarbotvale o CDN (NS) 240-241 P 4
Tarcoola o AUS 178-179 C 6
Tardie o AUS 176-177 D 3
Tardoki-Jani, gora ▲ RUS 122-123 H 4
Tardun o AUS 176-177 C 4
Taree o AUS 178-179 M 6
Tareja ~ RUS 108-109 Z 4
Taremert-n-Alki, Oued ~ DZ 190-191 E 8
Tarempa, Pulau ⌐ RI 162-163 G 3
Tärendö o S 86-87 L 3
Ṭarfa, Ra's aṭ- ▲ KSA 132-133 C 5
Ṭarfāwī, Bi'r < IRQ 128-129 K 6
Tarfaya o MA 188-189 E 7
Targa < RN 198-199 B 4
Targap o KA 146-147 B 4
Targhalāt, Wādī ~ LAR 192-193 F 1
Targhee Pass ▲ USA (ID) 252-253 G 2
Târgoviște o BG 102-103 E 6
Targuist o MA 188-189 J 3
Tarhaouhaout ∴ DZ 190-191 E 9
Tarhatine, Tizi-n ▲ MA 188-189 H 5
Tarhovo o RUS 116-117 E 7
Tarhūnah ◘ LAR 192-193 E 1
Tarhūnah ☆• LAR 192-193 E 1
Tari o PNG 183 B 3
Tari, Mutungu- o ZRE 216-217 D 3
Tariat = Horgo o MAU 148-149 D 3
Tarib o KSA 132-133 C 4
Tariba o YV 60-61 E 4
Tarica o PE 64-65 D 6
Ṭarīf o UAE 134-135 E 6
Tarifa o E 98-99 E 6
Tarija o BOL 76-77 E 1
Tarija, Río ~ BOL 76-77 E 1
Tarikere o IND 140-141 F 4
Tariku ~ RI 166-167 J 3
Tariku (Rouffaer) ~ RI 166-167 J 3
Tarim o• Y 132-133 F 5
Tarim Basin = Tarim Pendi ⊥ VRC 146-147 E 6
Tarime o EAT 212-213 E 4
Tarim He ~ VRC 146-147 E 5
Tarımı Milli Parkı ⊥ TR 128-129 F 3
Tarimoro o MEX 52-53 D 1
Tarim Pendi ⊥ VRC 146-147 E 6
Taring o RI 162-163 B 3
Taripa o RI 164-165 G 4
Tarira o BR 66-67 C 2
Tarit, Oued ~ DZ 190-191 D 8
Taritatu ~ RI 166-167 L 3
Taritatu (Idenburg) ~ RI 166-167 K 3
Tarka ~ ZA 220-221 G 6
Tarkastad o ZA 220-221 H 6
Tarkio o USA (MO) 274-275 C 4
Tarkio o USA (MT) 250-251 E 4
Tarkio River ~ USA (IA) 274-275 C 4
Tarko-Sale ☆ RUS 114-115 O 2
Tarkwa o GH 202-203 K 7
Tarlac ☆ RP 160-161 D 5
Tarlton Downs o AUS 178-179 D 2
Tarma o PE 64-65 E 7
Tarmaber Pass ▲ ETH 208-209 D 4
Ṭarmīdā o KSA 130-131 J 5
Tarn ~ F 90-91 H 10
Tarn, Gorges du ∪• F 90-91 J 9
Tärnaby o S 86-87 G 4
Tarnak Rūd ~ AFG 134-135 M 2
Tarnogskij Gorodok o RUS 94-95 S 1
Tarnopol o CDN (SAS) 232-233 N 3
Tarnów ☆• PL 92-93 Q 3
Taroa o CO 60-61 F 1
Tarobi o PNG 183 F 3
Taro Co ⊖ VRC 144-145 E 5
Taroko o RC 156-157 M 4
Taroko National Park ⊥• RC 156-157 M 4
Taron o PNG 183 G 3
Taronggo o RI 164-165 G 4
Taroom o AUS 178-179 K 3
Taroudannt ☆• MA 188-189 G 5
Taroum o RN 204-205 E 1
Tarpley o USA (TX) 266-267 H 4
Tarpon Springs o USA (FL) 286-287 G 3
Tarquinia o I 100-101 C 3
Tarrafal o CV 202-203 B 5
Tarrafal o CV 202-203 C 6
Tarrafal o CV 202-203 B 5
Tarragona o AUS 178-179 H 2
Tarragona o• E 98-99 H 4
Tarrajäkkå ~ S 86-87 H 3
Tarraleah o AUS 180-181 J 7
Tarrant City o USA (AL) 284-285 D 3
Tarras o NZ 182 B 6
Tàrrega o E 98-99 H 4
Tar River ~ USA (NC) 282-283 K 5
Tarso Emissi ▲ TCH 198-199 J 2
Tarsu Musa ▲ TCH 198-199 J 2
Tarsus ☆• TR 128-129 F 4
Tartagal o RA 76-77 F 2
Tartagal, Río ~ RA 76-77 F 2
Ṭarṭār, Buhairat aṭ- < IRQ 128-129 K 5
Ṭarṭār, Nahr aṭ- < IRQ 128-129 K 6
Tartaruga o BR 72-73 L 2
Tartarugalzinho o BR 62-63 J 5
Tartarugas, Cachoeira das ~ BR 68-69 D 4
Tartas ~ RUS 114-115 O 7
Tartrat, Hassi < DZ 188-189 H 7
Tartu ☆• EST 94-95 K 2
Ṭarṭūs ☆• SYR 128-129 F 5
Taruca o PE 70-71 C 5
Tarucani o PE 70-71 B 5
Tarum ~ RI 168 B 3
Taruma o BR 70-71 J 6
Tarusa ☆• RUS 94-95 P 4
Tarusan o RI 162-163 D 5
Tārūt, Wādī ~ LAR 192-193 E 4
Tarutung o RI 162-163 C 3
Tarutyne ☆ UA 102-103 F 4
Tarvagatajn Nuruu ▲ MAU 148-149 D 3
Tarversville o USA (GA) 284-285 G 4
Tarves o AUS 178-179 H 3
Tarvo, Río ~ BOL 70-71 G 4
Ṭarwāniya o UAE 132-133 J 2
Taryng-Ėrge ~ RUS 120-121 E 4
Tarzan o USA (TX) 264-265 C 6
Tasabo < WAN 204-205 G 6
Tašāk, Kūh-e ▲ IR 134-135 D 4
Tašanta o RUS 124-125 Q 4
Tašauz = Dažhovuz ☆ TM 136-137 F 4
Tašauzskaja oblast' ◘ TM 136-137 E 4
Tasböget ☆ KA 124-125 D 6
Taschereau o CDN (QUE) 236-237 K 4
Tascosa o USA (TX) 264-265 B 3
Tase o VRC 144-145 F 6
Tas-Ėėkit ~ RUS 110-111 P 4
Taseeva ~ RUS 116-117 G 7
Taseko Lakes ⊖ CDN (BC) 230-231 F 2
Taseko River ~ CDN (BC) 230-231 F 2
Tasermiut ≈ 28-29 S 6
Tasersiaq ≈ 28-29 P 3
Tasersuaq ≈ 28-29 P 3
Taserssuaq o GRØ (VGR) 28-29 P 4
Taserssuaq o GRØ (VGR) 28-29 Q 5
Taserssuatsiaq o GRØ 28-29 P 4
Tāsgaon o IND 140-141 F 2
Taš Guzar o AFG 136-137 K 6
Tashiding o• IND 142-143 F 2
Tashigang o BHT 142-143 G 2
Tashkent = Toškent ☆ •• US 136-137 L 4
Tashota o CDN (ONT) 234-235 Q 4
Tasialaujjuaq, Lac ⊖ CDN 36-37 O 5
Tasiat, Lac ⊖ CDN 36-37 M 5
Tasik Bera ⊖ MAL 162-163 E 3
Tasik Chini ⊖ MAL 162-163 E 3
Tasik Kenyir ⊖ MAL 162-163 E 2
Tasikmalaya o RI 168 C 3
Tasik Temengur ⊖ MAL 162-163 D 2
Tašina ~ RUS 122-123 D 3
Tašir o AR 128-129 L 2
Tasiussaq o GRØ 26-27 X 7
Tasiussarssuaq ≈ 28-29 P 4
Tas-Jurjah o RUS 118-119 F 5
Taskan o RUS 120-121 O 2
Taskan ~ RUS 120-121 O 3
Taškent = Toškent ☆ •• US 136-137 L 4
Taškentskaja oblast' ◘ US 136-137 L 4
Taškepri o TM 136-137 H 6
Taškeprinskoe vodohranilišče < TM 136-137 H 6
Tasker o RN 198-199 E 5
Taskesken o KA 124-125 M 5
Taşköprü ☆ TR 128-129 F 2
Taskul o PNG 183 F 2
Taš-Kumyr o KS 136-137 N 4
Tas-Kystabyt, hrebet ▲ RUS 110-111 Y 7
Tašla ☆ RUS 96-97 H 8
Tasman Abyssal Plain ≃ 13 G 6
Tasman Basin ≃ 13 G 7
Tasman Bay ≈ 182 D 4
Tasman Head ▲ AUS 180-181 J 7
Tasman Highway II AUS 180-181 K 6
Tasmania ⌐ AUS 180-181 H 6
Tasman Mountains ▲ NZ 182 D 4
Tasman Peninsula ∪•• AUS 180-181 J 7
Tasman Point ▲ AUS 174-175 D 4
Tasman Sea ≈ 13 G 6
Tasmate o VAN 184 II a 2
Tāşnad o RO 102-103 C 4
Taşova ☆ TR 128-129 G 2
Tāšqorğān = Hūlm o• AFG 136-137 K 6
Tassara o RN 198-199 B 4
Tassa-Takorat < RN 198-199 B 4
Tassedjefit, Erg ∴ DZ 190-191 D 8
Tasserest < RMM 196-197 M 7
Tassialouc, Lac ⊖ CDN 36-37 N 5
Tassiné ~ DY 204-205 E 3
Tasso Fragoso o BR 68-69 F 6
Taštagol ☆ RUS 124-125 P 2
Tastau, gora ▲ KA 124-125 N 5
Tastop o KA 136-137 K 3
Tastöp o KA 136-137 K 3
Tastuba o RUS 96-97 K 6
Taštyp ☆ RUS 124-125 Q 2
Tasty-Taldy ☆ KA 124-125 E 3
Tasu o CDN (BC) 228-229 C 4
Tasūğ o IR 128-129 L 3
Tasūki o• IR 134-135 J 3
Tata o H 92-93 P 5
Tata ☆ MA 188-189 H 6
Tatabánya o H 92-93 P 5
Tatachikapika River ~ CDN (ONT) 236-237 G 4
Ta Ta Creek o CDN (BC) 230-231 O 4
Tata d'Albouri Ndiaye ∴• SN 196-197 C 7
Tataguine o SN 202-203 B 2
Tatajachura, Cerro ▲ RCH 70-71 C 6
Tatajuba o BR 64-65 F 5
Tatali o GH 202-203 L 5
Tatalrose o CDN (BC) 228-229 H 3
Tatam o RI 164-165 L 3
Tatamagouche o CDN (NS) 240-241 M 5
Tata Mailau, Gunung ▲ RI 166-167 C 6
Tatamba o SOL 184 I d 3
Tatan o KA 124-125 K 4
Tataouine ☆• TN 190-191 H 4
Tatarbunary ☆ UA 102-103 F 5
Tatarsk ☆ RUS 114-115 N 7
Tatarskij proliv ≈ 122-123 J 3
Tatarskiy Proliv = Tatarskij proliv ≈ RUS 122-123 J 3
Tatarstan = Respublika Tatarstan ◘ RUS 96-97 F 6
Tatau o MAL 162-163 K 3
Tatau Island ⌐ PNG 183 F 2
Tatawa o RI 166-167 H 3
Tatéma o RG 202-203 D 5
Tate River ~ AUS 174-175 G 5
Tateyama o J 152-153 H 7
Tate-yama ▲ J 152-153 G 6
Tathlina Lake ⊖ CDN 30-31 L 5
Tathra o AUS 180-181 K 4
Tathra National Park ⊥ AUS 176-177 C 4
Tati ~ RB 218-219 D 5
Tâtîlt < RIM 196-197 C 5
Tatinnai Lake ⊖ CDN 30-31 V 5
Tatiščevo o RUS 96-97 D 8
Tatitlek o USA 20-21 R 6
Tat Kha o THA 158-159 F 2
Tatkon o MYA 142-143 K 5
Tatla Lake o CDN (BC) 230-231 E 2
Tatla Lake ⊖ CDN (BC) 230-231 E 2
Tatlanika Creek ~ USA 20-21 Q 4
Tatlatui Provincial Park ⊥ CDN 32-33 G 3
Tatlayoko Lake o CDN (BC) 230-231 E 2
Tatlayoko Lake ⊖ CDN (BC) 230-231 E 2
Tatlīt ◘ KSA 132-133 C 4
Tatlīt, Wādī ~ KSA 132-133 C 3
Tatlmain Lake ⊖ CDN 20-21 X 5
Tatlow, Mount ▲ CDN (BC) 230-231 F 2
Tatnam, Cape ▲ CDN 34-35 L 2
Tatokou o RN 198-199 D 5
Tatra = Tatry ▲ SK 92-93 P 4
Tatry ▲ SK 92-93 P 4
Tatsfield o CDN (SAS) 232-233 J 3
Tatshenshini-Alsek Kluane National Park ⊥•• CDN 20-21 U 6
Tatshenshini River ~ CDN 20-21 W 7
Tatta ~ RUS 120-121 E 2
Tattakarai o IND 140-141 G 5
Tattannagaripalli o IND 140-141 G 4
Tatu, Cachoeira do ~ BR 62-63 H 5
Tatuí o BR 72-73 G 7
Tatul, Sierra de ▲ RCH 76-77 B 5
Tatum o USA (NM) 256-257 M 5
Tatum o USA (TX) 264-265 K 6
Tatumville o USA (TN) 276-277 F 4
Tatvan ☆• TR 128-129 K 3
Tau o N 86-87 B 7
Ta'u o USA 184 V c 2
Tauá o BR 68-69 H 4
Tauari o BR 68-69 E 2
Taubaté o BR 72-73 H 7
Tauberbischofsheim o• D 92-93 K 4
Tauca o PE 64-65 C 6
Taufikia o SUD 206-207 K 4
Ta'u Island ⌐ USA 184 V c 2
Tauj ~ RUS 120-121 N 4
Taujskaja guba ≈ 120-121 N 4
Taukum ∪ KA 124-125 J 6
Taulihawa o NEP 144-145 D 7
Tauliya o IRQ 128-129 J 6
Taumarunui o NZ 182 E 3
Taumaturgo o BR 64-65 F 6
Taum Sauk Mountain ▲ USA (MO) 276-277 E 3
Taunay, Cachoeira ~ BR 70-71 G 2
Taung o ZA 220-221 G 3
Taungbon o MYA 142-143 J 4
Taungdwingyi o MYA 142-143 J 5
Taunggyi ☆ MYA 142-143 K 5
Taungtha o MYA 142-143 J 5
Taungthônlôn ▲ MYA 142-143 J 3
Taungup o MYA 142-143 J 6
Taunsa o PK 138-139 C 4
Taunton ☆ GB 90-91 F 6
Taunton o USA (MA) 278-279 K 7
Taupo o NZ 182 F 3
Taupo, Lake ⊖ NZ 182 E 3
Tauragė ☆• LT 94-95 H 4
Tauranga o NZ 182 F 2
Taureau, Réservoir ⊖ CDN (QUE) 238-239 M 2
Tauria o USA (MO) 276-277 B 4
Tauri River ~ PNG 183 C 4
Tauroa Point ▲ NZ 182 D 1
Taurova o RUS 114-115 M 5
Taurus Mountains = Toros Dağları ▲ TR 128-129 D 4
Taus = Domažlice o CZ 92-93 M 4
Tau Šalkarnür ▲ KA 126-127 P 3
Tauste o E 98-99 G 4
Taušyk o KA 126-127 J 5
Taušyk o KA 126-127 P 2
Tauta o PNG 183 C 3
Tavai o PY 76-77 K 4
Tavajvaam ~ RUS 112-113 T 4
Tavan Bogd ▲ MAU 146-147 H 1
Tavanei River ~ PNG 183 E 6
Tavani, Mount ▲ VAN 184 II b 3
Tavara o SOL 184 I c 3
Tavas ☆ TR 128-129 C 4
Tavda ☆ RUS (SVR) 114-115 H 5
Tavda ~ RUS 114-115 G 5
Tavda ~ RUS 114-115 J 6
Taverner Bay ≈ 28-29 D 3
Tavernier o USA (FL) 286-287 J 7
Taveta o EAK 212-213 F 5
Taveta o EAT 214-215 H 5
Taveuni ⌐ FJI 184 III c 2
Tavira o• P 98-99 D 6
Tavoliere ∪ I 100-101 E 4
Távora, Rio ~ P 98-99 D 4
Tavoy o MYA 158-159 E 4
Tavričeskoe ☆ RUS 124-125 H 1
Tavşanlı ☆ TR 128-129 C 3
Tavua o FJI 184 III a 2
Tavuki o FJI 184 III b 3
Tavul Point ▲ PNG 183 G 3
Tavu Na Sici ⌐ FJI 184 III c 3
Tawaeli o RI 164-165 F 4
Tawakoni, Lake ⊖ USA (TX) 264-265 H 6
Tawali o RI 168 D 7
Tawallah o AUS 174-175 C 5
Tawallah Range ▲ AUS 174-175 C 5
Tawang o• IND 142-143 G 2
Tawa Reservoir < IND 138-139 F 8
Tawargeri o IND 140-141 G 3
Tawas City o USA (MI) 272-273 F 3
Tawau o MAL 160-161 B 10
Tawau Hills Park ⊥ MAL 160-161 B 10
Ṭawīl, aṭ- ▲ KSA 130-131 F 3
Ṭawīla, aṭ- o Y 132-133 C 6
Ṭawīla, Ğazīrat ⌐ ET 194-195 F 4
Tawilah o SUD 200-201 B 6
Tawitawi Island ⌐ RP 160-161 C 10
Tawlokehn o LB 202-203 F 7
Tawma o MYA 142-143 K 4
Tawu o RC 156-157 M 5
Ṭāwūq ☆ IRQ 128-129 L 5
Ṭāwūq Čāy ~ IRQ 128-129 L 5
Tāwurghā' o LAR 192-193 F 1
Tāwurghā', Sabkhat ⊖ LAR 192-193 F 1
Taxco o• MEX 52-53 E 2
Taxco de Alarcon = Taxco o• MEX 52-53 E 2
Taxi o VRC 150-151 F 3
Taxila o•• PK 138-139 D 3
Taxkorgan o VRC 146-147 B 7
Tay ~ GB 90-91 F 3
Tay, Lake ⊖ AUS 176-177 F 6
Tayabamba o PE 64-65 D 6
Tayabas Bay ≈ 160-161 D 6
Tayahua o MEX 50-51 H 6
Tayan o RI 162-163 J 5
Tayandu, Kepulauan ⌐ RI 166-167 F 4
Tayandu, Pulau ⌐ RI 166-167 G 4
Tayebād o• IR 134-135 J 1
Tayeeglow o SP 208-209 G 6
Tayin, Wādī ~ OM 132-133 L 2
Taykah o LAR 192-193 J 2
Taylor o CDN 32-33 K 3
Taylor o USA (AK) 20-21 H 4
Taylor o USA (AR) 276-277 B 7
Taylor o USA (AZ) 256-257 E 4
Taylor o USA (NE) 262-263 G 3
Taylor o USA (TX) 266-267 K 3
Taylor, Mount ▲ USA (NM) 256-257 H 3
Taylor Canyon o USA (NV) 246-247 J 2
Taylor Head ▲ CDN (NS) 240-241 N 6
Taylor Highway II USA 20-21 T 5
Taylor Lake ⊖ CDN 30-31 P 4
Taylor Mountains ▲ USA 20-21 M 6
Taylor Park o USA (CO) 254-255 J 5
Taylor River ~ USA (CO) 254-255 J 5
Taylors Falls o USA (MN) 270-271 F 5
Taylors Island o USA (MD) 280-281 K 5
Taylorsville o USA (GA) 284-285 F 2
Taylorsville o USA (KY) 276-277 K 2
Taylorsville o USA (MS) 268-269 L 5
Taylorsville o USA (NC) 282-283 F 5
Taylorsville Lake ⊖ USA (KY) 276-277 K 3
Taylorville o USA (IL) 274-275 J 5
Taylorville, Lake ⊖ USA (IL) 274-275 J 5
Taymyr, Ozero = Tajmyr, ozero ⊖ RUS 108-109 d 4
Taymyr Autonomous District = Tajmyrskij avtonomnyj okrug ◘ RUS 108-109 a 4
Taymyr Peninsula = Tajmyr, poluostrov ∪ RUS 108-109 Y 4
Tây Ninh ☆• VN 158-159 J 5
Tayoltita o MEX 50-51 G 5
Tayota, Rio ~ BOL 70-71 E 4
Tay River ~ CDN 20-21 Y 5
Tây So'n o VN 158-159 K 4
Tay Sound ≈ 24-25 g 4
Taytay o RP 160-161 C 7
Taytay Bay ≈ 160-161 C 7
Ta Yü ⌐ RC 156-157 L 5
Tayu o RI 168 D 3
Tayuling o RC 156-157 M 4
Tayyāl, Wādī ~ KSA 130-131 F 3
Tayyāna o SYR 128-129 J 5
Tayyibah o SUD 200-201 F 5
Taz ~ RUS 108-109 S 8
Taz ~ RUS 114-115 R 2
Taza ☆ MA 188-189 J 3
Tāzah = Taza ☆ MA 188-189 J 3
Tazawa-ko ⊖ J 152-153 J 5
Tazenakht o MA 188-189 H 5
Tazerzaït ∴ RN 198-199 B 3
Tazewell o USA (TN) 282-283 D 4
Tazewell o USA (VA) 280-281 E 6
Tazgun o VRC 146-147 C 6
Taziet, Bi'r < LAR 192-193 E 5
Tazin Lake ⊖ CDN 30-31 P 6
Tazin River ~ CDN 30-31 O 5
Tāzirbū o LAR 192-193 J 5
Tazlina Lake ⊖ USA 20-21 R 6
Tazna, Cerro ▲ BOL 70-71 D 7
Tazolé < RN 198-199 D 4
Tazovskaja guba ≈ 108-109 Q 7
Tazovskij ☆ RUS 108-109 S 8
Tazovskij poluostrov ∪ RUS 108-109 Q 7
Tazrouk o DZ 190-191 F 9
Tazzarine o MA 188-189 J 5
Tazzeka, Ibel ▲ MA 188-189 J 3
Tbilisi ★• GE 126-127 F 7
Tchabal Gangdaba ▲ CAM 204-205 K 5
Tchabal Mbabo ▲ CAM 204-205 K 5
Tchad, Lac ⊖ 198-199 F 6
Tchad, Plaine du ∴ CAM 206-207 B 3
Tchadaoua o RN 198-199 C 6
Tchamba o CAM 204-205 K 4
Tchamba o RT 202-203 L 5
Tchangsou o TCH 206-207 B 4
Tchaourou o DY 204-205 E 4
Tchatchou o DY 204-205 E 4
Tchentlo Lake ⊖ CDN 32-33 H 4
Tchériba o BF 202-203 J 3
Tchetti o DY 202-203 L 6
Tchibanga ☆ G 210-211 C 5
Tchibemba o ANG 216-217 C 7
Tchie < TCH 198-199 J 4
Tchigai, Plateau du ▲ RN 198-199 G 2
Tchilounga o RCB 210-211 C 6
Tchin-Tabaradene o RN 198-199 B 5
Tchissakata o RCB 210-211 D 6
Tchizalamou o RCB 210-211 C 6
Tcholliré o CAM 206-207 B 4
Tchula o USA (MS) 268-269 K 3
Tczew o• PL 92-93 P 1
Teá, Rio ~ BR 66-67 E 3
Teacapan o MEX 50-51 G 6
Teague o USA (TX) 266-267 L 2
Teague, Lake ⊖ AUS 176-177 F 2
Te Anau o NZ 182 A 6
Te Anau, Lake ⊖ NZ 182 A 6
Teano Range ▲ AUS 176-177 D 2
Teapa o MEX 52-53 H 3
Teapot Dome ⊥ USA (WY) 252-253 M 3
Te Araroa o NZ 182 G 2
Te Aroha o NZ 182 E 2
Te Awamutu o NZ 182 E 3
Teba o RI 166-167 J 2
Tebaga, Jebel ▲ TN 190-191 G 4
Tebaram o RN 198-199 B 5
Tébe o G 210-211 D 4
Tebedu o MAL 162-163 J 4
Tebenkopf Bay ≈ 32-33 C 3
Tebenkopf Bay Wilderness ⊥ USA 32-33 C 3
Teben'kova, vulkan ▲ RUS 122-123 M 6
Tebensaj ~ KA 126-127 N 3
Teberda o RUS 126-127 D 6
Teberdinskij zapovednik ⊥ RUS 126-127 D 6
Tebesjuak Lake ⊖ CDN 30-31 U 4
Tébessa ☆• DZ 190-191 G 3
Tebez, köl ⊖ KA 126-127 N 3
Tebicuary, Río ~ PY 76-77 J 4
Tebingtinggi o RI 162-163 G 2
Tebingtinggi o RI 162-163 E 6
Tebingtinggi o RI (SUU) 162-163 C 3
Tebo ~ RI 162-163 D 5
Tébourba o TN 190-191 G 2
Téboursouk o TN 190-191 G 2
Tecalitlán o MEX 52-53 C 2
Tecamachalco o MEX 52-53 F 2
Tecámbaro de Collados o MEX 52-53 D 2
Tecate o• MEX 50-51 A 1
Tecer Dağları ▲ TR 128-129 G 3
Techerène, In- < RMM 196-197 K 4
Techia o MA 196-197 C 4
Techiman o GH 202-203 K 6
Techimpolo ~ ANG 216-217 D 8
Techirimba o ANG 216-217 C 5
Techissanha o ANG 216-217 D 7
Techongolola o ANG 216-217 D 4
Tecka o RA 78-79 D 7
Tecka, Río ~ RA 78-79 D 7
Tecoh o MEX 52-53 K 1
Tecojate o GCA 52-53 J 5
Tecolote, El o MEX 50-51 J 5
Tecoman o MEX 52-53 C 2
Tecopa o USA (CA) 248-249 H 4
Tecozautla o MEX 52-53 E 1
Tecpan de Galeana o MEX 52-53 D 3
Tecpatán o MEX 52-53 H 3
Tecuala o MEX 50-51 G 6
Tecuan, El o MEX 52-53 B 1
Tecuci o RO 102-103 E 5
Tecumseh o CDN (ONT) 238-239 C 6
Tecumseh o USA (MI) 272-273 F 6
Tecumseh o USA (NE) 262-263 K 4
Tecumseh o USA (OK) 264-265 H 3
Ted o SP 208-209 F 6
Tedecha Melka o ETH 208-209 D 4
Tédéini, In- < RN 198-199 D 4
Tedi River ~ PNG 183 A 3
Tedjorar, Adrar ▲ DZ 190-191 E 9
Tedžen o TM 136-137 G 6
Tedžen ~ TM 136-137 G 6
Tedžen ~ TM 136-137 G 7
Tedženstroj o TM 136-137 G 6
Teebinga Conservation Park ⊥ AUS 180-181 F 3
Teec Nos Pos o USA (AZ) 256-257 F 2
Teeli ☆ RUS 116-117 E 10
Teepee o CDN 20-21 X 7
Tees o CDN (ALB) 232-233 E 3
Tees ~ GB 90-91 F 4
Teeswater o CDN (ONT) 238-239 D 5
Tefé o BR 66-67 E 4
Tefé, Lago ⊖ BR 66-67 E 4
Tefé, Rio ~ BR 66-67 D 5
Tefedest ▲ DZ 190-191 E 8

Tefenni ★ TR 128-129 C 4
Tegaham, Enneri ~ TCH 198-199 H 3
Tegal ○ RI 168 C 3
Tegalombo ○ RI 168 D 4
Tegernsee ○ D 92-93 L 5
Tegguidda-n-Tessoum ○ RN 198-199 C 4
Tegheri, Bi'r < LAR 190-191 H 7
Teghra ○ IND 142-143 D 3
Tegina ○ WAN 204-205 G 3
Tegineneng ○ RI 162-163 F 7
Tegissor, köl ○ KA 126-127 P 3
Tégouma ~ RN 198-199 E 5
Tegua, Arroyo de ~ RA 78-79 G 2
Tegua = Île Teguan ⌒ VAN 184 II a 1
Teguan, Île = Tegua ⌒ VAN 184 II a 1
Tegucigalpa ★ •• HN 52-53 L 4
Tegul'det ○ 114-115 U 6
Teg Wani ~ ZW 218-219 D 4
Tehachapi ○ USA (CA) 248-249 F 4
Tehachapi Mountains ⛰ USA (CA) 248-249 F 5
Tehachapi Pass ▲ USA (CA) 248-249 F 4
Te Hapua ○ NZ 182 D 1
Te Haroto ○ NZ 182 F 3
Tehek Lake ○ CDN 30-31 W 3
Tehema-Colusa-Canal < USA (CA) 246-247 C 4
Teheran = Tehrān ★ •• IR 136-137 B 7
Tehery Lake ○ CDN 30-31 X 3
Téhini ○ CI 202-203 J 5
Tehrān ◘ IR 136-137 C 7
Tehrān ★ •• IR 136-137 B 7
Tehri ○ IND 138-139 G 4
Tehuacan ○ • MEX 52-53 F 2
Tehuantepec, Golfo de ≈ 52-53 G 4
Tehuantepec, Istmo de ∸ MEX 52-53 G 3
Tehuantepec, Río ~ MEX 52-53 G 3
Tehuantepec Ridge ≃ 4 E 7
Tehumardi ○ EST 94-95 H 2
Teide, Parque Nacional del ⊥ E 188-189 C 6
Teide, Pico de ▲ E 188-189 C 6
Teima, Oulad- ○ MA 188-189 G 5
Teiskot < RMM 196-197 L 6
Teiti ○ SUD 200-201 E 3
Teixeira ○ BR 68-69 K 5
Teixeira de Freitas ○ BR 72-73 L 4
Teixeira Soares ○ BR 74-75 E 5
Teja ~ RUS 116-117 F 6
Tejakula ○ RI 168 B 7
Tejar, El ○ RA 78-79 J 3
Tejira ○ RN 198-199 D 5
Tejkovo ★ RUS 94-95 R 3
Tejo, Rio ~ BR 64-65 F 6
Tejo, Rio ~ P 98-99 C 5
Tejon Pass ▲ USA (CA) 248-249 F 5
Tejupilco de Hidalgo ○ MEX 52-53 D 2
Tekadu ○ PNG 183 D 4
Te Kaha ○ NZ 182 F 2
Tekamah ○ USA (NE) 262-263 K 3
Tékane ○ RIM 196-197 C 6
Tekapo, Lake ○ NZ 182 C 5
Tekax de Álvaro Obregón ○ MEX 52-53 K 1
Teke, köli ○ KA 124-125 H 2
Tekeim ○ SUD 206-207 K 3
Tekek, Kampung ○ • MAL 162-163 F 3
Tekeli ○ KA 124-125 L 6
Tékélit, I-n- < BF 202-203 L 2
Tekes ○ VRC 146-147 E 4
Tekes He ~ VRC 146-147 E 4
Teketau ⛰ KA 126-127 P 2
Tekezē Wenz ~ ETH 200-201 J 6
Tekhammalt, Oued ~ DZ 190-191 D 9
Tekhammat, Oued ~ DZ 190-191 G 7
Tekirdağ ★ TR 128-129 B 2
Tekit ○ MEX 52-53 K 1
Tekkali ○ IND 142-143 D 6
Teklatnika River ~ USA 20-21 Q 4
Tekman ★ TR 128-129 J 3
Teknaf ○ BD 142-143 H 5
Tekoa ○ USA (WA) 244-245 H 3
Tėkodel'ka ~ RUS 114-115 Q 2
Tekom ○ MEX 52-53 K 1
Tekouiat, Oued ~ DZ 190-191 D 9
Tékro ○ TCH 198-199 K 3
Teku ○ RI 164-165 H 4
Te Kuiti ○ NZ 182 E 3
Tela ○ HN 52-53 L 4
Tela ○ ZRE 214-215 E 7
Telaga ○ RI 168 C 3
Telagapulang ○ RI 162-163 K 6
Telan, ostrov ⌒ RUS 120-121 S 3
Telanskij, mys ▲ RUS 120-121 S 3
Telaqua Lake ○ USA 20-21 N 6
Telarah ○ AUS 178-179 J 2
Telares ○ RA 76-77 F 5
Tel Ashqelon ∴ • IL 130-131 D 2
Télatai ○ RMM 196-197 L 6
Telavi ○ GE 126-127 F 7
Tel Aviv-Yafo ★ IL 130-131 D 1
Telč ○ ••• CZ 92-93 N 4
Telchac ○ MEX 52-53 K 1
Telde ○ E 188-189 D 7
Tele ~ ZRE 210-211 K 2
Télé, Lac ○ RMM 196-197 J 6
Teleckoe, ozero ○ • RUS 124-125 P 3
Telefomin ○ PNG 183 A 3
Telegootherra, Mount ▲ AUS 176-177 D 3
Telegraph ○ USA (TX) 266-267 H 3
Telegraph Creek ○ CDN 32-33 E 3
Telegraph Range ⛰ CDN (BC) 228-229 L 3
Telekitonga ⌒ TON 184 IV a 2
Telekól ○ KA 124-125 E 6
Telekól kanal < KA 124-125 E 6
Telêmaco Borba ○ BR 74-75 E 5
Télemsès ○ RN 198-199 B 5
Telemzane < DZ 190-191 E 4
Telen ~ RI 164-165 E 3
Teleneşt' = Teleneşti ★ MD 102-103 F 4
Teleneşti ★ MD 102-103 F 4
Telenešty = Teleneşti ★ MD 102-103 F 4
Teleorman ~ RO 102-103 D 5
Telerghma ○ DZ 190-191 F 2
Telerhteba, Djebel ▲ DZ 190-191 F 8
Teles Pires ou São Manuel, Rio ~ BR 70-71 K 4
Telfer ○ • AUS 172-173 F 6
Telfordville ○ CDN (ALB) 232-233 D 2
Telhāra ○ IND 138-139 F 9
Télimélé ○ RG 202-203 D 4
Teljo, Ǧabal ▲ SUD 200-201 B 5
Telkwa ○ CDN (BC) 228-229 G 2
Telkwa River ~ CDN (BC) 228-229 G 2
Tell ○ USA (TX) 264-265 D 4
Tell Atlas = Atlas Tellien ⛰ DZ 190-191 B 3
Tell City ○ USA (IN) 274-275 M 7
Teller ○ USA 20-21 G 4
Telli, I-n- < RMM 196-197 M 6
Tellico Lake < USA (TN) 282-283 C 5
Tellis < TCH 198-199 H 5
Tello, Chute du ~ • CAM 204-205 K 5
Telloh ∴ • IRQ 128-129 M 7
Telluride ○ USA (CO) 254-255 H 6
Tèlmen = Övögdij ○ MAU 148-149 C 3
Tèlmèn nuur ○ MAU 148-149 C 3
Telmet, Col de ▲ DZ 190-191 E 3
Telogia Creek ~ USA (FL) 286-287 E 1
Teloloapan ○ MEX 52-53 E 2
Telouèt ○ • MA 188-189 H 5
Telpani ○ NEP 144-145 C 6
Telpoziz, gora ▲ RUS 114-115 E 3
Telsang ○ IND 140-141 F 2
Telsen ○ RA 78-79 F 7
Telšiai ★ •• LT 94-95 H 4
Telteté ○ ETH 208-209 C 6
Teltsch = Telč ○ CZ 92-93 N 4
Telukan ○ RI 168 C 7
Telukbatang ○ RI 162-163 H 5
Telukbayur ○ RI (KTI) 164-165 E 2
Telukbayur ○ RI (SUB) 162-163 D 5
Telukbetung = Bandar Lampung ★ RI 162-163 F 7
Telukdalam ○ RI 162-163 B 4
Teluk Intan ○ • MAL 162-163 D 2
Teluk Kumbar ○ MAL 162-163 D 2
Teluklembu, Ujung ▲ RI 162-163 D 5
Teluknibung ○ RI 162-163 C 3
Teluk Penarik ≈ 162-163 G 3
Telukpulaidalem ○ RI 162-163 C 3
Teluk Sinabang ≈ 162-163 B 3
Teluku ○ RI 164-165 H 5
Tely ~ ZRE 212-213 A 2
Tem ○ RN 202-203 L 2
Téma ○ BF 202-203 K 3
Téma ○ • GH 202-203 K 7
Temacine ○ DZ 190-191 F 4
Temagami ○ CDN (ONT) 236-237 J 5
Temagami, Lake ○ CDN (ONT) 238-239 E 2
Temanggung ○ RI 168 D 3
Temascal, El ○ MEX 50-51 K 5
Temascaltepec ○ MEX 52-53 D 2
Temax ○ MEX 52-53 K 1
Temazcal ○ MEX 52-53 F 2
Temazcaltepec ○ MEX 52-53 F 3
Temba ○ ZA 220-221 J 2
Tembagapura ○ RI 166-167 J 4
Tembe Elefant Reserve ⊥ ZA 220-221 L 3
Tembeling ○ • MAL 162-163 E 2
Tembenči ~ RUS 116-117 J 3
Tembenči, ozero ○ RUS 116-117 G 2
Tembesi ~ RI 162-163 E 6
Tembilahan ○ RI 162-163 E 5
Tembito ○ RI 164-165 G 3
Tembladera ○ PE 64-65 C 5
Temblador ○ YV 60-61 K 3
Tembladeras, Laguna ≈ 52-53 H 4
Temblor Range ⛰ USA (CA) 248-249 D 4
Tembo ○ ZRE 216-217 D 3
Tembo, Chutes ~ ZRE 216-217 D 3
Tembo Aluma ○ ANG 216-217 D 3
Tembwe ○ Z 214-215 G 6
Temcha ~ ETH 208-209 C 3
Témegui, I-n- < RMM 196-197 K 6
Temelon ○ GQ 210-211 C 3
Téméra ○ RMM 196-197 K 6
Temerloh ○ • MAL 162-163 E 3
Teminabuan ○ RI 166-167 F 2
Temir ~ KA 126-127 M 3
Temirlan ★ KA 136-137 L 3
Temirovka ○ KS 146-147 C 4
Temirtau ○ KA 124-125 H 3
Temirtau = Temirtau ○ KA 124-125 H 3
Témiscamie, Rivière ~ CDN 38-39 H 3
Témiscaming ○ CDN (QUE) 238-239 F 2
Témiscamingue, Lac ○ CDN (QUE) 236-237 J 5
Témiscouata, Lac ○ CDN (QUE) 240-241 G 3
Temki ○ TCH 206-207 D 3
Temnik ~ RUS 116-117 M 10
Temnikov ○ RUS 94-95 S 4
Temnyj, mys ▲ RUS 112-113 Q 6
Temo ○ MEX 52-53 H 3
Temon ○ RI 168 D 3
Temora ○ AUS 180-181 J 3
Témoris ○ MEX 50-51 E 4
Tempe ○ USA (AZ) 256-257 D 5
Tempe, Danau ○ RI 164-165 F 6
Tempeh ○ RI 168 E 4
Temperance ○ USA (MI) 272-273 F 6
Tempestad ○ PE 64-65 E 2
Témpio Pausânia ○ I 100-101 B 4
Templadera del Derrumbe, La ○ MEX 50-51 F 5
Temple ○ USA (OK) 264-265 F 4
Temple ○ USA (TX) 266-267 K 2
Temple Bay ≈ 174-175 G 3
Templeman ○ USA (VA) 280-281 K 5
Templer Bank ≃ 160-161 B 7
Temple Terrace ○ USA (FL) 286-287 G 3
Templeton ○ USA (CA) 248-249 D 4
Templo de Viracocha • PE 70-71 B 4
Tempoal de Sánchez ○ MEX 50-51 K 7
Tempué ○ ANG 216-217 E 6
Temrjuk ○ RUS 102-103 K 5
Temrjukskij zaliv ≈ 102-103 K 5
Temuco ★ RCH 78-79 C 5
Temuka ○ NZ 182 C 6
Ten ○ CO 60-61 E 5
Tena ★ EC 64-65 D 2
Tenabó ○ MEX 52-53 J 1
Ténado ○ BF 202-203 J 3
Tenaghau = Aola ○ SOL 184 I e 3
Tenaha ○ USA (TX) 268-269 F 5
Tenakee Springs ○ USA 32-33 C 3
Tenali ○ IND 140-141 J 2
Tenamatua, Gunung ▲ RI 164-165 G 4
Tenancingo ○ MEX 52-53 E 2
Tenasserim = Tanintharı ○ MYA 158-159 E 4
Tenasserim Island ⌒ MYA 158-159 D 4
Tenasserim = Tanintharı ~ MYA 158-159 E 4
Tenau ○ RI 166-167 B 7
Tenaún ○ RCH 78-79 C 7
Tenby ○ • GB 90-91 E 6
Tendaba ○ WAG 202-203 C 3
Tendaho ○ ETH 208-209 E 3
Ten Degree Channel ≈ 140-141 L 4
Tendik ○ KA 124-125 J 3
Tendjedj ⛰ DZ 190-191 F 9
Tendō ○ J 152-153 J 5
Tendouk ○ SN 202-203 B 3
Tendoy ○ USA (ID) 252-253 E 2
Tendrara ○ MA (Fig) 188-189 L 4
Tendrivs'ka Kosa ∸ UA 102-103 G 4
Tendūkheda ○ IND 138-139 G 8
Téné ○ RMM 202-203 H 3
Tenemejai, Tanjung ▲ RI 164-165 G 5
Ténenkou ○ RMM 202-203 H 2
Tenente Marques, Rio ~ BR 70-71 G 2
Ténentou ○ RMM 202-203 G 4
Ténéré ∸ RN 198-199 E 4
Ténéré, Erg du ∸ RN 198-199 E 4
Ténéré du Tafassasset ∸ RN 198-199 E 2
Tenerife ⌒ E 188-189 C 6
Ténès ○ DZ 190-191 C 2
Tengah, Kampung ○ MAL 162-163 F 4
Tengah, Kepulauan ⌒ RI 168 C 6
Tengahdai ○ RI 166-167 B 6
Tengchong ○ VRC 142-143 L 3
Tenggara, Kepulauan ⌒ RI 166-167 F 5
Tenggarong ○ • RI 164-165 E 4
Tengger Shamo ∸ VRC 154-155 D 2
Tenggol, Pulau ⌒ MAL 162-163 E 2
Tengiz, köli ○ KA 124-125 F 3
Tengiz-Kürgalža ojpaty ∸ KA 124-125 F 3
Teng Kangpoche ▲ NEP 144-145 F 7
Tengréla ★ CI 202-203 G 4
Teng Xian ○ VRC 156-157 G 5
Tengzhou ○ VRC 154-155 K 4
Tenharim/ Igarapé Prêto, Área Indígena ✗ BR 66-67 G 7
Tenharim/ Transamazônica, Área Indígena ✗ BR 66-67 F 7
Teniente 1° Alfredo Stroessner ○ PY 76-77 G 2
Teniente Enciso, Parque Nacional ⊥ PY 76-77 G 2
Teniente General J.C. Sánchez ○ RA 76-77 H 3
Teniente Matienzo ○ ARK 16 G 31
Tenika • RM 222-223 D 9
Tenille ○ USA (FL) 286-287 F 2
Tenindewa ○ AUS 176-177 C 4
Tenino ○ USA (WA) 244-245 C 4
Tenis, ozero ○ RUS 114-115 M 6
Teniz, köli ○ KA 124-125 D 1
Tenja Seda, gora ▲ RUS 88-89 V 2
Tenkanyj, hrebet ⛰ RUS 112-113 Y 3
Tenkāsi ○ IND 140-141 G 6
Tenke ○ ZRE 214-215 D 6
Tenkeli ○ RUS 110-111 Y 4
Tènkèrgynpil'gyn, laguna ≈ 112-113 V 2
Tènki ~ RUS 110-111 T 5
Tenkiller Lake ○ USA (OK) 264-265 K 3
Tenkodogo ★ • BF 202-203 K 4
Tenlāu ○ IND 140-141 L 6
Tenmile Creek ~ USA (LA) 268-269 H 6
Ten Mile Lake ○ CDN (NFL) 242-243 M 1
Ten Mile Pond ○ CDN (NFL) 242-243 P 3
Tennant Creek ○ • AUS 174-175 C 6
Tennent Islands ⌒ CDN 24-25 Y 6
Tennessee ○ USA (TX) 268-269 E 5
Tennessee ◘ USA (TN) 276-277 F 5
Tennessee Ridge ○ USA (TN) 276-277 H 4
Tennessee River ~ USA (TN) 276-277 H 5
Tennessee River ~ USA (TN) 282-283 C 5
Tennille ○ USA (GA) 284-285 H 4
Tennyson ○ USA (TX) 266-267 G 2
Teno ~ FIN 88-89 J 2
Teno, Río ~ RCH 78-79 D 3
Tenochtitlán ○ MEX 52-53 G 3
Tenom ○ MAL 160-161 A 10
Tenosique de Pino Suárez ○ MEX 52-53 J 3
Tenouchfi, Djebel ▲ DZ 188-189 L 3
Tenoûmer ▲ RIM 196-197 E 3
Tenryu-gawa ~ J 152-153 G 7
Tensas River ~ USA (LA) 268-269 J 4
Tensas River National Wildlife Refuge ⊥ USA (LA) 268-269 J 4
Tensaw River ~ USA (AL) 284-285 C 6
Tensed ○ USA (ID) 250-251 C 4
Tensift, Oued ~ MA 188-189 G 5
Ten Sleep ○ USA (WY) 252-253 L 2
Tenstrike ○ USA (MN) 270-271 D 3
T'enta ○ ETH 208-209 D 3
Tente ○ RI 168 D 7
Tentek ~ KA 124-125 M 6
Tenteksor ∸ KA 96-97 H 10
Tenteksor köl ○ KA 124-125 C 2
Tentena ○ RI 164-165 G 4
Tenterfield ○ AUS 178-179 M 5
Ten Thousand Islands ⌒ USA (FL) 286-287 H 6
Tentolotianan, Gunung ▲ RI 164-165 G 3
Tentugal ○ BR 68-69 E 2
Tenuchchad, Oued ~ MA 188-189 G 7
Teo-Ašuu, pereval ▲ KS 136-137 N 3
Teocaltiche ○ MEX 50-51 H 7
Teocuitatlán de Corona ○ MEX 52-53 C 1
Teodoro Sampaio ○ BR (BAH) 72-73 L 2
Teodoro Sampaio ○ BR (PAU) 72-73 D 7
Teodoro Schmidt ○ RCH 78-79 C 5
Teófilo Otoni ○ BR 72-73 K 4
Teofipol' ★ UA 102-103 E 3
Teos • TR 128-129 B 3
Teotepec, Cerro ▲ MEX 52-53 D 3
Teotihuacán ∴ ••• MEX 52-53 E 2
Teotitlán del Camino ○ MEX 52-53 F 2
Tepa ○ GH 202-203 J 6
Tepalcatepec ○ MEX 52-53 C 2
Tepatitlán ○ MEX 52-53 C 1
Tepeaca ○ MEX 52-53 F 2
Tepechitlán ○ MEX 50-51 H 7
Tepecoacuilco ○ MEX 52-53 E 2
Tepehuanes ○ MEX 50-51 G 5
Tepehuanes, Río los ~ MEX 50-51 F 5
Tepeji del Río ○ MEX 52-53 E 2
Tepelenë ★ •• AL 100-101 H 4
Tepere ○ MOC 218-219 K 1
Tepetzintla ○ MEX 50-51 L 7
Tēpī ○ ETH 208-209 B 5
Tepic ★ MEX 50-51 G 7
Tepich ○ MEX 52-53 K 1
Teplice ○ CZ 92-93 M 3
Teplitz = Teplice ○ CZ 92-93 M 3
Teploe ★ RUS 94-95 P 5
Teploključenka ○ KS 146-147 D 4
Tëplyj Ključ ○ RUS 120-121 G 2
Tepoca, Bahía de ≈ 50-51 C 2
Tepoca, Cabo ▲ MEX 50-51 C 3
Teptep ○ PNG 183 D 3
Tepuxtla ○ MEX 50-51 F 6
Tequeje, Río ~ BOL 70-71 D 3
Tequendama, Salto ~ CO 66-67 B 3
Teques, Los ★ YV 60-61 H 2
Tequesquite Creek ~ USA (NM) 256-257 M 3
Tequila ○ • MEX 52-53 C 1
Tequisquiapan ○ MEX 52-53 E 1
Téra ○ RN 202-203 L 2
Tera, Río ~ E 98-99 E 4
Teradomari ○ J 152-153 H 6
Terakeka ○ SUD 206-207 K 6
Téramo ★ I 100-101 D 3
Terán ○ CO 64-65 C 1
Terang ○ AUS 180-181 G 5
Terapo ○ PNG 183 D 5
Teratani ~ PK 138-139 B 5
Teratyn ○ PL 102-103 C 2
Terbanggibesar ○ RI 162-163 F 7
Terbang Selatan, Pulau ⌒ RI 166-167 E 5
Terbjas ○ RUS 118-119 K 3
Tercan ★ TR 128-129 J 3
Terceira ⌒ P 6-7 E 6
Terceiro Acampamento ○ BR 62-63 H 5
Tercero, Río ~ RA 78-79 H 2
Terchicherin, Erg in ∸ RMM 196-197 K 4
Tere ~ RUS 116-117 G 4
Terebija ~ UA 102-103 C 3
Terebo ○ PNG 183 B 2
Terebovlja ★ UA 102-103 D 3
Terek ○ RUS 126-127 F 6
Terek ~ RUS 126-127 G 6
Terekhol ○ IND 140-141 E 3
Terekli-Mekteb ○ RUS 126-127 F 5
Térékolé ~ RMM 202-203 F 2
Terekti ○ KA 124-125 F 4
Tèrèlž ○ MAU 148-149 H 4
Terence Bay ○ CDN (NS) 240-241 M 6
Teren'ga ★ RUS 96-97 F 7
Terengganu ◘ MAL 162-163 E 2
Terengganu, Kuala ★ • MAL 162-163 E 2
Terenni ∴ • RIM 196-197 F 6
Terenos ○ BR 70-71 K 7
Terepaima, Parque Nacional ⊥ YV 60-61 G 3
Teresén ○ YV 60-61 K 2
Teresina ★ BR 68-69 G 4
Tereška ~ RUS 96-97 E 7
Teresópolis ○ BR 72-73 J 7
Terezinha de Goiás ○ BR 72-73 G 2
Terezy Klavenes, zaliv ≈ 108-109 f 3
Teriberka ○ RUS 88-89 N 2
Teriberka ~ RUS 88-89 N 2
Teridgerie Creek ~ AUS 178-179 K 6
Terina ~ RUS 116-117 J 6
Terin Kōt ★ AFG 134-135 L 2
Terisakkan ~ KA 124-125 E 3
Terlingua ○ USA (TX) 266-267 D 4
Terlingua Creek ~ USA (TX) 266-267 D 4
Terma, Ra's ▲ ER 200-201 L 6
Terma do Quilombo • BR 72-73 F 7
Termas de Chillán ○ RCH 78-79 D 4
Termas del Flaco ○ RCH 78-79 D 3
Termas de Pemehue ○ RCH 78-79 D 5
Termas Talacasto • RA 76-77 C 6
Terme ★ TR 128-129 G 2
Termessó ○ RG 202-203 D 3
Termez ★ • US 136-137 K 6
Termiang, Pulau ⌒ RI 162-163 F 4
Términi Imerese ○ I 100-101 D 6
Términi Imerese, Golfo di ≈ 100-101 D 5
Terminillo, Monte ▲ • I 100-101 D 3
Términos, Laguna de ≈ 52-53 J 2
Termit < RN 198-199 E 4
Termit, Massif de ⛰ RN 198-199 E 4
Termit-Kaoboul ○ RN 198-199 E 5
Térmoli ○ I 100-101 E 3
Term Point ▲ CDN 30-31 X 4
Ternate ○ • RI 164-165 K 3
Ternay, Lac ○ CDN 38-39 K 2
Ternej ○ RUS 122-123 G 6
Terni ★ I 100-101 D 3
Ternopil' ★ UA 102-103 D 3
Ternopol' = Ternopil' ★ UA 102-103 D 3
Terolak, Kampung ○ MAL 162-163 D 2
Terou ~ DY 202-203 L 5
Terowie ○ AUS 180-181 E 2
Terpenija, mys ▲ RUS 122-123 L 4
Terpenija, poluostrov ⌵ RUS 122-123 L 4
Terpenija, zaliv ≈ 122-123 K 4
Terpjaj-Tumsa, poluostrov ⌵ RUS 110-111 M 3
Terra Alta ○ BR 68-69 E 2
Terra Bella ○ USA (CA) 248-249 E 4
Terra Boa ○ BR 72-73 D 7
Terra Branca ○ BR 72-73 J 4
Terrace ○ CDN (BC) 228-229 F 2
Terracebaai ○ NAM 216-217 B 9
Terrace Bay ○ CDN (ONT) 234-235 Q 6
Terrace Mountain ▲ USA (UT) 254-255 B 2
Terraces, The ⛰ AUS 176-177 F 4
Terracina ○ I 100-101 D 4
Terra de Areia ○ BR 74-75 E 7
Terra Firma ○ ZA 220-221 F 2
Terråk ○ N 86-87 F 4
Terral ○ USA (OK) 264-265 G 5
Terralba ○ I 100-101 B 5
Terra Nivea ⛰ CDN 36-37 Q 3
Terra Nova ○ BR (ACR) 66-67 C 7
Terra Nova ○ BR (PER) 68-69 J 6
Terra Nova ○ CDN (NFL) 242-243 O 4
Terra Nova do Norte ○ BR 70-71 K 2
Terra Nova National Park ⊥ CDN (NFL) 242-243 O 4
Terra Preta ○ BR 66-67 H 6
Terra Preta, Igarapé ~ BR 66-67 H 5
Terra Vermelha ○ BR 76-77 J 1
Terrebonne ○ CDN (QUE) 238-239 M 3
Terrebonne ○ USA (OR) 244-245 D 6
Terrebonne Bay ≈ USA 268-269 K 7
Terre Haute ○ USA (IN) 274-275 L 5
Terrell ○ USA (TX) 264-265 H 6
Terrenate ○ MEX 52-53 F 2
Terrenceville ○ CDN (NFL) 242-243 O 5
Terre Noire Creek ~ USA (AR) 276-277 B 6
Terreton ○ USA (ID) 252-253 F 3
Terrier Rouge ○ RH 54-55 K 5
Terril ○ USA (IA) 274-275 D 1
Terry ○ USA (MT) 250-251 O 5
Terry Hie Hie ○ AUS 178-179 L 5
Tersakan Gölü ○ TR 128-129 E 3
Tersakkan ~ KA 124-125 E 4
Terschelling ⌒ NL 92-93 H 2
Tersef ○ TCH 198-199 H 6
Terskej Ala-Too', hrebet ⛰ KS 146-147 C 4
Terskenespe ~ KA 124-125 E 5
Terskij bereg ⌵ RUS 88-89 O 3
Tersko-Kumskij kanal < RUS 126-127 F 5
Terter ~ AZ 128-129 M 2
Terter = Tartar ○ AZ 128-129 M 2
Tertež ○ RUS 116-117 F 8
Teruel ○ CO 60-61 D 6
Teruel ○ ••• E 98-99 G 4
Terujak ○ RI 162-163 B 2
Tervel ○ BG 102-103 E 6
Tervo ○ FIN 88-89 J 5
Tervola ○ FIN 88-89 H 3
Tes' ○ RUS 116-117 E 8
Tes, Lake = Letas, Lac ○ VAN 184 II a 2
Tes = Zur ○ MAU 116-117 G 11
Tesalia ○ CO 60-61 D 6
Teschen = Český Těšín ○ CZ 92-93 P 4
Tescott ○ USA (KS) 262-263 J 5
Tésécau, Lac ○ CDN 38-39 G 3
Teselima ○ GH 202-203 J 5
Teseny ○ ER 200-201 H 5
Tès gol ~ MAU 116-117 F 10
Tès gol ~ MAU 148-149 C 3
Teshekpuk Lake ○ USA 20-21 O 1
Tes-Hem ~ RUS 116-117 G 10
Teshikaga ○ J 152-153 L 3
Teshio-santi ⛰ J 152-153 J 3
Teslin ○ CDN 20-21 Y 6
Teslin Lake ○ CDN 20-21 Y 7
Teslin River ~ CDN 20-21 X 6
Tesouras, Rio ~ BR 72-73 E 3
Tessalit ○ RMM 196-197 L 4
Tessaoua ○ RN 198-199 D 6
Tessaout, Oued ~ MA 188-189 H 5
Tesselamane < RMM 196-197 M 6
Tessema ~ RUS 108-109 e 3
Tesseralik ○ CDN 36-37 R 2
Tesséroukane < RN 198-199 C 3
Tessier, Lac ○ CDN (QUE) 236-237 N 4
Tessik Lake ○ CDN 36-37 M 2
Tessiner Alpen = Alpi Ticinese ⛰ CH 92-93 K 5
Tessit ○ RMM 202-203 L 2
Tessounfat < RMM 196-197 L 4
Test, Tizi-n ▲ MA 188-189 G 5
Teste, la ○ F 90-91 G 9
Testerazo, El ○ MEX 50-51 A 1
Testigos, Islas Los ⌒ YV 60-61 K 2
Testour ○ TN 190-191 G 2
Tesuque Indian Reservation ✗ USA (NM) 256-257 K 3
Têt ~ F 90-91 J 10
Tetachuck Lake ○ CDN (BC) 228-229 J 3
Tètanto, ozero ○ RUS 108-109 O 7
Tetas, Punta ▲ RCH 76-77 B 2
Tetcela River ~ CDN 30-31 H 5
Tete ◘ MOC 218-219 F 2
Tete ★ MOC (Tet) 218-219 G 3
Tété ~ RCA 206-207 E 4
Tetebatu ○ • RI 168 C 7
Tête d'Ours, Lac ○ CDN 30-31 O 4
Tetehui ○ PNG 183 C 4
Teteja ~ RUS 116-117 M 5
Tête Jaune Cache ○ CDN (BC) 228-229 P 4
Tetepare ⌒ SOL 184 I c 3
Tètèrè ~ RUS 116-117 L 5
Te Te Re ○ SOL 184 I e 4
Teteriv ~ UA 102-103 G 2
Teterow ○ • D (MVP) 92-93 M 2
Teteven ○ BG 102-103 D 6
Tethul River ~ CDN 30-31 O 5
Tetijiv ★ UA 102-103 F 3
Tétini ⛰ RG 202-203 F 5
Tetjuši ★ RUS 96-97 F 6
Tetlin Junction ○ USA 20-21 T 5
Tetlin Lake ○ USA 20-21 T 5
Tetlin River ~ USA 20-21 T 5
Tetonia ○ USA (ID) 252-253 G 3
Teton River ~ USA (MT) 250-251 H 4
Teton Village ○ USA (WY) 252-253 H 3
Tétouan = Tiṭwān ★ • MA 188-189 J 3
Tetovo ○ • MK 100-101 H 3
Tetris, Monte ▲ RA 80 D 4
Tetulia ~ BD 142-143 G 4
Teturi ○ ZRE 212-213 B 3
Teuco, Río ~ RA 76-77 F 2
Teulada ○ I 100-101 B 5
Teulada, Capo ▲ I 100-101 B 5
Teulon ○ CDN (MAN) 234-235 F 4
Teun, Pulau ⌒ RI 166-167 E 5
Teuquito, Arroyo ~ RA 76-77 G 3
Teuri-tō ⌵ J 152-153 J 2
Teutoburger Wald ⛰ D 92-93 J 2
Teutônia ○ BR 74-75 E 7
Teutonic Mining Centre ○ AUS 176-177 F 4
Tévere ~ I 100-101 D 3
Teverya ★ IL 130-131 D 1
Tevi, mys ▲ RUS 120-121 T 4
Tevriz ★ RUS 114-115 M 6
Te Waewae Bay ≈ 182 A 7
Tewah ○ RI 162-163 K 5
Tewantin ○ AUS 178-179 M 4
Têwo ○ VRC 154-155 C 4
Tewure ○ WAN 204-205 F 4
Texada Island ⌒ CDN (BC) 230-231 E 4
Texana, Lake < USA (TX) 266-267 L 5
Texarkana ○ USA (AR) 276-277 B 7
Texas ○ AUS 178-179 L 5
Texas ◘ USA (TX) 266-267 D 3
Texas City ○ USA (TX) 268-269 F 7
Texas Downs ○ AUS 172-173 J 4
Texas Point ▲ USA (TX) 268-269 G 7
Texcoco ○ MEX 52-53 E 2
Texel ⌒ NL 92-93 H 2
Texhoma ○ USA (TX) 264-265 C 2
Texiguat ○ HN 52-53 L 5
Texline ○ USA (TX) 264-265 A 2
Texola ○ USA (OK) 264-265 E 3
Texoma, Lake ○ USA (OK) 264-265 H 5
Texon ○ USA (TX) 266-267 F 2
Teyateyaneng ○ LS 220-221 H 4
Teymurlu ○ IR 128-129 L 4
Teyune •• CO 60-61 E 2
Tezejol ○ TM 136-137 G 6
Teziutlán ○ MEX 52-53 F 2
Tezpur ○ • IND 142-143 H 2
Tezzeron Creek ~ CDN (BC) 228-229 K 2
Tezzeron Lake ○ CDN (BC) 228-229 K 2
Tfaritiy ○ MA 188-189 F 7
Tha-Anne River ~ CDN 30-31 V 5
Thaba Nchu ○ ZA 220-221 H 4
Thaba Putsoa ⛰ LS 220-221 H 5
Thaba Tseka ○ LS 220-221 J 4
Thabazimbi ○ ZA 220-221 H 2
Thabeikkyin ○ MYA 142-143 J 4
Tha Bo ○ THA 158-159 G 2
Tha Champa ○ THA 158-159 H 2
Thach An ○ VN 156-157 E 5
Tha Chana ○ THA 158-159 E 6
Thạch Bi ○ VN 158-159 K 3
Thạch Tru ○ VN 158-159 K 3
Thackaringa ∴ AUS 180-181 F 2
Thādiq ○ KSA 130-131 J 5
Thafmakó ○ GR 100-101 J 5
Thagaya ○ MYA 142-143 K 6
Thái Bình ★ VN 156-157 E 6
Thái Hòa ★ VN 156-157 D 7
Thailand, Gulf of ≈ 158-159 F 5
Thailand = Muang Thai ■ THA 158-159 E 2
Thái Nguyên ★ VN 156-157 D 6
Thakadu ○ RB 218-219 D 5
Thakaundrove Peninsula ⌵ FJI 184 III b 2
Thakurgaon ○ BD 142-143 F 2
Thal ○ PK 138-139 C 3
Thala ○ TN 190-191 G 3
Thalang ○ THA 158-159 E 6
Thalberg ○ CDN (MAN) 234-235 G 4
Thalbitzer, Cape ▲ CDN 24-25 h 6
Thal Canal < PK 138-139 C 4
Thale Luang ≈ 158-159 F 7
Thalia ○ USA (TX) 264-265 E 5
Thallon ○ AUS 178-179 K 5
Thalpar ○ IND 138-139 E 2
Thamad al Qaṭṭār < LAR 192-193 F 3
Thamad Bū Hashishah < LAR 192-193 H 4
Thamad Qabr Ṣāliḥ < LAR 192-193 D 2
Thamaga ○ RB 220-221 G 2
Tha Mai ○ THA 158-159 G 4
Thames ~ GB 90-91 G 6
Thames River ~ CDN (ONT) 238-239 D 6
Thames River ~ USA (CT) 280-281 O 2
Thamesville ○ CDN (ONT) 238-239 D 6
Tham Than National Park ⊥ THA 158-159 E 3
Thana ○ IND 138-139 D 10
Thanatpin ○ MYA 158-159 D 2
Thanbyuzayat ○ MYA 158-159 D 3
Thăng Bình ○ VN 158-159 K 3
Thangoo ○ AUS 172-173 F 5
Thanh Hóa ○ VN 158-159 J 2
Thanh Hóa ★ VN 156-157 D 7
Thành Phố Hồ Chí Minh ★ • VN 158-159 J 5
Thanh Sơn ★ VN 156-157 D 6
Thanjavur ○ ••• IND 140-141 H 5
Thankot ○ NEP 144-145 E 7
Than Kyun ⌒ MYA 158-159 E 6
Thanlwin Myit ~ MYA 142-143 K 6
Thāno Būla Khān ○ PK 134-135 M 6
Than Uyên ★ VN 156-157 C 6
Thanyit ○ MYA 142-143 J 3
Thanze ○ MYA 158-159 C 2
Thaoge ~ RB 218-219 B 4
Thaolintoa Lake ○ CDN 30-31 V 5
Thảo Phi Tung ○ VN 156-157 D 5
Tha Pla ○ THA 158-159 F 2
Thap Put ○ THA 158-159 E 6
Thap Sakae ○ THA 158-159 E 5
Thap Than ○ THA 158-159 E 3
Thar ∸ IND 138-139 C 6
Tharād ○ IND 138-139 C 7
Tharaka ○ EAK 212-213 G 4
Tharb ○ KSA 130-131 G 5
Thar Desert ∸ PK 138-139 B 6
Thargomindah ○ AUS 178-179 G 5
Tharp Fracture Zone ≃ 14-15 O 13
Thárros • I 100-101 B 5
Tharsis ○ E 98-99 D 6
Tha Sae ○ THA 158-159 E 5
Tha Sala ○ THA 158-159 E 6
Tha Song Yang ○ THA 158-159 E 2
Thássos ○ GR 100-101 K 4
Thássos ⌒ GR 100-101 K 4
Thatcher ○ USA (AZ) 256-257 F 6
Thatcher ○ USA (CO) 254-255 L 6
Thất Khê ★ VN 156-157 E 5
Thaton ○ MYA 158-159 D 2
That Phanom ○ THA 158-159 H 2
Thatta ○ ••• PK 134-135 M 6
Tha Tum ○ THA 158-159 G 3
Thaungdut ○ MYA 142-143 J 3
Tha Uthen ○ THA 158-159 H 2
Tha Wang Pha ○ THA 142-143 M 6
Thayawthadangyi Kyun ⌒ MYA 158-159 D 4
Thayer ○ USA (KS) 262-263 L 7
Thayer ○ USA (MO) 276-277 D 4
Thayetmyo ○ MYA 142-143 J 6
Thayne ○ USA (WY) 252-253 H 4
Theba ○ USA (AZ) 256-257 C 6
The Beaches ○ CDN (NFL) 242-243 M 3
The Berkshire ⛰ USA (MA) 278-279 H 6
Thebes ∴ ••• ET 194-195 F 5
The Brothers = Lloyd Rock ⌒ BS 54-55 H 3
The Current ○ BS 54-55 G 2
Thedford ○ USA (NE) 262-263 F 3
Theewaterskloof Dam < ZA 220-221 D 7
The Forks ○ USA (ME) 278-279 M 3
The Gap ○ USA (AZ) 256-257 D 2
The Grenadines ⌒ WV 56 E 5
Theinkun ○ MYA 158-159 E 5
Thekkadi ○ IND 140-141 G 6
Thekulthili Lake ○ CDN 30-31 P 5
Thelon River ~ CDN 30-31 R 4
Thenia ○ DZ 190-191 D 2
Theniet El Had ○ DZ 190-191 D 3
Thenzawl ○ IND 142-143 H 4
Theo, Mount ▲ AUS 172-173 K 6
The Oaks ○ USA (CA) 248-249 F 5
Theodore ○ AUS 178-179 L 3
Theodore ○ CDN (SAS) 232-233 Q 4
Theodore ○ USA (AL) 284-285 B 6
Theodore Roosevelt Lake < USA (AZ) 256-257 D 5
Theodore Roosevelt National Park North Unit ⊥ USA (ND) 258-259 D 4
Theodore Roosevelt National Park South Unit ⊥ USA (ND) 258-259 D 5
Theodosia ○ USA (MO) 276-277 C 4
Thep Sa Thit ○ THA 158-159 F 3
Therhi ○ PK 138-139 B 6
Thermaïkós Kólpos ≈ 100-101 J 4
Thermal City ○ USA (NC) 282-283 F 5
Thermopolis ○ USA (WY) 252-253 K 3
Theron Range ⛰ ARK 16 E 0
The Settlement ○ GB (VI) 286-287 R 2
The Shoals Provincial Park ⊥ CDN (ONT) 236-237 E 5
Thesiger Bay ≈ 24-25 K 5
The Slot = New Georgia Sound ≈ 184 I c 2
Thessalía ⌵ GR 100-101 H 5
Thessalía ◘ GR 100-101 H 5
Thessalon ○ CDN (ONT) 238-239 B 2
Thessaloníki ★ ••• GR 100-101 J 4
Thetford ○ GB 90-91 H 5
Thetford Mines ○ CDN (QUE) 238-239 O 2
Thetis Island ○ CDN (BC) 230-231 F 5
Theunissen ○ ZA 220-221 H 4
Thevenard Island ⌒ AUS 172-173 B 6
The Village ○ USA (OK) 264-265 G 3
The Village of Soya Atlas (Victoria Fort) ∴ • RI 166-167 E 3
The Wash ≈ 90-91 H 5
Thiamis ○ GR 100-101 H 5
Thibodaux ○ USA (LA) 268-269 K 7
Thicket Portage ○ CDN 34-35 H 3
Thickwood Hills ⛰ CDN (SAS) 232-233 L 2
Thief Lake Wildlife Refuge ⊥ USA (MN) 270-271 C 2
Thief River Falls ○ USA (MN) 270-271 B 2
Thiel Mountains ⛰ ARK 16 E 0
Thiès ★ • SN 202-203 B 2
Thika ○ EAK 212-213 F 4
Thillé Boubakar ○ SN 196-197 C 6
Thilogne ○ SN 196-197 D 7
Thimphu ★ • BHT 142-143 F 2
Thingsat ○ IND 142-143 H 3
Thionville ○ F 90-91 L 7
Thíra ○ GR 100-101 K 6
Thíra ⌒ •• GR 100-101 K 6
Thirsk ○ GB 90-91 G 4
Thirsty, Mount ▲ AUS 176-177 F 6
Thirtymile Creek ~ USA (MT) 250-251 L 3
Thirty Mile Lake ○ CDN 30-31 V 4
Thiruvallar Temple • IND 140-141 H 5
Thiruvarur ○ IND 140-141 H 5
Thisbi ○ GR 100-101 J 5
Thisted ○ DK 86-87 D 8
Thistle Island ⌒ AUS 180-181 D 3
Thitani ○ EAK 212-213 F 4
Thiva ○ GR 100-101 J 5
Thị Xã Sơn Tây ★ VN 156-157 D 6
Thlewiaza River ~ CDN 30-31 V 5
Thoa River ~ CDN 30-31 Q 5
Thổ Chu, Hòn ⌒ VN 158-159 G 6
Thoen ○ THA 158-159 E 2
Thoeng ○ THA 142-143 M 6
Thohoyandou ★ ZA 218-219 F 6
Thomas ○ USA (OK) 264-265 F 3
Thomas ○ USA (SD) 260-261 J 2
Thomas ○ USA (WV) 280-281 G 4
Thomas Hill Reservoir ○ USA (MO) 274-275 F 5

Thomas Hubbard, Cape ▲ CDN 26-27 C 3
Thomas Lake, J.B. ⊙ USA (TX) 264-265 C 6
Thomas-Müntzer-Stadt Mühlhausen = Mühlhausen o • D 92-93 L 3
Thomas Pass ▲ USA (UT) 254-255 B 4
Thomas River ~ AUS 176-177 D 2
Thomassique o RH 54-55 K 5
Thomaston o USA (AL) 284-285 C 4
Thomaston o USA (GA) 284-285 F 4
Thomaston Corner o CDN (NB) 240-241 H 5
Thomasville o USA (AL) 284-285 C 5
Thomasville o USA (GA) 284-285 G 6
Thomasville o USA (NC) 282-283 G 5
Thom Bay o CDN 24-25 a 5
Thomonde o RH 54-55 K 5
Thompson o CDN 34-35 H 3
Thompson o USA (ND) 258-259 K 4
Thompson Falls o USA (MT) 250-251 D 4
Thompson Island ⌒ CDN (ONT) 234-235 O 6
Thompson Pass ▲ USA 20-21 S 6
Thompson Peak ▲ USA (CA) 246-247 C 2
Thompson River ~ CDN (BC) 230-231 H 3
Thompson River ~ USA (MO) 274-275 E 4
Thompson River ~ USA (MT) 250-251 D 4
Thompson River, North ~ CDN (BC) 230-231 K 2
Thompson Sound o CDN (BC) 230-231 C 3
Thomsen River ~ CDN 24-25 M 4
Thomson o USA (GA) 284-285 H 3
Thomson Dam < AUS 180-181 J 4
Thomson River ~ AUS 178-179 G 3
Thong Pha Phum o THA 158-159 E 3
Thongwa o MYA 158-159 D 2
Thôn Hai o VN 158-159 J 2
Thonon-les-Bains o • F 90-91 L 8
Thorburn o CDN (NS) 240-241 N 5
Thoreau o USA (NM) 256-257 G 3
Thornapple River ~ USA (MI) 272-273 D 5
Thornburg o USA (IA) 274-275 F 3
Thornbury o CDN (ONT) 238-239 E 4
Thorndale o USA (TX) 266-267 K 3
Thorndale o ZA 218-219 E 6
Thorne o CDN (ONT) 238-239 F 2
Thorne o USA (NV) 246-247 G 5
Thorne River ~ CDN 34-35 L 3
Thornhill o CDN (BC) 228-229 F 2
Thorn Hill o USA (TN) 282-283 D 4
Thornlea o CDN (NFL) 242-243 P 5
Thornloe o CDN (ONT) 236-237 J 5
Thornton o USA (AR) 276-277 C 7
Thornton o USA (IA) 274-275 E 2
Thornton o USA (WA) 244-245 H 3
Thorntonia o AUS 174-175 E 6
Thorntown o USA (IN) 274-275 M 4
Thorp o USA (WI) 270-271 H 6
Thorpe Reservoir < USA (NC) 282-283 D 5
Thorsby o CDN (ALB) 232-233 E 2
Thorshavn = Tórshavn ☆ FR 90-91 D 1
Thors Land ∸ GRØ 28-29 U 5
Thốt Nốt o VN 158-159 H 5
Thou o BF 202-203 J 3
Thouars o F 90-91 G 8
Thouet ~ F 90-91 G 8
Thouin, Cape ▲ AUS 172-173 D 6
Thourout = Torhout o B 92-93 G 3
Thousand Oaks o USA (CA) 248-249 F 5
Thousand Palms o USA (CA) 248-249 H 6
Thousand Springs o USA (NV) 246-247 L 2
Thrakiko Pelagos ≈ 100-101 K 4
Three Creek o USA (ID) 252-253 C 4
Three Creeks o USA (AR) 276-277 C 7
Three Forks o USA (MT) 250-251 H 6
Three Graces • AUS 174-175 C 4
Three Hills o CDN (ALB) 232-233 E 4
Threehills Creek ~ CDN (ALB) 232-233 E 3
Three Hummock Island ⌒ AUS 180-181 H 6
Three Lakes o USA (MI) 270-271 K 4
Three Lakes o USA (WI) 270-271 J 5
Three Mile Beach ∸ AUS 176-177 C 4
Three Mile Rock o CDN (NFL) 242-243 L 3
Three Point o USA (CA) 248-249 F 5
Three Rivers o AUS 176-177 E 2
Three Rivers o USA (MI) 272-273 D 6
Three Rivers o USA (NM) 256-257 J 5
Three Rivers o USA (TX) 266-267 J 5
Three Rocks o USA (CA) 248-249 D 3
Three Sisters ▲ AUS 178-179 F 3
Three Sisters ▲ USA (OR) 244-245 D 6
Three Sisters o ZA 220-221 F 5
Three Sisters, The ⌒ AUS 174-175 G 2
Three Sisters Islands = Olu Malua ⌒ SOL 184 I f 4
Three Springs o AUS 176-177 C 4
Three Valley o CDN (BC) 230-231 L 3
Three Ways Roadhouse o AUS 174-175 C 6
Throat River ~ CDN (ONT) 234-235 K 3
Throckmorton o USA (TX) 264-265 E 5
Throne o CDN (ALB) 232-233 G 3
Throssel, Lake ⊙ AUS 176-177 G 3
Throssell Range ▲ AUS 172-173 E 6
Thua ~ EAK 212-213 G 4
Thuận Châu ☆ VN 156-157 C 6
Thubun Lake ⊙ CDN 30-31 O 5
Thubun River ~ CDN 30-31 O 5
Thuburbo Majus ∴ • TN 190-191 G 2
Thuchonilini Lake ⊙ CDN 30-31 V 5
Thucúc o VN 156-157 C 6
Thu Cúc o VN 156-157 D 6
Thủ Dầu Một ☆ VN 158-159 J 5
Thud Point ▲ AUS 174-175 F 3
Thủ Đức o VN 158-159 J 5
Thuillier, Mount ▲ IND 140-141 L 6
Thul o PK 138-139 B 5
Thule = Qaanaaq ☆ GRØ 26-27 Q 5
Thuli o ZW (Mas) 218-219 E 5
Thuli ~ ZW 218-219 E 5
Thuli Safari Area ⊥ ZW 218-219 E 5
Thundelarra o AUS 176-177 D 4
Thunder Bay o CDN (ONT) 234-235 O 6
Thunder Bay ⊙ CDN (ONT) 234-235 O 6
Thunder Bay ⊙ USA (MI) 272-273 F 3
Thunder Bay ⊙ USA (MI) 272-273 F 2
Thunder Bay River ~ USA (MI) 272-273 F 2
Thunderbird, Lake < USA (OK) 264-265 G 3
Thunderbold o USA (GA) 284-285 J 4
Thunder Butte o USA (SD) 260-261 E 1
Thunderchild Indian Reservation ⚔ CDN (SAS) 232-233 K 2
Thunder Creek o CDN (SAS) 232-233 M 5
Thunder Hawk o USA (SD) 260-261 D 1
Thunder Mount ▲ USA 20-21 K 2
Thunder River o CDN (BC) 228-229 P 4
Thung Muang o THA 142-143 M 6
Thung Salaeng Luang National Park ⊥ THA 158-159 F 2
Thung Song o THA 158-159 E 6
Thung Wa o THA 158-159 E 7
Thung Yai o THA 158-159 E 6
Thung Yai Naresuan Wildlife Reserve ⊥ ••• THA 158-159 E 3
Thunkar o BHT 142-143 G 2
Thuraiyur o IND 140-141 H 5
Thüringen ▫ D 92-93 L 3
Thüringer Wald ▲ D 92-93 L 3
Thurles = Durlas o IRL 90-91 D 5
Thurlow o CDN (BC) 230-231 D 3
Thurmont o USA (MD) 280-281 J 4
Thurnwald, Pegunungan ▲ RI 166-167 L 4
Thursday Island o •• AUS 174-175 G 2
Thurso o GB 90-91 F 2
Thurston Island ⌒ ARK 16 F 27
Thury, Rivière de ~ CDN 36-37 O 5
Thury-Harcourt o F 90-91 G 7
Thutade Lake ⊙ CDN 32-33 G 3
Thyavanagi o IND 140-141 F 3
Thyborøn o DK 86-87 D 8
Thylungra o AUS 178-179 G 4
Thymania o AUS 178-179 G 2
Thyolo o MW 218-219 H 3
Thyou o BF 202-203 J 4
Thysville = Mbanza-Ngungu o ZRE 210-211 E 6
Tiabaya o PE 70-71 B 5
Tiabiga, Mare ⊙ • DY 202-203 L 4
Tiago o BR 62-63 F 6
Tiahualilo de Zaragoza o MEX 50-51 H 4
Tiahuanaco • BOL 70-71 C 5
Tiahuanacu o BOL 70-71 C 5
Tianamé o RMM 196-197 L 6
Tianbanjie o VRC 156-157 K 2
Tianchang o VRC 154-155 L 5
Tianchi • VRC 146-147 J 4
Tiandong o VRC 156-157 E 5
Tian'e o VRC 156-157 E 4
Tiangol Latiéouol ~ SN 202-203 C 2
Tiângol Louggueré ~ SN 202-203 C 2
Tianguel-Bory o RG 202-203 D 4
Tian Head ▲ CDN (BC) 228-229 A 3
Tianjin ☆ VRC 154-155 K 2
Tianjin Shi ▫ VRC 154-155 K 2
Tianjun o VRC 144-145 M 2
Tiankoura o BF 202-203 J 4
Tianlin o VRC 156-157 E 4
Tianmen o VRC 154-155 H 6
Tianmu Shan ▲ VRC 154-155 L 6
Tianmushan • VRC 154-155 L 6
Tianmushan Z.B. ⊥ • VRC 154-155 L 6
Tiansheng o VRC 154-155 E 6
Tianshui o VRC 154-155 D 4
Tianshuihai o VRC 144-145 B 3
Tiantai o VRC 156-157 M 2
Tiantaishan • VRC 156-157 M 2
Tiantangzhai ▲ VRC 154-155 J 6
Tianyahaijao • VRC 156-157 F 7
Tianyang o VRC 156-157 E 5
Tianzhu o VRC (GAN) 154-155 C 3
Tianzhu o VRC (GZH) 156-157 F 3
Tianzhushan • VRC 154-155 K 6
Tiaraçu o BR 76-77 K 6
Tiaret ☆ • DZ 190-191 C 3
Tias o E 188-189 E 6
Tiaski o SN 202-203 C 2
Tiassale o CI 202-203 H 7
Tibaji o BR 74-75 E 5
Tibaji, Rio ~ BR 72-73 E 7
Tibana o CO 60-61 E 5
Tibati o CAM 204-205 K 5
Tibaú o BR 68-69 K 4
Tibau, Gunung ▲ RI 164-165 D 3
Tibaú do Sul o BR 68-69 L 5
Tibba o PK 138-139 C 5
Tibbobura o AUS 178-179 F 5
Tiberghamine o DZ 190-191 C 6
Tibesti ▲ TCH 198-199 H 2
Tibesti, Sarir ∸ LAR 192-193 G 5
Tibet = Xizang Zizhiqu ▫ VRC 144-145 E 5
Tibi, Pulau ⌒ RI 164-165 E 2
Tibiri o RN (DOS) 198-199 B 6
Tibiri o RN (MAR) 198-199 C 6
Tibirica, Rio ~ BR 72-73 E 6
Tibles, Muntii ▲ RO 102-103 C 4
Tibni o SYR 128-129 H 5
Tibo o BF 202-203 J 2
Tibo o RI 164-165 F 5
Tibo o ZRE 212-213 A 2
Tibung o RI 164-165 F 5
Tiburon o •• RH 54-55 H 5
Tiburón, Isla ⌒ MEX 50-51 C 3
Tica o MOC 218-219 H 4
Ticaboo o USA (UT) 254-255 E 6
Ticao Island ⌒ RP 160-161 E 6
Ticao Pass ≈ 160-161 E 6
Ticatica o BOL 70-71 D 7
Tice o USA (FL) 286-287 H 5
Tichet < RMM 196-197 L 5
Tichît o RIM 196-197 F 5
Tichît, Dahr ∸ RIM 196-197 F 5
Tichka, Tizi-n- ▲ MA 188-189 H 5
Tichkatine, Oued ~ DZ 198-199 B 2
T'icho o ETH 208-209 D 5
Ticho Brahe, Kap ▲ GRØ 28-29 V 4
Tickera o AUS 180-181 D 2
Tickfaw River ~ USA (LA) 268-269 K 6
Ticonderoga o USA (NY) 278-279 H 5
Ticonderoga, Fort • USA (NY) 278-279 H 5
Ticsani, Volcán ▲ PE 70-71 B 5
Ticul o MEX 52-53 K 1
Tidal River o AUS 180-181 J 5
Tidangpala o RI 164-165 E 2
Tiddim o MYA 142-143 H 4
Tiddis ∴ • DZ 190-191 F 2
Tiderídjaouine, Adrar ▲ DZ 190-191 C 9
Tiderméné o RMM 196-197 M 6
Tidewater o USA (LA) 268-269 L 7
Tidewater o USA (OR) 244-245 B 6
Tidi Dunes ∸ RN 198-199 G 2
Tidikelt, Plaine du ∸ DZ 190-191 C 7
Tidirhine, Ibel ▲ MA 188-189 J 3
Tidjidit, Erg ∸ DZ 190-191 C 9
Tidjikja ☆ RIM 196-197 E 5
Tidnish o CDN (NS) 240-241 L 5
Tidore, Pulau ⌒ •• RI 164-165 K 3
Tidore = Soa-Siu o RI 164-165 K 3
Tidra, Île ⌒ RIM 196-197 B 5
Tidsit, Sebkhet ⊙ MA 196-197 C 3
Tiébissou o CI 202-203 H 6
Tiéblé o • BF 202-203 K 4
Tiéboro o TCH 198-199 H 2
Tiefa o VRC 150-151 D 6
Tiéfora o BF 202-203 H 4
Tiegba o CI 202-203 H 7
Tiel o SN 202-203 C 2
Tiel, Mayo ~ CAM 204-205 K 4
Tieli o VRC 150-151 G 4
Tieling o VRC 150-151 D 6
Tielong o VRC 144-145 B 3
Tielongtan o VRC 144-145 B 3
Tielt o B 92-93 G 3
Tiéma o CI 202-203 G 5
Tiemba ~ CI 202-203 G 5
Tiémé o CI 202-203 G 5
Tiémélékro o CI 202-203 H 6
Tiene o LB 202-203 E 6
Tiéningboué o CI 202-203 H 5
Tienko o CI 202-203 G 4
Tientsin = Tianjin ☆ VRC 154-155 K 2
Tiên Yên ☆ VN 156-157 E 6
Tiéré o RMM 202-203 H 4
Tierfontein o ZA 220-221 H 3
Tieri o AUS 178-179 K 2
Tierra Amarilla o USA (NM) 256-257 J 2
Tierra Blanca o MEX 52-53 F 2
Tierra Blanca Creek ~ USA (TX) 264-265 B 4
Tierra Colorada o MEX 52-53 E 3
Tierra Colorado, Bajo de la ∸ RA 78-79 F 7
Tierra del Fuego ⌒ 5 E 10
Tierra del Fuego ▫ RA 80 F 6
Tierra del Fuego, Isla Grande del ⌒ 80 F 6
Tierra del Fuego, Parque Nacional ⊥ RA 80 F 7
Tierradentro, Parque Archipiélago • CO 60-61 C 6
Tierralta o CO 60-61 C 3
Tie Siding o USA (WY) 252-253 N 5
Tiêtar, Río ~ E 98-99 E 5
Tietê o BR 72-73 G 7
Tietê, Rio ~ BR 72-73 G 7
Tie-Tree Roadhouse o AUS 178-179 B 2
Tiev, Shangev- o WAN 204-205 H 5
Tieyon o AUS 176-177 M 3
Tifernine, Erg ∸ DZ 190-191 F 7
Tiffin o USA (OH) 280-281 C 2
Tiffin River ~ USA (OH) 280-281 B 2
Tiflet o MA 188-189 H 4
Tiflis = Tbilisi ★ • GE 126-127 F 7
Tifore, Pulau ⌒ RI 164-165 K 3
Tifrirt < RIM 196-197 D 4
Tifton o USA (GA) 284-285 G 5
Tifu o RI 166-167 D 3
Tiga, Pulau ⌒ MAL 160-161 A 10
Tigalda Island ⌒ USA 22-23 O 5
Tigapulan, Pegunungan ▲ RI 162-163 E 5
Tiga Reservoir < WAN 204-205 H 3
Tiga Tarok o MAL 160-161 B 9
Tiger o USA (WA) 244-245 H 2
Tiger Island ⌒ GUY 62-63 E 2
Tighanimines, Gorges de • DZ 190-191 F 3
Tighenif o DZ 190-191 C 3
Tigi, Danau ⊙ RI 166-167 J 4
Tigil' ☆ RUS 120-121 S 5
Tigil' ~ RUS 120-121 S 5
Tignall o USA (GA) 284-285 H 3
Tignère o CAM 204-205 K 5
Tignirè < RIM 196-197 C 5
Tignish o CDN (PEI) 240-241 L 4
Tignuan o RP 160-161 D 5
Tigray ▫ ETH 200-201 J 6
Tigre o RA 78-79 K 3
Tigre, Arroyo el ~ RA 76-77 H 6
Tigre, Cordillera del ▲ RA 78-79 E 2
Tigre, El o CO 60-61 D 4
Tigre, El ∴ • MEX 52-53 J 2
Tigre, El o YV 60-61 J 3
Tigre, Isla ⌒ PE 66-67 B 4
Tigre, Lago del ⊙ GCA 52-53 J 3
Tigre, Río ~ PE 64-65 E 3
Tigre, Río ~ YV 60-61 K 3
Tigre, Sierra del ▲ RA 76-77 C 6
Tigre de San Lorenzo, El o PA 52-53 D 8
Tigres, Peninsula dos ⌣ ANG 216-217 A 8
Tigris ~ 134-135 B 2
Tigris = Diğla ~ IRQ 128-129 M 6
Tigrito, El = San José de Guanipa o YV 60-61 J 3
Tiguent o RIM 196-197 C 6
Tiguézéfene o RN 196-197 M 7
Tiguili o TCH 206-207 D 3
Tigzerte, Oued ~ MA 188-189 G 6
Tigzirt o DZ 190-191 E 2
Tihaja ~ RUS 120-121 R 5
Tihāma ∸ Y 132-133 C 6
Tihāmat aš-Šām ∸ KSA 132-133 B 4
Tihodaïne, Erg ∸ DZ 190-191 F 8
Tihoreck o RUS 102-103 M 5
Tihosuco o MEX 52-53 K 1
Tihuatlán o • MEX 52-53 F 1
Tihvin ☆ RUS 94-95 N 2
Tihvinskaja grjada ▲ RUS 94-95 N 2
Tijamuchi, Río ~ BOL 70-71 E 4
Tijāra o IND 138-139 F 6
Tijeras o USA (NM) 256-257 J 3
Tijí o LAR 192-193 D 2
Tijo, Tanjung ▲ RI 162-163 F 5
Tijoca, Ilha ⌒ BR 68-69 E 2
Tijuana o • MEX 50-51 A 1
Tijucas o BR 74-75 F 6
Tijucas, Ensenada de ≈ 74-75 F 6
Tijucu, Rio ~ BR 72-73 F 5
Tika o CDN (QUE) 242-243 C 2
Tikal o GCA (ELP) 52-53 K 3
Tikal ∴ •• GCA (ELP) 52-53 K 3
Tikal, Parque Nacional ⊥ ••• GCA 52-53 K 3
Tikamgarh o IND 138-139 G 7
Tikanlik o VRC 146-147 H 5
Tikaré o BF 202-203 K 3
Tikem o TCH 206-207 B 4
Tiki Basin ≃ 14-15 P 9
Tikiklut o USA 20-21 M 1
Tikkerutuk, Lac ⊙ CDN 36-37 L 6
Tiko o CAM 204-205 H 6
Tikota o IND 140-141 F 2
Tikša o RUS 88-89 M 4
Tikšeozero ⊙ RUS 88-89 L 3
Tiksi ☆ RUS 110-111 R 4
Tiksi, buhta ⊙ RUS 110-111 R 4
Tiku o RI 162-163 C 5
Tikuna de Feijoal, Área Indígena ⚔ BR 66-67 C 5
Tikuna São Leopoldo, Área Indígena ⚔ BR 66-67 C 5
Tiladummati Atoll ⌒ MV 140-141 B 4
Tilaiya ⊙ IND 142-143 D 3
Tilakvāda o IND 138-139 D 9
Tilāl an-Nūba ▲ SUD 200-201 E 6
Tilama o RCH 78-79 D 2
Tilamuta o RI 164-165 H 3
Tilantongo o MEX (OAX) 52-53 F 3
Tilantongo ∴ • MEX (OAX) 52-53 F 3
Tilarán o CR 52-53 B 6
Tilburg o NL 92-93 H 3
Tilbury o CDN (ONT) 238-239 C 6
Tilchuse River ~ CDN 30-31 L 2
Tilden o USA (NE) 262-263 J 2
Tilden o USA (TX) 266-267 J 5
Tilden Lake o CDN (ONT) 238-239 F 2
Tilemsen o MA 188-189 F 6
Tilemsi, Vallée du ∸ RMM 196-197 L 5
Tilford o USA (SD) 260-261 C 2
Tilia, Oued ~ DZ 190-191 C 7
Tiličiki ☆ RUS 112-113 O 6
Tiline o USA (KY) 276-277 G 3
Tiljuga ~ IND 142-143 E 2
Tillabéri ☆ RN 202-203 L 2
Tillamook o USA (OR) 244-245 B 5
Tillamook Bay ≈ 40-41 C 3
Tillamook Bay ≈ USA 244-245 B 5
Tillanchang Dwip ⌒ IND 140-141 L 5
Tillery, Lake < USA (NC) 282-283 G 5
Tilley o CDN (ALB) 232-233 G 5
Tillman o USA (SC) 284-285 J 4
Tillsonburg o CDN (ONT) 238-239 E 6
Tilly, Lac ⊙ CDN 38-39 G 2
Tilney o CDN (SAS) 232-233 N 5
Tiloa o RN 204-205 E 1
Tilopozo o RCH 76-77 C 2
Tilos ⌒ GR 100-101 L 6
Tilpa o AUS 178-179 H 6
Tilrempt o DZ 190-191 D 4
Tilston o CDN (MAN) 234-235 B 5
Tiltil o RCH 78-79 D 2
Tīmā o ET 194-195 E 4
Timahdite o MA 188-189 J 4
Timalchara o RCH 70-71 C 6
Timampuu o RI 164-165 G 5
Timane, Río ~ PY 70-71 G 7
Timanfaya, Parque Nacional de ⊥ E 188-189 E 6
Timanskij bereg ◡ RUS 88-89 U 3
Timanskij krjaž ▲ RUS 88-89 U 3
Timanskiy Kryazh = Timanskij krjaž ▲ RUS 88-89 U 3
Timare o RI 166-167 J 4
Timargarha o • PK 138-139 C 2
Timaru o NZ 182 C 6
Timaševsk o RUS 102-103 L 5
Timau o EAK 212-213 F 3
Timba o CO 60-61 C 6
Timbalier Bay ≈ 44-45 M 5
Timbalier Bay ≈ USA 268-269 K 7
Timbalier Island ⌒ USA (LA) 268-269 K 7
Timbang, Pulau ⌒ MAL 160-161 C 10
Timbaúba o BR 68-69 L 5
Timbavati Game Reserve ⊥ ZA 220-221 K 2
Timbedgha o RIM 196-197 F 6
Timber o USA (OR) 244-245 B 5
Timber Creek o AUS 172-173 K 3
Timber Creek Lake ⊙ USA (KS) 262-263 K 7
Timber Lake o USA (SD) 260-261 E 1
Timberlin Lodge Ski Area ⊥ USA (OR) 244-245 D 5
Timber Mill o AUS 172-173 K 2
Timber Mountain ▲ USA (NV) 246-247 K 5
Timberon o USA (NM) 256-257 K 6
Timberville o USA (VA) 280-281 H 5
Timbiras o BR 68-69 G 4
Timbó o BR 74-75 F 6
Timbo o RG 202-203 E 4
Timboon o AUS 180-181 G 5
Timboroa o EAK 212-213 E 3
Timbotuba, Ilha do ⌒ BR 66-67 D 4
Timboy o BOL 76-77 E 1
Timbuktu = Tombouctou o ••• RMM 196-197 J 6
Timbulun o RI 162-163 D 5
Timbuni ~ RI 166-167 G 2
Timbunke o PNG 183 B 3
Timbun Mata, Pulau ⌒ MAL 160-161 C 10
Timeldjame, Oued ~ DZ 190-191 D 6
Timelloutine o DZ 190-191 G 6
Timétrine, Djebel ▲ RMM 196-197 K 5
Timgad o ••• DZ 190-191 F 3
Timia o RN 198-199 D 3
Timiaouine o RMM 196-197 L 4
Timika o RI 166-167 J 4
Timimoun o • DZ 190-191 C 6
Timimoun, Sebkha de ⊙ DZ 188-189 L 6
Timirist, Râs ▲ RIM 196-197 B 5
Timiş ~ RO 102-103 C 5
Timiskaming, Lake= Témiscamingue, Lac ⊙ CDN (QUE) 236-237 J 5
Timişoara ☆ • RO 102-103 B 5
Timissit, Oued ~ DZ 190-191 G 6
Timkinskaja ~ RUS 112-113 K 2
Timmerkpuk Mountain ▲ USA 20-21 J 2
Timmiarmiut o GRØ 28-29 U 5
Timmins o CDN (ONT) 236-237 G 4
Timmonsville o USA (SC) 284-285 L 2
Timms Hill ▲ USA (WI) 270-271 H 5
Timna' ∴ • IL 130-131 D 3
Timoforo ~ RI 166-167 G 2
Timok ~ YU 100-101 J 2
Timon o BR 68-69 G 4
Timonha, Rio ~ BR 68-69 H 3
Timonium o USA (MD) 280-281 K 4
Timor ⌒ RI 166-167 C 6
Timor, Laut ≈ 166-167 D 7
Timor Sea ≈ 172-173 H 2
Timor Trough ≃ 166-167 C 7
Timote o RA 78-79 H 3
Timóteo o BR 72-73 J 5
Timoudi o DZ 188-189 L 6
Timpahute Range ▲ USA (NV) 248-249 J 2
Timpanogos Cave National Monument ∴ USA (UT) 254-255 D 3
Timpas o USA (CO) 254-255 M 6
Timpaus, Pulau ⌒ RI 164-165 H 4
Timpson o USA (TX) 268-269 F 5
Timpton ~ RUS 118-119 N 6
Timra o S 86-87 H 5
Tim Raré o RMM 196-197 J 6
Tims Ford Lake ⊙ USA (TN) 276-277 J 5
Timun o RI 162-163 E 4
Timur, Banjaran ▲ MAL 162-163 E 2
Timur Digul ~ RI 166-167 L 4
Timurni o IND 138-139 F 8
Timur Timor ▫ RI 166-167 C 6
Tina ~ ZA 220-221 J 5
Tin Abunda, Bi'r < LAR 192-193 E 4
Tinaca Point ▲ RP 160-161 F 10
Tinaco o YV 60-61 G 3
Ti-n-Aguelhaj o RMM 196-197 J 6
Tinaja, La o MEX 52-53 F 2
Tinaja, Punta ▲ PE 70-71 A 5
Ti-n-Akof o BF 202-203 K 2
Tin Alkoum < DZ 190-191 H 8
Tinambung o RI 164-165 F 5
Ti-n-Amzag < RMM 196-197 H 6
Tin Amzi, Oued ~ DZ 198-199 B 2
Tinangkong o RI 164-165 H 4
Tinaroo Falls Reservoir < AUS 174-175 H 5
Ti-n-Azabo o RMM 196-197 L 6
Ti-n-Bessais < RIM 196-197 F 3
Ti-n-Brahim < RIM 196-197 C 5
Tindangou o BF 202-203 L 4
Tinderry Range ▲ AUS 180-181 K 3
Tindila o RG 202-203 F 4
Tindivanam o IND 140-141 H 4
Tindjassé o RT 202-203 L 5
Tindouf ☆ • DZ 188-189 G 7
Tindouf, Hamada de ∸ DZ 188-189 G 7
Tindouf, Sebkha de ⊙ DZ 188-189 H 7
Tineba, Pegunungan ▲ RI 164-165 G 4
Ti-n-Eguelai o RMM 196-197 J 6
Tineo = Tinéu o E 98-99 D 3
Ti-n-Essako o RMM 196-197 M 5
Tinfouchy o DZ 188-189 J 6
Tin Fouye o DZ 190-191 F 6
Tingal ▲ SUD 200-201 E 6
Tingambato o MEX 52-53 D 2
Tinggi, Pulau ⌒ MAL (KED) 162-163 F 3
Tinghert, Hamâdat ∸ LAR 190-191 F 6
Tinglayan o RP 160-161 D 4
Tingmiarmiut ⌒ GRØ 28-29 U 5
Tingmiarmiut Fjord ≈ 28-29 T 5
Tingo Maria, Parque Nacional ⊥ PE 64-65 D 6
Tingong o VRC 156-157 F 4
Tingri o VRC 144-145 F 6
Tingsryd ☆ S 86-87 G 8
Tingstäde o S 86-87 J 8
Tinguá, Parque Nacional de ⊥ BR 72-73 J 7
Tingvoll ☆ N 86-87 D 5
Tingwon Group ⌒ PNG 183 E 2
Tingya o SUD 206-207 L 3
Tin Hadjène, Oued ~ DZ 190-191 F 8
Tinharé, Ilha de ⌒ BR 72-73 L 2
Tinherir o MA 188-189 J 5
Tinh Gia ☆ VN 156-157 D 7
Tini o SUD 198-199 L 5
Ti-n-Idnâne < RMM 196-197 J 6
Tinigart < RIM 196-197 F 5
Tiniroto o NZ 182 F 3
Tinis, Wādī ~ LAR 192-193 D 5
Tinitan o RP 160-161 C 7
Tiniteqilaaq o GRØ 28-29 W 4
Tinitonito Bay ≈ 36-37 N 2
Tinjil, Pulau ⌒ RI 168 A 3
Tinkisso ~ RG 202-203 F 4
Ti-n-Medjouf < RIM 196-197 C 5
Tin Merzouga ∸ DZ 190-191 H 9
Tin Mountain ▲ USA (CA) 248-249 G 3
Tinnie o USA (NM) 256-257 K 5
Tinogasta o RA 76-77 D 5
Tinombo o RI 164-165 G 3
Tinompo o RI 164-165 G 5
Tinos o GR 100-101 K 6
Tinos ⌒ GR 100-101 K 6
Ti-n-Oufart < RMM 196-197 K 6
Tinputz o PNG 184 I b 1
Tin Rerhoch < DZ 198-199 B 2
Tinrhert, Hamada de ∸ DZ 190-191 F 6
Tinrhert, Plateau du ▲ DZ 190-191 E 7
Tinsman o USA (AR) 276-277 C 7
Tin Tadjant ~ DZ 196-197 L 4
Tintagel o CDN (BC) 228-229 J 2
Tintah o USA (MN) 270-271 B 4
Tințâne o RIM 196-197 E 6
Tin Tarabine < DZ 190-191 F 9
Tin Tarabine, Oued ~ DZ 190-191 F 9
Ti-n-Tehoun < RMM 196-197 J 6
Tintejert, Adrar ▲ DZ 190-191 D 8
Tintern Abbey •• GB 90-91 F 6
Ti-n-Tijot < RMM 196-197 H 6
Tintina o RA 76-77 F 4
Tintinara o AUS 180-181 F 4
Tintioulen o RG 202-203 F 4
Tin Toumma ∸ RN 198-199 F 4
Tiny o CDN (SAS) 232-233 Q 4
Ti-n-Zaouâtene o RMM 196-197 M 5
Tin-Zawatine o DZ 196-197 M 5
T'i'o o ER 200-201 K 5
Tiobraid Árann = Tipperary o IRL 90-91 C 5
Tioga o USA (ND) 258-259 E 3
Tioman, Pulau ⌒ MAL 162-163 F 3
Tionesta o USA (PA) 280-281 G 2
Tionesta Lake ⊙ USA (PA) 280-281 G 2
Tioor, Pulau ⌒ RI 166-167 F 4
Tiop o RI 162-163 D 6
Tioribougou o RMM 202-203 G 3
Tioroniaradougou o CI 202-203 H 5
Tiou o BF 202-203 J 3
Tioughnioga River ~ USA (NY) 278-279 E 6
Tiouilît o RIM 196-197 B 5
Tiouki o RMM 202-203 H 2
Tioussiana o BF 202-203 H 4
Tipaza ☆ ••• DZ 190-191 D 2
Tipitapa o • NIC 52-53 L 5
Tipitapa, Rio ~ NIC 52-53 L 5
Tipolo o RP 160-161 F 7
Tippecanoe River ~ USA (IN) 274-275 M 3
Tipperary o AUS 172-173 K 2
Tipperary = Tiobraid Árann o IRL 90-91 C 5
Tipton o USA (CA) 248-249 E 3
Tipton o USA (IA) 274-275 G 3
Tipton o USA (IN) 274-275 M 4
Tipton o USA (MO) 274-275 F 6
Tipton o USA (OK) 264-265 E 4
Tipton, Mount ▲ USA (AZ) 256-257 A 3
Tiptonville o USA (TN) 276-277 F 4
Tip Top Mountain ▲ CDN (ONT) 236-237 B 4
Tiptur o IND 140-141 G 4
Tipuani, Río ~ BOL 70-71 C 4
Tipuru o GUY 62-63 E 4
Tiputini o EC 64-65 E 2
Tiquaruçu o BR 72-73 L 2
Tiquicheo o MEX 52-53 D 2
Tiquié, Rio ~ BR 66-67 C 2
Tiquillaca o PE 70-71 B 4
Tira, Boľšaja ~ RUS 116-117 M 7
Tiracambu, Serra do ▲ BR 68-69 E 4
Tiradentes o BR 72-73 H 6
Tirahart, Oued ~ DZ 190-191 D 9
Tirān, Ğazirat ⌒ KSA 130-131 D 4
Tirana, La o RCH 70-71 C 7
Tiranë ☆ • AL 100-101 G 4
Tirangole o SUD 206-207 L 6
Tiraouene < RN 198-199 C 3
T'irarè Shet' ~ ETH 200-201 J 6
Tirari Desert ∸ AUS 178-179 E 5
Tirasberge ▲ NAM 220-221 C 2
Tiraspol ☆ MD 102-103 F 4
Tirau o NZ 182 E 2
Tirband-e Torkestān, Selsele-ye Kūh-e ▲ AFG 136-137 H 7
Tire ☆ TR 128-129 B 3
Tire, Kōtal-e ▲ AFG 138-139 B 3
Tirebolu o TR 128-129 H 2
Tirecatinga, Área Indígena ⚔ BR 70-71 H 3
Tiree ⌒ GB 90-91 D 3
Tirehtjah ~ RUS 110-111 a 7
Tirehtjah ~ RUS 110-111 P 6
Tirere o PNG 183 B 5
Tîrgovişte ☆ • RO 102-103 D 5
Tîrgu Frumos o RO 102-103 E 4
Tirgui < TCH 198-199 J 3
Tîrgu Jiu ☆ RO 102-103 C 5
Tîrgu Mureş ☆ • RO 102-103 D 4
Tîrgu Secuiesc o RO 102-103 E 4
Tirhatimine < DZ 190-191 D 8
Tirhemar, Oued ~ DZ 190-191 F 7
Tiri Aguge ~ TCH 192-193 H 6
Tiriri o EAU 212-213 D 3
Tiririca o BR 68-69 G 7
Tiririne, Oued ~ DZ 190-191 G 9
Tiriro o RG 202-203 F 4
Tiris Zemour ▫ RIM 196-197 E 2
Tîrnăveni o RO 102-103 D 4
Tiro o RG 202-203 E 5
Tirol ▫ A 92-93 L 5
Tiros o BR 72-73 H 5
Tiroungoulou o RCA 206-207 F 4
Tirreno, Mar ≈ 100-101 D 5
Tirso ~ I 100-101 B 5
Tirso = Lago Omodeo ⊙ I 100-101 B 4
Tirthahalli o IND 140-141 F 4
Tiruchchendūr o • IND 140-141 H 6
Tiruchchirāppalli o • IND 140-141 H 5
Tiruchengodu o IND 140-141 G 5
Tiruganna o IND 140-141 F 4
Tirukkalukkunram o • IND 140-141 J 4
Tirukkoyilūr o IND 140-141 H 5
Tirumakudal o IND 140-141 G 4
Tirumala o • IND 140-141 H 4
Tirumangalam o IND 140-141 H 6
Tirumullaivāsal o IND 140-141 H 5
Tirunelveli o • IND 140-141 G 6
Tiruntan o PE 64-65 E 5
Tirupati o • IND 140-141 H 4
Tirupparangunram • IND 140-141 H 6
Tiruppattūr o IND 140-141 H 5
Tiruppattūr o IND 140-141 H 4
Tiruppporur o IND 140-141 J 4
Tiruppur o IND 140-141 G 5
Tirupuvanam o IND 140-141 H 6
Tirutturaippūndi o IND 140-141 H 5
Tiruvalaru o IND 140-141 H 5
Tiruvalla o IND 140-141 G 6
Tiruvannāmalai o • IND 140-141 H 4
Tiruvattiyur o IND 140-141 J 4
Tiruvūru o IND 142-143 B 7
Tirvyjaha ~ RUS 108-109 O 6
Tis o IR 134-135 J 6
Tis ~ RUS 116-117 E 6
Tisa ~ UA 102-103 C 3
Tisa ~ YU 100-101 H 2
Tisaiyanvilai o IND 140-141 G 6
Tisdale o CDN (SAS) 232-233 O 3
Tisgaon o IND 138-139 E 10
Tisgui-Remz o MA 188-189 G 6
Tishomingo o USA (OK) 264-265 H 4
Tishomingo National Wildlife Refuge ⊥ USA (OK) 264-265 H 4
Tišina ~ RUS 122-123 D 3
T'is Isat Fwafwatē = Blue Nile Falls ~ •• ETH 208-209 C 3
Tiska, Pic ▲ DZ 190-191 G 9
Tisnaïet, Oued ~ DZ 190-191 E 6
Tissa ~ RUS 116-117 J 9
Tissamaharama o CL 140-141 J 7
Tissān, Hasy < LAR 192-193 E 3
Tissemsilt ☆ DZ 190-191 C 3
Tista ~ BD 142-143 F 2
Tisul' ☆ RUS 114-115 U 7
Tisza ~ H 92-93 Q 5
Tit o DZ (ADR) 190-191 C 7
Tit o DZ (TAM) 190-191 E 9
Tit, Suon- o RUS 118-119 L 6
Titaluk River ~ USA 20-21 N 2
Titao o BF 202-203 J 3
Tit-Ary o RUS (SAH) 110-111 Q 3
Tit-Ary o RUS (SAH) 118-119 N 5
Tite o GNB 202-203 C 4
Titicaca, Lago ⊙ PE 70-71 C 4
Titicaca, Reserva Nacional ⊥ PE 70-71 B 4
Titigading o RI 162-163 D 4
Titiwaifuru o RI 166-167 K 3
Titiwan, Banjaran ▲ MAL 162-163 D 3
Titler o USA (OR) 244-245 C 8
Titograd = Podgorica ☆ YU 100-101 G 3
Titova Mitrovica = Kosovska Mitrovica o YU 100-101 H 3
Titov Drvar o BIH 100-101 F 2
Titovo Užice = Užice o YU 100-101 H 3
Titov Veles o • MK 100-101 H 4
Ti-Tree o AUS 178-179 B 2
Titu o RO 102-103 D 5
Titule o ZRE 210-211 K 2
Titumate o CO 60-61 C 3
Titusville o USA (FL) 286-287 J 3
Titusville o USA (PA) 280-281 G 2
Titwān ☆ • MA 188-189 J 3
Tiung, Tanjung ▲ RI 162-163 G 5
Tiva ~ EAK 212-213 G 4
Tivaouane o SN 202-203 B 2
Tivoli o I 100-101 D 4
Tivoli o USA (TX) 266-267 L 5
Tivtejjaha ~ RUS 108-109 N 6
Tiwāl, aṭ- o KSA 132-133 C 5
Tiwi o EAK 212-213 G 6
Tiwori, Teluk ≈ 164-165 G 4
Tiworo, Kepulauan ⌒ RI 164-165 H 6
Tiworo, Selat ≈ 164-165 H 6
Tixmul ∴ • MEX 52-53 K 2
Tixtla de Guerrero o MEX 52-53 E 3
Tiya ••• ETH 208-209 C 5
Tiyāb o IR 134-135 G 5
Tiyo, Pegunungan ▲ RI 166-167 H 4
Tizayuca o MEX 52-53 E 2
Tizimín o MEX 52-53 K 1
Tizi Ouzou ☆ DZ 190-191 E 2
Tiznados, Río ~ YV 60-61 H 3
Tiznit ☆ MA 188-189 G 6
Tižtiž o IR 128-129 M 5
Tjaneni o SD 220-221 K 2
Tjanja o RUS 118-119 J 6
Tjanja ~ RUS 118-119 K 6
Tjater ~ RUS 96-97 J 7
Tjatino o RUS 122-123 M 6
Tjatja, vulkan ▲ RUS 122-123 M 6
Tjažin ~ RUS 114-115 U 6
Tjažinskij ☆ RUS 114-115 U 6
Tjeggelvas ⊙ S 86-87 H 3
Tjera o BF 202-203 H 4
Tjörn ∸ S 86-87 E 8
Tjugël'saj o KS 146-147 B 5
Tjugjuène ~ RUS 118-119 K 4
Tjuhtet ☆ RUS 114-115 U 6
Tjukalinsk ☆ RUS 114-115 M 7
Tjukjan ~ RUS 110-111 L 7
Tjukjan ~ RUS 110-111 M 7
Tjukjan ~ RUS 118-119 J 4
Tjulender araly ⌒ KA 126-127 J 5
Tjulenij, mys ▲ AZ 128-129 O 2
Tjul'gan ☆ RUS 96-97 K 7
Tjuli o RUS 114-115 K 4
Tjumen' ☆ RUS 114-115 H 6
Tjung ~ RUS 110-111 M 6
Tjung ~ RUS 110-111 K 6
Tjung ~ RUS 110-111 M 7
Tjung ~ RUS 118-119 K 4
Tjungjulju o RUS 118-119 P 4
Tjup o KS 146-147 D 4
Tjup ~ KS 146-147 D 4
Tjuvfjorden ≈ 84-85 M 4
Tkvarčeli o GE 126-127 D 6
Tlacoapa o MEX 52-53 E 3
Tlacolula o • MEX 52-53 F 3
Tlacotalpan o • MEX 52-53 G 2
Tlacotepec o MEX 52-53 F 2
Tlaculilotepec o MEX 52-53 E 1
Tlahuac o MEX 52-53 E 2
Tlahuiltepa o MEX 52-53 E 1
Tlākshīn, Bi'r < LAR 192-193 E 2
Tlalchapa o MEX 52-53 D 2
Tlalnepantla o MEX 52-53 E 2

Tlalpan = Tlalnepantla o MEX 52-53 E 2
Tlaltenango o MEX 50-51 H 7
Tlapacoyan o MEX 52-53 F 2
Tlapa del Comonfort o MEX 52-53 E 3
Tlapaneco, Río ∼ MEX 52-53 E 3
Tlaquepaque o · MEX 52-53 C 1
Tlaxcala ◘ MEX 52-53 E 2
Tlaxcala ☆ · MEX (TLA) 52-53 E 2
Tlaxiaco o MEX 52-53 F 3
Tlell o CDN (BC) 228-229 C 3
Tlemcen ☆ ·· DZ 188-189 L 3
Tlemcen, Monts de ▲ DZ 188-189 L 3
Tleta-de-Sidi-Bouguedra o MA 188-189 G 4
Tlevak Strait ≈ 32-33 D 4
Tlhakgameng o ZA 220-221 G 3
Tljarata o RUS 126-127 G 6
Tlokoeng o LS 220-221 J 4
Tmassah o LAR 192-193 F 4
Tmeïmîchât o RIM 196-197 C 4
Tne Haven o ZA 220-221 J 6
Tnèkveem ∼ RUS 112-113 T 4
To o BF 202-203 J 4
Toa Baja o USA (PR) 286-287 P 2
Toade, Kepulauan ⌒ RI 164-165 J 2
Toad River ∼ CDN 30-31 G 6
Toak o VAN 184 II b 3
Toamasina ◘ RM 222-223 F 6
Toamasina ☆ RM (TMA) 222-223 F 7
Toano o USA (VA) 280-281 K 6
Toari o BR 66-67 D 6
Toaupulai o IND 140-141 G 6
Toaya o RI 164-165 F 4
Toba o CDN (BC) 230-231 E 3
Toba o J 152-153 G 7
Toba o VRC 144-145 L 5
Toba, Arroyo el ∼ RA 76-77 G 5
Toba, Isla ⌒ RA 80 H 2
Tobacco Range ⌒ BH 52-53 K 3
Tobago ⌒ TT 60-61 L 2
Toba Inlet ≈ 32-33 H 6
Toba Inlet ≈ CDN 230-231 E 3
Toba Kâkar Range ▲ PK 134-135 M 3
Tobalai, Pulau ⌒ RI 164-165 L 4
Tobalai, Selat ≈ 164-165 L 4
Tobamawu o RI 164-165 G 4
Toba River ∼ CDN (BC) 230-231 E 3
Tobarra o E 98-99 G 5
Toba Tek Singh o PK 138-139 D 4
Tobe o USA (CO) 254-255 M 6
Tobeatic Game Sanctuary ⊥ CDN (NS) 240-241 K 6
Tobejuba, Isla ⌒ YV 60-61 L 3
Tobelo o RI 164-165 K 3
Tobelombang o RI 164-165 G 4
Tobermorey o AUS 178-179 D 2
Tobermory o · CDN (ONT) 238-239 D 3
Tobermory o · GB 90-91 D 3
Tobias Barreto o BR 68-69 J 7
Tobin, Kap = Uunarteq o GRØ 26-27 p 8
Tobin, Mount ▲ USA (NV) 246-247 H 3
Tobin Lake ∼ AUS 172-173 G 6
Tobin Lake o CDN (SAS) 232-233 P 2
Tobin Lake ∼ CDN (SAS) 232-233 P 2
Tobique 20 Indian Reserve ✗ · CDN (NB) 240-241 H 4
Tobique River ∼ CDN (NB) 240-241 H 3
Tobishima ⌒ J 152-153 H 5
Toboali o RI 162-163 G 6
Tobol o KA 124-125 C 2
Tobol ∼ RUS 114-115 H 7
Tobol ∼ RUS 114-115 J 6
Tobol ∼ RUS 124-125 B 3
Tobol o RI 164-165 G 4
Tobol'sk ☆ · RUS 114-115 K 5
Tobol'skij materik, vozvyšennost' ▲ RUS 114-115 K 5
Tobré o DY 204-205 E 3
Tobseda o RUS 88-89 W 2
Toby = Morarano o RM 222-223 E 8
Tobyčan ∼ RUS 110-111 X 7
Tobyš ∼ RUS 88-89 V 4
Tobyš' ∼ RUS 88-89 W 5
Tobyšskaja vozvyšennost' ▲ RUS 88-89 V 3
Toca o CO 60-61 E 5
Tocache Nuevo o PE 64-65 D 6
Tocaima o CO 60-61 D 5
Tocancipa o CO 60-61 E 5
Tocantinia o BR 68-69 D 6
Tocantinópolis o BR 68-69 E 5
Tocantins ◘ BR 68-69 D 7
Tocantins, Rio ∼ BR 62-63 K 6
Tocantins, Rio ∼ BR 68-69 E 5
Toccoa o USA (GA) 284-285 G 2
Točes ∼ RUS 114-115 U 4
Tochatwi Bay ⊂ CDN 30-31 O 4
Tochcha Lake ⊂ CDN (BC) 228-229 J 2
Tochi ∼ PK 138-139 B 3
Toch'o Do ⌒ ROK 150-151 E 10
Toco o ANG 216-217 B 7
Toco o RCH 76-77 C 2
Toco o TT 60-61 L 2
Tocoa River ∼ USA (GA) 284-285 F 2
Toconquis, Cerros de ▲ RA 76-77 D 3
Tocopilla o RCH 76-77 B 2
Tocopuri, Cerros de ▲ BOL 76-77 D 2
Tocota o RA 76-77 C 6
Tocumwal o AUS 180-181 H 3
Tocuyito o YV 60-61 G 2
Tocuyo, El o YV 60-61 G 3
Tocuyo, Río ∼ YV 60-61 G 2
Toda-saki ▲ J 152-153 K 5
Todd River ∼ AUS 178-179 C 3
Todeli o RI 164-165 J 4
Todenyang o EAK 212-213 E 1
Tödi ▲ CH 92-93 K 5
Todi o · I 100-101 D 3
Todin o BF 202-203 J 3
Todlo o RI 166-167 F 2
Todmorden o AUS 178-179 C 4
Todos los Santos, Lago ⊂ RCH 78-79 C 6
Todos os Santos, Baía de ≈ 72-73 L 2
Todos os Santos, Rio ∼ BR 72-73 K 4
Todos Santos o BOL 70-71 E 5
Todos Santos o MEX 50-51 D 6
Todra, Gorges du · MA 188-189 J 5
Todža, ozero = ozero Azas ⊂ RUS 116-117 H 9
Todžinskaja kotlovina ⊥ RUS 116-117 H 9
Toéguin o BF 202-203 K 3
Toekomstig-stuwmeer ⊂ SME 62-63 F 3
Toéni o BF 202-203 J 3
Toéssé o BF 202-203 K 4
Toez o CO 60-61 C 6
Toffo o DY 204-205 E 5
Tofield o CDN (ALB) 232-233 F 2
Tofino o CDN (BC) 230-231 D 4
Töfsingdalens nationalpark ⊥ S 86-87 F 5
Toga, Île = Toga ⌒ VAN 184 II a 1
Toga = Île Toga ⌒ VAN 184 II a 1
Togafo o RI 164-165 K 3
Toganaly o AZ 128-129 M 2
Tōgane o J 152-153 J 7
Togba < RIM 196-197 E 6
Togdheer ◘ SP 208-209 G 4
Tog Dheer, toga ∼ SP 208-209 H 4
Togi o J 152-153 G 6
Togiak o USA 22-23 Q 3
Togiak Bay ≈ 22-23 Q 3
Togian, Kepulauan ⌒ RI 164-165 G 4
Togian, Pulau ⌒ RI 164-165 G 4
Togme o VRC 144-145 H 4
Togni o SUD 200-201 G 3
Toro o CDN (SAS) 232-233 R 4
Togo o PNG 183 B 5
Togo ■ RT 204-205 D 4
Togo o USA (MN) 270-271 E 3
Togo, Lac ⊂ RT 202-203 L 6
Togoba o PNG 183 C 3
Togobala o CI 202-203 G 5
Togo Hills ▲ GH 202-203 L 6
Togolika ∼ RUS 114-115 T 5
Togoromá o CO 60-61 C 5
Togou o RMM 202-203 H 3
Tögrög o MAU 146-147 L 2
Togtoh o VRC 154-155 G 1
Togučin ☆ RUS 114-115 S 7
Toguéré-Koumbé o RMM 202-203 H 2
Togul ☆ RUS 124-125 P 2
Tog Wajaale o SP 208-209 F 4
Togwotee Pass ▲ USA (WY) 252-253 H 3
Togyzak ∼ KA 124-125 C 2
Tohāna o IND 138-139 E 5
Tohareu, poluostrov ⌒ RUS 122-123 H 2
Tohatchi o USA (NM) 256-257 G 3
Tohiatoš o US 136-137 F 3
Tohma Çayı ∼ TR 128-129 H 3
Tōhoku o J 152-153 J 4
Töhöm o MAU 148-149 J 5
Tohomo ∼ RUS 116-117 G 5
Tohopekaliga, Lake ⊂ USA (FL) 286-287 H 3
Tohoun o RT 202-203 L 6
Toibalewe o IND 140-141 L 4
Toili o RI 164-165 H 4
Toineke o RI 166-167 C 7
Toison, La o RH 54-55 K 5
Toivala o FIN 88-89 J 5
Tojo o J 152-153 E 7
Tojoku o RUS 118-119 K 4
Tojtepa o US 136-137 L 4
Tok ∼ RUS 96-97 H 7
Tok ∼ RUS 118-119 O 8
Toka o GUY 62-63 E 4
Tokachi-dake ▲ J 152-153 K 3
Tokachi-gawa ∼ J 152-153 K 3
Tōkamachi o J 152-153 H 6
Tokapalle o IND 140-141 H 3
Tōkar o SUD 200-201 H 3
Tokara-kaikyō ≈ 152-153 C 9
Tokara-rettō ⌒ J 152-153 C 10
Tokat ☆ · TR 128-129 G 2
Tŏkchŏkto ⌒ ROK 150-151 E 9
Tokchon o DVR 150-151 F 8
Tok Do ⌒ ROK 150-151 H 9
Tokeland o USA (OR) 244-245 A 4
Tokelau Islands ⌒ NZ 13 K 3
Toki o TCH 206-207 C 4
Tokio o BOL 70-71 C 2
Tokio o USA (TX) 264-265 B 5
Tok Junction o USA 20-21 T 5
Tokko o RUS (SAH) 118-119 K 6
Tokko ∼ RUS 118-119 J 6
Tokko ∼ RUS 118-119 J 7
Toklat River ∼ USA 20-21 P 4
Tokma o RUS 116-117 M 6
Tokmak o KS 146-147 B 4
Tokmak o UA 102-103 J 4
Tokoro o J 152-153 L 2
Tokoroa o NZ 182 E 3
Tokounou o RG 202-203 F 5
Tokrau ∼ KA 124-125 J 4
Toksovo o RUS 94-95 M 1
Toksum o VRC 146-147 J 4
Toktogul o KS 136-137 N 4
Toktogul'skoje vodohranilišče < KS 136-137 N 4
Tokuma o RUS 110-111 U 6
Tokunoshima o J 152-153 C 11
Tokuno-shima ⌒ J 152-153 C 11
Tokur-Jurjah ∼ RUS 112-113 J 4
Tokushima ☆ J 152-153 F 7
Tokuyama o J 152-153 D 7
Tokwe ∼ ZW 218-219 F 5
Toky, Chute ∼ ZRE 212-213 B 3
Tōkyō ★ · J 152-153 H 7
Tōkyō-wan ≈ 152-153 H 7
Tōkyusan National Park ⊥ · ROK 150-151 F 10
Tol o PNG 183 G 3
Tola, La o EC 64-65 C 1
Tolabit o RI 164-165 K 3
Tolaga Bay o NZ 182 G 3
Tolala o RI 164-165 G 5
To' Lan o VN 158-159 K 5
Tôlanaro o · RM 222-223 E 10
Tolapalca, Río ∼ BOL 70-71 D 6
Tolar o USA (NM) 256-257 M 4
Tolar, Cerro ▲ RCH 76-77 B 1
Tolbazy ☆ RUS 96-97 J 6
Tolbo o MAU 146-147 K 1
Tolbo nuur ⊂ MAU 146-147 J 1
Tolbuhin = Dobrič o BG 102-103 E 6
Tolbuzino o RUS 118-119 M 9
Toldi o GH 202-203 K 5
Tolé o PA 52-53 D 7
Tolé o RCA 206-207 B 5
Toledo o BOL 70-71 D 6
Toledo o BR 74-75 D 5
Toledo o CDN (ONT) 238-239 K 4
Toledo o ··· E 98-99 E 5
Toledo o USA (OH) 280-281 C 2
Toledo o USA (OR) 244-245 B 6
Toledo, Montes de ▲ E 98-99 E 5
Toledo Bend Reservoir < USA (TX) 268-269 G 5
Toledo City o RP 160-161 E 7
Tolga o DZ 190-191 E 3
Tolhuaca, Parque Nacional ⊥ RCH 78-79 D 5
Tolhuin o RA 80 G 7
Toli o VRC 146-147 F 3
Toliara ◘ RM 222-223 C 9
Toliara ☆ · RM (Tla) 222-223 C 9
Tolima A o CO 64-65 F 2
Tolimán o MEX 52-53 E 1
Tolisain o NEP 144-145 C 6
Tolitoli o RI 164-165 G 3
Tol'jatti = Stavropol'-na-Volgi ☆ RUS 96-97 F 7
Tol'ka ∼ RUS 114-115 Q 3
Tolland o CDN (ALB) 232-233 H 2
Tolleson o USA (AZ) 256-257 C 5
Tolley o USA (ND) 258-259 F 3
Tollhouse o USA (CA) 248-249 E 2
Tollja, zaliv ≈ 108-109 d 3
Tolmačovo o RUS 94-95 L 2
Tolo ⌒ ZRE 210-211 G 5
Tolo, Teluk ≈ 164-165 G 5
Tolode o LB 202-203 F 6
Tolofu o RI 164-165 K 3
Tolokiwa Island ⌒ PNG 183 D 3
Tololalai (Muslim Tombs) o · RI 168 D 7
Tolon o · RUS 120-121 E 3
Tolongoina o RM 222-223 E 8
Tolono o USA (IL) 274-275 K 5
Tolonuu, Pulau ⌒ RI 164-165 L 3
Tolosa o E 98-99 F 3
Tolovana River ∼ USA 20-21 Q 4
Tolsan Do ⌒ ROK 150-151 F 10
Tolsmaville o CDN (MAN) 234-235 G 5
Tolstovo, mys ▲ RUS 110-111 V 2
Tolstyj, mys ▲ RUS 120-121 W 6
Toltén o RCH 78-79 C 5
Toltén, Río ∼ RCH 78-79 C 5
Tolu o CO 60-61 D 3
Toluca ☆ · MEX 52-53 E 2
Toluca de Lerdo = Toluca ☆ · MEX 52-53 E 2
Toluk o KS 136-137 N 4
Toluviejo o CO 60-61 D 3
Tolwe o ZA 218-219 E 6
Tol'yatti = Stavropol'-na-Volgi ☆ RUS 96-97 F 7
Tölz, Bad o D 92-93 L 5
Tom' ∼ RUS 114-115 S 7
Tom' ∼ RUS 122-123 D 3
Tom ∼ RUS 122-123 D 3
Tom' ∼ RUS 124-125 P 1
Tom o US 136-137 J 5
Tom o USA (OK) 264-265 K 5
Toma o BF 202-203 J 3
Toma, La o RA 78-79 G 2
Toma, Río la ∼ RA 76-77 D 4
Tomah o USA (WI) 270-271 H 7
Tomahawk o USA (WI) 270-271 J 5
Tomakomai o J 152-153 J 3
Tomales Bay ≈ 40-41 C 6
Tomales Bay ≈ USA 246-247 B 5
Tomali o RI 164-165 G 4
Tomani o MAL 160-161 A 10
Tomanivi ▲ FJI 184 III b 2
Tomar o BR 66-67 F 3
Tomar o ··· P 98-99 C 5
Tomara, Talahini- o CI 202-203 J 5
Tomari o RUS 122-123 K 5
Tomarovka o RUS 102-103 K 2
Tomarza ☆ TR 128-129 F 3
Tomas o PE 64-65 E 8
Tomás Garrido o MEX 52-53 K 2
Tomásia o BR 68-69 E 6
Tomaszów Lubelski o PL 92-93 R 3
Tomaszów Mazowiecki o PL 92-93 P 3
Tomat o SUD (Kas) 200-201 G 5
Tomat o SUD (NR) 206-207 H 3
Tomatán o MEX 50-51 B 3
Tomatlán o MEX 52-53 B 2
Tombador, Serra do ▲ BR 70-71 J 2
Tombali, Rio ∼ GNB 202-203 C 4
Tomball o USA (TX) 268-269 E 6
Tombe o ANG 216-217 D 6
Tombe du Camerounais ▲ TCH 198-199 H 3
Tombel o CAM 204-205 H 6
Tombetsu, Hama- o J 152-153 K 2
Tombetsu, Nako- o J 152-153 K 2
Tombetsu, Shō- o J 152-153 K 2
Tombigbee River ∼ USA (AL) 284-285 B 4
Tombigbee River ∼ USA (AL) 284-285 B 5
Tombigbee River ∼ USA (MS) 268-269 M 2
Tombo, Punta ▲ ·· RA 80 H 2
Tomboco o ANG 216-217 B 3
Tombokro o CI 202-203 H 6
Tombolo o RI 164-165 F 6
Tombouctou o ··· RMM 196-197 J 6
Tombstone o USA (AZ) 256-257 E 7
Tombua o ANG 216-217 A 7
Tomé o RCH 78-79 C 4
Tome o USA (NM) 256-257 J 4
Tomea, Pulau ⌒ RI 164-165 H 6
Tomé-Açu o BR 68-69 D 3
Tomelloso o E 98-99 F 5
Tomi ∼ RCA 206-207 D 6
Tomichi Creek ∼ USA (CO) 254-255 J 5
Tomiko o CDN (ONT) 238-239 F 2
Tomina, Río ∼ BOL 70-71 E 6
Tominé ∼ RG 202-203 D 4
Tomingley o AUS 180-181 K 2
Tomini o RI 164-165 G 3
Tomini, Teluk ≈ 164-165 G 4
Tominián o RMM 202-203 J 3
Tomioka o J 152-153 H 6
Tomkinson Ranges ▲ AUS 176-177 K 3
Tomma ⌒ N 86-87 F 3
Tommot o RUS 118-119 N 6
Tommotskij massiv ▲ RUS 110-111 W 5
Tomo, Río ∼ CO 60-61 G 5
Tomochic o MEX 50-51 F 3
Tomohon o RI 164-165 J 3
Tomori o RCA 210-211 E 2
Tomorrit, Mali i ▲ AL 100-101 H 4
Tompira o RI 164-165 G 5
Tompi Seleka o ZA 220-221 J 2
Tompkins o CDN (SAS) 232-233 K 5
Tompkinsville o USA (KY) 276-277 K 4
Tompo o RI 164-165 G 3
Tompo o RUS 120-121 F 2
Tompo ∼ RUS 120-121 H 1
Tom Price o AUS 172-173 C 7
Tom Price, Mount ▲ AUS 172-173 C 7
Tompuda ∼ RUS 118-119 E 8
Tomsk ☆ · RUS 114-115 S 6
Toms River o USA (NJ) 280-281 M 4
Tom Steed ⊂ USA (OK) 264-265 E 4
Tomtor o RUS (SAH) 110-111 T 6
Tomtor o RUS (SAH) 120-121 E 2
Tomu o RI 166-167 G 3
Tomur Feng ▲ VRC 146-147 E 4
Tomu River ∼ PNG 183 B 4
Tom White, Mount ▲ USA 20-21 T 6
Tonalá o MEX (JAL) 52-53 C 1
Tonalá o · MEX (CHI) 52-53 H 3
Tonami o J 152-153 G 6
Tonantins o BR 66-67 D 4
Tonasket o USA (WA) 244-245 F 2
Tonate o F 62-63 H 3
Tonawanda Indian Reservation ✗ USA (NY) 278-279 C 5
Tonb-e Bozorg, Ğazire-ye ⌒ IR 134-135 F 5
Tonb-e Kuček, Ğazire-ye ⌒ IR 134-135 F 5
Tonda o PNG 183 A 5
Tondano o RI 164-165 J 3
Tondano, Danau ⊂ RI 164-165 J 3
Tonde o Z 218-219 E 1
Tønder o · DK 86-87 D 9
Tondi o IND 140-141 H 6
Tondibi o RMM 196-197 K 6
Tondidji o RMM 202-203 K 2
Tondigamé Goulbi ∼ RN 204-205 E 2
Tondi Kiwidi o RN 204-205 E 1
Tondon o RG 202-203 D 4
Tondong o RI 164-165 F 5
Toné o BF 202-203 J 4
Tone-gawa ∼ J 152-153 H 6
Tonekābon o IR 136-137 B 6
Tong o SUD 206-207 J 5
Tong ∼ SUD 206-207 J 5
Tonga o CAM 204-205 J 6
Tonga o SUD 206-207 K 4
Tonga ■ TON 184 IV a 1
Tongaat o ZA 220-221 K 4
Tongaland ⌒ ZA 220-221 L 3
Tong'an o VRC 156-157 L 4
Tonga Ridge ≃ 184 IV a 2
Tongariki ⌒ VAN 184 II b 3
Tongariro National Park ⊥ ··· NZ 182 E 3
Tongatapu ⌒ TON 184 IV a 2
Tongatapu Group ⌒ TON 184 IV a 2
Tonga Trench ≃ 13 K 4
Tongbai o VRC 154-155 H 5
Tongbai Shan ▲ VRC 154-155 H 5
Tongcheng o VRC (ANH) 154-155 K 6
Tongcheng o VRC (HUB) 156-157 H 2
Tongchon o DVR 150-151 F 8
Tongchuan o VRC 154-155 F 4
Tongdao o VRC 156-157 F 3
Tongde o VRC 154-155 B 4
T'ongdo Sa · ROK 150-151 G 10
Tongehatan Point ▲ RP 160-161 D 10
Tongerai, Tanjung ▲ RI 166-167 G 3
Tonggu o VRC 156-157 J 2
Tongguan o VRC 154-155 G 4
Tongguzbasti o VRC 146-147 E 6
Tongguo Zhang ▲ VRC 156-157 K 4
Tonghae o ROK 150-151 G 9
Tonghai o VRC 156-157 C 4
Tonghaiko o VRC 154-155 H 6
Tonghe o VRC 150-151 E 5
Tonghua o VRC 150-151 E 7
Tong Island ⌒ PNG 183 D 2
Tongjiang o VRC (HEI) 150-151 J 4
Tongjiang o VRC (SIC) 154-155 E 6
Tongjosŏn Man ≈ 150-151 F 8
Tongko o RI 164-165 G 4
Tongkomanino o RI 164-165 G 5
Tongku o RI 164-165 G 4
Tongliang o VRC 156-157 E 2
Tongliao o VRC 150-151 D 6
Tongling o VRC 154-155 K 6
Tonglu o VRC 156-157 L 2
Tongmu o VRC 156-157 J 4
Tongnan o VRC 154-155 D 6
Tongo o RCB 210-211 F 4
Tongoa ⌒ VAN 184 II b 3
Tongobory o RM 222-223 D 9
Tongomayél o BF 202-203 K 2
Tongren o VRC (GZH) 156-157 F 3
Tongren o VRC (QIN) 154-155 B 4
Tongsa o BHT 142-143 G 2
Tongshan o VRC 156-157 J 2
Tongshi o · VRC 156-157 F 7
Tongtian He ∼ VRC 144-145 L 4
Tongue o · GB 90-91 E 2
Tongue River ∼ USA (MT) 250-251 N 6
Tonguo ∼ RUS 118-119 K 4
Tonguro, Rio ∼ BR 72-73 D 2
Tongxiang o VRC 154-155 M 6
Tongxin o VRC 154-155 D 3
Tongyu o VRC (JIL) 150-151 D 5
Tongyu o VRC (SHA) 154-155 H 3
Tongzi o VRC 156-157 E 2
Tonhil = Zujl o MAU 146-147 L 2
Tonichi o MEX 50-51 E 3
Tonila o MEX 52-53 C 2
Tonimuca, Raudal ∼ CO 66-67 B 3
Tonina o CO 60-61 H 6
Toniná ∴ · MEX 52-53 H 3
Tonk o IND 138-139 E 6
Tonka o RMM 196-197 J 6
Tonkawa o USA (OK) 264-265 G 2
Tonkensval ∼ SME 62-63 F 3
Tonki Cape ▲ USA 22-23 V 3
Tonkin o CDN (SAS) 232-233 Q 4
Tonkin, Gulf of ≈ 156-157 E 6
Tonkui, Mont ▲ CI 202-203 G 6
Tônlé Sab ⊂ K 158-159 H 4
Tonnerre o F 90-91 J 8
Tōno o J 152-153 J 5
Tonoda ∼ RUS 118-119 G 6
Tonono o RA 76-77 F 2
Tonopah o USA (AZ) 256-257 C 5
Tonopah o USA (NV) 246-247 H 5
Tonopah Test Range Atomic Energy Commission xx USA (NV) 248-249 H 2
Tonoro o YV 60-61 K 3
Tonosí o PA 52-53 D 8
Tonosyō o J 152-153 F 7
Tonotha o RB 218-219 D 5
Tonquil Island ⌒ RP 160-161 D 10
Ton Sai o THA 158-159 F 7
Tønsberg ☆ N 86-87 E 7
Tonsina o USA 20-21 S 6
Tonstad ☆ N 86-87 C 7
Tontado, Caleta ≈ 76-77 B 5
Tontal, Sierra del ▲ RA 76-77 C 6
Tontelbos o ZA 220-221 E 5
Tonto, Rio ∼ MEX 52-53 F 2
Tonto Basin o USA (AZ) 256-257 D 5
Tonto National Monument · USA (AZ) 256-257 D 5
Tonumea ⌒ TON 184 IV a 2
Tonya ☆ TR 128-129 H 2
Tony Creek ∼ CDN (ALB) 228-229 R 2
Tonzona River ∼ USA 20-21 O 5
Toobanna o AUS 174-175 J 6
Toobli o LB 202-203 F 6
Toodyay o AUS 176-177 D 5
Tooele o USA (UT) 254-255 C 3
To Okena o PNG 183 D 4
Toolebuc o AUS 178-179 F 2
Toolik River ∼ USA 20-21 Q 2
Toolondo o AUS 180-181 F 4
Tooloombilla o AUS 178-179 K 3
Toompine o AUS 178-179 H 4
Toomula o AUS 174-175 J 6
Tooncatchyin Creek ∼ AUS 178-179 E 5
Toora-Hem ☆ RUS 116-117 H 9
Toormt o MAU 116-117 F 10
Toornaarsuk ⌒ GRØ 28-29 Q 6
Toowoomba o AUS 178-179 L 4
Top, Ozero = Topozero ⊂ RUS 88-89 M 4
Topagoruk River ∼ USA 20-21 N 1
Topanga o USA (CA) 248-249 F 5
Topar o KA 124-125 J 6
Topasovèj, ostrov ⌒ RUS 108-109 M 7
Topawa o USA (AZ) 256-257 D 7
Topaz o USA (CA) 246-247 F 5
Topaz Lake ⊂ USA (NV) 246-247 F 5
Topeka ☆ USA (KS) 262-263 L 5
Topia o MEX 50-51 F 5
Topia ∼ RCA 206-207 C 6
Topía, Quebrada ∼ MEX 50-51 F 5
Topko, gora ▲ RUS 120-121 G 5
Topley o CDN (BC) 228-229 H 2
Topley Landing o CDN (BC) 228-229 H 2
Toplița o · RO 102-103 D 4
Topocalma, Punta ▲ RCH 78-79 C 3
Topock o USA (AZ) 256-257 A 4
Top of the World Provincial Park ⊥ CDN (BC) 230-231 O 4
Topografičeskaja, grjada ▲ RUS 108-109 Z 4
Topol o RUS 116-117 G 7
Topola o · YU 100-101 H 2
Topoli o ZRE 212-213 A 2
Topolinoe o RUS 120-121 F 1
Topolobampo o MEX 50-51 E 5
Topolovgrad o BG 102-103 E 6
Topolovka o RUS 120-121 T 3
Topozero o RUS 88-89 M 4
Toppenish o USA (WA) 244-245 E 4
Toppi-misaki ▲ J 152-153 C 9
Toprakkale ∴ · TR 128-129 K 3
Tops, Mount ▲ AUS 178-179 B 1
Topsfield o USA (ME) 278-279 O 3
Top Springs o AUS (NT) 172-173 K 4
Top Springs o AUS (NT) 174-175 C 5
Topura o PNG 183 F 6
Topyrakkala · US 136-137 G 4
Toquerville o USA (UT) 254-255 B 6
Tor o ETH 208-209 A 5
Toramarkog o VRC 144-145 L 4
Torata o PE 70-71 B 5
Torbanlea o AUS 178-179 M 3
Torbat-e Ğām o · IR 136-137 G 7
Torbat-e Heidariye o · IR 136-137 F 7
Torbay o AUS 176-177 D 7
Torbay o CDN (NFL) 242-243 Q 5
Tor Bay ≈ CDN 242-241 O 5
Torbay o GB 90-91 F 6
Torboy o USA (WA) 244-245 G 2
Torch River ∼ CDN (SAS) 232-233 P 2
Tordenskjold, Kap ▲ GRØ 28-29 T 6
Tordesillas o E 98-99 E 4
Töre o S 86-87 L 4
Torej, Zun, ozero ⊂ RUS 118-119 H 10
Torell Land ⊥ N 84-85 K 4
Torelló o E 98-99 J 3
Torenur o IND 140-141 F 4
Toreo Bugis o RI 164-165 H 5
Torğaj o KA (KST) 126-127 P 3
Torğaj ∼ KA 124-125 D 3
Torğaj ∼ KA 126-127 P 3
Torğaj kolaty ⌒ KA 126-127 P 3
Torğaj üstirti ▲ KA 124-125 B 3
Torgau o · D 92-93 M 3
Torgun ∼ RUS 96-97 E 8
Torhout o B 92-93 G 3
Tori o RMM 202-203 J 3
Toribio o CO 60-61 C 6
Tori-Bossito o DY 204-205 E 5
Torino ☆ · I 100-101 A 2
Torino, Cachoeira do ∼ BR 62-63 F 6
Tori-shima ⌒ J 152-153 C 11
Torit o SUD 206-207 L 6
Toritama o BR 68-69 K 6
Toriu o PNG 183 F 3
Toriud o IR 136-137 D 7
Torje, Barun, ozero ⊂ RUS 118-119 G 10
Torkamān o IR 128-129 M 4
Torkemān, Bandar-e o IR 136-137 D 6
Torlu River ∼ PNG 183 F 3
Tormèmtor, ozero ⊂ RUS 114-115 P 4
Torment, Point ▲ AUS 172-173 F 4
Tormes, Río ∼ E 98-99 E 4
Tormosin o RUS 102-103 N 3
Tornado Mountain ▲ CDN (BC) 230-231 P 4
Torneälven ∼ S 86-87 L 3
Torneträsk ⊂ · S 86-87 J 2
Torngat Mountains ▲ CDN 36-37 R 5
Tornik ▲ YU 100-101 G 3
Tornio o FIN 88-89 H 4
Tornionjoki ∼ FIN 88-89 G 3
Tornquist o RA 78-79 F 5
Toro o E 98-99 E 4
Toro o EAU 212-213 C 3
Toro, Cerro del ∼ RA 76-77 C 5
Toro, Isla del ⌒ MEX 50-51 L 7
Toro, Lago del ⊂ RCH 80 D 5
Toro, Punta ▲ RCH 78-79 D 2
Torobuku o RI 164-165 H 6
Torodi o RN 202-203 L 3
Toro Doum < TCH 198-199 H 4
Toro Game Reservat ⊥ EAU 212-213 C 3
Torokina o PNG 184 I b 2
Toro Kinkéné o CI 202-203 H 5
Torokoroba o RMM 202-203 G 3
Törökszentmiklós o H 92-93 Q 5
Torola, Río ∼ ES 52-53 K 5
Torom o RUS 120-121 F 6
Torom ∼ RUS 120-121 F 6
Toro Negro, Sierra del ▲ RA 76-77 C 5
Toronto ☆ · CDN (ONT) 238-239 F 5
Toronto o USA (KS) 262-263 L 7
Toronto Lake ⊂ USA (KS) 262-263 L 7
Toropec ☆ RUS 94-95 M 3
Toroq o IR 136-137 F 6
Tororo o EAU 212-213 E 3
Torqabe o IR 136-137 F 6
Torquato Severo o BR 76-77 K 6
Torquay o CDN (SAS) 232-233 P 6
Torquinie, Lake o AUS 178-179 E 3
Torrabaai o NAM 216-217 B 10
Torrance o USA (CA) 248-249 F 6
Torrão o P 98-99 C 5
Torrealba o YV 60-61 J 3
Torre del Greco o I 100-101 E 4
Torre de Moncorvo o P 98-99 D 4
Torrelaguna o E 98-99 F 4
Torrelavega o E 98-99 E 3
Torremolinos o E 98-99 E 6
Torrens, Cape ▲ CDN 24-25 a 2
Torrens, Lake o AUS 178-179 D 6
Torrens Creek o AUS 174-175 H 7
Torrens Creek ∼ AUS 178-179 H 2
Torrens River ∼ CDN (ALB) 228-229 P 2
Torreón o MEX 50-51 H 5
Torreon o USA (NM) 256-257 H 3
Torre-Pacheco o E 98-99 G 6
Torres o · BR 74-75 F 7
Torres, Îles = Torres Islands ⌒ VAN 184 II a 1
Torres del Paine o RCH 80 D 5
Torres del Paine, Parque Nacional ⊥ ·· RCH 80 D 5
Torres Islands = Îles Torres ⌒ VAN 184 II a 1
Torres Martinez Indian Reservation ✗ USA (CA) 248-249 H 6
Torres Novas o P 98-99 C 5
Torres Selat ≈ 183 A 5
Torres Strait ≈ 174-175 F 1
Torres Vedras o P 98-99 C 5
Torrevieja o E 98-99 G 6
Torrey o USA (UT) 254-255 D 5
Torricelli Mountains ▲ PNG 183 B 2
Torrijos o E 98-99 E 5
Torrington o CDN (ALB) 232-233 E 4
Torrington o USA (CT) 280-281 N 2
Torrington o USA (WY) 252-253 O 4
Torrock o TCH 206-207 B 4
Torrön ⊂ S 86-87 F 5
Torsås ☆ S 86-87 H 8
Torsby ☆ · S 86-87 F 6
Torset, Oued ∼ DZ 190-191 G 8
Tórshavn ☆ FR 90-91 D 1
Torsö ⌒ S 86-87 F 7
Torssuqatak ≈ 28-29 P 2
Tortas, Cachoeira das ∼ BR 70-71 J 4
Tortel o RCH 80 D 3
Tortiya o · CI 202-203 H 5
Törtköl o KA 136-137 L 3
Tortola ⌒ GB 56 C 2
Tortola ⌒ GB (VI) 286-287 R 2
Tórtoles de Esgueva o E 98-99 E 4
Tortona o I 100-101 B 2
Tortosa o E 98-99 H 4
Tortosa, Cabo de ▲ E 98-99 H 4
Tortue, Île de la ⌒ RH 54-55 J 4
Tortuga, Isla ⌒ MEX 50-51 D 4
Tortuga, Isla La ⌒ YV 60-61 J 2
Tortuguero, Parque Nacional ⊥ CR 52-53 C 6
Tortuguilla o C 54-55 H 5
Tortum ☆ TR 128-129 J 2
Torue o RI 164-165 G 4
Torul ☆ TR 128-129 H 2
Toruń ☆ ·· PL 92-93 P 2
Torup o S 86-87 F 8
Tõrva o ·· EST 94-95 J 2
Torwood o AUS 174-175 G 5
Tory o RUS 116-117 L 10
Tory Hill o CDN (ONT) 238-239 G 4
Toržkovskaja grjada ▲ RUS 94-95 O 3
Toržok ☆ RUS 94-95 O 3
Torzym o PL 92-93 N 2
Tosagua o EC 64-65 B 2
Tosari o RI 168 E 3
Tosa-shimizu o J 152-153 E 8
Tosa-wan ≈ 152-153 E 8
Tosca o ZA 220-221 F 2
Toscana ◘ I 100-101 C 3
Toscas, Las o RA (BUA) 78-79 J 3
Toscas, Las o RA (SAF) 76-77 H 5
Toscas, Las o ROU 78-79 M 2
Toshām o IND 138-139 E 5
Toshima ⌒ J 152-153 H 7
Toshino-Kumano National Park ⊥ J 152-153 G 7
Tosi o SUD 206-207 K 3
Toškent ★ ·· US 136-137 L 4
Toškuduk, kumlik ⊥ US 136-137 G 3
Toškürgon o US 136-137 K 5
Tosno ☆ RUS 94-95 M 2
Tosoncengel o MAU 148-149 D 3
Toson Hu ⊂ VRC 144-145 L 2
Tostado o RA 76-77 G 5
Tõstamaa o EST 94-95 H 2
Toston o USA (MT) 250-251 H 5
Tošviska o RUS 88-89 W 3
Tosya ☆ TR 128-129 F 2
Tot o EAK 212-213 E 3
Totaranui o NZ 182 D 4
Toteng o RB 218-219 B 5
Tôtes o F 90-91 H 7
Totias o SP 212-213 J 2
Tot'ma o RUS 94-95 S 2
Totnes o CDN (SAS) 232-233 K 4
Totnes Fiord ≈ 28-29 J 3
Totness ☆ SME 62-63 F 3
Toto o ANG 216-217 C 3
Toto o WAN 204-205 G 4
Totogan Creek ∼ CDN (ONT) 234-235 O 2
Totogan Lake ⊂ CDN (ONT) 234-235 O 2
Totoglag o VAN 184 II a 1
Totok o RI 164-165 J 3
Totolán o MEX 52-53 C 1
Totolapan o MEX 52-53 F 3
Totomai, Monts ▲ RN 198-199 G 2
Totonicapán ☆ · GCA 52-53 J 4
Totora o BOL (COC) 70-71 E 5
Totora o BOL (ORU) 70-71 C 5
Totoral o RCH 76-77 B 4
Totoral, Quebrada del ∼ RCH 76-77 B 5
Totoralejos o RA 76-77 E 5
Totoras o RA 78-79 J 2
Totota o LB 202-203 F 6
Totoya ⌒ FJI 184 III c 3
Totta ∼ RUS 120-121 G 5
Tottan Range ▲ ARK 16 F 35
Totten Glacier ⊂ ARK 16 G 12
Tottenham o AUS 180-181 J 2
Tottenham o CDN (ONT) 238-239 F 4
Tottori ☆ J 152-153 F 7
Totumito o YV 60-61 F 4
Totydèottajaha, Bol'šaja ∼ RUS 108-109 T 8
Touâjîl o RIM 196-197 D 3
Touak Fiord ≈ 36-37 S 2
Touâret < RN 198-199 D 2
Touaris, Djebel ▲ DZ 188-189 K 6
Touat ⊥ DZ 188-189 L 7
Touba o CI 202-203 G 5
Touba o · SN 202-203 C 2
Toubacouta o SN 202-203 B 3
Toubéré Bafal o SN 202-203 D 2
Toubkal, Ibel ▲ MA 188-189 H 5
Touboro o CAM 206-207 B 5
Touboutou, Chutes de ∼ · RCA 206-207 B 6
Toucha, Djebel ▲ DZ 188-189 L 5
Touchet o USA (WA) 244-245 G 4
Toucy o F 90-91 J 8
Toueyyirât < RMM 196-197 J 5
Tougan o BF 202-203 J 3
Tougé o RG 202-203 E 4
Tougourt o · DZ 190-191 F 4
Tougnifili o RG 202-203 C 4
Tougouri o BF 202-203 K 3
Tougoutaou < RN 198-199 C 5
Touijinet < RIM 196-197 F 5
Touil, Hâssi < RIM 196-197 H 6
Touila, Bir < TN 190-191 G 4
Toujî o RIM 196-197 E 7
Toukoto o RMM 202-203 F 3
Toukountouna o DY 202-203 L 4
Toul o F 90-91 K 7
Touléplеu o CI 202-203 F 6
Touliu o RC 156-157 M 5
Toulnustouc, Rivière ∼ CDN 38-39 K 4
Toulon ☆ F 90-91 K 10
Toulon o USA (IL) 274-275 J 3
Toulou, Abri des · RCA 206-207 E 4
Toulounga o TCH 206-207 D 4
Toulouse ☆ ·· F 90-91 H 10
Toumbélaga < RN 198-199 C 5
Toumodi o CI 202-203 H 6
Toumoundjila o RN 202-203 F 4
Tounassine, Hamada ⊥ DZ 188-189 H 6
Tounfafi o RN 198-199 B 5
Toungo o WAN 204-205 K 4
Toungoo o MYA 142-143 K 6
Toungour < TCH 198-199 J 4
Toura ∼ BF 202-203 K 3
Toura o DY 204-205 E 3
Touragondi o AFG 136-137 H 7
Tourassinne < RIM 196-197 E 2
Tourba o TCH 198-199 G 6
Tourcoing o F 90-91 J 6
Touré Kounda o SN 202-203 D 3
Tour Ham o AFG 138-139 C 2
Touriñán, Cabo ▲ E 98-99 C 3
Tourine o RIM 196-197 E 3
Tournai o · B 92-93 G 3
Tournavista o PE 64-65 E 6
Tournde, Oued ∼ DZ 190-191 H 9
Tourni o BF 202-203 H 4
Tournus o F 90-91 K 8
Touros o BR 68-69 L 4
Tourou ▲ CAM 204-205 K 3
Touroua o CAM 204-205 K 4
Tourougoumbé o RMM 202-203 F 2
Touroug o MA 188-189 J 5
Touroukoro o BF 202-203 H 4
Tours o F 90-91 H 8
Tour Village, De o USA (MI) 272-273 F 2

Touside, Pic ▲ TCH 198-199 H 2
Toussoro, Mont ▲ RCA 206-207 F 4
Toutes Aides o CDN (MAN) 234-235 D 3
Toutoukro o CI 202-203 H 5
Touwsrivier o ZA 220-221 E 6
Touwsrivier ~ ZA 220-221 E 6
Tōv ◘ MAU 148-149 G 4
Tovar o YV 60-61 F 3
Tovar Donoso o EC 64-65 C 1
Tovarkovskij o RUS 94-95 Q 5
Tovdalselva ~ N 86-87 D 7
Tovuz o AZ 128-129 L 2
Tow o USA (TX) 266-267 J 3
Towada o J 152-153 J 4
Towada-Hachimantai National Park ⊥ J 152-153 J 4
Towada Hachimantai National Park ⊥ J 152-153 J 5
Towada-ko • J 152-153 J 4
Towakaima o GUY 62-63 D 2
Towanda o USA (KS) 262-263 K 7
Towanda o USA (PA) 280-281 K 2
Towaoc o USA (CO) 254-255 G 6
Towari o RI 164-165 G 6
Towe o LB 202-203 F 6
Tower o USA (MN) 270-271 F 3
Towera o AUS 176-177 C 1
Towerhill Creek ~ AUS 178-179 H 1
Tower Peak ▲ AUS 176-177 G 6
Tower-Roosevelt o USA (WY) 252-253 H 2
Towla o ZW 218-219 E 5
Town Creek o USA (AL) 284-285 C 2
Town Creek ~ USA (AL) 284-285 C 2
Town Creek ~ USA (AL) 284-285 D 2
Town Creek Indian Mound • USA (NC) 282-283 H 5
Towne Pass ▲ USA (CA) 248-249 G 3
Towner o USA (CO) 254-255 N 5
Towner o USA (ND) 258-259 G 3
Townley o USA (AL) 284-285 C 3
Townsend o USA (GA) 284-285 J 5
Townsend o USA (MT) 250-251 H 5
Townsend o USA (WI) 270-271 K 5
Townsend Lake o CDN 30-31 W 4
Townsend Ridges ▲ AUS 176-177 J 3
Townshend o USA (VT) 278-279 J 5
Townshend Island ⌒ AUS 178-179 L 2
Towns River ~ AUS 174-175 C 4
Townsville o•• AUS 174-175 J 6
Towson o USA (MD) 280-281 K 4
Towuti, Danau o RI 164-165 G 5
Toxkan He ~ VRC 146-147 D 5
Toyah o USA (TX) 266-267 D 2
Toyah, Lake o USA (TX) 266-267 D 2
Toyah Creek ~ USA (TX) 266-267 D 2
Toyahvale o USA (TX) 266-267 D 3
Tōya-ko o J 152-153 J 3
Toyama ☆ J 152-153 G 6
Toyama-wan ≈ 152-153 G 6
Toyo o J 152-153 F 8
Toyohashi o J 152-153 G 7
Toyokawa o J 152-153 G 7
Toyooka o J 152-153 F 7
Toyota o J 152-153 G 7
Toyotomi o J 152-153 J 2
Tozer, Mount ▲ AUS 174-175 G 3
Tozeur ☆• TN 190-191 G 4
Tozitna River ~ USA 20-21 O 4
Trabária, Bocca ▲ I 100-101 D 3
Trà Bồng o VN 158-159 K 3
Trabzon ☆•• TR 128-129 H 2
Tracadie o CDN (NB) 240-241 L 3
Tracadie o CDN (PEI) 240-241 O 4
Trácino o I 100-101 D 6
Tracy o CDN (NB) 240-241 J 5
Tracy o USA (AZ) 256-257 C 6
Tracy o USA (CA) 248-249 C 2
Tracy o USA (MN) 270-271 C 6
Tracy Arm Fords Terror Wilderness ⊥• USA 32-33 D 3
Tracy City o USA (TN) 276-277 K 5
Tradewater River ~ USA (KY) 276-277 H 3
Trading River ~ CDN (ONT) 234-235 O 3
Traditional Villages • RI 168 D 7
Tradit. Villages o• RI 168 D 7
Traela, Punta de ▲ RCH 78-79 D 2
Trænstaven ⌒ N 86-87 E 3
Traer o USA (IA) 274-275 F 2
Tragacete o E 98-99 G 4
Traiguén o RCH 78-79 C 5
Traiguen, Isla ⌒ RCH 80 D 2
Trail o CDN (BC) 230-231 M 4
Trail o USA (MN) 270-271 C 3
Trail o USA (OR) 244-245 C 8
Trail City o USA (SD) 260-261 F 1
Traill Ø ⌒ GRØ 26-27 o 7
Traine River ~ AUS 172-173 H 4
Traipu o BR 68-69 K 6
Traíra, Serra do ▲ BR 66-67 C 3
Trairão, Rio ~ BR 68-69 C 5
Trairi o BR 68-69 J 3
Trajgorodskaja ~ RUS 114-115 P 4
Trakai ☆ LT 94-95 J 4
Trakan Phut Phon o THA 158-159 H 3
Trakošćan • HR 100-101 E 1
Trakt o RUS 88-89 V 5
Tralee = Trá Lí ☆ IRL 90-91 C 5
Trá Lí = Tralee ☆ IRL 90-91 C 5
Trallwng = Welshpool o• GB 90-91 F 5
Tramandaí o BR 74-75 E 7
Tramanu ~ RI 166-167 B 6
Trammel Fork ~ USA (KY) 276-277 J 4
Trampa, La o PE 64-65 B 5
Tramping Lake o CDN (SAS) 232-233 K 3
Tramping Lake o CDN (SAS) 232-233 K 3
Trà My o VN 158-159 K 3
Trân o BG 102-103 C 6
Tranås ☆ S 86-87 G 7
Tranche-sur-Mer, la o F 90-91 G 8
Trang o THA 158-159 E 7
Trangan, Pulau ⌒ RI 166-167 H 5
Trảng Bàng o VN 158-159 J 5
Trangie o AUS 180-181 J 2
Tranomaro o RM 222-223 E 10
Tranoroa o RM 222-223 D 10
Tranqui, Isla ⌒ RCH 78-79 C 7
Tranquille o CDN (BC) 230-231 J 3
Trans Africa Route = Route transafricaine II WAN 204-205 G 5
Trānsāh o IR 128-129 M 4
Trans-Amazon Highway = Transamazônica II BR 66-67 H 6
Transamazônica II BR 66-67 H 6
Trans-Australian-Railway II AUS 176-177 K 5
Trans-Canada-Highway • CDN 230-231 H 3
Transhimalaya = Gangdisê Shan ▲ 144-145 C 5
Transkei (former Homeland, now part of East-Cape) ◘ ZA 220-221 H 5
Transsib II• RUS 118-119 E 10
Transsua o CI 202-203 J 6
Transylvania = Transilvani, Podişul ◡ RO 102-103 C 4
Transylvanian Alps = Carpaţii Meridionali ▲ RO 100-101 J 2
Tranum o MAL 162-163 D 3
Tranzitnyj o RUS 112-113 V 3
Trà Ôn o VN 158-159 H 6
Trapalco, Cerro ▲ RA 78-79 E 6
Trapalcó, Salinas o RA 78-79 F 5
Trápani o I 100-101 D 5
Traralgon o AUS 180-181 J 5
Traras, Monts des ▲ DZ 188-189 L 3
Trarza ◘ RIM 196-197 C 5
Trârza ∴ RIM 196-197 C 6
Trasimeno, Lago o I 100-101 D 3
Traskwood o USA (AR) 276-277 C 6
Trás os Montes e Alto Douro ∴ P 98-99 D 4
Trat o THA 158-159 G 4
Trautenau = Trutnov o CZ 92-93 N 3
Trautfetter ~ RUS 108-109 d 4
Travaillant Lake o CDN 20-21 Z 3
Travelers Rest o USA (SC) 284-285 H 2
Traveler's Rest State Historic Site • USA (GA) 284-285 G 2
Travellers Lake o AUS 180-181 F 2
Travellers Rest • USA (MT) 250-251 E 5
Travemünde o D 92-93 L 2
Traverse, Lake o USA (SD) 260-261 K 1
Traverse City o USA (MI) 272-273 D 3
Traverse Peak ▲ USA 20-21 L 4
Travers Reservoir o CDN (ALB) 232-233 F 5
Travesía del Tunuyán ∴ RA 78-79 F 2
Travesía Puntana ∴ RA 78-79 F 3
Travessia de Caju ~ BR 68-69 D 5
Travessia do Jacuzao ~ BR 68-69 D 5
Trà Vinh o VN 158-159 J 6
Travis, Lake < USA (TX) 266-267 K 3
Travka ~ RUS 112-113 P 4
Trawas o RI 162-163 E 6
Trayning o AUS 176-177 D 5
Traynor o CDN (SAS) 232-233 K 3
Trbovlje o SLO 100-101 E 1
Tre ⌒ VN 158-159 K 4
Treasure Beach o JA 54-55 G 6
Treasure Island o USA (FL) 286-287 G 4
Treasury Islands ⌒ SOL 184 I b 2
Třebíč o CZ 92-93 N 4
Trebinje o BIH 100-101 G 3
Trebisacce o I 100-101 F 5
Trebitsch = Třebíč o CZ 92-93 N 4
Treelon o CDN (SAS) 232-233 K 6
Tree River ~ CDN 20-21 Y 3
Tree River ~ CDN 30-31 O 2
Treesbank o CDN (MAN) 234-235 D 5
Trees Point ▲ CDN 26-27 J 3
Trego o USA (MT) 250-251 E 3
Trego o USA (WI) 270-271 G 5
Trehbugornyj, mys ▲ RUS 108-109 P 7
Treherne o CDN (MAN) 234-235 E 5
Treinta y Tres ☆ ROU 78-79 M 2
Trelew o RA 78-79 G 7
Trelleborg o S 86-87 F 9
Tremblant, Mont ▲ CDN (QUE) 238-239 L 2
Trembleur Lake o CDN (BC) 228-229 J 2
Tremen, Volcán ▲ RA 78-79 D 4
Trémiti, Ísole ⌒ I 100-101 E 3
Tremont o USA (PA) 280-281 K 3
Tremonton o USA (UT) 254-255 C 2
Tremp o E 98-99 H 3
Trena o ETH 208-209 E 3
Trenary o USA (MI) 270-271 M 4
Trenche, Rivière o CDN (QUE) 236-237 P 4
Trenčín o SK 92-93 P 4
Trenčín = Trentschin o SK 92-93 P 4
Trenggalek o RI 168 D 4
Trenque Lauquen o RA 78-79 H 3
Trent ~ GB 90-91 F 5
Trent o USA (TX) 264-265 D 6
Trente-et-un Milles, Lac des o CDN (QUE) 238-239 K 2
Trentino -Alto Adige ◘ I 100-101 C 1
Trento ☆• I 100-101 C 1
Trenton o CDN (ONT) 238-239 H 4
Trenton o USA (FL) 286-287 G 2
Trenton o USA (GA) 284-285 E 2
Trenton o USA (IL) 274-275 J 6
Trenton o USA (MI) 272-273 F 5
Trenton o USA (MO) 274-275 E 4
Trenton o USA (NC) 282-283 K 5
Trenton o USA (NE) 262-263 E 4
Trenton o USA (TN) 276-277 G 5
Trenton ☆ USA (NJ) 280-281 M 3
Trent River ~ CDN (ONT) 238-239 H 4
Trent River ~ USA (NC) 282-283 K 5
Trepassey o CDN (NFL) 242-243 P 6
Trepassey Bay ≈ 38-39 S 5
Trepassey Bay ≈ CDN 242-243 P 6
Trephina Gorge ⊥ AUS 178-179 C 2
Tréport, Le o F 90-91 H 6
Tres Altilos, Cerro ▲ RA 78-79 E 2
Tres Arboles o• ROU 78-79 F 2
Tres Arroyos o RA 78-79 J 5
Três Barracas, Cachoeira ~ BR 66-67 G 7
Três Bicos o BR 74-75 E 5
Tres Bocas o RA 78-79 K 2
Três Casas o BR 66-67 F 6
Três Cerros ▲ RA 78-79 D 7
Três Corações o BR 72-73 H 6
Tres Cruces o BOL 70-71 F 5
Tres Cruces, Arroyo ~ ROU 76-77 J 6
Tres Cruces, Cerro ▲ MEX 52-53 H 4
Tres Cruces, Cerro ▲ RCH 76-77 C 4
Três de Maio o BR 76-77 K 4
Tres Esquinas o CO 64-65 E 1
Três Ilhas, Cachoeira das ~ BR 66-67 J 7
Três Irmãos, Cachoeira dos ~ BR 70-71 H 2
Três Irmãos, Serra dos ▲ BR 66-67 E 7
Tres Isletas o RA 76-77 G 4
Treska ~ MK 100-101 H 4
Três Lagoas o BR 72-73 E 6
Tres Lagos o RA 80 E 4
Tres Mapejos o BOL 70-71 E 2
Três Marias o BR 72-73 H 5
Três Marias, Represa < BR 72-73 H 5
Tres Matas, Las o YV 60-61 J 3
Tres Mojones o RA 76-77 G 4
Tres Montes, Cabo ▲ RCH 80 C 3
Tres Montes, Península ◡ RCH 80 C 3
Tres Morros o RA 76-77 E 2
Tres Palacios ~ USA (TX) 266-267 L 5
Tres Palmas o CO 60-61 D 3
Três Palmeiras o BR 74-75 D 6
Tres Palos, Laguna o MEX 52-53 E 3
Três Passos o BR 74-75 D 6
Tres Picos, Cerro ▲ RA 78-79 J 5
Tres Piedras o USA (NM) 256-257 K 2
Três Praias o BR 66-67 D 7
Tres Puntas ▲ GCA 52-53 K 4
Tres Puntas, Cabo ▲ RA 80 H 3
Três Ranchos o BR 72-73 G 5
Três Rios o BR 72-73 J 7
Tres Unidos o PE 64-65 E 4
Tres Valles o MEX 52-53 F 2
Três Vendas o BR 76-77 K 6
Tres Virgenes, Volcán de las ▲ MEX 50-51 C 4
Tres Zapotes ∴• MEX 52-53 G 2
Tretes o• RI 168 E 3
Tretij, ostrov ⌒ RUS 120-121 U 3
Tret'jakovo o RUS 124-125 M 3
Treuburg = Olecko o PL 92-93 R 1
Treuenbrietzen o D 92-93 M 2
Treuer Range ▲ AUS 172-173 K 7
Tréve, Lac la o CDN (ONT) 236-237 N 3
Trevelín o RA 78-79 D 7
Treviglio o I 100-101 B 2
Treviso o BR 74-75 F 7
Treviso ☆ I 100-101 D 2
Trevlac o USA (IN) 274-275 M 5
Trewdate o CDN (SAS) 232-233 M 5
Triabunna o AUS 180-181 J 7
Triang o MAL 162-163 E 3
Triangle o CDN 32-33 M 4
Triangle o USA (ND) 282-283 F 5
Triangle o ZW 218-219 F 5
Triángulos, Arrecifes ⌒ MEX 52-53 H 1
Trianon o RH 54-55 J 5
Tribugá o CO 60-61 C 5
Tribugá, Golfo de ≈ 60-61 C 5
Tribune o CDN (SAS) 232-233 P 6
Tribune o USA (KS) 262-263 E 6
Tricase o I 100-101 G 5
Trichur o• IND 140-141 G 5
Trici o BR 68-69 H 4
Tri City o USA (KY) 276-277 G 4
Trida o AUS 180-181 H 2
Tridell o USA (UT) 254-255 F 3
Trident o USA (MT) 250-251 H 6
Trident Peak ▲ USA (NV) 246-247 G 2
Trier o••• D 92-93 J 4
Trieste ☆• I 100-101 D 2
Trieste, Golfo di ≈ 100-101 D 2
Trieste, Gulf of = Trieste, Golfo di ≈ I 100-101 D 2
Triglav ▲ SLO 100-101 D 1
Triglavski Narodni Park ⊥ SLO 100-101 D 1
Trigo, El o RA 78-79 K 3
Trigonon o GR 100-101 H 4
Trikala o• GR 100-101 H 5
Trikkandiyur o IND 140-141 F 5
Trikonamadu o CL 140-141 J 6
Trillbar o AUS 176-177 D 2
Trilsbeck Lake o CDN (ONT) 236-237 D 2
Trim = Baile Átha Troim ☆• IRL 90-91 D 5
Trimble o USA (MO) 274-275 D 5
Trincheras, Las o YV 60-61 J 4
Trincomalee o• CL 140-141 J 6
Trindade o BR (GOI) 72-73 F 4
Trindade o BR (PER) 68-69 H 5
Trindade o BR (ROR) 62-63 D 5
Tring o PNG 183 B 2
Trinidad ☆ BOL 70-71 E 4
Trinidad o••• C 54-55 F 4
Trinidad o CO 60-61 F 5
Trinidad o••• PY 76-77 K 4
Trinidad ☆ ROU 78-79 L 2
Trinidad ⌒ TT 60-61 L 2
Trinidad o USA (CA) 246-247 A 2
Trinidad o USA (CO) 254-255 L 6
Trinidad, Golfo ≈ 80 C 4
Trinidad, Isla ⌒ RA 78-79 J 5
Trinidad, Laguna o PY 70-71 G 7
Trinidad and Tobago ■ TT 60-61 L 2
Trinidad de Arauca, La o YV 60-61 G 4
Trinidade o BR 68-69 D 3
Trinidade, Ilha da ⌒ BR 66-67 H 4
Trinitaria, La o MEX 52-53 H 3
Trinity o CDN (NFL) 242-243 P 4
Trinity o USA (TX) 268-269 E 6
Trinity Bay ≈ 38-39 S 5
Trinity Bay ≈ CDN 242-243 P 5
Trinity Center o USA (CA) 246-247 C 3
Trinity East o CDN (NFL) 242-243 P 4
Trinity Islands ⌒ USA 22-23 T 4
Trinity Range ▲ USA (NV) 246-247 F 4
Trinity River ~ USA (CA) 246-247 B 3
Trinity River ~ USA (TX) 264-265 H 6
Trinity River ~ USA (TX) 266-267 L 2
Trinity River ~ USA (TX) 268-269 F 6
Trinity Site • USA (NM) 256-257 J 5
Trinkat Island ⌒ IND 140-141 L 5
Triolet o MS 224 C 7
Trion o USA (GA) 284-285 E 2
Trios o BR 62-63 G 4
Tripoli o GR 100-101 J 6
Tripoli = Tarābulus o• RL 128-129 F 5
Tripolis = Tarābulus ★ LAR 192-193 E 1
Tripolitania = Tarābulus ∴ LAR 192-193 D 2
Tripp o USA (SD) 260-261 J 3
Tripton o USA (UT) 254-255 D 5
Tripura ◘ IND 142-143 G 4
Tristan da Cunha Fracture Zone ≃ 6-7 G 12
Tristao, Iles ⌒ RG 202-203 C 4
Triste, Golfo ≈ 60-61 H 2
Triste, Monte ▲ RA 78-79 G 7
Tristeza, Cuchilla de la ▲ RA 78-79 E 3
Trisul ▲ IND 138-139 G 4
Trisuli ~ NEP 144-145 E 7
Trisuli Bazar o NEP 144-145 E 7
Triton, Teluk ≈ 166-167 H 3
Triton Island = Zhongjian Dao ⌒ VRC 158-159 L 3
Triune o USA (TN) 276-277 J 5
Triunfo o BR 74-75 E 7
Triunfo, El o MEX 52-53 J 3
Triunfo, Igarapé ~ BR 68-69 B 5
Triunvirato o RA 78-79 J 3
Trivalea-Moşteni o RO 102-103 D 5
Trivandrum ☆• IND 140-141 G 6
Trnava o SK 92-93 O 4
Trobriand Islands ⌒ PNG 183 F 5
Trocana, Ilha ⌒ BR 66-67 H 5
Trocatá, Área Indígena X BR 68-69 D 3
Trochu o CDN (ALB) 232-233 E 4
Trocoman, Río ~ RA 78-79 D 4
Troebratskij o KA 124-125 E 1
Trofors o N 86-87 F 4
Trogir o•• HR 100-101 F 3
Troick o RUS 116-117 G 7
Troick ☆ RUS (CEL) 96-97 M 6
Troickij o RUS 114-115 G 6
Troicko-Pečorsk ☆ RUS 114-115 D 3
Trois Fourches, Cap des ▲ MA 188-189 K 3
Trois-Îlets, Les o F 56 E 4
Trois-Pistoles o CDN (QUE) 240-241 F 2
Trois-Rivières o CDN (QUE) 238-239 N 2
Trois Rivières, les o RCA 206-207 G 5
Trois Rivières, Les ~ RH 54-55 J 5
Trois Sauts o F 62-63 H 4
Trojan o BG 102-103 D 6
Trojes, Las o HN 52-53 B 4
Trojnoj, ostrov ⌒ RUS 108-109 U 4
Trolla < TCH 198-199 B 6
Trollhättan ☆ S 86-87 F 7
Trolltindane ▲•• N 86-87 C 5
Tromai, Baía do ≈ 68-69 F 2
Tromai, Rio ~ BR 68-69 F 2
Trombetas, Rio ~ BR 62-63 F 5
Trom"egan ~ RUS 114-115 M 3
Tromelin, Île ⌒ F 12 D 6
Trompsburg o ZA 220-221 G 5
Tromsø ☆• N 86-87 J 2
Trona o USA (CA) 248-249 G 4
Tronador, Cerro ▲ RCH 78-79 C 6
Troncal, La o EC 64-65 C 3
Troncos, Los o BOL 70-71 F 5
Troncoso o MEX 50-51 H 6
Trondheim ☆•• N 86-87 E 5
Trondheimsfjorden ≈ 86-87 D 5
Troodos ▲ CY 128-129 E 5
Troodos, Kirchen von = Ekklisía ••• CY 128-129 E 5
Tropas, Rio das ~ BR 66-67 J 6
Tropea o I 100-101 E 5
Tropêco Grande, Cachoeira do ~ BR 72-73 F 2
Tropia, Ponta ▲ BR 68-69 H 3
Tropico, El o C 54-55 E 3
Tropic of Cancer 6-7 D 6
Tropic of Cancer Monument • MEX 50-51 E 6
Tropic of Capricorn 6-7 H 11
Tropojë o AL 100-101 H 3
Troppau = Opava o CZ 92-93 O 4
Trosna o RUS 94-95 O 5
Trostjanec' o UA 102-103 J 2
Trotters o USA (ND) 258-259 D 4
Troubador Shoal ≃ 166-167 E 6
Troughton Island ⌒ AUS 172-173 H 2
Trouin o RH 54-55 J 5
Troup o USA (TX) 264-265 J 6
Trousdale o USA (TN) 276-277 K 5
Troutbeck o ZW 218-219 G 4
Trout Creek o CDN (ONT) 238-239 F 3
Trout Creek o USA (MT) 250-251 D 4
Trout Creek ~ USA (AZ) 256-257 B 3
Trout Lake o CDN (BC) 230-231 M 3
Trout Lake o CDN (NWT) 30-31 J 5
Trout Lake o CDN (BC) 230-231 M 3
Trout Lake o CDN (NWT) 30-31 J 5
Trout Lake o CDN (ONT) 234-235 K 3
Trout Lake o USA (MI) 270-271 N 4
Trout Lake o USA (WA) 244-245 D 5
Trout River o CDN (NFL) 242-243 K 3
Trout River ~ CDN 30-31 J 5
Trout River ~ CDN 30-31 G 6
Trout River ~ CDN 32-33 N 3
Troux aux Cerfs • MS 224 C 7
Trovoada, Cachoeira da ~ BR 66-67 K 5
Trowulan o RI 168 E 3
Troy o USA (AL) 284-285 E 5
Troy o USA (ID) 250-251 C 5
Troy o USA (IN) 274-275 M 7
Troy o USA (KS) 262-263 L 5
Troy o USA (MO) 274-275 H 6
Troy o USA (MT) 250-251 D 3
Troy o USA (NC) 282-283 H 5
Troy o USA (NY) 278-279 H 6
Troy o USA (OH) 280-281 B 3
Troy o USA (OR) 244-245 H 5
Troy o USA (PA) 280-281 K 2
Troya, Río de la ~ RA 76-77 C 5
Troya, Río la ~ RA 76-77 C 4
Troyes ☆• F 90-91 K 7
Troy Peak ▲ USA (NV) 246-247 K 5
Trpanj o HR 100-101 F 3
Trstenik o YU 100-101 H 3
Truandó, Río ~ CO 60-61 C 4
Truant Island ⌒ AUS 174-175 D 2
Trubčevsk o RUS 94-95 N 5
Truchas o USA (NM) 256-257 K 2
Truckee o USA (CA) 246-247 E 4
Truckee River ~ USA (NV) 246-247 F 4
Truck Island ⌒ FSM 13 G 2
Trucu o BR 68-69 J 5
True, Cape ▲ CDN 36-37 R 3
Truesdale o USA (MO) 274-275 G 6
Trufanova o RUS 88-89 S 4
Truite, Lac-à-la- o CDN (QUE) 236-237 K 5
Trujillo o• E 98-99 E 5
Trujillo ☆ HN 54-55 C 7
Trujillo ☆• PE 64-65 C 6
Trujillo o USA (NM) 256-257 L 3
Trujillo ☆ YV 60-61 F 3
Truman o USA (MN) 270-271 D 7
Trumann o USA (AR) 276-277 E 5
Truman National Historic Site, Harry S. • USA (MO) 274-275 D 5
Trumbull, Mount ▲ USA (AZ) 256-257 B 2
Trumon o RI 162-163 B 3
Trùng Khánh ☆ VN 156-157 E 5
Trung Liên o VN 156-157 C 5
Trường Lớn, Hòn ⌒ VN 158-159 J 6
Trunkey Creek o AUS 180-181 K 2
Truro o CDN (NS) 240-241 M 5
Truro o USA (IA) 274-275 E 3
Trusan o MAL 164-165 D 1
Truscott o USA (TX) 264-265 E 5
Trus Madi, Gunung ▲ MAL 160-161 B 10
Trutch o CDN 32-33 J 3
Truth or Consequences o USA (NM) 256-257 H 5
Trutnov o CZ 92-93 N 3
Truva (Troja) ∴•• TR 128-129 B 3
Truxno o USA (LA) 268-269 H 4
Truxton o USA (AZ) 256-257 B 3
Tryon o USA (NE) 262-263 F 3
Tryon Island ⌒ AUS 178-179 L 2
Tryphena o NZ 182 E 2
Trzebnica o• PL 92-93 O 3
Trzemeszno o PL 92-93 O 2
Tsacha Lake o CDN (BC) 228-229 K 3
Tsadumu o IND 140-141 H 4
Tsagaan ▲ MAU 148-149 E 2
Tsala Apopka Lake o USA (FL) 286-287 G 3
Tsalwor Lake o CDN 30-31 P 6
Tsama I o RCB 210-211 E 4
Tsamai o WAN 198-199 B 6
Tsandi o NAM 216-217 C 8
Tsangano o MOC 218-219 H 2
Tsanyawa o WAN 198-199 C 6
Tsaramandroso o RM 222-223 E 6
Tsaranonenana o RM 222-223 F 5
Tsaratanana o RM (MJG) 222-223 E 6
Tsaratanana ▲ RM 222-223 F 4
Tsarisberge ▲ NAM 220-221 C 2
Tsarishoogte Pass ▲ NAM 220-221 C 2
Tsau o RB 218-219 B 5
Tsauchab ~ NAM 220-221 B 2
Tsavo o EAK 212-213 G 5
Tsavo ~ EAK 212-213 G 5
Tsavo East National Park ⊥ EAK 212-213 G 5
Tsavo Safari Camp o EAK 212-213 G 5
Tsavo West National Park ⊥ EAK 212-213 F 5
Tsawah o LAR 192-193 E 4
Tsawwassen o CDN (BC) 230-231 F 4
Tsazar o IND 138-139 F 3
Tschida, Lake o USA (ND) 258-259 F 5
Tseikuru o EAK 212-213 G 4
Tselinograd = Akmola o KA 124-125 G 3
Tsembo o RCB 210-211 D 5
Tseminyu o IND 142-143 J 3
Tses o NAM 220-221 D 2
Tsévié o RT 202-203 L 6
Tshabong ☆ RB 220-221 F 3
Tshako o ZRE 214-215 B 5
Tshala o ZRE 214-215 B 5
Tshane o RB 220-221 E 2
Tshela o ZRE 210-211 D 6
Tshenga-Oshwe o ZRE 210-211 J 5
Tshesebe o RB 218-219 D 5
Tshibala o ZRE 216-217 F 3
Tshibamba o ZRE 214-215 B 5
Tshibambula o ZRE 210-211 J 6
Tshibeke o ZRE 212-213 B 5
Tshibuka o ZRE 216-217 F 3
Tshibwika o ZRE 216-217 F 3
Tshidilamolomo o ZA 220-221 G 2
Tshie o ZRE 214-215 B 5
Tshikapa o ZRE 216-217 F 3
Tshikapa ~ ZRE 216-217 F 3
Tshikula o ZRE 214-215 B 4
Tshilenge o ZRE 214-215 B 4
Tshimbalanga o ZRE 214-215 B 5
Tshimboko o ZRE 214-215 C 4
Tshimbulu o ZRE 214-215 B 5
Tshimbungu o ZRE 214-215 B 5
Tshintshanku o ZRE 214-215 B 4
Tshipise o ZA 218-219 F 6
Tshisenda o ZRE 214-215 D 7
Tshisenge o ZRE 216-217 F 3
Tshisonge o ZRE 214-215 B 5
Tshitadi o ZRE 216-217 F 3
Tshitanzu o ZRE 214-215 B 5
Tshkheenickh River ~ CDN (BC) 228-229 E 2
Tshofa o ZRE 210-211 K 6
Tshokwane o ZA 220-221 K 2
Tsholotsho o ZW 218-219 D 4
Tshongwe o ZRE 214-215 C 4
Tshootsha = Kalkfontein o RB 216-217 F 11
Tshopo ~ ZRE 210-211 L 3
Tshuapa ~ ZRE 210-211 H 4
Tshunga, Chutes ~ ZRE 210-211 K 3
Tsiafajavona ▲ RM 222-223 E 7
Tsiaki o RCB 210-211 D 5
Tsianaloka o RM 222-223 D 8
Tsiazompaniry o RM 222-223 E 7
Tsimafana o RM 222-223 D 7
Tsimanampetsotsa, Farihy o RM 222-223 C 10
Tsimazava o RM 222-223 D 8
Tsimlyanskoye Vodokhranilishche = Cimljanskoe vodohranil. < RUS 102-103 N 4
Tsimpsean Indian Reserve X CDN (BC) 228-229 D 2
Tsineng o ZA 220-221 F 3
Tsingtao = Qingdao ☆ VRC 154-155 M 3
Tsingy de Bamaraha Strict Nature Reserve ⊥••• RM 222-223 D 7
Tsiningia o RM 222-223 E 5
Tsinjoarivo o RM 222-223 E 7
Tsinjomitondraka o RM 222-223 E 5
Tsinjomorona ~ RM 222-223 F 5
Tsintsabis o NAM 216-217 D 9
Tsiombe o RM 222-223 D 10
Tsiribihina ~ RM 222-223 D 7
Tsiroanomandidy o RM 222-223 E 7
Tsitondroina o RM 222-223 E 8
Tsitsikamma National Park ⊥ ZA 220-221 G 7
Tsitsutl Peak ▲ CDN (BC) 228-229 J 4
Tsivory o RM 222-223 E 10
Tsoe o RB 218-219 C 5
Tsogstsalu o IND 138-139 G 2
Tsolo o ZA 220-221 J 5
Tsomo o ZA (CAP) 220-221 H 6
Tsomo ~ ZA 220-221 H 6
Tso Morari o IND 138-139 G 3
Tsu ☆ J 152-153 G 7
Tsubata o J 152-153 G 6
Tsuchiura o J 152-153 J 6
Tsugaru Quasi National Park ⊥ J 152-153 J 4
Tsugaru Strait = Tsugaru-kaikyō ≈ J 152-153 J 4
Tsu Lake o CDN 30-31 N 5
Tsuli o RB 218-219 D 4
Tsumbiri o ZRE 210-211 F 5
Tsumeb ☆ NAM 216-217 D 9
Tsumkwe ☆ NAM 216-217 F 9
Tsuruga o J 152-153 G 7
Tsurugi-san ▲ J 152-153 F 8
Tsurui o J 152-153 L 3
Tsuruoka o J 152-153 H 5
Tsushima ⌒ J 152-153 C 7
Tsuyama o J 152-153 E 7
Tswaane o RB (GHA) 216-217 F 11
Tswaane o RB (KWE) 218-219 B 6
t-Tarfa, Wādī ~ ET 194-195 E 3
t-Tartar, Wādī ~ IRQ 128-129 K 5
t-Tartar, Wādī ~ IRQ 128-129 K 5
Ttati, Laguna o RA 76-77 H 5
t-Tawīl, Wādī ~ IRQ 128-129 J 5
t-Tūbal, Wādī ~ IRQ 128-129 K 6
Tu ~ RUS 118-119 N 9
Tua, Tanjung ▲ RI 162-163 F 7
Tuaim = Tuam o IRL 90-91 C 5
Tual o RI 166-167 G 4
Tuam = Tuaim o IRL 90-91 C 5
Tuambli o CI 202-203 F 6
Tuameseh, Tanjung ▲ RI 166-167 C 6
Tuam Island ⌒ PNG 183 E 3
Tuamotu Archipel ⌒ F 13 N 4
Tuamotu Archipelago = Tuamotu, Îles ⌒ F 13 N 4
Tuần Giáo ☆ VN 156-157 C 6
Tuangku, Pulau ⌒ RI 162-163 B 3
Tuanxi o VRC 156-157 E 3
Tuapse o RUS 126-127 C 5
Tuaran o MAL 160-161 B 9
Tuare o RI 164-165 G 4
Tua River ~ PNG 183 C 4
Tuba ~ RUS 116-117 F 9
Ṭūbā, Qaṣr at- ∴• JOR 130-131 E 2
Tubac o USA (AZ) 256-257 D 7
Tuba City o USA (AZ) 256-257 D 2
Tubaiq, Ǧabal at- ▲ KSA 130-131 E 3
Tuban o RI 168 E 3
Tubarão o BR 74-75 F 7
Tubarão Latunde, Área Indígena X BR 70-71 G 3
Tūbās o WB 130-131 D 1
Tubau o MAL 162-163 K 3
Tubbataha Reefs ⌒••• RP 160-161 C 8
Tubek Bŭzačy ◡ KA 96-97 G 10
Tubek Bŭzačy ◡ KA 126-127 J 5
Tubek Tub-Karagan ◡ KA 126-127 J 5
Tubeya o ZRE 214-215 B 4
Ṭubǧa, Wādī ~ KSA 130-131 F 5
Tubili Point ▲ RP 160-161 D 6
Tübingen o•• D 92-93 K 4
Tubisyimita o RI 166-167 G 2
Tubkaragan, mujisi ▲ KA 126-127 J 5
Tubmanburg o LB 202-203 E 6
Tubo, River ~ WAN 204-205 G 3
Tuborg Fondets Land ∴ GRØ 26-27 o 4
Ṭubruq ◘ LAR 192-193 K 2
Ṭubruq ☆ LAR 192-193 K 1
Tubuai Islands = Australes, Îles ⌒ F 13 M 5
Tuburan o RP 160-161 E 7
Tucacas o YV 60-61 G 2
Tucano o BR 68-69 J 7
Tucapel, Punta ▲ RCH 78-79 C 4
Tucavaca, Río ~ BOL 70-71 H 6
Tucha River ~ CDN 30-31 E 6
Tucheng o VRC 156-157 D 3
Tuchitua o CDN 30-31 E 5
Tuchola o PL 92-93 O 2
Tuchol'ka o UA 102-103 C 3
Tuckanarra o AUS 176-177 E 3
Tucker o USA (AR) 276-277 D 6
Tucker o USA (TX) 268-269 E 5
Tucker Bay ≈ 16 F 18
Tuckerman o USA (AR) 276-277 D 5
Tuckerton o USA (NJ) 280-281 M 4
Tuckfield, Mount ▲ AUS 172-173 G 5
Tucson o• USA (AZ) 256-257 E 6
Tucuco, Río ~ YV 60-61 E 3
Tucum, Corredeira do ~ BR 70-71 J 4
Tucumã o BR 66-67 H 6
Tucumán ◘ RA 76-77 E 4
Tucumari Mountain ▲ USA (NM) 256-257 M 3
Tucumcari o USA (NM) 256-257 M 3
Tucuña o CO 66-67 B 2
Tucunare, Raudal ~ CO 66-67 B 2
Tucupido o YV 60-61 J 3
Tucupita ☆ YV 60-61 K 3
Tucuriba o BR 66-67 H 5
Tucuriba, Corredeira ~ BR 66-67 H 5
Tucuruí o BR 68-69 D 3
Tucuruí, Represa de < BR 68-69 D 4
Tucutibapo o CO 66-67 D 2
Tucu-Tucu o RA 80 E 4
Tūdakŭl, kŭli o US 136-137 J 5
Tudela o• E 98-99 G 3
Tudela o RP 160-161 E 8
Tudu o EST 94-95 K 2
Tudun Wada o WAN 204-205 H 3
Tuekta o RUS 124-125 O 3
Tuena o AUS 180-181 K 3
Tueré, Rio ~ BR 68-69 C 4
Tuetue o RI 164-165 H 6
Tufanbeyli ☆ TR 128-129 G 3
Tuffnell o CDN (SAS) 232-233 P 4
Tufi o PNG 183 E 5
Tug o VRC 154-155 F 2
Tugaloo Lake < USA (GA) 284-285 G 2
Tugaloo River ~ USA (GA) 284-285 G 2
Tugaske o CDN (SAS) 232-233 M 5
Tugela ~ ZA 220-221 K 4
Tugela Ferry o ZA 220-221 K 4
Tug Fork ~ USA (WV) 280-281 E 6
Tug Hill ▲ USA (NY) 278-279 F 5
Tugidak Island ⌒ USA 22-23 T 4
Tugtorqortôq ⌒ GRØ 26-27 W 7
Tugtulik ⌒ GRØ 28-29 O 2
Tugu o GH 202-203 K 5
Tuguegarao ☆ RP 160-161 D 4
Tugulym ☆ RUS 114-115 H 6
Tugur o RUS 122-123 G 2
Tugur ~ RUS 122-123 G 2
Tugurskij poluostrov ◡ RUS 122-123 G 2
Tugurskij zaliv ≈ 122-123 G 2
Tuguttur ~ RUS 110-111 F 4
Tugyi o MYA 158-159 C 2
Tuhan, Wādī ~ Y 132-133 D 7
Tuhsigat ~ RUS 114-115 O 5
Tui o•• E 98-99 C 3
Tuichi, Río ~ BOL 70-71 C 4
Tuina o RCH 76-77 C 2
Tuineje o E 188-189 D 6
Tuisen o IND 142-143 H 4
Tuitán o MEX 50-51 G 5
Tuiué o BR 66-67 F 5
Tuj ~ RUS 114-115 M 6
Tujau, Tanjung ▲ RI 166-167 D 5
Tujmazy ☆ RUS 96-97 H 6
Tujn gol ~ MAU 148-149 E 5
Tujun ~ RUS 122-123 E 3
Tukalan ~ RUS 108-109 e 7
Tukan ~ RUS 114-115 M 5
Tukangbesi, Kepulauan ⌒ RI 164-165 H 6
Tukarak Island ⌒ CDN 36-37 K 6
Tukayel o ETH 208-209 G 4
Tuki o SOL 184 I c 2
Tukola Tolha o VRC 144-145 K 3
Tukosmera ▲ VAN 184 II b 4
Tükrah o• LAR 192-193 J 1
Tuktoyaktuk o CDN 20-21 Y 2
Tukulan ~ RUS 120-121 E 2
Tukums ☆• LV 94-95 H 3
Tukuringra, hrebet ▲ RUS 118-119 M 8
Tukuyu o EAT 214-215 G 5
Tula o EAK (COA) 212-213 G 4
Tula ~ EAK 212-213 G 4
Tula o MEX 50-51 K 6
Tula ☆•• RUS 94-95 P 4
Tulā o Y 132-133 C 6
Tulach Mhór = Tullamore o IRL 90-91 D 5
Tula de Allende o• MEX 52-53 E 1
Tuladenggi o RI 164-165 G 3
Tula Hill ▲• WAN 204-205 J 4
Tulak o• AFG 134-135 K 2
Tulalip Indian Reservation X USA (WA) 244-245 C 2
Tulameen o CDN (BC) 230-231 J 4
Tulameen River ~ CDN (BC) 230-231 J 4
Tulancingo o MEX 52-53 E 1
Tulare o USA (CA) 248-249 E 3
Tulare o USA (SD) 260-261 H 2
Tulare Lake o USA (CA) 248-249 E 4
Tularosa o USA (NM) 256-257 J 5
Tularosa Basin ◡ USA (NM) 256-257 J 6
Tularosa River ~ USA (NM) 256-257 G 5
Tulate o GCA 52-53 J 4
Tula Yiri o WAN 204-205 J 4
Tulbagh o• ZA 220-221 D 6
Tulcan ☆ EC 64-65 D 1
Tulcea ☆• RO 102-103 F 5
Tul'čyn ☆ UA 102-103 F 3
Tule, El o MEX 50-51 J 3
Tule, Estero del ~ MEX 50-51 F 5
Tuléar = Toliara ☆• RM 222-223 C 9
Tulebaevo o KA 124-125 L 5
Tule Creek ~ USA (TX) 264-265 C 4
Tulehu o RI 166-167 E 3
Tulelake o USA (CA) 246-247 D 2
Tule Lake o USA (CA) 246-247 D 2
Tule Lake National Wildlife Refuge ⊥ USA (CA) 246-247 D 2
Tulema Lake o CDN 30-31 U 4
Tulen' o RUS 116-117 H 7
Tule River Indian Reservation X USA (CA) 248-249 F 3
Tuleta o USA (TX) 266-267 K 5
Tulia o USA (TX) 264-265 C 4
Tuli Block Farms ∴ RB 218-219 D 6
Tulik Volcano ▲ USA 22-23 M 6
Tulipan o MEX 52-53 J 3
Tuljāpur o IND 140-141 G 2
Tullahoma o USA (TN) 276-277 J 5
Tullamore o AUS 180-181 J 2
Tullamore = Tulach Mhór o IRL 90-91 D 5
Tulle ☆• F 90-91 H 9
Tullibigeal o AUS 180-181 J 2

Tullos o USA (LA) 268-269 H 5
Tullulah Falls o USA (GA) 284-285 G 2
Tullus o SUD 206-207 G 3
Tully o AUS 174-175 H 5
Tully Range ▲ AUS 178-179 G 2
Tuloma ∼ RUS 88-89 M 2
Tulppio o FIN 88-89 K 3
Tulsa o• USA (OK) 264-265 J 2
Tulsequah o CDN 32-33 D 2
Tulsipur o IND 142-143 C 2
Tulu o PNG 183 D 1
Tulua o CO 60-61 C 5
Tulu Ămara Terara ▲ ETH 208-209 C 4
Tulu Bolo o ETH 208-209 D 4
Tuluca o BR 66-67 C 2
Tuluksak o USA 20-21 K 6
Tülūl al-Ašaqif ▲ JOR 130-131 E 1
Tulúm o MEX (QR) 52-53 L 1
Tulúm ∴•• MEX (QR) 52-53 L 1
Tulumayo, Río ∼ PE 64-65 E 7
Tulume o ZRE 214-215 B 4
Tulun ✩ RUS 116-117 K 8
Tulungagung o RI 168 D 4
Tulungselapan o RI 162-163 F 6
Tulu Welel ▲ ETH 208-209 B 4
Tulvinskaja vozvyšennost' ▲ RUS 96-97 K 5
Tuma o RUS 94-95 R 4
Tuma, Río ∼ NIC 52-53 B 5
Ṭūma, Wādī ∼ IRQ 128-129 K 6
Tumacacori National Monument • USA (AZ) 256-257 D 7
Tumaco o CO 60-61 B 7
Tumaco, Ensenada de ≈ 60-61 B 7
Tumagabok o RP 160-161 D 6
Tumair o KSA 130-131 J 5
Tuma Island ⌒ PNG 183 F 5
Tumalin o RP 160-161 D 5
Tumalo o USA (OR) 244-245 D 6
Tuman Gang ∼ DVR 150-151 G 6
Tumannyj o RUS 88-89 N 2
Tumanšet ∼ RUS 116-117 H 8
Tumanskij hrebet ▲ RUS 120-121 Q 3
Tumara ∼ RUS 118-119 P 3
Tumat o RUS 110-111 W 4
Tumat, Khor ∼ SUD 208-209 B 3
Tumatskaja, protoka Bol'šaja ∼ RUS 110-111 Q 3
Tumba ✩ S 86-87 H 7
Tumba o ZRE 210-211 J 5
Tumbanglahung o RI 164-165 D 4
Tumbarumba o AUS 180-181 J 3
Tumbengu ∼ ZRE 210-211 J 4
Tumbes ✩ PE 64-65 B 3
Tumbes, Bahía de ≈ 64-65 B 3
Tumbes, Península de ∪ RCH 78-79 C 4
Tumbes, Punta ▲ RCH 78-79 C 4
Tumbler Ridge o CDN 32-33 K 4
Tumbu o RI 164-165 F 5
Tumbwe o ZRE 214-215 D 6
Tumby Bay o AUS 180-181 D 3
Tumd Youqi o VRC 154-155 G 1
Tumd Zuoqi o VRC 154-155 G 1
Tumen o VRC 150-151 G 6
Tumèncogt = Hanhöhij o MAU 148-149 L 4
Tumen Jiang ∼ VRC 150-151 G 6
Tumeremo o YV 62-63 D 2
Tumgaon o IND 142-143 C 5
Tumindao Island ⌒ RP 160-161 C 10
Tumkūr o IND 140-141 G 4
Tumlingtar o NEP 144-145 F 7
Tumnin ∼ RUS 122-123 H 4
Tumoiscatio del Ruiz o MEX 52-53 C 2
Tumpang o• RI 168 E 4
Tumpu, Gunung ▲ RI 164-165 H 4
Tumputiga, Gunung ▲ RI 164-165 H 4
Tumrok, hrebet ▲ RUS 120-121 S 6
Tumsar o IND 138-139 G 9
Tumu o GH 202-203 K 4
Tumucumaque, Parque Indígena do ✕ BR 62-63 G 4
Tumucumaque, Serra do ▲ BR 62-63 G 4
Tumul o RUS 118-119 P 4
Tumupasa o BOL 70-71 D 4
Tumureng o GUY 62-63 D 2
Tumut o AUS 180-181 K 3
Tumwater o USA (WA) 244-245 C 3
Tuna o GH 202-203 J 5
Tu Na, Đèo ▲ VN 158-159 K 4
Tuna Gain o RI 166-167 G 3
Tunago Lake ⊖ CDN 30-31 G 2
Tunaida o ET 194-195 D 5
Tunajča, ozero ⊖ RUS 122-123 K 5
Tūnali Sālang • AFG 136-137 L 7
Tunapa, Cerro ▲ BOL 70-71 D 6
Tunapuna o TT 60-61 L 2
Tunas, Las ✩ C 54-55 G 4
Tunas, Sierra de las ▲ RA 78-79 J 4
Tunas de Zaza o C 54-55 F 4
Tunas Grandes, Lagunas las ⊖ RA 78-79 H 3
Tunaydibah o SUD 200-201 G 6
Tunceli ✩ TR 128-129 H 3
Tunchang o VRC 156-157 G 7
Tuncurry o AUS 180-181 M 2
Tunda, Pulau ⌒ RI 168 B 2
Tundak ∼ RUS 118-119 H 8
Tund las Raices • RCH 78-79 D 5
Tundulu o Z 214-215 E 5
Tunduma o EAT 214-215 G 5
Tunduru o EAT 214-215 J 6
Tundyk ∼ KA 124-125 K 4
Tundža ∼ BG 102-103 E 6
Tunertooq ⌒ GRØ 28-29 P 2
Tunga o WAN 204-205 H 4
Tungabhadra ∼ IND 140-141 G 3
Tungabhadra Reservoir ⊖ IND 140-141 G 3
Tungaru o SUD 206-207 K 3
Tungawan o RP 160-161 E 9
Tungaztarim o VRC 144-145 D 2
Tungho o RC 156-157 M 5
Tungi o BD 142-143 G 4
Tungir ∼ RUS 118-119 K 8
Tungirskij, hrebet ▲ RUS 118-119 J 8
Tungkaranasam o RI 164-165 E 5
Tungku o MAL (SAB) 160-161 C 10
Tungku o MAL (SAR) 162-163 K 3
Tungokočen o RUS 118-119 G 9
Tungor o RUS 122-123 K 2
Tungshih o RC 156-157 M 4
Tungsten o CDN 30-31 E 5
Tungurahua, Volcán ▲ EC 64-65 C 2
Tungurča ∼ RUS 118-119 K 7
Tunguru o EAT 212-213 D 5
Tunguskaja vozvyšennost' ▲ RUS 88-89 M 4
Tungusskoe-Centraľno, plato ⩦ RUS 116-117 K 5
Tunguwatu o RI 166-167 H 4
Tunhèl o MAU 148-149 H 3
Tuni o IND 142-143 C 7
Tunia, La o CO 64-65 F 1
Tunica o USA (MS) 268-269 K 2
Tunis ★··· TN 190-191 H 2
Tunis o USA (TX) 266-267 L 3
Tunis, Golfe de ≈ 190-191 H 2
Tunisia = Tunisiyah ■ TN 190-191 G 4
Tunja ✩ CO 60-61 E 5
Tunkal ∼ RI 162-163 E 5
Tunkhannock o USA (PA) 280-281 L 2
Tunku Abdul Rahman National Park ⊥ MAL 160-161 A 9
Tunnel Creek National Park ⊥ AUS 172-173 G 4
Tunnsjøen ⊖ N 86-87 F 4
Tunqiu o VRC 156-157 F 4
Tuntum o BR 68-69 F 4
Tuntutuliak o USA 20-21 J 6
Tunu = Østgrønland □ GRØ 26-27 d 8
Tunuí, Cachoeira ∼ BR 66-67 C 2
Tunulic, Rivière ∼ CDN 36-37 Q 5
Tunulliarfik ≈ 28-29 R 6
Tununak o USA 20-21 H 6
Tunungayualok Island ⌒ CDN 36-37 T 6
Tununuk o CDN 20-21 Y 2
Tunuyan o RA 78-79 E 2
Tunuyán, Río ∼ RA 78-79 F 2
Tunuyan, Sierra de ▲ RA 78-79 E 2
Tunuyánviejo, Río ∼ RA 78-79 F 2
Tuoa Creek ∼ PNG 183 C 4
Tuobuja o RUS 118-119 L 4
Tuo Jiang ∼ VRC 156-157 D 2
Tuokechikemili o VRC 144-145 E 4
Tuolba ∼ RUS 118-119 L 5
Tuolbačan ∼ RUS 118-119 L 5
Tuŏl Kruŏs o K 158-159 G 4
Tuolumne o USA (CA) 248-249 D 2
Tuolumne River ∼ USA (CA) 248-249 D 2
Tu'o'ng Du'o'ng ✩ VN 156-157 D 7
Tuora ∼ RUS 118-119 M 6
Tuora-Sis, hrebet ▲ RUS 110-111 Q 4
Tuostah ∼ RUS 110-111 V 6
Tuotuo He ∼ VRC 144-145 H 3
Tuotuo Heyan o VRC 144-145 J 3
Tupã o BR 72-73 E 6
Tupaciguara o BR 72-73 F 5
Tupambaé o ROU 78-79 M 2
Tupana, Rio ∼ BR 66-67 G 5
Tupanaci o BR 68-69 J 6
Tupanatinga o BR 68-69 K 6
Tupanciretã o BR 74-75 D 7
Tuparrilo, Caño ∼ CO 60-61 G 5
Tuparrito, Caño ∼ CO 60-61 G 5
Tuparro, Río ∼ CO 60-61 G 5
Tupé II o BR 66-67 D 2
Tupelo o USA (AR) 276-277 D 5
Tupelo o USA (MS) 268-269 M 2
Tupelo o USA (OK) 264-265 H 4
Tupelo National Battlefield ∴ USA (MS) 268-269 M 2
Tupik ✩ RUS 118-119 J 8
Tupilco o MEX 52-53 H 2
Tupim, Rio ∼ BR 72-73 K 2
Tupinambarana, Ilha ⌒ BR 66-67 J 4
Tupinier, Kap ▲ GRØ 28-29 b 2
Tupiratins o BR 68-69 D 6
Tupitina o MEX 52-53 C 2
Tupiza o BOL 76-77 E 1
Tupiza, Río ∼ BOL 76-77 E 1
Tupper o CDN 32-33 K 4
Tupper Lake o USA (NY) 278-279 G 4
Tupran o IND 140-141 H 2
Tupungato o RA 78-79 E 2
Tupungato, Cerro ▲ RA 78-79 E 2
Tupure o YV 60-61 F 2
Tuquan o VRC 150-151 C 5
Tuque, La o CDN (QUE) 240-241 C 3
Tuquerres o CO 64-65 D 1
Tuqu Gang ▲ VRC 156-157 F 7
Tūr, aṭ- o Y 132-133 C 6
Tura o IND 142-143 G 3
Tura ∼ PA 52-53 F 8
Tura ✩ RUS (EVN) 116-117 K 3
Tura ✩ RUS 96-97 L 4
Tura ∼ RUS 114-115 H 6
Tura ∼ RUS 114-115 J 6
Tura ∼ RUS 118-119 F 10
Tura o VRC 144-145 F 2
Turaba o KSA (HAI) 130-131 H 3
Turaba o KSA (MAK) 132-133 B 3
Turagua, Serrania ▲ YV 60-61 J 4
Ṭuraif o KSA 130-131 F 2
Ṭuraif o SYR 128-129 H 5
Turakurgan o US 136-137 M 4
Turama ∼ RUS 116-117 H 5
Turama River ∼ PNG 183 B 4
Turan ✩ RUS 116-117 F 9
Turangi o NZ 182 E 3
Turan Lowland = Turan persligi ∪ TM 10-11 F 4
Turan Lowland = Turanskaja nizmennost' ∪ 136-137 F 5
Tūran ojlety = Turan persligi = Turon Pasttekisligi ∪ KA 136-137 F 5
Turan persligi = Turon Pasttekisligi = Tūran ojlety ∪ TM 136-137 F 5
Turāq al-'Ilab ▲ SYR 128-129 H 6
Turba o EST 94-95 J 2
Turba, at- o Y 132-133 D 7
Turba, at- o Y 132-133 C 7
Turbaco o CO 60-61 D 2
Turbat o PK 134-135 K 6
Turbeville o USA (SC) 284-285 K 3
Turbihal o IND 140-141 G 3
Turbio, El o RA 80 D 5
Turbio, Río ∼ RA 80 E 5
Turbio, Río ∼ RCH 76-77 C 4
Turbio, Río ∼ RCH 76-77 B 5
Turbo o CO 60-61 C 3
Turbón, Raudal el ∼ CO 66-67 B 2
Turco o BOL 70-71 C 6
Turco, Río ∼ BOL 70-71 C 6
Turda o RO 102-103 C 4
Tūrda < SUD 206-207 J 3
Turee Creek o AUS (WA) 176-177 E 1
Turee Creek ∼ AUS 176-177 D 1
Turek o PL 92-93 P 2
Turen o RI 168 E 4
Turgen ∼ KA 146-147 C 4
Türgen ▲ MAU 116-117 E 11
Turgeon, Rivière ∼ CDN (QUE) 236-237 J 3
Turgut o TR 128-129 D 3
Turgutlu ✩ TR 128-129 B 3
Turhal ✩• TR 128-129 G 2
Türi o EST 94-95 J 2
Turi, Igarapé ∼ BR 66-67 D 3
Turia, Río ∼ E 98-99 G 4
Turiaçu o BR 68-69 F 2
Turiaçu, Baía de ≈ 68-69 F 2
Turiaçu, Rio ∼ BR 68-69 F 3
Turiamo o YV 60-61 H 2
Turiančaj ∼ AZ 128-129 M 2
Turiani o EAT 214-215 J 4
Túriba o YV 60-61 H 4
Turin o CDN (ALB) 232-233 F 6
Turin o USA (IA) 274-275 C 2
Turin = Torino ✩• I 100-101 A 2
Turinsk ✩ RUS 114-115 G 5
Turinskaja ravnina ∪ RUS 114-115 G 6
Turinskaja Sloboda ✩ RUS 114-115 H 6
Tur'ja o RUS 88-89 V 5
Turka o RUS 116-117 O 9
Turka ∼ RUS 118-119 E 9
Turka ✩ UA 102-103 C 3
Turkana ⩦ EAK 212-213 E 2
Turkana, Lake ⊖ EAK (Es) 212-213 F 2
Turkestan o KA 136-137 L 3
Turkestanskij hrebet ▲ US 136-137 K 5
Turkestanskij kanal < KA 136-137 L 3
Turkey o USA (TX) 264-265 D 4
Turkey = Türkiye ■ TR 128-129 C 3
Turkey Creek o AUS 172-173 J 4
Turkey Creek o USA (LA) 268-269 H 6
Turkey Creek ∼ USA (NE) 262-263 J 4
Turkey Creek ∼ USA (OK) 264-265 G 2
Turkey Creek ∼ USA (SC) 284-285 J 2
Turkey Flat o USA (AZ) 256-257 F 6
Turkey Mountain ▲ AUS 178-179 L 4
Turkey Point o CDN (ONT) 238-239 E 6
Turkey River ∼ USA (IA) 274-275 G 2
Turkistan ✩ KA 136-137 L 3
Türkmen Dağı ▲ TR 128-129 D 3
Turkmenistan = Türkmenistan ■ TM 136-137 D 5
Turkmen-Kala o TM 136-137 H 6
Turkmenskij zaliv ≈ 136-137 C 5
Türkoğlu ✩ TR 128-129 G 4
Turks and Caicos Islands ⌒ GB 54-55 K 3
Turks Islands ⌒ GB 54-55 K 4
Turku = Åbo ✩• FIN 88-89 G 6
Turkwel ∼ EAK 212-213 E 2
Turkwel Gorge Reservoir < EAK 212-213 E 3
Turlock o USA (CA) 248-249 D 2
Turmalina o BR 72-73 J 4
Turmantas o LT 94-95 K 4
Turn o USA (NM) 256-257 J 4
Turnagain, Cape ▲ NZ 182 F 4
Turnagain Arm ≈ 20-21 P 6
Turnagain Island ⌒ AUS 174-175 G 1
Turnagain Point ▲ CDN 24-25 R 6
Turnagain River ∼ CDN 30-31 E 6
Turneffe Islands ⌒ BH 52-53 L 3
Turner o USA (ME) 278-279 L 4
Turner o USA (MT) 250-251 L 3
Turner o USA (OR) 244-245 C 6
Turner Lake ⊖ CDN 32-33 Q 3
Turner Ø ⌒ GRØ 28-29 d 2
Turner River ∼ AUS 172-173 D 6
Turners Peninsula ∪ WAL 202-203 D 6
Turnersville o USA (TX) 266-267 K 2
Turner Turnpike II USA (OK) 264-265 G 3
Turner Valley o CDN (ALB) 232-233 D 5
Turnerville o USA (SD) 260-261 K 2
Turnhout o B 92-93 H 3
Turnpike Creek ∼ USA (GA) 284-285 H 5
Turnu Măgurele o RO 102-103 D 6
Turočak ✩ RUS 124-125 P 2
Turon o USA (KS) 262-263 H 7
Turon Pasttekisligi = Turan persligi = Tūran ojlety ∪ US 136-137 F 5
Turpan o VRC 146-147 J 4
Turpan Pendi ⩦ VRC 146-147 J 4
Turpin o USA (OK) 264-265 D 2
Türpsal = Järve o EST 94-95 K 2
Tura • SUD 200-201 B 6
Turrell o USA (AR) 276-277 E 5
Turrialba o CR 52-53 C 7
Tursāq o IRQ 128-129 L 6
Tursuntskij Tuman, ozero ⊖ RUS 114-115 G 4
Tursunzade o TJ 136-137 L 5
Turt o MAU 148-149 E 2
Turt (Hanh) o MAU 148-149 E 2
Turtas ∼ RUS 114-115 K 5
Türtkŭl ✩ US 136-137 G 4
Turtle Creek Reservoir ⊖ USA (IN) 274-275 L 5
Turtle Farm • GB 54-55 E 5
Turtleford o CDN (SAS) 232-233 K 2
Turtle Head Island ⌒ AUS 183 B 6
Turtle Islands ⌒ RP 160-161 C 9
Turtle Islands Marine Park ⊥ MAL 160-161 C 9
Turtle Lake o CDN (SAS) 232-233 K 2
Turtle Lake o USA (ND) 258-259 G 4
Turtle Lake o USA (WI) 270-271 F 5
Turtle Mountain ▲ CDN (MAN) 234-235 C 5
Turtle Mountain Indian Reservation ✕ USA (ND) 258-259 H 3
Turton Lake ⊖ CDN 30-31 G 3
Turu ∼ RUS 116-117 M 3
Turu, Wangasi- o GH 202-203 K 5
Turu Cay Island ⌒ AUS 183 A 5
Turuchipa, Río ∼ BOL 70-71 E 6
Turugart Shankou ▲ VRC 146-147 B 5
Turuhan ∼ RUS 108-109 V 8
Turuhan ∼ RUS 114-115 T 2
Turuhansk o RUS 114-115 T 2
Turuhanskaja nizmennost' ∪ RUS 114-115 T 2
Turuktah, mys ▲ RUS 110-111 W 4
Turuna, Rio ∼ BR 62-63 F 5
Turuntaevo o RUS (TOM) 114-115 T 6
Turuntaevo ✩ RUS (BUR) 116-117 N 9
Turvânia o BR 72-73 E 4
Turvo, Rio ∼ BR 72-73 E 4
Turvo, Rio ∼ BR 72-73 F 6
Turvolândia o BR 72-73 H 6
Turwi ∼ ZW 218-219 F 5
Tūs o IR 136-137 F 6
Tušama ∼ RUS 116-117 K 7
Tuscaloosa o USA (AL) 284-285 C 3
Tuscaloosa, Lake < USA (AL) 284-285 C 3
Tuscània o• I 100-101 C 3
Tuscarora o USA (NV) 246-247 J 2
Tuscola o USA (IL) 274-275 K 5
Tuscola o USA (TX) 264-265 E 6
Tusculum o USA (TN) 282-283 E 4
Tuscumbia o USA (AL) 284-285 B 2
Tuscumbia o USA (MO) 274-275 F 6
Tusenøyane ⌒ N 84-85 M 4
Tushar Mountains ▲ USA (UT) 254-255 C 5
Tušig=Zëltėr o MAU 148-149 G 2
Tuskegee o• USA (AL) 284-285 E 4
Tuskegee Institute National Historic Site • USA (AL) 284-285 E 4
Tustumena Lake ⊖ USA 20-21 P 6
Tutaev ✩·· RUS 94-95 Q 3
Tutak ✩ TR 128-129 K 3
Tuticorin o IND 140-141 H 6
Tutóia o BR 68-69 G 3
Tutoko, Mount ▲ NZ 182 B 6
Tutončana ∼ RUS 116-117 F 2
Tutong o BRU 164-165 D 1
Tutrakan o BG 102-103 E 5
Tuttle o USA (ND) 258-259 H 4
Tuttle o USA (OK) 264-265 G 3
Tuttle Creek Lake ⊖ USA (KS) 262-263 K 5
Tuttle Town o USA (CA) 246-247 E 5
Tuttosoni, Nuraghe • I 100-101 B 4
Tutuaca o MEX 50-51 F 3
Tutuala o RI 166-167 D 6
Tutuba ⌒ VAN 184 II a 2
Tutuila Island ⌒ USA 184 V b 2
Tutukpene o GH 202-203 L 5
Tutume o RB 218-219 D 5
Tutup, Tanjung ▲ MAL 160-161 C 10
Tutupa o RI 164-165 K 4
Tutura o RUS 116-117 M 8
Tutura ∼ RUS 116-117 M 8
Tutwiler o USA (MS) 268-269 K 3
Tuul gol ∼ MAU 148-149 G 4
Tuusniemi o FIN 88-89 K 5
Tuva = Tuva, Respublika □ RUS 116-117 F 10
Tuvšinširèè = S èrgèlèn o MAU 148-149 K 4
Tuwaiq, Ǧabal ▲ KSA 130-131 J 5
Tuwaiq, Ǧabal ▲ KSA 132-133 D 3
Tūwal o KSA 130-131 F 6
Tuxcueca o MEX 52-53 C 1
Tuxedni Bay ≈ 20-21 O 6
Tuxford o CDN (SAS) 232-233 N 5
Tuxpan o MEX (NAY) 50-51 G 7
Tuxpan o• MEX (JAL) 52-53 C 2
Tuxpan, Río ∼ MEX 52-53 F 1
Tuxpan de Rodríguez Cano o MEX 52-53 F 1
Tuxtla, Sierra de los ▲ MEX 52-53 G 2
Tuxtla Gutiérrez ✩• MEX 52-53 H 3
Tuy, Río ∼ YV 60-61 H 2
Tuya River ∼ CDN 32-33 E 2
Tuyên Quang ✩ VN 156-157 D 6
Tuy Hòa o VN 158-159 K 4
Tuy Phong o VN 158-159 K 5
Tuyserkān o• IR 134-135 C 1
Tüzdyköl ⊖ KA 136-137 M 3
Tuz Gölü ⊖ TR 128-129 E 3
Ṭūz Ḫurmātū ✩ IRQ 128-129 L 5
Tuzigoot National Monument • USA (AZ) 256-257 D 4
Tuzla o• BIH 100-101 G 2
Tuzla Çayı ∼ TR 128-129 J 3
Tuzluca ✩ TR 128-129 K 2
Tuzule o ZRE 214-215 B 4
Tværá o FR 90-91 D 1
Tveitsund o N 86-87 D 7
Tver' ✩·· RUS 94-95 P 3
Tverrfjelli ∪ N 86-87 D 5
TV Tower • USA (MN) 270-271 A 3
Tweed o CDN (ONT) 238-239 H 4
Tweed ∼ GB 90-91 F 4
Tweed Heads o AUS 178-179 M 5
Tweedsmuir Provincial Park ⊥ CDN (BC) 228-229 H 3
Tweefontein o ZA 220-221 D 6
Tweeling o ZA 220-221 J 3
Twee Rivier o NAM 220-221 D 2
Twee Rivieren o ZA 220-221 E 3
Tweespruit o ZA 220-221 H 4
Twelve Apostles, The ·· AUS 180-181 G 5
Twentynine Palms o USA (CA) 248-249 H 5
Twentynine Palms Indian Reservation ✕ USA (CA) 248-249 H 5
Twentynine Palms Marine Corps Base xx USA (CA) 248-249 H 5
Twilight Cove ≈ 176-177 H 6
Twillingate o CDN (NFL) 242-243 O 3
Twin Bridges o USA (MT) 250-251 G 6
Twin Butte o CDN (ALB) 232-233 E 6
Twin Buttes Reservoir < USA (TX) 266-267 G 2
Twin City o CDN (ONT) 234-235 O 6
Twin City o USA (GA) 284-285 H 4
Twin Falls o USA (ID) 252-253 D 4
Twingge o MYA 142-143 K 4
Twingi o Z 214-215 E 6
Twin Mount ▲ USA 20-21 T 4
Twin Mountain o USA (NH) 278-279 K 4
Twin Oaks Reservoir ⊖ USA (TX) 266-267 L 2
Twin Peaks o AUS 176-177 C 3
Twin Sisters o USA (TX) 266-267 J 3
Twin Summit ▲ USA (NV) 246-247 J 3
Twin Valley o USA (MN) 270-271 C 3
Twisp o USA (WA) 244-245 E 2
Twitty o USA (TX) 264-265 D 3
Twitya River ∼ CDN 30-31 E 4
Twizel o NZ 182 C 6
Two Brothers ⌒ CDN 36-37 J 5
Two Buttes o USA (CO) 254-255 N 6
Two Buttes Creek ∼ USA (CO) 254-255 N 6
Two Creeks o CDN (MAN) 234-235 B 4
Two Creeks o USA (WI) 270-271 L 6
Twodot o USA (MT) 250-251 J 5
Twofold Bay ≈ 180-181 K 4
Two Harbors o USA (MN) 270-271 G 3
Two Headed Island ⌒ USA 22-23 U 4
Two Hills o CDN (ALB) 232-233 G 2
Two Inlets o USA (MN) 270-271 C 3
Two Medicine River ∼ USA (MT) 250-251 F 3
Twopete Mountain ▲ CDN 20-21 Y 5
Two Rivers o USA (WI) 270-271 L 6
Two Rocks o AUS 176-177 C 5
Twyfelfontein • NAM 216-217 C 10
Tyara, Cayo ⌒ NIC 52-53 C 5
Tybee Island o USA (GA) 284-285 K 4
Tyčany ∼ RUS 116-117 H 5
Tychy o PL 92-93 P 3
Tydyotta ∼ RUS 114-115 O 2
Tye o CDN (BC) 230-231 N 4
Tyélé o RMM 202-203 G 3
Tygart Lake ⊖ USA (WV) 280-281 F 4
Tygart River ∼ USA (WV) 280-281 F 4
Tygarts Creek ∼ USA (KY) 276-277 M 2
Tygda o RUS 118-119 N 9
Tygda ∼ RUS 118-119 N 9
Tyger River ∼ USA (SC) 284-285 J 2
Tygh Valley o USA (OR) 244-245 D 5
Tyiebas, cyganak ≈ 126-127 N 4
Tyľ ∼ RUS 120-121 F 6
Tylawa o PL 92-93 Q 4
Tyler o USA (TX) 264-265 J 6
Tyler o USA (WA) 244-245 H 3
Tyler o USA (WV) 280-281 F 4
Tylertown o USA (MS) 268-269 K 5
Tylgovajam ∼ RUS 112-113 O 6
Tylihul ∼ UA 102-103 F 4
Tylihul's'kyj lyman ≈ 102-103 G 4
Tylnoj ∼ RUS 112-113 M 5
Tym ∼ RUS 114-115 T 4
Tym ∼ RUS 114-115 Q 5
Tym' ∼ RUS 122-123 K 3
Tym, Ust'- o RUS 114-115 Q 5
Tymerokan ∼ RUS 116-117 F 2
Tymlat ✩ RUS 120-121 U 4
Tymna ∼ RUS 118-119 O 8
Tymna, laguna ≈ 112-113 U 4
Tymovskoe ✩ RUS 122-123 K 3
Tympyčan, Uèľ ∼ RUS 118-119 E 5
Tympylykan ∼ RUS 118-119 L 3
Tymtej ∼ RUS 120-121 L 2
Tynda ✩ RUS 118-119 M 8
Tynda ∼ RUS 118-119 N 9
Tyndall o CDN (MAN) 234-235 G 4
Tyndall o USA (SD) 260-261 J 4
Tyndall Air Force Base xx USA (FL) 286-287 D 1
Tyndik ∼ KA 124-125 K 3
Tyndrum o GB 90-91 E 3
Tyne ∼ GB 90-91 G 4
Tynep ∼ RUS 114-115 U 3
Tyner o USA (KY) 276-277 M 3
Tyne Valley o CDN (PEI) 240-241 M 4
Tynset ✩ N 86-87 E 5
Typical Torajan Villages ✕·· RI 164-165 F 5
Typtygir, köli ⊖ KA 124-125 D 2
Tyr ∴··· RL 128-129 F 6
Tyrifjorden ⊖ N 86-87 E 6
Tyrkan ∼ RUS 120-121 E 5
Tyrma o RUS (HBR) 122-123 E 3
Tyrma ∼ RUS 122-123 D 3
Tyrma ∼ RUS 122-123 E 4
Tyrnyauz o RUS 126-127 E 6
Tyro o USA (AR) 276-277 D 7
Tyrone o USA (GA) 284-285 H 3
Tyrone o USA (NM) 256-257 G 6
Tyrone o USA (OK) 264-265 C 2
Tyrone o USA (PA) 280-281 H 3
Tyrrell, Lake ⊖ AUS 180-181 G 3
Tyrrell Lake ⊖ CDN 30-31 R 4
Tyrrhenian Basin ≃ 100-101 C 5
Tyrrhenian Sea ≈ 100-101 C 5
Tyrs Bjerge ▲ GRØ 28-29 U 5
Tyrtova, ostrov ⌒ RUS 108-109 b 3
Tyry ∼ RUS 120-121 H 2
Tyškanbaj o KA 126-127 P 2
Tysnesøy ⌒ N 86-87 B 6
Tytyľ, ozero ⊖ RUS 112-113 P 3
Tyumen' = Tjumen' ✩ RUS 114-115 H 6
Tzaneen o ZA 218-219 F 6
Tzinteel o MEX 52-53 H 3
Tziscao o MEX 52-53 J 3
Tzonconejo, Río ∼ MEX 52-53 J 3
Tzucacab o MEX 52-53 K 1

U

Uaçá, Área Indígena ✕ BR 62-63 J 4
Uacaca, Cachoeira ∼ CO 66-67 C 2
Uachtar Ard = Oughterard o IRL 90-91 C 5
Uaco Cungo o ANG 216-217 C 5
Uacuru, Cachoeira ∼ BR 70-71 G 2
Ua'ili, Wādī al- ∼ KSA 130-131 F 2
Uala, zaliv ⊖ RUS 120-121 V 3
Uamba o ANG 216-217 D 3
Uanda o AUS 178-179 H 1
Uanga ∼ RUS 122-123 K 2
Uangando ∼ ANG 216-217 D 8
Uape o MOC 218-219 K 3
Uapuí, Cachoeira ∼ BR 66-67 C 2
Uarges ▲ EAK 212-213 F 3
Uar Igarore < SP 212-213 J 3
Uarini o BR 66-67 E 4
Uarini, Rio ∼ BR 66-67 D 5
Uaroo o AUS 172-173 B 7
Uati-Paraná, Área Indígena ✕ BR 66-67 D 4
Uatuma, Rio ∼ BR 66-67 H 4
Uauá o BR 68-69 J 6
Uauaretê o BR 66-67 C 2
Uaupés, Rio ∼ BR 66-67 D 2
Uaus, Ra's ▲ OM 132-133 J 5
Uavala ∼ ANG 216-217 D 8
Uaxactún ∴• GCA 52-53 K 3
Uaza ▲ ETH 200-201 J 6
Ub o YU 100-101 H 2
Ubá o BR 72-73 J 6
Uba ∼ KA 124-125 N 3
Uba o WAN 204-205 K 3
Ubagan ∼ KA 124-125 D 2
Ubaí o BR 72-73 H 4
Ubai o PNG 183 F 3
'Ubaid < SUD 200-201 B 6
Ubaila o IRQ 128-129 J 6
'Ubaila, al- o KSA 132-133 G 2
Ubaitaba o BR 72-73 L 3
Ubajay o RA 76-77 H 6
Ubaldino Taques o BR 74-75 E 6
Ubangi ∼ ZRE 210-211 F 3
Ubangui ∼ ZRE 206-207 D 6
Ubaporanga o BR 72-73 J 5
Ubar ∴• OM 132-133 H 4
Ubarc' ∼ BY 94-95 K 6
Ubatã o BR 72-73 L 3
Ubate o CO 60-61 E 5
Ubatuba o BR 72-73 H 7
Ubauro o PK 138-139 B 5
'Ubayyid, Wādī l- ∼ IRQ 128-129 J 7
Ube o J 152-153 D 8
Úbeda o E 98-99 F 5
Ubehebe Crater • USA (CA) 248-249 G 3
Ubekendt Ejland ⌒ GRØ 26-27 Y 8
Uberaba o BR 72-73 G 5
Uberaba, Lago ⊖ BR 70-71 J 5
Uberaba, Rio ∼ BR 72-73 F 5
Uberlândia o BR (MIN) 72-73 F 5
Uberlândia o BR (ROR) 62-63 E 5
Ubia, Gunung (Gunung Leonard Darwin) ▲ RI 166-167 J 4
Ubiaja o WAN 204-205 G 5
Ubina o BOL 70-71 D 7
Ubinskoe o RUS 114-115 P 7
Ubinskoe, ozero ⊖ RUS 114-115 P 7
Ubirajara o BR 72-73 F 7
Ubirr o AUS 172-173 L 2
Ubit < WAN 204-205 H 6
Ubojnaja ∼ RUS 108-109 U 5
Ubol Rat Reservoir ⊖ THA 158-159 G 2
Ubombo ▲ ZA 220-221 L 3
Ubon Ratchathani o THA 158-159 H 3
Ubovka o RUS 122-123 F 6
Ubundu o ZRE 210-211 K 4
Uč-Adži o TM 136-137 H 5
Učaly ✩ RUS 96-97 L 6
Učami ∼ RUS 116-117 F 4
Ucapinima o CO 66-67 C 2
Ucaral o KA 124-125 M 5
Ucayali, Río ∼ PE 64-65 F 4
Učdepe o TM 136-137 H 6
Uch o·· PK 138-139 C 5
Ucharonidge o AUS 174-175 C 5
Uchee Creek ∼ USA (AL) 284-285 E 4
Uchiura-wan ≈ 152-153 J 3
Uchiza o PE 64-65 D 6
Učkeken o RUS 126-127 E 6
Učkuduk ✩ US 136-137 H 3
Učkurgan o US 136-137 N 4
Ucluelet o CDN (BC) 230-231 D 5
Učničhilja ∼ RUS 112-113 P 5
Ucross o USA (WY) 252-253 M 2
Učsaj o US 136-137 F 3
Učtagankum ⩦ TM 136-137 E 4
Úcua o ANG 216-217 C 4
Učur ∼ RUS 120-121 F 6
Uda ∼ RUS 116-117 O 10
Uda ∼ RUS 116-117 J 8
Uda ∼ RUS 118-119 E 9
Uda ∼ RUS 120-121 D 6
Udačnyj o RUS 110-111 J 6
Udagamandalam o IND 140-141 G 5
Udaipura o IND 142-143 E 5
'Udaib, al- o KSA 130-131 E 4
'Udaiba, 'Uqlat al- o IRQ 130-131 K 3
'Udaid, al- o UAE 134-135 D 6
Udaipur o IND (RAJ) 138-139 D 7
Udaipur o IND (TRI) 142-143 G 4
Udaiyarpalaiyam o IND 140-141 H 5
Udaquiola o RA 78-79 K 4
Udayagiri o IND 140-141 H 3
Udbina o HR 100-101 E 2
Uddeholm o• S 86-87 F 6
Uddevalla ✩ S 86-87 E 7
Uddjaure ⊖ S 86-87 H 4
Udè, Ulan ✩• RUS 116-117 N 10
Udegi o WAN 204-205 G 4
Udgir o IND 138-139 F 10
Udhampur o IND 138-139 E 3
Udi o WAN 204-205 G 5
Údine ✩• I 100-101 D 1
Udinsk o RUS 122-123 H 2
Udintsev Fracture Zone ≃ 14-15 N 13
Udispattu o CL 140-141 J 7
Udja ∼ RUS 110-111 L 4
Udmurtia = Udmurtskaja Respublika □ RUS 96-97 H 5
Udobnaja o RUS 126-127 D 5
Udobnaja, buhta ⊖ RUS 108-109 b 2
Udokan, hrebet ▲ RUS 118-119 J 7
Udon Thani o THA 158-159 G 2
Udova ∼ RUS 120-121 R 6
Udpūdi o IND 140-141 F 2
Udskaja guba ⊖ RUS 120-121 F 6
Udskoe o RUS 120-121 F 6
Udubaddawa o CL 140-141 H 7
Udumalaippettai o IND 140-141 G 5
Udupi o IND 140-141 F 4
Udu Point ▲ FJI 184 III c 2
Udy ∼ RUS 102-103 K 2
Udyhyn ∼ RUS 120-121 D 6
Udyľ, ozero ⊖ RUS 122-123 H 2
Udzhar = Ucar o AZ 128-129 M 2
Uebonti o RI 164-165 G 4
Ueca ▲ ETH 208-209 C 4
Ueda o J 152-153 H 6
Uedinenija, ostrov ⌒ RUS 108-109 U 3
Uekuli o RI 164-165 G 4
Uèle ∼ RUS 110-111 K 3
Uele ∼ ZRE 210-211 J 2
Uèlen o• RUS 112-113 a 3
Uelgi, ozero ⊖ RUS 96-97 M 6
Uèľ-Siktjah ∼ RUS 110-111 P 5
Uèľ-Tympyčan ∼ RUS 118-119 E 5
Uelzen o D 92-93 L 2
Uembje, Lagoa ⊖ MOC 220-221 L 2
Ueno o J 152-153 G 7
Uere ∼ ZRE 206-207 H 6
Ueré, Rio ∼ BR 66-67 D 5
Ufa ✩ RUS (BAS) 96-97 J 6
Ufa ∼ RUS 96-97 K 5
Ufeyn o SP 208-209 J 3
Ufimskoe plato ▲ RUS 96-97 K 6
Uftjuga ∼ RUS 88-89 T 6
Ugab ∼ NAM 216-217 D 9
Ugahan o RUS 118-119 G 6
Ugak Island ⌒ USA 22-23 U 4
Ugāle o LV 94-95 H 3
Ugalla o EAT 212-213 C 6
Ugalla ∼ EAT 212-213 C 6
Ugalla River Game Reserve ⊥ EAT (TAB) 212-213 C 6
Ugamak Island ⌒ USA 22-23 O 5
Uganda ■ EAU 212-213 C 2
Uganik Island ⌒ USA 22-23 U 4
Ugarit ∴·· SYR 128-129 F 5
Ugashik Bay ≈ 22-23 R 4
Ugashik Lake ⊖ USA 22-23 S 4
Ugatkyn ∼ RUS 112-113 Q 3
Ugba o WAN 204-205 H 5
Ugbala o WAN 204-205 H 5
Ugbenu o WAN 204-205 F 5
Ugep o WAN 204-205 H 6
Ughelli o WAN 204-205 F 6
Ugie o ZA 220-221 J 5
Ugjokfok Bay ≈ 36-37 T 7
Ugjut o KS 146-147 B 5
Uglegorsk o RUS 122-123 K 4
Ugleural'skij o RUS 96-97 K 4
Uglič ✩·· RUS 94-95 Q 3
Uglovoe o RUS 122-123 C 3
Uglovoe, ozero ⊖ RUS 108-109 Z 1
Ugo o WAN 204-205 G 5
Ugojan o RUS 118-119 M 6
Ugoľnaja ∼ RUS 108-109 c 4
Ugoľnaja, buhta ⊖ RUS 112-113 U 5
Ugoľnoe o RUS 110-111 b 7
Ugoľnye Kopi o RUS 112-113 T 4
Ugoľnyj o RUS 118-119 M 7
Ugoľnyj, mys ▲ RUS 120-121 U 3
Ugra o RUS 94-95 O 4
Ugssugtussoq ≈ 28-29 V 4
Uḫaiḍir ∴• IRQ 128-129 K 6
Uhen o WAN 204-205 F 5
Uherské Hradiště o CZ 92-93 O 4
Uhi o WAN 204-205 G 5
Uhiere o WAN 204-205 F 5
Úhlava ∼ CZ 92-93 M 4
Uhlenhorst o NAM 220-221 C 1
Uhma ∼ RUS 88-89 W 5
Uholovo ✩ RUS 94-95 R 5
Uhrichsville o USA (OH) 280-281 E 3
Uhta o RUS (KOM) 88-89 W 5
Uhta ∼ RUS 88-89 W 5
Uhuru Peak ▲ EAT 212-213 F 5
Uib o NAM 216-217 D 9
Uige □ ANG 216-217 C 3
Uige ✩ ANG (UIG) 216-217 C 3
Uiha ⌒ TON 184 IV a 1
Uijŏngbu o ROK 150-151 F 9
Uiju o DVR 150-151 E 7
Uinskoe ✩ RUS 96-97 K 5
Uintah and Ouray Indian Reservation ✕ USA (UT) 254-255 E 3
Uinta Mountains ▲ USA (UT) 254-255 E 3
Uinta River ∼ USA (UT) 254-255 E 3
Uiraponu o BR 70-71 H 4
Uiraúna o BR 68-69 J 5
Uis Myn o NAM 216-217 C 10
Ŭisŏng o ROK 150-151 G 9
Uitenhage o ZA 220-221 G 6
Uivak, Cape ▲ CDN 36-37 S 5
Uivaq ⌒ GRØ 28-29 U 5
Uizèn o MAU 148-149 H 5
Uj ∼ RUS 96-97 L 6
Uj ∼ RUS 114-115 K 6
Uj ∼ RUS 114-115 G 7
Ujali o WAN 204-205 G 5
Ujaly o KA (KZL) 126-127 O 5
Ujaly o KA (MNG) 126-127 L 5
Ujaly o TJ 136-137 L 5
Ujan ∼ RUS 120-121 E 5
Ujana ∼ RUS 120-121 F 2
Ujandina ∼ RUS 110-111 Z 5
Ujar ✩ RUS 116-117 G 8
Ujdah ✩ MA 188-189 L 3
Ujelang ⌒ MAI 13 H 2
Uji o J 152-153 F 7
Uji-guntō ⌒ J 152-153 C 9
Ujiji o• EAT 212-213 B 6
Ujil ∼ KA 96-97 H 9
Ujil ∼ KA 126-127 L 3
Ujir, Pulau ⌒ RI 166-167 H 4
Ujjain o IND 138-139 E 8
Ujmen' ∼ RUS 124-125 P 3
Ujohbilang o RI 164-165 D 3
Ujskoe o RUS 96-97 M 6
Ujuk o KA 136-137 M 3
Ujuk ∼ RUS 116-117 F 10
Ujukskij, hrebet ▲ RUS 116-117 F 10
Ujungbatu o RI 162-163 D 4

Ujungberung ○ RI 168 B 3
Ujung Kulon Game Park ⊥ RI 168 A 3
Ujung Kulon National Park ⊥ ••• RI 168 A 3
Ujunglamuru ○ RI 164-165 F 6
Ujung Pandang ☆ RI 164-165 F 6
Ujvinvyvajam ~ RUS 120-121 V 3
Ujyk ○ KA 136-137 M 3
Uka ~ RUS 120-121 T 5
Ukara Island ⌒ EAT 212-213 D 4
'Ukāš, Tulūl al- ▲ IRQ 128-129 K 7
Ukata ○ WAN 204-205 F 3
Ukatnyj, ostrov ⌒ RUS 126-127 H 5
Ukdungle ○ IND 138-139 G 3
Ukehe ○ WAN 204-205 G 5
Ukėlajat ~ RUS 112-113 R 6
Ukėlajat, hrebet ▲ RUS 112-113 Q 6
Ukerewe Island ⌒ EAT 212-213 D 5
Ukhrul ○ IND 142-143 J 3
Ukhta = Uhta ○ RUS 88-89 W 5
Ukiah ○ USA (CA) 246-247 B 4
Ukiah ○ USA (OR) 244-245 G 5
Uki Ni Masi Island ⌒ SOL 184 I e 4
Ukinskaja guba ○ RUS 120-121 U 5
Ukkusissat ○ GRØ 26-27 Z 8
Uklāna ○ IND 138-139 E 5
Ukmergė ☆ •• LT 94-95 J 4
Ukolnoi Island ⌒ USA 22-23 Q 5
Ukraina ○ CDN (MAN) 234-235 C 3
Ukraine = Ukrajina ■ UA 102-103 E 3
Ukšum ~ RUS 118-119 G 8
Uktym ~ RUS 88-89 U 5
Ukukit ~ RUS 110-111 L 5
Uku-shima ⌒ J 152-153 C 8
Ukwatutu ○ ZRE 206-207 H 6
Ul ~ RUS 122-123 H 2
Ula ☆ TR 128-129 C 4
'Ulā, al- ○ •• KSA 130-131 E 4
Ulaanbaatar ★ MAU 148-149 H 4
Ulaan-Ėrėg ○ MAU 148-149 J 4
Ulaangom ☆ MAU 116-117 F 11
Ulaanhudag ○ MAU 148-149 G 4
Ulaan nuur ○ MAU 148-149 F 5
Ulaanšivėėt ○ MAU 148-149 F 4
Ulaan Tajga ⩡ MAU 148-149 D 2
Ulagan, Ust'- ☆ RUS 124-125 Q 3
Ulah-An ○ RUS 118-119 O 5
Ulahan-Bom, hrebet ▲ RUS 120-121 G 2
Ulahan-Botuobuja ~ RUS 118-119 E 5
Ulahan-Jurjah ~ RUS 110-111 O 3
Ulahan-Kjuėgjuljur ~ RUS 110-111 T 4
Ulahan-Kjuėl' ○ RUS (SAH) 110-111 V 6
Ulahan-Kjuėl' • RUS (SAH) 110-111 a 7
Ulahan-Murbajy ~ RUS 118-119 F 5
Ulahan-Siligile ~ RUS 120-121 D 4
Ulahan-Sis, hrebet ▲ RUS 110-111 b 5
Ulahan Taryn • RUS 110-111 Z 7
Ulahan-Taryn-Jurjah ~ RUS 110-111 Y 7
Ulahan-Tirentjah ~ RUS 110-111 P 5
Ulahan-Vava ~ RUS 116-117 N 3
Ulah-Tas, gora ▲ RUS 110-111 d 4
'Ulaim az-Zama ▲ KSA 130-131 G 3
Ulak Island ⌒ USA 22-23 G 7
Ulamona ○ PNG 183 F 3
Ulan ○ VRC 144-145 M 2
Ulan Bator = Ulaanbaatar ★ MAU 148-149 H 4
Ülanbel ○ KA 124-125 G 6
Ulan-Burgasy, hrebet ▲ RUS 116-117 O 9
Ūlang, Daryā-ye ~ AFG 134-135 K 2
Ulanhot ○ VRC 150-151 D 4
Ulanlinggi ○ VRC 146-147 H 4
Ulansuhai Nur ○ VRC 154-155 F 1
Ulan Tohoi ○ VRC 148-149 E 7
Ulan-Udė ☆ • RUS 116-117 N 10
Ulan Ude = Ulan-Udė ☆ • RUS 116-117 N 10
Ulan Ul Hu ○ VRC 144-145 H 3
Ulapara ○ BD 142-143 F 3
Ulapes, Sierra de ▲ RA 76-77 D 6
Ularbemban ○ RI 162-163 E 4
Ulaş ☆ TR 128-129 G 3
Ulawa Island ⌒ SOL 184 I e 3
Ulawun, Mount ▲ PNG 183 F 3
Ulaya ○ EAT 214-215 J 4
Ulbanep, Mount ▲ PNG 183 B 2
Ul'banskij zaliv ≈ 122-123 G 2
Ul'beja ~ RUS 120-121 K 3
Ul'beja ~ RUS 120-121 L 4
Ulcinj ○ YU 100-101 G 4
Ulco ○ ZA 220-221 G 4
Ul'durga ~ RUS 118-119 G 9
Uleåborg ☆ FIN 88-89 H 4
Ulefoss ☆ N 86-87 D 7
Ulemaririvier ~ SME 62-63 G 4
Ulete ○ EAT 214-215 H 5
Uliaga Island ⌒ USA 22-23 M 6
Uliastaj ☆ MAU 148-149 C 4
Uliga ★ MAI 13 J 2
Ulindi ~ ZRE 210-211 L 4
Ulindi ~ ZRE 212-213 B 5
Ul'inskij, hrebet ▲ RUS 120-121 H 5
Ul'ja ○ RUS 120-121 J 4
Ul'ja ~ RUS 120-121 H 4
Uljagan ~ RUS 112-113 L 4
Uljanivka ☆ UA 102-103 G 3
Ul'janovka ○ RUS 94-95 M 2
Ul'janovo ○ RUS 94-95 H 4
Ul'janovo ○ US 136-137 L 4
Ul'janovsk = Simbirsk ☆ RUS 96-97 F 6
Ul'janovskij ○ KA 124-125 H 3
Uljatuj ○ RUS 118-119 H 10
Uljin ○ ROK 150-151 G 9
Uljuveem ~ RUS 112-113 X 3
Uljuveemskaja vpadina ⩡ RUS 112-113 X 3
Ülkajyk ~ KA 126-127 P 2
Ülkajyk ~ KA 126-127 P 3
Ul'kan ~ RUS 116-117 N 8
Ul'kan ~ RUS 120-121 H 5
Ülken Acbolat, köli ○ KA 124-125 K 2
Ülken-Aktau, tau ▲ KA 136-137 L 3
Ülken Borsyk, kùm ⩡ KA 126-127 N 4
Ülken Cobda ~ KA 126-127 L 2
Ülken-Karoj, köli ○ KA 124-125 G 2
Ülken Özen ~ KA 96-97 F 9
Ülken Šagan ○ KA 96-97 G 8
Ülken sor ⩡ KA 126-127 J 5
Ulla, Río ~ E 98-99 C 3
Ulladulla ○ AUS 180-181 L 3
Ullahan-Kjuel', ozero ○ RUS 110-111 P 6
Ullāl ○ IND 140-141 F 4
Ullånger ○ S 86-87 J 5
Ullapool ○ • GB 90-91 E 3
Ulla Ulla ○ BOL 70-71 C 4
Ulla Ulla, Reserva Faunística ⊥ BOL 70-71 C 4
Ullawarra ○ AUS 176-177 D 1
Ulloma ○ BOL 70-71 C 5
Ullsfjorden ≈ 86-87 J 2
Ullŭng ○ ROK 150-151 H 9
Ullŭng Do ⌒ ROK 150-151 H 9
Ulm ○ • D 92-93 K 4
Ulm ○ USA (AR) 276-277 D 6
Ulm ○ USA (MT) 250-251 H 4
Ulm ○ USA (WY) 252-253 M 2
Ul'ma ~ RUS 122-123 D 3
Ul'ma ~ RUS 122-123 D 3
Ulmer ○ USA (SC) 284-285 J 3
Ulongwé ○ MOC 218-219 H 2
Uloowaranie, Lake ○ AUS 178-179 E 4
Ulricehamn ☆ S 86-87 F 8
Ulsan ○ ROK 150-151 G 10
Ultima ○ AUS 180-181 G 3
Ulu ○ MYA 158-159 E 5
Ulu ○ RI 164-165 J 2
Ulu ○ RUS (SAH) 118-119 N 5
Ulu ~ RUS 118-119 N 5
Ulu ○ SUD 208-209 A 3
Ulúa, Río ~ HN 52-53 K 4
Uluaa ○ GRØ (VGR) 26-27 X 7
Uluaa ⌒ GRØ (VGR) 26-27 X 7
Ulubat Gölü ○ TR 128-129 C 2
Uluçınar ○ TR 128-129 F 4
Uludağ ▲ TR 128-129 C 2
Uludere ☆ TR 128-129 K 4
Uludoruk Tepe ▲ TR 128-129 K 4
Ulugqat ○ VRC 146-147 B 6
Uluguru Mountains ▲ EAT 214-215 J 4
Ului Island ⌒ AUS 183 B 6
Uluinggalau ▲ FJI 184 III b 2
Ulujami ○ RI 168 C 3
Ulujul ~ RUS 114-115 T 6
Uluksan Peninsula ⌣ CDN 24-25 d 4
Ulungur He ~ VRC 146-147 H 2
Ulungur Hu ○ VRC (XUZ) 146-147 H 2
Ulungur Hu • VRC (XUZ) 146-147 H 2
Ulupalakua Ranch ○ USA (HI) 288 J 4
Uluputur ○ PNG 183 G 2
Uluru National Park ⊥ ••• AUS 176-177 L 2
Ulut ~ RP 160-161 F 7
Ulu Tiram ○ MAL 162-163 E 4
Ulva ○ AUS 178-179 H 1
Ulveah = Lopevi ⌒ VAN 184 II b 3
Ulverstone ○ AUS 180-181 H 6
'Ulyā, Wādī l- ○ OM 132-133 K 2
Ulysses ○ USA (KS) 262-263 E 7
Ulysses ○ USA (NE) 262-263 J 3
Ūly-Taldyk ~ KA 126-127 N 3
Ūlytau, tau ▲ KA 124-125 E 5
Ūly-Žylancyk ~ KA 124-125 D 4
Ulz gol ~ MAU 148-149 L 3
Uma ~ ZRE 210-211 L 3
Umadam ○ SUD 200-201 H 4
Umair ○ KSA 132-133 C 5
Umaish ○ WAN 204-205 G 4
Umaki ○ CO 60-61 F 2
Umak Island ⌒ USA 22-23 J 7
Umala ○ BOL 70-71 C 5
Umal'ta, Ust'- ○ RUS 122-123 E 3
Umán ○ MEX 52-53 K 1
Uman' ☆ UA 102-103 G 3
Umanak = Uummannaq ○ GRØ 28-29 O 1
Umanak Fjord ≈ 26-27 Y 8
Umanaq ○ GRØ 28-29 P 4
Umangcinang, Tanjung ▲ RI 164-165 E 5
Umarga ○ IND 140-141 G 2
Umari, Rio ~ BR 66-67 E 7
Umaria ○ IND 142-143 B 4
Umarkhed ○ IND 138-139 F 10
Umarkot ○ PK 138-139 B 7
Umaroona Lake ○ AUS 178-179 D 4
Umatilla ○ USA (FL) 286-287 H 3
Umatilla ○ USA (OR) 244-245 F 5
Umatilla Indian Reservation ⅩUSA (OR) 244-245 G 5
Umatilla River ~ USA (OR) 244-245 F 5
Umba ~ EAT 212-213 G 6
Umba ○ RUS 88-89 N 3
Umbakumba ⅩAUS 174-175 D 3
Umbarger ○ USA (TX) 264-265 B 4
Umbe ○ PE 64-65 D 6
Umbeb Bay ≈ 184 II a 3
Umbelasha ~ SUD 206-207 F 4
Umboi Island ⌒ PNG 183 D 3
Umbozero ○ RUS 88-89 N 3
Umbraj ○ IND 140-141 F 2
Umbria □ I 100-101 C 3
Umbukul ○ PNG 183 E 2
Umbulan Gayohpecoh ○ RI 162-163 F 6
Umbuluzi ~ MOC 220-221 L 3
Umbumbulu ○ ZA 220-221 K 5
Umburanas ○ BR 68-69 H 7
Umbuzeiro ○ BR 68-69 L 5
Umeå ☆ • S 86-87 K 5
Umeälven ~ S 86-87 J 4
Umfolozi Game Reserve ⊥ ZA 220-221 K 4
Umiat ○ USA 20-21 O 2
Umiivik Bugt ≈ 28-29 U 4
Umirim ○ BR 68-69 J 3
Umitker ○ KA 124-125 J 3
Umkomaas ○ ZA (NTL) 220-221 K 5
Umkomaas ~ ZA 220-221 K 5
Umlekan ○ RUS 118-119 N 9
Umm al 'Abīd ○ LAR 192-193 F 4
Umm al Aranib ○ LAR 192-193 F 4
Umm al-Ǧimāl ∴ • JOR 130-131 E 1
Umm al-Hait, Wādī = Ibn Ḥautar, Wādī ~ OM 132-133 J 4
Umm al 'Izām, Sabkhat ○ LAR 192-193 F 2
Ummannarsuaq = Kap Farvel ▲ GRØ 28-29 T 7
Umm ar Rizam ○ LAR 192-193 K 1
Umm Ašar Aš-Šarqīyā ○ KSA 130-131 J 4
Umm Ba'ānib, Ǧabal ▲ ET 194-195 F 4
Umm Badr ○ SUD 200-201 C 5
Umm Barbit ○ SUD 206-207 L 3
Umm Bel ○ SUD 200-201 D 6
Umm Buru ○ SUD 198-199 L 5
Umm Būshah ○ SUD 200-201 E 6
Umm Dafag ○ SUD 206-207 F 3
Umm Dam ○ SUD 200-201 E 6
Umm Defeis ○ SUD 200-201 D 6
Umm Digulgulaya ○ SUD 206-207 G 3
Umm Dubban ○ SUD 200-201 D 5
Umm Durmān = Omdurman ○ •• SUD 200-201 F 5
Umm Gamāla ○ SUD 206-207 J 3
Umm Gederri ○ SUD 206-207 F 3
Umm Harāz ○ SUD 206-207 F 3
Umm Ḥawsh ○ SUD 200-201 C 6
Umm Hibāl, Bi'r < ET 194-195 F 6
Umm Hitan ○ SUD 206-207 K 3
Ummi, Godār-e ▲ IR 134-135 H 1
Umm 'Illah, Sarir ⩡ LAR 192-193 F 4
Umm Inderaba ○ SUD 200-201 E 5
Umm Kaddādah ○ SUD 200-201 C 6
Umm Marahik ○ SUD 200-201 B 6
Umm Mirdi ○ SUD 200-201 F 3
Umm Naqqāt, Ǧabal ▲ ET 194-195 G 5
Umm Qasr ○ IRQ 130-131 K 2
Umm Qozein ○ SUD 200-201 C 5
Umm Qurein < SUD 200-201 D 4
Umm Rumetla < SUD 200-201 E 4
Umm Ruwābah ○ SUD 200-201 E 6
Umm Sa'ad ○ LAR 192-193 L 2
Umm Sagura ○ SUD 206-207 J 4
Umm Sa'īd = Musai'īd ○ Q 134-135 D 6
Umm Sayyālah ○ SUD 200-201 E 5
Umm Segeiti ○ SUD 200-201 E 6
Umnak ○ USA 22-23 M 6
Umnak Island ⌒ USA 22-23 M 6
Umnak Pass ≈ 22-23 N 6
Umniati ○ ZW 218-219 E 4
Umpaqua River ~ USA (OR) 244-245 B 7
Um Phang ○ THA 158-159 E 3
Umpuhua ○ MOC 218-219 K 2
Umran ○ KSA 130-131 L 5
Umrer ○ IND 138-139 G 9
Umsini, Gunung ▲ RI 166-167 G 2
Umtata ☆ ZA 220-221 J 5
Umtentu ○ ZA 220-221 K 5
Umuahia ○ WAN 204-205 G 6
Umuarama ○ BR 72-73 D 7
Umuda Island ⌒ PNG 183 B 5
Umu-Duru ○ WAN 204-205 G 6
Umunede ○ WAN 204-205 G 5
Umutina, Área Indígena Ⅹ BR 70-71 J 4
Umutu ○ WAN 204-205 G 6
Umvukwe Range ▲ ZW 218-219 F 3
Umvurudzi Safari Area ⊥ ZW 218-219 F 3
Umzimkulu ○ ZA 220-221 J 5
Umzimkulu ~ ZA 220-221 K 5
Umzimvubu ~ ZA 220-221 J 5
Umzingwani ~ ZW 218-219 E 5
Umzinto ○ ZA 220-221 K 5
Una ○ BR 72-73 L 3
Una ○ IND 138-139 F 4
Una ○ RUS 88-89 P 4
Una ○ USA (AR) 276-277 D 5
Una, Reserva Biológica de ⊥ BR 72-73 L 3
Una, Rio ~ BR 68-69 K 6
Unadilla ○ USA (GA) 284-285 G 4
Unaha ~ RUS 118-119 N 8
Unaí ○ BR 72-73 G 4
Unaiza ○ JOR 130-131 D 2
'Unaiza ○ KSA 130-131 J 4
Unalakleet ○ USA 20-21 K 5
Unalakleet River ~ USA 20-21 K 5
Unalaska ○ USA 22-23 N 6
Unalaska Bay ≈ 22-23 N 6
Unalaska Island ⌒ USA 22-23 N 6
Unalga Island ⌒ USA 22-23 N 6
Unango ○ MOC 214-215 H 7
Unare, Río ~ YV 60-61 J 3
Unari, Corredeira ~ BR 66-67 C 2
Unauna ○ RI 164-165 G 4
Unauna, Pulau ⌒ RI 164-165 G 4
Unawari ○ RI 166-167 H 3
Unbunmaroo, Mount ▲ AUS 178-179 F 2
Uncas ○ CDN (ALB) 232-233 E 2
Unčen' = Ungheni ☆ MD 102-103 E 4
Unčeny = Ungheni ☆ MD 102-103 E 4
Uncompahgre Peak ▲ USA (CO) 254-255 H 5
Uncompahgre Plateau ▲ USA (CO) 254-255 G 5
Uncompahgre River ~ USA (CO) 254-255 H 5
Unda ~ RUS 118-119 H 10
Undandita Ⅹ AUS 176-177 M 1
Underberg ○ ZA 220-221 J 4
Underbool ○ AUS 180-181 F 3
Underground River • RP 160-161 C 7
Underwood ○ USA (ND) 258-259 F 4
Underwood ○ USA (WA) 244-245 D 5
Undjuljung ~ RUS 110-111 P 6
Undozero, ozero ○ RUS 88-89 P 5
Undu, Tanjung ▲ RI 168 E 8
Unduma, Rio ~ BOL 70-71 D 3
Undur ○ RI 166-167 F 3
Unea Island ⌒ PNG 183 E 3
Uneča ○ RUS 94-95 N 5
Uneí, Igarapé ~ BR 66-67 D 3
Uneiuxi, Área Indígena Ⅹ BR 66-67 D 3
Uneiuxi, Rio ~ BR 66-67 D 3
Uneiuxi, Serra de ▲ BR 66-67 D 3
Unga Island ⌒ USA 22-23 Q 5
Ungalik ○ USA 20-21 K 4
Ungalik River ~ USA 20-21 K 4
Ungarie ○ AUS 180-181 J 2
Ungarra ○ AUS 180-181 D 3
Unga Strait ≈ 22-23 Q 5
Ungava, Péninsule d' ⌣ CDN 36-37 L 4
Ungava Bay ≈ 36-37 P 5
Ungerem ○ PNG 183 A 4
Ungheni ☆ MD 102-103 E 4
Ungjuèle ~ RUS 118-119 O 6
Ungo ~ RUS 118-119 D 10
Ungra ~ RUS 118-119 L 7
Unguz ⩡ TM 136-137 F 5
Ungwana Bay ≈ 212-213 H 5
Unhe ○ ANG 216-217 F 8
Uni ☆ RUS 96-97 G 5
Unia, Lac ○ ZRE 210-211 K 5
Uniab ~ NAM 216-217 B 9
União ○ BR (AMA) 66-67 C 4
União ○ BR (AMA) 66-67 B 6
União ○ BR (GSU) 70-71 K 5
União ○ BR (MAR) 68-69 F 2
União ○ BR (PIA) 68-69 G 4
União da Vitória ○ BR 74-75 E 6
União dos Palmares ○ BR 68-69 K 6
Uniāra ○ IND 138-139 F 7
Unicoi Mountains ▲ USA (TN) 282-283 C 5
Unimak ○ USA 22-23 O 5
Unimak Bight ≈ 22-23 O 5
Unimak Island ⌒ USA 22-23 O 5
Unimak Pass ≈ 22-23 O 5
Unini, Rio ~ BR 66-67 F 3
Unión ○ RA 78-79 G 3
Union ○ USA (MI) 272-273 D 6
Union ○ USA (MO) 274-275 G 6
Union ○ USA (MS) 268-269 L 4
Union ○ USA (OH) 280-281 B 4
Union ○ USA (OR) 244-245 H 5
Union ○ USA (SC) 284-285 J 2
Union ○ USA (TX) 264-265 D 6
Union ○ USA (WV) 280-281 F 6
Unión, Bahía ≈ 78-79 H 5
Unión, La ○ CO (NAR) 64-65 D 1
Unión, La ○ CO (VCA) 60-61 C 5
Unión, La ○ E 98-99 G 6
Unión, La ○ EC 64-65 B 2
Unión, La ☆ ES 52-53 L 5
Unión, La ○ HN 52-53 L 4
Unión, La ○ MEX 52-53 K 3
Unión, La ○ MEX 52-53 D 3
Unión, La ○ PE 64-65 D 6
Unión, La ○ RCH 78-79 C 6
Union, Mount ▲ USA (AZ) 256-257 C 4
Unión, Río La ~ MEX 52-53 D 2
Union Bay ○ CDN (BC) 230-231 E 4
Union Church ○ USA (MS) 268-269 K 5
Union City ○ USA (CA) 248-249 C 2
Union City ○ USA (IN) 274-275 O 4
Union City ○ USA (MI) 272-273 D 5
Union City ○ USA (PA) 280-281 G 2
Union City ○ USA (TN) 276-277 F 4
Union Creek ○ USA (OR) 244-245 C 8
Uniondale ○ ZA 220-221 F 6
Unión de Tula ○ MEX 52-53 B 2
Union Gap ○ USA (WA) 244-245 E 4
Unión Hidalgo ○ MEX 52-53 G 3
Union Island ⌒ WV 56 E 5
Unión Juárez ○ MEX 52-53 H 4
Union National Monument, Fort • USA (NM) 256-257 K 3
Union Pass ▲ USA (AZ) 256-257 A 3
Union Point ○ USA (GA) 284-285 G 3
Union Springs ○ USA (AL) 284-285 E 4
Uniontown ○ USA (AL) 284-285 C 4
Uniontown ○ USA (PA) 280-281 G 4
Unionville ○ USA (IL) 274-275 J 3
Unionville ○ USA (MO) 274-275 E 4
Unionville ○ USA (NV) 246-247 G 3
Unipouheos Indian Reserve Ⅹ CDN (ALB) 232-233 H 2
Unita ○ PE 64-65 D 3
United Arab Emirates = Daul.al-Im.al-'Ara. Al-Muttaḥida ■ UAE 132-133 H 2
United Kingdom ■ GB 90-91 H 4
United States Air Force Academy ×× USA (CO) 254-255 L 5
United States Atomic Energy Reserve ×× USA (CO) 254-255 G 5
United States Military Academy • USA (NY) 280-281 M 2
United States Naval Ammunition Depot (Crane) ×× USA (IN) 274-275 M 6
United States of America ■ USA 244-288 K 6
United States Range ▲ CDN 26-27 J 3
Unity ○ CDN (SAS) 232-233 J 3
Unity ○ USA (ME) 278-279 M 4
Unity ○ USA (OR) 244-245 G 6
Universal City ○ USA (TX) 266-267 J 4
Universitetskij, lednik ⊂ RUS 108-109 c 2
University City ○ USA (MO) 274-275 H 6
University of Virginia ••• USA (VA) 280-281 H 6
University Park ○ USA (NM) 256-257 J 6
Unmet ○ VAN 184 II a 3
Unnāo ○ IND 142-143 B 2
Unnejvajam ~ RUS 112-113 O 6
Uno ○ GNB 202-203 B 4
Uno, Ilha de ⌒ GNB 202-203 B 4
Unpongkor ○ VAN 184 II b 4
Unsan ○ DVR 150-151 E 7
Unskaja guba ≈ 88-89 P 4
Untor, ozero ○ RUS 114-115 H 3
Unturán, Sierra de ▲ YV 66-67 E 2
Unuk River ~ CDN 32-33 E 3
Unwin ○ CDN (SAS) 232-233 J 3
Ünye ☆ TR 128-129 G 2
Unža ~ RUS 94-95 S 3
Unža ~ RUS 96-97 D 4
Unzen Amakusa National Park ⊥ J 152-153 D 8
Uojan, Novyj ○ RUS 118-119 E 7
Uol'can ~ RUS 110-111 Y 7
Uŏng Bí ☆ VN 156-157 E 6
Uoro o Mbini, Río ~ GQ 210-211 C 3
Uozo ○ J 152-153 G 6
Upala ○ CR 52-53 B 6
Upata ○ YV 60-61 K 3
Upatoi River ~ USA (GA) 284-285 F 4
Upemba, Lac ○ ZRE 214-215 D 5
Upemba, Parc National de l' ⊥ ZRE 214-215 D 5
Upernagssivik ⌒ GRØ 28-29 U 4
Upernavik ○ GRØ (VGR) 26-27 W 7
Upernavik ⌒ GRØ (VGR) 26-27 Y 8
Upernavik Kujalleq = Søndre Upernavik ○ GRØ 26-27 X 7
Uphan ○ USA (ND) 258-259 G 3
Upi ○ RP 160-161 F 9
Upington ○ ZA 220-221 E 4
Upolokša ○ RUS 88-89 L 3
'Upolu Island ⌒ WS 184 V b 1
Upolu Point ▲ USA (HI) 288 K 4
Uporovo ☆ RUS 114-115 J 6
Upper Arrow Lake ○ CDN (BC) 230-231 M 3
Upper Canada Village • CDN (ONT) 238-239 K 4
Upper East Region □ GH 202-203 K 4
Upper Ferry ○ CDN (NFL) 242-243 J 5
Upper Forster Lake ○ CDN 34-35 D 2
Upper Fraser ○ CDN (BC) 228-229 N 2
Upper Hat Creek ○ CDN (BC) 230-231 H 3
Upper Humber River ~ CDN (NFL) 242-243 L 3
Upper Indian Pond ○ CDN (NFL) 242-243 M 3
Upper Karoo = Hoë Karoo ⩡ ZA 220-221 D 5
Upper Klamath Lake ○ USA (OR) 244-245 D 8
Upper Lake ○ USA (CA) 246-247 C 4
Upper Lake ○ USA (CA) 246-247 E 2
Upper May ~ PNG 183 A 3
Upper Musquodoboit ○ CDN (NS) 240-241 N 5
Upper Ouachita National Wildlife Refuge ⊥ USA (LA) 268-269 H 4
Upper Peninsula ⌣ USA (MI) 270-271 M 4
Upper Rawdon ○ CDN (NS) 240-241 M 5
Upper Red Lake ○ USA (MN) 270-271 D 2
Upper Sandusky ○ USA (OH) 280-281 C 3
Upper Sioux Indian Reservation Ⅹ USA (MN) 270-271 C 6
Upper Souris National Wildlife Refuge ⊥ USA (ND) 258-259 F 3
Upper Three Runs Creek ~ USA (SC) 284-285 J 3
Upper Twin Lake ○ CDN (ONT) 236-237 B 2
Upper West Region □ GH 202-203 J 4
Uppland ⩡ S 86-87 H 7
Uppsala ○ •• S 86-87 H 7
Upright, Cape ▲ USA 112-113 Y 6
Upsala ○ CDN (ONT) 234-235 N 5
Upsalquitch River ~ CDN (NB) 240-241 J 3
Upshi ○ IND 138-139 F 3
Upstart, Cape ▲ AUS 174-175 J 6
Upstart Bay ≈ 174-175 J 6
Upton ○ USA (KY) 276-277 K 3
Upton ○ USA (WY) 252-253 O 2
Upuí, Corredeira ~ BR 66-67 H 6
'Uqair, al- ○ KSA 134-135 D 6
'Uqlat aṣ-Ṣuqūr ○ KSA 130-131 H 5
'Uqlat Ibn Ǧabrain ○ KSA 130-131 G 4
Ur ∴ •• IRQ 130-131 K 2
Ura ~ RUS 118-119 H 5
Urabá, Golfo de ≈ 60-61 C 3
Uracoa ○ YV 60-61 K 3
Urad Houqi ○ VRC 148-149 H 7
Urad Qianqi ○ VRC 154-155 F 1
Urad Zhongqi ○ VRC 148-149 J 7
Uraguba ○ RUS 88-89 M 2
Urahoro ○ J 152-153 K 3
Uraim, Rio ~ BR 68-69 E 3
Uraj ○ RUS 114-115 H 4
Urak ~ RUS 120-121 J 4
Urakawa ○ J 152-153 K 3
Urakskoe plato ▲ RUS 120-121 J 4
Ural ~ RUS 96-97 L 7
Uralla ○ AUS 178-179 L 6
Ural Mountains = Ural'skij hrebet ▲ RUS 10-11 E 3
Ural'skij, Kamensk- ☆ RUS 96-97 M 5
Ural-Tau hrebet ▲ RUS 96-97 K 7
Ural üstirti ▲ KA 124-125 B 2
Urama ○ YV 60-61 G 2
Uran ○ IND 138-139 D 10
Urana ○ AUS 180-181 J 3
Urana, Lake ○ AUS 180-181 J 3
Urandangi ○ AUS 178-179 E 1
Urandi ○ BR 72-73 J 3
Uranie, Pulau ⌒ RI 166-167 F 1
Uranium City ○ CDN 30-31 P 6
'Uraq ○ SUD 200-201 F 5
Uraria, Paraná ~ BR 66-67 H 4
Uraricuera, Rio ~ BR 62-63 D 4
Ura-Tjube ○ • TJ 136-137 L 5
Uravakonda ○ IND 140-141 G 3
Urawa ☆ J 152-153 H 7
'Urayyiḍa, Bi'r < ET 194-195 E 3
Urbana ○ USA (IL) 274-275 K 4
Urbana ○ USA (OH) 280-281 C 3
Urbana, La ○ YV 60-61 H 4
Urbandale ○ USA (IA) 274-275 E 3
Urbank ○ USA (MN) 270-271 C 4
Urbano Noris ○ C 54-55 G 4
Urbano Santos ○ BR 68-69 G 3
Urbi ○ SUD 200-201 E 3
Urbinasopon ○ RI 166-167 F 2
Urbino ○ I 100-101 D 3
Urcos ○ PE 70-71 B 3
Urcubamba, Rio ~ PE 64-65 C 4
Urdaneta ○ RP 160-161 D 5
Urd gol ○ MAU 146-147 L 2
Urdinarrain ○ RA 78-79 K 2
Urdjužskoe, ozero ○ RUS 88-89 V 3
Urd Tamir gol ~ MAU 148-149 E 4
Ure ○ WAN 204-205 G 4
Ureca ○ GQ 210-211 B 2
Ureliki ○ RUS 112-113 Y 4
Urema ~ RI 166-167 H 3
Uren ○ CDN (SAS) 232-233 M 5
Uren' ○ RUS 96-97 D 5
Urenga hrebet ▲ RUS 96-97 L 6
Urengoj ○ RUS 114-115 P 2
Ureparapara ⌒ VAN 184 II a 1
Urer'jaha ~ RUS 88-89 Y 3
Ures ○ MEX 50-51 D 3
Urewera National Park ⊥ NZ 182 F 3
Urfa = Şanlı Urfa ☆ • TR 128-129 H 4
Urfa Yaylâsı ▲ TR 128-129 H 4
Urgal ○ RUS 122-123 E 3
Urgal ~ RUS 122-123 E 3
Urgamal = Hungij ○ MAU 146-147 M 1
Urganč ☆ US 136-137 G 4
Urganch = Urganč ☆ US 136-137 G 4
Urgenč = Urganč ☆ US 136-137 G 4
Ürgüp ☆ •• TR 128-129 F 3
Urgut ☆ US 136-137 K 5
Urho ○ VRC 146-147 G 2
Urho Kekkosen kansallispuisto ⊥ FIN 88-89 J 2
Uri ○ IND 138-139 E 2
Uri ○ TCH 198-199 J 2
Uriah ○ USA (AL) 284-285 C 5
Uriangato ○ MEX 52-53 D 1
Uribante, Río ~ YV 60-61 F 4
Uribe ○ CO 60-61 C 6
Uribe, La ○ CO (MET) 60-61 D 6
Uribe, La ○ CO (VCA) 60-61 C 5
Uribia ○ CO 60-61 E 2
Uribicha ○ BOL 70-71 F 4
Uribici ○ BR 74-75 F 7
Urica ○ YV 60-61 J 3
Urich ○ USA (MO) 274-275 D 6
Urickij ☆ KA 124-125 D 2
Urickoe ○ RUS 118-119 L 5
Urik ~ RUS 116-117 K 9
Uril ~ RUS 122-123 D 4
Uriman ○ YV 60-61 K 5
Urimará ○ BR 68-69 J 6
Urin ○ PNG 183 E 3
Urique, Río ~ MEX 50-51 F 4
Urjah, Kurun- ○ RUS 120-121 G 4
Urjum, ozero ○ RUS 124-125 L 1
Urjumkan ~ RUS 118-119 J 10
Urjumkanskij, hrebet ▲ RUS 118-119 J 10
Urjup ~ RUS 114-115 U 7
Urjupino ○ RUS 118-119 J 9
Urjupinsk ○ RUS 102-103 N 2
Urka ~ RUS 118-119 L 9
Urkan ~ RUS 118-119 M 9
Urkan ~ RUS 118-119 O 8
Urla ☆ TR 128-129 B 3
Urla-Burtja ~ RUS 96-97 K 8
Urluk ○ RUS 116-117 N 10
Urmatau hrebet ▲ RUS 96-97 K 7
Urmetan ○ TJ 136-137 L 5
Urmi ~ RUS 122-123 E 4
Urna ~ RUS 114-115 M 5
Urnes ○ N 86-87 C 6
Urnes, Stavkirke ••• N 86-87 C 6
Uročišče "Kontugaj" • RUS 96-97 K 8
Uroh ~ RI 164-165 F 5
Uromi ○ WAN 204-205 G 5
Uroševac ○ • YU 100-101 H 3
Urov ~ RUS 118-119 J 10
Urquhart Lake ○ CDN 20-21 Z 2
'Urr, al- ○ Y 132-133 C 6
Urre Lauquén, Laguna ○ RA 78-79 G 5
Urru Co ○ VRC 144-145 F 5
Ursano ○ RI 166-167 E 3
Ursine ○ USA (NV) 248-249 K 2
Ursulo Galván ○ MEX 52-53 K 2
Urt ○ MAU 148-149 E 6
Urtaovul ○ US 136-137 L 4
Urṭayyān ○ KSA 130-131 G 3
Uru ~ ZRE 210-211 L 4
Uru, Rio ~ BR 68-69 F 3
Uru, Rio ~ BR 72-73 F 3
Uruaçu ○ BR 72-73 F 2
Uruanã ○ BR 72-73 F 3
Uruapan del Progreso ○ • MEX 52-53 C 2
Uruara, Rio ~ BR 68-69 B 3
Uruaru, Cachoeira ~ BR 68-69 C 3
Urubamba ○ PE 64-65 F 8
Urubamba, Río ~ PE 64-65 F 8
Urubaxi, Rio ~ BR 66-67 E 3
Urubu, Cachoeira do ~ BR 72-73 F 2
Urubu, Ilha ⌒ BR 66-67 J 4
Urubu Grande, Rio ~ BR 68-69 D 7
Uruburetama ○ BR 68-69 J 3
Urucará ○ BR 66-67 J 4
Uruçu, Cachoeira do ~ BR 66-67 F 2
Urucu, Rio ~ BR 66-67 E 5
Urucu, Rio ~ BR 66-67 H 6
Uruçuca ○ BR 72-73 L 3
Uruçuí ○ BR 68-69 F 5
Uruçuí, Serra do ▲ BR 68-69 F 6
Urucuia ○ BR 72-73 H 4
Urucuia, Rio ~ BR 72-73 H 4
Uruçuí Preto, Rio ~ BR 68-69 F 6
Uruçuí Prêto, Rio ~ BR 68-69 F 5
Uruçuí Vermelho, Rio ~ BR 68-69 F 6
Urucum, Monte do ▲ BR 70-71 J 6
Urucuri, Ilha ⌒ BR 62-63 H 6
Urucuriana, Igarapé ~ BR 62-63 G 5
Uruena, Río ~ RA 76-77 E 4
Uru-Eu-Wau-Wau, Área Indígena Ⅹ BR 70-71 F 2
Uruguai, Rio ~ BR 74-75 D 6
Uruguaiana ○ BR 76-77 J 5
Uruguay ■ ROU 78-79 L 2
Uruguay, Río ~ RA 78-79 K 2
Uruguinha ○ BR 62-63 J 5
Uruk = Erech ∴ • IRQ 128-129 L 7
Uruljunguj ~ RUS 118-119 J 10
Uruma ○ RI 166-167 H 4
Uruma (Omba) ~ RI 166-167 H 4
Urumaco ○ YV 60-61 F 2
Urum aṣ-Ṣuġrā ○ SYR 128-129 G 4
Ürümqi ☆ VRC 146-147 H 4
Urungwe Safari Area ⊥ ZW 218-219 E 3
Urup ~ RUS 126-127 D 5
Urup, ostrov ⌒ RUS 122-123 O 6
Urup, proliv ○ RUS 122-123 O 5
Urupá, Rio ~ BR 70-71 F 2
Urupadi, Rio ~ BR 66-67 J 4
Urupês ○ BR 72-73 F 6
Urupuca, Rio ~ BR 72-73 J 5
'Urūq al-Awārik ⩡ KSA 132-133 E 4
'Urūq ar-Rumaila ⩡ KSA 132-133 E 3
'Urūq Hibāka ⩡ KSA 132-133 F 3
'Urūq Subai' ⩡ KSA 130-131 H 6
Ürür gol ~ MAU 148-149 E 2
Uruša ○ RUS 118-119 L 8
Uruša ~ RUS 118-119 L 9
Urus-Martan ○ RUS 126-127 F 6
Urussu ○ RUS 96-97 H 6
Urusta, Moj- ○ RUS 120-121 N 3
Urutaí, Ilha ⌒ BR 62-63 J 6
Uru Uru, Lago ○ BOL 70-71 D 6
Uruwira ○ EAT 214-215 F 4
Urville, Île d' ⌒ ARK 16 G 31
Urville, Mer d' ≈ 16 G 15
Uryū-gawa ~ J 152-153 K 2
Urziceni ○ RO 102-103 E 5
Uržum ☆ RUS 96-97 G 5
Us ~ RUS 116-117 F 9
Usa ○ J 152-153 D 8
Usa ~ RUS 88-89 Y 4
Usa ~ RUS 108-109 J 8
Usa ~ RUS 114-115 U 7
Usa, Bol'šaja ~ RUS 108-109 L 8
Ušačy ○ BY 94-95 L 4
Usagara ○ EAT 212-213 D 5
'Usaila ○ KSA 130-131 J 5
'Ušaira ○ KSA 130-131 J 5
Uşak ☆ TR 128-129 C 3
Usakos ○ NAM 216-217 C 11
Ušakova, ostrov ⌒ RUS 84-85 q 2
Ušakovskoe ○ RUS 112-113 V 1
Usalgin ~ RUS 122-123 G 2
Usalin ○ RI 166-167 B 7
Usambara Mountains ▲ EAT 212-213 G 6
Usa River ○ EAT 212-213 F 5
Usauer ○ RI 166-167 H 2
Uš-Bel'dir ○ RUS 116-117 J 10
Usborne, Mount ▲ GB 78-79 L 6
Uščal ○ US 136-137 F 3
Ušće ○ YU 100-101 H 3
Usedom ⌒ D 92-93 M 1
Useless Loop ○ AUS 176-177 B 3
Usemuare ○ RI 166-167 H 3
U.S. Energy Research and Development Administration ×× USA (WA) 244-245 F 4
Usengi ○ EAK 212-213 E 4
'Usfān ○ KSA 132-133 A 3
Ušh ~ RUS 120-121 R 5
Ushaa ○ Z 218-219 B 2
Ushagat Island ⌒ USA 22-23 U 3
Usherville ○ CDN (SAS) 232-233 Q 3
Ushibuka ○ J 152-153 D 8
Ushuaia ☆ RA 80 F 7
Usilampatti ○ IND 140-141 G 6
Usim ○ RI 166-167 G 2
Usina Apiacás ○ BR 70-71 J 2
Usina São Francisco ○ BR 66-67 H 5
Usine ○ RN 198-199 C 3
Usino ○ PNG 183 C 3
Usinsk ☆ RUS 88-89 Y 4
Ušišir, ostrova ⌒ RUS 122-123 P 5
Usk ○ CDN (BC) 228-229 F 2
Usk ○ USA (WA) 244-245 H 2
Uškanij krjaž ▲ RUS 112-113 U 4
Uški, zaliv ○ RUS 120-121 M 4
Us-Kjuėl' ○ RUS 118-119 P 4
Üsküdar ○ TR 128-129 C 2
Usmat ○ US 136-137 K 5
Ūsmat ☆ US 136-137 K 5
U.S.Navy's Srategic Radio and Communications Base • AUS 172-173 B 6
Usoke ○ EAT 212-213 D 6
Usol'e-Sibirskoe ☆ RUS 116-117 L 9
Usolka ~ RUS 116-117 H 7
Usol'e ☆ RUS 114-115 D 5
Usol'ye Sibirskoye = Usol'e-Sibirskoe ☆ RUS 116-117 L 9
Uson ○ RP 160-161 E 6
Uspallata ○ RA 78-79 E 2
Uspallata, Sierra de ▲ RA 78-79 E 2
Uspanapa, Río ~ MEX 52-53 G 3
Uspero ○ MEX 52-53 C 2
Usquil ○ PE 64-65 C 5
Ussel ○ F 90-91 J 9
Ussuri ~ RUS 122-123 F 7
Ussurijsk ○ RUS 122-123 E 7
Usta ○ USA (SD) 260-261 D 1
Usta Muhammad ○ PK 138-139 B 5
Ustamurot ○ US 136-137 J 3
Ust'-Barguzin ○ RUS 116-117 O 9
Ust'-Belaja ○ RUS 112-113 R 4
Ust'-Bel'skie gory ▲ RUS 112-113 R 4
Ust'-Bol'šereck ☆ RUS 122-123 R 2
Ust'-Cil'ma ○ RUS 88-89 W 4
Ust-Džeguta ○ RUS 126-127 D 5
Ust'-Džilinda ○ RUS 118-119 E 9
Ust'e ○ RUS 94-95 Q 2
Ust'e ○ RUS 116-117 G 7
Ust'-Elegest ○ RUS 116-117 G 10
Ust'-Hajrjuzovo ○ RUS 120-121 R 5
Ust'-Hakčan ○ RUS 120-121 M 2
Ustica, Isola di ⌒ I 100-101 D 5
Ust'-Ilga ○ RUS 116-117 M 8
Ust'-Ilimsk ☆ RUS 116-117 L 7
Ust'Ilimsk = Ust'-Ilimsk ☆ RUS 116-117 L 7
Ústí nad Labem ○ CZ 92-93 N 3
Ustinov = Iževsk ☆ RUS 96-97 H 5
Üstirt Šakyraj ▲ KA 126-127 M 4
Ust'-Išim ○ RUS 114-115 L 6
Ust'-Jansk ○ RUS 110-111 V 4
Ustjurtdagi Komsomol'sk ○ US 136-137 F 2
Ustjužina ○ RUS 94-95 P 2
Ustka ○ • PL 92-93 O 1
Ust'-Kada ○ RUS 116-117 K 8
Ust'-Kalmanka ○ RUS 124-125 N 2
Ust'-Kamčatsk ☆ RUS 120-121 U 5
Ust'-Kamenogorsk = Öskemen ○ KA 124-125 N 4
Ust'-Kan ○ RUS 116-117 F 7
Ust'-Kan ○ RUS 124-125 O 3
Ust'-Kara ○ RUS 108-109 L 7
Ust'-Karenga ○ RUS 118-119 H 8
Ust'-Karsk ○ RUS 118-119 J 9
Ust'-Koksa ○ RUS 124-125 O 3
Ust'-Kujga ○ RUS 110-111 U 4
Ust'-Kulom ○ RUS 96-97 H 3
Ust'-Kut ☆ RUS 116-117 M 7

Ust'-Labinsk o RUS 102-103 L 5
Ust'-Lenskij zapovednik (učastok Del'tevyj) ⊥ RUS 110-111 P 3
Ust'-Lenskij zapovednik (učastok Sokol) ⊥ RUS 110-111 Q 3
Ust'-Luga o RUS 94-95 L 2
Ust'-Lyža o RUS 88-89 Y 4
Ust'-Maja o • RUS 120-121 F 3
Ust'-Mil' o RUS 120-121 E 4
Ust'-Nem o RUS 96-97 J 3
Ust'-Nera ☆ • RUS 110-111 Y 7
Ust'-Njukža o RUS 118-119 K 7
Üštöbe o KA 124-125 K 6
Ust'-Olenëk o RUS 110-111 M 3
Ust'-Omčug ☆ RUS 120-121 N 3
Ust'-Ordynsk Buryat Autonomous District = Ust'-O.B avt.okrug □ RUS 116-117 L 9
Ust'-Ordynskij ☆ RUS 116-117 M 9
Ust'-Pinega o RUS 88-89 Q 4
Ust'-Pit o RUS 116-117 E 6
Ust'-Reka o RUS 88-89 O 6
Ustrzyki Dolne o • PL 92-93 R 4
Ust'-Sobolevka o RUS 122-123 H 5
Ust'-Srednekan o RUS 120-121 P 2
Ust'-Tym o RUS 114-115 Q 5
Ust'-Uda ☆ RUS 116-117 L 8
Ust'-Ulagan ☆ RUS 124-125 Q 3
Ust'-Umal'ta o RUS 122-123 E 3
Ust'-Vaen'ga o RUS 88-89 R 5
Ust'-Vaga o RUS 88-89 R 5
Ust'-Voja o RUS 114-115 D 2
Ust'-Voja o RUS (KOM) 88-89 Y 4
Ust'-Vyjskaja o RUS 88-89 T 5
Ust'-Vym' o RUS 88-89 V 5
Ust'-Zolotaja o RUS 116-117 F 9
Usu o RI 164-165 G 5
Usu o VRC 146-147 G 3
Usu, Chutes ~ ZRE 210-211 K 2
Usuaiuk o CDN 28-29 G 3
Usugli, Verhnie ☆ RUS 118-119 G 9
Usui-tōge ▲ J 152-153 H 6
Usuki o J 152-153 D 8
Usuktuk River ~ USA 20-21 M 1
Usulután ☆ ES 52-53 K 5
Usumacinta, Río ~ MEX 52-53 J 3
Usumun ~ RUS 110-111 K 5
Usun-Kjuël' o RUS 118-119 H 4
Uš-Urëkčen, hrebet ▲ RUS 112-113 K 3
Usu-san ▲ J 152-153 J 3
Usutu o ZA 218-219 E 6
Us'va o RUS 96-97 K 4
Usvjaty ☆ RUS 94-95 M 4
Ušycja ~ UA 102-103 E 3
Uta o RI 166-167 J 4
Uta ~ RI 166-167 J 4
Uta, Pulau ⌒ RI 166-167 E 1
Utaatap ~ RUS 112-113 Y 4
Utačan ~ RUS 110-111 W 7
Utah □ USA (UT) 254-255 C 4
Utah Lake o AUS 178-179 H 6
Utah Lake ⊂ USA (UT) 254-255 D 3
Utaitjiya o KSA 130-131 J 5
Utan o RI 168 C 7
Utara Baliem ~ RI 166-167 K 4
Utarupa, Canal ≈ 80 C 2
Utatlán ∴ • GCA 52-53 J 4
'Utayyiq o KSA 130-131 L 4
Ute o USA (IA) 274-275 C 2
Ute Creek ~ USA (NM) 256-257 M 2
Utegi o EAT 212-213 E 4
Utembo ~ ANG 216-217 F 8
Ute Mountain Indian Reservation ✕ USA (CO) 254-255 G 6
Utena ☆ • LT 94-95 J 4
Utengule o EAT 214-215 H 5
Uteni o RUS 118-119 K 8
Ute Peak ▲ USA (CO) 254-255 G 6
Utera o E 98-99 E 6
Utete o EAT 214-215 K 4
Uthal o PK 134-135 M 6
Utholok ~ RUS 120-121 R 5
Utholokskij, mys ▲ RUS 120-121 R 5
U Thong o THA 158-159 E 3
U Thumphon o LAO 158-159 H 2
Utiariti o BR 70-71 H 3
Utiariti, Área Indígena ✕ BR 70-71 H 3
Utica o CO 60-61 D 5
Utica ∴ • TN 190-191 H 2
Utica o USA (KY) 276-277 H 3
Utica o USA (MO) 274-275 E 5
Utica o USA (MS) 268-269 K 4
Utica o USA (MT) 250-251 J 5
Utica o USA (NY) 278-279 F 5
Utica o USA (OH) 280-281 D 3
Utica o USA (SD) 260-261 J 4
Utiel o E 98-99 G 5
Utik Lake ⊂ CDN 34-35 H 3
Utikuma Lake ⊂ CDN 32-33 N 4
Utikuma River ~ CDN 32-33 N 3
Utila o HN 52-53 L 3
Utila, Isla de ⌒ HN 52-53 L 3
Utinga o BR 72-73 K 2
Utinga, Rio ~ BR 72-73 K 2
Utiruyacu, Río ~ PE 64-65 E 4
Utl'uks'kyj lyman ≈ 102-103 J 4
Utnūr o IND 138-139 G 10
Utopia o AUS 178-179 C 2
Utopia o USA (TX) 266-267 H 4
Utopia Aboriginal Land ✕ AUS 178-179 C 2
Utorgoš o RUS 94-95 M 2
Utracán, Valle de ⊻ RA 78-79 G 4
Utraula o IND 142-143 C 2
Utrecht ☆ • NL 92-93 H 2
Utrecht o ZA 220-221 K 3
Utsjoki o FIN 88-89 J 2
Utsunomiya ☆ J 152-153 H 6
Uttangarai o IND 140-141 H 4
Uttaradit o THA 158-159 E 2
Uttaramerūr o IND 140-141 H 4
Uttarkashi o IND 138-139 G 4
Uttar Pradesh □ IND 138-139 G 5
Utterson o CDN (ONT) 238-239 F 3
Utu o PNG 183 C 3
Utuado o USA (PR) 286-287 P 2
Utuana o EC 64-65 C 4
Utubulak o VRC 146-147 H 2
Utue < WAN 204-205 H 6
Utukok River ~ USA 20-21 K 2
Utulik ~ RUS 116-117 L 10
Uturnbuwe ~ RI 166-167 K 4
Ututwa o EAT 212-213 D 5
Utva ~ KA 96-97 H 8
Uukusigssat Fjord ≈ 26-27 Y 7
Uumaanaq = Griffenfelds Ø ⌒ GRØ 28-29 U 5
Uumaanaq = Griffenfels Ø ⌒ GRØ 28-29 U 5
Uummannaq o GRØ 26-27 Q 5
Uummannaq = Umanak o GRØ 28-29 O 1
Uunarteq = Kap Tobin o GRØ 26-27 p 8
Uurainen o FIN 88-89 H 5
Uurèg o MAU 116-117 E 10
Uurèg nuur ⊂ MAU 116-117 E 10
Uusikaarlepyy = Nykarleby o FIN 88-89 G 5
Uusikaupunki o • FIN 88-89 F 6
Uusimaa ⊥ FIN 88-89 H 6
Uva ☆ RUS 96-97 H 5
Uvá, Río ~ CO 60-61 F 6
Uvada o USA (UT) 254-255 A 6
Uvalda o USA (GA) 284-285 H 4
Uvalde o USA (TX) 266-267 H 4
Uvareja, hrebet ▲ KA 96-97 L 6
Uvarovka o RUS 94-95 O 4
Uvarovo o RUS 102-103 N 2
Uvat o RUS 114-115 K 5
Uvdlorsivtit ⌒ GRØ 28-29 T 5
Uvel'skij ☆ RUS 96-97 M 6
Uveral o YV 60-61 J 3
Uverito o YV 60-61 J 3
Uviéu = Oviedo ☆ • E 98-99 E 3
Uvil'dy, ozero ⊂ RUS 96-97 M 6
Uvinza o EAT 212-213 C 5
Uvira o ZRE 212-213 B 5
Uvita, La o CO 60-61 E 4
Uvol o PNG (ENB) 183 F 3
Uvol o PNG (WNB) 183 F 4
Uvs □ MAU 116-117 E 11
Uvs nuur ⊂ MAU 116-117 F 10
Uvungu o ZRE 210-211 K 5
'Uwaināt, Tall o IRQ 128-129 K 4
'Uwaiqila, al- o KSA 130-131 H 2
Uwajima o J 152-153 E 8
Uwa-kai ≈ 152-153 E 8
Uwakeka o RI 166-167 D 5
Uwapa o RI 166-167 H 3
Uwimmerah ~ RI 166-167 L 5
Uxbridge o CDN (ONT) 238-239 F 4
Uxin Ju o VRC 154-155 F 2
Uxin Qi o VRC 154-155 F 2
Uxmal ∴ • MEX 52-53 K 1
'Uyaina, al- o KSA 130-131 K 5
Uyak Bay ≈ 22-23 T 4
Uyedineniya, Ostrov = Uedinenija, ostrov ⌒ RUS 108-109 U 3
Uyilankulam o CL 140-141 H 6
Uyo ☆ WAN 204-205 G 6
'Uyūn o KSA 130-131 L 5
'Uyun al-Ǧiwā' o KSA 130-131 H 4
Uyuni o BOL 70-71 D 7
Uyuni, Salar de ⊂ BOL 70-71 D 7
Uz ~ UA 102-103 F 2
Uz ~ UA 102-103 C 3
Uza ~ RUS 96-97 D 7
'Uzaim, al- o IRQ 128-129 K 5
'Uzair, al- o IRQ 128-129 M 7
Uzbekistan = Ŭsbekiston ■ US 136-137 E 3
Uzbel Shankou ▲ KA 136-137 N 5
Uzboj ~ TM 136-137 E 4
Uzcátegui o YV 60-61 F 4
Uzebba o WAN 204-205 F 5
Uzerche o • F 90-91 H 9
Uzgen o KS 136-137 N 4
Uzhcurrumi o EC 64-65 C 3
Uzhhorod = Užhorod ☆ UA 102-103 C 3
Užhorod ☆ UA 102-103 C 3
Užice o YU 100-101 G 3
Uzjan o RUS 96-97 K 7
Uzkij, proliv ⊂ RUS 108-109 d 2
Uzlovaja ☆ • RUS 94-95 Q 5
Uzon, vulkan ▲ RUS 120-121 S 6
Üzümlü ☆ TR 128-129 H 3
Uzuncaburç o TR 128-129 E 4
Uzunköprü o TR 128-129 B 2
Užur ☆ RUS 114-115 U 7

V

Vaala o FIN 88-89 J 4
Vaalajärvi o FIN 88-89 J 3
Vaalbos National Park ⊥ ZA 220-221 G 4
Vaaldam < ZA 220-221 J 3
Vaal Dam Nature Reserve ⊥ ZA 220-221 J 3
Vaalplaas o ZA 220-221 J 2
Vaalrivier ~ ZA 220-221 H 3
Vaalwater o ZA 220-221 J 2
Vaam"ëčgyn, ozero ⊂ RUS 112-113 T 5
Vaasa ☆ FIN 88-89 F 5
Vabalninkas o LT 94-95 J 4
Vača ~ RUS 118-119 G 6
Vaca Guzman o BOL 70-71 F 6
Vacaria o BR 74-75 E 7
Vacaria, Rio ~ BR 72-73 J 4
Vacaria, Rio ~ BR 76-77 K 1
Vacas Helados, Paso de ▲ RA 76-77 C 5
Vacaville o USA (CA) 246-247 C 5
Vacha o MOC 218-219 J 2
Vache, Ile-à- ⌒ RH 54-55 J 5
Vacherie o USA (LA) 268-269 K 7
Vachon, Rivière ~ CDN 36-37 N 4
Vači o RUS 126-127 G 6
Vāda o IND 138-139 D 10
Vādāsinor o IND 138-139 D 8
Vader o USA (WA) 244-245 C 4
Vadodara o IND 138-139 D 8
Vado del Yeso o C 54-55 G 4
Vadsø o N 86-87 O 1
Vadstena ☆ • S 86-87 G 7
Vadul lui Voda o MD 102-103 F 4
Vaduz ☆ • FL 92-93 K 5
Vadvetjåkka nationalpark ⊥ S 86-87 J 2
Vaegi ~ RUS 112-113 Q 5
Vaen'ga ~ RUS 88-89 R 5
Værøy ⌒ N 86-87 F 3
Vaga o RCB 210-211 E 4
Vaga ~ RUS 88-89 R 6
Vaga ~ RUS 94-95 R 1
Vågaholmen o N 86-87 F 3
Vagaj ☆ RUS (TMN) 114-115 K 6
Vagaj ~ RUS 114-115 K 6
Vågåmo ☆ N 86-87 D 6
Vaghena Island ⌒ SOL 184 I c 2
Vagis, gora ▲ RUS 122-123 K 2
Vagø = Vagár ⌒ FR 90-91 D 1
Vågsfjorden ≈ 86-87 H 2
Vah ~ RUS 114-115 Q 4
Vah ~ RUS 114-115 O 4
Vah ~ RUS 114-115 S 4
Vaha o SOL 184 I d 2
Vāhān o AFG 136-137 N 6
Vāhān, Daryā-ye ~ AFG 136-137 N 6
Vahanskij hrebet ▲ AFG 136-137 N 6
Vahruši o RUS 96-97 G 4
Vahš o • TJ 136-137 L 6
Vahš ~ TJ 136-137 L 5
Vai o GR 100-101 L 7
Vaiaku ★ TUV 13 J 3
Vaiden o USA (MS) 268-269 L 3
Vaikam o • IND 140-141 G 6
Vail o USA (CO) 254-255 J 4
Vailala River ~ PNG 183 C 4
Vaisāli o • IND 142-143 D 2
Vaitarna ~ IND 138-139 D 10
Vajegskij hrebet ▲ RUS 112-113 Q 5
Vajgac, mys ▲ RUS 108-109 f 2
Vajgač, ostrov ⌒ RUS 108-109 G 6
Vajmuga ~ RUS 88-89 Q 5
Vajvida ~ RUS 116-117 G 2
Vakaga □ RCA 206-207 F 4
Vakaga ~ RCA 206-207 F 4
Vakarel o BG 102-103 C 6
Vaku o ZRE 210-211 D 6
Vakunajka ~ RUS 118-119 D 5
Vakuta o PNG 183 F 5
Vakuta Island ⌒ PNG 183 F 5
Val o RUS 122-123 K 2
Vala ~ RUS 96-97 H 5
Valaam, ostrov ⌒ • RUS 88-89 L 6
Valachchenai o CL 140-141 J 7
Valadeces o MEX 50-51 K 4
Valaginskij hrebet ▲ RUS 120-121 S 7
Valašské Meziříčí o CZ 92-93 O 4
Valavanur o IND 140-141 H 5
Vălčedrăm o BG 102-103 C 6
Valcheta o RA 78-79 F 6
Valcheta, Arroyo ~ RA 78-79 F 6
Vălčidol o BG 102-103 E 6
Valdaj o RUS (KAR) 88-89 N 5
Valdaj ☆ • RUS (TVR) 94-95 N 3
Valdajskaja vozvyšennost' ▲ RUS 94-95 N 3
Val-David o CDN (QUE) 238-239 L 2
Valdayskaya Vozvyshennost' = Valdajskaja vozvyšennost' ▲ RUS 94-95 N 3
Valdemarsvik ☆ S 86-87 H 7
Valdepeñas o • E 98-99 F 5
Valderaduey, Río ~ E 98-99 E 4
Valdés, Península ⊻ • RA 78-79 H 7
Val-des-Bois o CDN (QUE) 238-239 K 3
Valdez o USA 20-21 R 6
Valdieri, Parco Nazionale di ⊥ I 100-101 A 2
Val-d'Isère o • F 90-91 L 9
Valdivia o CO 60-61 D 4
Valdivia o RCH 78-79 C 5
Valdivia Fracture Zone ≃ 5 B 9
Val-d'Or o CDN (QUE) 236-237 L 4
Valdosta o USA (GA) 284-285 G 6
Valdres ⊻ N 86-87 D 6
Vale o USA (OR) 244-245 H 7
Vale de Guaporé, Área Indígena ✕ BR 70-71 G 3
Vale do Javari, Áreas Indígenas do ✕ BR 66-67 B 5
Valemount o CDN (BC) 228-229 P 4
Valença o BR 72-73 L 2
Valença do Piauí o BR 68-69 H 5
Valence ☆ • F 90-91 K 9
Valence-sur-Baïse o F 90-91 H 10
Valência o E 98-99 G 5
Valencia o RP 160-161 F 9
Valencia ☆ YV 60-61 G 2
Valencia, Golfo de ≈ 98-99 H 5
Valencia, Lago de ⊂ YV 60-61 H 2
Valencia de Alcántara o E 98-99 D 5
Valencia de Don Juan o E 98-99 E 3
Valenciana □ E 98-99 G 5
Valenciennes o F 90-91 J 6
Valentia o CDN (ONT) 238-239 G 4
Valentim, Serra do ▲ BR 68-69 G 4
Valentim Gentil o BR 72-73 E 6
Valentine o USA (NE) 262-263 F 2
Valentine o USA (TX) 266-267 C 2
Valentine National Wildlife Refuge ⊥ USA (NE) 262-263 F 2
Valera o PE 64-65 D 5
Valera o USA (TX) 266-267 H 2
Valera o YV 60-61 F 3
Valerie Jean o USA (CA) 248-249 H 6
Valerio o MEX 50-51 F 4
Valesdir o VAN 184 II b 3
Valga ☆ • EST 94-95 K 3
Val Gagne o CDN (ONT) 236-237 H 4
Valhalla Provincial Park ⊥ CDN (BC) 230-231 M 4
Valier o USA (MT) 250-251 G 3
Valiyannur o IND 140-141 F 5
Val'ja ~ RUS 114-115 F 3
Valjala o EST 94-95 H 2
Val-Jalbert o CDN (QUE) 240-241 C 2
Val-Jalbert • CDN (QUE) 240-241 C 2
Valjean o CDN (SAS) 232-233 M 5
Valjevo o YU 100-101 G 2
Valka ☆ • LV 94-95 K 3
Val'kakynmangkak, laguna ≈ 112-113 T 2
Val'karkaj o RUS 112-113 Q 1
Valkeakoski o FIN 88-89 H 6
Val'kumej o RUS 112-113 Q 2
Vallabhīpur o IND 138-139 C 9
Valladolid o • E 98-99 E 4
Valladolid o EC 64-65 C 4
Valladolid o • MEX 52-53 K 1
Vallam o IND 140-141 H 5
Vallard, Lac ⊂ CDN 38-39 K 2
Vall d'Uixó, la o E 98-99 G 5
Valle o LV 94-95 J 3
Valle o USA (AZ) 256-257 C 3
Valle, El o PA 52-53 D 7
Valle, El o PE 64-65 D 5
Valle, Río del ~ RA 76-77 F 3
Vallecillos o MEX 50-51 K 4
Valle d'Aosta = Vallé d'Aoste ⊻ I 100-101 A 2
Valle de Allende o MEX 50-51 G 4
Valle de Bravo o • MEX 52-53 D 2
Valle de Guadalupe o MEX 52-53 C 1
Valle de Guanape o YV 60-61 J 3
Valle de la Luna, Reserva Nacional ⊥ • RA 76-77 C 6
Valle de La Pascua o YV 60-61 J 3
Valle del Encanto, Parque Nacional ⊥ RCH 76-77 B 6
Valle del Rosario o MEX 50-51 F 4
Valle de Santiago o MEX 52-53 D 1
Valle de Zaragoza o MEX 50-51 G 4
Valledupar ☆ CO 60-61 E 2
Vallée d'Aoste = Valle d'Aosta ⊻ I 100-101 A 2
Vallée de Mai National Park ⊥ ••• SY 224 D 2
Vallée du Serpent ~ RMM 202-203 F 2
Vallée-Jonction o CDN (QUE) 240-241 E 4
Valle Fertil, Sierra de ▲ RA 76-77 C 6
Vallegrande o BOL 70-71 E 6
Valle Grande o RA 76-77 E 2
Vallehermoso o E 188-189 C 6
Valle Hermoso o MEX (QR) 52-53 K 2
Valle Hermoso o MEX (TAM) 50-51 L 5
Vallejo o USA (CA) 246-247 C 5
Valle Nacional o • MEX 52-53 F 3
Vallenar o RCH 76-77 B 5
Valles Calchaquies ⊥ • RA 76-77 D 3
Valletta ★ M 100-101 E 7
Valley o USA (AL) 284-285 E 4
Valley o USA (NE) 262-263 K 3
Valley o USA (WA) 244-245 H 2
Valley o USA (WY) 252-253 J 2
Valley, The ☆ GB 56 D 2
Valley Centre o CDN (SAS) 232-233 L 4
Valley East o CDN (ONT) 238-239 D 2
Valley Falls o USA (KS) 262-263 L 5
Valley Falls o USA (OR) 244-245 E 8
Valleyfield o CDN (NFL) 242-243 P 3
Valley Forge National Historic Park • USA (PA) 280-281 L 3
Valley Head o USA (WV) 280-281 G 5
Valley Junction o USA (OR) 244-245 B 5
Valley Mills o USA (TX) 266-267 K 2
Valley of 1000 Hills • ZA 220-221 K 4
Valley of Fire State Park • USA (NV) 248-249 K 3
Valley of the Kings ∴ ••• ET 194-195 F 5
Valley of Willow o USA 20-21 N 2
Valley Park o USA (MS) 268-269 K 4
Valley River o CDN (MAN) 234-235 C 3
Valley River ~ CDN (MAN) 234-235 B 3
Valley River Indian Reserve ✕ CDN (MAN) 234-235 B 3
Valley Springs o USA (CA) 246-247 E 5
Valley Station o USA (KY) 276-277 K 2
Valleyview o CDN 32-33 M 4
Valley Wells o USA (CA) 248-249 J 4
Vallgrund ⌒ FIN 88-89 F 5
Vallières o RH 54-55 K 5
Vallimanca, Arroyo ~ RA 78-79 J 4
Vallita, La o C 54-55 F 4
Vallo della Lucània o I 100-101 E 4
Valls o E 98-99 H 4
Valls Bluff, De o USA (AR) 276-277 D 6
Val Marie o CDN (SAS) 232-233 L 6
Valmeyer o USA (IL) 274-275 H 6
Valmiera ☆ • LV 94-95 J 3
Valmont o USA (NM) 256-257 K 6
Valmy o USA (NV) 246-247 H 3
Valod o IND 138-139 D 9
Valor o CDN (SAS) 232-233 M 6
Valožyn ☆ BY 94-95 K 4
Val-Paradis o CDN (QUE) 236-237 J 3
Valparai o IND 140-141 G 5
Valparaíso o BR 64-65 F 5
Valparaíso o BR 72-73 E 6
Valparaíso o CDN (SAS) 232-233 O 3
Valparaíso o CO 64-65 E 1
Valparaíso o MEX 50-51 H 6
Valparaíso ☆ • RCH 78-79 D 2
Valparaíso o USA (FL) 286-287 C 1
Valparaíso o USA (IN) 274-275 L 3
Valparaíso o USA (NE) 262-263 K 3
Valparaíso, Río ~ MEX 50-51 H 6
Valpoy o IND 140-141 F 3
Val Racine o CDN (QUE) 238-239 O 3
Val Rita o CDN (ONT) 236-237 F 3
Vals, Tanjung ▲ RI 166-167 J 6
Valsād o IND 138-139 D 9
Valse Pisang, Kepulauan ⌒ RI 166-167 F 3
Valset o N 86-87 D 5
Valsjöbyn o S 86-87 G 4
Valsrivier ~ ZA 220-221 H 3
Valterlândia o BR 66-67 D 7
Valtimo o FIN 88-89 K 5
Valujki o RUS 102-103 L 2
Valunnaja, gora ▲ RUS 112-113 N 4
Valverde o E 188-189 C 7
Valverde o USA (NM) 256-257 J 5
Valverde de Júcar o E 98-99 F 5
Valverde del Camino o E 98-99 D 6
Valverde del Fresno o E 98-99 D 4
Vàm Cỏ Đông, Sông ~ VN 158-159 J 5
Vammala o FIN 88-89 G 6
Vamori o USA (AZ) 256-257 D 7
Van ☆ TR 128-129 K 3
Van o USA (OR) 244-245 G 7
Van o USA (TX) 264-265 J 6
Vanalphensvlei o ZA 220-221 J 2
Van Alstyne o USA (TX) 264-265 H 5
Vananda o USA (MT) 250-251 N 5
Vanapa River ~ PNG 183 D 5
Vanasse, Lac ⊂ CDN 36-37 M 4
Vanatta o USA (OH) 280-281 D 3
Vanavara ☆ RUS 116-117 L 5
Van Buren o USA (AR) 276-277 A 5
Van Buren o USA (ME) 278-279 O 1
Van Buren o USA (MO) 276-277 D 4
Vân Canh o VN 158-159 K 4
Vanceboro o USA (ME) 278-279 O 3
Vanceburg o USA (KY) 276-277 M 2
Vancleave o USA (MS) 268-269 M 6
Van Cloon Shoal ⌒ AUS 172-173 H 2
Vancouver, Mount ▲ CDN 20-21 V 6
Vancouver o • CDN (BC) 230-231 F 4
Vancouver o USA (WA) 244-245 C 5
Vancouver, Cape ▲ USA 20-21 H 6
Vancouver Island ⌒ CDN (BC) 230-231 B 4
Vancouver Island Ranges ▲ CDN (BC) 230-231 B 3
Van Daalen ~ RI 166-167 J 3
Vandalia o USA (IL) 274-275 J 6
Vandalia o USA (IN) 274-275 M 5
Vandalia o USA (MO) 274-275 G 5
Vandavāsi o IND 140-141 H 4
Vandekerckhove Lake ⊂ CDN 34-35 F 2
Vandenberg Air Force Base ✕✕ USA (CA) 248-249 D 5
Vanderbijlpark o ZA 220-221 H 3
Vanderbilt o USA (MI) 272-273 E 2
Vandergrift o USA (PA) 280-281 G 3
Vanderhoof o CDN (BC) 228-229 K 2
Vanderlei o BR 72-73 J 2
Van-der-Linda, mys ▲ RUS 122-123 N 6
Vanderlin Island ⌒ AUS 174-175 D 4
Van der Meulen, Isla ⌒ RCH 80 C 4
Van de Wal ~ RI 166-167 K 3
Van Diemen, Cape ▲ AUS (NT) 172-173 K 1
Van Diemen, Cape ▲ AUS (QLD) 174-175 E 5
Van Diemen Gulf ≈ 172-173 K 1
Vandmtor, ozero ⊂ RUS 114-115 H 3
Vandúzi, Rio ~ MOC 218-219 G 4
Vandyke Creek ~ AUS 178-179 J 3
Vandyksdrif o ZA 220-221 J 3
Van"egan ~ RUS 114-115 O 4
Vänern ⊂ S 86-87 F 7
Vänersborg ☆ S 86-87 F 7
Vaneteze, Rio ~ MOC 220-221 L 2
Van Etten o USA (NY) 278-279 E 6
Vangaindrano o RM 222-223 E 9
Vangaš ~ RUS 116-117 F 6
Vangaži o LV 94-95 J 3
Van Gölü ⊂ TR 128-129 K 3
Vanguard o CDN (SAS) 232-233 L 6
Vanguard Bank ≃ 158-159 K 7
Van-Gun"egan ~ RUS 114-115 O 4
Vangunu ⌒ SOL 184 I d 3
Vanier Island ⌒ CDN 24-25 U 2
Vanimo ☆ PNG 183 A 2
Vanivilasa Sāgara o IND 140-141 G 4
Vāniyambādi o IND 140-141 H 4
Vankarem o RUS 112-113 X 3
Vankarem ~ RUS 112-113 W 3
Vankaremskaja nizmennost' ⊻ RUS 112-113 V 2
Van Keulenfjorden ≈ 84-85 J 4
Van'kina guba ≈ 110-111 W 3
Vankleek Hill o CDN (ONT) 238-239 L 3
Van Koenig Point ▲ CDN 24-25 b 5
Văn Lân o VN 158-159 K 5
Van Lear o USA (KY) 276-277 N 3
Van Mijenfjorden ≈ 84-85 J 4
Vanna ⌒ N 86-87 J 1
Vännäs o S 86-87 J 5
Vanne ~ F 90-91 J 7
Vannes ☆ • F 90-91 F 8
Van Ninh o VN 158-159 K 4
Vanoise, Parc National de la ⊥ • F 90-91 L 9
Van Reenen o ZA 220-221 J 4
Van Rees, Pegunungan ▲ RI 166-167 J 3
Vanrhynsdorp o ZA 220-221 D 5
Vanrook o AUS 174-175 F 5
Vānsada o IND 138-139 D 9
Vansbro o S 86-87 G 6
Vanscoy o CDN (SAS) 232-233 M 4
Vansittart Bay ≈ 172-173 H 3
Vansittart Island ⌒ CDN 36-37 G 2
Vanstadensrus o ZA 220-221 H 4
Vantaa o FIN 88-89 H 6
Vantage o CDN (SAS) 232-233 M 6
Vantage o USA (WA) 244-245 E 4
Van Tassell o USA (WY) 252-253 O 4
Vant's Drift o ZA 220-221 K 4
Vanttauskoski o FIN 88-89 J 3
Vanua Balavu ⌒ FJI 184 III c 2
Vanua Lava ⌒ VAN 184 II a 1
Vanua Levu ⌒ FJI 184 III b 2
Vanuatu ■ VAN 184 II b 3
Vanua Vatu ⌒ FJI 184 III c 3
Van Vert o USA (OH) 280-281 B 3
Van Vleck o USA (TX) 268-269 E 7
Van Wyksdorp o ZA 220-221 E 6
Van Wyksvlei o ZA 220-221 E 5
Vanzevat o RUS 114-115 J 2
Vanžil' ~ RUS 114-115 S 4
Van Zylsrus o ZA 220-221 F 3
Vao, Nosy ⌒ RM 222-223 C 6
Vapanajvaam ~ RUS 112-113 R 3
Vapor, El o MEX 52-53 J 2
Vara ☆ S 86-87 F 7
Varadero o • C 54-55 E 3
Varalé o CI 202-203 J 5
Varāmīn o • IR 136-137 B 7
Vārānasi o •• IND 142-143 C 3
Varandej o RUS 108-109 H 7
Varangerfjorden ≈ 86-87 O 1
Varangerhalvøya ⊻ N 86-87 O 1
Varas o AFG 134-135 M 1
Varas, Las o MEX (CHA) 50-51 F 3
Varas, Las o MEX (NAY) 50-51 G 7
Varavani o IND 140-141 H 6
Varaždin o HR 100-101 F 1
Varazze o I 100-101 B 2
Varberg ☆ • S 86-87 F 8
Varčato, ozero ⊂ RUS 108-109 K 8
Vardaman o USA (MS) 268-269 L 3
Vardar ~ MK 100-101 H 4
Vardāvard o IR 136-137 B 7
Varde o DK 86-87 D 9
Vardenis o AR 128-129 L 2
Vardenis, gora ▲ AR 128-129 L 3
Vardenisskij hrebet ▲ AR 128-129 L 3
Vardin o IR 128-129 M 3
Vardø o N 86-87 P 1
Varejonal, El o MEX 50-51 F 5
Varela o GNB 202-203 B 3
Varela o RA 78-79 F 3
Varela, Baía de ≈ 202-203 B 3
Varela, Sierra de ▲ RA 78-79 F 3
Varėna ☆ LT 94-95 J 4
Varese ☆ I 100-101 B 2
Vårgårda ☆ S 86-87 F 7
Vargem Alegre o BR 72-73 J 5
Vargem Alta o BR 72-73 K 6
Vargem Bonita o BR 72-73 G 6
Vargem Grande o BR 68-69 G 3
Varginha o BR 72-73 H 6
Varhalamskaja guba ⊂ RUS 120-121 S 3
Varhalamskij, mys ▲ RUS 120-121 S 3
Variata National Park ⊥ PNG 183 D 5
Varillas o RCH (ANT) 76-77 B 3
Varillas o RCH (ANT) 76-77 C 3
Varillas, Las o RA 76-77 F 6
Varita, Pampa de la ⊥ RA 78-79 F 3
Varka-Syl'ky ~ RUS 114-115 Q 2
Varkaus o FIN 88-89 J 5
Varmahlið o IS 86-87 d 2
Värmland ⊥ S 86-87 F 7
Varna ☆ BG 102-103 E 6
Varna ☆ RUS 124-125 B 2
Värnamo ☆ S 86-87 G 8
Varnek o RUS 108-109 J 7
Varngèjaha ~ RUS 108-109 U 7
Varnville o USA (SC) 284-285 J 4
Varnjany o BY 94-95 K 4
Varón, Cerro de ▲ MEX 52-53 B 2
Varradero o USA (NM) 256-257 L 3
Varsaǧ o AFG 136-137 M 6
Varsinais Suomi ⊥ FIN 88-89 F 6
Varto ☆ TR 128-129 J 3
Varvarco o RA 78-79 D 4
Varvarinskij o RUS 118-119 F 8
Varžane o IR 134-135 E 2
Varzarin, Kūh-e ▲ IR 134-135 B 2
Várzea Alegre o BR 68-69 J 5
Várzea da Ema o BR 68-69 J 6
Várzea da Palma o BR 72-73 H 4
Várzea do Poço o BR 68-69 H 7
Várzea Grande o BR 68-69 G 5
Várzea Grande o BR 70-71 J 4
Varzeão o BR 74-75 F 5
Varzelândia o BR 72-73 H 3
Várzeo o BR 68-69 H 3
Varzuga ~ RUS 88-89 O 3
Varzuga, Bol'šaja ~ RUS 88-89 O 3
Vasa = Vaasa ☆ FIN 88-89 F 5
Väsad o IND 138-139 D 8
Vasai o IND 138-139 D 10
Vasconcelos o MEX 52-53 G 3
Vasil'eva, zalev ⊂ RUS 122-123 Q 3
Vasil'evka o RUS 122-123 F 5
Vasilija, mys ▲ RUS 112-113 U 4
Vāšir o AFG 134-135 K 2
Vasjugan ~ RUS 114-115 Q 5
Vasjuganskaja ravnina ⊻ RUS 114-115 N 6
Vaška ~ RUS 88-89 T 5
Vaslui ☆ RO 102-103 E 4
Vass o USA (NC) 282-283 H 5
Vassako ~ RCA 206-207 D 4
Vassar o CDN (MAN) 234-235 H 5
Vassar o USA (MI) 272-273 F 4
Vassouras o BR 72-73 J 7
Västbacka o S 86-87 G 6
Västerås ☆ S 86-87 H 7
Västerbotten ⊥ S 86-87 K 4
Västergötland ⊥ S 86-87 F 7
Västerhaninge o S 86-87 J 7
Västervik ☆ • S 86-87 H 8
Vasto o I 100-101 E 3
Vašutkiny ozero ⊂ RUS 108-109 J 7
Vasvár o H 92-93 O 5
Vasylivka o UA 102-103 J 4
Vasyl'kiv o UA 102-103 G 2
Vasyl'kivka o UA 102-103 K 3
Vaté, Île = Éfaté ⌒ VAN 184 II b 3
Vat"egan ~ RUS 114-115 N 3
Vatican City = Città del Vaticano ★ ••• SCV 100-101 C 4
Vaticano, Capo ▲ I 100-101 E 5
Vatilau Island = Buena Vista Island ⌒ SOL 184 I d 3
Vatinskij Egan ~ RUS 114-115 N 4
Vat Luang Temple • LAO 158-159 H 3
Vatnajökull ⊂ IS 86-87 e 2
Vatolatsaka o RM 222-223 D 9
Vatomandry o RM 222-223 F 7
Vatondrangy ▲ RM 222-223 E 8
Vat Phu Temple • LAO 158-159 H 3
Vatra Dornei o • RO 102-103 D 4
Vatrak ~ IND 138-139 D 8
Vattaikundu o IND 140-141 G 5
Vättern ⊂ S 86-87 G 7
Vatu-i-ra Channel ≈ 184 III b 2
Vatukoula o FJI 184 III a 2
Vatulele ⌒ FJI 184 III a 3
Vatu Vara ⌒ FJI 184 III c 2
Vatyl'ka ~ RUS 114-115 Q 3
Vatyna ~ RUS 112-113 R 6
Vatyna, hrebet ▲ RUS 112-113 Q 6
Vaughan Springs o AUS 172-173 K 7
Vaughn o USA (MT) 250-251 H 4
Vaughn o USA (NM) 256-257 K 4
Vaughn o USA (WA) 244-245 C 3
Vaupés, Río ~ CO 66-67 C 2
Vauxhall o CDN (ALB) 232-233 F 5
Vavatenina o RM 222-223 F 6
Vava'u ⌒ TON 184 IV b 1
Vava'u Group ⌒ TON 184 IV a 1
Vavenby o CDN (BC) 230-231 K 2
Vavilova, lednik ⊂ RUS 108-109 a 2
Vavkavysk o BY 94-95 J 5
Vavkavyskoe vzvyšša ▲ BY 94-95 J 5
Vavoua o CI 202-203 G 6
Vavož ☆ RUS 96-97 G 5
Vavuniya o CL 140-141 J 6
Vawn o CDN (SAS) 232-233 K 2
Växjö ☆ S 86-87 G 8
Vaya Chin o USA (AZ) 256-257 C 6
Vaygach, Ostrov = Vajgač, ostrov ⌒ RUS 108-109 H 6
Vaza Barris, Rio ~ BR 68-69 J 6
Vāzaḥā o AFG 138-139 B 3
Vazante o BR 72-73 G 4
Vazante Grande ou Funda ~ BR 70-71 J 6
Važgort o RUS 88-89 T 4
Vazobe ▲ RM 222-223 E 7
Vázquez o C 54-55 G 4
Veado, Cachoeira ~ BR 72-73 F 3
Veblen o USA (SD) 260-261 J 1
Vecumnieki o LV 94-95 J 3
Vedāranniyam o IND 140-141 H 5
Vedel, Kap ▲ GRØ 28-29 b 2
Vedel Fjord ≈ 28-29 b 2
Vedia o RA 78-79 J 3
Vedrovo o RUS 94-95 S 3
Vefsna ~ N 86-87 F 4
Vega ⌒ N 86-87 E 4
Vega o USA (TX) 264-265 B 3
Vega, La o CO 60-61 C 6
Vega, La ☆ • DOM 54-55 K 5
Vega, mys ▲ RUS 108-109 e 3
Vega Baja o USA (PR) 286-287 P 2
Vega de Alatorre o MEX 52-53 F 1
Vega Point ▲ USA 22-23 E 7
Vega Sund ≈ 26-27 o 7
Vegoritis, Limni ⊂ GR 100-101 H 4
Vegreville o CDN (ALB) 232-233 F 2
Vegueta o PE 64-65 D 7
Veguita, La o YV 60-61 F 3
Vehowa o PK 138-139 C 4
Veimandu Channel ≈ 140-141 B 7
Veintiocho de Mayo o EC 64-65 C 3
Veiru o PNG 183 C 4
Veis o IR 134-135 C 3
Vejer de la Frontera o E 98-99 E 6
Vejle o DK 86-87 D 9
Vekšino o RUS 94-95 M 3
Vela, Cabo de la ▲ CO (GUA) 60-61 E 1
Vela, Cabo de la ▲ CO (GUA) 60-61 E 1
Vela de Coro, La o YV 60-61 G 2
Vela Luka o HR 100-101 F 3
Velāpur o IND 140-141 F 2
Velasco, Sierra de ▲ RA 76-77 D 5
Velasco Ibarra ⊂ EC (GUA) 64-65 C 2
Velasco Ibarra < EC (MAN) 64-65 C 2
Velāyat o IR 134-135 E 4
Vélaz o RA 76-77 H 4
Velazquez o ROU 78-79 M 3
Velcho, Río ~ RCH 78-79 C 7
Velddrif o ZA 220-221 D 6
Velebitski kanal ≈ 100-101 E 2
Vélez o CO 60-61 E 4
Vélez Rubio o E 98-99 F 6
Velha Boipeba o BR 72-73 L 2
Velha Goa o •• IND 140-141 E 3
Velhas, Rio das ~ BR 72-73 H 4
Velia • I 100-101 E 4
Velikaja o RUS (NAO) 88-89 T 3
Velikaja ~ RUS 112-113 S 5
Velikaja Guba o RUS 88-89 N 5
Velikaja Kema o RUS 122-123 G 6
Velikan, gora ▲ RUS 112-113 P 2
Veliki Đerdap •• YU 100-101 J 2
Velikie Luki ☆ RUS 94-95 M 3
Velikij, ostrov ⌒ RUS 88-89 M 3
Velikij Ustjug o RUS 96-97 E 3
Velikiye Luki = Velikie Luki ☆ RUS 94-95 M 3
Velikoe, ozero ⊂ RUS 94-95 P 3
Velikonda Range ▲ IND 140-141 H 4
Veliko Plana o YU 100-101 H 2
Veliko Tărnovo o BG 102-103 D 6
Velille o PE 70-71 B 4
Velimlje o YU 100-101 G 3
Vélingara o SN (CAS) 202-203 C 3
Vélingara o SN (DIO) 202-203 C 2
Velingrad o BG 102-103 C 6
Velíž ☆ RUS 94-95 M 4
Vel'ju ~ RUS 88-89 X 5
Vel' Kal' o RUS 112-113 V 4
Vella Lavella ⌒ SOL 184 I c 2
Vellankulam o CL 140-141 J 6
Velloor o NAM 220-221 D 4
Vellore o • IND 140-141 H 4
Velloso o RA 78-79 K 4
Vel'maj ~ RUS 112-113 U 3
Vel'mo ~ RUS 116-117 G 5
Velo Troglav ▲ YU 100-101 F 3
Velsen o NL 92-93 H 2
Vel'sk o RUS 88-89 R 6
Velt' ~ RUS 88-89 V 3
Velva o USA (ND) 258-259 G 3
Velyka Lepetycha o UA 102-103 H 4
Velyka Pysarivka o UA 102-103 J 2
Velykyj Bereznyj o UA 102-103 C 3
Velykyj Byčkiv o UA 102-103 D 3
Velykyj Dobron' = Dobron' o UA 102-103 C 3
Vema Fracture Zone ≃ 5 G 3
Vembanad Lake o IND 140-141 G 6
Vempalle o IND 140-141 H 3
Vemsdalen o S 86-87 F 5
Venado, El o CO 60-61 H 6
Venado, Isla del ⌒ NIC 52-53 C 6
Venado Tuerto o RA 78-79 J 2
Venamo, Río ~ YV 62-63 D 2
Venâncio Aires o BR 74-75 D 7
Venango o USA (NE) 262-263 D 4
Venavena o PNG 183 A 4
Venceslau Brás o BR 72-73 F 7
Venda (former Homeland, now part of North-Transvaal) □ ZA 218-219 D 6
Venda Nova do Imigrante o BR 72-73 K 6
Vendas Novas o P 98-99 C 5
Vendôme o F 90-91 H 8
Vendom Fiord ≈ 24-25 e 2
Veneral o CO 60-61 C 6
Veneta o USA (OR) 244-245 B 6
Venetie o USA 20-21 R 3
Véneto □ I 100-101 C 2
Venev ☆ • RUS 94-95 Q 4

Venézia ☆··· I 100-101 D 2
Venézia, Golfo di ≈ 100-101 D 2
Venezuela ■ YV 60-61 F 3
Venezuela, Golfo de ≈ 60-61 F 2
Venezuela Basin ≃ 5 E 3
Vengurla o IND 140-141 E 3
Veniaminof Volcano ▲ USA 22-23 R 4
Venice o USA (FL) 286-287 G 4
Venice o USA (LA) 268-269 L 7
Venice, Gulf of = Venézia, Golfo di ≈ I 100-101 D 2
Venice = Venézia ☆··· I 100-101 D 2
Venjan o S 86-87 F 6
Venkatagiri o IND 140-141 H 4
Venlo o NL 92-93 J 3
Venray o NL 92-93 H 3
Venta o LT 94-95 H 3
Venta, La o MEX (TAB) 52-53 G 2
Venta, La ∴ • MEX (TAB) 52-53 G 2
Venta de Baños o E 98-99 E 4
Ventana o USA (AZ) 256-257 C 6
Ventana, La o MEX 50-51 J 6
Ventanas o EC 64-65 C 2
Ventanas, Las o YV 60-61 H 4
Ventania o BR 74-75 E 5
Ventas con Peña Aguilera, Las o E 98-99 E 5
Ventersburg o ZA 220-221 H 4
Ventersdorp o ZA 220-221 H 3
Venterstad o ZA 220-221 G 5
Ventisquero, Cerro ▲ RA 78-79 D 6
Ventosa, La o MEX 52-53 G 3
Ventoux, Mont ▲ F 90-91 K 9
Ventspils ☆·· LV 94-95 G 3
Ventuari, Río ~ YV 60-61 H 5
Ventura o • USA (CA) 248-249 E 5
Venjueuo o RUS 108-109 O 6
Venus o USA (FL) 286-287 H 4
Venus o USA (NE) 262-263 H 2
Venustiano Carranza o MEX 52-53 H 3
Venustiano Carranza, Presa o MEX 50-51 J 4
Venustiono Carranza o MEX 52-53 C 2
Veppur o IND 140-141 H 5
Ver, Horej- o RUS 88-89 Y 3
Vera o BR 70-71 K 3
Vera o CDN (SAS) 232-233 J 3
Vera o RA 76-77 G 5
Vera o USA (TX) 264-265 E 5
Vera, Bahía ≈ 80 H 2
Vera, Cape ▲ CDN 24-25 b 2
Vera, Laguna o PY 76-77 J 4
Veracruz o MEX (BCN) 50-51 B 1
Veracruz o • MEX 52-53 F 2
Veracruz ■ MEX 52-53 E 1
Verada da Redenção ~ BR 68-69 G 7
Verada do Buriti ~ BR 68-69 G 7
Verada Tábua ou Rio Salitre ~ BR 68-69 H 7
Verado de Côcos ~ BR 72-73 H 2
Veranópolis o BR 74-75 E 7
Verao = Île Moso ⌒ VAN 184 II b 3
Verãval o IND 138-139 C 9
Verbano = Lago Maggiore o I 100-101 B 2
Verbena o USA (AL) 284-285 D 4
Verbljud, gora ▲ RUS 108-109 f 3
Verbrande Berg • NAM 216-217 C 10
Verchères o CDN (QUE) 238-239 M 3
Verchivceve o UA 102-103 J 3
Verchnie Jamki o RUS 112-113 L 2
Verchnjadzvinsk ☆ BY 94-95 K 4
Verchn'odniprovs'k o UA 102-103 J 3
Verdalsøra o N 86-87 E 5
Verde, Arroyo ~ RA 78-79 G 6
Verde, Bahía ≈ 78-79 H 5
Verde, Cay ⌒ BS 54-55 H 3
Verde, Laguna o RA 78-79 E 7
Verde, Península ⌣ RA 78-79 H 5
Verde, Punta ▲ EC 64-65 C 1
Verde, Rio ~ BR 70-71 K 3
Verde, Rio ~ BR 72-73 D 6
Verde, Rio ~ BR 72-73 E 5
Verde, Rio ~ BR 72-73 G 4
Verde, Río ~ MEX 50-51 K 7
Verde, Río ~ MEX 52-53 C 1
Verde, Río ~ MEX 52-53 F 3
Verde, Río ~ PY 70-71 J 6
Verde, Río ~ PY 76-77 H 2
Verde Hot Springs o USA (AZ) 256-257 D 4
Verde Island ⌒ RP 160-161 D 6
Verde Island Passage ≈ 160-161 D 6
Verde River ~ USA (AZ) 256-257 D 4
Verdigre o USA (NE) 262-263 H 2
Verdigris Lake o CDN (ALB) 232-233 F 6
Verdigris River ~ USA (KS) 262-263 L 7
Verdigris River ~ USA (OK) 264-265 J 2
Verdinho, Rio ~ BR 72-73 E 4
Verdon ~ F 90-91 L 10
Verdon-sur-Mer, le o F 90-91 G 9
Verdun o • F 90-91 K 7
Verdun o ROU 78-79 M 2
Verdun, Pampa ⊥ RA 80 E 3
Vereda Pimenteira ~ BR 68-69 G 6
Vereeniging o ZA 220-221 H 3
Veregin o CDN (SAS) 232-233 Q 4
Verena o ZA 220-221 J 2
Vereščagino o RUS 114-115 T 2
Vereščagino ☆ RUS (PRM) 96-97 J 4
Verestovo, ozero o RUS 94-95 P 3
Vergara o ROU 74-75 D 9
Vergareña, La o YV 60-61 K 4
Vergas o USA (MN) 270-271 C 4
Vergel, El o MEX 50-51 F 4
Vergeleë o ZA 220-221 G 2
Vergement o AUS 178-179 G 2
Vergennes o USA (VT) 278-279 H 4
Vergi o EST 94-95 K 2
Vergne, La o USA (TN) 276-277 J 4
Verhalen o USA (TX) 266-267 D 2
Verhnee Ondomozero o RUS 88-89 P 3
Verhneimbatsk o RUS 114-115 U 3
Verhnejarkeevo ☆ RUS 96-97 J 6
Verhnekamskaja vozvyšennosť ▲ RUS 96-97 H 4
Verhnekarahbahskij kanal < AZ 128-129 M 2
Verhnekarelina o RUS 116-117 N 7
Verhnekolymskoe, nagor'e ▲ RUS 120-121 M 2
Verhnespasskoe o RUS 96-97 D 4
Verhne tazovskaja vozvyšennosť ▲ RUS 114-115 Q 3
Verhnetazovskij, zapovednik ⊥ RUS 114-115 R 3
Verhnetulomskij o RUS 88-89 L 2
Verhnetulomskoe Vodohranilišče < RUS 88-89 L 2
Verhneural'sk ☆ RUS 96-97 L 7
Verhneural'skoe vodohranilišče < RUS 96-97 L 7
Verhnevažskaja vozvyšennosť ▲ RUS 94-95 R 1
Verhneviljujsk ☆ RUS 118-119 K 4
Verhnevym'skaja grada ▲ RUS 88-89 V 4
Verhnezejsk o RUS 118-119 O 8
Verhnezejskaja ravnina ⌣ RUS 118-119 N 8
Verhnie Kigi ☆ RUS 96-97 L 6
Verhnie Tatyšly ☆ RUS 96-97 J 5
Verhnie Usugli ☆ RUS 118-119 G 9
Verhnij Balygyčan o RUS 112-113 H 5
Verhnij Baskunčak o RUS 96-97 E 9
Verhnij Enisej ~ RUS 116-117 F 10
Verhnij Kužebar o RUS 116-117 F 9
Verhnij Meľgin ~ RUS 122-123 D 3
Verhnij Paren' o RUS 112-113 M 5
Verhnij Suzun ~ RUS 124-125 N 2
Verhnij Toguzak ~ RUS 124-125 B 2
Verhnij Turukan ~ RUS 116-117 L 3
Verhnij Ufalej o RUS 96-97 M 5
Verhnij Uslon ☆ RUS 96-97 F 6
Verhnjaja Agapa ~ RUS 108-109 W 6
Verhnjaja Amga o RUS 118-119 M 7
Verhnjaja Angara ~ RUS 118-119 E 7
Verhnjaja Baiha ~ RUS 114-115 S 2
Verhnjaja Čunku ~ RUS 116-117 J 4
Verhnjaja Kočoma ~ RUS 116-117 N 5
Verhnjaja Kuènga o RUS 118-119 H 9
Verhnjaja Larba ~ RUS 118-119 L 8
Verhnjaja Mokla ~ RUS 118-119 J 8
Verhnjaja Pyšma ☆ RUS 96-97 M 5
Verhnjaja Salda ☆ RUS 96-97 M 4
Verhnjaja Sarčiha ~ RUS 114-115 U 3
Verhnjaja Tajmyra ~ RUS 108-109 a 4
Verhnjaja Tomba ~ RUS 116-117 M 2
Verhnjaja Viljujka ~ RUS 116-117 M 2
Verhnjaja Zolotica o RUS 88-89 Q 4
Verhojansk o RUS 110-111 T 6
Verhojanskij hrebet ▲ RUS 110-111 Q 5
Verhotupova, ostrov ⌒ RUS 120-121 V 4
Verhotur'e ☆ RUS 96-97 M 4
Véria o • GR 100-101 J 4
Verín o E 98-99 D 4
Verkhoyanskiy Khrebet = Verhojanskij hrebet ▲ RUS 110-111 Q 5
Verkola o RUS 88-89 S 5
Verkykerskop o ZA 220-221 J 3
Verlegenhuken ▲ N 84-85 K 2
Vermasse o RI 166-167 D 6
Vermelha, Serra ▲ BR 68-69 F 6
Vermelha, Serra ▲ BR 72-73 E 7
Vermelho, Rio ~ BR 68-69 E 6
Vermelho, Rio ~ BR 68-69 D 5
Vermelho, Rio ~ BR 68-69 C 5
Vermelho, Rio ~ BR 68-69 J 7
Vermelho, Rio ~ BR 72-73 E 3
Vermilion o CDN (ALB) 232-233 H 2
Vermilion o USA (OH) 280-281 D 2
Vermilion, Lake o USA (IL) 274-275 L 4
Vermilion Bay ≈ 44-45 L 5
Vermilion Bay o CDN (ONT) 234-235 K 5
Vermilion Bay ≈ USA 268-269 H 7
Vermilion Hills ▲ CDN (SAS) 232-233 M 5
Vermilion Lake o CDN (ONT) 234-235 L 4
Vermilion Lake o USA (MN) 270-271 F 3
Vermilion River ~ CDN (ALB) 232-233 G 2
Vermilion River ~ USA (LA) 268-269 H 7
Vermillion o USA (SD) 260-261 K 4
Vermillion River ~ CDN (ONT) 238-239 C 2
Vermillion River ~ USA (IL) 274-275 J 3
Vermillion River ~ USA (SD) 260-261 J 3
Vermillon, Rivière ~ CDN (QUE) 236-237 P 5
Vermont o USA (IL) 274-275 H 4
Vermont ■ USA (VT) 278-279 J 5
Vernal o USA (UT) 254-255 F 3
Vernalis o USA (CA) 248-249 C 2
Verner o CDN (ONT) 238-239 E 2
Verneuil-sur-Avre o F 90-91 H 7
Verneuk Pan o ZA 220-221 E 4
Vernia, La o USA (TX) 266-267 J 4
Vernoe o RUS 122-123 C 3
Vernon o CDN (BC) 230-231 K 3
Vernon o F 90-91 H 7
Vernon o USA (AL) 284-285 B 3
Vernon o USA (AZ) 256-257 F 4
Vernon o USA (CT) 280-281 O 2
Vernon o USA (FL) 286-287 D 1
Vernon o USA (IN) 274-275 N 6
Vernon o USA (LA) 268-269 H 4
Vernon o USA (OH) 280-281 F 2
Vernon o USA (TX) 264-265 E 4
Vernon o USA (UT) 254-255 C 3
Vernon, Lake < USA (LA) 268-269 G 5
Vernon Bridge o CDN (PEI) 240-241 N 4
Vernon Center o USA (MN) 270-271 D 7
Vernon Creek ~ USA (IN) 274-275 N 5
Vernon Hill o USA (VA) 280-281 G 7
Vernonia o USA (OR) 244-245 B 5
Vernon Islands ⌒ AUS 172-173 K 2
Vero Beach o USA (FL) 286-287 J 4
Verona o CDN (ONT) 238-239 J 4
Verona ☆·· I 100-101 C 2
Verona o USA (ND) 258-259 J 5
Verónica o RA 78-79 L 3
Veron Range ▲ PNG 183 G 3
Verret, Lake o USA (LA) 268-269 J 7
Versailles ☆··· F 90-91 J 7
Versailles o USA (IN) 274-275 N 5
Versailles o USA (KY) 276-277 L 2
Versailles o USA (MO) 274-275 F 6
Versailles o USA (OH) 280-281 B 3
Versalles o CO 60-61 C 5
Veršina-Tuojdah, gora ▲ RUS 110-111 W 7
Veršino-Darasunskij o RUS 118-119 G 9
Veršiny, Čelno- ☆ RUS 96-97 G 6
Versteende Woud • NAM 216-217 C 10
Vert, Cap ▲ SN 202-203 B 2
Verte, Rivière ~ CDN (QUE) 240-241 G 3
Vertentes o BR 68-69 L 5
Vertientes o C 54-55 F 4
Vertijievka o UA 102-103 G 2
Vert Island ⌒ CDN (ONT) 234-235 P 6
Vértiz o RA 78-79 H 3
Verulam o ZA 220-221 K 4
Verviers o B 92-93 H 3
Verwoert Tunnels II ZA 218-219 E 6
Verwood o CDN (SAS) 232-233 N 6
Vesali, Ruins of • MYA 142-143 H 5
Ves'egonsk o RUS 94-95 P 2
Vesele o UA 102-103 J 4
Veselovskoe o RUS 124-125 L 1
Veselovskoe vodohranilišče < RUS 102-103 M 4
Vesennij o RUS 112-113 N 3
Vešenskaja o RUS 102-103 M 3
Vesljana o RUS 88-89 V 5
Vesljana ~ RUS 88-89 V 5
Vesoul ☆ F 90-91 L 8
Vestaburg o USA (MI) 272-273 E 4
Vestbygd o N 86-87 C 7
Vesterålen ⌒ N 86-87 G 2
Vesterø Havn o DK 86-87 E 8
Vestfjorden ≈ 86-87 F 3
Vestfonna ⊂ N 84-85 L 3
Vestgrønland = Kitaa ■ GRØ 26-27 b 5
Vestmannaeyjar o IS (RAN) 86-87 c 3
Vestmannaeyjar ⌒ IS (RAN) 86-87 c 3
Vestnik, buhta ≈ RUS 122-123 R 3
Vestvågøy ⌒ N 86-87 F 2
Vesuvio ▲ I 100-101 E 4
Veszprém o H 92-93 O 5
Veta, La o USA (CO) 254-255 K 6
Vetal o USA (SD) 260-261 E 3
Vetauua ⌒ FJI 184 III c 1
Veteran o CDN (ALB) 232-233 G 4
Vetlanda ☆ • S 86-87 G 8
Vetluga o RUS (GOR) 96-97 D 5
Vetluga ~ RUS 96-97 E 4
Vetlužskij o RUS 96-97 D 5
Vetovo o BG 102-103 E 6
Vetrenyj pojas, krjaž ▲ RUS 88-89 N 5
Vetrivier ~ ZA 220-221 H 4
Vetryna o BY 94-95 L 4
Vetvejskij hrebet ▲ RUS 120-121 V 3
Vevay o USA (IN) 274-275 N 6
Vévi o GR 100-101 H 4
Veyo o USA (UT) 254-255 B 6
Vezdehodnaja ~ RUS 108-109 j 4
Vézelay o··· F 90-91 J 8
Vežen ▲ BG 102-103 D 6
Vézère ~ F 90-91 H 9
V. Gradište o YU 100-101 H 2
Vi o S 86-87 H 5
Viacha o BOL 70-71 C 5
Viahtu o RUS 122-123 K 3
Viahtu ~ RUS 122-123 J 3
Viai Island ⌒ PNG 183 C 2
Vialadougou o CI 202-203 G 5
Viale o RA 76-77 H 6
Viamão o BR 74-75 E 8
Vian o USA (OK) 264-265 K 3
Viana o ANG 216-217 B 4
Viana o BR (ESP) 72-73 K 6
Viana o BR (MAR) 68-69 F 3
Viana o BR (P) 62-63 J 6
Viana do Castelo o • P 98-99 C 4
Viangchan ★ LAO 158-159 G 2
Viangphoukha o LAO 156-157 B 6
Vianópolis o BR 72-73 F 4
Viar, Río ~ E 98-99 E 6
Viaréggio o I 100-101 C 3
Via River ~ PNG 183 E 3
Vibank o CDN (SAS) 232-233 P 5
Vibora, La o MEX 50-51 H 4
Viboras o USA (TX) 266-267 J 7
Viboras, Las o RA 76-77 E 3
Viborg o DK 86-87 D 8
Vic o E 98-99 J 4
Vicebck ☆ BY 94-95 M 4
Vic-en-Bigorre o F 90-91 H 10
Vicência o BR 68-69 L 5
Vicente Franco o BR 68-69 E 3
Vicente Guerrero o MEX 52-53 L 1
Vicente Guerrero o MEX (DGO) 50-51 H 6
Vicente Guerrero o MEX (TLA) 52-53 E 2
Vicente Noble o DOM 54-55 K 5
Vicenza ☆·· I 100-101 C 2
Viceroy o CDN (SAS) 232-233 N 6
Vicertópolis o BR 72-73 E 6
Vichada, Río ~ CO 60-61 G 5
Vichadero o ROU 76-77 K 6
Vichy o F 90-91 J 8
Vichy o USA (MO) 274-275 G 6
Vici o USA (OK) 264-265 E 2
Vicksburg o USA (AZ) 256-257 B 5
Vicksburg o USA (MS) 268-269 K 4
Vicksburg National Military Park • USA (MS) 268-269 K 4
Viçosa o BR (AL) 68-69 K 6
Viçosa o BR (MIN) 72-73 J 6
Victoire o CDN (SAS) 232-233 L 2
Victor o CDN (SAS) 254-255 K 5
Victor o USA (ID) 252-253 G 3
Victor o USA (MT) 250-251 E 5
Victor o USA (NY) 278-279 D 6
Victor o USA (SD) 260-261 K 1
Victor, Lac o CDN (QUE) 242-243 G 2
Victor, Mount ▲ AUS 180-181 E 2
Victor Emanuel Range ▲ PNG 183 A 3
Victor Harbor o AUS 180-181 E 3
Victoria ■ AUS 180-181 H 4
Victoria o BOL 70-71 D 2
Victoria o CDN (NFL) 242-243 P 5
Victoria o ☆ • CDN (BC) 230-231 F 5
Victoria o CO 60-61 D 5
Victoria ☆·· HK 156-157 J 5
Victoria o M 100-101 E 6
Victoria o RA 78-79 J 2
Victoria o RCH 78-79 C 5
Victoria o SME 62-63 G 3
Victoria ★ • SY 224 D 2
Victoria o USA (KS) 262-263 G 6
Victoria o USA (MS) 268-269 L 2
Victoria o USA (TX) 266-267 K 5
Victoria o USA (VA) 280-281 H 7
Victoria, Isla ⌒ RCH 80 C 2
Victoria, La o YV (APU) 60-61 F 4
Victoria, La o YV (ARA) 60-61 H 2
Victoria, Lake o AUS 180-181 F 3
Victoria, Lake o EAT 212-213 D 4
Victoria, Monte ▲ RCH 80 E 6
Victoria, Mount ▲ MYA 142-143 H 5
Victoria, Mount ▲ PNG 183 D 5
Victoria, Sierra de la ▲ RA 76-77 K 3
Victoria and Albert Mountains ▲ CDN 26-27 L 4
Victoria Beach o CDN (MAN) 234-235 G 4
Victoria Beach o CDN (NS) 240-241 K 6
Victoria Bridge o CDN (NS) 240-241 P 5
Victoria de Durango = Durango ☆ • MEX 50-51 G 5
Victoria Falls ~ ··· Z 218-219 C 3
Victoria Falls National Park ⊥ ZW 218-219 C 3
Victoria Fjord ≈ 26-27 a 2
Victoria Head ▲ CDN 26-27 N 4
Victoria Highway II AUS 172-173 J 3
Victoria Hill o BS 54-55 H 2
Victoria Island ⌒ CDN 24-25 O 5
Victoria Island ⌒ CDN (ONT) 234-235 O 6
Victoria Lake o CDN (NFL) 242-243 L 4
Victoria Land ⊥ ARK 16 F 16
Victoria Nile ~ EAU 212-213 C 2
Victoria Peak ▲ BH 52-53 K 3
Victoria Peak ▲ CDN (BC) 230-231 C 3
Victoria Peak ▲ USA (TX) 266-267 C 2
Victoria River o AUS (NT) 172-173 K 3
Victoria River ~ AUS 172-173 J 3
Victoria River ~ CDN (NFL) 242-243 M 4
Victoria River Downs o AUS 172-173 K 4
Victorias o RP 160-161 E 7
Victoria Strait ≈ 24-25 V 6
Victoria Vale o AUS 174-175 G 6
Victoriaville o CDN (QUE) 238-239 O 2
Victoria West o ZA 220-221 F 5
Victorica o RA 78-79 G 4
Victorino o C 54-55 G 4
Victor Rosales o MEX 50-51 H 6
Victorville o USA (CA) 248-249 G 5
Victory, Mount ▲ PNG 183 E 5
Vicuña ☆ RUS 94-95 R 3
Vicuña o RCH (COQ) 76-77 B 6
Vicuña o RCH (MAC) 80 F 7
Vicuña Mackenna o RA 78-79 G 2
Vicus • PE 64-65 B 4
Vida o USA (MT) 250-251 O 4
Vida o USA (OR) 244-245 C 6
Vidal o PE 64-65 F 3
Vidal o USA (CA) 248-249 K 5
Vidalia o USA (GA) 284-285 H 4
Vidalia o USA (LA) 268-269 J 5
Vidamlja o BY 94-95 H 5
Vidapanakallu o IND 140-141 G 3
Vidaurri o USA (TX) 266-267 K 5
Videira o BR 74-75 E 6
Vidhareiðhi = Viðareiði o FR 90-91 D 1
Vidim o RUS 116-117 L 7
Vidin o BG 102-103 C 6
Vidisha o IND 138-139 F 8
Vidor o USA (TX) 268-269 G 6
Vidora o CDN (SAS) 232-233 J 6
Vidzy o BY 94-95 K 4
Viedgesville o ZA 220-221 J 5
Viedma ☆ RA 78-79 H 6
Viedma, Lago o RA 80 D 4
Vieira Grande, Canal do ~ BR 62-63 J 6
Vieja, Punta la ▲ RCH 78-79 C 3
Vieja, Sierra ▲ USA (TX) 266-267 C 3
Viejitas, Caño las ~ CO 60-61 F 6
Viejo, El o NIC 52-53 L 5
Viejo, Mission o USA (CA) 248-249 G 6
Viejo, Río ~ RA 76-77 F 5
Vielha e Mijaran o E 98-99 H 3
Viella-Mitg Arán = Vielha e Mijaran o E 98-99 H 3
Vienna o USA (GA) 284-285 G 4
Vienna o USA (IL) 276-277 G 3
Vienna o USA (MD) 280-281 L 5
Vienna o USA (MO) 274-275 G 6
Vienna o USA (VA) 280-281 J 5
Vienna o USA (WV) 280-281 E 4
Vienna = Wien ★ ·· A 92-93 O 4
Vienne o F 90-91 K 9
Vienne ~ F 90-91 H 8
Vientiane = Viangchan ★ LAO 158-159 G 2
Viento, Cordillera del ▲ RA 78-79 D 4
Viento, Puerto del ▲ E 98-99 E 6
Vientos, Los o RCH 76-77 C 3
Vientos, Paso de los ≈ 54-55 H 5
Vieques, Isla de ⌒ USA (PR) 286-287 Q 2
Vieques Passage ≈ USA 286-287 Q 2
Vieremä o FIN 88-89 J 5
Vierwaldstätter See o CH 92-93 K 5
Vierzon o F 90-91 J 8
Viesca o MEX 50-51 H 5
Viesite o LV 94-95 J 3
Vieste o I 100-101 F 4
Vietas o S 86-87 J 3
Vietnam = Việt Nam ■ VN 158-159 K 2
Việt Trì ☆ VN 156-157 D 6
Viêt Vinh ☆ VN 156-157 D 5
Vieux-Comptoir, Lac du o CDN 38-39 F 2
Vieux-Comptoir, Rivière du ~ CDN 38-39 E 2
Vieux Fort o WL 56 E 5
View o USA (TX) 264-265 E 6
Vieytes o RA 78-79 L 3
Vigan ☆ RP 160-161 D 4
Vigan, le o F 90-91 J 10
Vigia o BR 62-63 K 6
Vigía, El o YV 60-61 F 3
Vigia Chico o MEX 52-53 L 2
Vigía de Curvaradó o CO 60-61 C 4
Vigía del Fuerte o CO 60-61 C 4
Vigil o USA (CO) 254-255 L 6
Vigo o E 98-99 C 3
Vihanti o FIN 88-89 H 4
Vihāri o PK 138-139 D 4
Vihorevka o RUS 116-117 K 7
Vihren ▲ BG 102-103 C 7
Vihti o FIN 88-89 H 6
Viisanmäki o FIN 88-89 J 5
Viitasaari o FIN 88-89 H 5
Viitna o·· EST 94-95 K 2
Vijayadurg o IND 140-141 E 2
Vijayanagar o IND 138-139 D 8
Vijayāpati o IND 140-141 G 6
Vijayapura o IND 140-141 G 4
Vijayapuri o IND 140-141 H 2
Vijayawada o • IND 140-141 J 2
Vik ☆ IS 86-87 d 3
Vik o N 86-87 C 6
Vikajärvi o FIN 88-89 J 3
Vikārābād o IND 140-141 G 2
Vikeke o RI 166-167 D 6
Vikenara Point ▲ SOL 184 I d 3
Vikersund ☆ N 86-87 D 7
Viking o CDN (ALB) 232-233 G 2
Vikna ⌒ N 86-87 E 4
Viksøyri ☆ N 86-87 C 6
Viktoria = Labuan o MAL 160-161 A 10
Viktorija, ostrov ⌒ RUS 84-85 U 2
Vikulova, mys ▲ RUS 108-109 H 4
Vila Aurora o BR 68-69 E 3
Vila Bela da Santíssima Trinidade o BR 70-71 H 4
Vila Coutinho o MOC 218-219 H 2
Vila de Ribeira Brava o CV 202-203 B 5
Vila de Sal-Rei o CV 202-203 C 5
Vila de Sena o MOC 218-219 H 3
Vila do Maio o CV 202-203 C 6
Vila dos Remédios o BR 68-69 L 1
Vila Flor o ANG 216-217 C 6
Vilafranca del Penedès o E 98-99 H 4
Vila Franca de Xira o P 98-99 C 5
Vilagarcía de Arousa o • E 98-99 C 3
Vila Gomes da Costa o MOC 220-221 L 2
Vilaine ~ F 90-91 G 8
Vila Ipixuna o BR 68-69 E 3
Vilakalaka o VAN 184 II a 2
Vila Maria Pia o CV 202-203 B 5
Vila Martins o BR 66-67 D 6
Vila Meriti o BR 66-67 H 5
Vilanandro, Tanjona ▲ RM 222-223 D 6
Vila Nazaré o BR 66-67 E 4
Vilanculos o MOC 218-219 H 5
Viljāni o·· LV 94-95 K 3
Vila Nova o ANG 216-217 D 6
Vila Nova o BR (PAR) 74-75 D 5
Vila Nova o BR (RSU) 74-75 D 8
Vila Nova da Fronteira o MOC 218-219 H 3
Vila Nova de Foz Côa o P 98-99 D 4
Vila Nova do Seles o ANG 216-217 C 5
Vilanova i la Geltrú o E 98-99 H 4
Vila Nova Laranjeiras o BR 74-75 D 5
Vila Nova Sintra o CV 202-203 B 6
Vila Porto Franco o BR 66-67 H 6
Vila-real o E 98-99 G 5
Vila Real o P 98-99 D 4
Vila Real de Santo António o P 98-99 D 6
Vilar Formoso o P 98-99 D 4
Vila Rica o BR 68-69 C 6
Vilarinho do Monte o BR 62-63 H 6
Vilas, Los o RCH 76-77 B 6
Vila Sagrado Coração de Jesus o BR 66-67 H 5
Vila Tambaquí o BR 66-67 E 4
Vila Tepequem o BR 62-63 D 4
Vila Velha o BR 62-63 J 4
Vila Velha o BR 72-73 K 6
Vila Velha de Ródão o P 98-99 D 5
Vilavila o PE 70-71 B 4
Vilca o PE 64-65 E 8
Vilcabamba o EC 64-65 C 4
Vilcabamba • PE 64-65 F 8
Vilcabamba, Cordillera ▲ PE 64-65 F 8
Vilcanota, Cordillera de ▲ PE 70-71 B 3
Vilcas Huaman o PE 64-65 F 8
Vilčeka, Zemlja ⌒ RUS 84-85 f 2
Vilches o E 98-99 F 5
Vilcún o RCH 78-79 C 5
Vilcún, Río ~ RCH 78-79 C 5
Vilejka ☆ BY 94-95 K 4
Vilelas o RA 76-77 F 4
Vilhelmina o • S 86-87 H 4
Vilhena o BR 70-71 G 3
Viliga ~ RUS 120-121 R 3
Viliginskij, mys ▲ RUS 120-121 R 3
Viljandi ☆ ·· EST 94-95 J 2
Viljoenskroen o ZA 220-221 H 3
Viljučinskaja buhta o RUS 120-121 S 7
Viljuj ~ RUS 116-117 M 3
Viljuj ~ RUS 118-119 D 3
Viljuj ~ RUS 118-119 G 4
Viljučan ~ RUS 118-119 G 4
Viljujsk ☆ • RUS 118-119 K 4
Viljujskoe vodohranilišče o RUS 118-119 E 4
Vil'kickogo, ostrov ⌒ RUS 108-109 Q 5
Vil'kickogo, proliv ≈ 108-109 d 3
Vilkija o LT 94-95 H 4
Vil'kitskogo, Proliv = Vil'kickogo, proliv ≈ RUS 108-109 d 3
Villa Abecia o BOL 70-71 E 7
Villa Ahumada o MEX 50-51 F 2
Villa Alcaraz o RA 76-77 H 6
Villa Alemana o RCH 78-79 D 2
Villa Ana o RA 76-77 H 5
Villa Angela o RA 76-77 G 4
Villa Atuel o RA 78-79 F 3
Villa Azueta o MEX 52-53 G 2
Villaba o RP 160-161 F 7
Villa Berthet o RA 76-77 G 4
Villablino o E 98-99 D 3
Villa Brana o RA 76-77 F 4
Villa Bruzual o YV 60-61 G 3
Villacañas o E 98-99 F 5
Villa Cañas o RA 78-79 J 3
Villa Candelaria o RA 76-77 F 5
Villa Carlos Paz o RA 76-77 E 6
Villacarrillo o E 98-99 F 5
Villach o A 92-93 M 5
Villa Constitución o RA 78-79 J 2
Villa Corona o MEX 52-53 C 1
Villa Coronado o MEX 50-51 G 4
Villa de Cazones o MEX 52-53 F 1
Villa de Cos o MEX 50-51 H 6
Villa de Cura o YV 60-61 H 2
Villa de García o MEX 50-51 J 5
Villa de Leiva o·· CO 60-61 E 5
Villa del Rosario o RA 76-77 F 6
Villa del Rosario o YV 60-61 E 2
Villa de Orestes o MEX 50-51 G 4
Villa de Reyes o MEX 50-51 J 7
Villa de Sari o MEX 50-51 D 3
Villadiego o E 98-99 E 3
Villa Dolores o RA 76-77 E 6
Villa Figueroa o RA 76-77 F 4
Villa Flores o MEX 52-53 H 3
Villafranca del Bierzo o E 98-99 D 3
Village Cove o CDN (NFL) 242-243 O 3
Village Creek ~ USA (TX) 268-269 F 6
Villa General Belgrano o RA 76-77 E 6
Villa General Güemes o RA 76-77 H 3
Villa General Roca o RA 78-79 F 2
Villa General San Martín o RA 76-77 C 6
Village of Yesteryear • USA (MN) 270-271 E 7
Villa Gesell o RA 78-79 L 4
Villa Gobernador Gálvez o RA 78-79 J 2
Villagran o MEX 52-53 D 1
Villaguay o RA 76-77 H 6
Villaguay Grande, Arroyo ~ RA 76-77 H 6
Villa Hermosa o MEX 52-53 C 1
Villahermosa o MEX (CAM) 52-53 K 3
Villahermosa ☆ • MEX (TAB) 52-53 H 3
Villa Hidalgo o MEX (DGO) 50-51 G 4
Villa Hidalgo o MEX (JAL) 50-51 H 7
Villa Hidalgo o MEX (SON) 50-51 E 2
Villa Huidobra o RA 78-79 G 3
Villa Insurgentes o MEX 50-51 D 5
Villa Joyosa o E 98-99 G 5
Villa Juárez o MEX 50-51 J 6
Villa Larca o RA 78-79 G 2
Villalba o E 98-99 D 3
Villalbin o PY 76-77 H 4
Villaldama o MEX 50-51 J 4
Villa Lola o YV 60-61 K 4
Villalonga o RA 78-79 H 5
Villalpando o E 98-99 E 4
Villa Mainero o MEX 50-51 K 5
Villa María o RA 78-79 H 2
Villa Martín o BOL 70-71 D 7
Villamartín o E 98-99 E 6
Villa Mascardi o RA 78-79 D 6
Villa Mazán o RA 76-77 D 5
Villa Media Agua o RA 76-77 C 6
Villa Mercedes o RA 78-79 G 2
Villa Mills o CR 52-53 C 7
Villamontes o BOL 76-77 F 1
Villanow o USA (GA) 284-285 E 2
Villanueva o CO 60-61 E 2
Villanueva o MEX 50-51 H 6
Villa Nueva o RA 76-77 C 6
Villanueva o USA (NM) 256-257 K 3
Villanueva de Córdoba o E 98-99 E 5
Villanueva de los Castillejos o E 98-99 D 6
Villanueva de los Infantes o E 98-99 F 5
Villanueva y Geltrú = Vilanova i la Geltrú o E 98-99 H 4
Villa Ocampo o MEX 50-51 G 4
Villa Ocampo o RA 76-77 H 5
Villa O'Higgins o RCH 80 D 4
Villa Ojo de Agua o RA 76-77 F 5
Villa Oliva o PY (CEN) 76-77 J 3
Villa Oliva o PY (NEE) 76-77 J 4
Villa Ortega o RCH 80 E 2
Villapinzon o CO 60-61 E 5
Villarcayo o E 98-99 F 3
Villard o RH 54-55 J 5
Villardecervos o E 98-99 D 4
Villa Reducción o RA 78-79 H 2
Villa Regina o RA 78-79 F 5
Villa Rica o USA (GA) 284-285 F 3
Villarpando o DOM 54-55 K 5
Villarreal de los Infantes = Vila-real o E 98-99 G 5
Villarrica ☆ PY 76-77 J 3
Villarrica o RCH 78-79 C 5
Villarrica, Lago o RCH 78-79 C 5
Villarrica, Parque Nacional ⊥ RCH 78-79 C 5
Villarrica, Volcán ▲ RCH 78-79 D 5
Villarrobledo o E 98-99 F 5
Villa Salvadorita o NIC 52-53 L 5
Villa San Martín o RA 76-77 E 5
Villa Santa Rita de Catuna o RA 76-77 D 6
Villasimius o I 100-101 B 5
Villa Talavera o BOL 70-71 E 6
Villa Toquepala o PE 70-71 B 5
Villatoya o E 98-99 G 5
Villa Tunari o BOL 70-71 E 5
Villa Unión o MEX 50-51 J 3
Villa Unión o MEX (DGO) 50-51 G 6
Villa Unión o MEX (SIN) 50-51 F 6
Villa Unión o RA 76-77 C 5
Villa Valeria o RA 78-79 G 3
Villa Vásquez o DOM 54-55 K 5
Villavicencio ☆ CO 60-61 E 5
Villaviciosa o E 98-99 E 3
Villazon o RA 76-77 E 2
Villebon, Lac o CDN (QUE) 236-237 L 5
Ville de Lameque o CDN (NB) 240-241 L 3
Villefranche-de-Rouergue o F 90-91 J 9
Villefranche-sur-Saône o F 90-91 K 9
Villeguera, La o YV 60-61 H 4
Ville-Marie o CDN (QUE) 236-237 J 5
Villemontel o CDN (QUE) 236-237 K 4
Villena o E 98-99 G 5
Villeneuve o CDN (ALB) 232-233 E 2
Villeneuve-sur-Lot o F 90-91 H 9
Ville Platte o USA (LA) 268-269 H 6
Villeroy o CDN (QUE) 238-239 O 2
Villeurbanne o F 90-91 K 9
Villicún, Sierra de ▲ RA 76-77 C 6
Villiers o ZA 220-221 J 3
Villisca o USA (IA) 274-275 D 4
Vilnes o N 86-87 B 6
Vilnius ★ ·· LT 94-95 J 4
Vil'njans'k o UA 102-103 J 4
Vil'nohirs'k o UA 102-103 J 3
Vilonia o USA (AR) 276-277 C 5
Vils ~ D 92-93 L 4
Vil'šany o UA 102-103 J 2
Vilyuyskoye Vodokhranilishche = Viljujskoe vodohranilišče < RUS 118-119 E 4
Vimieiro o P 98-99 D 5
Vimioso o P 98-99 D 4
Vimmerby ☆ • S 86-87 G 8
Vina ~ CAM 204-205 K 5
Vina o USA (AL) 284-285 B 2
Vina, Chute de la ~ • CAM 204-205 K 5
Viña, La o RA (CAT) 76-77 E 5
Viña, La o RA (SAL) 76-77 E 3
Viña del Mar o RCH 78-79 D 2
Vinalhaven o USA (ME) 278-279 N 4
Vinalhaven Island ⌒ USA (ME) 278-279 N 4
Vinanivao o RM 222-223 G 5
Vinaròs o E 98-99 H 4
Vinători o RO 102-103 C 5
Vincelotte, Lac o CDN 36-37 N 7
Vincennes o USA (IN) 274-275 L 6
Vincennes Bay ≈ 16 G 11
Vincent o USA (AL) 284-285 D 3
Vincent o USA (TX) 264-265 C 6
Vinces o EC 64-65 C 2
Vinchina o RA 76-77 C 5
Vinchina, Río ~ RA 76-77 C 5
Vindelälven ~ S 86-87 J 4
Vindeln o S 86-87 J 4
Vindhya Range ▲ IND 138-139 E 8
Vinegar Hill ▲ USA (OR) 244-245 G 6
Vine Grove o USA (KY) 276-277 K 3
Vineland o USA (CO) 254-255 L 5
Vineland o USA (NJ) 280-281 L 4
Viner Nejstadt, ostrov ⌒ RUS 84-85 f 2
Vingåker ☆ S 86-87 G 7
Vingerklip • NAM 216-217 C 10
Vinh ☆ VN 156-157 D 7
Vinhais o P 98-99 D 4
Vinh Bắc Bộ ≈ 156-157 E 6
Vinh Cam Ranh ≈ 158-159 K 5
Vinh Cây Dương ≈ 158-159 H 5
Vinh Diên Châu ≈ 156-157 D 7
Vinhedo o BR 72-73 G 7
Vinh Hy o VN 158-159 K 5
Vinh Kim o VN 158-159 K 3
Vinh Loc ☆ VN 156-157 D 6
Vinh Long o VN 158-159 H 5
Vinh Pham Thiêy ≈ 158-159 K 5
Vinh Yên ☆ VN 156-157 D 6
Vinita o USA (OK) 264-265 J 2
Vinju Mare o RO 102-103 C 5
Vinkovci o HR 100-101 G 2
Vinnica = Vinnycja ☆ UA 102-103 F 3
Vinnycja ☆ UA 102-103 F 3
Vinnytsya = Vinnycja ☆ UA 102-103 F 3
Vinson o USA (OK) 264-265 E 4
Vinson, Mount ▲ ARK 16 F 28
Vinstra ☆ N 86-87 D 6
Vinsulla o CDN (BC) 230-231 J 3
Vinter Øer ⌒ GRØ 26-27 W 6
Vinton o USA (IA) 274-275 F 2
Vinton o USA (LA) 268-269 G 6
Vinton o USA (OH) 280-281 D 5
Vinukonda o IND 140-141 H 2
Vinza o RCB 210-211 E 5
Vinzili o RUS 114-115 H 6
Viola o USA (IL) 274-275 H 3
Viola o USA (KS) 262-263 J 7
Viola o USA (WI) 274-275 H 1
Violaineville o G 210-211 C 3
Violeta, La o RA 78-79 J 2
Vioolsdrif o ZA 220-221 C 4
Viphya Mountains ▲ MW 214-215 G 7
Vipos, Río ~ RA 76-77 E 4
Vir o TJ 136-137 M 6
Virac ☆ RP 160-161 F 6
Viração, Cachoeira da ~ BR 62-63 G 6
Virac Point ▲ RP 160-161 F 6
Viradouro o BR 72-73 F 6
Vira-e-Volta, Cachoeira ~ BR 68-69 C 3
Viraganur o IND 140-141 H 5
Virago Sound ≈ CDN 228-229 B 2
Virамgām o IND 138-139 D 8
Viranşehir ☆ TR 128-129 H 4
Virapalle o IND 140-141 H 3
Virār o IND 138-139 D 10
Virarājendrapet o IND 140-141 F 4
Virāwah o PK 138-139 C 7
Virden o CDN (MAN) 234-235 C 5
Virden o USA (IL) 274-275 J 5
Virden o USA (NM) 256-257 G 6
Virei o ANG 216-217 B 7
Virgem da Lapa o BR 72-73 J 4
Virgen, La o NIC 52-53 B 6
Virgen de las Lajas, Santuario • CO 64-65 D 1
Virgen del Carmen, Canal < RA 76-77 F 3
Virgilina o USA (VA) 280-281 H 7
Virgin Gorda ⌒ GB 56 C 2
Virgin Gorda ⌒ GB (VI) 286-287 R 2
Virginia o AUS 180-181 E 3
Virginia o USA (IL) 274-275 H 5
Virginia o USA (MN) 270-271 F 3
Virginia ■ USA (VA) 280-281 G 6
Virginia o ZA 220-221 H 4
Virginia Beach o USA (VA) 280-281 L 7
Virginia City o USA (MT) 250-251 H 6
Virginia City o USA (NV) 246-247 F 4
Virginia Dale o USA (CO) 254-255 K 3
Virginia Falls ~ CDN 30-31 F 5
Virginiatown o CDN (ONT) 236-237 J 4
Virgin Islands ⌒ GB (VI) 286-287 R 2
Virgin Islands (United Kingdom) ■ GB (VI) 286-287 R 2

Virgin Islands (United States) ◘ USA (VI) 286-287 R 2
Virgin Islands National Park ⊥ USA (VI) 286-287 R 2
Virgin Mountains ⛰ USA (NV) 248-249 K 3
Virgin Passage ≈ 56 C 2
Virgin Passage ≈ USA 286-287 Q 2
Virgin River ∼ USA (NV) 248-249 K 3
Virgolândia ○ BR 72-73 J 5
Virihaure ⊖ S 86-87 H 3
Virojoki = Virolahti ○ FIN 88-89 J 6
Virolahti ○ FIN 88-89 J 6
Viroqua ○ USA (WI) 274-275 H 1
Virovitica ○ HR 100-101 F 2
Virrat ○ FIN 88-89 G 5
Virtsu ○ EST 94-95 H 2
Viru ○ PE 64-65 C 6
Virudó ○ CO 60-61 C 5
Virudunagar ○ IND 140-141 G 6
Virunga, Parc National des ⊥ ··· ZRE 212-213 B 4
Vis ○ HR 100-101 F 3
Vis ⌒ HR 100-101 F 3
Vis ∼ NAM 220-221 C 2
Visaginas ★ LT 94-95 K 4
Visalia ○ USA (CA) 248-249 E 3
Visayan Sea ≈ 160-161 E 7
Visayas ⌒ RP 160-161 E 7
Visby ★ ·· S 86-87 J 8
Viscount ○ CDN (SAS) 232-233 N 4
Viscount Melville Sound ≈ 24-25 P 3
Višegrad ○ · BIH 100-101 G 3
Višera ∼ RUS 88-89 V 5
Višera ∼ RUS 114-115 D 4
Viseu ★ · P 98-99 D 4
Vishākhapatnam ○ ·· IND 142-143 C 7
Visicsa, Río ∼ BOL 70-71 D 6
Visim ∼ RUS 114-115 F 3
Visimskij zapovednik ⊥ RUS 96-97 L 5
Visita ○ BR 66-67 H 6
Visite, La ○ RH 54-55 J 5
Višneva ○ BY 94-95 K 4
Višnevka ★ KA 124-125 H 3
Visočica ▲ HR 100-101 E 2
Visoko ○ BIH 100-101 G 3
Visrivier ○ ZA (CAP) 220-221 G 5
Visrivier ∼ ZA 220-221 E 5
Visrivierafgronde Park ⊥ NAM 220-221 D 3
Visriviercanyon ·· NAM 220-221 C 3
Visrivier Canyon Park, Ai-Ais and ⊥ NAM 220-221 C 3
Vista ○ CDN (MAN) 234-235 C 4
Vista ○ USA (CA) 248-249 G 6
Vista Alegre ○ ANG 216-217 C 4
Vista Alegre ○ BR (AMA) 66-67 E 3
Vista Alegre ○ BR (AMA) 66-67 C 6
Vista River ∼ CDN 24-25 c 4
Visuvisu Point ▲ SOL 184 I c 2
Visviri ○ RCH 70-71 C 5
Vit ∼ BG 102-103 D 6
Vita ○ CDN (MAN) 234-235 G 5
Vita ○ IND 140-141 F 2
Vitberget ▲ S 86-87 L 3
Vitebsk = Vicebck ○ BY 94-95 M 4
Viterbo ★ · I 100-101 D 3
Vitgenštejna, mys ▲ RUS 112-113 R 6
Vithalapur ○ IND 138-139 D 8
Vị Thanh ○ VN 158-159 H 6
Vitiaz Strait ≈ 183 D 3
Vitigudino ○ E 98-99 D 4
Viti Levu ⌒ FJI 184 III a 2
Vitim ○ RUS (SAH) 118-119 F 6
Vitim ∼ RUS 118-119 F 6
Vitimkan ∼ RUS 118-119 E 8
Vitimskij ○ RUS 118-119 F 6
Vitimskij zapovednik ⊥ RUS 118-119 H 7
Vitimskoe ploskogor'e ∸ RUS 118-119 F 9
Vitimskoye Ploskogor'ye = Vitimskoe ploskogor'e ∸ RUS 118-119 F 9
Vitiones, Lago de los ⊖ BOL 70-71 H 6
Vitolište ○ MK 100-101 H 4
Vitóna ○ BR 76-77 K 5
Vitor ○ PE 70-71 B 5
Vitoria ○ BR 68-69 B 3
Vitória ★ BR 72-73 K 6
Vitória da Conquista ○ BR 72-73 K 3
Vitória de Santo Antão ○ BR 68-69 L 6
Vitória do Mearim ○ BR 68-69 F 3
Vitoria-Gasteiz ○ · E 98-99 F 3
Vitória Seamount ≃ 72-73 M 6
Vitorino ○ BR 74-75 D 6
Vitorino Freire ○ BR 68-69 F 4
Vitoša, Naroden Park ⊥ BG 102-103 C 6
Vitré ○ F 90-91 G 7
Vitry-le-François ○ F 90-91 K 7
Vitshumbi ○ · ZRE 212-213 B 4
Vitsyebsk = Vicebck ○ BY 94-95 M 4
Vittangi ○ S 86-87 K 3
Vittel ○ · F 90-91 K 7
Vittichi, Río ∼ BOL 70-71 E 7
Vittória ○ I 100-101 E 6
Vittorio Vèneto ○ I 100-101 D 1
Vityaz Depth ≃ 122-123 O 6
Viuda, Isla La ⌒ PE 64-65 C 6
Viuda, La ○ YV 60-61 K 3
Viudas de Oriente ○ MEX 50-51 H 6
Vivario ○ F 98-99 M 3
Viveiro ○ E 98-99 D 3
Vivero, El ○ YV 60-61 H 4
Vivi ∼ RUS 116-117 H 4
Vivi ∼ RUS 116-117 G 2
Vivi, ozero ⊖ RUS 116-117 G 2
Vivian ○ CDN (MAN) 234-235 G 5
Vivian ○ USA (LA) 268-269 G 4
Vivian ○ USA (SD) 260-261 F 3
Vivo ○ ZA 218-219 E 6
Vivonne Bay ≈ 180-181 D 4
Vivoratá, Arroyo ∼ RA 78-79 L 4
Vivorillo, Cayos ⌒ HN 54-55 D 7
Viwa ⌒ FJI 184 III a 2
Vižas ∼ RUS 88-89 S 3
Vizcachas, Meseta de las ∸ RCH 80 D 5
Vizcachillas, Cerro ▲ BOL 76-77 D 2
Vizcaíno, Desierto de ∸ MEX 50-51 C 4
Vizcaino, Peninsula de ⌣ MEX 50-51 B 4
Vizcaíno, Reserva de la Biósfera El ⊥ ··· MEX 50-51 B 4
Vizcaya, Golfo de ≈ 90-91 G 10
Vizcaya, Golfo de ≈ 98-99 G 3
Vize, ostrov ⌒ RUS 84-85 p 3
Vizeu ○ BR 68-69 E 2
Vizianagaram ○ IND 142-143 C 6
Vizien, Rivière ∼ CDN 36-37 N 5
Vizille ○ F 90-91 K 9
Vizinga ○ RUS 96-97 G 3
Vizzini ○ I 100-101 E 6
Vjalozero ⊖ RUS 88-89 N 3
Vjartsilja ○ RUS 88-89 L 5
Vjatka ∼ RUS 96-97 H 4
Vjatskie Poljany ★ RUS 96-97 G 5
Vjazemskij ○ RUS 122-123 F 5
Vjaz'ma ★ RUS 94-95 O 4
Vjazniki ○ RUS 94-95 S 3
Vjosës, Lumi i ∼ AL 100-101 G 4
Vlaanderen ◘ B 92-93 H 3
Vladičin Han ○ YU 100-101 J 3
Vladikavkaz ★ RUS 126-127 F 6
Vladimir ★ ··· RUS 94-95 R 3
Vladimirovka ○ KA 124-125 F 2
Vladimirovka ○ RUS 122-123 K 3
Vladimirovo ○ RUS 122-123 K 4
Vladivostok ○ RUS 122-123 D 7
Vlaşca, Drăgăneşti- ○ RO 102-103 D 5
Vlasenica ○ BIH 100-101 G 2
Vlas'evo ○ RUS 122-123 J 2
Vlasovo ○ RUS 110-111 U 4
V. Lelija ▲ BIH 100-101 G 3
Vlieland ⌒ NL 92-93 H 2
Vliets ○ USA (KS) 262-263 K 5
Vlissingen ○ NL 92-93 G 3
Vlkolínec ○ ··· SK 92-93 P 4
Vlorë ★ ·· AL 100-101 G 4
Vltava ∼ CZ 92-93 N 4
Vnutrennjaja guba ⊖ RUS 120-121 T 3
Vobkent ○ US 136-137 J 4
Voč' ∼ RUS 96-97 J 3
Voca ○ USA (TX) 266-267 H 2
Vodla ∼ RUS 88-89 O 6
Vodlozero, ozero ⊖ RUS 88-89 O 5
Vodnyj ○ RUS 88-89 W 5
Vodopadnyj, mys ▲ RUS 120-121 U 3
Vogan ○ RT 202-203 L 6
Vogar ○ CDN (MAN) 234-235 E 4
Vogelkop = Doberai Peninsula ⌣ RI 166-167 F 2
Vogulka ∼ RUS 114-115 G 3
Vogul'skij Kamen', gora ▲ RUS 114-115 E 4
Vogvazdino ○ RUS 88-89 V 5
Vohémar = Iharana ○ RM 222-223 G 4
Vohilava ○ RM 222-223 F 8
Vohilengo ○ RM 222-223 F 6
Vohimena ○ RM 222-223 F 6
Vohimena ⛰ RM 222-223 E 10
Vohimena, Tanjona ▲ RM 222-223 D 10
Vohipeno ○ RM 222-223 E 9
Vohitra ∼ RM 222-223 F 7
Vohitraivo ○ RM 222-223 F 6
Võhma ○ EST 94-95 H 2
Võhma ○ ·· EST 94-95 J 2
Vohma ○ RUS 96-97 E 4
Voi ○ EAK 212-213 G 5
Voi ∼ EAK 212-213 G 5
Voi ○ VN 156-157 E 7
Voinjama ★ LB 202-203 F 5
Voiron ○ F 90-91 K 9
Voisey Bay ≈ 36-37 T 6
Voja, Ust'- ○ RUS 114-115 D 2
Voja, Ust'- ○ RUS (KOM) 88-89 Y 4
Vojampolka ○ RUS 120-121 S 4
Vojampolka (Matëraja) ∼ RUS 120-121 S 4
Vojampolka (Žilovaja) ∼ RUS 120-121 S 4
Vojejkov šel'fovyj lednik ⌒ ARK 16 G 13
Vojkarsyn'inskij massiv ⛰ RUS 114-115 F 2
Vojkor ∼ RUS 114-115 G 2
Vojnica ○ RUS 88-89 L 4
Vojvareto, ozero ⊖ RUS 108-109 P 7
Vojvož ○ RUS 88-89 X 5
Vokeo Island ⌒ PNG 183 C 2
Vokre, Hosséré ▲ CAM 204-205 K 4
Vol' ∼ RUS 88-89 W 5
Volborg ○ USA (MT) 250-251 O 6
Volcán ○ PA 52-53 C 7
Volcán ○ RA 76-77 E 2
Volcán, El ○ RCH 78-79 D 2
Volcán Barú, Parque Nacionale ⊥ ·· PA 52-53 C 7
Volcán de Colima, Parque Nacional ⊥ MEX 52-53 C 2
Volčanka ∼ RUS 108-109 Z 6
Volcano ○ USA (HI) 288 K 5
Volcans, Parc National des ⊥ ZRE 212-213 B 4
Volčansk ○ RUS 114-115 F 5
Volcán Tupungato, Parque Provincial ⊥ RA 78-79 E 2
Volčiha ★ RUS 124-125 M 3
Volda ★ N 86-87 C 5
Vol'dino ○ RUS 88-89 X 5
Volens ○ USA (VA) 280-281 G 7
Volga ∼ RUS 94-95 N 3
Volga ∼ RUS 96-97 E 8
Volga ∼ RUS 96-97 E 10
Volga ∼ RUS 96-97 F 10
Volga ∼ RUS 126-127 G 5
Volga-Baltic Waterway = Volgo-Baltijskij kanal < RUS 94-95 P 1
Volgo-Baltijskij kanal < RUS 94-95 P 1
Volgodonsk ○ RUS 102-103 N 4
Volgo-Donskoi kanal < RUS 102-103 N 3
Volgograd = Zarizyn ★ · RUS 96-97 D 9
Volgogradskoe vodohranilišče < RUS (SAR) 96-97 E 8
Volgogradskoe vodohranilišče < RUS (VLG) 96-97 D 9
Volgogradskoye Vodokhranilishche = Volgogradskoe vodohranil. < RUS 96-97 D 9
Volhov ○ RUS (LEN) 94-95 N 2
Volhov ∼ RUS 94-95 N 2
Volímes ○ GR 100-101 H 6
Volksrust ○ ZA 220-221 J 3
Volna, gora ▲ RUS 112-113 H 5
Volnovacha ○ UA 102-103 K 4
Voločanka ○ RUS 108-109 a 6
Voločys'k ★ UA 102-103 E 3
Volodarsk ★ KA 124-125 F 2
Volodarsk ○ RUS 94-95 S 3
Volodarskij ★ RUS 96-97 F 10
Volodino ○ RUS 114-115 S 6
Volodymyr-Volyns'kyj ○ UA 102-103 D 2
Vologda ★ · RUS 94-95 Q 2
Volokolamsk ○ · RUS 94-95 O 3
Volokonovka ○ RUS 102-103 K 2
Volokovaja ○ RUS 88-89 U 3
Volokvynejtkon, gora ▲ RUS 112-113 R 5
Volop ○ ZA 220-221 F 4
Vólos ○ · GR 100-101 J 5
Volosovo ★ RUS 94-95 L 2
Volot ○ RUS 94-95 M 3
Volquart Boon Kyst ∸ GRØ 26-27 o 8
Volšepahk, gora ▲ RUS 88-89 M 2
Vol'sk ★ RUS 96-97 E 7
Volstruisleegte ○ ZA 220-221 F 6
Volta ∼ GH 202-203 L 7
Volta Blanche ∼ BF 202-203 K 3
Voltaire, Cape ▲ AUS 172-173 G 3
Volta Lake < GH 202-203 K 5
Volta Noire ∼ BF 202-203 J 4
Volta Redonda ○ BR 72-73 H 7
Volta Region ◘ GH 202-203 L 5
Volta Rouge ∼ BF 202-203 K 4
Volterra ○ I 100-101 C 3
Volturino, Monte ▲ I 100-101 E 4
Volturno ∼ I 100-101 E 4
Voltzberg ▲ SME 62-63 F 3
Volubilis ∴ ·· MA 188-189 J 3
Vólvi, Límni ⊖ GR 100-101 J 4
Volyns'ka vysočyna ⛰ UA 102-103 D 2
Volyns'kyj, Novohrad- ○ UA 102-103 E 2
Volyns'kyj, Volodymyr- ○ UA 102-103 D 2
Volzhskiy = Volžskij ○ RUS 96-97 D 9
Volžsk ○ RUS 96-97 F 6
Volžskij ○ RUS 96-97 D 9
Volžsko-Kamskij zapovednik ⊥ RUS 96-97 F 6
Vom ○ WAN 204-205 H 4
Vonavona = Parara ⌒ SOL 184 I c 3
Vonda ○ CDN (SAS) 232-233 M 3
Vondanka ○ RUS 96-97 E 4
Vondrove ○ RM 222-223 D 8
Vondrozo ○ RM 222-223 E 9
Von Frank Mountain ▲ USA 20-21 N 5
Vónitsa ○ GR 100-101 H 5
Von Lindequist Gate < NAM 216-217 D 9
Von Ormy ○ USA (TX) 266-267 J 4
Vontimitta ○ IND 140-141 H 3
Voon, Tarso ▲ TCH 198-199 H 2
Voortrekker fort · ZA 220-221 K 2
Vopnafjarðurgrunn ≃ 86-87 g 1
Vopnafjörður ≈ 86-87 f 2
Vopnafjörður ○ IS 86-87 f 2
Voranava ★ BY 94-95 J 4
Voranga ∼ RUS 118-119 L 3
Vorarlberg ◘ A 92-93 K 5
Vordingborg ○ · DK 86-87 E 9
Vóreio Egéo ◘ GR 100-101 K 5
Vorenža ○ RUS 88-89 N 5
Vorgašor ○ RUS 108-109 K 8
Vóries Sporádes ⌣ GR 100-101 J 5
Vøringfossen ·· N 86-87 C 6
Vöring Plateau ≃ 6-7 K 2
Vor'ja ∼ RUS 114-115 G 3
Vorkuta ★ RUS 108-109 K 8
Vorkuta ∼ RUS 108-109 K 8
Vorma ∼ N 86-87 E 6
Vormamay ○ AFG 138-139 B 3
Vormsi saar ⌒ EST 94-95 H 2
Vorob'evo ○ RUS 114-115 O 6
Vorogovka ∼ RUS 116-117 E 5
Vorona ∼ RUS 94-95 S 5
Vorona ∼ RUS 102-103 N 2
Voroncovka ○ RUS 118-119 F 6
Voroncovo ○ RUS 108-109 U 6
Voroneț ○ ··· RO 102-103 D 4
Voronež ○ RUS 102-103 L 2
Voronež ∼ RUS 94-95 Q 5
Voronezh = Voronež ○ RUS 102-103 L 2
Voronina, ostrov ⌒ RUS 108-109 a 2
Voron'ja ∼ RUS 88-89 N 2
Voronov, mys ▲ RUS 88-89 R 3
Vorošilovgrad = Luhans'k ★ UA 102-103 L 3
Vorotan ∼ AR 128-129 L 3
Vorotynec ○ RUS 96-97 D 5
Vorožba ○ UA 102-103 J 2
Vorskla ∼ RUS 102-103 J 2
Vorsma ○ RUS 94-95 S 4
Vorstershoop ○ ZA 220-221 F 2
Võrtsjärv järv ⊖ EST 94-95 K 2
Võru ★ ·· EST 94-95 K 3
Vosburg ○ ZA 220-221 F 5
Vose ○ TJ 136-137 L 6
Vosges ⛰ F 90-91 K 8
Voskopojë ○ · AL 100-101 H 4
Voskresenovka ○ RUS 122-123 C 3
Voskresensk ★ · RUS 94-95 Q 4
Voskresenskoe ○ RUS 94-95 P 3
Voskresenskogo, buhta ⊖ RUS 108-109 X 4
Voss ○ USA (TX) 266-267 H 2
Vossavangen ○ · N 86-87 C 6
Vostočnaja, kosa ⌒ RUS 108-109 R 5
Vostočnaja Handyga ∼ RUS 120-121 G 2
Vostočnoe Munozero ○ RUS 88-89 N 3
Vostočno-Sahalinskie gory ⛰ RUS 122-123 K 3
Vostočnyj, proliv ≈ 110-111 H 2
Vostočnyj ○ RUS (CUK) 112-113 W 3
Vostočnyj ○ RUS (SHL) 122-123 K 4
Vostočnyj hrebet ⛰ RUS 120-121 S 7
Vostočnyj Kamennyj, ostrov ⌒ RUS 108-109 U 4
Vostočnyj Sinij, hrebet ⛰ RUS 122-123 E 7
Vostočnyj Tannu-Ola, hrebet ⛰ RUS 116-117 F 10
Vostok ○ ARK 16 F 11
Vostok ○ RUS 122-123 F 5
Votaw ○ USA (TX) 268-269 F 6
Votkinsk ★ RUS 96-97 J 5
Votkinskoe vodohranilišče < RUS 96-97 J 5
Votkinskoye Vodokhranilishche = Votkinskoe vodohranilišče < RUS 96-97 J 5
Vot Tande ⌒ VAN 184 II a 1
Votuporanga ○ BR 72-73 F 6
Vouga ○ ANG 216-217 D 6
Vouga, Rio ∼ P 98-99 C 4
Vouka ○ RCB 210-211 D 5
Vouliagméni ○ GR 100-101 J 6
Vouzela ○ P 98-99 C 4
Vovča ∼ UA 102-103 J 3
Vovča ∼ UA 102-103 K 3
Vovčans'k ○ UA 102-103 K 2
Vovodo ∼ RCA 206-207 G 5
Voxna ○ S 86-87 G 6
Voyageurs National Park ⊥ USA (MN) 270-271 F 2
Vože, ozero ⊖ RUS 94-95 Q 1
Vožega ○ RUS 94-95 R 1
Vožgora ○ RUS 88-89 U 4
Voznesens'k ○ UA 102-103 G 4
Voznesenskoe ○ RUS 94-95 S 4
Vozroždenie ○ RUS 96-97 F 7
Vozroždenije otasi ⌒ US 136-137 F 2
Vozvraščenija, gora ▲ RUS 122-123 K 4
vpadina Assake-Audan ⌣ US 136-137 E 3
Vraca ○ BG 102-103 C 6
Vrangelja, mys ▲ RUS 120-121 H 6
Vrangelja, ostrov ⌒ RUS 112-113 U 1
Vranica ▲ BIH 100-101 F 2
Vrăška čuka, Prohod ▲ BG 102-103 C 6
Vrbas ∼ BIH 100-101 F 2
Vrede ○ ZA 220-221 J 3
Vredefort ○ ZA 220-221 H 3
Vredenburg ○ ZA 220-221 C 6
Vredendal ○ ZA 220-221 D 5
Vredeshoop ○ NAM 220-221 D 3
Vreed-en-Hoop ○ GUY 62-63 E 2
Vreede Stein ○ GUY 62-63 E 2
Vriddhāchalam ○ IND 140-141 H 5
Vrigstad ○ S 86-87 G 8
Vríssa ○ GR 100-101 L 5
Vroolijk, Pulau ⌒ RI 164-165 L 4
Vršac ○ · YU 100-101 H 2
Vryburg ○ ZA 220-221 G 3
Vryheid ○ ZA 220-221 K 3
Vsesvjats'kyj kostel · UA 102-103 C 3
Vsevidof, Mount ▲ USA 22-23 M 6
Vsevidof Island ⌒ USA 22-23 M 6
Vsevoložsk ★ RUS 94-95 M 1
Vstrečnyj ○ RUS 112-113 N 3
Vtoroj Kuril'skij proliv ⊖ RUS 122-123 R 3
Vuadil' ○ US 136-137 M 4
Vube ○ ZRE 212-213 A 2
Vui-Uata Nova Itália, Área Indígena X BR 66-67 C 4
Vuka ∼ HR 100-101 G 2
Vukovar ○ · HR 100-101 G 2
Vuktyl ★ RUS 114-115 D 3
Vulavu ○ SOL 184 I d 3
Vulcan ○ CDN (ALB) 232-233 E 5
Vulcano, Ísola ⌒ I 100-101 E 5
Vulcan Shoal ⌒ AUS 172-173 G 2
Vulkannyj hrebet ⛰ RUS 112-113 N 3
Vulsinio = Lago di Bolsena ⊖ I 100-101 C 3
Vúlture, Monte ▲ I 100-101 E 4
Vulture Mine ○ USA (AZ) 256-257 C 5
Vul'vyveem ∼ RUS 112-113 T 3
Vumba Gardens ⊥ ZW 218-219 G 4
Vumba Mountains ▲ ZW 218-219 G 4
Vũng Hôn Khói ≈ 158-159 K 4
Vũng Lâng Mai ≈ 158-159 K 4
Vũng Tàu ★ · VN 158-159 J 5
Vunisea ○ FJI 184 III b 3
Vuokatti ○ FIN 88-89 K 4
Vuolijoki ○ FIN 88-89 J 4
Vuollerim ○ S 86-87 K 3
Vuolvojaure ⊖ S 86-87 J 3
Vuotso ○ FIN 88-89 J 2
Vuranggo ○ SOL 184 I c 2
Vurnary ○ RUS 96-97 E 6
Vuxikou ○ VRC 154-155 L 6
Vwaza Game Reserve ⊥ MW 214-215 G 6
Vya ○ USA (NV) 246-247 F 2
Vyaparla ○ IND 140-141 H 2
Vybor ○ RUS 94-95 L 3
Vyborg ★ · RUS 94-95 L 1
Vyčegda ∼ RUS 88-89 W 6
Vydrino ○ RUS 116-117 M 10
Vydropužsk ○ RUS 94-95 O 3
Vyezžij Log ○ RUS 116-117 F 8
Vygoniči ○ RUS 94-95 O 5
Vygozero ⊖ RUS 88-89 N 5
Vyhanaščanskoe, vozero ⊖ BY 94-95 J 5
Vyhodnoj, mys ▲ RUS 108-109 G 5
Vyja ∼ RUS 88-89 S 5
Vyksa ★ RUS 94-95 S 4
Vylkove ○ UA 102-103 F 5
Vym' ∼ RUS 88-89 V 4
Vym' ∼ RUS 88-89 V 5
Vyngajaha ∼ RUS 114-115 O 2
Vyngapurovskij ○ RUS 114-115 O 3
Vyra ○ RUS 94-95 L 2
Vys', gora ▲ RUS 112-113 H 5
Vyšhorod ○ UA 102-103 G 2
Vyšnij Voloček ★ RUS 94-95 O 3
Vysokae ○ BY 94-95 H 5
Vysokaja, gora ▲ RUS 122-123 N 6
Vysokaja Gora ★ RUS 96-97 F 6
Vysokaja gora ▲ RUS 120-121 V 4
Vysokaja Parma vozvyšennost' ⛰ RUS 114-115 E 4
Vysokij, mys ▲ RUS (KOR) 112-113 R 6
Vysokij, mys ▲ RUS (SAH) 110-111 a 2
Vysokogornyj ○ RUS 122-123 H 3
Vytegra ★ · RUS 88-89 O 6
Vyvenka ○ RUS (KOR) 120-121 V 3
Vyvenka ∼ RUS 112-113 P 6
Vyvenka ∼ RUS 120-121 V 3

W

Wa ○ CI 202-203 F 6
Wa ★ · GH 202-203 J 4
Waaheen, togga ∼ SP 208-209 G 3
Waajid ○ SP 212-213 J 2
Waal ∼ NL 92-93 H 3
Waangyi-Garawa Aboriginal Land X AUS 174-175 D 6
Waar, Pulau ⌒ RI 166-167 H 3
Waara ○ RI 164-165 H 6
Waarlangier, Tanjung ▲ RI 166-167 G 5
Waat ○ SUD 206-207 L 4
Wababimiga Lake ⊖ CDN (ONT) 236-237 B 2
Wabag ★ · PNG 183 B 3
Wabakimi Lake ⊖ CDN (ONT) 234-235 O 4
Wabakimi Provincial Park ⊥ CDN (ONT) 234-235 O 4
Wabamun ○ CDN (ALB) 232-233 D 2
Wabamun Lake ⊖ CDN (ALB) 232-233 D 2
Wabana ○ CDN (NFL) 242-243 Q 5
Wabasca Indian Reserve X CDN 32-33 O 4
Wabasca River ∼ CDN 32-33 N 3
Wabash ○ USA (IN) 274-275 N 4
Wabasha ○ USA (MN) 270-271 F 6
Wabash River ∼ USA (IL) 274-275 L 5
Wabash River ∼ USA (IL) 274-275 L 6
Wabash River ∼ USA (IN) 274-275 N 4
Wabash River ∼ USA (IN) 274-275 L 4
Wabassi River ∼ CDN (ONT) 234-235 R 3
Wabbaseka ○ USA (AR) 276-277 D 6
Wabbwood ○ CDN (ONT) 238-239 D 2
Wabē Shebelē Wenz ∼ ETH 208-209 E 5
Wabigoon Lake ⊖ CDN (ONT) 234-235 L 5
Wabimeig Lake ⊖ CDN 34-35 O 5
Wabinosh Lake ⊖ CDN (ONT) 234-235 O 4
Wabo ○ PNG 183 C 4
Wabowden ○ CDN 34-35 G 3
Wabron ○ CDN (BC) 230-231 K 2
Wabuda ○ PNG 183 B 5
Wabuda Island ⌒ PNG 183 B 5
Wabuk Point ▲ CDN 34-35 O 3
Waburton Bay ⊖ CDN 30-31 N 4
Wabuska ○ USA (NV) 246-247 F 4
Waccamaw, Lake ⊖ USA (NC) 282-283 J 6
Waccasassa Bay ≈ 48-49 G 5
Waccasassa Bay ≈ USA 286-287 G 2
Waccassa River ∼ USA (FL) 286-287 G 2
Wachapreague ○ USA (VA) 280-281 L 6
Wach'īlē ○ ETH 208-209 D 6
Waci ○ RI 164-165 L 3
Waco ○ CDN 38-39 M 3
Waco ○ USA (TN) 276-277 H 5
Waco ○ USA (TX) 266-267 K 2
Waco, Lake ⊖ USA (TX) 266-267 K 2
Waconda Lake ⊖ USA (KS) 262-263 H 5
Waconia ○ USA (MN) 270-271 E 6
Wacuach, Lac ⊖ CDN 36-37 Q 7
Wad ○ PK 134-135 M 5
Wada'ah ○ SUD 200-201 B 6
Wadalai ○ PNG 183 F 5
Wadamago ○ SP 208-209 H 4
Wad an-Nail ○ SUD 200-201 G 6
Wadau ○ PNG 183 D 3
Wadayama ○ J 152-153 F 7
Wad Bandah ○ SUD 200-201 C 6
Wad Ban Naqa ○ SUD 200-201 F 4
Wadbilliga National Park ⊥ AUS 180-181 K 4
Waddān ○ · LAR 192-193 G 3
Waddān, Jabal ⛰ LAR 192-193 G 3
Waddell Bay ≈ 36-37 Q 3
Waddenzee ≈ 92-93 H 2
Waddikee ○ AUS 180-181 D 2
Waddington, Mount ▲ CDN 230-231 D 2
Waddy Point ▲ AUS 178-179 M 3
Wade ○ USA (MS) 268-269 M 6
Wade Lake ⊖ CDN 36-37 R 7
Wadena ○ CDN (SAS) 232-233 P 4
Wadena ○ USA (MN) 270-271 C 4
Wadesboro ○ USA (NC) 282-283 G 6
Wadeye ○ AUS 172-173 J 3
Wad Ḥāmid ○ SUD 200-201 F 4
Wadham Islands ⌒ CDN (NFL) 242-243 P 3
Wad Hassib ○ SUD 206-207 H 3
Wadhope ○ CDN (MAN) 234-235 H 4
Wadi ○ IND 140-141 G 2
Wādī Ğimal, Ğazīrat ⌒ ET 194-195 G 5
Wādī Ḥalfā ○ SUD 200-201 E 2
Wādī Seidna ○ SUD 200-201 F 5
Wadley ○ USA (AL) 284-285 E 3
Wadley ○ USA (GA) 284-285 H 4
Wād Madanī ★ SUD 200-201 F 5
Wad Nafarein ○ SUD 200-201 F 6
Wadomari ○ J 152-153 C 11
Wad Rāwah ○ SUD 200-201 F 5
Wadsworth ○ USA (NV) 246-247 F 4
Wadsworth ○ USA (TX) 266-267 M 5
Waeldern ○ USA (TX) 266-267 K 4
Waenhuiskrans ○ ZA 220-221 E 7
Waeplau ○ RI 166-167 D 3
Waeputih ○ RI 166-167 D 3
Waerana ○ RI 168 E 7
Wafangdian ○ VRC 150-151 C 8
Wafra, al- ○ KWT 130-131 K 3
Wagait Aboriginal Land X AUS 172-173 K 2
Wagan ○ PNG 183 D 4
Waga River ∼ PNG 183 B 4
Wagau ○ PNG 183 D 4
Wagdari ○ IND 140-141 G 2
Wagener ○ USA (SC) 284-285 J 3
Wageningen ○ SME 62-63 F 3
Wager, Isla ⌒ RCH 80 C 3
Wager Bay ≈ 30-31 Z 3
Wageseri ○ RI 166-167 K 2
Wagga Wagga ○ AUS 180-181 J 3
Wağh, al- ○ KSA 130-131 E 4
Waghai ○ IND 138-139 D 9
Waghete ○ RI 166-167 J 4
Wağid, Ğabal al- ⛰ KSA 132-133 D 4
Wagin ○ AUS 176-177 D 6
Waglisla ○ CDN (BC) 228-229 F 4
Wagner ○ BR 72-73 K 2
Wagner ○ USA (SD) 260-261 H 3
Wagny = Ouana ∼ G 210-211 D 4
Wagoner ○ USA (OK) 264-265 J 3
Wagon Mound ○ USA (NM) 256-257 L 2
Wagontire ○ USA (OR) 244-245 F 7
Wagram ○ USA (NC) 282-283 H 6
Wągrowiec ○ · PL 92-93 O 2
Wagwalcook ○ CDN (NS) 240-241 P 4
Waha ○ RI 164-165 H 6
Waha ○ USA (ID) 250-251 C 5
Wahabu ○ GH 202-203 J 4
Wahai ○ RI 166-167 E 3
Wahala ○ RT 202-203 L 6
Wah Cantonment ○ PK 138-139 D 3
Wahi ○ PK 134-135 M 6
Wahiawa ○ USA (HI) 288 G 3
Wahlbergøya ⌒ N 84-85 L 3
Wahlebone Cape ▲ USA 22-23 N 6
Wahlenbergfjorden ≈ 84-85 L 3
Wahoo ○ USA (NE) 262-263 K 3
Wahpeton ○ USA (ND) 258-259 L 5
Wahrān ★ DZ 188-189 L 3
Wahroonga ○ AUS 176-177 C 2
Wai ○ IND 140-141 E 2
Waiakoa ○ USA (HI) 288 J 4
Waialua ○ USA (HI) 288 J 3
Waialua ○ USA (HI) 288 G 3
Waian ○ RC 156-157 L 5
Waianae ○ USA (HI) 288 G 3
Waiãpi, Área Indígena X BR 62-63 H 5
Waiau ○ NZ 182 D 5
Waibula ○ PNG 183 F 5
Waidhān ○ IND 142-143 C 3
Waidhofen an der Thaya ○ A 92-93 N 4
Waidu ○ WAL 202-203 E 5
Waigen Lakes ⊖ AUS 176-177 K 3
Waigeo, Pulau ⌒ RI 166-167 F 2
Waihau Bay ○ NZ 182 F 2
Waihi ○ NZ 182 E 2
Waiji, Pulau ⌒ RI 166-167 F 2
Waikabubak ○ · RI 168 D 7
Waikaia ○ NZ 182 B 6
Waikaremoana ○ NZ 182 F 3
Waikawa ○ NZ 182 B 7
Waikelo ○ RI 168 D 7
Waikerie ○ AUS 180-181 E 3
Waikii ○ USA (HI) 288 K 5
Waikiki Beach < · USA (HI) 288 H 3
Wailapa ○ VAN 184 II a 2
Wailea ○ USA (HI) 288 J 4
Wailebe ○ RI 166-167 B 6
Wailua ○ USA (HI) 288 F 2
Wailua Falls ∼ · USA (HI) 288 J 4
Wailuku ○ · USA (HI) 288 J 4
Waimanalo Beach ○ USA (HI) 288 H 3
Waimanguar ○ RI 168 D 7
Waimate ○ NZ 182 C 6
Waimea ○ USA (HI) 288 G 3
Waimea Canyon ⌣ · USA (HI) 288 F 2
Waimenda ○ RI 164-165 G 5
Waimiri Atroari, Área Indígena X BR 62-63 D 6
Wainganga ∼ IND 138-139 G 9
Waingapu ○ RI 168 E 7
Waini River ∼ GUY 62-63 E 1
Wainwright ○ CDN (ALB) 232-233 H 3
Wainwright ○ USA 20-21 L 1
Waiouru ○ NZ 182 E 3
Waipa ○ RI 166-167 J 3
Waipah ○ USA (HI) 288 G 3
Waipara ○ NZ 182 D 5
Waipawa ○ NZ 182 F 3
Waipio ○ USA (HI) 288 K 4
Waipoua Kauri Forest · NZ 182 D 1
Waipukang ○ RI 166-167 B 6
Waipukurau ○ NZ 182 F 4
Wair ○ RI 166-167 G 4
Waira ○ PNG (GUL) 183 B 4
Waira ○ PNG (GUL) 183 C 4
Wairaha ∼ SOL 184 I e 3
Wairoa ○ NZ 182 F 3
Wairunu ○ RI 166-167 B 6
Waisa ○ PNG 183 C 4
Waitakaruru ○ NZ 182 E 2
Waitaki ○ NZ 182 C 6
Waitaki River ∼ NZ 182 C 6
Waitangi ○ ·· NZ 182 E 1
Waitara ○ NZ 182 E 3
Waitati ○ NZ 182 C 6
Waite ○ USA (ME) 278-279 O 3
Waitomo Caves · NZ 182 E 3
Waitsburg ○ USA (WA) 244-245 G 4
Waitville ○ CDN (SAS) 232-233 N 3
Waiuku ○ NZ 182 E 2
Waiwa ○ PNG 183 E 5
Waiwai ○ GUY 62-63 E 5
Waiwerang ○ RI 166-167 B 6
Waje ○ WAN 204-205 G 4
Wajima ○ J 152-153 G 6
Wajir ○ EAK 212-213 H 3
Waka ○ ETH 208-209 C 5
Waka ○ RI 168 E 7
Waka ○ USA (TX) 264-265 D 2
Waka ○ ZRE (EQU) 210-211 H 3
Waka ○ ZRE (EQU) 210-211 H 4
Waka, Tanjung ▲ RI 166-167 D 3
Wakaf Tapai ○ MAL 162-163 E 2
Wakami Lake Provincial Park ⊥ CDN (ONT) 236-237 F 5
Wakamoek ○ RI 166-167 F 2
Wakarusa River ∼ USA (KS) 262-263 L 6
Wakasa-wan ≈ 152-153 F 7
Wakasawan Quasi National Park ⊥ J 152-153 F 7
Wakatin ○ RI 166-167 D 3
Wakatipu, Lake ⊖ NZ 182 B 6
Wakaw ○ CDN (SAS) 232-233 N 3
Wakay ○ SME 62-63 F 3
Wakaya ⌒ FJI 184 III b 2
Wakayama ★ J 152-153 F 7
Wakde, Pulau ⌒ RI 166-167 K 2
Wakeeny ○ USA (KS) 262-263 G 5
Wakefield ○ CDN (QUE) 238-239 K 3
Wakefield ○ NZ 182 D 4
Wakefield ○ USA (MI) 270-271 J 4
Wakefield ○ USA (NE) 262-263 K 2
Wakefield ○ USA (RI) 278-279 K 7
Wakefield ○ USA (VA) 280-281 K 7
Wakefield River ∼ AUS 180-181 E 3
Wake Forest ○ USA (NC) 282-283 J 5
Wakeham, Rivière ∼ CDN 36-37 N 4
Wakeman River ∼ CDN (BC) 230-231 C 2
Wakingku ○ RI 164-165 H 6
Wakinosawa ○ J 152-153 J 4
Wakkanai ○ J 152-153 J 2
Wakkerstrom ○ ZA 220-221 K 3
Waklarok ○ USA 20-21 H 5
Wako ○ PNG 183 E 4
Wakomata Lake ⊖ CDN (ONT) 238-239 B 2
Wakonassin River ∼ CDN (ONT) 238-239 C 2
Wakonda ○ USA (SD) 260-261 J 3
Wakoo ○ AUS 180-181 H 3
Wakool River ∼ AUS 180-181 G 3
Wakopa ○ CDN (MAN) 234-235 D 5
Wakulla Springs · USA (FL) 286-287 E 1
Wakunai ○ PNG 184 I b 1
Wakusimi River ∼ CDN (ONT) 236-237 F 4
Wakwayokwastic River ∼ CDN (ONT) 236-237 H 3
Wala ∼ EAT 212-213 D 6
Walachia ∸ RO 102-103 D 6
Wālājāpet ○ IND 140-141 H 4
Walakpa ○ USA 20-21 M 1
Walambele ○ GH 202-203 K 4
Wálamo, El ○ MEX 50-51 F 6
Walanae ∼ RI 164-165 G 6
Wal Athiang ○ SUD 206-207 J 5
Wałbrzych ★ · PL 92-93 O 3
Walbundrie ○ AUS 180-181 J 3
Walcha ○ AUS 178-179 L 6
Walckenaer, Teluk ≈ 166-167 K 3
Walcott ○ CDN (BC) 228-229 H 2
Walcott ○ USA (WY) 252-253 M 5
Walcott Inlet ≈ 172-173 G 4
Wałcz ○ · PL 92-93 O 2
Waldburg ○ AUS 176-177 D 2
Waldburg Range ⛰ AUS 176-177 D 2
Waldeck ○ CDN (SAS) 232-233 L 5
Walden ○ CDN (ONT) 238-239 D 2
Walden ○ USA (CO) 254-255 J 3
Walden ○ USA (NY) 280-281 M 2
Waldenburg ○ USA (AR) 276-277 E 5
Walden Ridge ⛰ USA (TN) 276-277 K 5
Waldersee ○ CDN (MAN) 234-235 D 4
Waldheim ○ CDN (SAS) 232-233 M 3
Waldo ○ USA (AR) 276-277 B 7
Waldo ○ USA (FL) 286-287 G 2
Waldo ○ USA (OH) 280-281 C 3
Waldorf ○ USA (MD) 280-281 K 5
Waldport ○ USA (OR) 244-245 A 6
Waldron ○ CDN (SAS) 232-233 Q 5
Waldron ○ USA (AR) 276-277 A 6
Walea, Selat ≈ 164-165 H 4
Waleabahi, Pulau ⌒ RI 164-165 H 4
Waleakodi, Pulau ⌒ RI 164-165 H 4
Waleri ○ RI 168 D 3
Wales ◘ GB 90-91 E 5
Wales ○ USA 20-21 F 4
Wales ○ USA (UT) 254-255 D 4
Wales Island ⌒ CDN 24-25 c 6
Wales Island ⌒ CDN (BC) 228-229 D 2
Walewale ○ GH 202-203 K 4
Walfe, Chute ∼ ZRE 210-211 J 6
Walgett ○ AUS 178-179 K 6
Walgra ○ AUS 178-179 E 1
Walgreen Coast ⌣ ARK 16 F 26
Walhalla ○ USA (MI) 272-273 C 4
Walhalla ○ USA (ND) 258-259 K 3
Walhalla ○ USA (SC) 284-285 G 2
Walhalla Historic Site ∴ USA (ND) 258-259 K 3
Walikale ○ ZRE 212-213 B 4
Walir, Pulau ⌒ RI 166-167 G 4
Walis Island ⌒ PNG 183 B 2
Walk = Valga ★ ·· EST 94-95 K 3
Walker ○ USA (IA) 274-275 G 2
Walker ○ USA (MI) 272-273 D 4
Walker ○ USA (MN) 270-271 D 3
Walker ○ USA (SD) 260-261 E 1
Walker, Mount ▲ CDN 24-25 Z 4
Walker Baldwin Range ⛰ CDN 24-25 S 3
Walker Bay ≈ 24-25 N 5
Walker Bay ≈ 220-221 D 7
Walker Creek ∼ AUS 176-177 M 2
Walker Lake ⊖ CDN (MAN) 34-35 H 3
Walker Lake ⊖ CDN (NWT) 30-31 Y 2
Walker Lake ⊖ USA (AK) 20-21 N 3
Walker Lake ⊖ USA (NV) 246-247 G 5
Walker Mountains ⛰ ARK 16 F 26
Walker Pass ▲ USA (CA) 248-249 F 4
Walker River ∼ AUS 174-175 C 3
Walker River ∼ USA (NV) 246-247 F 5
Walker River Indian Reservation X USA (NV) 246-247 G 4
Walkerston ○ AUS 178-179 K 1
Walkerton ○ CDN (ONT) 238-239 D 4
Walkerton ○ USA (IN) 274-275 M 3
Walkerville ○ AUS 180-181 H 5
Walkerville ○ USA (MI) 272-273 C 4
Wall ○ USA (SD) 260-261 D 2
Wall ○ USA (TX) 266-267 G 2
Wall, Mount ▲ AUS 172-173 C 7
Wallabi Group ⌒ AUS 176-177 B 4
Wallace ○ CDN (NS) 240-241 M 5
Wallace ○ USA (ID) 250-251 D 4
Wallace ○ USA (NC) 282-283 K 6
Wallace ○ USA (NE) 262-263 E 4
Wallaceburg ○ CDN (ONT) 238-239 C 6
Wallace River ⊖ CDN 30-31 W 5
Wallachisch Meseritsch = Valašské Meziříčí ○ CZ 92-93 O 4
Wallal Downs ○ AUS 172-173 E 5
Wallambin, L. ⊖ AUS 176-177 D 5
Wallam Creek ∼ AUS 178-179 J 5
Wallareenya ○ AUS 172-173 D 6
Wallaroo ○ AUS 180-181 D 2

Walla Walla o USA (WA) 244-245 G 4
Wallekraal o ZA 220-221 C 5
Wallenpaupack, Lake ⊖ USA (PA) 280-281 L 2
Wallhallow o AUS 174-175 C 5
Wallingford o USA (VT) 278-279 J 5
Wallis o USA (TX) 266-267 L 4
Walliser Alpen ⛰ CH 92-93 J 5
Wallis Lake ⊖ AUS 180-181 M 2
Wallkill River ~ USA (NY) 280-281 M 2
Walløe, Kap ▲ GRØ 28-29 T 6
Wallonie ◘ B 92-93 H 3
Wallowa o USA (OR) 244-245 H 5
Wallowa Mountains ▲ USA (OR) 244-245 H 5
Walls of China, The • AUS 180-181 G 2
Wallula o USA (WA) 244-245 G 4
Wallumbilla o AUS 178-179 K 4
Walmanpa-Warlpiri Aboriginal Land ✕ AUS 172-173 K 5
Walnut o USA (CA) 248-249 B 2
Walnut o USA (IL) 274-275 J 3
Walnut o USA (MS) 268-269 M 2
Walnut Canyon National Monument ∴ USA (AZ) 256-257 D 3
Walnut Cove o USA (NC) 282-283 G 4
Walnut Creek o USA (AZ) 256-257 C 4
Walnut Creek ~ USA (KS) 262-263 G 6
Walnut Grove o USA (MN) 270-271 C 6
Walnut Grove o USA (MO) 276-277 B 3
Walnut Grove o USA (TN) 276-277 G 5
Walnut Hill o USA (AL) 284-285 E 4
Walnut Ridge o USA (AR) 276-277 E 4
Walnut River ~ USA (KS) 262-263 J 7
Walparous o CDN (ALB) 232-233 D 4
Walpeup o AUS 180-181 G 3
Walpole o AUS 176-177 D 7
Walpole o CDN (SAS) 232-233 R 6
Walpole Island Indian Reserve ✕ CDN (ONT) 238-239 C 6
Walrus Island ⌒ USA 22-23 Q 4
Walrus Islands ⌒ USA 22-23 Q 3
Walrus Islands State Game Sanctuary ⊥ USA 22-23 Q 3
Walsall o GB 90-91 G 5
Walsenburg o USA (CO) 254-255 L 6
Walsh o CDN (ALB) 232-233 H 6
Walsh o USA (CO) 254-255 N 6
Walsh River ~ AUS 174-175 H 5
Walsingham, Cape ▲ CDN 28-29 K 3
Walsrode o D 92-93 K 2
Walterboro o USA (SC) 284-285 K 4
Walterhill o USA (TN) 276-277 J 5
Walter James Range ⛰ AUS 176-177 K 2
Walters o USA (OK) 264-265 F 4
Waltershausen Gletscher ⊂ GRØ 26-27 n 6
Walthall o USA (MS) 268-269 L 3
Waltham Station o CDN (QUE) 238-239 J 3
Walthill o USA (NE) 262-263 K 2
Waltman o USA (WY) 252-253 L 3
Walton o CDN (NS) 240-241 L 5
Walton o USA (IN) 274-275 M 4
Walton o USA (KY) 276-277 L 2
Walton o USA (NY) 278-279 F 6
Walton, Mount ▲ AUS 176-177 F 5
Walue o RI 164-165 H 6
Walungu o ZRE 212-213 B 5
Walvisbaai ≈ 220-221 B 1
Walvisbaai = Walvis Bay ☆• NAM 220-221 B 1
Walvis Bay ☆• NAM 220-221 B 1
Walvis Ridge ≃ 6-7 K 11
Walworth o USA (WI) 274-275 K 2
Wamal o RI 166-167 K 6
Wamala, Lake ⊖ EAU 212-213 C 3
Wamanfo o GH 202-203 J 6
Wamar, Pulau ⌒ RI 166-167 H 4
Wamaza o ZRE 210-211 L 6
Wamba o EAK 212-213 F 3
Wamba ∸ WAN 204-205 H 4
Wamba o ZRE 212-213 B 2
Wamba ~ ZRE 216-217 D 3
Wamba-Luadi o ZRE 216-217 D 3
Wamba Mountains ⛰ WAN 204-205 J 5
Wamdé Tabal ▲ BF 202-203 K 2
Wamego o USA (KS) 262-263 K 5
Wamena o RI 166-167 K 4
Wamera Island ⌒ PNG 183 F 5
Wami ~ EAT 214-215 K 4
Wamis o LAR 192-193 E 2
Wamoi Falls ~ PNG 183 B 4
Wamonket, Tanjung ▲ RI 166-167 F 2
Wampembe o EAT 214-215 F 4
Wamsutter o USA (WY) 252-253 L 5
Wamtakin, Mount ▲ PNG 183 A 3
Wāna o PK 138-139 B 3
Wanaaring o AUS 178-179 H 5
Wanaka o NZ 182 B 6
Wanaka, Lake ⊖ NZ 182 B 6
Wanapitae Lake ⊖ CDN (ONT) 238-239 E 2
Wanapitei o CDN (ONT) 238-239 E 2
Wanapitei River ~ CDN (ONT) 236-237 G 5
Wanapitei River ~ CDN (ONT) 238-239 E 2
Wanasabari o RI 164-165 H 6
Wanau o RI 166-167 G 2
Wanblee o USA (SD) 260-261 E 3
Wanbu o VRC 156-157 J 2
Wanci o RI 164-165 H 6
Wandagee o AUS 176-177 C 1
Wandai (Homeyo) o RI 166-167 J 3
Wandamen, Teluk ≈ 166-167 H 3
Wandamen Peninsula ⌒ RI 166-167 H 3
Wandao Shan ⛰ VRC 150-151 H 5
Wandel, Kap ▲ GRØ 28-29 X 3
Wandering River ~ CDN 32-33 O 4
Wanderlândia o BR 68-69 E 5
Wandiang o VRC 142-143 L 3
Wando o PNG 183 A 5
Wando o ROK 150-151 F 10
Wandoan o AUS 178-179 K 4
Wandokai o PNG 183 D 4
Wanesabe o RI 168 C 7
Waneta o CDN (BC) 230-231 M 4
Wanfotang Shiku • VRC 150-151 C 7
Wang o PNG 183 G 2
Wanga o ZRE 212-213 B 2
Wanga Mountains ⛰ WAN 204-205 J 5
Wanganui o NZ 182 E 3
Wanganui River ~ NZ 182 E 3
Wangaratta o AUS 180-181 J 4
Wangary o AUS 180-181 C 3
Wangasi-Turu o GH 202-203 K 5
Wangcang o VRC 154-155 E 5
Wangcheng o VRC 156-157 H 2
Wangdi Phodrang o BHT 142-143 F 2
Wangerooge ⌒ D 92-93 J 2
Wanggamet, Gunung ▲ RI 168 E 8
Wanggao o VRC 156-157 G 4
Wanggar o RI 166-167 H 3
Wanggar ~ RI 166-167 H 3
Wangi o AUS 172-173 K 2
Wāngi o IND 138-139 E 10
Wangianna o AUS 178-179 D 5
Wangiwangi, Pulau ⌒ RI 164-165 H 6
Wangjiang o VRC 154-155 K 6
Wangjie o VRC 156-157 B 5
Wangki, Río = Coco o Segovia ~ HN 52-53 B 4
Wangmo o VRC 156-157 E 4
Wang Nam Yen o THA 158-159 G 4
Wangon o RI 168 C 3
Wangpan Yang ≈ 154-155 M 6
Wang Sam Mo o THA 158-159 G 2
Wang Saphung o THA 158-159 F 2
Wang Thong o THA 158-159 F 2
Wang Wiset o THA 158-159 E 7
Wangziguan o VRC 154-155 D 5
Wanham o CDN 32-33 L 4
Wan Hsa-la o MYA 142-143 L 5
Wanhuayan • VRC 156-157 H 4
Wani o IND 138-139 G 9
Wanie-Rukula o ZRE 210-211 K 3
Wanigela o PNG 183 E 5
Wānkāner o IND 138-139 C 8
Wanless o CDN 34-35 F 3
Wanleweeyn o SP 212-213 K 2
Wan Long o MYA 142-143 L 4
Wanlong o VRC 154-155 E 6
Wanna o AUS 176-177 D 1
Wanna Lakes ⊖ AUS 176-177 K 4
Wannarra o AUS 176-177 D 4
Wannaska o USA (MN) 270-271 C 2
Wannian o VRC 156-157 K 2
Wannian Temple o VRC 156-157 C 2
Wannianxue ⛰ VRC 154-155 C 6
Wanning o VRC 156-157 G 7
Wannon River ~ AUS 180-181 F 4
Wannoo o AUS 176-177 C 3
Wanparti o IND 140-141 H 2
Wan Pong o MYA 142-143 L 5
Wanqing o VRC 150-151 G 6
Wanshan Qundao ⌒ VRC 156-157 J 6
Wansra o RI 166-167 H 2
Wantang o VRC 156-157 C 5
Wantoat o PNG 183 D 4
Wan Xian o VRC 154-155 F 6
Wanyuan o VRC 154-155 F 5
Wanzai o VRC 156-157 J 2
Waogena o RI 164-165 H 6
Wapah o CDN (MAN) 234-235 E 3
Wapakoneta o USA (OH) 280-281 B 3
Wapanucka o USA (OK) 264-265 H 4
Wapaseese River ~ CDN 34-35 L 3
Wapato o USA (WA) 244-245 E 4
Wapawekka Hills ⛰ CDN 34-35 D 3
Wapawekka Lake ⊖ CDN 34-35 D 3
Wapella o CDN (SAS) 232-233 R 5
Wapello o USA (IA) 274-275 G 3
Wapenamanda o PNG 183 B 3
Wapet Camp o AUS 172-173 B 6
Wāpi o IND 138-139 D 9
Wapikopa Lake ⊖ CDN (ONT) 234-235 P 2
Wapi Pathum o THA 158-159 G 3
Wapiti o CDN (ALB) 228-229 P 2
Wapiti o USA (WY) 252-253 J 2
Wapoga ~ RI 166-167 J 3
Wapomaru o RI 164-165 H 6
Wapotih o RI 166-167 D 3
Wappapello o USA (MO) 276-277 E 4
Wappapello, Lake ⊖ USA (MO) 276-277 E 4
Waprak o RI 166-167 H 3
Wapsipinicon River ~ USA (IA) 274-275 G 2
Wapta Icefield ⊂ CDN (ALB) 232-233 B 4
Wapuli o GH 202-203 L 5
Wapumba Island ⌒ PNG 183 B 5
Waputik Icefield ⊂ CDN (ALB) 232-233 B 4
Wara o WAN 204-205 F 3
Waradi < EAK 212-213 H 3
Warakaraket, Pulau ⌒ RI 166-167 F 3
Warakurna ✕ AUS 176-177 K 2
Warambif o PNG 183 G 3
Warandab o ETH 208-209 G 5
Waranga Basin < AUS 180-181 H 4
Warangal o• IND 138-139 G 10
Wararisbari, Tanjung ▲ RI 166-167 J 2
Waratah o AUS 180-181 H 6
Wara Wara Mountains ⛰ WAL 202-203 E 5
Warbreccan o AUS 178-179 G 3
Warburg o CDN (ALB) 232-233 D 2
Warburton o AUS (VIC) 180-181 H 4
Warburton ✕ AUS (WA) 176-177 J 3
Warburton o ZA 220-221 K 3
Warburton Creek ~ AUS 178-179 E 4
Warburton Range ⛰ AUS 176-177 J 3
Warburton Range Aboriginal Land ✕ AUS 176-177 J 2
Ward o NZ 182 E 4
Warda o USA (TX) 266-267 L 3
Wardak ◘ AFG 138-139 B 2
Wardang Island ⌒ AUS 180-181 D 3
Ward Cove o USA 32-33 E 4
Wardé o RMM 202-203 G 2
Warden o USA (WA) 244-245 F 4
Warden o ZA 220-221 J 3
Wardha o IND (MAH) 138-139 G 9
Wardha ~ IND 138-139 G 9
Wardha ~ IND 138-139 G 10
War Dhugulle < SP 212-213 K 2
Ward Hunt, Cape ▲ PNG 183 E 5
Ward Hunt Island ⌒ CDN 26-27 N 2
Ward Hunt Strait ≈ 183 F 5
Ward Inlet ≈ 36-37 Q 3
Wardlaw, Kap ▲ GRØ 26-27 p 8
Wardlow o CDN (ALB) 232-233 G 5
Wardner o CDN (BC) 230-231 O 4
Wardo o RI 166-167 H 2
Ware o CDN 32-33 H 3
Wareham o USA (MA) 278-279 L 7
Waren o RI 166-167 J 3
Waren ~ RI 166-167 J 3
Waren (Müritz) o• D 92-93 M 2
Warenda o AUS 178-179 F 2
Wares Crossroads o USA (VA) 280-281 J 5
Warfallah, Ra's ⛰ LAR 192-193 F 3
War Galoh o SP 208-209 H 5
Wariai, Tanjung ▲ RI 166-167 F 2
Warialda o AUS 178-179 L 5
Waria River ~ PNG 183 D 4
Wāri Godri o IND 138-139 E 10
Wari Island ⌒ PNG 183 F 6
Warilau o RI 166-167 H 4
Warilau, Pulau ⌒ RI 166-167 H 4
Warin Chamrap o THA 158-159 H 3
Waring Mountains ⛰ USA 20-21 K 3
Wario River ~ PNG 183 B 3
Wāris Aliganj o IND 142-143 D 3
Warkopi o RI 166-167 H 2
Warkworth o NZ 182 E 2
Warman o CDN (SAS) 232-233 M 3
Warmandi o RI 166-167 G 2
Warmbad o NAM 220-221 D 4
Warmbad o ZA 220-221 J 2
Warm Baths = Warmbad o ZA 220-221 J 2
Warm Creek Ranch o USA (NV) 246-247 K 3
Warming Land ∸ GRØ 26-27 Y 3
Warminster o USA (PA) 280-281 L 3
Warm Springs o USA (NV) 246-247 J 5
Warm Springs o USA (OR) 244-245 D 6
Warm Springs o USA (VA) 280-281 G 5
Warm Springs Indian Reservation ✕ USA (OR) 244-245 D 6
Warnemünde o D 92-93 M 1
Warner o CDN (ALB) 232-233 F 6
Warner o USA (OK) 264-265 J 3
Warner o USA (SD) 260-261 H 1
Warner Pass ▲ USA (OR) 244-245 E 8
Warner Range ⛰ USA (CA) 246-247 E 2
Warner Robins o USA (GA) 284-285 G 4
Warner Springs o USA (CA) 248-249 H 6
Warnes o RA 78-79 J 3
Warning, Mount ▲ AUS 178-179 M 5
Warnock o USA (KY) 276-277 N 2
Warnow ~ D 92-93 L 2
Waromge, Teluk ≈ 166-167 F 2
Warooka o AUS 180-181 D 3
Waroona o AUS 176-177 C 6
Waropen, Teluk ≈ 166-167 J 2
Waropko o RI 166-167 L 4
Warora o IND 138-139 G 9
Warra o AUS 178-179 L 4
Warrabri ✕ AUS 178-179 C 1
Warracknabeal o AUS 180-181 G 4
Warragul o AUS 180-181 H 5
Warrakalanna, Lake ⊖ AUS 178-179 E 5
Warrakunta Point ▲ AUS 174-175 C 4
Warralakin o AUS 176-177 E 5
Warral Island ⌒ AUS 183 B 6
Warrandirinna, Lake ⊖ AUS 178-179 D 4
Warrawagine o AUS 172-173 E 6
Warrego Highway II AUS 178-179 J 4
Warrego Mine • AUS 174-175 B 6
Warrego Range ⛰ AUS 178-179 H 3
Warrego River ~ AUS 178-179 H 4
Warren o AUS 178-179 J 6
Warren o CDN (MAN) 234-235 F 4
Warren o USA (AR) 276-277 C 7
Warren o USA (AZ) 256-257 F 7
Warren o USA (ID) 250-251 D 6
Warren o USA (IL) 274-275 H 2
Warren o USA (IN) 274-275 N 4
Warren o USA (MI) 272-273 F 5
Warren o USA (MN) 270-271 B 2
Warren o USA (MT) 250-251 L 6
Warren o USA (NH) 278-279 K 5
Warren o USA (OH) 280-281 F 2
Warren o USA (PA) 280-281 G 2
Warren o USA (TX) 268-269 F 6
Warrendale o USA (PA) 280-281 F 3
Warrender, Port o AUS 172-173 G 3
Warren Point ▲ CDN 20-21 Y 2
Warrensburg o USA (MO) 274-275 E 6
Warrensburg o USA (NY) 278-279 H 5
Warrens Landing o CDN 34-35 H 4
Warrenton o USA (GA) 284-285 H 3
Warrenton o USA (OR) 244-245 B 4
Warrenton o USA (VA) 280-281 J 5
Warrenton o ZA 220-221 G 4
Warren Vale o AUS 174-175 F 6
Warri o WAN 204-205 F 6
Warriedar o AUS 176-177 D 4
Warriedar Hill ▲ AUS 176-177 D 4
Warriner Creek ~ AUS 178-179 D 5
Warrington o USA (FL) 286-287 B 1
Warrington Bay ≈ 24-25 N 3
Warrior o USA (AL) 284-285 D 3
Warrior Creek ~ USA (GA) 284-285 G 5
Warrior Reefs ⌒ AUS 174-175 G 2
Warri River ~ WAN 204-205 F 6
Warri Warri Creek ~ AUS 178-179 F 5
Warrnambool o AUS 180-181 G 5
Warroad o USA (MN) 270-271 C 2
Warrumbungle National Park ⊥ AUS 178-179 K 6
Warrumbungle Range ⛰ AUS 178-179 K 6
Warruwi ✕ AUS 174-175 B 2
Warsa o RI 166-167 H 2
Warsaw o USA (IN) 274-275 N 3
Warsaw o USA (KY) 276-277 L 2
Warsaw o USA (MO) 274-275 E 6
Warsaw o USA (NC) 282-283 J 6
Warsaw o USA (NY) 278-279 C 6
Warsaw = Warszawa ★ ··· PL 92-93 Q 2
Warshi o IND 138-139 F 10
Warshiikh o SP 212-213 K 2
Warszawa ★ ··· PL 92-93 Q 2
Warta ~ PL 92-93 O 2
Wartburg o USA (TN) 282-283 C 4
Wartime o CDN (SAS) 232-233 K 4
Warton, Monte ▲ RCH 80 D 6
Waru o RI (JTI) 168 E 3
Waru o RI (KTI) 164-165 E 4
Waru o RI (MAL) 166-167 F 3
Warud o IND 138-139 G 9
Waruta ~ RI 166-167 L 3
Warwick o AUS 178-179 L 5
Warwick o CDN (ALB) 232-233 F 2
Warwick ☆• GB 90-91 G 5
Warwick o USA (GA) 284-285 G 5
Warwick o USA (ND) 258-259 J 4
Warwick o USA (NY) 280-281 M 2
Warwick o USA (OK) 264-265 H 3
Warwick Channel ≈ 174-175 D 4
Warwick Downs O.S. o AUS 178-179 E 1
Waryori ~ RI 166-167 G 2
Warzazāt = Ouarzazate ☆ MA 188-189 H 5
Wasa o CDN (BC) 230-231 O 4
Wasaga Beach o CDN (ONT) 238-239 E 4
Wasagaming o CDN (MAN) 234-235 D 4
Wasagu o WAN 204-205 F 3
Wasai o RI 166-167 F 2
Wasalangka o RI 164-165 H 6
Wasatch Plateau ⛰ USA (UT) 254-255 D 4
Wasatch Range ⛰ USA (ID) 252-253 G 4
Wasatch Range ⛰ USA (UT) 254-255 D 4
Wasco o USA (CA) 248-249 E 4
Wasco o USA (OR) 244-245 E 5
Wase o WAN 204-205 H 4
Wase, River ~ WAN 204-205 H 4
Waseca o CDN (SAS) 232-233 J 2
Waseca o USA (MN) 270-271 E 6
Wasel o CDN (ALB) 232-233 F 2
Washakie Wilderness Area ⊥ USA (WY) 252-253 J 3
Washago o CDN (ONT) 238-239 F 4
Washakie Needles ▲ USA (WY) 252-253 J 3
Washāp o PK 134-135 K 5
Washburn o USA (ME) 278-279 N 2
Washburn o USA (ND) 258-259 G 4
Washburn o USA (TX) 264-265 C 3
Washburn o USA (WI) 270-271 H 4
Washburne Lake ⊖ CDN 24-25 S 5
Washi Lake ⊖ CDN (ONT) 234-235 Q 3
Wāshīm o IND 138-139 F 9
Washington o USA (AR) 276-277 B 7
Washington o USA (GA) 284-285 H 3
Washington o USA (IA) 274-275 G 3
Washington o USA (IL) 274-275 J 4
Washington o USA (IN) 274-275 L 6
Washington o USA (KS) 262-263 J 5
Washington o USA (MO) 274-275 G 6
Washington o USA (MS) 268-269 J 5
Washington o USA (NC) 282-283 K 5
Washington o USA (NE) 262-263 K 3
Washington o USA (NJ) 280-281 M 3
Washington o USA (OH) 280-281 C 4
Washington o USA (PA) 280-281 F 3
Washington o USA (UT) 254-255 B 6
Washington o USA (WI) 270-271 M 5
Washington ◘ USA (WA) 244-245 B 4
Washington ★• USA (DC) 280-281 J 5
Washington, Mount ▲ USA (NH) 278-279 K 4
Washington/ Slagbaai, National Reservaat ⊥ NL 60-61 G 1
Washington Birthplace National Monument, George • USA (VA) 280-281 K 5
Washington Island ⌒ USA (WI) 270-271 M 5
Washington Land ∸ GRØ 26-27 R 3
Washington National Monument, Booker T. • USA (VA) 280-281 G 6
Washington Pass ▲ USA (WA) 244-245 E 2
Washita o USA (AR) 276-277 B 6
Washita, Fort ∴ USA (OK) 264-265 H 4
Washita River ~ USA (OK) 264-265 G 4
Washita River ~ USA (TX) 264-265 D 3
Washougal o USA (WA) 244-245 C 5
Washow Bay ⊖ CDN (MAN) 234-235 G 3
Washowng ☆ MYA 142-143 K 3
Washpool National Park ⊥ AUS 178-179 M 5
Washtucna o USA (WA) 244-245 G 4
Wāshūk o PK 134-135 L 5
Wasian o RI 166-167 G 2
Wasile o RI 164-165 K 3
Wasilla o USA 20-21 Q 6
Wasimi o WAN 204-205 E 4
Wasini Island ⌒ EAK 212-213 G 6
Wasini Marine National Park ⊥ EAK 212-213 G 6
Wāsiqa, al- o KSA 132-133 B 4
Wasir, Pulau ⌒ RI 166-167 H 4
Wāsiṭ ◘ IRQ 128-129 L 6
Wāsiṭ ∴• IRQ 128-129 M 6
Wāsiṭa, al- o KSA 130-131 F 6
Waskaganish = Fort Rupert o CDN 38-39 E 3
Waskahigan River ~ CDN (ALB) 228-229 R 2
Waskaiowaka Lake ⊖ CDN 34-35 H 2
Waskesiu Lake o CDN (SAS) 232-233 M 2
Waskesiu Lake ⊖ CDN (SAS) 232-233 M 2
Waskom o USA (TX) 264-265 K 6
Wasletan o RI 166-167 F 6
Wasola o USA (MO) 276-277 C 4
Waspam o NIC 52-53 B 4
Waspuk, Río ~ NIC 52-53 B 4
Wassadou o SN 202-203 C 3
Wassamu o J 152-153 K 2
Wassaw Island ⌒ USA (GA) 284-285 K 5
Wassaw Sound ≈ USA 284-285 K 5
Wasserburg am Inn o D 92-93 M 4
Wassou o RG 202-203 D 4
Wasta o USA (SD) 260-261 D 2
Wasu o PNG 183 D 3
Wasua o PNG 183 B 5
Wasum o PNG 183 E 4
Waswanipi o CDN (ONT) 236-237 M 3
Waswanipi, Lac ⊖ CDN (QUE) 236-237 M 3
Waswanipi, Rivière ~ CDN (QUE) 236-237 M 3
Waswanipi Indian Réserve ✕ CDN (QUE) 236-237 M 3
Wata o RI 164-165 G 5
Waṭā, al- ∸ OM 132-133 K 3
Watalgan o AUS 178-179 M 3
Watam o PNG 183 C 2
Watam o RI 164-165 L 3
Watambayoli o RI 164-165 G 4
Watampone o RI 164-165 G 6
Watamu Marine National Park ⊥ EAK 212-213 G 5
Watansoppeng o RI 164-165 F 6
Watar o IND 140-141 F 2
Watarais o PNG 183 D 4
Watarrka National Park ⊥ •• AUS 176-177 L 2
Watauga Lake ⊖ USA (TN) 282-283 F 4
Watawa o RI 166-167 D 3
Watee o SOL 184 I f 4
Waterberge ⛰ ZA 220-221 H 2
Waterberg Plateau Park ⊥ NAM 216-217 D 10
Waterbury o USA (CT) 280-281 N 2
Waterbury o USA (VT) 278-279 J 4
Waterbury Lake ⊖ CDN 30-31 R 6
Water Cay ⌒ BS 54-55 H 3
Water Cay ⌒ GB 54-55 J 4
Wateree Lake < USA (SC) 284-285 K 2
Wateree River ~ USA (SC) 284-285 K 2
Waterford o AUS 178-179 E 2
Waterford o ZA 220-221 G 6
Waterford = Port Láirge ☆• IRL 90-91 D 5
Waterfound River ~ CDN 30-31 R 6
Watergap o USA (KY) 276-277 N 3
Waterhen o CDN (MAN) 234-235 D 3
Waterhen Indian Reserve ✕ CDN (MAN) 234-235 D 3
Waterhen Lake ⊖ CDN (MAN) 234-235 D 2
Waterhen Lake ⊖ CDN (SAS) 32-33 Q 4
Waterhen River ~ CDN 32-33 Q 4
Waterhouse River ~ AUS 174-175 B 4
Waterloo o AUS 172-173 J 4
Waterloo o B 92-93 H 3
Waterloo o CDN (ONT) 238-239 E 5
Waterloo o CDN (QUE) 238-239 N 3
Waterloo o USA (AL) 284-285 B 2
Waterloo o USA (IA) 274-275 F 2
Waterloo o USA (IL) 274-275 H 6
Waterloo o USA (NY) 278-279 E 6
Waterloo o WAL 202-203 D 5
Waterman o USA (OR) 244-245 G 5
Waterport o ZA 218-219 E 6
Waterproof o USA (LA) 268-269 J 5
Waters o USA (MI) 272-273 E 3
Watersmeet o USA (MI) 270-271 J 4
Waterton Glacier International Peace Park ⊥ USA (MT) 250-251 E 3
Waterton Lakes National Park ⊥ CDN (ALB) 232-233 D 6
Waterton Park o CDN (ALB) 232-233 E 6
Waterton River ~ CDN (ALB) 232-233 E 6
Watertown o USA (MN) 270-271 E 6
Watertown o USA (NY) 278-279 F 5
Watertown o USA (SD) 260-261 J 2
Watertown o USA (TN) 276-277 J 4
Watertown o USA (WI) 274-275 K 1
Waterval-Boven o• ZA 220-221 K 2
Water Valley o CDN (ALB) 232-233 D 4
Water Valley o USA (MS) 268-269 L 2
Water Valley o USA (TX) 266-267 G 2
Waterville o CDN (QUE) 238-239 O 3
Waterville o USA (KS) 262-263 K 5
Waterville o USA (ME) 278-279 M 4
Waterville o USA (MN) 270-271 E 6
Waterville o USA (WA) 244-245 E 3
Waterville = An Coireán o IRL 90-91 B 6
Watervliet o USA (MI) 272-273 C 5
Watford o CDN (ONT) 238-239 D 6
Watford o GB 90-91 G 6
Watford City o USA (ND) 258-259 D 4
Wathaman Lake ⊖ CDN 34-35 D 2
Watheroo o AUS 176-177 D 5
Watheroo National Park ⊥ AUS 176-177 C 5
Watino o CDN 32-33 M 4
Watkin Bjerge ▲ GRØ 28-29 a 2
Watkins Glen o USA (NY) 278-279 E 6
Watkinsville o USA (GA) 284-285 G 3
Watkins Woolen Mill State Historic Site • USA (MO) 274-275 D 5
Watmuri o RI 166-167 F 5
Watnil o RI 166-167 G 4
Watoa Island ⌒ PNG 183 F 5
Watom Island ⌒ PNG 183 G 3
Watonga o USA (OK) 264-265 F 3
Watpi o PNG 183 G 3
Watri o RMM 202-203 F 2
Watrous o CDN (SAS) 232-233 N 4
Watrous o USA (NM) 256-257 L 3
Watrupun o RI 166-167 F 5
Watsa o ZRE 212-213 B 2
Watseka o USA (IL) 274-275 L 4
Watsi o ZRE 210-211 H 4
Watsikengo o ZRE 210-211 H 4
Watson o AUS 176-177 L 5
Watson o CDN (SAS) 232-233 O 3
Watson o USA (AR) 276-277 D 7
Watson Lake o CDN 30-31 E 5
Watson River ~ AUS 174-175 F 3
Watsonville o USA (CA) 248-249 C 3
Watt, Mount ▲ CDN (BC) 228-229 O 4
Watta, Hiré- o CI 202-203 H 6
Wattegama o CL 140-141 J 7
Watterson Lake ⊖ CDN 30-31 U 5
Watt Hills ⛰ AUS 176-177 F 5
Wattiwarriganna Creek ~ AUS 178-179 C 5
Watts Bar Lake ⊖ USA (TN) 282-283 C 5
Wattsview o CDN (MAN) 234-235 B 4
Wattsville o USA (VA) 280-281 L 6
Watubela, Kepulauan ⌒ RI 166-167 F 4
Watukebo, Tanjung ▲ RI 166-167 G 4
Watumanuk, Tanjung ▲ RI 168 E 7
Watumohai, Gunung ▲ RI 164-165 H 6
Watunea o RI 164-165 H 6
Watupati, Tanjung ▲ RI 166-167 E 6
Watutau o RI 164-165 G 4
Wau o PNG 183 D 4
Wau o RI 166-167 G 2
Wāu o SUD 206-207 H 5
Wāu ~ SUD 206-207 H 5
Waubaushene o CDN (ONT) 238-239 F 4
Waubay o USA (SD) 260-261 J 1
Waubra o AUS 180-181 G 4
Wauchope o AUS (NSW) 178-179 M 6
Wauchope o AUS (NT) 174-175 C 7
Wauchope o CDN (SAS) 232-233 R 6
Wauconda o USA (WA) 244-245 G 2
Waukaringa o AUS 180-181 E 2
Waukarlycarly, Lake ⊖ AUS 172-173 E 6
Waukegan o USA (IL) 274-275 L 2
Waukena o USA (CA) 248-249 E 3
Waukesha o USA (WI) 274-275 K 1
Waukon o USA (IA) 274-275 G 1
Wauneta o USA (NE) 262-263 E 4
Waupaca o USA (WI) 270-271 J 6
Waupun o USA (WI) 270-271 K 7
Waurika o USA (OK) 264-265 G 4
Waurika Lake ⊖ USA (OK) 264-265 F 4
Wausau o USA (WI) 270-271 J 6
Wausaukee o USA (WI) 270-271 L 5
Wautoma o USA (WI) 270-271 J 6
Wauwatosa o USA (WI) 274-275 K 1
Wave Hill o AUS 172-173 K 4
Waverley o CDN (NS) 240-241 M 6
Waverley Game Sanctuary ⊥ CDN (NS) 240-241 M 6
Waverly o USA (GA) 284-285 J 5
Waverly o USA (IA) 274-275 F 2
Waverly o USA (IL) 274-275 J 5
Waverly o USA (MO) 274-275 E 5
Waverly o USA (NE) 262-263 K 4
Waverly o USA (NY) 278-279 E 6
Waverly o USA (OH) 280-281 D 4
Waverly o USA (TN) 276-277 H 4
Waverly o USA (VA) 280-281 J 6
Waverly Hall o USA (GA) 284-285 F 4
Wave Rock •• AUS 176-177 E 6
Wawa o CDN (ONT) 236-237 D 5
Wawa o WAN 204-205 E 4
Wawa, Río = Río Huahua ~ NIC 52-53 B 4
Wawagosic, Rivière ~ CDN (QUE) 236-237 K 3
Wawalalindu o RI 164-165 H 5
Wāw al Kabīr o LAR 192-193 G 5
Wawan o RP 160-161 D 6
Wawanesa o CDN (MAN) 234-235 D 5
Wawawai o USA (WA) 244-245 H 4
Wawiwa Island ⌒ PNG 183 F 5
Wawo o RI 164-165 G 5
Wawoi River ~ PNG 183 B 4
Wawolandawe o RI 164-165 H 5
Waworada o RI 168 D 7
Waworada, Teluk ≈ 168 D 7
Wawota o CDN (SAS) 232-233 Q 6
Wawotobi o RI 164-165 H 5
Wawousu o RI 164-165 H 6
Waxahachie o USA (TX) 264-265 H 6
Waxxari o VRC 146-147 H 6
Way, Lake ⊖ AUS 176-177 F 3
Waya ⌒ FJI 184 III a 2
Wayabula o RI 164-165 L 2
Wayag, Pulau ⌒ RI 166-167 F 1
Wayamli o RI 164-165 L 3
Wayamli, Tanjung ▲ RI 164-165 L 3
Wayaua o RI 164-165 K 4
Waycross o USA (GA) 284-285 H 5
Wayerton o CDN (NB) 240-241 K 3
Waygay o RI (MAL) 164-165 J 4
Waygay o RI (MAL) 164-165 J 5
Wayhaya o RI 164-165 J 4
Waykadai o RI 164-165 J 4
Waykilo o RI 164-165 J 4
Wayland o USA (KY) 276-277 N 3
Wayland o USA (MI) 272-273 D 5
Wayland o USA (NY) 278-279 D 6
Wayne o CDN (ALB) 232-233 F 4
Wayne o USA (AL) 284-285 C 4
Wayne o USA (MI) 272-273 F 5
Wayne o USA (NE) 262-263 J 2
Wayne o USA (WV) 280-281 D 5
Wayne City o USA (IL) 274-275 K 6
Waynesboro o USA (GA) 284-285 H 3
Waynesboro o USA (MS) 268-269 M 5
Waynesboro o USA (PA) 280-281 J 4
Waynesboro o USA (TN) 276-277 H 5
Waynesboro o USA (VA) 280-281 H 5
Waynesburg o USA (KY) 276-277 L 3
Waynesburg o USA (PA) 280-281 F 4
Waynesville o USA (GA) 284-285 J 5
Waynesville o USA (MO) 276-277 C 3
Waynesville o USA (NC) 282-283 E 5
Waynoka o USA (OK) 264-265 F 2
Wayongon o MYA 142-143 J 3
Wayside o USA (NE) 262-263 C 2
Wayside o USA (VA) 280-281 J 6
Waza o CAM 206-207 B 3
Waza, Parc National de ⊥ CAM 206-207 B 3
Wāzaḥwa = Vāzaḥā o AFG 138-139 B 3
Wazān = Ouezzane o MA 188-189 J 3
Wāzin o LAR 190-191 H 5
Wazirābād o PK 138-139 E 3
W du Niger, Parc National du ⊥ BF 204-205 E 2
We o CAM 204-205 J 5
Weagamow Lake o CDN (ONT) 234-235 M 2
Weagamow Lake ⊖ CDN (ONT) 234-235 M 2
Weald o CDN (ALB) 232-233 B 2
Weam o PNG 183 A 5
Weasua o LB 202-203 E 6
Weatherall Bay ≈ 24-25 S 2
Weatherford o USA (OK) 264-265 F 3
Weatherford o USA (TX) 264-265 G 6
Weaton o USA (MD) 280-281 J 4
Weaver o USA (MN) 270-271 G 6
Weaver Lake ⊖ CDN (MAN) 234-235 G 2
Weaverville o USA (CA) 246-247 C 3
Weaverville o USA (NC) 282-283 E 5
Webb o CDN (SAS) 232-233 K 5
Webb o USA (TX) 266-267 H 6
Webb, Mount ▲ AUS 172-173 J 7
Webb City o USA (MO) 276-277 A 3
Webbers Falls Lake < USA (OK) 264-265 J 3
Webb Gemstone Deposit • AUS 176-177 E 3
Webbville o USA (KY) 276-277 N 2
Webequie o CDN (ONT) 234-235 Q 2
Weber o NZ 182 F 4
Weber o USA (AR) 276-277 D 6
Webster o USA (MA) 278-279 K 6
Webster o USA (ND) 258-259 J 3
Webster o USA (NY) 278-279 D 5
Webster o USA (SD) 260-261 J 1
Webster City o USA (IA) 274-275 E 2
Webster Reservoir o USA (KS) 262-263 G 5
Webster Springs o USA (WV) 280-281 F 5
Webuye o EAK 212-213 E 3
Wech'echa ▲ ETH 208-209 D 4
Weches o USA (TX) 268-269 E 5
Wecho Lake ⊖ CDN 30-31 N 4
Wecho River ~ CDN 30-31 M 4
Weda o RI 164-165 K 3
Weda, Teluk ≈ 164-165 L 3
Wedangkau o RI 166-167 F 5
Weddell Island ⌒ GB 78-79 K 6
Weddell Sea ≈ ARK 16 F 32
Wedderburn o AUS 180-181 G 4
Weddin Mountain National Park ⊥ AUS 180-181 K 2
Wedel Jarlsberg Land ∸ N 84-85 J 4
Wedgefield o USA (SC) 284-285 K 3
Wedge Island ⌒ AUS 176-177 C 5
Wedge Mountain ▲ CDN (BC) 230-231 G 3
Wedge Point o CDN (NS) 240-241 K 7
Wednesday Island ⌒ AUS 183 B 6
Wedowee o USA (AL) 284-285 E 3
Weduar o RI 166-167 G 4
Weduar, Tanjung ▲ RI 166-167 G 4
Wedweil o SUD 206-207 H 4
Weebubbie Caves ⊥ AUS 176-177 K 5
Weed o USA (CA) 246-247 C 2
Weed o USA (NM) 256-257 K 6
Weed Patch Hill ▲ USA (IN) 274-275 M 5
Weedville o USA (PA) 280-281 H 2
Weeim, Pulau ⌒ RI 166-167 F 2
Weekes o CDN (SAS) 232-233 Q 4
Weeki Wachee Spring • USA (FL) 286-287 G 3
Weeks o USA (LA) 268-269 J 7
Weelarrana o AUS 176-177 F 1
Weelhamby Lake ⊖ AUS 176-177 D 4
Weemarie, Lake ⊖ AUS 178-179 E 3
Weenen o ZA 220-221 K 4
Weeping Water o USA (NE) 262-263 K 4
Weesatche o USA (TX) 266-267 K 5
Weethalle o AUS 180-181 J 2
Wee Waa o AUS 178-179 K 6
Wegdraai o ZA 220-221 E 4
Wegener-Inlandeis ⊂ ARK 16 F 36
Węgorzewo o• PL 92-93 Q 1
Weh, Pulau ⌒ RI 162-163 A 2
Wehni o ETH 200-201 H 6
Weichang o VRC 148-149 N 7
Weiden in der Oberpfalz o D 92-93 M 4
Weidman o USA (MI) 272-273 E 4
Weifang o VRC 154-155 L 3
Weihai o VRC 154-155 N 3
Wei He ~ VRC 154-155 E 4
Wei He ~ VRC 154-155 J 4
Weihui o VRC 154-155 J 4
Weila o GH 202-203 K 5
Weilmoringle o AUS 178-179 J 5
Weimar o• D 92-93 L 3
Weimar o USA (TX) 266-267 L 4
Wein, Bur ▲ EAK 212-213 H 2
Weinan o VRC 154-155 F 4
Weiner o USA (AR) 276-277 E 5
Weinert o USA (TX) 264-265 E 5
Weining o VRC 156-157 D 3
Weipa o AUS 174-175 F 3
Weipa South ✕ AUS 174-175 F 3
Weirdale o CDN (SAS) 232-233 N 2
Weir River ~ AUS 178-179 K 5
Weir River o CDN (MAN) 34-35 J 2
Weir River ~ CDN 34-35 K 2
Weirton o USA (OH) 280-281 F 3
Weiser o USA (ID) 252-253 B 2
Weiser River ~ USA (ID) 252-253 B 2
Weishan o VRC 154-155 K 4
Weishan Hu ~ VRC 154-155 K 4
Weishi o VRC 154-155 J 4
Weiss o USA (LA) 268-269 K 6
Weiss Lake < USA (AL) 284-285 E 2
Weitchpec o USA (CA) 246-247 B 2
Weitou o VRC 156-157 L 4
Weixi o VRC 142-143 L 2
Wei Xian o VRC 154-155 J 3
Weixin o VRC 156-157 D 3
Weiya o VRC 146-147 M 5
Weiyuan o VRC (GAN) 154-155 D 4
Weiyuan o VRC (SIC) 156-157 D 2
Weizhou Dao ⌒ VRC 156-157 F 6
Wekakura Point ▲ NZ 182 D 4
Weko o ZRE 210-211 K 3
Wekusko o CDN 34-35 G 3
Wekusko Lake ⊖ CDN 34-35 G 3
Welab o RI 166-167 K 6
Welanpela o CL 140-141 J 7

Welatam ○ MYA 142-143 L 2
Welbedacht Dam < ZA 220-221 H 4
Welby ○ CDN (SAS) 232-233 R 5
Welch ○ USA (OK) 264-265 J 2
Welch ○ USA (TX) 264-265 B 6
Welch ○ USA (WV) 280-281 E 6
Welchman Hall Gully • BDS 56 F 5
Weldiya ○ ETH 208-209 D 3
Weldon ○ USA (NC) 282-283 K 4
Weldon River ∼ USA (MO) 274-275 E 4
Weldon Spring ○ USA (MO) 274-275 H 6
Weld Range ▲▲ AUS 176-177 D 3
Weleetka ○ USA (OK) 264-265 H 3
Welega □ ETH 208-209 B 4
Welench'iti ○ ETH 208-209 D 4
Weligama ○ • CL 140-141 J 8
Welisara ○ CL 140-141 H 7
Wel Jara < EAK 212-213 H 4
Welk'itē ○ ETH 208-209 C 4
Welkom ○ ZA 220-221 H 3
Well ○ USA (KY) 276-277 K 3
Welland ○ CDN (ONT) 238-239 F 6
Wella-Sofon-Gari ○ RN 204-205 E 1
Wellawaya ○ CL 140-141 J 7
Wellesley Basin ⩡ CDN 20-21 U 5
Wellesley Islands ⌒ AUS 174-175 E 5
Wellesley Lake ⊖ CDN 20-21 V 5
Welling ○ CDN (ALB) 232-233 F 6
Wellington ○ AUS 180-181 K 2
Wellington ○ CDN (NS) 240-241 M 6
Wellington ○ CDN (ONT) 238-239 H 5
Wellington ★ NZ 182 E 4
Wellington ○ USA (AL) 284-285 E 3
Wellington ○ USA (CO) 254-255 K 3
Wellington ○ USA (KS) 262-263 J 7
Wellington ○ USA (NV) 246-247 F 5
Wellington ○ USA (OH) 280-281 D 2
Wellington ○ USA (TX) 264-265 D 4
Wellington ○ USA (UT) 254-255 E 4
Wellington ○ ZA 220-221 D 6
Wellington, Isla ⌒ RCH 80 C 4
Wellington, Lake ⊖ AUS 180-181 J 5
Wellington Bay ≈ 24-25 S 6
Wellington Caves • AUS 180-181 K 2
Wellington Channel ≈ 24-25 Z 3
Wellington Range ▲▲ AUS 176-177 F 3
Wellman ○ USA (TX) 264-265 B 5
Wells ○ CDN (BC) 228-229 N 3
Wells ○ USA (MN) 270-271 E 7
Wells ○ USA (NV) 246-247 L 2
Wells ○ USA (TX) 268-269 F 5
Wells, Lake ⊖ AUS 176-177 G 3
Wellsford ○ NZ 182 E 2
Wells Gray Provincial Park ⊥ CDN (BC) 228-229 O 4
Wells Lake ⊖ CDN 34-35 F 2
Wellstead ○ AUS 176-177 E 7
Wellston ○ USA (MI) 272-273 D 3
Wellston ○ USA (OH) 280-281 D 4
Wellsville ○ USA (MO) 274-275 G 5
Wellsville ○ USA (NY) 278-279 D 6
Wellsville ○ USA (UT) 254-255 D 2
Wellwood ○ CDN (MAN) 234-235 D 4
Welmel Shet' ∼ ETH 208-209 E 6
Wel Meret < EAK 212-213 H 2
Wels ○ A 92-93 N 4
Welsford ○ CDN (NB) 240-241 J 5
Welsford, Cape ▲ CDN 36-37 G 2
Welsh ○ USA (LA) 268-269 H 6
Welshpool ○ CDN (NB) 240-241 J 6
Welshpool ○ • GB 90-91 F 5
Welshpool, Port ○ AUS 180-181 J 5
Welton ○ USA (AZ) 256-257 B 6
Welutu ○ RI 166-167 F 5
Welwel ○ ETH 208-209 G 5
Welwyn ○ CDN (SAS) 232-233 R 5
Wema ○ ZRE 210-211 H 4
Wembere ∼ EAT 212-213 E 6
Wembi ○ RI 166-167 L 3
Wembley ○ CDN 32-33 L 4
Wemindji ○ CDN 38-39 E 2
Wen ○ SUD 206-207 H 4
Wenago ○ ETH 208-209 D 5
Wenaha Tucannon Wilderness Area ⊥ USA (WA) 244-245 H 4
Wenasaga River ∼ CDN (ONT) 234-235 K 4
Wenatchee ○ USA (WA) 244-245 E 3
Wenatchee Mountains ▲▲ USA (WA) 244-245 E 3
Wenceslao Escalante ○ RA 78-79 H 2
Wenchang ○ VRC (HAI) 156-157 G 7
Wenchang ○ VRC (SIC) 154-155 E 6
Wenchi ○ GH 202-203 J 6
Wenchiki ○ GH 202-203 L 4
Wench'īt Shet' ∼ ETH 208-209 D 3
Wenchuan ○ VRC 154-155 C 6
Wendell ○ USA (ID) 252-253 D 4
Wenden ○ USA (AZ) 256-257 B 5
Wendeng ○ VRC 154-155 N 3
Wendesi ○ RI 166-167 H 3
Wendi ○ RI 164-165 J 4
Wendi ○ VRC 156-157 G 6
Wendo ○ ETH 208-209 D 5
Wendou Borou ○ RG 202-203 D 4
Wendover ○ USA (UT) 254-255 A 3
Wendover Range ✕✕ USA (UT) 254-255 B 3
Wenebegon Lake ⊖ CDN (ONT) 236-237 E 5
Wenga ○ ZRE 210-211 G 3
Weng'an ○ VRC 156-157 E 3
Wenge ○ ZRE 210-211 K 3
Weni ○ NEP 144-145 D 6
Wenlock ∴ AUS 174-175 G 3
Wenlock River ∼ AUS 174-175 F 3
Wenona ○ USA (IL) 274-275 J 3
Wenona ○ USA (MD) 280-281 L 5
Wenquan ○ VRC 144-145 H 4
Wenshan ○ VRC 156-157 D 5
Wen Shang ○ VRC 154-155 K 4
Wenshui ○ VRC (GZH) 156-157 E 2
Wenshui ○ VRC (SHA) 154-155 G 3
Wentworth ○ AUS 180-181 F 3
Wentworth ○ USA (SD) 260-261 K 3
Wentworth Centre ○ CDN (NS) 240-241 M 5
Wentworth Springs ○ USA (CA) 246-247 E 4
Wentzel Lake ⊖ CDN (ALB) 30-31 M 6
Wentzel Lake ⊖ CDN (NWT) 30-31 M 2
Wentzel River ∼ CDN 30-31 M 6
Wentzville ○ USA (MO) 274-275 H 6
Wenxi ○ VRC 154-155 G 4
Wen Xian ○ VRC 154-155 D 5
Wenzhen ○ VRC 156-157 K 2
Wenzhou ○ VRC 156-157 M 2
Wenzhou Wan ≈ 156-157 M 3
Weohyakapka, Lake ⊖ USA (FL) 286-287 H 4
Weott ○ USA (CA) 246-247 B 3
Wepener ○ ZA 220-221 H 4
Wer ○ IND 138-139 F 6
Werda ○ RB 220-221 F 2
Werdēr ○ ETH 208-209 G 5
Were Īlu ○ ETH 208-209 D 3
Wemadinga ○ AUS 174-175 E 6
Werner Lake ○ CDN (ONT) 234-235 J 4
Werota ○ ETH 208-209 C 3
Wer Ping ○ SUD 206-207 J 4
Werra ∼ D 92-93 L 3
Werribee ○ AUS 180-181 H 4
Werrikimbie National Park ⊥ AUS 178-179 M 6
Werris Creek ○ AUS 178-179 L 6
Wertach ∼ D 92-93 L 4
Wesel ○ D 92-93 J 3
Weser ∼ D 92-93 K 2
Weskan ○ USA (KS) 262-263 E 6
Weslaco ○ USA (TX) 266-267 J 7
Weslemkoon ○ CDN (ONT) 238-239 H 4
Weslemkoon Lake ⊖ CDN (ONT) 238-239 H 3
Wesley ○ USA (ME) 278-279 O 4
Wesleyville ○ CDN (NFL) 242-243 P 3
Wessel, Cape ▲ AUS 174-175 D 2
Wessel Islands ⌒ AUS 174-175 D 2
Wesselsbron ○ ZA 220-221 H 3
Wessington ○ USA (SD) 260-261 H 2
Wessington Springs ○ USA (SD) 260-261 H 2
Wesson ○ USA (MS) 268-269 K 5
West ○ USA (MS) 268-269 L 3
West ○ USA (TX) 266-267 K 2
West = Ouest □ CAM 204-205 J 6
West Amatuli Island ⌒ USA 22-23 V 3
West Arm ○ CDN (ONT) 238-239 E 2
West Baines River ∼ AUS 172-173 J 4
Westbank ○ CDN (BC) 230-231 K 4
West Bay ≈ 48-49 D 5
West Bay ○ CDN (NS) 240-241 O 5
West Bay ○ CDN (ONT) 238-239 C 3
West Bay ○ • GB 54-55 E 5
West Bay ≈ USA 286-287 D 1
West Bend ○ CDN (SAS) 232-233 P 4
West Bend ○ USA (IA) 274-275 D 2
West Bend ○ USA (WI) 274-275 K 1
West Bengal □ IND 142-143 E 4
West Berlin ○ CDN (NS) 240-241 L 6
West Bijou Creek ∼ USA (CO) 254-255 L 4
West Blocton ○ USA (AL) 284-285 C 3
Westboro ○ USA (WI) 270-271 H 5
Westbourne ○ CDN (MAN) 234-235 E 4
West Branch ○ USA (IA) 274-275 G 3
West Branch ○ USA (MI) 272-273 E 3
Westbridge ○ CDN (BC) 230-231 L 4
West Brook ∼ CDN (NFL) 242-243 M 1
Westbrook ○ USA (ME) 278-279 L 5
Westbrook ○ USA (MN) 270-271 C 6
Westbrook ○ USA (TX) 264-265 C 6
West Burke ○ USA (VT) 278-279 K 4
Westbury ○ AUS 178-179 H 2
West Butte ▲ USA (MT) 250-251 H 3
Westby ○ USA (MT) 250-251 P 3
Westby ○ USA (WI) 270-271 H 7
West Caicos ⌒ GB 54-55 J 4
West Canada Creek ∼ USA (NY) 278-279 G 5
West Cape Howe ▲ AUS 176-177 D 7
West-Cape Province □ ZA 220-221 D 6
West Channel ∼ CDN 20-21 X 2
West Chester ○ USA (OH) 280-281 E 3
West Chichagof Yakobi Wilderness ⊥ • USA 32-33 B 3
Westcliffe ○ USA (CO) 254-255 K 5
West Coast National Park ⊥ ZA 220-221 D 6
West Columbia ○ USA (SC) 284-285 J 2
West Columbia ○ USA (TX) 268-269 E 7
West Cote Blanche Bay ≈ USA 268-269 J 7
West Covina ○ USA (CA) 248-249 G 5
West Des Moines ○ USA (IA) 274-275 E 3
West End ○ BS 54-55 F 1
West End ○ GB 54-55 F 5
Westerberg ○ ZA 220-221 F 4
Westerland ○ D 92-93 K 1
Westerly ○ USA (RI) 278-279 K 7
Western □ EAK 212-213 E 3
Western □ EAU 212-213 C 3
Western □ PNG 183 A 4
Western ○ USA (NE) 262-263 J 4
Western □ Z 218-219 B 2
Western Australia □ AUS 176-177 F 1
Western Creek ∼ AUS 178-179 L 4
Western Desert = Ṣaḥrā' al-Garbīa, as- ⩡ ET 194-195 B 4
Western Entrance ≈ 184 I b 2
Western Ghāts ⩡ IND 10-11 G 7
Western Head ▲ CDN (NS) 240-241 K 7
Western Island ⌒ PNG 183 C 2
Western Kentucky Parkway II USA (KY) 276-277 H 3
Western Plains Zoo • AUS 180-181 K 2
Westernport ○ USA (MD) 280-281 G 4
Western Region □ GH 202-203 J 6
Western River ∼ CDN 30-31 Q 2
Western Sahara ■ WSA 196-197 C 2
Western Samoa ⌒ WS 184 V a 1
Western Samoa = Sāmoa-i-Sisifo ■ WS 184 V b 1
Western Sayan Mountains = Zapadnyj Sajan ▲▲ RUS 116-117 D 9
Western Tasmania National Parks ⊥ ··· AUS 180-181 H 7
Western Thebes ∴ ·· ET 194-195 F 5
Western Waigeo Pulau Reserve ⊥ • RI 166-167 F 2
Western Yamuna Canal < IND 138-139 F 5
Westerschelde ≈ 92-93 G 3
Westerville ○ USA (NE) 262-263 G 3
Westerville ○ USA (OH) 280-281 D 3
Westerwald ▲▲ D 92-93 J 3
West Falkland ⌒ GB 78-79 L 6
Westfall ○ USA (OR) 244-245 H 7
West Fargo ○ USA (ND) 258-259 L 5
Westfield ○ CDN (NB) 240-241 J 5
Westfield ○ USA (MA) 278-279 J 6
Westfield ○ USA (ND) 258-259 G 5
Westfield ○ USA (NY) 278-279 B 6
West Fork ∼ USA (MO) 274-275 G 5
West Fork ∼ USA (MT) 250-251 N 3
West Fork Big Blue River ∼ USA (NE) 262-263 H 4
West Fork des Moines ∼ USA (IA) 274-275 D 1
West Fork Grand River ∼ USA (IA) 274-275 D 4
West Fork River ∼ USA (WV) 280-281 F 4
West Fork Trinity ∼ USA (TX) 264-265 F 5
West Frankfort ○ USA (IL) 276-277 G 3
West Frisian Islands = Waddeneilanden ⩡ NL 92-93 H 2
Westgard Pass ▲ USA (CA) 248-249 F 2
Westgate ○ AUS 178-179 J 4
Westgate ○ CDN (MAN) 234-235 B 2
West Glacier ○ USA (MT) 250-251 F 3
West Gletscher ⊂ GRØ 26-27 I 8
West Group ⌒ AUS 176-177 F 6
West Hamlin ○ USA (WV) 280-281 D 5
West Haverstraw ○ USA (NY) 280-281 M 2
West Hawk Lake ○ CDN (MAN) 234-235 H 5
West Helena ○ USA (AR) 276-277 E 6
West Hobolochitto Creek ∼ USA (MS) 268-269 L 6
Westhoff ○ USA (TX) 266-267 K 4
West Holothuria Reef ⌒ AUS 172-173 G 2
Westhope ○ USA (ND) 258-259 F 3
West Ice Shelf ⊂ ARK 16 G 9
West Indies ⩡ 4 G 6
West Island ⌒ AUS (NT) 174-175 D 4
West Island ⌒ AUS (WA) 176-177 F 6
West Jordan ○ USA (UT) 254-255 C 3
West Kettle River ∼ CDN (BC) 230-231 K 4
West Lafayette ○ USA (IN) 274-275 M 4
Westlake ○ USA (LA) 268-269 G 6
Westland National Park ⊥ ··· NZ 182 C 5
West Levant ○ USA (ME) 278-279 N 4
West Liberty ○ USA (IA) 274-275 G 3
West Liberty ○ USA (KY) 276-277 M 3
West Liberty ○ USA (OH) 280-281 C 3
West Linn ○ USA (OR) 244-245 C 5
Westlock ○ CDN 32-33 O 4
West Lorne ○ CDN (ONT) 238-239 D 6
West Lunga ∼ Z 214-215 C 7
West Lunga National Park ⊥ Z 214-215 C 7
Westmar ○ AUS 178-179 K 4
Westmeath ○ CDN (QUE) 238-239 J 3
West Memphis ○ USA (AR) 276-277 E 5
Westminster ○ USA (CO) 254-255 K 4
Westminster ○ USA (MD) 280-281 K 4
Westminster ○ USA (SC) 284-285 G 2
Westminster ○ ZA 220-221 H 4
Westmond ○ USA (ID) 250-251 C 3
West Monroe ○ USA (LA) 268-269 H 4
Westmoreland ○ AUS 174-175 E 5
Westmoreland ○ USA (KS) 262-263 K 5
Westmoreland ○ USA (TN) 276-277 J 4
Westmorland ○ USA (CA) 248-249 J 6
Westmount ○ CDN (NS) 240-241 P 4
West Mount Barren ▲ AUS 176-177 E 7
West Nicholson ○ ZW 218-219 E 5
Weston ○ USA (FL) 286-287 J 5
Weston ○ USA (ID) 252-253 G 4
Weston ○ USA (OR) 244-245 G 5
Weston ○ USA (WV) 280-281 F 4
Weston ○ USA (WY) 252-253 N 2
Weston-Super-Mare ○ GB 90-91 F 6
West Ossipee ○ USA (NH) 278-279 K 5
West Palm Beach ○ ·· USA (FL) 286-287 J 5
West Plains ○ USA (MO) 276-277 D 4
West Point ▲ AUS (SA) 180-181 C 3
West Point ▲ AUS (TAS) 180-181 H 6
West Point ○ CDN (PEI) 240-241 L 4
Westpoint ○ GB 78-79 K 6
West Point ○ USA (IA) 274-275 G 4
West Point ○ USA (MS) 268-269 M 3
West Point ○ USA (NE) 262-263 K 3
West Point ○ USA (NY) 280-281 N 2
West Point ○ USA (TX) 264-265 B 5
West Point ○ USA (VA) 280-281 K 6
West Point ▲ USA (AK) 20-21 S 4
West Point ▲ WAN 204-205 H 6
West Point Lake < USA (GA) 284-285 E 3
West Poplar ○ CDN (SAS) 232-233 M 6
Westport ○ CDN (NFL) 242-243 M 3
Westport ○ CDN (ONT) 238-239 J 4
Westport ○ NZ 182 C 4
Westport ○ USA (CA) 246-247 B 4
Westport ○ USA (OR) 244-245 B 4
Westport ○ USA (WA) 244-245 A 4
Westport = Cathair na Mart ○ • IRL 90-91 C 5
West Prairie River ∼ CDN 32-33 M 4
Westpunt ○ NL 60-61 G 1
Westray ○ CDN 34-35 F 4
Westray ⌒ GB 90-91 F 2
Westree ○ CDN (ONT) 236-237 G 5
West Richland ○ USA (WA) 244-245 F 4
West River ∼ CDN 24-25 H 6
West River ∼ USA (VT) 278-279 J 5
West Road River ∼ CDN (BC) 228-229 K 3
West Saint-Modeste ○ CDN (NFL) 242-243 M 1
West Salem ○ USA (IL) 274-275 K 6
West Salem ○ USA (OH) 280-281 D 3
West Scotia Ridge ≃ 6-7 D 14
West Sepik □ PNG 183 A 2
West Siberian Plain = Zapadno-Sibirskaja ravnina ⩡ RUS 114-115 J 2
Westside ○ USA (MS) 268-269 J 5
West Springfield ○ USA (PA) 280-281 F 2
West Taghkanic ○ USA (NY) 278-279 H 6
West Thumb ○ USA (WY) 252-253 H 2
West Travaputs Plateau ▲▲ USA (UT) 254-255 E 4
West Union ○ USA (IA) 274-275 G 2
West Union ○ USA (IL) 274-275 L 5
West Union ○ USA (OH) 280-281 C 5
West Union ○ USA (WV) 280-281 F 4
West Unity ○ USA (OH) 280-281 B 2
West Valley City ○ USA (UT) 254-255 C 3
West Vancouver ○ CDN (BC) 230-231 F 4
Westview ○ CDN (BC) 230-231 E 4
Westville ○ USA (IL) 274-275 L 4
Westville ○ USA (IN) 274-275 M 3
Westville ○ USA (OK) 264-265 K 3
Westville • USA (GA) 284-285 F 4
West Virginia □ USA (WV) 280-281 F 4
West Warwick ○ USA (RI) 278-279 K 7
West Wendover ○ USA (NV) 246-247 L 3
Westwold ○ CDN (BC) 230-231 K 3
Westwood ○ AUS 178-179 L 2
Westwood ○ USA (CA) 246-247 E 3
West Wyalong ○ AUS 180-181 J 2
West Yellowstone ○ USA (MT) 250-251 H 7
West York Island ⌒ 160-161 A 7
Wetalltok Bay ≈ 36-37 K 7
Wetan, Pulau ⌒ RI 166-167 E 5
Wetar, Pulau ⌒ RI 166-167 D 5
Wetar, Selat ≈ 166-167 C 6
Wetaskiwin ○ CDN (ALB) 232-233 E 3
Wete ○ EAT 212-213 G 6
Wete ○ ZRE 210-211 K 6
Wetetnagami, Lac ⊖ CDN (QUE) 236-237 M 4
Wetetnagami, Rivière ∼ CDN (QUE) 236-237 M 4
Wetherell, Lake ⊖ AUS 180-181 G 2
Wetmore ○ USA (CO) 254-255 K 5
Wetmore ○ USA (MI) 270-271 M 4
Wet Mountains ▲▲ USA (CO) 254-255 K 6
Weto ○ WAN 204-205 G 5
Wetonka ○ USA (SD) 260-261 H 1
Wettlet ○ MYA 142-143 J 4
Wet Tropics of Queensland ⊥ ··· AUS 174-175 H 5
Wetumka ○ USA (OK) 264-265 H 3
Wetumpka ○ USA (AL) 284-285 D 4
Wetzlar ○ • D 92-93 K 3
Wevok ○ USA 20-21 G 2
Wewahitchka ○ USA (FL) 286-287 D 1
Wewak ☆ PNG 183 B 2
Wewela ○ USA (SD) 260-261 G 3
Wewoka ○ USA (OK) 264-265 H 3
Wexford = Loch Garman ☆ IRL 90-91 D 5
Weyakwin ○ CDN 34-35 D 3
Weyburn ○ CDN (SAS) 232-233 P 6
Weyland, Point ▲ AUS 180-181 C 2
Weymontachie Indian Reservation ✕ • CDN (QUE) 236-237 P 5
Weymouth ○ CDN (NS) 240-241 K 6
Weymouth ○ • GB 90-91 F 6
Weymouth, Cape ▲ AUS 174-175 G 3
Weymouth Bay ≈ 174-175 G 3
Whakatane ○ NZ 182 F 2
Whalan ○ USA (MN) 270-271 G 7
Whalan Creek ∼ AUS 178-179 K 5
Whaleback Mining Area, Mount • AUS 176-177 E 1
Whale Bay ≈ 32-33 C 3
Whale Bay ≈ 158-159 E 5
Whale Cay ⌒ BS 54-55 G 2
Whale Channel ≈ CDN 228-229 E 3
Whale Cove ○ CDN 30-31 X 4
Whale Island ⌒ USA 22-23 U 4
Whale Point ▲ CDN 36-37 F 2
Whaletown ○ CDN (BC) 230-231 E 3
Whangamata ○ NZ 182 E 2
Whanganui National Park • NZ 182 E 3
Whangarei ○ NZ 182 E 1
Wharfe ∼ GB 90-91 F 4
Wharton ○ USA (TX) 266-267 L 4
Wharton, Peninsula ∼ RCH 80 C 4
Wharton Lake ⊖ CDN 30-31 T 3
Whatshan Lake ⊖ CDN (BC) 230-231 L 3
Wheatland ○ CDN (MAN) 234-235 C 4
Wheatland ○ USA (CA) 246-247 D 4
Wheatland ○ USA (NM) 256-257 M 4
Wheatland ○ USA (WY) 252-253 O 4
Wheatland Reservoir No.2 < USA (WY) 252-253 N 5
Wheatley ○ CDN (ONT) 238-239 C 6
Wheaton ○ USA (IL) 274-275 K 3
Wheaton ○ USA (MN) 270-271 B 5
Wheeler ○ USA (TX) 264-265 D 3
Wheeler ○ USA (WI) 270-271 G 5
Wheeler Lake < USA (AL) 284-285 C 2
Wheeler National Wildlife Refuge ⊥ USA (AL) 284-285 D 2
Wheeler Peak ▲ USA (NM) 256-257 K 2
Wheeler Peak ▲ USA (NV) 246-247 L 5
Wheeler Ridge ○ USA 248-249 E 4
Wheeler River ∼ CDN 34-35 D 2
Wheelers Point ○ USA (MN) 270-271 D 2
Wheeling ○ USA (IN) 274-275 M 4
Wheeling ○ USA (WV) 280-281 F 3
Wheelock ○ USA (TX) 266-267 L 3
Whela Creek ∼ AUS 176-177 D 3
Whelan, Mount ▲ AUS 178-179 E 2
Whewell, Mount ▲ ARK 16 F 17
Whidbey Island ⌒ USA (WA) 244-245 C 2
Whidbey Isles ⌒ AUS 180-181 C 3
Whim Creek ○ AUS 172-173 C 6
Whirlwind Lake ⊖ CDN 30-31 P 5
Whiskey Gap ○ CDN (ALB) 232-233 E 6
Whiskey Jack Lake ⊖ CDN 30-31 T 6
Whiskeytown ⊥ USA (CA) 246-247 C 3
Whisky Chitto Creek ∼ USA (LA) 268-269 G 6
Whispering Pines ○ USA (CA) 246-247 C 5
Whistler ○ CDN (BC) 230-231 G 3
Whitbourne ○ CDN (NFL) 242-243 P 5
Whitby ○ CDN (ONT) 238-239 G 5
Whitby ○ • GB 90-91 G 4
Whitchurch ○ GB 90-91 F 5
White ○ USA (GA) 284-285 F 2
White, Lake ⊖ AUS 172-173 J 6
White, Mount ▲ AUS 176-177 F 3
White Bay ≈ 38-39 Q 3
White Bay ≈ CDN 242-243 M 2
White Bear ○ CDN (SAS) 232-233 K 5
White Bear Lake ○ USA (MN) 270-271 E 5
Whitebear Point ▲ CDN 24-25 U 6
White Bear River ∼ CDN (NFL) 242-243 L 4
White Bird ○ USA (ID) 250-251 C 6
White Bluff ○ USA (TN) 276-277 H 4
White Butte ▲ USA (ND) 258-259 D 5
White Cape Mount ▲ USA (ME) 278-279 M 3
White Castle ○ USA (LA) 268-269 J 6
White Cay ⌒ BS 54-55 H 2
White City ○ CDN (SAS) 232-233 O 5
White City ○ USA (KS) 262-263 K 6
Whiteclay ○ USA (NE) 262-263 D 2
Whiteclay Lake ⊖ CDN (ONT) 234-235 P 4
White Cliff ▲ BS 54-55 J 3
White Cliffs ○ • AUS 178-179 G 6
Whitecourt ○ CDN 32-33 N 4
White crowned pigeons • BS 54-55 G 2
White Deer ○ USA (TX) 264-265 C 3
Whitedog ○ CDN (ONT) 234-235 J 4
White Earth ○ USA (MN) 270-271 C 3
White Earth ○ USA (ND) 258-259 E 3
White Earth Indian Reservation ✕ USA (MN) 270-271 C 3
Whiteface ○ USA (MN) 270-271 F 3
Whiteface ○ USA (TX) 264-265 B 5
Whitefish ○ CDN (ONT) 238-239 D 2
Whitefish ○ USA (MT) 250-251 E 3
Whitefish Bay ⊖ USA (MI) 270-271 O 4
Whitefish Falls ○ CDN (ONT) 238-239 D 2
Whitefish Lake ⊖ CDN 30-31 Q 4
Whitefish Lake ⊖ USA (AK) 20-21 L 6
Whitefish Lake ⊖ USA (MN) 270-271 D 4
Whitefish Lake Indian Reserve ✕ CDN (QUE) 238-239 D 2
Whitefish Point ○ USA (MI) 270-271 O 4
Whitefish Point ▲ USA (MI) 270-271 O 4
Whitefish Range ▲▲ USA (MT) 250-251 E 3
Whitefish River ∼ CDN 30-31 H 3
Whitefish River ∼ USA (MI) 270-271 M 4
Whitefish River Indian Reservation ✕ CDN (ONT) 238-239 D 2
Whiteflat ○ USA (TX) 264-265 D 4
White Fox ○ CDN (SAS) 232-233 O 2
White Goat Wilderness ⊥ CDN (ALB) 232-233 B 3
Whitegull, Lac ⊖ CDN 36-37 R 7
Whitehall ○ USA (AR) 276-277 E 6
White Hall ○ USA (IL) 274-275 H 5
Whitehall ○ USA (IN) 274-275 M 5
Whitehall ○ USA (MI) 272-273 C 4
Whitehall ○ USA (MT) 250-251 G 6
Whitehall ○ USA (NY) 278-279 H 5
Whitehall ○ USA (WI) 270-271 G 6
White Hall State Historic Site • USA (KY) 276-277 L 3
White Handkerchief, Cape ▲ CDN 36-37 S 5
Whitehaven ○ USA (MD) 280-281 L 5
White Haven ○ USA (PA) 280-281 L 2
Whitehead ○ CDN (NS) 240-241 O 5
White Hills ▲ USA 20-21 Q 2
Whitehills Lake ⊖ CDN 30-31 W 3
Whitehorse ☆ • CDN 20-21 X 6
Whitehorse ○ USA (SD) 260-261 F 1
White Horse Pass ▲ USA (NV) 246-247 L 3
Whitehouse ○ USA (TX) 264-265 J 6
White Island ⌒ CDN 36-37 G 2
White Island ⌒ NZ 182 F 2
White Lady • NAM 216-217 C 10
White Lake ⊖ AUS 176-177 F 2
White Lake ⊖ CDN (ONT) 236-237 C 4
White Lake ⊖ CDN (ONT) 238-239 J 3
White Lake ○ USA (SD) 260-261 H 3
White Lake ○ USA (WI) 270-271 K 5
White Lake ⊖ USA (LA) 268-269 H 7
White Lakes ○ USA (NM) 256-257 K 3
Whitelaw ○ CDN 32-33 L 3
Whitelock Mountains ▲▲ USA (AZ) 256-257 F 6
Whitely ○ USA (TX) 264-265 C 4
Whiteman Range ▲▲ PNG 183 E 3
Whitemark ○ AUS 180-181 K 6
White Mountain ○ USA 20-21 J 4
White Mountains ▲▲ USA 20-21 R 4
White Mountains ▲▲ USA (CA) 248-249 F 2
White Mountains ▲▲ USA (NH) 278-279 K 4
Whitemouth ○ CDN (MAN) 234-235 H 5
Whitemud River ∼ CDN 32-33 L 3
White Nile = al-Baḥr al-Abyaḍ ∼ SUD 206-207 K 4
White Oak Creek ∼ USA (TX) 264-265 K 5
White Oak Lake < USA (AR) 276-277 B 7
White Oak Mountain ▲▲ USA (AR) 276-277 B 6
White Oaks ○ USA (NM) 256-257 K 5
White Otter Lake ⊖ CDN (ONT) 234-235 M 5
White Owl ○ USA (SD) 260-261 D 2
White Pass ▲ CDN 20-21 X 7
White Pass ▲ USA (WA) 244-245 D 4
White Pigeon ○ USA (MI) 272-273 D 6
White Pine ○ USA (MI) 270-271 J 4
White Pine ○ USA (TN) 282-283 D 4
White Plains ○ LB 202-203 E 6
White Plains ○ USA (NY) 280-281 N 3
White River ○ CDN (ONT) 236-237 C 4
White River ∼ CDN 20-21 U 5
White River ∼ CDN (BC) 230-231 O 3
White River ∼ CDN (ONT) 236-237 B 4
Whiteriver ○ USA (AZ) 256-257 F 5
White River ○ USA (SD) 260-261 F 3
White River ∼ USA (SD) 260-261 G 3
White River ∼ USA (AR) 276-277 D 5
White River ∼ USA (AZ) 256-257 E 5
White River ∼ USA (CO) 254-255 G 3
White River ∼ USA (IN) 274-275 N 4
White River ∼ USA (IN) 274-275 L 6
White River ∼ USA (IN) 274-275 M 4
White River ∼ USA (IN) 274-275 M 5
White River ∼ USA (MI) 272-273 C 4
White River ∼ USA (NV) 246-247 K 5
White River ∼ USA (TX) 264-265 C 5
White River ∼ USA (VT) 278-279 J 5
White River ∼ USA (WA) 244-245 D 3
White River Junction ○ USA (VT) 278-279 J 5
White River Lake < USA (TX) 264-265 C 5
White River National Wildlife Refuge ⊥ USA (AR) 276-277 D 6
White Rock ○ CDN (BC) 230-231 G 4
White Rock ○ USA (NM) 256-257 J 3
White Rock ○ USA (SD) 260-261 K 1
Whitesail Lake ⊖ CDN (BC) 228-229 G 3
White Salmon ○ USA (WA) 244-245 D 5
Whitesand River ∼ CDN (SAS) 232-233 Q 4
White Sands Missile Range ✕✕ USA (NM) 256-257 J 5
White Sands National Monument ∴ USA (NM) 256-257 J 6
White Sands Space Harbor ✕✕ USA (NM) 256-257 J 5
Whitesboro ○ USA (TX) 264-265 H 5
Whites Brook ○ CDN (NB) 240-241 H 3
Whitesburg ○ USA (GA) 284-285 F 3
Whitesburg ○ USA (KY) 276-277 N 3
Whites City ○ USA (NM) 256-257 L 6
White Sea = Beloe more ≈ RUS 88-89 O 4
White Sea-Baltic Canal = Belomorsko-Baltijskij kanal < RUS 88-89 N 4
White Settlement ○ USA (TX) 264-265 G 6
Whiteshell Provincial Park ⊥ ·· CDN (MAN) 234-235 H 4
Whiteside, Canal ≈ 80 E 6
White Signal ○ USA (NM) 256-257 G 6
White Springs ○ USA (FL) 286-287 G 1
White Spruce ○ CDN (SAS) 232-233 Q 4
Whitespruce Rapids ∼ CDN 30-31 T 6
White Star ○ USA (MI) 272-273 E 4
Whitestone River ∼ CDN 20-21 V 4
White Strait ≈ 36-37 O 3
White Sulphur Springs ○ USA (MT) 250-251 J 5
White Sulphur Springs ○ USA (WV) 280-281 F 6
White Swan ○ USA (WA) 244-245 E 4
Whiteswan Lake Provincial Park ⊖ CDN (BC) 230-231 O 3
Whitetail ○ USA (MT) 250-251 O 3
White Tank Mountains ▲▲ USA (AZ) 256-257 C 5
White Umfolozi ∼ ZA 220-221 K 4
Whiteville ○ USA (NC) 282-283 J 6
Whiteville ○ USA (TN) 276-277 F 5
White Volta ∼ GH 202-203 K 5
Whitewater ○ CDN (MAN) 234-235 C 5
Whitewater ○ USA (CO) 254-255 G 5
Whitewater ○ USA (KS) 262-263 J 7
Whitewater ○ USA (MT) 250-251 M 3
Whitewater ○ USA (WI) 274-275 K 2
Whitewater Baldy ▲ USA (NM) 256-257 G 5
Whitewater Bay ≈ 48-49 H 7
Whitewater Bay ≈ USA 286-287 H 6
Whitewater Creek ∼ CDN (SAS) 232-233 L 6
Whitewater Lake ⊖ CDN (ONT) 234-235 O 4
Whitewater River ∼ USA (MO) 276-277 F 3
White Woman Creek ∼ USA (KS) 262-263 E 6
Whitewood ○ AUS 178-179 G 1
Whitewood ○ CDN (SAS) 232-233 Q 5
Whitewood ○ USA (SD) 260-261 C 2
Whitewright ○ USA (TX) 264-265 H 5
Whitfield ○ AUS 180-181 J 4
Whitharral ○ USA (TX) 264-265 B 5
Whitianga ○ NZ 182 E 2
Whiting ○ USA (IN) 274-275 L 3
Whiting River ∼ USA 32-33 D 2
Whitkow ○ CDN (SAS) 232-233 L 3
Whitla ○ CDN (ALB) 232-233 G 6
Whitlash ○ USA (MT) 250-251 H 3
Whitley City ○ USA (KY) 276-277 L 4
Whitman ○ USA (NE) 262-263 E 2
Whitmann Mission National Historic Site • USA (WA) 244-245 G 4
Whitmire ○ USA (SC) 284-285 J 2
Whitmore Mountains ▲▲ ARK 16 E 0
Whitney ○ CDN (ONT) 238-239 G 3
Whitney ○ USA (NE) 262-263 C 2
Whitney ○ USA (TX) 266-267 K 2
Whitney, Lake < USA (TX) 264-265 G 6
Whitney, Lake < USA (TX) 266-267 K 2
Whitney, Mount ▲ USA (CA) 248-249 F 3
Whitney Point ○ USA (NY) 278-279 F 6
Whitney Turn ○ JA 54-55 G 5
Whitsett ○ USA (TX) 266-267 J 5
Whitsunday Island ⌒ AUS 174-175 K 7
Whitsunday Island National Park ⊥ AUS 174-175 K 7
Whitsunday Passage ≈ 174-175 K 7
Whittemore ○ USA (MI) 272-273 F 3
Whittier ○ USA 20-21 Q 6
Whittle, Cap ▲ CDN (QUE) 242-243 H 2
Whittlesea ○ AUS 180-181 H 4
Whittlesea ○ ZA 220-221 H 6
Whitula Creek ∼ AUS 178-179 G 3
Whitwell ○ USA (TN) 276-277 K 5
Whitworth ○ CDN (QUE) 240-241 F 3
Wholdaia Lake ⊖ CDN 30-31 R 5
Whonnock ○ CDN (BC) 230-231 G 4
Why ○ USA (AZ) 256-257 C 6
Whyalla ○ AUS 180-181 D 2
Whycocomagh ○ CDN (NS) 240-241 O 5
Whycocomagh Indian Reserve ✕ • CDN (NS) 240-241 O 5
Whymper, Mount ▲ CDN (BC) 230-231 E 5
Wiang Chai ○ THA 142-143 L 6
Wiang Sa ○ THA 142-143 M 6
Wiang Sa ○ THA 158-159 E 6
Wiarton ○ CDN (ONT) 238-239 D 4
Wiawer ○ EAU 212-213 D 2
Wia-Wia, National Reservaat ⊥ SME 62-63 G 2
Wiawso ○ GH 202-203 J 6
Wibaux ○ USA (MT) 250-251 P 5
Wichaway Nunataks ▲▲ ARK 16 E 0
Wichita ○ USA (KS) 262-263 J 7
Wichita Falls ○ USA (TX) 264-265 F 5
Wichita Mountains ▲▲ USA (OK) 264-265 F 4
Wichita Mountains National Wildlife Refuge • USA (OK) 264-265 F 4
Wichita River ∼ USA (TX) 264-265 F 5
Wichita River, North ∼ USA (TX) 264-265 E 5
Wichita River, South ∼ USA (TX) 264-265 E 5
Wick ○ GB 90-91 F 2
Wickenburg ○ • USA (AZ) 256-257 C 5
Wickepin ○ AUS 176-177 D 6
Wickersham Dome ▲ USA 20-21 Q 4
Wickes ○ USA (AR) 276-277 A 6
Wickett ○ USA (TX) 266-267 E 2
Wickham ○ AUS 172-173 C 6
Wickham, Cape ▲ AUS 180-181 G 5
Wickham River ∼ AUS 172-173 K 4
Wickliffe ○ USA (KY) 276-277 F 4
Wicklow = Cill Mhantáin ☆ IRL 90-91 D 5
Wicklow Mountains ▲▲ IRL 90-91 D 5
Wide Bay ≈ 22-23 S 4
Wide Bay ≈ 183 G 3
Widen ○ USA (WV) 280-281 F 5
Widener ○ USA (AR) 276-277 E 5
Wide Opening ≈ 54-55 F 2
Wide Ruins ○ USA (AZ) 256-257 F 3
Widgeegoara Creek ∼ AUS 178-179 J 5
Widgee Mountain ▲ AUS 178-179 M 4
Widi, Kepulauan ⌒ RI 164-165 L 4
Widjefjorden ≈ 84-85 J 3
Wi Do ⌒ ROK 150-151 F 10
Widyān, al- ⩡ IRQ 128-129 J 6
Widyan, al- ▲▲ KSA 130-131 G 2
Wielbark ○ PL 92-93 Q 2
Wieliczka ○ ··· PL 92-93 Q 4
Wieluń ○ • PL 92-93 P 3
Wien ★ ·· A 92-93 O 4
Wiener Neustadt ○ A 92-93 O 5
Wieprz ∼ PL 92-93 R 3
Wierden ○ NL 92-93 J 2
Wiesbaden ☆ • D 92-93 K 3
Wieskirche ·· D 92-93 L 5
Wiga Hill ▲ WAN 204-205 K 3
Wiggins ○ USA (CO) 254-255 L 3
Wiggins ○ USA (MS) 268-269 L 6
Wignes Lake ⊖ CDN 30-31 R 5
Wigwam River ∼ CDN (BC) 230-231 P 4
Wigwascence Lake ⊖ CDN (ONT) 234-235 O 2
Wikieup ○ USA (AZ) 256-257 B 4
Wikki warm Spring ∼ • WAN 204-205 J 4
Wik'ro ○ ETH 200-201 J 6
Wikwemikong ○ CDN (ONT) 238-239 D 3
Wikwemikong Indian Reserve ✕ CDN (ONT) 238-239 D 3
Wilber ○ USA (NE) 262-263 K 4
Wilberforce ○ CDN (ONT) 238-239 G 3
Wilberforce, Cape ▲ AUS 174-175 D 2
Wilbert ○ CDN (SAS) 232-233 J 3
Wilbrunga Range ▲▲ AUS 172-173 J 6
Wilbur ○ USA (WA) 244-245 G 3
Wilburton ○ USA (OK) 264-265 J 4
Wilcannia ○ AUS 178-179 G 6
Wilcock, Peninsula ∼ RCH 80 C 5
Wilcox ○ CDN (SAS) 232-233 O 5
Wilcox ○ USA (NE) 262-263 G 4
Wildcat Hill ▲ CDN (SAS) 232-233 Q 2
Wildcat Hill Wilderness Area ⊥ CDN (SAS) 232-233 P 2
Wildcat Peak ▲ USA (NV) 246-247 J 4
Wildcat River ∼ USA (IN) 274-275 M 4
Wild Cove ○ CDN (NFL) 242-243 M 3
Wild Cove Pond ⊖ CDN (NFL) 242-243 M 3
Wilde ○ CDN 34-35 H 3
Wilder ○ USA (ID) 252-253 B 3
Wilderness Area ⊥ USA (MT) 250-251 H 6
Wilderness Area ⊥ USA (MT) 250-251 F 4
Wilderness Area ⊥ USA (MT) 250-251 H 5
Wilderness Area ⊥ USA (OR) 244-245 G 6
Wilderness Area ⊥ USA (UT) 254-255 D 4
Wilderness Corner ○ USA (VA) 280-281 J 5
Wilderness National Park ⊥ ZA 220-221 F 6
Wilderville ○ USA (OR) 244-245 B 8
Wildhay River ∼ CDN (ALB) 228-229 Q 3
Wild Horse ○ CDN (ALB) 232-233 H 6

Wild Horse ○ USA (CO) 254-255 N 5
Wild Horse ○ USA (NV) 246-247 K 2
Wildhorse Creek ~ USA (OK) 264-265 G 4
Wild Lake ⬭ USA 20-21 P 3
Wildlife Area ⊥ USA (MN) 270-271 B 5
Wildlife Refuge ⊥ USA (MN) 270-271 E 5
Wildlife Refuge ⊥ USA (ND) 258-259 H 3
Wildman Lagoon ○ AUS 172-173 K 2
Wildorado ○ USA (TX) 264-265 B 3
Wild Rice River ~ USA (MN) 270-271 B 3
Wild Rogue Wilderness Area ⊥ USA (OR) 244-245 B 8
Wildrose Station ○ USA (CA) 248-249 G 3
Wildwood ○ CDN (ALB) 232-233 C 2
Wildwood ○ USA (FL) 286-287 G 3
Wildwood ○ USA (NJ) 280-281 M 5
Wilge ~ ZA 220-221 J 3
Wilgus ○ USA (OH) 280-281 D 5
Wilhelm, Mount ▲ PNG 183 C 3
Wilhelmina Gebergte ⛰ SME 62-63 F 4
Wilhelmøya ⌒ N 84-85 M 3
Wilhelm-Pieck-Stadt Guben = Guben ○ D 92-93 N 3
Wilhelmshaven ○ D 92-93 K 2
Wilhelmstal ○ NAM 216-217 D 10
Wilhoit ○ USA (AZ) 256-257 C 4
Wilkes ○ ARK 16 G 12
Wilkes-Barre ○ USA (PA) 280-281 L 2
Wilkes Fracture Zone ≃ 14-15 R 8
Wilkes Land ∸ ARK 16 F 12
Wilkes Rise ≃ 222-223 E 2
Wilkie ○ CDN (SAS) 232-233 K 3
Wilkinson Lakes ⬭ AUS 176-177 M 4
Wilkins Strait ≈ 24-25 P 1
Will, Mount ▲ CDN 32-33 F 3
Willacoochee ○ USA (GA) 284-285 G 5
Willamette River ~ USA (OR) 244-245 C 6
Willamette River ~ USA (OR) 244-245 B 7
Willandra Creek ~ AUS 180-181 H 2
Willandra Lakes Region ⊥··· AUS 180-181 H 2
Willandra National Park ⊥ AUS 180-181 H 2
Willapa Bay ≈ 40-41 B 2
Willapa Bay ≈ USA 244-245 A 4
Willapa Hills ⛰ USA (WA) 244-245 B 4
Willard ○ USA (MO) 276-277 B 3
Willard ○ USA (NM) 256-257 J 4
Willard ○ USA (OH) 280-281 D 2
Willare Bridge Roadhouse ○ AUS 172-173 F 4
Willcox ○ USA (AZ) 256-257 F 6
Willcox Playa ⬭ USA (AZ) 256-257 F 6
Willem Pretorius Wildtuin ⊥ ZA 220-221 H 4
Willemstad ☆ NL 60-61 G 1
Willen ○ CDN (MAN) 234-235 B 4
Willenberg ○ PL 92-93 Q 2
Willeroo ○ AUS 172-173 K 3
Willet ○ USA (NY) 278-279 F 6
William, Mount ▲ AUS 180-181 G 4
William A. Switzer Provincial Park ⊥ CDN (ALB) 228-229 R 3
William "Bill" Dannelly Reservoir ⬭ USA (AL) 284-285 C 4
Williambury ○ AUS 176-177 C 1
William Creek ○ AUS 178-179 D 5
Williamez Peninsula ⌣ PNG 183 F 3
William H. Harsha Lake < USA (OH) 280-281 B 4
William Lake ⬭ CDN 34-35 G 3
William Lambert, Mount ▲ AUS 176-177 H 2
William Point ▲ CDN 30-31 P 6
William River ~ CDN 30-31 P 6
Williams ○ AUS 176-177 D 6
Williams ○ USA (AZ) 256-257 C 3
Williams ○ USA (CA) 246-247 C 4
Williams ○ USA (MN) 270-271 D 2
Williamsburg ○ USA (IA) 274-275 G 3
Williamsburg ○· USA (VA) 280-281 K 6
Williams Island ⌒ BS 54-55 F 2
Williams Junction ○ USA (AR) 276-277 C 6
Williams Lake ○ CDN (BC) 228-229 M 4
Williamson ○ USA (WV) 280-281 D 6
Williams Peninsula ⌣ CDN 36-37 R 3
Williamsport ○ CDN (NFL) 242-243 M 2
Williamsport ○ USA (AK) 22-23 U 3
Williamsport ○ USA (MD) 280-281 J 4
Williamsport ○ USA (PA) 280-281 J 2
Williams River ~ AUS 174-175 F 7
Williamston ○ USA (MI) 272-273 E 5
Williamston ○ USA (NC) 282-283 K 5
William's Town ○ BS 54-55 H 3
Williamstown ○ USA (KY) 276-277 L 2
Williamstown ○ USA (MA) 278-279 H 6
Williamsville ○ USA (MO) 276-277 E 4
William Weatherford Monument · USA (AL) 284-285 C 5
Willibert, Mount ▲ CDN 32-33 E 3
Willimantic ○ USA (CT) 280-281 O 2
Willingdon ○ CDN (ALB) 232-233 F 2
Willis ○ USA (NE) 262-263 K 2
Willis Group ⌒ AUS 174-175 L 5
Williston ○ USA (FL) 286-287 G 2
Williston ○ USA (ND) 258-259 D 3
Williston ○ USA (SC) 284-285 J 3
Williston ○ ZA 220-221 E 5
Williston Lake ⬭ CDN 32-33 J 4
Willits ○ USA (CA) 246-247 B 4
Willmar ○ CDN (SAS) 232-233 Q 6
Willmar ○ USA (MN) 270-271 C 5
Willmore Wilderness Provincial Park ⊥· CDN (ALB) 228-229 P 3
Willochra ∴ AUS 180-181 E 2
Willochra Creek ~ AUS 178-179 D 6
Willow ○ USA 20-21 Q 6
Willow ○ USA (OK) 264-265 E 3
Willowbrook ○ CDN (SAS) 232-233 Q 4
Willow Bunch ○ CDN (SAS) 232-233 N 6
Willow Bunch Lake ⬭ CDN (SAS) 232-233 N 6
Willow City ○ USA (ND) 258-259 G 3
Willow Creek ○ CDN (SAS) 232-233 J 6
Willow Creek ~ CDN (ALB) 232-233 E 5
Willow Creek ○ USA (CA) 246-247 B 3
Willow Creek ○ USA (OR) 244-245 H 6
Willow Creek ~ USA (MT) 250-251 H 3
Willow Creek ~ USA (OR) 244-245 F 5
Willow Creek Pass ▲ USA (CO) 254-255 J 3
Willowdale ○ USA (OR) 244-245 E 6
Willow Lake ⬭ CDN 30-31 K 4
Willowlake River ~ CDN 30-31 H 4
Willowmore ○ ZA 220-221 F 6
Willow Point ○ CDN (BC) 230-231 M 4
Willowra ○ AUS 172-173 L 6
Willowra Aboriginal Land Trust X AUS 172-173 L 6
Willow Ranch ○ USA (CA) 246-247 E 2
Willow River ~ CDN 32-33 N 4
Willow River ~ CDN (BC) 228-229 M 3
Willow River ○ USA (MN) 270-271 F 4
Willows ○ CDN (SAS) 232-233 N 6
Willows ○ USA (CA) 246-247 C 4
Willow Springs ○ USA (MO) 276-277 D 4
Willowvale ○ ZA 220-221 J 6
Willow Valley ○ USA (IN) 274-275 M 6
Will Rogers Memorial · USA (OK) 264-265 J 2
Wills, Lake ⬭ AUS 172-173 J 6
Willsboro ○ USA (NY) 278-279 H 4
Wills Creek ~ AUS 178-179 E 2
Wills Creek Lake ⬭ USA (OH) 280-281 E 3
Wills Point ○ USA (TX) 264-265 J 6
Willwood ○ USA (WY) 252-253 K 2
Wilma ○ USA (FL) 286-287 E 1
Wilmer ○ USA (AL) 284-285 B 6
Wilmington ○ AUS 180-181 E 2
Wilmington ○ USA (DE) 280-281 L 4
Wilmington ○ USA (IL) 274-275 K 3
Wilmington ○ USA (OH) 280-281 C 4
Wilmington ○ USA (VT) 278-279 J 6
Wilmington ○· USA (NC) 282-283 K 6
Wilmore ○ USA (KY) 276-277 L 3
Wilmot ○ USA (AR) 276-277 D 7
Wilmot ○ USA (OH) 280-281 E 3
Wilmot ○ USA (SD) 260-261 K 1
Wilpattu National Park ⊥ CL 140-141 H 6
Wilpena Creek ~ AUS 178-179 E 6
Wilpena Pound · AUS 178-179 E 6
Wilsall ○ USA (MT) 250-251 J 6
Wilshaw Ridge ≃ 224 B 7
Wilson ∴ AUS 178-179 E 6
Wilson ○ CDN (ALB) 232-233 F 6
Wilson ○ USA (AR) 276-277 E 5
Wilson ○ USA (NC) 282-283 K 5
Wilson ○ USA (OK) 264-265 G 4
Wilson ○ USA (TX) 264-265 C 5
Wilson, Monte ▲ PE 64-65 D 9
Wilson, Mount ▲ CDN 30-31 E 4
Wilson, Mount ▲ USA (OR) 244-245 D 5
Wilson Bay ≈ 30-31 X 4
Wilson Buff Old Telegraph Station · AUS 176-177 K 5
Wilson Creek ○ USA (WA) 244-245 F 3
Wilson Creek ~ USA (WA) 244-245 G 3
Wilson Island ⌒ CDN (ONT) 234-235 Q 6
Wilson Island ⌒ IND 140-141 L 3
Wilson Lake ⬭ USA (KS) 262-263 H 6
Wilson Lake < USA (AL) 284-285 C 2
Wilson River ~ AUS 172-173 H 4
Wilson River ~ AUS 178-179 G 4
Wilson River ~ CDN 30-31 X 4
Wilson's Creek National Battlefield Park ∴· USA (MO) 276-277 B 3
Wilson's Mills ○ CDN (QUE) 238-239 O 2
Wilsons Promontory National Park ⊥ AUS 180-181 J 5
Wilsonville ○ USA (NE) 262-263 F 4
Wilton ○ USA (AR) 276-277 A 7
Wilton ○ USA (ME) 278-279 L 4
Wilton ○ USA (ND) 258-259 G 4
Wilton ○ USA (WI) 270-271 H 7
Wiltondale ○ CDN (NFL) 242-243 L 3
Wilton River ~ AUS 174-175 C 4
Wiluna ○ AUS 176-177 F 3
Wimbledon ○ USA (ND) 258-259 J 4
Wimborne ○ CDN (ALB) 232-233 E 4
Wimico, Lake ⬭ USA (FL) 286-287 D 2
Wimmera ⌣ AUS 180-181 G 4
Wimmera River ~ AUS 180-181 F 4
Winamac ○ USA (IN) 274-275 M 3
Winam Bay ≈ 212-213 E 4
Winburg ○ ZA 220-221 H 4
Winchelsea ○· AUS 180-181 G 5
Winchester ○ CDN (ONT) 238-239 K 3
Winchester ○· GB 90-91 G 6
Winchester ○ USA (ID) 250-251 C 5
Winchester ○ USA (IL) 274-275 H 5
Winchester ○ USA (IN) 274-275 O 4
Winchester ○ USA (KY) 276-277 L 2
Winchester ○ USA (OR) 244-245 B 7
Winchester ○ USA (TN) 276-277 J 5
Winchester ○ USA (VA) 280-281 H 4
Winchester ○ USA (WI) 270-271 J 4
Winchester ○ USA (WY) 252-253 K 3
Winchester Bay ○ USA (OR) 244-245 A 7
Winchester Inlet ≈ 30-31 Z 4
Windabout Lake ⬭ AUS 178-179 D 6
Windamere, Lake < AUS 180-181 K 2
Windarra Mine, Mount · AUS 176-177 G 4
Windber ○ USA (PA) 280-281 H 3
Wind Cave National Park ⊥ USA (SD) 260-261 C 3
Winder ○ USA (GA) 284-285 G 3
Winderie ○ AUS 176-177 C 2
Windermere ○ CDN (BC) 230-231 O 3
Windermere Lake ⬭ CDN (ONT) 236-237 E 5
Windham ○ USA 32-33 D 3
Windhoek ★ NAM 216-217 D 11
Windidda ○ AUS 176-177 G 3
Windigo Bay ⬭ CDN (ONT) 234-235 P 4
Windigo Lake ⬭ CDN (ONT) 234-235 M 2
Windigo River ~ CDN 34-35 L 4
Windigo River ~ CDN (ONT) 234-235 M 2
Winding Stair Mountain ⛰ USA (OK) 264-265 J 4
Windjana Gorge National Park ⊥ AUS 172-173 G 4
Windom ○ USA (MN) 270-271 C 7
Windom Peak ▲ USA (CO) 254-255 H 6
Windorah ○ AUS 178-179 G 3
Window on China · RC 156-157 M 4
Wind River ~ CDN 20-21 X 4
Wind River ○ USA (WY) 252-253 K 4
Wind River ~ USA (WY) 252-253 J 3
Wind River Indian Reservation X USA (WY) 252-253 J 3
Wind River Peak ▲ USA (WY) 252-253 J 4
Wind River Range ⛰ USA (WY) 252-253 J 3
Windsor ○ AUS 176-177 E 4
Windsor ○ CDN (NFL) 242-243 N 4
Windsor ○ CDN (NS) 240-241 L 6
Windsor ○ CDN (ONT) 238-239 C 6
Windsor ○ CDN (QUE) 238-239 N 3
Windsor ○ GB 90-91 G 6
Windsor ○ USA (CO) 254-255 L 3
Windsor ○ USA (IL) 274-275 K 5
Windsor ○ USA (MA) 278-279 H 6
Windsor ○ USA (MO) 274-275 E 6
Windsor ○ USA (NC) 282-283 L 4
Windsor ○ USA (NH) 278-279 J 5
Windsor ○ USA (SC) 284-285 J 3
Windsor, Mount ○ AUS 178-179 F 2
Windsor Ruins · USA (MS) 268-269 J 5
Windsorton ○ ZA 220-221 G 4
Windsorton Road ○ ZA 220-221 G 4
Windthorst ○ CDN (SAS) 232-233 Q 4
Windthorst ○ USA (TX) 264-265 F 5
Windward Islands ⌒ 56 E 4
Windward Passage = Vent, Passe du ≈ 54-55 H 5
Windy Bay ⬭ CDN 30-31 M 5
Windy Corner ▲ AUS 176-177 H 1
Windygate ○ CDN (MAN) 234-235 E 5
Windygates ○ CDN (MAN) 234-235 E 5
Windy Harbour ○ AUS 176-177 D 7
Windy Lake ⬭ CDN 30-31 T 5
Windy River ~ CDN 30-31 T 5
Winefred Lake ⬭ CDN 32-33 P 4
Winefred River ~ CDN 32-33 P 3
Winejok ○ SUD 206-207 H 4
Winesap ○ USA (WA) 244-245 E 3
Winfield ○ CDN (ALB) 232-233 D 3
Winfield ○ CDN (BC) 230-231 K 4
Winfield ○ USA (AL) 284-285 C 3
Winfield ○ USA (IA) 274-275 G 3
Winfield ○ USA (KS) 262-263 K 7
Wing ○ USA (ND) 258-259 G 4
Wingard ○ CDN (SAS) 232-233 M 3
Wingate ○ USA (TX) 264-265 D 6
Wingate Mountains ⛰ AUS 172-173 K 3
Winger ○ USA (MN) 270-271 C 3
Wingfield Petroglyhps ∸ KAN 56 D 3
Wingham ○ AUS 178-179 M 6
Wingham ○ CDN (ONT) 238-239 D 5
Wingham Island ⌒ USA 20-21 S 6
Wingon ○ MYA 142-143 J 4
Winifred ○ USA (MT) 250-251 K 4
Winifred, Lake ⬭ AUS 172-173 F 7
Winiperu ○ GUY 62-63 E 2
Winisk ○ CDN 34-35 O 3
Winisk Lake ⬭ CDN (ONT) 234-235 Q 2
Winisk River ~ CDN 34-35 O 3
Winisk River ~ CDN (ONT) 234-235 P 2
Winisk River Provincial Park ⊥ CDN 34-35 N 4
Wink ○ USA (TX) 266-267 D 2
Winkelmann ○ USA (AZ) 256-257 E 5
Winkler ○ CDN (MAN) 234-235 F 5
Winlock ○ USA (WA) 244-245 C 4
Winneba ○ GH 202-203 K 7
Winnebago ○ USA (MN) 270-271 D 7
Winnebago ○ USA (NE) 262-263 K 2
Winnebago, Lake ⬭ USA (WI) 270-271 K 6
Winnebago Indian Reservation X USA (NE) 262-263 K 2
Winnecke Creek ~ AUS 172-173 K 5
Winnemucca ○ USA (NV) 246-247 H 3
Winnemucca Lake ⬭ USA (NV) 246-247 F 3
Winnepegosis ○ CDN (MAN) 234-235 D 3
Winner ○ USA (SD) 260-261 G 3
Winnett ○ USA (MT) 250-251 L 5
Winnfield ○ USA (LA) 268-269 H 5
Winnibigoshish Lake ⬭ USA (MN) 270-271 D 3
Winnie ○ USA (TX) 268-269 F 7
Winning ○ AUS 176-177 C 1
Winnipeg ☆· CDN (MAN) 234-235 F 5
Winnipeg, Lake ⬭ CDN 34-35 G 4
Winnipeg, Lake ⬭ CDN (MAN) 234-235 G 4
Winnipeg Beach ○ CDN (MAN) 234-235 G 4
Winnipegosis, Lake ⬭ CDN 34-35 F 4
Winnipesaukee, Lake ⬭ USA (NH) 278-279 K 5
Winnsboro ○ USA (LA) 268-269 J 4
Winnsboro ○ USA (SC) 284-285 J 2
Winnsboro ○ USA (TX) 264-265 J 6
Winona ○ USA (AZ) 256-257 D 3
Winona ○ USA (KS) 262-263 E 5
Winona ○ USA (MI) 270-271 K 4
Winona ○ USA (MN) 270-271 G 6
Winona ○ USA (MO) 276-277 D 3
Winona ○ USA (MS) 268-269 L 3
Winooski River ~ USA (VT) 278-279 J 4
Winschoten ○ NL 92-93 J 2
Winslow ○ USA (AR) 276-277 A 5
Winslow ○ USA (AZ) 256-257 E 3
Winsted ○ USA (CT) 280-281 N 2
Winston ○ USA (NM) 256-257 H 5
Winston ○ USA (OR) 244-245 B 7
Winston-Salem ○ USA (NC) 282-283 G 4
Winter ○ CDN (SAS) 232-233 J 3
Winterberg ○ D 92-93 K 3
Winterberge ⛰ ZA 220-221 G 6
Winter Brook ○ CDN (NFL) 242-243 P 4
Winter Garden ○ USA (FL) 286-287 H 3
Winter Harbour ≈ 24-25 R 3
Winter Harbour ○ CDN (BC) 230-231 A 3
Winterhaven ○ USA (CA) 248-249 K 7
Winter Haven ○ USA (FL) 286-287 H 3
Wintering Lake ⬭ CDN 34-35 H 3
Wintering Lake ⬭ CDN (ONT) 234-235 Q 5
Winter Island ⌒ CDN 24-25 e 7
Winter Lake ⬭ CDN 30-31 N 3
Winterland ○ CDN (NFL) 242-243 N 5
Winter Park ○ USA (CO) 254-255 K 4
Winter Park ○ USA (FL) 286-287 H 3
Winterport ○ USA (ME) 278-279 N 4
Winters ○ USA (CA) 246-247 D 5
Winters ○ USA (TX) 266-267 H 2
Winterset ○ USA (IA) 274-275 D 3
Winter Springs ○ USA (FL) 286-287 H 3
Winterthur ○ CH 92-93 K 5
Winterton ○ ZA 220-221 J 4
Winterveld ∸ ZA 220-221 F 5
Winterville ○ USA (NC) 282-283 K 5
Winterville State Historic Site · USA (MS) 268-269 J 3
Winthrop ○ USA (ME) 278-279 M 4
Winthrop ○ USA (MN) 270-271 D 6
Winthrop ○ USA (WA) 244-245 E 2
Winton ○ AUS 178-179 G 2
Winton ○ NZ 182 B 7
Winton ○ USA (MN) 270-271 G 3
Winton ○ USA (NC) 282-283 L 4
Wintua ○ VAN 184 II a 3
Winyah Bay ≈ USA 284-285 L 3
Winyaw ○ MYA 158-159 E 3
Wipim ○ PNG 183 B 5
Wiradesa ○ RI 168 C 3
Wirawila ○ CL 140-141 J 7
Wiriagar ~ RI 166-167 G 2
Wirliyajarrayi Aboriginal Land X AUS 172-173 L 6
Wirmaf ○ RI 166-167 F 4
Wirrabara ○ AUS 180-181 E 2
Wirrulla ○ AUS 180-181 C 2
Wiscasset ○ USA (ME) 278-279 M 4
Wisconsin ▫ USA (WI) 270-271 G 6
Wisconsin Dells ○· USA (WI) 274-275 J 7
Wisconsin Rapids ○ USA (WI) 270-271 J 6
Wisconsin River ~ USA (WI) 270-271 J 5
Wisconsin River ~ USA (WI) 274-275 H 1
Wisdom ○ USA (MT) 250-251 F 6
Wisdom, Lake ⬭ PNG 183 D 3
Wisemans Ferry ○ AUS 180-181 L 2
Wisemen ○ USA 20-21 P 3
Wise River ○ USA (MT) 250-251 F 6
Wiseton ○ CDN (SAS) 232-233 L 4
Wishart ○ CDN (SAS) 232-233 P 4
Wishaw ○ GB 90-91 F 4
Wishek ○ USA (ND) 258-259 H 5
Wisil ○ SP 208-209 J 6
Wisła ○ PL (BIE) 92-93 P 4
Wisła ~ PL 92-93 P 1
Wiślany, Zalew ≈ 92-93 P 1
Wisłoka ~ PL 92-93 Q 3
Wismar ○· D 92-93 L 2
Wismar ○ GUY 62-63 E 2
Wisner ○ USA (LA) 268-269 J 5
Wisner ○ USA (NE) 262-263 K 3
Wistaria ○ CDN (BC) 228-229 H 3
Wister ○ USA (OK) 264-265 K 4
Wister Lake < USA (OK) 264-265 K 4
Witagron ○ SME 62-63 F 3
Witbank ○ ZA 220-221 J 2
Witbooisvlei ○ NAM 220-221 D 2
Witchecan Lake ⬭ CDN (SAS) 232-233 L 2
Witchekan Lake Indian Reservation X CDN (SAS) 232-233 L 2
Witfonteinrand ⛰ ZA 220-221 H 2
Withfish River ~ CDN (ONT) 236-237 H 4
Withington, Mount ▲ USA (NM) 256-257 H 5
Withlacoochee River ~ USA (GA) 284-285 G 6
Witjira National Park ⊥ AUS 178-179 C 4
Wit Kei ~ ZA 220-221 H 5
Witkoppies ▲ ZA 220-221 J 3
Witkransnek ▲ ZA 220-221 G 5
Witless Bay ○ CDN (NFL) 242-243 Q 5
Witney ○ GB 90-91 G 6
Witputz < NAM 220-221 C 3
Witrivier ○ ZA 220-221 K 2
Witsand ○ ZA 220-221 E 7
Witt, De ○ USA (AR) 276-277 D 6
Witt, De ○ USA (IA) 274-275 H 3
Wittabrenna Creek ~ AUS 178-179 F 5
Witteberge ⛰ ZA 220-221 F 6
Witteberge ⛰ ZA 220-221 E 6
Witteberge ⛰ ZA 220-221 H 4
Witteklip ○ ZA 220-221 G 6
Witten ○ USA (SD) 260-261 F 3
Wittenberg ○ USA (WI) 270-271 J 6
Wittenberge ○ D 92-93 L 2
Wittenoom ○ AUS 172-173 D 7
Wittenoom Gorge · AUS 172-173 D 7
Wittingen ○ D 92-93 L 2
Wittlich ○ D 92-93 J 4
Wittman ○ USA (AZ) 256-257 C 5
Witts Springs ○ USA (AR) 276-277 C 5
Wittstock ○· D 92-93 M 2
Witu ○ EAK 212-213 H 5
Witu ○ PNG 183 E 3
Witu Islands ⌒ PNG 183 E 3
Witvlei ○ NAM 216-217 E 11
Witwater ○ NAM 220-221 B 2
Witwater ○ ZA 220-221 D 5
Witwatersberge ▲ NAM 216-217 C 11
Witwatersrand ⛰ ZA 220-221 H 2
Wivenhoe, Lake < AUS 178-179 M 4
Wizzard Breakers ⌒ SY 224 B 4
Wladiwostok = Vladivostok ○ RUS 122-123 J 2
Władysławowo ○· PL 92-93 P 1
Wlingi ○ RI 168 E 4
Włocławek ☆· PL 92-93 P 2
Włodawa ○ PL 92-93 R 3
Włoszczowa ○ PL 92-93 P 3
Woburn ○ CDN (QUE) 240-241 E 5
Woden ○ USA (IA) 274-275 E 1
Woe ○ GH 202-203 L 7
Woëvre ∸ F 90-91 K 7
Wofikehn ○ LB 202-203 G 7
Wogadjina Hill ▲ AUS 176-177 F 1
Woganakai ○ PNG 183 F 3
Wogerlin Hill ▲ AUS 176-177 D 6
Wohlthat Mountains = Wohlthatmassivet ⛰ ARK 16 F 2
Woinui, Selat ≈ 166-167 H 2
Woitape ○ PNG 183 D 5
Wokam, Pulau ⌒ RI 166-167 H 4
Woko National Park ⊥ AUS 178-179 L 6
Wolbach ○ USA (NE) 262-263 H 3
Wolcott ○ USA (CO) 254-255 J 4
Wolcott ○ USA (NY) 278-279 E 5
Woleai ⌒ FSM 13 F 2
Woleu ~ G 210-211 C 3
Wolf ○ USA (OK) 264-265 E 4
Wolf, Isla ⌒ EC 64-65 B 9
Wolf, Volcán ▲ EC 64-65 B 9
Wolf Bay ○ CDN (QUE) 242-243 H 2
Wolf Creek ~ AUS 172-173 H 5
Wolf Creek ○ USA (MT) 250-251 G 5
Wolf Creek ○ USA (OR) 244-245 B 8
Wolf Creek ○ USA (TN) 282-283 E 5
Wolf Creek ~ USA (MT) 250-251 D 3
Wolf Creek ~ USA (TX) 264-265 D 2
Wolf Creek Meteorite Crater National Park ⊥ AUS 172-173 H 5
Wolf Creek Pass ▲ USA (CO) 254-255 J 6
Wolf Creek Reservoir ⬭ USA (KS) 262-263 L 6
Wolfeboro ○ USA (NH) 278-279 K 5
Wolfe City ○ USA (TX) 264-265 H 5
Wolfe Island ⌒ CDN (ONT) 238-239 J 4
Wolfenbüttel ○·· D 92-93 L 2
Wolfforth ○ USA (TX) 264-265 B 5
Wolf Hole ○ USA (AZ) 256-257 B 2
Wolf Lake ⬭ CDN 20-21 Z 6
Wolf Lake ○ USA (IN) 274-275 N 3
Wolford ○ USA (ND) 258-259 H 3
Wolf Point ○ USA (MT) 250-251 O 3
Wolf Rapids ~ CDN 30-31 V 2
Wolf River ~ CDN 20-21 Y 6
Wolf River ~ CDN 32-33 P 4
Wolf River ~ CDN (ALB) 232-233 B 2
Wolf River ~ USA (MS) 268-269 L 6
Wolf River ~ USA (TN) 276-277 F 5
Wolf River ~ USA (WI) 270-271 J 5
Wolf Rock, Pulau ⌒ RI 164-165 K 3
Wolfsburg ○ D 92-93 L 2
Wolfville ○ CDN (NS) 240-241 L 5
Wolgast ○ D 92-93 M 1
Wolgograd = Zarizyn ☆· RUS 96-97 D 9
Wolin ⌒ PL 92-93 N 2
Wolkefit Pass ▲ ETH 200-201 H 6
Wollaston, Islas ⌒ RCH 80 G 7
Wollaston Forland ∸ GRØ 26-27 p 6
Wollaston Lake ○ CDN (SAS) 30-31 S 6
Wollaston Lake ⬭ CDN (SAS) 34-35 E 2
Wollaston Peninsula ⌣ CDN 24-25 O 6
Wollemi National Park ⊥ AUS 180-181 L 2
Wollogorang ○ AUS 174-175 D 5
Wollomombi ○ AUS 178-179 M 6
Wollondilly River ~ AUS 180-181 L 3
Wollongong ○ AUS 180-181 L 3
Wolmaransstad ○ ZA 220-221 G 3
Wolo ○· RI 166-167 K 3
Wologizi Range ∸ LB 202-203 F 5
Wolong Daxiongmao Reserves ⊥ VRC 154-155 C 6
Wolong Xiongmao Baohuqu ⊥· VRC 154-155 C 6
Wołów ○ PL 92-93 O 3
Wolowaru ○ RI 168 E 7
Wolseley ○ CDN (SAS) 232-233 P 5
Wolseley ○ ZA 220-221 D 6
Wolseley Bay ○ CDN (ONT) 238-239 E 2
Wolsey ○ USA (SD) 260-261 H 2
Wolstenholme, Cap ▲ CDN 36-37 L 3
Wolstenholme Fjord ≈ 26-27 Q 5
Wolstenholme Ø ⌒ GRØ 26-27 P 5
Wolsztyn ○· PL 92-93 O 2
Wolverhampton ○ GB 90-91 F 5
Wolverine River ~ CDN 20-21 a 2
Wolverine River ~ CDN 30-31 V 6
Wolwefontein ○ ZA 220-221 G 6
Woman River ○ CDN (ONT) 236-237 F 5
Woman River ~ CDN (ONT) 236-237 F 5
Wombil Downs ○ AUS 178-179 J 5
Wonderfontein ○ ZA 220-221 J 2
Wonder Gorge ⌣· Z 218-219 E 2
Wondinong ○ AUS 176-177 E 3
Wondiwoi, Pegunungan ⛰ RI 166-167 H 3
Wonegizi Mountain ⛰ LB 202-203 F 6
Wonenara ○ PNG 183 C 4
Wongalarroo Lake ⬭ AUS 178-179 H 6
Wongan Hills ○ AUS 176-177 D 5
Wonganoo ○ AUS 176-177 F 3
Wonga Wongué ○ G 210-211 B 4
Wonga-Wongué, Parc National du ⊥ G 210-211 B 4
Wonga Wongué, Réserve de ⊥ G 210-211 B 4
Wongoondy Wheat Bin ○ AUS 176-177 C 4
Wŏnju ○ ROK 150-151 F 9
Wonnangatta River ~ AUS 180-181 J 4
Wono ○ RI 164-165 F 5
Wonogiri ○ RI 168 D 3
Wonoka ○ AUS 178-179 E 6
Wonosari ○ RI 168 D 3
Wonosobo ○ RI 168 C 3
Wonreli ○ RI 166-167 D 6
Wonsan ○ DVR 150-151 F 8
Wonthaggi ○ AUS 180-181 H 5
Wonyulgunna Hill ▲ AUS 176-177 E 2
Wood ○ USA (SD) 260-261 F 3
Wood, Isla ⌒ RA 78-79 H 5
Wood, Islas ⌒ RCH 80 F 7
Wood, Mount ▲ USA (MT) 250-251 K 6
Woodall Mountain ▲ USA (MS) 268-269 M 2
Woodanilling ○ AUS 176-177 E 6
Wood Bay ≈ 16 F 17
Wood Bay ≈ 24-25 G 6
Woodbine ○ USA (GA) 284-285 J 6
Woodbine ○ USA (IA) 274-275 C 3
Woodbridge ○ AUS 180-181 J 7
Woodbı.dge ○· GB 90-91 H 5
Wood Buffalo National Park ⊥··· CDN 30-31 N 6
Wood Buffalo River ~ CDN 32-33 O 3
Woodburn ○ AUS 178-179 M 5
Woodburn ○ USA (IN) 274-275 O 3
Woodburn ○ USA (OR) 244-245 C 5
Woodburry ○ USA (GA) 284-285 F 4
Woodbury ○ USA (GA) 284-285 F 4
Woodbury ○ USA (TN) 276-277 J 5
Wood Creek ~ CDN 34-35 N 3
Woodenbong ○ AUS 178-179 M 5
Woodfjorden ≈ 84-85 H 3
Woodford ○ AUS 178-179 M 4
Woodfords ○ USA (CA) 246-247 F 5
Woodgate ○ AUS 178-179 M 3
Woodgreen ○ AUS 178-179 C 2
Wood Islands ⌒ AUS 172-173 G 4
Wood Islands ○ CDN (PEI) 240-241 N 5
Woodi Woodi Mining Centre · AUS 172-173 E 6
Woodlake ○ USA (CA) 248-249 E 3
Wood Lake ○ USA (NE) 262-263 F 2
Woodland ○ USA (CA) 246-247 D 5
Woodland ○ USA (ME) 278-279 O 3
Woodland ○ USA (TX) 264-265 J 5
Woodland ○ USA (WA) 244-245 C 5
Woodland Beach ○ USA (DE) 280-281 L 4
Woodland Caribou Provincial Park ⊥ CDN (ONT) 234-235 H 3
Woodland Park ○ USA (CO) 254-255 K 5
Woodlands ○ AUS 176-177 E 2
Woodlark Island = Murua Island ⌒ PNG 183 G 5
Woodlawn ○ CDN (ONT) 238-239 J 3
Woodleigh (Old Homestead) ○ AUS 176-177 C 3
Wood Mountain ○ CDN (SAS) 232-233 M 6
Wood Mountain ▲ CDN (SAS) 232-233 M 6
Woodnorth ○ CDN (MAN) 234-235 B 5
Woodridge ○ CDN (MAN) 234-235 G 5
Wood River ~ CDN (BC) 228-229 Q 4
Wood River ~ CDN (SAS) 232-233 L 6
Wood River ○ USA (NE) 262-263 H 4
Wood River ~ USA 20-21 Q 4
Woodroffe, Mount ▲ AUS 176-177 L 3
Woodrow ○ CDN (SAS) 232-233 M 6
Woodrow ○ USA 20-21 Q 6
Woodruff ○ USA (SC) 284-285 H 2
Woodruff ○ USA (UT) 254-255 D 2
Woodruff ○ USA (WI) 270-271 J 5
Woodruff Lake ⬭ CDN 30-31 R 5
Woods, Cape ▲ CDN 26-27 G 2
Woods, Lake ⬭ AUS 174-175 B 5
Woods, Lake of the ⬭ CDN (ONT) 234-235 J 5
Woodsboro ○ USA (TX) 266-267 K 5
Woodsfield ○ USA (OH) 280-281 E 4
Woodside ○ CDN (MAN) 234-235 E 4
Woods Lake ⬭ CDN 36-37 R 7
Woods Lake < USA (TN) 276-277 J 5
Woods Landing ○ USA (WY) 252-253 M 5
Woodson ○ USA (TX) 264-265 E 5
Woods Peak ○ AUS 174-175 H 5
Woodstock ○ AUS (QLD) 174-175 J 6
Woodstock ○ AUS (QLD) 178-179 F 2
Woodstock ○ CDN (NB) 240-241 H 4
Woodstock ○ CDN (ONT) 238-239 E 5
Woodstock ○ USA (AL) 284-285 C 3
Woodstock ○ USA (IL) 274-275 K 2
Woodstock ○ USA (NY) 278-279 G 6
Woodstock ○ USA (VA) 280-281 H 5
Woodstock ○ USA (VT) 278-279 J 5
Woodstock 23 Indian Reserve X· CDN (NB) 240-241 H 4
Woodstock Dam < ZA 220-221 J 4
Woodstown ○ USA (NJ) 280-281 L 4
Woodsville ○ USA (NH) 278-279 J 4
Woodville ○ CDN (ONT) 238-239 G 4
Woodville ○ NZ 182 E 4
Woodville ○ USA (AL) 284-285 D 2
Woodville ○ USA (FL) 286-287 E 1
Woodville ○ USA (MS) 268-269 J 5
Woodville ○ USA (OH) 280-281 C 2
Woodville ○ USA (TX) 268-269 F 6
Woodward ○ USA (IA) 274-275 E 3
Woodward ○ USA (OK) 264-265 E 2
Woodward ○ USA (SC) 284-285 J 2
Woodworth ○ USA (ND) 258-259 H 4
Woody Island ⌒ USA 22-23 U 4
Woody Island Coulee ~ USA (MT) 250-251 L 3
Woody Point ○· CDN (NFL) 242-243 L 3
Woogi ○ RI 166-167 K 3
Wooi ○ RI 166-167 H 2
Woolfield ○ AUS 178-179 G 1
Woolgoolga ○ AUS 178-179 M 6
Wooli ○ AUS 178-179 M 5
Woollett, Lac ⬭ CDN 38-39 H 3
Woolly Hollow State Park ⊥ USA (AR) 276-277 C 5
Woolner ○ AUS 172-173 K 2
Woolnorth Point ▲ AUS 180-181 H 6
Woolocutty ○ AUS 176-177 E 6
Woolyeenyer Hill ▲ AUS 176-177 F 6
Woomelang ○ AUS 180-181 G 3
Woomera ○ AUS 178-179 D 6
Woomerangee Hill ▲ AUS 176-177 B 3
Woomera Prohibited Area X AUS 178-179 B 6
Woonsocket ○ USA (SD) 260-261 H 2
Woonsucket ○ USA (RI) 278-279 K 7
Woorabinda X AUS 178-179 K 3
Wooramel Raodhouse ○ AUS 176-177 C 2
Wooramel River ~ AUS 176-177 C 2
Woorkabing Hill ▲ AUS 176-177 D 6
Woorndoo ○ AUS 180-181 G 4
Wooster ○ USA (OH) 280-281 E 3
Wopasali ○ PNG 183 C 4
Wopmay Lake ⬭ CDN 30-31 L 3
Wopmay River ~ CDN 30-31 L 3
Woqooyi Galbeed ▫ SP 208-209 F 3
Woraksan National Park ⊥· ROK 150-151 G 9
Worcester ☆· GB 90-91 F 5
Worcester ○ USA (MA) 278-279 K 6
Worcester ○ ZA 220-221 D 6
Worcester Range ⛰ ARK 16 F 17
Worden ○ USA (MT) 250-251 L 6
Worden ○ USA (OR) 244-245 D 8
Wordie Bay ≈ 28-29 D 2
Wordie Gletscher ⊂ GRØ 26-27 o 6
Wordsworth ○ CDN (SAS) 232-233 Q 6
Wori ○ RI 164-165 J 3
Worin ○ PNG 183 D 4
Workai, Pulau ⌒ RI 166-167 H 5
Work Channel ≈ CDN 228-229 D 2
Workington ○ GB 90-91 F 4
Worland ○ USA (WY) 252-253 L 2
World's Largest Mineral Hot Springs · USA (WY) 252-253 K 3
Worms ○· D 92-93 K 4
Wortham ○ USA (TX) 266-267 L 2
Worthington ○ CDN (ONT) 238-239 D 2
Worthington ○ USA (MN) 270-271 C 7
Worthington ○ USA (OH) 280-281 C 3
Worthville ○ USA (KY) 276-277 K 2
Wosi ○ RI 164-165 K 4
Wosimi ○ RI 166-167 H 3
Wosnesenski Island ⌒ USA 22-23 Q 5
Wostok ○ CDN (ALB) 232-233 F 2
Wosu ○ RI 164-165 G 5
Wotap, Pulau ⌒ RI 166-167 F 5
Wotu ○ RI 164-165 G 5
Woumbou ○ CAM 206-207 B 6
Wounded Knee ○ USA (SD) 260-261 D 3
Wounded Knee Battlefield · USA (SD) 260-261 D 3
Wour ○ TCH 198-199 G 2
Wouri ~ CAM 204-205 H 6
Wouri, Wādī ~ TCH 198-199 G 2
Wowoni, Pulau ⌒ RI 164-165 H 6
Woyamdero Plain ∸ EAK 212-213 G 3
Wozhang Shan ▲ VRC 156-157 C 4
Wrangel Island = Vrangelja, ostrov ⌒ RUS 112-113 U 1
Wrangell ○ USA 32-33 D 3
Wrangell, Cape ▲ USA 22-23 C 6
Wrangell Island ⌒ USA 32-33 D 3
Wrangell Mountains ⛰ USA 20-21 T 6
Wrangell-St. Elias N.P. & Preserve & Glacier Bay N.P. ⊥··· USA 20-21 T 6
Wray ○ USA (CO) 254-255 N 3
Wreck Cove ○ CDN (NS) 240-241 P 4
Wren ○ USA (OR) 244-245 B 6
Wrens ○ USA (GA) 284-285 H 3
Wrentham ○ CDN (ALB) 232-233 F 6
Wrexham ○ GB 90-91 F 5
Wriedijk ○ SME 62-63 G 3
Wright ○ RP 160-161 F 7
Wright ○ USA (KS) 262-263 G 7
Wright ○ USA (WY) 252-253 N 3
Wright Brothers National Memorial · USA (NC) 282-283 M 5
Wright City ○ USA (OK) 264-265 J 4
Wrightson, Mount ▲ USA (AZ) 256-257 E 7
Wrightsville ○ USA (AR) 276-277 C 6
Wrightsville ○ USA (GA) 284-285 H 4
Wrightsville Beach ○ USA (NC) 282-283 K 6
Wrightwood ○ USA (CA) 248-249 G 5
Wrigley ○ CDN 30-31 H 4
Wrigley Gulf ≈ 16 F 24
Writing Rock ∴ USA (ND) 258-259 D 3
Wrocław ☆·· PL 92-93 O 3
Wrotham Park ○ AUS 174-175 G 5
Wrottesley, Cape ▲ CDN 24-25 L 3
Wrottesley Inlet ≈ 24-25 Y 5
Wroxton ○ CDN (SAS) 232-233 R 4
Września ○ PL 92-93 O 2
Wschowa ○· PL 92-93 O 3
Wu'an ○ VRC 154-155 J 3
Wuasa ○ RI 164-165 G 4
Wubin ○ AUS 176-177 D 5
Wubu ○ VRC 154-155 G 3
Wuchang ○ VRC (HEI) 150-151 F 5
Wuchang ○ VRC (HUB) 154-155 J 6
Wuchiu Yü ⌒ RC 156-157 L 4
Wuchuan ○ VRC (GDG) 156-157 G 6
Wuchuan ○ VRC (GZH) 156-157 E 2
Wuchuan ○ VRC (NMZ) 148-149 K 7
Wuda ○ VRC 154-155 E 2
Wudalianchi ○ VRC (HEI) 150-151 F 3
Wudalianchi · VRC (HEI) 150-151 F 3
Wudang Shan ⛰ VRC 154-155 G 5
Wudangshan · VRC 154-155 G 5
Wudang Zhao · VRC 154-155 G 1
Wudan Shan ▲ VRC 154-155 G 5
Wudaogou ○ VRC 150-151 F 2
Wuday'ah ○ KSA 132-133 E 5
Wudil ○ WAN 204-205 H 3
Wuding ○ VRC 156-157 C 4
Wuding He ~ VRC 154-155 F 2
Wudu ○ VRC 154-155 D 5
Wufeng ○ VRC 154-155 G 6
Wugang ○ VRC 156-157 G 3
Wugong ○ VRC 154-155 F 4
Wugong Ci · VRC 156-157 G 7
Wugong Shan ▲ VRC 156-157 J 3
Wuhai ○ VRC 154-155 E 2
Wuhan ☆· VRC 154-155 J 6
Wuhe ○ VRC 154-155 K 5
Wuhu ○ VRC 154-155 L 6
Wuhua ○ VRC 156-157 J 5
Wŭjang ○ VRC 144-145 B 4
Wuji ○ VRC 154-155 J 2
Wu Jiang ~ VRC 156-157 F 2
Wukari ○ WAN 204-205 H 5
Wulai · RC 156-157 M 4

Wulff Land ∸ GRØ 26-27 a 2
Wulgo ○ WAN 198-199 G 6
Wuli ○ VRC 144-145 J 3
Wulian ○ VRC 154-155 L 4
Wulian Feng ▲ VRC 156-157 C 3
Wuliaru, Pulau ⌒ RI 166-167 F 5
Wulichuan ○ VRC 154-155 G 5
Wulik River ~ USA 20-21 J 3
Wuling Shan ▲ VRC 156-157 F 3
Wulingshan Z.B. ⊥ • VRC 154-155 K 1
Wulingyuan ••• VRC 156-157 G 2
Wulo Kode ○ ETH 208-209 C 5
Wulong ○ VRC 156-157 E 2
Wuluhan ○ RI 168 E 4
Wulur ○ RI 166-167 E 5
Wum ○ CAM 204-205 J 5
Wumeng Shan ▲ VRC 156-157 C 4
Wuming ○ VRC 156-157 F 5
Wundanyi ○ EAK 212-213 G 5
Wundowie ○ AUS 176-177 D 5
Wunen ○ RI 166-167 K 3
Wuning ○ VRC 156-157 J 2
Wunna ~ IND 138-139 G 9
Wunnummin Lake ⬭ CDN 34-35 M 4
Wunnummin Lake ⬭ CDN (ONT) 234-235 O 2
Wun Rog ○ SUD 206-207 J 4
Wun Shwai ○ SUD 206-207 J 4
Wuntau ○ SUD 206-207 L 3
Wuntho ○ MYA 142-143 J 4
Wupatki National Monument ∴ USA (AZ) 256-257 D 3
Wuping ○ VRC 156-157 K 4
Wuppertal ○ D 92-93 J 3
Wuppertal ○ ZA 220-221 D 6
Wuqi ○ VRC 154-155 F 3
Wuqia ○ VRC 146-147 B 6
Wurarga ○ AUS 176-177 D 4
Wurno ○ WAN 198-199 B 6
Wurtele ○ CDN (ONT) 236-237 G 3
Wuruma Reservation < AUS 178-179 L 3
Würzburg ○•• D 92-93 K 4
Wuse ○ WAN 204-205 H 4
Wushan ○ VRC (ANH) 154-155 K 5
Wushan ○ VRC (GAN) 154-155 D 4
Wushan ○ VRC (SIC) 154-155 F 6
Wushao Ling ▲ VRC 154-155 C 3
Wusheng Guan ▲ VRC 154-155 J 6
Wushi ○ VRC (GDG) 156-157 F 6
Wushi ○ VRC (XUZ) 146-147 D 5
Wushishi ○ WAN 204-205 G 4
Wushizen ○ VRC 156-157 F 6
Wuskwatim Lake ⬭ CDN 34-35 G 3
Wusuli Jiang ~ VRC 150-151 K 4
Wutai ○ VRC 154-155 H 2
Wutaishan ▲ VRC 154-155 H 2
Wutan ○ VRC 156-157 G 2
Wutongqiao ○ VRC 156-157 C 2
Wutung ○ PNG 183 A 2
Wuwei ○ VRC (ANH) 154-155 K 6
Wuwei ○ VRC (GAN) 154-155 C 3
Wuwu ○ PNG 183 D 4
Wuxi ○ VRC (JIA) 154-155 M 6
Wuxi ○• VRC (SIC) 154-155 F 6
Wuxu ○ VRC 156-157 F 5
Wuxuan ○ VRC 156-157 F 5
Wuxue ○ VRC 156-157 J 2
Wuyang ○ VRC 154-155 H 5
Wuyi ○ VRC 156-157 C 3
Wuyiling ○ VRC 150-151 G 3
Wuyishan ○ VRC (FUJ) 156-157 L 3
Wuyi Shan ▲ VRC 156-157 K 3
Wuyishan • VRC (FUJ) 156-157 K 3
Wuyishan Z.B. ⊥ • VRC 156-157 K 3
Wuyunan ○ VRC 148-149 J 7
Wuzhai ○ VRC 154-155 G 2
Wuzhi ○ VRC 154-155 H 4
Wuzhi Shan ▲ VRC 156-157 F 7
Wuzhi Shan ▲ VRC 156-157 F 7
Wuzhong ○ VRC 154-155 E 2
Wuzhou ○ VRC 156-157 G 5
Wyaaba Creek ~ AUS 174-175 G 5
Wyabing ○ AUS 176-177 E 6
Wyaconda River ~ USA (MO) 274-275 G 4
Wyagamack, Lac ⬭ CDN (QUE) 240-241 C 3
Wyalkatchem ○ AUS 176-177 D 5
Wyalusing ○ USA (PA) 280-281 K 2
Wyandotte Caves ∴ • USA (IN) 274-275 M 6
Wyandra ○ AUS 178-179 H 4
Wyangala, Lake ⬭ AUS 180-181 K 2
Wyara, Lake ⬭ AUS 178-179 H 5
Wyarno ○ USA (WY) 252-253 M 2
Wycheproof ○ AUS 180-181 G 4
Wyemandoo Hill ▲ AUS 176-177 E 4
Wyena ○ AUS 178-179 J 1
Wyeville ○ USA (WI) 270-271 H 6
Wylie Scarp ∸ AUS 176-177 G 6
Wyllie's Poort ○ ZA 218-219 E 6
Wyloo ○ AUS 172-173 C 7
Wymark ○ CDN (SAS) 232-233 L 5
Wymer ○ USA (WA) 244-245 E 4
Wymore ○ USA (NE) 262-263 K 4
Wynbring ○ AUS 176-177 M 5
Wyndham ○ AUS 172-173 J 3
Wyndmere ○ USA (ND) 258-259 K 5
Wynndel ○ CDN (BC) 230-231 N 4
Wynne ○ USA (AR) 276-277 E 5
Wynnewood ○ USA (OK) 264-265 G 4
Wynniatt Bay ≈ 24-25 Q 4
Wynot ○ USA (NE) 262-263 J 2
Wynyard ○ AUS 180-181 H 6
Wynyard ○ CDN (SAS) 232-233 O 4
Wyola ○ USA (MT) 250-251 M 6
Wyola Lake ⬭ AUS 176-177 L 4
Wyoming ○ CDN (ONT) 238-239 C 6
Wyoming ○ USA (IL) 274-275 J 3
Wyoming ○ USA (MI) 272-273 D 5
Wyoming ○ USA (MN) 270-271 E 5
Wyoming ◘ USA (WY) 252-253 J 4
Wyoming Peak ▲ USA (WY) 252-253 H 4
Wyoming Range ▲ USA (WY) 252-253 H 3
Wyperfeld National Park ⊥ AUS 180-181 F 3
Wyralinu Hill ▲ AUS 176-177 G 6
Wyseby ○ AUS 178-179 K 3
Wysokie ○ PL 102-103 C 2
Wyszków ○ PL 92-93 Q 2
Wytheville ○ USA (VA) 280-281 E 7
Wyżyna Małopolska ⌣ PL 92-93 Q 3

X

Xaafuun = Dante ○ SP 208-209 K 3
Xaafuun, Raas ▲ SP 208-209 K 3
Xagquka ○ VRC 144-145 J 5
Xaidulla ○ VRC 138-139 F 1
Xainza ○ VRC 144-145 G 5
Xai-Xai ★ MOC 220-221 L 2
Xakriabá, Área Indígena X BR 72-73 H 3
Xalin ○ SP 208-209 J 4
Xalpatláhuac ○ MEX 52-53 E 3
Xa Mát ○ VN 158-159 J 5
Xambioá ○ BR 68-69 D 5
Xambrê, Rio ~ BR 72-73 D 7
Xam Hua ○ LAO 156-157 D 6
Xamindele ○ ANG 216-217 B 3
Xá-Muteba ○ ANG 216-217 D 4
Xandel ○ ANG 216-217 D 4
Xangongo ○ ANG 216-217 C 8
Xánthi ○ GR 100-101 K 4
Xanthos ••• TR 128-129 C 4
Xanxerê ○ BR 74-75 D 6
Xapuri ○ BR 70-71 C 2
Xapuri, Rio ~ BR 70-71 C 2
Xarar < SP 208-209 G 4
Xarardheere ○ SP 208-209 H 6
Xarlag ○ VRC 154-155 F 2
Xar Obot ○ VRC 148-149 O 5
Xarrama, Rio ~ P 98-99 C 5
Xassengue ○ ANG 216-217 E 5
Xateturu, Cachoeira ~ BR 68-69 B 5
Xátiva ○ E 98-99 G 5
Xau, Lake ⬭ RB 218-219 C 5
Xaudum ~ RB 216-217 F 9
Xavante ou Rio das Vertentes, Rio ~ BR 68-69 C 7
Xavantes, Represa de < BR 72-73 F 7
Xavantes, Serra dos ▲ BR 72-73 F 2
Xavantina ○ BR 72-73 D 6
Xavantinho, Rio ~ BR 68-69 C 7
Xayar ○ VRC 146-147 F 5
Xebert ○ VRC 150-151 D 5
Xêgar ○ VRC 144-145 F 6
Xeitongmoin ○ VRC 144-145 G 6
Xel-Há ∴ • MEX 52-53 L 1
Xenia ○ USA (IL) 274-275 K 6
Xenia ○ USA (OH) 280-281 C 4
Xerente, Área Indígena X BR 68-69 D 6
Xeriuni, Rio ~ BR 66-67 F 3
Xerokambos ○ GR 100-101 L 7
Xert ○ E 98-99 H 4
Xeruã, Rio ~ BR 66-67 C 6
Xiabande ○ VRC 150-151 E 5
Xiachuan Dao ⌒ VRC 156-157 H 6
Xiahe ○ VRC 154-155 C 4
Xiamen ○• VRC 156-157 L 4
Xi'an ☆•• VRC 154-155 F 4
Xianfen ○ VRC 154-155 G 4
Xianfeng ○ VRC 156-157 F 2
Xiangcheng ○ VRC (HEN) 154-155 H 5
Xiangcheng ○ VRC (HEN) 154-155 J 5
Xiangcheng ○ VRC (SIC) 144-145 M 6
Xianger Shan ▲ VRC 154-155 G 4
Xiangfan ○ VRC 154-155 H 5
Xianggang = Hong Kong ◘ HK 156-157 J 5
Xianghuang Qi ○ VRC 148-149 L 6
Xiang Jiang ~ VRC 156-157 H 3
Xiangkhoang ○ LAO 156-157 C 7
Xiangmihu • VRC 156-157 H 5
Xiang Ngeun ○ LAO 156-157 C 7
Xiangning ○ VRC 154-155 G 4
Xiangshan ○ VRC 156-157 M 2
Xiangsha Wan • VRC 154-155 F 1
Xiangshui ○ VRC 154-155 L 4
Xiangtan ○ VRC 156-157 H 3
Xiangtangshan Shiku • VRC 154-155 J 3
Xiangxiang ○ VRC 156-157 H 3
Xiangyin ○ VRC 156-157 H 2
Xiangyn ○ VRC 156-157 H 2
Xiangzhou ○ VRC 156-157 F 5
Xianju ○ VRC 156-157 M 2
Xianning ○ VRC 156-157 J 2
Xianshan Gang ~ VRC 156-157 M 2
Xiantao ○ VRC 154-155 H 6
Xianxia Ling ▲ VRC 156-157 L 2
Xianyang ○ VRC 154-155 F 4
Xianyou ○ VRC 156-157 L 4
Xiaochi ○ VRC 156-157 J 2
Xiaogan ○ VRC 154-155 H 6
Xiaohe ○ VRC 154-155 F 5
Xiaojiahe ○ VRC 150-151 J 4
Xiaojin ○ VRC 154-155 C 6
Xiaokouzi • VRC 154-155 D 2
Xiaomei Guan ▲ VRC 156-157 J 4
Xiaonanchuan ○ VRC 144-145 K 3
Xiaoniao Tiantang • VRC 156-157 H 5
Xiaoshan ○ VRC 154-155 M 6
Xiao Shan ▲ VRC 154-155 G 4
Xiaowutai Shan ▲ VRC 154-155 J 2
Xiao Xian ○ VRC 154-155 K 4
Xiapu ○ VRC 156-157 L 3
Xiasi ○ VRC 156-157 E 4
Xia Xian ○ VRC 154-155 G 4
Xiaxiyu ○ VRC 154-155 J 2
Xiayi ○ VRC 154-155 K 4
Xiazhai ○ VRC 156-157 D 4
Xiazhifu ○ VRC 144-145 C 5
Xiazhuang ○ VRC 154-155 J 5
Xiazi ○ VRC 156-157 E 3
Xichang ○ VRC (GXI) 156-157 F 6
Xichang ○ VRC (SIC) 156-157 C 3
Xichong ○ VRC 154-155 D 6
Xichou ○ VRC 156-157 D 5
Xichuan ○ VRC 154-155 G 5
Xicoténcatl ○ MEX 50-51 K 6
Xicotepec de Juárez ○ MEX 52-53 F 1
Xide ○ VRC 156-157 C 2
Xie, Rio ~ BR 66-67 D 2
Xiezhou Guandi Miao • VRC 154-155 G 4
Xifeng ○ VRC (GAN) 154-155 E 4
Xifeng ○ VRC (GZH) 156-157 E 3
Xigangzi ○ VRC 150-151 F 3
Xigazê ○•• VRC 144-145 G 6
Xigaze Shannan ▲ VRC 144-145 F 6
Xihua ○ VRC 154-155 J 5
Xiis ○ SP 208-209 H 3
Xiji ○ VRC 154-155 D 4
Xi Jiang ~ VRC 156-157 G 5
Xijin SK ~ VRC 156-157 F 5
Xijir Ulan Hu ⬭ VRC 144-145 H 3
Xijishui ○ VRC 154-155 D 3
Xikou ○ VRC (JXI) 156-157 J 2
Xikou ○ VRC (ZHE) 156-157 M 2
Xilamuren Caoyuan • VRC 148-149 K 7
Xi Liao He ~ VRC 150-151 D 6
Xilin ○ VRC 156-157 D 4
Xilinhot ○ VRC 148-149 N 6
Xilinji = Mohe ○ VRC 150-151 D 1
Xilitla ○ MEX 50-51 K 7
Xime ○ GNB 202-203 C 4
Xin'anjiang Sk. ⬭ VRC 156-157 L 2
Xin Barag Youqi ○ VRC 148-149 N 3
Xin Barag Zuoqi ○ VRC 150-151 B 3
Xinbin ○ VRC 150-151 E 7
Xincai ○ VRC 154-155 J 5
Xinchang ○ VRC 156-157 M 2
Xincheng ○ VRC 154-155 J 2
Xinchuan ○ VRC 154-155 M 5
Xindeng ○ VRC 156-157 L 2
Xindong ○ VRC 156-157 G 5
Xinduqiao ○ VRC 154-155 B 6
Xinfeng ○ VRC 156-157 J 4
Xinfengjiang SK ⬭ VRC 156-157 J 5
Xing'an ○ VRC 156-157 G 4
Xingan ○ VRC 156-157 J 3
Xingcheng ○ VRC 150-151 C 7
Xinge ○ ANG 216-217 E 4
Xingguo ○ VRC 156-157 J 3
Xinghua ○ VRC 154-155 L 5
Xingjiejie ○ VRC 156-157 E 5
Xingkai Hu ⬭ VRC 150-151 J 5
Xinglong ○ VRC 154-155 K 1
Xinglong ○ VRC 156-157 G 7
Xinglong-Shan Z.B. ⊥ • VRC 154-155 C 4
Xingning ○ VRC 156-157 J 4
Xingod ○ SP 208-209 J 5
Xingpan ○ VRC 156-157 F 6
Xingren ○ VRC 156-157 D 4
Xingrenbu ○ VRC 154-155 D 3
Xingshan ○ VRC 154-155 G 6
Xingtai ○ VRC 154-155 J 3
Xingtang ○ VRC 154-155 J 2
Xingu, Parque Indígena do X BR 68-69 B 7
Xingu, Rio ~ BR 68-69 B 5
Xingu, Rio ~ BR 72-73 D 2
Xinguara ○ BR 68-69 D 5
Xingwen ○ VRC 156-157 D 2
Xing Xian ○ VRC 154-155 G 2
Xingxingxia ○ VRC 146-147 M 5
Xingxiuhai • VRC 144-145 L 3
Xingyi ○ VRC 156-157 D 4
Xinhe ○ VRC 146-147 F 5
Xinhuang ○ VRC 156-157 F 3
Xining ☆ VRC 154-155 B 3
Xiniujiao ○ VRC 156-157 F 6
Xinji ○ VRC 154-155 J 3
Xinjie ○ VRC 156-157 D 5
Xinjin ○ VRC (LIA) 150-151 C 8
Xinjin ○ VRC (SIC) 154-155 C 6
Xinlong ○ VRC 154-155 B 6
Xinmin ○ VRC 150-151 D 7
Xinning ○ VRC 156-157 G 3
Xinping ○ VRC 156-157 E 3
Xinshao ○ VRC 156-157 C 4
Xintai ○ VRC 154-155 K 4
Xintian ○ VRC 156-157 H 4
Xinxiang ○ VRC 154-155 H 4
Xinxim, Rio ~ BR 68-69 B 6
Xinxing ○ VRC 156-157 H 5
Xinxing ○ VRC 156-157 F 7
Xinxu ○ VRC 156-157 E 5
Xinye ○ VRC 154-155 H 5
Xinyi ○ VRC (GDG) 156-157 G 5
Xinyi ○ VRC (JIA) 154-155 L 4
Xinying ○ VRC 156-157 F 7
Xinyu ○ VRC 156-157 J 3
Xinyuan ○ VRC 146-147 F 4
Xinzhao Shan ▲ VRC 154-155 E 2
Xinzhelin SK ⬭ VRC 156-157 J 2
Xinzheng ○ VRC 154-155 H 4
Xinzhou ○ VRC 154-155 H 2
Xinzuotang ○ VRC 156-157 J 5
Xiongyuecheng ○ VRC 150-151 D 7
Xipamanu, Rio ~ BR 70-71 C 2
Xipaotai • VRC 150-151 D 7
Xipembe, Rio ~ MOC 218-219 G 5
Xiping ○ VRC (HEN) 154-155 G 5
Xiping ○ VRC (HEN) 154-155 H 5
Xique-Xique ○ BR 68-69 G 7
Xishan • VRC (HUB) 154-155 J 6
Xishan • VRC (YUN) 156-157 C 4
Xishaqundao (Paracel Island) ≃ 158-159 L 2
Xishuangbanna • VRC 142-143 M 4
Xishuangbanna Z.B. ⊥ • VRC 142-143 M 5
Xishui ○ VRC (GZH) 156-157 E 2
Xishui ○ VRC (HUB) 154-155 J 6
Xistral ▲ E 98-99 D 3
Xi Taijnar Hu ⬭ VRC 144-145 H 2
Xiti ○ VRC 144-145 D 4
Xitole ○ GNB 202-203 C 4
Xituo ○ VRC 154-155 F 6
Xi Ujimqin Qi ○ VRC 148-149 N 5
Xiuning ○ VRC 156-157 L 2
Xiushan ○ VRC 156-157 F 2
Xiushui ○ VRC 156-157 J 2
Xiuwen ○ VRC 156-157 E 3
Xiuwu ○ VRC 154-155 H 4
Xiuyan ○ VRC 150-151 D 7
Xiuying ○ VRC 156-157 G 7
Xiwu ○ VRC 144-145 L 4
Xixabangma Feng ▲ VRC 144-145 E 6
Xi Xian ○ VRC 154-155 G 3
Xixiang ○ VRC 154-155 E 5
Xixia Wangling • VRC 154-155 D 2
Xixón = Gijón ○ E 98-99 E 3
Xixona ○ E 98-99 G 5
Xiyang ○ VRC 154-155 H 3
Xlacah ∴ • MEX 52-53 K 1
Xochiapa ○ MEX 52-53 G 3
Xochicalco ∴ • MEX 52-53 E 2
Xochimilco ○•• MEX 52-53 E 2
Xochob ∴ • MEX 52-53 K 2
Xom Đôn ○ VN 158-159 H 2
Xom Thôn ○ VN 158-159 H 2
Xopoto, Rio ~ BR 72-73 J 6
X-Pichil ○ MEX 52-53 K 2
Xpuji' ○ MEX (CAM) 52-53 K 2
Xpujil ∴ • MEX (CAM) 52-53 K 2
Xuân Đài, Vũng ≈ 158-159 K 4
Xuan'en ○ VRC 154-155 F 6
Xuanhan ○ VRC 154-155 E 6
Xuanhua ○ VRC 154-155 J 1
Xuankong Si • VRC 154-155 H 2
Xuân Lộc ○ VN 158-159 J 5
Xuanwei ○ VRC 156-157 D 3
Xuanzhong Si • VRC 154-155 H 3
Xuanzhou ○ VRC 154-155 L 6
Xuchang ○ VRC 154-155 H 4
Xuddur ☆ SP 208-209 F 6
Xudun ○ SP 208-209 H 4
Xuebao Ding ▲ VRC 154-155 C 5
Xuefeng Shan ▲ VRC 156-157 G 3
Xueshan ▲ VRC 154-155 D 3
Xufeng Shan ▲ VRC 156-157 G 3
Xugana Lodge ○ RB 218-219 B 4
Xumishan Shiku • VRC 154-155 D 3
Xunantunich ∴ • BH 52-53 K 3
Xungru ○ VRC 144-145 E 6
Xun He ~ VRC 154-155 F 5
Xunhua ○ VRC 154-155 C 4
Xun Jiang ~ VRC 156-157 G 5
Xunke ○ VRC 150-151 G 3
Xunwu ○ VRC 156-157 J 4
Xun Xian ○ VRC 154-155 J 4
Xunyang ○ VRC 154-155 F 5
Xunyi ○ VRC 154-155 F 4
Xupu ○ VRC 156-157 G 3
Xuro Co ⬭ VRC 144-145 F 5
Xushui ○ VRC 154-155 J 2
Xuwan ○ VRC 156-157 J 3
Xuwen ○ VRC 156-157 G 6
Xuyi ○ VRC 154-155 L 5
Xuyong ○ VRC 156-157 D 2
Xuzhou ○ VRC 154-155 K 4

Y

Yaak ○ USA (MT) 250-251 D 3
Yaak River ~ USA (MT) 250-251 D 3
Yaamba ○ AUS 178-179 L 2
Ya'an ○ VRC 156-157 C 2
Yaaq Braaway ○ SP 212-213 J 3
Yaba-Hita-Hikosan Quasi National Park ⊥ J 152-153 D 8
Yabassi ○ CAM 204-205 H 6
Yabayo ○ CI 202-203 G 7
Yabe ○ J 152-153 D 8
Yabebyry ○ PY 76-77 J 4
Yabebyry, Arroyo ~ PY 76-77 J 4
Yabelo ○ ETH 208-209 D 6
Yabelo Wildlife Sanctuary ⊥ ETH 208-209 D 6
Yabia ○ ZRE 210-211 J 2
Yabiti ~ DY 202-203 L 4
Yabo ○ YV 60-61 K 3
Yabrin ○ KSA 130-131 L 6
Yabucoa ○• USA (PR) 286-287 Q 2
Yabuli ○ VRC 150-151 G 5
Yabus ~ ETH 208-209 B 4
Yabuyanos ○ PE 64-65 F 2
Yacambú, Parque Nacional ⊥ YV 60-61 G 3
Yacaré Norte, Riacho ~ PY 76-77 H 2
Yachats ○ USA (OR) 244-245 A 6
Yacheng ○ VRC 156-157 F 7
Yachting Region •• 56 E 5
Yacimiento Río Turbio ○ RA 80 D 5
Yaciretá, Ilha ⌒ PY 76-77 J 4
Yacoraite, Río ~ RA 76-77 E 2
Yacuiba ○ BOL 76-77 F 1
Yacuma, Río ~ BOL 70-71 D 4
Yadat, Wādī ~ SUD 200-201 G 4
Yadé, Massif du ▲ RCA 206-207 B 5
Yadgir ○ IND 140-141 G 2
Yadibikro ○ CI 202-203 H 6
Yadiki ○ IND 140-141 G 3
Yadkin River ~ USA (NC) 282-283 G 4
Yadkin River ~ USA (NC) 282-283 G 5
Yadma ○ KSA 132-133 D 4
Yadong ○ VRC 144-145 G 7
Yadua ⌒ FJI 184 III b 2
Yaeng ○ THA 158-159 F 2
Yafase ○ RI 166-167 L 3
Yafo, Tel Aviv- ☆ IL 130-131 D 1
Yafran ◘ LAR 192-193 E 2
Yafran ☆•• LAR 192-193 E 1
Yagati ○ IND 140-141 G 4
Yaghan Basin ≃ 5 E 10
Yagishiri-tō ⌒ J 152-153 J 2
Yagoua ○ CAM 206-207 B 3
Yagradagzê Shan ▲ VRC 144-145 K 3
Yaguachi Nuevo ○ EC 64-65 C 3
Yaguajay ○ C 54-55 F 3
Yagual, El ○ YV 60-61 G 4
Yaguaraparo ○ YV 60-61 K 2
Yaguari, Arroyo ~ RA 76-77 H 5
Yaguarón, Río ~ ROU 74-75 D 9
Yaguas ○ CO 66-67 B 4
Yaguas, Río ~ PE 66-67 B 4
Yahekou ○ VRC 154-155 H 5
Yahk ○ CDN (BC) 230-231 N 4
Yahualica ○ MEX 50-51 H 7
Yahuma ○ ZRE 210-211 J 3
Yahyalı ☆ TR 128-129 F 3
Yaibrai ○ VRC 154-155 C 2
Yaita ○ J 152-153 H 6
Yajalón ○ MEX 52-53 H 3
Yajiang ○ VRC 154-155 B 6
Yaka ○ RCA 206-207 D 6
Yakabindie ○ AUS 176-177 F 3
Yakak, Cape ▲ USA 22-23 H 7
Yakamul ○ PNG 183 B 2
Yakana ○ ZRE 210-211 J 3
Yakassé-Attobrou ○ CI 202-203 J 6
Yakatograk ○ VRC 146-147 H 6
Yakawlang ○ AFG 134-135 M 1
Yakeshi ○ VRC 150-151 C 3
Yakfıkebir ☆ TR 128-129 H 2
Yakima ○ USA (WA) 244-245 E 4
Yakima Firing Center xx USA (WA) 244-245 E 4
Yakima Firing Range • USA 244-245 E 4
Yakima Indian Reservation X USA (WA) 244-245 D 4
Yakima River ~ USA (WA) 244-245 E 3
Yakmach ○ PK 134-135 K 4
Yako ○ BF 202-203 J 3
Yakobi Island ⌒ USA 32-33 B 2
Yakoma ○ ZRE 206-207 F 6
Yakoun River ~ CDN (BC) 228-229 B 3
Yaku ○ J 152-153 D 9
Yakumo ○ J 152-153 J 3
Yaku-shima ⌒ J 152-153 D 9
Yaku-shima National Park ⊥ ••• J 152-153 D 9
Yakutat ○ USA 20-21 V 7
Yakutat Bay ≈ 20-21 V 7
Yakutsk = Jakutsk ☆•• RUS 118-119 O 4
Yala ○ EAK 212-213 E 3
Yala ~ EAK 212-213 E 4
Yala ○ GH 202-203 K 4
Yala ○ THA 158-159 F 7
Yalaki ○ ZRE 210-211 J 3
Yalakom River ~ CDN (BC) 230-231 G 2
Yalape • PE 64-65 D 5
Yalardy ○ AUS 176-177 C 3
Yalata X AUS 176-177 L 5
Yalata Aboriginal Lands X AUS 176-177 L 5
Yalbalgo ○ AUS 176-177 C 2
Yalbyn ~ RUS 118-119 O 7
Yale ○ CDN (BC) 230-231 H 4
Yale ○ USA (MI) 272-273 G 4
Yale ○ USA (OK) 264-265 H 2
Yale ○ USA (WA) 244-245 C 4
Yaleko ○ ZRE 210-211 K 3
Yale Point ▲ USA (AZ) 256-257 F 2
Yalewa Kalou ⌒ FJI 184 III a 2
Yalgoo ○ AUS 176-177 D 4
Yalgorup National Park ⊥ AUS 176-177 C 6
Yali ~ BF 202-203 L 3
Yali ○ CO 60-61 D 4
Yali ○ NIC 52-53 L 5
Yaligimba ○ ZRE 210-211 J 2
Yalinga ○ RCA 206-207 F 5
Yallalong ○ AUS 176-177 C 3
Yalleroi ○ AUS 178-179 H 3
Yallingup Caves • AUS 176-177 C 6
Yallo ○ BF 202-203 J 3
Yalogo ○ BF 202-203 K 3
Yaloké ○ RCA 206-207 C 6
Yalong Jiang ~ VRC 144-145 M 4
Yalong Jiang ~ VRC 156-157 B 2
Yalongwa ○ ZRE 210-211 J 3
Yaloogarrie Creek ~ AUS 172-173 K 6
Yalova ☆ TR 128-129 C 2
Yaltubung ○ RI 166-167 E 5
Yalufi ○ ZRE 210-211 K 3
Yalu Jiang ~ VRC 150-151 E 7
Ya'lujiang Kou ≈ 150-151 E 8
Yālūr ○ AFG 136-137 M 6
Yamada ○ J 152-153 J 5
Yamagata ☆• J 152-153 J 5
Yamaguchi ☆ J 152-153 D 7
Yamakawa ○ J 152-153 F 7
Yamal, Poluostrov = Jamal, poluostrov ⌣ RUS 108-109 N 7
Yamal Nenets Autonomous District = Jam.-Neneckij avt.okrug ◘ RUS 108-109 N 7
Yamanashi ○ J 152-153 H 7
Yamarna X AUS 176-177 G 4
Yamarna Aboriginal Land X AUS 176-177 G 3
Yamasá ○ DOM 54-55 K 5
Yamasaki ○ J 152-153 F 7
Yamato Rise ≃ 152-153 F 5
Yamatosammyaku ▲ ARK 16 F 4
Yamatsuri ○ J 152-153 J 6
Yamba ○ AUS 178-179 M 5
Yamba ○ BF 202-203 L 3
Yambacoona ○ AUS 180-181 G 5
Yambah ○ AUS 176-177 M 1
Yambala ○ RCA 206-207 E 5
Yamba Lake ⬭ CDN 30-31 O 3
Yambala Koudouvélé ○ RCA 206-207 E 5
Yambata ○ ZRE 210-211 H 2
Yamba-Yamba ○ ZRE 210-211 L 6
Yambéring ○ RG 202-203 D 4
Yambio ○ SUD 206-207 J 6
Yambuya ○ ZRE 210-211 K 3
Yamdena, Pulau ⌒ RI 166-167 F 5
Yame ○ J 152-153 D 8
Yamethin ○ MYA 142-143 K 5
Yam Hamelah = Bahret Lut ⬭ JOR 130-131 D 2
Yamin ○ IRQ 130-131 K 2
Yam Kinneret ⬭ IL 130-131 D 1
Yamma Yamma Lake ⬭ AUS 178-179 F 4
Yamon ○ PE 64-65 C 5
Yamoussoukro ★• CI 202-203 H 6
Yampa ○ USA (CO) 254-255 J 3
Yampa River ~ USA (CO) 254-255 G 3
Yampi Sound Mining Area • AUS 172-173 F 4
Yamsay Mountain ▲ USA (OR) 244-245 D 8
Yamtu, Cape ▲ RI 166-167 F 2
Yamuna ~ IND 138-139 G 4
Yamuna ~ IND 138-139 G 6
Yamuna ~ IND 138-139 G 6
Yamuna ~ IND 142-143 B 3
Yamunanagar ○ IND 138-139 F 4
Yamur, Danau ⬭ RI 166-167 H 3
Yamzho Yumco ⬭ VRC 144-145 H 6
Yan ○ MAL 162-163 D 2
Yana ○ WAL 202-203 D 5
Yanaba Island ⌒ PNG 183 F 5
Yanac ○ AUS 180-181 F 4
Yanachaga-Chemillen, Parque Nacional ⊥ PE 64-65 E 7
Yanacu Grande, Río ~ PE 64-65 E 4
Yanadani ○ J 152-153 E 8
Yanagawa ○ J 152-153 D 8
Yanahuanca ○ PE 64-65 D 7
Yanai ○ J 152-153 E 8
Yanam ○ IND 140-141 K 2
Yan'an ○ VRC 154-155 F 3
Yanaoca ○ PE 70-71 B 4
Yanatili, Río ~ PE 64-65 F 8
Yanayacu ○ PE 64-65 E 4
Yanbu' al-Bahr ○ KSA 130-131 F 5
Yanbu' an-Nahl ○ KSA 130-131 F 5
Yancannia ○ AUS 178-179 G 6
Yancannia Creek ~ AUS 178-179 G 6
Yancannia Range ▲ AUS 178-179 G 6
Yancey ○ USA (TX) 266-267 H 4
Yanceyville ○ USA (NC) 282-283 H 4
Yanchang ○ VRC 154-155 G 3
Yancheng ○ VRC 154-155 M 5
Yanchep Beach ○• AUS 176-177 C 5
Yanchep National Park ⊥ AUS 176-177 C 5
Yanchi ○ VRC 154-155 E 3
Yanco Creek ~ AUS 180-181 H 3
Yanco Glen ○ AUS 178-179 F 6
Yanda Creek ~ AUS 178-179 H 6
Yandama Creek ~ AUS 178-179 F 5
Yandang Shan ▲ VRC 156-157 L 3
Yandangshan • VRC 156-157 M 2
Yandaxkak ○ VRC 146-147 J 6
Yandeearra ○ AUS 172-173 D 6
Yandeearra Aboriginal Land X AUS 172-173 D 6
Yandev ○ WAN 204-205 H 5
Yandina ○ SOL 184 I d 3
Yandon ○ MYA 158-159 C 2
Yandongi ○ ZRE 210-211 J 2
Yandun ○ VRC 146-147 M 4
Yanfeng ○ VRC 156-157 C 2
Yanfolila ○ RMM 202-203 F 4
Yang ○ THA 158-159 G 3
Yanga ○ CAM 210-211 E 2
Yanga ○ TCH 206-207 D 4
Yanga, Komin- ○ BF 202-203 L 4
Yangalia ○ RCA 206-207 E 5
Yangambi ○ ZRE 210-211 K 3
Yangara ~ TCH 198-199 J 2
Yangas ○ PE 64-65 D 7
Yangasso ○ RMM 202-203 H 3
Yangbajain ○ VRC (XIZ) 144-145 H 5
Yangbajain • VRC (XIZ) 144-145 H 5
Yangcheng ○ VRC 154-155 H 4
Yangchun ○ VRC 156-157 G 5
Yangcun ○ VRC 156-157 J 5
Yangdok ○ DVR 150-151 F 8
Yanggandu ○ RI 166-167 L 6
Yangjiang ○ VRC 156-157 G 6
Yanglin ○ VRC 156-157 C 4
Yangling ○ VRC 154-155 J 4
Yangmingshan National Park ⊥ • RC 156-157 M 4
Yangon ★•• MYA 158-159 D 2
Yangoru ○ PNG 183 B 2
Yangouali, Mare ⬭ DY 202-203 L 4
Yangpu Gang ≈ 156-157 F 7
Yangquan ○ VRC 154-155 H 3
Yangquangu ○ VRC 154-155 G 3
Yangqu Shan ▲ VRC 154-155 H 3
Yangshan ○ VRC 156-157 H 4
Yangshaocun Yizhi ∴ VRC 154-155 G 4
Yangshuo ○• VRC 156-157 G 4
Yangtze = Chang Jiang ~ VRC 154-155 L 6
Yangxi ○ VRC 156-157 G 6
Yangxin ○ VRC 156-157 J 2
Yang-Yang ○ SN 202-203 C 2
Yangyuan ○ VRC 154-155 J 1
Yangzhou ○• VRC 154-155 L 5
Yangzi'e Z.B. ⊥ • VRC 154-155 L 6
Yanhe ○ VRC 156-157 F 2
Yanhu ○ VRC 144-145 D 4
Yanhuqu ○ VRC 144-145 D 4
Yanji ○ VRC 150-151 G 6
Yanjin ○ VRC 156-157 D 2
Yankari Game Reserve ⊥ WAN 204-205 J 4
Yankee ○ USA (NM) 256-257 L 2
Yankoman ○ GH 202-203 J 7
Yankton ○ USA (SD) 260-261 J 4
Yankton Indian Reservation X USA (SD) 260-261 H 3
Yanmen G ▲ VRC 154-155 H 2
Yannarie River ~ AUS 176-177 C 1
Yanomami, Parque Indígena X BR 60-61 K 6
Yanonge ○ ZRE 210-211 K 3
Yan Oya ~ CL 140-141 J 6
Yanqi ○ VRC 146-147 H 4
Yanqing ○ VRC 154-155 J 1
Yanqul ○ OM 132-133 K 2
Yanrey ○ AUS 172-173 B 7
Yanshan ○ VRC (HEB) 154-155 K 2
Yanshan ○ VRC (YUN) 156-157 D 5
Yanshiping ○ VRC 144-145 J 4
Yanshou ○ VRC 150-151 G 5
Yansoribo ○ RI 166-167 G 2
Yantai ○ VRC 154-155 M 3
Yantakkeqik ○ VRC 146-147 J 6
Yantara, Lake ⬭ AUS 178-179 G 5
Yanting ○ VRC 154-155 D 6
Yantis ○ USA (TX) 264-265 J 6
Yantou ○ VRC 156-157 M 2
Yantzaza ○ EC 64-65 C 3
Yanuca ⌒ FJI 184 III c 2
Yanwodao • VRC 150-151 J 4
Yanzikou ○ VRC 156-157 D 3
Yaodian ○ VRC (GAN) 154-155 E 4
Yaodian ○ VRC (SXI) 154-155 F 3
Yaolin D. • VRC 156-157 L 2
Yaoundé ★• CAM 210-211 C 2
Yaowang Gang ○ VRC 154-155 M 5
Yaowang Hill ○ VRC 154-155 F 4
Yao Xian ○ VRC 154-155 F 4
Yapacana, Parque Nacional ⊥ YV 60-61 H 6
Yapacani, Río ~ BOL 70-71 E 5
Yapacárai ○ PY 76-77 J 3
Yapen, Pulau ⌒ RI 166-167 J 2
Yapen, Selat ≈ 166-167 H 2
Yapero ○ RI 166-167 J 4
Yapeyú ○• RA 76-77 J 5
Yappar River ~ AUS 174-175 F 6
Yappirāla ○ IND 140-141 H 3
Yapui ○ IND 142-143 J 1
Yaputih ○ RI 166-167 E 3
Yaqaga ⌒ FJI 184 III b 2
Yaqeta ⌒ FJI 184 III a 2
Yaque del Norte, Río ~ DOM 54-55 K 5
Yaqui ○ MEX 50-51 D 4
Yaqui, Boca del ≈ 50-51 D 4
Yaqui, Río ~ MEX 50-51 E 3
Yar ≈ 166-167 K 5
Yar < RN 198-199 F 2
Yara ○ C 54-55 G 4
Yaraka ○ AUS 178-179 H 3
Yaraligöz Dağı ▲ TR 128-129 F 2
Yaras, Las ○ PE 70-71 B 5
Yarbo ○ CDN (SAS) 232-233 R 5
Yardarino Gas and Oil Field • AUS 176-177 C 4
Yarden, ha ~ IL 130-131 D 1
Yardımcı Burnu ▲ TR 128-129 D 4
Yaré Lao ○ SN 196-197 C 6
Yaren ★ NAU 13 H 3
Yargatti ○ IND 140-141 F 3
Yarí, Río ~ CO 64-65 F 1
Yarim ○ Y 132-133 D 6
Yaritagua ○ YV 60-61 G 2
Yarkant He ~ VRC 138-139 F 1
Yarkant He ~ VRC 146-147 D 6
Yarkhun ~ PK 138-139 D 1
Yarle Lakes ⬭ AUS 176-177 L 5
Yarlung Zangbo Jiang ~ VRC 144-145 H 6
Yarmouth ○ CDN (NS) 240-241 J 7
Yarmouth ○ USA (ME) 278-279 L 5
Yarnell ○ USA (AZ) 256-257 C 4
Yaro Lund ○ PK 138-139 B 6
Yaroslavl' = Jaroslavl' ☆•• RUS 94-95 Q 3
Yaroupi ~ F 62-63 H 4
Yarra ○ DY 204-205 E 3
Yarrabubba ○ AUS 176-177 E 3
Yarralin ○ AUS 172-173 K 4
Yarraloola ○ AUS 172-173 B 6
Yarram ○ AUS 180-181 J 5
Yarraman ○ AUS 178-179 L 4
Yarra Yarra Lakes ⬭ AUS 176-177 C 4
Yarrie ○ AUS 172-173 E 6
Yarronvale ○ AUS 178-179 H 4
Yarrowitch ○ AUS 178-179 L 6
Yarrowmere ○ AUS 178-179 H 1
Yarumal ○ CO 60-61 D 4
Yarvicoya, Cerro ▲ RCH 70-71 C 7
Yarysah ~ RUS 110-111 P 5
Yasa ○ ZRE 210-211 H 5
Yāsāt, al- ⌒ UAE 134-135 E 6
Yasawa ⌒ FJI 184 III a 2
Yasawa Group ⌒ FJI 184 III a 2
Yashan ○ VRC 144-145 C 5
Yashi ○ WAN 198-199 C 6
Yashikera ○ WAN 204-205 E 4
Yasothon ○ THA 158-159 H 3
Yass ○ AUS 180-181 K 3
Yassıhöyük (Gordion) ☆•• TR 128-129 E 3
Yass River ~ AUS 180-181 K 3
Yāsūj ☆• IR 134-135 D 3
Yasun Burnu ▲ TR 128-129 G 2
Yasuni, Parque Nacional ⊥ EC 64-65 D 2
Yasuni, Río ~ EC 64-65 D 2
Yata ○ BOL 70-71 D 3
Yata ~ RCA 206-207 F 4
Yata, Río ~ BOL 70-71 E 3
Yatağan ☆ TR 128-129 C 4
Yatako ○ BF 202-203 L 2
Yata-Ngaya, Réserve de faune de la ⊥ RCA 206-207 F 4
Yates ○ CDN (ALB) 232-233 B 2
Yates Center ○ USA (KS) 262-263 L 7
Yates River ~ CDN 30-31 L 6
Yatesville ○ USA (GA) 284-285 F 4
Yathkyed Lake ⬭ CDN 30-31 U 4
Yatolema ○ ZRE 210-211 K 3
Yatsushiro ○ J 152-153 D 8
Yatsushiro-kai ≈ 152-153 D 8
Yatsu-take ▲ J 152-153 H 7
Yatta ○ EAK 212-213 F 4
Yatta Gap ▲ EAK 212-213 G 5
Yatta Plateau ▲ EAK 212-213 G 5
Yatúa, Río ~ YV 66-67 D 2
Yauca ○ PE 64-65 E 9
Yauca, Río ~ PE 64-65 E 9
Yauco ○ USA (PR) 286-287 P 2
Yauhannah ○ USA (SC) 284-285 L 3
Yauli ○ PE 64-65 E 8
Yauri ○ PE 70-71 B 4
Yaurisque ○ PE 70-71 B 3
Yauyos ○ PE 64-65 E 8
Yāval ○ IND 138-139 E 9
Yavapai Indian Reservation • USA (AZ) 256-257 C 4
Yavari, Río ~ PE 64-65 F 4
Yavari Mirim, Río ~ PE 64-65 F 4
Yávaros ○ MEX 50-51 E 4
Yavatmāl ○ IND 138-139 G 9
Yavero ó Paucartambo, Río ~ PE 64-65 F 8
Yaví, Cerro ▲ YV 60-61 J 5
Yavineto, Río ~ PE 64-65 E 2
Yavita ○ YV 60-61 H 6
Yaviza ○ PA 52-53 F 7
Yavuzeli ☆ TR 128-129 G 4
Yawatahama ○ J 152-153 E 8
Yawatongguzlangar ○ VRC 144-145 D 2
Yawatoutou, Mont ▲ RT 202-203 L 6
Yawgu ○ GH 202-203 L 4
Yawimu ○ RI 166-167 K 5
Yawkey ○ USA (WV) 280-281 E 5
Yawngo ○ MYA 142-143 L 4
Yawri Bay ≈ 202-203 D 5
Yaxcaba ○ MEX 52-53 K 1
Yaxchilan • MEX 52-53 J 3
Yaxia ∴• GCA 52-53 K 3
Yaxing ○ VRC 156-157 F 7
Yayama ○ ZRE 210-211 J 4
Yazd ◘ IR 134-135 E 3

Yazd ☆• IR (YAZ) 134-135 F 3
Yazdān ○ IR 134-135 J 2
Yazdavān, Rūd-e ∼ AFG 134-135 L 2
Yazlıca Dağı ▲ TR 128-129 K 4
Yazmān ○ PK 138-139 C 5
Yazoo City ○ USA (MS) 268-269 K 4
Yazoo National Wildlife Refuge ⊥ USA (MS) 268-269 K 3
Yazoo River ∼ USA (MS) 268-269 K 3
Yby Yaú ○ PY 76-77 J 2
Ycliff ○ CDN (ONT) 234-235 M 4
Ydžidnjur, boloto ⊶ RUS 88-89 V 5
Ydžidparma vozvyšennost' ▲ RUS 114-115 E 3
Ydžyd-Patok ∼ RUS 114-115 E 2
Ye ○ MYA 158-159 D 3
Yea ○ AUS 180-181 H 4
Yebawmi ○ MYA 142-143 J 3
Yebbi-Bou ○ TCH 198-199 J 2
Yebbi Souma ○ TCH 198-199 H 2
Yébenes, Los ○ E 98-99 F 5
Yébigué ∼ TCH 198-199 H 2
Yébigué, Enneri ∼ TCH 192-193 G 6
Yebok ○ MYA 142-143 H 6
Yebya ○ MYA 142-143 J 5
Yecheng ○ VRC 146-147 C 7
Yecla ○ E 98-99 G 5
Yécora ○ MEX 50-51 E 3
Yedseram ∼ WAN 198-199 G 6
Yedseram, River ∼ WAN 204-205 K 3
Yeed ○ SP 208-209 F 6
Yeehaw Junction ○ USA (FL) 286-287 J 4
Yeelanna ○ AUS 180-181 C 3
Yeelirrie ○ AUS 176-177 F 3
Yegguebo < RN 198-199 F 3
Yegros ○ PY 76-77 J 4
Yegua Creek ∼ USA (TX) 266-267 L 3
Yegua Creek, Middle ∼ USA (TX) 266-267 K 3
Yeguada ○ PA 52-53 D 7
Yégué ○ RT 202-203 L 5
Yegyi ○ MYA 158-159 C 2
Yeha ○ ETH 200-201 J 5
Yei ○ SUD (SR) 206-207 K 6
Yei ∼ SUD 206-207 K 6
Yeï Lulu, Col de ▲ RN 198-199 G 2
Yeji ○ GH 202-203 K 5
Yeji ○ VRC 154-155 J 6
Yekaterinburg = Ekaterinburg ☆ RUS 96-97 M 5
Yekebaierqier ○ VRC 144-145 M 3
Yekepa ○ LB 202-203 F 6
Yekia < TCH 198-199 H 4
Yekokora ∼ ZRE 210-211 H 3
Yelahanka ○ IND 140-141 G 4
Yele ○ WAL 202-203 E 5
Yelets = Elec ○ RUS 94-95 Q 5
Yélimané ○ RMM 202-203 E 2
Yelkaturti ○ IND 138-139 G 10
Yell ⌒ GB 90-91 G 1
Yellabinna Regional Reserve ⊥ AUS 176-177 M 5
Yellāpur ○ IND 140-141 F 3
Yellow Creek ○ CDN (SAS) 232-233 N 3
Yellow Creek ○ USA (PA) 280-281 H 3
Yellow Creek ∼ USA (AL) 284-285 B 3
Yellow Creek ∼ USA (MO) 274-275 E 5
Yellowdine ○ AUS 176-177 E 5
Yellow Grass ○ CDN (SAS) 232-233 O 6
Yellowhead Highway II CDN (ALB) 228-229 R 3
Yellowhead Pass ▲ CDN (BC) 228-229 Q 4
Yellow Jacket Pass ▲ USA (CO) 254-255 H 3
Yellowknife ☆• CDN 30-31 M 4
Yellowknife Bay ⊶ CDN 30-31 M 4
Yellowknife Highway II CDN 30-31 L 5
Yellowknife River ∼ CDN 30-31 N 4
Yellow Mission ○ PNG 183 A 2
Yellow Mountain, The ▲ AUS 180-181 J 2
Yellow Pine ○ USA (ID) 252-253 C 2
Yellow River ∼ PNG 183 A 2
Yellow River ∼ USA (AL) 284-285 D 5
Yellow River ∼ USA (FL) 286-287 C 1
Yellow River ∼ USA (GA) 284-285 G 3
Yellow River ∼ USA (WI) 270-271 H 6
Yellow River = Huang He ∼ VRC 154-155 G 3
Yellow Sea ≈ 150-151 D 10
Yellowstone Lake ⊶ USA (WY) 252-253 H 2
Yellowstone National Park ⊥ ••• USA (WY) 252-253 H 2
Yellowstone River ∼ USA (MT) 250-251 P 4
Yellville ○ USA (AR) 276-277 C 4
Yelm ○ USA (WA) 244-245 C 4
Yelrandu ○ IND 142-143 B 7
Yelvertoft ○ AUS 174-175 E 7
Yelvertone Bay ≈ 26-27 J 2
Yelvertone Inlet ≈ 26-27 J 2
Yelwa ○ WAN (PLA) 204-205 H 4
Yelwa ○ WAN (SOK) 204-205 F 3
Yema ○ ZRE 210-211 D 6
Yema Manshan ▲ VRC 146-147 N 6
Yemassee ○ USA (SC) 284-285 K 4
Yembo ○ ETH 208-209 C 4
Yemen = al-Yaman ■ Y 132-133 E 6
Yemnu ○ PNG 183 B 2
Yen ○ CAM 210-211 D 2
Yên, Mūi ▲ VN 158-159 K 4
Yenagoa ○ WAN 204-205 G 6
Yenakiyeve = Jenakijeve ○ UA 102-103 L 3
Yenangyaung ○ MYA 142-143 J 5
Yên Bái ☆ VN 156-157 D 6
Yên Châu ○ VN 156-157 D 6
Yenda ○ AUS 180-181 J 3
Yendé Millimou ○ RG 202-203 E 5
Yendéré ○ BF 202-203 H 4
Yendi ○ GH 202-203 K 5
Yên Định ☆ VN 156-157 E 6
Yénéganou ○ RCB 210-211 D 5
Yenge ∼ ZRE 210-211 H 4
Yengema ○ WAL 202-203 E 5
Yengil ○ IND 142-143 H 2
Yengisar ○ VRC 146-147 C 6
Yengo National Park ⊥ AUS 180-181 L 2
Yên Hưng ○ VN 156-157 C 6
Yenice Irmağı ∼ TR 128-129 E 2
Yenihisar ☆ TR 128-129 B 4
Yenişehir ☆ TR 128-129 C 2
Yenkis ○ PNG 183 B 3
Yên Ly ○ VN 156-157 D 7
Yéno ○ G 210-211 C 4
Yên So'n ○ VN 156-157 D 6
Yentna River ∼ USA 20-21 P 5
Yeoford ○ CDN (ALB) 232-233 D 2
Yeola ○ IND 138-139 E 9
Yeo Lake ⊶ AUS 176-177 H 4
Yeoval ○ AUS 180-181 K 2
Yeovil ○ GB 90-91 F 6
Yeppoon ○ AUS 178-179 L 2
Yerba Buena ○ PE 70-71 B 5
Yercaud ○ IND 140-141 H 5
Yerevan = Erevan ★ AR 128-129 L 2
Yergara ○ IND 140-141 G 2
Yergeni = Ergeni ▲ RUS 96-97 D 9
Yeriho = Arīḥā ☆•• AUT 130-131 D 2
Yerington ○• USA (NV) 246-247 F 5
Yerköy ○ TR 128-129 F 3
Yermala ○ IND 138-139 E 10
Yerupaja, Cerro ▲ PE 64-65 D 7
Yesan ○ ROK 150-151 F 9
Yesanpo • VRC 154-155 J 2
Yeshin ○ MYA 142-143 J 4
Yesildağ ○ TR 128-129 D 4
Yeşildağ ○ TR 128-129 D 4
Yeşilhisar ☆ TR 128-129 F 3
Yesilırmak ∼ TR 128-129 G 2
Yeşilırmak ∼ TR 128-129 G 2
Yeşilova ☆ TR 128-129 C 4
Yeso ○ USA (NM) 256-257 L 4
Yeso Arroyo ∼ USA (NM) 256-257 L 4
Yesterday River ∼ CDN (ONT) 236-237 H 2
Yet ○ ETH 208-209 F 6
Yetman ○ AUS 178-179 L 5
Yetti ⩦ RIM 196-197 G 2
Ye-u ○ MYA 142-143 J 4
Yeu, Île d' ⌒ F 90-91 F 8
Yevpatoriya = Jevpatorija ☆• UA 102-103 H 5
Yewa, River ∼ WAN 204-205 E 5
Yew Mountain ▲ USA (WV) 280-281 F 5
Ye Xian ○ VRC 154-155 H 5
Yeyik ○ VRC 144-145 D 2
Yganija ∼ RUS 110-111 W 4
Yguazú, Río ∼ PY 74-75 L 3
Ygyatta ∼ RUS 118-119 H 4
Yhú ○ PY 76-77 K 3
Yi'an ○ VRC 150-151 E 4
Yibin ○ VRC 156-157 D 2
Yichang ○ VRC 154-155 G 6
Yicheng ○ VRC (HUB) 154-155 H 6
Yicheng ○ VRC (SHA) 154-155 G 4
Yichuan ○ VRC (HEN) 154-155 H 4
Yichuan ○ VRC (SXI) 154-155 G 4
Yichun ○ VRC (HEI) 150-151 G 4
Yichun ○ VRC (JXI) 156-157 J 3
Yiğilca ☆ TR 128-129 D 2
Yihuang ○ VRC 156-157 K 3
Yijun ○ VRC 154-155 F 4
Yilan ○ VRC 150-151 G 4
Yıldız Dağları ▲ TR 128-129 B 2
Yıldızeli ☆ TR 128-129 G 3
Yilehuli Shan ▲ VRC 150-151 D 2
Yiliang ○ VRC (YUN) 156-157 D 3
Yiliang ○ VRC (YUN) 156-157 C 4
Yilingyan • VRC 156-157 F 5
Yilong ○ VRC 154-155 E 6
Yilou ○ BF 202-203 K 3
Yima ○ VRC 154-155 G 4
Yimen ○ VRC 156-157 C 4
Yimni River ∼ PNG 183 B 2
Yimuhe ○ VRC (NMZ) 150-151 C 1
Yinan ○ VRC 154-155 L 4
Yinchuan ☆• VRC 154-155 E 2
Yindarlgooda, Lake ⊶ AUS 176-177 G 5
Yindi ○ AUS 176-177 G 5
Yingawunarri Aboriginal Land ⅩAUS 172-173 K 4
Yingcheng ○ VRC 154-155 H 6
Yingde ○ VRC 156-157 H 4
Yinggehai ○ VRC 156-157 F 7
Ying He ∼ VRC 154-155 J 5
Yingjing ○ VRC 156-157 C 2
Yingkou ○ VRC 150-151 D 7
Yingkou (Dashiqiao) ○ VRC 150-151 D 7
Yingshan ○ VRC (HUB) 154-155 H 6
Yingshan ○ VRC (SIC) 154-155 E 6
Yingshang ○ VRC 154-155 K 5
Yingtan ○ VRC 156-157 K 2
Yingui ○ CAM 204-205 J 6
Ying Xian ○ VRC 154-155 H 2
Yingxian Muta • VRC 154-155 H 2
Yining ○ VRC 146-147 E 4
Yinjiang ○ VRC 156-157 F 2
Yinnietharra ○ AUS 176-177 D 2
Yin Shan ▲ VRC 148-149 J 7
Yinxu ⛬• VRC 154-155 J 3
Yi'ong Co • VRC 144-145 K 5
Yi'ong Zangbo ∼ VRC 144-145 K 5
Yipinglang ○ VRC 156-157 B 4
Yiqikai ○ VRC 144-145 M 3
Yirga Alem ○ ETH 208-209 D 5
Yirga Ch'efē ○ ETH 208-209 D 5
Yirol ○ SUD 206-207 K 5
Yirrkala Ⅹ AUS 174-175 D 3
Yirshi ○ VRC 150-151 B 4
Yirūb = Ġarūb ○ Y 132-133 H 5
Yishan ○ VRC 156-157 F 4
Yishui ○ VRC 154-155 L 4
Yismala Giyorgis ○ ETH 208-209 C 3
Yitong ○ VRC 150-151 E 6
Yitulihe ○ VRC 150-151 C 2
Yity ○ OM 132-133 L 2
Yiwu ○ VRC (XUZ) 146-147 M 4
Yiwu ○ VRC (ZHE) 156-157 M 2
Yiwulüshan • VRC 150-151 C 7
Yiwulüshan Z.B. ⊥• VRC 150-151 C 7
Yi Xian ○ VRC (HEB) 154-155 J 2
Yi Xian ○ VRC (LIA) 150-151 C 7
Yixing ○ VRC 154-155 L 6
Yiyang ○ VRC (HUN) 156-157 H 2
Yiyang ○ VRC (JXI) 156-157 K 2
Yiyuan ○ VRC 154-155 L 3
Yizhang ○ VRC 156-157 H 4
Yizheng ○ VRC 154-155 L 5
Ylämaa ○ FIN 88-89 J 6
Ylikiiminki ○ FIN 88-89 J 4
Yli-Kitka ⊶ FIN 88-89 K 3
Ylitornio ○ FIN 88-89 G 3
Ylivieska ○ FIN 88-89 H 4
Yllymah ○ RUS 118-119 N 6
Ylöjärvi ○ FIN 88-89 G 6
Ymer Nunatakker ▲ GRØ 26-27 n 5
Ymer Ø ⌒ GRØ 26-27 n 7
Ymir ○ CDN (BC) 230-231 M 4
Ynahsyt ○ RUS 118-119 J 4
Yoa, Lac ⊶ TCH 198-199 K 3
Yoakum ○ USA (TX) 266-267 K 4
Yobe, Komadougou ∼ 198-199 F 6
Yoboki ○ DJI 208-209 F 3
Yockanookany River ∼ USA (MS) 268-269 L 4
Yoco ○ YV 60-61 K 2
Yocona River ∼ USA (MS) 268-269 L 2
Yoder ○ USA (CO) 254-255 L 5
Yoder ○ USA (WY) 252-253 O 5
Yof ○• SN 202-203 B 2
Yofor ○ RI 166-167 J 4
Yogan, Cerro ▲ RCH 80 F 7
Yogoum < TCH 198-199 J 4
Yog Point ▲ RP 160-161 F 5
Yogyakarta ☆ RI 168 D 3
Yohnnybli ○ LB 202-203 F 7
Yoho ○ CDN (BC) 230-231 N 2
Yoho National Park ⊥ ••• CDN (BC) 230-231 N 2
Yoichi ○ J 152-153 J 3
Yoichi-dake ▲ J 152-153 J 3
Yokadouma ○ CAM 210-211 E 2
Yokena ○ USA (MS) 268-269 K 4
Yokkaichi ○ J 152-153 G 7
Yoko ○ CAM 204-205 K 6
Yokoate-shima ⌒ J 152-153 C 10
Yokoboué ○ CI 202-203 H 7
Yokohama ○ J (AOM) 152-153 J 4
Yokohama ☆• J (KAN) 152-153 H 7
Yokosuka ○ J 152-153 H 7
Yokote ○ J 152-153 J 5
Yola ○ CAM 206-207 B 6
Yola ☆ WAN 204-205 K 4
Yolla ○ AUS 180-181 H 6
Yolombo ○ ZRE 210-211 J 4
Yombi ○ G 210-211 C 4
Yomblon ○ PE 64-65 C 5
Yomou ○ RG 202-203 F 6
Yomuka ○ RI 166-167 K 5
Yonago ○ J 152-153 E 7
Yoneshiro-gawa ∼ J 152-153 J 4
Yonezawa ○ J 152-153 J 6
Yong'an ○ VRC 156-157 K 4
Yongchang ○ VRC 154-155 B 2
Yongcheng ○ VRC 154-155 K 5
Yongchuan ○ VRC 156-157 D 2
Yongdeng ○ VRC 154-155 C 3
Yongding ○ VRC 156-157 K 4
Yŏngdŏk ○ ROK 150-151 G 9
Yongfeng ○ VRC 156-157 J 3
Yongfu ○ VRC 156-157 F 4
Yongjing ○ VRC 154-155 C 4
Yongji Qiao • VRC 156-157 F 4
Yŏngju ○ ROK 150-151 G 9
Yongkang ○ VRC 156-157 L 2
Yongle Gong • VRC 154-155 G 4
Yongle Qundao ⌒ VRC 158-159 L 2
Yongling ○ VRC 150-151 E 7
Yongning ○ VRC (GXI) 156-157 F 5
Yongning ○ VRC (NIN) 154-155 E 2
Yongofondo ○ RCA 206-207 F 6
Yong Peng ○ MAL 162-163 E 3
Yongping ○ VRC 154-155 F 3
Yongren ○ VRC 156-157 B 3
Yongshun ○ VRC 156-157 F 2
Yongtai ○ VRC 156-157 L 4
Yongxin ○ VRC 156-157 J 3
Yongxing ○ VRC 156-157 H 3
Yongxiu ○ VRC 156-157 J 2
Yong Yap, Gunung ▲ MAL (KEL) 162-163 D 2
Yonibana ○ WAL 202-203 D 5
Yonkers ○ USA (NY) 280-281 N 3
Yonne ∼ F 90-91 J 7
Yonoféré ○ SN 202-203 C 2
Yop, Pulau ⌒ RI 166-167 H 3
Yopal ○ CO 60-61 E 5
Yopales ○ YV 60-61 K 3
Yopei = Tamala ○ GH 202-203 K 5
Yopie ○ LB 202-203 F 6
Yopurga ○ VRC 146-147 C 6
Yorito ○ HN 52-53 L 4
York ○ AUS 176-177 D 5
York ○ GB 90-91 G 5
York ○ USA (AL) 284-285 B 4
York ○ USA (MT) 250-251 H 5
York ○ USA (ND) 258-259 H 3
York ○ USA (NE) 262-263 J 4
York ○ USA (PA) 280-281 K 4
York ○ USA (SC) 284-285 J 2
York ○ WAL 202-203 D 5
York, Cape ▲ AUS 174-175 G 2
York, Kap ▲ GRØ 26-27 R 6
Yorke Peninsula ⌣ AUS 180-181 D 3
Yorketown ○ AUS 180-181 D 3
Yorkeys Knob ○ AUS 174-175 H 5
York Factory (abandoned) ○ CDN 34-35 K 2
York Haven ○ USA (PA) 280-281 K 3
Yorkrakine ○ AUS 176-177 D 5
York River ∼ CDN (ONT) 238-239 H 3
York River ∼ USA (VA) 280-281 K 6
Yorkshire Dales National Park ⊥ GB 90-91 F 4
Yorkshire Downs ○ AUS 174-175 F 7
York Sound ≈ 172-173 G 3
Yorkton ○ CDN (SAS) 232-233 Q 4
Yorktown ○ USA (TX) 266-267 K 5
Yorktown ○ USA (VA) 280-281 K 6
Yorkville ○ USA (IL) 274-275 K 3
Yoro ☆ HN 52-53 L 4
Yoro, Montaña de ▲ HN 52-53 L 4
Yorobougoula ○ RMM 202-203 G 4
Yoron ○ J 152-153 C 11
Yoron-shima ⌒ J 152-153 C 11
Yorosso ○ RMM 202-203 H 3
Yorubaland, Plateau of ▲ WAN 204-205 E 4
Yosemite ○ USA (KY) 276-277 L 3
Yosemite National Park ⊥ ••• USA (CA) 248-249 E 2
Yosemite Village ○ USA (CA) 248-249 E 2
Yoseravi ○ BOL 70-71 F 6
Yoshii-gawa ∼ J 152-153 F 7
Yoshino-gawa ∼ J 152-153 F 7
Yos Sudarso, Teluk ≈ 166-167 L 3
Yŏsu ○ ROK 150-151 F 10
Yosua ○ PNG 183 B 3
Yotefa Nature Reserve ⊥• RI 166-167 L 3
Yōtei-san ▲ J 152-153 J 3
Youangarra ○ AUS 176-177 E 4
Youbou ○ CDN (BC) 230-231 E 5
Youdunzi ○ VRC 146-147 K 6
Youghal = Eochaill ○ IRL 90-91 D 6
Youghiogheny River Lake ⊶ USA (PA) 280-281 G 4
Yougzhou ○ VRC 156-157 G 3
You Jiang ∼ VRC 156-157 E 5
Youkounkoun ○ RG 202-203 D 3
Young ○ AUS 180-181 K 3
Young ○ CDN (SAS) 232-233 N 4
Young ○ ROU 78-79 L 2
Younghusband, Lake ⊶ AUS 178-179 D 6
Younghusband Peninsula ⌣ AUS 180-181 E 4
Youngou ∼ RCA 206-207 E 5
Youngs Cove ○ CDN (NB) 240-241 K 5
Youngstown ○ CDN (ALB) 232-233 G 4
Youngstown ○ USA (FL) 286-287 D 1
Youngstown ○ USA (NY) 278-279 B 5
Youngstown ○ USA (OH) 280-281 F 2
Young Sund ≈ 26-27 p 6
Yountville ○ USA (CA) 246-247 C 5
Youssef Ben Tachfine, Barrage < MA 188-189 G 6
Youssoufia ○ MA 188-189 G 4
Youvarou ○ RMM 202-203 H 2
You Xian ○ VRC 156-157 H 3
Youyang ○ VRC 156-157 F 2
Youyi Feng = Tavan Bogd ▲ VRC 146-147 H 1
Youyiguan ○ VRC 156-157 E 5
Yowa ∼ ZRE 210-211 H 2
Yowah Creek ∼ AUS 178-179 H 4
Yoya, Pampa de la ⩦ PE 70-71 B 5
Yoyo National Park ⊥ GH 202-203 J 7
Yozgat ☆ TR 128-129 F 3
Ypsilanti ○ USA (MI) 272-273 F 5
Yreka ○ USA (CA) 246-247 C 2
Yrgyz ☆ KA (AKT) 126-127 O 3
Yrgyz ∼ KA 126-127 O 3
Yrgyz ∼ KA 126-127 O 2
Yr Wyddfa = Snowdon ▲ GB 90-91 E 5
Ysabel Channel ≈ 183 E 1
Ystad ○• S 86-87 F 9
Ystannah-Hočo ○ RUS 110-111 N 3
Yštyk ○ KS 146-147 D 5
Ysyk-Köl ○ KS 146-147 C 4
Ysyk-Köl, ozero ⊶ KS 146-147 C 4
Ytar, Sylgy- ○ RUS 112-113 H 3
Ytterhogdal ○ S 86-87 G 5
Yttygran, ostrov ⌒ RUS 112-113 Y 4
Ytyk-Kjuël' ☆• RUS 120-121 E 2
Ytymdža ∼ RUS 118-119 N 7
Yu, Pulau ⌒ RI 166-167 E 2
Yu'alliq, Ġabal ▲ ET 194-195 F 2
Yuanbao Shan ▲ VRC 156-157 F 4
Yuanjiang ○ VRC 155-155 G 4
Yuanjiang ○ VRC (HUN) 156-157 H 2
Yuanjiang ○ VRC (YUN) 156-157 B 5
Yuan Jiang ∼ VRC 156-157 C 5
Yuan Jiang ∼ VRC 156-157 G 2
Yuanling ○ VRC 156-157 G 2
Yuanmou ○ VRC 156-157 B 4
Yuanping ○ VRC 154-155 H 2
Yuanshangdu Yizhi ⛬• VRC 148-149 N 6
Yuantan ○ VRC 154-155 K 6
Yuanyang ○ VRC 156-157 C 5
Yuat River ∼ PNG 183 B 3
Yuba ○ USA (OK) 264-265 H 5
Yuba City ○ USA (CA) 246-247 D 4
Yuba Pass ▲ USA (CA) 246-247 E 4
Yūbari ○ J 152-153 J 3
Yūbari-gawa ∼ J 152-153 K 3
Yūbari-santi ▲ J 152-153 K 3
Yuba River ∼ USA (CA) 246-247 D 4
Yubdo ○ ETH 208-209 B 4
Yūbetsu ○ J 152-153 K 2
Yubetu-dake ▲ J 152-153 J 3
Yucaipa ○ USA (CA) 248-249 G 5
Yucatán ○ MEX 52-53 L 1
Yucatán ◘ MEX 52-53 K 1
Yucatán Basin ≃ 54-55 C 4
Yucatán Channel ≈ 54-55 B 3
Yucatán Peninsula = Yucatán, Península de ⌣ MEX 52-53 J 2
Yucca ○ USA (AZ) 256-257 A 4
Yucca House National Monument • USA (CO) 254-255 G 6
Yucca Valley ○ USA (CA) 248-249 H 5
Yuci ○ VRC 154-155 H 3
Yucumo ○ BOL 70-71 D 4
Yudu ○ VRC 156-157 J 4
Yuechi ○ VRC 154-155 E 6
Yuelai ○ VRC 154-155 E 6
Yuelong ○ VRC 156-157 H 2
Yuelushan • VRC 156-157 H 2
Yuendumu Ⅹ AUS 172-173 K 7
Yuendumu Aboriginal Land Ⅹ AUS 172-173 K 7
Yuenkotang ○ VRC 144-145 C 4
Yueqing ○ VRC 156-157 M 2
Yuexi ○ VRC 154-155 K 6
Yueyang ○ VRC 156-157 H 2
Yueyaqan Mingshashan • VRC 146-147 M 5
Yueyoquan • VRC 146-147 M 5
Yufengshan • VRC 156-157 F 4
Yüğlük Dağı ▲ TR 128-129 E 4
Yugorskiy Shar, Proliv = Jugorskij Šar, proliv ≈ RUS 108-109 H 7
Yugoslavia = Jugoslavija ■ YU 100-101 G 3
Yuhe ○ VRC (SXI) 154-155 F 3
Yuhe ○ VRC (YUN) 156-157 D 3
Yuhua D. • VRC 156-157 K 3
Yuin ○ AUS 176-177 D 3
Yuinmery ○ AUS 176-177 E 4
Yu Jiang ∼ VRC 156-157 F 5
Yuki ○ ZRE 210-211 G 5
Yuki River ∼ USA 20-21 M 4
Yukon ○ USA (OK) 264-265 G 3
Yukon-Charley-Rivers National Preserve ⊥ USA 20-21 T 4
Yukon Delta ≈ 20-21 H 5
Yukon Delta National Wildlife Refuge ⊥ USA 20-21 H 5
Yukon Flats ⊥ USA 20-21 S 3
Yukon Plateau ▲ CDN 20-21 V 5
Yukon River ∼ USA 20-21 P 4
Yukon Territory ◘ CDN 30-31 E 4
Yüksekova ☆ TR 128-129 L 4
Yukuhashi ○ J 152-153 D 8
Yulara ○ AUS 176-177 L 2
Yule, Mount ▲ PNG 183 D 5
Yuleba ○ AUS 178-179 K 4
Yulee ○ USA (FL) 286-287 H 1
Yule Island ⌒ PNG 183 D 5
Yule River ∼ AUS 172-173 D 6
Yuli ○ RC 156-157 M 5
Yuli ○ VRC 146-147 H 5
Yuli ○ WAN 204-205 J 4
Yuli, River ∼ WAN 204-205 J 4
Yulin ○ VRC (GXI) 156-157 G 5
Yulin ○ VRC (SHA) 154-155 F 2
Yulin Ku • VRC 146-147 M 5
Yulong Xue Shan ▲ VRC 142-143 M 2
Yulton, Lago ⊶ RCH 80 D 2
Yuluí ○ PNG 183 B 2
Yuma ○ USA (AZ) 256-257 A 6
Yuma ○ USA (CO) 254-255 N 3
Yuma Proving Ground ✕✕ USA (AZ) 256-257 A 5
Yumariba ○ YV 60-61 K 5
Yumbarra Conservation Park ⊥ AUS 176-177 M 5
Yumbe ○ EAU 212-213 C 2
Yumbel ○ RCH 78-79 C 4
Yumbi ○ ZRE (Ban) 210-211 F 4
Yumbi ○ ZRE (KIV) 210-211 L 4
Yumbo ○ CO 60-61 C 6
Yumen ○ VRC 146-147 N 6
Yumenguan ○ VRC (GAN) 146-147 L 5
Yumenguan • VRC (GAN) 146-147 L 5
Yumen Zhen ○ VRC 148-149 C 7
Yumin ○ VRC 146-147 F 2
Yumtang ○ BHT 142-143 F 2
Yuna ○ AUS 176-177 C 4
Yuna, Río ∼ DOM 54-55 L 5
Yunak ☆ TR 128-129 D 3
Yunan ○ VRC 156-157 G 5
Yunaska Island ⌒ USA 22-23 L 6
Yuncheng ○ VRC (SHA) 154-155 G 4
Yuncheng ○ VRC (SHD) 154-155 J 4
Yundamindera ○ AUS 176-177 G 4
Yunfu ○ VRC 156-157 H 5
Yungang Shiku • VRC 154-155 H 1
Yungas ⩦ BOL 70-71 D 5
Yungay ○ PE 64-65 D 6
Yungay ○ RCH 78-79 D 4
Yungui Gaoyuan ⩦ VRC 156-157 C 4
Yunguyo ○ PE 70-71 C 5
Yungyang ○ VRC 154-155 H 5
Yunhe ○ VRC 156-157 L 2
Yunkai Dashan ▲ VRC 156-157 F 5
Yunkanjini Aboriginal Land Ⅹ AUS 172-173 K 7
Yun Ling ▲ VRC 142-143 L 2
Yunlong ○ VRC 142-143 L 3
Yunmeng ○ VRC 154-155 H 6
Yunnan ◘ VRC 142-143 L 2
Yunomae ○ J 152-153 D 8
Yuntaishan • VRC 154-155 L 4
Yunwu Shan ▲ VRC 156-157 G 5
Yunwu Shan ▲ VRC 148-149 N 7
Yun Xian ○ VRC (HUB) 154-155 G 5
Yun Xian ○ VRC (YUN) 142-143 M 3
Yunxiao ○ VRC 156-157 K 5
Yuping ○ VRC 156-157 F 3
Yupurari, Raudal ∼ CO 66-67 B 2
Yuqian ○ VRC 154-155 L 6
Yuqing ○ VRC 156-157 E 3
Yuquanshan • VRC 154-155 G 6
Yura ○ PE 70-71 B 5
Yura, Río ∼ BOL 70-71 E 7
Yura-gawa ∼ J 152-153 F 7
Yurayaco ○ CO 64-65 D 1
Yuraygir National Park ⊥ AUS 178-179 M 5
Yurécuaro ○ MEX 52-53 C 1
Yurimaguas ○ PE 64-65 D 4
Yuriria ○ MEX 52-53 D 1
Yurua, Río ∼ PE 64-65 F 6
Yuruan, Río ∼ YV 62-63 D 2
Yurubí, Parque Nacional ⊥ YV 60-61 G 2
Yurungkax He ∼ VRC 144-145 C 2
Yusala, Lago ⊶ BOL 70-71 D 4
Yuscarán ☆ HN 52-53 L 5
Yu Shan ▲ RC 156-157 M 5
Yushan ○ VRC 156-157 L 2
Yushan National Park ⊥• RC 156-157 M 5
Yushe ○ VRC 154-155 H 3
Yushu ○ VRC (JIL) 150-151 F 5
Yushu ○ VRC (QIN) 144-145 L 4
Yūsuf, Baḥr < ET 194-195 E 3
Yusufeli ☆ TR 128-129 J 2
Yusun Shoal ≃ 158-159 K 5
Yusupalik Tag ▲ VRC 146-147 J 6
Yutian ○ VRC 144-145 C 2
Yuto ○ RA 76-77 E 2
Yuwang ○ VRC 154-155 E 3
Yuxi ○ VRC 156-157 C 4
Yu Xian ○ VRC 154-155 H 2
Yuyao ○ VRC 154-155 M 6
Yuzawa ○ J 152-153 J 5
Yuzhno Sakhalinsk = Južno-Sahalinsk ☆ RUS 122-123 K 5
Yuzhnyy Ural = Južnyj Ural ▲ RUS 96-97 K 8
Yuzhou ○ VRC 154-155 H 4
Yvetot ○ F 90-91 H 7
Ywathit ○ MYA 142-143 J 4
Ywathit ○ MYA 142-143 J 6

Z

Za, Oued ∼ MA 188-189 K 3
Zaachila ○ MEX (OAX) 52-53 F 3
Zaachila ⛬• MEX (OAX) 52-53 F 3
Zaalajskij hrebet ▲ TJ 136-137 M 5
Zaamar = Bat-Öldzijt ○ MAU 148-149 G 3
Zaamin ○ US 136-137 L 5
Zaanstad ○ NL 92-93 H 2
Zab, Monts du ▲ DZ 190-191 E 3
Zabadānī, az- ○ SYR 128-129 G 6
Žabaj ∼ KA 124-125 F 3
Zabajkal'sk ☆ RUS 118-119 H 11
Zabarġad, Ġazīrat ⌒ ET 194-195 H 6
Žabasak ○ KA 126-127 O 2
Zabid ○• Y 132-133 C 6
Zabid, Wādī ∼ Y 132-133 C 6
Žabljano ○ BG 102-103 C 6
Zābol ◘ AFG 134-135 M 2
Zābol ○• IR 134-135 J 3
Zāboli ○ IR 134-135 L 5
Zabré ○ BF 202-203 K 4
Zaburun'e ○ KA 96-97 G 10
Zaburunje cyganaky ≈ 96-97 G 10
Zabūt ○ Y 132-133 H 6
Žabysaj ∼ KA 126-127 O 3
Zabzugu ○ GH 202-203 L 5
Zacapa ☆ GCA 52-53 K 4
Zacapa ○ HN 52-53 K 4
Zacapu ○ MEX 52-53 D 2
Zacatal ○ MEX 52-53 J 2
Zacatecas ◘ MEX 50-51 H 6
Zacatecas ☆• MEX (ZAC) 50-51 H 6
Zacatecoluca ☆ ES 52-53 K 5
Zacatepec ○ MEX 52-53 E 2
Zacatlán ○ MEX 52-53 F 2
Zachariaes Bræ ⊂ GRØ 26-27 p 4
Zachary ○ USA (LA) 268-269 J 6
Zachidnyj Buh ∼ UA 102-103 C 2
Zachidnyj Buh ∼ UA 102-103 D 3
Zacoalco de Torres ○ MEX 52-53 C 1
Zacualpan ○ MEX 52-53 E 2
Zacualtipán ○ MEX 52-53 E 1
Zaculeu ⛬• GCA 52-53 J 4
Zad, Col du ▲ MA 188-189 J 4
Zadar ○• HR 100-101 E 2
Zadetkale Kyun ⌒ MYA 158-159 E 5
Zadetkyi Kyun ⌒ MYA 158-159 E 6
Zadgaj ○ MAU 148-149 D 4
Zadié ∼ G 210-211 D 3
Zadoi ○ VRC 144-145 K 4
Zadonsk ○ RUS 94-95 Q 5
Zadonsk, Severo- ○ RUS 94-95 Q 4
Zaër-Zaïa ⩦ MA 188-189 H 4
Za'farāna ○ ET 194-195 F 3
Za'farāna, Ra's ▲ ET 194-195 F 3
Zafarqand ○ IR 134-135 E 2
Zafarwāl ○ PK 138-139 E 3
Zafra ○•• E 98-99 D 5
Zafra, az- ⩦ UAE 132-133 J 2
Zagai Island ⌒ AUS 174-175 G 1
Żagań ○• PL 92-93 N 3
Zagaoua ⩦ TCH 198-199 K 5
Žagarė ○•• LT 94-95 H 3
Zagastajn davaa ▲ MAU 148-149 C 3
Zagatala = Zaqatala ○• AZ 128-129 M 2
Zāge ○ IR 134-135 C 2
Zaghouan ☆ TN 190-191 H 2
Zaghouan, Jebel ▲ TN 190-191 H 2
Zagné ○• CI 202-203 G 6
Zagora ○ MA 188-189 J 5
Zagorsk = Sergiev Posad ☆••• RUS 94-95 Q 3
Zagreb ★• HR 100-101 E 2
Zagros Mountains = Zāgros, Kūhhā-ye ▲ IR 128-129 M 5
Zagustaj ○ RUS 118-119 E 10
Zaharenko ○ RUS 110-111 Y 7
Zaharodze ⩦ BY 94-95 J 5
Zaharovka ○ KA 124-125 G 4
Zaharovo ○ RUS 118-119 D 10
Zāhedān ○ IR (FAR) 134-135 E 4
Zāhedān ☆ IR (SIS) 134-135 J 4
Zāhira, az- ⩦ OM 132-133 K 4
Zahirābād ○ IND 140-141 G 2
Zahir Pir ○ PK 138-139 C 5
Zahl ○ USA (ND) 258-259 D 3
Zahla ☆ RL 128-129 F 6
Zahmet ○ TM 136-137 H 6
Zahrān al-Ġanūb ○ KSA 132-133 C 5
Zāhū ☆ IRQ 128-129 K 4
Zaidiya, az- ○ Y 132-133 C 6
Zaigraevo ☆ RUS 116-117 O 10
Zaila ○ ZRE 214-215 C 5
Zainsk ☆ RUS 96-97 H 6
Zaio ○ MA 188-189 K 3
Zaire ◘ ANG 216-217 B 3
Zaire ∼ ZRE 210-211 G 3
Zaire ∼ ZRE 210-211 F 4
Zaire = Zaire ■ ZRE 210-211 G 5
Zaječar ○ YU 100-101 J 3
Zajsan ○ KA 124-125 O 5
Zajsan, köli ⊶ KA 124-125 N 4
Zajyndy ∼ KA 126-127 M 4
Zaka ○ ZW 218-219 F 5
Zakamensk ☆ RUS 116-117 L 10
Zakèt, In- < RMM 196-197 K 6
Zaki Biam ○ WAN 204-205 H 5
Zákinthos ○ GR 100-101 H 6
Zákinthos ⌒ GR 100-101 H 6
Zakobjakino ○ RUS 94-95 R 2
Zakopane ○•• PL 92-93 P 4
Zakouma ○ TCH 206-207 D 3
Zakouma, Parc National de ⊥ TCH 206-207 D 3
Zakou Shankou ▲ VRC 144-145 M 2
Žaksybaj ∼ KA 96-97 J 9
Žaksybaj, köli ⊶ KA 124-125 C 3
Žaksybutaly, tau ▲ KA 126-127 N 4
Žaksy-Kargaly ∼ KA 126-127 M 2
Žaksy-kön ∼ KA 124-125 F 4
Žaksy-Kylyc kölder ⊶ KA 126-127 P 4
Zala ○ ANG 216-217 C 3
Zala ○ ETH 208-209 C 5
Zalaa ○ MAU 148-149 D 5
Zalābiya ⛬• SYR 128-129 H 5
Zalaegerszeg ○ H 92-93 O 5
Zalaf, az ○ SYR 128-129 G 6
Zalamea de la Serena ○• E 98-99 E 5
Zalanga ○ WAN 204-205 J 3
Zalari ☆ RUS 116-117 L 9
Zalău ☆ RO 102-103 C 4
Žalauly, köli ⊶ KA 124-125 J 2
Žaldama ∼ KA 124-125 D 3
Zalegošč' ○ RUS 94-95 P 5
Zaleščyky ☆ UA 102-103 D 3
Zalesovo ☆ RUS 114-115 S 7
Zalesskij, Pereslavl'- ○• RUS 94-95 Q 3
Zalim ○ KSA 130-131 H 6
Zalingei ○ SUD 198-199 L 6
Zaliouan ○ CI 202-203 G 6
Zaliv ○ RUS 116-117 F 7
Zalki ○ IND 140-141 F 2
Zallūm, az- ○ KSA 130-131 G 2
Žalma', Ġabal az- ▲ KSA 130-131 F 4
Zaltan ○ LAR 192-193 H 3
Zaltan, Bi'r < LAR 192-193 H 3
Žaltyr ○ KA 124-125 F 3
Žaltyr, köl ⊶ KA 96-97 G 10
Žaltyrköl ⊶ KA 96-97 G 9
Zaluč'e ○ RUS 94-95 M 3
Zalut ○ MYA 158-159 E 4
Zal'vjanka ∼ BY 94-95 J 5
Zama ○ RN 204-205 E 1
Zamak ○ Y 132-133 E 5
Zama Lake ⊶ CDN 30-31 K 6
Žamanajrykty, tau ▲ KA 126-127 L 5
Žaman-Kön ∼ KA 124-125 F 4
Zamantı Irmağı ∼ TR 128-129 G 3
Zamantı Irmagı ∼ TR 128-129 F 4
Zamay ○ CAM 204-205 K 3
Žambaj aral ⌒ KA 96-97 F 10
Zambales Mountains ▲ RP 160-161 D 5
Žambejti ☆ KA 96-97 H 8
Zambéndé ○ BF 202-203 L 4
Zambeze ∼ ANG 214-215 B 6
Zambeze, Rio ∼ MOC 218-219 H 3
Zambezi ○ Z 218-219 B 1
Zambezi ∼ Z 218-219 E 2
Zambézia ◘ MOC 218-219 H 3
Zambezi Deka < ZW 218-219 D 4
Zambezi Escarpment ⩦ ZW 218-219 E 3
Zambezi National Park ⊥ ZW 218-219 C 3
Zambi, Rapids de ∼• ZRE 210-211 D 6
Zambia ■ Z 218-219 C 2
Zamboanga City ○• RP 160-161 E 9
Zamboanga Peninsula ⌣ RP 160-161 E 9
Zamboanguita ○ RP 160-161 E 8
Zambrano ○ HN 52-53 L 4
Zambrów ○ PL 92-93 R 2
Zambué ○ MOC 218-219 F 2
Žambyl ○ KA 124-125 G 5
Zamfara ∼ WAN 198-199 B 6
Zamīnān ○ IR 134-135 B 5
Zamlat Amagraj ⩦ MA 196-197 D 2
Zamora ○•• E 98-99 E 4
Zamora ☆ EC 64-65 C 4
Zamora ○ MEX 52-53 C 1
Zamora, Punta ▲ PE 64-65 C 6
Zamora, Río ∼ EC 64-65 C 3
Zamość ☆••• PL 92-93 R 3
Zāmurān Pass ▲ PK 134-135 K 5
Zamuro, Punta ▲ YV 60-61 G 2
Zamuro, Sierra del ▲ YV 60-61 K 5
Zamyn-Üüd = Borhojn Tal ○ MAU 148-149 K 6
Zamza ∼ RCA 206-207 E 5
Zamzam, Wādī ∼ LAR 192-193 F 2
Zan ○ TCH 206-207 D 3
Zanaaul ○ KA 124-125 O 4
Žanadar'ja ∼ KA 136-137 H 3
Zanaga ○ RCB 210-211 D 5
Žanakala ☆ KA 96-97 G 9
Žana Kazan ○ KA 96-97 F 9
Žanakorgan ☆ KA 136-137 K 3
Žanaortalyk ○ KA 124-125 J 5
Žanatas ○ KA 136-137 L 3
Žanatas ○ KA 136-137 L 3
Zanda ○ VRC 144-145 B 5
Zandamela ○ MOC 220-221 M 2
Zanderij ○ SME 62-63 G 3
Zandvoort ○ NL 92-93 H 2
Zane Hills ▲ USA 20-21 M 3
Zanelli, Cerro ▲ RCH 80 D 6
Zanesville ○ USA (OH) 280-281 D 4
Zanfla ○ CI 202-203 H 6
Zangān ◘ IR 128-129 M 4
Zangān ☆• IR (ZAN) 128-129 N 4
Zangāreddigūdem ○ IND 142-143 B 7
Zangasso ○ RMM 202-203 H 3
Zangdo ○ VRC 144-145 F 5
Zangğān Rūd ∼ IR 128-129 N 4
Zangguy ○ VRC 144-145 B 2
Zangitas ○ RA 78-79 F 2
Zango ○ WAN 198-199 D 6
Zanna, Ġabal az- ○ UAE 134-135 E 6
Zanpiéla ○ RMM 202-203 G 4
Zanré ○ BF 202-203 K 3
Zanskar ∼ IND 138-139 F 3
Zanskar Mountains ▲ IND 138-139 F 2
Zanthus ○ AUS 176-177 G 5
Zantiebougou ○ RMM 202-203 G 4
Zanuľe ○ RUS 96-97 F 3
Zanvar Čāy ∼ IR 128-129 L 3
Žanybek ☆ KA 96-97 E 9
Zanzibar ☆•• EAT 214-215 K 4
Zanzibar ○ RB 218-219 E 6
Zanzibar and Pemba ◘ EAT 214-215 K 3
Zanzibar Channel ≈ 214-215 K 3
Zanzibar Island ⌒ EAT 214-215 K 4
Zanzra ○ CI 202-203 G 6
Zaokskij ☆ RUS 94-95 P 4
Zaonežskij zaliv ⊶ RUS 88-89 N 5
Zao Quasi National Park ⊥ J 152-153 J 5
Zaoro-Songou ○ RCA 206-207 C 6
Zao-san ▲ J 152-153 J 5